NINTH EDITION

SCHROEDER'S
ANTIQUES
PRICE GUIDE

Edited by Sharon & Bob Huxford

COLLECTOR BOOKS
A Division of Schroeder Publishing Co., Inc.

The current values in this book should be used only as a guide. They are not intended to set prices, which vary from one section of the country to another. Auction prices as well as dealer prices vary greatly and are affected by condition as well as demand. Neither the Editors nor the Publisher assumes responsibility for any losses that might be incurred as a result of consulting this guide.

On the cover, clockwise from left:

Walt Disney Thumper ceramic figure, $75.00. Courtesy of *Stern's Guide to Disney Collectibles, Second Series*.

Music Master 1925 table model radio, $250.00. Courtesy of *The Collector's Guide to Antique Radios* by Marty & Sue Bunis.

Madame Alexander Gibson Girl doll, 10" hard plastic, 1962, $1,200.00. Courtesy of *Madame Alexander Collector's Dolls Price Guide #15* by Patricia Smith.

Mahogany and veneer Empire sofa with tufted back and serpentine front, 83" wide, $1,950.00. Courtesy of *Collector's Encyclopedia of American Furniture, Volume I : The Dark Woods of the Nineteenth Century* by Robert W. and Harriett Swedberg.

Majolica Etruscan Shell and Seaweed cuspidor, $595.00. Courtesy of *Majolica Pottery, Second Series* by Mariann Katz-Marks.

Heisey Twist green cocktail shaker, $400.00. Courtesy of *Very Rare Glassware of the Depression Years* by Gene Florence.

Additional copies of this book may be ordered from:

COLLECTOR BOOKS
P.O. Box 3009
Paducah, Kentucky 42002-3009

@$12.95. Add $2.00 for postage and handling.

Introduction

As the editors and staff of *Schroeder's*, our goal is to compile the most useful, comprehensive, and accurate background and pricing information possible. Our guide encompasses nearly 700 categories, many of which you will not find in other price guides. Our sources are varied; we use auction results, dealer lists, trade paper ads, and we consult with national collectors' clubs, recognized authorities, researchers, and appraisers. We have by far the largest Advisory Board of any similar publication on the market. Each year we add several new advisors and now have more than 250 who cover almost 500 categories. They go over our computer print-outs line by line, deleting listings that are misleading or too vague to be of merit; they often send background information and photos. We appreciate their assistance very much – only through their expertise and experience in their special fields are we able to offer with confidence what we feel are useful, accurate evaluations that provide a sound understanding of the dealings in the market place today. Correspondence with so large an advisory panel adds months of extra work to an already monumental task, but we feel that to a very large extent this is the foundation that makes *Schroeder's* the success that it has become.

Our Directory, which you will find in the back of the book, lists each contributor by state. These are people who have allowed us to photograph various examples of merchandise from their show booths, sent us pricing information, or in any way have contributed to this year's book. Feel free to contact them; many will be glad to ship you the merchandise you need. If you happen to be traveling, consult the Directory for shops along your way. We also list clubs who have worked with us and auction houses who have agreed to permit us the use of photographs from their catalogs. Our Advisory Board lists only names and home states, so check the Directory for addresses and telephone numbers should you want to correspond with one of our experts. Remember that when you do, if you expect an answer from either an advisor or a contributor, please send a SASE (self-addressed, stamped envelope).

To be used to your best advantage, this guide should be regarded as a basic tool, a rule of thumb, only one source of the information you need to digest in order to become a knowledgeable dealer or collector. Antique shows, trade papers, collectors' books, and association with others sharing the same interests all contribute toward making you more keenly aware of market trends and thus educate you toward becoming a wise and confident buyer.

We have organized our topics alphabetically, following the most simple logic, usually either by manufacturer or by type of product. If you have difficulty in locating your subject, consult the index. Our guide is unique in that much more space has been allotted to background information than any other publication of this type, and it is easier to read due to the larger-than-average print. Our readers tell us that these are features they enjoy. To be able to do this, we have adopted a format of one-line listings wherein we describe the items to the fullest extent possible by using several common-sense abbreviations; they will be easy to read and understand if you will first take the time to quickly scan through them.

The Editors

Listing of Standard Abbreviations

The following is a list of abbreviations that have been used throughout this book in order to provide you with the most detailed descriptions possible in the limited space available. No periods are used after initials or abbreviations. When two dimensions are given, height is noted first. If only one dimension is listed, it will be height, except in the case of bowls, dishes, plates, or platters, when it will be diameter. The standard two-letter state abbreviations apply.

For glassware, if no color is noted, the glass is clear. Hyphenated colors, for example blue-green, olive-amber, etc., describe a single color tone; colors divided by a slash mark indicate two or more colors, i.e. blue/white. A number following the last comma in a listing indicates how many items are included in the lot price. Teapots, sugar bowls, and butter dishes are assumed to be 'with cover.' Condition is extremely important in determining market value. This year, in order to conserve space, the condition line has been left out of the narrative, except when our advisors requested that it remain, or when the category contained items of such a varied nature that we felt it advantageous to leave the line in to avoid confusion. Common sense suggests that art pottery, china, and glassware values would be given for examples in pristine, mint condition, while suggested prices for utility wares such as Redware, Mocha, and Blue and White Stoneware, for example, reflect the the probability that since such items were subjected to everyday use in the home they may show minor wear (which is acceptable) but no notable damage. Values for other categories reflect the best average condition in which the particular collectible is apt to be offered for sale without the dealer feeling it necessary to mention wear or damage. For instance, advertising items are assumed to be in excellent condition since mint items are scarce enough that when one is offered for sale the dealer will most likely make mention of that fact. The same holds true for Toys, Banks, Coin-Operated Machines, and the like. Paper ephemera is evaluated as if in very good to excellent condition unless otherwise noted. A basic rule of thumb is that an item listed as VG (very good) will bring 40% to 60% of its mint price (a first-hand, personal evaluation will enable you to make the final judgment); EX (excellent) is a condition midway between mint and very good, and values would correspond.

Am	American	dvtl	dovetail
app	applied	drw	drawer
att	attributed to	ea	each
bk	back	emb	embossed, embossing
bsk	bisque	embr	embroidered
b3m	blown 3-mold	eng	engraved, engraving
bl	blue	EX	excellent
brn	brown	ext	exterior
bulb	bulbous	ft, ftd	foot, feet, footed
cb	cardboard	fr	frame, framed
CI	cast iron	Fr	French
C	century	G	good
ca	circa	grad	graduated
compo	composition	grpt	grain painted
c	copyright	gr	green
cr/sug	creamer and sugar	HP	hand painted
X, Xd	cross, crossed	hdl, hdld	handle, handled
c/s	cup and saucer	imp	impressed
cvd	carved	ind	individual
cvg	carving	int	interior
dk	dark	irid	iridescent
dtd	dated	Invt T'print	Inverted Thumbprint
decor	decoration	lg	large
dia	diameter	lav	lavender
Dia Quilt	Diamond Quilted	ldgl	leaded glass
dbl	double	L	length, long
dmn	diamond	lt	light

litho	lithograph	rpr	repaired
mahog	mahogany	rpl	replaced
mk	mark	rstr	restored
MIG	Made in Germany	rtcl	reticulated
M	mint	rvpt	reverse painted
MIB	mint in box	rnd	rnd
MOP	mother-of-pearl	s&p	salt and pepper
mt, mtd	mount, mounted	sgn	signed
mc	multicolor	SP	silverplated
NE	New England	sz	size
NM	near mint	sm	small
NP	nickel plated	sq	square
opal	opalescent	std	standard
orig	original	str	straight
o/w	otherwise	trn	turned, turning
pnt	paint	turq	turquoise
pr	pair	uphl	upholstered
pat	patented	VG	very good
ped	pedestal	Vict	Victorian
pc	piece	wht	white
pk	pink	W	wide, width
pt	pint	w/	with
prof	professional	w/o	without
porc	porcelain	yel	yellow
rfn	refinished		
re	regarding		
rpt	repainted		

A B C Plates

Children's plates featuring the alphabet as part of the design were popular from as early as 1820 until after the turn of the century. The earliest English creamware plates were decorated with embossed letters and prim moralistic verses; but the later Staffordshire products were conducive to a more relaxed mealtime atmosphere – often depicting playful animals and riddles or scenes of pleasant leisure-time activities. They were made around the turn of the century by American potters as well. All featured transfer prints, but color was sometimes brushed on by hand to add interest to the design. Braille plates were made for the blind, but these are rather scarce and therefore usually more valuable. You may also find an occasional bowl or mug. . . a matching set is rare.

Ceramic

Acrobatic monkeys, 7" 45.00
American Sports, Baseball, Caught on the Fly, 7¼" 250.00
B Is for Bobby's Breakfast & Bessie's Bread & Milk 95.00
Baker, worker putting loaves in oven, Staffordshire, 7" 135.00
Bowl, girl & boy play doctor, mc transfer, scalloped, 8½" 70.00
Boys in sailor hats fishing, Staffordshire, 5" 110.00
Boys in soldier hats play cards, tents at bk, Staffordshire, 5" 110.00
Canary, bullfinch, goldfinch, mc transfer, 6¾" 55.00
Children playing leapfrog, Powell & Bishop, 6¼" 125.00
Crusoe on the Raft, BP Co, 8" 125.00
Dancing pigs, 8" 30.00
Elephant, Wild Animal Series, 7¼" 100.00

Pranksters knock hat off of sleeping man, 7", $95.00.

Evening Bathing Scene at Manhattan Beach, 7½" 85.00
F Is for Frank Who a Sailor Would Be, Staffordshire, 7¾" 125.00
Famous Places, Capitol at Washington, flower rim, BP Co..........125.00
Gen McClellan on horsebk w/Union troups, 7", EX 225.00
Handling the Ware, ladies w/pottery, Staffordshire, 7" 125.00
Harvest Home, Meakin, 5½" 65.00
Highland Dance, blk transfer w/mc enamel, 5½" 98.00
Japanese, Nations of the World, BP Co 7¼" 90.00
Lamb, Syracuse 25.00
Mother & Daughter Dear to Each..., Elsmore & Forster, 7" 195.00

Mug, C Is for..., mulberry transfer, Staffordshire, 3" 58.00
Mug, Crusoe at Work, Brownhills, 1877 ....55.00
Mug, D...for dog, red transfer, Staffordshire, 3", EX 125.00
Mug, Houlette Shepherd's Crook, red/gr/yel, M 55.00
Mug, W&X w/mc religious figures, Staffordshire, 2½" 65.00
Niagara from Edge of American Falls, Staffordshire, 7¼" 125.00
Now I Have a Cow, Franklin Maxim, 5⅛" 100.00
Punch & Judy, Staffordshire, 7½" 45.00
Quartermaster & Trumpeter, 2 soldiers, Staffordshire, 5¼" 165.00
Reflections on the Beauty of Nature 95.00
Sacred History of Joseph & His Brethren, 7" 40.00
Silks & Satins, Franklin Maxim, 6¼" 175.00
Uncle Tom's Cabin, Vision of Uncle Tom, 8" 70.00

Glass

American Flag center 75.00
Cane, basketweave center, 6" 30.00
Christmas Eve, Santa in chimney, 6¼" 60.00
Clock center, 6" 55.00
Elephant w/howda & riders, ABC rim, 6" 150.00

Centennial Exposition, 1876, 6¾", $120.00.

Independence Hall, 1766-1876, L-33, ABC rim 125.00
Rabbit in grass, house behind 65.00
Stork, clear/frosted, ABC rim, 6" 95.00
1000 Eye, clock center, amber, 6" 65.00

Tin

Brownies, ABC Rim, 1896, EX 150.00
Girl swinging, 6¼" 45.00
Hey Diddle Diddle, 8" 55.00
Jumbo, 6¼", EX 85.00
Mary Had a Little Lamb, 8" 85.00
Washington & 3 Stars, 5½" 90.00
Who Killed Cock Robin?, 7¾" 65.00

Abingdon

From 1934 until 1950, the Abingdon Pottery Co. of Abingdon, Ill., made a line of art pottery with a white vitrified body decorated with various types of glazes in many lovely colors. Novelties, cookie jars, utility ware, and lamps were made in addition to several lines of simple yet striking art ware. Fern Leaf, introduced in 1937, featured molded vertical feathering. La Fleur, in 1939, consisted of flowerpots and flower-arranger bowls with rows of vertical ribbing. Classic, 1939-40, was a line of vases, many with evidence of Chinese influence. Several marks were used, most of which employed the company name. In 1950 the company reverted to the manufacture of sanitary ware that had been their mainstay before the Art Ware Division was formed.

Highly decorated examples and those with black, bronze, or red glaze usually command at least 25% higher prices.

#102, vase, Beta, maroon, 10" **40.00**
#109, vase, Alpha, wht matt, 5" **18.00**
#110, vase, Beta, lt bl, 6" **30.00**
#126, candlestick, Classic, wht, pr **32.00**
#142, vase, Classic, bl, mini, 5" **28.00**
#202, pitcher, chartreuse, ice lip, 1940-1941, 1-pt............**38.00**
#302-L, lamp base, Lunge, wht, brass fittings **175.00**
#305, bookend, sea gull, pk, pr **50.00**
#310, vase, Chang, copper brn, 1934-1936, rare............**275.00**
#310, vase, Chang, wht matt, 1934-1936, 10½"...........**245.00**
#312, vase, Han, ftd, Regency gr, older style **40.00**
#314, vase, Swedish, lt gr, 1934-1936, 8" **135.00**
#315, vase, Athenia Classic, wht, 1934-1936, 9".............**32.00**
#322, goblet, Swedish, gr **45.00**
#322, goblet, Swedish, wht, 1934-1936 ....**75.00**
#353, vase, Penthouse, peachbloom pk, 1935-1938.........**95.00**
#375, wall pocket, dbl morning-glory, deep red **55.00**
#375, wall pocket, dbl morning-glory, wht **40.00**
#377, wall pocket, morning-glory, pk, 1937-1950 ....**15.00**
#379, wall pocket, daisy, yel & brn, 1936-1941 ....**40.00**
#383, bowl, sunflower, turq matt, 1936-1938, 9½".........**75.00**
#390, vase, morning-glory, turq, 1936-1939, 10"............**55.00**
#3905b, chessman, bishop, bronze/blk, 1937, rare........**235.00**
#3906, shepherdess & fawn, yel w/gold traces.................**95.00**
#395, flower ring, wht, 2-pc, 1936-1938, 11½" dia **75.00**
#401, tea tile, coolie, wht matt, paper label **65.00**
#402, vase, box form, wht, 1937-1938, 5½" **65.00**
#408, bowl, leaf form, beige, 1937, 6½" **65.00**
#412, vase, Volute, wht, 1937-1940, lg............................**125.00**
#416, peacock, turq gloss **40.00**
#416, peacock, wht, 1937-1938 & 1942 ....**35.00**
#420, vase, Fern Leaf, turq matt, 1937-1938, 8" **75.00**
#427, vase, bud; Fern leaf, lt gr, 1937-1938, 5½" **70.00**
#430, pitcher, Fern Leaf, wht, 1937-1938, 8"..................**135.00**
#441, bookends, horse head, wht, pr **50.00**
#442, vase, Laurel, red, 1938-1939, 5½" **45.00**
#442, vase, Laurel, turq matt, 1938-1939, 5½" **33.00**
#451, candle holder, dbl, Astor, wht, 1936-1938, pr.......**44.00**
#468, vase, sea gull, decor, wht & bl, 1946-1947 ....**35.00**
#470, Dutch girl figure, gr or red matt, ea **50.00**
#483D, vase, bud; Petit, decor **30.00**
#486, vase, acanthus, gray, 11" **35.00**
#487, vase, floor; egret, chartreuse **85.00**
#488, ash tray, box form, turq, 1936-1938 ....**42.00**
#492, vase, bowl form, gr, 1940, sm **20.00**
#493, wall pocket, dbl, turq, 1940, 8"................................**65.00**
#496, vase, hollyhock, decor, 1940, 1946-1947 ....**36.00**
#504, vase/planter, shell, wht, 7".......................................**15.00**
#509, ash tray, elephant, wht, scarce **95.00**
#510, ash tray, donkey, blk, scarce.....................................**95.00**
#511, vase, Ionic, wht, bowl form **25.00**
#517, vase, Arden, gr, 1940-1950...**20.00**
#525, bowl, gray, oblong, flared, 1940-1950 ....**20.00**
#527, bowl, hibiscus, pk, 1941-1948, sm **28.00**
#528, bowl, hibiscus, yel, 1941-1949, lg **45.00**
#565, cornucopia, blk, 1942-1947 ....**25.00**
#566D, vase, pk, scalloped, decor, 8".................................**35.00**
#568, compote, pk, ftd, 1942-1947 ....**24.00**
#569, cornucopia, bl **20.00**
#569, cornucopia, decor...**25.00**

#571, goose, wht **25.00**
#572, pelican, gr **30.00**
#572D, pelican, decor, scarce **40.00**
#586D, wall pocket, calla lily, decor **65.00**
#593D, cache pot, bl & decor..**25.00**
#599, vase, quilted, wht, 9" **30.00**
#604D, vase, tulip, wht, decor **48.00**
#637, vase, pk, oblong, 9" **35.00**
#648, wall pocket, acanthus, wht, rare **55.00**
#649, wall shelf, acanthus, wht, rare **65.00**
#660, ash tray, leaf, blk & yel, 5" dia **35.00**
#661, swan, chartreuse **35.00**
#666, jam jar, cherry top, bl **9.00**
#670, planter, pooch, chartreuse **22.00**
#698, vase, Chinese Terrace, yel, 6" **25.00**
#705, vase, Modern, bl gloss **25.00**
#711, wall pocket, carriage, chartreuse...............................**35.00**
#713, console bowl, star, chartreuse **25.00**
#714, candlestick, star, gr..**8.00**
#716, candlestick, Bamboo, decor, pr **25.00**
#9-4, vase, Rope, chartreuse, 25" **150.00**
Cookie jar, #471, Black Lady, decor..................................**110.00**
Cookie jar, #471, Old Lady, decor **60.00**
Cookie jar, #495, Fat Boy, beige **60.00**
Cookie jar, #549, Hippo, no decor, 8" **50.00**
Cookie jar, #561, Baby..**55.00**
Cookie jar, #588, Money Sack **45.00**
Cookie jar, #602D, Rocking Horse, decor, 11"...............**135.00**
Cookie jar, #611, Jack-in-the-Box, no decor, 11" **40.00**
Cookie jar, #651, Locomotive, cream w/red & blk **55.00**
Cookie jar, #653D, Cookie Time...**35.00**
Cookie jar, #662, Little Miss Muffet....................................**60.00**
Cookie jar, #663, Humpty Dumpty, decor...........................**45.00**
Cookie jar, #663, Humpty Dumpty, no decor, 10¼" **35.00**
Cookie jar, #664, Pineapple, decor **45.00**
Cookie jar, #664, Pineapple, no decor **30.00**
Cookie jar, #674, Pumpkin **45.00**
Cookie jar, #677D, Daisy, brn **25.00**
Cookie jar, #694, Little Bo Peep..**65.00**
Cookie jar, #695D, Mother Goose, bl ruffles, goose by side............**95.00**
Vase, what not (A); bl & wht, sm hdl, 3½".........................**75.00**

What-Not Vases, 3½" to 5½", $75.00-85.00.

Vase, what not (A); gr & wht, squatty, 3½", rare **75.00**
Vase, what not (A); leaf motif, bl & wht, 3½", rare **75.00**
Vase, what not (A); wht matt, 3½", rare **75.00**
Vase, what not (B); bl & wht, hdld, rare **85.00**
Vase, what not (C); floral motif, rose & wht, 5" **85.00**
Vase, what not (C); wht, medallion in center, 4½" **85.00**

Adams

Wm. Adams, whose potting skills were developed under the tutelage of Josiah Wedgwood, founded the Greengates Pottery at Tunstall, England, in 1769. Many types of wares including basalt, ironstone, parian, and jasper were produced; and various impressed or printed marks were employed. Until 1800 'Adams Co.' or 'Adams' impressed in block letters identified the company's earthenwares and a fine type of jasper similar in color and decoration to Wedgwood's. The latter mark was used again from 1845 to 1864 on parian figures. Most examples of their product found on today's market are transfer-printed dinnerwares with ornate backstamps which often include the pattern name and the initials 'W.A. & S.' This type of product was made from 1820 until about 1920. After 1890 the word 'England' was included in the mark; 'Tunstall' was added after 1896. From 1914 through 1940, a printed crown with 'Adams, Estbd 1657, England' identified their products. From 1900 to 1965, they produced souvenir plates with transfers of American scenes, many of which were marketed in this country by Roth Importers of Peoria, Illinois. In 1965 the company affiliated with Wedgwood. Although there were other Adams potteries in Staffordshire, their marks incorporate either the first name initial or a partner's name and so are easily distinguished from those of this company. See also Spatter; Staffordshire; Adam's Rose.

Bowl, Cries of London, 7½" **45.00**
Bowl, vegetable; Columbus Discovers Am, gr transfer, 11" L **150.00**
Creamer, birdcage, dk bl transfer, prof lip rpr **85.00**
Cup & saucer, handleless; stick spatter w/gaudy floral, EX **45.00**
Plate, Columbia, red transfer, mk, 10¾" **30.00**

Plate, Palestine, red transfer border, green center, 9½", $65.00.

Plate, Mt Washington Steamer, bl transfer, 8" **30.00**
Plate, Seasons (Winter), pk transfer, 9½" **55.00**
Plate, The Sea (shipwreck), pk transfer, 9½", NM **55.00**
Plate, toddy; horses, dk bl transfer, minor edge wear, 4⅝" **55.00**
Platter, 2 stags/3 does, bl transfer, 1850s, 16" **275.00**
Soup plate, Oriental scenery, dk bl transfer, 10½", NM **150.00**

Urn, cobalt w/wht coat of arms, miniature, 2½" **75.00**

Adams' Rose, Early and Late

In the second quarter of the 19th century, the Adams and Son Pottery produced a line of hand-painted dinnerware decorated in large, red brush-stroke roses with green leaves on whiteware, which collectors call Adams' Rose. Later, G. Jones and Son (and possibly others) made a similar ware with less brilliant colors on a gray-white surface.

Bowl, early, rare size, 9", M **450.00**
Bowl, vegetable; late, 10¾", M **125.00**
Creamer, early, 5¾", M **285.00**
Pitcher, early, stains/minor flakes, 7" **205.00**
Pitcher, late, 6¾", M **175.00**
Plate, early, emb scalloped rim, 10½", NM **125.00**
Plate, early, 9", M **190.00**
Plate, late, 8¾", EX **110.00**
Plate, late, 9½", EX **110.00**
Platter, late, 12", EX **125.00**
Soup plate, early, wear/minor stains/glaze flakes, 9" **80.00**
Soup plate, early, 10", M **150.00**
Sugar bowl, late, M **175.00**
Sugar bowl, w/lid, early, M **350.00**
Tea bowl & saucer, early, M **195.00**
Tea bowl & saucer, late, M **95.00**
Teapot, early, dome lid, rpr, 11½" **550.00**
Teapot, late, M **300.00**

Advertising

The advertising world has always been a fiercely competitive field. In an effort to present their product to the customer, every imaginable gimmick was put into play. Colorful and artfully decorated signs and posters, thermometers, tape measures, fans, hand mirrors, and attractive tin containers – all with catchy slogans, familiar logos, and often-bogus claims – are only a few of the many examples of early advertising memorabilia that are of interest to today's collectors.

Porcelain signs were made as early as 1890 and are highly prized for their artistic portrayal of life as it was then . . . often allowing amusing insights into the tastes, humor, and way of life of a bygone era. As a general rule, older signs are made from a heavier gauge metal. Those with three or more fired-on colors are especially desirable.

Tin containers were used to package consumer goods ranging from crackers and coffee to tobacco and talcum. After 1880 can companies began to decorate their containers by the method of lithography. Though colors were still subdued, intricate designs were used to attract the eye of the consumer. False labeling and unfounded claims were curtailed by the Pure Food and Drug Administration in 1906, and the name of the manufacturer as well as the brand name of the product had to be printed on the label. By 1910 color was rampant with more than a dozen hues printed on the tin or on paper labels. The tins themselves were often designed with a second use in mind – as canisters, lunch boxes, even toy trains. As a general rule, tobacco-related tins are the most desirable, though personal preference may direct the interest of the collector to peanut butter pails with illustrations of children, or talcum tins with irresistible babies or beautiful ladies. Coffee tins are popular, as are those made to contain a particularly successful or well-known product.

Perhaps the most visual of the early advertising gimmicks were the character logos – the Fairbank Company's Gold Dust Twins, the goose trademark of the Red Goose Shoe Company, Nabisco's ZuZu Clown and Uneeda Kid, the Campbell Kids, the RCA dog Nipper, and Mr. Peanut, to name only a few. Any example of these brings high prices on the market today.

Our listings are alphabetized by company name or, in lieu of that information, by word content or other pertinent description. When no condition is indicated, the items listed below are assumed to be in excellent condition, except glass and ceramic items, which are assumed mint. Remember that condition greatly effects value. For instance, a sign in excellent or mint condition may bring twice as much as the same one in only very good condition.

We have several advertising advisors; Allen Smith specializes in Buster Brown, Pepsi-Cola, Planters Peanuts, and Red Goose Shoes. He is listed in the Directory under Texas. See also Advertising Dolls; Advertising Cards; Coca-Cola; Banks; Calendars; Cookbooks; Paperweights; Posters; Sewing Items.

Key:
cb — cardboard	ps — porcelain sign
cl — celluloid	sf — self-framed
lcs — litho on canvas	tc — tin container
pp — pre-prohibition	ts — tin sign

A&P Baking Powder, tc, red label, 2-lb 15.00
Activator Shoes, clock, lights up, Pam Clocks, EX 250.00
Adamant Floor Paint, tip tray, room interior, EX 75.00
Adams Pepsin Tutti-Frutti Gum, display tin, '17, 6x7x5", EX......150.00
Admiration Cigars, cast plaster sign, wall hanging, VG...............135.00
Advance Thresher Co, sf tin sign, knight/flag, 1900, 26x18" 575.00
Akron Brewing, tray, lady/tiger, Kauffman/Strauss, '10, 13".........250.00
Allen's Red Tame Cherry, syrup bottle, 5¢, glass label, NM 1,500.00
Angelus Marshmallows, pocket mirror, winged cherubs, EX..........85.00
Anheuser-Busch, tin sign, lady/eagle, 36x39", EX 325.00
Anheuser-Busch, tray, lady/cherubs, oval, EX.............................585.00
Apollinaris Waters, tip tray, 1920, NM....................................70.00
Arm & Hammer, blotter, church, 1880s, VG 5.00
Arm & Hammer, canvas sign, ducks/pond, 1905, EX....................105.00
Armour Bacon, mc tin sign, 19x12", EX 68.00
Atkinson's Perfume, pocket mirror, mc w/bottle.........................55.00
B-1 Lemon-Lime Soda, sf tin sign, gr bottle, 1940, NM 45.00
Bachelor Cigars, display case, ca 1915, 10x12x8", EX..................300.00
Bagdad Coffee, tc, American Can Co litho, 5-lb, EX...................100.00
Baker's Breakfast Cocoa, tray, lady/home, '15, 6½" dia, NM 200.00
Baker's Chocolate, box, emb aluminum, 2x3", EX.......................30.00
Baker's Cocoa, sf tin sign, girl holds tray, 28x22", EX.................850.00
Baker's Extracts, blotter, celluloid bk, EX................................30.00
Ballantine Brewery, sf ts, Meek litho, 1909, 23x31", VG 700.00
Banquet Tea, teapot, porc, emb letters, 1920s, 11", EX 75.00
Barnum's Animal Crackers, trolly card, 1924, 11x32, NM...........300.00
Bauer Whiskey, fr cb sign, gambling, 1870s, 28x21", EX 1,250.00
Beck's Hunting Tobacco, tin sign, yel/blk, 1890s, 6x13", VG 22.00
Beechnut Chewing Tobacco, banner, oilcloth, 3½x10", EX 75.00
Beechnut Peanut Butter, fr cb sign, Billy/kids, '05, 24x14" 155.00
Beechnut Tobacco, sign, Rockwell litho, 1940s, 20x31", NM 650.00
Benrus Watches, electric store display, '40s, 23x21", VG.............250.00
Berina Malted Milk, porc sign, 10-color, 24x60", EX 440.00
Berry Bros Varnishes, pocket mirror, kids/wagon, EX 175.00
BF Goodrich, Tumblin' Tire Man, promo toy, M in pkg..................45.00
Bickmore Gall Salve, sample tin 10.00
Biff Cigars, tip tray, stogie, EX 65.00

Biscuit Tins

Gray Dunn & Co, Concertina, 1903 ....185.00

Huntley & Palmer, Arabian, natives on side & bottom, 1891 ....185.00
Huntley & Palmer, athletes running/etc, triangular, 1892 ....225.00
Huntley & Palmer, Book, 1930...100.00
Huntley & Palmer, Bookstand, dtd 1905 ....225.00
Huntley & Palmer, Chinese Vase, 1928 ....125.00
Huntley & Palmer, florals w/gold on red, 1½x7x10" 145.00
Huntley & Palmer, Geo V & Mary, Silver Jubilee 1935 ....235.00
Huntley & Palmer, golf scene on lid, Paris Exposition 95.00
Huntley & Palmer, Inkstand, w/porc inkwell, 1928 ....185.00
Huntley & Palmer, Locket, 1912 ....335.00
Huntley & Palmer, marble pillar form, VG 225.00
Huntley & Palmer, Nanking bls/wht/blk, 7", NM 85.00
Huntley & Palmer, Nautical, Xmas tin, 1895...........................225.00
Huntley & Palmer, Olympian, Greek & Roman figures, 1892.....145.00
Huntley & Palmer, Princess Mary, emb brass, Xmas 1914, sm 60.00
Huntley & Palmer, Queen Victoria, military heroes 65.00
Huntley & Palmer, Queen Victoria's Golden Jubilee, 1887.........165.00
Huntley & Palmer, Robinson Crusoe, ca 1890 ....100.00
Huntley & Palmer, Seaside, children at beach, 1890 ....45.00
Huntley & Palmer, twilight nature scene.................................45.00
McFarlane, Lang, & Co, Trunk, 1913 ....95.00
McFarlane, Lang, & Co, Yule Log, w/hatchet hdl, 1910 ....135.00
Preek, Frean & Co, Castle, 1923..160.00
W&R Jacobs & Co, Coronation Coach, w/orig box, 1936 ....350.00
W&R Jacobs & Co, Houseboat, Waterwitch, ca 1923................300.00
Wm Crawford & Sons, Globe, 1938.......................................75.00

Black Cat, tin sign, blk/gr/yel, 20x27", NM..............................45.00
Black Cat Stove Polish, bill holder, EX 55.00
Bliss Native Herbs, tin match holder, Capitol bldg, EX 185.00
Blue Seal Grain Products, porc sign, farm animals, EX 110.00
Borden's, post card, Elsie Says, EX..15.00
Borden's Ice Cream, bowl, Elsie..25.00
Bowman's Pure Malt, paper sign, wood fr, 1902, 26x18", EX 425.00
Brother Long Cut Tobacco, lunch pail, EX...............................35.00
Brotherhood Overalls, pocket mirror, semi-nude in overalls 145.00
Buckeye Reapers & Mowers, cb sign, purse shape, 1890s, 11x7"....95.00
Buckingham Bros Cigars, celluloid note pad, flags/stag, 1900 ....85.00
Buckingham Tobacco, pocket tin, EX.....................................38.00
Budweiser, sleeping bag, cotton, red lining, 76x34", NM..............35.00
Bugler Cigarettes, paper sign, EX color, 1940s, 20x14" 30.00
Bull Durham Cigars, clock, copper, Louisville KY, 12" 650.00

Bull Durham sign, ca 1909, original frame, 27" x 45", $825.00.

Buster Brown

Buster Brown was the creation of cartoonist Richard Felton; his comic strip first appeared in the *New York Herald* on May 4, 1902. Since then Buster and his dog Tige(short for Tiger) have adorned sundry commercial products but are probably best known as the trademark for the Brown Shoe Company established early in this century. Today hundreds of Buster Brown premiums, store articles, and advertising items bring substantial prices from many serious collectors.

Bank, BB & Tige, M-241, CI, worn gold/red pnt, 5⅛", EX 135.00
Bank, BB & Tige w/horse & Good Luck, CI, EX pnt, Arcade 200.00
Bill holder, Vacation Days, EX...40.00
Bowl, cereal; porc, BB transfer, 2x4" 40.00
Cigar band...8.50
Color/comic book, BB & His Pets, 1913, EX...............................50.00
Comic book, 1908, VG..65.00
Flashlight, BB Health Shoes..30.00
Flyer, shows 4 BB cl items, Whitehead/Hoag, sq, 6"..................30.00
Game, Pin the Tie on Buster, EX 295.00
Hobby horse, EX orig...225.00
Knife, hunting; etched blade, mk hdl, EX.....................................50.00
Mask, BB Shoes, cb, NM...25.00
Match holder, BB Bread, 6¾x2¼"...425.00
Pencil case, pencil form, 1930s, EX...65.00
Pin-bk button, for BB Bread, lg, early 30.00
Plate, BB w/Tige doing trick, 4¾"..40.00
Play money, $5, $1, 50¢, set for..10.00
Playing cards, BB & Tige, 52 cards, 1906, EX in box....................65.00
Playing cards, mini, complete 60.00
Pocket mirror, BB Carnival Days, BB & Tige 55.00
Pocket mirror, Brunner's BB Bread, BB/Tige as bakers, 1907 ....100.00
Post card, BB w/Blk boy eating watermelon, Outcault, 1906 ....45.00
Post card, Outcault, 1908, EX 20.00
Poster, linen, BB & Tige, Outcault illus, Selchow, 17x24" 40.00
Ring, brass, Tige 65.00
Rocking horse, wood fr w/springs front & bk, 34x34x17", EX 135.00
Shoe box, EX 15.00
Shoe brush, brn w/cream bristles, wood hdl, 8½" 20.00
Shoe stretcher 35.00
Sign, BB Bread, tin litho, BB/Tige/wheat, 1920s, 23x31", VG.....350.00
Sign, Brown's Bread, die-cut tin, 1920s, 12x14", NM 100.00
Snow King Baking Powder, die-cut cb sign, 1900, 24x36", NM...350.00

C.D. Kenny

C.D. Kenny was determined to be a successful man, and he was. Between 1890 and 1934, he owned seventy-five groceries in fifteen states. He realized his success in two ways: fair business dealings and premium giveaways. These ranged from trade cards and advertising mirrors to tin commemorative plates and kitchen items. There were banks and toys, clocks and tins. Today's collectors are finding scores of these items, all carrying Kenny's name.

Bank, Dime Savings, clear glass, metal top 75.00
Coffee tin, Mammy's Favorite, Mammy serves coffee, 4-lb, VG ..140.00
Figurine, Indian in canoe, ceramic...27.50
Match holder, elephant form, gr..25.00
Mirror, Dutch family drinks coffee w/in cup & saucer, oval 250.00
Plate, boy & dog, holly trim, tin 125.00
Plate, Christmas girl in red & wht w/wreath, tin.........................125.00
Plate, Santa & sleeping child, tin, 9½", M 125.00
Pocket mirror, folding, metal case 35.00
Portrait, George Washington, tin litho, 5x7"..............................100.00

Tape measure, retractable 45.00
Tip tray, flag, 1914 Centennial...65.00
Tip tray, George Washington, 1920s, NM 85.00
Tip tray, Thanksgiving Greetings, boy delivers turkeys.............145.00
Toothpick holder 35.00
Trivet, advertising forms top, ftd, 5" 100.00
Whistle, early auto, tin litho, child's..75.00

Cabello Cigars, tray, long-haired brunette, oval, 17", EX 165.00
Cactus Brand Coffee, tc, faded paper label, w/lid, 9x7½"..............18.00
Camel Cigarettes, tin sign, red w/pack on right, 32" L, NM 55.00
Campbell's Soup, cup, plastic, Campbell Kid.................................2.50
Canada Dry, clock, metal fr, lights up, EX 75.00
Canada Dry, clock, plastic face, metal fr, 16x16", EX 40.00
Canada Dry, rvpt sign, red/silver crown, 8" dia, VG.....................20.00
Cannon Bros Vanilla Beans, tin sign, wood fr, 20x30", EX...........95.00
Carnation Milk, tip tray, cows grazing, EX...................................75.00
Central Union Tobacco, lunch box, tall...60.00
Ceresota Flour, pocket mirror, boy cuts bread, EX 75.00
Champ Pomade, tin container, boxer in ring, oval, 4", VG 45.00
Champagne Velvet, tray, oval, ca 1910, 15x12", EX 200.00
Che-On Tea, tip tray, Victorian girl in gr dress, EX......................85.00
Checkers Tobacco, upright pocket tin 225.00
Chesterfield Cigarettes, flange sign, bl banner on red, EX 65.00

Chicken Cock Whiskey, tin sign, framed, 29" x 23", NM, $2,100.00.

Chief 2 Moon Bitter Oil, folding display sign, 1900s, 40" 130.00
Clabber Girl Baking Powder, tin sign, dbl-sided, 12x34", EX.........50.00
Clabber Girl Baking Powder, tin sign, 1952, 12x30", EX 25.00
Clark Candy Bars, thermometer, wood, mc, NM 325.00
Clark's Thread, cabinet, walnut, 6-drw, 24x25x19", NM 600.00
Clark's Thread, spool cabinet, 2-drw, VG....................................125.00
Cleveland's...Baking Powder, fr paper sign, '20s, 18x25" 45.00
Club House Cigars, cb sign, 1885, 23x17", VG 200.00
Clysmic, King of Table Waters, tip tray, 1910, 6¼x4½", EX 80.00
Cobbs Creek...Whiskey, thermometer, 1936, 38x8", EX 40.00
Coleman's Ginger Ale, tin sign, Ask for..., 18x36", EX...............32.00
Colgate's Cold Cream, tin sign, 1915, 7½x6", NM 350.00
College Mixture Tobacco, tc, 1930s, 5½x3", EX 70.00
Columbia Ice Cream, tray, Loyal Friends, 1913, 16x13", NM 350.00
Columbus Brewing, tip tray, Columbus portrait, pre-pro..............115.00

Concord Cigars, fr cb sign, girl/cherub, 1910, 27x21", EX 450.00
Concordia Fire Insurance, porc sign, bl/wht, early, 20x14" 85.00
Cook's Beer, sf tin sign, ca 1935, 18x14", VG 85.00
Copenhagen Snuff, paper sign, orig fr, ca 1900, EX.....................250.00
Cottolene Shortening, tip tray, Blks in field, 1910, NM 110.00
Country Club Tobacco, tin lunch box, EX 165.00
Culp Co Furniture, tip tray, couple by bookcase, EX 75.00
Dad's Root Beer, blackboard, Press Signs, 28x20", NM 65.00
Dad's Root Beer, thermometer, gold/red/bl, 26x10", EX 60.00
Dartmouth Chocolate, canvas banner, 6-color, '20s, 16x46" 125.00
DeLaval Separators, match holder, figural, 6½", EX 95.00
DeLaval Separators, tin sign, maid/cow, '15, 40x29", EX......... 2,200.00
DeLaval Separators, tip tray, mother/child, 1915, NM.................130.00
Detroit Brewing, tray, Invitation, 1911, 13" dia, NM...................200.00
Devoe Paints, tin sign w/gr neon clock, 13x29", EX....................185.00
Dewars Whiskey, tray, tin litho, early, 16x12", VG 500.00
Diamond Dye, cabinet, children/balloon, 1910, 25x15x6", EX ...950.00
Diamond Dye, cabinet, court scene, 1905, 30x21x9", VG 850.00
Diamond Dye, cabinet, evolution of woman, 30x21x9", EX ... 1,500.00
Diamond Dye, cabinet, governess litho on tin/wood case, 30"... 1,500.00
Diamond Dye, cabinet, mansion litho, 1904, 24x15x8", VG.......750.00
Diamond Horseshoes, tin sign, horses/wagon, 1920s, 36x24" 375.00
Doans, porc thermometer, 1910s, 23x7", EX 95.00
Dolly Varden Chocolates, cb stand-up sign, 8½x5½", EX............110.00
Domestic Sewing Machine, sign, Little Savage, 1885, M 650.00
Don Digo Cigars, glass change receiver, man/palms, EX 30.00
Donald Duck Cola, cb sign, Donald w/bottle, 26x21", EX 50.00
Dorn's Carnation Chewing Gum, tip tray, ca 1910, NM................80.00
Dr Caldwell's Rheumatism Cures, pamphlet, 1906, VG.................12.00
Dr Claris' Veterinary Medicine, cabinet, oak, 1900, VG 450.00
Dr Daniels' Veterinarian Products, ts, 1900, 22x15", EX 450.00
Dr Hess' Louse Killer, tc, child w/dog, 6½x3" dia, NM...................30.00
Dr Jaynes' Sedative Pills, rvpt sign, fr, 1900, 4x10", NM 125.00
Dr Jaynes' Tonic Vermifuge, rvpt sign, fr, 1900, 6x10", NM 180.00

Dr Pepper

A young pharmacist, Charles C. Alderton, was hired by W.B. Morrison, owner of Morrison's Old Corner Drug Store in Waco, Texas, around 1884. Alderton, an observant sort, noticed that the drugstore's patrons could never quite make up their minds as to which flavor of extract to order. He concocted a formula that combined many flavors, and Dr Pepper was born. The name was chosen by Morrison in honor of a beautiful young girl with whom he had once been in love. The girl's father, a Virginia doctor by the name of Pepper, had discouraged the relationship due to their youth, but Morrison had never forgotten her. On December 1, 1885, a U.S. patent was issued to the creators of Dr Pepper.

Ad, cb, full color, 1948, 15x25", set of 4, EX 50.00
Bottle, clear, AM&B Co, circle A, EX...25.00
Bottle, syrup; King of Beverages, EX...200.00
Calendar, 1938, lady in yel gown, NM..250.00
Calendar, 1950, girl w/half-mask, complete, NM 50.00
Clock, brick wall effect, blk on beige, lt gr fr, rnd, 15" 100.00
Fan, cb, 6-pack, gr/red, VG..50.00
Fountain glass, Dr Pepper etched in wht rectangle, M 10.00
Match holder, 1930s, M..68.00
Post card, 10¢ coupon, M 5.00
Radio, AM, cooler form, wood case, gr pnt, 1940, 12x7x7".........250.00
Sign, tin, cut-out cap, 28", NM...50.00
Syrup dispenser, china w/metal legs, cylindrical, 18", VG 800.00

Tray, roses, King of Beverages, Vienna Art...................................250.00
Watch fob, Billiken, brass, EX..100.00

Drake Grain Beer, porc sign, Friendly, neon border, EX..............400.00
Dress Tomahawk Cut Plug, die-cut sign, Indians, 1885, EX 1,450.00
Duchess Trousers, tin sign, comic, 1910, 20x25", NM..................85.00
Dueber Watch Co, pocket mirror..45.00
Duffy's Whiskey, pocket mirror, chemist at work, EX 55.00
Dunlap Tires, tin sign, red/blk/wht, AM Signs, 59x14", EX 45.00
Dupont Powders, sf tin sign, 2 hunting dogs, 1903, 28x23" 1,200.00
Duralene Motor Oil, celluloid pin-bk, oval, 1938, EX....................22.00
Durr's Foods, fr tin sign, Chief/maid/teepee, 1920s, 27x20" 225.00
Dutch Java Coffee, pocket mirror, Dutch boy & girl kiss 65.00
Dyer's Beans, tin sign, Am Art litho, 1920s, 11x8", NM 125.00
Eatonia Allspice, tin container, camel scene, EX 22.00
Echo Spring Sour Mash, sf tin sign, 1905, VG 200.00
El Rocco Cigars, porc over steel sign, 12x27½", EX.......................85.00
El Verso Cigars, tip tray, Edwardian man in interior, '20, M.......100.00
Elgin, fr wood sign, My Elgin's All Right, 1920, 23x16", EX........175.00
Elliot Ear Plugs, celluloid display, 1906, 7½x9½", M 75.00
Emerson Fans, tin sgn, mc, 2 men, 1 w/fan, 1920, EX..................275.00
Empire Soap, paper sign, Blk children, 1915, 24x17", NM..........950.00
Empress Marmalade, tin container, mc ship, 5x5" dia, EX 30.00
Eye-Fix, tip tray, cherub gives drops to girl 150.00
Fast Mail Chewing Tobacco, pocket tin, flat, 1890s, G 120.00
Fehr's Beer, sf tin sign, lady, man in rocker, '10, 28x21"........... 1,500.00
Fels-Naptha, soap grater, 1930s, EX 10.00
Fink Brewing, tray, Right to the Point, 1914, 15x13", NM..........350.00
Five Roses Tea, porc thermometer, red/wht, 39x8", EX.................120.00
Florida Brewing, tray, tin, dog smoking, 1910, 11x13", VG 125.00
Fordson Tractor, brochure, color pictures, 1940s 5.00
Frank Jones Brewery, tray, monk, Vienna Art, pre-pro.................175.00
Freymeyer Cakes, tip tray, brunette w/scarf, EX.............................65.00
Friday Liquors & Cigars, pocket mirror, man frowns/smiles 45.00
Friedman-Keiler Distillers, fr tin sign, 1900, 38x28", EX 190.00
Frisco Line, pocket mirror, train by waterfall 65.00
Frontenac Peanut Butter, pail, red/gold/wht/blk, 3½x3", NM 27.00
Frostee, tin sign, bottle cap form, 3-color, 28", EX 175.00

Hartford Fire Insurance Company sign, painted and molded, in gilt-frame marked Hartford, 26" x 32", $1,400.00.

Fry's Caracas Chocolate, tin ruler, folding, 1915, 12x3¾" 25.00
Game Fine Cut Tobacco, store bin, birds, 1920s, 7x11x8", VG ...250.00
Ganong's Chocolates, fr cb sign, Deco picnic, 1920s, 22x13" 95.00
Garland Stoves, pocket mirror, factory scene, EX.........................65.00
Glendora Coffee, tc, Bertel litho, '30, 8x6½x6½", EX 200.00
Globe Ranges, die-cut bookmark, EX.......................................11.00
Goebel Beer, tip tray, old European man drinking.......................125.00
Golden Eagle Tobacco, cb sign, eagle/flag/shield, '10, 16x10" 100.00
Good Honest Coffee, tin container, 1920, 5½x4½x4½", EX 650.00
Good Luck Baking Powder, tc, horseshoe/clovers, red, 1901, M 25.00
Gooderman & Warts, paper under glass sign, Night Cap, 18x21"..48.00
Goodwin's Tobacco, tin container, paper label, early, 10½" 135.00
Grand Council Cigars, fr cb sign, soldiers, 1870s, 17x14" 170.00
Grant's Cherry Whiskey, tin sign, 2 men/lady, 1910, 13x9", EX .500.00
Grape Cola, syrup bottle, recessed label under glass, 11" 350.00
Grape Nuts, tin sign, To School..., 1900s, 23x20", VG 1,000.00
Grapette, tin sign, purple oval on wht, Stout, 12x24", M 55.00
Grapette, tin sign, 3-color, oval, emb border, 16x27", EX 45.00
Green River Whiskey, tin sign, wood fr, 1899, 42x33", EX 1,500.00
Guernsey's, celluloid pin-bk, pewter pitcher, 1930s, EX 30.00
Gulf Oil, celluloid tape measure, M 30.00
H-O Oats, Bobby Benson code book & code rule, 1935, EX..........40.00
Hamilton-Brown Shoes, cb sign, metal fr, flapper, 1925, VG.........80.00
Hampden Beer, tip tray, handsome waiter, EX............................85.00
Hartford Fire Insurance, plaque, bronze & oak, dtd 1909.............125.00
Hartford Fire Insurance, tin sign, stag, 19x11", NM....................100.00
Helmar Cigarettes, sf tin sign, girl w/pack, 1900, 28x22" 1,200.00
Hercules Powder, tin sign, eastern market, fr, '22, 19x13", EX......40.00
Hershey, tin sign, Drink a Hershey, 6 bottles, 19x55", VG 45.00
Hiawatha Beer, emb tin sign, mc, 1901, 14x10", EX 1,500.00
Hiawatha Tobacco, tin box, gr, sm 65.00

Hires

Charles E. Hires, a drugstore owner in Philadelphia, became interested in natural teas. He began experimenting with roots and herbs and soon developed his own special formula. Hires introduced his product to his own patrons and soon began selling concentrated syrup to other soda fountains and grocery stores. Samples of his 'root beer' were offered for the public's approval at the 1876 Philadelphia Centennial. Today's collectors are often able to date their advertising items by observing the Hires boy on the logo. From 1891 to 1906 he wore a dress; until 1914 he was shown in a bathrobe. From 1915 until 1926, he was depicted in a dinner jacket. The apostrophe may or may not appear in the Hires name; this seems to have no bearing on dating an item.

Booklet, advertising, 1894 ....10.00
Booklet, Merry Rhymes for Thirsty Times 25.00
Buckle, belt; Drink Hires Root Beer.......................................5.00
Checkerboard, 1892 ....145.00
Coaster, ceramic, Mettlach, rare, 4¾", EX...............................110.00
Dispenser, Drink...It's Pure, nickel lid, spigot, ca 1920 ....800.00
Dispenser, syrup; Muniemaker, brass/marble/glass, 35½" 2,300.00
Glass, soda; Enjoy Nature's..., syrup line, NM..........................45.00
Mug, blk or gray stoneware, block letters, EX 40.00
Mug, frosted glass, Drink Hires Root Beer, lg 6.00
Pocket mirror, Put Roses in Your Cheeks, NM...........................175.00
Pushbar, tin, bl/red/dk bl, 3x30", NM...................................75.00
Sign, celluloid on metal, Drink Hires, girl, 10x7", EX...................375.00
Sign, curved porc over steel, bottle figural, 29x8", NM.................45.00
Sign, paper, pop-eyed soda jerk, 5x13" 125.00
Sign, tin, bl & wht w/brn bottle, 18x56", VG 40.00
Sign, tin, bl/wht striped ground, brn bottle, 11x32", M................55.00

Sign, tin, bottle figural, brn w/orange label, 58x16", M 135.00
Sign, tin, Drink Hires in Bottles, girl, 9x6½", EX 150.00
Sign, tin, It's High Time for..., 1930s, 42x14", NM.....................65.00
Sign, tin, red/bls/wht, 1940s, 19x28", NM 55.00
Sign, window; paper, Thirsts...Suffocated..., 7x22", M.................75.00
Tire cover, canvas, for spare, 29" dia, EX................................200.00
Tray, Just What the Doctor..., 1914, EX.................................400.00

Holland's Ice Cream, tray, windmill, rectangular, EX 25.00
Holsome Bread, tie clasp, 50th Anniversary, 1915-1965, M 15.00
Home Light & Stove Co, tip tray, Victorian lady in kitchen.........75.00
Honey Sweet Cones, tc, Wheeling Can Co, 15x12" dia, EX 250.00
Hood's Sarsaparilla, stand-up counter display, owls, 19x14"........280.00
Horlacher Brewing, cb sign, Betsy Ross/flag, 1908, EX 250.00
Hotel Lee, porc sign, 1915, 10x8½", M.................................275.00
Howard Johnson's Ice Cream, plate, china, 1940s, NM 20.00
Howell's Orange Julep, paper sign, 1920s, 9x28", NM...............225.00
Howell's Orange Julep, syrup bottle, label under glass, 13" 550.00
Howell's Root Beer, tin sign, 12x23½", NM.............................40.00
Hubig's Pies, tip tray, factory scene, 1906, EX..........................75.00
Hudson Bay Tea, tin container, red ground, 3x3x5½", EX 95.00
Hudson Insurance, flat silver metal sign, early, 20x14", EX............50.00
Hunter Cigars, tin sign, wood fr, fox hunters, 1910, 31x23" 250.00
Hyroler Whiskey, tip tray, man in tuxedo, EX 55.00
Indian Crown Cigars, tin sign, 1912, 13x19", EX.....................550.00
Indianapolis Brewing, tray, 3 old men at fireplace, EX 125.00
Iroquois Beer, shopping bag, Indian, 1930s, M 10.00
Iroquois Brewery, tip tray, Indian in headdress, 1910, NM 120.00
Ivory Soap, metal & glass soap dispenser, 1923, 5½x6½x3".........45.00
Jam Boy Coffee, tc, Continental Can litho, '30, 5x4x4", VG......130.00
Jap Rose Soap, fr cb sign, doll gets bath, 1910, 28x38", EX.........285.00
JB Pace Scroll Cut Twist, tin container, 1880s, 4x6", G..............65.00
JH Cutter Whiskey, tray, From Sunrise..., ship, '15, 17x14".........325.00
Johnson's, first-aid manual, 140-pg, 1918, 6x8½", M.................40.00
JP Coats, wooden wagon, buckboard seat, 32x25x43", EX 825.00
JP Coats Spool Cotton, paper litho sign, 1895, 23x17", EX 165.00
JP Coats Thread, spool cabinet, oak, swivel base, '10, 23"....... 1,200.00
Kansas City Brewing, tray, blonde w/tray, pre-pro, EX 225.00
Keen's Mustard, wooden box, 12x22x4½", EX...........................44.00
Keen's Mustard, wooden box, 7x12x11", EX.............................20.00
Kelly Tires, tin sgn, lady w/head through tire, mc, EX..................875.00
Kendall's Spavin Cure, paper sign, 1890s, 42x28", EX 275.00
Kentucky Dew Whiskey, shot glass, cut panels, etched 12.50
Keystone Mincemeat, bucket, 1918, 9½x13x13", NM................100.00
Kik Cola, palm press, tin, red/wht/blk, Fr, 10x3½", EX 35.00
Kill-Em-Quick Gopher Poison, tin sign, 1920s, EX....................18.00
King Cole, palm press, porc, 9-color, 8x3", VG.........................90.00
King Cole, porc pushbar, yel/blk/red, minor chips, 3x30"............45.00
King Cole Coffee, tc, Am Can litho, 1930, 6x4x4", EX..............200.00
Kist, tray, sailor girl by giant bottle, 1930s, EX 115.00
Kodak, cb sign, canoe scene, blk/wht, 18x24", EX 110.00
La Belle Chocolatiere, fr tin sign, ca 1910, 39x27", EX..............750.00
La Corona, rvpt sign, blk w/gold, 11" dia, EX 65.00
Laflin & Rand, fr cb sign, 4 soldiers, 1900s, 24x43", EX.............295.00
Lambertville Rubber, paper sign, ca 1920, 41x28½", EX.............250.00
Lash's Lemonade, paper sign, 1920s, 8x14", NM 100.00
Laurier Cigars, sf tin sign, 1915, EX 440.00
LC Tiffany, fr tin sign, ca 1900, 13x15", EX............................275.00
Lee Union Overalls, cb sign, Nat'l Printing, 22x44", VG 295.00
Lighthouse Cleanser, tin sign, 1920s, 13x9", M........................300.00
Lion Coffee, wooden bin, lift top, 1900, 27x21x20", NM...........550.00

Lipton Tea, tin sign, wood fr, ca 1910, 13", EX.................................45.00

Log Cabin Syrup

Log Cabin Syrup tins have been made since the 1890s in variations of design that can be attributed to specific years of production. Until about 1914, they were made with paper labels. These are quite rare and highly prized by today's collectors. Tins with colored lithographed designs were made after 1914. When General Foods purchased the Towle Company in 1927, the letters 'GF' were added.

A cartoon series, illustrated with a mother flipping pancakes in the cabin window and various children and animals declaring their appreciation of the syrup in voice balloons, was introduced in the 1930s. A Frontier Village series followed in the late 1940s. A schoolhouse, jail, trading post, doctor's office, blacksmith shop, inn, and private homes were also available. Examples of either series today often command prices of $75.00 to $200.00 and up.

Bank, glass cabin figural, EX 32.00
Can opener, Towle's, metal..12.00
Syrup tin, bear in door, cartoon ends, Towle's, 5-lb.....................140.00
Syrup tin, blacksmith, 33-oz...135.00
Syrup tin, boy w/lasso, 1-lb..110.00
Syrup tin, cartoon all sides, sm...110.00
Syrup tin, children, man by pump, Towle's, 33-oz.........................150.00
Syrup tin, children playing, Towle's, 33-oz, NM............................135.00
Syrup tin, Dr RU Well, cartoon style, rare......................................150.00
Syrup tin, Express Office, coach, Towle's, 33-oz............................150.00
Syrup tin, Frontier Inn, cowboys & horse, 5-lb..............................220.00
Syrup tin, Frontier Jail, 12-oz...68.00
Syrup tin, hand w/finger pointing on top, Towle's, med sz...........165.00
Syrup tin, Home Sweet Home, 12-oz...75.00
Syrup tin, red, 5-lb..50.00
Syrup tin, Stockade School, Towle's, 33-oz....................................150.00
Syrup tin, Wigwam, 1-lb, 4x3¼x3½"...175.00
Syrup tin (bank), woman & girl in door, 1-lb, EX.............................45.00
Teaspoon...17.50

Log Cabin Chewing Tobacco, tin sign, cabin, 1907, EX...............225.00
Louis Berdgoll Brewing, goblet, founder/logo.................................30.00
Lowney's Chocolates, die-cut tin sign, couple, '10, 27x20".........575.00
Lowney's Cocoa, trolly card, cb litho, 1920s, 11x21", EX............225.00
Lucas Paint, window sign, Makes Pretty Homes, 16x15", pr..........50.00
Luden's Cough Drops, tip tray, 5¢ box, Shonk litho, 1920, NM....80.00
Luxor Certified Talcum Powder, tin container, 1920s, 5x3¼".........20.00
Mail Pouch Tobacco, porc sign, 1930s, 4x15", EX...........................75.00
Mail Pouch Tobacco, store bin, bl, rectangular, EX.......................175.00
Mail Pouch Tobacco, tin container, 10x13x11", EX.......................125.00
Majestic Hams, sf tin sign, cook/ham, 1905, 38x25", EX.........1,450.00
Maple Nut Fudge, tin container, 1⅛x4", EX.....................................12.00
Marseilles Wht Soap, cb sign, Victorian lady, 29x13", EX...........250.00
Marven's Biscuits, porc pushbar, red/wht/blk, 3x30", EX..............65.00
Max Frey, Justice of the Peace, pocket mirror, stag........................55.00
Maxwell House Coffee, cup & saucer, ceramic, Good to..., EX......32.00
Mayo's Cut Plug, porc sign, crowing rooster, 13x6½", EX...........325.00
Mayo's Tobacco, lunch box, collapsible, EX..................................145.00
McClary's Stoves & Ranges, porc flange sign, 12x15", EX.............75.00
McVitie & Price's Biscuits, tin sign, mom/kids, '39, 19x14".........150.00
Mellwood Whiskey, tip tray, shows bottle, EX................................55.00
Mennen's Talcum, pocket mirror, violets, EX..................................55.00
Merit Brand Clothing, emb tin sign, men models, mc, 1910.......475.00

Merrick Thread, spool cabinet, 6-drw, 28x18x17", EX.................200.00
Michelin Tires, Michelin Man ash tray..55.00
Midwest Ice Cream, flange sign, dbl-sided, 12x19", VG................35.00
Miller Beer, neon sign, High Life, On Tap, 3-color...........................50.00
Miller Beer, tip tray, mansion scene, 1940s, NM.............................28.00
Milward's Needles, cabinet, oak, 1-drw, '15, 3x15x12", EX...........50.00

Milwaukee Binders and Mowers match holder, 5" x 3", $95.00.

Mission of CA Orange, tin sign, marching bottles, 12x30", EX......60.00
Mitchell Car, emb tin sign, cars/tires, 1915, 20x14"...................350.00
Mobil Gas, glass tumbler, flying red horse.......................................10.00
Mobil Oil, porc over steel sign on CI stand, early, 24".................245.00
Mogen David, shakers, depression glass, EX, pr..............................15.00
Moldacot Sewing Machines, tin container, 8x2½x1½", EX.............15.00
Monarch Cocoa Tin, Am Can litho, 1925, 1-lb, VG.........................15.00
Monarch Coffee, thermos, Good Pilots..., 1920s, VG......................50.00
Monarch Peanut Butter, pail, Teenie Weenies, '25, 10-oz, EX........65.00
Monarch Tea, cb container w/tin top & bottom, 1925, 8-oz, EX....20.00
Monarch Teenie Weenie, peanut butter can, 55-lb.......................350.00
Monarch Teenie Weenie Toffies, tc, 1928, 1-lb, EX.....................120.00
Monroe Brewing, tray, king w/goblet, pre-pro, EX........................195.00
Monticello Whiskey, tip tray, fox hunters at Monticello, EX..........65.00

Moxie

The Moxie Company was organized in 1884 by George Archer of Boston, Massachusetts. It was at first touted as a 'nerve food' to improve the appetite, promote restful sleep, and in general to make one 'feel better!' Emphasis was soon shifted, however, to the good taste of the brew, and extensive advertising campaigns rivaling those of such giant competitors as Hires and Coca-Cola resulted in successful marketing through the 1930s. Today the term Moxie has become synonymous with courage and audacity, traits displayed by the company who dared compete with such well-established rivals. For more information we recommend *The Book of Moxie* by Frank N. Potter, available at your local bookstore or from Collector Books.

Baseball, Moxie League, Moxie boy..35.00
Bottle, King Size, paper label, orig, 16-oz......................................10.00
Bottle, Moxie, lt gr, 1914 paper label, 7-oz......................................7.50
Bottle, Moxie Nerve Food, Lowell MA, paper seal over cork......100.00
Candy tin, Moxiemobile...100.00
Crate, wood, yel w/red lettering, 1950s, EX....................................45.00
Display, cb diecut, man points finger, 1920, 41x20", G...............125.00
Display, diecut, man sits on case, 1920, 41x20", VG....................125.00
Fan, cb, Eileen Percy, EX..20.00

Fan, cb, girl & soda jerk, sm 37.00
Fan, cb, Lillian MacKenzie, 1919, 8½" 30.00
Gravy boat, girl's face w/banner, swag border, 8", EX 85.00
Match holder, die-cut bottle, VG.................................300.00
Photo, children atop Horsemobile, orig.......................100.00
Plate, Moxie girl, china, NM.......................................60.00
Platter, girl's face w/banner, swag border, 13½x10", EX 60.00
Post card, Moxie Horsemobile.....................................20.00
Sheet music, Just Make It Moxie for Mine, 1904, EX......30.00
Sheet music, Moxie Song, blk/wht cover, 1921 ....8.00
Sign, cb, Moxie boy w/feather, Learn To Drink..., 37x20" ...600.00
Sign, cb, Uncle Sam/2 men (1 soldier) drink, 1940s, 38x29"...500.00
Sign, cb diecut, Moxie boy bending, sm 500.00
Sign, cb diecut, Moxieland, home of Moxie, 29x38", EX 225.00
Sign, tin, bottle shape, ca 1905, 20½" dia 95.00
Sign, tin, Braces First-Chases Thirst, 7x20", EX 135.00
Sign, tin, Drink Moxie 100%, 1920s, 21¼x19⅛", VG 150.00
Sign, tin, Eclipse, 1930s, 54x19", VG 400.00
Sign, tin, hand w/bottle, Drink..., 1950s, 40x20", EX 145.00
Sign, tin, Learn To Drink..., ca 1905, 20x14", VG 500.00
Sign, tin, Moxie boy pointing, 1930s, 41x15", VG 140.00
Sign, tin, Moxie car, lady on horse behind, 1933, 12x17" ...500.00
Sign, tin, Moxie Nerve Food, early Moxie girl, 23x32" 950.00
Sign, tin, Yes! We Sell..., ca 1903, 27½x18¾", EX 150.00
Thermometer, Remember Those Days, orange, rnd 20.00
Thermometer, tin w/wood bk, boy on top, 1914, 38x11½" ...140.00
Thermometer sign, tin, It's Always a Pleasure, 1940s, 24x9"...90.00
Tip tray, Moxie Nerve Food, Moxie girl w/purple sash, 6"...600.00
Tray, girl's face w/banner, swag border, 9¼x5", VG 100.00
Tumbler, Licensed Only for Serving, glass, 4", NM 40.00

Murad Cigarettes, cb sign, c Anadgyros, 1920s, 9x14", VG ...125.00
Nabisco, cb, trolly card, Zu Zu, fr, 1919, 11x21", NM 350.00
Nabisco, die-cut cb display, Zu Zu, w/box, 1919, 12x6", NM...160.00
Nat'l Biscuit, booklet, Inner Seal logo, 1921, 3x6", NM ...40.00
Nat'l Biscuit, cracker box, tin litho, hinged, 7x10x7", VG ...50.00
Nat'l Biscuit, display case, etched glass, 1897, 32x24x24"...500.00
Nehi, flange sign, 2-sided metal diecut, 12x18", EX 60.00
Nesbitt's, porc pushbar, yel/blk/orange/wht, 3x30", NM...50.00
Nesbitt's, tin sign, bottle on blk/wht stripes, 10x28", VG ...40.00
Nestles, store case, rvpt front, 1900, 36x23x23", EX 800.00
New England Furniture, tip tray, maid of New England ...75.00
New Home Sewing Machines, paper sign, ca 1910, 41x28", EX ..100.00
New Home Sewing Machines, tip tray, grandma/boy........125.00
Nichol Cola, tin sign, drum major marching, 28x20", EX ...70.00
Nigger Hair Tobacco, tin pail w/lid, 1890s, 6½x5x5", EX ...150.00
Nova Scotia Fire Ins, porc sign, purple/wht, 12x19", NM ...65.00
Nu-Grape Soda, tin chalkboard, mc w/bottle, EX 32.00
Nu-Grape Soda, tin sign, yel/bl, dtd Mar 9, 1920, NM 100.00
Nu-Grape Soda, tray, flapper in pk w/bottle, VG 50.00
Nunn Busch Shoes, neon sign, 7½x27", NM.................75.00
Nursery Candies, lunch pail, animals/castle, 1-lb 200.00
OFC Bourbon, fr cb sign, hunters/stag, 1890s, 31x22", EX ...250.00
Old Barbee Whiskey, sf tin sign, man/2 girls, 1905, 38x26" ...850.00
Old Crow Rye, sf tin sign, monk w/basket, 1903, 28x22", EX...775.00
Old Dutch Root Beer, tin sign, windmill, 17½x35½", EX ...45.00
Old English Tobacco, fr cb sign, men at fire, 1900, 31x24" ...175.00
Old Master Coffee, tc, Myers litho, 1930, 5x4x4", NM ...170.00
Old Overholt Rye, canvas sign, wood fr, 1913, 37x27", VG ...400.00
Old Overholt Whiskey, fr tin sign, men/dog, 1900, 35x26", EX ..650.00
Old Pepper Whiskey, tray, Rev War soldiers/flag, oval, 17", EX...300.00

Old Reliable Coffee, pocket mirror, man by lg box, 1¾" ...50.00
Old Reliable Coffee, tip tray, portrait, 1910, 4½", NM ...150.00
Old Sarasota Whiskey, tin tray, 1905, 12½" 85.00
Orange Crush, bottle, orig contents & cap, 6-oz 10.00
Orange Crush, bottle, 10-oz, scarce, EX.........................15.00
Orange Crush, fountain glass, etched, syrup line, NM 40.00
Orange Crush, tin blackboard, Stout, 28x19", EX 50.00
Orange Crush, tin pushbar, expandable, orange/gr/wht, EX...55.00
Orange Crush, tin sign, lg bottle, 1920, 14½x19½", VG....200.00
Orange Crush, tin thermometer, mc on lt bl, 16x6", EX ...35.00
Oscar Mayer, weiner mobile, NM 195.00
Pabst Beer, tray, 2 monks in cellar, oval, pre-pro, 18½" ...300.00
Pabst Blue Ribbon, blackboard, cb, bartender, 26x17", EX ...35.00
Pan's Red Pack Candy, wood store canister, 12x10" 125.00
Parcel Lockers, porc flange sign, bl/wht, 9x16½", EX 95.00
Parliament Cigarettes, tin sign, bl/brn/wht, 12x24", VG ...24.00
Patterson's Tuxedo Tobacco, pocket tin, man smokes, NM ...30.00
Paul Jones Whiskey, sf tin sign, Comrades for 81 Yrs, lg, VG ...250.00
Paul Jones Whiskey, sf tin sign, farmer, 1900, 28x22", NM...950.00
Pear's Soap, die-cut bookmark, EX 18.00
Penn Beverage, tin sign, Deco bathing beauty, 24x18", EX...85.00
Penn's Tobacco, tin container, red, 6½x6½x3", NM 75.00
Penzoil, tin sign, mc, 11x35", EX 42.00
Peoples Clothing, pocket mirror, topless woman, EX........125.00

Pepsi-Cola

Pepsi-Cola was first served in the early 1890s to customers of Caleb D. Bradham, a young pharmacist who touted his concoction to be medicinal as well as delicious. It was first called 'Brad's Drink,' but was renamed Pepsi-Cola in 1898.

Ad, newspaper; Pepsi & Pete, 1939, NM 20.00
Bank, vending machine w/6 bottles & cb carrier, Marx, MIB ...40.00
Bottle, dbl-dot logo at top, 1st no return, 1948.............25.00
Bottle, orig paper label, ca 1910 ....30.00
Bottle opener, bottle form, metal 15.00
Clock, glass face w/convex cover, rnd, NM 200.00
Display rack, metal, bottle cap in center, 63x9", EX.......45.00
Fan, Pepsi & Pete, NM 30.00
Jug, syrup; emb glass, ca 1910, 1-gal 300.00
Pencil, mechanical; EX..30.00
Radio, bottle form, decals ea side, 7", VG 12.50
Sign, bottle hangs from thread, war label on bk, 16x9", NM ...55.00
Sign, cb cutout, Pepsi & Pete, beach girl, 12x8½", EX....175.00
Sign, dbl-sided flange, colon between Pepsi & Cola, early ...75.00
Sign, Pepsi Patrol, 2-sided figural standup, 69x30", VG ...295.00
Sign, plastic w/aluminum fr, lights up, NM..................50.00
Sign, plastic 3-D cap, easel bk, minor crack, EX............20.00
Sign, porc, Enjoy..., mc, 1950s, 30x12", NM.................45.00
Sign, tin, early carton & bottles w/paper labels, 1920 .....295.00
Soda machine, bl enameled metal, red/wht logo, 32x43", VG...100.00
Tip tray, Victorian lady in soda fountain, 1890, 7x5", EX ...220.00
Tray, map, MIB 400.00
Tray, 1906 ....450.00
Watch fob, New Bern NC 90.00

Perfection Dyes, cabinet, oak, dbl doors, 25x16x6", EX....220.00
Perfection Java Coffee, store bin, picnic scene, 1900, VG ...150.00
Peter Rabbit Baby Powder, tc, Deco style, '20s, 4x4", EX...50.00
Philips Choice Vegetable Seeds, box, label, 4x29x9", NM ...125.00

Piedmont Cigarettes, chair, wood w/dbl-sided porc insert, 31" ...**155.00**
Pillsbury, tin sign, Germos Flour, 6x13", VG **65.00**
Pioneer Chain Saws, porc pushbar, yel/gr, minor chips **58.00**

Planters Peanuts

Mr. Peanut, the dashing peanut man with the top hat, spats, monocle, and cane, has represented the Planters Peanut Company from 1916 to 1961 when the company was purchased by Standard Brands. He promoted the company's product by appearing on premium giveaways, store displays, jars, scales, and in special promotional events. Among the favored treasures of collectors today are the glass display jars. They come in a variety of styles – they are square, some hexagonal, some barrel-shaped, and others are round. The earliest, issued in 1926, was octagonal and is usually referred to as the 'pennant' jar. Although later reproduced, these are marked 'Made in Italy' on the bottom. The original is embossed on the back panel 'Sold Only in Printed Planters Red Pennant Bags.' In a second octagonal style, this embossed message was replaced with a paper label.

In 1930 a 'fishbowl' jar was introduced, and in 1932 a 'four-corner peanut' jar was issued. The rarest jar of all, the 'football' jar, was also used during the early 1930s. The Planters' square jar followed in the 1930s and was replaced by the 'barrel' jar. The six-sided jar with Mr. Peanut decals and the 'pickle' jar were later. All in all, more than fifteen different styles were developed.

In the late 1930s, premiums such as glass and metal figural paperweights, pens, and pencils were distributed. Post-war items were often made of plastic – Mr. Peanut salt and pepper shakers, mugs, and banks were popular. Today's collectors find a treasure trove of advertising memorabilia depicting that debonair gentleman, Mr. Peanut.

Alarm clock, Mr Peanut **75.00**
Ball, beach; plastic blow-up, Mr Peanut..................**22.00**
Bank, Mr Peanut, 1950s, EX..................**15.00**
Belt, Mr Peanut, MIB **28.00**
Book, color; Mr Peanut, 1968..................**7.00**
Book, color; Mr Peanut & Smokey the Bear..................**20.00**
Book, color; Presidents, Mr Peanut..................**8.00**
Book, paint; Entertaining & Educational, 1950, M..................**16.00**
Booklet, Our Fighting Forces, VG..................**20.00**
Booklet, Your Victory Garden, 1943, EX..................**28.00**
Bookmark, cb, Mr Peanut, 7¾x3"..................**8.00**
Box, cb, Mr Peanut..................**35.00**
Case cutter, Mr Peanut..................**10.00**
Champagne glass, gr plastic..................**10.00**
Cigarette lighter, Bic, Mr Peanut..................**20.00**
Cookie cutter, Mr Peanut, pr..................**20.00**
Costume, Mr Peanut Parade Man, rare..................**950.00**
Coupon, for Planters figural lighter, 1940s..................**8.00**
Doll, cloth, yel/blk, 19", NM..................**20.00**
Golf ball, 3 in box..................**18.00**
Hat, paper, Mr Peanut..................**25.00**
Hat, vendor's, early graphics, unused..................**45.00**
Jar, Barrel, running Mr Peanut, paper label..................**225.00**
Jar, chocolate-covered cashews, paper label, 1944, 4½-oz..................**25.00**
Jar, Clipper, orig lid..................**75.00**
Jar, Fish Bowl, rectangular label..................**100.00**
Jar, Fish Bowl, sq paper label..................**125.00**
Jar, Football, peanut finial..................**300.00**
Jar, frosted label, big knob, rnd..................**45.00**
Jar, Leap Year, orig lid..................**50.00**
Jar, mixed nuts, paper label, orig lid, 1950s, 4½-oz..................**15.00**
Jar, octagon, Pennant 5¢, 7 sides emb..................**200.00**

Jar, octagon, Pennant 5¢, 8 sides emb..................**250.00**
Jar, peanut butter, early Mr Peanut on tin lid, scarce..................**25.00**
Jar, Pennant 5¢, paper label..................**175.00**
Jar, sq, peanut finial, Planters emb ea side, 1934..................**150.00**
Jar, Streamline, tin lid..................**65.00**
Jar, 4-corner, lg blown-out peanut ea corner, M..................**300.00**
Jar, 6-sided, printed yel label..................**60.00**
Mr Peanut, cb figure, 10"..................**6.00**
Mr Peanut, cb figure, 36"..................**15.00**
Mug, pewter, Mr Peanut..................**20.00**
Peanut butter maker, Mr Peanut, plastic, 12¼", NM..................**18.00**
Pencil, mechanical; bl w/Mr Peanut figural top, MIB..................**18.00**
Pin, anniversary; Mr Peanut..................**15.00**
Pin, 70th Anniversary, enameled..................**15.00**
Pin-bk, colorful plastic, set of 5..................**15.00**
Plate, pewter, Mr Peanut, Wilton, ltd ed..................**35.00**
Playing cards, Mr Peanut..................**15.00**
Profit chart, old Mr Peanut..................**25.00**
Radio, figural peanut can, MIB..................**45.00**
Razor, Bic, Mr Peanut..................**15.00**
Spoon, Mr Peanut, gold wash..................**22.00**
Thermos, Mr Peanut..................**25.00**
Tin container, Chopped Peanuts, red, 1952, scarce..................**90.00**
Train set, Mr Peanut, MIB..................**45.00**
Wagon, plastic Mr Peanut, 1950s, M..................**165.00**
Whistle, gr/red, 3½"..................**10.00**

Plow Boy Tobacco, tin lunch box, paper label, EX..................**40.00**
Poll Parrot Shoes, clicker toy, tin litho, old, EX..................**7.50**
Poll Parrot Shoes, parrot statuette, 12", M..................**70.00**
Poll Parrot Shoes, tin whistle, mc, 2", VG..................**15.00**
Popper's Ace Cigars, tc, biplane, oval, 1910, 5½x3", EX..................**160.00**
Post Toasties, cut-out store sign, '15, 10x4", NM..................**1,000.00**
Prestone, porc thermometer, red/wht/bl, 10", NM..................**75.00**
Pride of Virginia, pocket tin, 4½", VG..................**15.00**
Puritan Tobacco, pocket tin, lg..................**100.00**

RCA Victor

Nipper, the RCA Victor trademark, was the creation of Francis Barraud, an English artist. His pet's intent fascination with the music of the phonograph seemed to him a worthy subject for his canvas. Although he failed to find a publishing house who would buy his work, the Gramaphone Co. saw its potential and adopted Nipper to advertise their product. The company eventually became the Victor Talking Machine Co. and was purchased by RCA in 1929. Nipper's image appeared on packaged accessories, in ads and brochures. If you are very lucky you may find a life-size statue of him – but all are not old, they have been reproduced! Except for the years between 1971 and 1981, Nipper has seen active duty; and, with his image spruced up only a bit for the present day, the ageless symbol for RCA still listens intently to 'His Master's Voice.'

Clock, His Master's Voice, rotating, 1950s..................**80.00**
Doll, RCA Majorette, wooden, jtd, 1920s, EX..................**650.00**
Doll, RCA Radiotrons, wooden, jtd, by Parrish..................**750.00**
Nipper, chalk, 4½"..................**35.00**
Nipper, papier-mache, glass eyes, 44", EX..................**1,500.00**
Nipper, stuffed plush, mk collar, 1950s..................**145.00**
Puzzle, opera scene, record shape, early..................**45.00**
Radio tube w/Nipper on all 4 sides, MIB..................**15.00**

Record book, Little Blk Sambo, Nipper, 1940 ....35.00
Record duster, Nipper figural hdl 12.50
Record duster, RCA & Nipper 20.00
Shakers, plastic, Nipper figural, 1950s, MIB, pr..........................15.00
Sign, wooden, phonograph & dog..185.00
Watch fob, EX 20.00

R&H Beer, tray, gold letters on woodgrain, 12" dia, EX 75.00
Rainbow Dyes, cabinet, dbl-sided, 1915, 19x12x6¼", VG...........225.00
Ramon's Pills, thermometer, wood, wht ground, 21" 275.00
Ramsay's Biscuits & Chocolates, cb sign, 24x36", EX 250.00
Rand McNally Children's Books, tin sign, dbl-sided elf, M 20.00
Randolf's Macon Cigars, sf ts, couple in reserve, 24x20"..............550.00
Ranier Beer, tray, girl w/arm on bear's head, 13", EX 250.00
Red Dot Cigars, tc, red-faced lady on sides/lid, 5x5x5", EX 60.00

Red Goose Shoes

Realizing that his last name was difficult to pronounce, Herman Giesecke, a shoe company owner, determined to give the public a modified, shortened version that would be better suited to the business world. The results suggested the use of the goose trademark, with the last two letters, 'ke,' represented by the key that this early goose held in his mouth. Upon observing an employee casually coloring in the goose trademark with a red pencil, Giesecke saw new advertising potential and renamed the company Red Goose Shoes. Although the company has changed hands down through the years, the Red Goose emblem has remained. Collectors of this desirable fowl increase in number yearly, as do prices. Beware of reproductions – new chalkware figures are prevalent.

Address book, EX... 6.00
Bank, goose, CI/red pnt, Red Goose School Shoes, 3¾"...............225.00
Bank, M-1585, Save w/Shoes...Kid, tin/worn pnt, 5⅝" 45.00
Bank, M-610, CI/worn red & gold pnt, 3¾" 165.00
Bank, tin, gr w/paper label, rnd, old, 2½", EX 125.00
Clicker, yel, Red Goose logo, 1950s, M..12.00
Figure, goose, chalk, red on gr base, 12", EX 55.00
Marbles, early logo, cb box of 5, EX 50.00
Mirror, floor; shoe store, sm decal, 15½x23" 150.00
Pencil box, wood, sliding top, old, 2x9", EX 85.00
Pencil holder, pencil shape, early, EX..50.00
Puzzle, cb, chain, ca 1925, 3½x6¼", EX 30.00
Shoe holder, wood, 18"..200.00
Shoe horn 12.00
Sign, diecut, boy w/goose by neck, ca 1910, EX............................275.00
Sign, diecut, porc/neon/red pnt, 24", EX 1,400.00
Sign, wood, lights up, goose shape, EX color, NM........................650.00
Tablet, school; Red Goose Rodeo, ca 1935, VG 12.50
Whistle, tin, red/bl/yel..15.00

Red Raven, tray, bird by bottle, sq, 13", EX 150.00
Red Raven Splits, tip tray, It's a Dream, mc, VG 85.00
Red Raven Splits, ts, nude child/dresser, 1900, 27x19"............. 3,500.00
Red Rose Coffee, tin container, full color, 19x27", NM 48.00
Red Rose Tea, tin pushbar, EX 35.00
Red Rose Tea, tin sign, red/gr/wht, 4x23", NM 32.00
Repeater Tobacco, tin container, horseman, 3x3½", NM................20.00
Resinol Soap & Ointment, tip tray, lady's portrait, 1910, 4" 35.00

Richardson's Root Beer, barrel w/spigot, 26x14½", EX.................150.00
Richardson's Root Beer, mug, clear, 5½" 24.00
Rockford Watches, tin sign, girl w/watch, 1900, 23x17", EX.......575.00
Rockford Watches, tip tray, girl in flimsy gown by tree, EX 65.00

Rising Sun Stove Polish paper sign, 29" x 21", $285.00.

Roly Poly

The Roly Poly tobacco tins were patented on November 5, 1912, by Washington Tuttle and produced by Tindeco of Baltimore, Maryland. There were six characters in all – Satisfied Customer, Storekeeper, Mammy, Dutchman, Singing Waiter, and Inspector. Four brands of tobacco were packaged in selected characters; some tins carry a printed tobacco box on the back to identify their contents. Mayo and Dixie Queen Tobacco were packed in all six; Red Indian and U.S. Marine Tobacco in only Mammy, Singing Waiter, and Storekeeper. Of the set, the Inspector is considered the rarest and in mint condition may fetch as much as $1,000 on today's market.

Dutchman, Mayo, EX..400.00
Dutchman, Mayo, NM..550.00
Inspector from Scotland Yard, Mayo, NM.................................. 1,000.00
Singing Waiter, Mayo, EX..600.00
Singing Waiter, US Marine, VG 400.00
Storekeeper, Mayo, NM 650.00

Roly Poly Scotland Yard Inspector, Mayo, EX, $725.00; Mammy, Mayo, EX, $600.00.

Round Trip Cut Plug Tobacco, tc, 1915, 3¼x6¼x5", VG 75.00
Royal Crown Cola, calendar, happy couple, 1945, NM.................30.00

Royal Crown Cola, ts, bottle form, Nehi Corp, 1936, 30" L 40.00
Royal Crown Cola, ts, bottle form, 1936, 58x15", M 135.00
Royal Crown Cola, ts, Enjoy, rectangular, NM 45.00
Royal Purple Poultry Conditioner, tc, mc, 8x6x8", VG.................35.00
Royal Shield Tea, tin container, mc on bl, 9x9x5", EX 48.00
Royal Talcum Powder, tin container, ca 1922, 8x3", EX 25.00
Salada Tea, porc over steel sign, 2-sided teapot, 30x42".........150.00
Salada Tea, porc palm press, mc, 10x2½", NM 95.00
Salada Tea, porc sign, bl/wht, 10x19", VG 50.00
Salada Tea, porc sign, 4-color, rstr..65.00
Salzburger Beer, metal sign, lobster/beer, 1900, 24" dia, EX 550.00
Sanderson's Whiskey, dispenser, glass w/NP spigot, 15½" 475.00
Satin Skin Powder, tin sign, 1903, 44x30", EX 40.00
Sauer's Extracts, cabinet, tin front, 1920, 26x12x8", VG.............500.00
Scandinavian-American Lines, sf tin sign, 22x30", EX...............750.00
Schaefer Beer, rvpt sign, orig fr, 1930s, 13½x21½", NM 200.00
Schlitz Beer, tin litho, winged nymph, EX 275.00
Schlitz on Tap, neon sign, red light, 12x23", EX 135.00
Schuhle's Pure Grape Juice, tin on cb sign, 6¼x9½", EX 75.00
Scotch Gall Cure, tin container, yel/blk, 3½x1" 12.00
Seagram's Whiskey, paper under glass sign, 1904, 34x47", EX 900.00
Sedgwick Rye, fr cb sign, Blks gamble, 1925, 22x13", EX 200.00
Senour's Floor Paint, tin sign, room interior, 1915, 20x14"..........100.00
Silver Gem Chewing Gum, tc, label in lid, Holmwood, 2x5x7" 85.00
Simon Pure Beer, tray, winged hops, post-pro, 13" dia, EX 80.00
Simon's Roosevelt Tobacco, tc, portrait, 1930s, 5x3½", VG 75.00
Smith Kirk Candy, pocket mirror, girl in low-cut dress 95.00
Spider Cigar, flanged tin sign, 1920s, 9½x13", NM....................100.00
Spokane Brewing, tray, stag, pre-pro, EX 140.00
Sprite, Sprite Boy truck, yel w/decals, 1940s, 20", EX 250.00
Squire's Hams, sf tin sign, pig portrait, 1906, 19x14", EX 1,250.00
Squirrel Brand Peanut Butter, tc, Canada Nut Co, 27-oz, EX......150.00
Squirt, display, boy w/bottle, Just Call Me..., 1947, 13", EX 75.00
Squirt, tin blackboard, boy w/bottle, 1950, 28x20", EX................70.00
St Lawrence Flour, porc thermometer, red/gr/wht, 30x8", EX 80.00
Stag Tobacco, tin canister, sm...125.00
Star Soap, paper sign, Sipple litho, ca 1900, 21x13", NM...........550.00
Star Weekly, porc palm press, 11x3", VG....................................38.00
Sultana Peanut Butter, tin container, bail hdl, 1-lb.....................110.00
Sun Insurance, Animal Jingle Book, promo giveaway, 1900s, EX ..10.00
Sunny Monday Soap, cb & wood 3-D sign, 1920, 30x39", VG....150.00
Sweet Caporal, canvas banner, red/wht/gr/blk, 36x50", EX...........22.00
T Eaton, needle tin, 3-color, concave, NM 30.00
Texaco, medallion, 2 scotties/logo, 1940s, 1" dia 17.50
Thompson's Corsets, paper sign under glass, 1902, 10x14", M....325.00
Tip Top Bread, geography wheels, Know Your States 10.00
Toyland Peanut Butter, tin pail, mc litho, 1920s, 2-lb, VG..........130.00
Traveler's Insurance, pocket mirror, train, EX............................75.00
Turkey Coffee, tc, American Can litho, 1910, 3-lb, EX 550.00
Tuxedo Tobacco, tc, man smokes, 1906, 5x4x3", EX...................135.00
Tuxedo Tobacco, tc, 50th Anniversary, ca 1906, 1-lb, VG 150.00
Uneeda Bakers, bulk cookie box, w/price card, 1923, EX.............30.00
Uneeda Bakers, cb sign, Closed on..., boy, 1926, 14x13", EX.........30.00
Uneeda Bakers, cb display, Uneeda Boy, '26, 50x21", EX...........350.00
Uniform Cut Plug, tc, Am Can litho, 1910s, 3x6x3½", G.............25.00
United Happiness, candy lunch pail, elephant people, 1-lb 250.00
Upper 10, tin sign, Donaldson Art, 12x30", M............................35.00
US Ammunition, sf tin sign, rifle team, 1908, 23x27"............. 1,250.00
US Standard Beer, cb sign, EX color, 1904, 25x20", EX 525.00
Use Beautyskin, pocket mirror, girl in low-cut dress, EX...............75.00
Vaseline, cb sign, Toonerville Town comic, 1930s, 17x10", EX 75.00
Venus Pencils, tin container, pencil/Venus, 10", EX.....................22.00
Viceroy Cigarettes, tin sign, mc on wht, 19x17, NM....................25.00

Veda Biscuits paper on cardboard sign, 17" x 22", $300.00.

Washington's Coffee, flange sign, dbl-sided, 4-color, VG...............45.00
Waterman's Fountain Pens, cb stand-up sign, 1903, 12x14" 80.00
Welsbach Lighting, tip tray, mother reads to child, EX 65.00
Wessen Oil, bl-banded beater jar 55.00
White Rock Table Water, tip tray, draped nude on rock 110.00
White Rose, porc flange sign, 2-sided, 4-color, 18", EX.................30.00
Whitebread Extra Stout, sf tin sign, product, '36, 14x9", EX 250.00
Will's Cigarettes, rvpt mirror, tin bk, 8x6", EX 35.00
William Tell Flour, tip tray, Meek litho, 1907, NM......................35.00
Winchester Cigarettes, golf game, 3-fold, 19x12", EX...................14.00
Winner Tobacco, lunch box, EX 165.00
Winston Cigarettes, thermometer, king-sz pack, 13x5", EX...........28.00
Winthrop M Baker Chocolates, cabinet, 27x18x7", EX................275.00
Wise Potato Chips, tin door push, 3½x6½", NM 165.00
WPG Tribune, porc thermometer, yel/blk, 39x8", EX 160.00
Wrigley's Spearmint Gum, tin sign, Shonk Works, 14x20", VG..160.00
Yellow Kid, button, w/top hat & cane, 1915, 1¼", VG.................25.00
Yellow Kid, cigarette button, 2 for 35.00
7-Up, blackboard, emb tin, gr/wht, Nothing Does It..., VG 20.00
7-Up, opener, heavy brass, EX 18.00
7-Up, pushbar, porc, Fresh Up w/..., 3x30", NM.........................25.00
7-Up, tin blackboard, emb, 5-color, 27x18½", EX.......................55.00
7-Up, tin sign, convex, blk/wht, Stout, 36x32", VG 280.00
7-Up, tin sign, Family Pack, Stout, 30", VG................................25.00
7-Up, tumbler, dk gr glass, M 25.00

Walter Baker's Breakfast Cocoa tin sign, ca 1901, framed, 20" x 13", NM, $2,250.00.

Advertising Cards

Advertising trade cards enjoyed a heyday during the last quarter of the 19th century when the printing process known as chromolithography was refined and put into popular use. The purpose of the trade card was to acquaint the public with a place of business, a product, or a service. Most trade cards range in size from 2" x 3" to 3" x 5"; however, some are found in both smaller and larger sizes. Four categories of particular interest to collectors are:

Mechanical – those which achieve movement through the use of a pull tab, fold-out side, or rotating disk.

Metamorphic – cards that transform a person or a thing from a 'before' to an 'after' condition, which of course represents a marked improvement immediately upon use of the featured product.

Hold-to-light – cards that reveal their design only when viewed before a strong light.

Diecuts – cards in figural forms such as the Heinz pickle series. Diecuts are usually in the shape of the advertised product or a theme-related object. For a more thorough study of the subject, we recommend *The Advertising Trade Card* by Kit Barry; his address can be found in the Directory under Vermont. When no condition is indicated, the items listed below are assumed to be in near-mint condition.

Sarica Coffee, 5" x 8", $4.00.

Acme Soap, girl in gr coat skating	5.00
Adams Westlake Oil Stove, 2 rats, 'Jim, it's the boss'	7.00
Anderson Co, Solace Plug Tobacco, package & flowers	8.00
AT Co Battle Ax Tobacco, die-cut hand & plug	12.00
Barrett Co Bandit King, woman holding horse's head	7.00
Bay State Fertilizer, carrot man w/top hat	9.00
Bay State Fertilizer, turnip man w/hat	9.00
Beckwith Round Oak Stoves, boy w/umbrella	7.00
Best Tonic, Mrs Grover Cleveland	7.00
Boss Watch Case, boat, deep-sea diver, sunken ship	6.00
Boss Watch Case, man playing banjo	8.00
Bowker Fertilizer Co, carnation	5.00
Burley & Tyrrell Pottery, die-cut 2-hdld urn	8.00
Burt Shoes, boy in lady's shoe, 2 girls	5.00
Bussy, McLeod Stove Co, 1887 gold coin in tree	8.00
Capadura Tobacco, woman leaning on chair	9.00
Celluloid Collars, Chinese girl smoking pipe	6.00
Celluloid Eye Glasses, specs, old couple, pallet	7.00

Chanfraus Kit, 2 men arm in arm	8.00
Charter Oak Range, girl & boy by fence	5.00
Child's Tiger Rake, man on horse-drawn rake	12.00
Clarks ONT Thread, drummer boy	4.00
Clarks ONT Thread, sailor boy hoisting flag	5.00
Coats Thread, butterfly & thread spool	4.00
Coats Thread, Little Maid	4.00
Corrugated Elbow Co, before & after kitchen scene	9.00
Cribben Universal Stoves, man waving out window	4.00
Davis as Alvin Joslin, man w/hoe over pumpkin	8.00
Dinsmore's Cough & Croup Balsam, baby's head, flowers	4.00
Eclipse Wringer, girl, doll w/parasol in carriage	5.00
Emory's Standard Cure, girl holding branch	6.00
Empire Wringer, 3 dressed foxes w/baby fox	5.00
Florence Oil Stove, 12 people on a picnic	8.00
French Co Pottery, artist painting vase	12.00
Guy Brothers Crockery Importers, pitcher diecut	6.00
Hartshorn's Cough Balsam, birds in old tree	5.00
Hub Gore Shoe Elastic, Uncle Sam automation	15.00
Indian Queen Perfume, Indian maid among flowers	9.00
Ivers & Pond Pianos, girl in muff & pk coat skating	4.00
Ivorine Cleanser, 3 kids w/pots & pans instruments	5.00
Keystone Watch Case, lawyer holding book	8.00
Kineo Stoves, 2 girls skating together, boy falling	4.00
Kirk Soap, Black w/cotton over his shoulder	6.00
Kirk Soap, Columbia w/eagle	5.00
Lavine Soap, 7 Chinamen dancing around box	7.00
Libby Prison War Museum, picture of the prison	12.00
Lovell Mfg Co, Adams Wringer, boy & girl w/wringer	6.00
Magee Furnace, girl in yel dress eating cookies	6.00
Magee Furnace, 2 child chefs carring cake in kitchen	9.00
Maillard Chocolate, boy lifting boy into cupboard	6.00
Marks Chair Co, Columbus, Brownies & Uncle Sam	15.00
Marsh, J Co, Boston, French soldier w/sword	5.00
Marshes Fine Soaps, 'The Duel About the Twins'	8.00
Merchants Gargling Oil, baseball, A Close Affair	10.00
Merchants Gargling Oil, baseball, Put It There	10.00
Merrick Thread, 2 boys, 2 girls at tug-of-war	5.00
Michigan Stove Co, Garland Stove, baby in highchair	6.00
Milwaukee Harvester, girl in wheat holding flowers	6.00
Morse's Pills, Indian on horseback spearing bear	9.00
NY Miniature Opera Co, Splendid Fellow	12.00
People's Church, Boston, pictures 1 brick	5.00
Portland Stoneware Co, 5 pcs of pottery	7.00
Reynolds Shoes, girl & fish pond	4.00
Rice's Seeds, 'A Corned Indian'	10.00
Rice's Seeds, couple in bed, lg tomato	8.00
Rice's Seeds, Irish potato-man w/pipe	10.00
Sine's Tar, Cherry & Hoarhound, Turkish ladies	9.00
Standard Sewing Machine, boy w/girl in wheelbarrow	5.00
Strasser Co Silk Segars, roses in urn	4.00
Union Web Hammock, man in hammock reading newspaper	9.00
Vanity Fair Cigarettes, 4 packages of cigarettes	10.00
Vienna Spring Mold, chef w/mold & plate of cakes	8.00
Williams & Clark Fertilizer, potato-man in tree	10.00
Willimantic Thread, bird carrying spool under wing	5.00

Advertising Dolls

Whether your interest in ad dolls is fueled by nostalgia or strictly because of their amusing, often clever advertising impact, there are several points that should be considered before making your purchases.

Condition is of utmost importance; never pay book price for dolls in poor condition, whether they are cloth or of another material. Restoring fabric dolls is usually unsatisfactory and involves a good deal of work – seams must be opened, stuffing removed, the doll washed and dried, and then reassembled. Washing old fabrics may prove to be disastrous – colors may fade or run, and most stains are totally resistant to washing. It's usually best to leave the fabric doll as it is.

Watch for new dolls as they become available. Save related advertising literature, extra coupons, etc., and keep these along with the doll to further enhance your collection. Old dolls with no marks are sometimes challenging to identify. While some products may use the same familiar trademark figures for a number of years – the Jolly Green Giant, Pillsbury's Poppin' Fresh, and the Keebler Elf, for example – others appear on the market for a short time only and may be difficult to trace. Most libraries have reference books with trademarks and logos that might provide a clue in tracking down your doll's identity. Children see advertising figures on Saturday morning cartoons that are often unfamiliar to adults, or other ad doll collectors may have the information you seek.

Advertising dolls are still easy to find and relatively inexpensive, ranging in cost from $1.00 to $100.00, with the average price at about $10.00. They are popular with children as well as adults. For a more thorough study of the subject, we recommend *Advertising Dolls*, by Joleen Robison and Kay Sellers. Joleen is our advisor; she is listed in the Directory under Kansas.

A&W Restaurant, teddy bear	15.00
Allied Van Lines, girl, orange jumper, brn hair, 1970s, 17"	12.00
Anahist, Hello Dolly, 12"	10.00
Aunt Jemima, Diana, cloth, ca 1905, 15"	65.00
Aunt Jemima, Wade, cloth, ca 1924	60.00
Bear Brand Hosiery, Mama Bear, cloth, bl/yel skirt, 9"	95.00

Bear Brand Hosiery Bears, painted cloth, 9½", $100.00 each.

Beaver Enterprises, beaver, felt/plastic/cloth, 12"	10.00
Big Boy Restaurant, Dolly, cloth, red dress, mk, 1978, 14"	8.00
Big Boy Restaurant, Nugget, tan, mk on collar, 1978, 14"	8.00
Blue Bonnet Margarine, Bl Bonnet Sue, plastic, bl dress, 8"	8.00
Buddy Lee, compo, dungaree trousers, plaid shirt, 12½"	150.00
Buddy Lee, Minute Men, plastic, station uniform, 12"	200.00
Bumble Bee Tuna, Yum Yum Bumble Bee, inflatable plastic, 24"	5.00
Burger King, Magician, MIB	10.00
Campbell Kids, compo, Horseman, 1947, 14", pr, M	400.00
Campbell's, cheerleader, vinyl, 1957-1961, 9½", M	35.00
Campbell's, chef, vinyl, unmk, 1966-1968, 10", M	30.00

Ceresota, boy, uncut cloth, 1920s	200.00
Collingbourne Cotton, Happy Family, cutout	135.00
Cream of Wheat, Blk chef, cloth, 1930, 20"	65.00
Cream of Wheat, man, cloth, hat/apron, 1920s premium	75.00
Douglas Gas, Freddy Fast, MIB	15.00
Dy-O-La Dye, girl, uncut cloth, 1920s	125.00
Eskimo Pies, boy, brn parka/pants, unmk, 1964, 15", VG	12.00
Farmer's Sweet Corn, barefoot farm boy in bibs & hat, cloth	85.00
General Electric, Bandy, Maxfield Parrish, Cameo Doll Co, M	450.00
General Food, minx, stuffed cloth, 1953	25.00
Gerber, baby, flirty eyes, anniversary, blk, MIB	40.00
Gerber, baby, vinyl, yel hair, 1972, 11"	22.00
Green Giant, Little Green Sprout, vinyl	8.00
Hostess Bakery, Happy Ho Ho, inflatable, 1970s, 48"	8.00
Just Rite Restaurant, Li'l Miss Rite, jtd vinyl, 1965, 8"	35.00
Kellogg's, Chiquita Banana, uncut cloth, 1940s	32.00
Kellogg's, Dig 'Em Frog, 1973, G	15.00
Kellogg's, Jack Spratt, cloth litho, early 1900s, 14"	80.00
Kellogg's, Papa Bear & Baby, uncut cloth, 1920s, ea	75.00
Kellogg's, Pop, hard vinyl, 8", EX	15.00
Kellogg's, Snap puppet, EX	15.00
Kellogg's, Tom the Piper's Son, stuffed	90.00
Kentucky Fried Chicken, Colonel, nodder, mk, 7"	18.00
Magic Chef, chef in tuxedo, EX	20.00
McDonald's Corp, Hamburger Cop, knob moves head, jtd, 7"	15.00
MD Bathroom Tissue, Cheshire Cat, cloth litho, unmk, 11"	15.00
Miss Revlon, hard plastic, EX clothes, 18"	50.00
Mohawk Carpet, Mohawk Tommy, Indian, cloth, 16"	15.00
Nestle, rabbit, brn/tan plush, vinyl eyes/teeth, 1976	10.00
Old Crow Whiskey, hard plastic, unmk, 1950, 4½"	12.00
Pepperidge Farm, goldfish, gold cotton, stuffed, 16"	8.00
Peters' Weatherbird Shoes, cloth, compo head/arms, 1920, 22"	150.00
Quaker Crackle, boy, dtd 1930, uncut, rare	125.00
Seiko Watch, robot, inflatable, 21"	8.00
Sweets Candy, Peppermint Pattie, bean bag, 1973, 10"	15.00
Trix, rabbit, vinyl	18.00
Vermont Maid Syrup, girl, jtd vinyl, 15", M	50.00
Vlasic Pickles, Vlasic Stork, inflatable, 1977, 53"	10.00

African Art

These artifacts of the African nation are a unique form of folk art, of interest not only in relation to the craftsmanship evident in their making, but because of the culture they represent.

Axe, openwork iron blade w/incising, wood/copper hdl, 17"	250.00
Bronze, Dahomey, 2 carry male figure on litter, eng, 14" L	300.00
Crook, Dogon, hooked form, pierced crest, wood, 29"	325.00
Cvg, Zaire, ivory, relief lizard/bands, cowrie shells, 6"	175.00
Figure, Ashanti, wood, female nursing child, 1935, 15x6"	200.00
Figure, Bambara, wood, standing female, tack eyes, rpr, 25"	475.00
Figure, Bobo, female w/conical breasts, scarification, 9½"	275.00
Figure, Cameroon Grasslands, wood, monkey on stool, 14"	400.00
Figure, Dogon, wood, male equestrian/upright female, 21"	550.00
Figure, Lunca/Chokwe, wood, female, scarifications, 12"	550.00
Figure, Mambila, abstract male w/exaggerated features, 14"	300.00
Figure, Nanji, wood/glass bead eyes, stylized human, 11"	450.00
Figure, Yoruba, wood, female twins, cvd/rpt, 1950s, 9½"	400.00
Fly whisk, Ashanti, giltwood/goat hair, much cvg, 1950, 11"	375.00
Funerary head, Ashanti, earthenware, lg features, 7¾"	160.00
Lock, door; Dogon, 2 female figures on block form, 9"	225.00
Lock, granary; Bambara, 2-part human form, incising, 16½"	130.00

Mask, ceremonial; cvd/pnt, 1900, 8x4½" 125.00
Mask, dance; Dogon, kanaga face, pierced eyes, lozenges, 30" 600.00
Mask, Gabon, wood/pnt, wht face w/pierced eyes, 15" 850.00
Mask, Lega Fence; Congo, wood/fibre/wht pnt, 7" 300.00
Mask, Liberia, wood/fur, exaggerated nose/brows, hinged jaw......350.00
Mask, Mama, antelope w/slender horn, flared mouth, 23½" 300.00
Mask, pendant; Bapende, lead, tripartite hair, 1½", pr 110.00
Mask, Pende, wood/cloth/hair/feathers/raffia, 7x12" 225.00
Mask, Senufo, cvd wood, open jaws, bared teeth, pnt, 26" 700.00
Mask, water spirit; Ijo, lizard on forehead, lineation, 27" 180.00

Punu 'White Face' mask, remains of white kaolin and red pigment, 13", $2,000.00.

Staff, Basonge, cvd wood, maternity group on grip, 12" 375.00
Staff, Mendi, wood, cvd human head finial, 26" 550.00
Stool, Bambara-Bobo, wood, kneeling human form, 5¼" H 120.00
Tambourine beater, Baule, antelope head form, worn pnt, 10" 150.00

Agata

Agata is New England peachblow (the factory called it 'Wild Rose') with an applied metallic stain which produces gold tracery and dark blue mottling. The stain is subject to wear, and the amount of remaining stain greatly affects the value. It is especially valuable (and rare) when found on peachblow of intense color. Caution – be sure to use only gentle cleaning methods.

Currently rare types of art glass have been realizing erratic prices at auction; until they stablize, we can only suggest an average range of values. In the listings that follow, examples are glossy unless noted otherwise. See also Green Opaque.

Finger bowl, fluted, EX color 875.00
Finger bowl, ruffled, 5", +crimped-edge underplate, 6" 1,450.00
Spooner, crimped top, allover mottling, matt, 5"...................... 1,500.00
Toothpick holder, bulbous, ruffled rim, VG mottling.................375.00
Toothpick holder, sq top, EX color & mottling 675.00
Toothpick holder, tricorn, EX mottling, 2¼"..............................575.00
Tumbler, EX color & mottling, 4" 785.00
Tumbler, NM mottling, 4¾"...950.00
Vase, lily form, 6" 1,750.00
Vase, pyriform base w/cup-like neck, slender form, 7" 1,300.00

Vase, stick neck, mottling at base, 8½" 750.00

Tumbler, allover mottle, 3¾", $785.00; Bowl (or lady's spittoon), 2¾" x 5", $600.00.

Akro Agate

The Akro Agate Co. founded in 1914 primarily as a marble maker, operated in Clarksburg, West Virginia, until 1951. Their popular wares included children's dishes, powder jars, flowerpots, and novelty items along with the famous 'Akro Aggies.' Much of their glass was produced in the distinctive marbleized colors they called Red Onyx, Blue Onyx, etc.; solid opaque and transparent colors were also produced. Most of the wares are marked with their trademark, a crow flying through the letter 'A' holding an Aggie in its beak and one in each claw. Other marks include 'J.P.' on children's pieces, 'J.V. Co., Inc,' 'Braun & Corwin,' 'N.Y.C. Vogue Merc Co. U.S.A,' 'Hamilton Match Co.,' and 'Mexicali Pickwick Cosmetic Corp.' on novelty items. In 1936 Akro obtained the moulds from the Balmer-Westite Co. of Weston, West Virginia. Westite produced a similar line of products for several years. Their ware is drab in color when compared to Akro and is generally unmarked. The embossed Westite logo does appear occasionally on the bottom of some pieces. Westite is commonly accepted as a companion collectible of Akro.

Chiquita

Chiquita tea set, fired-on blue, $28.00.

Creamer, baked-on colors, 1½"..8.00
Creamer, opaque gr, 1½" 5.00
Creamer, opaque turq, lav, or caramel, 1½" 12.00
Creamer, transparent cobalt, 1½"..10.00
Cup, opaque gr, 1½"...4.00
Cup, opaque turq, lav, or caramel, 1½" 15.00
Cup, transparent cobalt, 1½"..7.00

Plate, baked-on colors, 3¾" 4.00
Plate, transparent cobalt, 3¾" 6.00
Saucer, baked-on colors, 3⅛" 1.50
Saucer, gr opaque, 3⅛" 1.00
Saucer, opaque lav, caramel, or yel, 3¼" 7.00
Saucer, transparent cobalt, 3⅛" 2.00
Set, 16-pc, baked-on colors 70.00
Set, 16-pc, opaque colors other than gr 125.00
Set, 16-pc, opaque gr 47.00
Set, 16-pc, transparent cobalt 105.00
Sugar bowl, baked-on colors, open, 1½" 8.00
Sugar bowl, opaque turq, lav, or caramel, open, 1½" 12.00
Sugar bowl, transparent cobalt, open, 1½" 10.00
Teapot, baked-on colors, w/lid, 3" 12.00
Teapot, opaque gr, w/lid, 3" 9.00
Teapot, opaque turq or lav, w/lid, 3" 35.00
Teapot, transparent cobalt, w/lid, 3" 25.00

Concentric Rib

Creamer, opaque colors other than gr or wht, 1¼" 7.50
Creamer, opaque gr or wht, 1¼" 5.00
Cup, opaque colors other than gr or wht, 1¼" 5.00
Cup, opaque gr or wht, 1¼" 3.00
Plate, opaque colors other than gr or wht, 3¼" 3.00
Plate, opaque gr or wht, 3¼" 2.00
Saucer, opaque gr or wht, 2¾" 1.50
Sugar bowl, opaque colors other than gr or wht, 1¼" 7.50
Sugar bowl, opaque gr or wht, 1¼" 4.50
Teapot, opaque colors other than gr or wht, w/lid, 3⅜" ...10.00
Teapot, opaque gr or wht, w/lid, 3½" 9.00

Concentric Ring

Cereal, lg, solid opaque colors, 3⅜" 18.00
Cereal, lg, transparent cobalt, 3⅜" 28.00
Creamer, lg, marbleized bl, 1⅜" 45.00
Creamer, lg, transparent cobalt, 1⅜" 25.00
Creamer, sm, marbleized bl, 1¼" 35.00
Creamer, sm, solid opaque colors, 1¼" 14.00
Cup, lg, opaque lav or yel, 1⅜" 30.00
Cup, lg, opaque marbleized colors 30.00
Cup, lg, opaque pumpkin, 1⅜" 20.00
Cup, sm, transparent cobalt, 1¼" 24.00
Plate, lg, solid opaque colors, 4¼" 6.00
Plate, lg, transparent cobalt, 4¼" 12.00
Plate, sm, solid opaque colors, 3¼" 5.00
Plate, sm, transparent cobalt, 3¼" 12.00
Saucer, lg, solid opaque colors, 3⅛" 4.00
Saucer, lg, transparent cobalt, 3⅛" 6.00
Saucer, sm, solid opaque colors, 2¾" 3.00
Set, 16-pc, solid opaque colors, sm 105.00
Set, 21-pc, marbleized bl, lg 460.00
Sugar bowl, lg, solid opaque colors, w/lid, 1⅞" 18.00
Sugar bowl, lg, transparent cobalt, w/lid, 1⅞" 45.00
Teapot, lg, marbleized bl, w/lid, 3¾" 65.00
Teapot, lg, solid opaque colors, w/lid, 3¾" 35.00

Interior Panel

Cereal, lg, azure bl or yel, 3⅜" 18.00
Cereal, lg, marbleized gr/wht, 3⅜" 20.00
Creamer, lg, marbleized bl/wht, 1⅜" 25.00

Creamer, lg, pk or gr lustre, 1⅜" 14.00
Creamer, sm, azure bl or yel, 1¼" 27.00
Creamer, sm, pk or gr lustre, 1¼" 22.00
Cup, lg, marbleized red/wht, 1⅜" 25.00
Cup, sm, marbleized red/wht, 1¼" 20.00
Cup, sm, pk or gr lustre, 1¼" 8.00
Cup, sm, pumpkin, 1¼" 20.00
Pitcher, sm, transparent gr or topaz, 2⅞" 11.00
Plate, lg, azure bl or yel, 4¼" 12.00
Plate, sm, marbleized bl/wht, 3¾" 7.00
Plate, sm, pk or gr lustre, 3¾" 5.00
Saucer, sm, azure bl or yel, 2⅜" 5.50
Saucer, sm, marbleized red/wht, 2⅜" 5.00
Set, lg, 21-pc, marbleized bl/wht 325.00
Set, lg, 21-pc, pk or gr lustre...................................175.00
Set, sm, 16-pc, marbleized red/wht, MIB 220.00
Set, sm, 16-pc, pk or gr lustre, MIB...........................125.00
Set, sm, 8-pc, marbleized bl/wht, MIB 105.00
Set, sm, 8-pc, transparent gr or topaz 40.00
Sugar bowl, lg, lemonade/oxblood, w/lid, 1⅞" 47.00
Sugar bowl, lg, transparent gr or topaz, w/lid, 1⅞" 20.00
Sugar bowl, sm, azure bl or yel, 1¼" 27.00
Sugar bowl, sm, marbleized bl/wht, 1¼" 25.00
Teapot, lg, lemonade/oxblood, w/lid, 3¾" 47.00
Teapot, sm, azure bl or yel, w/lid, 3⅜" 40.00
Teapot, sm, marbleized bl/wht, w/lid, 3⅜" 40.00
Tumbler, sm, opaque, 2" 40.00
Tumbler, sm, transparent gr or topaz, 2" 6.00

J.P. (Made for J. Pressman Company)

Cup, baked-on colors, 1½".. 4.00
Cup, transparent cobalt w/ribs, 1½" 4.00
Cup, transparent gr, 1½" 25.00
Cup, transparent red or brn, 1½" 30.00
Plate, transparent gr, 4¼" 8.50
Plate, transparent red or brn, 1½" 30.00
Saucer, baked-on colors, 3¼" 1.50
Saucer, transparent cobalt w/ribs, 3¼" 4.00
Set, 17-pc, transparent gr 185.00
Set, 21-pc, baked-on colors 105.00
Sugar bowl, baked-on colors, w/lid, 1½" 10.00
Sugar bowl, transparent gr, w/lid, 1½" 25.00
Teapot, baked-on colors, w/lid, 1½" 13.50
Teapot, transparent gr, w/lid, 1½" 30.00

Miss America

Creamer, forest gr or marbleized orange/wht................39.00
Creamer, wht..35.00
Cup, forest gr or marbleized orange/wht......................32.00
Cup, wht 27.00
Plate, forest gr or marbleized orange/wht 20.00
Plate, wht..15.00
Saucer, forest gr or marbleized orange/wht..................11.00
Saucer, wht..10.00
Sugar bowl, forest gr or marbleized orange/wht, w/lid ...48.00
Teapot, forest gr or marbleized orange/wht, w/lid 90.00

Octagonal

Cereal, lg, dk gr, bl, or wht, 3⅜" 6.00
Cereal, lg, lemonade/oxblood, 3⅜" 20.00

Creamer, lg, beige, pumpkin, or lt bl, closed hdl, 1½" 12.00
Creamer, lg, dk gr, bl, or wht, closed hdl, 1½"...............................5.00
Creamer, sm, dk gr, bl, or wht, 1¼"...10.00
Plate, sm, dk gr, bl, or wht, 3⅜"...4.00
Saucer, sm, yel or lime gr, 3⅜"...5.00
Set, lg, 21-pc, dk gr, bl, or wht..90.00
Set, lg, 21-pc, lemonade/oxblood, closed hdls, MIB.................300.00
Sugar bowl, sm, dk gr, bl, or wht, 1¼"...8.00
Teapot, lg, bl or gr...14.00
Tumbler, sm, pumpkin, yel, or lime gr, 2" 12.00

Raised Daisy

Creamer, yel, 1¾"...35.00
Cup, bl, 1¾"...35.00
Cup, gr, 1¾"...15.00
Plate, bl, 3" 8.00
Saucer, beige, 2½" 6.00
Sugar bowl, yel, 1¾"...35.00
Teapot, bl, 2⅜"...57.00
Teapot, yel, 2⅜"..40.00
Tumbler, bl (no embossed pattern), 2"..55.00
Tumbler, yel or beige, 2" 18.00

Stacked Disc

Creamer, opaque colors other than gr or wht, 1¼" 7.50
Creamer, pumpkin, 1¼"..12.00
Cup, opaque gr or wht, 1¼" 5.00
Pitcher, opaque colors other than gr or wht, 2⅞" 12.00
Pitcher, opaque gr, 2⅞"..8.00
Plate, opaque bl, 3¼"...4.00
Set, 21-pc, opaque colors other than gr or wht 90.00
Set, 21-pc, opaque gr or wht...60.00
Sugar bowl, opaque colors other than gr or wht, 1¼" 7.50
Sugar bowl, pumpkin, 1¼"...14.00
Teapot, opaque colors other than gr or wht, 3⅜" 10.00
Teapot, opaque gr or wht, 3⅜"...9.00
Teapot, pumpkin, 3⅜"..20.00
Tumbler, opaque gr or wht, 2" 5.00
Tumbler, pumpkin, 2" 25.00

Stacked Disc and Interior Panel

Cereal, lg, marbleized bl, 3⅜" 35.00
Cereal, lg, transparent gr, 3⅜"...17.00
Creamer, lg, opaque solid colors, 1⅜"...12.00
Creamer, lg, transparent gr or cobalt, 1⅜".....................................25.00
Creamer, sm, opaque solid colors, 1¼"..10.00
Cup, lg, transparent cobalt, 1⅜"..18.00
Cup, sm, marbleized bl, 1¼"...18.00
Pitcher, sm, transparent gr, 2⅞"..12.00
Plate, lg, opaque solid colors, 4¾" 7.00
Set, lg, 21-pc, opaque solid colors, MIB.......................................225.00
Set, lg, 21-pc, transparent cobalt, MIB...350.00
Set, sm, 8-pc, opaque solid colors, MIB...65.00
Set, sm, 8-pc, transparent cobalt, MIB...115.00
Sugar bowl, lg, marbleized bl, w/lid, 1⅞".......................................40.00
Sugar bowl, sm, transparent gr, open, 1¼".....................................20.00
Teapot, lg, transparent gr, w/lid, 3¾" 35.00
Teapot, sm, transparent gr, w/lid, 2"..17.00
Tumbler, sm, opaque solid colors, 2"..20.00
Tumbler, sm, transparent cobalt, 2" 8.00

Stippled Band

Creamer, lg, transparent gr, 1½" 15.00
Creamer, sm, transparent amber, 1¼"..8.00
Cup, lg, transparent azure, 1½" 18.00
Cup, sm, transparent amber, 1¼" 5.00
Pitcher, sm, transparent amber, 2⅞"..10.00
Plate, lg, transparent amber, 4¼"...7.00
Plate, lg, transparent azure, 4¼"...10.00
Plate, sm, transparent gr, 3¼"...4.00
Saucer, lg, transparent gr, 3¼"...2.00
Set, lg, 17-pc, transparent amber 150.00
Set, sm, 8-pc, transparent gr, MIB...35.00
Sugar bowl, lg, transparent amber, w/lid, 1⅞"................................18.00
Sugar bowl, sm, transparent amber, open, 1¼" 8.00
Tumbler, sm, transparent amber, 1¾"...6.00
Tumbler, sm, transparent gr, 1¾"..7.00

Miscellaneous

Ash tray, bl, Hotel Lincoln..20.00
Ash tray, custard, Hamilton Match Co, w/matches..........................35.00
Ash tray, marbleized bl & wht, scalloped shell 4.00
Ash tray, sq, heavy, unmk, lg 24.00

Ash tray, embossed Akro Agate Ware, 4", $65.00.

Bowl, gr, Graduated Darts, #320...10.00
Bowl, pumpkin, tab hdld, #321 ....18.00
Bowl, yel, Stacked Disc...18.00
Candlestick, custard, assembled lamp parts, pr 15.00
Candlestick, marbleized gr & wht, 3¼", pr....................................65.00
Cornucopia, marbleized bl & wht, #765 ....5.00
Cornucopia, marbleized orange & wht, hand held, #766 ....12.00
Cup & saucer, demitasse; marbleized bl & wht................................10.00
Cup & saucer, demitasse; yel...15.00
Flowerpot, marbleized bl & wht, ribbed top, #293..........................10.00
Flowerpot, marbleized blk & wht, Banded Dart, #301.....................35.00
Flowerpot, pumpkin, #1311, mk Made in USA 45.00
J Vivaudou, apothecary jar, blk 20.00
J Vivaudou, mortar & pestle jar, pk..8.00
Jardiniere, cobalt, bell shaped, 8 darts...24.00
Jardiniere, pumpkin, Graduated Darts, #306 ....18.00
Jardiniere, yel, rectangular, tab hdld, #314....................................16.00
Lamp, boudoir; bl 45.00
Lamp, custard, wall hanging..15.00
Lamp, desk; crystal...18.00
Planter, bl, oval, #654, 6" 5.00
Planter, cobalt, rectangular, #653, 8"...20.00

Planter, pumpkin, Graduated Darts, Japanese garden style.............**65.00**
Powder jar, Apple, gr **125.00**
Powder jar, Colonial Lady, cobalt **100.00**
Powder jar, Colonial Lady, wht...**35.00**
Powder jar, Ivy design, marbleized bl & wht, #323 ....**35.00**
Powder jar, Scotty dog, pk...**40.00**
Powder jar, Scotty dog, transparent ice bl..**125.00**
Tire, pen holder, Goodrich Tires, marbleized orange & wht **8.00**
Westite, pot, gr, mk A Magnum Product, 2¾" **8.00**
Westite, pot, marbleized brn & wht, plain band, unmk, 6" **18.00**
Westite, vase, marbleized brn & wht, tab hdls, unmk, 6" **12.00**
Westite, vase stand, bl, 4" sq...**10.00**

Alexandrite

Alexandrite is a type of art glass introduced around the turn of the century by Thomas Webb and Sons of England. It is recognized by its characteristic shading – pale yellow to rose and blue. Although it was also produced by other companies, only examples made by Webb command premium prices. Prices for Alexandrite (as well as many other types of fine art glass) have been erratic for several months; values suggested below are average.

Bowl, irregular ruffled rim, 3x5" **650.00**
Compote, Optic Dia Quilt, sapphire-bl rim, Webb, 1⅝x5¾" **985.00**
Finger bowl, swirled, 5¼", +6½" underplate **835.00**
Goblet, floriform, irreg stem/ribbed petal bowl, Webb, 9" **1,750.00**
Toothpick holder, ruffled edge, Webb.. **1,000.00**
Vase, Honeycomb, ruffled, slim ribbed neck, 12¾"................... **1,200.00**
Vase, jack-in-the-pulpit; Honeycomb, crimped, 4x3½" **925.00**
Vase, 2 lilies on S-curve metal branch w/3 leaves, 9" L **1,500.00**

Alhambra China

A line of dinnerware made in Vienna during this century, the Alhambra pattern is strongly geometric with bold colors and gold trim. It is marked with the line name and the country of origin.

Candy bowl, folded rim, 4 shell ft, 8½x6" **40.00**
Creamer & sugar bowl, w/lid, 2½", 4¾" **110.00**
Cup & saucer, bouillon; dbl hdls **58.00**
Jam jar, hdls, Austria, w/lid & underplate.....................................**110.00**
Pitcher, 8½x4¾" **135.00**
Plate, 6" **20.00**
Plate, 8" **30.00**
Teapot, openwork, scalloped top, 4½" **135.00**

Almanacs

The earliest evidence indicates that almanacs were used as long ago as Ancient Egypt. Throughout the Dark Ages they were circulated in great volume and were referred to by more people than any other book except the Bible. *The Old Farmer's Almanac* first appeared in 1793 and has been issued annually since that time. Usually more of a pamphlet than a book (only a few have hard covers), the almanac provided planting and harvesting information to farmers, weather forecasts for seamen, medical advice, household hints, mathematical tutoring, postal rates, railroad schedules, weights and measures, 'receipts,' and jokes. Before 1800 the information was unscientific and based entirely on astrology and folklore. The first almanac in America was printed in 1639 by William Pierce Mariner; it contained data of this nature. One

of the best-known editions, Ben Franklin's *Poor Richard's Almanac*, was introduced in 1732 and continued to be printed for twenty-five years.

By the nineteenth century, merchants saw the advertising potential in a publication so widely distributed, and the advertising almanac evolved. These were distributed free of charge by drug stores and mercantiles, and were usually somewhat lacking in information, containing simply a calendar, a few jokes, and a variety of ads for quick remedies and quack cures.

Today their concept and informative, often amusing text make almanacs popular collectibles that may usually be had at reasonable prices. Because they were printed in such large numbers and often saved from year to year, their prices are still low – most fall within a range of $4 to $15. Those printed before 1860 are especially collectible. Quite rare and highly prized are the Kate Greenaway 'Almanacks,' printed in London from 1883 to 1897. These are illustrated with her drawings of children, one for each calendar month.

1810, Howe's, Greenwich, 32-pg, EX..**100.00**
1812, Howe's, Greenwich, 32-pg, EX...**75.00**
1816, Howe's, Greenwich, 30-pg, VG..**20.00**
1819, Howe's, Enfield, 32-pg, EX...**30.00**
1830, New England Anti-Masonic, Boston, Marsh & Co, VG **45.00**
1831, New England Anti-Masonic, Boston, Marsh & Co, VG......**30.00**
1833, New England Anti-Masonic, Boston, Souther, 48-pg, G **27.00**
1851, Cultivator, illus, 32-pg **3.00**
1868, Scovill Farmer's/Mechanics **10.00**
1870, Herricks, EX **8.00**
1885, Green's Diary, Woodbury, NJ, color, 18-pg, VG...................**10.00**
1890, Engleside, EX...**10.00**
1892, Shaker, NY, 32-pg, EX..**30.00**
1905, Armour, EX...**12.00**
1913, Internat'l Harvester, EX.. **6.00**
1914, Calumet, EX.. **5.00**
1921, Foley's, EX **5.00**
1923, Spalding Official Athletic, EX... **7.50**
1923, Velvet Joe's Tobacco, VG..**25.00**
1930, Dawn's Directory, EX.. **3.00**
1936, Lum & Abner, EX..**20.00**
1938, Illinois Herb Co, Indian cover, EX...**15.00**
1938, Kellogg's Housewives', EX... **3.00**
1939, Dr Miles', EX.. **3.00**
1940, Dr Jayne..**5.00**
1941, DeLaval, EX **10.00**

Aluminum

Aluminum, though being the most abundant metal in the earth's crust, always occurs in combination with other elements. Before a practical method for its refinement was developed in the late 19th century, articles made of aluminum were very expensive. After the process for commercial smelting was perfected in 1916, it became profitable to adapt the ductile, non-tarnishing material to many uses.

By the late thirties, novelties, trays, pitchers, and many other tableware items were being produced. They were often hand-crafted with elaborate decoration. Russel Wright designed a line of lovely pieces such as lamps, vases, and desk accessories that are becoming very collectible. Many who crafted the ware marked it with their company logo, and these signed pieces are attracting the most interest. In general, 'spun' aluminum is from the thirties or early forties, and 'hammered' aluminum is from the fifties. See also Russel Wright.

Bowl, emb florals, dbl-loop hdl, Cromwell, lg **30.00**

Butter dish, dbl-loop finial, glass insert, unmk..................14.00
Candy container, box shape, 3-section glass insert, 7½" dia...........30.00
Celery tray, World, handmade, fluted, 13" 15.00
Cigarette case, Park 8.00
Nut dish, rnd, unmk, 11".....................................7.50
Plaque, Will Rogers, detailed profile, 1967, 10x16"..................45.00
Scoop, Bl Diamond-Sunbeam Best Coffees, 4½x12" 25.00
Shakers, hammered, pr 12.00
Tray, Buenilum, hand wrought, hdls, 11" dia 10.00
Tray, Farberware, morning-glories, ceramic insert, 11½"...............12.50

AMACO, American Art Clay Co

AMACO is the logo of the American Art Clay Co. Inc., founded in Indianapolis, Indiana, in 1919, by Ted O. Philpot. They produced a line of art pottery from 1931 through 1938 that is today beginning to interest collectors. The company is still in business but now produces only supplies, implements, and tools for the ceramic trade.

Values for AMACO have risen sharply, especially those for figurals, items with Art Deco styling, and pieces with uncommon shapes.

Our advisor for this category is Virginia Heiss; she is listed in the Directory under Indiana.

Figure, #144, Deco head, wht, 6½" 125.00
Figure, #158, Deco head, bright bl, 8".......................185.00
Figure, #158, Deco head, wht, 8"............................150.00
Figure, #211, resting fawn, bright bl, 4½x6¼" 135.00
Figure, seated puma, bright bl, 4¾".........................80.00
Temple jar, #130, yel gloss, w/lid, 11½" 110.00
Vase, #S-3, bl/cream, 3"....................................24.00
Vase, #121, Deco, deep red w/wht int, 7" 85.00
Vase, #13, deep red, early mk, 8x7½"........................95.00
Vase, #4, matt gr, 4½" 30.00
Vase, #42, matt gr w/metallic streaks, 6½" 75.00
Vase, #74, matt gr, stick neck w/wide base, 8" 80.00
Vase, #75, yel, stick neck w/wide base, 5" 55.00
Vase, #86, matt gr w/metallic streaks, 9x8½"................125.00

Vase, #41, ivory with blue rim (rare hand decoration), 9½", $125.00. Same, with no hand work, $95.00.

Amberina

Amberina, one of the earliest types of art glass, was developed in 1883 by Joseph Locke, of the New England Glass Company. The trademark was registered by W.L. Libbey, who often signed his name in script within the pontil.

Amberina was made by adding gold powder to the batch, which produced glass in the basic amber hue. Part of the item, usually the top, was simply reheated to develop the characteristic deep red or fuchsia shading. Early amberina was mold-blown, but cut and pressed amberina was also produced. The rarest type is plated amberina, made by New England for a short time after 1886. It has been estimated that less than 2,000 pieces were ever produced. Other companies, among them Hobbs and Brockunier, Mt. Washington Glass Company, and Sowerby's Ellison Glassworks of England, made their own versions, being careful to change the name of their product to avoid infringing on Libbey's patent. Prices have been erratic at auction for several months; values given below are in the average range. See also Libbey.

Bowl, Daisy & Button, sq, flint, 5½"........................125.00
Bowl, Daisy & Button, sq, 9"................................325.00
Bowl, Invt T'print, flint, NE Glass, 1880s, 3x8"............545.00
Butter dish, Dia Quilt, NE Glass...........................675.00
Canoe, Daisy & Button, Hobbs Brockunier & Co, 8".........285.00
Celery vase, Dia Quilt, fuchsia, sq top, 6"................325.00
Celery vase, Invt T'print, 6½x3¾"..........................350.00
Celery vase, scalloped top, Mt WA, 6½" 400.00
Cordial, trumpet-shaped bowl, 4½"..........................325.00
Creamer, reeded hdl, tricorner top, Mt WA, 3½" 300.00
Cruet, Swirl, amber hdl, cut amber stopper, Mt WA, 6"......365.00
Cruet, T'print, amber hdl, faceted stopper, Mt WA, 5½" 345.00
Cruet, Venetian Dmn, NE Glass..............................350.00
Decanter, gold floral/hdl, ribbed, clear stopper, 9".......350.00
Finger bowl, Honeycomb, scalloped, 5" 150.00
Finger bowl, Invt T'print, florals/ferns, reversed, +plate.............400.00
Finger bowl, ruffled, 2¾x5", NE Glass, +7" plate 350.00
Finger bowl, scalloped, NE Glass, 5½" 170.00

Inverted Thumbprint by Mt. Washington: Spooner, 4", $300.00; Creamer, 5", $350.00.

Pitcher, appl amber ribbed hdl, 7½".........................275.00
Pitcher, bulbous, sq mouth, NE Glass, 6½"..................350.00
Pitcher, Dia Quilt, amber hdl, 4½" 175.00
Pitcher, Drape, sq mouth, bulbous, 7⅛x5½" 295.00
Pitcher, Hobnail, sq mouth, child's sz, 3¾"................195.00
Pitcher, HP florals, jewels, bulbous, clear hdl, 7¾".......245.00
Pitcher, Invt T'print, crimped, gr hdl, 7½" 195.00
Pitcher, Invt T'print, NE Glass, 6½"........................400.00
Pitcher, Invt T'print, ruffled, amber hdl, 5" 125.00
Pitcher, T'print, sq top, clear rope hdl about neck, 5½"...............220.00

Pitcher, tankard; blown, vertical swirl, 13" 65.00
Plate, Dia Quilt, fuchsia, 7" 100.00
Punch cup, Dia Quilt...95.00
Punch cup, Venetian Dmn, barrel form, NE Glass, 2¾x2¼" 125.00
Punch cup, Wheeling 50.00
Spooner, Honeycomb, scalloped, 5" 70.00
Sugar bowl, Daisy & Button, w/lid, 5½" 550.00
Toothpick holder, fuchsia, sq top, 2½" 150.00
Tumbler, Dia Quilt, gold floral/vines, 4" 80.00
Tumbler, juice; vertical ribs, corset shape, NE Glass 185.00
Tumbler, ribbed, EX color 125.00
Tumbler, Swirl, EX color 110.00
Tumbler, Venetian Dmn, EX fuchsia, 6" 135.00
Vase, flared, appl amber ruffle, 10⅛x7⅝"...............................350.00
Vase, lily; EX fuchsia, thin w/vertical ribs, 12" 495.00
Vase, lily; fuchsia, 6", in SP Greenaway holder 400.00
Vase, lily; Mt WA, 9" 350.00
Vase, lily; ribbed, folded top, NE Glass, 7" 330.00
Vase, lily; ribbed, 12x5" 500.00
Vase, lily; 7" 275.00
Vase, stylized floral, swirled, amber petal ft, 11".......................350.00
Wine, fuchsia, ribbed, 4¾" 325.00

Plated Amberina

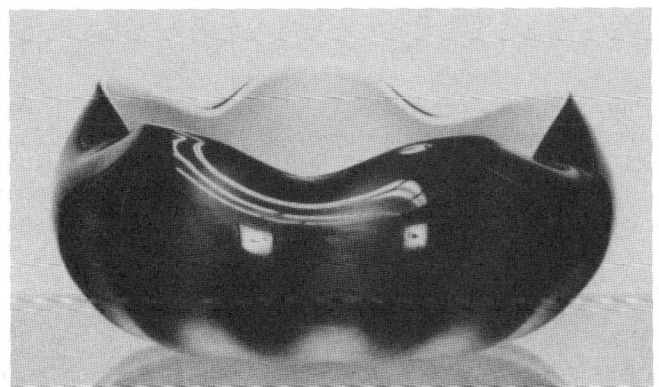

Bowl, turned-in rim, 3½" x 8", $4,700.

Bowl, deeply scalloped/incurvate rim, 3½x8" 4,700.00
Creamer, deep ribbing, amber hdl, EX color 3,650.00
Cruet, amber hdl, tricorn, rnd stopper, EX ribbing, 7" 1,800.00
Cruet, amber hdl/faceted stopper, EX color, 6½", NM 1,700.00
Pitcher, amber hdl, tricorn, EX color & ribbing, 4½" 4,750.00
Punch cup, slightly ribbed top, amber hdl, EX color, 3¾" 1,800.00
Tumbler, EX ribbing & color 1,500.00
Tumbler, lemonade; deep ribbing, amber hdl, EX color 2,500.00

American Encaustic Tiling Co.

A.E. Tile was organized in 1879 in Zanesville, Ohio. Until its closing in 1935, they produced beautiful ornamental and architectural tile equal to the best European imports. They also made vases, figurines, and novelty items with exceptionally fine modeling and glazes.

Inkwell, pk, 6x9" 95.00
Jar, temple; blk, w/lid, 9" 150.00
Lamp base, dk bl, 12+" 125.00
Tile, advertising, 1898 calender affixed to bk, mk on face.............85.00
Tile, Alexander G Bell portrait, bl, mk, dtd 1897, 3" 65.00
Tile, dedication souvenir, bl, 4" 75.00

Tile, HP on cream, sgn Rhead, fr, 6" 135.00
Tile, knight, mc, 10x14x1" 600.00
Tile, McKinley, bl, 3" 65.00
Tile, parrot, 3-color, 12x6" 225.00
Tile, stylized Indian in headdress holds shield, mc, 12x8" 385.00

Tile picture, raised figure of a woman, blue gloss, framed, 3-pc., 18" x 5½", $135.00.

American Indian Art

That time when the American Indian was free to practice the crafts and culture that was his heritage has always held a fascination for many. They were a people who appreciated beauty of design and colorful decoration in their furnishings and clothing; and because instruction in their crafts was a routine part of their rearing, they were well accomplished. Several tribes developed areas in which they excelled. The Navajo were weavers and silversmiths; the Zuni, lapidaries. Examples of their craftsmanship are very valuable. Today even the work of contemporary Indian artists – weavers, silversmiths, carvers, and others – is highly collectible. For a more thorough study we recommend *North American Indian Artifacts* by Lar Hothem; you will find his address in the Directory under Ohio.

Key:
bw — beadword   NE — Northeastern
dmn — diamond   S — Southern
E — Eastern   W — Western

Apparel and Accessories

Before the white traders brought the Indian women cloth from which to sew their garments and beads to use for decorating them, clothing was made from skins sewn together with sinew, usually made of buffalo tendon. Porcupine quills were dyed bright colors and woven into bags and armbands and used to decorate clothing and moccasins. Examples of early quillwork are scarce today and highly collectible.

Early in the 19th century, beads were being transported via pony pack trains. These 'pony' beads were irregular shapes of opaque glass imported from Venice. Nearly always blue or white, they were twice as large as the later 'seed' beads. By 1870 translucent beads in many sizes and colors had been made available, and Indian beadwork had become commercialized. Each tribe developed its own distinctive methods and preferred decorations, making it possible for collectors today to determine the origin of many items. Soon after the turn of the century, the craft of beadworking began to diminish.

Arm bands, Nez Perce, full bw w/florals, 1920, 10x3" **45.00**
Breastplate, Crow, hairpipe/fringe/beads, 1880, 15x13" **550.00**
Breastplate, Sioux, bones/Crow beads/tin cones, 1960, 40x9" **150.00**
Cape, Sioux child's, velvet w/bw eagle, cowrie shells, 1910 ....**35.00**
Coat, Athabascan Chief's, bw florals on hide, fringe, 1890 ....**225.00**
Cuffs, dance; Crow, full bw w/fringe, 1930, 8x6½" **140.00**
Dress, full pony bw yoke, bw fringe/brass thimbles, 1860......... **4,250.00**
Dress, Navajo lady's, woven panel, 4-color terraces/solids **1,100.00**
Dress, Warm Springs girl's, buckskin w/full bw yoke, 1940 ....**350.00**
Gauntlets, Blackfoot, floral bw, fringed, 1880s **375.00**
Gauntlets, Nez Perce, bow/arrow bw on buckskin, 1935, 11" **45.00**
Gauntlets, Yakima, elk/floral bw, buckskin, high tops, 1920.... **1,900.00**
Leggings, Sioux, geometric sinew-sewn bw, gr/bl/red on wht **550.00**
Leggings, Sioux lady's, buffalo hide w/bw, 1880, 18x7" **650.00**
Moccasins, Apache, hide soles/toes, tall muslin tops, 1890............**60.00**
Moccasins, Arapaho, full bw, buffalo hide/sinew sewn, 1880 ....**600.00**
Moccasins, Cheyenne, full bw geometrics, EX work, 1935 ....**300.00**
Moccasins, Cheyenne, full bw geometrics, hide soles, 1900 ....**160.00**
Moccasins, Comanche, hide w/star & cross motif, 1890 ....**45.00**
Moccasins, Crow, buffalo hide w/bw toe & trim, 1880................**175.00**
Moccasins, Iroquois child's, EX pony bead designs, 5½" **90.00**
Moccasins, Kootenai, geometric bw, buckskin/high-tops, 1935 .....**45.00**
Moccasins, Santee Sioux lady's, floral bw/hard sole, 1890 ....**125.00**
Moccasins, Sioux, buffalo hide w/full sinew-sewn bw, 1885 ....**400.00**
Moccasins, Sioux, buffalo hide w/geometric bw toes, 1880 ....**75.00**
Moccasins, Sioux lady's, quillwork on buffalo hide, 1880.............**250.00**
Moccasins, Tlingit, sealskin w/bw on toe, low-tops, 1935 ....**40.00**
Moccasins, Yakima, geometric bw, soft soles, 1930 ....**95.00**

Nez Perce, fully-beaded Dreamer Society vest with florals, ca 1900, $800.00.

Sash, Pueblo, hand woven, fringe, 1950, 4x50" **250.00**
Shirt, Kiowa, pnt Ghost Dance symbols, fringed, 1890, 42" **675.00**
Snowshoes, Athabascan, bentwood/basketry, fancy/pnt, 1880 ....**475.00**
Vest, Crow, EX bw/pnt/ermine & bead fringe on antelope skin ..**550.00**
Vest, Nez Perce, EX bw florals & binding, 1920, lg....................**350.00**
Vest, Nez Perce, floral bw front & bk on elk hide, 1910, M.........**750.00**

Arrowheads and Points

Relics of this type usually display characteristics of a general area, time period, or a particular location. With study, those made by the Plains Indians are easily discerned from those of the West Coast.

Because modern man has imitated the art of the Indian by reproducing these artifacts through modern means, use caution before investing your money in 'too good to be authentic' specimens.

Agate Basin, wht, IL, 6½" **195.00**
Breckenridge Dalton, tan, MO, 4" **30.00**
Bulverde, tan/pk stone, Brewster Co, TX, 2" **10.00**
Clovis, gray, classic, MO, 3¾" **100.00**
Dalton, tan, AR, 3¼", NM **110.00**
Dickson, wht/gray, Scott Co, IA, 2¾", VG **35.00**
Motley, wht, Hale Co, AL, pre-historic, 2¼" **10.00**
Nebo Hill, wht, MO, 4⅛" **35.00**
Pedernales, tan, 3", EX **25.00**
St Charles Dovetail, dk gray, IL, 3" **95.00**
Trinity, blk stone, Cass Co, TX, 3¼".......................................**25.00**

Arts and Crafts

Box, Navajo, silver, stamped, turq cab, sgn M, 1950, 6" L **250.00**
Canoe model, Chippewa, birch bark, 1910, 26" L **35.00**
Cvg, ivory shaman, abalone inlay, wood base, 1900, 4x2"...........**200.00**
Etching, NW Coast, by Ace Powell, 1975, 7x5".............................**55.00**
Frog dish, Kwakiutl, cvd wood, lid on bk, 1985, 9x7" **110.00**
Ledger drawing, Indians on horsebk, 1885, 12x15" **50.00**
Painting, Blue Horse, by Bobby Hicks, mat/fr, 1961, 11x8" **125.00**
Painting, Winter/teepees, Robert Redbird, 1975, fr, 18x24" **235.00**
Print, Arrow Top, by Winold Reiss, mat/fr, 1915, 13x16" **15.00**
Salt & pepper shakers, Paiute, red/wht bw, 1940, 3", pr **5.00**
Toy moccasins, Cheyenne, full bw, 1930, 2x1¾" **20.00**
Weaving, Germantown, geometrics/Xs, 1900, 40x22" **125.00**
Weaving, Navajo, pictorial, eagle & Vallero Star, 70x40" **850.00**
Weaving, Navajo, sandpnt pictorial, Shiprock, 1961, 54x46" **600.00**
Weaving, Navajo, 2 Gray Hills, tight/soft wool, '20, 54x28" **250.00**

Bags and Cases

The Indians used bags for many purposes, and most display excellent form and workmanship. Of the types listed below, many collectors consider the pipe bag to be the most desirable form. Pipe bags were long, narrow, leather and bead or quillwork creations made to hold tobacco in a compartment at the bottom and the pipe, with the bowl removed from the stem, in the top. Long buckskin fringe was used as trim and complemented the quilled and beaded design to make the bag a masterpiece of Indian Art.

Arapaho, knife case, hide w/geometric bw, 9x3", +knife..............**125.00**
Arapaho, quiver, hide, 1880, 30x5", +2 arrows **75.00**
Athabascan, gun case, hide, embr floral, fringe, 1920, 50"...........**200.00**
Blackfoot, medicine pouch, parfleche, blk pnt/fringe, 15x9"........**475.00**
Blackfoot, parfleche, pnt rawhide, choice, 1880, 19x11x8" **800.00**
Blackfoot, rifle case, EX full bw, long fringe, 1800, 49" **3,100.00**
Blackfoot, saddlebags, buffalo hide w/pony beads, 1860, 102" **550.00**
Cheyenne, bw/fringe/tin cones, 1901, 15x9" **600.00**
Cheyenne, peace medal pouch, buffalo hide w/bw, 1880, 4x3½" ...**60.00**
Cheyenne, pouch, quills/tin cones/bw on rawhide, 1800, 7x5"......**75.00**
Chippewa, bandolier, floral bw, 1890, 42x14" **550.00**
Cigarette case, Lucky Strike logo in bw, 1935, 3x2½" **125.00**
Crow, bonnet case, elk hide, pnt/long fringe, 1890, 19" **650.00**
Crow, bw geometrics/pnt, fringe, drawstring, 1900, 10x2" **150.00**
Crow, knife case, sinew-sewn/bw geometrics on hide, 9x3" **180.00**
Crow, medicine pouch, bw geometrics on hide, 1880, 3x2½" **125.00**
Crow, parfleche, elk hide, bl-outline motif, 1880, 28", pr **700.00**
Crow, parfleche, pnt geometrics, 1900, 29x12" **300.00**

Crow, parfleche, red/gr pnt motif, long fringe, 13x12" 210.00
Dakota, pipe, sinew motif/quilled fringe, 1885, 38x7" 1,250.00
Kootenai, parfleche, pnt on elk hide, 1890, 27x12", EX 400.00
Mandan, knife case, red/wht/purple quillwork, 1870, 9x1" 390.00
Mandan, medicine pouch, pony beads, 1870, 4x4" 75.00
Mandan, quiver, rawhide w/bw top, 1850, 17x3" 300.00
N Plains, bow case/quiver, bw/fringe, 1880, +bow & arrows .. 1,100.00
Nez Perce, belt pouch, corn husk w/geometrics, 1890, 3x3" 65.00
Nez Perce, belt pouch, corn husk w/subtle motif, 1890, 5x5".........90.00
Nez Perce, bow case/quiver, fur w/pony beads, 48", +bow 200.00
Nez Perce, corn husk, EX geometrics, 1900, 18x15" 700.00
Nez Perce, corn husk, geometric/floral, EX work, 1910, 7x7" 375.00
Nez Perce, corn husk, geometrics, 1890, 16x13" 400.00
Nez Perce, corn husk, subtle geometrics, 1890, 17x12" 425.00
Nez Perce, dreamer, all orig bw/bking, 1890, 12x11"..................700.00
Nez Perce, sheath, bw florals, 1920, 15", +knife 160.00

Great Lakes loom-beaded cloth bandolier bag, late 1900s, minor damage, 36" long, $850.00.

Plains, knife case, bw Am flag on hide, 24", +knife 175.00
Plains, knife case, bw on hide, 1920, 10", +handmade knife..........75.00
Plains, parfleche, pnt on rawhide, folded flap, 1900, 25x11" 300.00
Plateau, bw apaloosa, w/30" string of wampum, 1880, 11x10". 1,400.00
Plateau, bw Smowhalla Ghost Dance symbols, 1890, 9x7" 1,200.00
Plateau, Chinese pheasant bw/stroud cloth bk, 1910, 14x12" . 1,000.00
Plateau, Elk Dreamer Society, full contour bw, 1880, 14x11".. 1,200.00
Potawatomi, pipe, geometric/floral bw, fringe, 1890, 26x7" 500.00
Sioux, bow case, quill trim/fringe on buckskin, 1890, 38x6".........200.00
Sioux, pipe, geometric bw on hide, fringe, 1870, 34x7" 500.00
Sioux, pipe, hide w/lg geometric bw section, 1890, 33x8" 1,000.00
Tlingit, 'octopus' w/bw & red wool tassels, 1920, 18x9" 450.00
Tlingit, pouch, seal fur w/bw fir trees, 1920, 4x3½".....................50.00
Wasco, sally bag, twined, band designs, 1900, 12x6" 75.00
Wasco, sally bag, waterbug motif, 1840, 5x5½" 150.00
Yakima, bw feathers/arrows, 1920, 12x10" 425.00
Yakima, cloth w/bw flower, rnded, 1920, 6x5" 45.00
Yakima, corn husk, trade yarn butterfly/floral, 1910, 10x9" 725.00
Yakima, full bw w/contour florals, 1910, 15x13"......................300.00
Yakima, purse, full bw florals, metal top, 1925, 10x6½" 175.00

Yakima, sally bag, mc corn husk geometrics, 1900, 10x7" 325.00

Baskets

In the following listings, examples are basket form and coiled unless noted otherwise. The given dimension is diameter for bowls and round trays; for rectangular items, length is given.

Apache, bowl, dbl checkerboard star motif, 1930, 5x15" 1,050.00
Apache, bowl, whirlwinds/human/animals, 1920, 2½x18½" ... 1,400.00
Apache, burden, twined, line decor, 1890, 12½x14"...............600.00
Apache, dogs/birds/swastikas/arrowheads, 1935, 10x7" dia 500.00
Apache, olla, EX blk motif, 1930, 12x12", M 1,800.00
Apache, olla, geometrics/stairsteps, 1935, 11x13" 950.00
Apache, tray, blk-line design, 1920, 12" dia 150.00
Apache, tray, many dogs/swastikas, 1910, 6x24" 1,050.00
Apache, water basket, pitched, 1890, 12x8"..............................260.00
Chehailis, gr/blk geometrics, oval, w/lid, 1920, 8x7" 60.00
Chemeuvi, bowl, connecting dmns, fine work, 1925, 1½x7" 325.00
Chemeuvi, bowl, dbl-rattlesnake motif, 1930, 3x12", NM 110.00
Chemeuvi, bowl, stairsteps, 1910, 3x13", M 1,500.00
Chemeuvi, bowl, vertical rattlesnake motif, 1910, 3x11" 650.00
Chilkotin, storage, mc dmns, wire at top, 1880, 12x12x25" 300.00
Cowlitz, allover dmns, finger-woven trumpline, 1880, 28x18" . 2,900.00
Cowlitz, burden, snowflake motif, 1900, 16x15", M 1,400.00
Cowlitz, lines of Xs, rim loops, 1900, 5x8x10".........................275.00
Cowlitz, mc geometrics, hard sides, EX work, 1920, 14x10" 600.00
Cowlitz, zigzags, rim loops, by M Kioma, 1920, 3½x8"..............175.00
Haida, bowl, twined, openwork, shouldered, 1920, 6x4" 125.00
Hopi, plaque, w/Kachina face, 1960, 25" dia 650.00
Hupa, bowl, twined, brn geometrics, 1940, 2x3" 65.00
Hupa, bowl, twined, red/blk geometrics, 1920, 4x6" 200.00
Hupa, twined, blk/red geometrics, 1890, 9x12" 800.00
Hupa, woman's hat, twined, geometrics, 1910, 6x3" 225.00
Klamath, bowl, twined, brn/yel quillwork, 1910, 4x8½" 125.00
Klamath, gambling tray, EX lightening bolt motif, 1880, 14" 450.00
Klamath, hat, twined, diagonal stairsteps, 1910, 6x5" 175.00
Klamath, twined, w/lid & carrying hdl, 1910, 7½x11"................175.00
Klamath, twined, yel quillwork/brn hourglasses, 1900, 8x4"........175.00
Klickitat, animals/humans, minor damage, 1870, 15x12" 100.00
Klickitat, berry basket, hard sided/mc motif, 1870, 7½x8" 55.00
Klickitat, stairsteps, conical/hard, rim loops, 1880, 9x9"..............145.00

Southwestern coiled olla, Apache, human figures and geometrics, minor rim damage, 21", $675.00.

Klickitat, storage, geometrics/rim loops, 1890, 16x10", VG.........**200.00**
Maidu, mush cooker, red stairsteps/feathers, 1890, 12x21" **600.00**
Makah, bottle & lid covered w/twined basketry, 1920, 9x3" **55.00**
Makah, finely twined, birds/geometrics, w/lid, 1920, 5x6" **175.00**
Makah, lg basketry-covered abalone shell, 1920, 2x6x5" **45.00**
Makah, mc sea monsters, w/lid, 1930, 4x7" dia **150.00**
Mission, bowl, connecting sqs, 1900, 3x5" dia **140.00**
Mission, bowl, stairsteps, 1920, 4x11"..**250.00**
Mission, bowl, star/corn stalks, by Ramona, 1910, 13" **1,500.00**
Mission, bowl, yel stars, 1920, 7x4" **175.00**
Modoc, lady's cap, purple/gr dmn motif, 1880, 7½x4"...............**115.00**
Mono, bowl, blk arrows/stairsteps, 1840, 5x9" **400.00**
Mono, bowl, blk radiating stairsteps, 1910, 4x12" **350.00**
Mono, bowl, blk rattlesnake motif, mk Chemeuvi, 1935, 6x14"..**700.00**
Navajo, wedding, spirit release line, Ute-made, 1935, 3x11".......**175.00**
Nootka, mc whaling scenes, w/lid, 1910, 11x9" dia **225.00**
Paiute, twined/conical burden type, red lines, 1900, 12x10"..........**60.00**
Panamint, goblet form, red/brn butterflies, 1920, 4x6" **800.00**
Papago, bowl, Man in Maze motif, 1945, 3x10" **200.00**
Papago, dbl-snake motif, 1975, 3x27" **700.00**
Pima, bowl, intertwined blk frets, fine work, 1935, 6x16" **925.00**
Pima, bowl, whirlwind motif, 1940, 3x14"..................................**350.00**
Pima, humans/gila monster/Xs, 1920, 14x11"...........................**850.00**
Pima, tray, 2 rows rattlesnakes, oval, 1930, 7x4½" **130.00**
Pit River, basketry-covered whiskey bottle, 1900, 10", NM **100.00**
Pit River, bowl, twined, 1910, 2x3"...**70.00**
Pit River, twined, red arrowheads, 1890, 7x4" dia **100.00**
Pomo, bowl, geometrics, clamshell bead decor, 1890, 8x21" ..**1,500.00**
Pomo, bowl, rattlesnake motif, single-rod, 1920, 3x9" **350.00**
Pomo, bowl, red diagonals, single-rod, 1900, 3x6" **250.00**
Pomo, geometrics/clamshell beads, single-rod, 1880, 10x19" ..**1,300.00**
Pomo, treasure, 3-color feathers, shells/beads, 1920, 2x5" **1,900.00**
Quinault, raffia, geometrics, hdl, oval, 1930, 12x16" **35.00**
Salish, mc stars, w/lid & hdls, 1935, 4x9½".............................**110.00**
Salish, storage trunk, mc dmn, w/lid, 1910, 12x18" **175.00**
Salish, tray, mc geometrics, hdls, 1910, 21" L............................**160.00**
Salish, tray, 2 concentric mc stars, hdls, 1910, 20" dia **200.00**
Salish, trunk, geometrics, w/lid, 1910, 4x8x4"...........................**225.00**
Siletz, carrying, twined, w/hdl, 1920, 5x7".................................**50.00**
Siletz, storage, twined, brn-line motif, 1930, 14x11" **75.00**
Sioux, lady's gambling, w/3 plum seed mks, 1840, 9" dia............**550.00**
Skokomish, bowl, row of dogs at top, rim loops, 1920, 8x10" **150.00**
Skokomish, twined, gold zigzags, 1890, 7x7½"..........................**160.00**
Skokomish, utility, cedar bark, rim loops, 1900, 15x12" **175.00**
Tlingit, mat, circular designs, fine work, oval, 1890, 11" **115.00**
Tlingit, mat, twined, oval, 1910, 10" **95.00**
Tlingit, mc florals/geometrics, ped ft, 1910, 4x4" **275.00**
Tlingit, orange/blk fret motif, str sided, 1880, 6x4" **100.00**
Tlingit, rattle top, finely twined, brn frets, 1910, 5x3½" **325.00**
Tlingit, rattle top, twined, EX 2-tone motif, 1920, 6x5½" **300.00**
Tlingit, storage, twined/gold geometrics, w/lid, 1910, 6x8"..........**250.00**
Tlingit, twined, pk/brn dmn edges, superfine, 1910, 3x4"...........**275.00**
Tulare, bowl, 2 red/blk motif bands, incurvate, 1930, 4x9".........**850.00**
Tulare, rattlesnake motif, shouldered, 1920, 5½x8" **600.00**
Washo, bowl, red butterflies, 1920, 4x8"...................................**145.00**
Yurok, bowl, brn/blk motif, 1920, miniature, 2x3"........................**85.00**
Yurok, burden, brn motif, conical, 1890, 7x4", M **500.00**
Yurok, twined, openwork w/cross-motif bands, 1910, 7½x7" **275.00**

Blankets, Navajo

Pueblo Indians first made blankets centuries ago, but today most are made by Navajo Indians. Blankets were still made into the 1800s, when Pendleton and Hudson's Bay blankets became widely available. Around the turn of the century, rugs were developed because tourists were more likely to buy them as floor coverings and wall-hangings. Rugs or blankets are made in various regional styles; an expert can usually identify the area where it was made – sometimes even the individual who made it. The colors of wool are natural (gray-white, brown-black), vegetal (from plant dyes), or artificial (aniline, from synthetic chemicals.) Value factors include size, tightness of weave, artistry of design, and condition. Examples by artists whose names are well known command the higher prices.

Navajo transitional, woven in chief's variant pattern, two 'Church of Taos' devices, 67" x 56", $2,500.00.

Pictorial transitional, Xs/animals/bars, JB Moore, 86x40" **350.00**
Saddle, Chief's, vegetable dye, 1910, 33x26"...............................**100.00**
Saddle, Chief's style, striped, 1890, 30x30" **110.00**
Saddle, Germantown, hourglass columns/etc on red, 40x21".......**400.00**
Saddle, natural wool, 1920, 38x24"..**30.00**
Saddle, pulled warp diagonal weave, 1900, 46x30".......................**50.00**
Saddle, red/tan twill w/bl center stripe, tassels, 24x33" **60.00**
Sunday saddle, Eyedazzler on red, minor wear, 32x26"................**900.00**
Transitional, central lozenge/sawtooth dmns, 1910, 64x40" **300.00**
Wearing type, zigzags/Xs, 3 red panels on brn-blk, 70x47" **1,000.00**

Ceremonial Items

Amulet, shaman's; Tlingit, fossil ivory, abalone inlay, 2½" **210.00**
Amulet, Tlingit, ivory frog, 1870, 3x1¼"......................................**75.00**
Cradle, Hupa, twined, dentellium shells, 1880, 22x7" **175.00**
Dance kilt, Hopi, classic motif, hand woven, 1910, 96"..............**450.00**
Dance wand, N Plains, horn w/full bw hdl, 29x1" **300.00**
Doll, medicine; Crow, bw, many medicine balls, 1880, 20".........**425.00**
Drum, hand; Plains, faded pnt, 1890, 2x10" dia...........................**85.00**
Feast dish, Haida, cvd/pnt, trade bead inlay, 1930, 3x5x11" **105.00**
Fetish, Kiowa, oval, umbilical cord, bw, 3½x1"............................**50.00**
Fetish, Plains, turtle form, full bw bk, 5½x4" **75.00**
Fetish, Sioux, umbilical lizard, 1870, 7x2".................................**200.00**
Fetish, Zuni, brn serpentine bear, 1940, 2x1½" **30.00**
Mask, Husk Face Society, braided/fringed corn husks **350.00**
Mask, Iroquois, False Face Society, metal eyes, 1880, 11" **350.00**
Mask, Iroquois, False Face Society turtle, hair drops, 1850 ....**275.00**
Mask, NW Coast, hair/pnt/abalone inlay on hide, 10x7" **200.00**
Medicine man's cloth, pnt Yei/Healing Chant, 1890, 60x34" **200.00**
Medicine pc, Blackfoot, bw/fringe/feathers on ermine, 1870 ....**700.00**

Rattle, Blackfoot, pnt hide, Medicine Society, 1910, 12x2"............85.00
Rattle, Iroquois, turtle shell, 17"...225.00
Rattle, medicine; Horn Society, ochered/incised, 1870, 10".........350.00
Rattle, NW Coast, human head effigy, pnt/inlaid hide, 1870......300.00
Soul catcher, Tlingit, fossil ivory, totemic cvg, 1870, 2".............100.00
Speaker's staff, NW Coast, cvd/pnt/inlay, sgn LaValle, '75..........450.00
Spoon, Haida, bent horn, totemic-cvd hdl/abalone inlay, 11".....400.00
Spoon, Haida, mtn goat horn, many totemic cvgs, 1900, 11".....300.00
Spoon, Plains, bent horn w/geometric bw on border, 9x2".........145.00
Spoon, Tlingit, blk mtn goat horn, cvd totemics, 1870, 6½".......275.00
Spoon, Tlingit, blk mtn goat horn, totemics/inlay, 1900, 8".........550.00
Totem pole, argilite, raven/shaman, R Moody, 1930, 6½"...........300.00
Totem pole, Haida, argelite, female shaman/eagle, 1920, 9½".....350.00
Totem pole, Kwakiult, eagle on beaver, EX cvg, 1970, 22x4"......105.00
Totem pole, Tlingit, climbing side: 4 bears+dog, 1890, 52".........750.00

Dolls

Comanche, male in buckskin w/bw & fringe, 1935, 14".............250.00
Crow, dress w/bw, ear drops/horsehair braids, 1880, 11"..............350.00
Kachina, bear track symbols/pop eyes, cottonwood, 9"...............900.00
Kachina, Eagle Dancer, on cvd base, 1945, 19x19".......................125.00
Kachina, Maiden, cvd wood/mc pnt, feather trim, 11"..................195.00
Kachina, Owl, in dancing posture, EX cvg, 1945, 19"..................175.00
Kachina, Parrot, fine cvg/pnt, sgn Kayovoftewa, 1965, 14"........200.00
Kachina, Warrior, w/helmet & fur trim, 1930, 18x9"...................150.00
NW Coast, dancer, full costume, by E Graham, 1975, 30"...........375.00
Plains, bw dress/mocs/pants/necklace, human hair, 1910, 12".....400.00
Sioux, buckskin/bw clothes & mocs, hair braids, 1890, 11".........700.00
Sioux, much bw/quills/fringe/horsehair, earrings/boots, 18".... 1,400.00

Crow doll with hide face, ca 1980, 18", $300.00.

Domestics

Blanket chest, Kwakiult, totem corners/cvg, 1880, 12x20"..........375.00
Bowl, NW Coast, mtn sheep horn, cvd wolf/etc, 9" L, EX...... 5,500.00
Bowl, Woodlands, burl, w/hdls, heavy, 1870, 3x7".....................110.00
Cradle, Apache, willow & canvas w/ochre pnt, 1890, 12x24"......70.00
Cradle, Nez Perce, camas flower contour bw, 1875, 39x14".... 2,600.00
Cradle, Nez Perce, contour floral bw, orig brd, 1890, 40"....... 1,000.00
Kettle, brass, type traded to NW Coast, 1880, 12x18".................150.00
Ladle, Haida, cvd mtn sheep horn, 1870, 12"..............................85.00

Ladle, Mesa Verde, pottery w/blk on wht motif, pre-historic.......150.00
Mortar, Wasco, basalt, turtle form, Columbia River, 7x4"............600.00
Mortar, Wasco, basalt, w/owl face, Columbia River, 3x3"............225.00
Mortar, Yurok, hand-hewn wood, Klamath River, 1890, 9x8".......75.00
Mortar & pestle, gray stone, Dalles OR, pre-historic, 12x10".......600.00
Mortar & pestle, Wasco, stone, excavated, 1700, 11x4¾"..........115.00
Teepee rest, Cheyenne, Willow, old style, 1930, 86x35"..............215.00
Teepee rest, N Plains, willow w/canvas trim, 1900, 78x40".........250.00
Toy cradle, Arapaho, hide w/bw & pnt, 1870, 18", +wood doll...525.00
Toy cradle, Crow, bw geometrics, 1910, 15x5"............................650.00
Toy cradle, Crow, 3 bw flaps/bw top/fringe, 1880, 25", NM 1,900.00
Toy cradle, Flathead, mtn sheep hide/contour bw, 1870, 21"... 1,000.00
Toy cradle, Nez Perce, bw florals, 1890, 10x4".............................300.00
Toy cradle, Nez Perce, floral bw top & flap, 1920, 15x5".............340.00
Toy cradle, Paiute, sinew sewn, bw/basketry, 1890, 7x3".............400.00
Toy cradle, Sioux, full bw, w/brds, 1910, 14x5"...........................500.00

Jewelry

As early as 500 A.D., Indians in the Southwest drilled turquoise nuggets and strung them on cords made of sinew or braided hair. The Spanish introduced them to coral, and it became a popular item of jewelry; abalone and clam shells were favored by the Coastal Indians. Not until the last half of the 19th century did the Indians learn to work with silver. Each tribe developed its own distinctive style and preferred design, which until about 1920 made it possible to determine tribal origin with some degree of accuracy. Since that time, because of modern means of communication and travel, motifs have become less distinct.

Quality Indian silver jewelry may be antique or contemporary age, though certainly to be considered, is not as important a factor as fine workmanship and good stones. Pre-1910 silver will show evidence of hammer marks, and designs are usually simple. Beads have sometimes been shaped from coins. Stones tend to be small; when silver wire was used, it is usually square. To insure your investment, choose a reputable dealer.

Belt, Navajo, concho, 13 silver ovals w/turq cab, 41" 175.00
Bola, Eagle Dancer, turq/coral inlay, sgn, 1985, 4x5" 170.00
Bola, pottery turtle & tips by F Naranjo, 1950, 3x1" 50.00
Bola, silver arrowhead w/turq cab, 1970, 4x2" 75.00
Bracelet, full bw geometrics, 1910, 2" W 45.00
Bracelet, Haida, hammered copper, eng totem, 1930, 1" W.........105.00
Bracelet, hammered silver w/totemic eng, sgn Sitka, 1940 ....125.00
Bracelet, Navajo, hammered coin silver/1 turq, 1935, 3" W 300.00
Bracelet, Navajo, lg oval turq cab+26, 1935, 7x2½" 275.00
Bracelet, Navajo, sandcast, crude, 1930, 1" W 45.00
Bracelet, Navajo, sandcast naja form w/lg turq, 1970, 6x2"..........65.00
Bracelet, Navajo, sandcast w/5 oval turq cabs, 1935, 2" W..........275.00
Bracelet, Navajo, silver w/3 turq cabs, 1960, 1" W 55.00
Bracelet, Navajo, silver w/3 turq cabs, 1970, 2" W 75.00
Bracelet, Navajo, silver w/5 #8 spider-web cabs, 1965, ¾" 175.00
Bracelet, Navajo, 2¾" oval turq cab, 1935................................170.00
Bracelet, Navajo, 3 ovals, ea w/lg turq slab fr by sm cabs 400.00
Bracelet, Navajo, 7 turq cabs, 1930...150.00
Bracelet, Tlingit, hammered coin silver w/cvd eagle, 1900 ....90.00
Bracelet, Tlingit, hammered silver/totemic, mk Haines, '45........100.00
Bracelet, Zuni, 1½" cuff type w/mc inlay buffalo etc, 1935 ....500.00
Bracelet, Zuni, 10 rows of 17 sm turq sqs, 1935, 3" W 1,200.00
Buckle, Navajo, sandcast w/turq cab, 1935, 3x3½"......................50.00
Comb, Navajo, silver w/turq cab, 1935, 3¼" W 200.00
Concho belt, hammered silver on leather, heavy, '35, 42x5"... 1,000.00
Concho belt, Navajo, sandcast wing dancers/turq cabs, 1955......475.00
Concho belt, Zuni, 7 inlaid dancers, 1940, 48x4"....................... 1,500.00

Earrings, Sioux, dentellium shells/beads, 1880, 5½" 75.00
Earrings, Zuni, Knife Wing Dancer inlay, 1930, 1½x1½" 400.00
Necklace, Blackfoot, full bw rope, red/wht/bl, 1890, 24"................60.00
Necklace, lg turq nuggets/coral, 1965, 16" 85.00
Necklace, Navajo, box & bow 18-turq, squash blossom, 1915. 1,400.00
Necklace, Navajo, squash blossom, nuggets/beads/naja, '50 ....125.00
Necklace, Navajo, squash blossom, sandcast naja, 1935, 24"........400.00
Necklace, Navajo, squash blossom, turq/quarters, 1935, 34"........600.00
Necklace, Navajo, squash blossom, 15 turq cabs, 1960, 28" 245.00
Necklace, Navajo, 8-strand coral tubes/silver beads, 1935 ....675.00
Necklace, Navajo, 9-strand shell heishi/turq nuggets, 1940........250.00
Necklace, Plateau, clamshell wampum beads, 1850, 36" 35.00
Necklace, turq nuggets, 1970, 16" 55.00
Necklace, turq nuggets on heishi w/silver beads, 1935, 24" 400.00
Necklace, 6 strands tiny turq nuggets/heishi, 1975, 30" 150.00
Pendant, Zuni, inlaid shell, 2 silver snakes, 1935, 4x3½"............300.00
Pin, Navajo, silver w/9 turq stones, 1940, 4½" dia 35.00
Pin, Zuni, Kachina Dancer w/wht fox, inlay, 1935, 3½" 3,500.00
Pin, Zuni, mc inlay horse, 1975, 3x4" 135.00
Ring, Zuni, Pluto (dog figure), mc inlay, 1970..............................115.00
Trade beads, bl tile, 1880, 10 strands, ea 31" 225.00
Trade beads, chevrons, mixed shape, 1800, huge, 22" 275.00
Trade beads, cobalt, oval/rnd, Peking, 1880, 36" 230.00
Trade beads, cobalt, Peking, 1880, very lg, 24" 70.00
Trade beads, cobalt & clear, Dutch, 1800s, 30" 100.00
Trade beads, faceted cobalt & several in gold, Russian, 26" 250.00
Trade beads, red w/yel core, 'chief' type, 1820, 24"......................75.00
Trade beads, swirled/striped disks, Venetian, 1820, 24" 55.00
Trade beads, 21-strand red cornaline de leppos, 18" 150.00

Knives and Chipped Blades

The knife was an indispensable tool to the Indian whether he was in battle, hunting game, or doing chores at the campsite. Before the white man's metal blades, all were made of copper, obsidian, flint, or chert. Knife cases, fashioned of leather with intricate decorations of quilling or beadwork, were first worn suspended from the neck; later they were attached to the belt.

Archaic, Edwards Plateau chert, dbl-pointed, 4" 50.00
Archaic, gray turkey tail, MN, 2x6" 60.00
Archaic, moss agate, triangular, Blanco Canyon, 3½" 50.00
Archaic, oolitic chert/lt inclusions, side notch, 3" 40.00
Dk gray stone, Columbia River, pre-historic, 14x4" 250.00
Edwards Plateau chert, hafted, base tang, 4¾" 165.00
Fighting, Tlingit, ivory raven/octopus hdl, 1870, 20x2½"............900.00
Gr jade, rare, 1800, 6½x¾" 145.00
Jasper, high-grade, cache-found, oval, VA, 5¼" 75.00
NW Coast, cvd animal head hdl, 1975, +15" pnt/wood sheath 95.00
Paleo, banded agate, sturdy/well made, OR, 4" 40.00
Paleo, yel-brn jasper, base/side ground, PA, 3¼"..........................150.00
Pk flint, translucent, Table Rock type, Midwest, 4"........................55.00
Stilwell, flint, hafted/resharpened, AR, 3¼x1½" 125.00
Tan grave-deposit chert, EX chipping, TX, 6" 300.00
Torugas, Edwards Plateau flint, TX 3¼"..150.00
Woodland, layered flint, strong hafting, 3½" 45.00
Woodland, pk/tan flint, hafted, notched, 2⅞" 25.00
Yurok, blk obsidian, point ea end, pre-historic, 11x1½"................100.00

Pipes

Pipe bowls were usually carved from soft stone, such as catlinite or pipestone, an argilaceous sedimentary rock composed mainly of clay.

Granite was also used. Some ceremonial pipes were simply styled, while others were intricately designed naturalistic figurals, sometimes in bird or frog forms called effigies. Their stems, made of wood and often covered with leather, were sometimes nearly a yard in length.

Athabascan, cvd wood bowl/stem, brass trim, 1880, 1¼x7"..........30.00
Cherokee, ant effigy, cvd/inlaid gray stone, 1800, 2x10"..............50.00
Haida, steatite dbl-bird form bowl, 1970, 2x2" 75.00

Haida argillite portrait pipe carved in the form of a white sea captain's head, Indian dugout canoe with human figure and frog as stem surmount, 8½", $1,950.00.

Hopewell, sacrificial, 2 human forms, IL provenance, 7x8" 275.00
Mound Builder, blk stone, bird effigy, pre-historic, 10½" 165.00
Mound Builder, cvd stone effigy platform type, OH, 2x3"..............80.00
NW Coast, cvd kneeling human, metal bowl, 1975, 2½x3" 100.00
Pipe tomahawk, narrow head, tacked/file-burnt hdl, 1870, 21" ...150.00
Pipe tomahawk, Plains, pnt traces/file-burnt hdl, 1870, 18" 200.00
Pipe tomahawk, Plains, presentation, appl fox/moon/etc, 25". 2,500.00
Sioux, blk stone T-bowl w/inlay, bw/tacked stem, 2x6x40"..........275.00
Sioux, blk stone T-bowl w/inlay, tacked corkscrew stem, 31".......360.00
Sioux, blk stone T-bowl w/inlays, dtd 1880, 2x7x21"..................125.00
Sioux, blk stone T-bowl w/much inlay, bw stem, 2x6x28" 300.00
Sioux, red catlinite T-bowl, cvd wood stem, 1890, 2x19" 135.00
Sioux, red catlinite T-bowl, 1890, 4x16" 125.00
Sioux, red catlinite T-bowl & stem, 1890, 4x21" 225.00
Tlingit, cvd ivory 'animal,' abalone inlay eyes, 1850, 4½" 75.00
Trade pipe, wht clay, Hudson Bay, 1870, 1x2x5"..........................35.00
Wasco, gray stone L-bowl, from Columbia River, 1800, 2x2½" 55.00

Pottery

Indian pottery is nearly always decorated in such a manner as to indicate the tribe which produced it or the pueblo in which it was made. For instance, the designs of Cochiti potters were usually scattered forms from nature or sacred symbols. The Zuni preferred an ornate repetitive decoration of a closer configuration. They often used stylized deer and bird forms, sometimes in dimensional applications.

Acoma, basket, braid hdl, 1930, 4x3" 20.00
Acoma, olla, fine lines, 1950s, 15x9" 90.00
Anasazi, bowl, blk on wht motif, pre-historic, 3½x8" dia 130.00
Anasazi, duck effigy, red, pre-historic, 2½x4" 100.00
Casas Grandes, olla, geometrics, sgn F Ortiz, '86, 14x12" 200.00
Casas Grandes, parrot effigy pot, excavated, 9x9" 100.00
Casas Grandes, seated human effigy, excavated, 8x8" 150.00
Casas Grandes, 2-faced human effigy, mc, pre-historic, 8x8".......150.00
Chaco, bowl, checkerboard int, blk/wht, pre-historic, 9"............115.00
Chaco, bowl, geometrics, blk on wht, pre-historic, 2x6" 80.00
Chaco, effigy, blk on wht, trilobed, pre-historic, 2½" 95.00

Chaco, jar, blk on wht, pre-historic, 3½x3" 60.00
Chaco, pitcher, blk on wht, pre-historic, 8" 200.00
Ho Ho Kam, bowl, red on buff, flared, pre-historic, 7x14" 350.00
Hopi, bowl, birds/feathers, Nampeyo, 1920, 3x9" 800.00
Hopi, bowl, symbols, red/blk on wht, minor wear, 2x5½" 475.00
Hopi, canteen, stylized birds, Nampeyo, 1925, 4x3½" 150.00
Hopi, jar, EX mc motif, sgn Chakastewa, 1945, 8½x15" 700.00
Jar, mc/red, sgn S Suazo, 1975, 3x2½"..35.00
Santa Clara, child figure, sgn Margaret & Luther, 1955, 2" 85.00
Santa Clara, clown, sgn Margaret & Luther, 1965, 1½"................40.00
Santa Clara, dish, blk/blk, heavy braided hdls, 1930, 3x8" 85.00
Santa Clara, jar, birds/snakes, Margaret & Luther, 1960, 7" 325.00
Santa Clara, plate, snake/turkey, Lela & Luther, 1955, 10" 500.00
Santa Clara, racoon, EX pnt, sgn Margaret & Luther, 3½"..........100.00
Santa Clara, wedding vase, blk/cvd, Margaret Tafoya, 22" 2,250.00
Santo Domingo, bowl, blk on cream geometrics, 1945, 9x13"...375.00
Santo Domingo, bowl, leaves/turkey, sgn M Coriz, 1955, 13"......250.00
Santo Domingo, dough bowl, blk on cream motif, 1900, 6x13" ..550.00
Santo Domingo, dough bowl, blk on cream motif, 1910, 8x14" ..600.00
Sitkyatki style, seed jar, EX mc motif, rim rpr, 21" dia 275.00
St Johns, bowl, mc swirls on int, pre-historic, 3½x7" 100.00
St Johns, bowl, mc swirls/geometrics, pre-historic, 12" 200.00
Tonto, bowl, blk on cream motif, pre-historic, 8x15"...................225.00
Wingate, bowl, blk on red w/swirls, pre-historic, 6x12" 120.00
Zuni, olla, fine lines/curves, 1880, 7½x11"............................... 2,100.00

Zuni polychrome ceremonial jar with two sculptured frog effigies and two painted heartline deer, ca 1870, 4½" x 8", EX, $500.00.

Pottery, San Ildefonso

  The pottery of the San Ildefonso pueblo is especially sought after by collectors today. Under the leadership of Maria Martinez and her husband Julian, experiments began about 1918 which led to the development of the 'black-on-black' design achieved through exacting methods of firing the ware. They discovered that by smothering the fire at a specified temperature, the carbon in the smoke that ensued caused the pottery to blacken. Maria signed her work from the late teens to the 1960s; she died in 1980. Today a piece with her signature may bring prices in the $500 to $3,500 range.

Bowl, allover shiny blk, sgn Maria Poveka, 1965, 4x6" 900.00
Bowl, blk/blk, feather motif, Maria Poveka, 1965, 3x5½"............550.00
Bowl, blk/blk, sgn Blue Corn, 1965, 3x6" 250.00
Bowl, blk/blk feathers, sgn Santana & Adam, 1965, 3x4½" 250.00

Jar, blk/blk, avian abstractions, Marie & Julian, 8" dia 2,500.00
Jar, blk/blk, pointed swags, sgn Marie, 5" dia 425.00
Jar, blk/blk, water serpent/rain clouds, sgn Marie, 9" dia 3,000.00
Jar, buff on red, serpents, sgn H Gutuierez, 1976, 6x4" 50.00
Olla, blk/blk, Santana & Adam, 1975, 3½".....................................200.00
Plate, blk/blk, feathers, Marie & Santana, 6" 425.00
Vase, blk/blk, feather motif, Maria Poveka, 1960, 5½x7" 700.00
Vase, blk/blk, feathers/etc, Marie & Santana, 12" 3,000.00
Vase, blk/blk, sgn Marie, 1925, 6x6"..125.00

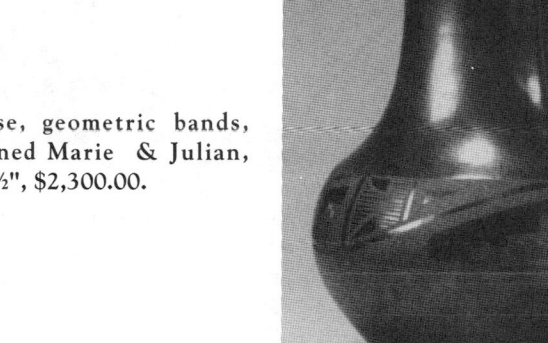

Vase, geometric bands, signed Marie & Julian, 11½", $2,300.00.

Rugs, Navajo

American flag, 48-star, 1965, 40x28"...250.00
Bird pictorial, tapestry weave, 1975, 31x21"................................250.00
Chief's 3rd Phase, dmns/stripes, 5-color, 85x60" 2,750.00
Classic, 5-color on red, handspun/commerical, 82x50" 3,000.00
Crystal, central lozenge/fishhooks, 1930, 81x53", NM................600.00
Crystal, striped, vegetal, 1945, 49x29"..200.00
Crystal, stripes/geometrics, vegetal, 1940, 75x46"......................875.00
Ganado, unusual geometrics, 1920, 54x31"..................................250.00
Ganado Red, 'railroad track' lozenge/dmn, 1930, 76x42" 250.00
Ganado Red, central lozenge, 1975, 65x56" 1,200.00
Ganado Red, geometrics, 1940, 59x37"...300.00
Geometrics, brn/gray/wht, natural wool, 1935, 50x26" 70.00
Germantown, corn stalks/birds, 3-color on red, 50x40" 2,000.00
Germantown, sharp/mc designs, superfine, 1910, 36x24" 300.00
Human/dmn bands, 4-color on wht, homespun, 66x40", NM 700.00
Hunting Chant, sand-pnt motif, New Mexico, '65, 45x38".........300.00
Pictorial, animals/cowbows/chickens/etc, 6-color, 84x52" 3,600.00
Pictorial, bird & tree, 1965, 52x30"..200.00
Pictorial, feathers/birds/etc, 'SUGAR' border, 76x51"............. 1,700.00
Regional, serrated field, 3-color on lt brn, 80x50" 1,300.00
Regional, Xs in terraces, 3-color on red, 98x64" 1,200.00
Saddle, natural wool, ca 1940, 29x27" 35.00
Serrated centipede motif, 4-color on wht, 70x41"........................500.00
Storm, mc geometrics, 1930, 96x58", NM....................................900.00
Terraced designs, red/blk, 1935, 50x28".......................................175.00
Transitional, serrated medallion, 2-color on red, 62x43" 700.00
Transitional, 4 bands of serrated dmns/stripes, 98x67" 700.00
Transitional Chief's, 5 Xs/stripes, 5-color, 65x55"................... 1,700.00
W Reservation, central lozenge/outlined dmns, 1935, 72x56".....650.00
W Reservation, sawtooth/dmn motif, 1935, 56x38"....................150.00
Weaving, Navajo, 4-figure Yei, pastels, 1945, 42x27" 400.00

Yei, 10-color, 69x43" **600.00**
2 Gray Hills, geometrics, natural wool, 1920, 70x55" **425.00**
2 Gray Hills, geometrics/Xs, bl/brn/tan, 80x51"......................**1,200.00**
2 Gray Hills, natural wool, classic, 1950, 58x38".....................**525.00**
2 Gray Hills, optical geometrics, EX work, natural, 83x51" **950.00**
2 Gray Hills, Xs/geometrics, natural wool, 1925, 70x56" **400.00**

Teec Nos Pos with outline diamond and triangle pattern, ca 1955, 66" x 38", $400.00.

Tools

Axe, blk stone, fully grooved, Columbia River, 6x3"......................**40.00**
Axe, gr jadite, ¾-grooved, pre-historic **150.00**
Axe, Ho Ho Kam, brn stone, from AZ, pre-historic, 7x3½" **20.00**
Axe, mottled blk stone, ¾-grooved, pre-historic, 7x4½"..............**100.00**
Celt, greenstone, EX lines, AL, 7x2x⅝" **200.00**
Celt, jade, fine work, from Columbia River, pre-historic **200.00**
Chisel, slate, Midwest, 7x1¾" **50.00**
Gouge, E Woodlands, dk brn stone, hollowed/tapered, 8x1½" **125.00**
Mat creaser, Salish, wood, bird head ends, 1870, 6¾x3" **175.00**
Paddle, NW Coast, cvd wood, 1880, 32x4"................................**105.00**

Weapons

Arrow, Plains, 1870, 28", group of 8...**250.00**
Axe, iron head: tacks/file mks, bw/wire-wrap hdl, 1880...............**450.00**
Bow, NW Coast, cvd, rawhide hand hold, wide, 1870, 52x1" **200.00**
Bow, NW Coast, wood, sinew string/sealskin wrap, 1890, 50" **75.00**
Bow, Plains, wood, narrow, 1870, 57"..**45.00**
Bow, Plains, wood, sinew string, recurved, 1900, 48" **150.00**
Club, gunstock; Plains, file brands/tacks/iron blade, 1870 ....**500.00**
Club, Iroquois, wood, face cvg/antler blade, 1860, 22x7"............**225.00**
Club, N Plains, full bw hdl/horsehair dangles, 29x1" **300.00**
Club, pipe tomahawk; Plains, file brands/tacks/iron blade **900.00**
Club, Plains, bw/fringe/hide-covered hdl, 1880, 21" **250.00**
Club, Plains, quillwork on rawhide-wrap hdl, 1870, 23" **60.00**
Club, Plains, red stone w/full bw hdl, bw drop, 33x5" **550.00**
Club, Sioux, brn stone head/full bw on wood hdl, 1860, 18" **100.00**
Club, Sioux, gray stone head, hide on wood hdl, 1870, 30x5" **115.00**
Club, Sioux, pnt wood/metal blades/hair dangles, 1870, 31" **175.00**
Club, Sioux, red stone egg-form head, full bw hdl, 28x5" **250.00**
Slave killer, gr slate, 4-leg animal silhouette form, 1880 ....**400.00**
Tomahawk, Crow, iron w/X cutout, bw hdl added later, 1870 .....**200.00**
Tomahawk, Plains, iron w/heart cutout, decor hdl, 1880, 22"........**80.00**

Miscellaneous

Blanket, Haida, pearl buttons/sitting figure, 1920, 56x56"...........**600.00**

Blanket, Kwakiult, pearl buttons/thunderbird, cloth, 1920 ....**450.00**
Blanket, Pendelton, wool, bl w/lg geometrics, 1940, lg **65.00**
Blanket, Pendleton, mc stripes, 1890, 74x62" **135.00**
Blanket, Pendleton, wool, striped, 1910, 48x38".........................**50.00**
Blanket, Rio Grande, mc stripes, short fringe, 1890, 82x50".........**75.00**
Blanket, saddle; Crow, bw on stroud cloth, muslin bk, 1870........**300.00**
Blanket, saddle; Sioux, bw/fringe/bells, 1890, 66x26" **1,900.00**
Boatstone, slate, hole drilled ea end, IN, pre-historic, 3" **110.00**
Box, Plains, parfleche w/mc geometric pnt, 1885, 6x3½" **110.00**
Box, Sioux, parfleche, pnt/blk-lined designs, 1890, 18x10" **500.00**
Box, tobacco; Neskapi, etched bark/wood, 1870, 3x2x1" **200.00**
Buttons, made from 'Shield' silver dollar, 1907, 4 for **35.00**
Canteen, tobacco; Zuni, silver w/mc inlay, 1940, 2½x3x4"...........**500.00**
Container, Woodlands, hunter/animals/etc on birch bark, 13"....**275.00**
Discoidal, Mound Builder, flecked gray stone, 2x4" dia................**50.00**
Flute, 'Love'; Cheyenne, cvd/pnt bird form, 1900, 24" **75.00**
Hat band, Plains, braided horsehair w/eng silver ornaments........**175.00**
Hat rack, buffalo horns, trade cloth/hide trim, 1880, 20" **55.00**
Medal, Andrew Johnson, silver, on 3-strand bone choker............**250.00**
Medal, Geo Washington, silver, 1¼", on 24" bone necklace........**200.00**
Medal, John Tyler, silver, drilled, 1841, 3" dia **225.00**
Medal, Thos Jefferson, silver, drilled, 1801, 3" dia......................**300.00**
Panel, saddle; Flathead, bw on stroud cloth, 1875, 13x11" **600.00**
Pincushion, Iroquois, EX horse/floral bw, 1880, 10x8" **70.00**
Quirt, Blackfoot, antler w/brass tacks, 1890, 18x3" **200.00**
Quirt, Crow, cvd wood w/bw, braided rawhide ends, 37" **70.00**
Quirt, Crow, horn hdl, full bw arm band holder, 1920, 36" **125.00**
Vase, Paiute, glass w/full bw geometrics, 1940, 7x3"....................**35.00**

Amphora

The Amphora Porcelain Works in the Teplitz-Turn area of Bohemia, produced Art Nouveau-styled vases and figurines during the latter part of the 1800s through the first few decades of the 20th century. They marked their wares with various stamps, some incorporating the name and location of the pottery with a crown or a shield. Because Bohemia was part of the Austro-Hungarian empire prior to WWI, some examples are marked Austria; items marked with the Czechoslovakia designation were made after the war.

Our advisor for this category is Jack Gunsaulus; he is listed in the Directory under Michigan.

Bowl, girl in long gown stands on ruffled rim, #1324, 9x7".........**275.00**
Bowl, water lilies emb, oval, lobed ft, leaf hdls, RS&K, 13".........**300.00**
Bust: Sappho, maid looks down, wreath in hair, RS&K, 17" ... **1,200.00**
Dish, formed by brunette's bl dress, gilt leaves, RS&K, 11".........**600.00**
Ewer, poppies/webs, red on cream/lav, root base, RS&K, 11".......**285.00**
Figurine, bearded man on camel peers into distance, 25" **1,200.00**
Figurine, Nouveau-style peasant girl w/baskets, 17½" **450.00**
Planter, cubist cat figural, Louis Waine, Imperial, 11" **2,400.00**
Umbrella stand, leaves/pods hang from rim, mc on tan, 16" **475.00**
Vase, abstract vines, pk/gr on cream, leafy hdls, RS&K, 10"........**300.00**
Vase, blown-out florals, Deco border, 6½" **40.00**
Vase, blown-out florals (mc), ftd, hdls, Austria, 6x11½" **110.00**
Vase, butterflies/webs/jewels, dbl-gourd form, RS&K, 6"............**600.00**
Vase, butterflies/webs/jewels on dk gr, bulbous, RS&K, 9" ... **1,000.00**
Vase, dandelions/leaves, gold/gr on cream, RS&K, 13"................**800.00**
Vase, gold/purple irid, 4 long wax-like runs at neck, 12"............**500.00**
Vase, grapes, 3-color on gr irid, rim forms 4 hdls, 9"..................**150.00**
Vase, grapes on irid gr, arching wing-like hdls, RS&K, 15".........**350.00**
Vase, grapes/vines appl on gr, bulbous rim, 16" **300.00**
Vase, grapes/vines appl on irid gr gourd form, RS&K, 11"..........**250.00**
Vase, lady's portrait, red St K mk, 7"..**575.00**

Vase, lg gr-dotted parrot on limb on beige, neck hdls, 16" 495.00
Vase, lg leaf-molded ft, fantasy flowers, RS&K, 7¾" 525.00
Vase, lioness atop tan gourd-shaped bowl, purple neck, 9" 850.00
Vase, magnolia bands on gr/purple texture, RS&K, 13" 400.00
Vase, maid in veil/jeweled tiara, trees bkground, RS&K, 12".. 1,500.00
Vase, maid/flowers in hair, forest bkground, RS&K, 13" 1,000.00
Vase, mc gems/bl trailings/gilt bubbles on cream, RS&K, 12" 550.00
Vase, oak twigs appl on gr/purple gourd form, RS&K, 12" 700.00
Vase, panel w/lav & gold forest, floral border, RS&K, 7".............500.00
Vase, peacock on cobalt, 12x9"..195.00
Vase, profile of maid in gilded helmet, spherical, RS&K, 6"........900.00
Vase, random mc jewels/bubbles, ornate hdls/neck, RS&K, 6"....400.00
Vase, random mc jewels/bubbles, sqd cylinder, RS&K, 10" 285.00
Vase, stylized incised vulture/branches, ftd pear, RS&K, 20".......600.00

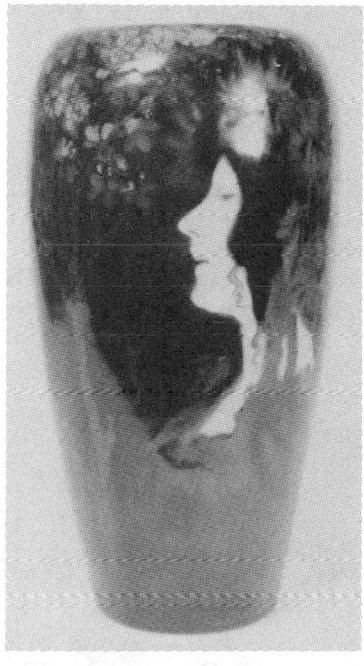

Vase, profile of a lady among stylized trees, #637, 11", $700.00.

Bird w/berry, milk glass, Greentown 300.00
Bird w/berry, Nile gr, Greentown.. 1,600.00
Boar's head, ribbed base, milk glass, Atterbury 1888, 9½"...........975.00
Cat, rectangular lacy base, milk glass, Westmoreland....................95.00
Cat on hamper, Nile gr, Greentown 1,200.00
Chick on vertical egg, milk glass, unmk, 6½" 85.00
Chicks in oblong basket, milk glass, unmk, 2¼x4¼"......................75.00
Cow, split-rib base, milk glass, mk McKee, 5½".............................875.00
Dog, bl opaque, milk glass head, Westmoreland, 5¼" 90.00
Dog, milk blass w/bl head, Westmoreland, 5¼".............................90.00
Dolphin, serrated rim, chocolate, Greentown 195.00
Dolphin, serrated rim, clear or color transparent, Greentown 350.00
Duck, cattail base, milk glass, unmk, 5½"......................................185.00
Duck, milk glass, Atterbury, dtd 1887, 11" 275.00
Duck, milk glass w/amethyst head, Atterbury 1887, 11" 500.00
Duck, split-rib base, milk glass, mk McKee, 5½".........................350.00
Duck, swimming, yel opaque, Vallerysthal, 5"................................65.00
Eagle w/young, colored opaque, Westmoreland..............................75.00
Elephant, standing, clear, unmk, 9"..45.00
Elephant w/rider, milk glass, Vallerysthal, 7"...............................250.00
Fish, collared base, clear frosted, unmk......................................150.00
Fish, Entwined; milk glass, red eyes, Atterbury, dtd, 6" 165.00
Fish, flat, gr transparent, unmk..75.00
Fox on ribbed lid, lacy base, milk glass, 6¼" 165.00
Hand & dove, milk glass, Atterbury, no date................................50.00
Hen, cattail base, milk glass, unmk, 5½".......................................95.00
Hen, diamond basketweave, colored, Westmoreland Specialty 45.00
Hen, Dominecker; milk glass, pnt eyes, Challinor-Taylor, 8".......250.00
Hen, lacy base, milk glass w/bl head, Atterbury 225.00
Hen, milk glass, mk Hazel Atlas, sm 15.00
Hen, str headed, bl carnival, Indiana Glass 15.00
Hen w/chicks, milk glass, unmk McKee, 5½" 265.00
Horse, split-rib base, milk glass, mk McKee, 5½" 275.00
Jack rabbit, oval ribbed base, clear, att Flaccus 150.00
Lamb, picket base, milk glass, Westmoreland 85.00
Lamb, split-rib base, milk glass, 2 McKee mks, 5½" 425.00
Lion, British; milk glass, unmk, 6¼" 195.00

Animal Dishes with Covers

Covered animal dishes have been produced for nearly two centuries and are as varied as their manufacturers. They were made in many types of glass – slag, colored, clear, and milk glass – as well as china and pottery. On bases of nests and baskets, you will find animals and birds of every sort. The most common was the hen.

Some of the smaller versions made by McKee, Indiana Tumbler and Goblet Company, and Westmoreland Glass of Pittsburgh, Pennsylvania, were sold to food-processing companies who filled them with prepared mustard, baking powder, etc. Occasionally one will be found with the paper label identifying the product and processing company still intact.

Many of the glass versions produced during the latter part of the 19th century have been recently reproduced. As late as the 1960s, the Kemple Glass Company made the rooster, fox, lion, cat, lamb, hen, horse, turkey, duck, dove, and rabbit on split-ribbed or basketweave bases. They were made in amethyst, blue, amber, and milk glass, as well as a variegated slag. It is sometimes necessary to compare items in question to verified examples of older glass in order to recognize reproductions.

For more information, we recommend *Covered Animal Dishes* by our advisor, Everett Grist, whose address is in the Directory under Illinois. In the listings below, when only one dimension is given, it is length.

Lion on ribbed base, Atterbury, milk glass with glass eyes, lid dated Aug. 6, 1889, $150.00.

Lion, picket base, bl w/wht head, Westmoreland 125.00
Lion on ribbed lid, lacy base, milk glass, Atterbury 1889 ....175.00
Pintail duck, bl opaque, unmk, 5½" 75.00
Quail, scroll base, milk glass, unmk, 5½" 65.00
Rabbit, Dome; chocolate, Greentown 375.00
Rabbit, Mule-eared; picket base, bl opaque, Westmoreland.........100.00
Rabbit, split-rib base, milk glass, mk McKee, 5½" 325.00
Rabbit emerging from horizontal egg, milk glass, unmk 295.00
Rat on egg, milk glass, Vallerysthal, lg or sm.................225.00
Robin, ped base, bl opaque, unmk.............................15.00
Robin, ped base, milk glass, mk Vallerysthal 75.00
Robin on nest, milk glass, ftd, unmk, 6½".....................15.00
Rooster, basketweave base, milk glass, Westmoreland, sm 225.00
Rooster, milk glass w/bl head, Westmoreland Specialty, 5" 75.00
Rooster, wide-rib base, goofus on milk glass, unmk..............75.00
Rooster, wide-rib base, milk glass, Westmoreland Specialty...........65.00
Squirrel, split-rib base, milk glass, unmk McKee, 5½"................145.00
Swan, Block; milk glass, Challinor-Taylor, 7" 295.00
Swan, clear frosted, mk Vallerysthal, 5½"....................95.00
Swan, closed neck, milk glass, Westmoreland Specialty 75.00
Swan, head down, milk glass, 2 McKee mks, 5½" 475.00
Turkey, ribbed base, milk glass, mk McKee, 5½" 295.00
Turkey, standing, milk glass 85.00
Turtle, amber, unmk 85.00
Turtle, scroll base, hdls, milk glass, unmk, 7½".............165.00

Appliances, Electric

Collectors of Americana enjoy vintage appliances such as those used in the kitchen – toasters, coffee makers, etc. – as well as early TV sets, vacuum cleaners, short-lived innovations, and examples with particularly distinctive Deco styling. Currently, items from the '50s are especially sought-after.

Torrid toaster, catalog number, T-70, NM, $60.00.

Blender, Knapp-Monarch Liquidizer, Deco style, 1940s, EX 55.00
Fan, General Electric, brass blade, 12", EX.................150.00
Fan, Ribbonaire, table sz 150.00
Fan, Robbing & Myers, brass blade, EX 125.00
Fan, Westinghouse, 4 brass blades, brass cage, 3-speed, 13" 125.00
Foot massager, Dr Scholl's, enamel/metal, chrome base 40.00

Iron, American Beauty #66AB, 6½", EX 24.00
Iron, General Electric, Deco style, 1930s, EX in orig box 45.00
Iron, Pelouze, porc screw-in plug, 6", EX....................150.00
Iron, Sunbeam, late 1800s, 1st elecric model.................85.00
Toaster, Dominion, #48, EX 45.00
Toaster, Fitzgerald, #529, M................................85.00
Toaster, Fitzgerald, #75000 ....75.00
Toaster, Hotpoint, #125T17, NM.............................65.00
Toaster, L&H, #202, EX 50.00
Toaster, Sunbeam, #T-9, EX 95.00
Toaster, Sunbeam, horizontal, NM..........................75.00
Toaster, Toastalator, NM 175.00
Toaster, Toastmaster, #1A1, EX 75.00
Toaster, Toastqueen, EX.....................................20.00
Toaster, Universal, #E941, EX 65.00
Toaster, Universal, #E946, EX 50.00
Toaster, Universal, #7722, VG 45.00

Arequipa

The Arequipa Pottery operated from 1911 until 1918 at a sanitorium near Fairfax, California. Its purpose was two-fold – therapy for the patients and financial support for the institution. Frederick H. Rhead was the originator and director. The ware, made from local clays, was often hand thrown, simply styled and decorated. Marks were varied but always incorporated the name of the pottery and the state. A circular arrangement encompassing the negative image of a vase beside a tree is most common.

Bowl, lt lav, emb foliage, 10" 500.00
Bowl, lustre, appl seashells, 2x6" 200.00
Vase, bl, incurvate, baluster, 3⅜" 200.00
Vase, gr, bulbous, mk, #d, 5" 250.00
Vase, gr lava, early Rhead period mk, 8" 695.00
Vase, plum matt, 7½" 350.00

Argy-Rousseau, G.

Gabriel Argy-Rousseau produced both fine art glass and quality commercial ware in Paris, France, in 1918. He favored Art Nouveau as well as Art Deco and in the twenties produced a line of vases in the Egyptian manner, made popular by the discovery of King Tut's tomb. One of the most important types of glass he made was pate-de-verre. Most of his work is signed. Items listed below are pate-de-verre unless noted otherwise.

Bowl, geometrics/scrolling cartouches, gr/bl, 7" H 7,000.00
Bowl, Les Ramiers, gray pigeons, wine lappet border, 5½"......20,000.00
Bowl, poppies, red/wht/blk on purple mottle, 3x4½" 4,750.00
Bowl vase, red berries/gr & brn leaves on lav mottle, 2½"....... 3,250.00
Lamp, La Danse, 3 dancers, orange/yel/gr, lily finial, 29".........13,500.00
Pendant, flower fr by stems/buds, purple/bl/gr, 1⅞" dia............ 2,400.00
Pendant, lg cicada in oval, gr/purple/mauves, sgn, 3" 1,800.00
Plaque, Madonna/lilies, ivory w/yel halo on gray, 3½x2½" 500.00
Tray, fish/waves, gr w/ochre, 7½" L......................... 6,700.00
Vase, faceted kite forms, yel/amber/brn/orange, 6½"............... 3,600.00
Vase, fan-form flowers, aqua/turq/purple on gray, 11" 7,000.00
Vase, Farniente, nude reserve ea side, lozenge bands, 6".......12,000.00
Vase, flowers on long stems, gr/red on celery, mold sgn, 6"...... 4,000.00
Vase, pk floral band on gr/purple mottle, cylinder, 2¾" 2,400.00
Vase, vine/berry band, gadrooned base, mottled brns, 4x6"..... 4,800.00

Vase, vines, gray streaked w/rose/purple/lav, 5½" **3,000.00**
Vase, violets/brn stems on semi-opaque wht, 5¾" **3,000.00**
Veilleuse, dome shade: red/purple star-center flowers, 6" **9,000.00**

Veilleuse, sunburst motif in orange/red mottle and purple, molded signature, on wrought iron base, 6", $6,000.00.

Figural bronze lamps: Nude with greyhound, 'Guilford CT 1939' on label, 7", $135.00; Figure on horseback, 6½", $120.00.

Art Deco

To the uninformed observer, 'Art Deco' evokes images of chrome and glass, streamlined curves and aerodynamic shapes, mirrored prints of pink flamingos, and statues of slender nudes and greyhound dogs. Though the Deco movement began in 1925 at the Paris International Exposition and lasted to some extent into the 1950s, within that period of time the evolution of fashion and taste continued as it always has, resulting in subtle variations.

The French Deco look was one of opulence – exotic inlaid woods, rich material, lush fur and leather. Lines tended toward symmetrical curves. American designers adapted the concept to cover every aspect of fashion and home furnishings from small inexpensive picture frames, cigarette lighters, and costume jewelry to high-fashion designer clothing and exquisite massive furniture with squared or circular lines. Vinyl was a popular covering, and chrome-plated brass was used for chairs, cocktail shakers, lamps, and tables. Dinnerware, glassware, theaters, and train stations were designed to reflect the new 'Modernism.'

The Deco movement made itself apparent into the fifties in wrought iron lamps with stepped pink plastic shades and Venetian blinds. The sheer volume of production during those twenty-five years provides collectors today with fine examples of the period that can be bought for as little as $10 or $20 up to the thousands. Chrome items signed 'Chase' are prized by collectors, and blue glass radios and tables with blue glass tops are high on the list of desirability in many areas.

Those interested in learning more about this subject will want to read *Collector's Guide to Art Deco* by our advisor, Mary Frank Gaston. She is listed in the Directory under Texas. See also Bronzes; Chase; Frankart; Furniture; Jewelry; Lalique; Radios; etc.

Ash tray, bl glass, chrome sailboat at side, FD Co, 5" dia **40.00**
Ash tray, lady's profile, ceramic, Japan, 6" **20.00**
Box, powder; ceramic, wht dancing nude on lid, Germany............**65.00**
Box, powder; gr frosted glass, semi-nude figural, 8½".................**65.00**
Chair, tub; lacquered wood, leather uphl, no mk, 31".............. **1,400.00**
Cigarette case, Bakelite & pigskin, Rolinx, England......................**70.00**
Clock, wood/chrome/enamel, triangular, Karl Schewiger, 17" **440.00**
Cocktail shaker, figural 5" glass pianist on 8" shaker **75.00**

Compact, chrome, bl Greek Key decor, Woolworth, 1916, 3¼" **50.00**
Compact, gold & silver geometrics, Elgin, 4" dia, NM..................**35.00**
Compact, mc enamel sections w/HP roses & brass-plated trim......**55.00**
Compact, silver/blk medallion on gr w/brass trim, 8-sided **30.00**
Decanter, clear to gr, notched/beaded ribs, 11", +5 shots **60.00**
Dish, brn/blk marble, bronze dachshund sits on edge, 10" **600.00**
Elevator light, 3-sided bronze, gr slag glass, 3-way switch **145.00**
Figurine, lady in sarong, Clarke, East Palestine OH, 1940s..........**125.00**
Figurine, lady w/fan, porc on metal base, unmk, 12" **125.00**
Figurine, seated pottery nude, Guiraud-Riviere, 21" L **2,600.00**
Hairbrush, brn plastic, stepped shape **6.00**
Lamp, boudoir; gr-pnt pot metal, dancing nude figural **125.00**
Lamp, metal, kneeling maids uphold amber shade/drape, 21" **1,500.00**
Lamp, pyramid geometric frosted shade; wrought base, Degue.....**900.00**
Piano, gray/blk lacquer, line detail, Monington/Weston, 57" .. **3,300.00**
Pipe stand, nude diving figure, bronze, unmk **100.00**
Pitcher, HP metal, Normandie, by P Muller-Munk, 12".......... **2,800.00**
Sconce, chrome top over cluster of glass slabs, Perzel, 24"....... **2,500.00**

Textile, black with gold geometrics, 50" square, $550.00.

Torchere, glass plaque w/nude; appl grapes on 3-strap std **2,800.00**
Tumbler, cobalt glass insert in chrome holder, 2½" **12.00**
Tumbler, sterling, flared mouth, lg rnd base, Cartier, 3" **50.00**
Vase, copper, 4-color abstraction, ovoid, Camille Faure, 7" **2,000.00**
Vase, metal, scrolls/garlands, 3-color on mc, C Faure, 3" **600.00**

Art Glass Baskets

A popular novelty and gift item during the Victorian era, these one-of-a-kind works of art were produced in just about any type of art glass in use at that time. They were never marked, since these were not true production pieces but 'whimsies' made by glassworkers to relieve the tedium of the long work day. Some were made as special gifts. The more decorative and imaginative the design, the more valuable the basket.

Aquamarine with white interior, Diamond Quilted, 7½", $275.00.

Amberina, swirled, gilt floral/criss-Xs, V-hdl/rigaree, 16" **750.00**
Amberina overshot, ruffled, thorn hdl, 7½" dia **200.00**
Bl opal, butterflies/ribbons, ruffled; amber V-hdl, 8x6" **400.00**
Bl spangle, clear thorn hdl, 7½x4¾" **175.00**
Butterscotch/opal spangle, crimped, clear V-hdl, 13" dia.............**275.00**
Cranberry, clear appl leaf ft, clear hdl, 7x5¼".............................**145.00**
Cranberry, sq, clear ruffle, sq thorn hdl, 6x5½" **165.00**
Cream opaque, appl red cherries, amber hdl, 5¼x3⅝" **195.00**
Frosted overshot w/lt amethyst rosettes at base of hdl, 7"..............**90.00**
Gr opal to red spatter, clear twist hdl, 6½x6" **135.00**
Gr opal w/appl florals on vaseline branch, twist hdl, 6x5" **145.00**
Melon Rib & Swirl, bl opal, ruffled, sq thorn hdl, 7½x5" **265.00**
Opal w/pk int, 3-color appl leaf ft, amber X-hdl, 13" H **700.00**
Orange overlay, 8-crimp, clear thorn hdl, ftd, 8¼x5¼".................**165.00**
Pk & wht spatter, Invt T'print, clear thorn hdl, 7x4¼" **135.00**
Pk candy stripe, crimped, clear thorn hdl, oval, 7x6" **145.00**
Pk opal, sq vaseline hdl, 5½"...**125.00**
Pk opal to vaseline, drape mold, thorn hdl, 7½x5½x7".................**195.00**
Pk opal w/clear appl leaves, twist hdl, 7x4"................................**165.00**
Pk overlay, clear appl wide ruffle/reeded hdl/ft, 7½x3⅝"..............**165.00**
Pk spangle, folded in, pleated, clear thorn hdl, 7x8" **200.00**
Pk spangle w/Hobnail ruffled rim, clear twist hdl, 9" L **350.00**
Pk striped opal, appl flowers, vaseline twist hdl, 6x5" **140.00**

Rose overlay, amber ruffle, amber criss-cross hdl, 8x6¼".............**195.00**
Rose overlay, Hobnail edge, twisted thorn hdl, 7x7"...................**195.00**
Rose to wht w/mica, twist/loop clear hdl, 8".............................**175.00**
Spatter overlay, wht int, HP florals, clear hdl, 7½x4¾" **165.00**
Tortoise shell, appl amber thorn twist hdl, 8x5" **90.00**
Wht opaque Hobnail, apricot int, clear thorn hdl, 5½x5¼" **175.00**
Wht w/rose int, crystal edge, thorn hdl, 9x9x10½" **225.00**
Yel opaque, wht spatter int, gold trim, thorn hdl, 5¾x4⅜" **95.00**

Art Nouveau

From the famous 'L'Art Nouveau' shop in the rue de Provence in Paris, 'New Art' spread across the continent and belatedly arrived in America in time to add its curvilineal elements and asymmetrical ornamentation to the ostentatious remains of the Rococo revival of the 1880s. Nouveau manifested itself in every facet of decorative art. In glassware Tiffany turned the concept into a commercial success that lasted well into the second decade of this century and created a style that inspired other American glassmakers for decades. Furniture, lamps, bronzes, jewelry, and automobiles were designed within the realm of its dictates. Today's market abounds with lovely examples of Art Nouveau, allowing the collector to choose one or several areas that hold a special interest. See also Bronzes; Jewelry; Tiffany; Silver; specific manufacturers; etc.

Bottle, scent; yel metal, from chatelaine, ca 1870s........................**32.00**
Box, gilt bronze, maid w/swirling hair on lid, leaf ft, 6"...............**465.00**
Box, gilt metal, nymph's face in corner/foliage, sq, 8x8" **375.00**
Box, pill; sterling, chased scrolls, England, 1⅞"..........................**150.00**
Box, SP, emb leaves/branches, probably Austrian, 8x8" **400.00**
Box, SP, interlaced foliage, openwork ft, WMF, 7" L...................**265.00**

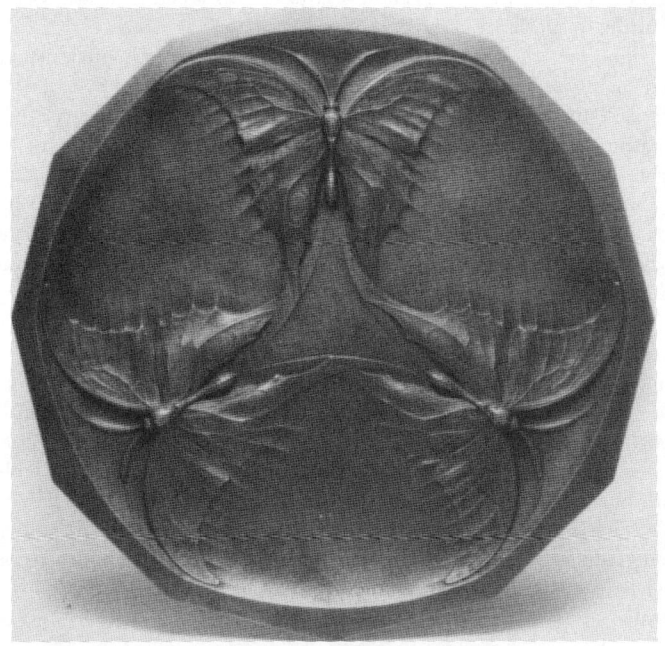

Bronze platter, after Henry Miault, early 20th century, 14", $650.00.

Candlestick, bronze, nude & lotus bobeche, Bouval, 3x6"...........**600.00**
Candlestick, silvered metal, tree form w/3 branch arms, 12" **350.00**
Candlestick, SP, branch ea side of maid, WMF, 11", pr **2,000.00**
Centerpc, silver metal fairy above glass 'pond,' WMF, 24" **1,500.00**
Charger, pottery, blonde in profile, gladiola rim, MS, 14"............**300.00**

Clock, gilt bronze, emb florals, bl enamel face, 14" 900.00
Compact, SP, chatelaine loop, hallmk, mini...................................60.00
Compote, silver metal, robed maid std, shell bowl, WMF, 18".....800.00
Dish, silvered metal, semi-nude, fountain mask ends, 12"............550.00
Figurine, silver metal, nymph beside harp, att WMF, 12".............300.00
Jardiniere, metal, conch shell, mermaid on rim, WMF, 12"..... 1,300.00
Mirror, hand; gilt metal, rtcl hdl w/face of nymph, 12" 200.00
Mirror, metal/patina, satyr mask/ivy, nude aside, Lucy, 17"..........600.00
Vase, gilt bronze, cherub on side, 1-hdl, Mingiot, 13", pr........ 1,300.00
Vase, pewter, maid hugs ea side, vine hdls, AK & Cie, 14" 600.00
Vase, pottery, Queen Anne's Lace bouquet form, Fr, 12" 900.00
Vase, pottery w/gilt-bronze dragonfly mtd ea side, MB, 7" 2,000.00

Arts and Crafts

The Arts and Crafts movement began in England during the last quarter of the 19th century, and its influence was soon felt in this country. Among its proponents in America were Elbert Hubbard (see Roycroft) and Gustav Stickley (see Stickley.) They rebelled against the mechanized mass production of the Industrial Revolution and against the cumulative influence of hundreds of years of man's changing taste. They subscribed to the theory of purification of the styles – that designs be geared strictly to necessity. At the same time they sought to elevate these basic ideals to the level of accepted 'art.' Simplicity was their virtue; to their critics it was a fault.

The type of furniture they promoted was squarely built of heavy oak, and so simple was its appearance that as a result many began to copy the style which became known as 'Mission.' Soon factories had geared production toward making cheap copies of their designs. In 1915 Stickley's own operation failed, forced into bankruptcy by the machinery he so despised. Hubbard lost his life that same year on the ill-fated *Lusitania.* Within the decade the style had lost its popularity. See also Furniture, Roycroft, Silver, Stickley, and specific manufacturers.

Andirons, wrought iron, ball atop sq post, 2-ftd, 17x9x20"..........700.00
Book, Friar Jerome's Beautiful..., Houghton/Mifflin, 1896 ....150.00
Bowl, hammered copper, wide, raised ft, KF Leinonen, 9½" 150.00
Bowl, sterling, monogram in shield, hoop hdl, Le Bolt, 5" 375.00
Candle holder, copper, lily pad w/lily cup, Lebolt, 6", pr..............165.00
Candlestick, bronze, Delta, orig bobeche, Jarvie, 1905, 15" 1,400.00
Candlestick, bronze patina, elongated cup, Jarvie/'I,' 14" 4,750.00
Candlestick, nickel-plated, slim std, Jarvie, 12", pr, EX 425.00
Chandelier, oak/slag glass w/leaded yel geometrics, 23" 550.00
Chandelier, slag glass w/8 metal-screened panels, 21" 495.00
Clock, tall case; beveled glass/cane panels, Crafters, 70" 1,000.00
Coat tree, wood, Xd ft, sq post, str wood hooks, varnished 100.00
Compote, sterling, Arthur Stone, 2½x4" 170.00
Cup, pewter, For Old Times Sake, Tudric, 2-hdl, 8" 225.00
Dresser set, sterling, tortoise shell comb+4 pcs, Kalo, VG 500.00
Fireplace hood, hammered copper, flaring, riveted, 43x36" 900.00
Jardiniere, hammered copper, relief panels, Randall, 8x11".........475.00
Lamp, hammered copper/4-panel mica 11" shade, D Van Erp. 6,500.00
Lamp, mica-panel cone shade; copper vase-form std, 25x19" . 2,750.00
Lamp, 3-panel shade w/mica, vasiform std, Kopperkraft, 13"... 4,100.00
Mirror, scooped bk, vertical slat ea side, Limbert, 23x38"........ 1,700.00
Pitcher, hammered copper w/repousse, straw-wrap hdl, 7x7" 375.00
Rug, dk/lt brn, Craftsman style, 46x26", VG 100.00
Rug, Drugget, geometrics, 4-color, 96x96", VG 1,000.00
Table runner, stylized silk embr work on ivory, 48x15", EX..........200.00
Tablecloth, linen w/3-color needlepoint motif, 32x32", VG 95.00
Teapot, hammered silver/ivory mts, #453/mk Kalo, 9x8", EX . 1,450.00

Table lamp, Dirk Van Erp, hammered copper and mica, marked with windmill, 'D'Arcy,' and signature, 16" x 14½", $1,100.00.

Trivet, hammered copper, irid inlay, rivets, Burdick, 5½" 325.00
Vase, copper, fluted, cylindrical, Karl Kipp/#218, 6½" 275.00
Vase, hammered bronze w/enamel-like finish, H Dixon, 8" 2,400.00
Vase, hammered copper, cylinder w/3 buttresses, mk, 7", EX .. 1,100.00
Vase, hammered copper, Dirk Van Erp, open box mk, 4x3", EX .475.00
Vase, hammered copper, Dirk Van Erp, rpr seam, 3½x5", VG.....500.00
Vase, hammered copper, flared/fluted cylinder, Avon Co, 9" 70.00
Vase, hammered copper, incurvate, Harry Dixon, 5½", EX· 550.00
Vase, hammered copper, tree-in-circle mk/BM, 4x5", VG 230.00
Vase, hammered copper, 3 vertical ribs, D'arcy Gaw, 5x6" 450.00
Vase, hammered copper/orig patina, D Van Erp, mk, 8" 1,700.00

Aurene

Aurene, developed in 1904 by Frederick Carder of the Steuben Glass Works, is a metallic iridescent glassware similar to some of Tiffany's. Usually a rich lustrous gold or blue, green and red may also be found on rare occasion. It was used alone and in combination with calcite, a cream-colored glass with a calcium base also developed by Carder. Decorated examples are very rare. It is usually marked Aurene or Steuben, sometimes with the factory number added, etched into the glass by hand. Paper labels were also used. See also Steuben.

Bonbon, bl, stretched/crimped/extended rim on rnd bowl, 6". 1,300.00
Bottle, scent; bl, teardrop stopper, slender, #1414, 6¾"................750.00
Bottle, scent; gold, slim w/flared base, 'gem' finial, 10"................450.00
Bowl, centerpc; brn 445.00
Bowl, gold, 3 appl ft, incurvate, sgn/#2586, 2¼x10" 275.00
Bowl, gold, 3 appl prunts form ft, incurvate, sgn, 2x8" 225.00
Candlestick, gold, twist stem, sgn/#686, 8", pr............................800.00
Candlestick, gold, 4 rosettes on ring stems, sgn/#d, 4", pr............750.00
Compote, bl, twist stem w/4 prunts, sgn/#2604, 7x8" 1,250.00
Compote, gold, twist stem w/prunts, sgn/#2604, 5¾x6¾" 850.00
Finger bowl, gold, ribbed, sgn, +underplate 300.00

Compote, gold, 4", $495.00; Salt cellar, blue, $300.00; Vase, gold, #355, 6", $450.00.

Nut dish, gold, stretched/ruffled rim, #699, 3½" 215.00
Pitcher, bl, sgn/#3005, 5" 1,000.00
Pitcher, gold, low/triangular, sgn/#2670, 2½x4" 300.00
Rose jar, bl-gold, 3 openings in lid, sgn/#2412, 6" 700.00
Shade, bl, silver leaves/vines, 4½x4", pr.................................. 1,400.00
Shade, pk, silver leaves/vines, 4½x4" 1,250.00
Tazza, gold, sgn/#5066, 6¼x5½" 500.00
Vase, bl, flared rim, sgn/#2619, 3½x5½" 900.00
Vase, bl, flared/crimped rim, sgn, 6" 900.00
Vase, bl, hearts/threaded vines at shoulder, #297, 6½" 2,750.00
Vase, bl, ped ft, stretched top, sgn/#312, 17" 1,350.00
Vase, bl, slim form w/flared top, 7" 450.00
Vase, bl, stick neck, sgn/#2556, 8" 225.00
Vase, bl, 3-branch stump, sgn/#2744, 6" 900.00
Vase, bl-gold, ped ft, sgn/#6165, 12" 575.00
Vase, gold, bulbous classic form, sgn/#2683, 8" 850.00
Vase, gold, Dia Quilt top, ruffled/flared, sgn/#277, 13"............ 1,050.00
Vase, gold, flared/ruffled, sgn, 8" 650.00
Vase, gold, ftd trumpet form, sgn, 10" 750.00
Vase, gold, leaves at top, sgn/#219, 8½" 1,800.00
Vase, gold, miniature, sgn/#2648, 2½" 425.00
Vase, gold, pulled feathers, sgn, 2½" 800.00
Vase, gold, ribbed trumpet form, sgn, 5½" 495.00
Vase, gold, stick neck, sgn/#2556, 8" 160.00
Vase, gold, urn form, sgn/#3064, 6" 850.00
Vase, jack-in-the-pulpit; gold, sgn/#2699, 6¼" 775.00
Vase, opal w/red leaves, gold lily pads & int, sgn/#d, 6" 12,000.00

Austrian Ware

From the late 1800s until the beginning of WWI, several companies were located in the area known at the turn of the century as Bohemia. They produced hard-paste porcelain dinnerware and decorative items primarily for the American trade. Today examples bearing the marks of these firms are usually referred to by collectors as Austrian ware, indicating simply the country of their origin. Of those various companies, these marks are best known: M.Z. Austria; Victoria, Carlsbad, Austria (Schmidt and Company); and O. & E.G. (Royal) Austria.

Though most of the decorations were transfer designs which were sometimes signed by the original artist, pieces marked Royal Austria were often hand painted and so indicated alongside the backstamp.

Of these three companies, Victoria, Carlsbad, Austria is the most

highly valued. Collectors should note that in our listings transfer decorations showing 'signatures' (sgn), such as 'Wagner,' 'Kauffmann,' 'LeBrun,' etc., were not actually painted by those artists but were merely based on their original paintings.

Bowl, portraits, mc, sq fluted rim, 10" **95.00**
Chamberstick, roses, pk on gr, gold hdl, ball ft, 3⅛x3¼"...............**65.00**
Charger, lady's portrait, gilt border, mk Zdekauer, 12½"..............**300.00**
Compote, Gothic figures, gr & wht w/gold, ftd, beehive mk, 3" ...**60.00**
Creamer, HP violets, gold hdl, dtd 1911, mk MZ Austria **20.00**
Cup & saucer, 4 ladies w/pitcher & fruit w/gold, Carlsbad **38.00**
Ewer, Kauffman scene on turq w/gold, Carlsbad, 9½" **125.00**
Pitcher, tankard; HP purple grapes w/gr vines, Vienna, 14".........**195.00**
Plate, birds in Baroque reserves on gr, in fr, 10" **90.00**
Plate, dog portrait, Rococo edge, 13" **225.00**
Plate, lady's portrait, Kauffman, Victoria, 10"...............................**85.00**
Tray, 3 draped ladies/cherub, sgn, Carlsbad, 12x7½" **95.00**
Vase, birds & branches, yel/gr/gold, hdls, 11x7" **55.00**
Vase, florals on burmese, flask form, sgn/#d, Carlsbad, 13" **550.00**
Vase, girl's portrait, ornate gold hdls, Victoria, 12" **275.00**
Vase, mc florals, gourd shape w/stick neck, Carlsbad, 12½" **225.00**
Vase, 4 Grecian figures, ornate hdls, Victoria Carlsbad, 10" **75.00**

Vases, figures in reserves, 14", $575.00 for the pair.

Autographs

Philography is defined as the practice of collecting autographs or, literally translated, the 'love of writing.' It is estimated that two million Americans own autographs of famous people, and of these at least twenty thousand are serious collectors. In recent years, autograph collecting has grown both from a standpoint of popularity as well as investment. Examples which only fifteen years ago sold for $5 to $10 now command prices in the hundreds. For example, in 1970 a Clark Gable signature was valued at about $15; today it would bring approximately ten times that amount. Knowledgeable collectors watch the market for the opportunity of purchasing a rare item that within a few years can be turned over at a substantial gain. In one instance, a collector purchased a handwritten letter of James 'Wild Bill' Hickok for $2,500—within five years he had turned down two different offers of $25,000 for the same letter.

The law of supply and demand is the foremost consideration in placing a value on an autograph. In most cases, age is not relevant. The greater the supply, the lower the value; when demand is great, the price goes up. Since the supply of signatures of persons no longer living is obviously stable, as more people become collectors, their values increase. Some celebrities are known to have signed their autographs thousands of times – others only a few, thus limiting their availablitiy. With fewer to go around, the cost to the collector would be higher.

The least desirable type of autograph is the simple signature signed on a card. The most desirable and valuable autograph is generally a handwritten letter signed in full. In between come signed photos, signed documents, signed typewritten letters, and various other types of autographs. In a letter, the content is important. Those conveying personal thoughts on or indicating involvement in issues relating to their participation in matters of public interest are more highly valued.

The beginning collector can add to his collection by corresponding with current celebrities. Most will respond to a letter when a self-addressed, stamped envelope is included. Because of their willingness to sign, the value of these autographs rarely exceed a few dollars. There are exceptions: Bush's signature is worth around $100, Reagan's about $75, Carter's about $40, Nixon's about $35, and Ford's around $25. Even more valuable – simply because they refuse to sign, or letters requesting signatures never reach them – are Greta Garbo, Idi Amin, and Muhammar Khadafy, whose mere signature could easily bring $500 on today's autograph market. As a rule of thumb, signed glossy black and white photographs of recent movie stars sell in the range of $5.00 to $15.00.

Philography can be a fun and rewarding hobby – often all it takes to start is the address of someone you admire. In the listings below, photos are assumed black and white unless noted color.

Our advisor for autographs is Tim Anderson; he is listed in the Directory under Utah.

Key:
ADS — handwritten document signed
ALS — handwritten letter signed
ANS — handwritten note signed
AQS — autograph quotation signed
CS — countersigned
ins — inscription
DS — document signed
LH — letterhead
ISP — inscribed signed photo
PLH — personal letterhead
LS — signed letter, typed or written by someone else
SP — signed photo
sig — signature

Agar, John; ISP, from Hold Bk Tomorrow, EX 20.00
Albert, Prince Consort of England, sig on LH, +photo card 65.00

Abigail Adams, signed letter, 1815, $4,750.00.

Autry, Gene; sig on post card, NM 10.00
Bailey, F Lee; ANS, on 3x5" card, NM 15.00
Bates, Katherine Lee; sig on printed form, 1898, EX 18.00
Benton, Thomas H; sig cut from envelope.................................15.00

Lilly Pons, inscribed signed photograph, 1930, 9" x 7", $550.00.

Bentson, Lloyd; ISP, w/memo on US Senate LH 20.00
Beston, Henry; sig on card, EX...15.00
Bolger, Ray; SP, as Scarecrow, glossy blk/wht, 8x10" 75.00
Boyle, John J; ANS, congratulations, NY, 1905, EX 16.00
Bradley, Omar N; LS, will sgn photo, CA, 1955, 1-pg..................50.00
Brown, Joe E; autograph endorsement w/sig, 1930s.......................17.50
Buchanan, James; ALS, appreciation of loyalty, 1848, 3-pg 800.00
Cagney, James; SP, bold sig, glossy blk/wht, 1930s, EX..................75.00
Cantor, Eddie; sig on card...22.00
Chapman, Oscar; sig on lg card, Sec of Interior under Truman......15.00
Charles II, DS, receipt for taxes, detailed account, 1661 ....50.00
Chiang Kai-shek, Madame; LS, enjoyed book, 1982, EX 35.00
Conner, James (CSA General); sig cut from envelope, EX............35.00
Conrad, Charles M; Sec of War, sig from free frank 16.00
Coolidge, Grace Goodhue; sig on White House card, EX..............70.00
Coolidge, Grace; ALS, cherishes gift, 1929, 2-pg, EX................110.00
Cromwell, Oliver; rental receipt for lands, 1653, 1-pg, EX 75.00
Dafoe, Allan Roy; LS, quint's guardianship, 1938, 1-pg................40.00
Daley, Richard; sig on City of Chicago card, 5x3" 27.50
Davis, Bette; SP, in evening gown, early, 8x10"..............................40.00
Day, William R; sgn check, from City Nat'l, Canton OH, 1892 ....15.00
Dietrich, Marlene; sig on program, 1972, EX................................48.00
Dix, Dorothy; sig on card, EX 15.00
Douglas, Wm O; sig on card..15.00
Du Maurier, Daphne; bold sig on typescript, 1-pg.........................17.50
Earhart, Amelia; sig on Waldorf Astoria menu, 4½x3½" 200.00
Eddy, Nelson; ISP, sepia, ca 1935, EX 50.00
Edison, Thomas A; fine sig on gold-edged card, EX 120.00
Einstein, Albert; sig on card, dtd 1946...300.00
Eisenhower, Mamie; LS, White House LH, thank you, '60, 1-pg...45.00
Ferber; Edna; LS, writing plans, 1947, 2-pg 50.00
Fillmore, Millard; full sig cut from DS, EX 100.00
Fish, Hamilton; ALS, as Sec of State, NY, 1838...........................22.00
Ford, Betty; sig on White House card 70.00
Ford, Gerald; ISP, color, as president...80.00
Funicello, Annette; SP, blk/wht, 1967 Disney stamp.......................20.00
Gage, Thomas; ALS, to Gov of RI, Mar 1764, 1-pg, EX.............350.00
Garson, Greer; ISP, matt portrait, ca 1940, M 27.50

Gehrig, Lou; ALS, hotel stationery, baseball plans, 1-pg 8,500.00
Gershwin, George; insc & sig on 3x5" card, EX 380.00
Gingold, Hermione; SP, 8x10", EX 32.00
Gleason, Jackie; bold sig on card 37.50
Graziano, Rocky; ISP, glossy blk/wht, 8x10", EX 25.00
Greenaway, Kate; sketch w/sig on 5¼x4" paper.......................235.00
Greene, Nathaniel; ALS, introduction for friend, 1785, 2-pg......500.00
Haley, Alex; sig on card, NM 15.00
Hammett, Dashiell; sig on album page, EX................................235.00
Harlow, Jean; ALS, butterfly stationery, 1930s, 1-pg................ 1,200.00
Hayes, Helen; SP, early, 8x10" 30.00
Heston, Charlton; SP, as Ben Hur, glossy blk/wht, 8x10" 30.00
Hill, Grace Livingston; LS, appreciation, 1940, 1-pg 17.50
Hilton, Conrad; SP, photo by F Bachrach, 8x10" 28.00
Hinton, Walter; ANS, ca 1919, 2x6"..130.00
Hoover, Herbert; ALS, accepts directorship, 1909, 1-pg 1,400.00
Howard, Leslie; LS, LH, thank you, 1936, 1-pg..........................325.00
Hughes, Rupert; LS, ordering 3 books, 1935, 1-pg......................17.50
Irving, Washington; ALS, Sec of US Legation in London, 1-pg..100.00
Jefferson, Joseph; sig on card, ca 1900, EX 15.00
Johnson, Lady Bird; SP, 1960s, NM 100.00
Kelly, Patsy; sig from contract, EX..15.00
Kennedy, Jacqueline Bouvier; bold sig on envelope 100.00
Lafayette, Marquis de; ALS, to Gen Pepe of Italy, 1831, 1-pg 450.00
Langley, Samuel Pierpont; sig on album pg, 1889.......................88.00
Lee, Gypsy Rose; bold sig on paper, ca 1940, w/photo...................38.00
Lee, Robert E; ALS, rprs at Fort Miffin, PA, 1844, ½-pg 2,000.00
Leonard, Sugar Ray; SP, action pose, 8x10", NM 37.50
Liberace, sig on card, NM 32.00
Lincoln, Abraham; sig on endorsement, 1861, 1-pg, VG 2,500.00
Lincoln, Robert T; sig on album leaf, as Sec of War 28.00
Lindbergh, Charles A; sig on portrait, ca 1927............................775.00
London, Jack; ADS, printed check, endorsed by wife, 1906 ....365.00
Long, Huey P; DS, LH, 1928, 15x9½" 300.00
Luce, Clare Booth; full sig on card, EX 15.00
Madison, James; ADS, as president, ship's passport, 1810............850.00
Marshall, George C; bold sig on card, 3x5", NM 38.00
McKinley, Wm; sig on Executive Mansion Washington card 235.00
Mix, Tom; sig & date in pencil on sm paper 88.00
Monet, Claude; LS, to receive friend, French, 1-pg.....................285.00
Monroe, James; ADS, as Sec of State, 1812, 2-pg, EX 600.00
Morris, Robert; ALS, land speculation, 1794, 2-pg, EX 450.00
Murphy, Audie; sig in book: To Hell & Back, 1949, EX.............275.00
Musial, Stan; sig on baseball card, 1962, 3½x2½" 15.00
Mussolini, Benito; cut sig, early 185.00
Nicklaus, Jack; SP, glossy blk/wht, NM 12.00
O'Brien, Pat; DS, membership application, 1941, EX 22.50
Owens, Jesse; sig on card, 1936, NM..25.00
Parker, Dorothy; LS, political views, 1942, 1-pg..........................55.00
Post, Wiley; sig on pencil sketch, 6x4" 285.00
Presley, Elvis; ISP, 8x10"...495.00
Quasimodo, Salvatore; sig on card 20.00
Reagan, Ronald; DS, presidential candidate, 1980, 1-pg...........110.00
Reagan, Ronald; 3 sm drawings, sgn in initials, 1974, EX 800.00
Rinehart, Mary Roberts; cut sig, Paris, 1919..............................27.50
Rogers, Richard; LS, to Pearl Buck, 1963, 1-pg.........................150.00
Roosevelt, Franklin; DS, Sec of Navy LH, 1-pg..........................350.00
Roosevelt, James; sig on calling card 14.00
Roosevelt, Theodore; ISP, platinum, oval, 1903, 6½x5¼.............600.00
Russell, Jane; ISP, glossy blk/wht, early, NM 28.00
Ruth, Babe; sgn menu, from Newhaven 1923 Baseball Dinner....600.00
Sadat, Anwar; ISP, standing pose, 7x9½" 145.00
Sandburg, Carl; LS, thanks for book, 1-pg..................................75.00

Spock, Dr Benjamin; SP, blk/wht, 5x3½" 17.50
Stein, Gertrude; sig on post card to collector, 1936....................188.00
Stewart, James; SP, ca 1940, EX 27.50
Taft, Wm H; DS, Sec of War LH, 1904, 1-pg, EX 170.00
Taft, Wm; LS, Supreme Court LH, thank you, 1928, 1-pg, EX ...380.00
Truman, Bess Wallace; LS, LH, sending husband's photo, 1976.....78.00
Truman, Bess; bold sig on sheet of 8¢ commemorative stamps.....100.00
Tutu, Desmond; SP, 8x10", NM 110.00
Vallee, Rudy; LS, invitation, 1942, 1-pg.....................................20.00
Van Buren, Martin; DS, military appointment, 1839, 1-pg..........600.00
Van Dyke, Henry; sig on card, Hague, 1916, EX 15.00
Vance, Bert; sig on card..15.00
Vance, Vivian; LS, bold sig on personalized post card 38.00
Wallace, Lew; sig cut from check, EX 18.00
Warren, Earl; SP, as Gov of CA, 1952, EX................................100.00
Wellington, Duke of; ALS, last 4 lines, sgn Wellington 78.00
Wells, Orson; sig in pencil on card...15.00
West, Adam; SP, sgn as Batman, glossy blk/wht, 8x10" 20.00
West, Mae; ISP, sexy pose, glossy blk/wht, 1930s, EX 38.00
Westinghouse, George; LS, business matter, 1897, 1-pg 220.00
Whitman, Walt; sig on 2x4" paper, dtd '86, EX 355.00
Wilson, Edith Bolling; sig on sm wht card, EX 38.00
Wilson, Woodrow; early sig cut from DS 45.00
Young, Cy; sig on card 47.50
Young, Loretta; SP, glossy blk/wht, ca 1945, EX 15.00

Automobilia

While some automobilia buffs are primarily concerned with restoring vintage cars, others concentrate on only one area of collecting. For instance, hood ornaments were often quite spectacular. Made of chrome or nickel plate on brass or bronze, they were designed to represent the 'winged maiden' Victory, flying bats, sleek greyhounds, soaring eagles, and a host of other creatures. Today they bring prices in the $75 to $200 range. R. Lalique glass ornaments go much higher!

Horns, radios, clocks, gear shift knobs, and key chains with company emblems are other areas of interest. Generally, items pertaining to the classics of the thirties are most in demand. Paper advertising material, manuals, and catalogs in excellent condition are also collectible.

License plate collectors search for the early porcelain-on-cast-iron examples. First year plates – e.g., Massachusetts, 1903; Wisconsin, 1905; Indiana, 1913 – are especially valuable. The last of the states to issue regulation plates were South Carolina and Texas in 1917, and Florida in 1918. While many northeastern states had registered hundreds of thousands of vehicles by the 1920s making these plates relatively common, those from the southern and western states of that period are considered rare. Naturally, condition is important. While a pair in mint condition might sell for as much as $100 to $125, a pair with chipped or otherwise damaged porcelain may sometimes be had for as little as $25 to $30. See also Gas Globes and Panels.

Ash tray, Diamond Tires, tire form w/glass insert, 1905..................50.00
Ash tray, Goodrich, gr glass..15.00
Badge, plant; Texaco...8.00
Book, cartoon; Think Volkswagen, 1967, 70-pg, EX....................10.00
Book, instruction; Model A Ford, 1928 ....10.00
Book, reference; Ford Deluxe V-8, complete, 1940, EX 5.00
Booklet, Kansas Motor Vehicle Laws, 1919................................27.50
Booklet, Presidential, Skelly, 1960 ....8.00
Booklet, Studebaker, Care of Truck in Wartime, 1940s................45.00
Bottle, Shell Oil emb, tall, 1930s, 16 in orig case......................350.00
Box, Puritan Inner-Tube, Hood Rubber Co 10.00

Brochure, Buick, 1940, fold-out, open: 33½x11" 12.50
Brochure, Hudson, color, 1932, 24-pg...............................15.00
Brochure, Packard, color, fold-out, 1936................................ 8.00
Buckle, Mobil Oil 12.00
Carrier, AF coil; Mobil Oil, for filpruf bottles, 8-qt 75.00
Catalog, Ford Hardware & Trim Supplies, 1936, 84-pg, VG 25.00
Container, Mobil Permazone, 1-gal, empty................................15.00
Emblem, door; Chevrolet Bel Aire...24.00
Flashlight, Shamrock Oil Co, gr..15.00
Headlamp, Ford, copper, kerosene burner, M 125.00
Headlight lens, CM Hall Lamp Co, Detroit MI, ca 1948, pr..........35.00
Hood ornament, Hudson, 1949...85.00
Hood ornament, leaping greyhound, Ford, 1933, on base 120.00
Horn, Overland, brass 30.00
Hubcap, Ford Model B, brass..18.00
Key chain w/knife, Tenneco 5.00
Knife, Cities Service 18.00
Lamp kit, Eveready Mazda, tin, red/bl, 4 lights, 5x2½" 22.00
License tag attachment, Putnam Oil..10.00
Lighter, Skelly Zippo, M 15.00
Lighter, Texaco 10.00
Lug wrench, Ford Motor Co, 1920s, EX....................................25.00
Manual, Chevrolet, 1934, rprs...25.00
Manual, Ford operator's; 1948, EX...18.00
Manual, Ford owner's, 1964, M in orig envelope 4.00
Medallion, Ford Motor Co, brass, 30-yr...................................35.00
Mirror, rear-view; ornate scrollwork, 1921 ....35.00
Money clip, Skelly 8.50
Pail, Run Easy Axle Grease, tin, fine graphics...........................45.00
Pin, Kaiser 5-yr, EX..10.00
Post card, Chrysler-Plymouth, Hopalong Cassidy, 1942 ....10.00
Poster, Employer's Mutuals, car safety, 1930s, 11x17" 6.00
Promotional car, 1959 Mercury convertible, EX 50.00
Promotional car, 1961 Ford Galaxy, 2-door, hard top, M 50.00
Promotional car, 1962 Falkon Futura, sport coupe, M..................50.00
Rack, Gargoyle Mobiloil, Authorized Quart Service, 1920s 395.00
Radiator cap, Chevrolet Viking, 1929 ....175.00
Spray washer dispenser, windshield; Mobil 20.00
Tag, Auto Owners' Protective Exchange, aluminum, 3x2" 8.00
Tie clasp, Exxon... 8.50
Tie clasp, Skelly-Getty...12.00
Tin container, Indian Head Radiator Cement, M 10.00
Tire breaker, CI, 1920s..20.00
Token, So-Vis D, oil pour can on front...................................... 8.00
Valve grinder, Model T Ford 35.00
Valve stem, brass, Michelin, Milltown NJ, Pat 2/28/05 ....15.00
Watch chain, Dodge Bros, enamel & gold.................................85.00

Autumn Leaf

In 1933 the Hall China Company designed a line of dinnerware for the Jewel Tea Company, who offered it to their customers as premiums. Although you may hear the ware referred to as 'Jewel Tea,' it was officially named 'Autumn Leaf' in the 1940s. In addition to the dinnerware, frosted Libbey glass tumblers, stemware, and a melmac service with the orange and gold bittersweet pod were available over the years, as were tablecloths, plastic covers for bowls and mixers, and metal items such as cake safes, hot pads, coasters, waste baskets, and canisters. Even shelf paper and playing cards were made to coordinate. In 1958 the International Silver Company designed silverplated flatware in a pattern called 'Autumn' which was to be used with dishes in the Autumn Leaf pattern. A year later, a line of stainless flatware was introduced.

These accessory lines are prized by collectors today.

One of the most fascinating aspects of collecting the Autumn Leaf pattern has been the wonderful discoveries of previously unlisted pieces. Among these items are two different bud-ray lid one-pound butter dishes; most recently a one-pound butter dish in the 'Zephyr' or 'Bingo' style; a miniature set of the 'Casper' salt and pepper shakers; coffee, tea, and sugar canisters; a pair of candlesticks; an experimental condiment jar; and a covered candy dish. All of these china pieces are attributed to the Hall China Company. Other unusual items have turned up in the accessory lines, as well, and include a Libbey frosted tumbler in a pilsner shape, a wooden serving bowl, and an apron made from the oilcloth (plastic) material that was used in the 1950s tablecloth. These latter items appear to be professionally done, and we can only speculate as to their origin. Collectors believe that the Hall items were sample pieces that were never meant to be distributed.

Hall discontinued the Autumn Leaf line in 1978. At that time the date was added to the backstamp to mark ware still in stock in the Jewel warehouse. A special promotion by Jewel saw the reintroduction of basic dinnerware and serving pieces with the 1978 backstamp. These pieces have made their way into many collections. Additionally, in 1979 Jewel released a line of enamel-clad cookware and a Vellux blanket made by Martex which were decorated with the Autumn Leaf pattern. They continued to offer these items for a few years only, then all distribution of Autumn Leaf items was discontinued.

It should be noted that the Hall China Company has produced three limited edition items for the National Autumn Leaf Collectors Club (NALCC): a New York-style teapot (1984), a vase (1987 – different than the original shape), and candlesticks (1988). All of these are plainly marked as having been made for the NALCC and are appropriately dated.

Range style or 'Casper' shakers, either pair: $18.00.

Baker, oval, Fort Pitt...75.00
Batter bowl, Saf-Hdl 1,250.00
Bean pot, 1-hdl..300.00
Bean pot, 2-hdl, 2 ¼-qt 85.00
Bowl, cereal; 6" 8.00
Bowl, coupe soup 10.00
Bowl, cream soup; 2-hdl 18.00
Bowl, fruit; 5½" 3.00
Bowl, metal, enamelware, set of 3 ....75.00
Bowl, mixing; set of 3: 6¼", 7½", 9".......................................35.00
Bowl, Royal Glas-Bake, set of 4...45.00
Bowl, salad 14.00

Bowl, stackette; set of 3: 18-oz, 24-oz, 34-oz, w/lid 60.00
Bowl, vegetable; divided, 10½" 65.00
Bowl, vegetable; oval, w/lid, 10" 35.00
Bowl, vegetable; oval, 10½" 12.00
Bowl, vegetable; rnd, 9" 65.00
Bowl cover set, plastic, 8-pc: 7 assorted covers in pouch 50.00
Bread box, metal..125.00
Butter dish, 1-lb 165.00
Butter dish, ¼-lb 125.00
Butter dish, ¼-lb, Square Top 400.00
Butter dish, ¼-lb, Wings 450.00
Cake plate, 9½" 10.00
Cake safe, metal, motif on top & sides, 5" 25.00
Cake safe, metal, side decor only, 4½x10½"....................................22.00
Cake stand, metal base, orig box 125.00
Candy dish..300.00
Canister, metal, rnd, w/coppertone lid, set of 4 ....125.00
Canister, metal, rnd, w/ivory plastic lid 10.00
Canister, metal, rnd, w/matching lid, 6" 15.00
Canister, metal, rnd, w/matching lid, 7" 25.00
Canister, metal, rnd, w/matching lid, 8¼" 35.00
Canister, metal, sq, set of 4: 8½", 4½" 115.00
Casserole, Royal Glas-Bake, deep, w/clear glass lid...........................25.00
Casserole, Royal Glas-Bake, shallow, w/clear glass lid 20.00
Casserole, Tootsie-hdl, w/lid 18.00
Casserole/souffle, swirl, 3-pt 12.00
Casserole/souffle, 10-oz 8.00
Casserole/souffle, 2-pt 65.00
Cleanser can, metal, sq, 6" 250.00
Clock, orig works 350.00
Coaster, metal, 3⅛" 4.00
Coffee dispenser/canister, metal, wall type, 10½x19" dia 125.00
Coffee maker, 5-cup, all china, w/china insert...............................175.00
Coffee maker, 9-cup, w/metal dripper, 8" 35.00
Coffee percolator, electric, all china 225.00
Coffee percolator/carafe, Douglas, w/warmer base, MIB 200.00
Cookie jar, Tootsie...100.00
Creamer, New Style 8.00
Creamer, Old Style, 4¼" 15.00
Cup & saucer 8.00
Cup & saucer, St Denis..18.00
Custard cup 4.00
Flatware, silverplate, ea 15.00
Flatware, stainless, ea...10.00
Fruit cake tin, metal 10.00
Golden Ray base, to use w/candy dish or cake plate, pr.................50.00
Gravy boat 15.00
Hot pad, metal, red or gr felt-like backing, rnd..............................12.00
Hot pad, oval 10.00
Hurricane lamp, Douglas, w/metal base, pr 400.00
Kitchen utility chair, metal 450.00
Marmalade jar, 3-pc 45.00
Mixer cover, Mary Dunbar, plastic 25.00
Mug, beverage 45.00
Mug, Irish coffee 85.00
Mustard jar, 3½"..45.00
Napkin, ecru muslin...25.00
Pickle dish or gravy liner, oval, 9" 18.00
Picnic thermos, metal 250.00
Pie baker, 9½" 18.00
Pitcher, beverage jug; 5½-pt 18.00
Pitcher, utility; 2½-pt, 6" 12.00
Place mat, paper, scalloped 22.00

Place mat, set of 8, in orig package 195.00
Plate, 10" 10.00
Plate, 6" or 7", ea 4.00
Plate, 8" 8.00
Plate, 9" 7.00
Platter, 11½" 14.00
Platter, 13½" 16.00
Playing cards, regular or Pinochle 110.00
Range set, shakers & covered drippings jar 32.00
Sauce dish, serving; Douglas, Bakelite hdl 125.00
Shakers, range, hdl, pr 18.00
Sugar bowl, New Style 12.00
Sugar bowl, Old Style, 3½" 18.00
Tablecloth, cotton sailcloth w/gold stripe, 54x54"...........................60.00
Tablecloth, cotton sailcloth w/gold stripe, 54x72"...........................70.00
Tablecloth, ecru muslin, 56x81"...150.00
Tablecloth, plastic...125.00
Teakettle, metal enamelware 75.00
Teapot, Aladdin 38.00
Teapot, long spout, 7" 45.00
Teapot, Newport 115.00
Teapot, Newport, dtd 1978 ....90.00
Toaster cover, plastic, fits 2-slice toaster 25.00
Towel, dish; pattern & clock motif..45.00
Towel, tea; cotton, 16x33" 35.00
Trash can, metal, red 65.00
Tray, glass, wood hdl, 19½x11¼" 95.00
Tray, metal, oval 55.00
Tray, red w/allover red & yel design, red border..............................65.00
Tray, tidbit; 2-tier 35.00
Tray, tidbit; 3-tier 45.00
Tumbler, Brockway, 13-oz 15.00
Tumbler, Brockway, 16-oz 18.00
Tumbler, Brockway, 9-oz 14.00
Tumbler, frosted, 14-oz, 5½" 11.00
Tumbler, frosted, 9-oz, 3¾" 18.00
Tumbler, gold frost etched, flat, 10-oz 30.00
Tumbler, gold frost etched, flat, 15-oz 45.00
Tumbler, gold frost etched, ftd, 10-oz 45.00
Tumbler, gold frost etched, ftd, 6½-oz 45.00
Vase, bud; 6" 150.00
Warmer base, oval 100.00
Warmer base, rnd..90.00
Warmer base, rnd, w/4 orig candles, orig mk box 110.00

Aviation

Aviation buffs are interested in any phase of flying – from early developments with gliders, balloons, airships and flying machines to more modern innovations. Books, catalogs, photos, patents, lithographs, ad cards, and posters are among the paper ephemera they treasure alongside models of unlikely flying contraptions, propellers and rudders, insignia and equipment from WWI and WWII, and memorabilia from the flights of the Wright Brothers, Lindbergh, Earhart, and the Zeppelins. See also Militaria.

Ash tray, Pan Am.. 3.00
Book, Boys Book of Airships, Delacomb, 1909, EX 88.00
Book, Conquest of Air by Airships & Flying Machines, 1910 ......55.00
Book, Lindbergh the Lone Eagle, 1927, VG 35.00
Book, Lone Eagle, Lindbergh's Flight, 1928, EX 22.00

Booklet, Of Men & Wings, United Airlines, 1945........................ **5.00**
Coin, Charles Lindbergh, 1st Non-Stop Flight NY to Paris, 1927.**18.00**
Envelope, First Flight of the Zeppelin, hand stamped, 1928 ....**30.00**
Knife, steak; United, SP **16.00**
Medallion, Eastern, 50th Anniversary, bronze oval, 6-oz **25.00**
Model of triplane, wood/metal fittings, dtd 1917, 95" W **1,400.00**

Photograph of Graf Zeppelin, ca 1930s, Frankfurt, Germany, in original die-cut envelope, $15.00. (Photo courtesy Hake's Americana, York, PA.)

Pin, lapel; ALPA, gilt wing w/star **12.50**
Pin, lapel; AVIO Pilot **18.00**
Pin, lapel; TWA silver 4-engine plane **12.50**
Pin-bk button, Welcome Lindy, 1927, 1¼"...**26.00**
Ramekin, CP Air, porc **11.00**
Shot glass, DC3, Fly Southern, yel, 2nd year.......................................**37.50**
Shot glass, 20 Years of Hospitality Southern Style, M **12.50**
Tag, Delta, suede **2.00**
Timetable, Hindenberg, pictures, 3-fold, French, 4x8½" **20.00**
Wing, Air Atlanta Agent, ½-wing, gold **27.50**
Wing, Delta flight attendant, gold w/red/wht/bl enamel, '72 ....**36.00**
Wing, hat badge; Delta, gold w/bl & wht enamel, 1929-1953 ....**110.00**
Wing, Horizon Air Jr Pilot, plastic, mc, 1986 .... **4.00**
Wing, McClain flight attendant, gold & blk, M **38.00**
Wing, Pan Am Jr Airline Pilot, metal, gold & bl **12.00**
Wing, Pan Am Jr Clipper Pilot, metal, gold & bl, M **5.50**
Wing, United Future Stewardess, plastic, gold/red/bl, M.................. **2.50**
Wings, presentation; Pan Am Airways, 10k gold, 1930s, MIB **495.00**

Avon

The California Perfume Company, the parent of the Avon Co., was founded in 1886. Although an 'Avon' line was introduced by the company in the mid-twenties, not until 1939 did it become known as Avon Products, Inc. Collectible Avon items include not only figural bottles and jars, but jewelry, awards, product samples, magazine ads, and catalogs as well. For more information concerning the Avon Collectors Club, see the Clubs, Newsletters, and Catalogs section of the Directory. See also California Perfume Company.

In the listings that follow, unless noted MIB, prices are for bottles only.

Ammoniated Toothpaste, 1949-55, gr & wht tube **10.00**

Autumn Harvest Pomander, 1979-80, yel & gr wax, 10" L **10.00**
Baked w/Love Plate, porc, 1982-83, 9" **20.00**
Big Mack, 1973-75, gr glass w/beige bed, 6-oz, MIB **7.00**
Christmas Bells, 1979-80, red glass, silver cap, 1-oz **5.00**
Christmas Call Set, 1965, 2 4-oz bottles **3.95**
Christmas Plate, porc, 1983-85, 9"..**25.00**
Clearfire Tulip Cup Candle, 1986, clear glass, 4" **8.00**
Collector's Pipe, 1973-74, brn glass w/blk stem, 3-oz, MIB............. **6.00**
Corncob Pipe, 1974-75, amber glass w/blk stem, 3-oz.................... **5.00**
Cuticle Softener, 1936-39, bottle w/turq cap, 1.2-oz **22.00**
Doubly Yours Set, 1956, bl & gold box, MIB..................................**23.00**
Felix Fox Wall Hook, 1982-83, wht & tan plastic **4.00**
Flowertime Set, 1949-52, turq & gold box w/satin lining, 4-oz **65.00**
Harvest Time Fragrance Candle, 1980-81, tan candle, 6" **12.00**
Iron Horse Mini Stein, ceramic, 1985, 5¼" **8.00**
John Wayne Figurine, porc, 1985, 7¼"..**20.00**
Kitten's Hideaway, 1974-76, amber basket, wht kitten, 1-oz **6.00**
Lady Bug Perfume, 1975-76, frosted glass, gold cap, ⅛-oz............... **7.00**
Liquid Milk Bath, 1975-76, frosted bottle, gold cap, 6-oz **5.00**
Liquid Shampoo, 1930-36, metal cap, 1-pt......................................**43.00**
Love Song, 1973-75, frosted glass, gold cap, 6-oz, MIB **5.00**
Moonlight Glow Annual Bell, 1981-82, glass bell, 3-oz **9.00**
Nail Beauty, 1954-57, wht jar w/wht lid, 1-oz **6.00**
Pipe Dream Clear Test, 1967, clear glass bottle, 6-oz **255.00**
Regal Peacock, 1973-74, bl glass, gold cap, 4-oz, MIB **10.00**
Rollin' Great Roller Skate, 1980-81, glass red top, 2-oz **6.00**
Royal Vase, 1970, bl cologne bottle, 3-oz, MIB **5.00**
Sapphire Swirl, 1973-74, bl glass, gold cap, 5-oz **3.00**
Sea Horse, 1970-72, clear glass, gold cap, 6-oz, MIB **7.00**
Sea Spirit, 1973-76, gr glass w/gr tail, 5-oz, MIB............................. **6.00**
Sharing the Christmas Spirit Figurine, 1981, 6", MIB....................**50.00**
Sniffy Skunk, 1978-80, blk glass/wht trim, 1.25-oz, MIB.............. **8.00**
Snuggly Mouse Candle Holder, ceramic, 1983, base, 4¼" W **15.00**
Soft Musk Candle, 1985, sm tin candle w/lid.................................. **6.00**
Special Nail Care Set, 1955-57, red & wht box, MIB **13.00**
Sporting Miniature Stein, ceramic, 1983-84, 5" **10.00**
Vase, florals, bl w/gr leaves & yel center, 5"....................................**70.00**
Victoriana Soap Dish, 1978, bl marbleized glass **7.00**
Wishful Thoughts, porc figurine, 1982-83, bl/wht, 5½" **13.00**

Baccarat

The Baccarat Glass company was founded in 1765 near Luneville, France, and continues to this day to produce quality crystal tableware, vases, perfume bottles, and figurines. The firm became famous for the high-quality millefiori and caned paperweights produced there from 1845 until about 1860. Examples of these range from $300 to as much as several thousand. Since 1953 they have resumed the production of paperweights on a limited edition basis. See also Paperweights.

Bottle, scent; Coque D'Or, cobalt/gilt, bow tie form, +box..........**600.00**
Bottle, scent; Rose Tiente Swirl, 6¾x2⅞".....................................**110.00**
Box, Rose Tiente Swirl, lift-off lid, 2x3" dia **70.00**
Candle holder, Rose Tiente Swirl, spherical, 1½x1¾", pr **95.00**
Celery vase, Rose Tiente Swirl, 9½"...**75.00**
Cruet, Rose Tiente Swirl, Reed & Barton SP base **165.00**
Decanter, chipped ice w/gilt swags, ftd, 11", +2 cordials **575.00**
Decanter, cranberry shaded to yel, 9" **95.00**
Fairy lamp, Rose Tiente Swirl, saucer base, 4x5¼" **235.00**
Jar, Swirl, sapphire bl, 6x3" dia **75.00**
Perfume, turtle form, gray-wash flippers, cut stopper, 5" **700.00**
Vase, cameo trees/butterflies, amber on frost, fan form, 5" **400.00**

Vase, frosted w/HP purple violets, gilt, sq cylinder, 8" **550.00**
Vase, Rose Tiente Swirl, red marble base w/bronze dolphin **165.00**

Badges

The breast badge came into general usage in this country about 1840. Since most are not marked and styles have changed very little to the present day, they are often difficult to date. The most reliable clue is the pin and catch. One of the earliest types, used primarily before the turn of the century, involved a 't-pin' and a 'shell' catch. In a second style, the pin was hinged with a small square of sheet metal, and the clasp was cylindrical. From the late 1800s until about 1940, the pin and clasp were made from one continuous piece of thin metal wire. The same type, with the addition of a flat back plate, was used a little later. There are exceptions to these findings, and other types of clasps were also used. Hallmarks and inscriptions may also help pinpoint an approximate age.

Badges have been made from a variety of materials, usually brass or nickel silver; but even solid silver and gold were used for special orders. They are found in many basic shapes and variations – stars with five to seven points, shields, disks, ovals, and octagonals being most often encountered. Of prime importance to collectors, however, is that the title and/or location appear on the badge. Those with designations of positions no longer existing (City Constable, for example) and names of early western states and towns are most valuable.

Badges are among the most commonly-reproduced (and faked) types of antiques on the market. At any flea market, ten fakes can be found for every authentic example. Genuine law badges start at $30.00 to $40.00 for recent examples (1950-1970); earlier pieces (1910-1930) usually bring $50.00 to $90.00. Pre-1900 badges often sell for more than $100.00. Authentic gold badges are usually priced at a minimum of scrap value (karat, weight, spot price for gold); fine gold badges from before 1900 can sell for $400.00 to $800.00, and a few will bring even more. A fire badge is usually valued at about half the price of a law badge from the same circa and material.

Our advisor for this category is Gene Matzke; he is listed in the Directory under Wisconsin.

14k yellow gold Deputy Commissioner's badge, name and address on back, 2½", $500.00.

Chauffer's, IN, brass, 1927, EX **10.00**
Deputy Sheriff Wayne County, bronze tone, ca 1900, 2½" **45.00**
Deputy Sheriff's Assoc, MA, bl & gold cloisonne, rnd pin-bk **15.00**
Deputy US Marshal AZ District, SP nickel, LAS&SCo, 2½x2" .**110.00**
Deputy US Marshal New Mexico, brass, hallmk, 1910, 2" **65.00**
Patrolman, Mt Vernon OH, chrome plate, screw bk, early, EX **10.00**
Police, Hartford CT, eagle/stars/seal, silver, 1860s, EX **200.00**
Police Sergeant, TN Hwy Patrol, 1930s **85.00**
Special Police, Glenn Falls NY, shield, gold plate, VG **35.00**

Yel Cab, chrome, yel/blk, EX...**55.00**

Banks

Collectors of mechanical and still banks have seen considerable change in the pricing picture in the past few years. An increasing number of banks are appearing in general auctions, and some auctions are now devoted entirely to banks and toys. Often the prices realized at auction varies greatly from advertised prices. This can sometimes be attributed to 'auction fever,' but it may also represent buyers with specific knowledge concerning the banks they are bidding on. Condition has become an important price-determining factor. A pristine bank will frequently sell for two to four times the price realized by the same bank in only 'good' condition. Always look for examples in the best-possible condition. They will cost more, but they will be the best investment for you. Banks should always be complete with all parts present, original, and in good working condition (if it is a mechanical). Replaced parts or retouched paint lessen a bank's value. Rarity is also an important factor in pricing banks – almost as important as condition.

Still banks are found in nearly every shape and size, and many types of material have been used in their making. Exactly how many styles were made is unknown; but about three thousand have been identified, and there are thousands more that are unlisted in any book. Cast iron examples are the most popular, but there is an increasing interest in the early tin and pottery banks made in the United States.

The category of mechanical banks is unique. Along with cast iron bell toys, they are among the most outstanding products of the Industrial Revolution and are recognized as some of the most successful of the mass-produced products of the nineteenth century. The earliest mechanicals were made of wood or lead; but when John Hall introduced Hall's Excelsior, a cast iron mechanical bank, it was an immediate success. J. and E. Stevens produced the bank for Hall and soon began to make their own designs. Several companies followed suit, most of which were already in the hardware business. They used newly-developed iron-molding techniques to produce these novelty savings devices for the emerging toy market. Mechanical banks reflect the social and political attitudes of the times, racial prejudices, the excitement of the circus, and humorous everyday events. Their designers made the most of simple mechanics to produce banks with captivating actions that served not only to amuse but to promote the concept of thrift to the children. The quality of detail in the castings are truly fine examples of industrial art. The most collectible examples were made during the period of 1870 to 1900; however, they continued to be made until the early days of World War II. J. and E. Stevens, Sheppard Hardware, and Kyser and Rex are some of the more well-known manufacturers – most made still banks as well.

While the cast iron banks dominate the market, there are examples made from many other materials. Combinations of tin and cardboard and banks made from tin alone are very collectible. Some of the European tin banks are quite rare; England made some fine cast iron mechanicals and many aluminum examples. The popularity of old mechanicals has created a market for reproductions and fakes. Reproductions may have minor value as such, but not as true collectibles. A few of the fakes have attained collectible status but are still not regarded as true mechanical banks.

As both value and interest continue on the increase, it becomes even more important to educate one's self to the fullest extent possible. We recommend these books for your library: *The Dictionary of Still Banks* by Long and Pitman, *The Penny Bank Book* by Moore, and *The Bank Book* by Norman. If you are primarily interested in mechanicals, *Penny Lane*, a new book by Davidson, is considered the most complete reference available. It contains a cross-reference listing of numbers from all other publications on mechanical banks.

In the listings that follow, banks are identified by L for Long, G for Griffith, M for Moore, N for Norman, D for Davidson, and W for Whiting.

Key:
CI — cast iron   NPCI — nickel-plated cast iron
EPCI — electroplated cast iron

Advertising

Atlantic Premium Motor Oil, tin litho, 2⅞"	18.50
Betsy Ross Tea, tin & paper, EX	15.00
Bokar Coffee, tin	12.00
Budweiser Beer, tin, M	10.00
Calumet Baking Powder, L-1231, can figural	95.00
Chevrolet Car, 1953	65.00
Cincy Stove, CI, lt bl porc enamel, nickel grill, 3½"	45.00
Decker's Iowana, M-603, pig, CI, gold pnt, 4⅜" L, EX	90.00
Eureka Gas Heater, M-1350, tin, minor wear, 5¼"	60.00
Fidelity Trust Vaults, M-903, CI, old rpt, 6½"	225.00
GE Refrigerator, M-1331, CI, wht & bl pnt, 4¼"	115.00
Gem Furnace, M-1364, CI, worn blk pnt, 4⅝"	105.00
Gem Heaters, Abendroth...NY, #1364, CI, bronze pnt, 4⅝"	165.00
Grapette, clown	16.00
Howard Johnson's Restaurant, CI, dk patina, modern, 4¾" L	45.00
Invest in Pork, L-267, pig, CI, worn blk pnt, 6¾" L	155.00
La Rosa Pizza Sauce, tin, M	10.00
Majestic Ice Box, M-1332, CI & sheet metal	250.00
Mellon Furnaces, furnace, M-1363, worn bronze finish, 3⅝"	115.00
N&Co Hdwe Chicago, Gypsy Money Pot, CI, no pnt, 5¼"	125.00
Old Dutch Cleanser, tin, NM	35.00
Patton Paints, tin litho, EX color, sm	35.00
Peter's Weatherbird Shoes, M-160, tin & paper, 2"	25.00
Radiation Stoves, L-1018, tin, minor wear, 5¼"	135.00

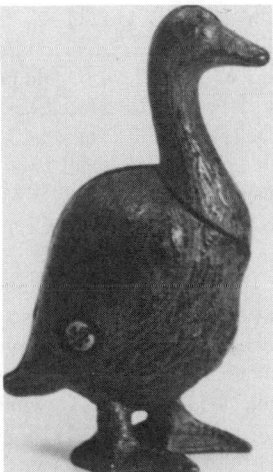

Red Goose Shoes, 4", $150.00.

Rival Dog Food, tin	12.50
RL Berry's Piano, M-840, sheet steel, bronze pnt, 5⅛", VG	100.00
Rochester Trust & Save, M-965, clock, bronze, orig pnt, 5"	100.00
Roper Range, M-1341, CI, mc pnt, Arcade, 4"	300.00
Roper Stove, M-1342, CI, gr pnt, lt rust, Arcade decal, 4"	115.00
San Gabriel Mission CSMS, M-957, CI, mc pnt, 4¾", EX	975.00
Save Your Money...Gas Stove, M-1349, tin, bronze pnt, 5½"	80.00
Sinclair Power X, EX	12.00
Sunoco Synalube Motor Oil, tin, EX	12.50

United Banking & Trust Co, M-1100, CI, worn gold pnt, 2¾"	65.00
Universal Stoves & Ranges, tin, revolving globe	235.00
West Chemical Products, tin, NM	22.00
Western Reserve, M-965, clock, bronze, orig pnt, 4⅞"	100.00
White City Puzzle..., M-94, NPCI, 3¼", EX	100.00
Worcester Salt, M-451, elephant, wht metal, gr patina, 4¼"	35.00
York Stove, M-1351, CI, bronze finish, 4"	225.00
Zenith Radio, M-823, wht metal, gold w/paper dial, 3½", EX	45.00

Mechanical

Always Did 'Spise a Mule, D-250, bench, EX	850.00
Always Did 'Spise a Mule, D-251, jockey, pat 1897	1,250.00
Artillery, N-1060-D, CI, mc pnt, minor wear, 6"	1,100.00
Bad Accident, N-1150-A, CI, worn mc pnt, 10¼", VG	1,200.00
Bamboula, D-21	1,000.00
Bird on Roof, D-36, CI	2,300.00
Bismark, D-37, man sits w/in lg pig, 8", VG	4,000.00
Boy Stealing Watermelon, D-53, pnt CI, EX	1,150.00

Butting Ram, D-92, 4", NM, $10,540.00.

Butting Buffalo, D-90, NM	3,200.00
Calamity, D-94	6,500.00
Cat & Mouse, D-104, CI, worn pnt, 8¼", G	1,150.00
Cat & Mouse, N-1700-S, CI, mc pnt, rpl trap, 11¼", EX	850.00
Clown on Globe, D-127, pnt CI, 9", G	1,400.00
Creedmore, N-2000, CI, very worn mc pnt, 6½"	600.00
Cross-legged Minstrel, D-142	2,000.00
Dark Town Battery, D-146, CI, worn pnt, 9⅞"	2,950.00
Dina, N-2150, CI, mc pnt, Made in England, 6½", EX	400.00
Fisherman, CI, mc pnt, modern, 12¼"	95.00
Freedman's Bureau, D-149, EX	4,000.00
Girl Skipping Rope, D-217, pnt CI, EX	1,500.00
Hall's Excelsior, N-2710, CI, worn mc pnt, 5", VG	250.00
Humpty Dumpty, D-248, CI, mc rpt, minor wear, 7½", EX	750.00
Indian & Bear, N-2980-A, CI, mc pnt, rpr/rpl, 7½", VG	375.00
Joe Socko, D-262	750.00
Jolly Nigger, N-3230, CI, worn mc pnt, 5¾"	125.00
Jolly Nigger, N-3270, aluminum w/zinc hat, 6½"	275.00
Jolly Nigger, N-3330-A, Shepard Hdw, CI, mc pnt, 6¾", EX	300.00
Leap Frog, D-292, EX	2,100.00
Lion & Monkeys, N-3650-A, CI, old rpt, pat '83, 9"	850.00
Little Mo, D-306, moves straw hat & arms, pnt CI, EX	2,750.00
Little Red Riding Hood, D-412	22,000.00
Mason, D-321, pnt CI, 7½", EX	4,000.00
Organ Bank, D-370, pnt CI, miniature	750.00

Owl, D-375, CI, EX pnt, J&E Stevens/pat 1880, 7⅝" 300.00
Pelican w/Arab, D-381, pnt CI, EX 3,700.00
Rabbit in Cabbage, D-408, 4½", NM.....................................350.00
Safety Locomotive, D-422 ....2,000.00
Speaking Dog, N-5170-C, CI, mc pnt, pat 1885, 7"...................950.00
Strike, CI, mc pnt, modern, 11½" 95.00
Tammany, N-5420-A, CI, old rpt, 5¾" 275.00
Tommy, D-477...5,500.00
Trick Dog, N-5620, CI, mc pnt, rpl hoop, pat 1888, 8¾" L 350.00
Trick Dog, N-5630-A, CI, mc pnt, Hubley, USA, 8¾" L.............325.00
Uncle Sam, N-5740, CI, worn mc pnt, pat 1886, 11¼" 1,000.00
Watchdog Safe, D-560, pnt CI, EX.......................................550.00
Wireless, D-569, electric, minor wear, 4¾", EX 150.00
World's Fair, N-6040-A, Columbus, CI, old pnt, 8¼", VG 600.00
Zoo, D-576, building w/animals in windows, EX 1,000.00
2 Frogs, D-200, CI, VG pnt, J&E Stevens/pat 1822, rpr, 8¾" . 1,200.00

Panorama Bank, J. & E. Stevens, 6½", EX paint, $19,800.00.

Registering

Astronaut Daily Dime 20.00
B&R Mfg, NY, 10¢ register 10.00
Bean Pot, M-951, 5¢ register, pnt CI, nickeled top, 4"...........155.00
Beehive Savings, M-681, NPCI, pnt traces, 5¼" 125.00
Daily Dime Clown..16.00
Honeycomb, C-105, 5¼" 100.00
Jr Cash, M-930, worn NPCI, lt rust, 4¼" 65.00
Jr Cash, M-931, nickeled steel, EX......................................65.00
Kettle, pnt NPCI, 5¢ register, 3½" 20.00
Popeye, 10¢ register, EX 30.00
Prudential, NPCI, pat Feb 25, 1890, worn label, 7¼", EX 425.00
Spinning Wheel, tin litho w/2 scenes, sq, W Germany, 4½"........25.00
Statue of Liberty 10.00
Trunk, Phoenix, M-947, 10¢ register, NPCI, worn blk pnt, 5".....95.00
Wee Folks Money Box, tin litho, sq, English, 5"...................50.00

Still

Aberdeen Angus Bull, M-555, aluminum, blk pnt, 7½" L, EX.......75.00
Air Mail, M-848, CI, mc pnt, minor wear, 6⅜" 350.00
Alice in Wonderland, M-1323, emb brass, 4¼", VG 85.00
Amish Boy, M-195, wht metal, mc pnt, minor wear, 4½" 65.00
Apple, L-904, CI, yel pnt, 5½" 750.00
Apple, pottery, orig yel & red pnt, 3"...................................175.00
Armored Bank Truck, M-1499, sheet metal/wood wheels, 6", EX..45.00
Aunt Jemima, CI, mc pnt, modern, 12", NM 50.00
Aunt Jemima, M-256, CI, mc pnt, minor wear, modern, 8¼"........25.00
Baby, M-348, celluloid, 5¼" 15.00
Baby in Egg, M-261, lead, wht pnt w/mc trim, 7", EX.................150.00
Bank Building, L-419, CI, bronze finish traces, 3⅜"..................115.00
Bank Building, M-1125, CI, dk pnt, worn gold trim, 5½" 145.00
Bank Building, M-1180, CI, gold & silver pnt, 3" 20.00
Barrel, M-916, Puzzle...#3, NPCI, worn, 5⅛" 85.00
Baseball Player, L-640, CI, pnt traces, 5¾" 135.00
Basket, M-917, CI, bronze finish, sm chip on base, 3⅛" 65.00
Battle of Gettysburg, M-1194, CI, mc pnt, modern, 4⅝" 450.00
Battleship Maine, M-1439, CI, mc pnt, minor wear, 10¼" 350.00
Bear, Cinnamon; M-706, wht metal, mc pnt, minor wear, 4".........65.00
Bear, Grisly; M-703, lead, bright copper pnt, 2¾" 35.00
Bear, L-15, w/staff, bronze foundry pattern, inscribed, 6" 90.00
Bear, M-1683, stands, CI, brn pnt, minor wear, 6⅜" 250.00
Bear, M-711, stands, aluminum, pnt traces, 6" 35.00
Bear, M-712, brass, worn blk pnt, foundry pattern, 5⅞" 115.00
Bear, M-713, stands, CI, brn pnt, minor wear, 5½"....................85.00
Bear Stealing Honey, M-1308, CI, japanning w/gold, 7", EX 175.00
Bed Post, M-1304, brass, 7½", EX 75.00
Bed Post, M-1305, brass, 5⅛", EX 65.00
Beehive bank/string holder, M-684, CI, NP brass finial, 5½".......450.00
Beggar Boy, L-643, boy kneels, holds hat, 7", EX......................65.00
Beggerman, M-55, silvered lead, German inscription, 7½", VG 80.00
Bethel College Admin Bldg, M-1196, CI, silver, modern, 5¼" 40.00
Billiken, M-74, Good Luck, CI, gold pnt w/red, minor wear, 4" ...85.00
Billiken, M-81, Good Luck, CI, old red & gold rpt, 6½" 35.00
Billy Can, M-79, CI, gold/bl/red pnt, minor wear, 5" 700.00
Bird, M-644, CI, worn gold pnt, 4¾" 270.00
Black Boy, M-82, 2-faced, CI, worn mc pnt, rpl screw, 4" 100.00
Black Boy, M-83, 2-faced, CI, mc pnt, minor wear, 4⅛" 150.00
Black Boy on Pot, chalkware, 13", M....................................30.00
Blackpool Tower, M-984, CI, brn japanning, 7⅛", EX 150.00
Boston Bulldog, M-413, CI, mc pnt, minor wear, 4⅜" 145.00
Boy Scout, L-654, CI, 8" 500.00
Boy Scout, M-45, CI, gold pnt, minor wear, 5⅞" 135.00
Boy Scout, M-45, CI, old tan rpt, minor wear, 5⅞" 95.00
Buffalo, M-537, CI, dk brn pnt w/blk highlights, 8"..................135.00
Buffalo, M-560, CI, gold rpt, 4⅜"...50.00
Bull, M-537, on base, CI w/mc pnt, minor pitting, 6" L 125.00
Bullet, M-1413, 1914-1918, brass & NPCI, no trap, 6¾"..............15.00
Bungalow, M-999, CI, bronze finish, 3¾", EX 150.00
Camel, M-767, CI, worn gold pnt w/mc trim, 7¼" 195.00
Camel, M-768, CI, worn mc pnt, 4¾" 45.00
Camel, W-202, sm 235.00
Capitol, Washington DC, M-1054, lead, bronze pnt, 4½" L 25.00
Captain Kidd, M-38, CI, worn pnt, 5¾".................................300.00
Carpet Bag, C-352, bronze, 3½", EX 45.00
Carriage Clock, M-1551, bronzed steel w/brass trim, 5⅜", EX 105.00
Castle, M-1114, 2 towers, CI, brn japanning, minor wear, 7" 400.00
Cat, C-146, stands, tail up, bow at neck, 4½"..........................75.00
Cat, M-366, seated, CI, worn mc pnt, 4⅛" 145.00
Cat & Ball, M-353, CI, worn gold pnt, 5⅝" L 300.00

Champion Thrift, CI, worn red & bl pnt, 4" 30.00
Charlie McCarthy, M-209, papier-mache, minor wear, 9¼" 85.00
Chest, Jewel; M-952, CI, worn bronze pnt, brass dial, 6⅜" L 225.00
Chest, Jewel; M-952, worn NPCI, 6⅜" L...........................60.00
Chest, Pirate; M-936, lead, bronze pnt, 2⅝", VG 12.50
Chest, Treasure; M-928, CI, worn gold pnt, 2¾" L, EX 85.00
Chest, Treasure; M-929, CI, gold pnt, modern, 4", EX 15.00
Chick Bank '84, aluminum, mc pnt, modern, 4⅛", NM 25.00
Church, M-982, CI, gr & wht pnt, modern, 5¾" L, EX 120.00
Clown, M-211, CI, worn silver pnt w/red trim, 6⅛" 85.00
Clown, M-212, brass, wht pnt, foundry pattern, 6" 215.00
Cockatoo, M-648, w/ball, lead & tin, EX mc pnt, 2⅞" 175.00
Cockatoo, M-656, wht metal, mc pnt, minor wear, 5" 255.00
Colonial House, M-992, CI, silver pnt, bl roof, 4" 40.00
Colonial House, M-993, CI, gold & gr pnt, minor wear, 3" 95.00
Colonial Woman, M-312, Staffordshire, mc pnt, hairline, 2¼" 55.00
Columbia Bank, M-1070, NPCI, Kenton, 6".......................235.00
Columbia Bank, M-1077, CI, worn wht pnt, no trap, 7"............225.00
County Bank, M-1110, CI, japanning traces, rpl screw, 4¼" 135.00
Cow, M-540, nickeled steel, mc pnt, 7" L, EX 195.00
Cow, M-544, CI, blk & wht pnt, 4⅝" 135.00
Cow, M-545, CI, blk pnt, minor wear, 4⅝" L 215.00
Cow, M-553, CI, worn gold pnt, 5⅜" L............................135.00
Crown, M-1226, CI, worn brn japanning w/gold, 3⅝" 100.00
Cupola Bank, M-1147, CI, worn mc pnt, lt rust, 3¼" 125.00
Davenport House, M-1107, pewter, 4¼"...........................100.00
Deer, L-59, 6¼" 75.00
Devil, L-695, 2-faced, CI, red/blk/wht pnt, 4¼" 500.00
Dog, M-443, on pillow, CI, pnt traces, 5½" 90.00
Dog w/Lighthouse, tin & lead, Germany, minor pnt wear, 4" 115.00
Dolphin, M-33, CI, pnt traces, 4½" 300.00
Dome Bank, M-1183, CI, silver & gold pnt, minor wear, 4¾" 55.00
Donkey, M-493, lead, tan harness, blk hooves, 3⅞", EX 55.00
Donkey, M-498, hinged saddle & padlock, CI, worn pnt, 3½".....45.00
Donkey, M-499, CI, worn gr pnt, 4¼", EX 80.00
Donkey, M-500, CI, mc pnt, minor wear, 7" 215.00
Donkey, M-502, on base, CI, worn mc pnt, 7½".................425.00
Dr's Bag, L-1432, 'MD,' nickel on brass, 5⅜"....................90.00
Dreadnought Bank, M-1314, CI, worn pnt, 7⅛"..................510.00
Duck, M-624, CI, mc pnt, minor wear, 5" 150.00
Dutch Boy, M-255, CI, factory doorstop conversion, rpt, 8¼" 200.00
Eagle, L-358, w/shield, 4" 600.00
Eagle, M-677, CI, gold pnt, minor wear, modern, 5¾" 15.00
Eiffel Tower, M-1074, CI, bronze & gold pnt, 9" 650.00
Elephant, M-1666, raised trunk, silvered lead, 6" L, VG............75.00
Elephant, M-446, w/howdah, wheels, CI, EX gold pnt, 4" 225.00
Elephant, M-447, CI, worn gr pnt, 4" L..........................315.00
Elephant, M-450, GOP, CI, red & gold pnt, 4", EX 155.00
Elephant, M-457, w/howdah, CI, gold pnt, 2⅜", EX 55.00
Elephant, M-459, w/howdah, CI, gr pnt, minor wear, 4" L.........22.50
Elephant, M-461, wht metal, worn blk pnt, 5" 20.00
Elephant, M-470, CI, gray pnt w/gold & red, 3⅜", EX 95.00
Elephant, M-474, w/howdah, CI, worn gold rpt, 6⅜" L...........55.00
Elephant, M-476, w/howdah, CI, gray/gold/silver pnt, 6⅝" L 75.00
Elephant, M-477, w/howdah, CI, mc pnt, minor wear, 5" L 85.00
Elephant, M-479, missing chariot, CI, worn pnt, 6⅞".............95.00
Elephant, M-480, w/howdah, CI, gray w/red & wht, 7" L 165.00
Elephant, M-481, converted doorstop, CI, gray/wht pnt, 7¼" L 85.00
Elephant, M-483, on tub, CI, gold pnt, minor wear, 5½" 135.00
Elephant, M-483, on tub, CI, rpl screw, 5½", VG.................85.00
Elf, M-309, CI, mc rpt, 9¾"....................................300.00
Empire Bank, M-1320, CI, brn japanning w/gold, 6¾", EX 135.00
Feed My Sheep, M-596, lamb, lead, minor wear, 2⅞", EX............55.00

Fez, M-1394, aluminum, red & blk pnt, minor wear, 5⅜" 65.00
Fidelity Safe, M-864, CI, dk brn japanning w/gold, 3", EX 95.00
Fort Dearborn, L-507, CI, 5¾"..................................175.00
Foxy Grandpa, M-320, CI, mc pnt, minor wear, 5½" 150.00
Frog, M-692, Iron Art, CI, gr pnt, 7" L..........................55.00
Frowning Face, M-12, CI, no pnt, 5¾"...........................550.00
Garage, M-1010, 2-car, CI, worn silver & bl pnt, 2½"..............85.00
Gen Pershing, M-151, CI, bronze finish, 7¾", EX 100.00
Gen Sheridan, M-50, on base, CI, old gold rpt, 6", EX 400.00
German Shepherd, bronze foundry pattern, 7¼" L 200.00
Give Me a Penny, M-15, pnt CI, minor wear, 4¾" 275.00
Globe, M-791, paper-covered steel, wooden base, 4⅜", EX............25.00
Globe, M-812, CI, bronze stripe finish, nickel dial, 5¼" 125.00
Golliwog, M-86, aluminum, unpnt, 6"............................95.00
Good Luck, M-508, CI bell form, blk & gold pnt, 4¼", EX 100.00
Goose, M-615, CI, gold pnt, 5", NM 150.00
Graf Zeppelin, L-1539, CI, aluminum & gr pnt, 6¾" L............200.00
Graf Zeppelin, M-1431, CI, silver pnt, nickel wheels, 7⅞", EX ...265.00
Gun Boat, M-1462, CI, bl/wht/brn, 8½", EX 850.00
Hall Clock, M-1547, lead, bronze pnt, rpl trap, 7½" 65.00
Harleysville Bank, M-1017, CI, wht & red pnt, modern, 5¼" L 30.00
High Rise, M-1219, CI, EX silver & gold pnt, 5½" 65.00
Home, M-1019, CI, bright bronze finish, 4⅛", EX 150.00
Home Savings, M-1201, worn NPCI, 10½".......................425.00
Horse, M-506, prancing, CI, gold pnt, minor wear, 4¾" 185.00
Horse, M-510, on tub, CI, worn silver pnt, 5½" 175.00
Horse, M-512, on wheels, CI, gold & silver pnt, 5⅛", EX 265.00
Horse, M-513, prancing, oval base, CI, gold rpt, 5"...............35.00
Horse, M-514, rearing, CI, worn blk & gold pnt, 4¾" 325.00
Horse, M-520, prancing, CI, blk pnt, minor wear, 7¼" 85.00
Horse, M-520, prancing, CI, old gold rpt, 7¼", EX 85.00
Horse, M-521, rearing, CI, gold pnt, minor wear, 7⅜" 85.00
Horse, M-531, My Pet, CI, blk pnt w/mc trim, lt wear, 4½" 125.00
Horse, M-532, CI, gold pnt, 3"..................................115.00
Horse, M-533, CI, worn bronze finish, 4⅞" L.....................35.00
Ideola Juke Box, M-1580, colored plastic, 6", EX 35.00
Independence Hall, M-1244, CI, old bl rpt w/bronze, 9", VG 200.00
Indian, M-228, CI, brn pnt w/worn mc trim, 6" 185.00
Indian, M-237, arms Xd, CI, mc pnt, 4⅛", EX 80.00
Jackie Robinson, metal...150.00
Japanese Safe, M-883, worn NPCI, lt rust, 5⅜"...................65.00
Jumbo, CI, gold & red pnt, NP wheels, 3⅞"......................155.00
Kewpie, M-292, papier-mache, worn mc pnt, no trap, 5" 35.00
Keyless Safety Deposit, L-1432, NPCI, 5⅞" 185.00
Kitty, M-349, CI, worn mc pnt, 4¾" 50.00
Liberty Bell, M-793, steel w/wood yoke, orig finish, 3¾" 15.00
Liberty Bell, M-809, CI, bronze pnt, 3⅜", EX 20.00
Liberty Bell, M-816, wht metal w/dk pnt, wood base, 7"..........125.00
Lindbergh Bust, L-779, aluminum, 6¼" 50.00
Lion, M-742, CI, gold pnt, minor wear, 2⅝" 55.00
Lion, M-747, on tub, CI, worn gold pnt, 4⅛".....................85.00
Lion, M-754, CI, worn bl pnt, 5" 60.00
Lion, M-755, CI, gold pnt, minor wear, 5" L 30.00
Lion, M-755, CI, worn gold pnt, 5" L............................20.00
Lion, M-757, CI, gold pnt, minor wear, 4½" L 35.00
Lion, M-759, CI, worn silver rpt, 4⅜" L..........................15.00
Lion, M-760, on wheels, CI, worn gold pnt, 4½" 225.00
Lion, M-760, on wheels, CI, worn silver rpt, 4¾"................65.00
Lion, M-764, CI, gold pnt, 5" L, EX 45.00
Lion, M-765, CI, gold pnt, minor wear, 5⅛" L 55.00
Log Cabin, M-1021, ...Lincoln Was Born..., ceramic, 3¾" L..........12.50
Log Cabin, M-1030, CI, mc pnt, modern, 6" L, NM 45.00
Lost Dog, M-407, CI, no pnt, 5⅜" 575.00

Main Street Trolly, L-1603, w/people, pnt CI, Wms, 6½" L..........220.00
Main Street Trolly, M-1469, CI, gold pnt, 6⅝" L, EX 375.00
Main Street Trolly, M-1474, worn NPCI, 5⅛" 285.00
Mammy, M-168, CI, worn mc pnt, rpl screw, 5¾" 115.00
Mantel Clock, M-1550, lead, bronze pnt, brass trim, 7" L, VG......35.00
Mark Twain, M-246, SBCCA 1982, CI, mc pnt, modern, 5¼" 65.00
Merry-Go-Round, M-1611, NP, 4¾" 175.00
Mickey Mouse w/Mandolin, M-203, wht metal, worn pnt, 4⅝" ..145.00
Milk Can, M-1310, brass, 3⅓", VG......................................30.00
Money Saver, M-1544, CI, blk & gold pnt, minor wear, 3½".........65.00
Monkey, M-744, wht metal, mc pnt, minor wear, rpl trap, 4¼" 75.00
Monkey, M-778, CI, doorstop conversion, mc pnt, 8⅝", VG.........95.00
Mosque, M-1177, worn NPCI, key trap, 4¼"............................90.00
Mourner's Purse, L-1481, lead, 1902, 5" 50.00
Mutt & Jeff, M-157, CI, gold pnt, minor wear, 5⅛" 140.00
My Pet, M-531, CI, blk rpt, 4¼", EX 65.00
New Deal, M-148, Roosevelt bust, bronze, minor wear, 4¾" 200.00
North Pole, M-1372, brass, foundry pattern, 4¼" 375.00
Old Liberty Bell, M-807, gr patina, worn NP base, label, 4½" 85.00
Old South Church, M-988, CI, old gold rpt, rpt, 9¾".................575.00
Organ Grinder, M-216, CI, steel base, worn pnt, 6½".................150.00
Oriental Boy, M-186, on pillow, CI, mc pnt, minor wear, 5¼" 175.00
Our Kitchener, M-1313, CI, 6½" 145.00
Owl, M-597, CI, mc pnt, 4¼", NM 135.00
Ox, M-536, CI, factory conversion, blk & wht rpt, 6¾" 145.00
Pagoda, M-1153, CI, silver w/worn gold overpnt, 5"..................265.00
Palace, M-1116, CI, blk & gold pnt, minor damage, 7½" 175.00
Peach on Stand, CI, mc pnt, Gaffney, modern, 6", EX..................65.00
Pig, M-579, grin on face, lead, bronze pnt, 4¼" L....................25.00
Pig, M-584, nickeled CI, 6⅞" L 65.00
Pig, M-608, CI, bronze finish, 7⅜" L....................................85.00
Pig, M-609, Wise, partial rpt, 6¾", EX 55.00
Pig, M-617, Wise, CI, wht pnt, minor wear, 6⅝" 40.00
Pig, M-621, ceramic, 2-tone, clear/brn marbleized, 4" L...............17.50
Pig, M-621, chalkware, old rpt, leg rpr, 7⅛" L, VG 45.00
Pirate, M-341, wht metal, mc pnt, minor wear, 5⅞"....................35.00

Policeman, EX paint, 6", $235.00.

Porky Pig by Barrel, L-826, pot metal, 4½" 60.00
Presto, M-1167, CI, silver w/gold dome, minor wear, 4⅛" 65.00
Pug Dog, M-405, CI, worn gold pnt, 3½" 95.00
Pump, M-1253, lead, wht w/brn pnt, crack in tub, 4½"..............65.00
Punch & Judy, M-1299, tin, 4⅜", EX 70.00
Rabbit, L-291, recumbent, ears back, CI, 2¼" 350.00

Rabbit, M-565, CI, gold pnt traces, 5¼" 375.00
Rabbit, M-568, CI, rpt traces, 3¾"......................................65.00
Rabbit, M-571, silvered lead, 4⅜" L....................................145.00
Rabbit, M-574, CI, gold pnt, 6½", EX 175.00
Radio, M-821, CI, bl pnt w/gold trim, 3¼", EX 100.00
Radio, M-827, CI, bronze finish, 4½"....................................30.00
Radio, M-830, CI, lt bl pnt w/gold, NP door, 6¼" L 135.00
Radio, M-833, CI, red pnt, NP door, minor wear, 4½" 80.00
Recording Bank, M-1062, worn NPCI, 6⅝"..........................170.00
Retriever, M-436, CI, pnt traces, casting hole, 3⅝"....................25.00
Rhino, M-721, CI, dull gold pnt, minor wear, 5"....................315.00
Roof Bank, M-1124, CI, bronze finish, lt wear & rust, 5¼".........125.00
Round Duck, M-619, CI, mc pnt w/G color, rpl trap, 4" 125.00
Round Duck, M-619, CI, yel pnt w/red & blk trim, 4", EX.........275.00
Rumplestiltskin, L-832, CI, 6", VG....................................325.00
Safe, Jewel; M-896, nickeled CI, sm crack, 5½" 100.00
Safe, M-869, CI, mc pnt, minor wear, 3¼" 35.00
Sailor, M-29, CI, worn wht pnt, 5¾"....................................45.00
Santa, M-104, at chimney, lead, mc pnt, 4½", EX 125.00
Santa, M-61, w/tree, CI, VG pnt, 5¾" 335.00
Satchel, M-1268, CI, bronze pnt, 5⅞" L 175.00
Save Your Pennies..., M-1545, CI, gold pnt, minor wear, 3½" 125.00
Savings, M-874, glass, sm chip, 3⅞"......................................25.00
Scottie, M-426, papier-mache, mc pnt, minor wear, 5⅛" 25.00
Scottie, M-430, CI, blk pnt, 2⅞", EX....................................60.00
Seal, M-732, CI, blk & silver pnt, minor wear, 3⅜" 300.00
Share Cropper, M-173, CI, pnt traces, 5⅛"............................125.00
Shell Out, L-1178, CI, 2½" 350.00
Skyscraper, M-1241, CI, worn silver & gold pnt, 6¾"................115.00
Snoopy, ceramic..25.00
Soldier, M-45, CI, gold & red pnt, minor wear, 6" 145.00
Space Heater, M-1094, CI, blk pnt, 6½", EX 85.00
Spitz Dog, M-409, CI, layers of worn gold pnt, 5" L................210.00
St Bernard, M-437, w/pack, CI, brn japanning, 5½", EX 65.00
Stag, M-737, NPCI, worn pnt, 9½", EX................................65.00
State Bank, M-1080, CI, mc metallic pnt, 5¾", EX 120.00
State Bank, M-1083, CI, mc metallic pnt, 4⅛", VG 45.00
Statue of Liberty, M-1164, CI, worn gold pnt, 6" 115.00
Stop-Save, M-1481, CI, lt wear on pnt, 5½" 200.00
Stove, L-1032, CI, worn wht pnt, Arcade, 3¾" 85.00
Sun Bonnet Sue, M-257, CI, mc pnt, minor wear, modern, 7⅜" ..75.00
Tally-Ho, M-535, CI, worn brn japanning w/gold, lt rust, 4½" 75.00
Tank, M-1414, CI, dk patina, lt rust, 7¼" L..........................275.00
Tank, M-1419, CI, brn japanning w/gold, rpl screw, 8¼" L..........225.00
Tank M-1437, USA, CI, gold pnt, minor wear, 4⅜" L 115.00
Teddy (Roosevelt), M-120, CI, gold pnt, minor wear, 5" 150.00
Time Around World, L-1506, japanned CI, cb inserts, 4", VG....250.00
Time Safe, M-895, NPCI, lt rust, 7⅛"..................................185.00
Tole House, L-523, CI, bl pnt w/silver, minor wear, 4⅛" 65.00
Top Hat, M-1391, tin, blk pnt, College on band, 4¼", EX..........200.00
Top Hat, M-1397, tin, blk w/gold band, minor wear, 3½" 70.00
Tower, M-1208, CI, brn japanning, minor wear, 8⅞"..................250.00
Truck, M-1514, sheet metal, red pnt, NP grill, 6¼" L................60.00
Turkey, M-587, CI, old blk rpt, 3½"....................................40.00
Turkey, M-587, CI, worn brn japanning w/red, 3½" 125.00
US Air Mail, M-841, CI, gr pnt w/gold, Hubley decal, 5½" 90.00
US Mail, M-838, CI, silver & red pnt, minor wear, 3⅜"................30.00
US Mail, M-842, CI, gr & gold pnt, minor wear, 3¾" 25.00
US Mail, M-856, CI, red & gold pnt, minor wear, 5¼" 45.00
US Mail, M-856, CI, red pnt traces, 5¼" 22.50
US Mint, M-839, CI, red & gold pnt, minor wear, 3½" 40.00
Villa, M-1179, CI, brn japanning, gold trim, red finial, 5½"........185.00
Villa, M-959, 1882, CI, dk brn japanning w/gold, 5½" 175.00

Virserums Sparbank, M-1513, bus, wht metal, minor wear, 6" L....30.00
Von Hindenburg, M-152, lead, dk brn pnt, 9¼", EX....................350.00
Washington Bell, M-786, CI, red & gold pnt, minor wear, 2⅞".....75.00
Washington Monument, M-1048, CI, EX gold pnt, 6⅛" 125.00
Westminster Abbey, M-974, CI, gold traces, 6⅝" 155.00
Whippet, M-362, on base, conversion, CI, gold pnt, 5" L, EX.....135.00
Wolf, M-1658, CI, mc pnt, minor wear, 4½" 35.00
Woolworth Building, M-1042, CI, worn gold pnt, 5¾" 55.00
Wurlitzer Jukebox, M-1581, wht metal, EX mc pnt, 3⅛" 50.00
Yel Cab, L-1570, CI, 4", VG 400.00
1876 Bank, M-1012, CI, pnt traces, 2⅞" 100.00
2 Kids, M-594, CI, blk/gr/silver pnt, some wear, 4⅜" 775.00
3 Monkeys, M-743, See No..., CI, bronze & gold pnt, 3¼".........305.00
4 Tower, M-1121, CI, brn japanning w/gold, 5¾", EX 185.00

Barber Shop Collectibles

Even for the stranger in town, the local barber shop was easy to find, its location vividly marked with the traditional red and white striped barber pole that for centuries identified such establishments. As far back as the twelfth century, the barber has had a place in recorded history. At one time he not only groomed the beards and cut the hair of his gentlemen clients, but was known as the 'blood letter' as well – hence the red stripe for blood and the white for the bandages. Many early barbers even pulled teeth! Later, laws were enacted that divided the practices of barbering and surgery.

The Victorian barber shop reflected the charm of that era with fancy barber chairs upholstered in rich wine-colored velvet; rows of bottles made from colored art glass held hair tonics and shaving lotion. Backbars of richly carved oak with beveled mirrors lined the wall behind the barber's station. During the late nineteenth century, the barber pole with a blue stripe added to the standard red and white as a patriotic gesture came into vogue.

Today the barber shop has all but disappeared from the American scene, replaced by modern unisex salons. Collectors search for the barber poles, the fancy chairs, and the tonic bottles of an era gone but not forgotten. See also Bottles; Razors; Shaving Mugs.

Blade bank, barber pole w/styptic pencil & brush, 6½" 25.00
Blade bank, Dandy Dan, celluloid, mc, w/tool holder, 6½" 15.00
Blade bank, donkey figural, ceramic, Listerine, 2½x4" 12.50
Blade bank, frog figural, porc, Listerine, EX 35.00
Blade bank, man's head w/derby hat figural, porc, EX 26.00
Bottle, Wildroot w/Oil, red/wht enamel on gr, rubber spout, 9".....30.00
Cabinet, sterilizer; NP, 23-compartment, porc lined, 10x4x6" 50.00
Chair, Berninghause, Cincinnati, rstr upholstery, EX....................550.00
Chair, Kern, St Louis 'America,' oak, leather upholstery, EX.......550.00
Chair, Koken, CI w/oak wood, rstr upholstery, 42", EX 895.00
Chair, Koken, Congress model, EX...650.00
Chair, Koken, porc trim, rstr leather, 49x24x43", NM.................950.00
Chair, Ransom & Randolf Toledo-Indianapolis, 1870s, 40", EX..300.00
Jar, Gauze, oval underglass label, Glasco, 7x4½", EX...................12.00
Neck duster, SP, ornate emb floral, twist hdl, 11", EX 85.00
Pole, CI & sheet metal w/worn rpt, 90" 175.00
Pole, laminated wood w/3-color rpt & 'Joe's,' 65" 165.00
Pole, leaded glass, Koken, 1890s, 32", VG 350.00
Pole, orig porc finish, for sidewalk, 90" 2,000.00
Pole, trn, knob in middle, block base, 3-color, 1890s, 78"...........600.00
Pole, wood, mk Rochester NY, 1920, 34" 285.00
Rack, mug; 35-hook, oak w/blk pnt, cvd gallery, 54x29x6".........350.00
Strop, horsehide, unused, NM..15.00
Strop, Kanner's Slyde-Stroke, NP brass & leather, EX 20.00
Strop, Kriss Kross Stropper, VG in orig cb box 22.00

Barometers

Barometers are instruments designed to measure the weight or pressure of the atmosphere in order to anticipate approaching weather changes. Those made around the turn of the century – earlier in England and on the continent – were beautifully housed in period cases of mahogany, rosewood, walnut, or cherry, often with brass trim. These quality pieces bring high prices on today's market.

Aneroid, cvd oak, 1900, 26"..145.00
Cairns, mahog stick type w/foliate cvg, temp, gimbal, 37" 2,500.00
Fitzroy, temp/wind direction, tells weather changes, 41" 1,350.00
Geo III style, oak, thermometer above, HP porc face, 34"...........650.00
German, aneroid, wood, wall mt, 6", EX......................................50.00
Mahog w/inlay, eng silvered brass face & trim, rpr, 38"...............165.00
P Catanio, cvd crest, bevelled glass face, stick type, 42" 500.00
Simmons, rosewood veneer, appl moldings, pat 1861, 38"...........400.00
Simmons, walnut case, appl moldings, pat 1861, 38" 325.00

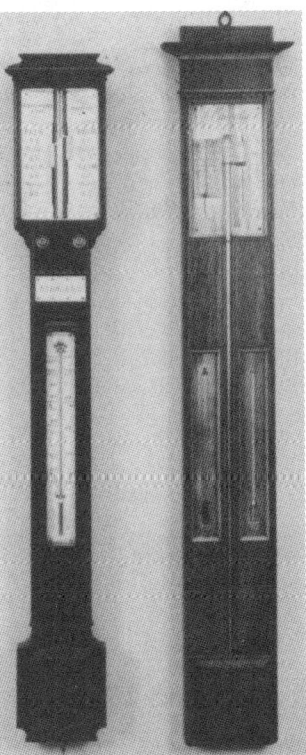

Standard, by D. Bonangaro & Son, engraved ivory dials, thermometer, 40", $1,350.00; Chevallier, silvered dials, two thermometers, 41", $950.00.

Baskets

Basket weaving is a craft as old as ancient history. Baskets have been used to harvest crops, for domestic chores, and to contain the catch of fishermen. Materials at hand were utilized, and baskets from a specific region are often distinguishable simply by analyzing the natural fibers used in their construction. Early Indian baskets were made of corn husks or woven grasses. Willow splint, straw, rope, and paper are only a few of the materials that have been used. Until the invention of the veneering machine in the late 1800s, splint was made by water-soaking a split log until the fibers were softened and flexible. Long strips were pulled out by hand and, while still wet and pliable, woven into baskets in either a cross-hatch or hexagonal weave.

Most handcrafted baskets on the market today were made between 1860 and the early 1900s. Factory baskets with a thick, wide splint cut by machine are of little interest to collectors. The more popular baskets are those designed for a specific purpose, rather than the more commonly-found utility baskets that had multiple uses. Among the most costly forms are the Nantucket Lighthouse baskets, which were basically copied from those made there for centuries by aboriginal Indians. They were designed in the style of whale oil barrels and named for the South Shoal Nantucket Lightship where many were made during the last half of the nineteenth century. Cheese baskets (used to separate curds from whey), herb-gathering baskets, and finely woven Shaker miniatures are other highly-prized examples of the basket weaver's art.

In the listings that follow, assume that each has a center bentwood handle (unless handles of another type are noted) that is not included in the height. Unless another type of material is indicated, assume that each is made of splint. See also American Indian; Eskimo; Sewing; Shaker.

Bentwood, oval, miniature, 3⅜" L......................................95.00
Bushel, bentwood rim hdls, minor damage, 12x19" dia..................85.00
Bushel, bentwood rim hdls, well made, 12x21" dia 150.00
Bushel, staved, wood rim w/bentwood hdls, varnish, 11x18" 145.00
Buttocks, EX age & color, 3¼x4½".....................................140.00
Buttocks, EX color, well shaped, 16" L...............................240.00
Buttocks, EX color & construction, 9" L 190.00
Buttocks, Eye of God at hdl, EX color, 12" L 200.00
Buttocks, good age, 6½x8" L 215.00
Buttocks, gr pnt w/red & blk floral, 12½x15"........................325.00
Buttocks, high rim w/3 wide horizontal splints, 8" L, NM 100.00
Buttocks, minor rim damage, 14" L 175.00
Buttocks, purple-dyed stripes, some age, 9½x14x16" 150.00
Buttocks, some age, miniature, 3x4¾x5", EX 155.00
Buttocks, some age, 17" L 175.00
Buttocks, well made, EX color, 13" L, EX............................300.00
Buttocks, well made, late, 4x7½' 55.00
Buttocks, well made, some age, 8x13x13½"............................150.00
Buttocks, zigzags in worn red & gr pnt on hdl, 8x14x15"...........165.00
Cotton-picking, leather strap, minor damage, 18" H 200.00

Double-handled splint basket, iron-tacked swing handles, 20" long, EX, $400.00.

Egg, radiating ribs, varnish, minor damage, 8½x14x15"................85.00
Egg, radiating ribs, 5x10x11" 165.00
Egg, well made, gr/blk pnt, 7x12x15" 550.00
Egg, 2¼"+bentwood hdl 165.00
Export, dbl lids hinge in center at hdl, miniature, 4½" L 45.00
Gathering, high arched woven hdl, worn bl pnt, 2x12x13".........175.00
Goose feather, wide splint, tall/ovoid, 25" 225.00
Goose feather, woven splint, w/lid, 22".............................195.00
Laundry, splint, bentwood rim hdls, worn pnt, 14x22", EX.........235.00

Market, fixed hdl, rectangular, 20½" L 50.00
Market, fixed hdl, 16½" dia..70.00
Market, swing hdl, dome bottom, 16" dia.............................225.00
Melon rib, rim hdls, oval, 9x16x18"..................................225.00
Melon rib, scrubbed finish, 11" L, EX 195.00
Nantucket, oval, late, 8" L, EX 500.00
Nantucket, rstr, 5" dia, EX 500.00
Nantucket, sgn/dtd 1909, 6½" dia, NM................................600.00
Nantucket, slight reweaving, 13" dia, EX.......................... 1,200.00
Nantucket, swing hdl, by Ferdinand Sylvaro, 13" dia, NM 1,250.00
Nantucket, swing hdl, well rstr, early, 7½" dia.....................650.00
Nantucket, swing hdl, 8¾" dia.......................................700.00
Nantucket, w/hdl, sgn Ferdinand Sylvaro, 11½" dia, M 1,400.00
Nantucket, 5" dia, EX...600.00
Nantucket, 9¾", M.. 1,400.00

Nantucket Lightship basket, 14" tall, $7,750.00.

Pie, splint w/curliques, wht pnt, w/lid, 12" dia, VG.................65.00
Rye straw, beehive shape, minor wear, 11x13½".....................155.00
Rye straw, bowl form, bentwood base, woven hdl, 9x18" 400.00
Rye straw, bowl form, minor wear, 5½x12" 75.00
Splint, bentwood hdl, 1800s, 12x8½" dia, VG.........................175.00
Splint, block design in rim, fine weave, no hdl, 2⅜" dia.............145.00
Splint, brass label: Guy C Maxwell, Malta OH, 8x13x16", VG.....65.00
Splint, cvd hdl, dk gr pnt, kicked-up bottom, 10" dia 150.00
Splint, cvd hdl, 1800s, EX patina, miniature, 2x2", EX 275.00
Splint, dbl-wrapped rim, fixed hdl, Am, 1890s, 13½x14½" 175.00
Splint, hdl attaches outside rim, EX patina, 6x12x11", EX 225.00
Splint, radiating ribs, rope twist sapling hdl, 11x18x32" 130.00
Splint, radiating ribs, salmon pnt, 14x19" L, EX....................210.00
Splint, radiating ribs, well made, minor damage, 3x5x5½"..........210.00
Splint, radiating ribs, worn gr-gray rpt, 6x11x12", EX...............200.00
Splint, radiating ribs, 7½x12x15", EX................................125.00
Splint, rectangular, 14x11x12", VG...................................100.00
Splint, swivel hdl, primitive, 6x9¾" 125.00
Splint, unusual vertical shape, EX detail, 8½" 450.00
Splint, w/lid, 1800s, weathered, 19x15", EX.........................100.00
Splint, well made, EX color, oval, 6x10x12", VG.....................125.00
Splint, well made, EX patina, 7¾x10½x16½" 200.00
Splint, wide stripes, red-brn pnt, 8x11x16" 115.00
Splint, wide strips, minor wear, 14x24" L 115.00
Splint, worn bl-blk stain, miniature, 2½x4x5½" 125.00
Splint, woven bl bands, 4x7¾" dia...................................65.00

Splint, woven foot, fixed/cvd hdl, Am, 1900, 3¾x7½" 300.00
Splint, 6½x13" dia 185.00
Splint w/sweet grass rim, Indian, miniature, 2½x4" 65.00
Swivel hdl, EX color, minor damage, 9x16" dia 250.00
Swivel hdl, kick-up in bottom, well made, 8x14" dia 725.00
Swivel hdl, rnd, minor damage, 7x11" dia 180.00
Swivel hdl, well made, EX age & color, 8x14" dia 345.00
Swivel hdl, wood bottom, 10x15x16" 175.00
Twig, cylinder held by wire & wood rim, pnt, 22x21", EX 145.00

Batchelder

Ernest A. Batchelder was a leading exponent of the Arts and Crafts movement in the United States. His influential book, *Design in Theory and Practice*, was originally published in 1910. He is best known, however, for his artistic tiles which he first produced in Pasadena, California, from 1909 to 1916. In 1906 the business was relocated to Los Angeles where it continued until 1932, closing because of the Depression.

In 1938 Batchelder resumed production in Pasedena under the name of 'Kinneola Kiln.' Output of the new pottery consisted of delicately cast bowls and vases in an Oriental style. This business closed in 1951. Tiles carry a die-stamped mark; vases and bowls are hand incised.

Our advisor for this category is Jack Chipman; he is listed in the Directory under California.

Bowl, gr, 3x11" 95.00
Bowl, Kinneola Kiln mk, gr, scalloped, 3x10½" 100.00
Bowl, Pasadena mk, rose, oval, 4x12x7" 135.00
Tile, scenic w/lg tree, brn, mk, 7¾" 175.00
Tile, stylized ivy, tan & bl, 7", VG 45.00
Vase, lime gr, 6" 125.00

Tile, La Mayan, terra cotta, 3½" square, $60.00.

Battersea

Battersea is a term that refers to enameling on copper or other metal. Though originally produced at Battersea, England, in the mid-eighteenth century, the craft was later practiced throughout the Staffordshire district. Boxes are the most common examples – some are figurals, and many bear an inscription. Values are given for examples with only minimal damage, which is normal.

Tapersticks, florals on white, probably Bilston, ca 1780, cracks/chips, 6½", $1,500.00 for the pair.

Box, Admiral Lord Nelson on lid, 1¾" dia, EX 400.00
Box, bird firm, bird & fruit on lid, 1½", EX 800.00
Box, dog's head, minor retouching, sm 425.00
Box, Reward of Virtue, yel, dtd 1768, 1¾" 585.00
Box, Trifle from London, floral garland, 1½" L, EX 350.00
Knob, Hope resting on anchor, ship in bkground, EX 150.00
Knob, 18th Century lady, oval, pr 275.00
Locket, ship, bk: clock face, EX 265.00

Bauer

Originally founded in Paducah, Kentucky, in 1885, the J.A. Bauer Company moved to Los Angeles where it was re-established in 1909. Until the 1920s, their major products were terra cotta gardenware, flowerpots, and stoneware and yellowware bowls. During prohibition they produced crocks for home use. A more artful form of product began to develop with the addition of designer Louis Ipsen to the staff in 1915. Some of his work – a line of molded vases, flowerpots, bowls, etc. – was awarded a bronze medal at the Pacific International Exposition the following year.

In 1930 the first of many dinnerware lines was tested on the market. Their initial pattern, Plain Ware, was well accepted and led the way to the introduction of the most popular dinnerware in their history and with today's collectors – Ring Ware. It was produced from 1932 into the early 1960s in solid colors of jade green, royal blue, Chinese yellow, light blue, orange-red, and (in very limited quantities) black or white. Its simple pattern was a design of closely-spaced concentric ribs, either convex or concave. Over the years, more than one hundred shapes were available. Some were made in limited quantities, resulting in rare items to whet the appetites of Bauer buffs today. Other patterns were La Linda, produced during the 1940s and 1950s, and Monterey Moderne, introduced in 1948 and remaining popular into the 1950s (made in pink, black, gray, brown, and green.)

After WWII a flood of foreign imports drastically curtailed their sales, and the pottery began a steady decline that ended in failure in 1962. Prices listed below reflect the California market. For more information, we recommend *The Complete Collector's Guide to Bauer Pottery* by Jack Chipman, our advisor for this category, and Judy Stangler. Mr Chipman's address may be found in the Directory under California.

Ash tray, Monterey, all colors but wht 67.50
Ash tray, plain, blk, sq, 3" 50.00
Ash tray, Ring, orange-red or dk bl, 2" 25.00
Bean pot, plain, all colors but blk, hdls, 2-qt 50.00
Bowl, batter; La Linda, burgundy or dk brn, 2-qt............40.00
Bowl, berry; Ring, yel or lt bl, 4" 10.00
Bowl, cereal; Ring, dk bl or ivory, 4½" 18.00
Bowl, fruit; Monterey, all colors but wht, 6" 10.00
Bowl, fruit; Monterey Moderne, all colors but blk, 4¼" 7.50
Bowl, mixing; La Linda, gr, yel, or turq, #36, 1-pt 9.00
Bowl, ramekin; La Linda, burgundy or dk brn...................8.00
Bowl, salad; Ring, dk bl or wht, low, 12" 60.00
Bowl, soup/cereal; Al Fresco, speckled, gr, or gray, 5½" 4.50
Bowl, vegetable; Al Fresco, coffee brn or Dubonnet, rnd, 9½" 18.00
Bowl, vegetable; Contempo, all colors, 9½" 13.00
Bowl, vegetable; Ring, turq or red-brn, oval, 8"...............27.50
Butter dish, Al Fresco, speckled, gr, or gray 20.00
Butter dish, Monterey Moderne, all colors but blk, rnd 30.00
Butter dish, Ring, ivory or wht, w/lid, rnd 70.00
Cake plate, Monterey, wht, ped ft, 10½" 100.00
Candlestick, Monterey, wht 30.00
Canister, flour; coffee brn or Dubonnet 30.00

Carafe, Ring Ware, light green, 6-cup, $25.00.

Casserole, Al Fresco, speckled, gr, or gray, 2-qt 7.50
Casserole, Ring, yel, lt bl, or gray, ind, 5½" 55.00
Cigarette/cigar jar, Ring, blk, 4"................................200.00
Coffee server, Ring, dk bl, wht, or ivory, 6-cup...............40.00
Coffeepot, plain, all colors but blk, ind, 2-cup...............40.00
Cookie jar, La Linda, pk, gray, or ivory 45.00
Cookie jar, Ring, yel, olive, or gray 75.00
Creamer, Al Fresco, coffee brn or Dubonnet, jumbo 7.50
Creamer, Contempo, all colors 4.00
Creamer, La Linda, burgundy or dk brn, old shape 10.00
Creamer, Monterey, all colors but wht, midget 10.00
Creamer, plain, blk, 1-pt 30.00
Cup, El Chico, all colors 35.00
Egg cup, Ring, turq, yel, or jade gr..............................60.00

Figurine, hippo, mouth open, wht matt, 4" 100.00
Figurine, striding horse, wht matt, 4" 50.00
Flowerpot, Ring & Gardenware, speckled or turq, 10".......60.00
Goblet, Ring, chartreuse, turq, or red-brn......................45.00
Gravy boat, Contempo, all colors.................................8.00
Gravy boat, La Linda, burgundy or dk brn 20.00
Mug, Al Fresco, speckled, gr, or gray, hlds, 12-oz 9.00
Mug, Monterey Moderne, blk, 10-oz 30.00
Pitcher, cream; plain, all colors but blk, 1-pt 30.00
Pitcher, La Linda, gr, yel, or lt brn, 1½-pt 18.00
Pitcher, low Dutch; plain, all colors but blk, 3-qt 50.00
Pitcher, Monterey Moderne, all colors but blk, 1-qt 24.00
Pitcher, Ring, burgundy, wht, or dk bl, ball form, 1½-qt ...80.00
Plate, bread & butter; Ring, blk, 5" 40.00
Plate, chop; Monterey Moderne, blk, 13" 45.00
Plate, chop; plain, all colors but blk, 14½"....................50.00
Plate, dinner; Al Fresco, speckled, gr, or gray, 10" 4.50
Plate, grill; La Linda, chartreuse or turq, 10" 15.00
Plate, salad; El Chico, all colors, 7½" 15.00
Plate, salad; Monterey, all colors but wht, 7½" 10.00
Plate, salad; Monterey Moderne, blk, 7½" 15.00
Plate, salad; plain, blk, 7½" 32.00
Platter, Monterey, wht, oval, 17" 35.00
Platter, Monterey Moderne, gr or pk, oval, 10" 12.00
Platter, Ring, yel, lt bl, or red-brn, oval, 12" 22.50
Relish, Monterey, burgundy or red-brn, oval, 10½".........137.50
Saucer, El Chico, all colors..10.00
Shakers, Ring, blk, low, pr 30.00
Sugar bowl, Monterey Moderne, all colors but blk, low 15.00
Sugar bowl, plain, all colors but blk, midget 20.00
Teapot, Monterey, all colors but wht, new shape, 6-cup.....45.00
Teapot, plain, all colors but blk, 6-cup 90.00
Teapot, Ring, burgundy or wht, 6-cup...........................60.00
Tumbler, Monterey, wht, 8-oz.....................................20.00
Tumbler, Ring, orange-red, or burgundy, 6-oz 15.00
Vase, Ring & Gardenware, speckled or burgundy, 6" 30.00
Water jug, Ring, turq or red-brn, open...........................37.50

Bavaria

Bavaria, Germany, was long the center of that country's pottery industry; in the 1800s, many firms operated in and around the area. Chinaware vases, novelties, and table accessories were decorated with transfer prints as well as by hand by artists who sometimes signed their work. The examples here are marked with 'Bavaria' and the logos of some of the various companies which were located there. See also Children's Things, China.

Bowl, nasturtiums, HP, gold scalloped edge, 10"...........135.00
Cookie jar, roses, pk on gr shaded w/gold, mk, 7½x5½" ...100.00
Creamer & sugar bowl, roses on gr band w/gold 35.00
Cup & saucer, Dresden Flowers, Schumann 25.00
Pitcher, tankard; grapes w/gold, Guillaume, 11¼" 110.00
Plate, lady's portrait, lacy gold rim, 6½" 30.00
Plate, pk roses/leaves, gold border, artist sgn, 7½".........10.00
Shelf sitter, boy fishing, gr hat, orange pants 45.00
Teapot, alternating panels w/gold, +6 c/s 175.00

Beer Cans

When the flat-top can was first introduced in 1934, it came with printed instructions on how to use the triangular punch opener. Cone-top cans, which are rare today, were patented in 1935 by the Continental Can Company. By the 1960s, aluminum cans with pull tabs had made both types obsolete.

The hobby of collecting beer cans has been rapidly gaining momentum over the past ten years. Series types, such as South African Brewery, Lion, and the Cities Series by Schmit and Tucker, are especially popular.

Condition is an important consideration when evaluating market price. Grade 1 must be in like-new condition with no rust. However, the triangular punch hole is acceptable. Grade 2 cans may have slight scratches or dimples but must be free of rust. For Grade 3, light rust, minor scratching, and some fading may be acceptable. When these defects are more pronounced, a can is defaulted to Grade 4. Those in less-than-excellent condition devaluate sharply. In the listings that follow, cans are arranged alphabetically by brand name, not by brewery. Unless noted otherwise, values are for cans in Grade 1 condition.

Our advisor for this category is Lowell Owens; he is listed in the Directory under New York.

ABC, pull top, red & wht, 12-oz	3.00
Alpine, flat top, 12-oz	45.00
American, pull top, red, wht, & gold, 12-oz	10.00
Atlas Prager, flat top, red & wht, 12-oz	14.00
Ballantine, pull top, gold & wht, 12-oz	3.00
Bavarian, pull top, bl & wht, 12-oz	1.00
Berghoff, flat top, red & wht, 12-oz	70.00
Best, flat top, wht & gold, 12-oz	30.00
Big Mac, flat top, wht & gold, 12-oz	100.00
Black Horse Ale, pull top, wht, gold, & blk, 12-oz	2.00
Blatz Bock, pull top, red & gold, 12-oz	10.00
Breunig's, pull top, red & wht, 12-oz	1.00
Brown Derby, flat top, wht & gold, 12-oz	14.00
Budweiser, flat top, red & wht, 12-oz	6.00
Bull Dog ML, flat top, wht, gold, & bl, 12-oz	12.00
Burger, flat top, red & wht, 12-oz	10.00
Busch Bavarian, pull top, wht & bl, 12-oz	2.00
Butte Lager, flat top, red, wht, & gold, 12-oz	25.00
Canadian Ace Premium, flat top, wht & gold, 12-oz	7.00
Cascade, pull top, bl & wht, 12-oz	1.00
Circle, flat top, red & wht, 12-oz	10.00
Club Special, pull top, wht, 12-oz	50.00
Colt Beer, pull top, wht & bl, 12-oz	10.00
Coors, flat top, gold & blk, 12-oz	65.00
Crystal Rock, flat top, wht & bl, 12-oz	35.00
Denver, flat top, bl, 12-oz	30.00
Dodger, flat top, wht & red, 12-oz	50.00
Drewry's, flat top, wht & bl, 12-oz	20.00
Drewry's Extra Dry, flat top, wht, 12-oz	7.00
DuBois, pull top, gold & wht, 12-oz	5.00
Duquesne, flat top, wht, red, & blk, 12-oz	22.00
Eastern, flat top, wht & red, 12-oz	75.00
Eastside Old Tap, flat top, red & wht, 12-oz	12.00
Edelweiss, pull top, 12-oz	1.50
Fabacher Brau, pull top, blk, 12-oz	5.00
Falstaff, flat top, wht & gold, 12-oz	4.00
Fischer's, flat top, red, blk, & gold, 12-oz	25.00
Fitger's, flat top, blk, gold, & wht, 12-oz	6.00
Fox DeLuxe, flat top, wht & gold, 12-oz	8.00
Fox Head Bock, flat top, wht, red, & gold, 12-oz	17.00
Garten Brau, pull top, gold & wht, 12-oz	5.00
Genesee, flat top, red & wht, 12-oz	10.00
Gold Crest, flat top, red & wht, 12-oz	55.00
Red Top Ale, cone top, NM	60.00

Similar, flat top, red, 12-oz 8.00

Yuengling & Son, Inc.; cone top, yellow and white on red, 3¾", $58.00.

Belleek, American

From 1883 until 1930, several American potteries located in New Jersey and Ohio manufactured a type of china similar to the famous Irish Belleek soft-paste porcelain. The American manufacturers identified their porcelain by using 'Belleek' in their marks. American Belleek is considered the highest achievement of the American porcelain industry. Production centered around artistic cabinet pieces and luxury tablewares. Many examples emulated Irish shapes and decor with marine themes and other naturalistic styles. While all are highly collectible, some companies' products are rarer than others. The best-known manufacturers are Ott and Brewer, Willets, The Ceramic Art Company (CAC), and Lenox. You will find more detailed information in those specific categories. For a more thorough study of the subject, we recommend you refer to *American Belleek* by our advisor Mary Frank Gaston; you will find her address in the Directory under Texas.

Key:
AAC — American Art China   CAP — Columbian Art Pottery
                                                      Works

Cream soup, Bouquet, Coxon, w/underplate	125.00
Cup & saucer, Boulevard, Coxon	125.00
Cup & saucer, demitasse; magenta w/gold, mk Gordon	75.00
Cup & saucer, morning-glories, Morgan	120.00
Gravy boat, Boulevard, attached underplate, Coxon	425.00
Mug, Indian portrait, sgn E Lee/June 8, 1900, 1-pt	150.00
Pitcher, HP grapes, dtd 1904, 14", M	175.00
Pitcher, tankard; blkberries, gold dragon hdls, 15", +6 mugs	950.00
Plate, Boulevard, Coxon, 10½"	200.00
Plate, Boulevard, Coxon, 7¼"	125.00
Plate, bread & butter; etched gold rim w/cobalt band, Morgan	12.50
Plate, floral, gold rim, mk Coxon, #S-115, 10½"	200.00
Platter, Boulevard, oval, Coxon, 17½"	300.00
Tureen, Boulevard, Coxon, w/underplate	900.00

Belleek, Irish

Belleek is a very thin translucent porcelain that takes its name from the district in Ireland where it originated in 1857. The glaze is a creamy ivory color with a pearl-like lustre. Tablewares, baskets, figurines, and vases have been produced; Shamrock, Tridacna, Echinus, and Lotus are but a few of the many patterns.

It is possible to date an example to within twenty to thirty years of manufacture by the mark. Pieces with an early stamp often bring prices nearly triple that of a similar but current item. With some variation, the marks have always incorporated the wolfhound, castle, harp, and shamrock. The first three marks (usually in black) were used from 1863 to 1946. A series of green marks has been in use since 1946; the most current mark is gold.

Vase, applied florals, 2nd green mark, 12", $995.00.

Aberdeen, vase, 2nd blk mk, florals, lustre finish, 9"	225.00
Aberdeen, vase, 3rd gr mk, florals, 6", pr	225.00
Artichoke, plate, 1st blk mk, 8¼"	125.00
Basketweave, egg cup, 1st blk mk, w/holder, 6 for	1,195.00
Bust, Clytie, 3rd gr mk, pearl & bsk finish, 10¾"	400.00
Bust, Queen of the Hops, 1st blk mk, pearl & bsk finish	3,500.00
Celtic, bread plate, 3rd blk mk	325.00
Celtic, candlestick holder, 3rd gr mk, pearl finish, 5½", pr	700.00
Celtic, cup & saucer, 3rd blk mk, lg	160.00
Celtic, teapot, 3rd blk mk, med sz	600.00
Chinese, teapot, 1st blk mk, gold trim, 9"	1,500.00
Cottage, butter dish, 1st gr mk, yel lustre, 6½x5¾"	165.00
Daisy w/Shamrocks, spill vase, 3rd blk mk	100.00
Dolphin, spill vase, 3rd gr mk, cobalt lustre, 6"	60.00
Echinus, egg cup, 3rd gr mk, cobalt lustre, 2½"	22.50
Echinus, teapot, 1st red mk	900.00
Erne, basket, 4-strand, Belleek & Co Fermanagh mk, 6"	475.00
Erne, tray, 2nd blk mk, pearl finish, 17"	450.00
Erne, tray, 2nd blk mk, yel trim, 17½" dia	550.00
Fan, cup & saucer, 2nd blk mk, gold trim, tea sz	80.00
Fan, trinket box, 2nd blk mk, red tint	335.00
Fern, flowerpot, 1st blk mk, cobalt lustre, 8"	1,250.00
Figure, Affection, 2nd blk mk, pearl finish, 15"	800.00
Figure, collie, 3rd gr mk, 5½"	120.00
Figure, Meditation, 1st blk mk, rstr base, 14"	1,300.00
Flying Fish, vase, 2nd blk mk, pk trim, 4⅜"	425.00
Grass, bread plate, 1st blk mk, gold trim, 11½" dia	300.00
Grass, honey pot, 1st blk mk, bl wings	900.00
Grass, mug, 3rd blk mk, 2¾"	125.00
Grass, plate, 1st blk mk, gold trim, 8", 6 for	300.00
Harp & Shamrock, bell, 3rd gr mk, 4¼"	40.00
Harp & Shamrock, vase, 2nd blk mk, 6½"	145.00

Hexagon, tray, 2nd blk mk, floral decor, gold trim, 16½"	1,300.00
Honeysuckle & Shamrock, vase, 3rd gr mk, 6½"	45.00
Institute, cup & saucer, breakfast; 1st blk mk, pearl lustre	400.00
Ivy, creamer & sugar bowl, 1st gr mk	95.00
Ivy, creamer & sugar bowl, 3rd blk mk	90.00
Ivy, cup & saucer, 3rd blk mk, cobalt lustre	130.00
Lily, creamer & sugar bowl, 1st gr mk	95.00
Lily of the Valley, vase, 2nd gr mk, 6½"	95.00
Limpet, bread plate, 3rd gr mk	92.00
Limpet, cup & saucer, 1st gr mk	60.00
Limpet, cup & saucer, 3rd blk mk	75.00
Limpet, jug, milk; 2nd gr mk	85.00
Limpet, plate, 3rd blk mk, 7"	45.00
Lotus, creamer & sugar bowl, 1st gr mk	70.00
Lotus, creamer & sugar bowl, 3rd blk mk	125.00
Mask, powder bowl, 3rd blk mk, Cyril Arnold, 5¼"	350.00
Neptune, teapot, unmk, 5"	120.00
Neptune, teapot, 3rd gr mk	150.00
Princess, vase, 2nd blk mk, 9x4½"	795.00
Ribbon, creamer & sugar bowl, 1st gr mk	110.00

Sea horse spill vase, 2nd black mark, $295.00.

Shamrock, basket, 3-strand, Belleek & Co Fermanagh mk, 4¾"	450.00
Shamrock, coffeepot, 1st gr mk, 7"	175.00
Shamrock, creamer, 2nd blk mk, brn twig hdl, 3-ftd	75.00
Shamrock, creamer & sugar bowl, 1st gr mk, lg	50.00
Shamrock, creamer & sugar bowl, 3rd blk mk, 3¾"	120.00
Shamrock, creamer & sugar bowl, 3rd gr mk, 3-legged, hdls	48.00
Shamrock, cup & saucer, 2nd gr mk, low	55.00
Shamrock, cup & saucer, 3rd blk mk, tall w/twig hdl	80.00
Shamrock, dejeuner set, 2nd blk mk, 8-pc	1,000.00
Shamrock, honey pot, on stand, 3rd gr mk	110.00
Shamrock, jug, milk; 3rd blk mk, 4"	100.00
Shamrock, mug, 3rd blk mk, twig hdl	75.00
Shamrock, plate, 3rd gr mk, 10½"	55.00
Shamrock, plate, 3rd gr mk, 8"	38.00
Shamrock, trinket box, 3rd blk mk, 2¼"	225.00
Shamrock Basketweave, jug, milk; 3rd blk mk, 4"	135.00
Shamrock Basketweave, plate, 2nd blk mk, 6¼"	35.00
Shamrock Basketweave, plate, 3rd blk mk, 8½", 8 for	500.00
Shamrock Basketweave, plate, 3rd gr mk, 10½"	42.50
Shamrock Basketweave, teapot, 3rd blk mk	295.00
Shell, biscuit jar, 1st gr mk, pearl finish, 7¾"	120.00
Shell, creamer & sugar bowl, 1st gr mk, child's sz	120.00
Shell, creamer & sugar bowl, 3rd blk mk	120.00
Shell, flowerpot, 2nd blk mk, ftd, pearl finish, 9"	1,600.00
Shell, plateaux, 3rd blk mk, 4¼"	50.00
Shell & Coral, biscuit jar, 3rd blk mk, pearl lustre, 7¼"	425.00

Sydenham, basket, 4-strand, Belleek & Co Fermanagh, 10¼".....700.00
Thorn, ash tray, 3rd gr mk, cobalt lustre, sq, 4" 25.00
Thorn, bowl, 2nd blk mk, florals, 6¾" 650.00
Toy Shell, creamer & sugar bowl, 1st gr mk.............................110.00
Tridacna, cake plate, 2nd gr mk, yel..100.00
Tridacna, creamer & sugar bowl, 2nd blk mk 150.00
Tridacna, creamer & sugar bowl, 3rd blk mk 125.00
Tridacna, cup & saucer, 2nd blk mk...115.00
Tridacna, cup & saucer, 3rd gr mk 50.00
Tridacna, jug, milk; 2nd gr mk, cobalt lustre, 5½" 70.00
Tridacna, mustard, 3rd gr mk, cobalt lustre, 2¾" 35.00
Tridacna, plate, 2nd blk mk, 8" 45.00
Tridacna, plate, 3rd blk mk, pk trim, 8" 44.00
Tridacna, teapot, 1st blk mk, tinted, 3¾".................................350.00
Tridacna, teapot, 1st blk mk, 3¼"..225.00
Vase, shell forms vase on fish's bk, 2nd blk mk, 2⅜x4⅜" 425.00
Vase, triple fish, 1st blk mk/imp mk, 15¾", NM 3,250.00
Vase, triple tulip, 2nd blk mk, rstr, 9" 650.00

Bells

The earliest form of bell, the crotal or closed-mouth, is most familiar to us today as the sleigh bell. Rattles, hollow forms containing stones or seed pods, are also of this type of construction. Gongs, most often associated with the Orient, have no clapper and must be struck to sound. The more common forms of bells are made with a flaring shape and a freely-moving interior clapper that causes the bell to ring as it is swung. Bells come in many shapes and serve many uses. They have been used throughout history to sound an alarm, call a congregation, announce dinnertime, or signal a victory. School bells called children in from recess, and cow bells made the herd easier to locate. Bells have been made in brass, glass, china, bronze, and cast iron; in simple as well as elaborately embossed forms; and in amusing figurals. See also Schoolhouse Collectibles.

Church bell, made by Meneeley Bell Co., Troy, NY; signed/dated 1911, with mounting bracket, 20" diameter, $300.00.

Brass, lady in full dress, hand up, head turned, 5" 65.00
Brass, lady in hoop skirt, low-cut bodice, holds fan, 7" 95.00
Brass, Lucy Locket, fancy clothes & hat, 4¾x2⅛"..........................65.00
Brass, pilgrim lady in full dress & cap w/hair down, 5" 55.00
Brass, Queen Elizabeth I, high ruff collar, crown, 5½" 65.00
CI, turtle, ring by pressing on head or tail, 6½" L......................200.00
Glass, bl, wht int, ruffled, appl red cherries/leaves, 6½" 45.00
Glass, cranberry, wht opaque edge, clear hdl, 15" 200.00
Gong, brass, dome form on lamp-base std, 16" 75.00
Gong, Veiled Prophet, St Louis, dtd 1903, EX.............................125.00
Sheep, smooth heavy brass w/iron clapper, 3½x3½"......................27.50
Silver, cherub figural, hallmk 145.00
Sleigh, brass, graduated, 15 on orig 56" leather strap, EX..............40.00
Sleigh, brass, 1¼" dia, 30 on leather strap, EX...........................175.00
Sleigh, brass, 47 on orig leather strap..260.00
Sleigh, NP brass, Droschky, upright fr, 12x13" 150.00
Tap, NP brass, in yoke on std, dtd 1882, 6"..................................50.00
Tap, SP, mushroom, CI octagonal base, pat 1883, 6" 55.00
Tea, silver, winged angel figural hdl, mk 800 ....70.00

Bennington

Although the term has become a generic one for the mottled brown ware produced there, Bennington is not a type of pottery, but rather a town in Vermont where two important potteries were located. The Norton Company, founded in 1793, produced mainly redware and salt-glazed stoneware; only during a brief partnership with Fenton (1845-47) was any Rockingham attempted. The Norton Company endured until 1894, operated by succeeding generations of the Norton family. Fenton organized his own pottery in 1847. There he manufactured not only redware and stoneware, but more artistic types as well – graniteware, scroddled ware, flint enamel, a fine parian, and vast amounts of their famous Rockingham. Though from an esthetic standpoint his work rated highly among the country's finest ceramic achievements, he was economically unsuccessful. His pottery closed in 1858.

It is estimated that only one in five Fenton pieces were marked; and although it has become a common practice to link any fine piece of Rockingham to this area, careful study is vital in order to be able to distinguish Bennington's from the similar wares of many other American and Staffordshire potteries. Although the practice was without the permission of the proprietor, it was nevertheless a common occurrence for a potter to take his molds with him when moving from one pottery to the next, so particularly well-received designs were often reproduced at several locations. Of eight known Fenton marks, four are variations of the '1849' impressed stamp – 'Lyman Fenton Co., Fenton's Enamel Patented 1849, Bennington, Vermont.' These are generally found on examples of Rockingham and flint enamel. A raised, rectangular scroll with 'Fenton's Works, Bennington, Vermont,' was used on early examples of porcelain. From 1852 to 1858, the company operated under the title of the United States Pottery Company. Three marks – the ribbon mark with the initials USP, the oval with a scrollwork border and the name in full, and the plain oval with the name in full – were used during that period.

Among the more sought-after examples are the bird and animal figurines, novelty pitchers, figural bottles, and all of the more finely-modeled items. Recumbent deer, cows, standing lions with one forepaw on a ball, and opposing pairs of poodles with baskets in their mouths and 'coleslaw' fur were made in Rockingham, flint enamel, and occasionally in parian. Numbers in the listings below refer to the book *Bennington Pottery and Porcelain* by Barret.

Key: c/s — cobalt on salt glaze

Book flask, Bennington Bible, flint enamel, B 411-B, pt, EX.......750.00
Book flask, Bennington Companion, flint enamel, 2-qt, M.........950.00
Book flask, Bennington Companion, flint enamel, 4-qt, M 1,500.00
Book flask, Departed Spirits, flint enamel, B 411-D, pt, M.........550.00
Book flask, Ladies Companion, flint enamel, pt, M 800.00
Book flask, Suffering of Kossuth, flint enamel, pt, NM 800.00
Bowl, mixing; flint enamel, 1849 mk, B 149-A, 10" dia, NM .. 1,000.00
Bowl, mixing; Rockingham, B 149-A, minor crazing, 5x11" 300.00
Bowl, vegetable; flint enamel, 1849 mk, oval, 11", EX 500.00
Candlestick, flint enamel, B 198-B, 8" 600.00
Candlestick, flint enamel, gr w/bl & orange flecks, 8" 600.00
Candlestick, flint enamel w/bl flecks, B 198-A, 9½", pr 1,500.00
Candlestick, Rockingham, B 197-C, 9", pr 1,500.00
Candlestick, Rockingham, B 197-D & E, rpr to neck, 9", pr .. 1,200.00
Candlestick, Rockingham, B 198-D, 9½" 350.00

Candlesticks, Rockingham glaze, B 197-D and E (rare form), 9", M, $2,000.00.

Chamberstick, Rockingham, yel-brn mottle, B 195-A, 3x4½". 1,600.00
Coachman, Rockingham, oval 1848 mk, B 421-3, rstr, 11" 425.00
Coachman, Rockingham, 1849 mk, B 419-B, M 695.00
Creamer, flint enamel, Tulip & Heart, B 30-A, 6", NM...............525.00
Creamer, toby, Rockingham, faint 1849 mk, B 416-E, M............695.00
Creamer, toby, Rockingham, 1849 mk, B 416-E, glaze bubble 500.00
Cuspidor, scroddled ware, scalloped rib, 9" dia 625.00
Cuspidor, Shell, side vents, 8½" 90.00
Figurine, parian, Autumn, EX orig gold, 12¾", EX 125.00
Foot warmer, flint enamel, B 183-2, spout rpr, 11" 400.00
Foot warmer, Rockingham, B 183-C, EX...................................350.00
Lamp, fluid; flint enamel std/base, eng globe, prisms, 21".. 3,500.00
Lamp, fluid; flint enamel std/base, prisms missing, 15", M....... 2,300.00
Mold, Rockingham, B 145-E, 8¾", M......................................150.00
Mug, Rockingham, 1849 mk, B 133-E 550.00
Picture fr, Rockingham, B 8-F, oval, 9½x8½" 450.00
Pie pan, flint enamel, 1849 mk, B 146-A, minor crazing, 11"......395.00
Pie pan, Rockingham, 9", NM 150.00
Pipkin, Rockingham, Alternate Rib, mk, no lid, B 143-E, 6" 900.00
Pitcher, Rockingham, emb floral panels, N&F mk, B 23-C, 9"....675.00
Snuff jar, toby, flint enamel, B 417-C 725.00
Snuff jar, toby, flint enamel, gr/cream/brn, mk, B 417-C 1,100.00
Snuff jar, toby, gr, orig hat lid, 1849 mk, B 418-B 1,100.00
Snuff jar, toby, Rockingham, orig lid, B 418-B, NM....................850.00
Soap dish, flint enamel, oblong, open, 5" 90.00
Soap dish, flint enamel, scalloped, att......................................95.00
Sugar bowl, flint enamel, 1849 mk, B 135-2, w/lid, 8", EX 1,100.00
Teapot, Rockingham, squat pear form, att, 4"............................425.00
Tile, flint enamel, lattice design, 1849 mk, 8½x7", EX 140.00
Tobacco jar, Rockingham, Alternate Rib, w/lid, mk, B 129-C.....850.00

Toothbrush holder, flint enamel, Alternate Rib, B 164-B............500.00
Vase, belleek, eagle form, B 401-B, 9", NM...............................200.00
Wash bowl, flint enamel, mk, rare sm sz, B 169, 13½"............ 1,200.00
Wash bowl, flint enamel, paneled, B 167, 13½", EX 350.00
Wash bowl & pitcher, flint enamel, Alternate Rib, B 169....... 2,500.00

Stoneware

Batter jug, Albany slip, orig lid, bail hdl, B 155-D, 1-gal 250.00
Crock, floral, c/s, E&LP, 3-gal...350.00
Crock, 2 pheasants on limb, c/s, J Norton, lug hdls, 12½"....... 1,760.00
Jar, bird on twig, c/s, J&E Norton, 1-gal, NM 300.00
Jar, flower/dots/tendrils, c/s, J&F, ½-gal 125.00
Jug, Albany slip, E&LP, 9"...55.00
Jug, bird on branch, c/s, Norton & Co, hairlines, 14" 400.00
Jug, bird on stump looks bk, c/s, J&E, mfg flaw, 15"................ 2,200.00
Jug, floral, brushed, c/s, Norton & Fenton, 13" 175.00
Jug, floral, c/s, L Norton, ovoid, 18", NM................................350.00
Jug, IWC/squiggle, c/s, JF Norton, hdl reattached, 1-gal.............150.00
Jug, long-tailed bird on branch, c/s, J Norton & Co, 14" 600.00
Pitcher, Albany slip, E&LP, 1½-gal 300.00

Jar, J. Norton & Co., extensive floral in cobalt, 13", EX, $450.00; Jug, N.B. Norton & Son, leafy flourishes centering a flying onion with whirlwind over initials 'C.H.,' 18", NM, $1,000.00.

Big Little Books

The first Big Little Book was published in 1933 and copyrighted in 1932 by the Whitman Publishing Company of Racine, Wisconsin. Its hero was Dick Tracy. The concept was so well accepted that others soon followed Whitman's example; and, though the 'Big Little Book' phrase became a trademark of the Whitman Company, the formats of its competitors – Saalfield, Goldsmith, Van Wiseman, Lynn, and World Syndicate – were exact copies. Today's Big Little Book buffs collect them all.

These hand-sized sagas of adventure were illustrated with full-page cartoons on the right-hand page and the story narration on the left. Colorful cardboard covers contained hundreds of pages, usually totaling over an inch in thickness. Big Little Books originally sold for 10¢ at the dime store; as late as the mid-1950s when the popularity of comic books caused sales to decline signaling an end to production, their price had risen to a mere 20¢. Their appeal was directed toward the pre-teens who bought, traded, and hoarded Big Little Books. Because so many were stored in attics and closets, many have survived. Among the super heroes are G-Men, Flash Gordon, Tarzan, the Lone Ranger, and Red Ryder; in a lighter vein, you'll find such lovable characters as Blondie and Dagwood, Mickey Mouse, Little Orphan Annie, and Felix the Cat.

In the early to mid-1930s, Whitman published several Big Little Books as advertising premiums for the Coco Malt Company, who packed them in boxes of their cereal. These are highly prized by today's collectors, as are Disney stories and super-hero adventures.

Our advisor for this category is Ron Donnelly; he is listed in the Directory under Florida.

Ace Drummond, Rickenbacker, 1935, EX 19.00
Adventures of Huckleberry Finn, 1948, VG 15.00
Air Fighters of America, 1941, VG 15.00
Alley Oop & Dinny, 1935, EX 20.00
Andy Panda & Presto the Pup, NM..15.00
Apple Mary & Dennie's Lucky Apples, 1939, VG....................12.00
Betty Boop, Snow White, Whitman, 1934, EX 60.00
Blaze Brandon, Foreign Legion, 1938, G...............................12.00
Blondie, Count Cookie In Too, EX...22.00
Blondie, Fun for All, EX..22.00
Blondie, Papa Knows Best, 1945, NM....................................25.00
Blondie, Who's Boss, 1942, EX...15.00
Blondie & Baby Dumpling, 1939..20.00
Blondie & Dagwood, Everybody's Happy, EX.........................22.00
Brer Rabbit, Song of the South, 1945-1947, EX.....................25.00
Buck Jones, Fighting Rangers, 1936, EX 30.00
Buck Jones, Killers of Crooked Butte, 1940, EX 25.00
Buck Rogers, Depth Men of Jupiter, 1935, VG.......................45.00
Buck Rogers, Doom Comet, EX 35.00
Buck Rogers, Planetoid Plot, EX 55.00
Buck Rogers, War w/Planet Venus, VG 35.00
Buck Rogers, 25th Century AD, 1933, NM.............................75.00
Bugs Bunny & the Giant Brothers, 1949, G 6.00
Capt Frank Hawks, Air Ace & League of 12, 1938, EX 12.00
Captain Midnight, Secret Squadron, EX 20.00
Charlie Chan Solves a New Mystery, EX 25.00
Charlie McCarthy, 1938, VG..25.00
Chester Gump at Silver Creek Ranch, 1933, G 15.00
Clyde Beatty, Lions & Tigers, EX 30.00
Coach Bernie Bierman's Brick Barton & the Winning Eleven, G .10.00
Dan Dunn & the Border Smugglers, 1938, NM 30.00
Danger Trails in Africa, NM...20.00
David Copperfield, 1934, hard or soft cover, VG....................25.00
Dick Tracy, Adventures of; 1st Big Little Book, rare, NM............100.00
Dick Tracy, Bicycle Gang, EX..25.00
Dick Tracy, Boris Arson Gang, 1935, EX 40.00
Dick Tracy, On the Trail of Larceny Lu, 1935, EX..................25.00
Dick Tracy, Out West, EX..45.00
Dick Tracy, Racketeer Gang, 1936, VG 27.00
Dick Tracy & Dick Tracy Jr, VG 40.00
Dog Stars of Hollywood, 1936..35.00
Donald Duck, Ghost Morgan's Treasure, EX..........................35.00
Donald Duck Says Such a Life, 1939, VG...............................23.00
Ella Cinders & the Mysterious House, 1934 ....50.00
Erik Noble & the Forty Niners, 1934, EX...............................15.00
Flash Gordon, Ice World of Mongo, 1942, EX 50.00
Flash Gordon, Jungles of Mongo, EX 40.00
Flash Gordon, Power Men of Mongo, 1943, EX 50.00
Flash Gordon, Tyrant of Mongo, 1938, EX 40.00
Flash Gordon, Water World of Mongo, EX 35.00
Flash Gordon, Witch Queen of Mongo, EX............................60.00
Flying the Sky Clipper w/Winsie Atkins, NM.........................20.00
Frank Buck Presents Ted Towers Animal Master, EX 15.00

Felix the Cat, Whitman, VG, $24.00; Li'l Abner in New York, Whitman, VG, $30.00.

G-Man VS the Fifth Column, VG 15.00
G-Men Alien, 1939, NM 20.00
Gene Autry, Cowboy Detective, EX 25.00
Gene Autry, Land Grab Mystery, EX 25.00
Gene Autry, Law of Range, 1939, VG...................................20.00
Gene Autry, Raiders on the Range, EX 25.00
Gene Autry, Red Bandit's Ghost, EX....................................20.00
Inspector Wade, Red Aces, 1937, VG...................................17.00
Jack Armstrong, Mystery of Iron Key, EX.............................30.00
Jim Craig State Trooper, Kidnapped Governor, EX 17.50
Jim Craig State Trooper, Kidnapped Governor, 1938, VG 13.00
Jim Starr of Border Patrol, 1937, G......................................12.00
Joe Lewis, Brown Bomber, 1936, VG 40.00
Jungle Jim, Vampire Woman, 1937, EX................................35.00
Ken Maynard, Gun Justice, 1934, G 22.00
King Royal Mounted, Cocomalt giveaway, 1935, EX 30.00
Li'l Abner Among the Millionaires, 1939, EX........................50.00
Little Orphan Annie, Ghost Gang, premium, 1935, EX 60.00
Little Orphan Annie, Gooneyville Mystery, EX.....................22.00
Little Orphan Annie & Sandy, #716, VG...............................40.00
Lone Ranger, Vanishing Herd, 1936, VG..............................30.00
Mandrake & the Midnight Monster, EX................................30.00
Mickey Mouse, Bell Boy Detective, VG 25.00
Mickey Mouse, Electro Box, 1946, VG.................................40.00
Mickey Mouse, Foreign Legion, EX......................................45.00
Mickey Mouse, Lazy Day Mystery, EX 22.00
Mickey Mouse & the Bat Bandit, EX....................................40.00
Mickey Mouse Sails for Treasure Island, 1933, VG 35.00
Mickey Rooney, Judy Garland, 1941, VG 28.00
Mr District Attorney on the Job, 1941, NM 25.00
Paramount, Newsreel, Admiral Byrd, 1934, VG....................25.00
Phantom, Desert Justice, 1941, EX 19.00
Phantom & the Girl of Mystery, EX......................................30.00
Plainsman, 1936 ....35.00
Powder Smoke Range, 1935, VG...20.00
Red Ryder, Circus Luck, EX..22.00
Red Ryder, Rimrock Killers, EX..20.00
Red Ryder, Squaw-Tooth Rustlers, EX.................................20.00
Roy Rogers, Range Detective, EX..10.00
Roy Rogers, Robber's Roost, VG...12.50
Roy Rogers & the Gopher Creek Gunman...............................20.00
Roy Rogers at Crossed Feather Ranch, 1945, EX 25.00
Shadow, Ghost Makers, NM 45.00
Shadow, Living Death, 1940, VG 20.00
Shooting Sheriffs, Wild West, 1936, VG................................14.00

Skippy, Story of; 1934, EX 75.00
Smitty, Golden Gloves, Cocomalt giveaway, 1934, G 22.00
Son of Mystery, 1939, NM 18.00
Speed Douglas, Mole Gang, 1941, VG 15.00
Tailspin Tommy, Lost Transport, 1940, G 15.00
Tarzan, Beast of; 1937, NM 55.00
Tarzan, Fearless, EX 50.00
Tarzan, Land of the Giant Apes, 1949, EX 25.00
Tarzan, Twins, 1934, rare, NM 175.00
Tarzan of the Apes, 1933, EX 60.00
Terry & the Pirates, Giants Vengeance, VG 20.00
Terry & the Pirates, Mountain Stronghold, 1941, VG 20.00
Texas Kid, 1937, VG 15.00
Timid Elmer, Disney, 1939, NM 30.00
Tom Beatty, Ace of the Service, 1934 ....15.00
Tom Mix, Fighting Cowboy, 1935, G 17.00
Tom Mix & His Circus on Barbary Coast, 1940, EX 30.00
Treasure Island, 1934, EX 35.00
We 3 Barrymores, 1935, G 12.00
Wells Fargo, 1938, VG 18.00
Will Rogers, The Story of 1935 ....25.00

Bing and Grondahl

In 1853 brothers M.H. and J.H. Bing formed a partnership with Frederick Vilhelm Grondahl in Copenhagen, Denmark. Their early wares were porcelain plaques and figurines designed by the noted sculptor Thorvaldsen of Denmark. Dinnerware production began in 1863, and by 1889 their underglaze color 'Copenhagen Blue' had earned them worldwide acclaim. They are perhaps most famous today for their Christmas plates, the first of which was made in 1895. See also Limited Edition Plates.

Figurine, boy playing accordion, #1661, 9" 175.00
Figurine, Cocker Spaniel, tan & wht, #2172, 4½" 40.00
Figurine, Colonial man playing cello, #2032 ....250.00
Figurine, Come to Mom, #2324 ....140.00
Figurine, duck, #1/1507 ....125.00
Figurine, girl & butterfly, #2125, 7½" 245.00
Figurine, girl mending, #1879, 7¾" 160.00
Figurine, girl w/puppy & kitten, #2333 ....125.00
Figurine, Gold-crested Kinglet 50.00
Figurine, Goose Girl, #2254 ....275.00
Figurine, mandolinist sits on stool, gray/wht, #1600, 11" 325.00
Figurine, Pickie, #1636 ....135.00
Figurine, Siamese cat, #2464, wht, 5½" 85.00
Figurine, squirrel w/acorn, #2177 ....75.00
Figurine, Youthful Boldness, #2162 ....185.00
Shakers, bl & wht floral w/gold, pr 20.00
Vase, rtcl wht seed pods at neck, bulbous brn base, 4½" 1,650.00

Birdcages

Birdcages can be found in various architectural styles and in a range of materials – wood, wicker, brass, and gilt metal with ormolu mounts. Those that once belonged to the wealthy are sometimes inlaid with silver or jewels. In the 1800s, it became fashionable to keep birds, and some of the most beautiful examples found today date back to that era. Musical cages that contained automated bird figures became popular; today these command prices of several thousand dollars. In the latter 1800s, wicker styles came into vogue. Collectors still appreciate their graceful lines and find they adapt easily to modern homes.

Brass, Hendryx, w/stand, EX 68.00
Model of Crystal Palace, brass/glass, 8-leg stand, 78x43" 4,600.00
Tin/wire, trn wood finial, pnt, 21" 125.00
Twig work, on stand, 54" 250.00
Wood & wire, red/wht/bl, house shape, 21", EX 400.00

Victorian wire and bentwood cage, ca 1880s, 77" x 44", $5,000.00.

Bisque

Bisque is a term referring to unglazed earthenware or porcelain that has been fired only once. During the Victorian era, bisque figurines became very popular. Most were highly decorated in pastels and gilt and demonstrated a fine degree of workmanship in the quality of their modeling. Few were marked. See also Heubach; Nodders; Dolls; Piano Babies.

Pair of children, one with puppy, one with kittens, applied flowers, 11", $595.00.

Baby girl in hat & yel gown holds puppy, no mk, 18" 95.00
Baby girl sits on floral plinth, basket ea side, 8x11" 85.00
Boy & girl, ea w/flower basket, Continental, 1800s, 17", pr.........245.00
Boy & girl sell flowers from basket & tray, pk & bl, 6¾", pr 145.00
Boy carrying basket, bl shorts/lav shirt, German, 14" 225.00
Boy w/basket, girl w/doll, EX detail, Rudolstadt, 15", pr 950.00
Busts of Spring & Autumn, sgn L Kley, ped base, 10", pr.............325.00
Cherub seated, writing table on knee, ped ft, German, 13½" 300.00
Couple at well w/bucket on string, gold trim, 5¾" 110.00
Cupids support rtcl vase, gold trim, 9" 175.00
Dog, sad face, gray w/blk, on tan/brn/gr base, 6⅜x4⅞".............145.00
Girl w/doll, French, 1850s, 17" 150.00
Peasant couple, she w/dog in apron, Germany, 13", pr................325.00
Renaissance couple gathers flowers, mc, Austrian, 22", pr 600.00
Renaissance lady, Continental, 1890s, 14" 150.00
Romeo & Juliet holding hands, flower base, 13" 275.00

Black Americana

Black memorabilia is without a doubt a field that encompasses the most widely-exploited ethnic group in our history. But within this field there are many levels of interest – arts and achievements such as folk music and literature, caricatures in advertising, souvenirs, toys, fine art, and legitimate research into the days of their enslavement and enduring struggle for equality. The list is endless.

In the listings below are some with a derogatory connotation. Thankfully, these are from a bygone era and represent the mores of a culture that existed nearly a century ago. They are included only to convey the fact that they are a part of this growing area of collecting interest.

Our advisor for this category is Linda Rothe; she is listed in the Directory under Washington. Black Americana catalogs featuring a wide variety of items for sale are published quarterly. See the Directory under Clubs, Newsletters, and Catalogs for more information. See also Post Cards; Posters, Minstrel; Sheet Music.

Ash tray, Coon Chicken Inn, glass w/decal 35.00
Ash tray, Uncle Mose, pnt CI, Hubley, NM 95.00
Book, comic; Story of Little Blk Sambo, 1921, EX 65.00
Book, Little Blk Sambo Magic Drawing, 1928, unused 35.00
Book, Little Brn KoKo's Pets & Playmates, Hunt, c 1959, NM......28.00
Book, Peter's Wagon, Biesterveld, 1968, EX 12.00
Book, Tambo, His Jokes & Funny Sayings, NY, 1882, 64-pg, M 22.00
Bottle stopper, man's head, bsk..55.00
Cigarette keeper, 3 children on clothesline, ceramic......................20.00
Clothes brush, porter figural hdl, boar bristles, EX 24.00
Clothespin bag, cloth w/stuffed mammy's head, 17", EX 32.00
Cookie jar, Mammy, red dress, plastic, minor wear, 10"................145.00
Cracker jar, Mammy, wicker hdl, orange/bl/gr, 7¼", NM..............385.00
Creamer & sugar, Aunt Jemima/Uncle Mose, gr, F&F..................165.00
Creamer & sugar, Aunt Jemima/Uncle Mose, yel, F&F 85.00
Creamer & sugar, minstrel, stacking, ceramic, 8", EX....................88.00
Cup & saucer, Coon Chicken Inn, Inca Ware 125.00
Decanter, butler, full figure, corked neck, 8", NM 185.00
Decanter, clown on keg, ceramic, hat stopper, 7", NM...................38.00
Decanter, man plays drum & cymbals, cork in hat, Italy, 10".........85.00
Doll, Topsy, blk compo, 3 pigtails, 10" 65.00
Doll, Topsy, rubber, Japan, 5", M in orig pkg 17.50
Egg, Blk child hatching, bl base, bsk, 3½" 120.00
Fan, Coon Chicken Inn 20.00
Figurine, boy by fence w/monkey, Germany, 3¼x2¾" 145.00
Figurine, boy w/watermelon, fruit basket at ft, bsk, 8" 150.00
Figurine, man w/drum, mc w/gold tie, porc, 6½".............................28.00

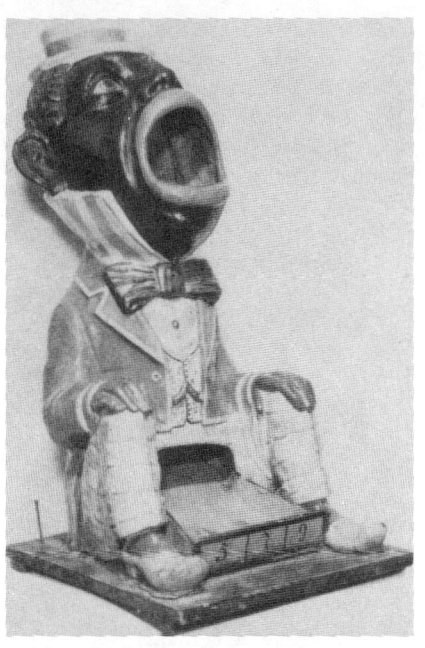

Darkie Game, German composition ball toss, 20", EX, $3,000.00.

Figurine, Red Cap w/bags, cast lead, Barclay 32.00
Figurine, sleeping baby, pants down in bk, chalkware, 4" L............27.50
Figurine, Soldier Joe Crap Shooter, w/orig dice, 3½", pr 55.00
Fishing lure, man wearing barrel, old, 3" 18.50
Humidor, boy w/watermelon, ceramic, 11" 650.00
Humidor, jockey w/pk & yel cap, gr bow tie, ceramic, 4½".........200.00
Lamp, boy kneeling, Royal Copley, 12½" 78.00
Lapel pin, man w/watermelon slice, metal, 1900s, ⅝x½" 75.00
Matchbook, Coon Chicken Inn, w/10 figural matches, EX 35.00
Memo holder, Mammy, compo, Hampton Novelty, w/pencil, M ...50.00
Mug, man, rolling pin/arm forms hdl, ceramic, Japan, 4½" 45.00
Nodder, embarassed girl w/pants down, Japan, 6½", EX...............100.00
Nodder, lady w/exaggerated features, compo, 6½" 50.00
Noisemaker, clown form, tongue rolls when cranked, 8" 15.00
Paperweight, CI, Mammy figural...45.00
Pincushion, boy by walnut shell cushion, 2¾x3½" 18.00
Pitcher, Blk Sambo & 4 tigers, frosted glass, plastic top, M 130.00
Pitcher, Mammy figural, F&F Dieworks, NM...................................27.50
Planter, butler by fence, ceramic, 4½x4½", M...............................120.00
Planter, girl in pk w/watermelon, Interco, 5½" 45.00
Planter, Mammy, bl dotted dress, red scarf, ceramic, 4" 50.00
Plaque, Mammy, brn kerchief w/yel dots, wide smile, 7¾" 38.00
Plate, boy attacked by goose, mk, 7", EX 38.00
Plate, Coon Chicken Inn, 5½" 95.00
Platter, Coon Chicken Inn, 11" 175.00
Post card, Jocular Jinks of Kornelia Kinks, 6 for 40.00
Pretzel holder, man w/tray form, vents at top, ceramic, M 75.00
Rack, towel; Mammy holds bar, pnt wood, 11x12", EX..................50.00
Shakers, babies in basket, mc, ceramic, EX....................................38.00
Shakers, boy & girl, googly eyes, ceramic, 3½", pr 24.00
Shakers, boy & girl w/watermelon, ceramic, 4", pr 55.00
Shakers, boy w/watermelon, mc clothes, ceramic, 4½", pr.............66.00
Shakers, Chef & Maid, red lips, ceramic, 3", pr.............................22.00
Shakers, girl w/knees up, seated boy, ceramic, 3", pr 25.00
Shakers, Mammy, F&F Dieworks for Luzianne Coffee, 5¼", pr......88.00
Shakers, Mammy, S&P on aprons, gr/wht, ceramic, 6½", pr..........48.00
Shakers, Mammy & Butler, F&F Dieworks, sm 22.50
Shakers, Mammy & Chef, ceramic, 8", pr.......................................88.00
Shakers, Mammy & Chef, mc clothes, ceramic, 2¾", pr 65.00
Shakers, Mammy & Chef, no gold, ceramic, 5", pr, +drip jar........85.00
Shakers, Mammy & Chef, roly poly, chalkware, 2¾", pr, EX........26.50

Shakers, Mammy seated, hands on hips, chalkware, 2¼", pr..........32.00
Shakers, milkmaid w/bucket shakers on pole, ceramic, 5", pr........66.00
Shakers, Red Cap, suitcase shakers, ceramic, 4½", pr....................55.00
Shopping board, Mammy, We Needs?, 11x7", M..........................65.00
Soap dish, pnt CI Mammy w/basket (soap dish) on head, 5"......150.00
Spoon rest, musician trio, ceramic, 2x3¼"..................................35.00
Sprinkler bottle, Mammy ironing, Pfaltzgraff, 7", M...................95.00
String holder, Bellhop, mk Fredericksburg, 1930s, EX................120.00
String holder, Butler, ceramic, 6½x3".......................................200.00
String holder, lady w/bl bandana & red bowl, Japan, 6¾"............75.00
String holder, Mammy, pottery, mk Nat'l Silver.........................100.00
Teapot, boy on elephant, bamboo hdl, Japan, 8x6", EX................85.00
Teapot, Mammy, ceramic, 4x5", +boy & girl cr/sug, M...............185.00
Thermometer, Dapper Dan, syrocco wood, 1949, 5½", EX............55.00
Tire patch kit, MO'E Patch, Yowsah Ah's Good, 3½x2¼"............35.00
Toby, Chef, full figure, blk trim, ceramic, 3½"............................65.00
Toby, Mammy, full figure, EX pnt details, ceramic, 4½"..............70.00
Toothpick holder, Coon Chicken Inn..195.00
Wall hanger, Chef on scoop, mc w/gold, ceramic, 5½x3".............50.00
Wall pocket, lady & man, ceramic, England, 5½", M, pr..............75.00

Mammy soap dish, painted cast iron, 2-piece, 5", $150.00.

Black Cats

The main producer of the 'Black Cats' collectibles was the Shafford Company, although occasionally pieces will be found bearing the marks of other firms. Wood and Sons, Ltd., in Burslem, England, produced an 8" figural teapot as part of a novelty line marketed in this country by Fondeville of New York. Other items have been found marked 'Wales,' 'Empress,' and 'Napco Ceramics, Japan.' Black Cat collectors usually prefer to limit their 'litter' to those kittens with a shiny black glaze and styling similar to the Shafford cats.

Ash tray, full figure, flat, 'Ashes' in body, 2½x3¾"........................14.00
Bookends, cat on book, fluffy hair, 5½"..30.00
Condiment set, 2 heads, bow finials, gr eyes, 4"...........................30.00
Cookie jar, head w/red ribbon 60.00
Creamer, seated, paw spout, red bow, yel eyes, 6".......................15.00
Cruet, seated, gold bow w/red dots, Relco label, 7".....................12.00
Cruet, seated, red bow on head, droopy eyes, Shafford, 8"..........14.00
Decanter, sq, upright, head stopper, 6 hooks on bk, 11⅜"...........40.00
Figurine, reclining kitten, wht eyes, red ears, 1¾".........................6.00
Letter holder, recumbent w/wire holder in bk, 3¼x6½"..............12.00
Shakers, kittens in shoe, wht eyes, 3", pr....................................12.00
Shakers, seated, bl eyes, Enesco label, 5¾", pr............................17.00
Shakers, seated, gold bow, red dots, 3⅛", pr...............................16.00
Shakers, seated, joined at base, gold bows w/red dots, 4", pr........12.00
Shakers, seated/recumbent, lg heads, Japan, 1¾", 3", pr..............12.00

Sugar bowl, full figure, seated, gr eyes, red bow, 4⅞" 18.00
Teapot, full figure, head forms lid, gr eyes, red bow, 6½" 35.00
Teapot, head only, dbl spout/chambers, wicker hdl, 4" 45.00
Teapot, w/creamer & sugar bowl, stacking....................................35.00

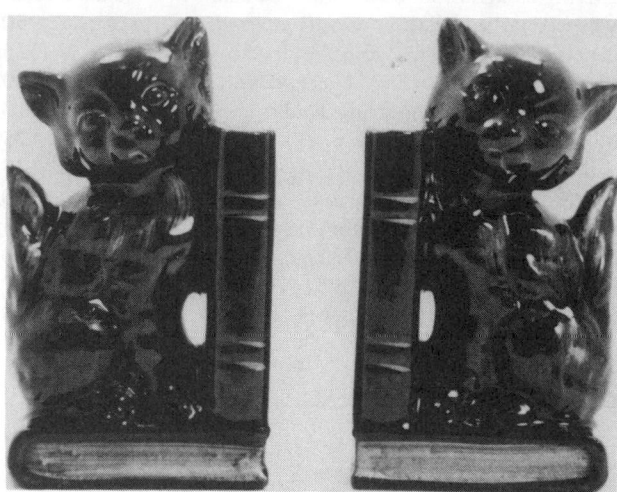

Bookends, 7", $25.00 for the pair.

Black Glass

Black glass is a type of colored glass that when held to strong light usually appears deep purple – though since each glasshouse had its own formula, tones may vary. It was sometimes etched or given a satin finish; and occasionally it was decorated with silver, gold, enamel, coralene, or any of these in combination. The decoration was done either by the glasshouse or by firms that specialized in decorating glassware. Crystal, jade, colored glass, or milk glass was sometimes used with the black as an accent. Black glass has been made by many companies since the seventeenth century. Contemporary glasshouses produced black glass during the Depression, seldom signing their product. It is still being made today.

To learn more about the subject, we recommend *A Collector's Guide to Black Glass*, written by our advisor, Marlena Toohey; she is listed in the Directory under Kansas. See also Tiffin and specific manufacturers.

Vase, nude in relief, 8½", $50.00.

Box, patch; mc florals w/wht dots, hinged lid, 1x2" dia...............100.00
Butter dish, Tiara 40.00

Candle holders, Tiara, pr 25.00	
Candy dish, tall ped, Tiara, 16" 25.00	
Creamer & sugar bowl, Tiara 20.00	
Doorstop, bulldog, US Glass 425.00	
Hat, pontil on base, 7x11" 150.00	
Ice bucket, Tiara 25.00	
Ice bucket, Tiara, +6 tumblers 75.00	
Pitcher, Tiara, +4 goblets..65.00	
Shakers, Tiara, pr 10.00	
Vase, Bird & Greek Key, toed, 3½" 20.00	
Vase, emb flower, 8½"...35.00	
Vase, HP stork/water plants, pilgrim flask w/rnd ft, 9x6½" 80.00	
Vase, 6-color floral, ringed neck, rnd base, 15", pr 175.00	

Sugar bowl, cobalt, solid finial/base, ps on ea pc, 6½" 275.00
Tumbler, honey-amber, 16 swirled ribs, 4" 50.00
Vase, aqua, heavy appl bulbous base, 12" 55.00
Vase, hyacinth; cobalt, lg ps, 7¾" 55.00
Wine, air-twist stem, dome ft, 1750s, 6¾" 200.00
Wine, stem w/lg trapped bubble, folded ft/tooled lip, 1-pc...........150.00

Blown Glass

Blown glass is rather difficult to date; eighteenth and nineteenth century examples vary little as to technique or style – it ranges from the primitive to the sophisticated. But the metallic content of very early glass caused tiny imperfections that are obvious upon examination, and these are often indicative of age.

In America, Stiegel introduced the English technique of using a patterned, part-size mold, a practice which was generally followed by many glasshouses after the Revolution. From 1820 to about 1850, glass was blown into full-size 3-part molds. In the listings below, glass is assumed clear unless color is mentioned. Numbers refer to a standard reference book, *American Glass* by George and Helen McKearin. See also Bottles and specific manufacturers.

Our advisor for this category is Mark Vuono; he is listed in the Directory under Connecticut.

Key: ps — pontil scar

Bird drinking font, mold blown, cobalt ball top/rim, 4½" 200.00
Bottle, globular, gr-aqua, 24 vertical ribs, VG imp, 7¾" 525.00
Bottle, nursing; gr-aqua, 24 vertical ribs, flake/wear, 6" 55.00
Bowl, amethyst, lily pad type, crimp ft, att Clevenger, 12" 140.00
Bowl, aqua, appl flared ft, folded rim on lip/ft, 9x8" 50.00
Bowl, cobalt, folded rim, 5x6½" 165.00
Bowl, yel-gr, plain rim, polished pontil, 3½x4⅜" 55.00
Canister, lt gr, folded lip, tin lid, 6½" 250.00
Christmas light, plum amethyst w/amber rim, 12-dmn, 2¾" 80.00
Christmas light, sapphire, 16-rib swirl to right, 3⅞" 70.00
Compote, 12-rib, solid stem, folded rim, 1830s, 5x5" 195.00
Cruet, hollow hdl w/rigaree attachment, 8" 150.00
Cup, Dia Quilt bowl, ear hdl, 3¼", pr 20.00
Decanter, cut panels, 3 appl rings, matching stopper, 8" 125.00
Hat, gold-amber, rolled/tooled rim, rough ps, 3⅜" 275.00
Hat, red threading overall, tubular ps, att Sandwich, 2x4" 170.00
Lamp, rnd font, 4-knop std w/wafer, petticoat base, 9" 900.00
Mug, freeblown, bbl form, 1800s, 4¾" 125.00
Pan, aqua, folded rim, 2½x10" 200.00
Pan, aqua, folded rim, 5x10" 275.00
Pan, aqua, folded rim & spout, 7x21" 325.00
Pipe whimsey, lt yel opal w/appl clear yel lip on bowl, 16" 165.00
Pipe whimsey, med opaque bl w/wht lip on bowl, chipped, 19" ...125.00
Pitcher, hollow hdl, ogee sides, ca 1830s, 6", MN 150.00
Pitcher, pillar mold, appl hdl, ground pontil, 9" 375.00
Pitcher, solid hdl w/curl, 3 tooled bands at wide mouth, 8" 210.00
Rolling pin, dk gold-amber, solid, 1 end rnd/1 sheared, 12" 90.00
Rolling pin, steel bl, 2 knob ends drawn from body, 1 open.........130.00
Salt, steel bl, flared cylinder on solid stem, ps, 2½" 400.00
Spitton, deep amber, folded lip, 1830s, 5¼" dia...................245.00

Blown Three-Mold Glass

A popular collectible in the 1920s, '30s, and '40s, blown three-mold glass has again gained the attention of many. Produced from approximately 1815 to 1840 in various New York, New England, and Midwestern glasshouses, it was a cheaper alternative to the expensive imported Irish cut glass.

Distinguishing features of blown three-mold glass are the three distinct mold marks and the concave-convex appearance of the glass. For every indentation on the inner surface of the ware, there will be a corresponding protuberance on the outside. Blown three-mold glass is most often clear with the exception of inkwells and a few known decanters. Any colored three-mold glass commands a premium price.

The numbers in the listings that follow refer to the book *American Glass*, by George and Helen McKearin.

Our advisor for this category is Mark Vuono; he is listed in the Directory under Connecticut.

Blown 3-mold decanters: GV-8, sapphire-blue, open pontil, tooled flared lip, small potstone in shoulder, 7½", $750.00; GV-13, faint citron color, open pontil, tooled flared lip, 7", M, $450.00.

Bottle, toilet; GI-7, deep violet, no stopper 160.00
Bottle/decanter, GII-7, barrel, med olive gr, 1-pt....................3,000.00
Bowl, GI-6, shallow...140.00
Celery vase, GII-18 ....1,100.00
Creamer, GI-30, brilliant aquamarine 4,000.00
Creamer, GII-18, tooled flared mouth, solid hdl, 2⅞" 120.00
Decanter, GII-10, w/stopper, 1-qt 550.00
Decanter, GII-33, 1-qt...250.00

Decanter, GII-7, barrel, sea gr, orig stopper **4,000.00**
Decanter, GIII-16, olive-amber, 1-pt **450.00**
Decanter, GIII-19, olive-amber, 1-qt **900.00**
Decanter, GIII-2, olive gr, 1-pt **2,200.00**
Decanter, GIII-2, olive gr, 1-qt **4,000.00**
Decanter, GIV-7, emb GIN, w/stopper **350.00**
Dish, GII-22 ....**50.00**
Dish, GII-24, shallow **65.00**
Dish, GIII-24, shallow **75.00**
Flip, grayish tint, pontil, NE, 1835, 6½" **175.00**
Hat, GII-45 ....**275.00**
Hat, GIII-23, cobalt, tooled folded lip, pontil, 2¼" **700.00**
Hat, GIII-3 ....**50.00**
Hat, GIII-7, folded rim, ray base w/pontil, 2¼x2¾" **95.00**
Inkwell, GII-18, amber **130.00**
Inkwell, GII-2, olive gr **160.00**
Tumbler, GI-6 ....**250.00**
Wine, button-knop stem, tooled lip/pontil, NE, 3¾" **350.00**
Wine, GII-19 ....**350.00**

Blue and White Stoneware

Blue and white stoneware, much of which was decorated with such in-mold designs as grazing cows and Dutch children, was made by practically every American pottery from the turn of the century until the mid-1930s. Crocks, pitchers, wash sets, rolling pins, and canisters are only a few of the items that may be found in this type of 'country' pottery that has become one of today's popular collectibles.

Roseville, Brush-McCoy, Uhl Co., and Burley Winter were among those who produced it; but very few pieces were ever signed. Naturally, condition must be a prime consideration, especially if one is buying for resale; pieces with good, strong color and fully-molded patterns bring premium prices. Normal wear and signs of age are to be expected since this was utility ware and received heavy use in busy households. In the listings that follow, crocks and jars are assumed without lids unless noted otherwise. See also specific manufacturers.

Bean pot, Boston Baked Beans, Flemish, w/lid 290.00
Bowl, Apricot, 9½" 85.00
Bowl, Daisy on Waffle, 10¾" 95.00
Bowl, Daisy on Waffle, 9½" 90.00
Bowl, dough; dk bl, scalloped rim, lg 85.00
Bowl, mixing; Feathers, 10½" 125.00
Bowl, plain, 11" 70.00
Bowl, Wedding Ring, 10" 125.00
Butter crock, Apple Blossom, orig lid & bail 155.00
Butter crock, Apricot, orig lid & bail 200.00
Butter crock, Apricots w/Honeycomb, orig lid & bail 225.00
Butter crock, Butterfly, orig lid & bail, 6½" 120.00
Butter crock, Cow, stenciled, orig lid & bail 120.00
Butter crock, Cows & Columns, orig lid & bail 250.00
Butter crock, Daisy & Trellis, orig lid & bail, 4½" 175.00
Butter crock, Diffused Bl, orig lid & bail, 4x4½", 1-lb 95.00
Butter crock, Dutch Couple, orig lid & bail, lg 155.00
Butter crock, Eagle, orig lid & bail...450.00
Butter crock, Indian Good Luck Sign, orig lid & bail 125.00
Butter crock, Wildflower, orig lid & bail 150.00
Canister, Basketweave, Coffee, orig lid 185.00
Canister, Basketweave, Raisins, orig lid 225.00
Canister, Diffused Bl, Tea, orig lid..125.00
Canister, Snowflake, Rice, orig lid 110.00
Canister, Wildflower, Crackers, orig lid 175.00
Coffeepot, devil on body, emb Blanke's Coffeepot on lid, 9½" 350.00

Cookie jar, Basketweave, Put Your Fist In, orig lid, 7½" 325.00
Cookie jar, Brickers, orig lid...245.00
Cookie jar, Flying Birds, orig lid..350.00
Cup & saucer, Flowerpot, deep, ca 1820..125.00
Humidor, stippled w/bird dog on side, flower finial, w/lid 150.00
Mug, advertising 150.00
Mug, Basketweave 95.00
Mug, Cattails 125.00
Mug, Diffused Bl 75.00
Mug, Flying Bird 175.00
Mug, golfer, bl/gray, Robinson Clay Products 150.00
Mug, plain..65.00
Mug, Windy City (Fannie Flagg), Robinson Clay Products.........150.00
Pickle crock, Bl Bands, advertising, bail hdl, 5-gal 150.00
Pie plate, Star Mfg 145.00
Pitcher, Acorns 115.00
Pitcher, American Beauty Rose, 10" 175.00
Pitcher, Apricot, 8" 150.00
Pitcher, Barrel, +6 mugs 395.00
Pitcher, Basketweave & Flowers 175.00
Pitcher, Bl Band, plain..80.00
Pitcher, Bl Band Scroll 160.00

Pitcher, Swan, 8", M, $250.00; Pitcher, Butterfly, 9", M, $250.00.

Pitcher, Bl Sawtooth, Wht Hall..95.00
Pitcher, Bow Tie 135.00
Pitcher, Butterfly, 4¾" 245.00
Pitcher, Butterfly, 9x7" 250.00
Pitcher, Castle & Fishscale, 8" 195.00
Pitcher, Cattails, 7½" 160.00
Pitcher, Cattails, 9" 155.00
Pitcher, Cattails & Butterfly 150.00
Pitcher, Cherry Cluster..225.00
Pitcher, Cosmos 195.00
Pitcher, Cow 175.00
Pitcher, Diffused Bl, 8¾", M...100.00
Pitcher, Doe & Fawn...225.00
Pitcher, Dutch Boy & Girl 160.00
Pitcher, Dutch Landscape, stenciled, tall 150.00
Pitcher, Eagle...425.00
Pitcher, Eagle w/Shield & Arrows, rare 495.00
Pitcher, Edelweiss, flower on gray bkground, M..............................90.00
Pitcher, Edelweiss, no flower 175.00
Pitcher, Fishscale & Wild Rose, sm...95.00
Pitcher, flat iron bldg/girl, Robinson Clay Products, 8½" 185.00
Pitcher, Flowers, stenciled 100.00
Pitcher, Flying Bird...495.00
Pitcher, Grape Cluster on Trellis, 8½" 155.00

Pitcher, Grapes on Waffle 165.00
Pitcher, Grapes w/Rickrack, 8" 150.00
Pitcher, Hunting Scene, rare 300.00
Pitcher, Indian Boy & Girl...225.00
Pitcher, Indian Head in War Bonnet, waffled body, 8", EX..........250.00
Pitcher, Leaping Deer 200.00
Pitcher, Lincoln w/Log Cabin 450.00
Pitcher, Lovebird, arc bands, deep color, 8½" 325.00
Pitcher, Lovebird, pale color, 8½" 175.00
Pitcher, Morning-Glory..150.00
Pitcher, Poinsettia, 6½" 250.00
Pitcher, Rose & Fishscale, 6" 165.00
Pitcher, Scroll & Leaf, advertising 250.00
Pitcher, Stag & Pine Trees, 9" 295.00
Pitcher, Swan, long beak, arched neck, deep color, 8½" 250.00
Pitcher, Swirl 155.00
Pitcher, Tulip 225.00
Pitcher, Wild Rose 275.00
Pitcher, Wildflower, stenciled 295.00
Pitcher, Windmill & Bush, 7" 165.00
Potty, Beaded Rose 110.00
Rolling pin, Wildflower 200.00
Salt crock, Apricot, orig lid 135.00
Salt crock, Blackberry, orig lid 145.00
Salt crock, Butterfly, orig lid...185.00
Salt crock, Daisy on Snowflakes, orig lid 220.00
Salt crock, Eagle w/Arrow, orig lid...325.00
Salt crock, Flying Bird, orig lid 300.00
Salt crock, Grape on Basketweave, orig lid................................150.00
Salt crock, Oak Leaf, orig lid...125.00
Salt crock, Peacock, orig lid 300.00
Salt crock, Wildflower, orig lid..250.00
Slop jar, Bow Tie 125.00
Slop jar, Fishscale & Wild Rose 150.00
Soap dish, Beaded Panels w/Open Rose....................................125.00
Soap dish, Beaded Rose 120.00
Soap dish, Fishscale w/Wild Rose...95.00
Soap dish, Flower Cluster w/Fishscale 115.00
Soap dish, Indian in War Bonnet...195.00
Spittoon, Peacock & Fountain..245.00
Toothbrush holder, Bow Tie, stenciled flower............................50.00
Toothbrush holder, Fishscale & Wild Rose 70.00
Umbrella stand, oak leaves/animals emb, 21", NM....................350.00
Vase, Swirl, cone shape 300.00
Wash set, Bow Tie, 2-pc 350.00
Wash set, Fishscale & Wild Rose, 5-pc 600.00
Wash set, Rose on Trellis, 2-pc..300.00
Water cooler, Apple Blossom 500.00
Water cooler, Bl Band, orig lid 150.00
Water cooler, Cupid, orig lid 600.00
Water cooler, Polar Bear, orig lid...500.00
Water cooler, Rachel at the Well, orig lid...................................500.00

Blue Ridge

Blue Ridge dinnerware was produced by Southern Potteries of Erwin, Tennessee, from the late 1930s until 1956 in eight basic styles and eight hundred different patterns, all of which were hand decorated under the glaze. Vivid colors lit up floral arrangements of seemingly endless variation, fruit of every sort from simple clusters to lush assortments, barnyard fowl, peasant figures, and unpretentious textured patterns. Although it is these dinnerware lines for which they are best known, collectors prize the artist-signed plates from the forties and the

limited line of character jugs made during the fifties most highly. Examples of the French Peasant pattern are valued at double the prices listed below; very simple patterns will bring 25% to 50% less.

Our advisors, Betty and Bill Newbound, have compiled a lovely book, *Blue Ridge Dinnerware*, Revised Third Edition, with beautiful color illustrations and current market values. They are listed in the Directory under Michigan. For information concerning the National Blue Ridge Newsletter, see the Clubs, Newsletters, and Catalogs section of the Directory.

Ash tray, advertising, w/rest 50.00
Ash tray, individual 12.00
Bonbon, divided, center hdls, china 75.00
Bowl, cereal/soup; 6" 8.00
Bowl, divided, 8" 15.00
Bowl, fruit; 5" 3.50
Bowl, mixing; 8½" 25.00
Bowl, rnd, 8" 12.00
Bowl, salad; 10½" 40.00
Bowl, salad; 11½"...40.00
Bowl, soup; flat, 8" 9.00
Bowl, vegetable; divided, oval, 9" 20.00
Bowl, vegetable; oval, 9" 18.00
Box, candy; rnd w/lid 85.00
Box, cigarette 60.00
Box, cigarette; w/4 trays 100.00
Box, raised or sculptured designs 75.00
Breakfast set..300.00
Butter dish, ¼-lb, w/lid..35.00
Butter pat/coaster..15.00
Cake lifter 20.00
Carafe, w/lid 55.00
Casserole, w/lid..35.00
Celery, leaf shape, china 30.00
Celery, Skyline shape 25.00
Child's cereal bowl..25.00
Child's feeding dish, deep 25.00
Child's feeding dish, divided 25.00
Child's mug 15.00
Child's plate 25.00

Pitcher, girl figural, 9", $95.00.

Child's play set..225.00
Chocolate pot, pedestal, china...........................125.00
Coffeepot..90.00
Creamer, china...40.00
Creamer, demitasse..45.00
Creamer, regular..10.00
Cup & saucer, demitasse; china............................25.00
Cup & saucer, regular...12.00
Dish, baking; 13x8"...24.00
Egg cup, dbl..18.00
Egg dish, deviled...30.00
Gravy boat...17.00
Gravy tray..15.00
Jug, batter; w/lid..60.00
Jug, character; china...400.00
Jug, syrup; w/lid...70.00
Lamp, china...100.00
Pie baker...20.00
Pitcher, fancy, china...85.00
Plate, aluminum edge, 12".................................17.50
Plate, artist sgn, china.......................................425.00
Plate, cake; 10½"..25.00
Plate, Christmas or Turkey...................................55.00
Plate, dinner; 10"...15.00
Plate, dinner; 9½"...9.00
Plate, party; w/cup well & cup.............................20.00
Plate, salad; bird decor, 8½".................................45.00
Plate, salad; 8½"..6.00
Plate, snack; 3-compartment................................15.00
Plate, sq, 7½"..7.50
Plate, 11½"..25.00
Plate, 6"..2.50
Platter, artist sgn, 17½".......................................700.00
Platter, Thanksgiving Turkey.............................175.00
Platter, Turkey w/Acorns....................................175.00
Platter, 11"...10.00
Platter, 12½"..15.00
Platter, 13"...15.00
Platter, 15"...20.00
Ramekin, w/lid, 5"...20.00
Ramekin, w/lid, 7½"...30.00
Relish, deep shell, china.......................................45.00
Relish, heart shape, sm...30.00
Relish, loop hdl, china..60.00
Relish, Maple Leaf, china......................................40.00
Relish, Martha, 3-compartment, china.................70.00
Relish, T-hdl, china...35.00
Salad fork...25.00
Salad spoon..25.00
Server, center hdl..25.00
Shakers, Apple, pr..10.00
Shakers, Blossom Top, pr.......................................30.00
Shakers, Bud Top, pr..30.00
Shakers, Chickens, pr..80.00
Shakers, ftd, china, tall, pr....................................40.00
Shakers, mallards, pr...135.00
Shakers, Moderne, pr...25.00
Shakers, Range, pr...30.00
Shakers, regular, short, pr.....................................18.00
Sugar bowl, demitasse..25.00
Sugar bowl, ped or flare, china.............................40.00
Sugar bowl, regular, w/lid.....................................12.00
Tea tile, rnd or sq..30.00

Teapot, china...75.00
Teapot, demitasse..70.00
Teapot, earthenware..65.00
Tidbit, 2-tier..25.00
Tidbit, 3-tier..30.00
Toast, covered..80.00
Tray, chocolate pot; china...................................350.00
Tray, flat shell, china..50.00
Vase, boot, 8"...65.00
Vase, bud...75.00
Vase, hdls, china, 7¼"..60.00
Vase, rnd, china, 5½"...55.00
Vase, ruffled top, 9¼"..70.00
Vase, tapered...75.00

Bluebird China

Made from 1910 to 1934, Bluebird china is lovely ware decorated with bluebirds flying among pink flowering branches. It was inexpensive dinnerware and reached the height of its popularity in the second decade of this century. Several potteries produced it; shapes differ from one manufacturer to another, but the decal remains basically the same. Among the backstamps you'll find W.S. George, Cleveland, Carrolton, Homer Laughlin, and Limoges China of Sebring, Ohio . . . and there are others.

Bowl, fruit; Deerwood, 5½".....................................12.50
Bowl, fruit; Hopewell China, 5"..............................10.00
Bowl, gravy; w/saucer, Hopewell China....................50.00
Bowl, sauce; SP Co, 4½"..10.00
Bowl, soup; PMC Co, 8"..25.00
Butter dish, 4½" holder w/in 7" dia dish, Steubenville.....85.00
Casserole, w/lid, Ostro China, 10½" dia....................95.00
Casserole, w/lid, SP Clinchfield, 8½" dia..................85.00
Creamer & sugar bowl, w/lid, Homer Laughlin...........45.00
Cup, coffee; unmk, 3½"...25.00
Plate, dessert; Limoges, 6".......................................8.00
Plate, Homer Laughlin, 8½".....................................10.00
Plate, National China, 8"...10.00
Plate, rtcl, sq, unmk, 9"..35.00
Platter, Homer Laughlin, 15½"x10½"........................75.00
Platter, Hopewell China, 17½"x13"...........................95.00
Platter, Steubenville, 12¾"x9½"...............................55.00
Platter, unmk, 9x7"...35.00
Sauce ladle, gold scrolling.......................................25.00
Teapot, ELP Co, 8½"x8½".......................................125.00

Boch Freres

Founded in the early 1840s in La Louviere, Boch Freres Keramos became the foremost producer of art pottery in Belgium. Though primarily they served a localized market, in 1844 they earned world wide recognition for some of their sculptural works on display at the International Exposition in Paris.

In 1907 Charles Catteau of France was appointed head of the art department. Before that time, the firm had concentrated on developing glazes and perfecting elegant forms. The style they pursued was traditional, favoring the re-creation of established 18th-century ceramics. Catteau brought with him to Boch Freres the New Wave (or Art Nouveau) influence in form and decoration. His designs won him international acclaim at the Exhibition d'Art Decoratif in Paris in 1925, and it is for his work that Boch Freres is so highly regarded today. He occasionally signed his work as well as that of others who under his direct supervision carried out his preconceived designs. He was associated with the company until 1950 and lived the remainder of his life in Nice, France, where he died in 1966. The Boch Freres Keramos factory continues to operate today, producing bathroom fixtures and other utilitarian wares. A variety of marks have been used, all incorporating some combination of 'Boch Freres,' 'Keramos,' 'BFK,' or 'Ch Catteau.'

Mirror, fr w/ladies by drapery & plant in relief, mc, 17x13"	**1,300.00**
Vase, Chinese bl crackle, ovoid, 11", pr	150.00
Vase, deer/mtns/tree on wht crackle, Keramos, 13½"	**1,650.00**
Vase, exotic mc foliage scrolls overall, spherical, 8"	385.00
Vase, frieze of deer, crackle glaze, Catteau, baluster, 14"	**1,300.00**
Vase, frieze of deer, crackle glaze, Catteau, bulbous, 15"	**2,200.00**
Vase, stags/doe, bl/blk on crazed cream, Catteau, 12½"	800.00
Vase, 3-color vertical floral stripes, crazed glaze, 10½"	**245.00**

Vase, incised and painted with stylized fan shapes in red and black on crazed cream, marked Keramos, 14", $600.00.

Boehm

Boehm sculptures were the creation of Edward Marshall Boehm, a ceramic artist who coupled his love of the art with his love of nature to produce figurines of birds, animals, and flowers in lovely background settings accurate to the smallest detail. Sculptures of historical figures and those representing the fine arts were also made and along with many of the bird figurines, have established secondary-market values many times their original prices. His first pieces were made in the very early 1950s in Trenton, New Jersey, under the name of Osso Ceramics. Mr. Boehm died in 1969, and the firm has since been managed by his wife. Today known as Edward Marshall Boehm, Inc., the private family-held corporation produces not only porcelain sculptures but collector plates as well. Both limited and non-limited editions of their works have been issued. Examples are marked with various backstamps, all of which have incorporated the Boehm name since 1951. 'Osso Ceramics'

in upper case lettering was used in 1950 and 1951. Values listed below represent prices realized at auction.

American Avocet, #40134	1,250.00
Blue Jays, #466, pr	9,800.00
Blue Nile Rose, #300-80	1,450.00
Brindle Boxer dog, 5x4½"	200.00

Brown Pelican, #40161, 21", $1,000.00.

California Quail, #433, pr	1,750.00
Canada Geese, #408-E, oblong bsk base, 5x7", pr	1,200.00
Capped Chickadee, #438, 9"	450.00
Common Tern, #497	4,000.00
Fledgling Eastern Bluebird, #442	135.00
Golden-Crowned Kinglets, #419	1,800.00
Grace de Monaco Rose, #300-71	1,900.00
Green Jays, #486, pr	3,200.00
Lady Helen Rose, #30070	1,500.00
Lapwing, #100-14	1,800.00
Lark Sparrow, #400-35	2,750.00
Magnolia Grandiflora, #300-12	1,500.00
Mearns Quail, #467, pr	2,700.00
Nonpareil Buntings, #446	1,250.00
Northern Water Thrush, #490	1,700.00
Painted Bunting, #400-38	700.00
Pascali Rose, #30093	1,500.00
Ptarmigans, #463, pr	2,800.00
Road Runner, #493	3,400.00
Rose-Breasted Grosbeak, no decor	1,200.00
Roy Hartley Begonia, #300-41	1,500.00
Ruby-Crowned Kinglets, #434	975.00
Ruffed Grouse, #456, pr	3,250.00
Stone Chats, #100-71	1,750.00
Towhee, #471E	2,000.00
Tumbler Pigeons, #416	750.00
Varied Buntings, #481	4,800.00
Western Bluebirds, #400-01	5,800.00
Wood Thrushes, #485	6,200.00

Young American Eagle, #498..................................... 1,300.00

Bohemian Glass

The term 'Bohemian glass' has come to refer to a type of glass developed in Bohemia in the late sixth century at the Imperial Court of Rudolf II, the Hapsburg Emperor. The popular artistic pursuit of the day was stone carving, and it naturally followed to transfer familiar procedures to the glassmaking industry. During the next century, a formula was discovered that produced a glass with a fine crystal appearance which lent itself well to deep, intricate engraving, and the art was further advanced.

Although many other types of art glass were made there, collectors today use the term 'Bohemian glass' to most often indicate clear glass overlaid with color through which a design is cut or etched. Red on crystal is common, but other colors may also be found. Another type of Bohemian glass involves cutting through and exposing three layers of color in patterns that are often very intricate. Items such as these are sometimes further decorated with enamel work.

Bottle, scent; red, cut bands, 4⅞x2⅛"..68.00
Bottle, scent; red, gold decor, 7½"...110.00
Bottle, scent; red, gold trim, cut panel stopper, 6½"....................145.00
Bowl, cobalt, hobstars & diamonds, 5" 75.00
Box, red, ferns & flowers, octagonal, 3" H...90.00
Compote, red, scrolls & flowers, irreg cut rim, 5½x5½"..............110.00
Cruet, red, stag & castle, dtd 1887, red cut stopper.....................115.00
Decanter, red, deer & bird, 11"..115.00
Decanter, red, deer & castle, 10" 110.00
Decanter, red, vintage, orig cut stopper, 6½" 55.00
Dresser jar, red, frosted flower/gold, cut/HP, 6½x4", pr..............100.00
Lamp, red, deer & castle, drilled for electricity, 20" 350.00

Goblets, stags in landscape reserve, ruby etched to clear, 6½", $45.00 each.

Lamp, red, vintage, kerosene burner, iron base..............................180.00
Lustre, red, floral panels w/gold, clear prisms, 12", pr..................995.00
Stein, red, cathedral arches, pewter mts, 6¾x3"............................245.00
Vase, amber, deer & castle, fan form, 11¼".....................................115.00
Vase, gr, florals, cut/HP, 8¼"...145.00

Vase, red, deer & bird, 4" 37.50
Vase, red, deer & castle, 5"..50.00
Vase, red, floral medallions, elaborate/EX cutting, 11" 475.00
Vase, red, flowers & geese, ped ft, 16"...600.00
Vase, red, triple diamond cutting, scalloped, 10" 75.00
Vase, red cut to amber, florals, ftd, 9½" 120.00

Bookends

Though a few were produced before 1880, bookends became a necessary library accessory and a popular commodity after the printing industry was revolutionized by Mergenthaler's invention, the linotype. Books became abundantly available at such affordable prices that almost every home suddenly had need for bookends. They were carved from wood, cast in iron, bronze, or brass, or cut from stone. Today's collectors may find such designs as ships, animals, flowers, and children. Patriotic themes, art reproductions, and those with Art Nouveau and Art Deco styling provide a basis for a diverse and interesting collection.

Nude atop open book, painted metal, $175.00.

Angelus, copper flashed, mk V, pr 35.00
Cat, metal, Nuart, pr 35.00
Caterpillar dozer w/man, pr..75.00
Dartmoor Pixie in high relief, bronze, dtd 1923, 6", pr 115.00
Drunkard, bronzed metal, pr...15.00
Dutch boy & girl, bronze, Vienna, 4¾x3", pr..................................175.00
Elephant, copper over metal, 3x3¼", pr...35.00
End of Trail, metal, dtd 1930, pr 30.00
English cottage, syrocco, pr...15.00
Eve (nude), CI, copper plated, Verona, 7¼", pr 75.00
Flowers, chalkware, pr...15.00
Gazelle, leaping, bronze, M Osmond, gr marble base, 8", pr 285.00
Girl w/doll, spelter, Nuart, worn, pr 35.00
Hartford Fire Ins Co, bronze, dtd 1935, pr......................................100.00
Indian & youth w/bow & arrow in relief, bronze, WB, 6"............280.00
Indian chief, full headdress, copper flashed, pr 40.00
Indian chief kneels w/peace pipe, metal on plaster, 8½", pr.........150.00
Indian chief's head, bronze over plaster, 8", pr 150.00
Lindbergh, bronze-washed iron, dtd 1929, 6", pr...........................95.00
Lion, roaring, paw raised, metal, pr...30.00
Nouveau nude butterfly, metal, pr..150.00
Nude holds drapery overhead, bronze/marble, H Molins, 8", pr...350.00
Owl, CI, #587, pr 75.00
Pharaoh, seated, copper w/gr patina, mk, 7", pr.............................85.00

Pouter pigeon on perch, silvered bronze, mk Bouraine, 6", pr......900.00
Setter dog lying by gate, metal, pr.....................................25.00
Thinker, bronzed spelter, pr...45.00
WWI Doughboy, American Legion, bronze, pr 80.00

Bootjacks and Bootscrapers

Bootjacks were made from metal or wood – some were fancy figural shapes, others strictly business! Their purpose was to facilitate the otherwise awkward process of removing one's boots. Bootscrapers were handy gadgets that provided an effective way to clean the soles of mud and such.

Bootjacks

Am Bull Dog, CI, pistol shaped, folding, blk pnt, 8" 75.00
Beetle-shaped jaws, CI, no pnt, ca 1880 ....38.00
Boss emb on shaft, lacy CI, 15" L 135.00
Heart figural, scalloped sides, CI, 13" L 130.00
Mermaid form, CI...80.00
Naughty Nellie, CI, no pnt, 9½" 65.00
Naughty Nellie, CI w/worn mc pnt, 9½" 150.00
Pine w/sq nails, lg, early...65.00
Stylized fish, cvd wood, worn finish, 22" L 115.00
Try Me, CI, openwork, no pnt, 1890s, 12x4"..............................68.00

Bootscrapers

CI, base pushes into ground, Holcroft & Sons label, 19" L 45.00
Dachshund, CI, old dk gr pnt, 21" L...................................260.00
Duck, full bodied, scraper on bk, CI, 14½" L..........................350.00
Plain, emb P&C Darain #33 ....28.00
Wrought iron, knob finials, in marble block, 14" 65.00
Wrought iron, ram's horn scrolls, in marble block 135.00

Boru, Sorcha

Sorcha Boru was the professional name used by California ceramist Claire Stewart. She was a founding member of the Allied Arts Guild of Menlo Park (California) where she maintained a studio from 1932 to 1938. From 1938 until 1955, she operated Sorcha Boru Ceramics, a production studio in San Carlos. Her highly-acclaimed output consisted of colorful, slip-decorated figurines, salt and pepper shakers, vases, wall pockets, and flower bowls. Most production work was incised 'S.B.C.' by hand.

Our advisor for this category is Jack Chipman; he is listed in the Directory under California.

Bowl, blue to lavender with applied white lily, 6½", $90.00.

Bowl, horse motif, 7" 37.50
Bowl, maroon, appl peony on lid, 6" 55.00
Figurine, Penelope, fawn, 6" 35.00
Figurine, 2 girls dancing, hands clasped 145.00
Pitcher, robin's egg bl, w/underplate 175.00
Shakers, boy & girl, pr 50.00
Sugar shaker, lady figural, 6"...85.00

Bottles and Flasks

As far back as the first century B.C., the Romans preferred blown glass containers for their pills and potions. Though you're not apt to find many of those, you will find bottles of every size, shape, and color made to hold perfume, ink, medicine, soda, spirits, vinegar, and many other liquids. American business firms preferred glass bottles in which to package their commercial products and used them extensively from the late eighteenth century on. Bitters bottles contained 'medicine' (actually herb-flavored alcohol); and, judging from the number of these found today, their contents found favor with many! Because of a heavy tax imposed on the sale of liquor in seventeenth-century England by King George, who hoped to curtail alcohol abuse among his subjects, bottlers simply added 'curative' herbs to their brew and thus avoided taxation. Since gin was taxed in America as well, the practice continued in this country. Scores of brands were sold; among the most popular were Dr. H.S. Flint & Co. Quaker Bitters, Dr. Kaufman's Anti-Cholera Bitters, and Dr. J. Hostetter's Stomach Bitters. Most bitters bottles were made in shades of amber, brown, and aquamarine. Clear glass was used to a lesser extent, as were green tones. Blue, amethyst, red-brown, and milk glass examples are rare.

Perfume or scent bottles were produced abroad by companies all over Europe from the late sixteenth century on. Perfume making became such a prolific trade that as a result, beautifully decorated bottles were fashionable. In America they were produced in great quantities by Stiegel in 1770 and by Boston and Sandwich in the early nineteenth century. Cologne bottles were first made in about 1830 and toilet-water bottles in the 1880s. Rene Lalique produced fine scent bottles from as early as the turn of the century. The earliest were one-of-a-kind creations with silver casings. He later designed bottles for the Coty Perfume Company with a different style for each Coty fragrance.

Spirit flasks from the nineteenth century were blown in specially designed molds with varied motifs including political subjects, railroad trains, and symbolic devices. The most commonly-used colors were amber, dark brown, and green.

From the twentieth century, early pop and beer bottles are very collectible, as are nearly every extinct commercial container.

Bottles may be dated by the methods used in their production. For instance, a rough pontil indicates a date before 1845. The iron pontil, used from then until about 1860, left a metallic residue on the base of the bottle, which is evident upon examination. A seam that reaches from base to lip marks a machine-made bottle from after 1903, while an applied or hand-finished lip points to an early mold-blown bottle. The Industrial Revolution saw keen competition between manufacturers; and, as a result, scores of patents were issued. Many concentrated on various types of closures; the crown bottle cap, for instance, was patented in 1892. If a manufacturer's name is present, consulting a book on marks may help you date your bottle.

Among our advisors for this category are Madeleine France (see the Directory under Florida), Mark Vuono (Connecticut), and Steve Ketcham (Minnesota). In the listings that follow (most of which have been taken from auction catalogs), glass is assumed to be clear unless color is indicated. Numbers refer to a standard reference book, *American Glass*, by George and Helen McKearin. See also Advertising, various companies; Avon; Barber Shop Collectibles; Blown Glass; Blown

Three-Mold Glass; California Perfume Company; Czechoslovakia; De Vilbiss; Fire Fighting; Lalique; Medical Collectibles; Steuben.

Key:
am — applied mouth	GW — Glass Works
bbl — barrel	ip — iron pontil
bt — blob top	PS — pontil scar
b3m — blown 3-mold	rm — rolled mouth
cm — collared mouth	sm — smooth base
fm — flared mouth	sl — sloping
gm — ground mouth	sm — sheared mouth
gp — graphite pontil	tm — tooled mouth

Barber

Amethyst, mc butterflies/flowers, melon base, 8½" 55.00
Amethyst, mc florals, rolled lip, exposed pontil, 8" 100.00
Bl irid, mc florals, melon base, twist neck, 8½", NM......................55.00
Bl opal w/vertical stripes, melon base, grd, 7½" 105.00
Clear opal w/stripes, rolled lip, 7".......................................55.00
Cobalt, mc flowers, sm/exposed pontil, 7½", NM 60.00
Cranberry, mc florals, cylindrical, rm, 9", NM............................110.00
Cranberry opal w/vertical stripes, melon base, 7½" 100.00
Daisy & Fern, bl opal, melon base, rm, 7½" 125.00
Milk glass, Hair Tonic w/mc flowers, rm, 9", EX...........................110.00
Stars & Stripes, cranberry opal, 7" 250.00

Bitters Bottles

Am Stomach.../Buffalo NY USA, med amber, am/sb, 11", NM ..110.00
Am Stomach...EA Meyer....Pro, med amber, am/sb, 12", NM 190.00
Baker's Orange Grove, yel, am/sb, NM labels, 9½".......................425.00
Begg's Dandelion...Sioux City, amber, am/sb, 9½".......................165.00
Bourbon Whiskey, dk amethyst, bbl form, cm/sb, 9", EX 240.00
Bourbon Whiskey, strawberry-amber, bbl, flat cm, 9¼", NM 60.00
Bourbon Whiskey, strawberry-puce, bbl form, sq cm, 9", EX 170.00
Brand Bros Co Eigenthumer, amber, tm/sb, foil neck, 10".............55.00
Brown & Lyon's Blood...Binghamton, med amber, am/sb, 10" 210.00
Brown's Celebrated Indian Herb, gold-amber, tm, 12" 340.00
Brown's Celebrated Indian Herb, honey-amber, sb, 12", NM 210.00
Brown's Celebrated Indian Herb, yel-amber, maid form, 12" 375.00
Buhrer's Gentian...S Buhrer Prop, med amber, am/sb, 9" 150.00
C Gates/Life of Man, lt to med sapphire, am, NM label, 8" 350.00
Constitution, dk gold-yel, rectangular, sl cm/sb, 9" 650.00
David Andrews Vegetable Jaundice, aqua, am/ps, 8" 525.00
Doctor Fisch's/WH Ware Pat 1866, amber, fish form, rm, 12" 160.00
Dr Ball's Vegetable Stomachic...Northboro, aqua, am/ps, 7"..........95.00
Dr Bell's Blood Purifying...English Remedy, amber, 9½" 100.00
Dr Blake's Aromatic...NY, dk aqua, am/ps, 7½" 230.00
Dr Geo Pierce's Indian Restorative, aqua, am, 8¾" 40.00
Dr Hoofland's German...Liver Complaint Dyspepsia, aqua, 7".......45.00
Dr J Hostetter's Stomach, dk olive-amber, am, 9½"......................70.00
Dr J Hostetter's Stomach, olive-gr (rare), 9" 130.00
Dr J Hostetter's Stomach/S McKee (base), yel-amber, am, 9" 55.00
Dr Langley's Root & Herb/Union St Boston, aqua, am/sb, 7" 20.00
Dr Lovegood's Family, dk gold-amber, cabin form, 10", NM.... 1,100.00
Dr Skinner's Celebrated 25 Cent/So Reading, aqua, am, 8½"........90.00
Dr Skinner's Sherry Wine/So Reading MA, aqua, am/ps, 8½" 110.00
Dr Wilkinshaw's Curative, amber, sq, EX label, sl cm, 10" 325.00
Drake's 1868 Plant'n/Pat 1862, med puce, sl cm/sb, 10".............100.00
Drake's 1869 Plant'n, med amber 5-log, am, lt stain, 9¾" 195.00
Eagle Angostura Bark/Eagle...Distilleries, amber, tm, 7"...............65.00
Excelsior Herb, amber, sq cm/sb, 10", NM 300.00
Geo Benz Appetine, amber, sq w/scrolls, sl cm/sb, 8", NM 145.00

Digestine Bitters, P.J. Bowlin Liquor Co., Sole Proprietors; amber, tooled lip, minor inside stain, rare, $400.00.

Geo C Goodwin Indian Vegetable/Sarsaparilla, gr-aqua, 8½" 375.00
Great Tonic Caldwell's Herb, amber, am/ip, 12½" 170.00
Greeley's Bourbon, copper-amber, bbl form, sq cm/sb, 9", NM 125.00
Greeley's Bourbon, copper-puce, am/sb, 9", NM 130.00
Greeley's Bourbon, copper-puce, bbl form, sq cm/sb, 9", NM.........95.00
Greeley's Bourbon, olive-gr, bbl form, flat cm/sb, 9", NM 320.00
Greeley's Bourbon, smoky amber, bbl, thick flange lip, 9½" 110.00
HH Warner's Tippecanoe, dk gold-amber, mushroom mouth, 9" ..90.00
Holtzermann's Pat Stomach, amber, 2-roof, am/sb 625.00
Homo FH Grau Buffalo NY, amber, am/sb, EX label, 9½".............75.00
Hop & Iron/Utica NY, amber, am/sb, NM labels, 8½" 220.00
HP Herb Wild Cherry/Reading PA, amber, am/sb, 10", NM 180.00
HP Herb Wild Cherry/Wild Cherry (tree), amber, tm, 9" 425.00
Kelly's Old Cabin, dk gold-amber, cabin form, sl cm, 9", NM......350.00
Kelly's Old Cabin, red-amber, cabin form, sm/sb, 9½", NM.........450.00
Kelly's Old Cabin Pat 1863 (twice), amber, cabin, am/sb 600.00
Kimball's Jaundice, lt olive-amber, beveled corners, 7" 300.00
Kimball's Jaundice...Troy NH, lt amber, sl cm/ip, 7" 275.00
King's 25 Cent, aqua, am/sb, 6¾" 130.00
Litthauer Stomach/Invented 1864, milk glass, 9½", NM 65.00
Mishler's Herb/Dr SB Hartman & Co, yel w/olive, am/sb, 9" 80.00
National Bitters, gold-yel, corn form, am w/ring, sb, 12½" 300.00
Old Homestead Wild Cherry, gold-amber, cabin form, cm, 10" ...250.00
Old Sachem/& Wigwam Tonic, dk strawberry-puce, bbl, 9½".....300.00
Old Sachem/Wigwam Tonic, gr-aqua, bbl form, sq cm, 9½" ... 1,400.00
Old Sachem/Wigwam Tonic, lt gold-yel, bbl form, 9½", EX........500.00
Orig Pochontas, aqua, bbl form, cm/sb, 9" 1,100.00
Poor Man's Family, aqua, am/sb, 6½" 25.00
Red Jacket/Bennett Pieters & Co, yel-olive, 9½", EX 90.00
Royal Italian, amethyst, sq sm/sb, 13½", NM 450.00
Sazarac Aromatic, milk glass, lady's leg form, 12", NM 350.00
Schroeder's, gold-amber, lady's leg, tm/sb, 5¼", NM 290.00
Simon's Centennial, gold-amber, Geo WA bust, dbl cm, 10" 900.00
ST Drake's 1860 Plant'n X 1862, amber, 4 label panels, 10"........145.00
ST Drake's 1860 Plant'n X 1862, amber, 4-log, am/sb..................50.00
ST Drake's 1860 Plant'n X 1862, amber, 6-log, am/sb, 10" 60.00
ST Drake's 1860 Plant'n X 1862, dk pk-puce, 6-log, am, 10".......160.00
ST Drake's 1860 Plant'n X 1862, yel-amber, 6-log, 9¾", NM......150.00
Suffolk, lt gold-amber, pig form, dbl cm/sb, 10½" 450.00
Warner's Safe, dk gold-amber, dbl cm/sb, 9½", NM 325.00

Willard's Golden Seal, aqua, am/sb, 7½"..**45.00**
Wm Allen's Congress, dk aqua, am/sb, 10", NM2 ....**75.00**

Blown Glass

Amethyst w/wht looping, blown-in-mold, pewter lip, 7½" **850.00**
Aqua, club shape, minor wear & sickness, 7¾"...........................**95.00**
Aqua, cylindrical w/long neck, folded/fm, wear, 7"......................**25.00**
Chestnut flask, aqua, appl ring below sm/ps, 1750s, 3½".............**100.00**
Chestnut flask, aqua, 18 swirled ribs, 6¾" **95.00**
Chestnut flask, lt olive-gr, freeblown, cm/ps, 5½", NM **80.00**
Chestnut flask, yel-olive, r-cm, ps, NE, 1800s, 5¾" **140.00**
Condiment, GII-44, 4⅜", +stopper....................................**100.00**
Decanter, GI-27, b3m, flanged mouth, smooth base w/ps **95.00**
Decanter, GII-16, b3m, type 24 stopper, tm/ps, pt **140.00**
Decanter, GII-16, olive-gr, sm/ps, Keene, pt................................**375.00**
Decanter, GII-18, b3m, 3 appl rings on neck, stopper, 8".............**275.00**
Decanter, GII-2, type 2, yel-olive, fm/ps, Mt Vernon, pt......... **2,100.00**
Decanter, GII-22, b3m, pressed lollipop stopper, ps....................**120.00**
Decanter, GV-12, b3m, orig hollow ribbed stopper, ps.................**350.00**
Decanter, GV-8, sapphire, b3m, matching plain stopper, EX . **3,100.00**
Demijohn, olive-amber, str-sided cylinder, sm/ps, 18x9" **50.00**
Dk amber, ovoid, appl lip, 5¼"...**150.00**
Gr-aqua, cylindrical w/bulbous lip, 8"......................................**85.00**
Honey-amber, globular w/kick-up, minor scratches, 8½"..............**375.00**
Ludlow, gr, 10" **125.00**
Ludlow, lt gr, minor residue, 7"..**85.00**
Ludlow, lt olive-amber, 5"..**135.00**
Olive-gr, GIII-16, b3m, 7"...**525.00**
Olive-gr, octagonal, am, 6"...**425.00**
Pitkin, lt olive-gr, broken left swirl, ½-pt....................................**275.00**
Pitkin, lt yel-olive, 36-rib, right swirl, sm/ps, 5½", NM...............**270.00**
Pitkin, olive-amber, 36-rib, sm/ps, sm potstone, 5½"...................**250.00**
Pitkin, olive-gr, ribs, right swirl, ½-post, ½-pt **225.00**
Pitkin, olive-gr, 30-rib, left swirl, wear, 6½".............................**325.00**
Pitkin, olive-yel, 24-rib broken swirl, sm flakes, 5" **600.00**
Pumpkin flask, olive-gr, 20-rib, crude am/ps, NE, pt **400.00**
Snuff, emerald gr, freeblown, 4-sided, att Willington, 6x3".........**325.00**
Snuff, olive-amber, freeblown/paddled, tm/ps, NE, 4½"...............**260.00**
Toilet, cobalt, paneled, collared, lollipop stopper, 7"..................**275.00**
Toilet, G-7-II, purple, flared mouth, ps, collared neck **100.00**
Toilet, GI-3-II, dk cobalt, b3m, swirl rib, ringed base, ps **125.00**
Toilet, GI-7, cobalt, hollow tam stopper, ps, 7", EX **195.00**
Whiskey flask, clambroth, 2-part mold, slanted collar, 7½" **25.00**

Cologne or Perfume Bottles

A'suma, floral stopper, spherical, Coty, in 3" box.........................**220.00**
Amber, dbl, brass flip tops, stoppers missing, ca 1850, 5" **140.00**
Amethyst, 12-sided, tm/sb, att Sandwich, 7"...............................**160.00**
Amethyst, 8-sided hourglass form, tm/ps, Sandwich type, 6".......**550.00**
Burmese color w/gold-traced ferns, spherical, 4¼"........................**725.00**
Charley Ross, rm/sb, 4¾"..**60.00**
Citron, blown, waisted hexagon w/matching stopper, 4½" **450.00**
Cobalt cut to yel, lattice/floral intaglio, 5" **795.00**
Cranberry, mc florals, neck cuttings, clear cut stopper, 7½"..........**135.00**
Cranberry w/mica flecks, laydown, London, 1884, 8" **375.00**
Dancing Indian, emb on aqua, rm/ps, 5"..................................**90.00**
Dk amethyst, 12-sided, Sandwich, 11", NM **290.00**
Dk pk & wht w/ovals & panels cut to clear w/gilt, 8" **525.00**
Electric bl, hexagonal w/emb dmns, +stopper, NE Glass, 4½" . **1,100.00**
Emerald gr cut to clear, waisted, eng metal top, 1860, 3" **150.00**
Gr to clear, prism & mirror cut, faceted stopper, 6x3".................**125.00**

Gr/wht swirl candy cane Venetian, emb brass top, 1920, 3¾" **225.00**
Guerlain, clear/ribbed, in leather case, 3½" **60.00**
Ivory satin, mc/gold florals/branches, Webb, silver top, 5½"........**400.00**
Med amethyst, 12-sided, tm/sb, Sandwich type, 7" **275.00**
Miss Worth, Deco, dmn form, MIB...**35.00**

Sandwich colognes: Sapphire-blue, square with herringbone corners, tooled lip, 11", $2,300.00; Bright green, 12-sided, 6", $375.00; Orange-amber, square with thumbprint, tooled flared lip, 5½", $425.00.

Pk shaded overlay, mc florals/branches, silver top, 4¼".................**225.00**
Scroll, blown, flanged lip/ps, 4" **95.00**
Teal-gr, 12-sided, tm, Sandwich, 4¼", NM...............................**275.00**
Threaded, eng silver flip top, Dutch, 3½", NM **275.00**
Vaseline, cut, bbl form, mk top, London, 1861, 1¾", NM **125.00**

Figural Bottles

Cleveland bust, clear/frost, tm/ps, Am, 1880-1900, 10"...............**140.00**
Geo Washington bust, Simon's Centennial Bitters, aqua, 11".....**275.00**
Girl standing on head, clear/frosted, tm, minor stain, 14"...............**65.00**
Man on bbl, lt olive-yel, whiskey w/shot glass stopper, 14".........**100.00**
National Bitters, ear of corn, lt amber, am w/ring, 12".................**325.00**
Pear, yel opaque, bl-gr/pk/yel flecks, 5¼" **120.00**
Rosenbaum Bros Old KY Whiskies, pig, tan pottery, 7" L............**350.00**
Seated bear, dk red-amethyst, flat cm/sb, 1880s, 11" **40.00**
W&C Co/NY, pineapple, olive-yel, whiskey, dbl cm/ip, 8½".......**650.00**

Flasks

Adams/Jefferson, GI-114, gold-amber, sm/ps, NE, ½-pt **135.00**
Army Officer/Lg Flower, GXIII-15, lt bl-gr, qt calabash...............**210.00**
Ben Franklin/TW Dyott, GI-96, aqua, sm/ps, Kensington, qt **140.00**
Cannon/Little More Grape Capt Bragg, GX-4, aqua, pt, NM **285.00**
Cannon/Little More Grape Capt Bragg, GX-6, aqua, ½-pt..........**250.00**
Clasped Hands/Eagle, GXII-15, yel w/olive tone, cm, qt **450.00**
Clasped Hands/Eagle, GXIII-33, gold-amber, sm/sb, ½-pt **125.00**
Clyde GW/NY, aqua, am/sb, qt, NM **35.00**
Columbia/Eagle, GI-117, aqua, sm/ps, Kensington, pt, NM........**150.00**
Columbia/Eagle, GI-121, aqua, sm/ps, 1830s, pt........................**230.00**

Columbia/Eagle, GI-121, gr-aqua, sm/ps, pt................................350.00
Cornucopia, GIII-14, emerald, tm/tubular pontil, ½-pt 350.00
Cornucopia/Urn, GII-12, gold-amber w/olive tone, ½-pt 110.00
Cornucopia/Urn, GIII-10, yel-olive, sm/ps, lt imp, ½-pt 75.00
Cornucopia/Urn, GIII-13, aqua, sm/ps, Lancaster, ½-pt............120.00
Cornucopia/Urn, GIII-17, dk bl-gr, sm/ps, Lancaster, pt 190.00
Cornucopia/Urn, GIII-4, yel-olive, sm/ps, Coventry, pt..............65.00
Cornucopia/Urn, GIII-7, olive-amber, sm/ps, NE, ½-pt 85.00
Dbl Eagle, GII-108, dk aqua, am w/ring, sb, lt stain, pt 75.00
Dbl Eagle, GII-108, olive-gr, am w/ring, Pittsburgh, pt 110.00
Dbl Eagle, GII-31, emerald, Louisville GW, qt, EX 900.00
Dbl Eagle, GII-71, olive-amber, sm/ps, ½-pt, NM 110.00
Dbl Eagle, GII-88, olive-gr, sm/ps, ½-pt, NM 90.00
Dbl Eagle, GIII-40, aqua, short neck, sm/ps, pt...........................90.00
Dbl Eagle/Louisville KY GW, GII-114, yel-gr, 8⅝".....................750.00
Dbl Eagle/Pittsburgh PA in Oval, lt yel-gr, 7⅝" 55.00
Eagle, GI-45, aqua, sm/tm/ps, ½-pt 85.00
Eagle & Keene/Masonic, GIV-17, olive-gr, 7½"..........................145.00
Eagle & TWD/Washington, GI-14, aqua, 7"..................................95.00
Eagle/Cornucopia, GII-11, aqua, sm/ps, Pittsburgh, ½-pt..........225.00
Eagle/Cornucopia, GII-72, dk olive-gr, sm/ps, pt, EX 75.00
Eagle/Cornucopia, GII-73, dk forest gr, sm/ps, Keene, pt 150.00
Eagle/Flag, GII-48, aqua, sm/ps, Coffin & Hay, qt 125.00
Eagle/Flag, GII-52, gr-aqua, sm/ps, pt, NM 60.00
Eagle/Flag, GII-54, dk striated olive-amber, sm/ps, pt............. 2,000.00
Eagle/Frigate, GII-42, aqua, sm/ps, lt stain, pt 160.00
Eagle/Grapes, GII-55, aqua, sm/ps, lt stain, qt 100.00
Eagle/Louisville KY GW, GII-35, dk aqua, rnd cm/sb, qt 110.00
Eagle/Louisville KY GW, GII-36, aqua, am w/ring, sb, pt............165.00
Eagle/Morning-Glory, GII-19, dk aqua, sm/ps, pt, EX 300.00
Eagle/Oak Tree, GII-60, dk gold-amber, sm/ps, ½-pt 1,300.00
Eagle/Tree, GII-41, aqua, sm/ps, Kensington GW, pt 125.00
Eagle/Tree, GII-47, aqua, sm/ps, lt stain, qt 425.00
Eagle/Willington GW, GII-61, dk gr w/olive tone, qt 170.00
Eagle/Willington GW, GII-61, red-amber, dbl cm/sb, qt 225.00
Flora Temple (horse)/bk: plain, GXIII-19, puce-amber, qt...........250.00
Flora Temple (horse)/bk: plain, GXIII-19, strawb'y puce, qt........300.00
For Pike's Peak Prospector/Hunter, GXI-52, dk aqua, ½-pt.........170.00
For Pike's Peak/Eagle & Ceredo, GXI-35, lt yel-gr, 7⅞" 500.00
For Pike's Peak/Eagle & Pittsburgh PA, GXI-9, aqua, 7⅝" 60.00
Gen Lafayette/Eagle, GI-90, aqua, sm/ps, lt imp, pt 160.00
Gen Washington/Eagle, GI-1, lt bl-gr, sm/ps, minor wear, pt.......550.00
Gen Washington/Eagle, GI-14, gr-aqua, sm/ps, Kensington, pt ...200.00
Gen Washington/Eagle, GI-16, aqua, sm/ps, Kensington, pt 110.00
Gen Washington/Eagle, GI-3, aqua, sm/ps, Pittsburgh, pt 600.00
Granite Glass Co Stoddard NH, GXV-7, yel-amber/olive, pt......160.00
Great Western Trapper/Stag, GX-30, aqua, am w/ring, sb, pt 375.00
Horse & Cart/Eagle, VG-9, olive-gr, sm/ps, Coventry, pt.............270.00
Hunter/Fisherman, GXIII-4, gold-amber, sl cm/ip, calabash 150.00
Jenny Lind/Factory, GI-99, emerald, sl cm-bevel/ps, pt...............650.00
Jenny Lind/Glassworks, GI-104, sapphire, qt calabash, NM.... 2,200.00
Jenny Lind/Lyre, GI-110, lt bl-gr, sm/ps, qt, NM........................750.00
Kossuth/Frigate, gold-amber, sl cm/ip, NJ, qt calabash............. 1,700.00
Kossuth/Sloop, GI-111, aqua, sm/ps, lt stain, pt 175.00
Kossuth/Tree, GI-113, olive-yel, sl cm/ps, qt calabash.................300.00
Lafayette/DeWitt Clinton, GI-80, lt olive-amber, sm/ps, pt..........375.00
Lafayette/DeWitt Clinton, GI-80, olive-amber, sm/ps, pt............475.00
Lafayette/Eagle, GI-90, aqua, sm/ps, Kensington, pt, NM...........135.00
Lafayette/Liberty Cap, GI-86, olive-amber, sm/ps, ½-pt..............400.00
Louisville KY/GW Scroll, GIX-8, gr-aqua, sm/ip, pt....................110.00
Masonic, GIV-24, olive-amber, sm/ps, Keene NH, ½-pt................80.00
Masonic/Eagle, GIV-19, olive-amber, sm/ps, Keene, pt...............140.00
Masonic/Eagle, GIV-24, olive-amber, sm/ps, lt imp, ½-pt 130.00

Masonic/Eagle, GIV-32, lt bl-gr, sm/ps, Wht GW, pt...................210.00
Masonic/Eagle, GIV-7, med olive-gr, tm/ps, pt, NM 550.00
Masonic/Frigate, GVI-34, aqua, sm/ps, Kensington, pt 250.00
Pantaloon Eagle/Cornucopia, GII-75, dk olive, sl cm/ps, pt 2,200.00
Railroad, GV-1, cornflower bl/bl-aqua, sm/tm, pt 400.00
Roosevelt/TVA, GI-129, aqua, sl cm/sb, qt calabash 120.00
Scroll, GIX-1, dk yel-gr, flat cm/ps, qt 800.00
Scroll, GIX-11, dk gold-yel, sm/ip, pt, EX 125.00
Scroll, GIX-12, gold-amber, sm/ps, pt, EX 160.00
Scroll, GIX-2, moonstone w/amethyst tint, sm/ps, qt...................475.00
Scroll, GIX-32, dk aqua, collared rm/ip, ½-pt...............................100.00
Scroll, GIX-35, citron, sm/ps, Am, 1845-1860, ½-pt...................425.00
Scroll, GIX-38, lt yel-gr, BP&B, 5⅞" 1,200.00
Seeing Eye Masonic, GIV-43, olive-amber, sm/ps, pt...................150.00
Sheaf of Wheat/Sheets & Duffy Star, GXIII-41, aqua, qt 150.00
Sheaf of Wheat/Star, GXIII-39, bright yel-gr, dbl cm/sb, pt..........200.00
Sheaf of Wheat/Star, GXIII-45, gold-amber, hdld qt calabash.....325.00
Sheaf of Wheat/Westford Glass, GXIII-37, red-amber, ½-pt 150.00
Soldier/Ballet Dancer, GXIII-11, lt gr-bl, sm/ps, pt 150.00
Soldier/Lg Daisy, GXIII-15, aqua, sl cm/ip, qt calabash, NM.......100.00
Spring Garden/GW, Anchor & Cabin, GXIII, aqua, sm/sb, pt...120.00
Success to RR, CV-5, dk emerald, sm/ps, pt 275.00
Success to RR, GV-2, aqua, rare, 6½"...275.00
Success to RR, GV-3, olive-amber, sm/ps-crude shearing, pt.......180.00
Success to RR, GV-4, lt olive-amber, sm/ps, Keene, pt 310.00
Success to RR/Eagle, GV-8, olive-amber, sm/ps, pt 225.00
Summer Tree/Winter Tree, GX-15, aqua, sl cm/sb, pt....................75.00
Summer/Winter, med olive-yel, dbl cm/smooth base, pt, NM 325.00
Sunburst, GVIII-14, bright gr, sm/ps, Keene, ½-pt................. 1,300.00
Sunburst, GVIII-14A, med gr, sm/ps, att Keene, ½-pt 1,200.00
Sunburst, GVIII-16, olive-amber, sm/ps, ½-pt..............................300.00
Sunburst, GVIII-2, apple gr, heavy, 8" 275.00
Sunburst, GVIII-25, aqua, sm/ps, ½-pt 275.00
Sunburst, GVIII-8, olive-amber, Keene, pt, NM 350.00
Sunburst, GVIII-8, olive-gr, sm/ps, Keene, pt 400.00
Sunburst, GVIII-9, gold-amber, sm/ps, Keen NH, ½-pt 190.00
Taylor/Masterson & Eagle, GI-77, lt gr-bl, sm/ps, qt 700.00
Traveler's Companion/Ravenna GW, GIV-3, gold-amber, pt 400.00
Traveler's Companion/Wheat Sheaf, GXIV-1, olive-amber, qt ..160.00

Union, Clasped Hands; back: Cannon, GXIII-41, amber, $180.00.

Union & Clasped Hands/Eagle & Banner, GXII-29, amber, 6" ...**100.00**
Union & Clasped Hands/Old Rye & Eagle, GXIII-25, aqua, 7½" .**45.00**
Union & Clasped Hands/Wm Frank & Sons, GXII-38, aqua, 9"...**65.00**
Urn/Cornucopia, GII-7, olive-amber, 5" **65.00**
Urn/Cornucopia, GIII-4, olive-gr, 6¾" **55.00**
Washington Monument/Corn for World, GVI-4, ice bl, qt **150.00**
Washington Monument/Corn for World, GVI-6, aqua, pt..........**110.00**
Washington/Baltimore GW Monument, GI-18, yel-gr/olive, pt . **3,100.00**
Washington/Classical Bust, GI-22, gr-aqua, sm/ps, qt **200.00**
Washington/Eagle, GI-16, aqua, sm/ps, int stain, pt...................**155.00**
Washington/Jackson, GI-31, lt yel-amber, lt imp, pt...................**100.00**
Washington/Jackson, GI-31, yel-olive, sm/ps, Keene, pt, NM **90.00**
Washington/Jackson, GI-34, yel-olive, sm/ps, lt imp, ½-pt.........**130.00**
Washington/Sheaf of Rye, GI-57, aqua, dbl cm, lt stain, qt **40.00**
Washington/Taylor, GI-43, smoky mauve, sm/ps, qt **1,100.00**
Washington/Taylor, GI-50, dk forest gr, sl cm/ps, pt...................**550.00**
Washington/Tree, GI-35, aqua, sl cm/ps, lt stain, qt....................**50.00**
Wm Jenning Bryan/Eagle, GI-126, clear, coin shape, ½-pt **700.00**

Food Bottles and Jars

Freeblown, milk glass, cylindrical, fm/ps, Am, 1850s, 8½" **675.00**
Peppersauce, aqua, cathedral arches, am/sb, 8¾"........................**45.00**
Peppersauce, aqua, rnded 8-panel body, am/ip, 8¾"...................**30.00**
Peppersauce, lt gr, rope corners, 4 panels w/stars, 8½".................**150.00**
Pickle, aqua, cathedral, 6-sided, fancy arches, cm/sb, 14" **130.00**
Pickle, aqua, ps, 7½" **40.00**
Pickle, gr, cathedral arches w/scrollwork, r-cm, sb, 12" **250.00**
Preserves, dk gold-amber, dbl cm/smooth base, 11" **350.00**
Vinegar, cobalt, GI-3, b3m, right swirl, period stopper **300.00**

Ink Bottles

Allings High School/Rochester, aqua, domical, tm/sb, 1⅞".........**130.00**
Butler's/Cincinnati, aqua, 12-sided, rm/ps, 3" **150.00**
B3m, olive/honey-amber, ps, Keene GW, 2x2½"...........................**175.00**
Cone, dk olive-amber, sm/ps, att Stoddard, 2¼" **100.00**
Cone, lt bl-gr, rm/ps, 2⅜" **20.00**
Cottage, aqua, am/sb, Patd Mar 14, 1871, 2½" **400.00**
E Waters, aqua, ribbed, A on bk, rectangular, tm/ps, 3" **200.00**
GE Hatch Pat Dec 27 1875, milk glass, emb pear/leaves, 2½" **170.00**
James Masons & Co, aqua, 8-sided cone, rm/ps, 2⅜" **185.00**
JS Dunham, lt-med gr, 8-sided, rm/ps, lt stain, 2⅜" **575.00**
NE Plus Ultra Fluid, dk aqua, cottage, unfinished lip, 2⅝" **145.00**
Patterson's Excelsior, aqua, 8-sided, rm/ps, 2½" **350.00**
Pitkin, olive-amber, 36-rib, left swirl, folded lip, 2x1¾" **260.00**
Pitkin, yel-olive, right swirl, disk mouth, 1⅝x2¼" **350.00**
RF, dk amethyst, cylindrical, rm/ps, 2x2⅜" **200.00**
S Fine Blk Ink, gr, cylindrical, rm/ps, minor stain, 3" **175.00**
Teakettle, amethyst, 8 cut/polished panels, neck ring, 1⅝" **450.00**
Teakettle, med yel-gr, gm/sb, 2"...**575.00**
Teakettle, yel-amber, s-gm/sb, ribbed sides, 2⅛" **750.00**
Umbrella, citron, 8-sided, r-cm, ps, lt stain, 2¼" **250.00**
Umbrella, dk cobalt, 8-sided, rm/sb, 1½".....................................**450.00**
Umbrella, med amber, 8-sided, rm/ps, 2½" **120.00**
Umbrella, med cobalt, 8-sided, rm/ps, 1850s, 2½" **500.00**
Warren's Congress, aqua, 8-sided, sm/ps, prof cleaned, 2⅞" **140.00**

Medicine Bottles

ABL Myers AM Rock Rose New Haven, emerald, bt/ip, 9½" **500.00**
Am Compound Coventry/Auburn NY, aqua, am/ps, 7" **60.00**
Bach's Am Compound Auburn NY, aqua, am/ps, 7" **75.00**

Balsam of Wild Cherry & Tar/Barnes & Park, aqua, am/ps, 7½"....**65.00**
Carter's Spanish Mixture, olive-amber, am/ip, 8" **215.00**
Clark's Syrup, med gr, am/sb, 9¾", NM......................................**55.00**
Craig Kidney Cure Co, amber, am/sb, minor stain, 9½"..............**115.00**
Doct Curtis' Cherry Syrup, clear, am/ps, 7½" **45.00**
Doct Fowler's Anti/Epicholic, aqua, am/ps, 6" **120.00**
Dr Atherton's Wild Cherry Syrup/EW Hall, aqua, am, 5", NM ..**110.00**
Dr Craig's Cough & Consumption Cure, orange-amber, am, 8" .**625.00**
Dr Ford's Pectoral Syrup, aqua, am/ps, 5⅝" **85.00**
Dr Hershey's Worm Syrup, aqua, rm/ps, 5½".................................**95.00**
Dr JS Wood's Elixir Albany NY, emerald, am/ip, bubbly, 8¾" . **1,100.00**
Dr Mitchel's Ipecac Syrup/Perry NY, aqua, rm/ps, 5" **70.00**
Dr Perkin's Syrup Albany, bl-gr, am/ip, bubbly, 9½", NM **450.00**
Dr White's Dandelion Alternative/Indy, dk aqua, am, 9", EX........**55.00**
GW Merchant Chemist Lockport NY, emerald, am/sb, 7½".......**140.00**
Hopkins' Chalybeate Baltimore, bright yel-gr, am, pt, NM............**85.00**

Fulton's Radical Cure Remedy, Sure Kidney Liver and Dyspepsia Cure, amber, 9", $375.00; Germ, Bacteria, or Fungus Destroyer, Wm Radam's Microbe Killer Cures All Diseases, Trademark Dec. 13, 1887, yellow, 10", $110.00.

Houses Indian Tonic, dk aqua, emb Indian, rm/ps, 5½" **700.00**
Jenk's Vegetable Extract, aqua, rm/ps, wide mouth, 4" **60.00**
JL Curtis Syrup of Sassafras, aqua, rm/ps, 4¼" **90.00**
JR Spalding's Rosemary & Castor Oil, aqua, rm/ps, 5" **25.00**
MB Robert's Vegetable Embrocation, emerald, am/ps, 5½" **130.00**
Moore's Revealed (RMR monogram in shield), amber, 9" **40.00**
Mrs MN Gardner's Indian Balsam..., aqua, hat whimsey, 1x2½" .**800.00**
PB Wait & Co/Stanley's Celery Malt, yel-amber, 8", NM............**80.00**
Prepared by Dr C Freeman...For Coughs, aqua, fm/ps, 5" **150.00**
Sanford's Radical Cure, cobalt, am/sb, 7⅝", NM **25.00**
Swaim's Panacea Philada, olive, am/ps, crude, 7⅞" **180.00**
Vaughn's Vegetable Lithontriptic Mixture, dk aqua, ip, 8" **210.00**

Milk Bottles

Ayrhill Farms, Adams Mass, 1-qt **7.00**

Borden's, Elsie the Cow, ½-pt 12.50
Brookfield, 'baby face,' ½-pt 75.00
Butler Dairy, Willimantic CT, 1-qt 12.00
Maplewood Dairy, Fairhaven VT/Hudson Falls NY, amber, 1-qt ...10.00
Springdale Farms, Millington New Jersey, cream top, 1-qt.............18.00
VM&CI Co's in circle, amber, pt 18.00

Mineral Water and Soda Bottles

Adirondack Spring Whitehall NY, emerald, am/sb, pt, NM 100.00
Alpena Magnetic Spring Co, amber, am/sb, qt, NM 350.00
Artesian Spring Co AS (monogram) Ballston NY, olive, am 130.00
Avon Spring, aqua, am/sb, qt 350.00
Avon Spring/CH Nowlen Avon NY, emerald, am/sb, pt, EX 110.00
Deep Rock Spring Oswego NY-D, aqua, am/sb, pt 210.00
Deep Rock Spring/Trade/Deep Rock/Mark/Oswego, aqua, qt......110.00
E Smith Elmira NY, cobalt, cylindrical, lg cm/ip, ½-pt, EX 300.00
Eureka Spring Co, emerald, torpedo form, sl cm w/ring, pt 500.00
Excelsior Spring Saratoga NY, emerald, am/sb, qt......................180.00
Gettysburg Katalysine Water, emerald, am/sb, qt 20.00
Highrock Congress Spring 1767 (rock) C&W, amber, am, pt......210.00
J Lake Schenectady NY, cobalt, 10-pin form, lg cm/ip, 8" 3,000.00
Massena Spring (monogram) Water, teal bl, am/sb, qt, NM 120.00
Oak Orchard Acid Springs Address GW Merchant, yel-gr, qt.....130.00
Oak Orchard Acid Springs Alabama Genesse, dk bl-gr, qt 325.00
Oak Orchard Acid Springs HW Bostwick Agt #574, amber, qt.....80.00
Oak Orchard Acid Springs HW Bostwick Agt #574, bl-gr, qt 160.00
Oswego Deep Rock/This Bottle Must Be..., aqua, am/sb, qt.........135.00
Poland Water, aqua, Moses figural, sm/sb, 11" 60.00
Quaker Springs/IW Meader & Co, emerald, am/sb, pt 650.00
Richfield Springs NY Sulphur Water, aqua, am/sb, pt, NM 150.00
St Regis Water Massena Springs, teal bl, am/sb, qt, NM..............150.00
Superior Soda Water/Eagle & Shield, cobalt, sl cm/ip, ½-pt........475.00
Syracuse Springs Excelsior, yel-amber, am/sb, pt 130.00
Washington Lithia Well/Ballston Spa, aqua, am/sb, pt, NM........135.00
Washington Spring (bust of WA) Ballston Spa, emerald, pt........425.00

Sarsaparilla Bottles

Cornell & Folsom Wahoo & Sarsaparilla, NY, aqua,
iron pontil, rare, possibly unique, 9½", $475.00;
Dr. Russell's Balsam of Horehound and Sarsaparilla,
aqua, open pontil, very rare, 9", $235.00.

Bristol's Extract/Buffalo, dk aqua, am/ps, 5¾" 80.00
Bristol's Genuine/NY, aqua, am/ps, 10½" 425.00
CD Co's...Resolvent, amber, tm/sb, 8½" 50.00
Dr Townsend's/Albany NY, dk olive-amber, ps, 9⅝" 145.00
JL Kelley & Co, aqua, am/ps, 8", EX..100.00
Masury's Cathartic, aqua, sq cm/ps, rectangular, Am, 6¾" 100.00
Old Dr Townsend's/NY, emerald, am/ip, 10" 250.00
Quaker, clear, tm, full label, rectangular, 8" 70.00

Spirits Bottles

Bennett & Carroll/#120 Wood..., gold-amber, am/ip, 8", NM 225.00
Bininger's Regulator, yel-amber, clock form, dbl cm, pt 250.00
Case gin, olive-amber, blown, flared am/ps, 9" 85.00
Charles' London Cordial Gin, med bl-gr, am/sb, 8" 75.00
Duffy's Malt Whiskey 1860 Boston, hdld decanter, disk body......125.00

E.G. Booz's Old Cabin
Whiskey cabin bottle,
GVIII-3, honey amber,
qt, $1,000.00.

EG Booz's Old Cabin Whiskey, amber, 2 dots by St, 7½", NM 500.00
EG Booz's Old Cabin Whiskey, gold-amber, 2 dots by St, qt 600.00
EG Booz's Old Cabin Whiskey, honey-amber, cabin form, qt.. 1,000.00
Forest Lawn JVH, dk yel-olive, bulbous, emb seal, fm/ip, 8".........100.00
Fortune Sequattir, dk olive-gr w/seal, am w/string, 9", NM..........225.00
NE Glass Bottle Co, dk olive-gr (blk), sl cm/ps, 8½" 225.00
Slater's Premium Bourbon/John Sroufe..., gold-amber, 12" 425.00
Star, gold-amber, conical hdld jug form, dbl cm w/spout, 8" 250.00
Swan Brewery Co, yel-olive, Never Sold, ½-pt, EX........................75.00
Udolpho Wolfe's Schiedam...Schnapps, olive-amber, 10", NM 30.00
Wharton's Chestnut Grove Whiskey 1850, cobalt, teardrop, 5"..200.00

Miscellaneous

Lavender Salts, Goetting & Co, see California Perfume Co.
Liniment, Genessee, aqua, rm/ps, 5½" 65.00
Liniment, JR Burdsall's Arnica, aqua, am/ps, 5½" 45.00
Nursing, aqua, 21 vertical ribs, bubbly/scratches, 6⅜" 25.00
Nursing, gr-aqua, 14 vertical ribs, 6⅜" 75.00
Poison, amber, triangular, tm/sb, 10½" 200.00
Poison flask, aqua, emb cow & sheaf of wheat, 5" 125.00
Snuff, E Roome Troy NY, olive-amber, sq w/bevel corners, 4" 150.00
Snuff, JJ Mapes #61 Front St N York, dk olive-amber, 4½"..........800.00

Soda, J Wismann Dayton OH, lt-bl paneled, ip, 8", EX..............150.00
Sweet 16, Goetting & Co, see California Perfume Co.

Osborn's Liquid Polish, olive-yellow, open pontil, 3¾", $400.00.

Boxes

Boxes have been used by civilized man since ancient Egypt and Rome. Down through the centuries, specifically designed containers have been made from every conceivable material. Precious metals, papier-mache, battersea, Oriental lacquer, and wood have held riches from the treasuries of kings, snuff for the fashionable set of the last century, China tea, and countless other commodities. See also Toleware; specific manufacturers.

Beech, bl pnt w/wht birds & flowers, dome top, 12" L.................500.00
Bentwood, burnt-wood, wood spring latch lid, 9" L, VG 75.00
Bentwood, dk pnt, wood hdl on wire bail, 12" dia.......................175.00
Bentwood, gray pnt, wood hdl on wire bail, worn, 7x12"............225.00
Bentwood, red pnt, wood hdl on wire bail, 5x9" dia 200.00
Bentwood, rpt, 2-finger base, 1 on lid, iron tacks, 7" L 275.00
Bible, oak, cvd front panel, dtd 1676, 23" L, EX 550.00
Bible, pine, grpt over orig bl, sgn/1828, age split, 13" L 150.00
Blanket, dvtl, bracket base, leather hinges, 1840s, 4x7x4"..........600.00
Bride's, pine w/bl pnt, mc floral/verse, 17 L", EX 1,000.00
Butternut, wide dvtl, appl moldings, strap hinges, 16" L..............350.00
Candle, brass, cylindrical w/3-scallop crest, 12" L, EX 140.00
Candle, fruitwood, dvtl, sliding lid, 20" L...................................600.00
Candle, oak, dvtl, shaped bk brd w/hanging hole, 17" L..............175.00
Candle, pine, simple crest, hinged lid, wall mt, 13" L 275.00
Candle, pine, simple crest, 1-drw, natural/weathered, 16" L........400.00
Candle, tin, cylindrical, shield bk, wire hangers, 12" L...............265.00
Document, dome top, pine w/EX orig red pnt, 12" L 135.00
Document, leather-covered, 1809 newspaper liner, 13½" L.........295.00
Document, pine, dvtl, EX old brn pnt, 1780s, 15" L 150.00
Glass, amethyst, Dia Quilt, HP florals, hinged, 3⅝x3x4¾"..........245.00
Glass, amethyst, HP florals, brass rings, hinged, 3⅝" dia.............175.00
Glass, bl w/floral branch & bird, 4 brass claw ft, 6" dia 200.00
Jewel, burl, fancy brass mts, Continental, 1800s, 8½" L..............200.00
Knife, figured mahog veneer w/inlay, Hplwht, 13" L, VG...........650.00
Knife, mahog, dvtl, scrolled edges, divider w/hdl, 9x15"............135.00
Knife, mahog w/inlay Hplwht, shaped front, 1700s, 15½" L........650.00
Knife, pine, old worn red pnt, crack in trn hdl, 8¾x12½" 145.00
Knife, walnut, shaped divider w/cut-out hdl, 9½x13"....................75.00
Pantry, copper tacks, ca 1870s, 3" dia 165.00
Pantry, lapped wood, natural patina, 6½" dia...............................85.00
Pantry, wood, orig red pnt, stenciled name, 11x18", EX..............175.00
Pine, later mc floral, dvtl, 13" L...225.00

Pine, well-shaped crest, lift lid, wall mt, European, 9" L.............150.00
Porc, lovers in woods, sgn, bronze ormolu fr, Fr, 7x8½"................250.00
Shell art, chest of drw w/mirror figural, minor damage, 9" 35.00
Spice, bentwood, w/8 orig canisters w/tin edging, 9" dia..............325.00
Spice, poplar w/old red, simple crest, lift lid, 11x11", EX............200.00
Sterling w/ivorene sphinx finial, Bakelite/inlay bottom, 4" 495.00
Walnut w/cherry & maple inlay, dvtl, no hasp, 14" L, EX..............85.00

Painted and decorated box, Maine, ca 1840, 10" long, $6,000.00.

Bradley and Hubbard

The Bradley and Hubbard Mfg. Company was a firm which produced metal accessories for the home. They operated from about 1860 until the early part of this century, and their products reflected both the Arts and Crafts and Art Nouveau influence. Their logo was a device with a triangular arrangement of the company name containing a smaller triangle and an Aladdin lamp.

Reverse-painted glass and patinated metal table lamp, signed base and shade, 22", $1,045.00.

Clock, Geo WA figural, pnt CI, 17"	1,100.00
Lamp, slag glass 12" 8-sided cone shade; mk base, 18"	575.00
Lamp, slag panel 15½" shade w/filigree band; #1773 std	525.00
Letter opener, brass, sgn	275.00
Mirror, brass easel bk w/openwork & mythological mask, 12"	175.00

Brass

Brass is an alloy consisting essentially of copper and zinc in variable proportions. It is a medium that has been used for both utilitarian items and objects of artistic merit. Today, with the inflated price of copper and the popular use of plastics, almost anything made of brass is collectible. Our advisor, Mary Frank Gaston, has compiled a lovely book, *Antique Brass*, with full-color photos; you will find her address in the Directory under Texas. See also Candlesticks.

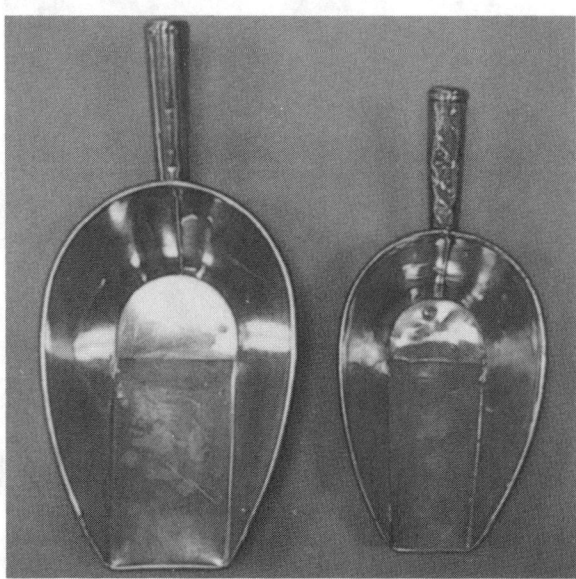

Brass scoops for grain or sugar, marked Patented Dec. 8, 1868, $75.00 and $55.00.

Candle sconce, cast, urn & Minerva head detail, 20", pr	175.00
Compote, satyr scene in center, classical detail, 12" dia	95.00
Doorknob, hand figural w/cross bar, ca 1820, EX	150.00
Grater, pierced, on wrought iron fr, twisted arch hdl, 15x6"	295.00
Kettle, apple butter; forged iron bell hdl, 10½x16"	185.00
Kettle, jam; Am Brass Kettle Co, 11" dia	80.00
Kettle, jam; iron bail hdl, heavy, 10"	90.00
Kettle, jam; spun, mk Hiram W Hayden, pat 1851, 11", NM	125.00
Kettle, wrought iron bail, 7x12", EX	150.00
Ladle, iron hdl, mk FBS Canton O, 13½", EX	75.00
Ladle, ornate wrought iron hdl, eng/copper-filled 1847, 21"	325.00
Ladle, Richard Lee str-line touch mk, 10", NM	650.00
Ladle, wrought iron hdl w/hook end, 13⅜"	150.00
Match box, high hinged lid, 3⅝" H	28.00
Pail, spun, Ansonia Brass Co, minor edge split, 19" dia	175.00
Pail, spun, brass bail, sm dents, 15" dia	125.00
Pail, spun, Hayden's Pat Ansonia Brass Co, 9x13½"	150.00
Propeller, Dyna Jet, 12" dia	25.00
Sconce, 3 candle arms, Rococo style, 18", pr	270.00
Skimmer, str-line touch mk of Richard Lee	675.00
Skimmer, wrought iron hdl, finely made, 11"	150.00
Spatula, wrought iron hdl w/open heart end, sgn Shaak, 15"	275.00
Spit jack, clock work, 14"	30.00
Steam pressure gauge, Ashton Boston, 6" dia	20.00

Stencil, barrel; High Grade...Corn, ca 1875, 8½x11"	65.00
Trammel, sawtoothed w/bird-head ratchet, 18"	95.00

Brastoff, Sascha

The son of immigrant parents, Sascha Brastoff was encouraged to develop his artistic talents to the fullest – encouragement that was well taken, as his achievements aptly attest. Though at various times he has been a dancer, sculptor, Hollywood costume designer, jeweler, and painter, it is his ceramics that are today becoming highly-regarded collectibles.

Brastoff began his career in the United States in the late 1940s. In a beautiful studio built for him by his friend and mentor, Winthrop Rockefeller, he designed innovative wares that even then were among the most expensive on the market. All designing was done personally by Brastoff; he also supervised the staff which at the height of production numbered approximately 150. Wares signed with his full signature were personally crafted by him and are valued much more highly than those signed 'Sascha B.,' indicating work done under his supervision. Sascha Brastoff still resides in Los Angeles, California, at present producing 'Sascha Holograms,' which are distributed by the Hummelwerk Company.

Another medium he used in his work was resin, and such pieces are also very collectible, though extremely scarce. In the listings below, all items are signed 'Sascha B.' unless otherwise indicated (full signature).

Our advisor for this category is Jack Chipman; he is listed in the Directory under California.

Ash tray, ceramic, bird motif on gray, 8x5"	22.00
Ash tray, enamel, amber tones, 6"	25.00

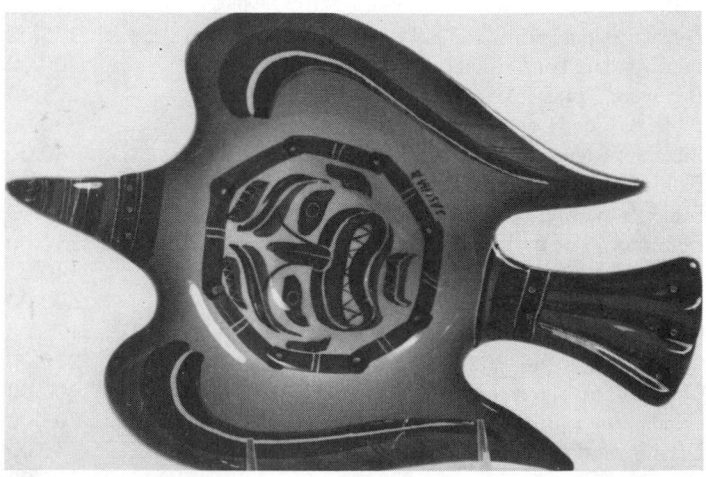

Bird-form tray, mask face in center, signed Sascha B., 11", $65.00.

Bowl, ceramic, yel w/gold, 2x6"	20.00
Figurine, cat, bl translucent resin, 10"	200.00
Figurine, hippopotamus, bl resin, 4½x10"	175.00
Figurine, pelican, bl resin, 10½"	150.00
Pitcher, ceramic, prancing horse on gray, 15½"	125.00
Plaque, enamel, leaves/jewels in rust & orange, 12"	45.00
Plate, ceramic, florals, bl & gray, full signature, 10½"	125.00
Plate, ceramic, poodle sitting up, mc, 11½"	85.00
Plate, ceramic, stylized lion, blk, full signature, 10"	175.00
Table lighter, ceramic, abstract flowers, full signature	38.00
Tile, ceramic, brn, 8x21"	200.00
Vase, ceramic, poodle, sgn Sasha B, 8½x6"	75.00

Brayton, Laguna

Durlin E. Brayton made hand-crafted vases, lamps, and dinnerware in a small kiln at his Laguna Beach, California, home in 1927. He soon married; and, with his wife, Ellen Webster Grieve, as his partner, the small business became a successful commercial venture. They are most famous for their amusing, well-detailed figurines, some of which were commissioned by Walt Disney Studios. Though very successful even through the Depression years, with the influx of imported novelties that deluged the country after WWII, business began to decline. By 1968 the pottery was closed.

Our advisor for this category is Jack Chipman; he is listed in the Directory under California.

Candy jar, Coachman, Disney	125.00
Cookie jar, Red Riding Hood, jar & basket at ft	225.00
Cookie jar, Scandanavian woman, much decor	175.00
Cookie jar, Wolf, yel base	225.00
Figurine, Basset Hound, gold label	30.00
Figurine, cow, purple, 8" L	45.00
Figurine, Dutch girl, 7"	30.00
Figurine, goose, turq, 7"	24.00
Figurine, lady singer, Deco style, 8"	45.00
Figurine, man pushing cart, mc, 6"	60.00
Figurine, peasant woman, w/open baskets, 8"	45.00
Figurine, Sally, flower holder	25.00
Figurine, Seashore Honeymoon, Gay '90s Series	45.00
Figurine, Siamese cat, lg, pr	125.00

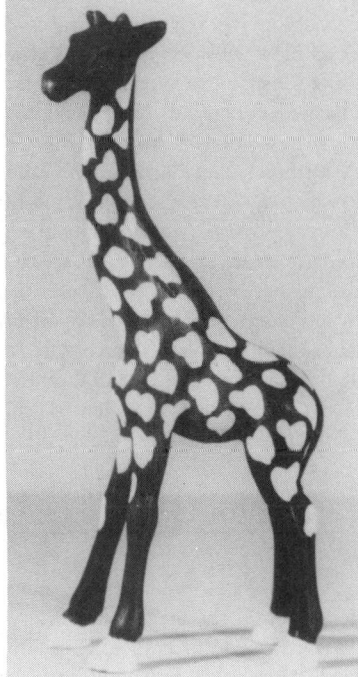

Giraffe, wood-tone bisque with glossy white spots, 8½", $45.00.

Pencil holder, Gingham Dog	45.00
Planter, organ grinder & monkey, 11"	60.00
Planter, peasant woman w/shawl & wicker basket, 11"	60.00

Bread Plates and Trays

Bread plates and trays have been produced not only in many types of glass but in metal and pottery as well. Those considered most col-lectible were made during the last quarter of the nineteenth century from pressed glass with well-detailed embossed designs, many of them portraying a particularly significant historical event. A great number of these plates were sold at the 1876 Philadelphia Centennial Exposition by various glass manufacturers who exhibited their wares on the grounds. Among the themes depicted are the Declaration of Independence, the Constitution, McKinley's memorial 'It Is God's Way,' Remembrance of Three Presidents, the Purchase of Alaska, and various presidential campaigns, to mention only a few.

'L' numbers correspond with a reference book by Lindsey; 'S' refers to a book by Stuart.

Balky Mule	85.00
Beaded Grape, sq	30.00
Beehive, Be Industrious, deer on border	95.00
Bible, Give Us This Day, 10¾x8"	45.00
Bishop, L-201	200.00
Black Builders of Bicentennial, 1776-1976	35.00
BPOE clock in center, Cervus Alces border, clear/frosted	125.00
Bunker Hill, Prescott/1776/Stark, L-44, 13¼x9"	100.00
California Bear, 1894 Expo, L-104	140.00
Classic Warrior, 11"	100.00
Constitution, L-43	45.00
Continental Hall, hand hdls, 12¾" L	75.00
Cupid & Venus, hdls, 10½" dia	45.00
Deer & Pine Tree	48.00
Dewdrop w/Sheaf of Wheat, Give Us This Day, S-7, 11"	25.00
Eagle & Constitution, Give Us This Day	100.00
Eggs In Sand, 12¼x7¾"	45.00
Egyptian, Cleopatra center, 13" L	50.00
Egyptian, Mormon Temple center	325.00
Eureka, w/motto, L-103	45.00
Faith, Hope, & Charity, hdls, 11½"	45.00
Feather Duster	22.00
Frosted Lion, hdls	60.00
Frosted Stork w/101 border, 11½x8"	55.00
GAR, L-505, 11" L	85.00
Garden of Eden, Give Us This Day, 12½x9"	35.00
Garfield Memorial, L-302, 10" L	55.00
Give Us This Day, rosettes in center & border, rnd	65.00
Golden Rule, Do Unto Others	55.00
Heroes of Bunker Hill	70.00
Horseshoe, dbl horseshoe hdls, 13" L	85.00
Horseshoe, single hdls, 13" L	50.00
It Is Pleasant To Labor for Those We Love, hdls, 12½"	55.00
Kayak, 11"	20.00
Knights of Labor, bl, ca 1889	200.00
Knights of Labor, L-513	60.00
Last Supper, goofus	35.00
Lattice, Waste Not Want Not, 11½" L	32.00
Liberty & Freedom, w/eagle, 12" L	75.00
Liberty Bell, John Hancock signature, milk glass, hdls	260.00
Liberty Bell, Signers	85.00
Liberty Bell, 13 Colonies	45.00
Liberty Bell, 200 Yrs, recent	30.00
Lotus & Serpent	45.00
Maple Leaf, vaseline, oval, 13x9½"	45.00
McKinley, His Will Be Done, clear/frosted	48.00
McKinley, It Is God's Way, 10½" L	60.00
Memorial Hall	60.00
Nelly Bly, L-136, 12" L, NM	170.00
Niagara Falls, milk glass, 2 American flags	55.00
Old State House, sapphire bl, L-31, rare	175.00
Oregon	32.00

Prescot Stark	90.00
Railroad w/Engine, L-134, 9x12"	85.00
Retriever, milk glass	80.00
Rock of Ages, milk glass, clear rim, pat dtd, oval	150.00
Ruth the Gleaner, Gillinder	135.00
Scroll w/Flowers, 12" dia	35.00
Star Rosetted, S-71	25.00
Stippled Cherry, Our Daily Bread, 9½"	40.00
Teddy Roosevelt, dancing bears, L-357, 10" L	140.00
Texas Centennial, Alamo center	85.00
Union Pacific RR	80.00
US Grant, Let Us Have Peace, amber, 10½" dia	85.00
Wheat	30.00
Wheat & Barley, milk glass	60.00
Wildflower, sq	28.00
Wm J Bryan, milk glass	39.00
101 w/Implements, Give Us This Day, 10¾x8"	45.00
3 Presidents	130.00

McKinley 'Gold Standard,' 10½", $250.00; Nellie Bly, 11", NM, $170.00.

Bride's Baskets and Bowls

Victorian brides were showered with gifts, as brides have always been; one of the most popular gift items was the bride's basket. Art glass inserts from both European and American glasshouses, some in lovely transparent hues with dainty enameled florals, others of Peachblow, Vasa Murrhina, satin or cased glass were cradled in complementary silverplated holders. While many of these holders were simply engraved or delicately embossed, others such as those from Pairpoint and Wilcox were wonderfully ornate, often with figurals of cherubs or animals. The bride's basket was no longer in fashion after the turn of the century.

Watch for 'marriages' of bowls and frames. To warrant the best price, the two pieces should be the original pairing. If you can't be certain of this, at least check to see that the bowl fits snugly into the frame. Beware of later-made bowls (such as Fenton's) in Victorian holders.

In the listings that follow, if no frame is described, the price is for a bowl only.

Apricot w/gold edge, gold/red/bl motif, ruffled; SP fr, 10", M	875.00
Cranberry shaded, appl rim; ped base, sgn, fair SP, 8"	125.00
Cranberry to mauve overlay, HP decor, Rococo, 11½"	115.00
Gr shaded overlay, HP florals, 16 scallops, 11¼"	95.00

Gold coralene on bright blue; Wilcox silver-plated frame, #5599, 12", M, $1,200.00.

Hobnail, pk satin, floral int, scalloped; Poole fr, 12"	175.00
Hobnail, pk satin w/bl edge, Mt WA; rstr SP fr, 14"	550.00
Invt T'print, amberina, scalloped, NE; ornate fr, 8"	595.00
MOP Dia Quilt, bl, darker int, appl/crimped edge, sq, 10"	300.00
MOP Herringbone, pk w/gold floral, lime int; gold-tone fr	1,350.00
Nile gr opal, HP decor, melon ribbed, ruffled, 11"	100.00
Peach to bl to yel opaque, HP decor, crimped, 8"	70.00
Peachblow satin Dia Quilt w/roses; Barbour Bros fr, 8x11"	700.00
Peachblow w/fish & dragonflies, flowers, Webb; fr, 8"	575.00
Pk & yel spatter overlay, clear thorn hdl, 5⅝x5⅛"	150.00
Pk cased, gold floral, Webb; Middletown fr w/apples on hdls	1,050.00
Pk satin w/florals & leaves, ruffled, 2½x10"	225.00
Pk satin/yel ext w/decor & gilt; Wilcox fr w/6" cherubs, EX	1,800.00
Pk shaded w/florals, scalloped; tall Meriden fr w/6" figural	350.00
Pk w/wht overlay, amber crimped edge; ornate Wilcox fr, EX	250.00
Red to custard overlay, beads, clear rim, 10"	75.00
Robin's egg bl shaded, portrait, clear ruffled rim, 12¼"	200.00
Rose shaded satin, crimped edge; mini 5" Pairpoint fr	165.00
Rubena, HP florals & dots; ornate Meriden fr, 12½"	495.00
Teal-bl satin w/coralene floral & insect; ornate fr, 10"	200.00
Wht satin w/pk int, box-pleated top; compote ft w/peacocks	395.00
Wht w/gold rim, florals, Webb; SP fr, 12" dia	185.00

Bristol Glass

Bristol is a type of semi-opaque opaline glass whose name was derived from the area in England where it was first produced. Similar glass was made in France, Germany, and Italy. In this country, it was made by the New England Glass Company and to a lesser extent by its contemporaries. During the eighteenth and nineteenth centuries, Bristol glass was imported in large amounts and sold cheaply, thereby contributing to the demise of the earlier glasshouses here in America. It is very difficult to distinguish the English Bristol from other opaline types. Style, design, and decoration serve as clues to its origin; but often only those well versed in the field can spot these subtle variations.

Biscuit jar, pk overlay, mc florals, SP rim/lid/hdl, 6½"	145.00
Biscuit jar, wht, brn leaves/wht flowers, self lid, 6½"	150.00
Bottle, scent; bl, gold bands, bl stopper, 7½"	85.00

Bottle, scent; bl, mc florals w/gold, bl stopper, 6½" **95.00**
Bottle, scent; bl, mc florals w/gold panels, 3¾x1½" **85.00**
Bottle, scent; gr, gold Roman Key decor, gr ball stopper, 6" **88.00**
Bottle, scent; wht, bl bow & ornate gold trim, 7½" **125.00**
Bowl, lt bl, cupid plays mandolin, gold trim **32.00**
Box, bl, mc florals, gold bands, 2x2¼" dia **85.00**
Box, pk, mc florals, ormolu trim w/rings, ball ft, 5x5¼" **375.00**
Box, turq w/gold bands & florals, wht dots, 2x2¼" **85.00**
Jar, powder; ivory, mc pansies, bl rim, hinged lid **62.00**
Lamp, beige, florals on ball form, brass hardware, mini **60.00**
Lustre, pk overlay, mc florals w/gold, prisms, 15⅝x6¼", pr **850.00**
Mug, wht, eagle/'Liberty,' 5", VG **375.00**
Salt cellar, gray, mc florals, scuttle form, 2½x3⅛" **50.00**
Vase, aqua, birds/flowers, flat-sided, 13½", pr...................**525.00**
Vase, bl, wht flowers/beading; in SP Webster holder, 15" **225.00**
Vase, cream, pk & gold fuchsias, ftd, 12⅛x3" **95.00**
Vase, custard, mc florals, aqua & gold flower prunt, 7¼" **60.00**
Vase, flowers overall, goat's head hdls, ruffled top, 8½"...........**60.00**
Vase, pk, boy & girl w/lamb on gold, ornate urn form, 18" **550.00**
Vase, pk, butterflies/flowers, 8", pr **150.00**
Vase, pk, florals, trumpet form, in ormolu holder, 10", pr **200.00**
Vase, tan, coralene florals/butterflies, gold trim, 11", pr...............**300.00**
Vase, turq, gold bands, yel florals, wht dots, 5⅛x2½" **65.00**
Vase, wht, mums, brn/tan w/olive leaves, 10", pr **100.00**

Vase, coralene flowers on pink, 11", $75.00.

British Royalty Commemoratives

While most modern-day commemorative collectors start their collections with souvenirs issued during Queen Victoria's reign, interest in royal commemorative collecting has been evident for centuries. A commemorative medal was issued for Edward VI's 1547 coronation. Ceramics are the most popular type of commemoratives. Food tins are gaining in popularity – so are glass, paper, and metal souvenirs. Since commemoratives have always been a commercial endeavor, nearly any item with room for a portrait and an inscription has been manufactured as a souvenir; thus a wide variety is available in all price ranges. Since royal events are an ongoing state of affairs, it is possible to choose almost any time in British history as a commemorative starting point. Even present-day souvenirs make a good, inexpensive beginning collection. Today's events will be tomorrow's history!

For further study we recommend *British Royal Commemoratives*, by

our advisor for this category, Audrey Zeder; she is listed in the Directory under California.

Key:
anniv — anniversary	Jub — Jubilee
chr — christening	LE — limited edition
com — commemorative	mem — memorial
cor — coronation	wed — wedding

Beaker, Edward VII 1902 King's Dinner, Doulton/Song Sheet.....**100.00**
Beaker, Edward VIII cor, pk w/wht portrait relief, Johnson **40.00**
Beaker, Victoria 1897 Jub, cobalt, stoneware, Doulton **190.00**
Beaker, Victoria 1897 Jub, enamel w/color portrait & decor........**125.00**
Bust, Charles/Diana, wht china, 5", pr.................................**95.00**
Bust, Edward VII/Alexandra, parian, pr...............................**250.00**
Bust, Edward VIII, soapstone, 4½" **75.00**
Bust, Elizabeth, creamware, 5"...**75.00**
Cup & saucer, Charles/Diana wed, portraits w/St Paul's.............**30.00**
Cup & saucer, Edward VII cor, sepia transfer/portrait on wht......**150.00**
Cup & saucer, Elizabeth cor, sepia portrait w/children **150.00**
Cup & saucer, George V cor, mc portrait on wht, Doulton..........**100.00**
Cup & saucer, George VI Canada/US visit, ornate design **50.00**
Cup & saucer, Princess Elizabeth/Margaret, miniature...................**40.00**
Cup & saucer, Victoria 1897 Jub, brn transfer on wht **150.00**
Ephemera, Andrew/Sara wedding booklet **5.00**
Ephemera, Charles/Diana booklet.......................................**5.00**
Ephemera, Charles/Diana paperdolls, M **5.00**
Ephemera, Charles/Diana wed, matchbook, unused **2.00**
Ephemera, Edward VII cor, NY Times, Aug 10, 1902..................**50.00**
Ephemera, Elizabeth, 1977 Jub calendar, unused **20.00**
Ephemera, George V Official Jub program.............................**25.00**
Ephemera, George VI 1923 wed, Illus London News **30.00**
Ephemera, Princess Mary 1922 marriage, Illus London News **35.00**
Ephemera, Victoria 1901, Illus London News Record No...........**125.00**
Ephemera, Victoria 1901, The Graphic.................................**50.00**
Figural, Victoria & Prince of Wales, Staffordshire, 18"............ **1,200.00**
Figural, William IV bust, 1831, by Sam Parker, 5¾" **425.00**
Loving cup, Charles/Diana wed, enamel decor, Paragon, 5½".........**75.00**
Loving cup, Edward VII mem, HP, LE-100, Copeland, 7" **1,100.00**
Loving cup, Elizabeth cor, relief decor, Doulton, 10½" **900.00**
Loving cup, Elizabeth 60th birthday, Trooping colors, 3½" **40.00**
Loving cup, George VI cor, relief decor, Doulton, 10½" **1,000.00**
Loving cup, Victoria 1887 Jub, blk transfer on wht, 8x5" **525.00**
Medal, Victoria 1837 visit to London, portrait, 2⅜" **100.00**
Medal, Victoria 1897 Jub, brass, relief portrait & inscribed **25.00**
Medal, Victoria/Albert 1851, portraits, Crystal Palace, 2" **75.00**
Miniature, Charles/Diana tea set, mc portrait, 7-pc **55.00**
Miniature, Charles/Diana teapot, mc portrait, 2" **20.00**
Miniature, Charles/Diana wed, photo album w/pictures, 1½x1" **18.00**
Miniature, Charles/Diana/Wm/Henry tea set, mc portrait, 7-pc....**55.00**
Miniature, Elizabeth basket, mc portrait/relief decor, 2½" **20.00**
Miniature, Elizabeth/Philip tea set, mc portrait, 7-pc.....................**55.00**
Miniature, Princess Elizabeth/Margaret plate, lustre, 3¼" **30.00**
Mug, Charles/Diana wed, enamel design, Hammersley **30.00**
Mug, Charles/Diana wed, engagement portrait.............................**30.00**
Mug, Charles/Diana 650th Duke of Cornwall anniv **65.00**
Mug, Diana's 21st birthday **40.00**
Mug, Edward VII cor, correct Aug date, mc transfer, Doulton **225.00**
Mug, Edward VII cor, portrait relief on yel stipple, 4¾" **60.00**
Mug, Elizabeth cor, mc transfer, crown-shape hdl....................**45.00**
Mug, Elizabeth cor, mc transfer, official design **30.00**
Mug, George V cor, mc King/Queen portrait, gold hdl...................**90.00**
Mug, George V 1893 marriage, sepia transfer, Doulton...............**200.00**

Mug, George VI cor, official design, British Pottery Mfg...............45.00
Mug, Prince Henry christening, family portrait 25.00
Mug, Prince William christening, mc family portrait 40.00
Mug, Princess Beatrice birth, wht w/gold, LE-2000, Wedgwood....60.00
Mug, Victoria 1897 Jub, blk transfer, inscription 175.00
Novelty, Charles/Diana, 'Splitting Image' slippers, M 35.00
Novelty, Charles/Diana, pendant, mc portrait, China.................10.00
Novelty, Charles/Diana, potpourri, mc portrait, hanging..............20.00
Novelty, Charles/Diana, potpourri holder/brewer, china.................25.00
Novelty, Charles/Diana, purse mirror w/felt holder, 3".................20.00
Novelty, Charles/Diana, ring holder, mc portrait, china 20.00
Novelty, Charles/Diana, tree ornament, mc portrait, china 20.00
Novelty, Charles/Diana, watch, portrait face, quartz 60.00
Novelty, Charles/Diana wed, audio 33⅓ post card 10.00
Novelty, Charles/Diana wed, coaster, leather, set of 6 .... 5.00
Novelty, Charles/Diana wed, Coca-Cola bottle, unopened............75.00
Novelty, Charles/Diana wed, irid decal, 5½x5" 5.00
Novelty, Charles/Diana wed, pin-bk 5.00
Novelty, Charles/Diana/William/Henry, baby shoe, mc portrait....25.00
Novelty, Charles/Diana/William/Henry, spoon, SP, mc portrait 10.00
Novelty, Edward VII cor, pin-bk, mc portrait/design 25.00
Novelty, Edward VIII cor, Deco-style pin w/photograph, 2" 25.00
Novelty, Elizabeth cor, hatpin w/red/wht/bl braid, 5½" 25.00
Novelty, Elizabeth cor, knife, 2-blade, mc transfer, 3" 25.00
Novelty, Elizabeth Jub, charm, sterling w/relief portrait 20.00
Novelty, Elizabeth Jub, playing cards, sealed, M 20.00
Novelty, George V cor, compact, mc portrait on blk......................40.00
Novelty, George V cor, tray, mc portrait/design, 11½" 225.00
Novelty, George VI cor, box, rnd, plastic, relief portrait 35.00
Novelty, George VI visit to US, spoon, SP 25.00
Novelty, Princess Diana, spoon, SP, mc portrait 10.00
Novelty, Princess Diana, watch w/portrait face, quartz.................60.00
Novelty, Princess Diana, 10-pack notepaper w/portrait 20.00
Novelty, Victora pendant w/photograph, ¾" 50.00
Novelty, Victoria 1887 wooden box w/appl portrait 85.00
Pitcher, Edward VII cor, mc portrait & decor, 5½".......................125.00
Pitcher, Edward VIII cor, Deco style w/maize portrait, 6½" 75.00
Pitcher, George V cor, mc portrait in military attire, 8" 195.00
Pitcher, Victoria 1897 Jub, full-length mc portrait, 8½" 295.00
Pitcher, Victoria 1897 Jub, gr w/portrait, Copeland-Spode 290.00
Plate, Andrew/Sarah wed, portrait in wedding clothes, 8¼" 50.00

**Plate, George V Coronation, Royal Doulton, 10½",
$225.00.**

Plate, Charles/Diana, portrait, she in pk/he in red coat, 8" 30.00
Plate, Charles/Diana wed, enamel portrait, Wedgwood, 10" 75.00
Plate, Charles/Diana wed, mc portrait, china, Coalport, 10" ...150.00
Plate, Elizabeth Australian bi-centenary LE-500, 10½".................85.00
Plate, Elizabeth Canada visit, portraits, 22k gold trim, 10" 85.00
Plate, Elizabeth w/husband & young children, 4½" 50.00
Plate, Geo V cor, mc portraits, ribbon edge 145.00
Plate, George VI Canada visit, portraits, relief rim, 10" 95.00
Plate, George VI cor, sepia protrait, mc design, sq......................30.00
Plate, Prince Henry birth, parents & baby portrait, 10½" 35.00
Plate, Prince Henry chr, Eliz/Chas/Diana/Wm/Henry portrait.......35.00
Plate, Victoria, relief portrait, ribbon edge, milk glass 100.00
Plate, Victoria 1840-1850, emb head & design, clear, 3½" 190.00
Plate, Victoria 1887 Jub, mc portrait & design, 9" 195.00
Plate, Victoria 1897 Jub, gr transfer, made for Harrods 150.00
Post card, Charles/Diana Australian royal tour, portraits/map 4.00
Post card, Charles/Diana honeymoon, portraits/route plans 4.00
Post card, Charles/Diana wed, distributed by London Zoo 4.00
Post card, Charles/Diana wed, LE... 4.00
Post card, Charles/Diana wed, peel-off pictures, M....................... 4.00
Post card, Charles/Diana wed, set of 60, M...............................40.00
Post card, Charles/Diana wed, wedding clothes, mc 3.00
Post card, Charles/Diana 1987 German trip 6.00
Post card, Edward VII mem, blk portrait & border, M..................15.00
Post card, Edward VII w/ruling monarchs of the time 25.00
Post card, Elizabeth China visit, set of 5 w/China stamps 35.00
Post card, Elizabeth w/President Reagan riding horseback 4.00
Post card, George V cor, blk/wht, ornate, Tuck, M 10.00
Post card, George V cor, Durbar Delhi, blk/wht, M 10.00
Post card, George V cor, mc portrait w/crown & ermine robe........20.00
Post card, George V w/future Edward VIII, blk/wht 15.00
Post card, George VI cor, King in cor robe w/family.....................15.00
Post card, George VI w/Queen & Princess Elizabeth, blk/wht 10.00
Post card, Princess Beatrice birth, LE...................................... 4.00
Post card, Princess Diana 21st birthday, LE............................... 6.00
Post card, Princess Elizabeth & Princess Margaret 10.00
Post card, Princess Elizabeth/Philip betrothal, blk/wht, M...........15.00
Post card, Princess Mary wed, M 10.00
Post card, Queen Elizabeth w/children, blk/wht 10.00
Post card, Queen Mother 85th birthday, LE, M 4.00
Post card, Queen Mother 87th birthday, M 3.00
Post card, Victoria 1901 mem, blk portrait/border, M 30.00
Teabag holder, Charles/Diana, mc portrait, teapot shape 20.00
Teapot, Charles/Diana, mc portrait, china, 2-cup, 6" 45.00
Teapot, Elizabeth cor, relief decor, aluminum/blk hdl, 1-cup..........25.00
Teapot, George V Jub, mc portrait on creamware, 4-cup 100.00
Tin, Charles/Diana, mc portraits on royal bl, octagonal 30.00
Tin, Charles/Diana wed, engagement portrait, w/30 tea bags.........25.00
Tin, Charles/Diana wed, mc portraits w/St Paul's, 2x9" dia...........30.00
Tin, Edward VI, 3 generations shown, octagonal, 7x7x7" 165.00
Tin, Elizabeth cor, mc portrait, Huntley-Palmers, 1¼x5" dia.........25.00
Tin, Elizabeth cor, mc portrait, octagonal, hinged 35.00
Tin, Elizabeth cor, mc portrait on bl, hinged, 3x5" 30.00
Tin, Elizabeth Jub, mc portrait, flat, ¾x7x3".............................15.00
Tin, George V, King & 3 future monarchs, hinged 100.00
Tin, George V Jub, watercolor-like portraits, hinged.....................40.00
Tin, George VI cor, mc portrait on gold tone, hinged 35.00
Tin, Prince of Wales (future Edward VIII) Oct 1929 exhibition ...50.00
Tin, Prince Philip in Naval uniform, ships on sides......................30.00
Tin, Prince William birth, unopened tea tin, hinged......................30.00
Tin, Princess Mary wed, mc portraits, hinged 60.00
Tin, Victoria, 1900 South Africa war gift for troops......................90.00
Toby mug, Queen Mary, mc, EX detail 225.00

Broadsides

Webster defines a broadside as simply a large sheet of paper printed on one side. During the 1880s, they were the most practical means of mass-communication. By the middle of the century they had become elaborate and lengthy with information, illustrations, portraits, and fancy border designs.

Champions of Freedom, Greely/Sumner/Seward/Whitter, 14x10"..**150.00**
Columbian Tragedy: Bloody Indian Battle, 1791, 61x22", VG ...**900.00**
Declaration of Independence, vellum, Stone, 1823, 35x29" ..**17,000.00**
Draft...Bounty to Volunteers $285.00, PA, 1862, 24x18", EX **280.00**
Epistles from G Fox's Collection..., ca 1715, sm folio, EX............**300.00**
Estate sale of slaves, 18 listed by name/age, 1858, 10x8" **600.00**
Great...Speech of Hon AH Stephens, VP Confederacy, 19x11"..**120.00**
Jackson Ticket, 3-column text/portraits, 1828, 22x15", EX **2,000.00**
John Jay for Gov of NY, 2 columns of text, 1795, 17x11", EX.....**220.00**
Maungwudas...Indians, lecture on manners, etc, 1849, 18x8"........**80.00**
Notice Wheelmen, bicycling rules, cloth, 1870s, 20x15"............**550.00**
Olympic Circus, lists acts, linen, Jan 1816, 20x6", VG...............**140.00**
Parliamentary summons, Oliver Cromwell, London, 1651, EX ...**200.00**
Programme of Exercises..., Ohio church, 1871, 8½x5½".................**10.00**
Runaway, $100 reward for Negro man, MD, 1853, 10x12", EX ...**350.00**
Runaway, $50 Reward, Negro Woman, MD, 1854, 15x12"..........**450.00**
Victory, Clear Track...Springfield, Whig news, 1840, 18x12"......**350.00**
Volunteers Wanted, fine graphics, IL, Feb 1864, 16x12", EX......**600.00**
Willard Elmer Shoes, woodcut of shoes, IL, 1847, 24x18½" **280.00**
WW Gavitt's Medical System Regulator, 1880s, 15x5½", VG.......**15.00**

Civil War Naval Broadside, General Order, Navy Dept., Dec. 23, 1861, 44" x 30", EX, $4,200.00.

Bronzes

Thomas Ball, George Bessell, and Leonard Volk were some of the earliest American sculptors who produced figures in bronze for home decor during the 1840s. Pieces of historical significance were the most popular, but by the 1880s a more fanciful type of artwork took hold. Some of the fine sculptors of the day were Daniel Chester French, Augustus St. Gaudens, and John Quincy Adams Ward. Bronzes reached the height of their popularity at the turn of the century. The American West was portrayed to its fullest by Remington, Russell, James Frazier, Hermon MacNeil, and Solon Borglum. Animals of every species were modeled by A.P. Proctor, Paul Bartlett, and Albert Laellele, to name but a few.

Art Nouveau and Art Deco influenced the medium during the twenties, evidenced by the works of Allen Clark, Harriet Frishmuth, E.F. Sanford, and Bessie P. Vonnoh.

Be aware that recasts abound. While often esthetically satisfactory, they are not original and should be priced accordingly. In much the same manner as prints are evaluated, the original castings made under the direction of the artist are the most valuable. Later castings from the original mold are worth less. A recast is not made from the original mold. Instead, a rubber-like substance is applied to the bronze, peeled away, and filled with wax. Then, using the same 'lost wax' procedure as the artist uses on completion of his original wax model, a clay-like substance is formed around the wax figure and the whole fired to vitrify the clay. The wax, of course, melts away – hence the term 'lost wax.' Recast bronzes lose detail and are somewhat smaller than the original due to the shrinkage of the clay mold.

Isidore-Jules Bonheur (1827-1902), tiger on marble base, 16", $1,000.00.

Alonzo, D; Lecture, lady on wht onyx stair w/book, 13".......... **1,000.00**
Austrian, table lamp, palm w/camel & Arab, 1900, unmk, 14" ...**550.00**
Barthelemy, L; Dutch girl, ivory limbs, gilded, 9" **450.00**
Becquerel, Andre-Vincent; 2 lovebirds, silvered, 13" **500.00**
Becquerel, pr of lions, gr patina, blk stone base, 16" L............. **1,400.00**
Botello, young girl's head, sgn/#9, 12½".......................................**300.00**
Bouraine, Marcel; woman w/coffer, X-legged on tall ped, 16" . **1,200.00**
Bouvral, Maurice; semi-nude holds drape to form basket, 11". **1,500.00**
Brault, javelin thrower, after Antique, marble base, 20" **550.00**
Bureau, Leon; pheasant, on rockwork base, gilt, 22" **900.00**
Canova (after), draped cherub, rockwork base, 9", pr **495.00**
Chiparus, Foile de Printemps, harem dancer, gilt/mc, 13" **2,400.00**
Chiparus, Vedette, dancer w/arms extended, onyx base, 20" .. **4,100.00**
Cognel (after), bust of lady in feather hat, on plinth, 11"............**300.00**
Colinet, CJR; nude, arms outstretched, marble base, 13".............**550.00**
Colombier, Amelie; Carmencita dancing flamenco, 22", EX .. **1,500.00**
Daen, Lindsay; Girl Skipping Rope No VI, 29"............................**400.00**
David, Fernand; seated nude holds garland overhead, 21"....... **1,800.00**
Dejean, Louis; lady, flaring cape/wide-brim hat, 13" **495.00**

Descomps, Jean-Bernard; elegant Victorian lady, 1904, 25" ... **1,200.00**

Descomps, Joe; maid in fancy dress holds feather fan, 28" **4,000.00**

Drouot, E; Indian warrior, semi-prone, w/bow, 20" L..................**800.00**

Eriksen, Edvard; Little Mermaid, sits on rock, 9" **1,400.00**

Erte, An Evening in 1922, RKP Int Corp, 1980, 17" **2,800.00**

Erte, Autumn, nude stands on leaf, Fine Arts, 15" **2,300.00**

Erte, L'Amour, chained to red heart on her chest, 21" **2,800.00**

Fayral, Deco nude holds scarf & mirrored tambourine, 23" **1,200.00**

Fournier, Paul; Shakespeare holds book, sq base, 21" **600.00**

French, Venus, standing near column, 1880s, 20" **700.00**

Gallo, I; woman in short toga runs w/greyhound, 19" **1,200.00**

Gardent, George; 2 long-tailed birds on tree branch, 9¾" **1,000.00**

Gautherin, Jean; mother holds infant, title plaque, 27" **1,000.00**

Gilbert, Andre; 2 maids hold hands/dance, on onyx base, 18".. **3,800.00**

Gillemin (after), Early Explorers, silvered, 9", pr.......................**550.00**

Gladenbeck, Oscar; nude boy fishing, gold/brn patina, 6¾" **495.00**

Gladenbeck, Oscar; peasant traveler w/cane, waving, 10½" **300.00**

Gregory (after), Apollo embraces Diana, dk brn patina, 20" ... **1,400.00**

Guiraud-Riviere, Foemina, smiling nude, 16" **2,200.00**

Guiraud-Riviere, 2 nude men strain to pull rope, 36" L..........**15,000.00**

Herbert, Emile; Thetis dons her armor, ft on helmet, 15" **495.00**

Jacquement, Henri Alfred-Marie; egret w/frog in beak, 12" **385.00**

Joerning, L; 2 cherubs walk hand in hand, marble base, 9" **350.00**

Jonchery, Charles; Carmen, hand on hip/2nd to shoulder, 13" **465.00**

Kinsburger, Sylvain; woman w/fur muff bends forward, 27" **1,800.00**

Korschann, Charles; bust: Nouveau maid, foliate ped, 7" **465.00**

Koster, E; nude dancer leans left, left leg raised, 18"....................**500.00**

Kowalizewski, PL; Dutch boy stand on rock, marble base, 12".....**300.00**

Kuba, Carl; Die Fromme Helene, girl, hands on hips, 6".............**200.00**

Lambeaux, Jef; bust: Nouveau maid, self-ped base, 24" **400.00**

Le Faguays, Pierre; Diana lifts bow, gr patina, 27" **1,500.00**

Le Faguays, Pierre; nude, tiptoe, dove in raised hand, 31" **3,000.00**

Ledru, Eve; plate, despairing nude/thistles, 13½", pr **550.00**

Leisek, Georg; lady in riding habit w/dog, marble ped, 27"...... **3,000.00**

Leonard, Agathon (after); Batwoman, gilded, 13" **3,300.00**

Liebermann, F; nude riding ostrich, 24" L **3,600.00**

Linder, Henry; Little Queen, sits on high platform, 13" **1,200.00**

Lorenzl, dancer, bat-wing sleeves, 11"......................................**385.00**

Lorenzl, female jester, arms akimbo, mc, onyx base, 13" **1,320.00**

Lorenzl, semi-nude in feathered headdress, head bk, 14½" **450.00**

Lorenzl, woman kneels, w/lg alabaster bowl, gr patina, 8½" **500.00**

Lormier, J; woman in short dress runs w/2 whippets, 32" L **2,000.00**

Mane-Katz, bass player, blk patina, sgn/#d, 11½"..................... **1,900.00**

Marin (after), bust of maid, upswept hair, on ped, 18" **495.00**

Masse, C; dueling gentleman, 13", pr **1,500.00**

Mazura, group of sparrows, stepped ped, 1920, 8½" **700.00**

Moigniez, Jules; 2 sheep, brn patina, self base, 12" L................ **1,000.00**

Moreau, Mathurian; Venus w/hand mirror by pedestal, 19" **1,000.00**

Perelmagne, Vladimir; lady in slim gown/fluffy stole, 20" **900.00**

Perl, Karl; Loie Fuller, skirts swirling, gr patina, 13" **1,300.00**

Peyre, Raphael; vase, 2 nudes play about irises, 18" **3,500.00**

Philippe, Paul (att); yawning nude, gilt, marble base, 18"............**600.00**

Philippe, Russina Dancer, blk stone socle, sgn, 23".................. **2,400.00**

Poertzel, Otto; turbanned African child sells flowers, 12"...........**800.00**

Pompon, Francois; walking panther, blk patina, 6x19" **8,000.00**

Preiss, Ferdinand; girl en pointe, gold/gr tutu, 7" **1,200.00**

Rosse, F; winged nymph amidst poppies, blk stone socle, 16" **500.00**

Sandoz, EM; bunny, 1 ear up, Susse Fres Edts Paris, 2½" **600.00**

Schmidt-Felling, warrior on horse extends arm bk, 20" **900.00**

Schott, Walter; Joueuse De Boules, nude w/ball, 17" **1,200.00**

Somme, dancer, dragonfly at feet, ivory face/arms, 14" **1,800.00**

Stotenberg, Hans; vase of Loie Fuller, 6" **1,400.00**

Terescuk, boy/girl kiss by screen, 2nd girl spies, 7" **600.00**

Terescuk, girl in long dress w/parasol, ivory face, 6" **550.00**

Villanis, Emmanuel; bust: Nouveau maid, ped base, 11" **260.00**

Villanis, Emmanuel; Favorite, bust of lady in tiara, 22"........... **1,200.00**

Volti, Antoniucci; reclining nude, brn patina, 10" L............... **7,000.00**

Zach, Bruno; dancer, skirts to side, head bk, Austria, 6½" **385.00**

Zach, Bruno; female fencer, semi-nude, marble base, 29".......**14,000.00**

Zach, Bruno; girl w/cigarette in leather suit, 28" **800.00**

Zelikson, Serge; man w/broken wrist shackles kneels, 24" L **700.00**

Brownies by Palmer Cox

Created by Palmer Cox in 1883, the Brownies charmed children through the pages of books and magazines, as dolls on their dinnerware, in advertising material, and on souvenirs. Each had his own personality – among them The Bellhop, The London Bobby, The Chairman, and Uncle Sam. But the oversized, triangular face with the startled expression, the protruding tummy, and the spindlelegs were characteristics of them all. They were inspired by the Scottish legends related to Cox as a child by his parents, who were of English descent. His introduction of the Brownies to the world was accomplished by a poem called *The Brownies Ride*. Books followed in rapid succession – thirteen in the series, all written as well as illustrated by Palmer Cox.

By the late 1890s, the Brownies were active in advertising. They promoted such products as games, coffee, toys, patent medicines, and rubber boots. 'Greenies' were the Brownies' first cousins, created by Cox to charm and to woo through the pages of the advertising almanacs of the G.G. Green Company of New Jersey. Perhaps the best-known endorsement in the Brownies' career was for the Kodak Brownie, which became so popular and sold in such volume that their name became synonymous with this type of camera.

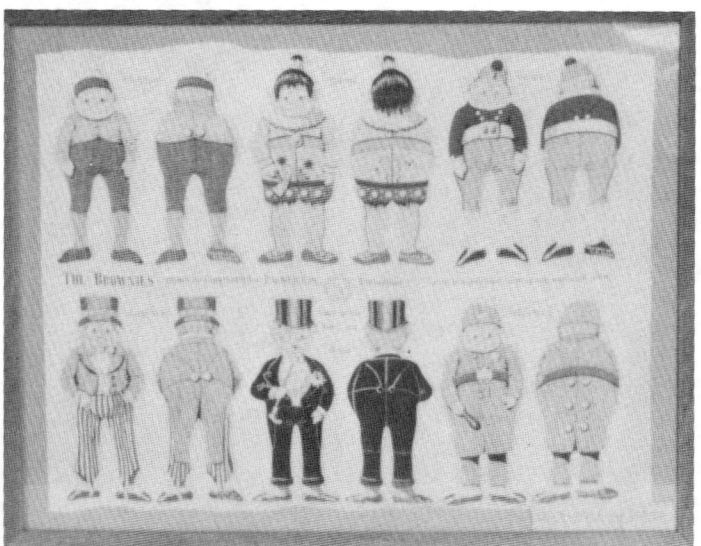

Uncut sheet of Brownie dolls, Arnold Print Works, copyright January 15, 1892, 18" x 24", $500.00.

Basket, SP, Brownies w/chocolate advertising, Tufts **140.00**

Book, Brownies, Other Stories, Cox illus, Donohue, undtd, EX ...**45.00**

Book, Brownies Around the World, DeBinne Press, NY, 1894......**75.00**

Book, Brownies' Kind Deed, WB Conkey, Chicago, 1903, VG **25.00**

Book, Monkey Jack, Cox illus, 1902 ....**25.00**

Book, Palmer Cox Brownie Primer, c 1909 & 1933, G **50.00**

Book, Queer People, Palmer Cox, 1894, EX.............................**45.00**

Book, The Brownies, Their Book, 1897, EX..............................**175.00**

Box, Log Cabin Brownies, cabin form, Nat'l Biscuit Co, '20s......**125.00**

Brownie Portrait Cubes, McLoughlin Bros, c Palmer Cox 1892 ..300.00
Cup & saucer, china 50.00
Game, Brownie Horseshoes, early, complete in box 50.00
Game, Jump-Up, EX in box........................50.00
Ice cream sandwich bag, Brownies, 5¢, 1920s, EX 15.00
Match holder, Brownie on striker, majolica 155.00
Paper doll, w/Lion Coffee advertising on bk 15.00
Paperweight, Brownie figural, SP 110.00
Pin tray, Brownie figural, SP, Pairpoint 125.00
Sheet music, Dance of the Brownies 25.00
Stamps, wood & rubber, orig pad & box, set of 6........................25.00
Tin container, Brownie Ointment, 1924, MIB 40.00

Brush

George Brush began his career in the pottery industry in 1901 working for the J.B. Owens Pottery Co. in Zanesville, Ohio. He left the company in 1907 to go into business for himself, only to have fire completely destroy his pottery less than one year after it was founded. Brush became associated with J.W. McCoy in 1909 and for many years served in capacities ranging from General Manager to President. (From 1911 until 1925, the firm was known as The Brush-McCoy Pottery Co.; see that section for information.) After McCoy died, the family withdrew their interests, and in 1925 the name of the firm was changed to The Brush Pottery. The era of hand-decorated art pottery had passed for the most part and would soon be completely replaced by the production of commercial lines. Of all the wares bearing the later Brush script mark, their figural cookie jars are the most collectible. See also Brush-McCoy.

Cookie Jars

Antique Touring Car 95.00
Boy w/Balloons 110.00
Chick in Nest 85.00
Cinderella Pumpkin 95.00
Circus Horse 110.00
Clown, yel pants 95.00
Clown Head........................95.00
Cookie House........................55.00
Covered Wagon 150.00
Cow, w/cat on bk, brn 65.00
Cow, w/cat on bk, purple 300.00
Davy Crockett 95.00
Dog w/Basket 85.00
Donkey & Cart 110.00
Elephant, w/monkey on bk........................200.00
Elephant w/Baby Bonnet 125.00
Fish........................95.00
Formal Pig 75.00
Granny 75.00
Hen on Basket 65.00
Hill Billy Frog 250.00
Hobby Horse........................110.00
Humpty Dumpty, w/beanie & bow tie 95.00
Humpty Dumpty, w/peaked hat........................85.00
Lantern, brn/cream, mk K1 ....55.00
Laughing Hippo 85.00
Little Angel 125.00
Little Boy Blue 95.00
Little Girl........................95.00
Little Red Riding Hood, basket in arm, mk K24 ....95.00
Nite Owl........................65.00

Old Clock 65.00
Old Shoe 65.00
Panda 85.00
Peter Pan 125.00
Peter Peter Pumpkin Eater, boy/girl/pumpkin, mk W24................75.00
Puppy Police 95.00
Raggedy Ann 85.00
Sitting Hippo 75.00
Sitting Pig 65.00
Smiling Bear 85.00
Squirrel in Top Hat........................65.00
Squirrel on Log 45.00
Stylized Owl........................65.00
Stylized Siamese........................75.00
Teddy Bear, feet apart 65.00
Teddy Bear, feet together 55.00
Treasure Chest 75.00

Miscellaneous

Bowl, console; Princess, 13" L 9.00
Bowl, Majolica, Amaryllis mold, 7½" 45.00
Bowl, Pastel Ware, Amaryllis mold, 6" 22.00
Clock, Jugtime, Onyx, brn, 7" 85.00
Clock, Lux Sweetheart, pendulum........................95.00
Hanging basket, Stardust, flying saucer form, 1957 ....45.00
Jardiniere, Majolica, Amaryllis mold, #252, 8" H........................80.00
Jug, Pastel Kitchen Ware, pk tulip on lt gr, w/lid, 5" 20.00
Lamp, Wise Birds, owl figural, 8" 150.00
Planter, train engine, airbrushed lt gr/yel/brn, 1956 ....15.00
Planter, turtle form, gr/blk on wht, late, 7" 12.00
Spooner, lady's face in flower-petal surround, 1950s........................12.50
Vase, lt bl, ovoid, 1940s, miniature 8.00
Vase, Onyx, brn, slim w/str sides, #041, 10" 27.50
Vase, V for Victory, eagle on orb, wht, 8" 40.00

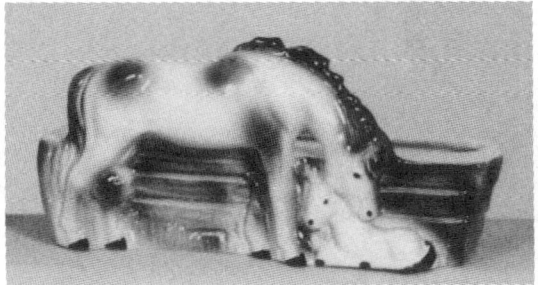

Mare and colt planter, 1958, $14.00.

Brush-McCoy

The Brush-McCoy Pottery was formed in 1911 in Zanesville, Ohio, an alliance between George Brush and J.W. McCoy. Brush's original pottery had been destroyed by fire in 1907; McCoy had operated his own business there since 1899. After the merger, the company expanded and produced not only their staple commercial wares, but also fine artware. Lines such as Navarre, Venetian, Persian, Oriental, and Sylvan were of fine quality equal to that of their larger competitors. Because very little of the ware was marked, it is often mistaken for Weller, Roseville, or Peters and Reed.

In the twenties, after a fire in Zanesville had destroyed the manufacturing portion of that plant, all production was contained in their Roseville (Ohio) plant #2. A stoneware type of clay was used there; and as a result, the artware lines of Jewell, Zuniart, King Tut, Florastone, and Panel-Art are so distinctive that they are more easily recognizable. Examples of these lines are unique and very beautiful – also quite rare and highly prized!

The Brush-McCoy Pottery operated under that name until after J.W. McCoy's death when it became the Brush Pottery. The Brush-Barnett family retained their interest in the pottery until 1981 when it was purchased by the Dearborn Company. See also Brush.

Bowl, Navarre, gr w/wht Nouveau lady, 4½x8" 150.00
Candlestick, Zuniart, 10¼", pr 325.00
Ferner, Zuniart, w/liner, 5" 150.00
Jar, Nurock, emb peacocks, w/lid, sm flake, 5x6½" 150.00
Umbrella stand, Onyx, #74, 22½" 250.00
Vase, Chrome Art, road & trees, 8½" 150.00
Vase, Jetwood, baluster, 10½" 375.00
Vase, Navarre, gr w/wht Nouveau lady, w/hdls, 8½" 275.00
Vase, Onyx, baluster, 8" 35.00
Vase, Sylvan, dk gr gloss, trees, bulbous top, 10" 75.00

Woodland jardiniere and pedestal, signed A. Cusick, 28" overall, $450.00.

Buffalo Pottery

The founding of the Buffalo Pottery in Buffalo, New York, in 1901, was a direct result of the success achieved by John Larkin through his innovative methods of marketing 'Sweet Home Soap.' Choosing to omit 'middle-man' profits, Larkin preferred to deal directly with the consumer and offered premiums as an enticement for sales. The pottery soon proved a success in its own right and began producing advertising and commemorative items for other companies, as well as commercial tableware. In 1905 they introduced their Blue Willow line after extensive experimentation resulted in the development of the first successful underglaze cobalt achieved by an American company. Between 1905 and 1909, a line of pitchers and jugs were hand decorated in historical, literary, floral, and outdoor themes. Twenty-nine styles are known to have been made. These have been found in a wide array of color variations.

Their most famous line was Deldare Ware, the bulk of which was made from 1908 to 1909. It was hand decorated after illustrations by

Cecil Aldin. Views of English life were portrayed in detail through unusual use of color against the natural olive-green cast of the body. Today the 'Fallowfield Hunt' scenes are more difficult to locate than 'Scenes of Village Life in Ye Olden Days.' A Deldare calendar plate was made in 1910. These are very rare and are highly valued by collectors. The line was revived in 1923 and dropped again in 1925. Every piece was marked 'Made at Ye Buffalo Pottery – Deldare Ware Underglaze.' Most are dated, though date has no bearing on the value. Emerald Deldare, made with the same olive body and on standard Deldare Ware shapes, featured historical scenes and Art Nouveau decorations. Most pieces are found with a 1911 date stamp. Production was very limited due to the intricate, time-consuming detail. Needless to say, it is very rare and extremely desirable.

Abino Ware, most of which was made in 1912, also used standard Deldare shapes, but its colors were earthy and the decorations more delicately applied. Sailboats, windmills, and country scenes were favored motifs. These designs were achieved by overpainting transfer prints and were often signed by the artist. The ware is marked 'Abino' in handprinted block letters. Production was limited; and as a result, examples of this line are scarce today. Prices only slightly trail those of Emerald Deldare Ware.

The many uncataloged items that have been found over the years indicate that Buffalo Pottery decorators were free to use their own ideas and talents to create many beautiful one-of-a-kind pieces.

Our advisors for this category are Ruth and Dale Van Kuren; they are listed in the Directory under New York. Assistance was also provided by Schrader's Antiques; see California. See also Willow Ware.

Abino

Bowl, fruit; windmills & pond, 9" 825.00
Pitcher, lighthouse scene, 9" 925.00
Plaque, orig Stuart scene, sgn, 12¼" 1,600.00
Plaque, The Waning Day, 13½" 1,490.00
Plate, Portland ME, Portland Head Light, 8½" 510.00
Plate, yachting scene, 7" 285.00
Tankard, millpond & boat scene, 10½" 1,130.00
Tankard, sailing scene, 6½" 775.00
Tray, millpond & boat scene, 12½x9" 1,100.00

Deldare

Bowl, fruit; Emerald, Dr Syntax Reading His Tour, 9" 800.00
Bowl, fruit; Ye Village Tavern, 9" 450.00
Bowl, punch; untitled Fallowfield Hunt scenes, 15" 3,700.00
Bowl, relish; Fallowfield, The Dash, 12x6½" 435.00
Bowl, sauce; Fallowfield, Breaking Cover, 5" 160.00
Bowl, sauce; Ye Olden Days, 6½" 150.00
Bowl, soup; Fallowfield Hunt, 9" 265.00
Candle holder/match holder, untitled..465.00
Candlestick, Emerald, Dr Syntax 950.00
Candlestick, untitled, 9½" 325.00
Creamer, Emerald, Dr Syntax..325.00
Creamer, Fallowfield Hunt, Breaking Cover 215.00
Creamer & sugar bowl, Ye Olden Days, w/lid................................375.00
Cup, punch; untitled 150.00
Cup & saucer, demitasse; Ye Olden Days.......................................245.00
Cup & saucer, Emerald, Dr Syntax scenes & verse........................385.00
Cup & saucer, Fallowfield Hunt..235.00
Egg cup, untitled 195.00
Hair Receiver, Emerald, Art Nouveau decor 650.00
Hair Receiver, Ye Village Street..320.00
Humidor, Emerald, Dr Syntax, 7" 610.00

Humidor, Emerald, There Was an Old Sailor, 8" 800.00
Humidor, The Fallowfield Hunt, 7" 735.00
Humidor, Ye Lion Inn, 7" 525.00
Humidor, Ye Lion Inn, 8" 550.00
Mug, Emerald, Dr Syntax, I Give the Law..., 2¼" 450.00
Mug, Emerald, Dr Syntax Again Filled..., 4¼" 450.00
Mug, Fallowfield Hunt, At Three Pigeons, 4½" 450.00
Mug, Fallowfield Hunt, Breaking Cover, 3½" 300.00
Mug, Fallowfield Hunt, 2½" 325.00
Mug, Scenes of Village Life, 2½" 285.00
Mug, Ye Lion Inn, 3½" 235.00
Mug, Ye Lion Inn, 4½" 285.00

Charger, Ye Lion Inn, 12", $395.00.

Pin tray, Ye Olden Days, 6¼x3½" 300.00
Pitcher, Emerald, Dr Syntax Bound to a Tree, 8" 700.00
Pitcher, Emerald, Dr Syntax Stopt by Highway Men, 6".....635.00
Pitcher, tankard; The Fallowfield Hunt Supper, 12½" 825.00
Pitcher, tankard; The Great Controversy, 12½" 800.00
Pitcher, tankard; Ye Lion Inn, 6¾" 415.00
Pitcher, The Fallowfield Hunt, Breaking Cover, 10" 625.00
Pitcher, The Fallowfield Hunt, The Return, 8" 495.00
Pitcher, Their Manner of Telling Stories, 6".......................395.00
Pitcher, To Demand My Annual Rent, 8" 495.00
Pitcher, Ye Old English Village, 10" 600.00
Plaque, Emerald, Art Nouveau geometric design, 12" 495.00
Plaque, Emerald, Dr Syntax Sketching..., 12" 1,075.00
Plaque, Fallowfield Hunt, Breakfast at Three Pigeons, 12" 525.00
Plaque, Ye Lion Inn, 12"...475.00
Plate, At Ye Lion Inn, 6¼" 85.00
Plate, Calendar, 9½" 1,300.00
Plate, Emerald, Art Nouveau geometric design, 8¼" 325.00
Plate, The Fallowfield Hunt, Breaking Cover, 10" 245.00
Plate, The Fallowfield Hunt, The Start, 9¼".......................200.00
Plate, The Fallowfield Hunt, 6½" 125.00
Powder jar, Ye Village Street, w/lid 310.00
Sugar bowl, Scenes of Village Life, w/lid 210.00
Sugar bowl, untitled, village life scenes, open, 6-sided............160.00
Tea tile, Dr Syntax Takes Possession, 6" 490.00
Tea tile, The Fallowfield Hunt, 6" 295.00
Tea tile, Traveling in Ye Olden Days, 6" 275.00
Teapot, Scenes of Village Life, 5¾"....................................385.00
Teapot, The Fallowfield Hunt, Breaking Cover, 3¾" 350.00

Tray, calling card; The Fallowfield Hunt, 7¾" 335.00
Tray, calling card; Ye Lion Inn, 7¾" 300.00
Tray, tea; Heirlooms, 12x10½" 615.00
Vase, untitled, depicts fashionable man & woman, 8" 850.00
Vase, untitled, Village Scenes, 9" 300.00

Miscellaneous

Ash tray, Sea Cave, Multifleure Lamelle, rnd, 4"................35.00
Ash tray, Tahoe Tavern, Rouge Ware, rnd, 4"....................29.50
Bouillon cup, Artic Club 15.50
Bowl, Tom & Jerry, 11½" 85.00
Canister, bl & wht, no lid, 7½" 65.00
Creamer, Roosevelt Bears, 3½" 125.00
Cup & saucer, Bluebird..18.00
Cup & saucer, Vienna...12.00
Dish, child's feeding; Campbell Kids, 7½" 75.00
Dish, child's feeding; Campbell Kids w/alphabet, 7½".......110.00
Dish, child's feeding; Roosevelt Bears, 7½" 110.00
Gravy boat, Bonrea...22.50
Mug, Arroyo Seco (over) #137, 4½" 65.00
Mug, Celebration, 4½" 85.00
Mug, Tom & Jerry, 3½" 25.00
Pitcher, Cinderella, 6" 450.00
Pitcher, Gaudy Willow, 7½" 285.00
Pitcher, George Washington, 7½" 550.00
Pitcher, Geranium, bl-gr, 4" 150.00
Pitcher, Geranium, mc, 6½" 245.00
Pitcher, Gloriana, 9¼" 425.00
Pitcher, John Paul Jones, 9¼" 460.00
Pitcher, Pilgrim, mc, 9" 590.00
Pitcher, Robin Hood, 8¼" 400.00
Pitcher, Roosevelt Bears, 5"...150.00
Pitcher, Sailor, 9¼" 600.00
Pitcher, Triumph, 7" 430.00
Plate, advertising, Advance, 7¼" 75.00
Plate, Atlantic salmon, 9" 75.00
Plate, Caribou deer, 9" 50.00
Plate, Christmas, 1950-1960, 9½", ea 50.00
Plate, Commemorative; Hudson Terminal Bldg, 7½" 75.00
Plate, Commemorative; IOOF, 7½" 65.00
Plate, Commemorative; White House, Washington DC, 7½" 65.00
Plate, Historical; The White House, Washington, 10"...........65.00
Plate, Indian Tree, 10½" 35.00
Plate, Mandalay, 10" 35.00
Plate, Roycroft Inn, 10" 150.00
Plate, Sea Cave, Multifleure Lamelle, 10" 95.00
Platter, deer in forest setting, 11x15"................................150.00
Platter, small-mouth blk bass, 11x15" 150.00
Platter, Vienna, 9x11" 55.00
Rose bowl, mc geraniums, 3½" 100.00
Sauce boat, harvest scene, Colorido body 60.00
Teapot, Argyle; w/orig infuser 185.00
Teapot, Gaudy Willow, 4½" 225.00
Teapot, Japan pattern, 6½" 75.00
Vase, for shaving brush, wht w/gold trim, 4" 35.00
Vase, Geranium, mc, 3¾" 125.00
Vase, sprays of roses w/gold decor......................................75.00

Burmese

Burmese glass is opaque, in soft shades of yellow shading to pink. It was patented in 1885 by Frederick Shirley of the Mt. Washington Glass

Co. The formula he developed contained gold which reacted with the fire to produce the delicate pink blush. It was made in both a glossy and satin finish. Some pieces were decorated by hand or gilded. Similar glass was later produced by Webb in England; it was reissued by Gunderson-Pairpoint and in 1978 by Bryden at the Sagamore Pairpoint factory. The items below are assumed satin unless noted otherwise. See also Lamps.

Our advisors for this category are Betty and Clarence Maier; they are listed in the Directory under Pennsylvania.

Biscuit jar, floral/butterfly, Queen's, Webb, 6" dia **900.00**
Biscuit jar, wild roses in gray & blk, Queen's, Webb, 6x6" **825.00**
Bowl, Dia Quilt, roses/Thos Hood poem, rigaree, 4x4" **1,750.00**
Bowl, flared rim w/2 spouts, ped ft, Mt WA, 2½x4" **945.00**
Bowl, leaves/berries, ftd, hexagonal, 3x3½" **400.00**
Bowl, rectangular top, Mt WA, 2x5x4½" **435.00**
Bowl, ruffled top, 3-ftd, berry pontil, Mt WA, 7½" **1,500.00**
Bowl, slightly ribbed, shallow, 4½"...**275.00**
Candlestick, ruffled, Gunderson, 5½", pr....................................**450.00**
Castor set, ribbed, 4-bottle, in Pairpoint holder, 7" **900.00**
Celery vase, flared top, Mt WA, in SP Rogers base, 8½" **750.00**
Creamer & sugar bowl, Webb, SP mts, 7¼" & 3½" **795.00**
Creamer & sugar bowl (open)..**550.00**
Cruet, ribbed, w/ribbed stopper, 6½" **1,185.00**
Cup & saucer, angular hdl, delicate, Mt WA................................**400.00**
Hat, Dia Quilt, flared brim, Gunderson, 3½".............................**385.00**
Jar, rose; burmese lid w/ silver insert, Mt WA, 5½x4" **1,100.00**
Marmalade, butterfly/floral, gold-tone bail/lid, Webb, 4" **750.00**
Marmalade, shiny, floral band at top, silver apple lid, 4½"..........**225.00**

Pitcher, enameled berries and leaves, original Webb label, $1,185.00.

Pitcher, Hobnail, appl yel hdl, Mt WA, 5½x3¼" **1,550.00**
Pitcher, pansies & gold decor, crimped, 5½" **1,100.00**
Pitcher, shiny, Hobnail, slim form, 6" **650.00**
Pitcher, tankard; shiny, 9" **525.00**
Pitcher, tankard; 7"...**425.00**
Plate, floral, Queen's, 6"... **1,000.00**
Plate, Gunderson, 9" **300.00**
Plate, Mt WA, 9¾"..**375.00**
Plate, pansies, Mt WA, EX art, 9" **1,300.00**
Saucer, shiny, Mt WA, 5"...**165.00**
Shakers, ribbed, SP lids, Mt WA, 4", pr......................................**345.00**
Sugar shaker, autumn leaves/flowers, egg shaped, 4" **195.00**

Sugar shaker, florals, pat Dec 31, 1889, Mt WA, eagle on lid **425.00**
Syrup, mums/gold-lined leaves, hinged lid, Mt WA, 5¾" **2,500.00**
Toothpick holder, crimped **325.00**
Toothpick holder, Dia Quilt, sq top **225.00**
Toothpick holder, flowers/vines, tricorner **475.00**
Toothpick holder, shiny, Dia Quilt, sq top..................................**350.00**
Toothpick holder, tricorner **200.00**
Tumbler, fern leaves..**750.00**
Vase, acorns/leaves, unmk Webb, 3¾x2¾" **325.00**
Vase, astors, gourd form, decor att to Steffin, Mt WA, 12"...... **1,850.00**
Vase, baluster, crimped, 4½" **125.00**
Vase, berries, folded petal top, Queen's, Webb, 3¼"....................**500.00**
Vase, bulbous, crimped, 3" **250.00**
Vase, bulbous, flared rim, Mt WA, 5½" **545.00**
Vase, bulbous, ruffled top, Pairpoint, 1920s, 6x7" **400.00**
Vase, dainty floral in bl, gold on base/rim, slender, 9½" **900.00**
Vase, florals, beaded top, stick neck, 8" **525.00**
Vase, florals, collared 6-sided top, 3⅜x3" **295.00**
Vase, florals, fold-down top, 3¼" **400.00**
Vase, florals, gourd shape, Mt WA, 12" **1,850.00**
Vase, florals, pinched sides, stick neck, 6" **300.00**
Vase, florals, ruffled, 5", in 3-ftd metal holder **300.00**
Vase, florals, star-shaped top, Webb, 3¼x2½" **485.00**
Vase, florals, stick neck, Mt WA, 10x5½" **1,250.00**
Vase, florals, 4-petal top, Webb, 4¼x2½" **365.00**
Vase, florals/foliage, bulbous w/narrow base, 7"....................... **1,100.00**
Vase, florals/foliage, star-shaped top, unmk Webb, 3x2½" **325.00**
Vase, gourd shape, Mt WA, 10¼x5½" **975.00**
Vase, gr ivy, ball base, att Webb, 3⅛x3¼" **325.00**
Vase, gr ivy, shield-shape top, att Webb, 3¼x3⅛" **185.00**
Vase, jack-in-pulpit; appl base, Pairpoint, 8x7" **700.00**
Vase, jack-in-pulpit; not crimped, Mt WA, 10x4¼"......................**735.00**
Vase, jack-in-pulpit; ruffled, Mt WA, 1880s, 8x3½" **750.00**
Vase, jack-in-pulpit; ruffled, 7" **725.00**
Vase, lily; Gunderson, 1940s, 9½"..**365.00**
Vase, lily; ruffled, Mt WA, 1880s, 9¾x4½" **635.00**
Vase, maidenhair fern, mc/gold, petticoat form, Mt WA, 11" . **1,750.00**
Vase, ovoid, Mt WA, 9¼x4¾" **975.00**
Vase, Queen's, bottle form, Webb, 10" **975.00**
Vase, Queen's, Egyptian Urn, sq hdls, 7" **3,550.00**
Vase, shiny, scrolled hdls, 10" **950.00**
Vase, shouldered, ovoid, Mt WA, 1880s, 9½x4¾"........................**975.00**
Vase, stick neck w/flat top, Mt WA, 7x5¼" **955.00**
Vase, swallows, dbl-gourd shape, Mt WA, 8x5" **1,200.00**
Vase, tea roses, reeded shell hdls, 4¾x6" **1,150.00**
Vase, yel hdls, Queen's, Webb, 5x3" **695.00**
Vase, 4 swallows on yel to pk, dbl gourd form, 8x5"................. **1,200.00**
Water set, Egyptian-style 7" pitcher+6 4" tumblers, Mt WA .. **2,245.00**
Wine, Mt WA, 4¼" **325.00**

Butter Molds and Stamps

The art of decorating butter began in Europe during the reign of Charles II. This practice was continued in America by the farmer's wife who sold her homemade butter at the weekly market to earn extra money during hard times. A mold or stamp with a special design, hand carved either by her husband or a local craftsman, not only made her product more attractive but also helped identify it as hers. The pattern became the trademark of Mrs. Smith, and all who saw it knew that this was her butter. It was usually the rule that no two farms used the same mold within a certain area, thus the many variations and patterns available to the collector today. The most valuable are those which have animals, birds, or odd shapes. The most sought-after motifs are the eagle, cow, fish, and rooster. These works of early folk art are quickly disappearing from the market.

Our advisor for this category is Rosella Tinsley; she is listed in the Directory under Kansas.

Molds

Acorn/2 oak leaves, 3½" dia	175.00
Anchor/rope, rnd, ½-lb	269.00
Beaver, 3½" dia	165.00
Berry, lg/flanked by 2 leaves, 4" dia, EX	125.00
Cow, 2-part, crimped, oval, rare, 10½x5¼"	475.00
Eagle encircled by wreath, weathered, 4¼" dia	200.00
Eagle w/emblem in breast, fine cvg, 3½" dia	950.00
Eagle/stars/foliage, primitive, 3½" dia	250.00
Flower, lg/stylized, w/leaves, 3⅞" dia	175.00
Flowering plant w/star above & 'JR' brand, 3" dia	225.00
Foliage, lg 'W,' 3½" dia	70.00
Hen, detailed cvg, rare, 3½" dia	425.00
Lamb/foliage, 3⅜" dia, EX	375.00
Pears on branch, rectangular, 4½x7"	60.00
Pineapple, EX cvg, 4⅜"	325.00
Pineapple w/leaves, deep cvg, primitive	95.00
Rose, deep cvg	95.00
Sheaf of wheat, EX cvg, 4¼" dia	120.00
Sheaf of wheat, plunger type, 1880s, 1-lb	85.00
Sheaf of wheat w/rosettes & foliage, EX cvg, 5"	275.00
Strawberries/lg leaf, 1-lb	85.00
Strawberry, EX cvg, 1½" dia	65.00
Strawberry, EX cvg, 4" dia	300.00
Strawberry/3 leaves, EX cvg, 3⅜" dia	300.00
Swan, detailed cvg, ca 1830, ½-lb	220.00
Thistle, 3⅝" dia	100.00
5-sided, ea w/cvg, cow/farmer & wife/etc, 3¾x3¾x4"	400.00

Butter molds: Eagle with emblem in breast, 3½", $950.00; Strawberry and three leaves, 3¼", $300.00.

Stamps

Acorn, X-hatching & leaves, knob hdl, 3¼" dia	220.00
Beetle/6-pointed star, 2-sided, 4½"	325.00
Bow tie/leaves above heart, knob hdl, ca 1830, 2⅝" dia	220.00
Cow, elongated knob hdl, ca 1800, 1⅝"	190.00
Cow, primitive, lollipop, scrubbed, 9"	450.00
Cow w/gate & tree branch, trn hdl, few worm holes, 4¾" dia	200.00
Cow w/tree, screw-in trn hdl, 4" dia	225.00
Eagle, rnd, 1-pc, knob hdl, ca 1850, 3"	350.00
Floral, bk: fish, almond-shaped, branded mk, 6" L	220.00
Floral, stylized, scrubbed finish, semicircular, 3½x7"	215.00
Floral, stylized/primitive, concave, knob hdl, 5" dia	190.00
Foliage, EX detail, knob hdl, 4" dia	105.00

Pear, trn hdl, short age crack, 3" dia	200.00
Pineapple, geometric border, cvd pine, ca 1800, EX	125.00
Quail, trn screw-in hdl, wear/age cracks, 4" dia	500.00
Roller in yoke, floral designs, 5" L	350.00
Roses/foliage ea side, lollipop, primitive, worn, 9"	345.00
Sheaf of wheat, sickle in rope tie, dia quilt ground, 5x7"	275.00
Sheaf of wheat, trn hdl, EX color, 4½" dia	125.00
Stag beside tree, 1-pc trn hdl, scrubbed, wear, 3½" dia	575.00
Star w/tree & stars between points, 1800s, 3½x7", EX	395.00
Starflower, octagonal, ca 1840, 4¾x5", EX	140.00
Swirls w/flower center, trn hdl, 3½" dia	135.00
Thistle, trn hdl, minor edge chips, 4" dia	75.00
Thistle, trn hdl, 2½" dia	45.00
Thistles w/X-hatching & border, deep cvg, 1700s, 5"	350.00
Tulip, primitive, 4" dia	200.00

Buttonhooks

Buttonhooks were made from around the mid-1800s when high-button shoes made of stiff leather became fashionable and continued to be used to some extent until 1935. They were made of bone, brass, iron, or silver – simple utilitarian no-nonsense styles, fold-up styles with jeweled gold handles, and combination styles with built-in gadgets – all designed to ease the struggle of buttoning high-top shoes, long kid gloves, and stiffly starched collars. While most do have a hook end, some were made with a wire loop instead. Study the construction; quality workmanship is an important worth-assessing factor in addition to the more obvious elements of material and design.

Brass, repousse, folding type, 2 hooks	27.00
Celluloid, gr w/marble overlay, 7"	9.00
Glove, crescent moon MOP figural hdl, 2¾"	35.00
Glove, gold-washed metal, 1" pearl hdl, 2½"	22.50
Glove, ivory hdl, 2½"	25.00
MOP teardrop-shaped hdl, 3½"	12.50
Plique-a-jour, HP floral, gold on silver, Shiebler, 3¼"	165.00

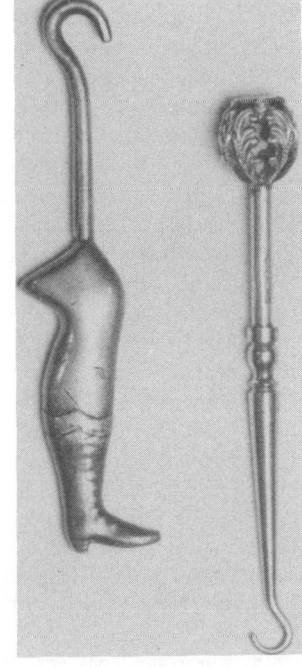

Lead lady's leg, $40.00; Sterling with faux gem, $30.00.

Sterling, Art Nouveau, repousse, dtd 1893, 6¼", EX 70.00
Sterling, Nouveau lady's head, flowing hair forms hdl, 6½" 65.00
Sterling hdl, 6" 25.00
Tower of Jewels, tower emb on shield at end of hdl......................16.00

Bybee

The Bybee Pottery was founded in 1809 in the small town of Bybee, Kentucky. Their earliest wares were primarily stoneware churns and jars. Today the work is carried on by sixth-generation Cornelison potters who still use the same facilities and production methods to make a more diversified line of pottery. From a fine white clay mined only a few miles from the potting shed itself, the shop produces vases, jugs, dinnerware, and banks in a variety of colors, some of which are shipped to the larger cities to be sold in department stores and specialty shops. The bulk of their wares, however, is sold to the thousands of tourists who are attracted to the pottery each year.

Candle holder, bl gloss, saucer base, hdl 35.00
Candlestick, gr mottle, spiral-twist stem, 6" 25.00
Jug, gr, w/lid, 9" 35.00
Lamp, gr mottle, triple hdl, 7" 55.00
Mug, olive gloss..14.00
Vase, grasses relief, matt gr, flared rim, 11" 200.00

Calendar Plates

Calendar plates were advertising give-aways most popular from about 1906 until the late twenties. They were decorated with colorful underglaze decals of lovely ladies, flowers, animals, birds – and, of course, the twelve months of the year of their issue. During the late thirties they came into vogue again, but never to the extent they were originally. Those with exceptional detailing, or those with scenes of a particular activity are most desirable – so are any from before 1906.

1903, harvesting scene, Lowel Fertilizer............................27.50
1908, Souvenir, Altona NY, gr border, 9¼" 32.00
1909, flowers & holly, Compliments of Creston State Bank, WA .24.00
1909, Gibson Girl, Tower Mercantile, Peterson IA, 9½" 35.00
1909, outdoor scenes, ...General Merchandise, OR, 8½" 36.00
1910, Compliments of the Cash Store, Silver Lake OR, 8½"......22.00
1910, country scene, Durkee Mercantile, Durkee OR, 8½" 24.00
1910, Gibson Girl, Carnation, mk McNichol 30.00
1910, Gibson Girl & horse head, Athena OR, 8¾" 27.50
1910, High School in center, bell border 32.00
1910, peacock 30.00
1911, horseshoe w/ribbons, Cocoanut Palm Ave, FL, 8½" 24.00
1912, fruit & berries, months on rim, Woodburn OR, 8¼" 24.00
1913, boy in rags under arch, mtn scene, scalloped, 7¼"........28.00
1913, irises, 8" 28.00
1914, pear & 3 plums, ribbon connects months, gilt rim, 7" 25.00
1915, Panama Canal, Am flag, gilt rim, 6" 20.00
1918, For Right & Freedom, Allied flags, gilt rim, 8¼" 38.00
1919, Betsy Ross sewing flag..38.00
1919, US/Belgium/English flags, wht dove, 8¼" 32.00
1920, US/French/British coat of arms, dk border w/roses, 8 ....38.00
1920, Victory, globe..34.00
1921, Peace, Dove, & Flags 34.00
1922, hunting scene w/dog, 9" 35.00
1924, flower bouquet, holly & berries, San Francisco, 9" 35.00
1928, deer in field, 8¾"..35.00
1929, automobile, 8½"...30.00

1930, Dutch boy & dog, 9" 45.00
1931, automobile, 8½"...30.00
1976, Bicentennial 15.00

Calendars

Calendars are collected for their colorful prints, often attributed to a well-recognized artist of the period. Advertising calendars from the turn of the century often have a double appeal when representing a company whose products are themselves collectible. See also Parrish, Maxfield; Prints; and Rockwell, Norman.

Perpetual, brass, Statue of Liberty form, pat 1928...................30.00
1884, Hood's Sarsaparilla, die-cut top, VG..........................80.00
1893, Prudential Insurance, colorful, EX 135.00
1895, Hood's Sarsaparilla, heart shape, EX 50.00
1899, Dutton-Nister, Shakespeare characters, EX 30.00
1900, Bells of the Year, EX 20.00
1900, Fairy Soap, patriotic child, M....................................135.00
1901, Fairbanks fairies, VG 65.00
1901, Hood's Sarsaparilla, w/date pads, EX 35.00
1904, Equitable, Maude Humphrey, children, 6-pg, VG 125.00
1904, Gibson Girls, complete, 12 lg sheets, EX 300.00
1905, New Home Sewing Machines, M 27.50
1906, Peters Cartridges, hunters w/moose, EX......................950.00
1906, Where Violets Blow, VG...15.00
1909, Strauss Bros & Co, Lincoln & Contraband, 16x21" 125.00
1909, WB Thompson Florist, die-emb flower basket, 16x11½" 25.00
1911, Zula Kenyon, 6-pg (1 for ea 2 months), EX 35.00

Swift & Co., 1902, 25", $395.00.

1912, NY Telephone Co, sm, EX 15.00
1916, Mary Pickford for Pompeian beauty products, 27x8", EX.....30.00
1917, Buffalo Typewriter Exchange, cowgirl, EX 35.00
1918, Winchester Repeating Arms, top only, 23x18", VG 55.00
1919, Indian Maiden Laughing Water, 18x11", EX.................75.00
1920, Peters Cartridge, hunter w/dogs, 1-sheet, G 250.00
1924, Remington, Old Mike painting decoys, fr, EX 950.00
1926, Atkins Silver Steel Saws, EX....................................22.00
1928, Peters Cartridges, pointer in field, full pad, EX................185.00

1932, Hercules Powder, Stowaways, Humphrey, 18x12", G 40.00
1932, Mother & Child, Earl Christy, 14x21", EX 95.00
1938, Internat'l Harvester, EX...20.00
1941, Sanitary Dairy, baby w/horn & dog, Becker, 13x15".............75.00
1943, Esquire, Vargas girl...20.00
1944, Esquire, Vargas girl...15.00
1945, American Way, Rockwell, 23x11", EX...............................60.00
1947, Dionne Quints, Everybody Helps, complete.......................10.00
1952, Royal Crown Cola, Loretta Young, 24x11½", EX 40.00
1953, Moorman's Feed, complete 5.00
1956, Esquire, Petty art, EX...20.00
1966, Union Pacific RR, complete.. 5.00

California Faience

California Faience was the trade name used by William V. Bragdon and Chauncy R. Thomas on vases, bowls, and other artware produced at their pottery known as 'The Tile Shop' in Berkeley, California, from 1920 to 1930. Faience tile was the principal product of the business during these years and is the favorite with today's collectors. Items in a glossy glaze are rare and therefore more valuable. Tiles were marked 'California Faience' with a die stamp.

Our advisor for this category is Jack Chipman; you will find him listed in our Directory under California.

Candle holders & curved bowl, bl gloss, 3-pc set..........................125.00
Pitcher, gr, 8½" 125.00
Tile, cobalt matt, border for 5" dia tile, 2x4"....................................10.00
Tile, fruit basket, 6-color, mk, 5" 325.00
Tile, galleon, 5-color, 5½x5½" 375.00
Tile, gr, for corner, sq w/rnd corner, 4½x4½" 15.00
Tile, turq, ½-octagon form, 6½", pr..27.50
Vase, bl alligatored matt, 5" 160.00
Vase, bl gloss, 4½" 125.00
Vase, purple & gray matt, cylindrical, 4" 175.00
Vase, red bsk, 3¼" 95.00
Vase, rose gloss, mk, 7" 225.00

California Perfume Company

D.H. McConnell, Sr., founded the California Perfume Company (C.P. Company; C.P.C.) in 1886 in New York City. He had previously been a salesman for a book company, which he later purchased. His door-to-door sales usually involved the lady of the house, to whom he presented a complimentary bottle of inexpensive perfume. Upon determining his perfume to be more popular than his books, he decided that the manufacture of perfume might be more lucrative. He bottled toiletries under the name 'California Perfume Company' and a line of household products called 'Perfection' until 1929, when 'Avon Products, Inc.' appeared on the label. In 1939 the C.P.C. name was entirely removed from the product. The success of the company is attributed to the door-to-door sales approach and 'money back' guarantee offered by his first 'Depot Agent,' Mrs. P.F.E. Albee, known today as the 'Avon Lady.'

The company's containers are quite collectible today, especially the older, hard-to-find items. Advanced collectors seek bottles and other items labeled Goetting & Co., New York; Goetting's; or Savoi Et Cie, Paris. Such examples date from 1871 to 1896. The Goetting Company was at one time owned by D.H. McConnell; Savoi Et Cie was a line which they imported to sell through department stores. Also of special interest are packaging and advertising with the Ambrosia or Hinze Ambrosia Company label. This was a subsidiary company whose objective seems to have been to produce a line of face creams, etc., for sale through drugstores and other such commercial outlets. They operated in New York from about 1875 until 1954. Because very little is known about these companies, and since only a few examples of their product containers and advertising material have been found, market values for such items have not yet been established. Other examples of rare items sought by the collector include products marked Gertrude Recordon; Marvel Electric Silver Cleaner; Easy Day Automatic Clothes Washer; pre-1930 catalogs; and California Perfume Company 1909 and 1910 calendars.

There are hundreds of local clubs throughout the world that are supported by the National Association of Avon Collectors Inc. Organization. Those wishing to join (as well as those seeking additional information concerning California Perfume Company and its products) may contact our advisor, Dick Pardini, who is listed in the Directory under California.

American Ideal Lipstick, 1929, CPC on tube, M 40.00
American Ideal Perfume, in wood box, introductory sz, M..........225.00
American Ideal Perfume, 1929, gr satin box, 1-oz, MIB 140.00
Ariel Perfume, 1930, glass stopper, 1-oz, MIB 125.00
Ariel Toilet Water, 1930-1935, 2-oz 105.00
Baby Set, 3-pc, w/box, 1916, MIB...350.00

Baby set, 1916, complete and mint, $350.00.

Bandoline Hair Dressing, 1923, 4-oz...65.00
Bay Rum, 4-oz, 1908, M 120.00
Boudoir Manicure Set, 4-pc, w/booklet, 1929 ....150.00
California Tooth Tablet, metal lid, glass bottom, ca 1900 ....90.00
Carnation Sachet, bottle, 1915 ....60.00
Catalog, color, w/tabs, 1920s 90.00
CPC Sample Case, basketweave w/label, 1915.............................100.00
Cut Glass Perfume, 1915, 2-oz 225.00
Daphne Bath Salts, 1925, glass jar w/gold label, MIB....................70.00
Daphne Talcum Powder, tin container, 1923, 4-oz 65.00
Depilatory, 1915, 1-oz...100.00
Easy Day/Simplex Auto Clothes Washer, '18, zinc, 11x9", MIB..100.00
Eau De Quinine, 1923, 6-oz 90.00
Elite Powder, Perfect Foot Powder, oval can, 1923, sm 35.00
Elite Powder, Perfect Foot Powder, tin can, 1923, 1-lb..................75.00
Gentleman's Shaving Set, 7-pc, w/box, 1917 ....400.00
Gertrude Recordon's Introductory Facial Treatment Set 300.00
Juvenile Set, 1915 ....435.00
Lavender Salts, gr glass, 1910...225.00

Lemonal Cleansing Cream, jar, 1926 ....**65.00**
Lilac Vegetal, ribbed glass, 1925, 2-oz........................**65.00**
Liquid Shampoo, 1923, 6-oz..**85.00**
Little Folks Set, 4 bottles, 1937 ....**175.00**
Lotus Cream, 1917, 12-oz..**160.00**
Lotus Cream, 1925, 4-oz, MIB.......................................**90.00**
Marvel Electric Silver Cleaner, 1918, Pat Jan 11, 1910, MIB **100.00**
Massage Cream, jar, 1916 ....**125.00**
Mission Garden Compact, brass, 1922 ....**45.00**
Nail Cream, tin container, 1924....................................**15.00**
Narcissus Perfume, 1925, 1-oz....................................**120.00**
Narcissus Perfume, 1929-30, mc box, 1-oz, MIB **160.00**
Natoma Rose Perfume, 1914-15, glass bottle w/stopper, ½-oz......**160.00**
Natoma Rose Perfume, 1916, ½-oz, M.........................**150.00**
Natoma Rose Talcum, squaw, triangular, tin container, 1914 ......**110.00**
Natoma Rose Talcum Powder, tin container, '11, 3 ½-oz, MIB ...**160.00**
Perfection, Auto Lustre, can, 1930, 1-pt......................**80.00**
Perfection, Baking Powder, can, 1931, 1-lb....................**20.00**
Perfection, Coloring, bottle, 1934, ½-oz.......................**15.00**
Perfection, Coloring Set, 5 bottles in wood box, 1920 ....**250.00**
Perfection, Furniture Polish, can, 1916, 12-oz **70.00**
Perfection, Kwick Cleaning Polish, can, 1922, 8-oz **50.00**
Perfection, Laundry Crystals, in box, 1931 ....**40.00**
Perfection, Liquid Shoe White, sample, 1935, ½-oz.........**40.00**
Perfection, Liquid Shoe White, 1931, 4-oz **20.00**
Perfection, Liquid Spots Out, 1925, 4-oz **45.00**
Perfection, Mending Cement, tube, 1933 ....**15.00**
Perfection, Mothicide, can, 1925, ½-lb..........................**40.00**
Perfection, Olive Oil, can, 1931, 1-pt............................**40.00**
Perfection, Powdered Cleaner, can, 1934, 16-oz.............**12.00**
Perfection, Prepared Starch, can, 1931, 6-oz..................**25.00**
Perfection, Savoury Coloring, 1941, 4-oz.......................**12.00**
Perfection, Silver Cream Polish, can, 1931, ½-lb **20.00**
Perfume Sample Set, 1931...**300.00**
Powder Sachets, 1890s **90.00**
Powder tin, 2 nude babies playing w/giant rose ea side, 1912.......**100.00**
Radiant Nail Powder, tin container, 1923........................**40.00**
Rose Pomade, jar, milk glass, 1914 ....**65.00**
Shampoo Cream, milk glass, 1908, 4-oz **75.00**
Sweet Sixteen Face Powder, paper container, 1916.........**50.00**
Tooth Tablet, aluminum lid, clear or milk wht bottom, 1920s.......**50.00**
Tooth Wash, emb bottle w/label, 1915 ....**105.00**
Trailing Arbutus Face Powder, paper container, 1925 .....**40.00**
Trailing Arbutus Talcum, tin container, 1914, sample sz.......**85.00**
Trailing Arbutus Talcum, tin container, 1920, 1-lb **70.00**
Verna Talc, 1928, mc container, MIB.............................**95.00**
Vernafleur Face Powder, tin container, 1925 ....**20.00**
Vernafleur Perfume, 1923, 1-oz, MIB............................**140.00**
Vernafleur Toilet Soap, 3 bars in turq/wht paper box, 1936..........**60.00**
Violet Almond Meal, tin container, 1923, 4-oz, EX **70.00**
Witch Hazel Cream, 1904, 2-oz tube, MIB.....................**50.00**

Calling Cards, Cases, and Receivers

The practice of announcing one's arrival with a calling card borne by the maid to the mistress of the house was a social grace of the Victorian era. Different messages – condolences, a personal visit, or a good-by – were related by turning down one corner or another. The custom was forgotten by WWI. Fashionable ladies and gents carried their personally engraved cards in elaborate cases made of such materials as embossed silver, mother-of-pearl with intricate inlay, tortoise shell, and ivory. Card receivers held cards left by visitors who called while the mistress was out or 'not receiving.' Calling cards with fringe, die-cut

flaps that cover the name, or an unusual decoration are worth about $3.00 to $4.00, while plain cards usually sell for around $1.00.

Cases

Gold, 14k, Art Nouveau **650.00**
Ivory, cvd figures in gardens, 1800s, 3¼x2¾" **195.00**
MOP, cvd cameo & monogram, 3⅝" **75.00**
MOP, deer relief, grape & leaf cvg, hinged lid **65.00**
Silver, 4-petal floral & scroll decor, hinged lid, unmk **75.00**
Sterling, eng name amid emb florals, hinged, 4x2½" **250.00**
Tin, vertical strap, weekdays in French on pockets, 2x11" **35.00**
Tortoise shell, cvd intricate Oriental relief, 3x4½" **250.00**

Receivers

Brass tray w/Nouveau scrolled edge, 4¼x6¼" **45.00**
Gold-washed metal, swans hold shell-shaped dish.............**35.00**
Pewter, 3-D lady on ladder in apple tree, oval, 6¼x4½" **68.00**
Pewter tray, Nouveau lady at side, 4¼x7" **75.00**
Porc, bust of armored knight, Derby, 3¾x5" **60.00**
SP, Greenaway girl & dog on rnd tray w/hdl, Derby **225.00**

Camark

The Camden Art and Tile Company of Camden, Arkansas, was organized in 1926. John Lessell and his wife were associated with the company only briefly before he died that same year. After his death, his wife stayed on and continued to decorate wares very similar to those he had made for Weller. Le-Camark closely resembled Weller LaSa; Lessell was almost a duplication of Marengo. Perhaps the most outstanding was a mirror black line with lustre decoration. Naturally, examples of these lines are very rare. The company eventually became known as Camark and began production of commercial ware of the type listed below.

In 1986 the pottery was purchased and reopened, but according to the new owners the old molds will not be used.

Pitcher with parrot handle, 6½", $40.00.

Cat, glossy wht, wall mt, 15", pr **45.00**
Pitcher, bl w/parrot hdl, gold mk, 6" **40.00**
Sign, state of Arkansas, yel, 6½" **50.00**
Vase, bl, lily form, 11" **8.00**
Vase, blk, #288, 10x12" **7.50**
Vase, cornucopia; wht **5.00**

Vase, orange & gr, 3½" 10.00
Wall pocket, window box form, #218............................ 7.50

Cambridge Glass

The Cambridge Glass Company began operations in 1901 in Cambridge, Ohio. They made primarily crystal dinnerware and well-designed accessory pieces until the 1920s when they introduced the concept of color that was to become so popular on the American dinnerware market. Always maintaining high standards of quality and elegance, they produced many lines that became best-sellers; through the twenties and thirties they were recognized as the largest manufacturer of this type of glassware in the world.

Of the various marks the company used, the 'C in triangle' is the most familiar. Production stopped in 1958. For a more thorough study of the subject, we recommend *Colors in Cambridge Glass*, by the National Cambridge Collectors, Inc.; their address may be found in the Directory under Clubs. See also Carnival Glass.

Animals and Birds

Bluejay, flower frog 125.00
Bluejay, peg base, crystal.....................................100.00
Bluejay, peg base, gr 295.00
Eagle, bookend, ea...85.00
Heron, lg 125.00
Heron, sm, 9" 75.00
Lion, bookend, ea 90.00
Pouter Pigeon, bookend, ea 75.00
Scottie, bookend, ea 75.00
Scottie, ebony, ea...120.00
Sea gull, flower frog 50.00
Swan, candlestick, milk glass, 4½", pr 175.00
Swan, carmen, 3½"...125.00

Swan, carmen, 6½", $235.00.

Swan, carmen, 8½"..255.00
Swan, Crown Tuscan, 3½"..35.00
Swan, Crown Tuscan, 8½" 150.00
Swan, ebony, 10½"...300.00
Swan, ebony, 12½"...350.00
Swan, ebony, 3½"..60.00
Swan, ebony, 4½"..85.00
Swan, ebony, 6½"..100.00

Swan, ebony, 8½" 125.00
Swan, emerald, 3½" 35.00
Swan, emerald, 6½" 95.00
Swan, emerald, 8½" 125.00
Swan, milk glass, 3½" 60.00
Swan, milk glass, 4½" 75.00
Swan, milk glass, 6½" 125.00
Swan, milk glass, 8½" 350.00
Turkey, amber, w/lid...450.00
Turkey, bl, w/lid 500.00
Turkey, gr, w/lid 450.00
Turkey, pk, w/lid 400.00

Apple Blossom, colors; bowl, bonbon, hdls, 5¼" 17.50
Apple Blossom, colors; bowl, low ftd, 11" 45.00
Apple Blossom, colors; bowl, oval, 4-ftd, 12" 60.00
Apple Blossom, colors; bowl, pickle; 9".......................20.00
Apple Blossom, colors; creamer, ftd...........................17.50
Apple Blossom, colors; pitcher, #3025, 64-oz 200.00
Apple Blossom, colors; plate, bread & butter; sq 9.00
Apple Blossom, colors; plate, dinner; 9½" 55.00
Apple Blossom, colors; plate, grill; 10".......................45.00
Apple Blossom, colors; plate, salad; sq 16.00
Apple Blossom, colors; stem, #3025, 10-oz 27.00
Apple Blossom, colors; stem, sherbet; #3025, high ft, 7-oz.....18.00
Apple Blossom, colors; stem, water; #3130, 8-oz...............26.00
Apple Blossom, colors; tumbler, #3025, 12-oz..................30.00
Apple Blossom, crystal; bowl, baker; 10"......................25.00
Apple Blossom, crystal; bowl, cereal; 6" 14.00
Apple Blossom, crystal; bowl, 13".............................35.00
Apple Blossom, crystal; pitcher, #3130, 64-oz 100.00
Apple Blossom, crystal; pitcher, 76-oz........................100.00
Apple Blossom, crystal; plate, sandwich; tab hdls, 11½" 30.00
Apple Blossom, crystal; plate, tea; 7½".......................7.00
Apple Blossom, crystal; shakers, pr...........................37.50
Apple Blossom, crystal; stem, cocktail; #3130, 3-oz...........18.00
Apple Blossom, crystal; sugar bowl, ftd 9.00
Apple Blossom, crystal; tumbler, #3025, 4-oz..................12.00
Apple Blossom, crystal; tumbler, #3130, ftd, 10-oz 13.00
Apple Blossom, crystal; tumbler, #3135, ftd, 8-oz 12.00
Apple Blossom, crystal; vase, 2 styles, 8"....................30.00
Apple Blossom, crystal; vase, 5" 22.00
Caprice, bl; ash tray, #216, 5" 17.50
Caprice, bl; bonbon, #155, oval, ftd, 6" 30.00
Caprice, bl; bowl, #65, oval, 4-ftd, hdls, 11" 60.00
Caprice, bl; bowl, relish; #120, hdls, 2-part, 6½" 30.00
Caprice, bl; candlestick, #74, 3-light........................42.50
Caprice, bl; cigarette box, w/lid, #207, 3½x2¼" 27.50
Caprice, bl; creamer, #40, ind................................16.00
Caprice, bl; ice bucket, #201 ....125.00
Caprice, bl; mayonnaise, #129, 3-pc set, 6½"..................67.50
Caprice, bl; stem, claret; #5, 4½-oz 60.00
Caprice, bl; tumbler, #12, ftd, 3-oz 40.00
Caprice, bl; vase, #249, 3½" 100.00
Caprice, bl; vase, #340, 9½" 135.00
Caprice, crystal; ash tray, #214, 3" 6.00
Caprice, crystal; bonbon, #154, sq, hdls, 6" 10.00
Caprice, crystal; bowl, #49, 4-ftd, 8" 30.00
Caprice, crystal; bowl, jelly; #151, hdls, 5" 10.00
Caprice, crystal; bowl, pickle; #102, 9" 15.00
Caprice, crystal; bowl, punch; ftd 1,500.00
Caprice, crystal; bowl, salad; #57, 4-ftd, 10" 32.50

Caprice, crystal; candlestick, #67, 2½", ea 12.00
Caprice, crystal; coaster, #13, 3½" 12.00
Caprice, crystal; comport, #130, low ftd, 7" 17.50
Caprice, crystal; creamer, #41, lg 10.00
Caprice, crystal; cup, #17 ....12.00
Caprice, crystal; plate, #22, 8½" 14.00
Caprice, crystal; shakers, #96, flat, pr 22.00
Caprice, crystal; stem, wine; #6, 3-oz 27.50
Caprice, crystal; sugar bowl, #38, med 8.00
Caprice, crystal; tumbler, #10, ftd, 10-oz 18.00
Caprice, crystal; vase, #345, 5½" 40.00
Chantilly, crystal; bowl, bonbon; hdls, ftd, 7" 20.00
Chantilly, crystal; bowl, 4-ftd, flared, 10" 40.00
Chantilly, crystal; bowl, 4-ftd, oval, 12" 45.00
Chantilly, crystal; candlestick, 5" 17.50
Chantilly, crystal; creamer 14.50
Chantilly, crystal; decanter, ftd 140.00
Chantilly, crystal; plate, bread & butter; 6½" 6.50
Chantilly, crystal; plate, dinner; 10½" 60.00
Chantilly, crystal; plate, salad; 8" 10.00
Chantilly, crystal; stem, claret; #3600, 4½-oz 30.00
Chantilly, crystal; stem, cocktail; #3775, 3-oz 20.00
Chantilly, crystal; stem, cordial; #3600, 1-oz 42.50
Chantilly, crystal; stem, cordial; #3779, 1-oz 50.00
Chantilly, crystal; stem, sherbet; #3600, tall ftd, 7-oz 17.50
Chantilly, crystal; stem, sherbet; #3625, low ftd, 7-oz 15.00
Chantilly, crystal; stem, water; #3625, 10-oz 22.50
Chantilly, crystal; tumbler, juice; #3600, ftd, 5-oz 15.00
Chantilly, crystal; tumbler, juice; #3625, ftd, 5-oz 15.00
Chantilly, crystal; tumbler, juice; #3779, ftd, 5-oz 14.00
Chantilly, crystal; tumbler, water; #3625, ftd, 10-oz 16.00
Chantilly, crystal; vase, bud; 10" 30.00
Chantilly, crystal; vase, keyhole base, 9" 35.00
Cleo, all colors; bowl, bonbon; hdls, Decagon, 5½" 20.00
Cleo, all colors; bowl, comport; 4-ftd, 6" 35.00
Cleo, all colors; bowl, fruit; 5½" 15.00
Cleo, all colors; bowl, oval, 11½" 40.00
Cleo, all colors; creamer, Decagon 17.50
Cleo, all colors; cup, Decagon 15.00
Cleo, all colors; ice pail 65.00
Cleo, all colors; mayonnaise, ftd 30.00

Cleo, all colors; plate, 7" 10.00
Cleo, all colors; platter, 12" 45.00
Cleo, all colors; stem, cordial; #3077, 1-oz 95.00
Cleo, all colors; stem, fruit; #3115, 6-oz 14.00
Cleo, all colors; stem, sherbet; #3077, tall ftd, 6-oz 15.00
Cleo, all colors; tray, service; oval, Decagon, 12" 40.00
Cleo, all colors; tumbler, #3077, ftd, 8-oz 22.00
Cleo, all colors; vase, 11" 100.00
Cleo, all colors; vase, 5½" 50.00
Crown Tuscan, bowl, flying nude, #3011/40 ....195.00
Crown Tuscan, bowl, seashell, #18, 3-toed, 10" 60.00
Crown Tuscan, candlestick, dolphin, shell, ftd, 4", pr 100.00
Crown Tuscan, candy dish, #3500/57, 3-part, w/lid 65.00
Crown Tuscan, compote, nude stem, gold trim w/roses, 7" 150.00
Crown Tuscan, compote, nude stem, 7" 100.00
Crown Tuscan, compote, seashell, floral decor, 7" 100.00
Crown Tuscan, dish, shell, 3-ftd, 11" 60.00
Crown Tuscan, flower holder, seashell 58.00
Crown Tuscan, vase, centerpiece; shell, ftd, 8" 75.00
Crown Tuscan, vase, cornucopia; #3900/575, 10" 55.00
Decagon, cobalt; bowl, almond; ftd, 6" 35.00
Decagon, cobalt; plate, bread & butter; 6¼" 5.00
Decagon, cobalt; stem, water; 9-oz 30.00
Decagon, cobalt; tray, celery; 11" 20.00
Decagon, cobalt; tumbler, ftd, 12-oz 30.00
Decagon, pastels; bowl, almond; ind, 2½" 16.00
Decagon, pastels; bowl, vegetable; oval, 9½" 18.00
Decagon, pastels; creamer, ftd 9.00
Decagon, pastels; plate, grill; 10" 15.00
Decagon, pastels; tray, pickle; 9" 12.00
Decagon, red; bowl, cereal; belled, 6" 12.50
Decagon, red; comport, low ftd, 6½" 25.00
Decagon, red; plate, salad; 8½" 10.00
Decagon, red; stem, cordial; 1-oz 50.00
Decagon, red; sugar bowl, ftd 20.00
Decagon, red; tray, service; oval, 15" 35.00
Decagon, red; tumbler, ftd, 5-oz 15.00
Diane, crystal; basket, hdls, ftd, 6" 20.00
Diane, crystal; bowl, baker; 10" 40.00
Diane, crystal; bowl, berry; 5" 16.00
Diane, crystal; bowl, bonbon; hdls, 5¼" 18.00
Diane, crystal; bowl, oval, 4-ftd, 12" 42.00
Diane, crystal; bowl, 4-ftd, 11" 40.00
Diane, crystal; cabinet flask 150.00
Diane, crystal; candlestick, 5" 17.50
Diane, crystal; comport, blown, 5⅜" 35.00
Diane, crystal; comport, 5½" 25.00
Diane, crystal; pitcher, Doulton 200.00
Diane, crystal; plate, bonbon; hdls, ftd, 8" 16.00
Diane, crystal; plate, bread & butter; sq, 6" 7.00
Diane, crystal; shakers, flat, pr 30.00
Diane, crystal; stem, cocktail; #1066, 3-oz 20.00
Diane, crystal; stem, wine; #3122, 2½-oz 25.00
Diane, crystal; tumbler, ftd, 8-oz 20.00
Diane, crystal; tumbler, juice; #3122, 5-oz 16.00
Diane, crystal; tumbler, water; #1066, 9-oz 20.00
Diane, crystal; vase, flower; 13" 75.00
Diane, crystal; vase, keyhole base, 9" 40.00
Elaine, crystal; bowl, bonbon; hdls, 5¼" 16.00
Elaine, crystal; candlestick, 5" 17.50
Elaine, crystal; comport, 5½" 35.00
Elaine, crystal; pitcher, Doulton 200.00
Elaine, crystal; plate, bread & butter; 6½" 7.00

Crown Tuscan candlesticks, nude stem, 8½", $300.00 for the pair.

Elaine, crystal; shakers, pr..30.00
Elaine, crystal; stem, parfait; #3500, low ftd, 5-oz.......35.00
Elaine, crystal; tumbler, water; #1402, ftd, 9-oz 17.00
Elaine, crystal; vase, ftd, keyhole, 9" 40.00
Elaine, crystal; vase, ftd, 6" 22.00
Gloria, colors; bowl, cereal; rnd, 6" 17.50
Gloria, colors; bowl, fruit; hdls, 11"..............................55.00
Gloria, colors; cake plate, ftd, sq 125.00
Gloria, colors; candlestick, 6", ea 32.50
Gloria, colors; cup, 4-ftd, sq...40.00
Gloria, colors; plate, bread & butter; 6" 10.00
Gloria, colors; plate, salad; sq 14.00
Gloria, colors; saucer, rnd 5.00
Gloria, colors; stem, sherbet; #3120, tall ftd, 6-oz........20.00
Gloria, colors; stem, water; #3135, 8-oz.......................26.00
Gloria, colors; sugar bowl, ftd 18.00
Gloria, colors; tumbler, water; #3135, 10-oz.................20.00
Gloria, colors; vase, keyhole base, 10".........................75.00
Gloria, colors; vase, 11" 80.00
Gloria, crystal; bowl, bonbon; hdls, 5½" 16.00
Gloria, crystal; bowl, nut; ind, 4-ftd, 3" 30.00
Gloria, crystal; bowl, oval, 4-ftd, 12" 40.00
Gloria, crystal; bowl, vegetable; hdls, 9½" 55.00
Gloria, crystal; comport, 4-ftd, 5" 20.00
Gloria, crystal; plate, hdls, 6" 12.00
Gloria, crystal; shakers, short, pr 35.00
Gloria, crystal; stem, cocktail; #3035, 3½-oz 20.00
Gloria, crystal; tumbler, #3120, ftd, 5-oz 15.00
Imperial Hunt Scene, colors; bowl, cereal; 6" 25.00
Imperial Hunt Scene, colors; bowl, 8" 37.50
Imperial Hunt Scene, colors; creamer, ftd 24.00
Imperial Hunt Scene, colors; ice bucket 75.00
Imperial Hunt Scene, colors; stem, cordial; #3077, 1-oz....95.00
Imperial Hunt Scene, colors; stem, wine; #1402, 2½-oz....55.00
Imperial Hunt Scene, colors; sugar bowl, ftd 24.00
Imperial Hunt Scene, colors; tumbler, #1402, flat, 15-oz....35.00
Imperial Hunt Scene, colors; tumbler, #1402, flat, 2½-oz....35.00
Mt Vernon, amber; ash tray, #63, 3½" 10.00
Mt Vernon, amber; bowl, #136, oval, 4-ftd, 11" 35.00
Mt Vernon, amber; bowl, pickle; #65, 8" 15.00
Mt Vernon, amber; cake stand, #150, ftd, 10½" 50.00
Mt Vernon, amber; candlestick, #35, 8" 35.00
Mt Vernon, amber; comport, #77, hdls, 5½" 15.00
Mt Vernon, amber; creamer, ftd, 8"...............................10.00
Mt Vernon, amber; cup, #7 ....10.00
Mt Vernon, amber; pitcher, #90, 50-oz 75.00
Mt Vernon, amber; saucer, #7...7.50
Mt Vernon, amber; shakers, #28, pr 40.00
Mt Vernon, amber; stem, claret; #25, 4½-oz 12.50
Mt Vernon, amber; stem, water; #1, 10-oz.....................12.50
Mt Vernon, amber; sugar bowl, #86 ....10.00
Mt Vernon, amber; tumbler, #59, tall, 14-oz..................18.00
Mt Vernon, amber; vase, #50, ftd, 6" 25.00
Mt Vernon, crystal; bonbon, #10, ftd, 7" 12.50
Mt Vernon, crystal; bowl, finger; #23 ....10.00
Mt Vernon, crystal; cigarette holder, #66 ....20.00
Mt Vernon, crystal; comport, #33, 4½".........................12.00
Mt Vernon, crystal; decanter, #47, 11-oz......................40.00
Mt Vernon, crystal; pitcher, #91, 86-oz........................100.00
Mt Vernon, crystal; plate, dinner; #40, 10½"..................25.00
Mt Vernon, crystal; sugar bowl, #8, ftd 10.00
Mt Vernon, crystal; tumbler, #21, ftd, 5-oz...................12.00
Mt Vernon, crystal; vase, #42, 5" 15.00

Mt Vernon, crystal; vase, #54, ftd, 7" 35.00
Portia, crystal; basket, hdl, 7" 125.00
Portia, crystal; bowl, bonbon; ftd, tab hdld, 7" 20.00
Portia, crystal; candlestick, 3-light, 6" 35.00
Portia, crystal; comport, 5½" 27.50
Portia, crystal; cup, ftd, sq 18.00
Portia, crystal; pitcher, Doulton 195.00
Portia, crystal; plate, dinner; 10½" 55.00
Portia, crystal; stem, claret; #3121, 4½-oz 30.00
Portia, crystal; stem, claret; #3124, 4½-oz 19.00
Portia, crystal; stem, goblet; #3126, 9-oz 18.00
Portia, crystal; stem, sherbet; #3130, tall ftd, 7-oz 15.00
Portia, crystal; sugar bowl, ind 15.00
Portia, crystal; tray, celery; 11" 30.00
Portia, crystal; tumbler, water; #3130, 10-oz.................16.00
Portia, crystal; vase, bud; 10" 35.00
Portia, crystal; vase, ftd, 6" 30.00
Rosalie, colors; bowl, bouillon; hdls 15.00
Rosalie, colors; bowl, console; 13"................................37.50
Rosalie, colors; bowl, cream soup 17.50
Rosalie, colors; bowl, fruit; 5½" 12.50
Rosalie, colors; comport, 5¾" 22.00
Rosalie, colors; creamer, ftd 12.50
Rosalie, colors; ice tub 45.00
Rosalie, colors; mayonnaise, ftd, w/liner 37.50
Rosalie, colors; plate, hdls, 7" 12.50
Rosalie, colors; platter, 12" 40.00
Rosalie, colors; stem, cocktail; #3077, 3½-oz 17.50
Rosalie, colors; sugar bowl, ftd.....................................12.00
Rosalie, colors; tumbler, #3077, ftd, 5-oz.....................16.00
Rosalie, colors; vase, ftd, 5½" 32.50
Rose Point, crystal; ash tray, #721, sq, 2½" 40.00
Rose Point, crystal; basket, #119, hdl, 7" 325.00
Rose Point, crystal; bowl, #3900/54, flared, 4 tab ft, 10" 60.00
Rose Point, crystal; bowl, nappy, #3400/56, 5½"...........32.50
Rose Point, crystal; bowl, soup; #381, 8½"..................100.00
Rose Point, crystal; candlestick, #3900/68, 5"...............32.50
Rose Point, crystal; coaster 35.00
Rose Point, crystal; comport, #3400/74, 4-ftd, 5" 35.00
Rose Point, crystal; creamer, #3900/41, ftd 20.00
Rose Point, crystal; creamer, flat 125.00
Rose Point, crystal; pitcher, #3900/115, 76-oz 175.00
Rose Point, crystal; pitcher, #3900/117, 20-oz 225.00
Rose Point, crystal; plate, bread & butter; #3900/20, 6½"....13.00
Rose Point, crystal; plate, breakfast; #3400/62, 8½" 17.50
Rose Point, crystal; plate, canape; 6⅛".........................75.00
Rose Point, crystal; plate, dinner; #3400/64, 10½" 105.00
Rose Point, crystal; punch bowl, Martha, #478, 15" 2,000.00
Rose Point, crystal; shakers, #1468, egg shape, pr........70.00
Rose Point, crystal; stem, cordial; #3121, 1-oz..............67.50
Rose Point, crystal; stem, parfait; #3121, low ftd, 5-oz....65.00
Rose Point, crystal; stem, water; #3121, 10-oz..............26.50
Rose Point, crystal; stem, wine; #3121, 3½-oz...............52.50
Rose Point, crystal; sugar bowl, flat.............................125.00
Rose Point, crystal; tumbler, #3900, 5-oz 40.00
Rose Point, crystal; vase, #1237, keyhole, ftd, 9" 75.00
Rose Point, crystal; vase, #1301, ftd, 10".....................75.00
Rose Point, crystal; vase, #6004, ftd, 5" 45.00
Rose Point, crystal; vase, #797, flared, flat, 8" 100.00
Valencia, crystal; ash tray, #3500/126, rnd, 4" 15.00
Valencia, crystal; bowl, #1402/82, 10"..........................40.00
Valencia, crystal; bowl, #3500/49, hdld, 5"...................18.00
Valencia, crystal; bowl, finger; #3500, ftd....................27.50

Valencia, crystal; comport, #3500/37, 7" 50.00
Valencia, crystal; ice pail, #1402/52 ....55.00
Valencia, crystal; plate, #3500/39, ftd, 12" 35.00
Valencia, crystal; plate, salad; #3500/167, 7½" 10.00
Valencia, crystal; saucer, #3500/1 .... 5.00
Valencia, crystal; shakers, #3400/18 ....45.00
Valencia, crystal; stem, claret; #1402 ....25.00
Valencia, crystal; stem, claret; #3500, 4½-oz 30.00
Valencia, crystal; stem, cordial; #1402 ....55.00
Valencia, crystal; stem, sherbet; #1402, low....................................15.00
Valencia, crystal; stem, sherbet; #1402, tall 18.00
Valencia, crystal; tumbler, #3400/92, 2½-oz...................................25.00
Valencia, crystal; tumbler, #3500, ftd, 10-oz 18.00
Valencia, crystal; tumbler, #3500, ftd, 12-oz 20.00
Valencia, crystal; tumbler, #3500, ftd, 2½-oz 18.00
Wildflower, crystal; basket, hdls, ftd, 6" 22.00
Wildflower, crystal; bowl, bonbon; hdls, 7".....................................20.00
Wildflower, crystal; bowl, flared, 4-ftd, 10" 40.00
Wildflower, crystal; bowl, flared, 4-ftd, 12" 45.00
Wildflower, crystal; candlestick, 3-light, ea 32.00
Wildflower, crystal; candlestick, 5"..25.00
Wildflower, crystal; comport, 5½" 30.00
Wildflower, crystal; creamer, ind 15.00
Wildflower, crystal; pitcher, Doulton 185.00
Wildflower, crystal; plate, bread & butter; 6½" 8.00
Wildflower, crystal; plate, salad; 8" 11.00
Wildflower, crystal; plate, service; 4-ftd, 12" 40.00
Wildflower, crystal; shakers, pr 30.00
Wildflower, crystal; stem, claret; #3121, 4½-oz 30.00
Wildflower, crystal; stem, cordial; #3121, 1-oz...............................47.50
Wildflower, crystal; stem, sherbet; #3121, tall, 6-oz 17.50
Wildflower, crystal; stem, water; #3121, 10-oz 20.00
Wildflower, crystal; sugar bowl 12.50
Wildflower, crystal; tumbler, water; #3121, 10-oz 17.50
Wildflower, crystal; vase, keyhole ft, 9" 45.00

Cameo

The technique of glass carving was perfected 2,000 years ago in ancient Rome and Greece. The most famous ancient example of cameo glass is the Portland Vase, made in Rome around 100 A.D. After glass blowing was developed, glassmakers devised a method of casing several layers of colored glass together, often with a light color over a darker base, to enhance the design. Skilled carvers meticulously worked the fragile glass to produce incredibly detailed classic scenes. In the eighteenth and nineteenth centuries Oriental and Near-Eastern artisans used the technique more extensively. European glassmakers revived the art during the last quarter of the nineteenth century. In France, Galle and Daum produced some of the finest examples of modern times, using as many as five layers of glass to develop their designs, usually scenics or subjects from nature. Hand carving was supplemented by the use of a copper engraving wheel, and acid was used to cut away the layers more quickly.

In England, Thomas Webb and Sons used modern machinery and technology to eliminate many of the problems that plagued early glass carvers. One of Webb's best-known carvers, George Woodall, is credited with producing over four hundred pieces. Woodall was trained in the art by John Northwood, famous for reproducing the Portland Vase in 1876. Cameo glass became very popular during the late 1800s, resulting in a market that demanded more than could be produced, due to the tedious procedures involved. In an effort to produce greater volume, less elaborate pieces with simple floral or geometric designs were made, often entirely acid etched with little or no hand carving. While very

little cameo glass was made in this country, a few pieces were produced by James Gillender, Tiffany, and the Libbey Glass Company. Though some continued to be made on a limited scale into the 1900s, for the most part, inferior products caused a marked reduction in its manufacture by the turn of the century. See also specific manufacturers.

Our advisor for this category is Don Williams; he is listed in the Directory under Iowa.

Vase, red floral bough on shaded yellow to red, gold highlights, Honesdale, American, 11½", $550.00.

English

Biscuit jar, berries, wht on vaseline frost, SP lid/hdl, 6½"........ 2,000.00
Biscuit jar, floral, red on wht, SP lid/rim/hdl, 6x4¾" 2,500.00
Finger bowl, floral, red on wht, 5⅛", +5¼" plate.........................995.00
Perfume, lay down; floral, wht on red, hallmk top, 6½" 1,600.00
Rose bowl, wild rose/lg butterfly, wht on olive, 3" H 1,100.00
Tumbler, top panel: daisies/leaves/scallops, wht on citron..........475.00
Vase, Christmas rose/butterfly/dragonfly, wht on bl, 8" 2,000.00
Vase, clematis vines, geometric bands, wht on red, 22½"........ 6,500.00
Vase, floral clusters/butterfly, wht on red, 9" 2,300.00
Vase, insect/wild roses, wht on citron, 9½" 1,300.00
Vase, morning-glories, wht on red to pk, camphor hdls, 12" ... 4,000.00
Vase, wild roses, leafy band at top, wht on citron, 7"............... 1,600.00

French

Bowl, floral, brn on gold frost, Banz, 2¼x5" 125.00
Cordial, floral, cranberry on frost, Vessiere, Nancy, 5"................350.00
Cordial, floral in gr on frosted stem/base, Vessiere, 3½".............375.00
Vase, bud; pods/heron in marsh, Raspellen-Strasbourg, 7"..........650.00
Vase, floral, burgundy on red/yel spatter, D'Aurys, 4½" 350.00
Vase, floral, red w/burgundy leaves on gr, Degue, 5x10" 625.00
Vase, grapes, purple to orange on yel, Charder, 9½"....................925.00
Vase, lake/man in sailboat on citron, Michel, 12½" 2,000.00
Vase, leaves/berries, brn pnt on gold frost, Chouvenin, 10".........225.00
Vase, leaves/pods, gr on polished gold, ftd, J Lusca, 7" 600.00
Vase, long-petal flowers, brn on yel, Ciriama, 6" 170.00
Vase, phlox, lav/gr on peach frost to lav, Arsall, 12" 1,200.00

Vase, roses, red on red & gold, blk base sgn Nicolas, 20" **7,500.00**
Vase, sailboats/mtns on frost, Michel, 8½" **1,600.00**
Vase, scenic, dk gr on orange frost texture, Chouvenin, 8"..........**300.00**
Vase, trees/castle, floral band, dk brn on yel, Michel, 8" **1,500.00**
Window plaque, mtn path w/figure, R Boutille, fr, 10x13"...........**650.00**

Canary Lustre

Canary lustre was produced from the late 1700s until about the mid-nineteenth century in the Staffordshire district of England. The body of the ware was of yellow clay with a yellow overglaze; more often than not, copper or silver lustre trim was added. Decorations were usually black-printed transfers, though occasionally hand-painted polychrome designs were also used.

Bowl, mc florals, minor wear, 3⅜x6¼" **575.00**
Creamer, mc florals, 4¼", EX **350.00**
Cup & saucer, mc florals, minor wear, mini **525.00**
Figurine, cat, back arched, full bodied, 8" L **525.00**
Figurine, swan, gr sponging, prof rpr to neck, 3½" **1,500.00**
Flowerpot, floral, rust border, w/underplate **550.00**
Gravy boat, duck form, mc brush strokes, sm prof rpr, 3½"...... **2,200.00**
Invalid feeder, flower basket, floral wreath, 7¼", NM **1,800.00**
Ladle, mc brush strokes, pierced flower bowl, prof rpr hdl **1,600.00**
Mug, child sleeping on drum w/dog, red transfer, 2¼", EX **135.00**
Mug, child's name & floral sprays, 2½", NM **300.00**
Mug, grapevines, brn bands, brushed decor on hdl, 2½", M.........**235.00**
Pitcher, Dia Quilt w/sunbursts, squat, 5½", NM **1,100.00**
Salt cellar, stylized flowers in orange & gr, ftd, 1¾", M **500.00**
Sauce boat, swags at rim, dragon's head hdl, 7¼" H **2,200.00**
Saucer, land owner talks to workers, blk transfer, 4½" **110.00**
Sugar bowl, mc geometrics, lion's head hdls, w/lid, 6", VG..........**275.00**
Teapot, Oriental scene, swan finial, octagonal, 6¼", M **1,700.00**
Teapot, stylized flowers on lid & body, 3½" **550.00**
Vase, flowers & vines, sq, silver lustre base, 6", NM **950.00**

Candle Holders

The earliest type of candlestick, called a pricket, was constructed with a sharp point on which the candle was impaled. The socket type, first used in the sixteenth century, consisted of the socket and a short stem with a wide drip pan and base. These were made from sheets of silver or other metal; not until late in the seventeenth century were candlesticks made by casting. By the 1700s, styles began to vary from the traditional fluted column or baluster form and became more elaborate. A Rococo style with scrolls, shellwork, and naturalistic leaves and flowers came into vogue that afforded the individual silversmith the opportunity to exhibit his skill and artistry. The last half of the eighteenth century brought a return to fluted columns with neoclassic motifs. Because they were made of thin sheet silver, weighted bases were used to add stability. The Rococo styles of the Regency period were heavily encrusted with applied figures and flowers. Candelabra with six to nine branches became popular. By the Victorian era when lamps came into general use, there was less innovation and more adaptation of the earlier styles. See also Silver; specific manufacturers.

Key: QA — Queen Anne

Brass, Adam, stop fluting, 1780s, normal wear, 10", pr.................**350.00**
Brass, altar type, twist shaft, circular base, 20", pr...........................**45.00**
Brass, beehive & Dia Quilt, w/push-up, polished, 10", pr **150.00**

Brass, capstan, early, 10¼", EX **1,000.00**
Brass, capstan, early, 4⅝" **325.00**
Brass, chamberstick, w/ejector & snuffer, 5x6", NM **175.00**
Brass, church pricket, late, 7", pr...**75.00**
Brass, EX detail, dome base, early, minor lip damage, 8" **350.00**
Brass, EX detail, scalloped base/lip, push-up, 7½", pr **375.00**
Brass, pricket, Italian style, 24", pr...**245.00**
Brass, Queen Anne, stem resoldered to base, 7¼" **350.00**
Brass, scalloped mid-drip pan, early, 11", EX **325.00**
Brass, side ejector, minor dents, 7"..**80.00**
Brass, sq base, paw ft, early, 7½" **100.00**

Empire-style bronze 3-light candelabra, French, 1875, 26", $950.00 for the pair.

Brass, w/push-up, Victorian, 7½" **75.00**
Glass, caryatid (draped lady), pat 1870 for NE, 9¾", NM............**350.00**
Glass, clambroth base, bl petal socket, hexagonal, 8¼" **525.00**
Glass, dk amethyst, hexagonal, 6¾" **425.00**
Iron, hogscraper, brass stem & socket, pat 1853, 3½"...................**175.00**
Iron, hogscraper, wrought, 1700s, 5½", +hook & lift.....................**95.00**
Iron, spiral adjustment, hdl & ornamental hanger, 1800, 8" **250.00**
Iron, spiral std, adjustable, on wood base, early, 7¾" **75.00**
Iron, sq base w/hanger hook & open hdl for pole mt, 11½" **250.00**
Iron, Sticking Tommy, wrought, 10" L...**85.00**
Iron, taper stick, early, 6"...**200.00**
Steel, hogscraper, brass wedding band,'Bellow' on tab, 7½".........**325.00**
Steel, hogscraper, brass wedding band, sgn SH, 6½" **250.00**
Steel, hogscraper, pat 1853 on tab, 5"..**175.00**
Steel, hogscraper, pat 1863 on tab, 4"..**125.00**
Steel, hogscraper, sgn'Bellow' on tab, 14", NM **675.00**
Steel, hogscraper, sgn'Robin' on tab, 7½", VG **200.00**
Steel, hogscraper, 13", EX **350.00**
Tin, conical base, adjustable, minor rust, 1800s, 11" **130.00**
Wood, trn w/tin socket, blk pnt, minor damage, 23", pr **120.00**

Candlewick

Candlewick crystal was made by the Imperial Glass Corporation, a division of Lenox Inc., Bellaire, Ohio. It was introduced in 1936; and, though never marked except for paper labels, it is easily recognized by the beaded crystal rims, stems, and handles inspired by the tufted needlework called candlewicking, practiced by our pioneer women. During its production, more than 741 items were designed and produced. In September 1982 when Imperial closed its doors, thirty-four pieces were still being made.

Identification numbers and mold numbers used by the company help collectors recognize the various styles and shapes. Most of the pieces are from the #400 series, though other series numbers were also used. Stemware was made in eight styles – five from the #400 series made from 1941 to 1962, one from #3400 series made in 1937, another from #3800 series made in 1941, and the eighth style from the #4000 series made in 1947. In the listings that follow, some #400 items lack the mold number because that information was not found in the company files.

A few pieces have been made in color or with a gold wash. At least two lines, Valley Lily and Floral, utilized Candlewick with floral patterns cut into the crystal. These are scarce today. Other rare items include gifts such as the desk calendar made by the company for its employees and customers; the dresser set comprised of a mirror, clock, puff jar, and cologne; and the chip and dip set.

Ash tray, eagle form, #1776/1, 6½" 35.00
Ash tray, heart form, #400/172, 4½" 9.00
Ash tray, ind 5.00
Ash tray, rnd, #400/19, 2¾" 4.50
Basket, hdld, #400/40/0, 6½" 27.50
Basket, hdld, #400/73/0, 11" 95.00
Bell, #400/108, 5" 35.00
Bowl, belled, #400/106B, 12" 75.00
Bowl, bouillon; hdls, #400/126 ....17.50
Bowl, deep, hdls, #400/113A, 10" 40.00
Bowl, finger; #3800 ....13.50
Bowl, finger; ftd, #3400 ....13.50
Bowl, fruit; #400/1F, 5" 9.00
Bowl, hdld, #400/113B, 12" 27.50
Bowl, heart form, #400/53H, 5½" 12.50
Bowl, oval, #400/124A, 11" 30.00
Bowl, relish; #400/60, 7" 20.00
Bowl, rnd, #400/10F, 9" 30.00
Bowl, rnd, hdls, #400/42B, 4¾" 10.00
Bowl, rnd, hdls, #400/52, 6" 20.00
Bowl, salad; #400/75B, 10½" 35.00
Bowl, shallow, #400/17F, 12" 40.00
Bowl, sq, #400/231, 5" 30.00
Bowl, sq, #400/233, 7" 50.00
Bowl, 3-ftd, #400/182, 8½" 55.00
Bowl, 3-ftd, #400/183, 6" 27.50
Butter dish, rnd, w/lid, #400/144, 5½" 27.50

Center-handle tray, etched florals, 11½", $85.00.

Cake stand, low ft, #400/670, 10" 45.00
Calendar, desk; 1947...80.00

Candle holder, flat, #400/280, 3½" 13.00
Candle holder, mushroom form, #400/86 ....17.50
Candle holder, rolled edge, #400/79R, 3½" 10.50
Candle holder, 2-light, #400/100....................................16.00
Candy box, rnd, #400/59, 5½" 30.00
Cigarette box, w/lid, #400/134 ....22.00
Cigarette holder, beaded ft, #400/44, 3" 20.00
Coaster, #400/78, 4" 5.00
Compote, #400/63B, 4½" 12.50
Compote, 4 beaded stems, #400/45, 5½" 18.00
Creamer, domed ft, #400/1835 ....35.00
Cruet, oil; beaded base, #400/166, 6-oz 37.50
Cup, coffee; #400/37 .... 7.50
Cup, punch; #400/211 .... 6.00
Deviled egg server, center hdl, 12" 75.00
Egg cup, beaded ft, #400/19 ....30.00
Ice tub, hdls, #400/168, 7" 85.00
Jar tower, 3-part, #400/655 ....75.00
Knife, butter; #4000..110.00
Pitcher, low ft, #400/19, 16-oz......................................125.00
Pitcher, plain, #400/416, 20-oz.......................................25.00
Pitcher, plain, #400/424, 64-oz.......................................30.00
Plate, bread & butter; #400/1D, 6" 6.50
Plate, hdls, #400/145D, 12" 22.50
Plate, hdls, #400/420, 5½" 6.50
Plate, hdls, #400/62D, 8½" 12.00
Plate, luncheon; #400/7D, 9" 12.50
Plate, oval, #400/124, 12½" 35.00
Plate, oval, #400/169, 8" 12.00
Plate, salad; #400/3D, 7" 8.00
Plate, salad; oval, #400/38, 9" 15.00
Plate, service; #400/13D, 12" 22.00
Plate, torte; #400/20D, 17" 42.50
Sauce boat liner, #400/169 ....30.00
Shakers, beaded ft, str side, chrome top, #400/247 ....16.00
Shakers, bulbous w/beaded ft, chrome top, #400/96 .....12.50
Stem, claret, #3800...30.00
Stem, cocktail, #3400, 4-oz 14.00
Stem, cordial, #400/190, 1-oz 65.00
Stem, sherbet, #400/190, 6-oz 12.00
Stem, sherbet, low, #3400, 5-oz 10.00
Stem, wine, #3400, 4-oz..24.00
Sugar bowl, domed ft, #400/18 ....35.00
Tray, #400/29, 6½" 15.00
Tumbler, cocktail; #400/18, 3 ½-oz...............................35.00
Tumbler, ftd, #3400, 9-oz 14.00
Tumbler, juice; #3800, 5-oz 16.00
Tumbler, juice; #400/18, 5-oz 32.00
Tumbler, wine; ftd, #400/19, 3-oz 14.00
Vase, bud; ftd, #400/186, 7"...45.00
Vase, ftd, #400/193, 10" 110.00
Vase, ivy bowl, #400/74J, 7" 45.00

Candy Containers

Figural glass candy containers have been made in many different styles since 1876 when the Liberty Bell and Independence Hall were created for our country's centennial celebration. The production of these glass toys launched an industry that lasted until the mid-1960s.

Candy containers include automobiles, animals, doll furniture, telephones and other household items, comic characters, guns, and hundreds of other intriguing designs. The oldest containers (prior to 1920) were usually handpainted and often contained extra metal parts in addition to the metal strip or screw closures. During the 1950s, these metal parts were replaced with plastic, a practice that continued until candy containers met their demise in the 1960s. While predominately clear, nearly all colors of glass can be found including milk glass, green, amber, pink, emerald, cobalt, ruby flashed, and light blue. Usually the color was intentional, but leftover glass was often used resulting in unplanned colors – light blue, for instance. Various examples are found in light or ice blue, and new finds are always being discovered. Production of the glass portion of candy containers was centered around the western Pennsylvania city of Jeannette. Major producers include Westmoreland Glass, West Bros., Victory Glass, J.H. Millstein, J.C. Crosetti, L.E. Smith, Jack Stough, and T.H. Stough. While 90% of all glass candies were made in the Jeannette area, other companies such as Eagle Glass, Play Toy, and Geo. Borgfeldt Co. have a few to their credit as well.

Buyer beware! Many candy containers have been reproduced. Some, for instance the Rabbit Pushing Wheelbarrow, come already painted from distributors. The following list should alert you to possible reproductions:

#12 — Chicken on Nest
#24 — Dog (clear and cobalt)
#38 — Mule and Waterwagon
#47 — Rabit Pushing Wheelbarrow (eggs are speckled on the repro; solid on the original.)
#55 — Peter Rabbit Rocking Horse
#76 — Independence Hall (original is rectangular; repro has off set base with red felt-lined closure.)
#89 — Happifats on Drum (no notches on repro for closure to hook into.)
#90 — Jackie Coogan (marked inside 'B.')
#91 — Kewpie (must have Geo. Borgfeldt on base to be original.)
#94 — Naked Child
#103 — Santa (original has plastic head; repro is all glass and opens at bottom.)
#114 — Mantel Clock
#144 — Amber Pistol (first sold full in the 1970s.)
#168 — Uncle Sam's Hat
#233 — Santa's Boot
#238 — Camera (original must say Pat Appld For; repro says B Shakman or could be ground off.)
#254 — Mailbox
#255 — Drum Mug
#268 — Safe
#289 — Piano
#352 — Auto
#377 — Auto
#378 — Station Wagon
#386 — Fire Engine
Others are possible.

Those who desire further information on candy containers may contact Candy Collectors of America Club listed in our Directory under Clubs, Newsletters, and Catalogs. A bimonthly newsletter offers insight on new finds, reproductions, updates, and articles from over two hundred collectors and members, including all authors of books on candy containers.

Numbers used in this category refer to a standard reference series, *An Album of Candy Containers*, Vols 1 and 2, by Jennie Long. Values are given for undamaged examples with original paint and metal parts when applicable or unless noted otherwise. Repaired pieces (often repainted) are worth only a small fraction of one that is perfect. The symbol (+) at the end of some of the following lines was used to indi-

cate items that have been reproduced.

Taxi, 12-Vent, marked V.G. Co., no paint, original closure, $90.00; With 100% paint (yellow, orange, or green), $125.00.

Acorn, #221	600.00
Airplane, Army Bomber, w/paper label prop, #328	25.00
Airplane, P-38, cb closure, #326	100.00
Airplane, P-51, #327	35.00
Airplane, Passenger; #323	225.00
Airplane, Spirit of Goodwill, #320	80.00
Airplanc, US Army B-5-1, no wings, #591	20.00
Airplane, US Army B-5-1, w/wings, #591	45.00
Amos & Andy, #77	425.00
Barney Google on Pedestal, w/pnt, #78	190.00
Baseball, frosted, no decals, #222	20.00
Basket, flower design, #224	35.00
Basket, grape design, #223	25.00
Bear in Auto, #2	135.00
Bear on Circus Tub, orig blades, #1	300.00
Bear on Circus Tub, rpl blades	200.00
Bear Sitting, #454	175.00
Bell, Hand, wood hdl, #494	150.00
Bell, Liberty; #1, pewter top, paper label, #227	75.00
Bell, Liberty; #2, incised for slot, emb closure, #229 (+)	50.00
Bird, metal head, #643	55.00
Black Cat for Luck, #4	600.00
Boat, w/photograph, #594	85.00
Bottle, Apothecary; #62 or #63	10.00
Bottle, Baby Dear, #64	10.00
Bottle, Rnd Nurser, #70	17.50
Bottle, Waisted Nurser, complete w/contents, #71	15.00
Bus, Jitney; closure, #340	350.00
Bus, Rapid Transit; G pnt, #345	500.00
Bus, Rapid Transit; no pnt	400.00
Candelabrum, #202	40.00
Candlestick, hdls, #203	175.00
Cannon, cobalt bbl, orig carriage, #534	450.00
Cannon, cobalt bbl, rpl carriage, #534	300.00
Cannon, Quick Firer; #537	1,000.00
Cannon, sm barrel, orig carriage, #535	475.00
Car, Auto w/Tassels #2, #360	120.00
Car, Electric Coupe #1, #354	55.00
Car, Electric Coupe #2, closure, #356 (+)	50.00
Car, Limousine, 4-door, G pnt, #348	500.00
Car, Ribbed-Top Sedan, #375	20.00
Car, Ribbed-Top Sedan, closurc, #376	25.00
Charlie Chaplin, Smith, G pnt, #84	350.00
Charlie Chaplin by Barrel, Borgfeldt, closure, orig pnt, #83	125.00

Chick in Egg Shell Auto, closure, orig pnt, #7 ....275.00
Chicken on Oblong Basket, closure, gr, #10 ....45.00
Circus Wagon, #644 ....100.00
Clock, Alarm #11; #549 ....80.00
Clock, Mantel; #2, closure, paper face, orig pnt, #116 ....125.00
Clock, Mantel; octagon, paper face, #117..............................165.00
Clock, Mantel; rnd top, #113 ....200.00
Clock, Oval, pnt milk glass, closure, G pnt, #114 (+)..................155.00
Coal Car, w/tender, #402 ....170.00
Cruet, #615 ....20.00
Dog, lg glass hat, #22 ....22.00
Dog, Mutt, #20..50.00
Dog, Mutt #11, #476..25.00
Dog, Scotty, #17...12.00
Dog by Barrel, closure, orig pnt, #13 ....200.00
Dog w/Top Hat, #480..22.00
Drum, milk glass w/emb cannon & flag, orig lid, 2⅞" dia 425.00
Duckling, closure, orig pnt, #30..70.00
Fire Engine, bl glass, #381 ....100.00
Fire Engine, Little Boiler, #383...50.00
Fire Engine, Stough's 1914, closure, orig wheels, #379-A..............85.00
Flatiron, orig pnt, closure, #249 ....375.00
Flatiron, orig pnt, no closure, #249 ....300.00
Fort, #510..275.00
Gas Pump, #316...180.00
Gasoline Truck, #609...45.00
Gun, metal, #157...75.00
Gun, Victory Glass, #541, tiny...45.00
Happifats on Drum, orig pnt, #89 (+)...................................200.00
Hot Doggie, bl glass, #14 ....450.00
Hot Doggie, clear w/pnt, #14 ....375.00
House, closure, orig pnt, #75 ....150.00
Independence Hall, #74 (+)..265.00
Jack-O'-Lantern, open top, #552...125.00
Jackie Coogan, #1, G pnt, #90 ....950.00
Jackie Coogan, #521 (+)...1,000.00
Kettle, orig closure/hdl, #251..30.00
Kettle, ruby flashed, #252 ....30.00
Kiddies' Band, complete, #277...135.00
Kiddies' Breakfast Bell, #18..20.00
Lamp, Hobnail, w/shade, #209...125.00
Lamp, Hurricane; mini, #211...65.00
Lamp, Novelty, complete, #205 ....500.00
Lamp, Valentine, #556 ....325.00
Lantern, beveled glass globe, gilt/ruby flashed, #175 ....55.00
Lantern, brass cap, #184..15.00
Lantern, crossette-ribbed base, #198....................................15.00
Lantern, fancy trim, #190...20.00
Lantern, glass reflector, #185..18.00
Lantern, Japanese paper type, #572......................................300.00
Lantern, K-600, #187..20.00
Lantern, Little Ball, Signal, bl-gr globe, #181 ....25.00
Lantern, oval panels, #570..30.00
Lantern, Stough's #3, lg, #196..12.00
Lantern, Victory Glass #1, #191 (+ by Avon) 10.00
Little Gem, #588..400.00
Locomotive, dbl rectangular windows, closure, #413.....................75.00
Locomotive, litho, no wheels, #395......................................50.00
Locomotive, litho, orig wheels, #395....................................125.00
Locomotive, screw cap, #411...135.00
Locomotive, Stough's #5, w/whistle......................................25.00
Mailbox, silver pnt, #254 (+)...115.00
Mug, Child's Tumbler, closure, #256.....................................125.00

Naked Child w/Derby, #95..45.00
Owl, closure, glass eyes, #37 ....100.00
Owl, pewter head, #645..55.00
Parlor Stove, pewter top/base, #644 ....85.00
Phonograph, glass record, orig horn, #288 ....275.00
Pipe, open bowl, #264 ....115.00
Play Nursing Set, complete, #259 ....130.00
Pocket Watch, 'Jeanette' on paper face, #457...........................350.00
Rabbit Begging, closure, orig pnt, #50..................................75.00
Rabbit Family, M pnt, #43...675.00
Rabbit in Egg Shell, gold pnt, #48......................................55.00
Rabbit on Dome, gold pnt, #46 ....275.00
Rabbit Pushing Cart, G pnt, #44...325.00
Rabbit Running on Log, gold pnt, #42....................................175.00
Rabbit w/Layed-Bk Ears, #40...65.00
Rabbit w/Paws Together, #52...55.00
Rainbow Condiment Set, #503...115.00
Refrigerator, Victory Glass Co, #266 ....1,250.00
Rooster Crowing, orig pnt, #56, EX......................................175.00
Safe, ruby flashed, #268..70.00
Sand Bucket, #236...25.00
Soldier by Tent, #108 ....2,300.00
Suitcase, clear, #217...30.00
Suitcase, milk glass, no pnt, #216......................................85.00
Swan, #492..125.00
Telephone, lg glass receiver, bl glass, #580...........................85.00
Telephone, Redlich's #4, paper sticker, #295 ....60.00
Telephone, Stough's #3, #308..20.00
Telephone, Stough's #5, #310..15.00
Telephone, Victory Glass #1, #298 ....175.00
Telescope, #270...600.00
Telescope, magnifying lens, #632..125.00
Train, Overland Limited, #394, 4-pc, EX.................................900.00
Trophy Cup, #634..125.00
Trunk, #218...85.00
Ugly Duckling, G pnt, #28 ....100.00
Village Buildings, no glass inserts, #76, ea............................20.00
Volkswagon, #373..25.00
Windmill, pewter top, all orig, #443...................................400.00
Windmill, shaker top, #445..150.00

Papier-Mache, Composition

Boot, papier-mache, Germany, 1920s, 5½" 35.00
Chick, cloth-covered compo, glass eyes, head removes, 3"...............85.00
Chick in egg, papier-mache, mc pnt, 5½" 95.00
Dog, wht rabbit fur, glass eyes, head removes, 9x8½" 335.00
Duck, papier-mache, cb base, Germany, 1920s, 3½".......................65.00
Football, emb lacing, Germany, EX 65.00
Gnome, compo face, cotton clothes, Germany, 3¾" 85.00
Hen, papier-mache, mc pnt, 5½", NM 85.00
Rabbit, brn woolly fur, glass eyes, 4½", EX............................110.00
Rabbit, celluloid face, tan mohair, head removes, 4¾".................135.00
Rabbit, compo, pulls moss & wood cart, 6½", M.........................195.00
Rabbit, compo, spring ears, Germany, 5½"...............................85.00
Rabbit, papier-mache, brn glass eyes, head removes, 15x15" 625.00
Rabbit, papier-mache, mc pnt clothes, 8"...............................145.00
Rabbit, papier-mache, spring ears, Germany, 1910s, 8" 50.00
Rabbit on log, papier-mache, 4½x3".....................................95.00
Rabbit pulling wooden cart w/cb wheels, 8½" L, NM 150.00
Radio, emb cb w/metal trim, 1¾x3½", EX.................................95.00
Turkey, compo, hair wattle, head removes, Germany, 7½" 175.00
Turkey, papier-mache, bottom closure, 5", VG 55.00

Canes

Fancy canes and walking sticks were once the mark of a gentleman. Hand-carved examples are collected and admired as folk art from the past, and the glass canes that never could have been practical as unique whimseys of the glass-blower's profession.

Canes

Bamboo, curved hdl, finished end, incised circles, 35½" 25.00
Bamboo, cvd netsuke-type animals overall, Japan, 35" 85.00
Bamboo root hdl, rattan wrapped, horn end, rope ferrule, 37".......50.00
Bamboo/thornwood, sterling ferrule, horn hdl, brass tip, 36".......100.00
French ivory, nude on bear rug, gold ferrule, horn tip, 38"...........400.00
Glass, aqua-gr, 4-rib, twist hdl, str body, crook hdl, 57".................75.00
Glass, cobalt/maroon/wht/clear swirled stripes, 35", M 135.00
Horn hdl w/cvd florals, sterling tip/ferrule, horn tip, 36" 300.00
Ivory, baboon & young hdl, gold ferrule, Japan, 35½"................400.00
Ivory tip & hdl, gold ferrule w/1872 presentation eng, 32" 100.00
Silver fox head hdl, teeth bared, wood shaft, 35" 1,000.00
Silver Punch's head hdl, pointed hat forms crook, detailed..... 1,200.00
Walnut, fine grained, curved hdl, simple style, 36" 30.00
Wood, cvd allover w/animals etc, 4-color, 36", EX 45.00
Wrapped sheet metal, curved hdl, advertising, 34½" 45.00

Walking Sticks

Ash, spiraling snake, blk & red ink-drawn scales, 36", EX 100.00
Burl root hdl, 3 cvd roosters on shank, red stain, 36" 85.00
Composition ivory hdl w/stag & dogs relief, 35"............................65.00
Ebonized, trn bone hdl w/simple eng, age cracks, 32"....................12.00
Glass, aqua w/amber stripe & twisted detail, 43" 65.00
Glass, aqua w/2 amber stripes & twisted detail, 31"......................55.00
Glass, clear w/twisted detail, 52½" 35.00
Glass, cobalt/clear swirl, 46"..150.00
Glass, red/wht/bl spirals in clear, sq w/twist ea end, 41" 150.00
Glass, red/wht/bl/pk/yel/clear spiral, 47"....................................300.00
Man's head cvd at tip, silver collar w/initials, dtd 1849, EX 195.00
Snake, natural growth of limb, pnt/inscription, 38" 20.00
Tiger maple, tapered & trn, inlaid knob hdl & collar, 33" 85.00

Silver-mounted walking sticks with portrait handles, each 35", left: $250.00; right: with bust of Shakespeare, $300.00.

Walnut, folk-art cvd face, spade, hearts, eagle, 36" 175.00
Wood, cvd camel's head hdl, Jerusalem souvenir, 38"....................45.00
Wood, cvd fist w/scroll hdl, dtd 1931 in relief, 39".......................175.00
Wood, cvd gold floral knob, dtd Dec 1890 ....150.00
Wood, cvd Indian head hdl w/mc pnt, 1900s, 37", EX...................100.00
Wood, cvd lion hdl, primitive, worn finish, 38" 35.00
Wood, cvd snake w/bird in its mouth, gray/yel pnt, 40" 200.00
Wood, cvd vines & Xmas 1898, varnished, 33½", EX.....................125.00
Wood, cvd w/2 spiraling blk-pnt snakes, trn hdl, 34" 115.00

Canton

From the last part of the eighteenth century until the early 1900s, porcelain was made in and around Canton, China, expressly for western export. This pattern, whose name was borrowed from the city of its manufacture, is decorated in blue on a white ground with a scene containing a bridge, willow trees, birds, and a teahouse, all within a rain and cloud border. The popularity of Canton (porcelain) prompted potteries in England and the U.S. to adapt the pattern to earthenware dinner services which are referred to as Willow Ware today.

See listings for specific values.

Bowl, fruit; scalloped, shallow, 1880s, 4x10x13" 1,200.00
Bowl, salad; deep, shaped rim, 1800s, 9" 900.00
Bowl, scalloped, 1800s, 10", NM..350.00
Bowl, vegetable; knob finial, 1800s, w/lid, 10½" L 475.00
Bowl, warming; Rain Cloud border, 1800s, 9" dia 350.00
Bowl, 6 high lobes, Rain Cloud border, 1880s, 3x10" 1,000.00
Box, pounce; diaper border, perforated depressed top, 2x2"..... 1,300.00
Candlestick, cylindrical w/wide base, 1800s, 8", pr..................... 1,900.00
Creamer, helmet form, twig hdl, emb tassels on base, 4¾"...........550.00
Creamer, 3⅞", VG..135.00
Cuspidor, individual, 3¼" 525.00
Dish, leaf form, Rain Cloud border, 1800s, 8x6", pr 400.00
Dish, shrimp; scalloped leaf form w/wide shaped hdl, 10x10" 600.00
Fruit basket, rtcl, Rain Cloud border, 4x9", +11" tray, EX 700.00
Fruit basket, rtcl, Rain Cloud border, 9x11", +11" tray, EX 900.00
Ginger jar, now lamp, 1800s...200.00
Pitcher, dog finial on lid, 5½", EX..500.00
Pitcher, ovoid, 1880s, 8", NM 700.00
Plate, chop; late, 14" dia...300.00
Plate, chop; Rain Cloud border, 1880s, 12" 800.00
Plate, chop; 1800s, 14½" dia 950.00
Platter, canted corners, late, 19x15½" 475.00
Platter, canted corners, Rain Cloud border, 15", NM...................350.00
Platter, canted corners, Rain Cloud border, 18½", EX 500.00

Platter, canted corners, Rain Cloud border, 19" **700.00**
Punch bowl, Rain Cloud border, mk China, 6¾x16" **1,600.00**
Salt cellar, scalloped, high base, Nanking border, 3x4", pr...........**550.00**
Sauce boat, scalloped, 8", +spoon & 7½" tray **400.00**
Soap dish, low dome lid, rtcl liner, 1800s, 5¾" L **1,700.00**
Spittoon, deep wide rim, Rain Cloud border, 7½", EX **1,800.00**
Tea canister, sq, 1800s, 5½", NM...**1,200.00**
Teapot, dome lid w/ball finial, 1800s, 8½", NM **950.00**
Teapot, urn form, scroll spout, high dome lid, 1870s, 8" **700.00**
Tray, bulb; flat hdls, floral sprig decor on sides, 14" L **1,900.00**
Tureen, cut corners, boar hdls, 1800s, rstr finial, 13" W **650.00**
Tureen, dome lid w/flower finial, twisted twig hdls, 13½" **1,900.00**
Tureen, dome lid w/leaf finial, boar's head hdls, 9x12"................**950.00**
Tureen, stem finial, boar's head hdls, 7", + 7" tray......................**900.00**
Tureen, stem finial, boar's head hdls, 9", +12" tray.....................**950.00**

Capo-Di-Monte

Established in 1743 near Naples and sponsored by Charles II, who was King of Naples at that time, Capo-Di-Monte produced soft-paste porcelain figurines and dinnerware usually marked with a 'crown over N' device, though a fleur-de-lis was used on occasion. The factory was closed throughout the 1760s but reopened in 1771 in the city of Naples. There both hard- and soft-paste porcelains were made, sometimes decorated with applied florals in high relief. Their technique as well as their marks were blatantly copied. As a result, this type of encrusted decoration is often referred to today as Capo-Di-Monte. The original factory closed in 1821. Some of their molds were purchased by the Docceia Porcelain factory in Florence which continues to operate to the present time. Most examples on the market today are of fairly recent manufacture. Capo-Di-Monte type wares have been made in Hungary and Germany, as well as France and Italy. Many of these pieces continue to bear the 'crown over N' gold stamp. As more collectors recognize and appreciate the quality of the older ware, buyer demand drives prices higher.

Our advisor for this category is William T. Brinkley; he is listed in the Directory under Illinois.

Tray, swags around central cartouch, 12x15", $1,200.00.

Box, scene w/Bacchus, lion finial, 8" L **235.00**
Cup & saucer, chocolate; cupid finial **135.00**
Figurine, African Crowned Crane, foot up, Armani, 14", NM ...**150.00**

Figurine, aristocrat mtd on mtn goat, 7x6½", NM **425.00**
Figurine, buccaneer on rock base draws sword, Colle, 12x6" **175.00**
Figurine, Captain w/shell & pearl, Bonalberti, 9½x7".................**175.00**
Figurine, dandy w/flowers in right hand, floral vest, 8" **160.00**
Figurine, fisherman, man mending nets, Armani, 10½" **250.00**
Figurine, girl & boy on seesaw, Xd feathers/B Martino, 11" L **150.00**
Figurine, girl in wide hat holds flowers, basket at ft, 10" **125.00**
Figurine, girl sits, boy kneels w/camera, Armani, 8½x9½" **150.00**
Figurine, Last Cab, old man/horse-drawn cab, Armani, 17" L **350.00**
Figurine, man in bl coat/striped pants, w/flowers, Crown/N, 8" ...**160.00**
Figurine, man in gr coat w/top hat & flowers, Crown/N, 8" **160.00**
Figurine, Pan sits on sq pyramid, gold trim, 8½".........................**325.00**
Plaque, throng surrounds man on throne, ornate fr, 10x14" ... **1,000.00**
Triptych, coronation of Chas the Great in cathedral, 16x20" . **1,200.00**
Tureen, cherub/Pan on lid & body sides, +12" tray w/crest **650.00**
Urn, cherubs/grapes/florals in relief, Bacchus hdls, 18", pr...........**425.00**

Carlton

Carlton Ware was the product of Wiltshaw and Robinson, who operated in the Staffordshire district of England from about 1890. During the 1920s, they produced ornamental ware with enameled and gilded decorations such as flowers and birds, often on a black background. In 1958 the firm was renamed Carlton Ware Ltd. Their trademark was a crown over a circular stamp with 'W & R, Stoke on Trent' surrounding a swallow. 'Carlton Ware' was sometimes added by hand.

Ash tray, Rouge Royale, Oriental scene, sq, 4¾" **25.00**
Biscuit jar, florals on cream w/gold, SP lid/rim/hdl, 7x5½" **110.00**
Biscuit jar, pk, bird/floral reserves, SP lid/rim/hdl, 6½" **118.00**
Bowl, Rouge Royale, gold Deco trim, 10½" L **115.00**
Ginger jar, birds & flowers w/gold on cobalt.................................**95.00**
Pitcher, Australian design, emb decor, 7½" **38.00**
Sugar shaker, fruit basket figural, mc, mk, 5¼x2½" **45.00**
Sugar shaker, tree figural, mc, mk, 4⅝x2⅞" **45.00**
Vase, Rouge Royale, pk lustre int, gold hdls, 7".............................**175.00**

Carnival Collectibles

Carnival items from the early part of this century represent the lighter side of an America that was alternately prospering and sophisticated or devastated by war and domestic conflict. But whatever the country's condition, the carnival's thrilling rides and shooting galleries were a sure way of letting it all go by . . . at least for an evening.

For further information on chalkware figures, we recommend *The Carnival Chalk Prize* by Thomas G. Morris, who is listed in the Directory under Oregon.

Chalkware figure, Bell Hop, c Jenkins, 1946, 13" **25.00**
Chalkware figure, Bell Hop, c Rainwater, 1936, 14¼"....................**75.00**
Chalkware figure, Bell Hop, Jenkins style, 1934, 11½" **35.00**
Chalkware figure, Cowboy, 1940s, 12" **30.00**
Chalkware figure, Indian, 1935-1945, 9" **35.00**
Chalkware figure, Little Cowboy, ca 1940, 8½" **15.00**
Chalkware figure, Miss Malibu, c Jenkins, 1933, 25½"...................**95.00**
Chalkware figure, Miss Victory, Multi Plastic Co, 1942, 11¼" **25.00**
Chalkware figure, Paul Revere, 1935-1945, 14½" **20.00**
Chalkware figure, Sailor Boy, Jenkins, 1934, 9" **25.00**
Chalkware figure, Sailor Girl, c Jenkins, 1934, 13½" **35.00**
Chalkware figure, Snuffy Smith, King Features, 1934-1945, 9¼" ..**55.00**
Chalkware figure, sunbonnet lady, Mama on base, 10½" **100.00**
Shooting gallery target, bear, CI w/worn yel pnt, 5" **65.00**

Shooting gallery target, donkey, kicks, worn pnt, 22½" 350.00
Shooting gallery target, duck on bracket, CI w/rpt, 5¾" 35.00
Shooting gallery target, elephant, CI w/worn pnt, 9", EX 95.00
Shooting gallery target, Indian in canoe, CI w/worn pnt, 9" 200.00
Shooting gallery target, muskrat, CI w/rpt, 9" 25.00
Shooting gallery target, quail, CI w/worn wht pnt, rust, 4" 50.00

Chalkware figure, Ferdinand, 9½", $25.00.

Carnival Glass

Carnival glass is pressed glass that has been coated with a sodium solution and fired to give it an exterior lustre. First made in America in 1905, it was produced until the late 1920s and had great popularity in the average American household; for unlike the costly art glass produced by Tiffany, carnival glass could be mass-produced at a small cost. Colors most found are marigold, green, blue, and purple; but others exist in lesser quantities and include white, clear, red, aqua opalescent, peach opalescent, ice blue, ice green, amber, lavender, and smoke.

Acanthus (Imperial), plate, marigold, 10" 155.00
Acorn (Fenton), bowl, gr, 7"-8½" 70.00
Acorn & File, compote, pastel, ftd, rare.................................. 1,000.00
Acorn Burrs (Northwood), bowl, amethyst, flat, 5" 50.00
Acorn Burrs (Northwood), tumbler, gr...85.00
Age Herald (Fenton), bowl, amethyst, scarce, 9¼" 985.00
Apple Blossom Twigs (Dugan), bowl, peach opal 165.00
Apple Blossoms (Dugan), plate, marigold, 8¼" 95.00
Apple Tree (Fenton), pitcher, vase whimsey, bl, rare............... 1,200.00
Arcadia Baskets, plate, marigold, 8"..50.00
Arcs (Imperial), bowl, gr, 8½" 45.00
Art Deco (English), bowl, marigold, 4"..32.00
Asters, bowl, marigold, 6"..58.00
Aurora, bowl, amethyst, w/decor, 8½" 150.00
Australian Swan (Crystal), bowl, marigold, 5" 38.00
Autumn Acorns (Fenton), plate, amethyst, rare 900.00
Aztec (McKee), creamer, marigold 200.00
Aztec (McKee), rose bowl, pastel..350.00
Ball & Swirl, mug, marigold...90.00
Balloons (Imperial), cake plate, marigold 60.00
Banded Diamonds (Crystal), bowl, amethyst, 10".........................110.00
Banded Grape (Fenton), pitcher, water; marigold.........................210.00

Banded Grape & Leaf (English), tumbler, marigold, rare...............90.00
Banded Portland (US Glass), puff jar, marigold.............................60.00
Basketweave (Fenton), vase whimsey, bl, rare..............................625.00
Basketweave & Cable (Westmoreland), sugar bowl, gr, w/lid 85.00
Beaded Acanthus (Imperial), pitcher, milk; marigold 75.00
Beaded Bull's Eye (Imperial), vase, amethyst, 8"-14"....................40.00
Border Plants (Dugan), bowl, amethyst, flat, 8½" 60.00
Bouquet (Fenton), tumbler, marigold..35.00
Boutonniere (Millersburg), compote, gr 160.00
Bow & English Hob (English), nut bowl, bl 55.00
Brocaded Summer Gardens, bonbon, pastel 62.00
Brocaded Summer Gardens, vase, pastel 90.00
Broken Arches (Imperial), bowl, marigold, 8½"-10" 42.00
Brooklyn, bottle, w/stopper, amethyst 90.00
Brooklyn Bridge (Dugan), bowl, marigold, scarce 320.00
Bubbles, lamp chimney, pastel 45.00
Bull Dog, paperweight, marigold...250.00
Bull's Eye (US Glass), oil lamp, marigold 185.00
Bull's Eye & Loop (Millersburg), vase, gr, rare, 7"-11" 300.00
Bull's Eye & Spearhead, wine, marigold 48.00
Bumblebees, hatpin, amethyst...26.00
Bunny, bank, marigold 30.00
Butterflies (Fenton), card tray, marigold 35.00
Butterflies & Bells (Crystal), compote, amethyst 125.00
Butterfly, pin tray, marigold 35.00
Butterfly & Berry (Fenton), pitcher, bl..520.00

Butterfly & Berry (Fenton), vase, pastel, rare..............................400.00
Butterfly & Fern (Fenton), tumbler, amethyst...............................47.00
Butterfly & Tulip (Dugan), bowl, marigold, ftd, scarce, 10½"......475.00
Butterfly Bower (Crystal), compote, amethyst 115.00
Buttress (US Glass), pitcher, marigold, rare 300.00
Buzz Saw (Cambridge), cruet, gr, rare, 6" 385.00
Canada Dry, bottle, marigold 14.00
Cane (Imperial), bowl, marigold, 7½"-10"....................................30.00
Cane (Imperial), pickle dish, pastel 45.00
Cane & Daisy Cut (Jenkins), vase, marigold 90.00
Cane & Scroll (Sea Thistle), rose bowl, bl....................................70.00
Cannonball VT, pitcher, pastel 300.00
Capitol (Westmoreland), mug, marigold, sm 75.00
Captive Rose (Fenton), plate, gr, 9"...225.00
Carnival Honeycomb (Imperial), plate, amethyst, 7"....................80.00
Caroline (Dugan), bowl, marigold, 7"-10" 52.00
Cartwheel #411 (Heisey), goblet, marigold 60.00
Cathedral (Sweden), creamer, marigold, ftd 45.00
Central Shoe Store (Northwood), bowl, amethyst, 6"-7" 285.00
Chain & Star (Fostoria), tumbler, marigold, rare 750.00
Chatelaine (Imperial), pitcher, amethyst, rare 2,500.00
Chatham (US Glass), compote, marigold 65.00
Checkerboard (Westmoreland), cruet, pastel, rare......................600.00
Checkerboard Bouquet, plate, amethyst, 8" 50.00
Checkers, bowl, marigold, 9"...32.00

Checkers, plate, marigold, 7" 50.00
Cherry (Dugan), plate, amethyst, 6" 125.00
Cherry (Millersburg), plate, marigold, rare, 6" 525.00
Cherry (Millersburg), powder jar, gr, rare 1,250.00
Cherry & Cable (Northwood), spooner, marigold, rare 175.00
Cherry & Daisies (Fenton), banana boat, bl................960.00
Cherry Blossoms, pitcher, bl...95.00
Cherry Chain (Fenton), plate, pastel, 7"-9" 150.00
Cherry Circles (Fenton), bonbon, amethyst 60.00
Cherry Smash (US Glass), butter dish, marigold 110.00
Cherub, lamp, pastel, rare 425.00
Chrysanthemum Drape, oil lamp, pastel, rare................900.00
Circle Scroll (Dugan), bowl, amethyst, 10" 75.00
Circle Scroll (Dugan), tumbler, marigold, rare.................300.00
Circle Scroll (Dugan), vase whimsey, amethyst 140.00
Classic Arts (Czech), rose bowl, marigold 260.00
Classic Arts (Czech), vase, marigold, 7" 245.00
Cleopatra, bottle, marigold 100.00
Cobblestones (Dugan), bowl, amethyst, 5" 40.00
Cobblestones (Imperial), bonbon, marigold 40.00
Cobblestones (Imperial), bowl, gr, 5" 45.00
Coin Dot (Fenton), tumbler, bl 100.00
Coin Dot VT (Westmoreland), bowl, aqua opal 195.00

Colonial Lady (Imperial), vase, amethyst......................800.00
Columbus, plate, marigold, 8" 38.00
Concave Flute (Westmoreland), vase, gr 65.00
Concord (Fenton), bowl, bl, scarce, 9" 95.00
Cone & Tie (Imperial), tumbler, amethyst, rare............550.00
Connie (Northwood), pitcher, pastel 650.00
Coral (Fenton), bowl, marigold, 9" 65.00
Corinth (Dugan), bowl, peach opal, 9" 170.00
Corinth (Westmoreland), bowl, bl..60.00
Cornucopia (Fenton), vase, marigold, 5" 65.00
Cosmos & Cane, pitcher, marigold, rare............................665.00
Cosmos & Cane, rose bowl, pastel 165.00
Country Kitchen (Millersburg), bowl, marigold, rare, 9" 250.00
Country Kitchen (Millersburg), spooner, gr 550.00
Country Kitchen (Millersburg), vase whimsey, marigold, rare 500.00
Covered Little Hen, miniature, pastel, rare, 3½" 90.00
Crab Claw (Imperial), pitcher, marigold, scarce...........295.00
Crackle (Imperial), bowl, gr, 9" 27.00
Crackle (Imperial), candlestick, marigold, 3½" 25.00
Crackle (Imperial), spittoon, marigold, lg.........................38.00
Crystal Cut (Crystal), compote, marigold.........................50.00
Cut Arches (English), banana bowl, marigold.................50.00
Cut Crystal (US Glass), water bottle, marigold..............165.00
Cut Flowers (Jenkins), vase, pastel, 10" 95.00
Cut Ovals (Fenton), bowl, red, 7"-10" 385.00
Dahlia (Dugan), sugar bowl, amethyst..............................100.00
Dahlia (Dugan), tumbler, pastel, rare 150.00

Daisy (Fenton), bonbon, bl, scarce.....................................95.00
Daisy & Cane (English), decanter, marigold, rare 75.00
Daisy & Plume (Northwood), rose bowl, bl, 2 shapes 75.00
Daisy Block (English), rowboat, marigold, scarce............265.00
Daisy Web (Dugan), hat, peach opal, rare 85.00
Dance of The Veils (Fenton), vase, marigold, rare 2,650.00
Dandelion (Northwood), pitcher, gr.................................650.00
Deep Grape (Millersburg), compote, bl, rare................. 2,000.00
DeVilbiss, perfumer, marigold 40.00
Diamond & Daisy (US Glass), pitcher, bl, rare 350.00
Diamond & File, banana bowl, marigold 55.00
Diamond & Rib (Fenton), vase whimsey, gr....................600.00
Diamond & Sunburst (Imperial), bowl, gr, 8" 48.00
Diamond & Sunburst (Imperial), decanter, marigold 100.00
Diamond Checkerboard, bowl, marigold, 5" 25.00
Diamond Checkerboard, butter dish, marigold.................70.00
Diamond Flutes (US Glass), parfait, marigold 40.00
Diamond Lace (Imperial), bowl, amethyst, 5" 37.00
Diamond Ovals (English), creamer, marigold 35.00
Diamond Point Columns (Imperial), compote, marigold............26.00
Diamond Points (Northwood), vase, gr, 7"-14" 37.00
Diamond Ring (Imperial), bowl, amethyst, 5" 28.00
Diamond Star, vase, marigold, 8" 60.00
Diamond Vane (English), creamer, marigold, 4" 35.00
Diamonds (Millersburg), pitcher, gr.................................265.00
Dog, ash tray, marigold 65.00
Dogwood Sprays (Dugan), bowl, peach opal, 9" 165.00
Dorsey & Funkenstein (Northwood), plate, amethyst 235.00
Dotted Daisies, plate, marigold, 8" 65.00
Double Dolphins (Fenton), bowl, pastel, ftd, 9"-11" 110.00
Double Dolphins (Fenton), compote, pastel 60.00
Double Dutch (Imperial), bowl, gr, ftd, 9" 60.00
Double Loop (Northwood), creamer, bl.............................100.00
Double Star (Cambridge), pitcher, marigold, scarce...................500.00
Double Star (Cambridge), spittoon whimsey, gr, rare 1,500.00
Double Star (Cambridge), tumbler, amethyst, scarce........110.00
Dragon & Lotus (Fenton), bowl, marigold, 9" 48.00
Dragon & Strawberry (Fenton), bowl, gr, flat, scarce, 9" 325.00
Drapery (Northwood), candy dish, marigold 55.00
Drapery (Northwood), rose bowl, bl....................................85.00
Drapery VT (Fenton), pitcher, marigold, rare 485.00
Dutch Mill, ash tray, marigold..35.00
Dutch Twins, ash tray, marigold 45.00
Eagle Furniture (Northwood), plate, amethyst 260.00
Ebon, vase, amethyst...90.00
Elks (Millersburg), bowl, amethyst, rare 1,050.00
Elks (Millersburg), paperweight, gr, rare 1,200.00
Embroidered Mums (Northwood), plate, bl.....................175.00
Emu (Crystal), bowl, marigold, rare, 5" 60.00
Enamelled Grape (Northwood), pitcher, bl......................240.00
English Button Band (English), sugar bowl, marigold 38.00
English Hob & Button (English), bowl, gr, 7"-10".............90.00
Engraved Floral (Fenton), vase, marigold, 8" 40.00
Estate, Stippled; (Westmoreland), vase, peach opal, 3".............85.00
Estate (Westmoreland), perfumer, pastel...........................95.00
Exchange Bank (Northwood), plate, amethyst, 6" 200.00
Fanciful (Dugan), plate, bl, 9"..175.00
Fancy Flowers (Imperial), compote, gr 110.00
Fashion (Imperial), bowl, gr, 9" 75.00
Fashion (Imperial), tumbler, marigold 20.00
Feather Stitch (Fenton), bowl, marigold, 8½"-10" 50.00
Feather Swirl (US Glass), butter dish, marigold...............110.00
Feathered Serpent (Fenton), bowl, gr, 10" 65.00

Feathers (Northwood), vase, amethyst, 7"-12" **40.00**
Feldman Brothers (Northwood), bowl, amethyst **150.00**
Fentonia, pitcher, bl **560.00**
Fentonia Fruit (Fenton), bowl, bl, ftd, 10"..................................**150.00**
Fern (Northwood), bowl, amethyst, 6½"-9".....................................**50.00**
Fern Brand Chocolates (Northwood), plate, amethyst **245.00**
Field Flower (Imperial), tumbler, gr, scarce..................................**70.00**
Field Thistle (US Glass), bowl, pastel, 6"-10" **250.00**
Field Thistle (US Glass), plate, marigold, rare, 6" **180.00**
Field Thistle (US Glass), spooner, marigold, rare **70.00**
File (Imperial & English), pitcher, amethyst, rare **435.00**
File (Imperial & English), sugar bowl, marigold **120.00**
File (Imperial & English), vase, pastel **50.00**
File & Fan, bowl, peach opal, ftd, 6" **156.00**
Fine Cut Flower & VT (Fenton), compote, marigold.....................**50.00**
Fine Cut Flower & VT (Fenton), goblet, marigold.........................**50.00**
Fine Cut Rings (English), celery, marigold **58.00**
Fine Cut Rings (English), creamer, marigold **45.00**
Fine Rib (Northwood & Fenton), bowl, amethyst, 9"-10" **60.00**
Fine Rib (Northwood & Fenton), bowl, gr, 5"................................**36.00**
Fishscale & Beads (Dugan), bowl, peach opal, 6"-8"...................**150.00**
Fishscale & Beads (Dugan), plate, marigold, 7" **40.00**
Flannel Flower (Crystal), cake stand, amethyst **175.00**
Flared Panel, shade, peach opal **50.00**
Flared Wide Panel, atomizer, marigold, 3½" **90.00**
Fleur-De-Lis (Jenkins), vase, marigold..**195.00**
Fleur-De-Lis (Millersburg), bowl, gr, ftd, 8½" **450.00**
Floral, hatpin, pastel **50.00**
Floral & Grape (Dugan), tumbler, amethyst **35.00**
Floral & Optic (Imperial), bowl, pastel, flat, 8"-10" **20.00**
Floral & Wheat (US Glass), compote, bl..**42.00**
Floral Oval (Hig-bee), bowl, marigold, 8" **45.00**
Flower & Beads, plate, marigold, rnd, 8½".....................................**75.00**
Flowering Dill (Fenton), hat, gr **42.00**
Flowers & Spades (Dugan), bowl, peach opal, 10" **195.00**
Flute (Fenton), toothpick holder, marigold **75.00**
Flute (Millersburg), bowl, marigold, 10" **65.00**
Flute (Millersburg), vase, amethyst, rare **300.00**
Flute (Northwood), bowl, marigold, 10"...**45.00**
Flute & Cane (Imperial), tumbler, marigold, rare.......................**350.00**
Flute #3 (Imperial), bowl, amethyst, 10" **220.00**
Flute #3 (Imperial), pitcher, gr...**495.00**
Flute #3 (Imperial), tumbler, bl **85.00**
Flying Bat, hatpin, gr, scarce..**58.00**
Footed Drape (Westmoreland), vase, pastel **50.00**
Forget-Me-Not (Fenton), tumbler, gr...**48.00**
Forks (Cambridge), cracker jar, gr, rare.......................................**495.00**
Fostoria #1231, (Fostoria), rose bowl, pastel **100.00**
Fostoria #600 (Fostoria), napkin ring, marigold...........................**75.00**
Four Flowers (Finland), bowl, amethyst, 6¼"................................**38.00**
Four Flowers (Finland), plate, peach opal, 9"-10½" **475.00**
Four Flowers VT (Westmoreland), bowl, gr, 9"-11".......................**65.00**
Frolicking Bears (US Glass), pitcher, gr, rare **8,700.00**
Frosted Block (Imperial), bowl, marigold, 9" **32.00**
Frosted Block (Imperial), plate, pastel, 7½" **60.00**
Frosted Block (Imperial), rose bowl, pastel **75.00**
Frosted Buttons (Fenton), bowl, pastel, ftd, 10" **175.00**
Fruit & Flowers (Northwood), banana plate, gr, rare, 7".............**110.00**
Fruit & Flowers (Northwood), fruit bowl, marigold, 10" **56.00**
Garden Mums (Northwood), bowl, amethyst, 8½"-10"...................**65.00**
Garden Path (Dugan), fruit bowl, amethyst, 10" **95.00**
Garden Path (Dugan), fruit bowl, marigold, 10".............................**85.00**
Garden Path VT (Dugan), bowl, peach opal, 9" **165.00**

Garland (Fenton), rose bowl, amethyst, ftd **70.00**
Garland (Fenton), rose bowl, bl, ftd...**65.00**
Georgia Belle (Dugan), compote, amethyst, ftd **75.00**
Georgia Belle (Dugan), compote, gr, ftd **80.00**
God & Home (Dugan), pitcher, bl, rare...**985.00**
Goddess of Harvest (Fenton), bowl, bl, rare, 9½" **4,100.00**
Goddess of Harvest (Fenton), bowl, marigold, rare, 9½" **4,300.00**
Golden Cupids (Crystal), bowl, pastel, rare, 9" **265.00**
Golden Harvest (US Glass), wine, amethyst **35.00**
Golden Harvest (US Glass), wine, marigold **28.00**
Golden Honeycomb (Imperial), bowl, marigold, 5" **25.00**
Good Luck (Northwood), plate, amethyst, 9"................................**285.00**
Good Luck (Northwood), plate, gr, 9"...**500.00**
Goodyear, ash tray in tire, marigold **50.00**
Gothic Arches, vase, amethyst, rare, 8"-12" **60.00**
Gothic Arches, vase, gr, rare, 8"-12" **70.00**
Grand Thistle (Finland), tumbler, bl, rare....................................**550.00**
Grape, Heavy (Dugan), bowl, amethyst, rare, 5"..........................**155.00**
Grape, Heavy (Dugan), bowl, peach opal, rare, 5".......................**375.00**
Grape, Heavy (Imperial), custard cup, gr.......................................**35.00**
Grape, Heavy (Imperial), nappy, amethyst.....................................**38.00**
Grape, Heavy (Imperial), nappy, marigold.....................................**35.00**
Grape, Heavy (Imperial), plate, amethyst, 8" **70.00**
Grape, Heavy (Imperial), plate, pastel, 8" **90.00**

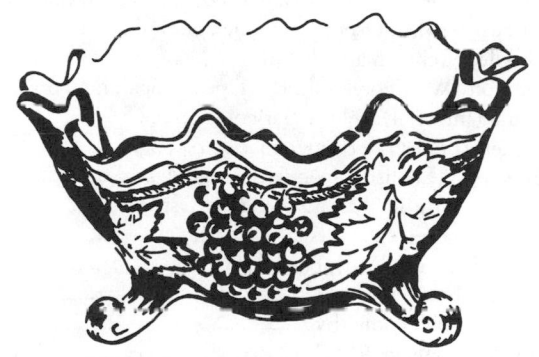

Grape (Fenton's Grape & Cable), bowl, gr, ftd, 8¾" **67.00**
Grape (Fenton's Grape & Cable), plate, gr, ftd, 9".....................**160.00**
Grape (Fenton's Grape & Cable), plate, marigold, ftd, 9".............**80.00**
Grape (Imperial), bowl, marigold, 5" **18.00**
Grape (Imperial), milk pitcher, amethyst **225.00**
Grape (Imperial), milk pitcher, gr...**200.00**
Grape (Imperial), pitcher, gr **170.00**
Grape (Imperial), pitcher, marigold **97.00**
Grape (Imperial), plate, gr, 7"-12"..**160.00**
Grape (Northwood's Grape & Cable), compote, gr, open............**490.00**
Grape (Northwood's Grape & Cable), compote, pastel, open **750.00**
Grape (Northwood's Grape & Cable), orange bowl, gr, ftd **195.00**
Grape (Northwood's Grape & Cable), pin tray, gr **145.00**
Grape & Gothic Arches (Northwood), pitcher, marigold **200.00**
Grape Arbor (Dugan), bowl, marigold, ftd, 9½"-11" **50.00**
Grape Arbor (Northwood), pitcher, amethyst................................**540.00**
Grape Delight (Dugan), nut bowl, amethyst, ftd, 6"......................**75.00**
Grape Frieze (Northwood), bowl, pastel, rare, 10½" **450.00**
Grape Leaves (Millersburg), bowl, gr, rare, 10" **800.00**
Grape Leaves (Northwood), bowl, gr, 8¾".......................................**75.00**
Grape Wreath (Millersburg), bowl, marigold, 5" **38.00**
Grapevine Lattice (Dugan), bowl, bl, 8½"......................................**60.00**
Grapevine Lattice (Dugan), bowl, pastel, 5"...................................**52.00**
Grapevine Lattice (Fenton), pitcher, marigold, rare **220.00**
Greek Key (Northwood), plate, gr, rare, 9"-11"............................**390.00**
Greek Key VT, hatpin, amethyst...**28.00**

Harvest Flower (Dugan), tumbler, gr 400.00
Harvest Poppy, compote, peach opal 160.00
Hattie (Imperial), bowl, marigold 38.00
Hawaiian Lei (Higbee), sugar bowl, marigold 65.00
Heart & Horseshoe (Fenton), bowl, marigold, 8½" 700.00
Heart & Trees (Fenton), bowl, gr, 8¾" 195.00
Hearts & Flowers (Northwood), bowl, bl, 8½" 58.00
Heavy Diamond (Imperial), bowl, marigold, 10" 32.00
Heavy Diamond (Imperial), vase, gr 48.00
Heavy Hobnail (Fenton), vase, amethyst, rare 475.00
Heavy Shell (Fenton), bowl, pastel, 8¼" 92.00
Heavy Web (Dugan), bowl, peach opal, rare, 10" 8.00
Heinz, bottle, pastel 36.00
Heisey #357, tumbler, marigold 42.00
Heron (Dugan), mug, amethyst, rare 265.00
Hobnail, Miniature; pitcher, marigold, rare, 6" 210.00
Hobnail, Miniature; tumbler, marigold, 2½" 48.00
Hobnail (Fenton), vase, pastel, 5"-11" 75.00
Hobnail (Millersburg), tumbler, gr, rare 1,000.00
Hobnail Panels (McKee), vase, pastel, 8¾" 65.00
Hobstar (Imperial), butter dish, amethyst 195.00
Hobstar & Arches (Imperial), bowl, gr, 9" 57.00
Hobstar & Cut Triangles (English), bowl, gr 58.00
Hobstar & Cut Triangles (English), plate, amethyst.............95.00
Hobstar & Cut Triangles (English), rose bowl, marigold.......45.00
Hobstar & Feather (Millersburg), spooner, gr, rare..............800.00
Hobstar & File, pitcher, marigold, rare........................... 1,500.00
Hobstar & Fruit (Westmoreland), bowl, peach opal, rare, 6" 90.00
Hobstar Band (Imperial), celery, marigold 85.00
Hobstar Panels (English), creamer, marigold 45.00
Hobstar Reversed (English), spooner, marigold 45.00
Hobstar Whirl (Whirligig), compote, amethyst, 4½" 58.00
Holiday, bottle, pastel...67.00
Holly, Panelled (Northwood); bowl, gr 65.00
Holly (Fenton), bowl, marigold, 8"-10" 36.00
Holly (Fenton), goblet, amethyst 36.00
Holly (Fenton), plate, gr, 9" 400.00
Holm Spray, atomizer, marigold, 3" 45.00
Homestead, shade, marigold 40.00
Honeycomb Ornament, hatpin, amethyst.............................70.00
Horses Heads (Fenton), bowl, gr, flat, 7½" 80.00
Horses Heads (Fenton), bowl, marigold, flat, 7½" 57.00
Horses Heads (Fenton), rose bowl, gr, ftd 125.00
Horseshoe, shot glass, marigold 42.00
Hyacinth, lamp, marigold 1,900.00
Illinois Daisy (English), bowl, marigold, 8".........................40.00
Illusion (Fenton), bonbon, bl 65.00
Imperial #5 (Imperial), bowl, marigold, 8".........................40.00
Indiana Statehouse (Fenton), plate, bl, rare 335.00
Intaglio Daisy (English), bowl, marigold, 7½" 48.00
Intaglio Ovals (US Glass), bowl, pastel, 7" 65.00
Intaglio Ovals (US Glass), plate, pastel, 7½".......................80.00
Interior Poinsettia (Northwood), tumbler, marigold, rare 465.00
Interior Swirl, spittoon, bl 95.00
Interior Swirl, spittoon, peach opal....................................95.00
Interior Swirl, vase, marigold, ftd, 9"..................................37.00
Inverted Coin Dot (Northwood-Fenton), bowl, gr...............67.00
Inverted Coin Dot (Northwood-Fenton), bowl, marigold.............38.00
Inverted Coin Dot (Northwood-Fenton), pitcher, amethyst 450.00
Inverted Coin Dot (Northwood-Fenton), pitcher, bl 400.00
Inverted Feather (Cambridge), compote, marigold 100.00
Inverted Feather (Cambridge), cup, gr, rare........................85.00
Inverted Feather (Cambridge), spooner, amethyst, rare 320.00

Inverted Feather (Cambridge), spooner, marigold, rare 290.00
Inverted Strawberry, bowl, amethyst, 5" 50.00
Inverted Strawberry, tumbler, gr, rare...............................375.00
Inverted Strawberry, tumbler, marigold, rare.....................325.00
Inverted Thistle (Cambridge), bowl, amethyst, rare, 5" 85.00
Inverted Thistle (Cambridge), bowl, gr, rare, 5" 95.00
Inverted Thistle (Cambridge), bowl, gr, rare, 9" 200.00
Inverted Thistle (Cambridge), pitcher, marigold, rare 2,700.00
Iris (Fenton), compote, marigold 47.00
Jack-in-the-Pulpit (Dugan), vase, bl 80.00
Jackman, whiskey bottle, marigold......................................30.00
Jacob's Ladder, perfume, marigold 47.00
Jacob's Ladder VT (US Glass), rose bowl, marigold 52.00
Jewel Box, inkwell, marigold...75.00

Jewelled Heart (Dugan), bowl, amethyst, 5"........................42.00
Jewelled Heart (Dugan), plate, marigold, 6"......................125.00
Jewels (Imperial), vase, amethyst 150.00
Kangaroo (Australian), bowl, marigold, 9½" 70.00
Kingfisher & VT (Australian), bowl, amethyst, 5"................50.00
Kittens, bottle, pastel...52.00
Kittens (Fenton), plate, marigold, scarce, 4½" 128.00
Kittens (Fenton), vase, bl, 3" 215.00
Kiwi (Australian), bowl, amethyst, rare, 10" 300.00
Knotted Beads (Fenton), vase, gr, 4"-12" 40.00
Kookaburra & VTs (Australian), bowl, marigold, 10" 80.00
Lacy Dewdrop (Westmoreland), banana boat, pastel 350.00
Large Kangaroo (Australian), bowl, amethyst, 10" 85.00
Lattice & Daisy (Dugan), bowl, marigold, 5"........................30.00
Lattice & Grape (Fenton), pitcher, gr 385.00
Lattice & Leaves, vase, bl, 9½" 67.00
Lattice & Sprays, vase, marigold, 10½" 40.00
Laurel & Grape, vase, marigold, 6" 110.00
Laurel Band, tumbler, marigold 42.00
LBJ Hat, ash tray, marigold..26.00
Leaf & Beads (Northwood-Dugan), bowl, gr, 9" 85.00
Leaf Chain (Fenton), bowl, bl, 7"-9" 48.00
Leaf Column (Northwood), vase, marigold 35.00
Leaf Swirl (Westmoreland), compote, amethyst....................55.00
Leaf Tiers (Fenton), bowl, marigold, ftd, 5" 30.00
Leaf Tiers (Fenton), tumbler, bl, ftd, rare 95.00
Lily of the Valley (Fenton), tumbler, bl, rare.....................450.00
Little Beads, bowl, marigold, 8" 18.00
Little Darling, bottle, marigold..52.00
Little Fishes (Fenton), plate, bl, rare, 10½" 450.00
Little Flowers (Fenton), bowl, marigold, 5½" 28.00
Little Stars (Millersburg), bowl, gr, rare, 4" 375.00
Loganberry (Imperial), vase, amethyst, scarce 385.00
Long Hobstar, compote, marigold 65.00
Long Prisms, hatpin, amethyst 35.00
Long Thumbprint (Dugan), bowl, marigold, 8¾"..................30.00

Long Thumbprint (Dugan), compote, amethyst............................39.00
Lotus & Grape (Fenton), bonbon, bl.......................................42.00
Lotus & Grape (Fenton), bowl, marigold, ftd, 7"......................48.00
Louisa (Westmoreland), bowl, amethyst, ftd.............................50.00
Lucky Bell, bowl, marigold, rare, 8¾".....................................40.00
Luster, tumbler, marigold 40.00
Lustre & Clear (Fenton), fan vase, gr......................................55.00
Lustre & Clear (Imperial), bowl, marigold, 5" 20.00
Lustre & Clear (Imperial), wall pocket, marigold.......................30.00
Lustre Flute (Northwood), bowl, marigold, 5½" 36.00
Lustre Rose (Imperial), butter dish, pastel 100.00
Lustre Rose (Imperial), pitcher, marigold...............................85.00
Lutz (McKee), mug, marigold, ftd 45.00
Magnolia Drape, pitcher, marigold 140.00
Magpie (Australian), bowl, amethyst, 6"-10".............................56.00
Malaga (Dugan), bowl, marigold, scarce, 9"..............................70.00
Maple Leaf (Dugan), butter dish, bl......................................118.00
Maple Leaf (Dugan), pitcher, bl...300.00
May Basket (English), basket, marigold, 7½"............................46.00
Mayan (Millersburg), bowl, gr, rare, 9"..................................140.00
Mayan (Millersburg), bowl, gr, 7½".......................................130.00
Mayflower, shade, marigold 30.00
Maypole, vase, gr, 6¼" 56.00
Melon Rib (Imperial), tumbler, marigold.................................24.00
Memphis (Northwood), bowl, gr, 10".....................................100.00
Miniature Bell, paperweight, marigold, 2½" 45.00
Mirrored Lotus (Fenton), bowl, bl, 7"-8½"...............................50.00
Mirrored Lotus (Fenton), plate, marigold, rare, 7½" 145.00
Mirrored Peacocks, tumbler, marigold, rare 150.00
Mitered Diamond & Pleats (English), bowl, bl, shallow, 8½" 40.00
Moonprint (English), compote, marigold 45.00
Moonprint (English), vase, marigold.......................................50.00
Morning Glory (Imperial), vase, gr 70.00
Moxie, bottle, pastel, rare 78.00
Multi-Fruits & Flowers (Millersburg), tumbler, amethyst.............950.00
Napoleon, bottle, pastel...70.00
Near Cut (Cambridge), decanter w/stopper, gr, rare 2,200.00
Near Cut Souvenir (Cambridge), tumbler, marigold, rare...........210.00
Near Cut Wreath (Millersburg), mug, marigold 65.00
Nesting Swan (Millersburg), bowl, marigold, ruffled, 10" 165.00
Nippon (Northwood), bowl, gr, 8½".......................................56.00
Nippon (Northwood), plate, gr, 9" 375.00
Northern Star (Fenton), card tray, marigold, 6" 38.00
Northern Star (Fenton), plate, marigold, rare, 6½" 70.00
Northwood Jester's Cap, vase, bl, ...58.00
Northwood's Nearcut, compote, marigold 85.00
Northwood's Poppy, bowl, bl, 7"- 8¾"....................................58.00
Nu-Art Chrysanthemum (Imperial), plate, gr, rare 950.00
Number 2176 (Sowerby), lemon squeezer, marigold....................50.00
Number 2351 (Cambridge), punch bowl, amethyst 65.00
Number 270 (Westmoreland), compote, amethyst.......................70.00
Number 4 (Imperial), bowl, pastel, ftd....................................36.00
Octagon (Imperial), butter dish, gr 126.00
Octagon (Imperial), creamer or spooner, marigold......................48.00
Octet (Northwood), bowl, amethyst, 8½" 60.00
Ohio Star (Millersburg), vase, gr, rare....................................900.00
Oklahoma (Mexican), shade, pastel, rare...................................87.00
Oklahoma (Mexican), tumble-up, marigold, complete 175.00
Olympic, shade, marigold 50.00
Olympic (Millersburg), compote, gr, rare, sm 1,000.00
Omnibus, tumbler, marigold, rare...275.00
Open Flower (Dugan), bowl, gr, flat or ftd, 7" 38.00
Open Rose (Imperial), plate, amethyst, 9" 290.00

Optic & Buttons (Imperial), pitcher, marigold, rare, sm 185.00
Optic Flute (Imperial), compote, marigold 55.00
Optic 66 (Fostoria), goblet, marigold 45.00
Orange Peel (Westmoreland), punch bowl, pastel, w/base..........165.00
Orange Tree (Fenton), butter dish, bl 150.00
Orange Tree (Fenton), creamer or spooner, marigold....................45.00
Orange Tree (Fenton), cup, pastel 38.00
Orange Tree (Fenton), hatpin holder whimsey, bl, rare 2,500.00
Orange Tree & Scroll (Fenton), tumbler, gr 85.00
Orange Tree Orchard (Fenton), tumbler, amethyst......................48.00
Oriental Poppy (Northwood), pitcher, pastel 1,800.00
Ostrich (Australian), cake stand, marigold, rare 160.00
Oval Prisms, hatpin, amethyst 32.00
Oval Star & Fan (Jenkins), rose bowl, amethyst.........................57.00
Owl Bank, marigold..38.00
Owl Bottle, pastel 65.00
Painted Pansy, fan vase, marigold 42.00
Palm Beach (US Glass), banana bowl, amethyst........................220.00
Panelled Dandelion (Fenton), tumbler, bl 70.00
Panelled Diamond & Bows (Fenton), vase, gr, 7"-14"..................38.00
Panelled Palm (US Glass), mug, marigold, rare 90.00
Panelled Smocking, sugar bowl, marigold 47.00
Panelled Swirl, rose bowl, marigold..65.00
Panels & Beads, shade, pastel 44.00
Pansy (Imperial), creamer or sugar bowl, amethyst 40.00
Panther (Fenton), whimsey bowl, bl, 10½" 900.00
Paperweight, flower-shaped, pastel, rare 195.00
Parlor, ash tray, bl 95.00
Pastel Panels (Imperial), tumbler, pastel 70.00
Peach (Northwood), pitcher, bl...585.00
Peach & Pear (Dugan), banana bowl, marigold..........................70.00
Peaches, wine bottle, marigold..37.00
Peacock, Strutting; (Westmoreland), creamer, gr, w/lid...............60.00
Peacock (Millersburg), bowl, gr, 5"...58.00
Peacock & Dahlia (Fenton), plate, bl, rare, 8½".......................210.00
Peacock & Urn (Fenton), bowl, amethyst, 8½" 67.00
Peacock & Urn (Northwood), bowl, gr, 9"...............................100.00
Peacock & Urn & VTs (Millersburg), compote, gr, rare 995.00
Peacock & Urn & VTs (Millersburg), plate, marigold, 10½" .. 2,600.00
Peacock at the Fountain (Dugan), pitcher, bl.............................350.00

Peacock at the Fountain (Northwood), cup, amethyst..................35.00
Peacock at the Fountain (Northwood), sugar bowl, gr 95.00
Peacock at the Fountain (Northwood), tumbler, marigold 36.00
Peacock Lamp, carnival base, amethyst 300.00
Peacock Tail (Fenton), compote, bl...48.00
Peacock Tail (Fenton), plate, marigold, 9"...............................195.00
Peacock Tail VT (Millersburg), compote, gr, scarce 85.00
Pearl & Jewels (Fenton), basket, pastel, 4"..............................190.00
Pearl #37 (Northwood), shade, pastel......................................60.00
Pearl Lady (Northwood), shade, pastel 55.00

Perfection (Millersburg), tumbler, gr, rare 650.00
Persian Garden (Dugan), bowl, ice cream; bl, 6" 90.00
Persian Medallion (Fenton), bonbon, amethyst 48.00
Petal & Fan (Dugan), bowl, marigold, 8½" 50.00
Petals (Dugan), compote, pastel 80.00
Pickle, paperweight, amethyst, 4½" 45.00
Pillar & Drape, shade, peach opal 65.00
Pin-Ups (Australian), bowl, marigold, rare, 8¾" 90.00
Pineapple (English), butter dish, marigold.....................................85.00
Pinwheel (English), bowl, marigold, rare, 8" 65.00
Plaid (Fenton), plate, bl, rare, 9" 185.00
Plain Jane (Imperial), basket, marigold...60.00
Pleats & Hearts, shade, pastel 70.00
Polo, ash tray, marigold..40.00
Pony (Dugan), bowl, amethyst, 8½" 120.00
Poppy (Millersburg), salver, gr, rare 1,450.00
Poppy Show (Imperial), hurricane whimsey, pastel 1,600.00
Poppy Show (Northwood), plate, gr, rare, 9" 900.00
Prayer Rug (Fenton), bonbon, peach opal, rare 645.00
Premium (Imperial), underplate, pastel, 14"................................130.00

Pretty Panels (Fenton), pitcher, pastel, w/lid................................490.00
Pretty Panels (Northwood), tumbler, gr...70.00
Primrose (Millersburg), bowl, ice cream; gr, scarce, 9" 150.00
Princely Plumes, candle holder, amethyst.....................................260.00
Prism, hatpin, amethyst...40.00
Prism & Daisy Band (Imperial), bowl, marigold, 8" 30.00
Prism Band (Fenton), pitcher, gr, w/decor 375.00
Propeller (Imperial), compote, marigold...30.00
Proud Puss (Cambridge), bottle, marigold......................................80.00
Pulled Loop (Dugan), vase, bl 30.00
Quartered Block, sugar bowl, marigold 50.00
Queen's Lamp, gr, rare... 1,600.00
Question Marks (Dugan), cake plate, amethyst, stemmed, rare...450.00
Quill (Dugan), tumbler, marigold, rare 375.00
Rainbow (Northwood), compote, gr..145.00
Ranger (Mexican), nappy, marigold 80.00
Raspberry (Northwood), pitcher, amethyst 220.00
Rays & Ribbons (Millersburg), banana bowl, gr, rare....................900.00
Red Panels (Imperial), shade, red 160.00
Rib & Panel (Fenton), vase, marigold 45.00
Ribbed Elipse, mug, pastel, rare..90.00
Ribbon & Block, lamp, marigold, complete 500.00
Ribbon & Fern, atomizer, marigold, 7" 75.00
Ribbon Tie (Fenton), bowl, gr, 8¾" 60.00
Rings, vase, marigold, 8" 55.00
Rising Sun (US Glass), butter dish, marigold................................150.00
Rock Crystal (McKee), cup, amethyst 45.00
Rococo (Imperial), vase, gr, 5½" 160.00
Roll, tumbler, marigold..38.00
Rose & Greek Key, plate, pastel, sq, rare 6,000.00

Rose Bouquet, creamer, marigold 54.00
Rose Garden (Sweden), letter vase, bl 55.00
Rose Panels (Australian), compote, marigold, lg...........................120.00
Rose Pinwheel, bowl, gr, rare 2,000.00
Rose Show (Northwood), bowl, pastel, 8¾" 265.00
Rose Spray (Fenton), compote, marigold.......................................160.00
Rosetime, vase, marigold 68.00
Rosettes (Northwood), bowl, amethyst, ftd, 7" 95.00
Royalty (Imperial), cup, marigold 28.00
S-Band (Australian), compote, amethyst..65.00
S-Repeat (Dugan), cup, amethyst, rare 110.00
S-Repeat (Dugan), tumbler, marigold 45.00
Sailboats (Fenton), goblet, gr..260.00
Sailing Ship, plate, marigold, 8" 40.00
Salamanders, hatpin, amethyst 45.00
Salt Cup, marigold...45.00
Satin Swirl, atomizer, pastel 65.00
Scale Band (Fenton), pitcher, bl..210.00
Scales (Westmoreland), bonbon, aqua opal....................................300.00
Scroll (Westmoreland), pin tray, marigold 45.00
Scroll Embossed (Imperial), plate, marigold, 9"..............................58.00
Seagulls, bowl, marigold, scarce, 6½" 65.00
Seagulls, vase, marigold, rare..750.00
Seaweed (Millersburg), bowl, gr, rare, 5" 400.00
Sharp, shot glass, pastel 60.00
Shell, shade, pastel...65.00
Shell & Balls, perfumer, marigold, 2½" 48.00
Sheraton (US Glass), butter dish, pastel...120.00
Ship & Stars, plate, marigold, 8" 30.00
Shrine (US Glass), champagne, pastel...90.00
Silver & Gold, tumbler, marigold...25.00
Silver Queen (Fenton), pitcher, marigold.......................................175.00
Singing Birds (Northwood), mug, bl...280.00
Single Flower (Dugan), hat, gr...35.00
Six Petals (Dugan), hat, peach opal 70.00
Ski-Star (Dugan), bowl, gr, 5" 50.00
Small Blackberry (Northwood), compote, gr 57.00
Small Palms, shade, marigold...34.00
Small Thumbprint, creamer, marigold 60.00
Smooth Panels (Imperial), vase, pastel 58.00
Smooth Rays (Imperial), bonbon, pastel...24.00
Smooth Rays (Northwood), bonbon, gr..50.00
Smooth Rays (Westmoreland), compote, amethyst 50.00
Snow Fancy (McKee), bowl, gr, 5"..40.00
Soda Gold (Imperial), bowl, marigold, 9" 45.00
Soda Gold Spears (Dugan), plate, pastel, 9" 160.00
Soutache (Dugan), bowl, peach opal, 10".......................................365.00
Souvenir Banded, mug, marigold..70.00
Souvenir Mug (McKee), any lettering, marigold 52.00
Souvenir Vase (US Glass), vase, marigold, rare, 6½" 90.00
Sphinx (English), paperweight, pastel, rare 475.00
Spiderweb (Northwood), candy dish, pastel, w/lid 35.00
Spiralled Diamond Point, vase, marigold, 6" 38.00
Split Diamond (English), butter dish, marigold, scarce 70.00
Spring Basket (Imperial), basket, pastel, 5" 48.00
Springtime (Northwood), bowl, gr, 9" 120.00
Square Diamond, vase, bl, rare..125.00
Stag & Holly (Fenton), plate, bl, ftd, 9" 1,000.00
Standard, vase, marigold, 5½" 48.00
Star (English), bowl, marigold..35.00
Star & Diamond Point, hatpin, amethyst 40.00
Star & Fan, vase, bl, rare, 9½"..200.00
Star & File (Imperial), compote, pastel...56.00

Star & File (Imperial), sherbet, marigold 32.00
Star & Medallion (Imperial), tumbler, pastel 52.00
Star & Nearcut, hatpin, amethyst 38.00
Star Center (Imperial), plate, amethyst, 9" 65.00
Star Medallion (Imperial), butter dish, marigold................85.00
Star of David (Imperial), bowl, gr, scarce, 8¾" 75.00
Star Spray (Imperial), bowl, marigold, 7" 28.00
Starbright, vase, amethyst, 6½" 42.00
Starburst, perfumer, marigold, w/stopper............................50.00
Starflower, pitcher, bl, rare 1,800.00
Starlyte (Imperial), shade, marigold.....................................28.00
Stippled Diamond Swag (English), compote, bl..................56.00
Stippled Flower (Dugan), bowl, peach opal, 8½" 80.00
Stippled Petals (Dugan), bowl, amethyst, 9".......................80.00
Stippled Rays (Fenton), plate, gr, 7" 45.00
Stippled Rays (Imperial), sugar bowl, gr, stemmed 46.00
Stippled Rays (Northwood), compote, marigold 45.00
Stippled Strawberry (Jenkins), butter dish, marigold..........90.00
Stork & Rushes (Dugan), mug, amethyst 58.00
Strawberry (Dugan), epergne, amethyst, rare 795.00
Strawberry (Fenton), bonbon, amethyst 45.00
Strawberry (Millersburg), gravy boat whimsey, pastel 275.00
Strawberry Intaglio (Northwood), bowl, marigold, 5½".......25.00
Strawberry Point, tumbler, marigold 100.00
Strawberry Scroll (Fenton), tumbler, bl, rare 175.00
Strawberry Spray, brooch, bl 170.00
Stream of Hearts (Fenton), compote, pastel, rare 70.00
Studs (Imperial), tumbler, juice; marigold 30.00
Sun Punch, bottle, pastel 26.00
Sunflower (Millersburg), pin tray, gr, rare...........................275.00
Sunken Daisy (English), sugar bowl, bl................................36.00
Sunray, compote, amethyst 38.00
Sweetheart (Cambridge), tumbler, marigold, rare 600.00
Swirl (Northwood), mug, marigold, rare................................65.00
Swirl Hobnail (Millersburg), spittoon, gr, rare 1,050.00
Swirl VT (Imperial), epergne, gr...170.00
Swirled Ribs (Northwood), pitcher, marigold 165.00
Sword & Circle, tumbler, marigold, rare 85.00
Target (Fenton), vase, gr, 7"-11"...48.00
Ten Mums (Fenton), pitcher, bl, rare...................................875.00
Texas, giant tumbler, bl 185.00
Thistle, shade, marigold...40.00

Thistle (English), vase, marigold, 6" 30.00
Thistle (Fenton), compote, bl 58.00
Thistle & Lotus (Fenton), bowl, gr, 7".................................58.00
Three Diamonds (Dugan), vase, amethyst, 6"-10"...............46.00
Three Fruits (Northwood), bowl, gr, 5"................................30.00
Three Fruits VT (Dugan), plate, gr, 12-sided.....................200.00
Three Monkeys, bottle, pastel, rare.......................................75.00
Three Row (Imperial), vase, amethyst, rare.........................950.00

Three-In-One (Imperial), bowl, gr, 8¾" 36.00
Thumbprint & Spears, creamer, marigold..............................50.00
Thunderbird (Australian), bowl, amethyst, 5".......................45.00
Tiger Lily (Imperial), pitcher, gr...300.00
Tiny Hobnail, lamp, marigold..95.00
Top Hat, vase, pastel 45.00
Top O' the Morning, hatpin, amethyst 26.00
Tornado VT (Northwood), vase, marigold, rare................1,200.00
Toy Punch Set (Cambridge), bowl only, marigold, ftd.........48.00
Tree Bark, (Imperial), candy jar, marigold, w/lid 30.00
Tree of Life (Imperial), tumbler, marigold............................22.00
Treebark VT, candle holder on stand, marigold 85.00
Triad, hatpin, amethyst..27.00
Triands (English), spooner, marigold 48.00
Triplets (Dugan), bowl, gr, 6"- 8"..42.00
Tulip (Millersburg), compote, gr, rare, 9"...........................950.00
Tulip Scroll (Millersburg), vase, gr, rare, 6"- 12" 240.00
Tumble-Up (Fenton-Imperial), plain, marigold, complete 55.00
Twins (Imperial), bowl, gr, 5"...30.00
Two Flowers (Fenton), rose bowl, bl, rare 147.00
Two Fruits (Northwood), sugar bowl, bl, rare 450.00
Umbrella Prisms, hatpin, amethyst, lg 30.00
Urn, vase, marigold, 9"...40.00
Utility, lamp, marigold, complete, 8" 75.00
Valentine, ring tray, marigold..80.00
Venetian (Cambridge), butter dish, marigold, rare 600.00
Victorian, bowl, amethyst, rare, 10"-12".............................250.00
Vineyard & Fishnet (Imperial), vase, red, rare 550.00
Vining Twigs (Dugan), hat, pastel 55.00
Vintage (Fenton), card tray, marigold 36.00
Vintage (Millersburg), bowl, gr, rare, 9" 650.00
Vintage (US Glass), wine, amethyst 48.00
Vintage Banded (Dugan), mug, marigold 30.00
Vintage VT (Dugan), plate, amethyst 385.00
Votive Light (Mexican), candle vase, marigold, rare, 4½"...........265.00
Waffle Block (Imperial), nappy, pastel 40.00
Waffle Weave, inkwell, marigold..85.00
War Dance (English), compote, marigold, 5" 65.00
Washboard, creamer, marigold, 5½".....................................42.00
Water Lily (Fenton), bowl, gr, ftd, 10".................................46.00
Water Lily & Cattails (Fenton), bowl, bl, 5".........................50.00
Water Lily & Cattails (Northwood), tumbler, bl 2,700.00
Wavey Satin, hatpin, amethyst 25.00
Western Daisy (Westmoreland), hat, amethyst 45.00
Wheels (Imperial), bowl, marigold, 9" 45.00
Whirling Hobstar (US Glass), cup, marigold.........................16.00
Whirling Star (Imperial), compote, gr 62.00
White Elephant, ornament, pastel, rare................................350.00
White Oak, tumbler, marigold, rare 250.00
Wide Panel (US Glass), salt, marigold 38.00
Wide Panel (Westmoreland), bowl, pastel, 8¼" 62.00
Wide Panel Bouquet, basket, marigold, 3½".........................65.00
Wide Panel VT (Northwood), pitcher, tankard; gr 260.00
Wide Rib (Dugan), vase, peach opal 60.00
Wild Berry, jar, marigold, w/lid..75.00
Wild Fern (Australian), compote, amethyst 165.00
Wild Loganberry (Westmoreland), goblet, peach opal.........100.00
Wild Loganberry (Westmoreland), wine, marigold................85.00
Wild Rose (Millersburg), lamp, marigold, rare, lg 1,500.00
Wild Strawberry (Dugan), bowl, amethyst, rare, 6" 65.00
Windflower (Dugan), plate, bl, 9".......................................160.00
Windmill (Imperial), fruit bowl, gr, 10½" 40.00
Windmill (Imperial), milk pitcher, amethyst........................135.00

Windsor (Imperial), flower arranger, pastel, rare 85.00
Wine & Roses (Fenton), wine, bl...80.00
Winged Heavy Shell, vase, pastel, 3½" 95.00
Wise Owl, bank, marigold 46.00
Wishbone (Northwood), pitcher, gr, rare..............................985.00
Wisteria (Northwood), pitcher, pastel, rare........................... 4,000.00
Woodlands, vase, marigold, rare, 5" 75.00
Woodpecker (Dugan), wall pocket, pr 75.00
Wreath of Roses (Fenton), bonbon, bl..................................40.00
Wreath of Roses VT (Dugan), compote, gr...............................60.00
Wreathed Cherry (Dugan), butter dish, amethyst 160.00
Zig Zag (Fenton), tumbler, bl, decorated..............................50.00
Zig Zag (Millersburg), card tray, gr, rare.............................750.00
Zip Zip (English), flower frog holder, marigold 54.00
Zipper Loop (Imperial), hand lamp, pastel, rare 500.00
474 (Imperial), bowl, marigold, 8"-9" 60.00
474 (Imperial), goblet, gr...65.00
49'er (Imperial), wine, marigold...50.00

Carousel Figures

Who can forget the dazzle of the merry-go-round – lights blinking, animals prancing proudly by to the waltzes that bellowed from the band organ . . .

Gustav Dentzel, a German woodworker, created one of the first carousels in America in 1867. By the turn of the century, his animals had evolved from horses with a military bearing to fanciful creatures in various postures with garlands of flowers, exotic saddles, and other adornment. Dentzel was followed in the business by his son William, and both are noted for the exacting perfection of their carving and painting. The Philadelphia Toboggan Company, established in 1903, is famous today for its superior chariot designs. In 1901 Marcus Charles Illions formed his company, M.C. Illions and Sons. Illions' carvings became more intricate with the growth of his company, and those from the twenties are generally valued more highly than those from between 1901 and 1910. The largest carousels were produced by the Artistic Carousel Manufacturers of Brooklyn, Harry Goldstein and Solomon Stein. Charles Carmel and Daniel Muller are both exquisite carvers whose work is today very highly regarded. Other builders whose works are also very valuable (though much less intricate) are The Herschell – Spillman Company; American Merry-Go-Round and Novelty Company; Charles Dare of the New York Carousel Manufacturing Company; and Charles Parker.

Until the 1930s, carousels were found in nearly every fair and amusement park in the country. One by one, as they fell into disrepair, many have been dismantled and junked or sold at auction. Today these hand-carved creatures are respected examples of American folk art and often bring prices well into the thousands. Price is based on a number of factors, the most important of which are: carver (with Dentzel, Looff, PTC, Carmel, Illions, and Muller the most valued), type of animal (some species are rarely encountered), and intricacy of carving. Also to be considered are size, wood and paint condition, where the figure was located on the carousel, whether it stands or jumps, and in some cases its age. Because there are so many factors to consider and since no two figures are identical, exact pricing is difficult. Condition can affect the price of an animal as much as $3,000 for the more elaborate pieces and up to 50% for the lower-priced animals.

Key:
IR — inside row
MR — middle row
OR — outside row
PP — park paint

PR — paint removed
PTC — Philadelphia Toboggan Company
MR — middle row

SEC — Spillman Engineering Corp.   OR — outside row

Bayol, pig, tongue out, PP, M 2,950.00
Carmel, OR jumper, star gazer, mirrors/jewels, PR 10,500.00

Carmel star gazer, park paint, 45" x 45", $8,800.00.

Dentzel, deer, OR prancer, closed mouth/eagle saddle, rstr 17,500.00
Dentzel, MR jumper, mare style w/roached mane, PR 7,500.00
Herschell-Spillman, zebra, rstr, 1902 .... 4,450.00
Looff, goat, PR, sm 9,000.00
Looff, stander, parrot saddle, EX rstr....................................12,000.00
Muller, MR jumper, PR 8,000.00
Muller Dentzel, MR jumper, PR 7,500.00
PTC, OR stander, head down, tassels, VG PP, 1922...............15,000.00
PTC, OR stander, jeweled, w/wooden tail, 1932, PR 11,000.00
PTC, stander, tassels/owls behind cantle, tongue out, EX 12,750.00
Spillman, jumper, PR, sm... 3,750.00

Carpet Balls

Carpet balls are glazed china spheres decorated with intersecting lines or other simple designs, that were used for indoor games in the British Isles during the early 1800s. Mint condition examples are rare; listings are for those with minimal damage.

Carpet balls, 1 of cloth, 1 of wicker, 2 of ceramic, each in VG condition, lot of 4: $125.00.

Bl w/wht polka dots, 3", EX...80.00
Blk & bl circles around bull's eye on wht, 3", VG 50.00

Blk w/blk dots w/in wht frilly circles, 3⅜", NM 60.00
Brn w/brn dots w/in wht frilly circles, 4", EX 68.00
Gr & blk stripes wrap around 3 ways on wht, 2⅝", VG 100.00
Gr stripes wrap around 3 ways on wht, 3", EX 45.00
3 bands of pk stripes wrap around 3 ways on wht, 3¼", VG 50.00

Cartoon Art

Collectors of cartoon art are interested in many forms of original art – animation cels, sports, political or editorial cartoons, syndicated comic strip panels, and caricature. To produce even a short animated cartoon strip, hundreds of original drawings are required, each showing the characters in slightly advancing positions. Called 'cels' because those made prior to the 1950s were made from a celluloid material, collectors often pay hundreds of dollars for a frame from a favorite movie. Prices of Disney cels with backgrounds vary widely. Background paintings, model sheets, storyboards, and preliminary sketches are also collectible   so are comic book drawings executed in India ink and signed by the artist. Daily 'funnies' originals, especially the earlier ones portraying super heroes, and Sunday comic strips, the early as well as the later ones, are collected. Cartoon art has become recognized and valued as a novel yet valid form of contemporary art.

Animation Cel-Full Color

Alice in Wonderland, alarmed amid flowers, '51, 10x13" **1,650.00**
Bambi, w/3 rabbits, gouache ground, Disney, '42, 9x13" **1,870.00**
Briar Rose, Sleeping Beauty, full cell, NM....................................115.00
Cat in the Hat, Dr Seuss, full cell, NM..145.00
Cinderella, Gus the mouse w/corn kernels, 1950, fr, 8x10" 800.00
Cinderella, stepmother & sisters on stairs, '50, 11x16" 660.00
Donald Duck, hand colored, inscribed, 1940s, full cell, NM........275.00

Donald Gets Drafted, Courvoisier background, 6¾" x 6¼", $1,100.00.

Dr Ages, Secret of Nimh, full cell, fr & matted...........................275.00
Dumbo, flying, airbrushed ground, Disney, 1941, 7x8½" **4,125.00**
Dumbo, Mouse, gouache, Courvoisier ground, '55, 8x10" **1,600.00**
Fantasia, baby Pegasus flying, 1940, fr, 4x6" **1,000.00**
Fred Flintstone, dressed as Santa, matted 125.00

Fred Flintstone, 4 characters, fr & matted 275.00
Jungle Book, King Louie, printed ground, '67, fr, 9x12" 900.00
Jungle Book, Shere Khan & tiger, matted, 1967, 10x13" 550.00
Little Hiawatha, bow/arrow, Disney, 1937, matted, 9x10" **1,000.00**
Peter Pan, Tiger Lily, watercolor ground, matted, '53, 8x9" 715.00
Pinocchio, Giddy & Foulfellow, Disney, inscribed, '39, 7x8".... **1,870.00**
Popeye, on ship's deck, HP bkground, matted, EX 185.00
Snow White & 7 Dwarfs, Grumpy, starred ground, fr, 7x5" 825.00
Tinkerbell, w/wand on starry ground, Disney, 1955, fr, 7x8".... **1,000.00**
Wizard of Oz, entire cast, 1973, matted, w/stamp, NM 225.00
101 Dalmations, Pongo/Badun Bros, gouache, 1961, 12x15".......500.00

Animation Drawing

Canine Caddy, Mickey Mouse playing golf, pencils, '41, 9x10" ...**900.00**
Dognapper, M Mouse & D Duck, graphite/crayon, '34, 8x12".....**900.00**
Lady & Tramp, Jock & Scamp, HP ground, pr 245.00
Mickey's Circus, MM as ringmaster, pencils, '36, 8x7" 600.00
Pinocchio, Stromboli gesturing, pencils, 1940, fr, 7x10" 400.00
Snow White, in princess clothes w/cape, pencils, '38, 7½x8" 700.00

Model Sheets

Bell Boy Donald, Senator Pete/son/Donald+more, 1942 ....300.00
Early to Bed, Donald Duck getting ready, 1940, 22x14" 235.00
Jungle Book, vultures & Mowgli, varied poses, rare 365.00
Mickey's Grand Opera, Donald Duck & frog, 1936, 13x16"........230.00
Peter Pan, Wendy, Peter, all the boys, 1953, 14¼x17" 400.00

Sunday Newspaper Comics

Buster Brown, NY Herald, 1902, EX 60.00
Dick Tracy, w/BO Plenty & 2-way wrist radio, Jan 1946, ½-pg 18.00
Flash Gordon, Lands of Mongo, 2nd strip, full pg.........................40.00
Krazy Cat, no other characters, Feb 13, 1938, 11x16" 16.00
Little Orphan Annie, lost infant, Dec 4, 1927, lg panel, EX..........10.00
Mandrake the Magician, w/Narda, magic panels, Dec 2, 1945 ......12.50
Pogo, bear as Santa, Pogo, & turtle w/reins, '53, 11x14" 12.50
Prince Valiant, Valiant & Gawain, June 1954, full pg...................10.00
Superman, Clark/Superman/Lois, Aug 9, 1942, full pg.................12.50
Superman, Tokyo Rose/Japs/Superman/Lois, Sept 9, 1945, full pg.17.50
Tarzan, Execution Chamber, trimmed margins, Aug 26, 1934 ......10.00

Ink cartoon drawing, Maggie and Jiggs, George McManus, 8" x 13", $400.00.

Cartoon Books

'Books of cartoons' were printed during the first decade of the twentieth century and remained popular until the advent of the modern comic book in the late thirties. Cartoon books, printed in both color and black and white, were merely reprints of current newspaper comic strips. The books, ranging from thirty to seventy pages and in sizes from 3½" x 8" up to 11" x 17", were usually bound with cardboard covers and were often distributed as premiums in exchange for coupons saved from the daily paper. One of the largest of the companies who printed these books was Cupples and Leon, producer of nearly half of the two hundred titles on record. Among the most popular sellers were Mutt and Jeff, Bringing Up Father, and Little Orphan Annie.

Bringing Up Father, 1st Series, EX, $60.00; 2nd Series, NM, $60.00; The Gumps, 1925, VG, $45.00; Keeping Up with the Joneses, 2nd Series, EX, $35.00.

Barney Google & Spark Plug, #4, EX......................32.00
Bringing Up Father, McManus, #14, 1928, EX...............25.00
Bringing Up Father, McManus, #20, EX....................55.00
Bringing Up Father, McManus, #20, VG....................20.00
Bringing Up Father, McManus, #5, EX.....................40.00
Bringing Up Father, McManus, #7, NM.....................68.00
Bringing Up Father, McManus, #9, EX.....................36.00
Hans Und Fritz, R Dirks, Saalfield, Book 193, 1917........60.00
Mutt & Jeff, Ball, #1, EX..............................185.00
Mutt & Jeff, Ball, #4, VG...............................75.00
Mutt & Jeff, Ball, #5, EX..............................100.00
Mutt & Jeff, Bud Fisher, #12, 1937......................35.00
Mutt & Jeff Big Book #2.................................40.00
Skeezix & Uncle Walt, King, 1924, NM....................40.00
Toonerville Trolley, Cupples & Leon, #1, 1921, NM 75.00

Cash Registers

Cash registers are being restored, rebuilt, and used as they were originally intended, in businesses ranging from eating establishments to antique stores. Their brass and marble construction has made them almost impervious to aging, and with just a bit of polish and shine they bring a bit of the grand Victorian era into modern times.

Antique cash registers are categorized as either restored or unrestored. A restored register is one where the cabinet has been stripped, polished, and lacquered; indicators are free of dust, dirt, and visible signs of wear; key arms are rust-free, plated or painted; and key checks and rings are new, used, or originals. The drawer has been stripped and revarnished, and the rails are in good condition. All mechanisms are completely reworked; broken parts are replaced, oiled, and working per-

fectly. Prices for registers in unrestored condition vary greatly. Unrestored registers are classed as either working or non-working. Values for those with missing major parts are much lower. In the listings that follow, M condition refers to fully-restored cash registers; VG condition is for registers in original unrestored working condition. For further information we recommend the highly-informative books, *Antique Cash Registers 1880 - 1920*, by Bartsch and Sanchez (Mr. Bartsch's address may be found in our Directory under Oregon); and *The Incorruptible Cashier Vol. 1*, which is currently available from our advisor, John Apple, who is listed in the Directory under Wisconsin.

American, 50-key register, copper plated, 212-lb, M..............1,800.00
American, 50-key register, copper plated, 212-lb, VG................900.00
McCaskey Alliance, metal, 1-drw, blk w/gold, 22x21x18", VG...100.00
Michigan #1, 22-key, M...500.00
Michigan #1, 22-key, VG..200.00
Michigan #7, 9-key, M..750.00
Michigan #7, 9-key, VG...450.00
NCR #1000 class, autographic box attachment, 1910, M.......1,200.00
NCR #1000 class, autographic box attachment, 1910, VG........600.00
NCR #13, nickeled CI, Ionic pattern, continuous cap, M.......1,100.00
NCR #13, nickeled CI, Ionic pattern, continuous cap, VG........600.00
NCR #130, barber shop, keyed from 5¢ to $1, VG.................800.00
NCR #2, inlayed wood, VG.....................................2,000.00
NCR #210 or #211, 11-key, fleur-de-lis pattern, M, ea..........1,500.00
NCR #210 or #211, 11-key, fleur-de-lis pattern, VG, ea.........1,000.00
NCR #226, keyed from 5¢ to $1, unplated bronze, M............1,100.00
NCR #226, keyed from 5¢ to $1, unplated bronze, VG.............600.00
NCR #3, inlayed wood, M......................................3,000.00
NCR #311, copper, ca 1915, VG 750.00
NCR #312 or #313, dolphin pattern, 1908-1916, M, ea.........1,200.00
NCR #312 or #313, dolphin pattern, 1908-1916, VG, ea...........750.00

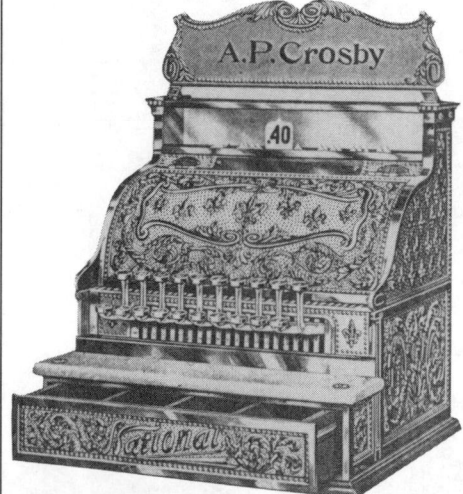

National Cash Register Co., Model #317, registers 5¢ to $1.00, marble change shelf, with printer, 16", EX, $1,200.00.

NCR #322, 15-key, extended base, M.......................... 1,600.00
NCR #322, 15-key, extended base, VG......................... 1,100.00
NCR #327, brass, barber shop, extended base, VG.................900.00
NCR #332, brass, top sign, rstr............................. 1,000.00
NCR #333, ornate brass, 14" W, VG 500.00
NCR #349-2-2, 2-counter, 2-drw, 1910, M.................... 1,800.00
NCR #349-2-2, 2-counter, 2-drw, 1910, VG................... 1,000.00
NCR #360 to #367, 37-key, personalized top sign, M, ea........950.00
NCR #360 to #367, 37-key, personalized top sign, VG, ea.......600.00
NCR #4, 40-key 'Signature Model,' 1892, M 2,500.00
NCR #4, 40-key 'Signature Model,' 1892, VG 1,000.00
NCR #442, crank machine, rstr............................. 1,000.00
NCR #442, crank machine, VG 600.00

NCR #444, check-numbering device, 1910, M 1,200.00
NCR #444, check-numbering device, 1910, VG...................700.00
NCR #452-2, crank style, 2-drw oak base, VG.....................850.00
NCR #522 Class, 2-drw, requires electricity, 1906, M............. 2,400.00
NCR #522 Class, 2-drw, requires electricity, 1906, VG 1,500.00
NCR #582-5E, bronze/panelled oak, 8-drw floor model, VG . 2,500.00
NCR #593-E-L, 9-drw, floor cabinet, 460+ lbs, 67¾", M......... 5,000.00
NCR #593-E-L, 9-drw, floor cabinet, 460+ lbs, 67¾", VG 2,500.00
NCR #71 to #99½, 79 Principle, 1892 scroll pattern, M, ea.... 1,800.00
NCR #71 to #99½, 79 Principle, 1892 scroll pattern, VG, ea 900.00
Peninsula, Muren, nickel plated, ca 1912, M....................500.00
Peninsula, Muren, nickel plated, ca 1912, VG 200.00

Cast Iron

In the mid-1800s, the cast iron industry was raging in the United States. It was recognized as a medium extremely adaptable for uses ranging from ornamental architectural filigree to actual building construction. It could be cast from a mold into any conceivable design that could be reproduced over and over at a relatively small cost. It could be painted to give an entirely versatile appearance. Furniture with openwork designs of grapevines and leaves and intricate lacy scrollwork was cast for gardens as well as inside use. Figural doorstops of every sort, bootjacks, trivets, and a host of other useful and decorative items were made before the 'ferromania' had run its course. See also Kitchen, Cast Iron Bakers and Kettles; and other specific categories.

Architectural finial, eagle on base dtd 1912, 31" W, pr.................450.00
Basin, early, 11½" 65.00
Bench, Classical design, old pnt, 35" L...................................200.00
Carriage step, CI & wrought, 1870s, EX 20.00
Chair, foliage design, pnt layers, sm 75.00
Cookie mold, Grecian urn, rectangular, 3x4" 175.00
Dumbbells, ca 1880, 4-lb, pr...25.00
Factory torch, dbl spout, screw-on lid, 7½" 60.00
Fence, spear point finials, gr pnt, 4 sections, 43x70" 245.00
Figurine, horse & foal, on wood base, orig pnt, 5¾".................105.00
Fountain ornament, theater mask form, 1800s, 12".....................200.00
Hitching post, Blk jockey on 6-sided base, pnt, 1900s, 36".........225.00
Hitching post, horse head atop, fluted, w/lion's heads, 70" 475.00
Hitching post, horse head atop spiral std, 39", VG..................150.00
Hook, drag; 4 stubby hooks, old, 17" 18.00
Kettle, apple butter; ring on hdl for hanging, sm 65.00
Kettle, hog scalding; hdls, 17x27" 355.00
Magazine rack, Chanticleer in Rococo pattern, ftd 135.00
Mailbox, Standard, scrollwork, peephole.....................................48.00
Plate, 1700s, 7¾" 130.00
Plug cutter, HB Rouse, Chicago USA, lift hdl, 1895-1900, 12½"..35.00
Posnet, str sprue, 1800s, 4¾x6¾" 95.00
Settee, 3-section bk, ea w/crest, scrollwork, 45" L......................400.00
Snow bird, eagle w/worn pnt, 6½", pr 70.00
Spider, str sprue, 1800s, 4½x9" 95.00
Teakettle, gooseneck, brass lid/hdl, mk #4 8-Pints.......................75.00
Teakettle, gooseneck, 3 legs, wrought pouring lever, 9½".............700.00
Teakettle, partial label: Alkiry #1, wrought hdl, 7" 175.00
Top hat, pnt hat band & bow, wht pnt int, worn, 7" 225.00
Umbrella stand, Rococo, 1870s, 27x13x10" 150.00
Urn, EX detail, 32", pr...850.00
Urn, foliage & scroll details, openwork hdls, Kramer, 27", EX 600.00
Urn, foliage detail, sq base, wht pnt, 43x36" dia 650.00
Urn, lg ear hdls w/pierced foliage, sq plinth, 31x18" 225.00
Urn, on sq base, worn pnt, 10" 85.00
Urn, ribbed, scalloped short ped base, 7x10", pr...........................130.00

Urn, sawtooth flange, sq ped ft, 20x21", pr....................................450.00
Urn, swan base, wht rpt, 38½", VG, pr..900.00
Vise, Columbia, Cleveland O, USA, 1800s, EX............................125.00
Wall bracket, flower form, mk Pat 1868, 6½", pr..............................75.00

State seal of New York, eagle and inscription, gilded, 35" x 34" $2,200.00.

Castor Sets

Castor sets became popular during the early years of the eighteenth century and continued to be used through the late Victorian era. Their purpose was to hold various condiments for table use. The most common type was a circular arrangement with a center handle on a revolving pedestal base that held three, four, five, or six bottles. Some had extras; a few were equipped with a bell for calling the servant. Frames were made of silverplate, glass, or pewter. Though most bottles were of pressed glass, some of the designs were cut; and occasionally colored glass with enameled decorations was used. To maintain authenticity and value, castor sets should have matching bottles. Prices listed below are for those with matching bottles and in frames with plating that is in excellent condition (unless noted otherwise).

Watch for new frames and bottles in both clear and colored glass – these have recently been appearing on the market.

Silverplated pewter stand by Roswell Gleason, doors of each compartment close by turning knob on top, 6 cut bottles, 16½", $1,500.00.

3-bottle, American Shield, mini, child's sz............................75.00
4-bottle, cranberry, orig stoppers; glass holder 225.00
4-bottle, Gothic Arch; pewter fr 115.00
4-bottle, King's Crown; SP fr 150.00
4-bottle, Venecia, rubena; glass fr, NM............................145.00
5-bottle, Bellflower, pressed stoppers; pewter fr w/ped, 11"............275.00
5-bottle, cut; 18" Rogers & Bro ornate fr, VG 150.00
5-bottle, etched amberina, cut amberina stoppers; gilt fr, EX . 2,000.00
5-bottle, etched wreath/polka dots; rib trim on fr, NM 150.00
5-bottle, Honeycomb; ornate Wilcox fr, EX 250.00
6-bottle, cut; SP pewter mechanical-door housing, Gleason ... 1,500.00
6-bottle, Daisy & Button, vaseline; lg Gleason fr, call bell...........700.00
6-bottle, eng; tiered Simpson-Hall-Miller fr revolves 165.00
6-bottle, etched wreath; lg Reed & Barton fr w/cupid................350.00
6-bottle, pressed; 18" Simpson-Hall-Miller fr w/VG SP 125.00
6-bottle, Sawtooth; ornate Meriden fr, call bell, dtd 1888, EX 395.00

Catalina Island

Catalina Island pottery was made on the island of the same name, which is about twenty-six miles off the coast of Los Angeles. The pottery was started in 1927 at Pebble Beach, by Wm Wrigley, Jr., who was instrumental in developing and using the native clays. Its principal products were brick and tile to be used for construction on the island. Garden pieces were first produced, then vases, bookends, lamps, ash trays, novelty items, and finally dinnerware. The ware became very popular and was soon being shipped to the mainland as well.

Some of the pottery was hand thrown; some was made in molds. Most pieces are marked Catalina Island or Catalina with a printed incised stamp, or handwritten with a pointed tool. Cast items were sometimes marked in the mold; a few have an ink stamp, and a paper label was also used.

The color of the clay can help to identify approximately when a piece was made: 1927 to 1932 – brown to red clay; 1931 to 1932 – an experimental period with various colors; 1932 to 1937 – mainly white clay, but tan to brown were also used on occasion.

See also Gladding McBean and Company.

Dinnerware

Catalina Island, bowl, berry............................18.00
Catalina Island, candle holder, low 55.00
Catalina Island, carafe, yel gloss 50.00
Catalina Island, cup & saucer 35.00
Catalina Island, custard cup 20.00
Catalina Island, plate, bread & butter; rimmed, 6½"............................15.00
Catalina Island, plate, dinner; 10"............................20.00
Catalina Island, plate, dinner; 11"............................25.00
Catalina Island, plate, luncheon; 8"............................15.00
Catalina Island, sugar bowl............................20.00
Catalina Island, tumbler, lg............................18.00
Catalina Island, wine cup, hdld............................13.00
Rope Edge, cup............................20.00
Rope Edge, plate, bread & butter 10.00
Rope Edge, plate, chop; 12"............................60.00
Rope Edge, plate, dinner............................20.00
Rope Edge, saucer 10.00

Miscellaneous

Ash tray, bear novelty, rare............................200.00
Ash tray, cowboy hat 65.00
Bowl, flower or fruit; 3½x10"............................95.00

Box, cigarette; horse's head 150.00
Candelabrum, 3-hole, half-circle............................95.00
Flower frog, crane............................75.00
Plate, Mexican scene, sgn FA Graham 350.00
Shakers, cactus, pr............................50.00
Shakers, tulip, pr............................65.00
Vase, bud; 5"............................45.00
Vase, flared top, 7½"............................85.00
Vase, shell shape, 6"............................125.00
Vinegar bottle, gourd-shape............................75.00

Catalogs

Catalogs are not only intriguing to collect on their own merit, but for the collector with a specific interest, they are often the only remaining source of background information available, and as such they offer a wealth of otherwise unrecorded data. The mail-order industry can be traced as far back as the mid-1800s. Even before Aaron Montgomery Ward began his career in 1872, Laacke and Joys of Wisconsin and the Orvis Company of Vermont, both dealers in sporting goods, had been well established for many years. The E.C. Allen Company sold household necessities and novelties by mail on a broad scale in the 1870s. By the end of the Civil War, sewing machines, garden seed, musical instruments – even medicine – were available from catalogs. In the 1880s, Macy's of New York issued a 127-page catalog; Sears and Spiegel followed suit in about 1890. Craft and art supply catalogs were first available about 1880 and covered such varied fields as china painting, stenciling, wood burning, brass embossing, hair weaving, and shellcraft. Today, some collectors confine their interests not only to craft catalogs in general, but often to one subject only. Examples may range from $1 to as much as $25 for the larger, color-illustrated versions.

AC Becken, watches/clocks/sterling/etc, 1909, 712-pg, EX 135.00
Astronomical Telescopes & Transit Instruments, 1890, 40-pg.......35.00
Baird-North, Providence RI, jewelry, illus, 1914, EX 15.00
Barlow Hardware, Corry PA, 1906, 252-pg, 5½x8" 30.00
Bramhall Galley Equipment, NY, 1919, 24-pg, 6x9" 25.00
Brown & Sharpe, machinery/tools, RI, 1920, 609-pg, 3½x6".........25.00
Buffalo Stoves, blk/wht illus, 1894, 54-pg, 5¼x8"........................35.00
Champion Harvesting Machines, 1901, EX 25.00
Chas William Stoves, color illus, 1922, EX............................75.00
Climax Ensilage Cutters, 16-pg, 1900, EX 15.00
Corn King Manure Spreader, 24-pg, 1905, G 10.00
Darly Municipal Equipment, 1920s, 27-pg, 8½x11", EX 22.50
Disston Saws, Tools, Files, 48-pg, 1924 .... 8.00
Dixie Stoves & Ranges, ca 1930, 68-pg 25.00
Endicot Johnson Shoes, full color, 1913, 79-pg, 8x10½" 40.00
Enterprise Food Choppers, 1927, 78-pg 45.00
F Stewart Electric Household Supplies, 1904, 72-pg 65.00
Fairbanks Scales, 1914, 914-pg, 4½x7", EX 45.00
Fisher Stringed Instruments, Boston, 1902, 120-pg, 9½x12".........95.00
Ford Business Trucks, 1921, 54-pg, 6x9", EX 25.00
Frances Brundage's Baby Book, 4 color pgs 100.00
Furst Parlor Clocks, Baltimore MD, 1893, 95-pg, VG 25.00
Garage Equipment Mfg, Milwaukee, 1910, EX 28.00
Gearhart's Improved Knitters, 12-pg, 1906, EX 12.50
Gellman Bros, MN Novelty & Premium Mdse, 1932, 320-pg 22.00
Gimson & Coltman Hosiery Machinery, 16-pg, 1880s, VG...........14.00
Gleeson Jewelry, hardbound, 1932, 172-pg............................65.00
Goldblatt's Mason's Tools, 48-pg, 1913, VG 9.00
Gummey, McFarland Tinners' Supplies, 156-pg, 1913, VG 14.00
Hajoca Vitreous China, 1928, 6x9" 25.00
Heaney Magical Goods, 96-pg, 1924, G 14.00

Heddon Fishing Tackle, 1954, EX..20.00
Hodges Kitchen Tinware, 1929, 107-pg, EX 30.00
Hyde Exploring Expedition of Indian Goods, NY, 1903 ....125.00
John Pritzlaff Hdwe Mechanics' & Edge Tools, 326-pg, 1913 ....30.00
Johnson Soap Premiums, 16-pg, 1890s, VG.................................. 8.00
JS Wodehouse Agricultural Implements, 1914, 81-pg, 7x10"........37.50
Kelly Bros Water Closets, Chicago, 1919, 40-pg, 6½x10" 35.00
Kodak Cameras, 1911, 64-pg, 5½x8", EX....................................35.00
L&C Mayers, 5th Ave, NY, jewelry, 1932, 436-pg, EX................100.00
Lehigh Plumbing & Heating, PA, hardback, 1925, 336-pg, 8x11".35.00
Leonard Cleanable Refrigerators, 96-pg, 1915, EX 15.00
Lewis Ross Shoes, 1909, 72-pg, 6x9½" 35.00
Marine Hardware, NY, 1912, 280-pg, EX....................................40.00
Marsten & Wells Fireworks, 1907, 84-pg, 4x5½", NM..................40.00
McAlear Steam Heating Specialties, 96-pg, 1910s, G.................... 6.00
Merritt Elliot Shoes, 1903, 64-pg, 7x10"....................................35.00
Mickey Mouse Merchandise, 98-pg, 1939, VG 180.00
Missouri Tent & Awning, 1894..35.00
Montgomery Ward, Christmas, 1961, EX 25.00
Montgomery Ward Fishing & Hunting Supplies, 1951, EX 25.00
Montgomery Ward...Sale of House Furnishings, 1911, EX 12.50
Moon Bros Carriages, St Louis, 1899, 48-pg, 6x9½", EX..............40.00
Murray Carriages, 1911, 176-pg, 8x10", EX.................................55.00
Nice Business Advertising Calendars, 14-pg, 1931, EX..................10.00
Olson Rugs, 51-pg, 1931, VG... 6.00
Oshkosh Trunks & Luggage, 55-pg, 1941, VG 6.00
Parry Buggies, Indianapolis IN, 1914, 106-pg, EX 55.00
Peters & Reed Pottery, Moss Aztec & Landsun Ware, OH, 1920 ..65.00
Pexto Machines & Tools for Sheet Metal Work, 404-pg, 1920 .....16.00
Ranger Bicycles, 1918, 64-pg, EX..65.00
Rawlings Sports Equipment, 64-pg, 1932-1933, EX.....................12.50
Sears, 1936, G..25.00
Sears Roebuck Sporting Goods, 1908, EX....................................45.00
Seattle Tents & Awnings, 1912, 120-pg, 6x9½", EX.....................55.00
Sedgwick Machines, elevators/dumbwaiters, NY, 1927, 32-pg 25.00
Shimer Cutter Heads, 224-pg, 1910, VG 12.00
Silent Motion Projectors, 1913, 8-pg, 6x8", EX............................75.00
Skinner-Steenman Sideboards & Buffets, 48-pg, 1904, VG...........15.00
Starret Tools, 383-pg, 1920, EX..40.00
Stockman-Farmer Supply, western wear, 1941-1942, 50-pg 22.50
Studebaker Automobiles, 1910s, 20-pg, EX..................................60.00
Sylvania Radio & Picture Tubes, 150-pg, 1953, G......................... 8.00
T Kelly Bros Water Closets, ca 1919, 40-pg..................................40.00
Terrestrial Telescopes & Accessories, 1892, 25-pg 45.00
Thompson Boats, 32-pg, 1928, EX 26.00
Toy Guidance Council, 1952, 63-pg 25.00
Trolley Car Air Brakes, 1903, 56-pg, EX......................................35.00
Uhlen Baby Carriages, NY, 1928, 88-pg.......................................45.00
United Cigar Stores Premiums, 48-pg, 1927, G............................. 8.00
US Cream Separator, EX color, 1900s, 48-pg, 6x9" 25.00
Waddel Showcases, 1920, 16-pg, 8x10" 15.00
Western Auto, 1937, 32-pg 5.00
Western Cartridge, ammunition, 1935, EX....................................25.00
White Appliances, colored illus, 1912, EX 75.00
Williamson Warm Air Furnaces, Cincinnati, 1923, 32-pg, EX 12.50
Wm Johnson Mason's Tools, 4-pg, 1890s, EX 7.00
Wodehouse Agricultural Implements, illus, 1914, 80-pg, EX 35.00

Caughley Ware

The Caughley Coalport Porcelain Manufactory operated from about 1775 until 1799 in Caughley, near Salop, Shropshire, in England. The owner was Thomas Turner, who gained his potting experience from his association with the Worcester Pottery Company. The wares he manufactured in Caughley are referred to as 'Salopian.' He is most famous for his blue-printed earthenwares, particularly the Blue Willow pattern, designed for him by Thomas Minton. For a more detailed history, see Coalport.

Creamer, Classical motif, mc, scalloped rim, 2¾", NM 160.00
Creamer, Oriental decor, 4¾" 300.00
Creamer/sugar bowl/2 cups & saucers, maid & cow, mc, NM 650.00
Sugar bowl, Classical figures, mc, acorn finial, 6", VG 160.00
Tankard, fisherman scene, bl transfer, 1780, bl S mk, 5½" 250.00
Tea bowl & saucer, Classical figures, mc on lt brn, EX................110.00
Teapot, emb ribs, florals w/gilt, 5¾", EX....................................475.00
Teapot/dregs bowl/cup & saucer, cottage, gray monochrome.......175.00

Ceramic Art Company

Jonathan Coxon, Sr., and Walter Scott Lenox established the Ceramic Art Company in 1889 in Trenton, New Jersey, where they produced fine belleek porcelain. Both were experienced in its production, having previously worked for Ott and Brewer. They hired artists to hand paint their wares with portraits, scenes, and lovely florals. Today, artist-signed examples bring the highest prices. Several marks were used, three of which contain the 'CAC' monogram. A green wreath surrounding the company name in full was used on special-order wares, but these are not often encountered. Coxon eventually left the company, and it was later reorganized under the Lenox name. See also Lenox.

Our advisor for this category is Mary Frank Gaston; she is listed in the Directory under Texas.

Box, floral, bl w/gold, oval, gr mk, 3¾x2⅜" 48.00
Box, trinket; lav Delft-style scene, artist sgn, mk, 5¼" 185.00
Creamer, gold florals & rim, palette mk, 3½" 120.00
Cup & saucer, demi; floral, gold on bl, gold hdl, brn mk.............125.00
Mug, monk holds open box on brn, gr mk, 5¾".............................85.00

Mug, man with mug and verse: 'Who loves not women...,' signed F.A., 7½", $795.00.

Pitcher, berries, maroon hdl, gold spout, palette mk, 12½" 195.00
Pitcher, berries w/gold, maroon rim/hdl, CAC palette mk, 12" ...195.00
Pitcher, cider; mc grapes, palette mk 145.00
Sherbet, gold paste florals, ped ft, mk, 3¼"................................130.00
Vase, couple by stream w/swans decal, mk, 11" 125.00
Vase, poppies, gold on gr, baluster form, mk, 12" 115.00
Vase, portrait, blossoms & gold trim, palette mk, 10" 325.00

Ceramic Arts Studio, Madison

The Ceramic Arts Studio Company began operations sometime prior to the 1940s; but it was about then that Betty Harrington started marketing her goods through this company. Betty Harrington is the designer primarily responsible for creating the line of figurines and knick-knacks that have recently become so popular with collectors. There were two others – Ulli Rebus, who designed several of the animals; and Ruth Planter, who worked there for only a short time. About 65% of these items are marked, but even unmarked items become easily recognizable after only a brief study of their distinctive styling and glaze colors. Those that are marked carry either the black ink stamp or the incised mark: 'Ceramic Arts Studio, Madison, Wisc.'; a paper sticker was also used.

After the 1955 demise of the company in Madison, the owner (Ruben Sand) went to Japan where he continued production under the same name using many of the same molds. After a short time, the old molds were retired and new and quite different items were produced. All of the Japan pieces can be found with a Ceramic Arts Studio backstamp. The Japan identification was on a paper label and is often missing. Japan pieces are never marked Madison, Wisc., but not all Madison pieces are either. Red or blue backstamps are exclusively Japanese.

Another company that also produced figurines operated at about the same time as the Madison studio. It was called Ceramic Art (no 's') Studio; do not confuse the two.

A second and larger building in the C.A.S. complex in Madison was for the exclusive production of metal accessories. The creator and designer of this related line was Zona Liberace, Liberace's stepmother. These pieces are rising fast in value and because they weren't marked can sometimes be found at bargain prices. They were so popular that other ceramic companies bought them to complement their lines as well, so they may also be found with ceramic figures other than C.A.S.'s.

For those seeking additional information, a price guide and accompanying video tapes (Series 1 and 2) are available from the author, BA Wellman, whose address can be found under Massachusetts. Mr. Wellman will also send a series of articles written for *The Daze* to those who will include a large SASE with their requests.

Bank, razor disposal, Tony, 4¾"	45.00
Bank, Skunky, 4"	48.00
Bowl, scalloped, oval, 3½"	20.00
Candle holder/vase, Hear/See/Speak No Evil, cherub, ea	30.00
Figurine, Adam & Eve, 12"	265.00
Figurine, adult band, 6-pc	295.00
Figurine, Annie & Bennie, pr	45.00
Figurine, Beth & Bruce, 5" & 6½", pr	65.00
Figurine, Betty, 5½" L	65.00
Figurine, birchbark canoe, 8" L	38.00
Figurine, blk panthers, 8½" L, pr	125.00
Figurine, Carmin & Carmelita, pr	42.00
Figurine, Cinderella, 6½"	65.00
Figurine, colts, Balky & Frisky, 3¾", pr	45.00
Figurine, Comedy, dk gr, 10"	65.00
Figurine, Dutch man & woman kissing, 5", pr	25.00
Figurine, fighting stallions, Thunder & Lightning, 5½", pr	95.00
Figurine, Fire man & woman, 11¼", pr	95.00
Figurine, goat w/beard, 4"	25.00
Figurine, harem girls, 1 sitting/1 lying down, pr	55.00
Figurine, Harry & Lillibeth, 6½", pr	45.00
Figurine, Jim & June, pr	32.00
Figurine, Lady Rowena on horsebk, 8¼"	75.00
Figurine, Little Bo Peep, 5¾"	25.00

Figurine, man w/guitar, Poncho, 4"	15.00
Figurine, Mary & lamb w/bow, 6¼" & 3¾"	38.00

Modern Dance man and woman, $95.00 for the pair.

Figurine, pekingese, 3"	20.00
Figurine, Peter Pan & Wendy, 5¼", pr	65.00
Figurine, Pied Piper, 6¼"	35.00
Figurine, Praise & Blessing, pr	48.00
Figurine, Promenade man & woman, 7¾", pr	48.00
Figurine, puma, Cubist	40.00
Figurine, Rebecca, 12"	65.00
Figurine, schoolboy & girl, Spring Sue & Autumn Andy, 5", pr	38.00
Figurine, Shepherd & Shepherdess, pr	65.00
Figurine, Summer Sally, 3½"	35.00
Figurine, Swish & Swirl, rare	65.00
Figurine, Temple Dancers, man & woman, 6¾", pr	125.00
Figurine, Ting-a-Ling & Sung-Tu, pr	25.00
Figurine, Toby the Horse, 2¾"	22.00
Figurine, tortoise w/cane, 3¼"	30.00
Figurine, Water man & woman, 11½", pr	95.00
Jug, Toby, 3½"	35.00
Lamp, Aphrodite & Adonis, rotating disk	325.00
Lamp, flutist on base	95.00
Planter, Bamboo, no figure, 2"	24.00
Planter, Bamboo, w/sitting Chinese boy	25.00
Planter, Barbie, 7"	35.00
Planter, Becky, 5¼"	32.00
Planter, Bonnie, 7"	38.00
Planter, Lotus & Manchu, 7½", pr	90.00
Planter, Svea & Sven, pr	75.00
Plaque, Chinese Lantern man & woman, 8", pr	65.00
Plaque, Comedy & Tragedy masks, 5¼", pr	65.00
Plaque, Greg & Grace, 9", pr	65.00
Plaque, Mary Contrary, rare, 5"	50.00
Plaque, Shadow Dancers, 7", pr	65.00
Plaque, Zor & Zorina, 9", pr	48.00
Shakers, Chirp & Twirp, 4", pr	28.00
Shakers, clown & dog, 3¾", pr	30.00
Shakers, cow & calf, 5¼", pr	28.00

Shakers, donkey & elephant, Dem & Rep, 4½", pr 25.00
Shakers, elf & mushroom, pr 20.00
Shakers, Gingham Dog & Calico Cat, pr 25.00
Shakers, Mr & Mrs Penguin, pr 25.00
Shakers, Sambo & Tiger, rare, pr...65.00
Shakers, sea horse & seaweed, 4", pr 25.00
Shakers, Siamese cat & kitten, pr 28.00
Shakers, skunk mother & baby, pr 35.00
Shakers, snuggle monkeys, pr 30.00
Shakers, Sootie & Taffy, pr...28.00
Shakers, Waldo & Sassy, pr 25.00
Shelf sitter, Berty, 4½" 65.00
Shelf sitter, Dutch couple, bl, pr...35.00
Shelf sitter, farm girl, bl 25.00
Shelf sitter, Japanese man & woman, pr 35.00
Shelf sitter, Little Jack Horner 25.00
Shelf sitter, Maurice & Michele, 7", pr 48.00
Shelf sitter, Pete & Polly, 7½", pr 48.00
Shelf sitter, Pudgie & Budgie, 5", pr 38.00
Vase, Becky, 5¼"...40.00
Vase, bud; Bamboo, no figure, 6" 22.00
Vase, roses, rnd, 2¼"...15.00

Metal Accessories

Arched window, for Madonna w/child.....................................30.00
Artist palette, left & right, 12", pr 32.00
Artist palette w/shelves, left & right, 12", pr 38.00
Bean stalk for Jack, rare 35.00
Birdcage w/perch, 14" 30.00
Diamond shadow box, for Attitude & Arabesque 22.00
Frame w/shelf 25.00
Free form, left & right, pr 32.00
Free form w/shelf, left & right, pr...45.00
Pyramid shelves, ea...28.00
Shadow box, w/wood, sq, 13" 28.00

Metal sofa for Maurice and Michele, designed by Zona Liberace, $32.00.

Star, for angel trio, 9"..15.00
Triple ring shelves, ea 28.00

Chalkware

Chalkware figures were a popular commodity from approximately 1860 until 1890. They were made from gypsum or plaster of Paris

formed in a mold and then hand painted in oils or watercolors. Items such as animals and birds, figures, banks, toys, and religious ornaments modeled after more expensive Staffordshire wares were often sold door to door. Their origin is attributed to Italian immigrants. Today regarded as a form of folk art, nineteenth century American pieces bring prices in the hundreds of dollars. Carnival chalkware from this century is also collectible, especially figures that are personality related. For those, see Carnival Collectibles.

Bank, dove, very little pnt, 9½", EX 325.00
Cat, seated, curled tail, red/yel/brn pnt, 5½" 600.00
Cat, seated, red/yel/smoked grain decor, 11" 2,400.00
Cat, seated, w/mouse, octagonal base, rprs/pnt rstr, 10" 450.00

Cat, brown-spotted, wearing red collar, on round brown base, 15", $8,750.00.

Dog, seated, orig mc pnt, 5", EX 500.00
Dog, sitting King Chas spaniel, gold/blk pnt, 14" 1,050.00
Dog, sitting King Chas spaniel, on base, 3-color pnt, 8½" 700.00
Dog, standing spaniel, VG red/blk pnt, base rprs, 7" 225.00
Dove on stump w/cherries & leaves, rpr/pnt rstr, 12", pr.............525.00
Garniture, fruit basket, sq base, 4-color pnt, sm hole, 15"...........700.00
Garniture, fruit in urn on sq plinth, red/yel/blk pnt, 12".............900.00
Garniture, leafy pomegranate on pedestal, 3-color pnt, 11".........800.00
Horse, raised foreleg on shrubbery base, rpr/rstr pnt, 10" 285.00
Parrot on ball perch, worn orig pnt, wht base, 8½" 400.00
Rabbit, crouching, red/yel/gr pnt, 5½" 700.00
Squirrel, orig mc pnt, minor wear, 6¾" 525.00
Stag, recumbent, 1 open leg, gr/yel/red pnt/smoke, 5½" 750.00
Stag, recumbent on rectangular base, pnt details, rpr, 16" 400.00
Watch stand, recumbent dog atop rectangle base, EX pnt, 11"....900.00

Champleve

Champleve, enameling on brass, differs from cloisonne in that the design is depressed or incised into the metal, rather than being built up with wire dividers as in the cloisonne procedure. The cells, or depressions, are filled in with color, and the piece is then fired.

Clock, Louis XVI style, onyx/ormolu mts, 20x12x7" 1,400.00

Floor lamp, floral bands, 3-section baluster form, 62", EX 275.00
Inkwell, in the form of Louis XVI bureau, ormolu mts, 6" 800.00
Jardiniere, mums/scrolls, bud hdls, 3 short ft, 10" dia 235.00
Lamp, sq baluster, demon mask/ring hdls, Chinese, 1900, 15" 475.00
Mirror, foliate band, flower crest, cherub ft, 18x14" 2,000.00
Urn, bronze w/2 flower & leaf bands, foo dog hdls, 12x7½"........350.00
Urn, marble, champleve band top/base, ormolu mask hdls, 19"...450.00
Vase, floral medallions on honeycomb bronze, mask hdls, 12" 250.00
Vase, Hu-form w/demon head hdls, Chinese, 1900s, 10", pr........275.00
Vase, porc w/HP cherub, champleve socle, onyx base, 8", pr.......700.00
Vase, set w/sardonyx etc, ring/mask hdls, 1800s, 9½"..................250.00

Bronze and champleve floor vase, 1800s, restorations, 35", $1,000.00.

Chase Brass & Copper Company

The Chase Brass and Copper Company of Waterbury, Connecticut, recognized the demand for Art Deco-style products influenced by the Hollywood spectaculars of the 1930s and became the nation's pioneer and major producer of machine-made, Art Deco-styled housewares, accessories, and lamps during the depression era.

Harry L. Layon, a now-retired designer of the Chase Company, joined his talents with other designers outside the company such as Russel Wright, Rockwell Kent, Walter von Nessen, Lauelle Guild, and Gerth & Gerth to design Chase housewares which, though in the Hollywood style, could be mass-produced and sold at reasonable prices. Emily Post, the highly-regarded home economist of the 1930s, strongly endorsed Chase products and used the mass media to encourage a nationwide movement toward inexpensive and infomal dining using Chase products. The Art Deco housewares line was discontinued with the advent of World War II and was not resumed after the war.

The company was able to minimize consumer costs by purchasing its own raw materials, operating mills which produced the sheet brass and copper used in its products, and by performing the complete manufacturing process at its facilities in Waterbury.

Chase products are gaining in popularity and are eagerly sought after by collectors. Thousands of pieces were sold during the 1930s, and most are still available in good condition at reasonable prices. Although the designers of many pieces are still unknown, Harry Laylon has been able to provide that information for a great many previously unidentified examples. Research by collectors also continues in an effort to identify other 'designer' pieces. As the designer is identified, the demand (and hence the value) for these pieces is greatly increasing.

For a more thorough study of this subject, we recommend that you refer to *Art Deco Chrome, The Chase Era,* by Richard J. Kilbride, and *Art Deco Chrome, Book 2,* recently published by Kilbride in collaboration with Harry L. Laylon. Our advisor, Mr. Kilbride, is listed in the Directory under Connecticut.

In the listings that follow, the finish is polished unless noted satin.

Ash receiver, chrome or copper, flip top, #871, 2⅞x3¼" 31.00
Bookends, brass w/plastic crescents, #90137, 4⅝", pr 132.00
Bowl, chrome, lotus form, #17045, 3¼x6", +ladle & tray 75.00
Bowl, flower; chrome or copper, #15005, 10" dia...........................46.00
Box, 3-tray, chrome or copper, #17105, 6¾x4¾" 56.00
Candelabrum, chrome, brass or satin silver, #17114, 13½" 72.00
Coaster, chrome or copper, #17072, 3¾" dia, 4 for 47.00
Coffee service, chrome, oval/fluted, blk plastic mts, 4-pc 465.00
Coffee set, ind; chrome, stacks w/cr/sug, #90073, 3-pc..................84.00
Creamer & sugar bowl, chrome or copper, #26007, 2¼", pr...........37.00

Creamer and sugar bowl, #17089, polished chromium with white plastic handle and knob, designed by Walter von Nelson, $125.00.

Crumber, chrome or copper, half-circle form, #90147, +brush.......52.00
Cup, cocktail; chrome/bl glass, #90067, 3½" 23.00
Ice bucket, chrome, Bacchic frieze, Rockwell Kent, 9½" 350.00
Ice crusher/tongs, chrome, #90135, 6" 32.00
Jelly dish, chrome or copper, glass insert, #90062, 5½" dia.............38.00
Ladle, chrome, wht plastic knob, #17081, 9¾" 56.00
Lamp, boudoir; metal drum majorette w/3-color enamel, 9"........225.00
Lamp, brass or English bronze, parchment shade, #6179, 17" 55.00
Lamp, brass or nickel w/plastic crescent stem, #6156, 11½" 63.00
Lamp, desk; chrome or brass w/blk plastic, #6320, 9¼" 85.00
Pitcher, chrome, strainer at spout, #17091, 1-qt, 8⅝" 150.00
Pitcher, water; Sparta, chrome or copper, #9004, 2-qt, 8" 72.00
Relish, Fairfax, chrome, glass liner, #90128, 1x8½".......................35.00
Spoon & fork, chrome, plastic hdls, #90076, 10⅛", pr..................45.00
Sugar shaker, chrome, spherical, #90078, 2⅞x2⅝" 175.00
Syrup, Jubilee, chrome/clear ribbed glass, #26004, 4¼" 40.00
Tea ball, chrome, #90118, 5"...60.00

Tray, cocktail; chrome, #09013, 15⅞x5⅜" 25.00
Tray, incidental, chrome or copper, #09015, 8¼" dia....................25.00
Wall bracket, nickel or brass w/glass mirror, #04005, 10¾" 48.00
Watering can, brass & copper, #05004, 8⅜x4½" 45.00
Weathervane, brass, sailboat, #90136, 15½x9¾" 110.00
Wine coaster, copper/brass, cherub panel, sgn RK, 4½" dia 165.00

Chelsea

The Chelsea Porcelain Works operated in London from the middle of the eighteenth century, making porcelain of the finest quality. In 1770 it was purchased by the owner of the Derby Pottery and for about twenty years operated as a decorating shop. Production periods are indicated by trademarks: 1745-1750 – incised triangle, sometimes with 'Chelsea' and the year added; early 1750s – raised anchor mark on oval pad; 1752-1756 – small painted red anchor, only rarely found in blue underglaze; 1756-1769 – gold anchor; 1769-84 – Chelsea Derby mark with the script 'D' containing a horizontal anchor. Many reproductions have been made; be suspicious of any anchor mark larger than ¼".

Our advisor for this category is William J. Brinkley; he is listed in the Directory under Illinois.

Bottle, scent; cupid at altar, appl florals, 1760s, 3", NM **2,400.00**
Bowl, florals/foliage, scalloped, swirled ribs, mk, 8¾" **575.00**
Plate, mc floral w/gold, scalloped rim, gold anchor mk, 8½"........**450.00**
Platter, stag-head crest/ 'Duem Cole Regem Serva,' late, 16".......**500.00**
Seal, dog, mtd w/carnelian intaglio of Aristotle, 1¼"....................**500.00**
Teapot, mc floral w/gold, sm flake, D w/anchor mk, 6¼" **750.00**

Figurines, gold anchor mark, very slight chips to foliage on backside, 9¾", $350.00 for the pair.

Chelsea Dinnerware

Made from about 1830 to 1880 in the Staffordshire district of England, this white dinnerware is decorated with lustre embossings in the grape, thistle, sprig, or fruit and cornucopia patterns. The relief designs vary from lavender to blue, and the body of the ware may be porcelain, ironstone, or earthenware. Because it was not produced in Chelsea as the name would suggest, dealers often prefer to call it 'Grandmother's Ware.'

Grape, bowl, 8" 30.00
Grape, coffee cup 22.50

Grape, coffeepot, 2-cup, stick hdl, 7" 40.00
Grape, creamer..30.00
Grape, pitcher, milk; 40-oz 38.00
Grape, plate, 6" 15.00
Grape, plate, 7" 18.00
Grape, plate, 8" 20.00
Grape, sugar bowl, w/lid 32.00
Grape, teacup 22.00
Grape, teapot, 2-cup 38.00
Sprig, plate, cake; 9" 35.00
Sprig, plate, dinner 25.00
Sprig, plate, 7" 18.00
Thistle, cup & saucer 25.00

Thistle pattern plate, 7", $14.00.

Chelsea Keramic Art Works

Established in 1872 in Chelsea, Massachusetts, by several members of the Robertson family who later formed the Dedham Pottery, this firm is most noted for its experiments in attempting to re-create the ancient Oriental oxblood-red glaze. They succeeded in this in 1885 and also developed several other outstanding glazes as a result of their perseverance. One was their Oriental crackle glaze which they ultimately used in the manufacture of the very successful Dedham dinnerware. Though their very early artware utilized a redware body, by the late 1870s it was replaced with yellow- or buff-burning clay. A line called Bourgla-Reine (underglaze slip-decorated ware with primarily blue and green backgrounds) was produced, though not to any great extent. Other pieces were designed in imitation of metalware, even to the extent that surfaces were 'hammered' to further enhance the effect. Occasionally live flora were pressed into the damp vessel walls to leave a decorative impression. The pottery closed in 1889. Early wares were not marked; those made from 1875 to 1880 were marked with either two or three lines containing 'Chelsea Keramic Art Works, Robertson and Son,' the 'C-KA-W' cipher, or 'CPUS' in a 4-leaf clover. These were used up to 1889. A paper label was used for a short time on the crackleware. See also Dedham.

Bowl, plain crackleware, wide-mouth/bulbous, CPUS, 4½x5½"..**500.00**

Cake plate, clover rim in bl on wht crackle, CPUS, 10½".........600.00
Cup plate, florals in border, bl on wht crackle, CPUS, 4" 900.00
Cup plate, Pineapple, bl on wht crackle, mk CPUS, 4½".........550.00
Pitcher, olive-gr gloss, pinched rim, mk CKAW, 6" 425.00
Plate, clover emb rim, wht/bl crackle, CPUS, 8¾", EX.............325.00
Vase, allover honeycomb w/stippled floral, bulbous, HR, 12"......450.00
Vase, celadon gr matt w/gr crackle ft ring, stick neck, 10" 2,800.00
Vase, iris, bl/wht on bl, no mk, hairlines, 7"...........................550.00
Vase, oxblood, bulbous w/cylinder neck, presentation, 4½".... 1,300.00
Vase, oxblood irid, bulbous shoulder, no mk, 8" 1,400.00
Vase, turq gloss, flat-side ovoid, lion/ring hdls, 12½"..................550.00
Wall pocket, lt gray-bl, man's grinning face form, 6" 700.00

Vase, 4-sided, applied birds or flowers in each panel, marked, 7", EX, $225.00.

Chicago Crucible

For only a few years during the 1920s, the Chicago (IL) Crucible Company made a limited amount of decorative pottery in addition to their regular line of architectural wares. Examples are very scarce today; they carry a variety of marks, all with the company name and location.

Ash tray, ochre, 5" 50.00
Vase, floral, stylized/upright, mint gr on texture, 9x5½" 450.00
Vase, gr/brn/gr crystalline drip, dbl gourd/akimbo hdls, 7"...........370.00
Vase, mottled, 5½x3½" 275.00
Vase, upright emb leafage, mustard/olive, ovoid, mk, 5½"...........385.00

Children's Books

Children's books, especially those from the Victorian era, are charming collectibles. Colorful lithographic illustrations that once delighted little boys in long curls and tiny girls in long stockings and lots of ribbons and lace have lost none of their appeal. Some collectors limit themselves to a specific subject, while others may be far more interested in the illustrations. First editions are more valuable than later issues, and condition and rarity are very important factors to consider before making your purchase.

Across Canada, Bice, Macmillan, 1st printing, 1949, EX...............12.00
Baby Bunting ABC, cloth, McLoughlin, 1911 ....30.00
Bamby, 1st Am edition, 1928, VG...20.00
Book of Fables, FT Cooper, Hampton, color illus, 1921, VG 28.00
Childs Garden of Verses, Stevenson, Scribner, 1929, EX.............55.00
Christmas Carol, Dickens, Crowell, 1st ed, 1924, EX...................35.00
Dr Dolittle's Circus, Lofting, Stokes, 2nd printing, 1924, EX 22.00
Father Goose His Book, Frank Baum, 1900, EX 75.00
Fun w/Dick & Jane, 1946-1947 ed...40.00

Grimm's Fairy Tales, Brundage, 1925, EX.................................15.00
Happy Jack, Burgess, Little Brown, 8 color plates, 1920, VG.........28.00
Horton Hatches Egg, Seuss, 1940, EX.....................................22.50
House That Grew, Molesworth, Macmillan, 1902, EX..................14.00
Life on Mississippi, Twain, Harper, blk/wht illus, 1917, VG 15.00
Little Mother Goose, McLoughlin, 1907, NM 30.00

Little People of the Snow, by W.C. Bryan, blue cloth covers, illustrated by A. Fredericks, engraved by A. Bobbett, NY, 1873, VG condition, $40.00.

Mademoiselle Misfortune, Brink, Macmillan, 1st ed, 1946, EX 25.00
Mother Goose Rhymes, cloth, Saalfield, 1909, EX.......................20.00
Nonsense ABCs, Lear, 1936, EX 20.00
Our 4-Footed Friends, linen, McLoughlin, 1899, 12x10", EX 20.00
Peter Rabbit, Donahue, 1913, EX..30.00
Pinocchio, Brundage illus, 1924, EX...25.00
Poetic Parrot, MacKay, Day, 1st ed, 1951, VG............................12.00
Raggedy Andy Stories, Gruelle, 1948, EX..................................10.00
Raggedy Ann in Cookie Land, 1931, EX 12.50
Runaway Rhymes, Higgins, Wise-Parslow, color illus, 1942, EX....16.00
Sevenfold Trouble, Pansy, Lathrop, 1st ed, 1889, EX 22.00
Six to Sixteen, Ewing, Bell, color illus, 1st ed, 1908, VG..............16.00
Story of Bo Peep & Boy Blue, Queen Holden, 1929, EX...............25.00
Story of Peter Rabbit, Whitman, #723, EX.................................10.00
Tale of Benjamin Bunny, London, 1904, EX...............................85.00
Tale of Peter Rabbit, London, Racquet Press, EX 85.00
Tales Told in Holland, Miller, Bookhouse, color illus, 1948, EX....20.00
Tanglewood Tales, N Hawthorne, Crowell, 1897, VG 15.00
Tawnymore, Shannon, Doubleday Doran, 1st ed, 1931, EX 28.00
Three Little Kittens, McLoughlin Bros, ca 1892, EX 25.00
Through the Looking Glass, Lewis Carroll, 1897, VG 45.00
Tiger in the Bed, Catto, 1st ed, 1963, EX 6.00
Tin Woodman of Oz, Baum, Reilly & Lee, blk/wht illus, '18, EX .55.00
Tony Sarg's Surprise Book, 1941, G 25.00

Children's Things

Nearly every item devised for adult furnishings has been reduced to child's size – furniture, dishes, sporting goods, even some tools. All are very collectible. During the late seventeenth and early eighteenth centuries, miniature china dinnerware sets were made both in China and in England. They were not intended primarily as children's playthings, however, but instead were made to furnish miniature rooms and cabinets that provided a popular diversion for the adults of that period. By the nineteenth century, the emphasis had shifted, and most of the small-scaled dinnerware and tea sets were made for children's play.

Late in the nineteenth century and well into the twentieth, toy pressed glass dishes were made, many in the same pattern as full-scale glassware. Today these toy dishes often fetch prices in the same range as those for the 'grown-ups'!

One of our advisors for this category is Rosella Tinsley; she is listed in the Directory under Kansas. Authorities Margaret and Kenn Whitmyer have compiled a lovely book, *Children's Dishes*, with full-color photos and current market values; you will find their address in the Directory under Ohio. We also recommend *Children's Glass Dishes, China, and Furniture*, by Doris Anderson Lechler, available at your local bookstore or public library. See also A B C Plates; Canary Lustre; Willow Ware.

Key:
Co — country   Vict — Victorian
Emp — Empire

China

Bowl, Nursery Rhyme Scenes, Tom Tom, The Pipers Son, 5⅜"	10.00
Casserole, Bl Willow, Made in Japan, 5"	22.00
Casserole, florals w/lacy border on wht, Made in Japan, 6⅝"	15.00
Creamer, Roman Chariots, Cauldon, England, 2"	30.00
Cup, tan & gray lustre, Phoenix China, Made in Japan, 1½"	7.50
Cup & saucer, flowers on fence, Made in Japan	9.00
Cup & saucer, Silhouette, Noritake, saucer: 3¾"	15.00
Cup & saucer, Sunset, Made in Japan, saucer: 3⅜"	6.00
Gravy boat, Bl Marble, England, 1½"	38.00
Mug, A Mother's Affection, girl in swing, bl on wht, 2⅝"	75.00
Mug, Blacksmith Shop, mc, Staffordshire	45.00
Mug, children playing, bird whistle hdl, Germany, 1900s	40.00
Mug, copper lustre, floral in high relief	55.00
Mug, For Age & Want..., lav transfer, Staffordshire, 2⅝", EX	110.00
Mug, For Loving a Book, canary lustre, 2¼", M	250.00
Mug, Gift From a Friend, gr transfer, Staffordshire, 2½"	160.00
Mug, History o/t House Jack Built, Staffordshire, 2½", EX	60.00
Mug, Keep Thy Shop..., brn-red transfer/lustre, EX	180.00
Mug, Make Hay While Sun Shines, farm scene in carmine, EX	110.00
Mug, Present for John, brn on buff, Staffordshire, 2⅝", EX	210.00
Mug, Prosper Freedom, eagle on bk, mulberry on wht, 2½"	200.00
Mug, The Path of Truth Is Plain & Safe, 2⅝"	75.00
Mug, When I Take My Walks Abroad..., brn transfer, 2", EX	85.00
Plate, History of Joseph, decal, emb flower rim, 7½", 6 for	350.00
Plate, I Lay My Body Down To Sleep..., Staffordshire, 6"	55.00
Plate, Oriental scene, chinoiserie, mc transfer, 6⅛"	60.00
Rolling pin, Mary Had a Little Lamb, w/advertising, 9"	25.00
Sugar bowl, pk lustre, Merry Christmas, Germany, w/lid, 3⅝"	30.00
Tea set, Christmas, Germany, ca 1900, serves 6	350.00
Tea set, Oriental Youth, England, 1850s, 3-pc	350.00
Teapot, children, pastels on wht, Sarreguemines, 5½"	115.00
Teapot, May, bl on wht, Staffordshire, England, 5"	40.00
Teapot, Silhouette Children, Victoria Czecho-Slovakia, 3⅝"	20.00

Furniture

Examples with no dimensions given are child's size unless noted doll size.

Armchair, ladderbk, splint seat, rstr/rfn, EX	250.00
Armchair, Windsor, bamboo trn, spindle bk/arms, pnt, 21"	300.00
Baby bed, cherry, trn posts/spindle rails, 43x54x29"	200.00
Baby bed, curly maple, EX trn, rfn, 48x28x52"	1,750.00
Bed, walnut Victorian, orig mattress, 1850, 27" L	100.00
Blanket chest, poplar, dvtl, simple molding, 17x21"	475.00

Bureau, mahog Empire, bird's eye maple facings, 25" W	1,500.00
Bureau, mahog Empire, 2-drw superstructure, 30" W	375.00
Chair, ladderbk, worn yel pnt w/VG stencil, 14"	135.00
Chair, ladderbk arm, rush seat, 1700s, rpt, VG	200.00

Ladderback armchair, New England, ca 1800, 27½", $375.00.

Chair, ladderbk side, splint seat, Am, 1820s, rfn, EX	75.00
Chair, side, sausage-bk Hitchcock, rush seat, re-decor, EX	110.00
Chair, Windsor, fan-bk arm, Stickley label, 22", EX	575.00
Chaise, Louis XVI style, wht pnt, fluted seat rail, uphl	440.00
Chest, cherry Co Chippendale, trn ft, 3-drw, 25x24", EX	1,650.00
Chest, cherry/curly maple Empire, rfn, 25x22"	2,050.00
Chest, oak/cherry w/pnt traces, 5 dvtl drw, 20"	250.00
Cradle, brn w/yel striping & mc rose stencil, 19" L	150.00
Cradle, cherry/pine, hooded, Am, 1800, 43" L	500.00
Cradle, hardwood, arched hood, pnt ext, 42" L	225.00
Cradle, pine, old gr pnt, 14¼", EX	145.00
Cradle, slat-sided w/bentwood fr, swinging, 48" L	125.00
Cradle, walnut, EX scroll detail/heart cutout, 19"	300.00
Cradle, walnut, scalloped rim, 8x13" L	85.00
Cupboard, pine, 2 4-pane doors, base drw, cut-out ft, 25"	500.00
Cupboard, walnut/burl veneer Vict, step-bk, arch doors, 31"	975.00
Highchair, ladderbk, trn detail, scalloped slats, 37", EX	325.00
Highchair, oak press-bk, w/tray, shaped seat, 1920s, NM	250.00
Highchair, plank seat, 3-spindle bk, worn red rpt, 35"	135.00
Rocker, adirondack, w/arms, 11"	125.00
Rocker, Boston, orig stencil decor, 1850s, EX	200.00
Rocker, oak press-bk w/curving arms, trn bk spindles, NM	200.00
Rocker, short 8-spindle bk, w/arms, plank seat, 1915, 25"	375.00
Rocker, 2-slat bk, w/arms, splint seat, primitive, 19"	55.00
Table, mahog, ped base, rfn, 5x8"	90.00
Table, walnut, trn legs, 8" drop leaves, 11x20" top	500.00
Walker, wood, 4 trn legs w/in bentwood ring, 1900, 16", EX	165.00

Glassware

Acorn, creamer, clear	90.00
Acorn, sugar bowl, frosted, w/lid	295.00
Amazon VT, butter dish, clear	75.00
Austrian, butter dish, clear	195.00
Austrian, spooner, clear	100.00

Austrian, sugar bowl, chocolate, w/lid, 3¾" 550.00
Baby Flute, bowl, berry; clear, sm 20.00
Baby Thumbprint, cake stand, clear, lg 150.00
Baby Thumbprint, compote, clear, w/lid 225.00
Bead & Scroll, butter dish, color 295.00
Beaded Swirl VT, spooner, color 100.00
Beaded Swirl VT, sugar bowl, clear, w/lid 35.00
Braided Belt, spooner, clear or milk glass 90.00
Braided Belt, sugar bowl, color, w/lid 200.00
Bread & Scroll, creamer, clear 60.00
Bread & Scroll, sugar bowl, flashed, w/lid 150.00
Bucket, spooner, clear 150.00
Bucket, sugar bowl, clear, w/lid 200.00
Button Arches, creamer, clear 60.00
Button Arches, sugar bowl, clear 60.00
Button Panel, butter dish, clear, gold flashed 110.00
Button Panel, sugar bowl, clear, w/lid 85.00
Buzz Star (Whirligig), punch cup, clear 6.00
Buzz Star (Whirligig), spooner, clear 25.00
Chateau, punch bowl, clear 300.00
Chimo, sugar bowl, clear, w/lid 75.00
Clambroth Scenery, creamer, clear or milk glass 75.00
Clambroth Scenery, sugar bowl, clear or milk glass, w/lid 95.00

Clear and Diamond Panels, large-size butter dish, $100.00.

Clear & Diamond Panels, creamer, clear 20.00
Clear & Diamond Panels, sugar bowl, color, w/lid 48.00
Cloud Band, creamer, clear or milk glass 70.00
Cloud Band, sugar bowl, clear or milk glass, w/lid 115.00
Colonial, punch cup, clear 10.00
Colonial, tumbler, clear 5.00
D&M #42, butter dish, clear 175.00
D&M #42, spooner, clear 45.00
Deep Stars & Octagons, pitcher, clear or milk glass 45.00
Dewdrop, butter dish, color 165.00
Dewdrop, sugar bowl, clear, w/lid 75.00
Doyle #500, butter dish, clear 60.00
Doyle #500, tray, color 95.00
Drape, castor set, clear 100.00
Drum, butter dish, clear 120.00
Drum, creamer, clear 60.00
Dutch Boudoir, candlestick, milk glass 120.00
Dutch Boudoir, pitcher, bl opaque 150.00
Euclid, butter dish, clear 30.00

Euclid, cake salver, clear 32.00
Fine Cut & No 379, bowl, master berry; clear 55.00
Fine Cut Star & Fan, butter dish, clear 32.00
Fine Cut Star & Fan, creamer, clear 17.50
Flattened Diamond, punch bowl, clear 40.00
Flattened Diamond, sugar bowl, color, w/lid, old 48.00
Galloway, pitcher, clear 28.00
Grape Vine w/Ovals, butter dish, clear 80.00
Grape Vine w/Ovals, creamer, color 30.00
Hawaiian Lei, butter dish, clear 35.00
Hawaiian Lei, creamer, clear 25.00
Hobnail w/Thumbprint Base, butter dish, color 85.00
Hobnail w/Thumbprint Base, tray, clear 55.00
Horizontal Threads, spooner, clear 40.00
Horizontal Threads, sugar bowl, clear, w/lid 55.00
Kittens, bowl, cereal; clear 95.00
Kittens, vase, marigold 120.00
Lacy Daisy, bowl, amber or mint gr, lg 70.00
Lamb, creamer, clear 75.00
Lamb, creamer, milk glass 195.00
Lamb, sugar bowl, milk glass, w/lid 195.00
Large Block, butter dish, color 80.00
Liberty Bell, butter dish, clear 185.00
Liberty Bell, creamer, milk glass 285.00
Liberty Bell, mug, milk glass 165.00
Lion, cup & saucer, frosted 95.00
Little Jo, tumbler, lt gr or amber 75.00
Michigan, pitcher, clear or milk glass w/flashing 35.00
Nursery Rhyme, pitcher 115.00
Nursery Rhyme, punch bowl, bl opaque, +6 cups 575.00
Oval Star, butter dish, clear 22.00
Oval Star, tray, clear 70.00
Pattee Cross, pitcher, clear 65.00
Pennsylvania, butter dish, color 195.00
Pennsylvania, sugar bowl, clear or milk glass, w/lid 60.00
Pert, spooner, clear 65.00
Petite Square, pitcher, clear 75.00
Petite Square, vase, frosted 80.00
Pointed Jewel, butter dish, clear 150.00
Pointed Jewel, spooner, clear 75.00
Rex, creamer, clear 25.00
Rex, tumbler, clear 12.50
Rooster, nappy, clear 185.00
Sandwich, decanter, clear 365.00
Sandwich, tumbler, clear 20.00
Sawtooth, sugar bowl, clear, w/lid 45.00
Sawtooth Band, butter dish, clear w/EX gold 165.00
Sawtooth Band, creamer, flashed 85.00
Steigel (type), pitcher, clear 38.00
Stippled Dewdrop & Raindrop, sugar bowl, color, w/lid 125.00
Stippled Diamond, butter dish, clear 95.00
Stippled Diamond, sugar bowl, color, w/lid 145.00
Stippled Forget-Me-Not, butter dish, color 385.00
Stippled Forget-Me-Not, creamer, clear 195.00
Stippled Hearts, butter dish, clear 25.00
Sultan (Wild Rose w/Scrolling), butter dish, frosted 145.00
Sultan (Wild Rose w/Scrolling), creamer, clear 75.00
Sultan (Wild Rose w/Scrolling), spooner, color 95.00
Sunbeam, creamer, clear 65.00
Tappan, butter dish, color 40.00
Tappan, spooner, clear 25.00
Tulip & Honeycomb, butter dish, clear, sm 55.00
Tulip & Honeycomb, creamer, clear 20.00

Twist, creamer, color	75.00
Twist, vase, clear or milk glass	25.00
Two Band, sugar bowl, clear, w/lid	48.00
Wabash Series, fish plate, clear, oval	300.00
Wabash Series, plate, clear, rnd, sm	70.00
Wee Branches, plate, clear or milk glass	60.00
Wild Rose, butter dish, milk glass	65.00
Wild Rose, candlestick, clear	95.00
Wild Rose, spooner, milk glass	35.00

Miscellaneous

Brush, sterling, Victorian children playing on bk	35.00
Fork, Peter Rabbit, ABCs, tin	10.00
Kaleidoscope, CG Bush, leatherized cb, wood base, 14", VG	500.00
Lamp, hand; tin, alphabet-emb rim, 'Jumbo'/elephant, 3½"	150.00
Mannequin, knit over papier-mache, CI hi-button shoes, 40"	300.00

Tin mug, gold lettering on orange, ca 1870, 2½", $95.00.

Push cart, metal fr/wire wheels/wood seat, bk adjusts, 57"	125.00
Puzzle cube, all wood, Rubic type, 4x4x7¾"	65.00
Rocking horse, spindle-side chair/horse head mtd in frwork	250.00
Rocking horse, 2 pnt wood cutouts joined by seat, 32", EX	250.00
Silverware set, 'Like Mother's,' 1930s, service for 6, VG	75.00
Sled, Dictator, lettering on bl pnt, 1800s, EX	350.00
Sled, horse's head/scrolls/pinstripes on red, 45x12"	650.00

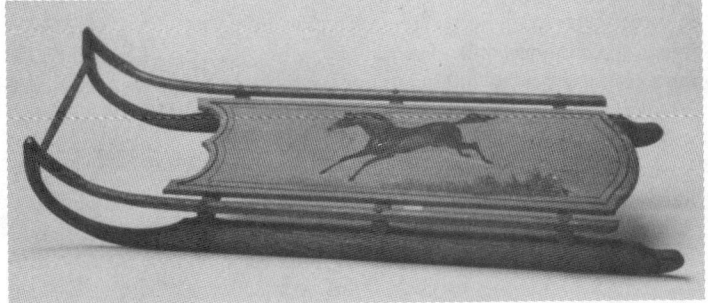

Oak and maple snow sled, painted green with horse depicted on seat, New Hampshire, ca 1900, large, NM condition, $1,000.00.

Sled, walnut & oak w/iron runners, 72"	110.00
Sled, wood w/worn yel rpt, iron-tipped wood runners, 40"	100.00
Sleigh, dog; curved iron runners, wood deck rpl, 53" L	475.00
Sleigh, pnt wood, tufted upholstered seat, 43", EX	660.00
Wagon, wood bed w/worn red & gr pnt, CI wheels, 28" L	250.00
Washboard, redware insert, scrubbed wood fr, 14x7", EX	295.00
Washboard, wood, grooved surface, 9¼x6¼"	45.00

Wheelbarrow, poplar, gr & yel stripes/stencils, '1896,' 28"	175.00
Wheelbarrow, wood w/factory-printed fox, SA Smith, 34"	155.00
Wheelbarrow, wood w/worn bl rpt, 33" L	85.00

Chocolate Glass

Jacob Rosenthal developed chocolate glass, a rich shaded opaque brown sometimes referred to as caramel slag, in 1900 at the Indiana Tumbler and Goblet Company of Greentown, Indiana. Later, other companies produced similar ware. Only the latter is listed here. See also Greentown.

Bowl, Geneva, oval, 8¼x5¼"	110.00
Bowl, Geneva, 8⅜" dia	185.00
Butter dish, Geneva	385.00
Compote, Melrose, scalloped, 4¾x6"	195.00
Compote, Melrose, scalloped, 8½" dia	285.00
Creamer, Strigal, tankard form, 6"	90.00
Cruet, Wild Rose w/Bow Knot	350.00
Nappy, Masonic, w/hdl	125.00
Pitcher, water; Feather	500.00
Sauce, Wild Rose w/Bow Knot	75.00
Spooner, Geneva	115.00
Tray, dresser; Wild Rose w/Bow Knot, 10¼x8"	250.00
Vase, Wild Rose w/Bow Knot, 10"	265.00

Christmas Collectibles

Christmas past . . . lovely mementos from long ago attest to the ostentatious Victorian celebrations of the season.

St. Nicholas, better known as Santa, has changed much since 300 A.D. when the good Bishop Nicholas showered needy children with gifts and kindnesses. During the early eighteenth century, Santa was portrayed as the kind gift-giver to well-behaved children and the stern switch-bearing disciplinarian to those who were bad. In 1822 Clement Clark Moore, a New York poet, wrote his famous *Night Before Christmas*, and the Santa he described was jolly and jovial – a lovable old elf who was stern with no one. Early Santas wore robes of yellow, brown, blue, green, red, or even purple. But Thomas Nast, who worked as an illustrator for Harper's Weekly, was the first to depict Santa in a red suit instead of the traditional robe, and to locate him the entire year at the North Pole headquarters.

Today's collectors prize early Santa figures, especially those in robes of fur or mohair or those dressed in an unusual color. Some early examples of Christmas memorabilia are the pre-1870 ornaments from Dresden, Germany. These cardboard figures – angels, gondolas, umbrellas, dirigibles, and countless others – sparkled with gold and silver trim. Late in the 1870s, blown glass ornaments were imported from Germany. There were over 6,000 recorded designs – all painted inside with silvery colors. From 1890 through 1910, blown glass spheres were often decorated with beads, tassels, and tinsel rope.

Christmas lights, made by Sandwich and some of their contemporaries, were either pressed or mold-blown glass shaped into a form similar to a water tumbler. They were filled with water and then hung from the tree by a wire handle; oil floating on the surface of the water served as fuel for the lighted wick.

Kugels are glass ornaments that were made as early as 1820 and as late as 1890. Ball-shaped examples are more common than the fruit and vegetable forms and have been found in sizes ranging from 1" to 14" in diameter. They were made of thick glass with heavy brass caps, in cobalt, green, gold, silver, and occasionally in amethyst.

Although experiments involving the use of electric lightbulbs for the Christmas tree occured before 1900, it was 1903 before the first manufactured socket set was marketed. These were very expensive and often proved a safety hazard. In 1921 safety regulations were established, and products were guaranteed safety approved. The early bulbs were smaller replicas of Edison's household bulb. By 1910 G.E. bulbs were rounded with a pointed end, and until 1919 all bulbs were hand blown. The first figural bulbs were made around 1910 in Austria. Japan soon followed, but their product was never of the high quality of Austrian wares. American manufacturers produced their first machine-made figurals after 1919. Today, figural bulbs – especially character-related examples – are very popular collectibles. Bubble lights were popular from about 1945 to 1960 when miniature lights were introduced. These tiny lamps dampened the public's enthusiasm for the bubblers, and manufacturers stopped providing replacement bulbs.

Feather trees were made from 1850 to 1950 – all are collectible. Watch for newly-manufactured feather trees that have lately been reintroduced.

Bulbs

Andy Gump, gr pants/blk coat/pk head, milk glass, NM	85.00
Angel, orange hair, molded wings, clear, Japan	35.00
Apricot, yel w/orange, clear, EX	15.00
Baby in basket, tan, striped blanket, celluloid, NM	95.00
Baby in red stocking, milk glass, EX	45.00
Battleship, mc pnt, US flag, NM	100.00
Bear in pajamas, pk, celluloid, EX	75.00
Betty Boop, pk & red dress, blk hair, milk glass, NM	70.00
Birdcage w/2 red birds, milk glass	12.00
Boy playing concertina, mc pnt, milk glass, EX	60.00
Boy w/egg basket, mc pnt, celluloid, 3"	90.00
Bunny, sitting, pk pnt, milk glass, NM	68.00
Candy cane, red & wht, milk glass, 3", NM	35.00
Car, gr & wht pnt, clear, NM	95.00
Cat, bright colors, milk glass, 4"	35.00
Cat w/bowl of cherries, wht/pk/gr pnt, milk glass, NM	65.00
Chick in egg, yel/tan/red, milk glass, NM	125.00
Circus elephant, 3-color, celluloid, 2½", EX	85.00
Cross & flowers, 2-sided, yel disk, milk glass, NM	25.00
Dick Tracy, EX pnt, milk glass, 3"	135.00
Dismal Desmond, polka dots, red/yel/tan, milk glass, M	45.00

Disney characters, $25.00 each.

Dog, brn & red, milk glass, 4"	45.00
Dog hockey player w/stick, milk glass	65.00
Drama face, 2-sided, clear w/red & wht, Germany, NM	245.00
Drummer boy, red/gr/orange, milk glass, NM	45.00
Duckling, mc pnt, milk glass, sm, NM	45.00
Ear of corn, pearly wht w/pk/bl, 3½", EX	48.00
Father Christmas, European, mc pnt, milk glass, NM	200.00
Father Christmas, Japan, 9", in orig box	100.00
Father Christmas w/tree, red robe/gold staff, Hungary, NM	135.00
Frog, gr & yel, 3"	65.00
Girl w/fruit basket, mc pnt, celluloid	95.00
Holly ball, gr & red pnt, milk glass, NM	22.00
Horse's head in shoe, pk horse, red halter, milk glass, 3"	110.00
Hound dog, gr bow at neck, pk tones, milk glass, NM	40.00
Humpty Dumpty on wall, mc pnt, milk glass, EX	65.00
Indian's head, matt face, blk hair & bonnet, milk glass	95.00
Jack & Jill, pails behind bks, mc pnt, milk glass, M	265.00
Jack-O'-Lantern, EX pnt, milk glass	55.00
Kewpie doll, pk pnt, milk glass, EX	65.00
Keystone Cop, mc pnt, milk glass, EX	45.00
Lantern, molded swirls, mc pnt, clear, Germany, NM	45.00
Lantern, VG pnt, milk glass, Japan, lg	22.00
Lion w/pipe, milk glass, G	55.00
Little Bo Peep, mc pnt, wht lamb, milk glass, M	250.00
Little Jack Horner w/bowl, mc pnt, milk glass, M	245.00
Lucky Lindy, purple & pk w/gold plane, milk glass, NM	50.00
Matchless Star, clear w/gr center, 2"	10.00
Minstrel, wht & yel w/orange & red horn, Germany	60.00
Monkey, sitting, mc pnt, frosted glass, NM	90.00
Moon Mullins, G pnt, milk glass, VG	95.00
Ocean liner, mc pnt, gold anchor, milk glass, NM	225.00
Owl, mc pnt on clear, Germany	65.00
Owl, yel & gray, milk glass, 3"	115.00
Pelican, bl & yel w/red bill, milk glass, EX	65.00
Pig, bl tie, gr jacket, yel pants, milk glass, 3"	110.00
Pig in chimney, yel & pk, milk glass, NM	88.00
Queen of Hearts w/2 blk birds, milk glass, EX	55.00
Rooster, roly poly, yel/red/gr, milk glass, EX	65.00
Rose bud, pk pnt, milk glass, sm	25.00
Santa, bright colors, milk glass, 9"	115.00
Santa, red w/wht pnt, milk glass, Mazda, EX	45.00
Santa, 2-faced, red pnt, milk glass, 3"	28.00
Santa at door, children in window, EX pnt, milk glass	75.00
Santa atop chimney, milk glass	65.00
Santa on disk, 2-sided, full figure, yel pnt, milk glass, NM	88.00
Santa on roof, mc pnt, milk glass, NM	65.00
Santa walking up to house, mc pnt, milk glass, NM	35.00
Seashell w/roses, tan w/bl flowers, milk glass, EX	65.00
Smitty, milk glass, VG	85.00
Snowman, red hat, brn switches, milk glass, European, EX	65.00
Squirrel, paw to mouth, tan & red pnt, milk glass, NM	45.00
Star, Noma, 7", EX in orig box	45.00
Star, red on yel disk, milk glass, EX	45.00
Stop watch, red trim, milk glass, NM	45.00
Three Men in a Tub	85.00
Turkey, orange/yel/bl, milk glass, NM	80.00
Woman in shoe, mc pnt, milk glass, NM	75.00

Candy Containers

Banjo, Dresden, 3-D, silver/gold/brn/red, 3½x1½", EX	165.00
Basket, Dresden, corrugated/patterned, EX	145.00
Drum, Dresden, vertical gold stripes, silver star, 2½x3"	95.00

House, cb litho, 1930s, Japan, 5x3¾x3" 35.00
House, glass, red brick, gr roof, 3" 75.00
Irish heart, Dresden, gr w/opal stone, 2" 115.00
Opera glasses, Dresden, dbl, old resilvering, 2x3" 185.00
Santa, compo, red coat, bl pants, 4½" 65.00
Santa, nodder, paper w/plastic face, fur trim, 14", EX......65.00
Santa, papier-mache, felt robe, Germany, 7¾" 575.00
Santa, pressed cb, red/wht/flesh, VG............................45.00
Santa in basket, plaster hands, Japan, 5" 110.00
Santa in chimney, fireplace below, papier-mache, 5½" 385.00
Santa on sled, red & wht, mk Germany, 3", EX 150.00
Sled, die-cut Santa on top, Germany, 3¾".....................120.00
Snowball, celluloid, 2"...35.00
Snowman, cotton body, cb top hat, 7".............................55.00
Snowman, papier-mache on cb box, Germany, 7½" 65.00
Snowman, papier-mache w/cb hat, comic, 7½" 55.00

Snowman, unmarked Japan, ca 1930s, 4¾", $35.00.

Snowman's head, musical, US Zone Germany, 6x3", EX 75.00
Top hat, Dresden, red silk w/silver rosettes, 2", EX.............245.00
Tree, gr velour on wood base, beaded branches, 1930s, 14" 65.00
Violin case w/wood violin, Dresden, 3" L........................200.00
Wreath, Dresden, 4¼" 135.00

Ornaments

Alice in Wonderland, blown, silver/yel/red/bl, 3¼", EX 110.00
Angel, blown, pearly wht face, gold hair & wings, 3" 125.00
Angel, cotton w/die-cut face, Dresden rosettes, early, 6" 175.00
Angel, wax, spun glass wings, mesh skirt, sm.......................95.00
Angel's head, blown, pearly wht & orange, early, 2½", EX............65.00
Apple, blown, silver w/blk leaves, 3½" 55.00
Baby in sack, blown, pearly wht w/red bow, 3½" 110.00
Baby Jesus on leaf, blown, mc pnt, silvered, EX...................265.00
Baby w/pacifier, blown, pearly wht, 3" 185.00
Balloon, blown, dbl, wire-wrapped, w/boy diecut, 5½".............150.00
Balloon, blown, pk, w/bl scrap Santa, 8", EX.....................135.00
Balloon, blown, red/wht/gold, wire-wrapped, girl w/arrows, 9" 135.00
Balloon, blown, swirled color, wire-wrapped, angel diecut 85.00
Balloon, pk cotton w/colored scrap, 13"..........................120.00
Bear, blown, gold w/blk features, 2½" 110.00
Bear, blown, standing, hump on bk, silvered, rare, 4½" 435.00

Beetle, blown, pearly wht, bl wings, unsilvered, NM..............85.00
Bell, blown, red/wht/bl, Merry Christmas, clapper, early.........35.00
Bird, blown, angel hair tail, metal clip, 6⅝", EX................30.00
Bird, blown, unsilvered, glass eyes, ca 1910, 5"................25.00
Bird, bsk w/spun glass wings, 4".................................25.00
Bird, mc, angel hair tail, metal clip, some flaking, 4" 5.00
Birds in nest, blown, pearly wht, yel nest, pk & bl birds, 3" 100.00
Boot, Victorian lady's, Dresden, foil paper at top, 9", EX........575.00
Boy in cap, blown, pearly wht/gold/gr, early, 3¼", EX...........135.00
Boy w/hands in pockets, pearly wht/pk/gold, blown, 3½", EX.......85.00
Brownie, blown, gr pants, pk tie, blk hat, unsilvered, 5" 385.00
Buffalo, Dresden, dk brn shading, 2⅛"...........................350.00
Butterfly, blown, red, 3" 70.00
Camel, Dresden, gold w/red blanket, flat, EX 65.00
Camel rider, Dresden, 1-hump camel/Blk rider, 3¼x3½" 385.00
Car, blown, red & wht, 3" 185.00
Car (coupe), blown, dk red, 1930s, 2½", VG 85.00
Carousel, pearly wht w/gold & pk, blown, on clip, 3½" 100.00
Carrot, blown, orange w/gr, EX..................................135.00
Carrot, pressed cotton, orange, 3½" 55.00
Cat, Dresden, gold w/gr & red, flat, EX..........................110.00
Cat in bag, blown, pearly pk/wht/aqua/red, early, 4", NM.........135.00
Charlie Chaplin, blown, pearly wht, blk hair, 3½" 285.00
Cherries in cluster, blown, maroon, silvered, wire-wrapped 45.00
Cherries on ball, blown, pearly wht/red/gr, '20s, 2¾", EX 20.00
Child w/clown hat, silver w/red & gold, blown, 3⅝" 85.00
Clock, wall; blown, paper face, detailed molding, early, EX 80.00
Clown, blown, appl legs, ca 1900, 3½".............................35.00
Clown, blown, molded inscription: My Darling, flaking, 4¼" 15.00
Clown, blown, pearly wht/gr/red, 2½"..............................80.00
Clown, blown, silver & red, 4½", EX...............................40.00
Clown, blown, wht face, red cb hat, 3¼" 100.00
Coal hod, Sebnitz, wire-wrapped, cotton base, EX.................150.00
Cockatoo, blown, mc, on metal clip, 3¼" L.........................55.00
Cockatoo in hoop, Dresden, gold & rose irid, 3½", EX.............175.00
Dachshund, Dresden, brn w/red bow on collar, 4½"................250.00
Devil's head, blown, molded horns, gr eyes, gold hair, 2½" 225.00
Doe, leaping, Dresden, 3-D, brn/cream/red, EX 120.00
Dog, blown, red w/wht details, 4".................................95.00
Dog, Dresden, 3-D, sitting, silver, 3x3".........................285.00
Doll's head, blown, silver curls, matt face, glass eyes, 2½".......100.00
Dutch girl's head, blown, flesh/gold/pk, 3½", EX.................200.00
Elephant, blown, pearly wht w/gold blanket, 2½", NM.............150.00
Elephant, circus; blown, silver/red/gold, 3" 165.00
Elf, blown, mc, 4⅝", EX..50.00
Elf in tree, blown, silver/bl/gr, 3" 75.00
Elf on toadstool, blown, pearly wht/orange/red/gr, early.........135.00
Explorer, blown, wht frosted hood, gold suit, 4", EX.............120.00
Father Christmas, blown, pearly wht w/gold robe, 2¾" 65.00
Father Christmas, red w/silver, heavy glass, early................88.00
Fish, blown, silver w/pk & gr fins, blk eyes, 3½".................45.00
Flapper's head, blown, pearly wht/gold/bl, 1920s, 3¼", EX........125.00
Flower w/girl's face, blown, flesh w/gold, 3" 95.00
Foxy Grandpa, blown, gold coat & legs, yel vest, 4½"............275.00
Frog, blown, gr & red, early, some flaking, 4"....................85.00
Frog, blown, yel/blk/red, 4", EX..................................95.00
Girl, pressed cotton, 3-D, brn paper face/paper dress, 5" 185.00
Girl in flower, blown, silver face w/yel & pk, 4", EX 135.00
Girl w/purse, blown, pearly wht & pk, 3¾".........................85.00
Girl's face, blown, glass eyes, minor flaking, 3¼" 65.00
Gnome, blown, gr, 3½"..60.00
Gnome w/pipe, blown, gr/silver/red, 3½", EX......................120.00
Gnome w/shovel, blown, pk/pearly wht w/gold shovel, 3", EX 125.00

Goat, Dresden, blk/tan/wht, 2x2⅜" 185.00
Goat pulls 2-wheel basket cart, Dresden, 3¾" 450.00
Goldilocks, blown, pearly wht face, gold hair, pk ribbon 150.00
Grape cluster w/face & red tassel, blown, ca 1910, 4½" 150.00
Guitar, Dresden, Santa scrap, 1900s, 4", EX 145.00
Happy Hooligan, blown, peach coat, yel legs, 4½", EX...............300.00
Hatbox, Dresden, tan, 2" 130.00
Horn, blown, pearly wht/pk/gold/aqua, emb flowers, 4", EX 30.00
Horn, blown, silver/red/bl, 5½", EX 25.00
House, blown, gold w/wht frosted roof, 3", EX 25.00
House, Sebnitz, die-cut stork & baby, metal house, EX 95.00
House w/turkey in front, blown, yel/silver/red, 3⅛", EX..............65.00
Hummingbird, blown, unsilvered turq, tinsel tail & wings, 10" ..120.00
Hummingbird, blown, 4-color, spun glass wings & tail, 1x4" 65.00
Imp, blown, pearly wht w/blk features, 3", EX 300.00
Indian bust, blown, pearly pk w/pnt features, ca 1910, 3½" 245.00
Indian in canoe, blown, pearly wht w/pk & red, EX 175.00
Indian on horse, pnt cotton & paper, Germany, EX...............375.00
Jack-O'-Lantern, blown, gr w/wht, unsilvered, EX..............165.00
Jester on stick, bsk head w/worn cloth costume, 10" 135.00
Jockey on horse, Dresden, 3-D, EX mc pnt, 3x3" 285.00
Joey Lewis, blown, pk hat, yel ruffle, 6" 265.00
Kite face, pearly wht w/gold, spun glass tail, 1800s, 5½" 250.00
Kugel, ball, cobalt, Baroque cap, 2½" 60.00
Kugel, ball, cobalt, swirl leaf-end brass hanger, 4" 95.00
Kugel, ball, cobalt, 8-petal hanger, 1½" 45.00
Kugel, ball, gold, mercury lined, orig hanger, 8" 150.00
Kugel, ball, gr, brass fastener, Made in France, 7½" 475.00
Kugel, ball, med gr, 2½" 65.00
Kugel, ball, red, Baroque hanger, 2" 90.00
Kugel, ball, red, brass fastener, 4¼" 450.00
Kugel, ball, red/silver/wht stripes, brass cap, 1890s, 2¾" 225.00
Kugel, ball w/stem, amethyst, cork hanger, 4" 200.00
Kugel, grapes, bl, 6", EX 200.00
Kugel, grapes, cobalt, brass hanger, 4"..........................250.00
Kugel, grapes, gr, brass hanger, 4½"...........................225.00
Kugel, grapes, silver, brass clip, 5" 225.00
Kugel, grapes, silver, emb brass hanger, 7" 285.00
Kugel, grapes, silver w/gr, 8-petal cap, ca 1890, 4" 235.00
Kugel, pear, emerald gr, Baroque brass hanger, 3¾" 250.00
Kugel, pear, silver, brass hanger, 9½".........................250.00
Kugel, ribbed sphere, cobalt, common hanger, 1⅝"...............250.00
Kugel, teardrop, silver, Baroque hanger, 2¾" 185.00
Kugel, teardrop, silver, Baroque hanger, 3½"...................225.00
Kugel, turnip, silver, metal holder, lg..........................250.00

Little Miss Muffet, blown glass, 3½", $95.00.

Lady in cart, chenille, die-cut face/crepe paper skirt, 4½" 150.00
Lady's face, Dresden, flat, mc pnt, mk Paris, 3½" 95.00
Lady's hat, Dresden, gold w/red feather & bl bow.................110.00
Lion, Dresden, tan & brn w/red mouth, EX.......................255.00
Los Angeles Zeppelin, blown, pearly wht/red/gold, label 285.00
Man's head, blown, pearly wht & pk, red mouth & flower, 3½" ..125.00
Mickey Mouse, blown, blk & wht, pipe cleaner tail, 1931, EX 95.00
Miss Muffett, blown, pearly wht/red/gr, 3¼", EX 80.00
Moose, Dresden, 3-D, brn, 2¼x2¼", EX 88.00
Mountain climber, blown, flesh face, mc clothes, 6" 85.00
Mr Apple, molded face & arms, pearly gold w/red, 2¼", EX 150.00
Mrs Claus, blown, pearly wht w/red, early, 4¼", EX 265.00
Nude on bell, matt w/gold curls, red bell, ca 1915, 3" 225.00
Oil lamp, blown, gold w/milk glass shade, 1930s, 4½", EX............45.00
Oil lamp, blown, silver w/red shade, 1930s, 4", EX................45.00
Owl, blown, gold, 3¾", EX 45.00
Owl, blown, pk & silver w/yel eyes, 3⅝", EX 75.00
Owl, Dresden, gold w/brn features, 6" 130.00
Owl, pearly cream/gr/pk, spun glass tail, hanger, early, EX 50.00
Parasol, blown, aqua, unsilvered, wire-wrapped, 8½"...............45.00
Parrot, blown, lav & wht w/angel hair tail, metal clip, 6" 75.00
Parsnip w/face, blown, pearly wht w/gr leaves, 4¼", EX 265.00
Peacock on ball, blown, bl/silver/red, early, 1910, 5" 40.00
Pear, blown, yel w/red blush, unsilvered, 3½" 55.00
Pear, pressed cotton, wht w/hanger, 3", EX 20.00
Pickle, blown, pearly gr, 4" 95.00
Pine cone, blown, gr, 2¾", EX.....................................35.00
Pine cone, blown, pk w/frost & needles, 1900, M..................65.00
Pipe, blown, metal reed for whistle, gr & silver, 1920s, EX 35.00
Policeman, blown, flesh face, bl uniform, 4"......................185.00
Professor, compo face, paper vest, Dresden trim, 4¾", EX...........250.00
Purse, Dresden, red, 1½" 95.00
Rattle, baby's, Dresden, wood stick w/gold, early, 4½", EX 95.00
Retriever w/riding crop & gloves, Dresden, 2¾", EX 300.00
Ringmaster's head, blown, mc pnt, unsilvered, 1910, 2¼" 250.00
River boat, Dresden, EX silver, smoke stack w/cotton, EX...........300.00
Rooster, blown, red, 3"...85.00
Rooster, blown, wht w/blk hat & red coat, on clip, 4½" 300.00
Rooster, Dresden, mc pnt, silk bag at bk, EX 225.00
Salamander, Dresden, 3-D, tan w/dk shading, 4⅛" 250.00
Santa, blown, chenille legs, compo boots, mc pnt, 4½" 145.00
Santa, blown, pearly gold robe, w/tree, early, 2¾", EX 30.00
Santa, blown, red w/gold molded legs & tree, 4½" 55.00
Santa, blown, yel w/gr hat & silver face, 3" 60.00
Santa, bsk, Japan, ca 1930, 4" 40.00
Santa, celluloid, Irwin, made in USA, 5", EX......................12.00
Santa in automobile, celluloid, 3¾", EX 85.00
Santa in basket, blown, red w/gold, 3" 80.00
Santa in fireplace, blown, EX pnt, lg 50.00
Santa's head, blown, 2-sided, pearly wht/red/silver, 3"................85.00
Scallop shell, blown, red, 2¾", EX 55.00
Scotty, blown, gold w/wht spots, 3¾" 75.00
Scotty, blown, pk w/wht spots & collar, 3".........................65.00
Serpent, blown, pearly gold/red, molded scales, early, 5", EX 200.00
Ship, Dresden, flat, EX details, 1½x1¼", NM 85.00
Smitty, blown, pearly wht/yel/bl, 5", EX 345.00
Spaniel, blown, silver w/gr ears & legs, red bow, 3" 85.00
Sparrow, blown, unsilvered wht, spun glass tail, 1920s, sm.............15.00
Squirrel, blown, pearly gold w/red details, 2½", EX 75.00
Star, Dresden, flat, 2-sided, gold, 2x2", EX 45.00
Star, tin, silver w/red center, faceted, 3¾"........................55.00
Strawberry, blown, yel/pk/wht frost, 5"............................70.00
Swan, blown, pearly wht/red/bl, tinsel tail, 1930s, 8"................65.00

Teddy, blown, gold pnt, 3½" **65.00**
Truck, blown, gold/silver/red, minor wear, 2¾" **150.00**
Turk's head, 2-sided, red & gold, early, 3" **175.00**
Umbrella, blown w/wire mesh, bl, 6⅝", EX **85.00**
Victorian girl, blown, silver/gold/red, 3¼", VG **65.00**
Walnut, blown, orange, unsilvered, 2½" **40.00**
Windmill, Sebnitz, metal fr, foil/wire blades, die-cut child **165.00**
Witch's head, blown, pk face, blk glasses, ca 1900, 2" **200.00**

Santa with toys, embossed paper Santa with cotton skirt and crepe paper trim, 20", VG, $275.00.

Miscellaneous

Bank, Santa, carnival chalkware, EX pnt, 9" **65.00**
Banner, star w/Merry Xmas in tail, German diecut, '20s, 19" **45.00**
Book, Doings of Kriss Kringle, McLoughlin, 7x8½", EX **60.00**
Book, Night Before Christmas, house diecut, Graham, 6½" **65.00**
Book, Visit from Santa Claus, McLoughlin, 1899, EX **90.00**
Bookmark, Noel/elves/etc, woven silk, EX..................................**65.00**
Boot, Sebnitz, cotton-covered wire fr, metal overlay, 1800s..........**135.00**
Bottle, liquor; Father Christmas, ceramic, Germany, early, 5" **150.00**
Candelabrum, Father Christmas figural, brass, English **80.00**
Candle holder, blown head, pnt features, clip-on, 1900, 3" **165.00**
Candle holder, cherub, gr, tin, clip-on, 2"...............................**95.00**
Candle holder, counter-balance style, bl clay ball, 5½" **25.00**
Candle holder, lantern form w/glass panes, 1880s, 8x3x3", EX **88.00**
Candle holder, tin, clip-on, ca 1900, set of 20 ....**60.00**
Church, cork, gelatin windows, ca 1910, 7½x5x6", EX................**65.00**
Cornucopia, red paper/gold foil, scrap Santa decor, 8½" **75.00**
Costume, Santa suit w/hooded mask, 1930s **120.00**
Cow, Putz, brn, 2½x3½", EX **45.00**
Donkey, Putz, gray & blk, 3½"..**30.00**
Father Christmas, Belsnickle, gr w/feather tree, 7", EX...............**495.00**
Father Christmas, Belsnickle, wht w/red chenille, 9½", EX **675.00**
Fence, feather, Evergreen Hedge, Germany, 65", EX **525.00**
Fence, wood, gr pnt, 3¼x27" sq, EX in orig box **90.00**
Fence, wood, pie-wedge shape, picket style, varnished, 62" **175.00**
Fence, wood, red & gr pnt, gate at front, 4x19" sq, EX.................**90.00**
Fence, wood, 4-section, brn/gr, Germany, 56" L, EX **65.00**
Fence, wood, 5-section, brn/gr, Germany, 91" L, EX **88.00**
Fence, wood, 6-section, wicker uprights, 24" sq, EX....................**145.00**
Garland, bl glass beads, 2 strands, 152", EX **55.00**
Garland, gr & gold glass beads, 112", EX **45.00**
Garland, paper bells, Father Xmas litho, '20s, Germany, 120" **45.00**

Garland, silver beads/celluloid bells/red clappers, lg, 108"..............**45.00**
Girl, cotton w/compo face on cb sled covered w/mica flakes, 3" **65.00**
House, paper, wht/pk/red/silver, snow covered, 4x4½" **45.00**
Lamb, compo w/wood legs, gr color, 3½", NM **85.00**
Lamb, compo w/wood legs, woolly covering, 5½", EX **75.00**
Lamb, woolly, wht, Germany, 2½x2½", EX................................**45.00**
Lantern, Santa figural globe, red, battery-op, 6", NMIB.................**65.00**
Manger, wood w/cotton on roof & bk, Germany, 8½x10" **65.00**
Music box, wooden church, paper roof, 1930s, 14x8½x8", EX **65.00**
Nativity scene, fold-out cb litho, Germany, 1900, 20x15x14" **65.00**
Pin-bk, Santa's head/Merry Christmas, 1¼", NM **30.00**
Print, Santa in snow w/children, ca 1895, 6½x9½", EX **55.00**
Ram, compo w/wood legs, cb horns, woolly, Japan, 3¼" **45.00**
Ram, wood w/metal horns, Germany, 3½", EX **75.00**
Rattle, Santa on barrel figural, cb, 2-sided, 1930s, 6", EX **28.00**
Santa, Belsnickle, bl, Germany, 7¼", EX..................................**695.00**
Santa, Belsnickle, wht w/bl trim, 8" **425.00**
Santa, celluloid face, papier-mache boots, Japan, 6½", EX...........**135.00**
Santa, clay face, cloth suit, cb sleigh, '30s, Japan,14x15x3" **95.00**
Santa, compo, by cb castle, mica snow, Japan, '30s, 7x6x4" **55.00**
Santa, mask face, compo boots, fur beard, 30" **225.00**
Santa, papier-mache face & boots, Japan, 10", EX **95.00**
Santa, papier-mache face & boots, Japan, 6½", EX **65.00**
Santa, wooden cutout, mc pnt, 1930s, 28x14x1", EX **85.00**
Santa in car, celluloid, mc, 3x4½" **100.00**
Santa in sleigh w/reindeer, bsk, 3", EX....................................**110.00**
Santa on skis, celluloid, 1930s, 4", VG **65.00**
Santa on skis, clay face, 1930s, Japan, 4", EX **70.00**
Santa w/deer, celluloid, mechanical, mc pnt, 3½x6", EX **125.00**
Shade, revolves, Merry Glo Lites, EX, 5 for **85.00**
Shepherd, compo, 2¼", +3 woolly 2¼" sheep+2" dog, EX **145.00**
Snowman, papier-mache, cotton carrot nose, Germany, 5½" **145.00**
Spoon, Santa/sleigh/deer in bowl, SP, child's, 4¼" **65.00**
Star, treetop, tin, gold & red pnt, pat 1926, 8½x3" **50.00**
Stocking, felt, stamped Santa face, 10¾", EX **65.00**
Stocking, gold silk w/HP cherries, dtd 1882, 6", EX **88.00**
Tree, feather, trn wood base, Germany, early, 32", EX **255.00**
Tree base, musical, electric, Gilbert, EX **150.00**
Tree stand, CI, EX 3-color pnt, Santa's head relief, 5x11" **265.00**
Tree stand, CI, inverted cone on tripod ft, 1920s, 15x18x18".......**65.00**
Tree stand, rotating/musical, Swill windup, electrified................**235.00**
Tree stand, trn wood, tripod legs, old gr pnt, 18½x16" **75.00**
Tree stand, trn wood, w/tramp art fence, old pnt, 5x11x11" **150.00**

Chrysanthemum Sprig, Blue

This is the blue opaque version of Northwood's popular pattern, Chrysanthemum Sprig. Though collectors often refer to it as 'blue custard,' in the strictest sense it is not. It was made at the turn of the century and is today very rare, as its values indicate.

Bowl, berry; sm **125.00**
Butter dish **800.00**
Celery vase, NM gold & decor...**1,200.00**
Compote, jelly **475.00**
Condiment tray, rare, VG gold **675.00**
Creamer **350.00**
Cruet **775.00**
Pitcher, water..**900.00**
Sauce dish, EX gold **145.00**
Shakers, pr **450.00**
Spooner...**250.00**
Sugar bowl, open **300.00**

Sugar bowl, w/lid 425.00
Toothpick holder 450.00
Tumbler..200.00

Circus Collectibles

The 1890s – the Golden Age of the circus. Barnum and Bailey's parades transformed mundane city streets into an exotic never-never land inhabited by trumpeting elephants with jeweled gold headgear strutting by to the strains of the calliope that issued from a fine red- and gilt-painted wagon extravagantly decorated with carved wooden animals of every description. It was an exciting experience – is it any wonder that collectors today treasure the mementos of that golden era?

See also posters.

Key:
B&B — Barnum & Bailey   RB — Ringling Bros.

Annual, RB, 1901..195.00
Book, Jungle Performers, Clyde Beatty, 1941, 1st ed, EX 80.00
Holster, RB B&B, leather, sm.......................................35.00
Magazine, RB B&B, Daily Review, Wallendas article, 1932 ....32.00
Magazine, RB B&B, 100th Anniversary Souvenir, 1971................25.00
Menu, Greatest Show on Earth, mc w/gilt, 1898 ....85.00
Post card, B&B, Germany, ca 1910 ....20.00
Program/magazine, RB B&B, 1942, EX....................................12.00
Route book, B&B, 1906, EX 195.00
Sign, baby elephant, pnt wood cutout, trunk up, 72" 235.00
Ticket, RB B&B, filming of Greatest Show on Earth, 1950s............ 3.00
Wallet, B&B stamped on leather, w/early business cards, EX 65.00

Clambroth

Clambroth is a term that refers to a type of glass popular during the Victorian period. It was semi-opaque and gray-white in color, said to resemble the broth of the clam. See also Sandwich.

Candlestick, sq base, fluted std, petal socket, 8¾" 95.00
Cruet, lt bl cuttings in paneled body, step-cut lip, 7" 700.00
Epergne, 1-lily, ftd/ruffled bowl: 6¼x4½" 125.00
Pitcher, appl hdl, 10½" 70.00
Toothpick holder, Button Arches..20.00
Toothpick holder, floral at rim, Sandwich, 2" 95.00

Clarice Cliff

Between 1928 and 1935, in Burslem, England, as the director and part owner of Wilkinson and Newport Pottery Companies, Clarice Cliff and her 'paintresses' created a body of hand-painted pottery whose influence is felt to the present time.

The name for the oevre was Bizarre Ware, and the predominant sensibility, style, and appearance was Deco. Almost all pieces are signed and include the pattern names. There were over 160 patterns and more than 400 shapes, all of which are illustrated in A Bizarre Affair – the Life and Work of Clarice Cliff, published by Harry N. Abrams, Inc., written by Len Griffen and our advisors, Susan and Louis Meisel, whose address is listed in the Directory under New York.

Clarice Cliff died in 1972, shortly after the Victoria and Albert Museum showed her work in retrospect, and collectors (primarily in England) began seeking and admiring her work. In September of 1982, the Metropolitan Museum of Art in New York acquired and placed on view a selection of six pieces.

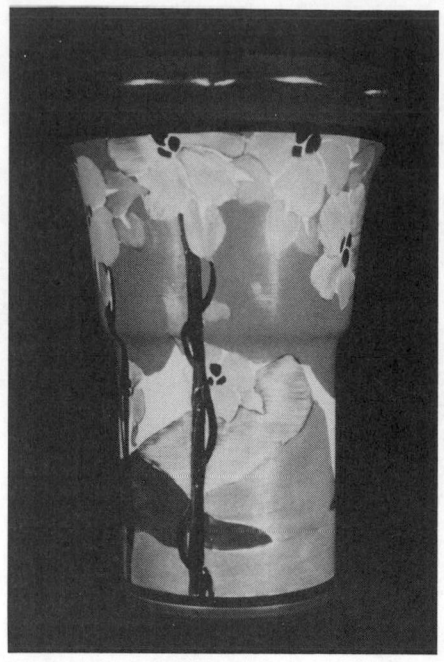

Applique Palermo pattern on Archaic shape vase, ca 1932, 12", $7,500.00.

Biscuit Barrel, Geometric, 8" 1,400.00
Biscuit Barrel, Honolulu, 8"... 1,700.00
Bowl, Autumn, 10" 1,200.00
Bowl, Umbrellas, 10"..900.00
Charger, Latona Floral, 18"...15,000.00
Charger, Sunray, 18" 12,000.00
Charger, Umbrellas, 18"... 9,000.00
Coffee set, Lugano, 3-pc... 4,000.00
Conical sugar sifter, Blue Chintz 650.00
Conical sugar sifter, Crocus 300.00
Conical sugar sifter, Gibralter 1,200.00
Honey pot, Stripes, Beehive..300.00
Honey pot, Windbells, Beehive 500.00
Isis jug, Geometric, 10"... 3,000.00
Isis jug, Inspiration, 10"... 2,400.00
Jam pot, Melon, cylindrical..400.00
Jam pot, Trees & House, cylindrical....................................600.00
Lotus jug, Blue W, 12" 7,500.00
Lotus jug, Farmhouse, 12" 5,000.00
Lotus jug, Geometric, 12" 4,200.00
Plate, Blue Firs, rectangular, 9" 1,100.00
Plate, Citrus Delicia, 10"...300.00
Plate, Honolulu, octagonal, 8½" 800.00
Plate, Secrets, 10"...475.00
Plate, Windmill, 9" 6,800.00
Vase, Baluster, Gardenia, 9" 1,600.00
Vase, Cylinder, Geometric, 7" 1,000.00
Vase, Globe, Geometric, 4" 3,200.00
Vase, Triangle, Oranges, 8".. 1,200.00

Cleminson

A hobby turned to enterprise, Cleminson is one of several California potteries whose clever hand-decorated wares are attracting the attention of today's collectors. The Cleminsons started their business at their El Monte home in 1941 and were so successful that eventually they expanded to a modern plant that employed more than 150 workers. They produced not only dinnerware and kitchen items such as cookie jars, canisters, and accessories, but novelty wall vases, small trays, plaques, etc., as well. Though nearly always marked, Cleminson wares are easy to spot as you become familiar with their distinctive glaze colors. Their grayed-down blue and green, berry red, and dusty pink say 'Cleminson' as clearly as their trademark. Unable to compete with foreign imports, the pottery closed in 1963.

Our advisor for this category is Jack Chipman; he is listed in the Directory under California.

Butter dish, Distlefink..**25.00**
Canister, tree branches w/apples, red/gr on wht...........**15.00**

Cookie jar, potbellied stove, $75.00.

Creamer & sugar bowl, King & Queen of Hearts **35.00**
Gravy boat, Distlefink, w/ladle...................................**20.00**
Plaque, pear & cherries on gr **8.50**
Plaque, People Will Say We're in Love, heart form **18.50**
Shakers, Distlefink, lg, pr..**15.00**
Shakers, girl & boy, 6" **18.00**
Spoon rest, leaf form **12.50**
Sprinkler, Chinese boy **15.00**
Wall pocket, mortgage bank......................................**12.00**

Clewell

Charles Walter Clewell was a metal worker who perfected the technique of plating an entire ceramic vessel with a thin layer of copper or bronze treated with an oxidizing agent to produce a natural deterioration of the surface. Through trial and error, he was able to control the degree of patina achieved. In the early stages, the metal darkened and, if allowed to develop further, formed a natural turquoise-blue or green corrosion. He worked alone in his small Akron, Ohio, studio from about 1906, buying undecorated pottery from several Ohio firms, among them Weller, Owens, and Cambridge. His work is usually marked. Clewell died in 1965, having never revealed his secret process to others.

Bowl, bulbous w/3 scroll ft, sgn/1931-421-26, 2½x5½" **110.00**
Candlestick, dk metallic w/gr on base, #4115-2-6, 10", pr **475.00**

Jug, bronze patina, wheat motif, #820, 6½" **450.00**
Mug, orig patina, 4½"..**210.00**

Pitcher, 10", and four mugs, riveted, $750.00.

Vase, brn striations on brass wash, cylindrical, 19" **850.00**
Vase, brn/gr/orange patina on bronze, bulbous, #459-21, 8" **450.00**
Vase, copper patina, rolled rim/cylinder neck, #458, 6½" **375.00**
Vase, EX orig patina, #444-26, crack in metal, 6½" **450.00**
Vase, EX patina, mk/#323-1-6, several metal cracks, 10".............**550.00**
Vase, orange/gr patina, flange rim, wide body, 7" **375.00**
Vase, rust/gr patina, flaring neck, rnd ft, 7" **575.00**
Vase, rusty orange to gr, elongated teardrop, #357-2-7, 11½" **600.00**

Clews

Brothers Ralph and James Clews were potters who operated in Cobridge in the Staffordshire district from 1817 to 1835. They are best known for their blue and white transfer-printed earthenwares, which included American Views, Moral Maxims, Picturesque Views, and English Views. A series called *Three Tours of Dr. Syntax* contained nearly eighty different scenes with each piece bearing a descriptive title. Two other popular series were *Don Quixote* with twenty prints and *Pictures of Sir David Wilkie* with twelve. Both printed and impressed marks were used, often incorporating the pattern name as well as the pottery. See also Staffordshire, Historical.

Bowl, Christmas Eve, dk bl transfer, 5½" **195.00**
Cup & saucer, Christmas Eve, dk bl transfer, Wilkie series, EX ...**165.00**
Cup & saucer, Water Girl, dk bl transfer, EX................................**145.00**
Plate, American & Independence, bl on wht, 8¾" **250.00**
Plate, Christmas Eve, dk bl transfer, 9" **165.00**
Plate, Don Quixote, Curious Impertinent..., dk bl, 5½" **165.00**
Plate, Don Quixote & Sancho Panza, dk bl transfer, 9" **150.00**
Plate, Don Quixote & Sancho Panza, gr transfer, 8¾" **65.00**
Plate, Dr Syntax, Drawing After Nature, dk bl transfer, 10¼" **145.00**
Plate, Dr Syntax Mistakes a Gent's House..., 10", NM.................**150.00**
Plate, Dr Syntax Returned from His Tour, dk bl transfer, 8" **165.00**
Plate, Dr Syntax Taking Possession..., dk bl transfer, 10" **225.00**
Plate, Escape of the Mouse, dk bl transfer, 10" **165.00**
Plate, Meeting of Sancho & Dapple, dk bl transfer, 9" **150.00**
Plate, river scenery, lt bl transfer, glaze wear, 9¾"..........................**40.00**
Plate, Sancho, the Priest & Barber, dk bl transfer, 7⅝" **145.00**

Plate, Sancho Panza's Debate w/Teresa, dk bl transfer, 9" 165.00
Platter, Don Quixote, Knight o/t Woods..., dk bl, 17" 495.00
Platter, Don Quixote, Teresa Pansa & Messenger, dk bl, 15" 495.00
Platter, Dr Syntax, Advertisement for a Wife, dk bl, 15" 550.00
Platter, Sancho Panza & the Duchess, ca 1820, 18½" 650.00
Platter, still life w/bird, med bl transfer, 19", EX..........................250.00
Soup plate, English Cathedral, dk bl transfer, 10", NM 100.00

Clifton

Clifton Art Pottery of Clifton, New Jersey, was organized ca 1903. Until 1911 when they turned to the production of wall and floor tile, they made artware of several varieties. The founders were Fred Tschirner and William A. Long. Long had developed the method for underglaze slip painting that had been used at the Lonhuda Pottery in Steubenville, Ohio, in the 1890s. Crystal Patina, the first artware made by the small company, utilized a fine white body and flowing, blended colors, the earliest a green crystalline. Indian Ware, copied from the pottery of the American Indians, was decorated in black geometric designs on red clay. Robin's Egg Blue, pale blue on the white body, and Tirrube, a slip-decorated matt ware, were also produced.

Bowl, Indian Ware, Greek Key design, blk glossy int, 3x6" 55.00
Jug, Indian Ware, Greek Key design, rnd, imp mk, 4½" 55.00
Lamp, Crystal Patina base, copper/abalone shell Valk shade... 4,000.00

Crystal Patina teapot, 5½", $100.00.

Vase, Crystal Patina, lime/silver flambe, #156, 9x4½" 200.00
Vase, Indian Ware, brns & blk, 9x12" 325.00
Vase, Indian Ware, narrow neck on squat bulb, sgn S/#29, 6" 60.00
Vase, Indian Ware, squatty, incised at shoulder, #d, 2½x3½" 50.00
Vase, matt gr, slim neck, dtd 1906, 10"..175.00
Vase, Tirrube, floral HP on red, 8½"...150.00
Vase, Tirrube, stork & foliage, #257, 12x7" 325.00

Clocks

In the early days of our country's history, clock makers were influenced by styles imported from Europe and Germany. They copied their cabinets and re-constructed their movements. But needed materials

were in short supply; modifications had to be made. Of necessity was born mainspring motive power and spring clocks. Wooden movements were made on a mass-production basis as early as 1808. Before the middle of the century, metal movements had been developed.

Today's collectors prefer clocks from the eighteenth and nineteenth centuries with pendulum-regulated movements. Bracket clocks made during this period utilized the shorter pendulum improvised in 1658 by Fromentiel, a prominent English clock maker. These smaller square-face clocks usually were made with a dome top fitted with a handle or a decorative finial. The case was usually walnut or ebony and was sometimes decorated with pierced brass mountings. Brackets were often mounted on the wall to accommodate the clock, hence the name. The banjo clock was patented in 1802 by Simon Willard. It derived its descriptive name from its banjo-like shape. A similar but more elaborate style was called the lyre clock. Twentieth century novelty clocks, such as the animated examples in the listings that follow, are becoming very popular collectibles, as their values indicate. Our advisor is Bruce A. Austin; he is listed in the Directory under New York. Our novelty clock advisors are DLK Nostalgia and Collectibles; they are listed in the Directory under Pennsylvania.

Key:
esc — escapement   T&S — time and strike
mvt — movement   wt — weight
pnd — pendulum   2nds — seconds
reg — regulator

Art Nouveau bronze and onyx mantel clock, ca 1890, 18½", $1,400.00.

A Willard, banjo, eglomise panels, dial sgn, ca 1825, 36" 3,000.00
Am Clock Co, regulator, battery impulse, oak case 450.00
Anniversary, brass, glass dome, 11"...130.00
Ansonia, Apex, crystal regulator 2,700.00
Ansonia, Arcadia, swing arm, bronze statue, rpr, 1890, 31½".. 3,000.00
Ansonia, Capitol, porc dial, time only, spring, mahog case..........950.00
Ansonia, Crystal Palace, orig oval dome, #1 Extra 800.00
Ansonia, Floral, crystal regulator... 1,400.00

Ansonia, General, regulator, 8-day wt, 18" dial, mahog, 68" ... **3,200.00**
Ansonia, Gilmore, kitchen, oak, 8-day/T&S, alarm **190.00**
Ansonia, Jupiter, crystal regulator, glass columns.................... **1,800.00**
Ansonia, Lucia, crystal regulator **900.00**
Ansonia, mantel, blk marble, 4-pillar, Boston model..................**165.00**
Ansonia, Marchioness, crystal regulator **950.00**
Ansonia, Queen Mary, 8-day/T&S, walnut case **750.00**
Ansonia, Regis, crystal regulator **475.00**
Ansonia, siren statue, visible esc, porc dial, 1906.................**450.00**
Ansonia, wall, mk Scott & Kikley, Ainwick, 8-day/T&S **220.00**
Arcadia, swing arm, bronze statue, rpr, ca 1890, 31½"............. **3,000.00**
Atkins & Downs for Geo Mitchell, pillar/scroll, wood dial **1,250.00**
Aulding, carriage, brass, enamel dial, 8-day, leather case, 6½".....**450.00**
Austrian, Vienna regulator, T&S, mirror bk, 37".................**700.00**
Banjo, gilt mahog, pnt iron dial, rvpt floral, 8-day/T, 33" **900.00**
Banjo, mahog, timepc mvt, ball/eagle finial, ca 1820, 34" **2,150.00**
Banjo, mahog/giltwood, rvpt badminton scene, 40" **1,350.00**
Banjo, mahog/giltwood Fed presentation, 1820, rstr, 40".......... **1,800.00**
Banjo, rnd mvt, T&S, New Haven, miniature, 18"......................**300.00**
BB Lewis, #2, calendar, 12" time/9" calendar dial, rosewood **650.00**
Birge & Fuller, Empire, 8-day/T&S, 33" **425.00**
Birge & Mallory, rfn mahog case, rpl weights/hands **350.00**

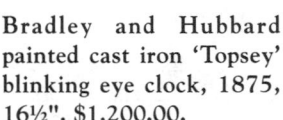
Bradley and Hubbard painted cast iron 'Topsey' blinking eye clock, 1875, 16½", $1,200.00.

Brewster & Ingraham, steeple, mahog, 8-day, T&S w/alarm........**375.00**
C Jerome, ogee, walnut, 30-hr, rpt zinc dial, 26" **160.00**
C Jerome, shelf, gilt columns, rosewood case, 18¼" **150.00**
Carriage, drum case, w/alarm, 1880 ....**170.00**
Carriage, gilt brass, cylinder esc, 30-hour, 6" **175.00**
Chas Oudin, traveling, brass/glass, leather case, 3½" **385.00**
Chelsea, banjo, rvpt: Perry's Victory at Lake Erie, 31", M **575.00**
Chelsea, desk, brass, beveled glass, 4½" **500.00**
China, bracket, MOP moldings, crown-wheel esc, 1840s, 14" . **1,550.00**
Concord MA, banjo, eagle atop & in rvpt glass, 1830s, 34" **700.00**
Couaillet, carriage, pediment, 5" oblong gilt dial, 1890 ....**175.00**
Desbois, bracket, gilt/eng dial, ebony pagoda case, 10" **2,700.00**
Drocourt, carriage, repeater, anglaise riche, 1880, 7" **800.00**
Dutch, wall, mahog, brass decor, Atlas finial, 19" **100.00**
E Downs, pillar & scroll, mahog, 30-hr, ca 1815-1840, 31" **800.00**
E Howard, #5, banjo, dial sgn, numbered mvt, rosewood **1,800.00**
Elmer Stennes, mahog pillar & scroll, rvpt, 31" **900.00**
Elnathan Taber, mahog/brass urn, rectangular wall mt, 35" **8,000.00**
EN Welch, Sinico, walnut regulator, 8-day/T&S **1,100.00**
EN Welch, steeple, rpl dial, mahog/rosewood, 8-day/T&S.........**225.00**

English, bracket, mahog, appl cvd decor, ca 1820-1830, 16"........**975.00**
English, gallery, brass bezel, brass fusee mvt, 21" **550.00**
English, mantel, Art Deco, T&S...**75.00**
Forestville, octagon wall, rosewood, 8-day/T&S, 25x16½".........**325.00**
French, china w/ormolu & HP cherubs, decor dial, 18", M **800.00**
French, chinoiserie, pierced brass sheet, 1920, 10½"...............**115.00**
French, mantel, Chas X, wht marble w/bronze mts, 20".............**700.00**
French, mantel, crystal regulator, gilt, 8-day, 11" **900.00**
French, mantel, crystal regulator, mercury pnd, 6½" **700.00**
French, mantel, gr onyx, putto atop, ornate gilt mts, 25" **1,200.00**
French, mantel, HP porc side panels & urn surmount, 16" **1,600.00**
French, mantel, onyx w/gilt-bronze garlands, mk JED, 17" **375.00**
French, marquetry w/ormolu mts, open brass face, T&S, 18½" ..**350.00**
French, pottery, orb w/gilt dial, lg lion figure aside, 13" **800.00**
G Becker, mahog shelf, Westminster chime, Germany **400.00**
G Becker, walnut, 2-weight, fancy face, 47" **750.00**
G Becker, walnut, 2-weight, fancy porthole style, pnd, 50" **950.00**

John Willats George II mahogany bracket clock, double fusee movement with rack striking the hours, 1760s, 21", $2,000.00.

German, mantel, rosewood, ormolu mtd, triple fusee, 17"....... **1,300.00**
German, wall, mahog, 1-weight, 2nds bit, 45"..........................**550.00**
German, wall, walnut, open pnd, spring, 8-day/T&S **475.00**
Gilbert, #11, oak, 2-weight w/spring strike.............................. **1,800.00**
Gilbert, #3, weight regulator, rosewood case, 1897, M **1,400.00**
Gilbert, #6, weight drive, wall type **1,100.00**
Gilbert, #64, oak regulator, weight drive **800.00**
Gilbert, cottage, emb molding, 8-day, pat 1882, 16" **250.00**
Gilbert, Lake #4, kitchen, oak, 8-day/T&S **175.00**
Gilbert, mantel, blk wood, ornate columns/mts, 8-day/T&S........**150.00**
Gilbert, Occidental, parlor, walnut w/mirror sides **350.00**
Gilbert, Tuscan, crystal regulator **900.00**
H&H France, carriage, brass, wht enamel face, key, 4⅜" **375.00**
Hingham, mahog Fed banjo, pnt metal dial/flat moldings, 32"....**650.00**
Horlogerie J, Paris, blk onyx w/ormolu, urn finial, 15½"..............**225.00**

Ingraham, Colby, mantel, blk..**50.00**
Ingraham, Dew Drop, 8-day/T...250.00
Ingraham, Gila, kitchen, calendar mvt, 8-day/T&S......................275.00
Ingraham, Ionic, mosaic case, 8-day/T, w/label, rstr, 22" 400.00
Ingraham, store regulator, calendar, orig glass.............................475.00
International, master, walnut, 2-weight.....................................950.00
Ithaca, Brisbane, dbl dial calendar... 3,200.00
Ithaca, calendar, mahog, cvd/ebonized architecture, 20" 1,650.00
JE Caldwell & Co, bracket, inlaid mahog, brass mts, T&S, 14" ..200.00
Jerome-Gilbert-Grant, mahog Empire ogee shelf, 30-hr/T&S.....125.00
John Sawin, mahog banjo, 2 rvpt: floral/Father Time, 32" 2,100.00
John Sawin, mahog/veneer banjo, pnd/brass works, rstr, 33" 810.00
Julien Leroy, Louis XVI style, marble, bronze child/goat 1,300.00
Junghans, bracket, inlaid mahog, w/chimes, brass face, 17" 400.00
Kenzle Uhren, key wind, rod chime, 40" 425.00
Kroeber Saxonia, CI, gladiator statue, gargoyle sides, 20"............450.00
Le-Coulture, mantel, brass/glass cased, French, 9", EX 300.00
Mark Leavenworth, pillar & scroll, wood works, rvpt, 30" 1,050.00
New Haven, Elfrida, oak regulator, weight drive......................1,250.00
New Haven, Mission oak, mantel, 8-day 75.00
New Haven, office regulator, oak, w/calendar, rstr, 43"................650.00
New Haven, schoolhouse, dk wood, 1880, M...............................350.00
Riley Whiting, mahog Emp, acanthus/eagle cvg, 1825, 30" 250.00
Seikosha, shelf, oak, Japan, 8-day/T&S 75.00
Sessions, banjo, rvpt Colonial scene, 27" 60.00

Eli Terry & Sons Federal mahogany and mahogany veneer pillar and scroll shelf clock, 1830, restoration, 32", $950.00.

Seth Thomas, #18, regulator, weight driven............................ 2,200.00
Seth Thomas, #50, Sonora, w/chimes, 5 bells 475.00
Seth Thomas, #6, office calendar, 8" dial, strike 1,100.00
Seth Thomas, Adamantine, mantel, marbleized, 8-day/T&S......225.00
Seth Thomas, cottage, rosewood, 30-hr, T&S, alarm.................185.00
Seth Thomas, Gothic, rosewood, ripple front, 8-day/T&S 350.00
Seth Thomas, Lincoln, oak, weight driven 1,100.00
Seth Thomas, mantel, dbl dial calendar, walnut, 8-day, 20" 850.00
Seth Thomas, mantel, glass/brass, molded cornice, 1900, 9½" 130.00
Seth Thomas, mantel, ornate case, porc dial, bell strike 165.00
Seth Thomas, parlor shelf, burled walnut, 8-day/T&S.................250.00
Seth Thomas, Queen Anne, walnut, time only..........................900.00
Seth Thomas, regulator, bl label, ca 1854, 34" 1,800.00
Seth Thomas, shelf, mahog, 8-day/T&S, alarm...........................160.00

Seth Thomas, shelf, ogee fr, 30-hr/T&S, weight driven, 26" 125.00
Seth Thomas, time clock, oak, orig fancy case, 60", M 800.00
Seth Thomas, time clock, 30-day, nickel bob/mvt, ca 1900.........650.00
Simon Willard, banjo, eagle atop/rvpt, 8-day/T, 34" 1,900.00
Simon Willard, banjo, mahog, ca 1802-1805, 34¼"................. 7,500.00
Standard, regulator w/program, oak, 1915, 60" 600.00
Tiffany, mantel, crystal regulator, brass, 8-day, 8¼" 900.00
Vicenti, mantel, ormolu, boy on ladder/tree, 1855, 16" 485.00
Vienna, mantel, HP panels, dome surmount, 4-column, 18"... 1,500.00
Vienna, wall, gilt cast bezel, wht porc dial, ca 1850, 38" 2,575.00
W&H, bracket, inlaid mahog, brass ft/door/face, T&S, 15".........425.00
Wag on wall, brass gears w/wood plates/case/pnt face, 8x5" 175.00
Waltham, chronometer, up/down indicator, 8-day 650.00
Waterbury, #53, oak, rfn.. 1,600.00
Waterbury, apple form, pnt cast aluminum, windup, 4½", VG.......60.00
Waterbury, Duxbury, mantel...80.00
Waterbury, kitchen, golden oak, ornate......................................150.00
Waterbury, Rochester, walnut, rfn, simple calendar 450.00
Waterbury, rosewood veneer, rvpt floral, 30-hr, 26x16" 165.00
Waterbury, steeple, rfn pine case, 30-hr, T&S 110.00
Welch, #5, regulator, dbl dial calendar..................................... 1,950.00
Welch, mantel, iron, side urns/statue atop, 8-day/T&S...............550.00
Welch Spring & Co, Patti, shelf, rosewood, rstr dial, 19" ... 1,250.00
Welch/Spring Co Bristol, BB Lewis's perpetual calendar, 44".. 2,100.00
Westclox, Ironclad, CI, alarm 80.00
Willard, banjo, mahog w/inlay, rvpt, brass works, 33" 3,000.00
Wm Gilbert, steeple, paper label, rosewood case, 17¼" 140.00
Wurttemburg, Victorian house, mahog, 1900, 18" 225.00

Novelty

Art Nouveau, digital, NM...125.00
Barbie, 3", NM..100.00
Batman Talking Clock, NM...125.00
Bird Song, bird on top, alarm 30.00
Blessing, duck w/rocking butterfly, sm letters................................40.00
Blessing, paddle boat, paddle turns, late 1960s 45.00
Bradley & Hubbard, Geo Washington figure, pnt CI, 17" 1,200.00
Bugs Bunny, figural, talking clock, M 100.00
Chicken pecks at ground, ceramic, 1970s.....................................140.00
Deer, eye moves, ceramic..45.00
Diamond, dragon, head rocks, Shanghai, China.............................45.00
GE, dog w/ball on nose, ball rolls to top of nose 160.00
German, blksmith elf, arm w/hammer lifts, 1920s.......................300.00
German, windmill, beveled glass, pre-WWII, 1920s 280.00
God Bless America, animated flags, 1940s....................................100.00
Indian Head, Iroquois Beer-Ale Clock..90.00
Ingraham, Roy Rogers 100.00
Ives, Blk man w/banjo (dial), rolling eyes, pnt CI, 16" 1,200.00
Jerger, men's arms strike alarm bells, 1960s...................................30.00
Keebler, bulldog w/kitten, EX 30.00
Keebler, Martha & Geo Washington, kissing bird.........................80.00
Keebler, quail cuckoo, 8-day mvt, 8x7½"....................................250.00
Lux, Blk man organ grinder, VG...125.00
Lux, clown w/seals, animated, NM 260.00
Lux, cottage shape, VG...40.00
Lux, dog w/wagging tongue 87.50
Lux, Lindbergh, airplane shape, NM...55.00
Lux, mechanical bell, digital, G 35.00
Lux, organ grinder w/monkey, arm turns, 1930s 150.00
Lux, showboat, paddle turns, 1950 ....90.00
Lux, train, steam engine, 1970 ....50.00
Lux, Village Mill, figural, alarm, 1920, EX...................................49.50

Master Crafters, church figural, animated/electric, 12", EX	10.00
Mouse & bird, bird pecks, ceramic	45.00
Musical alarm w/ballerina, animated, NM	40.00
Powder box, musical, metal, WWI	130.00
Raggedy Ann, talking clock	20.00
Roosevelt, Spirit of USA, w/Johnson & Perkins, 10"	135.00
Smith, bookie, dbl animation, arm & numbers	410.00
Smith, boxing dog & bear, arms move, 1960s	105.00
Smith, rooster pecks ground, sq case, late 1950s	210.00
Tiempo, horse race, horse rocks, Brazil	45.00
Tiempo, police, police car rocks, Brazil	45.00
UEC, Bartender, arm moves, 1933	125.00
UEC, Roosevelt Band Leader, 1934	90.00
UEC, Spirit of '76 Drummer	100.00
Windmill, animated, alarm, 5" sq celluloid face	20.00
Woodcutter, cuckoo, people saw & chop wood, music box, M	125.00

Cloisonne

Cloisonne is a method of decorating metal with enameling. Fine metal wires are soldered onto the metal body following the lines of a predetermined design. The resulting channels are filled in with enamels of various colors, and the item is fired. The final step is a smoothing process that assures even exposure of the wire pattern. The art is predominately Oriental and has been practiced continuously, except during war years, since the sixteenth century. The most excellent examples date from 1865 until the turn of the century. The early twentieth century export variety is usually lightweight and the workmanship inferior. Modern wares are of good quality and are produced in Taiwan as well as China.

Several variations of the basic art include plique-a-jour, achieved by removing the metal body after firing, leaving only the transparent enamel work; foil cloisonne, using transparent or semi-translucent enameling over a layer of embossed silver covering the metal body of the vessel; wireless cloisonne, made by removing the wire dividers prior to firing; and cloisonne executed on ceramic, wood, or lacquer rather than metal.

Apple box, floral/bird panels, 5-color, 5x5"	80.00
Apple box, florals, pk/red on beige, 5x3½"	60.00
Bowl, cherry blossoms on royal bl w/gold scrolls, lid, 4½x5"	85.00
Bowl, cloud scrolls on wht, mc peonies, short ped ft, 10"	350.00
Bowl, dragons w/in & w/out, folded rim, mk, 2½x8"	210.00
Bowl, peonies/bird, gold on royal bl, 10"	150.00
Bowl, peonies/birds, bl/yel on lt gr, scalloped, 3x9"	135.00
Bowl, peonies/butterfly on royal bl, divided, 4x8"	325.00
Box, duck form, yel/pk flowers on med bl, 5x4½", pr	250.00
Box, egg form, cloud scrolls, gold on red, wht flowers, 6"	60.00
Box, egg form, clouds in gold on beige, lav peonies, 5½"	60.00
Box, florals overall, hinged lid, ftd, early, unmk, 4x3"	85.00
Box, quail form, wings form lid, gilt beak/ft, 6¾", pr	300.00
Brush washer, group of various fruits form, 4x5½"	125.00
Cache pot, birds/trees on T-fretted turq, quatrefoil, 11"	250.00
Compote, floral, mc on bl, ped ft, scalloped, 5½x9½"	225.00
Figurine, bird, plique-a-jour, 2½x4½", pr	175.00
Figurine, court lady, ivory face/turq jeweled hairband, 10"	360.00
Figurine, dog, bl w/flowers, 15" L	900.00
Figurine, Gods of Good Fortune (3), ivory hands/faces, 14"	2,150.00
Figurine, Snow Queen, ivory face, brn robe, gold branch, 9"	225.00
Goblet, goldfish, mc on bl, gr/pk seaweed, 3x2½"	45.00
Jardiniere, red roundels w/masks on ochre, dragons, 13" dia	385.00
Mirror, lotus, mc on lt bl, swivels, on rnd ped ft, 18"	375.00
Snuff bottle, floral/bird panels, bl on blk, oval, 3½" EX	80.00

Snuff bottle, floral/butterfly panels, mc on bl on blk, 3"	80.00
Teapot, floral, gr & orchid foil, ftd, unmk, 3¾x5¾"	225.00
Teapot, floral, red/pk on bl, 2½x4½"	70.00
Teapot, vines/Tao-tieh masks on tan, curved hdl/spout, 6½"	150.00
Vase, bird/florals on bark texture, globular, 1890s, 8½"	400.00
Vase, cloud scrolls on lt bl, yel dragon/red flames, 8½", pr	250.00
Vase, clouds, gold on chartreuse, 5-claw mc dragon, 11", pr	225.00
Vase, clouds on lt gr, pk/wht cherry blossoms, 8½", pr	180.00
Vase, florals/fruits in panels, dbl-gourd form, 9½", pr	350.00

Vase, florals on green ground, silverplated rim and base, Japanese, 10", $600.00; Teapot, phoenix birds on red and cobalt, ca 1900, Japanese, 5", $400.00.

Vase, girl/trees on 2-color ground in panel, 8½"	125.00
Vase, mums, pk on dk gr, Japanese, 9½"	250.00
Vase, peonies, pk/wht on med gr, yel bird, bulbous, 10", pr	250.00
Vase, peonies on blk, panels w/waterfalls/etc, 9½x8"	185.00
Vase, prunus tree, wht/pk/yel flowers on royal bl, 12", pr	375.00
Vase, 2 bands/3 sections w/magnolias in purple & wht, 10"	250.00
Vase, 2 deer-&-geese panels, mc floral panel, 7½", pr	295.00

Clothing and Accessories

'Second-hand' or 'vintage'? It's all a matter of opinion. But these days it's considered good taste – downright fashionable – to wear clothing from Victorian to World War II styles. Jackets with padded shoulders from the thirties are 'trendy.' Jewelry from the Art Deco era is just as beautiful and often less expensive than current copies. Victorian blouses on models with Gibson Girl hair styles are pictured in leading fashion magazines – but why settle for new when the genuine article can be bought for the same price with exquisite lace that no reproduction can rival! When once the 'style' of the day was so strictly obeyed, today – in New York and the larger cities of California and Texas, in particular – nothing well-designed and constructed is 'out of style.' And though in recent days costumes by such designers as Chanel, Fortuny, and Lanvin may bring four-figure prices at fine auction houses, as a general rule, prices are very modest considering the wonderful fabrics one may find in vintage clothing, many of which are no longer available.

Cashmere coats, elegant furs, and sequined or beaded gowns can be bought for only a small fraction of today's retail. Though some are strictly collectors, many do buy their clothes to wear. Care must be given to alterations, and gentle cleaning methods employed to avoid damage that would detract from their value.

Our advisor for this category is Ruth Osborne; she is listed in the Directory under Ohio.

Key:

cap/s — cap sleeves	n/s — no sleeves
embr — embroidery	plt — pleated
hs — hand sewn	s/p — shoulder pads
lgth — length	s/s — short sleeves
l/s — long sleeves	/s — sleeves
ms — machine sewn	

Apron, gr/wht checked cotton, early, hs 40.00
Apron, printed corded lawn, lace trim, full length, EX 25.00
Apron, tea style, pk silk, embr violets, lace trim 15.00
Bathing tunic, sateen, 1915 ....35.00
Blouse, blk lace, l/s, 1920s, NM 25.00
Blouse, wht nylon, satin trim, l/s, 1930s 15.00
Bodice, blk lace, wht silk lined, EX 45.00
Bonnet, baby's, ecru embr, ca 1870, EX 35.00
Bonnet, baby's, wht organdy w/bl ribbons & trim, old, M 18.00
Camisole, crochet, EX 25.00
Cape, bl & blk silk w/velvet, full length, 1920s, EX 130.00
Cape, blk beaded, hs, short, 1800s, VG 85.00
Cape, blk crochet wool w/sequins, 1950s, EX 24.00
Cape, blk plush, monkey fur trim, EX 40.00
Coat, Battenburg lace, crochet buttons, 1910s, EX 500.00
Coat, blk crepe w/sm dots, fox trim, fringed neck, 1920s 225.00
Coat, blk velvet, pleated collar, leg-o-mutton/s, EX 50.00
Coat, blk velvet, wht fur collar & sleeves, 1930s 75.00
Coat, blk vinyl, fake fur lining, collar, & cuffs, EX 15.00
Collar, blk jet overall beading, lg, NM 50.00
Collar, blk velvet w/rhinestones/beads/pearls, 1930s, EX 30.00
Dress, baby's, wht w/cross-over smocking, EX 18.00
Dress, blk chiffon, sequin trim, flapper style, EX 45.00
Dress, blk crepe, s/s, V neck, rosette front, 1930s 55.00
Dress, blk georgette, overall blk beads, EX 200.00
Dress, blk net, chemise, embr w/sequins & beads, 1920s 175.00
Dress, blk net, tunic, sequinned florals, 1920s 150.00
Dress, blk velvet, l/s, jewel neck, 1920s, EX 65.00
Dress, blk velvet, strapless, tulip skirt, Ciel Chapman, 1950s 55.00
Dress, child's, ecru lace net, lace trim, 1920s, EX 45.00
Dress, child's, ivory linen w/red embr, red sash 45.00
Dress, christening; lace, eyelet inserts, ca 1900, EX 75.00
Dress, christening; Swiss embr trim & tucks, button bk, EX 75.00
Dress, christening; wht cotton batiste, lace tiers, EX 35.00
Dress, cotton, Irish lace, embr flowers, summer, 1910s 110.00
Dress, cream crepe, rhinestones at top, 1930s, EX 60.00
Dress, cream lace w/matching jacket, l/s, 1910s, EX 500.00
Dress, cream lawn, net lined, lace inserts, floral embr, EX 175.00
Dress, cream lawn, pin tucks, lace inserts, 1910, EX 125.00
Dress, cream linen, lace inserts, crochet buttons, 1915, EX 80.00
Dress, embr blk silk w/gold & silver collar, 1910s, EX 80.00
Dress, georgette chemise, jet beads/embr, 1920s, EX 85.00
Dress, gold lace, chemise, embr designs, gold lace slip, '20s 300.00
Dress, gray metallic lace, gr velvet trim, flapper style, EX 125.00
Dress, gray net, rhinestones/beads, long skirt, lined, 1920s 245.00
Dress, lace, silk-lined, beads/sequins, l/s, jewel neck, '50s 65.00
Dress, mourning; blk silk, Victorian style, EX 175.00
Dress, orange georgette, chemise, embr paisley, 1920s 110.00

Dress, rose & cream silk lace, chemise style, 1920s, EX 65.00
Dress, satin, chemise, beads/rhinestones in dmn shapes, '20s 150.00
Dress, satin, Empire waist, train skirt, beads, 1915, EX 175.00
Dress, satin w/lace & floral satin overlay, long skirt, '30s 30.00
Dress, silk faille, n/s, self bow at neck, 1950s, EX 45.00
Dress, striped silk, steel buttons, blk velvet ribbons, 1880s 250.00
Dress, wedding; batiste, lace & tucks, high neck, Victorian 375.00
Dress, wedding; georgette in pastel flowers, netting, 1920s 125.00
Dress, wedding; ivory lace, taffeta slip, '20s, +silk hose 250.00
Dress, wht embr net, lace panel & sleeves, 1920s 225.00
Dress, wht lawn, chemise, flower embr, lace trim, 1920s 125.00
Dress, wht lawn, chemise style, embr, lace inserts, 1920s 125.00
Dress, wht lawn, high neck, train skirt, Irish lace, 1910 ....350.00
Dress, wht lawn, over-bodice ties, embr & lace, 1910s, EX 165.00
Dressing gown, lady's, red satin, ruffled edges, 1920s, EX 65.00
Fur bolero, leopard skin, 18" L 225.00
Fur cape/stole, ocelot, EX lining, 15" L, EX 250.00
Fur coat, brn Persian lamb, mink trim, long, EX 200.00
Fur coat, dk brn Persian lamb w/mink trim, EX 250.00
Fur coat, leopard w/fox collar & cuffs, short, EX 350.00
Fur coat, mouton, detailed cuffs/lapel/collar, EX lining, 38" 50.00
Fur hat, mink, autumn haze, designer label, EX 25.00
Fur stole, silver fox, 10x72" 85.00

Edwardian gown, black net trimmed with beaded lace and fringe over ivory and black satin, ca 1910, $400.00.

Hat, lady's, blk velvet, 1939, MIB 27.50
Hat, pillbox, simulated Persian lamb, EX 5.00
Hat, silk, carnival glass beads, Victorian, +matching belt 125.00
Jacket, blk taffeta/velvet, fitted waist, ca 1900, EX 65.00
Nightgown, silk, embr, lace-edged neckline, long, 1930s 85.00
Pantaloons, lace trim, EX 30.00
Pantaloons, wht crochet border, 1800s, EX 35.00
Petticoat, wht w/crochet insert, Victorian, EX 45.00
Shawl, blk lace, 1925, 12x66" 45.00
Shawl, blk wool, blk satin embr, long silk fringe, EX 75.00

Shawl, gr, full embr, fringed, 1925, lg, M 75.00
Shawl, Kashmir, paisley in rose colors, gr center 225.00
Shawl, silk, embr pastel florals, China 95.00
Shirt, lady's, western style, gabardine, l/s, 1940s, EX 40.00
Shirt, man's, wht, pique front, narrow pleats, Victorian, EX..........24.00
Shoes, high button; blk leather, EX, pr 55.00
Shoes, high button; wht satin, EX 75.00
Skirt, wht, Victorian walking style, EX.........................100.00
Slip, baby's, wht cotton w/lace trim 24.00
Suit, wool gabardine, dbl-breasted, str skirt, Adrian, 1940s 150.00
Sweater, bolero style, lilac & gray wool.........................12.50
Sweater, heavily beaded, pk-lined 50.00
Teddy, rose print on wht, wide French lace yoke 35.00
Waist, purple silk taffeta, 20+ marcasite buttons, 1800s, EX..........65.00

Cluthra

The name Cluthra is derived from the Scottish word 'clutha,' meaning cloudy. Glassware by this name was first produced by J. Couper and Sons, England. Frederick Carder developed Cluthra while at the Steuben Glass Works, and similar types of glassware were also made by Durand and Kimball. It is found in both solid and shaded colors and is characterized by a spotty appearance resulting from small air pockets trapped between its two layers.

Bowl, strawberry, #6885, att Steuben, 4x12" 450.00
Finger bowl, pk, hexagonal, Steuben, 2x4½" 475.00
Vase, gr, sgn Steuben, fleur-de-lis mk, 7½" 450.00
Vase, lime/wht, unsgn Steuben, 13" 400.00
Vase, mauve/wht, classic form, #K-1710-4-Dec-100, 4½".........300.00
Vase, med bl to wht, classic form, drilled, Steuben, 11" 785.00
Vase, orange/gray, polished pontil, Kimball, 1910-6, 7x5" 625.00
Vase, wht, Steuben, fleur-de-lis mk, #2683, 8" 1,300.00

Vase, blue mottled, stamped Steuben, 9", $700.00.

Coalport

In 1745 in Caughley, England, Squire Brown began a modest business fashioning crude pots and jugs from clay mined in his own fields. Tom Turner, a young potter who had apprenticed his trade at Worcester, was hired in 1772 to plan and oversee the construction of a 'proper' factory. Three years later he bought the business, which he named Caughley Coalport Porcelain Manufactory. Though the dinnerware he produced was meant to be only everyday china, the hand-painted flo-

rals, birds, and landscapes used to decorate the ware were done in exquisite detail and in a wide range of colors. In 1780 Turner introduced the Willow pattern which he produced using a newly-perfected method of transfer printing. (Wares from the period between 1775 and 1799 are termed 'Caughley' or 'Salopian' – see section on Caughley.) John Rose purchased the Caughley factory from Thomas Turner in 1799, adding that holding to his own pottery which he had built two years before in Coalport. (It is from this point in the pottery's history that the wares are termed 'Coalport.') The porcelain produced there before 1814 was unmarked with very few exceptions. After 1820 some examples were marked with a '2' with an oversize top loop. The term 'Coalbrookdale' refers to a fine type of porcelain decorated in floral bas relief, similar to the work of Dresden.

After 1835 highly-decorated ware with rich ground colors imitated the work of Sevres and Chelsea, even going so far as to copy their marks. From about 1895 until the 1920s, the mark in use was 'Coalport' over a crown with 'England, A.D. 1750' indicating the date claimed as the founding, not the date of manufacture. From the 1920s until 1945, 'Made in England' over a crown and 'Coalport' below was used. Later, the mark was 'Coalport' over a smaller crown with 'Made in England' in a curve below. In 1926 the Coalport Company moved to Shelton in Staffordshire and today belongs to a group headed by the Wedgwood Company. See also Indian Tree.

Basket, encrusted flowers/foliage, pierced inner lid, 5".................350.00
Box, bl studs on gilt, lid w/marbled cartouch, shaped, 4" 1,500.00
Box, marbled medallion on floral lid, jewels/gilt, 1900, 5"...........600.00
Cup & saucer, allover gold decor on yel, miniature......................100.00
Cup & saucer, demitasse; Cairo.........................22.50
Cup & saucer, marbled cartouches on lime, ftd, 1900, 6" 700.00
Ewer, jeweled geometric reserve on pk, lg hdls, 1900, 7½"..........300.00
Ewer, lg medallion w/hexagon & teardrops on pk, 2-hdl, 7½" 330.00
Figurine, Stella, gr & lav gown, late, 8¼" 75.00
Loving cup, maid's portrait, sgn Sutton, ornate hdls, 11" 1,200.00
Potpourri, appl flowers, scrolled leaf hdls, leafy lid, 8" 750.00
Sugar bowl, bl-studded collar on yel w/gilt, 1900, 6" 385.00
Tea caddy, red jewels on circles w/allover gilt, mk, 5½" 175.00
Toast rack, semi-porc, Roman Key w/florals, crown mk 135.00
Vase, appl flowers/HP birds, hdls, Coalbrookdale, 10", EX 200.00

Coalbrookdale vase, applied and hand-painted florals and gilt, damage and repairs, 16", $400.00.

Vase, landscape, bl studs on cream, 3-hdl, ftd, 1900, 7" **550.00**
Vase, maid's portrait, gr w/waisted pk neck, hdls, 1900, 10" **650.00**
Vase, mtn view on dk bl, gilt lion-mtd hdls/paw ft, 1900, 5" **350.00**
Vase, named view on pk, gilt lion-mtd hdls/paw ft, lid, 13" **950.00**

Cobalt Glass

Cobalt glass is characterized by its deep transparent blue color obtained by mixing cobalt oxide and alumina to the batch. It may be found in free-blown, mold-blown, and pressed glassware. See Blown Glass.

Bottle, scent; cut decor, Germany, 6" **125.00**
Chamberstick, saucer base, free-form rigaree, appl hdl, 5" **195.00**
Figurine, Collie dog **18.00**
Match striker, mother cat & kitten, mk, 3¾x3¾" **100.00**
Mustard pot, ball shape, pewter base & hinged lid **110.00**
Pipe whimsey, blown, 18" L **200.00**
Pitcher, gold panels & enameled scrolls, 2x1½" **55.00**
Vase, gold band w/mc florals, ewer form, 5¼x1⅜" **75.00**

Coca-Cola

J.S. Pemberton, creator of Coca-Cola, originated his world-famous drink in 1886. From its inception the Coca-Cola Company began an incredible advertising campaign which has proven to be one of the most successful promotions in history. The quantity and diversity of advertising material put out by Coca-Cola in the last one hundred years is literally mind-boggling. From the beginning, the company has projected an image of wholesomeness and Americana. Beautiful women in Victorian costumes, teenagers and schoolchildren, blue- and white-collar workers, the men and women of the Armed Forces – even Santa Claus – have appeared in advertisements with a Coke in their hands. Some of the earliest collectibles include trays, syrup dispensers, gum jars, pocket mirrors, and calendars. Many of these items fetch prices in the thousands of dollars. Later examples include radios, signs, lighters, thermometers, playing cards, clocks, and toys – particularly toy trucks.

In 1970 the Coca-Cola Company initialed a multi-million dollar 'image refurbishing campaign,' which introduced the new 'Dynamic Countour' logo, a twisting white ribbon under the Coca-Cola and Coke trademarks. The new logo often serves as a cut-off point to the purist collector. Newer and very ardent collectors, however, relish the myriad of items marketed since that date, as they often cannot afford the high prices that the vintage pieces command. For more information we recommend *Petretti's Coca-Cola Collectibles Price Guide*; you may order a copy from Nostalgia Publications, Inc., whose address is listed under Auction Houses in the Directory.

Beware of reproductions – prices are given for the genuine original articles, but the symbol (+) at the end of some of the following lines indicate items that have been reproduced. Watch for frauds: genuinely old celluloid items ranging from combs, mirrors, knives and forks to doorknobs that have been recently etched with a new double-lined trademark. Still another area of concern deals with reproduction and fantasy items. A fantasy item is a novelty made to appear authentic with inscriptions such as 'Tiffany Studios,' 'Trans Pan Expo,' 'World's Fair,' etc. In reality, these items never existed as originals. For instance, don't be fooled by a Coca-Cola cash register – no originals are known to exist! Large mirrors for bars are being reproduced and are often selling for $10.00 to $50.00.

Of the hundreds of reproductions (designated 'R' in the following examples) and fantasies (designated 'F') on the market today, these are the most deceiving.

Reproductions and Fantasies

The following items have been reproduced and are among the most deceptive of all:
Pocket mirrors from 1905, 1906, 1908, 1909, 1910, 1911, 1916, and 1920.
Trays from 1899, 1910, 1913, 1914, 1917, 1920, 1923, 1925, 1926, 1934, and 1937.
Tip trays from 1907, 1909, 1910, 1913, 1914, 1917, and 1920.
Knives: many versions of the German brass model.
Cartons: wood versions, yellow with logo.

Belt buckle, no originals thought to exist (F), up to **5.00**
Bottle, dk amber, w/arrows, heavy, narrow spout (R) **10.00**
Bottle carrier, wood, yel w/red logo, holds 6 bottles (R) **10.00**
Clock, mantel; brass, battery-op, 1908, 6x9" (R) **100.00**
Cooler, Glascock Jr, made by Coca-Cola USA (R) **200.00**
Doorknob, glass w/etched trademark (F)...**3.00**
Knife, bottle shape, 1970s (F)...**5.00**
Knife, fork, or spoon w/celluloid hdl, newly-etched TM (F) **5.00**
Knife, pocket; yel & red, 1933 World's Fair (F) **2.00**
Letter opener, stamped metal, CC 5¢ (F)..**3.00**
Sign, cb, lady w/fur, dtd 1911, 9x11" (F) **3.00**
Sign, oval, girl w/fur, 1970s (R) **10.00**
Soda fountain glass holder, word 'Drink' not on orig (R) **5.00**
Thermometer, bottle figural DONASCO, 17" (R) **5.00**
Trade card, copy of 1905 'Bathtub' foldout, emb 1978 (R) **3.00**
Vanity pc (mirror/brush/etc), celluloid, newly-etched TM (F) **5.00**
Watch, pocket; often old watch w/new face (R) **10.00**

These items are currently being marketed:
Brass button, 18", Taiwan (R)
Brass thermometer, bottle shape, 24", Taiwan
Cast iron toys (none ever made)
Cast iron door pull, bottle shape, made to look old
Poster, Yes Girl (R)
Button sign, 12", has 1 round hole while original has 4 slots (R)
Bullet trash receptacles (old cans with decals)
Paperweight, rectangular, with Pepsin Gum insert
1949 cooler radio (new)
Countless trays

Centennial Items

1986 was the year for the Coca-Cola Company to celebrate her 100th birthday; and amidst all the fanfare comes many new collectible items, all sporting the 100th anniversary logo. These items are destined to become an important part of the total Coca-Cola Collectible spectrum. The following pieces are among the most popular centennial items.

Bottle, gold dipped, in velvet sleeve, 6½-oz....................................**50.00**
Bottle, Hutch, amber, Root Co, 6½-oz, 3 in case...........................**150.00**
Bottle, International, set of 9 in plexiglas case **175.00**
Bottle, leaded crystal, 100th logo, 6½-oz, MIB **100.00**
Medallion, bronze, w/box, 3" dia **50.00**
Pin set, wood fr, 101 pins...**250.00**
Scarf, silk, 30x30" **35.00**
Thermometer, glass cover, 14" dia, M **22.00**

Coca-Cola Originals

Ad, 1907, man at fountain, blk/wht, Massengale, EX....................**25.00**
Ad, 1911, Del Howard, blk/wht, newspaper, EX.............................**8.00**

Sales kit, cooler with leatherette carrying carrying case, 1939, 12" long, in NM condition, $3,100.00.

Ad, 1916, golfing couple, blk/wht, Massengale, EX	8.00
Ad, 1931, Your Presence..., blk/wht, newspaper, NM	15.00
Ash tray, 1950s, glass, octagonal, M	10.00
Ash tray, 1950s, ruby glass, card suit shapes, set of 4, M	250.00
Blotter, 1910, Absolute Sanitary, rare, EX	275.00
Blotter, 1923, Drink CC, Delicious..., 2 fountain glasses, NM	125.00
Blotter, 1927, couple leans on open icebox, NM	35.00
Blotter, 1931, Natural Refreshment, girl in swimsuit, EX	65.00
Blotter, 1931, Pause That Refreshes, woman w/bottle, EX	115.00
Blotter, 1935, A Home Run..., NM	40.00
Blotter, 1939, Drink Everybody Knows, NM	10.00
Blotter, 1944, 3 ladies, How About a Coke, EX	3.00
Blotter, 1956, Friendliest Drink, NM	3.00
Book, 1958-1961, Pause for Living, EX	5.00
Booklet, 1940s, Know Your War Planes, EX	35.00
Bookmark, 1905, Delicious & Refreshing, 5¼x2¼", NM	400.00
Bookmark, 1906, celluloid, owl, 3⅛x1½", EX	500.00
Bottle, Cadada misprint, aqua, EX	20.00
Bottle, Canada, Property of..., script, aqua, str sides, EX	10.00
Bottle, Chattanooga, misspelled, Hutchinson block, Coco-Cola	500.00
Bottle, Indiana PA, lt amber, str sides	40.00
Bottle, Morgantown WV, med amber, logo at top/str sides, NM	25.00
Bottle, Portland OR, dk amber, str sides, rare, NM	100.00
Bottle, seltzer; gr, etched, Property of CC, PA, 12½", NM	160.00
Bottle, syrup; 1900s, label under glass, w/cap, NM	450.00
Bottle, water; ship, block letters, clear, NM	65.00
Bottle, 1920s, Christmas display, w/cap, 20", M	250.00
Bottle rack, 1930s, Drink...at Home, 60", NM	145.00

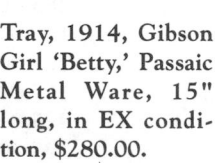

Tray, 1914, Gibson Girl 'Betty,' Passaic Metal Ware, 15" long, in EX condition, $280.00.

Bumper sticker, 1970s, Look Up America, M	2.50
Business card, 1908, 2x3½", EX	20.00
Calendar, 1914, Betty, complete, full pad, NM	700.00
Calendar, 1916, girl w/rose basket, top only, EX	200.00
Calendar, 1921, Autumn girl, glass, 1 pg on pad, 12x32", EX	275.00
Calendar, 1931, Rockwell art, boy & dog, 12x24", full pad, NM	400.00
Calendar, 1951, girl & confetti, complete, NM	50.00
Calendar, 1955, complete, 6-pg, 22x13", EX	45.00
Calendar, 1957, complete, 6-pg, 14x14", M	27.50
Calendar, 1963, lady at mirror, 6-pg, complete, EX	20.00
Calendar, 1976, Olympic, 4-pg, 12x9", NM	7.50
Cap, 1940s, cloth, soda jerk, EX	15.00
Cap, 1950s, cb, visor style, EX	7.50
Cap, 1959, beanie, M	20.00
Case, 1920s, wood, EX pnt & logo	45.00
Case, 1940s, wood, EX pnt & logo	25.00
Case, 1950s, wood, EX pnt & logo	25.00
Change purse, 1908, triangular shape, snap closure, VG	50.00
Chinese checkers, 1940s, wood/cb, 16½" sq, complete, EX	50.00
Christmas card, 1920s, verse, hand holds bottle, EX	7.50
Christmas card, 1936, Santa, Christmas Greetings, NM	5.00
Clock, 1905-1907, Regulator, printed dial, Ingraham, EX	1,750.00
Clock, 1916, Gilbert, In Bottles, EX	850.00
Clock, 1930, mantel, brass, windup, Germany, 6x9", NM	750.00
Clock, 1939, Coca-Cola in bottles, wood fr, 16x16"	250.00
Clock, 1941, neon, octagonal, 18", NM	1,500.00
Clock, 1942, neon, w/bottle, 16x16", NM (+)	450.00
Clock, 1950s, sq face, lights up, NM	150.00
Clock, 1960s, fishtail, red/gr/wht, sq, NM	60.00
Clock, 1970s, battery, hanging, mini regulator, 27x12", NM	125.00
Clock, 1974, plastic, Betty, M	35.00
Convention badge, 1959, Altoona PA, EX	30.00
Cooler, 1929, Glascock, single case, jr sz, NM (+)	500.00
Cooler, 1929, table top sz, w/faucet, no legs	750.00
Cooler, 1950s, picnic, red aluminum hdl, regular 1 case sz	55.00
Coupon, 1890s, Seth W Fowle & Sons, 1½x3⅜", EX	150.00
Coupon, 1905, Lillian Nordica, 6½x9½", NM	125.00
Coupon, 1939, bottle in hand, 2½x4", EX	4.00
Cribbage board & cards, 1940s, NM	65.00
Dart board, 1940s, silhouette girl, 18x18", M	65.00
Door pull, 1940, plastic/metal, bottle shape, NM (+)	125.00
Envelope, 1904, Montgomery AL, CC Bottling Co, EX	20.00
Envelope, 1908, NY, CC Co, VG	7.50
Fan, 1920s, baby w/toys, paddle shape, EX	20.00
Fan, 1950s, cb foldout, flower basket, EX	20.00
Fan, 1950s, wicker, EX	20.00
Fly swatter, 1920s, wood hdl, EX	20.00
Glass, 1930s, bell, trademark in tail, etched, 4-oz, M	40.00
Glass, 1930s, pewter, etched logo, 6-oz, in leather case	350.00
Glass, 1976, Olympic, Montreal Expo	5.00
Gum wrapper, 1910s, Peppermint Pepsin, EX	200.00
Hatpin, (for route drivers), 1930s, enamel style, 1⅛x2", M	150.00
Jar, 1912, CC Pepsin Gum, beveled corners, w/lid, NM	600.00
Jar, 1916-24, CC Chewing Gum, paper label, NM (+)	1,200.00
Jump rope, 1920s, Sure As Sunlight, whistle in hdl, rare, NM	185.00
Letterhead, 1916, Franklin-Caro Mfg Co, rare	120.00
Match safe, 1910, Drink CC, duster girl, celluloid, NM	450.00
Match striker, 1938, porc, red/yel/blk/wht, 4½x4½", M	150.00
Match striker, 1939, porc, Drink CC, Strike...Here, EX	85.00
Matchbook, 1936, Delicious, Refreshing, EX	4.00
Matchbook holder, 1910, Sold Everywhere, EX	75.00
Menu, 1904, Lillian Nordica, 6½x4⅛", NM	400.00
Menu board, 1934, tin, Deco lines, NM	75.00
Menu board, 1939, tin, silhouette girl, NM	75.00

Menu board, 1950s, cb, 2 bottles, M	40.00
Menu board, 1950s, tin, Canada, M	40.00
Menu board, 1960s, plastic in chrome fr, fishtail, decal, EX	50.00
Menu board, 1960s, tin, Sign of Good Taste, fishtail, EX	35.00
Mirror, 1930s, metal fr, 14¼x10¼", M	185.00
Needle case, 1924, NM	35.00
Opener, Drink 'Over the Top,' M	20.00
Opener, syrup can; Coca-Cola, NM	10.00
Paddle ball, 1950, NM	35.00
Palm press, 1940s, Fr Canadian, red/yel/wht, 4x11½", NM	65.00
Palm press, 1950s, porc, Iced CC Here, NM	125.00
Pencil holder, 1978, sm ceramic dispenser, NY 75th Anniv, NM	60.00
Plate, sandwich; 1930s, china, lt wear, 7¼", EX	125.00
Plate, sandwich; 1930s, china, 8¼", NM	450.00
Playing cards, 1943, ballerinas, complete, w/box	90.00
Playing cards, 1943, girl w/leaves, Coke bottle, MIB	75.00
Playing cards, 1963, girl w/Cokes on tray, unopened	32.00
Playing cards, 1971, Boy Scouts Jamboree, MIB	75.00
Pocket mirror, 1909, JB Carroll Chicago, oval, NM	300.00
Pocket mirror, 1910, H King/JB Carroll Chicago, oval, NM (+)	200.00
Pocket mirror, 1911, H King/Whitehead-Hoag, oval, NM (+)	200.00
Pocket mirror, 1936, 50th Anniv, rectangular, M in package	150.00
Popcorn holder, 1950, M	5.00
Post card, 1908, bridge on Potomac, Relieves Fatigue, NM	15.00
Post card, 1910, Hamilton King CC Girl, EX	350.00
Post card, 1920s, Atlanta GA, Home of CC, EX	75.00
Post card, 1964, World's Fair, Coke Pavilion, EX	2.50
Pretzel dish, 1930s, aluminum, NM	125.00
Pushbar, 1930, porc, 12" bottle, EX	75.00
Pushplate, 1930s, porc, red/yellow, Call Again, oval, M	85.00
Rack, display; 1930s, 6-pack, EX	125.00
Rack, drink; 1940s, 4 top hooks, 60" H, EX	175.00
Radiator plate, 1920s, chrome, CC in bottles, script, NM	245.00
Radio, can figural, EX (+)	12.50
Radio, 1950, cooler figural, 7x12x9½", NM	450.00
Record, 1950, Learn To Dance, A Capps, 45 rpm, M	5.00
Record, 1982, Coke Is It, Penn State, 45 rpm, M	5.00
Road map, 1926, Rand McNally, EX	22.00
Score card, 1942, St Louis Browns, EX	10.00
Score card, 1950, Chicago Cubs, Wrigley Field, EX	7.50
Sheet music, 1940s, Rum & CC, Jeri Sullivan, 13x10½", NM	25.00
Sheet music, 1970s, Look Up America, M	5.00
Sheet music, 1972, Country Sunshine, M	2.50
Sign, curb; 1939, tin, Delicious & Refreshing, gr, 19x28"	115.00
Sign, 1906, tin, sf, Relieves Fatigue, 27x18½", EX	3,250.00
Sign, 1914, cb cutout, couple w/umbrella, 35x30", EX	2,500.00
Sign, 1920s, cb, Delicious..., 2 bottles/metal fr, 21x60", EX	450.00
Sign, 1924, cb, CC girls, picnic scene, 14x24", NM	775.00
Sign, 1927, tin, Drink CC, 10½x31", NM	275.00
Sign, 1927, tin, girl w/bottle, 8½x11", NM	700.00
Sign, 1930s, tin, Christmas bottle, Delicious, 24x58", EX	150.00
Sign, 1933, tin, Ice Cold, w/bottle, vertical, 54x19", EX	200.00
Sign, 1934, cb, Joan Crawford, 24x14", EX	325.00
Sign, 1934, tin, wht ground, Sold Here...Ice Cold, 19x28", EX	225.00
Sign, 1936, cb, snowman w/2 bottles, Ice Cold, 30x14", M	125.00
Sign, 1936, cb cutout, Santa, train, doll, 36x40", EX	250.00
Sign, 1940s, porc, Drink CC, Sold Here Ice Cold, 12x29", NM	300.00
Sign, 1941, masonite, couple, 20x28", EX	200.00
Sign, 1941, masonite, girl w/bottle, vertical, 19x54", NM	225.00
Sign, 1946, cb standup, Santa, 12x6", EX	35.00
Sign, 1948, tin, w/bottle, 40x16", w/18" button sgn, NM	110.00
Sign, 1948, tin, w/6-pack, 40x16", w/18" button sgn, NM	165.00
Sign, 1950s, celluloid, w/bottle, 9", M	125.00
Sign, 1950s, glass front, lights up, 8x18", NM	150.00
Sign, 1950s, tin, button form, 12", M (+)	75.00
Sign, 1950s, tin, Ice Cold, w/bottle, Robertson, NM	50.00
Sign, 1960, tin, fishtail, vertical or horizontal, 18x54", NM	60.00
Sign, 1960s, metal, lights up, 'wall basket,' 12", NM	75.00
Sign, 1960s, plastic front, fishtail, 8x18", NM	50.00
Sign, 1962, cb cutout, Santa w/train set, 47x32", EX	50.00
Sign, 1963, tin, fishtail, 11x28", M	60.00
Sign, 1963, tin, fishtail, 54x18", EX	60.00
Stock certificate, 1934, CC Bottling Sales Co, M	50.00
Straw box, 1940s, unopened, M	55.00
Thermometer, 1905, wood, heavy wear, 15x4", NM	375.00
Thermometer, 1915, wood, 5x21", NM	300.00
Thermometer, 1930s, tin, w/gold bottle, red, oval, 16x7", EX	125.00
Thermometer, 1939, tin, silhouette girl, 6½x16", NM	125.00
Thermometer, 1940, porc, silhouette girl, 18x6", NM	225.00
Thermometer, 1941, tin, twin bottles, 16x7", EX	85.00
Thermometer, 1944, masonite, 17x7", NM	150.00
Thermometer, 1950s, glass front, bottle, Drink, 12" dia, NM	150.00
Thermometer, 1950s, tin, red/wht, oval, 30", EX	90.00
Thermometer, 1960s, plastic, Sprite, NM	12.50
Tip tray, 1906, Juanita, Delicious, Refreshing, 4" dia, NM	400.00
Tip tray, 1913, Hamilton King girl, 4½x6", NM	275.00
Tip tray, 1914, Betty, 4¼x6", EX	75.00
Tip tray, 1916, girl w/rose basket, 4¼x6", NM	125.00
Tip tray, 1917, Elaine w/Coke, 8½x19", NM	200.00
Tip tray, 1920, garden girl, 4¼x6", NM	250.00
Tip tray, 1969, Swedish smoke glass, CC in wreath, 8x6", NM	30.00
Toy Booma plane, Go w/Coke, NM	10.00
Toy car, 1970s, Buddy-L Racer, 2½", EX	18.00
Toy hamburger stand, 1950s, Playtown, complete	150.00
Toy train, 1930s, Am Flyer #6073, tin litho, 13-pc, w/o box	2,000.00
Toy train, 1950, tin, windup, 4-pc, 14", EX	165.00
Toy truck, 1950, Marx #21, NM	125.00
Toy truck, 1965, Dinky #402, red/wht, MIB	250.00
Toy truck, 1970, plastic/tin friction, Japan, EX	45.00
Toy truck, 1973, Big Wheel, 3 versions/battery operated, MIB	50.00
Trade card, 1901, Hilda Clark, great logo, rare, NM	575.00
Trade card, 1910, bottle, str sides, folding, EX	200.00
Tray, 1914, Betty, 10½x13¼", EX	260.00
Tray, 1914, Betty, 10½x13¼", NM	345.00
Tray, 1920, garden girl, 10½x13¼", NM	425.00
Tray, 1920, garden girl, 10½x13¼", VG	200.00
Tray, 1921, autumn girl, 10½x13¼", NM	450.00
Tray, 1922, summer girl, 10½x13¼", NM	450.00
Tray, 1922, summer girl, 10½x13¼", VG	250.00
Tray, 1923, flapper girl, 10½x13¼", EX	125.00
Tray, 1923, flapper girl, 10½x13¼", NM	225.00
Tray, 1924, smiling girl, 10½x13¼", NM	375.00
Tray, 1925, girl w/fur, 10½x13¼", NM (+)	250.00
Tray, 1927, bobbed-hair girl, 10½x13¼", EX	200.00
Tray, 1927, curb-side service, 10½x13¼", M	325.00
Tray, 1928, Soda Jerk, Coke, 10½x13¼", NM	285.00
Tray, 1930, bathing beauty, 10½x13¼", EX	150.00
Tray, 1930, bathing beauty, 10½x13¼", NM	200.00
Tray, 1930, telephone girl, 10½x13¼", NM	175.00
Tray, 1931, Rockwell boy w/sandwich & dog, 10½x13¼", NM	425.00
Tray, 1933, Francis Dee, 10½x13¼", NM	275.00
Tray, 1934, Weissmuller & O'Sullivan, 10½x13¼", M (+)	450.00
Tray, 1935, Madge Evans, 10½x13¼", NM	200.00
Tray, 1936, hostess, 10½x13¼", EX	120.00
Tray, 1936, hostess, 10½x13¼", M	175.00
Tray, 1937, running girl, 10½x13¼", NM (+)	125.00
Tray, 1938, girl in afternoon, 10½x13¼", NM	85.00
Tray, 1939, springboard girl, 10½x13¼", NM	125.00

Tray, 1940, sailor girl, 10½x13¼", EX 60.00
Tray, 1941, skater girl, 10½x13¼", EX 85.00
Tray, 1942, roadster girls, 10½x13¼", NM 85.00
Tray, 1948, girl w/wind in hair, 10½x13¼", M 50.00
Tray, 1948, girl w/wind in hair, 10½x13¼", VG 35.00
Tray, 1950, menu girl, 10½x13¼", EX 15.00
Tray, 1950, menu girl, 10½x13¼", M 30.00
Tray, 1957, birdhouse, 10½x13¼", EX 50.00
Tray, 1957, birdhouse, 10½x13¼", M 85.00
Tray, 1957, rooster, 10½x10¼", NM 85.00
Tray, 1957, rooster, 10½x13¼", EX 50.00
Tray, 1957, umbrella girl, Fr, 10½x13¼", M 175.00
Tray, 1957, umbrella girl, 10½x13¼", NM 185.00
Tray, 1957, 6 sandwiches/6 Cokes, 10½x13¼", NM 60.00
Tray, 1960, fishtail, Drive In for Coke, rare, NM 125.00
Tray, 1961, pansy garden, 10½x13¼", EX 10.00
Tray, 1970, Santa, not Long John Silver, 10½x13¼", NM 10.00
Tray, 1972, girl in duster, EX... 8.00
Tray, 1976, Canadian Olympics, NM 10.00
Tray, 1978, Capt Cook, 10½x13¼", NM 8.00
Tray, 1982, Nashville Fair, rnd, M 5.00
Uniform patch, 1950s, Drink CC in Bottles, rnd, NM.................... 4.50
Uniform patch, 1960s, Drink CC in Bottles, lg, M......................... 5.00
Uniform patch, 1960s, Things Go Better w/Coke, sq, M 3.00
Uniform patch, 1970s, Enjoy CC, sq, M 1.00
Wallet, 1920s, leather, tri-fold style, EX.......................................20.00
Watch fob, 1910, celluloid, Gibson Girl, bk: Drink CC, NM 450.00
Watch fob, 1920s, Coke bulldogs, 1½x1", EX 100.00
Watch fob, 50th Anniversary, NM...10.00

Machines

Interest in Coca-Cola machines of the 1949 – 1959 era has risen dramatically. The major manufacturers of these curved top, 5¢ and 10¢ machines were Vendo (V), Vendorlator (VMC), Cavalier (C or CS), and Jacobs. Market forecasters foresee tremendous investment potential over the next five years. In the following listings, 'VG' values are for machines in clean, original condition.

Cavalier, model #CS72, M rstr 3,500.00
Cavalier, model #CS72, VG 350.00
Cavalier, model #C27, M rstr 3,000.00
Cavalier, model #C27, VG..350.00
Cavalier, model #C51, M rstr 2,500.00
Cavalier, model #C51, VG..250.00
Jacobs, model #26, M rstr 4,500.00
Jacobs, model #26, VG 750.00
Vendo, model #23, M rstr 2,000.00
Vendo, model #23, VG 250.00
Vendo, model #39, M rstr 2,500.00
Vendo, model #39, VG 350.00
Vendo, model #44, M rstr 5,000.00
Vendo, model #44, VG 750.00
Vendo, model #56, M rstr 4,500.00
Vendo, model #56, VG 500.00
Vendo, model #80, M rstr 2,250.00
Vendo, model #80, VG 250.00
Vendo, model #81, M rstr 4,500.00
Vendo, model #81, VG 500.00
Vendorlator, model #27, M rstr 3,000.00
Vendorlator, model #27, VG...500.00
Vendorlator, model #27A, M rstr 3,500.00
Vendorlator, model #27A, VG..500.00
Vendorlator, model #33, M rstr 3,500.00

Vendorlator, model #33, VG...500.00
Vendorlator, model #44, M rstr 5,000.00
Vendorlator, model #44, VG...750.00
Vendorlator, model #72, M rstr 3,500.00
Vendorlator, model #72, VG...500.00

Coffee Grinders

The serious collector of kitchenwares and country store items rank coffee mills high on the list of desirable examples. A trend is developing toward preferring items whose manufacturers are easily identifiable. Names to look for include Adams, Arcade, Baldwin Bros., Daisy, Elgin National, Elma, Enterprise, Lane Bros., Parker, Regal, and Sun Mfg. Co.; there are many others. Any of these marks found on coffee mills represent companies who were in business at or before the turn of the century.

Side mills usually have a brass tag located on the tin hopper. If the hopper was made of cast iron, the name was usually cast into the metal. Some of the less expensive versions had no identification. Decals were often used on the front of lap mills and table styles, though sometimes you will find these decals on the inside of the drawer. Because decals are prone to flaking off and fading, and since they are often destroyed when the mill is being refinished, lap and table mills are the most difficult types to attribute to a specific manufacturer. Canister mills had names and patent dates molded into the cast iron housing or on the canister itself. Commercial mills used in country and general stores were made of cast iron. Important information such as manufacture and patent dates were usually cast into the wheels, housing, or base of the mill. Such identification helps determine date of manufacture and contributes considerably toward value.

Good examples of early coffee mills are rapidly becoming difficult to find. Beware of the many imported imposters that are on the market today.

Key: adj   adjustment

A Kendrick & Sons No 1, lap, CI w/brass hopper 95.00
American Beauty, canister, w/orig cup & papers............................40.00
Arcade, Crystal No 3, canister, CI w/glass hopper, ca 1910............65.00
Arcade, Crystal No 44, CI w/glass hopper, orig lid & glass.............75.00
Arcade, Favorite, lap, fancy CI top & hopper..............................95.00
Arcade, Favorite No 27, side, CI, orig CI lid 65.00
Arcade, Favorite No 7, side, CI, grind adj front...........................60.00
Arcade, Imperial, lap, wood & CI, 11" 75.00
Arcade, Imperial, table, 2-lb, wood & CI, 13" 75.00
Arcade, Imperial No 200, lap, oak, CI eagle, Pat 1888-1889 ....95.00
Arcade, IXL, table, fancy CI top, wood box, crank hdl, 10½" 135.00
Arcade, Jewel, canister, rectangular w/glass hopper.......................75.00
Arcade, Sunbeam, canister, CI w/glass hopper, tin lid 75.00
Arcade, table, 1-lb, w/decal, Pat 6/5/1884, 7x7x12½" 90.00
Arcade No 147, lap, fancy CI closed top, wood box 85.00
Arcade No 700, lap, w/dust cover, Sears, ca 1908........................90.00
Blacksmith made, wall, funnel hopper, ca 1790 ....180.00
Brighton, Wrights Hdwe, table, 1-lb, 8"......................................75.00
Bronson Walton, canister, tin & CI, Pat 1911...............................75.00
C Ibach stamped on hdl, dvtl walnut, iron hopper.......................145.00
Canister, boy & girl decal, miniature, 5½x1½" 85.00
Caravan, canister, CI works, tin hopper, ca 1910 ....60.00
Chas Parker No 350, side, CI, Pat 4/1876....................................65.00
Chas Parker No 5005, counter, CI, 12½" wheels, 17" 475.00
Clevis Walton, canister, orig cup, Pat 7/9/1901 ....60.00
Coffee bean roaster, tin cylinder & holder, CI/wood hdl 125.00
Coles Mfg No 7, counter, CI, Pat 1887, 16" wheels, 27" 475.00
Common, lap, wood w/box joints, CI open hopper 75.00

Common unmk, lap, decals, box joints, CI hopper, 8x6½x6½" 65.00
Common unmk, 1-lb, wood & CI 65.00
DeVe, Holland, lap, 1950s, 4¾x5⅛x8⅛" 45.00
Elgin National No 40, counter, CI, 2 wheels.........................325.00
Elgin National No 44, orig CI w/eagle, 15" wheels, 24" 375.00
Elgin National No 48, 2 wheels w/eagle, orig lily decal.........425.00
Elma, counter, CI w/wooden drw, 10¾" single wheel, 17" 85.00
Enterprise, counter, CI, eagle on hopper, 2 wheels, Pat 1873......475.00
Enterprise, counter, closed hopper, blk hdl, Pat 1873, 12" 180.00
Enterprise, floor, eagle at top, Pat 1873, 39" wheels, 72" 3,500.00
Enterprise, table, CI, brass hopper, Pat 1873, 6" wheels.............395.00
Enterprise, table, CI w/CI cup, orig gold decal 45.00

Enterprise, eagle finial, NM original 3-color paint, replaced drawer, 24", $500.00; Charles Parker Co. #200, EX original 3-color paint, 12", $375.00.

Enterprise No 1, counter, open hopper, Pat 1873, 11" hdl 180.00
Enterprise No 12, counter, 2 lg wheels w/eagle, Pat 1898 ....625.00
Enterprise No 216, floor, CI hopper, decals, Pat 1898 .... 2,600.00
Enterprise No 7, counter, CI, 17" wheels w/eagle.........................475.00
Enterprise No 9, CI, brass eagle, Pat 1898, 19" wheels, 28" 525.00
Euclid No 4, counter, CI w/aluminum hopper, 2 10" wheels........385.00
Fairbanks Morse, floor, CI, brass hopper, 72" 1,300.00
Golden Rule, canister, CI w/glass front, wood box 235.00
Grand Union Tea, canister, red, orig writing, Pat 1910..................85.00
Grand Union Tea, table, CI, sq base, rnd hopper 95.00
J Fisher, Warranted, lap, dvtl mahog, pewter hopper....................145.00
J Fisher, Warranted, lap, dvtl walnut, brass hopper 150.00
K&M, lap, maple box, clips on drw, aluminum hopper 45.00
KM Geschmiedetes und Gefrates Mahlwerk, brass hopper 55.00
L&S, side, CI, mtd on orig board 65.00
L'il Tot, orig drw, miniature, 4x2¾x2¾" 80.00
Landers, Frary & Clark, canister, tin & CI, Pat 1905 ....65.00
Landers, Frary & Clark, counter, CI, #50 drw, 12" wheels 425.00
Landers, Frary & Clark, lap, fancy CI top, wood box 95.00
Landers, Frary & Clark, Regal No 44, canister, tin & CI 80.00
Landers, Frary & Clark, table, CI, Pat Feb 14, 1905......................55.00
Landers, Frary & Clark, Universal No 14, table, Pat 1905 ....55.00
Lap, CI, octagon shape, open hopper, 4x4x4"...............................75.00
Lees, canister, CI works, rnd glass hopper 65.00
Lightning, canister, CI works, tin hopper 70.00
Logan & Strobridge, Franco American, lap, CI & wood...............90.00
National, coffee & spice, counter, 12" wheels, 25".......................425.00
National, coffee & spice, counter, 17" wheels, 28".......................425.00

National Specialty Mfg, Philadelphia PA, CI, 25" wheels 575.00
New Home, table, 1-lb, CI top, enclosed hopper, wood box 75.00
New Model, lap, CI w/CI drw, 5½x4½x5½" 75.00
None Such, Bronson Co, Cleveland OH, table, tin 50.00
Parker, side, CI, grind adj on front, Pat 1876..............................60.00
Parker Eagle No 144, canister, tin hopper 65.00
Parker No 2, counter, CI w/orig decals, 9" wheels 375.00
Parker No 449, canister, CI works, rnd w/glass hopper 75.00
Parker No 5000, counter, CI, Pat 1897, 12" wheels, 17" 275.00
Parker No 60, side, eagle on tin hopper, Parker lid.......................60.00
Persepolis, table, CI & brass 155.00
Peugeot Freres, lap, wood box, tin-covered hopper 40.00
Primitive, lap, brass/iron/dvtl walnut, handmade 160.00
Primitive, lap, dvtl cherry, brass hopper, 4x4"............................155.00
Primitive, lap, red buttermilk pnt, pewter hopper, ca 1850..........150.00
PS&W No 3500, side, CI..65.00
Putz stamped on hdl, lap, walnut, brass hopper 150.00
Queen, child's miniature, wood w/CI hopper & drw front 80.00
Rock Hard, Garant-Sewaarborge, lap, 4¾x4¾x5½" 40.00
Royal, side, CI w/CI cup, open hopper, Pat Apr 15, 1890 ....65.00
RR Kreiterr, Lewisberry, York County PA, dvtl, pewter hopper ...155.00
Russer, canister, porc top 55.00
S&H, counter, CI w/drw, 19" wheels, 21".....................................425.00
Star, canister, tin w/CI works, Pat 1910 ....65.00
Starr, floor, CI, lg wheels, 72"...975.00
Sun Mfg, rnd table, 1-lb, wood, 13" 195.00
Sun Mfg, table, 1-lb, orig decal, screw lid, 12" 75.00
Sun Mfg No 1080, Challenge Fast Grind, Columbus OH, 1-lb......75.00
Swift, side, CI, Pat 1845, Pat ext Aug 16, 1859 ....75.00
Swift No 13, orig metal drw, Pat 1885, 12" wheels, 19"................325.00
Swift No 15, CI, orig decals, Pat 1875, 19" wheels.......................875.00
Telephone, canister, wood w/no CI, ca 1900-1910 ....65.00
Turkish, brass cylinder, folding hdl, old 55.00
Turkish, table, primitive, 13x7½" sq box on 28" board................155.00
W Cross & Sons, lap, CI w/orig CI drw, brass hopper 75.00
WW Weaver, lap, primitive, dvtl walnut, pewter hopper 155.00
X-Ray, canister, glass front, wood hopper, 1908.............................70.00

Coin Operated Machines

Coin-operated machines may be the fastest-growing area of collector interest in today's market. Many machines are bought, restored, and used for home entertainment. Older examples from the turn of the century and those with especially elaborate decoration and innovative accessories are most desirable, often bringing prices in excess of $7,000.00.

Vending machines sold a product or a service. They were already in common usage by 1900 selling gum, cigars, matches, and a host of other commodities. Peanut and gumball machines are especially popular today. The most valuable are those with their original finish and decals. Older machines made of cast iron are especially desirable, while those with plastic globes have little or no collector value. When buying unrestored peanut machines, beware of salt damage.

The coin-operated phonograph of the early 1900s paved the way for the jukeboxes of the twenties. Seeburg was first on the market with an automatic 8-tune phonograph. By the 1930s, Wurlitzer was the top name in the industry with dealerships all over the country. As a result of the growing ranks of competitors, the forties produced the most beautiful machines made. Wurlitzers from this era are probably the most popularly sought-after models on the market today. The model 1015 of 1946 is considered the all-time classic, and often brings prices in excess of $6,000.

Coin-Op Newsletter; Jukebox Collectors' Newsletter; Chicagoland

Antique Advertising, Slot Machine, and Jukebox Gazette; and *Loose Change Magazine* are all excellent publications for those interested in coin-operated machines; see the Clubs, Newsletters, and Catalogs section of the Directory for publishing information.

    Jackie and Ken Durham are our advisors (for all but Jukeboxes); they are listed in the Directory under the District of Columbia.

Arcade Machines

Booze 5¢ Meter, EX	150.00
Mercury 1¢ Strength Tester, EX	125.00
Munves Love Tester	900.00
Munves Reel Peep Show, EX	900.00
Mutascope 2¢ Hockey, orig marquee, early, EX orig	1,200.00
Mutoscope Iron Claw, digger, walnut floor model, EX	2,500.00
Mutoscope Peep Show, tin floor model, EX orig	995.00
Scotch 1¢ Golf, rstr	350.00
Seeburg Coon Hunt, rstr, w/manuals	1,800.00
Wee Gee 1¢ Fortune Telling, 8x17", EX	350.00
Williams 10 Strike, bowling, EX	750.00

Jukeboxes

Wurlitzer Model #1015 jukebox, restored, $9,500.00.

AMI Model A, rstr	3,000.00
AMI Model C	800.00
AMI Model D-40	650.00
AMI Model H-200, 1957, VG orig	750.00
Cremona G, rstr	11,500.00
Mills, novelty Ferris Wheel type, 78 rpm, EX orig	200.00
Mills Carousel, 5¢ coin slot, 12-selection, 1933, VG orig	800.00
Mills Throne of Music, EX orig	750.00
Rockola #1422, 1946, EX	1,700.00
Rockola #1428, EX orig	2,000.00
Rockola #1434, 78-rpm, EX orig	700.00
Rockola Empress, 1959, EX orig, +records	1,325.00

Rockola Princess, EX orig	800.00
Seeburg #100-G, EX	1,300.00
Seeburg #146, EX orig	1,200.00
Seeburg B, EX orig	1,150.00
Seeburg B, rstr	2,250.00
Seeburg B, VG orig	700.00
Seeburg Barrel, EX	775.00
Seeburg C, EX orig	1,750.00
Seeburg C, VG orig	1,075.00
Seeburg E, oak w/xylophone, EX orig	6,500.00
Seeburg HF-100R, M orig	2,000.00
Seeburg Q, EX orig	650.00
Seeburg R, 1954, rstr	3,900.00
Seeburg VL-200, EX orig	2,000.00
Wurlitzer #1015, 1946, EX orig	6,500.00
Wurlitzer #1100, EX orig	2,200.00
Wurlitzer #1100, M	4,500.00
Wurlitzer #1700, all orig	2,000.00
Wurlitzer #1900	600.00
Wurlitzer #24, EX orig	1,750.00
Wurlitzer #24, rstr	2,250.00
Wurlitzer #2500, NM	950.00
Wurlitzer #4002, speaker model, EX	275.00

Slot Machines

Bally G 5¢-25¢ Dbl Bell, EX orig	3,000.00
Bally Hold & Draw, EX orig	500.00
Bally Poker Spinner, EX	2,000.00
Bally 10¢ Super Bars, 4-reel, rvpt glass, 64x24", EX	175.00
Bally 5¢ 8 Ball, EX orig	1,500.00
Berkely 10¢, 3-reel, gr metal case w/chrome, EX	500.00
Buckley 5¢, blk & gold case w/red trim, EX	950.00
Buckley 5¢ Bonanza, 1940s, rstr	800.00
Caille Commander-Streamline, yel, 1930s, EX	675.00
Caille 1¢, gumball, center pull	2,795.00
Caille 10¢ Playboy, red, 1930, NM	700.00
Caille 25¢ Superior, EX orig	1,100.00
Caille 5¢ Silent Sphinx, 3-reel, EX orig	1,200.00
Caille 5¢ Silver Cup, EX orig	9,700.00
Columbia 10¢, red & bl, compact, 1930s, NM	595.00
Jennings Chief 5¢ Tic Tac Toe, wood & chrome case, EX	1,995.00
Jennings Sportsman, 1938, EX orig	2,100.00
Jennings 10¢ Standard Chief, wood/chrome case, 3-reel, EX	1,795.00
Jennings 25¢ Dutch Boy & Girl, 1930s, EX orig	1,800.00
Jennings 5¢ Export Chief, M rstr	1,400.00
Jennings 5¢ Victoria, mints, rstr	1,700.00
Jennings 5¢ Victory Chief, 1941, rstr	1,700.00
Keeney Bonus Super Bell, 3-reel, formica case, 67x28", EX	995.00
Mills Bell Boy, w/marquee, rstr	1,750.00
Mills 10¢ Bell-Fruit-Gum, 1910, payout printed on front, VG	675.00
Mills 10¢ Hi Top, cvd Indian w/headdress, 1940, EX	2,200.00
Mills 10¢ War Eagle, rstr	2,000.00
Mills 25¢ Hi Top, EX orig	1,700.00
Mills 5¢ Black Cherry, EX orig, w/orig manual	1,500.00
Mills 5¢ Bonus Horse Head, ca 1939, EX	2,495.00
Mills 5¢ Brown Front, orig jackpot, EX orig	1,795.00
Mills 5¢ Bursting Cherry, 1940s, EX orig	1,600.00
Mills 5¢ Lion Front, EX orig	1,750.00
Mills 5¢ Poinsettia, EX orig	1,650.00
Mills 5¢ QT Smoker, 1930s, scarce	1,100.00
Mills 5¢ Torch Front, EX orig	1,500.00
Pace All Star Comet, EX orig	1,500.00

Pace 1¢ Bantam, 1928, EX orig 1,200.00
Sega 10¢, blk & gold, marquee, 1940, EX.................................650.00
Watling 1¢ Treasury, EX 3,850.00
Watling 5¢ Lincoln Deluxe, EX orig 2,000.00
Watling 5¢ Lincoln DeLuxe, VG 1,700.00
Watling 5¢ Rol-A-Top, coin front, EX orig 3,000.00

Trade Stimulators

Best Hand Poker, ca 1935, 20x13x8", EX 395.00
Bluebird 1¢ Penny Flip, w/gumball dispenser, 17x12x8", EX 250.00
Bomb Hitler, penny drop, ca 1940s, 16x12x6", EX 550.00
Burlesque 1¢ Skill, 11x15x9", w/lock & key, EX orig 99.00
Caille Jumbo, EX reels 2,000.00

Caille, 1¢ gumball trade stimu-
lator, all original, 18", EX,
$375.00.

Daval's Poker, 5-reel, 1940s, EX....................................350.00
Griswold Wheel of Fortune, wood case, 16½x15x4", EX 795.00
Jennings Grand Stand, EX orig 395.00
Keeney's Spinner Winner, w/gumball vendor at left, 7x16x12" ...375.00
King 6 Jr, BA Withey Co, dice game 500.00
Mills Little Perfection, 4-reel, oak cabinet, 1926, 16", EX...........595.00
Mills 5¢ Vest Pocket, 3-reel, 1933, VG 400.00
Nat'l Penny Flip 275.00
Over the Top 1¢ Skill game, penny push-up, 8x20" 395.00
Pace 25¢ Races, rstr... 8,900.00
Penny Ante Draw Poker, 1930s, 10x9x8", EX rstr.....................315.00
Pok-O-Reel 1¢, payout card on front, EX 495.00
Puritan Baby Bell 3¢ Fortune, Daval, 1931, EX 450.00
Rockola 1¢ Official Sweepstakes Horse Race, w/vendor, EX 995.00
Scramball Gambling, mc balls on ramps, 19x14x9", EX 155.00
Seeburg Shoot the Bear, EX orig, w/manuals 1,500.00
Skill Cards 5¢ Poker, EX orig 275.00
Skilltest 1¢, oak cabinet 225.00
Sparky 5¢ Poker, 5-reel, flat top, 6x15x11", EX orig 165.00
Spin It, EX orig...125.00
Waddell 1893 Bicycle, NM.. 3,000.00
Whiz-Ball, baseball skill game, countertop, 1930s 365.00
Wings 5¢, 5-reel, cigarette advertising, EX............................225.00

Vendors

Acorn 5¢, all purpose, Oak Mfg, 1940, EX orig 65.00
Ad-Lee EZ, gumball, orig pnt, 1908, EX.................................475.00
Adams 1¢, chewing gum, gold & silver metal, 22½x10x4", VG 95.00
Advance Big Mouth, peanuts, 1923, EX orig 175.00
Advance D, gumball, EX..150.00
American Flags 1¢, gumball, 1930, EX....................................175.00

Asco, hot nuts, EX orig..325.00
Atlas Master, glass globe, gumball, 1954 ....95.00
Atlas Master, gumball, 1923, rstr 150.00
Atlas 10¢ Master Deluxe 40.00
Atlas 5¢ Bantam, w/decals, lock & key, 11x7", EX........................95.00
Baseball Flip, gumball, w/key, 1958, EX.................................150.00
Bozo, balloons, w/pump to blow up balloons, 1960, 60", M 125.00
Burnham & Mills 1¢, gumball, rstr 1,250.00
Columbus A 1¢, peanuts, 1910, NM.....................................250.00
Columbus D, EX orig..550.00
Columbus K, gumball, EX orig..350.00
Columbus M Bulk, nuts, 1920s, EX orig 165.00
Columbus Slug Rejector, EX..95.00
Dean 1¢, gum, metal case w/glass panels, 13x7x8", VG 60.00
Dexter 5¢, RG Sullivan Cigars, brn metal case, G 75.00
Diamond 1¢, matches, 13", EX 395.00
Eat 'Em, hot nuts, 1934, w/orig glass cup dispenser, EX...............275.00
Exhibit Rotary Merchandiser.. 1,900.00
Exhibit Supply Cards, 1930s, w/cards, EX................................95.00
Ford 1¢, gumball, chrome, 1940, EX......................................35.00
Ford 1¢, gumball, 1920s, NM...125.00
Fortune 1¢, napkins, EX orig..75.00
Hershey 1¢, candy bars, blk metal case, 18x3½", EX 125.00
Hershey 5¢, candy bars, tan/brn/wht/silver, 28x9x8", VG.............50.00
Hilo 1¢, gum, blk-pnt cast metal, glass top, 17", VG...................165.00
Jacob's 5¢, cigars, holds 3 kinds, pat 1907, 36" W 1,400.00
Lion Puritan 1¢, gumball, w/payout card on front, EX 375.00
Masters 1¢, gumball, 1923, EX 175.00
Mills, gumball, 6-column automatic tab, 1936, rstr....................150.00
Mr Cornet's US Standard 5¢, aspirin, St Louis MO, VG 210.00
Northwestern #33, peanuts, EX orig 125.00
Northwestern OH 1¢, matches, gray metal case, decal, 14x4" 80.00
Northwestern Tab, gumball, w/key...45.00
Northwestern 49er, peanuts...65.00
Northwestern 5¢, package gum 45.00
Noveltone Distributing 25¢, prophylactics, 31x4", VG.................60.00
Oak Vista, gumball, unused, M 40.00
Philadelphia Phillies 10¢, cigars, hanging, 29x8x7", VG 120.00
Pulver 1¢, gum, Stop & Go Policeman, orange case, rare 875.00
Scoopy Gum, clockwork, man drops gum from scoop, 20" 2,500.00
Select-O-Vend 1¢, chocolate & gum, rotates, 18x7x8", VG 55.00
Shipman Mfg 10¢, postage cards, 3 cards for 10¢, VG.................60.00
Silver King, gumball, EX...65.00
Silver King, hot nuts, EX orig 125.00
Silver Queen, NM 55.00
Victor Baseball Flip, gumball, all orig 125.00
Victor Halfback, gumball, 1950, EX orig 40.00
Victor Selectorama, early capsule machine, EX 80.00
Victor Topper, EX 125.00
Victor 10¢, capsule machine w/coin slide 65.00
Wrigley's 1¢ Win A Chew, gum, EX orig 225.00
Zeno, collar buttons..750.00
Zeno, gum, yel porc, G 425.00
20th-Century Novelty Co Spiral, 1906, EX orig 2,700.00

Miscellaneous

Bally Fireball, pinball, NM 1,700.00
Bally 4 Million BC, pinball, M 1,000.00
Chicago Coin Steam Shovel 600.00
Genco Subway 5¢, pinball, 1934, 43x37x18", EX 600.00
Genco 5¢ Baseball, pinball, 1953, M 1,200.00
Jennings Indian 1¢ Hit the Target, EX orig 500.00
Watling 1¢ Scale, Philadelphia, 1918, 73x29x20", EX................700.00

Comic Books

Public acceptance of the cartoon book as an enjoyable form of entertainment caused printing companies to experiment with size and format; by the early 1930s, the comic book as we know it today had evolved – 7" x 9" paper-back books stapled together and selling for 10¢. Each unfolded a new saga of adventure as experienced by detective extraordinare Dick Tracy; super-heroes like Batman and Robin, Superman and Wonderwoman, Tarzan, and The Lone Ranger; or the science fictional characters Flash Gordon and Captain Midnight.

Today first issues in excellent condition may bring prices as high as $300 or over. Though values on the majority of comic books are still modest, Marvel Comics #1, published in 1938, has sold for the astounding price of $35,000. Rarity, age, and quality of artwork are prime factors in determining comic book values. Condition is also important – prices below reflect examples in fine condition unless otherwise noted.

A-1 Comics, #11, Teena, EX 7.50
Abe Lincoln's Life Story, #1, VG 15.00
Action Comics, #252, Supergirl, EX 95.00
Action Comics, #33, Mister America, VG 65.00
Adventure Comics, #256, Green Arrow, VG 14.00
Adventures into Terror, #43, 1950, EX 22.00
Adventures of Alice, #2, Through the Magic Looking Glass, M....25.00
Adventures of the Fly, #14, Fly Girl, VG 2.00
Adventures of the Fly, #2, VG 25.00
Alien Encounters, #14, mature reading, 1987, NM 2.00
All Sport Comics, #3, VG 7.50
Amazing Ghost Stories, #14, St John, VG...............................25.00
Amazing Spider-Man, #5, Marvel, VG 28.00
American Library, #3, Look to Mountain, McKay, VG 12.00
Andy Panda, #4, Dell, VG.. 2.00
Archie's Madhouse, #6, EX...14.00
Archie's Pal, Jughead, #18, VG 12.50
Atom-Age Combat, #3, St John, VG......................................10.00
Badmen of the West, #3, NM..32.00
Barbie & Ken, #2, Dell, EX 9.00
Battle Cry, #11, Stanmor, EX 6.00
Ben Casey, #10, photo cover, M 12.00
Bewitched, #22, Dell, NM..8.00
Big Shot Comics, #88, Columbia, EX 5.00
Blackstone the Magician, #3, Marvel, VG...............................25.00
Blazing West, #5, American, VG 3.00
Blondie, #34, VG..18.00
Bob Steel Western, #5, Fawcett, photo cover, NM......................44.00
Bouncer, #12, Fox Features, EX...15.00
Brides in Love, #9, Charlton Comics, M................................. 4.50
Bugs Bunny, #48, Dell, M.. 3.50
Bugs Bunny Beach Party, #32, Dell Giant, M..........................16.00
Buz Sawyer, #2, Standard, EX...14.00
Captain Atom, #79, Charlton, NM.. 7.50
Captain Gallant, #2, Charlton, EX 6.50
Captain Marvel & Good Humor Man, Fawcett, 1950, VG...........25.00
Caught, #5, Atlas, EX...10.00
Charlie Chan, #2, Dell, NM.. 7.00
Cinderella Love, #12, St John, EX 5.00
Classics Illustrated, #167, Crime & Punishment, VG 2.00
Classics Illustrated, #78, Joan of Arc, 1950, NM.....................25.00
Comics on Parade, #47, Nancy & Fritzi, United Features, VG 7.50
Cowgirl Romances, #2, Fiction House, VG 14.00
Crime Reporter, #3, St John, EX..28.00
Daredevil Comics, #31, Death of the Claw, Gleason, VG 48.00
Dear Lonely Heart, #4, Artful, EX... 8.00

Dell Junior Treasury, #5, Wizard of Oz, M 25.00
Dennis the Menace Television Special, #2, Fawcett, M 10.00
Detective Eye, #2, Centaur, VG...78.00
Dinky Duck, #3, St John, M 5.00
Durango Kid, #2, photo cover, Magazine Enterprises, VG 48.00
Ellery Queen, #2, Superior, EX...32.00
Escape from Fear, Planned Parenthood of America, 1969, M 25.00
F-Troop, #5, photo cover, Dell, NM....................................... 5.00
Family Funnies, #2, Harvey, EX.. 6.00
Famous Stars, #3, Ziff-Davis, VG..22.00
Farmer's Daughter, #2, Stanhall, EX......................................10.00
Fawcett's Funny Animals, #3, VG..10.00
Fighting Fronts, #2, Harvey, NM...12.50
Flash Gordon, #10, King, M 7.50
Forbidden Worlds, #63, American, VG 5.00
Four Color, #124, Roy Rogers, photo cover, NM 75.00
Four Color, #305, Woody Woodpecker, Lantz, EX 7.50
Four Color, #419, Sergeant Preston, VG.................................. 6.00
Four Color, #628, Elmer Fudd, M 5.00
Four Color, #963, Johnny Mack Brown, photo cover, M...............18.00
Four Favorites, #2, Black Ace, Ace Magazines, M....................100.00
Frankie Comics, #4, Marvel, EX..10.00
Funny Tunes, #17, USA Comics Magazine, EX 5.00
GI Combat, #2, Quality Comics Group, VG.............................15.00
GI Joe, Real American Hero, #11, Marvel, NM.........................12.00
Going Steady, #14, St John, VG...15.00
Green Mask, #7, Fox Features, VG...25.00
Gunsmoke Western, #32, Atlas, M...20.00
Harvey Hits, #45, Harvey Toon, M.. 5.00
Horrors, #11, Horrors of War, Star, EX...................................12.50
House of Mystery, #2, Nat'l Periodical, VG..............................35.00
I Love Lucy, #22, Dell, NM..28.00
Intimate Confessions, #4, Realistic, EX...................................32.00
Josie & the Pussycats, #46, Archie, M 4.00
Journey into Unknown Worlds, #27, Atlas, EX.........................10.00
Justice League of America, #250, Nat'l Periodical, M 2.00
Ken Maynard Western, #5, photo cover, Fawcett, VG 75.00
King Comics, #21, David McKay, VG 50.00
Krazy Komics, #12, Timely, VG..20.00
Leave It to Beaver, #912, 4-color, Dell, VG..............................20.00
Life w/Archie, #42, Archie, NM 2.50
Little Dot, #4, Harvey, NM..80.00
Little Orphan Annie, #5, Never Say Die, Cupples & Leon, NM...65.00
Looney Tunes, Merrie Melodies, #19, VG................................45.00
Lost Worlds, #5, Standard, VG 36.00
Magic Comics, #62, McKay, EX.. 8.00
March of Comics, #277, Daffy Duck, KK, NM 10.00
Marvel Super Heroes, #18, Guardians of Galaxy, M..................... 2.00
Master Comics, #5, Fawcett, VG...45.00
Maverick, #16, Kelly/Moore photo cover, Dell, VG 8.00
Mickey Mouse March of Comics, #60, KK, VG........................48.00
Miracle Comics, #3, Hillman, VG 28.00
Monkeyshines Comics, #8, Ace, NM...................................... 7.00
Mopsy, #13, St John, VG...12.00
Movie Comics, Goodbye, Mr Chips, O'Toole photo cover, EX 10.00
Murderous Gansters, #2, Baby Face Nelson, Avon, EX 30.00
Mystery in Space, #53, Nat'l Periodical, VG.............................65.00
New Funnies, #55, Dell, VG...35.00
New Terrytoons, #10, Dell, M 6.50
No Time for Sergeants, #3, Dell, EX.......................................15.00
Our Gang Comics, #8, Benny Burro, Dell, VG.........................68.00
Out of the Shadows, #9, Standard, VG 6.00
Pebbles & Bamm Bamm, #7, Charlton, M 2.50
Petticoat Junction, #4, Dell, EX... 7.50

Pictorial Love Stories, #22, Charlton, VG 15.00
Popular Comics, #46, Dell, VG 36.00
Power Pack, #27, mutants, Marvel, M.......................................2.50
Rangers Comics, #13, Fiction House, G 15.00
Rat Patrol, #4, photo cover, Dell, VG 3.50
Return of the Outlaw, #3, Toby Press, VG 4.00
Richie Rich Fortunes, #11, Harvey, EX 3.00
Ricky Nelson, Dell, #998, VG...18.00
Rocky Lane Western, #8, Fawcett, VG.....................................20.00
Sad Sack & Sarge, #12, Harvey, M..5.00
Scooby Doo, #23, Gold Key, M 3.00
Sergeant Bilco, #4, Nat'l Periodicals, VG 25.00
Shadow, #4, DC, M 2.50
Snagglepuss, #2, Gold Key, EX 5.00
Strange Fantasy, #3, Farrell, NM..20.00
Tales of Asgard, #1, Marvel, NM...2.00
Thrilling Comics, #4, Better, VG...25.00
Transformers, #1, Marvel, M 5.00
Uncle Milty, #2, Victoria, EX...25.00
Victory Comics, #2, Hillman, NM..225.00
War Comics, #4, Dell, NM..48.00

Compasses

ES Ritchie & Sons, brass gimball, 9¾" dia, EX in box 100.00
Keffel & Esser, pocket-watch type, EX 20.00
Pike, Philadelphia, surveyor's, w/case.......................................800.00
Thaxter & Son, surveyor's, brass, mahog case, complete.............425.00
Travel, dry card, mtd in rnd holly wood box, 1825, 2½" 250.00
Wittnauer US, closed case 12.50

Consolidated Lamp and Glass

The Consolidated Lamp and Glass Company of Coraopolis, Pennsylvania, was incorporated in 1894. For many years their primary business was the manufacture of lighting glass such as shades, globes, and table lamps. In the mid-1920s Consolidated introduced their Martele line, a type of 'sculptured' ware intended to resemble Lalique glassware of France. (Compare Consolidated's 'Lovebirds' vase with the Lalique 'Perruches' vase.) It is this line of vases, lamps, and tableware which is often mistaken for a very similar type of glassware produced by the Phoenix Glass Company, located nearby in Monaca, Pennsylvania. For example, the so-called Phoenix 'Grasshopper' vases are actually Consolidated's 'Katydid' vases.

Items in the Martele line were produced in blue, pink, green, crystal, white, or custard glass decorated with various fired-on color treatments or a satin finish. For the most part, their colors were distinctively different from those used by Phoenix. Although not foolproof, one of the ways of distinguishing Consolidated's wares from those of Phoenix is that perhaps 80% of the time Consolidated applied color to the raised portion of the design leaving the background plain, while Phoenix usually applied color to the background leaving the raised surfaces undecorated. This is particularly true of those pieces in white or custard glass.

Consolidated closed its doors for good in 1964. Subsequently a few of the molds passed into the hands of other glass companies who later produced certain patterns in plain white milk glass or colors such as custard or green.

Key: mg — milk glass

Bird of Paradise, vase, amber or crystal, ftd fan form, 7" 60.00
Bird of Paradise, vase, pk on crystal, oblong, 9" 140.00

Bittersweet, gold berries/vines/leaves on milk glass, 10" 90.00
Catalonian, bowl, salad; amber on crystal, flared, 10" 35.00
Catalonian, plate, wht on crystal, 8" 8.00
Catalonian, sundae, gr on crystal, conical, 7-oz............................15.00
Catalonian, vase, bl on crystal, fan form, 8" 50.00
Catalonian, vase, gr, rose jar form w/flared rim, 7" 90.00
Catalonian, vase, 4-lobed nasturtium, lavender on crystal 70.00
Cockatoo, vase, bl birds/brn/coral on custard, rnd, 10" 195.00
Con-Cora, Quilt, cracker jar, HP violets/gold buttons on mg, 9"...50.00
Dancing Girl, vase, pk nudes/Pan on wht satin, 11".....................325.00
Dancing Nymphs, plate, crystal, 10" 65.00
Dancing Nymphs, sherbet, pk 50.00
Dancing Nymphs, tumbler, crystal nudes on satin, 3½"................40.00
Dogwood, vase, coral flowers/gr leaves/brn limbs on wht, 10" 140.00
Dragonfly, vase, aqua wings, gr/brn cattails on custard, 6"............90.00
Fish, bowl, amethyst on crystal, shallow, 15" 200.00
Florette, mustard pot, pk satin cased over wht.............................135.00
Florette, pitcher, pk satin cased over wht, 7"...............................150.00
Flower & Leaf, bowl, console; ftd, 11", +tall candlestick 130.00
Flower & Leaf, jug, gr on crystal, ½-gal.......................................150.00
Foxglove, vase, coral flowers/aqua leaves on wht satin 95.00
Fruit & Leaf, plate, gr on crystal, 8" 25.00
Fruit & leaf, pound box, milk glass, oval, scalloped, 7" L 40.00
Goldfish, vase, lavender fish on gr, milk glass, oblong, 9" 140.00
Katydids, vase, amber on crystal, fan form, 8"..............................80.00
Katydids, vase, amethyst on crystal, ovoid, 7"..............................125.00
LeFleur, vase, russet on crystal...125.00
Lovebirds, vase, bl birds on custard satin, 11"..............................160.00
Martele Fairy, bowl, bl, flared, 13" 115.00
Olive, bowl, crystal satin olives on gr ground, 3½x9" 40.00
Owls, vase, aqua pattern on wht satin, 6" 65.00
Peony, lamp, bl flowers/gr leaves on wht satin, 12" base..............145.00
Peony, vase, crystal flowers on cranberry, 9" 95.00
Pine Cone, vase, brn cones/limbs, gr needles on custard, 7"........120.00
Ruba Rombic, console set, smoke, 12" L bowl, +candlesticks......525.00
Ruba Rombic, whiskey, cased yel 50.00
Santa Maria, cigarette jar, orchid on crystal, ship finial 80.00
Swallows, bowl, gr on crystal, low/flared, 9" 80.00
Two-Bird, vase, bl pattern on wht satin, oblong, 6½".....................70.00

Cookbooks

Cookbooks from the nineteenth century, though often hard to find, are a delight to today's collectors both for their quaint formats and printing methods as well as for their outmoded, often humorous views on nutrition. Recipes required a 'pinch' of salt, butter 'the size of an egg' or a 'walnut,' or a 'handful' of flour. Collectors sometimes specialize in cookbooks issued as advertising premiums. Especially desirable are the figurals that were shaped like a jar, a slice of bread, or some other form relative to the product. Others with unique features such as illustrations by well-known artists or references to famous people or places are priced in accordance. Cookbooks written earlier than 1874 are the most valuable and when found command prices as high as $200; figurals usually sell in the $10 to $15 range.

Key: CB — Cookbook

American Woman's CB, 1947, 823-pg, EX 17.50
Best of Bake-Off Collection, 1959, EX 36.00
Better Homes & Gardens, ring binder, gold cover, 1965, NM 25.00
Better Homes & Gardens, 1968, G 10.00
Betty Crocker, ring binder, 1973, EX 45.00
Betty Crocker's Picture CB, 1950, EX..15.00
Blue Ribbon, illus, 1907, G 20.00

Boston Cooking School, Fanny Farmer, 1928 ....10.00
Boston Cooking School CB, 1918, 656-pg, EX.........................17.50
Buttery Shelf CB, Tasha Tudor illus, EX 16.00
Cooking the French Way, London, 1953 ....6.00
Cutco, meat, 1961 ....2.50
Family Circle Cake & Cookie Book, 1953, EX..........................10.00
Gone w/the Wind, Pebeco premium, Scarlett on cover 40.00
Household Searchlight Homemaking Guide, 1937, VG 25.00
Joy of Cooking, hard bk, 1946, EX 12.00
Joy of Cooking, 1962 ....10.00
Let's Cook It Right, Adele Davis, 1st edition, 1947, EX...............12.00
Look No Further, R Hougan of Boone Tavern, 1954, EX 7.50
Mary Arnold's Century CB, 1895, VG.....................................22.50
Pillsbury Grand Nat'l, 3rd edition 15.00
Plan-Ahead CB, D Dyer, 1969, 233-pg, NM.............................6.00
Practical Housekeeping, 1883, G 15.00
Science in the Kitchen, 1893, EX...25.00
Service CB, Allen, pub for Woolworth, 1933 ....5.00
Sour Cream Cookery, B Brown, 1947, 235-pg 12.00
White House CB, 1889, VG..10.00
White House CB, 1926, EX...38.00
Woman's Home Companion CB, 1955, 987-pg, EX.....................15.00
365 Ways To Cook Hamburger, 1960, EX.................................12.00

Cookie Cutters

Early hand-fashioned cookie cutters have recently been commanding stiff prices at country auctions, and the ranks of interested collectors are growing steadily. Especially valuable are the figural cutters; and the more complicated the design, the higher the price. A follow-up of the carved wooden cookie boards, the first cutters were probably made by itinerant tinkers from left-over or recycled pieces of tin. Though most of the eighteenth-century examples are now in museums or collections, it is still possible to find some good cutters from the late 1800s when changes in the manufacture of tin resulted in a thinner, less expensive material. The width of the cutting strip is often a good indicator of age – the wider the strip, the older the cutter. While the very early cutters were 1" to 1½" deep, by the twenties and thirties, many were less than ½" deep. Crude, spotty soldering indicates an older cutter, while a thin line of solder usually tends to suggest a much later manufacture. The shape of the backplate is another clue. Later cutters will have oval, round, or rectangular backs, while on the earlier type the back was cut to follow the lines of the design. Cookie cutters usually vary from 2" to 4" in size, but gingerbread men were often made as tall as 12". Birds, fish, hearts, and tulips are common; simple versions can be purchased for as little as $12.00 to $15.00. The larger figurals, especially those with more imaginative details, often bring $75.00 and up.

Amish man, full figure 65.00
Bull w/horns, 4½" 50.00
Cornucopia, rolled edges, strap hdl, 3½".................................25.00
Dog, 4½" L 45.00
Dove, stylized, 4¾" L 25.00
Duck, 3½" L 18.00
Fish, crimped all around, 4½" L..35.00
Fish, crimped fins, strap hdl, 7¼" L.....................................250.00
Fish, lg tail, 5" 38.00
Goose, standing, 1800s, 4x4x½"...25.00
Hatchet, rolled edges, strap hdl, 1830s, 6½x8½" 85.00
Horse, prancing, bobtail, 6½" L 250.00
Horse, trotting, 6"..78.00
Horse & rider, primitive, 7", EX...180.00

Lady w/shaped hair & apron, strap hdl, 8" 550.00
Lady w/sm arms & full skirt, 4"..25.00
Man in top hat & tails, 6" 165.00
Star, 3" 15.00

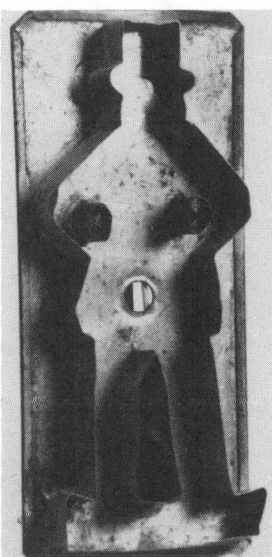

Man in top hat, 7",
$75.00.

Cookie Jars

The appeal of the cookie jar is universal; folks of all ages, both male and female, love to collect 'em! The early thirties' heavy stoneware jars of a rather nondescript nature quickly gave way to figurals of every type imaginable. Those from the mid to late thirties were often decorated over the glaze with 'cold paint,' but by the early forties underglaze decorating resulted in cheerful, bright, permanent colors and cookie jars that still have a new look forty years later.

Unmarked jars, unless properly identified and rare, bring the lowest prices, while cookie jars trimmed in gold are usually highly valued. The examples listed below were made by companies other than those found elsewhere in this book; see also specific manufacturers. For further study, we recommend *An Illustrated Guide to Cookie Jars* by Ermagene Westfall, and *The Collector's Encyclopedia of Cookie Jars*, by Fred and Joyce Roerig.

See specific manufactures such as Brush, Metlox, and McCoy.

Albert Apple, PD Co, 1942 ....85.00
Angel Face, You're an Angel/Have One, mk LE...........................80.00
Animal Cookies, mk USA American Bisque 20.00
Aunt Jemima, plastic, Quaker Oats premium, lt wear..................110.00
Baby Bear, sleeping, bow at neck, American Bisque 45.00
Balloon Lady, Pottery Guild, NM 85.00
Barefoot Boy, made for Gem Refractories, NM 250.00
Bear on ABC Blocks, Starnes of CA, orig label, lt wear.................80.00
Bear on Stump w/Sucker, Twin Winton 30.00
Bear w/Cookie, American Bisque, M 40.00
Betty Boop, w/bear, early '80s, scarce 225.00
Blackboard Little Girl, mk USA American Bisque 42.00
Blackboard Schoolboy, mk USA American Bisque 45.00
Blk Granny, watermelons on dress, w/24k gold, Gifford USA 130.00
Blk Little Girl, w/cookie, pk or wht dress, Sears 450.00
Blk Mammy, brn/red dots, lid in tummy, Rockingham 175.00
Blk Topsy Girl, red, bl, or yel dots, Metlox................................110.00
Boots, mk USA, American Bisque...90.00
Boy, red hair, gr hat, Robinson Ransbottom 30.00
Brownie, Robinson Ransbottom 45.00

Buck Lamb, American Bisque 80.00
Bunny Rabbit Sheriff, Twin Winton 20.00
Bus, Disney characters in windows, Walt Disney............225.00
Campbell Kid, nodding head, mk DA-AR in oval w/V 300.00
Captain, Robinson Ransbottom 80.00
Casper the Ghost, Harvey, M....................................650.00
Cat on Beehive, American Bisque, NM............................32.00
Cat w/Mouse on Bk, Treasure Craft 30.00
Century 21 House, For Sale, people allover, M 225.00
Cheerleaders, #802 USA Corner Cookie Jar, American Bisque .100.00
Chef, Nat'l Silver, M 200.00
Chef, Pearl China 400.00
Chicken, Twin Winton...20.00
Churn, American Bisque...85.00
Clown on Stage, mk 805 USA American Bisque 70.00
Collegiate Owl, cap w/tassel, mk USA American Bisque...........40.00
Cookie Cop, Pfaltzgraff..35.00
Cookie Truck, American Bisque, lg, NM 65.00
Cookie Truck, sm USA, American Bisque 50.00
Cookies w/Nut, LA Potteries....................................30.00
Cooky Girl, O's in 'Cooky' are eyes, braids & bow 25.00
Cottage, Twin Winton CA USA 40.00
Cow Jumped Over the Moon, gold trim, Robinson Ransbottom .120.00
Cow Jumped Over the Moon, no gold, Robinson Ransbottom......70.00
Cow Jumped Over the Moon, yel or gr, Doraine, NM...............125.00
C3PO, orig movie jar, 1977, M 110.00
Davy Crockett, in bushes, American Bisque 250.00
Davy Crockett, w/bear, Sierra Vista 400.00
Dennis the Menace, standing....................................300.00
Donald Duck, Disney, hand in cookie jar, MIB 98.00
Donkey w/Milk Wagon, American Bisque...........................50.00
Dove, gr or pk, Fapco 18.00
Dumbo, 4-way, Walt Disney Turnabout 125.00
Dutch Boy, Pottery Guild 50.00
Dutch Girl, Pottery Guild 50.00
Ee-Yore, Disney..125.00
Elephant, brn, wht sailor hat, Twin Winton 25.00
Elephant, sitting up, American Bisque 52.00
Elf Bakery Tree Stump, Keebler.................................38.00
Elf Head, various colors, unmk.................................55.00
Elsie the Cow, Pottery Guild, NM...............................112.00
Farmer Pig, American Bisque....................................30.00
Flasher Clown, American Bisque.................................70.00
Frogs, legs Xd, #106 USA.......................................50.00
Fruit & Vegetable Bowl, LA Pottery, M 75.00
German Man's Head, West Germany 225.00
Gingerbread House, Twin Winton 42.00
Glamour Boy Rooster, Artcraft of CA 40.00
Goldilocks, Regal China 125.00
Granny, w/gold, American Bisque................................150.00
Howdy Doody, M...450.00
Hubert the Lion, Regal China...................................225.00
Indian, arms folded, sucker in hand, tongue to side, unmk 30.00
Jack-in-the-Box, American Bisque...............................45.00
Kitten on Beehive, American Bisque.............................25.00
Kittens w/Ball of Yarn, American Bisque........................35.00
Kraft Bear, Regal China, lg....................................100.00
Lady w/Muffler, gray goat, hands in muffler, old, EX 90.00
Little Lamb, American Bisque, M 47.00
Majorette, Regal China, gold trim, lt wear 118.00
Majorette, unmk American Bisque 65.00
Mammy, Mosaic Tile, lg, NM 395.00
Mammy, Pearl China, M 480.00
Mammy, yel, red, or bl dots, Metlox............................120.00

Mammy, National Silver, $210.00.

Mouse w/Cheese, gray w/yel cheese, Lefton, M 42.00
Noah's Ark, w/30 animals, ramp, USA-881, 11½x11½" 75.00
Old King Cole, Robinson Ransbottom 200.00
Olive Oyl, w/daisy in hat 550.00
Oscar the Grouch 45.00

Peek-a-Boo, Van Telligen, $375.00.

Pillsbury Doughboy, American Bisque 35.00
Pinocchio, long nose, gr hat, C26 USA, M 65.00
Pixie Head, various colors, unmk...............................55.00
Poodle, American Bisque 40.00
Popeye, w/pipe, American Bisque................................425.00
Puss 'N Boots, gold trim, decals, fish on hat, not Shawnee, M 175.00
Quaker Oats, oatmeal box form, Regal China, M 105.00
Rabbit in Hat, American Bisque.................................40.00
Rabbit w/Bowl 58.00
Raccoon, Twin Winton 35.00

Raccoon in Tree Stump, M	32.00
Rag Doll, polka dot dress, hands up, Starnes of CA, M	85.00
Red Riding Hood, Pottery Guild, M	85.00
Ring for Cookies, American Bisque	25.00
Rooster, Sierra Vista, M	45.00
R2D2, orig movie jar, bl & wht, M	90.00
Saddle w/Blackboard, American Bisque	110.00
Santa, Blk, sitting, 24k gold trim, Gifford USA, M	175.00
Santa in Rocker, Lefton China	85.00
Seal on Igloo, USA American Bisque	40.00
Sheriff, no hole in hat	30.00
Smiley Pig, Terrace Ceramics	28.00
Spaceship, American Bisque	50.00
Stagecoach, plastic windows, Sierra Vista	250.00
Sweet Pea, crawling	710.00
Tattle Tale Woman, holding up finger	160.00
Tigger Tiger, Disney, EX	80.00
Tom & Jerry, MGM, 1981, M	160.00
Tug Boat, mk California	30.00
Tweedle Dee, Disney	35.00
Winnie the Pooh, Disney, dk yel & red, M	90.00
Wooden Soldier, American Bisque	30.00
Yogi Bear, felt tongue, Hanna Barbara	160.00
Zoo, animals in relief on gr, Ace Hardware, M	40.00

Cooper, Susie

Bowl, Parrot Tulip, w/lid	65.00
Breakfast-in-bed set, Kestral shape, mushroom glaze, 17-pc	175.00
Cup & saucer, orange w/blk bands	27.00

Coors

The firm that became known as Coors Porcelain Company in 1920 was founded in 1908 by John J. Herold, originally of the Roseville Pottery in Zanesville, Ohio. Though still in business today, they are best known for their artware vases and Rosebud dinnerware produced before 1939.

Baker, Rosebud, 4¾" dia	12.50
Baking pan, Rosebud, rectangular, 2x12x8"	22.00
Baking pan, Rosebud, 10¾x6¾"	17.50
Bowl, fruit; Rosebud, 5"	7.50
Bowl, mixing; Rosebud, hdld, 3½-cup	15.00
Bowl, pudding; Rosebud, early, lg	20.00
Bowl, pudding; Rosebud, 2-pt, sm	12.50
Cake knife, Rosebud, 10"	22.50
Casserole, Dutch; Rosebud, 3½-cup	25.00
Casserole, Rosebud, w/lid, 14-cup	38.00
Cookie jar, HP decor, lg	35.00
Creamer, Rosebud, 3"	14.00
Egg cup, Rosebud, 6-oz	15.00
Honey pot, Rosebud, w/lid & ladle	50.00
Muffin set, Rosebud, 8" plate+5½" dome lid	40.00
Planter, orange matt, 3-legged, 8¾"	25.00
Plate, Rosebud, 7¼"	6.00
Plate, Rosebud, 9"	10.00
Plate, soup; Rosebud, 4"	14.00
Saucer, Rosebud, 5½"	6.00
Shakers, Rosebud, str sides, 4½", pr	12.50
Shakers, Rosebud, 2½", pr	24.00
Tumbler, Rosebud, ftd, no hdl, 12-oz	22.50
Tumbler, Rosebud, hdl, 8½-oz	20.00

Underplate, Rosebud, 7"	7.50
Vase, coral/gr matt, ped ft, 5"	25.00
Vase, yel, imp design, 5½"	30.00

Vase, Art Deco, orange matt, 9", $45.00.

Water server, Rosebud, Commemorative, corked stopper, 3-pt	88.00
Water server, Rosebud, corked stopper, 6-cup	36.00

Copper

Hand-crafted copper was made in America from early in the eighteenth century until about 1850, with the center of its production in Pennsylvania. Examples have been found signed by such notable coppersmiths as Kidd, Buchanan, Babb, Bently, and Harbeson. Of the many utilitarian items made, teakettles are the most desirable. Early examples from the eighteenth century were made with a dovetailed joint which was hammered and smoothed to a uniform thickness. Pots from the nineteenth century were seamed. Coffeepots were made in many shapes and sizes and along with mugs, kettles, warming pans, and measures are easiest to find. Stills ranging in sizes of up to fifty-gallon are popular with collectors today.

Our advisor, Mary Frank Gaston, has compiled a lovely book, *Antique Copper*, with many full-color photos and current market values; you will find her address in the Directory under Texas.

Bed warmer, engr floral lid, spiral grpt hdl, 45", EX	375.00
Coal scuttle, helmet form, bail hdl, hand-hold at bk, 20"	285.00
Fish poacher, dvtl, wrought hdls, lift-out liner, DH&M, 22"	300.00
Flagon, baluster form w/stepped hinged lid, rnd ft, 14"	250.00
Jar, hammered, dvtl seams, Middle Eastern, 9x11¼"	35.00
Kettle, dvtl, rnded bottom, wrought side hdls, 12x24"	200.00
Kettle, rolled rim, CI swing hdl, dome lid, mk IS, 18x15"	265.00
Pitcher, tapered cylinder, rolled oval rim, C-hdl, 15"	300.00
Pot, Gaillard Paris, iron hdls, 1-gal	300.00
Pot, w/C-form bell-metal hdls ea mk #18, 1800s, 8x22" L	200.00
Saucepan, dvtl, 8" wrought copper hdl, battered, 8½" dia	60.00
Saucepan, French, 1880s, w/lid, set of 4, largest: 8½"	375.00
Skillet, dvtl, wrought iron hdl, Smith & Anthony, MA, 11½"	105.00
Skillet, wrought steel hdl, Colony RI, 10½" dia	85.00
Skimming spoon, trn mahog hdl, Am, 1800, 26", NM	200.00
Teakettle, dvtl, gooseneck, sgn JMWE, EX	150.00
Teakettle, dvtl, gooseneck, sgn W Morrison, 6-qt, VG	165.00
Teakettle, gooseneck, acorn finial, 11½", EX	300.00
Teakettle, gooseneck, oval strap hdl, sgn J Geddes, 11"	850.00
Teakettle, gooseneck, sgn (unreadable), minor denting, 8"	275.00
Teakettle, gooseneck, sgn J Bollinger, minor dents, 12"	500.00

Teakettle, gooseneck, sgn J Kiersted, minor dents, 10" 350.00
Teakettle, gooseneck, sgn Wm A Lewis Phila, 11", EX...............450.00
Teakettle, handmade, to set on iron range, Am, 2-gal 500.00
Teakettle, S-curve spout, flat curved swing hdl, sgn, 6" 800.00

Teakettles: Signed, small, $150.00; With acorn finial, large, $200.00.

Copper Lustre

Copper lustre is a term referring to a type of pottery made in Staffordshire after the turn of the nineteenth century. It is finished in a metallic rusty-brown glaze resembling true copper. Pitchers are found in abundance, ranging from simple styles with dull bands of color to those with fancy handles and bands of embossed, polychromed flowers. Bowls are common; goblets, mugs, teapots, and sugar bowls much less so. It's easy to find, but not in good condition. Pieces with hand-painted decoration and those with historical transfers are the most valuable.

Our advisor for this category is Richard Marden; he is listed in the Directory under New Hampshire.

Teapot, floral band, marked Made in England, 5¾", $125.00.

Bowl, Friendly Society of Cordwainers of England, 8" 66.00
Coffeepot, ribbed & beaded, Georgian style, 10½" 375.00
Cup, Satyr, w/frog inside, 5" 95.00
Goblet, Faith & Hope, purple transfer on wht band, 4½" 55.00
Mug, bl band, purple lustre rim, 2½"...45.00
Mug, child's, floral in high relief 55.00

Mug, wide agate band, ca 1800, 2¾" 75.00
Pitcher, allegorical scenic mc panels, 4⅝" 75.00
Pitcher, children & dog relief, mc highlights, 3¼" 35.00
Pitcher, dancing girls relief, bl enameling, 1890, 7½" 65.00
Pitcher, grapevines relief w/bl highlights, paneled, 5¾" 45.00
Pitcher, London scenes, 7½" 75.00
Pitcher, mc emb floral on bl band, fish hdl/mask spout, 7".............85.00
Pitcher, mc enameling, faceted, 6½" 55.00
Pitcher, mc floral relief, Bacchus spout, 6" 65.00
Plate, leaf chain, gr on oatmeal band, mks, 8½" 15.00
Teapot, floral spray, bl trim, faceted sides, 7", NM 125.00
Tumbler, gr band, 3¼" 50.00

Coralene Glass

Coralene is a unique type of art glass easily recognized by the tiny grains of glass that form its decoration. Lacy allover patterns of seaweed, geometrics, and florals were used, as well as solid forms such as fish, plants, and single blossoms. It was made by several glasshouses both here and abroad. Values are based to a considerable extent on the amount of beading that remains.

Our advisors for this category are Betty and Clarence Maier; they are listed in the Directory under Pennsylvania.

Bowl, Dia Quilt, yel w/bl int, butterfly/floral motif, 8" 685.00
Bowl, fruit; orange w/fruits & flowers, Meriden SP fr 550.00
Ewer, Herringbone, yel to wht, floral motif, ruffled, 8¾" 275.00
Jar, peachblow, roses/leaves motif, 7¾" 250.00
Shakers, wht frost w/orange seaweed motif, pr 300.00
Tumbler, bl shaded overlay, overall yel motif, 4" 265.00
Tumbler, Dia Quilt, bl MOP w/orange coral motif, 4".................335.00
Vase, Dia Quilt, pk MOP w/stars & diamond motif, 4½x3⅜" 475.00
Vase, Dia Quilt, pk MOP w/yel wheat motif, 10½" 1,065.00

Vase, Diamond Quilted, pink with gold coralene, 4½", $550.00.

Vase, Herringbone, bl, short neck, lobed/tapered form, 8" 600.00
Vase, lt bl Bristol, bird on floral branch motif, 1900, 5½"............195.00
Vase, peachblow colored w/yel seaweed motif, bulbous, 4½" 250.00
Vase, pk to bl w/beaded designs in irregular panels, 6x5" 375.00
Vase, Snowflake, yel MOP, yel wheat motif, 5½x3⅝" 495.00
Vase, unsgn Moser, peacock decor.. 1,250.00

Coralene, Oriental

Fine chinaware decorated in the same manner as coralene glass was produced in Japan during the early 1900s. Many items are marked 'Patent Pending' or with a specific patent date.

Bowl, plums, purple on bl, 8" 165.00
Plate, florals, pk on gr bsk, much gold, 7¾" 85.00
Plate, poppy, pk on gr w/gold beaded rim, mk pat, 7¾" 100.00
Vase, florals, gr/yel beads on bl, 1909, 9" 298.00
Vase, iris, pk/lav on gr, cobalt & gold trim, 9x3½" 455.00
Vase, water lily, lav/pk on bl/pk mottle w/gold, hdls, 4" 250.00

Cordey

The Cordey China Company was founded in 1942 in Trenton, New Jersey, by Boleslaw Cybis. The operation was small with less than a dozen workers. They produced figurines, vases, lamps, and similar wares, much of which was marketed through gift shops both nationwide and abroad. Though the earlier wares were made of plaster, Cybis soon developed his own formula for a porcelain composition which he called 'Papka.' Cordey figurines and busts were characterized by old-world charm, Rococo scrolls, delicate floral appliques, ruffles, and real lace which was dipped in liquified clay to add dimension to the work.

Although on rare occasions some items were not numbered or signed, the 'basic' figure was cast both with numbers and the Cordey signature. The molded pieces were then individually decorated and each marked with its own impressed identification number as well as a mark to indicate the artist-decorator. Their numbering system began with 200 and in later years progressed into the 8000s. As can best be established, Cordey continued production until sometime in the mid-1950s. Boleslaw Cybis died in 1957, his wife in 1958.

Key: ff — full figure

Bird, #2307, blk & gray w/red breast, perched on stump, 8½" 110.00
Bluebird, #6004, perched on stump, 10" 110.00
Bust, #5009, girl w/hat, 6" 65.00
Bust, #5014, Junior Prom, ringlets, scrolled base, 7" 48.00
Clock, mantel; #914, Rococo, Lanshire, electric, 9½" 225.00
Lady, #300, ruffled bosom, holds fan, ff, 15½" 195.00
Lady, #302, brimmed hat, ff, 16½" 225.00
Lady, #4158, gold headband, much lace, 13¼" 185.00
Lady, #5054, flowers in hair, bustle, skirt forms base, 9¼" 70.00
Lady, #5082, ringlets, lace kerchief, 10¾" 100.00
Lady, #5084, upswept hair, scrolled base, 11¾" 100.00
Lady, #5089, ringlets, bustle, ff, 10¾" 100.00
Lamb, #5024, scrolled base 135.00
Lamp, dbl figure (man & lady), #5041/#5084, pr 150.00
Lamp, dbl figure (man & lady), #5044P/#5044B, 11½", pr 175.00
Lamp, floor; gold metal base, milk glass torchere, 60" 265.00
Lamp, lady on scrolled base, lace & ruffles, 11" 100.00
Lamp, Madam Dubarry bust, gold lace, Rococo base, 18" 250.00
Man, #303, plumed hat, ff, 16" 195.00
Man, #305, grape harvester, ff, 16" 195.00
Man, #4153, lg hat, gold trim, ff on scrolled base, 14" 150.00
Man, #5042, ff on scrolled base, 10½" 85.00
Man & Lady, #304/#305, ff, 16", pr 190.00
Neopolitan Boy, #5046, ff, 9½" 90.00
Plaque, #902, lady's face, ringlets, 10" 225.00
Plaque, advertising, 4½x3" 100.00
Teapot, #631, 7¼", w/creamer (#633) & sugar bowl (#632) 250.00
Vase, #7061, birds on leaf, roses appl ea side, 8¾" 145.00

Vase, #7094, Orientals in relief, appl flowers, 8" 140.00
Wall shelf, #7028, Art Nouveau nude w/cornucopia, 8x6½" 95.00
Yorkshire girl, #5047, jug on shoulder, grapes in dress, 10" 90.00

Figure of a man, 15½", $80.00.

Corkscrews

The history of the corkscrew dates back to the mid-1600s, when wine makers concluded that the best-aged wine was that stored in smaller containers, either stoneware or glass. Since plugs left unsealed were often damaged by rodents, corks were cut off flush with the bottle top and sealed with wax or a metal cover. Removing the cork cleanly with none left to grasp became a problem. The task was found to be relatively simple using the worm on the end of a flintlock gun rod – and the corkscrew evolved. Endless patents have been issued for mechanized models; handles range from figural ivories (lady's legs are popular) to repousse silver, carved bone, wood, and porcelain.

Our advisor for this category is Roger Baker; he is listed in the Directory under California.

Anheuser Busch, bottle figural, 1897, EX 50.00
Boar's tusk, cvd, Nouveau decor, sterling end cap, 9½" 325.00
Bruxelles, naughty boy figural, brass, sm 7.50
Carter's Ink, folding, pat 1894 ....12.00
CI bottle holder, wooden T hdl, 5½" 10.00
Coney's Pat, walnut & brass, ca 1884 ....225.00
CT Winn & Timmins, steel eyebrow hdl, center worm, 1880s 38.00
E-Z Cork Puller Pat Pending on 4-barb shaft, EX 25.00
England, brass, semi-modern, 2-finger pull 10.00
England, burl walnut hdl, steel shaft, bulbous end w/teeth 95.00
England, dumbbell-type wood hdl, center worm, early, EX 20.00
England, ebonized wood hdl, tapered sq shaft, fluted 15.00
England, ivory hdl, lady's scent bottle corkscrew, 1700s 100.00
England, rosewood hdl, sq shaft, center worm, 1880s, EX 20.00
England, stag hdl, trn steel shaft, serrated, 1880, 3½" 40.00
England, steel shaft w/4 teeth, ca 1880, EX 45.00
England, swivel-over collar, bronze finish on steel, VG 40.00

England, traveling, registry mk 1927, sleeve becomes hdl, EX 80.00
Equinox, champagne, late 1800s...45.00
France, wood hdl, metal ends, dimpled shaft, ca 1875, EX.............30.00
France, wood hdl, steel ends/band/shaft, center worm, 1880s 45.00
France, wood hdl, steel shaft, metal end caps, center worm, 1870.15.00
Germany, spring-covered shaft, open bbl, VG.........................20.00
Germany, spring-covered shaft, wood hdl, VG........................40.00
Germany, spring-release helix worm, steel cage, 1880s 45.00
Geschutz, nude, bent at waist, mermaid-like, celluloid 325.00
Good Luck Pixie, brass, cyphered center worm, EX 38.00
Heeley's A-1 Dbl Lever, bronze finish, pat 1888, EX...................115.00
Heeley's Orig Patent, Pulleze, Made in England, EX 75.00
Lever Signet, Wolverson 1873 Tangent Lever, helix worm, EX.....60.00
London Rack, rack & pinion actions, unmk English, 1800s 150.00
Lund Patentee London, emb crest, no finish 95.00
Lund Patentee London, lever, 2-part, orig bronze finish 100.00
Lund's Lever 1855 Patent, 2-finger hdl, helix worm, EX 60.00
Magic Lever Cork Drawer, pat appl for, ca 1925, VG....................45.00
Man, 2-sided, SP, w/jigger/opener/spoon, dtd 1932 ....110.00
Old Snifter, Senator Volstead, brass, fixed hat, w/opener 200.00
Old Snifter, Senator Volstead, gray metal, pnt hat, VG................75.00
Old Snifter, Senator Volstead, thermoplastic w/mc pnt 225.00
Parrot form, metal hdl, aluminum finish....................................20.00
Perpetual, dbl-threaded shaft, automatic reverse, unmk.................75.00
Staghorn hdl, helix worm, sm, VG 10.00
Thomason Dbl Action, bone hdl w/brush & cap, 1820s, 6¼".......265.00
Waiter's, lever, lifter, 2½" blade, fluted helix, 1920s.......................10.00
Walker's 1893 Pat on sterling bell cap, 8½" boar's tusk 125.00
Walker's 1900 Pat, fruitwood hdl, bell cap, long center worm 15.00
Walnut hdl, rnd shaft, center worm, gilt metal, EX......................... 7.50
Weir's Patent 12804 25, Sept, 1884, VG bronze finish 120.00
Williamson 1900 Pat, bullet form, worm folds into top 40.00
Yankee #7 RB Gilchrist's 1913 Pat, clamp type 125.00

Cosmos

Cosmos, sometimes called Stemless Daisy, is a patterned glass tableware produced from 1894 through 1915 by Consolidated Lamp and Glass Company. Relief-molded flowers on a fine cross-cut background were painted in soft colors of pink, blue, and yellow. Though nearly all were made of milk glass, a few items may be found in clear glass with the designs painted on. In addition to the tableware, lamps were also made.

Miniature lamp, 7", $325.00.

Bottle, scent, pk & bl floral, orig stopper, M 135.00
Butter dish, 7½" dia..225.00
Condiment set, 3-pc on glass stand, complete............................395.00
Creamer 150.00
Lamp, banquet; kerosene, 24" 475.00
Lamp, banquet; slender base, rnd globe, all orig, 16" 450.00
Lamp, 10" 400.00
Pickle castor, dbl, mk SP fr..500.00
Pickle castor, single, ftd SP fr 350.00
Pitcher, milk; 5" 170.00
Pitcher, syrup 200.00
Pitcher, 8¾"...250.00
Shakers, tall, orig lids, pr 135.00
Spooner...125.00
Sugar bowl, open 150.00
Sugar bowl, w/lid 185.00
Tumbler, 3¾"...65.00

Cottageware

You'll find a varied assortment of novelty dinnerware items – all styled as cozy little English cottages or huts with cone-shaped roofs; some may have a waterwheel or a windmill alongside. Marks will vary. English-made Price Brothers or Beswick pieces are valued in the same range as those marked Occupied Japan, while items marked simply Japan are considered slightly less pricey.

Our advisor for this category is Grace Klender; she is listed in the Directory under Ohio.

Butter dish, English, $45.00.

Chocolate pot, English 75.00
Condiment set, pr shakers+mustard on tray, English....................25.00
Cookie jar, Japan, sm 35.00
Cookie jar, Japan, 7" 40.00
Creamer & sugar bowl, English, 2½", 4½" 20.00
Cup & saucer, English 30.00
Pitcher, water; English...90.00
Teapot, English or Occupied Japan, 6½" 50.00
Teapot, Japan, 6½" 35.00
Tumbler, Japan, 3½", set of 6..40.00

Coverlets

The Jacquard attachment for hand looms represented a culmination of weaving developments made in France. Introduced to America by the early 1820s, it gave professional weavers the ability to easily create complex patterns with curved lines. Those who could afford the new loom adaptation could now use hole-punched pasteboard cards to weave floral patterns that before could only be achieved with intense labor on a draw-loom.

Before the Jacquard mechanism, most weavers made their coverlets in geometric patterns. Use of indigo-blue and brightly-colored wools often livened the twills and overshot patterns available to the small-loom home weaver. Those who had larger multiple-harness looms could produced warm double-woven, twill-block, or summer-and-winter designs.

While the new floral and pictorial patterns' popularity had displaced the geometrics in urban areas, the mid-Atlantic, and the Midwest by the 1840s, even factory production of the Jacquard coverlets was disrupted by cotton and wool shortages during the Civil War. A revived production in the 1870s saw a style change to a center-medallion motif, but a new fad – for white 'Marseilles' spreads – soon halted sales of Jacquard-woven coverlets. Production of Jacquard carpets continued to the turn of the century.

Rural and frontier weavers continued to make geometric-design coverlets through the 19th century, and local craft revivals have continued this tradition through this century. All-cotton overshots were factory-produced in Kentucky from the 1940s, and factories and professional weavers made cotton-and-wool overshots during the past decade.

Many Jacquard-woven coverlets have dates and names of places and people (often the intended owner – not the weaver) woven into corners or borders.

In the listings that follow, examples are blue and white unless noted otherwise.

Jacquard

Red and white jacquard weave with wreath, eagles, and building; dated 1850, NM condition, $1,200.00.

Bird borders, corners sgn/1842, 5-color w/yel, bk: w/gr 900.00
Birds feed young, Christian/Heathen border, 78x88", EX 600.00
Centennial, Memorial Hall 1776-1786, 5-color, 76x82", EX.......950.00
Floral, bird borders, 4-color, sgn Lichty/1848, EX.....................475.00
Floral medallion center, eagle spandrels, 5-color, label 500.00
Floral medallion center, scroll border, 5-color, wear/faded 200.00

Floral medallion on checked bkground, 4-color, wear/faded 200.00
Floral medallions, bird/vintage borders, sgn, 2-pc single 350.00
Floral medallions, dbl-headed eagle border, sgn Lorenz, NM 550.00
Floral medallions, 5-color, sgn P Siebert Easton/1852, VG 395.00
Floral medallions w/strawberries, 4-color, 78x86", NM 650.00
Floral medallions/border, teal/navy/pk/wht, sgn Lorenz, EX.........800.00
Floral sqs/border, sgn Seibert/1853, 2-pc dbl, 74x88", EX 500.00
Floral urns/stars/4 rose medallions, 5-color, sgn/dtd, VG 650.00
Floral/foliage, vintage border, navy/teal/red/wht, NM 525.00
Floral/star medallions, bird border, 4-color, sgn/1842, NM 475.00
Floral/vintage border, 2-tone bl/red/wht, sgn Lorenz/1839 ....800.00
Florals/birds, red/wht, 1-pc dbl, minor stains, 78x88"....................275.00
Lacy foliage, 4-color, 1-pc single, some wear/stains 150.00
Leaf medallions, grapevine border, 4-color, fringed, VG 350.00
Medallions/bird border, 4-color, sgn Lorenz/1841, VG.................200.00
Pineapple/leaf medallions, 72x84" 150.00
Rows of lg flowers on vining stems, red/bl/gr/wht, NM 400.00
Star center, floral/vintage border, red/gr/orange/wht, NM 325.00
Star medallions, bird border, sgn Sheaffer/1839, NM...................760.00
Stars in ovals, 3-color, corners dtd 1863, 1-pc single, EX.............400.00
Stylized floral, rose border, 4-color, sgn Staudt/1842, EX 700.00
Tree/bldg borders, eagle corners, labeled/1868, EX......................600.00

Overshot

Bl sqs w/in red/gr/wht bar & sqs frwork, 72x86" 300.00
Dmns w/in sqs, bl/wht, minor wear, 70x98" 225.00
Intricate optical pattern, pk/blk/natural, wear, 66x82"..................160.00
Optical, 4 bl sqs in wht geometric frwork, fringe added, VG 150.00
Plaid motif, minor moth damage, 85x105" 85.00
Sqs, lines, 9-star sqs, navy/tomato/natural, 71x89", EX................350.00
Unusual design w/sm oval components, navy on wht, 64x96" 345.00
9 red elements form sq w/in wht frwork w/bl corners, VG 180.00

Cowan

Guy Cowan opened a small pottery near Cleveland, Ohio, ca 1912, where he made tile and artware on a small scale from the natural red clay available there. He developed distinctive glazes – necessary, he felt, to cover the dark red body. After the war and a temporary halt in production, Cowan moved his pottery to Rocky River, where he made a commercial line of artware utilizing a highly-fired white porcelain. Although he acquiesced to the necessity of mass-production, every effort was made to insure a product of highest quality. Fine artists, among them Waylande Gregory, Thelma Frazier Winter, and Viktor Schreckengost, molded figurines which were often produced in limited editions, some of which sell today for prices in the thousands. Most of the ware was marked 'Cowan' or 'Lakewood Ware,' not to be confused with the name of the 1927 mass-produced line called 'Lakeware.' Falling under the crunch of the Great Depression, the pottery closed in 1931.

Bookend, horse, turq, 9½" 375.00
Bookends, elephant figurals, Push/Pull, blk, pr............................500.00
Bottle, burnt orange, ribbed, w/stopper, 10½" 125.00
Bowl, console; bl/gr mottled, sea horse ea side, 17" 110.00
Bowl, console; turq, lg...42.00
Bowl, copper lustre, flared top, 4x8" 40.00
Bowl, yel lustre, monogram, #555, 3x5" 65.00
Candle holder, ivory, vine decor, curved, 3-light, pr 68.00
Candle holder, leaping gazelle, caramel gloss, 5¾" 135.00
Candle holder, nude, ivory, 12½", pr..600.00

Candle holder, sea horse, gr, 4", pr 35.00
Candle holder, triple; cream, 3½x7½" 85.00
Cigarette holder, sea horse base, Delft bl 30.00
Compote, pk on ivory, #C838 ....35.00
Decanter, King & Queen, Oriental red, pr.......................... 1,200.00
Decanter, rose, narrow paneled shape, 12" 225.00
Figurine, Spanish Dancer, male & female, mc, pr 750.00
Flower frog, nude, ivory, #698, 6½" 135.00
Hot plate, ivory, fish decor 165.00
Jar, ginger; purple, lustre, w/lid, 5½" 150.00
Lamp, pk lustre, candlestick shape, #L31, 8", pr.......................110.00
Lamp, russet, allover star-shaped flowers, ovoid, 21" 110.00

Plaque, Thunderbird Limited Edition, melon crackle glaze, 15½", $550.00.

Punch bowl, Jazz, bl/blk, sgn Schreckengost, 8" H 15,000.00
Tea set, yel, melon rib, 3-pc, ea w/lid...225.00
Trivet, fish, bl, imp mk, 5½"..250.00
Trivet, floral relief, 5-color, 6-sided, mks 325.00
Vase, bl lustre, Logan Award pc, hdls, #649B 65.00
Vase, bl lustre, pillow form, mk, 8" 75.00
Vase, blk satin, ftd, V-form, 6½" 70.00
Vase, brn crystalline, paneled fan form, 8"..................................60.00
Vase, Chinese bird, bl, fan form, 11½" 475.00
Vase, flying fish decor, silver-gray crystalline on wht, 11"............595.00
Vase, gunmetal irid drip over orange lustre, 13½x7".................400.00
Vase, lav irid over beige, ribbed, trumpet form, 9½".....................90.00
Vase, Oriental red, classic form, 9" 165.00
Vase, Oriental red, cylindrical, 10" 185.00
Vase, Oriental red, mk, 5½"...110.00
Vase, purple, in metal holder, 4" 65.00
Vase, sea horse base, ivory, fan form, 7" 45.00
Vase, sea horse base, turq/gr, unmk, sm......................................35.00

Cracker Jack

Kids have been buying Cracker Jack since it was first introduced in the 1890s. By 1912 it was packaged with a free toy inside. Before the first kernel was crunched, eager fingers had retrieved the surprise from the depth of the box – actually no easy task, considering the care required to keep the contents so swiftly displaced from spilling over the side! Though a little older, perhaps, many of those same kids still are

looking – just as eagerly – for the Cracker Jack prizes. Point of sale, company collectibles, and the prizes as well have over the years reflected America's changing culture. Grocer sales and incentives from around the turn of the century – paper dolls, post cards and song books – were often marked Rueckheim Brothers (the inventors of Cracker Jack) or Reliable Confections. The first loose-packed prizes were toys made of wood, clay, tin, metal, and lithographed paper. Plastic toys were introduced in 1948. Paper wrapped for safety purposes in 1933, subjects echo the 'hype' of the day – Yo-Yos, tops, whistles, and sports cards in the simple, peaceful days of our country, propaganda and war toys in the forties, games in the fifties, and space toys in the sixties. Few of the estimated 15 billion prizes were marked. Advertising items from Angelus Marshmallow and Checkers Confections (cousins of the Cracker Jack family) are also collectible. When no condition is indicated, the items listed below are assumed to be in excellent condition. 'CJ' indicates that the item is marked.

Our advisor for this category is Wes Johnson; he is listed in the Directory under Kentucky.

Cast Metal Prizes

Badge, shield, CJ Jr Detective, silver, 1931, 1¼"............................35.00
Badge, 6-point star, mk CJ Police, silver, 1931, 1¼" 35.00
Button, stud bk, Me for Cracker Jack, boy & dog 18.00
Button, stud bk, Xd bats & ball, CJ pitcher/etc series, 1928..........78.00
Dollhouse items: lantern, mug, candlestick, etc; no mk, ea............ 6.50
Horse & wagon, CJ, 3-D, silver or gold, early, 2½", ea 150.00
Pistol, soft lead, inked, CJ on barrel, early, rare, 2⅛"..................180.00
Rocking horse, no rider, 3-D, inked, early, 1⅛"............................. 7.50
Rocking horse w/boy, 3-D, inked, early, 1½"................................22.00
Tootsie Toy series: boats, cars, animals; ¾"-1½", ea 7.00

Dealer Incentives

Cart w/2 movable wheels, wood dowel tongue, CJ 28.00
Jigsaw puzzle, CJ or Checkers, 1 of 4, 7x10", in envelope 35.00
Magic puzzle, metal, CJ/Angelus, 1 of 15, 1934, ea........................14.00
Mask, Halloween; paper, CJ, 10" or 12", ea...................................15.00
Palm puzzle, mirror bk, CJ, mk Germany/RWB, 1910-14, 1½".......78.00
Post card, bear, 1 of 16, CJ, 1907..22.00

Packaging

Box, popcorn; red scroll border, CJ, ca 1920..................................85.00
Box, popcorn; store display, CJ, 1923, no contents.........................65.00
Canister, tin, CJ Candy Corn Crisp, 10-oz 75.00
Canister, tin, CJ Coconut Corn Crisp, 1-lb 55.00
Canister, tin, CJ Coconut Corn Crisp, 10-oz 65.00
Crate, shipping; wood, CJ, early, lg...150.00

Paper Prizes

Baseball CJ score counter, 3⅜" L..45.00
Book, Animals (or Birds), to color, Makatoy, CJ, 1949, mini.........35.00
Book, Bess & Bill on CJ Hill, series of 12, 1937, mini....................65.00
Book, Birds We Know, CJ, 1928, mini 45.00
Book, drawing w/tracing paper, CJ, 1920s, mini 85.00
Book, Twigg & Sprigg, CJ, 1930, mini...65.00
Booklet, stickers/wise cracks/riddles, Borden, CJ, 1965 on............. 1.00
Decal, cartoon or nursery rhyme figure, 1947-49, CJ.....................26.00
Disguise, ears, red (punch out from carrier), 1950, pr....................20.00
Disguise, glasses, hinged, cellophane lenses, CJ, 1933 ....65.00
Disguise, glasses, hinged, w/eyeballs, 1933 .... 6.00
Disguise, mustache, blk/brn, in carrier, CJ, 1949 ....45.00

Fortune wheel, 2-pc litho, turn for fortune, CJ, 1¾" **43.00**
Game, Midget Auto Race, wheel spins, CJ, 1949, 3⅜" H **20.00**
Game spinner, ...baseball at home, rectangle, CJ, 2¾" W **110.00**
Game spinner, ...baseball at home, unmk, 1946, 1½" dia **40.00**
Hat, fold out, More You Eat/More You Want, CJ, early **55.00**
Magic game book, erasable slate, series of 13, 1946, ea **27.00**
Movie, boy at blkboard, turn wheel: draws/erases, CJ, '31, 2" **55.00**
Movie, Goofy Zoo, turn wheel(s): change animals, 1939 ....**12.00**
Movie, pull tab for 2nd picture, series, CJ, 1943, 1¼", ea **45.00**
Movie, pull tab for 2nd picture, yel, early, 3", in envelope **85.00**
Palm puzzle, ball(s) roll into holes, plastic dome, from 1966 .... **1.00**
Riddle card, 2 series of 20, in pkg/from factory, CJ, ea.....................**7.00**
Sand picture, sand pours for action, series of 14, 1967, ea...............**9.00**
Top, golf game, wood stick center, CJ, 1933 ....**35.00**
Transfer, iron on, sport figure or patriotic, CJ, 1939, ea..................**26.00**

Whistle, Razz Zooka, C. Carey Cloud design, CJ, 1949, $24.00.

Plastic Prizes

Animals, standup, letter on bk, series of 26, Nosco, 1953, ea **3.50**
Animals, standup on base, assorted, Nosco or CJ, 1947 on, ea........ **1.00**
Badge, pin-bk, celluloid, pretty lady, CJ label, 1¼"..........................**35.00**
Baseball players, 3-D, bl or gray team, 1958, 1½", ea.....................**8.00**
Disc, emb comic character, series of 12, 1954, 1½" dia **12.00**
Disc, emb fish plaque, oval, series of 10, 1956, ea...........................**9.00**
Dog, 3-D, hollow base, series of 10, CJCO, 1954, ea **4.50**
Figure, circus; stands on base, 1 of 12, Nosco, 1951-54 .... **1.75**
Figure on rocking base, semi-flat, 1 of 9, Cloud design, '56............. **3.00**
Fob, alphabet letter w/loop on top, 1 of 26, 1954, 1½" **2.25**
Magnifying glass, many designs/shapes, from 1961, ea.................... **1.00**
Pinball game, lever shoots ball/score in holes, 1964 to recent......... **2.00**
Signs, road; Stop, Caution, etc, yel, series of 10, 1954-60, ea.......... **2.50**
Spinner, varied colors, 10 designs, from 1948, ea **1.50**
Toys, take apart/assemble, variety, from '62, assembled, ea.............. **1.00**
Toys, take apart/assemble, variety, from '62, unassembled, ea **2.25**
Whistle, tube w/animals on top, CJ, 1 of 6, 1950-53, 1⅜"............. **8.50**

Premiums

Bat, baseball; wood, Hillerich & Bradsby, CJ, full sz **125.00**
Book, pocket; jester on cover, CJ **40.00**
Book, pocket; riddle/sailor boy/dog on cover, RWB, CJ **30.00**
Harmonica, full scale, emb CJ, early, rare, 5⅛"...........................**185.00**
Recipe book, Angelus, 1930s...**22.00**
Wings, air corps type, silver or blk, stud-bk, CJ, '30s, 3", ea............**42.00**

Tin Prizes

Bank, 3-D book form, red/gr/or blk, CJ Bank, early, 2" **95.00**
Boy & dog, diecut, complete w/bend over tab, CJ........................**110.00**
Boy & dog, diecut, w/o tab at top **65.00**
Clicker, 'Noisy CJ Snapper,' pear shape, aluminum, 1949.............**25.00**
Doll dishes, tin plated, CJ, '31, 1¾", 1⅝", & 2⅛" dia, ea...............**25.00**
Fortune Wheel, 2-pc litho, CJ, 1939-41, 1¾".................................**37.00**
Helicopter, yel propellor, wood stick, 1937, 2⅝"........................... **9.00**
Horse & wagon, litho diecut, CJ & Angelus, 2⅛" **35.00**
Horse & wagon, litho diecut, gray/red mks, CJ, 1914-23, 3⅛" **250.00**
Model T Ford, License: NY 1915 #999, blk/wht, CJ, rare, 2".......**350.00**
Oval stand up, Am flag, 1 of 4, unmk, 1936-46 .... **9.00**
Oval stand up, comic character, 1 of 10, CJ, 1936-46....................**65.00**
Pocket watch, silver of gold, CJ as numerals, 1931, 1½".................**35.00**
Sled, tin plated, CJ, 1931, 2" L..**20.00**
Soldier, litho, die-cut standup, officer/private/etc, 1939, ea **17.00**
Tall box shape: 'Frozen Foods' locker freezer, 1947, 1¾"...............**48.00**
Tall box shape: 'Refrigerator Car, CJ 2006,' 1947, 1¾" L **65.00**
Tall box shape: grandfather clock, unmk, 1947, 1¾" **35.00**
Tall box shape: radio, tune in w/CJ, brn/yel, 1939, 1¾" **95.00**
Toonerville Trolly, litho engine/coach, 2-pc, 1941, 2⅜" L.............**17.00**
Wagon shape: Caterpillar tractor, unmk, 1931, 1¾" L....................**25.00**
Wagon shape: CJ Shows Circus, 1947...**95.00**
Wagon shape: Playtime Trailer (auto trailer), unmk, 1947.............**20.00**
Wagon shape: tank, orange/red/gr camouflage.................................**65.00**
Wagon shape: Tank Corps No 57, gr & blk, 1941 ....**20.00**
Wheelbarrow, tin plated, bk leg in place, 1931, 2½" L.....................**22.00**

Miscellaneous

Ad, comic book, CJ, ea.. **9.00**
Ad, Saturday Evening Post, mc, 1919, 11x14"..................................**18.00**
Hat, ball park vendor cap, 1930s..**25.00**
Sign, bathing beauty, 5-color cb, CJ, early, 17x22".......................**150.00**
Sign, boy or girl w/box of CJ, 5-color cb, early, 17x22", ea...........**150.00**
Sign, Jack & Bingo, die-cut litho, easel standup, CJ, early...........**135.00**
Sign, Santa & prizes, mc cb, CJ or Angelus, early, lg **110.00**

Crackle Glass

    Crackle glass (or craquelle) was made during the 1800s in America as well as abroad. The name is derived from the texture of the ware, achieved by first plunging the hot glass into cold water, then reheating and reblowing the vessel, thereby producing ware with a crackled appearance.

Cruet, lt bl w/HP floral, 7" **175.00**
Pitcher, cranberry, appl hdl, 7" **125.00**
Pitcher, med gr, clear hdl, 5"..**20.00**
Pitcher, water; clear, w/lid..**55.00**
Tumbler, ruby w/HP floral, 4" **40.00**
Vase, cranberry flashed, clear base, braided stem, ftd, 10"..............**50.00**

Cranberry

    Cranberry glass is named for its resemblance to the color of cranberry juice. It was made by many companies both here and abroad, becoming popular in America soon after the Civil War. It was made in free-blown ware as well as mold-blown. Today, cranberry glass is being reproduced, and it is sometimes difficult to distinguish the old from the new. Ask a reputable dealer if you are unsure. See also Cruets; Salts; Sugar Shakers; Syrups.

Bell, wht edging, clear hdl w/cranberry finial, 15" 200.00
Biscuit jar, gold-traced ivy, gilt mts w/emb ivy.............................300.00
Box, florals & foliage, hinged lid, 2⅝x4⅛" dia 225.00
Box, forget-me-nots & scrolls, ormolu mts, sq, 4½" 275.00
Box, gold bands & flowers, 3½x3½" dia 225.00
Box, gold bands w/yel florals, lift-off lid, 1¾x2¾" 110.00
Box, patch; lacy brass filigree allover, 1x2" dia 135.00
Creamer, appl amber flower w/stem as hdl, 4¾" 100.00
Decanter, florals, 7¾x3¼", +4 1⅝" mugs, +8" tray 265.00
Decanter, Invt T'print, waisted, Mt WA, 11½" 375.00
Decanter, wine; rtcl pewter band/hdl/ft, cut stopper, 16" 395.00
Lemonade set, Invt T'print, pitcher+6 tumblers 150.00
Pipe whimsey, 2-part, 21" L 130.00
Pitcher, florals & garlands w/gold, bulbous, 3½x2⅝" 75.00
Pitcher, florals w/gold leaves & branches, 6½x3" 80.00
Pitcher, Invt T'print, clear rope hdl about neck, 6"..................100.00
Pitcher, Invt T'print, daisies/wheat, sq hdl, water sz................200.00
Tumbler, Baby Invt T'print, mc floral 40.00
Vase, berries/birds, heavy enamel, slim form, 16", pr 600.00
Vase, bl/wht flowers w/gold, 3x1⅛" 69.00
Vase, clear rigaree, clear stem, 9¼x4 " 175.00
Vase, clear ruffled rim, 3 clear leaf ft, 4½x3" 65.00
Vase, daisies, 9x3½", pr...245.00
Vase, emb Fleurette pattern, petal top, 4½x3¾", pr 165.00
Vase, florals, gold berries, appl shell trim, 13x5¼" 225.00
Vase, florals w/gold, sm wht tassels, 4¾x3" 60.00
Vase, grapes/leaves, wht scallops, gold ft, 5¾x3", pr.................225.00
Vase, sanded gold scrolls, florals, 3½x2½" 55.00
Wine, gold leaves, clear stem, 5x2⅝" 55.00

Creamware

Creamware was a type of earthenware developed by Wedgwood in the 1760s and produced by many other Staffordshire potteries, including Leeds. Since it could be potted cheaply and was light in weight, it became popular abroad as well as in England, due to the lower freight charges involved in its export. It was revived at Leeds in the late nineteenth century, and the type most often reproduced was heavily reticulated or molded in high relief. These later wares are easily distinguished from the originals since they are thicker and tend to craze heavily. See also Leeds.

Puzzle jug, impressed verse 'gentlemen come try your skill...,' Leeds mark, 6¾", $400.00; Tea caddy, modeled bust of George III, back: Queen Charlotte, 5¾", EX condition, $400.00.

Chestnut basket, rtcl, Mayer, 11" L, +insert/lid/tray, VG 4,600.00
Coffeepot, brn/bl granite w/wht bands, dog finial, rpr, 10"...........700.00
Creamer, gr feather edge, 4" 35.00
Mug, child's, May Success Attend Our Agriculture..., NM...........550.00
Pepper pot, bl feather edge, HP star on top, 4½", NM................90.00
Pepper pot, 3-leaf clover & flowers, maroon band, 4", EX 75.00
Plate, fluted shoulders, rtcl rim, mk Leeds, 9", VG....................100.00
Plate, leaf & acorn border, mk Spode #15, 10" 50.00
Platter, bl feather edge, T Mayer, 1830s, 17½", EX 80.00
Sweetmeat, bird finial above 4-leaf tray, rtcl sq base, 4" 150.00
Sweetmeat, lady sits above 2 5-shell tiers, Leeds type, 10"...........600.00
Tea set, heron, mc in brn circle, 8-pc, miniature, EX 2,900.00
Teapot, mc florals, plain hdl, emb flower finial, 4½" 700.00
Teapot, mc florals, rope hdl, appl flower finial, 4⅝" 750.00
Teapot, ribbed, rope hdl w/floral ends, dome lid, 9", EX 800.00
Urn, rtcl ½-fluted body, rtcl lid/base band, rpr, 11", pr 1,300.00

Credit Cards and Charge Coins

Charge coins were first issued in the 1890s with some stores continuing to use them as late as 1959. Coins were issued in various shapes and sizes. Some, from clothing stores, came in shapes such as shirts, socks, or hats. Coins were made of different materials such as copper, brass, German silver, steel, fiber, and celluloid. All coins have the store's name or monogram along with a number for indentification. None ever had the name of the individual to whom the coin was issued. When making a purchase, the salesperson would check a master list to compare the number of the coin and the name of the person presenting the coin to see if they matched. If they didn't, the coin would be confiscated until the rightful owner could be located. Most coins had holes so they could be put on a key chain. Often ladies wore their coins on necklaces as a status symbol.

In the 1930s, stores began using the metal charge plates. These plates looked like military dog tags. The front of the plate, in raised letters, contained the person's name, address, and account number. The back had a cardboard mount where the cardholder could sign his name. Metal plates were generally discontinued in the 1950s.

Paper credit cards were used in the early 1900s, but it was not until the 1940s that they began to be more common. By the early 1950s, they were being issued by many companies. Because paper was easily worn and damaged through everyday use, a clear plastic laminate was eventually added. By the late 1950s, companies began using the plastic credit card we know today.

Our advisor for this category is Greg Tunks; he is listed in the Directory under Texas.

Cards

American Express, violet on wht...60.00
BankAmericard, 1970s.. 6.00
Bell System, paperboard, 1965 .... 5.00
Diners' Club, 1964...55.00
Frederick's of Hollywood 15.00
Hilton, paperboard, 1958...15.00
Hotel Roosevelt, paper, calendar on bk, 1946............................15.00
Lit Brothers, metal w/case...16.00
Master Charge, 1970s 6.00
MasterCard, pre-hologram, 1980s 3.00
Midwest Bank Card, 1960s..15.00
Mobilgas, paperboard, 1951..65.00
Pan Am Take Off Card, 1971..12.00
Pure Oil, red firebird on top, 1965 ....10.00

Sinclair, paperboard, 1942................................115.00
Standard Oil, 1967 ....12.00
Texaco, paperboard, 1957..............................60.00
TWA, swim-suited couple, 1975 ....7.00
Visa, pre-hologram, 1980s 3.00

Gulf Travel card, land, sea, and air, $8.00.

Charge Coins

Filene's, Boston 15.00
Hilton Hotels 20.00
Lit Brothers, Philadelphia...............................10.00
Neill, Philadelphia..10.00
Partridge Company, Boston 10.00
Plotkin Brothers, Boston 10.00

Crown Milano

Crown Milano was introduced in 1884 by the Mt. Washington Glass Company. When the company merged with Pairpoint in 1894, it continued to be one of their best sellers. It is an opaque, highly-decorated ware with gold or colored enamels in intricate designs on pale backgrounds. Many pieces were marked 'CM' with a crown. Since it is nearly always found in a satin finish, in the listings that follow, satin is assumed unless glossy is indicated.

Our advisors for this category are Betty and Clarence Maier; they are listed in the Directory under Pennsylvania.

Biscuit jar, apple blossoms on peach, lid mk P in dmn, 7" 650.00
Biscuit jar, bamboo, gold & brn on burmese color, 6" 1,150.00
Biscuit jar, beaded floral/gilt/peach shadow leaves, ribbed 500.00
Biscuit jar, Colonial children/gold scrolls, mk Mt WA lid 1,200.00
Biscuit jar, floral/gold scrolls, opal to tan, acorn finial 1,000.00
Biscuit jar, leaves/vines, gold on cream, sq, SP mts, label 1,000.00
Biscuit jar, oak leaves/acorns/gilt on burmese color, 8" 450.00
Bottle, scent; violets on wht base, pk at neck, 9½" 550.00
Bowl, daisies on cream, beaded top, 4½x5" 345.00
Bowl vase, thistles, gold-traced on amber leaves, 4½" 800.00
Bride's basket, pansies, crimped; ornate base w/3 ft, 12½" 2,100.00
Ewer, cherubs/gilt floral, gold twist hdl, dome lid, 19" 4,500.00
Jar, florals, gold scrolls, appl scroll hdls, mk, 8½x5" 1,300.00
Jar, gilt roses on bl/wht 'ribbons,' turtle finial, 5"....................475.00
Jar, swirled pinwheels on yel/wht 'ribbons,' turtle finial..............400.00
Jardiniere, autumn leaves, gold-lined on cream, 6x7" dia 425.00
Lamp base, asters on squat ribbed form, orig fittings, 11"..........650.00

Mustard, emb/HP florals on opal, SP hdl & mk lid, 3"................215.00
Mustard, pansies on burmese color, melon shape, SP hdl, 3¼" 425.00
Sweetmeat, emb tan swirls/gold-lined leaves, emb SP top, 4"......300.00
Sweetmeat, floral, emb X-bars, hallmk lid, 3¾" 800.00
Sweetmeat, forget-me-nots, emb X-bars, lid mk: Sant Co Epns...325.00
Sweetmeat, jeweled starfish on gold star-texture, 4x6" 1,050.00
Sweetmeat, jeweled starfish on lt pk w/emb X-bars, 4x6" 800.00
Sweetmeat, oak leaves, gold-lined on lt gold Dia Quilt, 5" 600.00
Syrup, oak leaves/acorns on ribbed burmese color, 6" 1,000.00
Vase, bats, gold scrolls/etc, bulbous w/tri-lobe top, 15" 1,750.00
Vase, beaded floral/gold leaves/etc, spiral neck, hdls, 12"........2,750.00
Vase, cactus/floral, mc/gold on swirls, 4-lobe rim, 7x7" 1,200.00
Vase, children/flowers in gray on wht, gray 4-lobe rim, 10" 500.00
Vase, cupid reserve on gilt scrolls, extended rim hdls, 9"...........1,000.00
Vase, florals, mc/gold, lav shadow leaves, scroll hdls, 10" 1,300.00
Vase, gold rose bouquets on gold-tan 'shadows,' 14x9" 1,475.00
Vase, lg mums w/gold on lt gold, sm neck/4-lobe top, 13½" 2,300.00
Vase, mc pansies w/gold, 3 leaf hdls, triangular, 8" 1,870.00
Vase, oak leaves/acorns, gold-lined on cream, 9" 375.00
Vase, pk flamingos/palm fronds, cup-shape top, hdls, 9½".......1,500.00
Vase, roses, gold scrolls, leaf hdls, 5x6½" 955.00
Vase, thistles, gr/purple w/gold tracing, pk/gr leaves, 10" 1,475.00
Vase, Venetian gondola scene/gold scrolls, hdls, 16" 2,600.00
Vase, wild roses, gold on cream, stick neck, 12x8".....................650.00

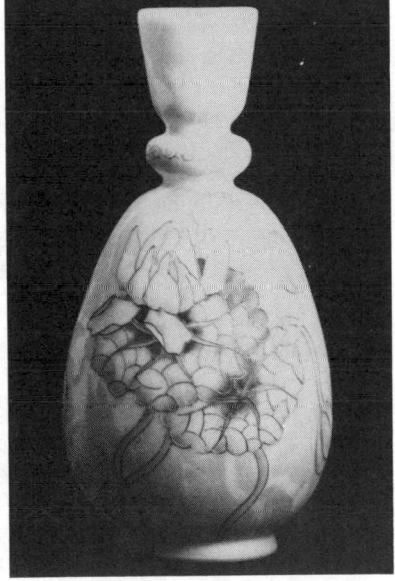

Vase, water lilies and gold tracing on cream, no mark, 9½", $950.00.

Cruets

Cruets, containers made to hold oil or vinegar, are usually bulbous with tall narrow throats and a stopper. During the nineteenth century and for several years after, they were produced in abundance in virtually every type of glassware available. Those listed below are assumed to be with stopper and mint unless noted otherwise.

Alaska, gr w/wht leaves 200.00
Alaska, vaseline opal, clear faceted stopper...............................250.00
Amazon, amethyst, matching hand-&-bar stopper 170.00
Amber, bl hdl & stopper, sq bulbous form, 3-petal top, 7¾" 135.00
Amberina, swirled, amber bulbous stopper 300.00
Argonaut Shell, clear opal, paneled stopper 150.00
Bag Ware, amber, amber pressed-stars stopper 70.00
Beaded Circle, apple gr w/mc flowers, faceted stopper 145.00

Beaded Oval, gr, matching stopper 175.00
Beaded Swag, etched, ruby stain w/EX gold 195.00
Beaded Swag, milk glass w/cornflowers, milk glass stopper 135.00
Big Button, amber & clear, faceted stopper 105.00
Big Button, ruby flashed & clear, flashed/faceted stopper ...125.00
Blocked T'print, ruby flashed/enamel band, cut stopper 125.00
Bubble Lattice, bl satin, pressed faceted stopper 235.00
Bulbous Base Optic, cranberry, cut faceted stopper 160.00
Bulging Loops, bl, clear faceted stopper, rare 300.00
Cased wht w/pk liner, HP rosebud, cut faceted stopper 135.00
Champion (Fans & Crossbar), clear & ruby flashed 170.00
Circled Scroll, gr opal, faceted stopper, rare 450.00
Clear, gold/etched vintage, ftd, etched stopper 70.00
Co-Op Block, ruby stained & clear, cut faceted stopper 130.00
Column Block, bl, matching design stopper 140.00
Cone, bl satin, clear faceted stopper 225.00
Cone, pk overlay, cut faceted stopper 225.00
Cord Drapery, amber, 5½" 325.00
Cord Drapery, bl, 5½" 650.00
Cranberry, clear twisted rope hdl, star cut base, 8⅞" 145.00
Criss-Cross Consolidated, cranberry, very rare 650.00
Daisy & Button, amber-stained panel, rare 250.00
Daisy & Button w/Crossbar, amber, lg amber faceted stopper 115.00
Daisy & Fern, Apple Blossom mold, wht opal, clear stopper 115.00
Dewey, gr, matching stopper 195.00
Dewey, vaseline, matching stopper 135.00
Dia Quilt, amberina w/berries, amber reeded hdl, 6½" 290.00
Dia Quilt MOP, bl, cut faceted stopper 550.00
Dia Quilt MOP, lemon satin, cut faceted stopper 600.00
Dia Quilt MOP, wht, faceted stopper 500.00
Dice & Block, bl, matching design stopper 115.00
Esther, emerald gr, matching stopper, lg......................250.00
Everglades, bl opal, step-paneled clear stopper, rare 435.00
Everglades, clear opal, clear faceted stopper 205.00
Everglades, vaseline opal, clear faceted stopper 400.00
Famous, apple gr, matching pressed stopper..................195.00
Feather, emerald gr, gr faceted stopper 300.00
Fern, cranberry opal, clear hdl & faceted stopper 350.00
Florida (Emerald Green Herringbone), matching stopper 110.00
Geneva, custard..400.00
Herringbone Buttress, emerald gr, gr stopper, rare 400.00
Hobnail, canary opal, matching faceted stopper.............250.00
Idyll, gr, pressed stopper..150.00
Intaglio, custard w/gr stain, custard stopper 350.00
Invt Fan & Feather, custard, custard stopper 675.00
Invt T'print, amber w/wht flowers, sq w/pinched sides 140.00
Invt T'print, amberina w/forget-me-nots, amber stopper 515.00
Invt T'print, cranberry w/mc flowers, cut faceted stopper 350.00
Invt T'print, cranberry/wht spatter, matching stopper 150.00
Invt T'print, peacock bl w/flowers, cut faceted stopper 190.00
Iris w/Meander, bl opal, clear paneled stopper...............400.00
Jackson, bl opal...165.00
Jeweled Heart, apple gr, matching ribbed stopper...........195.00
Kings 500, cobalt, matching swirl stopper, very rare.........600.00
Leaf Mold, cranberry satin spatter, clear cut stopper 350.00
Leaf Mold, vaseline spatter, matching faceted stopper 345.00
Leaf Umbrella, bl overlay, very rare, 6½" 595.00
Leaf Umbrella, cranberry, cut stopper, very rare 575.00
Leaf Umbrella, Rose DuBarry overlay, faceted stopper, rare 550.00
Leaf Umbrella, topaz overlay, clear hdl, cut stopper, rare 535.00
Louis XV, custard, faceted stopper 235.00
Louis XV, emerald gr, EX gold 255.00
Majestic, ruby stained, pressed faceted stopper 145.00
Mary Gregory, clear 135.00

Medallion Sprig, amethyst, amethyst stopper................235.00
Medallion Sprig, bl, cut faceted stopper......................275.00
Medallion Sprig, cranberry, cut faceted stopper.............325.00
Millard, ruby flashed/clear, pressed stopper.................165.00
Nester, apple gr, clear faceted stopper 175.00
Netted Oak, milk glass w/pk & gr leaves, matching stopper 150.00
Palm Beach, red grapes/gr leaves on clear, clear stopper.....125.00
Peacock bl, mc florals, ribbed, amber hdl & stopper 160.00
Pioneer, amber satin, matching stopper......................150.00
Pleat & Panel, apple gr, matching acorn stopper, Heisey.....100.00
Radiant Daisy, clear w/amber stain 175.00
Radiant Daisy, frosted w/amber stain 175.00
Regal, gr opal, 6"...200.00
Reverse Swirl, vaseline opal 175.00
Ribbed Drape, custard w/HP rose, very rare.................400.00
Ribbed Opal Lattice, clear opal, cut stopper.................135.00
Ribbed Opal Lattice, cranberry 350.00
Ribbed Pillar, pk/wht satin spatter, ribbed satin stopper 225.00
Satina Swirl, amber overlay, cut amber stopper, rare........450.00
Satina Swirl, bl, cut bl stopper, very rare 550.00
Scroll w/Acanthus, bl opal, paneled stopper.................185.00
Seaweed, cranberry opal, clear hdl & faceted stopper 425.00
Spatter, pk cased, cut faceted stopper.......................135.00
Spatter, pk/gr/wht, swirl overlay, cut faceted stopper.......175.00
Stars & Bars, bl, hobstar block stopper.......................100.00
Stars & Stripes, cranberry opal...............................375.00
Sunk Honeycomb, ruby stained, pointed/paneled stopper, sm 115.00
Swag w/Brackets, amber opal, matching stopper 160.00
Swag w/Brackets, amethyst, matching stopper 175.00
Swirl, cranberry opal, clear hdl & faceted stopper...........275.00
Tiny Optic, amethyst w/floral, cut faceted teardrop stopper.........90.00
Tokyo, apple gr, clear paneled stopper 130.00
Tortoise Shell, swirled, dk amber stopper 325.00
Truncated Cube, ruby flashed & clear, pressed cube stopper........135.00
US Rib, emerald gr, matching ribbed stopper...............115.00
Vesta, amber, amber stopper..................................150.00
Wild Bouquet, bl opal 325.00
Wild Bouquet, custard, faceted custard stopper, very rare 650.00
Winged Scroll, emerald gr, cut faceted stopper..............300.00
Zipper Diamond, clear hdl/faceted stopper 50.00

Windows, cranberry opalescent, cut stopper, 6¾", $375.00.

Cup Plates, Glass

Before the middle 1850s, it was socially acceptable to pour hot tea into a deep saucer to cool. The tea was sipped from the saucer rather than the cup, which frequently was handleless and too hot to hold. The cup plate served as a coaster for the cup. It is generally agreed that the first examples of pressed glass cup plates were made about 1826 at the Boston and Sandwich Glass Co. in Sandwich, Cape Cod, Massachusetts. Other glassworks in three major areas – New England, Philadelphia, and the Midwest (especially Pittsburgh) – quickly followed suit.

Antique glass cup plates range in size from 2⅝" up to 4¼" in diameter. The earliest plates had simple designs inspired by cut glass patterns, but by 1829 they had become more complex. The span from then until about 1845 is known as the 'Lacy Period,' when cup plate designs and pressing techniques were at their peak. To cover pressing imperfections, the backgrounds of the plates were often covered with fine stippling which endowed them with a glittering brilliance called 'laciness.' They were made in a multitude of designs – some purely decorative, others commemorative. Subjects include the American eagle, hearts, sunbursts, log cabins, ships, George Washington, the political candidates Clay and Harrison, plows, beehives, etc. Of all the patterns, the round George Washington plate is the rarest and most valuable – only three are known to exist today.

Authenticity is most important. Collectors must be aware that contemporary plates which have no antique counterparts and fakes modeled after antique patterns have had wide distribution. Condition is also important, though it is the exceptional plate that does not have some rim roughness. More important considerations are scarcity of design and color.

Our advisor for this category is John Bilane; he is listed in the Directory under New Jersey. The book *American Glass* by George and Helen McKearin has a section on glass cup plates. A more definitive book is *American Glass Cup Plates*, by Ruth Webb Lee and James H. Rose. Numbers in the listings that follow (computer sorted) refer to the latter. When no condition is indicated, the examples listed below are assumed to have only minor rim roughness as is normal. See also Staffordshire; Pairpoint.

R-101, scarce, G	35.00
R-101, scarce, VG	52.00
R-102, scarce, VG	50.00
R-104, G	26.00
R-105, scarce, VG	48.00
R-107, rare, VG	68.00
R-124, VG	36.00
R-124A, VG	36.00
R-13C, G	28.00
R-145, G	22.00
R-147, scarce, VG	40.00
R-147A, scarce, VG	40.00
R-148, VG	32.00
R-149, VG	29.00
R-154, EX	37.00
R-154B, EX	37.00
R-158B, scarce, VG	44.00
R-159, VG	29.00
R-162, VG	33.00
R-172A, EX	37.00
R-172B, EX	37.00
R-176A, VG	30.00
R-176B, VG	32.00
R-179A, rare, EX	77.00

R-203, scarce, G	35.00
R-216, VG	65.00
R-217A, VG	67.00
R-22, VG	28.00
R-226C, VG	28.00
R-229A, rare, G	64.00
R-229B, scarce, VG	44.00
R-235, G	22.00
R-236, G	32.00
R-242A, VG	34.00
R-243, bl opal, scarce, VG	140.00
R-243, VG	36.00
R-246, VG	34.00
R-247, med gr, att Sandwich, NM	350.00
R-255A, scarce, VG	35.00
R-257A, VG	32.00
R-268, G	28.00
R-269, VG	30.00
R-27, G	24.00
R-272, VG	30.00
R-275, VG	38.00
R-277, scarce, VG	48.00
R-279, VG	34.00
R-28, G	19.00
R-291, G	22.00
R-293, scarce, G	42.00
R-311, G	17.00
R-322, VG	19.00
R-323, bl opal, VG	38.00
R-324, bl opal, EX	36.00
R-328, VG	21.00
R-333, G	15.00
R-334, G	16.00
R-340, G	15.00
R-37, scarce, VG	42.00
R-376, VG	15.00
R-38, VG	28.00
R-391, EX	14.50
R-393, G	10.00
R-402, VG	14.00
R-439C, peacock bl, att Sandwich, NM	200.00
R-441, G	34.00
R-441A, VG	32.00
R-444, EX	41.00
R-447, VG	26.00
R-458, scarce, VG	28.00
R-46, lav, NM	300.00
R-46, VG	27.00

R-465E, opalescent, EX condition, $65.00; R-222, moonstone, M condition, $450.00.

R-465F, G 16.00
R-465L, VG 19.00
R-465O, G 18.00
R-467A, G 17.00
R-476, VG 19.00
R-479, G 15.00
R-49, G 26.00
R-500, very rare, G 40.00
R-500, very rare, VG 48.00
R-501, G 11.00
R-509, G 9.00
R-52, scarce, G 36.00
R-522, red-amber, att Sandwich, NM 120.00
R-526A, VG 21.00
R-53, scarce, G 46.00
R-531, VG 25.00
R-537, G 12.00
R-538, scarce, VG 28.00
R-546, bl, sunburst, VG 50.00
R-561, Washington, octagonal, Midwestern, NM 3,700.00
R-562, very rare, G 325.00
R-562A, very rare, G 325.00
R-564, VG 28.00
R-565, G 28.00
R-565A, VG 30.00
R-566B, rare, VG 70.00
R-575, scarce, EX 75.00
R-592, extremely rare, VG 265.00
R-593, scarce, G 38.00
R-605, scarce, VG 135.00
R-605A, scarce, G 95.00
R-605A, scarce, VG 135.00
R-610D, G 35.00
R-612, rare, VG 255.00
R-612A, rare, VG 255.00
R-619, VG 40.00
R-619B, rare, G 98.00
R-624A, VG 65.00
R-628, scarce, VG 60.00
R-632, VG 45.00
R-640, G 18.00
R-641, G 14.00
R-642, G 18.00
R-643A, G 20.00
R-643A, VG 23.00
R-65, scarce, EX 50.00
R-654A, very rare, G 225.00
R-662, G 31.00
R-665A, G 32.00
R-666, G 30.00
R-666, VG 36.00
R-670, scarce, G 47.00
R-670A, G 30.00
R-676C, scarce, G 49.00
R-676C, scarce, VG 55.00
R-679, VG 30.00
R-680B, VG 35.00
R-691, scarce, VG 80.00
R-693, scarce, VG 55.00
R-695, G 36.00
R-76, scarce, VG 55.00
R-78, scarce, G 48.00
R-891, G 10.00
R-95, opal opaque, rare, VG 150.00

R-97, scarce, VG 48.00
R-98, rare, VG 70.00

Custard

As early as the 1880s, custard glass was produced in England. Migrating glassmakers brought the formula for the creamy ivory ware to America. One of them was Harry Northwood, who in 1898 founded his company in Indiana, Pennsylvania, and introduced the glassware to the American market. Soon other companies were producing custard, among them Heisey, Tarentum, Fenton, and McKee. Not only dinnerware patterns but souvenir items were made. Today, custard is the most expensive of the colored pressed glassware patterns. The formula for producing the luminous glass contains uranium salts which imparts the cream color to the batch and causes it to glow when it is examined under a black light.

Argonaut Shell, bowl, master berry; gold & decor, 10½" L 225.00
Argonaut Shell, butter dish, gold & decor 300.00
Argonaut Shell, butter dish, no gold.......................................245.00
Argonaut Shell, compote, jelly; gold & decor, scarce................135.00
Argonaut Shell, creamer 110.00
Argonaut Shell, creamer, gold & decor 125.00
Argonaut Shell, cruet, gold & decor 450.00
Argonaut Shell, pitcher, water; gold & decor 335.00
Argonaut Shell, sauce, ftd, gold & decor 65.00
Argonaut Shell, spooner, gold & decor 115.00
Argonaut Shell, sugar bowl, w/lid, gold & decor 160.00
Argonaut Shell, tumbler, gold & decor 85.00
Bead Swag, goblet, floral & gold 60.00
Bead Swag, sauce, floral & gold...45.00
Bead Swag, tray, pickle; floral & gold, rare 260.00
Bead Swag, wine, floral & gold..58.00
Beaded Circle, bowl, master berry; floral & gold 225.00
Beaded Circle, butter dish, floral & gold 325.00
Beaded Circle, creamer, floral & gold 135.00
Beaded Circle, cruet, floral & gold, rare 750.00
Beaded Circle, pitcher, water; floral & gold..............................495.00
Beaded Circle, shakers, floral & gold, pr 250.00
Beaded Circle, spooner, floral & gold 135.00
Beaded Circle, sugar bowl, w/lid, floral & gold.........................200.00
Beaded Circle, tumbler, floral & gold, very rare 100.00
Cane Insert, berry set, 7-pc...365.00
Cane Insert, table set, 4-pc...425.00
Cherry & Scales, bowl, master berry; nutmeg stain 130.00
Cherry & Scales, butter dish, nutmeg stain 225.00
Cherry & Scales, creamer, nutmeg stain 115.00
Cherry & Scales, pitcher, water; nutmeg stain, scarce 325.00
Cherry & Scales, spooner, nutmeg stain, scarce..........................85.00
Cherry & Scales, sugar bowl, w/lid, nutmeg stain, scarce...........125.00
Cherry & Scales, tumbler, nutmeg stain, scarce..........................50.00
Chrysanthemum Sprig, bowl, master berry; gold & decor 225.00
Chrysanthemum Sprig, bowl, master berry; no gold...................175.00
Chrysanthemum Sprig, butter dish, gold & decor 250.00
Chrysanthemum Sprig, celery vase, gold & decor, rare 850.00
Chrysanthemum Sprig, compote, jelly; gold & decor 115.00
Chrysanthemum Sprig, compote, jelly; no decor 75.00
Chrysanthemum Sprig, condiment: shakers/t'pick/cruet/base .. 1,250.00
Chrysanthemum Sprig, creamer, gold & decor...........................105.00
Chrysanthemum Sprig, cruet, gold & decor, 6¾" 290.00
Chrysanthemum Sprig, pitcher, water; gold & decor 425.00
Chrysanthemum Sprig, sauce, ftd, gold & decor 50.00
Chrysanthemum Sprig, shakers, gold & decor, pr.......................225.00

Chrysanthemum Sprig, spooner, gold & decor 105.00
Chrysanthemum Sprig, spooner, no gold 70.00
Chrysanthemum Sprig, toothpick holder, gold & decor..............275.00
Chrysanthemum Sprig, toothpick holder, no decor.....................165.00
Chrysanthemum Sprig, tumbler, gold & decor 55.00
Dandelion, mug, nutmeg stain 165.00
Delaware, creamer, breakfast; pk stain.................................70.00
Delaware, sauce, pk stain 65.00
Delaware, tray, pin; gr stain 75.00
Delaware, tumbler, pk stain 55.00
Diamond w/Peg, bowl, master berry; roses & gold.....................215.00
Diamond w/Peg, butter dish, roses & gold 200.00
Diamond w/Peg, creamer, ind; souvenir 45.00
Diamond w/Peg, creamer, roses & gold 75.00
Diamond w/Peg, mug, souvenir 50.00
Diamond w/Peg, napkin ring, roses & gold, rare.........................150.00
Diamond w/Peg, pitcher, 5½" 175.00
Diamond w/Peg, sauce, roses & gold 40.00
Diamond w/Peg, shakers, souvenir, pr 135.00
Diamond w/Peg, sugar bowl, w/lid, roses & gold........................160.00
Diamond w/Peg, toothpick holder, roses & gold.........................90.00
Diamond w/Peg, tumbler, roses & gold 50.00
Diamond w/Peg, water set, souvenir, 7-pc................................500.00
Diamond w/Peg, wine, roses & gold 55.00
Diamond w/Peg, wine, souvenir 40.00
Everglades, bowl, master berry; gold & decor 215.00
Everglades, butter dish, gold & decor......................................365.00
Everglades, creamer, gold & decor 145.00
Everglades, sauce, gold & decor..60.00
Everglades, shakers, gold & decor, pr 325.00
Everglades, spooner, gold & decor 130.00
Everglades, sugar bowl, w/lid, gold & decor 175.00
Everglades, tumbler, gold & decor 100.00
Fan, bowl, master berry; good gold 185.00
Fan, butter dish, good gold 210.00
Fan, creamer, good gold...110.00
Fan, ice cream set, good gold, 7-pc...500.00
Fan, pitcher, water; good gold...275.00
Fan, sauce, good gold 55.00
Fan, spooner, good gold 95.00
Fan, sugar bowl, w/lid, good gold 135.00
Fan, tumbler, good gold 75.00
Fan, water set, good gold, 7-pc 700.00
Fine Cut & Roses, rose bowl, fancy int, nutmeg stain..................100.00
Fine Cut & Roses, rose bowl, plain int.....................................85.00
Geneva, bowl, master berry; floral decor, ftd, oval, 8½"L.............90.00
Geneva, bowl, master berry; floral decor, rnd, 9" 120.00
Geneva, butter dish, floral decor 175.00
Geneva, butter dish, no decor 125.00
Geneva, compote, jelly; floral decor...85.00
Geneva, creamer, floral decor 90.00
Geneva, cruet, floral decor 325.00
Geneva, pitcher, water; floral decor 225.00
Geneva, sauce, floral decor, oval 45.00
Geneva, sauce, floral decor, rnd..45.00
Geneva, shakers, floral decor, pr 175.00
Geneva, spooner, floral decor 85.00
Geneva, sugar bowl, open, floral decor.....................................75.00
Geneva, sugar bowl, w/lid, floral decor 135.00
Geneva, syrup, floral decor..350.00
Geneva, toothpick holder, floral w/M gold 175.00
Geneva, tumbler, floral decor 50.00
Georgia Gem, bowl, master berry; good gold 115.00
Georgia Gem, bowl, master berry; gr opaque 90.00

Georgia Gem, butter dish, good gold 190.00
Georgia Gem, celery vase, good gold 145.00
Georgia Gem, creamer, good gold 75.00
Georgia Gem, creamer, no gold 50.00
Georgia Gem, mug, good gold 45.00
Georgia Gem, powder jar, w/lid, good gold 60.00
Georgia Gem, shakers, good gold, pr..95.00
Georgia Gem, spooner, souvenir 55.00
Georgia Gem, sugar bowl, w/lid, no gold 60.00
Grape (& Cable), bottle, scent; orig stopper, nutmeg stain 525.00
Grape (& Cable), bowl, master berry; nutmeg stain, ftd, 11".......265.00
Grape (& Cable), bowl, nutmeg stain, 7½" 50.00
Grape (& Cable), butter dish, nutmeg stain..............................235.00
Grape (& Cable), compote, jelly; open, nutmeg stain....................95.00
Grape (& Cable), compote, nutmeg stain, 4½x8" 250.00
Grape (& Cable), cracker jar, nutmeg stain 600.00
Grape (& Cable), creamer, breakfast; nutmeg stain 75.00
Grape (& Cable), humidor, bl stain, rare...................................600.00
Grape (& Cable), humidor, nutmeg stain, rare 650.00
Grape (& Cable), nappy, nutmeg stain, rare...............................45.00
Grape (& Cable), pitcher, water; nutmeg stain 375.00
Grape (& Cable), plate, nutmeg stain, 8" 55.00
Grape (& Cable), powder jar, nutmeg stain 300.00
Grape (& Cable), punch bowl, w/base, nutmeg stain 1,000.00
Grape (& Cable), sauce, nutmeg stain, ftd 45.00
Grape (& Cable), spooner, nutmeg stain...................................95.00
Grape (& Cable), sugar, breakfast; open, nutmeg stain 75.00
Grape (& Cable), sugar bowl, w/lid, nutmeg stain 150.00
Grape (& Cable), tray, dresser; nutmeg stain, scarce, lg..............325.00
Grape (& Cable), tray, pin; nutmeg stain..................................125.00
Grape (& Cable), tumbler, nutmeg stain....................................75.00
Grape & Gothic Arches, bowl, master berry; pearl w/gold 200.00
Grape & Gothic Arches, butter dish, pearl w/gold......................200.00
Grape & Gothic Arches, creamer, pearl w/gold, rare 90.00
Grape & Gothic Arches, favor vase, nutmeg stain.......................80.00
Grape & Gothic Arches, goblet, pearl w/gold.............................60.00
Grape & Gothic Arches, pitcher, water; pearl w/gold..................275.00
Grape & Gothic Arches, spooner, pearl w/gold...........................80.00
Grape & Gothic Arches, sugar bowl, w/lid, pearl w/gold.............125.00
Grape & Gothic Arches, tumbler, pearl w/gold...........................65.00
Grape Arbor, vase, hat form 90.00
Heart w/T'print, creamer..80.00
Heart w/T'print, lamp, good pnt, scarce, 8" 325.00
Heart w/T'print, sugar bowl, ind 75.00
Honeycomb, wine...65.00
Horse Medallion, bowl, gr stain, 7" 70.00

Intaglio, master berry bowl, 9" diameter, $250.00.

Intaglio, butter dish, gold & decor, scarce 300.00
Intaglio, compote, jelly; gold & decor 125.00
Intaglio, creamer, gold & decor 100.00
Intaglio, cruet, gold & decor 350.00
Intaglio, pitcher, water; gold & decor 345.00
Intaglio, sauce, gold & decor 48.00
Intaglio, shakers, gold & decor, pr 200.00
Intaglio, spooner, gold & decor 110.00
Intaglio, sugar bowl, w/lid, gold & decor 145.00
Intaglio, tumbler, gold & decor 75.00
Inverted Fan & Feather, bowl, master berry; gold & decor 215.00
Inverted Fan & Feather, butter dish, gold & decor 295.00
Inverted Fan & Feather, compote, jelly; gold & decor, rare 410.00
Inverted Fan & Feather, creamer, gold & decor 130.00
Inverted Fan & Feather, cruet, gold & decor, scarce, 6½" 675.00
Inverted Fan & Feather, pitcher, water; gold & decor 450.00
Inverted Fan & Feather, punch cup, gold & decor 250.00
Inverted Fan & Feather, sauce, gold & decor 65.00
Inverted Fan & Feather, shakers, gold & decor, pr 450.00
Inverted Fan & Feather, spooner, gold & decor 130.00
Inverted Fan & Feather, sugar bowl, w/lid, gold & decor 185.00
Inverted Fan & Feather, tumbler, gold & decor 85.00
Jackson, bowl, master berry; good gold, ftd 125.00
Jackson, creamer, good gold 85.00
Jackson, pitcher, water; good gold 250.00
Jackson, pitcher, water; no decor 150.00
Jackson, sauce, good gold 45.00
Jackson, shakers, good gold, pr 135.00
Jackson, tumbler, good gold 45.00
Louis XV, berry set, w/nutmeg, 7-pc 375.00
Louis XV, bowl, master berry; good gold 165.00
Louis XV, butter dish, good gold 200.00
Louis XV, creamer, good gold 80.00
Louis XV, cruet, good gold 250.00
Louis XV, pitcher, water; good gold 225.00
Louis XV, sauce, good gold, ftd 47.00
Louis XV, spooner, good gold 80.00
Louis XV, sugar bowl, w/lid, good gold 150.00
Louis XV, tumbler, good gold 65.00
Maple Leaf, bowl, master berry; gold & decor, scarce 300.00
Maple Leaf, butter dish, gold & decor 255.00
Maple Leaf, compote, jelly; gold & decor, rare 455.00
Maple Leaf, creamer, gold & decor 110.00
Maple Leaf, cruet, gold & decor, rare 1,500.00
Maple Leaf, pitcher, water; gold & decor 345.00
Maple Leaf, sauce, gold & decor, scarce 95.00
Maple Leaf, shakers, gold & decor, pr 550.00
Maple Leaf, spooner, gold & decor 115.00
Maple Leaf, sugar bowl, w/lid, gold & decor 175.00
Maple Leaf, tumbler, gold & decor 85.00
Panelled Poppy, lamp shade, nutmeg stain, scarce 850.00
Peacock & Urn, bowl, ice cream; nutmeg stain, sm 80.00
Peacock & Urn, bowl, ice cream; nutmeg stain, 10" 310.00
Punty Band, shakers, pr 110.00
Punty Band, spooner, floral decor 60.00
Punty Band, tumbler, floral decor, souvenir 65.00
Ribbed Drape, butter dish, scalloped, roses & gold 280.00
Ribbed Drape, compote, jelly; roses & gold, rare 200.00
Ribbed Drape, creamer, roses & gold, scarce 125.00
Ribbed Drape, cruet, roses & gold, scarce 395.00
Ribbed Drape, pitcher, water; roses & gold, rare 345.00
Ribbed Drape, sauce, roses & gold 40.00
Ribbed Drape, shakers, roses & gold, pr, rare 235.00
Ribbed Drape, spooner, roses & gold 115.00

Ribbed Drape, toothpick holder, roses & gold 200.00
Ribbed Drape, tumbler, roses & gold 65.00
Ribbed T'print, wine, floral decor 75.00
Ring Band, bowl, master berry; roses & gold 135.00
Ring Band, butter dish, roses & gold 200.00
Ring Band, compote, jelly; roses & gold, scarce 165.00
Ring Band, creamer, roses & gold 90.00
Ring Band, cruet, roses & gold 300.00
Ring Band, pitcher, roses & gold, 7½" 240.00
Ring Band, sauce, roses & gold 40.00
Ring Band, shakers, roses & gold, pr 115.00
Ring Band, spooner, roses & gold 95.00
Ring Band, syrup, roses & gold 335.00
Ring Band, toothpick holder, roses & gold 110.00
Ring Band, tray, condiment; roses & gold 175.00
Singing Birds, mug, nutmeg stain 85.00
Tarentum's Victoria, bowl, master berry; gold & decor 200.00
Tarentum's Victoria, butter dish, gold & decor, rare 275.00
Tarentum's Victoria, celery vase, gold & decor, rare 225.00
Tarentum's Victoria, creamer, gold & decor, scarce 115.00
Tarentum's Victoria, pitcher, water; gold & decor, rare 365.00
Tarentum's Victoria, spooner, gold & decor 115.00
Tarentum's Victoria, sugar bowl, w/lid, gold & decor 160.00
Tarentum's Victoria, tumbler, gold & decor 70.00
Vermont, butter dish, bl decor 185.00
Vermont, toothpick holder, bl decor 115.00
Vermont, vase, floral decor, jeweled 75.00
Wide Band, bell, roses 175.00
Wild Bouquet, butter dish, gold & decor, rare 400.00
Wild Bouquet, creamer, no gold 145.00
Wild Bouquet, cruet, no decor, w/clear stopper 300.00
Wild Bouquet, sauce, gold & decor 60.00
Wild Bouquet, spooner, gold & decor 145.00
Wild Bouquet, tumbler, no decor 55.00
Winged Scroll, bowl, master berry; gold & decor, 11"L 140.00
Winged Scroll, butter dish, good gold 185.00
Winged Scroll, butter dish, no decor 150.00
Winged Scroll, celery vase, good gold, rare 400.00
Winged Scroll, cigarette jar, scarce 155.00
Winged Scroll, compote, ruffled, rare, 6¾x10¾" 495.00

Winged Scroll, creamer and sugar bowl, $265.00.

Winged Scroll, cruet, good gold, clear stopper 235.00
Winged Scroll, hair receiver, good gold 120.00
Winged Scroll, pitcher, water; bulbous, good gold 300.00
Winged Scroll, sauce, good gold 35.00
Winged Scroll, shakers, bulbous, good gold, rare, pr 350.00
Winged Scroll, shakers, str sides, good gold, pr 165.00
Winged Scroll, sugar bowl, w/lid, good gold 150.00
Winged Scroll, syrup, good gold 365.00
Winged Scroll, tumbler, good gold 75.00

Cut Glass

The earliest documented evidence of commercial glass cutting in the United States was in 1810; the producers were Bakewell and Page of Pittsburgh. These first efforts resulted in simple patterns with only a moderate amount of cutting. By the middle of the century, glass cutters began experimenting with a thicker glass which enabled them to use deeper cuttings, though patterns remained much the same. This period is usually referred to as Rich Cut. Using three types of wheels – a flat edge, a mitered edge, and a convex edge – facets, miters, and depressions were combined to produce various designs. In the late 1870s, a curved miter was developed which greatly expanded design potential. Patterns became more elaborate, often covering the entire surface. The Brilliant Period of cut glass covered a span from about 1880 until 1915. Because of the pressure necessary to achieve the deeply cut patterns, only glass containing a high grade of metal could withstand the process. For this reason and the amount of handwork involved, cut glass has always been expensive.

Our advisors for this category are Jeanette and Marvin Stofft; they are listed in the Directory under Indiana. See also specific manufacturers.

Key:
dmn — diamonds
strw — strawberry
X-cut — cross-cut
X-hatch — crosshatch

Atomizer, Harvard, sq, 8x2½" 80.00
Boot, X-hatch/T'print/stars, 11" 350.00
Bottle, birds/ferns eng, faceted stopper, 7½" 115.00
Bottle, bull's eyes/fleur-de-lis, cobalt to clear, 8" 135.00
Bottle, scent; stars/fans/fine cuts, faceted stopper, 6½" 100.00
Bottle, scent; T'prints/notches, faceted stopper, 5½" 150.00
Bowl, allover hobstars/buttons in dmn field, serrated, 8" 175.00
Bowl, allover hobstars/X-cut dmn, scalloped/serrated, 10" 400.00
Bowl, buzz star center, hobstar corners, serrated, sq, 7" 195.00
Bowl, cane/X-hatch/hobstars, star base, sq, serrated, 12" 450.00
Bowl, chain of hobstars border, prism body, serrated, 8" 350.00
Bowl, fern motif at rim, rayed hobstar center, tricorn, 10" 300.00
Bowl, flashed star base, pinwheels/hobstars/fans, 8" 200.00
Bowl, floral/hobstars, Harvard border, serrated, 10" 175.00
Bowl, frosted buzz stars w/fine cut dmn panels, 8½"........................80.00
Bowl, hobstar band/dmn points & fan, scalloped, shallow, 9" 125.00
Bowl, hobstar w/in star, hobstars by star points, 9" 100.00
Bowl, hobstars, scalloped/serrated, Egginton, 8", NM 100.00
Bowl, hobstars w/split vesicas, serrated, Hoare, 7" 130.00
Bowl, hobstars/bands of canes/X-hatches, Hoare, 9" L 450.00
Bowl, hobstars/fans, serrated, 8" 150.00
Bowl, hobstars/X-hatches in dmn fields, Clarke, 8½"...................210.00
Bowl, lg hobstar w/hobstars by points, serrated, 6" 70.00
Bowl, Pineapple & Fan, blown-out corners, serrated, 9" 300.00
Bowl, Pinwheel, 8¼" 145.00
Bowl, Russian, hobstar base, red to clear, serrated, 8½".............550.00
Bowl, Russian, low ped ft, scalloped, 10" 550.00
Bowl, Russian, Persian buttons, shell shape, 10½" L 550.00
Bowl, Star of David variant, scalloped/serrated, 8".....................650.00
Bowl, sunburst effects/cane, sq, serrated/scalloped, 11" 575.00
Bowl, 20-point hobstar/hobstars/cane/fan, 2-fold rim, 10" L........400.00
Butter dish, buzz stars, mini, 3¾x5"....................................115.00
Butter dish, hobstars & florals, dome lid, 7½" dia 195.00
Butter dish, hobstars/nailheads, serrated, faceted knob, 9"...........350.00
Candy dish, buzz stars/fans, scalloped, 6" 40.00
Candy dish, stars/florals, serrated, sgn Hoare, 6" dia...................50.00
Carafe, radiant star, notched prism/fans, notched neck, 8" 90.00

Celery tray, Chrysanthemum, 12" 225.00
Chalice, snowflakes, gr to clear, dbl-cut knob stem, 10"...............90.00
Cigarette box, top is ash tray, buzz stars, 3x4" L.........................45.00
Claret, Almond T'print, 4 for 60.00
Compote, Creswick, notched teardrop stem, Eggington, 7x6" 400.00
Compote, Expanding Star variant, 4-section, 7x8" 350.00
Compote, Hart, T'print stem, star base, Parsche, 9" H 150.00
Compote, hobstars/fan, scalloped folded rim, 9x6½" 190.00
Compote, hobstars/fans, notched 6-side stem, ray base, 9x5" 200.00
Compote, zipper-cut ped ft w/rays, buzz stars/fans, 8x6" 150.00
Compote, 4 pinwheels in panels, boat shape w/ped ft, 8x6" 75.00
Cookie jar, hobstars/fan/nailhead lozenges, sterling lid 850.00
Cracker jar, pinwheels, very heavy, 9½x6½".................................80.00
Creamer, dainty stars/fans/dmns, clear hdl, rayed base, 4½"...........30.00
Creamer & sugar, hobstar/flashed fans, serrated, ped ft 550.00
Cruet, cane/fans, fluted top, cut stopper, sgn Hoare 175.00
Decanter, hobstar fans, hdl, 10½" 275.00
Decanter, hobstars/fans/dmn points, 11½"..................................350.00
Decanter, strw dmn, notched paneled neck, w/stopper, 12".........110.00
Dresser tray, Russian, 2 sides folded in, 8" dia............................225.00
Fernery, bands of hobstars/cane, 3-ftd, 8" dia.............................125.00
Flask, Cane, silver top w/monogram, 10", in orig bag...................325.00
Humidor, hobstars/fans, lg hobstar/punty top, 8" 475.00
Ice bucket, strw dmn/cane & fans, hdls, serrated, 6" dia 350.00
Jug, paneled, gr to clear, faceted stopper, 6" 225.00
Knife rest, faceted knobs, 5" L 25.00
Knife rest, fans/X-hatching, tapered ends, 4" 25.00
Ladle, hobstars/X-hatch hdl, SP bowl sgn JD Bergen Co 500.00
Lamp, lg hobstars/cane/flashed fans, cut dome shade, 23x11" . 3,300.00
Lamp, ovals/circles, cobalt to clear bullet font, 11" 1,000.00

Table lamp, cut with pinwheels, leaves, daisies, etc.; minor roughage, 20" x 11", $1,500.00.

Loving cup, cut florals, gold trim, 3-hdl, 3½" 100.00
Loving cup, dmn point blocks, 3-hdl, 10"...................................950.00
Mayonnaise jar, zippers/dmns, faceted finial, w/spoon, 4½" 45.00
Nappy, pinwheels, 6¼" 20.00
Pitcher, buzz stars/fans, squat/bulbous, 8x7½"...........................150.00
Pitcher, etched panels w/roses, dmns/fans, 5x7" 75.00

Pitcher, facets/dmns, star-cut bottom, bulbous, 8" 200.00
Pitcher, hobstars w/palm trees of flashed fans & cane, 6" 400.00
Pitcher, hobstars/cane/nailheads/fans, hobstar base, 12" 575.00
Pitcher, pineapple/fans, very heavy, serrated, 8½" 250.00
Pitcher, Pinwheel, 10" 225.00
Punch bowl, Newport, 2-pc, ea sgn Hoare, 13x12½" 1,500.00
Punch bowl, pinwheels/feathering/fans, compote ft, 16x14" ... 1,200.00
Rose bowl, Star & Feather, serrated rim, Hoare, 5" 145.00
Tankard, Bull's Eye, Dmn Point Hobnail Cross, 11" 350.00
Tankard, Hobstar Dmn Point w/canes & fans, Hoare, 11" 275.00
Tray, allover cluster of hobstars/cane & fan, serrated, 14" 950.00
Tray, celery; block/fan, serrated folded edge, 12" L 85.00
Tray, floral center, Harvard border, 12" dia 400.00
Tray, hobstar clusters, 13½" 375.00
Tray, hobstars/fan, 'club' shape, serrated, 6" L.............................135.00
Tray, ice cream; bands of hobstars/strw dmn, Hoare, 9x13" 190.00
Tray, ice cream; clusters of hobstars/bands of cane, 14" L............210.00
Tray, ice cream; hobstar/fan/cane, scalloped/serrated, 14"............220.00
Tray, ice cream; hobstars/bars of X-hatches, 10x18" 475.00
Tray, Russian, scalloped/serrated, 9½" dia 275.00
Tumbler, buzz stars/fans/dmns, 4" 20.00
Tumbler, pineapples, 4" 25.00
Vase, allover flowers/leaves on flowing stems, waisted, 14" 180.00
Vase, fine-cut cane/hobstars/X-hatching, on low std, 13" 250.00
Vase, hobstar/prisms/nailheads, 24-point star base, 12½".............300.00
Vase, octagon panel Button & Star, cranberry to clear, 13".........160.00
Vase, rose/leaf, vertical cut ribs, cobalt to clear, 11"....................150.00
Vase, stemmed daisies, 2 Harvard rim panels, slim form, 12".........75.00
Vase, stemmed roses, ea w/hobstar center, serrated, 12"................225.00
Vase, 16-point hobstar base, hobstars/dmns/fans/vesicas, 6" 75.00
Vase, 3 ea floral/dmn X-hatch panels, marble/bronze ft, 14"..........90.00
Wine, Bengal, Sinclaire, pr...40.00

Zipper pattern vase, signed Hoare, 9¾", $260.00.

Cut Velvet

Cut Velvet glassware was made during the late 1800s. It is characterized by the effect achieved through the application of relief-molded patterns, often ribbing or diamond quilting, which allows its white inner casing to show through the outer pastel layer.

Biscuit jar, Ribbon, gr, SP bail & lid, 7x5".............................295.00

Bowl, Dia Quilt, rose, clear ruffle/ft, 4½x6½" 215.00
Ewer, Dia Quilt, bl, appl frosted leaf/berry, Mt WA, 8" 265.00
Ewer, Dia Quilt, bl, stick neck, Mt WA, 7¾" 265.00
Ewer, Dia Quilt, med bl, frosted leaf/berry, Mt WA, 8" 275.00
Pitcher, Dia Quilt, pk, sq top, clear reeded hdl, 8" 300.00
Rose bowl, Dia Quilt, med bl, 4-crimp, 3x3½" 165.00
Rose bowl, Dia Quilt, rose pk, 4-crimp, 3½x3½" 175.00
Rose bowl, Dia Quilt, rose pk, 8-crimp, 3⅝x3½".........................185.00
Vase, Dia Quilt, bl, bottle form, 10½x5¼" 175.00
Vase, Dia Quilt, bl, pinched rim, 4"...135.00
Vase, Dia Quilt, olive gr, stick neck, 10" 145.00
Vase, Dia Quilt, rose pk, ruffled top, 6⅛x3⅛".............................165.00

Vase, Diamond Quilted, rose, $145.00.

Vase, Ribbed, pk, ruffled top, 6⅛x3⅛".......................................165.00
Vase, Ribbed, pk, 9⅞x4⅛" 225.00
Whiskey, Dia Quilt, burmese color, 2¾" 250.00

Cybis

Boleslaw Cybis was a graduate of the Academy of Fine Arts in Warsaw, Poland, and was well recognized as a fine artist by the time he was commissioned by his government to paint murals in the Polish Pavillion's Hall of Honor at the 1939 World's Fair. Finding themselves stranded in America at the outbreak of WWII, the Cybises founded an artists' studio, first in Astoria, New York, and later in Trenton, New Jersey, where they made fine figurines and plaques with exacting artistry and craftsmanship entailing extensive handwork. The studio still operates today producing exquisite porcelains on a limited edition basis. Our advisor is William T. Brinkley; he is listed in the Directory under Illinois.

Ballerina on Cue, wht bsk, blk wood base 450.00
Blue Betty 200.00
Emily Ann 175.00
Funny Face w/Holly, 10"..125.00
Goldilocks, holding panda bear 300.00
Indian boy, w/full headdress, bust..625.00
Little Princess 550.00
Matchgirl 195.00
Mr Snowball Bunny 65.00
Owl 85.00
Pollyanna 350.00

Red Riding Hood..150.00
Seal, wht, 4x5"..150.00
Suzanne w/Kitten 225.00
Wendy 120.00

Goldilocks and Panda Bears, $495.00 for the set.

Czechoslovakian Collectibles

Czechoslovakia came into being as a country in 1918. Located in the heart of Europe, it was a land with the natural resources necessary to support a glass industry that dates back to the mid-fourteenth century. This ware has recently captured the attention of today's collectors, and for good reason. There are beautiful vases – cased, ruffled, applied with rigaree or silver overlay – fine enough to rival those of the best glasshouses. Czechoslovakian art glass baskets are quite as attractive as Victorian America's, and the elegant cut glass perfumes made in colors as well as crystal are unrivaled. There are also pressed glass perfumes, molded in lovely Deco shapes, of various types of art glass. Some are overlaid with gold filigree set with 'jewels.' Jewelry, lamps, porcelains and fine art pottery are also included in the field.

More than thirty-five marks have been recorded, including those in the mold, ink stamped, acid etched, or on a small metal name plate. The newer marks are incised, stamped 'Royal Dux made in Czechoslovakia' (see Royal Dux), or simply a paper label which reads 'Bohemian Glass made in Czechoslovakia.' For a more thorough study of the subject, we recommend you refer to the book *Made in Czechoslovakia*, by Ruth A. Forsythe; she is listed in the Directory under Ohio. In the listings that follow when one dimension is given, it refers to height; decoration is enamel unless noted otherwise.

Candy Baskets

Blk w/silver mica, bl int, blk hdl, 8".................................95.00
Cased 3-color mottle, blk rim & hdl, 7" 160.00
Hobnail, red w/blk rim, plain crystal hdl, 6½" 110.00
Mc mottle, flat-top crystal thorn hdl, 6½" 110.00
Pk w/pale pk streaks, matching hdl, 8"..........................98.00
Red & yel mottle, flat-top crystal hdl, 8½" 85.00
Red & yel mottle, ruffled rim, plain crystal hdl, 6½".....................98.00
Red & yel mottle, twisted crystal thorn hdl, 7"..........125.00

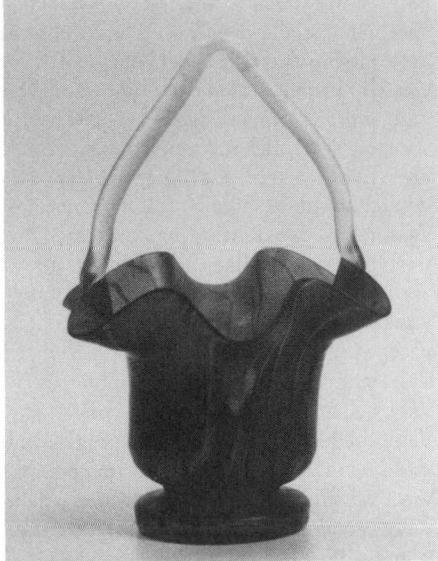

Streaky blue, yellow, and black in red, clear handle, 9½", $95.00.

Yel w/blk rim, plain crystal hdl, 6½" 70.00

Cased Art Glass

Bowl, cameo-cut vine, dk gr on lt orange, ftd, 5½" 400.00
Bowl, red, blk/wht flower basket reserves, ftd, 6¾".........80.00
Box, mc mottle, rnd, 3 blk buttressed ft, 8" 125.00
Candlestick, orange w/mc mottle at base, 10¼" 32.00
Candy jar, yel, appl flower, no lid, 3¾" 35.00
Cocktail, gr, mc rooster, 3½" 32.50
Mayonnaise, mc mottle, rnd form w/stem finial, 4¼" 70.00
Pitcher, orange w/exotic bird, blk hdl, 11½"...............165.00
Tumbler, orange, w/exotic bird, 5¼" 45.00
Vase, bl, pk int, ruffled top, ftd, 8½" 85.00
Vase, bl, rose int, ruffled top, rnd, 6"...........................85.00
Vase, bl w/mc mottle at base, shouldered, ftd, 6¼" 50.00
Vase, blk, silver-deposit bands & clover, squat, ftd, 7¼" 75.00
Vase, blk, silver-deposit bird, flared neck, 6½" 60.00

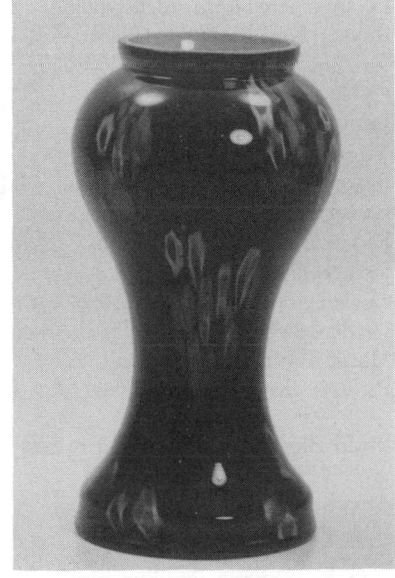

Vase, black with millefiori, red interior, 9½", $145.00.

Vase, bud; mc mottle, slim w/wide base, 8¼"................45.00
Vase, bud; yel, silver-deposit bird/tree, slim w/blk ft, 9½" 32.50

Vase, gr, blk streaks extend upward from base, 8¼" 60.00
Vase, HP medallions, blk on orange, blk-lined rim/ft, 8½" 60.00
Vase, jack-in-the-pulpit; yel w/mc mottle at base, 7½" 55.00
Vase, lt bl w/blk ruffled rim, slim w/flared base, 8¼" 40.00
Vase, lt gr, 3 bl angle hdls, bl rim, 8¼"....................................350.00
Vase, mc swirl, classic form, 8" 70.00
Vase, mottled, appl wht serpentine decor, 9⅝"..........................95.00
Vase, mottled, hexagonal, ftd, short neck, 4" 60.00
Vase, mottled, red int, appl blk rim, ftd, 7" 50.00
Vase, paperweight-like canes, red int, ftd, wide rim, 6".............125.00
Vase, paperweight-like canes, red int, squat, 5½" 125.00
Vase, pk, appl pk hdls, ewer form, 7½" 60.00
Vase, wht, crystal hdls, classic form, 7½" 50.00
Vase, wht, rose int, ruffled top, spherical, 5½" 70.00
Vase, yel, appl blk serpentine decor, 9" 85.00
Vase, yel, blk clover, 3 blk angular hdls, wide base, 3½"..............50.00
Vase, yel mottle w/blk trim, ftd trumpet form, 6¾" 50.00
Vase, yel w/blk trim, ruffled rim, slim w/flared base, 8½" 38.00
Vase, yel w/mc mottle at base, ftd, short neck, 8" 46.00
Wine, red w/blk stem, silver trim, 7½" 35.00

Cut Glass Perfume Bottles

Amber, sm neck, wide base, clear figural stopper, 5½"...................225.00
Amethyst, gold jewels, amethyst floral stopper, 5¾"....................210.00
Blk transparent, clear floral stopper, 5½" 125.00
Crystal, diamond cuttings, red fan stopper, 3½"..........................60.00
Crystal, lt bl lovebirds intaglio stopper, 4¾" 110.00
Crystal, overall cuttings, crystal rectangular stopper, 4" 50.00
Crystal, stepped base, crystal triangular stopper, 5¾" 72.00
Crystal, Triomphe on red sq stopper, 3¾" 90.00
Crystal, wide base, crystal & frosted floral stopper, 7⅛" 98.00
Crystal, 2 on tray, ring relief, pk base & stoppers, 4⅛" 135.00
Crystal & frosted, dome base, frosted peacock in stopper, 8" 225.00
Crystal & frosted, frosted head in stopper, 5¾"..........................90.00
Gr, fancy cuttings, gr cut stopper, 5⅜"......................................90.00
Gr, jeweled, tall gr stopper, 4½"..120.00
Gr, narrow neck, wide base, gr fan stopper, 4⅞" 78.00
Gr, sq base, long tapered crystal stopper, 6¼" 125.00
Gr & crystal, 2-pc bottle, gr frosted stopper, 5¾" 185.00
Pk, shouldered form, ftd, crystal floral stopper, 5¾"....................90.00
Rose-amber, allover cuts, fan stopper, 4¾" 75.00
Vaseline, cornucopia form, cut stopper, 10"...............................225.00

Lamps

Basket, bl beaded, red-beaded fruit, gold trim, 8" 400.00
Basket, crystal beads, amber glass nuts, 7½"..............................525.00
Basket, crystal beads, glass nuts & fruit, gold trim, 10¾" 520.00
Desk, acid-cut shade, 10" 160.00
Goebel girl in glass flower dress, 10¼" 585.00
HP decor w/gold on milk glass, kerosene, 12¾" 110.00
Mottled satin base & shade, 12½"..180.00
Perfume, frosted glass w/HP dots, 6" 135.00

Mold Blown and Pressed Bottles

Amethyst & crystal, HP daisies, 7" 95.00
Bl, nude & butterfly relief, rare, 5¼" 385.00
Crystal, blk & red bands, slim form, 7¾"....................................65.00
Crystal, gold decor w/red jewels, 4¾".......................................185.00
Frosted crystal, HP daisies, ftd, 6½"..95.00
Gr, appl blk serpentine decor, atomizer, 8".................................90.00
Gr, low shoulders, orange stopper, 7⅛" 40.00

Gr, overall gold & jewel decor, 2⅜" 85.00
Orange cased, blk ft & stopper, 6½"..55.00
Orange cased, HP blk bands, bulbous, atomizer, 5" 55.00
Purple lustre, squat teardrop form, flower stopper, 4½"...............85.00
Topaz tinted, pillow form, jet stopper, 5"...................................25.00

Opaque, Crystal, Colored Transparent Glass

Candlestick, pk, appl leaf & vine decor, 8" 45.00
Decanter, gr bubbly glass, HP equestrian, 9⅝"..........................125.00
Pitcher, bl, HP exotic bird, 11¼" 185.00
Pitcher, bl bubbly glass, tall matching stopper, 8⅝"....................85.00
Tumbler, amber, yel overlay, quilted, 4½" 45.00
Tumbler, orange & gr, stacked cone form, 4⅞"...........................20.00
Vase, canes, mottled, red trailings on clear, hdls, 7"...................300.00
Vase, cobalt cut to clear, floral etch, 10¼"...............................150.00
Vase, crystal w/red & blk pull-ups, ftd U-form, 8¼" 110.00
Vase, dk bl lustre, U-form on dome base, 5⅞".............................250.00
Vase, golden topaz, orange pull-ups, fan form, 8" 95.00
Vase, pk lustre, lustre threading at top, ftd, 9⅜"........................200.00

Pottery, Porcelain, Semi-Porcelain

Bowl, blk w/mc Deco-style floral vine, wht int, 3" 55.00
Coffeepot, Art Deco peasant w/HP flowers, 7" 85.00
Creamer, pk lustre, 3¼" 20.00
Figurine, Deco lady w/hand to head, wht, 9¾" 85.00
Figurine, elephant, blk w/yel saddle blanket, 4½".......................45.00
Plate, wht, yel chicks in center, 6½" 25.00
Sauce bowl, lobster head forms lid, red, 3½" 15.00
Teapot, girl finial, skirt forms body of pot, 8" 85.00
Wall pocket, bird at bird house form, 5½" 25.00
Wall pocket, bird at side of pineapple form, 7" 45.00
Wall pocket, bl w/mc peacock, 7¼" 45.00

D'Argental

D'Argental cameo glass was produced in France from the 1870s until about 1920 in the Art Nouveau style. Browns and tans were favored colors used to compliment florals and scenic designs developed through acid cuttings.

Our advisor for this category is Don Williams; he is listed in the Directory under Iowa.

Cameo

Bottle, floral, red on polished gold frost, wood lid, 6"..................575.00
Vase, bldg/trees, lt/dk brn on mottle, bulbous base, 13".......... 1,500.00
Vase, castle/trees, brn/gold/wht, sgn, 14½".......................... 1,800.00
Vase, floral, lav on yel/brn mottle, 6" 250.00
Vase, lake scene fr w/vines, burgundy/gold-tan, 7½"...................850.00
Vase, locust pods, polished red on gold to red frost, 9½"............950.00
Vase, mtn cottage w/barn & pine forest w/in geometrics, 10" . 1,000.00
Vase, starflowers, wine on amber frost, wine neck, 4" 650.00
Vase, summer scene w/trees, gr on yel, 13½"....................... 2,550.00
Vase, trees/foliage/man in field/mtns, gourd shape, 10" 1,000.00
Vase, trees/lake, plum on burnt orange, 8" 500.00
Vase, trees/mtns on frost, 3-layer, 7½" 650.00

Daum Nancy

Daum was an important producer of French cameo glass, operating from the late 1800s until after the turn of the century. They used various techniques – acid cutting, wheel engraving, and handwork – to create beautiful scenic designs and nature subjects in the Art Nouveau manner. Virtually all examples are signed.

Our advisor for this category is Don Williams; he is listed in the Directory under Iowa.

Cameo

Bowl, berries/leaves, orange/gold on yel/wht mottle, 4x6"	1,700.00
Bowl, nasturtiums, red/olive on mustard mottle, 11"	1,800.00
Box, floral branches, salmon/wine on citron, dome lid, 6"	1,900.00
Card holder, summer scene, 1¼x3½"	1,550.00
Chandelier, floral, red on red/gold, 16" dia+3 6" shades	16,500.00
Creamer, sweet peas, red/gr HP on orange/clear frost, NM	1,250.00
Cruet, floral, red/gold on cranberry frost texture, 4½"	1,500.00
Cruet, pods, gold on gr, gold-tone filigree base, 7"	1,250.00
Jam jar, violets, sq, 4½"	800.00
Lamp, floral, burgundy on gold frost, 8" tricorn shade, 17"	9,500.00
Lamp, ships/trees, purple/yel, 9" shade, 22"	16,000.00
Tumbler, violets, red/bl/yel mottle, sgn, 4¾"	450.00
Vase, berries/fronds, gr/yel on orange mottle, 13"	1,100.00
Vase, birch trees/hills on bl to gr, HP details, 17½"	4,000.00
Vase, bleeding hearts, cvd/HP on yel/amber/gr mottle, 8¾"	2,500.00
Vase, bleeding hearts/leaves, yel/gr on red mottle, sq, 2"	1,500.00
Vase, floral branches, wht/amber/gr mottle w/HP detail, 5"	750.00
Vase, floral on aqua w/gilt, sq, 4¾"	300.00
Vase, floral/tendrils, dk gr on turq martele, wide base, 7"	3,200.00
Vase, lg birch tree/lake, ftd baluster, 9x3"	2,100.00
Vase, morning-glories, cvd/HP on mottle, bulbous top, 4½"	1,200.00
Vase, pines/birds/marsh, bl on yel frost, slender, sgn, 10"	625.00
Vase, rain scene, blk trees on gr, pk to frosted top, 8"	3,400.00
Vase, sailboats/trees, brn on orange mottle, 5½"	1,500.00
Vase, sm floral, cvd/HP on tan/yel mottle, shouldered, 5½"	2,300.00
Vase, spring scene on gr/bl mottle frost, ftd, 6½"	2,750.00
Vase, sweet peas, pk on frost, 4¾"	700.00
Vase, trees/branches, gr/brn on orange & yel mottle, 7"	1,300.00
Vase, trees/river, wine/brn on orange mottle, can neck, 11"	3,250.00
Vase, violets, lav on textured frost, stick neck, 4¾"	700.00
Vase, winter scene on mottled gold, pillow form, 4"	1,900.00
Vase, winter scene/pine cones on frost w/yel, slim form, 6"	1,350.00
Vase, winter: cvd/HP birds in snow-covered trees, 6x8"	7,000.00
Vase, woodland scene/mtns, 4-layer, frosted ground, 13"	3,500.00

Vase, winter landscape, enameled details inside and out on acid-etched clear glass, ca 1910, signed with the Croix de Lorraine, 4½", $1,500.00.

Enameled Glass

Salt cellar, winter scene on yel, bucket form, 1⅜"	700.00
Vase, Dutch riverscape w/sailboats & windmills, 4½x10"	1,100.00
Vase, floral, yel/red on lt orange mottle, slim form, 5"	900.00
Vase, rampant lion on smoked glass, 4½"	975.00
Vase, ships/rocky coastline on yel, 3"	700.00

Miscellaneous

Bowl, gold-spangled yel mottle; in wrought cage-like mt, 8"	1,500.00
Bowl, red/wht/bl, French coin in base, ped ft, dtd 1872, 4x9"	300.00
Box, powder; lt gray, etched concentric circles, 1½x5"	500.00
Charger, lt gr w/bubble inclusions, 15"	500.00
Ferner, amber mottle frost w/gold scrolls, 4 appl ft, 9" L	185.00
Inkwell, red/orange mottle, clear insert, sq, 4¾"	1,700.00
Lamp, 12" shade/ball base w/wht-on-wht lines & dots, 12"	9,000.00
Paperweight, pate-de-verre, mouse form, gr/brn, 3½" L	3,400.00
Pitcher, clear to gr, etch/gilt floral, silver lid/hdl, 12"	800.00
Sculpture, pate-de-verre, clock/coat hanger, Dali, 30"	7,900.00
Sculpture, pate-de-verre, Cyclops, royal bl, Dali, 1968	4,000.00
Tazza, flat bubbly bowl w/bl rim, bronze/marble ped ft, 8"	325.00
Vase, acid-etched intaglio circles, conical/ftd, 1925, 9"	3,000.00
Vase, aqua, lines/roundels, cut/etched/polished, thick, 5"	700.00
Vase, gold-yel w/etched banding, conical, 12"	1,800.00
Vase, gr w/internal bubbles, rose jar form, 8"	400.00
Vase, jade w/appl blk spiral & ft banding, ftd sphere, 6"	550.00
Vase, lt aqua w/etched circles & stripes, sq baluster, 14"	2,500.00
Vase, lt tan, etched Deco bands, spherical, 7½"	300.00
Vase, rose etched w/gold floral, trapezoidal, 7"	525.00
Vase, wht cased in clear, 4 appl bl 'leaves,' 6"	1,300.00
Vase, wht opal w/etched/gilt daisies, waisted, 16"	700.00

Davis, Lowell

Figurines, plates, bells, and ornaments painted by Lowell Davis and produced by Border Fine Arts, Schmid Sculptured Porcelain, capture the heritage of rural America.

Lowell Davis, known better as Mr. Lowell to his farm animals, is described by many as 'just a country farmer from Missouri' fulfilling his dreams of preserving rural America as he knew it in the 1930s.

A Secondary Market Price Guide is published by Rosie Wells Enterprises for his collectibles. She is listed in the Directory under Clubs, Newsletters, and Catalogs. Items below are assumed to be in mint condition with box.

Country Road	575.00
Country Store	1,000.00
Ignorance Is Bliss	875.00
Mad As a Wet Hen	435.00
Milking Time	175.00
RFD Counter Sign	115.00
Studio Mouse	200.00
Surprise in the Cellar	875.00
Up To No Good, 6¼"	875.00
1983 Christmas	575.00

De Vez

De Vez was a type of acid-cut French cameo glass produced by Cristallerie de Pantin in Paris around the turn of the century.

Our advisor for this category is Don Williams; he is listed in the Directory under Iowa.

Cameo

Box, butterflies/sm flowers, bl on irid frost, 3x3½" dia	575.00
Compote, water/mtns/bldgs, rust/brn on yel, clear int, 4"	1,100.00
Vase, bent tree/branches fr mtns/island on frost, 3½x9" L	650.00
Vase, birds/mtns, orange/dk bl on pk, trumpet form, 6"	800.00
Vase, body: harbor, stick neck: vines, red/wine on gr, 9½"	1,100.00
Vase, branches/fruit, olive/ochre on lime, 16"	800.00
Vase, castle on mtn/lake & trees in bl, 9"	1,250.00
Vase, girl w/sheep & cow, bk: shepherd, 1920, 12"	1,700.00
Vase, lake/mtns, dk gr on gold to red, slim form, 12"	1,050.00
Vase, landscape, bl on bl to yel, 5"	675.00
Vase, man fishes from hillside/snow-capped mtns, 6"	1,200.00
Vase, mtns/cattle in stream, bl/gr, 5"	1,200.00
Vase, Venetian scene fr w/vines, man/gondolas/bldgs, 12"	1,800.00

De Vilbiss

Perfume bottles, atomizers, and dresser accessories marketed by the De Vilbiss Company are appreciated by collectors today for the various types of lovely glassware used in their manufacture, as well as for their pleasing shapes. Various companies provided the glass, while De Vilbiss made only the metal tops. They marketed their merchandise not only here but in Paris, England, Canada, and Havana as well. Their marks were acid stamped, ink stamped, in gold script, molded in, or on paper labels. One is no more significant than another. For more information we recommend *Bedroom and Bathroom Glassware of the Depression Years* by Margaret and Kenn Whitmyer; their address is listed in the Directory under Ohio.

Atomizer, amethyst flashed, w/cord & netted bulb, med sz	95.00
Atomizer, bl transparent, 3"	45.00
Atomizer, blk w/crystal stem & foot, 4¼"	50.00
Atomizer, blk w/gold encrusted stem & ft, crystal base, 7"	100.00
Atomizer, clear, brass top w/coral jewel, 2¼", orig box	42.00
Atomizer, clear cut 'doorknob' base, bl pyramid stopper, 5"	95.00
Atomizer, clear frosted flatiron shape w/ridges, 2¼"	35.00
Atomizer, clear/etched ovoid on blk base, 7½"	65.00
Atomizer, clear/frost fluted cylinder, blk spray button, 6½"	38.00
Atomizer, cranberry stain, gold decor, mesh bulb & cord, 7"	95.00

Atomizer, ruffled tiers of clear and opalescent glass, paper label, 4½", $45.00.

Atomizer, emerald gr w/gold, 7¾"	110.00
Atomizer, enameled dk gr w/blk florals, octagonal, 5½"	50.00

Atomizer, gold w/gold matt motif, squat disk form, 1¾"	42.00
Atomizer, orange stain on crystal base, 6"	75.00
Bottle, scent; blk w/chrome neck	45.00
Bottle, scent; smoke gray, hand blown, sm	15.00
Dresser set, HP flowers w/gold, mk, 7-pc	400.00
Perfume dropper, crystal w/bl florals	20.00
Perfume dropper, orange enamel, 5⅝"	45.00
Vanity set, orange enamel w/blk & gold decor, 3-pc	165.00

Decanters

Ceramic whiskey decanters were brought into prominence in 1955 by the James Beam Distilling Company. Few other companies besides Beam produced these decanters during the next ten years or so; however, other companies did eventually follow suit, so that today there are at least twenty prominent companies and several on a lesser scale that make these decanters.

We have tried to list those brands that are the most popular with collectors. Likewise, individual decanters listed are the ones (or representative of the ones) most commonly found. These are a small fraction of the several thousand different decanters that have been produced. These decanters come from all over the world. While Jim Beam owns its own china factory in the U.S., some of the others import from Mexico, Taiwan, Japan and elsewhere. They vary in size from miniatures (approximately 2 oz.) to gallons. Values range from a few dollars to more than $3,000 per decanter. A mint condition decanter is one with no chips or cracks and all labels intact. Whether a decanter is full or not has no bearing on the value, nor does a missing federal tax stamp. It is advisable to empty the contents of a ceramic decanter, otherwise the thin inner glaze could crack, allowing the contents to seep through the porous body, thus ruining the decanter. An (m) behind a listing indicates a miniature. All others are fifth or 750 ml unless noted otherwise.

Animals, Domestic

Beam, Cats, Burmese, Siamese, or Tabby, ea	10.00
Beam, Dog, Great Dane	10.00
Beam, Dog, Poodle, gray or wht	10.00
Beam, Dog, St Bernard	22.00
Beam, Horse, Apaloosa	10.00
Beam, Horse, Mare & Foal	45.00
Beam, Horse, Stallion, rearing, blk/brn/or gray, '61 or '62, ea	20.00
Grenadier, Horse, Arabian	20.00
Hoffman, Cat, 6 different, ea	12.00
Hoffman, Dog, mini set #2	15.00
Hoffman, Horse, 6 different, (m), ea	10.00
Old Bardstown, Dog, Bulldog	75.00
Old Bardstown, Horse, Citation	150.00
Old Commonwealth, Dog, Golden Retriever	30.00
Old Commonwealth, Horse, Tennessee Walking	28.00
Ski Country, Dog, Bassett Hound	60.00
Ski Country, Dog, Labrador w/pheasant	75.00

Animals, Wild

Beam, Doe	20.00
Brooks, Fox, Redtail	40.00
Brooks, Lion, African	25.00
Brooks, Raccoon	32.00
Brooks, Tiger, Bengal	30.00
Cyrus Noble, Elk, Bull	45.00
Cyrus Noble, Walrus	45.00

Famous Firsts, Panda..50.00
Hoffman, Doe & Fawn..30.00
Old Bardstown, Tiger..22.00
Old Bardstown, Wildcat #1..60.00
Ski Country, Bobcat & Chipmunk..................................55.00
Ski Country, Deer, Wht Tail...100.00
Ski Country, Fox & Butterfly...65.00
Ski Country, Raccoons (wall plaque)..............................60.00
Ski Country, Sheep, Rocky Mountain............................60.00
Ski Country, Skunk Family...55.00
Ski Country, Squirrels (wall plaque).............................100.00

Automotive

ASI, Cadillac, 1903, bl or wht.......................................40.00
ASI, Chevrolet, 1914..45.00
ASI, Oldsmobile...75.00
Beam, Chevy, 1957 Bel Air, turq....................................60.00
Beam, Chevy, 1978 Corvette, red, yel, or wht 60.00
Beam, Duesenberg, Convertible Coupe.........................140.00
Beam, Duesenberg, 1934, lt or dk bl.............................110.00
Beam, Fire Engine, 1867 Mississippi Pumper................100.00
Beam, Ford, Woodie Station Wagon...............................50.00
Beam, Ford, 1903 Model A, blk or red............................40.00
Beam, Ford, 1913 Model T, blk or gr..............................45.00
Beam, Ford, 1928 Fire Chief's Car 125.00
Beam, Ford, 1928 Model A..65.00
Beam, Ford, 1929 Phaeton..48.00
Beam, Ford, 1929 Police Car...90.00
Beam, Ford, 1930 Fire Truck, Model A..........................120.00
Beam, Ford, 1964 Mustang, blk.....................................110.00
Beam, Ford, 1964 Mustang, wht 55.00
Beam, Jewel Tea Wagon 78.00
Beam, Mack, 1917 Fire Truck..120.00
Beam, Mercedes, bl or red...40.00
Beam, Oldsmobile, 1904...45.00
Beam, Racecar, Unser Olsonite Eagle 60.00
Beam, Stutz Bearcat, 1914, gray or yel............................50.00
Beam, Thomas Flyer, 1907, bl or cream 75.00
Beam, Volkswagen, red or bl...40.00
McCormick, Packard, 1937, blk or cream........................40.00
Pacesetter, Fire Truck #1, LaFrance................................45.00
Pacesetter, Fire Truck #2, Pirsch....................................50.00
Pacesetter, Tractor #1, John Deere................................125.00
Pacesetter, Tractor #2, Green Machine 75.00
Pacesetter, Tractor #4, Ford 60.00

Birds and Waterfowl

Beam, Blue Jay 9.00
Beam, Cardinal, female...12.00
Beam, Cardinal, male 30.00
Beam, Ducks Unlimited #1, Mallard 45.00
Beam, Ducks Unlimited #2, Wood Duck........................45.00
Beam, Ducks Unlimited #3, Mallard Hen 40.00
Beam, Ducks Unlimited #4, Mallard Head 35.00
Beam, Owl, red or gray...15.00
Beam, Pheasant...10.00
Brooks, Baltimore Oriole..30.00
Brooks, Duck, Canadian Loon..30.00
Brooks, Macaw...35.00
Brooks, Owl #2, Eagle 60.00
Brooks, Snow Egret..25.00
Cyrus Noble, Penguin Family..45.00

Lionstone, Duck, Canvasback...40.00
Lionstone, Goose, Canadian...50.00
Lionstone, Goose, Snow...65.00
Lionstone, Pheasant...50.00
Ski Country, Dove 60.00
Ski Country, Duck, King Eider 50.00
Ski Country, Duck, Mallard, 1980..................................60.00
Ski Country, Duck, Pintail...75.00
Ski Country, Eagle, Harpy 110.00
Ski Country, Eagle on Water...100.00
Ski Country, Falcon, Gyrafalcon.....................................50.00
Ski Country, Falcon, Wht...85.00
Ski Country, Gamecocks, Fighting 125.00
Ski Country, Grouse, Ruffed...45.00
Ski Country, Hawk, Redtail..90.00
Ski Country, Owl, Barn..65.00
Ski Country, Owl, Horned..85.00
Ski Country, Owl, Saw-whet...50.00
Ski Country, Pheasant, Fighting......................................90.00
Ski Country, Pheasant in Corn 55.00
Wild Turkey, Series I, #1..250.00
Wild Turkey, Series I, #2..160.00
Wild Turkey, Series I, #3..70.00
Wild Turkey, Series I, #4..70.00
Wild Turkey, Series I, #5..30.00
Wild Turkey, Series I, #6..20.00
Wild Turkey, Series I, #7..20.00
Wild Turkey, Series I, #8..35.00

People

McCormick, Elvis, Gold..195.00
McCormick, Elvis, Karate 125.00
McCormick, Elvis, Karate, (m) 50.00
McCormick, Elvis, Sergeant..200.00
McCormick, Elvis, Sergeant, (m)....................................35.00
McCormick, Elvis, Silver...125.00
McCormick, Elvis #1..75.00
McCormick, Elvis #1, (m)...35.00
McCormick, Elvis #2..45.00
McCormick, Elvis #2, (m)...25.00
McCormick, Elvis #3..45.00
McCormick, Elvis #3, (m)...28.00
McCormick, Hank Williams, Jr......................................90.00
McCormick, Hank Williams, Sr......................................45.00

Vocations — Coalminers

Old Bardstown, Surface Miner.......................................20.00
Old Commonwealth, Miner #1, (m).................................20.00
Old Commonwealth, Miner #1, w/Shovel.......................100.00
Old Commonwealth, Miner #2, (m).................................20.00
Old Commonwealth, Miner #2, w/Pick............................50.00
Old Commonwealth, Miner #3, (m).................................25.00
Old Commonwealth, Miner #3, w/Lump of Coal..............35.00
Old Commonwealth, Miner #4, (m).................................20.00
Old Commonwealth, Miner #4, Lunch Time 35.00
Old Commonwealth, Miner #5, (m).................................20.00
Old Commonwealth, Miner #5, Coal Shooter 35.00

Vocations — Firefighters

Lionstone, #1, w/Hose 110.00

Lionstone, #2, w/Child..100.00
Lionstone, #3, Down Pole 80.00
Lionstone, #6, Hydrant..60.00
Lionstone, #7, Helmet..75.00
Lionstone, #9, Fire Extinguisher.............................55.00
Old Commonwealth, Professional #1, Modern Hero.....................35.00
Old Commonwealth, Professional #2, Nozzleman.........................40.00
Old Commonwealth, Professional #3, On Call............................45.00
Old Commonwealth, Professional #4, Fallen Comrade.................45.00
Old Commonwealth, Professional #5, Harmony..........................45.00
Old Commonwealth, Volunteer #2, Volunteer 50.00
Old Commonwealth, Volunteer #3, Valiant Volunteer 50.00
Old Commonwealth, Volunteer #4, Heroic Volunteer.............55.00
Old Commonwealth, Volunteer #5, Lifesaver 45.00
Old Commonwealth, Volunteer #6, Breaking Through.............45.00

Vocations — Railroad

Beam, Train, Baggage Car...55.00
Beam, Train, Boxcar, yel or brn 50.00
Beam, Train, Caboose, red 60.00
Beam, Train, Coal Tender..25.00
Beam, Train, Dining Car 80.00
Beam, Train, Grant Locomotive 70.00
Beam, Train, JB Turner Locomotive 85.00
Beam, Train, Log Car...40.00
Beam, Train, Lumber Car 30.00
Beam, Train, Observation Car..................................35.00
Beam, Train, Passenger Car 50.00
Beam, Train, Wood Tender.......................................30.00

Decoys

American colonists learned the craft of decoy making from the Indians who used them to lure birds out of the sky as an important food source. Early models were carved from pine, cedar, balsa, etc., and a few were made of canvas or papier-mache. There are two basic types of decoys: water floaters and shorebirds (also called 'stick-ups'). Within each type are many different species, ducks being the most plentiful since they migrated along all four of America's great waterways. Market hunting became big business around 1880, resulting in large-scale commercial production of decoys which continued until about 1910 when such hunting was outlawed by the Migratory Bird Treaty.

Today, decoys are one of the most collectible types of American folk art. The most valuable are those carved by such artists as Laing, Crowell, Ward, and Wheeler, to name only a few. Each area, such as Massachusetts, Connecticut, Maine, the Illinois River, and the Delaware River, produces decoys with distinctive regional characteristics. Examples of commercial decoys produced by well-known factories – among them Mason, Stevens, and Dodge – are also prized by collectors. Though mass-produced, these nevertheless required a certain amount of hand carving and decorating. Well-carved examples, especially those of rare species, are appreciating rapidly, and those with original paint are more desirable. Writer Carl F. Luckey has compiled a fully-illustrated identification and value guide, *Collecting Antique Bird Decoys*; you will find his address in the Directory under Alabama.

In the listings that follow, all decoys are solid-bodied unless noted hollow.

Key:
OP— original paint   RP— repaint
ORP— old repaint   WOP— worn original paint
OWP— original working paint   WRP— working repaint

Black Duck pair, carved by Charles Thomas, painted by Joseph Lincoln, glass eyes, lead weights, loss to original paint, shot scars, 18" long, $550.00.

Black Duck, Harry V Shourds, hollow, 1900, EX **5,000.00**
Black Duck, Jos Kupper OH, hollow, cvd detail, NM OP, 20" **300.00**
Black Duck, Ken Anger, hollow, trn head, NM **1,200.00**
Black Duck, Mason's Challenge, snakey head, NM **3,000.00**
Black Duck, Mason's Challenge, 1905, sm rpr, VG................. **1,250.00**
Black Duck, Mason's Premier, hollow, tail rpr, 1910, EX **2,250.00**
Black Duck, Mason's Premier, snakey head, rpr, 1900, EX....... **2,250.00**
Black Duck, Southwestern Ontario, tack eyes, shot scar, OP.......**150.00**
Bluebill, Art Herron, Ontario, simple relief detail, OP............**125.00**
Bluebill, Sam Denny, VG detail, glass eyes, WOP, 15" **175.00**
Bluebill drake, Adam Anger, EX detail, glass eyes, OP, 13"............**85.00**
Bluebill drake, Arthur Wellington, glass eyes, EX OP, 15" **175.00**
Bluebill drake, Ben Schmidt, sgn, glass eyes, WRP, crack **275.00**
Bluebill drake, Ed Kellie, glass eyes, worn OP, half-sz................**350.00**
Bluebill drake, Evans Decoy Co, glass eyes, OP, minor wear........**195.00**
Bluebill drake, Lake St Clair, glass eyes, WOP, 14" **175.00**
Bluebill drake, Mason's Premier, low head, hollow, EX **2,750.00**
Bluebill drake, MI, EX cvd detail, glass eyes, RP, 13" **180.00**
Bluebill drake, Peterson, Detroit, 1875, NM........................... **1,250.00**
Bluebill drake, WI, well-sculpted/exaggerated, WRP, 1920s **375.00**
Bluewing Teal pr, Mason's Standard, glass eyes, 1910, EX **3,250.00**
Brant, Lloyd Parker, hollow, 1910, bill/neck rpr, EX OP.......... **2,250.00**
Brant, Rowley Horner, hollow, swimming, orig weight, NM ... **3,750.00**
Broadbill pr, Mason's Standard, tack eyes, NM **1,250.00**
Bufflehead drake, Mason's Standard, glass eyes, EX OP **2,000.00**
Canada Goose, Geo Bowker, hollow, high head, WRP, rpr, 23" ..**825.00**
Canada Goose, hollow, glass eyes, old pnt, folky, 22½" **200.00**
Canada Goose, Jessie Birdsall, hollow, WRP, rpr, 1918, 22" **1,225.00**
Canvasback drake, Bob McGaw, 1940, all orig, EX **1,500.00**
Canvasback drake, IL River, hollow, drilled eyes, WOP, 17".........**85.00**
Canvasback drake, Mason's Premier, lightly shot, NM OP...... **2,250.00**
Canvasback drake, Mason's Premier, snakey head, 1895, NM. **2,750.00**
Canvasback drake, Mason's Premier, 1910, NM orig............... **1,700.00**
Canvasback drake, Ontario, hollow, glass eyes, rpr, EX OP **105.00**
Canvasback drake, R Madison Mitchell, his rpt, early, 16" **275.00**
Canvasback drake, Ralph Malpage, EX detail, varnish, 12".........**100.00**
Canvasback pr, Mason's Seneca Lake, 1910, EX orig **2,750.00**
Coot, Herter's, canvas-covered cork, 1940s, M **275.00**
Coot, Mason's Challenge, 1910, sm rprs, EX OP **2,250.00**
Goldeneye drake, Harry Norman, cvd wings, glass eyes, WOP **95.00**
Goldeneye pr, Madison Mitchell, 1960, NM **1,500.00**
Goldeneye pr, Southwestern Ontario, glass eyes, WRP, '50s **70.00**
Greater Yellowlegs, NJ, elongated body, 1910, EX **950.00**
Hudsonian Curlew, NJ, orig sickle bill, 1900, EX **1,100.00**
Mallard drake, Bert Graves, swimmer, 1935, EX OP, rare **650.00**
Mallard drake, Bert Graves, 1928, sm rpr, VG OP................... **1,100.00**
Mallard drake, John McLoughlin, hollow, sgn/dtd, NM **2,000.00**
Mallard drake, Mason's Challenge, hollow, EX OP style, rstr.. **1,650.00**
Mallard hen, CA, lt/hollow, tack eyes, EX OP, ca 1930s...............**145.00**
Mallard hen, David Simandl, glass eyes, OP, 1950s, 18" **200.00**

Mallard hen, Heck Whittington, 1929, orig weight, EX.......... **1,350.00**
Mallard hen, Herter's balsa/pine kit, glass eyes, OP, 16" **45.00**
Mallard hen, Ignatious Valentine Stachowik, down to OP..........**250.00**
Mallard pr, Mason's Standard, glass eyes, 1910, VG OP **950.00**
Merganser drake, Knots Island VA, glass eyes, 1900, OP.............**150.00**
Merganser hen, Mason's Standard, tack eyes, 1905, NM......... **2,000.00**

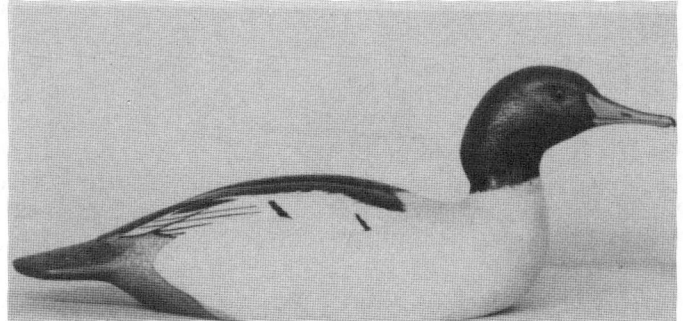

American Merganser drake by Joe Wooster, inscribed by the artist and dated 1975, EX, $1,400.00.

Pintail drake, Chas Perdew, pnt by Edna, minor rstr, 1927 ..... **5,500.00**
Pintail drake, Mason's Standard, glass eyes, EX OP **1,350.00**
Pintail drake, Robert Elliston, EX OP, rare............................. **3,500.00**
Pintail pr, Madison Mitchell, 1960, M **1,500.00**
Pintail pr, Mason's Premier, bold feathering, 1905, EX OP **9,000.00**
Pintail pr, Wildfowler, Old Saybrook, balsa, EX **550.00**
Redbreasted Merganser pr, Eugene Hendrickson, 1965, EX........**850.00**
Redhead drake, Mason's Premier, 1910, EX dry OP **1,500.00**
Redhead drake, Thos Chamber, sm filled chip, EX................. **1,350.00**
Sanderling Peep, Jim Slack, Pekin IL, orig pnt, 7" **125.00**
Scaup drake, Reg Culver, hollow, orig weight, NM **3,500.00**
Shorebird, primitive, made from 1 pc wood, tack eyes, EX **95.00**
Shoveler drake, Hurley Conklin, 1965, M....................................**750.00**
Wood Duck drake, Ken Harris, 1940, unused, NM **750.00**

Dedham Art Pottery

In 1895 the Chelsea Pottery moved to Dedham, changing its name to indicate the new locality and to avoid confusion with the Chelsea companies of England. Though their primary product was the blue-printed crackle-glazed dinnerware, two types of artware were also produced: crackle glaze and flambe. Their notable volcanic ware was a type of the latter. The mark is incised and often accompanies the cipher of Hugh Robertson. See also Chelsea Keramic Art Works.

Bowl, moss gr mottled drip, 4 arched ft, sgn HR, 8¾" **300.00**
Vase, celadon, tapered bulbous form, sgn HR, 8" **850.00**
Vase, gloss w/dragon's blood/moss/bl/rust, HCR, 15", EX **4,250.00**
Vase, olive gloss, cylindrical, sgn HCR, 10" **325.00**
Vase, oxblood, bulbous, wide mouth/short neck, label, 6½".... **2,500.00**
Vase, oxblood/bl/gr 'leopard skin' experimental, HCR, 11" ... **4,100.00**
Vase, red/burnt brn drip, short neck, sgn HR, 9", EX **2,000.00**
Vase, sang de boeuf w/gr blush, classic form, 13", NM **6,750.00**
Vase, volcanic gray/bl/brn, wide mouth, sgn HR, 10", EX....... **1,000.00**
Vase, wht iris on bl crackle, sgn/#34, 7½", NM **2,200.00**

Dedham Dinnerware

Originally founded in Morrisville, Pennsylvania, as the Chelsea Keramic Works, the name was changed to Dedham Pottery in 1895

after the firm relocated in Dedham, near Boston, Massachusetts. The move was effected to make use of the native clay deemed more suitable for the production of the popular dinnerware designed by Hugh Robinson, founder of the company. The ware utilized a gray stoneware body with a crackle glaze and simple cobalt border designs of flowers, birds, and animals. Decorations were brushed on by hand using an ancient Chinese method which suspended the cobalt within the overall glaze. There were thirteen standard patterns, among them Magnolia, Iris, Butterfly, Duck, Polar Bear, and the Rabbit, the latter of which was chosen to represent the company on their logo. On the very early pieces the rabbits face left; decorators soon found the reverse position easier to paint, and the rabbits were turned to the right. In addition to the standard patterns, other designs were produced for special orders. These and artist signed pieces are highly valued by collectors today.

The firm was operated by succeeding generations of the Robertson family until it closed in 1943. See also Chelsea Keramic Works.

Ash tray, Dutch Boy, unmk, 4⅞", EX **2,000.00**
Ash tray, Elephant, in central medallion, stamped, 4", EX **275.00**
Ash tray, Rabbit, stamped/registered, 4" **325.00**
Bowl, Grape, 1897 rabbit mk, 3¼x7" **350.00**
Bowl, Horse Chestnut, rabbit mk, 7", EX **450.00**
Bowl, lg 3-petal flower, cut corners, registered, 3½x9" **1,000.00**
Bowl, Magnolia, registered, 6", EX...**350.00**
Bowl, Rabbit, bl mk/incised mk, 5⅜", EX **400.00**
Bowl, Rabbit, button finial on dome lid, stamped, 7½"..............**475.00**
Bowl, Rabbit, flared rim, bl rabbit mk, 9½", EX **400.00**
Bowl, Rabbit, lotus edge, stamped/registered/impressed, 9"........**750.00**
Bowl, Rabbit, registered, dtd 1931, 8¼", EX...............................**700.00**
Bowl, Rabbit, registered, 12½", EX **750.00**
Bowl, Rabbit, registered, 5½", EX **350.00**
Bowl, Rabbit, registered, 5¾", ...**450.00**
Bowl, Rabbit, registered, 8", EX **300.00**
Bowl, Rabbit, registered, 9" **550.00**
Bowl, Rabbit, shallow, registered, hairline, 9¼"..........................**100.00**
Bowl, Rabbit, stamped, w/lid, 6x9½" L **900.00**
Bowl, Rabbit, stamped, 4½", EX **300.00**
Bowl, Rabbit, stamped, 7", EX **400.00**
Bowl, rabbits in row of ovals, stamped, hairline, 2½x4¾" **650.00**
Bowl, stylized flowers, cut corners, stamped, 8" **950.00**
Bowl, Swan, bl rabbit mk, 6", EX **500.00**
Bowl, Turkey, registered, 5½" **350.00**
Butterpat, Pansy, stamped, 3½" **275.00**
Butterpat, Primrose, stamped, 3½" **225.00**
Candlestick, Rabbit, stamped/registered, 1½x3½", pr **375.00**
Chamberstick, Rabbit, registered, 1½", pr **750.00**
Child's dish, Rabbit (center medallion/rabbit rim), 8"............. **1,000.00**
Creamer, Elephant, bulbous, cylinder neck, factory flaw, 3".........**500.00**
Creamer, Grape, stamped/incised D9, 5" **325.00**
Creamer, Magnolia, bl rabbit mk, hairline, 2¼" **125.00**
Creamer, Night & Morning, bl rabbit mk, 4⅞", EX **700.00**
Creamer, Night & Morning, mk, 5"..**950.00**
Creamer, Night & Morning, unmk, glaze bubbling, 4⅞".............**475.00**
Creamer, Rabbit, bl rabbit mk, 3¼", EX **325.00**
Creamer, Rabbit, bulbous w/cylinder neck, stamped, 5½" **325.00**
Creamer, Rabbit, registered, 3⅜" **375.00**
Creamer, Rabbit, 3⅜", EX **325.00**
Creamer, tankard; Rabbit, imp, 5" **375.00**
Cup & saucer, Crab, stamped/registered/dtd 1931, 6" dia............**700.00**
Cup & saucer, Rabbit, registered, M **275.00**
Cup plate, Rabbit, registered, 4⅜", EX **425.00**
Dish, Rabbit, ruffled, stamped, 9"..**650.00**
Dish, Rabbit, 5-sided, stamped, 7" **550.00**
Egg cup, Rabbit, dbl, ftd, unsgn, 3x3½" **250.00**

Flower arranger, rabbit form, unmk, 6⅛", EX 850.00
Jar, Scottie Dog, dome lid, stamped/registered, rpr, 6" 1,200.00
Knife rest, Rabbit, stamped, 2½" 425.00
Marmalade, Azalea, cylindrical, stamped, 4½" 475.00
Marmalade, Grape, spherical, stamped/sgn B, 5" 475.00
Mug, Rabbit, registered, dtd 1931, 3⅜", EX 575.00
Paperweight, rabbit form, registered, 3½" 500.00
Paperweight, turtle, stamped, 3½" L 500.00
Pitcher, Oak Block, stamped/registered, 5½" 1,300.00
Pitcher, Rabbit, pear shape w/angle hdl, stamped, 7" 500.00
Pitcher, tankard; Rabbit, registered/dtd 1931, sm crack, 6⅞".......350.00
Plate, Azalea, 2 imp mks/registered, 8½", EX 250.00
Plate, Azalea, 2 incised mks/registered, 9⅝", EX 450.00

Azalea plate, stamped, 9¾", EX, $450.00; Rabbit sugar and creamer, stamped, 4½", $700.00.

Plate, Bird in Potted Orange Tree, imp, 10¼", NM.....................800.00
Plate, Butterfly, experimental, stamped, 6" 700.00
Plate, Crab, impressed/stamped/registered, 12" 1,100.00
Plate, Crab, stamped/impressed, 6" 500.00
Plate, Crab w/Waves, 2 incised mks/registered, 8⅝", EX 750.00
Plate, Day Lily, stamped, sm age line, 6¼" 475.00
Plate, Dolphin, CPUS mk/incised, 10⅛", EX..........................1,500.00
Plate, Dolphin, stamped, 6½"..........................650.00
Plate, Duck, bl rabbit mk, age line, 10" 250.00
Plate, Duck, bl rabbit mk, 6⅛", EX 300.00
Plate, Duck, imp/stamped, 8⅜", EX 375.00
Plate, Duck, registered, 6⅜", EX 350.00
Plate, Duck, sgn Maud Davenport 'O,' imp/stamped, 8½" 275.00
Plate, Fish, moulded rim, tercentenary mk, 8⅞" 2,300.00
Plate, Fly & Moth variant, bl rabbit mk, 6⅛", EX..........................200.00
Plate, Flying Woodcock, stamped, rim chip, 8½" 650.00
Plate, Grape, stamped, 8½"..........................225.00
Plate, Horse Chestnut, imp/stamped, 6", EX 200.00
Plate, Horse Chestnut, registered, 8½", EX 250.00
Plate, Horse Chestnut, sgn M Davenport, imp/stamped, 8½" 300.00
Plate, Horse Chestnut, 10", EX..........................350.00
Plate, Iris, stamped, 8½" 300.00
Plate, lg standing bird in center, stamped, 8½" 1,700.00
Plate, Lobster, impressed/stamped, 6" 750.00
Plate, Lobster & Wave, 2 imp mks/registered, 7½" 750.00
Plate, Magnolia, imp/stamped, 6⅛", EX..........................175.00

Plate, Magnolia, imp/stamped, 8½", EX..........................200.00
Plate, Moth, imp/stamped, rstr, 8½"..........................275.00
Plate, Mushroom, imp/stamped, 6", NM..........................325.00
Plate, Mushroom, stamped, 6"..........................450.00
Plate, Mushroom, 10"..........................495.00
Plate, Owl, bl rabbit mk, rough glaze, 6⅛" 825.00
Plate, Pineapple, imp, 10⅛", NM..........................800.00
Plate, Polar Bear, stamped, 6"..........................550.00
Plate, Pond Lily, bl rabbit mk, 8½", EX..........................250.00
Plate, Pond Lily, CPUS mk, 10¼", EX 2,500.00
Plate, Pond Lily, imp, 8⅝", EX 300.00
Plate, Pond Lily, incised, 10¼", EX..........................350.00
Plate, Poppy, 5-cornered, registered, 7⅜", EX..........................475.00
Plate, Poppy (in center), wht on bl, 8¾", VG..........................400.00
Plate, Rabbit, bl rabbit mk, 6⅛", NM 195.00
Plate, Rabbit, bl rabbit mk, 8½", EX..........................225.00
Plate, Rabbit, imp, 10⅛", EX..........................275.00
Plate, Rabbit, stamped/incised, 10⅜", EX..........................300.00
Plate, Rabbit, 2 imp mks/registered, 9¾", EX 175.00
Plate, Scottie Dog, stamped/registered, 8¾"..........................1,800.00
Plate, Scottie Dog, stamped/registered/dtd, 8½"..........................1,700.00
Plate, Snow Tree, sgn Maud Davenport 'O,' bl mk, 6⅛", EX.......250.00
Plate, Snow Tree, sgn Maud Davenport 'O,' incised, 11", EX......450.00
Plate, Snow Tree, stamped, 10"..........................400.00
Plate, Snow Tree, 2 imp mks/stamped, 6"..........................175.00
Plate, Strawberry, imp rabbit mk, 6"..........................1,500.00
Plate, stylized floral border, bsk fired, rabbit mk, 8½"..................650.00
Plate, Swan, bl rabbit mk, 6", EX 575.00
Plate, Swan, imp/stamped/registered 1931, 7½" 350.00
Plate, Tapestry Lion, stamped, 8½" 1,700.00
Plate, Tufted Duck, imp, 10⅛", EX..........................350.00
Plate, Tufted Duck, incised, 8¾", EX..........................275.00
Plate, Turkey, imp/stamped, 8½", EX..........................350.00
Plate, Turkey, incised/registered, 6⅜", EX 425.00
Plate, Turkey, registered, 10", EX..........................475.00
Plate, Turkey, sgn Maud Davenport 'O,' bl mk, 8⅜", EX.............425.00
Plate, Turkey, 2 imp mks/registered, 6¼", EX 400.00
Plate, Turkey, 2 imp mks/registered, 8½", EX 425.00
Plate, Turkey (turned left), sgn Robertson, imp, 8⅝".............. 1,600.00
Plate, Turtle, Double; stamped/B1, 6" 850.00
Plate, Turtle, stamped, dtd 2/17/16, 8½"..........................750.00

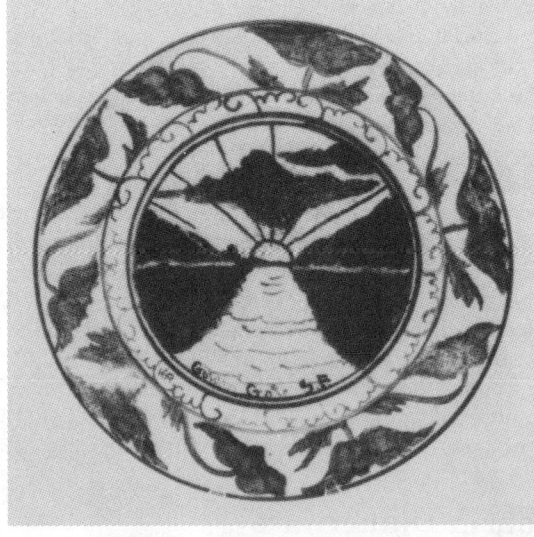

Plate, Golden Gate, San Francisco, sgned HCR, impressed/stamped, 10", $2,200.00.

Platter, Rabbit, stamped, 14x8½"	700.00
Saucer, Horse Chestnut, registered, 5", EX	125.00
Shaker, Baby Elephant, 2¾", EX	625.00
Shakers, Rabbit, DP mk, 3¾", EX, pr	450.00
Sugar bowl, Rabbit, registered, w/lid, 2¾", EX	300.00
Sugar bowl, Rabbit, squat/bulbous, unmk, 3"	275.00
Sugar bowl, Rabbit, 4", EX	275.00
Tea tile, Rabbit, stamped, 6" dia	400.00
Tea tile, Rabbit, stamped, 7⅝"	375.00
Teapot, Rabbit, ovoid, dome lid, stamped, 7", EX	450.00
Tray, celery; Rabbit, registered, sm chip, 9¾"	150.00
Tray, celery; Rabbit, 2 imp mks/registered, 9⅝", EX	375.00
Tray, celery; Swan, rectangular, imp/registered, 1931, 9¾"	700.00
Tray, Rabbit, stamped, minor bubble bursts, 13"	550.00

Degenhart

The Crystal Art Glass factory in Cambridge, Ohio, opened in 1947 under the private ownership of John and Elizabeth Degenhart. John had previously worked for the Cambridge Glass Company and was well known for his superior paperweights. After his death in 1964, Elizabeth took over management of the factory, hiring several workers from the defunct Cambridge Company, including Zack Boyd. Boyd was responsible for many unique colors, some of which were named for him. From 1964 to 1974, more than twenty-seven different moulds were created, most of them resulting from Elizabeth Degenhart's work and creativity, and over 145 official colors were developed. Elizabeth died in 1978, requesting that the ten moulds she had built while operating the factory were to be turned over to the Degenhart Museum. The remaining moulds were to be held by the Island Mould and Machine Company, who (complying with her request) removed the familiar 'D in heart' trademark. The factory was eventually bought by Zack's son, Bernard Boyd. He also acquired the remaining Degenhart moulds, to which he added his own logo.

In general, slags, jades, and opaques should be valued 15% to 20% higher than crystals in color.

Baby Shoe Toothpick, Milk Blue	20.00
Beaded Oval Toothpick, Lemon Custard	32.00
Bell, Blue Fire	8.00
Bell, Crown Tuscan	8.00
Bell, Custard	7.50
Bell, Heatherbloom	7.50
Bell, Lime Ice	16.00
Bell, Misty Brown	7.50
Bell, Rose Marie Pink	6.00
Bell, Vaseline	7.50
Bird Salt, Amberina	16.00
Bird Salt & Pepper, Milk Blue	40.00
Bow Shoe, Blue Marble Slag	20.00
Buzz Saw Wine, Amberina	42.00
Buzz Saw Wine, Cobalt	40.00
Buzz Saw Wine, Light Custard #5	34.00
Candy Dish, Amethyst, unmk	30.00
Candy Dish, Cobalt, unmk	22.00
Candy Dish, Crown Tuscan, unmk	23.00
Candy Dish, Crystal, unmk	17.50
Centennial Bell, Amethyst	5.00
Centennial Bell, Opal	15.00
Chick, Cobalt, 2"	28.00
Chick, Lemon Custard, 2"	50.00
Child's Mug, Apple Green	12.50
Child's Mug, Opal	12.50

Coaster, Amber	10.00
Colonial Drape Toothpick, Light Custard	18.00
Daisy & Button Salt, Custard, unmk	10.00
Daisy & Button Salt, Light Amberina	12.50
Daisy & Button Salt, Vaseline	22.00
Daisy & Button Toothpick, Lime Ice	20.00
Daisy & Button Toothpick, Light Amberina	16.00
Dog, April Green	12.50
Dog, Bittersweet	16.00
Dog, Bittersweet Slag	66.00
Dog, Daffodil	12.50
Dog, Fantastic	28.00
Dog, Fawn	25.00
Dog, Gray Marble	16.00
Dog, Green Opal	12.50
Dog, Heatherbloom	22.00
Dog, Milk Blue	12.50
Dog, Old Lavender	12.50
Dog, Peach Opal	12.50
Dog, Persimmon, inside mk	22.00
Dog, Red	15.00
Dog, Taffee	12.50
Dog, Tangerine	27.50
Dog, Tomato	85.00
Forget-Me-Not Toothpick, Caramel	30.00
Forget-Me-Not Toothpick, Custard	16.00
Forget-Me-Not Toothpick, Dark Chocolate Creme	17.50
Forget-Me-Not Toothpick, Lavender Blue	17.50
Forget-Me-Not Toothpick, Milk Blue	12.50
Gypsy Pot Toothpick, Amethyst	15.00
Gypsy Pot Toothpick, Canary	24.00
Hand, Crown Tuscan	15.00
Hand, Persimmon	10.00

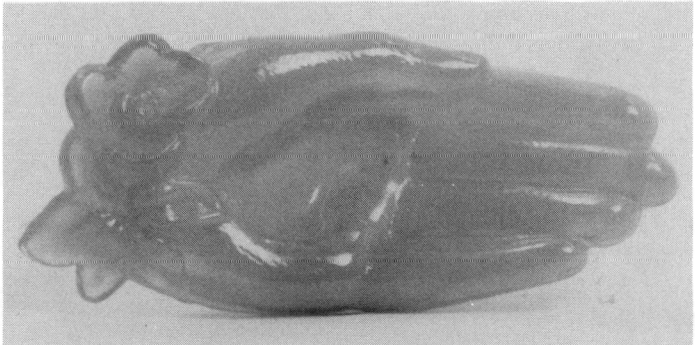

Hand, Tomato, 5", $60.00.

Hat, Vaseline, unmk	17.00
Heart Box, Baby Pink	24.00
Heart Box, Brown	22.00
Heart Box, Chocolate	32.00
Heart Box, Light Chocolate Creme	24.00
Heart Box, Milk Blue	24.00
Heart Toothpick, Amethyst	18.00
Hen, Amberina, unmk, 3"	22.00
Hen, Brown Sparrow Slag, 3"	55.00
Hen, Canary, 3"	28.00
High Boot, Crystal	15.00
Hobo Shoe, Brown Sparrow Slag	23.00
Jewel Box, Baby Green	30.00
Mini Pitcher, Opal	25.00
Mug, Amberina	15.00

Mug, Heather...12.50
Owl, Blue-Green..72.50
Owl, Bluebell..32.00
Owl, Cobalt..22.00
Owl, Custard..30.00
Owl, Custard Opal..55.00
Owl, Dark Blue Fire..27.50
Owl, Fog Opaque..60.00
Owl, Heliotrope..80.00
Owl, Mauve..35.00
Owl, Milk Blue...25.00
Owl, Mystery Surprise 135.00
Owl, Peach Glo...22.00
Owl, Pigeon Blood 34.00
Owl, Sunset..25.00
Owl, Violet #1..27.50
Pooche, Buttercup Slag..40.00
Pooche, Gray Marble Opal...30.00
Pooche, Milk White 20.00
Pooche, Tomato Slag...45.00
Priscilla, Fawn..60.00
Priscilla, Jade Green 100.00
Priscilla, Smokey Blue...95.00
Priscilla Doll, Daffodil...88.00
Priscilla Doll, Jade..88.00
Priscilla Doll, Periwinkle..75.00
Robin, Crown Tuscan, unmk, 5" 36.00
Seal of Ohio Cup Plate, Colored Crystals............................10.00
Skate Shoe, Sapphire, unmk...34.00
Star & Dewdrop Salt, Custard, unmk..................................10.00
Star & Dewdrop Salt, Heatherbloom 12.50
Tomahawk, Emerald Green 23.00
Tramp Shoe, Rosemary Pink 10.00
Turkey, Amethyst..60.00
Turkey, Gray Slag, unmk 80.00
Wildflower Candy Dish, Twilight Blue 40.00

Delatte

Delatte was a manufacturer of French cameo glass. Founded in 1921, their style reflected the influence of the Art Deco era with strong color contrasts and bold design.

Our advisor for this category is Don Williams; he is listed in the Directory under Iowa.

Cameo

Vase, bleeding heart, brn on mottled orange, ovoid, 6" 550.00
Vase, irises, bl/purple on wht, narrow neck, 8" 600.00
Vase, maple branches, red on wht, 9" 800.00
Vase, roses, purple on pk, pear form, 8" 800.00
Vase, wisteria, bl tones on frost & bl, 10"................................1,250.00

Delft

Old Delftware, made as early as the 16th century, was originally a low-fired earthenware coated in a thin opaque tin glaze with painted-on polychrome designs. It was not until the last half of the 19th century, however, that the ware became commonly referred to as Delft, acquiring the name from the Dutch village that had become the major center of its production. English, German, and French potters also produced Delft, though with noticeable differences both in shape and decorative theme.

In the early part of the 18th century, the German potter, Bottger, developed a formula for porcelain; in England, Wedgwood began producing creamware – both of which were much more durable. Unable to compete, one by one the Delft potteries failed. Soon only one remained. In 1876 De Porcelyne Fles reintroduced Delftware on a hard white body with blue and white decorative themes reflecting the Dutch countryside, windmills by the sea, and Dutch children. This manufacturer is the most well known of several operating today. Their products are now produced under the Royal Delft label. Examples listed here are blue on white unless noted otherwise. See also specific manufacturers.

Pastille burner, Germany, 6", $135.00.

Bowl, floral, hairline, 3½x7⅝", EX 600.00
Canteen, floral/windmill/man & harp, bl/wht/blk, sgn AK, 7" 250.00
Clock, Germany, kitchen type, 4-lobed, 8-day, 8½" 95.00
Jar, apothecary; coat of arms, labels, rpr ft, 4 ½", pr 750.00
Jar, birds/flowers, mk, minor chips, 9¾"...................................650.00
Jar, herons/flowers/pines, mk, minor chips, 9¾" 650.00
Pastille burner, Germany, Tapperij Curacau, 2-pc, 6"..................135.00
Plaque, portrait, after Rembrandt, fruit borders, 15" dia 250.00
Plate, building/trees, minor wear, 8¾" 400.00
Plate, floral, bl/wht, yel rim, sgn BPJ, 9", EX 175.00
Plate, floral, sm rim chip, 10¾"...350.00
Plate, Oriental motif, yel rim, minor wear, 9"..............................250.00
Plate, pancake; Dutch, people/view, 1720, 10", EX 150.00
Plate, ship/castle/etc, minor wear, 9" 350.00
Tankard, Oriental motif, pewter base & lid, 1719, 8½" 1,500.00
Thermometer, Dutch, Grandfather's clock form, 7" 125.00
Tile picture, Dutch, river/boat/horse, manganese, 17x12"...........400.00
Tile picture, Dutch, Wm II on horsebk, 15x10" 90.00
Vase, floral, sgn BP, 8", EX 275.00

Denver

The Denver China and Pottery Company began production in 1901 in Denver, Colorado. The founder, William A. Long, used materials native to Colorado and produced underglaze-decorated brownware as well as other artware lines. Several marks were used: an impressed 'Denver' (often with the Lonhuda Faience cipher inside a shield), an imprinted 'Denaura,' and an arrow mark. Pieces were sometimes dated.

Jar, bl, lightly cvd banded motif in wht, mk, 5x4"......................250.00
Vase, bl w/wht decor, Denver Wht, 5"..250.00

Vase, emb violets/leaves, lt gr, Denaura, 2¼x5½" **475.00**
Vase, gray matt, no decor, mk Denver Wht 1916, 4¾" **140.00**

Vase, blue matt with sgraffito band, 6", $195.00.

Depression Glass

Other than coins and stamps, colored glassware produced during the Depression era is probably the most sought-after collectible in the field today. There are literally thousands of collectors in the United States and Canada buying, selling, and trading 'Depression Glass' on today's market.

Depression Glass is defined by Gene Florence, author of several best-selling books on the subject, as 'the inexpensive glassware made primarily during the Depression era in the colors of amber, green, pink, blue, red, yellow, white, and crystal.' This glass was mass produced, sold through five-and-dime stores and mail-order catalogs, and given away as premiums with gas and food products.

The listings in this book are far from being complete. If you want a more thorough presentation of this fascinating glassware, we recommend *The Collector's Encyclopedia of Depression Glass, Pocket Guide to Depression Glass,* and *Very Rare Depression Glass, Vol. II,* by Gene Florence, whose address is listed in the Directory under Kentucky.

Adam, ash tray, pk, 4½" 23.00
Adam, bowl, cereal; pk, 5¾" 30.00
Adam, bowl, dessert; pk, 4¾" 10.00
Adam, bowl, gr, oval, 10" 19.00
Adam, bowl, gr, w/lid, 9" 65.00
Adam, bowl, gr, 7¾" 15.00
Adam, bowl, pk, w/lid, 9" 42.00
Adam, cake plate, ftd, 10" 14.00
Adam, candlesticks, pk, 4", pr 60.00
Adam, candy jar, w/lid, 2½" 75.00
Adam, coaster, gr, 3¾" 13.00
Adam, creamer, pk 13.00
Adam, cup, pk 28.00
Adam, lamp, pk or gr 225.00
Adam, pitcher, gr, 32-oz, 8" 32.50
Adam, plate, dinner; gr, sq, 9" 16.00
Adam, plate, dinner; pk, sq, 9" 17.00

Adam, plate, grill; gr, 9" 13.00
Adam, plate, salad; pk, sq, 7¾" 8.00
Adam, plate, sherbet; pk, 6" 4.00
Adam, platter, pk, 11¾" 15.00
Adam, shakers, pk, 4", pr 42.50
Adam, sherbet, gr, 3" 28.00
Adam, tray, relish; gr, divided, 8" 12.50
Adam, tumbler, gr, 4½" 16.00
Adam, tumbler, iced tea; pk, 5½" 43.00
Adam, vase, gr, 7½" 35.00
American Pioneer, bowl, console; gr, 10⅜" 50.00
American Pioneer, bowl, gr, w/lid, 8¾" 85.00
American Pioneer, bowl, pk, hdls, 5" 12.50
American Pioneer, bowl, pk, hdls, 9" 15.00
American Pioneer, candlesticks, pk, 6½", pr 50.00
American Pioneer, candy jar, gr, w/lid, 1½-lb 95.00
American Pioneer, candy jar, pk, w/lid, 1-lb 65.00
American Pioneer, coaster, gr, 3½" 18.00
American Pioneer, creamer, pk, 3½" 16.00

American Pioneer, cup, gr 9.00
American Pioneer, cup, pk 7.00
American Pioneer, goblet, water; pk, 8-oz, 6" 27.00
American Pioneer, goblet, wine; gr, 3-oz, 4" 40.00
American Pioneer, ice bucket, pk, 6" 35.00
American Pioneer, lamp, pk, 8½" 75.00
American Pioneer, mayonnaise, gr, 4¼" 75.00
American Pioneer, pitcher, gr, w/lid, 7" 175.00
American Pioneer, pitcher, pk, w/lid, 5" 110.00
American Pioneer, plate, gr, hdls, 11½" 14.00
American Pioneer, plate, pk, 8" 6.00
American Pioneer, sherbet, gr, 3½" 16.00
American Pioneer, sherbet, pk, 4¾" 22.00
American Pioneer, sugar bowl, gr, 2¾" 17.00
American Pioneer, sugar bowl, pk, 3½" 16.00
American Pioneer, tumbler, gr, 12-oz, 5" 40.00
American Pioneer, tumbler, gr, 8-oz, 4" 27.50
American Pioneer, tumbler, juice; pk, 5-oz 17.50
American Pioneer, tumbler, pk, 12-oz, 5" 25.00
American Pioneer, whiskey, pk, 2-oz, 2¼" 32.50
American Sweetheart, bowl, berry; monax, 9" 38.00
American Sweetheart, bowl, cereal; pk, 6" 9.50
American Sweetheart, bowl, console; monax, 18" 275.00
American Sweetheart, bowl, cream soup; pk, 4½" 30.00
American Sweetheart, bowl, soup; monax, 9½" 40.00
American Sweetheart, cup, pk 9.50
American Sweetheart, pitcher, pk, 80-oz, 8" 360.00
American Sweetheart, plate, luncheon; monax, 9" 8.00
American Sweetheart, platter, pk, oval, 13" 20.00
American Sweetheart, sherbet, monax, ftd, 4¼" 13.00
American Sweetheart, tumbler, pk, 9-oz, 4¼" 45.00
Anniversary, bowl, berry; pk, 4⅞" 3.00

Anniversary, bowl, soup; crystal, 7⅜".............................. 4.00
Anniversary, cake plate, crystal, 12½"............................ 5.50
Anniversary, candy jar, pk, w/lid.................................30.00
Anniversary, cup, pk... 4.50
Anniversary, dish, pickle; crystal, 9"............................ 3.50
Anniversary, plate, cake; crystal, 12½"........................... 5.50
Anniversary, plate, dinner; pk, 9"................................ 5.50
Anniversary, plate, sherbet; pk, 6¼".............................. 2.00
Anniversary, sherbet, crystal, ftd................................ 2.50
Anniversary, vase, pk, 6½".......................................15.00
Aunt Polly, bowl, berry; bl, lg, 7⅞".............................22.00
Aunt Polly, bowl, berry; gr, 4⅜".................................. 6.00
Aunt Polly, bowl, gr, oval, 8⅜"..................................30.00
Aunt Polly, creamer, gr..22.00
Aunt Polly, pitcher, bl, 48-oz, 8"..............................135.00
Aunt Polly, plate, sherbet; gr, 6"................................ 4.00
Aunt Polly, sherbet, gr... 7.50
Aunt Polly, sugar bowl, bl.......................................25.00
Aunt Polly, tumbler, bl, 8-oz, 3¾"...............................20.00
Aunt Polly, vase, bl, ftd, 6½"...................................30.00
Aurora, bowl, cobalt, 5⅜"... 8.00
Aurora, creamer, cobalt, 4½".....................................10.00
Aurora, cup, cobalt... 6.00
Aurora, plate, cobalt, 6½".. 4.00
Aurora, tumbler, cobalt, 4¾".....................................13.00
Avocado, bowl, relish; pk, ftd, 6"...............................15.00
Avocado, bowl, salad; gr, 7½"....................................40.00
Avocado, creamer, pk, ftd..25.00
Avocado, cup, gr, ftd..26.00
Avocado, pitcher, pk, 64-oz.....................................425.00
Avocado, plate, cake; pk, hdls, 10¼".............................25.00
Avocado, saucer, pk..18.00
Avocado, sherbet, gr...45.00
Avocado, sugar bowl, gr, ftd.....................................27.50
Avocado, tumbler, pk...85.00
Beaded Block, bowl, gr, plain edge, 7½".......................... 7.50
Beaded Block, bowl, gr, 6¼"....................................... 6.50
Beaded Block, bowl, jelly; gr, hdls, 4½".......................... 6.00
Beaded Block, bowl, opal, hdl, 5½"...............................10.00
Beaded Block, bowl, opal, sq, 5½"................................. 8.50
Beaded Block, creamer, gr..12.50
Beaded Block, plate, gr, sq, 7¾".................................. 5.00
Beaded Block, plate, opal, 8¾"...................................15.00
Beaded Block, sugar bowl, opal...................................20.00
Beaded Block, vase, opal, 6".....................................18.00
Block Optic, bowl, berry; gr, 4¼"................................. 5.00
Block Optic, bowl, berry; pk, lg, 8½"............................12.00
Block Optic, bowl, cereal; pk, 5¼"................................ 6.00
Block Optic, candlestick, gr, 1¾", pr............................50.00

Block Optic, candy jar, pk, w/lid, 2¼"...........................32.50
Block Optic, creamer, pk, 3 styles, ea........................... 9.50
Block Optic, cup, gr, 4 styles, ea............................... 5.00
Block Optic, goblet, wine; gr, 9-oz, 5¾".........................17.00
Block Optic, ice bucket, pk......................................22.50
Block Optic, plate, dinner; gr, 9"...............................13.50
Block Optic, plate, dinner; pk, 9"...............................17.00
Block Optic, plate, luncheon; gr, 8".............................. 3.00
Block Optic, plate, sherbet; gr, 6"............................... 1.50
Block Optic, shakers, pk, ftd, pr................................45.00
Block Optic, sherbet, gr, 5½-oz, 3¼".............................. 4.50
Block Optic, tumbler, gr, flat, 14-oz............................20.00
Block Optic, tumbler, gr, ftd, 9-oz..............................13.50
Block Optic, tumbler, pk, flat, 9-oz.............................10.00
Block Optic, whiskey, pk or gr, 2-oz, 2¼"........................16.00
Bowknot, bowl, cereal; gr, 5½"...................................12.00
Bowknot, cup, gr.. 5.00
Bowknot, plate, salad; gr, 7".................................... 7.50
Bowknot, tumbler, gr, 10-oz, 5"..................................11.00
Bubble, bowl, berry; crystal, 4"................................. 3.50
Bubble, bowl, cereal; bl, 5¼"..................................... 8.00
Bubble, bowl, soup; crystal, 7¾"................................. 5.00
Bubble, creamer, bl..21.00
Bubble, cup, bl... 3.00
Bubble, pitcher, red, ice lip, 64-oz.............................37.50
Bubble, plate, dinner; bl, 9⅜"................................... 5.00
Bubble, platter, crystal, oval, 12".............................. 4.00
Bubble, sugar bowl, crystal...................................... 3.00
Bubble, tumbler, iced tea; red, 12-oz............................ 9.00
Bubble, tumbler, water; red, 9-oz................................ 6.00
Cameo, bowl, berry; gr, 8¼"......................................24.00
Cameo, bowl, salad; gr, 7¼"......................................35.00
Cameo, bowl, vegetable; yel, oval, 10"...........................30.00
Cameo, candlesticks, gr, 4", pr..................................75.00
Cameo, creamer, gr, 4¼"..17.50
Cameo, creamer, yel, 3¼"...12.50
Cameo, cup, yel, 2 styles, ea.................................... 6.50
Cameo, goblet, water; gr, 6".....................................37.50
Cameo, jam jar, gr, w/lid, 2"...................................120.00
Cameo, plate, dinner; gr, 9½"....................................12.00
Cameo, plate, grill; gr, closed hdls, 10½".......................50.00
Cameo, plate, grill; gr, 10½"..................................... 7.50
Cameo, plate, luncheon; gr or yel, 8"............................. 7.50
Cameo, plate, sherbet; gr or yel, 6".............................. 2.00
Cameo, sherbet, gr, 4⅞"..24.00
Cameo, sugar bowl, yel, 3¼"......................................10.00
Cameo, tumbler, gr, flat, 10-oz, 4¾".............................20.00
Cameo, tumbler, yel, ftd, 9-oz, 5"...............................12.00
Cameo, vase, gr, 8"..17.50
Cherry Blossom, bowl, berry; gr, 4¾".............................12.00
Cherry Blossom, bowl, berry; pk or gr, 8½".......................20.00
Cherry Blossom, bowl, cereal; pk, 5¾"............................22.00
Cherry Blossom, butter dish, gr, w/lid...........................65.00
Cherry Blossom, coaster, pk......................................10.00
Cherry Blossom, cup, gr..16.00
Cherry Blossom, mug, pk, 7-oz...................................160.00
Cherry Blossom, plate, dinner; pk, 9"............................12.00
Cherry Blossom, plate, grill; gr, 9".............................18.00
Cherry Blossom, plate, sherbet; pk or gr, 6"..................... 5.00
Cherry Blossom, platter, gr, oval, 11"...........................22.00
Cherry Blossom, saucer, gr....................................... 3.00
Cherry Blossom, sherbet, gr......................................12.00
Cherry Blossom, sugar bowl, pk...................................10.00
Cherry Blossom, tray, sandwich; pk, hdls, 10½"...................10.00

Cherry Blossom, tumbler, pk, ftd, 4½" 23.00
Chinex Classic, bowl, cereal; ivory, 5¾" 4.00
Chinex Classic, creamer, ivory 4.50
Chinex Classic, cup, ivory 3.50
Chinex Classic, plate, dinner; ivory, decor, 9¾" 5.00
Christmas Candy, plate, bread & butter; teal, 6" 8.00
Christmas Candy, plate, dinner; crystal, 9⅝" 7.00
Christmas Candy, plate, sandwich; crystal, 11¼" 10.00
Christmas Candy, sugar bowl, teal 13.00
Circle, bowl, gr, 8" 7.50
Circle, cup, pk... 3.00
Circle, plate, dinner; pk, 9½" 6.00
Circle, sugar bowl, gr.. 5.00
Circle, tumbler, water; pk, 8-oz... 5.00
Cloverleaf, bowl, cereal; gr, 5"..20.00
Cloverleaf, bowl, dessert; gr, 4"...12.50
Cloverleaf, candy dish, gr, w/lid 40.00
Cloverleaf, creamer, yel, ftd, 3⅝".......................................12.50
Cloverleaf, cup, gr... 6.00
Cloverleaf, plate, luncheon; gr, 8" 5.00
Cloverleaf, saucer, yel 3.00
Cloverleaf, sugar bowl, gr, ftd, 3⅝" 7.50
Cloverleaf, tumbler, gr, flat, 10-oz, 4"...............................28.00
Cloverleaf, tumbler, yel, ftd, 10-oz, 5¾"............................20.00
Colonial, bowl, berry; gr, 4½" 9.00
Colonial, bowl, cereal; pk, 5½" 35.00
Colonial, bowl, soup; gr, 7" 40.00
Colonial, bowl, vegetable; gr, oval, 10" 22.00
Colonial, cup, pk or gr 9.00
Colonial, goblet, wine; gr, 2½-oz, 4½" 20.00
Colonial, plate, dinner; gr, 10"..47.50
Colonial, plate, luncheon; pk, 8½" 6.00
Colonial, plate, sherbet; gr, 6" 4.00
Colonial, platter, pk, oval, 12"..20.00
Colonial, shakers, pk, pr 100.00
Colonial, sherbet, pk 7.50
Colonial, tumbler, gr, 10-oz..33.00
Colonial, tumbler, iced tea; pk, 12-oz...............................33.00
Colonial, tumbler, juice; pk, 5-oz, 3".................................11.00
Colonial, tumbler, water; gr, 9-oz, 4".................................16.00
Colonial, whiskey, pk, 1½-oz, 2½"..................................... 7.00
Colonial Block, bowl, pk, 4" 5.00
Colonial Block, butter dish, gr 30.00
Colonial Block, candy dish, gr, 8½" 27.50
Colonial Block, creamer, pk 8.50
Colonial Block, pitcher, gr...27.50
Colonial Fluted, bowl, cereal; gr, 6" 6.00
Colonial Fluted, cup, gr 3.50
Colonial Fluted, plate, luncheon; gr, 8" 3.25
Colonial Fluted, plate, sherbet; gr, 6" 1.50
Colonial Fluted, sugar bowl, gr 3.00
Columbia, bowl, cereal; crystal, 5" 10.00
Columbia, cup, crystal 4.50
Columbia, plate, luncheon; pk, 9½" 17.50
Columbia, saucer, pk... 7.00
Columbia, tumbler, crystal.. 9.00
Coronation, bowl, berry; red, 4¼" 5.00
Coronation, bowl, berry; red, 8"...12.00
Coronation, bowl, nappy, pk, 6½" 3.50
Coronation, cup, pk... 3.50
Coronation, plate, luncheon; red, 8½" 6.00
Coronation, tumbler, pk, ftd, 10-oz, 5"...............................12.00
Cremax, bowl, vegetable; ivory, 9" 5.50
Cremax, cup, ivory w/decor 3.50

Cremax, plate, bread & butter; ivory, 6¼" 1.50
Cremax, plate, dinner; ivory w/decor, 9¾".......................... 6.00
Cremax, sugar bowl, ivory 3.00
Cube, bowl, dessert; pk, 4½" 4.00
Cube, bowl, salad; gr, 6½" 12.00
Cube, creamer, gr, 3" 6.00
Cube, cup, gr 7.00
Cube, pitcher, pk, 45-oz, 8¾"..140.00
Cube, plate, luncheon; gr, 8" 4.50
Cube, shakers, pk, pr 25.00
Cube, sherbet, gr, ftd 6.00
Cube, tumbler, pk, 9-oz, 4" 35.00
Daisy, bowl, cereal; amber, 6" 20.00
Daisy, bowl, cream soup; amber, 4½" 7.50
Daisy, creamer, crystal, ftd 4.50
Daisy, plate, dinner; crystal, 9⅜" 3.50
Daisy, plate, luncheon; amber, 8⅜" 5.50

Daisy, plate, salad; crystal, 7⅜" 2.00
Daisy, platter, crystal, 10¾".. 5.00
Daisy, sherbet, amber, ftd.. 7.00
Daisy, tumbler, crystal, ftd, 9-oz.. 5.00
Diamond Quilted, bowl, cereal; gr, 5" 4.00
Diamond Quilted, candlesticks, gr, 2 styles, pr................... 8.50
Diamond Quilted, creamer, bl 9.50
Diamond Quilted, goblet, wine; gr, 3-oz............................ 8.00
Diamond Quilted, ice bucket, bl 55.00
Diamond Quilted, plate, luncheon; bl, 8"........................... 9.50
Diamond Quilted, plate, sherbet; gr, 6" 2.00
Diamond Quilted, punch bowl w/stand, gr 350.00
Diamond Quilted, sherbet, bl 8.00
Diamond Quilted, sugar bowl, gr.. 5.50
Diamond Quilted, tumbler, gr, ftd, 9-oz............................. 8.50
Diamond Quilted, tumbler, water; gr, 9-oz 6.00
Diamond Quilted, whiskey, gr, 1½-oz................................. 6.00
Diana, ash tray, pk, 3½"... 3.00
Diana, bowl, salad; pk, 9" 6.50
Diana, coaster, pk, 3½".. 3.00
Diana, cup, pk.. 4.00
Diana, plate, dinner; pk, 9½"... 6.00
Diana, sherbet, amber 8.00
Diana, tumbler, amber, 9-oz, 4⅛"......................................18.00
Dogwood, bowl, berry; gr, 8½"...75.00
Dogwood, bowl, cereal; pk, 5½"...16.00
Dogwood, bowl, fruit; pk, 10¼"...210.00
Dogwood, creamer, gr, 3½"..40.00
Dogwood, cup, pk 10.00
Dogwood, plate, bread & butter; gr, 6"............................... 5.50
Dogwood, plate, dinner; pk, 9¼"..17.50
Dogwood, plate, luncheon; gr, 8" 5.00
Dogwood, saucer, gr 5.00
Dogwood, sherbet, gr, ftd 60.00

Dogwood, tumbler, pk, 10-oz, 4"..............................25.00
Doric, bowl, berry; gr, 4½" 5.50
Doric, bowl, vegetable; gr, oval, 9" 17.00
Doric, cake plate, pk or gr, 3-leg...........................12.50
Doric, coaster, pk, 3" 10.00
Doric, cup, gr.. 6.50
Doric, pitcher, pk, 48-oz, 7½"..............................300.00
Doric, plate, dinner; gr, 9"..................................10.00
Doric, plate, salad; pk, 7"..................................12.50
Doric, plate, sherbet; gr, 6" 3.00
Doric, platter, pk, oval, 12"................................12.50
Doric, serving tray, pk, sq, 8" 7.50
Doric, shakers, pk, pr.......................................25.00
Doric, sugar bowl, gr 10.00
Doric & Pansy, bowl, berry; pk, 4½"......................... 6.50
Doric & Pansy, bowl, berry; ultramarine, lg, 8".............60.00
Doric & Pansy, butter dish, ultramarine 400.00
Doric & Pansy, child's set, ultramarine, 14-pc.............190.00
Doric & Pansy, creamer & sugar bowl, ultramarine, child's sz 30.00
Doric & Pansy, cup, pk, child's sz..........................20.00
Doric & Pansy, cup, ultramarine 15.00
Doric & Pansy, plate, sherbet; pk, 6" 5.00
Doric & Pansy, saucer, ultramarine 3.00
Doric & Pansy, shakers, ultramarine, pr...................300.00
Doric & Pansy, tray, ultramarine, hdls, 10".................15.00
Doric & Pansy, tumbler, ultramarine, 9-oz, 4½" 37.50
English Hobnail, bowl, cream soup; pk 13.50
English Hobnail, bowl, relish; gr, oval, 12"................18.00
English Hobnail, candlesticks, gr, 8½", pr..................45.00
English Hobnail, celery dish, pk, 9"........................20.00
English Hobnail, cup, pk 12.00
English Hobnail, egg cup, gr................................32.50
English Hobnail, goblet, pk, 8-oz, 6¼".....................20.00
English Hobnail, grapefruit, pk or gr, flange rim, 6½" 14.00
English Hobnail, pitcher, gr, 23-oz........................135.00
English Hobnail, plate, pie; gr, 7¼" 4.00
English Hobnail, shakers, pk, rnd base......................67.50
English Hobnail, sherbet, gr................................12.50
English Hobnail, sugar bowl, pk, ftd........................20.00
English Hobnail, tumbler, gr, ftd, 7-oz.....................13.50
English Hobnail, whiskey, gr, 3-oz..........................22.00
Fire-King Alice, cup, jadite................................ 1.25
Fire-King Alice, plate, jadite, 8½"......................... 5.00
Fire-King Jane Ray, bowl, oatmeal; jadite, 5⅞" 2.00
Fire-King Jane Ray, bowl, vegetable; jadite, 8¼"............ 4.00
Fire-King Jane Ray, plate, dinner; jadite, 9⅛" 2.50
Fire-King Jane Ray, sugar bowl, jadite 1.50
Fire-King Oven Glass, baker, bl, 2-qt......................10.00
Fire-King Oven Glass, cup, measuring; bl, 8-oz 10.00
Fire-King Oven Glass, custard cup, bl, 5-oz 2.50
Fire-King Oven Glass, plate, pie; bl, 8⅜"................... 7.00
Fire-King Oven Glass, plate, pie; bl, 9⅝".................. 9.00
Fire-King Oven Glass, roaster, bl, 10⅜" 50.00
Fire-King Oven Glass, roaster, bl, 8¾" 30.00
Fire-King Philbe, bowl, salad; bl, 7¼" 40.00
Fire-King Philbe, cup, pk..................................90.00
Fire-King Philbe, plate, grill; crystal, 10½"..............30.00
Fire-King Philbe, plate, sherbet; gr, 6"...................30.00
Fire-King Philbe, sugar bowl, pk, ftd, 3¼".................65.00
Fire-King Philbe, tumbler, bl, ftd, 10-oz, 5¼".............50.00
Fire-King Philbe, tumbler, iced tea; gr, ftd, 15-oz, 6½"....45.00
Fire-King Square, bowl, dessert; jadite, 4¾"............... 3.00
Fire-King Square, cup, wht................................. 2.25
Fire-King Square, plate, dinner; wht, 9¼"................. 3.75

Fire-King Swirl, cup, pk or bl.............................. 2.50
Fire-King Swirl, plate, dinner; jadite, 9⅛"................ 2.75
Fire-King Swirl, platter, jadite, 12" 7.50
Fire-King Swirl, sugar bowl, wht w/gold decor 2.00
Fire-King Turquoise Blue, bowl, cereal; 5" 4.50
Fire-King Turquoise Blue, bowl, mixing; rnd, 3-qt 6.00
Fire-King Turquoise Blue, bowl, mixing; tear form, 1-pt.... 4.00
Fire-King Turquoise Blue, cup 2.00
Fire-King Turquoise Blue, plate, 9"........................ 4.00
Fire-King Turquoise Blue, plate 10"........................ 8.00
Fire-King Turquoise Blue, sugar bowl 3.75
Floragold, bowl, fruit; irid, ruffled, 5½" 4.50
Floragold, bowl, salad; irid, 9½"..........................27.50
Floragold, creamer, irid 6.25
Floragold, cup, irid 4.50
Floragold, plate, irid, 13½"...............................12.50
Floragold, platter, irid, 11¼".............................14.00
Floragold, sherbet, irid, ftd, low 8.00
Floragold, tumbler, irid, ftd, 10-oz 12.50
Floragold, vase or celery, irid 155.00
Floral, bowl, vegetable; gr, oval, 9" 13.00
Floral, candlesticks, pk, 4", pr...........................50.00
Floral, cup, gr 8.50
Floral, plate, dinner; pk, 9".............................11.00
Floral, platter, gr, oval, 10¾"............................12.50
Floral, shakers, pk, ftd, 4", pr...........................35.00
Floral, sugar bowl, gr 8.50
Floral, tumbler, lemonade; pk, ftd, 9-oz, 5¼" 32.00
Floral, tumbler, water; gr, ftd, 7-oz, 4¾" 15.00
Floral & Diamond Band, bowl, berry; gr, 4½".............. 6.00
Floral & Diamond Band, bowl, berry; pk, 8"................ 9.50
Floral & Diamond Band, creamer, gr, 4¾"..................15.00

Floral & Diamond Band, sherbet, pk........................ 5.00
Floral & Diamond Band, sugar bowl, gr, sm 8.00
Floral & Diamond Band, tumbler, iced tea; pk, 5"..........16.00
Floral & Diamond Band, tumbler, water; gr, 4" 14.00
Florentine No 1, bowl, berry; yel, 5" 12.00
Florentine No 1, bowl, cereal; gr, 6" 15.00
Florentine No 1, cup, yel 8.00
Florentine No 1, plate, dinner; gr, 10" 10.00
Florentine No 1, plate, salad; yel, 8½" 9.50
Florentine No 1, plate, sherbet; gr, 6" 3.00
Florentine No 1, sherbet, gr, ftd, 3-oz.................... 6.00
Florentine No 1, tumbler, water; yel, ftd, 10-oz, 4¾" 15.00
Florentine No 2, bowl, berry; gr, 8" 15.00
Florentine No 2, bowl, cream soup; yel, 4¾" 15.00
Florentine No 2, candlesticks, gr, 2¾", pr................35.00
Florentine No 2, gravy boat, yel..........................35.00
Florentine No 2, pitcher, gr, 54-oz, 7½"..................40.00
Florentine No 2, plate, dinner; yel, 10"..................12.00
Florentine No 2, plate, salad; gr, 8½" 6.00

Florentine No 2, sherbet, yel, ftd........................ 8.00
Florentine No 2, sugar bowl, gr........................... 6.50
Flower Garden w/Butterflies, bowl, console; pk, ftd, 10" 77.50
Flower Garden w/Butterflies, candlesticks, pk, 8", pr 85.00
Flower Garden w/Butterflies, candy dish, blk, open, 6" 25.00
Flower Garden w/Butterflies, cup, amber 50.00
Flower Garden w/Butterflies, plate, gr, 2 styles, 8" 16.00
Flower Garden w/Butterflies, saucer, bl-gr...............20.00
Flower Garden w/Butterflies, shakers, gr, 4", pr 45.00
Flower Garden w/Butterflies, sugar bowl, amber 65.00
Flower Garden w/Butterflies, tray, pk, 11¾x7¾"..........60.00
Forest Green, ash tray, dk gr 3.00
Forest Green, cup, dk gr.................................... 2.50
Forest Green, plate, dinner; dk gr, 10" 8.50
Forest Green, sugar bowl, dk gr, flat 4.50
Forest Green, tumbler, dk gr, 5-oz....................... 2.00
Forest Green, vase, dk gr, 6⅜" 3.50
Fortune, bowl, berry; pk, 4" 3.00
Fortune, bowl, berry; pk, 7¾" 8.00
Fortune, cup, pk 3.00
Fortune, tumbler, water; pk, 9-oz, 4" 4.50
Fruits, bowl, cereal; pk, 5"..............................11.00
Fruits, cup, gr... 4.50
Fruits, pitcher, gr, flat 45.00
Fruits, plate, luncheon; pk, 8".......................... 4.00
Fruits, sherbet, pk 5.50
Fruits, tumbler, gr, 12-oz, 5" 40.00
Fruits, tumbler, juice; gr, 3½" 8.00
Georgian, bowl, berry; gr, 4½" 5.50
Georgian, bowl, vegetable; gr, oval, 9" 47.50
Georgian, cup, gr 7.50
Georgian, plate, luncheon; gr, 8" 5.50
Georgian, sherbet, gr 8.00
Georgian, sugar bowl, ftd, 3" 7.50
Georgian, tumbler, gr, flat, 9-oz, 4" 37.50
Harp, cake stand, crystal, 9" 16.50
Harp, plate, crystal, 7" 4.50
Harp, vase, crystal, 6" 10.00
Heritage, bowl, berry; crystal, 5"....................... 4.50
Heritage, cup, crystal 4.00
Heritage, plate, dinner; crystal, 9¼" 7.00
Heritage, saucer, crystal 2.00
Hex Optic, bowl, berry; pk, lg, 7½" 5.00
Hex Optic, cup, gr, 2 styles 4.00
Hex Optic, pitcher, gr, ftd, 48-oz, 9" 30.00
Hex Optic, plate, luncheon; pk, 8"...................... 4.50
Hex Optic, tumbler, gr, 9-oz, 3¾" 4.00
Hex Optic, whiskey, pk or gr, 1-oz, 2" 5.00
Hobnail, bowl, cereal; crystal, 5½"...................... 2.50
Hobnail, pitcher, crystal, 67-oz.........................20.00
Hobnail, tumbler, iced tea; crystal, 15-oz 5.00
Hobnail, whiskey, crystal, 1½" 4.00
Holiday, bowl, berry; pk, 5⅛"............................ 7.00
Holiday, bowl, soup; pk, 7¾" 27.50
Holiday, butter dish, pk 30.00
Holiday, cup, pk, 2 sizes, ea 5.00
Holiday, plate, dinner; pk, 9" 9.50
Holiday, sugar bowl, pk 5.00
Holiday, tumbler, pk, ftd, 4" 27.50
Homespun, bowl, cereal; pk, 5" 12.50
Homespun, cup, crystal................................... 4.50
Homespun, tumbler, iced tea; pk, 13-oz, 5¼" 20.00
Homespun, tumbler, pk, ftd, 5-oz, 4" 5.00
Homespun, tumbler, pk, 5-oz, 4" 5.00

Indiana Custard, bowl, berry; ivory, 4⅞" 7.00
Indiana Custard, bowl, soup; ivory, 7½" 25.00
Indiana Custard, bowl, vegetable; ivory, oval, 9½" 20.00
Indiana Custard, cup, ivory 32.00
Indiana Custard, plate, dinner; ivory, 9¾" 13.50
Indiana Custard, plate, salad; ivory, 7½" 8.50
Indiana Custard, sugar bowl, ivory 7.50
Iris, bowl, cereal; crystal, 5" 35.00
Iris, bowl, salad; irid, 9½"............................. 8.00
Iris, bowl, soup; irid, 7½"..............................30.00
Iris, candlesticks, irid, pr 22.50
Iris, coaster, crystal...................................32.50
Iris, cup, demi; crystal 20.00
Iris, cup, irid 7.50
Iris, goblet, crystal, 4-oz, 5¾" 16.00
Iris, goblet, wine; irid, 4" 17.00
Iris, plate, dinner; crystal, 9" 30.00
Iris, saucer, irid 4.00
Iris, sherbet, crystal, ftd, 4" 12.50
Iris, tumbler, crystal, ftd, 6½" 12.00
Iris, vase, irid, 9" 14.00
Jubilee, candlesticks, topaz, pr 75.00
Jubilee, cup, topaz 10.00
Jubilee, goblet, topaz, 10-oz, 6" 25.00
Jubilee, plate, salad; topaz, 7" 6.50
Jubilee, sherbet, topaz, 4¾".............................25.00
Jubilee, tray, cake; topaz, hdls, 11" 30.00
Lace Edge, bowl, salad; pk, 6⅜"..........................15.00
Lace Edge, candlesticks, pk, pr 135.00
Lace Edge, cookie jar, pk, w/lid 45.00
Lace Edge, cup, pk 16.50
Lace Edge, fish bowl, crystal, 1-gal+8-oz 17.50
Lace Edge, plate, dinner; pk, 10½".......................19.00
Lace Edge, plate, salad; pk, 7¼".........................14.00
Lace Edge, saucer, pk 7.50
Lace Edge, sugar bowl, pk 15.00
Lace Edge, vase, pk, 7".................................245.00
Laced Edge, bowl, fruit; bl, 4½".........................15.00
Laced Edge, bowl, salad; pk, 7¾".........................15.00
Laced Edge, bowl, vegetable; gr, 9".....................45.00

Laced Edge, creamer, gr 20.00
Laced Edge, plate, dinner; gr, 10" 27.50
Laced Edge, plate, salad; bl, 8" 15.00
Laced Edge, sugar bowl, bl 19.00
Laced Edge, tumbler, bl, 9-oz 27.50
Laced Edge, vase, bl or gr, 5½" 40.00
Lake Como, bowl, cereal; wht, 6" 12.00
Lake Como, bowl, vegetable; wht, 9¾" 20.00
Lake Como, cup, wht 12.00
Lake Como, plate, dinner; wht, 9¼" 12.50
Lake Como, platter, wht, 11" 22.50

Laurel, bowl, cereal; gr, 6" 5.00
Laurel, bowl, vegetable; ivory, oval, 9¾" 15.00
Laurel, candlesticks, ivory, 4", pr 25.00
Laurel, cup, child's, gr 20.00
Laurel, cup, gr 6.00
Laurel, plate, grill; ivory, 9⅛" 7.50
Laurel, plate, salad; gr, 7½" 8.00
Laurel, shakers, ivory, pr 35.00
Laurel, sherbet, ivory 9.50
Laurel, tumbler, gr, flat, 9-oz, 4½" 35.00
Lincoln Inn, bowl, fruit; pk, 5" 7.00
Lincoln Inn, bowl, gr, ftd, 9¼" 15.00
Lincoln Inn, comport, crystal 12.00
Lincoln Inn, goblet, water; bl 20.00
Lincoln Inn, plate, blk, 12" 10.00
Lincoln Inn, sherbet, pk, 4¾" 10.00
Lincoln Inn, sugar bowl, red 16.50
Lincoln Inn, vase, bl or red, ftd, 12" 95.00
Lorain, bowl, cereal; gr, 6" 27.50
Lorain, bowl, vegetable; yel, oval, 9¾" 37.50
Lorain, cup, gr 8.50
Lorain, plate, luncheon; gr, 8⅜" 13.00
Lorain, plate, salad; yel, 7¾" 12.00
Lorain, platter, yel, 11½" 30.00
Lorain, saucer, gr 3.50
Lorain, sugar bowl, gr, ftd 10.00
Madrid, bowl, salad; amber, 8" 11.50
Madrid, bowl, vegetable; amber, oval, 10" 12.50
Madrid, creamer, gr, ftd 8.50
Madrid, cup, amber 5.00
Madrid, pitcher, amber, ice lip, 80-oz, 8½" 50.00
Madrid, plate, dinner; gr, 10½" 30.00
Madrid, plate, luncheon; amber, 8⅞" 6.00
Madrid, shakers, gr, ftd, 3½", pr 77.50
Madrid, sugar bowl, amber 6.50
Madrid, tumbler, amber, ftd, 10-oz, 5½" 20.00
Manhattan, ash tray, crystal, rnd, 4" 8.00
Manhattan, bowl, berry; crystal, lg, 7½" 8.50
Manhattan, bowl, fruit; crystal, 9½" 17.50
Manhattan, bowl, sauce; pk, 4½" 6.00
Manhattan, candlesticks, crystal, sq, 4½", pr 12.00
Manhattan, compote, crystal, 5¾" 15.00
Manhattan, cup, pk 95.00
Manhattan, pitcher, crystal, 42-oz 15.00
Manhattan, plate, salad; crystal, 8½" 7.50
Manhattan, plate, sherbet; pk, 6" 25.00
Manhattan, sherbet, crystal 6.50
Manhattan, wine, crystal, 3½" 5.00
Mayfair, bowl, cereal; pk, 5½" 17.50
Mayfair, bowl, fruit; bl, 12" 52.50
Mayfair, bowl, vegetable; bl, oval, 9½" 40.00
Mayfair, bowl, vegetable; bl, 10" 40.00
Mayfair, bowl, vegetable; pk, 10" 16.00
Mayfair, bowl, vegetable; pk, 7" 17.50
Mayfair, celery dish, bl, divided, 10" 35.00
Mayfair, cookie jar, pk, w/lid 32.50
Mayfair, creamer, pk, ftd 15.00
Mayfair, cup, bl 35.00
Mayfair, decanter, pk, w/stopper, 32-oz 110.00
Mayfair, goblet, water; 9-oz, 5¾" 45.00
Mayfair, pitcher, bl, 60-oz, 8" 110.00
Mayfair, pitcher, pk, 37-oz, 6" 32.00
Mayfair, pitcher, pk, 80-oz, 8½" 62.50
Mayfair, plate, cake; pk, ftd, 10" 18.00

Mayfair, plate, dinner; pk, 9½" 36.00
Mayfair, plate, grill; pk, 9½" 25.00
Mayfair, plate, sherbet; pk, rnd, 6½" 9.00
Mayfair, platter, bl, open hdls, 12" 35.00
Mayfair, relish, pk, 4-part, 8⅜" 20.00
Mayfair, shakers, bl, flat, pr 190.00
Mayfair, shakers, pk, flat, pr 42.50
Mayfair, sherbet, pk, ftd, 3" 12.00
Mayfair, sugar bowl, pk, ftd 17.50
Mayfair, tumbler, iced tea; pk, 13½-oz, 5¼" 33.00
Mayfair, tumbler, water; bl, 9-oz, 4¼" 65.00
Mayfair, vase, pk 105.00
Mayfair, whiskey, pk, 1½-oz, 2¼" 50.00
Mayfair Federal, bowl, cereal; amber, 6" 14.00
Mayfair Federal, cup, gr 6.50
Mayfair Federal, plate, dinner; gr, 9½" 10.00
Mayfair Federal, platter, amber or gr, oval, 12" 20.00
Miss America, bowl, berry; pk, 6¼" 12.50
Miss America, bowl, vegetable; crystal, oval, 10" 10.00
Miss America, compote, crystal, 5" 11.00
Miss America, creamer, crystal, ftd 6.50
Miss America, cup, pk 16.00
Miss America, goblet, water; pk, 10-oz, 5½" 35.00
Miss America, pitcher, crystal, ice lip, 65-oz, 8½" 57.50
Miss America, plate, cake; pk, ftd, 12" 27.50
Miss America, plate, grill; crystal, 10¼" 7.50

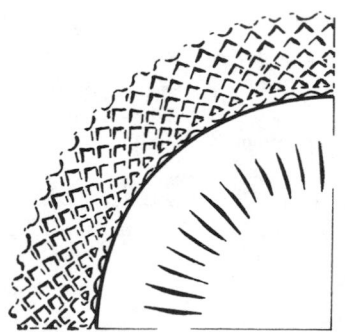

Miss America, plate, salad; pk, 8½" 14.00
Miss America, relish, crystal, rnd, divided, 11¾" 15.00
Miss America, saucer, pk 4.00
Miss America, sherbet, pk 10.00
Miss America, tumbler, iced tea; pk, 14-oz, 5¾" 47.50
Miss America, tumbler, juice; crystal, 5-oz, 4" 14.00
Moderntone, ash tray, bl, w/match holder center, 7¾" .110.00
Moderntone, bowl, berry; amethyst, 5" 12.00
Moderntone, bowl, cereal; bl, 6½" 42.50
Moderntone, bowl, soup; amethyst, 7½" 45.00
Moderntone, butter dish, bl, w/metal cover 65.00
Moderntone, creamer, bl 7.50
Moderntone, cup, amethyst 5.00
Moderntone, plate, dinner; amethyst, 8⅞" 7.50
Moderntone, plate, salad; amethyst, 6¾" 6.00
Moderntone, plate, sherbet; amethyst, 5¾" 3.75
Moderntone, platter, bl, oval, 12" 35.00
Moderntone, shakers, bl, pr 27.50
Moderntone, sherbet, bl 8.50
Moderntone, sugar bowl, amethyst 6.50
Moderntone, tumbler, amethyst, 5-oz 15.00
Moderntone, tumbler, bl, 12-oz 55.00
Moderntone, whiskey, bl, 1½-oz 15.00
Moondrops, ash tray, red 30.00
Moondrops, bl or red, 5", pr 65.00

Moondrops, bowl, berry; pk, 5¼" 5.00
Moondrops, bowl, casserole; red, w/lid, 9¾" 100.00
Moondrops, bowl, console; pk, rnd, 3-ftd, 12" 25.00
Moondrops, bowl, pickle; bl, 7½" 17.00
Moondrops, bowl, relish; red, divided, 3-leg, 8½" 22.00
Moondrops, bowl, soup; red, 6¾" 12.00
Moondrops, bowl, vegetable; amethyst, oval, 9¾" 20.00

Moondrops, butter dish, gr, w/lid 200.00
Moondrops, candlesticks, bl or red, 3-light, 5¼", pr 75.00
Moondrops, candy dish, blk, ruffled, 8" 15.00
Moondrops, compote, bl or red, 4" 17.50
Moondrops, compote, colors other than bl or red, 11½" 10.00
Moondrops, creamer, colors other than bl or red, 3¾" 7.50
Moondrops, cup, colors other than bl or red 7.50
Moondrops, goblet, blk, 5-oz, 4¾" 12.00
Moondrops, goblet, wine; pk, w/metal stem, 5½" 8.50
Moondrops, mug, colors other than bl or red, 12-oz, 5⅛" 20.00
Moondrops, plate, dinner; red, 9½" 15.00
Moondrops, plate, luncheon; bl, 8½" 11.00
Moondrops, plate, salad; red, 7⅛" 9.00
Moondrops, plate, sandwich; red, hdls, 14" 30.00
Moondrops, plate, sherbet; gr, 6⅛" 2.50
Moondrops, platter, red, oval, 12" 20.00
Moondrops, sugar bowl, bl, 2¾" 9.00
Moondrops, sugar bowl, colors other than bl or red, 4" 7.00
Moondrops, tumbler, juice; red, ftd, 3-oz, 3¾" 11.50
Moondrops, tumbler, red, 12-oz, 5⅛" 20.00
Moondrops, vase, red, flat, ruffled top, 7¾" 50.00
Moonstone, bowl, berry; opal, 5½" 9.00
Moonstone, bowl, divided relish; opal, 7¾" 7.50
Moonstone, creamer, opal 6.00
Moonstone, cup, opal 6.00
Moonstone, goblet, opal, 10-oz 15.00
Moonstone, plate, luncheon; opal, 8" 8.50
Moonstone, sherbet, ftd, opal 6.00
Moonstone, vase, bud; opal, 5½" 8.50
Moroccan Amethyst, bowl, cereal; amethyst, 5¾" 4.50
Moroccan Amethyst, cup, amethyst..................................... 3.00
Moroccan Amethyst, plate, dinner; amethyst, 9⅜" 4.00
Moroccan Amethyst, plate, sandwich; amethyst, 12" 6.00
Moroccan Amethyst, tumbler, iced tea; amethyst, 16 oz 8.00
Moroccan Amethyst, tumbler, water; amethyst, 11-oz, 4½" ... 5.50
Mt Pleasant, creamer, cobalt 12.50
Mt Pleasant, cup, cobalt 8.50
Mt Pleasant, plate, cobalt, sq, 8" 11.00
Mt Pleasant, plate, grill; cobalt, 9" 8.50
Mt Pleasant, sherbet, cobalt 12.50
Mt Pleasant, sugar bowl, cobalt 12.50
Mt Pleasant, vase, cobalt, 7¼" 20.00
New Century, bowl, berry; gr, 4½".................................... 5.00
New Century, butter dish, gr 47.50

New Century, cup, gr 5.00
New Century, decanter, gr, w/stopper.................................40.00
New Century, goblet, wine; gr, 2½-oz.................................14.00
New Century, plate, dinner; gr, 10" 10.00
New Century, plate, salad; gr, 8½" 6.00
New Century, plate, sherbet; gr, 6".................................... 2.25
New Century, platter, gr, oval, 11" 11.00
New Century, sherbet, gr, 3" 6.00
New Century, sugar bowl, gr 5.00
New Century, tumbler, gr, ftd, 5-oz, 4" 10.00
New Century, tumbler, gr, 10-oz, 5" 10.00
New Century, tumbler, gr, 5-oz, 3½".................................. 8.00
New Century, whiskey, gr, 1½-oz, 2½"...............................12.00
Newport, bowl, berry; cobalt, lg, 8¼"................................30.00
Newport, bowl, berry; cobalt, 4¼".....................................10.00
Newport, bowl, cream soup; amethyst, 4¾" 12.00
Newport, creamer, cobalt...10.00
Newport, plate, luncheon; cobalt, 8½".............................. 7.50
Newport, plate, sandwich; cobalt, 11½" 25.00
Newport, platter, amethyst, oval, 11¾"...............................23.00
Newport, sugar bowl, cobalt 10.00
Newport, tumbler, amethyst, 9-oz, 4½"..............................20.00
No 610 Pyramid, bowl, berry; pk, 4¾".................................14.50
No 610 Pyramid, bowl, yel, oval, 9½" 45.00
No 610 Pyramid, creamer, pk 18.00
No 610 Pyramid, ice tub, yel 175.00
No 610 Pyramid, pitcher, pk..200.00
No 610 Pyramid, sugar bowl, yel 25.00
No 610 Pyramid, tumbler, pk, ftd, 8-oz................................20.00
No 610 Pyramid, tumbler, yel, ftd, 11-oz.............................55.00
No 612 Horseshoe, bowl, berry; gr, 4½" 16.00
No 612 Horseshoe, bowl, salad; gr, 7½" 14.00
No 612 Horseshoe, bowl, vegetable; yel, oval, 10½" 18.00
No 612 Horseshoe, bowl, vegetable; yel, 8½" 22.50
No 612 Horseshoe, creamer, gr, ftd......................................11.50
No 612 Horseshoe, cup, yel 7.50
No 612 Horseshoe, plate, dinner; yel, 10⅜" 18.00
No 612 Horseshoe, plate, grill; yel, 10⅜" 25.00
No 612 Horseshoe, plate, luncheon; gr, 9⅜" 8.00
No 612 Horseshoe, plate, salad; gr, 8⅜" 6.00
No 612 Horseshoe, plate, sherbet; yel, 6" 4.50
No 612 Horseshoe, saucer, gr.. 3.00
No 612 Horseshoe, sugar bowl, yel, open.............................10.50
No 612 Horseshoe, tumbler, gr, 12-oz, 4¾" 85.00
No 612 Horseshoe, tumbler, yel, ftd, 12-oz 90.00
No 616 Vernon, creamer, gr, ftd..20.00
No 616 Vernon, cup, gr 13.50
No 616 Vernon, plate, luncheon; yel, 8"............................. 6.50
No 616 Vernon, saucer, yel.. 4.50
No 616 Vernon, sugar bowl, yel, ftd....................................17.50
No 616 Vernon, tumbler, gr, ftd 25.00
No 618 Pineapple & Floral, ash tray, crystal, 4½"................13.00
No 618 Pineapple & Floral, bowl, amber, 4¾"......................14.00
No 618 Pineapple & Floral, bowl, cereal; crystal, 6" 18.50
No 618 Pineapple & Floral, bowl, vegetable; amber, oval, 10" 20.00
No 618 Pineapple & Floral, cream soup, crystal 18.00
No 618 Pineapple & Floral, cup, amber 7.00
No 618 Pineapple & Floral, plate, dinner; amber, 9⅜".........12.50
No 618 Pineapple & Floral, plate, salad; crystal, 8⅜" 5.00
No 618 Pineapple & Floral, plate, sandwich; crystal, 11½".........12.50
No 618 Pineapple & Floral, platter, amber, hdls, 11" 12.00
No 618 Pineapple & Floral, saucer, crystal 3.00
No 618 Pineapple & Floral, sugar bowl, amber, dmn shaped.......... 8.50
No 618 Pineapple & Floral, tumbler, crystal, 12-oz, 5"..........30.00

No 622 Pretzel, bowl, berry; crystal, 9⅜" 10.00
No 622 Pretzel, bowl, soup; crystal, 7½" 7.50
No 622 Pretzel, cup, crystal 3.50
No 622 Pretzel, plate, dinner; crystal, 9⅜" 4.00
No 622 Pretzel, plate, salad; crystal, 8⅜" 3.00
No 622 Pretzel, tumbler, water, crystal, 9-oz 12.00
Normandie, bowl, berry; amber, 5" 4.00
Normandie, bowl, cereal; pk, 6½" 12.00
Normandie, bowl, vegetable; amber, oval, 10" 12.00
Normandie, cup, pk 6.50
Normandie, plate, dinner; amber, 11" 17.50
Normandie, plate, luncheon; pk, 9¼" 9.50
Normandie, plate, sherbet; amber, 6" 2.00
Normandie, platter, amber, 11¾" 11.00
Normandie, shakers, pk, pr 55.00
Normandie, sherbet, amber 5.00
Normandie, sugar bowl, pk 6.00
Normandie, tumbler, water; amber, 9-oz, 4¼" 11.00
Old Cafe, bowl, berry; pk, 3¾" 2.00
Old Cafe, bowl, cereal; red, 5½" 8.50
Old Cafe, cup, pk 3.00
Old Cafe, pitcher, pk, 80-oz..75.00
Old Cafe, plate, dinner; pk, 10" 16.00
Old Cafe, tumbler, juice; red, 3" 7.50
Old Cafe, tumbler, water; pk, 4" 6.00
Old Cafe, vase, red, 7¼" 13.50
Old English, bowl, berry; gr, 4" 12.00
Old English, bowl, fruit; pk, ftd, 9" 22.50
Old English, candlestick, amber, 4", pr 22.50
Old English, creamer, gr 14.00
Old English, goblet, gr, 8-oz, 5¾" 22.50
Old English, pitcher, pk 50.00
Old English, sugar bowl, amber 12.00
Old English, vase, amber, fan form, 7" 35.00
Old English, vase, gr, ftd, 12" 40.00
Ovide, bowl, berry; blk, lg, 8" 14.00
Ovide, cocktail, fruit; blk, ftd 3.00
Ovide, creamer, gr.. 2.50
Ovide, cup, blk 5.00
Ovide, plate, luncheon; gr, 8" 1.50
Ovide, plate, sherbet; blk, 6" 2.50
Ovide, shakers, gr, pr 10.00
Ovide, sherbet, blk... 5.00
Oyster & Pearl, bowl, fruit; pk, deep, 10½" 16.00
Oyster & Pearl, bowl, pk, deep, hdls, 6½" 8.00

Oyster & Pearl, bowl, red, rnd or hdls, 5¼" 9.50
Oyster & Pearl, candle holder, red, 3½", pr 32.50
Oyster & Pearl, plate, sandwich; red, 13½" 27.50
Oyster & Pearl, relish, pk, oval, 10¼" 7.00
Parrot, bowl, berry; amber, lg, 8" 60.00
Parrot, bowl, berry; gr, 5" 12.50

Parrot, creamer, gr, ftd..20.00
Parrot, jam dish, amber, 7" 25.00
Parrot, plate, dinner; gr, 9" 30.00
Parrot, plate, sherbet; amber, 5¾" 11.00
Parrot, platter, gr, oval, 11¼" 27.50
Parrot, saucer, amber 8.50
Parrot, sugar bowl, amber 25.00
Parrot, tumbler, amber, ftd, 5¾" 110.00
Parrot, tumbler, gr, 10-oz, 4¼" 95.00
Patrician, bowl, berry; amber, lg, 8½" 32.00
Patrician, bowl, berry; gr, 5"... 8.50
Patrician, bowl, cream soup; amber, 4¾" 11.00
Patrician, creamer, amber, ftd 7.00
Patrician, cup, gr 8.50
Patrician, plate, grill; amber, 10½" 9.00
Patrician, plate, luncheon; amber, 9" 7.50
Patrician, plate, sherbet; amber, 6" 7.00
Patrician, platter, gr, oval, 11½" 17.00
Patrician, shakers, amber, pr 42.50
Patrician, sugar bowl, gr, w/lid 42.50
Patrician, tumbler, amber, 14-oz, 5½" 28.00
Patrician, tumbler, gr, ftd, 8-oz, 5½" 40.00
Patrick, bowl, console; pk, 11" 25.00
Patrick, candlestick, yel, pr 35.00
Patrick, creamer, yel 11.00
Patrick, cup, pk 8.00
Patrick, goblet, water; pk, 10-oz, 6" 22.50
Patrick, mayonnaise, pk, 3-pc 40.00
Patrick, plate, luncheon; pk, 8" 6.50
Patrick, plate, sherbet; yel, 7" 5.00
Patrick, sugar bowl, pk 10.00
Petalware, bowl, cereal; monax, 5¾" 4.50
Petalware, bowl, cream soup; pk, 4½" 5.00
Petalware, creamer, pk, ftd 3.50
Petalware, cup, monax 4.50
Petalware, plate, salver; monax, 11" 6.50
Petalware, plate, sherbet; monax, 6" 2.00
Petalware, sherbet, pk, ftd... 3.50
Petalware, sugar bowl, monax, ftd 4.50
Primo, bowl, gr, 4½" 8.00
Primo, cake plate, gr, 3-ftd, 10" 15.00
Primo, coaster/ash tray, yel 6.50
Primo, cup, yel 6.50
Primo, plate, dinner; gr, 10" 10.00
Primo, plate, gr, 7½" 5.00
Primo, saucer, yel 2.00
Primo, sugar bowl, gr 7.50
Primo, tumbler, gr, 9-oz, 5¾" 12.00
Princess, ash tray, gr, 4½"...60.00
Princess, bowl, berry; pk, 4½" 12.50
Princess, bowl, cereal; gr, 5"..22.00
Princess, bowl, vegetable; pk, oval, 10" 15.00
Princess, cake stand, gr, 10" 15.00
Princess, creamer, pk, oval 9.00
Princess, cup, gr 9.00
Princess, pitcher, pk, 60-oz, 8" 35.00
Princess, plate, dinner; gr, 9" 19.00
Princess, plate, grill; pk, 9"... 7.00
Princess, relish, pk, divided, 7½" 14.00
Princess, sherbet, pk, ftd..11.00
Princess, sugar bowl, gr 8.50
Princess, tumbler, gr, ftd, 10-oz, 5¼" 22.50
Princess, tumbler, iced tea; pk, 13-oz, 5¼" 16.50
Princess, tumbler, pk, ftd, 12½-oz, 6½" 40.00

Princess, tumbler, water; gr, 9-oz, 4" 20.00
Princess, vase, pk, 8" 18.00
Queen Mary, ash tray, pk, oval, 2x3¾" 3.50
Queen Mary, bowl, berry; crystal, lg, 8¾" 6.00
Queen Mary, candlesticks, dbl-branch; crystal, 4½", pr 14.00
Queen Mary, coaster, pk, 3½" 2.50
Queen Mary, coaster/ash tray, crystal, sq, 4¼" 4.00
Queen Mary, compote, pk, 5¾" 9.00
Queen Mary, cup, pk 5.00
Queen Mary, plate, dinner; crystal, 9¾" 11.00
Queen Mary, relish tray, crystal, 4-part, 14" 8.00
Queen Mary, shakers, pk, pr 15.00
Queen Mary, tumbler, juice; pk, 5-oz, 3½" 6.00
Queen Mary, tumbler, pk, ftd, 10-oz, 5" 25.00
Queen Mary, tumbler, water; crystal, 9-oz, 4" 4.00
Radiance, bonbon, red, ftd, 6" 13.00
Radiance, bowl, crystal, crimped, 10" 15.00
Radiance, bowl, pickle; amber, 7" 10.00
Radiance, bowl, relish; bl, 3-part, 8" 22.50
Radiance, butter dish, red..350.00
Radiance, candlestick, amber, 8", pr....................................27.50
Radiance, comport, red, 6" 12.50
Radiance, creamer, bl 12.50
Radiance, cup, red...10.00
Radiance, lamp, amber, 12"...42.50
Radiance, punch cup, amber, flat 5.00
Radiance, punch ladle, cobalt 75.00
Radiance, sugar bowl, crystal 10.00
Radiance, tray, amber 95.00
Radiance, tumbler, amber, 9-oz...12.50
Raindrops, bowl, berry; gr, 7½"...25.00
Raindrops, bowl, cereal; gr, 6" 4.00
Raindrops, bowl, fruit; gr, 4½" 3.00
Raindrops, creamer, gr 5.00
Raindrops, plate, luncheon; gr.. 3.50
Raindrops, shakers, gr, pr..150.00
Raindrops, sherbet, gr 5.00
Raindrops, sugar bowl, gr 4.50
Raindrops, whiskey, gr, 1⅞" 4.00
Ribbon, bowl, berry; blk, lg, 8" 17.50
Ribbon, bowl, berry; gr, 4" 4.00
Ribbon, cup, gr.. 3.50
Ribbon, plate, luncheon; blk, 8"...10.00
Ribbon, shakers, blk, pr 35.00
Ribbon, sherbet, gr, ftd... 4.00
Ribbon, tumbler, gr, 10-oz, 5½" 10.00
Ring, bowl, berry; crystal, lg, 8" 5.00
Ring, butter tub or ice bucket, gr..17.50
Ring, cup, gr 3.50
Ring, decanter & stopper, crystal 15.00
Ring, goblet, gr, 9-oz, 7"-8" 12.50
Ring, pitcher, crystal, 80-oz, 8½" 12.00
Ring, pitcher, gr, 60-oz, 8" 15.00
Ring, plate, luncheon; gr, 8" 3.00
Ring, shakers, gr, 3", pr 25.00
Ring, sugar bowl, crystal, ftd.. 3.00
Ring, tumbler, crystal, 12-oz, 5⅛" 4.00
Ring, tumbler, water; crystal, ftd, 5½" 4.00
Ring, vase, gr..27.50
Ring, whiskey, gr 5.50
Rock Crystal, bonbon, crystal, scalloped edge, 7½" 15.00
Rock Crystal, bowl, celery; red, oval, 12"............................47.50
Rock Crystal, bowl, crystal, 13" 25.00

Rock Crystal, bowl, relish; crystal, 2-part, 11½" 27.00
Rock Crystal, bowl, salad; crystal, scalloped, 7" 17.50
Rock Crystal, cake stand, crystal, ftd, 2¾x11" 20.00
Rock Crystal, candlesticks, crystal, tall, 8½", pr 60.00
Rock Crystal, candlesticks, red, 5½", pr..............................100.00
Rock Crystal, cup, crystal, 7-oz...12.00
Rock Crystal, cup, red, 7-oz...55.00
Rock Crystal, goblet, iced tea; red, low ftd, 11-oz................55.00
Rock Crystal, lamp, electric, crystal 85.00
Rock Crystal, pitcher, crystal, lg..125.00
Rock Crystal, salt dip, crystal 25.00
Rock Crystal, sherbet, crystal, ftd, 3½-oz 12.00
Rock Crystal, sundae, crystal, low ftd, 6-oz 9.50
Rock Crystal, tumbler, juice; crystal, 5-oz 12.00
Rock Crystal, tumbler, old fashioned; red, 5-oz...................35.00
Rose Cameo, bowl, berry; gr, 4½" 4.50
Rose Cameo, sherbet, gr 8.00
Rose Cameo, tumbler, gr, ftd, 5" 11.00
Rosemary, bowl, berry; amber, 5" 4.00
Rosemary, bowl, cereal; gr, 6" 20.00
Rosemary, bowl, vegetable; amber, oval, 10"....................... 9.00
Rosemary, cup, amber 4.00
Rosemary, plate, dinner; gr...10.00
Rosemary, plate, grill; amber 6.00
Rosemary, plate, salad; gr, 6¾".. 6.00
Rosemary, saucer, gr 3.50
Rosemary, sugar bowl, amber, ftd....................................... 6.50
Rosemary, tumbler, gr, 9-oz, 4¼"...22.50
Roulette, bowl, fruit; gr, 9" 10.00
Roulette, pitcher, pk, 64-oz, 8" 22.50
Roulette, sherbet, gr 4.50
Roulette, tumbler, gr, ftd, 10-oz, 5½" 15.00
Roulette, tumbler, iced tea; gr, 12-oz, 5⅛" 16.50
Roulette, tumbler, juice; pk, 5-oz, 3¼" 6.00
Roulette, tumbler, water; pk, 9-oz, 4⅛" 10.00
Roulette, whiskey, pk, 1½-oz, 2½" 6.50
Round Robin, bowl, berry; gr, 4" 4.25
Round Robin, creamer, gr, ftd 5.00
Round Robin, cup, irid, ftd... 5.00
Round Robin, plate, luncheon; gr, 8"................................... 2.50
Round Robin, plate, sandwich; irid, 12" 6.00
Round Robin, sugar bowl, irid 5.00
Roxana, bowl, berry; yel, 5 " 4.00
Roxana, plate, sherbet; yel, 6 " 2.50
Roxana, sherbet, yel, ftd 4.00
Roxana, tumbler, yel, 9-oz, 4"..10.00
Royal Lace, bowl, berry; bl, 5"..30.00
Royal Lace, bowl, berry; pk, 10"..18.00
Royal Lace, bowl, cream soup; pk, 4¾"................................12.00
Royal Lace, bowl, vegetable; pk, oval, 11" 18.00

Royal Lace, candlesticks, bl, str edge, pr 77.50
Royal Lace, cookie jar, pk, w/lid 37.50
Royal Lace, cup, bl 23.50
Royal Lace, pitcher, bl, 86-oz, 8" 135.00
Royal Lace, plate, grill; bl, 9⅞" 22.50
Royal Lace, plate, sherbet; pk, 6" 3.50
Royal Lace, saucer, bl 7.50
Royal Lace, tumbler, bl, 12-oz, 5⅜" 45.00
Royal Lace, tumbler, pk, 9-oz, 4⅛" 11.00
Royal Robin, bowl, bl, 3-leg, str edge, 10" 42.50
Royal Ruby, ash tray, red, sq, 4½" 2.50
Royal Ruby, bowl, berry; red, 4¼" 4.00
Royal Ruby, bowl, vegetable; red, oval, 8" 27.50
Royal Ruby, creamer, red, flat 6.00
Royal Ruby, lamp, red 20.00
Royal Ruby, plate, luncheon; red, 7¾" 4.00
Royal Ruby, plate, red, 13¾" 15.00
Royal Ruby, plate, salad; red, 7" 3.50
Royal Ruby, sherbet, red, ftd 6.50
Royal Ruby, sugar bowl, red, ftd 5.00
Royal Ruby, tumbler, iced tea; red, 13-oz 9.50
Royal Ruby, tumbler, juice; red, 2 styles, 5-oz 5.00
Royal Ruby, tumbler, water; red, 9-oz 5.00
S Pattern, bowl, cereal; amber, 5½" 3.50
S Pattern, cup, amber, thick or thin 3.50
S Pattern, plate, dinner; crystal, 9¼" 3.50
S Pattern, plate, luncheon; amber, 8" 2.50
S Pattern, sherbet, amber, low ftd 6.00
S Pattern, tumbler, amber, 9-oz, 4" 5.50
S Pattern, tumbler, crystal, 12-oz, 5" 7.50
Sandwich, bowl, berry; crystal, 4⅞" 4.00
Sandwich, bowl, console; crystal, 9" 15.00
Sandwich, bowl, crystal, oval, 8¼" 6.00
Sandwich, bowl, crystal, smooth or scalloped, 6½" 6.00
Sandwich, bowl, pk, 8¼" 10.00
Sandwich, bowl, salad; gr, 7" 40.00
Sandwich, butter dish, pk, domed, w/lid 150.00
Sandwich, candlesticks, crystal, 7", pr 38.00
Sandwich, cookie jar, crystal, w/lid 30.00
Sandwich, creamer, gr 15.00
Sandwich, cruet, crystal, 6½" 37.50
Sandwich, cup, crystal 4.50
Sandwich, cup, tea or coffee; gr 15.00
Sandwich, custard cup, crystal 3.50
Sandwich, decanter, pk 65.00
Sandwich, goblet, pk, 9-oz 12.00
Sandwich, pitcher, crystal, 68-oz 45.00
Sandwich, pitcher, juice; crystal, 6" 42.50
Sandwich, plate, crystal, 8" 3.00
Sandwich, plate, dinner; gr, 9" 49.50
Sandwich, plate, dinner; pk, 10½" 12.00
Sandwich, plate, sandwich; crystal, 13" 6.00
Sandwich, plate, sherbet; pk, 6" 2.50
Sandwich, sandwich server, pk, center hdl 25.00
Sandwich, sherbet, crystal, ftd 6.00
Sandwich, sugar bowl, crystal, w/lid 12.50
Sandwich, tumbler, cocktail; crystal, ftd, 3-oz 15.00
Sandwich, tumbler, water; crystal, 9-oz 6.50
Sharon, bowl, berry; amber, lg, 8½" 4.50
Sharon, bowl, cereal; pk, 6" 15.00
Sharon, bowl, cream soup; amber, 5" 17.50
Sharon, bowl, fruit; pk, 10½" 22.00
Sharon, cake plate, amber, ftd, 11½" 16.00
Sharon, candy jar, pk 33.00

Sharon, cup, amber 8.00
Sharon, jam dish, pk, 7½" 100.00
Sharon, pitcher, amber, w/ice lip, 80-oz 100.00
Sharon, plate, dinner; pk, 9½" 10.00
Sharon, plate, salad; pk, 7½" 16.50
Sharon, saucer, pk 5.50
Sharon, sherbet, amber, ftd 9.00
Sharon, sugar bowl, amber 6.50
Sharon, tumbler, pk, ftd, 15-oz, 6½" 32.50
Sierra, bowl, cereal; pk, 5½" 7.00
Sierra, bowl, vegetable; gr, oval, 9½" 50.00
Sierra, creamer, pk 10.00
Sierra, pitcher, gr, 32-oz, 6½" 75.00
Sierra, plate, dinner; pk, 9" 10.50
Sierra, platter, gr, oval, 11" 30.00
Sierra, saucer, gr 4.00
Sierra, sugar bowl, gr 15.00
Spiral, bowl, berry; gr, 4¾" 4.00
Spiral, pitcher, gr, 58-oz, 7⅝" 24.00
Spiral, plate, luncheon; gr, 8" 2.50
Spiral, shakers, gr, pr 17.50
Spiral, sugar bowl, gr, flat or ftd 5.00
Spiral, tumbler, water; gr, 9-oz, 5" 4.00
Starlight, bowl, cereal; pk, 5½" 5.00
Starlight, bowl, pk, closed hdls, 8½" 9.00
Starlight, bowl, salad; crystal, 11½" 14.00
Starlight, creamer, crystal, oval 3.00
Starlight, plate, sandwich; pk, 13" 8.50
Starlight, shakers, crystal, pr 16.00
Starlight, sherbet, crystal 8.00
Strawberry, bowl, berry; gr, 4" 7.00
Strawberry, bowl, salad; pk, deep, 6½" 15.00
Strawberry, creamer, gr, lg, 4⅝" 17.50
Strawberry, pickle dish, gr 10.00
Strawberry, plate, sherbet; pk, 6" 5.00
Strawberry, sherbet, gr 6.50
Strawberry, tumbler, pk, 9-oz, 3⅝" 22.50
Sunflower, ash tray, gr, center design only, 5" 7.00
Sunflower, cup, pk 8.00
Sunflower, plate, dinner; gr, 9" 12.00
Sunflower, saucer, gr 4.00
Sunflower, sugar bowl, gr 13.00
Sunflower, tumbler, pk, ftd, 8-oz, 4¾" 15.00
Swirl, ash tray, pk, 5⅜" 6.00
Swirl, bowl, cereal; ultramarine, 5¼" 8.00
Swirl, butter dish, pk 135.00
Swirl, candy dish, pk, open, 3-leg 6.00
Swirl, creamer, pk, ftd 6.50

Swirl, cup, ultramarine 8.50
Swirl, plate, salad; pk, 8" 6.00
Swirl, plate, sherbet; ultramarine, 6½" 3.50

Swirl, sugar bowl, pk, ftd.. 6.50
Swirl, tumbler, pk, ftd, 9-oz 12.50
Swirl, vase, ultramarine, ftd, 8½" 17.50
Tea Room, bowl, celery; gr, 8½" 25.00
Tea Room, creamer, gr, 4" 12.50
Tea Room, goblet, gr, 9-oz 60.00
Tea Room, mustard, gr 95.00
Tea Room, parfait, pk 45.00
Tea Room, plate, sherbet; gr, 6½" 20.00
Tea Room, relish, gr, divided 16.00
Tea Room, sugar bowl, gr, 4" 13.50
Tea Room, sugar bowl, pk, flat 80.00
Tea Room, tumbler, gr, ftd, 6-oz 25.00
Tea Room, vase, gr, 9" 50.00
Thistle, bowl, cereal; gr, 5½" 16.00
Thistle, cup, gr, thin 17.50
Thistle, plate, grill; pk, 10¼" 12.50
Thistle, plate, luncheon; pk, 8" 8.00
Thistle, saucer, gr 7.50
Twisted Optic, bowl, cereal; gr, 5" 3.00
Twisted Optic, bowl, cream soup; pk, 4¾" 7.00
Twisted Optic, creamer, gr 6.00

Twisted Optic, cup, pk.. 2.50
Twisted Optic, plate, gr, oval, 9½x7"......................... 4.00
Twisted Optic, plate, sherbet; pk, 6" 1.50
Twisted Optic, sherbet, gr 4.00
Twisted Optic, tumbler, gr, 9-oz, 4½" 4.50
Twisted Optic, tumbler, pk, 12-oz, 5¼" 6.50
US Swirl, bowl, berry; gr, 4⅜" 4.50
US Swirl, bowl, berry; pk, 7⅛" 12.00
US Swirl, bowl, gr, oval, 8¼" 12.50
US Swirl, butter bottom, pk 52.50
US Swirl, butter dish, pk, complete 70.00
US Swirl, butter top, gr 10.00
US Swirl, creamer, gr 10.00
US Swirl, plate, sherbet; gr, 6⅛"................................ 1.50
US Swirl, shakers, pk, pr 35.00
US Swirl, sugar bowl, pk..30.00
US Swirl, tumbler, gr, 12-oz, 4⅝" 8.50
US Swirl, vase, gr, 6½" 12.50
Victory, bonbon, bl, 7" 15.00
Victory, bowl, cereal; pk, 6½" 7.50
Victory, bowl, vegetable; pk, oval, 9" 25.00
Victory, creamer, pk 10.00
Victory, goblet, pk, 7-oz, 5" 17.50
Victory, plate, bread & butter; bl, 6" 8.00
Victory, platter, bl, 12" 45.00
Victory, sugar bowl, pk 10.00
Vitrock, bowl, cereal; milk glass, 7½" 3.00
Vitrock, bowl, fruit; milk glass, 6" 4.00
Vitrock, plate, dinner; milk glass, 10" 4.00

Vitrock, plate, luncheon; milk glass, 8¾".................... 2.00
Waterford, ash tray, crystal, 4" 6.00
Waterford, bowl, berry; crystal, 8¼" 6.00
Waterford, bowl, cereal; crystal, 5½" 9.00
Waterford, coaster, pk, 4"... 5.00
Waterford, creamer, crystal, oval 2.50
Waterford, cup, pk 10.00
Waterford, pitcher, juice; crystal, tilted, 42-oz 17.50
Waterford, plate, salad; pk, 7⅛" 4.50
Waterford, plate, sandwich; crystal, 13¾" 5.00
Waterford, saucer, pk 3.50
Waterford, sugar bowl, pk 6.50
Waterford, tumbler, crystal, ftd, 10-oz, 4⅞" 8.50
Windsor, ash tray, crystal, 5¾"..................................11.50
Windsor, bowl, berry; pk, 4¾".................................... 5.00
Windsor, bowl, cereal; crystal, 5⅛" or 5⅜"................. 5.00
Windsor, bowl, cream soup; pk, 5" 12.50
Windsor, butter dish, crystal 22.50
Windsor, cake plate, pk, thick, 13½"..........................11.50
Windsor, candlesticks, crystal, 3", pr.........................15.00
Windsor, coaster, crystal, 3¼" 2.50
Windsor, compote, pk..12.00
Windsor, creamer, pk 7.50
Windsor, pitcher, crystal, 52-oz, 6¾" 11.00
Windsor, plate, chop; pk, 13⅝" 20.00
Windsor, plate, sandwich; crystal, hdls, 10¼" 4.00
Windsor, plate, sherbet; pk, 6"................................... 3.50
Windsor, platter, crystal, oval, 11½" 4.50
Windsor, sherbet, crystal, ftd 2.50
Windsor, sugar bowl, pk...17.50
Windsor, tumbler, crystal, 5-oz, 3¼" 6.00

Derby

William Duesbury operated in Derby, England, from about 1755, purchasing a second establishment, The Chelsea Works, in 1769. During this period fine porcelains were produced which so impressed the King that in 1773 he issued the company the Crown Derby patent. In 1810, several years after Duesbury's death, the factory was bought by Robert Bloor. The quality of the ware suffered under the new management, and the main Derby pottery closed in 1848. Within a short time, the work was revived by a dedicated number of former employees who established their own works on King Street in Derby.

The earliest-known Derby mark was the crown over a script 'D'; however this mark is rarely found today. Soon after 1782, that mark was augmented with a device of crossed batons and six dots, usually applied in underglaze blue. During the Bloor period, the crown was centered within a ring containing the words 'Bloor' above and 'Derby' below the crown, or with a red printed stamp – the crowned Gothic 'D.' The King Street plant produced figurines that may be distinguished from their earlier counterparts by the presence of an 'S' and 'H' on either side of the crown and crossed batons.

In 1876 a new pottery was constructed in Derby, and the owners revived the earlier company's former standard of excellence. The Queen bestowed the firm the title Royal Crown Derby in 1890; it still operates under that name today. See also Royal Crown Derby.

Candlestick, Captivity, female w/cage, sheep at ft, 12", EX 450.00
Cup & saucer, floral, 3-color+underglaze bl, red crown mk 95.00
Cup & saucer, handleless; vines, underglaze bl, ribbed, mk..........215.00
Figurine, Autumn w/fruit, Winter w/kindling, 7", pr, EX 400.00
Figurine, lady flower seller on scroll base, 1825, 5", EX 240.00
Flowerpot & stand, florals/gold bands/scroll hdls, 1810, VG........160.00

Vase, gilt flowers and leaves on dark blue, reticulated handles and finial, dome lid, 12", $1,800.00.

Vase, floral reserves, scroll hdls, ftd, 1820s, 9", VG......................220.00

Desert Sands

As early as the 1850s, the Evans family living in the Ozark Mountains of Missouri produced domestic clay products. Their small pot shop was passed on from one generation to the next. In the 1920s it was moved to North Las Vegas, Nevada, where the name Desert Sands was adopted. Succeeding generations of the family continued to relocate, taking the business with them. From 1937 to 1962 it operated in Boulder City, Nevada; then it was moved to Barstow where it remained until it closed in the late 1970s.

Desert Sands pottery is similar to Mission Ware by Niloak. Various mineral oxides were blended to mimic the naturally occuring sand formations of the American West. A high-gloss glaze was applied to add intensity to the colorful striations that characterize the ware. Not all examples are marked, making it sometimes difficult to attribute. Marked items carry an ink stamp with the Desert Sands designation. Paper labels were also used.

Bowl, swirled colors, 4½"..10.00
Tumbler, swirled colors 10.00
Vase, swirled colors, cactus ink mk, 7"....................................28.00
Vase, swirled colors, 3½x3" 15.00

Devon, Crown Devon

Devon and Crown Devon were trade names of S. Fielding and Company, Ltd., an English firm founded about 1879. They produced majolica, earthenware mugs, vases, and kitchenware. In the 1930s, they manufactured an exceptional line of Art Deco vases that have recently been much in demand.

Dish, fuchsias, pk emb on gray, leaf form, mk, 5¼x3¾"..................20.00
Jug, musical, John Peel, fox hdl, 8"..................................185.00
Pitcher, fuchsias, pk/purple emb on lt gray, mk, 6¾x4½"..............45.00
Vase, fantasy forest/spider webs, w/gilt, urn form, 6½".................110.00
Vase, Mattajade, dragon on turq w/gilt, 10½"..............................300.00

Dickota

The Dickota Pottery, a name coined from Dickinson, North Dakota, where it was founded as a brickyard, began operations in the early 1930s. In 1934 potters formerly associated with the North Dakota School of Mines and Charles Hyten from Niloak began their own operation there. Hyten developed a line of swirled ware which was marked

'Dickota Badlands.' Vases, bowls, and ash trays in a mottled glaze were also made. A variety of marks were used, all of which contain the Dickota name. The company closed in the late 1930s.

Ash tray, advertising, creamery products, horseshoe form..............38.00
Bookends, ram form, pr 90.00
Vase, mc swirls, ovoid, 6"..65.00
Vase, mc swirls, sgn Howard Lewis, 6¾" 250.00

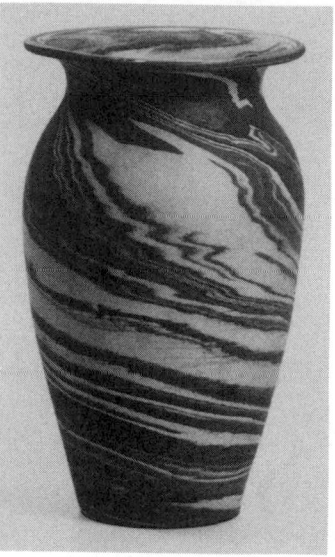

Vase, swirled multicolor clay, 6½", $65.00.

Documents

Although the word 'document' is defined in the general sense as 'anything printed or written, etc., relied upon to record or prove something. . .,' in the collectible market, the term is more diversified with broadsides, billheads, checks, invoices, letters and letterheads, land grants, receipts, and waybills some of the most sought after. Some documents in demand are those related to a specific subject such as advertising, mining, railroads, military, politics, banking, slavery, nautical, or legal (deeds, mortgages, etc.). Other collectors look for examples representing a specific period of time such as colonial documents, Revolutionary, or Civil War documents, early western documents or those from a specific region, state, or city.

Aside from supply and demand, there are five major factors which determine the collector-value of a document. These are:

1) Age – Documents from the eastern half of the country can be found that date back to the 1700s or earlier. Most documents sought by collectors usually date from 1800 to 1900. Those with twentieth century dates are still abundant and not in demand unless of special significance or beauty.

2) Region of origin – Depending on age, documents from rural and less-populated areas are harder to find than those from major cities and heavily populated states. The colonization of the West and Mid-West did not begin until after 1850, so while an 1870s billhead from New York or Chicago is common, one from Albuquerque or Phoenix is not, since most of the Southwest was still unsettled.

3) Attractiveness – Some documents are plain and unadorned, but collectors prefer colorful, profusely illustrated pieces. Additional artwork and engravings add to the value.

4) Historical content – Unusual or interesting content, such as a letter written by a Civil War soldier giving an eye-witness account of the Battle of Gettysburg or a western territorial billhead listing numerous animal hides purchased from a trapper, will sell for more than one with mundane information.

5) Condition – Through neglect or environmental conditions, over many decades paper articles can become stained, torn, or deteriorated. Heavily damaged or stained documents are generally avoided altogether while those with minor problems are more acceptable, although their value will decrease anywhere from 20% to 50% depending upon the extent of damage. Avoid attempting to repair tears with scotch tape – sell 'as is' so that the collector can take proper steps toward restoration.

Foreign documents are plentiful; and, though some are very attractive, resale may be difficult. The listings that follow are generalized; prices are variable depending entirely upon the five points noted above. Values here are based upon examples with no major damage.

Our advisor for this category is Warren Anderson; he is listed in the Directory under Utah.

Key: illus — illustrated   vgn — vignette

Application, US citizenship, ca 1900	7.50
Bill of sale, New Orleans, slave, describes talents, 1853	40.00
Commission, NJ, state seal/emblem, sgn GF Fort, 1852, 13x17"	30.00
Confederate bill, $10, Gen Bragg Artillery vgn, 1864, EX	10.00
Deed, PA, emb printed parchment, wax seal, 1796, VG	100.00
Exemption petition, lists ailment, bk: not approved, 1860s	15.00
Fractional note, 10¢, gr print, US Treasury, 1873, EX	8.50
General court martial, drunkenness, Potomac, 1863, 1-pg, EX	15.00
General orders, Hooker in command, 3-pg, 1863, EX	10.00
Invoice, wine from France to Phila, sgn GW Roosevelt, 1882	24.00
Land grant, Richland Co OH, sgn Andrew Jackson, 1833, fr	300.00
Letter, Confederate officer's, war news, MS, 1864, 2-pg	75.00
Letter, to Confederate soldier from wife, 1862, 2-pg, EX	30.00
Letter, WV, Gov Stevenson to Gov Jacob, handwritten, 1871	35.00
Lottery ticket, GA, blk & red on wht, state seal, dtd 1845	8.00
Manifest, shipment of sugar/etc from Cuba to Phila, 1869, EX	17.50
Note, State of VA, blk/wht, 2½x4¾", EX	12.50
Oath of Allegiance, Bedford County VA, 1861, 5x8", EX	48.00
Pass, HQ Dept of WA, sgn loyalty oath on bk, 1864, 4x6"	50.00
Passport, mtd in folding case w/emb eagle, dtd 1860, EX	45.00
Promisory certificate, Edison Storage Battery Co, 1921	25.00
Receipt, PA, payment of horse, sgn Thomas Penn	95.00
Receipt for impressment, oats/hay, VA, 1864, 3x8"	22.00
Slave, levy against slave & delivery bond, TN, 1833, 1-pg	32.00
Slave, tax receipts, printed, 1860, 10 sheets for	25.00
Slave, 5 charged w/murder, 1-pg, 1835, 7x8", EX	50.00
Summons for arrest, CT, sgn by Wm Williams, 1762	110.00
Tax certificate, Sheboygan Co WI, 1860, fr	15.00
Telegram, US Military, requiring reports, GA, 1864, 5x8", EX	30.00
Voucher, salary Walla Walla chief sgn by Indian agent, 1870	68.00
Voucher, Union Military pay & rations, 11x17", EX	8.00

Dollhouses and Furnishings

Dollhouses were introduced commercially in this country late in the 1700s by Dutch craftsmen who settled in the East. By the mid-1800s, they had become meticulously detailed, divided into separate rooms, and lavishly furnished to reflect the opulence of the day. Originally intended for the amusement of adults of the household, by the latter 1800s their status had changed to that of a child's toy. Though many early dollhouses were lovingly hand-fashioned for a special little girl, those made commercially by such companies as Bliss and Schoenhut are highly valued.

Furniture and furnishings in the Biedermeier style featuring stenciled Victorian decorations often sell for several hundred dollars each. Other early pieces made of pewter, porcelain, or papier-mache are also quite valuable. Certainly less expensive but very collectible, nonetheless, is the quality, hallmarked plastic furniture produced during the forties by Renwal and Acme, and the 1960s Petite Princess line produced by Ideal. In the listings that follow, dollhouses are litho paper on wood, unless otherwise noted. When no manufacturer or country of origin is noted, examples are German, turn of the century.

Our advisor for this category is Barbara Rosen; she is listed in the Directory under New Jersey. See also Miniatures.

Furnishings

Bed, brass, minor bending to posts, 3", G	60.00
Bed, iron, tubular, VG pnt	50.00
Bed, oak, simple style, minor wear, EX	25.00
Bed, ormolu head & ft, 3½x5", EX	275.00
Bedroom set, wooden, Donna Lee, MIB	15.00
Bird stand w/bird, brass, ornate style, early, G	575.00
Bird stand w/bird, brass, simple style, early, VG	200.00
Birdcage w/bird, brass, Adrian Cook, VG	60.00
Buffet, Tootsie Toy	15.00

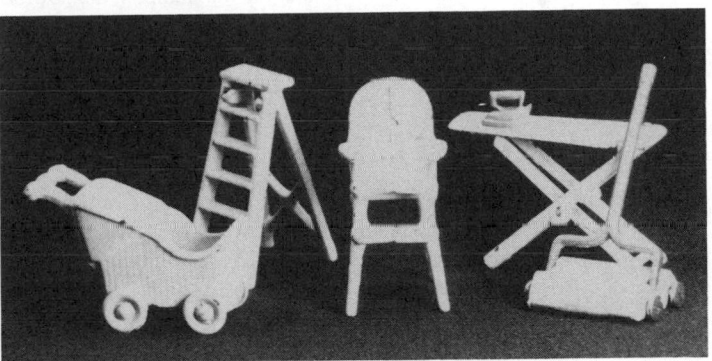

Kilgore cast iron furnishings: Buggy, 2", $40.00; Highchair, 3", $40.00; Ironing board and iron, 2", $50.00; Ladder, 3", $40.00; Sweeper, 2¼", $35.00.

Bureau, oak, marble top, 3-drw, rprs, EX	150.00
Cabinet, oak, mirrored bk, VG	75.00
Candelabrum, brass, wall hanging, VG, pr	250.00
Candelabrum, metal & glass, EX, pr	50.00
Carriage, lead, mc pnt, VG	175.00
Castor set, 4-bottle, gilt fr, VG	40.00
Chair, living room; gold, Tootsie Toy	12.00
Chair, side; ormolu, G	25.00
Chamberstick, brass, EX	25.00
Chandelier, metal & glass, 3 for	25.00
Chifferobe, Mattel	5.00
Clock, Grandfather; Petite Princess, w/screen	28.00
Clock, shelf; gilt w/porc dial, VG	125.00
Clock, wall regulator; ormolu, EX	80.00
Coal hod, pnt metal, VG	40.00
Cradle, mahog, hooded, EX	90.00
Cupboard, kitchen; Petite Princess	45.00
Desk, ormolu, bow legs, 4⅜", EX	200.00
Dining set, extension table & 4 chairs, wood, EX	60.00
Dining set, oak, table, 4 chairs, & china cabinet, EX	90.00
Dresser, 3-drw, dk wood, mirror-bk, EX	45.00
Fantasy Telephone, Petite Princess, in box	10.00
Fireplace, tin litho, marble top, VG	30.00
Fireplace, wood & metal, w/3 tools, EX	35.00
Frame, gilt, stand-up, G	10.00
Highchair, bentwood oak, EX	225.00

Ice box, tin, orig grain pnt, EX..................................225.00
Lamp, banquet; brass, glass shade, G......................250.00
Mirror, hall; ormolu, 5½", EX..................................150.00
Parlor set, bentwood, settee, rocker, & armchair, EX 225.00
Parlor set, oak, sofa, armchairs, 4 side chairs, 7-pc, EX 400.00
Piano, upright; oak, minor rpr, EX.............................50.00
Piano/bench, Tootsie Toy 20.00
Rack, towel; brass, G..70.00
Radiator, lead, gilt pnt, VG..................................25.00
Royal Candelabra, Petite Princess, in box 15.00
Server, oak, marble top, VG...................................75.00
Stove, Dutch, ceramic, EX 70.00
Stove, Eclipse, CI, EX..175.00
Stove, Little Fanny, CI, minor rust, EX 300.00
Stove, Little Willie, CI, EX..................................75.00
Table, coffee; Salon, Petite Princess, in box 12.00
Table, dining; w/picture, Petite Princess, in box 12.00
Table, drop leaf; oak, EX.....................................40.00
Tea cart, brn, Tootsie Toy....................................20.00
Television, Petite Princess...................................60.00
Umbrella stand, brass, G......................................30.00
Vase, brass, long neck, hdls, VG, pr..........................25.00
Wash stand, ormolu, 3¼", VG 175.00
Wash stand, pnt tin, VG 30.00

Houses

Bliss, cottage, 2-story/2-room, paper on wood, 11x7½x5", EX 500.00
Bliss, 2-story, chimney/pitched roof/steps/porch, 18x10" 900.00
Bliss type, 2-story/2-room, gabled roof/porch, 18x11x8" 880.00
Bliss type, 2-story/3-room, paper ext, rpt/rpl, 18x12" 385.00

German Blue-Roofed 2-story, lithographed paper on wood, painted wood foundation, metal porch railing, 25" x 18" x 11", NM, $1,100.00.

German Red-Roof Series, 3-story/8-room, rpt, 1920s, 40" 550.00
Log cabin, 3-room, battery lights, furnished, 1930s, 18x25" 850.00
McLoughlin, folding, opens to 4 rooms, 1894, 12x12", w/box 400.00
Schoenhut, NJ farm, 2-story/6 furnished rooms, clapboard 3,000.00
Schoenhut, 2-story/2-room, furnished, ca 1915, 14x10x9" 800.00
Victorian, 3-story/3-room, columned porch, 25x22x14", EX.......660.00
2-story, wood w/brick paper, front opens, 1920s, 16x14", EX 85.00

Dolls

Collecting dolls of any sort is one of the most rewarding hobbies in the United States. The rewards are in the fun, the search, and the finds – plus there is a built-in factor of investment. No hobby, be it dolls, glass, or anything else, should be based completely on investment; but any collector should ask: 'Can I get my money back out of this item if I should ever have to sell it?' Many times we buy on impulse rather than with logic, which is understandable; but by asking this question we can save ourselves a lot of 'buyer's remorse' which we have all experienced at one time or another.

Since we want to learn to invest our money wisely while we are having fun, we must become aware of defects which may devaluate a doll. In bisque, watch for eye chips, hairline cracks and chips, or breaks on any part of the head. Composition should be clean, not crazed or cracked. Vinyl and plastic should be clean with no pen or crayon marks. Though a quality replacement wig is acceptable for bisque dolls, composition and hard plastics should have their originals in uncut condition. Original clothing is a must except in bisque dolls, since it is unusual to find one in its original costume. However, they should be well dressed and ready for your collection.

A price guide is only that – a guide. It suggests the average price for each doll. Bargains can be found for less-than-suggested values, and 'unplayed-with' dolls in their original boxes may cost more. Dealers must become aware of condition so that they do not over-pay and therefore over-price their dolls – a common occurrence across the country. Quantity does not replace quality, as most find out in time. A faster turnover of sales with a smaller margin of profit is far better than being stuck with an item that does not sell because it is over-priced. It is important to remember that prices are based on condition and rarity. When no condition is noted, dolls are assumed to be in excellent condition with the exceptions of Armand Marseille, Madame Alexander, and Effanbee dolls, which are priced in mint condition. In relation to bisque dolls, excellent means having no cracks, chips, or hairlines, being nicely dressed, shoed, wigged, and ready to to be placed into a collection. For a more thorough study of the subject, we recommend you refer to the many lovely doll books written by authority Pat Smith, available at your favorite bookstore or public library.

Key:
bjtd — ball-jointed	OC — original clothes
blb — bent limb body	p/e — pierced ears
bsk — bisque	pnt — painted
c/m — closed mouth	pwt — paperweight eyes
hh — human hair	RpC — replaced clothes
hp — hard plastic	ShHd — shoulder head
jtd — jointed	ShPl — shoulder plate
MIG — Made In Germany	SkHd — socket head
NC — no clothes	str — straight
o/c — open closed	trn — turned

Armand Marseille

A 0 ½ M, 300n, Armand Marseille, adult, SkHd, 15½" 350.00
A 10/0 M, 324, Germany, Armand Marseille, pnt eyes, 7"..........465.00
A 10/0 M, 390, SkHd, 1900, 18"....................................400.00
A 11 M, DRGM, Germany, SkHd, 26"................................575.00
A 11 M, DRGM 276/1, Germany, SkHd, 26".........................575.00
A 11 M, G 327 B, Germany, SkHd, 1914, 20" 585.00
A 11 M, 1894, ShPl, 26" 550.00
A 11/0 M, 255, DRGM, Germany, SkHd, intaglio eyes, 7½" 425.00
A 11/0 M, 323, Germany, SkHd, glass eyes, 7½"...................625.00
A 11/0 M, 395, Germany, SkHd, Heidi, 1920, 9" 225.00
A 11/0 M, 500, MIG, molded hair, Infant Berry, 1908, 5" 300.00
A 12 M, 390n, Germany, SkHd, Louisa, 1915, 27" 575.00
A 12/0 M, MIG, SkHd, o/c eyes, 7" 125.00
A 2/0 M, DRGM 201013, Germany, trn ShHd, talks, 16"..........425.00

A 2/0 M, G 329 B, Germany, SkHd, girl, 9" 250.00
A 2/0 M, 500, DRGM, molded hair, Infant Berry, 1908, 10" 450.00
A 3/0 M, 990, SkHd, baby, 8" 145.00
A 30/0 M, MH, Germany, SkHd, c/m, lady, dimples, 1913, 10" ..950.00
A 4 M, 347, Germany, SkHd, 1909, 16" 475.00
A 4/0 M, 320, Germany, SkHd, c/m, pnt eyes, 6½" 400.00
A 4/0 M, 323, Germany, SkHd, googly eyes, 11" 1,200.00
A 450 M, 1 ½, Germany, SkHd, c/m, provincial attire, 19" 850.00
A 5 M, 590, DRGM, o/c eyes & mouth, Hoopla Girl, 16" 1,700.00
A 5/0 M, 402, Germany, SkHd, pnt bsk, 14" 250.00
A 6 M, 550, DRGM, Germany, SkHd, c/m, 16" 2,900.00
A 6/0 M, G 327B, DRGM 259, Germany, SkHd, 1914, 12" 185.00
A 7 M, Germany, SkHd, 17" 295.00
A 7 M, 257, Germany, SkHd, baby, 1914, 22" 450.00
A 7 M, 390, MIG, SkHd, 23" 425.00
A 7/0 M, MIG, ShHd, boy, 14" 385.00
A 7/0 M, 390, MIG, SkHd, 9½" 145.00
A 9 M, CM Bergmann, MIG, SkHd, 24" 525.00
A 985 M, 3, Germany, SkHd, baby, 13½" 375.00
Alma 10/0/Germany, ShHd, 26" 525.00
Alma 14/0, ShHd, 26" 525.00
Alma 3/0, ShHd, 12" 165.00
Alma 9/0, ShHd, 15" 250.00
AM Darling Baby, 1906, 12" 325.00
AM DEP, MIG, SkI Id, 16" 225.00
AM DEP, 3/0, MIG, SkHd, 1894, 14" 300.00
AM DEP, 3200, ShHd, some trn, 1898, 16" 375.00
AM G 327 B, DRGM, SkHd, baby, fur hair, 1914, 12" 325.00
AM G 328 B, Germany, SkHd, closed dome, 1922, 14" 350.00
AM 0 ½ DEP, 3200, MIG, ShHd, 1898, 14" 285.00
AM 1 ½, DEP, SkHd, wht, 1894, 16½" 375.00
AM 11 DEP, 3200, ShHd, some trn, 26" 600.00
AM 12, Germany, flange neck, baby, 1907, 16" 475.00
AM 1894, DEP, Germany, SkHd, blk, 12" 425.00
AM 2 1/2k, Germany, SkHd, o/m, blk, 12" 425.00
AM 2/0, DEP, 3500, MIG, ShHd, 17" 400.00
AM 2/0 DEP, 370, MIG, ShHd, 19½" 325.00
AM 20/0, Germany, SkHd, o/c, Indian, 1890s, 8" 400.00
AM 3 DEP, 370, MIG, ShHd, fur eyebrows, 22½" 425.00
AM 3k, 362, Germany, SkHd, closed dome, baby, wht, 15" 400.00
AM 341, Germany, flange, c/m, My Dream Baby, 1924, 7" 165.00
AM 341 7, Germany, flange, c/m, My Dream Baby, 18" 600.00
AM 341/Ok, Germany, SkHd, c/m, My Dream Baby, 16" 500.00
AM 341/10, Germany, flange, c/m, My Dream Baby, 21" 675.00
AM 341/3, Germany, socket & flange, c/m, baby, wht, 8" 185.00
AM 341/4, Germany, flange, c/m, My Dream Baby, 15" 450.00
AM 351 10/0, Germany, w/rubber body, Wee One, 7" 165.00
AM 351 17/0, Germany, socket & flange, o/m, 6" 145.00
AM 351/4k, Germany, socket & flange, o/m, wht, 22" 800.00
AM 351/6, Germany, socket & flange, o/m, 26" 1,200.00
AM 352 10, Germany, flange, Baby Love, 1914, 19" 675.00
AM 3524, 7, Germany, flange neck, baby, Baby Gloria, 18" 1,000.00
AM 390, MIG, SkHd, My Dearie, 1908-1922, 18½" 375.00
AM 4/0x DEP, 370, MIG, ShHd, 16½" 275.00
AM 5 DEP, 3200, ShHd, some trn, 15" 325.00
AM 5/0x, 370, MIG, ShHd, c/m, 15½" 250.00
AM 500, DRGM, Germany, Infant Berry, 1908, 8" 300.00
AM 6/0 DEP, 370, ShHd, 15" 250.00
AM 600, DRGM, Germany, flange, SkHd, c/m, 1910, 10" 700.00
AM 7/0 DEP, MIG, SkHd, 1894, 12" 275.00
AM 8 DEP, 3200, trn ShHd, 22" 500.00
AM 800, 'Mama,' talker in head, Baby Sunshine, 1925, 16" ... 1,900.00
AM 83115, SkHd, 8" 165.00
AM 917, Germany, SkHd, baby, Mobi, 1921, 16" 400.00

AM 95 6 DEP, Armand Marseille, trn ShHd, 20" 425.00
AM 966 3, MIG, SkHd, baby, flirty eyes, 14" 450.00
AM 980, Germany, SkHd, baby, 14" 350.00
Armand Marseille, A 0 1/2 M, 990, Germany, SkHd, 13" 400.00
Armand Marseille, A 1 M, 390, SkHd, 16" 425.00
Armand Marseille, A 11 M, 990, SkHd, Happy Tot, 1910, 21" ..675.00
Armand Marseille, A 11/0 M, 390, Germany, o/c mouth, 7½" 125.00
Armand Marseille, A 2 M, 390n, Germany, Patrice, SkHd, 18" ..500.00
Armand Marseille, A 2/0 M, 995, Germany, SkHd, 12" 350.00
Armand Marseille, A 2/0 M, 996, Germany, SkHd, baby, 15" 425.00
Armand Marseille, A 4 ½ M, 990, Germany, SkHd, 1910, 16" ...450.00
Armand Marseille, A 4/0x M, 390n, Germany, SkHd, 1915, 11" .275.00

Armand Marseille, 17" shoulder plate, marked A. 4/0, MIG, 17", **$400.00.**

Armand Marseille, A 6 M, 390, MIG, SkHd, walks, 22" 525.00
Armand Marseille, A 6 M, 390, SkHd, 21" 425.00
Armand Marseille, A 7 M, 390, Germany, SkHd, 22" 485.00
Armand Marseille, A 7 M, 992, Germany, SkHd, 1914, 22" 750.00
Armand Marseille, A 9 M, 390, SkHd, pnt bsk, 9" 165.00
Armand Marseille, A 975 M, 13, Germany, SkHd, 1914, 24" 700.00
Armand Marseille, A 975 M, 2/0, Germany, SkHd, 1914, 9" 165.00
Armand Marseille, AM 10/0 DEP, 370, MIG, ShHd, 12" 195.00
Armand Marseille, AM 7/0 DEP, 370n, MIG, ShHd, 12" 195.00
Armand Marseille, Germany, SkHd, c/m, 14" 600.00
Armand Marseille, 390, MIG, SkHd, 24" 500.00

Armand Marseille, 560a, DRGM 232, Dorothy, 1912, 15" **475.00**
Columbia, MIG, ShHd, 1904, 24" **600.00**
Fany, A 11 M, 231, DRGM 248/1, baby, c/m, 1913, 25" **8,300.00**
Floradora, A 0 M, MIG, SkHd, 17" **325.00**
Floradora, A 1 M, MIG, ShHd, 20" **365.00**
Floradora, A 11 M, MIG, SkHd, 27" **575.00**
Floradora, A 3 M, MIG, ShHd, 23" **475.00**
Floradora, A 4 M, SkHd, 23" **450.00**
Floradora, A 5 M, Germany, ShHd, 24" **500.00**
Floradora, A 77 M, MIG, SkHd, 15" **300.00**
Floradora, A 9/0 M, MIG, SkHd, 12" **225.00**
Floradora, 1347, ShHd, fur eyebrows, 21" **425.00**
Floradora, 2/0x AM, ShHd, 21½" **400.00**
Floradora, 3740, 30, 1374, ShHd, 21" **450.00**
GB, A 5/0 M, DRGM 248/1, SkHd, o/m, 1912, 10" **165.00**
GB 250, A 1 M, Germany, SkHd, c/m, molded hair, 10½" **375.00**
Googly, A 11/0 M, 254, SkHd, molded hair, 8" **550.00**
Googly, A 12/0 M, 210, Germany, SkHd, pnt eyes, 6" **500.00**
Googly, A 253 M, 5/0, DRGM, Germany, SkHd, 1915, 16".... **1,600.00**
Googly, A 3/0 M, G 252 B, DRGM, SkHd, 1915, 9½" **825.00**
Googly, A 3/0 M, 200, DRGM 213, SkHd, 11½" **2,200.00**
Googly, A 6/0 M, SB 252, DRGM, Germany, SkHd, 10" **795.00**
Googly, AM, 353, 5/0, SkHd, 6½" **600.00**
Googly, AOM, 253 SB, DRGM, Germany, SkHd, 8" **725.00**
Kiddiejoy, A 3 M, 997, Germany, SkHd, 14" **475.00**
Kiddiejoy, AM, 991, Germany, SkHd, 14" **375.00**
Kiddiejoy, AOM, Germany, ShHd, 9" **165.00**
Kiddiejoy, 3/0, Germany, ShHd, cloth body, c/m, girl, 20" **1,900.00**
Kiddiejoy, 372, Germany, ShHd, molded hair, 1926, 9" **285.00**
Kiddiejoy, 375 6, Germany, c/m, molded hair, girl, 20" **1,800.00**
Lily, 4/0, MIG, ShHd, 1913, 17" **375.00**
Mabel, 131, Germany, ShHd, 1898, 17" **375.00**
Mabel, 3/0, Germany, ShHd, 1898, 15" **400.00**
My Dearie, A 2M, DRGM 246/1, SkHd, 1908, 14" **325.00**
My Playmate (Baby), AM Germany, closed dome, c/m, 18".... **1,400.00**
Otto Gans, A 5 M, 970, Germany, Lady Marie, 1916, 20" **525.00**
Otto Gans, A 7 M, 975, Germany, SkHd, Sadie, 1914, 17".........**450.00**
Queen Louise, Germany, SkHd, 1910, 22" **550.00**
Queen Louise, 100, Germany, SkHd, 1910, 12" **300.00**
Queen Louise, 100, SkHd, 1910, 18½" **425.00**
Queen Louise, 315, Germany 12, SkHd, 27" **850.00**
Rosebud, A 4/0 M, MIG, ShHd, 1902, 15".............................**365.00**
Roseland, AOM, 1910, 18" **475.00**
Sunshine, 1910, Germany, ShHd, 24" **525.00**
Wonderful Alice, DRGM 377439, SkHd, fur eyebrows, 26" **600.00**

Barbie Dolls and Related Dolls

   Though the face has changed three times since 1959, Barbie is still as popular today as she was when she was first introduced. Named after the young daughter of the first owner of the Mattel Company, the original Barbie had a white iris but no eye color. These dolls are nearly impossible to find, but there is a myriad of her successors and related collectibles just waiting to be found. When no condition is indicated, the dolls listed below are assumed to be nude and in excellent condition unless otherwise specified. For further information, we recommend *An Illustrated Price Guide to Collectible Barbie Dolls* by Paris, Susan, and Carol Manos; and *The Collector's Encyclopedia of Barbie Dolls and Collectibles* by Sibyl DeWein and Joan Ashabraner.

Barbie, 1959, #1, blond, swimsuit, holes in feet, MIB **1,500.00**
Barbie, 1960, #3, bl eyes, curved brows, ivory skin, MIB.............**300.00**
Barbie, 1960, #4, vinyl plastic, tan skin **200.00**
Barbie, 1961, #5, hollow body, curly bangs, MIB.......................**125.00**

Barbie, 1961, Bubble Cut, MIB **150.00**
Barbie, 1963, Fashion Queen, w/3 wigs, swimsuit, MIB **200.00**
Barbie, 1964, Ponytail Swirl, no curly bangs............................**200.00**
Barbie, 1965, Color 'N Curl, 2 heads & accessories, MIB **300.00**
Barbie, 1967, standard, str legs, pnt lashes **65.00**
Barbie, 1968, Spanish Talking, MIB **185.00**
Barbie, 1969, Twist 'N Turn...**85.00**
Barbie, 1972, Busy, long blond hair.......................................**85.00**
Barbie, 1972, Ward's Anniversary, 100th Anniversary.................**185.00**
Barbie, 1973, Quick Curl, blond, bendable knees.......................**85.00**
Barbie, 1974, Sun Valley, w/ski accessories, MIB.......................**75.00**
Barbie, 1974, Sweet Sixteen, Barbie's birthday, MIB.................**85.00**
Barbie, 1975, Free Moving, blond, MIB **65.00**
Barbie, 1975, Funtime, bendable knees, twist waist, MIB **65.00**
Barbie, 1975, Gold Metal Skater, w/skates & stand **40.00**
Barbie, 1975, Hawaiian, str hair, grass skirt, MIB.....................**65.00**
Barbie, 1976, Ballerina, blond ponytail, wht tutu, MIB...............**40.00**
Barbie, 1976, Beautiful Bride, bendable knees, w/gown, MIB **85.00**
Barbie, 1976, Plus 3, in package, M..**65.00**
Barbie, 1977, Hawaiian Super Star, Canada, MIB **75.00**
Barbie, 1978, Beautiful Bride, MIB **45.00**
Barbie, 1978, Fashion Photo, remote control play camera, MIB....**55.00**
Barbie, 1978, Super Size Bridal, MIB.....................................**95.00**
Barbie, 1978, Super Star, In the Spotlight, w/3 outfits, MIB.........**85.00**
Barbie, 1979, Kissing, w/2 gowns, lipstick, & stand, MIB.............**50.00**
Barbie, 1979, Pretty Changes, w/lamp base **50.00**
Barbie, 1980, Beauty Secrets, MIB **25.00**
Barbie, 1981, Western, MIB...**25.00**
Barbie, 1983, Twirly Curls..**25.00**
Brad, 1970, Talking, Black, pnt hair, MIB................................**85.00**
Cara, 1975, Free Moving, Black, long hair w/bows, MIB **55.00**
Cara, 1976, Ballerina, Black, swivel head & arms, blk hair...........**45.00**
Carla, 1965, Black, blk ponytail w/wht ribbon, MIB....................**45.00**
Casey, 1975, Baggie, blond, str legs, swimsuit, MIB........................**30.00**
Christie, 1969, Talking, Black..**55.00**
Christie, 1971, Live Action, Black, bendable knees, MIB..............**75.00**
Christie, 1979, Kissing, w/lipstick, MIB **45.00**
Christie, 1980, Golden Dream, 2nd issue, MIB **40.00**
Curtis, 1976, Free Moving, MIB..**60.00**
Francie, 1966, bendable knees **60.00**
Francie, 1966, str legs, pnt lashes, swimsuit **90.00**
Francie, 1967, Black, 1st issue, brn eyes/red oxidized hair...........**300.00**
Francie, 1970, Hair Happenin's, 4 blond hairpieces, MIB............**150.00**
Francis, 1978, Malibu, MIB..**30.00**
Ginger, 1976, Growing Up Ginger, brunette **30.00**
Guardian Goddess, Sun Spell, MIB...**150.00**
Julia, 1969, Twist 'N Turn, 2-pc nurse's uniform, MIB **150.00**
Ken, 1961, Flocked Hair, movable head, arms, & legs....................**70.00**
Ken, 1969, Talking, bendable knees, jacket & shorts, MIB...........**125.00**
Ken, 1970, Spanish Talking, bl & orange outfit, MIB..................**150.00**
Ken, 1972, Walk Lively, pnt hair, MIB **95.00**
Ken, 1974, Ward's Dressed, bl & blk tuxedo, mod hair, MIB **125.00**
Ken, 1976, Funtime, bl trunks, MIB..**50.00**
Ken, 1976, Gold Medal Skier, w/skis & ski poles, MIB **50.00**
Ken, 1977, Super Star, w/free gift, MIB...................................**75.00**
Ken, 1978, Malibu, MIB..**25.00**
Ken, 1981, Western, MIB...**25.00**
Ken, 1982, All Star, MIB..**30.00**
Kitty O'Neil, MIB **45.00**
Kristie McNichol, MIB **40.00**
Midge, 1965, bendable legs, bouffant hair **150.00**
Miss America, 1972, Kellogg's Walk Lively, wht gown, MIB.......**200.00**
Miss America, 1974, Kellogg's Blond Quick Curl, MIB.................**85.00**
PJ, 1970, Twist 'N Turn, blond..**45.00**

PJ, 1971, Live Action PJ on Stage 95.00
PJ, 1975, Gold Medal Gymnast, w/balance beam.......................40.00
PJ, 1976, Free Moving, MIB...45.00
Ricky, 1965, red hair, str legs, freckles 45.00
Skipper, 1967, Funtime, blond, bendable knees 45.00
Skipper, 1970, Pose 'N Play, MIB..................................40.00
Skipper, 1976, Growing Up, MIB....................................40.00
Skipper, 1979, Super Teen, MIB....................................25.00
Skipper, 1981, Western, MIB.......................................25.00
Skooter, 1965, str legs, pigtails & freckles.....................40.00
Stacey, 1968, Talking, British accent, w/plastic box.............75.00
Steffie, 1972, Busy Talking, blond................................85.00
Tiff, 1972, Pose 'N Play, swing-free arms 65.00
Truly Scrumptious, 1969, Talking, bendable legs..................175.00
Twiggy, 1967, blond, bendable knees, mini dress, MIB 145.00

Barbie Gift Sets and Related Accessories

When no condition is indicated, the items listed below are assumed to be mint and in the original box.

Barbie & Skipper Living Room Furniture Group, MIB 60.00
Barbie Baby-Sitting Room, Canada, 1976-1986, MIB................75.00
Barbie Beach Party Play Set, w/doll, 1976-1986, M 50.00
Barbie Country Living House, M 30.00
Barbie Diary, 1963, M 25.00
Barbie Dream Kitchen & Dinette, #4095, 1964, MIB..............100.00
Barbie Fashion Stage, MIB 30.00
Barbie Goes Traveling Carrying Case, M.........................65.00
Barbie Hot Rod, Irwin Corp, MIB...............................100.00
Barbie Lawn Swing & Planter, Mattel, MIB.......................75.00
Barbie Make-Up Case, 1963, M...................................25.00
Barbie Olympic Ski Village, MIB................................35.00
Barbie Photo Album, 1963, M....................................35.00
Barbie Queen Size Bed, Suzy Goose, M...........................60.00
Barbie Record Player, Vanity Fair, 1961, M.....................50.00
Barbie Roller Gift Set, Spain 85.00
Barbie Snow Princess Dog Sled, Sweden, MIB....................200.00

Barbie Sparkling Pink Gift Set #1011, 1953, MIB, $300.00.

Barbie Star Cycle, 1976-1986, MIB 30.00
Barbie Story Book, World of Barbie, Random House, M............20.00
Barbie Thermos Bottle, 1961, M.................................20.00
Barbie Travelin' Trailor, 1976-1986, MIB.......................50.00
Clothes, Bicentennial Dress, 1976-1986, M......................60.00
Clothes, Dreamtime, #1909, (1963 booklet) 20.00
Clothes, Enchanted Evening, #983, (#2 1958 booklet)............85.00
Clothes, Fashion Fantasy, M....................................20.00
Clothes, Fun at the Fair, #1624, (1964 booklet)................50.00
Clothes, Golden Glory, #1645, (1965 booklet) 40.00
Clothes, Ice Empress, M..45.00
Clothes, Lace Pace, #1216, (1967 booklet) 40.00
Clothes, Outdoor Life, #1637, (1964 booklet)...................40.00
Clothes, Riding in the Park, #1668, (1965 booklet).............45.00
Clothes, Ship Ahoy, #1918, (1964 booklet) 40.00
Clothes, Sugar Plum Fairy, 1976-1986, MIB 65.00
Dallas, Barbie's Horse, Germany, 1976-1986, MIB................75.00
Francie House, #3302, 1966, M 40.00
Francie Mod a Go-Go Bedroom Furniture, by Susy Goose, M.....200.00
Honey, Skipper's Horse, 1976-1986, MIB 30.00
Pink & Pretty Barbie Gift Set, England........................250.00
Skipper 'N Skooter Double Bunk Beds & Ladder...................45.00
Walking Jamie Strollin' in Style Gift Set, #1247, 1972........450.00

Belton

Concave head, 2 or 3 hole, EX bsk, o/c or c/m w/wig, 10" .. **1,400.00**
Concave head, 2 or 3 hole, EX bsk, o/c or c/m w/wig, 13" .. **1,800.00**
Concave head, 2 or 3 hole, EX bsk, o/c or c/m w/wig, 15" **2,100.00**
Concave head, 2 or 3 hole, EX bsk, o/c or c/m w/wig, 16" **2,200.00**
Concave head, 2 or 3 hole, EX bsk, o/c or c/m w/wig, 17" **2,300.00**
Concave head, 2 or 3 hole, EX bsk, o/c or c/m w/wig, 20" **2,900.00**
Concave head, 2 or 3 hole, EX bsk, o/c or c/m w/wig, 22" **3,100.00**
Concave head, 2 or 3 hole, EX bsk, o/c or c/m w/wig, 23" **3,200.00**
Concave head, 2 or 3 hole, EX bsk, o/c or c/m w/wig, 26" **3,600.00**
Concave head, 2 or 3 hole, EX bsk, o/c or c/m w/wig, 8" **975.00**

Bru

Closed mouth, all kid body, bisque lower arms; Bru, 16".......... **9,000.00**
Closed mouth, all kid body, bisque lower arms; Bru, 18" **12,000.00**
Closed mouth, all kid body, bisque lower arms; Bru, 21" **18,000.00**
Closed mouth, all kid body, bisque lower arms; Bru, 26" **24,000.00**
Closed mouth, kid/wood body, bsk lower arms; Bru Jne, 12" .**20,000.00**
Closed mouth, kid/wood body, bsk lower arms; Bru Jne, 14" .**18,000.00**
Closed mouth, kid/wood body, bsk lower arms; Bru Jne, 16" .**20,000.00**
Closed mouth, kid/wood body, bsk lower arms; Bru Jne, 20" .**24,000.00**
Closed mouth, kid/wood body, bsk lower arms; Bru Jne, 25" .**30,000.00**
Closed mouth, kid/wood body, bsk lower arms; Bru Jne, 28" .**36,000.00**
Closed mouth, kid/wood body, bsk lower arms; Bru Jne, 32" .**42,000.00**
Closed mouth, mk Bru, circle dot, 16" **22,000.00**
Closed mouth, mk Bru, circle dot, 19" **25,000.00**
Closed mouth, mk Bru, circle dot, 23" **29,000.00**
Closed mouth, mk Bru, circle dot, 26" **32,000.00**
Open mouth, comp walker's body, throws kisses, 18"............... **5,600.00**
Open mouth, comp walker's body, throws kisses, 22".............. **6,400.00**
Open mouth, comp walker's body, throws kisses, 26".............. **7,300.00**
Open mouth, nursing (Bebe), high color, late SFBJ, 12" **1,900.00**
Open mouth, nursing (Bebe), high color, late SFBJ, 15" **2,800.00**
Open mouth, nursing (Bebe), high color, late SFBJ, 18" **3,400.00**
Open mouth, nursing Bru (Bebe), early, EX bsk, 12" **5,600.00**
Open mouth, nursing Bru (Bebe), early, EX bsk, 15" **7,800.00**
Open mouth, nursing Bru (Bebe), early, EX bsk, 18" **9,700.00**
Open mouth, socket head, compo body; Bru, R, 14", EX bsk .. **4,800.00**

Open mouth, socket head, compo body; Bru, R, 17", EX bsk .. **6,000.00**
Open mouth, socket head, compo body; Bru, R, 22", EX bsk .. **8,200.00**
Open mouth, socket head, compo body; Bru, R, 25", EX bsk .. **8,200.00**
Open mouth, socket head, compo body; Bru, R, 28", EX bsk .. **9,000.00**

Bru Jne R/12, human hair, blue paperweight eyes, pierced ears, closed mouth, ball-jointed body, original shoes, re-dressed, 26", $8,200.00.

Dolly Madison, modeled ribbon & bow, RpC, 1870-80s, 14" **250.00**
Dolly Madison, modeled ribbon & bow, RpC, 1870-80s, 18" **475.00**
Dolly Madison, modeled ribbon & bow, RpC, 1870-80s, 21" **525.00**
Flat Top, blk hair, mid-part/short curls, RpC, ca 1860, 17" **225.00**
Flat Top, blk hair, mid-part/short curls, RpC, ca 1860, 20" **285.00**

Flat top with sausage curls, cloth body, china legs and arms, possibly original clothes, 16", $285.00.

Glass Eyes, various hairstyles, RpC, 1840s-70s, 14" **1,800.00**
Glass Eyes, various hairstyles, RpC, 1840s-70s, 22" **2,800.00**
Japanese, blk or blond hair, mk or unmk, RpC, 1910-20s, 14".....**125.00**
Japanese, blk or blond hair, mk or unmk, RpC, 1910-20s, 17".....**165.00**
Man or Boy, glass eyes, side part, RpC, 14" **1,400.00**
Man or Boy, pnt eyes, side part, RpC, 16" **1,400.00**
Peg Wood Body, early hairdo, 16", EX................................ **2,800.00**
Pet Name, molded shirtwaist w/name on front, RpC, 1905, 19"..**325.00**
Pet Name, molded shirtwaist w/name on front, RpC, 1905, 8"....**125.00**
Pierced Ears, various hairstyles, RpC, 14"...............................**550.00**
Pierced Ears, various hairstyles, RpC, 18"...............................**800.00**
Snood/Combs, any appl hair decor, RpC, 14" **550.00**
Snood/Combs, any appl hair decor, RpC, 17" **800.00**
Spill Curls, w/or w/out head band, RpC, 14"..............................**400.00**
Spill Curls, w/or w/out head band, RpC, 22"..............................**725.00**
Wood Body, articulated/slim hips, RpC, 1840s-50s, 12" **1,400.00**
Wood Body, articulated/slim hips, RpC, 1840s-50s, 17" **4,000.00**
Wood Body, jtd hips, covered-wagon hairdo, 1840s-50s, 12" **950.00**

Bye-Lo

#1269, compo, SkHd, K&W, 14" **1,000.00**
#1360/30, compo, jtd, o/c eyes, Grace S Putnam, RpC, 11" **475.00**
Bsk, pnt eyes, molded hair, jtd hips/shoulders, 8" **625.00**
Bsk/cloth, o/c eyes, cm, c Grace Putnam, MIG, RpC, 11" **475.00**
Cloth w/celluloid hands, 15" bsk head, o/c eyes, OC, 18" **1,000.00**
Frozen bsk, lying on bk, arms/legs raised, 3½" **350.00**
O/c eyes, cloth w/compo hands, str legs, 1923, Putnam, 12"........**475.00**
Vinyl/cloth, pnt eyes, molded hair, Grace Storey Putnam, 16"....**300.00**

China, Unmarked

Adelina Patti, center part, curls at temples, 1860s, 14"................**325.00**
Adelina Patti, center part, curls at temples, 1860s, 18"................**465.00**
Adelina Patti, center part, curls at temples, 1860s, 22"................**625.00**
Biedermeier or Bald Head, takes wig, RpC, 14" **800.00**
Biedermeier or Bald Head, takes wig, RpC, 20" **1,100.00**
Brown Eyes (pnt), any hairstyle or date, 16"...........................**600.00**
Brown Eyes (pnt), any hairstyle or date, 20" **1,000.00**
Common Hairdo, blond or blk hair, RpC, after 1905, 12" **145.00**
Common Hairdo, blond or blk hair, RpC, after 1905, 23" **200.00**
Common Hairdo, blond or blk hair, RpC, after 1905, 8"............**85.00**
Covered Wagon Style, sausage curls, RpC, 1840s-70s, 12" **425.00**
Covered Wagon Style, sausage curls, RpC, 1840s-70s, 24" **700.00**
Curly Top, loose ringlet curls, RpC, 1845-60s, 16"......................**625.00**
Curly Top, loose ringlet curls, RpC, 1845-60s, 20".....................**750.00**

Cloth

Alabama, baby, bare ft w/stitched toes, RpC, 24" **3,600.00**
Art Fabric, litho on muslin, cotton stuffed, RpC, 26" **650.00**
Babyland topsy-turvy, muslin, mitt hands, early, OC, 12"...........**450.00**
Bruckner topsy-turvy, mitt hands, pnt mask faces, OC, 12" **375.00**
Chase, Geo Washington, molded/pnt face, jtd, OC, 25" **1,800.00**
Columbian, jtd knees, sewn fingers, curly-Q nose, RpC, 19" .. **4,100.00**
Cotton, cotton stuffed, jtd, embr face, hair wig, 1900s, 21" **125.00**
Muslin, cotton stuffed, jtd hips/shoulders, 1850s, 17" **225.00**
Oil pnt on muslin, appl nose, mitt hands, 1850s, RpC, 17" **625.00**
Philadelphia Baby, stockinet, sewn fingers, RpC, 20" **2,400.00**

Effanbee

Bernard Fleischaker and Hugo Baum became business partners in

1910; and, after two difficult years of finding toys to buy and a retail market to sell them in, they decided to manufacture dolls of their own. Their lovely dolls were a decided success largely because of their dedication to their work and the mutual trust and respect they held for each other. This is reflected in the Effanbee trademark – Eff stands for Fleischaker and bee for Baum. The company still exists today.

Americana Collection, 1975-1977, ea	55.00
Baby Grumpy, compo/cloth, unmk, RpC, 14"	265.00
Bedtime Story Collection, 1972, ea	55.00
Black Little Boy, hp, o/c eyes, caracul wig, OC, 20"	450.00
Bright Eyes, vinyl/cloth, flirty eyes, 22"	365.00
Button Nose, compo, OC, 9"	175.00
Button Nose Betty, 1943, 8"	175.00
Candy Kid, blk compo, 12"	285.00
Candy Kid, compo, jtd, o/c eyes, molded hair, OC, 13"	285.00
Carnegie Hall, 1980	95.00
Charlie McCarthy, compo/cloth, OC, 19"	400.00
Colonial Prosperity, Historical Series, pnt eyes, OC, 14"	1,100.00
Compo/cloth, ShHd, tin o/c eyes, human hair wig, 24"	250.00
Cunning Baby, compo/hard rubber, tin o/c eyes, RpC, 16"	145.00
Currier & Ives Collection, 1978-80, ea	65.00
Fluffy, vinyl, jtd neck/shoulders/hips, rooted hair, RpC, 10"	45.00
Four Seasons, 1976-1980, ea	70.00
Happy Boy, 1959-1965, 11"	70.00
Ice Queen, compo, o/m, OC, 17"	750.00
John Wayne, vinyl, carries rifle, 1981, OC, 17"	125.00
Lee, compo/cloth, OC, 18"	95.00
Little Boy Blue, 1912, 12"	125.00
Little Lady, compo/cloth, pnt eyes, rpl wig, RpC, 17"	295.00
Little Lady, compo/rubber w/pnt, o/c eyes, yarn hair, 27"	500.00
Lovems, compo, o/c eyes, o/m w/teeth, molded hair, 18"	245.00
Mae Starr, compo/cloth, ShHd, orig wig, RpC, 30"	450.00
Mary Jane, vinyl, flirty eyes, walker, RpC, 30"	285.00
Noma Electronic Talker, 1949-1951, 30"	150.00
Patricia, compo, o/c eyes, brn human hair wig, OC, 15"	385.00

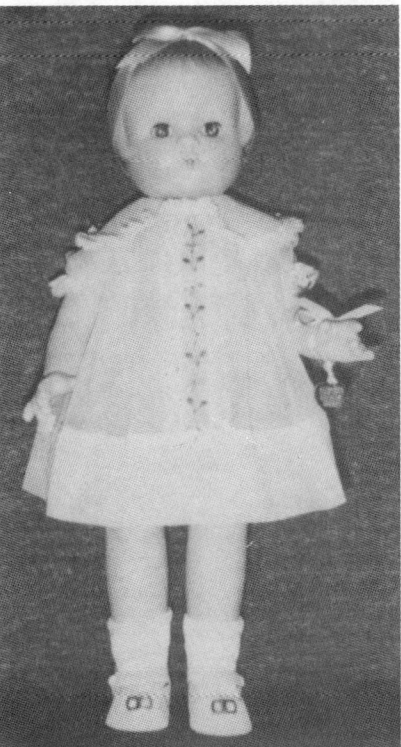

Patsy, limited edition of 1976, 16", $365.00.

Patsy, rigid vinyl, jtd, o/c eyes, rooted hair, OC, 15"	300.00
Patsy Baby, compo, celluloid over tin o/c eyes, c/m, 10"	285.00
Patsy Baby, compo/cloth, o/c eyes, molded/pnt hair, RpC, 10"	245.00
Patsy Joann, compo, o/c eyes, molded hair, OC, 16"	385.00
Patsy Lou, compo, o/c eyes, bent left arm, molded hair, 22"	465.00
Patsy Lou, compo, o/c eyes, bent left elbow, wig, 22"	465.00
Patsy Ruth, compo, jtd, glass eyes, heart bracelet, RpC, 26"	725.00
Regal Heirloom collection, 1976-1978, ea	95.00
Rootie Kazootie, vinyl head/limbs, pnt eyes, RpC, 21"	175.00
Rosemary, compo/cloth, ShPl, o/c eyes, o/m w/teeth, 24"	265.00
Strolling in the Park, 1982-1983	55.00
Sugar Plum Fairy, plastic/vinyl, o/c eyes, OC, tag, 11"	65.00
Suzie Sunshine, blk plastic/vinyl, rooted hair, RpC, 18"	75.00
Sweetie Pie, compo, strung limbs/head, o/c eyes, wig, 16"	185.00
Tommy Tucker, compo/cloth, flirty eyes, 22"	365.00
Twinkie, vinyl, o/c eyes, o/m nurser, molded hair, 16"	35.00
Twinkie, vinyl (thin), o/c eyes, o/m nurser, 1980, OC, 16"	35.00
Victorian Lady, 1976-1977, ea	185.00
WC Fields, compo/cloth, 22"	425.00

Half Dolls

Half dolls, lovely porcelain figures awaiting attachment to secure bases, were never meant to be objects of play. Most of these lovely ladies were firmly sewn into pincushion bases that were beautifully decorated and served as the skirt of their gown. Other skirts were actually covers for items on milady's dressing table. Some were used for parasol or brush handles or for tops to candy containers or perfume bottles. Most popular from 1900 to about 1930, they will most often be found marked with the country of their origin – Bavaria, Germany, France, and Japan. You may also find some fine quality pieces marked Goebel, Dressel and Kester, and Heubach.

For further information we recommend *The Collector's Encyclopedia of Half Dolls* by Frieda Marion and Norma Werner, available at your local bookstore or from Collector Books.

Arms & hands away from body, china or bsk, 12"	900.00
Arms & hands away from body, china or bsk, 5"	300.00
Arms & hands away from body, china or bsk, 8"	425.00
Arms & hands to body, china, 3"	25.00
Arms & hands to body, china, 5"	35.00
Arms & hands to body, china, 8"	50.00
Arms & hands to body, papier-mache or compo, 3"	15.00
Arms & hands to body, papier-mache or compo, 5"	22.00
Arms away, hands to body, china or bsk, 3"	60.00
Arms away, hands to body, china or bsk, 5"	70.00
Arms away, hands to body, china or bsk, 8"	95.00
Arms away, hands to body, papier-mache or compo, 4½"	20.00
Arms away, hands to body, papier-mache or compo, 6½"	65.00
Child or man, jtd shoulders, 3"	60.00
Child or man, jtd shoulders, 5"	90.00
Child or man, jtd shoulders, 7"	145.00
Child or man, 3"	40.00
Child or man, 5"	65.00
Child or man, 7"	95.00
Japan, mk, 3"	15.00
Japan, mk, 5"	28.00
Japan, mk, 7"	45.00
Jtd shoulders, china or bsk, 12"	145.00
Jtd shoulders, china or bsk, 5"	95.00
Jtd shoulders, china or bsk, 8"	110.00
Jtd shoulders, papier-mache, 4"	28.00
Jtd shoulders, papier-mache, 7"	70.00

Jtd shoulders, wax over papier-mache, 4" **38.00**
Jtd shoulders, wax over papier-mache, 7" **90.00**
Lady w/animal, 5" **80.00**
Lady w/animal, 8" **150.00**

Handwerck

#10, compo, jtd, o/c eyes, p/e, 18" **425.00**
#109, bjtd, orig wig, OC, 18" **1,200.00**
#139, brn eyes, new body/wig, 28" **900.00**
Bebe Elite, brn o/c eyes, old clothes, 20" **550.00**
Bsk, SkHd, o/c eyes, o/m w/teeth, p/e, orig wig, RpC, 32" **950.00**
Child, bsk, bjtd, glass eyes, o/m, wig, after 1885, RpC, 18" **375.00**

Heubach

#10633, Dainty Dorothy, o/m, glass eyes, RpC, 16" **500.00**
#5730, Santa, child body, o/c eyes, jtd, 20" **2,500.00**
#6790, boy, intaglio eyes, c/m, OC, 12" **1,500.00**
#7604, laughing child, compo, glass eyes, 15" **1,400.00**
#7604, laughing child, compo, intaglio eyes, 18" **2,000.00**
#7634, crying baby, o/c eyes, RpC, 15" **1,200.00**
#7788, Coquette, tilted head, intaglio eyes, RpC, 12" **975.00**
#7977, Baby Stuart, bsk bonnet, glass eyes, RpC, 12" **1,600.00**
#7977, Baby Stuart, bsk bonnet, intaglio eyes, RpC, 12" **1,200.00**
#8774, Whistling Jim, eyes to side, puckered mouth, 16" **1,000.00**
Character boy, bsk, dome SkHd, intaglio eyes, o/c mouth, 14" **850.00**

Heubach-Koppelsdorf

#250, jtd, o/c eyes, o/m, OC, 20" **425.00**
#275, bsk SkHd, o/c eyes, o/m w/teeth, mohair, kid body, 12" **145.00**
#275, bsk/cloth, ShHd, o/m, RpC, 24" **500.00**
#342-2, bsk/papier-mache, o/c eyes, 5-pc toddler, RpC, 22" **725.00**
Newborn, compo/cloth, o/c eyes, c/m, pnt hair, 16" **600.00**

Horsman

Ella Cinders, compo/cloth, pnt eyes, molded hair, RpC, 18" **575.00**
Peterkin, compo, pnt eyes, molded hair, character face, 11" **325.00**
Pram Baby, vinyl, glass o/c eyes, c/m, trns head/coos, 19" **65.00**
Ronald Reagan, 17", M **55.00**
Ruthie, vinyl, glass o/c eyes, cm/, jtd, walks/talks, 16" **22.00**

Ideal

Baby Jane, compo, o/c eyes, o/m w/teeth, orig wig, RpC, 18" **225.00**
Betsy Wetsy, compo w/rubber body, molded hair, 14" **120.00**
Betty Jane, compo, o/c eyes, o/m w/teeth, OC, 18" **245.00**
Deanna Durbin, compo, o/c eyes, o/m w/teeth, OC, 14" **425.00**
Jiminy Cricket, compo & wood, 9" **200.00**
Miss Revlon, hp/plastic, rooted hair, o/c eyes, c/m, OC, 17" **165.00**
Pinocchio, compo & wood, molded head, pnt features, 10½" **235.00**
Saralee, vinyl/cloth, o/c eyes, o/c mouth, RpC, 18" **135.00**

Jumeau

Emile Jumeau took over his father's doll company sometime in the 1870s. He brought many new innovations and ideas to the business. One fascination Jumeau had concerned dolls' eyes and led to the patents for eyelids that dropped over the eye itself; a second type allowed the doll to 'sleep.' Jumeau's distaste for German dolls is apparent in the booklets that were packaged with his dolls. These booklets referred to the German dolls as cheap and ugly and and as having 'stupid' faces. In reality, these less-expensive dolls were the downfall of the French doll manufacturers, and in 1899 the Jumeau company had to combine with several others in an effort to save the French doll industry from the German competition.

Closed mouth, mk EJ (incised) Jumeau, 10" **5,200.00**
Closed mouth, mk EJ (incised) Jumeau, 14" **5,700.00**
Closed mouth, mk EJ (incised) Jumeau, 16" **6,200.00**
Closed mouth, mk EJ (incised) Jumeau, 19" **6,600.00**
Closed mouth, mk EJ (incised) Jumeau, 21" **7,200.00**
Closed mouth, mk Tete Jumeau, 10" **3,600.00**
Closed mouth, mk Tete Jumeau, 14" **3,300.00**
Closed mouth, mk Tete Jumeau, 16" **3,800.00**
Closed mouth, mk Tete Jumeau, 19" **4,200.00**
Closed mouth, mk Tete Jumeau, 21" **4,800.00**
Closed mouth, mk Tete Jumeau, 23" **5,300.00**
Closed mouth, mk Tete Jumeau, 25" **5,500.00**
Closed mouth, mk Tete Jumeau, 28" **6,400.00**
Closed mouth, mk Tete Jumeau, 30" **7,000.00**
Depose/Tete Jumeau, swivel head, p/e, long curls, 18" **6,200.00**
Depose/Tete Jumeau, swivel head, p/e, long curls, 28" **9,200.00**

Closed outlined mouth, paperweight eyes, pierced ears, marked Depose Tete Jumeau, Bte SGDG/4, 14", $2,950.00.

E 6 J/Jumeau, swivel head, inset eyes, kid body, 16" **5,800.00**
E 6 J/Jumeau, swivel head, inset eyes, kid body, 20" **6,600.00**
EJ/Depose Brevete, swivel head, inset eyes, 'mama/papa,' 16". **5,800.00**
Jumeau 1907, SkHd, appl ears, o/m, 18" **2,400.00**
Jumeau 1907, swivel head, o/m, o/c eyes, p/e, 18" **2,400.00**
Jumeau 1907, swivel head, o/m, o/c eyes, p/e, 23" **2,800.00**
Jumeau 1909, swivel head, o/m, inset eyes, p/e, 21" **2,600.00**
Long face, c/m, 21" **23,000.00**
Long face, c/m, 30" **26,000.00**
Mechanical/musical, cm, p/e, pwt eyes, hh, 12" on 4" box **3,800.00**
Open mouth, mk Tete Jumeau, 10" **995.00**
Open mouth, mk Tete Jumeau, 14" **1,400.00**
Open mouth, mk Tete Jumeau, 16" **1,600.00**
Open mouth, mk Tete Jumeau, 19" **1,900.00**
Open mouth, mk Tete Jumeau, 21" **2,400.00**
Open mouth, mk Tete Jumeau, 23" **2,800.00**
Open mouth, mk Tete Jumeau, 25" **4,000.00**
Open mouth, mk Tete Jumeau, 28" **4,800.00**

Open mouth, mk Tete Jumeau, 30"	**5,200.00**
Open mouth, mk 1907 Jumeau, 14"	**1,400.00**
Open mouth, mk 1907 Jumeau, 17"	**1,700.00**
Open mouth, mk 1907 Jumeau, 20"	**2,000.00**
Open mouth, mk 1907 Jumeau, 25"	**2,500.00**
Open mouth, mk 1907 Jumeau, 28"	**3,000.00**
Open mouth, mk 1907 Jumeau, 32"	**3,400.00**
Phonograph in body, o/m, 20"	**3,400.00**
Phonograph in body, o/m, 25"	**4,800.00**
Portrait Jumeau, c/m, 16"	**5,800.00**
Portrait Jumeau, c/m, 20"	**7,400.00**

Kammer and Reinhardt

#101, boy or girl w/glass eyes, 12"	**1,600.00**
#101, boy or girl w/glass eyes, 16"	**4,200.00**
#101, boy or girl w/glass eyes, 20"	**4,600.00**
#101, boy or girl w/glass eyes, 9"	**1,300.00**
#101, boy or girl w/pnt eyes, 12"	**1,200.00**
#101, boy or girl w/pnt eyes, 16"	**2,400.00**
#101, boy or girl w/pnt eyes, 20"	**3,200.00**
#101, boy or girl w/pnt eyes, 9"	**1,200.00**
#109, rare, w/glass eyes, 15"	**14,000.00**
#109, rare, w/glass eyes, 18"	**20,000.00**
#109, rare, w/pnt eyes, 15"	**14,000.00**
#109, rare, w/pnt eyes, 18"	**19,000.00**
#112, rare, w/glass eyes, 15"	**14,000.00**
#112, rare, w/glass eyes, 18"	**17,000.00**
#112, rare, w/pnt eyes, 15"	**9,500.00**
#112, rare, w/pnt eyes, 18"	**12,000.00**
#114, rare, w/glass eyes, 15"	**6,000.00**
#114, rare, w/glass eyes, 18"	**7,000.00**
#114, rare, w/pnt eyes, 15"	**5,800.00**
#114, rare, w/pnt eyes, 18"	**5,600.00**
#115, closed mouth, 15"	**3,300.00**
#115, closed mouth, 18"	**4,600.00**
#115, closed mouth, 22"	**5,000.00**
#115, open mouth, 15"	**1,300.00**
#115, open mouth, 18"	**1,900.00**
#115, open mouth, 22"	**2,500.00**
#115a, closed mouth, 15"	**3,300.00**
#115a, closed mouth, 18"	**4,600.00**
#115a, closed mouth, 22"	**5,000.00**
#115a, open mouth, 15"	**1,300.00**
#115a, open mouth, 18"	**1,900.00**
#115a, open mouth, 22"	**2,300.00**
#116, closed mouth, 15"	**2,400.00**
#116, closed mouth, 18"	**3,200.00**
#116, closed mouth, 22"	**4,000.00**
#116, open mouth, 15"	**1,300.00**
#116, open mouth, 18"	**1,900.00**
#116, open mouth, 22"	**2,300.00**
#116a, closed mouth, 15"	**2,400.00**
#116a, closed mouth, 18"	**3,200.00**
#116a, closed mouth, 22"	**4,000.00**
#116a, open mouth, 15"	**1,300.00**
#116a, open mouth, 18"	**1,900.00**
#116a, open mouth, 22"	**2,000.00**
#117, closed mouth, 18"	**4,600.00**
#117, closed mouth, 24"	**6,400.00**
#117, closed mouth, 30"	**7,400.00**
#117a, closed mouth, 18"	**4,800.00**
#117a, closed mouth, 24"	**7,000.00**
#117a, closed mouth, 30"	**8,800.00**

Dolly face, open mouth, mold #400-403-109, etc, 16"	**550.00**
Dolly face, open mouth, mold #400-403-109, etc, 20"	**650.00**
Dolly face, open mouth, mold #400-403-109, etc, 24"	**750.00**
Dolly face, open mouth, mold #400-403-109, etc, 28"	**875.00**
Dolly face, open mouth, mold #400-403-109, etc, 38"	**2,300.00**
Dolly face, open mouth, mold #400-403-109, etc, 40"	**2,500.00**

Kestner

Johannes D. Kestner made buttons at a lathe in a Waltershausen factory in the early 1800s. When this line of work failed, he used the same lathe to turn doll bodies. Thus the Kestner company began. It was one of the few German manufacturers to make the complete doll. By 1860 with the purchase of a porcelain factory, Kestner made doll heads of china and bisque as well as wax, worked-in-leather, celluloid, and cardboard. In 1895 the Kestner trademark of a crown with streamers was registered in the U.S. and a year later in Germany. Kestner felt the mark was appropriate since he referred to himself as the 'king of German dollmakers.'

Character 'Hilda' socket head incised K/Made in 14/Germany/JDK.237, open mouth with teeth, 19", $4,600.00. She holds a Gebruder Heuback socket head baby with molded bonnet incised 7877-81, intaglio eyes, closed mouth, 5-piece body, 8", $750.00.

A, ShHd, o/m, MIG/Kestner, 19"	**550.00**
A/5, ShHd, o/c mouth, 23"	**2,400.00**
B/6, ShHd, kid w/bsk ½-arms, o/m w/teeth, o/c eyes, 19"	**550.00**
B/6, SkHd, jtd compo, o/m w/2 teeth, set eyes, 22"	**600.00**
Bergmann, SkHd, made for CM Bergmann, o/m, JDK/CM, 14"	**400.00**
Bergmann, SkHd, made for CM Bergmann, o/m, JDK/CM, 17"	**475.00**
Bergmann, SkHd, made for CM Bergmann, o/m, JDK/CM, 20"	**550.00**
Century Doll Co, flanged closed dome, c/m, 15"	**675.00**
D/8, SkHd & ShHd, kid w/bsk ½-arms, c/m, 15"	**1,000.00**
E/9, ShHd, o/m, MIG, 26"	**1,000.00**
E/9, SkHd, o/m, 1892, 26"	**900.00**
G/11, SkHd, brn, o/m, 16"	**500.00**

G/8, trn ShHd, o/m, MI/JDK, 19" **550.00**
Grace Putnam, bsk, 1-pc pnt eyes, 10/10/COPR, 6" **650.00**
Grace Putnam, bsk, 1-pc body & head, 1/COPR, 1923, 6" **650.00**
Grace Putnam, Bye-Lo baby, 6 12/COPR, 1927, 16" **525.00**
H 1/2, ShHd, o/m, 23" **625.00**
H/12, SkHd, o/c mouth, JDK, 1892, 23" **2,500.00**
Handwerck, SkHd, made for Handwerck, o/m, JDK/H/12, 23" ...**625.00**
Handwerck, SkHd, made for Handwerck, o/m, JDK/H/12, 27" **750.00**
I/13, SkHd, o/m, JDK, 1892, 16" **450.00**
I/13, SkHd, o/m, JDK, 1892, 26" **900.00**
J/13, SkHd, o/m, 1896, 27" **950.00**
JDK, bsk head on celluloid, R Gummi Co, turtlemark, 18" **600.00**
K/12, ShHd, made for Century, o/c mouth, molded hair, 21" . **2,000.00**
Kewpie, bsk, Rose O'Neill/10 945G, 1913, 8" **350.00**
KK/14 1/2d, o/m, 1896, 26" **850.00**
L 1/2/15 1/2, SkHd, c/m, 14" **1,600.00**
L/15, SkHd, c/m, 21" **2,100.00**
L/15, SkHd, swivel, ShPl, c/m, 21" **2,100.00**
L/3, ShHd, o/c mouth w/molded teeth, 23" **2,300.00**
N/17, SkHd, o/m, 1892, 17" **475.00**
SkHd, Oriental, o/m, JDK/Kestner, 14" **4,600.00**
SkHd, pnt eyes, JDK/3 4/0, 8" **500.00**
Trn ShHd, Kidoline w/bsk ½-arms, o/c eyes, G/MIG, 16" **650.00**
10, SkHd, bsk ShPl, c/m, 21" **2,000.00**
10, SkHd, o/c mouth w/2 teeth, JDK/MIG, 12" **600.00**
10/G, SkHd, c/m, JDK, 1912, 12" **600.00**
1070, SkHd, o/m, G11/237 15/JDK Jr 1914 HILDA/GES, 16". **3,400.00**
11, SkHd, o/c mouth, pnt eyes to side, JDK/MIG, 11" **600.00**
12, SkHd, 5-pc baby, o/c eyes, o/m/2 teeth, JDK/MIG, 15" **575.00**
13, SkHd, o/m, JDK/MIG, 18" **500.00**
143, ShHd, kid w/bsk ½-arms, o/m, 17" **675.00**
145, ShHd, kid w/bsk ½-arms, o/c mouth, 15" **1,200.00**
145, SkHd, c/m, MI/O/G/18, 14" **1,100.00**
145, SkHd, c/m, 143/4/0/JDK, 11" **600.00**
146, SkHd, swivel, on ShPl, o/m, JDK, 18" **550.00**
147, trn ShHd, o/m, JDK, 25" **675.00**
148, ShHd, kid w/bsk ½-arms, o/m, 7 1/2, 18" **450.00**
148, ShHd, kid w/bsk ½-arms, o/m, 7 1/2, 21" **500.00**
150.1, bsk, Kestner seal on body, 8" **350.00**
151, SkHd, 5-pc baby, intaglio eyes, o/m/teeth, MIG/5, 12" **425.00**
151, SkHd, 5-pc baby, intaglio eyes, o/m/teeth, MIG/5, 16" **575.00**
151, SkHd, 5-pc baby, intaglio eyes, o/m/teeth, MIG/5, 20" **675.00**
152, SkHd, made for Wolf, o/m, LW & CO 12, 1916, 20" **750.00**
154, SkHd/ShHd, kid w/bsk ½-arms, o/m/teeth, DEP, 14" **465.00**
154, SkHd/ShHd, kid w/bsk ½-arms, o/m/teeth, DEP, 17" **675.00**
154, SkHd/ShHd, kid w/bsk ½-arms, o/m/teeth, DEP, 20" **775.00**
154, SkHd/ShHd, kid w/bsk ½-arms, o/m/teeth, DEP, 26" **1,000.00**
16, SkHd, o/m, JDK/MIG, 21" **575.00**
16/GES#1, ShHd, o/c mouth, molded boy's hair, 16" **1,800.00**
167, SkHd, jtd compo, o/m, p/e, F 1/2/MI6 1/2/G, 16" **475.00**
167, SkHd, jtd compo, o/m, p/e, F 1/2/MI6 1/2/G, 20" **575.00**
168, SkHd, o/m, MID/G7, 26" **800.00**
169, SkHd, jtd compo, c/m, o/c eyes, B 1/2/BI6 1/2G, 16" **1,800.00**
169, SkHd, jtd compo, c/m, o/c eyes, B 1/2/BI6 1/2G, 18" **2,500.00**
171, SkHd, jtd compo, o/m, o/c eyes, 'Daisy,' F/M110, 15" **450.00**
171, SkHd, jtd compo, o/m, o/c eyes, 'Daisy,' F/M110, 18" **600.00**
171, SkHd, jtd compo, o/m, o/c eyes, 'Daisy,' F/M110, 22" **700.00**
172, ShHd, ball, kid fashion, bsk arms, c/m, p/e, 14" **1,800.00**
180 12/Ox/Crown seal, SkHd, o/m, 16" **450.00**
201, ShHd, celluloid on kid, o/m, set eyes/lashes, JDK, 19" **425.00**
211, SkHd, 5-pc baby, o/c mouth, o/c eyes, MI10/G/JDK, 12" **500.00**
211, SkHd, 5-pc baby, o/c mouth, o/c eyes, MI10/G/JDK, 15" **675.00**
215, SkHd, jtd compo, fur eyebrows, o/m, MI9/GJDK, 21" **575.00**
217A/Kestner, bsk, c/m smile, googly pnt eyes, 12" **2,000.00**

221/GES/GESCH, SkHd, c/m smile, googly eyes, G/JDK, 21". **7,500.00**
235, toddler, kid body, 16" **675.00**
245, SkHd, 5-pc baby, G/MIG/11/JDK Jr/1914 Hilda, 14" **2,700.00**
245, SkHd, 5-pc baby, G/MIG/11/JDK Jr/1914 Hilda, 17" **3,600.00**
257, SkHd, 5-pc baby, o/m, G/JDK, 10" **400.00**
257, SkHd, 5-pc baby, o/m, G/JDK, 16" **600.00**
257, SkHd, 5-pc baby, o/m, G/JDK, 20" **800.00**
257, SkHd, 5-pc baby, o/m, G/JDK, 24" **1,200.00**
26, K&Co/JDK/MIG/81, 16" **425.00**
270, SkHd, o/m, made for Carl Trautman, CP/39, 38" **2,400.00**
639, trn ShHd, closed dome, c/m, G/6, 18" **800.00**
7 1/2/B, ShHd, kid w/bsk ½-arms, o/m w/teeth, o/c eyes, 14" **350.00**

Lenci

Eleanora Scavani, separated from her husband who was in the service of Italy during WWI, found herself painfully alone after the death of her baby. With her brother as her partner, this talented artist began designing lovely felt-covered dolls with beautiful hand-painted features. These dolls became her children, and she regarded them as a tribute to her lost daughter.

Following the war, her husband returned and joined the firm as a partner. The Lenci firm (a name he used as a term of endearment for his wife) soon became well-known in the doll-making industry. Great care was taken in every detail. Characteristics of Lenci dolls include seamless, steam-molded felt heads, quality clothing, childishly plump bodies, and painted eyes that glance to the side. Fine mohair wigs were used, and the middle and fourth fingers were sewn together. Look for the factory stamp on the foot, though paper labels were also used. Dolls under 10" are known as mascots and usually sell for $125.00 to $150.00. The Lenci factory continues today, producing dolls of the same high quality.

#109, jtd, swivel head, cloth torso, RpC, 16" **850.00**
Boy, all felt, eyes to left, blond wig, RpC, 12" **235.00**
Boy, swivel neck/jtd body, mohair, sailor outfit, 17" **850.00**
Chinaman, w/opium pipe, 1920s, 12½", M **1,600.00**
Girl in sailor dress, blond wig, 1920s, boxed, 20", M **900.00**
Glass eyes, braided bun, canvas-type body/limbs, 18" **1,800.00**
Glass eyes, jtd, holds dog, OC, 20" **2,600.00**
Indian lady w/papoose, jtd, pnt features, OC, 18" **3,000.00**

**Lenci tea cosy, English coachman with whip, 17",
$1,800.00.**

Surprised eyes, jtd, swivel head, OC, 20" **2,600.00**

Madame Alexander

Beatrice Alexander founded the Alexander Doll company in 1923 using a lovely doll that was designed after her daughter Mildred. With the help of her three sisters, the company prospered; and by the late 1950s there were three factories with over six hundred employees making Madame Alexander dolls. The company still produces these lovely dolls today.

Abigail Adams, President's Ladies, 1976-78, 1st set 150.00
Agatha, hp, Wendy Ann, 1953-54, 8"... **1,100.00**
Alice in Wonderland, compo, Little Betty, 9" 200.00
Alice in Wonderland, compo, swivel waist, Wendy Ann, 13" 400.00
Alice in Wonderland, compo, Wendy Ann, 11-14" 350.00
Amanda, hp, Wendy Ann, 1961 Americana Group, 8"........... **1,550.00**
American Babies, cloth, 18"..500.00
Amish Girl, HP, bend knee, Wendy Ann, 1966-69, 8" 500.00
Annie Laurie, compo, Wendy Ann, 1937, 14" 500.00
Argentine Boy, hp, bend knee walker, Wendy Ann, 1965, 8"......525.00
Aunt Agatha, hp, Wendy Ann, 1957, 8" **1,500.00**
Babs, hp, Maggie, 1949, 20" 475.00
Babs Skater, compo, Margaret, 18" 500.00
Baby Betty, compo, 1935-36, 10-12"..175.00
Baby Ellen (Black Sweet Tears), 1965-72, 14".........................165.00
Baby Genius, compo/cloth, 11-12"..135.00
Baby Lynn, cloth/vinyl, 1973-76, 20"..125.00
Ballerina, compo, Wendy Ann, 1936-38, 11-14" 350.00
Barbara Jane, cloth/vinyl, 1952, 29"...385.00
Beauty Queen, hp, Cissette, 1961 ....245.00
Birthday Doll, compo, Tiny Betty, 7" 225.00
Blue Boy, cloth, 16" 600.00
Bobby, hp, Wendy Ann, 1957, 8" **1,300.00**
Bobby Q, cloth, 1940 ....475.00
Brenda Star, hp, 1964, 12"..200.00
Bride, hp, Cissy, 1956-57, 20" 450.00
Bride, hp, Lissy, 12" 375.00
Bride, plastic/vinyl, Polly, 1965-70, 17" 300.00
Bridesmaid, compo, Wendy Ann, 15" 350.00
Brigitta, Sound of Music, sailor suit, 14"...................................300.00
Buck Rabbit, cloth/felt, 1930s..600.00
Butch, compo/cloth, 14-16"..350.00
Camille, compo, Wendy Ann, 1938, 21" **1,600.00**
Caroline, vinyl, riding clothes, 15"..400.00
Cherry Twins, hp, Wendy Ann, 1957, 8" 750.00
Cinderella, hp, Margaret, 18" 650.00
Cissy, hp, street dress, 20"...350.00
Clover Kid, compo, 7" 200.00
Cuddly, cloth, 1942, 10½"..195.00
Cynthia, hp, Black Margaret, 1952, 15" 650.00
Czechoslovakia, compo, Tiny Betty, 1935-37, 7"........................175.00
Debutant, hp, Maggie, 1953, 18" 800.00
Ding Dong Dell, compo, Tiny Betty, 1937, 7" 175.00
Dionne Quints, compo, toddlers, 16-17", ea................................550.00
Doris Keane, cloth...500.00
Dutch Girl, hp, bend knee walker, 1961-72, 8" 350.00
Edith, the Lonely Doll, plastic/vinyl, 22"...................................425.00
Edwardian, hp, Margaret, 1953, 8" 900.00
Elise Ballerina, hp/vinyl arms, 1957-60, 16½"...........................450.00
Enchanted Doll, eyelet pinafore, 1981, 8" 300.00
Eva Lovelace, compo, Tiny Betty, 1935, 7" 200.00
Fairy Queen, compo, Wendy Ann, 18"..485.00
First Communion, hp, Wendy Ann, 1957, 8"...............................675.00

Dionne quints on seesaw, each doll 8" long, $1,250.00 for the set.

Florence Nightingale, 1986-87, 14"..100.00
French, hp, bend knee, Wendy Ann, 1965-72, 8" 135.00
Gibson Girl, hp, eyeshadow, Cissette, 1962, 10".................... **1,200.00**
Gidget, plastic/vinyl, Mary Ann, 1966, 14"................................400.00
Godey, hp/vinyl str arms, Cissy, 1961, 21"................................550.00
Godey Bride, hp, Margaret, 18"...750.00
Goldilocks, cloth, 1930s, 18" 550.00
Graduation, hp, Wendy Ann, 1957, 8" **1,300.00**
Groom, compo, 18-21"..650.00
Guardian Angel, hp, Wendy Ann, 1954, 8".............................. **1,100.00**
Hawaiian, hp, bend knee, Wendy Ann, 1966-69, 8"....................550.00
Honeyette Baby, compo/cloth, 1940, 16" 185.00
Hungarian, hp, bend knee walker, Wendy Ann, 1962-65, 8" 350.00
Indian Boy, hp, bend knee, Wendy Ann, discontinued 1966, 8" .550.00
Ingres, plastic/vinyl, 1987 only, 14" 85.00
Israeli, hp, bend knees, Wendy Ann, 1965-72, 8".......................135.00
Jacqueline, hp/vinyl arms, ballgown, 1961-62, 21" 900.00
Jamie Ballerina, plastic/vinyl, 1965 only 375.00
Jeannie Walker, compo, 18"...600.00
Jenny Lind, hp/vinyl arms, Jacqueline, 1969, 21" **1,000.00**
Judy, compo, Wendy Ann, 1945, 21" **1,600.00**
June Bride, compo, 21" **1,000.00**
Karen Ballerina, compo, Margaret, 1947, 15"............................450.00
Kathryn Grayson, hp, Margaret, 1949, 20-21"...........................750.00
Kathy Tears, vinyl, 1959-62, 15" 100.00
Kitten Kries, cloth/vinyl, 1967, 20"...150.00
Korea, hp, bend knee, Maggie Mixup, 8"....................................525.00
Lady Hamilton, hp, Cissette, 1957, 11" 575.00
Laughing Allegra, cloth..550.00
Lazy Mary, compo, Tiny Betty, 1936, 7"....................................175.00
Lissy Bride, hp, jtd knees & elbows, 1956-58, 11½-12"...............325.00
Little Angel, latex/vinyl, 9" 185.00
Little Bo Peep, hp, bend knee walker, Wendy Ann, 1962-64, 8".425.00
Little Boy Blue, compo, Tiny Betty, 1937, 7"..............................185.00
Little Colonel, compo, Betty, 11-13"..625.00
Little Genius, compo/cloth, 18-20" 235.00
Little Jack Horner, compo, Tiny Betty, 1937, 7".........................185.00
Little Lord Fauntleroy, cloth 600.00
Little Nell, cloth, Dickens Character, 16"..................................600.00
Little Southern Girl, hp, Wendy Ann, 1953, 8" **1,000.00**
Little Women, compo, Tiny Betty, 1937-39, 9", ea 265.00
Little Women, hp, bend knee walker, Wendy Ann, 1950s, 8", ea..185.00
Littles Kittens, vinyl, 1963, 8" 185.00
Lola Bridesmaid, compo, Tiny Betty, 1938, 7"............................185.00
Looby Loo, hp, ca 1951-54, 15½"...475.00
Lucinda, plastic/vinyl, Mary Ann, 1971-82, 14" 125.00

Lucy Bride, compo, Wendy Ann, 21" **1,600.00**
Madelaine, compo, Wendy Ann, 1940, 14".....................350.00
Maggie Mixup, hp/vinyl, Elise body, 1960, 16½" 375.00
Maggie Mixup Angel, hp, 1961, 8"............................ **1,300.00**
Maid of Honor, compo, Wendy Ann, 18"......................500.00
Majorette, compo, Wendy Ann, 14-17".......................650.00
Margot, hp, Cissette, formal, 10-11"..........................425.00
Marine, compo, 14"...475.00
Mary Cassatt Baby, cloth/vinyl, 1969-70, 14"..............125.00
Mary Martin, hp, Margaret, 1949, 14".......................600.00
Mary Sunshine, plastic/vinyl, 1961, 15".....................475.00
Molly Cottontail, cloth/felt, 1930s 600.00
Mrs Buck Rabbit, cloth/felt....................................550.00
Nina Ballerina, compo, Tiny Betty, 7" 175.00
Norwegian, compo, Tiny Betty, 1936, 7-8" 175.00
Nurse, hp, Wendy Ann, 1956, 8".............................600.00
Orphan Annie, plastic/vinyl, Mary Ann, 1965, 14"........400.00
Pamela, hp, Lissy, takes wigs, 1962, 12" 500.00
Patty Pigtails, hp, 1949, 14" 550.00
Penny, cloth/vinyl, 1951, 34"..................................385.00
Peter Pan, hp, Wendy Ann, 1953, 8" **1,300.00**
Pinky, cloth, 16" 450.00
Pocahontas, hp, bend knee, Wendy Ann, 1967-70, 8" 575.00
Polly Ballerina, plastic/vinyl, Maria, 1965, 17"...............350.00
Portugal, hp, bend knees, Wendy Ann, 1968-72, 8" 135.00
Prince Charles, hp, Wendy Ann, 1957, 8"............... **1,200.00**
Princess Ann, hp, Wendy Ann, 1957, 8" **1,250.00**
Princess Elizabeth, compo, c/m, 13"..........................400.00
Princess Margaret Rose, hp, Margaret, 1949-53, 14"........400.00
Pumpkin', cloth/vinyl, rooted hair, 1976 only, 24"........225.00
Queen, hp, Wendy Ann, red velvet robe, 1955, 8"......... **1,100.00**
Queen, hp/vinyl arms, Cissy, wht gown, 1957-58, 10" 600.00
Quiz-kins Groom, hp, Wendy Ann, 1953, 8".................800.00
Red Riding Hood, compo, Little Betty, 1939, 9" 200.00
Riley's Little Annie, plastic/vinyl, Mary Ann, 1967, 14" 450.00
Romance, compo, Wendy Ann, 1945, 21" **1,600.00**
Rosebud, cloth/vinyl, 1952-53, 16".............................95.00
Rumania, hp, bend knees, Wendy Ann, 1968-72, 8" 135.00
Scarlet O'Hara, compo, Tiny Betty, 1936-38, 7" 225.00
Scarlet O'Hara, hp, Lissy, 1963, 12" **1,400.00**
Scottish, hp, bend knee walker, Wendy Ann, 1964-65, 8"........350.00
Shari Lewis, 1958-59, 14" 365.00
Sleeping Beauty, compo, Princess Elizabeth, 1938, 15-16"........425.00
Snow White, hp, Margaret, 21" 600.00
Sonja Henie, compo, Wendy Ann, 11" 350.00
Southern Belle, hp, Wendy Ann, 1954, 8"............... **1,250.00**
Spanish Girl, hp, bend knee, 1965-72, 8"....................135.00
Suellen, compo, Wendy Ann, 1937, 14-17" 475.00
Sunflower Clown, flower eyes, 1951, 40".....................450.00
Suzy, plastic/vinyl, Janie, 1970, 12" 450.00
Sweet Tears, vinyl, in window box, 1965-74, 14" 165.00
Teeny Twinkle, cloth, flirty eyes 550.00
Tippy Toe, cloth, 16" 600.00
Tommy Bangs, hp, Maggie, 1952, 12".......................750.00
Tyrolean Boy, hp, bend knee walker, Wendy Ann, 1962-65, 8"...350.00
United States, hp, str legs, Wendy Ann, 1974-75, 8" 65.00
Victoria, compo, Flavia, 1945, 21" **1,600.00**
Victorian, hp, Margaret, 1953, 18"..............................75.00
Virginia Dare, compo, Little Betty, 1940, 9"................225.00
3 Little Pigs & Wolf, compo, 1938, ea 425.00

Papier-Mache

Greiner, molded hair, pnt eyes, cloth w/kid arms, 23" **1,400.00**

Greiner, molded hair, pnt eyes, cloth w/kid arms, 29" **1,850.00**
Greiner, ShHd, molded hair/features, cloth w/kid limbs, 24" .. **1,100.00**
Man, molded/pnt head, cloth w/wood arms, suit/hat, 10" 500.00
Milliner's model, OC, 9½" 365.00
Molded long curls, ShHd, kid body, wood limbs, 13".............. **1,300.00**
Molded/pnt hairdo & features, kid w/wood limbs, OC, 8" 250.00
Motschmann type, pnt overlay, muslin body, glass eyes, 5" 145.00
Puff curls, cloth w/wood limbs, ca 1840s, 24" **2,300.00**
ShHd, pnt hair, glass eyes, o/m, kid body, 26" **1,400.00**
Sonneberg type, ShHd, pnt eyes, c/m, RpC, 15" 225.00
Stationary glass eyes w/no pupils, o/m, 4 bamboo teeth, 28" ... **1,600.00**
Trn SkHd, glass eyes, c/m, cloth/kid body, 22"................950.00

Parian

Bald bsk head, orig wig, pnt eyes, cloth body/legs, 17" 950.00
Blonde w/molded center part, swivel neck, p/e, 16"................ **2,500.00**
Blonde w/sausage curls, flat face, pnt eyes, 1850s, 16".............400.00
Brn molded hair w/head band, glass eyes, 14".................825.00
Bsk, kid body, parian arms, pnt eyes w/red liner, 14" 475.00
Bsk, kid body, pnt eyes, molded yoke/collar/tie, 16" 685.00
Countess Dagmar, porc, pnt eyes, unmk, 18"....................775.00
Molded braid wrapped around head, p/e, pnt eyes, 18" 725.00
Ribbon entwined in molded hair, 14" 600.00

Schoenhut

Albert Schoenhut left Germany in 1866 to go to Pennsylvania to work as a repairman for toy pianos. He eventually applied his skills to wooden toys and later designed an all-wood doll which he patented on January 17, 1911. These uniquely jointed dolls were painted with enamels and came with a metal stand. Some of the later dolls had stuffed bodies, voice boxes, and hollow heads; some were made with heads of imitation bisque. These innovations influenced the development of the popular Bye-Lo Baby which was introduced in 1924. Due to the changing economy and fierce competition, the company closed in the mid-1930s.

Baby head, o/c eyes, o/m w/teeth, jtd, OC, 14"............................700.00
Baby head, pnt hair & eyes, o/c mouth, jtd, 16" 750.00
Character, cvd hair w/bow, intaglio eyes, jtd, OC, 14" **2,100.00**
Child, cvd hair w/comb mks/etc, c/m, spring jtd, OC, 16" **1,800.00**
Compo, molded hair, pnt eyes, c/m, jtd neck, 1924, RpC, 13".....425.00
Dolly face, decal eyes, pnt teeth, jtd, mohair wig, OC, 21".........875.00
Dolly face, o/ or c/m, pnt eyes, wig, spring jtd, OC, 17" 675.00
Girl, brn o/c eyes, OC, 19", M....................................950.00
Girl, cvd hair w/comb mks, intaglio brn eyes, RpC, 19" **2,000.00**
Girl, smiling o/m w/teeth, brn hair, pat Jan 17, '11, 18" 750.00
Pouty, orig paper label, 1919, 11½"...............................550.00
Sailor boy, spring jtd, OC, 15", VG 550.00
Walker, bl pnt eyes, c/m, mohair wig, mk head/body, 16½"..... **1,000.00**
Walker, pnt eyes, o/c mouth, OC, 17" **1,000.00**

SFBJ

By 1895 Germany was producing dolls of good quality at much lower prices than the French dollmakers because of lower wages in German factories. This was a serious threat to the French companies; and, in a supreme effort to save the doll industry, several leading French manufacturers united to form one large company in the hope they could combine their strengths to save the French market. Bru, Raberry and Delphieu, Pintel and Godshaux, Fleischman and Bodel, and Jumeau united to form the company today known as SFBJ. Their dolls did well while Germany was otherwise occupied with WWII, but after the war German doll production proved to be too strongly competitive, and SFBJ closed in 1958.

Bebe Parisiana, bsk head, c/m, inset eyes, 1902, 16"	2,600.00
Celestine, bsk SkHd on papier-mache, o/m, inset eyes, 18"	800.00
SkHd, jtd papier-mache/wood body, o/m, o/c eyes, 30"	2,200.00
Tete Jumeau, p/e, o/m, o/c eyes/lashes, 18"	1,250.00
11, compo w/bsk swivel head, c/m, inset eyes, 16"	650.00
20, molded ptd shoes & eyes, 5-pc body, Paris/12, 10"	350.00
203, 1900 bsk head on compo, o/c mouth, inset eyes, 20"	2,500.00
215, bsk swivel on compo, c/m, inset eyes, 15"	1,800.00
223, bsk, closed dome, o/m/8 teeth, molded hair, 17"	2,000.00
227, brn swivel closed dome head, animal skin wig, 15"	1,800.00
227, brn swivel closed dome head, animal skin wig, 18"	2,000.00
227, closed dome, o/m, inset eyes, pnt hair, 15"	1,800.00
228, toddler, papier-mache body, c/m, inset eyes, 16"	1,800.00
229, compo w/swivel head, o/c mouth, inset eyes, 18"	3,500.00
229, wood walker, o/c mouth, inset eyes, 18"	2,000.00
230, compo walker, p/e, o/m, inset eyes, 16"	1,300.00
230, SkHd, p/e, o/m, o/c eyes, 23"	2,200.00
235, closed dome, molded hair, o/c mouth & eyes, 16"	2,100.00
235, closed dome, molded hair, o/c mouth & eyes, 8"	650.00
236, laughing Jumeau, o/m, o/c eyes, dbl chin, 12"	1,500.00
236, laughing Jumeau, o/m, o/c eyes, dbl chin, 20"	2,300.00
238, compo w/swivel head, o/m, inset eyes, Paris 6, 15"	3,000.00
239, Poulbot, c/m, street urchin, red wig, 14"	16,000.00
239, Poulbot, c/m, street urchin, red wig, 17"	19,000.00
245, boy, o/c mouth, lg glass eyes, googly, pnt shoes, 12"	2,600.00
245, boy, o/c mouth, lg glass eyes, googly, pnt shoes, 8"	1,000.00
247, toddler, o/c mouth/2 inset teeth, 16"	4,000.00
247, toddler, o/c mouth/2 inset teeth, 20"	5,000.00
247, toddler, o/c mouth/2 inset teeth, 24"	5,400.00
247, Twirp, SkHd, o/c mouth & eyes/2 teeth, 21"	2,800.00
251, toddler, 25"	2,900.00
251, 1099 character baby, o/c mouth, eyes, hair lashes, 16"	1,300.00
251, 1099 character baby, o/c mouth, eyes, hair lashes, 18"	1,700.00
252, pouty, c/m, inset eyes, papier-mache body, 18"	5,400.00
252, pouty, c/m, inset eyes, papier-mache body, 22"	7,900.00
257, 1900 toddler, o/c mouth, inset eyes, 16"	2,300.00
266, character, bsk head, closed dome, o/c mouth, 20"	3,600.00
301, bsk SkHd on compo, o/m, inset eyes, 16"	625.00
301, bsk SkHd on compo, o/m, inset eyes, 22"	875.00
301, bsk SkHd on compo, o/m, inset eyes, 30"	1,500.00
60, French WWI nurse, 5-pc body, SFBJ/13/0, 8½"	300.00
60, kiss-blower, cryer/walker, 22"	1,800.00
60, SkHd, compo w/str legs, o/m, curved arms, 15"	650.00
60, SkHd, papier-mache/compo, plunger cryer, o/m, 1-pc, 11"	400.00

Shirley Temple

Bsk, Japan, 7½"	245.00
Compo, 11", cowboy outfit, orig pin, EX	650.00
Compo, 11", in trunk, EX	750.00
Compo, 13", tagged bl/wht dress w/pin, 1930s, all orig	625.00
Compo, 15", OC, Ideal	550.00
Compo, 16", red dotted dress, velvet coat/hat, all orig	625.00
Compo, 18", OC, EX	675.00
Compo, 20", Ideal	725.00
Compo, 20", OC, NM	725.00
Compo, 20", tagged clothes, all orig, orig box	725.00
Compo, 22", teeth, orig bl dress w/daisies, Ideal, 1934, NM	750.00
Compo, 25", sailor suit, EX	850.00
Compo, 27", flirty eyes, orig, EX	1,100.00
Vinyl, 12", complete w/4 outfits, Ideal, 1957, MIB	250.00

Vinyl, 12", gr/wht dress, slip, complete, Ideal, 1957, MIB	150.00
Vinyl, 14", Montgomery Ward's, 1972, MIB	140.00
Vinyl, 15", Heidi outfit, w/pin & tag, 1957	275.00
Vinyl, 15", RpC, Ideal	245.00
Vinyl, 16", Rebecca, Ideal, 1972	245.00
Vinyl, 16", red polka dress/Captain Jan outfit, 1973, MIB	95.00
Vinyl, 16", Stand Up & Cheer dress, 1973, MIB	245.00
Vinyl, 17", Heidi outfit, w/pin, MIB	395.00
Vinyl, 19", flirty eyes, all orig, 1957	350.00
Vinyl, 36", OC, EX	1,500.00
Vinyl, 8", Stowaway, Ideal, 1982	45.00

Simon and Halbig

Simon and Halbig was a large German doll firm that operated from ca 1870 until the 1930s. They were a popular supplier of bisque heads to French dollmakers of the 1870s and '80s. This company made dolls for such famous companies as Gimbel Bros., Jumeau, Kammer and Reinhardt, as well as many others. Halbig became the sole owner of the company in 1895 but did not register 'S&H' as his trademark until ten years later.

AW, SkHd, o/m, SH/13, 21"	600.00
Baby Blanche, SkHd, o/m baby, S&H, 16"	750.00
Baby Blanche, SkHd, o/m baby, S&H, 21"	900.00
CM Bergmann, SkHd, o/m, Simon & Halbig, 3 1/2, 18"	500.00
CM Bergmann, SkHd, o/m, 1895, Halbig/S&H5, 30"	1,100.00
CM Bergmann, SkHd, o/m, 1897, S&H6, 12"	350.00
Elenore, SkHd, o/m, CMB/Simon & Halbig, 18"	500.00
G68, SkHd, flirty eyes, 1908, S&H/K*R, 16"	550.00
Handwerck, SkHd, o/m, G/Halbig, 4, 26"	850.00
Handwerck, SkHd, o/m, 1893, 16"	450.00
Handwerck, SkHd, o/m, 1895, G/S&H/1, 16"	450.00
S&H3, all bsk, c/m, inset eyes, molded-on shoes, 6"	185.00
10, SkHd, o/m, G/Halbig/S&H, 16"	450.00
10, SkHd, o/m, G/Halbig/S&H, 19"	550.00
10, SkHd, o/m, G/Halbig/S&H, 22"	650.00
10 1/2, SkHd, o/m, flirty o/c eyes, S&H, 18"	550.00
100, SkHd, o/m, Simon & Halbig/S&C/G, 15"	425.00
100, SkHd, o/m, Simon & Halbig/S&C/G, 22"	650.00
101, SkHd, c/m, Simon & Halbig/K*R, 16"	4,200.00
1039, SkHd, o/m w/teeth, p/e, jtd arms/wrists, hh, 22"	650.00
1059, SkHd, swivel on ShPl, wood w/kid fashion, o/m, 19"	2,600.00
109, SkHd, o/m, 1895, Handwerck/G/Halbig, 23"	675.00
114, SkHd, c/m, glass eyes, Simon & Halbig K*R/L, 14"	4,200.00
114, SkHd, c/m, glass eyes, Simon Halbig K*R/L, 20"	6,200.00
114, SkHd, c/m, Simon & Halbig K*R/L, 9"	1,200.00
115, SkHd, c/m, 1912, K*R/Simon & Halbig, 16"	2,500.00
115a, SkHd, c/m pouty, K*R/Simon & Halbig, 15"	2,400.00
1159, SkHd, adult, 1905, G/Simon & Halbig/S&H7, 14"	1,000.00
1159, SkHd, adult, 1905, G/Simon & Halbig/S&H7, 18"	1,500.00
1159, SkHd, adult, 1905, G/Simon & Halbig/S&H7, 24"	2,400.00
116a, SkHd, c/m, K*R/Simon Halbig, 17"	2,300.00
116a-38, SkHd, 2 teeth, tongue, K*R/Simon & Halbig, 17"	2,200.00
117, SkHd, c/m, 1919, Simon & Halbig/K*R, 16"	3,200.00
117, SkHd, c/m, 1919, Simon & Halbig/K*R, 20"	4,400.00
117a, SkHd, c/m, K*R/Simon & Halbig, 16"	3,200.00
117a, SkHd, c/m, K*R/Simon & Halbig, 20"	4,400.00
117n, SkHd, o/m, Simon & Halbig/K*R, 20"	2,000.00
119, SkHd, o/m, 13/Handwerck 5/Halbig, 16"	550.00
121, SkHd, o/c mouth/teeth, flirty o/c eyes, 1920, K*R, 16"	1,200.00
121, SkHd, o/c toddler, 16"	1,200.00
121, SkHd, o/m, 1920, K*R/Simon & Halbig, 14"	950.00
121, SkHd, o/m, 1920, K*R/Simon & Halbig, 19"	1,500.00

122, SkHd, 1920, K*R/Simon & Halbig, 14" 850.00
126, SkHd, o/c mouth, SH, 23" 825.00
126, SkHd, o/m, Simon & Halbig/K*R, 14" 475.00
126, SkHd, o/m, Simon & Halbig/K*R, 19" 650.00
127, SkHd, o/m, K*R/Simon & Halbig, 18" 600.00

Socket head with sleep eyes, open mouth with 2 teeth, dimples, and jointed body; marked S&H/DEP/1279, 7½", $1,800.00.

128, SkHd, o/m, K*R/Simon & Halbig, 14" 600.00
128, SkHd, o/m, K*R/Simon & Halbig, 19" 850.00
1296, SkHd, 1911, FS&Co/Simon & Halbig, 14" 425.00
1329, SkHd, o/m, olive, G/Simon & Halbig/SH, 14" 1,800.00
151, SkHd, o/c mouth, pnt eyes, S&H/1, 16" 5,500.00
156, SkHd, 1925, S&H, 18" 500.00
156, SkHd, 1925, S&H, 22" 650.00
159, SkHd, o/m, Simon & Halbig, 16" 475.00
179, SkHd, o/m, Simon & Halbig S11H DEP, 20" 600.00
1848, SkHd, o/m, Jutta Simon & Halbig, 16" 475.00
191, SkHd, o/m, Bergmann/CB, 18" 500.00
1923, SkHd, o/m, SH Sp 53/4/G, 14" 400.00
1923, SkHd, o/m, SH Sp 53/4/G, 21" 550.00
1923, SkHd, o/m, SH Sp 53/4/G, 26" 850.00
246, SkHd, o/m, 1900, K*R/Simon & Halbig, 18" 550.00
282, SkHd, o/m, SH, 14" 375.00
282, SkHd, o/m, SH, 18" 500.00
282, SkHd, o/m, SH, 22" 650.00
383, SkHd, flapper body, S H, 14" 900.00
402, SkHd, o/m, K*R SH, 16" 550.00
403, SkHd, o/c mouth, K*R, Simon & Halbig, 20" 2,800.00
403, SkHd, o/m, walker, K*R SH, 21" 1,400.00
409, SkHd, o/m, S&H, 24" 600.00
409, SkHd, o/m, S&H, 26" 750.00

409, SkHd, o/m, S&H, 30" 1,400.00
48m SkHd, o/m, 1905, Simon & Halbig/K*R, 27" 950.00
50, SkHd, c/m, Simon & Halbig, 16" 1,600.00
50, SkHd, o/m, 1900, K*R/Simon & Halbig, 14" 400.00
53, SkHd, c/m, brown bsk, Simon & Halbig/K*R, 16" 1,600.00
530, SkHd, o/m, G/Simon & Halbig, 21" 600.00
540, SkHd, o/m, G/Halbig/S&H, 16" 750.00
540, SkHd, swivel on bsk ShPl, o/m, S&H, G, 16" 750.00
550, SkHd, o/m, Simon & Halbig/S&H, 16" 450.00
570, SkHd, o/m, Halbig S&H/G, 18" 500.00
570, SkHd, o/m, walking, head turns, G/Halbig S&H, 18" 750.00
576, SkHd, o/m, Simon & Halbig, 16" 450.00
612, SkHd, o/m, MIG/S&H/CM Bergmann, 16" 475.00
670, SkHd, o/m, Simon & Halbig, 16" 475.00
70, SkHd, o/m, 1896, Halbig/K*R, 26" 850.00
719, SkHd, c/m, S&H DEP, 16" 1,800.00
719, SkHd, swivel, ShPl, c/m, S&H, DEP, 20" 2,300.00
739, SkHd, c/m, brn, S 5 H DEP, 14" 1,400.00
739, SkHd, c/m, brn, S 5 H DEP, 18" 2,200.00
759, SkHd, o/m, brn, S 10 H DEP, 20" 650.00
769, SkHd, c/m, S&H DEP, 17" 1,800.00
905, SkHd, swivel on ShPl, c/m, SH, 21" 2,200.00
908, SkHd, swivel on ShPl, c/m, SH, 16" 2,300.00
929, SkHd, c/m, S&H, DEP, 20" 2,300.00
929, SkHd, c/m, S&H, DEP, 25" 3,200.00
939, SkHd, c/m, S 11H DEP, 17" 2,500.00
939, SkHd, c/m, S 11H DEP, 23" 2,500.00
939, SkHd, o/c eyes, o/m, S16H, 30" 3,600.00
940, SkHd, closed dome, o/c mouth, S 2 H, 26" 3,200.00
940, SkHd, swivel on ShPl, o/c mouth, S 2 H, 14" 1,400.00
945, SkHd, c/m, S 2 H DEP, 16" 2,000.00
99, SkHd, o/m, 1899, 11 1/2 Handwerck/Halbig, 16" 450.00

Steiner

Jules Nicholas Steiner established one of the earliest French doll manufactories in 1855. Having been a clockmaker, he began with mechanical dolls and his patents grew to include walking and talking dolls. In 1880 he registered a patent for a doll with moving eyes. This doll could be put to sleep by turning a rod that operated a wire attached to its eyes. Though these new innovations brought much acclaim to the Steiner company, it closed around 1910 because it could not compete with the less-expensive German dolls that were flooding the market at that time.

A Series, wire eyes, c/m, jtd, RpC, 16" 4,800.00
A Series child, c/m, o/c eyes, jtd, cb pate, RpC, 12" 3,000.00
A Series child, c/m, o/c eyes, jtd, cb pate, RpC, 16" 3,800.00
A Series child, c/m, o/c eyes, jtd, cb pate, RpC, 20" 5,300.00
A Series child, c/m, o/c eyes, jtd, cb pate, RpC, 25" 6,600.00
A Series child, o/m, o/c eyes, jtd, cb pate, RpC, 16" 2,200.00
A Series child, o/m, o/c eyes, jtd, cb pate, RpC, 20" 2,800.00
A Series child, o/m, o/c eyes, jtd, cb pate, RpC, 26" 3,800.00
Bourgoin, c/m, pwt eyes, 1870s, RpC, 16" 4,600.00
Bourgoin, c/m, pwt eyes, 1870s, RpC, 20" 6,000.00
Bourgoin, c/m, pwt eyes, 1870s, RpC, 25" 7,200.00
Bourgoin, wire eyes, c/m, jtd, RpC, 16" 4,700.00
Bourgoin, wire eyes, c/m, jtd, RpC, 20" 5,800.00
C Series, wire eyes, c/m, RpC, 16" 4,700.00
C Series child, c/m, rnd face, pwt eyes, RpC, 16" 4,600.00
C Series child, c/m, rnd face, pwt eyes, RpC, 20" 6,000.00
Le Parisien, A Series, 1892, 16" 3,800.00
Mechanical, key wind, kicks/cries, teeth, RpC, 18" 1,800.00
Motschmann style, bsk, RpC, 18" 5,200.00

Unmk, early wht bsk, o/m w/teeth, jtd, RpC, 18" **5,900.00**
Unmk, early wht bsk, rnd face, o/m w/teeth, jtd, RpC, 14" **4,200.00**

Shoulder head, station-
ary glass eyes, closed
mouth, blond mohair,
wax over composition,
minor damage, replaced
shoes, 24", $2,100.00.

Vogue

Baby, vinyl/cloth, pnt eyes, rooted hair, 1961, 12"..........................**45.00**
Baby Dear, vinyl/cloth, pnt eyes, rooted hair, 1964, 12", M...........**50.00**
Brickette, vinyl, flirty o/c eyes, jtd waist, 1960, OC, 22"................**95.00**
Brickette, vinyl, o/c eyes, curly hair, 1978, OC, 16" **65.00**
Ginny, Bo Peep, hp, o/c eyes, pnt lashes, '52, OC, 8", M.............**250.00**
Ginny, Ginger, hp, orig red velvet dress, 8" **300.00**
Ginny, hp, molded lashes, walker, OC, 8" **165.00**
Ginny, Toddles, compo, OC, 7½", M..**265.00**
Ginny Crib Crowd, bent-leg baby, lamb's wool wig, NM.............**600.00**
Ginny Hawaiian, hp, brn skin tones, OC, 16" **1,500.00**
Hug A Bye Baby, vinyl, OC, 16" **35.00**
Little Imp Country Cousin, hp, o/c eyes, freckles, OC, 10½" **65.00**
Littlest Angel, plastic/vinyl, o/c eyes, OC, 1965, 15" **65.00**
Miss 1920, hp, orig taffeta dress/hat/shoes, 1950, 8", EX **400.00**
Wee Imp, vinyl, red wig, OC, 8" **400.00**

Wax, Poured Wax

Over compo, c/m, glass eyes, cloth body, wig, RpC, 29"...............**300.00**
Over compo, ShHd, o/c eyes, auburn hair, orig dress, 18" **300.00**
Over compo, ShHd, set eyes, molded hair, cloth body, 15"..........**250.00**
Over compo, slit head, blk eyes, cloth body, 14" **325.00**
Over papier-mache, jtd wooden body, wire-eyed, all orig, 11" **400.00**
Poured, bl pwt eyes, England, OC, 24" **2,200.00**
Poured, glass eyes, set-in hair, cloth body, 19"..........................**1,400.00**

Door Knockers

Door knockers, those charming precursors of the door bell, come
in an intriguing array of shapes and styles. The very rare ones come
from England. Cast iron examples made in this country were often produced in forms similar to the more familiar doorstop figures.

Amish man, CI, orig mc pnt, 4¼" **45.00**
Basket of flowers, CI, mc pnt, 3¾" **45.00**
Devil's head, brass, old...**60.00**
Foo dog, bronze, lg..**100.00**
House w/trees, lane, etc, CI, VG pnt **65.00**
Kissing couple w/roses, brass, 5½" **50.00**

Monkey, brass **35.00**
Napoleon, brass..**20.00**
Oliver Twist, brass..**20.00**
Parrot, CI, gr & gold pnt **75.00**
Parrot on leafy branch, pnt CI..**45.00**
Wolf's head, brass, English...**45.00**
Woman's hand, brass **20.00**
Woodpecker, tree bkplate, pnt CI **55.00**

Flowers in yellow bas-
ket, cast iron with
excellent paint, 4",
$45.00.

Doorstops

Although introduced in England in the mid-1800s, cast iron
doorstops were not made to any great extent in this country until after
the Civil War. Once called 'door porters,' their function was to keep
doors open to provide better ventilation. They have been produced in
many shapes and sizes, both dimensional and flat backed, and in the
past few years have become a popular, yet affordable collectible. While
cast iron examples are the most common, brass, wood, and chalk were
also used. An average price is in the $40 to $50 range, though some are
valued at more than $200. Doorstops retained their usefulness and
appeal well into the thirties.

The prices below reflect market values in the east where doorstops
are now at a premium. For other areas of the country, it may be necessary to adjust prices down about 25%. In the listings below, items are
assumed flat backed unless noted full figured and cast iron unless noted
otherwise.

Key: ff — full figured

Ally Sloper, man w/lg nose, umbrella, & dog, English, 11⅛" **300.00**
Amish Man, wide-brimmed hat, hand in pocket, ff, 8½x3¾" **175.00**
Apple Blossoms, in woven basket, Hubley #329, 7⅝x5⅜" **75.00**
Aunt Jemima, wht apron, red dress, 13¼x8" **275.00**
Basket of Kittens, M Rosenstein, c 1932, 10x7" **300.00**
Beagle Pup, sitting, ff, 8x7½" **275.00**
Bellhop, bl & red uniform, #1244, 8⅞x4⅝"..................................**200.00**
Blk jockey w/brass ring, ff, 11½" **175.00**
Blk Man on Cotton Bale, wht clothes, top hat, 6⅞x6⅞" **500.00**
Bloodhound, long face & ears, sm body, ff, 6¾x4¼" **125.00**
Blowfish, rests on fins & tail, ff, Hubley, 8x7¼" **225.00**
Bobby Blake, boy in short pants w/teddy, Hubley, 9½x5¼" **350.00**
Boston Bulldog, glass eyes, Greenblatt Studios, 13x5½" **150.00**

Boston Terrier Begging, paws & face lifted, ff, 8¾x5" 225.00
Boston Terrier w/Paw Up, faces right, ff, 9½x7" 250.00
Bronze Dog, sits, faces right, 9¼x6" 125.00
Buddha, sitting figure, worn pnt, ff, 7x5¾" 175.00
Buster Brown, boy in short sailor suit, 7¾x5¼" 350.00
Camel, 2 humps, walking, ff, 7x9" 250.00
Cat, comic form w/red bow tie, Eastern Specialty #62, 7x4½" 200.00
Cat, licking bk, Sculptured Metal Studios, 10¾x7½" 350.00
Chamelion, tail curled to side, Sherwin Williams, 1¼x8" 75.00
Charleston Dancers, c Fish, Hubley, 8⅞x5⅜" 550.00
Child, reaching, nude bkside, Elba Road label, 17x7" 500.00
Clown, wide collar, red suit, faces right, 10x4½" 550.00
Cocker Spaniel, stands, faces right, ff, Hubley, 6¾x11" 175.00
Colonial Dame, w/flowers/hat/shawl, Hubley, 8x4½" 150.00
Colonial Lady, ruffled skirt, Nat'l Foundry, 4⅝x3⅜" 75.00
Colonial lady w/hat & purse, poor pnt, Littco, 10¼x5¾" 85.00
Colonial Lawyer, yel coat, gr pants, WS mk, 9⅝x5¼" 325.00
Colonial Pilgrim, right arm out, 8¾x5⅜" 275.00

Colonial Woman, Littco Products, 10", $125.00.

Columbia, draped lady, ff, 16½x4½" 550.00
Conestoga Wagon, w/oxen team, c 64, 6¼x10¼" 125.00
Dog, seated, 'Mutt & His Bone,' minor wear, 8½" 175.00
Dutch Girl, ff, worn pnt, 6x3¾" 150.00
Dutch Girl w/Big Shoes, hands on hips, EX pnt, 9¾x9¼" 275.00
Dutch Woman, ff, worn pnt, 4x2⅜" 100.00
El Capitan, soldier marches to left, 7¾x5¼" 150.00
Elephant, mk B&H, worn pnt, 10½" 175.00
Elephant by Palm, trunk up, long tusk, wedge, 13¾x10¼" 200.00
Fawn, stylized form, faces right, c Taylor Cook 1930, 10x6" 150.00
Fireside Cat, recumbent, faces right, ff, Hubley, 5⅝x11" 125.00
Fox Terrier, sm collar, faces left, 10⅜x10½" 175.00
French Basket, mc flowers, woven basket, Hubley #69, 11x6¾" 75.00
Frog w/Blk Boy, boy on frog's bk, poor pnt, ff, 5½x6½" 150.00
Geisha, kneels w/instrument, ff, Hubley, 7x6" 175.00
George Washington, left hand at hip, ff, 16x6½" 400.00
German Shepherd, faces left, ff, Hubley, 9¼x10" 75.00
Girl w/Beanie, red hair, bl dress, ff, 8¾x3¼" 300.00
Gnome, pointed red hat, beard, ff, 10x4" 225.00
Halloween Girl, holds pumpkin, worn pnt, 13¾x9¾" 500.00
Horse, realistic pnt, ff, Hubley, 10x12" 100.00
Horse, w/bridle & saddle, faces left, Nat'l Foundry, 8x10" 125.00
Horse Jumping Fence, rider, Eastern Specialty #79, 8x12" 300.00

Humpty Dumpty, on gray brick wall, ff, #661, 4½x3½" 200.00
Imp w/Bone, mk GR-1421, worn mc pnt, 5" 135.00
Iris, 3 lg blossoms, Hubley #469, 10⅝x6¾" 175.00
Jill, girl in bonnet & apron w/pail, Hubley, 8¾x5¾" 300.00
Judy w/child, holds skirt, English, 12x7½" 300.00

Kitten, Hubley, 8"x6", $150.00.

Koala, crawling on log, c Taylor Cook 1930, 7¼x5½" 350.00
Lady Holding Flowers, wht bonnet/red dress, 8½x4¾", EX 85.00
Lady in Ruffled Dress, holds fan, ff, Pat Appld For, 6¼" 150.00
Lady w/Hatbox, wide skirt, worn pnt, 6¾x5¼" 125.00
Lady w/Ruffled Skirt, holds flower basket, worn pnt, 6⅜x5" 125.00
Lafayette, sword in right hand, ruffle at neck, 11⅝x6⅜" 375.00
Lambs Under Tree, willow w/2 recumbent lambs, 7¼x6⅜" 200.00
Latin Gent, Derby-type hat, CI w/mc pnt, 16" 350.00
Lil Red Riding Hood, w/basket, worn pnt, Hubley, 9½x5" 350.00
Lil Red Riding Hood & Wolf, Nat'l Foundry, 7¼x5⅜" 275.00
Lion, stands, faces left, aluminum, old gold pnt, 7" 35.00
Log Cabin, trees at sides, Nat'l Foundry, 4⅝x10" 100.00
Mad Hatter, blk hat, red bow tie, ff, #666, 6⅝x2⅞" 225.00
Maid, curtsying, worn pnt, #1242, 8⅞x4⅞" 225.00
Maid of Honor, w/bouquet, skirt held aside, Hubley, 8¼x5" 175.00
Man in Chair, cup in hand, tam hat, English, 10⅛x6" 225.00
Man w/Cane, long plaid coat, faces right, 10x4⅞" 325.00
Mary Quite Contrary, waters flowers, Littco, 11⅜x9⅝" 550.00
Messenger Boy, w/bouquet, c Fish, Hubley, 10x5⅜" 375.00
Modernistic Cat, angular form, ff, Hubley, 9¾x5" 325.00
Monkey, sits w/arms & legs Xd, ff, 7x5" 150.00
Old Mill, log building w/wheel at side, 6¼x8¼" 200.00
Old Salt, man in yel slicker, 14½x6½" 300.00
Oriental Child, sits on pillow, worn mc pnt, 5" 140.00
Owl, perched on stump, realistic details, 10x6" 200.00
Owl on Books, Eastern Specialty, 9¼x6½" 375.00
Pan & Nymph, facing figures, EX pnt, 9¼x14" 550.00
Peacock, tail spread wide, 6¼x6¼" 125.00
Peacock by Urn, draped tail, Hubley #208, 7½x4¼" 150.00
Pekingese, stands, faces left, ff, Hubley, 14½x9" 350.00
Penguin w/Top Hat, blk & wht pnt, ff, Hubley, 10½x3¾" 225.00
Percheron, realistic pnt, ff, Hubley, 9x7¾" 150.00
Pheasant, faces right, grassy base, Hubley, 8½x7½" 200.00
Pirate w/Chest, sword in left hand, red cape, 9¾x6" 175.00
Polly, parrot on perch, Hubley #180, 8⅛x5¼" 75.00
Popeye, ff, Hubley, King Features c 1929, 9x4½" 550.00
Primrose, lg blossoms in sm vase, Hubley #448, 7⅜x6¼" 100.00

Punch, seated, faces right, English, 12x9" 425.00
Quail, realistic pr on grassy base, Hubley, 7¼x6¼" 250.00
Rabbit Eating Carrot, red sweater, 8⅛x4⅞" 300.00
Rhumba Dancer, thin figure in ruffled skirt, 11⅛x6⅝" 400.00
Rooster, crowing, blk w/red comb, ff, 15⅜x6⅛" 250.00
Safety First Policeman, by fire plug, 9½x5⅝" 550.00
Sax Player, Blk man in red jacket w/instrument, 6⅞x6" 350.00
Scottish Highlander, in kilt, w/spear, 15½x13" 250.00
Shore Bird, wings up, faces left, 10x6½" 225.00
Skier, lady holds skis at side, ff, 12½x5" 375.00
Sleeping Cat, curled position, ff, 4½x13" 500.00
Spanish Girl, Pat Appld For, WS mk, EX pnt, 9½x5¼" 175.00
Sunbonnet Girl, faces right, worn pnt, 9x5½" 300.00
Swallows, pr on berry branches, Hubley, 8½x7½" 250.00
Terrier w/Bushes, stands w/tail up, c 1929 PAL, 8x7" 125.00
Toby, yel vest, striped pants, T Kennedy, ff, 16x8⅜" 550.00
Turtle, crawling, head out, ff, 4¼x17" 275.00
Uncle Sam, hands at waist, rnd base, 12x5½" 550.00
Washington, leans on left elbow/hat in right hand, 12¼x6⅜" 375.00
West Wind, English, EX pnt, 18x7" 275.00
Wine Man, man w/many bottles, unmk, 9½x7" 550.00
Wolfhound, blk & wht w/red collar, wedge, Spencer, 6½x3½" 125.00
Woman w/Hooped Dress, unmk, worn pnt, 7x5¼" 85.00

Dorchester Pottery

Taking its name from the town in Maine where it was organized in 1895, the Dorchester Pottery Company made primarily utilitarian wares, though other types of items were made as well. By 1940 a line of decorative pottery was introduced, some of which was painted by hand with scrollwork or themes from nature. The buildings were destroyed by fire in the late 1970s and the pottery was never rebuilt.

Bowl, bl swirls on cream, 5⅞", EX 75.00
Plate, floral border, bl & wht, 9⅞", EX 125.00
Vase, bl, flared-out top, orig paper label, 6½", EX 60.00

Dorflinger

C. Dorflinger was born in Alsace, France, and came to this country when he was ten years old. When still very young, he obtained a job in a glass factory in New Jersey. As a young man, he started his own glassworks in Brooklyn, New York, opening new factories as profits permitted. During that time he made cut glass articles for many famous people including President and Mrs. Lincoln, for whom he produced a complete service of tableware with the United States Coat of Arms. In 1863 he sold the New York factories because of ill health and moved to his farm near White Mills, Pennsylvania. His health returned, and he started a plant near his home. It was there that he did much of his best work, making use of only the very finest materials. Christian died in 1915, and the plant was closed in 1921 by consent of the family.

Dorflinger glass is rare and often hard to identify. Very few pieces were marked – many only carried a small paper label which was quickly discarded.

Bottle, scent; gr to clear, hobnail base, 4¾x2" 350.00
Bowl, Prince of Wales, plumes motif, knob stem, 7x9" 385.00
Ice bucket, Marlboro, tab hdls, +underplate 1,400.00
Nappy, cranberry to clear, X-cut dmn, strawberry dmn, 6½" 475.00
Parfait, Kalana Lily, 6" 75.00
Plate, Picket Fence, 6¼" 35.00
Vase, Kalana Geranium, 7½" 85.00

Vase, Kalana Pansy, 6" 75.00

Doulton, Royal Doulton

The range of wares produced by the Doulton Company since its inception in 1815 has been vast and varied. Their earliest wares produced in the tiny pottery in Lambeth, England, were salt-glazed pitchers, plain and fancy figural bottles – all utility-type stoneware geared to the practical need of everyday living. The original partners, John Doulton and John Watts, saw the potential for success in the manufacture of drain and sewage pipes and during the 1840s concentrated on this highly lucrative type of commercial ware. Watts retired from the company in 1854, and Doulton began experimenting with a more decorative style of product. As time went by, many glazes and decorative effects were developed, among them Faience, Impasto, Silicon, Carrara, Marqueterie, Chine, and Rouge Flambe. Tiles and architectural terra cotta were an important part of their manufacture. Late in the nineteenth century at the original Lambeth location, fine artware was decorated by such notable artists as Hannah and Arthur Barlow, George Tinworth, and J.H. McLennan. Stoneware vases with incised animal drawings, gracefully-shaped urns with painted scenes, and cleverly-modeled figurines rivaled the best of any competitor.

In 1882 a second factory was built in Burslem which continues even yet to produce the famous figurines, character jugs, series ware, and table services so popular with collectors today. Their Kingsware line, made from 1899 to 1946, featured flasks and flagons with drinking scenes, usually on a brown-glazed ground, some of which were limited editions while others were commemorative and advertising items. The Gibson Girl series, twenty-four plates in all, was introduced in 1901. It was drawn by Charles Dana Gibson and is recognized by its blue and white borders and central illustrations, each scene depicting a humorous or poignant episode in the life of 'The Widow and Her Friends.' Dickensware, produced from 1911 through the early 1940s, featured illustrations by Charles Dickens, with many of his famous characters. The Robin Hood series was introduced in 1914; the Shakespeare series #1, portraying scenes from the Bard's plays, was made from 1914 until World War II. The Shakespeare series #2 ran from 1906 until 1974 and was decorated with featured characters. The Nursery Rhymes series was produced first in earthenware in 1903 and later in bone china. In 1933 a line of decorated children's ware, the Bunnykins series, was introduced and continues to be made to the present day. About 150 'bunny' scenes have been devised, the earliest and most desirable being those signed by the artist Barbara Vernon.

The value of a figurine is appreciated by age, because of a limited production run, or by exceptional color and detail. Those signed by the artist or marked 'Potted' (indicating pre-1939 origin) are also more valuable. After 1920 wares were marked with a lion – with or without a crown – over a circular 'Royal Doulton.'

Our advisor (for all but the Flambe section) is Nicki Budin; she is listed in the Directory under Ohio.

Animals and Birds

Dog, #2654, w/slipper in mouth 65.00
Dog, Bull Terrier, K-14 ....140.00
Dog, Chow Chow, K-15, standing, 2¼" 45.00
Dog, Cocker Spaniel, #1000, blk, lg 245.00
Dog, Collie, #2958, med sz 125.00
Dog, Dachshund, K-17, 2⅜" 45.00
Dog, Doberman Pinscher, #2645 ....135.00
Dog, Greyhound, #1077, brn, sm 300.00
Dog, Irish Setter, #1055, med sz 150.00
Dog, St Bernard, K-19 ....40.00

Dog, Welsh Corgi, K-16, standing, 2¼" 50.00
Elephant, #2644, 5½" 95.00
Kitten, #2581, sleeping 40.00
Kitten, #2583, licking paw..40.00
Leopard, #2638, on rock 1,800.00
Magpie, K-34 ....150.00
Mallard, K-26 ....50.00
Mare & Foal, #3524..295.00
Penguin & Chick, K-20, 2¼" 125.00
Pig, #800, asleep, med sz 200.00
Polar Bear, #119..145.00
Puppies, #2588, in basket 65.00
Sea gull, #2574 ....135.00
Snowy Owl, #2670, 16" 1,700.00
Tiger, #2646 ....900.00
Winter Wren, #3505, 4¾" 3,500.00
Yel-Throated Warbler, K-27 ....125.00

Character Jugs

Ann Boleyn, D6650, sm 57.50
Apothecary, D6581, miniature...................................50.00
Aramis, D6508, miniature 40.00
Ard of 'Earing, D6591, sm 675.00
Arry, D6235, sm, A..80.00
Arry, D6249, miniature..75.00
Arry, D6255, tiny 195.00
Artful Dodger, tiny 40.00
Athos, D6452, sm 40.00
Auld Mac, D5823, lg, A 95.00
Auld Mac, D5824, sm, A 45.00
Auld Mac, D6250, miniature......................................40.00
Auld Mac, D6257, tiny 225.00
Bacchus, D6521, miniature 40.00
Beefeater, D6206, ER hdl, lg......................................75.00
Beefeater, D6233, GR hdl, sm, A 60.00
Beefeater, D6251, GR hdl, miniature 65.00
Bill Sykes, tiny 40.00
Blacksmith, D6585, miniature....................................45.00
Bootmaker, D6570, sm...65.00
Bootmaker, D6586, miniature 55.00
Cap'n Cuttle, D5842, sm, A..95.00
Captain Ahab, D6500, lg..95.00
Captain Ahab, D6522, miniature 45.00
Captain Henry Morgan, D6510, miniature..................45.00
Captain Hook, D6601, sm...350.00
Captain Hook, D6605, miniature 345.00
Cardinal, D5614, lg...155.00
Cardinal, D6033, sm...75.00
Catherine of Aragon, D6657, sm 50.00
Cavalier, D6114, lg..150.00
Cavalier, D6114, lg, A..160.00
D'Artagnan, D6691, lg..95.00
Dick Turpin, D6128, gun hdl, miniature.....................70.00
Dick Turpin, D6528, horse hdl, lg 110.00
Dick Turpin, D6542, horse hdl, miniature 45.00
Don Quixote, D6455, lg..95.00
Drake, D6115, lg, A...160.00
Drake, D6174, sm, A...75.00
Fagin, tiny 40.00
Falconer, D6547, miniature 40.00
Falstaff, D6385, sm...45.00
Falstaff, D6519, miniature 40.00
Farmer John, D5788, lg...165.00

Farmer John, D5789, 1941, sm 85.00
Fat Boy, D6139, miniature 75.00
Fortune Teller, D6497, lg 550.00
Fortune Teller, D6523, miniature 350.00
Friar Tuck, D6321, lg 450.00
Gaoler, D6570, lg 100.00
Gaoler, D6584, miniature 55.00
Gardner, D6630, lg...150.00
Gardner, D6638, miniature 65.00
George Washington, D6669, lg...................................95.00
Gladiator, D6550, lg...500.00
Golfer, D6623, lg 95.00
Gondolier, D6589, lg..575.00
Gondolier, D6595, miniature......................................365.00
Gone Away, D6538, sm...60.00
Gone Away, D6545, miniature 50.00
Granny, D5521, toothless, lg 1,000.00
Granny, D6520, miniature..45.00
Guardsman, D6568, lg..100.00
Gulliver, D6566, miniature 375.00
Gunsmith of Williamsburg, D6573, lg........................100.00
Henry Morgan, D6467, lg...95.00
Henry Morgan, D6510, miniature 55.00
Henry VIII, D6648, miniature....................................45.00
Jane Seymour, D6646, lg...95.00
Jarge, D6288, lg...295.00
Jester, D5556, sm 125.00
Jockey, D6625, lg..375.00
John Barleycorn, D5327, lg..165.00
John Barleycorn, D6041, miniature............................70.00
John Peel, D5612, lg...160.00
John Peel, D6259, tiny 225.00
Johnny Appleseed, D6372, lg.....................................350.00
Lawyer, D6524, miniature 45.00
Little Nell..45.00
Lobster Man, D6620, sm...50.00
Long John Silver, D6386, sm......................................50.00
Lumberjack, D6613, sm..65.00
Mad Hatter, D6602, sm..75.00
Mae West, D6688, lg...100.00
Mark Twain, D6694, sm...50.00
Merlin, D6543, miniature...45.00
Mikado, D6501, lg..550.00
Mikado, D6525, miniature...350.00
Mine Host, D6468, lg..95.00
Mr Bumble, tiny..40.00
Mr Micawber, D5842, sm, A 75.00
Mr Pickwick, D6060, lg, A 160.00
Mr Pickwick, D6245, miniature 65.00
Night Watchman, D6576, sm......................................65.00
Old Charley, D5420, lg..95.00
Old Charley, D5527, sm, A..55.00
Old Charley, D6046, miniature, A...............................45.00
Old King Cole, D6037, yel crown, sm 4,500.00
Old Salt, D6554, sm..50.00
Paddy, D5753, lg, A..160.00
Paddy, D5768, sm...60.00
Paddy, D6145, tiny..95.00
Parson Brown, D5529, sm...65.00
Pearly Boy, D6207, brn 1,800.00
Pied Piper, D6462, sm..60.00
Poacher, D6515, miniature 45.00
Porthos, D6516, miniature 45.00
Punch & Judy Man, D6593, sm...................................375.00

Punch & Judy Man, D6596, miniature 350.00
Regency Beau, D6562, sm 675.00
Regency Beau, D6565, miniature 650.00

Regency Beau, D6559, 7", $995.00.

Rip Van Winkle, D6463, sm 50.00
Robin Hood, D6252, no feather, sm 50.00
Robin Hood, D6252, sm 65.00
Robinson Crusoe, D6546, miniature 45.00
Romeo, D6670, lg 95.00
Sairey Gamp, D6045, miniature 45.00
Sam Weller, D5841, sm, A 85.00
Sam Weller, D6064, lg 160.00
Sam Weller, D6140, miniature 55.00
Sancho Panza, D6456, lg 110.00
Sancho Panza, D6461, sm 65.00
Santa Claus, D6690, stocking hdl, lg 110.00
Scaramouche, D6561, sm 425.00
Scaramouche, D6564, miniature 345.00
Scrooge, tiny 40.00
Sleuth, D6631, lg 95.00
Sleuth, D6635, sm 50.00
Sleuth, D6639, miniature 40.00
St George, D6621, sm 165.00
Tam O'Shanter, D6640, miniature 55.00
Toby Philpots, D5736, lg 150.00
Toby Philpots, D5737, sm, A 65.00
Toby Philpots, D6043, miniature 50.00
Tony Weller, D5530, sm 55.00
Tony Weller, D6044, miniature, A 45.00
Touchstone, D5613, lg, A 250.00
Trapper, D6609, lg 110.00
Ugly Duchess, D6599, lg 460.00
Ugly Duchess, D6607, miniature 285.00
Uncle Tom Cobbleigh, D6637, lg 425.00
Vicar of Bray, D5615, lg, A 225.00
Viking, D6526, miniature 125.00
Walrus & Carpenter, D6604, sm 65.00
WC Fields, D6674, lg 125.00

Figurines

Affection, HN2236 ....100.00
Afternoon Call, HN82, lav coat 2,400.00
Alchemist, HN1259, red hat 1,500.00
Alfred Jingle, HN541, blk jacket, 3¾" 55.00

All Aboard, HN2940 ....150.00
Amy, HN2958, wht dress 95.00
And One for You, HN2970 ....80.00
Annabella, HN1875, red dress 500.00
Antoinette, HN2326 ....140.00
As Good As New, HN2971 ....85.00
Autumn Breezes, HN1934, red dress 195.00
Baba, HN1244, yel & gr pants 750.00
Babette, HN1424, bl cloak 750.00
Balloon Man, HN1954 ....295.00
Balloon Seller, HN479 ....1,200.00
Bather, HN781, bl & gr robe 1,200.00
Beachcomber, HN2487 ....175.00
Beat You to It, HN2871 ....250.00
Bell o' the ball, HN1997 ....250.00
Betty, HN1435, mc dress 425.00
Betty, HN438, gr skirt 1,800.00
Biddy, HN1500, yel dress 2,200.00
Biddy, HN1513, red dress 165.00
Blossom, HN1667, orange shawl 1,250.00
Bluebeard, HN1528 ....850.00
Bo-Peep, HN1202 ....875.00
Bon Jour, HN1879, gr dress 675.00
Bonnie Lassie, HN1626 ....250.00
Boudoir, HN2542 ....350.00
Boy w/Turban, HN662, blk & wht 750.00
Bride, HN1600, yel roses 695.00
Bride, HN2873 ....130.00
Bunny, HN2214 ....150.00
Buttercup, HN2309 ....155.00
Butterfly, HN1203, gold wings 950.00

Cobbler, HN1706, 8", $275.00.

Captain, HN2260 ....250.00
Carmen, HN2545, bl skirt 250.00
Cassim, HN1231, bl hat & pants 750.00
Catherine, HN2395 ....200.00

Charley's Aunt, HN640	750.00
Charmian, HN1568	575.00
Chelsea Pair, HN579	575.00
Cherie, HN2341, bl dress	100.00
Child Study, HN604A	350.00
China Repairer, HN2943	140.00
Chloe, M10	285.00
Christine, HN2792, bl dress	250.00
Cissie, HN1809, red dress	100.00
Clare, HN2793	150.00
Clarinda, HN2724	150.00
Clarissa, HN1525	150.00
Cleopatra, HN2868	1,250.00
Clown, HN2890	275.00
Cobbler, HN542, yel shirt	850.00
Colonel Fairfax, HN2903	650.00
Contemplation, HN2213, wht	75.00
Coralie, HN2307	185.00
Country Lass, HN1991	115.00
Courtier, HN1338	875.00
Cradle Song, HN2246, gr dress	395.00
Crinoline, HN21A, yel skirt	1,250.00
Cup of Tea, HN2322, blk dress	135.00
Curtsey, HN371, yel dress	1,300.00
Daisy, HN1575	550.00
Dancers of the World, Chinese Dancer, HN2840	595.00
Dancers of the World, West Indian, HN2384, mc costume	595.00
Darling, HN1371, gr nightshirt	175.00
Dawn, HN1858A, no headdress	650.00
Deauville, HN2344	150.00
Derrick, HN1398	475.00
Detective, HN2359	195.00
Dinky Do, HN2120, red	75.00
Dorcas, HN1490, beige dress	450.00
Drummer Boy, HN2679	350.00
Eleanor of Provence, HN2009	550.00
Elegance, HN2264, gr dress	150.00
Embroidering, HN2855	295.00
Enchantment, HN2178	150.00
Eugene, HN1520	650.00
Eventide, HN2814	155.00
Fagin, HN534	50.00
Fair Lady, HN2193	160.00
Fairy, HN1393	950.00
Falstaff, HN2054, red jacket	150.00
Falstaff, HN609	1,650.00
Fiddler, HN2171	750.00
First Waltz, HN2862	190.00
Flower Seller, HN789	750.00
Foaming Quart, HN2162	185.00
Fortune Teller, HN2159	425.00
Forty Thieves, HN497	950.00
Forty Winks, HN1974, wht apron	195.00
Friar Tuck, HN2143	450.00
Frodo, HN2912	85.00
Geisha, HN1321, gr kimono	1,200.00
Geisha, HN634, blk & wht kimono	1,500.00
Georgina, HN2377	95.00
Gillian, HN1670, pk dress	795.00
Giselle, Forest Glade, HN2140	375.00
Giselle, HN2139, bl dress	350.00
Gnome, HN319	950.00
Goody Two Shoes, HN2037, red dress	95.00
Grandma, HN2052, bl shawl	350.00
Granny, HN1832, yel dress	675.00
Grief, HN595	995.00
Griselda, HN1993	425.00
Happy Anniversary, HN3097	165.00
Happy Birthday, HN3095	165.00
Harlequin, HN2186	225.00
Harlequinade, HN711	675.00
Harmony, HN2824	175.00
Hazel, HN1796	395.00
Heidi, HN2975	75.00
Helen, HN2994	50.00
Helen of Troy, HN2387	950.00
Helmsman, HN2499	195.00
Her Ladyship, HN1977	295.00
Hilary, HN2335	150.00
Honey, HN1910, gr dress	550.00
Hostess of Williamsburg, HN2209	175.00
Hunts Lady, HN1201	1,250.00
Innocence, HN2842	150.00
Irishman, HN1307, gr jacket	1,250.00
Jack Point, HN85	2,250.00
Janice, HN2165	455.00
Jasmine, HN1862, floral jacket	675.00
Jester, HN308	1,350.00
Jester, HN630	1,200.00
Jester, HN71	1,100.00
Judge, HN2443	200.00
Juliet, HN2968	295.00
June, M65	450.00
Katharine, HN341, red dress	1,250.00
Kathleen, HN1291	650.00
Kirsty, HN2381, orange dress	200.00
Ko-Ko, HN2898	600.00
Lady April, HN1958	295.00
Lady Clown, HN770	1,350.00
Lady Diana Spencer, HN2885	400.00
Lady of the Elizabethan Period, HN73	1,400.00
Lady of the Fan, HN53A	1,400.00
Lady Pamela, HN2718, pk dress	155.00
Ladybird, HN1638	800.00
Last Waltz, HN2315, peach dress	195.00
Lavinia, HN1955, red dress	95.00
Leap, HN3522	85.00
Leisure Hour, HN2055	400.00
Lily, HN1795, pk dress	135.00
Linda, HN2106, red cloak	125.00
Lisette, HN1684	650.00
Little Bridesmaid, M30	250.00
Little Lady Make Believe, HN1870	375.00
Little Nell, M-51	55.00
Lori, HN2801, wht dress	95.00
Louise, HN2869	95.00
Lucy, HN2863	95.00
Lute, HN2431	995.00
M'Lady's Maid, HN1795	1,200.00
Madonna of the Square, HN27	1,350.00
Magpie Ring, HN2978	95.00
Make Believe, HN2225	95.00
Margaret, HN2397	100.00
Margaret, 1989	350.00
Margot, HN1636	625.00
Marguerite, HN1946	550.00
Marietta, HN2699	550.00
Marigold, HN1555	425.00

Mary Had a Little Lamb, HN2048	135.00
Mask, HN729	1,250.00
Mask Seller, HN2103, gr coat	200.00
Masquerade, HN637, gold dress	725.00
Matilda, HN2011	525.00
Maureen, HN1770, bl dress	225.00
Meditation, HN2330	295.00
Memories, HN1857	475.00
Memories, HN2030	400.00
Meriel, HN1932	950.00
Michelle, HN2234	150.00
Milkmaid, HN2057A	145.00
Miss Demure, HN1499, pk dress	375.00
Miss Muffet, HN1936, red coat	160.00
Miss Winsome, HN1665	450.00
Modena, HN1845, bl dress	1,500.00
Monica, HN1467, red hat	95.00
Monte Carlo, HN2332	150.00
Mother's Help, HN2151, blk dress	195.00
Mr Micawber, HN532	295.00
Mr Pickwick, HN2099	295.00
Mrs Bardell, M86	60.00
Musicale, HN2756	75.00
My Teddy, HN2177	495.00
Negligee, HN1219, bl hairband	800.00
Nell, HN3014, pk dress	95.00
Nelson, HN2928, ship's head, limited edition	750.00
Nicola, HN2839, lav dress	250.00
Officer of the Line, HN2733, red coat	175.00
Old Balloon Seller, HN1315, red jacket	200.00
Old King, HN358	1,200.00
Old Lavender Seller, HN1492, 1939	675.00
Olga, HN2463, gr dress	175.00
Olivia, HN1995	450.00
Once Upon a Time, HN2047	450.00
Orange Lady, HN1759, 1953	225.00
Orange Lady, HN1953, yel dress, gr shawl	225.00
Orange Vendor, HN508, purple coat	900.00
Paisley Shawl, HN1392	325.00
Paisley Shawl, HN1987	250.00
Pan on Rock, HN622	1,250.00
Pantalettes, M31, bl suit	395.00
Parisian, HN2445	150.00
Parson's Daughter, HN1356	450.00
Patricia, HN1431, pk & bl dress	450.00
Patricia, HN2715	100.00
Paula, HN2906	150.00
Pauline, HN2441	135.00
Peace, HN2433	80.00
Pearly Boy, HN1482	275.00
Pecksniff, HN535	250.00
Peggy, HN1941	250.00
Peggy, HN2038, red dress	95.00
Penelope, HN1901	295.00
Pensive Moments, HN2704	185.00
Phyllis, HN1486	575.00
Pied Piper, HN2102	250.00
Piper, HN2907	225.00
Please Keep Still, HN2967	75.00
Poacher, HN2043, gray jacket	225.00
Polly Peachum, HN589	325.00
Potter, HN1493	300.00
Premiere, HN2343	175.00
Pretty Lady, HN565	875.00
Pretty Polly, HN2768	125.00
Prince of Wales, HN2883, blk suit	350.00
Prince of Wales, HN2884	575.00
Proposal, HN1209, man in bl coat	750.00
Proposal, HN725, red coat	775.00
Quality Street, HN1211	700.00
Queen of the Ice, HN2435	135.00
Rachel, HN2919	175.00
Rendezvous, HN2212	350.00
Rest Awhile, HN2728	175.00
River Boy, HN2128	135.00
Robin, M38	450.00
Rocking Horse, HN2072	1,750.00
Rosabell, HN1620	650.00
Rose, HN1368	95.00
Rose, HN2123	75.00
Rosemary, HN2091	395.00
Rosina, HN1556	700.00
Rumplestiltskin, HN3025	150.00
Rustic Swain, HN1745	1,450.00
Sairey Gamp, HN1896	450.00
Sandra, HN2275	145.00
Santa Claus, HN2725	175.00
Saucy Nymph, HN1539	475.00
Scrooge, M87	55.00
Secret Thoughts, HN2382, gr dress	175.00
Serena, HN1868	725.00
Shadowplay, HN3526	85.00
Shepherd, HN709	695.00
Siamese Cat, Chatcull series, HN2660, lg	110.00
Sibell, HN1735	425.00
Silk & Ribbons, HN2017, gr dress	135.00
Simone, HN2378	135.00
Sir Ralph, HN2371, gray armor	350.00
Sir Thomas, HN2372	350.00
Sleepy Darling, HN2953	185.00
Solitude, HN2810	250.00
Sonia, I IN1692	650.00
Southern Belle, HN2229	175.00
Spring, HN2085	350.00
Spring Flowers, HN1807	275.00
Stayed at Home, HN2207	150.00
Stop Press, HN2683	150.00
Suitor, HN2132	350.00
Sunday Best, HN2206	195.00
Susan, HN2056	350.00
Suzette, HN1696, gr dress	650.00
Sweet & Twenty, HN1549	495.00
Sweet Anne, HN1496	195.00
Swimmer, HN1270	995.00
Taking Things Easy, HN2677	150.00
Teatime, HN2255, red dress	150.00
Teresa, HN1682, red dress	1,150.00
Thanks Doc, HN2731	185.00
Tiny Tim, HN539	85.00
Tom, HN2864	125.00
Tony Weller, HN346	1,200.00
Top O' the Hill, HN1833	195.00
Top O' the Hill, HN1834, red dress	175.00
Tracy, HN2736	95.00
Treasure Island, HN2243	135.00
Twilight, HN2256	175.00
Uncle Ned, HN2094, brn jacket	425.00
Veneta, HN2722	125.00

Veronica, HN1517, red & wht dress 350.00
Victorian Lady, HN1345 .... 295.00
Viking, HN2375 .... 295.00
Vivienne, HN2073 .... 285.00
Wee Willie Winkie, HN2050 .... 350.00
Wendy, HN2109, wht dress 85.00
Windflower, HN1920 .... 375.00
Windmill Lady, HN1400 .... 3,500.00
Wistful, HN2396 .... 225.00
Wizard, HN2877 .... 185.00
Wood Nymph, HN2192 .... 250.00
Yeoman of the Guard, HN688 .... 750.00
Young Master, HN2872 .... 250.00
Yum-Yum, HN1268 .... 750.00

Sweet Anne, HN1318, 7½", $375.00.

Flambe

Bowl, cockerel, 8" 190.00
Bulldog, 2¾" 145.00
Cat, #9, sitting, 5" 125.00
Cup & saucer, demitasse 50.00
Cup & saucer, woodcut, sm 65.00
Dragon, 14" 500.00
Duck, #112, sitting, 1½" 80.00
Duck, swimming, 1½x3" 75.00
Elephant, trunk up, 5" 250.00

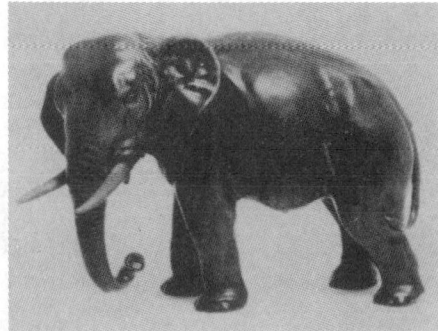

Elephant, signed Noke, 12", NM, $600.00.

Foo Dog 185.00
Fox, recumbent, #14, 4" 75.00

Hare, #330, ear up, 2½" 95.00
Hare, #656 .... 110.00
Owl 325.00
Rhinoceros, 19" 350.00
Tiger, crouching, sgn FM, 9½" 395.00
Tiger, sgn Noke, 14" 650.00
Tiger, stalking, 6x13" 1,000.00
Vase, Chang, crazed colors, sgn Noke, cylindrical, 9" 1,200.00
Vase, countryside scene, 6" 175.00
Vase, cows, woodcut, 1930s, 7" 50.00
Vase, deer, 7" 165.00
Vase, man fishing in stream, #1616, 13¼" 280.00
Vase, Sung, florals, mc on violet, sgn Noke, 8½x4½" 550.00
Vase, Veined Sung, fish, sgn FM, 8½" 200.00
Vase, Veined Sung, ovoid, 10" 225.00
Vase, woodcut, #1603, 7¼" 95.00

Series Ware

Ash tray, Welsh Ladies, rectangular, mk, 3½x4" 45.00
Biscuit jar, Royal Mail Coach, 8" 160.00
Biscuit jar, Sir Roger de Coverley, SP lid/rim/hdl, mk, 6¾" 225.00
Bowl, Coaching Days, coach departing, 8" 130.00
Bowl, Gaffers, oval, 11" 110.00
Bowl, Historic England, Dr Johnson at Temble Bar 45.00
Bowl, Nursery Series, girl by seashore 50.00
Bowl, Robin Hood, low ped ft, mk, 3¾x7½" 120.00
Bowl, Welsh Ladies, rnd, fluted rim, mk, 5½" 65.00
Box, Robin Hood, rectangular, mk, 2x4½x3⅝" 98.00
Box, Robin Hood, rectangular, 3x3½x4½" 125.00

Bread tray, Falstaff, 15" long, $100.00.

Child's set, Nursery Rhymes, bowl/plate/mug, ca 1909 .... 115.00
Coffeepot, Dickensware, Tony Weller, 7¼x3¾" 185.00
Cup & saucer, Dickensware, Adam, reg sz 45.00
Cup & saucer, Dickensware, sm 75.00
Cup & saucer, Don Quixote 100.00
Cup & saucer, Nursery Rhymes, Mother Goose 35.00
Cup & saucer, Robin Hood, mk, 2⅜x3⅜", & 5¾" 65.00
Dish, child's feeding; Shakespeare, Shylock, mk, 1½x8" 95.00
Dish, John Peel, 6", in silver stand 70.00
Flask, Kingsware, Dewars, Bonnie Prince Charlie 200.00
Jardiniere, Welsh Ladies, going to church, mk, 7¼x4¼" 325.00
Match striker, Dutch People, couple w/crying child, mk, 3" 145.00
Mug, Jackdaw of Rheims 75.00
Mug, Kingsware, Drink Wisely 185.00
Mug, shaving; Kingsware, sterling rim 550.00
Mug, Welsh Ladies, 3 ladies & child, mk, 1⅜x1⅜" 70.00

Pitcher, Arabian Nights, Ali Baba w/treasure, 6" **285.00**
Pitcher, Coaching Days, innkeeper talks to driver, 6" **120.00**
Pitcher, Dickensware, Curiosity Shop, sq **165.00**
Pitcher, Dutch People, emb children & windmill, mk, 6¼x4" **135.00**
Pitcher, Dutch People, 2 ladies, boy on bk, mk, 2x1¾" **85.00**
Pitcher, hot water; Shakespeare, Orlando, 7" **120.00**
Pitcher, Moorish Gate, 2 Arabs by gate, mk, 4¾x4" **80.00**
Pitcher, Old Curiosity Shop **145.00**
Pitcher, Old Moreton Hall, 2 courtiers at hall, cream sz **30.00**
Pitcher, Old Sea Dogs, Jack's the Boy for Play, 6" **125.00**
Pitcher, Shakespeare, Portia, mk, 6⅜x4⅝" **100.00**
Pitcher, Shakespeare, Romeo, 4½" **85.00**
Pitcher, Skating, Greek Key borders, cream sz **70.00**
Pitcher, Williamsburg, Bootmaker..**75.00**
Plate, Automobile Series, Deaf, scarce, 10⅜" **250.00**
Plate, Babes in Woods, girl w/basket & flowers, 8¾" **230.00**
Plate, Cavaliers, lion/cross/shield border, 10" **225.00**
Plate, Coaching Days, William, Ye Driver, 10" **65.00**
Plate, Eglington Tournament, knights in combat, 10"................**65.00**
Plate, Gibson Girl, Miss Babbles, the Authoress, 10" **85.00**
Plate, Gibson Girl, She Longs for Seclusion **95.00**
Plate, Gibson Girl, They Take a Morning Run..........................**110.00**
Plate, Golfers, Every Dog Has His Day, 10½" **175.00**
Plate, Gondoliers, ca 1940, 10" **55.00**
Plate, Old English Inns, King's Head, Chigwell, 10" **40.00**
Plate, Old English Proverbs, Fine Feather **50.00**
Plate, Shakespeare, Merry Wives of Windsor, bl & wht, 9"..........**65.00**
Plate, The Admiral, #TC1045..**68.00**
Plate, The Jester, 10" **60.00**
Plate, Treasure Island, Long John Silver w/crew, 13" **90.00**
Plate, Windsor Castle, 10½"..**40.00**
Sugar bowl, Fox Hunting, John Peel, men lead horses **40.00**
Teapot, Fisherwomen, mk, 5½" **195.00**
Teapot, Monks, bl & wht **185.00**
Teapot, Robin Hood, Little John, & Friar Tuck, 5½" **195.00**
Toothpick holder, sunset scene, 2-hdl **85.00**
Tray, Dickensware, Barnaby Rudge, 5⅜x4" **80.00**
Tray, Rustic England, hounds leap at fence, 5x10½" **60.00**
Tray, Shakespeare, Katharine, 15½" **95.00**
Vase, Babes in Woods, flow bl w/gold, 6⅜x4⅜".......................**245.00**
Vase, Babes in Woods, girl w/flower basket, mk, 7⅛" **195.00**
Vase, Babes in Woods, 2 girls/pixie, gold trim hdls, 8x3½" **265.00**
Vase, Babes in Woods, 3 girls & dog under tree, 6" **250.00**
Vase, Dickensware, Artful Dodger, mk, 3x1½" **95.00**
Vase, Dickensware, Barnaby Rudge, early mk, 4¾x2⅛" **75.00**
Vase, Dickensware, Barnaby Rudge, mk, 4¾" **70.00**
Vase, Dickensware, Cap'n Cuttle, early mk, 4⅝x2"...................**75.00**
Vase, Dickensware, Sydney Carton, hdls, 7" **175.00**
Vase, Dutch People, girl on rock, gold trim, mk, 5½" **125.00**
Vase, Isle of Man, man w/cane, mk, 3½x1¾"............................**75.00**
Vase, Robin Hood, flattened sq form, 5½x2x4".........................**95.00**
Vase, Shakespeare, Romeo & Juliet, mk, 11⅞x3⅛", pr **425.00**
Vase, Shakespeare, Shylock, 7x4" **135.00**
Vase, Warwick Castle, flow bl, 8¾" **110.00**
Vase, Welsh Ladies, 2 ladies by fence, mk, 3⅜x2⅝" **100.00**
Vase, Welsh Ladies, 2¾x2¼" **85.00**

Stoneware

Ash tray, Courage's Ale **45.00**
Beaker, hunting scene, brass rim, 5" **60.00**
Ducklings, M Marshall, 4½", pr **250.00**
Ewer, Cerrara, M Marshall, 7" **135.00**
Jug, hallmk silver rim, sgn Miss J Lasham, ca 1898.................**180.00**

Jug, Leatherware w/motto, SP rim, 8¼x6" **135.00**
Jug, puzzle; writings/sayings, Lambeth, 9" **225.00**
Lawn fountain, pelican figural, 15", EX **265.00**
Teapot, floral on tapestry, bl/wht on beige, mk, 5x4½" **125.00**
Tray, Kaola figure at bk, leaves at rim, Lambeth, 10½x5¼" **275.00**
Vase, goats, Hanna Barlow, 8½" **250.00**
Vase, horses/sheep, Hanna Barlow, 12" **325.00**
Vase, hunting scene, Coleman, miniature **35.00**
Vase, Nouveau birds, sq, FC Pope, 9" **80.00**

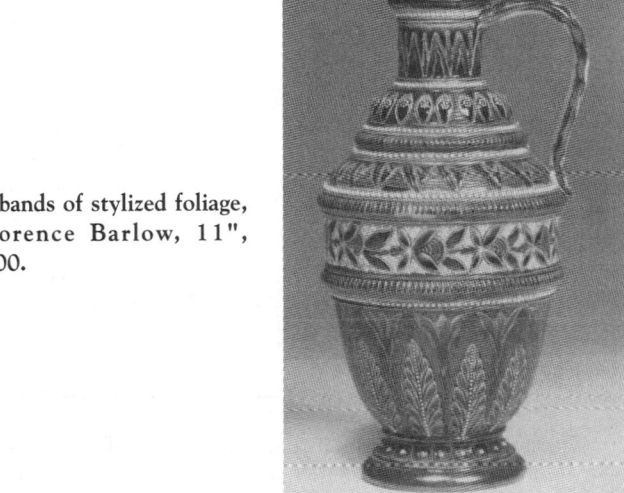

Ewer, bands of stylized foliage, by Florence Barlow, 11", $650.00.

Toby Jugs

Best Is None Too Good, D6107, 4½"..**275.00**
Charrington, One Toby Leads to Another **345.00**
Cliff Cornell, tan, 9"..**425.00**
Double XX, D6088, 6½"...**300.00**
Falstaff, 8½"..**95.00**
Fat Boy, D6264, 4½"...**225.00**
George Roby **2,750.00**
Honest Measure, D6108, 4½"...**80.00**
Huntsman, D6320, 7½" **95.00**
Jolly Toby, D6109, 6½" **85.00**
Sairey Gamp, D6263 ....**295.00**
Sir Winston Churchill, D6172, 5½"..**70.00**

Miscellaneous

Ash pot, Farmer John, D6007 ....**120.00**
Beaker, Wedding, A Princess for Wales, 1981 ....**30.00**
Biscuit jar, HP florals, SP lid/rim/hdl, Burslem, 6¼x5¾"............**145.00**
Bottle, whiskey; Scotsman in relief..**275.00**
Bottle, Zorro, red, 4" **32.00**
Cigarette Lighter, Beefeater...**95.00**
Jug, Pickwick Papers, D5756 ....**165.00**
Lighter, Poacher..**85.00**
Match holder, Mr Squeers, 2" **90.00**
Pitcher, Dewars Whiskey, Sporting Squire, 8¼" **265.00**
Pitcher, floral on cream, turq jewels, Burslem, #139596, 5" **225.00**
Teapot, Tony Weller **1,500.00**
Vase, children's portrait on cobalt/gold, Burslem, 10¼".............**260.00**
Vase, floral panels separated by branches, #8751, 1930, 14" **400.00**
Vase, Japanese iris, sgn Ethel Beard, 1925, 14½" **400.00**
Vase, lav, checked gray neck, cylindrical, 8" **200.00**

Vase, maple/beech impressions & sgraffito, 1880s, 18", pr 650.00
Vase, tapestry w/floral, banded ft & rim, Slater's Pat, 7" 170.00

Dragon Ware

An undulating moriage dragon with a fierce expression decorates shaded gray bisque backgrounds in this type of ware that was very popular as gift-shop items during the forties and fifties. It was produced in Japan and may sometimes be found with the Nippon mark. Only unmarked items are listed here.

Castor set, 6-pc on 10" tray 80.00
Cup & saucer, nude lithophane 25.00
Demitasse set, lithophane, 16-pc 130.00
Plate, 8" 18.00
Saucer, brn rim.. 3.00
Tea set, lithophane, 13-pc, serves 5...125.00
Tea set, pearlized cups, 11-pc, serves 4 ....65.00
Teapot, gold hdl, 7"..35.00
Vase, gold trim, bulbous, 6"..85.00
Vase, orange lustre, hdls, 9"..95.00
Vase, slender form, 6"..50.00

Dresden

The term Dresden is used today to indicate the porcelains that were produced in Meissen and Dresden, Germany, from the very early 18th century well into the next. John Bottger, a young alchemist, discovered the formula for the first true porcelain in 1708 while being held a virtual prisoner at the palace in Dresden because of the King's determination to produce a superior ware. Two years later a factory was erected in nearby Meissen with Bottger as director. There fine tableware, elaborate centerpieces, and exquisite figurines with applied details were produced. In 1731, to distinguish their product from the wares of such potters as Sevres, Worcester, Chelsea, and Derby, Meissen adopted their famous crossed swords trademark. During the next century, several potteries were producing porcelain in the 'Meissen style' in Dresden itself. Their wares were marked with their own logo and the Dresden indication. Those listed here are from that era. See the Meissen section for examples with the crossed swords marking.

Our advisor for this category is William Brinkley; he is listed in the Directory under Illinois.

Box, maid peering into pool, reserved on green with fired gold, 30" x 6½", $600.00.

Basket, rtcl w/appl flowers, 4 Baroque ft, floral hdl, 5x7" 125.00

Bowl, appl florals, int: HP floral, openwork, 4-ftd, 4x9" 175.00
Bowl, appl florals on front, int: HP floral, boat form, 17"............325.00
Bowl, fruit; mc florals, open lattice rim, mk, 5x8½" 350.00
Compote, rtcl bowl, appl roses on 3-ftd std, hdls, 8x8" 265.00
Compote, rtcl bowl, floral transfers, appl roses, 12x9"................275.00
Cup & saucer, 1700s couple in garden, gold trim, boat shape 55.00
Figurine, ballerina, Popplesdorf mk, 7", M............................150.00
Figurine, ballerina, red/wht dress w/appl flowers, 6½" 250.00
Figurine, ballerina, 4" 85.00
Figurine, chess game, man in red coat/lady in bl, 6½x5½"............450.00
Figurine, Dame de la Courde Francois I, C Thieme, 1875, 8"......350.00
Figurine, dancing couple, appl flowers, crown mk/MZ, 6x5" 225.00
Figurine, French boy & girl, bsk, sgn Colbert, 13"........................145.00
Figurine, group of musicians, 19" 775.00
Figurine, lady on a couch, pk, 7x4" 375.00
Figurine, lady w/instrument, man w/music book, 9½x9" 975.00
Figurine, man plays guitar, girl in chair, basket at ft, 13" 1,150.00
Figurine, Monika, 5½"..95.00
Figurine, Ring Around the Rosie, 3 girls, pk, 7x7" 275.00
Figurine, 17th-century girl, 5" 75.00
Figurine, 2 male violinists, 1 sitting, lady at piano, 10" 1,050.00
Figurine, 2 women/man at tea table, appl roses, 12" L 950.00
Floor lamp, spirals/emb leaves, 3 acanthus ft, 61"....................1,500.00
Lamp, HP flowers on ftd chalice form, sgn, 1860s, 12" 950.00
Pen holder, pk w/gold, ftd boat shape 68.00
Plate, Winter, maid in gr cape/hood w/sparrow, after Mucha.......600.00
Table, 19" dia top: floral w/cobalt band, leaf-cast tripod.......... 1,900.00
Urn, floral panels, goat hdls, ftd boat shape, Thieme, 10"............650.00
Urn, portraits, appl florals, sq base, 8", pr 165.00
Urn, 4 panels w/garden scenes, gold scrolls, 13½" 275.00

Dresser Accessories

All those lovely items that graced milady's dressing table – dresser sets, ring trees, figural or satin pincushions, manicure sets – were at the same time decorative as well as functional. Today they appeal to collectors for many reasons. The Victorian era is well represented by repousse silver-backed mirrors and brushes and pincushions that were used to display ornamental pins for the hair, hats, and scarves. The hair receiver – similar to a powder jar but with an opening in the lid – was used to hold the lovely strands of hair retrieved from the comb or brush. These were wound around the finger and tucked in the opening to be used later for hair jewelry and pictures, many of which survive to the present day. (See Hair Weaving.)

Celluloid dresser sets were popular during the late 1800s and early 1900s. Some included manicure tools, pill boxes, and buttonhooks, as well as the basic items. Because celluloid tends to break rather easily, a whole set may be hard to find today. (See also Plastics.) With the current interest in anything Art Deco, sets from the thirties and forties are especially collectible. These may be made of crystal, Bakelite, or silver, and the original boxes just as lavishly appointed as their contents.

Bonnet brush, repousse hollow hdl, mk sterling, EX.......................30.00
Case, blk leather, fitted, +8 toilet articles, Cartier, 13" 550.00
Compact, silver w/stylized deer & foliage, sgn CJ, 4" dia 75.00
Glove hook, Whiting, Lily of the Valley, 1885 ....48.00
Hair receiver, SP, vintage relief, ftd, Victorian 45.00
Hairbrush, sterling, Nouveau lady & flowers, EX 150.00
Jar, powder; Cubist, transparent pk, Jeannette......................17.50
Jar, powder; graduation hat form, pk frost 20.00
Jar, powder; military hat form, cobalt, Paden City, 5"....................45.00
Jar, powder; rose blossom form, frosted pk....................................40.00
Jar, powder; sailboat finial lid, transparent gr................................60.00

Dresser set, Art Nouveau silver, Wm. Kerr & Co., $700.00.

Jar, powder; treasure chest form, gr frost, 4-ftd 40.00
Manicure set, Fr ivory, 17-pc in leather case, EX 65.00
Nail file, sterling, repousse 25.00
Set, celluloid, HP bl & peach flowers, 3-pc 45.00
Set, celluloid, pk/blk Deco decor on tan, glass tray, 10-pc 195.00
Set, pearlized gr celluloid, 12-pc in blk case, EX 115.00
Set, red/blk/pearl plastic, Art Deco geometrics, 6-pc, EX 125.00
Wig curler, wrought iron, scissors shape, ball ends, 10" L...............65.00

Dryden

James Dryden opened his pottery in Ellsworth, Kansas, in 1946. Within a year, he was producing 2,000 pieces per week, and the pottery continued to grow. During the 1950s some of the pottery was subcontracted to Van Briggle. In 1956 Dryden moved to Hot Springs, Arkansas.

Ellsworth clay was dark tan, while pieces made in Hot Springs were of white clay. This helps to date the ware, all of which is marked. Various marks were used, but all include either the words 'Dryden' or 'Ozark Frontier.'

Ewer, tan & gr mottled, Ozark Frontier sticker, 7½".....................15.00
Figurine, elephant, mk 'Souvenir,' 3x4" 18.00
Pitcher, bl, #92, 6" 10.00
Pitcher, brn, bird hdl, #94, w/sticker, 6½" 25.00
Spittoon vase, brn/bl, sgn ARS, gold sticker, lg............................45.00
Teapot, bl, w/lid, sm 28.00
Vase, bl/gr, #LOL-77, 3½x3¼" 15.00
Vase, blk, #104 ....12.00
Vase, boot form, bl, 5" 12.50

Duncan and Miller

The firm that became known as the Duncan and Miller Glass Company in 1900 was organized in 1874 in Pittsburgh, Pennsylvania, a partnership between George Duncan, his sons Harry and James, and his son-in-law Augustus Heisey. John Ernest Miller was hired as their designer. He is credited with creating the most famous of all Duncan's glassware lines, Three Face. (See Pattern Glass.) The George Duncan and Sons Glass Company, as it was titled, was only one of eighteen companies that merged in 1891 with U.S. Glass. Soon after the Pitts-

burgh factory burned in 1892, the association was dissolved, and Heisey left the firm to set up his own factory in Newark, Ohio. Duncan built his new plant in Washington, Pennsylvania, where he continued to make pressed glassware in such notable patterns as Bagware, Amberette, Duncan Flute, Button Arches, and Zippered Slash. The firm was eventually sold to U.S. Glass in Tiffin, Ohio, and officially closed in August, 1955.

In addition to the early pressed dinnerware patterns, today's Duncan and Miller collectors enjoy searching for opalescent vases in many patterns and colors, frosted 'Satin Tone' glassware, acid-etched designs, and lovely stemware such as the Rock Crystal cuttings. Milk glass was made in limited quantity and is considered a good investment. Ruby glass, Ebony (a lovely opaque black glass popular during the twenties and thirties), and, of course, the glass animal and bird figurines are all highly valued examples of the art of Duncan and Miller.

Expect to pay at least 25% more than values listed for 'color' for ruby and cobalt and as much as 50% more in the Georgian, Pall Mall and Sandwich lines. Pink, green, and amber Sandwich is worth approximately 30% more than the same items in crystal. Milk glass examples of American Way are valued up to 30% higher than color, 50% higher in Pall Mall. Add approximately 40% to listed prices for opalescent items. Etchings, cuttings and other decorations will increase values by about 50%. For further study, we recommend *The Encyclopedia of Duncan Glass*, by Gail Krause; she is listed in the Directory under Pennsylvania.

Animals and Birds

Donkey..475.00
Goose, fat...225.00
Heron, 7" 115.00
Pheasant..475.00
Ruffled Grouse 500.00
Swan, bl opal, W&F, spreadwing, 10x12½" 225.00
Swan, crystal w/gray cut, 10½" 150.00
Swan, gr opal, W&F, spreadwing, 10x12½" 200.00
Swordfish 145.00

American Way, crystal/frost; vase, 9½" 45.00
Astaire, ruby; champagne 12.00
Astaire, ruby; cocktail, 3-oz 12.00
Astaire, ruby; cordial..28.00
Canterbury, color; basket, oval, 10" 110.00
Canterbury, color; candlestick, 6", pr 38.00
Canterbury, color; candy dish 65.00
Canterbury, color; compote 35.00
Canterbury, color; flower arranger, 5½"...45.00
Canterbury, color; tray, oval 12.00
Canterbury, color; vase, crimped, 4" 16.00
Canterbury, color; violet vase, crimped, 2¾" 14.00
Canterbury, crystal; bowl, dessert 6.00
Canterbury, crystal; bowl, oval, 9"...25.00
Canterbury, crystal; bowl, 10½"..25.00
Canterbury, crystal; candlestick, low 12.00
Canterbury, crystal; celery, hdls 18.00
Canterbury, crystal; cigarette box, SP lid 45.00
Canterbury, crystal; compote, high ft 20.00
Canterbury, crystal; creamer & sugar bowl, ind, +tray 22.00
Canterbury, crystal; gardenia bowl, 7½"...13.00
Canterbury, crystal; goblet, water 10.00
Canterbury, crystal; pitcher, martini 295.00
Canterbury, crystal; relish, 2-part, hdls, 7" 12.00
Canterbury, crystal; tray, 4-part 14.00
Canterbury, crystal; tray, 5" 12.00

Canterbury mayonnaise, 3-piece set, $45.00.

Caribbean, color; bowl, oval, hdls, 7" 75.00
Caribbean, color; bowl, 9" 95.00
Caribbean, color; cheese compote 35.00
Caribbean, color; finger bowl 45.00
Caribbean, color; flower bowl, 12" 60.00
Caribbean, color; goblet, water 40.00
Caribbean, color; nappy, hdls, 7" 55.00
Caribbean, color; pitcher, milk; 16-oz, 4¾" 125.00
Caribbean, color; plate, torte 55.00
Caribbean, color; plate, 7½" 28.00
Caribbean, color; relish, 5-compartment 95.00
Caribbean, color; saucer 15.00
Caribbean, color; shakers, 3", pr 85.00
Caribbean, color; sherbet, low 15.00
Caribbean, color; syrup, 8" 250.00
Caribbean, crystal; champagne 15.00
Caribbean, crystal; cocktail 18.00
Caribbean, crystal; old fashioned 25.00
Caribbean, crystal; relish, 5-part, 12" 40.00
Caribbean, crystal; sherbet, low 10.00
Caribbean, crystal; tray, center hdl, 8" 50.00
Feathers, color; vase, cornucopia 65.00
First Love, crystal; candlestick, dbl, #30, pr 52.00
First Love, crystal; candlestick, dbl, 8½", pr 150.00
First Love, crystal; candy dish, 3-compartment 70.00
First Love, crystal; champagne 25.00
First Love, crystal; cheese stand 30.00
First Love, crystal; compote 30.00
First Love, crystal; decanter, w/stopper, 32-oz 250.00
First Love, crystal; goblet, tall, 10-oz 25.00
First Love, crystal; plate, bread & butter 9.00
First Love, crystal; plate, sandwich; hdls, 11" 60.00
First Love, crystal; relish, 2-compartment, 6" 22.00
First Love, crystal; relish, 3-compartment, 7" 22.00
First Love, crystal; relish, 3-compartment, 8" 30.00
First Love, crystal; vase, #117, 8" 70.00
First Love, crystal; vase, cornucopia 95.00
Hobnail, color; basket, 10" 125.00
Hobnail, color; candy dish 125.00
Hobnail, color; champagne 22.50
Hobnail, color; flip vase, crimped, 8" 68.00
Hobnail, color; goblet, water; 9-oz 18.00
Hobnail, color; iced tea, flat 30.00
Hobnail, color; pitcher, 64-oz 250.00
Hobnail, color; sugar bowl, 5-oz 12.00

Hobnail, crystal; bowl, centerpiece; crimped, 12" 25.00
Hobnail, crystal; bowl, deep, 9" 20.00
Hobnail, crystal; cake plate, ftd, 10" 45.00
Hobnail, crystal; candlestick 12.00
Hobnail, crystal; candy basket, hdl, 5" 22.50
Hobnail, crystal; champagne 8.00
Hobnail, crystal; cocktail 8.00
Hobnail, crystal; comport 24.00
Hobnail, crystal; creamer & sugar bowl, +tray 25.00
Hobnail, crystal; flip vase, 8" 20.00
Hobnail, crystal; goblet, water 10.00
Hobnail, crystal; hat vase, 6x9" 47.00
Hobnail, crystal; mug, cobalt hdl, 3¾" 15.00
Hobnail, crystal; nappy, 6" 10.00
Hobnail, crystal; punch bowl, w/underplate & 8 cups 125.00
Hobnail, crystal; relish, oval, 12" 22.00
Hobnail, crystal; top hat, 4" 30.00
Hobnail, crystal; violet vase, 7½" 40.00
Language of Flowers, crystal; bowl, 11½" 35.00
Language of Flowers, crystal; candlestick, dbl, #30, 6x8", pr ...63.00
Language of Flowers, crystal; candy dish 30.00
Language of Flowers, crystal; creamer & sugar bowl 27.50
Language of Flowers, crystal; mayonnaise, ftd 25.00
Mardi Gras, crystal; gas shade 27.00
Mardi Gras, crystal; punch cup 5.50
Pall Mall, color; swan, 10½" 80.00
Pall Mall, color; swan, 7" 50.00
Pall Mall, crystal; swan, silver overlay, 7" 35.00
Pall Mall, crystal; swan, 3½" 25.00
Pall Mall, crystal; swan, 7" 30.00
Passion Flower, crystal; vase, cornucopia; 8" 38.00
Sandwich, color; bowl, ice cream; 4¼" 16.00
Sandwich, color; finger bowl 18.00
Sandwich, color; goblet, 6" 22.00
Sandwich, color; shaker, ind 12.00
Sandwich, crystal; ash tray, ind 10.00
Sandwich, crystal; basket, high, 7" 90.00
Sandwich, crystal; basket, low, 6½" 45.00
Sandwich, crystal; bonbon, heart shape, ring hdl 15.00
Sandwich, crystal; bowl, flared, 11½" 55.00
Sandwich, crystal; bowl, 5" 9.00
Sandwich, crystal; cake salver, 13" 70.00
Sandwich, crystal; candelabrum, 1-light, 10", pr 110.00
Sandwich, crystal; candlestick & bobeche, no prisms, 10" 70.00
Sandwich, crystal; candlesticks, 4", pr 29.00
Sandwich, crystal; candy dish, ftd, 8½" 60.00
Sandwich, crystal; coaster 7.00
Sandwich, crystal; cocktail 10.00
Sandwich, crystal; compote, 5½" 20.00
Sandwich, crystal; creamer & sugar bowl 25.00
Sandwich, crystal; cup & saucer 12.00
Sandwich, crystal; epergne, flower & fruit, tall, 3-pc 175.00
Sandwich, crystal; flower bowl, 12" 60.00
Sandwich, crystal; goblet, 9-oz, 6" 12.00
Sandwich, crystal; jelly dish, 3" 10.00
Sandwich, crystal; mayonnaise, ftd, 5" 22.00
Sandwich, crystal; mint dish, hdl, 7" 22.00
Sandwich, crystal; oil cruet, 5¾" 30.00
Sandwich, crystal; pitcher, ice lip 125.00
Sandwich, crystal; plate, torte; cupped, 14" 60.00
Sandwich, crystal; plate, 12" 35.00
Sandwich, crystal; plate, 7" 11.00
Sandwich, crystal; plate, 8" 10.00
Sandwich, crystal; syrup 50.00

Sandwich, crystal; tray, divided, oval, 7".........................15.00
Sandwich, crystal; tray, pickle; oval, 7" 15.00
Sandwich, crystal; tray, relish; oblong, 3-compartment, 10"..........37.00
Sandwich, crystal; tumbler, flat, 4¼".............................12.00
Sandwich, crystal; tumbler, juice; ftd, 5-oz......................12.00
Sandwich, crystal; vase, fan form, ftd, 5"........................30.00
Sandwich, crystal; vase, ftd, 10".................................42.00
Sandwich, crystal; wine...14.00
Sanibel, color; bookend vase......................................60.00
Sanibel, color; float garden, oval, 13"...........................45.00
Sanibel, color; hors d'oeuvres, 14"...............................90.00
Sanibel, color; nappy, fruit; 6½".................................20.00
Sanibel, color; plate, salad; 8½".................................28.00
Sanibel, color; relish, 3-compartment, oval, 12"..................40.00
Spiral Flutes, color; baked apple, 7½"............................20.00
Spiral Flutes, color; bowl, flanged, 8½"..........................17.50
Spiral Flutes, color; compote, 4½x5¼".............................25.00
Spiral Flutes, color; compote, 5¾x6½".............................30.00
Spiral Flutes, color; cruet......................................100.00
Spiral Flutes, color; cup, seafood................................15.00
Spiral Flutes, color; cup & saucer................................15.00
Spiral Flutes, color; iced tea, flat..............................40.00
Spiral Flutes, color; oyster plate, 3-flange......................12.00
Spiral Flutes, color; plate, 8½"...................................6.00
Spiral Flutes, color; platter, 11"................................45.00
Spiral Flutes, color; sherbet.....................................10.00
Spiral Flutes, color; sugar bowl..................................10.00
Spiral Flutes, color; sweetmeat, open.............................25.00
Spiral Flutes, color; sweetmeat, w/lid...........................125.00
Spiral Flutes, color; tumbler, ftd, 5"............................17.50
Spiral Flutes, color; vase, 10½"..................................40.00
Spiral Flutes, color; vase, 8¾"...................................30.00
Spiral Flutes, color; wine..15.00
Sylvan, bl opal; swan, 12½".......................................195.00
Sylvan, color; bowl, leaf form, 6"................................12.00
Sylvan, yel opal; swan, 5½".......................................150.00
Tear Drop, crystal; ash tray, rnd, ind, 3¼".........................6.00
Tear Drop, crystal; bonbon, hdld, 6"..............................20.00
Tear Drop, crystal; butter dish, SP lid, ¼-lb....................17.50
Tear Drop, crystal; candlesticks, pr..............................47.00
Tear Drop, crystal; champagne......................................6.00
Tear Drop, crystal; cheese compote................................20.00
Tear Drop, crystal; claret, 4-oz, 5½".............................14.00
Tear Drop, crystal; cup, ftd.......................................9.00
Tear Drop, crystal; gardenia bowl, label, 11½"....................32.00
Tear Drop, crystal; ice bucket, ftd, monogram.....................37.00
Tear Drop, crystal; iced tea, ftd, 5½"............................12.50
Tear Drop, crystal; marmalade, 4".................................35.00
Tear Drop, crystal; mustard.......................................20.00
Tear Drop, crystal; olive dish, 2-compartment, 6"..................7.00
Tear Drop, crystal; preserve dish, hdls...........................25.00
Tear Drop, crystal; tumbler, flat, 12-oz..........................12.00
Tear Drop, crystal; wine, 4⅞".....................................14.00
Terrace, color; ash tray, sq, lg..................................40.00
Terrace, color; ash tray, sq, sm..................................28.00
Terrace, color; plate, dinner; sq.................................65.00
Terrace, color; plate, sq, 6".....................................16.50
Willow, crystal; sherbet/champagne, 4¾"...........................14.00

Durand

Durand Art Glass was a division of Vineland Glass Works in Vineland, New Jersey. Created in 1924, it was geared specifically toward the manufacture of fine handcrafted artware. Iridescent, opalescent, and cased glass was used to create such patterns as King Tut, reminiscent of Tiffany and Steuben. Production halted in 1931 after the death of Victor Durand. Very few examples are signed, and unmarked pieces are often mistaken for Steuben or Quezal. Unmarked items are often hard to sell, sometimes bringing only about half the price of a similar but signed piece.

Compote, feathers, wht on ruby to clear, canary ped, 4½x6"......550.00
Cordial, ruby bowl/base, amber stem, ribbed......................190.00
Ginger jar, gold w/gold threading, rosette on lid, 7½"..........1,000.00
Ginger jar, heart leaves/vines, bl/gold, rosette on lid, 7".......2,300.00
Ginger jar, King Tut, bl/gr irid, amber prunt on lid, 7"..........1,900.00
Goblet, feathers, wht on ruby/clear, cut rim, amber ped ft.......500.00
Goblet, feathers on cobalt, amber stem & base, unsgn.............275.00
Lamp, table; vine & leaf on irid baluster base, cloth shade......575.00
Mug, gold, wht int, appl amber hdl, unsgn........................140.00
Plate, amber w/cut flowers in center, threaded border, 11".......125.00
Plate, gr cut to clear roses in border, feather center, 8".......450.00
Plate, red, scalloped/ribbed, 7".................................200.00
Powder jar, King Tut, gold/bl-gr, orange int, star-cut lid......1,150.00
Rose bowl, clear bl-amber, floral/leaf cuttings, ftd, 5".........475.00
Shade, feathers/threading, gold/wht/bl, unsgn, 8", pr............400.00
Shade, feathers/threading, 7½", in mk EPNS stand, 12"............125.00
Tazza, ruby w/Spanish yel twist stem, ribbed optic, 4x7½".......225.00

Vase, 10-ribbed bottle form in cobalt with silver-blue lustre, 2 factory labels, 12", $1,400.00.

Vase, bl irid on amber irid base, 8½"............................300.00
Vase, bl w/bl-gold threading, flared rim, 6¾"...................550.00
Vase, bl-gold, bulbous w/flared top, sgn/#1490-6, 6"............700.00
Vase, bl/purple/gr irid, ribbed, #1926-7, 6¾"...................900.00
Vase, bronze, pearl int, sgn/#1812-6, 6½".......................450.00
Vase, burnt orange lustre, sgn, #1722 ½-6, 6x3".................370.00
Vase, feathers, gr & amber, orange int, ftd, unsgn, 7"..........600.00
Vase, feathers, ruby/wht, bulbous w/cone ft, unsgn, 9½".........900.00
Vase, feathers, ruby/wht, ruby cut to clear floral, 9½".......1,200.00
Vase, feathers, ruby/wht, sgn/#19127, 6"........................950.00
Vase, feathers/threading, orange/wht/bl, unsgn, 8¾", NM.........450.00
Vase, feathers/threading, 3 gold lions' heads, unsgn, 10".......600.00
Vase, heart leaves, bl-gold on opal, gold threads/int, 12"......900.00
Vase, heart leaves/vines, bl on red, ovoid, unsgn, 6½"..........525.00
Vase, heart leaves/vines, dk bl irid, cylindrical, 7½"..........550.00
Vase, heart leaves/vines, gold on irid opal, 6".................375.00

Vase, heart leaves/vines, wht on dk bl, sgn/#1710-4, 4" **1,150.00**
Vase, King Tut, orange & gr, sgn/#1710-4, 4" **475.00**
Vase, King Tut, orange & gr, sgn/#1812-6, 6½" **125.00**
Vase, King Tut, pk irid 'Lady Gay Rose,' low ft, 12½" **2,300.00**
Vase, King Tut, pk/gold, orange rim/cream int, ftd, sgn, 7" **1,300.00**
Vase, King Tut, pk/gold, orange rim/cream int, unsgn, 10" **1,500.00**
Vase, lt/dk gr vertical bars, opal int, ribbed, ftd, 8½"................**900.00**
Vase, lt/dk ruby vertical bars, orange int, sgn/#, 12½" **3,500.00**
Vase, swirls, wht on gold, flared, 7" **400.00**
Wine, feathers, ruby/wht, cut rim, amber stem, unsgn **250.00**
Wine, feathers, wht/gr on gr transparent, lt gr ped ft....................**275.00**

Durant Kilns

The Durant Pottery Company operated in Bedford Village, New York, in the early 1900s. Its founder was Mrs. Clarence Rice; she was aided by L. Volkmar to whom she assigned the task of technical direction. (See also Volkmar.) The artware and table ware they produced was simple in form and decoration. The creative aspects of the work were carried on almost entirely by Volkmar himself, with only a minimal crew to help with production. After Mrs. Rice's death in 1919, the pottery was purchased by Volkmar, who chose to drop the Durant name by 1930. Prior to 1919 the ware was marked simply 'Durant' and dated. After that time a stylized 'V' was added.

Bowl, bl & blk, flared scalloped, dtd 1914, 4x6" **250.00**
Bowl, Chinese plum, bl crackle int, oval, dtd 1917, 4x8x7" **295.00**
Bowl, crazed bright aqua, low, dtd 1917, 15" **495.00**
Vase, cobalt, exposed ft, flanged U-form, 1917, 6x7½" **175.00**

Easter

Eggs, bunnies, chicks, and baskets have all become basic elements of our Easter celebrations; and the older, more interesting examples are being collected, often for nostalgic reasons, and displayed during the holidays to make the festivities brighter.

Box, Fanny Farmy, children's illus, 1930s **18.00**
Candy container, duck, papier-mache, Germany, 1920s, 5", EX ..**175.00**
Candy container, duck, wax, 5½", EX..**55.00**
Candy container, egg, tin, mc pnt, Chein, 1930s, 4½x5" **45.00**
Candy container, rabbit, pressed cb, molded clothes, 8", EX..........**75.00**
Candy container, rabbit w/carrot, compo, head removes, 5" **65.00**
Candy container, 2" cotton chicken on crepe-lined box, EX **24.00**
Egg, paper, Art Deco florals on purple, 5", EX **35.00**
Egg, paper, child painting/egg-hatching scenes, 3½" **25.00**
Egg, paper, children w/rabbit & chicken, minor wear, 3½" **30.00**
Egg, paper, rabbits on red, minor wear, 2¾" **25.00**
Figurine, rabbit w/carrot, papier-mache, 5"....................................**35.00**
Plate, Easter Chicks, milk glass, 7"...**38.00**
Plate, Easter Rabbits, milk glass, old pnt, 6¼" **42.00**

Elfinware

Made in Germany from about 1920 until the 1940s, these miniature vases, boxes, salt cellars, and miscellaneous novelty items are characterized by the tiny applied flowers that often cover their entire surface. Pieces with animals and birds are the most valuable, followed by the more interesting examples such as diminutive grand pianos, candle holders, etc. See also Salts, Open.

Bottle, cologne; appl roses, gr lustre, 8½".......................................**45.00**

Box, appl flowers, oval, brass hinge, 4x3" **75.00**
Box, HP florals on fan form, orig label, 2¼x3" **30.00**

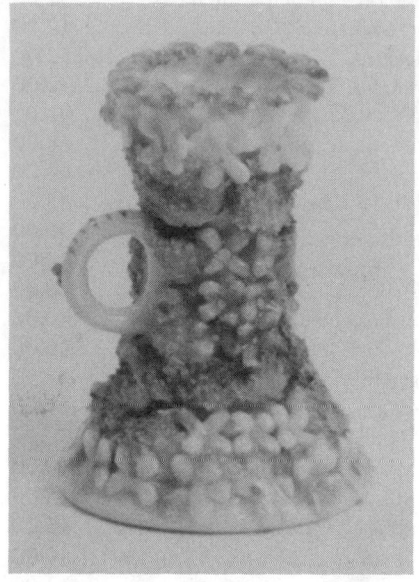

Candlestick, 2½", $50.00.

Figurine, pig, 1⅞x1¾"...**70.00**
Inkwell, 3x3¾" **35.00**
Salt cellar, swan **55.00**
Slipper, 2¼"..**35.00**
Teapot...**35.00**
Vase, allover florals, cylindrical, 2¾"..**40.00**

Epergnes

Popular during the Victorian era, epergnes were fancy centerpieces often consisting of several tiers of vases (called lilies), candle holders, or dishes, or a combination of components. They were made in all types of art glass, and some were set in ornate plated frames.

Amethyst swirl w/gold festoons, 1-lily in fluted bowl **295.00**
Bl rim 11" bowl w/1 opal hobnail lily; SP dtd 1895 std, 11".........**400.00**
Bl satin Dia Quilt, 3 bowls, lily in 1; SP ft dtd 1914, 24" **1,000.00**
Cranberry bowl, 1-lily, wht serpentine decor, 15"....................**325.00**
Cranberry, clear ft/scallops, 1-lily, 9¾x7¼"..............................**265.00**
Cranberry opal, 2 hanging baskets, 9½" dia **1,000.00**
Fireglow w/flowers, 1-lily, crimped; ornate ftd fr, 19x11" **275.00**

George III silver epergne by George Ashforth & Co., Sheffield, 1801, 11½", $1,700.00.

Gr opal bowl w/emb sqs, 1-lily; metal ft/mts, 13½" **195.00**
Orange to clear, overall threading, 3-lily, Webb, 15x9½" **675.00**
Pk frosted bowl, sq ruffled lily; metal ft/mts, 12" **225.00**
Pk ruffled rim 10" bowl; Pairpoint SP fr w/beaded hdl **190.00**
Pk w/gr rims & rigaree, 3 hanging baskets, 15" dia base **725.00**
Rubena, 3-lily; metal ft & mts, 18x10¼" **375.00**
Vaseline opal, 3-lily, appl vaseline spiral trim, 17½" **365.00**
Vaseline w/rigaree & pk opal rims, 3 baskets+lily, 10" base **400.00**

Erickson

Carl Erickson of Bremen, Ohio, produced hand-formed glassware from 1943 until 1960 in artistic shapes, no two of which were identical. One of the characteristics of his work was the air bubbles that were captured within the glass. Though most examples are clear, colored items were also made. Rather than to risk compromising his high standards by selling the factory, when Erickson retired, the plant was dismantled and sold.

Bottle, caramel cased, clear bubble stopper, signed, 9", $275.00.

Bowl, paperweight, amber over crystal, 8" **58.00**
Bowl, pk, bubble ball center, 13", +pr 5" sticks **100.00**
Candle holder, purple, bubble designs, 2", pr **90.00**
Cruet, crystal, ground stopper, 9½" **60.00**
Vase, gray, controlled bubble base, fan form, unmk......................**125.00**
Vase, smoke, Art Deco, sq base..**95.00**

Eskimo Artifacts

While ivory carvings made from walrus tusks or whale teeth have been the most emphasized articles of Eskimo art, basketry and wood-working are other areas in which these Alaskan Indians excell. Their designs are effected through the application of simple yet dramatic lines and almost stark decorative devices. Though not pursued to the extent of American Indian art, the unique work of this northern tribe is beginning to attract the serious attention of today's collectors.

Adze, whalebone/antler hdl, excavated, pre-historic, 11x10" **250.00**
Basket, baleen, woven motif, ivory lid w/wolf surmount, 4"..........**900.00**
Basket, carrying; twined, red/bl design, Aleut, 1880, 10x5" **160.00**
Basket, coiled, gr/orange sqs, w/lid, Hooper Bay, 1940, 7x9"..........**95.00**
Basket, coiled, red/blk crosses, w/lid, 1900, 5x8" **90.00**

Basket, coiled bowl form w/crosses, 1920, 4x9½" dia.....................**55.00**
Basket, geometrics/'Alaska,' coiled, w/lid, 1920, 15x14" **300.00**
Basket, rye grass/silk embr, openwork edge/swing hdl, 3½" **425.00**
Basket, storage; bw heart/floral, oval w/lid, 1920, 11x9" **150.00**
Basket, twined, red wool florals, w/lid, 1890, 9x7"........................**275.00**
Bowl, stone, cvd tab hdls, Arctic Circle, pre-historic, 11" **300.00**
Bracelet, expansion; fossil ivory, 2 seals in center, 1930 ....**45.00**
Bracelet, fossil ivory, full rnd form, 1800, 1½" wide **200.00**
Comb, ivory, 4-prong, fish finial, 3" H...**100.00**
Cribbage board, ivory, cvd walrus scenes, 1910, 15x1½" **275.00**
Cribbage board, ivory, eng foliage/2 seals, 3 pegs, 5" L **100.00**
Cribbage board, ivory, etched/inlay genre scenes, 1910, 18"........**175.00**
Cribbage board, ivory, 4 high-relief creatures+mc eng, 13"..........**900.00**
Cup & saucer, finely coiled basketry, 1910, 5" dia **90.00**
Cvg, blk stone man w/windblown parka, 1920, 7x4" **100.00**
Cvg, caribou horn w/igloo+3 human faces, 1910, 12x9" **60.00**
Cvg, gr stone, standing man, 1930, 4x1¾"...**75.00**
Cvg, ivory, human effigy, Punuk culture, pre-historic, 3" **145.00**
Cvg, ivory, seal effigy, Punuk culture, pre-historic, 3½" **120.00**
Cvg, soapstone, polar bear w/seal, by Ashoona, 1984, 9x10" .. **1,300.00**
Cvg, walrus tusk, dog sled+5 huskies, 12½", NM **225.00**
Doll, fossil ivory w/inlaid eyes, pre-historic, 1¾" **115.00**
Doll, ivory, human form, inlaid features, 1800, 4½" **300.00**
Doll, wood, lady/baby on bk, hide/cloth dress, jtd, 16" **800.00**
Drum, hide-covered/trade bead suspensions, 1860, 3x11x7"........**110.00**
Gun case, seal skin, 1890, 46" **275.00**
Harpoon, pnt wood, 3-prong bone tip, sinew wrap, 55" **150.00**
Harpoon, wood, bone head/tip, guide/bladder float, 1870, 43" ...**325.00**
Harpoon, wood, bone head/tip, sinew/rawhide wrap, 1850, 61" ..**300.00**
Harpoon, wood, ivory & bone tip, 1870, 66x1" **85.00**
Harpoon, wood, ivory head, sinew wrap, 1850, 55x1"...................**155.00**
Harpoon, wood, stone point/pnt rings/ivory toggle, 1850, 65".....**160.00**
Harpoon, wood, triple ivory tips, 1870, 50x¾" **95.00**
Knife, cvd/eng bone animal head hdl, stone blade, 1870, 11"......**200.00**
Knife rest, ivory, bar w/bear head ea end, baleen inlay, 9"............**120.00**
Lamp, oil; compressed clay/seal blood, excavated, 6" dia **200.00**
Lure, cvd/pnt ivory fish shape, 1800, 3½x½", 4 for........................**60.00**
Necklace, fossil ivory beads, St Lawrence Island, 1880, 32".........**110.00**
Necklace, ivory beads, graduated, 1900, 16" **60.00**
Pipe, cvd ivory, sailor's pipe form, 1800, 5" **60.00**
Pipe, gray stone, rawhide-wrap wood hdl, 1840, 11x2" **200.00**
Shakers, cvd/pnt ivory, stylized seal heads, 1920, 3", pr **80.00**

Miniature sled, baleen and ivory, built to scale, 28" long, $2,300.00.

Snow goggles, wood, visor-like rim above viewing slit, 6" **400.00**
Sword, steel w/cvd ivory hdl, fish skin wraps, 1880, 42x2" **250.00**
Toggle, fossil ivory, 'eye' motif, sinew string, 4x1" **70.00**
Umiak, child's toy, hide covered, 1880, 32" long...........................**125.00**

Fabris Porcelain

Similar in quality, workmanship, and design, fine Fabris porcelain sculptures might easily be confused with Meissen and Dresden pieces; only the red-iron anchor mark denotes the difference.

The French sculptor, Jean-Pierre Varion, formerly of the Vincennes factory, settled in Este, Italy, during the 1750s. He died soon after developing his own formula for porcelain. His wife, Fiorina, and a partner, Antonio Costa, formed a business and manufactured the first Fabris sculptures at Bassano del Grappa in 1875. Many of the figurines and groupings were after paintings by 18th-century artists such as Fragonard, the Rococo decorator; Longhi; and the playwright, Carlo Goldoni. Most of the figures and groups were of a limited production; strict attention was given to detail.

The Museum Collection, a 1980-1982 re-issue, utilized the very early molds. A gold anchor mark was used on this limited line only; after this period, they reverted back to the red-iron anchor. Items listed here bear the red mark unless noted otherwise.

Aunt, aunt on sofa chaperoning 2 lovers, 9x16" **2,000.00**
Beauties, 2 ladies on flowered balcony, 8½x10" 650.00
Cecilia, girl w/wht skirt, 2 flower baskets, 4½x5¼" 300.00
Coppersmith, man sits/mends copper pot, tricorn hat, 5½x8" 325.00
Flamenco Dancer, girl in red bodice & lace dress, 13½" 950.00
Gertrude, flowered dress, knitting bag, 6x7" 425.00
Girl in pk lace skirt, holding basket of flowers, 5x8½" 550.00
Harlequin's Love, girl & clown in costume, seated, 11x15" **2,700.00**
Lady Beatrice, wht skirt, fashion magazine in lap, 7½x7½" 550.00

Lovers, 9" x 7", $750.00.

Margarita, girl w/ft on bl pillow, wht skirt, 6x6" 350.00
Melon Vendor, brn pants, wht apron, & melons, 5½x10½" 350.00
Musical, 2 figures: man at a piano, woman singing, 6½x8½" 550.00
Rug Vendor, long bl coat, rugs over shoulder, 10" 550.00
Swing, girl on a swing in floral & leaf arbor, 10x11½" **1,500.00**
2-Faced Woman, young girl on 1 side, old hag on other, 9" 450.00

Face Jugs, Contemporary

Grotesque, often humorous faces are the subject for handcrafted stoneware jugs made by various country potters, many of whom work in the southern states.

Appl features, gr ash glaze, Reggie Meaders, 15½" 65.00
Appl features, porc teeth, redware, Rinhardt, 1900, 7", EX..... **1,400.00**
Brn, molded features, wht eyes/teeth, John Brock 10/50, 1-gal 60.00
Brn alkaline, china teeth, stone eyes, Chester Hewell, 1-gal 45.00
Brn/gr alkaline, appl lizard hdl, Chester Hewell, 1-gal 25.00
Brn/tan, wht eyes/teeth, appl hdl, Marie Rogers, 1½" 55.00

Devil mask, brown glaze with red streaks, signed BH, inscribed 'beautiful day, Oct. 8,' early 20th century, 19", $600.00.

Brn/wht diagonals, wht eyes/teeth, appl brows/hdl, mk CL, 1-qt...**45.00**
Gray, bl incised/molded hair & brows, Jerry Brown 6-88, 1-gal **45.00**
Inset teeth, lg modeled ears, 2-hdl, HB Craig, 17" 300.00
Lg ears/lips/nose, gr ash glaze, Lanier Meaders, 9" 320.00
Wht eyes/row of teeth, gr ash glaze, Chester Hewell, 8½".............65.00

Fairings

Fairings, small chinaware figural groups that portray amusing (if not risque) scenes of courting couples, marital woes, and family feuds, were popular purchases and prizes at 19th-century English fairs. From 1840 through the 1850s, their bases were embossed with marks that identified the manufacturer as well as the artist who applied the polychrome enameling. From 1860 until 1870, they were no longer marked and became smaller in size. During the 1870s, they retained their smaller size but once again were marked in relief, indicating manufacturer and artisan. Through the 1880s, all marks were omitted; but the bases were much more shallow than those from the 1860s. About 1890, the Staffordshire potters sold the molds to German manufacturers who marked their product with the name of their country until about 1900. Examples from this period are most commonly encountered. Fairings made in Germany in the early 20th century often have two holes in their bases.

Generally, the more complex groups and those that are marked bring the higher prices. Earlier examples from the sixties and seventies are of better quality. Similiar items such as small boxes and match holders with much the same type of theme and figural decoration are also listed here.

Before Marriage, couple on sofa 245.00
Box, child asleep in highchair, Staffordshire, 3⅜" 115.00
Box, child w/trumpet, doll in basket, Staffordshire, 3¾" 175.00
Box, dressing table w/mirror, various adornments, 3½" 100.00
Box, girl putting on stockings, #107, 4x3½x2" 150.00
Box, piano figural, 2⅜" 80.00
Box, 3 children play on oval lid, Staffordshire, 4⅝" 200.00
Delights of Matrimony 200.00
Last in Bed To Put Out the Light, 3½" 225.00
Looking Down on His Luck 225.00
Nip on the Sly 225.00
Robbing the Mail 225.00

12 Months After Marriage, unmk, 3½x3½"................265.00
3 O'Clock in the Morning, 2¾x3¼".........................225.00

The Last in Bed To Put Out the Light, First series, ca 1840, 3½", $225.00: Second series, ca 1860s, 3", $325.00.

Fans

The Japanese are said to have invented the fan. From there it went to China, and Portuguese traders took the idea to Europe. Though usually considered milady's accessory, even the gentlemen in 17th-century England carried fans! More fashionable than practical, some were of feathers and lovely hand-painted silks with carved ivory or tortoise sticks. Some French fans had peepholes. There are mourning fans, calendar fans, and those with advertising.

Fine antique fans (pre-1900) of ivory or mother of pearl have recently escalated in value. Our advisor for this category is Vicki Flanigan; she is listed in the Directory under Virginia.

Ivory, cvd flower in high relief, silk, 9" L.....................200.00
Ivory brise, HP florals, French, 1860 ....500.00
Leather, pierced, on cvd horn fr, 11x7", VG................150.00
Ostrich feathers, cvd blk wood sticks, 11x23", EX 95.00
Ostrich feathers, HP ivory sticks 150.00

Paper with Oriental figures, Treaty Port of Whampoa on the back, ivory sticks, Mandarin, 1850s, $2,750.00.

Red silk, HP florals & birds, wood slats, 16x8", VG.........125.00
Rtcl French paper, aristocratic scenes, MOP sticks, 14x8" 500.00
Satin, HP florals, MOP sticks, Tiffany & Co, rare 700.00
Satin, HP florals, Victorian style, wood sticks.............100.00
Tuck illus, poem, ribbon laced, Made in England, 12" 125.00

Farm Collectibles

Country living in the 19th century entailed plowing, planting, and harvesting; gathering eggs and milking; making soap from lard rendered on butchering day; and numerous other tasks performed with primitive tools of which we in the 20th century have had little first-hand knowledge. For more information on this subject, we recommend *Collecting Farm Antiques*, an identification and value guide by our advisor for this category Lar Hothem; his address is listed in the Directory under Ohio. See also Cast Iron; Woodenware; Wrought Iron.

Basket, horse feeding; rnd bottom/bentwood hdl, 16x13"...........55.00
Blueberry picker, tin/sheet iron, slide lid, pat 1914 ....45.00
Bucket, feed; leather, red/gold shield, MIE for Brooks, 12".........110.00
Chicken catcher, wire w/wood hdl, scarce 40.00
Corn husker, A&O, brass, dtd 1862, EX....................22.00
Corn sheller, Fulton, hand crank 35.00

Cotton gin, homemade, $50.00.

Crackling squeezer, wood w/leather hinge, 21½" L............28.00
Ear marker, Stay There, Wilcox & Harvey, w/tag pliers, pr 15.00
Grain flail...45.00
Harness hook, iron, 10"...................................12.50
Hay rake, all wood, 62".................................200.00
Hay rake, hickory w/traces of old red, well made, 71" 200.00
Hog ringer, Hill's Hog Ringer Pat Aug 1872, screw adjust 18.00
Hoof cleaner, CI w/hdl, pat 1899 ....18.00
Hoof cleaner, Pioneer, wood hdl, EX 20.00
Implement seat, Bonanza, EX............................125.00
Implement seat, Bradley's Mower, CI.....................100.00
Implement seat, Deere & Co, CI 115.00
Implement seat, Empire, CI.................................40.00
Implement seat, Fuller & Johnson, CI....................150.00
Implement seat, Jenkins, CI.................................55.00
Implement seat, Milwaukee, CI 40.00
Implement seat, Peerless, CI...............................165.00
Implement seat, Walter A Wood, CI 40.00
Manual, operator's; Case, Model F combine, EX 5.00
Medallion, dealer's, John Deere, 100th Anniv, 1937 ....125.00
Operator's manual, McCormick-Deering, 1-row picker..........10.00
Ox yoke, tiger maple, red wash, full sz, EX 225.00
Pitch fork, oak, 3-prong, 60" 225.00
Shovel, grain; maple, made from 1 pc, 1800s, 36".........325.00
Shovel, grain; wood, cvd initials/1910, EX cvg, 36" 285.00
Shovel, grain; wood, dk patina, 37" 185.00
Steam gauge, JI Case......................................25.00
Tray, tobacco drying; weathered gray surface, 26x39"..........75.00
Wagon jack, wood/wrought iron, 1800s, 30" 45.00
Wagon seat, trn posts & arms w/spindle bk, 34" W, VG 375.00
Wheelbarrow, wood w/iron wheel, rpt, primitive, 67" L 95.00
Yoke, cow; bentwood, 26x13" +heavy wood pc at bottom..........50.00
Yoke, oxen training; all orig, 34", EX......................60.00

Yoke, wood w/traces of old bl, primitive, 39" W 25.00

Fenton

Frank and John Fenton were brothers who founded the Fenton Art Glass Company in 1906 in Martin's Ferry, Ohio. The venture, at first only a decorating shop, began operations in July of 1905 using blanks purchased from other companies. This operation soon proved unsatisfactory, and by 1907 they had constructed their own glass factory in Williamstown, West Virginia. John left the company in 1909 and organized his own firm in Millersburg, Ohio.

The Fenton Company produced over 130 patterns of carnival glass. They also made custard, chocolate, opalescent, and stretch glass. This company has always been noted for its various colors of glass and has continually changed its production to stay attune with current tastes in decorating. In 1925 they produced a line of 'handmade' items that incorporated the techniques of threading and mosaic work. Because the process proved to be unprofitable, the line was discontinued by 1927. Even their glassware made in the past twenty-five years is already regarded as collectible. Various paper labels have been used since the 1920s; only since 1970 has the logo been stamped into the glass.

For information concerning Fenton Art Glass Collectors of America, Inc., see the Clubs, Newsletters, and Catalogs section of the Directory. See also Carnival Glass; Custard Glass; Stretch Glass.

Aqua Crest, basket, #1923, 10" 70.00
Aqua Crest, bonbon, ruffled, 6" 12.00
Aqua Crest, cake stand, 13" 65.00
Aqua Crest, candlestick, #1523, 5", pr 55.00
Aqua Crest, candlestick, cornucopia, pr 45.00
Aqua Crest, epergne, lily insert, 6" 50.00
Aqua Crest, plate, 11¼" 35.00
Aqua Crest, vase, #210, 4" 15.00
Aqua Crest, vase, #36, 4" 25.00
Aqua Crest, vase, triangular, 6½" 35.00
Basketweave, basket, ruby, cupped bowl, 6" dia 22.50
Basketweave, bowl, French opal, cupped, 6" 20.00
Basketweave, bowl, Mandarin red, shallow, 8" 85.00
Beaded Melon, basket, gold overlay, 7" 78.00
Beaded Melon, bottle, scent; gr cased, 3¼" 50.00
Beaded Melon, bowl, bl overlay, 7" 32.00
Beaded Melon, rose bowl, bl overlay, 6" 35.00
Beaded Melon, rose bowl, dk gr overlay, 3½" 35.00
Beaded Melon, vase, gold overlay, tulip form, 9¼" 60.00
Beaded Melon/Ivy, tulip vase, #711, 5½" 40.00
Big Cookies, hat basket, Mandarin red 95.00
Black Rose, basket, blk hdl, #7237, 7" 120.00
Black Rose, hurricane lamp, #7398 ....115.00
Black Rose, vase, hand at base, #5155, 10½" 100.00
Blue Overlay, basket, #1924, 7" dia 40.00
Blue Overlay, basket, #203, 7¼" 55.00
Blue Overlay, vanity set, #192-A, 5½" bottle+jar 65.00
Blue Overlay, vanity set, 3-pc 85.00
Blue Overlay, vase, #3160, 5" 32.00
Bookend, peacock figural, lt gr satin, #711, ca 1935, 5¾" 80.00
Bubble Optic, vase, honey amber, 8½" 60.00
Burmese, basket, 6¾x7¾" 55.00
Burmese, vase, jack-in-the-pulpit; 11" 65.00
Burmese, vase, rose decor, sq w/rnd crimped top, 7½" 55.00
Coin Dot, basket, cranberry opal, #1925, 10½" 100.00
Coin Dot, bowl, honeysuckle opal, #203, 6" 45.00
Coin Dot, candy box, cranberry opal, #1522 ....90.00

Coin Dot, candy jar, bl opal, #91 ....50.00
Coin Dot, creamer, cranberry opal, #1924, 4" 40.00
Coin Dot, creamer & sugar bowl, bl opal 80.00
Coin Dot, hat, cranberry opal, 3½" 48.00
Coin Dot, lamp, w/chimney, French opal, 11" 200.00
Coin Dot, pitcher, cranberry opal, sm 65.00
Coin Dot, pitcher, gr opal, water sz 200.00
Coin Dot, pitcher, lime opal, lg 125.00
Coin Dot, vase, bl opal, #208, 5½" 40.00
Coin Dot, vase, bl opal, hdls, #1353, 9" 85.00
Coin Dot, vase, bl opal, tulip form, 10½" 40.00

Coin Dot vase, clear with opalescence, 11", $95.00.

Coin Dot, vase, cranberry opal, dbl-crimped top, 6¾" 60.00
Coin Dot, vase, cranberry opal, hdls, #194, 11" 78.00
Coin Dot, vase, French opal, #1925, 6" 45.00
Colonial Blue, candy dish, #1780 ....45.00
Crystal Crest, vase, tulip form, 8" 45.00
Daisy & Button, basket, Colonial bl, #1900, 7½" 50.00
Daisy & Button, bottle, scent; French opal 22.00
Daisy & Button, bowl, milk glass, oval, #1929, 11" 25.00
Daisy & Button, top hat, bl opal, #1900, 3¾" 38.00
Daisy & Button, vase, rose pastel, #1957, 8" 40.00
Daisy & Fern, pitcher, water; cranberry opal 250.00
Dancing Ladies, vase, Mongolian gr, flared, #901, 8½" 180.00
Dancing Ladies, vase, periwinkle bl, #901, ca 1935, 9" ...175.00
Dancing Ladies, vase, royal bl, #901, 8½" 200.00
Dancing Ladies, vase, ruby, #901, ca 1933, 9" 200.00
Diamond Lace, console set, bl opal, 3-pc 80.00
Diamond Lace, console set, French opal, #1948, 3-pc 80.00
Diamond Lace, epergne, French opal, #1948 ....95.00
Diamond Optic, basket, ruby, 7" 35.00
Diamond Optic, candy dish, gr, dolphin, 4" 55.00
Diamond Optic, creamer & sugar bowl, rose, 3½" 40.00
Diamond Optic, pitcher, ruby overlay, #192, 8" 55.00
Diamond Optic, vase, cranberry opal, ca 1951-54, 7½" 80.00
Diamond Optic, vase, ruby overlay, dbl crimp, 8½" 40.00
Diamond Rib, vase, cranberry satin, #1925 ....95.00
Dolphin, bonbon, ruby, #1621 ....35.00
Dolphin, bowl, blk, oval, #1608, 10" 70.00
Dolphin, bowl, gr, hdls, 6½" 30.00
Dolphin, bowl, jade gr, hdls, #1504A 40.00
Dolphin, bowl, jade gr, oval, #1608, 10" 55.00
Dolphin, bowl, moonstone, oval, #1608, 10" 90.00

Dolphin, candlestick, rose, #1623, 3½" 20.00
Dolphin, candlestick, ruby, 3½" 20.00
Dolphin, compote, ruby, #1533, 6" 55.00
Dolphin, plate, sandwich; pk, center hdl 40.00
Dolphin, vase, topaz stretch, fan form, 5" 62.50
Dot Optic, bowl, topaz opal, 10½" 50.00
Dot Optic, pitcher, bl opal, 4" 35.00
Dot Optic, pitcher, lime opal, blk hdl, #1352, rare............175.00
Dot Optic, tumbler, cranberry opal, flat, #1353, 4" 25.00
Dot Optic, vase, bl opal, crimped top, 8" 98.00
Drapery Optic, water set, gr opal, 7-pc............150.00
Ebony, candy bowl, w/lid, #844, 6¼" 75.00
Ebony, candy jar, ca 1925, ½-lb, 9" 75.00
Ebony, tray, 6½" 15.00
Emerald Crest, bowl, soup; 6" 22.00
Emerald Crest, creamer, #7261 ....25.00
Emerald Crest, cruet 40.00
Emerald Crest, epergne, lg............175.00
Emerald Crest, flowerpot w/attached saucer, #401, 4½" 75.00
Emerald Crest, plate, 12" 30.00
Emerald Crest, vase, #36, 6" 30.00
Emerald Crest, vase, rnd, 4½" 18.00
Epergne, vaseline opal, 3-lily............300.00
Flame, candlestick, #549, ca 1924-26, 8", pr 165.00
Flame Crest, bowl, crimped, 9" 55.00
Flame Crest, cake plate, stem 145.00
Florentine, bonbon, gr stretch, ftd, #643 ....38.00
Flowering Dill, bonbon, amethyst opal, #1606 ....48.00
Georgian, claret, ruby, #1611, 4½-oz............18.00
Georgian, cocktail, amber, #1611 ....25.00
Georgian, creamer & sugar bowl, ruby, #1611, pr............35.00
Georgian, cup & saucer, ruby, #1611 ....18.00
Georgian, goblet, ruby, #1611, water sz 12.00
Georgian, shakers, ruby, orig top, 4½", pr 65.00
Georgian, tumbler, moonstone, #1611............20.00
Georgian, tumbler, royal bl, #1611, 9-oz............27.50
Georgian, tumbler, ruby, 2½"............ 5.00
Georgian, tumbler, ruby, 9-oz 7.50
Georgian, whiskey, gr 8.00
Gold Crest, bonbon, sq, #36, 5½" 8.00
Gold Crest, bowl, 10" 30.00
Gold Crest, bowl, 6" 10.00
Gold Crest, bowl vase, ribbed, dbl crimped, 5¼x6"............22.00
Gold Crest, plate, 6¾" 12.50
Gold Crest, vase, #1523, 4" 20.00
Gold Crest, vase, dbl-crimped top, #201, 5" 20.00
Grape & Cable, humidor, ebony 85.00
Halo etched, bonbon, 3 ftd, #1800, ca 1937, 7"............45.00

Hanging Heart vase, black on bittersweet, ca 1976, 7¾", $200.00.

Hobnail, ash tray, French opal, 5¼" 22.00
Hobnail, basket, bl opal, #3834, 4½" 40.00
Hobnail, basket, bl opal, #3837, 7" 65.00
Hobnail, basket, cranberry opal, #248 ....45.00
Hobnail, basket, cranberry opal, #3837, 7" 65.00
Hobnail, basket, milk glass, 10" 35.00
Hobnail, bonbon, French opal, oval, 6" 17.50
Hobnail, bottle, scent; French opal, w/stopper 32.00
Hobnail, bowl, bl opal, #3827, 7" 27.50
Hobnail, bowl, bl opal, oval, crimped top, #389, 7"............36.00
Hobnail, bowl, cranberry opal, fluted, 10" 90.00
Hobnail, bowl, cranberry opal, 11" 90.00
Hobnail, bowl, gr opal, ftd, #3923, 11" 110.00
Hobnail, bowl, topaz opal, crimped, 9½" 30.00
Hobnail, candlestick, cranberry opal, hdl, 3½x4", pr............65.00
Hobnail, candlestick, gr opal, #389 ....22.50
Hobnail, candlestick, turq pastel, #3974, 4½" 20.00
Hobnail, candy jar, gr pastel, #3883, 5½" 40.00
Hobnail, compote, plum opal, w/lid, #3887 ....80.00
Hobnail, compote, yel opal, dbl-crimped top, #1948, 6½" 25.00
Hobnail, creamer & sugar bowl, bl opal 35.00
Hobnail, creamer & sugar bowl, vaseline opal, child's sz 40.00
Hobnail, cruet, cranberry opal, w/stopper, 6" 67.50
Hobnail, epergne, bl opal, 3-lily, 7" 130.00
Hobnail, epergne, French opal 95.00
Hobnail, goblet, bl opal, #3845, 5½" 17.50
Hobnail, lamp, table; cranberry opal............250.00
Hobnail, mayonnaise, bl opal 25.00
Hobnail, mustard, bl opal 25.00
Hobnail, mustard, topaz opal 25.00
Hobnail, nappy, ruby overlay, 5"............22.00
Hobnail, pitcher, bl opal, #3967, 80-oz, 8" 100.00
Hobnail, pitcher, cranberry opal, 80-oz, 8" 200.00
Hobnail, pitcher, topaz opal, 5½" 48.00
Hobnail, plate, bl opal, 8" 17.50
Hobnail, rose bowl, gr opal, 4½"............40.00
Hobnail, shakers, bl opal, flat, pr............55.00
Hobnail, shakers, cranberry opal, #3806, 3½", pr 65.00
Hobnail, shakers, French opal, flat, pr............40.00
Hobnail, sherbet, French opal, 4" 15.00
Hobnail, tray, bl opal, fan form, 10½" 28.00
Hobnail, tumbler, bl opal, 4¼" 17.50
Hobnail, tumbler, French opal, #3945, 5-oz, 3½" 14.00
Hobnail, tumbler, French opal, #3949, 9-oz............16.00
Hobnail, vase, bl opal, fan form, 8¼" 55.00
Hobnail, vase, cornucopia/candlestick; bl opal, #389, 6" 42.00
Hobnail, vase, cranberry opal, #3856, 5½" 55.00
Hobnail, vase, cranberry opal, #3859, 8½" 65.00
Hobnail, vase, cranberry opal, 4" 32.00
Hobnail, vase, French opal, fan form, #389, 8¼" 27.50
Hobnail, vase, gold overlay, #3856, 5½" 40.00
Hobnail, vase, gr opal, #389, 6" 40.00
Hobnail, vase, gr opal, flared, 3½" 25.00
Hobnail, vase, gr opal, tricorn, mini 20.00
Hobnail, vase, peachblow, dbl-crimped top, 5¾" 32.00
Ivory Crest, bowl, console; #1522, 10½"............48.00
Ivory Crest, candle holder, cornucopia form, 6¼"............32.00
Ivory Crest, vase, #1923, 7½"............38.00
Ivory Crest, vase, cornucopia; #1523, pr............135.00
Ivy, rose bowl, gr/wht, #711, 5"............55.00
Ivy, vase, gr/wht, #194, 11"............45.00
Jade Green, bowl, flower; elephant form, #1618, ca 1928, 7"............275.00
Jade Green, candy dish, ftd............36.00
Jade Green, ice bucket, #1616, 6½" 55.00

Jade Green, vase, #184, 12" **75.00**
Jade Green, vase, cylindrical, 8" **32.00**
Jamestown Blue, vase, 12" **88.00**
Lamb's Tongue, candy jar, pastel bl, #4381, 5½" **38.00**
Lamb's Tongue, candy jar, turq pastel, #4381, 5½" **35.00**
Leaf Tiers, bowl, milk glass, #1790, 10" **35.00**
Lilac Cased, vase, fan form, #857, 8" **125.00**
Lilac Cased, vase, 8" **60.00**
Lincoln Inn, cup & saucer, aquamarine bl, #1700 ....**37.50**
Lincoln Inn, goblet, water; cobalt, 6" **28.00**
Lincoln Inn, sherbet, gr **17.50**
Lincoln Inn, sherbet, ruby **18.00**
Lincoln Inn, wine, cobalt **23.00**
Lincoln Inn, wine, jade gr, #1700, ca 1931, 4" **32.00**
Mandarin Red, candlestick, #318, 3" **40.00**
Mandarin Red, ginger jar, #893, rare **265.00**
Mandarin Red, macaroon jar, #1681, ca 1933, 7" **195.00**
Mandarin Red, vase, fan form, 6" **75.00**
Melon Rib, vase, bl overlay, 6" **35.00**
Melon Rib, vase, pk overlay, 8" **55.00**
Ming, bowl, pk, deep, 3-toe, 7" **30.00**
Ming, candelabra, #2000, 5" **32.00**
Mongolian Green, vase, 8½" **90.00**
Orange Tree, goblet, rose, #1412, 5" **20.00**
Orchid, ice pail, #1616, 5¾" **50.00**
Orchid, vase, fan form, #349, w/orig label, 8" **65.00**
Peach Crest, basket, milk glass hdl, 6½" **55.00**
Peach Crest, bowl, shell form, #9020, 10¼" **85.00**
Peach Crest, candlestick, #1523, 4½", pr **48.00**
Peach Crest, top hat, 3¼" **30.00**
Peach Crest, vase, crimped tricorn rim, #186, 8" **47.50**
Peach Crest, vase, roses & violets w/gold, dbl crimped, 6½" **55.00**
Peach Crest, vase, tricorn rim, #187, 5" **50.00**
Pekin Blue, bowl, oval, #1663, 12½" **78.00**
Pekin Blue, candlestick, #318, 3" **30.00**
Pekin Blue, candlestick, #549, ca 1924, 8" **145.00**
Pekin Blue, pitcher, #192, 6" **35.00**
Periwinkle Blue, bottle, whiskey; elephant form, ca 1935 ....**285.00**
Periwinkle Blue, vase, flared, ca 1935, 8½" **30.00**
Persian Medallion, compote, vaseline opal **25.00**
Petal, candle holder, blk amethyst, 3-legged **12.00**
Pineapple, compote, pk satin, #2000, 5¼" **28.00**
Plymouth, champagne, crystal, tall..............................**16.00**
Plymouth, champagne, ruby, 4" **18.00**
Plymouth, plate, French opal, #1620, 8" **25.00**
Plymouth, shot glass, ruby **14.00**
Plymouth, tumbler, juice; ruby **12.00**
Poinsettia, basket, etched, #1616, ca 1939, 6½x9½" ...**55.00**
Poinsettia, bowl, etched, #349, 10½" **40.00**
Poinsettia, vase, etched, #183, 6½" **40.00**
Polka Dot, butter dish, cranberry opal, milk glass base **115.00**
Polka Dot, ivy ball, cranberry opal, #2221, 9" **78.00**
Polka Dot, pitcher, cranberry opal, #2267, 9" **130.00**
Polka Dot, shakers, cranberry opal, 2¾", pr **50.00**
Polka Dot, sugar shaker, cranberry opal, #2293, 4½" ...**65.00**
Priscilla, bowl, emerald gr, #1890, 9"..........................**32.00**
Rib Optic, creamer & sugar bowl, gr opal, #1604 ....**85.00**
Rib Optic, cruet, cranberry opal, #1669, 7" **125.00**
Rib Optic, top hat, French opal, #1922, 6x9"..............**100.00**
Rib Optic, wine, gr opal, #1647, 4" **32.00**
Rib Optic, wine bottle, cranberry opal, #1667, 13½" ...**85.00**
Ring, pitcher, French opal, 7".......................................**78.00**
Rosalene, basket, threaded **55.00**
Rosalene, candle holder, fairy light, owl **45.00**

Rose Crest, basket, #36, 4½" **55.00**
Rose Crest, basket, 10" **88.00**
Rose Crest, plate, 12"..**42.00**
Rose Crest, vase, 6½" **50.00**
Rose Overlay, basket, 7½" **50.00**
Rose Overlay, pitcher, #192, 5½" **40.00**
Rose Overlay, pitcher, #192, 8" **50.00**
Rose Pastel, epergne, 4-pc **40.00**
Royal Blue, bowl, flower form, #848, ca 1932, 9" dia....**28.00**
Ruby, creamer, #1639, 4" **32.00**
Ruby, ivy ball, #705, 5" dia **42.50**
Ruby, plate, #1639, 12" **65.00**
Ruby, tumbler, #1933, 4¼" **15.00**
San Toy, bowl, #349, 8½" **40.00**
September Morn, flower frog, blk opaque **175.00**
September Morn, flower frog, crystal **90.00**
September Morn, flower frog, lt gr, blk base **130.00**
Sheffield, bowl, French opal, crimped, #1800, 12" **38.00**
Sheffield, plate, Silvertone etching, 3-ftd, #1800, 8".....**22.00**
Sheffield, shakers, ruby, pr **55.00**
Sheffield, tumbler, amber, #1800, 4¼" **15.00**
Silver Crest, bowl, crimped, 7" **15.00**
Silver Crest, bowl, dessert; #680 .... **9.00**
Silver Crest, bowl, fruit; ftd, sq, 8" **40.00**
Silver Crest, bowl, 3¾x7" **10.00**
Silver Crest, cake plate, low, ftd, 13" **30.00**
Silver Crest, cup & saucer **27.50**
Silver Crest, mayonnaise, w/underplate & milk glass ladle **22.50**
Silver Crest, pitcher, 9" **22.00**
Silver Crest, plate, torte; 15¼" **55.00**
Silver Crest, plate, 10½" **18.00**
Silver Crest, relish, hdl **17.00**
Silver Crest, sandwich server, hdls **22.00**
Silver Crest, tray, chrome center hdl, 5½" **15.00**
Silver Crest, tray, tidbit; 3-tier, #680 ....**32.00**
Silver Turquoise, hurricane lamp, #7398.....................**70.00**
Snow Crest, hat, ruby overlay, 5" **65.00**
Spanish Lace, syrup, cranberry opal **95.00**
Spiral, vase, cranberry opal, #3253, 6½" **50.00**
Spiral Optic, cruet, cranberry opal, clear twist reeded hdl............**90.00**
Spiral Optic, vase, bl opal, dbl crimped, #1924, 3½" ...**30.00**
Spiral Optic, vase, bl opal, hdls, #194, 6½" **38.00**
Spiral Optic, vase, cranberry opal, #3253, 6½" **65.00**
Spiral Optic, vase, cranberry opal, #894, 10" **90.00**
Stars & Stripes, pitcher, cranberry opal **125.00**
Swirl, basket, cranberry opal, clear hdl........................**42.00**
Swirl, cruet, ruby overlay, w/stopper **30.00**
Swirled Feather, hurricane chimney, gr opal, #2098, 7½" ...**65.00**
Teardrop, candy box, milk glass, #6985, ca 1955, 6" ...**28.00**
Thumbprint, compote, pk..**15.00**
Turquoise Pastel, vase, 6½" **20.00**
Velva Rose, fan vase, Spirit of St Louis, #562 ....**125.00**
Velvatone, bonbon, #846, 5" **65.00**
Velvatone, compote, #574, crimped **32.00**
Velvatone, vase, triangular, #1934, 5" **50.00**
Waffle, sugar bowl, milk glass, #6180, ca 1960............**25.00**
Water Lily & Cattail, bowl, amethyst opal, 10" **75.00**

Fiesta

Fiesta is a line of dinnerware produced by the Homer Laughlin China Company of Newell, West Virginia, from 1936 until 1973. It was made in eleven different solid colors with over fifty pieces in the assortment. The pattern was developed by Frederic Rhead, an English Stoke-on-Trent potter who was an important contributor to the art-pottery movement in this country during the early part of the century. The design was carried out through the use of a simple band-of-rings device near the rim. Fiesta Red, a strong red-orange glaze color, was made with depleted uranium oxide. It was more expensive to produce than the other colors and sold at higher prices. Today's collectors still pay premium prices for Fiesta Red pieces. During the fifties the color assortment was gray, rose, chartreuse, and dark green. These colors are relatively harder to find and along with Fiesta Red and medium green (new in 1959) command the higher prices.

Fiesta Kitchen Kraft was introduced in 1939; it consisted of seventeen pieces of kitchenware such as pie plates, refrigerator sets, mixing bowls, and covered jars in four popular Fiesta colors.

As a final attempt to adapt production to modern-day techniques and methods, Fiesta was restyled in 1969. Of the original colors, only Fiesta Red remained. This line, called Fiesta Ironstone, was discontinued in 1973.

Two types of marks were used: an ink stamp on machine-jiggered pieces and an indented mark molded into the hollowware pieces.

In 1986 HLC reintroduced a line of Fiesta dinnerware in five colors: black, white, pink, apricot, and cobalt (darker and denser than the original shade). Yellow was added in 1989. However, collectors feel the new ware will pose no threat to their investment.

In the listings below, 'original colors' indicates only four of the original six – ivory, light green, turquoise, and yellow. Red and cobalt values are listed separately. For more information we recommend *The Collector's Encyclopedia of Fiesta, Harlequin, and Riviera* by Sharon and Bob Huxford, now in its sixth edition. Available at your local bookstore or from Collector Books.

Dinnerware and Accessories

Ash tray, '50s colors	45.00
Ash tray, orig colors	30.00
Ash tray, red or cobalt	35.00
Bowl, covered onion soup; cobalt	225.00
Bowl, covered onion soup; red	250.00
Bowl, covered onion soup; turq	700.00
Bowl, covered onion soup; yel, lt gr, or ivory	200.00
Bowl, cream soup; '50s colors	35.00
Bowl, cream soup; med gr	550.00
Bowl, cream soup; orig colors	25.00
Bowl, cream soup; red or cobalt	30.00
Bowl, dessert; '50s colors, 6"	30.00
Bowl, dessert; med gr, 6"	180.00
Bowl, dessert; orig colors, 6"	22.00
Bowl, dessert; red or cobalt, 6"	28.00
Bowl, fruit; '50s colors, 4¾"	20.00
Bowl, fruit; '50s colors, 5½"	22.00
Bowl, fruit; med gr, 4¾"	165.00
Bowl, fruit; med gr, 5½"	50.00
Bowl, fruit; orig colors, 11¾"	95.00
Bowl, fruit; orig colors, 4¾"	15.00
Bowl, fruit; orig colors, 5½"	15.00
Bowl, fruit; red or cobalt, 11¾"	125.00
Bowl, fruit; red or cobalt, 4¾"	20.00
Bowl, fruit; red or cobalt, 5½"	18.00
Bowl, ftd salad; orig colors	145.00
Bowl, ftd salad; red or cobalt	180.00
Bowl, ind salad; med gr, 7½"	55.00
Bowl, ind salad; red, turq, & yel, 7½"	45.00
Bowl, nappy, '50s colors, 8½"	32.00
Bowl, nappy, med gr, 8½"	50.00

Bowl, nappy, orig colors, 8½"	22.00
Bowl, nappy, orig colors, 9½"	25.00
Bowl, nappy, red or cobalt, 8½"	30.00
Bowl, nappy, red or cobalt, 9½"	35.00
Bowl, Tom & Jerry, ivory w/gold letters	100.00
Bowl, unlisted; red or cobalt	150.00
Bowl, unlisted; yel	45.00
Candle holder, bulb; orig colors, pr	45.00
Candle holder, bulb; red or cobalt, pr	60.00
Candle holder, tripod; orig colors, pr	180.00
Candle holder, tripod; red or cobalt, pr	200.00
Carafe, orig colors	100.00
Carafe, red or cobalt	120.00
Casserole, '50s colors	150.00
Casserole, French; standard colors	250.00
Casserole, French; yel	150.00
Casserole, med gr	200.00
Casserole, orig colors	65.00
Casserole, red or cobalt	110.00
Coffeepot, '50s colors	145.00
Coffeepot, demi; orig colors	110.00
Coffeepot, demi; red or cobalt	150.00
Coffeepot, orig colors	85.00
Coffeepot, red or cobalt	110.00
Compote, orig colors, 12"	65.00
Compote, red or cobalt, 12"	80.00
Compote, sweets; orig colors	30.00
Compote, sweets; red or cobalt	35.00

Compote, turquoise, $65.00.

Creamer, '50s colors	15.00
Creamer, ind; red	80.00
Creamer, ind; turq	150.00
Creamer, ind; yel	35.00
Creamer, med gr	30.00
Creamer, orig colors	11.00
Creamer, red or cobalt	15.00
Creamer, stick hdld, orig colors	18.00
Creamer, stick hdld, red or cobalt	20.00
Cup, demi; '50s colors	90.00
Cup, demi; orig colors	30.00
Cup, demi; red or cobalt	35.00
Egg cup, '50s colors	80.00
Egg cup, orig colors	30.00
Egg cup, red or cobalt	35.00
Gravy boat, '50s colors	38.00
Gravy boat, med gr	45.00
Gravy boat, orig colors	25.00
Gravy boat, red or cobalt	35.00
Lid, for mixing bowl #1-#3, any color	200.00
Lid, for mixing bowl #4, any color	225.00

Marmalade, orig colors..95.00
Marmalade, red or cobalt.......................................125.00
Mixing bowl, #1, orig colors 45.00
Mixing bowl, #1, red or cobalt.................................70.00
Mixing bowl, #2, orig colors 35.00
Mixing bowl, #2, red or cobalt.................................40.00
Mixing bowl, #3, orig colors 40.00
Mixing bowl, #3, red or cobalt.................................50.00
Mixing bowl, #4, orig colors 45.00
Mixing bowl, #4, red or cobalt.................................55.00
Mixing bowl, #5, orig colors 52.00
Mixing bowl, #5, red or cobalt.................................60.00
Mixing bowl, #6, orig colors 68.00
Mixing bowl, #6, red or cobalt.................................75.00
Mixing bowl, #7, orig colors 120.00
Mixing bowl, #7, red or cobalt................................135.00
Mug, Tom & Jerry; '50s colors 55.00
Mug, Tom & Jerry; ivory w/gold letters.....................40.00
Mug, Tom & Jerry; orig colors 32.00
Mug, Tom & Jerry; red or cobalt..............................50.00
Mustard, orig colors...85.00
Mustard, red or cobalt...120.00
Pitcher, disk juice; gray 300.00
Pitcher, disk juice; other standard colors.................300.00
Pitcher, disk juice; red 150.00
Pitcher, disk juice; yel 25.00
Pitcher, disk water; '50s colors..............................135.00
Pitcher, disk water; med gr 300.00
Pitcher, disk water; orig colors 50.00
Pitcher, disk water; red or cobalt 75.00
Pitcher, ice; orig colors 50.00
Pitcher, ice; red or cobalt 70.00
Pitcher, jug, 2-pt; '50s colors...................................60.00
Pitcher, jug, 2-pt; orig colors...................................35.00
Pitcher, jug, 2-pt; red or cobalt 40.00
Plate, '50s colors, 10"..30.00
Plate, '50s colors, 6"... 4.50
Plate, '50s colors, 7".. 8.50
Plate, '50s colors, 9"..13.00
Plate, cake; lt gr or yellow 250.00
Plate, cake; red or cobalt 300.00
Plate, calendar; 1954 or 1955, 10"...........................30.00
Plate, calendar; 1955, 9" 35.00
Plate, chop; '50s colors, 13" 35.00
Plate, chop; '50s colors, 15" 40.00
Plate, chop; med gr, 13"..55.00
Plate, chop; orig colors, 13" 20.00
Plate, chop; orig colors, 15" 22.00
Plate, chop; red or cobalt, 13" 22.00
Plate, chop; red or cobalt, 15" 25.00
Plate, compartment; '50s colors, 10½" 28.00
Plate, compartment; orig colors, 10½" 18.00
Plate, compartment; orig colors, 12" 22.00
Plate, compartment; red or cobalt, 10½"..................20.00
Plate, compartment; red or cobalt, 12" 25.00
Plate, deep; '50s colors..30.00
Plate, deep; med gr..50.00
Plate, deep; orig colors..20.00
Plate, deep; red or cobalt 30.00
Plate, med gr, 10"..45.00
Plate, med gr, 6" 8.00
Plate, med gr, 7" 13.00
Plate, med gr, 9" 30.00
Plate, orig colors, 10" 17.00

Plate, orig colors, 6" 3.00
Plate, orig colors, 7" 5.00
Plate, orig colors, 9" 6.50
Plate, red or cobalt, 10" 25.00
Plate, red or cobalt, 6" 4.50
Plate, red or cobalt, 7" 7.50
Plate, red or cobalt, 9" 13.00
Platter, '50s colors..28.00
Platter, med gr...50.00
Platter, orig colors...18.00
Platter, red or cobalt..25.00
Saucer, '50s colors... 4.00
Saucer, demi; '50s colors 35.00
Saucer, demi; orig colors 9.00
Saucer, demi; red or cobalt 10.00
Saucer, med gr... 7.00
Saucer, orig colors... 2.00
Saucer, red or cobalt 3.00
Shakers, '50s colors, pr..22.00
Shakers, med gr, pr..40.00
Shakers, orig colors, pr...14.00
Shakers, red or cobalt, pr..18.00
Sugar bowl, ind; turq...150.00
Sugar bowl, ind; yel..60.00
Sugar bowl, w/lid, '50s colors, 3¼x3½" 32.00
Sugar bowl, w/lid, med gr, 3¼x3½" 45.00
Sugar bowl, w/lid, orig colors, 3¼x3½" 18.00
Sugar bowl, w/lid, red or cobalt, 3¼x3½".................28.00
Syrup, orig colors...150.00
Syrup, red or cobalt 175.00
Teacup, '50s colors..25.00
Teacup, med gr..28.00
Teacup, orig colors..18.00
Teacup, red or cobalt 22.00
Teapot, lg; orig colors..70.00
Teapot, lg; red or cobalt 85.00
Teapot, med; '50s colors 140.00
Teapot, med; med gr...225.00
Teapot, med; orig colors...60.00
Teapot, med; red or cobalt......................................80.00

Teapot, rose, medium size, $140.00.

Tray, figure-8; cobalt 40.00
Tray, figure-8; turq 125.00
Tray, figure-8; yel 135.00
Tray, relish; gold decor..120.00
Tray, relish; mixed colors, no red.................................100.00
Tray, utility; orig colors 20.00
Tray, utility; red or cobalt 25.00
Tumbler, juice; chartreuse, Harlequin yel or dk gr 100.00
Tumbler, juice; orig colors..18.00
Tumbler, juice; red or cobalt 25.00
Tumbler, juice; rose...25.00
Tumbler, water; orig colors..32.00
Tumbler, water; red or cobalt 40.00
Vase, bud; ivory...60.00
Vase, bud; orig colors...32.00
Vase, bud; red or cobalt 45.00
Vase, orig colors, 10" 350.00
Vase, orig colors, 12" 400.00
Vase, orig colors, 8" 275.00
Vase, red or cobalt, 10"..400.00
Vase, red or cobalt, 12"..500.00
Vase, red or cobalt, 8"...325.00

Kitchen Kraft

Bowl, mixing; lt gr or yel, 10" 55.00
Bowl, mixing; lt gr or yel, 6" 30.00
Bowl, mixing; lt gr or yel, 8" 45.00
Bowl, mixing; red or cobalt, 10" 65.00
Bowl, mixing; red or cobalt, 6" 40.00
Bowl, mixing; red or cobalt, 8" 55.00
Cake plate, lt gr or yel...30.00
Cake plate, red or cobalt 38.00
Cake server, lt gr or yel 50.00
Cake server, red or cobalt 60.00
Casserole, ind; lt gr or yel...85.00
Casserole, ind; red or cobalt 95.00
Casserole, lt gr or yel, 7½"...55.00
Casserole, lt gr or yel, 8½"...60.00
Casserole, red or cobalt, 7½"..65.00
Casserole, red or cobalt, 8½"..70.00
Covered jar, lg; lt gr or yel.......................................150.00
Covered jar, lg; red or cobalt 175.00
Covered jar, med; lt gr or yel......................................140.00
Covered jar, med; red or cobalt 160.00
Covered jar, sm; lt gr or yel.......................................135.00
Covered jar, sm; red or cobalt......................................150.00
Covered jug, lt gr or yel 125.00
Covered jug, red or cobalt 150.00
Fork, lt gr or yel...40.00
Fork, red or cobalt..45.00
Metal frame for platter..20.00
Pie plate, lt gr or yel, 10" 30.00
Pie plate, lt gr or yel, 9" 25.00
Pie plate, red or cobalt, 10" 35.00
Pie plate, red or cobalt, 9" 32.00
Shakers, lt gr or yel, pr 55.00
Shakers, red or cobalt, pr 65.00
Spoon, lt gr or yel..40.00
Spoon, red or cobalt...45.00
Stacking refrigerator lid, lt gr or yel..............................35.00
Stacking refrigerator lid, red or cobalt.............................45.00
Stacking refrigerator unit, lt gr or yel 22.00
Stacking refrigerator unit, red or cobalt 28.00

Finch, Kay

Kay Finch and her husband, Braden, operated a small pottery in Corona Del Mar, California, from 1939 to 1963. The company remained small, employing from twenty to forty local residents who Kay trained in all but the most requiring tasks, which she herself performed. The company produced animal and bird figurines, most notably dogs, Kay's favorites. Figures of 'Godey' type couples were also made, as were tableware (consisting of breakfast sets) and other artware. Most pieces were marked.

Our advisor for this category is Jack Chipman; he is listed in the Directory under California.

Figurine, angel, 4½" 35.00
Figurine, bear, 9" 65.00
Figurine, dove, 2¾"..15.00
Figurine, duck, 3¾"..20.00
Figurine, Gay Nineties couple, 7", ...55.00

Girl with bowed head, 7",
$42.00.

Figurine, man holding bouquet, 9" 65.00
Figurine, owl, 6" 40.00
Figurine, Pekingese, seated, tan w/mc details, 4½" 45.00
Shakers, turkey, pr 25.00
Vase, Santa figural, 4" 45.00

Findlay Onyx and Floradine

Findlay, Ohio, was the location of the Dalzell, Gilmore, and Leighton Glass Company, one of at least sixteen companies that flourished there between 1886 and 1901. Their most famous ware, Onyx, is very rare. It was produced for only a short time beginning in 1889 due to the heavy losses incurred in the manufacturing process.

Onyx is layered glass, usually found in creamy white with a dainty floral pattern accented with metallic lustre that has been trapped between the two layers. Other colors found on rare occasions include a light amber (with either no lustre or with gilt flowers), light amethyst (or lavender), and rose. Although old tradepaper articles indicate the company originally intended to produce the line in three distinct colors, long-time Onyx collectors report that aside from the white, production was very limited. Other colors of Onyx are very rare, and the few examples that are found tend to support the theory that production of colored Onyx ware remained for the most part in the experimental stage. Even three-layered items have been found (they are extremely rare) decorated with three-color flowers. As a rule of thumb, using white Onyx prices as a basis for evaluation, expect to pay two to three times more for colored examples.

Floradine is a separate line that was made with the Onyx molds. A single-layer rose satin glassware with white opal flowers, it is usually priced in the general range of colored Onyx.

Our advisors for this category are Betty and Clarence Maier; they are listed in the Directory under Pennsylvania.

Floradine

Box, dresser; sm crack in lid liner, 5½" dia	650.00
Creamer	945.00
Mustard	850.00
Spooner, 4¼"	925.00
Sugar bowl, w/lid, 3¾x4½"	950.00
Sugar shaker	1,250.00
Toothpick holder	1,100.00
Tumbler, 3¾", NM	550.00

Onyx

Box, wht w/silver decor, 5½" dia	600.00
Butter dish, wht w/silver decor	1,250.00
Celery vase, wht w/silver decor, 6½"	425.00
Creamer, wht w/silver decor, 4½"	450.00
Creamer & sugar, w/lid, wht w/silver decor, 5½"	950.00
Jam jar, wht w/silver decor	450.00

Pitcher, Onyx, white with silver flowers, 8", $1,200.00.

Spoon holder, wht w/silver decor, 3¾x3⅞"	225.00
Sugar shaker, wht w/silver decor, 5¼"	475.00
Syrup, wht w/silver decor, 7"	750.00
Toothpick holder, wht w/silver decor, 2½"	375.00

Fire Fighting Collectibles

Fire fighting antiques from the 19th century reflect the feeling of pride the men had in their companies and in their role as volunteer fire fighters. Dress uniforms, fancy helmets, and presentation trumpets full of flowers recall the charisma of the 'Laddies' on parade. Leather buck-

ets, bed keys, rattles, torches, lanterns, and riveted hose serve as reminders of their dedication to service.

In the 1860s the old volunteer units gave way to paid municipal fire departments. Sophisticated alarm equipment began to evolve at about this time also. Hand and horse-drawn apparatuses began to give way to self-propelled machines soon after the turn of the century. Many cities were totally 'motorized' after WWI, although sleighs were kept by many northern cities long after the horses were gone. Today many collectors find a fascination with these fire-fighting relics of the past.

Our advisor for this category is H. Thomas Laun; he is listed in the Directory under New York.

Alarm, Farady, heavy red metal box, silver emb letters, M	35.00
Alarm box, CI pedestal, ornate	650.00
Alarm box, Gamewell, CI, Excelsior, telegraph door	300.00
Alarm box, Gamewell, CI, slant fist w/telegraph door	175.00
Alarm box, Holtzer Cabot, CI/brass, local	55.00
Alarm box, Safa, aluminum, complete	75.00
Alarm box, Utica FA+T, CI, Excelsior, rare	500.00
Alarm box, Utica FA+T, CI, full sz, complete	300.00
Badge, Fire Marshall, NJ, rodium-plated w/blk enamel	18.00
Badge, Fireman Engine #1 Franklin NH, blk letters, 1900, 2"	35.00
Badge, Kearney & Trecker Fire Brigade, celluloid, 2¼"	10.00
Badge, life member of Union Hose & Engine Co, gold filled	45.00
Badge, Milwaukee Fire Dept, nickel, stamped	65.00
Badge, PC FD, Columbia E&HL Co, eagle on shield, nickel	75.00
Badge, presentation; LA Fire Dept, gold	125.00
Badge, Providence RI FD, nickel, stamped	65.00
Badge, Redding FD #1173, gold-plated metal, ca 1920s, 2"	35.00
Badge, Somerville MA FD, cross, nickel	37.50
Badge, toy; Fire Chief, Occupied Japan, M	20.00
Bell alarm, Gamewell, center wind	225.00
Bell alarm, Gamewell, chain wind,	165.00
Bell alarm, Gamewell, fancy oak case, w/indicator, 18"	5,000.00
Bell alarm, Gamewell, fancy oak case, 15"	2,900.00
Bell alarm, Gamewell, M Crane type, walnut w/feather, 15"	2,500.00
Bell alarm, Gamewell, oak case, Excelsior, 15"	2,350.00
Bell alarm, Gamewell, oak case, Excelsior, 6"	650.00
Bell alarm, Gamewell, oak case, 10"	1,200.00
Bell apparatus, American/La France w/eagle, complete, 12"	475.00
Bell apparatus, New Departure, rotary, hand crank	425.00
Bell apparatus, nickel/brass, complete, 10"	350.00
Bell apparatus, nickel/brass, complete, 12"	400.00
Bell apparatus, Seagrave, complete, 12"	425.00
Bell apparatus, 1949 Seagrave, complete, EX	425.00
Book, Bucket Brigade to Flying Squadron, Jenness, EX	75.00
Book, rules, Sheboygan Fire Dept, leather bk, 1901, EX	5.00
Booklet, Engine Engine, Currier & Ives cover, 1939, 64-pg	35.00
Bucket, #1, leather, orig pnt w/eagle	650.00
Bucket, galvanized, red, rnd bottom, EX	17.50
Bucket, leather, blk/wht pnt: W Dobbins, worn, 13"	200.00
Bucket, leather, gr rpt w/name, minor wear, 12"+hdl	275.00
Bucket, leather, pnt name/# in reserve, dtd 1803, 12", EX	1,300.00
Bucket, leather, rpt gold eagle/name/address, 14", VG	175.00
Bucket, leather, rpt Victory hose	450.00
Bucket, leather, worn gr pnt w/yel name, 12", EX	400.00
Bucket, rubberized canvas, overhaul type	65.00
Buckle, belt; San Francisco Fire Brigade, CA, brass, VG	45.00
Catalog, American/La France Fire Equipment, #10, 1926	100.00
Catalog, Darley, magazine type	25.00
Catalog, Gamewell alarm equipment, 1880s	350.00
Extinguisher, Badgers, copper/brass, 2½-gal	35.00
Extinguisher, Badgers, emb brass label, pony sz	110.00
Extinguisher, Badgers, pnt label, pony sz	65.00

Extinguisher, Hardens, quilted, sq, lt bl 65.00
Extinguisher, Phister #1B, red pnt, w/gauge, EX 25.00
Extinguisher, Richmond, tin cylinder, EX..........................60.00
Grenade, Am Fire Ext, clear, quilted/ftd, 4-panel (1 emb) 425.00
Grenade, Autofyrstop, EX 28.00
Grenade, Harden's, teal bl, full, lip chips, 6" 50.00
Grenade, Harden's #1, bl quilted, hand held, pat 1883, 6" 75.00
Grenade, Harden's Star, lt bl 65.00
Grenade, Harkeness...Destroyer, sapphire w/blk streaks, 6" 400.00
Grenade, Red Comet, w/bracket 15.00
Helmet, brass, orig leather, English, 13½" 125.00
Helmet, Chief E Rockaway, leather shield on tan, low front, VG .75.00
Helmet, leather, Cairns New Yorker, low front 85.00
Helmet, leather, Cairns Volunteer, low front 95.00

Helmet, black leather, lion front holder, red panels and white letters, Chelton and Cheever of Boston, VG, $425.00.

Helmet, leather, Olsen, high eagle, 7 Comb, TFD 200.00
Helmet, leather, Steamer 1 RFD, high eagle, 48 Comb 335.00
Helmet, plastic, Cairns 770, red, blk, etc 30.00
Helmet, tin, blk w/gold trim/high eagle, ca 1900, G 95.00
Helmet, tin, Senator, low front 35.00
Inkwell set, Chief of Dept, brass, steamer broadside 375.00
Lantern, brass, Adams & Westlake Queen, eng globe 675.00
Lantern, brass, Ham's #6, 2-color globe 675.00
Lantern, Dietz King, Am La France Fire Engine Co, tin, Pat 07 .210.00
Lantern, Dietz King, Am La France Foamite Co, tin, Pat 07 ......250.00
Lantern, Dietz King, brass, mk Dietz, Pat 07 ....225.00
Lantern, Dietz King, brass, tubular w/slide over cage, Pat 89 ......275.00
Lantern, Dietz King, mk Seagrave Co, brass, Pat 93 ....375.00
Lantern, Dietz King, tin w/copper tank, Pat 07 ....135.00
Magazine, Playboy, fireman on cover, March 1976 ....6.50
Medal, 6-pointed star, gilt w/red & bl, NY VF, 4" dia, EX 25.00
Nozzle, Akron, brass playpipe, hard rubber hdls, 2½" 175.00
Nozzle, bayonet applicator, low velocity fog, 1½" 25.00
Nozzle, bayonet applicator, piercing..............................35.00
Nozzle, Callaghan 1883 Pat playpipe, leather hdls, 2½" 235.00
Nozzle, Larkin, brass playpipe, leather hdls, 2½" 225.00
Nozzle, Rockwood, aluminum, combination str spray/fog, 2½" 25.00
Nozzle, Rockwood, brass, combination str spray/fog, 1½" 35.00
Nozzle, Underwriters, brass, string wrap, w/tip, short, 2½" 60.00
Nozzle, Underwriters, brass, string wrap, w/tip, 2½" 40.00
Painting, Ed Wynn fire chief, oil on canvas, 1930s 85.00
Statuary, fireman, SP pot metal, Braxmar, 1890s, 17" 625.00
Tank, chemical; copper, hand drawn, 350-lbs, EX 200.00

Torch, parade; NP burner on swivel, wood hdl......................100.00
Trophy, Waterman FD, Field Day, June 1930, SP, EX 20.00
Trumpet, brass, eng scene/inscriptions/1870, SP traces, 21"........75.00
Trumpet, brass, quality reproduction, 21" 75.00
Trumpet, nickel/brass, engr, working, 17" 450.00
Trumpet, SP/brass, engr presentation, 11" 800.00
Trumpet, SP/brass, presentation, pie-crust bell, 21" 950.00
Trumpet, 2 appl helmets, Goodwille Hose #2, PA, lg, NM **1,850.00**

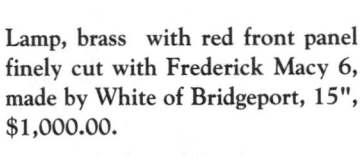

Lamp, brass with red front panel finely cut with Frederick Macy 6, made by White of Bridgeport, 15", $1,000.00.

Fire Marks

During the early 18th century, insurance companies used fire marks — signs of insurance — to indicate to the volunteer fire fighters which homes were covered by their company. Handsome rewards were promised to the brigade that successfully extinguished the blaze, so competition was fierce between rivals and sometimes resulted in an altercation at the scene to settle the matter of which brigade would be the one to fight the fire! Fire marks were originally made of cast iron or lead; later examples were sometimes tin or zinc. They were used abroad as well as in this country, and those from England tended to be much more elaborate. When municipal fire departments were organized in the mid- to late 1860s, volunteer departments and fire marks became obsolete.

Fire Association of Philadelphia, CI, oval 150.00
Mutual Assurance Co, Philadelphia, CI, oval, ca 1827..............700.00
Reliance Marine Fire Ins Co, Liverpool England, tin, M...........145.00
Securitas Anterpen, Belgium, tin, oval, M 135.00
St Paul Fire & Marine, tin, some rust, 3x6" 290.00
Union Fire Insurance, CI, ca 1870 ....850.00

Fireglow

A type of art glass attributed to Mt. Washington, fireglow is an opaque cafe au lait that glows with rich red 'fire' when held to a strong source of light.

Creamer & sugar bowl, florals, 3" 150.00

Epergne, 1-lily, HP flowers, crimped, ornate silver fr, 19" 275.00
Garniture, 2 10" vases+13" urn, exotic florals, Sandwich 650.00
Rose bowl, bl daisies, 4½" dia 125.00
Tumbler, narrow ribs, M 110.00
Vase, asters/ferns in bl & brn, mk Durand-Kimberly, 16".............225.00
Vase, flowers/leaves in bl, corset waist, 4¼" 125.00
Vase, mc flowers, ornate brass holder, 7½" 150.00
Vase, mc wild roses, bulbous, 5½"...150.00
Vase, stick neck, 7½"..110.00

Fireplace Implements

In the colonial days of our country, fireplaces provided heat in the winter and were used year round to cook food in the kitchen. The implements that were a necessary part of these functions were varied and have become treasured collectibles, many put to new use in modern homes as decorative accessories. Gypsy pots may hold magazines; copper and brass kettles, newly polished and gleaming, contain dried flowers or green plants. Firebacks, highly ornamental iron panels that once reflected heat and protected masonry walls, are now sometimes used as wall decorations.

By Victorian times, the cookstove had replaced the kitchen fireplace, and many of these early utensils were already obsolete. But as a source of heat and comfort, the fireplace continued to be used for several more decades. See also Wrought Iron.

Andirons, brass, ball finial, spur legs, Whittingham, 17" 900.00
Andirons, brass, ball finial, spur legs, 1820s, 17" 325.00
Andirons, brass, beehive design, w/log stops, 1880, 20"........... 2,000.00
Andirons, brass, EX trn stds, 3-spur legs, 1820s, rpr, 22" 325.00
Andirons, brass, Fed, acorn finial, spur legs, ball ft, 21"........... 1,400.00
Andirons, brass, Transitional QA/Chippendale, c/b ft, 20" 4,250.00
Andirons, bronze, cactus form, Van Eckhardt/Reusser, 18" 650.00

Andirons, bronze, Neo-Egyptian style, 1875, 39", $1,400.00.

Andirons, CI, comic Blk man, mk Foran Fdry 1929, 17" 400.00
Andirons, CI, Hessian soldier form, 1800s, 22" 300.00
Andirons, CI, owl form w/glass eyes, c Sept 14, 1887, 16" 450.00
Andirons, CI, seated cat form, yel glass eyes, 17" 120.00
Andirons, CI, standing baseball player, 1800s, 20" 4,800.00
Andirons, wrought iron, gooseneck finials, 19"..............................175.00
Andirons, wrought iron, penny ft, faceted finials, 15"...................200.00
Bellows, dome top, brass mts, orig leather, VG pnt 165.00

Bellows, turtle-bk, gr pnt w/floral stencil, worn, 18".......................55.00
Bellows, turtle-bk, orig bronze-powder stencil, 18" L 195.00
Broiler, wrought iron wheel shape, 3-ftd, 1700s, EX....................250.00
Broom, birch splint, ca 1840, 10½" 90.00
Crane, wrought iron, curved brace, 1700s, 34x26" 150.00
Fan, brass, pierced, 26", EX...300.00
Fender, brass, pierced, English, 1820s, 43" L 275.00
Firebk, CI, emb portrait of Major Gen Wolfe/cannons, 46" 2,700.00
Firescreen, sm faceted opal/amber glass sqs w/in brass fr 2,000.00
Kettle shelf, wrought horseshoe w/sm brass heart, 13" L 150.00
Kettle shelf, wrought iron/brass, Masonic design/'Comfort' 150.00
Mantle, pine Federal, appl eagle/acorns/ram's heads, 58x67"... 2,500.00
Mantle, pine Federal, rpt, minor wear/losses, 61x70" 225.00
Mantle, pine Federal w/pnt traces, EX cvgs w/eagle, 57x86"........900.00
Pot, cooking; cast bronze, 3 short legs, IH3 on 8" hdl 145.00
Roaster, wrought iron, circular form w/24½" hdl..........................500.00
Skewer, iron 85.00
Skillet, iron, twist hdl, early, well preserved 950.00
Skillet, iron, 3-leg, long hdl, sgn WJ Bach, VG.............................400.00
Spider, wrought, half-rnd ball form, ftd, 5½x7½", 11" hdl 350.00
Spit, iron, standing, tension adjustment, scroll ft, 26"................750.00
Toaster, star shape, wire w/wood hdl, 1900, EX 40.00
Toaster, wire forms Maltese cross, wood hdl....................................35.00
Tongs, ember; wrought iron, scissors form, 1700s, 11½" L............130.00
Tongs, wrought iron w/brass hdl, 23½"..25.00
Trammel, wrought, sawteeth, movable ring hdl, for crane, 32"....120.00

Fisher, Harrison

Harrison Fisher (1875-1934), noted illustrator and creator of the Fisher Girl, was the son of landscape artist, Hugh Antoine Fisher. His career began in his teens in San Francisco where he did artwork for the Hearst papers. Later in New York, his drawings of beautiful American women attracted much attention and graced the covers of the most popular magazines of the day – *Puck, Ladies' Home Journal, Saturday Evening Post,* and *Cosmopolitan.* He also illustrated novels, and his art books were treasured. His drawings appeared on thousands of post cards and on advertising items such as candy tins, pocket mirrors, calendars, and posters. His creation of the Fisher Girl, and his panel of six scenes of the *Greatest Moments in a Woman's Life* made him the most sought-after and well-paid illustrator of his day.

The Harrison Fisher Society, founded in 1977, maintains a communications network of collectors and dealers and also publishes a yearly exchange letter. The Society is listed under Clubs, Newsletters, and Catalogs.

Art book, A Dream of Fair Women, 1907, EX 150.00
Art book, A Girl's Life & Other Pictures, 1913, EX....................395.00
Art book, American Beauties, 1909, EX 195.00
Art book, American Belles, 11", EX...250.00
Art book, American Girls in Miniature, 1912, w/box, EX 250.00
Art book, Bachelor Belles, 1907, EX..150.00
Art book, Beauties, 1913, EX...285.00
Art book, Fair Americans, 1911, EX, ...185.00
Art book, Hiawatha, Special Edition, 1906, EX 95.00
Art book, Maidens Fair, 1912, EX...285.00
Art book, The American Girl, 1909, w/box, EX 425.00
Art book, The Harrison Fisher Book, 1907, EX............................195.00
Art book, The Little Gift Book, 1913, EX....................................185.00
Banner, Red Cross, nurse, w/Foringer's Madonna, 41½x8½", EX ..95.00
Book, Heart & Masks, 10 illus, 1905, VG......................................10.00
Bookplate, from American Beauties, fr 65.00
Candy tin, Dancing Girl, Tindeco, 2½x7" dia 40.00

Candy tin, Dancing Girl, Tindeco, 2¾x10" dia **70.00**
Candy tin, His Pledge, heart shaped, Tindeco, 2x8½x8½"..............**70.00**
Candy tin, Snowbird, Tindeco, 1⅜x4" dia **40.00**
Magazine cover, Cosmopolitan, ea...**20.00**
Magazine cover, Ladies' Home Journal, ea.....................................**22.00**
Magazine cover, Saturday Evening Post, ea **18.00**
Magazine print, Debutant, 1918, 10x14", EX **55.00**
Post card, Artist, lady w/violin, p/Reinthal-Newman, VG.............**15.00**
Post card, Autumn's Beauty, lady artist, Reinthal-Newman, EX **20.00**
Post card, Greatest Moments, set of 6 in orig matting & fr............**95.00**
Post card, Six Senses, set of 6 in orig matting & fr......................**125.00**
Poster, Have You Answered...Red Cross Christmas Roll Call **125.00**
Print, All Mine, girl w/puppy, fr **35.00**
Print, Danger, ca 1908, in old fr **85.00**
Print, Evening Hour, original fr, 8x11" **45.00**
Print, King of Hearts, orig fr, 11x13"..**65.00**
Prints, orig, old & unmatted, 11x14", ea...**35.00**
Tin container, Tindeco, Coquette masquerade girl, 6½" **45.00**

Fishing Collectibles

Collecting old fishing tackle is becoming more popular every year.
Though at first most interest was geared toward old lures and some
reels, rods, advertising, and miscellaneous items are quickly gaining
ground. Values are given for examples in excellent or better condition
and should be used only as a guide. For more information contact our
advisor Randy Hilst, an appraiser and collector whose address and
phone number are listed in the Directory under Illinois.

Catalog, Creek Chub, 1941 ....**35.00**
Catalog, Heddon, 1946 ....**35.00**
Lure, Creek Chub #100 Wiggler, glass eyes, wood..........................**20.00**
Lure, Creek Chub #200 Wiggler, glass eyes, wood..........................**20.00**
Lure, Creek Chub Castrola, glass eyes, wood..................................**75.00**
Lure, Creek Chub Crawdad, bead eyes, wood **12.50**
Lure, Creek Chub Gar Minnow, glass eyes, wood **225.00**
Lure, Creek Chub Husky Injured Minnow, glass eyes, wood..........**50.00**
Lure, Creek Chub Husky Pikie Minnow, glass eyes, wood **9.00**
Lure, Creek Chub Injured Minnow, glass eyes, wood **10.00**
Lure, Creek Chub Jigger, glass eyes, wood **100.00**
Lure, Creek Chub Jointed Pikie Minnow, glass eyes, wood............ **8.00**
Lure, Creek Chub Lucky Mouse, bead eyes, wood **50.00**
Lure, Creek Chub Midget Pikie Minnow, glass eyes, wood **7.00**
Lure, Creek Chub Plunker, glass eyes, wood **6.00**
Lure, Creek Chub Sarasota, glass eyes, wood................................**160.00**
Lure, Creek Chub Snook Pikie, glass eyes, wood............................**10.00**
Lure, Creek Chub Weed Bug, glass eyes, wood..............................**100.00**
Lure, Eger Dillinger, pnt eyes, wood..**15.00**
Lure, Heddon #00 Underwater Minnow, glass eyes, wood **125.00**
Lure, Heddon #150 Underwater Minnow, glass eyes, wood **65.00**
Lure, Heddon #20 Underwater Minnow, glass eyes, wood.............**65.00**

Lure, Heddon #300 Surface Minnow, glass eyes, wood.................**100.00**
Lure, Heddon #70, Stanley Pork-Rind, glass eyes, pyralin.............**25.00**
Lure, Heddon #800 Swimming Minnow, glass eyes, wood **250.00**
Lure, Heddon River Runt, glass eyes, wood **25.00**
Lure, Heddon SOS Wounded Minnow, glass eyes, wood **25.00**
Lure, Heddon Torpedo, glass eyes, wood.......................................**50.00**
Lure, Heddon Walton Feather Tail, glass eyes, wood.....................**75.00**
Lure, Heddon Weedless Widow, no eyes, wood **25.00**
Lure, Helga-Devil, no eyes, plastic **10.00**
Lure, Pflueger Scoop, glass eyes, wood **35.00**
Lure, Pflueger Neverfail, glass eyes, wood......................................**40.00**
Lure, Pflueger Peerless, no eyes, wood..**10.00**
Lure, Pflueger Wizard, glass eyes, wood...**30.00**
Lure, Rush Tango, no eyes, wood **50.00**
Lure, Shakespeare Bass-a-lure, glass eyes, wood............................**35.00**
Lure, Shakespeare Little Joe, glass eyes, wood **30.00**
Lure, Shakespeare Revolution, no eyes, metal...............................**135.00**
Lure, South Bend Babe Oreno, glass eyes, wood **6.00**
Lure, South Bend Combination Minnow, glass eyes, wood **65.00**
Lure, South Bend Crippled Minnow, glass eyes, wood...................**50.00**
Lure, South Bend Tease Oreno, glass eyes, wood...........................**30.00**
Lure, South Bend Vacuum Bait, glass eyes, wood **75.00**
Lure, South Bend Woodpecker, no eyes, wood **25.00**
Lure, True Temper Crippled Shad, pnt eyes, plastic.......................**10.00**
Match safe, NP brass, fishing scene on sides **40.00**
Minnow trap, glass, unmk..**25.00**
Reel, Pflueger Supreme, level wind **25.00**
Reel, Winchester #4161, non-level wind.......................................**150.00**
Rod, Hendryx, metal, 3-pc **25.00**

Flags of the United States

The brevity and imprecise language of the first Flag Act of 1777
allowed great artistic license for our early flag makers. As a result, vast
and varied interpretations were produced until 1912 when stringent
design standards were established for the new 48-star flag. Early patterns ranged from 'scatter' arrangements to elaborate wreaths and
'Great Stars.' Most surviving vintage flags are of the 'generic' variety,
devoid of any special pedigree or proven history. Nevertheless, these
cherished artifacts continue to be avidly collected on the basis of age,
scarcity, configuration, craftsmanship, and aesthetic merit.

Pre-Civil War flags of 33 stars or less are very scarce and usually
surface as 'big ticket' items. Civil War-era flags of 34 and 35 stars – also
fairly scarce – are in great demand and are priced accordingly. Although
36 and 37 star flags have less broad-based appeal, both vintages can
fetch respectable prices. Flags of 38 stars and the unofficial vintages of
39, 40, and 42 stars provide a popular, moderately-priced marketplace
for journeyman collectors, while the elusive 43-star flag is sought by
nearly everyone. Flags of 44, 45, and 46 stars are commonly available,
appealing largely to junior collectors. Ordinary 48-star flags have no
serious value or market appeal, but the scarcer 49-star flag may attract
modest attention. 13-star flags surface in all forms and must be judged
on a case-by-case basis. Many flag buffs favor flag sizes that are
manageable for wall display, and most will make allowances for normal
wear and tear. Modern-day flag repros of any vintage are of little or no
interest to the serious collector.

The dollar value of a flag is by no means based on age alone. The
wide price swings in the listings that follow are the result of a variety of
special considerations and features. Mass-printed flags, for instance, are
generally not the equal of hand-crafted flags, nor do unions with con-
ventional rows of stars compare to the remarkable 'Great Star' and
wreath patterns of the past. In fact, almost any special feature that
stands out as unusual or distinctive is a potential asset. Imprinted flags

**Heddon #209F Surface Bait in Frog finish, L-rig, with original box
and pocket catalog, $100.00.**

and inscribed flags; 8-pointed stars, gold stars, and added stars; extra stripes, missing stripes, tri-color stripes, and war stripes are all part of the pricing equation. And while political and military flags may rank above all others in terms of prestige and price, any flag with a significant and well-documented historical connection has 'star' potential (pardon the pun).

Our advisor for this category is Robert Banks; he is listed in the Directory under Maryland.

13 stars, Betsy Ross flag, by grandaughter, 1903, 8x12"	500.00
13 stars, Civil War boat ensign, USS Wabash, 44x64"	1,000.00
13 stars, in semi-wreath, hand-sewn, 1870s, 54x102"	140.00
13 stars, printed w/advertisement, 1880s, 4x7"	18.00
13 stars, US Navy boat ensign, dtd Sept 1904, 44x78"	75.00
13 stars, 3rd MD pattern, hand-sewn, 1840s, 32x45"	445.00
19 stars, 16 orig+3, sewn scrap fabric, 39x66"	660.00
23 stars, Civil War related, home-sewn muslin, 48x96"	200.00
25 stars, stenciled burlap on 24" wood tripod pole, 5x7"	170.00
26 stars, Great Star, embr on sewn silk, 30x43"	630.00
31 stars, Great Star, Lincoln related, printed, 11x14"	145.00
31 stars, Great Star, 14 stripes, hand-sewn, 39x69"	550.00
32 stars, dbl wreath of inset stars, hand-sewn, 36x48"	335.00
33 stars, hand- & machine-sewn wool bunting, 66x92"	275.00
33 stars, printed wreath pattern, glazed muslin, 16x22"	50.00
33 stars, wreath w/10 stripes, hand-sewn, 77x127"	380.00
34 stars, dbl-wreath pattern, printed silk, 18x28"	120.00
34 stars, Garfield campaign legend, printed, 24x48"	225.00

34-star hand and machine-stitched in the 'Great Star' pattern, wool and cottons, 92" x 154", $460.00.

34 stars, pattern variation, hand-sewn, damaged, 48x117"	180.00
34 stars, pattern variation, stitched cotton, 76x136"	260.00
35 stars, recruiting flag, sewn bunting, 50x116"	245.00
36 stars, Civil War, 8-pointed sewn wreath, 78x90"	720.00
36 stars, hand-sewn wool bunting, 68x85"	185.00
36 stars, hand/machine-sewn bunting, damaged, 62x96"	135.00
36 stars, sewn pattern variation, deteriorating, 110x168"	65.00
36 stars, 11 tri-color stripes, hand-sewn, 51x99"	230.00
37 stars, hand/machine-sewn wool bunting, 48x69"	195.00
37 stars, printed silk, 32x40"	40.00
37 stars, wreath pattern, hand-sewn cotton, 72x106"	290.00
38 stars, Blaine campaign, printed cotton, 17x27"	250.00
38 stars, Centennial 1886, printed cotton, 15x24"	48.00
38 stars, clamp-dye printed wool bunting, 48x78"	55.00
38 stars, double-wreath pattern, sewn muslin, 87x128"	160.00
38 stars, flag of the SS America, sewn bunting, 68x108"	320.00

38 stars, Great Star, printed silk, gold fringe, 12x17"	40.00
38 stars, pattern variation, hand-sewn, 96x164"	80.00
38 stars, pattern variation, hand/machine-sewn, 48x95"	66.00
38 stars, pattern variation, printed/sized muslin, 19x28"	28.00
38 stars, triple-wreath pattern, sewn bunting, 76x136"	240.00
38 stars, Union on red war stripe, homemade, 44x84"	75.00
39 stars, clamp-dye printed wool bunting, 56x117"	95.00
39 stars, originally 34 Great Star, sewn, 69x129"	310.00
39 stars, scatter pattern, hand-sewn, 78x120"	170.00
39 stars, unofficial silk flag, printed, 12x16"	32.00
40 stars, printed heavy-gauge bunting, 43x64"	55.00
40 stars, unofficial, hand/machine-sewn, 61x115"	90.00
40 stars, wreath-in-box pattern, hand-sewn, 43x82"	140.00
42 stars, minor pattern variation, sewn bunting, 96x138"	68.00
42 stars, printed cotton, unhemmed, 18x24"	22.00
42 stars, Union scatter pattern, hand-sewn, 48x72"	114.00
42 stars, unofficial, machine/hand-sewn, 120x180"	89.00
43 stars, machine-sewn bunting, extremely rare, 29x70"	382.00
44 stars, family flag w/history, machine-sewn, 84x156"	75.00
44 stars, hand-sewn bunting, 70x144", EX	85.00
44 stars, machine-sewn cotton bunting, 53x82"	45.00
45 stars, machine-sewn cotton bunting, 80x108"	24.00
45 stars, modified 38-star, hand-sewn, 120x192"	110.00
45 stars, printed silk, 33x48"	11.00
45 stars, triple-wreath GAR flag, printed muslin, 11x16"	40.00
45 stars, Union, hand-sewn wool bunting, 92x135"	30.00
45 stars, Union Jack, machine-sewn bunting, 50x76"	37.00
46 stars, machine-sewn cotton bunting, 96x142"	28.00
46 stars, printed silk, in baton-type carrying tube, 12x17"	17.00
46 stars, random pattern, machine-sewn, 40x100"	55.00
47 stars, unofficial sewn bunting, 108x137"	95.00
48 stars, embr on machine-sewn rayon, 23x38"	6.00
48 stars, machine-sewn cotton bunting, 60x96"	12.00
48 stars, modified 44-star flag, hand-sewn, 60x90"	60.00
48 stars, sewn canton resting on red war stripe, 41x61"	35.00
48 stars, staggered rows, printed muslin, 13x23"	4.00
48 stars, Whipple Peace Flag, printed silk, 14x24"	160.00
49 stars, embr w/sewn stripes, cotton bunting, 24x36"	8.00
49 stars, embr w/sewn stripes, gold fringe, 48x72"	30.00
49 stars, machine-sewn cotton bunting, 36x60"	15.00
49 stars, Navy Jack, machine-sewn nylon, 32x48"	12.00
50 stars, Carter's campaign flag, printed plastic, 12x18"	15.00
50 stars, unauthorized pattern, printed acetate, 4x6"	3.00

Florence Ceramics

Figurines marked 'Florence Ceramics' were produced in the forties and fifties in Pasadena, California. The quality of the ware and the attention given to detail are prompting a growing interest among today's collectors. The names of these lovely ladies, gents, and figural groups are nearly always incised into their bases. The company name is ink-stamped. Because this is a relatively new area of collecting and the rarity of many items has yet to be determined, examples are evaluated by size and the intricacy of design.

Our advisor for this category is Jack Chipman; he is listed in the Director under California.

Abigail, 8¼"	95.00
Angel, wht w/gold trim, 7¾"	95.00
Ava, wht blouse, gr skirt, blk hair, 10½"	125.00
Boy w/ice cream cone, 7¼"	65.00
Chinese lantern boy, bl & wht	50.00
Choir boy, blk & wht robe, 6"	50.00

Clarissa, pk w/gold trim, 7¾" 125.00
Delia, maroon, 8" 100.00
Diane, 7¾" 115.00
Douglas, gray-bl clothes, 8¼" 95.00
Elaine, wht, 6" 75.00
Elizabeth, seated on couch, elaborate, 8¼x7" 200.00
Ellen, bl, 6½" 70.00
Ethel, 7¼" 115.00
Irene, gray, 5½" 65.00
Jeanette, gr top w/peplum over cream skirt, gold trim, 7¾" 115.00
Jeanie 115.00
Jennifer, 8" 125.00
Kiu & She-Ti, Oriental couple, pr 200.00
Madelyn..135.00

Martin, 10½", $125.00.

Matilda, gray w/gr trim, 8¼" 75.00
Melanie, 7" 75.00
Mermaid Betty, purple 115.00
Sue Ellen, gold trim, 8¼" 95.00

Florentine Cameo

Although its appearance may look much like English cameo, the decoration on this type of glass is not wheel cut or acid etched. Instead, a type of heavy paste – usually a frosty white – is applied to the surface to create a look very similar to true cameo. It was produced in France as well as England; it is sometimes marked 'Florentine.'

Pitcher, basketweave cut, yel chinoiserie on bl satin, 8" 195.00
Pitcher, bird/flowers, wht on bl frost, clear frost hdl, 8" 195.00
Tumbler, floral, wht on red, 3¾" 100.00
Vase, floral, wht on lt bl, stick neck, 8½" 75.00
Vase, floral/bird, wht on red, stick neck, 9" 100.00
Vase, florals/leaves, wht on cranberry, 9¼".................160.00
Vase, 3 cameos, ea w/lady, wht on dk bl, stick neck, 7"................200.00

Flow Blue

Flow Blue ware was produced by many Staffordshire potters; among the most familiar were Meigh, Podmore and Walker, Samuel Alcock, Ridgway, John Wedge Wood (who often signed his work Wedgwood), and Davenport. It was popular from about 1825 through 1860 and again from 1880 until the turn of the century. The name describes the blurred or flowing affect of the cobalt decoration, achieved through the introduction of a chemical vapor into the kiln. The body of the ware is ironstone, and Oriental motifs were favored. Later issues were on a lighter body and often decorated with gilt.

Our advisor, Mary Frank Gaston, has compiled a lovely book, *The Collector's Encyclopedia of Flow Blue China*, with full-color illustrations and current market values; you will find her address in the Directory under Texas.

Abbey, teapot, Geo Jones 325.00
Alaska, platter, 14" 100.00
Albany, bowl, vegetable; hdls, Grindley, 9¼" 85.00
Aldine, butter pat, Grindley..12.00
Aldine, platter, Grindley, 18x13".................................225.00
Amoy, bowl, Davenport, ca 1844, 6x8" 200.00
Amoy, creamer, Davenport..250.00
Amoy, cup & saucer, handleless; Davenport 125.00
Amoy, plate, Davenport, 1844, 10½" 90.00
Amoy, plate, Davenport, 9¼" 85.00
Amoy, plate, dessert; Davenport.....................................55.00
Amoy, platter, Davenport, 14¾" 275.00
Amoy, platter, Davenport, 16x12" 385.00
Amoy, sauce, Davenport, 5" 60.00
Amoy, saucer, Davenport..40.00
Arabesque, cup & saucer, Mayer 85.00
Arabesque, platter, Mayer, 13" 125.00
Arabesque, platter, Mayer, 16" 150.00
Arabesque, soup, Mayer, 1845 ....80.00
Argyle, bone dish, Grindley...48.00
Argyle, bowl, vegetable; final rpr, Grindley 125.00
Argyle, butter pat, Grindley 30.00
Argyle, creamer, Grindley 125.00
Argyle, flanged soup, Grindley 70.00
Argyle, gravy boat, Grindley 125.00
Argyle, plate, Grindley, 10" 70.00
Argyle, plate, Grindley, 8" 50.00
Argyle, plate, Grindley, 9" 60.00
Argyle, platter, Grindley, 17½x12" 160.00
Ashburton, bowl, vegetable; oval, 10" 75.00
Ashburton, butter dish, Grindley, 3-pc........................200.00
Ashburton, platter, 20x15"..250.00
Ashburton, soup tureen, finial rpr................................195.00
Astoria, plate, New Wharf Pottery, ca 1891, 9" 70.00
Astoria, platter, 12" 85.00
Athens, bowl, vegetable; w/lid 400.00
Athens, teapot, Meigh 400.00
Baltic, plate, Grindley, ca 1891, 10" 60.00
Beaufort, platter, Grindley, 16x11¼" 175.00
Beauties of China, plate, 8½" 75.00
Bentick, butter dish, Cauldon 148.00
Bentick, platter, Cauldon, 15".......................................135.00
Bentick, soup, rimmed, Cauldon 45.00
Blue Danube, butter pat, Johnson Bros 30.00
Blue Danube, plate, Johnson Bros, 10" 45.00
Blue Danube, platter, Johnson Bros, 18x13" 175.00
Brazil, plate, 9" 42.00
Burleigh, bowl, vegetable; w/lid, Wedgwood, 12" 145.00
Burleigh, bowl, vegetable; w/lid, 10" 145.00
Burleigh, butter dish w/drainer, Wedgwood 250.00
Burleigh, sugar bowl, w/lid, Wedgwood 125.00
Burleigh, waste bowl, Wedgwood....................................80.00

Cambridge, platter, Meakin, 14" 185.00
Candia, plate, 7" 45.00
Canton, platter, Maddock, 13¼" 275.00
Canton, platter, Maddock, 17½" dia 450.00
Cashmere, creamer 285.00
Cashmere, cup & saucer, Morley 125.00
Cashmere, plate, Morely, 10⅝" 130.00
Chapoo, plate, 9⅜" 90.00
Chapoo, platter, 13½x10¼" 350.00
Chapoo, teapot 350.00
Chelsea, bowl, vegetable; w/lid, Weatherby & Sons ...195.00
Chen-Si, bowl, vegetable; Maier, 9" 132.00
Chen-Si, cup & saucer, Maier 80.00
Chen-Si, plate, Maier, 1835, 8¾" 80.00
Chinese, platter, Wedgwood, 17x14" 325.00
Chusan, butter dish, Podmore Walker, 1845 ....125.00
Chusan, pitcher, water; Fell 395.00
Chusan, pitcher, Wedgwood, 7½" 295.00
Chusan, plate, Clementson, 7¾" 45.00
Chusan, teapot, Fell 350.00
Claremont, ale tankard, 6¾" 325.00
Claremont, sugar bowl, w/lid, Johnson Bros 148.00
Clarence, bone dish, Grindley, ca 1900 ....32.00
Clarence, bowl, dessert; Grindley 32.00
Clarence, pitcher, Grindley, 8" 145.00
Clarence, plate, Grindley, 10" 50.00
Clarence, soup tureen 240.00
Clayton, waste bowl, Johnson Bros 140.00
Clifton, soup plate, Grindley 55.00
Coburg, creamer, Edwards 185.00
Coburg, soup, Edwards, 10½" 88.00
Colonial, pitcher, Meakin, 6" 140.00
Colonial, sauce 27.00
Colonial, soup tureen, w/lid, Meakin 325.00
Columbia, sugar bowl, Clementson 250.00
Constance, plate, 9" 25.00
Conway, bowl, New Wharf Pottery, 8½" 75.00
Conway, cup & saucer, New Wharf Pottery 65.00
Conway, plate, New Wharf Pottery, 9" 55.00
Conway, platter, New Wharf Pottery, 10" 60.00
Conway, soup, New Wharf Pottery, 9" 45.00
Conway, waste bowl, New Wharf Pottery 100.00
Corey Hill, cup & saucer 90.00
Corey Hill, ladle, 9" 250.00
Corey Hill, sugar bowl 175.00
Cows, pitcher, 12" 225.00
Crumlin, gravy boat, w/underplate, Myott 98.00
Crumlin, plate, Myott, 9" 30.00
Crumlin, tureen, w/lid, Myott, 12" 265.00
Dainty, cup, demitasse; Burgess & Leigh 50.00
Dainty, sauce 30.00
Daisy, cup, demitasse; Burgess & Leigh 55.00
Daisy, plate, Burgess & Leigh, 10" 44.00
Davenport, bowl, vegetable; w/lid, Wood & Sons 130.00
Davenport, creamer, Wood & Sons 75.00
Davenport, gravy boat, Wood & Sons 80.00
Davenport, plate, Wood & Sons, 8" 34.00
Del Monte, creamer, Johnson Bros 85.00
Del Monte, plate, 9" 40.00
Delamere, cup & saucer, Alcock 65.00
Delaware, plate, 10½" 48.00
Delaware, platter, Meakin, 20" 260.00
Denton, egg cup, sm. 40.00
Denton, platter, 14" 105.00

Devon, bowl, oval, w/lid, Ford & Sons 110.00
Devon, gravy boat 35.00
Doreen, bowl, Grindley, 5½x18" 135.00

Doreen, covered chamber, Grindley, $475.00.

Dorothy, bone dish, Johnson Bros 40.00
Dorothy, platter, 17" 135.00
Dorothy, sauce, Johnson Bros, 6" 18.00
Duchess, bone dish, Grindley 40.00
Duchess, bowl, w/lid, 5½x11" 130.00
Duchess, tureen, Grindley, 8" 110.00
Fairy Villas, bowl, vegetable; rectangular, Adams, 11x8" ...110.00
Fairy Villas, cup & saucer, Adams 60.00
Fairy Villas, plate, Adams, 10" 80.00
Fairy Villas, plate, Adams, 7" 28.00
Fairy Villas, plate, Adams, 8" 45.00
Fairy Villas, soup, flanged rim, Adams 50.00
Fleur-de-lis, bone dish 20.00
Florida, bowl, Grindley, 7½" 55.00
Florida, bowl, Johnson Bros, 7½" 58.00
Florida, butter dish, Grindley 295.00
Florida, gravy boat, Johnson Bros 60.00
Florida, plate, Grindley, 10" 60.00
Florida, plate, Grindley, 9" 45.00
Florida, platter, Grindley, 14x10" 200.00
Florida, saucer, Johnson Bros, 6" 15.00
Fuchsia, invalid feeder 350.00
Gem, gravy boat, w/underplate, Johnson Bros 40.00
Gem, soup plate, Johnson Bros 20.00
Geneva, pitcher, Doulton, 4" 115.00
Geneva, pitcher & bowl, Doulton 900.00
Geneva, plate, Doulton, 6½" 32.00
Georgia, bowl, Johnson Bros, 9" 50.00
Georgia, plate, Johnson Bros, 10" 45.00
Gironde, bowl, vegetable; w/lid, Grindley 75.00
Gironde, butter dish, Grindley 100.00
Gironde, butter pat, Grindley 18.00
Gironde, plate, Grindley, 7" 27.50
Glenwood, cup & saucer, Johnson Bros 65.00
Glenwood, plate, Johnson Bros, 10" 65.00
Glenwood, tureen, vegetable; w/lid, Johnson 225.00
Gothic, bowl, vegetable; 1850s, 9⅝" 110.00

Gothic, gravy boat, Mayer, ca 1845 ....210.00
Gothic, teapot, bulbous, Furnival, ca 1850 ....535.00
Hamilton, bowl, Maddock & Son, 10" 50.00
Hamilton, sauce ladle 75.00
Hampton Spray, bowl, gold trim, Grindley, 6" 30.00
Hindustan, cup plate 95.00
Holland, butter dish, Johnson Bros 130.00
Holland, egg cup, Johnson Bros 50.00
Holland, platter, Johnson Bros, lg 155.00
Honc, creamer, Regout 148.00
Honc, plate, Regout, 9" 75.00
Hong Kong, bowl, 12-sided, 10½" 275.00
Hong Kong, plate, Meigh, 10½" 100.00
Huron, vase, 5" 75.00
Idris, bone dish, Grindley 55.00
Idris, bouillon cup, hdls, w/underplate, Grindley 45.00
Idris, sugar bowl 150.00
Indian, platter, Pratt, 13½x10¼" 225.00
Indian Jar, gravy boat, Furnival 165.00
Indian Jar, platter, Furnival, 14" 300.00
Indian Jar, sugar bowl, rpl lid 275.00
Indian Jar, teapot, octagonal, Furnival 380.00
Ivanhoe, plate, Wedgwood, 10¼" 75.00
Janette, tureen, vegetable; w/lid, Grindley 200.00
Jeddo, relish dish, 5x7½" 50.00
Keele, platter, Grindley, 9" 115.00
Kenworth, bowl, vegetable; w/lid, Johnson Bros 125.00
Kenworth, butter dish 150.00
Knox, pitcher, 6" 155.00
Knox, platter, New Wharf Pottery, 10½" 100.00
Knox, sauce, New Wharf Pottery, 5" 22.00
Korea, cup & saucer, handleless 65.00
Kyber, charger, Adams, 12" 130.00
Kyber, plate, Adams, 10" 100.00
Kyber, plate, Adams, 8" 65.00
Kyber, plate, 9" 75.00
Kyber, platter, 10x7¼" 145.00
La Belle, bowl, scalloped, lg 165.00
La Belle, bowl, vegetable; sq 65.00
La Belle, cup & saucer 45.00
La Belle, spittoon, hairline, rare 575.00
La Belle, sugar bowl, open 85.00
La Francais, bowl, cereal 18.00
La Francais, bowl, 8½" 20.00
La Francais, butter pat 6.00
La Francais, gravy boat 45.00
La Francais, platter, 12½x9½" 60.00
Lahore, creamer, Philips & Son 185.00
Lahore, plate, Philips & Son, 7½" 50.00
Lahore, platter, Philips & Son, 16x12" 280.00
Lakewood, bowl, vegetable; Wood 65.00
Lakewood, butter pat, Wood 25.00
Lancaster, cup & saucer, New Wharf Pottery 60.00
Lancaster, gravy boat, New Wharf Pottery 65.00
Lancaster, plate, New Wharf Pottery, 10" 60.00
Lancaster, plate, New Wharf Pottery, 9" 50.00
Lancaster, sauce 30.00
Le Pavot, platter, oval, Grindley, 18x13" 175.00
Linda, butter dish, Maddock & Son 75.00
Linda, plate, bread & butter; Maddock & Son 20.00
Linda, plate, Maddock & Son, 10" 45.00
Lorne, bowl, Grindley, 10" 48.00
Lorne, bowl, vegetable; w/lid, Grindley 250.00
Lorne, creamer, Grindley 80.00

Lorne, cup & saucer, Grindley 55.00
Lorne, gravy boat, Grindley 70.00
Lorne, plate, Grindley, 10" 55.00
Lorne, plate, Grindley, 9" 45.00
Lorne, platter, Grindley, 16" 100.00
Lotus, cup & saucer, Grindley 50.00
Lotus, plate, Grindley, 9" 45.00
Lotus, platter, Grindley, 16x12" 120.00
Lustre Band, cookie plate 90.00
Madras, bowl, vegetable; rnd, w/lid, Doulton 240.00
Madras, cup, bouillon; w/underplate, Doulton 75.00
Madras, pitcher, Doulton, 8" 365.00
Madras, plate, dinner; Doulton 65.00
Madras, plate, luncheon; Doulton 45.00
Madras, platter, Alcock, 13½" 145.00
Madras, soup plate, Alcock, 10¼" 65.00
Madras, tureen, vegetable; Doulton, EX 300.00
Magnolia, creamer & sugar bowl, Johnson Bros 225.00
Manhattan, bowl, Alcock, 9" 48.00
Manhattan, creamer, Alcock, ind sz 105.00
Manhattan, cup & saucer, Alcock 50.00
Manhattan, teapot, Alcock 260.00
Manilla, bowl, vegetable; w/lid 475.00
Manilla, gravy boat, Podmore Walker 125.00
Manilla, plate, Podmore Walker, 10" 100.00
Manilla, platter, Podmore Walker, 16x13" 325.00
Manilla, sugar bowl, lion hdls, Podmore Walker 275.00
Manilla, teapot, prof rpr 300.00
Manilla, waste bowl 150.00
Marechal Niel, bowl, vegetable; w/lid, Grindley 160.00
Marechal Niel, gravy boat, Grindley 80.00
Marechal Niel, soup, flanged, Grindley, 8½" 58.00
Marechal Niel, sugar bowl, Grindley 125.00
Marechal Niel, teapot, Grindley 300.00
Marguerite, platter, Grindley, 1891, 18" 120.00
Marguerite, tureen, vegetable; w/lid 195.00
Marie, gravy boat, Grindley 70.00
Marie, pitcher, Grindley, 6½" 75.00
Marie, platter, Grindley, 16" 150.00
Marlborough, plate, Grindley, 9" 45.00
Marquis, cup & saucer, Grindley 55.00
Marquis, plate, 6" 25.00
Marquis, plate, 9" 30.00
May, tureen, w/lid, Grindley, 8½" 110.00
Melbourne, egg cup, Grindley 45.00
Melbourne, gravy boat, hdls, attached tray, Grindley ...200.00
Melbourne, platter, Grindley, 11" 125.00
Melbourne, platter, Grindley, 16" 185.00
Melbourne, platter, Grindley, 18" 245.00
Melbourne, sugar bowl, hdls 45.00
Millais, bowl, 8" 30.00
Millais, plate, 9" 32.00
Mongolia, bowl, vegetable; oval, Johnson Bros, 10" ...65.00
Mongolia, plate, Johnson Bros, 7" 25.00
Mongolia, platter, Johnson Bros, 12" 80.00
Muriel, gravy boat, Hanley 65.00
Muriel, sugar bowl, w/lid, Hanley 135.00
Muriel, teapot, +cr/sug, Hanley 650.00
Nankin, pitcher, Doulton, 7½" 175.00
Nankin, plate, Doulton, 9" 57.00
Ning-Po, butter dish, Hall 395.00
Ning-Po, plate, 9½" 95.00
Non Pareil, bowl, vegetable; w/lid, Burgess & Leigh ...225.00
Non Pareil, butter pat 25.00

Non Pareil, charger, 13" 295.00
Non Pareil, plate, Burgess & Leigh, 7" 42.00
Non Pareil, sugar bowl, w/lid, Burgess & Leigh 175.00
Oregon, cup & saucer, handleless; Mayer 88.00
Oregon, sauce, Mayer, ca 1845, 5" 60.00
Oregon, teapot 495.00
Oriental, butter dish, w/insert, Ridgway 225.00
Oriental, plate, Ridgway, 9" 40.00
Oriental, plate, 7½" 35.00
Osborne, bowl, vegetable; rnd, w/lid, 7½" 180.00
Osborne, gravy boat 65.00
Osborne, platter, Grindley, 14x10¼" 165.00
Osborne, teapot, Ridgway 150.00
Oxford, bowl, oval, Johnson Bros, 7¾" 25.00
Oxford, butter pat, Johnson Bros 20.00
Oxford, plate, Johnson Bros, 8¾" 45.00
Oxford, platter, Ford & Sons, 15½" 95.00
Oxford, platter, Johnson Bros, 14" 125.00
Paris, bowl, 7" 35.00
Paris, plate, Johnson Bros, 10" 45.00
Paris, plate, New Wharf Pottery, 9" 55.00
Paris, platter, New Wharf Pottery, 14½" 140.00
Peach, bowl, vegetable; oval, w/lid, Johnson Bros, 8x6" 135.00
Peach, platter, Johnson Bros, 14" 100.00
Peach, soup, flanged, Johnson Bros 36.00
Peking, teapot, +cr/sug, Podmore Walker, ca 1840 ....900.00
Pelew, bowl, Challinor, 10" 110.00
Pelew, cup & saucer, handleless; Challinor 95.00
Pelew, plate, Challinor, 9½" 100.00
Pelew, platter, 10" 165.00
Pelew, sugar bowl, w/lid, Challinor 250.00
Pelew, teapot 550.00
Pelew, tureen, w/lid, Challinor, 6½x10" 350.00
Petunia, platter, 14x10" 85.00
Poppy, bowl, Bennett, 8½" 50.00
Poppy, gravy boat, Grindley 85.00
Poppy, plate, dinner; Grindley, 1890s, 10" 30.00
Poppy, soup, flat rim, Grindley 25.00
Poppy, teapot, A Wood 150.00
Portman, bowl, vegetable; oval, 8" 80.00
Primrose, pitcher, Wood & Sons, 7½" 140.00
Raleigh, bowl, Burgess & Leigh, 8" 40.00
Raleigh, casserole, w/lid, Burgess & Leigh 225.00
Raleigh, cup & saucer, Burgess & Leigh 40.00
Raleigh, pie plate, Burgess & Leigh, 6" 18.00
Raleigh, plate, Burgess & Leigh, 8½" 30.00
Raleigh, plate, Burgess & Leigh, 9½" 42.50
Raleigh, platter, Burgess & Leigh, 13" 125.00
Raleigh, platter, Burgess & Leigh, 17½x14½" 195.00
Raleigh, soup, Burgess & Leigh, 9" 27.50
Regent, bowl, vegetable; w/lid, 12" 185.00
Rhine, cup plate 65.00
Richmond, bowl, vegetable; w/lid, Johnson Bros 215.00
Richmond, butter dish, Johnson Bros 98.00
Richmond, plate, Johnson Bros, 8" 40.00
Richmond, platter, Johnson Bros, 15" 100.00
Richmond, sauce, Johnson Bros 28.00
Romantic, pitcher & bowl, rectangular 750.00
Rose, butter dish, Grindley 85.00
Rose, gravy goat, w/underplate, Grindley 120.00
Royal Blue, egg cup, Burgess & Campbell 65.00
Saskia, wash bowl & pitcher, Ridgway, ca 1841 ....625.00
Savoy, gravy boat 105.00
Savoy, sugar bowl, w/lid 115.00

Scinde, bowl, vegetable; w/lid, oval, rpr finial, Alcock 365.00
Scinde, cup plate, Alcock 85.00
Scinde, gravy boat, Alcock 200.00
Scinde, pitcher, Alcock, 1840s, 10" 500.00
Scinde, pitcher, milk; Alcock, 8" 395.00
Scinde, plate, Alcock, 10¼" 135.00
Scinde, platter, Alcock, 16x12½" 375.00
Scinde, platter, Walker, 15½" 300.00
Scinde, relish, Alcock 100.00
Scinde, soup, Alcock, 10½" 80.00
Scinde, teapot, Alcock, lg 485.00
Sefton, gravy boat 85.00
Segapore, pitcher, water 395.00
Shanghae, creamer, Furnival 125.00
Shanghae, plate, Furnival, 9" 100.00
Shanghai, cup & saucer, bouillon; Grindley 70.00
Shanghai, plate, Adams, 9" 70.00
Shanghai, plate, England, 9¾" 65.00
Shanghai, plate, Grindley, 10" 100.00
Shanghai, sugar bowl, Grindley 125.00
Shell, creamer 250.00
Shell, relish 235.00
Shell, sugar bowl 225.00
Shell, teapot, +cr/sug, prof rpr 850.00
Singan, plate, Goodfellow, ca 1840, 8¼" 65.00
Spinach, cup & saucer, Libertos 75.00
Stanley, bowl, berry; 10" 45.00
Stanley, cup & saucer 45.00
Stanley, gravy boat w/stand, Johnson Bros 130.00
Stanley, pitcher, 6" 85.00
Stanley, plate, 7" 25.00
Stanley, plate, 9" 30.00
Stanley, platter, Johnson Bros, 12½x9½" 88.00
Star, bowl, vegetable; Grimwade, w/lid 195.00
Sweet Pea, toothbrush holder, Grimwade, 5½" 110.00
Sydney, platter, 14" 150.00
Temple, cup & saucer, handleless 125.00
Temple, plate, 10" 100.00
Temple, plate, 9" 80.00
Temple, saucer, Podmore Walker 35.00
Togo, creamer 85.00
Togo, sugar bowl, w/lid 105.00
Tonquin, plate, Adams, ca 1845, 7½" 60.00
Tonquin, plate, Adams, 9½" 100.00
Tonquin, plate, Heath, 7½" 60.00
Tonquin, plate, Heath, 9½" 95.00
Tonquin, soup, Heath, 10½" 125.00
Tonquin, wash bowl & pitcher, Adams, ca 1845 ....950.00
Touraine, bowl, Stanley, 1898, 9" 45.00
Touraine, bowl, vegetable; oval, w/lid, lg 250.00
Touraine, cup & saucer, Alcock 65.00
Touraine, cup & saucer, Stanley 65.00
Touraine, pitcher, water; Stanley 300.00
Touraine, plate, Stanley, 10" 80.00
Touraine, platter, 15x11½" 250.00
Touraine, sugar bowl, w/lid, Alcock 125.00
Trilby, cake plate, advertising, 10½" 55.00
Troy, plate, Meigh, 1845, 8¼" 50.00
Tulip, pitcher, 6" 225.00
Turin, bowl, w/lid, Johnson Bros, 11" 155.00
Turin, plate, Johnson Bros, 10" 55.00
Turin, plate, Johnson Bros, 9" 45.00
Turin, platter, Johnson Bros, 14½x10½" 135.00
Turin, platter, Johnson Bros, 16x12" 150.00

Turin, soup, Johnson Bros	35.00
Turkey, game set, platter+4 plates	475.00
Tyrolean, charger, Ridgway, 12¼"	160.00

Valencia, platter, 10", $80.00.

Vermont, plate, 10"	48.00
Verona, pickle dish, Ridgway, 5x8½"	50.00
Verona, platter, 11¾x9½"	125.00
Virginia, platter, emb hdls, Maddock, 18x15"	325.00
Wagon Wheel, plate, 5½"	40.00
Waldorf, plate, New Wharf Pottery, 9"	50.00
Waldorf, platter, 10½x8"	140.00
Watteau, bowl, oval	95.00
Watteau, compote, rtcl, Doulton, 6½"	88.00
Watteau, cup, Doulton	65.00
Watteau, platter, Doulton, 13½x11"	275.00
Watteau, platter, 11x8"	185.00
Watteau, punch bowl, Doulton, rare	1,095.00
Watteau, soup, flanged, Doulton, 8½"	75.00
Weir, tureen, vegetable; w/lid, Ford & Sons, 7x11"	135.00
Wentworth, bone dish	40.00
Windsor Wreath, compote, oval, hdls, tall ped	225.00

Flue Covers

When spring house cleaning started and the heating stove was taken down for the warm weather season, the unsightly hole where the stovepipe joined the chimney was hidden with an attractive flue cover. They were made with a colorful litho print behind glass with a chain for hanging. Although scarce today, some scenes were actually reverse painted on the glass itself. The most popular motifs were florals, children, and lovely ladies. Square, rectangular, or diamond shapes are more valuable than oval or round covers, especially when Victorian ladies or children are pictured. Occasionally flue covers were made in sets of three – one served a functional purpose, while the other two were added to provide a more attractive wall arrangement. They range in size from 7"-8" to 13"-14", but 9" is the average.

Floral medallion w/palmetto surround, CI, 16"	30.00
Roman lady's profile, gold emb paper	24.00
Victorian children, under glass, 9"	35.00
Victorian girl in pk dress, 8¾"	38.00
Victorian lady in lg hat, under glass, 9½"	30.00

Vintage car, under glass	45.00
Winter country scene, brass fr, sgn	30.00

Folk Art

That the creative energies of the mind ever spark innovations in functional utilitarian channels as well as toward playful frivolity is well documented in the study of American folk art. While the average early settler rarely had free time to pursue art for its own sake, his creative energy exemplified itself in fashioning useful objects carved or otherwise ornamented beyond the scope of pure practicality. After the advent of the Industrial Revolution, the pace of everyday living became more leisurely, and country folk found they had extra time. Not accustomed to sitting idle, many turned to carving, painting, or weaving. Whirligigs, imaginative toys for the children, and whimsies of all types resulted. Though often rather crude, this type of early art represents a segment of our heritage and as such has become valued by collectors. See also Baskets; Decoys; Frakturs; Samplers; Trade Signs; Weathervanes; Wood Carvings.

Back scratcher, cvd ivory hand mtd on 15½" stick, from NH	22.00
Birdhouse, log-cabin form, weathered pnt, 19"	250.00
Broom holder, wall mt, cvd/pnt as shield, wire/wood	28.00
Calligraphy, alligator & sm Blk boy, 10x21"	2,000.00
Calligraphy, dragon/tree/Am flag, ink/crayon, 1880, 25x31"	375.00
Calligraphy, family record, last date 1895, 21x30"	65.00
Calligraphy, leaping deer, sgn, stained, 20x28"	100.00
Cvg, head of man w/mustache, sandstone w/mc pnt, 10", EX	90.00
Cvg, pig, sandstone, sgn E Reed 1982, 18"	425.00
Kaleidoscope, tiger maple, red & mustard pnt, early, 9½"	165.00
Paper cutout, altar-like w/crucifixion, lamb, etc, 10x13"	165.00
Paper cutout, leaf form, minor damage, in fr, 9x12"	95.00
Puzzle chain, cvd wood, sailor's, 1800s, 24"	175.00
Sheep, cvd & pnt, ca 1900, 5¾x9¼", 3⅝x4¾", pr	875.00
Snake, made from coiled vine growth, cvd head, blk pnt, 10"	225.00
Theorem on velvet, bird/foliage wreath, 4x5" in 8x10" fr	110.00
Theorem on velvet, detailed flowers, gold-leaf fr, 16x20"	1,100.00
Theorem on velvet, flowers, orig gold-leaf fr, 11½x10¼"	345.00
Theorem on velvet, fruit, Am, 1800s, fr, 10½x12"	880.00
Theorem on velvet, fruit basket/bird/butterfly, late, 18x22"	150.00

Molded and painted tin whirligig, Vermont, early 1900s, 33" long, $2,200.00.

Whirligig, smithy w/hammer & anvil, wood, mc pnt, 1930s, 28"	45.00
Whirligig, Indian in canoe, EX cvg, tack/leather trim, 18"	600.00
Whirligig, man & kicking mule, wood, mc pnt, 1900s, 29", EX	225.00

Whirligig, man cutting wood, wood, mc pnt, 1920, 12x16", EX **70.00**
Whirligig, man milking, wood, worn pnt, 1900s, 22" L.................**65.00**
Whirligig, organ grinder/monkey by tree, mc pnt, 13½x22" **75.00**
Whirligig, rooster, sheet metal & wood, worn pnt, 22" **55.00**
Whirligig, soldier, pnt/cvd, w/metal arm blades, 8", EX **550.00**
Whirligig, washerwoman, wood, mc pnt, 1920s, 12x16", EX **60.00**
Whirligig, 2 sm men saw wood, pnt wood, 1900s, 39" H **115.00**
Wood cutout, Blk boy w/rod & fish, mc pnt, 1950s, 28" **55.00**

Fostoria

The Fostoria Glass Company was built in 1887 at Fostoria, Ohio, but by 1891 it had moved to Moundsville, West Virginia. During the next two decades, they produced many lines of pressed patterned tableware and lamps. Their most famous pattern, American, was introduced in 1915 and has been produced continuously since that time in well over two hundred different pieces. From 1920 to 1925, top artists designed tablewares in colored glass – canary (vaseline), amber, blue, orchid, green, and ebony – in pressed patterns as well as etched designs. By the late thirties, Fostoria was recognized as the largest producer of handmade glassware in the world. The company ceased operations in Moundsville in 1986.

Our advisor for this category is Michael Baker; he is listed in the Directory under West Virginia. We are assisted in our listings by the Fostoria Glass Society of America, Inc., whose mailing address may be found in the Directory under Clubs, Newsletters, and Catalogs.

Animals and Birds

Colts, sitting..**35.00**
Colts, sitting, bl...**30.00**
Deer, sitting or standing **40.00**
Deer, sitting or standing, milk glass **35.00**
Deer, sitting or standing, silver mist...**40.00**
Duck w/3 ducklings, amber, set...**50.00**
Eagle, bookend...**95.00**
Elephant, bookends, blk, pr **75.00**
Frog **85.00**
Goldfish, tail up **95.00**
Horse, bookends, blk, pr **75.00**
Horse, bookends, pr **45.00**
Owl, bookend, scarce..**100.00**
Pelican **50.00**
Pelican pr w/clock & night light...**275.00**
Penguin **25.00**
Polar bear **35.00**
Pony, bl **20.00**
Sea horse, bookend..**75.00**
Seal...**85.00**
Seal, frosted **60.00**
Seal, wisteria **85.00**
Squirrel...**20.00**
Squirrel, frosted **20.00**
Whale **20.00**

American, ash tray, oval, 5½"..**12.00**
American, ash tray, sq, 2⅞"..**6.00**
American, basket, 10" **25.00**
American, bonbon, 3-ftd, 6"...**15.00**
American, bottle, cologne; w/stopper, 6-oz, 5¾"......................**50.00**
American, bottle, water; 44-oz, 9¼" **275.00**
American, bowl, centerpiece; 11" **40.00**
American, bowl, deep, 10" **16.75**

American, bowl, finger; smooth edge, 4½" **20.00**
American, bowl, float; oval, 10"...**32.50**
American, bowl, float; 11½"..**47.50**
American, bowl, fruit; shallow, 13"...**50.00**
American, bowl, nappy, 7"..**22.50**
American, bowl, olive; oblong, 6" **9.00**
American, bowl, oval, 4½"...**7.00**
American, bowl, pickle; oblong, 8"..**13.00**
American, bowl, punch; w/low ftd base, 14" **160.00**
American, bowl, shrimp; 12¼"..**250.00**
American, bowl, vegetable; oval, 9"...**25.00**

American, wedding bowl, 8", $85.00.

American, box, hairpin; w/lid, 3½x1¾".................................**125.00**
American, candlestick, rnd ft, 3" **13.50**
American, coaster, 3¾" **5.00**
American, compote, jelly; 4½" **8.00**
American, compote, w/lid, 5"...**22.50**
American, creamer, ind, 4¾-oz **7.50**
American, cup, ftd, 7-oz **9.00**
American, hat, tall, 3" **22.50**
American, ice dish insert **5.00**
American, jam pot, w/lid..**40.00**
American, lamp, hurricane; base..**42.50**
American, lamp, hurricane; complete, 12" **120.00**
American, mayonnaise, w/liner & ladle.....................................**30.00**
American, napkin ring **5.00**
American, oil, 7-oz..**22.00**
American, plate, cake; hdld, 10" **16.00**
American, plate, salad; 7" **8.50**
American, plate, salad; 8½"..**8.00**
American, plate, torte; oval, 13½" **30.00**
American, platter, oval, 12"..**47.50**
American, sauce boat, w/liner **52.50**
American, shaker, 3", ea..**9.50**
American, toothpick **17.50**
American, tray, appetizer; w/6 inserts, 10½" **190.00**
American, tray, oval, hdld, 10½x5" **40.00**
American, tray, oval, hdld, 6"...**35.00**
American, tray, relish; 4-part, 6½x9" **35.00**
American, tray, sq, 10"..**115.00**
American, tray, sq, 4-part, 10" **75.00**
American, tray, sq, 4-part, 10¾"...**90.00**

American, tumbler, juice; #2056½, str sides, 5-oz....12.00
American, urn, sq, ped ft, 7½"....30.00
American, vase, flared, 10"....85.00
American, vase, flared, 8"....77.50
American, vase, str side, 12"....100.00
American, vase, str side, 6"....25.00
Baroque, bl; ash tray....15.00
Baroque, bl; bowl, pickle; 8"....16.50
Baroque, bl; bowl, vegetable; oval, 9½"....45.00
Baroque, bl; bowl, 3-ftd, 7"....25.00
Baroque, bl; candlestick, 4"....15.00
Baroque, bl; creamer, ind, 3¼"....11.00
Baroque, bl; cup, punch; 6-oz....17.50
Baroque, bl; plate, torte; 14"....30.00
Baroque, bl; plate, 8"....11.00
Baroque, bl; platter, oval, 12"....40.00
Baroque, bl; rose bowl, 3¾"....40.00
Baroque, bl; sherbet, 5-oz, 3¾"....17.50
Baroque, bl; sugar bowl, ftd, 3½"....12.00
Baroque, bl; tray, oval, 11"....21.50
Baroque, bl; tumbler, juice; 5-oz, 3¾"....30.00
Baroque, bl; vase, 6½"....38.00
Baroque, crystal; bowl, celery; 11"....12.00
Baroque, crystal; bowl, fruit; 5"....9.00
Baroque, crystal; bowl, punch; ftd....250.00
Baroque, crystal; candlestick, 3-light, 6"....15.00
Baroque, crystal; compote, 4¾"....9.00
Baroque, crystal; mayonnaise, w/liner, 5½"....15.00
Baroque, crystal; sugar bowl, ind, 3"....5.00
Baroque, crystal; tray, oval, 11"....10.00
Baroque, crystal; vase, 7"....15.00
Baroque, yel; ash tray....13.00
Baroque, yel; bowl, celery; 11"....20.00
Baroque, yel; bowl, cereal; 6"....23.50
Baroque, yel; candelabrum, 2-light, 16-lustre, 8¼"....40.00
Baroque, yel; cup....11.00
Baroque, yel; oil, w/stopper, 5½"....235.00
Baroque, yel; plate, cake; 10"....20.00
Baroque, yel; sherbet, 5-oz, 3¾"....15.50
Baroque, yel; tumbler, tea; 14-oz, 5¾"....30.00
Baroque, yel; vase, 7"....37.50
Century, ash tray, 2¾"....5.00
Century, bowl, cereal; 6"....10.00

Century, bowl, footed, 11", $35.00.

Century, candlestick, 4½"....12.00
Century, creamer, 4¼"....6.00
Century, plate, dinner; 9½"....17.50
Century, plate, salad; 7½"....4.00
Century, tray, muffin; hdld, 9½"....22.00
Century, tumbler, juice; ftd, 5-oz, 4¾"....10.00
Century, vase, oval, 8½"....40.00
Chintz, bowl, finger; #869, 4½"....18.00
Chintz, bowl, fruit; #2496, 5"....11.00
Chintz, candlestick, #2496, 5½"....17.50
Chintz, ice bucket, #2496....50.00
Chintz, plate, dinner; #2496, 9½"....22.50
Chintz, saucer, #2496....3.50
Chintz, sugar bowl, #2496, ftd, 3½"....8.00
Chintz, tumbler, juice; #6026, ftd, 5-oz....13.00
Chintz, vase, #4143, ftd, 6"....45.00

Colony, vase, footed, 7½", $40.00.

Coin, amber; ash tray, 7"....22.00
Coin, amber; bowl, oval, 9"....45.00
Coin, amber; candlestick, 4", pr....30.00
Coin, amber; candy box....32.00
Coin, amber; candy jar, w/lid....32.00
Coin, amber; cigarette urn, ftd....32.00
Coin, amber; compote, ftd, 8½"....40.00
Coin, amber; compote, jelly....20.00
Coin, amber; creamer....22.00
Coin, amber; lamp, coach....165.00
Coin, amber; lamp, finger; #310....110.00
Coin, amber; nappy, hdl , 5"....18.00
Coin, amber; pitcher, qt....55.00
Coin, amber; shakers, pr....30.00
Coin, amber; sugar bowl, w/lid....32.50
Coin, amber; vase, bud; 8"....20.00
Coin, bl; ash tray, oblong, 4"....20.00
Coin, bl; ash tray, 8"....15.00
Coin, bl; candlestick, 4½", pr....30.00
Coin, bl; sugar bowl, w/lid....35.00
Coin, crystal; ash tray, 10"....18.00
Coin, crystal; ash tray, 3"....8.00
Coin, crystal; ash tray, 7"....14.00
Coin, crystal; bowl, oval, 9"....35.00
Coin, crystal; bowl, wedding; w/lid....55.00
Coin, crystal; bowl, 7"....18.00
Coin, crystal; cake salver....125.00
Coin, crystal; candlesticks, 4½", pr....24.00
Coin, crystal; candy box, w/lid....38.00

Coin, crystal; candy jar, w/lid	35.00
Coin, crystal; cigarette urn	25.00
Coin, crystal; compote, ftd, 8½"	85.00
Coin, crystal; condiment set, cruet & shakers on tray	95.00
Coin, crystal; condiment set, 5-pc	135.00
Coin, crystal; creamer	25.00
Coin, crystal; decanter	95.00
Coin, crystal; highball, 12-oz	35.00
Coin, crystal; iced tea, 14-oz	35.00
Coin, crystal; pitcher, 1-qt	82.50
Coin, crystal; shakers, pr	32.00
Coin, crystal; sugar bowl, w/lid	29.00
Coin, crystal; tumbler; water, 9-oz	32.00
Coin, crystal; urn, ftd, w/lid, tall	65.00
Coin, crystal; vase, bud; ftd, 8"	17.50
Coin, emerald gr; ash tray, 5"	50.00
Coin, emerald gr; bowl, oval, 9"	165.00
Coin, emerald gr; candy box, w/lid	145.00
Coin, emerald gr; candy jar, w/lid	125.00
Coin, emerald gr; compote, fruit; ftd, 8"	225.00
Coin, emerald gr; condiment set, 5-pc	300.00
Coin, emerald gr; urn, w/lid, tall	250.00
Coin, emerald gr; vase, bud; 8"	75.00
Coin, olive gr; ash tray, raised center, 10"	40.00
Coin, olive gr; ash tray, raised center, 7"	25.00
Coin, olive gr; ash tray, 5"	19.00
Coin, olive gr; bowl, oval, 9"	45.00
Coin, olive gr; bowl, wedding; w/lid	75.00
Coin, olive gr; cake salver	80.00
Coin, olive gr; candlestick, 4½", pr	37.00
Coin, olive gr; candlestick, 8", pr	65.00
Coin, olive gr; candy box, w/lid	35.00
Coin, olive gr; cigarette urn, ftd	30.00
Coin, olive gr; compote, fruit; ftd, 8"	52.50
Coin, olive gr; compote, jelly	20.00
Coin, olive gr; condiment set, 4-pc	80.00
Coin, olive gr; condiment set, 5-pc	135.00
Coin, olive gr; condiment tray	15.00
Coin, olive gr; creamer	25.00
Coin, olive gr; goblet, water	55.00
Coin, olive gr; pitcher, qt	65.00
Coin, olive gr; shakers, pr	30.00
Coin, olive gr; sugar bowl, w/lid	29.00
Coin, olive gr; wine	45.00
Coin, red; ash tray, 8"	50.00
Coin, red; bowl, oval, 9"	45.00
Coin, red; bowl, wedding; w/lid	85.00
Coin, red; candlestick, 8", pr	57.50
Coin, red; candy jar, tall	60.00
Coin, red; compote, ftd, 8½"	60.00
Coin, red; compote, jelly	20.00
Coin, red; creamer	27.00
Coin, red; goblet	95.00
Coin, red; nappy	29.00
Coin, red; shakers, 4", pr	55.00
Coin, red; urn, w/lid, tall	125.00
Coin, red; vase, bud; ftd	40.00
Colony, ash tray, rnd, 6"	15.00
Colony, ash tray, 3½"	10.00
Colony, bowl, finger; 4¾"	9.00
Colony, bowl, oval, ftd, 11"	32.50
Colony, bowl, pickle; 9½"	10.00
Colony, bowl, rnd, 5"	7.50
Colony, bowl, salad; 7¾"	20.00
Colony, bowl, sq, 5½"	10.00
Colony, candlestick, 7"	15.00
Colony, compote, 4"	15.00
Colony, creamer, ind, 3¼"	5.50
Colony, ice bucket	45.00
Colony, mayonnaise, 3-pc	32.50
Colony, plate, dinner; 9"	17.50
Colony, plate, salad; 7"	7.00
Colony, platter, 12"	35.00
Colony, tumbler, ftd, 5-oz, 4½"	12.50
Colony, vase, cupped, 7"	35.00
Colony, vase, str, 12"	145.00
Fairfax, amber; bouillon, ftd	35.00
Fairfax, amber; bowl, lemon; hdls, 9"	6.00
Fairfax, amber; compote, 7"	10.00
Fairfax, amber; platter, oval, 12"	20.00
Fairfax, amber; stem, wine; 3-oz, 5½"	22.50
Fairfax, bl; ash tray	20.00
Fairfax, bl; bonbon	12.50
Fairfax, bl; creamer, ftd	11.00
Fairfax, bl; ice bucket	40.00
Fairfax, bl; mayonnaise	12.00
Fairfax, bl; plate, dinner; 10¼"	21.00
Fairfax, bl; platter, oval, 12"	32.00
Fairfax, bl; sauce boat	30.00
Fairfax, bl; stem, cordial; ¾-oz, 4"	40.00
Fairfax, bl; sugar bowl, ftd	10.00
Fairfax, bl; tumbler, ftd, 9-oz, 5¼"	13.50
Fairfax, bl; whipped cream pail	40.00
Fairfax, gr; bowl, centerpc; oval, 13"	22.50
Fairfax, gr; bowl, nappy, rnd, 8"	14.00
Fairfax, gr; oil, ftd	90.00
Fairfax, gr; stem, claret, 4-oz, 6"	18.00
Fairfax, orchid; bowl, dessert; lg, hdld	17.00
Fairfax, orchid; bowl, fruit; 5"	8.50
Fairfax, orchid; plate, cake; 10"	17.50
Fairfax, orchid; plate, luncheon; 9½"	12.00
Fairfax, orchid; plate, salad; 8"	9.00
Fairfax, orchid; tray, relish; 11½"	15.00
Fairfax, orchid; tumbler, ftd, 12-oz, 6"	15.00
Fairfax, orchid; tumbler, ftd, 5-oz, 4½"	12.00
Fairfax, rose; candlestick, flattened top	10.00
Fairfax, rose; platter, oval, 15"	27.00
Fairfax, topaz; ice bucket	35.00
Fairfax, topaz; plate, salad; 7"	3.50
Fairfax, topaz; stem, wine, 3-oz, 5½"	22.50
Fairfax, topaz; tumbler, ftd, 12-oz, 6"	14.00
June, bl; bowl, baker, oval, 9"	65.00
June, bl; bowl, lemon	25.00
June, bl; candlestick, 2"	20.00
June, bl; goblet, claret; 4-oz, 6"	55.00
June, bl; ice dish	42.50
June, bl; mayonnaise w/liner	45.00
June, bl; plate, canape	18.00
June, bl; plate, chop; 13"	44.00
June, bl; plate, luncheon; 8¾"	12.00
June, bl; sugar pail	150.00
June, bl; vase, 8"	165.00
June, crystal; ash tray	23.00
June, crystal; bowl, cereal; 6"	15.00
June, crystal; bowl, nappy, ftd, 6"	10.00
June, crystal; bowl, whipped cream	10.00
June, crystal; decanter	150.00
June, crystal; ice bucket	47.50

June, crystal; parfait, 5¼" 22.50
June, crystal; plate, salad; 7½" 5.00
June, crystal; sauce boat 35.00
June, crystal; sugar bowl, ftd 12.00
June, crystal; tray, center hdld, 11" 20.00
June, crystal; tumbler, ftd, 12-oz, 6" 17.50
June, crystal; whipped cream pail 65.00
June, rose; bowl, bouillon; ftd 20.00
June, rose; compote, 5" 27.50
June, rose; plate, grill; 10" 27.50
June, rose; tumbler, ftd, 5-oz, 4½" 22.50
June, topaz; candlestick, 5" 22.50
June, topaz; goblet, wine; 3-oz, 5½" 45.00
Kashmir, gr; bowl, baker, 9" 37.50
Kashmir, gr; bowl, cream soup 22.00
Kashmir, gr; bowl, fruit; 5" 13.00
Kashmir, gr; candlestick, 2" 15.00
Kashmir, gr; cup 15.00
Kashmir, gr; pitcher, ftd 350.00
Kashmir, gr; plate, salad; sq, 7" 6.00
Kashmir, gr; saucer, rnd 5.00
Kashmir, gr; sherbet, high ft, 6-oz 17.50
Kashmir, gr; stem, wine; 2½-oz 32.00
Kashmir, yel; ash tray 25.00
Kashmir, yel; bowl, cereal; 6" 22.00
Kashmir, yel; bowl, finger 15.00
Kashmir, yel; candy dish, w/lid 65.00
Kashmir, yel; compote, 6" 35.00
Kashmir, yel; ice bucket 65.00
Kashmir, yel; oil, ftd 250.00
Kashmir, yel; plate, bread & butter; 6" 5.00
Kashmir, yel; plate, grill; 10" 22.00
Kashmir, yel; plate, luncheon; 9" 9.00
Kashmir, yel; sauce boat, w/liner 75.00
Kashmir, yel; saucer, sq 5.00
Kashmir, yel; shakers 90.00
Kashmir, yel; stem, claret; 4-oz 28.00
Kashmir, yel; stem, cocktail; ftd, 3½-oz 22.00
Kashmir, yel; stem, cordial; ¾-oz 85.00
Kashmir, yel; stem, juice; ftd, 5-oz 15.00
Kashmir, yel; stem, whiskey; ftd, 2-oz 25.00
Kashmir, yel; sugar bowl, ftd 15.00
Kashmir, yel; vase, 8" 85.00
Navarre, bowl, finger; #869, 4½" 18.00
Navarre, bowl, nut; #2496, 3-ftd, 6¼" 17.50
Navarre, candlestick, #2496, 4" 13.50
Navarre, candlestick, #2496, 5½" 20.00
Navarre, creamer, #2440, ftd, 4¼" 9.00
Navarre, pitcher, #5000, ftd, 48-oz 195.00
Navarre, plate, cracker; #2496, 11" 40.00
Navarre, plate, salad; #2440, 7½" 7.50
Navarre, sauce, #2496, 6½x5¼" 35.00
Navarre, stem, cocktail; #6106, 3½-oz, 6" 20.00
Navarre, sugar bowl, #2440, ftd, 3⅝" 8.00
Navarre, vase, #4121, 5" 45.00
Royal, amber; ash tray, #2350, 3½" 22.50
Royal, amber; bowl, #2267, ftd, 7" 28.00
Royal, amber; bowl, #2315, ftd, 10½" 40.00
Royal, amber; bowl, bouillon; #2350, flat 10.00
Royal, amber; bowl, cream soup; #2350, flat 12.50
Royal, amber; candlestick, #2324, 4" 14.00
Royal, amber; candlestick, #2324, 9" 40.00
Royal, amber; cup, #2350, flat 12.00
Royal, amber; egg cup, #2350 ....18.00

Royal, amber; mayonnaise, #2315 ....25.00
Royal, amber; plate, chop; #2350, 15" 38.00
Royal, amber; plate, dinner; #2350, 10½" 22.00
Royal, amber; sauce boat, w/liner 70.00
Royal, amber; tumbler, #859, flat, 9-oz 25.00
Royal, gr; bowl, baker, #2350, oval, 9" 28.00
Royal, gr; bowl, console; #2329, 13" 30.00
Royal, gr; bowl, finger; #869, 4½" 15.00
Royal, gr; bowl, fruit; #2350, 5½" 10.00
Royal, gr; bowl, nappy, #2350, 8" 28.00
Royal, gr; compote, jelly; #1861½, 6" 25.00
Royal, gr; creamer, #2315½, ftd 18.00
Royal, gr; ice bucket, #2378 ....40.00
Royal, gr; pitcher, #1236 ....295.00
Royal, gr; plate, salad; #2350, 7½" 4.00
Royal, gr; platter, #2350, 15½" 55.00
Royal, gr; stem, cocktail; #869, 3-oz 22.50
Royal, gr; stem, cordial; #869, ¾-oz 50.00
Royal, gr; stem, parfait; #869, 5½-oz 25.00
Royal, gr; sugar bowl, #2350½, ftd 12.00
Royal, gr; tumbler, #869, ftd, 5-oz 14.00
Trojan, rose; ash tray, lg 27.50
Trojan, rose; bowl, baker; 9" 45.00
Trojan, rose; bowl, bouillon; ftd 16.00
Trojan, rose; bowl, cereal; 6" 22.00
Trojan, rose; bowl, cream soup; ftd 18.00
Trojan, rose; bowl, fruit; 5" 15.00
Trojan, rose; bowl, whipped cream 11.00
Trojan, rose; bowl, 10" 30.00
Trojan, rose; candlestick, 5" 19.50
Trojan, rose; cheese & cracker set 45.00
Trojan, rose; creamer, ftd 17.50
Trojan, rose; cup, ftd 16.00
Trojan, rose; goblet, cordial; ¾-oz, 4" 65.00
Trojan, rose; goblet, wine; 3-oz, 5½" 40.00
Trojan, rose; ice bucket 65.00
Trojan, rose; parfait 37.00
Trojan, rose; pitcher 265.00
Trojan, rose; plate, bread & butter; 6" 5.00
Trojan, rose; plate, cream soup; w/liner, 7½" 7.50
Trojan, rose; plate, grill; rare, 10¼" 35.00
Trojan, rose; plate, luncheon; 8¾" 10.00
Trojan, rose; plate, salad; 7½" 7.50
Trojan, rose; platter, 12" 42.00
Trojan, rose; sauce boat 60.00
Trojan, rose; shakers, ftd, pr 70.00
Trojan, rose; sugar bowl, ftd 17.50
Trojan, rose; tray, service 27.50
Trojan, rose; tumbler, ftd, 12-oz, 6" 20.00
Trojan, rose; tumbler, ftd, 2½-oz 30.00
Trojan, rose; tumbler, ftd, 5-oz, 4½" 22.50
Trojan, topaz; ash tray, sm 22.50
Trojan, topaz; bowl, bonbon 13.00
Trojan, topaz; bowl, mint; 3 ftd 17.00
Trojan, topaz; bowl, soup; 7" 23.00
Trojan, topaz; candlestick, 2" 15.00
Trojan, topaz; compote, 6" 25.00
Trojan, topaz; ice dish 30.00
Trojan, topaz; mayonnaise, w/liner 30.00
Trojan, topaz; pail, whipped cream 100.00
Trojan, topaz; plate, canape 15.00
Trojan, topaz; plate, dinner; 10¼" 32.50
Trojan, topaz; platter, 15" 65.00
Trojan, topaz; sauce plate 20.00

Trojan, topaz; sherbet, high ft, 6"	20.00
Trojan, topaz; vase, 2 styles, 8", ea	120.00
Versailles, bl; bowl, baker, 9"	55.00
Versailles, bl; bowl, cereal; 6"	30.00
Versailles, bl; bowl, finger; w/liner	32.00
Versailles, bl; candlestick, 2"	20.00
Versailles, bl; compote, 6"	35.00
Versailles, bl; compote, 8"	75.00
Versailles, bl; goblet, cocktail; 3-oz, 5¼"	35.00
Versailles, bl; parfait	35.00
Versailles, bl; plate, canape; 6"	65.00
Versailles, bl; plate, chop; 13"	40.00
Versailles, bl; plate, dinner; sm, 9½"	20.00
Versailles, bl; shakers, ftd, pr	110.00
Versailles, bl; tumbler, ftd, 2½-oz	40.00
Versailles, bl; vase, 8"	150.00
Versailles, gr; ash tray	24.00
Versailles, gr; bowl, cream soup; ftd	16.00
Versailles, gr; candlestick, 5"	20.00
Versailles, gr; goblet, cordial; ¾-oz, 4"	75.00
Versailles, gr; ice bucket	62.50
Versailles, gr; pitcher	250.00
Versailles, gr; plate, salad; 7½"	6.00
Versailles, gr; platter, 15"	60.00
Versailles, gr; sherbet, high ft, 6"	20.00
Versailles, gr; tumbler, ftd, 12-oz, 6"	22.50
Versailles, gr; tumbler, tea; flat	80.00
Versailles, pk; bowl, bonbon	13.00
Versailles, pk; bowl, mint; 3-ftd	16.00
Versailles, pk; bowl, whipped cream	12.00
Versailles, pk; bowl, 10"	30.00
Versailles, pk; creamer, ftd	15.00
Versailles, pk; goblet, wine; 3-oz, 5½"	35.00
Versailles, pk; plate, bread & butter; 6"	4.00
Versailles, pk; plate, dinner; 10¼"	35.00
Versailles, pk; sugar bowl, ftd	15.00
Versailles, yel; bowl, bouillon; ftd	17.50
Versailles, yel; bowl, centerpc; 11"	35.00
Versailles, yel; bowl, fruit; 5"	16.00
Versailles, yel; cheese & cracker set	52.00
Versailles, yel; cup, ftd	19.00
Versailles, yel; ice dish	30.00
Versailles, yel; pail, whipped cream	85.00
Versailles, yel; plate, grill; 10"	25.00
Versailles, yel; plate, luncheon; 8¾"	9.00
Versailles, yel; sauce boat	60.00
Versailles, yel; sherbet, low ft, 4¼"	22.00
Versailles, yel; tray, service	35.00
Versailles, yel; tumbler, ftd, 5-oz, 4½"	22.00
Vesper, amber; bowl, finger	17.50
Vesper, amber; bowl, 8"	25.00
Vesper, amber; candy jar, w/lid	80.00
Vesper, amber; cheese dish, ftd	20.00
Vesper, amber; creamer, ftd	16.00
Vesper, amber; cup	14.00
Vesper, amber; ice bucket	60.00
Vesper, amber; plate, bread & butter; 6"	5.00
Vesper, amber; plate, chop; 13"	37.50
Vesper, amber; plate, luncheon; 8½"	8.50
Vesper, amber; platter, 10½"	25.00
Vesper, amber; saucer, after dinner	9.00
Vesper, amber; shakers, 2 styles, pr	75.00
Vesper, amber; sherbet	16.00
Vesper, amber; stem, cocktail; 3-oz	25.00

Vesper, amber; stem, cordial; ¾-oz	70.00
Vesper, amber; stem, parfait	27.50
Vesper, amber; tumbler, ftd, 5-oz	15.00
Vesper, amber; vase, 8"	75.00
Vesper, bl; bowl, cereal; 6½"	22.00
Vesper, bl; bowl, fruit; 5½"	16.00
Vesper, bl; candlestick, 3"	30.00
Vesper, bl; compote, 6"	35.00
Vesper, bl; compote, 8"	50.00
Vesper, bl; sugar bowl, fat, ftd	25.00
Vesper, gr; ash tray	25.00
Vesper, gr; bowl, bouillon; ftd	12.00
Vesper, gr; bowl, console; 11"	25.00
Vesper, gr; bowl, cream soup	12.50
Vesper, gr; candlestick, 9"	30.00
Vesper, gr; dish, celery	15.00
Vesper, gr; pitcher, ftd	275.00
Vesper, gr; plate, dinner; 10½"	23.00
Vesper, gr; plate, salad; 7½"	6.00
Vesper, gr; platter, 15"	50.00
Vesper, gr; sauce boat, w/liner	75.00
Vesper, gr; stem, cocktail, 3-oz	22.50
Vesper, gr; stem, water	22.50
Vesper, gr; stem, wine; 2¾-oz	27.50
Vesper, gr; sugar bowl, ftd	14.00
Vesper, gr; tumbler, ftd, 12-oz	18.00
Vesper, gr; urn, sm	60.00
Vesper, gr; vase, 8"	70.00

Fraktur

Fraktur is a German style of black letter text type. To collectors the fraktur is a type of hand-lettered document used by the people of German descent who settled in the areas of Pennsylvania, New Jersey, Maryland, Virginia, North and South Carolina, Ohio, Kentucky, and Ontario. These documents recorded births and baptisms and were used as bookplates and as certificates of honor. They were elaborately decorated with colorful folk-art borders of hearts, birds, angels, and flowers. Examples by recognized artists and those with an unusual decorative motif bring prices well into the thousands of dollars. Frakturs made in the late 1700s after the invention of the printing press provided the writer with a prepared text that he needed only to fill in at his own discretion. The next step in the evolution of machine-printed frakturs combined woodblock-printed decorations along with the text which the 'artist' sometimes enhanced with color. By the mid-1800s, even the coloring was done by machine. The vorschrift was a handwritten example prepared by a fraktur teacher to demonstrate his skill in lettering and decorating. These are often considered to be the finest of frakturs. Those dated before 1820 are most valuable.

The practice of fraktur art began to diminish after 1830 but hung on even to the early years of this century among the Pennsylvania Germans ingrained with such customs.

Our advisor for this category is Pastor Frederick S. Weiser; he is listed in the Directory under Pennsylvania.

Key:
brd — board	p/i — pen and ink
lp — laid paper	wc — watercolored
pr — printed	wp — wove paper

Birth Record

P/i/pr/wc, hearts/florals, 1794, Jungman & Gruber, 17x21" **1,000.00**

P/i/wc, heart/vines/tulips, 1779, 8x13", EX..............................800.00
P/i/wc/wp, flowers/form in English (not filled in), 12x16" 250.00
P/i/wc/wp, flowers/tulips, faded color/stain, 13x17"......................400.00
Pr/wc, angels, 1832 birth, Grater & Blumer, 16x19", NM 155.00
Pr/wc, angels, 1863 birth, Hager & Leifenring, 17x20", EX 125.00
Pr/wc, angels/birds, Blumer, Allentown, 1838, fr, 19x15" 325.00
Pr/wc, birds/flowers w/'Columbian,' 15x17", VG............................550.00
Pr/wc, Herman, Lancaster OH, 1827, fr, 16x13", EX.....................625.00
Pr/wc, JS Weistling, PA, 1817, old fr, 20x16¾", EX 300.00
Pr/wc, Lebanon County, 1818, Baumann, Ephrata, 19x16" 300.00
Pr/wc, Peters, Harrisburg, 1832, gilt fr, 18x14½", EX 75.00
Pr/wc, sgn Rev Long, 1825, JS Weistling, 17¾x13¾" 175.00
Pr/wc/lp, Cumberland Co, 1798, 16⅜x18⅝", EX 325.00
Pr/wc/lp, 3 hearts, stylized florals, F Krebs, 17x20", EX 390.00

Miscellaneous

P/i (3-color), bookplate, EX work, 1787, tramp art fr, 6x9" 750.00
P/i/lp, drawing, stylized flowers, 2-color, 3x5½", EX 675.00
P/i/lp, lg lettering/flowers, 10x14", EX.......................................85.00
P/i/wc, bookplate, trees/Property of...1865, damage, 6x6" 100.00
P/i/wc, drawing, Griest/1839, old fr, 5x7⅝", EX.........................400.00
P/i/wc, Family Record, stylized trees/etc, old fr, 9x11", EX..........650.00
P/i/wc, vorchrift, florals, att Detweiler/1808, fr, 8x10" 1,550.00
P/i/wc/lp, vorchrift, lg letters, 8x12", VG.................................200.00
P/i/wc/wp, fruit tree/inscription, 1830, 4x6½", EX 1,175.00
Pr/wc, house blessing, J Ritter, Reading PA, 19½x15½"..............300.00

Watercolor and ink birth and baptismal certificate, dated 1818, in grain-painted frame, 17"x19", $3,000.00.

Frames

Styles in picture frames have changed with the fashion of the day, but those that especially interest today's collectors are the deep shadow boxes made of fine woods such as walnut or cherry, those with Art Nouveau influence, and the oak frames decorated with molded gesso and gilt from the Victorian era.

Bird's eye veneer, 1¾" W, 14¾x11⅞", EX....................................145.00
Brass, florals/leaves, oval, French, 1860, 6x4½", EX.....................50.00
CI, swivels in ftd fr, ornate, wht pnt, 18" 25.00
Curly maple, rfn, 15x19" 150.00
Garnets, prong set, 1¾" dia 125.00
Silver, branch/bird, eng/repousse, shaped top, English, 9"............800.00

Miniature mosaic frame, 3" x 2", $30.00.

Silver, shagreen w/strapwork & flowerheads, hall mk, 7" 1,800.00
Sterling, basketweave w/iris, Birmingham A & JZ, 12x10"..........600.00
Tin, scrollwork, rectangular, easel bk, 6x3" 32.00
Walnut Victorian, cvd branch & leaf decor, 39x33", pr 400.00
Walnut Victorian crisscross, cvd leaves at corners, 22x18"..........150.00
Walnut Victorian crisscross, cvd leaves/porc buttons, 15x16" 90.00
Walnut Victorian shadow box, oval, 32x23" 335.00

Frances Ware

Frances Ware, produced in the 1880s by Hobbs, Brockunier and Company of Wheeling, West Virginia, is a clear or frosted tableware with amber-stained rim bands. The most often found pattern is Hobnail, but Swirl was also made.

Hobnail, clear; bowl, 7½" 55.00
Hobnail, clear; butter dish..85.00
Hobnail, clear; creamer 50.00
Hobnail, clear; finger bowl, 4"..35.00
Hobnail, clear; pitcher, 8½" 95.00
Hobnail, clear; spooner..40.00
Hobnail, frosted; bowl, ftd, berry pontil, 6x10" 150.00
Hobnail, frosted; bowl, oblong, 8"..70.00
Hobnail, frosted; bowl, sq, 7½"..70.00
Hobnail, frosted; bowl, 2½x5½"...40.00
Hobnail, frosted; bowl, 4½"...30.00
Hobnail, frosted; bowl, 8"..75.00
Hobnail, frosted; bowl, 9"..85.00
Hobnail, frosted; butter dish 120.00

Frosted Hobnail celery vase, 6", $75.00.

Hobnail, frosted; creamer	75.00
Hobnail, frosted; finger bowl, 4"	30.00
Hobnail, frosted; marmalade	125.00
Hobnail, frosted; plate, sq, 5¾"	25.00
Hobnail, frosted; sauce dish, sq, 4"	25.00
Hobnail, frosted; shakers, pr	75.00
Hobnail, frosted; spooner	70.00
Hobnail, frosted; sugar bowl, w/lid	80.00
Hobnail, frosted; syrup	150.00
Hobnail, frosted; syrup, pewter lid	165.00
Hobnail, frosted; toothpick holder	60.00
Hobnail, frosted; tray, cloverleaf, 12"	125.00
Hobnail, frosted; tray, oblong, 14"	150.00
Hobnail, frosted; tumbler	45.00
Hobnail, frosted; water pitcher, sq top	165.00
Swirl, clear; shakers, pr	55.00
Swirl, clear; syrup	90.00
Swirl, frosted; cruet	175.00
Swirl, frosted; cruet, orig stopper, miniature	260.00
Swirl, frosted; mustard jar	140.00
Swirl, frosted; shakers, pr	75.00
Swirl, frosted; sugar shaker, orig lid	125.00
Swirl, frosted; syrup, pat dtd	145.00
Swirl, frosted; tumbler	35.00

Franciscan

Franciscan is a trade name used by Gladding McBean and Co., founded in northern California in 1875. In 1923 they purchased the Tropico plant in Glendale where they produced sewer pipe, gardenware, and tile. By 1934 the first of their dinnerware lines, El Patio, was produced. It was a plain design but made in bright, attractive colors. El Patio Nouveau followed in 1935, glazed in two colors – one tone on the inside, a contrasting hue on the outside. Coronado, a favorite of today's collectors, was introduced in 1936. It was styled with a wide, swirled border and was made in pastels in both a satin and glossy finish. Before 1940 fifteen patterns had been produced. The first hand-decorated lines were introduced in 1937, the ever-popular Apple pattern in 1940, Desert Rose in 1941, and Ivy in 1948. Many other hand-decorated and decaled patterns were produced there from 1934 to 1984.

Dinnerware marks before 1940 include 'GMcB' in an oval, 'F' within a square, or 'Franciscan' with 'Pottery' underneath (which was later changed to 'Ware.') A circular arrangement of 'Franciscan' with 'Made in California USA' in the center was used from 1940 until 1949. At least forty marks were used before 1975; several more were introduced after that. At one time, a paper label was used.

The company merged with Lock Joint Pipe Company in 1963, becoming part of the Interpace Corporation. In July of 1979, Franciscan was purchased by Wedgwood Limited of England, and the Glendale plant closed in October 1984.

Our advisor, authority Delleen Enge, has compiled an informative book, *Franciscan Ware*, with current values. You will find her address in the Directory under California. See also Gladding McBean.

Coronado

Bowl, cereal	10.50
Bowl, cream soup	13.00
Bowl, vegetable; serving, oval	25.00
Bowl, vegetable; serving, rnd	13.00
Candlesticks, pr	25.00
Candy dish, rnd, w/lid	45.00
Casserole, w/lid	25.00

Cigarette box	35.00
Coffeepot, demitasse	45.00
Creamer & sugar bowl, w/lid	28.00
Cup & saucer	10.00
Cup & saucer, demitasse	20.00
Gravy boat, w/attached plate	25.00
Nut cup, ftd	14.00
Plate, chop; 12"	20.00
Plate, chop; 14"	30.00
Plate, 6½"	7.00
Plate, 7½"	8.50
Plate, 8½"	9.50
Platter, 11½"	20.00
Platter, 15½"	30.00
Saucer, cream soup	5.50
Shakers, pr	13.00
Sherbet	9.00
Teapot	35.00

El Patio

Bowl, cereal	10.00
Bowl, fruit	9.00
Bowl, salad; 3-qt	22.00
Bowl, vegetable; oval	28.00
Butter dish	28.00
Creamer	8.00
Cup	8.00
Cup, jumbo	16.00
Gravy boat, w/attached underplate	24.00
Plate, bread & butter	6.00
Plate, 10½"	12.00
Plate, 8½"	10.00
Saucer	3.00
Saucer, jumbo	6.00
Sherbet	9.00
Sugar bowl, w/lid	15.00
Teapot, w/lid, 6-cup	35.00

Franciscan Fine China

The main line of fine china was called Masterpiece. There were at least four marks used during its production from 1941 to 1977. Almost every piece is clearly marked. This china is true porcelain, the body having been fired at a very high temperature. Many years of research and experimentation went into this china before it was marketed. Production was temporarily suspended during the war years. More than 170 patterns and many varying shapes were produced. All are valued about the same with the exception of the Renaissance group, which is 25% higher.

Bowl, vegetable; serving, oval	45.00
Cup	15.00
Plate, bread & butter	15.00
Plate, dinner	25.00
Plate, salad	18.00
Saucer	10.00

Hand-Painted Embossed Earthenware

Values listed here apply to these patterns: Apple, Desert Rose, Ivy, Meadow Rose, Forget-Me-Not, October, Strawberry, Fresh Fruit, and other hand-painted lines.

Ash tray, ind	10.00

Bowl, batter..45.00
Bowl, lug hdl, sm 14.00
Bowl, soup; flat 14.00
Bowl, vegetable; sm 12.00
Bowl, vegetable; w/lid................................45.00
Bowl, 7½"...25.00
Bowl, 8¼"...35.00
Casserole, stick hdls, 12-oz 20.00
Coaster, 3¾"..15.00
Coffeepot 65.00
Compote, lg..35.00
Creamer, lg...14.00
Cup & saucer, demitasse, ea 20.00
Cup & saucer, jumbo 25.00
Egg cup..14.00
Goblet..22.00
Mug..18.00
Pickle dish, 10¼"..28.00
Pitcher, water...50.00
Pitcher, 1-pt 22.00
Plate, chop; 14"..50.00
Plate, grill; 10¾" 30.00
Plate, 10½"..20.00
Plate, 6½" 10.00
Plate, 8½" 14.00
Plate, 9½" 18.00
Platter, 12½" 30.00
Platter, 19½" 95.00
Relish, 3-part, 11"...30.00
Shakers, Rosebud, pr....................................18.00
Shakers, tall, pr 30.00
Sugar bowl, open, sm...................................25.00
Sugar bowl, w/lid, lg.....................................28.00
Tray, 3-tier..35.00
Tumbler, 5⅛"..15.00

Apple, turkey platter, 19½", $95.00.

Frankart

During the 1920s, Frankart, Inc., of New York City, produced a line of accessories that included figural nude lamps, bookends, ash trays, etc. These white metal composition items were offered in several finishes including verde green, jap black, and gun-metal gray. The company also produced a line of caricatured animals, but the stylized nude figurals have proven to be the most collectible today. With few excep-

tions, all pieces were marked 'Frankart, Inc.' with a patent number or 'pat. appl. for.' All pieces listed are in very good original condition unless otherwise indicated.

Our advisor for this category is Walter Glenn; he is listed in the Directory under Georgia.

Ash tray, dancing nude holds tray to side, box on base, 10".........425.00
Ash tray, dolphin, tail holds glass insert, 6" 185.00
Ash tray, goose, upright wings hold cigarette pack, 6" 210.00
Ash tray, nude on horseshoe base holds tray aloft, 23"................485.00
Ash tray, seated nude w/match box holder, 5½" 360.00
Bookends, dancing nudes, frog on base, 10", pr...........................385.00
Bookends, ladies w/fans, 10", pr 365.00
Bookends, standing nudes peeking around books, 8", pr 275.00
Lamp, dancing nude silhouettes before glass panel, 11" 625.00
Lamp, nude stands, silhouettes against amber glass fan, 10" 950.00
Lamp, seated nude, leg extended, 2" cylinder on ea side, 8" 725.00
Lamp, silhouette nudes sit before 3 sq glass cylinders, 12" 785.00
Lamp, 2 nudes stand either side of sq glass cylinder, 13" 785.00

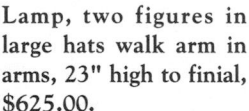
Lamp, two figures in large hats walk arm in arms, 23" high to finial, $625.00.

Lighter, seated nude, arms around lighter, 6" 425.00
Mirror, kneeling nude holds 6" gold-bk mirror, 11".....................485.00
Smoker's stand, nude sits atop wrought iron stand, 36"...............515.00

Frankoma

The Frank Pottery, founded in Oklahoma in 1933 by John Frank, became known as Frankoma in 1934. The company produced decorative figurals, vases, and such, marking their ware from 1936-38 with a pacing leopard 'Frankoma' mark. These pieces are highly sought. The entire operation was destroyed by fire in 1938, and new molds were cast – some from surviving pieces – and a similar line of production was pursued. The body of the ware was changed in 1954 from a honey tan to a red brick clay, and this, along with the color of the glazes (over forty have been used), helps determine the period of production. A Southwestern theme has always been favored in design as well as in color selection.

In 1965 they began to produce a limited-edition series of Christmas plates, followed by a bottle vase series in 1969. Considered very collectible are their political mugs, bicentennial plates, Teenagers of the Bible plates, and the Wildfire series. Their ceramic Christmas cards are also very popular items with today's collectors.

Frankoma celebrated their 50th Anniversary in 1983. On September 26 of that same year, Frankoma was again destroyed by fire. Because of a fire-proof wall, master molds of all 1983 production items were saved, allowing plans for rebuilding to begin immediately. 'Grand Opening' was celebrated in July, 1984.

For a more thorough study of the subject, we reommend that you refer to *Frankoma Treasures* by Phyllis and Tom Bess, our advisors; you will find their address in the Directory under Oklahoma.

Ash tray, Art Deco, Ada clay, #456	10.00
Ash tray, bl, w/magazine rack, #36-M	60.00
Ash tray, Cocker Spaniel, Desert Gold, Ada clay, unmk, 3"	50.00
Ash tray, elephant, #459, 1951-1952, 6½"	75.00
Ban-O-Bug, 1965-1967	15.00
Bank, dog, 7½"	40.00
Bolo tie, 4-leaf clover, complete	25.00
Bookend, Irish Setter, Ada clay, blk, pr	200.00
Bookend, Leopard, Prairie Gr, Ada clay, #421, pr	250.00
Bookend, Mountain Girl, Ada clay, #425, 5¾", ea	125.00
Bookend, Rearing Clydesdale, #431, pr	250.00
Bookend, Sea Horse, rare, ea	225.00
Bookend, Walking Ocelot, #424, ea	225.00
Bowl, ball form, ped ft, #42, 6½"	25.00
Bowl, Gracetone, Pine Cone, Jade	30.00
Bowl, Knobby Cactus, Ada clay, #203	25.00
Bowl, rectangular, flat, #206, 7"	15.00
Bowl, 4-leaf clover, Clay Bl, #223	8.00
Candelabrum, #306, 11¾"	48.00
Candle holder, #307, 3", pr	35.00
Candle holder, blk onyx high gloss, dbl, #304, pr	20.00
Candle holder, Dusty Rose, Ada clay, dbl, #304, pr	30.00
Candle holder, Monks, #308, pr	225.00
Candle holder, Oral Roberts	10.00
Canteen, Thunderbird, #59, 6½"	10.00
Carafe, w/lid, all colors	20.00
Christmas card, 1947-1948	75.00
Christmas card, 1950-1951	70.00
Christmas card, 1952, Donna Frank	60.00
Christmas card, 1953-1954	75.00
Christmas card, 1955-1956	70.00
Christmas card, 1958	60.00
Christmas card, 1960	60.00
Christmas card, 1967-1968	40.00
Christmas card, 1972	20.00
Christmas card, 1973-1974	25.00
Christmas card, 1975, bird in hand, Grace Lee, rare	100.00
Christmas plate, 1966	75.00
Christmas plate, 1968	35.00
Christmas plate, 1971-1973, ea	22.50
Christmas plate, 1977-1980	20.00
Cornucopia, tall, Ada clay, #56, 1942-1949, 7"	30.00
Cornucopia, Wht Sand, Ada clay, #57, 9½"	25.00
Creamer, Prairie Gr, pacing leopard mk, 3½"	45.00
Creamer, Silver Sage, pacing leopard mk, #42	50.00
Donkey mug, 1975, Autumn Yel	25.00
Donkey mug, 1976, Centennial Red	25.00
Donkey mug, 1978, Woodland Moss	20.00
Donkey mug, 1980, Terra Cotta	20.00
Elephant mug, 1968, Wht Sand	85.00
Elephant mug, 1969, Nixon/Agnew, Flame	85.00
Elephant mug, 1970, bl	55.00
Elephant mug, 1972, Prairie Gr	40.00
Flower frog, Mermaid, 7"	1,000.00

Flower frog, Royal Bl, Ada clay, #400	35.00
Flower holder, Boot, stars on sides, Ada clay, #507, 3½"	10.00
Flower holder, Duck, #184, 3¾"	135.00
Flower holder, Hobby Horse, #182, 3½"	135.00
Flowerabrum, Wht Sand, Ada clay	65.00
Grease jar, w/lid, #46, 1938, 3¾"	20.00
Honey jug, Swirl, w/orig waxed cork, #833	35.00
Honey pot, beehive, w/bee finial, Flame Red	5.00
Jug, Golda's Corn, brn, dtd 1951	20.00
Jug, Uncle Slug, Peacock Bl, Ada clay, #561	15.00
Lazy susan, Wagon Wheel, Desert Gold	75.00
Marionette head, rare	65.00
Mask, Indian Head, Ada clay, #135, 3¾"	15.00
Mask, Oriental Man or Woman, #134/#133, ea	125.00
Medallion, woman's profile, oval, 1⅞"	85.00
Pipe rest, #454, 2x6½x6½"	75.00
Pitcher, Autumn Yel, 2-qt	10.00
Pitcher, batter; Dusty Rose, Ada clay, #87	25.00
Pitcher, Fireside, #77-A	65.00
Pitcher, Guernsey, Prairie Gr, lg	25.00
Pitcher, jug form, w/stopper, #86, 1½-gal, 7"	35.00
Pitcher, jug form, w/stopper, 1934-1935, 3-cup, 5"	50.00
Pitcher, Red Bud, #87A	15.00
Pitcher, Wagon Wheel, brn & cream, #94-D, 2-qt	25.00
Pitcher, Widow Maker, blk, 1½-qt	75.00
Planter, log, #9-L, 11"	10.00
Planter, Madonna of Grace, #231-B, 6"	50.00
Planter, swan, turq, Ada clay, middle sz	60.00
Plaque, Will Rogers, lt bsk, borderless, imp mk, 4¾x4"	38.00
Plaque, Will Rogers, w/border, Prairie Gr, Ada clay	25.00
Plate, AAUW, 1976	24.00
Plate, chop; fish, #T-8	50.00
Plate, Easter, wht, 7½"	15.00
Plate, Wildlife, Buffalo	50.00
Pow Wow Pot, #829, complete w/12 skewers, 1957-1961	45.00

Gardener Boy, bibbed overalls, Prairie Green, $100.00.

Sculpture, Amazon Woman, mk Frank Potteries, #101, 6¼x8"	350.00
Sculpture, Amazon Woman, mk Taylor, 6¼x8"	350.00
Sculpture, Charger Horse, Ada clay	100.00
Sculpture, Charger Horse, Norman glaze	115.00
Sculpture, Circus Horse, Cherokee Red, #138, 4½"	85.00
Sculpture, Cowboy Boot, mk Frankoma Pottery	15.00
Sculpture, Donna Ruth, pacing leopard mk, #113, 7¾"	175.00

Sculpture, Dreamer Girl, Sorghum 125.00
Sculpture, English Setter, #163, 2⅞" 40.00
Sculpture, Fawns, #100/#101, 8", pr 50.00
Sculpture, Gardener Boy, Prairie Gr, belted, #702 ....90.00
Sculpture, Gardener Girl, Prairie Gr...............................85.00
Sculpture, Harlem Hoofer, #127, 13"...............................600.00
Sculpture, Indian Bowl Maker, discontinued glaze, #123, 6"...........40.00
Sculpture, Indian Chief, Ada clay, #142 ....90.00
Sculpture, Pacing Leopard, #104-L, 15".............................200.00
Sculpture, Pekingese Dog, #112, 7¾".............................300.00
Sculpture, Prancing Colt, #117, 8" 485.00
Sculpture, Prancing Percheron, #108, 4¾".............................200.00
Sculpture, Rearing Clydesdale, Osage Brn, Ada clay, #107..........175.00
Sculpture, Reclining Puma, Ada clay...............................85.00
Sculpture, Seated Puma, Ada clay, #114, 1934-1963, 7½" 85.00
Sculpture, Terrier, #161, 2⅞"...............................75.00
Sculpture, Torch Singer, #126, ca 1934, 13½"...............................600.00
Sculpture, Walking Elephant, #169, 1¾".............................75.00
Sculpture, Wedding Bell, rare 50.00
Shakers, Bull, #166, 2", pr...............................55.00
Shakers, Gracetone, Cinnamon, egg form, 3½", pr 15.00
Shakers, Snail, Desert Gold, Ada clay, #558-H, pr 10.00
Shakers, Teepee, #47, 1942-1960, 2⅞", pr.............................10.00
Shakers, Wheat Shock, Ada clay, #48-H, pr 15.00
Sign, Pacing Leopard, 8⅝" L 450.00
Sugar bowl, w/lid, Ada clay 10.00
Swan, #229, 1950-1963, 9" 40.00
Swan, Norman glaze, #168, miniature, 3" 40.00
Teapot, w/lid, gr, 2-cup...............................8.00
Tray, Mayan, Desert Gold, 9"...............................3.00
Tray, Palm Leaf, #T-11, 1962-1967, 17"...............................35.00
Trivet, Cherokee, brn, 5" 5.00
Trivet, Lazybones, Prairie Gr, #4-TR...............................40.00
Tumbler, Bamboo, #T-2, 1962-1976, 14-oz 12.00
Vase, #78, 9"...............................35.00
Vase, bottle form, Chinese Red, #14, 9½"...............................200.00
Vase, bottle form, Peach Glow, 9" 25.00
Vase, brn, Ada clay, #506, miniature 10.00
Vase, bud; Crocus, Ada clay, #43, 8"...............................15.00
Vase, bud; ivory, scalloped...............................25.00
Vase, Cactus, Red Bud 30.00
Vase, Cockatoo, pacing leopard mk, 5x8" 110.00
Vase, collector; V-1, Prairie Gr, 1969, 15" 70.00
Vase, collector; V-10, Morning-Glory Bl, wht int, 11½" 35.00
Vase, collector; V-11, Morning-Glory Bl, 1979, 11½" 35.00
Vase, collector; V-12, 1980 ....40.00
Vase, collector; V-13, blk & Terra Cotta, 1981, 13"...............40.00
Vase, collector; V-14, Flame Red & blk, 1982...............................55.00
Vase, collector; V-15, 2-pc, last of series...............................50.00
Vase, collector; V-2, turq, 1970, 12" 55.00
Vase, collector; V-3, red & blk, 1971, 12" 70.00
Vase, collector; V-4, blk & Terra Cotta, 1972 ....65.00
Vase, collector; V-5, Flame Red, 1973, 13"...............................70.00
Vase, collector; V-8, Freedom Red & wht, 1976 ....60.00
Vase, Cross, #804, 1955-1961, 6½"...............................25.00
Vase, Fan Shell, Ada clay, #54, 6"...............................20.00
Vase, Flying Goose, #60-B, 6" 20.00
Vase, leaf hdls, early glaze, #71, 1942, 10" 60.00
Vase, Modeled, #74, 8½"...............................50.00
Vase, pacing leopard mk, #502, 3"...............................60.00
Vase, Ram's Head, pacing leopard mk, #38, 1934-1949, 6"..........60.00
Vase, Ram's Head, pacing leopard mk, 9¼"...............................100.00
Vase, Reed, Prairie Gr, #61, made in 1942 only...............................35.00
Vase, scalloped top, #79, 1934-1938, 7"...............................125.00

Vase, spiral cvd, #73, 12"...............................85.00
Vase, Stove Pipe, #72, 9" 65.00
Vase, Swan, #168, 3"...............................75.00
Vase, Wagon Wheel, #94, 1942-1961, 7"...............................25.00
Wall pocket, Acorn, #190, 6"...............................15.00
Wall pocket, Boot, gr, Ada clay, 7"...............................15.00
Wall pocket, Negro, late 1930s, 2½"...............................110.00
Wall pocket, Phoebe, bsk, HP features & hair...............................125.00
Wall pocket, Phoebe, Prairie Gr, Ada clay, #730...............................75.00

Fraternal Organizations

Fraternal memorabilia is a vast and varied field. Emblems representing the various organizations have been used to decorate cups, shaving mugs, plates, and glassware. Medals, swords, documents, and other ceremonial paraphernalia from the 1800s and early 1900s are especially prized.

Elks

Book, Authentic History of..., C Ellis, 1910, 700-pg, VG 35.00
Earrings, symbols, ceramic, pr...............................7.00
Money case, sterling, w/cut-out letters: BPOE 15.00
Plate, metal, 1907 reunion 32.00

Masons

Bandana, 10+ symbols in red & wht, ca 1817, 22x26", EX 900.00
Bible, leather binding, gold stamping, ca 1931, 12x10"...............50.00
Breast pin, lady's, gold & pearl enamel, 1880s, EX 25.00
Chocolate pot, china, platinum trim, lodge name/roster...............85.00
Emblem, cvd wood, 4½" dia 28.00
Gavel, ivory & silver, presentation, 1910, M in case...............................175.00
Horseshoe, eagle atop, emblem in center, 4x6" 65.00
Match holder, walnut, pierced & cvd w/symbols, 11"...............65.00
Mug, ceramic, Atlantic City, 1904 ....50.00
Pencil box, wood, cvd insignia, sliding lid, 7" L 85.00
Penny, Bristol VT, dtd 1872, EX 18.00
Plate, Huntington WV, Commandery, 1908 ....35.00
Plate, Medina Temple, 1901...............................30.00
Sign, rvpt, convex, MOP & silver foil, EX 85.00

Wall shelf, brass and wood, 1850s, 7"x12", $400.00.

Shrine

Champagne, Rochester, 1911	85.00
Champagne, symbols, 4 leaves at base, Louisville, 1909	65.00
Champagne, Syria, Pittsburgh PA, tobacco leaf	75.00
Cup & saucer, glass, Los Angeles, 1906	70.00
Goblet, gold scimitars/etc, St Paul, 1908, M	65.00
Goblet, ruby flashed, scimitars/etc, St Paul, 1908	50.00
Goblet, silver symbols on ruby, St Paul, 1908	55.00
Horseshoe, brass, eagle atop, emblem in center, 4x6"	68.00
Mug, glass, Atlantic City, 1904	85.00
Mug, glass, Indian head relief, scimitar hdl, Saratoga, '03	65.00
Shot glass, cranberry w/gold, 1908	195.00
Tumbler, lady crying 'I want to be a Shriner,' 1897, M	135.00

Miscellaneous

Knights of Columbus, souvenir plate, china, Vienna Art	25.00
Knights of Columbus, sword w/brass eagle, 1840s, +scabbard	500.00
Knights of Pythias, goblet, gr, 1900	55.00
Knights of Pythias, shaving mug, gold name, Limoges, M	115.00
Odd Fellows, watch, symbols on dial, silver case, Waltham	200.00

Fraunfelter

Charles Fraunfelter organized his company in Zanesville, Ohio, in 1915. It was known as the Ohio Pottery Company until 1923. During this period their main product was a line of utilitarian articles for chemical laboratories made of hard paste porcelain. In 1918 they used the same body to produce a brown and white line called 'Petrascan.' By 1920 a line of hotel ware was added. The company organized in 1923 and became known as Fraunfelter China Company; but after the death of Fraunfelter in 1925, the business fell into hard times and eventually closed altogether in 1939.

Coffeepot, tulips decal, dripolator	45.00
Custard	2.50
Teapot, ribbed	10.00
Vase, acorns, gray/rose lustre, sgn Lessell, mk, 4½"	375.00
Vase, florals on pk lustre, sgn Lessell, 4½"	375.00

Fruit Jars

As early as 1829, canning jars were being manufactured for use in the home preservation of foodstuffs. For the past twenty-five years, they have been sought as popular collectibles. At the last estimate, over four thousand fruit jars and variations were known to exist. Some are very rare, perhaps one-of-a-kind examples known to have survived to the present day. Among the most valuable are the black glass jars, the amber Van Vliet, and the cobalt Millville. These often bring prices in excess of $3,000.00 when they can be found. Aside from condition, values are based on age, rarity, color, and special features.

Our advisor for this category is John Hathaway; he is listed in the Directory under Maine.

A Kline Pat'd Oct 27 1863 (on glass stopper), aqua, qt	23.00
Agnew & Co Pittsburgh, Patd Appl for 1887, b3m, clear, qt	78.00
Atlas E-Z Seal, cornflower bl, pt	15.00
Atlas E-Z Seal Trademark Reg (base only), aqua, qt	6.00
Atlas Good Luck, clear, ½-pt	11.00
Atlas Mason's Patent, aqua, ½-gal	4.00
Atlaz E-Z Seal, apple gr, aqua lid, qt	5.00

Ball (underlined) Perfect Mason, gripper ribs, bl, qt	9.00
Ball Eclipse Wide Mouth, clear, ½-gal	6.00
Ball Ideal Pat'd July 14 1908 (all on front), bl, pt	4.00
Ball Perfect Mason, clear, ½-pt	3.00
Ball Perfect Mason (italic & block letters), clear, qt	8.00
Baltimore Glass Works, aqua, qt	275.00
Beaver (beaver), aqua, midget	85.00
Canton Manufacturing Co Boston (base), amber, pt	6.00
Clyde (script in circle), clear, lid not emb, qt	9.00
Conserve Jar, clear, qt	7.00
Crown Mason Ribbed, clear, ½-pt	6.00
Cunningham & Co, Pittsburgh PA (base), aqua, qt	33.00
Daisy FE Ward & Co (in circle), aqua, qt	9.00
Dexter (circled by fruits & vegetables), aqua, qt	58.00
Diamond symbol on front, aqua, ½-gal	23.00
Doolittle (script), clear, pt	43.00
Doolittle Patented Dec 3 1910 on lid, clear, ½-gal	28.00
Drey Pat'd 1920 Improved Everseal, clear, glass ears, pt	9.00
Durham (in circle), aqua, pt	23.00
Eagle, aqua, ½-gal	125.00
EC Hazard & Co Schrewbury NJ (base), aqua, tall, qt	10.00
Electric (world globe) Fruit Jar, aqua, qt	108.00
Electric Trademark (script in circle), aqua, ½-gal	15.00
Empire (in stippled cross), clear, ½-gal	15.00
Everlasting Jar (word jar in flag), aqua, pt	23.00
Flaccus Bros Steershead Fruit Jar, clear, pt	58.00
Franklin Dexter Fruit Jar, aqua, ½-gal	33.00

Fridley & Cornman's Patent Oct 25th 1859 Ladies' Choice, aqua pint, M, $1,000.00.

Fruit Keeper GCCo, aqua, qt	38.00
Gem, reverse: Hourglass, aqua, ½-gal	18.00
GJCo (monogram), aqua, domed milk glass lid, pt	38.00
Haines Combination, aqua, qt	138.00
Hansee's Place Home Jar, clear, qt	68.00
Helme's Railroad Mills, dk amber, pt	18.00
Hero, aqua, qt, w/correct tin lid	38.00
Honest Mason Jar Pat 1858, clear, qt	12.00
HW Pettit Westville NJ (base), aqua, pt	10.00
Improved Everlasting Jar (in oval, 14 panels), clear, qt	18.00
Independent Jar, clear, midget	75.00
J&B (in octagon) Fruit Jar Pat'd July 14th 1898, aqua, qt	38.00
JE Taylor & Co Pure Food Santa Ana, Cal, aqua, qt	18.00
Jewell Jar Made in Canada, clear, ½-gal	10.00
K&O Queen Trademark Wide Mouth Adjustable, clear, qt	14.00
Kerr Economy Trademark, base: Chicago Ill, clear, qt	8.00
Kerr Self-Sealing Mason, amber, qt	18.00

Kilner Jar Improved Regd, clear, qt 10.00
King (on banner below king's head), clear, side clamps, pt 15.00
Klines Patent Oct 27 63 (on blown stopper), aqua, qt 123.00
Lustre RE Tongue & Bros Co Inc Phila (in circle), bl, pt...........10.00
Mason (shepherd's crook), aqua, pt 15.00
Mason Fruit Jar, amber, pt 98.00
Mason Fruit Jar (3 lines), aqua, pt 10.00
Mason Jar of 1872, aqua, qt 33.00
Mason's (cross) Improved, aqua, pt 10.00
Mason's (cross) Patent Nov 30th 1858, amber, qt 123.00
Mason's (cross) Patent Nov 30th 1858, amber, ½-gal 133.00
Mason's (keystone in circle) Patent Nov 30th 1858, aqua, qt......... 7.00
Mason's CFJCo Improved, amber, ½-gal.............................148.00
Mason's CFJCo Improved, aqua, midget 14.00
Mason's CJF Improved, reverse: Clyde NY, aqua, qt 6.00
Mason's IV Patent Nov 30th 1858, aqua, qt 20.00
Mason's LGW Improved, clear, qt......................................20.00
Mason's Patent Nov 30th 1858 (2 reversed N's), clear, qt.............15.00
Mason's Patent Nov 30th 58, aqua, midget.............................58.00
Mason's Patent 1858, aqua, pt 15.00
Mason's 2 Patent Nov 30th 1858, aqua, ½-gal 15.00
Mason's 4 Patent Nov 39th 1858, aqua, midget......................28.00
Model (underlined w/tail of l) Mason, clear, qt......................23.00
My Choice, aqua, lid not emb, ½-gal.................................198.00
P Lorillard Co (on base), amber, pt 9.00
Pansey (paneled), clear, qt 198.00
Patented Columbia Dec 29 1896 (on lid), clear, ½-pt 35.00
Patented July 27th 1886 (base), emerald gr Greek Key, ½-gal 348.00
Patented Oct 29 1868 (on lid), aqua, qt 43.00
Potter & Bodine Air-Tight Fruit Jar, aqua, qt 48.00
Princess (in shield & fr), clear, qt.....................................23.00
Protector (arched), aqua, qt 48.00
Protector (recessed panels), aqua, qt 55.00
Putnam Glass Works Zanesville O (base), aqua, qt 33.00
Queensland (pineapple) Fruit Jar, gr, qt................................123.00

Reservoir—To Open Admit Air by Inserting a Penknife Blade Between the Rubber and Glass, aqua quart, original clear glass stopper, embossed Mrs. G.E. Haller Patd Feb 25-73, M, $475.00.

Rose, clear, ½-gal 42.00
Royal (in crown) TM Registered Full..., amber, clear lid, qt 58.00
S McKee & Co (base), aqua, wax sealer, qt 23.00
Safety Valve Patd May 21 1895 (base), aqua, ¾-qt 10.00

SAMCO (in circle) Genuine Mason, clear, pt 2.00
Schaffer Jar Rochester NY, aqua, qt, bruise on lid 198.00
Silicon Glass Company Pittsburgh Penna (in circle), aqua, pt 15.00
Simplex (in diamond on side), clear, ½-pt 9.00
Smalley's Nu-Seal (in diamond), clear, ½-pt 45.00
Southern Double Seal Mason, clear, ½-gal 38.00
Square (G in sq) Mason, clear, ½-gal 10.00
Standard, reverse: Erased Mastadon, WMcC & Co, aqua, qt.........18.00
Standard (over shepherd's crook), aqua, qt 23.00
Standard (underlined w/loop), clear, qt 22.00
Star (below stippled star) clear, aqua insert, qt 33.00
Swasey Double Safety (in fr), clear, pt 12.00
Swayzee's Improved Mason, aqua, qt 8.00
The Burlington BG Co R'D 1975, clear, ½-gal 58.00
The Howe Jar Scranton PA, aqua, qt.................................48.00
The Ideal Imperial, aqua, qt 23.00
Thrift Buck Glass Co Baltimore MD, clear, qt......................14.00
TM Lightning Reg US Patent Office, amber, ½-gal 65.00
Trade Mark Keystone Registered, clear, qt 7.50
Trade Mark Lightning Putnam (all on base), aqua, pt 4.00
Trade Mark the Dandy, amber, qt.....................................133.00
Trade Mark the Dandy, clear, pt..63.00
Trade Mark the Smalley Self Sealer (in circle), clear, pt 5.00
United Drug Co Boston Mass (in fr), clear, qt......................12.00
Veteran (bust of veteran), clear, pt 18.00
Victory (in shield on lid), clear, twin wire clamps, ½-pt 12.00
Victory (in shield), The Victory Jar (on lid), clear, ½-pt 9.00
Victory 1 (circled by patent dates), aqua, qt 48.00
Wears (in circle), aqua, qt 15.00
Wears (on banner below crown), clear, side clamps, pt 15.00
Wears (on banner below crown), clear, side clamps, qt 14.00
Wears Jar (in stippled oval), clear, pt 9.00
Western Pride, no N in star, aqua, rpl clamp, qt, EX 150.00
Widemouth Famous Jar (in circle), aqua, pt 18.00
Widemouth Telephone Jar TM Reg, aqua, ½-gal 14.00
Winslow Jar, aqua, pt 98.00
Zinc, gray w/copper plate imp 'No 1,' dents, 5¼" 150.00

Fry

Henry Fry established his glassworks in 1901 in Rochester, Pennsylvania. There, until 1933 when it was sold to the Libbey Company, he produced glassware of the finest quality. In the early years, they produced beautiful cut glass; and when it began to wane in popularity, Fry turned to the manufacture of occasional pieces and oven glassware. He is perhaps most famous for the opalescent pearl glass called 'Foval.' It was made in combination with crystal or colored trim; because it was in production for only a short time in 1926 and 1927, it is hard to find.

Collectors of depression-era glassware look for the opalescent reamers and opaque green kitchenware made during the early thirties. See also Kitchen Collectibles.

Ash tray, rose crystal, bowl form w/buttress ft, 4 rests 25.00
Baker, pearl ovenware, 6" dia 15.00
Basket, Foval, jade gr w/festooning, 12".............................525.00
Basket, unnamed floral cutting, slim base, flared rim 300.00
Butter tub, Sunbeam cutting, lug-type hdls, 2½x4¾"...................235.00
Cake plate, Pershing cutting, center hdl...............................285.00
Candle holders, amber w/gold trim, orig paper labels, pr...............45.00
Candy dish, Alexis cutting, serrated rim, ftd, 5" 100.00
Carafe, Rose etching, rpl stopper 50.00
Casserole, pearl ovenware, emb grapes on lid, sq, 7".................35.00
Casserole, pearl ovenware, flower etching, metal holder................30.00

Cruet, Nashville cutting, faceted stopper 155.00
Cup & saucer, Foval, pearl w/floral cutting, #2000.................85.00
Cup & saucer, Foval, wide gold overlay band, jade gr hdl...........100.00
Ferner, Albert cutting, smooth rim, 3-ftd 185.00
Finger bowl, Rose etching, w/underplate 15.00
Goblet, rose w/gold-etched band...................................15.00
Goblet, Vienna cutting, long stem 85.00
Meatloaf pan, pearl ovenware, emb grapes on lid, 9" L 25.00
Pitcher, Ivy cutting, jug style, 4-pt 235.00

Foval pitcher and lid, jade handle and finial, $200.00.

Plate, Flower Basket cutting, scalloped rim, 9"..................165.00
Plate, Foval, pearl w/jade gr trim, 7½" 30.00
Plate, grill; amber, 3-compartment................................25.00
Plate, grill; pearl ovenware, bl enamel band at rim, 10½" 20.00
Plate, Sunbeam cutting, scalloped rim, 8" 165.00
Teapot, Foval, pearl, #2002, 2-cup...............................145.00
Vase, amber, slim cylinder..45.00
Vase, bud; azure bl...25.00
Vase, bud; Foval, pearl, #814, 10" 110.00
Vase, Foval, rose festooning, cylindrical, 10"...................350.00
Vase, Ivy cutting, slim form, 10" 225.00
Vase, jack-in-the-pulpit; Foval, Delft bl trim, #821, 10" 200.00
Vase, tazza; Venetian cutting, 12"...............................325.00

Fulper

The Fulper Pottery was founded in 1899, after nearly a century of producing utilitarian stoneware under various titles and managements. Not until 1909 did Fulper venture into the art pottery field. Vasekraft, their first art line, utilized the same heavy clay body used for their utility ware. Although shapes were unadorned and simple, the glazes they developed were used with such flair and imagination (alone and in unexpected combined harmony) that each piece was truly a work of art. Graceful Oriental shapes were produced to compliment the important 'famille rose' glaze developed by W.H. Fulper, Jr. Other shapes and glazes were developed in line with the Arts and Crafts movement of the

same period.

During WWI, doll's heads and Kewpies were made to meet the demand for hard-to-find imports. Figural perfume lamps and powder boxes were made both in bisque and glazed ware. Examples prized most highly by collectors today are those made before a devastating fire destroyed the plant in 1929, resulting in an operations takeover by Martin Stangl later that same year.

Several marks were used: a vertical 'Fulper' in a line reserve, a horizontal mark, a Vasekraft paper label, 'Rafco,' 'Prang,' and 'Flemington.'

Fulper values are to a major degree determined by the desirability of the glazes and forms. And, of course, larger examples command higher prices as well. Lamps with colored glass inserts are rare and highly prized.

Bottle, brn, music box, 9½".....................................125.00
Bowl, bl flambe over cream, red highlights, fluted, 9"...........150.00
Bowl, bl mottle, flared, shallow, arched raised ft, 3x7½".........60.00
Bowl, brn & bl, crystalline int, 3-ftd, 2x6" 150.00
Bowl, brn matt, bl/gr flambe int, hdls support ring above 200.00
Bowl, gray w/streaky bl int, 4 ogee ft, 7½" 135.00
Bowl, hammered olive on lt gr, 3-scroll ft on platform, 11"..... 1,600.00

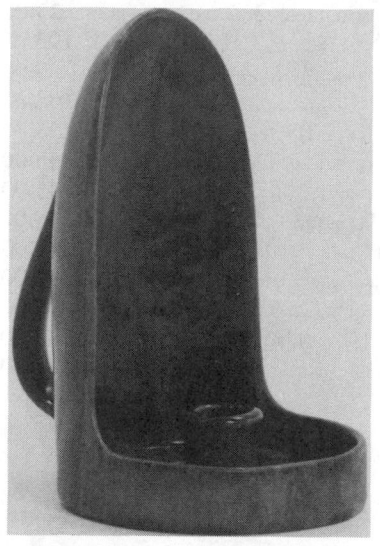

Shield-back candle holder, wisteria flambe, 8½", $145.00.

Candlestick, gr matt, slim std on bun base, 11",pr..............250.00
Cider pitcher, elephant's breath glaze, mk, 10", +6 mugs.........450.00
Lamp, 20 pcs ldgl in 9½" ceramic cone shade; ceramic std...... 3,500.00
Lamp, 24 pcs ldgl in 14" dome shade; flaring base, 17"......... 9,000.00
Perfume lamp, seated lady, pk floral dress, hat at ft, 7" 250.00
Perfume lamp, standing lady, purple/yel gown, 11½", NM 700.00
Pilgrim flask, lime/dk brn flambe, Chinese hdls, 10x8"..........400.00
Sugar bowl, gr, w/lid, early block mk, 3" 75.00
Tankard, gr frogskin w/crystalline, Prang mk, 7¾" 175.00
Vase, bl crystalline, brn/gr drip top, sq scroll hdls, 5x6".....200.00
Vase, bl crystalline drip on cream, ribbed, rnd ft, 10" 150.00
Vase, bl crystalline w/dk brn drip at top, squat, 4x5½".........80.00
Vase, bl flambe, appl serpent around slim neck, mk, 8" 450.00
Vase, bl flambe w/gr accents, 4 sm shoulder hdls, 13x14"....... 1,500.00
Vase, bl to streaky gray-gr, ovoid w/can neck, hdls, 7¾".......150.00
Vase, bl/gr flambe, appl dragon at stick neck, 8" 575.00
Vase, bl/gr flambe over dk bl, bulbous w/short neck, 9" 275.00
Vase, brn-gray drip over bl & wht w/pk flambe touches, 7x8".....475.00
Vase, brn/bl flambe over lav, ped ft, hdls, 9x9"................450.00
Vase, brn/mauve flambe/gr crystalline, sm rim, Prang, 8x6" 425.00
Vase, bud; dk bl crystalline, pencil neck, bun base, 8½" 135.00
Vase, bud; ivory/brn flambe w/bl, 4 base rings, 9"..............150.00

Vase, blue and ochre crystalline, 13", $395.00.

Vase, Chinese bl w/olive flambe top half, classic, 12" 425.00
Vase, copper dust crystalline, baluster, 8", pr.................................700.00
Vase, dove gray/tan gloss, ovoid w/flared neck, 7½".....................150.00
Vase, famille rose over gr matt bottom, shouldered/hdls, 6" 425.00
Vase, gr crystalline, 3-hdld, oval ink mk, 7" 195.00
Vase, gr crystalline/gun metal, hdls at bulb shoulder, 8" 275.00
Vase, gr/brn w/lt gr crystalline drip, buttressed, 9", NM 300.00
Vase, gr/gray crystalline mottle, sq/scalloped rim, 10"..................245.00
Vase, gun-metal crystalline, ovoid w/everted rim, 16½" 1,200.00
Vase, gun-metal crystalline/ochre mottle, in-mold hdls, 8" 225.00
Vase, indigo hi-gloss w/bl matt collar & loop hdls, 9x8".............550.00
Vase, lav w/lt bl highlights, 4-ftd fluted sq form, 8¾" 200.00
Vase, lime on floriform neck/hdls, med gr/mauve body, 9x12".....950.00
Vase, lt bl/olive flambe, incurvate, 5x6½" 200.00
Vase, lt gr crystalline over dk gr flambe, hdls, 6x7" 350.00
Vase, lt gr crystalline w/dk brn & gr, rim hdls, 9" 225.00
Vase, lt gr pools over matt mint gr, scroll hdls, 12½" 3,300.00
Vase, lt yel drips on bl/olive flambe, 3 horn hdls, 6x6" 450.00
Vase, matt bl, 8" 225.00
Vase, med grs & tans, paper & imp label, 4⅜", EX 150.00
Vase, mirror blk, rnd collar, 5" 145.00
Vase, olive flambe, Chinese bl around bottom, classic, 12" 210.00
Vase, olive w/bl crystalline drip, amphora w/loop hdls, 11" 375.00
Vase, pk flambe on dk brn/bl, yel top, emb mushrooms, 10" 650.00
Vase, rose over lime flambe, 6-side ogee form, 11x5½" 200.00
Vase, yel/gr flambe, gun-metal crystalline at neck, 8x6" 550.00

Furniture

From the cabinetmaker's shop of the early 1800s with apprentices and journeymen who learned every phase of the craft at the side of the master carpenter, the trade had evolved by the mid-century to one with steam-powered saws and turning lathes and workers who specialized in only one operation. By 1870 the Industrial Revolution was in progress, and large factories in the East and Midwest turned out increasingly elaborate styles, ornately machine carved and heavily inlaid. Rococo, Egyptian, and Renaissance Revival furniture adapted well to factory production. Eastlake offered a welcome respite from Victorian frumpery and a return to quality handcrafting. All of these styles remained popular until the turn of the century.

As early as 1880, factories began using oak; early mail-order catalogs offered oak furniture, simply styled and lighter in weight, since long-distance shipping was often a factor. Mission, or Craftsman, a style introduced around 1890, was simple to the extreme. Stickley and Hubbard were two of its leading designers. Other popular Victorian styles were Colonial Revival, Cottage, Bentwood, and Windsor. Prices are as variable as the styles.

To learn more about furniture, we recommend *The Collector's Encyclopedia of American Furniture* by Robert and Harriet Swedberg.

Key:
Am — American	G — good
brd — board	Geo — Georgian
Chpndl — Chippendale	grpt — grainpainted
Co — Country	hdbd — headboard
cvd — carved	hdw — hardware
cvg — carving	Hplwht — Hepplewhite
c&b — claw and ball	NE — New England
do — door	QA — Queen Anne
drw — drawer	trn — turning
Emp — Empire	Vict — Victorian
Fed — Federal	W/M — William and Mary
Fr — French	: — over (example: 1 do:2 drw —
ftbd — footboard	1 door over 2 drawers)

Bed

Victorian mahogany half-tester bed, ca 1850s, $3,000.00.

Brass, sq posts, cherub medallions on hd/ftbd, dbl sz 450.00
Maple Emp, bell & ball posts, pine hdbd, Am, 1820, 48" 250.00
Murphy, lg sq mirrored front, ornate cvgs, rstr/rfn 600.00
Murphy, oak, swivel mirror atop, rstr/rfn 550.00
Rope, cherry, trn posts w/cannonballs, EX detail, 61" 1,200.00
Rope, cherry Emp, pineapple cvg/cannonballs, scalloped hdbd ...700.00
Rope, hardwood post w/pineapple finials, scroll hd/ftbd 650.00
Rope, maple w/some curl, cherry hd/ftbd, goblet finials...............325.00
Rope, poplar w/cherry finish, cannonballs/trn posts, 54" 500.00
Rope, walnut, short chamfered posts, simple hd/ftbd, 36"...........325.00
Rope trundle, poplar w/old red, short trn posts w/knobs 325.00
Rope trundle, short posts w/trn ft & cannonballs, 38x60" 200.00
Tall post, cherry/poplar, EX trn, scroll hdbd, 83" 1,300.00

Tall post, cherry/poplar, sq tapered posts w/appl molding 850.00
Tall post, walnut, spool trn, ¾-sz, 81", EX 500.00
Tall post/rope, trn cherry posts/mahog veneer hdbd, 70" 450.00
Tester, cherry Sheraton, w/canopy, NM 1,250.00
Tester, fluted mahog & maple posts/pine hdbd Sheraton 2,400.00
Tester, maple Sheraton, reeded legs, urn finials, 1820, 73" 1,500.00
Tester, tiger maple Emp, bird's eye hdbd, Am, 1820s, 83"........ 2,000.00

Bench

Brn pnt w/yel striping & mc stenciled flowers, 73" L............. 1,000.00
Deacon's, chair-leg base, 1850s, rfn, 81" L 400.00
Deacon's, natural finish, Am, 1800s, 120" L................................100.00
Deacon's, pine/maple, trn spindles, plank seat, blk pnt, 71".........375.00
Kneeling, pine w/worn red flame grpt, 20" L 100.00
Limbert, flat top:arched apron, branded, varnished, 24" W 650.00
Onondaga, even-arm settle #743, slat bk/sides, 76" 4,750.00
Pine, bootjack brd ft mortised through top, old rfn, 18x97" 85.00
Pine, primitive, legs mortised through top, 61" L, VG 135.00
Settle, EX turn/plank seat, ½-arrow bk, wide crest, 74" 375.00
Settle, heavy gr rpt, trn detail/plank seat, 87" 175.00
Settle, pine w/worn red finish, brn grpt panels, late, 81" 1,000.00
Wash, pine, NE, 1800s, 76" L, EX...400.00
Wash, pine, primitive, 1800s, 66" L..300.00
Water, pine, primitive, step bk, damage/worn, 51x35"............675.00
Water, pine, scalloped bk brd, width reduced, 44x28", EX...........350.00
Water, pine Co, 3-shelf, 1-brd ends w/cut-out ft, 45x47"...........625.00
Water, pine Co w/gr rpt, bootjack ends, shelf & drw, 39x27".......800.00
Water, pine w/worn red & wht rpt, bootjack ends, 36" L.............425.00
Windsor, mammy's, rockers, 57" L...450.00
Windsor settle, plank seat, scroll arms, old finish, 78" 1,600.00

Blanket Chest

Cherry w/curly maple panels, trn ft, till, 20x38x17"....................325.00
Grpt Co Chpndl, 43" L 600.00
Pine, trn maple legs, 1-drw, 1800s, rfn, 36" W.............................425.00
Pine, 1-drw, Am, 1700s, rfn, 41" L...350.00
Pine, 3-drw, lift lid, Am, 1820s, 44x37", EX........................... 1,200.00
Pine, 6-brd, drw, 1700s, rfn/rpr, 28x43".................................400.00
Pine Co Chpndl, lift lid, 1-drw, NE, 1700s, old finish/hdw..........600.00
Pine Co w/bl rpt, 6-brd, scalloped ft, 44" 400.00
Pine w/dk red finish, 2-drw, 1700s, 39" W, EX 2,900.00
Pine w/orig bl, lg landscape/initials/1834, 46" L, EX 6,550.00
Pine w/orig bl pnt, NE, 1800, 44" L, NM.................................800.00
Pine w/red grpt on salmon, trn ft/dvtl case, 44" L, EX................950.00
Pine/poplar PA w/vinegar grpt, bl-sponge panels, 54" W......... 1,400.00
Pine/poplar w/orig flame grpt in bl tones, 1-brd top 700.00
Pine/poplar w/wht smoke grpt panels, red grpt rails, etc..............900.00
Poplar w/orig yel grpt, dvtl, trn ft, 48" W, M 525.00
Tiger maple Chpndl, 1-drw, lift top, Am, 1780s, rfn, 40" L 1,900.00
Walnut Co Chpndl VA Valley , walnut, 3 dvtl base drw, 51"... 2,100.00

Bookcase

Fruitwood/inlay Biedermeier, frieze drw:3 shelves, 33x42"........1,000.00
Limbert, #359, 3-do, no mk, rfn/minor rstr, 58x67" 1,500.00
Oak, drop-lid desk:3 drw, glass do, sm mirror, appl cvgs 750.00
Oak, sectional, 4-unit, 1920s, rstr/rfn.....................................500.00
Oak, 1-do, simple styling, 4-shelf, rfn/rstr................................300.00
Oak, 2 do:2, ldgl w/bevels, rfn/rstr 1,000.00
Oak, 2-do, simple styling, 4-shelf, rstr/rfn................................500.00
Oak, 3-do, cvd/trn posts, paw ft, rstr/rfn.................................950.00
Onondaga, #328 ½, 2-do, gallery/exposed tenons, 57x49"....... 4,750.00

Bureau, see Chest

Cabinet

China, curved glass front, mirror bk, very simple, NM 850.00
China, oak, curved glass front, EX cvg, paw ft, 45" W 1,600.00
China, oak, curved glass front, paw ft, cvd/mirrored crest 1,200.00
China, oak, ldgl sides/do, mirror bk, 1900s.................................900.00
Corner, pine, 2 arched glazed do:2 do, molding, pnt, 86x58" .. 1,000.00
Corner, 2 arched 2-panel do:2, rpt w/traces of orig, 79x42"..... 5,000.00
Corner china, oak, beveled mirror bk/ldgl do, 3-leg, paw ft..... 1,200.00
Corner china, oak, broken pediment, ball ft, glass sides/do 1,500.00
Kitchen, oak, 2 glass do:step bk shelf:2 drw:2 do, 1920s...............500.00
Liquor, Limbert #752, glass-lined tray, 1-drw/2-do, mk, 39" 2,400.00
Side, rosewood/marquetry Renaissance Revival, att Marcotte.. 3,100.00

Candlestand

Ash/hickory, Xd shoe ft, ratchet adjusts, 2-cup candle arm..........400.00
Birch Co Hplwht, spider legs, trn column 1-brd 16x17" top 450.00
Birch Co Hplwht, trn w/spider legs, 15x21" tilt top, VG 400.00
Cherry, tripod base w/snake ft, trn columns, rpl 19" top 225.00
Cherry Co, EX detail, trn column, 18" dia 2-brd top, 27"...........600.00
Cherry Co, stout trn column, delicate legs/ft, 19" dish top 425.00
Cherry Co, tripod base/snake ft, trn column w/18" dia top 325.00
Cherry Co Hplwht, spider legs, trn column, 16" W 1-brd top 500.00
Cherry QA, tilt top, snake ft, Am, 1700s, EX 550.00
Curly maple Co Empire, 2-brd 19" dia tilt top, scroll legs...........550.00
Curly maple Hplwht, birdcage under oval top, tripod base...... 1,650.00
Curly maple/bird's eye w/inlay star, 1880s.................................300.00
Mahog, trn tripod base, rpl 14x16" 1-brd tilt top 325.00

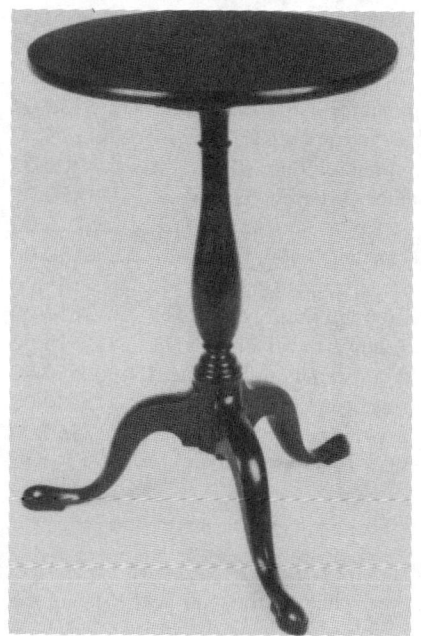

Mahogany tilt-top candle-stand, ca 1790, 28", $4,000.00.

Mahog w/ebony line inlay on spider legs, 18x20" tilt top.............225.00
Mahog w/string inlay Hplwht, tilt top, 1780s, EX 450.00
Poplar w/red re-grpt Co Hplwht, 20" sq top, EX.........................375.00
Red/blk grpt, tripod base, cut-out ft, 1-brd 18" dia top.................850.00

Chair

Armchair, banister-bk, dbl-trn stretchers/arm supports 850.00
Armchair, banister-bk, later rush seat, Am, 1700.........................250.00

Armchair, crest/arms/legs of longhorns, needs uphl, ca 1880... **1,000.00**
Armchair, fruitwood Transitional QA, EX trn, pierced splat... **2,500.00**
Armchair, library; Geo III, shell/acanthus cvd legs & knees.... **1,100.00**
Armchair, oak, basic Mission style, rfn/rstr.....................**150.00**
Armchair, Sheraton w/orig dk pnt & gold striping, trn **200.00**
Armchair, walnut Spanish Baroque, leather uphl, 1700, EX........**175.00**
Armchair, walnut Vict, grape-cvd crest EX **210.00**

Windsor fan-back writing armchair, red paint over old green, ca 1800, 45" high, $12,000.00.

Belter, Vict side, rose/grape-cvd crest, pr, NM **4,500.00**
Corner, Co style, sausage trn, scroll arm rail w/crest **1,000.00**
Corner, mahog Chpndl, sq legs, trn posts, vase splats, EX **800.00**
Corner, maple QA, traces of old red pnt, rpl seat, MS, 1720 ....**600.00**
Corner, walnut QA, 2 EX pierced/cvd splats, slip seat, EX **3,700.00**
Cube, oak, spindle sides & bk, Mission type, unsgn **225.00**
Cube, Oak Craft, slatted, thru tenons, rpl seat, 34x32" **1,000.00**
Cube, Oak Craft, thru tenons, label, rstr uphl, 34x32", EX **1,000.00**
Desk, oak, 4-leg swivel base, vertical slats in bk, w/arms..............**225.00**
Ladderbk arm, bold trn, 4 arched grad splats, rstr, EX **800.00**
Ladderbk arm, EX sausage trn/curved arms, orig finish, 45" ... **1,900.00**
Ladderbk side, EX orig blk pnt, 1780s, pr **350.00**
Ladderbk side, 4 arched splats, trn legs, bulbous stretcher...........**450.00**
Ladderbk ½-arm, EX trn, maple/worn rpt, EX turn, VG **425.00**
Lady's walnut Vict, finger-cvd fr/grape-cvd crest, EX **200.00**
Limbert, armchair #575, sq cutouts in bk & sides, label **3,200.00**
Lolling, mahog/inlay Sheraton, MS region, 1800, EX **5,750.00**
Morris, oak, bow arm, pegged bk, thru posts, rope seat, rfn...........**700.00**
Morris, oak, reclining, wide arms: 5-slat sides, rfn, 40x32"...........**800.00**
Rocker, banister-bk arm, old blk pnt, rpl rush seat, 1850s...........**250.00**
Rocker, ladderbk, rpt/re-stencil, rush seat **200.00**
Rocker, oak, no arms, simple style, 1920s, rstr/rfn **125.00**
Rocker, oak, T-bk 3-spindle sides, str armrest **200.00**
Rocker, oak press-bk, 3 trn spindles under curving armrest..........**350.00**
Rocker, oak w/tacked-on leatherette bk & seat, w/arms, NM **250.00**
Rocker, sewing; oak, 3-slat bk, swing-out tray under seat **200.00**
Rosewood Vict, shield-bk, finger-mold arms, cabriole legs **250.00**
Side, banister-bk, EX detail, paper rush seat, rpt/rpr.....................**275.00**
Side, Chpndl, red-brn pnt w/blk striping, rush seat, 1760s...........**250.00**
Side, Co QA, maple w/some curl in splat, bulb trn, seat..............**700.00**
Side, laminated rosewood Rococo, scroll bk, att Meeks **475.00**
Side, mahog Chpndl, ornate bk splat prof rpl, 1775 .... **1,500.00**
Side, mahog Chpndl ribbon-bk, Am, 1775, orig finish, EX **475.00**
Side, maple Co QA, trn legs/Spanish ft, EX trn, rush seat **800.00**
Side, maple Co QA, trn legs/Spanish ft, vase splat, VG **395.00**
Side, QA, yoke bk, bulbous trn, rpl rush seat, EX **100.00**

Side, rosewood Vict w/floral inlay, EX cvgs, VG **200.00**
Side, stenciled fruit/yel stripes on brn, ½-spindle bk **125.00**
Side, tiger maple, str crest rail, 1-slat bk, cane seat.....................**100.00**
Side, tiger maple Emp, vase splat/cane seat, 1830s, pr.................**350.00**
Side, walnut Biedermeier, incurvate bk supports, pr **1,750.00**
Windsor, bow-bk arm, Am, 1700s, rfn, NM.................................**400.00**
Windsor, bow-bk arm, oak, repro.................................**200.00**
Windsor, bow-bk arm, oval seat, trn legs, old rfn **750.00**
Windsor, bow-bk knuckle arm, trn legs/saddle seat, rstr........... **1,050.00**
Windsor, bow-bk side, 7-spindle, old blk pnt, 1 rpr, pr............. **2,000.00**
Windsor, bow-bk side, 9-spindle, branded Sanborn, rfn, EX **375.00**
Windsor, bow-bk side, 9-spindle, Samuel Tuck brand, NM **1,200.00**
Windsor, bow-bk side, 9-spindle, shaped seat, rpl/rfn, VG **375.00**
Windsor, bow-bk side, 9-spindle/saddle seat, 1780, cut down **450.00**
Windsor, brace-bk side, fine trn, wide splay legs, 1780s **1,100.00**
Windsor, brace-bk side, Wallace Nutting label, worn/split **250.00**
Windsor, cage-bk side, rpt over orig mustard yel, 1820s **250.00**
Windsor, comb-bk arm, bamboo trn, oval seat, rfn/rpr...............**450.00**
Windsor, comb-bk arm, 7-spindle, eared crest/bamboo trn, EX ...**700.00**
Windsor, continuous-arm Co, shaped seat, bamboo trn **375.00**
Windsor, fan-bk arm, saddle seat, EX ears, trn legs **1,750.00**
Windsor, fan-bk arm, Wallace Nutting label, NM orig............. **1,050.00**
Windsor, fan-bk arm, worn blk rpt, rpr crest/spindle................ **1,300.00**
Windsor, fan-bk side, red rpt w/blk striping, saddle seat **850.00**
Windsor, fan-bk side, saddle seat, Am, 1780s, EX **300.00**
Windsor, fan-bk side, trn legs/saddle seats, rfn, pr................... **1,500.00**
Windsor, fan-bk side, 7-spindle, saddle seats, mk LB, pr.......... **1,200.00**
Windsor, fan-bk side, 8-spindle, shaped crest, worn **550.00**
Windsor, side, bamboo trn, red over blk pnt, sgn, VG **225.00**
Windsor, writing arm, orig pnt stripes/flowers, oval seat **2,900.00**
Windsor, writing arm w/2 drws, bar crest, saddle seat, rpt........ **1,000.00**
Wingbk, custom Chpndl style, c/b front legs, EX **400.00**
Wingbk, cvd legs, c/b ft, re-uphl, 1920 ....**325.00**
Wingbk, mahog Geo w/leather uphl, English, 1700s, NM....... **1,400.00**
Wright, Russel; armchair, blond wood, blk leather uphl **600.00**

Chair Set

Ladderbk side, chrome yel decor, splint seat, 1840, 4 for **250.00**
Ladderbk side, curly maple, 4 shaped slats, EX trn, 6 for **1,800.00**
Ladderbk side, splint seat, orig red pnt, 4 for.....................**950.00**
Side, arrow half-bk, plank seat, rfn, 4 for.....................**340.00**
Side, Co Emp, trn legs, shaped splat, rfn/rpl seats, 6 for **680.00**
Side, golden oak Chpndl style, c/b ft, EX, 6 for.....................**575.00**
Side, gr w/freehand & stencil decor, plank seat, EX, 6 for **1,500.00**
Side, Hitchcock, plank seats, orig striping, EX, 5 for.....................**750.00**
Side, mahog Chpndl style, 1910s, set of 5+armchair **1,000.00**
Side, mahog Hplwht style, shield bk/spade ft, EX, 6 for **500.00**
Side, mahog QA style, slip seats, minor wear, 6 for **900.00**
Side, maple w/some curl & bird's eye, sabre leg, 4 for.....................**400.00**
Side, oak, press-cvd crest & splat, saddle seat, 4 for **500.00**
Side, oak kitchen type, 5-spindle (2 trn) bk, 1900s, 4 for **200.00**
Side, oak pressed bk, pressed cane bottom, rfn/rstr, 4 for.............**500.00**
Side, oak T-bk, leatherette seat, 4 for.................................**250.00**
Side, oak T-bk, plank seat, 4 for **200.00**
Side, orig florals, 4-color on salmon, EX, 6 for **1,800.00**
Side, rosewood Regency, brass ornaments, English, 8 for......... **4,750.00**
Side, Sheraton w/gr & gilt rpt, EX detail, 8 for.....................**240.00**
Side, Sheraton w/re-decor, minor rprs, 6 for.....................**1,050.00**
Side, stenciled Emp, rush seats, Am, orig finish, 5 for.................**400.00**
Side, Thonet, bentwood, interlaced splat, 6 for **1,200.00**
Side, thumb-bk, orig yel w/stencil, 1830s, 6 for.....................**1,300.00**
Side, walnut Vict, simple cvg, VG, 8 for.................................**725.00**
Side, Windsor step-down, orig floral on blk, 1820s, 6 for **5,100.00**

Chest

Apothecary, poplar w/rpt over red, 25 cock-beaded drw, 72"... 3,200.00
Birch Chpndl, swell front, ogee bracket base, rfn, 37" W 1,700.00
Birch Fed, 4 grad drw, rpl hdw/rfn, 42x37" 2,600.00
Birch Sheraton, 4-drw, orig hdw & red finish, 1810, 41" W ... 1,300.00

Country Federal birch chest, ca 1800, 40" x 36" x 19", $850.00.

Cherry Co Chpndl, appl edge beading, rpl hdw, 40x41" 1,300.00
Cherry Co Hplwht, top drw has 2 false fronts:5, pnt traces 1,650.00
Cherry Co Sheraton, sq posts/trn ft, 2-brd top, 40x40" 1,000.00
Cherry Hplwht, string/band inlay, bow front, rpl hdw, 38" 2,600.00
Cherry Hplwht, tiger maple molding, 4-drw, orig hdw, 41" W.. 2,400.00
Cherry w/inlay Co Sheraton, exaggerated scroll apron, 46" ... 1,150.00
Cherry w/mahog facings Chpndl, ogee bracket base, 38x45" .. 5,500.00
Cherry/bird's eye maple Sheraton bow front, 1800, 44" W...... 1,050.00
Cherry/curly maple Co Emp, trn ft/tapered pilasters, 52x43".......550.00
Cherry/poplar, red/blk pnt, stencil birds, Soap Hollow PA 5,000.00
Chest, mahog Geo III, molded top:4 grad drws, rstr, 1780s 800.00
Chest on chest, walnut Georgian, English, orig hdw, 73x40".. 1,200.00
Chest on fr, Co QA, pine/maple, EX cornice, losses, 40x36" .16,500.00
Mahog, rope post, bow front, 3-drw superstructure, tall.......... 1,300.00
Mahog Sheraton, bow front, rope posts, 2 drw:4, 40" W 1,100.00
Mahog Sheraton, bow front, trn/reeded legs, beading, 42" W . 1,850.00
Mahog w/band inlay, Sheraton, bow front, orig hdw, 40" W ... 2,900.00
Mahog w/figured veneer English Hplwht bow front, 42" W 1,000.00
Mahog WM IV, bowed top:2 short drw:3 grad, spool ft, 44"........550.00
Manog veneer on pine English Hplwht, rpl brasses/rfn/rpr 900.00
Maple Emp, 4-drw, cvd ½-columns, needs rfn, 49" 100.00
Maple w/curl Co Chpndl, 4-drw, rpl ft, edge damage, 40"............800.00
Mule, pine w/brn flame grpt, 2-drw +2 faux drw, 39x35" 675.00
Mule, walnut Co Sheraton, sq posts/trn ft, rfn/rpl, 47x43" 950.00
Oak Chas II, 3 grad drw, block ft, 1675, 31x34".......................1,000.00
Pine, 4-drw, blanket drw at top, Am, 1800, 39" W, EX 900.00
Pine Co Chpndl, 4-drw, rpl hdw, worn, 47x38" 1,250.00
Striped tiger maple-faced Sheraton, bow front, 42" W 3,500.00
Sugar, cherry, dvtl drw, panel sides, repro, 36x24" 300.00
Tiger maple, 3 drw:2:5, 1775, rfn, 62x38" 7,000.00
Tiger maple facings/maple sides/birch top Hplwht, bow front . 1,600.00
Tiger maple w/bird's eye drw facings Emp, 48x42", NM 1,350.00
Walnut Chpndl, 4 grad drw, ogee bracket base, 36" W............ 3,500.00
Walnut Co Hplwht, curly maple facings & scalloped apron'.... 1,000.00
Walnut Italian Renaissance, 3-drw/grotesque ea side, 33" 1,400.00
Walnut w/minor inlay Co Hplwht, scroll base, rfn, 44x40".... 1,300.00

Walnut w/simple inlay Co Hplwht, much rstr/rfn/rpl brasses.......875.00

Commode, see Washstand

Cupboard

Corner, cherry, high cut-out ft w/scrolled apron, 83x49" 2,350.00
Corner, curly maple, scrolled apron, bonnet top, repro, 85" 1,600.00
Corner, pine, 2 dbl-panel do:2 base do, NE, 1700s, 85x53" ... 1,600.00
Corner, pine, 2 6-pane do:2, old bl pnt, minor rstr, 74x50" 1,700.00
Corner, poplar, glaze 9-pane do:2 panel do, PA, 1780s, 92"..... 1,700.00
Corner/hanging, mahog, 1 bentwood do, 1820s, 27x19".............125.00
Corner/hanging, pine, panel rails/stiles/do, pegged, 40x23".........700.00
Corner/hanging, pine w/bl traces, panel do, 46x23" 400.00
Hanging, pine, 1 dbl-panel do, Am, 1800s, rfn, 30x24" 225.00
Hanging, walnut, base/cornice moldings/reeded stiles, 35x25" 525.00
Jelly, butternut, 1 do w/dbl panel, 55x41" 300.00
Jelly, pine w/bl rpt, simple crest/cut-out ft, 1-do, 60x47".............600.00
Pine w/yel rpt, 1-pc, appl moldings, fitted int, 64x26" 1,100.00
Poplar, primitive, 1 do:1, probably PA, 1800, 64x28" 1,500.00
Poplar, scroll bksplash, 2-drw:2 do, PA, 1835, 44x41", EX 400.00
Poplar, 2 9-pane do:2, PA, 1850s, rfn, 84x50½" 850.00
Poplar, 2-pc, panel do/3-drw/pie shelf, CI latches, 85x55" 2,600.00
Poplar w/dk red Co, 1-pc, renailed/rpl cornice, 84x48"................950.00
Walnut, 2-pc, 2 panel do:step bk:2 drws:2 do, simple, 80" 1,000.00

Desk

Butler's, curly maple w/cherry banding Hplwht, rpr, 41x48" ... 1,700.00
Cherry Chpndl, slant lid, 4 grad thumb-mold drw, 36" W....... 3,200.00
Cherry QA, 9 pigeonholes/13 drw, NE, 1750s, 36" W 1,600.00
Clerk's, pine w/red grpt over orig bl, on fr base, 52x37" 950.00
Curly maple, slant lid, Am, 1700s, rstr/rfn, 34" W.................... 2,200.00
Curly maple Co Chpndl, slant lid, EX rprs/rfn, 41x36" 3,500.00
Kneehole, mahog/walnut Geo III, bowed leather top, 38" 900.00
Lifetime, #927, flat top, cabinet do 1 side, ½-drw:1 .... 1,600.00
Limbert, partners, 3 drw ea side, arched kneehole, 48", EX..... 2,900.00
Limbert, slant top #713, copper strap hdw, sgn, 40" W, EX 1,600.00
Mahog Chpndl, oxbow, simple hdw, bracket base, 42" W............200.00
Mahog Chpndl, slant lid, NY, 1775, old rfn/minor rpl, 48" W 1,250.00
Mahog/inlay Hplwht, cylinder front, orig eagle hdw, 44" W .. 2,400.00
Maple (scrubbed) Co Chpndl, slant lid, well fitted, 40" W 3,700.00
Maple Co Chpndl, slant lid, Am, 1790s, rfn, rpl hdw, 36" W . 4,000.00
Maple Co Chpndl, slant lid, 4-drw, bracket base, 36" W......... 4,000.00
Maple w/some curl Co Chpndl, slant front, orig hdw, 42x36"...12,250.00
Oak, slant lid:drw, open base w/curved front legs & paw ft..........400.00

Victorian paneled oak roll-top desk, 60" wide, $1,500.00.

Roll top, oak, well-fitted top, 4-drw ea side base, 45" W **1,600.00**
Satinwood Edwardian Carlton House, superstructure, 38x36" . **2,600.00**
Schoolmaster's, cherry, 3 sm drw:1, trn legs, lift lid **450.00**
T Brooks, rosewood Renaissance Revival mirror-bk, 63x30" ... **1,600.00**
Tiger maple Chpndl, slant lid, EX figure, 1780s, 40" W, EX ... **4,000.00**
Travel, brass-bound mahog, all orig, open: 16" L **150.00**

Dresser

Limbert #492½ vanity, 1 drw: arched apron, branded, VG **1,400.00**
Oak, curved facade, swivel mirror, press/cvd decor **450.00**
Oak, swivel mirror, 2-drw, 1920s, sm **300.00**
Walnut Renaissance Revival/Eastlake, marble top **850.00**
Walnut Vict, candle shelves by mirror, marble top **1,300.00**

Dry Sink

Butternut, 3 panel do, sm dvtl drw, lift lid, rfn, 55" W **800.00**
Pine, panel do, top shelf w/sm drw, CI latches, 51x43" **1,050.00**
Pine w/yel pnt over blk, simple ft, 2 panel do, 43" L, EX **1,350.00**
Poplar, panel do, drw to side, bracket ft, 51" L, VG **575.00**
Poplar w/pnt layers, scalloped base, panel do, drw, 48" W **650.00**

Hall Piece

Console table, Louis XV-style giltwood, marble top, 71" **1,500.00**

Charles Limbert oak hall bench, unsigned, 40" long, $3,200.00.

Hall tree, oak, high-bk chair type w/mirror & coat hooks **700.00**
Oak Renaissance style, ornate cvg/mirror/lift seat, 91x53" **2,300.00**
Oak seat, lift lid/paw ft, +beveled mirror, simple, 36" W **750.00**
Oak seat, tall mirror bk, EX cvg on crest & bk, 47" W **1,000.00**
Stand, walnut Rococo, Blake & Davenport, marble top, 90" **800.00**
Stand, walnut/marble Renaissance, ornate cornice, 96" **800.00**

Highboy

Curly maple Co QA, flat top, rpr/more needed, rpl hdw, 73" .. **2,750.00**
Curly maple QA, NE, 1750s, rfn/rpl hdw, 69x38" **10,000.00**
Mahog QA style, fan cvg, handmade repro w/some age, 90" ... **1,500.00**
Maple Co QA, hidden cornice drw, rpl legs, rfn/rpr, 68" **3,250.00**
Oak English, molded cornice, cock-bead drw, orig hdw, 63" .. **2,000.00**

Lowboy

Birch/maple Co QA, highboy base w/added top, rfn, 36x40" .. **1,100.00**
Burled walnut w/inlay English QA, cock beading, 1700s, 28". **2,500.00**

Mahog English Chpndl, sq legs, 3-drw, scalloped apron, 32" ... **1,200.00**
Mahog English QA, elaborate apron, 3-drw, rpl/rstr, 26x28" ... **1,900.00**
Pine/hardwoods Co Chpndl, English, 1750s, 30" W, EX **450.00**

Pie Safe

Butternut/pine, yel re-grpt, scalloped apron/tin do, 58" W **1,500.00**
Butternut/poplar w/rpt over red, tin-panel do, 72x50" **800.00**
Hanging, pine/poplar, punched tin panels in do/ends, 19x21".. **1,250.00**
Poplar, 6 punched tin panels w/hex motif, rpl drw, 53x43" **250.00**
Poplar w/orig yel grpt & gr molding, screen do, 50x50" **475.00**
Poplar w/yel grpt, red grpt do panels, trn ft, tin sides **1,500.00**

Rack

Baker's, hardwood English, mortised, dowel shelves, 44x30" **175.00**
Limbert, luggage, 6-slat top, fully pegged, branded, 19x27" **500.00**
Limbert, magazine #302, branded, 28x28" W, EX **800.00**

Secretary

Butler's, cherry & mahog w/band inlay Hplwht, 86x41", NM. **4,500.00**
Curly maple, 2 glaze do:slant lid:3 drw, rfn/rpl, 90x43" **2,600.00**

Federal mahogany and veneer inlaid secretary, ca 1815, 76", $4,500.00.

Mahog Sheraton, 2 crotch grain do, drop writing lid, 41" **800.00**
Mahog w/flame grain veneer Emp, paw ft, open base, 80x38" **2,300.00**
Mahog w/inlay Hplwht, 2-pc, tambour do, rstr/rpl, 79x39" **2,600.00**
Mahog w/line & star inlay custom Chpndl-style, 94x42" **2,000.00**
Mahog/inlay, tambour front, urn finials, later copy, 75x18" **2,200.00**
Oak Continental, bombe style, ornate cvg, 1880s, 92x47" **2,000.00**
Walnut Vict, 2 glaze do:fall front, compartmented int, 83" **425.00**
Walnut w/burl veneer Eastlake, cylinder front, 84x39" **2,800.00**

Settee

Continental Rococo style, cherub/griffins/lions cvg, 60" **1,375.00**
Limbert #653, spade cut-out sides/bk slats, branded, 68" **1,600.00**
PA, 3 drws under seat, half spindles, 1800s, 72" L **350.00**
PA w/yel pnt & stencil, 1800s, minor wear, 72" **600.00**
Rosewood Rococo, shell in crest rail, serpentine seat, 57" **900.00**
Walnut Rococo Revival, grape cvg, curved seat, +2 chairs **575.00**
Walnut Vict, EX uphl, 54" L **350.00**
Walnut Vict, floral cvd crest, scroll arms/legs, EX uphl **375.00**
Walnut Vict, simple cvg, minor losses **275.00**
Windsor, plank seat, spindle bk, rfn, 40" L **800.00**

Shelf

Book, walnut Vict, 5-shelf, 60x31", EX 200.00
Cherry, cut-out ends, att Zoar OH, 22" L 200.00
Corner, walnut Vict what-not, jigsaw work, 23x8".............85.00
Pewter, pine, cut-out edges, shoe ft, 1800s, 45x33" 450.00
Pine, scalloped ends, wall mt, old repro, 27x31" 160.00
Pine, 2-tier w/plate bars, 2 dvtl base drw, re-grpt, 37x42" 400.00
Pine w/worn red pnt Co, shoe ft, mortised, rpl/rstr, 52x36" 265.00
Poplar, allover jigsaw cutouts, 4-shelf, triangular, 28" 100.00
Poplar, scalloped ends/crest, panel do, wire nails, 22x21" 165.00

Sideboard

Curly maple Co Emp, paneled cherry ends, gallery, 49x45" 750.00
Golden oak, elaborate cvd/beadwork, beveled glass, 54" L 450.00
Kittinger, mahog Hplwht style, 48" L, NM....................................750.00
Mahog Co Sheraton, allover reeded facade, gallery, 45" W 1,500.00
Mahog Emp, leaf-top fluted columns, orig hdw, 44x48" 500.00
Mahog w/inlay Georgian, English, 1780s, 51" W 1,500.00
Mahog w/some inlay Fed, trn/reeded legs, 5 dvtl drw, 58" 2,100.00
Oak, EX cvd crest & facade w/griffins, paw ft, marble top 5,000.00
Oak, gallery w/high shelf & beveled mirror, 1920s 350.00
Oak, gallery w/high shelf & mirror, simple, sm, 1900s 350.00
Oak, gallery w/shaped beveled mirror, paw ft, EX cvgs, 1900 .. 1,100.00
Oak, str bksplash:2 drw, open base w/cvd front legs, 1900s 400.00

Sofa

Emp, eagle-cvd legs, scroll arms, str crest, re-uphl 700.00
Geo-style camel bk, cabriole legs/shell knees, c/b ft, 84" 1,100.00
Mahog Duncan Phyfe style, reed lyre fr, re-uphl, 82" 175.00
Mahog Emp, acanthus cvd scrolls/arm facings, paw ft, 94" 500.00
Mahog Fed, arched crest continuing to shaped arms, 78" 2,500.00
Mahog Fed Duncan Phyfe, drapery/thunderbolt cvg, 79" 16,000.00
Mahog/inlay Sheraton, simple, NE, 1800, needs uphl, 73" 2,750.00

Victorian eagle-carved mahogany sofa, ca 1800s, $2,200.00.

Stand

Cherry, spool trn legs, 12" drop leaves, 2 dvtl drw, 24" W...........400.00
Cherry Co Hplwht, sq tapered legs, 1-brd 21x29" top, rfn...........175.00
Cherry Co Sheraton, ring-trn ankles, 20" 2-brd top, rpr/rfn 475.00
Cherry Co Sheraton, 1-drw, 1-brd 20x20" top, rpr, EX 300.00
Cherry w/line inlay, S-curve front legs/trn bk legs, 19" W 350.00
Cherry/walnut, 2 drw:1, 3-brd 20x21" top, cabriole legs...........1,600.00
Crock, pnt poplar w/old pnt traces, 3-tier, 40x48", VG 275.00

Curly maple Co Sheraton, 1-drw, 1-brd 18" top, sgn/dtd 1840 ....600.00
Emp mahog/figured veneer, paw ft, acanthus columns, 16x20"....425.00
Golden oak, trn splay legs, lower shelf, rstr/rfn 250.00
Hardwood w/cherry finish Co Hplwht, 1-brd 19" scrubbed top ...395.00
Limbert, magazine, branded, rfn, 29x16x10" 775.00
Limbert, plant, arched apron, shelf, mk, 27", VG 550.00
Limbert, plant, arched apron, shelf, mk, 33", VG 600.00
Pine w/orig red flame grpt, trn legs, nailed drw, 16" sq 240.00
Pine w/worn yel grpt, 4-tier, rpr, 48" W 175.00
Walnut, trn legs, 2-brd 20x29" top, att to Delaware Valley 350.00
Walnut Co Hplwht, slim splay legs, rpl 15" top............................350.00

Stool

Co Windsor, splay legs, rnd top, rpt, 30" H...................................175.00
Footstool, mahog, needlepoint cushions, pr.................................140.00
Harpsichord, Regency, uphl, adjustable, EX 100.00
Limbert #213¾, orig leather, varnished, 18x14" sq, EX 550.00
Pine w/red rpt, bootjack legs mortised through top, 6x15" 110.00
Poplar, sm drw under top w/curly maple front, 9x8x14" 275.00
Poplar w/gr pnt on ft, scroll aprons, 7x7x36" 225.00
QA, japanned/uphl seat, cabriole legs, shaped skirt, 24" L...........225.00
S Allman & Co NY, footstool, uphl, Victorian................................300.00
Windsor, English hardwood, trn splay legs, 16x12x9" 150.00

Table

Banquet, cherry Sheraton, reeded legs, shaped drop leaves 3,000.00
Banquet, figured veneer apron/top, demi-lune, 50" 100.00
Breakfast, burl walnut Vict, tilt top, leaf-cvd legs, 51" 450.00
Brooks, corbels under 18" 8-sided top, cut-out sides, rfn 300.00
Card, mahog Fed, fly leaf, leafy/gadroon cvd base, paw ft 850.00
Card, mahog w/inlay Hplwht, 1780s, EX 950.00
Card, mahog w/inlay Sheraton, lt wood panels, MS, 1800, EX .. 1,700.00
Card, mahog w/inlay Sheraton, reeded legs, 1800, EX............. 1,000.00
Card, mahog/inlay Hplwht, fly leaf, Am, 1700s, EX 3,200.00
Card, walnut Vict, scroll-cvd legs, shaped 36" top 350.00
Center, rosewood Rococo, 50" shaped marble top, att Meeks .. 3,000.00
Center, walnut/seaweed W/M style, cvd, 2-drw, 1800s, 47".....3,000.00
Console, rosewood Rococo, 17x40" marble top, att Meeks, pr . 7,250.00
Dining, golden oak, rnd-top pedestal w/paw ft, rfn/rstr 900.00
Dining, golden oak, rnd-top pedestal w/scroll legs, rfn.................550.00
Dining, golden oak, rope-trn legs, paw ft, extension 275.00
Dining, mahog, reeded tripod, brass paw ft, 2-part, 77" L 4,200.00
Dining, mahog/inlay, reeded ped & legs, top: 64x40"..................850.00
Dining, quartered oak, cvd/fluted legs, c/b ft, +leaves.................400.00

Neoclassical curly maple dressing table, 37" wide, $1,800.00.

Dressing, pine, high bksplash, orig decor, 1820s 850.00
Dressing, pine, scroll side/bksplashes, rpt, 25" W 250.00
Dressing, pine w/EX grpt, trn legs/dvtl drw/str crest, 33" 325.00
Dressing, pine w/flame grpt, trn legs/dvtl drw/scroll crest............175.00
Drop leaf, cherry, trn legs, Am, 1820s, opens to 54", EX............225.00
Drop leaf, cherry QA, Am, 1780s, opens to 37x36" 800.00
Drop leaf, curly maple, 6-leg, 19½" 1-brd leaves 1,650.00
Drop leaf, curly maple Co Hplwht, rfn/rstr, open: 45" L 1,100.00
Drop leaf, maple QA, minor rstr, rfn, opens to 42" 2,300.00
Drop leaf, walnut Chpndl, 29" W, opens to 60" 325.00
Drop leaf, walnut QA, rpl 37x40" (open) top, 1750s...............1,200.00
Drop-leaf work, bird's eye maple, 2-drw/trn legs, NM 1,450.00
Drop-leaf work, tiger maple Sheraton, 2-drw, trn legs, EX 850.00
Game, mahog Fed flip-top, paw ft, octagonal, 37" W 2,300.00
Hutch, pine Co, cut-out ends, removable seat, rpl top, sm 650.00
Hutch, pine/maple QA, rpl seat, orig red pnt, 49" dia 3,300.00
Library, golden oak, cvd top, 1-drw, bulb trn legs, EX 150.00
Library, golden oak, long drw, sq legs & stretcher........................175.00
Library, golden oak, lyre legs, trestle base...................................200.00
Library, oak, spiral-cvd legs/upper stretchers, 71" L 600.00
Lifetime, drop leaf #902, gate leg/D-leaf, mk, 40x44", VG 700.00
Lifetime, 2-tier, thru tenons, label, rfn, 18" top, VG 450.00
Limbert, #146, oval 45" top, sq cutouts in sides, branded 1,700.00
Limbert, lamp #251, 8-sided top, trapezoid cutouts...................1,900.00
Limbert, library #1163, 2 drw:2 corbels, brand, rfn....................425.00
Limbert, library #158, 36x48" oval top, 2nd tier below, mk.....8,000.00
Limbert, tabouret #191, rnd top/tapered legs, label, rfn 850.00
Limbert, turtle top #153, sq cutouts in sides, 30x48" 1,700.00
Marjorelle, fruitwood w/fruit & leaf inlay, 2-tier, 30x16".........5,000.00
Marjorelle, rectangle top w/rnd corners, arched apron, 36" 2,000.00
Marjorelle, 2-tier, inlaid clematis, 31x28x22" 2,420.00
Michigan Chair Co, tabouret, 18" dia leatherette top..................110.00
Pembroke, curly maple Co Hplwht, sq tapered legs, rpl/rfn 550.00
Pembroke, mahog English Chpndl, sq legs, 21x30", +9" leaves ...275.00
Pembroke, mahog Hplwht, 1-drw, 20x34" 1,000.00
Ponti, Gio; side, wood/glass, rvpt animals, 27" dia top 285.00
Refectory, oak Jacobean style, 6 cvd/fluted legs, 75" 200.00
Saarinen, Eero; coffee, oval marble top:steel mushroom ped 600.00
Sewing, cherry top/pine fr Sheraton, Am, 1800, rfn....................275.00
Sewing, mahog Emp, rope legs, 2-drw, bag drw, drop leaf............550.00
Sewing, mahog Emp, 2 swell-front drw, drop leaves, heavy.........550.00
Sewing, mahog Hplwht, 1780s, rfn...450.00
Sewing, pine Co Hplwht, 1780s, rfn..350.00
Sewing, tiger maple Hplwht, legs w/incised circles, rfn 400.00
Tavern, maple QA, duck ft, gr-pnt top, rpl braces, 34" L.........3,500.00
Tavern, maple/pine QA, splay leg, 30" L oval rpl top 1,500.00
Tavern, pine/hardwood, bl over orig red, washed top, 34" W ..1,500.00
Tavern, pine/maple, trn legs/stretcher base, oval, 37" L...........2,600.00
Tavern, Windsor, red pnt, EX trn, 30" dia 2-brd top 4,700.00
Tea, walnut, 30x23" tilt top, 1800, EX.......................................250.00
Tilt-top, walnut Chpndl, w/birdcage, snake ft, 35" dia.................900.00
Tilt-top, walnut Co Chpndl, birdcage, cvd details, 30" dia......1,600.00
Tobey, bungalow library, thru tenon, 1" thick top, rfn, 47" 575.00
Trestle, oak English Gothic, trefoil piercing, 27" dia....................350.00
Vitrine, walnut, rnd glass top:frieze, cvd legs, 1800s, 23" 350.00
Wheeler, Eldred; serving, cherry Chpndl, fluted legs, 40" 600.00
Work, bird's eye maple 2-drw, 4-leg walnut leaf-cvd base 4,000.00
Work, cherry top Co Sheraton, tiger maple legs/drw front...........300.00
Work, cleaned poplar top, sawbuck base, fully trn legs, 42" 225.00
Work, curly birch Co Hplwht, lacy Sandwich opal drw pull........575.00
Work, mahog Sheraton, fluted legs, 2-drw, rpl bag, NM 5,600.00
Wright, Frank Lloyd; oak, 2 shelves wrap right side, 22x38" ...3,500.00
Writing, mahog w/inlay English Hplwht, leather top, 24" W 725.00
2-tier Walnut Vict, old finish, 30" 125.00

Wardrobe

Armoire, burl walnut/rosewood Renaissance Revival, 15x13" 450.00
Armoire, mahog, leaf/scroll cvg atop pillars & at ft, 93" 1,700.00
Armoire, mahog Louis XVI style, bronze mts/2 do, 91" 2,200.00
Kas, walnut, Zoar OH, do w/4 raised panels, cornice, 74x46" . 3,800.00
Mahog Vict, do ea side mirror+3 drw, minor cvg.....................1,400.00
Oak English, A&C design, 1900s, 10x36".....................................425.00
Pine/poplar w/orig brn grpt do panels, scallop base, 87x51".........275.00
Poplar w/flame grpt, molded stiles/cornice, panel do, 71" 400.00

Washstand

Corner, cherry, bow front, trn legs, base drw, cut-out top.............300.00
Curly maple Co Sheraton, drw in base, dvtl gallery, 15" W 1,550.00
Mahog, hinged lid, 1 drw:do:base drw, English, 1800, 18" W 175.00
Mahog Emp, top bowed w/contour of cutout, 2 sm drw ea side....625.00
Mahog English Hplwht, gallery w/shelf, 3 false drw:shelf.............325.00
Mahog Sheraton, well trn legs, cut-out top, rpr/rpl, 16" W.........300.00

Federal mahogany and inlaid veneer corner washstand, ca 1800, 47" x 25" x 18", $1,600.00.

Oak, towel bar & mirror in harp fr, drw:2 do, rfn 300.00
Oak, towel bar in harp fr, serpentine drw:2 sm drw+sm do 250.00
Pine/poplar Co Sheraton, trn legs/posts, 1 drw, 17" W................175.00
Walnut, raised panel do & drw, ebony/gilt teardrop pulls 400.00
Walnut, trn side hdls & legs, lower shelf, drw, bksplash..............150.00
Walnut Am Sheraton, shaped bksplash & shelf, trn legs 190.00
Walnut Co, EX trn, dvtl base drw, scroll gallery, cutout..............280.00
Walnut Vict, marble top, finish wear, 31½" 550.00
Walnut Vict, marble top & bksplash, molded do panels, 30" 550.00
Yel w/stencil decor, scalloped sides, 1830, EX.............................350.00

Miscellaneous

Adirondack child's rocker, minor damage/rpr, 31"........................75.00
Adirondack child's rocker, w/arms, blk/red/silver pnt, 30" 120.00
Adirondack fern stand, blk/silver pnt, 14" sq top 65.00
Adirondack planter, blk/silver decor, on legs, 36" L 50.00
Adirondack planter, fancy, lime/orange pnt, on legs, 51" W........450.00
Bureau plat, brass-mtd mahog/fruitwood Louis XVI style, 51". 1,200.00
Chiffoniere, oak, sm swivel mirror, 5-drw, simple, NM 450.00
Chifforobe, oak, swivel mirror, drop-lid compartment, NM.........325.00
Chifforobe, oak, 1 long do beside hat do+5 short drw.................200.00
Dumbwaiter, mahog Geo III, dish top:2nd tier, 35" 900.00
Etagere, walnut Renaissance Revival, base drw w/marble top . 3,000.00
Love seat, rosewood Vict, cvd/pierced crest, cartouch bk........ 2,250.00

Victorian carved mahogany etagere, white marble insert, $1,500.00.

Pedestal, ebonized/gilded Eastlake-Vict, 34" 250.00
Pedestal, golden oak, cvd/shaped std w/sq base..................165.00
Pedestal, golden oak, sq top, str std w/scroll legs 125.00
Pedestal, gr marble, EX cvd details, 44", EX..................325.00
Pedestal, Limbert, long corbel ea side post, 13" top, 36" 1,800.00
Pedestal, mahog, open spiral stem, tripod base, 1920s, 56" 225.00
Pedestal, walnut Biedermeier style, ebonized trim, 14" sq 450.00
Reading stand, mahog Vict, 15" dia tilt top, tripod std 700.00
Screen, Vict, ebonized w/2 oil-on-canvas florals, 57" 250.00
Server, mahog English, 3-tier, mortised/dvtl, 41x23x28" 300.00

Galle

Emile Galle was one of the most important producers of cameo glass in France. His firm, founded in Nancy in 1874, produced beautiful cameo in the Art Nouveau style during the 1890s, using a variety of techniques. He also produced glassware with enameled decoration, as well as some fine pottery—animal figurines, table services, vases, and other objects d' art. In the mid-1880s, he became interested in the various colors and textures of natural woods and as a result began to create furniture which he used as yet another medium for expression of his artistic talent. Marquetry was the primary method Galle used in decorating his furniture, preferring landscapes, Nouveau floral and fruit arrangements, butterflies, squirrels, and other forms from nature. It is for his furniture and his cameo glass that he is best known today. All Galle is signed.

Our advisor for this category is Don Williams; he is listed in the Directory under Iowa.

Cameo

Bowl, fern fronds, dbl overlay, peaked rim, ftd, 6" 800.00
Bowl, ferns, olive-brn on lt gr frost, 5" 500.00
Bowl, floral, lav/gr on pk frost, int: pk floral, 7" L 850.00
Bowl, jasmine, lav/gr on texture, int: peach floral, 11" L.........2,450.00
Bowl, maidenhair fern, gr on gr frost, pinched ends, 10" L......1,350.00
Box, floral, shiny amber on gold frost lid & base, 4" dia 1,600.00
Dish, cherry boughs, rose/red on yel frost, 2¾x6½"..................1,700.00
Lamp, floral, red on gold frost, 8" dome shade, 14".................18,500.00
Lamp, grapevines on dome shade & vasiform std, 2 cuts, 24"..22,000.00

Lamp base, flowers/leaves, 3 cuts, brass mts, 10¼" 1,000.00
Perfume, berries, red/gold frost, gold-plate bulb mt, 11" 1,700.00
Perfume, bl floral/gr leaves, metal band/lid, 4" 700.00
Perfume, scene, brn/gr on gold frost, filigree lid, 7".................1,850.00
Perfume, trees/lake, dk gr/brn, gold-tone top, 7" 600.00
Sweetmeat, floral, pk on gr, gold-tone lid/bail, 7" dia 1,600.00
Vase, apple blossom, plum on cloudy bl, wide ft, 5"..................600.00
Vase, bamboo leaves/pods, 3-color gr on frost, 6-panel, 12" 1,250.00
Vase, blown-out cherries, bl/brn on gold frost, 11½" 10,000.00
Vase, blown-out grapes, purple/gr on amber frost, 11½" 10,000.00
Vase, bud; buds/blossoms, amber on frost, 3" 400.00
Vase, clematis, lav on gold frost, 9¾" 2,000.00
Vase, clematis, purple on frost, pillow form, 6x4½" 1,750.00
Vase, cottage/mtns, lav/brn on yel, pinched/sq neck, 4¾".......2,700.00
Vase, curled vines/blossoms, purple on amber, 2¾" 700.00
Vase, daisies, red on wht, polished, 2¾" 700.00
Vase, florals/birds, brn/pk/amber on orange, 18" 7,500.00
Vase, foliage, lt/dk gr on rose, 8¾" 1,800.00
Vase, freesia, orange on orange/frost mottle, low ft, 3½"..............375.00
Vase, grape clusters, amber on pk frost, 8" 2,000.00
Vase, grapes/leaves, lav on frost & lav, sgn w/star, 2½".............375.00
Vase, hydrangeas, lav on pk/orange/clear frost, star mk, 8" 1,500.00
Vase, leaves, gr on gr frost, stick form, 13" 1,500.00
Vase, leaves/berries, gold on gold frost, purple base, 5" 550.00
Vase, leaves/berries, lav on gr/clear frost, ovoid, 3" 225.00
Vase, leaves/pods, brn on gold frost, stick neck, 5"....................950.00
Vase, leaves/pods, gold on frost, 4" 400.00
Vase, leaves/pods, lt gr on frost to gold, 18" 2,600.00
Vase, man on bridge over river, brn/gold on gold to pk, 20"....4,500.00
Vase, maple leaves, dk/lt gr on pk frosted, waisted, 5" 1,300.00
Vase, morning-glories/tendrils, cobalt on pk/wht, 5" 850.00
Vase, mtns/pine trees, bl tones w/frosted top, 10" 5,000.00
Vase, orchids, lav on lt bl frost, polished, tapered, 5" 1,150.00
Vase, pond grasses, gr on pk frost, 2⅞".....................................400.00
Vase, pond lilies/flowers, purple/brn on wht to yel, 10" 1,900.00
Vase, poppies, pk/citron on 3-color mottle, low ft, 9".............1,500.00
Vase, riverbank scene, gr/brn on mottled peach, 14½"............4,000.00
Vase, spring flowers, lav on lt bl frost, ftd, 5½" 700.00
Vase, sweet peas, lav/purple on frost, flat-sided ovoid, 6" 1,000.00
Vase, sweet peas, lav/purple on pk/wht, bottle form, 11".........1,300.00
Vase, thistles, lime on pk/clear mottle, tumbler form, 4¾" 500.00

Vase, tree scenic, brown and green over salmon mottled and frosted glass, signed, 7¾", $2,500.00.

Vase, trees, brn-gold on gold frost, ped ft, star mk, 8½" 2,500.00
Vase, trees/flying birds, brn on gold frost, stick neck, 7" 900.00
Vase, trees/water, dbl overlay, baluster on ped ft, 8" 2,500.00

Vase, Vines & Cicada (inscribed), bl on ribbed bl-gr, 13" **11,500.00**
Vase, wisteria, brn on gold frost, 10" **850.00**
Vase, wisteria, brn on gold frost, 21½" **2,550.00**
Vase, wisteria, brn on tan frost, 21½" **2,100.00**
Vase, wisteria, brn-purple on pk frost, 8"......................................**1,750.00**
Vase, wisteria, lav on yel to wht, tapered cylinder, 14"............**2,400.00**
Vase, wisteria, shiny lav on lt gold to mottled lav, 12" **1,300.00**

Enameled Glass

Cup & saucer, floral on gr crystal w/int mottle..........................**750.00**
Cup & saucer, thistles/cross on lt amber, ftd **850.00**
Ewer, floral, mc/gold on lt amber w/foil inclusions, 8" **2,500.00**
Ewer, 3-color multifloral w/gilt, 11" **1,500.00**
Rose bowl, florals/intaglio florals on clear to bl opal................**1,700.00**
Tray, florals/insect on lt amber, rolled rim forms hdl, 12" **1,800.00**
Vase, etched flames, enameled LaLumiere d'Justice/1900, 4".. **1,800.00**

Vase, florals on amber with gilding, 13", $2,100.00.

Vase, grasshopper/branches on lt topaz, ruffled/ftd, 9" **2,500.00**
Vase, prunus/strapwork, appl prunts on lt tan, sgn, 10" **1,500.00**

Marquetry, Wood

Cabinet, frog ft/dragonfly gallery, inlay, 2 doors, 64" **15,000.00**
Nest of 4: ocean cliff/village/seashore/boatman, 27x23" **4,800.00**
Table, bats/crescent moon, 3 lobed tiers, vine legs, 42x25" **8,000.00**
Table, butterflies, QA Lace open-cvd legs, 2-tier, 30x16" **1,700.00**
Table, butterfly/mtns, lower cruciform shelf, 28x16" **3,000.00**
Table, card; thistles/suit symbols, cloth surface, 36"..................**1,300.00**
Table, card; wisteria/suit symbols, hinged, cabriole legs **1,900.00**
Table, vanity; mums, vine-cvd legs, drw/mirror, 33x28x16" ... **4,950.00**
Tray, penguins stand on icebergs, hdls, 27" L **1,300.00**
Vitrine, 2 upper glaze doors over 3 shelves, inlaid bk, 63" **12,000.00**

Pottery

Basket, floral panel, rtcl, 4-ftd, scroll hdls, 10" L **450.00**
Bowl, scenic reserve ea end, basket-like w/4-lobe rim, 8½" **450.00**
Candlestick, swirls, gray/rust on wht, leaf bobeche, 9", pr............**450.00**
Centerpc, florals, gr/red/brn on wht, basket form, 7½" L **300.00**
Centerpc, frog atop clam shell holds reins on fish, 13½" **2,200.00**

Charger, undulating stems/florals, brn/ochre w/foil, 18" **2,700.00**
Dish, shell form w/scenic in bl, 9½" L **350.00**
Figurine, cat in bonnet/brocade coat, dog on locket, 13".........**4,000.00**
Figurine, owl, earthen tones, on rnd base, 12¾" **4,000.00**
Platter, insects/grass on cream & gilt, turtle hdl, 12" L **700.00**
Vase, boats/fishermen/shell bands, 3-part overhead hdl, 9" **1,600.00**
Vase, grasshopper/leaves HP on dimpled cylinder, EFG, 8" **525.00**
Vase, rabbit reads in garden, disk w/stem & root base, 8" **1,000.00**
Vase, wintry harbor scene, swirled ribs, gilt borders, 4" **300.00**

Gambling Memorabilia

Book, Encyclopedia of Indoor Games, Hoyle, 1897, EX.................**25.00**
Book, Game of Billiards, 1st ed, Phelan, NY, 1857, EC **78.00**
Card press, 10-deck, dvtl wood partitions, 3x9½x4½", EX **150.00**
Chip, bone, blk numerals, hexagonal, EX.....................................**38.00**
Chip, ivory, eagle scrimshaw w/blk details, scalloped, EX **100.00**
Chip, polished bone, octagonal, 1850s, 1½" **35.00**
Chips, clay, emb style, various colors, 10 for.................................**12.00**
Chips, clay, inlaid style, various colors, 15 for **10.00**
Chips, clay, terrier's head, 6 ea: red, wht, bl, VG, 18 for................**25.00**
Chips, compo, emb horse & jockey, red, wht, bl, 24 for **15.00**
Chips, ivory, blk flowers, EX, 10 for...**140.00**
Chips, ivory, floral scrimshaw decor, EX, 4 for.............................**45.00**
Chips, ivory, red & wht concentric circles, VG, 2 for **24.00**
Chips, ivory, red flower center, VG, 12 for....................................**130.00**
Cuff holder, The Tip, steel cheating device, Pat Appl For **30.00**
Cuff holder, Wizard, NP brass cheating device, pr **30.00**
Dice, ivory, rnded corners, 1890s, ¾", pr......................................**17.50**
Dice cage, NP brass post, Rott Games, NYC, 12x4½", EX...........**100.00**
Dice cage, wire fr w/cb ends, gr felt lining, 11½" +dice.................**42.00**
Dice cup, leather professional type w/5 dice **35.00**
Knife, Bakelite hdl, fits in gambler's hat band, Germany, sm **25.00**
Layout, Chuck-A-Luck, gr felt, lg, EX...**26.00**
Marker, bone, octagonal, VG, pr..**25.00**
Markers, clay, rnd & rectangular, 1890s, 12 for.............................**45.00**
Markers, pearl, varied colors, set of 5, VG **50.00**
Rack, chip; revolves, wood w/metal hdl, G **15.00**
Roulette game, felt layout, ES Lower, c 1941, complete, EX..........**75.00**
Roulette wheel, Arcade, EX...**1,200.00**
Roulette wheel, Bestmaid, w/instructions, EX in box.....................**40.00**
Roulette wheel, Spin-er-ette, Louis Marx, EX...............................**40.00**
Roulette wheel, wood & metal, paper #s on spinner, 13", VG **75.00**
Wheel, wood, 9½" dia on wood stand for table, 12", EX **85.00**
Wheel, wood w/bird decals at center, complete, 24" dia.................**85.00**

Gameboards

Gameboards handmade in the 18th and 19th centuries have come to be regarded as highly-prized collectibles by devotees of Americana and folk art. Some are elaborately laid out and their bright primary colors as well chosen as a deliberate work of art – these often bring prices reaching upwards of a thousand dollars. Even those less imaginative are usually valued from a few to several hundred dollars.

Checkers, appl/raised molding, blk/wht w/wht border, 20" **1,500.00**
Checkers, bk: 2nd game, octagonal, worn, 27" **210.00**
Checkers, blk sqs on natural pine, maize bk, 1840s, 12", EX........**250.00**
Checkers, blk/wht, 2 sides w/grpt, batten edges, 16x21".........**1,800.00**
Checkers, oilcloth, intricate designs on blk, 26", VG **250.00**
Checkers, pine, wht & gr pnt, initialed, 12x18", VG...................**275.00**
Checkers, pine w/walnut edging, blk/wht, gr border, 15x15" **300.00**
Checkers, red/gr w/mustard border, appl/molded edge, 18" **2,600.00**

Checkerboard, multicolored with pinstriping and flourishes, decorated on the reverse with a brown horse, 1800s, 13½", $3,750.00.

Checkers, rvpt glass, flaking/wear, 20" sq 95.00
Checkers, tortoise shell pnt on raised blk sqs, appl edge 900.00
Checkers, 3-color chevron band, blk outer border, 1880s........ 3,000.00
Parchesi, 4-color pnt, folding, minor wear, 14" 3,000.00

Games and Puzzles

19th-Century games continue to be the stars of the board game field. The colorful, well-done lithography used during the last quarter of the 1800s seems to attract more buyers to this era than to games produced during the 1850s-1850s period. While more collectors look for games by W. B. Ives and several other early producers as well, they avidly pursue the works of such companies as McLoughlin. Interest in the 1920s-1940 period is increasing, and TV games are also drawing a following. Although not as spectacular as the large game boards, they too display quality artwork and printing methods.

Puzzles have been produced in large numbers since the mid-1850s. Many of the early puzzles and games were made to educate the youth. Originally the 'jig-saws' were made of wood and handcrafted. By the 1890s, die-cut cardboard puzzles were introduced and soon dominated the market. Though wood continued to be used, solid wood was eventually replaced by plywood. During the 1920s-1930s, jig-saw puzzles became a major form of home entertainment. Today, cube puzzle blocks from the turn of the century are bringing good prices. Scroll-type puzzles with good lithography have values that are consistent with board games. See also Personalities.

Games

Air Defense Target Shoot, tin, Wolverine, EX 35.00
American Football, American News, 1935, M 20.00
Annie Oakley, Milton Bradley, EX in orig box 25.00
Billionaire, 1973, MIB 15.00
Billy Whiskers, 1923, EX in box 40.00
Blocks, Blondie & Dagwood pictures, 1951, EX in orig box 85.00
Bobbsey Twins, 1957 ....25.00
Break the Bank, Bert Parks 25.00
Calling All Cars, Parker Bros, 1930s 25.00
Charlie Chan, Milton Bradley, 1937, EX 60.00

Chiromagica, card game, McLoughlin Bros, NMIB 250.00
Christmas Goose, board game, McLoughlin Bros, 1890, NMIB.....80.00
Chutes & Ladders, 1972, MIB...10.00
Clue, 1956...10.00
Columbo Detective, 1974, MIB..22.50
Craftsman & Printer, made in USA by T St Co, MIB 25.00
Cuckoo, JH Singer, ca 1880s, EX 190.00
Dark Shadows, Whitman, 1968, M...45.00
Doni Potato Race, Hasbro..15.00
Eddie Cantor's Tell It to the Judge, EX 28.00
Finance, 1936 ....20.00
Flinch, card game, Parker Bros, 1934, EX in orig box..................10.00
Flinch, card game, 1936... 7.50
Foolish Questions, Rube Goldberg, 1920s, VG.............................26.00
Frog Who Would A Wooing Go, United, VG 135.00
Fun w/Electricity, Thomas M St John, NYC, 1901, MIB 95.00
Game of Airmail, Milton Bradley, 1927, EX 35.00
Game of US, card game, educational, 1890s, 65 cards w/o box......18.00
Gold Medal Game Chest, boards/wood pcs, c 1937, complete........35.00
Government, Milton Bradley, 1939, Capitol on NM box 10.00
Hendrick Van Loom's Wide World Game, Parker Bros, 1933, EX.28.00
Highway Patrol, WWII, EX..45.00
House That Jack Built, card game, McLoughlin, 1890, EX 45.00
Jack Daw, Milton Bradley #4663, teddy bear cover, VG 58.00
Jr Combination Board, 1905, EX in box 400.00
Kentucky Derby, Whitman, 1950s, EX in box 40.00
Letters & Anagrams, ca 1900, VG in box.....................................30.00
Lindy, Parker, 1927, EX 20.00
Little Cowboy, Parker Bros, VG...130.00
Louisa, McLoughlin, 1888, EX...425.00
Magic Dots, 1907, EX..20.00
Mah Jong, teak & ivory, China, 1920, EX 450.00
Meet the Presidents, board game, Selchow & Righter, 1950, M....32.00
Monkeys Wild, 1958, M 25.00
Munsters, card game, EX...25.00
Partridge Family, board game, Milton Bradley, 1971, MIB.............36.00
Peanut the Elephant, Parker Bros...18.00
Pin the Tail on the Donkey, 1930s, M in envelope 10.00
Puppet Pinball, blk & wht marbles, Marx, MIB 50.00
Realistic Baseball, Patterson, tin litho, 1925, EX in box 100.00
Round the World w/Nelly Bly, McLoughlin Bros, 1890, EX 275.00
Shakespeare, card game, Cincinnati Game Co, 1901, EX..............25.00
Shoot the Bulldog, CI/wood, iron marbles, Arcade, 29" L...........150.00
Single Target, wooden balls, Milton Bradley, 15½x7¾", G 100.00
Sorry, 1950, complete in EX orig box...10.00
Star Wars, Escape from Death Star, Kenner, 1977, VG.................25.00
Ten Commandments, Cadaco, 1966, MIB.....................................17.50
Tom Barker Baseball, card game, 53 cards in case, EX 750.00

Toonerville Trolley, paper litho on cardboard, 17" long, EX, $80.00.

Touring, cards, Parker Bros, 1920s, VG..............................30.00
Travel America, Wiry Dan the Action Man, battery op, EX..........25.00
Treasure Hunt, 1941, in treasure chest box......................15.00
Trolley, card game, 1904, MIB 20.00
Twin Target, w/wooden balls, Milton Bradley, 13x13", EX 130.00
Uncle Wiggily, Milton Bradley, ca 1954, EX 20.00
US History, battleship cover, Parker Bros, 7¼x4½", G.............25.00
Where's Christopher Robin, EX 37.00
Why, Alfred Hitchcock, 1958, EX 40.00
World Educator, spools & cards, WS Reed, EX in box...............150.00
Yacht Race, Clark & Snowdon, ca 1890s, EX 140.00
Zip-Top, Deluxe Game Corp, MIB..................................65.00

Puzzles

Animal Antics Scroll, McLoughlin, 1894 ....450.00
Blocks, chromograph on wood, nested set of 8, EX 260.00
Changeable Charlie, dtd 1943....................................10.00
Dissected Map of US, McLoughlin, litho cover, EX................45.00
Fire Engine, Milton Bradley, 9x16", 1920, EX 75.00

Fire Engine picture puzzle, copyrighted 1887, McLoughlin, VG in original box, $425.00.

Flying Family, jigsaw, 1932, M in envelope......................30.00
Hood's Sarsaparilla, Rainy Day & Balloons, 1890s, 2 in box......50.00
Just Kids, 4 tray puzzles in cartoon box, 1932, EX..............35.00
Keep Going w/Kellogg's, boy w/baseball, 1933, 6x8" 25.00
Kellogg's for Crispness, girl w/flowers, 1933, 6x8", NM.........38.00
Kolynos Dental Cream, South Pole Flight, complete w/envelope..30.00
Model Ship, cb, Milton Bradley, 22x16½", EX in wooden box....100.00
Sliced Animals, Selchow & Righter, NY, 1900, EX in box..........95.00
Spiderman, 100-pc, Whitman, 1982, MIB 10.00
4-Footed Friends, cubes, McLoughlin, EX in box..................450.00

G. A. R. Memorabilia

The 'The Grand Army of the Republic' was first conceived by Chaplain W.J. Rutledge and Major B.J. Stephenson early in 1864 when they were tent-mates during our own Civil War. These men, deciding that if they were spared, vowed to each other to establish an organization that would preserve friendships and memories formed during this time. Shortly after the war ended, Rutledge and Stephenson made their desires a reality. The first National Convention of the Grand Army of the Republic was held in Indianapolis, IN, on November 20, 1866. The purpose of the organization was to provide aid and assistance to the widows and orphans of the fallen Union dead and to care for the hospitalized veterans as needed. The last comrade of the G.A.R. died in 1949.

Many items are surfacing from the early encampments, held at both the state and national level, which is due to the wide variety of souvenir items that were made.

Badge, Encampment, State & National, various dates/places 30.00
Badge, membership; cannon bronze, eagle/flag/star, 3rd issue 25.00
Badge, membership; nickel, eagle/flag/star, 2nd issue 50.00
Badge, membership; 3rd Battalion, 1st issue 60.00
Belt & buckle, EX 20.00
Button, uniform; brass, various mfgrs, coat/vest sz, ea.................... 1.50
Cane, Washington, Grant's bust at top, 1892, EX 50.00
Canteen, 1892 ....80.00
Canteen flask, china, Grant or Lee ea side, 5½x4½" 200.00
Casket, jewel; eng 1884 Pittsburgh 70.00
Cup, tin, souvenir, emb 25.00
Cup, tin, souvenir, printed in red & bl.................................20.00
Flag, GAR emblem in full color, 1880s, 24x24", EX 25.00
Flag stand, WRC, dtd 1888, EX 35.00
Goblet, pressed glass, souvenir 35.00
Grave marker, bronze, varied designs...................................20.00
Grave marker, CI, varied designs..25.00
Grave urn 22.00
Hat, CI, souvenir, blk & gold 20.00
Hat decoration, wreath w/GAR 10.00
Lamp globe, GAR symbol etched on frost, 4½x7"...........................75.00
Match safe, CI, lg wall type, w/logo & all corps insignia 200.00
Medal, Congressional Medal of Honor shape, early 30.00
Medal, Representative, bronze w/brooch bar, PA, 1928, EX 15.00
Membership application, information completed, 1890s, EX.........10.00
Paperweight, 28th Nat'l Encmpt 1894, eagle/flag, 3" dia, EX 100.00

Pocket flask, clear with under-glass label: 33rd National Encampment 1899 Phila PA, on back: US, original cap, 5", $650.00.

Ribbon, memorial to Gen Grant, 1800s.......................................35.00
Spoon, cannon bronze, souvenir 40.00
Spoon, sterling, varied dated & designs 55.00
Sword, ceremonial, w/scabbard, clean.......................................150.00
Tumbler, 1889 ....35.00
Walking stick, burl, cvd amber dog's head, sapling shank, 38" 90.00
Watch fob, 21st Nat'l Encampment, Louisville, 1934 ....30.00

Gas Globes and Panels

Gas globes and panels, once a common sight, have vanished from the countryside but are being sought by collectors as a unique form of advertising memorabilia. Early globes from the 1920s, now referred to as 'one-piece globes,' were made of molded milk glass and were globular in shape. The gas company name was etched or painted on the glass. Few of these were ever produced, and this type is valued very highly by collectors today.

A new type of pump was introduced in the early 1930s; the old 'visible' pumps were replaced by 'electric' models. Globes were changing at the same time. By the mid-thirties, a five-piece globe consisting of a pair of inserts, two retaining rings, and a metal body were being produced in both 15" and 16½" sizes. Collectors prefer to call globes that are not one-piece or plastic 'three-piece' glass' (Type 2) or 'metal body, glass inserts' (Type 3). Though metal body globes (Type 3) were popular in the 1930s, they were common in the 1920s, and some were actually made as early as 1915. Though rare in numbers, their use spans many years. In the 1930s, Type 2 and Type 3 globes became the replacements of the one-piece globe. The most recently manufactured gas globes, used since the late 1940s, are made with a plastic body that contains two 13½" glass lenses.

Note: Standard Crowns with raised letters are one-piece globes that were made in the 1920s; those made in the 1950s (no raised letters), though one-piece, are not regarded as such by today's collectors. Both variations are listed below.

Our advisor for this category is Scott Benjamin; he is listed in the Directory under California.

Standard Oil, embossed glass globe, 1-piece body, $300.00.

Type 1, Plastic Body, Glass Inserts—1931-1950s

Ashland Diesel	110.00
Champlin	125.00
Dixie, plastic band	125.00
DX Ethyl	100.00
DX Lubricating Gasoline, tan body	135.00
Falcon	300.00
Frontier Gas, Rarin' To Go, w/horse	225.00
Marathon, no runner	90.00
Never Nox Ethyl	150.00
Shamrock, oval body	125.00
Shamrock, w/clover	150.00
Spur	85.00
Texaco Sky Chief	100.00
Viking, pictures Viking ship	175.00
Wood River	110.00
66 Flite Fuel, Phillips, shield shape	150.00

Type 2, Glass Frame, Glass Inserts—1926-1940s

American	185.00
Atlantic Hi-Arc, glass gill body	175.00
Coltex Service Gasoline, unused	250.00
Derby	185.00
Esso	150.00
Frontier Gas, no horse	175.00
Gulf	250.00
Indian Gas, Red Dot	225.00
Koolmotor, clover shape	375.00
Mobil Gas	225.00
Pure	175.00
Shell, milk glass, clam shape	325.00
Sinclair H-C, narrow glass body, Red Dot	200.00
Sinclair Pennant	250.00
Skelly Anomarx w/Ethyl	250.00
Skelly Powermax	175.00
Spartan	210.00
Standard Blue Crown	300.00
Texaco Diesel Chief	250.00
Texaco Ethyl	250.00
Texaco Star, blk outline on 'T'	225.00
Trophy, Our Premium Gasoline	185.00
White Flash, gill body	185.00
WNAX	300.00

Type 3, Metal Frame, Glass Inserts—1915-1930s

Atlantic Ethyl, 16½"	350.00
Atlantic White Flash, 16½"	350.00
Essolene, 16"	250.00
Happy Gas, metal band, 16½"	325.00
Mobil Gas, winged horse, metal fr, NM	375.00
Mobilfuel Diesel, lg horse, high profile, metal band	350.00
Multipower (Marathon), 15"	900.00
Pure, porc body, 15"	400.00
Purol Gasoline, w/arrow, porc body	650.00
Purol Pep, porc body	450.00
Red Crown Ethyl	425.00
Richfield	375.00
Rocor, w/eagle, metal fr	450.00
Socony, milk glass inserts	650.00
Sunland Ethyl, 15"	350.00
Sunoco, 15", pr	300.00
Texaco Leaded, glass panels, in fr, pr	1,500.00
Tidex, 16"	325.00
Tydol, cast faces, 15"	500.00
Tydol, 16½"	350.00

Type 4, One-Piece Glass Globes, No Inserts, Co. Name Etched, Raised or Enameled—1914-1931

Atlantic, chimney cap	2,200.00
Champlin Gasoline	850.00
Diamond	500.00
Dixie, etched, 1-pc	900.00
Gasoline, etched	350.00
Good Gulf	550.00
Iowa Gas	750.00
Mobil Oil Gargoyle	700.00
Musgo	1,800.00
Pierce Pennant, etched	1,600.00
Red Crown, rnd, etched	1,800.00
Republic, English Globe, 1-pc	275.00
Shell, rnd, etched	450.00
Sinclair, etched, milk glass	650.00

Sinclair Aircraft, etched	2,200.00
Sinclair Aircraft, pnt.	1,500.00
Sinclair H-C, pnt	600.00
Skelly	600.00
Standard Crown, different colors	300.00
Standard Red Crown Ethyl, emb letters	600.00
Super Shell, clam shape	600.00
Super Shell, rnd, etched	1,300.00
Texaco, milk glass, emb letters, brass collar	500.00
Texaco Ethyl	650.00
That Good Gulf Gasoline, emb letters, orig pnt	650.00
White Eagle, eagle shape, blunt nose	750.00
White Rose, pnt	1,600.00

Gaudy Dutch

Inspired by Oriental Imari wares, Gaudy Dutch was made in England from 1800 to 1820. It was hand decorated on a soft-paste body with rich underglaze blues accented in orange, red, pink, green, and yellow. It differs from Gaudy Welsh in that there is no lustre (except on Water Lily). There are seventeen patterns, some of which are: War Bonnet, Grape, Dahlia, Oyster, Urn, Butterfly, Carnation, Single Rose, Double Rose, and Water Lily.

Butterfly, creamer	850.00
Butterfly, cup plate	675.00
Butterfly, pitcher, milk; 4", M	800.00
Butterfly, plate, 6½", M	650.00
Butterfly, plate, 9¾", M	800.00
Butterfly, sugar bowl, M	900.00
Butterfly, tea bowl & saucer, EX	650.00
Butterfly, teapot, squat baluster form, 5", M	1,400.00
Butterfly, waste bowl	900.00
Carnation, bowl, 8¼", NM	600.00
Carnation, plate, 8", EX	550.00
Carnation, plate, 9¾", EX	600.00
Carnation, tea bowl & saucer, M	450.00
Carnation, tea bowl & saucer, rstr	265.00
Dahlia, sugar bowl	850.00
Dahlia, tea bowl & saucer	650.00
Double Rose, creamer, M	500.00
Double Rose, plate, 10"	650.00
Double Rose, plate, 7", M	425.00
Double Rose, soup plate, 9", M	450.00
Double Rose, tea bowl & saucer, M	425.00
Double Rose, teapot, NM	1,200.00
Double Rose, waste bowl, 3x5½", EX	400.00

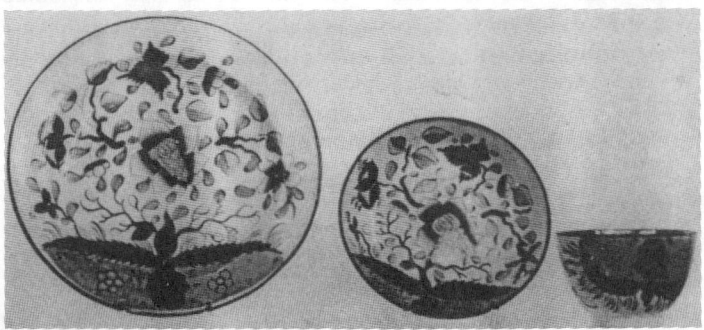

Dove, plate, 8", M, $450.00; Tea bowl and saucer, VG, $220.00.

Dove, plate, 10", M	550.00

Dove, sugar bowl, w/lid	650.00
Dove, tea bowl & saucer, M	500.00
Dove, waste bowl, M	570.00
Grape, creamer	600.00
Grape, plate, pnt flaking, 9¾"	250.00
Grape, plate, toddy, 5", NM	375.00
Grape, plate, wear/sm rpr, 8"	300.00
Grape, plate, 7", M	425.00
Grape, tea bowl & saucer, EX	250.00
Grape, teapot, hairlines/lt stains, 6½"	500.00
Grape, teapot, imperfections, 6½"	600.00
Oyster, plate, minor wear, 9¼"	475.00
Oyster, plate, 9½", NM	450.00
Oyster, soup plate, 8½", EX	450.00
Oyster, tea bowl & saucer, M	425.00
Single Rose, coffeepot, dbl gourd form, 10¾", M	1,200.00
Single Rose, plate, minor wear, 9¾"	425.00
Single Rose, plate, 7", M	410.00
Single Rose, plate, 8", M	450.00
Single Rose, sugar bowl, w/lid, M	575.00
Single Rose, tea bowl & saucer, M	425.00
Strawflower, creamer	750.00
Strawflower, plate, 8", M	650.00
Strawflower, tea bowl & saucer, M	650.00
Urn, creamer	600.00
Urn, plate, sectional border, 7"	500.00
Urn, plate, 5", M	450.00
War Bonnet, creamer, M	600.00
War Bonnet, plate, minor flaking, 8"	450.00
War Bonnet, plate, toddy; M	425.00
War Bonnet, plate, 7", M	650.00
War Bonnet, tea bowl & saucer, NM	475.00
War Bonnet, teapot	1,250.00
Water Lily, tea bowl & saucer, EX	725.00
Zinnia, plate, 8½", NM	725.00

Gaudy Ironstone

Gaudy Ironstone was produced in the mid-1800s in Staffordshire, England. Some of the ware was decorated in much the same colors and designs as Gaudy Welsh, while other pieces were painted in pink, orange, and red with black and light blue accents. Lustre was used on some designs, omitted on others. The heavy ironstone body is its most distinguishing feature.

Key:
pc — polychrome   ug bl — underglaze blue

Bowl, floral, purple lustre, ftd, 5x9¾", EX	195.00
Creamer, floral, 4"	40.00
Cup & saucer, floral, ug bl/red & gr enamel, Adams, EX	35.00
Cup & saucer, handleless; vintage, ug bl/pc/lustre, EX	50.00
Pitcher, emb tulips, ug bl/copper lustre, 6½", NM	75.00
Pitcher, floral, ug bl/pc/purple lustre, 8", NM	175.00
Pitcher, floral, ug bl/pc/worn lustre, 5⅝", EX	45.00
Plate, floral, ug bl/pc/purple lustre, 10-sided, 9½", NM	65.00
Plate, morning-glories/strawberries, 6", NM	50.00
Plate, Morning-Glory, ug bl/pc/lustre, stains, 8"	70.00
Plate, toddy; Urn, ug bl/pc/lustre, 4¾"	175.00
Plate, Urn, minor wear, 8"	60.00
Plate, Urn, 9½", NM	135.00
Plate, vintage, ug bl/pc/lustre, minor stains, 8"	60.00

Platter, marked Widdin #1151, 15" x 12", $110.00.

Platter, floral/strawberries, ug bl/pc/purple lustre, 13½" 200.00
Platter, Morning-Glory, ug bl/gr, red/blk enamel, 14", EX 250.00
Platter, Strawberry, ug bl/pc/worn lustre, 12⅜", EX.....................200.00
Teapot, floral, ug bl/pc/purple lustre, prof rpr lid, 9" 250.00
Waste bowl, floral, ug bl/pc/purple lustre, 5" 165.00

Gaudy Welsh

Gaudy Welsh was an inexpensive hand-decorated ware made in both England and Wales from 1820 until 1860. It is characterized by its colors – principally underglaze blue, orange-rust, and copper lustre – and by its uninhibited patterns. Accent colors may be yellow and green. (Pink lustre may be present, since lustre applied to the white areas appears pink. A copper tone develops from painting lustre onto the dark colors.) The body of the ware may be heavy ironstone, creamware, earthenware, or porcelain; even style and shapes vary considerably. Patterns, while usually floral, are also sometimes geometric and may have trees and birds.

Daisy & Chain, creamer..70.00
Daisy & Chain, cup & saucer...65.00
Daisy & Chain, sugar bowl, w/lid..120.00
Flower Basket, bowl, 10½"...165.00
Flower Basket, cup & saucer..40.00
Flower Basket, plate, 12-sided, purple lustre trim, 8⅞"..................75.00
Flower Basket, plate, 8½" 45.00
Flower Basket, sugar bowl, w/lustre, lion's-head hdls, lid..............140.00
Flower Basket, tea bowl & saucer..80.00
Grape, cup & saucer 70.00
Grape, mug, cobalt leaves/rust-colored vine, 2¼x2¼" 60.00
Grape, wash bowl & pitcher, vulture hdl, mk Stone China, M ...700.00
Grape II, mug, cobalt floral, orange petals, 2⅜x2⅛" 75.00
Morning-Glory, bowl, red/gr berries, octagonal, 8⅝", NM 85.00
Morning-Glory, bowl, shell form, 7½" L, EX 60.00
Morning-Glory, creamer, 5", EX...75.00
Morning-Glory, cup & saucer, 5", EX...60.00
Morning-Glory, pitcher, underglaze bl w/purple lustre, 8" 135.00
Morning-Glory, plate, toddy; 4⅜", EX..25.00
Morning-Glory, plate, 8", NM..60.00
Morning-Glory, platter, copper lustre, 14½", EX........................135.00
Morning-Glory, sugar bowl, w/lid..95.00

Morning-Glory, tea set, leaf hdls, pot: 6¼", 3-pc, EX 400.00
Oyster, bowl, ftd, 6x10½"...80.00
Oyster, bowl, 6"...65.00
Oyster, creamer, 1820s, 3¾", M 80.00
Oyster, cup & saucer...65.00
Oyster, jug, hot water..100.00
Oyster, pitcher, 4½x4½"..85.00
Oyster, plate, dessert; 5½"..40.00
Oyster, plate, 6"..25.00
Poppy, cup & saucer...65.00
Shanghai, creamer 90.00
Shanghai, plate, 5½"...60.00
Strawberry, creamer 85.00
Strawberry, mug, 4"...135.00
Strawberry, plate, 7¾"..50.00
Strawberry, plate, 8½"..65.00
Strawberry, tea bowl & saucer 90.00

Tulip, cup and saucer, $65.00.

Tulip, creamer..65.00
Tulip, mug, miniature, 1⅞"...25.00
Tulip, plate, 6"..25.00
Tulip, plate, 9"..65.00
Tulip, teapot, ca 1840...135.00
Tulip, waste bowl, 6½"..85.00
Wagon Wheel, cup & saucer 70.00
Wagon Wheel, mug, 2½"...65.00
Wagon Wheel, pitcher, 8½"..175.00
Wagon Wheel, plate, 5½"..32.00
Wagon Wheel, plate, 7½"..50.00
Wagon Wheel, plate, 8"..65.00
Wagon Wheel, tea set, flow bl, child's, complete 525.00

Geisha Girl

Upon the discovery of tea in China some four thousand years ago, civilization was beset with a small problem – what to use in serving this special beverage. One solution came in the form of 'Geisha Girl' porcelain. At the end of the 19th century, this lovely type of Japanese tea service found its way to the west. Produced in more than sixty-five patterns, this fine porcelain features geishas going about the everyday activities of Japanese life. Mt. Fuji is very often included in the background along with a wide variety of flora and fauna. Though some items were entirely hand painted and others were hand decorated over decals, most were made by the raised stencil method. Tea sets, snack sets, children's items, salt and pepper shakers, and even such items as mustache cups may be found. Pieces were bordered in one of many bright colors – red, yellow, blue, green, or brown. As interest continues to climb, so will the values. For further information, we recommend *The Collector's Encyclopedia of Geisha Girl Porcelain* by Elyce Litts, available at your local bookstore or from Collector Books.

Key:
#2 — Torii	#20 — Made in Japan
#4 — T in Cherry Blossom	#35 — Plum Blossom
#19 — Japan	#J16 — Kutani

Parasol: Plate, 7½", $8.50; Tray, $9.50; Mustard, $22.00; Butter pat, $4.50; Heart dish, $12.00; Creamer, 4¼", $18.00; Creamer, 2½", $9.00.

Bowl, berry; Boat Festival, pale cobalt, #35, ind 10.00
Bowl, berry; Fan Dance A, red w/gold, 9½" 35.00
Bowl, berry; Meeting B, 8-lobed, gr w/gold buds, ind 13.00
Bowl, berry; Paper Carp, ind 7.00
Bowl, berry; Pointing F, apple gr, ind...11.00
Bowl, Dragonboat, 6-lobed, bl w/gold, 7".....................................25.00
Bowl, Ikebana in Rickshaw, ftd, yel, 8" 40.00
Bowl, nappy; Leaving the Teahouse, mc border, #J16.....................22.00
Bowl, salad; Garden Bench A, 9-lobed, red, 7¼" 23.00
Cake platter, Parasol E, pale cobalt, #20, 11¼"............................30.00
Cocoa pot, Battledore, conical, yel/gr, 8".....................................55.00
Cocoa pot, Courtesan Processional, #J16......................................75.00
Cocoa pot, Footbridge A, fluted, #4 ....45.00
Cocoa pot, Lesson, fluted, cobalt w/gold lacing, 9½" 65.00
Cocoa pot, Oni Dance B, fluted, cobalt w/gold, #20, 9½" 65.00
Cocoa pot, Origami, fluted, red-orange w/gold buds, #20..............45.00
Creamer, Boy w/Scythe, cobalt w/gold, #20 ....15.00
Creamer, Geisha in Sampan B, cobalt.. 7.00
Creamer, Lantern A, red, #J16 ....15.00
Creamer & sugar bowl, Kite A, brn w/gold....................................30.00
Dish, Geisha Band, leaf-shaped, red/orange w/gold 15.00
Dish, master nut; Duck Watching A, ftd, red w/gold.....................28.00
Hatpin holder, Parasol E, brn, #19...35.00
Mug, Boy's Processional, red w/yel lacing, 5" 25.00
Mustard jar, Long-Stemmed Peony, red, 3⅝x2¾"...........................15.00
Pitcher, Garden Bench K, red, #20, 3¼" 10.00
Plate, Bamboo Tree, #19, 7¼" 10.00
Plate, Child's Play, cobalt w/gold buds, #19, 6½" 10.00
Sauce dish, Meeting B, dk apple gr 12.00
Shakers, Cherry Blossom Ikebana, red, pr......................................15.00
Shakers, Parasol I: Black Parasol, red/orange, pr 10.00
Teapot, Dressing, red w/gold...25.00

Teapot, Geisha in Cards, cobalt w/gold, 3" 40.00
Teapot, Porch, cobalt w/gold, #2 ....45.00
Toothpick holder, In a Hurry, scalloped, cobalt w/gold lacing 12.00
Trinket box, Koto, club-shaped, #J16...28.00
Vase, Geisha on Parade, bl/gr, 3⅜"..32.00

German Porcelain

Unless otherwise noted, the porcelain listed in this section is marked simply 'Germany.' Products of other German manufactures are listed in specific categories. See also Bisque; Pink Pigs; Elfinware.

Our advisor for this category is William Brinkley; he is listed in the Directory under Illinois.

Bottle, scent; appl florals on pear form, mc, 11" 250.00
Chocolate pot, lovers/garden, Kauffman, wht w/gold, 10" 150.00
Figurine, boy & girl w/basket & jugs, lav/wht, 9¾", pr 145.00
Figurine, boy & girl w/dogs, 9" 90.00
Figurine, boy & girl w/flower basket & tray, mc, 6¾x2", pr 145.00
Figurine, butterfly girl carries 3 flower baskets, 8" 375.00
Figurine, child in basket, pillow behind, mk, 5½x3¼" 70.00
Figurine, country boy & girl, ca 1900, 13" pr 160.00
Figurine, dancer in pleated skirt, ca 1915, 13"............................385.00
Figurine, dog, tan & wht w/blk face, collar, 8¼" 145.00
Figurine, Edwardian couple, ca 1870-1890, 10½", pr 325.00
Figurine, maid in toga w/mallet & chisel stands by ped, 8".........275.00
Figurine, peasant girl w/harmonica, Fisher, 10" 45.00
Figurine, 17th century gentleman, ca 1920, 6" 25.00

Plate, rabbit in a landscape, 9", $185.00.

Pitcher, floral sprigs w/in str panel sides, 9" 60.00
Plaque, maid in rust bodice, sgn R Salt, ornate fr, 20x16" 1,900.00
Plaque, 2 maids share songbook, after Riesel, 6x4"......................385.00
Schnapps set, seated dog bottle+6 dog head cups on 8" tray........495.00
Shelf sitter, Blk boy w/fishing pole, EX color 65.00
Toothpick holder, little girl w/basket on bk, 4x3".........................75.00

Gladding McBean and Company

This company was established in 1875 in Lincoln, California.

They first produced only clay drainage pipes, but in 1883 architectural terra cotta was introduced, which has been used extensively in the United States as well as abroad. Sometime later a line of garden pottery was added. They soon became the leading producers of tile in the country. In 1923 they purchased the Tropico Pottery in Glendale, California, where in addition to tile they also produced huge garden vases. Their line was expanded in 1934 to included artware and dinnerware.

At least fifteen lines of art pottery were developed between 1934 and 1942. For a short time they stamped their wares with the Tropico Pottery mark; but the majority was signed 'GMcB' in an oval. Later the mark was changed to 'Franciscan' with several variations. After 1937 'Catalina Pottery' was used on some lines. (All items marked 'Catalina Pottery' were made in Glendale.)

Bowl, Capistrano Art Ware, mauve satin, rectangular, 11¾x8" 20.00
Bowl, Coronado Art Ware, ivory satin, 9" 15.00
Bowl, Tropico Art Ware, yel, bulbous, sm... 7.50
Candlestick, Coronado Art Ware, coral satin, 6½" 14.00
Compote, Avalon Art Ware, turq & ivory, 8"....................................18.00
Cup & saucer, Ruby Art Ware..25.00
Flowerpot, bl, Tropico Art Ware, 6"..10.00
Jardiniere, Tropico Art Ware, turq 17.50
Lamp base, Ox Blood Art Ware, detached underplate 60.00

Glazed terra cotta faux granite Corinthian capital-form pedestal of the style made for Carnegie Hall, 29", $700.00.

Pitcher, bl, Tropico Art Ware, 5¾" 12.50
Shell, Nautical Art Ware, flat, lg 18.00
Vase, Bamboo, ivory/gr, cylindrical, 8" 45.00
Vase, bud; Encanto Art Ware, celadon.. 8.00
Vase, Catalina Art Ware, cornucopia form, bl & wht...................20.00
Vase, Coronado Art Ware, turq satin, 10½" 25.00
Vase, Encanto Art Ware, flambe, bulbous......................................25.00
Vase, Ox Blood Art Ware, wide flared shape, 9¼" 175.00
Vase, Ox Blood Art Ware, 11"..175.00
Vase, Ox Blood Art Ware, 5"...67.00

Glidden

Genius designer Glidden Parker established Glidden Pottery in 1940 in Alfred, New York, having been schooled at the unrivaled New York State College of Ceramics at Alfred University. Glidden pottery is characterized by a fine stoneware body, innovative forms, outstanding hand-milled glazes, and hand decoration which make the pieces individual works of art. Production consisted of casual dinnerware, accessories, and artware which was distributed internationally.

In 1949 Glidden Pottery became the second ceramic plant in the country to utilize the revolutionary Ram pressing machine. This allowed for increased production and for the most part eliminated the previously used slip-casting method. However Glidden stoneware continued to reflect the same superb quality of craftsmanship until the factory closed in 1957. Although the majority of form and decorative patterns were Mr. Parker's personal designs, Fong Chow and Sergio Dello Strologo also designed award-winning lines.

Glidden will be found marked on the unglazed underside with a signature that is hand incised, mold impressed, or ink stamped. Interest in this unique stoneware is growing as collectors discover that it embodies the very finest of Mid-Century High Style. Our advisor is David Pierce; he is listed in the Directory under Ohio.

See listings for values.

Boat, Sandstone, rust/wht/bl, #4034, 10x3½" (illus)....................100.00
Bowl, Sage & Sand, #17, 8x8x4¼"..25.00
Bowl, Turquoise Matrix, #38, oval, 7¼x3¾x2" 25.00
Box, Afrikans, blk/rust/wht, #223, 9x4x2" 125.00
Canister, Garden, #601, w/cover & bail, 5x5½" dia 40.00
Casserole, bl, 5x8½" 28.00
Casserole, gr spatter, #167, ind, 5½".. 5.00
Casserole, Mexican Cock, #163, 11x6½x5"...................................40.00
Charger, Leaf, dk cobalt, #68, 15" dia (illus) 125.00
Creamer, Pear, 6x3½x3¼" 30.00
Flowerpot, Charcoal & Rice, bird form, 4x5½" (illus) 60.00
Flowerpot, Sandstone, rust/wht/bl, #4030, 6" (illus) 85.00
Flowerpot, Yellowstone, #218, 4¼x4½x3¾" 15.00
Pitcher, Feather, wht englobe, #616, 2-qt 45.00
Plate, Canine, Great Dane, #35, 5½x5½".....................................75.00
Plate, Ric Rac, yel, #31-B, 9¾x9¾"...25.00
Plate, Snowdrop, wht/bl, #33, 8x8"..30.00
Plate, Viridian, #542, triangular 15.00
Server, Alfred Stoneware, saffron, oak hdl, #805, 21x11x4"........125.00
Teapot, Turquoise Matrix, #618, 9½x6½x3½"...............................50.00
Tray, Blackfish, w/metal stand, #200, 8x6" 100.00
Tray, Flourish, dk cobalt, #32, 9x6¾" 35.00
Vase, bl spatter, sq, #86, 7½" 10.00
Vase, bl speckled w/wht drip overglaze, tumbler form, 5½"...........22.00
Vase, Chinese bl to dk bl, rectangular, 8" 40.00
Vase, Cobalt, #2, 9x5"...40.00
Vase, Early Pink, ball form, #62, 4x3¾"..25.00
Vase, Gulfstream, turq/bl/blk, apple form, #4021, 15½x10½"......500.00

Vase, Loop Artware, rust/charcoal, #940, 9x9" dia **400.00**
Vase, Turquoise Matrix, #87, pillow form, 7½x4½x2¾" **30.00**

Goebel

F.W. Goebel founded the Hummelwork Porcelain Manufactory in 1871, located in Rodental, West Germany. They produced porcelain figurines, plates, and novelties, the most famous of which are the Hummel figurines (these are listed in a separate section). There were many other series produced by Goebel – Disney characters, birds, animals, Art Deco figurines, and the Friar Tuck Monks that are especially popular.

Friar Tuck Monks, small bee mark: Calendar, 4¼" across, $25.00; Egg timer, 3¼", $25.00.

Barometer, Cardinal, 3-line mk..**115.00**
Creamer, Friar Tuck Monks, 2½" **25.00**
Creamer & sugar bowl, Friar Tuck Monks, w/lid, on tray..............**70.00**
Decanter, comical man, hands in pockets, smokes cigar, 9½" **125.00**
Egg cup on 5" tray, Friar Tuck Monks, 3-line mk..........................**125.00**
Figurine, Center Court, #1903 ....**35.00**
Figurine, nude, seated, wht bsk, M **65.00**
Figurine, peacock, sgn, 1984, 11x16" **90.00**
Figurine, rabbit, brn w/ladybug on tail, 1959 mk **35.00**
Mustard jar, Friar Tuck Monks, stylized bee **25.00**
Night light, jester/devil/owl, Deco style, 1925, 10" **200.00**
Shakers, Friar Tuck Monks, pr **35.00**

Goldscheider

The Goldscheider family operated a pottery in Vienna for many generations before seeking refuge in the United States following Hitler's invasion of their country. They settled in Trenton, New Jersey, in the early 1940s where they established a new corporation, producing objects of art and tableware items. In 1946 Marcel Goldscheider established a pottery in Staffordshire where he manufactured bone china figures, earthenware, etc., marked with a stamp of his signature.

Bookends, seated nude, 1 reads/1 holds book, Austria, 9½" **825.00**
Bust, Madonna w/crown, 7" **85.00**
Bust, nude looks down/holds flower, tight curls, Wein, 14" **1,200.00**
Bust, Oriental man & lady, mk Goldcrest, 7", pr............................**95.00**
Bust, stylized lady, bl flower/yel shirt, curled hair, 7½" **350.00**
Figurine, April Showers..**50.00**
Figurine, butterfly girl, spider web tunic, 19" **3,000.00**
Figurine, Colonial lady w/fan, 10½"...**60.00**
Figurine, Colonial man, bl & gray, 9¼" **95.00**
Figurine, dancer, floral drape falling between ft, '20, 18" **1,500.00**
Figurine, lady, seated, wht & bl, 7½"..**150.00**
Figurine, Madam Pompadour, pk & wht, 6¼"..................................**95.00**

Lady with parasol, whippet by her side, #7723, 14", $850.00.

Figurine, maid in peach floral dress curtsies, Lorenzl, 13" **500.00**
Figurine, maid in purple floral dress/hat curtsies, USA, 15".........**350.00**
Figurine, mallard in flight, mc, 9" **125.00**
Figurine, matador embraces senorita, Karl Perl, 16½" **500.00**
Figurine, nude, red heels/pk plume/drape, Dakon, 13" **800.00**
Figurine, Oriental male guitarist/dancing lady, 10¼", pr.............**100.00**
Figurine, Oriental poet & guitarist, yel/gold, 7½", pr **125.00**
Figurine, Pierette, gr costume, holding mask, Wein, 12½"...........**700.00**
Figurine, Southern belle, rose gown, 10½"....................................**85.00**
Figurine, stylized bridal couple, 6"..**600.00**
Figurine, Wht Christmas, 6½" **125.00**
Figurine, Yankee Doodle, 7"...**65.00**
Figurine, 2 birds, bl & purple, 3" **150.00**
Mask, lady, blk ringlets, orange lips, mk Wein, 10" **300.00**
Mask, lady, curly hair, red lips, yel apple, mk Wein, 8" **400.00**
Mask, lady, gr curls, orange lips, yel flower by face, 8" **300.00**
Mask, lady, redhead w/orange lips, bl/blk hat, Wein, 8½"...........**300.00**

Gonder

Lawton Gonder grew up a ceramist. By the time he opened his own pottery in December, 1941, he had a solid background in both production and management. Gonder Ceramic Arts, Inc. purchased the old Peters and Reed – Zane Pottery in South Zanesville, Ohio. There they turned out quality commercial ware with graceful shapes in both Oriental and contemporary designs. Their greatest achievements were the development of their superior glazes: flambe; 24k gold crackle; and Chinese crackle glazes in celadon, ming yellow, and blue. Most of the ware is marked with 'Gonder' impressed in script and a mold number.

Ewer, gr matt, #H-73 USA, 7½"...**15.00**
Figurine, coolie, gray, 9" **15.00**
Figurine, deer w/long ears, turq, 10" **35.00**
Figurine, Oriental water carrier, 14½"..**45.00**
Figurine, sampan, bl, 10" **10.00**
Figurine, swan, bl/pk, #E-44, 5½"...**14.00**
Figurine, swan, gold crackle, #E-44, 5½".......................................**20.00**
Tea set, brn mottle, 3-pc **25.00**
Vase, bl/pk, #53 ....**8.00**
Vase, bl/pk, fan form, #E-5, 7½"..**15.00**
Vase, bud; turq, hdls, 6" **10.00**
Vase, emb flowers, #E-66, 6½" **9.00**
Vase, mauve, hdls, #E-48..**9.00**

Goofus Glass

Goofus was an inexpensive type of lustre-painted pressed glassware made by many companies during the first two decades of the 20th century. Bowls and trays are most common, and red and gold combinations are found more often than blues and greens. Authority Carolyn McKinley has compiled a lovely book, *Goofus Glass, An Illustrated Value Guide*, available at your favorite bookstore.

Bonbon, strawberry & flower pod, dome ft, orig pnt, 4" dia 40.00
Bowl, gr poppy, sgn Northwood, 2½x7", M 30.00
Bowl, Grape & Lattice, minor rstr, 2x6½" 40.00
Bowl, iris forms ruffles in rim, orig pnt, 3x7", M 25.00
Bowl, pine cones & roses, orig red/gold pnt, 2½x9½" 45.00
Candy dish, Grape & Cable, rpt, 5¼x2" 25.00
Coaster, floral on gold, orig pnt, 3", EX 10.00
Compote & saucer, poppy, crackle glass, orig pnt, 4" 25.00
Lamp, fairy; roses, flash-fired gr, 3 holes for smoke, 7" 35.00
Lamp, Nosegay, oil burning, #2, EX orig pnt 150.00
Nut dish, cherries, orig pnt, scalloped rim, 6½" 40.00
Plate, holly, opal w/orig pnt, 10½", NM 45.00
Powder box, basketweave, milk glass, orig pnt, rare, M 50.00
Syrup, Cabbage Rose, no pnt, 5½" 35.00
Vase, Cabbage Rose, milk glass, remains of orig pnt, 5½" 30.00
Vase, dogwood blossom, gold on milk glass, 6" 17.00
Vase, dogwood blossom cluster, EX orig pnt, 15" 55.00
Vase, draped nude, EX pnt, 12½" 95.00
Vase, lovebirds, orig pnt, rare, 10" 47.00
Vase, peacock, bl & gr, NM pnt, 10½" 75.00
Vase, rose, red on gold crackle, rpt, 14" 55.00
Water bottle, basketweave, orig wht pnt, 10" 40.00
Water bottle, grapes on crackle, no pnt, 7½" 35.00

Goss

William Henry Goss received his early education at the Government School of Design and as a result of his merit was introduced to Alderman William Copeland, who owned a large pottery firm. Under the influence of Copeland, Goss quickly learned the trade and soon became their chief designer. Little is known about this brief association, and in 1858 Goss left to begin his own business. After a short-lived partnership with a Mr. Peake, Goss opened a pottery on John Street, Stoke-on-Trent, but by 1870 he had moved his business to a location near London Road. This pottery became the famous Falcon Works.

Many of the early pieces made by Goss were left unmarked and are difficult to discern from products made by the Copeland factory, but after he had been in business for about fifteen years, all of his wares were marked. Today, unmarked items do not command the prices of the later marked wares.

Adulphus William Henry Goss joined his father's firm in the 1880s. He introduced cheaper lines, though the more expensive lines continued in production. Shortly after his father's death in 1906, Adulphus retired and left the business to his two younger brothers. The business suffered from problems created by a war economy, and in 1936 Goss assets were held by Cauldron Potteries Ltd. These were eventually taken over by the Coalport Group, who retained the right to use the Goss trademark. Messrs. Ridgeway Potteries bought all the assets in 1954, as well as the right to use the Goss trademark and name. Now it remains to be seen if Goss ware will ever be produced again.

Abbots cup, Fountains Abbey 25.00
Bottle, Sunderland, Sir William Wallace 32.00

Bowl, beer; dragon 25.00
Bowl, Scarlett, #38660 .... 35.00
Cup, St George, Wiltshire, Calne, 3-hdld 25.00
Ewer, Japan, Windsor crest 37.50
Huer's House 200.00
Irish Mather, Hastings 20.00
Jug, Kendall, Assyrian Armour 25.00
Jug, Litchfield, St Alban's Abbey 30.00
Jug, Newcastle Roman, Falmouth 32.00
Jug, St George 25.00
Look Out House 140.00
Manx Cottage 105.00
Milk can, Welsh, St Helena 25.00
Pipkin, Southampton, Blairgowrie 32.00
Rufus Stone 40.00
Shakespeare's House 100.00
St Nicholas Chapel 200.00
Urn, Mullelburg, Norway, Kirkpark 25.00
Vase, bud; St Andrews University, sm 28.00
Wall pocket, Christ Church, lg 32.00
Yorick's Skull 135.00
1st & Last House 135.00

Gouda

Since the 18th century the main center of the pottery industry in Holland was in Gouda. One of its earliest industries, the manufacture of clay pipes, continues to the present day. The artware so easily recognized by collectors today was first produced about 1885. It was decorated in the Art Nouveau manner. Stylized florals, birds, and geometrics were favored motifs; only rarely is the design naturalistic. The Nouveau influence was strong until about 1915. Art Deco was attempted but with less success. Though most of the ware is finished in a matt glaze, glossy pieces in both pastels and dark colors are found on occasion and command higher prices. Decoration on the glossy ware is usually very well executed. Most of the workshops failed during the depression, though earthenware is still being made in Gouda and carries the Gouda mark. Until very recently, Regina was still making a limited amount of the old Gouda-style pottery in a matt finish. Watch for the Gouda name, which is usually a part of the backstamp of the various manufacturers.

Basket, mc on blk, Regina, 6½" 135.00
Basket &flower frog, blk, Regina, #1168 .... 100.00
Bowl, blk w/rust/bl/cream border, house mk, #923, 8" 120.00
Bowl, florals, mc on brn w/gold, mk, 3¾x9" 135.00
Bowl, flower holder; florals, mc w/gold, mk, 3¼x12" 165.00
Candlestick, florals, yel on blk w/turq leaves, mk, 7¼", pr 145.00
Dutch shoe, Astri, mc, 7½" 69.00
Ewer, florals/scrolls, shiny, Zuid-Holland, 14" 450.00
Humidor, florals & scrolls, blk trim, house mk, 5¼x4½" 135.00
Inkwell, mc w/blk base, Damascus, 8½x5½" 110.00
Match striker, Deco motif, mc on blk, house mk, 2x2⅜" 40.00
Pitcher, sgn Holland Gouda Reba 976-ES, 9" 125.00
Tumbler, florals, mc on cream, house mk, 4⅜x3⅝" 55.00
Vase, bellflowers/exotic leaves, wine/gr on gr & tan, 11" 550.00
Vase, birds of paradise/floral clusters, ovoid, mk, 7" 135.00
Vase, floral, high gloss, mk Haas, 7½" 95.00
Vase, floral, mc on gray, mk, 7¼x3¾" 75.00
Vase, mc w/blk base & int, Regina, 8½" 140.00
Vase, pansies, house mk, 6" 48.00
Vase, red Deco florals, gold bands, 8" 40.00
Vase, stylized dotted lilies/foliage on blk & brn, 12" 385.00

Vase, stylized floral band on olive, hdls, sgn/1849, 7" 140.00
Wall pocket, florals, mc on blk, mk/#4262, 11½" 135.00

Pitcher, stylized peacock feathers, artist signed, house mark, #1721, 5½", $65.00.

Grand Feu

The Grand Feu Art Pottery operated from 1912 until about 1918 in Los Angeles, California. It was owned and operated by Cornelius Brauckman who developed a method of producing remarkably artistic glaze effects achieved by extremely high temperatures during the firing process. The body of the ware, as a result of the intense heat (2500 degrees), was vitrified as the glaze matured. Brauckman signed his ware, either with his name or 'Grand Feu Pottery, L.A. California'. His work is regarded today as being among the finest art pottery ever produced in the United States. Examples are rare and command high prices on today's market.

Bowl, lt mustard & terra cotta, bulbous, imp mk, 4" 850.00
Vase, brn/gr flambe w/pk splotches, dbl gourd, 8x4", NM 1,700.00
Vase, silver bl irid, mk, 6½" 1,400.00
Vase, yel/orange crystalline, LA/CA, 2½x3½" 1,800.00

Graniteware

Graniteware, made of a variety of metals with enamel coatings, derives its name from its appearance. The speckled, swirled, or mottled effect of the vari-colored enamels may look like granite – but there the resemblance stops. It wasn't especially durable! Expect at least minor chipping if you plan to collect.

Graniteware was featured in 1876 at Phily's Expo. It was mass-produced in quantity, and enough of it has survived to make at least the common items easily affordable. Color is an important consideration in evaluating an item; cobalt, brown, green swirl, or old red and white items are unusual, thus more expensive. Pieces of heavier weight, seam constructed, and those with wooden handles and tin lids are usually older.

In recent months, magazine articles featuring decorating ideas with an emphasis on the 'country look' have caused the price of graniteware to escalate – a trend which is likely to continue.

For further study, we recommend *The Collector's Encyclopedia of Graniteware – Colors, Shapes, and Values* by our advisor, Helen Greguire. She is listed in the Directory under New York. For the address of the National Graniteware Society, see the section on Clubs, Newsletters, and Catalogs.

Ash tray, red, Polar Ware advertising, 1928, M 165.00
Baking pan, bl & wht lg swirl, molded hdls, oblong, EX 85.00
Baking pan, bl & wht swirl, blk trim, appl hdls, oblong................145.00
Bedpan, gray & wht speckled, w/lid 30.00
Biscuit cutter, brn & wht, blk strap hdl, Onyx Ware, 2¼", NM ..425.00
Bowl, bl & wht lg swirl, rimmed, Columbian Ware, EX.................45.00
Bowl, bl & wht med swirl, blk trim, serving sz, NM 45.00
Bowl, dough; red & wht lg swirl, cobalt trim, 1960s, NM 55.00
Bowl, vegetable; red & wht lg swirl w/blk, oblong, 1950s, M.......135.00
Bread box, wht w/bl lines, rnd, hinged, NM 90.00
Bread box, wht w/blk trim & letters, vented top, rnd, EX............125.00
Bread pan, gray mottle, EX..32.00
Bread raiser, cobalt & wht med mottle, blk trim, ftd, sm, NM.....475.00
Bucket, berry; turq & wht swirl, w/lid, 2¼x3" 195.00
Bucket, water; bl & wht swirl, NM 90.00
Butter carrier, aqua & wht lg swirl, cobalt trim, oval, NM...........300.00
Cake turner, wht w/blk hdl, pierced, NM 35.00
Can, cream; bl & wht lg swirl, blk trim, wire bail, NM................175.00
Can, cream; gray lg mottle, wood bail, flat ears, M 155.00
Can, cream; solid brn, 1-pt, NM 58.00
Can, cream; solid red, w/lid & bail, 1-qt 20.00
Can, milk; blk & wht speckled, lock top, wire hdl, 8", EX 35.00
Can, milk; gr & wht lg swirl, bl trim, hdl, Emerald Ware, NM....350.00
Can, milk; gr shaded, matching lock lid, Shamrock Ware, M 160.00
Canister, Meal in wht on solid bl, wht int, EX 100.00
Chamber pot, bl & wht lg swirl, blk trim, wht int, NM 115.00

Chamber stick with push-up, gray mottle, 7", $285.00.

Churn, gr to wht shaded, floor-model dasher type, EX.................750.00
Clothes boiler, wht, red-brn letters & trim, w/lid, sm, NM..........215.00
Coffee biggin, bl & wht fine mottle, squatty, 3-pc, M 550.00
Coffee biggin, cobalt & wht checks w/red trim, 3-pc, M..............365.00
Coffee biggin, red & wht med mottle, 4-pc, NM 565.00
Coffee biggin, wht w/gold bands, hdld biggin, 4-pc, EX..............100.00
Coffee boiler, bl & wht lg swirl, EX 200.00
Coffee boiler, gr & wht lg swirl, Emerald Ware, NM...................400.00
Coffee boiler, red & wht lg swirl w/dk bl trim, old, NM..............850.00
Coffee boiler, wht w/blk, Belmont Stamping & Enameling, M ...125.00
Coffee carrier, bl & wht checks, red trim, tin lid, EX..................195.00
Coffee flask, gray & wht fine mottle, metal top, 4½x3½", M.......225.00
Coffee roaster, blk & wht med mottle, screen drum, lg, M...........425.00
Coffeepot, bl & wht swirl, 10", NM..185.00
Coffeepot, brn & wht mottle, metal lid, wood hdl/knob, M 275.00

Coffeepot, cream & gr, gr glass dome, EX 40.00
Coffeepot, dk gr & wht med swirl chrysolite, M...........................350.00
Coffeepot, gray, pewter trim, brass ring on base, NM 285.00
Coffeepot, lt gr & wht relish pattern, EX 215.00
Coffeepot, reverse cobalt & wht swirl, triple-coated, NM 285.00
Coffeepot, wht w/bl veins, chicken-wire pattern, EX...................195.00
Colander, bl & wht swirl, EX 68.00
Colander, cobalt & wht lg swirl, blk trim, ftd, deep, M................275.00
Colander, gr & ivory shaded, blk trim, Old Ivory Ware, NM 135.00
Colander, gr & wht lg mottle, cobalt trim, ftd, deep, NM............295.00
Creamer, dk gr shaded, wht int, Shamrock Ware, EX 185.00
Creamer, gray lg mottle, seamless, rolled hdl, squat, NM............225.00
Creamer, solid cobalt, squat, NM...135.00
Cup, brn & wht lg swirl, blk trim, NM 55.00
Custard cup, cobalt & wht lg swirl, blk trim, NM 85.00
Custard cup, lt bl & wht lg swirl, blk trim, wht int, NM................85.00
Dbl boiler, aqua & wht lg swirl, cobalt trim, flared, NM..............285.00
Dipper, bl & wht lg mottle int/ext, bl trim, flared, M..................110.00
Dipper, bl & wht lg swirl, blk trim, flat blk hdl, EX 75.00
Dipper, bl swirl Windsor...30.00
Dish pan, dk gr & wht lg chrysolite swirl, cobalt hdls, EX 140.00
Dust pan, dk bl w/blk appl hdl, seamless, NM 225.00
Egg cup, solid lt bl...28.00
Egg separator, solid bl int/ext, EX...395.00
Foot tub, cobalt & wht lg swirl, blk trim, oval, EX.......................195.00
Fruit jar filler, gray lg mottle, riveted strap hdl, EX.....................35.00
Fruit jar filler, wht & gr lg mottle, gr trim, Elite, EX..................140.00
Fry pan, bl & wht lg swirl, blk rim & hdl, sm, EX 165.00
Fry pan, gr & wht lg swirl, wht int, EX 195.00
Fry pan, lav & wht lg swirl, blk trim & hdl, wht int, EX..............165.00
Funnel, bl & wht fine mottle, wht specks, Elite Austria, EX..........65.00
Funnel, dk gr & wht fine mottle, wht int, mk Elite, EX..............125.00
Funnel, gray, seamed, riveted hanging ear, NM 45.00
Gravy boat, wht & lt bl lg mottle, cobalt trim, NM.....................595.00
Honey pot, lt gray, wht int, tin top, wht porc knob, NM.............215.00
Jug, batter; dk bl & wht relish pattern, tin lid, bail hdl, NM 275.00
Kettle, preserve; bl & wht lg swirl, lipped, wood bail, M 125.00
Kettle, preserve; lt gray, side hdls, 13x6", NM 30.00
Ladle, skimmer; lt & bl fine mottle, wht int, mk Elite, NM...........50.00
Ladle, soup; bl & wht med swirl, wht int, EX................................65.00
Ladle, soup; gray med mottle, blk trn wood hdl, NM 95.00

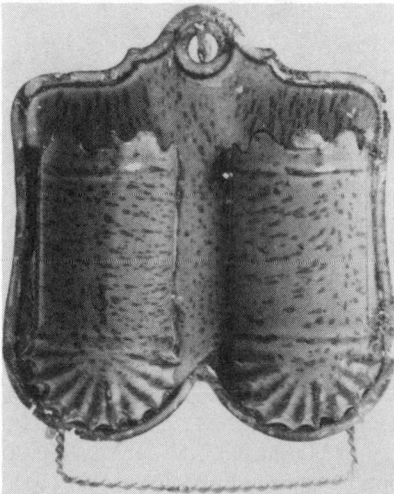

Double match safe, gray mottle, 5" wide, in good condition, $465.00.

Mold, gray lg mottle, ribbed tube, M...80.00
Mold, shell, brn to tan shaded, wht int, ring to hang, M 135.00
Mold, shell, wht, oblong, ring to hang, EX 85.00
Mug, bl & wht fine mottle w/blk trim, EX......................................55.00

Mug, cobalt & wht lg swirl, NM...60.00
Mug, gr & wht lg swirl w/blk trim, Emerald Ware, lg, EX 115.00
Mug, mush; bl & wht lg swirl, blk trim, M 185.00
Onion keeper, wht w/blk trim, mk Swiebln, hole to hang, NM...185.00
Pail, berry; gray mottle, tin lid, 6½x7½", NM.............................45.00
Pail, water; bl & wht lg swirl, blk trim, wood bail, sm, M 145.00
Pail, water; cobalt & wht lg swirl, blk trim, lg, M........................195.00
Pan, cornstick; solid red, cream int, Griswold, 7-stick, M............345.00
Pan, jelly roll; bl swirl 28.00
Pan, lady finger; lt & dk gray fine mottle, makes 6, NM 265.00
Pan, mining; gray, Opal Ironware, 16" 65.00
Pan, muffin; cobalt & wht lg swirl int/ext, 8-cup, M...................285.00
Pan, muffin; gray lg mottle, deep, 12-cup, NM 50.00
Pan, muffin; gray lg mottle, sq, 9-cup, EX 40.00
Pan, muffin; gray lg mottle, 6-cup, NM...50.00
Pan, pudding; cobalt & wht lg swirl w/blk trim, lg, EX...............110.00
Pie plate, brn & wht lg swirl, blk trim, wht int, NM......................65.00
Pie plate, cobalt & wht lg swirl, blk trim, wht int, M....................55.00
Pitcher, gray, ice lip, 11", M...110.00
Pitcher, milk; bl/orange/blk/gr/wht lg swirl, wht int, EX 650.00
Pitcher, molasses; wht w/cobalt trim, flared cylinder, M.............145.00
Pitcher, water; bl & wht med mottle, bl trim, EX.........................140.00
Pitcher, water; bl & wht wavy mottle, triple-coated, M...............365.00
Pitcher, water; brn shaded, blk trim & hdl, EX............................140.00
Pitcher, water; gr & wht lg swirl, bl trim, Emerald Ware, EX.......265.00
Pitcher, water; gray lg mottle, welded hdl, Nesco Ware, M 165.00
Pitcher, water; gray med mottle, riveted hdl, ftd, EX 155.00
Plate, gr, 9", NM 8.00
Plate, gray lg mottle, lg, M...40.00
Plate, red-brn & wht fine mottle, wht int, 12-sided, EX...............45.00
Plate, soup; lt bl & wht lg mottle int/ext, EX...............................45.00
Plate, wht w/bl trim, 8½"...15.00
Platter, gr & wht speckled, EX...30.00
Roaster, cobalt & wht lg swirl, flat top, 3-pc, NM.......................285.00
Roaster, gr shaded, flat top, 3-pc, Shamrock Ware, NM..............175.00
Roaster, gray, w/lid, lg...35.00
Roaster, violet shaded, wht int, 3-pc, Thistle Ware, EX...............120.00
Scoop, grocer's, gray lg mottle, open end hdl, rivets, EX 135.00
Scoop, thumb; gray lg mottle, EX...165.00
Skimmer, cobalt & wht med mottle w/gr veins, blk hdl, NM 150.00
Skimmer, gray med mottle, pierced, long hdl, NM........................35.00
Skimmer, wht, pierced diamond-shaped center, NM....................120.00
Soap dish, aqua & wht lg swirl, hanging, NM 125.00
Soap dish, cobalt & wht swirl, w/strainer, NM 95.00
Spatula, gray med mottle, sm, NM...65.00
Spatula, gray mottle, lg..85.00
Spoon, cobalt & wht med mottle int/ext, blk hdl, EX....................65.00
Spoon, cream & gr, long hdl, NM..25.00
Strainer, gray...18.00
Strainer, lt bl & wht speckled, 6x12", EX 35.00
Strainer, solid gray, pierced bottom, NM......................................60.00
Sugar bowl, gray mottle, pewter trim, w/lid, EX 295.00
Sugar bowl, lt bl & wht med mottle, blk trim/hdls, squat, EX......275.00
Tea steeper, bl & wht fine mottle, wht int, EX 150.00
Teakettle, bl & wht shaded, wood bail, Bluebelle Ware, NM 225.00
Teakettle, cobalt & wht lg swirl, blk trim, wood bail, EX.............395.00
Teakettle, gr & wht fine mottle, gr trim, NM...............................225.00
Teapot, bl & wht fine mottle, pewter trim, M Bowman, M...........285.00
Teapot, cobalt & wht lg swirl w/blk trim, gooseneck spout, M.....395.00
Teapot, dk gr, 1-cup, EX...55.00
Teapot, gray med mottle w/cobalt trim, M...................................135.00
Teapot, gray mottle, pewter trim, copper base, squat...................325.00
Teapot, red & wht red mottle, gooseneck spout, old, NM............495.00
Teapot, violet shaded, squat, Thistle Ware, sm, EX......................225.00

Teapot, wht w/gr veins, med swirl 'snow on mtn,' Elite, EX.........395.00
Tray, gray med mottle, oval, NM..145.00
Tray, red & wht mottle, dk bl trim, rnd, ltweight, '60s, NM...........85.00
Tumbler, dk solid bl w/blk trim, Ski Blu label, M 85.00
Wash basin, gray 15.00
Wash basin, lav & wht lg swirl, wht int, w/eyelet, NM 115.00
Wash bowl, old red & wht lg swirl, blk trim, lg, EX 295.00
Wash pitcher & bowl, red w/blk trim & hdl, squat, M.................100.00
Water carrier, gr & wht chrysolite swirl, wood bail, lg, EX...........460.00
Water cooler, bl/gray/wht lg swirl, 2-part, Lava Ware, NM 595.00

Green and Ivory

Green and ivory are the colors of a type of country pottery decorated with in-mold designs very similar to those of the more familiar blue and white wares. It is unmarked and was produced from about 1910 to 1935 by many manufacturers as part of their staple line of kitchenwares.

Bowl, Apricot, 9½" 75.00
Bowl, Daisy & Waffle, 10" 65.00
Butter crock, Apricots & Honeycomb, w/lid & bail 85.00
Butter crock, Daisy & Waffle, w/lid...95.00
Mug, Grape 40.00
Pitcher, Basketweave & Morning Glory, rope hdl, 9"...................150.00
Pitcher, Cow, EX color & detail, 7½" 150.00
Pitcher, Grape..95.00
Pitcher, Indian Head in War bonnet, waffle body, 8½", NM 165.00
Pitcher, Pine Cone, 9"...145.00
Spittoon, Cosmos, 6" 75.00
Toothpick holder, Swan..30.00
Umbrella stand, Irises, 20"..295.00

Green Opaque

Introduced in 1887 by the New England Glass Company, this ware is very scarce due to the fact that it was produced for less than one year. It is characterized by its soft green color and a wavy band of gold reserving a mottled blue metallic stain. It is usually found in satin; examples with a shiny finish are extremely rare.

Bowl, deep, 4" dia 275.00
Cruet, tricorn, 6"... 1,400.00
Shakers, squat form, EX mottling, 2¾", pr...................................475.00
Spooner, 4" 850.00
Toothpick, 2" 1,150.00
Tumbler, EX mottling & gold, 4" 425.00
Tumbler, M mottling, 4" 600.00
Tumbler, Optic Ribs, fine mottling, gold border 575.00
Vase, flared mouth, minor wear to mottling, 6"...........................700.00
Vase, NM mottling & gold, 3¾x4" 650.00

Greenaway, Kate

Kate Greenaway was an English artist who lived from 1846 to 1901. She gained world-wide fame as an illustrator of children's books, drawing children clothed in the styles worn by proper English and American boys and girls of the very early 1800s. Her book, *Under the Willow Tree*, published in 1878, was the first of many. Her sketches appeared in leading magazines, and her greeting cards were in great demand. Manufacturers of china, pottery, and metal products copied her characters to decorate children's dishes, tiles, and salt and pepper

shakers as well as many other items. See also Almanacs; Napkin Rings; Sewing.

Book, A Apple Pie, London, Warne, ca 1920, VG 35.00
Book, Almanack for 1884, London, VG.....................................60.00
Book, Almanack for 1887, London, Routledge, VG 95.00
Book, Almanack for 1927, London, VG.....................................50.00
Book, April Baby's Book of Tunes, Macmillan, 1st ed, 1900 ....35.00
Book, Day in a Child's Life, London, 1st edition, 1881, VG..........85.00
Book, Kate Greenaway's Birthday Book, Warne, reprint, EX.........27.50
Book, Language of Flowers, London, rebound, G 50.00
Book, Mother Goose, London, Routledge, 1st ed, 1881, VG.........95.00
Book, Mother Goose, NY/London, Warne, VG 65.00
Book, Mother Goose or Old Nursery Rhymes, London, 1st ed ...125.00
Book, Pied Piper of Hamelin, London, Warne, illus, VG 20.00
Book, Royal Progress of King Pepito, London, 1st issue, 1889 ....55.00
Book, Under the Window, early, EX 75.00
Book, Under the Window, London, illus, 1st edition, VG...........125.00
Book, Under the Window, NY, Routledge, 1st edition, 1878.........85.00
Book, 16 Examples in Colour of the Artist's Work, 1910, EX......120.00
Bowl, Daisy & Button, amber, girl/dog on Reed & Barton fr 525.00
Cup & saucer, pk lustre 125.00
Figurine, boy w/basket, proc, 1893 mk, 8½x4" 525.00
Plate, children at play, fruit, birds & flowers, 9" 100.00
Thimble holder, girl figural 130.00
Toothpick holder, girl sits on stump, basket on bk, bsk 40.00

Vase, three children in barrel, 4", $225.00.

Greentown Glass

Greentown glass is a term refering to the product of the the Indiana Tumbler and Goblet Company of Greentown, Indiana, ca 1894 to 1903. Their earlier pressed glass patterns were #1, a pseudo-cut glass design; #137, Pleat Band; and #200, Austrian. Another line, Dewey, was designed in 1898. Many lovely colors were produced in addition to crystal. Jacob Rosenthal, who was later affiliated with Fenton, developed his famous chocolate glass in 1900. The rich shaded opaque brown glass was an overnight success. Two new patterns, Leaf Bracket and Cactus, were designed to display the glass to its best advantage, but previously existing molds were also used. In only three years, Rosenthal developed yet another important color formula, golden agate. The Holly Amber pattern was designed especially for its production. The Dolphin covered dish with a fish finial is perhaps the most common and easily-recognized piece ever produced. Other animal dishes were also made; all are highly collectible. There have been many repros – not all are marked! See the Pattern Glass section for clear pressed glass, only colored items are listed here. See also Chocolate Glass; Animal Dishes with Covers.

Aldine, sugar bowl, w/lid, chocolate................................. 1,595.00
Austrian, bowl, rectangular, canary, 8" L 130.00
Austrian, cordial, canary 130.00
Austrian, spooner, canary 95.00
Austrian, sugar bowl, w/lid, chocolate, 2½".....................145.00
Austrian, tumbler, canary 125.00
Austrian, wine, canary..145.00
Brazen Shield, bowl, bl, 7½" dia..............................70.00
Brazen Shield, relish tray, bl...............................70.00
Brazen Shield, spooner, bl...................................78.00
Brazen Shield, sugar bowl, w/lid, bl........................145.00
Brazen Shield, tumbler, bl...................................50.00
Cactus, bowl, chocolate, 8".................................125.00
Cactus, butter dish, chocolate 190.00
Cactus, compote, chocolate, 7¼" dia........................190.00
Cactus, compote, chocolate, 9¼" dia........................225.00
Cactus, cracker jar, chocolate..............................230.00
Cactus, cracker jar, red agate..............................165.00
Cactus, creamer, chocolate..................................135.00

Cactus cruet, chocolate, 6½",
$195.00.

Cactus, mug, chocolate..60.00
Cactus, plate, chocolate, 7½"................................95.00
Cactus, syrup, w/metal lid, chocolate 175.00
Cactus, tumbler, chocolate 55.00
Cord Drapery, bowl, fluted, emerald gr, 6"..................135.00
Cord Drapery, cake plate, ftd, cobalt 165.00
Cord Drapery, compote, open, cobalt, 8½" dia...............175.00
Cord Drapery, creamer, emerald gr, 4¾" 130.00
Cord Drapery, pickle dish, amber............................90.00
Cord Drapery, pitcher, water; emerald gr....................225.00
Cord Drapery, spooner, cobalt 100.00
Cord Drapery, toothpick holder, amber 295.00
Cord Drapery, tray, water; cobalt...........................165.00
Cord Drapery, tumbler, cobalt...............................125.00
Cupid, butter dish, Nile gr.................................395.00
Cupid, spooner, Nile gr 295.00
Daisy, butter dish, chocolate 225.00

Daisy, sugar bowl, open, chocolate..........................100.00
Daisy, sugar bowl, w/lid, wht opaque 45.00
Dewey, butter dish, chocolate, 4" dia 150.00
Dewey, butter dish, chocolate, 5" dia 445.00
Dewey, creamer, amber, 5" 60.00
Dewey, creamer, emerald gr, 5"..............................70.00
Dewey, mug, Nile gr 175.00
Dewey, pitcher, amber 110.00
Dewey, pitcher, emerald gr 130.00
Dewey, shakers, amber, pr 100.00
Dewey, sugar bowl, chocolate................................100.00
Dewey, tray, serpentine, amber, lg 70.00
Dewey, tray, serpentine, emerald gr, sm 45.00
Dewey, tumbler, canary......................................55.00
Diamond Prisms, tumbler, chocolate 420.00
Dish, covered; cat on hamper, cobalt, 4½" 295.00
Dish, covered; hen on nest, canary 225.00
Early Diamond, pitcher, emerald gr..........................150.00
Fleur-de-lis, celery vase, chocolate, 5¾" 245.00
Fleur-de-lis, creamer, chocolate............................145.00
Fleur-de-lis, spooner, chocolate............................160.00
Geneva, creamer, chocolate 175.00
Greentown Daisy, mustard, w/lid, emerald gr frost 75.00
Herringbone Buttress, bowl, emerald gr, 7¼" dia.............180.00
Herringbone Buttress, cake stand, emerald gr................370.00
Herringbone Buttress, cruet, w/stopper, emerald gr 345.00
Herringbone Buttress, goblet, emerald gr....................200.00
Herringbone Buttress, pitcher 220.00
Herringbone Buttress, sugar bowl, w/lid, emerald gr.........220.00
Herringbone Buttress, syrup, chocolate 185.00
Holly Amber, bowl, oval, 7½"................................370.00
Holly Amber, bowl, 7½" 520.00
Holly Amber, bowl, 8½" 600.00
Holly Amber, butter dish 1,400.00
Holly Amber, cake stand 2,400.00
Holly Amber, compote, open, 4½" dia.........................850.00
Holly Amber, compote, w/lid, 6½" dia 1,445.00
Holly Amber, creamer 595.00
Holly Amber, cruet, 6½" 1,850.00
Holly Amber, plate, sq, 7½"................................745.00
Holly Amber, plate, 7¼" 650.00
Holly Amber, sauce dish, 4½" dia............................270.00
Holly Amber, shakers, orig caps, 3¼", pr 550.00
Holly Amber, sugar bowl, w/lid 750.00
Holly Amber, toothpick holder, lg 495.00
Holly Amber, toothpick holder, sm 375.00

Holly Amber tumbler, plain
rim, $350.00.

Holly Amber, tumbler, beaded rim........................500.00
Holly Amber, vase, 6"...550.00
Leaf Bracket, bowl, chocolate, 8" dia 70.00
Leaf Bracket, celery tray, chocolate, 11" 100.00
Leaf Bracket, cruet, chocolate 185.00
Leaf Bracket, nappy, chocolate 58.00
Leaf Bracket, relish, oval, chocolate, 7" 75.00
Leaf Bracket, salt shaker, chocolate........................90.00
Leaf Bracket, sugar bowl, w/lid, chocolate 145.00
Novelty, Dewey Bust, amber 160.00
Novelty, Dustpan, amber 75.00
Novelty, Trunk, wht opaque 135.00
Novelty, Wheelbarrow, teal bl 150.00
Pitcher, Ruffled Eye, amber 130.00
Pitcher, Ruffled Eye, chocolate 500.00
Pitcher, Running Deer, chocolate 450.00
Pitcher, Squirrel, chocolate 450.00
Pleat Band, cordial, canary 170.00
Sawtooth, tumbler, chocolate................................85.00
Shuttle, bowl, chocolate, 8¼" dia 405.00
Shuttle, butter dish, chocolate 800.00
Shuttle, punch cup, chocolate 95.00
Stein, deer & oak tree, chocolate 400.00
Stein, dog & child, Nile gr 320.00
Stein, outdoor drinking scene, castle, chocolate 135.00
Stein, outdoor drinking scene, Nile gr 120.00
Teardrop & Tassel, bowl, cobalt, 7¼" dia 95.00
Teardrop & Tassel, compote, w/lid, Nile gr, 4½" dia....300.00
Teardrop & Tassel, relish, oval, amber 100.00
Teardrop & Tassel, relish, oval, emerald gr 75.00
Teardrop & Tassel, sauce dish, chocolate, 4½" 165.00
Teardrop & Tassel, spooner, amber 85.00
Teardrop & Tassel, sugar bowl, w/lid, chocolate 470.00
Teardrop & Tassel, tumbler, cobalt.........................55.00
Teardrop & Tassel, tumbler, Nile gr 275.00
Toothpick holder, picture frame, amber 220.00
Toothpick holder, picture frame, chocolate 900.00
Toothpick holder, picture frame, teal bl 275.00
Toothpick holder, sheaf of wheat, amber 160.00
Toothpick holder, sheaf of wheat, teal bl 195.00
Tumbler, Uneeda Milk Biscuit, chocolate................125.00

Grueby

William Henry Grueby joined the firm of the Low Art Tile Works at the age of fifteen; and in 1894, after several years of experience in the production of architectural tiles, founded his own plant, the Grueby Faience Company, in Boston, Massachusetts. Grueby began experimenting with the idea of producing art pottery and had soon perfected a fine glaze – soft and without gloss – in shades of blue, gray, yellow, brown, and his most successful, cucumber green. In 1900 his exhibit at the Paris Exposition Universelle won him three gold medals.

Grueby pottery was hand thrown and hand decorated in the Arts and Crafts style. Vertically-thrust stylized leaves and flowers in relief were the most common decorative devices. Tiles continued to be an important product – unique (due to the matt glaze decoration) as well as durable. Grueby tiles were often a full inch thick. Obviously incompatible with the Art Nouveau style, the artware was discontinued soon after 1910. The ware is marked in one of several ways: 'Grueby Pottery, Boston, USA'; 'Grueby, Boston, Mass.'; or 'Grueby Faience.' The artware is often artist signed.

Bowl, gr & blk striations, low, incurvate rim, 2½" H....................350.00

Bowl, gr gloss, swirled, 1¼x7¾" 275.00
Bowl, gr mottle, 8 encircling tooled leaves, label, 3½x5"............600.00
Bust, Laughing Boy, gr mottle, after Donatello, 11"................ 1,800.00
Candlestick, mustard, tapered w/bulbous bobeche, 8¾"..............600.00
Paperweight, scarab, bl/brn, imp mk, 4".................400.00
Paperweight, scarab, gr mottle, imp logo/label, 4" 325.00
Tile, candle in holder/'Grueby Tile,' gr/yel, 6x5" 1,500.00
Tile, galleon in high seas, 7-color/EX detail, 9x9"................... 2,000.00
Tile, griffin, gray/gr, 8x8", EX 275.00
Tile, grove of pines/lake/mtns, 6-color/EX detail, 8x8" 2,750.00
Tile, mermaid w/mirror, orange/bl on red clay, 6x6x1" 250.00
Tile, seated monk w/viola, gr/blk on red clay, sgn MCM, 6" 275.00
Tile, star design, bl & unglazed, mk, 4"..................200.00
Tile, turtle, gr leaves on mustard, 6x6".................350.00
Tile, 2 geese entwined beneath trees, Kiichi Yameda, 4".............365.00
Vase, bl drip on sand-bsk, tooled leaves, experimental, 11" 4,000.00
Vase, bl wash on oatmeal, cylindrical, 8" 550.00
Vase, brn-gr semi-gloss, ribbed, bulbous, 21x20", EX..............4,500.00
Vase, butterscotch, wide leaves/buds, sgn Post/'06, 7x9" 6,500.00
Vase, gr, conical, 3¾" 475.00
Vase, gr, elongated leaves, cylindrical, sgn AL, 8½x4" 2,400.00
Vase, gr, leaves cvd at bulbous base, panels at neck, 8" 1,100.00
Vase, gr, long-stem buds, overlapping row of leaves, 13" 4,250.00
Vase, gr, repeating vertical lines, swollen cylinder, 7½".........1,200.00
Vase, gr, tooled leaves, encircling row of 7, #39/RE, 8x7" 2,600.00
Vase, gr, yel buds alternate w/wide leaves, shaped rim, 8" 2,400.00
Vase, gr, yel buds between wide leaves, sgn AL, 6x8", EX 3,300.00

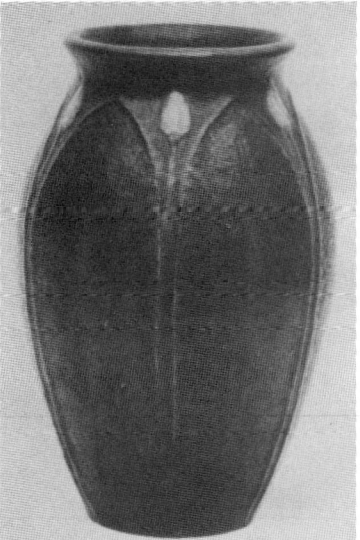

Vase, six yellow buds on green with broad leaves, artist initialed, 10", $3,000.00.

Vase, gr, 4-pinch rim, ovoid, early mk, 8"..................475.00
Vase, gr, 5 recessed panels on canister neck, 7x5", NM 450.00
Vase, gr (textured), 5 leaves cvd around bottom, 6½"................650.00
Vase, gr (thick/textured), leaves, bulbous, ftd, 3½"................475.00
Vase, gr w/yel bud & leaves, 5 repeats at rim, 12x5", NM 3,000.00
Vase, gr-gray, cylindrical, incised mk, 8½", EX...............600.00
Vase, lt bl, thrown/ribbed cylinder, imp mk, 7½"...........550.00
Vase, oatmeal, broad leaves, bulbous, artist sgn, 5", NM 7,500.00
Vase, yel, broad leaves, cylindrical neck, sgn CH, 7" 700.00
Vase, yel w/gr buds & stems, sgn ER/dtd '07, bulbous, 8½" 1,200.00
Vase/lamp base, gr, overlapping leaves, sgn, 6½x9½" 2,600.00

Gutta Percha

Gutta Percha is the plastic substance from the latex of several types of Malaysian trees. It resembles rubber but contains more resin. A patent for the use of this material in manufacturing an early type of plastic was issued in the 1850s, and it was used extensively for daguerreotype cases and picture frames. Numbers in the following listings refer to *American Miniature Case Art* by Rinhart, an excellent reference that is now out of print. When found, copies of this book usually sell for $100.00 to $150.00.

Our advisor for this category is Roberta Etter; she is listed in the Directory under England.

Case, Chess Players, 9th-plate, EX..50.00
Case, children, lady & pets, 4¾x3", EX 125.00
Case, geometrics, cavalry officer, 4th-plate, EX.............................350.00
Case, Habana, monument/palms/ships, 4th-plate, VG 85.00
Case, half-plate, Holy Family, EX 100.00
Case, jewel motif, 9th-plate, VG...20.00
Case, Mary & Her Lamb, Littlefield/Parsons, 1861, 9th-plate 45.00
Case, Masonic symbols, 6th-plate, VG 40.00

Case, The Pirate and the Lady, 4th plate, $85.00.

Case, Rob Roy design, w/2 daguerreotypes, 4x3¼x1", VG 40.00
Case, shield w/eagle/cannons/flags, 4th-plate, M...........................95.00
Case, Tryst, Rinhart #16, 4th-plate, M..95.00
Case, young farm couple, Rinhart #99, 6th-plate, EX 35.00
Frame, inner liner w/rnded corners, 15x15"..................................125.00
Pill box, warrior's head lid, 2½"..40.00
Token, Jefferson bust, Union Coffee Co, NY, 1½" 20.00

Hair Weaving

A rather unusual craft became popular during the mid-1800s. Human hair was used to make jewelry (rings, bracelets, lockets, etc.) by braiding and interlacing fine strands of hair into hollow forms with pearls and beads added for effect. Hair wreaths were also made, often using hair from deceased family members as well as the living. They were displayed in deep satin-lined frames along with mementoes of the weaver or her departed kin. The fad was abandoned before the turn of the century.

Our advisor for this category is Steven DeGenaro; he is listed in the Directory under Ohio. See also Mourning Collectibles.

Bracelet, hollow tube of woven hair w/gold mts, ca 1840 ....265.00
Brooch, coiled openwork w/14k fittings..245.00
Brooch, glass over braid, 32 seed pearls in gold fr, 1⅛"..................60.00
Charm, hair anchor w/gold wire spiral around shaft, 1½" 75.00
Charm, hair woven on fr to form cross, gold mts, ca 1840 ....95.00
Ring, 9k gold w/plaited hair band 125.00

Wreath, elaborate florals, 4-color hair, 27" fr, EX.........................135.00
Wreath, orig gilt shadow box fr, 1800s, 14x12" 125.00

Hall

The Hall China Company of East Liverpool, Ohio, was established in 1903. Their earliest product was whiteware toilet seats, mugs, jugs, etc. By 1920 their restaurant-type dinnerware and cookingware had become so successful that Hall was assured of a solid future. They continue today to be one of the country's largest manufacturers of this type of product.

Hall introduced the first of their famous teapots in 1920; new shapes and colors were added each year until about 1948, making them the largest teapot manufacturer in the world. These and the dinnerware lines of the thirties through the fifties have become popular collectibles. For more thorough study of the subject, we recommend *Hall China* by Margaret and Kenn Whitmyer; their address may be found in the Directory under Ohio.

Acacia, bowl, Radiance, 7½"..10.00
Acacia, bowl, salad; 12"...12.00
Acacia, casserole, Radiance...32.00

Blue Bell tea set: Pot, $60.00; Creamer & sugar bowl, $30.00.

Blue Blossom, batter jug, Sundial 125.00
Blue Blossom, bowl, thick rim, 7½" 30.00
Blue Blossom, casserole, oval, #100..40.00
Blue Blossom, cookie jar, Sundial 200.00
Blue Blossom, creamer, New York 25.00
Blue Blossom, teapot, Airflow 150.00
Blue Bouquet, bowl, cereal; 6"... 6.00
Blue Bouquet, bowl, fruit; 5½"... 4.00
Blue Bouquet, bowl, vegetable; rnd, 9¼" 22.00
Blue Bouquet, cup & saucer.. 8.00
Blue Bouquet, plate, 7¼"... 5.00
Blue Bouquet, platter, oval, 11¼"...16.00
Blue Bouquet, platter, oval, 13¼"...18.00
Blue Garden, batter jug, Sundial..110.00
Blue Garden, bowl, thick rim, 6"...20.00
Blue Garden, casserole, Sundial, #4..35.00
Blue Garden, custard, thick rim 10.00
Blue Garden, syrup, Sundial...90.00
Blue Garden, teapot, New York 95.00
Blue Willow, casserole, 5"...30.00
Blue Willow, casserole, 7½"..35.00

Bouquet (Zeisel), bowl, fruit; 5¾"	3.50
Bouquet (Zeisel), bowl, salad; lg, 14½"	14.00
Bouquet (Zeisel), butter dish	30.00
Bouquet (Zeisel), coffeepot, 6-cup	30.00
Cactus, ball jug, #3	45.00
Cactus, bowl, Radiance, 6"	12.00
Cactus, creamer, New York	15.00
Cactus, teapot, French	75.00
Cameo Rose, bowl, cream soup; 5"	12.00
Cameo Rose, bowl, vegetable; rnd, 9"	14.00
Cameo Rose, plate, 7¼"	4.00
Cameo Rose, platter, oval, 13¼"	14.00
Clover, ball jug, #3	35.00
Clover, bowl, Radiance, 6"	12.00
Clover, bowl, thick rim, 7½"	14.00
Clover, casserole, Radiance	30.00
Crocus, bowl, cereal; 6"	8.00
Crocus, bowl, fruit; 5½"	4.00
Crocus, bowl, oval	18.00
Crocus, gravy boat	20.00
Crocus, plate, 10"	15.00
Crocus, plate, 6"	3.00
Crocus, plate, 7¼"	6.00
Crocus, platter, oval, 13¼"	18.00
Fantasy, ball jug, #3	50.00
Fantasy, bean pot, New England, #4	70.00
Fantasy, casserole, Radiance	35.00
Fantasy, coffee server, Sundial	225.00
Fantasy, teapot, Streamline	175.00
Five Band, bowl, 6"	8.00
Five Band, carafe	70.00
Five Band, coffeepot	40.00
Five Band, cookie jar	40.00
Flamingo, cookie jar, Five Band	75.00
Flamingo, creamer, Viking	18.00
Flamingo, teapot, Streamline	110.00
Flareware, bowl, 6"	4.00
Flareware, coffee server, 15-cup	25.00
Flareware, teapot, 6-cup	35.00

Forman Family, Black & Gold: Casserole, $25.00; Tip-Pot, $55.00.

Heather Rose, bowl, oval, 9¼"	11.00
Heather Rose, bowl, soup; flat, 8"	7.00
Heather Rose, coffeepot, Terrace	30.00
Heather Rose, creamer	5.00
Heather Rose, pickle dish, 9"	8.00

Heather Rose, plate, 10"	5.50
Heather Rose, plate, 6½"	2.00
Heather Rose, platter, oval, 15½"	15.00
Heather Rose, teapot, London	20.00
Meadow Flower, ball jug, #3	45.00
Meadow Flower, bean pot, New England, #4	75.00
Meadow Flower, canister, Radiance	90.00
Meadow Flower, casserole, Radiance	28.00
Meadow Flower, custard, thick rim	10.00
Meadow Flower, teapot, Streamline	225.00
Morning Glory, bean pot, New England, #4	60.00
Morning Glory, bowl, cereal; 6"	6.00
Morning Glory, bowl, rnd, 9¼"	16.00
Morning Glory, bowl, thick rim, 7½"	14.00
Morning Glory, bowl, thick rim, 8½"	16.00
Morning Glory, casserole, Medallion	30.00
Morning Glory, casserole, thick rim	28.00
Morning Glory, cup, St Denis	14.00
Morning Glory, gravy boat	20.00
Morning Glory, platter, 13¼"	18.00
Morning Glory, pretzel jar	70.00
Morning Glory, teapot, Aladdin	65.00
Morning Glory, teapot, New York	50.00
Morning Glory, teapot, Rutherford	65.00
Mums, bowl, fruit; 5½"	4.00
Mums, bowl, oval, 10¼"	16.00
Mums, bowl, Radiance, 6"	8.00
Mums, bowl, soup; flat, 8½"	8.00
Mums, casserole, Medallion	35.00
Mums, coffeepot, Medallion	40.00
Mums, creamer, Art Deco	12.00
Mums, plate, 6"	3.50
Mums, platter, oval, 11¼"	14.00
Mums, platter, oval, 13¼"	16.00
Orange Poppy, bowl, cereal; 6"	10.00
Orange Poppy, bowl, fruit; 5½"	4.00
Orange Poppy, bowl, soup; flat, 8½"	12.00
Orange Poppy, bowl, vegetable; rnd, 9¼"	20.00
Orange Poppy, plate, 9"	10.00
Orange Poppy, platter, oval, 11¼"	16.00
Orange Poppy, platter, oval, 13¼"	18.00
Pastel Morning Glory, plate, 10"	11.00
Pastel Morning Glory, plate, 6"	3.00
Pine Cone, bowl, rnd, 9"	12.00
Pine Cone, plate, 6"	2.00
Primrose, bowl, fruit; 5¼"	2.50
Primrose, bowl, oval, 9¼"	12.00
Primrose, plate, 10"	5.00
Red Poppy, ball jug, #3	30.00
Red Poppy, bowl, cereal; 6"	8.00
Red Poppy, bowl, fruit; 5½"	4.00
Red Poppy, bowl, oval, 10¼"	16.00
Red Poppy, bowl, Radiance, 7½"	10.00
Red Poppy, bowl, rnd, 9¼"	18.00
Red Poppy, cake plate	12.00
Red Poppy, cake safe, metal	20.00
Red Poppy, casserole, Radiance	22.00
Red Poppy, coffee dispenser, metal	20.00
Red Poppy, creamer, Daniel	8.00
Red Poppy, cup	7.00
Red Poppy, gravy boat	20.00
Red Poppy, hot pad, metal	10.00
Red Poppy, jug, Radiance, #5	16.00
Red Poppy, plate, 10"	14.00

Red Poppy, plate, 6" 3.00
Red Poppy, plate, 7¼" 4.50
Red Poppy, platter, oval, 13¼" 18.00
Red Poppy, shakers, ea 6.00
Rose Parade, bowl, salad; 9" 25.00
Rose Parade, creamer, Pert.....................................12.00
Rose Parade, jug, Pert, 5"...20.00
Rose Parade, jug, Pert, 7½".......................................30.00
Rose Parade, teapot, Pert, 3-cup 25.00
Rose Parade, teapot, Pert, 6-cup 32.00
Rose White, bowl, Medallion, 6" 12.00
Rose White, bowl, Medallion, 7¼" 14.00
Rose White, bowl, salad; 9" 18.00
Rose White, creamer, Pert 10.00
Rose White, jug, Pert, 5" 13.00
Rose White, jug, Pert, 7½" 20.00
Rose White, teapot, Pert, 3-cup 20.00
Rose White, teapot, Pert, 6-cup 30.00
Royal Rose, ball jug, #3...30.00
Royal Rose, bowl, salad; 9" 20.00
Royal Rose, bowl, thick rim, 6" 10.00
Royal Rose, bowl, thick rim, 7½" 12.00
Royal Rose, casserole, thick rim 20.00
Royal Rose, teapot, Aladdin......................................95.00
Royal Rose, teapot, French..35.00
Sears' Arlington, bowl, fruit; 5¼" 2.50
Sears' Arlington, bowl, oval, 9¼" 12.00
Sears' Arlington, pickle dish, 9" 5.00
Serenade, bowl, cereal; 6" 5.50
Serenade, bowl, oval; 14.00
Serenade, platter, 11¼" 12.00
Serenade, saucer... 1.50
Shaggy Tulip, bean top, New England, #4................80.00
Shaggy Tulip, casserole, Radiance 28.00
Shaggy Tulip, pretzel jar 85.00
Shaggy Tulip, teapot, Radiance 125.00
Silhouette, ball jug, #3...50.00
Silhouette, bean pot, New England, #4 ....85.00
Silhouette, bowl, cereal; 6" 10.00
Silhouette, bowl, fruit; 5½"... 5.00
Silhouette, bowl, Medallion, 6" 11.00
Silhouette, bowl, oval 16.00
Silhouette, bowl, Radiance, 7½" 14.00
Silhouette, bowl, soup; flat, 8½" 12.00
Silhouette, casserole, Medallion................................30.00
Silhouette, creamer, Medallion 10.00
Silhouette, drip coffeepot, Medallion 135.00
Silhouette, gravy boat..22.00
Silhouette, jug, Medallion, #3 ....16.00
Silhouette, pie baker..20.00
Silhouette, plate, 7¼" 6.00
Silhouette, plate, 8¼" 7.00
Silhouette, plate, 9" 10.00
Silhouette, platter, oval, 13¼" 16.00
Silhouette, teapot, Medallion....................................35.00
Silhouette, teapot, New York.....................................85.00
Silhouette, teapot, Streamline...................................85.00
Spring (Zeisel), bowl, fruit; 5¾" 3.00
Spring (Zeisel), bowl, salad; lg, 14½" 12.00
Spring (Zeisel), coffeepot, 6-cup 30.00
Springtime, bowl, fruit; 5½" 3.50
Springtime, bowl, soup; flat, 8½".............................. 9.00
Springtime, platter, oval, 13¼"...................................14.00
Springtime, saucer.. 1.50

Stonewall, casserole, Radiance................................30.00
Stonewall, jug & cover, Radiance, #5 ....55.00
Stonewall, teapot, Radiance....................................110.00
Sunglow, ash tray 4.00
Sunglow, bowl, salad; 11¾" 9.00
Sunglow, gravy boat..10.00
Teapot, Airflow, cobalt w/gold floral 35.00
Teapot, Aladdin, Chinese red w/insert 50.00
Teapot, Automobile, maroon w/silver trim 350.00
Teapot, Basketball, Chinese red 350.00
Teapot, Connie, celadon gr 30.00
Teapot, Donut, cobalt w/gold trim 175.00
Teapot, Football, emerald gr w/gold trim 350.00
Teapot, Globe, maroon w/gold trim 65.00
Teapot, Melody, Chinese red.....................................95.00
Teapot, Murphy, turq bl, 1940s.................................35.00
Teapot, New York, cobalt w/gold trim, 6-cup............30.00
Teapot, New York, delphinium bl w/gold trim, 2-cup....22.00
Teapot, Surfside, yel w/gold trim 65.00
Teapot, World's Fair..250.00
Tulip, bowl, fruit; 5½" 4.00
Tulip, bowl, Radiance, 6" 9.00
Tulip, bowl, salad; 9" 14.00
Tulip, bowl, soup; flat, 8½" 9.00
Tulip, bowl, thick rim, 8½" 17.00
Tulip, cup 5.00
Tulip, gravy boat 20.00
Tulip, plate, 7" 5.00
Tulip, platter, 13¼" 16.00
Tulip, saucer, St Denis... 5.00
Wild Poppy, baker, oval...35.00
Wild Poppy, bean pot, New England, #3 ....75.00
Wild Poppy, bowl, Radiance, 6" 12.00
Wild Poppy, canister, Radiance 95.00
Wild Poppy, casserole, oval, #103 ....45.00
Wild Poppy, casserole, Sundial, #1 ....27.00
Wild Poppy, casserole, thick rim...............................35.00
Wild Poppy, custard, Radiance 8.00
Wild Poppy, drip jar, Radiance 25.00
Wild Poppy, teapot, French......................................125.00
Wild Poppy, teapot, Radiance 125.00
Wildfire, bowl, fruit; 5½" 3.50
Wildfire, bowl, salad; 9" 12.00
Wildfire, bowl, soup; flat, 8½" 10.00
Wildfire, bowl, thick rim, 6" 11.00
Wildfire, pie baker 16.00
Wildfire, plate, 6" 2.50
Wildfire, platter, 13¼"...15.00
Wildfire, teapot, Boston...75.00
Yellow Rose, bowl, fruit; 5½".................................... 3.50
Yellow Rose, bowl, Radiance, 7½".............................10.00
Yellow Rose, bowl, salad; 9"......................................12.00
Yellow Rose, bowl, soup; flat, 8½" 9.00
Yellow Rose, coffeepot, Norse 40.00
Yellow Rose, creamer, Norse.....................................10.00
Yellow Rose, plate, 8¼"... 4.00
Yellow Rose, platter, oval, 13¼" 14.00
Yellow Rose, teapot, New York 40.00

Hallmark

In 1973 Hallmark introduced a line of decorated molded-plastic ornaments that have recently become popular with collectors. Also of interest are their ball-type ornaments (especially those issued as part of a series) as well as their small plastic party-type favors now known as Merry Miniatures. A magazine edited by Rosie Wells, our advisor for this category, is available if you want more information; Rosie also publishes a yearly official Secondary Price Guide. Her address is listed in the Directory under Clubs, Newsletters, and Catalogs, and again under Illinois. Items listed below are assumed to be in mint condition and in the original box.

1973, Betsey Clark, #XHD110-2, ball ornament, 1st ed................95.00
1973, Betsey Clark Musicians, #XHD100-2, glass ball ornament...50.00
1974, Raggedy Ann & Andy, #QX114-1, ball ornament 50.00
1975, Adorable Santa, #QX155-1...235.00
1975, Betsy Clark Adorable ornament, #QX155-1 ....250.00
1977, Betsey Clark, #QX264-2, ball ornament, 5th ed 340.00
1980, Checking It Twice Santa, #QX158-4...............................165.00
1983, Rocking Horse, #QX417-7, 3rd ed 110.00
1985, Windows of the World, #QX490-2, 1st ed.........................75.00
1986, Twelve Days of Christmas, #QX378-6, acrylic 20.00
1988, Dated Daughter, #QX415-1...45.00

Halloween

The origin of Halloween can be traced back to the ancient practices of the Druids of Great Britain who began their New Year on the 1st of November. The Druids were pagans and their New Year's celebrations involved pagan rites and superstitions. They believed that as the old year came to an end the Devil would gather up all the demons and evil in the world and take them back to Hell with him. Witches were women who had sold their souls to the Devil and, with their black cat in attendance, flew up through their chimneys on brooms. When the Roman Catholic Church came into power in 700 A.D., they changed the holiday into a religious event called 'All Saints Day,' or 'Allhallows.' The evening before, October 31, became 'Allhallow's Eve' or 'Halloween.' Today Halloween is strictly a fun time, and Halloween items are fun to collect. Pumpkin-head candy containers of papier-mache or pressed cardboard, noisemakers, post cards with black cats and witches, costumes, and decorations are only a sampling of the variety available. See also Candy Containers.

Candy container, cat, pressed paper, 1930s, 3", VG 85.00
Candy container, jack-o'-lantern, compo, Germany, 3".............100.00

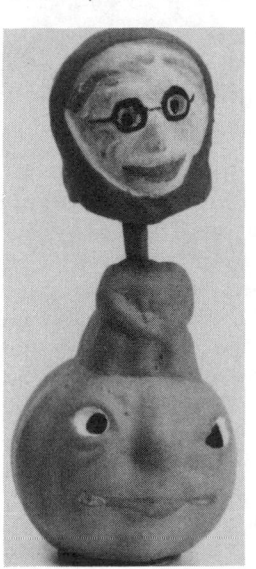

Candy container, nodding head of old lady on pumpkin face, Made in Germany, 6", NM, $245.00.

Candy container, pumpkin man, compo, 6" 165.00

Candy container, witch, cotton batting/crepe, Japan, '30s, 5" 265.00
Costume, Lucy, Peanuts character, c 1966, EX in box...................45.00
Costume, Superman, Ben Cooper, 1958, MIB.............................100.00
Decoration, cat in moon, cb, emb, 10", EX 45.00
Decoration, jack-o'-lantern, crepe paper, Dennison, M in pkg.......65.00
Decoration, skeleton, cb, metal rivet joints, old, 23x23" 65.00
Decoration, witch, diecut, Germany, 2".......................................35.00
Decoration, witch, paper, accordion type, USA, '30s, 27" 45.00
Figurine, pumpkinhead girl holds cat, wht bsk, 6" 45.00
Game, Halloween Pie, Stunt & Fortune, 6" dia............................45.00
Jack-O'-Lantern, papier-mache, 4½" 48.00
Jack-O'-Lantern, papier-mache, 6½" 55.00
Jack-O'-Lantern, pressed cb, orig face insert, 5", NM 65.00
Lantern, cat's face, blk pressed cb, orig insert, 6" 75.00
Lantern, cat's face, papier-mache, Germany, 6", EX 95.00
Nodder, ghost, compo, orange pumpkin face, Germany, 5½".......145.00
Noisemaker, blk devil, litho on tin, wood hdl, 5", EX 45.00
Noisemaker, Blk man w/guitar on paddle shape, EX.....................65.00
Noisemaker, cat face on front, litho on tin, wood hdl, 7" 45.00
Noisemaker, cb paddle w/2 witch clappers, Germany, EX 45.00
Noisemaker, children at fair, tin, wood hdl, Kirchhaf, 1928...........35.00
Noisemaker, clown & girl dance, metal w/wood hdl, rnd, USA 15.00
Noisemaker, clowns playing drums, litho on tin, USA..................20.00
Noisemaker, drum on stick w/rattles, wood/paper, 8", EX.............65.00
Noisemaker, lg clown, 2 clappers, pan shape, Kirchhaf USA 35.00
Noisemaker, sq w/hdl, 2 clappers w/wooden balls 20.00
Noisemaker, wood, rachet style, Germany, 6"..............................65.00
Noisemaker, wooden horn, Czechoslovakia, EX 35.00
Noisemaker, 3 boys & girl make noise, Kirchhaf USA..................25.00
Noisemaker, 5 girls in mc clothes, litho on tin, Barone.................15.00
Nut cup, crepe paper pumpkin w/face, 1940s, 3" 12.00
Nut cup, jack-o'-lantern, papier-mache 65.00
Nut cup, witch diecut on blk & orange paper...............................25.00
Seals, emb evil faces on lg sheet, early, M...................................25.00
Skull, porc, moveable jaw 135.00
Tambourine, pumpkin face, Chein, EX..55.00
Toy, witch, pot metal, Mother Witch, Tommy Toys, 2½", EX........45.00

Hampshire

The Hampshire Pottery Company was established in 1871 in Keene, New Hampshire, by James Scollay Taft. Their earliest products were redware and stoneware utility items such as jugs, churns, crocks, and flowerpots. In 1878 they produced majolica ware which met with such success that they began to experiment with the idea of manufacturing art pottery. By 1883 they had developed a Royal Worcester type of finish which they applied to vases, tea sets, powder boxes, and cookie jars. It was also utilized for souvenir items that were decorated with transfer designs prepared from photographic plates.

Cadmon Robertson, brother-in-law of Taft, joined the company in 1904 and was responsible for developing their famous matt glazes. Colors included shades of green, brown, red, and blue. Early examples were of earthenware, but eventually the body changed to semi-porcelain. Some of his designs were marked with an M in a circle as a tribute to his wife, Emoretta. Robertson died in 1914, leaving a void impossible to fill. Taft sold the business in 1916 to George Morton, who continued to use the matt glazes that Robertson had developed. After a temporary halt in production during WWI, Morton returned to Keene and re-equipped the factory with the machinery needed to manufacture hotel china and floor tile. Because of the expense involved in transporting coal to fire the kilns, Morton found he could not compete with potteries of Ohio and New Jersey who were able to utilize locally available natural gas. He was forced to close the plant in 1923.

Basket, creamware, triple hdl, red ink stamp, 4¾" **75.00**
Bowl, gr matt, block letters w/circle M mk, 2x4" **80.00**
Compote, gr matt, hdls, imp mk, 5½" **100.00**
Ewer, gr gloss, 6½" **95.00**
Ewer, gr matt, mk JST&Co, Keene NH, 9" **185.00**
Lamp, gr matt, hooded, electrified, circle M mk..........................**275.00**
Mug, gr matt, 6" **135.00**

Vase, antique green matt, 8½", $145.00.

Vase, feathered bl matt, leaves w/trailing stems, 8½" **450.00**
Vase, gr matt, Arts & Crafts design, hdls, ped ft, 5½" **140.00**
Vase, gr matt, bulbous base, inscised mk, 5" **160.00**
Vase, gr matt, emb lily pads at shoulder, squat, 6" dia **100.00**
Vase, gr matt, hdls spiral ¼-way around body, 15", NM.............**325.00**
Vase, gr matt, Indian motif, bowl form, artist sgn, 2x6" **95.00**
Vase, gr matt, molded leaves, hdls, 8".....................................**150.00**
Vase, gr matt, repeating tulips, tapered cylinder, 9", NM **350.00**
Vase, gr matt, vertical lotus leaves, 7" **175.00**
Vase, gr mottle, emb leaves/vines, ftd trumpet form, 15" **325.00**

Handel

Philip Handel was best known for the art glass lamps he produced at the turn of the century. His work is similar to the Tiffany lamps of the same era. Handel made gas and electric lamps with both leaded glass and reverse-painted shades. Chipped ice shades with a texture similar to overshot glass were also produced. Shades signed by artists such as Bailey, Palme, and Parlow are highly valued.

China and glassware decorated by Handel are rare and command high prices on today's market. Teroma is a term used to describe glassware decorated on the obverse (outside) with paint that has a sandy finish. Many of the chinaware blanks were supplied by Limoges.

Lamps

Boudoir, pnt 7" winter forest sgn sqd shade; gr-patina std........ **1,700.00**
Boudoir, rvpt fir trees/snow dome shade; unmk std, 14½" **900.00**
Boudoir, rvpt wisteria 6-sided 8" shade #6709; labeled std....... **2,000.00**
Boudoir, rvpt 7" Japanese-motif yel sgn shade; metal std **700.00**
Boudoir, rvpt 7" roses sgn shade; foliate-emb bronze std **2,100.00**
Boudoir, rvpt 7" winter forest unsgn sqd shade; bronzed std **1,100.00**
Boudoir, satin 7" bell-shape shade w/swags; floral-emb std..........**400.00**
Boudoir, Teroma 7" scenic sqd shade; #6154A bronze std, 16" . **1,850.00**
Desk, pnt 12" dragonflies open-top bell shade; slim std **1,600.00**
Desk, rvpt 18" mtn/trees sunset shade; sgn top/base, 24" **2,750.00**

Floor, rvpt 6" ribbed shade w/roses; sgn std w/3 petal ft **2,500.00**
Floor, Steuben dome shade suspended in bell-form fr, 56" **2,100.00**
Floor, unsgn art glass shade w/in harp std, sgn base, 57" **700.00**
Lily pond, lg & sm ldgl gr/wht lily shades; leafy base, 29"........ **1,200.00**
Night light, ribbed frosted crackle shade w/HP roses, 7" **200.00**
Piano, cylinder shade, filigree/brn slag, harp std, 14" **1,300.00**
Shade, Teroma 14" scenic sgn/#6192; metal rim **2,500.00**
Table, bronzed metal 14" octagonal shade; slim std, 21" **300.00**
Table, etched/HP 18" peacocks shade by Bedigie; 3-leg std **3,300.00**
Table, ldgl bud/leaf sgn cone shade; Hampshire base, 21"........ **2,750.00**
Table, ldgl 16" banded dogwood unsgn shade; bronze std, 22". **2,000.00**
Table, ldgl 16" floral-belted unsgn shade; bronze std, 23" **1,400.00**
Table, ldgl 16" hibiscus sgn shade; sgn std, 25".........................**2,600.00**
Table, ldgl 19" apple blossom sgn shade; sgn base, 24"............. **4,750.00**
Table, ldgl 20" simple geometric shade; slim sgn std, 21" **950.00**
Table, palm tree filigree over slag shade; sgn fluted base.......... **2,200.00**
Table, pine cone filigree, gr/tan slag shade; 'bamboo' std......... **2,700.00**
Table, pnt 14" landscape sgn shade; baluster std **1,500.00**
Table, pnt 14" scenic shade; floriform-base std, 17", EX **5,500.00**
Table, pnt 18" stylized floral sgn dome shade; baluster std....... **1,600.00**
Table, pnt 18" stylized floral sgn shade; bronze urn std **2,300.00**
Table, pnt 18" sunset forest sgn shade; baluster base **2,400.00**
Table, pnt 18" windmill/red sky sgn shade; copper-tone std..... **1,700.00**
Table, pnt/rvpt 18" pines & river sgn shade; Oriental std **3,700.00**
Table, rvpt 16" blkberry-border sgn shade; 3-scroll std **3,500.00**
Table, rvpt 16" winter dusk scene sgn shade; bronze std **1,900.00**
Table, rvpt 17" scenic shade; webb-molded hdld std, unmk **1,800.00**

Lamp, reverse-painted scenic unmarked shade, cloth label on base, 17", $1,870.00.

Table, rvpt 18" Art Deco sgn cone shade; hdld vasiform std ... **3,200.00**
Table, rvpt 18" autumn sunset sgn shade; textured std **5,600.00**
Table, rvpt 18" Blk-Eye Susan band sgn shade; bronze std....... **1,900.00**
Table, rvpt 18" floral tapestry sgn shade; 3-eagle std **1,800.00**
Table, rvpt 18" rose-border yel sgn shade; baluster std **1,600.00**
Table, rvpt 18" stylized floral shade; Persian tripod std **1,200.00**
Table, rvpt 18" trees/lake shade, dk gr/orange; mk std..................**950.00**
Table, Teroma 10" parrots shade; slender std #7073, 15" **8,500.00**
Table, Teroma 16" marsh shade sgn Bailey, 23" **3,000.00**
Table, Teroma 18" scenic shade; leaf-cast std #979664, 26"..... **3,850.00**
Torch, pnt flowers on yel 7" cylinder shade; std w/prisms **400.00**

Miscellaneous

Candlestick, copper, studs hold top/base to stem, 10", pr **550.00**
Humidor, dancing ballerina on gr/brn, metal lid w/pipe, #d........**550.00**

Humidor, horse head, pipe finial, flattened sphere, 6" dia............450.00
Humidor, no decor, melon lobed, squat 250.00
Humidor, owls, tapered form, 7" dia...600.00
Humidor, squirrel, pipe finial, flattened sphere, 6" dia 500.00
Humidor, stag, pipe finial, 5½" dia..525.00
Vase, Teroma, lake/mtns, artist sgn, cylindrical, 8" 2,200.00

Teroma vase, landscape with birds in fall trees, signed Handel, 11", $1,900.00.

Harker

The Harker Pottery was established in East Liverpool, Ohio, in 1840. Their earliest product was yellowware and Rockingham produced from local clay. After 1900 whiteware was made from imported materials. The plant eventually grew to be a large manufacturer of dinnerware and kitchenware, employing as many as three hundred people. It closed in 1972 after it was purchased by the Jeannette Glass Company. Perhaps their best-known lines were their Cameo wares, decorated with white silhouettes in a cameo effect on contrasting solid colors. Floral silhouettes are standard, but other designs were also used. Blue and pink are the most often found background hues; a few pieces are found in yellow.

Teapot, $40.00; Carafe with embossed florals, 7", $25.00; Tumbler in ash tray coaster, $15.00 – all in shaded medium green gloss.

Baker, Petit Point, 9" 17.50

Bean pot, Amy, ind..4.00
Bowl, Cameo, 6"...7.50
Bowl, Cameo, 7¾"..10.00
Bowl, Mallow, 6"..6.00
Bowl, mixing; Petit Point, nested set of 3: 6", 7", 8"...................27.50
Bowl, vegetable; Amy...10.00
Cake plate, Laurenton, lg 6.00
Cake plate, Modern Tulip, 10¾"..7.00
Cake plate, Petit Point 10.00
Casserole, Deco Dahlia, w/lid 15.00
Casserole, Jubilee, w/lid 12.00
Creamer, Cameo 6.00
Creamer, Chesterton...3.00
Creamer & sugar bowl, Orange Tulip w/Wheat, w/lid 12.00
Cup & saucer, Chesterton 5.00
Cup & saucer, Mallow 5.00
Cup & saucer, Petit Point 4.50
Custard, Deco Dahlia...4.00
Drip jar, Deco Dahlia, w/lid...15.00
Gravy boat, Chesterton 5.00
Jug, water; Orange Tulip w/Wheat, w/lid 25.00
Jug, water; Petit Point, w/lid...30.00
Jug, water; Rose Cameo, w/lid 30.00
Pie plate, Amy 10.00
Pie plate, Petit Point, 9"...16.00
Pie plate, Tulip 15.00
Pie server, Modern Tulip..12.50
Pie server, Petit Point 12.50
Pitcher, Rose Cameo, 5¾" 15.00
Plate, Deco Dahlia, 10"...7.50
Plate, Mallow, 7" 3.00
Plate, Petit Point, dinner sz 4.00
Plate, Springtime, tab hdls, 6¾"..3.00
Platter, Deco Dahlia, 13½" 11.00
Platter, Deco Dahlia, 15½" 15.00
Platter, Petit Point, 11¾" 10.00
Refrigerator set, Petit Point, 3-stack..45.00
Rolling pin, Amy...72.50
Rolling pin, Mallow..75.00
Rolling pin, Modern Tulip 60.00
Rolling pin, Orange Tulip w/Wheat 75.00
Rolling pin, Petit Point 75.00
Rolling pin, Red Apple...45.00
Rolling pin, Taverne...95.00
Shakers, Chesterton, pr 6.00
Shakers, Deco Dahlia, lg..14.00
Shakers, Orange Tulip, pr 6.00
Spoon, Mallow 16.00
Spoon, Petit Point 16.00
Spoon, Red Apple...12.00
Sugar bowl, Cameo, w/lid 7.50
Teapot, Deco Dahlia, 6-cup...20.00
Teapot, Modern Tulip...15.00
Teapot, Orange Tulip w/Wheat 15.00
Teapot, Rose Cameo 25.00

Harlequin

Harlequin dinnerware, produced by the Homer Laughlin China Company of Newell, West Virginia, was introduced in 1938. It was a lightweight ware made in maroon, mauve blue, and spruce green, as well as all the Fiesta colors except ivory (see Fiesta). It was marketed exclusively by the Woolworth stores, who considered it to be their all-time best seller. For this reason, they contracted with Homer Laughlin to reissue Harlequin to commemorate their 100th anniversary in 1979. Although three of the original glazes were used in the reissue, the few serving pieces that were made were restyled, and collectors found the new line to be no threat to their investments.

The Harlequin animals, including a fish, lamb, cat, penguin, duck, and donkey, were made during the early 1940s, also for the dime-store trade. Today these are very desirable to collectors of Homer Laughlin China.

In the listings that follow, the values designated 'high' are for these colors: maroon, gray, medium green, spruce green, chartreuse, dark green, rose, red, and light green, with the latter five perhaps 20% under listed prices. 'Low' listings are for examples in mauve blue, turquoise, and yellow. *The Story of Fiesta* by Sharon and Bob Huxford is available in its sixth edition and contains a more thorough study of this subject. Available from Collector Books or your local bookstore.

Animals, mavericks	25.00
Animals, non-standard colors	100.00
Animals, standard colors	50.00
Ash tray, basketweave, high	35.00
Ash tray, basketweave, low	22.00
Ash tray, regular, high	38.00
Ash tray, regular, low	25.00
Bowl, '36s oatmeal; high	10.00
Bowl, '36s oatmeal; low	7.00
Bowl, '36s; high	18.00
Bowl, '36s; low	10.00
Bowl, cream soup; high	12.00
Bowl, cream soup; low	9.00
Bowl, fruit; high, 5½"	7.00
Bowl, fruit; low, 5½"	4.00
Bowl, ind salad; high	15.00
Bowl, ind salad; low	10.00
Bowl, mixing; Kitchen Kraft, mauve bl, 8"	85.00
Bowl, mixing; Kitchen Kraft, red or spruce gr, 6"	55.00
Bowl, mixing; Kitchen Kraft, yel, 10"	85.00
Bowl, nappy; high, 9"	18.00
Bowl, nappy; low, 9"	11.00
Bowl, oval baker, high	18.00
Bowl, oval baker, low	13.00
Butter dish, high, ½-lb	70.00
Butter dish, low, ½-lb	55.00
Candle holder, high, pr	150.00
Candle holder, low, pr	120.00
Casserole, w/lid, high	65.00
Casserole, w/lid, low	45.00
Creamer, high lip, any color	40.00
Creamer, ind; high	13.00
Creamer, ind; low	11.00
Creamer, novelty, high	16.00
Creamer, novelty, low	11.00
Creamer, regular, high	9.00
Creamer, regular, low	7.00
Cup, demitasse; high	33.00
Cup, demitasse; low	21.00
Cup, lg, any color	65.00
Egg cup, dbl, high	16.00
Egg cup, dbl, low	11.00
Egg cup, single, high	19.00
Egg cup, single, low	13.00
Gravy boat, high	17.00
Gravy boat, low	11.00
Marmalade, any color	80.00

Nut dish, basketweave, orig color	6.50
Perfume bottle, any color	50.00
Pitcher, service water; high	41.00
Pitcher, service water; low	28.00
Pitcher, 22-oz jug, high	35.00
Pitcher, 22-oz jug, low	18.00
Plate, deep; high	16.00
Plate, deep; low	10.00
Plate, high, 10"	15.00
Plate, high, 6"	4.00
Plate, high, 7"	6.00
Plate, high, 9"	10.00
Plate, low, 10"	10.00
Plate, low, 6"	3.00
Plate, low, 7"	4.00
Plate, low, 9"	6.00
Platter, high, 11"	12.00
Platter, high, 13"	17.00
Platter, low, 11"	7.00
Platter, low, 13"	12.00
Saucer/ash tray, high	40.00
Saucer/ash tray, ivory	50.00
Saucer/ash tray, low	35.00
Shakers, high, pr	11.00
Shakers, low, pr	8.00
Sugar bowl, w/lid, high	13.00
Sugar bowl, w/lid, low	9.00

Syrup pitcher, any color, $120.00.

Teacup, high	8.00
Teacup, low	6.00
Teapot, high	55.00
Teapot, low	40.00
Tray, relish; mixed colors	140.00
Tumbler, high	32.00
Tumbler, low	23.00

Hatpin Holders

Most hatpin holders were made from 1860 to 1920 to coincide with the period during which hatpins were popularly in vogue. The taller types were required to house the long hatpins necessary to secure the large hats that were in style from 1890 to 1914. They were usually porcelain, either decorated by hand or by transfer with florals or scenics, although some were clever figurals. Glass examples are rare, and those of slag or carnival glass are especially valuable.

If you are interested in collecting or dealing in hatpins or hatpin holders, you will find that authority Lillian Baker has several fine books available on the subject, including *Hatpins and Hatpin Holders*, complete with beautiful color illustrations and current market values. She is listed in the Directory under California. For information concerning the International Club for Collectors of Hatpins and Hatpin Holders, see the Clubs, Newsletters, and Catalogs section of the Directory. Our advisor for this category is Robert Larsen; he is listed in the Directory under Nebraska.

Austria, HP florals, saucer type	**65.00**
Daisy & Button, silver top w/pinholes, rare, 8"	**300.00**
Germany, lustre roses, stick type, attached saucer	**65.00**
Jasperware, bl w/wht Grecian figures	**125.00**
Limoges, HP floral, rare, 9"	**350.00**
MZ Austria, floral, +stickpin holder & ring tree on tray	**325.00**
Nippon, Oriental figures, good mk, 4½"	**65.00**

Pickard, floral with gold trim, 4½", $135.00.

Rosenthall, gr china w/silver overlay	**225.00**
Royal Bayreuth, figural owl, shades of gray	**350.00**
Royal Bayreuth, roses, yel on gr, w/tray, mk	**175.00**
Royal Bayreuth, Santa figural, pin holes in bag, 4½"	**800.00**
RS Prussia, floral, 3-hdl, red mk, 3¾" base, 4"	**350.00**
RS Prussia, hanging basket decor, w/tray & lid	**225.00**
RS Prussia, roses on lustre, scalloped base, mk, 4¾"	**275.00**
Schafer & Vater, Nouveau lady's face, lav & gr bsk	**95.00**
Suhl Prussia, florals, gold border, 5"	**80.00**
Unmk china, bear figural by stump, HP, w/pin tray	**165.00**
Unmk china, dbl-face figural, lady 1 side, man on other	**250.00**

Hatpins

A hatpin was used to securely fasten a hat to the hair and head of the wearer. Hatpins, measuring from 4" to 12" in length, were worn from approximately 1850 to 1920. During the Art Deco period, hatpins became ornaments rather than the decorative functional jewels that they had been. The hatpin period reached its zenith in 1913 just prior to World War I, which brought about a radical change in women's headdress and fashion. About that time, women began to scorn the bonnet and adopt 'the hat' as a symbol of their equality. The hatpin was made of every natural and manufactured element in a myriad of designs that challenge the imagination. They were contrived to serve every fashion need and complement the milliner's art. Collectors often con-

centrate on a specific type: hand-painted porcelains, sterling silver, commemoratives, sporting activities, carnival glass, Art Nouveau and/or Art Deco designs, Victorian Gothics with mounted stones, exquisite rhinestones, engraved and brass-mounted escutcheon heads, gold and gems, or simply primitive types made in the Victorian parlor. Some collectors prefer the long pin-shanks while others select only those on tramblants or nodder-type pin-shanks.

If you are interested in collecting or dealing in hatpins, see the information in the Hatpin Holders introduction concerning reference books and a national collectors' club. Our advisor for this category is Robert Larsen; he is listed in the Directory under Nebraska.

Key: cab — cabochon

Art Nouveau, solid gold head & shank, 4 faces	**400.00**
Brass, leaf & flower mt, 22mm gr stone in powder lid, 9¾"	**250.00**
Brass, ornate filigree, vanity w/puff & mirror intact, 11½"	**295.00**
Carnival glass, butterfly, gr irid	**75.00**
Celluloid w/rhinestones	**12.50**

Plique-a-jour butterfly, blue and green, 1¼" wingspan, 6¼" shank, $475.00. Photo by Robert Larsen.

Eagle figural, nodder w/rhinestones, 1½" dia	**175.00**
Satsuma, rtcl, garden decor, 1¼" dia	**165.00**
Sterling, cherub, ¾" dia	**50.00**

Haviland

The Haviland China Company was organized in 1840 by David Haviland, a New York china importer. His search for a pure white, non-porous porcelain led him to Limoges, France, where natural deposits of suitable clay had already attracted numerous china manufacturers. The fine china he produced there was translucent and meticulously decorated, with each piece fired in an individual sagger.

It has been estimated that as many as 60,000 chinaware patterns were designed, each piece marked with one of several company backstamps. 'H. & Co.' was used until 1890 when a law was enacted making it necessary to include the country of origin. Various marks have been used since that time including 'Haviland, France'; 'Haviland & Co. Limoges'; and 'Decorated by Haviland & Co.' Various associations with family members over the years have resulted in changes in management as well as company name. In 1892 Theodore Haviland left the firm to start his own business. Some of his ware was marked 'Mont Mery.' Later logos included a horseshoe, a shield, and various uses of his initials and name. In 1941 this branch moved to the United States. Wares produced here are marked 'Theodore Haviland, N.Y.' or 'Made In America.'

Though it is their dinnerware lines for which they are most famous, during the 1880s and 1890s they also made exquisite art pottery using a technique of underglaze slip decoration called Barbotine, which had been invented by Ernest Chaplet. In 1885 Haviland bought the formula and hired Chaplet to oversee its production. The technique involved mixing heavy white clay slip with pigments to produce a compound of the same consistency as oil paints. The finished product actually resembled oil paintings of the period, the texture achieved through the application of the heavy medium to the clay body in much the same manner as an artist would apply paint to his canvas. Primarily the body used with this method was a low-fired faience, though they also produced stoneware.

Authority Mary Frank Gaston has compiled a lovely book, *Haviland Collectibles and Objects of Art,* with full-color illustrations and current values; you will find her address in the Directory under Texas. Numbers in the listings below refer to pattern books by Arlene Schleiger.

Ash tray, man in tux, Pigall's Paris-Montmartre, 4½x3" **48.00**
Basket, bonbon, Fantaisie Romeo form, 1904-1920s....................**135.00**
Basket, floral/clover, gold trim/hdl, 1893-1930, 4x5¼" **130.00**
Berry set, violets, 6-pc..**70.00**
Bouillon, florals w/gold, Crystal form, w/lid, 1893-1930................**95.00**
Bouillon, roses w/gold, Portia form, w/lid, 1893-1930 ....**200.00**
Bowl, vegetable; Ganga, w/lid, octagonal **145.00**
Bowl, vegetable; Princess, oval, w/lid...**40.00**
Box, crouching monkey figural, yel/wht, EM Sandoz, 7" **600.00**
Bust, Cavalier, bsk, sgn Champigny, 11½x10½" **4,500.00**
Butter pat, florals, Nenuphar form, 1876-1889, 3" sq **20.00**
Candlestick, Ranson shape, 1893-1930, 7".................................**115.00**
Chamberstick, rosebuds/flowers, Marseille form, 3x5½" **135.00**
Chocolate pot, Baltimore Rose, 1893-1930, 8" **485.00**
Chocolate pot, floral & gold, St Germaine form, 1903-25, 11" ...**165.00**

Chocolate pot, floral and gold decor on 'Star' form, 8", $175.00.

Chocolate pot, florals w/gold, Henry II form, 1876-1889, 8½" **165.00**
Chocolate pot, gold band/spout/hdl, 1876-1930, 5" **95.00**
Chocolate pot, mc florals, Epi Haut form, 1876-1889, 7¼"............**85.00**
Chocolate pot, pk florals w/gold, emb scallops, 1890s, 5¼" **80.00**
Chocolate pot, Star form, ca 1893-1930, 8" **160.00**
Chocolate set, Baltimore Rose, Ranson, 1893-1930, 12-pc.....**2,800.00**
Chocolate set, florals, Marseille, 1888-1896, 10-pc....................**850.00**
Coffeepot, floral sprays, Pompador, 1888-1896, 8½" **165.00**
Coffeepot, Norma, Ranson form, 1893-1930, 10½" **185.00**
Coffeepot, scalloped spout, gold trim, 1850s-1865, 8" **70.00**
Coffeepot, undecorated, ca 1850s-1865, rare, 10½" **425.00**

Coffeepot, wide gold bands, curved hdls, 1850s-1865, 9" **70.00**
Compote, lacy, rtcl, 2-pc, 1876-1889, 7½x9"............................**235.00**
Compote, rtcl, gold trim, 2 mks, ca 1880s, 5x9" **175.00**
Cracker jar, cobalt w/gold, Marseille, 1888-1896, 8" **175.00**
Creamer & sugar bowl, Cannele, w/lid, 4", 3½" **145.00**
Creamer & sugar bowl, dessert; roses w/gold, 1893-1930 ....**155.00**
Creamer & sugar bowl, Rosamonde **23.00**
Creamer & sugar bowl, wht w/gold band, 1850s-1865 ....**155.00**
Cup & saucer, demi; bird & floral, gold beads, 1876-1930............**50.00**
Cup & saucer, demi; floral w/gold, Silver form, 1893-1930 ....**50.00**
Cup & saucer, demi; florals, Cannele form, 1876-1889 ....**95.00**
Cup & saucer, Ganga **30.00**
Cup & saucer, gold swags, Crystal form, ped ft, 1893-1930 ....**95.00**
Cup & saucer, pk floral in center, Ranson form **80.00**
Cup & saucer, Rosalinde, French **30.00**
Dish, florals w/gold, leaf form, 1876-1889, 9¼" **70.00**
Dish, lobster amid 2 half shells form, 1893-1930, 11½" W **255.00**
Egg cup, florals w/gold at rim & ft, 1904-1920s, 3" **50.00**
Egg cup & saucer, Club Ware, US Navy emblem, 1880s-1890s **50.00**
Ewer, rose & daises HP over relief, 1865-1875, 8" **150.00**
Ferner, roses w/gold, 6-sided, w/liner, 1893-1930, 2½x7½" **250.00**
Figurine, cockatoo, preening, on perch, wht, EM Sandoz, 8".......**385.00**
Figurine, curled-up cat, yel/wht, EM Sandoz, 9½" L **1,300.00**
Footbath, ornate gold-trimmed hdls, 1850s-1865, 11x21x13" **625.00**
Gravy boat, #575 ....**35.00**
Hair receiver, florals w/gold, 4-lobed, 1893-1930, 5" **145.00**
Invalid feeder, no decor, whiteware, 1893-1930, 2¼x6½" **50.00**
Jardiniere, Terra Cotta, sculpted flowers, unsgn, 1873-1882....**1,600.00**
Jug, claret; florals/insects, Vermicella, 1876-1889, 5½"................**125.00**
Jug, stoneware, florals w/gold, sgn, 1880s, 5" **850.00**
Knife rest, Sandoz, fish figural, 1904-1920s, 5" L.......................**300.00**
Match box, florals, Marseille shape, 1888-1896, 1x5" **70.00**
Mayonnaise, leaf form w/gold, 1904-1920s, w/7" underplate **80.00**
Mustache cup & saucer, florals, Marseille form, 1876-1889 ....**125.00**
Mustard, florals, Ranson form, 1888-1896, w/underplate..............**115.00**
Mustard, florals, St Cloud form, early 1890s, w/underplate............**95.00**
Pancake dish, florals, Rouen form, w/lid, 1904-1920s, 10½" **120.00**
Pitcher, milk; Norma, Ranson form, 1893-1930, 7" **135.00**
Pitcher, Portia form, ca 1893-1930..**155.00**
Pitcher, red band w/gold, 1865-1875, 15", +12" bowl **900.00**
Pitcher, water & trees, Ranson, 1888-1896, 9" **175.00**
Plate, #24, Ranson blank, salad sz **10.00**
Plate, #856, dinner sz..**21.00**
Plate, Diana, 7½" **30.00**
Plate, fish center, F Bracquemond, 1876-1889, 8½", pr..............**165.00**
Plate, floral w/gold trim, HP, ca 1893-1930................................**60.00**
Plate, Grant's Tomb, Let Us Have Peace, 1880s-1890s, 9"...........**115.00**
Plate, huntsman on horsebk, sgn Jean Dufy, 9½" **140.00**
Plate, Montreux, Theo, luncheon sz **20.00**
Plate, oyster; marine decor, 1876-1880, 9" **85.00**
Plate, oyster; shell design, HP in factory, 1876-1880, 9" **110.00**
Plate, Rosalinde, American, dinner sz, 10¼" **18.00**
Plate, salad; Hotel China, kidney shape, 1925-1940s, 8¼" **80.00**
Plate, Silver Anniversary, dinner sz..**20.00**
Platter, floral, pk on wht, gold & wht bows, Limoges, 16x11"........**45.00**
Platter, floral, pk on wht w/gold stalks, Limoges, 11¼"..................**55.00**
Platter, Ganga, 14"...**75.00**
Platter, Princess, 12"...**35.00**
Platter, RR China, 2 narrow floral borders, 11½x7¾" **375.00**
Platter, Silver Anniversary, 14" **65.00**
Pudding dish, gold trim, hdld liner, 1904-1920s **165.00**
Ramekin, florals, Star, 1893-1930, 3½", +5½" saucer **45.00**
Salt cellar, Norma, Ranson form, 1893-1930, ⅝x2" **35.00**
Sardine box, HP, fish form hdl, ca 1888-1896, 1¼x4½" **90.00**

Spooner, Hotel China, for J Reed Whipple, 1893, 6".................135.00
Sugar bowl, #625A, w/lid 30.00
Tea set, forget-me-not/gold medallions, 1894 mk, for 10 .... 1,500.00
Teapot, emb decor, gold trim, bud finial, 1850s-1865 ....85.00
Teapot, penguin figural, artist sgn, Sandoz, 1904-20s, 5¾" 500.00
Teapot, pk floral/gr ivy, ca 1893-1930, 5".....................................70.00
Teapot, pk florals, Frank Haviland mk, 5", +cr/sug.......................300.00
Tray, Drop Rose, wht, ca 1876-1930, 15¾x10¾"..........................475.00
Tureen, Napkin Fold form, shell finial/hdls, 8¼x12½"..................175.00
Tureen, vegetable; gold wheat/bands, w/lid, 1865-70, 7x11".........115.00
Tureen, wht w/gold decor, Marseille form, 1888-1896, 9x12" 250.00
Vase, cobalt w/gold decor & hdls, Marseille form, 13¼" 900.00
Vase, cream bsk finish, Marseille form, 1876-1889, 8½" 250.00
Vase, grapes, sgn, non-factory decor, hdls, 1893-1930, 12".........200.00
Vase, HP florals ea side, 3-hdl, 1893-1930, 11"........................ 1,100.00
Vase, HP pk/bl marbled effect, ca 1893-1930, 7"............................85.00
Vase, sculpted florals, hdls, sgn Lindeneher, 16½" 3,200.00
Vase, Terra Cotta, gold/silver on blk lacquer, 12x13" 2,250.00
Vase, Terra Cotta, mc florals on brn, 3-ftd, 1873-1882, 5".........450.00
Vase, Terra Cotta, sculpted flowers, 12", pr............................. 1,000.00
Wash set, red bands w/gold trim, 7-pc 850.00

Hawkes

Thomas Hawkes established his factory in Corning, New York, in 1880. He developed many beautiful patterns of cut glass, two of which were awarded the Grand Prize at the Paris Exposition in 1889. By the end of the century, his company was renowned for the finest in cut glass production. The company logo was a trefoil form enclosing a hawk in each of the two bottom lobes with a fleur-de-lis in the center.

Our advisors for this catgory are Jeanette and Marvin Stofft; they are listed in the Directory under Indiana.

Bell, strw dmns...225.00
Bowl, band of hobstars/X-hatching/fan, serrated rim, 10" 295.00
Bowl, Brunswick, 10"...500.00
Bowl, celeste bl w/gold rim band, intaglio floral/swag, 8".............175.00
Bowl, chain-of-hobstar rim, allover mitre-cut panels, 8".............425.00
Bowl, Chrysanthemum, scalloped, shallow, att, 8" 275.00
Bowl, floral, octagonal, 7¾" 100.00
Bowl, hobstar band, star center, shallow, flared rim, 8" 155.00
Bowl, hobstar/X-hatches/fan, hobstar base, serrated rim, 8".........180.00
Bowl, hobstars/florals, serrated rim, 8" 100.00
Bowl, Russian w/3 bull's eyes ea end, serrated rim, 12" L 725.00
Bowl, sunburst center w/hobstars & florals, 8"............................145.00
Box, leaf/vine eng, apple gr, 3" dia 130.00
Carafe, hobstars/fans, 8" 150.00
Compote, bowl/bottom of base: Harvard, prism-cut stem, 8x7"...195.00
Compote, hobstars/X-hatch/fan, folded rim, cut stem, 9x7" 350.00
Creamer & sugar bucket, allover step cuttings 285.00
Cruet, floral eng, mk sterling/glass stopper, Pat 1910 ....145.00
Decanter, Harvard body, prism-cut stem, faceted stopper, 12" 395.00
Dish, florals, ftd, 2⅛x6", pr..125.00
Flower center, Gravic, allover florals, serrated rim, 7x9".............550.00
Goblet, pineapple & fan, knob stem, set of 6 ....300.00
Lamp, kero; Gravic, hobstar/floral chain, cut-out base, 8" 220.00
Pitcher, cocktail; flat dmn points, silver mts/stick, 8½"...............125.00
Tray, nut; intaglio flower baskets, set of 6 ....110.00
Vase, bl w/silver band, wheel cut, sgn, 10"................................275.00
Vase, Brunswick, trumpet form, 10"..450.00
Vase, Easter, scalloped/serrated rim, trumpet form, 10"...............400.00
Vase, exotic bird/flowers eng, lav frost, sgn, 8" 225.00
Vase, floral eng, apple gr, low ped ft, silver border, 5" 195.00

Heisey

A.H. Heisey began his long career at the King Glass Company of Pittsburgh. He later joined the Ripley Glass Company which soon became Geo. Duncan and Sons. After Duncan's death, Heisey became half-owner along with his brother-in-law, James Duncan. In 1895 he built his own factory in Newark, Ohio, starting production in 1896 and continuing until Christmas of 1957. At that time, Imperial Glass Corporation purchased some of the moulds. In 1968 they removed the old 'Diamond H' from any moulds they put into use.

During their highly successful period of production, Heisey made fine hand-crafted tableware with simple, yet graceful designs. Early pieces were not marked. After November 1901, the glassware was marked either with the 'Diamond H' or a paper label. Blown ware is often marked on the stem, never on the bowl or foot. For information concerning Heisey Collectors of America, see the Clubs, Newsletters, and Catalogs section of the Directory.

Animals and Birds

Airdale 450.00
Asiatic Pheasant..325.00
Bull, sgn 1,250.00
Chick, head down...60.00
Chick, head up...60.00
Clydesdale..425.00
Colt, kicking...190.00
Colt, rearing...195.00
Cygnet 185.00
Dolphin, candlestick, #110, pr..240.00
Dolphin, candlestick, moongleam, #110, pr 650.00
Donkey 235.00
Duck, ash tray 95.00
Duck, ash tray, flamingo 140.00
Duck, ash tray, moongleam 165.00
Duck, flower block...130.00
Duck, flower block, hawthorne 240.00
Elephant, lg..350.00
Elephant, med 275.00
Elephant, sm 195.00
Fish, candlestick 140.00
Fish, match holder 130.00
Fish, Tropical.. 1,200.00

Flying Mare, $1,800.00.

Frog, cheese plate, #1210, flamingo 125.00
Frog, cheese plate, marigold 300.00
Frog, cheese plate, moongleam 240.00
Gazelle 1,200.00
Giraffe, head bk 175.00
Giraffe, head to side 175.00
Goose, wings down 375.00
Goose, wings half 95.00
Goose, wings up 95.00
Hen 360.00
Horse head, bookend 125.00
Horse head, cigarette box, #1489, 4½x4" 65.00
Irish Setter, ash tray 30.00
Irish Setter, ash tray, flamingo 45.00
Irish Setter, ash tray, moongleam 55.00
Kingfisher, flower block, flamingo 225.00
Kingfisher, flower block, hawthorne 300.00
Kingfisher, flower block, moongleam 250.00
Mallard, wings down 250.00
Mallard, wings half 100.00
Mallard, wings up 150.00
Piglet, sitting 75.00
Piglet, standing 75.00
Plug Horse 85.00
Pouter Pigeon 600.00
Rabbit, paperweight 160.00
Ringneck Pheasant 135.00
Rooster, Fighting, 8" 150.00
Rooster, stem cocktail 55.00
Rooster, vase, 6½" 95.00
Rooster, 5⅜" 350.00
Rooster head, cocktail 40.00
Rooster head, cocktail shaker, 1-qt 95.00
Scotty 120.00
Show Horse 550.00
Sow 425.00
Sparrow 80.00
Swan, candlestick, 6½" 135.00
Swan, ind nut, #1503 ....18.00
Swan, master nut, #1503 ....45.00
Wood duck 500.00

Dinnerware

Adam, crystal; finger bowl, #3376 ....10.00
Adam, crystal; saucer champagne, #3376, 6-oz 20.00
Adam, flamingo; claret, #3376, 4-oz 40.00
Admiralty, crystal; claret, #3424, 4½-oz 40.00
Admiralty, crystal; cordial, #3424, 1-oz 100.00
Admiralty, crystal; goblet, #3424, 9-oz 50.00
Admiralty, crystal; oyster cocktail, #3424, 4½-oz 30.00
African, crystal; goblet, #3370, 8-oz 30.00
African, crystal; sherbet, #3370, 6-oz 25.00
African, flamingo; cocktail, #3370, 4-oz 45.00
Albemarle, crystal; comport, high ftd, #3368, 7" 45.00
Albemarle, crystal; parfait, #3368, 4½-oz 25.00
Albemarle, crystal; sherbet, #3368, 5-oz 15.00
Albemarle, flamingo; saucer champagne, #3368, 5-oz 50.00
Albemarle, flamingo; tumbler, ftd, #3368, 10-oz 20.00
Barbara Fritchie, crystal; cocktail, #3416, 3½-oz 40.00
Barbara Fritchie, crystal; goblet, #3416, 10-oz 60.00
Barbara Fritchie, crystal; saucer champagne, #3416, 6-oz ...40.00
Barbara Fritchie, crystal; sherbet, #3416, 6-oz 40.00
Barbara Fritchie, crystal; tumbler, ftd, #3416, 10-oz 15.00

Biltmore, crystal; goblet, #3316, 10-oz 15.00
Biltmore, crystal; saucer champagne, #3316, 6-oz 10.00
Biltmore, crystal; sherbet, #3316, 5½-oz 10.00
Carcassonne, crystal; cigarette holder, #3390 ....25.00
Carcassonne, crystal; oyster cocktail, #3390, 3-oz 20.00
Carcassonne, crystal; saucer champagne, #3390, 6-oz 20.00
Carcassonne, flamingo; sherbet, #3390, 6-oz 40.00
Carcassonne, sahara; goblet, tall, #3390, 11-oz 50.00
Carcassonne, sahara; vase, ftd, #3390, 8" 90.00
Charlotte, hawthorne; goblet, moongleam stem, #3361 ...500.00
Charter Oak, crystal; parfait, #3362, 4½-oz 17.00
Charter Oak, crystal; sherbet, #3362, 6-oz 15.00
Charter Oak, crystal; tumbler, iced tea; #3362, 12-oz 12.00
Charter Oak, moongleam; goblet, #3362, 8-oz 40.00
Charter Oak, moongleam; oyster cocktail, #3362, 3½-oz ...25.00
Coarse Rib, crystal; bowl, nappy, #406, 9" 25.00
Coarse Rib, crystal; bowl, nappy, #407, 9" 25.00
Coarse Rib, crystal; creamer, #407, hotel sz 20.00
Coarse Rib, crystal; jelly dish, high ftd, #407, 5" 25.00
Coarse Rib, crystal; pickle tray, #407, 6" 15.00
Coarse Rib, crystal; tumbler, #406, 8-oz 15.00
Coarse Rib, crystal; tumbler, ice tea; #406, 12-oz 18.00
Coarse Rib, flamingo; plate, #407, 8" 15.00
Coarse Rib, hawthorne; jelly dish, low ftd, #407, 5" 50.00
Coarse Rib, moongleam; celery tray, #407, 9" 30.00
Coarse Rib, moongleam; goblet, #407, 8-oz 40.00
Coleport, crystal; bowl, #1486, 8" 35.00
Coleport, crystal; ice tub, #1486 ....60.00
Coleport, crystal; saucer champagne, #1486, 5½-oz 30.00
Coleport, crystal; sherbet, #1486, 5½-oz 30.00
Comet Leaf, crystal; goblet, #1306, 9-oz 45.00
Comet Leaf, sahara; saucer champagne, #1306, 5-oz 50.00
Coronation, crystal; cocktail, ftd, #4054, 4-oz 25.00
Coronation, crystal; cocktail shaker, #4054, 28-oz 100.00
Coventry, crystal; oyster cocktail, #4090, 4½-oz 30.00
Coventry, crystal; sherbet, #4090, 6-oz 30.00
Coventry, zircon; cordial, #4090, 1-oz 300.00
Coventry, zircon; goblet, low ftd, #4090, 10-oz 130.00
Creole, alexandrite; cordial, #3381, 1-oz 350.00
Creole, alexandrite; goblet, tall, #3381, 11-oz 195.00
Creole, alexandrite; oyster cocktail, #3381, 5-oz 125.00
Creole, alexandrite; sherbet, #3381, 7-oz 150.00
Creole, alexandrite; tumbler, ftd, #3381, 10-oz 125.00
Delaware, crystal; parfait, #3324, 4½-oz 20.00
Delaware, crystal; saucer champagne, #3324, 6½-oz 20.00
Delaware, flamingo; oyster cocktail, #3324, 4-oz 30.00
Delaware, hawthorne; sherbet, #3324, 6½-oz 40.00
Diamond Rose, crystal; pilsner, #3386, 8-oz 45.00
Diamond Rose, crystal; saucer champagne, #3386, 6½-oz ...30.00
Diamond Rose, flamingo; sherbet, #3386, 7-oz 50.00
Diamond Rose, sahara; pilsner, #3386, 12-oz 125.00
Double Ring, crystal; goblet, #7005 ....150.00
Duquesne, crystal; cocktail, #3389, 3-oz 25.00
Duquesne, crystal; oyster cocktail, #3389, 4-oz 20.00
Duquesne, crystal; saucer champagne, #3389, 5-oz 25.00
Duquesne, sahara; parfait, #3389, 5-oz 40.00
Duquesne, sahara; sherbet, #3389, 5-oz 35.00
Empress, alexandrite; celery tray, #1401, 13" 175.00
Empress, crystal; bowl, nappy, #1401, 8" 15.00
Empress, crystal; comport, ftd, #1401, 6" 35.00
Empress, crystal; comport, sq, #1401, 6" 40.00
Empress, crystal; creamer, #1401, ind 15.00
Empress, flamingo; sherbet, #1401, 4-oz 30.00
Empress, moongleam; mint dish, ftd, #1401, 8" 45.00

Empress, sahara; ash tray, #1401 ....250.00
Empress, sahara; bowl, salad; #1401, 10" 50.00
Fairacre, crystal; claret, #3555, 4½-oz 15.00
Fairacre, crystal; iced tea, ftd, #3555, 12-oz 15.00
Fairacre, flamingo; saucer champagne, #3555, 6½-oz 30.00
Fairacre, moongleam; cordial, #3555, 1-oz 150.00
Fern, crystal; bowl, fruit; hdls, #1495, 13" 30.00
Fern, crystal; plate, sandwich; #1495, 13" 30.00
Fern, zircon; bonbon, hdls, #1495, 6" 55.00
Galaxy, moongleam; goblet, #8005 ....60.00
Gascony, crystal; creamer, #3397 ....40.00
Gascony, crystal; saucer champagne, #3397, 6-oz 50.00
Gascony, crystal; sherbet, #3397, 6-oz 25.00
Gascony, sahara; goblet, low ftd, #3397, 11-oz 120.00
Gascony, sahara; sugar bowl, #3397 ....80.00
Gayoso, crystal; cordial, #3312, 1-oz 35.00
Gayoso, crystal; parfait, #3312, 5-oz 15.00
Gayoso, flamingo; sherbet, #3312, 5½-oz 20.00
Ipswich, crystal; plate, sq, #1405, 8" 15.00
Ipswich, crystal; sherbet, #1405, 4-oz 12.00
Ipswich, crystal; tumbler, soda; ftd, #1405, 12-oz 20.00
Ipswich, moongleam; tumbler, #1405, 10-oz 40.00
Jamestown, crystal; sherbet, #3408, 6-oz 20.00
Jamestown, crystal; tumbler, ftd, #3408, 9-oz 12.00
Jamestown, sahara; cordial, #3408, 1-oz 250.00
Jamestown, sahara; saucer champagne, #3408, 6-oz 80.00
Kenilworth, crystal; cocktail, #4092, 3-oz 40.00
Kenilworth, crystal; comport, #4092, 5½-oz 75.00
Kenilworth, crystal; cordial, tall stem, #4092, 1-oz ..100.00
Kenilworth, crystal; goblet, #4092, 10-oz 50.00
Kenilworth, crystal; sherbet, #4092, 5½-oz 25.00
Kimberly, crystal; saucer champagne, #4091, 5½-oz 30.00
Kimberly, crystal; sherbet, #4091, 5½-oz 25.00
Kimberly, zircon; cordial, #4091, 1-oz 300.00
Kimberly, zircon; goblet, low ftd, #4091, 10-oz 130.00
King Arthur, crystal; goblet, #3357, 10-oz 20.00
King Arthur, crystal; saucer champagne, #3357, 6½-oz ..15.00
King Arthur, crystal; wine, #3357, 2½-oz 35.00
King Arthur, flamingo; sherbet, #3357, 6½-oz 30.00
King Arthur, moongleam; cordial, #3357, 1-oz 150.00
Kohinoor, crystal; floral bowl, #1488, 14" 50.00
Kohinoor, crystal; goblet, low ftd, #4085, 9-oz 35.00
Kohinoor, crystal; saucer champagne, #4085, 5½-oz 30.00
Kohinoor, zircon; ash tray, #1488 ....80.00
Kohinoor, zircon; bowl, fruit; #1488, 15½" 175.00
Kohinoor, zircon; bowl, salad; #4085, 11" 150.00
Kohinoor, zircon; cordial, #4085, 1-oz 250.00
Loren, crystal; goblet, #4067 ....175.00
Marriette, crystal; cordial, #3414, 1-oz 100.00
Marriette, crystal; goblet, #3414, 10-oz 60.00
Marriette, crystal; saucer champagne, #3414, 6-oz 40.00
Marriette, crystal; sherbet, #3414, 6-oz 40.00
Marriette, crystal; tumbler, ftd, #3414, 10-oz 15.00
Monte Cristo, crystal; comport, #3411, 7" 60.00
Monte Cristo, crystal; goblet, #3411, 9-oz 40.00
Monte Cristo, crystal; tumbler, ftd, #3411, 9-oz 15.00
Monte Cristo, sahara; cocktail, #3411, 3½-oz 80.00
Narrow Flute w/Rim, crystal; jelly dish, hdls, #473, 5" ...18.00
Narrow Flute w/Rim, crystal; pickle tray, #473, 6" 15.00
New Era, crystal; claret, #4044, 4-oz 25.00
New Era, crystal; cordial, #4044, 1-oz 65.00
New Era, crystal; saucer champagne, #4044, 6-oz 25.00
New Era, crystal; tumbler, ftd, #4044, 10-oz 25.00
New Era, crystal; wine, #4044, 3-oz 40.00

Octagon, crystal; bowl, ftd, #1229, 8" 20.00
Octagon, crystal; bowl, nappy, #500, 6" 15.00
Octagon, crystal; jelly dish, #1229, 5½" 10.00
Octagon, flamingo; basket, #500, 5" 110.00
Octagon, moongleam; bonbon, #1229, 6" 20.00
Octagon, sahara; creamer, #500 ....30.00
Octagon, sahara; mint dish, #1229, 6" 20.00
Old Dominion, crystal; claret, #3380, 4-oz 20.00
Old Dominion, crystal; cocktail, #3380, 3-oz 20.00
Old Dominion, crystal; tumbler, ftd, #3380, 10-oz 12.00
Old Dominion, flamingo; parfait, #3380, 5-oz 30.00
Old Dominion, sahara; comport, #3380, 7" 60.00
Old Dominion, sahara; cordial, #3380, 1-oz 180.00
Old Glory, crystal; cocktail, #3333, 3-oz 30.00
Old Glory, crystal; comport, high ftd, #3333, 6" 60.00
Old Glory, crystal; cordial, #3333, 1-oz 50.00
Old Glory, hawthorne; parfait, #3333, 4½-oz 55.00
Old Sandwich, crystal; beer mug, #1404, 14-oz 55.00
Old Sandwich, crystal; creamer, oval, #1404 ....20.00
Old Sandwich, crystal; goblet, low ftd, #1404, 10-oz ..20.00
Old Sandwich, flamingo; comport, #1404, 6" 80.00
Old Sandwich, moongleam; parfait, #1404, 4½-oz 40.00
Old Sandwich, sahara; cigarette holder, #1404 ....200.00
Old Sandwich, sahara; plate, sq, #1404, 6" 20.00

Butter dish, Orchid etching on Waverly shape, sea horse finial, $150.00.

Park Lane, crystal; claret, #4055, 4-oz 25.00
Park Lane, crystal; cordial, #4055, 1-oz 100.00
Park Lane, crystal; saucer champagne, #4055, 6-oz 30.00
Park Lane, crystal; sherbet, #4055, 6-oz 20.00
Penn Charter, crystal; claret, #3360, 4½-oz 20.00
Penn Charter, crystal; oyster cocktail, #3360, 4-oz ...20.00
Penn Charter, crystal; saucer champagne, #3360, 6-oz ..20.00
Penn Charter, flamingo; sherbet, #3360, 6-oz 40.00
Penn Charter, hawthorne; parfait, #3360, 5-oz 70.00
Plateau, crystal; oyster cocktail, #3359, 4-oz 12.00
Plateau, crystal; rose bowl, #3359, 6" 35.00
Plateau, flamingo; goblet, #3359, 8½-oz 35.00
Plateau, marigold; saucer champagne, #3359, 6½-oz 45.00
Pleat & Panel, crystal; bowl, vegetable; #1170, 9" 20.00
Pleat & Panel, crystal; goblet, #1170, 8-oz 15.00
Pleat & Panel, crystal; marmalade, #1170, 4¾" 12.00
Pleat & Panel, crystal; plate, #1170, 8" 12.00
Pleat & Panel, flamingo; creamer, #1170, hotel sz 25.00
Pleat & Panel, flamingo; sherbet, #1170, 5-oz 20.00
Pleat & Panel, moongleam; jelly dish, hdls, #1170, 5" .25.00
Pleat & Panel, moongleam; tumbler, #1170, 8-oz 35.00

Plymouth, crystal; parfait, #3409, 5-oz **45.00**
Plymouth, crystal; saucer champagne, #3409, 6-oz **35.00**
Plymouth, sahara; banquet goblet, #3409, 12-oz.................**225.00**
Plymouth, sahara; sherbet, #3409, 6-oz **80.00**
Portsmouth, crystal; sherbet, #3440, 7-oz **15.00**
Portsmouth, flamingo; goblet, #3440, 9-oz **35.00**
Quaker, crystal; bowl, nappy, #1463 ....**25.00**
Quaker, crystal; plate, #1463, 9" **25.00**
Quator, flamingo; bonbon, #355 ....**35.00**
Queen Guinevere, crystal; goblet, #8046..............................**100.00**
Rampul, crystal; goblet, #3325, 9-oz **30.00**
Rampul, flamingo; sherbet, #3325, 6-oz **25.00**
Ramshorn, crystal; parfait, #3365, 4½-oz **35.00**
Ramshorn, crystal; sherbet, #3365, 6-oz **20.00**
Ramshorn, flamingo; goblet, #3365, 9-oz **60.00**
Ramshorn, flamingo; saucer champagne, #3365, 6-oz **50.00**
Rib In Ring, moongleam; cocktail, #8021 ....**300.00**
Ribbed Octagon, crystal; celery tray, #1231, 9" **15.00**
Ribbed Octagon, crystal; platter, oval, #1231, 12¾"............**20.00**
Ribbed Octagon, flamingo; creamer, #1231, hotel sz **20.00**
Ribbed Octagon, moongleam; bowl, salad; #1231, 12½" **35.00**
Ridgeleigh, amber; shakers, #1469½ **350.00**
Ridgeleigh, crystal; ash tray, rnd, #1469 ....**20.00**
Ridgeleigh, crystal; bowl, fruit; #1469, 12" **45.00**
Ridgeleigh, crystal; bowl, nappy, #1469, 4½" **10.00**
Ridgeleigh, crystal; celery tray, #1469, 12" **25.00**
Ridgeleigh, crystal; creamer, #1469 ....**20.00**
Ridgeleigh, crystal; plate, #1469, 6" **15.00**
Ridgeleigh, crystal; plate, sq, #1469, 8" **30.00**
Ridgeleigh, crystal; shakers, #1469, pr **30.00**
Ridgeleigh, crystal; vase, #1469, 6" **20.00**
Rococo, crystal; bowl, shallow, hdls, #1447, 9½" **30.00**
Rococo, crystal; plate, #1447, 7" **20.00**
Rococo, crystal; shakers, #1447, pr......................................**65.00**
Rococo, sahara; bonbon, #1447 ....**50.00**
Rococo, sahara; comport, #1447, 6" **120.00**
Saturn, crystal; bowl, fruit; #1485, 12" **35.00**
Saturn, crystal; bowl, salad; #1485, 11" **35.00**
Saturn, crystal; creamer, #1485 ....**20.00**
Saturn, crystal; goblet, #1485, 10-oz **20.00**
Saturn, crystal; mayonnaise, #1485 ....**20.00**
Saturn, crystal; parfait, #1485, 5-oz **15.00**
Saturn, crystal; tumbler, #1485, 10-oz **15.00**
Saturn, zircon; bowl, #1485, 5"...**45.00**
Saturn, zircon; comport, #1485, 7"..**150.00**
Saturn, zircon; plate, #1485, 6" **40.00**
Saturn, zircon; sherbet, #1485, 4½-oz **40.00**
Saturn, zircon; sugar bowl, #1485 ....**60.00**
Savoy Plaza, crystal; claret, #3418, 4-oz **30.00**
Savoy Plaza, crystal; cordial, #3418, 1-oz **100.00**
Savoy Plaza, crystal; goblet, #3418, 10-oz **50.00**
Savoy Plaza, crystal; oyster cocktail, #3418, 3½-oz **30.00**
Saxony, crystal; cordial, #3394, 1-oz **110.00**
Saxony, crystal; oyster cocktail, #3394, 4-oz **20.00**
Saxony, crystal; wine, #3394, 2½-oz **45.00**
Saxony, sahara; saucer champagne, #3394, 5½-oz **40.00**
Spanish, crystal; cocktail, #3404, 3½-oz...............................**40.00**
Spanish, crystal; cocktail, #3404, 3½-oz...............................**40.00**
Spanish, crystal; saucer champagne, #3404, 5½-oz **40.00**
Spanish, crystal; sherbet, #3404, 5½-oz................................**30.00**
Spanish, crystal; tumbler, ftd, #3404, 10-oz.........................**30.00**
Stanhope, crystal; bowl, nappy, #1483, 4½" **15.00**
Stanhope, crystal; creamer, hdl, #1483.................................**25.00**
Stanhope, crystal; goblet, #4083, 10-oz................................**30.00**

Stanhope, crystal; plate, #1483, 7" **15.00**
Stanhope, crystal; shakers, #1483, pr **50.00**
Stanhope, crystal; sugar bowl, hdls, #1483...........................**25.00**
Stanhope, zircon; saucer champagne, #4083, 5½" **70.00**
Sussex, flamingo; cocktail, #419, 2½-oz................................**60.00**
Sussex, moongleam; goblet, #419, 8-oz.................................**75.00**
Trojan, crystal; parfait, #3366, 4½-oz **25.00**
Trojan, crystal; tumbler, ftd, #3366, 10-oz **10.00**
Trojan, flamingo; oyster cocktail, #3366, 3-oz......................**20.00**
Trojan, flamingo; saucer champagne, #3366, 5-oz................**35.00**
Trojan, hawthorne; comport, ftd, #3366, 7".............................**95.00**
Tudor, crystal, tumbler, #411, 8-oz.......................................**12.00**
Tudor, crystal; banana split, ftd, #412, 8" **25.00**
Tudor, crystal; bowl, nappy, #411, 8" **25.00**
Tudor, crystal; bowl, nut; #411, 4½" **25.00**
Tudor, crystal; celery tray, #411, 12" **25.00**
Tudor, crystal; goblet, #412, 7½-oz **20.00**
Tudor, crystal; jelly dish, hdls, #411, 5" **15.00**
Tudor, crystal; pickle tray, #411, 7" **20.00**
Tudor, crystal; plate, #411, 8" **10.00**
Tudor, crystal; saucer champagne, #411, 5½-oz **15.00**
Tudor, crystal; tumbler, #412, 8-oz.......................................**12.00**
Tudor, hawthorne; mint dish, hdls, #411, 6" **35.00**
Tudor, moongleam; bonbon, hdls, #411 ....**25.00**
Tudor, moongleam; cheese dish, hdls, #411, 6" **25.00**
Twentieth Century, crystal; pitcher, milk; #1415, 1-pt **40.00**
Twentieth Century, crystal; tumbler, ftd, #1415, 9-oz...........**20.00**
Twentieth Century, sahara; sherbet, ftd, #1415, 4-oz...........**35.00**
Twist, crystal; bonbon, hdls, #1252, 6" **12.00**
Twist, crystal; creamer, ind, #1252 ....**20.00**
Twist, crystal; goblet, #1252, 9-oz **20.00**
Twist, crystal; plate, sandwich; hdls, #1252, 12" **20.00**
Twist, flamingo; plate, #1252, 8" **15.00**
Twist, marigold; jelly dish, hdls, #1252, 6" **25.00**
Twist, marigold; plate, #1252, 7" **27.00**
Twist, moongleam; bowl, nappy, #1252, 8" **35.00**
Twist, moongleam; celery tray, #1252, 10" **35.00**
Twist, moongleam; cheese tray, hdls, #1252, 6" **20.00**
Universal, crystal; cocktail, #3304, 3½-oz.............................**15.00**
Universal, crystal; cordial, #3304, 1-oz.................................**30.00**
Universal, crystal; goblet, #3304, 10-oz................................**20.00**
Universal, crystal; saucer champagne, #3304, 5½-oz **20.00**
Velvedere, crystal; parfait, #3311, 7-oz **15.00**
Velvedere, crystal; saucer champagne, #3311, 5½-oz **15.00**
Velvedere, crystal; sherbet, ftd, #3311, 5½-oz **15.00**
Velvedere, crystal; tumbler, ftd, #3311, 10-oz **15.00**
Victorian, cobalt; cheese holder, #1425 ....**95.00**
Victorian, cobalt; saucer champagne, #1425, 5-oz................**110.00**
Victorian, crystal; bowl, nappy, #1425, 8"..............................**25.00**
Victorian, crystal; bowl, punch; #1425 ....**200.00**
Victorian, crystal; plate, cracker; #1425, 12" **30.00**
Victorian, crystal; vase, ftd, #1425, 6"...................................**35.00**
Victorian, sahara; plate, sandwich; #1425, 13" **65.00**
Victorian, sahara; shakers, #1425, pr **90.00**
Wabash, crystal; cordial, #3350, 1-oz **40.00**
Wabash, crystal; tumbler, ftd, #3350, 10-oz..........................**20.00**
Wabash, moongleam; claret, #3350, 4-oz..............................**25.00**
Wabash, moongleam; plate, #3350, 6"....................................**10.00**
Waldorf, crystal; goblet, #3318, 11-oz **25.00**
Waldorf, crystal; saucer champagne, #3318, 5-oz **20.00**
Waldorf, crystal; sherbet, low ftd, #3318, 5-oz **15.00**
Waldorf, crystal; wine, #3318, 2½-oz.....................................**25.00**
Yeoman, crystal; ash tray, 4-hdl **20.00**
Yeoman, crystal; bowl, fruit; oval, #1184, 9" **20.00**

Yeoman, crystal; jelly dish, low ftd, #1184, 5" **15.00**
Yeoman, crystal; plate, #1184, 9" **10.00**
Yeoman, crystal; tray, oblong, #1184, 12" **20.00**
Yeoman, crystal; tumbler, #1184, 8-oz **10.00**
Yeoman, flamingo; dish, vegetable; #1184, 6" **12.00**
Yeoman, moongleam; bonbon, hdls, #1184, 5½" **20.00**
Yeoman, moongleam; bowl, nappy, #1184, 4½" **12.00**
Yeoman, moongleam; bowl, nappy, deep, #1184, 8" **22.00**
Yeoman, sahara; goblet, #1184, 8-oz **25.00**

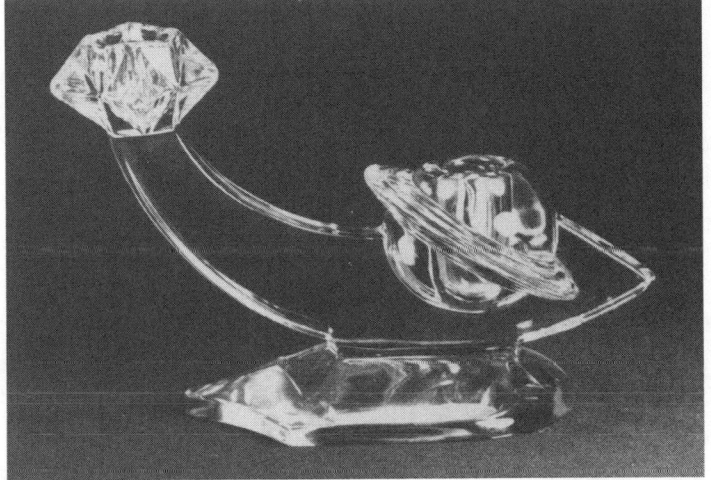

World, double candle holder, very rare, 6", $300.00.

Heubach

Gebruder Heubach is a German porcelain company that has been in operation since the 1800s producing quality figurines and novelty items. They are perhaps most famous for their doll heads and piano babies, most of which are marked with the circular rising sun device containing an 'H' superimposed over a 'G.'

Baby, bug on arm, 6" **300.00**
Baby crawling in wht gown, 5½x8" **415.00**
Baby in highchair, sm **165.00**
Baby lying on bk, plays w/toes, intaglio eyes, mk, 7" **350.00**
Baby on tummy, ft Xd, wht gown/pk trim, unsgn, 4" **175.00**
Baby w/grapes, reclining, intaglio eyes, mk, 8" **300.00**
Bear on step of outhouse **150.00**
Box, clown head finial, mk, 3½x2½" dia **150.00**

Box, Stowaways, 8½" long, $1,800.00.

Boy w/fish in net, intaglio eyes, cap, unmk, 11½" **150.00**
Bust, boy, quilted bib, metal fly on nose, unmk, 3½", MIB **265.00**
Dutch children, sitting, EX details, 6¾x4x5", pr **225.00**
Dutch children stand bk to bk, unmk, 7½x4¾" **145.00**
Girl dancer in tan ruffled dress, wht collar, mk, 6½" **90.00**
Girl in pk pleated skirt, gr shash, mk, 6¼" **120.00**
Girl lying on bk holding lg bl egg, 3¼" L **110.00**
Girl w/basket, intaglio eyes, ruffled bonnet, unmk, 11½" **150.00**
Girl w/sled, blk/wht pants, gr/wht sweater & cap, 8" **200.00**
Lady w/baby in arm, jug in hand, pastels, mk, 12½" **365.00**
Man w/ax wipes brow, mk, 12½" **365.00**
Mother mouse on shoe, baby peeks out, mk, 3¼x5" **165.00**
Planter, shepherdess w/flock figural, mk, 4x10¾x2¾" **195.00**
Spanish dancer w/fan, Deco attire, red shoes, mk, 7⅝" **240.00**

Hickman, Royal Arden

Born in Willamette, Oregon, Royal A. Hickman was a genius in all aspects of design interpretation. Mr. Hickman's expertise can be seen in the designs of the lovely Heisey figurines; Kosta crystal; Bruce Fox aluminum; Three Crowns aluminum; Vernon Kilns; and Royal Haeger Pottery as well as hand-crafted silver, furniture, and paintings.

Because Mr. Hickman moved around during much of his lifetime, his influence has been felt in all forms of the media. Designs from his independent companies include 'Royal Hickman Pottery and Lamps' (sold through Ceramic Arts, Inc., of Chattanooga, Tennessee), 'Royal Hickman's Paris Ware,' 'Royal Hickman—Florida,' and 'California Designed by Royal Hickman.' The following listings will give examples of pieces bearing the various trademarks. Our advisor for this category is Lee Garmon; she is listed in the directory under Illinois. See also Royal Haegar; Vernon Kilns, Melinda pattern.

Bruce Fox Aluminum

Banana leaf, mk Royal Hickman-RH 6, 22½" L **20.00**
Candle snuffer, sterling silver, sgn Royal Hickman, 12" **35.00**
Dish, lobster, lg **40.00**
Dish, 3-point leaf, sgn Royal Hickman, 15½" L..........................**20.00**
Platter, fish, EX detail, sgn Royal Hickman-RH 3, 13x9" **50.00**

California, Designed by Royal Hickman

Bowl, red w/blk highlights, #607, 9½"......................................**15.00**
Figurine, deer, apple gr w/wht spots, appl eyes, 15".....................**25.00**
Figurine, giraffe & young, pk w/blk spots & base, 11x7" **35.00**
Swan, red w/blk highlights, #643, 17" **40.00**

Miscellaneous Signatures

Sea horse vase, sgn Royal Hickman USA, #468, 8" **25.00**
Vase, fish figurine, 'petty crystal glaze,' #467 ....**25.00**
Vase, lg heart, sgn Royal Hickman, Italy, #3774.........................**35.00**

Royal Hickman–Florida

Vase, horse's head, gray w/wht mane, 13¾" **75.00**
Vase, modernistic free-form, #578, 14" **30.00**
Vase, sailfish, sgn Royal Hickman FL Pottery of FL Clay..............**25.00**

Historical Glass

Glassware commemorating particularly significant historical

events became popular in the late 1800s. Bread trays were the most common form; but plates, mugs, pitchers, and other items were also pressed in clear as well as colored glass. It was sold in vast amounts at the 1876 Philadelphia Centennial Exposition by various manufacturers who exhibited their wares on the grounds. It remained popular well into the 20th century.

In the listings that follow, L numbers refer to a book by Lindsey; M numbers correspond with a book by Marsh. Both are standard guides used by many collectors. See also Bread Plates; Pattern Glass.

Bowl, Industry, clear lacy Sandwich, L-267, minor nicks, 6¼", $200.00.

Bowl, Gen Grant, Patriot & Soldier, clear/frosted, 9⅜"	65.00
Bust, Dewey, frosted, after Lotto portrait, L-6, 5", NM	190.00
Bust, Geo Washington, clear/frosted, Gillinder 1876, L-259	35.50
Bust, Lincoln, clear/frosted, Gillinder, 6"	355.00
Calabash, Roosevelt-TVA, aqua, qt	60.00
Campaign hat, He's All Right	30.00
Covered dish, battleship Oregon, L-469, 6½" L, EX	75.00
Covered dish, locomotive, L-138, VG	150.00
Cup, McKinley, w/lid	42.00
Cup plate, Garfield, L-297	125.00
Goblet, Deer, Dog, & Hunter, U-shape, Gillinder	80.00
Goblet, Liberty Bell	37.50
Goblet, Philadelphia Centennial	45.00
Goblet, 3 Presidents	275.00
Jar, apothecary; Statue of Liberty, 1876 Philadelphia Expo, pr	275.00
Lamp chimney, Columbus, etched on frosted band, L-9, 8"	250.00
Mug, Bumper to the Flag, Union Forever, L-479	235.00
Mug, Centennial, snake hdl, Gillinder & Sons	295.00
Mug, Columbus & Washington busts, Worlds Expo 1893, L-2	95.00
Mug, E Pluribus Unum	45.00
Mug, Lincoln/Garfield Assassination	60.00
Mug, Martyrs, L-272	100.00
Mug, Peabody	70.00
Mug, Union Forever	215.00
Paperweight, Lincoln, clear/frosted, Gillinder, M-165	250.00
Paperweight, Lincoln, clear/frosted, Gillinder, M-166	200.00
Paperweight, Plymouth Rock, inscribed, 1620	75.00
Pitcher, Gridley, L-401	85.00
Pitcher, Lincoln Log, milk glass, rare	175.00
Pitcher, Texas Centennial, Alamo, 9"	80.00
Plaque, Lincoln Log, milk glass, L-278	195.00
Plate, Garfield, frosted center, star border, 5½"	30.00
Plate, It's Pleasure To Labor	60.00
Plate, McKinley, milk glass, M gold, 7½"	135.00
Plate, Pope Leo, milk glass, L-240	25.00
Plate, Protection & Plenty, clear/frosted, 7¼"	50.00
Plate, Washington, 13-star border, milk glass, M-90	45.00
Relish, 1876 Centennial, w/bear paws	40.00
Shaker, Benjamin Franklin, M-194	85.00

Shaker, Eagle	30.00
Shaker, Lighthouse	48.00
Shaving mug, Mr & Mrs Garfield, milk glass	125.00
Toothpick holder, Liberty Torch, bl	75.00
Trough, bl, L-151	20.00
Tumbler, Admiral Dewey, L-394	45.00
Tumbler, America, My Country Tis of Thee, L-458	40.00
Tumbler, Garfield, w/wreaths, L-296	45.00
Tumbler, Lincoln Tribute, L-282	20.00
Tumbler, Lord's Prayer, blown & etched	25.00
Tumbler, McKinley, Protection & Plenty, L-337	45.00
Tumbler, Mephistopheles	35.00
Tumbler, Motto, L-224	7.00
Tumbler, Protection, Sound Currency, McKinley & Hobart	55.00
Tumbler, Religious, L-224	7.00
Tumbler, Star Spangled Banner	30.00
Whiskey, Bumper to the Flag/Union Forever, flint	125.00

Plate, amber, cabin and Fort Meigs in center, Tippecanoe and Harrison in relief among acorn, vine, and oak leaf border, scalloped rim, 8", $150.00.

Hobbs, Brockunier, & Co.

Hobbs and Brockunier's South Wheeling Glass Works was in operation during the last quarter of the 19th century. They are most famous for their peachblow, amberina, Daisy and Button, and Hobnail pattern glass. The mainstay of the operation, however, was druggist items and plain glassware – bowls, mugs, and simple footed pitchers with shell handles. See also Frances Ware.

Bowl, Daisy & Button, shallow, sgn, 7"	325.00
Canoe, Daisy & Button, amberina, 8" L	285.00
Creamer, Hobnail, bl, sq rim, 4", EX	165.00
Goblet, Block, amber frost, rare	110.00
Pitcher, Hobnail, amber frost, ruffled/beaded rim, 8"	125.00
Pitcher, Hobnail, cranberry, +6 tumblers	550.00
Pitcher, Hobnail, cranberry opal, sq top, +4 tumblers	400.00
Pitcher, Optic, rubena, water sz	120.00

Homer Laughlin

The Homer Laughlin China Company of Newell, West Virginia, was founded in 1871. The superior dinnerware they displayed at the Centennial Exposition in Philadelphia in 1876 won the highest award of excellence. From that time to the present, they have continued to produce quality dinnerware and kitchenware, many lines of which are becoming very popular collectibles. Most of the dinnerware is marked with the name of the pattern and occasionally with the shape name as well. The 'HLC' trademark is usually followed by a number series, the first two digits of which indicate the year of its manufacture. See also Fiesta; Harlequin; Riviera.

Kitchen Kraft/Oven-Serve: Pie plate, $7.00; Cake server, $20.00; Platter, 12", $12.00; Plate, 10", $5.00; Bowl, 7½" oval, $8.50; Fruit, 5½", $4.00; Cup & saucer, $8.00.

Amberstone, ash tray	17.00
Amberstone, bowl, vegetable	8.50
Amberstone, casserole	30.00
Amberstone, creamer	6.50
Amberstone, dessert dish	3.00
Amberstone, jam jar, w/lid	35.00
Amberstone, pie plate	25.00
Amberstone, sauce boat stand	18.00
Amberstone, tea server	35.00
Americana, creamer	8.00
Americana, sauce boat, w/liner	22.00
Americana, sugar bowl, w/lid	10.00
Casualstone, bowl, salad; jumbo, 10"	12.00
Casualstone, bowl, vegetable; rnd	7.50
Casualstone, coffee server	20.00
Casualstone, cup & saucer	6.50
Casualstone, mug, jumbo	6.50
Casualstone, plate, salad	2.50
Casualstone, platter, oval, 13"	9.50
Casualstone, sauce boat	9.50
Casualstone, sugar bowl, w/lid	6.50
Conchita, bowl, fruit; 5"	7.00
Conchita, plate, deep; 8"	12.00
Conchita, platter, 11½"	13.50
Epicure, bowl, soup	6.00
Epicure, coffeepot	35.00
Epicure, creamer	8.00
Epicure, plate, 6½"	3.00
Epicure, shakers, pr	10.00
Epicure, teacup & saucer	10.00
Hacienda, bowl, vegetable; 8"	16.00
Hacienda, casserole, Nautilus	85.00
Hacienda, plate, 6"	4.00
Hacienda, platter, w/oval well, 13½"	18.00
Hacienda, sauce boat	18.00
Hacienda, teapot	55.00
Jubilee, bowl, fruit	3.50
Jubilee, bowl, mixing; Kitchen Kraft, 10"	90.00
Jubilee, casserole	22.00
Jubilee, cup & saucer	5.00
Jubilee, platter, 11"	3.00
Jubilee, sauce boat	6.00
Laughlin Art China, bowl, American Beauty, 10"	100.00
Laughlin Art China, jardiniere, flow blue, 10x14½"	400.00
Laughlin Art China, pot, demitasse; Currant	160.00

Laughlin Art China, vase, Currant, 16"	150.00
Mexicana, bowl, vegetable; 8½"	16.00
Mexicana, cup & saucer	13.50
Mexicana, egg cup, rolled edge	25.00
Mexicana, plate, deep; 8"	12.00
Mexicana, plate, 7"	5.50
Mexicana, platter, 10"	12.00
Mexicana, sauce boat	18.00
Priscilla, bowl, fruit; 9½"	12.00
Priscilla, creamer	6.00
Priscilla, plate, 8"	4.00
Priscilla, sauce boat, 8½"	7.50
Rhythm, bowl, fruit; 5½"	3.00
Rhythm, bowl, mixing; Kitchen Kraft, 6"	60.00
Rhythm, bowl, soup	7.00
Rhythm, cup & saucer	8.00
Rhythm, plate, 6"	2.00
Rhythm, plate, 9"	4.00
Rhythm, platter, 11½"	13.00
Rhythm, sauce boat, cobalt	14.00
Rhythm, spoon rest, gr	200.00
Rhythm, sugar bowl, w/lid	6.00
Rhythm Rose, bowl, nested, med	14.00
Rhythm Rose, casserole, Kitchen Kraft, 8½"	28.00
Rhythm Rose, creamer	6.00
Rhythm Rose, plate, 9"	5.00
Rhythm Rose, platter, 13"	9.00
Rhythm Rose, sugar bowl, w/lid	9.00
Serenade, bowl, nappy, 9"	8.00
Serenade, pickle dish	8.50
Serenade, plate, 10"	8.00
Serenade, shakers, pr	10.00
Serenade, sugar bowl, w/lid	10.00
Serenade, teapot	40.00
Tango, bowl, nappy, 8¾"	6.00
Tango, creamer	5.00
Tango, plate, deep	8.00
Tango, plate, 10"	8.00
Tango, sugar bowl, w/lid	7.50
Virginia Rose, bowl, nested, sm	12.00
Virginia Rose, bowl, vegetable; w/lid	40.00
Virginia Rose, bowl, vegetable; 7½"	9.00
Virginia Rose, butter dish, ½-lb	65.00
Virginia Rose, cake plate	15.00
Virginia Rose, pitcher, milk; 5"	14.00
Virginia Rose, plate, 10½"	10.00
Virginia Rose, sauce boat	12.00
Wells Art Glaze, bowl, nappy, 8"	8.50
Wells Art Glaze, casserole	32.00
Wells Art Glaze, pickle dish, w/hdls	9.00
Wells Art Glaze, platter, oval, 15½"	14.00
Wells Art Glaze, sauce boat	10.00
Wells Art Glaze, syrup, w/decals	30.00
Wells Art Glaze, teapot	35.00

Hull

The A.E. Hull Pottery was formed in 1905 in Zanesville, Ohio, and in the early years produced stoneware specialities. They expanded in 1907, adding a second plant and employing over two hundred workers. By 1920 they were manufacturing a full line of stoneware, art pottery with both air-brushed and blended glazes, florist pots, and gardenware. They also produced toilet ware and kitchen items with a white semi-porcelain body. Although these continued to be staple products, after the stock market crash of 1929, emphasis was shifted to tile production. By the mid-thirties interest in art pottery production was growing; over the next fifteen years, several lines of matt pastel floral-decorated patterns were designed, consisting of vases, planters, baskets, ewers, and bowls in various sizes.

The Red Riding Hood cookie jar, patented in 1943, proved so successful that a whole line of figural kitchenware and novelty items were added. They continued to be produced well into the fifties. Through the forties their floral artware lines flooded the market, due to the restriction of foreign imports. Although best known for their pastel matt-glazed ware, some of the lines were high gloss. Rosella, glossy coral on a pink clay body, was produced for a short time only; and Magnolia, although offered in a matt glaze, was produced in gloss as well.

The plant was destroyed in 1950 by a flood which resulted in a devastating fire when the floodwater caused the kilns to explode. The company rebuilt and equipped their new factory with the most modern machinery. It was soon apparent that the matt glaze could not be duplicated through the more modern processes, however, and soon attention was concentrated on high-gloss artware lines such as Parchment and Pine and Ebb Tide. Figural planters and novelties, piggy banks, and dinnerware were produced in abundance in the late fifties and sixties. By the mid-seventies dinnerware and florist ware were the mainstay of their business. The firm discontinued operations in 1986.

Our advisor, Brenda Roberts, has compiled a lovely book, *The Collector's Encyclopedia of Hull Pottery*, with full-color photos and current values which has been recently reprinted. You will find her address in the Directory under Missouri. Mark Supnick (see Directory under Florida) has written a new book, *Collecting Hull Pottery's Red Riding Hood*, published by L-W Sales.

Blossomflite, basket, T-9, 10" 65.00
Blossomflite, ewer, T-3, 8½" 45.00
Bow Knot, basket, B-12, 10½" 425.00
Bow Knot, basket, B-25, 6½" 115.00
Bow Knot, bowl, console; B-16, 13½"......................................165.00
Bow Knot, cornucopia, B-5, 7½" 70.00

Bow Knot jardiniere, 5¾", $65.00.

Bow Knot, teapot, B-20, 6" 225.00
Bow Knot, vase, B-14, 12½" 240.00
Bow Knot, vase, B-3, 6½"...60.00
Bow Knot, vase, B-9, 8½"..110.00
Calla Lily, bowl, #500/32, 10" 95.00
Calla Lily, ewer, #506, 10"...150.00

Calla Lily, vase, #530/33, pillow form, 9½"...............................150.00
Calla Lily, vase, #530/33, 5" 48.00
Calla Lily, vase, #540/33, 6" 48.00
Camellia, basket, #140, 10½" 230.00
Camellia, creamer, #111, 5" 32.00
Camellia, ewer, #128, 4¾" 38.00
Camellia, vase, #121, 6¼" 40.00
Camellia, vase, #123, 6½" 40.00
Crescent, bowl, B-1, gr/yel, 9½" 20.00
Crescent, cookie jar, B-8, yel, w/gr lid, 9½" 40.00
Crescent, creamer, B-15, yel w/gr hdl, 4¼" 10.00
Crescent, teapot, B-13, yel w/gr hdl, 7½" 45.00
Dogwood, cornucopia, #522, 3¾" 35.00
Dogwood, ewer, #505, pk, 8½" 115.00
Dogwood, ewer, #506, 11½" 175.00
Dogwood, ewer, #520, 4¾" 48.00
Dogwood, jardiniere, #514, 4" 42.00
Dogwood, vase, #503, 8½"...75.00
Dogwood, vase, #513, 6½"...65.00
Dogwood, vase, #517, 4¾"...35.00
Early Art, vase, semi-porcelain, turq, #660/33, 8"........................25.00
Early Art, vase, stoneware, #32, H in circle, 8"............................40.00
Early Art, vase, stoneware, turq w/bl & red, 5½"..........................35.00
Early Utility, bowl, #106, H in circle, gr, 5".................................15.00
Early Utility, bowl, #25, H in circle, gr, 7"..................................24.00
Early Utility, pitcher, #107, H in circle, yel w/brn, 4¾"..................32.00
Early Utility, pretzel jar, H in circle, 9½" 180.00
Ebb Tide, basket, E-11, 16½" 95.00
Ebb Tide, ewer, E-10, 14" 125.00
Iris, console, #409, 12" 155.00
Iris, ewer, #401, 8" 130.00
Iris, jardiniere, #413, 5½"...60.00
Iris, vase, #402, 7" 60.00
Iris, vase, #403, 4¾" 36.00
Iris, vase, #405, 10½"...155.00
Iris, vase, #406, 4¾" 36.00
Magnolia, glossy; basket, H-14, 10½" 110.00
Magnolia, glossy; candle holder, H-24, pk floral, 4"....................20.00
Magnolia, glossy; cornucopia, H-10, pk floral, 8½" 38.00
Magnolia, glossy; creamer, H-21, bl floral, 3¾"...........................22.00
Magnolia, glossy; vase, H-16, salesman's sample sticker, 12½" 95.00
Magnolia, matt; candle holder, #27, 4" 30.00
Magnolia, matt; console bowl, #26, 12" 85.00
Magnolia, matt; cornucopia, #19, 8½" 65.00
Magnolia, matt; dbl cornucopia, #6, 12" 95.00
Magnolia, matt; ewer, #14, 4¾" 32.00
Magnolia, matt; ewer, #18, 13½"..155.00
Magnolia, matt; ewer, #5, 7" 65.00
Magnolia, matt; sugar bowl, #25, open, 3¾" 32.00
Magnolia, matt; vase, #1, 8½"...60.00
Magnolia, matt; vase, #11, 6¼" 38.00
Magnolia, matt; vase, #13, 4¾" 28.00
Magnolia, matt; vase, #15, 6¼" 38.00
Magnolia, matt; vase, #16, side hdls, 15" 240.00
Magnolia, matt; vase, #20, side hdls, 15" 240.00
Magnolia, matt; vase, #3, side hdls, 8½" 60.00
Magnolia, matt; vase, #4, 6¼" 38.00
Magnolia, matt; vase, #7, 8½"..60.00
Magnolia, matt; vase, #9, 10½" 80.00
Magnolia, vase, #22, 12½"...125.00
Mardi Gras, ewer, #31, 10" 55.00
Mardi Gras, ewer, #66, 10" 55.00
Mardi Gras, vase, #216, 9"...25.00
Novelty, dancing girl, #955, 7"..30.00

Novelty, dish, #85, leaf form, 13" 16.00
Novelty, flowerpot, #95, 4½" 7.00
Novelty, vase, #108, 8" 22.00
Novelty, vase, #110, 9¼" 18.00
Orchid, basket, #305, 7" 165.00
Orchid, jardiniere, #310, 6" 90.00
Orchid, vase, #301, 10" 175.00
Orchid, vase, #303, 4¾" 42.00
Orchid, vase, #304, 6" 50.00
Orchid, vase, #307, 4¾" 42.00
Orchid, vase, #308, 4¼" 40.00
Parchment & Pine, bowl, console; 16" 50.00
Poppy, basket, #601, 12" 300.00
Poppy, basket, #601, 9" 195.00
Poppy, vase, #606, 10½" 160.00
Red Riding Hood, canister, cereal 300.00
Red Riding Hood, canister, tea, coffee, sugar, or flour; ea 225.00
Red Riding Hood, canister, tidbits 600.00
Red Riding Hood, casserole, red hdls, extremely rare 2,000.00
Red Riding Hood, cookie jar, open end basket, 13" 95.00
Red Riding Hood, cookie jar, rnd basket, 13" 150.00

Little Red Riding
Hood cracker jar,
8½", $195.00.

Red Riding Hood, creamer & sugar bowl, head pour, w/lid 200.00
Red Riding Hood, creamer & sugar bowl, side pour 70.00
Red Riding Hood, feeding dish, 3-compartment 2,000.00
Red Riding Hood, jar, cracker; skirt held wide, 8½" 195.00
Red Riding Hood, jar, dresser; w/bow, 9" 175.00
Red Riding Hood, matchbox, wall hanging 300.00
Red Riding Hood, mug, chocolate 400.00
Red Riding Hood, pitcher, batter 120.00
Red Riding Hood, pitcher, milk; ruffled skirt 1,500.00
Red Riding Hood, pitcher, milk; standing, 8" 95.00
Red Riding Hood, planter, standing 1,200.00
Red Riding Hood, shakers, lg, pr 35.00
Red Riding Hood, shakers, med, 4½", pr 200.00
Red Riding Hood, shakers, sm, pr 25.00
Red Riding Hood, spice jar (any) 285.00
Red Riding Hood, string holder, wall mt 315.00
Red Riding Hood, teapot or hot chocolate pot, ea 95.00
Red Riding Hood, wolf (any) 300.00

Rosella, creamer, R-3, open, 5½" 20.00
Rosella, ewer, R-11, 7" 45.00
Rosella, ewer, R-7, 9½" 140.00
Rosella, vase, R-2, 5" 22.00
Rosella, vase, R-5, 6½" 32.00
Serenade, ewer, S-2, 6½" 35.00
Serenade, ewer, S-21, pk w/gold, 10½" 60.00
Serenade, teapot, S-17, 5" 80.00
Serenade, vase, S-1, 6½" 25.00
Serenade, vase, S-4, 5¼" 35.00
Sueno Tulip, vase, #100/33, 10" 115.00
Sueno Tulip, vase, #107/33, 8" 75.00
Sun Glow, basket, #84, 6½" 32.00
Sun Glow, flowerpot, #97, 5½" 16.00
Sun Glow, pitcher, #52, 24-oz 24.00
Thistle, vase, #51, 6½" 30.00
Thistle, vase, #52, 6½" 30.00
Tokay, cornucopia, #10, shaded bkground, 11" 32.00
Tokay, vase, #4, shaded bkground, 8¼" 32.00
Tokay, vase, #8, shaded bkground, 10" 40.00
Tropicana, ewer, #56, 12½" 300.00
Tuscany, basket, #11, wht bkground, 10½" 40.00
Tuscany, urn, #5, wht bkground, 5½" 28.00
Water Lily, candle holder, L-22, 4½", pr 32.00
Water Lily, cornucopia, L-7, 6½" 45.00
Water Lily, creamer, L-19, apricot & walnut, 5" 32.00
Water Lily, dbl cornucopia, L-27, 12" 95.00
Water Lily, ewer, L-3, 5½" 40.00
Water Lily, jardiniere, L-23, 5½" 55.00
Water Lily, vase, L-A, 8½" 95.00
Water Lily, vase, L-10, 9½" 85.00
Water Lily, vase, L-11, 9½" 85.00
Water Lily, vase, L-12, 10½" 100.00
Water Lily, vase, L-13, 10½" 100.00
Water Lily, vase, L-16, apricot & walnut, 12½" 140.00
Water Lily, vase, L-4, 6½" 40.00
Water Lily, vase, L-6, 6½" 32.00
Water Lily, vase, L-8, 8½" 60.00
Wildflower, bowl, console; W-21, 12" 85.00
Wildflower, cornucopia, W-10, 8½" 65.00
Wildflower, cornucopia, W-7, 7½" 45.00
Wildflower, ewer, #55, 13½" 200.00
Wildflower, ewer, W-11, 8½" 80.00
Wildflower, ewer, W-2, 5½" 35.00
Wildflower, lamp base, W-17, 12½" 145.00
Wildflower, vase, #17, 12½" 110.00
Wildflower, vase, #52, 5¼" 45.00
Wildflower, vase, #59, 10½" 80.00
Wildflower, vase, #67, 8½" 145.00
Wildflower, vase, W-1, 5½" 28.00
Wildflower, vase, W-12, 9½" 75.00
Wildflower, vase, W-14, 10½" 80.00
Wildflower, vase, W-17, 12½" 110.00
Wildflower, vase, W-3, 5½" 30.00
Wildflower, vase, W-4, 6½" 42.00
Wildflower, vase, W-5, 6½" 45.00
Wildflower, vase, W-6, 7½" 42.00
Wildflower, vase, W-8, 7½" 45.00
Wildflower, vase, W-9, 8½" 60.00
Woodland, glossy; basket, W-22, 10½" 90.00
Woodland, glossy; bowl, console; W-29, 14" 55.00
Woodland, glossy; cornucopia, W-10, 11" 38.00
Woodland, glossy; cornucopia, W-2, 5½" 22.00
Woodland, glossy; ewer, W-3, 5½" 28.00

Woodland, glossy; jardiniere, W-7, 5½" 35.00
Woodland, glossy; tea set, W-26, W-27, & W-28, 3-pc 85.00
Woodland, glossy; teapot, peach 60.00
Woodland, glossy; vase, W-16, 8½" 40.00
Woodland, glossy; vase, W-17, 7½" 50.00
Woodland, glossy; vase, W-4, 6½" 24.00
Woodland, glossy; vase, W-8, 7½" 34.00
Woodland, matt; bowl, console; W-29, 14" 120.00
Woodland, matt; cornucopia, W-10, 11" 50.00
Woodland, matt; creamer, W-27, 3½" 40.00
Woodland, matt; ewer, W-3, 5½" 42.00
Woodland, matt; jardiniere, W-7, 5½" 70.00
Woodland, matt; teapot, W-26, 6½" 200.00
Woodland, matt; vase, W-16, 8½" 80.00
Woodland, matt; vase, W-4, 6½" 42.00

Hummel

Hummel figurines were created through the artistry of Berta Hummel, a Franciscan nun called Sister M. Innocentia. The first figures were made about 1935 by Franz Goebel of Goebel Art Inc., Rodental, West Germany. Plates, plaques, and candy dishes are also produced; and the older, discontinued editions are highly-sought collectibles. Generally speaking, an issue can be dated by the trademark. The first Hummels, from 1934-1950, were either incised or stamped with the 'Crown WG' mark. The 'full bee in V' mark was employed with minor variations until 1959. At that time the bee was stylized and represented by a solid disk with angled symmetrical wings completely contained within the confines of the 'V.' The three-line mark, 1964-1972, utilized the stylized bee and included a three-line arrangement, 'c by W. Goebel, W. Germany.' Another change in 1970 saw the 'stylized bee in V' suspended between the vertical bars of the 'b' and 'l' of a printed 'Goebel, West Germany.' Collectors refer to this mark as the 'last bee' or 'Goebel bee.' The current mark in use since 1979 omits the 'bee in V.' For a more thorough study of the subject we recommend *Hummel Figurines and Plates, A Collectors Identification and Value Guide*, by Carl Luckey, available at your local book dealer. Idiosyncrasies in the numerical order of the following listings are due to computer sorting.

Key:
ce — closed edition   GB — Goebel bee
CM — crown mark   SB — stylized bee
FB — full bee   LB — last bee

#III/53, Joyful, candy box, LB, 6¼" 115.00
#III/57, Chick Girl, candy box, LB, 5¼" 135.00
#III/58, Playmates, candy box, 3-line mk, 5¼" 135.00
#III/63, Singing Lesson, candy box, SB, 5¼" 210.00
#III/69, Happy Pastime, candy box, SB, 6" 300.00
#10/I, Flower Madonna, color, LB, 8¼" 195.00
#109/0, Happy Traveler, SB, 5" 88.00
#11/0, Merry Wanderer, LB, 4¾" 88.00
#110/I, Let's Sing, 3-line mk, 3⅞" 110.00
#110/0, Let's Sing, 3-line mk, 3¼" 75.00
#111/3/0, Wayside Harmony, LB, 3¾" 78.00
#113, Heavenly Song, candle holder, LB, 3½x4¾" 1,875.00
#115/#116/#117, Advent Group, candle holders, LB, 3½", set 120.00
#119, Postman, LB, 5¼" 110.00
#123, Max & Moritz, FB, 5¼" 145.00
#124/I, Hello, FB, 7" 200.00
#124/0, Hello, 3-line mk, 6¼" 110.00
#125, Vacation Time, plaque, LB, 4¼x4" 165.00
#126, Retreat to Safety, plaque, FB, 4¾x4¾" 225.00

#126, Retreat to Safety, plaque, SB, 4¾" 165.00
#129, Band Leader, LB, 5¼" 115.00
#13/V, Meditation, 3-line mk, 13¾" 1,250.00
#13/0, Meditation, FB, 6" 165.00
#131, Street Singer, FB, 5" 115.00
#132, Star Gazer, FB, 4¾" 210.00
#133, Mother's Helper, LB, 5" 115.00
#134, Quartet, plaque, FB, 6x6" 265.00
#134, Quartet, plaque, SB, 6x6" 245.00
#135, Soloist, LB, 4¾" 70.00
#136/I, Friends, SB, 5" 165.00
#136/V, Friends, 3-line mk, 10¾" 685.00
#137, Child-in-Bed, plaque, LB, 2¾" dia 38.00
#140, Mail Coach, plaque, 3-line mk, 4½x6¼" 195.00
#141/I, Apple Tree Girl, FB, 6" 195.00
#141/3/0, Apple Tree Girl, FB, 4" 135.00
#142/I, Apple Tree Boy, FB, 6" 195.00
#143/0, Boots, FB, 5¼" 165.00
#144, Angelic Song, LB, 4¼" 88.00
#146, Angel Duet, font, 3-line mk, 4¾x2" 36.00
#147, Devotion, font, 3-line mk, 5x3" 35.00
#15/1, Hear Ye Hear Ye, 3-line mk, 6" 155.00
#150/I, Happy Days, FB, 6" 400.00
#150/0, Happy Days, FB, 5¼" 225.00
#152/A/II, Umbrella Boy, FB, 8" 1,275.00
#152/A/II, Umbrella Boy, 3-line mk, 8" 945.00
#152/B/II, Umbrella Girl, SB, 8" 995.00
#153/0, Auf Widersehen, SB, 7" 185.00
#153/0, Auf Widersehen, 3-line mk, 5¼" 150.00
#154/I, Waiter, FB, 7" 185.00
#16/1, Little Hiker, FB, 5½" 160.00
#16/2/0, Little Hiker, LB, 4¼" 70.00
#163, Whitsuntide, LB, 7¼" 165.00
#164, Worship, font, 3-line mk, 4¾x2¾" 38.00
#167, Angel w/Bird, font, 3-line mk, 4¼x3¼" 32.00
#168, Standing Boy, plaque, SB, 5½x4⅛" 145.00
#169, Bird Duet, LB, 4" 88.00
#17/0, Congratulations, no socks, 3-line mk, 6" 120.00
#170/III, School Boys, LB, 10" 120.00
#171, Little Sweeper, SB, 4½" 98.00
#174, She Loves Me, She Loves Me Not, 3-line mk, 4¼" 115.00
#176, Happy Birthday, FB, 7" 365.00
#177/III, School Girls, FB, 9½" 1,800.00
#177/III, School Girls, 3-line mk, 9½" 1,350.00
#178, Photographer, 3-line mk, 4¾" 150.00
#180, Tuneful Goodnight, plaque, 3-line mk, 4¾x4" 160.00
#182, Good Friends, LB, 4" 110.00
#183, Forest Shrine, FB, 9x7" 1,150.00
#184, Latest News, SB, 5¼" 135.00
#185, Accordion Boy, SB, 5¼" 135.00
#186, Sweet Music, 3-line mk, 5¼" 110.00
#188, Celestial Musician, 3-line mk, 7" 185.00
#192, Candlelight, candle holder, long candle, FB, 6¾" 465.00
#193, Angel Duet, 3-line mk, 5" 120.00
#197/I, Be Patient, 3-line mk, 6¼" 155.00
#198, Home From Market, CM, 5¾" 385.00
#199/I, Feeding Time, FB, 5¾" 225.00
#199/0, Feeding Time, FB, 4¼" 200.00
#2/1, Little Fiddler, FB, 7½" 450.00
#20, Prayer Before Battle, LB, 4¼" 95.00
#20½0, Retreat to Safety, SB, 4" 130.00
#203/I, Signs of Spring, 3-line mk, 5" 150.00
#203/2/0, Signs of Spring, FB, 4" 165.00
#204, Weary Wanderer, FB, 6" 245.00

#206, Angel Cloud, font, FB, 4¾x2¼" 345.00
#206, Angel Cloud, font, 3-line mk, 4¾x2¼" 35.00
#207, Heavenly Angel, font, SB, 4¾x2" 40.00
#21/0, Heavenly Angel, 3-line mk, 4¼" 68.00
#21/1, Heavenly Angel, SB, 6¾" 155.00
#217, Boy w/Toothache, FB, 5½" 200.00
#219/2/0, Little Velma, FB, 4⅛" 3,750.00
#22/1, Angel w/Birds, font, FB, 4x3¼" 400.00
#222, Madonna, plaque, SB, 5x4" 825.00
#223, To Market, table lamp, FB, 9½" 400.00
#226, Mail Coach, 3-line mk, 4¼x6¼" 400.00
#23/III, Adoration, 3-line mk, 9" 350.00
#23/1, Adoration, SB, 6¼" 250.00
#235, Happy Days, table lamp, SB, 7¾" 450.00
#24/III, Lullaby, candle holder, FB, 6x8" 675.00
#240, Little Drummer, SB, 4¼" 100.00
#246, Holy Family, font, FB, 4x3" 120.00
#25, Angelic Sleep, candle holder, 3½x5" 150.00
#255, Stitch in Time, SB, 6¾" 235.00
#258, Which Hand?, 3-line mk, 5¼" 85.00
#26/0, Child Jesus, font, SB, 5x1½" 32.00
#262, Heavenly Lullaby, LB, 3½x5" 125.00
#27/III, Joyous News, LB, 4¼x4¾" 155.00
#28/II, Wayside Devotion, SB, 7½" 275.00
#28/III, Wayside Devotion, CM, 8½" 1,250.00
#30/OA&B, Ba-Bee Ring, plaques, 3-line mk, 5" dia, pr 135.00
#304, Artist, 3-line mk, 5¼" 355.00
#319, Doll Bath, SB, 5¼" 765.00
#32/1, Little Gabriel, LB, 5" 85.00
#327, Run-A-Way, 3-line mk, 5¼" 725.00
#33, Joyful, ash tray, 3-line mk, 3½x6" 78.00
#332, Soldier Boy, SB, 6" 825.00
#34, Singing Lesson, ash tray, 3-line mk, 3½x6¼" 125.00
#35/0, Good Shepherd, SB, 4¾x2¼" 32.00
#35/1, Good Shepherd, font, 5¾x2¾" 95.00
#36/0, Child w/Flowers, SB, 4x2¾" 38.00
#36/1, Child w/Flowers, font, LB, 4½x3½" 48.00
#37, Herald Angels, candle holder, FB, 2¼x4" 200.00
#4, Little Fiddler, 3-line mk, 4¾" 100.00
#42/0, Good Shepherd, SB, 6¼" 120.00
#43, March Winds, 3-line mk, 5" 80.00
#44/B, Out of Danger, SB, 9½" 300.00
#45/III, Madonna w/Halo, 3-line mk, 16¼" 120.00
#46/1, Madonna w/o Halo, FB, 11¼" 98.00
#47/3/0, Goose Girl, LB, 4" 98.00
#48/V, Madonna, plaque, SB, 8¼x10½" 995.00
#49/I, To Market, 3-line mk, 6¼" 275.00
#49/3/0, To Market, SB, 4" 150.00
#50/0, Volunteers, SB, 5½" 195.00
#51/0, Village Boy, CM, 6" 500.00
#51/3/0, Village Boy, 3-line mk, 4" 65.00
#52/I, Going to Grandma's, FB, 6" 495.00
#54, Silent Night, candle holder, 3-line mk, 4¾x5½" ...150.00
#55, St George, 3-line mk, 6¾" 235.00
#56/A, Culprits, 3-line mk, 6¼" 150.00
#56/B, Out of Danger, FB, 6¼" 275.00
#58/I, Playmates, SB, 4½" 180.00
#6/II, Sensitive Hunter, CM, 7½" 1,250.00
#60/A&B, Farm Boy & Goose Girl, bookends, FB, 6", pr 525.00
#62, Happy Pastime, ash tray, 3-line mk, 3½x6¼" 120.00
#64, Shepherd's Boy, LB, 5½" 115.00
#66, Farm Boy, FB, 5¼" 185.00
#68, Lost Sheep, FB, 5½" 185.00
#68/0, Lost Sheep, 3-line mk, 5½" 110.00

Village Boy, #51/3/0, crown mark, 4", $230.00.

#7/II, Merry Wanderer, 3-line mk, 9½" 850.00
#71, Stormy Weather, 3-line mk, 6¼" 300.00
#72, Spring Cheer, LB, 5" 55.00
#74, Little Gardener, FB, 4¼" 145.00
#75, Wht Angel Font, 3-line mk, 3½x1¾" 30.00
#78/II, Infant of Krumbad, 3-line mk, 3½" 40.00
#78/VI, Infant of Krumbad, SB, 10" 155.00
#81/0, School Girl, FB, 5¼" 155.00
#82/II, School Boy, FB, 7½" 500.00

Angel Serenade, #83, stylized bee, 5", $200.00.

#84/0, Worship, CM, 5" 385.00
#84/5, Worship, FB, 13" 1,450.00
#85/II, Serenade, FB, 7½" 450.00
#85/0, Serenade, FB, 4¾" 125.00
#87, For Father, LB, 5½" 95.00
#88/II, Heavenly Protection, SB, 9¼" 465.00
#89/II, Little Cellist, FB, 8" 455.00
#89/1, Little Cellist, 3-line mk, 6" 120.00
#91/A&B, Eventide & Adoration, bookends, FB, 4¾x2", pr 88.00

#92, Merry Wanderer, plaque, 3-line mk, 5⅛x4¾" 100.00
#94/I, Surprise, FB, 5½" 225.00
#95, Brother, LB, 5½" 88.00
#98/2/0, Sister, FB, 4¾" 110.00
#99, Eventide, FB, 4¾" 285.00

Hutschenreuther

Sources do not agree as to when the Carl Hutschenreuther factory was initially established in the Bavarian district of Germany. Most indicate a year near the middle of the 19th century. Carl's sons, Christian and Lorenz, later formed their own companies and operated independently until 1969. At that time Carl and Lorenz merged; and that firm is still in business today producing limited edition plates, figurines, dinnerware, and other fine china.

Our advisor for this category is Jack Gunsaulus; he is listed in the Directory under Michigan.

Cake plate, fruit, grape clusters at rim, hdls, mk, 11" 55.00
Figurine, ballerina w/arms behind, head bk, 7x9" 150.00
Figurine, bird, appl leaves, K Tutter, 6½" 60.00
Figurine, kneeling dancer in yel tunic, hands upraised, 11" 400.00
Figurine, nymph, 2 fighting brn bears, rock base, 12" 550.00
Figurine, polar bear on ball, wht w/gold 4" 95.00
Figurine, 2 geese, 14" 250.00
Figurine, 2 wht horses running, sgn MH Fritz, 11½x15" 500.00
Plate, Roses of Redonte, gold rim, 6¼", 8 for.............................260.00
Plate, 22k gold leaf rim decor, Selb Bavaria, 10¾", pr 45.00
Platter, Kensington, 15x11"..80.00
Teapot, Thistle, +cr/sug...95.00
Tray, seated elfin flutist, Tutter...135.00

Hyalyn

Organized in 1947 in Hickory, North Carolina, Hyalyn Porcelain, Inc., produced artware with a fine porcelain body made from material mined primarily in the southeastern states. Small sculptures, vases, and lamp bases made up the bulk of their output. Early examples carry the original shield logo, which was replaced later on with the outline of a vase within a rectangle. In 1973 the company was purchased by Hamilton-Cosco, and in the late 1970s by Robert Warmuth, an official of the Hyalyn company.

Lamp base, blk w/gold '50s design, sgn Briand, mk, 8" 75.00
Lamp base, blk w/gold '50s design, sgn Briand, 16" 175.00
Lamp base, blk w/stylized silver inlay, sgn G Briand, 16" 195.00
Vase, bl & gray w/gold '50s design, sgn G Briand, 12" 165.00
Vase, wht w/bold design, Briand, 1950s, 8" 150.00

Imari

Imari is a generic term which covers a broad family of wares. It was made in more than a dozen Japanese villages, but the name is that of the port from whence it was shipped to Europe. There are several types of Imari. The most common features a design with panels of birds, florals, or people surrounding a central basket of flowers. The colors used in this type are underglaze blue with overglaze red, gold, and green enamels. The Chinese also made Imari wares which differ from the Japanese type in several ways — the absence of spur marks, a thinner-type body, and a more consistent control of the blue. Imari-type wares were copied on the continent by Meissen and by English potters, among them Worcester, Derby, and Bow.

Bowl, birds/floral panels, shaped/scalloped, 1880, 11", NM 375.00
Cat, sleeping, late, 12½" L 375.00
Charger, ducks in pond w/iris near pavilion, gilt, 18"...................300.00
Charger, exotic bird center, paneled floral border, 24" 900.00
Charger, floral/fan medallion, scenes of cranes, 1890, 16" 275.00
Charger, woman in courtyard/elaborate florals, ruffled, 10" 750.00
Dish, bldgs/foliage reserves, boat form, 1800s, 13" 375.00
Jar, floral/bird panels, 1880s, no lid, 9½" 425.00
Jar, temple; panels of children or phoenix, dog finial, 19"............750.00
Jardiniere, florals, fluted body, 1880s, 6½" 300.00
Jardiniere, mums/honeycomb, incurvate, 8½x7½" 450.00
Punch bowl, flowerpot, floral medallions, ribbed, 14", EX 900.00
Punch bowl, vase in medallion/phoenix, int: same, 8x15" 3,600.00
Tankard, floral, peach-color accents, gilding, 1700s, 6" 750.00

Tray, dragon, bird, & florals on rim, central landscape with deer, 16" x 13½", $425.00.

Tray, mum garden, floral/tree-panel rim, sq, 1880s, 10"................150.00
Tray, 3 deer by stream center, w/gold, sq, 1800s, 16x13½" 425.00
Vase, floral panels, fluted w/wide mouth, 1800s, 8", NM.............275.00
Vase, floral panels, 1880s, 10" 275.00
Vase, overall florals, bulbous w/molded banding, 1800s, 12" 325.00
Vase, plain reserves/floral ground, ornate hdls, 1800s, 36" 1,500.00
Wash pitcher, foliage, gilt/orange/bl, 13", +18" basin..................700.00

Imperial Glass

Although the Imperial Glass Company was organized in 1901, it was not until three years later that they began to manufacture glassware. Their early products were jelly glasses, hotel tumblers, etc.; but by 1910 they were making a name for themselves by pressing quantities of Carnival Glass, the iridescent colored glassware that was popular during that time. From 1916 to 1920, they used the lustre process to make a line they called Imperial Jewels, now referred to as stretch glass. Opalescent glassware was introduced in the thirties and was made in Sea Foam, Harding Blue, Moss Green, and Burnt Almond. In contrast to their colored lines, Candlewick was a simple pattern in crystal glass, yet one for which the company is best known. (All of these types are listed by specific category in this book.) Free-Hand Ware, art glass made entirely by hand using no molds, was made for a short time only from about 1923 to 1928. Nu-Cut was made to imitate cut glass; it was produced in crystal as well as color and was introduced in 1914.

The company closed in 1931 but soon reorganized and reopened as the Imperial Glass Corporation. In 1940 they bought the molds and assets of the Central Glass Works of Wheeling, West Virginia, and in 1958 they purchased molds from Cambridge and Heisey. Although Imperial later used these molds to reproduce the older pieces, since

1951 they have indicated their issues with the 'I' superimposed over a 'G' trademark. The company sold out to Lenox in 1973 but continues today to make hand-pressed giftware items. See also Animal Dishes with Covers; Candlewick; Carnival Glass; Opalescent Glass; Stretch Glass.

Animals and Birds

Dog, Airdale, cobalt	35.00
Dog, Champ Terrier, caramel slag	200.00
Donkey, caramel slag, mk IG	50.00
Elephant, gr carnival, mk IG, ltd ed, med, scarce	100.00
Pony, standing/rearing/or kicking, ultra bl, mk IG, ea	30.00
Rabbit, paperweight, milk glass, mk IG	15.00
Swan, caramel slag, mk, 9¼"	95.00
Swan, purple slag, 4"	38.00
Wood duck, caramel slag	40.00

Ash tray, Cape Cod, 5½"	5.00
Bowl, console; Cape Cod, rolled rim, 13"	40.00
Bowl, Crocheted Crystal, 11" +2 4½" candle holders	15.00
Bowl, float; Cape Cod, 14"	45.00
Bowl, fruit; Cape Cod, ruby, 4½"	16.00
Bowl, fruit; Cape Cod, 4½"	4.00
Butter dish, Cape Cod, 2-hdl	25.00
Cake plate, Tradition, 72-candle, 13"	65.00
Cake stand, Crocheted Crystal, 12"	15.00
Candlestick, Cathay, woman, 9"	125.00
Candy dish, Cape Cod, ruby, 9¼"	42.00
Celery boat, Cape Cod, oval, 10½"	45.00
Celery tray, Pillar Flutes, bl, hdls	15.00
Coaster, Cape Cod, w/spoon rest	6.00
Cocktail, Cape Cod, 3½-oz	8.00
Compote, Cape Cod, 6"	20.00
Cordial, Cape Cod, 1½-oz	12.00
Creamer & sugar bowl, Cape Cod, ftd, on tray	30.00
Cruet, Cape Cod, amber, w/stopper	30.00
Cruet, Cape Cod, olive gr	35.00
Cup, Pillar Flutes, bl	6.00
Cup, punch; Cape Cod	7.00
Cup & saucer, Cape Cod	10.00
Cup & saucer, Niagara, ruby	8.00
Decanter, Cape Cod, rnd, 30-oz	48.00
Egg cup, Cape Cod	17.00
Epergne, Cape Cod, 2-pc	150.00

Crocheted Crystal: Epergne, $25.00; Vase, $20.00; Creamer & sugar bowl, $20.00.

Goblet, Cape Cod, gr	28.00

Goblet, Cape Cod, 8-oz	7.50
Hors d'ouvre, Crocheted Crystal, rnd, 4-part, 10½"	12.50
Horseradish, Cape Cod, w/stopper	68.00
Marmalade, Cape Cod, 4-pc	25.00
Martini mixer, Big Shot Series, red	80.00
Mayonnaise set, Crocheted Crystal, 5¼" bowl, 7½" plate	8.00
Old Fashioned, Cape Cod	15.00
Parfait, Cape Cod	12.00
Pepper mill, Cape Cod	28.00

Cape Cod pitcher, $65.00.

Pitcher, Tradition, ice lip, 54-oz	35.00
Plate, Cape Cod, cupped, 14"	20.00
Plate, Cape Cod, 10"	33.00
Plate, Cape Cod, 4½"	4.50
Plate, Cape Cod, 8"	9.00
Plate, Niagara, ruby	6.00
Punch set, Cape Cod, 15-pc	175.00
Relish, Cape Cod, oval, 3-part, 9½"	20.00
Relish, Cape Cod, 5-part, 11"	40.00
Relish, Pillar Flutes, bl, oval	14.00
Relish, Pillar Flutes, oval	12.50
Salt cellar, Cape Cod, ind, +glass spoon	10.00
Sherbet, Cape Cod, ftd, 5"	6.00
Sherbet, Cape Cod, gr, 6-oz	12.00
Stein, Cape Cod, 12-oz	45.00
Tumbler, Big Shot Series, red, 12-oz	15.00
Tumbler, Cape Cod, flat, 6-oz	6.00
Tumbler, Cape Cod, ftd, 8-oz	8.00
Tumbler, Cape Cod, 10-oz	10.00
Tumbler, iced tea; Cape Cod, gr	16.00
Tumbler, Pillar Flute	20.00
Vase, bud; Pillar Flutes, bl	20.00
Vase, Free-Hand, burgundy irid w/bl & silver, incurvate, 6"	175.00
Vase, Free-Hand, heart leaves, bl on opal, gold int, 11"	350.00
Vase, Free-Hand, heart leaves, wht on cobalt, gold int, 7"	250.00
Vase, Free-Hand, heart leaves on orange irid, bl int, 8x4"	275.00
Wine, Cape Cod, wafer stem, #150, 3¾"	8.00

Imperial Porcelain

The Blue Ridge Mountain Boys were created by cartoonist Paul

Webb and translated into three-dimension by the Imperial Porcelain Corporation of Zanesville, Ohio in 1947. These figurines decorated ash trays, vases, mugs, bowls, pitchers, planters, and other items. The Mountain Boys series were numbered 92 through 108, each with a different and amusing portrayal of mountain life. Imperial also produced American Folklore miniatures, twenty-three tiny animals one inch or less in size, and the Al Capp Dogpatch series. Because of financial difficulties, the company closed in 1960.

American Folklore Miniatures

Cat, 1½" 40.00
Cow, 1¾" 35.00
Hound dogs 35.00
Plaque, store ad, Am Folklore Porcelain Miniatures, 4½" 300.00
Sow 30.00

Blue Ridge Mountain Boys by Paul Webb

Ash tray, #101, man w/jug & snake 75.00
Ash tray, #103, hillbilly & skunk 75.00
Ash tray, #105, baby, hound dog, & frog............................110.00
Ash tray, #106, Barrel of Wishes, w/hound 75.00
Ash tray, #92, 2 men by tree stump, for pipes 125.00
Box, cigarette; #98, dog atop, baby at door, sq...............115.00
Decanter, #100, outhouse, man, & bird 75.00
Decanter, #104, Ma leaning over stump, w/baby & skunk 95.00
Decanter, man, jug, snake, & tree stump, Hispch Inc, 1946 ....75.00
Figurine, #101, man leans against tree trunk, 5" 90.00
Figurine, man on hands & knees, 3" 95.00
Figurine, man sitting, 3½" 95.00
Figurine, man sitting w/chicken on knee, 3"....................95.00
Jug, #101, Willie & snake 75.00
Mug, #94, Bearing Down, 6" 95.00
Mug, #94, dbl baby hdl, 4¼"...95.00
Mug, #94, ma hdl, 4¼" 95.00
Mug, #94, man w/bl pants hdl, 4¼".................................95.00
Mug, #94, man w/yel beard & red pants hdl, 4¼" 95.00
Mug, #99, Target Practice, boy on goat, farmer, 5¾" 95.00
Pitcher, lemonade 200.00
Plack, store ad, Handcrafted Paul Webb Mtn Boys, rare, 9" 500.00
Planter, #100, outhouse, man, & bird 75.00
Planter, #104, Ma leaning over stump, w/baby & skunk 95.00
Planter, #105, man w/chicken on knee, washtub 110.00
Planter, #110, man, w/jug & snake, 4½" 65.00
Planter, #81, man drinking from jug, sitting by washtub 75.00

Shakers, Ma & Old Doc, $95.00 for the pair.

Miscellaneous

Items in this section that are designated 'IP' are miscellaneous novelties made by Imperial Porcelain; the remainder are of interest to Paul Webb collectors, though made by an unknown manufacturer. Prints on calendars and playing cards are signed 'Paul Webb.'

Calendar, 1954, 12 sgn scenes, Brown & Bigelow, complete..........35.00
Figurine, cat in high-heeled shoe, 5½" L................................40.00
Hot pad, Dutch boy w/tulips, rnd, IP......................................30.00
Ink blotters, sgn scenes, ea.. 8.00
Mug, #29, man hdl, sgn Paul Webb, 4¾" 25.00
Planter, #106, dog sitting by tub, IP 75.00
Planter, #26, man & tree stump, sgn Paul Webb, bl 25.00
Planter, #27, man, jug, & barrel, sgn Paul Webb 25.00
Planter, #81, Uncle Rafe, dog by washtub, IP, 4" L...............75.00
Playing cards, ad: Rafe Oiling Gun, Brown & Bigelow, MIB 45.00
Shakers, pigs, 5", pr 95.00
Shakers, standing pigs, IP, 8", pr...95.00

Indian Tree

Indian Tree was a popular dinnerware pattern produced by various potteries since the early 1800s to recent times. Although backgrounds and borders vary, the Oriental theme is carried out with the gnarled, brown branch of a pink-blossomed tree. Among the manufacturers marks, you may find represented such notable firms as Coalport, S. Hancock and Sons, Soho Pottery, and John Maddock and Sons.

Bowl, vegetable; rnd, Meakin..20.00
Creamer, Meakin...10.00
Cup & saucer, Meakin..25.00
Cup & saucer, miniature..35.00
Plate, bread & butter; Meakin 4.00
Plate, dinner; Meakin 8.00
Plate, Maddock, 9¾"..12.00
Platter, Hancock & Sons, 12"..30.00
Platter, oval, Meakin...25.00
Soup/cereal, Meakin.. 6.00

Inkwells and Inkstands

Receptacles for various writing fluids have been used since ancient times. Through the years they have been made from countless materials – glass, metal, porcelain, pottery, wood, and even papier-mache. During the 18th century, gold or silver inkstands were presented to royalty; the well-known silver inkstand by Philip Syng, Jr., was used for the signing of the Declaration of Independence, and impressive brass inkstands with wells and a pounce pot (sander) were proud possessions of men of letters. When literacy vastly increased in the 19th century, the dip pen replaced the quill pen; and inkwells and inkstands were widely used and produced in a broad range of sizes in functional and decorative forms – from ornate Victorian to flowing Art Nouveau and stylized Art Deco designs. However, the acceptance of the ballpoint pen literally put inkstands and inkwells 'out of business.' But their historical significance and intriguing diversity of form and styling fascinate today's collectors.

Blown, amber, pontil, att Ellenville, sm bubbles, 1⅞" 100.00
Blown, aqua, door-knob form, rough pontil, from NY, 2½x3"........60.00
Blown, controlled bubbles, loose sterling lid, 5" dia 500.00
Blown, olive amber, GIII-29, disk mouth, pontil, 1½" 140.00
Blown, olive gr, GII-18, disk mouth, Coventry, 1½x2¼" 150.00
Blown, olive-gr, GII-18, 2¾" dia 150.00

Blown, pitkin-type 35-rib right swirl, conical, 2½" dia **275.00**
Brass, dual covered wells, orig glass inserts, 4¼x7" **95.00**
Brass, hinged lid, pen holder, glass insert **35.00**
Brass, mandolin & sheet music figural, EX **250.00**
Brass plated, emb Victorian carriage scenes, Japan, 3-pc...............**37.50**
Bronze, cupid sleeps in new moon w/mandolin, Dolivet, 7" **700.00**
Bronze, shepherdess & 2 sheep, sgn Korschamm, 6¾x8½" **650.00**
Bronze, Viking ships relief, Jenning Bros, 4½", +tray **95.00**
Bsk, owl figural, glass eyes **195.00**
Cameo, floral/berries, red/gold on olive, St Louis, 5" **550.00**

Arts & Crafts hammered copper inkstand with pine cones & brass trim, 4" x 10" x 5", $425.00.

Copper lustre, flowers on bl band, 5 quill holders, 3x4" **295.00**
Cut, gr, dbl, stag's head in center of SP fr, 4x7" **275.00**
Cut, sq w/brass partners lid, 2½" **250.00**
Cut, w/sterling hinged lid mk Unger.....................................**300.00**
Cut, 6-sided pyramid, hinged lid, starred base, 3¾x3" **150.00**
Glass, bl & wht nailsea, brass lid, 3½" dia **550.00**
Glass, cranberry w/wht overshot, ribbed, 'jockey hat' lid **300.00**
Glass, mug form, appl hdl, 10 vertical panels, 3¼" **80.00**
Glass, Safety Inkstand Pat Apl 3 66, 2¾x3¼" dia **45.00**
Glass, snail, in CI stand, revolves, 3x5x2" **160.00**
Glass, stack of cannonballs form, electric bl, att Sandwich..........**550.00**
Glass & Bakelite, self closing, Sengbusch **75.00**
Leather, glass insert, rectangular, EX..**65.00**
Mixed metal, Gorham Athenic silver on copper, 12" W **2,500.00**
Pewter, center cup insert w/5 quill holes, 1860s, 3½x4½"............**140.00**
Porc, floral, ribs, dbl hinged, attached tray, 2½x6x4" **125.00**
Porc, floral, sq form, loose lid, Nippon, 4" **250.00**
Pottery, boat shape, 2 quill holes, Rockingham glaze, 3" L...........**100.00**
Silvered metal, racing car w/2 drivers, well in boot, 15" **3,000.00**
Soapstone, ribbed dome/geometrics/quill holders, 1800s, 2½" **150.00**
SP, lady golfer putting...**250.00**
Staffordshire, bird's nest **225.00**
Stoneware, teakettle, brn-glaze, Josiah Johnson, 2½", NM..........**200.00**
Treen, worn brn grpt w/gold stencil, paper label, 3⅝" **165.00**
Wood, trn, brn flame grpt, blk trim, Silliman & Co, 3" dia **175.00**

Insulators

The telegraph was invented in 1844. The devices developed to hold the electrical transmission wires to the poles were called insulators. The telephone, invented in 1876, intensified their usefullness; and, by the turn of the century, thousands of varieties were being produced in glass of various colors, pottery, and wood. Many are embossed with patent dates.

Of the more than 3,000 types known to exist, today's collectors evaluate their worth by age and rarity of color. Aqua and green are the most common colors in glass, dark brown the most common in ceramic. Threadless insulators (CD #737) made between 1850 and 1870, bring prices well into the hundreds.

In the listings that follow, the CD numbers are from an identification system developed in the late 1960s by N.R. Woodward.

Those seeking additional information about insulators are encouraged to contact the National Insulator Association, whose address may be found in the Directory under Clubs, Newsletters, and Catalogs.

Key:
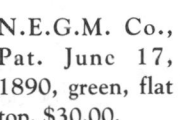

CB — corregated base	SDP — sharp drip points
CD — Consolidated Design	RB — rough base
SB — smooth base	RDP — round drip points

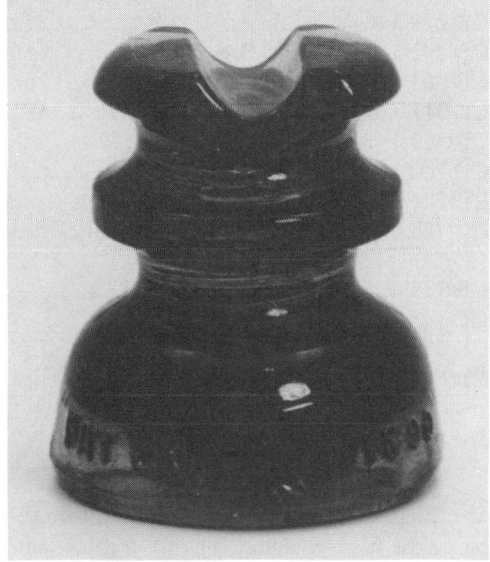

N.E.G.M. Co., Pat. June 17, 1890, green, flat top, $30.00.

CD #122.4, Pyrex, SB, lemon... **4.00**
CD 100, Surge, RDP, clear **2.00**
CD 1000, no name (Glass Block), lt gr **500.00**
CD 102, BGM Co, SB, purple...**18.00**
CD 102, California, SB, bl **15.00**
CD 102.2, Westinghouse, SB, bl..**130.00**
CD 104, Brookfield, SB, aqua.. **5.00**
CD 106, Ericson, RDP, clear, foreign......................................**10.00**
CD 106, Star, SB, olive gr **8.00**
CD 112, California, SB, smoke **6.00**
CD 112, New England Telegraph & Telephone, SB, gr **80.00**
CD 1130, California, purple..**150.00**
CD 115, Hemingray, CB, clear **1.00**
CD 121, Diamond, SB, purple, foreign **15.00**
CD 121, Maydwell, SDP, straw..**14.00**
CD 122, McLaughlin, RDP, apple gr **6.00**
CD 123, EC&M Co SF, SB, aqua w/olive streaks **80.00**
CD 124.6, Agee, SB, emerald gr, foreign **50.00**
CD 128, Hemingray E-14-B, SB, opal.....................................**50.00**
CD 130.7, AGM, SB, aqua, foreign **10.00**
CD 134, KCGW, SB, gr...**20.00**
CD 138, Kerr, SB, clear **4.00**
CD 141, no name (Hot Cross Bun,) SB, emerald gr......................... **9.00**
CD 143, Canadian Pacific, SB, royal purple, foreign......................**15.00**
CD 143, CNR, SB, aqua **10.00**
CD 145, Brookfield, SB, aqua.. **1.00**
CD 145, Hemingray, SDP, bl **1.00**
CD 150, Brookfield, SB, aqua **50.00**
CD 150.2, Telefonos Ericson, SB, lt gr, foreign.............................**30.00**

CD 152, Hemingray, SB or DP, aqua **1.00**
CD 155, Armstrong's DPL, SB, clear.. **1.00**
CD 162, Hemingray, DP, dk cobalt bl **125.00**
CD 162, SS&Co, SB, lime gr **75.00**
CD 168, Hemingray, SB, carnival **25.00**
CD 185, Jeffery, SB, aqua...**60.00**
CD 190/191, Am Telegraph & Telephone, SB, jade gr, 2-pc..........**35.00**
CD 190/191, AT&T, SB, aqua.. **8.00**
CD 201, California, SB, gr **600.00**
CD 203.2, Armstrong, SB, near clear **160.00**
CD 235, Pyrex, SB, carnival...**18.00**
CD 252, M&E, SB, aqua **40.00**
CD 257, Hemingray, DP, clear.. **4.00**
CD 263, Hemingray, SB, bl **80.00**
CD 267, NEGM, SB, yel-gr..**220.00**
CD 270, no name, SB, gr...**150.00**
CD 292.5, Boston, SB, dk gr..**95.00**
CD 303/310, Hemingray, RDP, lt gr **45.00**
CD 317, Chambers, SB, lime gr **150.00**
CD 320, Pyrex, SB, clear **9.00**
CD 700, no name (threadless egg), bl..**195.00**
CD 724, Chester, SB, dk cobalt, threadless **600.00**
CD 728, Boston Bottle Works, SB, lt aqua, threadless **60.00**
CD 731, McKee, SB, aqua, threadless..**130.00**
CD 733, Brookfield, SB, aqua, threadless **200.00**
CD 743, no name, SB, deep amber **400.00**
CD 743, no name, SB, deep amber, threadless **300.00**
CD 843, Verlica, SB, aqua **20.00**

Irons

Irons are available in great variety, with the sad iron (or flat iron) being the most common. The detachable-handled iron (invented by Mrs. Mary Florence Potts in 1871) prevented the hand of the user from becoming uncomfortably hot. The success of this invention led to the introduction of many variations of detachable handles, asbestos-lined hoods, heat shields, and other heat-modifying methods. The box iron was hollow and usually had a rear door through which a heated slug was inserted. Some of the earliest handmade irons were of this type. Slug irons continued to be made into this century.

Charcoal irons have been in use since the 1700s. They were simply small portable stoves. Burning coals supplied the heat, but flying sparks and ashes were a nuisance. Gasoline irons of the 20th century were a great improvement in convenience and comfort, but they were dangerous. A pump supplied pressure to the tank, and flare-ups were common. Alcohol and kerosene were also used as fuels.

Electric irons, though a 19th-century invention, did not achieve general use until electricity became widely available several decades later. Some of the most interesting collectible electric irons are from the Art Deco period. Almost every possible heating method has been used for ironing – including hot water. But some of the most fascinating devices used no heat at all. Such implements include smoothing boards, slickenstones, and linen presses.

In the listings that follow, prices are given for examples in very good to excellent condition. Damage, repairs, excessive wear, rust, and missing parts can dramatically reduce value. Our advisor for this category is The Iron Lady (Carol Walker and Jimmy Walker), whose address is listed in the Directory under Texas. See also Appliances.

Box, French, handmade, swing gate w/hook latch, 1700s, 6" **295.00**
Box, J&J Siddons, nickel shield, blk pnt, 5½" w/slug..................**175.00**
Box, lift gate at bk for iron slug, wrought hdl, 1850 ....**150.00**
Box, Scottish, ornate brass scrolling uprights, no slug, 1860s .. **1,000.00**

Charcoal, Eclipse, Pat Appl'd For 1902 ....75.00
Charcoal, Singapore, Kim Hiap Liong, polished brass, 8" 185.00
Charcoal, WD Cummings & E Bless, Pat 1852, tall chimney, 7"...75.00
Fluter, Crown, stencil & pnt, w/slugs, 1880s...............................125.00
Fluter, Johnson Transverse, brass bed, 4¼x3⅝", EX 300.00

Fluter, corrugated top and bottom, Patented Dec. (latter 1800s), $200.00.

Gasoline, Coleman #3, bl enamel hdl, NP 60.00
Goffering, A Kenrick & Son on base, 4¼" bbl, no heater 125.00
Sad iron, Le Parisien #6, coat of arms emb on face, 6½" 80.00
Sad iron, Mexico, Pagoel #7, 7⅝" 10.00
Sad iron, PW (Wintenberger), plain face, 2⅞"...............................75.00
Sad iron, raised star center, wood hdl, 2½" 95.00
Sad iron, Sensible #6, 4" 125.00
Sensible No 90, asbestos lined/hdl detaches, Pat/1908, 6½" 50.00
Sleeve, Hub, X-hatched iron hdl, 7" 45.00
Sleeve, Ober Mfg Chagrin Falls #801, 6¾" 95.00
Tailor's, CI w/twisted wrought & forged-on hdl, 1860s 45.00
Tailor's, smithy made, drawn-out hdl curves to bk, 7¼" 80.00
Tolliker, hat maker's, curved, shapes brims 130.00
Troy, shirt iron, diamond pattern on bottom, 4¼".......................130.00

Ironstone

During the last quarter of the 18th century, English potters began experimenting with a new type of body that contained calcinated flint and a higher china clay content, intent on producing a fine durable whiteware – heavy, yet with a texture that would resemble porcelain. To remove the last trace of yellow, a minute amount of cobalt was added, often resulting in a bluish-white tone. Wm. and John Turner of Caughley, and Josiah Spode II were the first to manufacture the ware successfully. Others, such as Davenport, Hicks and Meigh, and Ralph and Josiah Wedgwood, followed with their own versions. The latter coined the name 'Pearl' to refer to his product and incorporated the term into his trademark. In 1813 a 14-year patent was issued to Charles James Mason, who called his ware Patented Ironstone. Francis Morley, G.L. Asworth, T.J. Mayer, and other Staffordshire potters continued to produce ironstone until the end of the century. While some of these patterns are simple to the extreme, many are decorated with in-mold designs of fruit, grain, and foliage on ribbed or scalloped shapes. In the 1830s transfer-printed designs in blue, mulberry, pink, green, and black became popular; and polychrome versions of Oriental wares were manufactured to compete with the Chinese trade. See also Mason's Ironstone.

Our advice for this category comes from Home Place Antiques, whose address is listed in the Directory under Illinois.

Baker, Gothic, rectangular, Edwards, 3x13x10⅛" 35.00
Baker, Hebe, Alcock, 1¾x9⅜x7⅛" 50.00

Baker, Prairie, oval, Clementson, 1¾x9x6⅝" 22.00
Baker, Wheat, Turner & Goddard, 2⅛x10⅝x8¼" 55.00
Bowl, sauce; Baltic, oval, w/lid & ladle 85.00
Bowl, sauce; Leaf Fan, w/lid & base, Alcock, 7⅞" H 75.00
Bowl, vegetable; Memnon, oval, w/lid, J Meir & Son, 11½x6" ..125.00
Bowl, vegetable; Tiny Oak & Acorns, w/lid, Pankhurst, 11¾" L.125.00
Butter dish, Corn & Oats, w/liner, Wedgwood, 2¼x6½" 145.00
Butter pat, plain, unmk, 2½" 3.00

Cake stand, Anthony Shaw, Burslem, 13" diameter, NM, $145.00.

Creamer, Cable & Ring, bulbous, Burgess, 5½" 45.00
Creamer, Gothic, octagonal, ped ft, Challinor, 7" 65.00
Creamer, Gothic, ped ft, Edwards.................................55.00
Creamer, Grenade, bulbous, T&R Boote, 5½" 65.00
Creamer, Wheat & Clover, Turner & Tomkinson, 5¼" 65.00
Cup, handleless; Panelled Columbia, 1850s, child's, 1⅝"...........20.00
Cup, syllabub; Branch of 3 Leaves, 1860s, 3¼x2⅞".........20.00
Cup, syllabub; Columbia, ring hdl, 4x3⅛" 25.00
Cup & saucer, handleless; Ceres, Elsmore & Forster, tea sz...........45.00
Cup & saucer, handleless; Leaf Focus, Taylor Bros, 1860s, lg.........28.00
Cup & saucer, handleless; Octagon, T&R Boote....................32.00
Cup & saucer, handleless; Vintage, Challinor, 3⅛x3⅝"...........35.00
Cup & saucer, handleless; Wheat, Meakin 27.50
Cup plate, Paris, Alcock, 4⅛" 12.00
Cup plate, plain, Tomkinson Bros, 4¼".......................... 6.00
Gravy boat, Ceres, Elsmore & Forster, 5" H 55.00
Gravy boat, Fuchsia, bulbous, 1860s, 5¼" H 32.00
Gravy boat, Wheat & Blackberry, unmk, 1860s, 5" H 40.00
Nappy, Mocho 'Little Palm,' T&R Boote, 5" 18.00
Nappy, Sydenham, T&R Boote, 6" 20.00
Nappy, Vintage, Challinor, 5" 18.00
Pitcher, Ceres, Elsmore & Forster, 8½" 85.00
Pitcher, Sydenham, T&R Boote, 10¼" 185.00
Pitcher, Sydenham, T&R Boote, 7⅞" 165.00
Pitcher, syrup; Panelled Columbia 135.00
Pitcher, Wheat & Blackberry, Meakin, 11¾" 145.00
Plate, Bellflower, 1860s, 9¾" 18.00
Plate, Fluted Pearl, Wedgwood, 1847, 9½" 18.00
Plate, Forget-Me-Not, Alcock, child's, 4⅛" 12.50
Plate, New York, copper lustre trim, Clementson, 9⅝" 15.00
Plate, plain, Meakin, 9" 5.00
Plate, Prairie, Clementson, 6⅝" 10.00
Plate, Sydenham, T&R Boote, 6⅜" 12.00
Plate, Sydenham, T&R Boote, 9½" 18.00
Plate, Wheat, Meakin, 9¾" 18.00
Platter, Baltic, oval, 9¾x7", EX...................................24.00
Platter, Sydenham, oval, T&R Boote, 16x12" 55.00
Punch bowl, Berry Cluster, hdls, 1850s, 3-qt, 6½x9⅝".........145.00
Relish, Fluted Pearl, octagonal, rtcl hdls, Wedgwood, 7⅝" 40.00

Shaving mug, Block Optic, Meakin, 1880s, 3⅜x3¾" 50.00
Soap dish, Sharon Arch, gourd finial, unmk, 5⅜x4" 65.00
Soup plate, plain, Meakin, 9" 12.00
Soup plate, plain, Shaw, 9⅝" 12.00
Sugar bowl, Ceres, Elsmore & Forster, 7¼" 65.00
Teapot, Ceres, Elsmore & Forster, 9¾" 235.00
Teapot, Ceres, Turner, Goddard & Co, 10" 235.00
Teapot, Ivy Wreath, bulbous, J Meir & Son, 10"...........175.00
Teapot, Laurel, bulbous, Wedgwood, 9¾" 185.00
Teapot, Pearl Sydenham, bulbous, Meakin, 9¼" 125.00
Teapot, Sydenham, T&R Boote, 9¼" 145.00
Toothbrush holder, horizontal, w/lid, Burgess, 3¼x8⅜"............65.00
Tureen, chowder; Sharon Arch, w/lid, Wedgwood, 10¼" 185.00
Tureen, sauce; Ceres, oval, w/underplate, 6¾x6x4½"............180.00
Tureen, sauce; Columbia, rnd, Goodwin, +8" underplate 125.00
Tureen, sauce; Sydenham, w/base & ladle, T&R boot, 8" H........225.00
Tureen, vegetable; Ceres, Elsmore & Forster, 8⅝x6½" 125.00
Tureen, vegetable; Ceres, w/lid, Elsmore & Forster, 10x7½" 125.00
Tureen, vegetable; Ivy Wreath, oval, w/lid, 6¼x9⅝x6¾" 95.00
Tureen, vegetable; Octagon, w/lid, T&R Boote, 7⅜" H.............110.00
Tureen, vegetable; Sydenham, w/lid, T&R Boot, 9¼" base 150.00
Wash bowl & pitcher, Octagon, T&R Boote, 13¼" dia bowl 225.00
Waste bowl, Shaw's Fan, Shaw, 4¼x6¼".........................50.00
Waste bowl, Wheat & Clover, Turner & Tomkinson Bros, 5⅞" 55.00

Ivory

Technically, true ivory is the substance composing the tusk of the elephant; the finest type comes from those of Africa. However, tusks and teeth of other animals – the walrus, the hippopotamus, and the sperm whale, for instance – are similar in composition and appearance and have also been used for carving. The Chinese have used this substance for centuries, preferring it over bone because of the natural oil contained in its pores, which not only renders it easier to carve but also imparts a soft sheen to the finished product. Aged ivory usually takes on a soft caramel patina, but unscrupulous dealers sometimes treat new ivory to a tea bath to 'antique' it! A bill passed in 1978 reinforced a ban on the importation of whale and walrus ivory. All examples listed here are Oriental in origin unless noted otherwise.

Ancestor sits on throne, eng robes/headdress, 9", pr 700.00
Apple, leaf/stem, int: village w/2 figures under tree, 3" 125.00
Beauty w/lantern on cloud base, lantern in hand, mc, 13"...........350.00

Boat, carved and stained panels, seven household gods on deck, early 19th Century, needs restoration, 15"x12", $900.00.

Deity, multi-armed, sits on lotus, jewelry/headdress, 9" 300.00
Dragon w/turq eyes carries 3 gods w/instruments, 14" L...............895.00
Equestrian, court figure, stained/incised, 14½", pr.......................800.00
Female warrior, trumpet/sword, wood base, 1900, 10", EX...........225.00
Fisherwoman in lg floppy hat, seated, 1861, 6"..............................225.00
Foo dog, jeweled collar, coral eyes, lift-off heads, 5" 90.00
Girl holds lg rose in left hand, ribbon in right, 1880, 9" 250.00
Head of Kwan Yin, ornate headdress w/Buddha & phoenix, 8" ..325.00
Immortal, smiling, beard/fan/pot belly, 10", EX............................525.00
Immortal holds branch & fly wisk, wood stand, 12½" 250.00
Immortals, 2 astride fish, 1 w/basket, 2nd w/sm fish, 11" 385.00
Kwan Yin, reclines/holds peonies, precious stones inlay, 9" 350.00
Maid in kimono holds peony, rolled coiffure, 9"............................225.00
Pendant, man/mtns/trees, etched/4-color, heart form, 1½" 30.00
Peony bouquet, in ivory basket, on X-bar/ring chain, 12x10"......795.00
Phoenix bird in flower garden, wings up, red coral eyes, 5"..........275.00
Phoenix bird on high stump, long openwork tail, 8½" 225.00
Quanyin astride lion, boy attendant/cub, stained detail, 9" 250.00
Samurai in armor holds spear, quiver on bk, stained, 11".............350.00
Teapot, tree/crane, dragon spout/hdl, lid: squirrel, 4x5" 150.00
Tusk, cvd w/18 monks in mtn landscape, 1800s, 16" 1,200.00
Urn, relief figural scenes, lid: landscape cvg, 9", pr 495.00
Warrior in chain mail, sword at waist, shield on bk, 8" 175.00

French

Bust of armor-clad man w/mustache on plinth, 6"........................175.00
Cupid, hand to chin, stands in flowering plant, plinth, 9"...........600.00
Cupid pushes sleigh w/winged female, wood-grain base, 2¼".......220.00
Girl, long braids/simple dress, stone steps, plinth, 7"...................440.00
Lady feeds doves, 1700s costume/bonnet, holds basket, 9"...........700.00
Landsnacht, festive dress/plumed hat, w/tankard & cup, 9" ... 1,100.00
Lovers, provincial 1700s costume, rockwork base/plinth, 8"........600.00
Soldier rests against young attendant, rockwork base, 4" 350.00
3 Graces, sharing drape, huddled on oval plinth, 7½"..................800.00

Jack-in-the-Pulpit Vases

Popular novelties at the turn of the century, jack-in-the-pulpit vases were made in every type of art glass produced. Some were simple, others elaborately appliqued and enameled. They were shaped to resemble the lily for which they were named.

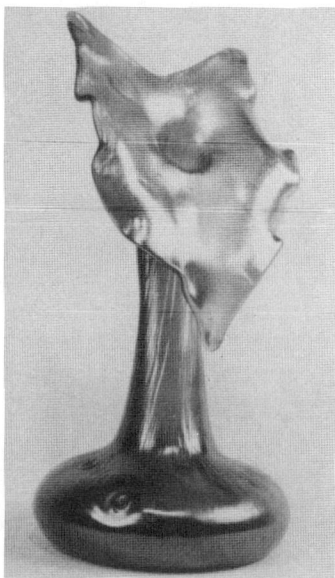

Iridescent silver-blue, bulbous iridescent green foot, attributed to Loetz, 12½", $850.00.

Cranberry, gold decor, 12½" 275.00
Gold stretch top, stem: bl/wht pulls on cobalt, 11" 225.00
Gr opaque w/maroon rim, hobnails, ruffled, 7¾x6⅝" 110.00
Maroon overlay, wht ext, ruffled top, 6x6" 110.00
Mc spatter overlay, clear wishbone ft, 8x4"...............................110.00
Opal, red ruffled edge, squatty, 4¾"..125.00
Pk opal/clear, striped/swirled, clear ruffled base, 12"..................250.00
Rainbow satin, star at upper edge, 5" 250.00
Rubena verde, 12½" 200.00
Wht, bl int, rigaree band, clear ruffled base, 9¼x5½"...................75.00
Wht opaque w/cranberry rim, 7x6⅛" 95.00

Jalan

During the second quarter of the century, both hand-thrown and molded pottery was produced by Manuele Jalanivich and Olsen Ingvardt, most of which was marked 'Jalan.' Their studio was located in San Francisco until the late thirties and after that in Belmont. Their wares were low-fired earthenware, and crackle glazes were favored.

Bowl, bl gloss, ped ft, mk/dtd 1928, 2x11" 150.00
Bowl, purple, Chinese bl crackle int, mk, 2x8"...........................190.00

Jewelry

Jewelry as objects of adornment has always been regarded with special affection. Whether it be a trinket or a costly ornament of gold, silver, or enameled work, jewelry has personal significance to the wearer. The art of the jeweler is valued as is any art object, and the names of Lalique or Faberge on collectible pieces bring prices demanded by the signed works of Picasso. Once the province of kings and noblemen, jewelry now is a legacy of all strata of society. The creativity reflected in the jeweler's art has resulted in a myriad of decorative adornments for men and women, and the modern usage of 'lesser' gems and base metals has elevated the value and increased the demand for artistic merit so that now it is considered by collectors to be on a par with intrinsic value. Luxuriously appointed pieces of Victorian splendor and Edwardian grandeur now compete with the unique, imaginative renditions of jewelry produced in the exciting Art Nouveau period as well as the adventurous translation of jewelry executed in man-made materials versus natural elements. Today prices for gems and gemstones crafted into antique and collectible jewelry are based on artistic merit, personal appeal, pure sentimentality, and intrinsic value. Note: Diamond prices vary greatly depending on color, clarity, etc. Values given here are for diamond jewelry with a standard commercial grade of diamonds that are most likely to be encountered.

Our advisor for this category is Rebecca Dodds; her address may be found in the Directory under Florida. If you are interested in collecting or dealing in jewelry, you will find that authority Lillian Baker has several fine books available on the subject – 100 Years of Collectible Jewelry: 1850-1950; Art Nouveau and Art Deco Jewelry; and Fifty Years of Collectible Fashion Jewelry: 1925-1975. These books are complete with beautiful full-color illustrations and current market values. Mrs. Baker is listed in the Directory under California. See also Plastics.

Key:
A/C — Arts and Crafts	gf — gold filled
AD — Art Deco	grad — graduated
AN — Art Nouveau	gp — gold plated
cab — cabochon	gw — gold washed
cl — clear	k — karat
comp — complementary	plat — platinum

ct — carat
dmn — diamond
dwt — penny weight
g'el-plt — gold electroplate
g-stn — gemstone
g-t — gold toned

r'stn — rhinestone
rdm — rhodium
stn — stone
tw — total weight
wg — white gold
yg — yellow gold

Bar pin, plat, 21 European dmn ea .10ct, EX quality, 64mm .. 1,100.00
Bracelet, bangle; 14k yg w/16 sapphires & 16 pearls 750.00
Bracelet, cultured pearl, 3-row, 7-7.5mm, +5 dmn-set bars 850.00
Bracelet, Georg Jensen, sterling links w/10 Jensen charms 300.00
Bracelet, hammered sterling, carnelian cabs/heart cutouts 300.00
Bracelet, Los Castillos/Taxco, silver zigzags w/gr stones 495.00
Bracelet, 14k yg, lg textured links, 81dwt................................. 1,300.00
Bracelet, 14k yg tennis style w/21 amethysts 500.00
Bracelet, 18k, chased, tricolor, wide, 88dwt 1,300.00
Bracelet, 18k, mtd w/line of 12 step-cut golden citrines..............650.00
Bracelet, 18k yg, 6 dmn tw 1.17ct 1,500.00
Brooch, g/f, jet cross on rnd bking, 1860s, 1"..............................90.00
Brooch, kilt; agate & silver, dirk form, 1850s, 4½"......................195.00
Brooch, stylized tree: cvd jade leaves+sm dmn at base of ea 400.00
Brooch, y/g, rope knot w/lg cab garnet, Victorian, 17.5dwt.........425.00
Brooch, y/g salamander w/emerald eyes, 16.5dwt.......................475.00
Brooch, 14k, artist's palette w/gems & synthetics, 19dwt.............325.00
Brooch, 14k yg flower form w/3 sm rubies, 7.2dwt.......................125.00
Brooch, 18k, flower mt pave-set w/dmn tw 9ct 9,000.00
Brooch, 18k, pearls, rock crystal over hair flower, 1x1½".............475.00
Brooch, 18k, tiger's eye w/sm dmns tw .50ct, 16dwt....................350.00

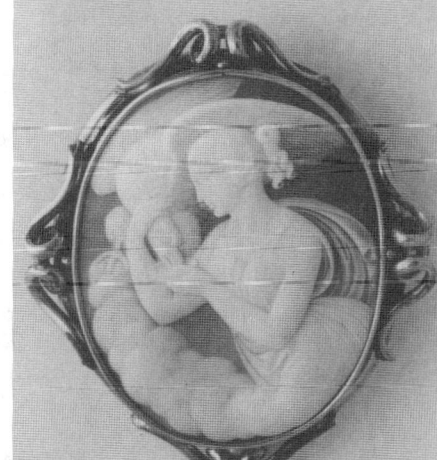

Shell cameo depicting Hebe feeding an eagle, gold-plated mount, large, $350.00.

Earrings, 14k, dmn .25ct w/2 kite-shape rubies+5 sm dmns.........300.00
Earrings, 14k yg, ea w/16 sm rubies+2 dmns.............................300.00
Earrings, 18k, dmn 1.80ct dropping from dmn-set mt, '20s 5,000.00
Locket, pinchbeck fr around hair bouquet, 1x¾".........................165.00
Muff chain, y/g, scroll mt set w/16 oval sapphires tw 25ct....... 1,500.00
Necklace, Antonio Pineda, silver links w/moonstone cabs..........400.00
Necklace, cultured pearls, 1-strand of 67, 5.5mm-9mm, EX 450.00
Necklace, cultured pearls, 2-strand of 84, clasp: 9 sm dmn...... 1,350.00
Necklace, cultured pearls, 2-strand 8-8.5mm, ruby/dmn clasp. 1,000.00
Necklace, cultured pearls, 7-7.5mm w/gold & dmn clasp, 35" 400.00
Necklace, Georg Jensen, silver & agate links, agate clasp 950.00
Necklace, Georg Jensen, sterling, links w/tulips & berries...........300.00
Necklace, hammered sterling Baroque pearl-mtd links/drop........250.00
Necklace, lapis lazuli, 72 matched beads, 26" 350.00
Necklace, Paul Lobel, sterling, open 'leaf' pendant, 1940s 125.00
Necklace, Wm Spratling, silver lacing w/6 amethyst drops..........825.00

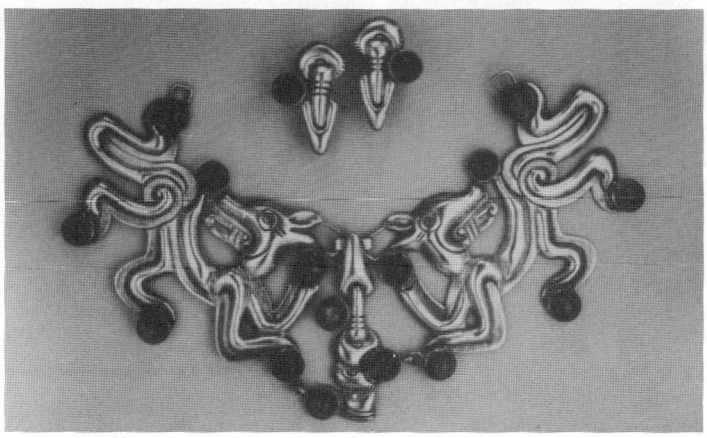

Silver and amethyst necklace and earrings by William Spratling, $880.00.

Necklace, yg, inflexible links form fr for aqua/garnet drop...........275.00
Necklace, yg, pk/gold topazes mtd in 17 drops, Victorian............700.00
Necklace, yg, 3 coral cabs in leaf/scrollwork w/enameling 425.00
Necklace, yg beads, Victorian, 18", 25 dwt.................................200.00
Necklace, 18k rope twist w/1904 $20 US gold pc.......................800.00
Necklace+earrings, Beto, silver, rectangle links w/scrolls............495.00
Pendant, pinchbeck, beveled glass bk/front opens, 2½x1½" 150.00
Pendant, yg, 6 sm pearls+1 sm dmn, on gold chain 60.00
Pendant, 14k, sapphire 3.5ct cushion on 5mm Baroque pearls 300.00
Pendant, 18k mt w/24 sm dmns around 1975 Krugerrand (1-oz) .800.00
Pin, Georg Jensen, geometric w/enameled blocks, 1¾" L.............200.00
Pin, Georg Jensen, silver w/lg bl sodalite cab, 2" 300.00
Pin, Georg Jensen, sterling, 2 birds on wheat shaft, 1½" 225.00
Pin, Kalo, sterling, dogwood blossom, 1¾" 175.00
Pin, Mary Gage, sterling, openwork maple leaves/beads, 2" 200.00
Pin, Mary Gage, sterling sabre, turq/coral-mtd hdl, 5" L.............150.00
Pin, plat, circlet w/28 dmn ea .10, EX quality, handmade 1,400.00
Pin, watch; 14k yg, 17-jewel Swiss w/9 dmn, ribbon-form top.....150.00
Pin, yg, star shape w/many sm pearls+1 sm dmn 150.00
Pin, 14k, potted flower form w/2 types semi-precious stones........140.00
Pin, 14k yg circlet w/tourmaline, peridot, garnets, etc 375.00
Pin, 14k yg crescent w/4 tourmaline & peridots.........................325.00
Pin & earrings, ivory flower on silver, marcasite/HP leaves 45.00
Ring, eternity; gold/plat w/line of 26 dmn tw 1.30ct...................900.00
Ring, plat, dmn pear-shape 8.09 ct+baguettes ea side.............35,000.00
Ring, plat, dmn 1.60ct European+20 baguettes & rnds, sgn.... 3,800.00
Ring, plat, dmn 1.75ct, 1.2ct dmn ea side, +10 single cut 4,600.00
Ring, plat, dmn 1ct in mound w/9 marquise tw 1.2, sgn mt..... 3,700.00
Ring, plat, 2 dmns ea .70, 18 full+16 single-cuts surround 1,400.00
Ring, silver, lg oval carnelian, mk Sterling 95.00
Ring, yg, oval moonstone..125.00
Ring, 14k, crisscross mt w/dmn cluster tw 1.95ct 2,000.00
Ring, 14k, dmn .33ct, simple mt...250.00
Ring, 14k, dmn cluster of 14 tw 3.5ct 2,500.00
Ring, 14k, dmns: 5 European cut tw .75ct set in cross mt 500.00
Ring, 14k, jade cab 10x15mm w/in ring of 48 tiny dmns 400.00
Ring, 14k, lg oval jade+6 sm dmns 250.00
Ring, 14k, sapphire 1.05 sq-cut flanked by 18 sm dmns 475.00
Ring, 14k, sapphire 5ct oval bordered w/sm dmn tw .95ct....... 1,900.00
Ring, 14k wg, lg oval peridot 450.00
Ring, 14k wg, med-sz emerald-cut aqua+12 sm dmn 375.00
Ring, 14k yg, emerald-cut 4.3ct aqua+6 sm dmn 250.00
Ring, 14k yg, oval 4.85 andalucite+6 sm dmn tw .33ct...............375.00
Ring, 14k yg, tiger's eye+6 sm dmn 200.00
Ring, 14k yg, 4 sm sapphires+13 sm dmn tw .31ct 350.00

Ring, 18k, dmn engagement style w/1.05ct **1,400.00**
Ring, 18k, 4 rubies tw 1.10ct in zigzag w/3 dmn tw .6ct **375.00**
Ring, 18k w/g, dmn European cut 1.30ct in flower mt, 1910 .. **1,600.00**
Ring, 18k yg dome w/36 full-cut sapphires **1,700.00**

Costume Jewelry

Bar pin, Joseff, oxidized brass w/chains & tassel, '45, 4½" **95.00**
Bracelet, Eisenberg, r'stn shapes in wide rhodium mt **125.00**
Bracelet, Eisenberg Ice, ½" rhodium mt w/lg & sm r'stn **110.00**
Bracelet, Renoir, hand-wrought copper links, wide, '55 ....**65.00**
Bracelet, Rosenstein, lg g-t ovals pave-set w/r'stn, '50 ....**125.00**
Bracelet, S Coventry, Harvest Wheat, wide antique g-t, '50 ....**35.00**
Bracelet, Trifari, rhodium/r'stn links w/enamel rose+buds **95.00**
Bracelet, Weiss, lg baguettes/sm rnd r'stn in wide mt, '60 ....**110.00**
Bracelet & earrings, S Coventry, modern style in r'dm, '50.............**35.00**
Bracelet & earrings, Weiss, prong-set aurora borealis, '60 ....**145.00**
Bracelet/necklace/earrings; Weiss, Parure: yel/clear stones...........**125.00**
Brooch, Castlecliff, g-el'plt coral branch w/lg pk pearl **85.00**
Brooch, Cini, hand-wrought sterling Baroque star, '40 ....**95.00**
Brooch, Danecraft, Nouveau openwork repousse grapevine, '50....**60.00**
Brooch, DeNicola, St Geo Killing Dragon, g-t w/r'stns etc **75.00**
Brooch, Kramer, mc faceted stone cluster, med sz, '50 ....**45.00**
Brooch, lg g-t sunburst w/lg & sm 3-color borealis & r'stn **85.00**
Brooch, M Haskell, lg crystals+r'stn cluster on g-el'plt **145.00**
Brooch, Rosenstein, rose quartz-petaled rose w/jade drop **135.00**
Brooch, Trifari, crown w/lg cab r'stn & sm mc stn, '60 ....**85.00**
Brooch, Weiss, lg butterfly in japanned mt w/lg r'stn, '50 ....**110.00**
Brooch & earrings, Eisenberg Ice, multiform r'stn, very lg **150.00**
Brooch & earrings, Emmons, g-t w/aurora borealis, 1960 ....**75.00**
Earrings, Chr Dior/Germany, faux jade & sapphire 'crowns' **65.00**
Earrings, Emmons, 3 faux pearls in rhodium mt, 1960s **15.00**
Earrings, H Carnegie, rhodium 'buckles' pave-set w/r'stns **95.00**
Earrings, Jomax, bl glass cabs & r'stn 'buttons,' '40 ....**55.00**
Earrings, Renoir, copper, Art Moderne styling, '55.....................**30.00**
Earrings, Trifari, rhodium apples w/baguette r'stns, '50 ....**35.00**
Fur clip, Trafari, fuchsia, 3-color enamel/pave-set r'stn **95.00**
Necklace, faceted beads & drops, cabs in g-t filigree, '25 ....**95.00**
Necklace, Monet, rhodium 3-bar Art Moderne-link choker..........**45.00**
Necklace, Trifari, 4-strand g-t chain, '65................................**65.00**
Necklace & earrings, Trifari, wht glass beads w/g-t leaves **55.00**
Pendant, Emmons, Regency cross, rhodium filigree, 1977 ....**20.00**
Pendant, Emmons, Royalty cross, faux turq/pearl, 1970s..............**35.00**
Pin, Boucher, Blkamoor, g-t turban/blk enamel face, mc stn..........**85.00**
Pin, Boucher, exotic fish, 2-tone gr enamel on g-t, '55..................**60.00**
Pin, Boucher, rhodium curled leaf w/allover r'stn, '60 ....**45.00**
Pin, Brooks, gilt brass flying bird w/pearl & r'stn, '60 ....**75.00**
Pin, BSK, g-t hand-cast cat w/mc stn eyes & collar, '60 ....**35.00**
Pin, Cadoro, g-t dbl bow, '55 ....**15.00**
Pin, Castlecliff, g-el'plt thistle mt w/lg faux pearl, '60 ....**55.00**
Pin, Chr Dior, 3 lg g-t leaves w/faux laips/turq 'berries' **85.00**
Pin, Cini for Gumps, handcrafed sterling 5-petal flower **95.00**
Pin, Coro, crown w/3 lg red & gr cab-cut stones+r'stn, '60 ....**45.00**
Pin, Coro, peacock on branch, enamel/r'stn on g-el'plt, '50...........**75.00**
Pin, Danecraft, sterling leaf form, '40....................................**50.00**
Pin, Danecraft, sterling shamrock w/mk mk casing, '60 ....**45.00**
Pin, DeNicola, g-t filigree dome, lg pk quartz center+r'stn **65.00**
Pin, Emmons, Bobcat, ltd ed, goldstone w/gr eyes, 1954 ....**45.00**
Pin, Emmons, Lambkin, oxidized brass & enamel, 1960 ....**15.00**
Pin, Emmons, Rainbow Star, g-t w/aurora borealis, '50 ....**30.00**
Pin, Emmons, Scarecrow, g-t tassel limbs, pearl face, '60 ....**35.00**
Pin, Emmons, Tinlizzy, rhodium car w/r'stn, '70........................**35.00**
Pin, Kramer, g-t butterfly set allover w/bl-tone stones...................**65.00**
Pin, Kramer, relief-pressed glass oval in g-el'plt, '65 ....**35.00**

Pin, Ledo, pave-set pear/baguette faux g'stn in g-t, '62 ....**35.00**
Pin, M Haskell, gilt brass flower mt w/2 tassel drops, '50...............**95.00**
Pin, Marvella, g-el'plt fan w/faux jade & eng spokes, '55 ....**55.00**
Pin, Mazer, gw sterling starburst, cultured pearls/sm r'stn **45.00**
Pin, Orig by Robert, g-el'plt vine w/2 enamel strawberries.............**85.00**
Pin, Theda, florentine sterling peacock at fountain, '50 ....**110.00**
Pin, Trifari, g-t flower mt w/aurora borealis, '55...........................**65.00**
Pin, Trifari, r'stn basket set w/topaz & cl r'stn, 1960s...................**45.00**
Pin, Trifari, sterling vermeil elephant w/r'stn accents.....................**95.00**
Pin, Trifari, stylized bird head w/red & cl r'stns, 1960...................**65.00**
Pin, Weiss, Christmas tree w/mc stns & r'stn candles, '60 ....**65.00**
Pin, Weiss, g-el'plt heart w/sm faux rubies allover, '50 ....**35.00**
Pin & earrings, S Coventry, Snowflake, r'stn, 1960 ....**65.00**
Pin & earrings, Trifari, rhodium leaf set w/r'stn, '50 ....**65.00**
Ring, Emmons, g-t kite form w/pave-set aurora borealis, '70..........**30.00**
Scarf pin, Accessocraft, g-el'plt lion's head w/loose ring.................**75.00**
Scarf pin, Emmons, rhodium shaft w/tassel ea end, '50 ....**35.00**
Scarf pin, Standard, rhodium open kite form set w/sm r'stn **25.00**

Judaica

The items listed below are representative of objects used in both the secular and religious life of the Jewish people. They are evident of a culture where silversmiths, painters, engravers, writers, and metal workers were highly gifted and skilled in their art. Most of the treasures shown in recently-displayed exhibits of Judaica were confiscated by the Germans during the late 1930s up to 1945; by then eight Jewish synagogues and fifty warehouses had been filled with Hitler's plunder.

Amulet case, Italian silver, cartouch form, ca 1800, 5¼" **3,000.00**
Bridal headdress, Moroccan silver wire/copper coins, 1700s.... **2,000.00**
Charity box, German sheet copper, cylindrical, 1800s, 5" **225.00**
Circumcision cup, Greek silver, cartouches, 1850s, 3½" **850.00**
Circumcision knife, Continental brass hdl, 1700s, 6¾" **700.00**
Etrog container, German silver, fruit form, ca 1880, 5½" **1,500.00**
Halitza shoe, E Europe, leather, typical design, 1800, EX **800.00**
Hanukah lamp, Dutch sheet brass, flowers/grapes, 1700s, 9" ... **1,100.00**
Hanukah lamp, Dutch silver, hearts/flowers, 1880, 3¼" **2,500.00**
Hanukah lamp, Indian brass, Star-of-David form, 1800s, 18" **550.00**
Havdalah compendium, German silver, rooster form, 1900, 7" ...**900.00**
Marriage cup, German silver, tulip form, 1890s, 7½", pr.......... **5,500.00**
Mezura, Sezalel silver cased, inscriptions, scroll w/in, 3½"........**600.00**
Passover plate, German pewter, lions/eagles, 1803, 12¼" **2,600.00**
Purim bowl, Russian silver, gilt int, Moscow, 1845, 6" dia....... **2,300.00**
Sabbath candlestick, German silver, 1860, 14½", pr **750.00**
Sabbath lamp, Dutch brass, hanging, ca 1700, 17" **1,850.00**
Spice container, Continental silver, fish form, 1800s, 13" **1,000.00**
Spice container, Dutch silver, rooster form, 1891, 11" **825.00**
Spice container, Turkish silver, fruit form, 1850s, 8" **1,100.00**
Spice tower, German pewter mtd wood, lion top, 1700s, 8" **1,300.00**
Spice tower, Russian silver, flags/bells/spire, 1800s, 8½" **475.00**
Synagogue laver, American SP, 3-hdl, Phila 1907, 6½" **450.00**
Tora finial, English silver, star, London/1943, 16", pr...................**550.00**
Torah binder, German, embr silk on linen, 1809, 142x7" **650.00**
Torah finial, N African silver/gold filigree, 1700, 10", pr......... **2,200.00**
Torah scroll, Continental, bone rollers, mantle, 1700s, 12" **1,600.00**
Wall sconce, Dutch chased brass, Tora Ark, 1800, 16", pr **700.00**

Jugtown

The Jugtown Pottery was started about 1920 by Juliana and Jacques Busbee, in Moore County, North Carolina. Ben Owen, a young descendant of a Staffordshire potter, was hired in 1923. He was the master potter, while the Busbees experimented with perfecting glazes and supervising design and modeling. Preferred shapes were those reminiscent of traditional country wares and classic Oriental forms. Glazes were various: natural clay oranges, buffs, 'tobacco-spit' brown, mirror black, white, 'frog-skin' green, a lovely turquoise called Chinese blue, and the traditional cobalt-decorated salt glaze. The pottery gained national recognition and as a result of their success, several other local potteries were established. Jugtown is still in operation, however they no longer use their original glaze colors which are now so collectible.

Bowl, burnt orange, hdls, imp mk, 3" H	40.00
Bowl, milk; redware w/yel slip bird, imp label, 3½x12"	95.00
Chamberstick, burnt orange, appl hdl, mk, NM	50.00
Cup, frogskin gr, sm	45.00
Inkwell vase, Chinese bl	95.00

Mug, tobacco spit brown, 4½", $95.00.

Pitcher, gr w/bl, bulbous w/pinched spout, 5½"	55.00
Vase, Chinese, bl & purple, bulbous, 7"	350.00
Vase, Chinese bl, lower part: brn clay w/clear glaze, 4"	225.00
Vase, Chinese bl, 4"	250.00
Vase, frogskin gr, imp mk, cabinet sz	75.00
Vase, gr, squat, mk, 4"	95.00
Vase, lt lav w/thick pooled aqua, ovoid, 6"	275.00
Vase, metallic glaze, 4 appl hdls, 8½"	75.00

K. P. M. Porcelain

Under the tutelage of Frederick the Great, King of Prussia, porcelain manufacture was instituted in Berlin in 1751 by William K. Wegeley. In jealous competition with Meissen, hard-paste porcelain was produced – dinnerware, figurines, vases, etc. – some of which were undecorated while other pieces were hand painted in Watteau scenes, landscapes, or florals. It soon became evident that the factory was unable to offer serious competition. The King withdrew his support, and the factory failed in 1757. In 1761 Johann Ernst Gotzkowsky bought the rights and attempted a similar operation which soon failed due to financial difficulties. Still determined to gain the same recognition enjoyed by Meissen, the King bought the plant in 1763 and ruled the operation with an iron hand, often assuring his success by taking advantage of his position. The King died in 1786, but production has continued and quality tableware and decorative porcelains are still being made on a commercial basis. Earliest marks were simply 'G' or 'W,' followed by the

sceptre mark. After 1830 'K.P.M.' with an orb or eagle was adopted.

Our advisor for this category is Don Williams; he is listed in the Directory under Iowa.

Bowl, 2 cherubs pull haycart, bl floral/wheat border, 12½"	200.00
Dish, florals/butterflies, burgundy border, 3-section, 12"	145.00
Figurine, merchant boy, lg basket on bk/sm 1 on arm, 11x3¾"	200.00
Figurine, stag, antlers touch bk, Wrobro, 5½"	300.00
Plaque, Chastity, maid/attendant child, Raupp, 9x6"	2,600.00
Plaque, classical male steals kiss, forest bkground, 9x6"	2,800.00
Plaque, Columbus, seated in chains, imp mk, 1900s, 20x16"	7,250.00
Plaque, group of cherubs carry fruit garland, 1920s, 10x16"	7,000.00
Plaque, maid sits on marble bench w/book, Muller, 16x10"	9,000.00
Plaque, Mary/Joseph/babies on donkey, angels, fr, 15x12"	3,700.00
Plaque, mother lifts child from crib, 1880s, 12x10"	6,000.00
Plaque, Music Hath Charms, man w/violin & gypsy, 15x12"	7,000.00
Plaque, peasant lady/son petting dog, 15x12"	6,000.00
Plaque, Romeo & Juliet, she on bench, wall between, 10x7"	2,600.00
Plaque, Venus & Cupid, dog/bird, after Titian, 6½x9½"	4,400.00
Plaque, Venus reclining on daybed, dog at ft, Titian, 6x9"	4,600.00
Plaque, 2 maids portraits, sgn Fratill, oval, 5x7"	550.00
Salt cellar, dbl, cherub, scalloped bowl ea side, 5"	175.00

Porcelain plaque of young woman, unframed dimensions: 7½" x 5¾", $1,300.00.

Kayserzinn Pewter

J.P. Kayser Sohn produced pewter decorated with relief-molded Art Nouveau motifs in Germany during the late 1800s and into the twentieth century. Examples are marked with 'Kayserzinn' and the mold number within an elongated oval reserve. Items with dimensional animals, insects, and birds, etc. are valued much higher than bowls, plates, and trays with simple embossed florals. These pieces are usually priced at $75.00 to about $150.00, depending on size.

Bowl, stylized floral, raised/shaped border, #4368, 17½"	250.00
Charger, 4-part, emb floral dividers, 14"	100.00
Inkwell, frog finial, 12" L	200.00
Pitcher, Mephistopheles, sgn/#d, 12"	350.00
Plaque, Warship SMP Aegir, sea gods, insignias, 20" dia	925.00
Punch bowl, claw & ball ft, cherub finial, heart reserve	550.00
Tray, lilies relief, 3-D dragonfly ea end, #4188, 18½"	700.00
Vase, Bismark bust, serpentine monster, Nouveau flowers, 12"	545.00
Vase, fish & flower decor, 3-ftd, #53, 7"	55.00
Water can, fish relief, snail finial, leaf hdl, #7-4203, 11"	1,300.00

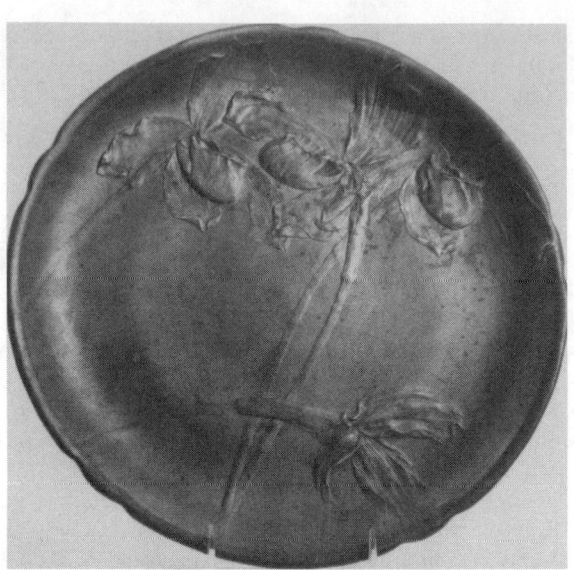

Plate, Nouveau flowers in relief, #4285, 13",
$165.00.

Keen Kutter

Keen Kutter was a brand name of E.C. Simmons Hardware, used from about 1870 until the mid-1930s. In 1923 Winchester merged with Simmons but continued to produce Keen Kutter marked knives and tools. The merger dissolved, and in 1940 the Simmons Company was purchased by Shapleigh Hardware. Older items are very collectible. For further study, we recommend *Keen Kutter Collectibles*, an illustrated price guide by Jerry and Elaine Heuring, available at your favorite bookstore or from Collector Books.

Our advisor for this category is Jim Calison; he is listed in the Directory under New York.

Auger bit, lg	25.00
Cake knife	7.50
Calendar, metal, 1940s	45.00
Calipers	22.00
Can opener, CI, dtd 1895, EX	30.00
Chopper, ball shape, 6 blades, mk wood hdl	22.50
Corkscrew	20.00
Food grinder, KK #21	25.00
Food grinder, KK #22	10.00
Hammer, riveting	20.00
Hammer, str claw, 7-oz	25.00
Hatchet, tack; claw, KK #5	32.50
Jar, beater; bl banded w/KK advertising	65.00
Knife, Boy Scouts, KK insignia in hdl	55.00
Knife, Congress; KK #16	75.00
Knife, KK #20	20.00
Knife, KK #255	25.00
Knife, KK #36	22.50
Knife, linoleum; M	25.00
Knife, Spirit of St Louis, ltd ed, MIB	165.00
Level, KK #13	25.00
Level, KK #3, brass end caps, 28"	45.00
Level, KK #5	18.00
Manicure set, EX	20.00
Monkey wrench, KK #95	20.00
Padlock	85.00
Plane, block; KK #102	20.00

Plane, block; KK #18	40.00
Plane, KK #3	45.00
Plane, KK #4	30.00
Plane, KK #5 ½	40.00
Pliers, fencing; cutters & hammer combination, 9"	22.50
Pliers, slip joint; 8"	20.00
Razor, KK #15, w/box	15.00
Razor, Safety Jr, w/box & blades, EX	35.00
Razor hone, EX in box	30.00
Razor strop, KK #94	25.00
Router, KK #71	45.00
Scissors, buttonhole; NM	10.00
Scissors, 8"	10.00

Hardware sign, 30" x 30", $100.00.

Skeleton key	10.00
Slaw cutter, lg, rare	45.00
Steel, butcher's	12.50
Tack puller	20.00
Thermometer, wood	95.00
Waffle iron	150.00
Waffle iron, miniature	150.00
Wrench, alligator; KK #40	60.00

Kelva

Kelva was a trademark of the C.F. Monroe Company of Meriden, Connecticut, used on an opaque mold-blown glassware that was hand decorated with pastel florals and often set in ormolu holders. It was very similar to the company's other lines, Nakara and Wave Crest; only those pieces bearing the Kelva mark are listed here. All three types were in production from about 1900 until WWI. Hand-painted pieces bring much higher prices than those with decals. For more information we recommend *Wave Crest, The Glass of C.F. Monroe* by Wilfred R. Cohen, available at your local bookstore or from Collector Books.

Biscuit jar, floral, wht on peach, SP lid & hdl, rare	800.00
Box, blown-out autumn maple leaf on bl, sq, 4"	850.00
Box, blown-out roses, 3" dia	450.00
Box, floral, mc on bl-gray, hinged, mk, 6½"	495.00
Box, orchids on pk, hinged w/brass fittings, mk, 5" dia	320.00

Box, petunias, pk on dk gr, mk, 8" dia................................**600.00**
Box, poppies, orange on gr mottle, hinged, 2¾x4¾" dia **295.00**
Box, roses, pk on lav-bl, swivel mirror in lid, 7½" dia **800.00**
Cigarette urn/match holder, wild rose, fitted brass tray **500.00**
Ferner, floral, bl & wht on dk pk, ftd, 6¼x7¾" **550.00**
Tray, floral, hexagonal, ormolu hdls......................................**235.00**
Tray, floral, pk on bl, 3x2¼" oval mirror, 6¼x4" **500.00**
Vase, floral, pk on gr, SP base/hdls, old rpr, 19".....................**925.00**
Vase, floral/beadwork on fuchsia, gilt ft, 6x2" **425.00**
Vase, lilies, pk on yel & gr, ormolu hdls/ft, 13" **1,250.00**

Vase, marked Kelva,
12¾", $625.00.

Kenton Hills

Kenton Hills Porcelain was established in 1940 in Erlanger, Kentucky, by Harold Boop, former Rookwood superintendent, and David Seyler, noted artist and sculptor. Native clay was used; glazes were very similar to Rookwood's of the same period. The work was of high quality; but because of the restrictions imposed on needed material due to the onset of the war, the operation failed in 1942. Much of the ware is artist signed and marked with the Kenton Hill name or cipher and shape number.

Bowl, oxblood aventurine, 8"...**250.00**
Flowerpot, lotus relief, bl matt, sgn AC/mk HB, 3½x5"..............**150.00**
Vase, gr adventurine w/lines & dots, Wm Hentschel, 6½" **325.00**
Vase, lady's head figural, pk gloss, 6½", EX....................................**275.00**
Vase, med bl gloss, mk, 4¼" **100.00**
Vase, oxblood gloss, #105, 4" **200.00**

Kentucky Derby Glasses

Since the 1940s, souvenir glasses have commemorated the famous Kentucky Derby; recently these have become popular collectibles, especially among race fans. Among the most valuable is the plastic Beetleware tumbler from the forties, the shorter version made in 1945, and the 1950 tumbler which is now valued over $100.00. On the Gold Cup glass from 1952, current winners are shown along with those from the previous year. There were two from 1958 – one was the Gold Bar tumbler and the other, called the Iron Liege, both were simply leftover '57 glasses with the 1958 winners added at the top.

1940s, aluminum **150.00**
1940s, plastic Beetleware **275.00**
1945, short **375.00**
1945, tall..**150.00**
1948 ....**48.00**
1949, He Has Seen Them All **48.00**
1950 ....**155.00**
1951 ....**125.00**
1952, Gold Cup...**45.00**
1953..**38.00**
1954..**35.00**
1955..**30.00**
1956..**30.00**
1957..**28.00**
1958, Gold Bar..**30.00**
1958, Iron Liege...**42.00**
1959-1960, ea **24.00**
1961..**20.00**
1962-1963, ea **18.00**
1964-1965, ea **18.00**
1966..**15.00**
1967-1968, ea **14.00**
1969..**13.00**
1970..**10.00**
1971..**9.00**
1972..**9.00**
1973..**7.00**
1974..**6.00**
1975..**5.00**
1976..**4.50**
1977-1978, ea **4.00**
1979-1980, ea **3.50**
1981-1982, ea **3.00**
1983..**2.50**
1984-1986, ea **2.00**
1987-1988, ea **2.00**

Kew Blas

Kew Blas was a trade name used by the Union Glass Company of Summerville, Massachusetts, for their iridescent, lustered art glass produced from 1893 until about 1920. The glass was made in imitation of Tiffany and achieved notable success. Some items were decorated with pulled leaf and feather designs while others had a monochrome lustre surface. The mark was an engraved 'Kew-Blas' in an arching arrangement.

Candlestick, gold irid, swirled stem, sgn, 8", pr **485.00**
Decanter, gr/gold, elongated neck, wide base, sgn, 13"................**350.00**
Finger bowl, amber irid, ribbed/scalloped, +6¾" underplate **325.00**
Tumbler, gold irid, pinched sides, mk, 4" **200.00**
Vase, gold irid, dbl gourd form, 8½x5½" **275.00**
Vase, gold irid, ribbed, ped ft, 4x5½" **300.00**
Vase, pulled feathers, gold on orange irid, 4-pointed rim, 7½" **775.00**
Vase, pulled feathers, gold on wht, gold int, sgn, 5½" **400.00**
Vase, pulled feathers, gr/gold on iridized opal, 4" **1,200.00**
Wine, gold, twisted stem, sgn, 4¾" **150.00**

King's Rose

King's Rose is a soft-paste ware that was made in Staffordshire, England, from about 1820 to 1830. It is closely related to Gaudy Dutch in body type as well as the colors used in its decoration. The pattern consists of a full-blown, orange-red rose with green, pink, and yellow leaves and accents. When the rose is in pink, the ware is often referred to as Queen's Rose.

Our advisor for this category is Richard Marden; he is listed in the Directory under New Hampshire.

Coffeepot, dome lid, minor wear, 11¾" 950.00
Creamer, emb shell & vine border, minor wear, 4¼"....................350.00
Creamer, solid border, minor wear, 4½" 450.00
Cup & saucer, solid border, M 250.00
Cup & saucer, vine border, minor wear 200.00
Cup plate, vine border, 3½", EX..90.00
Plate, Queen's, 8½", NM...40.00
Plate, sectional border, lt wear, 9¾"...325.00
Plate, solid border, 10", NM...325.00
Plate, soup; solid border, 9⅞" 325.00
Plate, 7½", M..115.00
Sugar bowl, emb shell & solid border, finial rpr, 5⅝" 200.00
Teapot, sectional border, lt wear, 5⅞" 400.00
Waste bowl, solid border, minor wear, 2¾x5⅝" 175.00

Assembled tea set, King's Rose and Queen's Rose patterns, with both vine and trellis borders, $1,700.00.

Kingwood Ceramics

Established in 1939 in East Palestine, Ohio, Kingwood Ceramics produced a line of 'weeping gold' serving items, novelty ware, and figural items that are today attracting collector interest. Marks usually incorporate the name of the company and/or a crown, with 'Weeping Bright Gold, 22K Gold, USA' below.

Bowl, weeping gold, 3-compartment, low, w/hdl 65.00
Pitcher, weeping gold, 8" 85.00

Kitchen Collectibles

During the last half of the 1850s, mass-produced kitchen gadgets were patented at an astonishing rate. Most were ingeniously efficient. Apple peelers, egg beaters, cherry pitters, food choppers, and such were only the most common of hundreds of kitchen tools well designed to perform only specific tasks. Today all are very collectible.

Our advisor for Cast Iron Bakers and Kettles is Denise Harned, who is the author of *Griswold Cast Collectibles*. She is listed in the Directory under Connecticut. See also Appliances; Molds; Primitives; Tinware; Wooden Ware.

Cast Iron Bakers and Kettles

Bean pot, Griswold #93, Erie, w/lid, 1-pt 30.00

Bread stick pan, Griswold #955, rolled hdls w/eye rings.................85.00
Broiler, Triumph #6, for wood cook stove, EX 38.00
Brownie pan, Griswold #19, 7¾x4⅝" 115.00

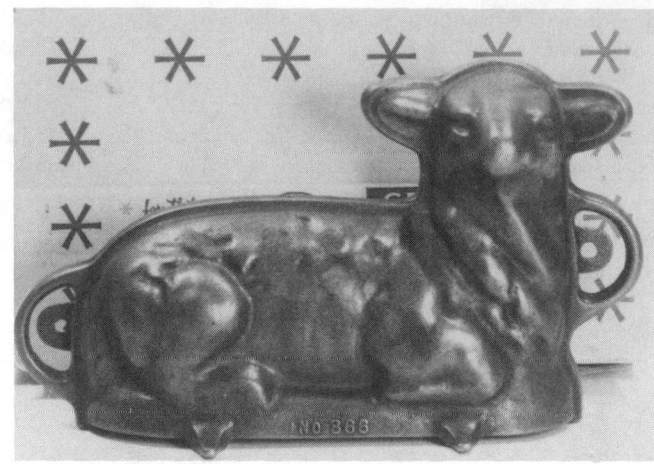

Griswold lamb cake mold in original box, $150.00.

Cake mold, Santa, Griswold, 4½x12x6¾" 295.00
Casserole, Griswold, lg emblem, 5" dia 22.50
Casserole, Griswold, 8" dia 24.00
Cinnamon crisp pan, Wagner Ware #30, 11 swirl forms, 10x7" 95.00
Corn stick pan, Griswold #262, 7 sticks, 8½x4¼" 95.00
Corn stick pan, Wagner, Jr Krusty Korn Kobs, Pat 1920 ....125.00
Corn stick pan, Wagner Krusty Korn Kobs, 13" 22.00
Corn stick pan, Wagner Krusty Korn Kobs, 16" 25.00
Danish cake pan/egg poacher, Griswold #32 ....49.00
Deep fryer, Griswold, #1003, 2½-qt 55.00
Dutch oven, Griswold #10 Chuck Wagon, w/lid, 8-qt 130.00
Dutch oven, Griswold #8, hinged lid, sm emblem, 4½ qt.............47.50
Dutch oven, Griswold #8, Tite Top, Erie, glass lid, 4x9" 48.00
Griddle, Griswold #110, lg emblem, 12¼" 85.00
Griddle, Griswold #6, rnd, w/hdl...48.00
Griddle, Wagner #6 ....66.00
Kettle, Griswold #8, flat bottom, lg emblem, 7-qt 60.00
Kettle, shallow, Vermont 1875 on bail hdl, 3-qt..........................50.00
Little Slam Bridge Pan, Wagner #1340, 11x8" 140.00
Meat loaf pan, Griswold, side hdl, 2¾x10⅛x5½" 45.00
Muffin pan, GF Filley #4, 8-mold, 14½x6½" 155.00
Muffin pan, GF Filley #7, 11 rectangle forms, hdls.....................100.00
Muffin pan, GF Filley #8, 11 trapezoid forms, hdls.....................100.00
Muffin pan, Griswold #140, Turk's head, 12½x8¼" 75.00
Muffin pan, N Waterman, Boston, dtd 1859 ....50.00
Muffin pan, WC Davis, 10 hexagonal forms, ring hdls 125.00
Platter, Griswold, Aristocraft, sm emblem, 11½x16" 55.00
Popover pan, Griswold #10, 11-part, 1890s, 11x7½" 55.00
Skillet, Griswold #10, Erie, smoke ring.....................................78.00
Skillet, Griswold #11, sm emblem, no smoke ring........................36.00
Skillet, Griswold #12, Erie, smoke ring.....................................150.00
Skillet, Griswold #12, sm emblem, no smoke ring........................44.00
Skillet, Griswold #13, lg emblem, no smoke ring 88.00
Skillet, Griswold #14, Erie, smoke ring.....................................150.00
Skillet, Griswold #168, diamond shape 45.00
Skillet, Griswold #2, lg emblem, smoke ring...............................80.00
Skillet, Griswold #2, sm emblem, no smoke ring.........................45.00
Skillet, Griswold #20, 2-hdl, no lid, 19" 140.00
Skillet, Griswold #26, sq, 7¾x7¾" 45.00
Skillet, Griswold #3, sm emblem, no smoke ring.........................12.50
Skillet, Griswold #5, lg emblem, smoke ring...............................60.00

Skillet, Griswold #5, sm emblem, no smoke ring 22.00
Skillet, Griswold #6, sm emblem, no smoke ring 28.00
Skillet, Griswold #6, Victor, smoke ring 55.00
Skillet, Griswold #7, lg emblem, smoke ring 50.00
Skillet, Griswold #7, Victor 55.00
Skillet, Griswold #8, lg emblem, smoke ring 40.00
Skillet, Griswold #9, sm emblem, no smoke ring 22.50
Skillet, Griswold #9, Victor, smoke ring 60.00
Skillet, Wagner #5 ....20.00
Skillet, Wagner #8 ....20.00
Skillet, Wagner #9 ....30.00
Skillet, Wapak #9, Indian head 150.00
Springerle iron, Wagner, 12 designs, 1850s, 10" 185.00
Teakettle, sliding lid w/vent, wrought hdl, 1880s, 7" dia 165.00
Teakettle, Wood Bishop & Co, Bangor ME, 1800s, 14" 100.00
Vienna roll pan, Griswold #6, Erie, PA 85.00
Waffle iron, Griswold #8, American, later version, +stand 130.00
Waffle iron, Wagner, Pat Feb 22, 1910, wood hdl, +stand 125.00
Wheat stick pan, Griswold #28, wheat-patterned mold, 12½x7".150.00

Glassware

Apothecary jar, gr transparent 25.00
Baker, sapphire bl, rnd or sq, Fire-King, 1-pt 3.50
Batter set, cobalt, New Martinsville 265.00
Beater bowl, Chalaine bl, w/spout, 4½" 32.00
Bottle, water; cobalt, Hazel Atlas, 64-oz, 10" 55.00
Bottle, water; gr clambroth 90.00
Bowl, gr jadite, vertical rib, Jeannette, 8" 12.50
Bowl, gr transparent, Crisscross, 5¼" 8.00
Bowl, mixing; blk, 7⅜" 30.00
Bowl, mixing; delphite, vertical ribs, Jeannette, 7" 22.50
Bowl, mixing; dk amber, US Glass, 8" 22.50
Bowl, mixing; Dots, gr on custard, McKee, 8" 12.50
Bowl, mixing; fruit on wht, Splash Proof, Fire-King, 4-qt 10.00
Bowl, mixing; gr transparent, 10½" 17.50
Bowl, mixing; gr transparent, 8" 12.50
Bowl, mixing; wht, Hocking Vitrock, 11¼" 16.00
Bowl, utility; sapphire bl, Fire-King, 8⅜" 10.00
Butter dish, amber, Federal, 1-lb 27.50
Butter dish, Chalaine bl, plain, no tabs 275.00
Butter dish, cobalt, emb lid, Hazel Atlas 155.00
Butter dish, cobalt, Hazel Atlas 155.00
Butter dish, delphite, Jeannette 150.00
Butter dish, gr transparent, Jeannette 32.50
Butter dish, lt gr jadite, Jeannette 32.00
Butter dish, pk transparent, bow-hdld top 48.00
Butter dish, Red Ships, McKee 20.00
Butter dish, red transparent w/clear top 95.00
Cake plate, cobalt, 3-ftd, Fry 80.00
Canister, delphite, McKee, 10-oz 35.00
Canister, gr transparent, emb Coffee 100.00
Canister, gr transparent, Hazel Atlas 40.00
Canister, yel opaque, McKee, 48-oz 50.00
Cocktail shaker, gr transparent, pinched-in sides 32.00
Cocktail shaker, gr transparent, Sweet Adeline pnt on side 22.50
Crock, gr transparent, 8" 35.00
Cruet, vinegar; jadite 110.00
Custard cup, Skokie gr, McKee 4.00
Dispenser, water; cobalt; LE Smith 250.00
Egg cup, Skokie gr, McKee 10.00
Ice bucket, amber, Party Line, Paden City 25.00
Ice bucket, gr, Hex Optic, w/reamer top, Jeannette 40.00
Ice bucket, gr, McKee 22.50

Jar, pretzel; pk transparent, Hocking 45.00
Jar, refrigerator; gr clambroth, 4¼x4¾" 20.00
Jug, batter; blk, McKee 60.00
Jug, batter; forest gr, New Martinsville 50.00
Jug, batter; red transparent, w/liner 135.00
Knife, clear, flowers on hdl 32.00
Knife, pk, plain hdl, 9¼" 25.00
Ladle, blk, rnd bottom 27.50
Ladle, forest gr 20.00
Ladle, pickle; wht 12.50
Measuring cup, caramel, 2-spout, McKee 150.00
Measuring cup, clear, Saginaw Milling Co 25.00
Measuring cup, pk transparent, 1-spout, US Glass 45.00
Measuring cup, ultramarine, Jeannette, 1-cup 37.50
Measuring mug, yel opaque, McKee, 4-cup 85.00
Measuring pitcher, Chalaine bl, 4-cup 165.00
Measuring pitcher, custard, McKee, 4-cup 28.00
Measuring pitcher, delphite, McKee, 2-cup 65.00
Mug, gr clambroth 27.50
Mug, gr transparent, Hocking 26.00
Mug, gr transparent, soda-fountain type 22.50
Mug, pk transparent, Adam's Rib 16.00
Pitcher, delphite, sunflower bottom, Jeannette, 2-cup 42.50
Pitcher, Dots, red on custard, Hazel Atlas, 2-cup 32.50
Pitcher, milk; cobalt, Hazel Atlas 55.00
Pitcher, Skokie gr, Mckee, 2-cup 12.50
Refrigerator dish, gr jadite, floral lid, Jeannette, 5x5" 18.00
Refrigerator dish, gr transparent, Tufglas, 5⅞" sq 22.50
Refrigerator dish, jadite, florals, 5x5" 18.00
Refrigerator dish, pk transparent, Federal, 3¾x5¾" 8.00
Refrigerator dish, pk transparent, Federal, 4x4" 7.50
Refrigerator dish, pk transparent, rnd, tab hdls 27.50
Refrigerator dish, Seville yel, 7¼x7¼" 32.50
Refrigerator dish, yel opaque, Hocking, 6x6" 18.00
Rolling pin, peacock bl 165.00
Rolling pin, wht clambroth, wood hdls 80.00
Salt box, clear 15.00
Salt box, clear, emb Salt on side, w/lid 16.00
Shaker, delphite, Jeannette, 8-oz 40.00
Shaker, gr transparent, Domino Sugar label, 8-oz 12.50
Shaker, lady w/apron on custard, McKee 15.00
Shaker, wht clambroth, ovoid, Owens-Illinois 6.50
Shakers, Panelled, fired-on bl, pr 18.00
Shakers, peacock bl, 8-oz, pr 95.00
Shakers, pk transparent, flat, Jennyware, pr 50.00
Shakers, red transparent, Wheaton Nuline, pr 45.00
Shakers, wht, sq, pr 15.00
Spoon, yel transparent, salad sz 32.00
Spoon holder, gr transparent 150.00

Sellers sugar canister in black: $70.00; Sugar shaker, $15.00.

Sugar canister, gr fired-on, Hazel Atlas 27.50
Sugar shaker, gr clambroth 27.50
Sugar shaker, gr transparent, Beehive, Lancaster.................135.00
Sugar shaker, gr transparent, Jeannette 50.00
Sugar shaker, red fired-on 17.50
Sugar shaker, red fired-on, Gemco 20.00
Sugar shaker, yel transparent 185.00
Syrup jug, amber, Cambridge 45.00
Syrup pitcher, gr transparent, Party Line, Paden City 35.00
Tray, dk amber, oval, Fry, lg 40.00
Tumbler, blk, McKee 17.50
Tumbler, gr clambroth, ftd...10.00
Tumbler, gr jadite, Jeannette, 12-oz..................................10.00

Apple peeler, cherry, well made, table clamp, 14" 275.00
Apple peeler, CI, rolls in half circle 85.00
Apple peeler, Goodell, CI, clamp-on, pat 1898 ....85.00
Apple peeler, Little Star 85.00
Apple peeler, Lockley-Howland, CI, dtd 1856....................55.00
Apple peeler, Reading Hardware, CI, pat Mar 5, 1862, EX 55.00
Apple peeler, Reading Hardware, CI, pat 1868-1875-1877, EX.....50.00
Biscuit cutter, Egg Baking Powder ad on tin, egg-shaped hdl 95.00
Biscuit pricker, wood hdl, iron spikes, 1¼" dia, 3⅛" H 75.00
Bread slicer, oblong wood box, iron slicer w/hdl at end.............110.00
Cherry seeder, Goodell, Antrim NH USA, CI, 1895, EX 35.00
Cherry seeder, Logan & Strobridge, New Brighton PA 32.00
Cherry seeder, New Standard, Mt Joy PA, CI, ca 1900, EX 36.00
Cherry seeder, Patd Nov 17, 1863, CI w/3 wrought legs, EX 48.00
Chopper, Enterprise #12...45.00
Chopper, NRS&Co #20, CI w/tin blades, pat May 2, '39.............35.00
Chopper, scrolled Queen Anne blade, scroll-end hdl 1,100.00
Churn, Dazey #10, 1-qt, EX...750.00
Churn, Dazey #20, dtd 2-14-22 ....160.00
Colander, brass, hdls, 1800s, minor solder rpr, 9" dia 150.00
Cream whip, Fries, churn form on legs, ca 1898, 9"................85.00
Dough scraper, iron, tooled brass hdl, blade mk PD/1850 ....350.00
Doughnut form, Ace, St Louis MO, CI, cloverleaf shape 145.00
Dredger, Kreamer, copper, punched star decor top...................38.00
Egg beater, Eagle Precision, chrome/red plastic, 12½" 14.00
Egg beater, Holts, flared dasher, dtd 1899 ....35.00
Funnel, Straiter, copper w/brass spout, dtd 1893, sm 45.00
Grater, Climax, CI, crank hdl, tin plates, 1932, NMIB 45.00
Grater, half-rnd pierced tin on hewn board, 1830s, 13" 85.00
Grater, nutmeg; CI, wood/brass fittings, pat June 1870, 3½".......195.00
Grater, nutmeg; CI pierced disk, pat Mar 9, 1896 ....295.00
Grater, nutmeg; Edgar, tin w/wood hdls, pat 1896, 5¼"...........65.00
Grater, nutmeg; punched tin w/sliding lid, fancy inlay, 7" 200.00
Grater, nutmeg; red & gr tole pnt w/flowers, early 275.00
Grater, nutmeg; screw-off ends, grater in top, EX trn/cvg 200.00
Grater, nutmeg; tin, oval, pocket-style compartment.................165.00
Grater, nutmeg; tin/wood, hand crank, primitive, 5" 145.00
Grater, nutmeg; trn wood, brass fittings, crank, 7¾" 325.00
Grater, punched tin half-cylinder, walnut star-cvd bk, 4x10" 420.00
Grater, punched tin in wood fr, mortised/trn hdl, 14" 85.00
Grinder, Griswold #1110, EX...35.00
Grinder, Levikin, CI, reg sz...20.00
Grinder, sausage; Enterprise, July 11 1876/1883, 28x9", EX...........45.00
Ice box, oak, 3-door, rstr/rfn 500.00
Ice shaver, Enterprise, CI 29.00
Iron, fritter; 6-pointed star figural, long hdl, 1800s, 17" 150.00
Knife, bread; Larkin...12.00
Kraut cutter, curly maple, heart in crest, 16" L, VG 225.00
Kraut cutter, maple w/sliding box, EX 60.00
Kraut cutter, walnut, tombstone arch top, 17" 50.00

Kraut cutter, wood w/some curl, iron latch on hopper feed 175.00
Lemon squeezer, LF&C, CI, long hdl, pour spout.....................22.00
Lemon squeezer, Pat 1868, CI w/wht ironstone center..................85.00
Lemon squeezer, Pearl, CI, sm 45.00
Lemon squeezer, Townsend, CI, Phila, pat May 30, 1866............50.00
Meat tenderizer, CI, wood hdl, ca 1850, 3x2½x3" 38.00
Nut cracker, Perfection, 1914 ....25.00
Oyster sheller, wrought brass, pliers form, early 47.50
Peach peeler, Sinclair Scott...100.00
Pie crimper, brass, wood hdl, early, EX 40.00
Pie crimper, Vaughn's, gr Catalin hdl, 1921 ....20.00
Pie crimper, 2 brass cutting wheels, lg iron crimper, 1886 ....95.00
Potato peeler, Hamlinite, tin, rough surface, oval, 1920............45.00
Press, fruit/lard; Griswold #2, CI 60.00
Raisin seeder, Everett, wire grid, wood hdl, ca 1893 ....65.00
Rolling pin, aqua glass, hollow w/tin screw cap 1 end 45.00
Rolling pin, aqua glass, miniature, 6" L 85.00
Rolling pin, dbl; 2 rollers on 1 hdl, pegged ends, early 185.00
Rolling pin, springerle, 12 designs, w/recipe for cookies 45.00
Sausage stuffer, Russell & Irwin New Britain CT, CI, 1886 ....35.00
Sausage stuffer, Wagner Stuffer, Silver Mfg Salem OR, 36" L......495.00
Scoop, flour; Heart of Value emblem 15.00
Spatula, Swansdown, metal 8.00
Springerle board, 6 cvd patterns, rectangular, early, 3¼x7"..........295.00
Taster, copper bowl, well-shaped wrought iron hdl, 10" 215.00
Waffle iron, bronze w/wrought hdls, star/sq motif, 17", VG 100.00

Knives

Knife collecting as a hobby began in earnest during the 1960s when government regulations required for the first time that knife companies mark their product with the country of origin. The few collectors and dealers cognizant of this change at once began stockpiling the older knives made before this law was enacted. Another impetus to the growing interest in this area came with the Gun Control Act of 1968, which severely restricted gun trading. Frustrated gun dealers transferred their attention to knives. Today there are collectors clubs in many of the states.

The most sought-after pocket knives are those made before WWII. However, Case, Schrade, and Primble knives of a more recent manufacture are also collected. Most collectors prefer knives 'as found.' Do not attempt to clean, sharpen, or in any way 'improve' on an old knife.

The prices quoted here are for knives in mint condition (except for those in the Miscellaneous section). If a knife has been used, sharpened, or blemished in any way, its value decreases – the newer the knife, the greater the reduction in value.

Our advisor for this category is Charles D. Stapp; he is listed in the Directory under Indiana.

Key:
bd — blade   p/b — push button

Case, C51050SAB, stag hdl, 1-bd, tested XX, 1920-40, 5⅛", M..750.00
Case, M100, gold hdl, 1-bd, tested XX, 1940-64, 3¼", M 163.00
Case, M3102R, metal hdl, 3-bd, tested XX, 1920-40, 2¾", M 115.00
Case, 11011, walnut hdl, 1-bd, 10-dot, 1970, M...................30.00
Case, 31048, yel compo hdl, 1-bd, tested XX, 1940-64, 4⅛", M 35.00
Case, 5299½, stag hdl, 2-bd, tested XX, 1920-40, 4⅛", M 265.00
Case, 5308, stag hdl, 3-bd, tested XX, 1920-40, 3¼", M 340.00
Case, 5332, stag hdl, 3-bd, 10-dot, 1970, 3⅝", M 50.00
Case, 61024, gr bone hdl, 1-bd, tested XX, 1920-40, 3", M 115.00
Case, 61024½; bone hdl, 1-bd, USA, 1965-69, 3", M................45.00
Case, 61048, red bone hdl, 1-bd, tested XX, 1940-64, 4⅛", M.......55.00

Case, 6106, gr bone hdl, 1-bd, tested XX, 2⅝", M 140.00
Case, 6111½-L, bone hdl, 1-bd, USA, 1965-69, M 62.00
Case, 61213, gr bone hdl, 1-bd, tested XX, 1920-40, 5⅜", M 505.00
Case, 6143, bone hdl, 1-bd, tested XX, 1940-64, 5", M 150.00
Case, 6294, gr bone hdl, 2-bd, tested XX, 1920-40, 4¼", M 355.00
Case, 6308, bone hdl, 3-bd, USA, 1965-69, 3¼", M 40.00
Case, 64047PU, bone hdl, 4-bd, XX, 1940-64, 4", M 65.00
Case, 7285, turq hdl, 2-bd, tested XX, 1920-40, 3⅝", M 415.00
Case, 91210½, onyx hdl, 1-bd, tested XX, 3⅜", M 380.00
Case, 9151, onyx hdl, 1-bd, tested XX, 1920-40, 5¼", M 555.00
Primble, Belknap Hdw, 5222, bone hdl, 2-bd, 3", M 35.00
Primble, Belknap Hdw, 5517, faux bone hdl, 4-bd, 4⅛", M 30.00
Primble, Belknap Hdw, 5733, bone hdl, 2-bd, 3⅛", M 27.00
Primble, Belknap Hdw, 902, peachseed bone hdl, 2-bd, 2⅞", M....40.00
Primble, Belknap Hdw, 909, peachseed bone hdl, 2-bd, 3", M.......40.00
Queen, Congress, 32, bone hdl, 4-bd, 4", M 47.00
Queen, Lockback, 36, bone hdl, 1-bd, 4½", M 90.00
Queen, 139, brn bone hdl, 2-bd, 3½", M 45.00
Queen, 15, winterbottom bone hdl, 2-bd, 3½", M 30.00
Queen, 36, Rogers bone hdl, 1-bd, 4½", M 105.00
Queen, 52, winterbottom bone hdl, 2-bd, 4½", M 45.00
Queen, 6105, stag hdl, 2-bd, 3½", M 40.00
Queen Steel, 60, bone hdl, 1-bd, 3½", M 35.00
Remington, RB43, brn bone hdl, 2-bd barlow, 3⅜", M 130.00
Remington, RS4233, scout knife, 3⅜", M 200.00
Remington, RS4373, girl scout knife, 3⅜", M 250.00
Remington, R1123, bullet, bone hdl, 2-bd, M 1,000.00
Remington, R2103, bone hdl, 2-bd, 3⅛", M 73.00
Remington, R228, cocobolo hdl, 2-bd, M 125.00
Remington, R263, bone hdl, 2-bd, 4", M 185.00
Remington, R31, redwood hdl, 1-bd, 3⅜", M 95.00
Remington, R3363, brn bone hdl, 2-bd, 3¾", M 255.00
Remington, R3393, bone hdl, 3¾", M 205.00
Remington, R3555G, pyremite hdl, 3-bd, 3⅞", M 255.00
Remington, R3685C, pyremite hdl, 3-bd, M 175.00
Remington, R3700BU, buffalo horn hdl, 4", M 235.00
Remington, R3735, pyremite hdl, 3⅞", M 250.00
Remington, R395, pyremite hdl, 2-bd, 3⅜", M 125.00
Remington, R4133, bone hdl, 3-bd, 3⅜", M 150.00
Remington, R4234, pearl hdl, M 305.00
Remington, R4283, bone hdl, 5-bd, 3¾", M 1,000.00
Remington, R4334, pearl hdl, 3-bd, 3½", M 255.00
Remington, R4336, stag hdl, 3½", M 230.00
Remington, R4353, brn bone hdl, 2-bd, 4¼", M 1,405.00
Remington, R4703, brn bone hdl, 2-bd, 4¼", M 255.00
Remington, R593, bone hdl, 2-bd, 3¼", M 165.00

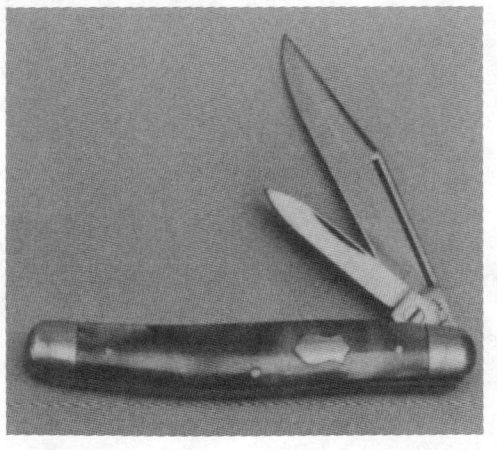

Remington, #R605, gold swirl pyremite, 3⅜", $125.00.

Remington, R6193, bone hdl, 3⅜", M 135.00

Remington, R6194, pearl hdl, 2-bd, 3⅜", M 180.00
Remington, R6694, brn bone hdl, 4-bd, 3⅛", M 205.00
Remington, R6872, blk hdl, 3", M 43.00
Remington, R6905, onyx hdl, 2-bd, 2½", M 65.00
Remington, R728, cocobolo hdl, 1-bd, 4½", M 85.00
Remington, R7343, brn bone hdl, 2-bd, 3⅛", M 130.00
Remington, R82, blk hdl, 2-bd, M 95.00
Remington, R982, blk hdl, 2-bd, 2⅞", M 85.00
Schrade Cut Co, B2153, bone hdl, 2-bd, 3⅜", M 55.00
Schrade Cut Co, F7423T, bone hdl, 3⅛", M 50.00
Schrade Cut Co, M7703T, bone hdl, 2⅞", M 45.00
Schrade Cut Co, SS7426B, mother of pearl hdl, 3⅛", M 65.00
Schrade Cut Co, 07404W, ivory celluloid hdl, 3⅜", M 100.00
Schrade Cut Co, 1001, cocobolo hdl, 4", M 45.00
Schrade Cut Co, 1147¾, bone hdl, 1-bd, 5", M 155.00
Schrade Cut Co, 1251, cocobolo hdl, 1-bd, 3¼", M 40.00
Schrade Cut Co, 2014S, tortoise celluloid hdl, 3⅝", M 95.00
Schrade Cut Co, 2019BR, brass hdl, 2-bd, 3⅝", M 95.00
Schrade Cut Co, 2063½, bone hdl, 3⅝", M 115.00
Schrade Cut Co, 2072¾, ebony hdl, 3⅝", M 50.00
Schrade Cut Co, 2211, cocobolo hdl, 3½", M 50.00
Schrade Cut Co, 2214BSD, blk celluloid hdl, 3⅝", M 50.00
Schrade Cut Co, 2221, cocobolo hdl, 3½", M 90.00
Schrade Cut Co, 2223¾, bone hdl, 3½", M 105.00
Schrade Cut Co, 2264W, ivory celluloid hdl, 3¼", M 65.00
Schrade Cut Co, 2813¾, bone hdl, 4", M 95.00
Schrade Cut Co, 7113SGB, bone hdl, 3⅜", M 55.00
Schrade Cut Co, 71145, tortoise celluloid hdl, 3⅜", M 50.00
Schrade Cut Co, 7404, bl pearl celluloid hdl, 3⅜", M 155.00
Schrade Cut Co, 7414S, tortoise celluloid hdl, 3⅜", M 180.00
Schrade Cut Co, 7424BT, blk celluloid hdl, 3⅛", M 45.00
Schrade Cut Co, 7439GM, metal hdl, 3⅛", M 40.00
Schrade Cut Co, 7444R, red celluloid hdl, p/b, 2⅞", M 115.00
Schrade Cut Co, 7494W, ivory celluloid hdl, 3½", M 45.00
Schrade Cut Co, 7503B, bone hdl, 2-bd, p/b, 3¾", M 180.00
Schrade Cut Co, 7504K, cream & brn pyralin hdl, p/b, 3¾", M..155.00
Schrade Cut Co, 8116, mother of pearl hdl, 3⅜", M 95.00
Schrade Cut Co, 8354K, cream & brn pyralin hdl, 3¼", M 70.00
Schrade Cut Co, 8853¼, bone hdl, 3¼", M 70.00
Schrade Cut Co, 9464US, celluloid hdl, 3⅝", M 155.00
Schrade Cut Co, 9604W, celluloid hdl, 2¼", M 45.00
Winchester, 1621, ebony hdl, 4¾", M 140.00
Winchester, 1920, bone hdl, 1-bd, 5⅜", M 1,000.00
Winchester, 1922, stag hdl, 3⅜", M 125.00
Winchester, 1936, brn bone hdl, 5", M 355.00
Winchester, 1938, brn bone hdl, 3⅜", M 130.00
Winchester, 1950, stag hdl, 1-bd, 5¼", M 1,200.00
Winchester, 2309, pearl hdl, 3", M 125.00
Winchester, 2317, pearl hdl, 3", M 130.00
Winchester, 2606, cocobolo hdl, 3⅜", M 125.00
Winchester, 2703, brn bone hdl, 3½", M 155.00
Winchester, 2852, stag hdl, 3", M 135.00
Winchester, 2875, stag hdl, 3¼", M 130.00
Winchester, 2878, stag hdl, 4¼", M 330.00
Winchester, 2999, wht smooth bone hdl, 3⅛", M 180.00
Winchester, 3002, gr celluloid hdl, 3¾", M 250.00
Winchester, 3006, blk celluloid hdl, 3⅜", M 200.00
Winchester, 3018, candystripe hdl, 3-bd, 4", M 330.00
Winchester, 3018, celluloid hdl, 4", M 250.00
Winchester, 3023, red celluloid hdl, 3⅝", M 300.00
Winchester, 3625, ebony hdl, 3⅝", M 155.00
Winchester, 3911, stag hdl, 3", M 205.00
Winchester, 3944, bone hdl, 3¼", M 255.00
Winchester, 4340, pearl hdl, 3¼", M 305.00

Miscellaneous

Bowie, Confederate brass D guard, hand forged, 18" **400.00**
Bowie, NP/silver/MOP hdl, 6¼" bd, Sheffield, EX......................**220.00**
Bowie, Sheffield, stag horn grip, 1850s, 7", EX............................**110.00**
Bowie, WM Jackson & Co, bd: Rio Grand Camp Knife **700.00**
Chinese Tong assassination, 7" bd, ivory hdl, 1850s, EX.............**150.00**
Hunting, J Lingard, Bowie style, emb eagle, 7½" bd **750.00**
Hunting, 6½" etched Herder/Solingen bd, 1900s, +sheath **50.00**
Thomas Short, Bowie style, 8" etched bd, ivory hdl, 1850s **3,500.00**

Kosta

Kosta glassware has been made in Sweden since the mid-1700s. Today they are one of that country's leading producers of quality art glass. Two of their most important designers were Elis Bergh (1929-1950) and Vicke Lindstrand, artistic director from 1950 to 1973. Lindstrand brought to the company knowledge of important techniques such as Graal, fine figural engraving, Ariel, etc. She influenced new artists to experiment with these techniques and inspired them to create new and innovative designs. Today's collectors are most interested in pieces made during the 1950s and '60s.

Decanter, etched figures, maypole stopper, Lindstrand, 13" **500.00**
Vase, clear w/int blk stripes, trumpet form, Lindstrand, 7" **285.00**
Vase, etched fisherman, cone w/angular rim, Lindstrand, 10" **200.00**
Wine, 6 cut panels, gr w/clear stem, 5", 6 for................................**125.00**

Vase, fishing nets and wooden boat, frosted, etched and cut on crystal, signed LC, ca 1950s, 12½", $200.00.

Kutani

Kutani, named for the Japanese village where it originated, was first produced in the 17th century. The early ware, Ko Kutani, was produced for only about thirty years. Several types were produced before 1800, but these are rarely encountered. In the 19th century, kilns located in several different villages began to copy the old Kutani wares. This later, more familiar type has large areas of red with gold designs on a white ground decorated with warriors, birds, and flowers in controlled colors of red, gold, and black.

Charger, water/rocks/dwellings, ext: 3 peonies, 1800s, 13" **495.00**

Chocolate pot, bird/floral panels, people in gardens, 9" 125.00
Cup & saucer, people/floral/trees/clouds w/gilt, late 25.00

Jar, warriors in fan-shaped reserves converse before battle, shishi finial, late 1800s, 21", $650.00.

Vase, figural scenes, cicada hdls, baluster, 1900, now lamp..........**500.00**
Vase, peacocks on rocks/peony bushes, mc/gilt, mk, 13"..............**220.00**

L. E. Smith

Perhaps best known for their line of black glass vases and novelty items, this 20th-century American glass company also made several patterns of colored depression-type dinnerware.

Bonbon, gr, #81 .... 7.50
Bookends, horse, rearing, clear, pr...45.00

Rearing horse bookends (two variations), black glass, 8", $50.00 each.

Bowl, fruit; blk, hdls, ftd 20.00
Candlesticks, blk w/silver band, pr..15.00

Candy dish, Moon & Stars, emerald gr, 6"	25.00
Figurine, Scotty, frosted	40.00
Plate, Block, amethyst, 7½"	7.50
Powder shaker, blk	14.00
Tray, cordial; pk, #381	10.00
Vase, blk, #1900, 7¼"	20.00
Vase, blk, #433, 7"	15.00
Vase, blk, #49, 6"	12.50
Vase, blk, terrier decal, #102, 6½"	15.00
Vase, cobalt, #711, 5½"	6.50
Window box, blk, #405, 7¾"	25.00
Window box, cobalt, oval, 6⅜"	9.00
Window box, wht, #405-10	12.00

Labels

Before the advent of the cardboard box, wooden crates were used for transporting products. Paper labels were attached to the crates to identify the contents and the packer. These labels often had colorful lithographed illustrations covering a broad range of subjects. Eventually the cardboard box replaced the crate, and the artwork was imprinted directly onto the carton. Today these paper labels are becoming collectible – primarily for the art, but also for their advertising appeal.

Apple, Appleton, lady, valley, & apples, 1915, CA	7.50
Apple, British Empire, red seal & apple	3.00
Apple, Columbia Belle, lady dressed in flag w/sword, 1940	3.00
Apple, Golden West, 4 apples on branch, 1910	20.00

Hunter Apples, ca 1930s, $5.00.

Apple, Red Diamond, lg diamond & apples, 1920s	4.00
Apple, SnoBoy, snowboy w/apple, 1930s, WA	4.50
Apple, U Like UM, Indian on horse, 1940s, WA	4.00
Apple, Uncle Sam, stone litho, man holding hat, 1920	7.50
Apricot, Golden Spike, lg golden spike	8.00
Asparagus, Grizzly Island, blk bear on lg rock, 1929	6.00
Asparagus, Pride of the River, Mississippi river boat, 1930	7.50
Cigar, Alexander the Great, portrait, 1910, 6½x10"	17.50
Cigar, Camel, Arab on camel in desert, 1920s, 7x9"	10.00
Cigar, First Cabinet, men in oval medallion, 1920s 7x8½"	12.00
Cigar, Irish Singer, man in gr, 1910s, 6½x8½"	9.00
Cigar, Memory, man beside fireplace, 1910s, 6x20"	17.50
Cigar, Surveyor, man beside horse, 1920s, 6½x8½"	10.00
Cigar, Two Wheelers, lady w/2 burros, 1910s, 6½x10"	17.50
Citrus, Dixie Delite, couple dancing, 1930s, 9x9"	6.00
Citrus, Eureka, Indian left of fruit, 1930s, 9x9"	6.00
Citrus, Taste It, grapefruit & oranges in bowl	2.50
Lemon, Comet, comet over orchard scene, 1930, CA	2.50
Lemon, Exposition, 1920s, 9x13"	4.00
Lemon, Goleta, sailing ship, 1940s, CA	2.50
Lemon, Helena, 2 lemons & triangle, 1930, CA	2.50
Lemon, Meteor, red & orange meteor & lemons, 1930, CA	5.00
Lemon, Tom Cat, cat on red pillow, 1930, CA	45.00

Orange, Altissimo, pk mtns, 1920s, CA	17.50
Orange, Cupid, cupid's face w/bl eyes, 1920s, CA	20.00
Orange, Dipper, half orange drips into dipper	6.50
Orange, Have One, hand holds orange, 1930s, CA	4.00
Orange, Homer, flying bird, 1940s, 10x11"	5.00
Orange, Lincoln, bust of president amid oranges, 1930s, CA	5.00
Orange, Preferred, lg orange & document, 1930s, CA	3.00
Orange, Victoria, Queen's portrait, 1930s, CA	4.00
Pear, American Maid, lady in bonnet silhouette, 1940	1.50
Pear, High Hand, hand holds 4 aces, 1930	4.00
Pear, Orchard, old truck & orchard, stone litho, 1920	4.00
Pear, Pinnacle, canyon scene, 1930	3.00
Sauerkraut, Home Plate, runner safe at home base	7.50
Tomato, Our Family, tomato people	6.50
Vegetable, Dominater, fighter plane, 1940	4.00
Vegetable, Safe Hit, ball player, 1940s, 9x7"	4.00
Vegetable, Santa Maria, train scene, 1940s, CA	4.00
Vegetable, Top Row, 3 crates of lettuce, 1930s	2.00
Yam, LaGrange Sweets, Louisiana map & capitol building	2.50
Yam, Pure Winner, 5 cards, royal flush of hearts	3.50

Labino

Dominick Labino was a glass blower who until mid-1985 worked in his studio in Ohio, blowing and sculpting various items which he signed and dated. A ceramic engineer by trade, he was instrumental in developing the heat-resistant tiles used in space flights. His glassmaking shows his versatility in the art. While some of his designs are free-form and futuristic, others are reminiscent of the products of older glasshouses. Because of problems with his health, Mr. Labino became unable to blow glass himself; he died January, 10, 1987. Work coming from his studio after mid-1985 will be signed 'Labino Studios, Baker,' indicating ware made by his prodigy, E. Baker O'Brien. In addition to her own compositions, she continues to use many of the colors developed by Labino.

Bowl, gold ruby, ftd, 1966, 4¾"	375.00
Bowl, gr festoons on rose, sgn/#12-1970, 4" H	250.00
Bowl, silver smeltz, flared, sgn/1968, 6½"	160.00
Decanter, smoky burgundy, w/stopper, sgn/#2-1974, 11½"	100.00
Dolphin, bl, sgn/#10-1971, 5"	235.00
Paperweight, Blue Aerial, w/irid, 1982, 2½" dia	200.00
Paperweight, Bronze Rose, 1982, 2¼" dia	275.00
Paperweight, Chambered Nautilus, #7-1980, 2½" dia	200.00
Paperweight, Draped Flower, orange on bl irid, 3" dia	195.00
Paperweight, Ring & Bubbles, 1977	200.00
Paperweight, 2 Pansies, 1970	225.00

Bird sculpture, medium blue, 6" x 7", $650.00.

Sculpture, Aerial, cased, bl w/clear, #10-1973, 3½x5" 600.00
Sculpture, Breakthrough, amber, hot glass, #4-1971, 7¾" 725.00
Sculpture, Faceted Fountain, Emergence Series, pk/gold, 6" ... **1,800.00**
Sculpture, Mt St Helens, cased, sgn/1980, 6" 550.00
Sculpture, Neutron Bombardment, #11-1982, 4" 450.00
Sculpture, Sea Kingdom, sgn/#2-1873, 8" **2,000.00**
Vase, air sculpture, crystalline irid, sgn/#8-1981, 4" 425.00
Vase, amber w/appl glass rim, 1963, 4" 475.00
Vase, bl-gr w/cased festoons under crystal, #8-1972, 5½" 650.00
Vase, bud; silver smeltz, clear base, sgn/#2-1978, 10½" 275.00
Vase, cased cadmium selenium, opal/yel motif in red, 5½" **1,000.00**
Vase, copper-red irid w/appl mc designs, #4-1984, 4" 400.00
Vase, German Half Post, gr, 1965, 5¾" 350.00
Vase, gold chrome deposit design in opal, sgn/#7-1972, 3½" 100.00
Vase, Harlequin, cased, red/yel/bl/gr, sgn/#1-1975, 6½" **1,600.00**
Vase, jade gr, flared, sgn/#6-1972, 7" 200.00
Vase, mingled yel/orange/cobalt, ovoid, 1983, 5¾" **1,500.00**
Vase, silver smeltz decor, #12-1976, 5" 350.00
Vase, silver smeltz opal, ovoid, sgn/#3-1971, 5" 400.00
Wine cup, burnt orange, molded sides, #10-1975, 2¼", pr 200.00
Wine cup, lt jonquil on clear, #7-1979, 2", pr......................250.00

Lace, Linens, and Needlework

It has been recorded that lace was found in the tombs of ancient Egypt. Lace has always been a symbol of wealth and fashion. Italian laces are regarded as the finest ever produced, but the differences between them and the laces of France are nearly indistinguishable. Needlework was revived during the 18th century and became the favorite of feminine pastimes. Examples of many forms are readily available today – tatting, embroidery, needlepoint, and crochet – and, though fragile in appearance, have withstood the ravages of time with remarkable durability.

Key:
embr — embroidered   ms — machine sewn
hs — hand sewn

Apron, ankle length, 7" crochet edge w/drawnwork sqs 65.00
Bedspread, Battenburg, embr/multi-drawn center, 78x92" 455.00
Bedspread, candlewick, bl flowers on wht, old, 74x80", NM 165.00
Bedspread, crewel, birds in center, ca 1900, full sz, NM 400.00
Bedspread, crochet, Popcorn design, 88x92" 185.00
Bedspread, crochet, Spoke, handmade, lg, M 175.00
Bedspread, ivory satin, Deco style, w/shams & heart pillows 195.00
Bedspread, linen, wht embr roses on wht, 1800s, 76x80", EX 185.00
Bedspread, net, ecru, floral machine filet inserts, lg, EX..............150.00
Bedspread, Tambour embr on net, ecru, French, lg, EX............150.00
Blanket, homespun, center seam, fringed, 1800s, lg 275.00
Blanket, homespun, 3-color plaid, 2 strips, 1830s, 64x72" 295.00
Blanket, wool, handwoven bl & wht, 1800s, 64x78", EX............75.00
Bolster, Battenburg ferns, 84x26", EX 98.00
Bolster, Irish linen, dbl, plain, 20x48"..............................85.00
Bolster, 9-patch in mc prints, PA, 55x16", EX 65.00
Centerpiece, Battenburg, drawnwork center, sq, 30" 50.00
Centerpiece, Battenburg, scalloped, 12" dia 65.00
Centerpiece, Battenburg, solid center, sq, 18" 45.00
Centerpiece, Battenburg, 8" sq plain center, 17x17", EX 40.00
Centerpiece, crochet, eagle/Liberty, 15" sq, EX....................55.00
Centerpiece, embr elephant in center, 8½x10", EX..................45.00
Centerpiece, Irish crochet, roses, daisies, bells, 38" dia 75.00
Centerpiece, 5½" Battenburg lace edge, octagonal, 17½" 45.00
Chair set, filet crochet, Am eagle, 3-pc................................65.00

Coverlet, dbl weave, mc geometrics, wool & cotton, 1840s, EX..285.00
Curtains, machine lace, ecru, 60x48", pr 65.00
Dresser scarf, linen, wht, openwork at border, scalloped 65.00
Lap robe, wool, bulldog center, floral/lattice border, 61x46" 165.00
Mat, bread tray; crochet, 'Bread' in center, 4½x11".................35.00
Mattress cover, homespun, bl & wht, machine sewn, 66x96" 200.00
Napkin, linen, gr roses on gr, 21x21", 6 for........................35.00
Napkin, linen, hemstitched, 16x16", 8 for.........................45.00
Napkin, linen, monogram, 26x26", 8 for 50.00
Napkin, linen, red & natural, set of 12.............................80.00
Needlework, Am eagle/shield/flags, silk embr, 24x28", EX 160.00
Needlework, fisherman returns to family, 1800s, fr, 17x21" 225.00
Needlework, girl feeds chickens, sgn J Sian, fr, 12x9" 575.00
Needlework, landscape/flowers, sgn, dtd 1838, 22x26" 350.00
Needlework, maiden in woodland, silk embr, oval, 15x12".........275.00
Needlework, Moses' Discovery, w/HP, sgn/1819, 20x25".............600.00

Needlework picture, English, 1700s, 14" x 16", $200.00.

Runner, Battenburg, drawnwork center sq, 48x16", EX 125.00
Runner, Battenburg, drawnwork insert center, 46x20"................85.00
Runner, crochet, cat center, 13x18"................................45.00
Runner, crochet, God Bless Our Home, ecru, 12x20", EX 45.00
Runner, crochet, initial center, scalloped, 10½x29" 35.00
Runner, crochet, rooster center, 10x13"............................45.00
Runner, crochet, Spirit of St Louis, plane center, 17x25" 68.00
Runner, linen, drawnwork, 22x92", EX...........................65.00
Runner, machine lace, ecru, 13x19"................................45.00
Runner, silk, red & blk embr on cream, fringed, 29x128" 65.00
Sham, Irish linen, Continental, cut/embr border, pr 55.00
Sham, linen, ivory embr, wide lace edge, 26", EX 75.00
Sham, red embr cupids on wht linen, lg, pr 55.00
Sham, red embr girl on pillow, Good Night, 29x32", EX 45.00
Sham, roses/ribbon/bow embr, initialed corners, lg.................65.00
Sheet, cotton homespun, embr initials, hs, 64x108" 85.00
Sheet & pillowcases, cotton w/crocheted trim, EX..................65.00
Tablecloth, Battenburg, sm plain center, 69" dia....................425.00
Tablecloth, Battenburg, 45" dia, M 185.00
Tablecloth, Battenburg, 56" dia, M 200.00
Tablecloth, Battenburg, 8-pointed star center, sq, 29" 165.00
Tablecloth, Battenburg grape border, embr center, 78x92" 475.00
Tablecloth, crochet, beige, 60x60", M 85.00
Tablecloth, crochet, dmn pattern, scalloped, 60x80"................70.00
Tablecloth, crochet, filet, heavy, 58" dia...........................85.00
Tablecloth, crochet, handmade, 76x76", M.........................135.00
Tablecloth, crochet, Pineapple, oval, 59x78", M....................75.00

Tablecloth, cross-stitch on ecru, Oriental garden, 50x50" **75.00**
Tablecloth, damask, gr, 92x70", +6 napkins, M **95.00**
Tablecloth, damask, house/trees, 84x66" **125.00**
Tablecloth, Irish linen, Shamrock pattern, 72x90", M **150.00**
Tablecloth, Irish linen damask, 108x72" **145.00**
Tablecloth, lace/cutwork/embr lawn, Queen's Motif, 59x104".....**250.00**
Tablecloth, linen, cutwork, 72x78", NM **100.00**
Tablecloth, linen, embr grapes on brn, crochet border, 33x33" **45.00**
Tablecloth, linen, embr/cutwork, ecru on wht, 54x60" **40.00**
Tablecloth, linen, gold embr, 45x45" **45.00**
Tablecloth, linen, gr embr on ecru, 57x75", M **45.00**
Tablecloth, linen, quad-drawn, Germany, 72x100" **135.00**
Tablecloth, linen, roses/leaves embr, 1800s, 36" dia, EX **85.00**
Tablecloth, linen homespun, 2-pc, ms, 64x90" **85.00**
Tablecloth, machine lace, floral, oval, scalloped, 60x108" **65.00**
Tablecloth, machine lace, floral w/scalloped border, 68x82".........**45.00**
Tablecloth, machine lace, rose pattern, 70" dia..........................**45.00**
Tablecloth, Quaker lace, floral, ecru, 68x88", EX **65.00**
Tablecloth, red chenille, pk flower center, fringe, sq, 45" **185.00**
Tablecloth, red embr flowers at center & border, 65x48" **95.00**
Towel, homespun, bl/wht checks, drawnwork, fringe, 38x17".......**180.00**
Towel, damask, red borders & fringe, 41x23".............................**65.00**
Towel, show; homespun, embr initials & 1798,, 51x16" **115.00**
Wall hanging, US map in silk piecework, Victorian **75.00**
Window hanging, filet crochet, birds & flowers, M **65.00**

Lachenal

Bowl, 6-point star, bl/olive on gr wash, 6½" **200.00**
Pitcher, naturalistic branch hdl, lt bl/brn drip, 16" **400.00**
Vase, cvd circles, orange-red/blk, tapered cylinder, 6½".............**600.00**
Vase, triangular panels, gr on flecked yel w/gilt, 7½" **700.00**

Lacy Glassware

Lacy glass became popular in the late 1820s after the development of the pressing machine. It was decorated with allover patterns – hearts, lyres, sheaves of wheat, etc. – and backgrounds were completely stippled. The designs were intricate and delicate, hence the term 'lacy.' Although Sandwich produced this type of glassware in abundance, it was also made by other eastern glassworks as well as in the midwest. By 1840 its popularity on the wane and a depressed economy forcing manufacturers to seek less expensive modes of production, lacy glass began to be phased out in favor of pressed pattern glassware. When no condition is indicated, the items listed below are assumed to be without obvious damage; minor roughness is normal. See also Sandwich Glass.

Plate, heart border, circle of hearts in center, att New England Glass Co, 12", NM, $2,700.00.

Bowl, heart & lyre border, att NE Glass Co, 9½", NM..................**50.00**
Bowl, lyre center, shallow, minor chips, 6⅜"..............................**35.00**
Dish, Leaf & Gothic Arch, rectangular, chips, 5x7"......................**45.00**
Dish, scrolls/leaves in leafy scroll border, shaped, 8" L **160.00**
Plate, bl, dmn center, ray border, plain edge, 4½" **110.00**
Plate, cobalt, 2 rows Roman Rosette, sunburst, 5", EX **375.00**
Plate, gold-amber, flower & ray, stippled/beaded border, 5"..........**30.00**
Plate, heart, 5½", NM..**50.00**
Plate, lyre & dmn border, flower center, 12-sided, 6" **25.00**
Plate, lyre & plant border, 12-sided, 5", NM...............................**50.00**
Plate, opal, Roman Rosette, 5½", EX.......................................**70.00**
Plate, toddy; heart border, NE Glass Co, 5", NM **40.00**
Plate, 8-point star, dmn-filled heart border, scalloped, 5"..............**30.00**
Sugar bowl, cobalt, octagonal, NM **800.00**

Lalique

Beginning his lengthy career as a designer and maker of fine jewelry, Rene Lalique at first only dabbled in glass, making small panels of pate-de-verre (paste-on-paste) and cire perdue (wax casting) to use in his jewelry. He also made small flacons of gold and silver with his glass inlays, which attracted the attention of M.F. Coty, who commissioned Lalique to design bottles for his perfume company. The success of this venture resulted in the opening of his own glassworks at Combs-la-Ville in 1909. In 1921 a larger factory was established at Wingen-sur-Moder in Alsace-Lorraine. By the thirties Lalique was world renown as the most important designer of his time.

Lalique glass is lead based, either mold blown or pressed. Favored motifs during the Art Nouveau period were dancing nymphs, fish, dragonflies, and foliage. Characteristically the glass is crystal in combination with acid-etched relief. Later, some items were made in as many as ten colors – red, amber, and green among them – and were occasionally accented with enameling. These colored pieces, especially those in black, are rare and highly prized by advanced collectors.

During the twenties and thirties, Lalique designed several vases and bowls reminiscent of American Indian art. He also developed a line in the Art Deco style decorated with stylized birds, florals, and geometrics. In addition to vases, clocks, automobile mascots, stemware, and bottles, many other useful objects were produced. Items made before his death in 1945 were marked 'R. Lalique'; later the 'R' was deleted even though some of the original molds were still used. Numbers found on the bases of some pieces are catalog numbers.

Our advisor for this category is John Danis; he is listed in the Directory under Illinois.

Key:
cl/fr — clear and frosted	RL — signed R. Lalique
L — signed Lalique	RLF — signed R. Lalique, France

Ash tray, Vezelay, fr opal w/gray wash, RL/#218, 4½x4½" **400.00**
Atomizer, Dahlia, amber wash/enamel, RLF, 7"............................**600.00**
Atomizer, frieze of nudes/garlands, amber wash, RL/MIF, 3" **385.00**
Atomizer, nudes/floral garlands, RL/MIF, 5" **600.00**
Atomizer, pr sparrows perched at shoulder, fr, RLF, 4" **1,800.00**
Bottle, display; Worth, emb stars, rnd stopper w/'W,' 10" **495.00**
Bottle, scent; Bouquet de Faunes, cl/fr, Guerlain Paris, 4" **350.00**
Bottle, scent; Telline, cl/fr, w/bl stain, RL/#508, 4" **800.00**
Bottle, scent; Tzigane, zigzag ridges/stopper, fr, RL, 4½" **350.00**
Bowl, Bol Fleur, enamel/amber wash, RLF, 4½"...........................**600.00**
Bowl, Coquilles, cl/fr, RL, 6½" **130.00**
Bowl, Coquilles, opal, RLF/#3201, 8" **500.00**
Bowl, fish leap amidst waves, opal, RLF, 12".................................**600.00**
Bowl, Jardiniere St Hubert, antelope hdls, RLF, cl/fr, 18½" **3,600.00**

Bowl, Lys, opal, eng RLF, 9½" 800.00
Bowl, Martigues, fish, amber opal, RL/inscr F, 14½" 1,900.00
Bowl, Nemours, gray, RLF, 10" 600.00
Bowl, Ondine Ouverte, opal, RLF, 8" 1,200.00
Bowl, palmettes/daisies, cl/fr, LF, 9½" 100.00
Bowl, peonies/broad leaves, brick-red wash, RLF/N-3210, 9" 495.00
Bowl, peonies/broad leaves, opal, RLF, 9" 275.00
Bowl, radiating tulips, cl/fr, RL, 9½" 300.00
Bowl, Volubilis, 3 blossoms form base, opal, RLF, 2¼x8½" 400.00
Box, Cigarettes Hirondelles, birds/chevrons, cl/fr, RLF/#54 .... 1,200.00
Box, Degas, gr wash, sgn L, 3" dia.......................... 1,000.00
Box, powder; floral relief, amber wash, D'Orsay/RL, 4" dia..........700.00
Box, powder; Rambouillet, bl tint, RL/France, 3½" dia...............400.00
Box, powder; 3 nudes on lid, fr, for Coty, RLF, 3¾" H.................385.00
Dish, spiraling fish/bubbles, opal, RLF, 11½" 385.00
Figurine, Cendrier, woman holding blossom, fr, RL, 4½" 375.00
Goblet, Hesperides, leafy fronds, fr, RLF/#3412, 5" 300.00
Inkwell, Colbert, birds/branches, cl/fr, w/tray, RL/#2, 11" 2,200.00
Inkwell, 3 mermaids, dk/opal butterscotch, 1932, 9½" dia 2,000.00
Lamp, seashell form, RL, 8" dia, mtd on ornate metal base 2,000.00
Luminaire, Suzanne, standing nude, opal/bronze, RL, 11"......11,000.00
Mascot, Coq Nain, rooster form, cl/fr, LF, 8" 275.00
Mascot, Horses, row of 5, cl, RLF, 6½" 8,000.00
Mascot, Perche, fish form, fr, LF, 7½" 2,000.00
Mascot, Petite Libellule, dragonfly, fr, RLF, 6" 5,000.00
Mascot, Tete d'Aigle, eagle's head, cl/fr, RL, mtd, 4¼" 2,500.00
Mascot, Tete d'Aigle, eagle's head, cl/fr, RLF, unmtd, 4½" 2,000.00
Mascot, Tete de Belier, ram's head, smoke, RFL, 3¾" 26,000.00
Mascot, Victorie, stylized woman's head, cl/fr, RLF, 5" 11,000.00
Necklace, Collier-Lierre, 19 opal/amber ivy leaves on cord..... 4,600.00
Paperweight, Moineaux Ailes Croisees, bird, cl/fr, RLF, 4½" 440.00
Paperweight, recumbent bull, Royal Dutch Mail, RLF, 3½".........700.00
Pendant, Cherries, electric bl, LF, 1½"....................................700.00
Perfume burner, artichoke leaves relief, gray, RL/MIF, 5" 800.00
Plate, dandelions radiate from center, amber wash, RLF, 12" 495.00

Vase, Gros Scarabees, clear with brown patina, signed Lalique, ca 1920, 11½", $3,500.00.

Vase, Actina, serrated curves, cl/fr, RL, 8½"..................................600.00
Vase, Bacchantes, opal w/bl wash, wheel-cut RLF, 9½"..........12,000.00
Vase, Beliers, charcoal gray, RL, 7½".................................. 1,900.00

Vase, Camargue, horses, brn wash, thick walled, RL, 11"........ 6,000.00
Vase, Ceylan, opal, RL, 9½", NM.................................... 2,900.00
Vase, Chamois, bl wash, RLF, 5"................................... 1,200.00
Vase, Charmille, gray fr, emb RL/eng France, 14"..................... 6,000.00
Vase, Dahlias, fr/blk enamel, RL, 5".............................. 1,400.00
Vase, Deux Mointeaux Dormant, sleeping birds, fr, RL, 8" 495.00
Vase, Druides, mistletoe, fr w/polished berries, RLF, 8¾"............600.00
Vase, Estrel, stylized leaves, fr/sandy wash, 6"............................650.00
Vase, Estrel, stylized leaves, opal, RLF/#941, ovoid, 6" 800.00
Vase, Ferns, cl/fr, spherical, RLF/#996, 7"...................................550.00
Vase, Ferrieres, cased/fr, RLF, 6½" 600.00
Vase, Formose, fish, fr/cased, RLF, 6¾"..................................... 1,000.00
Vase, Grenade, overlapping leaves, amber, RLF, 4½" 3,000.00
Vase, Gui, mistletoe/berries, fr, RLF, 6½" 600.00
Vase, Honfleur, cl w/amber wash, RLF/#994, 5½".......................500.00
Vase, Le Man's, roosters, gr cased opal, RLF, 4" 600.00
Vase, Lierre, cl w/pk wash, RLF, 6½" 500.00
Vase, Malesherbes, cased gr, RLF/#1014, 9" 3,700.00
Vase, Moissac, fr/gray wash, RL, 5"...600.00
Vase, Monnaie du Pape, cl/fr w/amber wash, RL, 9" 900.00
Vase, Oleran, fr, RLF/#1008, 3½" 500.00
Vase, Oursin, molded nodules, gray wash, RLF, 7" 800.00
Vase, Palmes, palm leaves, gr, RL, 4½" 2,400.00
Vase, sparrows nestling in brush, cl/fr, ovoid, RLF, 6½" 495.00
Vase, Spirales, opal w/translucent centers, RLF, 6½" 1,000.00
Vase, St Francois, high-relief birds, fr, RLF/#1055, 7"............. 1,000.00
Vase, Thistles, opal, traces of bl wash, RLF/#979, 8½" 1,000.00

Lamps

The earliest lamps were simple dish containers with a wick that hung over the edge or was supported by a channel or tube. Grease and oil from animal or vegetable sources were the first fuels used. Ancient pottery lamps, crusie, and Betty lamps are examples of these early types. In 1784 Swiss inventor Ami Argand introduced the first major improvement in lamps. His lamp featured a tubular wick and a glass chimney. During the first half of the 19th century, whale oil, burning fluid (a highly explosive mixture of turpentine and alcohol), and lard were the most common fuels used in North America. Many lamps were patented for specific use with these fuels.

Kerosene was the first major breakthrough in lighting fuels. It was demonstrated by Canadian geologist Dr. Abraham Gesner in 1846. The discovery and drilling of petroleum in the late 1850s provided an abundant and inexpensive supply of kerosene. It became the main source of light for homes during the balance of the 19th century and for remote locations until the 1950s.

Although Thomas A. Edison invented the electric lamp in 1879, it was not until two or three decades later that electric lamps replaced kerosene household lamps. Millions of kerosene lamps were made for every purpose and pocketbook. They ranged in size from tiny night or miniature lamps to tall stand or piano lamps. Hanging varieties for homes commonly had one or two fonts (oil containers), but chandeliers for churches and public buildings often had six or more. Wall or bracket lamps usually had silvered reflectors. Student lamps, parlor lamps (now called Gone-with-the-Wind lamps), and patterned glass lamps were designed to compliment the popular furnishing trends of the day. From about 1910, Aladdin lamps with a mantle became the mainstay of rural America, providing light that compared favorably with the electric light bulb. Gaslight, introduced in the early 19th century, was used mainly in homes of the wealthy and public places until the early 20th century. Most fixtures were wall or ceiling mounted although some table models were also used.

Few of the ordinary early electric lamps have survived. Many lamp manufacturers made the same or similar styles for either kerosene or electricity, sometimes for gas. Top-of-the-line lamps were made by Pairpoint, Phoenix, Tiffany, Bradley and Hubbard, and Handel. See also these specific sections.

For those seeking additional information on Aladdin Lamps, we recommend *Aladdin – The Magic Name in Lamps; Aladdin Electric Lamps;* and *A Collector's Manual and Price Guide,* all written by our advisor for Aladdins, J. W. Courter; he is listed in the Directory under Illinois.

Another of our lamp advisors is Ruth Osborne; she is listed under Ohio. See also specific manufacturers.

Aladdin Lamps

Alacite, G-17, opalique, boudoir, electric, 1938-1952, EX 60.00
Alacite, G-172, table lamp, electric, complete 50.00
Alacite, G-23, boudoir, electric, complete, NM 38.00
Alacite, G-318, Princess, electric, illuminated base 45.00
Alacite, G-349, planter lamp w/planter, electric, EX....................75.00
Alacite, G-351, wall medallion, electric, EX 40.00
Alacite, G-47C, Bullet, illuminated base, w/shade, NM 255.00
Bed lamp, #832-SS, Whip-o-lite pleated shade, NM 185.00
Beehive, B-82, dk amber, EX...100.00
Beehive, B-83, ruby, complete, EX 295.00
Boudoir, G-10, glass, electric, orig 8" shade, EX 50.00
Boudoir, G-22, electric, EX..25.00
Caboose lamp, #23, complete, EX 45.00
Caboose lamp, B, complete, NM 95.00
Candelabrum, G-211, alacite, electric, M......................................125.00
Cathedral, B-107, clear, complete, EX 80.00
Cathedral, B-111, gr moonstone, NM...170.00
Cathedral, B-112, rose moonstone, NM 200.00
Ceramic, P-401, table lamp, complete, EX 25.00
Ceramic, TV-386, TV lamp, planter, complete, EX 50.00
Cherry & brass, MT-520, touch lamp, NM.....................................215.00
Colonial, B-104, clear, complete, NM 95.00
Colonial, B-106, amber crystal, VG..100.00
Colonial, G-97, crystal, electric, complete, 15½".........................130.00
Colonial, M-59, modern candlestick, electric, 18", NM 27.50
Corinthian, B-103, clear, VG..55.00
Corinthian, B-114, wht moonstone, complete, NM......................95.00
Corinthian, B-125, wht moonstone font, gr moonstone ft, EX 95.00
Crystal Vase, #12, Venetian Art-Craft, red, 12", NM 225.00
Desk lamp, M-238, electric, plastic shade, EX 40.00
Florentine Vase, #12, gr moonstone, 8½", EX 720.00
Hanging, #1, w/shade #203, NM 600.00
Hanging, #5, w/shade #215, EX 275.00
Hanging, #9, w/orig shade, EX 220.00
Hanging, B, glass shade, NM...245.00
Horsehead, G-335C, orig shade, EX 365.00
Lincoln Drape, Short; B-60, alacite, EX 300.00
Lincoln Drape, Tall; B-74, clear, old, EX 1,600.00
Lincoln Drape, Tall; B-77, ruby, old, EX 385.00
Majestic, B-120, wht moonstone, complete, VG...........................100.00
Majestic, B-121, rose moonstone, VG 125.00
Majestic, B-122, gr moonstone, complete, M 200.00
Orientale, B-131, gr, VG 65.00
Orientale, B-133, silver, NM 150.00
Parlour lamp, #3, kerosene burner, EX 625.00
Pin-up lamp, G-352, alacite, M...40.00
Practicus, table lamp 225.00
Queen, B-94, wht moonstone, complete, VG................................75.00
Queen, B-98, rose moonstone, complete, NM 185.00
Quilt, B-91, wht moonstone font, rose moonstone ft, EX 140.00

Shade, #601S, cabin, EX 285.00
Shade, #681, dogwood on wht satin, EX 45.00
Shade, parchment, Whip-o-lite, florals, 14", EX 38.00
Shade, wht cased, English, 10" 35.00
Simplicity, B-26, alacite, decalcomania, M...................................275.00
Simplicity, B-27, alacite, gold lustre, EX......................................225.00
Solitaire, B-70, wht moonstone, EX 1,000.00
Table lamp, #1, kerosene burner, EX...450.00
Table lamp, #14, brass font, NM 100.00
Table lamp, #3, kerosene burner, NM 545.00
Table lamp, #8, kerosene burner, VG 150.00
Table lamp, G-195, alacite, electric, M...45.00
Table lamp, G-2, marble-like glass, electric, EX 175.00
Table lamp, G-213, alacite, electric, M..35.00
Table lamp, G-240, electric, NM 85.00
Table lamp, G-287C, alacite & metal, electric, M...........................75.00
Treasure, B-136, chromium, complete, NM..................................165.00
Venetian, #101, gr, VG 40.00
Venetian, #99, clear, NM..175.00
Vertique, B-88, yel moonstone, NM...385.00
Victoria, B-25, china w/floral decor, NM......................................325.00
Vogue Pedestal, E-201, bl electric, complete, EX 300.00
Washington Drape, B-40, gr, rnd base, EX 65.00
Washington Drape, B-48, gr, bell stem, EX 155.00
Washington Drape, B-50, clear, filigree stem, EX........................70.00
Washington Drape, B-53X, clear, no oil fill, plain stem, VG 40.00

Washington Drape, B-53, $90.00.

Chandeliers

Brass, 3-branch, frost/clear scalloped shades, electric, EX 375.00
Brass w/crimped pan, 4 sockets, hanging loop, dk patina, EX 205.00
CI, 4-branch, clear fonts, #2 burners, pearl-top chimneys 425.00
Copper, hammered, 4-branch, slag glass shades, 1910s................300.00
Cut crystal, 4-branch, w/cut pendant prisms, 42" 450.00
Gilt brass & ironstone, 5-branch, Victorian style, 25", EX 750.00
Gilt metal, 6-light, Renaissance style, 34" 2,200.00
Tole, gilt on maroon, Provincial Emp, 4 fluid lamps, 28" 1,800.00

Decorated Kerosene Lamps

Amethyst, looped font, octagonal std, sq base, 10", EX.................325.00

Cobalt cut to clear font, blk amethyst ft, 9½", EX 150.00
Cranberry pear-shaped threaded font, 8½" 265.00
Cut overlay, cobalt to clear, clear base, NE Glass, 11" 1,600.00
Cut overlay, gr to clear font, wht ft, gilt base, 9½", EX 300.00
Cut overlay, plum to wht to clear ovals/star bursts, 14"...............275.00
Cut overlay, wht to clear, gold scrolls, 2-tier base, 13" 375.00
Dbl cut overlay, pear font, jade gr std, Sandwich, 13", NM 2,300.00
Wht pear-shaped font w/gold leaves, sq base, 12".........................140.00
Yel cased satin, diamonds/X motif, dome shade, 16" 950.00

Sapphire bl, diamond cut, clear Clarke cup, 5" 145.00
Yel cased, Swirl overshot, clear Clarke base, 3½x2⅞" 95.00

Burmese shade, signed Clarke peg-lamp base, brass and copper figural dog, 13", EX, $550.00.

Cornelius & Co., Philadelphia, blown etched and frosted shade, faceted prisms, ca 1845, 26" x 13", $400.00.

Fairy Lamps

Amber Dia Point, mk Clarke Fairy Pyramid, 3¾"...........................65.00
Amber Dia Quilt, emb ribs, Clarke base, 4¾x3⅞"........................165.00
Bl Dia Quilt w/melon ribs, clear mk Clarke base, 4⅝" 145.00
Bl overshot, crown form, Queen Victoria 1877 Jubilee, 4½" 185.00
Bl verre moire, matching base, Clarke cup, 5x5½"........................425.00
Burmese, dome shade & bowl, Webb, Clarke cup, 6x4½"............550.00
Burmese, maple leaves, Clarke base 200.00
Burmese, no decor, sgn Clarke base, 3½" 150.00
Burmese, red berries/fall leaves, folded/ruffled, Webb, 5½"...... 1,800.00
Burmese, unmk Webb, clear mk Clarke base, 3¾x2⅞"...............165.00
Chartreuse gr overlay, melon ribs, clear Clarke base, 4⅝"..........175.00
Cranberry verre moire, dome shade, ruffled base, 5½x6½" 495.00
Cranberry verre moire, wht loops, Clarke base, 4½x3⅞" 175.00
Dk gr overlay, clear mk Clarke base, 4½x3⅞" 110.00
Gr verre moire, clear Clark base, 4½x3⅞" 175.00
Gray to wht overlay, ruffled top, clear mk Clarke base, 6¼" 195.00
Milk glass, Delft-style windmill & sailboat, 8" 350.00
Milk glass, Wm Henry Harrison/1892 commemorative, 9", NM.700.00
Nailsea, cranberry/wht satin, 4½", NM...300.00
Nailsea, wht frost on clear frost, matching base, 5" 300.00
Pk/wht mottled rib shade, clear base, 4½", NM.............................175.00
Rose Dia Quilt MOP, Clarke Cricklite base, 7x5½" 675.00
Rose Dia Quilt MOP, clear Clarke base, pyramid sz, 3½x2⅞" 145.00
Rose Swirl MOP satin, Clarke cup, brass base, 14" 375.00

Gone-with-the-Wind and Banquet Lamps

Bl satin, emb 'Baby Face' on shade & base, electrified, 24"..........600.00
Cherries on rose to yel 9" ball shade, brass base/hdls, 30" 450.00
Cut/frosted pyriform shade, prisms, marble plinth, 30" 850.00
Floral HP on milk glass w/emb decor, 9½" shade, 20", EX 550.00
Gr satin w/emb poppies on base & shade, 24" 350.00
Lions' heads blown out on 10" red satin glass shade, 23", EX.......800.00
Lt bl satin base/shade, brn eagle/World's Fair 1893, 20"..............550.00
Roses, pk w/gr & gold leaves on opal, flared base, 19".................250.00

Hanging Lamps

Amber hobnail 14" Francis Ware shade; ornate fr w/prisms 1,350.00
Clear textured shade, polished brass fr, VG 180.00
Coin Spot pk MOP satin, 8-sided shade, brass fittings 895.00
Cranberry Invt T'print w/flowers & butterflies, 14" 350.00
Floral, mc on milk glass, brass fr, electrified.................................140.00
Gr-cased shade. brass fr, 10", EX 125.00
Pk opal ribbed & paneled shade, brass fr, EX................................250.00
Pk satin, mc flowers in relief panels, vasiform, 18" 600.00
Roses HP on milk glass, clear font, brass fr, prisms, VG 250.00
Smoke bell, cut Gothic arch globe, emb brass fr, 20" 625.00
Smoke bell & frosted globe w/folded rims, brass trim, 27" 400.00
Store, patterned tin shade, polished brass font, M.......................200.00
Swirled Rib, pk opal, wrought & brass fr, 28", EX 135.00

Lanterns

Barn type, pine & hardwood w/old red, glass sides, 10½".............350.00

Brass w/amethyst glass globe, orig burner, bail hdl, 7" 325.00
Candle, tin, orig chimney & red pnt, 12½" 125.00
Dietz Jr, brass, orig globe w/label, cleaned, 12" 75.00
Dietz Sport..., tin, clear globe mk Scout, 7½" 55.00
Skater's, brass, bl chimney, minor dents, 7", EX 175.00
Skater's, brass, dmn-form frwork, pat 1867, 7½", NM 150.00
Skater's, brass, pat 1867, minor dent, 7½" 125.00
Skater's, brass, pat 1867, 9", EX 150.00
Skater's, brass, rare sz, 4½" 150.00
Steven's Pat 1875, tin, w/hanger & shutter, orig finish, 6" 225.00
Tin, curved glass, folding hdl, brn japanning, 5⅛" 55.00
Tin, pierced, crimped wafer, flat bail, ca 1800, 10½" 195.00
Tin, pierced, w/orig glass lamp, 12", VG 175.00
Tin w/onion globe, camphene burner, minor dents, 8", EX 275.00

Lard Oil/Grease

Betty, brass, long hanger, 1800s, 21½" L, NM 200.00
Betty, iron, rooster finial, hanger, French, 6½" W, EX 175.00
Betty, iron w/brass heart imp 'Boker,' w/hanger, 1800s, EX 400.00
Betty, tin, w/hanger & wick, 1800s, EX 70.00
Betty, tin, w/matching stand, 12", VG 250.00
Crusie, dbl, iron, English, 1700s, EX 200.00
Kettle, iron, 2-burner, 3-leg pencil std, 9" 550.00
Kettle, iron, 3-leg, EX detail, 1825, 10", NM 450.00
Kettle, iron/brass, pencil std, 3-ftd saucer base, 9" 275.00
Loom rush light/candle holder, iron, adjusts to 37" 400.00
Loom rush light/candle holder, iron, not adjustable, 20" 400.00
Pan, iron, long hook atop, 3-ftd, adjustable, 16", EX 550.00
Pan, iron, orig trammel, EX form, extends to 39" 850.00
Pan, iron, orig trammel, rare sz, extends to 13" 550.00
Pan, iron, orig trammel, 1700s, extends to 36", EX 225.00
Pan, iron, twisted wrought hanger, 1700s, 20" L 150.00
Phoebe, iron, distlefink decor, 1700s 245.00
Pottery, buff clay w/clear glaze, 2⅝" 475.00
Rush light, iron, standing, brass ornament, 3 spade ft, 55" 1,200.00
Rush light, iron, 3-leg, shoe ft, spring-operated, 9½" 450.00
Rush light, wrought iron on wood base, ca 1800, 9" 245.00

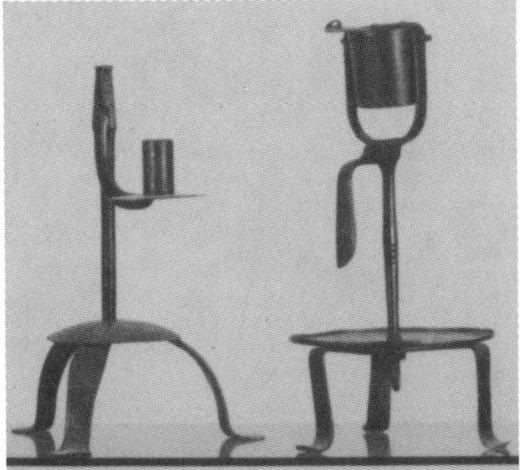

Iron rush light and candleholder with penny-foot base, 10", $300.00; Iron 3-legged kettle lamp, early 1800s, 10", $450.00.

Leaded Glass Lamps

Colonial 19" shade; swag-emb std, Duffner/Kimberly, 23" 4,900.00

Bigelow Kennard, stylized foliate band, 16" diameter shade, 19", $2,400.00.

Geometric/floral band 20" shade; Duffner/Kimberly, 24" 2,000.00
Intricate floral 16" metal-mtd shade; Bigelow Kennard, 19" ... 2,000.00
Paneled 25" shade; ldgl conical base w/chevrons, 32" 3,100.00
Scroll/floral 21" metal-mtd shade; Duffner/Kimberly, 30" 10,000.00
Stylized 22" cone shade; gilt leafy std, Duffner/Kimberly 2,700.00

Miniature Lamps, Kerosene

Acorn, blk opaque, HP daisies, orig burner 225.00
Aqua opaque in silver filigree, 2-pc, 7¼", M 900.00
Basket, milk glass, nutmeg burner, chimney, 7⅝", EX 100.00
Cased bl satin, rnd ruffled shade, acorn burner, 8⅞" 385.00
Clear, wide 16-panel font on hexagonal base, w/burner, 5" 150.00
Cosmos, cased yel, brass fixture, 4" 60.00
Cranberry ribbed, finger lamp, complete, 6" 145.00
Cranberry threads on clear, pewter fr & burner, 6" 395.00
Custard, smooth, appl gr ft, unmk brass burner, 8⅝", EX 275.00
Drape, cranberry w/amber scallops on ped base, 6¼" 300.00
Drape, red satin, 3¼" sq base, 9½" 200.00
Eagle in fired-on bl & yel on wht opaque, 7" 325.00
End of Day, purple/wht shade, finger lamp 85.00
Fire Fly, cobalt, 4" 225.00
Globular font, stepped base, Thos Cains, 6" 300.00
Gr to wht satin, nutmeg burner, chimney, 8¾", EX 1,550.00
Improved Banner, wht opaque, 5", pr 100.00
Invt T'print, gr, finger lamp, complete, 6¼" 75.00
Little Harry Night Lamp, cobalt, appl hdl, 4" 275.00
Marbled opaque bl base, clear fluted font, Sandwich, 4", pr 375.00
Milk glass, fleur-de-lis/florals, Hornet burner, 8⅝", EX 500.00
Optic panels, cranberry, Hornet burner, 8¼", EX 225.00
Porc, cat figural, tan w/bl ribbon, mk base, Fr, 4⅜", EX 500.00
Porc w/Delft-style cherubs, rpl burner, 6", EX 300.00
Queen's Necklace, Findlay, rare 225.00
Sapphire bl, emb stars, ball globe/squat bulbous base, 6¾" 375.00
Shoe form, clear, emb Patd June 30 1868, Atterbury, 3" 400.00
Spiral Beaded, ruby flashed, 8½" 395.00
Sweetheart, crystal, Findlay 140.00

Pattern Glass Lamps

Acanthus Leaf, bl opaque/wht, Sandwich, 11", EX 1,000.00
Acanthus Leaf, flint, all orig, rare sz, 9½", NM 250.00
Aquarius, vaseline, ftd, finger lamp 150.00

Beaded Hearts, gr & clear, finger lamp...................................275.00
Bellflower, fluid burning, scalloped ft, w/collar, 7", NM 200.00
Bull's Eye & Fleur-de-Lis, brass collar, att Sandwich, 9" 175.00
Bull's Eye & Fleur-de-Lis, flint, whale oil, hexagonal, 11"...........225.00
Bull's Eye & Fleur-de-Lis font, sq fiery opal base, 9½" 150.00
Bull's Eye & Invt Dia Point, flint, period burner, 10", pr............425.00
Centennial, finger lamp, 8"..235.00
Coin Spot, clear opal font, clear ft/hdl, finger lamp, 5⅜" 350.00
Dbl Wedding Ring, appl hdl, flint, finger lamp.......................95.00
Diamond & Fan, amber, flat finger lamp 125.00
Easton, clear opal font, blk ft, finger lamp, 5¼", EX.................325.00
Giant Sawtooth, flint, whale oil, 11", EX 150.00
Gothic Arch & T'print, cranberry, finger lamp, 3¼", EX 275.00
Harp, flint, whale oil, hexagonal, 10" 150.00
King Melon, clear w/opal spots, #1 burner, 9", EX 475.00
Loop, amethyst, w/hdl, orig burner/collar, att NE, 3", NM 375.00
Loop, fiery opal, appl hdl, octagonal, att NE Glass, 3" 600.00
Loop, fiery opal, hexagonal base, dbl drop burner, NE, 6" 700.00
Loop, flint, waisted, all orig, att NE Glass, 8½" 200.00
Moon & Star, early, w/hdl, 3⅝" 170.00
Optic, spatter font, end-of-day variant base, #2 burner, 9"..........500.00
Peacock Feather, bl, #1 burner, 9¼", EX............................235.00
Periwinkle, brass collar, scalloped ft, 6¾" 175.00
Polka Dot, bl opal, clear swirl stem & base, 8"......................450.00
Prince Edward, bl opaque, stand lamp................................475.00
Prince Edward, emerald gr, ftd, finger lamp 185.00
Quilt, yel, stand lamp, complete 675.00
Sheldon Swirl, wht opal, ftd, finger lamp 495.00
Star & Punty, dk bl opaque, camphene, att Sandwich, 11" 2,000.00
Star & Punty, flint, 10", EX...125.00
Sweetheart, flint, orig brass collar, Sandwich, 9", NM 150.00
Sweetheart, flint, whale oil, att Sandwich, 9¾" 200.00
Torpedo, orig burner, stand lamp, 10" 110.00
Tulip, flint, rnd base, period burner, 9", NM 150.00

Peg Lamps

Blown, brass collar, whale oil, 5¾" 135.00
Brass & tin, whale oil, 3"...315.00
Emb satin, mushroom shade in brass candlestick, 19" 495.00
Pk overlay, mushroom shade in brass candlestick, 21½"............395.00
Pk satin, matching 6" dia ruffled shade on long-stem base 350.00
Pk shaded, wht int, brass holder w/bearded head, 16" 825.00
Yel overlay font & shade, brass candlestick & mts, 15"..............495.00
8-sided, pewter color, brass/pewter burner, complete, VG............165.00

Reverse-Painted Lamps

Breaking waves 16" dia shade; gr-patina std, Pittsburgh........... 1,400.00
Butterflies on burnt orange 16" shade sgn on mt, Jefferson...... 1,600.00
Call of Wild 19" campsite shade; bronze std, Pittsburgh.......... 1,200.00
Clipper ship at sea 16" shade; 3-dolphin std, Jefferson............. 3,000.00
Country road 18" sgn shade; sgn baluster base, Jefferson 1,400.00
Floor, 10" orange scenic shade, emb trees, Classique #600 ..... 1,800.00
Houses/boats 12" shade; pot metal/openwork std, Phoenix..........475.00
Moon/lake 16" chipped-ice shade; 3-dolphin std, Pittsburgh .. 1,800.00
Moon/trees on 8" shade, bronze-washed std, Moe Bridges, 13" 800.00
Scenic 17" shade; polychrome metal base, 23", EX 700.00
Trees/lake 16" #872 shade; brn metal berry-leaf emb std.............475.00
6 panels: mill/stream, w/repousse strips, ornate std, 25" 2,250.00

Student Lamps, Kerosene

Brass, dbl, elaborate appl cable decor, rpl shades, 29" 1,800.00

Brass, dbl, wht-cased tan shades, late, needs rpr, 19" 275.00
Brass, gr cased ogee shade, polished/electrified, 21½" 425.00
Brass, milk glass shade, mk/1863 on burner, 19½", EX.............325.00
Brass, orig HP chimney & burner, miniature, 13" 700.00
Brass, vertical canister font, orig wht shade, 12" 425.00
German, milk glass shade, pat 1863/1873, 21" 325.00

Whale Oil/Burning Fluid

Acorn font, single ft, twin-tube burner, 8"...........................115.00
Beaded Loop font, 'Jenny Lind,' hex base, female std, 11" 300.00
Blackberry emb on clear globular font, milk glass base, 9" 100.00
Blown onion font, rnd ft, brass color base, 6" 125.00
Blown teardrop font, ornate 3-sided ftd base, Sandwich, 10".......525.00
Brass, acorn font, dbl drop burner, early, 8", NM, pr 750.00
Brass, fluted stem/marble base, Cornelius & Co, 12" 200.00
Brass, lemon font, EX quality, early, 8", pr......................... 1,600.00
Brass, lemon font, 6½", pr 600.00
Canister font att NE Glass, tall tin base, 7", EX 125.00
Conical font on heavy cup plate base, period burner, 7" 375.00
Conical font on sq plain lacy base, Sandwich, 7" 125.00
Cut/frosted globe, prisms, fluted brass/marble base, 20" 400.00
Cut/frosted shade, prisms, sq ped base, 18", pr.....................325.00
Globular font, high std, lacy acanthus base, Sandwich, 7" 400.00
Globular font, tin saucer base & cylinder std w/hdl, 7"..............100.00
Globular font mtd on cup plate base, period burner, 5½"............350.00
Globular font w/cut grapes att NE Glass, tin base w/hdl, 7".......275.00
Lacemaker's, Invt T'print, cranberry, brass base w/hdl, 18".........450.00
Loop, sapphire bl, shaped std on sq base, 10", pr 1,200.00
Overlay, bl floral-cut to clear, fluted brass std, Sandwich 1,800.00
Petticoat, tin, dbls as peg lamp, EX orig pnt, 3-burner, 5"............100.00

Printie pattern in amethyst, 8½", EX, $850.00 for the pair.

Rayo type, brass w/cased yel fluted shade, electrified, 21" 130.00
Sheffield, dbl-magnification lenses, worn SP, 11" 120.00
Shield-shape font, rpl collar, att Sandwich or NE, 6½" 50.00
Shield-shape font on stepped/scalloped pressed base, 7"..............100.00
Sparking, blown, w/hdl, period tin burner 150.00
Sparking, blown, wine-glass form, rnd ft, w/burner 175.00
Sparking, blown/swirl mold, appl crimped hdl, w/burner 800.00
Sparking, b3m, moonstone, period tin burner, waisted 650.00
Sparking, cup-plate base, period burner, NM 200.00
Teardrop font, cut/etched, scalloped/stepped base, 9", VG 175.00

Teardrop font, sq lacy base, 6" **250.00**
Teardrop font att to NE Glass, tin saucer w/hdl, 4" **200.00**
Teardrop font on lacy acanthus base, Sandwich, 7", NM **150.00**
Teardrop font on octagonal lacy acanthus base, Sandwich, 9" **275.00**
Tin, conical hinged burner, saucer base, hdl, 3½", pr **250.00**
Tin, saucer base w/hdl, 4¼" **120.00**
3-Printie, amethyst, shaped std, 6-sided dome base, 8", pr **1,100.00**

Miscellaneous

Float, Bristol cups: florals on pk, brass fr, mini....................**295.00**
Jones Utica Pat May 27, 1863, tole, saucer base **100.00**
Marriage, Ripley & Co Pat 1870, clear, 12¾", EX......................**675.00**
Miner's, wrought/CI, brass chicken finial & trim, 8"+hanger **225.00**
Sanford's Pat Safety Lamp, Feb'y 9, 1869, brass w/tin, 6" **125.00**
Vapo-Cresolene, 6", EX...**25.00**
Vapo-Cresolene, 6", NM in orig box......................................**80.00**

Lang, Anton

Anton Lang was a German potter who came to this country in 1923. His work, marked with his name in script, is scarce and highly valued.

Flowerpot, ochre, ribbed, w/saucer **20.00**
Goat, 5" **40.00**
Pitcher, bl stylized florals, sgn **60.00**
Pitcher, rust & gr banded, hand thrown, pinched sides, sgn...........**55.00**
Rooster, wht, hand modeled, 3x4"......................................**55.00**
Vase, squatty, bowl form, mk Oberammergau **45.00**

Latticinio

A type of art glass produced in this century as well as the last by glasshouses both here and abroad, latticinio glass is characterized by swirled, twisted ribbons of color within the glass itself. It is a technique often seen in paperweights and Venetian glass.

Bowl, bl/wht swirl, St Louis, 4¼", +6¾" tray **210.00**
Paperweight, whale form, mc bands/ribbons, 5½" L **50.00**
Tumbler, pk/wht swirl, appl latticinio ft, pontil, 6" **110.00**
Vase, wht/bl ribbons on clear, faceted finial, ftd, 15" **160.00**
Wine, swirled red/wht ribbons, clear section in base, 4½"............**210.00**

Le Verre Francais

Le Verre Francais was produced during the 1920s by Schneider at Epinay-sur-Seine in France. It was a commercial art glass in the cameo style composed of layered glass with the designs engraved by acid. Favored motifs were stylized leaves and flowers or geometric patterns. It was marked with the name in script or with an inlaid filigrane.

Our advisor for this category is Don Williams; he is listed in the Directory under Iowa.

Cameo

Bowl, stylized floral, gold/bl on gold mottle, ftd, 5x6" **450.00**
Bowl, vines/thistles, red on orange mottle, 8"..............................**800.00**
Bowl, zinnias, lav on flecked hot pk, incurvate, 6" H **800.00**
Ewer, floral, purple/orange on yel, 12" **900.00**
Ewer, ivy, burgundy/wht on orange, 8" **800.00**
Ewer, leaf/berry panels, purple on orange to wht, 14½" **1,800.00**

Lamp, base/12" shade: berries/leaves, red/brn on yel, 21" **4,400.00**
Vase, balloon-like floral, wide shoulder, bun ft, 19" **1,800.00**
Vase, Deco florals, 3-color, 3x9" dia **875.00**
Vase, fern fronds, orange on wht, blk hdls, Charder, 10" **700.00**
Vase, floral, burgundy on gold mottle, flared, 7½" **350.00**
Vase, floral, lav on pk mottled frost, 12½" **1,000.00**
Vase, floral, mottled plum on textured pk, slim/ftd, 11"...............**850.00**
Vase, floral, orange on mottled frost, ftd, 16"...........................**1,300.00**
Vase, foxglove, polished red on wht/pk mottle, ftd, 13" **900.00**
Vase, fruiting vines, orange to bl on yel, goblet form, 12"...........**800.00**
Vase, palm trees, bl on milky wht, bun ft, 16" **2,900.00**
Vase, Queen Anne's lace, wine to pk on wht speckled, 16" **800.00**
Vase, salamanders/dragonflies, bl/orange on yel, 6½" **600.00**
Vase, 3 long-stem florals, red/wine on yel/wht, bun ft, 9" **600.00**

Miscellaneous

Pitcher, red to orange & yel mottle, blk hdl, 12½" **550.00**

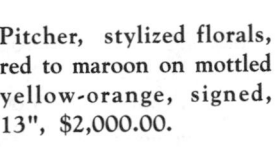

Pitcher, stylized florals, red to maroon on mottled yellow-orange, signed, 13", $2,000.00.

Vase, floral, rust HP on tangerine mottle, Charder, 14" dia.........**900.00**
Vase, Oriental seascape, bl HP on yel, ftd, can neck, 8½" **495.00**

Leeds, Leeds Type

The Leeds Pottery was established in 1758 in Yorkshire and under varied management produced fine creamware, often highly reticulated and transfer printed, shiny black-glazed Jackfield wares, polychromed pearlware, and figurines similar to those made in the Staffordshire area. Little of the early wares were marked; after 1775 the impressed 'Leeds Pottery' mark was used. From 1781 to 1820, the name 'Hartley Greens & Co.' was added. The pottery closed in 1898.

Today the term 'Leeds' has become generic and is used to encompass all polychromed pearlware and creamware – wherever its origin. Thus similar wares of other potters – Wood for instance – is often incorrectly called 'Leeds.' Unless a piece is marked or can be definitely attributed to Leeds by confirming the pattern to be authentic, 'Leeds-

Type' would be a more accurate nomenclature.

Key:
rtcl — reticulated   sp — soft paste

Bowl, creamware, British war ship/Chinese scenes, rpr, 11" **600.00**
Bowl, sp, rim motif in bl & yel, ftd, hairline, 6" **75.00**
Chamber pot, sp, gaudy bl/wht floral, leaf hdl, 3½" **315.00**

Coffeepot, blue transfer decoration, 11½", VG, $650.00.

Creamer, gaudy floral, cobalt trim, 3¼", EX **200.00**
Creamer, sp, bl/gr brushwork, emb leaf hdl, 4", EX **100.00**
Creamer, sp, gaudy bl/gr floral, stains/wear, 4" **115.00**
Cup & saucer, gaudy 4-color floral...**150.00**
Cup & saucer, handleless; florals, emb reeding, NM **125.00**
Cup & saucer, water bug & sunburst, 5-color, NM.......................**325.00**
Mug, sp, gaudy 4-color floral, 4⅝", EX **150.00**
Mug, 5-color floral, boy fishing, stains, 5¾"................................**400.00**
Pitcher, sp, Oriental motif, stains, 5⅞" **225.00**
Pitcher, yel & red flowers, 6-sided, 7½" **500.00**
Pitcher, 5-color gaudy floral, sm rpr at hdl, 9" **500.00**
Plate, gr feather edge, heart-shape rtcl border, 6", NM **110.00**
Plate, Oriental motif, bl feather edge, 9¾", EX **225.00**
Plate, pagoda in center, feather edge, bl on wht, rpr, 10" **275.00**
Sugar bowl, sp, Oriental motif, w/lid, 2⅞"x2¾" **300.00**
Sugar bowl, sp, 5-color floral, 5¼", EX **75.00**
Sugar bowl, 4-color motif, shell hdls, NM **225.00**
Teapot, sp, 2-color floral, hairline, 5"...**125.00**
Teapot, sp, 4-color house, rpl lid, 7¼", EX....................................**350.00**
Teapot, 3-color Oriental motif, stain/rpr, 5¾" **95.00**
Teapot, 5-color floral, rim rpr, 6"..**200.00**

Legras

Legras and Cie was founded in St. Denis, France, in 1864. Production continued until about 1914. In addition to their enameled wares, they made cameo art glass decorated with outdoor scenes and florals executed by acid cuttings through two to six layers of glass. Their work is signed 'Legras' in relief.

Cameo

Vase, berries/leaves, dk gr on pk & gr frost, 19" **1,600.00**

Vase, bridge/stream/bushes, tan/orange, flat sides, 4½" **600.00**
Vase, bud; snow scene, 7" **360.00**
Vase, floral, burgundy on cream, 14" **400.00**
Vase, floral, cobalt/yel, enamel details, 7" **395.00**
Vase, floral, shiny burgundy on textured frost, ovoid, 8" **300.00**
Vase, leaves & berries, bl & gold on dk gr, sgn, 7½" **475.00**
Vase, riverbank, wht/gr on lt gr, bulbous, 3½" **600.00**
Vase, sailing boats/lake, tan on shaded purple, 7" **750.00**
Vase, ships/lake, brn on lt pk & amber, ovoid, 3x4½" **300.00**
Vase, tree/lake, brn tones, sq top, 5½" **450.00**
Vase, trumpet vines, purple on clear frost, 19" **2,000.00**
Vase, woodland, brn/lt & dk gr on gr, oval rim/bun ft, 24" **2,200.00**

Vase, wooded landscape with foreground pool, dark and light greens and brown on shaded green, signed, 24", $1,800.00.

Miscellaneous

Bowl, HP winter scene in orange/wht/brn, 10" L **350.00**
Vase, etched stylized palms/fans on taupe, spherical, 9"..............**600.00**
Vase, etched/HP woods & lake at sunset, tapered, 14" **800.00**
Vase, HP autumn trees, orange/gold sky & lake, slim form, 16" .**500.00**
Vase, HP snow at base, trees extend up tall sq neck, 20", pr ... **1,300.00**
Vase, HP winter scene: trees/houses/lake, 3-crimp rim, 16".........**800.00**

Lenox

Walter Scott Lenox, former art director at Ott and Brewer, and Jonathan Coxon founded The Ceramic Art Company of Trenton, New Jersey, in 1889. By 1906 Cox had left the company and to reflect the change in ownership, the name was changed to Lenox, Inc. Until 1930 when the production of American-made Belleek came to an end, they continued to produce the same type of high-quality ornamental wares that Lenox and Coxon had learned to master while in the employ of Ott and Brewer. Their superior dinnerware made the company famous, and since 1917 Lenox has been chosen the official White House China.

Our advisor for this category is Mary Frank Gaston; she is listed in the Directory under Texas. See also Ceramic Art Company.

Bowl, fruit; Montclair..**18.00**
Bowl, salad; Lace Point...**15.00**

Tea set, gold floral trim on white belleek, green palette mark, pot: 10½", $350.00 for the three pieces.

Bowl, serving; Wyndcrest 75.00
Bowl, vegetable; Lace Point, oval 50.00
Box, cigarette; Lenox Rose, +3 ash trays.................58.00
Coffee set, Bl Wreath, silver overlay, 3-pc.............275.00
Coffeepot, Lace Point 85.00
Coffeepot, Lenox Rose, +teapot, creamer, & sugar bowl, set.......495.00
Creamer & sugar bowl, Colonial, gold trim 85.00
Creamer & sugar bowl, Lace Point.............................55.00
Cup, Repertoire 24.00
Cup, Terrace 15.00
Cup & saucer, Biltmore 40.00
Cup & saucer, Caribee 30.00
Cup & saucer, Country Garden 35.00
Cup & saucer, Fairfield 30.00
Cup & saucer, Flirtation 40.00
Cup & saucer, Lace Point 22.50
Cup & saucer, Lenox Rose 30.00
Cup & saucer, Mystic 35.00
Cup & saucer, Rhodora 40.00
Cup & saucer, Tuxedo 30.00
Cup & saucer, Wyndcrest 35.00
Dish, wht, dbl leaf form w/center hdl, 10½"............75.00
Figurine, First Waltz, ltd ed, 1984 ....125.00
Figurine, flapper's head, 4" 87.00
Figurine, penguin, 3-color, #1827, gr wreath mk 245.00
Figurine, seal on ledge, ivory, 6x4".........................150.00
Figurine, semi-nude lady w/greyhound, ivory, 13" 190.00
Flower holder, Lenox Rose, pierced shell 95.00
Gravy boat, Wyndcrest 95.00
Plate, bread & butter; Lace Point 10.00
Plate, bread & butter; Repertoire 12.50
Plate, bread; Country Garden.....................................20.00
Plate, bread; Lenox Rose 20.00
Plate, dinner; Amethyst...38.00
Plate, dinner; Country Garden 30.00
Plate, dinner; Meadow Song 38.00
Plate, dinner; Mystic 30.00
Plate, dinner; Repertoire 38.00
Plate, dinner; Snow Flower 30.00
Plate, dinner; Tuxedo 30.00
Plate, dinner; Wyndcrest 30.00
Plate, luncheon; Caribee 30.00
Plate, salad; Caribee 20.00
Plate, salad; Country Garden 25.00
Plate, salad; Fairfield 20.00

Plate, salad; Lenox Rose 20.00
Plate, salad; Montclair 12.00
Plate, salad; Mystic 22.00
Plate, salad; Repertoire 18.00
Plate, salad; Wyndcrest 25.00
Platter, Lace Point, oval, 16" 65.00
Platter, Wyndcrest, lg 135.00
Platter, Wyndcrest, sm 125.00
Saucer, Repertoire 12.50
Soup, Mystic 35.00
Toby, Wm Penn, Indian hdl 200.00
Vase, Empire, swan hdls, gr wreath mk, 10½".............65.00

Letter Openers

Brass, Grammes, Allentown PA, w/ruler 10.00
Brass, Napoleon figural, 6¾" 36.00
Celluloid, Capital National Bank, Indianapolis.............. 6.00
Metal, Cyprus Novelty, Brooklyn NY, w/ruler 13.50
Metal, Fuller Brush man figural, EX 10.00
Metal, Prudential life Insurance 14.00
Saber (Army, 1902), etched blade, NP scabbard, 9½"....45.00
SP, figural horse head hdl, Reed & Barton 85.00

Libbey

The New England Glass Company was established in 1818 in Boston, Massachusetts. In 1892 it became known as the Libbey Glass Company. At Chicago's Columbian Expo in 1893, Libbey set up a ten-pot furnace and made glass souvenirs. The display brought them worldwide fame. Between 1878 and 1918, Libbey made exquisite cut and faceted glass, considered today to be the best from the brilliant period. The company is credited for several innovations – the Owens bottle machine that made mass-production possible and the Westlake machine which turned out both electric light bulbs and tumblers automatically. They developed a machine to polish the rims of their tumblers in such a way that chipping was unlikely to occur. Their glassware carried the patented Safedge guarantee.

Libbey also made glassware in numerous colors – cobalt, ruby, pink, green, and amber. In 1935 it was bought by Owens-Illinois and remains a division of that company. See also Amberina and other specific types.

Bowl, amberina, Baby T'print, tri-fold top, 4½" 425.00
Bowl, cut, Anita, scalloped sawtooth edge, 8" 225.00
Bowl, cut, bl to clear, 4 hobstar vesicas, serrated, 6"....130.00
Bowl, cut, Gloria, scalloped/serrated, shallow, 9" 325.00
Bowl, cut, hobstars/fans, 3-fold serrated rim, 9x10"....500.00
Bowl, cut, hobstars/fans & dmn panels, sgn, 8½" 240.00
Bowl, cut, pinwheels/flashed star center, 4-section, 7"....200.00
Bowl, cut, scalloped rim w/flashed stars, lg hobstar, 8"....225.00
Box, floral on opal satin, ribbed, red circle mk, 3x3" dia.....275.00
Candlestick, intaglio florals/ferns, 10", pr...................200.00
Candlestick, Lightware, twist stems, #4093 eng, 10", pr 300.00
Cocktail, frosted kangaroo stem 110.00
Compote, amberina, Invt T'print, #3022, 4¼" 800.00
Compote, cut, flashed fans/nailheads, teardrop stem, 8½" 310.00
Compote, cut, florals/etc, hollow twisted stem, 9x5"....150.00
Compote, purple opal, ribbed, clear stem/base, 7x7"....950.00
Cordial, lily pads, cobalt in clear, ftd, 3" 115.00
Decanter, cut, sapphire to clear, split sqs/fan/prisms, 15"....175.00

Goblet, cat stem, water sz 125.00

**Cocktail glasses with frosted kangaroo stems, ca 1930s, 6",
$125.00 each.**

Maize, bowl, gr husks 175.00
Maize, celery vase, marigold irid w/bl husks.............195.00
Maize, cruet, clear w/lt bl husks, maize stopper, rare...........350.00
Maize, pickle castor, gr husks, SP fr 500.00
Maize, pitcher, clear w/amber irid, bl husks, clear hdl, 9"..........585.00
Maize, pitcher, wht w/gr husks, strap hdl, 8½x5½".....................450.00
Maize, shakers, bl husks, pr.................................350.00
Maize, sugar shaker, gr husks, 5½" 235.00
Maize, syrup, gr husks, scarce, 6" 350.00
Maize, toothpick holder, gold-traced gr husks, scarce 400.00
Maize, tumbler, 4½"...175.00
Nappy, cut, Anita, 6" 80.00
Pitcher, cut, dragonflies/cattails allover, 8½".........125.00
Pitcher, cut, florals in Harvard & cane borders, ftd, 14" 775.00
Pitcher, jade gr loops on clear, Nash design, 8½" 375.00
Pitcher, tankard; cut, bl to clear, hobstars/cane/fans, 9"..........200.00
Pitcher, tankard; cut, New Brilliant, 8" 285.00
Punch bowl, cut, hobstars/lg X-hatch dmns, 1-pc, 15" dia 800.00
Punch bowl, cut, pinwheels/fan/cane, serrated, 2-pc, 10" 825.00
Ring holder, kangaroo stem, opal...........................125.00
Tazza, cut, floral/vine eng, twist stem, eng base, 5½x7"...........325.00
Tray, cut, Gloria, hobstars/X-hatches, serrated, 14" dia 1,600.00
Tray, cut, intaglio floral/wreath border, hobstars/etc, 12" 500.00
Tray, ice cream; cut, hobstars/fern, serrated, 10x16" 400.00
Tumbler, cut, hobstars/fans/X-hatches, star base, 6 for 600.00
Tumbler, jade gr loops on clear, appl ft, Nash design, 5" 125.00
Vase, bud; amberina, bowl atop long slender stem, 11x3"...........800.00
Vase, Corinthian, 1896, sgn, 7" 195.00
Vase, cut, Wild Rose, vesicas/dmns, X-hatch rim band, ftd, 14"..950.00
Vase, jack-in-pulpit; amberina, sgn/#3014, 5x4"..................... 1,100.00
Vase, jack-in-pulpit; amberina, 16" 1,550.00
Wine, kangaroo stem, opal, 6" 100.00

Lightning Rod Balls

Amethyst, sun-colored 7.50

Bl opaque, Hawkeye...25.00
Bl opaque, swirl, Mast..30.00
Bl opaque, 10-sided, DUS......................................30.00
Cobalt, Nat'l...18.00
Dk gr, Thompson...10.00
Milk glass, Hawkeye...12.50
Milk glass, Moon & Stars, M...................................40.00
Milk glass, Nat'l 15.00
Wht swirl 12.00

Limited Edition Plates

Bing and Grondahl

1895, Behind the Frozen Window 3,500.00
1896, New Moon 2,250.00
1897, Christmas Meal of Sparrows.........................800.00
1898, Roses & Star 850.00
1899, Crows Enjoying Christmas 875.00
1900, Church Bells Chiming...............................800.00
1901, 3 Wise Men...425.00
1902, Gothic Church Interior.............................300.00
1903, Expectant Children 300.00
1904, View of Copenhagen from Fredericksberg Hill 120.00
1905, Christmas Night 195.00
1906, Sleighing to Church 100.00
1907, Little Match Girl 145.00
1908, St Petri Church 100.00
1909, Yule Tree 90.00
1910, Old Organist 100.00
1911, Angels & Shepherds.................................100.00
1912, Going to Church 125.00
1913, Bringing Home the Tree.............................110.00
1914, Amalienborg Castle.................................115.00
1915, Dog on Chain Outside Window 120.00
1916, Prayer of the Sparrows 85.00
1917, Christmas Boat.....................................90.00
1918, Fishing Boat 90.00
1919, Outside the Lighted Window 90.00
1920, Hare in the Snow...................................85.00
1921, Pigeons 85.00
1922, Star of Bethlehem..................................80.00
1923, Hermitage 85.00
1924, Lighthouse 85.00
1925, Child's Christmas..................................100.00
1926, Churchgoers 85.00
1927, Skating Couple 115.00
1928, Eskimos 80.00
1929, Fox Outside Farm 100.00
1930, Christmas Train 100.00
1931, Tree in Town Hall Square...........................90.00
1932, Lifeboat at Work...................................85.00
1933, Korsor-Nyborg Ferry 80.00
1934, Church Bell in Tower 80.00
1935, Lillebelt Bridge...................................85.00
1936, Royal Guard 90.00
1937, Arrival of Christmas Guests 115.00
1938, Lighting the Candles 150.00
1939, Old Lock-Eye, The Sandman..........................175.00
1940, Delivering Christmas Letters.......................215.00
1941, Horses Enjoying Meal...............................245.00
1942, Danish Farm on Christmas Night 245.00
1943, Ribe Cathedral.....................................200.00

1944, Sorgenfri Castle	100.00
1945, Old Water Mill	185.00
1946, Commemoration Cross	90.00
1947, Dybbol Mill	165.00
1948, Watchman	100.00
1949, Landsoldaten	75.00
1950, Kronborg Castle at Elsinore	125.00
1951, Jens Bang	120.00
1952, Old Copenhagen Canals & Thorsvaldsen Museum	80.00
1953, Snowman	115.00
1954, Royal Boat	125.00
1955, Kaulundorg Church	125.00
1956, Christmas in Copenhagen	160.00
1957, Christmas Candles	120.00
1958, Santa Claus	100.00
1959, Christmas Eve	110.00
1960, Village Church	120.00
1961, Winter Harmony	80.00
1962, Winter Night	65.00
1963, Christmas Elf	90.00
1964, Fir Tree & Hare	55.00
1965, Bringing Home the Tree	45.00
1966, Home for Christmas	42.50
1967, Sharing the Joy	30.00
1968, Christmas in Church	35.00
1969, Arrival of Guests	22.50
1970, Pheasants in Snow	20.00

M. I. Hummel

1971, Heavenly Angel	525.00
1972, Hear Ye, Hear Ye	65.00
1973, Glober Trotter	120.00
1974, Goose Girl	70.00
1975, Ride into Christmas	75.00
1976, Apple Tree Girl	75.00
1977, Apple Tree Boy	85.00
1978, Happy Pastime	75.00
1979, Singing Lesson	65.00
1980, School Girl	75.00

Royal Copenhagen

1908, Madonna & Child	1,950.00
1909, Danish Landscape	200.00
1910, Magi	165.00
1911, Danish Landscape	165.00
1912, Christmas Tree	175.00
1913, Frederik Church Spire	125.00
1914, Holy Spirit Church	200.00
1915, Danish Landscape	100.00
1916, Shepherd at Christmas	95.00
1917, Our Savior Church	115.00
1918, Sheep & Shepherds	150.00
1919, In the Park	100.00
1920, Mary & Child Jesus	120.00
1921, Aabenraa Marketplace	70.00
1922, 3 Singing Angels	85.00
1923, Danish Landscape	100.00
1924, Sailing Ship	125.00
1925, Christianshavn	90.00
1926, Christianshavn Canal	65.00
1927, Ship's Boy at Tiller	125.00

1928, Vicar's Family	70.00
1929, Grundtvig Church	125.00
1930, Fishing Boats	145.00
1931, Mother & Child	120.00
1932, Frederiksberg Gardens	120.00
1933, Ferry & Great Belt	165.00
1934, Hermitage Castle	100.00
1935, Kronborg Castle	175.00
1936, Roskilde Cathedral	185.00
1937, Main Street of Copenhagen	295.00
1938, Round Church of Osterlars	300.00
1939, Greenland Pack Ice	365.00
1940, Good Shepherd	275.00
1941, Danish Village Church	300.00
1942, Bell Tower	265.00
1943, Flight Into Egypt	525.00
1944, Danish Village Scene	195.00
1945, Peaceful Scene	320.00
1946, Zealand Village Church	200.00
1947, Good Shepherd	250.00
1948, Nodebo Church	175.00
1949, Our Lady's Cathedral	215.00
1950, Boeslunde Church	200.00
1951, Christmas Angel	255.00
1952, Christmas in Forest	80.00
1953, Frederiksberg Castle	100.00
1954, Amalienborg Palace	115.00
1955, Fano Girl	145.00
1956, Rosenborg Castle	110.00
1957, Good Shepherd	65.00
1958, Sunshine Over Greenland	125.00
1959, Christmas Night	60.00
1960, Stag	85.00
1961, Training Ship	100.00
1962, Little Mermaid	195.00
1963, Hojsager Mill	60.00
1964, Fetching the Tree	50.00
1965, Little Skaters	30.00
1966, Blackbird	24.00
1967, Royal Oak	22.50
1968, Last Umiak	18.00
1969, Old Farmyard	20.00
1970, Christmas Rose & Cat	38.00

Limoges

From the mid-18th century, Limoges was the center of the porcelain industry of France, where at one time more than forty companies utilized the local kaolin to make a superior quality china, much of which was exported to the United States. Various marks were used; some included the name of the American export company (rather than the manufacturer) and 'Limoges.' After 1891 'France' was added. Pieces signed by factory artists are more valuable than those decorated outside the factory by amateurs. For a more thorough study of the subject, we recommend you refer to *The Collector's Encyclopedia of Limoges Porcelain* by our advisor Mary Frank Gaston, who is listed in the Directory under Texas. Her book has beautiful color illustrations and current market values.

Bowl, int scene: Pierrot, hat in hands, at door, 16" dia	175.00
Box, roses, pk on cream w/gold, mk, 3¼x6"	60.00
Cake plate, cupid center, emb gold border, 15", +12 plates	700.00

Cake plate, roses, pk on plum & aqua, artist sgn 75.00
Candlestick, violets & leaves w/gold, factory decor, 5¾" 100.00
Celery tray, strawberries w/much gold 48.00
Charger, floral, sgn L Thomas, gilt edge, 13" 275.00
Chocolate pot, floral, burgundy top & hdl, ribbed, 9½" 175.00
Chocolate pot, panels of poppies alternate w/leaves, 10 ....250.00
Chocolate pot, roses front & bk, ribbed, H&Co/L, 9" 175.00
Coffeepot, roses, mc on gr to wht w/gold, mk, 10x6" 150.00
Cup & saucer, peaches, yel on ivory w/gold, T&V 30.00
Dish, floral, gold on cobalt, branch hdl, 3-section, 12" 165.00
Jardiniere, floral branch, wht on lt gr, gold rim, 10x13" 265.00
Jardiniere, yel rose/purple flower, floral Baroque ft, 5x9" 275.00
Pitcher, tankard; grapes, sgn Ariez, gold dragon hdl, 15" 450.00
Pitcher, tankard; grapes on shaded gr, mk, 12" 185.00
Pitcher, tankard; poppies, ribbed, gold S-hdl, T&V, 11".............375.00
Plaque, Arab on horse, artist sgn, gold Rococo rim, mk, 12½" 245.00
Plaque, farm scene, pastels, rectangular, T&V, 6x14" 100.00
Plaque, game birds, gold Rococo border, Coronet, 11½".............145.00
Plaque, grapes & watermelon, artist sgn, gold scallops, 11"............75.00
Plaque, lady's portrait, sgn LaPie, Coronet, 10¼" 125.00
Plaque, recumbent nymph/swirling drapery, sgn Muller, 14x6"....600.00
Plate, Boars in Snow, sgn Pradet, Coronet, 10" 135.00
Plate, brunette in profile after Mucha, R Ribble, 13" 400.00

**Plate, cardinals and raspberries, gold trim, JPL mark, 14",
$285.00.**

Plate, collie portrait, burgundy border, gold tracery, 7½" 55.00
Plate, ducks/fronds, sgn Max, gold Rococo rim, Coronet, 10".....95.00
Plate, flowers, yel/tan w/gr leaves, sgn Stafford, 9" 35.00
Plate, game bird, scalloped, B&M, 10" 85.00
Plate, game birds, sgn Dubois, Rococo rim, 12½" 225.00
Plate, girl w/lg hat, high collar, sgn Dussou, B&C, 15" 650.00
Plate, holly & berries, T&V, 9½" 40.00
Plate, hunter & dog, 13½", pr 650.00
Plate, pheasants & quail, gold Rococo rim, 10½", pr 350.00
Plate, roses, mc on shaded pk w/gold, mk, 18" 100.00
Platter, gr foliage, w/drain, 14" L 100.00
Punch bowl, grapes, mc on bl, Kimmel, 1907, mk, 8x14½" 375.00
Punch bowl, grapes/gold band, sgn Seger, 9x14", +6 tumblers. 1,150.00
Punch bowl, strawberries/gold, sgn LeRoy, scroll ft, 9" 800.00
Tray, Indian tents by stream/mtns, 16½" 275.00
Vase, named ladies as goddesses on pk, sgn Muller, 22" 300.00

Vase, tree bark on gr irid, twisted, 11" 275.00

Lithophanes

Lithophanes are porcelain panels with relief designs of varying degrees of thickness and density. Transmitted light brings out the pattern in graduated shadings – lighter where the porcelain is thin and shaded in the heavy areas. They were cast from wax models prepared by artists and depict views of life from the 1800s, religious themes, or scenes of historical significance. First made in Berlin about 1803, they were used as lamp shade panels, window plaques, or candle shields. Later, steins, mugs, and cups were made with lithophanes in their bases. Japanese wares were sometimes made with dragons or geisha lithophanes. See also Dragon Ware; Steins.

Candle lamp, 6 scenes, German, sm 285.00
Lamp, 3 sailing scenes on 11" shade, Doric column base, 21".. **1,865.00**
Mug, allover color w/wht pnt decor, HP monk reserve, 6½" 95.00
Panel, Christ holds orb w/cross, Inri/Die incised, 6½x8" 185.00
Panel, fishing boats/bldgs, 6½x5" 200.00
Panel, man talks to lady on bridge, brass mt, French, 4x4½"..........95.00
Shade, 4 hunt scenes, lg 285.00
Shade, 6 scenic trapezoid panels, sgn/#d, 6¼x12" 675.00
Stein, dancing couple lithophane, deer transfer, ½-L 100.00
Table screen, mother/child int scene, KPM, #184142, 20"...........500.00

Liverpool

In the late 1700s, Liverpool potters produced a creamy ivory ware, sometimes called Queen's Ware, which they decorated by means of the newly-perfected transfer print. Made specifically for the American market, patriotic inscriptions, political portraits, or other States themes were applied in black with colors sometimes added by hand. (Obviously their loyalty to the crown did not inhibit the progress of business!) Before it lost favor in about 1825, other English potters made a similar product; today Liverpool is a generic term used to refer to all ware of this type.

Our advisor for this category is Richard Marden; he is listed in the Directory under New Hampshire.

Jug, Am ship/Charity, rpr, 5¾" 150.00
Jug, Britannia in...Glory/Penelope, mc, 1-qt, NM 700.00
Jug, child w/grapes & verse, bk: harvesting, 5½", VG 150.00
Jug, Com Prebles Squadron/1804, bk: man, spout: eagle, 10".. **4,100.00**
Jug, Farmer's Arms/bk: rural scene, 7½", VG 300.00
Jug, Fayette, Nation's Guest/WA Co's Father, 4¾", EX 750.00
Jug, Geo WA, bk: ship, names of states, mc, rpr, 11" **3,000.00**
Jug, map of Eastern seabrd w/Liberty & WA, rstr, 11"............. **1,300.00**
Jug, Masonic poem, bk: symbols, spout: Holiness..., 10", EX........400.00
Jug, Masonic/Independence/WA/etc, 8", EX 850.00
Jug, Peace-Plenty..., bk: WA w/15 states, 10", NM **2,000.00**
Jug, Peace-Plenty.../WA in Glory, 9", EX 850.00
Jug, poem/names of states, bk: WA/Franklin, mc, 10", EX....... **3,900.00**
Jug, Ship Wrights Arms, bk: Ship Caroline, mc, 10½"................600.00
Jug, Success to Trade/Lord Nelson, rpr, 7" 350.00
Jug, Susan's Farewell/verse, bk: ship, 9½", NM **1,300.00**
Jug, WA/Liberty/Justice/Victory, bk: Masonic, rpr, 12" **1,600.00**
Jug, WA/slain British lion/troops/banner, 8", VG.......................650.00
Mug, Admiral Lord Nelson, pt, 4¾", NM 475.00
Mug, Geo Washington/Long Live..., 5⅞", EX **2,200.00**
Plate, Am ship, scalloped, 10", EX 210.00
Plate, ship w/British Jack, wear/chips, 10" 50.00

Mug, eagle with banner in its beak, linked-ring border with names of first 16 states, 4½", EX, $1,900.00.

Lladro

Lladro porcelains are currently being produced in Labernes Blanques, Spain. Their retired and limited edition figurines are popular collectibles.

Our advisor for this category is William Brinkley; he is listed in the Directory under Illinois.

Ballerina, #5054	145.00
Boy Graduate, #5918, tassel rpr	125.00
Bullfighter, #5116	150.00
Country Lass w/Dog	345.00
Courtship	350.00
Debutante	150.00
Donkey	115.00
Dressmaker	225.00
Flower Curtsy	295.00
Forgotten	145.00
Geisha, #4807	235.00
Girl Graduate, #5199	175.00
Girl w/Doll	300.00
Girl w/Parasol & Geese	155.00
Happy Birthday	110.00
Harlequin w/Guitar	375.00
Hindu Children	265.00
Lady of Taste	695.00
Lady w/Dog	175.00
Lover's Serenade	425.00
Lovers in the Park	950.00
Man w/Wine Bottle, #5165	150.00
Nuns, matt finish, #2075	165.00
Over the Threshold	165.00
Pensive Clown, w/base	285.00
Pilar	200.00
Plaque, Holy Family, wht, 1974, 5½x7"	225.00
Roaring '20s	185.00
Sad Sax	155.00
Sign, Collector's Society Dealer, wht bsk	65.00
Soccer Player, #4809	125.00
Spring Bouquet	450.00
Sunday in the Park	445.00
Sweet Scent	90.00
Viennese Lady	185.00

Winter Frost	275.00
Zapato Enanito, #79	195.00

Lobmeyer

J. and L. Lobmeyer, contemporaries of Moser, worked in Vienna, Austria, during the last quadrant of the 1800s. Most of the work attributed to them is decorated with distinctive enameling; favored motifs are people in 18th-century garb.

Bowl, mc floral w/curlique decor, 6"	245.00
Goblet, 18th-century lady, sgn	200.00
Punch cup, HP pk coral, 4-leaf clover shape, hdl, sgn	185.00
Salt, open; 18th-century man, 2¼"	145.00
Tumbler, maid w/parasol w/in mc florals, 12-panel, sgn	350.00

Tumbler, enameled floral sprigs and 18th-century man, 3", $250.00.

Locke Art

Joseph Locke already had proven himself many times over as a master glass maker, working in leading English glasshouses for more than seventeen years. He came to America and he joined the New England Glass Company. There he invented processes for the manufacture of several types of art glass – amberina, peachblow, pomona, and agata among them. In 1898 he established the Locke Art Glassware Co. in Mt. Oliver, Pittsburgh, Pennsylvania. Locke Art Glass was produced using an acid etching process by which the most delicate designs were produced on crystal blanks. Most examples are signed simply 'Locke Art,' often placed unobtrusively near a leaf or a stem. Other items are signed 'Jo Locke,' some are dated, and some are unsigned. Most of the work was done by hand. The business continued into the 1920s. See the Locke Art Glass listing in the Directory under Pennsylvania.

Champagne, Rose, coat-of-arms & May 1916, 6¾"	55.00
Cordial, Poppy, sgn, 3¼"	85.00
Cordial, Vintage, 2¼"	45.00
Sherbet, Aster, 4½"	125.00
Sherbet, Poinsettia, saucer base, sgn, EX	40.00
Sherbet, Poppy, w/saucer base, 3½"	160.00
Sherbet, Vintage, saucer base, sgn	175.00

Sherbet, Vintage, sgn, 4½" 75.00
Stein, Vintage, 5¼" 130.00
Tumbler, Vintage, sgn 70.00
Vase, Poppy, 6x3" 175.00
Vase, Sweet Pea, lt pk on clear, ribbed, flared, att, 5"....80.00
Vase, Violet, 4" 65.00

Locks

The earliest type of lock in recorded history was the wooden cross bar used by ancient Egyptians and their contemporaries. The early Romans are credited with making the first key-operated mechanical lock. The ward lock was invented during the Middle Ages by the Etruscans of Northern Italy; the lever tumbler and combination locks followed at various stages of history with varying degrees of effectiveness. In the 18th century, the first precision lock was constructed. It was a device that utilized a lever-tumbler mechanism. Two of the best-known of the early 19th century American lock manufacturers are Yale and Sargent, and today's collectors value Winchester and Keen Kutter locks very highly. Factors to consider are rarity, condition, and construction. Brass and bronze locks are generally priced higher than those of steel or iron.

Our advisor for this section is Joe Tanner; he is listed in the Directory under Montana.

Key:
bbl — barrel   st — stamped

Brass Lever Tumbler

Ames Sword Co, Perfection stamped on shackle, 2¾" 50.00
Bingham's Best Brand, BBB emb on front, 3¼" 150.00
Cleveland 4 Way, Cleveland 4 Way emb on front, 3⅝" 90.00
Crusader, shield, swords emb on body, 2¾" 40.00
Eagle Lock Co, word Eagle emb on front, scrolled, 3" 60.00
Jackson's, stamped Jackson's on front, 2½" 25.00
Keen Kutter, shape of KK emblem, KK emb on front, 4¾" 115.00
Mercury, Mercury emb on body, 2¾" 25.00
Motor, Motor emb on body, 3¼" 35.00
Our Very Best, OVB emb on body, 2⅞" 150.00
Romer & Co, Romer & Co stamped on dust cover, 3" 50.00
Ruby, Ruby emb in scroll on front, 2¾" 25.00
Safe, Safe emb in scroll on front, 2⅜" 20.00
Siberian, Siberian emb on shackle, 2½" 80.00
Sphinx, sphinx & pharaoh head emb on front, 2¾" 35.00
W Bohannan & Co, SW emb in scroll on front, 2⅜" 30.00
Winchester, Winchester emb on front, 3" 135.00

Combinations

Chicago Combination Lock Co, stamped on front, brass, 2¾".......80.00
Corbin Sesamee 4-Dial Brass Lock, stamped Sesamee, 2¾" 12.00
Edwards Mfg Co No-Key, stamped on lock, brass, 2¾" 60.00
Junkunc Bros Mfrs, all stamped on bk, brass, 1⅞".......................25.00
Karco stamped on body, 2½" 50.00
Number or letter disk type (4 disks), brass, 2¾".......................120.00
Sq lock case of steel, stamped Pat Germany, 4-wheel, 3¼" 110.00
Sutton Lock Co stamped on body, 3"...200.00
Your Own stamped on body, 3⅞" 325.00

Eight-Lever Type

Armory, brass, Armory 8-Lever stamped on front...........................20.00
Electric, steel, Electric stamped on front......................................20.00

Goliath, steel, Goliath 8-Lever stamped on front....................20.00
Miller, steel, Miller 8-Lever stamped on front 15.00
Samson, brass, 8-Lever stamped on front................................18.00

Iron Lever Tumbler

Bull, word Bull emb on front, 2⅝"...20.00
Bulldog, word Bulldog & face of dog emb on front, 2¾" 15.00
Dan Patch, Dan Patch emb on front, horseshoe on bk, 2¾" 130.00
Dragon, word Dragon & dragon emb on front, 2⅞" 25.00
Eagle, word Eagle emb on body, 4⅜" 40.00
Indian Head, Indian head emb on front, 3" 80.00
Jupiter, word Jupiter/star & moon emb on front, 3¼" 18.00
Karo, word Karo emb on front, CI, 3⅛" 25.00
King Korn, words King Korn emb on body, 2⅞" 20.00
Nineteen O Three, 1903 emb on front, iron, 3⅞" 90.00
Red Chief, words Red Chief emb on body, 3¾" 60.00
Rugby, football emb on body, 3" 20.00
Unique, word Unique emb on front, 3¼" 80.00
Yale & Towne, lion face emb on front, shackle mk Y&T, 3"........100.00

Lever Push Key

Champion, emb Champion 6-Lever, brass push-key type, 2¼" 25.00
Climax, emb Climax 6-Lever, iron push-key type, 2¼" 35.00
Columbia, emb Columbia 6-Lever, brass push-key type, 2¼" 35.00
Dash, emb Dash 6-Lever, iron push-key type, 2¼" 25.00
Excelsior, emb Excelsior 6-Lever, brass push-key type, 2¼" 25.00
Harvard, emb Harvard 4-Lever, brass push-key type, 2" 60.00
IXL, emb IXL on body, 2¼" 50.00
Keystone, emb Keystone 6-Lever, brass push-key type, 2¼" 40.00
McIntosh, emb McIntosh on body, 2¼" 90.00
SB Co, emb SB Co on body, 3¼" 40.00
Smith & Egge Mfg Co, Smith & Egge stamped on front, 3" 75.00
Ten Star, emb Ten Star 6-Lever, 2¼" 45.00

Logo-Special Made

Brass pancake push key emb US Internal Revenue, 2¼"..............175.00
Heart-shape brass lever type emb Shults Co, bbl key, 2¾" 45.00
Heart-shape brass lever type st Board Education, bbl key, 3½".......50.00
Sq brass pin-tumbler case st Regd US Mail, int counter, 2¾" 120.00
Sq Yale-type brass pin tumbler, em w/Texaco & star, 3" 25.00
Sq Yale-type brass pin tumbler, st Shell Oil Co on body, 3⅛" 15.00
Sq Yale-type brass pin tumbler, st US/A/tree/Forest Svc, 2⅞"......125.00

Pin-Tumbler Type

Corbin, brass, Corbin in oval stamped on body, 3⅝" 30.00
Eagle, brass, Eagle stamped on body, 2⅞" 20.00
Fulton, emb Fulton on body, 2⅝" 30.00
Hope, brass, emb Hope on body, 2½" 18.00
Il-A-Noy, emb Il-A-Noy on body, 2½" 40.00
Pearl, brass, emb Pearl on body, 2⅛" 16.00
Sargent, brass, emb Sargent on body, 3" 15.00
Segal, iron, emb Segal on shackle, 3¾" 40.00
Shapleigh, emb Shapleigh on body, 2⅝" 35.00
Yale, brass, emb Yale on body, Made in England on shackle, 3" 50.00
Yale, brass, emb Yale on body, Yale & Towne on shackle, 2⅝".......25.00

Scandinavian (Jail House) Type

JHW Climax Co, iron, 2⅞" 50.00
Star, emb line on bottom, iron, 3¾"..80.00

Star, iron, 2½"	**70.00**
99 Miller, emb 99, brass, 1¾"	**80.00**
999 Miller, emb 999, brass, 2½"	**70.00**

Six-Lever Type

Eagle, brass, Eagle Six Lever stamped on body	**15.00**
Edwards, iron, Edwards stamped on body	**15.00**
Safe, brass, Safe stamped on body	**18.00**
Yale, brass, Yale emb on front	**12.00**

Story and Commemorative

AYPEX Seattle (Alaska Yukon Pacific Expo), emb tin/iron, 3"	**125.00**
Canteen, US emb on lock, lock: canteen shape, 2"	**400.00**
CI, emb ornate scroll motif throughout body of lock, 3½"	**170.00**
CI, emb skull/X-bones w/florals, NH Co on bk, 3¼"	**275.00**
CQD/sinking ship Titanic & SOS waves emb on brass, 2¾"	**120.00**
Eagle/stars/shield & stars, emb CI, Eagle Liberty, 2½"	**250.00**
Mail Pouch, emb on lock, lock in shape of a mail pouch, 3⅛"	**200.00**
1901 Pan Am Expo, brass, emb w/buffalo, 2⅝"	**125.00**

Warded Type

Army, iron pancake ward key, emb letters, 2½"	**30.00**
Globe, iron sq lock case, emb US on bk, 2⅜"	**20.00**
Hex, iron, sq lock case, emb US on bk, 2⅛"	**95.00**
Navy, iron pancake ward key, bk: scrolled emb letters, 2½"	**25.00**
Red Cross, brass sq case, emb letters, 2"	**10.00**
Rex, steel case, emb letters, 2⅝"	**18.00**
Safe, brass sq case, emb letters, 1⅞"	**8.00**
Safety First, brass pancake type, emb letters, 2¾"	**15.00**
Secure, iron pancake type, emb letters, 2⅝"	**20.00**
Sprocket, brass oval shape, emb letters, 2⅛"	**55.00**
Try Me, iron pancake type, emb letters, 2½"	**25.00**
Winchester, brass sq case, stamped letters, 2¾"	**95.00**

Wrought Iron Lever Type (Smokehouse Type)

DM&Co, bbl key, 4¼"	**15.00**
MW&Co, bbl key, 2⅝"	**10.00**
MW&Co, flat key, 3½"	**20.00**
S&Co, bbl key, 3"	**8.00**

Loetz

The Loetz Glassworks was established in Klostermule, Austria, in 1840. After Loetz's death the firm was purchased by his grandson, Johann Loetz Witwe. Until WWII the operation continued to produce fine artware, some of which made in the early 1900s bears a striking resemblance to Tiffany's, with whom Loetz was associated at one time. In addition to the iridescent Tiffany-style glass, he also produced threaded glass and some cameo.

Our advisor for this category is Don Williams; he is listed in the Directory under Iowa.

Key:
att — attributed   o/l — overlay

Basket, gr irid, combed effect, appl prunts, clear hdl, 15"	**400.00**
Bowl, gr irid, ruffled, ornate metal stand, att, 7x7½"	**80.00**
Ewer, heavy metallic lustre exposing cobalt, metal mts, 11"	**425.00**
Inkwell, purple/gr irid, frost/shiny swags, Nouveau lid, 4"	**475.00**

Loving cup, cameo-cut clover, gold on textured amber, 3¾"	**300.00**
Pitcher, bl/irid splotches, pewter rim, dimpled, att, 10"	**800.00**
Spittoon, lady's, gr w/bl irid spots, 3½x6½"	**600.00**
Vase, amber/gold butterfly-wing irid, pinch-sided bulb, 9"	**1,300.00**
Vase, amber/gold butterfly-wing irid, tri-fold rim, 4¾"	**1,100.00**
Vase, amethyst w/bl irid spots, pinch-sided, metal rim, 9"	**275.00**
Vase, bl irid, pinched sides, ruffled, 13¾"	**350.00**
Vase, bl oil-spot irid, Nouveau florals, dbl gourd, 5x3"	**355.00**
Vase, bl-gold irid, lg appl leaf at base, floriform, 14"	**1,600.00**
Vase, bl-gr, pinched/twisted, att, 9½"	**100.00**
Vase, bl-gr w/purple irid, swirled, bulbous, 8½x6"	**685.00**
Vase, bronze Nouveau side mts, orange mottle on wht, 6½"	**450.00**
Vase, bronze/pk irid w/bl to purple feathers & dashes, 7"	**3,500.00**
Vase, cameo lilies, gr on yel, 13½"	**1,400.00**
Vase, coils/threads on amber irid, fan-pleated/conical, 13"	**600.00**

Vase, cream waves and gold on caramel transparent with silver floral overlay, $1,500.00; Vase, green waves and lozenges with gold iridescence on lime, silver floral overlay, 7", $2,850.00.

Vase, dk bl irid w/silver spots, swollen cylinder, att, 10"	**350.00**
Vase, floral silver rim-to-base hdls, pulled motif/irid, 6"	**600.00**
Vase, gold, flower form w/appl leaves & vines on stem, 13"	**2,000.00**
Vase, gold on clear textured, 3 appl snail prunts, 3½"	**225.00**
Vase, gold w/oil spots, tri-lobe rim, att, 11"	**375.00**
Vase, gr crackle w/raised brn streaks, orange at base, 9x4"	**135.00**
Vase, gr irid w/emb 'scales,' pinched bottle form, att, 8"	**85.00**
Vase, gr irid w/lt bl trailings, tapered cylinder, 3½"	**165.00**
Vase, gr irid w/silvery-purple trailings, att, 2¾x3¼"	**135.00**
Vase, gr irid/emb silver-bl swags, wide shoulder, att, 5"	**110.00**
Vase, gr to bl mottle irid, bulbous w/can neck, att, 9"	**300.00**
Vase, gr w/bl irid molded branches, 5"	**175.00**
Vase, gr w/gr & bl mottle irid, blown-out/swirled top, 8"	**675.00**
Vase, gr/purple/gold irid swirls, quatrelobed/pinched, 7"	**2,400.00**
Vase, iris silver o/l on irid, trefoil rim, att, 5¾"	**900.00**
Vase, jack-in-pulpit; amber irid, thick threading, 13"	**475.00**
Vase, lav/gold irid swirls, 5½"	**155.00**
Vase, olive-gr irid, 2-hdl basket shape, att, 10"	**75.00**
Vase, orange cased to clear w/internal bl & gr swirls, 10"	**3,100.00**
Vase, pk-spotted irid, metallic waves, pinched rim, att, 4"	**350.00**
Vase, pulled 'flames,' bl on amber/gold/opal, sq rim, 4"	**3,100.00**
Vase, purple irid, scalloped, 4x5½"	**140.00**
Vase, purple irid w/bl oil spots, ftd, flared rim, att, 6"	**800.00**
Vase, red crackle, att, 9¼"	**850.00**

Vase, silver o/l floral on purple irid, lobed rim, att, 11" **3,000.00**
Vase, silver o/l foliage on salmon w/irid waves, att, 9½" **2,400.00**
Vase, textured gr/irid striped effect, conical, att, 14½"................**250.00**
Vase, yel w/amber to purple oil spots, ftd cone, att, 10" **700.00**
Vase, yel w/pk & wht swags at rim, 4-lobe rim, att, 10" **1,300.00**

Lomonosov Porcelain

Founded in 1744, the Lomonosov porcelain factory produced exquisite porcelain miniatures for the Czar and other Russian nobility. One of the first factories of its kind, Lomonosov pieces consisted largely of vases and delicate sculptures. In the 1800s Lomonosov became closely involved with the Russian Academy of Fine Arts, a connection which has continued to this day, as the company continues to supply the world with these fine artistic treasures.

Figurine, Afghan hound, #3436, lg **38.00**
Figurine, bear, recumbent, #6570 ....**20.00**
Figurine, bullfinch, #9555, miniature **8.00**
Figurine, bullock, #6490 ....**23.50**
Figurine, ermine, standing, #6432 ....**24.00**
Figurine, Great Dane, #6467 ....**28.50**
Figurine, hedgehog, #2158 ....**12.50**
Figurine, Kazarka, #2157...**24.50**
Figurine, Nosey Bear, #2351 ....**21.00**
Figurine, otter, #6538...**31.00**
Figurine, penguin, #6581 ....**21.00**
Figurine, pointer dog, #6536..**40.00**
Figurine, puppy, #6549...**26.00**
Figurine, raccoon, standing, #6502...**11.50**
Figurine, spaniel, #6500...**20.50**
Figurine, Spitz dog, #9528, miniature **17.50**
Figurine, squirrel, #7404, miniature... **3.25**
Figurine, wild cat, #6563 ....**38.00**
Figurine, Yakut woman, #6194 ....**59.00**
Figurine, young elk, #6111..**65.00**

Longwy

The Longwy workshops were founded in 1798 and continue today to produce pottery in the north of France near the Luxembourg-Belgian border. The ware for which they are best known was produced during the Art Deco period, decorated in bold colors and designs. Earlier wares made during the first quarter of the 19th century reflected the popularity of Oriental art, cloisonne enamels in particular. The designs were executed by impressing the pattern into the moist clay and filling in the depressions with enamels. Examples are marked 'Longwy,' either impressed or painted under glaze.

Candelabrum, floral, mc on bl std, 3-arm, 10¾" **110.00**
Candlestick, mc florals on bl, brass std, prisms, 9¾", pr...............**185.00**
Charger, fawn in abstract landscape, Primavera, 1925, 14" **1,400.00**
Charger, stag in fanciful forest w/trees & mtns, 15".......................**600.00**
Charger, 3 dragons circle butterfly, mc on crazed aqua, 17" **600.00**
Charger, 3 nudes (2 Blk/1 wht)/exotic landscape, 1925, 15" ... **2,000.00**
Tile, bird on floral branch on bl, 6x6" in pewter fr **125.00**
Vase, Matisse nudes/exotic flora, att Catteau, bulbous, 12".....**4,000.00**

Lonhuda

William Long was a druggist by trade who combined his knowledge of chemistry with his artistic ability in an attempt to produce a type of brown-glazed slip-decorated artware similar to that made by the Rookwood Pottery. He achieved his goal in 1889 after years of long and dedicated study. Three years later he founded his firm, the Lonhuda Pottery Company. The name was coined from the first few letters of the last name of each of his partners, W.H. Hunter and Alfred Day. Laura Fry, formerly of the Rookwood company, joined the firm in 1892, bringing with her a license for Long to use her patented airbrush-blending process. Other artists of note, Sarah McLaughlin, Helen Harper, and Jessie Spaulding, joined the firm and decorated the ware with nature studies, animals, and portraits, often signing their work with their initials. Three types of marks were used on the Steubenville Lonhuda ware. The first was a linear composite of the letters 'LPCO' with the name 'Lonhuda' impressed above it. The second, adopted in 1893, was a die-stamp representing the solid profile of an Indian, used on ware patterned after pottery made by the American Indians. This mark was later replaced with an impressed outline of the Indian head with 'Lonhuda' arching above it. Although the ware was successful, the business floundered due to poor management. In 1895 Long became a partner of Sam Weller and moved to Zanesville where the manufacture of the Lonhuda line continued. Less than a year later, Long left the Weller company. He was associated with J.B. Owens until 1899, at which time he moved to Denver, Colorado, where he established the Denver China and Pottery Company in 1901. His efforts to produce Lonhuda utilizing local clay were highly successful. Examples of the Denver Lonhuda are sometimes marked with the LF (Lonhuda Faience) cipher contained within a canted diamond form.

Bowl, floral, brn, 3½" **145.00**
Bowl, floral, 3-ftd, sgn Jessie Spaulding, mk/1899, 7".................**250.00**
Ewer, branches/berries, sgn AH, #315, 3½" **165.00**
Jug, bull portrait, EX art, #806, 5"...**500.00**
Vase, floral, artist sgn, #248, 3x4½"...**150.00**
Vase, grapes, gray-bl w/gr & rust vine on brn bsk, 9½" **250.00**
Vase, lg fish/waves, integral hdls, 5x8½" **525.00**

Pillow vase, herd of steers, shield mark, 12", $4,000.00.

Lotton

Charles Lotton is a contemporary glass artist, living and working in Lansing, Illinois. Examples of his glass are much in demand and are on display in many major museums and other collections of distinction, among them the Smithsonian, The Art Institute of Chicago, The Corning Museum of Glass, and the Chrysler Museum.

For further information concerning this subject, we recommend the recently released *Lotton Art Glass*, co-authored by Charles Lotton and Tom O'Conner; see the Directory under Illinois.

Bottle, scent; floral, any sz 450.00
Bottle, scent; gold ruby, any sz.......................................600.00
Bowl, leaf & vine, cased, 10-12", ea, up to 800.00
Bowl, leaf & vine, cased, 6"...350.00
Paperweight, floral...135.00
Paperweight, floral, cased, David Lotton, lg 200.00
Paperweight, King Tut 70.00
Paperweight, web design, David Lotton 75.00
Persian water sprinkler (swan-neck vase), old or new 500.00
Vase, dbl multi-flora, cased, 6-7", ea 2,800.00
Vase, dbl multi-flora, cased, 8-12", ea, up to 3,600.00
Vase, floral, cased, 6-7", ea 800.00
Vase, floral, cased, 8-12", ea, up to 2,000.00
Vase, floral, 6-7", ea...450.00
Vase, floral, 8-12", ea, up to 700.00
Vase, leaf & vine, 4" 200.00
Vase, leaf & vine, 8" 250.00

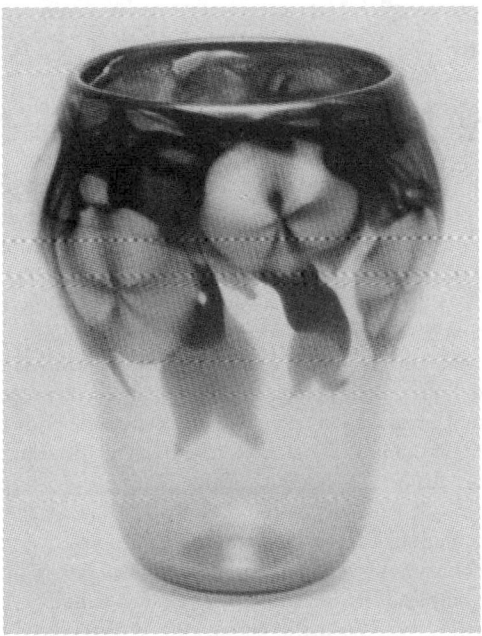

Vase, paperweight technique with white morning-glories, green and brown stems and leaves, amber-gold interior, signed/dated 1974, 7", $425.00.

Vase, web design, 4" 200.00
Vase, web design, 8" 250.00

Lotus Ware

Isaac Knowles and Issac Harvey operated a pottery in East Liverpool, Ohio, in 1853 where they produced both yellowware and Rockingham. In 1870 Knowles bought Harvey's interests and took as partners John Taylor and Homer Knowles. Their principal product was ironstone china, but Knowles was confident that American potters

could produce as fine a ware as the Europeans. To prove his point, he hired Joshua Poole, an artist from the Belleek Works in Ireland. Poole quickly perfected a Belleek-type china, but fire destroyed this portion of the company. Before it could function again, their hotel china business had grown to the point that it required their full attention in order to meet market demands. By 1891 they were able to try again. They developed a bone china, as fine and thin as before, which they called Lotus. Henry Schmidt from the Meissen factory in Germany decorated the ware, often with lacy filigree applications or hand-formed leaves and flowers to which he added further decoration with liquid slip applied by means of a squeeze bag. Due to high production costs resulting from so much of the fragile ware being damaged in firing and because of changes in tastes and styles of decoration, the Lotus Ware line was dropped in 1896. Some of the early ware was marked 'KT&K China'; later marks have a star and a crescent with 'Lotus Ware' added. For further study, we recommend *American Belleek* by our advisor, Mary Frank Gaston. She is listed in the Directory under Texas.

Bowl, gold fish net & prunus on cream, pk liner, 4x4¾" 375.00
Bowl, mc netting w/molded & HP flowers & insects, 5", EX.......170.00
Bowl, mums on wht, rtcl bosses ea end, sgn MIW-1894, 5" L 500.00

Bowl, shell form, pink with hand-painted floral, 5½", $95.00.

Bowl, wht, appl lotus bud in bowl, 3 ft: buds/twigs, 2x6" 3,100.00
Bowl, wht, appl porc pcs for texture, twig hdls, 11" L, EX....... 2,250.00
Bowl, wht, molded wht prunus flowers, beaded top, 4½" 300.00
Chocolate pot, ivory, relief daisies, 8"..250.00
Chocolate pot, yel orchids/gr & gold leaves, 8½" 650.00
Cookie jar, wild roses...600.00
Creamer, wht w/wht fish net, squatty, 3½" 250.00
Dresser jar, rtcl/jeweled lid & body, sgn MH '95, 5x4" 600.00
Ewer, dk gr, appl wht leaves/lotus, 6"... 1,500.00
Ewer, pk florals, gold-speckled twig hdl, 6½" 350.00
Ewer, rtcl, 9½" 700.00
Ewer, rtcl jeweled body decor, gold beading/hdl, 10"....................800.00
Ewer, wht, beaded spout/neck, 9" 185.00
Ewer, wht, plain w/ribbed neck, 9½" 100.00
Pitcher, textured leaf body design, w/bamboo hdl, squat............150.00
Pitcher, wht w/wht fish net, 4"...250.00
Pitcher, wild roses, dk gr spout, gold bamboo hdl, squat..............170.00
Relish tray, textured leaf body, twig ft, 6½"....................................60.00
Sachet container, disk body w/rtcl sides, 3½" 250.00

Sauce, textured leaf body, twig ft, 5¼" L 30.00
Teapot, tan, gold decor, oblong, 3½", +cr/sug 400.00
Urn, lady/cherub ea side, gr/gold rim decor, dbl hdls, 19" 1,500.00
Vase, dk gr, appl wht flowers, scroll hdls, 8" 2,800.00
Vase, gold hobs, 8 pastel rtcl panels at base, ball ft, 8" 1,100.00
Vase, lotus lily form, pk/bl leaves & vine base, 9" 700.00
Vase, lotus lily form, wht, openwork leaf ft, 9" 600.00
Vase, lt gr, appl wht flowers, hdld gourd form, 8", EX 800.00
Vase, rtcl/gilt arched panels, violets, 3 gold ball ft, 8" 1,350.00
Vase, wht, irreg flower petal top, wide rtcl leaf base, 9" 225.00
Vase, 2 mask faces/wild roses in pk on cream, gold hdls, 8" 450.00

Lu Ray Pastels

Lu Ray Pastels dinnerware was introduced in the early 1940s by Taylor, Smith, and Taylor of East Liverpool, Ohio. It was offered in assorted colors – Persian Cream, Sharon Pink, Surf Green, Windsor Blue, and Gray – in complete place settings as well as many service pieces. It was a successful line in its day and is once again finding favor with collectors of American dinnerware.

Bowl, berry; sm 6.00
Bowl, cream soup 17.50
Bowl, fruit; 5½" 4.50
Bowl, mixing; lg 45.00

Relish bowl with handle, 4-section, 10", $46.50.

Bowl, salad; lg 30.00
Bowl, soup; 9" 8.50
Bowl, tab hdl, 6" 10.00
Bowl, vegetable; oval 10.00
Bowl, vegetable; 9" 8.50
Butter dish, w/lid, ¼-lb 22.50
Casserole, w/lid 55.00
Coffeepot, demitasse; ovoid, w/lid 50.00
Coffeepot, demitasse; str sides, w/lid 85.00
Creamer 5.00
Creamer, demitasse; ovoid 20.00
Creamer, demitasse; str sides 40.00
Cup & saucer 7.50
Cup & saucer, demitasse 12.50
Egg cup 12.00
Egg cup, Chatham Gray, rare color 15.00
Epergne 50.00
Muffin cover, w/8" underplate 50.00
Pitcher, bulbous w/flat bottom 35.00
Pitcher, ftd 40.00
Pitcher, juice; ovoid 55.00

Pitcher, syrup 40.00
Plate, cake 15.00
Plate, Chatham Gray, rare color, 7" 6.00
Plate, chop; 14" 16.00
Plate, grill 11.00
Plate, serving; tab hdl 15.00
Plate, very rare, 8" 15.00
Plate, 10" 10.00
Plate, 6" 2.00
Plate, 7" 3.00
Plate, 9" 5.00
Platter, #1040, 9½" 6.00
Platter, oval, 11½" 8.00
Platter, oval, 12" 9.00
Platter, oval, 13" 10.00
Sauce boat, fast-stand 15.00
Sauce pitcher 15.00
Saucer, cream soup 12.50
Shakers, pr 8.50
Sugar bowl, w/lid 9.00
Sugar bowl, w/lid, demitasse; ovoid 20.00
Sugar bowl, w/lid, demitasse; str sides 40.00
Teapot, w/lid, curved spout 35.00
Teapot, w/lid, flat-top spout 45.00
Tidbit, 2-tier 18.00
Tray, pickle 12.00
Tumbler, juice 18.00
Tumbler, water 30.00

Lunch Boxes

Early 20th-century tobacco companies such as Union Leader, Tiger, and Dixie sold their products in square, steel containers with flat metal carrying handles. These were specifically engineered to be used as lunch boxes when they became empty. (See Advertising, specific companies.) By 1930 oval lunch pails with colorful lithographed decorations on tin were being manufactured to appeal directly to children. These were made by Ohio Art, Decoware, and a few other companies. In 1950 Aladdin Industries produced the first 'real' character lunch box – a Hopalong Cassidy decal-decorated steel container now considered the beginning of the kids' lunch box industry. The other big lunch box manufacturer, American Thermos (later King Seely Thermos Company) brought out its 'blockbuster' Roy Rogers box in 1953, the first fully-lithographed steel lunch box and matching bottle.

Other companies – ADCO Liberty; Landers, Frary & Clark; Ardee Industries; Okay Industries; Universal; Tindco; Cheinco – also produced character pails. With the publication of the book *Official Price Guide to Lunch Box Collectables* by Scott Bruce in 1988, the hobby has skyrocketed. Today's collectors often tend to specialize in those boxes dealing with a particular subject. Western, space, TV series, Disney movies, and cartoon characters are the most popular. There are well over five hundred different lunch boxes available to the astute collector.

Our advisor for this category is Alan Smith; he is listed in the Directory under Texas.

Adam-12, w/thermos, 1973, EX 75.00
Astronaut, dome top, 1960, EX 175.00
Barbie, vinyl, w/thermos, 1962, EX 150.00
Batman, w/thermos, 1966, EX 150.00
Battle Kit, 1965, VG 60.00
Beatles, bl tin, 1966, VG 375.00
Bonanza, brn rim, w/thermos, 1965, M 400.00

Captain Kangaroo, red vinyl, w/thermos, 1964, EX 600.00
Casper, vinyl, w/thermos, 1966, EX 600.00
Cowboy in Africa, w/thermos, 1968, EX 200.00
Dark Crystal, w/thermos, 1982, M 40.00
Dick Tracy, w/thermos, 1967, EX 275.00
Disney School Bus, dome top, 1961-1973, EX...........................25.00
Disneyland, monorail, 1960, VG 100.00
Dudley Do-Right, 1962, EX 600.00
Fireball XL-5, 1964, VG..100.00
Firehouse, dome top, w/thermos, 1959, EX...............................400.00
Flintstones, w/thermos, 1964, EX..250.00
Green Hornet, 1967, EX 120.00
Guns of Will Sonnett, w/thermos, 1968, EX 175.00
Gunsmoke, w/thermos, 1962, EX...275.00
Hogan's Heroes, dome top, 1966, VG..100.00
Hopalong Cassidy, 1950, EX 200.00
Howdy Doody, 1954, EX 600.00
Jetsons, dome top, 1963, EX 1,000.00
Kewtie Pie, vinyl, w/thermos, 1964, M 500.00
Land of the Lost, w/thermos, EX 45.00
Lawman, 1961, EX 125.00
Lost in Space, dome top, 1967, EX 400.00
Man From UNCLE, w/thermos, 1966, EX 200.00
Mickey Mouse, oval, 1935, VG 1,200.00
Mork & Mindy, 1980, EX 30.00
Munsters, 1965, EX 200.00
Peanuts, red, Charlie Brown pitching, 1976, VG 45.00
Popeye, 1964, VG..100.00
Rifleman, 1961, VG 90.00
Roy Rogers, 1st, 1953, VG 65.00
Soupy Sales, vinyl, 1965, EX..600.00
Star Trek, dome top, 1968, EX 400.00
Tom Corbett, full litho, w/thermos, 1954, EX 400.00
Wild Wild West, 1969, VG 75.00
Woody Woodpecker, 1972, EX 100.00
Yellow Submarine, 1969, EX...400.00

Lutz

From 1869 to 1888, Nicholas Lutz worked for the Boston and Sandwich Glass Company where he produced the threaded and striped art glass that was popular during that era. His works were not marked; and, since many other glassmakers of the day made similar wares, the term Lutz has come to refer not only to his original works but to any of this type.

Clear with pink threading: Tumbler, $75.00; Covered jar, $150.00; Pitcher, $150.00.

Bowl, clear w/wht threads, yel/gold stripes, rolled rim, 5" 75.00
Decanter, ruby, eng floral, bulbous w/bottle neck 500.00
Ewer, pk/wht/gold lattice, gold-flecked clear hdl, 12" 140.00
Tazza, cranberry/clear threads, ribbon candy ft/bowl, 3x6"...........150.00
Tumbler, lemonade; etched/clear, pk-threaded bottom half.........100.00
Whiskey, appl cranberry threading/etched lilies, att, 3⅜" 80.00
Wine, bl/wht opaque/clear swirl att 120.00

Maastricht

Maastricht, Holland, was the site of the De Sphinx Pottery, founded in 1836 by Petrus Regout. They made earthenware decorated with transfer prints as well as dinnerware with gaudy hand-painted designs. Potteries are still working in this area today.

Bowl, Oriental scene, 8" 35.00
Bowl, stick spatter, gaudy floral, 8", EX 25.00
Pitcher, milk; Canton, mc Oriental motif.....................................45.00
Plate, Abbey, 8" 20.00
Plate, Abe Lincoln, Petrus Regout, 9" 30.00
Plate, gaudy floral, Petrus Regout, heavy, 11" 20.00
Plate, parakeets, bl transfer, Petrus Regout, 8" 30.00
Plate, stick spatter, gaudy floral, 11", NM 42.50
Plate, stick spatter, gaudy floral, 7½"...20.00

Maddux of California

One of the California-made ceramics now so popular with collectors, Maddux was founded in the late 1930s and during the years that followed produced novelty items, TV lamps, figurines, planters, and tableware accessories.

Bull, red, head up/head down, #972/#973, 11", L, pr....................30.00

Figurine, cockatiel, 11", $25.00.

Chinese pheasant, air-brushed colors, #913/#912, 11", pr 25.00
Ducklings, 3 on grassy base..15.00

Planter, flamingo, pk, #515, 10½" 25.00
Planter, swan, blk, #510, 11" 18.00
Rooster, #932, tall 25.00
Stag, standing, natural colors, #914, 12½" 15.00
TV lamp, bassett hound, #896 ....35.00
TV lamp, prairie schooner (covered wagon), 11" 30.00
TV lamp, stallion, prancing, on base, 12" 35.00
TV lamp, swan, wht, #828P, 12" 35.00
Vase, swan, wht, #221, 12" 20.00

Magazines

Magazines are collected for their cover prints and for the information pertaining to defunct companies and their products that can be gleaned from the old advertisements. In the listings that follow, items are assumed to be in very good condition unless noted otherwise. See also Fisher, Harrison; Movie Memorabilia; and Parrish, Maxfield.

Key:

M –– mint condition, in original wrapper

EX — excellent condition, spine intact, edges of pages clean and straight

VG — very good condition, the average as-found condition

Atlantic, 100th Anniversary issue, Hemingway/Thurber/Frost 5.00
Boys Life, 1927, Lindbergh cover, VG 15.00
Collier's, 1904, June 25, EX.....................................12.50
Collier's, 1905, Oct 21, Gibson girl cover, VG 15.00
Delineator, 1909, June, color fashion plates, VG................20.00
Delineator, 1913, Jan, 2 pgs doll cutouts, VG 28.00
Good Housekeeping, Jan 1969, Caroline Kennedy cover, NM 5.00
Good Housekeeping, Nov 1969, Sophia Loren cover, M 7.00
Harper's, 1924, Feb, Koerner illus, EX......................... 8.00
Harper's, 1956, June, Faulkner article 10.00
Harper's Weekly, 1868, Aug 8, Maryland flood, 16-pg, VG 12.50
Harper's Weekly, 1872, Aug 17, Winslow Homer cover, EX 48.00
Harper's Weekly, 1872, Nov 2, Boston fire cover, VG.............12.50
Harper's Weekly, 1887, Mar 19, Funeral Rites of HW Beecher, G . 8.50
Harper's Weekly, 1889, May 25, City of Worcester, VG.............12.50
Harper's Weekly, 1890, Jan to June, bound, EX 125.00
Life, 1937, Jan 25, England's Royal Lion cover, M 30.00
Life, 1937, Nov, Greta Garbo cover, EX........................22.00
Life, 1938, Feb 14, Queen of Egypt cover, EX..................12.50
Life, 1938, July, Shirley Temple cover, EX 20.00
Life, 1938, Oct, Carole Lombard cover, EX 22.00
Life, 1939, July 3, Swim Suits in Pacific cover, EX 12.50
Life, 1940, Sept, Dionne Quints cover, EX 22.00
Life, 1961, July 14, Hemingway cover......................... 4.00
Life, 1963, Nov 22, Elizabeth Ashley cover, M 175.00
Look, 1965, Nov 30, Princess Margaret cover, M 5.00
Look, 1966, June 14, John Kennedy cover, EX 5.00
Look, 1971, Oct 19, Inside the White House cover, NM 6.00
Madd, 1955, EX 15.00
National Geographic, 1887-1889, ea 30.00
National Geographic, 1900-1905, ea 18.00
National Geographic, 1906-1908, ea 15.00
National Geographic, 1909-1910, ea 12.00
National Geographic, 1911-1915, ea 6.00
National Geographic, 1916-1920, ea 4.00
Paris Review, #1-#18, VG & EX, in wraps 125.00
People, 1973, Aug 20, pre-publication issue, M...............25.00
Playboy, 1965, Jan 1, holiday anniversary issue, EX......... 7.50
Playboy, 1968, July, Sex in Foreign Films article, NM 8.00

Playboy, 1976, Nov, Jimmy Carter interview, EX............... 5.00
Rolling Stone, 1974, June 20, James Dean, NM 2.00
Saturday Evening Post, 1922, Mar 11, Caddy's Diary story, VG.....12.00
Time, 1939, June 19, Lindbergh cover, EX.....................35.00
Time, 1964, July 17, Falkner cover, EX 6.00
Time, 1972, Empire Strikes Back cover, NM 10.00
Woman's Day, 1961, Aug, American Glass......................10.00
Woman's Home Companion, 1901, Mar, Harrison Fisher cover....15.00

Majolica

Majolica is a type of heavy earthenware, design-molded and decorated in vivid colors with either a lead or tin type of glaze. It reached its height of popularity in the Victorian era; examples from this period are found in only the lead glazes. Nearly every potter of note, both here and abroad, produced large majolica jardinieres, umbrella stands, pitchers with animal themes, leaf shapes, vegetable forms, and nearly any other nature theme that came to mind. Few, however, marked their ware. Among those who did were Minton, Wedgwood, and George Jones in England; Griffin, Smith and Hill (Etruscan) in Phoenixville, Pennsylvania; and Chesapeake Pottery (Avalon and Clifton) in Baltimore.

Asparagus server, asparagus center, Minton, 10¼x8¾" 600.00
Asparagus server, asparagus on ocean waves, 11"...........................350.00
Basket, Bamboo & Basketweave, Banks & Thorley 225.00
Basket, floral, gr on bl, pk int, brn hdl, 6-sided, 6" L.................250.00
Basket, Shell & Seaweed, rope hdl, 8½" L.............................275.00
Bowl, artichoke figural, bird finial, unmk, 7¼"........................180.00
Bowl, chestnut leaf on folded napkin int, G Jones, 2¾x9".............225.00
Bowl, Lettuce Leaf, Wannapee, 6½"..................................125.00
Bowl, Picket Fence w/florals, turq/brn/wht mottled int, 9" 200.00
Bowl, Pond Lily, leaf ftd, Holdcroft, 11" 175.00
Bowl, sauce; Daisy, mc w/gr, pk int, Etruscan, 8¼" L..................225.00
Bowl, Shell & Seaweed, Etruscan, 5"................................250.00
Bowl, sunflowers, yel on turq, lav int, Wardle, 10½"..................165.00
Bowl, vegetable; Bird & Fan, Wardle, 10" 165.00
Bowl, vining leaves border, twig ftd, Holdcroft, 10½" 260.00
Box, sardine; basket of fish figural, open hdls, 8½" L 345.00
Box, sardine; Conch Shell & Basketweave, shell finial, 8½" 275.00
Box, sardine; leafy garlands on cobalt, fish finial, 9½"...............350.00
Box, sardine; Pond Lily & Bamboo, VPC mk, 9" L.....................320.00
Box, sardine; seascape relief on sides, duck finial, 5¾".............350.00
Box, sardine; seaweed on cobalt, fish finial, 7½" 300.00
Box, sardine; swan finial, cobalt ground, dolphin ft, 6" 350.00
Butter dish, floral on cobalt, unmk, 7½"............................250.00
Butter dish, Shell, Seaweed & Waves, mc on turq, 7"................225.00
Butter dish, sunflower w/fly figural, gr & brn, unmk, 6¾" 225.00
Butter dish, Wild Rose w/rope trim on bl-gray, 6½" 175.00
Butter dish, yel & gr mottle, cow finial, Etruscan, 7¾" 600.00
Butter pat, floral on cobalt, unmk, 3" 35.00
Butter pat, horseshoe form w/turq center, Wedgwood, 3".............45.00
Butter pat, morning-glory on napkin, unmk Germany, 3" 25.00
Butter pat, Pansy, 5-color, Etruscan, 3" 45.00
Butter pat, 3 gr leaves, unmk, 3" 32.00
Cake stand, maple leaves, Etruscan..................................165.00
Cake stand, Shell & Seaweed, low, 2¼x8½" 295.00
Cake stand, snail shell amid fishnet, Fielding, 5¼x9½" 195.00
Cheese keeper, Dogwood/Woven Fence, G Jones, 10x12" 1,275.00
Cheese keeper, holly, gr on brn, 10½x10½"...........................650.00
Coffeepot, Hummingbird, bamboo hdl & finial, Fielding, 9" 295.00
Compote, Daisy, mc on wht, Etruscan, 5x9" 250.00
Compote, Pineapple, turq int, 4¾x9".................................200.00

Compote, shell form, ftd, turq w/lav int, att Morley, 6x9" 175.00
Compote, shell w/dolphin supports, Worcester, 7x9" 350.00
Creamer & sugar bowl, floral on branch on turq, twig hdls 150.00
Cup & saucer, Fan, bl on wht, Fielding, 7" saucer 130.00
Cup & saucer, Fern & Bamboo, Wardle 125.00
Cup & saucer, Pineapple, lav int, 5½" 135.00
Cup & saucer, Water Lily, 6½" saucer..125.00
Cuspidor, Fan, bl on brn, 6½" 210.00
Cuspidor, floral, waisted, sq w/canted corners, 5½" 150.00
Cuspidor, Sunflower, Etruscan, 6" 500.00
Jardiniere, Pond Lily, lav int, ftd, 8"..275.00
Match holder, elephant w/howdah figural, att England, 8" 235.00
Match holder, monkey in loincloth before holder, 7¾" 195.00
Mug, Acorn, Etruscan, 3½" 150.00
Mug, Fern on Bamboo, 2 figural frogs inside, 4½" 200.00
Mug, lilies, wht on turq, Holdcroft, 3½" 125.00
Mug, shaving; Pansy, divided lav int, att Fielding, 3½" 195.00
Mug, trailing ivy on cobalt, lav int, unmk, 4"............................150.00
Mustache cup, Sunflower & Classical Urn, S Lear, 6½" 200.00

**Parrot, marked Minton, 14",
$650.00.**

Pitcher, Albino Shell, Etruscan, 5¾" 130.00
Pitcher, Bird & Fan on wht, bamboo hdl, Wardle, 7¼" 180.00
Pitcher, Bird & Iris on turq, ftd, bamboo hdl, unmk, 4" 70.00
Pitcher, Blackberry, turq ground, lav int, yel rim, 8" 210.00
Pitcher, Blackberry & Picket Fence, mc on brn, unmk, 7" 85.00
Pitcher, Blackberry on wht, twig hdl, unmk, 7½" 100.00
Pitcher, butterfly & floral, mc on turq, unmk, 3½" 50.00
Pitcher, cobalt w/wicker hdl & lower half, att G Jones, 6"...........175.00
Pitcher, Corn, tan w/gold trim, 6¾" 75.00
Pitcher, Dogwood on turq, yel rim, lav int, G Jones, 5½" 130.00
Pitcher, ear of corn figural, pewter lid, England, 9½" 200.00
Pitcher, Egyptian Lotus, cobalt trim, Copeland, 6½" 450.00
Pitcher, elephant running in relief on yel, unmk, 7½" 165.00
Pitcher, English cottage figural, twig hdl, unmk, 7" 235.00
Pitcher, Fan & Scroll w/Insect, att Fielding, 5½" 130.00
Pitcher, Fern, wht ground, lav int, Etruscan, 8¼"........................275.00
Pitcher, Fern & Bamboo, Wardle, 7½" 150.00
Pitcher, Fern on Bark, pewter top, unmk, 7" 140.00
Pitcher, fish jumps from water, cobalt ground, JRL mk, 7" 195.00
Pitcher, floral, mc on brn wavy ground, gray emb hdl, 8"..............90.00

Pitcher, floral, winged dragon figural hdl, unmk, 8¼" 180.00
Pitcher, floral on bark ground, leaf spout, unmk, 7" 115.00
Pitcher, fruit in relief, mc on wht, Clifton, 6½"...........................130.00
Pitcher, Iris & Lily on cobalt, G Jones, 6¾" 500.00
Pitcher, mc floral medallion/florals in relief, English, 12" 195.00
Pitcher, Owl & Fan, mc on wht, triangular, bamboo hdl, 7½" 175.00
Pitcher, owl figural, wht ironstone, Morley, 8¼" 295.00
Pitcher, parrot figural, France, 11" 115.00
Pitcher, peas in pod over basketweave, pewter lid, unmk, 5½" 150.00
Pitcher, pig waiter figural, Frie Onnang, 10¾" 225.00
Pitcher, pineapple figural, leaves form spout, unmk, 8" 155.00
Pitcher, reindeer & leaves in relief on yel, unmk, 7½" 125.00
Pitcher, rooster figural, bright colors, France, 12".......................110.00
Pitcher, Seashell & Ocean Waves, sq form, unmk, 4" 75.00
Pitcher, Shell & Fishnet, coral figural hdl, Fielding, 7"................295.00
Pitcher, spaniel figural, unmk, 4½" 80.00
Pitcher, standing lady in shawl/hair forms hdl, Minton, 12" 450.00
Pitcher, Stork in Marsh on wht, eel hdl, unmk, 9½" 275.00
Pitcher, Sunflower, cobalt ground, Etruscan, 6½".......................275.00
Pitcher, Sunflower & Classical Urn, S Lear, 3½"..........................75.00
Pitcher, swan figural top, neck forms hdl, Bevington, 8½"...........350.00
Pitcher, water lily & dragonfly in relief, 7½" 150.00
Pitcher, 2-pelican figural, neck hdl, 9".......................................250.00
Plate, basketweave border, mottled center, Wedgwood, 9" 110.00

Basketweave and Floral plate, 10", $165.00.

Plate, bird in flight on turq, att Holdcroft, 8½" 135.00
Plate, Blackberry on turq basketweave, unmk, 10½"....................110.00
Plate, cake; Shell & Coral, open hdls, 11"..................................150.00
Plate, Cauliflower, Etruscan, 9"...125.00
Plate, Fan w/florals on wht, Fielding, 8¾" 95.00
Plate, fish & flower on brn w/bl border, Holdcroft, 8½" 90.00
Plate, floral on cobalt rim, mottled center, 8" 90.00
Plate, Lettuce Leaf, Wannapee, 8½" 90.00
Plate, Maple Leaf, wht ground, Etruscan, 8" 110.00
Plate, mottled center, rtcl border, Wedgwood, 8¾" 120.00
Plate, oyster; Shell & Seaweed, 6 bl shells, G Jones, 8¾" 195.00
Plate, oyster; 5 gr dolphins & 5 wht shells, Wedgwood, 9¼" 195.00
Plate, oyster; 6 sm/1 lg fish, cobalt center, unmk, 10" 150.00
Plate, Pond lily, wht flower amid lg gr leaves, unmk, 9" 90.00
Plate, portrait, floral swags on 8-sided rim, Wedgwood, 9"...........150.00
Plate, Shell & Seaweed, albino, Etruscan, 8"................................75.00

Plate, Strawberry on bl basketweave, Etruscan, 9" **125.00**
Plate, 3 pineapples in swirled leaf border, unmk, 9" **150.00**
Platter, Bamboo & Bow, cobalt center, oval, unmk, 13" **175.00**
Platter, Banana Leaves & Bows, gr on wht, unmk, 14½" **160.00**
Platter, Begonia Leaf on Bark, sq bark hdls, unmk, 12¼" **120.00**
Platter, cake; Shell, 8 scallops, Etruscan, 13½" **400.00**
Platter, Fan & Dragonfly w/cobalt, half-open fan form, 10½" **175.00**
Platter, ferns on wht, turq basketweave rim, unmk, 11¼" **150.00**
Platter, fish & coral w/waves on cobalt, Wedgwood copy, 13" **175.00**
Platter, floral, mc on wht, diamond shape, unmk, 12" **125.00**
Platter, Flying Crane & Water Lily on cobalt, unmk, 10½" **150.00**
Platter, geraniums, Etruscan **250.00**
Platter, Picket Fence w/florals, cobalt center, 14" **175.00**
Platter, Sunflower on wht, stem figural hdls, Wardle, 12½" **150.00**
Platter, Wild Rose on wht w/bl rim, eyelet hdls, unmk **85.00**
Spooner, Shell, albino, unmk Etruscan, 3½" **100.00**
Sugar bowl, Bird & Fan on cobalt, 4½" **150.00**
Sugar bowl, Cauliflower, Etruscan, w/lid...................................**175.00**
Sugar bowl, parrot on branch, 6-sided, unmk, 5½" **150.00**
Sugar bowl, Shell & Seaweed, fish finial & hdls, unmk, 5" **250.00**
Syrup, Blackberry on Basketweave, unmk, 6" **150.00**
Syrup, Sunflower, cobalt ground, Etruscan, pewter top, 8" **250.00**
Teapot, chick on nest figural, twig hdl, 6" **200.00**
Teapot, Flying Crane on wht, brn bamboo hdl, 6¾" **185.00**
Teapot, pyramid form, brn/yel/gr w/hieroglyphics, +cr/sug **250.00**
Teapot, Shell & Seaweed on wht, Wedgwood, 7" **340.00**
Teapot, Strawberry & Bow on turq, berry finial, 6" **200.00**
Teapot, Water Lily, brn rope hdl, 4" **150.00**
Tray, Begonia Leaf figural, Etruscan, 9" **200.00**
Tray, bread; Bamboo & Fern, cobalt center, Wardle, 13" **195.00**
Tray, fruit; acorns & oak leaves, Etruscan, 12" **300.00**
Vase, ferns up sides, cobalt at top, att G Jones, 9½" **400.00**
Vase, Pineapple & Hand figural, cuff at wrist, 7¼" **300.00**

Malachite

Malachite is a type of art glass that exhibits strata-like layerings in shades of green – similar to the mineral in its natural form.

Box, berries & bows, 1920s, 3½" dia **195.00**
Buddha, seated on lotus base, hand on leg, 7½x6"..........................**90.00**
Toothpick holder, diamond-point relief, flared/bulbous..................**25.00**
Vase, emb standing nudes & trees, 5" **220.00**
Vase, nudes/grapes relief, faceted base, flared rim, 9½" **295.00**

Mantel Lustres

Brass figural maid lies on marble base, prisms, 13", pr **350.00**
Bristol, pk overlay, heavy gold/florals, prisms, 16", pr..................**450.00**
Cranberry w/cut wht overlay, florals, 9-prism, 12½", pr **575.00**
Crystal, diamond/fan cutting, cut prisms, 13¾", pr **300.00**
Overlay, amber cut to clear, 10 ball/arrow prisms, 10", pr **300.00**
Overlay, wht cut to gr, petal cutting, gilt prisms, 22", pr **400.00**
Overlay, wht cut to pk, HP florals, prisms, 14½", pr **400.00**
Ruby glass, plain w/knop stem, prisms, 10½", pr, EX **240.00**
Spiral-cut cup/bobeche/base, beaded drops, 1820, 10", pr **750.00**

Mantua

A glasshouse was established in Mantua Township, Ohio, in 1821 for the purpose of manufacturing bottle-glass. Two years later, the proprietor David Ladd, left Mantua, re-establishing and enlarging his

glasshouse in Kent, Ohio. Besides bottle-glass, flint glass items such as bowls, pitchers, decanters, etc. were also blown in green, aquamarine, amber, and amethyst shades – some with decorative devices that were seldom attempted outside the area. Though plain ware was common, several patterns were used as well – 16-rib, 32-rib, broken rib, swirled, corrugated, and 15-diamond.

Bottle, club, aqua, 16-rib broken swirl, faint imp, 8" **130.00**
Bottle, club, gr-aqua, 16-rib, EX imp, kick-up, 8" **200.00**
Bottle, gr-aqua, 16-rib, cylindrical w/high neck, 9½" **250.00**
Bottle, nursing; aqua, 16 vertical ribs, ground lip, 7" **45.00**
Bottle, 16 vertical ribs, flanged lip, pontil, 3¼" **250.00**
Flask, chestnut; aqua, 16 vertical ribs, sheared mouth, 6" **110.00**
Pitkin, gr, 36 vertical ribs, tooled/sheared rim, 7" **325.00**
Pitkin, gr, 36-rib broken swirl to left, 6¾" **550.00**

Pitkin, yellow-green, Type-1, 16-rib swirled to right, attributed, 6", $650.00.

Maps and Atlases

Maps are highly collectible, not only for historical value but also for their sometimes elaborate artwork, legendary information, or data that has been proven erroneous. There are many types of maps including geographical, military, celestial, road, and railroad. The most valuable are those made before the mid-1800s.

Key:
hc — hand colored   p — publisher

Atlases

Asher & Adams...of US, hc, 60 maps, 1874, lg folio, EX.............**650.00**
Atlas of World War Edition, Geographical Pub, 1945, EX.............**12.00**
Collier's World Atlas & Gazetteer, hardbound, 1938, lg.................**20.00**
Collier's World Atlas & Gazetteer, 1944, EX..................................**10.00**
Colton's General, color, dbl-folio sheets, 212 maps, 1876 ....**550.00**
Complete Atlas, hc, Collins, London/Glascow, 120 maps **150.00**
Cummings' School, ancient/modern geography, 1822, VG............**85.00**
Gram's Universal, 1897, worn cover & binding **20.00**
Greece, maps/plans/views, 31 plates, Mills, Dublin, 1795, EX **85.00**

Johnson's New ...Family...of World, Johnson, 1868, lg folio.........**450.00**
Johnson's New Illustrated Family, hc, ornate borders, EX **485.00**
M Lavoisne, Phila, hc, M Carey & Son, 1820, lg folio, EX **1,350.00**
Mitchell's Ancient, color, E Butler, 1844, sm folio, VG **25.00**
Mitchell's New General, eng grape-cluster borders, 1872, VG **550.00**
Mobile, Alabama, from surveys/records, Hopkins, 1878, EX........**140.00**
New & Improved School, hc, Olney, Robinson, CT, 1837, VG **75.00**
New & Improved School, hc, Robinson & Prat, 1830, VG.........**125.00**
Tunison's Peerless Universal...World, hc, IL, 1887, VG **75.00**
Wisconsin, hc, HF Walling, 72 sm & lg folio maps, 1876............**265.00**
World, Premier Edition, Rand McNally, 1947, EX.........................**12.00**

Atlas, Ortelius, Abraham; Theatrum Orbis Terrarus, Antwerp, 1584, comprising 112 maps, brown leather binding, $10,000.00.

Maps

Alaska Territory, hc, fancy border, Colton, 1880, VG **30.00**
America, w/history & statistics, Matthew, 1820, 16x20" **115.00**
Baltick, copperplate, H Moll, London, 1709, 21x24", VG.............**80.00**
Boston street plans, 1860s, folio sheet.......................................**25.00**
Brittany, eng, hc, margins, Sanson, Paris, 1693, 21x32", VG.........**90.00**
Carricta Meridionalis, hc, Blaeu, Amsterdam, 1654, 15x21" **50.00**
Connecticut, hc, counties/etc, Asher/Adams, 1870s, 19x24" **60.00**
District of ME w/New Brunswick & Nova Scotia, Morse, 1796 ....**55.00**
Guinea, eng, hc, cartouch, Jansson, Amsterdam, 1645, 15x21".....**50.00**
IN, hc, colony west of Wabash, shows Indian lands, 1833 ....**75.00**
IN, hc, Indian territory/settlements, Finley, 1831, 9x11" **75.00**
Japan Empire & part of Korea, deVaugondy/Paris/1757, 19x22" .**115.00**
MA & RI, Boston inset, Cowperthwait, Phila, 1850, 16x12½" **40.00**
Maine, hc, counties, Mitchell, 1846, 16x12½", EX **35.00**
Mexico, hc, statistics/history, Carey & Lea, 1822, 16x20" **275.00**
Mexico, kingdoms as of 1521, hc, Conder, 1780, 12x15" **80.00**
Mexico or New Spain, hc, General Atlas, Carey, 15x17", VG ...**275.00**
Mexique, shows west coast of US, Duval/Paris/1670, 4x5", EX ...**110.00**
MI, color, unknown coastline, half settled, Bradford, 1838..........**100.00**
N America, hc, Texas apart, Bradford, Boston, 1838, 15x12" **40.00**
N America, unexplored west, Finley, Phila, 1824, 10x12" **45.00**
N America, western territories, Cowperthwait, 1850, 16x12½"......**45.00**
N&S Carolina/GA, copper eng, Conder/London/1788, 14x14"..**200.00**
New & Exact...France, eng, hc, H Moll, London, 1700, EX..........**85.00**
New York City, hc street plan, Cowperthwait, 1850, 16x12½" **50.00**
Norddeautscher Lloyd Bremen World, rolls, 1903, 30x41"..........**750.00**
OR, Upper CA, & NM; color, Mitchell, 1849, 12x15", EX **165.00**

Progress of Irrigation...US..., Blaisdell, 1891, 26x20", EX **25.00**
Prussia, hc, Finley, Phila, 1824, 10x12".......................................**25.00**
Russiae Magnae, hc, Homann, Nuremburg, 1700, 23x20", VG...**110.00**
S California, some of Nevada, hc, Asher/Adams, 1870s, 19x24" ...**20.00**
Scotland, hc, margins, cartouch, Morden, 1695, 18x14", EX **110.00**
Tabula Asiae II, Ptolemy, Venice, 1574, 6x10", VG **50.00**
Turkish Empire in Europe, Asia, Africa, H Moll, London, 1700....**60.00**
US, color, Mitchell, 1860, 13x21", EX **110.00**
US, color, vast territories, Colton, 1852, 16x26", EX **135.00**
US, hc, TX/Mexico, Carey French version, 1828, 17x21", VG ...**275.00**
US, Mitchell, colored borders, hc, Phila, 1846, 16x12½" **40.00**
Utriusque Castiliae, hc, Blaeu, Amsterdam, 1654, 16x20", VG.....**80.00**
Washington DC city plan, linen, Russell/London/1800, 15x21" .**475.00**
West Indies...Coasts, hc, cartouch, Bowen, 1750, VG **100.00**
WI, color, one-third settled, Mitchell, 1848, 13x16", EX..............**65.00**
World, ink/hc, schoolgirl's scroll, sgn, ME, 1820s, 20x29" **400.00**

Marblehead

What began as therapy for patients in a sanitarium in Marblehead, Massachusetts, has become recognized as an important part of the Arts and Crafts movement in America. Results of the early experiments under the guidance of Arthur E. Baggs in 1904 met with such success that by 1908 the pottery had been converted to a solely commercial venture. Simple vase shapes were often incised with stylized animal and floral motifs or sailing ships. Some were decorated in low relief; many were plain. Simple matt glazes in soft yellow, gray, wisteria, rose, tobacco brown, and their most popular, Marblehead blue, were used alone or in combination. The Marblehead logo is distinctive – a boat with full sail and the letters 'M' and 'P.' The pottery closed in 1936.

Bowl, bl-gr mottle w/lav int, flaring, ca 1915, 8¾" **175.00**
Bowl, dusty rose, 2⅛x8⅞", EX..**175.00**
Bowl, flowers at rim, dk bl/brn on med bl w/dk specks, 2x8" **550.00**
Bowl, purple, 2x4½" **95.00**
Bowl vase, floral band, bl/brn/gray on bl-specked gray, 3½".........**800.00**
Humidor, medallion/dot shoulder band, brn on gr, 4½x3½" **750.00**
Pitcher, marine bl, sgn AEB, bulbous, dtd 1933, 8x7".................**425.00**
Planter, lav, bulbous w/3 loop hdls, 4x6½" **90.00**
Tile, lake/trees, 4-/5-color, mk A-40/label, oak fr, 6½" **2,900.00**
Vase, bl, mk, 8"..**280.00**

Vase, floral band in light and dark blue on gray, artist initialed, 6", $850.00; Vase, floral panels in dark gray on slate gray, artist initialed, 3½", $500.00; Vase, stylized tree in olive on light green, 6", NM, $600.00.

Vase, bl, sgn, 11½"...**275.00**
Vase, bl textured, squat/bulbous w/flared rim, 4" **140.00**
Vase, dk bl, cylindrical, 4⅛", EX..**125.00**
Vase, floral band, bl on gray, sgn, minor scratch, 3½" **700.00**
Vase, floral band, 3-color, artist initialed, 6½" **1,500.00**
Vase, fruit trees, 5 repeats, 5-color, sgn H Tut, rpr, 7" **1,150.00**
Vase, lav, cylindrical, swelling toward base, 1910, 8" **225.00**
Vase, leaves/grapes cvd at rim, bl on bl-specked gray, 4½" **1,000.00**
Vase, long-stem stylized floral, 2-tone brn on gr, HT, 3½" **800.00**
Vase, mustard yel, cylindrical, imp mk, 4⅛", EX **125.00**
Vase, sm sqs at top over vertical panels, 4-color, HT, 9" **5,000.00**
Vase, stylized floral, bl/brn on lt gray-bl, squat, 3".......................**300.00**
Wall pocket, gray & brn, mk, 4" **125.00**

Marbles

Marbles have been popular with children since the mid-1800s. They've been made in many types from a variety of materials. Among some of the first glass items to be produced, the earliest marbles were made from a solid glass rod broken into sections of the proper length which were placed in a tray of sand and charcoal and returned to the fire. As they were reheated, the trays were constantly agitated until the marbles were completely round. Other marbles were made of china, pottery, steel, and natural stones.

Below is a listing of the various types, along with a brief description of each. When size is not otherwise indicated, prices are listed for mint condition marbles of average size, ½" to 1".

Agates: stone marbles of many different colors – bands of color alternating with white usually encircle the marble; most are translucent.

Ballot Box: handmade (with pontils), opaque white or black, used in lodge elections.

Bloodstone: green chalcedony with red spots, a type of quartz.

China: with or without glaze, in a variety of hand-painted designs – parallel bands or bull's-eye designs most common.

Clambroth: opaque glass with outer evenly spaced swirls of one or alternating colors.

Clay: one of the most common older types; some are painted while others are not.

Comic Strip: a series of twelve machine-made marbles with faces of comic strip characters, Peltier Glass Factory, Illinois.

Crockery: sometimes referred to as Benningtons; most are either blue or brown, although some are speckled. The clay is shaped into a sphere, then coated with glaze and fired.

End of the Day: single-pontil glass marbles – the colored part often appears as a multicolored blob or mushroom cloud.

Goldstone: clear glass completely filled with copper flakes that have turned gold-colored from the heat of the manufacturing process.

Indian Swirls: usually black glass with a colored swirl appearing on the outside next to the surface, often irregular.

Latticinio Core Swirls: double-pontil marble with an inner area with net-like effects of swirls coming up around the center.

Lutz Type: glass with colored or clear bands alternating with bands which contain copper flecks.

Micas: clear or colored glass with mica flecks which reflect as silver dots when marble is turned. Red is rare.

Onionskin: spiral type which are solidly colored instead of having individual ribbons or threads, multicolored.

Peppermint Swirls: made of white opaque glass with alternating blue and red outer swirls.

Ribbon Core Swirls: double-pontil marble – center shaped like a ribbon with swirls that come up around the middle.

Rose Quartz: stone marble, usually pink in color, often with frac-

tures inside and on outer surface.

Solid Core Swirls: double-pontil marble – middle is solid with swirls coming up around the core.

Steelies: hollow steel spheres marked with a cross where the steel was bent together to form the ball.

Sulfides: generally made of clear glass with figures inside. Rarer types have colored figures or colored glass.

Tiger Eye: stone marble of golden quartz with inclusions of asbestos, dark brown with gold highlights.

Vaseline: machine-made of yellowish-green glass with small bubbles.

For a more thorough study of the subject, we recommend *Antique and Collectible Marbles, Revised Second Edition*, an identification and value guide by Everett Grist; you will find his address in the Directory under Illinois.

Agate, contemporary, carnelian, 1¾"...........................**175.00**
Agate, gr & wht, ¾" **50.00**
Banded Opaque, gr & wht, 2" **375.00**
Banded Opaque, red & wht, 1¾" **500.00**
Banded Opaque, red & wht, ¾" **75.00**
Banded Transparent Swirl, bl, ¾" **40.00**
Banded Transparent Swirl, lt gr, 1¾" **300.00**
Bennington, bl, 1¾" **15.00**
Bennington, bl, ¾" **1.00**
Bennington, brn, 1¾" **10.00**
Bennington, fancy, 1¾" **20.00**
Bennington, fancy, ¾" **2.00**
China, decorated, glazed, apple, 1¾" **250.00**
China, decorated, glazed, rose, 1¾" **400.00**
China, decorated, glazed, wht w/geometrics, 1¾"............**65.00**
China, decorated, unglazed, geometrics & flowers, ¾".......**250.00**
Clambroth, opaque, bl & wht, 1¾"...............................**800.00**
Clambroth, opaque, bl & wht, ¾" **150.00**
Clear Swirl Lutz-type, clear w/wht & gold swirls, 1¾" **375.00**
Clear Swirl Lutz-type, clear w/wht & gold swirls, ¾".......**85.00**
Cloud, w/mica, red & wht, 1¼" **225.00**
Cloud, yel, rare, 1¾" **500.00**
Comic, Cotes Bakery, advertising **250.00**
Comic, Kayo, rare **55.00**
Comic, Little Orphan Annie **55.00**
Comic, Moon Mullins **55.00**
Comic, set of 12..**550.00**
Comic, Skeezix..**55.00**

Lobed Core Swirl: ¾", $250.00; 1¾", $150.00.

Cork Screw, machine-made...**3.00**
End of Day, bl & wht, 1¾" **300.00**
Goldstone, ¾"..**35.00**
Indian Swirl, 1¾"...**700.00**
Indian Swirl Lutz-type, gold flakes, ¾" **300.00**
Line Crockery, clay, wht w/zigzag gr & bl lines, ¾" **10.00**

Mica, bl, ¾"	25.00
Mica, gr, 1¾"	400.00
Onionskin, w/mica, 1¾"	500.00
Onionskin, w/mica, ¾"	75.00
Onionskin, 1¼"	75.00
Onionskin, 16-lobe, unusual, 2"	700.00
Onionskin, 2"	400.00
Onionskin, ¾"	50.00
Onionskin, 4-lobe, 1¼"	175.00
Onionskin Lutz-type, gold flakes, 1¾"	800.00
Opaque Swirl, gr, ¾"	35.00
Opaque Swirl Lutz-type, bl, yel, gr, or vaseline, ¾"	225.00
Peppermint Swirl, opaque, red, wht, & bl, 1¾"	450.00
Peppermint Swirl, opaque, red, wht, & bl, ¾"	65.00
Pottery, tan w/purple lines, 1¾"	15.00
Ribbon Core Lutz-type, transparent colors, 1¾"	800.00
Slag, machine-made, sm	1.00
Slag, machine-made, 2"	35.00
Solid Opaque, bl, ¾"	25.00
Solid Opaque, gr, 1¾"	300.00
Sulfide, alligator, 1¾"	160.00
Sulfide, baboon, 2⅛", NM	230.00

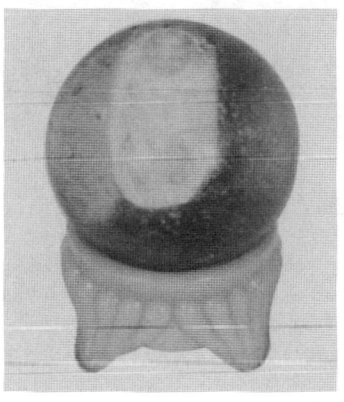

Sulphide, baby in basket, 1¾", VG, $500.00.

Sulfide, bear, sitting, 1⅝", EX	80.00
Sulfide, bear, standing, 1¾", M	140.00
Sulfide, bear, standing, 2¼"	250.00
Sulfide, bear, walking, 1", M	110.00
Sulfide, bird, flying, surface wear, 2 int bubbles, 1¼"	80.00
Sulfide, bird w/long feathers, 1½", M	150.00
Sulfide, camel, 2"	175.00
Sulfide, cat, 1¼"	75.00
Sulfide, child, seated, 1 lg int bubble, 1½"	240.00
Sulfide, child on stump, 1⅝", NM	350.00
Sulfide, child w/ball & mallet, 1¼"	250.00
Sulfide, child w/sailboat, 1¾"	650.00
Sulfide, coin w/number 7, 2"	350.00
Sulfide, cow, grazing, 2⅛", NM	225.00
Sulfide, cow, 1⅛"	100.00
Sulfide, dbl eagle, very rare, 1¾"	675.00
Sulfide, dog, begging, 2", NM	160.00
Sulfide, dog, bird in mouth, 2"	600.00
Sulfide, dog, long haired, 1¼", NM	135.00
Sulfide, dog, running, 1¾", M	170.00
Sulfide, donkey, 1⅝", NM	125.00
Sulfide, dove, 1⅝", M	160.00
Sulfide, dove on post, 1⅛"	278.00
Sulfide, eagle, 1⅝"	185.00
Sulfide, eagle on post, 2", EX	285.00
Sulfide, elephant, 1⅝", M	160.00

Sulfide, fish, 1½", NM	120.00
Sulfide, fish, 2⅛", M	200.00
Sulfide, fox, 1½", EX	130.00
Sulfide, goat, 1¾", M	190.00
Sulfide, goat, 2", M	225.00
Sulfide, hen, 1⅛"	65.00
Sulfide, hen on nest, 1½", M	120.00
Sulfide, horse, running, 1½", M	120.00
Sulfide, jackal, 1", EX	150.00
Sulfide, lamb, 1¼", EX	100.00
Sulfide, lamb, 1¾", M	140.00
Sulfide, lion, lt purple glass, 1⅝", EX	275.00
Sulfide, lion, 1⅝", NM	150.00
Sulfide, lion, 2", NM	200.00
Sulfide, llama, 1⅝", M	140.00
Sulfide, monkey, 1⅛"	95.00
Sulfide, owl, spread-winged, 2"	200.00
Sulfide, papoose, 1⅝"	300.00
Sulfide, papoose, 2"	350.00
Sulfide, pelican, 1¼"	275.00
Sulfide, pig, 1¼"	90.00
Sulfide, pig, 2", M	180.00
Sulfide, prairie chicken, 1¼", M	325.00
Sulfide, rabbit, running, 2"	140.00
Sulfide, rabbit, 1⅛"	65.00
Sulfide, raccoon, 2"	200.00
Sulfide, ram, 2"	175.00
Sulfide, rooster, lt yel glass, 1¾"	375.00
Sulfide, rooster, 1½", M	140.00
Sulfide, rooster, 2", M	180.00
Sulfide, Santa Claus, 2"	350.00
Sulfide, squirrel w/nut, 1½", M	125.00
Sulfide, squirrel w/nut, 2", EX	200.00
Sulfide, steer, 1⅝", M	125.00

Marine Collectibles

See also Steamship Collectibles, Scrimshaw, and Tools.

Anchor, fancy flutes, 1800s, 90+ lbs, 48"	85.00
Becket, fancy ropework, red/wht/bl pnt, 10", pr	230.00
Becket, for sea chest, 1800s, pr	175.00
Binnacle w/compass, brass, Bergen Nautik, 11½", VG	175.00
Binnacle w/compass, brass, mtd on mahog base, 21", NM	300.00
Binnacle w/compass, mahog w/brass & bronze, ES Ritchie, 49"	700.00
Binnacle w/compass, NP brass, complete, 11"	350.00
Chart roller, wood w/linen covering & ropework, early, 36"	400.00
Chronometer, Hamilton, pocket sz	140.00
Chronometer, J Sewell, brass-mtd coriander wood, 50-hr	1,500.00
Communicator, engine room; CI/brass, Chadburnes, 7x14½"	150.00
Fog horn, brass, oak/leather foot-operated bellows, 28"	300.00
Fog horn, pump type, brass, lg, EX	150.00
Harpoon toggle, rpl cone, minor rust, 30½"	225.00
Harpoon toggle, traces of orig red pnt, 33", EX	325.00
Hose nozzle, fire boat's; Capt Earl G Young & Son label, 45"	200.00
Lamp, cabin; brass, w/gimbal, elaborate brass holder, 18"	400.00
Lamp, Non-Sweating Adlake, copper, missing burner, 19", VG	100.00
Lance/killing iron, mtd on orig pole, from Nantucket, 140"	375.00
Lantern, cabin; brass, pat dtd burner, all orig, 9"	320.00
Lantern, dbl: Port/Starboard, brass, 10", NM	160.00
Lantern, gangway; brass, Perko, 13", EX	225.00
Lantern, signal/anchor; copper, 16", EX	120.00

Model, schooner, solid hull, 1900, 61x48" **600.00**
Quadrant, Norie & Co, ebony w/ivory label, in case, NM **1,500.00**
Rope server, whalebone, 1850s, shows wear, 5½" **100.00**
Ruler, navigator's; folding ivory **165.00**
Sailor's valentine, shellwork flower basket, wood case, 10" **1,100.00**
Sailor's valentine, shellwork starfish centers, hinged, 8"..........**1,500.00**
Sailor's valentine, 2 shellwork inscriptions, hinged, 9"............**1,900.00**
Seaman's chest, pnt pine w/becket hdls, ship pnt w/in, 34" **400.00**
Search light, brass, electric, 11" dia, EX....................................**70.00**
Sextant, AB Topping & Co, brass, portable, in case, 4x4"...........**135.00**
Sextant, brass w/inlaid silver scale, maker unknown, w/case **550.00**
Sextant, E Louieux Paris, brass, in case, minor losses...................**600.00**
Sextant, Gray-Strand, brass, in case, VG....................................**300.00**
Sextant, NV Observator Rotterdam, iron/brass, parts missing.....**250.00**
Sextant, OT Olsen, brass, in case, NM **550.00**

Ship's binnacle, brass on mahogany base, 20½", $300.00; Ship's bell, engraved 'USS Metacom, 1941,' 14½", EX, $400.00.

Ship's bell, w/mt bracket, 12" dia, NM **225.00**
Ship's clock, Seth Thomas, brass, time & strike, 7" dia................**250.00**
Ship's wheel, brass hub, laminated wood, needs rfn, 31"..............**135.00**
Stadimeter, Shick Inc, length of case: 12½" **325.00**

Martin Bros.

The Martin Bros. were studio potters who worked from 1873 until 1914, first at Fulham and later at London and Southall. There were four brothers, each of whom excelled in their particular area. Robert, known as Wallace, was an experienced stonecarver. He modeled a series of grotesque bird and animal figural caricatures. Walter was the potter, responsible for throwing the larger vases on the wheel, firing the kiln, and mixing the clay. Edwin, an artist of stature, preferred more naturalistic forms of decoration. His work was often incised or had relief designs of seaweed, florals, fish, and birds. The fourth brother, Charles, was their business manager. Their work was incised with their names, place of production, and letters and numbers indicating month and year.

Bird jar, head cocked, eyes open, EX detail, 1903, 10½".......... **8,000.00**
Bird jar, 1 eye partially open, sgn/1884, 13" **7,000.00**
Bust, Dr Edwin Cronin, terra cotta, rstr, 9¾" **700.00**
Face jug, realistically modeled, sgn/1898, 9½" **6,000.00**
Spoon holder, furry creature w/wide mouth form, 3-color, 6" . **2,800.00**
Vase, frieze of battling beasts, bl/blk/brns, 9½", NM................ **1,500.00**
Vase, incised stylized florals, bl band at shoulder, 6" **280.00**

Vase, leaves, gr/brn on buff mottle, brn neck band, 8" **850.00**
Vase, olive tea-dust w/bl rim, hexagonal ovoid, 10½".................**450.00**
Vase, ribbed lobes, dk brn/gr/cream, bl dot rim, 10", EX............**600.00**
Wine jug, bl/cream mottle, ovoid w/loop hdl, 8½"......................**150.00**

Bird jar, 9", $4,000.00.

Mary Gregory

Mary Gregory glass, for reasons that remain obscure, is the namesake of a Boston and Sandwich Glass Company employee who worked for the company for only two years in the mid-1800s. Although no evidence actually exists to indicate that glass of this type was even produced there, the fine colored or crystal ware decorated with figures of children in white enamel is commonly referred to as Mary Gregory. The glass, in fact, originated in Europe and was imported into this country where it was copied by several eastern glasshouses. It was popular from the mid-1800s until the turn of the century. It is generally accepted that examples with all-white figures were made in the U.S.A., while gold-trimmed items and those with children having tinted faces or a small amount of color on their clothing are European. Though amethyst is rare, examples in cranberry command the higher prices. Blue ranks next; and green, amber, and clear items are worth the least.

Bottle, barber; cobalt, child plays tennis, pontil, 8" **325.00**
Box, cobalt, children at tennis, ormolu mts, oblong, 5½" H ... **1,000.00**
Box, cobalt, girl & floral sprays, brass hinge/ft, 2½x3½" **225.00**
Box, cranberry, girl in flower garden, ormolu mts, 4" dia **275.00**
Box, dk amethyst, girl, brass mts, sq, 3" H **325.00**
Box, dresser; lime gr, lady w/harp, rnd, lg....................................**185.00**
Box, peacock bl, boy w/flowers, brass mts, rnd, 4½" H................**350.00**
Box, sapphire bl, 2 girls pick flowers, ormolu mts, 4x5" **395.00**
Cruet, emerald gr, girl/flowers, trilobed, flat sides, lg **275.00**
Cruet, gr, boy, matching stopper, 8¼" **275.00**
Decanter, cranberry, girl by swan in water, 9½" **300.00**
Decanter, wine; cranberry, girl/fence, bubble stopper, 11"............**365.00**
Ginger jar, cranberry, courting couple, ovoid, lg, pr **550.00**
Pin tray, gr opaque, girl w/basket, 3½" dia....................................**75.00**
Pitcher, amber, boy on tree limb, ruffled rim, 8½" **325.00**
Pitcher, bl, girl holds leaf, 2" **225.00**
Pitcher, bl, girl/trees, ribbed, 11"...**250.00**

Pitcher, gr, girl/trees, 6" 125.00
Pitcher, tankard; bl, girl w/staff, appl hdl, 10x4½" 235.00
Powder jar, gr, lady w/harp, much gilt, lg 145.00
Shot glass, cranberry, girl, 2⅛x2⅛" 85.00

Salt and pepper shaker on tray, dark amber, silverplated base with cupid figural, 7", $850.00.

Shot glass, lt amber, boy, 2x1⅞" 65.00
Toothpick holder, cranberry, girl w/flowers, gold rim 225.00
Tumbler, cranberry, boy & girl, 2½x1¾", pr 100.00
Tumbler, gr, girl holds flower, 4" 55.00
Tumbler, sapphire bl, girl, bbl shape, 4¼x2½" 68.00
Vase, amber, girl w/bouquet, 6¾" 95.00
Vase, amberina, boy in woods, ribbed/bulbous, 7" 175.00
Vase, apple gr, boy w/tray of flowers, 11⅛x4⅛" 235.00
Vase, bl, boy blowing horn, 8" 150.00
Vase, bl, girl w/basket, boy w/hat, 7⅝x3⅛", pr 335.00
Vase, cobalt, girl, scalloped top, 5⅝x2⅛" 115.00
Vase, cobalt, girl w/hat, 7⅜x3" 110.00
Vase, cranberry, boy w/tam, scalloped, 11¼x3⅞" 325.00
Vase, cranberry, girl w/book, bulbous, 4⅛x3¼" 145.00
Vase, cranberry, girl w/watering can, facing pr, 9" 395.00
Vase, gold-amber, child, ped ft, scroll hdls, 10", pr 450.00
Vase, gr, boy & girl play tennis, cylindrical, 8x5½" 125.00
Vase, gr Bristol, boy w/tray, emb bands, ruffled, ftd, 11" 225.00
Vase, honey-amber, boy & girl, appl scroll hdls, 10", pr 450.00
Vase, lime gr, boy w/cap, 6⅝x3⅜" 100.00
Vase, lime gr, girl, ruffled top, 6⅜x2⅝" 80.00
Vase, lime gr, girl at shore, sailboat, snail hdls, 11⅝" 275.00
Vase, lime gr frost, boy w/bird, 5⅞x3¼" 110.00
Vase, lt sapphire bl, girl, 11x4¼" 195.00
Vase, pk Bristol overlay, girls, facing pr, 9½" 325.00
Warming stand, ruby, figures in domestic settings, sq, 5x5" 375.00

Mason's Ironstone

In 1813 Charles J. Mason was granted a patent for a process said to 'improve the quality of English porcelain.' The new type of ware was in fact ironstone which Mason decorated with colorful florals and scenics, some of which reflected the Oriental taste. Although his business failed for a short time in the late 1840s, Mason re-established himself and continued to produce dinnerware, tea services, and ornamental pieces until about 1852 at which time the pottery was sold to Francis Morley. Ten years later, Geo. L. and Taylor Ashworth became owners. Both Morley and the Ashworths not only used Mason's molds and patterns but often his mark as well. Because the quality and the workmanship of the later wares do not compare with Mason's earlier product, collectors should take care to distinguish one from the other. Consult a good book on marks to be sure.

Jug, Bandana, gold/orange/blk/gr, mk, 1860, 4⅞" 195.00
Jug, Chrysanthemum, bl & orange, unmk, 1820, 3" 155.00
Jug, Imari, paneled, snake hdl, 8⅜" 300.00
Jug, Mazareen, bl chrysanthemums, unmk, 1820s, 8" 300.00
Jug, Mazareen, mc floral, sloped sides, unmk, 5¼" 235.00

Plate, birds and florals, 9½", $65.00.

Plate, chinoiserie, mc, mk, 6½" 125.00
Plate, Imari, mk, 8" 175.00
Tureen, vegetable; fruit finial, 1820s, 9½" 245.00

Massier

Clement Massier was a French artist-potter who in 1881 established a workshop at Golfe Juan, France, where he experimented with metallic lustre glazes. (One of his pupils was Jacques Sicardo, who brought the knowledge he had gained through his association with Massier to the Weller Pottery Company in Zanesville, Ohio.) The lustre lines developed by Massier incorporated nature themes with allover decorations of foliage or flowers on shapes modeled in the Art Nouveau style. The ware was usually incised with the Massier name, his initials, or the location of the pottery. Massier died in 1917.

Bowl, lizard/Greek Key border, metallic on lt red bsk, 6½" 1,300.00
Bowl, sea nymph/waves mold, irid, dtd 1901, rstr, 15" L 600.00
Charger, landscape, mc lustres, 14" 1,800.00
Vase, berries, mc irid, 3 rim-to-shoulder straps, 14" 1,600.00
Vase, floral, mc irid, baluster form w/hdls, 1900, 16", pr.... 1,200.00
Vase, floral, mc irid, coiled hdls w/snakes' heads, 18" 1,500.00

Match Holders

Before the invention of the safety match in 1855, matches were kept in matchboxes and carried in pocket-size match safes because they ignited so easily. John Walker, an English chemist, invented the match more than one hundred years ago – quite by accident. Walker was working with a mixture of potash and antimony, hoping to make a combustible that could be used to fire guns. The mixture adhered to the end of the wooden stick he had used for stirring. As he tried to remove it by scraping the stick on the stone floor, it burst into flames. The invention of the match was only a step away! From that time to the present, match holders have been made in amusing figural forms as well as simple utilitarian styles and in a wide range of materials. Most were wall-hanging; a few were table-top models – all designed to keep matches conveniently at hand. See also Advertising; Majolica.

Advertising, Philip Morris, Little Johnny tin litho, hanging..........**65.00**
Amber glass hook, striker on cover **50.00**

Bacchus face, cast iron, 6", $85.00.

Beetle, lead figural, 4¼" **22.00**
Blk boy sitting on log, bsk figural **85.00**
Boy w/basket mtd on ash tray w/matchbox holder, CI, Hubley ...**200.00**
Boy w/dog figural, mk Elbogen, ca 1890, 4x5" **125.00**
Chamberstick w/matchbox holder, Dresden **95.00**
Chicken in front of basket, bronze, 2½x3½" **150.00**
Columbus, pnt CI figural..**95.00**
Cone-shaped holder on tray w/floral decor, Limoges.............**95.00**
Englishman, tongue sticking out, chalkware, wall mt, 5½" **48.00**
Fairing, man on fainting couch, 2-pc, EX **150.00**
Flowers & scrolls in relief, dbl pocket, CI, 5½x6½" **75.00**
Girl in bonnet, bsk, Germany, EX.......................................**25.00**
Horse's hoof, brass, 3-D turtle on hinged lid, 4¾x4¾x6" **88.00**
Hunting pouch/hanging game, cast brass, 8½" **130.00**
India Wharf Brewing, Brooklyn, glass..................................**28.00**
Lady's bloomers, glass, 3" **135.00**
Log cabin figural, hinged roof, CI, orig pnt, 1860s, 4x2½" **130.00**
New Process Ranges, tin, 3½" **38.00**
Rifles & game, bag forms safes, CI, 10x6" **65.00**
Scrolls, CI, wall hanging **30.00**
Stoneware, cone shape on tray, brn glaze.............................**45.00**
Tin, cut-out decor, crimped crest, pnt traces, 4x7", EX **30.00**
Tin tray w/cone-shaped glass holder....................................**45.00**
Urn, dbl; lacy iron, hanging, dtd 1867, 5½x7½".................**75.00**
Victorian shoe, beads on cloth, 9x5" **85.00**
Wht Ribbon Temperance Beverage Co, Chicago, glass **30.00**

Match Safes

Match safes, aptly-named cases used to carry matches in the days before cigarette lighters, were used during the last half of the 19th century until about 1920. Some incorporated added features – hidden compartments, cigar cutters, etc. – some were figural, and others were used by retail companies as advertising give-aways. They were made from every type of material, but silverplated styles abound. See also Advertising.

Advertising, Anheuser Busch, repousse, eagle w/wings **95.00**
Advertising, Bl Union Label, celluloid & nickel, EX **75.00**
Advertising, Hanley's Peerless Ale, NP, pat 1904, VG **30.00**
Advertising, Internat'l Taylor Co, nickel, EX **75.00**
Advertising, Red Top Rye Distillers, gutta percha, EX **75.00**
Advertising, United Brewery Workman, OH, celluloid/nickel **60.00**
Advertising, 1st Nat'l of Blairsville, metal/celluloid......................**40.00**
Alligator, Monon Route **275.00**
Deer hoof, NP brass figural **80.00**
Fishing equipment eng on nickel/brass **35.00**
Horse's head, sterling figural, 2½x1½" **285.00**
Man's head, brass figural, 1½x2" **110.00**
Pig, SP figural, head opens, base striker, 1½x¾x2½" **85.00**
Repousse florals ea side, mk sterling **85.00**
SP, eng, w/coin & stamp holder/pencil/toothpick, unusual..........**250.00**
Trousers w/suspenders, SP figural, lid dtd Nov 9, '86 ....**145.00**
Walnut, SP figural, top opens, striker on bk, 1¼x1¾" **75.00**

McCoy

The third generation McCoy potter in the Roseville, Ohio, area was Nelson, who with the aid of his father, J.W., established the Nelson McCoy Sanitary Stoneware Company in 1910. They manufactured churns, jars, jugs, poultry fountains, and foot warmers. By 1925 they had expanded their wares to include majolica jardinieres and pedestals, umbrella stands and cuspidors, and an embossed line of vases and small jardinieres in a blended brown and green matt glaze. From the late twenties through the mid-forties, a utilitarian stoneware was produced, some of which was glazed in the soft blue and white so popular with collectors today. They also used a dark brown mahogany color and a medium to dark green – both in a high gloss. In 1933 the firm became known as the Nelson McCoy Pottery Company. They expanded their facilities in 1940 and began to make the novelty artware, cookie jars, and dinnerware that today are synonomous with 'McCoy.' To date more than two hundred cookie jars of every theme and description have been produced. Some are very common. Mammy, the Clown, and the Bear (although very old) are easy to find; while the Dalmations, Christmas Tree, and Kangaroo, for instance, (though not so old) are harder to locate. The Indian and the Tepee, both made in the fifties, are two of the most popular and some of the most expensive!

More than a dozen different marks have been used by the company; nearly all incorporate the name 'McCoy,' although some of the older items were marked 'NM USA.' For further information, consult *The Collector's Encyclopedia of McCoy Pottery* by Sharon and Bob Huxford, available at your local bookstore or public library.

Our McCoy cookie jar advisor is Judy Posner; she is listed in the Directory under Pennsylvania.

Cookie Jars

Animal Crackers...**75.00**

Apollo Age 250.00
Apple, 1950-64 ....25.00
Apple on Basketweave 30.00
Bananas 55.00
Barnum's Animals 130.00
Bear, cookie in vest 45.00
Bear, upside down, blk/wht 25.00
Betsy Baker 115.00
Black Kettle, w/immovable bail, HP flowers 25.00
Bobby Baker 40.00
Caboose 105.00
Chef 80.00
Chiffoniere, Early American Chest 75.00

Chinese Lantern, $40.00; Hillbilly Bear, $350.00 and up.

Chipmunk 70.00
Christmas Tree 300.00
Circus Horse 115.00
Clown Bust 70.00
Clown in Barrel 45.00
Clyde Dog 75.00
Coalby Cat 100.00
Coffee Grinder 25.00
Coffee Mug 25.00
Colonial Fireplace 80.00
Cookie Barrel 20.00
Cookie Boy 115.00
Cookie Cabin 50.00
Cookie Jug, dbl loop 20.00
Cookie Jug, single loop, 2-tone gr rope 18.00
Cookie Jug, w/cork stopper, brn & wht 15.00
Cookie Log 30.00
Cookie Safe 35.00
Cookstove 25.00
Corn 80.00
Covered Wagon 45.00
Cylinder, w/red flowers 20.00
Dalmations in Rocking Chair 175.00
Dog on Basketweave 45.00
Drum 50.00
Duck on Basketweave 40.00
Dutch Boy 30.00
Dutch Girl, boy on reverse 40.00
Dutch Treat Barn 50.00
Elephant 105.00
Elephant w/Split Trunk, rare 250.00
Engine, blk 115.00

Forbidden Fruit 50.00
Friendship 75.00
Frontier Family 40.00
Fruit in Bushel Basket 45.00
Gingerbread Boy 25.00
Globe 150.00
Grandfather Clock 45.00
Granny 50.00
Hamm's Bear 125.00
Happy Face 25.00
Hen on Nest 75.00
Hobby Horse 90.00
Honey Bear 50.00
Indian 185.00
Jack-O'-Lantern 200.00
Kangaroo, bl 195.00
Kettle, jumbo sz 25.00
Kissing Penguins 50.00
Kitten on Basketweave 45.00
Kittens on Ball of Yarn 65.00
Kookie Kettle, blk 20.00
Lamb on Basketweave 40.00
Leprechaun, M 400.00
Liberty Bell 35.00
Little Clown 60.00
Lollipop 40.00
Mac Dog 55.00
Mammy 115.00
Mammy w/Cauliflower, G pnt 350.00
Modern 30.00
Monk 30.00
Mother Goose 85.00
Mr & Mrs Owl 70.00
Oaken Bucket 20.00
Old Churn 20.00
Pears on Basketweave 30.00
Pelican 90.00
Pepper, yel 22.00
Picnic Basket 50.00
Pineapple 40.00
Pineapple, Modern 25.00
Pirates Chest 50.00
Pot Belly Stove, blk 25.00
Puppy, w/sign 70.00
Quaker Oats 200.00
Red Barn, cow in door, rare 135.00
Rooster, 1955-1957 ....85.00
Rooster, 1970-1974 ....45.00
Round w/HP Leaves 25.00
Sad Clown 40.00
Snoopy on Doghouse 125.00
Snow Bear 40.00
Strawberry, 1955-57 ....35.00
Strawberry, 1971-75 ....25.00
Teapot 25.00
Tepee 185.00
Tilt Pitcher, blk w/roses 26.00
Tomato 25.00
Touring Car 50.00
Tudor Cookie House 75.00
Tulip on Flowerpot 45.00
Turkey 115.00
Upside Down Bear, panda 25.00

WC Fields	120.00
Wedding Jar	55.00
Windmill	60.00
Wishing Well	30.00
Woodsy Owl	115.00
Wren House	60.00
Yosemite Sam	115.00

Miscellaneous

Basket, oak leaf & acorn decor	25.00
Bean pot, Suburbia Ware, mk, 1964, 2-qt	10.00
Beverage jug, Sunburst Gold, w/lid	40.00
Bookend/planter, violin, pr	22.00
Bowl, shoulder; bl, ringed, rectangular base, 9"	22.00
Coffee server & warmer, El Rancho Bar-B-Que	50.00
Coffeepot, Grecian, gr & gold, w/creamer & sugar bowl	55.00
Creamer, dog figural, 1950s	22.50
Creamer, stick hdl, 1945	4.00
Decanter, Jupiter 60, train set, 4-pc	200.00
Decanter, 1932 Pierce Arrow Sport Phantom	30.00
Dripolator, hexagonal shape, 1943	17.50
Elephant, Victory Depends on You, WWII era	20.00
Ice tub, El Rancho Bar-B-Que	30.00
Lamp, cowboy boots form, orig shade, lg	50.00
Lamp base, blk panther figural, 1950s	20.00
Lamp base, mermaid w/seashell figural	50.00
Mug, Campbell kids, mk USA, recent	2.00
Pitcher, chicken figural, unmk, 1943	14.00
Pitcher, curved top, flattened sides, 1950s	10.00
Pitcher, elephant figural, wht, 1940s, NM	20.00
Pitcher, water lily emb on gr, fish hdl, 1935	20.00
Planter, cat figural, bow at neck, 1953	8.00
Planter, conch-shell figural, unmk, 1954	10.00
Planter, cradle, unmk	6.00
Planter, Grecian, rectangular, 1958	22.50
Planter, Liberty Bell	60.00
Planter, rolling pin w/Boy Blue	18.00
Planter, stork beside basket, 1956	12.00
Planter, turtle figural, 1955	15.00
Planter, Village Smithy	14.00
Shakers, cabbage figural, 1954, pr	20.00
Spoon rest, penguin figural, 1953	35.00
Tea set, Two-Tone Green, 3-pc	50.00
Teapot, cat figural, paw spout, head forms lid	35.00
Teapot, Grecian, 1958	40.00
Teapot, Sunburst Gold, mk, 1957	32.00
Vase, feather shape, unmk, 1950s	8.00

McCoy, J. W.

The J.W. McCoy Pottery Company was incorporated in 1899. It operated under that name in Roseville, Ohio, until 1911 when McCoy entered into a partnership with George Brush, forming the Brush-McCoy Company. During the early years, McCoy produced kitchenware, majolica jardinieres and pedestals, umbrella stands, and cuspidors. By 1903 they had begun to experiment in the field of art pottery and, though never involved to the extent of some of their contemporaries, nevertheless produced several art lines of merit. Their first line was Mt. Pelee, examples of which are very rare today. Two types of glazes were used, matt green and an iridescent charcoal gray. Though the line was primarily mold formed, some pieces evidence the fact that while the clay remained wet and pliable it was pulled and pinched with the fin-

gers to form crests and peaks in a style not unlike George Ohr.

The company rebuilt in 1904 after being destroyed by fire, and other artware was designed. Loy-Nel Art and Renaissance were standard brown lines, hand decorated under the glaze with colored slip. Shapes and artwork were usually simple but effective. Olympia and Rosewood were relief-molded brown-glaze lines decorated in natural colors with wreaths of leaves and berries or simple floral sprays. Although much of this ware was not marked, you will find examples with the die-stamped 'Loy-Nel Art, McCoy' or an incised line identification.

Florastone, vase, unmk, 1923, 12"	165.00
Grape, bowl, cereal; w/lid, unmk, 1912	95.00
Grape, cuspidor, 1½"	45.00
Greystone, birdbath, shape #6, unmk, 27"	125.00
Loy-Nel-Art, bowl, 3½x9"	85.00
Loy-Nel-Art, jardiniere, 1905, 6"	100.00
Loy-Nel-Art, vase, unmk, 1905, 8"	115.00
Marble Ware, jardiniere & ped, unmk, 39"	300.00
Rosewood, vase, pre-1903, unmk, 3"	30.00
Sylvan, vase, unmk, 6"	30.00

Vase, Loy-Nel Art, floral, 8", $125.00.

McKee

McKee Glass was founded in 1853 in Pittsburgh, Pennsylvania. Among their early products were tableware of both the flint and non-flint variety. In 1888 the company relocated to avail themselves of a source of natural gas, thereby founding the town of Jeannette, Pennsylvania. One of their most famous colored dinnerware lines, Rock Crystal, was manufactured in the 1920s. During the thirties and forties, colored opaque dinnerware, Sunkist reamers, and 'bottoms up' cocktail tumblers were popular as well as a line of black glass vases, bowls, and novelty items. All are popular items with today's collectors. The company was purchased in 1916 by Jeannette Glass, under which name it continues to operate. See also Animal Dishes with Covers; Depression Glass; Kitchen Collectibles; Reamers.

Bottoms Up, butterscotch opal, 3¼"	60.00
Bottoms Up, frosted, w/coaster	75.00
Bowl, Flower Band, 9"	22.00
Bowl, Laurel, French ivory, 11"	17.50
Bowl, Red Ships, 4½"	12.00
Box, custard, 4x5"	15.00
Canister, Red Ships, 10-oz	15.00

Clock, Tambour, amber 375.00
Cocktail shaker, Bl Ships 30.00
Egg cup, Flower Band, jade...6.00
Pitcher, Red Ships, ice lip...40.00
Refrigerator jar, Red Ships, 4x5" 15.00
Tumbler, juice; Bl Ships, 3¾" 7.00

Medical Collectibles

The field of medical-related items encompasses a wide area from the primitive bleeding bowl to the X-ray machines of the early 1900s. Other closely related collectibles include apothecary and dental items. Many tools that were originally intended for the pharmacist found their way to the doctor's office, and dentists often used surgical tools when no suitable dental instrument was available. A trend in the late 1700s toward self-medication brought a whole new wave of home-care manuals and 'patent' medical machines for home use. Commonly referred to as 'quack' medical gimmicks, these machines were usually ineffective and occasionally dangerous.

Our advisor for this category is Jim Calison; he is listed in the Directory under New York.

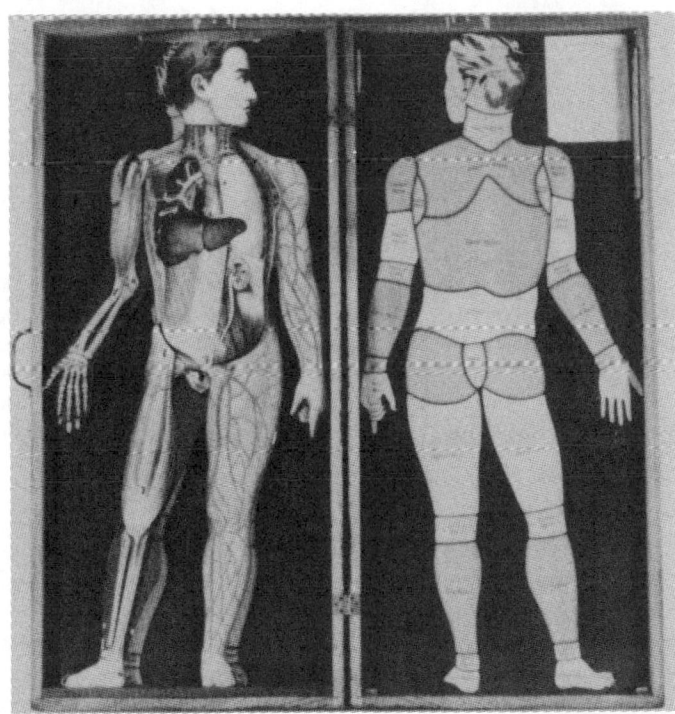

Anatomical teaching device, Smith's New Outline Map of the Human System, ca 1888, wood figures with applied lithos of the muscular and skeletal systems, 44" x 20", $900.00.

Bleeder, brass, single steel blade, Snowden, EX 225.00
Book, Diseases of Women & Children, Gunning, MD, 1860, EX .25.00
Book, Stammering, Its Cause & Cure, Bogue, 1939, VG 5.00
Bottle, Tr Cannab I, cobalt, label under glass, 9" 300.00
Case, medicine; fold-up leather, Cross, + vials/cup/spoon, VG 40.00
Eye cup, aluminum, flat, 1¼"...4.00
Eye cup, amber, 8-panel, 2½" 25.00
Eye cup, cobalt, 8-panel, mk M in circle, 2⅜" 15.00
Eye cup, John Bull, 2⅝" 25.00
Eye cup, milk glass, 8-panel, Westmoreland, 2½" 20.00
Eye cup, no panels, ball & pillar ped 9.00
Eye cup, Optrex Sight Safeguard, no ped, 1¼" 22.00

Jar, ironstone, mc HP label, gold 'Polvo De Opio,' 10", EX 145.00
Jar, ointment; wht w/gold trim, matching lid, 11½" 55.00
Journal, prescription, handwritten, 1920s, lg, 6 for....................25.00
Machine, pill; walnut, brass fittings, tray removes, 13x8" 95.00
Machine, pill; Wirz #384, pat 1867, 13x6½", EX 175.00
Machine, suppository; aluminum, Applebaum, 1924, 6", EX........200.00
Mold, suppository; brass, 3-part, 12-form, 4½" L, EX 25.00
Mold, suppository; brass, 3-part, 48-form, 22", VG 350.00
Otoscope, electrical, 1920s, EX in case 28.00
Quack machine, Challenge, Sears Roebuck, M in case.................40.00
Quack machine, David/Kidder's Pat Magneto 275.00
Quack machine, Electro-Medical Health Kit, 1921, EX in box...175.00
Quack machine, Master Violet Ray #11, EX in orig box...............40.00
Quack remedy, Baby's Ear Tucker, special bonnet, 1920s 10.00
Quack remedy, Dr Young's Rectal Dilators, 1920s, MIB.................30.00

Meissen

The Royal Saxon Porcelain Works was established in 1710 in Meissen, Saxony. Under the direction of Johann Freidrick Bottger, who in 1708 had developed the formula for the first true porcelain body, fine ceramic figurines with exquisite detail and tableware of the highest quality were produced. Although every effort was made to insure the secrecy of Bottger's discovery, others soon began to copy his ware; and in 1731 Meissen adopted the famous crossed sword trademark to identify their own work. The term 'Dresden ware' is often used to refer to Meissen porcelain, since Bottger's discovery and first potting efforts were in nearby Dresden. See also Onion Pattern.

Our advisor for this category is William Brinkley; he is listed in the Directory under Illinois.

Allegorical ewer, 'Fire,' late 1800s, 27", $1,300.00.

Bust, child, grapevines about shoulders/in hair, 10", EX 1,200.00
Cake plate, wht w/gold trim, X-swords 145.00
Candelabrum, 7-light, base w/3 figures, appl vines/etc, 23" 1,900.00
Candle holder, dbl, appl figures/roses, mirror bk, 14", pr.............650.00
Centerpiece, 3-tier, rtcl borders, lady atop, 1900, 21"............. 1,000.00
Compote, appl florals, branch hdls/ft, rtcl body, 14" L 600.00

Compote, bl/wht, lady & cupid, X-swords 675.00
Compote, cherub, wht w/gr & gold, scroll border, #447/old mk...175.00
Compote, floral emb center/edge, beading, gilt, mk, 6½x12" 350.00
Compote, rtcl floral bowl, std w/appl couple/florals, 20" 6,000.00
Compote, rtcl floral bowl, 3 Graces/appl roses on ped, 12"...... 1,300.00
Creamer & sugar bowl, wht w/gold trim, X-swords.........................85.00
Cup & saucer, harbor cartouches, quatrelobed, AR mk, 1800s...250.00
Figurine, Air: Cupid, bird in ea hand, cage at side, 5x4¾" 700.00
Figurine, cherub sits on sphinx w/lady's head, 9", EX 2,800.00
Figurine, cherub w/shovel, plants/rake, oval base, 5x4½"............495.00
Figurine, country boy & girl, ornate Rococo base, pr 725.00
Figurine, couple in 1700s attire, Cupid in tree, 1810s, 14"..........750.00
Figurine, Cupid holds floral garland, Je les Ramene, 5¾"............900.00
Figurine, Cupid w/baskets feeds birds, quiver on branch, 7".........800.00
Figurine, Cupid w/bellows & 2 flaming hearts, 1910, 7" 450.00
Figurine, Cupid w/cage, Je le Captive, 4½", NM 475.00
Figurine, Cybel on lion, 3 cherubs, rstr, 9", EX 1,400.00
Figurine, Diana leans over fallen Endymion, 12x5" 1,400.00
Figurine, girl on stool w/book, pk floral dress, 1860s, 6"..............750.00
Figurine, L'Econome, lady w/pen, marble-top table, 6", NM .. 1,500.00
Figurine, lady & flowers, X-swords, 9" 425.00
Figurine, lady & pets, X-swords, 9" 425.00
Figurine, lady at piano, 1700s attire, shaped base, 4¾x3½"..........550.00
Figurine, lady gardener w/basket of flowers, X-swords, 7" 575.00
Figurine, lady in lacy housecoat holds cat, 1870, 9", NM 1,400.00
Figurine, Leda & the Swan, w/cherubs & angels, 1900, 7½"........775.00
Figurine, Love: holds Cupid against hip/2nd at ft, 8½" 400.00
Figurine, lovers/lamb/dog sit beneath tree, 1850s, 9", EX 600.00
Figurine, male cherub puts floral crown on female, 5x4"..............600.00
Figurine, man gathers twigs, hat on trunk, 1870, 7½", EX 550.00
Figurine, man w/New Testament, cherub at side, 9x3"...............800.00
Figurine, Medici Venus, dolphin at side, stepped base, 10"..........700.00
Figurine, Night w/owl, Day w/torch, on plinth, 20", pr 4,400.00
Figurine, peasant figures, German, 11½", pr 475.00
Figurine, scarf dancer, breast bare, mk B-255, 10½" 1,700.00
Figurine, shepherd pets brn/wht dog, stepped base, 27x11" 3,850.00
Figurine, Silenus on donkey, man aside, lady ahead, 8", NM... 1,300.00
Figurine, Theatre: nymph, holds masks, cherub/monkey, 7".... 1,400.00
Figurine, Touch: maid on stool, bird in cage on table, 6" 700.00
Figurine, Venus attends seated nude Mars, 13x9" 1,700.00
Figurine, Water: cherub kneels by trap, fish in ea hand, 4".........400.00
Figurine, wine merchants, ea w/keg, she w/pitcher, 7", pr 1,300.00
Figurine, Zephyr & Flora embrace, sq/stepped base, 11x4½" ... 1,650.00
Figurine, 2 boys/2 girls frolic in ring, 1700s attire, 6" 1,100.00
Figurine, 2 children at play, pastels, X-swords, 5", pr....................375.00
Figurine, 2 hawks on wht rock ledge, 14" 350.00
Figurine, 2 sea nymphs/2 cherubs cast for baby tritons, 12" 1,700.00
Figurine, 3 cherubs, 1 w/page, 1 w/inkstand, 8x6¾" 900.00
Figurine, 3 Graces rob Cupid, rockwork/appl birds, 14x13" 4,600.00
Figurine, 4 cherubs around fire, 1 on stump, 7x7" 1,300.00
Figurine, 4 cherubs lead blindfolded Cupid, rock base, 7x9" ... 1,200.00
Figurine, 5 cherubs pull goddess of Athens, gold trim 750.00
Plate, pate-sur-pate, nude/2 swans, 4-color, 13" dia................ 2,200.00
Teapot, bouquets, gilt/porc hdl w/foliage terminals, 1850 .... 1,400.00
Tureen, finial: girl w/cornucopia, HP florals, hdls, 15" L.............800.00
Vase, HP florals, gold hdls & trim, X-swords, 1880s, 11" 400.00
Vase, wht w/gr leaves, X-swords, 9" 165.00

Mercury Glass

Mercury glass was popular during the 1850s and enjoyed a short revival at the turn of the century. It was made with two thin layers, either blown with a double wall or joined in sections, with the space between the walls of the vessel filled with a mixture of tin, lead, bismuth, and mercury. The opening was sealed to prevent air from dulling the bright color. Though most examples are silver, blue and gold can be found on occasion. Remember that the value of this type of glass hinges greatly upon condition of the mercury lining.

Vase, silver with enameled robin and nest, 12", $45.00.

Bowl, silver, 3 clear appl ft, 4¾x9½" 80.00
Candlestick, gold, dome base, 6", pr...75.00
Candlestick, 10"...30.00
Goblet, gold, wht enamel floral band, 5" 35.00
Mug, clear hdl, 3" 25.00
Pitcher, water; silver w/eng florals, clear hdl...............................225.00
Rolling pin 75.00
Salt cellar, silver, gold int, sgn on plug, 2½x3" 85.00
Vase, silver w/wht enamel birds, 7½"...45.00
Vase, wht florals, 12", pr..95.00

Merrimac

Founded in 1897 in Newburyport, Massachusetts, the Merrimac Pottery Company primarily produced tile and gardenware. In 1901, however, they introduced a line of artware that is now attracting the interest of collectors. Marked examples carry an impressed die-stamp or a paper label, each with the firm name and the outline of a sturgeon, the Indian word for which was Merrimac.

Note: the vase listed at $4,250.00 below was estimated to sell for $2,500.00 to $3,500.00 at auction.

Bowl, wht bsk, emb figures all around, 2½x6" 100.00
Mug, dk gr gloss, frog in bottom, 4½" 100.00
Vase, gr drip over olive, cylindrical, hairline, 11" 400.00
Vase, gr matt, swirling leaves, sgn ED/1903, 2¾x3½" 950.00
Vase, gr matt mottle, bulbous, incurvate, ca 1905, 6½" 475.00
Vase, gr matt mottle, squat/bulbous, wide neck, label, 4½" 450.00
Vase, gr semi-matt, 4-leaf clovers cvd at shoulder, 8x5" 4,250.00
Vase, mustard yel gloss, label, 3"...130.00

Metlox

The Metlox Manufacturing Company was founded in 1927 in

Manhattan Beach, California. Before 1934 when they began producing the ceramic housewares for which they have become famous, they made ceramic and neon outdoor advertising signs. The company went out of business in 1989.

Well-known sculptor Carl Romanelli designed artware in the late 1930s and early 1940s (and again briefly in the 1950s). His work is especially sought after today.

Our advisor for this category is Jack Chipman; he is listed in the Directory under California.

California Ivy, bowl, berry; 5" 6.00
California Ivy, bowl, cereal 8.00
California Ivy, bowl, 9½" 15.00
California Ivy, butter dish..25.00
California Ivy, celery tray 22.00
California Ivy, chop plate, 13"...25.00
California Ivy, creamer & sugar bowl, w/lid 15.00
California Ivy, gravy boat & underplate........................27.50
California Ivy, pepper mill 12.00
California Ivy, pitcher, ice lip 30.00
California Ivy, plate, 10¼" 10.00
California Ivy, plate, 6" 2.50
California Ivy, plate, 6¾" 3.50
California Ivy, plate, 8" 5.00
California Ivy, plate, 9½" 7.00
California Ivy, shakers, hdls, pr 10.00
California Ivy, teapot..30.00
California Ivy, tray, 2-tier 15.00
California Provincial, bowl, divided vegetable 30.00
California Provincial, bowl, salad serving.....................30.00
California Provincial, bowl, soup; rimmed 15.00
California Provincial, bowl, 5½" 6.00
California Provincial, bread tray 40.00
California Provincial, candle holders, pr 30.00
California Provincial, coffee server, wood hdl 30.00
California Provincial, creamer.. 5.00
California Provincial, cup & saucer 10.00
California Provincial, egg cup, dbl 15.00
California Provincial, mug..15.00
California Provincial, mug, beer.......................................17.50
California Provincial, pitcher, milk sz, 1-qt 35.00
California Provincial, plate, bread & butter....................5.00
California Provincial, plate, dinner; 9" 8.00
California Provincial, plate, salad...................................... 6.00
California Provincial, platter, rnd 25.00
California Provincial, server, divided, rectangular.......30.00
California Provincial, shakers, pr 14.00
California Provincial, sprinkler 30.00
California Provincial, sugar bowl 6.00
Cookie jar, Blk Mammy w/mixing bowl, M 100.00
Cookie jar, Clown 45.00
Cookie jar, Dog's Head, Cockapoo..................................30.00
Cookie jar, Kitten, wht 25.00
Cookie jar, Lion..35.00
Cookie jar, Owl...25.00
Cookie jar, Raggedy Andy...35.00
Cookie jar, Rose..35.00
Cookie jar, Squirrel on Pine Cone 40.00
Cookie jar, Squirrel on Stump 28.00
Homestead Provincial, bowl, divided vegetable; stick hdl..............27.50
Homestead Provincial, bowl, vegetable 22.00
Homestead Provincial, bread tray.....................................20.00
Homestead Provincial, canister set, fruits, wood lids, 4-pc............60.00

Homestead Provincial, cup & saucer 10.00
Homestead Provincial, jewelry box 30.00
Homestead Provincial, match holder, wall hanging 30.00
Homestead Provincial, mustard jug, w/lid......................22.00
Homestead Provincial, plate, 6" 4.00
Homestead Provincial, platter, rnd, 13".........................20.00
Homestead Provincial, server, 2-part 25.00
Provincial Fruit, bowl, vegetable; rnd 15.00
Provincial Fruit, coffeepot 35.00
Red Rooster Provincial, bowl, soup; flat..........................7.00
Red Rooster Provincial, bowl, tab hdls, 5" 12.00
Red Rooster Provincial, bowl, 5⅞" 6.00
Red Rooster Provincial, coffeepot 27.50
Red Rooster Provincial, creamer & sugar bowl.............15.00
Red Rooster Provincial, cup & saucer............................. 7.50
Red Rooster Provincial, egg cup.......................................22.00
Red Rooster Provincial, gravy boat 20.00
Red Rooster Provincial, match holder 26.00
Red Rooster Provincial, mug...15.00
Red Rooster Provincial, pitcher, milk 25.00
Red Rooster Provincial, plate, 10" 10.00
Red Rooster Provincial, plate, 6" 5.00
Red Rooster Provincial, platter, 13"................................18.00
Red Rooster Provincial, shakers, hdls, pr 12.00
Red Rooster Provincial, soup tureen.............................100.00
Red Rooster Provincial, teapot...27.50
Red Rooster Provincial, turkey platter............................45.00
Sculptured Daisy, bowl, vegetable; hdls, 8".................20.00

Sculptured Grape teapot, $35.00.

Sculptured Daisy, bowl, w/lid, 9" 35.00
Sculptured Daisy, coffeepot 40.00
Sculptured Daisy, creamer & sugar bowl 8.00
Sculptured Daisy, cup & saucer 7.50
Sculptured Daisy, mug, coffee 12.00
Sculptured Daisy, pitcher, 6" 30.00
Sculptured Daisy, pitcher, 9" 45.00
Sculptured Daisy, platter, 14" 28.00
Sculptured Daisy, shakers, pr 12.50
Sculptured Daisy, teapot 40.00
Sculptured Daisy, tumbler, 5¼" 12.50

Mettlach

In 1836 Nicholas Villeroy and Eugene Francis Boch, both of whom were already involved in the potting industry, formed a partnership and established a stoneware factory in an old restored abbey in Mettlach, Germany. Decorative stoneware with in-mold relief was their specialty, steins in particular. Through constant experimentation, they developed innovative methods of decoration. One process, called chromolith, involved inlaying colorful mosaic designs into the body of the ware. Later, underglaze printing from copper plates was used. Their stoneware was of high quality, and their steins won many medals at the St. Louis Expo and early World's Fairs. Most examples are marked with an incised castle and the name 'Mettlach.' The numbering system indicates size, date, stock number, and decorator. Production was halted by a fire in 1921 – the factory was not rebuilt.

Our advisor for this category is Ron Fox; he is listed in the Directory under New York.

Key:
L — liter   PUG — print under glaze
POG — print over glaze   tl — thumb lift

#1005, stein, relief, cavaliers, ½-L, M 275.00
#1032, coaster, PUG, 4¾", 6 for..525.00
#1044/264, plaque, PUG, Lohengrin, tiny rear flake, 17" 385.00
#1062, stein, glazed, mosaic, Pilsner shape, base rpr, ½-L..............440.00
#1068, stein, glazed, mosaic, ½-L, M...355.00
#1098, stein, Westerwald style, 1-L, M 440.00
#112, tray, PUG, man & barmaid, 18x12", M 385.00
#1154, stein, etched, hunters, 1-L, M 550.00
#1161, stein, etched, women & shields, crown lid, 7-L, EX 3,000.00
#1222, stein, glazed, mosaic, ½-L, M...350.00
#1300, stein, relief, brewery symbols, ½-L, M...............................380.00
#1403, stein, etched, bowling, ½-L, M..465.00
#1425, plaque, etched, woman w/plumed hat, 15½", M 800.00
#1474, plaque, etched, woman, 16x10½", M 2,100.00
#1526, stein, appl brass shield, shooting club award, 1-L 240.00
#1526, stein, enameled, dbl crest, ½-L, M...................................385.00
#1570, stein, glazed, mosaic, ½-L, M...350.00
#1608, compote, etched, harvest, 13", M....................................850.00
#1675, stein, etched, Heidelberg, ½-L, M....................................465.00
#1695, stein, etched, hunters, rabbit tl, ½-L, M 635.00
#1723, stein, etched, scene, Abbey inlay, ½-L, M.................... 1,700.00
#1769/#1770, plaques, Wilhelm Tell & Winkelried, 14½", pr. 4,300.00
#1786, stein, etched/glazed, St Florian, dragon tl, 1-L, M............900.00
#1819, stein, etched, masonic, ½-L, M 855.00
#1893, stein, etched, mosaic, 1-L, M 525.00
#1909, stein, PUG, Yale University, minor flakes, ½-L 385.00
#1909/1097, stein, PUG, drunks & night watchman, ½-L, M 275.00
#1909/1181, stein, PUG, young couple, ½-L, M 415.00
#1909/677, stein, PUG, 3 women talking, ½-L, M........................275.00
#1909/979, stein, PUG, Blk children in school, ½-L, M..............525.00
#1909/983, stein, PUG, Fallstaff, ½-L, M....................................300.00
#1932, stein, etched, cavaliers, ½-L, M.......................................550.00
#1999, stein, etched, men drinking, ½-L, M................................415.00
#2001K, stein, book, banking & commerce, ½-L, M 465.00
#2003, stein, etched, cavaliers, ½-L, M.......................................525.00
#2027, stein, etched, Gambrinus, band flake, 1-L 687.00
#2027, stein, etched, Gambrinus, minor flake rprs, ½-L..............525.00
#2030, stein, etched, military, ½-L, M..715.00
#2051, stein, etched, fraternal dueling students, ½-L, M 600.00
#2052, stein, etched, Munich child, ¼-L, M 495.00
#2082, stein, etched, Wilhelm Tell, ½-L, M............................ 1,155.00

#2083, stein, etched, boar hunt, .3-L, M......................................880.00
#2090, stein, etched, club scene, orig pewter lid, 1-L, M 500.00
#2093, stein, etched, cards, ½-L, M 635.00
#2103, stein, etched, cavalier, 1½-L, M......................................795.00
#2105, stein, etched, cavalier, ½-L, M..770.00
#2127, vase, etched, cherubs, minor chips, 12", pr......................770.00
#2140/881, stein, PUG, 10 Field Artl Hannover, ½-L, M...........525.00
#2143, plaque, etched, Von Moltke, 15", M 900.00
#2176, stein, etched, table scene, 1-L, M 660.00
#2192, stein, etched, Greek scene, ½-L, M..................................800.00
#2204, stein, color relief, Imperial eagle, 1-L, M 990.00
#2205, stein, etched, hunters, squirrel inlay lid, 5-L, NM 1,430.00
#22187, plaque, etched, Hohenzollern, chip on bk rim, 17" ... 2,090.00
#2227/900, stein, PUG, military, inlay lid, 4-L, NM................ 1,595.00
#2235, stein, etched, targets & barmaid, music box, ½-L, M.......700.00
#2255, stein, etched, wedding scene, 1-L, M........................... 1,100.00
#2263, stein, relief, cavaliers, ½-L, M 385.00
#2327, beaker, enameled, dueling fraternal crest, ¼-L, M...........160.00
#2327/427, beaker, PUG, Berlin, ¼-L, M 88.00
#2327/6137, beaker, Rookwood-style cavalier, ¼-L, NM............200.00
#2383, stein, etched, Diogenes, 4-L, M 2,860.00

Steins: #2065, inlaid lid, jeweled base, signed Schlitt, 2.4-L, $850.00 ; #1143, print under glaze, 1-L, 300.00.

#2388, stein, pretzel body & hdl, ½-L, M 330.00
#2391, stein, etched, Lohengrin, ½-L, M 660.00
#2401, stein, etched, cavalier & maid, ½-L, M 685.00
#2433, jug, etched, Art Nouveau, 8½", M...................................200.00
#2474, vase, etched, integral hdls, 3", M....................................195.00
#2482, stein, etched, target shooting, 1½-L, NM 880.00
#2484, plaque, etched, knight, 11½", M 495.00
#2504, vase, etched, Nouveau florals, base flakes, 9" 110.00
#2526, stein, relief/glazed, Kruessen style, chip rpr, 1-L 1,200.00
#2580, stein, etched, knights at castle, 1-L, M 900.00
#2581, stein, etched, singing women, ½-L, M 550.00
#2583, stein, etched, Egyptian, 1-L, M 1,430.00
#2583, stein, etched, Egyptian, ½-L, M................................... 1,020.00
#2585, stein, etched/color relief, Munich, ½-L, M......................495.00

#2585, stein, etched/color relief, 1-L, M **795.00**
#2635, stein, etched, woman bicyclist, ½-L, M **685.00**
#2640, stein, etched, cavalier & barmaid, ½-L, M **465.00**
#2690, stein, etched, cavaliers, 1½-L, M....................................**825.00**
#2717, stein, etched/glazed, target, sm chip rpr, 1-L **2,300.00**
#2718, stein, etched/glazed, David & Goliath, 1-L, M **2,530.00**
#2718, stein, etched/glazed, David & Goliath, ½-L, M **1,650.00**
#2749, plaque, etched, country church, 20", M **825.00**
#2755, stein, cameo, drinking scenes, ½-L, M **855.00**
#2764, stein, etched, knight on horse, inlay lid, 5-L, M **6,000.00**
#2775/1014, beaker, PUG, Munich child, ½-L, M......................**325.00**
#2775/1032, beaker, PUG, dwarfs, ½-L, M **235.00**
#2778, stein, etched, carnival scene, base flake, ½-L **850.00**
#2778, stein, etched, carnival scene, 1-L, M...........................**1,125.00**
#2778, stein, etched, carnival scene, ¼-L, NM **175.00**
#2780, stein, etched, mandolin player, 1-L, M **635.00**
#2788/6133, stein, Rookwood-type cavalier, ½-L, M **385.00**
#280, stein, enameled, fraternal crest, ½-L, M...........................**355.00**
#280C, stein, enameled, fraternal crest, ½-L, M **525.00**
#2801, stein, etched, Art Nouveau, 2½-L, M..............................**465.00**
#2811, stein, etched, Art Nouveau, ½-L, M................................**465.00**
#2829, stein, color relief, Rodenstein, inlay lid, ½-L, M..........**1,760.00**
#2833C, stein, etched, river scene, ½-L, M.................................**495.00**
#2835, stein, etched, men leave castle, turret lid, 3-L, EX.......**1,800.00**
#2844, stein, etched, farmer, ½-L, M.......................................**1,100.00**
#2869, stein, glazed relief, Munich, lion/shield lid, 3-L **3,400.00**
#2871, stein, etched, Cornell University, 1-L, M **900.00**
#2893/1290B, stein, PUG, Wurttemburg, 3-L, M.......................**465.00**
#2913, vase, etched, Nouveau florals at shoulders, 14", M **465.00**
#2938, stein, etched, hunter, base chip rpr, ½-L **355.00**
#2963, ash tray, etched, Nouveau florals, 6", M.........................**265.00**
#2990, tray, etched, 3-ftd, flake, 11" **150.00**
#3054, plate, etched, geometric decor, 6½", M............................**40.00**
#3090, stein, etched, guitarist, hdl chip rpr, 1-L **685.00**
#3091, stein, etched, drinking knight, flake, 1-L **825.00**
#3091, stein, etched, drinking knight, ½-L, M...........................**715.00**
#3099, stein, etched, Diogenes, 3½-L, M **1,540.00**
#3166, plaque, etched, Lohengrin, 17", M **1,200.00**
#3183, plaque, etched, Hohkonigsburg, 17", M **1,155.00**
#3225/1290, plaque, PUG, United States shield form, crazing **525.00**
#3321, cup & saucer, etched, Art Nouveau, M............................**120.00**
#3339, candlesticks, etched, Art Nouveau, sm chips, 8", pr.........**220.00**
#3344, stein, POG, students duel, inlay crest lid, ½-L, M...........**550.00**
#3363, bowl, etched, Nouveau florals, w/lid, 8x9½" **345.00**
#385, stein, enameled, fraternal crest, ½-L, M............................**465.00**
#4504, humidor, etched, Art Nouveau, lid rpr, 6½" **315.00**
#5013/5013, stein, faience, Rothenburg, dk crazing, 1-L..............**550.00**
#5013/5395, stein, Delft-type couple dancing, ½-L, M **965.00**
#5013/5444, stein, faience, chimney sweep, ½-L, M **965.00**
#5019/5030, stein, faience, Bayreuth, 1-L, M...........................**1,210.00**
#5019/5393, stein, faience, hunter, 1-L, M..............................**1,760.00**
#5020/5020, stein, faience type, Munich, 2½-L, M.....................**825.00**
#5022/5022, stein, faience, medallions, 1-L, M.......................**1,100.00**
#5230, plaque, relief, Delft-type cavalier/barmaid, 26x18" **4,500.00**
#7054/#7055, plaques, cameo, children, oval, 9", NM, pr............**525.00**

Midwestern Glass

As early as 1814, blown glass was made in Ohio. By 1835 glasshouses in Michigan were producing similar pattern-molded types that have long been highly regarded by collectors. During the latter part of the 19th century, all six of the states of the Northwest Territory were mass-producing the pressed glass tableware patterns that were then in vogue. Various types of art glass were produced in the area until after the turn of the century. Items listed here are attributed to the Midwest by certain physical characteristics known to be indigenous to that part of the country. See also Findlay Onyx; Greentown Glass; Libbey; Zanesville Glass.

Bottle, club, aqua, wear, 7⅝" **100.00**
Bottle, club, bright aqua, right swirl, collared mouth, 8"............**200.00**
Bottle, globular, amber, appl lip, some wear/sickness, 3½" **550.00**
Bottle, globular, aqua, 18-rib, appl collar, pontil, 7" **195.00**
Bottle, pocket; lt gr, 12-dmn, wide sheared mouth, 6", NM **150.00**
Bowl, 20-dmn, appl bl rim, solid base w/rough pontil, 4" **325.00**
Flask, chestnut; clear, 16 swirled ribs, 6" **135.00**
Flask, poison; yel-gr, lg raised dmns, flat collar, 4¾" **500.00**
Jug, amber, appl lip/hdl, int residue, 5" **525.00**
Jug, bright red-amber, 24-rib swirl w/popcorn effect, 6"..........**15,000.00**
Jug, puce, solid hdl w/curl, flat sloping collar, ovoid, 6" **210.00**
Jug, red amber, appl solid hdl w/curl, globular, trn lip, 5".........**1,600.00**
Paperweight, gold-amber, solid free-formed bird on dome, 2¾" ...**130.00**
Plate, lacy, floral center, octagonal, 5", NM **50.00**

Militaria

Because of the wide and varied scope of items available to collectors of militaria, most tend to concentrate mainly on the area or areas that interest them most or that they can afford to buy. Some items represent a major investment and because of their value have been reproduced. Extreme caution should be used when purchasing Nazi items. Every badge, medal, cap, uniform, dagger, and sword that Nazi Germany issued is being reproduced today. Some repros are crude and easily identified as fakes, while others are very well done and difficult to recognize as reproductions. Purchases from WWII veterans are usually your safest buys. Reputable dealers or collectors will normally offer a money-back guarantee on Nazi items purchased from them. There are a number of excellent Third Reich reference books available in bookstores at very reasonable prices. Study them to avoid losing a much larger sum spent on a reproduction.

Our advisor for this category is Ron Willis; he is listed in the Directory under Oklahoma.

Imperial German

Badge, Bavarian Aviation Observer, silver, 3-pc, EX...................**500.00**
Badge, wound; Kriegsmarine, gold, hollow stamped type, EX **60.00**
Bayonet, butcher; WWI, blued steel blade, 19½", +scabbard.........**48.00**
Buckle, Army, brass w/brass center, crown & motto **24.00**
Buckle, WWI, brass, 2-pc, EX **22.50**
Buckle, WWI, stamped steel, field gray pnt, 1-pc, EX....................**17.50**
Buckle, 1890-1910 Fireman, brass w/orig blk leather belt **48.00**
Cocard, helmet; Kurassiere, early pattern, 67mm, EX **28.00**
Flag, battle; eagle/gold crown/cross in corner, 60x90", VG **145.00**
Grenade, WWI, oyster type, inert, lt rust, scarce **38.00**
Grenade, WWI, wood hdl, steel head, EX **75.00**
Hat band, Navy, gilt wire Bevo-type embr on blk, EX....................**24.00**
Helmet, spike; Prussian, blk leather body, VG **100.00**
Helmet, WWI, M-16, missing liner, EX..**38.00**
Hemlet, WWI, Army, M-16, camo steel, w/liner, EX....................**120.00**
Matchbox holder, WWI, brass, crown buckle center, 2¼x1½" **12.00**
Medal, Baden 1907 Verdienst, wht metal, Fur Verdienst on bk.....**22.00**
Medal, Bavaria War, Mcrit Cross, 3rd Class, bronze, EX **28.00**
Medal, Franco-Prussian War, combatant, gilt bronze......................**18.00**
Medal, Iron Cross, 1st Class, domed, screwbk, complete..............**135.00**

Medal, Iron Cross, 2nd Class, no ribbon, EX 30.00
Medal, Kaiser Wilhelm Commemorative & Jubilee, bronze bust.... 8.00
Medal, pre-WWI, Baden Golden Erinnerungzeichen, cutouts........90.00
Medal, Wurttemburg Bravery & Loyalty, silver, Whilhem II 37.50
Medal, WWI, Oldenburg Friedrich August Cross, 2nd Class, EX..32.00
Medallion, WWI, gray metal, soldier silhouette, 1¾" dia..............18.00
Service bar, Landwehr 2nd Class, crossed swords, 1842-1913 ....14.00
Shoulderboards, Lieutenant, silver w/blk, slip-on, pr 30.00
Stein, Bavarian, 4th infantry regiment, ½-liter, EX 350.00
Stein, crockery, Naval, dtd 1908, 1-liter, EX 900.00
Tunic, pre-WWI, dress bl w/red, shoulderboards, EX 165.00

Third Reich

Armband, Wermacht, gold & orange w/embr, EX........................20.00
Armband, WWII, Hilfspolizei, blk silkscreen on wht, EX.............15.00

Armband, Hitler Youth, 4¼" x 6", $30.00.

Badge, Air Force ground combat, silver wreath, mk MUK5, EX..180.00
Badge, driver proficiency; WWII, gilt, oak leaves/wheel, EX 25.00
Badge, flak; Luftwaffe, NP silver, wreath/eagle/gun, Juncker........165.00
Badge, pin; WWII, Submarine, gilt, wreath/eagle, horizontal......135.00
Badge, sleeve; pre-WWI, Artillery Shooting, wreath/cannons 120.00
Badge, WWII, Hitler Youth Marksmanship, SP/enamel, EX 78.00
Badge, WWII, Kriegsmarine Auxiliary Cruiser, gilt wash, 2-pc 98.00
Badge, WWII, Kriegsmarine U-Boat Officer, flat gold bullion.......50.00
Badge, WWII, Luftwaffe Ground Combat, 1-pc, pot metal type....48.00
Banner, Hitler Youth, cloth, diamond/swastika, 24x40", NM 65.00
Bar, close combat; WWII, bronze, grenade/bayonet/eagle, EX.......90.00
Bayonet, WWII, K-98, Bakelite grips, +scabbard/leather frog 40.00
Book, Gegen England, plane/sub on cover, 1939, EX 45.00
Book, Mein Kampf, bl cover w/eagle/swastika, 1934, VG 95.00
Book, Mein Kampf, soft bound, 1933, VG..................................45.00
Book, Mein Kampf, Wedding edition, 1941, EX 145.00
Breech cover, WWII, Luftwaffe Paratrooper, K-98, canvas, EX 68.00
Buckle, WWII, Hitler Youth, chromed steel, 2-pc, EX..................20.00
Buckle, WWII, Kriegsmarine, aluminum, 2-pc, EX.....................24.00
Buckle, WWII, RAD, aluminum, Assmann, 1-pc, EX....................27.50
Canister, WWII, Bakelite, for 6 pistol flares, 4½x3¼"..................22.00
Canteen, WWII, Wehrmacht, Bakelite cup, w/strap, EX................28.00
Cap, over seas, WWII, Afrikakorps, eagle/cocard, red liner, EX 88.00
Cap, WWII, Luftwaffe, M-43, winter style, EX 88.00
Case, map; Wehrmacht, brn leather, pebbled finish, EX 36.00
Chevron, WWII, Kriegsmarine Able Seaman, gold braid on bl 5.00
Collar tab, WWII, Luftwaffe Flak Colonel, gull/wreath, pr 38.00

Collar tab, WWII, Luftwaffe Flying Personel, yel w/gull, pr..........24.00
Collar tab, WWII, Luftwaffe Lieutenant, gr, pr 24.00
Dagger, Army, SP fittings, wht hdl, Soligen, EX.........................200.00
Dagger, Luftwaffe, 1st type, NP/silver, gold swastikas, EX...........300.00
Dagger, Luftwaffe, 2nd type, wire wrap/wht grip, Horster.............200.00
Dog tag, WWII, Wehrmacht, blank, unissued, NM 12.00
Field pack, WWII, Wehrmacht, cowhide bk flap, mk/dtd, EX.......38.00
Flag, podium; swastika, wht border w/fringe, 40x39", EX.............78.00
Flag, SS Panzer, red/blk w/gold eagle/swastika/skull, 19x13" 25.00
Flag, WWII, red wool, blk swastika in wht circle, 30x55", EX.......70.00
Fork, mess; WWII, RAD, aluminum, mk ESM42, EX 7.00
Helmet, WWII, Fire Police, w/comb, orig decals, NM 90.00
Helmet, WWII, Luftschutz Gladiator, 3-pc style, NM...................78.00
Jacket, drill; WWII, Waffen SS, gr herringbone twill, EX.............90.00
Kit, rifle cleaning, WWII, Waffenampt, M-98, EX.......................18.00
Knife, pocket; WWII, Wehrmacht Swiss Army style, mk, EX 45.00
Knife, WWII, Hitler Youth, Solingen, +scabbard.........................75.00
Medal, Austrian Occupation, w/pin-bk ribbon, NM in case 48.00
Medal, Iron Cross, 1st Class, heavy silver, #800, VG 75.00
Medal, Italian Afrika Campaign, bronze, w/ribbon, EX.................48.00
Medal, Russian Front, rpl ribbon, EX 16.00
Medal, 18-year service; Police, silver, Maltese cross, EX................80.00
Medal, 25-Yr Faithful Service, SP metal/blk enamel, EX 22.50
Pennant, Hitler Youth, diamond/swastika/stripe, 6x10", NM 28.00
Photo, Hitler in uniform, #218, Berlin, 9½x6¾" 20.00
Pin, Nazi party membership, rnd, enamel, swastika center, EX 15.00
Radio, WWII, Luftwaffe, FM, AC/DC, dbl doors, 12x7x18", EX...95.00
Saber knot, WWII, Army NCO, gray leather & aluminum, NM ..14.00
Scarf, WWII, Wehrmacht, gray wool w/blk fringe, EX...................15.00
Shoulderboards, WWII, Luftwaffe Flak, red on bl-gray, pr 22.00
Shoulderboards, WWII, RAD Obertruppfuhrer, brn wool, pr........27.50
Sweater, WWII, Wehrmacht, gray wool w/gr stripe at collar 27.50
Sword, Police, eng, nickel fittings, eagle grip, Soligen, EX 925.00
Tunic, WWII, Army Strabzahmeister Service officer, EX 148.00
Tunic, WWII, Waffen SS Assault Gunner, Panzer cut, brn wool.745.00

Japanese

Badge, Reserve, gilt star, anchor/Xd swords, lg, EX.........................18.00
Badge, WWII, Army Field Artillery Observer, gilt mum/rams 75.00
Badge, WWII, Army General's College Graduation, silver oval..145.00
Bayonet frog, WWII, brn leather w/buckle & strap, EX 7.50
Blanket, WWII, Army, tan wool, issue tag, EX.............................36.00
Bowl, rice; WWII, wood, 4" dia, +pr wood chopsticks, EX 32.00
Breeches, WWII, Army, wool, 3-pocket, drawstring ankles, EX 22.00
Cap, field; WWII, Army officer, olive-drab wool, yel star 40.00
Cape, WWII, Army officer, olive-drab wool, Manchuria, EX 45.00
Chevrons, WWII, Police, Bevo-type embr wht mum on yel, pr 5.00
Collar tab, Army Private, olive drab wool, pr 8.00
Collar tab, WWII, Fire Police Commander, mums/gold braid, pr ..12.00
Flag, WWII, Army style, Rising Sun, red silk, 20x26", NM...........40.00
Hat, visor; WWII, Army, red band/piping, gilt star, VG 30.00
Helmet, post-WWII, Self-Defense Forces, steel, EX 32.00
Helmet, WWII, Army, steel, EX pnt 60.00
Helmet, WWII, Navy Landing Forces, no liner, VG......................75.00
Jacket, WWII, Navy officer, wht, brass anchor buttons, EX 40.00
License, driver's; WWII, Navy, w/photo, 2-pg, EX 24.00
Medal, WWII, Killed in Action, for next of kin, wht metal 15.00
Medal, WWII, Red Cross Ladies' Auxiliary, aluminum w/ribbon ..22.50
Rucksack, WWII, Navy Landing Forces, lt brn canvas, EX...........75.00
Sandals, WWII, tropics, olive-drab web strap, brn leather, pr 42.50
Shell casing, WWII, for 37mm cannon, brass, dtd '44, EX............20.00
Tunic, Army, tropics, khaki, Sergeant Major collartabs, NM.........40.00

Tunic, WWII, Army, M-1938, olive-drab wool, 4-pocket, EX **44.00**
Wing, WWII, Pilot, silver wire, yel wreath/gold star, NM.............**35.00**
Wings, WWII, Army Pilot, flat embr aluminum wire, ¾", pr.........**27.50**

United States

Bag, B4; WWII, Air Force Flyer, waterproof....................................**48.00**
Bag, duffel; WWII, Navy, olive-drab canvas, dtd 1944, EX............**10.00**
Belt, cartridge; WWII, M-2, 10-pocket, olive-drab canvas, EX......**22.00**
Belt plate, Civil War Confederate, Texas Lone Star, rare.............**450.00**
Bible, pocket; WWII, Army Air Corps, 3x4", EX **15.00**
Book, WWII, Army Songs, soft cover, 1941, 61-pg, EX **4.00**
Bracelet, WWII, Army Air Corps Pilot, sterling, sq links **38.00**
Breeches, riding; Army, zinc buttons/lace-up calves, '30s, EX **12.00**
Buckle, belt; Civil War, Confederate Navy, cast metal, 2" **48.00**
Canteen, Spanish-American War, missing strap, VG....................**20.00**
Canteen, WWII, Army, olive-drab canvas cover, w/cup, EX **12.50**
Cap, forage; bl wool w/gold braid, 1870s, EX................................**195.00**
Cap, overseas; Veterans of WWI Assoc, red/wht/bl, EX **5.00**
Chair, camp; Civil War officer, folds, cherry wood/carpet **145.00**
Cigarette case, WWII, Army officer, tooled leather cover, EX.......**15.00**
Epaulettes, WWII, Army Medical Corps Lt Colonel, dress bl, pr .**32.00**
Flag, WWI, Son in Service, red/wht/bl wool, 15x24", EX..............**12.00**
Flashlight, WWII, angle head, olive drab, TL-122D, EX **6.00**
Gas mask, WWI, Marine Corps, complete w/canister, rare, NM ...**75.00**
Goggles, WWII, variable sensity, for gunners, w/canister, NM.......**18.00**
Handkerchief, WWII, GI, olive-drab cotton, NM **5.00**
Hat, campaign; WWI, Marine Corps emblem **65.00**
Hat, campaign; WWII, Marine Corps, bronze globe/anchor, EX ...**30.00**
Hat, visor; WWII, Air Force Pilot's 50th Mission, khaki, EX **48.00**
Hat, visor; WWII, Marine Corps, dress gr cover, EX.....................**30.00**
Helmet, diving; WWII, bronze/copper, dtd 1941, EX **545.00**
Helmet, Kevlar, camo cover, modern, NM **125.00**
Helmet, pith; WWII, Army, tan cloth cover, w/liner, EX **32.00**
Holster, WWII, Army, 45 automatic, brn leather, Sears, EX **12.00**
Inkwell, WWII, Navy, glass, contract #/lot #, NM......................**12.50**
Jacket, combat; WWII, Marine Corps, herringbone, early, EX **25.00**
Jacket, WWII, Paratrooper, 4 slant pockets, EX **300.00**
Kepi, WWI, sky bl, grenade side buttons, gold strap, VG...............**65.00**
Kit, shaving; WWI, Army, olive-drab case, complete, NM............**15.00**
Knife, bloodletting; Civil War, bone hdl, rare **30.00**
Knife, WWII, Navy Mark 1, Camillus NY, 5" blade.....................**50.00**
Leggings, WWI, Army officer, brn leather, NM............................**15.00**
Letter opener, WWI, cast metal, rifle form, EX **10.00**
Life belt, WWII, M-26, inflates manually, 2-tube, EX...................**20.00**
Life preserver, WWII, Army Air Force Aviator, Mae West...........**55.00**
Log, WWII, Army Air Force Navigator, form #21A-1, 20x26", EX. **5.00**
Manual, WWII, Army Air Corps, ID of Aircraft, 145-pg, EX........**12.50**
Manual, WWII, War Dept, Browning Automatic Rifle, 225-pg **15.00**
Mask, oxygen; Army Air Force, A-14, sealed in bag, M.................**55.00**
Medal, WWII, Army Distinguished Service, gilt metal, NM.........**75.00**
Medal of Honor, Vietnam War, Air Force, w/neck ribbon, NM **300.00**
Microphone, WWII, Air Force Aviator, w/chest pack control **48.00**
Parka, WWII, snow camo, M-1943, EX...**36.00**
Pouch, WWII, Browning automatic rifle ammunition, mk/dtd, EX. **5.00**
Ring, WWII, Coast Gard, sterling, emblem/eagle, EX **20.00**
Shirt, fatigue; WWII, Air Force Colonel, sateen cotton **12.00**
Shirt, WWII, Army Sergeant, olive-drab wool, chevrons, EX **12.50**
Suspenders, ammo belt; WWII, olive-drab web, EX, pr **5.00**
Telephone, field; WWII, Army, complete, pr **45.00**
Tunic, WWI, winter wool, US collar/Signal Corps disks, EX **45.00**
Tunic, WWII, Army Air Corps Cadet, all insignias+patch, EX.....**22.50**
Tunic, WWII, Navy Aviator officer, dress bl, EX...........................**32.00**

Tunic, WWII, Navy Chief Radioman, dress bl, EX **24.00**
Tunic & pants, Vietnam War, Marine Corps officer, dress bl **70.00**
Uniform, WWI, Army, summer, 4-pc, EX.....................................**65.00**
Uniform, WWII, Marine Corps, lady's, 4-pc, NM **75.00**

Other Types

Australia, beret, WWII, Military Forces, bl w/brass badge **18.00**
Austria, medal, 1873 General Campaign, gilt bronze, EX **18.00**
British, beret, post-WWII, RAF, bl-gray, w/badge.........................**12.50**
British, medal, Baltic, 1854-1855, w/ribbon, EX............................**90.00**
British, wing, WWII, RAF Pilot, King's Crown I........................... **7.50**
British, WWII, Atlantic Star, NM **18.00**
Canada, wing, modern, Air Force Pilot, gilt metal/enamel, M.......**12.50**
Cuba, jacket & pants, Angola & Grenada, Army camo, EX **95.00**
Egypt, wing, Nassar period, Pilot, silver, 3-star shield, M **32.00**
Egypt, wing, WWII, Paratrooper, 4th Class, wht metal, EX...........**12.50**
France, haversack, WWI, red-tan canvas, w/strap, EX **15.00**
France, medal, Dardanelles Expedition, bronzed metal, NM..........**22.00**
France, medal, WWI, Cross of Combattant Volontaire, M **12.00**
France, overcoat, WWII, army, wool, no shoulderboards, EX **25.00**
Iran, wing, Shah of Iran period, gilt & wht metal, NM **12.00**
Italy, breeches, WWII, Artillery officer, gray w/blk/yel, EX **55.00**
Italy, tunic, WWII, 4-pocket, lined wool, EX **88.00**
Oman, wing, Paratrooper, silver & gold wire embr on bl, M **17.50**
S Africa, beret, Army Infantry, gi, Nat'l colors enamel bar **32.00**
Switzerland, hat, visor; WWI, Army officer, gray, EX...................**30.00**
Turkey, badge, WWII, Parachutist, wht metal, chute/star, M.........**10.00**
United Nations, wing, Pilot, gilt/enamel, UN emblem, M.............**32.00**

Milk Glass

Milk glass is the current collector's name for milk-white opaque glass. The early glassmaker's term was Opal Ware. Originally attempted in England in the 18th century with the intention of imitating china, milk glass was not commercially successful until the mid-1800s. Pieces produced in the U.S.A., England, and France during the 1870-1900 period are highly prized for their intricate detail and fiery, opalescent edges. Opaque glass produced in colors is often referred to as 'blue milk glass,' etc. See also Animal Dishes with Covers; Bread Plates; Historical Glass; Vallerysthal; Westmoreland.

Bowl, Daisy, mc enamelling, Challinor, 8" **75.00**
Bowl, florals, emb/HP, rtcl rim, 1880, 4½x8" **250.00**
Bowl, fruit; floral center, lattice edge, ftd **25.00**
Bowl, lacy edge, Atterbury, 2¾x10" **28.00**
Bowl, Tree of Life, crimped, 4x8" **55.00**
Box, 3 kittens, EX pnt, sq, 3½" **35.00**
Butter dish, Melon w/Leaf & Net, Atterbury................................**75.00**
Butter dish, Wild Iris, gold decor...**55.00**
Cake stand, Hand, 11-point star, Atterbury..................................**125.00**
Compote, Atlas, scalloped rim, Atterbury **100.00**
Compote, Jenny Lind, 7½"...**55.00**
Compote, lattice edge, basketweave, Atterbury, 7x8¼" **65.00**
Compote, latticework, blossoms/gr leaves, ftd, Atterbury, 7" H **85.00**
Covered dish, Baby Moses, cattail base, unmk 6½" **225.00**
Covered dish, Baby Moses, mk McKee, 5½" **850.00**
Creamer & sugar bowl, pheasant, w/lid **55.00**
Dish, covered; battleship, L-466, EX orig gilt, 8" L........................**75.00**
Dish, covered; drum, cannon finial, L-147, 4" dia, EX....................**60.00**
Dish, covered; log cabin, orig held mustard, orig pnt/label.............**95.00**
Dish, covered; Pope Leon XIII **100.00**
Dish, covered; sleigh, lg **90.00**

Dish, pin; fleur-de-lis shape, tinted rim **14.00**
Jar, Dutch girl mc/gold in raised panel on lid, sq, 3" **18.00**
Match holder, dog in house **20.00**
Match holder, Indian's head, 5x3¾" **130.00**
Pitcher, fish, Atterbury, 7" **200.00**
Pitcher, tankard; Scroll, att Atterbury, 12" **110.00**
Plate, Anchor & Belaying Pin **30.00**
Plate, Columbus, 1491-1892, lattice border, 9½" **45.00**
Plate, Eagle, Flag, & Star **30.00**
Plate, Easter Bunny & Egg **60.00**
Plate, Fan & Circle, 8" **15.00**
Plate, Fleur-de-Lis, dtd **35.00**
Plate, Frank Bros **45.00**
Plate, Indian, lacy edge **65.00**
Plate, lattice edge, enameled florals, 10" **60.00**
Plate, Marine border **40.00**
Plate, Owl Lovers, 7½" **50.00**
Plate, Rabbit & Horseshoe, EX pnt, 7½" **40.00**
Plate, Rock of Ages **145.00**
Plate, Scroll & Eye Variant, flower center **35.00**
Plate, US Battleship Maine transfer, Club & Shell border **30.00**
Plate, Yacht & Anchor **25.00**
Plate, 3 bears, 7¼" **30.00**
Plate, 3 kittens, orig gold **35.00**
Plate, 3 owls, gold trim, dtd **35.00**
Plate, 3 puppies w/squirrel **95.00**
Sugar bowl, Tree of Life, Challinor, w/lid **75.00**
Tray, pinwheel w/leaves, ftd, 2½x10½" dia **60.00**
Tumbler, emb Dutch boy w/wagon, 6" **15.00**

Millefiori

Millefiori was a type of art glass produced during the late 1800s. Literally, the term means 'thousand flowers,' an accurate description of its appearance. Canes, fused bundles of multicolored glass threads such as are often used in paperweights, were cut into small cross sections, arranged in the desired pattern, refired, and shaped into articles such as cruets, lamps, and novelty items. It is still being produced, and many examples found on the market today are of fairly recent manufacture. See also Paperweights.

Cruet, 6" **125.00**
Lamp, table; mushroom shade, dbl-gourd base, 18" **325.00**

Sugar shaker, 5", $200.00.

Pitcher, tricorner, 2¾" **135.00**
Spittoon, lady's, ruffled, 6" dia **60.00**
Tea set, child's, wht on cobalt, pot, cr/sug, 6 c/s **250.00**
Toothpick holder, hat form **50.00**
Tumbler, bl ground, 4" **125.00**
Vase, slim neck, appl hdls, 4" **125.00**

Miniatures

There is some confusion as to what should be included in a listing of miniature collectibles. Some feel the only true miniature is the salesman's sample; other collectors consider certain small-scale children's toys to be appropriately referred to as miniatures, while yet others believe a miniature to be any small-scale item that gives evidence to the craftsmanship of its creator. For salesman's samples, see specific category; other types are listed below. See also Dollhouses and Furnishings; Children's Things.

Ranking at the top of today's leading collectibles, scaled 1:12" miniatures represent the work of hundreds of artisans who supply local shops with highly prized one-of-a-kind articles and specialties, all scaled one inch to the foot. Many leading producers and distributors of collectibles have entered the field as well. Clubs for miniature enthusiasts have sprung up throughout the United States, Canada, and abroad. Authority Lillian Baker has compiled a lovely book, *Creative and Collectible Miniatures*, with many full-color photos; you will find her address in the Directory under California.

Mahogany chests of drawers, late 1800s: 16½" x 16", $900.00; 17" x 11", $700.00.

Andirons, CI, worn pnt, 3½" **75.00**
Armchair, English Windsor fan-bk, mk SK, 1900s, 12" **150.00**
Bed warmer, brass, wooden hdl, 9" **100.00**
Blanket chest, cherry w/tan pnt, w/scrollwork, 14½", EX **250.00**
Blanket chest, pine, EX detail, trn ft, 1800s, 10" L **325.00**
Book, snap-lock scrolls front & bk, 3 leaves, dtd 1896, 1x⅞" **28.00**
Bureau, mahog Empire, ½-columns, 3-drw, 1820s, 13" **325.00**
Cabinet, Provincial style w/ormolu mts, 1890s, 11x13½" **440.00**
Chamberstick, opal glass, ornate hdl, Sandwich, 2" **110.00**
Chest, mahog Hplwht bow front, Fr ft, 5-drw, nailed, 12" **750.00**
Chest, pine, serpentine front, 3 dvtl drw, 12x15", EX **1,000.00**
Cupboard, hanging; oak, molded base/cornice, 1890s, 19" **375.00**
Fire grate, CI, fruit/foliage, unicorn crest, 13" **100.00**
Ice tongs, wrought iron, 7" **30.00**
Mule chest, pine w/brn grpt over orig red, orig hdw, 13x14" **825.00**
Mule chest, rpt pine, bootjack ends, sq nails, 10x12" **275.00**
Rolling pin, blown glass, aqua, 6" L **85.00**

Table, tea; mahog w/line inlay, Mersman label, 5" dia	70.00
Teakettle, copper, gooseneck, brass lid/hdl, handmade, 4"	95.00
Wash set, florals w/gold on lt pk, 7-pc	195.00

Minton

Thomas Minton established his firm in 1793 at Stoke on Trent and within a few years began producing earthenware with blue-printed patterns similar to the ware he had learned to decorate while employed by the Caughley Porcelain Factory. The Willow pattern was one of his most popular. Neither this nor the porcelain made from 1798 to 1805 was marked (except for an occasional number series), making identification often impossible.

After 1805 until about 1816, fine tea services, beehive-shaped honey pots, trays, etc. were hand decorated with florals, landscapes, Imari-type designs, and Neoclassic devices. These were often marked with crossed 'L's. From 1816 until 1823, no porcelain was made. Through the twenties and thirties, the ornamental wares with colorful decoration of applied fruits and florals and figurines in both bisque and enamel were usually left unmarked. As a result, they have been erroneously attributed to other potters. Some of the ware that was marked bears a deliberate imitation of Meissen's crossed swords. From the late twenties through the forties, Minton made a molded stoneware line – mugs, jugs, teapots, etc. – with florals or figures in high relief. These were marked with an embossed scroll with an 'M' in the bottom curve. Fine parian ware was made in the late 1840s, and in the fifties Minton perfected and produced a line of quality majolica for which they gained widespread recognition. During the Victorian era, M.L. Solon decorated pieces in the pate-sur-pate style, often signing his work; these examples are considered to be the finest of their type. After 1862 all wares were marked 'Minton' or 'Mintons,' with an impressed year cipher. See also Majolica; Pate-Sur-Pate.

Plaque, enameled cupids in reserve, signed A. Boullemier, dated 1879, 9" x 14", $1,320.00.

Bowl, parian, water lily relief, ca 1849, +lid/tray	125.00
Cup & saucer, Persian Rose	40.00
Figurine, sitting dog, #1978, ca 1876, life size, 38", NM	7,000.00
Jardiniere, Seccessionist, wht flowers at rim on turq, 13"	900.00
Jardiniere & pedestal, lg floral, squeezebag, 1900, 41"	950.00
Plate, dinner; Persian Rose	38.00
Plate, Melrose, 10½", 12 for	250.00
Plate, salad; Persian Rose	22.00
Vase, Cupid on turq, rtcl neck, dolphin finial, 1873, 10"	1,600.00

Vase, Seccessionist, bl to gr, 4 upright rosette bands, 13"	385.00
Vase, Seccessionist, gr stars at base, wavy neck bands, 5"	240.00
Vase, trees/hills on bl, silver neck/overlay devices, 12"	4,600.00

Mirrors

The first mirrors were made in England in the 13th century of very thin glass backed with lead. Reverse-painted glass mirrors were made in this country as early as the late 1700s and remained popular throughout the next century. The simple hand-painted panel was separated from the mirrored section by a narrow slat, and the frame was either the dark-finished Federal style or the more elegant, often-gilded Sheraton.

Mirrors changed with the style of other furnishings; but whatever type you purchase, as long as the glass sections remain solid, even broken or flaking mirrors are more valued than replaced glass. Careful resilvering is acceptable if excessive deterioration has taken place.

Key:
Chpndl — Chippendale   Hplwht — Hepplewhite
Emp — Empire   QA — Queen Anne
Fed — Federal

Am convex, eagle flanked by dolphins in cvd/gilt crest, 35"	750.00
Am Sheraton over-mantle, gilded, 1920s, 28x78"	325.00
Chpndl, red pnt, fr w/shaped crest & pendant, rprs, 18x9"	1,800.00
Chpndl, shaped/pierced crest w/gilt medallion, orig, 38x20"	1,800.00
Chpndl mahog scroll, gilt liner, cvd/gilt phoenix, 33", VG	475.00
Chpndl mahog scroll, gilt liner/ornament, rpr/rpl, 40x21"	1,650.00
Chpndl mahog scroll, minor damage/old rprs & glass, 20x12"	375.00
Chpndl mahog scroll, molded fr, rpl crest/ears, 30x14"	375.00
Chpndl mahog w/appl gilt eagle, rpl ears, sm	110.00
Chpndl mahog/pine scroll, rpl glass, 17x29", VG	400.00
Chpndl walnut scroll, molded fr, cvd shell, losses/rpl, 37"	475.00
Chpndl-style mahog scroll, reeded fr, rpl glass/rpr, 19x12"	150.00
Co QA walnut on pine, scrolled crest w/1801, 21x11", EX	1,700.00
Courting, shaped mirror-insert crest, rvpt lady, Holland	1,600.00
Emp, half-columns & corner blocks w/brass rosettes, 12x11"	300.00
Emp architectural 2-part gilt fr, rpl rvpt, old mirror, 33"	175.00
Emp mahog/figured veneer, trn/rope-cvg, brass rosettes, 45"	225.00
Emp 2-part w/rvpt scene, gold/blk pnt on trn fr, 26x14"	375.00
Fed architectural mahog 2-part, eagle/floral inlay, 55x28"	3,200.00
Fed giltwood, cornice projects, gesso figural panel, 49"	2,300.00
Fed mahog w/gilt vase in broken ped, rpl glass, 49x21"	6,000.00
Golden oak, beveled glass, sq fr, 30x18"	100.00
Golden oak, floor standing, oval swivel fr	550.00
Golden oak, floor standing, swivel fr, rectangular glass	450.00
Hitchcock-type, half-column, blk/gold pnt, 12½x10½"	80.00
Plateau, beveled glass w/19 cut rosettes, ftd, 18"	185.00
Plateau, SP, emb florals, ball ft, bevelled glass, 10"	25.00
Plateau, SP, ftd gallery, cut-out sides, hdls, 14½"	60.00
Plateau, SP, Rococo border w/flowers, Eureka, 12"	125.00
Plateau, SP, shaped/beaded rim, A Risler & Carre, 23" L	850.00
Plateau, Victorian bronze, 4 fancy ft/scrolled hdls, 14x12"	200.00
QA figured walnut on pine, bird silhouette in crest, 30x14"	650.00
QA rfn pine, scrolled crest, beveled glass, 33x17"	400.00
QA walnut-faced, fancy crest, orig beveled glass, 27"	1,050.00
QA walnut-faced, gilt shell in crest, 1750, 28", EX	1,400.00
Regency pier giltwood, extended cornice w/rvpt ship, 37x18"	1,300.00
Rococo Revival giltwood, ornate crest, columns, 75x71"	1,500.00
Shaving, Hplwht mahog veneer w/inlay, maker's label, 16x15"	200.00
Shaving, mahog, arched beveled glass, scroll cvd ft, 33"	400.00
Shaving, mahog w/ebony inlay, trn bone knobs/ft, 22x21"	400.00

Shaving, walnut, mortised/pinned, beaded edge/shoe ft, 12" 250.00
Sheraton architectural, classic figures/flute cvg, 50" 600.00
Victorian, gold leaf, simple molding, 51x31"................................150.00
Victorian walnut, cvd oval w/leaf garlands, 31x16" 425.00
2-Part, gold/blk pnt trn columns/corner blocks, rvpt, 19" 275.00

Empire, reverse-painted soldier on horseback, American, ca 1830-40, 32" x 15", $500.00.

Mocha

Mocha Ware is a utilitarian pottery made principally in England (and to a lesser extent in France) between 1780 and 1840 on the then prevalent creamware and pearlware bodies. Initially, only those pieces decorated in the seaweed pattern were called 'Mocha,' while geometrically-decorated pieces were referred to as 'Banded Creamware.' Other types of decorations were called 'Dipped Ware.' During the last thirty to forty years the term 'Mocha' has been applied to the entire realm of 'Industrialized Slipware' – pottery decorated by the turner on his lathe using coggle wheels and slip cups.

Mocha was made in numerous patterns – Tree, Seaweed or Dandelion, Rope (also called Worm or Loop), Cat's-eye, Tobacco Leaf, Lollypop or Balloon, Marbled, Marbled and Combed, Twig, Geometric or Checkered, Banded, and slip decorations of rings, dots, flags, tulips, wavy lines, etc. It came into its own as a collectible in the latter half of the 1940s and has become increasingly popular as more and more people are exposed to the rich colorings and artistic appeal of its varied forms of abstract decoration.

The collector should take care not to confuse the early pearlware and creamware Mocha with the later kitchen yellowware, graniteware, and ironstone sporting mocha-type decoration that was produced in America by such potters as J. Vodrey, George S. Harker, Edwin Bennett, and John Bell. This type was also produced in Scotland and Wales and was marketed well into the 20th century.

Bowl, earthworm, late, 4x7½", VG...300.00
Bowl, earthworm on lt bl, brn stripes, 4x9½", EX 425.00
Bowl, earthworm on orange band, bl/wht stripes, 6½", NM 675.00
Bowl, emb geometrics, 4-color stripes, w/lid, 6x7¼", EX 2,000.00
Bowl, 2-row earthworm/emb border, 3¼x6¼", NM.....................800.00
Creamer, bl/wht stripes, late, 4", EX 35.00

Creamer, 4-color marbleized decor, w/strainer spout, 5" 1,000.00
Cup, earthworm in canary/brn/tan, canary int, sgn LL, 3" 700.00
Mug, bands/stripes, emb leaf hdl, hairline, late, 4¾" 70.00
Mug, brn & sanded bands, 3"..190.00
Mug, emb band/bl & mustard bands, leaf hdl, 2½", EX.............225.00
Mug, marbleized band, hairlines, 6"...325.00
Mug, polka-dot rim band on mustard, leaf hdl, 6", VG.............250.00
Mug, seaweed, bl bands, blk stripe, late, prof rpr, 5" 175.00
Mug, seaweed, olive band, bl stripes, Imperial, late, 5", EX 175.00
Mug, seaweed, stripes, emb crown/VR Imperial, late, 6", EX......150.00
Mug, seaweed, 3⅝", NM...325.00
Mug, seaweed on brn w/blk rim, leaf hdl, 4⅝", EX.....................400.00
Mug, seaweed/stripes on tan band, leaf hdl, 3½", EX 350.00
Mug, seaweed/stripes/emb band, leaf hdl, 6", G.........................325.00
Mustard pot, stripes, blk on lt bl, stains/chips, 2x3"...................285.00
Pepper castor, bands/rings, brn/yel/wht, minor wear, 4½" 245.00
Pepper castor, bl bands on wht, 4"...275.00
Pepper castor, seaweed/stripes, broken dome/stains, 4½" 260.00
Pitcher, bl/gray bands/brn stripes, leaf hdl, late, 7½", EX...........200.00
Pitcher, brn lines amid wide bl bands w/wavy lines, 6" 350.00
Pitcher, cat's eyes/stripes, leaf hdl, bulbous, 7", VG....................800.00

Pitcher, tobacco leaves, minor base chips, 9½", $6,000.00. (Pre-auction estimate: $1,500.00 – $2,500.00.)

Pitcher, earthworm, emb leaf hdl, 7¾", VG.................................600.00
Pitcher, earthworm, rpr hdl, 8"...550.00
Pitcher, earthworm/cat's eye bands, emb rim/hdl, 6", VG...........900.00
Pitcher, earthworm/loops on 2 wide bl bands, 6", EX.................550.00
Pitcher, earthworm/stripes, emb leaf hdl, 5", EX 450.00
Pitcher, seaweed, emb foliage spout, stained/chips, 7"................225.00
Pitcher, seaweed on orange w/gr/bl/cream bands, scroll hdl, 6"....700.00
Pitcher, stripes on wht ironstone, late, 5¾", NM 125.00
Salt cellar, bl band/blk stripes, EX...235.00
Salt cellar, emb band/bl & brn stripes, ftd, 3", NM 250.00

Molds

Food molds have become a popular collectible – not only for their value as antiques, but because they also revive childhood memories of elaborate ice cream Santas with candy trim, or barley sugar figurals adorning a Christmas tree. Ice cream molds were made of pewter and came in a wide variety of shapes and styles. Chocolate molds were made in fewer shapes but were more detailed. They were usually made of tin, copper, and occasionally of pewter. Hard candy molds were usually metal, although the primitive maple sugar molds (usually simple hearts, rabbits, and other animals) were carved from wood. Cake molds were made of cast iron or cast aluminum and were most common in the shape of a lamb, a rabbit, or Santa Claus.

Our advisors for this category are Dale and Ruth Van Kuren; they are listed in the Directory under New York.

Chocolate Molds

Alarm clock, much detail	48.00
Ballerina, med	48.00
Basketball	68.00
Bear, walking, lg	235.00
Bell, lg	55.00
Boar, lg	235.00
Boy holding book, 3x2½"	50.00
Bugs Bunny, tin, 2x5¼"	20.00
Bugle	88.00
Bulldog, 3x3"	50.00
Chicken on nest, 6½"	75.00
Cigar, sm	27.50
Clovers, 2 rows on 10x4" tray	48.00
Clown, 4½x2"	12.00
Clown boy w/heart on clothes, 7½x3¾"	62.00
Dog, begging, sm	55.00
Dutch boy, full-figure, hinged, Holland mk, 6½"	70.00
Dutch shoe, fancy, sm	78.00
Dutch shoe, lg	88.00
Easter basket, lg	75.00
Easter egg, 2-part, sits on 3 ft, early 1800s	95.00
Elephant, 4¼x6¼"	68.00
Father Christmas, lg	110.00
Father Christmas, sm	98.00
Father Christmas on donkey, sm	110.00
Fish, 7x14"	75.00
Football player, K-491	70.00
Girl riding scooter, 5x5½"	60.00
Grandma, sm	60.00
Hen, nesting, lg	66.00
Hound sits w/long ears, 2-pc, clamped, unmk, 4½x5½"	60.00
Lamb, aluminum, 7x6"	10.00
Pelican, 8x4¼"	75.00
Penguin, sm	45.00
Pig, 2½x4½"	58.00
Poodle, lg	235.00

Rabbit dressed w/umbrella, Antone Reiche #26012, 2-part, 4½"	65.00
Rabbit pulling chick in egg, 2½x5"	40.00
Rabbit running, metal fr w/clamps, 5"	25.00
Rabbit sitting, hinged, metal fr w/clamps, 9"	60.00
Rabbit sitting, hinged & clamped, 5"	40.00
Rabbit standing, 9½"	75.00
Rabbit w/pack, X-lg	195.00
Rooster, crowing, med	66.00
Rooster pulling chick in egg	78.00
Rooster pulling open wagon, 4¼x8"	60.00
Roosters, 12 in 2 rows on 8½x4½" tray	58.00
Santa, sm	66.00
Santa on horse above roof tops, tin, 2-pc, mk Holland, 6x8"	225.00
Snowman, lg	60.00
Telephone receiver	50.00
Thanksgiving turkey, sm	55.00
Weightlifter, sm	88.00
Yule log	60.00
3 hands & wrists, V Clad & Sons, Phila PA, 2-part	85.00

Hard Candy Molds

Am Eagle w/shields & cannon, TM-252, groove for stick, 2"	100.00
Canary, TM-219, groove for stick, 3" L	68.00
Donkey, TM-89, groove for stick, 1¾x1¾"	60.00
Fish over waves, TM-32, groove for stick, 1x2¼"	66.00
Lamb, TM-128, groove for stick, 1¼x2"	57.50
Lion w/cubs, TM-248, groove for stick, 2x2"	65.00
Ostrich, TM-179, groove for stick, 2x3"	78.00
Puss-in-Boots, TM-246, groove for stick, 2¼x2½"	48.00
Sprinkler can, TM-239, groove for stick, 1½x2"	48.00
Squirrel eating nut, TM-155, groove for stick, 2x2½"	65.00

Ice Cream Molds

Ace of Clubs, E-903	30.00
Airplane, 5¼"	55.00
American standard, swords, cannon, flags, E-1200	55.00
Apple, E-239	15.00
Apple, E-240	25.00
Army tent, WWI era, #515, 3"	55.00
Asparagus, 3⅝"	20.00
Automobile, S&Co, #562	60.00
Bell, #605	35.00
Cabbage w/bunny, 3⅝"	24.00
Calla lily, 3-part, E&Co, #354	55.00
Candlestick w/fingerhole, #932, 4"	60.00
Cherries, 4 in mold, E-340	20.00
Cherub riding rabbit, 4"	20.00
Chick, S-186	30.00
Chinaman, Palmer Cox Brownie, S-388	70.00
Columbus bust, #321, 4"	75.00
Cornucopia, 4⅜"	15.00
Cornucopia w/fruit, E&Co, #1004, ca 1880	55.00
Crab apple, CC-0001	25.00
Cradle, 3-pc, #344	37.50
Cucumber, E-226	22.00
Cupid in rose, E-959	50.00
Daisy, 3 in mold, E-349	25.00
Dove, S-347	50.00
Dove w/raised wings, 4½"	25.00
Doves cooing, E-665	45.00
Dude in tuxedo, Palmer Cox Brownie, S-406	70.00

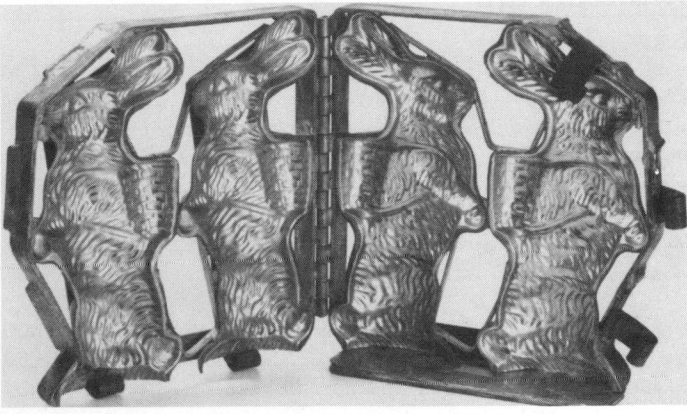

Rabbit with basket, double, 9½", $125.00.

Eagle, E&Co, #655	150.00
Ear of corn, 5"	10.00
Father Knickerbocker, symbol of NY state, S-504	88.00
Football, 3-pc, #381	32.00
Frog under toadstool, patd, 3"	35.00
Goose egg, #298	25.00
Grant bust in laurel leaf medallion, 3½" dia	95.00
Grape cluster, #159	35.00
Grapes on leaf, #580	38.00
Hat, Army campaign; K-618	48.00
Horse, E-639	45.00
Horseshoe, E-974	40.00
Irishman's head w/hat, S-384	75.00
Kewpie, E-1115	80.00
Lemon, #346, 3"	22.00
Letter w/heart & valentine, 4¼"	15.00
Log, #987, 5"	28.00
Love on 2 hearts, 4½" L	15.00
Man in moon, E&Co, c 1888, 5½"	70.00
Masonic emblem, Shrine, E-1081	35.00
Melon, E-204	18.00
Mikado, K-202	55.00
Mother scroll, E-1193	44.00
Odd Fellows Lodge emblem, triple links, K-577	25.00
Orange, #307, 3"	27.50
Orange, #357	20.00
Peach, #254, lg	28.00
Pear, E-250, sm	20.00
Pie slice, E-1097	30.00
Poinsettia, E-1144	68.00
Pork chop, 5"	45.00
Pumpkin, E-309	28.00
Rabbit w/cupid side-saddle on bk, K-561	68.00
Raspberries, 4 in mold, #1063, 4"	28.00
Rose bud, 2 in mold, 3"	22.00
Rotary Club emblem, E-1110	32.00
Shamrock, E-1039	35.00
Slipper, 3-pc, E-899A	38.00

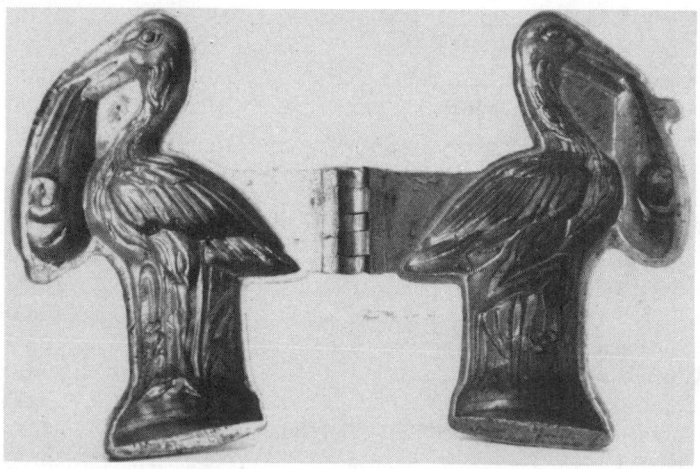

Stork, #1151, 5", $110.00.

Thistle, #820, 3"	22.00
Tomato, #208, lg	40.00
Tulip, E&Co, 4⅛"	32.00
Tulip, E-352	35.00
Uncle Sam, standing, #1073, 6"	75.00
Wedding bell w/cupid, E-1019	38.00

Yacht w/rudder showing waves, E-986	60.00
Yum Yum, K-201	58.00

Maple Sugar Molds

Fish & flower design, walnut wood, 3¼x11¾"	40.00
Heart, wood, cvd design, ca 1890, 8x3¼"	135.00
Openwork on rnd fluted cups, CI, 1840s, 12 in 11x16" fr	95.00
Rooster, deeply cvd pine, sq, 8½"	240.00
5 cvd shapes: 2 hearts, 3 rectangles, primitive, 29" L	65.00
8 fruit & vegetable sections, CI, bar hdls, 20x8"	145.00

Miscellaneous

Aluminum, bell, for cake, heavy	12.50
CI, basket of fruit & flowers, ca 1830s, 3½" L	130.00
CI, lamb, 2-part, 4x7x13"	120.00
Copper/NP top, eagle form, slight rust, 6" L	400.00
Copper/NP top, rabbit, minor rust, 4⅜", EX	125.00
Copper/tin, cat sitting, fluted skirt, 4½x3¼"	155.00
Copper/tin, fish, 3½"	40.00
Copper/tin, group of fruit, 7" L, EX	275.00
Copper/tin, pear, 3½"	40.00
Copper/tin, pineapple, fluted skirt, 6½x4⅞"	110.00
Copper/tin, rose, 5¾" L	150.00
Copper/tin, scalloped, rnd, sm	38.00
Copper/tin, seashell, curved, w/hook, 5"	45.00
Copper/tin, shell, 3½"	40.00
Copper/tin, starflower, 4"	40.00
Copper/tin, turtle, fluted skirt, 4½x3"	150.00
Copper/tin, 3 fruits, fluted, 2½x7"	40.00
Tin, fish form, EX details, 8", EX	36.00
Tin, melon-shaped top, 2-part, hdls	35.00
Tin, turtle in oval, 3x4"	165.00
Tin/NP copper top, bunch of grapes, minor rust, 5¾" L	80.00
Tin/NP copper top, lg rose w/stem & bud, 6⅝"	120.00
Tin/NP copper top, pineapple, minor rust, 7" L	150.00
Tin/NP copper top, thistle, 6½" L	170.00

Monart

Bowl, bl mottle center, goldstone flecks at rim, mk, 12"	165.00
Bowl, orange & gr w/gold flecks, paper label, 10x8"	150.00
Bowl, pk, w/flared aventurine rim, 10½"	100.00
Vase, bl shades to pk, gold flecks, bulbous, stick neck, 14"	650.00

Monmouth

The Monmouth Pottery Company was established in 1892 in Monmouth, Illinois. Their primary products were salt-glazed stoneware crocks, churns, and jugs, Bristol, spongeware, and brown glaze. In 1906 they were absorbed by a conglomerate called the Western Stoneware Company. Monmouth became their #1 plant and until 1930 continued to produce stoneware marked with their maple leaf logo. Items marked 'Monmouth Pottery Co.' were made before 1906; after the merger, 'Co.' was dropped, and 'Ill.' was substituted.

Bank, pig form, pierced eyes, spongeware, 3½"	125.00
Basket, emb bow, 7½"	18.50
Cookie jar, 'Cookies,' bail hdl	20.00
Mug, short squat, band around center, mk	5.00
Pitcher, brn, 6"	10.00

Pitcher, gr, ribbed, tall 15.00
Platter, brn, oval, lg... 8.00
Vase, brn mottle on orange, hdls, paper label, 8" 20.00
Vase, gr, hdls, #564, paper labels, 4½"... 8.00
Vase, Lotus, gray & bl, 8" 20.00

Jardiniere, Aztec, 7", $65.00.

Monot and Stumpf

The firm of Monot and Stumpf was organized in 1868, the merger of the E.S. Monot and F. Stumpf glassworks; it was located in Pantin, France. They produced fine art glass of various types until circa 1892, when the company reorganized and became known as the Cristallerie de Pantin.

Bowl, amberina opal, ruffled, 5" 170.00
Salt cellar, pk opal stripes, gold lustre int, ruffled, 1¼x2"...............65.00
Salt cellar, yel & pk irid, rnd, fluted top..50.00
Sauce dish, sq, EX color & opalescence, scarce, 4"........................185.00
Vase, cranberry irid int, swirled, 4½" 185.00

Mont Joye

Mont Joye was a type of acid-cut French cameo glass produced by Cristallerie de Pantin in Paris around the turn of the century. It is accented by enamels.

Our advisor for this category is Don Williams; he is listed in the Directory under Iowa.

Rose bowl, HP violets/gold leaves on swirl frost, 4" H 425.00
Vase, bird/insect/flowers on lt bl frost, gold leaves, 8" 550.00
Vase, frieze of oak leaves/acorns, gold on gr, 5½" 700.00
Vase, gold flowers & sm pearls on gr aventurine, 5¾"...................350.00
Vase, lg iris, lav w/gold on gr texture, 13½"..................................425.00
Vase, poppies, wht/gold on gr texture, 8" 350.00
Vase, vines/thistle blooms, red/gilt on purple, 12"........................750.00

Moorcroft

William Moorcroft was an English potter who worked for MacIntyre Potteries from 1897 to 1913, signing his pieces with his last name or 'W. M.' In 1913 he established a workshop in Burslem, England, where he produced tablewares and a line of fine Art Nouveau vases, bowls, etc., which until 1919 were marked with the printed or impressed block lettered 'Moorcroft, Burslem.' After that, the patented 'W. Moorcroft' signature mark was used, and after 1921 'Made in England' was added. Note: Except for pieces with the salmon-pink ground, all of William's work was signed. Those he refused to sign because he personally did not like them.

William Moorcroft died in 1945, and his son Walter continued in the business. Walter soon created his own designs, but he signed only the larger examples. Today W. Moorcroft Ltd. continues to use many of the same methods of hand-applied, slip-trailed decoration that William developed. Walter recently retired, and his brother William John is presently in charge of the company. He is developing his own designs that are introducing a new look to the Moorcroft line.

Our advisor for this category is Bob Haynes. He is listed in the Directory under Washington.

Key:
#1 — Potter to Her Majesty the Queen, Made in England
#2 — MacIntyre

Biscuit jar, buttercups in dk bl panels on wht, silver lid, #2..... 1,700.00
Biscuit jar, lilacs in oval gold panels on bl, silver mts, #2 .... 1,700.00
Bowl, Moonlit Bl, Landscape, imp mk/MIE, 3½x11"............... 1,250.00
Bowl vase, pomegranates, red/purple on dk bl, #1, 6x8"..............895.00
Box, orchids, 3-color on gr to bl, #1, 1½x4½" 225.00
Charger, Landscape, tree/field, red sky, silver rim, 12" 1,500.00
Creamer & sugar (open), mushrooms, red/gr on bl & gr mottle ..700.00
Cup & saucer, poppies, red on bl/gr, sgn WM/Potter/MIE, 2¼"...195.00
Ewer, Florian, trees, dk bl on lt bl sky, sgn WM des, 8".............1,000.00
Humidor, poppies, orange on stippled lt gr, sgn WM/#2, 3½" 900.00
Lamp base, orchid, mc on red/bl flambe, #2, 11" 900.00
Loving cup, buttercups on wht, sgn WM des/#2 .... 1,300.00
Plate, orchid, 3-color on red to bl flambe, imp mk/MIE, 9" 300.00
Sweetmeat, tulips/flowers, red/bl on cream, sgn WM/#2, 8" ... 1,850.00
Tea set, Florian, silver mts, sgn WM des, 4½", 3-pc............... 1,500.00
Tea set, orchids, mc on dk bl/cream, WM/Potter/MIE, 3-pc........895.00
Tray, grapes, red/bl/yel on red flambe, sgn WM/MIE, 11½" 995.00
Vase, anemones, red/bl/wht on dk bl, imp mk/#1, 5" 295.00

Vase, Hazeldene, in the 'Dawn' palette, signed in blue, dated 1926, 13", NM, $1,250.00.

Vase, anemones, red/yel on dk bl/gr, imp Moorcroft, 3½"............350.00
Vase, birds/gr trees on dk bl, WM label/sgn, 8½" 650.00
Vase, cornflower panels, yel/ochre/dk bl on lt bl, WM, 11" 1,350.00
Vase, Dawn, cylinder w/flared rim, imp mks, pewter ft, 9½" ...1,300.00
Vase, Florian, lilacs, dk bl/lav on lt/dk bl, WM des, 12" 1,550.00
Vase, Florian, peacock feathers, lt/dk bl on royal, 5" 1,200.00

Vase, Florian, peacock feathers, rust/gr on peach/dk gr, 5" 1,200.00
Vase, Florian, poppies, yel on lt/dk bl, ftd, WM des, 12" 1,400.00
Vase, Florian, tulips, yel/bl on lt to dk bl, hdls, 13" 1,500.00
Vase, King Geo V memorial, red rose bands on wht, 8" 800.00
Vase, leaves/berries on red flambe, squat, WM/#2, 3" 195.00
Vase, leaves/berries, red/purple on med to dk gr, #1, 5" 495.00
Vase, leaves/grapes, red/yel on red/bl flambe, MIE/#2, 7" 695.00
Vase, orchids, mc on gr mottle, sgn/#1, 7" 695.00
Vase, orchids, mc on wht to dk bl, Moorcroft/MIE, 3" 150.00
Vase, pansies, pk/purple on dk bl, imp mk/MIE, 8" 895.00
Vase, plums, red/bl/yel on dk bl to bl/gr, imp mk/MIE, 10" 995.00
Vase, pomegranates, mc on dk bl, imp WM, dtd, 7" 795.00

Morgan, Matt

From 1883 to 1885, the Matt Morgan Art Pottery of Cincinnati,
Ohio, produced fine artware, some of which resembled the pottery of
the Moors with intense colors and gold accents. Some of the later wares
were very similar to those of Rookwood, due to the fact that several
Rookwood artists were also associated with the Morgan pottery. Some
examples were marked with a paper label, others with either a two- or
three-line impression: 'Matt Morgan Art Pottery Co.,' with 'Cin. O.'
sometimes added.

Honey jug, leaves/butterfly cvg, Limoges style, Daly, 6½" 275.00
Honey jug, molded cornstalks, dk bl w/gold, chain/tag, 7" 350.00
Umbrella stand, florals in relief, bl w/gold, rtcl, 20½" 500.00
Vase, goose in reeds, Limoges style, flattened ovoid, 14½" 825.00
Vase, reeds/dragonflies, Limoges style, NJ Hirschfield, 4½" 200.00
Vase, textured gr w/gold, floral cvg exposes red clay, 5" 180.00

Moriage

The term 'moriage' refers to certain Japanese wares decorated with
applied slipwork designs. There are several methods used to achieve the
characteristic relief effect. The decorative devices may be designed separately and applied to the vessel, piped on in narrow ribbons of clay
(slip-trailed), or built up by brushing on successive layers of liquified
slip. See also Nippon.

Vase, orchids in slipwork, handles, 6", $150.00.

Ewer, florals w/allover scrolls & dots on beige, unmk, 3½" 70.00
Ewer, panels of roses, floral moriage/turq beads, 6x5½" 225.00
Pitcher, net over HP florals, 6" 75.00
Planter, HP poppies, brn moriage trim, ruffled, ftd, 5" 80.00
Spittoon, lady's, floral slip on tan, gr mk, 5" dia 225.00
Sugar shaker, roses, barrel shape 80.00
Teapot, gold panels w/roses alternate w/gr panels, 3¾" 85.00
Vase, floral panels, appl gr/wht leaves, pk/gr moriage, 7" 225.00
Vase, florals, lav on gr shaded, brn hdls, unmk, 3x1¾" 40.00
Vase, mc floral panels, 3 gr hdls w/dots, 5½x7" 240.00

Mortar and Pestle

Mortars are bowl-shaped vessels used for centuries for the purpose
of grinding drugs to a powder or grain into meal. The masher or grinding device is called a pestle.

Brass, flared rim, sm, w/4" brass pestle 50.00
Brass, heavy, hdl, 4½", w/9½" pestle 95.00
Brass, ped base, bell shape, 1700s, 5x6", w/7½" pestle 175.00
Brass, 2-hdl, #8, 5", w/pestle 15.00
Cast iron, 5½", w/pestle 35.00
Wood, cvd, 9x7", w/12½" trn pestle, EX 50.00
Wrought iron, boat form w/2 ft, animal head & tail, 17" L 450.00

Mortens Studio

Oscar Mortens was already established as a fine sculptural artist
when he left his native Sweden to take up residency in Arizona. During
the 1940s he developed a line of detailed animal figures which were distributed through the Mortens Studios, a firm he co-founded with Gun-
nar Thelin. Thelin hired and trained artists to produce Mortens' line,
which he called Royal Designs. More than two hundred dogs were
modeled and over one hundred horses. Cats and wild animals such as
elephants, panthers, deer, and elk were made, but on a much smaller
scale. Bookends with sculptured dog heads were shown in their catalogs, and collectors report finding wall plaques on rare occasions. The
material they used was a plaster-type composition with wires embedded
to support the weight. Examples were marked 'Copyright by the
Mortens Studio' either in ink or decal. Watch for flaking, cracks, and
separations – crazing seems to be present in some degree in many examples. When no condition is indicated, the items listed below are
assumed to be in near-mint condition, allowing for minor crazing.

Bear mother w/cubs 85.00
Boxer, med brn w/ivory & blk, standing, 5½x5½" 55.00
Chow pup, tan/brn, 3x3" 45.00
Cocker Spaniel, blk, brn details, recumbent, 3x6" 40.00
Collie, standing, 6x7" 75.00
Collie pup, recumbent 40.00
Dachshund, recumbent, 3½x4" 55.00
Doberman Pinscher, blk/tan, standing, 7½x8" 80.00
English Setter, ivory/charcoal, standing, paper label, 6x7" 75.00
English Setter, ivory/charcoal, standing, 6½x10½" 88.00
Fox Terrier, ivory/gray, standing, 5½x6¾" 75.00
French Poodle, ivory w/blk details, standing, 5x5" 75.00
German Shepherd, tan/charcoal, 7x8" 75.00
Pekingese, tan/charcoal, standing, label, 5x6½" 68.00
Plaque, Dachshund head 70.00
Scotch Terrier, blk/charcoal, paper label, 4½x5" 60.00
Spaniel pup, ivory w/blk spots, 3x3¾" 35.00
St Bernard, ivory/tan, standing, 6½x8½" 80.00

Wire-Haired Terrier...55.00
Wire-Haired Terrier pup, recumbent, 3x3¼" 37.50

Horse, rearing, 9",
$60.00.

Morton Pottery

Six potteries operated in Morton, Illinois, at various times from 1877 to 1976. Each traced its origin to six brothers who immigrated to America to avoid military service in Germany. The Rapp brothers established their first pottery near clay deposits on the south side of town where they made field tile and bricks. Within a few years, they branched out to include utility wares such as jugs, bowls, jars, pitchers, etc. During the ninety-nine years of pottery operations in Morton, the original factory was expanded by some of the sons and nephews of the Rapps. Other family members started their own potteries where artware, gift-store items, and special-order goods were produced. The Cliftwood Art Pottery and the Morton Pottery Company had showrooms in Chicago and New York City during the 1930s. All of Morton's potteries were relatively short-lived operations with the Morton Pottery Company being the last to shut down on September 8, 1976. For a more thorough study of the subject, we recommend *Morton's Potteries: 99 Years* by Doris and Burdell Hall; their address can be found in the Directory under Illinois.

In the listings that follow VP refers to Vincent Price National Treasures items which were made for Sears and Roebuck from 1967 to 1968.

Morton Pottery Company, Rockingham pitcher and bowl, Vincent Price mark, $135.00.

Morton Pottery Works – Morton Earthenware Co. (1877-1917)

Bean pot, ind, brn Rockingham, ¼-pt 15.00
Bean pot, ind, yellow ware, 1½-pt 30.00
Bowl, brn Rockingham, 10¼" dia 60.00
Bowl, brn Rockingham, 15¼" dia 85.00
Bowl, brn Rockingham, 5¼" dia 45.00
Jardiniere, dk gr, 7x7" 24.00
Milk boiler, brn, 1½-pt 40.00
Milk boiler, brn, 2½-pt 45.00
Milk boiler, brn, 3½-pt 55.00
Mug, yellowware w/wht slip bands 65.00
Teapot, brn, globe shape, ind, 1½-cup 25.00
Teapot, globe shape, brn, 5¼-pt 50.00

Cliftwood Art Potteries, Inc. (1920-1940)

Figurine, bulldog, Nero, bl-gray drip, 6½x11" 80.00
Figurine, elephant, gray, 7¼x13½" 80.00
Figurine, lion, tan w/brn mane, 9¼x16" 90.00
Figurine, tiger, tan w/brn stripes, 5x16" 70.00
Flower bowl, bl mulberry drip, ftd, deep, 8" dia 30.00
Flower bowl, brn chocolate drip, ftd, deep, 10" dia........35.00
Flower bowl, old rose, ftd, deep, 9" dia...........................20.00
Flower disc, bl mulberry drip, 3" dia 10.00
Flower disc, brn chocolate drip, 5" dia 14.00
Flower disc, old rose, 4" dia 7.00
Grease jar, pk/gr drip, w/lid, 3x5" 35.00
Lamp mt w/fixture, Chinese pagoda, brn chocolate drip, 22½"......80.00
Lamp mt w/fixture, donut clock in base, bl mulberry drip, 18" 95.00
Lamp mt w/fixture, owl on log, gr, 8½" 35.00
Lamp mt w/fixture, snakes swallow fish, cobalt, hdls, 30" 110.00
Matchbox holder, pk/gr drip, wall hanging, 5" 40.00
Pitcher, water, yel/gr drip, 1½-qt, 9" 25.00
Pretzel jar, gr, barrel form, 10" 30.00
Radio speaker, Megaphone, brn chocolate drip, 15" 95.00
Radio speaker, Sweetone, cobalt w/bronze spackling, 15" 95.00
Shakers, pk/orchid drip, 6", pr..24.00

Midwest Potteries, Inc. (1940-1944)

Figurine, blue jay on stump, 6½" 15.00
Figurine, cowboy on bronco, blk w/gold decor, 7½" 25.00
Figurine, Deco lady w/Russian wolfhound, gold/platinum, 11" 95.00
Figurine, deer, stylized antlers, brn-gray spray, 12½" 25.00
Figurine, road runner, wht w/gold decor, 8" 12.00
Figurine, tiger, yel w/blk stripes, 7x12" 40.00
Figurine, wild horse, gold, 14½" 40.00
Lamp, Art Deco, 13x4½" opening w/figurine, yel/gr drip, 20"......55.00
Mask, African female, blk w/gold turban neck rings, 8x4" 35.00
Planter, cat w/hole for tail, gr 4.00
Planter, colt in front of stump, bl.................................... 5.00
Planter, female duck, wht w/brn bonnet, gold decor......15.00
Planter, female duck, wht w/gr bonnet 12.00
Planter, male duck, wht w/brn top hat, gold decor 15.00
Planter, male duck, wht w/gr top hat...............................12.00
Planter, pear, yel w/gr leaves 6.00
Planter, stump w/kingfisher on branch, yel 4.50

Morton Pottery Company (1922-1976)

Baker, brn Rockingham, oval, 12x8½", VP.....................50.00

Canister set, gr, 9-qt descending to 1½-qt, set of 4 ....180.00
Canister set, resemble milk cans, bl spongeware, 4-pc, VP 140.00
Catalog, color centerfold, 1929, 16-pg, 4x6" 22.00
Cookie jar, jug form, brn Rockingham, VP.......................................38.00
Food mold, rnd grape cluster in bottom, dk gr, VP...........................45.00
Grass grower, wht bsk, Jake bust, handlebar mustache 22.00
Grass grower, wht bsk, Jiggs bust 20.00
Grass grower, wht bsk, pig...14.00
Grass grower, wht bsk, Sunny Jim bust 18.00
Grass grower, wht bsk, tree, cone shape 10.00
Iced tea set, pitcher w/6 beakers & coasters, gr..............................175.00
Incense burner, church, gr, 3½"...25.00
Incense burner, Oriental lady, brn Rockingham, 5½" 40.00
Incense burner, oven, open pipe on top, burgundy, 3x3x3"............12.00
Matchbox holder, gr, wall hanging, 6¾" 35.00
Meat tenderizer, wht, bell shape, wood hdl, VP..............................50.00
Planter, baby shoe w/buttons, bl, #572 .... 8.00
Planter, baby shoe w/shoestrings, pk, #313...................................... 6.00
Planter, cat, hole for tail, wht, #473, 3¾".. 4.00
Planter, lotus bowl, pk, #774, 6x2½" dia 8.00
Planter, stump w/appl mini kangaroo, #611....................................10.00
Potato masher, wht, ball shape, wood hdl, VP.................................40.00
Salt box, wood w/bl lid, wall hanger, 6¼".......................................50.00
Spice shaker, bl, 5"...20.00
Tea set, bl, teapot, creamer, sugar bowl & tea tile.........................100.00
Vase, bird in flight, pk, #493, 9"...16.00
Vase, bud; yel, #310, 6"... 5.00
Vase, heart w/Cupid's arrow, red, #428..10.00
Vase, lady w/muff, wht matt, #338, 10"...18.00
Vase, pitcher form w/hdls, fan decor, #492, burgundy 8.00
Vase, tree trunk, gr matt, #260, 8" 12.00

American Art Potteries (1947-1961)

Figurine, rooster, brn/burgundy spray, 8" 15.00
Lamp, TV; conch shell, pk/orchid spray, 7x10" 18.00
Lamp, TV; horse & colt running, brn/gr spray, 9x12"....................30.00
Lamp, TV; panther in slinking position, blk, 6x14" 20.00
Lamp, TV; titmouse on limbs, mauve/bl spray, 8x12" 18.00
Lamp base, semi-nude belly dancer, mc, 17"...................................30.00
Planter, bear, brn/gray spray 10.00
Planter, cowboy boot, gray/pk spray 12.00
Planter, rabbit at tree peeking through grass, natural colors 12.00
Ring holder, wht, hand appl flat saucer...18.00
Vase, bud; bl/rose spray, 6"... 8.00
Vase, dbl fern fronds, brn/gray spray, 11" 12.00
Vase, ewer form, bl/orchid sprays w/gold, paper label, 6" 18.00

Mosaic Tile Co.

The Mosaic Tile Company was organized in 1894, in Zanesville, Ohio, by Herman Mueller and Karl Langenbeck, both of whom had years of previous experience in the industry. They developed a faster, less-costly method of potting decorative tile, utilizing paper patterns rather than copper molds. By 1901 the company had grown and expanded with offices in many major cities. Faience tile was introduced in 1918, greatly increasing their volume of sales. They also made novelty ash trays, figural boxes, bookends, etc., though not to any large extent. Until they closed during the 1960s, Mosaic used various marks that included the company name or their initials – 'MT' superimposed over 'Co.' in a circle.

Card tray, blk & gr w/figural dog, 4" 175.00

Figurine, bear, 6x9" 115.00
Figurine, German Shepherd, tan, unmk, 9x8".................................110.00
Figurine, man in doghouse, dog on roof, brn & wht, 5x6x5" 175.00
Tile, Delft-like scene, bl & wht, on red clay, mk, 4" 60.00
Tile, Hispania, mc, 6x6", set of 3, MIB...150.00
Tile, 1898 Winton decal, blk & gr, 6" 50.00
Tile, 1903 Cadillac decal, gr, 6" 50.00

Cookie jar, Mammy, $200.00.

Moser

Ludwig Moser began his career as a struggling glass artist, catering to the rich who visited the famous Austrian health spas. His talent and popularity grew and in 1857 the first of his three studios opened in Karlsbad, Czechoslovakia. The styles developed there were entirely his own; no copies of other artists have ever been found. Some of his original designs include grapes with trailing vines, acorns and oak leaves, and richly enameled, deeply cut or carved floral pieces. Sometimes jewels were applied to the glass as well. Moser's animal scenes reflect his careful attention to detail. Famed for his birds in flight, he also designed stalking tigers – even elephants – all created in fine enameling.

Moser died in 1916, but the business was contined by his two sons who had been personally and carefully trained by their father. They merged with Meyer's Nephews Glassworks in 1921, and continued to produce quality glass until the Nazi invasion in 1938 when these fine Jewish artists were all placed in concentration camps.

When identifying Moser, look for great clarity in the glass; deeply carved, continuous engravings; perfect coloration; finely applied enameling (often covered with thin gold leaf); and well-polished pontils.

Our advisor for this category is Don Williams; he is listed in the Directory under Iowa. Items listed below are enameled unless noted otherwise.

Bowl, amber, gold leaves/appl acorns, lg/tall hdls, 4½"................450.00
Bowl, cameo, pods/leaves, smoke on texture, mk M-M, 5½x7" ...375.00
Box, cobalt w/scrolls & gilt, brass mts, rnd, 4½" H......................400.00
Box, sapphire, mc/gold florals & birds, ornate mts, 4½" H..........400.00
Cordial, amber, gold branches, mc leaves, appl acorns, sgn..........425.00
Cruet, amber, florals, clear hdl/stopper, sgn, 10".........................600.00
Cruet, amber, florals, sq w/bl twist hdl, faceted stopper 275.00
Cruet, cranberry, mc florals/gold leaves/4 bees, sgn, 11" 750.00

Cruet, emerald, florals & gold, ribbed, teardrop stopper 250.00
Cruet, lime, sapphire hdl/stopper, appl bird, foliage 875.00
Decanter, cranberry, florals/insects/acorns, sgn, 11" 1,000.00
Decanter, gr to clear, gold/silver vintage, cut stopper..................475.00
Dish, amberina, gold leaves/grapevines, leaf form, 5½" 175.00
Nut dish, rubena, allover gold decor, sawtooth rim, hdl..............585.00

Tumble up, cranberry with enameled florals, heavily applied pulled gold trim, signed, 10", $2,400.00.

Tumbler, bl to clear, red & gr jewels, sgn, 3⅝x2¼" 185.00
Tumbler, chipped ice w/dk bl bands & gold Grecian frieze 190.00
Tumbler, emerald gr, gold/yel Russian pattern, 3¾" 120.00
Tumbler, yel to clear, red & gr jewels, sgn, 3⅝x2¼" 185.00
Vase, Alexandrite, bl/lav, faceted/ftd, 6½" 175.00
Vase, amethyst, gold lovers scene, intaglio panels, unmk, 10" 400.00
Vase, amethyst, snake in tree, elaborate rigaree, sgn, 10"............400.00
Vase, amethyst to clear, appl berries/blossoms, jewels, 12" 1,400.00
Vase, amethyst to clear, gold butterfly, appl acorns, sgn, 4" 500.00
Vase, bl, gold leaves/3-color floral, cylindrical, sgn, 14"..............600.00
Vase, bud; cranbery w/gold, appl floral roundels, sgn, 10"...........500.00
Vase, clear to lime, rust/brn decor, trumpet form, sgn, 18"...........600.00
Vase, cobalt, band of gold cvd elephants & palms, sgn, 10".........575.00
Vase, cobalt (textured), gold elephants/palms, sgn, 4" 425.00
Vase, cranberry, gold floral, ribbed, sgn, 13½" 750.00
Vase, cranberry, icicles & florals, icicle ft/rigaree, 11".................600.00
Vase, crystal, button/star cutting, sq stepped base, 10"................150.00
Vase, flashed cranberry, dmn point cut, w/gilt, sgn, 5" 250.00
Vase, gr, portrait on 5" medallion, ped ft, sgn, 12", pr..................975.00
Vase, gr opal to clear, red/yel poppies, gold leaves, 11" 350.00
Vase, gr to clear, paneled, intaglio iris, sgn, 16"...........................600.00
Wine, chipped ice, cameo Nouveau motif & monogram, mk, 6" .225.00
Wine, purple to clear, eng grapevines/florals, sgn, 7x4"................115.00
Wine, Rhine, amber, star-cut amber ft, 8¼" 60.00

Moss Rose

Moss Rose was a favorite dinnerware pattern of many Staffordshire

and American potters from the mid-1800s. In America the Wheeling Pottery of West Virginia produced the ware in large quantities, and it became one of their best sellers, remaining popular well into the nineties.

Bone dish, unmk, gold edge..30.00
Bowl, vegetable; unmk, w/lid 50.00
Butter pat, sq, Meakin, EX 15.00
Coffee mug & saucer, Meakin 60.00
Coffeepot, Haviland, lg 65.00
Creamer & sugar bowl, unmk..20.00

Creamer and sugar bowl, Haviland & Co., 7" to finial, $65.00.

Egg cup, unmk, set of 6, MIB..28.00
Gravy boat, Meakin..30.00
Plate, dinner; unmk, 10"...15.00
Plate, Meakin, 9" 16.00
Plate, Powell & Bishop, 10" 20.00
Platter, rectangular, Meakin, 14x10".......................................30.00
Shaving mug, unmk 22.00
Tea set, American, 14-pc...125.00
Tea set, Japan, 16-pc+lids..60.00
Teapot, unmk, 8"...36.00
Tray, unmk, 8"...15.00
Wash set, unmk, 11" pitcher+13½" bowl.................................265.00

Mother-of-Pearl Glass

Mother-of-Pearl glass was a type of mold-blown satin art glass popular during the last half of the 19th century. A patent for its manufacture was issued in 1886 to Frederick S. Shirley, and one of the companies who produced it was the Mt. Washington Glass Company of New Bedford, Massachusetts. Another was the English firm of Stevens and Williams. Its delicate patterns were developed by blowing the gather into a mold with inside projections that left an intaglio design on the surface of the glass, then sealing the first layer with a second, trapping air in the recesses. Most common are the Diamond Quilted, Raindrop, and Herringbone patterns. It was made in several soft colors, the most rare and valuable is rainbow – a blend of rose, light blue, yellow, and white. Occasionally it may be decorated with coralene, enameling, or gilt.

Our advisors for this category are Betty and Clarence Maier; they are listed in the Directory under Pennsylvania.

Biscuit jar, Dia Quilt, rose, SP dome lid/bail/ft, 8¾" 735.00

Biscuit jar, Moire, red w/gold prunus, Webb, emb silver lid **650.00**
Bowl, bride's; Dia Quilt, bl shaded, sq, Mt WA, 9½" **585.00**
Bowl, Coin Spot, bl shaded, 3 frosted thorn ft, Webb, 5x7" **450.00**
Bowl, Dia Quilt, apple gr, appl ft, Webb, 4¼x4⅞" **550.00**
Bowl, Dia Quilt, bl, ftd tricorn, mk Patent, 4¼x5¼" **750.00**
Bowl, Dia Quilt, lt gold w/gold flowers, pk int, Webb, 9½" **800.00**
Bowl, Dia Quilt, pk, ruffled, 4x10" **400.00**
Bowl, Dia Quilt, pk shaded, Webb, 3¾x10" **800.00**
Bowl, Dia Quilt, rainbow, vaseline ft, tricorn, Patent, 5x5" **1,100.00**
Bowl, Dia Quilt, rainbow swirl, camphor petal base, 12½" **550.00**
Bowl, Dia Quilt, rose to wht, 8-pleat top, Webb, 3¾x10" **750.00**
Bowl, Dia Quilt, yel, folded-in pinched rim, 9" **225.00**
Bowl vase, Dia Quilt, shiny gr w/mica, Mt WA, 4x6½" **750.00**
Box, Dia Quilt, bl shaded, 3 scroll ft, 3½" dia...................**200.00**
Creamer, Ribbon, bl, frosted wafer ft, crimped, 2⅞x3¼" **235.00**
Epergne, Dia Quilt, pk, 9" ribbed bowl w/1 lily, 17" **1,550.00**
Ewer, Dia Quilt, bl, appl frosted hdl, Mt WA, 9½" **275.00**
Ewer, Herringbone, rose, ribbed, crimped, Mt WA, 7" **225.00**
Finger bowl, Dia Quilt, amberina, 2½x4½", +6½" plate **900.00**
Finger bowl, Herringbone, pk, clover-leaf shape, 3x4¼" **185.00**
Pitcher, Dia Quilt, bl, tricorn, frosted reeded hdl, 7" **250.00**
Pitcher, Dia Quilt, lemon to wht, frosted reeded hdl, 5" **120.00**
Pitcher, Dia Quilt, pk, sq top, frosted reeded hdl, 7x7" **400.00**

Pitcher, Raindrop, white, Boston & Sandwich, 9", $975.00

Pitcher, Herringbone, red to wht, frost hdl, sq, 6" **200.00**
Pitcher, Moire, apricot, frosted reeded hdl, sq mouth, 7½" **700.00**
Pitcher, Raindrop, med bl, reeded hdl, 4½" **225.00**
Pitcher, Raindrop, rainbow w/gold floral, high hdl, 6½" **250.00**
Rose bowl, Dia Quilt, bl, 8-crimp, 3½x4¼" **195.00**
Rose bowl, Dia Quilt, rainbow, mk Patent, 2⅜x4⅜" **950.00**
Rose bowl, Dia Quilt, rainbow w/clear stripes, 3½x4" **1,395.00**
Rose bowl, Moire, tan, metallic bird, 3 thorn ft, Webb, 6" **575.00**
Rose bowl, Peacock Eye, red, wht int, 3" **900.00**
Sweetmeat, Herringbone, pk/wht, roses/butterfly, Webb, 4" **350.00**
Sweetmeat, Moire, wht, gold prunus, sq/concave, Webb, 3½" **500.00**
Toothpick holder, Dia Quilt, yel, quatrelobe rim, 2½" **350.00**
Tumbler, Dia Quilt, bl w/orange coralene seaweed.......................**200.00**
Tumbler, Dia Quilt, dk pk w/bl daisies & mc leaves....................**190.00**
Tumbler, Dia Quilt, pk w/flowers & gold leaves **225.00**
Tumbler, Dia Quilt, rainbow, sq top...**300.00**
Tumbler, Dia Quilt, yel w/coralene seaweed **150.00**
Tumbler, Raindrop, rose to wht w/flowers & gold leaves.............**200.00**
Vase, Coin Spot, bl, 4-petal top, 7⅜x4" **195.00**

Vase, Coin Spot, bl/wht, metallic leaf/butterfly, Webb, 5".........**300.00**
Vase, Dia Quilt, apricot, ruffled, wishbone ft, 5x3" **225.00**
Vase, Dia Quilt, bl, frosted ruffled rim, 5½x4" **185.00**
Vase, Dia Quilt, bl, frosted ruffled rim, 7x4⅛" **210.00**
Vase, Dia Quilt, butterscotch shaded, ribbed, ruffled, 9" **525.00**
Vase, Dia Quilt, peach shaded, wht int, 10½x5" **225.00**
Vase, Dia Quilt, pk, ruffled, 8¼x4⅜" **465.00**
Vase, Dia Quilt, pk, tricorn ruffled top, ewer form, 12¾" **450.00**
Vase, Dia Quilt, pk & yel, appl ft, mk Patent, 6" **880.00**
Vase, Dia Quilt, rainbow, appl camphor ruffle, Mt WA, 8x4" . **1,750.00**
Vase, Dia Quilt, rainbow, 3-petal top, 6¼x3" **895.00**
Vase, Dia Quilt, yel, HP florals, frosted ruffle, 7¼x4" **495.00**
Vase, Drape, pk shaded, fan form, 6¼x3½" **210.00**
Vase, Federzeichnung, brn w/gilt tracery, quatrefoil, 6" **1,600.00**
Vase, Federzeichnung, gold enamel, 7" **1,215.00**
Vase, Herringbone, bl, ewer from, 8x3½" **195.00**
Vase, Herringbone, bl, frosted ft & hdls, 9¾x4½", pr.................**750.00**
Vase, Herringbone, pk, ribbed, frosted hdls, 7½" **245.00**
Vase, Herringbone, pk, ruffled, 5½" **175.00**
Vase, Herringbone, rose, appl crystal threads, Mt WA, 7½".... **1,000.00**
Vase, Moire, yel w/florals, turq beads, camphor hdls, 12" **200.00**
Vase, Peacock Eye, wht w/leaves & bugs, rnd w/sq rim, 7" **285.00**
Vase, Raindrop, wht, appl frosted rim, egg form, 6x3½" **275.00**
Vase, Swirl, rose shaded, wht int, 11¼x5"....................................**265.00**
Vase, Swirl, shaded burnt orange, ruffled, 8½" **325.00**
Vase, Swirl, yel shaded, flared, 5"...**100.00**

Mourning Collectibles

During the 18th and early 19th centuries, ladies made needlework pictures, samplers, paintings on ivory plaques, watercolor drawings, etc. to commemorate the death of a loved one. Elements contained in nearly all examples are the tomb, mourners, a weeping willow tree, and data relating to the deceased. Often plaits of hair were included. Today these are recognized and valued as a valid form of folk art.

Brooch, lady at tomb by willow, gold case dtd 1796, 1x1¾".........**250.00**
Needlework, silk embr, lady at stone, data, 1800s, 12x9" **275.00**
Needlework, silk embr, lady by willow, data, 1800s, 15x18".........**550.00**

Picture, silk embroidery on silk, signed and dated 1810, 15" x 14", $1,000.00.

Needlework, silk w/hair/watercolor/ink/etc, 21x27".....................**600.00**
Sampler, needlepoint, flowers/cherubs/tomb/etc, 1884, 30" **275.00**
Watercolor, dedication/1833 on monument, bldgs, 11x15"..... **1,650.00**

Movie Memorabilia

Movie memorabilia covers a broad range of collectibles, from books and magazines dealing with the industry in general to the various promotional materials which were distributed to arouse interest in a particular film. Many collectors specialize in a specific area – posters, pressbooks, stills, lobby cards, or souvenir programs (also referred to as premier booklets). In the listings below, a one-sheet poster measures approximately 27" x 41", three-sheet: 41" x 81", and six-sheet: 81" x 81". See also Autographs; Cartoon Art; Personalities.

Clark Gable M.G.M. Dressing room tag, brass, 2", $2,860.00.

Book, souvenir; Wings, Clara Bow & Buddy Rogers, 1924, rare **75.00**
Display card, Belle Starr, G Tierney, 1941, 22x28", EX **80.00**
Display card, Between 2 Women, Van Johnson, 1945, 22x28"......**32.00**
Display card, Bride of Vengeance, P Goddard, 1949, 22x28" **27.50**
Display card, Brother Rat, Ronald Reagan, 22x28" **100.00**
Display card, Deep Valley, Ida Lupino, 1947, 22x28"....................**40.00**
Display card, Desire Me, Greer Garson, 1947, 22x28" **32.00**
Display card, Farmer's Daughter, L Young, 1947, 22x28" **55.00**
Display card, Ganster's Boy, Jackie Cooper, 1938, 22x28".............**55.00**
Display card, Guns of Timberland, Alan Ladd, 1960, 22x28" **22.00**
Display card, Let's Go Collegiate, Gale Storm, 1940s, 22x28".......**28.00**
Display card, Lightnin' Bill Carson, Tim McCoy, 1938, 22x28" ..**120.00**
Display card, On the Sunnyside, R McDowell, 1940s, 22x28" **22.00**
Display card, Safari, D Fairbanks Jr, 1940, 22x28"..........................**65.00**
Display card, Southern Yankee, Red Skelton, 1948, 22x28" **35.00**
Insert card, Anna & King of Siam, Irene Dunn, 1946, 14x36" **37.50**
Insert card, Autumn Leaves, Joan Crawford, 14x36" **45.00**
Insert card, Between 2 Worlds, J Garfield, 1944, 14x36" **65.00**
Insert card, Bowery to Bagdad, Bowery Boys, 1954, 14x36"..........**22.00**
Insert card, Caretakers, Joan Crawford, 1963, 14x36" **17.50**
Insert card, Chapman Report, Jane Fonda, 1962, 14x36" **12.00**
Insert card, Flare-up, R Welch, 14x36" **35.00**
Insert card, Gentlemen Marry Brunettes, J Russell, 14x36" **40.00**
Insert card, Man in Middle, Robert Mitchum, 1964, 14x36" **12.50**
Insert card, Over My Dead Body, M Berle, 1942, 14x36" **42.50**
Insert card, Roman Spring of Mrs Stone, V Leigh, 14x36" **45.00**

Insert card, Streetcar Named Desire, V Leigh, 14x36" **115.00**
Insert card, The Man I Love, Ida Lupino, 14x36"............................**35.00**
Insert card, Without Love, K Hepburn, 1945, 14x36".....................**115.00**
Lobby card, Ambassador Bill, Will Rogers, 1936, 11x14"...............**65.00**
Lobby card, Blob, Steve McQueen, 1958, 11x14" **17.50**
Lobby card, Cardinal Richelieu, G Arliss, 1935, 11x14" **40.00**
Lobby card, Carnival, Jimmy Durante, 1935, 11x14" **37.50**
Lobby card, Delightfully Dangerous, R Ballamy, 1945, 11x14" **12.00**
Lobby card, Desire, Dietrich/Cooper, 1936, 11x14"......................**245.00**
Lobby card, Dog's Life, C Chaplin, bl/wht, 1918, 11x14" **325.00**
Lobby card, East of Eden, James Dean, 1955, 11x14" **65.00**
Lobby card, New Orleans, L Armstrong, 1947, 11x14"....................**38.00**
Lobby card, Nocturne, Geo Raft/Lynn Bari, 1946, 11x14"..............**25.00**
Lobby card, Peggy, Billie Burke, 1916, 11x14" **120.00**
Lobby card, Robin Hood of Texas, Autry, 1942, 11x14".................**25.00**
Lobby card, Trader Horn, Harry Carey, 1931, 11x14" **55.00**
Lobby card, Wht Zombie, Bela Lugosi, 2-tone, 11x14" **37.50**
Lobby card, Wife vs Secretary, Myrna Loy, 1936, 11x14"...............**75.00**
Lobby card, Yankee Doodle Dandy, Cagney, 1942, 11x14" **80.00**
Magazine, Modern Screen, Betty Grable, Aug 1951, EX.................. **8.00**
Magazine, Modern Screen, Peyton Place cover, Mar 1966, EX **4.00**
Magazine, Motion Picture, Gable in uniform, 1943, NM...............**35.00**
Magazine, Movie Life, Elvis cover, Jan 1959, EX.......................... **8.00**
Magazine, Movieland, Bette Davis cover, Feb 1945, EX.................**12.50**
Magazine, Movieland, Joan Leslie cover, Feb 1946, EX.................**12.00**
Magazine, Photoplay, Barbara Stanwyck cover, Jan 1967, EX **5.00**
Magazine, Photoplay, Garbo cover, Jan 1933, EX..........................**15.00**
Magazine, Photoplay, Norma Talmadge cover, July 1927, EX **16.00**
Magazine, Screen Stars, Grace Kelly cover, May 1955 .... **7.50**
Magazine, Screen Stars, Maureen O'Hara cover, Aug 1945, EX **12.50**
Magazine, Silver Screen, Marilyn Monroe cover, 1943, EX **35.00**
Photo, Garbo on skis from 2-Faced Woman, silver print, 13x10" .**20.00**
Photo, Garbo/Bickford in Anna Christie, silver print, 1930 ....**25.00**
Poster, Annie Hall, Woody Allen, 1977, 27x41" **20.00**
Poster, Apartment for Peggy, Jeanne Crain, 1948, 27x41" **27.50**
Poster, Battle Circus, Bogart, 1953, 41x81" **65.00**
Poster, Beguiled, Eastwood, 1971, 27x41"....................................**22.50**
Poster, Blues Brothers, John Belushi, 1980, 45x60" **27.50**
Poster, Chances Are, Cybil Shepherd, 27x41"................................**20.00**
Poster, Change of Habit, Presley/Tyler Moore, 1969, 27x41".........**22.00**
Poster, Cinderella, orig release, 1-sheet **350.00**
Poster, Daddy Long Legs, Fred Astaire, 1955, 22x28".....................**25.00**
Poster, Donovan's Reef, John Wayne, 1-sheet **50.00**
Poster, Giant, 1970, 27x41"...**65.00**
Poster, Girl from Jones Beach, R Reagan, 1-sheet **125.00**
Poster, Girls, Girls, Girls, Elvis Presley, 1962, EX **85.00**
Poster, Gone w/the Wind, 1954, 27x41", EX **300.00**
Poster, Her Cardboard Lover, N Shearer, 1942, 41x81" **165.00**
Poster, High & the Mighty, John Wayne, 1-sheet **100.00**
Poster, High Time, Bing Crosby, 1960, 27x41" **22.50**
Poster, Let's Make Love, Marilyn Monroe, 1960, 1-sheet.............**125.00**
Poster, Luck of the Irish, Tyrone Power, 1948, 1-sheet **40.00**
Poster, Man w/X-Ray Eyes, R Milland, 1963, 3-sheet.....................**25.00**
Poster, McLintock, Wayne/O'Hara, 1963, 27x41" **35.00**
Poster, Meet the Killer, Abbot & Costello, 1949, 27x41" **75.00**
Poster, Mickey's Christmas Carol/Rescuers, 1-sheet, NM...............**50.00**
Poster, Nutty Professor, Jerry Lewis, 1963, 27x41" **22.50**
Poster, Pardners, Martin & Lewis, 27x41" **17.50**
Poster, Raw Wind in Eden, Esther Williams, 27x41" **27.50**
Poster, Roman Spring of Mrs Stone, V Leigh, 1962, 27x41"...........**22.50**
Poster, Roots of Heaven, E Flynn, 1958, 27x41"............................**27.50**
Poster, Royal Wedding, Fred Astaire, 1951, 22x28" **60.00**
Poster, Scorpio, B Lancaster, 1973, 27x41" **15.00**
Poster, Shadow in the Sky, Nancy Davis, 1952, 1-sheet **40.00**

Poster, Mutiny on the Bounty, Laughton and Gable, 1956 (reissue), 22" x 28", $150.00.

Poster, Shane, A Ladd, 1-sheet **125.00**
Poster, Shepherd of the Hills, John Wayne, 1941, 1-sheet...........**300.00**
Poster, Showdown, Hopalong Cassidy, 1-sheet.............................**55.00**
Poster, The Bank, Charlie Chaplin, Essany, Central, 42x28" .. **8,500.00**
Poster, Thunder of Drums, C Bronson, 1961, 27x41" **10.00**
Poster, Torn Curtain, Paul Newman, 1966, 3-sheet........................**25.00**
Poster, Touch, Ingmar Bergman, 1971, 27x41"...............................**16.00**
Poster, Twilight in the Sierras, Roy Rogers, 1-sheet **50.00**
Poster, Verdict, Sidney Greenstreet, 1946, 27x41" **50.00**
Poster, War Lover, Steve McQueen, 1962, 27x41"...........................**22.50**
Poster, You Were Never Lovelier, R Hayworth, 1949, 1-sheet.......**95.00**
Poster, 2 Mules for Sister Sara, C Eastwood, 1-sheet **10.00**
Pressbook, Comanche, Randolf Scott, 1950, 4-pg, EX **5.00**
Pressbook, Cool Hand Luke, Newman/Kennedy, 1967, M.............**12.00**
Pressbook, Dbl Trouble, Presley, 1967, 12-pg, M **15.00**
Pressbook, Easy Rider, Fonda/Hopper/Nicholson, 1969, NM.........**14.00**
Pressbook, Flaming Lead, K Maynard, 1939, 8-pg, VG **65.00**
Pressbook, Glass Web, Edward G Robinson, 1953, 12-pg, EX........**17.50**
Pressbook, Hatari!, J Wayne, 1962, 32-pg, EX **25.00**
Pressbook, Johnny Come Lately, Cagney, 1943, 16-pg, EX **85.00**
Pressbook, Little Miss Marker, Temple, 1934, 20-pg, EX **365.00**
Pressbook, World Premiere, J Barrymore, 1941, 20-pg **35.00**
Program, Fantasia, 1940, 32-pg **65.00**
Program, Laurence of Arabia, Peter O'Toole, 2 maps, EX **40.00**
Still, Annie Oakley, Barbara Stanwyck, 1935.................................. **7.50**
Still, Good Sport, Boles/Watkins, 1930s, 8x10" **5.00**
Still, Little Minister, K Hepburn, 1934 .... **4.50**
Still, Secrets of Actress, Brent/Francis, 1938, 8x10" **7.50**
Still, World Gone Mad, Pat O'Brien, 1933 .... **5.00**
Title card, Son of Frankenstein, B Karloff......................................**65.00**
Trailer, Boeing-Boeing, Tony Curtis, 1965, 35mm **5.00**
Trailer, Finger on a Trigger, Rory Calhoun, 1965, 35mm................. **4.00**
Trailer, Operation Snafu, Sean Connery, 1965, 35mm **7.50**
Trailer, She, Ursula Andress, 1965, 35mm **6.00**
Trailer, Yel Canary, Pat Boone/Barbara Eden, 1963, 35mm............. **7.50**
Window card, A Star Is Born, J Garland, 1954, 14x22"................**100.00**
Window card, Chisum, John Wayne, 14x22" **175.00**
Window card, East of Eden, James Dean, 14x22" **175.00**
Window card, Gentlemen Prefer Blondes, M Monroe, 14x22"....**300.00**
Window card, I Was a Male War Bride, Grant, 1949, 14x22"........**38.00**
Window card, Lady of the Tropics, E Taylor, 1939, 14x22".........**145.00**
Window card, Last Time I Saw Paris, E Taylor, 14x22" **95.00**
Window card, Little Nelly Kelly, Judy Garland, 14x22" **45.00**
Window card, Quiet Man, Wayne/O'Hara, 14x22".......................**35.00**
Window card, Rebecca of Sunnybrook Farm, S Temple, 14x22" ...**400.00**
Window card, Sea Chase, John Wayne, 14x22" **35.00**
Window card, Tarzan & Lost Safari, G Scott, 1957, 14x22" **22.50**

Mt. Washington

The Mt. Washington Glass Works was founded in 1837 in South

Boston, Massachusetts, but moved to New Bedford in 1869 after purchasing the facilities of the New Bedford Glass Company. Frederick S. Shirley became associated with the firm in 1874. Two years later the company reorganized and became known as the Mt. Washington Glass Company. In 1894 it merged with the Pairpoint Manufacturing Company, a small Brittania works nearby, but continued to conduct business under its own title until after the turn of the century. The combined plants were equipped with the most modern and varied machinery available and boasted a working force with experience and expertise rival to none in the art of blowing and cutting glass. In addition to their fine cut glass, they are recognized as the first American company to make cameo glass, an effect they achieved through acid-cutting methods. In 1885 Shirley was issued a patent to make Burmese, pale yellow glassware tinged with a delicate pink blush. Another patent issued in 1886 allowed them the rights to produce Rose Amber, or amberina, a transparent ware shading from ruby to amber. Pearl Satin Ware and Peachblow, so named for its resemblance to a rosy peach skin, were patented the same year. One of their most famous lines, Crown Milano, was introduced in 1893. It was an opal glass either free-blown or pattern-molded, tinted a delicate color and decorated with enameling and gilt. Royal Flemish was patented in 1894 and is considered the rarest of the Mt. Washington art glass lines. It was decorated with raised, gold-enameled lines dividing the surface of the ware in much the same way as lead lines divide a stained glass window. The sections were filled in with one or several transparent colors and further decorated in gold enamel with florals, foliage, beading, and medallions.

Our advisors for this category are Betty and Clarence Maier; they are listed in the Directory under Pennsylvania. See also Cranberry; Salt Shakers; Burmese; Crown Milano; Royal Flemish; etc.

Atomizer, melon shape, HP pansies, rpl bulb...............................**145.00**
Biscuit jar, Albertine, pk/lav floral on burmese color, 7" **325.00**
Biscuit jar, blown-out/pulled drapery w/gold, burmese int **875.00**
Biscuit jar, floral, pk on wht, crab motif on lid sgn MW **650.00**
Bowl, floral band on cranberry to clear, 28-rib, 3½x9" **275.00**
Bowl vase, shiny gr MOP Dia Quilt w/silver mica, 4x6½" **750.00**
Box, blown-out roses/bows/medallion on gr w/gold, 4x7½" **1,245.00**
Box, glove; silver & gold flowers, emb pk borders, 9½x4½".........**575.00**
Box, Monk w/wine glass, gilt rim & hinge, 3¼x4½" dia...............**545.00**
Compote, cranberry cut to clear, 1870s, 7x8½" **325.00**
Condiment set, roses, red on yel, 3-bottle; Wilcox fr, 7½" **225.00**
Creamer & sugar (open), bridal wht satin, ribbed, peach int.......**180.00**
Decanter, Invt T'print, cranberry, corset form, 11½x4½" **375.00**
Humidor, spider mums, magenta on wht satin, SP lid, 8x5¾"......**435.00**
Jar, Napoli, Brownies/cats/gold webs, turtle finial, 3x5" **650.00**
Pitcher, fish, gold on bl, gold spout & rim, 5x5" **965.00**
Pitcher, Verona, naturalistic mums, 6x5½" **435.00**
Plate, roses, pk on lustreless wht, 1870, 10" **110.00**
Rose bowl, cherub in cape, bl shaded, 3½x4½" **175.00**
Rose bowl, clear, vertical ribs, 3¾x3¼" **115.00**
Rose bowl, cranberry to wht opal, appl rigaree, 4-ftd, 8x7" **150.00**
Rose bowl, florals front/bk on cream, dotted rim, 4x5" **235.00**
Rose bowl, lustreless wht, plain, 8-crimp, 5x5½" **65.00**
Sugar shaker, daisies on ribbed satin, ornate SP top, 5".............**200.00**
Sugar shaker, florals, yel & wht on bl, egg form, NM **375.00**
Toothpick, ribbed, beaded top, 2½" **100.00**
Vase, acid-etched florals on rubena, ribbed int, 6x4½" **265.00**
Vase, aquatic plants on craquelle, ball form, 4" **170.00**
Vase, chrysanthemums on yel opal, 9x7½" **375.00**
Vase, cranberry to clear, bulbous, 8x4" **275.00**
Vase, daffodils on crystal, triple-gourd form, ca 1895, 12".........**275.00**
Vase, ferns, gr & gold w/red berries on crystal, 8" **160.00**
Vase, florals, mc on yel, bulbous, 9x7½" **365.00**
Vase, Lava, blk w/mc chips, ca 1878, 10½x6½" **2,750.00**

Vase, Lava, blk w/mc chips, classical shape, 6" **1,550.00**
Vase, Lava, curled reeded hdls, short neck/bulbous, 3½" **1,500.00**
Vase, lt bl satin to wht, bulbous/ruffled, 8x4" **145.00**
Vase, Napoli, clear w/gold trim, ribbed/bulbous, 8½x5" **985.00**
Vase, Napoli, frog in rushes, ext w/gold decor, ribs, 9" **975.00**
Vase, roses, mc on gr shaded, 11x6½" **650.00**
Vase, roses, mc on pk opal, cylindrical, #d, 9½x3½" **375.00**
Vase, satin rainbow spatter, mc on wht, frost edge, 9x5" **400.00**

Chepstow platter, Woods & Sons, 10", $75.00.

Plate, church in a landscape on white, 12", $250.00.

Mulberry China

Mulberry china was made by many of the Staffordshire area potters from about 1830 until the 1850s. It is a transfer-printed earthenware or ironstone named for the color of its decorations, a purplish-brown resembling the juice of the mulberry. Shades vary; some pieces look almost gray with only a hint of purple. Some of the patterns – Corean, Jeddo, Pelew, and Formosa, for instance – were also produced in Flow Blue ware. Others seem to have been used exclusively with the mulberry color.

Our advisor for this category is Mary Frank Gaston; she is listed in the Directory under Texas.

Balmoral, soap dish, w/lid **75.00**
Beauties of China, plate, 9" **50.00**
Bleeding Heart, creamer **85.00**
British Scenery, soup, hdls, w/underplate, Booth **65.00**
Bryonia, sauce dish, 5" **8.50**
Calcutta, cup & saucer, handleless **150.00**
Caledonia, platter, 20" **100.00**
Charmontel, cup plate, Ridgway, 3⅞" **40.00**
Chusan, plate, Podmore Walker, 8¼" **25.00**
Cologne, bowl, vegetable; w/lid, Alcock, lg **175.00**
Corea, plate, 12-sided, Clementson, 9½" **60.00**
Corean, cup plate, 4 for **110.00**
Corean, sugar bowl, lion-head hdls **125.00**
Corean, teapot, Podmore Walker, 8" **225.00**
Corean, toothbrush box, w/lid **200.00**
Cyprus, plate, Davenport, 9" **66.00**
Cyprus, tureen, vegetable; w/lid **175.00**
Delhi, plate, 7¾" **30.00**

Delhi, relish dish, 5½x8½" **65.00**
Dora, plate, 9" **40.00**
Dresden, plate, 7¼" **25.00**
Foliage, creamer, Walley **85.00**
Foliage, cup & saucer, handleless **60.00**
Foliage, plate, soup; Walley, 9¼" **35.00**
Foliage, plate, 8¼" **22.00**
Foliage, plate, 9" **24.00**
Heath's Flower, platter, 13½" **95.00**
Hyson, cup & saucer, handleless **55.00**
Jardiniere, creamer, Villeroy & Boch **35.00**
Jeddo, bowl, vegetable; w/lid, Adams, ca 1845 .... **210.00**
Jeddo, compote, tall ped, Adams **350.00**
Jeddo, cup, handleless **125.00**
Jeddo, pitcher, Adams & Son, ca 1845, 7" **125.00**
Jeddo, pitcher, Adams & Son, ca 1845, 8" **135.00**
Jeddo, pitcher & bowl, Adams & Son, ca 1845 .... **675.00**
Jeddo, platter, ca 1845, 15½x12" **160.00**
Jeddo, teapot **250.00**
Leipzig, platter, ca 1850, 14x10" **75.00**
Loretta, bowl, vegetable; Alcock **145.00**
Marble, toothbrush holder, w/lid **40.00**
Mogul Scenery, platter, Mayer, 13¼" **65.00**
Neva, plate, Challinor, 9" **60.00**
Ning Po, cup plate **35.00**
Pelew, cup & saucer, Challinor **65.00**
Pelew, plate, Challinor, 9¾" **55.00**
Pelew, sugar bowl **45.00**
Peruvian, nappy, Wedgwood, 5⅛" **18.00**
Peruvian, plate, Wedgwood, 7½" **30.00**
Rhone Scenery, bowl, vegetable; w/lid, Mayer, ca 1855 .... **175.00**
Rhone Scenery, creamer, hexagonal, Mayer, 5¼" **110.00**
Rhone Scenery, relish dish, Mayer **20.00**
Rhone Scenery, sauce tureen, w/underplate **225.00**
Royal Rose, cup & saucer **45.00**
Scinde, plate, Podmore Walker, 7½" **30.00**
Seaweed, plate, w/shells, Ridgway, 10¾" **65.00**
Shapoo, waste bowl **95.00**
Singan, plate, Goodfellow, 9¼" **55.00**
Susa, cup & saucer, Meigh **55.00**
Tavoy, plate, Podmore Walker, 8¾" **30.00**
Temple, cup & saucer, handleless; Podmore Walker, 4" **100.00**
Temple, plate, Podmore Walker, 7" **22.00**
Temple, plate, Podmore Walker, 7¾" **35.00**

Temple, plate, Podmore Walker, 9½" 55.00
Temple, platter, 14x10½" 110.00
Tivoli, bowl, vegetable; rnd, open, 10" 75.00
Tonquin, bowl, vegetable; 7¾" 75.00
Tonquin, cup & saucer, Heath..75.00
Tonquin, plate, Heath, 6" 30.00
Tonquin, plate, 9½" 45.00
Tonquin, sauce..45.00
Ventura, plate, 10½" 45.00
Vincennes, plate, Alcock, 9½" 55.00
Vincennes, sauce tureen, w/ladle & tray, Alcock 395.00
Vincennes, sugar bowl, w/lid, Alcock 135.00
Washington Vase, creamer..175.00
Washington Vase, cup & saucer, handleless 65.00
Washington Vase, pitcher, milk; 7½" 250.00
Washington Vase, plate, 9" 40.00
Washington Vase, platter, 16x12"..160.00
Washington Vase, sugar bowl, lion head hdls, w/lid....................175.00
Wreath, plate, soup; Furnival, 10½" 35.00

Muller Freres

Henri Muller established a factory in 1900 at Croismare, France. He produced fine cameo art glass decorated with florals, birds, and insects in the Art Nouveau style. The work was accomplished by acid engraving and hand finishing. Usual marks were 'Muller,' 'Muller Croismare,' or 'Croismare, Nancy.' In 1910 Henri and his brother Deseri formed a glassworks at Luneville. The cameo art glass made there was nearly all produced by acid cuttings of up to four layers with motifs similar to those favored at Croismare. A good range of colors was used, and some pieces were gold flecked. Handles and decorative devices were sometimes applied by hand. In addition to the cameo glass, they also produced an acid-finished glass of bold mottled colors in the Deco style. Examples were signed 'Muller Freres' or 'Luneville.'

Our advisor for this category is Don Williams; he is listed in the Directory under Iowa.

Cameo

Chandelier, poppies, 3-color on gold, 17" +3 6" shades..........16,000.00
Lamp, dome shade/tall std: cupids among trees, 2 cuts, 17" 7,000.00
Plaque, trees/lady & child by lake, man in boat, 12x6" 2,900.00
Shade, poppies/foliage, pk/bl on amber/bl mottle frost, 16".....6,000.00
Vase, butterflies/floral on rainbow frost, 7½" 1,500.00
Vase, evergreens/mtns, bl/brn on lt yel, incurvate, 4½" 900.00
Vase, fern fronds/scroll panels, cobalt on wht/pk, 6" 800.00

Cameo vase, lake scene, red-brown on yellow mottle, signed Luneville, 14", $4,400.00.

Vase, lake scene, dk/lt orange on yel, 4" 700.00
Vase, lg trees by lakeside, wine on pk/amber mottle, 9" 850.00
Vase, man w/cattle in silhouette, 3 cuts, 4½x3¼" 395.00
Vase, pine trees/brook w/bridge, 3-color on mottle, 16" 4,000.00
Vase, pine trees/mtns/lake, 5-color on yel opal, ovoid, 18" 7,800.00
Vase, pond lilies, lime on wht, polished, 4¾"..............................165.00
Vase, riverbank, brn on orange, 10" 1,650.00
Vase, rose bushes, red/yel/pk on gray to amber, ovoid, 17" 4,000.00
Vase, sheep/mtns, wht/bl/lav on rose, indented lip, 13" 4,000.00
Vase, trees & lake/man & 2 cows, dk bl on orange, 4½" 1,000.00
Vase, trees/boat/man in boat, 5" 900.00
Vase, windmill/ships, brn on orange mottle, 7½" 800.00
Vase, winter scene on yel to purple, tumbler form, 5" 450.00
Vase, 2 birds on branch/river bkground, bulbous neck, 8" 1,700.00
Vase, 2 shepherds/sheep, brn on orange, hdls, slim, 14" 2,500.00
Vase, 3 cherubs w/garlands, 3 cuts, Luneville, 5x5¾" 1,650.00
Vase, 4 oval reserves/floral garlands, brn on orange, 13½" 800.00

Miscellaneous

Chandelier, cream/lav mottle, gilt floral mts, 14" dia..................800.00
Lamp, boudoir; purple/pk mottle shade; wrought std w/leaves. 1,200.00
Lamp, floor; mottled bowl form in wrought std w/ivy, 70" 3,000.00
Plant stand, mottled lily form in wrought leafy std, 24" 800.00
Vase, satin w/internal bl mottle w/gold, 6½" 250.00

Muncie

Muncie Pottery, established in Muncie, Indiana, by Charles O. Grafton, was produced from 1922 until about 1935. It is made of a heavier clay than most of its contemporaries; the styles are sturdy and simple. Early glazes were bright and colorful. In fact, Muncie was advertised as the 'rainbow pottery.' Later, most of the ware was finished in a matt glaze. The more collectible examples are those modeled after Phoenix Glass vases – sculptured with lovebirds, grasshoppers, and goldfish. Their line of Art Deco-style vases bear a remarkable resemblance to the Consolidated Glass Company's Ruba Rombic line. Vases, candlesticks, bookends, ash trays, bowls, lamp bases, and luncheon sets were made. A line of garden pottery was manufactured for a short time. Items were frequently impressed with MUNCIE in block letters. Letters such as A, K, E, or D and the numbers 1, 2, 3, 4, or 5 often found scratched into the base are finishers' marks.

Bowl, Ruba Rombic type, lavender and green, 8½", $65.00; Vase, lavender and green, 6", $35.00.

Candle holder, lt gr matt, mold pressed, 3-hdld, 2½", pr 35.00
Refrigerator jug, tan gloss, ball form, base cavity, mk, 7"...............65.00
Strawberry jar, wht matt, hanging, 6" 125.00

Vase, blk/rust high gloss, flared, 6" **35.00**
Vase, gr/lavender matt, corset shape, 12" **80.00**
Vase, gr/rose matt, stick shape, 8" **30.00**
Vase, lav/gr, ribbed, pillow form, 6" **30.00**
Vase, mocha gloss, corset shape, 6" **45.00**
Vase, mocha/beige/rust gloss, #181, 1926, 7½" **45.00**
Vase, Ruba Rombic type, turq, triangular panels, A mk, 7" **55.00**
Vase, yel tones w/wht drips, Oriental style, A mk, 6½"x4½"..........**65.00**

Musical Instruments

The field of automatic musical instruments covers many different categories ranging from tiny dolls and trinkets concealing musical movements to huge organs and orchestrions which weigh many tons. Music boxes, first made in the late 18th century by Swiss watchmakers, were produced in both disk and cylinder models. The latter type employs a cylinder studded with tiny projections. As the cylinder turns, these projections lift the tuned teeth in the 'music comb,' and the melody results. The value of the instrument depends upon the length of the cylinder and the quality of workmanship, though other factors must also be considered. Those in ornate cabinets or with extra features such as bells, mechanical birds, etc., often sell for much more. Units built into matching tables sell for about twice the amount they would bring otherwise. While small and medium size units are still being made today, most of the larger ones date from the 19th century. Disk-type music boxes utilize interchangeable steel disks with projecting studs, which by means of an intervening 'star wheel' cause a music comb to play. There are many different variations and mechanisms. Most were made in Germany, but some were produced in the United States. Among the most popular makes are Polyphon, Symphonion, and Regina. The latter was made in Rahway, New Jersey, from about 1894 through 1917.

Player pianos were made in a wide variety of styles. Early varieties consisted of a mechanism which pushed up to a piano and played on the keyboard by means of felt-tipped fingers. These use sixty-five note rolls. Later models have the playing mechanisms built in. At first these also used sixty-five note rolls, but those produced from about 1908 until 1940 use eighty-eight note rolls.

Coin-operated electric pianos are deluxe versions of player pianos. These incorporate expression mechanisms so that by using special-made rolls they can play the hand-recorded rolls of famous pianists. Popular makes include Ampico, Duo-Art, and Welte. Roll-operated organs were made in many forms, ranging from table-top models to large foot-pumped versions. Of the latter, the Aeolian Orchestrelle is considered to be one of the best.

Unless noted, prices given are for instruments in fine condition, playing properly, with cabinets or cases in well-preserved or refinished condition. In all instances, unrestored instruments sell for much less, as do pieces with broken parts, damaged cases, and the like. On the other hand, particularly superb examples in especially ornate case designs and pieces which have been particularly well restored often will command more.

Key:
c — cylinder   d — disk

Mechanical

Box, Bremond, 8" 4-tune c, single comb, tune card, 5x16" **400.00**
Box, Bremond, 9" c, 8-air **1,200.00**
Box, Britannia, 9" duplex comb, inlaid walnut case.................. **2,000.00**
Box, Capital Cuff Box B, mahog, EX orig **5,000.00**
Box, Empress Concert Grand, 18½" d, mahog console **9,500.00**

Swiss cylinder music box, rosewood veneer with exotic woods and marble inlay, B.A. Bremond, 13" cylinder, 8-air, bells and original sheet, 10" x 23", $3,000.00.

Box, Euphonia, 20½" d, w/matching oak base, +20 disks **6,800.00**
Box, Mandoline, 12½" c, 10-tune, EX orig **1,500.00**
Box, Mermond, oak case, 12-tune, w/orig card, ca 1895, EX .. **2,000.00**
Box, Polyphon, 11" d, EX orig **1,650.00**
Box, Polyphon, 15½" d, rosewood/walnut, 12-drw base, 34" ... **3,500.00**
Box, Polyphon, 19⅝" d, glass front, upright, walnut case **5,000.00**
Box, Regina, 15½" d, dbl comb, oak case, EX orig **3,500.00**
Box, Regina, 20¾" d, automatic changer, mahog case **18,000.00**
Box, Regina, 26" d, single comb, mahog, 17"..........................**15,000.00**
Box, Regina #1, dbl comb, upright, NM **8,500.00**
Box, Regina #2, 15½" dbl comb, mahog case........................... **4,000.00**
Box, Regina #20, 11" d, rstr, +18 disks **2,500.00**
Box, Regina #26, 20¾" d, fancy case, EX orig......................... **6,800.00**
Box, Regina #32, mahog, d changer **13,500.00**
Box, Regina #34, 27" changer **15,000.00**
Box, Regina #35, 15½" d, automatic changer, oak case **17,500.00**
Box, Regina #39, 20¾" d, serpentine mahog case **6,000.00**
Box, Regina #40, orig factory oil paintings, console **7,500.00**
Box, Regina #403, oak, EX orig **500.00**
Box, Regina #50, 15½" d, serpentine mahog case **5,000.00**
Box, Regina #51, 15½" d, coin op, mahog case, w/base **5,500.00**
Box, Regina Bell, mahog, EX orig **8,500.00**
Box, Regina Orchestral #4, fancy case, 80", NM **13,500.00**
Box, Stella, 17" d, dbl comb/metal bed, mahog, 1900, 28x21" . **4,000.00**
Box, Symphonion, 15¼" d, upright glass/walnut case w/base .**12,000.00**
Box, Symphonion, 9½" d, dbl comb, walnut case **1,250.00**
Box, 15½" d, oak bow front, coin-op changer.........................**15,000.00**
Harp, 2-tune music box, 22", NM...**950.00**
Nickelodeon, Capitol, violin pipes, EX orig.............................. **7,500.00**
Nickelodeon, Coinola, keyboard, 3 windows, rail, oak, EX **4,750.00**
Nickelodeon, Empress Electric, stained glass front, oak, EX.... **3,600.00**
Nickelodeon, Milton A, rstr... **6,500.00**
Nickelodeon, Seeburg E, w/reitterating xylophone, oak, NM .. **7,200.00**
Nickelodeon, Western Electric Mascot, oak, rstr..................... **7,500.00**
Nickelodeon, Western Electric Selectra-B, EX orig **7,000.00**
Orchestrion, Bejou, 20-key, paper rolls, EX orig.........................**750.00**
Orchestrion, Coinola Midget, style O, rstr..............................**18,000.00**
Orchestrion, Wurlitzer CX, automatic roll changer, NM **27,000.00**

Organ, Aeolian-Hammond, speaker cabinet, EX, +50 rolls..... **3,000.00**
Organ, band; Wurlitzer #105, orig drums, EX orig **12,500.00**
Organ, band; Wurlitzer #146B, dbl tracker, EX **21,000.00**
Organ, dance; Mortier, cafe style, oak & leaded glass, EX **22,000.00**
Organ, dance; Mortier, 84-key, 350 pipes, 180" W **35,000.00**
Organ, Gem Roller Cob, EX orig **450.00**
Piano, baby grand; Duo-Art, walnut, 1925, NM, +15 rolls..... **15,000.00**
Piano, grand; Apollo, cvd mahog art case, rstr, +bench........... **5,300.00**
Piano, grand; Chickering Ampico Centennial, mahog, 68" ... **12,500.00**
Piano, grand; Henry F Miller, walnut case, 1896, 70", EX **3,400.00**
Piano, grand; Knabe Ampichron B, mahog, 64", EX orig........ **9,000.00**
Piano, grand; Knabe Ampico, EX orig.. **3,500.00**
Piano, grand; Knabe Ampico, rstr **18,000.00**
Piano, grand; Mason & Hamlin Ampico, burl walnut, 64" **13,500.00**
Piano, grand; Mason & Hamlin Ampico A, rstr, +500 rolls ... **20,500.00**
Piano, grand; Steck Duo-Art, EX **3,000.00**
Piano, grand; Steinway Duo-Art XR, walnut, '28, 74", EX **9,000.00**
Piano, grand; Stroud Duo-Art, EX orig **2,200.00**
Piano, grand; Weber Duo-Art, walnut, 68", EX orig **8,500.00**
Piano, hurdy-gurdy street; Louis Casalini, 1881, 52x52x23".... **5,500.00**
Piano, Poppers Konsertist, EX, +39 rolls **2,500.00**
Piano, Red Welte, oak cabinet, EX orig **3,500.00**
Piano, upright; Capitol, violin pipes, A rolls, EX orig............. **7,500.00**
Piano, upright; Steinway Duo-Art, mahog, 1914, EX, +rolls... **3,400.00**
Piano, upright; Story & Clark Storytone, Deco, 1932-42, EX . **2,900.00**
Piano, upright; Wheelock Duo-Art, VG orig **1,500.00**
Violano, Mills, dbl, rstr **30,000.00**
Violano, Mills, single, mahog, EX orig, +14 rolls **9,500.00**
Violano, Mills, single, oak, EX orig **6,000.00**

Non-Mechanical

Accordion, Empress, Germany, ca 1890, sm, EX **65.00**
Accordion, Trafficanty, MOP inlay, Italy, orig case, EX **135.00**
Banjo, Gibson Mastertone Custom copy, 5-string, EX, +case **245.00**
Banjo-ukelele, Waverley, bird's eye maple, 1920s, EX orig **125.00**
Cello, stamped & labled: Ehrmann-Albany, ca 1870, EX **150.00**
Cornet, Conn, modified shepherd's crook, USN, 1917, EX **70.00**
Cornet, Solo, E flat alto, ca 1875, rare, EX **70.00**
Cornet, York, B flat, fingertip key change to A, NP **30.00**
Flute, dk stained fruitwood, blk mtd metal rings, VG................... **40.00**
Flute, sweet potato; stoneware, 1879 Sydney Expo, Austria **85.00**
Guitar, Fender, inlay on neck, electric/dbl pickups, '60s, VG **300.00**
Guitar, Gibson L-5, pearl inlaid fretboard, NM, +lined case........ **900.00**
Guitar, Vincenzo Miroglio, classical, orig label, 1920s, VG **30.00**
Harmonica, Hohner's Best, MIB **25.00**
Harmonica, Marine Band, sm, MIB **30.00**
Harmonica, Novophone, Germany, EX **12.50**
Horn, H Durand-Paris, E flat alto, all brass, 1920s, G **45.00**
Mandolin harp, eagle & crest on front, 32 strings, 13x19" **90.00**
Saxophone, baritone; Conn, SP, #12501, VG **50.00**
Saxophone, Beuscher, B flat tenor, #88511, EX, +worn case **80.00**
Tambourine, early HP birds & bumblebee on tree branch **68.00**
Violin, Antonio Papolo, Magini Brescia 1872, 2-pc maple bk....... **80.00**
Violin, Antonio Stradivarius, Germany, plain, ½-sz, VG............... **50.00**
Violin, Antonio Stradivarius Cermonesis...1737, EX.................... **190.00**
Violin, CH Hacket, 2-pc flamed maple bk & sides, ca 1906, EX.**100.00**
Violin, copy of Amiti, 1-pc maple bk & sides, spruce top, EX **20.00**
Violin, De Salzasrd, French, 1-pc maple bk & sides, EX................ **50.00**
Violin, J Guarnerius Cremona-Fecit IHS, 1-pc pearwood bk, EX..**55.00**
Violin, Jakobus Steiner, 2-pc maple bk & sides, ca 1925, EX.......... **45.00**
Violin, John Juzek, 24" +bow & case **85.00**
Violin, Laurent Storoni Fecit Cremona, 2-pc maple bk, EX **85.00**
Violin, N Gagliano Filius Alexandri...1730, 2-pc bk, EX.............. **50.00**

Violin, Nicholaus Amatus Fecit, Cremona Germany, 1690, VG ..**70.00**
Violin, Paris, 2-pc maple bk, machine head, spruce top, EX..........**70.00**
Violin, Salvadore de Durr, Germany, 1-pc maple bk, EX **95.00**

Nailsea

Nailsea is a term referring to clear or colored glass decorated in contrasting spatters, swirls, or loops. These are usually white but may also be pink or blue. It was first produced in Nailsea, England, during the late 1700s but was made in other parts of Britain and Scotland as well. Originally used for decorative novelties only, by 1845 pitchers, tumblers, and other practical items were being made from Nailsea-type glass. See also Lamps.

Bottle, gemel; clear w/rigaree & wht looping, bl rim, 8" **120.00**
Flask, chestnut; amethyst loops alternate w/wht, 4" **230.00**
Flask, clear bl w/cranberry looping & wht casing, 9"...................**185.00**
Flask, cobalt w/wht looping, 7" **170.00**
Flask, custard bl w/pk looping & vertical ribs, 6¾" **185.00**
Flask, pigeon blood shading to cranberry w/wht looping, 8".........**175.00**

Pocket flask, deep amber with white and green loopings, pontiled, sheared mouth, 5¾", $230.00.

Flask, red-amber w/irregular wht spirals, European, 4½" **200.00**
Flask, wht w/bright bl loops, teardrop form, pontil, 7½" **110.00**
Flask, wht w/red & bl alternating loops, pontil, 7".....................**130.00**
Pipe, clear w/wht looping, 24" L **200.00**

Nakara

Nakara was an opaque glassware made soon after the turn of the century by the C.F. Monroe Company. Though shapes were plainer and colors deeper, it was very similar to their famous Wave Crest line. Boxes of all sizes, pin trays, and dresser items of every sort were decorated with delicate hand-painted florals and 'squeeze-bag' lace reserves transfer printed with portraits of classical figures, birds, or Victorian ladies. Ormolu handles, bases, and collars, and scented satin box linings added opulence to the already elegant ware. The C.F. Monroe Company closed in 1916. For more information, we recommend *Wave Crest: The Glass of C. F. Monroe* by Wilfred R. Cohen, available from Collector Books or your local bookstore.

Biscuit jar, poppies, orange on bl spatter, SP mts, 6x6" **725.00**
Box, cherub & wild roses on bl, mk, 4½" dia...............................**650.00**
Box, daisies, bl on pk, sq, 3½" **325.00**
Box, lady's portrait on bl, mk, 4½" dia **475.00**

Box, medallions, pk on bl w/wht beads, hexagonal, mk, 3x4".......325.00
Box, portrait lid/enamel beading on pk, sq, 4"...........................700.00
Hair receiver, florals on gr, ormolu rosettes, 4" dia 350.00
Humidor, elk/BPOE, brass-tone lid, 7½"......................................550.00
Humidor, Indian in headdress/Cigars on olive gr, 5½"..............650.00

Humidor, owl on branch, 'Cigars' on lid, marked, 5½", $1,500.00.

Vase, florals front/bk on shaded gr, ormolu ft/rim, 11x6" 825.00
Vase, Indian portrait, brass rim, 5½"..395.00
Vase, iris in lav, beaded top, ormolu ftd base, 13½".....................785.00

Napkin Rings

Napkin rings became popular during the late 1800s. They were made from various materials. Among the most popular and collectible today are the large group of varied silverplated figural types made by American manufacturers.

When no condition is indicated, the items listed below are assumed to be all original and in very good to excellent condition. A timely warning: inexperienced buyers should be aware of excellent reproductions on the market, especially the wheeled pieces. However, these do not have the fine detail and patina of the originals and tend to have a more consistent, soft pewter-like finish. Over the past year, the larger figurals in excellent condition have appreciated considerably. Only those with a blackened finish, corrosion, or broken and/or missing parts have maintained their earlier price levels.

Key:
gw — gold washed   SH&M — Simpson, Hall, &
R&B — Reed & Barton   Miller

Barrel ring held by Xd branches & leaf..88.00
Beaver sits on leaves & branches, Toronto 75.00
Bird perched atop sq ring on ped..125.00
Boy dressed for winter w/book under arm stands by ring...............220.00
Boy in harness pulls ring on wheels..350.00
Boy on stool pulls off boot, eng ring, NM 225.00
Boys kick on ea side of filigree ring, Meriden #332 ....195.00
Camel on ftd base by ring on sm ped, Meriden............................250.00
Cavalry saddlebags & sabres hold ring, VG 150.00
Cherries hang from barrel ring, ped leaf-base, Toronto #733 ....150.00
Cherub atop ring guides butterfly on flower, SH&M #201 ....285.00
Cherub in soldier hat w/sword sits on turtle, Middleton 295.00
Cherub rides dolphin & holds spear, Meriden #157.....................295.00
Cherub w/ring on bk, scrolled base, ftd, Barbour.........................250.00

Cherubs aside ring, tiered base, R&B #1320................................300.00
Cherubs support ring w/bks, ped ft, Wilcox.................................220.00
Chick on wishbone, Rococo base, elevated ring, EX 85.00
Cockatoo on stem of leaf at side of ring.......................................135.00
Cockatoo w/tail spread atop ring, leafy base, flower at side..........160.00
Crocodile crawls w/ring on bk, unmk 235.00
Dog harnessed to sled that holds ring, Meriden...........................165.00
Dog on haunches tries to catch bird atop ring, Aurora #27 ....195.00
Dog w/bushy tail/paws on latticed ring, sq/ftd base, ball ft...........135.00
Dolphin w/ring on bk, Aurora #32, EX..250.00
Eagle perched on bar, holds ring w/wings, Rogers-Smith #203 ....295.00
Fox ea side, bird on nest atop ring, Meriden #01534...................195.00
Fox looks around ring held by oak tree, Derby #314 ....235.00
Fox pulling cart, wheels turn 295.00
Frog w/glass eyes on sm leaf, fly on hammered ring.....................295.00

Girl feeds begging dog, #199, Rogers & Bro., $295.00.

Goat beside ring, Rogers & Bro #195..200.00
Goat pulling wheels, Meriden #212 ....295.00
Grapes & leaf at side of ring, Toronto #733 ....85.00
Greenaway boy holds drumstick, ring is drum, Hartford #30 ......295.00
Greenaway boy kneels to look in nest of eggs beside ring 265.00
Greenaway boy lies on shield holding emb ring, Wilcox 350.00
Greenaway boy sits/reads book leans on ring, Aurora 425.00
Greenaway boy w/bat & ball...245.00
Greenaway girl leads goat w/rein, Meriden #0236.......................255.00
Greenaway girl w/hands on ring, Barbour Bros............................185.00
Greenaway girl w/rifle, ftd sq base, mk SHM...............................395.00
Griffins face out at ea side of ring, ring in hair, unmk 185.00
Horse pulls wheeled cart w/ring, Meriden #214..........................265.00
Hound w/ring on bk, SHM #610 ....175.00
Jack & Jill ready to climb hill, Tufts..395.00
Jester before ring points & holds torch, Meriden #0258 ....275.00
Lion lies on rectangular base w/ring at bk, Meriden #152...........195.00
Lion stands beside ring 175.00
Lotus bud & leaf base w/stem hold ring, Meriden.......................80.00
Man in turban sits w/legs Xd before ring, Webster 200.00
Monkey dressed as man, Tufts..300.00
Parakeet atop ring, SHM #810...135.00
Parrot w/glass eyes on loop hdl by ring, #4338............................185.00
Peacock atop ring, tail down bk, Meriden #234 ....200.00
Poodle on haunches aside floral ring, Tufts..................................145.00
Rabbits on sq grassy base, eng shells on ring, Pairpoint................395.00
Ring on sled, Wilcox #05176 ....185.00
Rip Van Winkle stands on rocky base, ring on shoulder 600.00

Rosebud w/3 leaves ea side of supported ring, unmk......................85.00
Squirrel eats nut atop log ring, acorns at sides, unmk..................200.00
Squirrel w/blk glass eyes blows horn beside ring, unmk...............265.00
Stork w/ring on bk, octagonal base, SH&M..220.00
Tennis racquet & ball support ring, EX..150.00
Turtle w/ring on bk, Meriden #284 ....195.00
Violin at side of ring, sheet music on base, Wilcox #4393 ....285.00
Wheelbarrow holds ornate ring, Pairpoint......................................185.00
3-leaf clover supports ring, Pairpoint #6 ....85.00

Nash

A. Douglas Nash founded the Corona Art Glass Company in Long Island, New York. He produced tableware, vases, flasks, etc. using delicate artistic shapes and forms. After 1933 he worked for the Libbey Glass Company.

Bowl, gold irid, cased, ribbed, scalloped, sgn, 8½"........................375.00
Compote, Chintz, gr, flange rim in red w/gray spirals, 5x8" 485.00
Finger bowl, clear smoke, ground pontil, sgn/#d, 3" H 100.00
Pitcher, gr loops on clear, 8½"..375.00
Plate, Chintz, tan/lime on clear, 6½" 150.00
Sherbet, pulled concentric lines, gr & bl on clear, +plate............250.00
Tumbler, Chintz, lt aqua, orange stripes, 6¼" 110.00
Tumbler, gr loops on clear, appl crystal ft, 5" 125.00
Vase, allover gold decor on dk bl, sgn, 8½" 675.00
Vase, bl & gr vertical stripes, bulbous, flared, sgn, 18" 600.00
Vase, bl feather strokes, lime streaks, bulbous, 6½" 395.00
Vase, bl/gr on gold, 4½x6½"..250.00
Vase, gold, curving sq rim, sgn/#539, 6¾", pr..............................400.00
Vase, gold, patterned lower body, scalloped, sgn, 4½" 225.00
Vase, gold w/bl irid, knopped trumpet form, ftd, #529, 9½" 600.00
Vase, gr/bl int vertical stripes, trumpet form, #84, 10" 250.00

Natzler, Gertrude and Otto

The Natzler's came to the United States from Vienna in the late 1930s. They settled in Los Angeles where they continued their work in ceramics, for which they were already internationally recognized. Gertrude created the forms; Otto formulated a variety of interesting glazes – among them volcanic, crystalline, and lustre.

Bowl, Bl Pompeian, fine volcanic gray/lime, 6½" 2,000.00
Bowl, bright lapis bl, thin walled, 3x5½".................................. 1,400.00
Bowl, cobalt crystalline, rnd/shallow, sgn, 12".......................... 1,200.00
Bowl, Sang glaze, ochre w/exposed blk, thin walled, 6" 1,000.00
Bowl, yel w/gray streaking to brn at rim, elongated, 8" 2,000.00
Vase, yel, 4x4½"..795.00

Netsukes

Netsukes are miniature Japanese carvings made with holes called Himitoshi, either channeled or within the carved design, that allow it to be threaded onto a waist cord and worn with the kimono. Because the kimono had no pockets, the Japanese man hung his tools, his pipe, tobacco pouch, and other daily necessities from his sash. The netsuke was the toggle that secured them all. Although most are of ivory, others were made of bone, wood, metal, porcelain, or semi-precious stones. Some were inlaid or lacquered. They are found in many forms, but figurals are the most common and desirable. They range in size from 1" up to 3", which was the maximum size allowed by law. Most netsukes rep-

resented the religion, mythology, and the habits of the average person; there was no written word, hence carvers depicted the daily life of the people.

Careful study is required to recognize the quality of the netsuke. Many have been made in Hong Kong in recent years; and even though some are very well carved, these are considered copies and avoided by the serious collector. There are many books that will help you learn to recognize quality netsukes, and most reputable dealers are glad to assist you. Use your magnifying glass to check for repairs. In the listings that follow, netsukes are ivory unless noted otherwise; 'stained' indicates a color wash.

Arhat w/scroll, wood, gold lacquer, Yoshihide, 1880s, 1¼"...... **4,620.00**
Baku, dk stain, sm age crack, unsgn, 1790s, 1⅜" **1,430.00**
Baku on haunches, wood, EX cvg/patina, unsgn, 1700s, 1⅝" . **7,150.00**
Bamboo, man w/scythe cvd w/in, wood, unsgn, 1880s, 1¾" .. **1,200.00**
Beetle on pomegranates, 2 stains, Gyokuyosai, 1800s, 1⅜".........**550.00**
Blind man crawling on raft, lt stain, Hikaku, 1850s, 1¾"............**990.00**
Cockerel, ebony wood, dbl inlaid eyes, M Mitsu, 1850s, 1¾" . **1,320.00**
Dragon ship w/Lady Murasaki & figures, Somei, 1880s, 1¾" **825.00**
Eagle w/fox in talons, inlaid eyes, Shokyusai, 1880s, 1½"........ **1,200.00**
Ebisu on fish, stain, sgn Toshimune in MOP plaque, 1880s, 2"....**660.00**
Frog on lotus leaf, wood, inlaid eyes, ca 1800, Issan, 1⅝" **1,430.00**
Goat, wood, inlaid eyes, EX patina, Masanao, 1850s, 1⅝"....... **3,850.00**
Hare, elongated body, inlaid eyes, Bishu, 1900s, 1¾".............. **1,100.00**
Horned beetle on branch, wood, Harumitsu, 1800s, 1⅝" **1,540.00**
Horse leaping, dbl inlaid eyes, Risshisai Kangyoku, 1900s, 2" .. **2,420.00**
Horse w/saddle, 3 inlaid pearls, Meigyokusai, 1900s, 1⅞"........ **1,650.00**
Kanyu, EX details, dk stain, Kinrusai, 1800s, 1½" **550.00**
Karako w/mask of Okame, gr stain, Hoko, ca 1880s, 1¼"........ **1,200.00**
Lantern ghost (Oiwa), wood, inlaid eyes, Kosei, 1970s, 3" **2,200.00**
Monkey w/mask, inlaid eyes, eng, Masatami, 1800s, 1⅝" **1,980.00**
Monkey wrestles octupus, stain, Ikkosai, late 1800s, 1⅜" **1,430.00**
Mushrooms, wood, naturalistic stain, Tomokazu, 1800s, 1½" **420.00**
Oni & lady in tub, wood, inlaid eyes, Shoku, 1880s, 1½"........ **1,430.00**
Oni Nembutsu & Fujihime, lt stain, Minkoku, 1800s, 1½" **800.00**
Oni w/rope, wood, EX patina, unsgn, 1700s, 2¼" **4,840.00**
Oshidori, wood, ittobori style, inlaid eyes, unsgn, 1800s, 2" **465.00**
Ox, recumbent, wood, stained, Ruyshin, 1800s, 1⅝"............... **1,800.00**
Persimmon, wood, stem forms himotoshi, Koichi, 1800s, 1½".....**770.00**
Puppy chewing on ball, fine patina, Gyokuyosai, 1850s, 1¼" **935.00**
Puppy w/sandal, wood, inlaid eyes, Hogen Tadashide, 1¾"...... **4,950.00**
Rat catcher w/rat on bk, inlaid eyes, Masayoshi, 1880s, 1¾" **880.00**
Rat w/walnut, wood, inlaid eyes, stain, Itten, 1800s, 1¼"........ **2,200.00**
Sparrow dancer w/shishi mask, unsgn, ca 1800, 2¾".............. **1,045.00**
Teakettle, badger study w/in, lacquered, Yasuaki, 1880s, 1"..... **1,980.00**
Teakettle, badger/octupus w/in, wood, Masanao, 1800s, 1½" .. **3,960.00**
Tennin w/flute in flight, Masatoshi, 1900s, 2¼"...................... **1,650.00**
Tiger, wood, fine patina, brass eyes, Minko, 1890s, 1⅝".............**825.00**
Toad on rock, wood, inlaid eyes, stain, Masanao, 1890s, 1⅜".. **1,320.00**
Toads, 1 sm on 2nd's bk, wood, inlaid eyes, Masanao, 1800s, 2" ..**880.00**
Trainer w/monkey on bk, stain, Kosen, 1880s, 1½" **550.00**
Turtle dove, dbl inlaid eyes, Shingetsu, 1900s, 2" **1,200.00**
2 Fugu-Fish w/3 eggplants, wood, stain, Tadayuki, 1800s, 1¾".. **3,080.00**
2 monkeys wrestle, EX details, stain, Ikkosai, 1800s, 1½"....... **1,200.00**
2 Shishi playfully fighting, stain, Tomochika, 1800s, 1⅝" **1,430.00**
3 Immortals in lg shell, stain, Shugetsu, 1880s, 1⅝" **600.00**
3 kittens in basket, dbl inlaid eyes, Godo, 1900s, 1¾" **440.00**

New England Glass Works

Founded in 1818 by Deming Jarves in Boston, Massachusetts, the New England Glass Company produced cut, blown-three-mold, freeblown, and pressed glass of the highest quality. They were recognized for their fine decorative accomplishments, using etching, gilding, and engraving to emphasize their wares. For more than fifty years they produced prize-winning pressed glass dinnerware sets. Because they refused to compromise the quality of their product by using the cheaper lime-based glass that flooded the market in the 1860s, the company fell into financial trouble and by 1877 was forced to close. However, William Libbey, who had been the sales manager there since 1870, leased the premises and resumed operations with his father Edward Drummond Libbey as full partner. In 1892 the firm became known as The Libbey Glass Company. See also Amberina; Libbey.

Candlestick, caryatid (draped lady), Whitney design, 10" 375.00
Sugar bowl, Beehive, top of finial ground, 7½" 950.00
Sugar bowl w/conical lid, eng grapes/acorns, 1830, 9½" 2,700.00
Vase, Loop, purple-bl, gauffered rim, marble base, 9½" 300.00
Vase, Swirl, pk/yel/gr, 3-ring neck, bulbous base, 11x5½" 125.00

New Geneva

In the early years of the 19th century, several potteries flourished in the Greensboro, Pennsylvania, area. They produced utilitarian stoneware items as well as tile and novelties for many decades; all failed well before the turn of the century.

Bank, floral, rust brushed on red bsk, dome top, 7", EX 350.00
Flowerpot, brushed brn floral, red clay, free-ring hdls, 8" 1,300.00
Flowerpot, brushwork/name, brn on tan, crimped rims, 6", VG ..275.00

Jar, floral on brushed cobalt on salt glaze, repaired, 12", EX, $3,000.00.

Jar, floral/foliage, brn on red clay, 10", NM 775.00
Jug, floral/inscription/1901, brn on red-gray clay, 5¾" 5,000.00
Pitcher, foliage, rust on red bsk, minor wear, 12" 550.00

New Hall

The New Hall Company was established in the early 1780s in the Shelton district of England. In the early years, they produced hardpaste dinnerware typically decorated with simple floral sprays, often assigning a number rather than a name to their patterns. By 1812, a bone china body was favored and styles revised to suit the fashion. Decorations

became more elaborate. Much of the ware was unmarked and is often attributed to Worcester. Occasionally a piece was marked 'New Hall' within a double circle. Production ceased by 1835.

Bowl, floral, mc, 2½x5", EX 35.00
Bowl, red transfer, mc florals, mk, 7¾" 250.00
Cup & saucer, pk/bl/gr floral+King's roses, pk border 110.00

Mother and Child tea service, ca 1800-1810, 59 pieces, $800.00.

New Martinsville

The New Martinsville Glass Company took its name from the town in West Virginia where it began operations in 1901. In the beginning years, pressed tablewares were made in crystal as well as colored and opalescent glass. Considered an innovator, the company was known for their imaginative applications of the medium in creating lamps made entirely of glass, vanity sets, figural decanters, and models of animals and birds. In 1944 the company was purchased by Viking Glass, who continued to use many of the old molds – the animal molds included. They marked their wares 'Viking' or 'Rainbow Art.' Viking recently ceased operations and has been purchased Kenneth Dalzell, President of the Fostoria Company; and they, too, are making the animal birds and animal models. Although at first they were not marked, future productions are to be marked with an acid stamp. Dalzell/Viking animals are in the $50.00 to $60.00 range. See also Depression Glass.

Bookends, Russian wolfhound, ea 75.00
Bookends, seal w/ball, lg, pr 110.00
Bookends, ship, pr..95.00
Bottle, scent; bl, octagonal stoppper 30.00
Bowl, Florentine, flared, 12" 15.00
Bowl, Meadow Wreath, #26 etch, crimped, 12" 45.00
Bowl, Sun Glow, ribbed, ruffled, 5"...65.00
Butter dish, Radiance, silver overlay 80.00
Cake plate, Prelude, ftd, 11¼" 48.00
Candlestick, Florentine, 5"...10.00
Candlestick, swan, dk gr, pr...25.00
Cocktail, rooster stem, 4-oz 10.00
Console set, gold Florentine etch, 3-pc...50.00
Console set, Swan, 3-pc..30.00
Cruet, Janice, bl 40.00
Cruet, Prelude, cobalt hdl, w/stopper 55.00
Decanter, Su Su Bird 15.00
Figurine, bear, papa...225.00
Figurine, chick 28.00
Figurine, duck, dk teal, Viking..35.00
Figurine, eagle, single, ea...65.00
Figurine, German Shepherd 65.00
Figurine, hen, mama 65.00
Figurine, pig, mama, scarce 350.00
Figurine, rooster, curved tail, 7½" 85.00

Figurine, rooster, gr, Viking Epic Line................................**50.00**
Figurine, rooster, ruby, Viking Epic Line............................**60.00**
Figurine, seal, w/candle holder, lg, pr.............................**140.00**
Figurine, squirrel, no base..**35.00**
Figurine, squirrel, on sq/flat base......................................**40.00**
Figurine, tiger, head down..**175.00**
Figurine, woodsman...**95.00**
Flower frog, dancing lady, pk...**450.00**
Goblet, Mt Vernon, golf ball stem, ruby, 6"......................**7.50**
Goblet, Prelude..**18.00**
Mayonnaise, Prelude, etched, 3-pc.....................................**35.00**
Mustard, Janice, bl...**30.00**
Plate, torte; Prelude, ftd, 11¼"..**55.00**
Powder jar, Queen Anne, Ritz Blue....................................**32.00**
Relish, Princess, Prelude etched, 3-part..............................**12.50**
Sherbet, Mt Vernon, golf ball stem, ruby...........................**7.50**
Sugar bowl, Meadow Wreath...**8.00**
Swan, gr, S-Line, 6"...**20.00**
Swan, Janice, cobalt neck & head, 10"...............................**35.00**
Swan, open, Prelude, 5"...**25.00**
Swan, S-Line, amber, 6"...**18.00**
Tumbler, Oscar, amber, platinum trim..................................**3.50**

Divided oval covered dish, black, 8", $47.50.

Newcomb

The Newcomb College of New Orleans, Louisiana, established a pottery in 1895 to provide the students with first-hand experience in the fields of art and ceramics. Using locally dug clays – red and buff in the early years, white-burning by the turn of the century – potters were employed to throw the ware which the ladies of the college decorated. Until about 1910, a glossy glaze was used on ware decorated by slip painting or incising. After that a matt glaze was favored. Soft blues and greens were used almost exclusively, and the decorative themes were chosen to reflect the beauty of the South. 1930 marked the end of the matt-glaze period and the art-pottery era.

Various marks used by the pottery include an 'N' within a 'C,' sometimes with 'HB' added to indicate a 'hand-built' piece. The potter often incised his initials into the ware, and the artists were encouraged to sign their work. Among the most well-known artists were Sadie Irvine, Henrietta Bailey, and Fannie Simpson.

Newcomb pottery is evaluated to a large extent by two factors: design and condition. In the following listings, items are assumed matt unless noted otherwise.

Bowl, floral rim, EX art, AF Simpson, 3½x8½"...........................**750.00**
Bowl, floral rim, red w/gr stems on bl, 6"....................................**650.00**
Box, flower on lid, vertical-rib base, S Irvine, 3½x5"................**600.00**
Jar, cvd morning-glories, cut-out ft, gr/bl matt, Mason, 4".......**1,250.00**

Jar, moss/trees, acorns on lid, AF Simpson, 7x5½"...................**1,900.00**
Loving cup, w/flowers, 3 hdls, 7x7"...**5,400.00**
Match urn, gr/bl matt, thrown by Meyer, 2½x3".........................**175.00**
Pitcher, sm floral neck band, bl on dk bl, S Irvine, 2½"..............**450.00**
Vase, alligator, bulbous, 8x12"...**17,600.00**
Vase, daffodils w/long stems, wht/yel on bl, HB, 8", NM...........**750.00**
Vase, elongated leaves from rim to base, lav/bl/gr, HB, 5".........**900.00**
Vase, floral neck band, S Irvine/JM/#173/RA24, 6"...................**600.00**
Vase, floral/berries in wide band at top, Irvine/Meyer, 9"..........**600.00**
Vase, florals on long stems, EX art, A Mason, #d, 7"................**1,600.00**
Vase, geometrics on bl matt, gourd shape, S Irvine, 6"..............**1,300.00**
Vase, iris band/dk bl bands on bl gloss, SE Wells, 10x4"...........**1,500.00**
Vase, jonquils, 4-color, allover decor, sgn AFS/JM, 8½".........**1,900.00**
Vase, leaves on body, pk-floral collar, hexagon neck, 6"............**700.00**
Vase, mistletoe, dk maroon, mk/1903, 3½"..................................**850.00**
Vase, moon/moss, S Irvine, 8"..**2,500.00**
Vase, moon/moss/oak trees, EX color, 6½x6".............................**1,400.00**
Vase, moon/moss/trees, AC Arbo/#V-30, potter Ford, 6"..........**900.00**
Vase, moon/moss/trees, cylindrical, AFS, 6½x3½".....................**725.00**
Vase, moon/moss/trees, cylindrical, artist initialed, 9½".........**1,600.00**
Vase, moon/moss/trees, JM & Sadie Irvine, EX cvg, 11".........**4,250.00**
Vase, moss/trees, lt yel sky, AFS/J/#49/JL86, 7".......................**2,300.00**

Vase, moon, moss, and oak trees, A.F. Simpson, 1922, 13", $3,500.00; Vase, moon, moss, two oak trees, and a fence against a morning sky, A.F. Simpson, 1920, 11", $4,400.00 at auction.

Vase, pine cones/branches, gr/pk on bl, H Bailey, 7½"...............**1,750.00**
Vase, snowdrops/leaves, gr/wht on bl, Alma Mason, 6¾"..........**1,300.00**
Vase, wide floral band, bl/wht gloss, L Nicholson, 4x5"............**1,100.00**
Vase, woodland scene, bl/gray, baluster, sgn AFS, 8½"............**1,150.00**
Vase, yel flowers, early, 9x3½"...**3,300.00**

Newspapers

In addition to historic content, there are other factors that can add or take away the value of an old newspaper. These factors are: whether or not the account is a 'first report' (the first time that the news appeared – a 'later-report' is a subsequent reporting); location of articles on the event (those with front-page articles are more highly valued); displayability (size of headlines, presence of photos or graphics to illustrate the event, etc.); whether the paper is from a small or large town; a daily or weekly; and charisma of the paper or event. Prices listed here are for a typical mid-sized town paper with front-page coverage and medium-size headlines.

Papers that do not cover a specific event are called 'atmosphere' newspapers. While these are not as valuable, they offer interesting insight into a particular era through ads for runaway slaves, ships' schedules, jobs wanted, etc. Many have interesting articles on topics such as mermaids, hangings, sea voyages, and a host of other topics.

For a more complete price guide and information on how to determine values as well as how to grade historic newspapers, detect reprints, where to buy and sell originals, and much more, the Newspaper Collectors Society of America offers a *Free Mini-Course About Historic Newspapers*. To obtain your copy of the 32-page primer and extensive price guide, send $1.00 to NCSA, Box 19134-S, Lansing, MI 48901. From it you will learn, for instance, how to recognize the original April 15, 1865, *New York Herald* version of the report of Lincoln's assassination from among the thousands of reprints which abound today. This booklet could save collectors from making bad investments and prevent dealers from loosing their honest reputation.

Our advisor for this category is Rick Brown; his name, address, and phone number are listed in the Directory under Michigan.

Key:
lr — letter   pub — publisher

1784-1799, Atmosphere papers	17.00
1800-1859, Atmosphere papers	5.00
1861, Civil War opens, first reports	115.00
1861, Civil War opens, later reports	65.00
1861-1865, Atmosphere papers, Confederate	50.00
1861-1865, Atmosphere papers, Union	4.00
1861-1865, Major battles of Civil War, Confederate titles	165.00
1861-1865, Major battles of Civil War, first reports	85.00
1861-1865, Major battles of Civil War, later reports	40.00
1862, Emancipation Proclamation	115.00
1863, Battle of Gettysburg, first reports	125.00
1863, Battle of Gettysburg, later reports	85.00
1863, Gettysburg address	165.00
1865, Capture & death of J Wilkes Booth	45.00
1865, End of Civil War, first reports	160.00
1865, End of Civil War, later reports	60.00
1865, Fall of Richmond	55.00
1865, Harper's Weekly, Apr 29 edition	125.00
1865, Leslie's Illustrated Newspaper, Apr 29 edition	165.00
1865, Lincoln assassination, NY Herald, Apr 15, 10 AM ed	1,200.00
1865, Lincoln assassination, NY Herald, Apr 15, 2 AM ed	600.00
1865, Lincoln assassination, NY Herald, Apr 15, 3 AM ed	450.00
1865, Lincoln assassination, other titles, first reports	125.00
1865, Lincoln assassination, other titles, later reports	50.00
1866-1900, Atmosphere papers	3.00
1871, Chicago fire, Chicago paper, 1st reports	400.00
1871, Chicago fire, later reports	40.00
1871, Chicago fire, other first reports	75.00
1872, Grant elected 2nd term	12.00
1876, Custer's Last Stand, first reports	145.00
1876, Custer's Last Stand, later reports	75.00
1876, Tilden defeats Hayes, lg graphics	80.00
1876, Tilden defeats Hayes, no graphics	35.00
1877, Hayes declared president	17.00
1880, Garfield elected	18.00
1881, Billy the Kid killed	185.00
1881, Garfield assassinated	30.00

1881, Gunfight at OK Corral	225.00
1882, Jesse James killed, first reports	215.00
1882, Jesse James killed, later reports	100.00
1884, Grover Cleveland elected	12.00
1885, Ulysses S Grant dies	40.00
1889, Johnstown flood	30.00
1892, Grover Cleveland re-elected 2nd term	17.00
1892, Lizzie Borden crime & trial	15.00
1898, Sinking of Maine, NY Journal or World	250.00
1898, Sinking of Maine, other titles	50.00
1898, Spanish American War begins	35.00
1898, Spanish American War ends	35.00
1900, James Jeffries defeats Jack Corbett to retain title	12.00
1900, McKinley elected 2nd term	17.00
1900-1945, Atmosphere papers	1.00
1901, McKinley assassinated	28.00
1903, Wright Brother's flight	450.00
1904, Teddy Roosevelt elected	17.00
1906, San Francisco earthquake, other titles	50.00
1906, San Francisco earthquake, San Francisco paper	185.00
1908, Taft elected	10.00
1912, Sinking of Titanic, first reports	215.00
1912, Sinking of Titanic, later reports	100.00
1912, Wilson elected	15.00
1914, WWI begins	30.00
1915, Lusitania sunk, first reports	85.00
1916, Woodrow Wilson elected	12.00
1917, US declares war	27.00
1918, November 11 Armistice	25.00

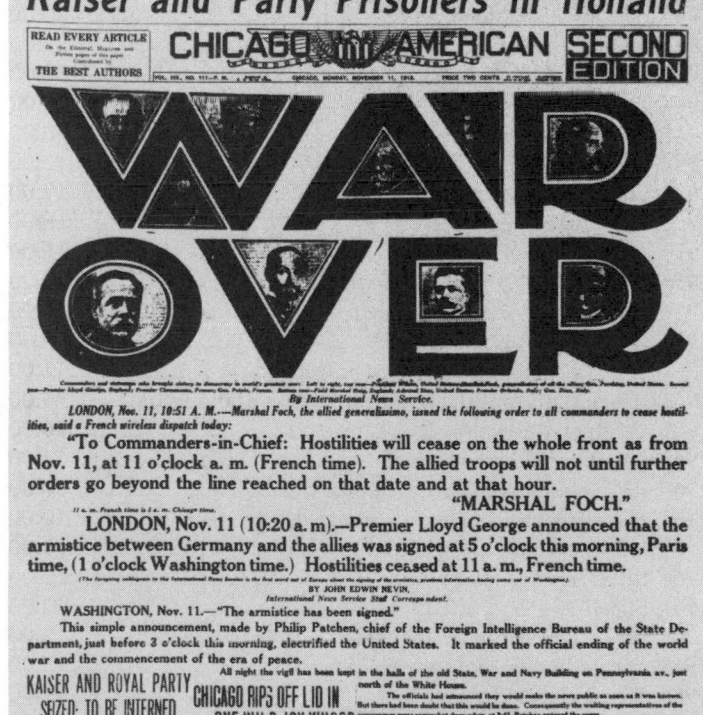

WWI paper, exceptional front-page graphics, $60.00. Courtesy R.S. Brown Archives.

1920, Harding elected	12.00
1920, Prohibition takes effect	22.00
1920, Women's Suffrage, 19th amendment	22.00

1924, Coolidge elected 12.00
1925, Scopes 'Monkey' trial verdict 22.00
1926, Tunney defeats Jack Dempsey 25.00
1927, Babe Ruth hits 60th home run..................................175.00
1927, Lindbergh in Paris, first reports 65.00
1927, Lindbergh in Paris, later reports 25.00
1928, Hoover elected..12.00
1929, Byrd flies to South Pole 15.00
1929, St Valentine's Day Massacre 115.00
1929, Stock Market crash...85.00
1931, Al Capone found guilty 45.00
1932, FDR elected 1st term 12.00
1932, Lindbergh baby found dead 20.00
1933, Prohibition repealed 18.00
1934, Bonnie & Clyde killed...35.00
1934, Dillinger killed, Chicago title 185.00
1934, Dillinger killed, other titles 95.00
1936, FDR elected 2nd term...10.00
1936, King Edward renounces crown 13.00
1937, Amelia Earhart vanishes 15.00
1937, Hindenbergh explodes, first reports 65.00
1937, Hindenbergh explodes, later reports 35.00
1939, Gone w/the Wind, either Atlanta title, Dec 17-19 ......17.00
1939-1945, Major battles in the war 18.00
1940, FDR elected 3rd term..12.00
1941, Pearl Harber attacked, Honolulu Star-Bulletin 750.00
1941, Pearl Harbor attacked, Dec 8 issues, first reports 25.00
1941, Pearl Harbor attacked, other titles w/lg headlines 40.00
1944, D-Day...20.00
1944, FDR elected 4th term 12.00
1945, FDR dies 12.00
1945, First atomic bomb dropped 25.00
1945, Japan surrenders 25.00
1945, VE-Day or VJ-Day 30.00
1948, Babe Ruth's death 100.00
1948, Dewey Defeats Truman, Chicago Daily Tribune 700.00
1950, US enters Korean War...12.00
1953, Truce signed to end Korean War 17.00
1956, Eisenhower elected 2nd term 8.00
1957, Soviets launch Sputnik...15.00
1958, Alaska joins Union, Alaska title 35.00
1959, Hawaii joins Union, Honolulu title 35.00
1960, JFK elected 8.00
1961, Alan Shepard, 1st American in space 12.00
1961, Roger Maris hits 61st home run, breaks Ruth's record..........85.00
1962, Death of Marilyn Monroe 20.00
1962, John Glenn orbits the earth 12.00
1963, JFK assassination, Nov 22, Dallas title 50.00
1963, JFK assassination, Nov 22, other titles 10.00
1963, JFK assassination, papers dtd Nov 23 to Nov 26.....................3.00
1964, LBJ elected 7.00
1967, Superbowl I 12.00
1968, Bobby Kennedy assassination 12.00
1968, Martin Luther King assassination................................15.00
1968, Nixon elected 1st term 5.00
1969, Moon landing 17.00
1973, Vietnam peace pacts signed 7.00
1974, Nixon resigns 12.00
1976, Carter elected 3.00
1977, Death of Elvis, Memphis paper...................................60.00
1977, Death of Elvis, other titles...10.00
1980, Chicago Sun-Times error: It's Reagan & Ford 3.00
1980, Death of John Lennon, NY title...................................12.00
1986, Challenger explodes 7.00

Nicodemus

Chester Nicodemus began making pottery items in 1937 in Columbus, Ohio, using a local red clay containing a large amount of iron and known for durability. From this clay he makes animal and bird sculptures, Christmas cards, nativity sets, and many other items as well. The line he produces is called Ferro-Stone. Many colors are used, some of which are turquoise, antique ivory, green mottle, and golden yellow – all shaded with the warm brown tones of the clay which he allows to show through the glaze. Examples are usually marked with his name incised into the clay. Paper labels are also found that read 'Nicodemus, Ferro-Stone.'

Cup & saucer, lt & dk gr...15.00
Figurine, bison 55.00
Vase, brn/yel, long hand-twisted hdl, 8", pr.......................95.00
Vase, lt & dk gr, loop hdls, 4"...20.00
Vase, pk-gray, Ferro-Stone, hdls, 3¾" 15.00
Vase, yel/brn, incised decor, 5"...30.00

Niloak

Benton, Arkansas, was an area rich with natural clay, high in quality and easily accessible. During the last half of the 1800s, a dozen potteries flourished there; but by 1898 the only one remaining was owned by Charles Dean Hyten. In 1909 he began to experiment, trying to preserve in his finished ware the many colors of the native clay. By 1912 he had perfected a method that produced the desired effect. He obtained a U.S. patent for his handcrafted Niloak Mission pottery, characterized by swirling layers of browns, blues, red, and buff clays. Only a few early pieces were glazed both inside and out; these are extremely rare. After the process was perfected, only the interior was glazed. The ware was marked 'Niloak,' the backward spelling of Kaolin, a type of fine porcelain clay. No sooner had production began than the pottery burned, but Hyten rebuilt and added a stoneware line called Eagle Pottery. Hywood, an inexpensive novelty ware, was introduced in 1929 in an attempt to boost sales during the onset of the depression years. Until 1934 when the management changed hands, the line was marked 'Hywood-Niloak.' After that, 'Hywood' no longer appeared on the ware. Hyten left the pottery in 1941; in 1946 the operation closed.

Our advisors for this category are Lila and Fred Schrader; they are listed in the Directory under California.

Ash tray, Mission Ware, w/metal pierced cap 85.00
Bowl, Mission Ware, brns/tans only, 3½x6" 75.00
Bowl, Mission Ware, flared, 3½x6".....................................65.00
Candlestick, Mission Ware, bl/brn/cream, 8", pr...............225.00
Creamer & sugar bowl, bl...15.00

Ewer, relief eagle, green and caramel, 10", $35.00.

Figurine, 'razor-back,' w/or w/o Arkansas emb, maroon **45.00**
Inkwell, Mission Ware, w/lid & insert, 3" **165.00**
Lamp base, Mission Ware, 9¼" **195.00**
Match holder/ash tray, Mission Ware, 3½" **65.00**
Pitcher, Mission Ware, lemonade style, 8½" **225.00**
Pitcher, Mission Ware, squat, 5½" **110.00**
Pitcher, yel, 5" **8.00**
Planter, bird, bl, 2" **20.00**
Planter, kangaroo, beige, 5" **45.00**
Planter, parrot, wht & orange, 4" **35.00**
Planter, pelican, wht & orange, 5" **35.00**
Tumbler, Mission Ware, 3¾", 4 for **255.00**
Vase, bl gloss, ftd, flared top, hdls, 6½" **20.00**
Vase, chartreuse, twist neck, hdls, melon base, 6½" **20.00**
Vase, Hywood, orange to gr, molded sides, pre-1930, 6½x5"..........**25.00**
Vase, maroon, hdls, 7" **16.00**
Vase, Mission Ware, brn/bl swirl, 4½"..................................**40.00**
Vase, Mission Ware, bulbous, 9½" **95.00**
Vase, Mission Ware, gray/bl/red, 4½" **65.00**
Vase, Mission Ware, simple form, 5½x6" **55.00**
Vase, Mission Ware, squat, 10" **120.00**
Vase, Mission Ware, 5-color, bulbous, sgn, label, 9" **135.00**
Vase, Mission Ware, 7½" **85.00**
Wall pocket, Mission Ware, inverted V-shape, 7½x3½" **95.00**
Wall pocket, stylized florals in relief, dusty rose.....................**35.00**

Nippon

Nippon generally refers to Japanese wares made during the period from 1891 to 1921, although the Nippon mark was also used to a limited extent on later wares (accompanied by 'Japan'). Nippon, meaning Japan, identified the country of origin to comply with American importation restrictions. After 1921 'Japan' was the acceptable alternative. The term does not imply a specific type of product and may be found on items other than porcelains.

Authority Joan Van Patten has recently released the third volume of her lovely series *The Collector's Encyclopedia of Nippon Porcelain*, with many full-color photos and current prices; you will find her address in the Directory under New York. In the following listings, items are assumed hand painted unless noted otherwise. Numbers included in the descriptions refer to these specific marks:

Key:
#1 — China E-OH	#5 — Rising Sun
#2 — M in Wreath	#6 — Royal Kinran
#3 — Cherry Blossom	#7 — Maple Leaf
#4 — Double T Diamond in Circle	#8 — Royal Nippon, Nishiki
	#9 — Royal Moriye Nippon

Ash tray, moose center, nuts at rim, hexagonal, #2, 6" **110.00**
Ash tray, playing cards, 3 indents, bl #2, 5" dia **140.00**
Ash tray, Wedgwood, ped base...**350.00**
Bonbon, river scene on lid, Imperial mk, 5" dia **140.00**
Bottle, scent; gold overlay on wht, gr #2, 5¼" **95.00**
Bowl, berry; medallions in wide gr band, #7, +8¾" plate **175.00**
Bowl, bird on branch, oval w/curled hdls, #2, 7½" **120.00**
Bowl, elk at river, earth tones, gr #2, 7¼" **80.00**
Bowl, floral medallions, 8-scallop rim, bl #7, 7½" **100.00**
Bowl, gold overlay on wht, beaded/scalloped rim, #7, 9¾"...........**125.00**
Bowl, Gouda-like decor on blk, hdls, #2, 9¼" **150.00**
Bowl, mc roses, ornate gold scalloped rim, bl #7, 12" **240.00**
Bowl, pastoral scene, moriage trim, squat, hdls, #7, 9" **400.00**
Bowl, peanuts relief, brn on lt shaded, hdls, #2, 7" **150.00**

Bowl, blown-out squirrel, 3-footed, 9", $450.00.

Bowl, river scene, bl floral border, gr #2, 7½" **135.00**
Bowl, river scene, sgn Kimu, oval, gr #2, 12½" **265.00**
Bowl, roses on wht, 3 lobes, center hdl, gr #2, 7" W.....................**80.00**
Bowl, swans on lake w/lily pads, gold rim, #7, 8½" **120.00**
Bowl, Wedgwood, cream on bl, hdls, gr #2, 7¼".........................**325.00**
Box, cigarette; sampan scene on lid, gr #2, 4¾"..........................**200.00**
Box, jewelry; iris, yel/wht on cream, sq, gr #2, 4¾" **140.00**
Box, powder; floral w/gold rim on wht, gr #2, 5½" **80.00**
Box, powder; river scene, gold beaded rim, #7, 5¾" dia **275.00**
Box, stamp; deer, earth tones, 2-compartment, gr #2, 2¾"..........**100.00**
Box, trinket; floral, piano form, #2, 2½x5" **265.00**
Box, trinket; floral, yel on wht, heart form, gr #2 ....**75.00**
Box, trinket; pastoral reserve, clover form, bl #7 ....**85.00**
Butter dish, roses, yel on cream shaded w/gold, #2, 7½"..............**150.00**
Cake plate, florals, mc on cream, gold rim, hdls, #2, 9¾" **150.00**
Cake plate, wide floral band, scalloped, hdls, #7, 11¼"................**250.00**
Cake set, florals, gold overlay on cobalt border, #7, 5-pc **500.00**
Calendar, desk; sampan scene, gr #2, 3x4½" **175.00**
Candlestick, floral, gold/red on blk, gr #2, 8", pr **325.00**
Candlestick, moriage w/HP violets, scalloped ft, unmk, 6¾" **325.00**
Candlestick, peacock/florals on wht w/gold, RC mk, 6", pr **240.00**
Candlestick, scenic w/moriage trim, triangular, #2, 10" **325.00**
Celery dish, 3 rose reserves, fancy gold/cobalt, #7, 13"...............**265.00**
Charger, birds & flowers, mc on blk, octagonal, mk, 18" **235.00**
Charger, palms scene, earth tones, gr #2, 14" **250.00**
Chocolate pot, floral medallion, gold overlay, bl #7, 9¾" **350.00**
Chocolate pot, floral w/gold, gr #2, 9", +6 c/s............................**400.00**
Chocolate pot, moriage dragons, HP mk, 9½", +4 c/s **400.00**
Chocolate pot, 3 figures in boat/mtn/florals, +6 c/s **150.00**
Cigar holder & tray, sampan scene, oval, gr #2 ....**150.00**
Cinnamon stick holder, river scene, gr #2, 4½" **200.00**
Coffeepot, roses, pk/wht on cream, gold overlay, bl #7, 8" **185.00**
Compote, Wedgwood, cream on bl, gr #2, 5¼" **400.00**
Cookie jar, floral, bl on wht, Greek Key border, #2, 9½" **235.00**
Cookie jar, gold overlay on wht, 6-sided, RC mk, 8"....................**325.00**
Cookie jar, peonies, pk on wht, gold overlay rim/hdl, #7, 9"........**275.00**
Cookie jar, roses, mc/gilt on shaded ground, ftd, #7, 7½"............**425.00**
Creamer & sugar bowl, geese by water, angle hdls, HP mk, pr.....**170.00**
Creamer & sugar bowl, mc roses, gold hdls, gr #2.........................**60.00**
Cup, bouillon; gold overlay on cobalt, #2, w/underplate...............**160.00**
Cup & saucer, bouillon; bluebird/flowers on wht, bl #7................**40.00**

Demitasse set, butterflies, blk on wht w/gold, #2, serves 6 ....225.00
Demitasse set, gold dragons on wht, gr #2, 9" pot+6 c/s 450.00
Dish, child's feeding; girl & puppy, pk rim, #5, 8" 80.00
Dresser set, berries, red on gr w/gold, 4-pc 215.00
Dresser set, geometric motif w/gold, bl #7, 5-pc 525.00
Dutch shoe, yel roses, gr #2, 3" 160.00
Egg warmer, roses, mc on shaded, 4-hole, gr #2, 5½" 150.00
Ewer, grapes allover, yel base, bl #6, 9½" 160.00
Ewer, mums reserve on gold, flared base, bl #7, 9¾" 350.00
Ewer, pastoral scene, moriage trim, ftd, bl #2, 7½" 450.00
Ewer, roses, mc on blk, cobalt & gold overlay, #6, 10" 240.00
Ewer, roses, pk on brn to wht, ornate hdl, bl #6, 9¼" 225.00
Ewer, roses at top, heavy gold overlay, bl #7, 10" 200.00
Ferner, Arab on camel scene, gold ft/hdls, #2, 5¾x10½" 400.00
Ferner, floral band, relief-molded hdls, gr #2, 3¾x8½" 275.00
Ferner, floral branches, blk ruffled rim, gr #2, 4¼x7¾" 300.00
Ferner, landscape reserve, canted corners, ftd, #2, 8" 200.00
Ferner, moriage dragons on earth tones, #7, 7½" 325.00
Ferner, scenic, jewels, octagonal, 3-ftd, gr #2 ....85.00
Hair receiver, roses, mc on dk shaded ground, bl #7, 5" 80.00
Hatpin holder, gold overlay on wht, RC mk, 4¾" 65.00
Hatpin holder, woodland scene, bl #7, 4¾" 150.00
Humidor, Am flag, roses, gold beadwork, gr #2, 7½" 600.00
Humidor, Am Indian reserve on tan, gr #2, 6" 625.00
Humidor, Arab on camel relief, earth tones, #2, 7½" 1,100.00
Humidor, collie relief, gr #2, 6" 750.00
Humidor, deer in woods, earth tones, gr #2, 5½" 350.00
Humidor, desert scene, hieroglyphic-style band, #2, 5½" 550.00
Humidor, Indian in canoe, earth tones, hexagonal, #2, 10" 525.00
Humidor, moriage owl on earth tones, gr #7, 6½" 1,000.00
Humidor, moriage pipes on shaded ground, #7, 7" 550.00
Humidor, mums on gold w/beads, bl #7, 5½" 600.00
Humidor, Nouveau florals, 6-sided, gr #2, 4½" 375.00
Humidor, owl on branch on shaded bl, 6-sided, #2, 6½" 500.00
Humidor, people in open car on cream, gr #2, 6½" 650.00
Humidor, playing cards on shaded bl, gr #2, 6½" 425.00
Humidor, relief-molded monks/priests/etc, #7, 7½" 1,300.00
Humidor, river scene, earth tones, knob finial, gr #2, 6¾" 350.00
Humidor, roses, mc on shaded ground, gold overlay, #7, 8¼" 425.00
Humidor, scenic tapestry w/gold, bl #7, 6½" 1,100.00
Humidor, 3 horses in profile in wide band, gr #2, 6¾" 450.00
Ink blotter, sampan scene, gr #2, 4¼" L 185.00
Jug, whiskey; full-blown mc roses w/gold, bl #7, 7" 425.00
Jug, whiskey; river scene reserve, keg form, gr #2, 5½" 650.00
Jug, whiskey; windmill & house, florals, jewels, 7½" 400.00
Jug, wine; desert scene, bl & gold bands, #2, 9½" 650.00
Jug, wine; monk portrait, vintage decor, gr #2, 9½" 650.00
Jug, wine; night village scene, slim form, bl #7, 11" 650.00
Lamp, candle; desert scene, earth tones, gr #2, 12½" 1,400.00
Lamp, candlestick; mums, gold overlay/beads, #7, 13" 325.00
Lamp, river scene, fancy gold base/hdls, gr #2, 13½" 275.00
Lamp, sampan in banded reserve on cobalt, unknown mk, 17" ..280.00
Lemon dish, bluebirds on wht, hdls, bl #5, 5½" 30.00
Letter holder, florals & scenic w/gold, gr #4 ....145.00
Matchbox holder, gold overlay on wht, wall mt, gr #2, 4½" 125.00
Mug, mc grapes w/gold, gr #7, 4¾" 235.00
Mug, shaving; Indian reserve, stylized band, gr #2, 3¾" 150.00
Mustache cup & saucer, floral, pk on wht, bl #5 ....170.00
Nappy, floral, gold overlay, 3-hdl, bl #7, 6¼" 100.00
Nut bowl, roses on shaded gr, gold rim, #2, 7", +4 3" bowls 180.00
Pancake server, roses, mc on shaded yel w/gold, #7, 8¾" 165.00
Pitcher, floral, gold overlay & beads, squat, #7, 6½".. ....150.00
Pitcher, floral, lt earth tones, bl #7, 5½" 150.00
Pitcher, gold overlay on wht, scalloped rim, gr #7, 7" 225.00

Pitcher, roses reserve on gold w/beads, cylindrical, mk, 4" 150.00
Pitcher, tankard; rose reserve on blk w/gold, bl #7, 14" 450.00
Planter, boat scene, decor at 4 holes for hanging, gr #2, 5x4" 350.00
Plaque, Am Indian decor, geometric rim, gr #2, 8" 275.00
Plaque, camel scene, gr #2, 10" 225.00
Plaque, castle by water scene, earth tones, gr #2, 10" 300.00
Plaque, Indian portrait reserve, fancy border, bl #7, 10" 800.00
Plaque, sheep scene, earth tones, gr #2, 10" 300.00
Plaque, squirrel w/nut relief, earth tones, #2, 10½" 950.00
Plaque, 2 dogs in relief, earth tones, gr #2, 10½" 950.00
Plate, berries, red on tan, Imperial mk, 10" 100.00
Plate, floral band w/gold reserves, gr #2, 10¼" 50.00
Plate, floral on wht, heavy gold overlay, #7, 8½" 225.00
Plate, mountain scene, fancy gold-on-cobalt rim, #7, 10" 300.00
Plate, red house in snow scene, HP mk, 6½" 60.00
Plate, windmill scene, gold-on-cobalt rim, #2, 6½" 165.00
Punch bowl, florals w/grapes, gold-banded rim, ftd, #2, 11" 250.00
Punch bowl, grapes on streaky brn, ftd/hdls, #2, 13x13" 900.00
Punch bowl, river scene, gold overlay on bl band, #2, 7x12" 335.00
Relish, river scene, 2-compartment, hdls, bl #7, 7½" 120.00
Salt cellar, roses, pk on wht, gold trim, gr #7, sm 20.00
Shakers, butterflies, gr w/gold trim, pr 30.00
Shakers, pk floral branches on bl, gr HP mk, pr 50.00
Shakers, roses, pk on shaded brn, bl #7, pr 40.00
Stein, cloisonne on porc, red florals on blk, #2, 7" 450.00
Stein, moose profile, earth tones w/gold, bl #7, 7¼" 400.00
Stein, sampan scene, pk shaded sky, gr #2, 7" 425.00
Stein, 2 people/houses, earth tones, gr #2, 7" 450.00
Sugar bowl, lady reserve, gold overlay on wht, hdls, #7, 6" 175.00
Sugar shaker, roses on wht w/gold, gr #7, 4" 110.00
Tea set, butterflies, bl on wht, #5, child's 4" pot+14 pcs...............260.00
Tea set, child's face, arm spout, Nippon, 3½" pot+4 cups.............125.00
Tea set, cranes, pagoda mk, 6½" pot, +cr/sug+6 c/s 350.00
Tea set, river scene, angle hdls, gr #2, 6½" pot+6 pcs 400.00
Tea set, roses, yel on peach, gold beads, #7, 15-pc 450.00
Teapot, scenic reserve, gold overlay on cobalt, gr #2, 8¾" 300.00
Tile, Egyptian lady, stylized mc band, octagonal, #2, 6¼" 120.00
Toothpick holder, river scene, earth tones w/gold, #2, 2" 75.00
Tray, Capitol Building, Washington DC, gold trim, #2, 8¾"........160.00
Trivet, river scene, earth tones, canted corners, #2, 5" 65.00
Urn, chrysanthemum reserve, fancy gold overlay, bl #7, 13"........650.00
Urn, lady in oval reserve, gold overlay on gr, #7, 14" 900.00
Urn, lilies on cream, gold overlay, 2-pc bolted, #2, 15¼" 950.00
Urn, river scenic band w/gold, 2-pc bolted, #2, 24½" 1,400.00
Urn, roses, wht on cream w/gold, 2-pc bolted, #2, 18" 575.00
Urn, roses reserve on gr w/gold, ornate hdls, #2, 15¼" 900.00
Urn, swan scene, gold overlay, ped base, gr #2, 19" 2,500.00
Urn, wide river-scenic band, gold beads, 4-ftd, unmk, 9¼" 450.00
Vase, bl butterflies, Toronto Exhibition, 1919, mk, 5¼" 65.00
Vase, camel scene, angle hdls, ftd, gr #2, 5½" 145.00
Vase, cloisonne on porc, red leaves on blk, bulb, Nippon, 4" 300.00
Vase, coralene floral on shaded brn, baluster, #5, 7" 350.00
Vase, exotic birds in panels, gold hdls, bl #2, 14" 400.00
Vase, fisherman scene relief, ftd, hdls, gr #2, 8¼" 1,500.00
Vase, floral, pk on lt bl, integral hdls, bl #7, 7½" 175.00
Vase, floral reserves, Greek Key trim, sq hdls, #2, 13½" 300.00
Vase, florals, mc on cobalt, long angle hdls, #6, 9½" 200.00
Vase, florals in relief, mc on shaded, baluster, #7, 9¾" 600.00
Vase, gold overlay mums on cobalt, tapered baluster, #7, 7" 400.00
Vase, gold overlay on cobalt, basket form, gr #2, 7¾" 375.00
Vase, gold overlay on shaded brn, cylindrical, #7, 7½" 225.00
Vase, gold reserve in band on cobalt, ftd/hdls, #7, 7½" 450.00
Vase, grapes tapestry w/gold, flared cylinder, bl #7, 9½" 600.00
Vase, house/river reserve, gold beads, hdls, spoke mk, 5½" 85.00

Vase, hunt scene relief, earth tones, sq hdls, #2, 6½" 600.00

Vase, Indian in reserve, 11", $495.00.

Vase, lady reserve, gold ring hdls, ftd, bl #7, 5½" 400.00
Vase, lady reserve band on cobalt, integral hdls, #7, 6¾"............300.00
Vase, lilies, pk on gr w/gold, ring hdls, gr #7, 9½" 350.00
Vase, lilies on shaded brn, sm hdls, bl #2, 9¾" 200.00
Vase, man on horse silhouette, sm hdls, Imperial mk, 12" 525.00
Vase, mc roses, ring hdls, ruffled neck w/gold, bl #7, 10" 325.00
Vase, moriage gulls on earth tones, hdls, bl #7, 4½" 300.00
Vase, open florals, Greek Key border, hdls, bl #2, 9¼" 200.00
Vase, pagodas/bridges/mtns, gold overlay on wht, #7, 11¼"........275.00
Vase, pastoral scene on cobalt, ftd baluster, #7, 9" 350.00
Vase, phoenix bird in peony bush/butterflies on blk, 10x6" 225.00
Vase, poppies, red on lav, angle hdls, bl #7, 10" 160.00
Vase, portrait reserve, gold overlay, bulbous, hdls, #7, 7½"........450.00
Vase, river reserve on turq, gold angle hdls, gr #2, 10½" 250.00
Vase, river scene, earth tones, 4 sm angle hdls, #2, 6¾" 250.00
Vase, rose medallions, gold beads, ring hdls, bl #7, 7¾" 275.00
Vase, rose tapestry w/gold, bulbous, bl #7, 6¼"..........................500.00
Vase, roses, gold integral hdls, sm neck, 3½x8½" 160.00
Vase, roses, mc on shaded bl, gold hdls, bl #7, 6¾" 75.00
Vase, roses, mc on shaded gr, cobalt top & hdls, #7, 6½"............100.00
Vase, roses, mc on shaded ground, baluster, hdls, #7, 12" 325.00
Vase, roses, pk on shaded gr, urn form, bl #7, 8¾" 200.00
Vase, roses, pk/yel, gold beading, hdls, 5" 90.00
Vase, roses on gold w/beads, basket form, unmk, 7" 350.00
Vase, roses reserve on gold w/beads, bulbous, hdls, #7, 7"..........425.00
Vase, roses reserve/medallions, integral hdls, unmk, 8½"............325.00
Vase, sailing ship scene, gold overlay, hdls, #2, 8½"....................250.00
Vase, silver overlay on cobalt, baluster, Nippon mk, 6½"............475.00
Vase, storks w/young, bulbous w/sm neck, gold hdls, #7, 8"........225.00
Vase, swan scenic, moriage trim, bulbous, hdls, #7, 9" 300.00
Vase, Wedgwood, cream on bl, classic form, hdls, gr #2, 8" 500.00
Vase, wide floral band on cobalt, baluster, bl #7, 6½" 225.00
Vase, wide river scenic band, ftd cylinder, gr #7, 9" 625.00
Vase, windmill scene, earth tones, loving cup form, #2, 5½".......100.00
Vase, winter scene in banded reserve, gold hdls, bl #7, 10" 300.00

Nodders

So called because of the nodding action of their heads and hands, nodders originated in China where they were used in temple rituals to

represent deity. Early in the 18th century, the idea was adapted by Meissen and by French manufacturers who produced not only china nodders but bisque as well. Most nodders are individual – couples are unusual. The idea remained popular until the end of the 19th century and was used during the Victorian era by toy manufacturers.

Boy w/shamrock on hat, wire cane, bsk, 4" 65.00
Cat, ceramic bank 25.00
Deco lady on couch in bikini, holds fan, 5½x2½" 85.00
Donkey, celluloid, 3" 20.00
Girl in pajamas kneeling, compo..45.00
Hawaiian Hula Dancer, ceramic 25.00
Lord Plushbottom, bsk, Germany 120.00
Man's head on book, jaw moves, bsk, toothpick holder................95.00
Oriental man, bsk, ca 1950, M 125.00
Oriental man, head & hand w/fan nods, on floral boat, 7½" 225.00
Oriental man or lady, parian, 7", pr..175.00

Pig couple, marked Patent T.T., Made in Japan, 4" x 4½", $45.00.

Shriner wearing fez, ceramic..45.00
Sultan, sitting, bsk, lt bl w/gold trim, Germany, 3¾x2½"..............85.00
Turtle, compo & fiberboard, tail & head move, EX pnt, 5" L 65.00
Uncle Bim, bsk, Germany..120.00
Uncle Walt, bsk, Germany..120.00
Winnie Winkle, bsk, Germany 120.00

Noritake

The Noritake Company was first registered in 1904 as Nippon Gomei Kaisha. In 1917 the name became Nippon Toki Kabushiki Toki. The 'M' in wreath mark is that of the Morimura Brothers, distributors with offices in New York. It was used until 1941. The tree crest mark is the crest of the Morimura family.

The Noritake Company has produced fine porcelain dinnerware sets and occasional pieces decorated in the delicate manner for which the Japanese are noted. Their Azalea pattern was produced exclusively for the Larkin Company, who gave the lovely ware away as premiums to club members and their home agents. From 1916 through the thirties, Larkin distributed the fine china which was decorated in pink Azaleas on white with gold tracing along edges and handles. Early in the thirties, six pieces of crystal hand painted with the same design were offered: candle holders, a compote, a tray with handles, a scalloped fruit bowl, a cheese and cracker set, and a cake plate. All in all, seventy different pieces of Azalea were produced. Some, such as the fifteen-piece child's set, bulbous vase, china ash tray, and the pancake jug, are quite rare. Marks varied over the years; the earliest was the blue rising sun Nippon mark, followed by the Noritake M in wreath with variations.

Later the ware was marked 'Noritake, Azalea, hand painted, Japan.'

Authority Joan Van Patten has compiled a lovely book, *The Collector's Encyclopedia of Noritake*, with many full-color photos and current prices; you will find her address in the Directory under New York. In the following listings, examples are hand painted unless noted otherwise. Numbers refer to these specific marks:

#1 — Komarn   #2 — M in Wreath
#3 — N in Wreath

Azalea

Basket, mint; Dolly Varden, #193	145.00
Bonbon, #184, 6¼"	45.00
Bowl, #12, 10"	32.00
Bowl, deep, #310	50.00
Bowl, fruit; shell form, #188, 7¾"	325.00
Bowl, oatmeal; #55, 5½"	18.00
Bowl, vegetable; divided, #439, 9½"	235.00
Bowl, vegetable; oval, #101, 10½"	40.00
Butter chip, #312, 3¼"	40.00
Butter dish, #314	90.00
Butter tub, w/insert, #54	44.00
Cake plate, #10, 9¾"	50.00
Candy jar, #313	525.00
Casserole, gold finial, w/lid, #371	420.00
Casserole, gold finial, w/lid, #372	450.00
Casserole, w/lid, #16	85.00
Celery tray, closed hdls, #444, 10"	240.00
Celery/roll tray, #99, 12"	50.00
Child's set, #253, 15-pc	1,500.00
Coffeepot, AD; #182	500.00
Compote, #170	70.00
Condiment set, #14, 5-pc	60.00
Creamer & sugar bowl, #122	115.00
Creamer & sugar bowl, #401	110.00
Creamer & sugar bowl, #449, ind.	130.00
Creamer & sugar bowl, #7	50.00
Creamer & sugar bowl, AD; open, #123	100.00
Cruet, #190	175.00
Cup & saucer, #2	17.50
Cup & saucer, AD; #183	25.00
Cup & saucer, bouillon; #124, 3½"	20.00
Egg cup, #120	40.00

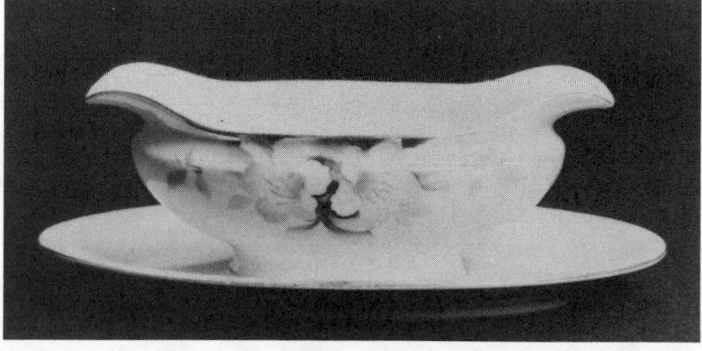

Gravy boat, attached undertray, 9" long, $40.00.

Jam jar set, #125, 3-pc	125.00
Mayonnaise set, scalloped, #453, 3-pc	440.00
Mustard jar, #191	47.50
Pitcher, milk jug; #100, 1-qt	175.00

Plate, #4, 7½"	10.00
Plate, bread & butter; #8, 6½"	10.00
Plate, breakfast; #99, 8½"	17.50
Plate, cream soup; #363	65.00
Plate, dinner; #13, 9¾"	20.00
Plate, grill; 3-compartment, #338, 10¼"	95.00
Plate, soup; #19, 7⅛"	18.00
Plate, sq, #315, 7⅝"	45.00
Platter, #17, 14"	55.00
Platter, #186, 16"	325.00
Platter, #311, 10¼"	180.00
Platter, #56, 12"	38.00
Refreshment set, #39, 2-pc	42.00
Relish, #194, 7⅛"	70.00
Relish, loop hdl, 2-part, #450	300.00
Relish, oval, #18, 8½"	17.50
Relish, 4-part, #119, 10"	110.00
Saucer, fruit; #9, 5¼"	10.00
Shakers, #126, ind, pr	32.00
Shakers, bell form, #11, pr	27.50
Shakers, bulbous, #89, pr	25.00
Snack set, #39, 2-pc	35.00
Spoon holder, #189, 8"	75.00
Syrup, #97, w/underplate	95.00
Tea tile, #169, 6"	45.00
Teapot, #15	80.00
Teapot, gold finial, #400	420.00
Toothpick holder, #192	90.00
Vase, bulbous, #452	925.00
Vase, fan form, ftd, #187	150.00
Whipped cream set, #3, 3-pc	35.00

Ash tray, lady in gr dress figural, gr #2, 5½"	120.00
Ash tray, nude at rim of flower form bowl, red #2, 7"	225.00

Ash tray, Harlequin figural on rim, 3½", $225.00.

Bowl, florals on bl, bird at rim, gr #2, 7½"	110.00
Bowl, iris on cream, bl rim, gold trim/hdls, gr #2, 10½"	40.00
Bowl, parrot on branch, blk border w/gold trim, #2, 10½"	40.00
Bowl, river scene, orange & bl lustre, hdls, red #2, 7"	40.00
Bowl, salad; yel w/vegetables on wht int, scalloped, #2, 10"	55.00
Box, elephant figural, ornate howdah, red #2, 6½"	225.00
Box, powder; bl w/cat finial, gr #2, 4½"	125.00
Box, puff; Deco lady in tricorner hat, bouffant dress, sgn	125.00

Butter dish, reserve on yel w/gr band, bud finial, #2, 6½" **40.00**
Cake plate, pheasants in lg medallion, pk/gold trim, #2, 8" **40.00**
Cake plate, sailboat & palms on bl & orange lustre, #2, 9¾" **35.00**
Candlestick, bird on branch on bl, decor base, #2, 8", pr **175.00**
Candlestick, bird/flower medallion, red/blk bands, #2, 9", pr **175.00**
Candlestick, man on camel, cobalt & gold, #1, 5¼" **125.00**
Candy dish, Deco lady on blk & red, red #2, 6½" dia...................**185.00**
Celery dish, fruit, goat's-head hdls, gr #2, 12½" **85.00**
Celery tray, ivory w/red trim, gr #2, 12½" **25.00**
Chamberstick, Egyptian motif, bl/orange lustre, #2, 6½", pr........**140.00**
Chamberstick, florals, orange lustre, ring hdls, #2, 2¼", pr **60.00**
Chip & dip set, water scene, earth tones, 2-tier, #2, 9¾" **65.00**
Chocolate set, floral on wht w/gold, hexagonal, #2, 9-pc...........**185.00**
Chocolate set, pyramids near river, #2, 13-pc **185.00**
Compote, florals at side on bl lustre rim, hdls, #2, 8½" **45.00**
Compote, 3 ladies support bowl, red #2, 7"...................................**250.00**
Condiment set, florals on yel w/gold, 3-pc on tray, #2 ....**75.00**
Condiment set, parrots on red, gold trim, gr #2, 4-pc **80.00**
Cookie jar, man on camel, cobalt & gold, #1, 7".........................**225.00**
Cookie jar, roses, lav on gray tones, ftd, gr #2, 8" **75.00**
Creamer, roses on cream w/orange lustre, gold hdl, #2, 5¾" **25.00**
Dish, man on camel, cobalt & gold, basket form, #2, 7½" **170.00**
Dish, serving; florals on brn, center ring hdl, #2, 5" **20.00**
Egg cup, flower baskets & gold bands on cream, #2, 3½" **20.00**
Egg warmer, florals w/pk band, gold center hdl, #2, 5½" **80.00**
Ferner, orange leaves/blkberries, triangular, #2, 6" W....................**90.00**
Flower holder, bird figural, bl w/orange lustre, #2, 4½" **175.00**
Humidor, horse w/in horseshoe relief, earth tones, #2, 7" **500.00**
Humidor, man playing golf, banded lid, gr #2, 6½" **325.00**
Inkwell, clown figural, red #2, 4"...**245.00**
Inkwell, owl form, orange lustre, gr #2, 3½" **225.00**
Jam jar, strawberries along sides, bud finial, gr #2, 5½" **45.00**
Jam jar, strawberries on lid, w/ladle, gr #2, 3½"..............................**60.00**
Lemon dish, lemons center, gold lustre rim, red #2, 6" **80.00**
Match holder, Deco girl smoking, red #2, 1¾"................................**75.00**
Match holder, florals on cream, wall mt, #2, 3½"............................**95.00**
Mustache cup & saucer, river scene, earth tones, #2, 5¾" **80.00**
Mustard, linear decor, gr #2, 7½"..**30.00**
Napkin ring, appl butterfly, gr #2, 2½"..**45.00**
Napkin ring, roses, yel on cream, gr #2, 2¼" W..............................**35.00**
Night light, lady figural, orange lustre dress, #2, 9¾" **850.00**
Night light, owl figural, gr #2, 7½"..**800.00**
Plaque, elk at water, relief molded, earth tones, gr #2, 10½"........**450.00**
Plaque, steamship, gold trim, #1, 10" **165.00**
Plaque, 3 brn/wht dogs in meadow, gr #2, 10½" **600.00**
Plate, game; ring-necked drake, fruit & swag rim, #2, 8½".............**85.00**
Plate, mc florals w/blk & orange rim, open hdls, 9¾"......................**15.00**
Plate, medallions/florals/geometrics, gr mk, 6¼", 6 for **50.00**
Playing card holder, river scenic, gr #2, 3¾" **110.00**
Potpourri jar, bl top over wht, red bud finial, #2, 6" **65.00**
Potpourri jar, floral spray, mc on bl, bud finial, #2, 6½" **65.00**
Punch bowl, Oriental motif on red, ftd, gold hdls, #2, 16"..........**450.00**
Punch bowl, peacock medallion w/gold, #2, 16", +8 cups **800.00**
Salt cellar, butterflies on basket form, hdls, #1, 2⅛" **10.00**
Sauce dish, flower form, bl w/ivory int, red #2, +plate **60.00**
Sauce dish, peacock & florals, gold lustre rim, #2, 4½" **40.00**
Smoke set, butterflies on gray, red #2, 3-pc on 7½" tray...............**375.00**
Smoke set, florals, blk on red w/gr band, #2, 8" tray+3 pcs **275.00**
Syrup, scenic, gold trim, gr #2, 2-pc **100.00**
Tea tile, river scene, sq w/canted corners, gr #2, 5" **30.00**
Teapot, exotic bird/floral on cobalt, #2, 6", +cr/sug **125.00**
Toast rack, bird finial, gr #2, 5½" L...**80.00**
Toothpick holder, Spanish dancer, 3-hdl, gr #2, 2¼" **50.00**
Tray, water scene, bl tones, canted corners, #1, 12" **55.00**

Trinket box, Deco lady & whippet on cream, ftd, gr #2, 3" **50.00**
Trinket dish, man on camel in desert, center hdl, #1, 2¼".............**15.00**
Urn, river reserve on red w/gold, red #2, 12" **250.00**
Urn, river/tree scene, cobalt w/gold, #1, 8¾"...............................**250.00**
Vase, bird & tree trunk figural, orange lustre, gr #2, 5¼" **195.00**
Vase, floral medallions on cream w/gold, angle hdls, #2, 7½" **250.00**
Vase, florals on bl to cream shaded, ftd, red #2, 5½" **125.00**
Vase, florals on cream shaded, gold hdls, gr #2, 11¼" **135.00**
Vase, florals on yel w/gr & ivory decor, fan form, #2, 6½" **85.00**
Vase, house/river/bridge, earth tones, bulbous, #2, 8¾" **80.00**
Vase, man on camel, cobalt & gold, squat, #1, 2½"........................**85.00**
Vase, peacock feathers, fluted top, #1, 8" **100.00**
Vase, red w/gold hdl & int, ruffled basket form, #2, 5½".............**110.00**
Vase, tulip figural, lav w/gr leaves, red #2, 5½" **195.00**
Wall pocket, appl butterfly/bee, red #2, 8¼"..................................**80.00**

Norse

The Norse Pottery was established in 1903 in Edgerton, Wisconsin, by Thorwald Sampson and Louis Ipson. A year later it was purchased by A.W. Wheelock and moved to Rockford, Illinois. The ware they produced was inspired by ancient bronze vessels of the Norsemen. Designs were often incised into the red clay body, dragon handles and feet were favored decorative devices, and they achieved a semblance of patina through the application of metallic glazes. The ware was marked with a stylized 'N' containing a vertical arrangement of the remaining letters of the name. Production ceased after 1913.

Bowl, incised rising sun, 2 dragon's-head hdls, #50 ....**125.00**
Candlestick, blk w/gold snake looped at base, #54, 12", pr **150.00**
Jar, incised scrollwork at shoulder, lid w/finial, 6½" **140.00**

Covered jar, 6½" diameter, $140.00.

Mug, incised decor, blk w/brn wash, #51, 5" **135.00**
Vase, blk, simple form w/minor decor at top, mk, 4¾" **60.00**
Vase, incised waves, 3 dragon's head ft, #8, 4x7½" **150.00**
Vase, incised/interlocking snakes & symbols, 8x9" **200.00**

North Dakota School of Mines

The School of Mines of the University of North Dakota was established in 1890, but due to a lack of funding, it was not until 1898 that Earle J. Babcock was appointed as Director, and efforts were made to produce ware from the native clay he had discovered several years earlier. The first pieces were made by firms in the east from the clay Babcock sent them. Some of the ware was decorated by the manufacturer; some was shipped back to North Dakota to be decorated by native artists. By 1909 students at the University of North Dakota were producing utilitarian items – tile, brick, shingles, etc. – in conjunction with a ceramic course offered through the Chemistry Department. By 1910 a ceramic department had been established, supervised by Margaret Kelly Cable. Under her leadership, fine artware was produced. Native flowers, grains, buffalo, cowboys, and other subjects indigenous to the state were incorporated into the decorations. Some pieces have an Art Nouveau – Art Deco style easily attributed to her association with Frederick H. Rhead, with whom she studied in 1911. During the twenties the pottery was marketed on a limited scale through gift and jewelry stores in the state. From 1927 until 1949 when Miss Cable announced her retirement, a more widespread distribution was maintained with sales branching out into other states. The ware was marked in cobalt with the official seal – 'Made at School of Mines, N.D. Clay, University of North Dakota, Grand Forks, N.D.' in a circle. Very early ware was sometimes marked 'U.N.D.' in cobalt by hand.

Bookends, half-bowl shape, sgn Grunefelter, pr	225.00
Bowl vase, bl gloss, vertically ribbed, artist sgn, 2x4"	150.00
Bowl vase, confronting buffalo panels, bl on cream, 3½"	475.00
Coaster, oxen pulling wagon, brn, sgn Huck, 4"	150.00
Figurine, wolf, sitting, yel matt, bl stamp mk, 3"	80.00
Pin tray, Indian bust relief, pearly gr, Taylor, #3-90, 5"	165.00
Pitcher, gr, dolphins/fish/shell, sgn, #d, mk, 7¼"	135.00
Rose bowl, cvd Indian motif, gray & brn, sgn JH, 4x6"	350.00
Vase, bl & violet, sgn Hall, 1942, 7x4"	175.00
Vase, bl gloss, slim, horizontal rings, 7¼"	95.00
Vase, bl gloss, squat, 4½x5½"	85.00

Vase, carved jonquil panels on tan, signed M Cable, 5½", $600.00.

Vase, cvd wheat, brn matt, 2x3½"	125.00
Vase, geometric band cvd at top, dk brn on gr, sgn, 6x7"	325.00
Vase, gr & blk drip, squat, 3x4"	100.00
Vase, tan & gr, sgn Hall, 1942, 5½"	150.00

North State

In 1924 the North State Pottery of Sanford, North Carolina, began small-scale production, the result of the extreme fondness Mrs. Rebecca Copper had for potting. With the help of her husband and the abundance of suitable local clay, the pottery flourished and became well known for lovely shapes and beautiful glazes. The pottery was in business for thirty-five years; most of its ware was sold in gift and craft shops throughout North Carolina.

Ash tray, burnt orange/gr, imp mk, 1¾" H, NM	25.00
Ewer, gr, 5¼"	25.00
Jug vase, Chinese red, sm	35.00
Pitcher, copper lustre, slender form, 6½"	25.00
Pitcher, red over gr, tall	58.00
Sugar bowl, yel, imp 1920s-1930s mk, 3" H	30.00
Vase, beige, fan form, 3¾"	25.00

Northwood

The Northwood Company was founded in 1896 in Indiana, Pennsylvania, by Harry Northwood, whose father, John, was the art director for Stevens and Williams, an English glassworks. Northwood joined the National Glass Company in 1899 but in 1901 again became an independent contractor and formed the Harry Northwood Glass Company of Wheeling, West Virginia. He marketed his first carnival glass in 1908, and it became his most popular product. His company was also famous for its custard, goofus, and pressed glass. Northwood died in 1923, and the company closed. See also Carnival; Custard; Goofus; Opalescent; Pattern Glass.

Bowl, berry; Royal Ivy, rubena frost, 7½", +6 sauces	350.00
Bowl, Palm & Scroll, bl opal, 3-toed, 9½"	70.00
Butter dish, Peach, gr w/gold, 5¾x7¾"	120.00
Butter dish, Peach, rubena w/gold	85.00
Butter dish, Royal Ivy, rubena	225.00
Butter dish, Royal Oak, frosted	150.00
Butter dish, Royal Oak, rubena	175.00
Butter dish, Royal Oak, rubena frost	200.00
Creamer, Peach, gr w/gold, 4¾x3¾"	75.00
Creamer, Royal Oak, clear frost	75.00
Cruet, Royal Ivy, clear frost, 6½"	110.00
Cruet, Royal Ivy, pk crackle, 6"	375.00
Cruet, Royal Ivy, rainbow cased, 6½"	425.00
Cruet, Royal Ivy, rubena, cut faceted stopper	220.00
Cruet, Royal Ivy, rubena frost, clear faceted stopper, 6½"	325.00
Cruet, Royal Oak, rubena, cut faceted stopper	375.00
Lamp, Leaf Umbrella, cranberry, wall bracket style	395.00
Pitcher, Leaf Umbrella, bl satin, water sz	350.00
Pitcher, Leaf Umbrella, cranberry spatter, 8¾"	330.00
Pitcher, Royal Ivy, rubena frosted, water sz	225.00
Pitcher, Royal Oak, clear frost	110.00
Pitcher, Wavering Quill, gr, water sz	45.00

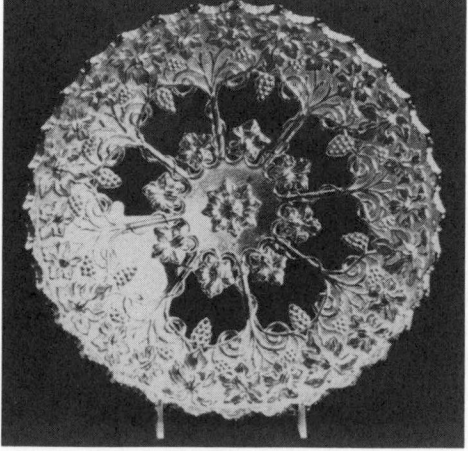

Plate, Grape Frieze, cobalt with heavy gold, 3-footed, 11", $225.00.

Plate, Paneled Grape, gr, 8"	40.00
Rose bowl, pull-up loops, mauve on beige, Patent mk, 3x4½"	895.00

Rose bowl, Royal Ivy, rubena frost..**95.00**
Shaker, Royal Ivy, rubena frost..**135.00**
Shaker, Royal Oak, rubena **160.00**
Spooner, Royal Ivy, rubena frost, 3½"..........................**110.00**
Spooner, Royal Oak, clear frost..**50.00**
Spooner, Royal Oak, rubena..**95.00**
Spooner, Shell, gr opal..**85.00**
Sugar bowl, Peach, gr w/gold, 6½x3¾"............................**90.00**
Sugar shaker, Leaf Mold, vaseline spatter **195.00**
Sugar shaker, Leaf Umbrella, lav opaque **275.00**
Sugar shaker, Royal Ivy, cranberry spatter........................**195.00**
Sugar shaker, Royal Ivy, rubena frost, 4½" **190.00**
Sugar shaker, Royal Oak, rubena frost **145.00**
Sweetmeat, Panelled Sprig, w/lid & hdl, resilvered....................**195.00**
Sweetmeat, pull-up, pk/yel, ornate bail/lid, 3¾x5" **475.00**
Syrup, Royal Ivy, rubena frost, frosted hdl, SP lid, 6½" **575.00**
Toothpick holder, Leaf Mold, cranberry spatter..........................**145.00**
Toothpick holder, Leaf Umbrella, mauve........................**155.00**
Toothpick holder, Royal Ivy, rubena frost **125.00**
Toothpick holder, Royal Oak, rubena **80.00**
Toothpick holder, Royal Oak, rubena frost **125.00**
Tumbler, Bloom & Blossom..**48.00**
Tumbler, Cherry Lattice..**37.50**
Tumbler, Panelled Cherry, clear frost **37.50**
Tumbler, Royal Ivy, rubena frost **70.00**
Tumbler, Royal Oak, rubena frost..**80.00**
Vase, pull-up, bl w/brn feathers, yel int, 6x6"..........................**1,250.00**
Vase, pull-up, brn on peach satin, bl int, 5½x3"........................**750.00**
Vase, pull-up, rust/yel on wht, HP florals, 13x6" **875.00**
Vase, pull-up, rust/yel on wht, HP jonquils/butterfly, 13" **850.00**
Water set, Flute, gr w/gold, 6-pc **200.00**
Water set, Memphis, gr w/gold, 7-pc....................................**300.00**
Water set, Peach, gr w/gold, 6-pc **325.00**

Nutcrackers

The nutcracker, though a strictly functional tool, is a good example of one to which man has applied ingenuity, imagination, and engineering skills. Though all were designed to accomplish the same end, hundreds of types exist in almost every material sturdy enough to withstand sufficient pressure to crack the nut. Figurals are popular collectibles, as are those with unusual design and construction. Patented examples are also desirable.

Admiral Dewey's head, brass, sgn TS Hitchcock, 1892, 5¾"........**225.00**
Alligator, CI, EX pnt, 13½" **85.00**
Alligator, CI, no pnt, 13½"..**45.00**
Bearded elf, CI, 10"..**285.00**
Dog, blk & wht porc over CI..**250.00**
Dog, St Bernard, bronze..**50.00**
Elephant, CI w/red/blk/ivory pnt, Art Deco, 4½x8½"..........**150.00**
Man w/walrus mustache, well-cvd wood, 8" **105.00**
Mythological birds, for betel nuts, brass, old....................**48.00**
Perfection, nickel-plated CI, mechanical, 1880s **25.00**
Reed's Rocket, CI, rocket shape on wood base, adjusts, MIB..........**20.00**
Santa Claus head, cvd wood, EX pnt, free-standing, 7½" **750.00**
Squirrel, CI, 1913, 5"..**25.00**
Wood, threaded screw device, 2-pc, early, EX................................**25.00**

Occupied Japan

Items marked 'Occupied Japan' have become popular collectibles in the last few years. They were produced during the period from the end of World War II until April 18, 1952, when the occupation ended. By no means was all of the ware exported during that time marked 'Occupied Japan' – some was marked 'Japan' or 'Made In Japan.' It is thought that because of the natural resentment felt by the Japanese toward the occupation, only a fraction of these wares carried the 'Occupied' mark. Even though you may find identical 'Japan'-marked items, because of its limited use, only those with the 'Occupied Japan' mark are being collected to any great extent. Values vary considerably based on the quality of workmanship. Generally, bisque figures command much higher prices than porcelain, since on the whole they are of a finer quality.

For those wanting more information, we recommend *The Collector's Encyclopedia of Occupied Japan Collectibles* by Gene Florence; he is listed in the Directory under Kentucky.

Our advisor for this category is Florence Archambault; she is listed in the Directory under Rhode Island. She represents the Occupied Japan Club, whose mailing address may be found in the Directory under Clubs, Newsletters, and Catalogs. All items in the listings that follow are assumed ceramic unless noted otherwise.

Ash tray, horse head in horseshoe fr, 4⅞" **7.00**
Ash tray, man w/fly on nose, 3"..**40.00**
Ash tray, Wedgwood type, sq, 2⅝" **6.00**

Celluloid toys: Bellhop, 4⅜", $85.00; Dancing couple, 4⅝", $65.00.

Bookends, penguins, 4", pr **35.00**
Bowl, fruit center, rtcl rim, 7"..**14.00**
Box, cigarette; pk florals on wht, 3¾x2¾" +3 trays **22.00**
Box, jewel; silver-toned metal, scrolling, ftd, 3½x4½"........**10.00**
Box, music; Geisha dancer, 5x12"..**155.00**
Candle holder, Colonial man & lady, 4", pr........................**50.00**
Candlestick, silver-toned metal, 5", pr................................**22.50**
Creamer, bird form, souvenir, 2¾"..**15.00**
Creamer, parrot figural, 2¾" **25.00**
Creamer & sugar bowl, silver-toned metal, on 7¾" tray............**22.50**
Cup, elephant w/flag, 1¾" **8.00**
Cup & saucer, bl & wht striped rim, florals, Ucagco **12.50**
Cup & saucer, desert scene, ornate hdl, Aurger design **18.00**
Cup & saucer, floral medallions on yel, Ohashi China................**16.00**
Cup & saucer, flow bl, Maruta China **18.00**
Cup & saucer, gr w/gold bands, Merit **10.00**
Cup & saucer, leaf shape, Merit **20.00**

Cup & saucer, pk w/floral int, Jyoto 10.00
Cup & saucer, pk w/gold stripe, blk int, Merit 14.00
Cup & saucer, Spring Violets, Rossetti, Chicago USA 12.50
Cup & saucer, tomato figural, child's sz 4.50
Dish, florals on wht, leaf form w/hdl, Ucagco, 6½" 10.00
Doll, celluloid, feather dancer, 13" 44.00
Doll, celluloid, Kewpie, 2¾" 15.00
Doll, celluloid, molded hair, nude, 4¾" 14.00
Doll, celluloid, Quints, 2¾", 5 in box 65.00
Fan, paper & wood, 7¾" spine 12.00
Fan, silky cloth, wood hdl, 13¼" 25.00
Figurine, ballerina, net dress, 5¾" 38.00
Figurine, bl jay, 2½" 5.00
Figurine, boy hiker, Hummel type, 4" 10.00
Figurine, boy skier, bl cap & pants, 4" 15.00
Figurine, boy w/books under arm, 4" 10.00
Figurine, child & seashell, bsk, mc w/gold, 5¾" 32.00
Figurine, Colonial couple, bsk, Royal Sealy, 9¼", pr 100.00
Figurine, Colonial couple at piano, 4" 15.00
Figurine, Colonial lady w/accordion, 9¼" 50.00
Figurine, Colonial lady w/flower basket, mc w/gold, 8" 34.00
Figurine, Colonial man in unform, 10⅜" 50.00
Figurine, Colonial man w/gray hair, floral vest, 6¼" 27.50
Figurine, Colonial man w/violin, bsk, 9" 55.00
Figurine, cowboy on horse jumping fence, 4⅞x4½" 25.00
Figurine, cowboy w/red bandana, brn holster & gun, 7⅛" 36.00
Figurine, cowgirl, bl vest, gr skirt, 5½" 20.00
Figurine, cowgirl, gr hat, bl skirt, red boots, 5" 20.00
Figurine, Dalmation, blk & wht, 2x3", MIB 10.00
Figurine, Deco dancing lady, mc, bsk, 6½" 50.00
Figurine, Deco lady w/purse, walking, 6½" 36.00
Figurine, Dutch girl w/flower basket, 3¾" 10.00
Figurine, Dutch water girl, 4" 12.00
Figurine, Eskimo couple, 3" & 2¾", pr 15.00
Figurine, Flamingo, grassy base, souvenir, 5½" 15.00
Figurine, flutist, gr coat, brn pants & hat, 4½" 8.00
Figurine, gaucho w/guitar, 6½" 20.00
Figurine, German Shepherd, brn & wht, 2⅝x2¾" 9.00
Figurine, girl dancer, bl & wht clothes, 3" 8.00
Figurine, girl golfer, red hat, bl bows, 5¼" 20.00
Figurine, girl w/basket, Hummel type, 5½" 20.00
Figurine, girl w/chicks in basket, 4" 15.00
Figurine, goose preening, 2½" 10.00
Figurine, horse, wht, 2¼" 8.00
Figurine, horse & sulky, silver-toned metal 24.00
Figurine, Indian Chief, 5½" 20.00
Figurine, Mexican lady w/basket on head, bsk, 6¼" 25.00
Figurine, Oriental couple, blk MIOJ mk, 6", pr 35.00
Figurine, Oriental dancer, gold pointed hat, 8¾", pr 95.00
Figurine, Oriental dancer, 5", pr 36.00
Figurine, Oriental dancer, 8⅛" 25.00
Figurine, Oriental girl reclines on rug, 3¼x3½" 10.00
Figurine, Oriental lady w/muff, 8" 25.00
Figurine, pig, bow on head, 2½x3½" 8.00
Figurine, pup beside lamp, 2" 4.00
Figurine, rabbit pulling egg cart, 1x2¼" 5.00
Figurine, seaman, bl & wht, 5" 20.00
Figurine, Spaniel, brn & wht, 4½x5½" 14.00
Figurine, tuba player, red pants & hat, brn coat, 5" 10.00
Figurine, villain in blk w/young lady, 7½" 40.00
Jar, powder; floral medallion on bl, 2½" 10.00
Lamp base, Colonial couple, metal base, 10½", pr 50.00
Lamp base, Colonial man & lady, mc clothes, bsk, 11", pr 110.00
Lamp base, musician & singer, 11½", pr 60.00

Lighter, gun figural, metal, 2" 16.00
Mug, barrel figural, man in nightshirt hdl, 4¼" 25.00
Mug, elephant, seated, brn, trunk is hdl, 4¾" 25.00
Mug, winking man figural w/squirrel hdl, 5" 25.00
Pencil holder, house figural w/dog at door, celluloid 18.00
Pincushion, cat figural, 3½x5¼" 16.00
Pincushion, tomato figural, 1¾x3" 7.50
Pitcher, florals on bl, Pico, 2½" 5.00
Planter, bird beside house, 3" 7.00
Planter, boy beside cactus, 4" 7.00
Planter, bug w/bonnet, 4x4½" 12.00
Planter, cat on shoe, 2x3" 20.00
Planter, couple w/rabbits, Paulux, bsk, 5¼x7¼" 145.00
Planter, elephant, brn & beige, 3¼x6¾" 18.00
Planter, frog in weeds, 3⅝x3" 15.00
Planter, girl in wht dress, w/flower basket, 7" 18.00
Planter, lady stands beside shell, bsk, 5½x6½" 47.50
Planter, Mexican w/guitar beside lg basket, 4¼" 12.50
Planter, rabbit pulls cart, bl, 2½x6" 14.00
Planter, rooster pulls cart, 3x4½" 7.50
Planter, seated pixie in front, 4¾x3¾" 25.00
Planter, shoe house, rooster on toe, 4¼x5" 16.00
Planter, swan, bsk, Lefton China, 4x5½" 35.00
Plaque, cup & saucer, 3¼" 6.50
Plaque, duck, wings wide, 6½" 22.00
Plaque, Dutch girl, 6¼x4" 22.50
Plaque, monkey, bsk, 5" 20.00
Plate, hibiscus center, rtcl rim, Rosetti, Chicago USA, 8¼" 25.00
Plate, mc florals on wht, sq, Ardalt Lenwile China #3160, 4½" 7.00
Shakers, bellhop w/suitcases, pr 20.00
Shakers, cottage & lighthouse, pr 20.00
Shakers, Donald Duck, 3⅜", pr 20.00
Shakers, frogs on lily pad, 2½x4", pr 20.00
Shakers, graduates, pr 18.00
Shakers, silver-toned metal, 2¼", pr 16.00
Shakers, teakettle, scenic, pr 15.00
Shelf sitter, Colonial musician, 3¼" 20.00
Teapot, brn, 3x6¼" 22.00
Teapot, tomato shape, +matching creamer & sugar bowl 60.00
Teapot, tomato shape, 3" 30.00
Tray, leaf form, metal, 5½" 5.00
Tray, souvenir of United Nations, metal, 2x4¾" 9.00
Tray, Statue of Liberty/Empire State Building, metal, 5¼" 14.00
Umbrella, paper & wood w/metal tip, closed: 18" 25.00
Vase, Colonial man at front, 4" 12.50
Vase, floral, pk on brn, low hdls, 4¼" 5.00
Vase, pagoda in relief, ftd, sm hdls, 5¼" 22.00
Vase, Wedgwood type, 6⅛" 30.00
Water lily, celluloid, MIB 8.00

Ohr, George

George Ohr established his pottery around 1893 in Biloxi, Mississippi. The unusual style of the ware he produced and his flamboyant personality earned him the dubious title of 'the mad potter of Biloxi.' Though acclaimed by some of the critics of his day to be perhaps the most accomplished thrower in the history of the industry, others overlooked the eggshell-thin walls of his vessels, each a different shape and contortion, and saw only that their 'tortured' appearance contradicted their own sedate preferences.

Ohr worked alone. His work was typically pinched and pulled, pleated, crumpled, dented, and folded. Lizards and worms were often applied to the ware, each with detailed, expressive features. He was well recognized, however, for his glazes, especially those with a metallic patina. The ware was marked with his name, alone or with 'Biloxi' added. Ohr died in 1918.

Our advisors for this category are Fer-Duc, Inc.; they are listed in the Directory under New York.

Bowl, brn/gold streaky gloss, severe crimps/pleats, 3½" W	**700.00**
Bowl, gr/brn flecked, boat form w/everted sides, 7" L	**400.00**
Creamer, cherry red gloss, 2½"	**265.00**
Creamer, cratered gray metallic, 3½"	**495.00**
Hat, brn, incised 'USS Winona/etc,' 5½" L	**400.00**
Hat, charcoal gray, curled brim, 3½" L	**385.00**
Inkwell, coiled serpent on artist's palette, brn, sgn, 7x6¾"	**500.00**
Jar, bsk, swirled in 2 colors, undulating shape, 4"	**750.00**
Mug, gun-metal streaks over yel-gr gloss, lg hdl, 5x5½"	**650.00**
Mug, puzzle; gr, script mk, 3½"	**600.00**
Pitcher, bl/gr, Grover Cleveland emb, wife on bk, 8", EX	**700.00**
Pitcher, dk brn gloss, dimpled, cut-out angular hdl, 3½"	**800.00**
Pitcher, dk gray gloss over dk brn clay, 4½"	**350.00**
Pitcher, violet w/bl mottle, cut-out hdl, pinched sides, 5"	**4,900.00**
Pitcher, yel w/brn & gr, chamber pot form, 2"	**350.00**
Vase, bl w/mc mottle, gr mottle int, 2 rim/body folds, 3"	**3,000.00**
Vase, bl/gr mottle, pinched/twisted rim & shoulder, 6x5"	**800.00**
Vase, blistered mauve, torn/crimped/twisted rim, slim, 5"	**1,000.00**
Vase, brn metallic mottle, dbl hdls, shoulder twist, 4"	**2,400.00**
Vase, crystalline speckled gr/brn/bl/beige, flared pear, 7"	**1,000.00**
Vase, curdled raspberry, bulbous w/central twist, 5x5"	**2,500.00**
Vase, dk bl-gr speckles on gold-yel, shoulder twist, 7x4½"	**2,000.00**
Vase, dk brn, crushed/twisted rim, waisted sphere, 3½"	**385.00**
Vase, dk gray metallic, pear form w/ruffled 'skirt,' 3"	**1,850.00**
Vase, gr w/brn flecks, pinched lateral folds, bulbous, 3"	**550.00**
Vase, gr-mottle metallic gray, pinched/undulating rim, 3½"	**700.00**
Vase, gr/bl volcanic, can neck/angle shoulder/rnd ft, 4"	**550.00**
Vase, gr/dk bl speckles on rose/buff, in-body twist, 4x3"	**1,800.00**
Vase, gray-blistered red bottom, twist in canister neck, 8"	**16,000.00**
Vase, gray-blistered red w/blk, bulbous/ped ft, 7x6", NM	**8,500.00**
Vase, gray/brn w/bl sponging, sq-top dents at shoulder, 4"	**1,600.00**
Vase, lapis bl gloss, ruffled, slim, low ft, 5¾"	**500.00**
Vase, lav semi-matt, hourglass form w/star-shape mouth, 5"	**400.00**
Vase, ochre w/gr & brn spots, pear form w/bulbous rim, 5½"	**400.00**
Vase, ochre/bl-gr w/brn specks, bulbous w/can neck, 4½"	**285.00**
Vase, olive & bl w/gun-metal runs, can neck/ring hdls, 9x6"	**7,000.00**
Vase, plum/dk teal on olive, crimped/ruffled rim, 5x5"	**2,750.00**
Vase, purple/dk gr, gun-metal runs, canister neck, 6½x4"	**1,100.00**
Vase, red w/cup-like red/gr/bl mottled neck, rnd ft, 5"	**495.00**

Vase, speckled ochre with dark brown splotches, twisted mid-section, 6½" x 4", $3,000.00.

Vase, unglazed, severe base twist, deeply pinched rim, 5"	**500.00**
Vase, yel w/gr speckles, severe rim manipulations, 5"	**2,800.00**
Vase, 3 areas of varied color, ruffled snake, crimped, 6x6"	**6,750.00**

Old Ivory

Old Ivory dinnerware was produced during the late 1800s in Selesia. The patterns are referred to by the numbers stamped on the bottom of each piece. The mark sometimes includes a crown and the name 'Selesia.' Patterns #16 and #84 are the easiest to find and come in a wide variety of table items. Values are about the same for both patterns. Other floral designs include pink, yellow, and orange roses; holly; and lavender flowers – all on the same soft ivory background.

Berry set, #16 or #84, 6½" master+6 ind	250.00
Berry set, #16 or #84, 9" master+6 ind	275.00
Berry set, #75, 6½" master+4 ind	180.00
Bowl, #15, oval, ftd, 4½x11x8"	200.00
Bowl, berry; #15, ind	15.00
Bowl, berry; #69, 10"	135.00
Bowl, berry; #75, ind	15.00
Bowl, oyster; #16 or #84	125.00
Cake plate, #16 or #84, pierced hdls	75.00
Cake plate, #6	100.00
Celery dish, #11, 11½"	60.00
Celery dish, Thistle, 12¾x5½"	55.00
Chocolate pot, #15, +4 c/s	785.00
Chocolate pot, #16 or #84, +6 c/s	900.00
Chocolate pot, Thistle	185.00
Cracker jar or biscuit jar, #16 or #84	325.00

Cracker or biscuit jar, #75, 6", $325.00.

Creamer & sugar bowl, #16 or #84	175.00
Creamer & sugar bowl, #16 or #84, oversz	300.00
Cup, chocolate; #28	40.00
Cup, demitasse; #13	15.00
Cup, tea; #73	18.00
Cup & saucer, #53, 6 for	385.00
Cup & saucer, chocolate; #10	55.00
Cup & saucer, coffee; #202	60.00
Cup & saucer, coffee; #28	60.00
Cup & saucer, demitasse; #200	60.00
Cup & saucer, tea; #28	40.00
Mustard jar, #16 or #84	200.00
Pitcher, water; #84	550.00
Plate, #10, 6¼"	28.00

Plate, #11, 6¼" 18.00
Plate, #15, 7½" 20.00
Plate, #16 or #84, 8½" 45.00
Plate, #16 or #84, 9½" 125.00
Plate, #19, 8" 75.00
Plate, #200, 6" 20.00
Plate, #22, Holly, 9½" 125.00
Plate, #73, 6¼" 18.00
Plate, #73, 8½" 27.50
Plate, #75, 7¾" 32.00
Relish, #15 ....36.00
Relish, #16 or #84, hdls, 6" dia 75.00
Shakers, #122, pr 95.00
Tea set, #204, teapot, cr/sug, & waste bowl 150.00
Tea tile, #16 ....65.00
Tray, dresser; #28 ....125.00
Tureen, vegetable; #84, w/lid & hdl 695.00

Old Paris

Old Paris porcelains were made from the late 18th century until about 1900. Seldom marked, the term refers to the area of manufacture rather than a specific company. In general, the ware was of high quality and characterized by classic shapes, colorful decoration, and gold application.

Bowl, gilt detail on emb wht, 1850, 9" 120.00
Cache pot, gilt foliage band, lion mask hdls, 7" ...175.00
Cake stand, buff w/gold motif, 3-tier, 17", pr 900.00
Compote, musical motifs, scroll/foliate hdls, ftd, 10" ...425.00
Desk set, 3 girls as cover, well & sander w/in, rstr, 8" ...300.00
Jardiniere, roses on wht, scalloped base/rim, hdls, 9", pr ...300.00
Tureen, cauliflower finial, leaf hdls, gold trim, 8" ...65.00
Vase, cherub/floral frieze on lt gr, ring hdls, ftd, 16", pr ...825.00
Vase, floral reserves, scroll hdls, sq base, gilt, 7½", pr ...200.00
Vase, gilt calla lilies/leaves w/mc floral panels, 8", pr ...375.00
Vase, leaf form, cobalt/gr/gilt decor, 10½", pr ...300.00
Vase, mc florals on wht, hdls, sq ped ft, 1880s, 16", pr ... 2,400.00

Vase, courting couples in reserve, branch handles, applied florals, ca 1850, repaired, 18", $500.00 for the pair.

Old Sleepy Eye

Old Sleepy Eye was a Sioux Indian chief who was born in Min-

nesota in 1780. His name was used for the name of a town as well as a flour mill. The Sleepy Eye Milling Company of Sleepy Eye, Minnesota, contracted the Weir Pottery Company of Monmouth, Illinois, to make steins, vases, salt crocks, and butter tubs which the company gave away to their customers in each bag of their flour. A bust profile of the old Indian and his name decorated each piece of the blue and gray stoneware. In addition to these four items, the Minnesota Stoneware Company of Red Wing made a mug with a verse which is very scarce today.

In 1906 Weir Pottery merged with six others to form the Western Stoneware Company in Monmouth. They produced a line of blue and white ware using a lighter body, but these pieces were never given as flour premiums. This line consisted of pitchers (five sizes), steins, mugs, sugar bowls, vases, trivets, and mustache cups. These pieces turn up only rarely in other colors and are highly sought by advanced collectors.

Advertising items such as trade cards, pillow tops, thermometers, paperweights, letter openers, post cards, cookbooks, and thimbles are considered very valuable.

The original ware was made sporadically until 1937. Brown steins and mugs were produced in 1952.

Barrel, grapevine-effect banding 1,200.00
Butter crock, Flemish 500.00
Calendar, 1904 ....350.00
Cookbook, Indian on cover, Sleepy Eye Milling Co, 4¾x4" ...55.00
Cookbook, loaf of bread shape, NM 250.00
Coupon, for ordering cookbook 60.00
Dough scraper, tin/wood, To Be Sure, EX 350.00
Fan, Indian chief, die-cut cb, 1900 ....175.00
Flour sack, cloth, mc Indian, red letters 275.00
Flour sack, paper, Indian in blk, blk lettering, NM ...100.00
Ink blotter 100.00
Label, barrel end; mc Indian portrait, 16", NM 125.00
Label, egg crate; Indian chief in color, 1930s, 9x11" ...25.00
Letter opener, bronze 850.00
Match holder, pnt 1,500.00
Match holder, wht 850.00
Milk carton 18.00
Mirror, advertising, 1935 ....35.00
Mug, bl & wht, 4¼" 175.00
Mug, verse, Redwing, EX 1,300.00
Paperweight, bronzed company trademk 450.00
Pillow cover, Sleepy Eye & tribe meet Pres Monroe ...600.00

Pitcher, #2, $200.00.

Pillow cover, trademk center w/various scenes, 22", NM 600.00
Pitcher, #1...150.00
Pitcher, #3, rare...250.00
Pitcher, #3, w/bl rim...350.00
Pitcher, #4...325.00
Pitcher, #5...350.00
Pitcher, gold & brn, 1981..125.00
Pitcher, standing Indian, good color, #5 size 1,250.00
Post card 90.00
Ruler, wooden 400.00
Salt crock, Flemish...450.00
Sign, tin, Sleepy Eye Flour & Cereal Products 3,500.00

Sign, $2,500.00.

Spoon, demitasse; emb roses in bowl, Unity SP 85.00
Spoon, Indian-head hdl...100.00
Stein, bl & wht, 7¾" 500.00
Stein, brn, 1952, 22-oz...350.00
Stein, brn & wht 900.00
Stein, brn & yel, Western Stoneware 900.00
Stein, cobalt 800.00
Stein, ltd edition, 1979-1984, ea 100.00
Sugar bowl, bl & wht, 3" 600.00
Tumbler, etched, 1979 commemorative..25.00
Vase, bl & wht, good color, 9" 425.00
Vase, brn on yel, rare color..800.00
Vase, Indian & cattails, Flemish, 8½"..375.00
Watch fob, Sleepy Eye Mills, Indian, M......................................50.00

Omar Khayyam Pottery

Oscar Louis Bachelder was an itinerate potter for several years before opening a small pottery of his own in Buncombe County, North Carolina, which he operated from about 1915 until 1935. He produced fine stoneware utilitarian items as well as decorative vases. Some of his ware is signed with a device formed by his co-joined initials.

Vase, Caneware, tan, broad shoulders, OLB mk, 4½" 350.00

Vase, dk bl volcanic, mottled, OL Batchelder, imp mks, 3¾" 450.00

O'Neill, Rose

Rose O'Neill's Kewpies were introduced in 1909 when they were used to conclude a story in the December issue of *Ladies' Home Journal*. They were an immediate success, and soon Kewpie dolls were being produced world-wide. German manufacturers were among the earliest and also used the Kewpie motif to decorate chinaware as well as other items. The Kewpie is still popular today and can be found on products ranging from Christmas cards and cake ornaments to fabrics and wall-paper.

In the following listings, 'sgn' indicates that the item is signed Rose O'Neill. Unsigned items are of little interest to collectors. Items marked 'Germany' are sometimes reproductions.

Bank, jasper, 6 Kewpies w/flag, flower border, ftd, 5x5½".............450.00
Bell, brass, Kewpie form, sm 65.00
Book, Sing-A-Song of Safety, O'Neill illus, 1937, EX 25.00
Bowl, cereal; 7 Kewpies, Royal Rudolstadt, 6¼" 120.00
Calendar plate, Kewpies, glass, 1975, rare....................................75.00
Christmas card, Kewpies, lacy fold-out 10.00
Clock, bl & wht jasper, Kewpies w/flowers, sgn, 3½x5" 585.00
Feeding dish, 7 Kewpies, sgn Rose O'Neill, Royal Rudolstadt 235.00

Jasperware desk clock, blue and white, German wind-up movement, repaired, 4" x 5", $450.00.

Kewpie, brass, 4" 40.00
Kewpie, bsk, holding cat, 4" 425.00
Kewpie, bsk, holding pen, 3" 365.00
Kewpie, bsk, in basket w/flowers, 3½".....................................600.00
Kewpie, bsk, jtd arms, 1-pc body, 9" 400.00
Kewpie, bsk, jtd arms & hips, 4" 465.00
Kewpie, bsk, jtd arms only, 1-pc body, 1½" 95.00
Kewpie, bsk, on stomach, 4"...425.00
Kewpie, bsk, seated at tea table, sgn 1,700.00
Kewpie, bsk, sits w/open book, sgn..850.00
Kewpie, bsk, w/broom, 4" 465.00
Kewpie, bsk, w/dog Doodle, 3½" 1,500.00
Kewpie, bsk, w/drawstring bag, 4½" 575.00
Kewpie, bsk, w/drum, sgn, 3½" 2,400.00

Kewpie, bsk, w/guitar stands beside pillar, sgn 600.00
Kewpie, bsk, w/helmet, 6" 700.00
Kewpie, bsk, w/outhouse, 2½"...1,100.00
Kewpie, bsk, w/teddy bear, 4" 750.00
Kewpie, bsk, w/umbrella & dog, 3½" 1,200.00
Kewpie, bsk shoulder head, cloth body, 6" 600.00
Kewpie, celluloid, jtd arms, 3" 60.00
Kewpie, celluloid, jtd arms, 9" 175.00
Kewpie, celluloid, 2" 40.00
Kewpie, sgn, 1¼", on heart-form amber ribboned pincushion 300.00
Kewpie, vinyl, Cameo, 16", MIB w/orig sticker 85.00
Kewpie Bride, Groom, & Minister, celluloid, Japan, sgn, 2½" 75.00
Kewpie Bride & Groom, bsk, sgn ft, sticker, 4"............................465.00
Kewpie Confederate Soldier, bsk, molded-on cap/rifle/sword, 6" .775.00
Kewpie Farmer, bsk, 4" 485.00
Kewpie Gardener, bsk, 4" 485.00
Kewpie Governor, bsk, 4" 400.00
Kewpie Hot 'N Tot, Blk, sgn ft, Cameo, MIB 89.00
Kewpie Santa, cb, Royal Society, 1913, 11½" 35.00
Kewpie Soaps, sgn, 4", pr 85.00
Kewpie Soldier, bsk, 4½" 500.00
Kewpie Traveler, bsk, sgn ft, sticker, 3½" 325.00
Kewpie Traveler, bsk, tan or blk suitcase, 3½" 325.00
Kewpie w/puppy, sgn..600.00
Kewpie w/umbrella & dog, sgn, rpr ft, 2⅜" 400.00
Letter opener, Kewpie figural hdl 65.00
Mug, Kewpies playing leap frog, china w/lustre, sgn, lg 135.00
Paper plate, Kewpies 4.00
Planter, bl jasper, tumbling Kewpies, sgn, 4½" 220.00
Plaque, jasper, 4 Kewpies, sgn, mk Germany, 4x3½" 265.00
Plate, 3 Kewpies on bench, c Rose O'Neill Wilson, Germany, 7" .75.00
Post card, Taking in Sights, c Rose O'Neill, ca 1915, VG 30.00
Purse, Kewpieville, child's..18.00
Shakers, Kewpies, SP, Sheffield, 3", pr 60.00
Sheet music, Songs of Safety, O'Neill illus, 1937 ....35.00
Stickpin, ¾" Kewpie on top..20.00
Talc shaker, Kewpie, compo & metal, sgn/1913, 7" 225.00
Thimble, Kewpie, metal, mk 35.00
Tie tack, Kewpie 18.00
Tray, bl jasper, 5 Kewpies, clover shape, sgn, 7x6¼" 395.00
Watch holder, pewter, Kewpie..125.00
Whistle, brass, Kewpie 35.00

Onion Pattern

The familiar pattern known to collectors as Onion acquired its name through a case of mistaken identity. Designed in the early 1700s by Johann Haroldt of the Meissen factory in Germany, the pattern was a mixture from earlier Oriental designs. One of its components was a stylized peach, which was mistaken for an onion; as a result, the pattern became known by that name. Usually found in blue, an occasional piece may also be found in pink. The pattern is commonly associated with Meissen, but it has been reproduced by many others including Villeroy and Boch and Royal Copenhagen.

Our advisor for this category is William Brinkley; he is listed in the Directory under Illinois.

Basket, rtcl, shallow, Meissen, 1890s, 7", pr 250.00
Bowl, scalloped, X-swords, 3¼x4¾" dia 120.00
Bowl, soup; lg 50.00
Butter chip 25.00
Cake plate, rnd, 10"..150.00

Canister, Germany, set of 4 ....165.00
Canister, Pepper, barrel form, 3½" 35.00
Canister, Reis, barrel form, w/lid 75.00

Casserole, Johnson Bros., England, 6" x 10", $145.00.

Canister, Zucker, stenciled, ped base 65.00
Cheese board, 9½" 75.00
Chop plate, Meissen, 12", ...185.00
Compote, twisted knopped stem, Meissen, 8¾x9" 375.00
Creamer, X-swords, late 75.00
Cruet, flow bl, pr 300.00
Cup & saucer, demitasse; mk Meissen in oval, Germany 30.00
Cup & saucer, Meissen 60.00
Funnel, w/leaves, lg 100.00
Funnel, w/1 flower, sm 50.00
Gravy boat, w/hdls, attached undertray, 10" 85.00
Meat tenderizer..120.00
Petit four, 2-tiered, pierced, boy or girl finial, 16½", pr............3,200.00
Pie crimper..60.00
Plate, fruit grouping, ca 1850, 9½" 150.00
Plate, X-swords, 10" 75.00
Plate, X-swords, 9½" 50.00
Platter, Meissen, 2 mks, 10½"..68.00
Platter, oval, 17" 295.00
Potato masher, orig wood hdl, 1800s..245.00
Rolling pin..225.00
Salt box, stenciled 120.00
Salt cellar, X-swords 75.00
Shakers, pr 40.00
Spoon, 10¼"..85.00
Sugar bowl, Meissen, ca 1900, w/lid..100.00
Tea ball stand, wire holder..90.00
Toothpick holder, 3-ftd, on ped base..95.00
Tureen, soup; cherub finial, Meissen, 1890s, rstr, 11"..................700.00
Vase, ftd, X-swords, 5" 85.00
Warming dish, flow bl 150.00
Whisk 100.00

Opalescent Glass

First made in England in 1870, opalescent glass became popular in America around the turn of the century. Its name comes from the milky-white opalescent trim that defines the lines of the pattern. It was produced in table sets, novelties, toothpick holders, vases, and lamps.

Alaska, banana boat, bl..250.00

Alaska, berry set, bl, 7-pc 275.00
Alaska, bowl, bl, sq, 8" 95.00
Alaska, butter dish, bl or vaseline 260.00
Alaska, butter dish, bl w/HP floral 295.00
Alaska, celery tray, bl 155.00
Alaska, celery tray, vaseline 145.00
Alaska, creamer, bl 70.00
Alaska, creamer, vaseline 60.00
Alaska, creamer, vaseline w/HP floral 70.00
Alaska, cruet, bl, w/stopper 265.00
Alaska, cruet, vaseline 250.00
Alaska, cruet, vaseline w/HP floral 265.00
Alaska, pitcher, water; bl 325.00
Alaska, pitcher, water; bl w/HP floral 450.00
Alaska, pitcher, water; clear 225.00
Alaska, pitcher, water; vaseline 350.00
Alaska, sauce, bl 25.00
Alaska, sauce, gr w/HP floral 30.00
Alaska, shakers, bl or vaseline, pr 65.00
Alaska, spooner, bl 65.00
Alaska, spooner, vaseline 45.00
Alaska, sugar bowl, bl, w/lid 150.00
Alaska, sugar bowl, vaseline, w/lid 130.00
Alaska, tumbler, vaseline 60.00
Arabian Nights, pitcher, water; cranberry 500.00
Arabian Nights, tumbler, bl 60.00
Arabian Nights, tumbler, cranberry 95.00
Argonaut Shell, berry set, clear, 7-pc 275.00
Argonaut Shell, butter dish, bl 275.00
Argonaut Shell, compote, jelly; vaseline 75.00
Argonaut Shell, creamer, bl 75.00
Argonaut Shell, cruet, bl 275.00
Argonaut Shell, pitcher, water; bl 350.00
Argonaut Shell, spooner, bl 150.00
Argonaut Shell, sugar bowl, bl, w/lid 200.00
Argonaut Shell, tumbler, vaseline 100.00
Astro, bride's bowl, bl, ruffled, 8" 35.00
Beaded Ovals in Sand, butter dish, gr 250.00
Beaded Ovals in Sand, creamer, bl 70.00
Beatty Rib, creamer, ind; clear 20.00
Beatty Rib, sugar bowl, bl, w/lid 125.00
Beatty Rib, table set, bl, 4-pc 265.00
Beatty Rib, toothpick holder, clear 24.00
Beatty Swirl, butter dish, bl 150.00
Beatty Swirl, celery vase, bl 75.00
Beatty Swirl, pitcher, water; bl 130.00
Beatty Swirl, syrup, bl, rare 200.00
Beatty Swirl, tray, water; vaseline 75.00
Bubble Lattice, pitcher, water; cranberry 325.00
Bubble Lattice, sugar bowl, bl, w/lid 160.00
Buttons & Braids, pitcher, water; bl 165.00
Buttons & Braids, pitcher, water; cranberry ...350.00
Buttons & Braids, tumbler, bl 35.00
Buttons & Braids, tumbler, cranberry 85.00
Chrysanthemum Base Reverse Swirl, mustard, bl 135.00
Chrysanthemum Base Reverse Swirl, sugar shaker, cranberry 245.00
Chrysanthemum Base Swirl, butter dish, cranberry 300.00
Chrysanthemum Base Swirl, spooner, bl 75.00
Chrysanthemum Base Swirl, syrup, bl 175.00
Chrysanthemum Base Swirl, toothpick holder, cranberry 125.00
Chrysanthemum Base Swirl, tumbler, cranberry 85.00
Circled Scroll, butter dish, bl 295.00
Circled Scroll, compote, gr 125.00

Circled Scroll, cruet, bl 350.00
Circled Scroll, shakers, bl, pr 175.00
Circled Scroll, sugar bowl, bl, w/lid 225.00
Circled Scroll, tumbler, gr 80.00
Coin Spot, celery vase, cranberry 150.00
Coin Spot, compote, peach 35.00
Coin Spot, creamer, bl 50.00
Coin Spot, pitcher, water; bl, 9" 120.00
Coin Spot, pitcher, water; clear 85.00
Coin Spot, pitcher, water; cranberry 250.00
Coin Spot, sugar shaker, bl, bulbous base 85.00
Coin Spot, sugar shaker, cranberry, ring neck 120.00
Coin Spot, tumble-up, cranberry 250.00
Coin Spot, tumbler, cranberry 45.00
Contessa, basket, amber, 4¼x7" 100.00
Criss Cross, finger bowl, cranberry 95.00
Daisy & Fern, cruet, Netted Blossom mold, bl 110.00
Daisy & Fern, pitcher, water; bl 165.00
Daisy & Fern, pitcher, water; clear 95.00
Daisy & Fern, pitcher, water; cranberry, solid hdl 225.00
Daisy & Fern, syrup, bl 120.00
Daisy & Fern, tumbler, cranberry 45.00
Daisy in Criss Cross, pitcher, water; bl 275.00
Daisy in Criss Cross, syrup, bl 245.00
Daisy in Criss Cross, syrup, cranberry 345.00
Diamond Spearhead, butter dish, gr 225.00
Diamond Spearhead, butter dish, vaseline 195.00
Diamond Spearhead, celery vase, bl 110.00
Diamond Spearhead, compote, bl 95.00
Diamond Spearhead, creamer, cobalt 125.00
Diamond Spearhead, cup, cobalt 75.00
Diamond Spearhead, goblet, bl 125.00
Diamond Spearhead, mug, bl 75.00
Diamond Spearhead, pitcher, water; cobalt 450.00
Diamond Spearhead, pitcher, water; gr 325.00
Diamond Spearhead, sugar bowl, cobalt, w/lid 175.00
Diamond Spearhead, sugar bowl, gr, w/lid 135.00
Diamond Spearhead, syrup, cobalt 450.00
Diamond Spearhead, tumbler, vaseline 45.00
Dolly Madison, butter dish, bl 290.00
Dolly Madison, creamer, bl 75.00
Dolly Madison, pitcher, water; gr 350.00
Dolly Madison, spooner, gr 75.00
Dolly Madison, sugar bowl, gr, w/lid 125.00
Dolly Madison, tumbler, bl 75.00
Double Greek Key, butter dish, bl 285.00
Double Greek Key, celery vase, bl 115.00
Double Greek Key, creamer, bl 65.00
Double Greek Key, shakers, bl, pr 180.00
Double Greek Key, spooner, bl 70.00
Double Greek Key, sugar bowl, bl, w/lid 150.00
Double Greek Key, toothpick holder, bl 225.00
Double Greek Key, tumbler, bl 65.00
Drapery, pitcher, water; bl 165.00
Drapery, rose bowl, aqua 95.00
Drapery, rose bowl, bl 65.00
Drapery, water set, bl, 7-pc 375.00
Drapery, water set, clear, 7-pc 250.00
Everglades, butter dish, bl w/gold 225.00
Everglades, butter dish, vaseline 275.00
Everglades, compote, jelly; bl w/gold 85.00
Everglades, compote, jelly; vaseline 110.00
Everglades, creamer, bl 80.00

Everglades, cruet, vaseline 395.00
Everglades, pitcher, water; vaseline 360.00
Everglades, spooner, vaseline 85.00
Everglades, sugar bowl, bl w/gold 150.00
Everglades, sugar bowl, vaseline, w/lid 150.00
Everglades, tumbler, bl 65.00
Everglades, tumbler, bl w/gold 75.00
Fern, shaker, cranberry 50.00
Fern, spooner, cranberry 120.00
Flora, bowl, master berry; vaseline 75.00
Flora, butter dish, bl 245.00
Flora, butter dish, vaseline 175.00
Flora, butter dish, vaseline w/gold 210.00
Flora, celery vase, bl 110.00
Flora, compote, jelly; bl, rare 135.00
Flora, creamer, vaseline 80.00
Flora, cruet, vaseline 375.00
Flora, pitcher, water; vaseline 450.00
Flora, shakers, bl, pr 350.00
Flora, shakers, vaseline, pr 300.00
Flora, spooner, vaseline 70.00
Flora, sugar bowl, vaseline, w/lid 110.00
Flora, toothpick holder, bl 400.00
Flora, toothpick holder, vaseline 300.00
Flora, tumbler, vaseline 75.00
Fluted Scrolls, bowl, master berry; bl 65.00
Fluted Scrolls, butter dish, bl w/HP decor 215.00
Fluted Scrolls, butter dish, vaseline 165.00
Fluted Scrolls, creamer, bl 55.00
Fluted Scrolls, creamer, vaseline 60.00
Fluted Scrolls, cruet, vaseline, orig stopper 175.00
Fluted Scrolls, dresser jar, vaseline, w/lid 55.00
Fluted Scrolls, pitcher, water; bl 225.00
Fluted Scrolls, pitcher, water; vaseline 195.00
Fluted Scrolls, puff box, bl 55.00
Fluted Scrolls, puff box, vaseline 50.00
Fluted Scrolls, spooner, bl 50.00
Fluted Scrolls, sugar bowl, vaseline, w/lid 88.00
Fluted Scrolls, water set, clear, 5-pc 225.00
Frosted-Leaf & Basketweave, butter dish, bl 250.00
Frosted-Leaf & Basketweave, creamer, bl 135.00
Frosted-Leaf & Basketweave, sugar bowl, bl, w/lid 165.00
Frosted-Leaf & Basketweave, sugar bowl, vaseline, w/lid 145.00
Hobnail, creamer, vaseline, bulbous, 4" 225.00
Hobnail, pitcher, bl, clear threaded hdl, 5½" 50.00
Hobnail, pitcher, cranberry, sq mouth, lg 185.00
Hobnail, pitcher, milk; vaseline, clear reeded hdl 115.00
Hobnail, pitcher, rubena, clear hdl, +6 tumblers 750.00
Hobnail, pitcher, yel, 7" 225.00

Swirled Honeycomb, pitcher, cranberry, 5½", $295.00.

Honeycomb & Clover, butter dish, bl 300.00
Honeycomb & Clover, pitcher, water; bl 350.00
Honeycomb & Clover, sugar bowl, bl, w/lid 200.00
Honeycomb & Clover, tumbler, bl 85.00
Idyll, butter dish, bl 325.00
Idyll, creamer, clear 36.00
Idyll, creamer, gr 85.00
Idyll, spooner, gr, 4½x3½" 70.00
Idyll, sugar bowl, bl, w/lid 175.00
Idyll, toothpick holder, bl 210.00
Idyll, tumbler, bl 90.00
Intaglio, bowl, master berry; bl 100.00
Intaglio, butter dish, bl 350.00
Intaglio, compote, jelly; bl 30.00
Intaglio, compote, jelly; vaseline 39.00
Intaglio, creamer, bl w/HP decor 55.00
Intaglio, creamer, clear 20.00
Intaglio, creamer, vaseline 45.00
Intaglio, cruet, bl, w/bl stopper 135.00
Intaglio, pitcher, water; bl 200.00
Intaglio, sugar bowl, vaseline, w/lid 90.00
Intaglio, tumbler, bl 100.00
Inverted Fan & Feather, creamer, bl 135.00
Inverted Fan & Feather, pitcher, water; bl 495.00
Inverted Fan & Feather, sugar bowl, bl, w/lid 200.00
Inverted Fan & Feather, tumbler, bl 75.00
Iris w/Meander, berry set, vaseline, 6-pc 220.00
Iris w/Meander, bowl, bl, 8½" 85.00
Iris w/Meander, bowl, master berry; bl, 10" 90.00
Iris w/Meander, butter dish, bl 265.00

Meander, bowl, green, 9", $55.00.

Iris w/Meander, compote, jelly; bl 45.00
Iris w/Meander, creamer, vaseline 75.00
Iris w/Meander, cruet, vaseline 350.00
Iris w/Meander, pitcher, water; bl 375.00
Iris w/Meander, pitcher, water; vaseline 300.00
Iris w/Meander, shakers, bl, pr 200.00
Iris w/Meander, spooner, bl 75.00
Iris w/Meander, sugar bowl, bl, w/lid 150.00
Iris w/Meander, sugar bowl, gr, w/lid 125.00
Iris w/Meander, toothpick holder, clear 45.00
Iris w/Meander, toothpick holder, vaseline 75.00
Iris w/Meander, tumbler, bl 75.00
Jackson, butter dish, bl 250.00
Jackson, butter dish, vaseline 225.00
Jackson, cruet, vaseline 165.00
Jackson, pitcher, water; vaseline 450.00
Jackson, powder box, bl 55.00

Jackson, shakers, vaseline, pr 175.00
Jackson, spooner, vaseline 60.00
Jackson, sugar bowl, bl, w/lid 110.00
Jackson, tumbler, vaseline 80.00
Jewel & Flower, butter dish, clear 95.00
Jewel & Flower, butter dish, vaseline 225.00
Jewel & Flower, creamer, vaseline 85.00
Jewel & Flower, cruet, bl 300.00
Jewel & Flower, pitcher, water; bl 450.00
Jewel & Flower, shakers, vaseline, pr 165.00
Jewel & Flower, sugar bowl, vaseline, w/lid 145.00
Jewel & Flower, tumbler, bl 80.00
Jeweled Heart, compote, bl 125.00
Jeweled Heart, cruet, bl 350.00
Jeweled Heart, nappy, clear, ruffled, 6" 22.00
Jeweled Heart, spooner, bl 110.00
Jeweled Heart, sugar bowl, bl, w/lid 175.00
Jeweled Heart, toothpick holder, bl 250.00
Leaf Chalice, rose bowl, gr, ped ft 45.00
Leaf Chalice, sugar bowl, gr, ped ft, w/lid 55.00
Lustre Flute, butter dish, bl 280.00
Lustre Flute, creamer, bl 85.00
Lustre Flute, pitcher, water; bl 325.00
Lustre Flute, spooner, bl 85.00
Lustre Flute, sugar bowl, bl, w/lid 175.00
Lustre Flute, tumbler, bl 65.00
Palm Beach, butter dish, bl 275.00
Palm Beach, compote, vaseline 175.00
Palm Beach, creamer & sugar bowl, bl, w/lid 195.00
Palm Beach, pitcher, water; bl 385.00
Palm Beach, pitcher, water; vaseline 350.00
Palm Beach, sauce, bl 25.00
Palm Beach, spooner, bl 85.00
Palm Beach, tumbler, bl 85.00
Paneled Holly, berry set, bl opal, 6-pc 350.00
Paneled Holly, butter dish, bl 300.00
Paneled Holly, creamer, bl 75.00
Paneled Holly, pitcher, water; bl 500.00
Paneled Holly, sauce bowl, bl w/gold 45.00
Paneled Holly, spooner, bl 65.00
Paneled Holly, sugar bowl, bl, w/lid 225.00
Paneled Holly, tumbler, bl 75.00
Poinsettia, bowl, clear, ruffled, 3-ftd 40.00
Poinsettia, pitcher, water; bl, tankard form 275.00
Poinsettia, sugar shaker, bl 150.00
Poinsettia, syrup, bl 300.00
Poinsettia, tumbler, bl 50.00
Queen's Crown, creamer, yel, 5" 80.00
Regal, butter dish, clear 95.00
Regal, butter dish, gr w/gold 235.00
Regal, celery vase, bl 125.00
Regal, cruet, bl 400.00
Regal, pitcher, water; bl 290.00
Regal, spooner, gr 55.00
Regal, sugar bowl, bl, w/lid 145.00
Reverse Swirl, creamer, bl 125.00
Reverse Swirl, pitcher, water tankard; cranberry 425.00
Reverse Swirl, spooner, bl 95.00
Reverse Swirl, spooner, cranberry 110.00
Reverse Swirl, sugar bowl, bl, w/lid 175.00
Reverse Swirl, syrup, vaseline 135.00
Ribbed Spiral, butter dish, bl 350.00
Ribbed Spiral, compote, bl 47.00
Ribbed Spiral, creamer, bl 50.00

Ribbed Spiral, plate, vaseline 35.00
Ribbed Spiral, shakers, vaseline, pr 185.00
Ribbed Spiral, sugar bowl, bl, w/lid 175.00
Ribbed Spiral, tumbler, bl 75.00
Scottish Moor, pitcher, water; cranberry 375.00
Scroll w/Acanthus, butter dish, bl 350.00
Scroll w/Acanthus, creamer, bl 60.00
Scroll w/Acanthus, cruet, bl, w/clear stopper 190.00
Scroll w/Acanthus, cruet, vaseline 350.00
Scroll w/Acanthus, pitcher, water; vaseline 350.00
Scroll w/Acanthus, spooner, bl 65.00
Scroll w/Acanthus, sugar bowl, vaseline, w/lid 125.00
Scroll w/Acanthus, tumbler, bl 75.00
Seaweed, rose bowl, vaseline, lg 48.00
Shell, butter dish, bl 450.00
Shell, compote, bl 110.00
Shell, cruet, bl 350.00
Shell, pitcher, water; bl 500.00
Shell, sauce, clear, 6 for 150.00
Shell, spooner, bl 95.00
Shell, toothpick holder, bl 400.00
Shell, tumbler, bl 75.00
Spanish Lace, pitcher, water; clear 95.00
Spanish Lace, rose bowl, clear 35.00
Spanish Lace, shakers, cranberry, pr 175.00
Spanish Lace, sugar shaker, bl 135.00
Spanish Lace, sweetmeat, cranberry, SP rim/lid/hdl, M 375.00
Spanish Lace, tumbler, cranberry 75.00
Sunburst on Shield, creamer, bl 125.00
Sunburst on Shield, cruet, vaseline 650.00
Sunburst on Shield, pitcher, water; bl 500.00
Sunburst on Shield, spooner, vaseline 85.00
Sunburst on Shield, sugar bowl, clear, w/lid 30.00
Sunburst on Shield, sugar bowl, vaseline, w/lid 175.00
Sunburst on Shield, tumbler, bl 100.00
Swag w/Brackets, berry set, gr, 7-pc 200.00
Swag w/Brackets, compote, gr 30.00
Swag w/Brackets, pitcher, water; vaseline 250.00
Swag w/Brackets, sauce, vaseline 25.00
Swag w/Brackets, shakers, bl, pr 175.00
Swag w/Brackets, spooner, gr 45.00
Swag w/Brackets, sugar bowl, gr, w/lid 75.00
Swag w/Brackets, toothpick holder, bl 300.00
Swag w/Brackets, tumbler, bl 60.00
Swag w/Brackets, tumbler, clear 30.00
Swirl, hat, clear, lg 75.00
Swirl, pitcher, water; bl 125.00
Swirl, pitcher, water; clear 60.00
Swirl, sugar shaker, cranberry 150.00
Swirl, toothpick holder, cranberry, scarce tumbler shape 65.00
Tokyo, compote, gr 33.00
Tokyo, creamer, bl 65.00
Tokyo, cruet, bl, w/clear stopper 175.00
Tokyo, pitcher, water; bl 300.00
Tokyo, shakers, bl, pr 180.00
Tokyo, sugar bowl, clear, w/lid 50.00
War of Roses, boat dish, vaseline, 3x7½x2½" 50.00
Water Lily & Cattails, bowl, master berry; clear, ruffled 35.00
Water Lily & Cattails, butter dish, bl 375.00
Water Lily & Cattails, creamer, bl 45.00
Water Lily & Cattails, pitcher, water; bl 395.00
Water Lily & Cattails, sugar bowl, bl, w/lid 175.00
Water Lily & Cattails, tumbler, bl 50.00
Wild Bouquet, berry set, clear, 6-pc 145.00

Wild Bouquet, butter dish, bl **400.00**
Wild Bouquet, compote, jelly; bl..**125.00**
Wild Bouquet, compote, jelly; clear **45.00**
Wild Bouquet, cruet, bl **325.00**
Wild Bouquet, pitcher, water; bl...**250.00**
Wild Bouquet, sugar bowl, bl, w/lid...**200.00**
Wild Bouquet, toothpick holder, bl...**275.00**
Wild Bouquet, tumbler, bl **100.00**
Wild Bouquet, tumbler, gr **60.00**
Wreath & Shell, bowl, master berry; bl..**85.00**
Wreath & Shell, butter dish, bl..**225.00**
Wreath & Shell, celery vase, bl..**165.00**
Wreath & Shell, cracker jar, bl..**695.00**
Wreath & Shell, pitcher, water; bl...**350.00**
Wreath & Shell, rose bowl, bl **75.00**
Wreath & Shell, salt dip, bl **135.00**
Wreath & Shell, sauce, vaseline..**18.00**
Wreath & Shell, spittoon, lady's, vaseline **90.00**
Wreath & Shell, spooner, bl..**75.00**
Wreath & Shell, spooner, vaseline **65.00**
Wreath & Shell, sugar bowl, vaseline, w/lid....................................**130.00**
Wreath & Shell, toothpick holder, bl...**225.00**
Wreath & Shell, toothpick holder, vaseline w/decor **250.00**
Wreath & Shell, tumbler, bl...**70.00**

Opaline

A type of semi-opaque opal glass, opaline was made in white as well as pastel shades and is often enameled. It is similar in appearance to English bristol glass, though its enamel or gilt decorative devices tend to exhibit a French influence.

Box, bl, brass mts, 7" L, fitted int w/2 enameled bottles **575.00**
Box, cigarette; wht, brass mts, French, 4x3½x5" **175.00**
Box, clambroth, egg form w/gilt brass 'nest,' 4" L **175.00**
Box, pk, egg form w/brass mts & stand, 5¼" H............................**200.00**
Cologne, bl, egg form, in gilt brass silk-lined basket, 3" **175.00**
Cologne, bl, panel cut, brass mts, litho scene in lid, 4½" **210.00**
Cologne, gr, alabaster base w/gilt mts & Paris litho, 7" **300.00**
Cologne, gr, fancy brass mts, litho of fountain in lid, 5".............**275.00**
Cologne, pk, 6⅝", +cut & enameled stopper................................**105.00**
Compote, clambroth, fancy brass mts, lion finial, 6x4" **225.00**

Openers

Around the turn of the century, manufacturers began to seal bottles with a metal cap that required a new type of bottle opener. Now the screw cap and the flip top have made bottle openers nearly obsolete. There are many variations, some in combination with other tools. Many openers were used as means of advertising a product. Various materials were used, including silver and brass.

A figural bottle opener is defined as a figure designed for the sole purpose of lifting a bottle cap. The actual opener must be an integral part of the figure itself. The major producers of iron figurals were Wilton Products, John Wright Inc., Gadzik Sales, and L & L Favors. Openers may be free-standing and three-dimensional, wall hung, or flat. They can be made of cast iron (often painted), brass, bronze, or aluminum.

Those seeking additional information concerning figural bottle openers are encouraged to contact the Figural Bottle Opener Collectors, whose address can be found in the Directory under Clubs, Newsletters, and Catalogs.

Alligator, mouth is opener, CI w/worn mc pnt, 6" L.....................**45.00**
Beaver, brass **105.00**
Canadian Goose, CI w/3-color pnt, 3⅝", VG................................**25.00**
Cocker Dog, CI, EX pnt **17.00**
Cowboy w/guitar, CI, EX **70.00**
Donkey, Democrat, CI, 1940s **12.50**
Donkey, Democrat, Des Moines IA, metal **45.00**
Donkey, sitting, mouth is opener, head bk, CI, EX pnt, 3⅝" **35.00**
Donkey's head & shoulders, mouth open/ears up, pnt CI, 3⅝" **20.00**
Elephant, Republican, CI, 1940s, EX..**12.50**
Goat, C-curved horns are opener, CI w/worn gr & wht pnt, 4½" ..**30.00**
Indian, Iroquois Beer, copper & steel, EX **40.00**
Lobster, CI, EX orig pnt..**20.00**
Lobster, CI w/worn red pnt, 3½" L **65.00**
Nude w/arms above head, brass, 4" **20.00**
Parrot, Deco style, CI, VG pnt..**20.00**
Parrot on perch, CI w/mc pnt, Delphos OH, 5", EX.....................**40.00**
Parrot on perch, lg beak, CI w/EX mc pnt, 5⅜"............................**30.00**
Peacock, brass **40.00**
Pelican, CI w/mc pnt, 3⅜", NM..**45.00**

Pelican, painted cast metal, 2½", $45.00.

Sea gull, CI, VG pnt..**45.00**
Setter, left leg raised, on point, CI w/rpt, 4½" L **50.00**
Squirrel on log, CI w/EX pnt, 1⅞" H **75.00**
Squirrel on log, CI w/worn gold rpt, 1⅞" H **45.00**

Optical Items

Collectors of Americana are beginning to appreciate the charm of antique optical items, and those involved in the related trade find them particularly fascinating. Anyone, however, can appreciate the evolution of technology apparent when viewing a collection of old eye wear and at the same time admire the primitive ingenuity involved in their construction.

Case, spectacles; sterling, etched decor, velvet lined, 2x4½" **75.00**
Microscope, Bausch & Lomb, brass, cherry case, 1900, 12" **475.00**
Microscope, C Zeiss, fancy brass, walnut case, 1880s **525.00**
Opera glasses, LeMaire, MOP, brass trim, 1890s **70.00**
Opera glasses, tortoise shell & silvered metal, long hdl, EX...........**55.00**
Spectacles, folding, silver fr w/sliding ear pcs, hall mk **100.00**
Spectacles, Pince Nez, gutta percha fr, cobalt lenses **25.00**
Spectacles, slightly wing shaped w/rhinestones, France, 1940s **35.00**

Tester, Test...Eyes Scientifically, lenses/frames/etc, case 75.00

Opera glasses, French enameling on cobalt, gold metal, 2¾", $585.00.

Orientalia

The art of the Orient is an area of collecting currently enjoying strong collector interest, not only in those examples that are truly 'antique' but in the 20th-century items as well. Because of the many aspects involved in a study of Orientalia, we can only try through brief comments to acquaint the reader with some of the more readily-available examples and suggest specialized reference sources for detailed information.

Celadon, introduced during the Ching Dynasty, is a green-glazed ware developed in an attempt to imitate the color of jade. Designs are often incised or painted on over glaze in heavy enamel applications. Chinese export ware was designed to appeal to Western tastes and was often made to order. During the 18th century, vast amounts were shipped to Europe and on westward. Many of these dinnerwares were given specific pattern names – Rose Mandarin, Fitzhugh, Armorial, Rose Medallion, and Canton are but a few of the more familiar. Cinnabar is carved lacquer work, often involving hundreds of layers built one at a time on a metal or wooden base. Later pieces are red; older examples tend to darken.

The Chinese were introduced to snuff in the 17th century, and their carved and painted snuff bottles typify their exquisite taste and workmanship. These small bottles, seldom measuring over 2½", were made of amber, jade, ivory, and cinnabar; tiny spoons were often attached to their stoppers. By the 18th century, some were being made of porcelain, others were of glass with delicate designs tediously reverse painted with minuscule brushes sometimes containing a single hair. Copper and brass were used but to no large extent.

Ojimes were small slides used in conjunction with the netsuke to adjust tension on the obi (sash) and as a means to secure it. Those described in our listings are signed unless noted otherwise. See also Canton; Champleve; Cloisonne; Coralene, Oriental; Dragon Ware; Geisha Girl; Imari; Ivory; Kutani; Moriage; Netsuke; Nippon; Noritake; Peking Glass; Rose Medallion; Satsuma; Soapstone.

Key:
Ch — Chinese	FV — Famille Verte
ctp — contemporary	E — export
cvg — carving	hdwd — hardwood
do — door	Jp — Japan
drw — drawer	Ko — Korean
Dy — Dynasty	lcq — lacquer
FJ — Famille Juane	rswd — rosewood
FN — Famille Noire	tkwd — teakwood
FR — Famille Rose	

Blue and White Porcelain

Blue and white porcelain garden seat, pierced medallions, stylized florals, 1800s, 19", $550.00.

Bottle, wine; mtns/bldgs, 1800s, 8½" 550.00
Bowl, pine tree border, phoenix medallion, Jp, 1890s, 12" 160.00
Bowl, rice; teatime in garden, Kangxi, 4" 450.00
Charger, figural court scenes, Qianlong, 19", EX.....................850.00
Coffeepot, E, scholar on bridge/pavilions, 1850s, 10" 275.00
Flask, moon; figure panels/florals, dragon hdls, 1800s, 10"...........450.00
Jar, waterway scene, ruyi/lappet band, foo dog finial, 31" 1,650.00
Jardiniere, emb dragons in clouds, Jp, 1880s, 7" 150.00
Jardiniere, flowering hawthorn trees, 14½" 225.00
Plate, scolars/immortals scene, brn rim, Ming Dy style, 13".........250.00
Umbrella stand, stylized foliage, Jp, 1880s, 24".......................... 300.00
Vase, courtyards, sq w/everted rnd rim, Cheng Hau, 21", EX.. 1,000.00
Vase, dragon/clouds reserve, dragon hdl, separate base, 19".........175.00
Vase, emb lizard, bk: birds/maids in garden, Canton, 14" 125.00
Vase, fisherman/river, bk: calligraphy, mk, 1800s, 14" 650.00
Wine pot, scenic, floral finial, Kangxi, 6" L 450.00

Bronze

Bronze vase, four relief owl faces, unsigned, late 1800s, 9", $325.00.

Bodhisattva on lotus throne w/foo dog support, 6½" 325.00
Buddha, seated on waisted lotus plinth, 1700s, 12½" 400.00
Bull, walking w/head lowered, 1800s, 13½x27" 1,200.00
Crane, beak open, well detailed, pr: 62" & 58" 1,200.00
Drum, sunburst/rings, frogs surmount, Shan States, 25", EX ... 1,400.00
Mirror, birds/flowers/horse, 8-sided, Tang Dy, 4½" 1,000.00
Planter, flanged band, S-curve/key-fret motif, Jp, 7" 300.00
Scholar, seated, Ch, 8" 220.00
Tsuba, gold inlay stream/trees, emb Jurojin w/scroll, 3x2½" 325.00
Urn, foo lion finial, kylin mask hdls, openwork top, 23"..............500.00
Urn, tiger relief, pear form, seal mk, cvd stand, Jp, 16" 325.00
Vase, eng/inlaid: gilt/silver/mc leaves on brn, 1900, 6" 275.00

Celadon

Bowl, globular w/ring ft, Longquan, Song Dy, 4¾" 600.00
Cup, flared rim, knop stem, Ming Dy 3,000.00
Dish, bubbly glaze, thick-walled, Ming Dy, 6" dia 600.00
Ginger jar, incised foliage, spherical, w/lid, 1700s, 6½"..............600.00
Plate, incised floral, ribbed, Longquan, crack, 13" 400.00
Vase, tall neck/flared mouth & base, Ming Dy, 20" 1,100.00

Furniture

Armchair, Ch, rswd, dragon arms & bk, brocade cushion 450.00
Armchair, Ch, rswd, 2 dragons form arms, tails form bk 1,000.00
Armchair, Ch E, rswd, prunus bk/apron, dragon arms, pr.............800.00
Armchair, cinnabar lacquer w/damask uphl, bamboo-cvd legs 550.00
Armchair, Near East, ivory/MOP inlay, parquetry.......................600.00
Bench, Ch, birds/flowers cvg, openwork crest/apron, 50" L 1,400.00
Cabinet, Ch E, lacquer, landscapes, 5 int drws, 1800s, 15" 725.00

Center table, Huang Huali, lobed marble top, ca 1900, 32" x 25", $900.00.

Desk, Ch, EX cvd crest/apron/curved legs, fitted top, 56" 1,600.00
Display stand, rswd, open shelves/scrolled terminals, 24" 165.00
Stool, Hongmu, galleried apron/scroll-end supports, 1800s 100.00
Table, altar; Ch, rswd, cvd as bamboo sections, 73" 500.00
Table, Ch, rswd, 3-leg claw-ft base w/3-D dragon, 22" dia 550.00

Table, Ch tkwd, caryatid legs/paw ft, marble top, 18" 350.00
Table, Ch tkwd, 21" marble top, rtcl apron, paw ft, 24" 400.00
Table, rswd, cloisonne insert, 5 legs on ring base, 16" 195.00
Taboret, Ch, rswd, cabriole legs, inset marble top, 18"................250.00

Hardstones

Amethyst, beauty in long robe holds peony, scarves, 5½" 150.00
Amethyst, incense burner, foo lion hdls/finial, 5½x4" 225.00
Amethyst, phoenix in peony bush w/sm bird, openwork, 7½" 325.00
Amethyst, vase, peonies, peony lid, dk color, 6x6"......................350.00
Coral, pk; God of Longevity holding pear, 2¼" 150.00
Coral, red; beauty w/gourd bottle, 2" 150.00
Gray/rust-flecked lt gr, urn: floral/bird, lid: bird, 7" 400.00
Jade, burmese; kylin, looks bk/tail along side, 5x5" 250.00
Jade, gray; turtle-form box, 5 terrapins on bk, 15½" L 1,100.00
Jade, lt gr; phoenix & sm bird, floral branch, 6x9½"...................350.00
Jade, lt gr; vase, dragon cvg & hdl, loose rings, lid, 9" 275.00
Jade, med gr w/wht flecks; 2 facing magpies on flowers, 6" 225.00
Jade, med gr; peonies on body & lid, 6½x4½" 350.00
Jade, wht, foo lion w/treasure box on bk, 1700s, 5½"................1,800.00
Malachite, horse, reclining on inlaid base, EX cvg, 4" L 175.00
Malachite, rabbit, ears laid bk/scratching, 2x3" L 185.00
Rose quartz, beauty holds flowering branch by tree, 5x5½" 195.00
Rose quartz, Guanyin, holds pearl/basket, bird at ft, 16" 700.00
Serpentine, 3 pheasants on rockwork, wood stand, 6½x11" 220.00
Turquoise, kylin, reclining, bl w/matrix, 3x4"..............................350.00

Inro

Blk lcq, Otsu-e symbols on ginji, 4-case, sgn, 1800s, 3⅛" 1,320.00
Gold & blk lcq, bamboo shape, Kanyosai, 1800s, 2" 550.00
Gold lcq, dragon amid clouds, 4-case, 1600s, 3", +manju........ 1,200.00
Gold/silver lcq, narcissus in bowl, 4-case, 1800s, 3" 1,980.00

Inro, Tsuishu red lacquer, relief Chinese gentlemen in a pine grove, 4-case, 3", with ivory ojime with dragon, netsuke in the form of Tsuishu gourd with carved floral and silver mounts, unsigned, $1,000.00.

Gold/silver lcq, toys among ferns, 4-case, 1800s, 3⅛" 8,250.00
Ivory, landscape, cvd/stained, 4-case, 3¼", +okume/manju 2,640.00
Ivory, salamander/toad, cvd/HP, 4-case, 1890s, 3¾" 1,100.00
Lcq w/coral inlay, crows in flight, sgn, 5-case, 1800s, 4" 3,520.00
Metal/gold lcq, dragon/phoenix, 2-case, 1800s, 3⅜", +ojime 990.00
MOP dragonflies inlay, 3-color lcq, 3-case, sgn, 1800s, 3" 2,860.00
MOP/hardstone inlay, gold lcq, birds, 5-case, 1800s, 3½" 1,650.00
MOP/ivory inlay, gold/silver lcq, 4-case, 1800s, 3½" 825.00
Red lcq, phoenix, 4-case, sgn, 1800s, 3¼", +ojime/netsuke 8,800.00
3-color lcq, crows on branch, 3-case, sgn, 1800s, 2¾" 3,300.00
3-color lcq, galleon on waves, 5-case, sgn, 1800s, 3¼" 3,740.00
3-color lcq, hare & 2 monkeys, 4-case, 1800s, 3⅝", +ojime 2,200.00
3-color lcq, samurai on horsebk, 4-case, 1800s, 3½" 1,760.00
3-color lcq, takamaki w/hat & drum, 4-case, 1800s, 2½" 1,980.00

Lacquer

Bowl, figural landscape frieze, red w/blk int, 7½" 425.00
Box, bird/tree/wind chime, gold dust finish, 5x13x15" 1,000.00
Box, cinnabar w/berries & butterflies, berry on lid, 8x11" 60.00
Box, sewing; gilt scenic, lobed rectangle, gilt paw ft, 14" 550.00
Box, travelers in river landscape, gilt on red, 15" L 200.00
Plate, cinnabar, 2 dragons/flames, floral border, 13" 400.00
Screen, 3-panel, red/gold hiramakie fish & flora, 44" 225.00
Tea caddy, dk brn w/gilt squirrels, ftd melon form, 7", EX............950.00
Tray, cinnabar, pagodas & bridge w/2 people, deep cvg, 14"...........85.00
Tray, cinnabar, wht figures in landscape, quatrefoil, 15" 600.00
Tray, genre scenes, mc/gilt on blk, minor wear, 16x20" 175.00
Vase, cinnabar, landscape w/figures & flowers, 12", pr 270.00
Vase, cinnabar, panels w/fish, seaweed, florals, 15" 500.00

Mud Figures

Elder carries yoke w/shield & water jug, 8", pr.............................180.00
Elder seated w/hat on bk, fishing, 4" 65.00
Elder seated w/pnt brush in hand, brn robe, 5" 50.00
Elder standing w/fish in hand, brn robe, 6" 50.00
Elder stands holding bl jar, 6" 50.00
Elder w/plate in hand, 5" 45.00
Lady seated, holds flower, wht robe, 4" 60.00

Ojimes

Awabi fishergirl, ivory, lt stain, 1800s, 1⅝"..................................935.00
Bird amid flowers, pierced/molded, gold, 1890s, ⅝" 770.00
Cricket on flowers, pierced/molded, gold, 1890s, ⅝" 990.00
Eggplant, ivory, stained, Mitsuhiro, 1850s, ⅞" 1,200.00
Peony blossoms, pierced & molded, gold, 1890s, ¾" 1,980.00
Quail amid flowers & ferns, pierced/molded, gold, 1890s, ½" 660.00
Rat curled in ball, ivory, inlaid eyes, ca 1800, ¾" 660.00
Spider mums & daisies, pierced/molded, gold, 1880s, ¾" 2,100.00
Tiger on haunches, ivory, inlaid eyes, 1800s, ¾" 1,760.00

Porcelain

Basin, E, Bl Fitzhugh, 1880s, 5½x16" 1,100.00
Bowl, E, floral sprays, 1820s, 11"..700.00
Bowl, hunters on horsebk/florals, bl on wht, 1700s, 7½"..............750.00
Buddha w/5 climbing children, pk/yel florals, 14" 325.00
Charger, FV, dragons/waves, faux Kangxi mk, 21" 200.00
Charger, FV, landscape w/in diaper borders, 1800s, 16" 500.00
Charger, peacock/florals int & ext, Ming, 12½", NM 700.00
Court Lady, bl floral dress/red coat, w/goat, 16" 350.00

Cup & saucer, E, genre scene, diaper border, 1700s.....................325.00
Fruit cooler, E, dk bl/gold on wht, gold hdls, 1700s, 10½" 900.00

Famille Rose vases, enameled winter scene, back: summer scene, on vine and palmette field painted in gilt and fuchsia, underglaze blue chop mark, 8¾", with pierced hardwood stands, $675.00 for the pair.

Garden seat, E, 2 rows bosses, cash medallions, rtcl, 18" 2,000.00
Goddess, 24-arm, w/attributes, on lotus throne, 16"....................350.00
Jardiniere, lotus/ducks, 1900s, 16" dia..100.00
Lamp, 2 panels: roosters/peonies, on mc floral ground, 24"..........175.00
Mandarin bows before Sacred Mtn, boy at side, 12" 75.00
Plate, Fitzhugh, red-orange, eagle/banner w/'BLP,' 16"................850.00
Plate, FV, figures border water scenes, foliage, etc, 11" 550.00
Plate, Precious Ornaments, central urn, 1850s, 9¾" 200.00
Platter, bl band w/gold stars, scenic center, 1780s, 12"................650.00
Platter, Bl Fitzhugh, 1800, 12x14½" 850.00
Platter, coastal village, underglaze bl, 1700s, 9½", EX.................350.00
Platter, E, flowers/insects in puce enamel, 1700s, 16½" 800.00
Platter, E, scattered florals, octagonal, 1800s, 17" 650.00
Siamese God, seated w/bl vase, bl/yel attire, 10" 125.00
Tankard, apple gr w/landscape, gold lizard hdl, 4¾" 400.00
Tankard, E, bl-fr panels w/bats, HP figural scene, 4¾" 450.00
Tankard, E, figural scene, gilt bkground, 1700s, 4½", EX 200.00
Teapot, mandarin in gr robe/cap figural, ca 1874, 7x5" 175.00
Tureen, E, garlands, turq/gold on wht, hdls, 13" L 700.00
Tureen, Nanking scene/butterfly, pig's head hdls, 7", +tray..........950.00
Vase, flowers/peacocks w/warriors reserves, 1880s, 30", pr....... 1,800.00
Vase, foo lions in red-orange, foo lion hdls, 1870, 23" 450.00
Vase, gr, brn crackle int, lion's head/ring hdls, 1800s, 9" 500.00
Vase, panel w/God of Longevity & Kwan Yin, bk: poem, 23"......450.00
Vase, peonies/deer/trees, bk: poem/script, 1861, 23" 450.00
Vase, scenes w/figures, diapering/florals, Canton, 10", pr............125.00
Wig stand, foo lions, rtcl cylinder, bl/manganese, 11"..................225.00

Pottery

Beggar kneeling w/bowl in hand, bl/wht robe, 7" 40.00

Censer, sang de boeuf, 3 mask/paw ft, 6¾", EX........................275.00
Cup, brn glaze, cylindrical, Tang Dy, 3½x3"........................500.00
Cup, iron red, dragons/flaming pearls, 1800s, 2", pr........200.00
Eagle, wings partially folded, on bl/gr perch, 7x7½"........45.00
Figure, guardian; straw glazed, full armor, Sui Dy, 12"........2,100.00
Jar, gr w/emb dragons, loop hdls, mtd as lamp, 23", pr........800.00
Lady, unglazed, wht slip decor, Tang Dy, 12"........750.00
Lady in shawl, unglazed/slip traces, Tang Dy, 12"........800.00
Moncy Boy, yoke on shoulders, w/cash & peach, 8"........40.00
Official, gr-glaze clothing w/wht slip traces, 14"........175.00
Planter, sang de boeuf, globular, flattened rim, 5"........200.00
Roof tile, w/3-D foo dog, gr on red clay, 12½"........95.00
Roof tile, warrior on deer, 1800s........300.00
Scholar on bench w/fan, books at side, 9½"........50.00
Tomb figure, hands folded on chest, slip traces, 11", pr........1,700.00
Vase, butterfly in gr/bl/purple, butterfly shape, 9x8"........30.00
Vase, powder bl, bulbous w/flared rim, 7"........350.00
Vase, sang de boeuf, baluster, 1910, 23", pr........1,400.00
Vase, scenic panels, elephant head hdls/finial, 1900, 20"........185.00
Vase, turq crackle, dragons emb, hexagonal baluster, 8½"........150.00
Water dropper, blk w/pigment traces, rat form, 1½x4½"........350.00

Bactrian camel, T'ang style, painted white, 13½", $800.00.

Snuff Bottles

Agate, carnelian inclusions, cvd as peach w/flowers etc, 2"........150.00
Agate, crazy lace, 2 bats w/coins, 3"........350.00
Agate, cvd as bamboo section w/flowers, 2½"........400.00
Amber, cvd tiger, bk: elephant, lt to dk, 2¼"........300.00
Amethyst, cvd Buddha on front, 2¼"........125.00
Cloisonne, allover floral on dk bl, 2½"........130.00
Cloisonne, hundred flower, mc on yel, 2½"........75.00
Copper, famille rose enamel, bl Qianlong 4-character mk........800.00
Horn, jeweled silver metal mtd, Mongolian, 1800s........150.00
Ivory, dragon fish form, stopper: flaming pearl water spout........85.00
Ivory, panels front/bk: 2 people under pine tree, 3"........75.00
Jadeite, cvd foo dog/ball, bk: foo dog, 2¾"........600.00
Malachite, cvd phoenix bird on front, 2½"........125.00
Marcasite, deer cvd 1 side, 2¾"........100.00
Mongolian silver, coral/turq insets, floral panels, 2¼"........100.00
Peking glass, flowers/vines, bl on wht, 3", NM........325.00

Porc, warrior w/sword & bat, orange/gr on wht, 2¾"........100.00
Sodalite, cvd w/bat, peaches etc, dk bl w/some wht, 2¼"........75.00

Sumida

Bowl, bl/wht/brn w/red lower half, no mk, 4½x3¼"........85.00
Bowl, 3 children on rim, red rope-like bottom half, 3x6"........210.00
Bowl, 3 ladies in kimonos on rim, gr int, sqd, 6x7"........300.00
Brush pot, appl monkeys, seal sgn, 4"........89.00
Incense burner, Oriental man in relief, mk, 2⅝x2⅞"........110.00
Mug, boy after nest of eggs, imp mks, 4⅝x3⅛"........88.00
Mug, boy in gr/blk robe, rope-like bottom half, 4½"........145.00
Mug, figure on front, mk, 4x2¾"........85.00
Mug, man holds bird on ledge, 5⅝"........165.00
Tankard, appl children, seal signature, 12½", +3 5" mugs........825.00

Tankard and six mugs, figures with baskets, 11½", 4½", $575.00 for the set.

Vase, boy on ledge w/bottle, brn/gray/blk over red, 8"........185.00
Vase, boy w/ball on front, imp mk, 6⅝x2⅞"........118.00
Vase, child on limb on side, red rope-like bottom half, 8"........165.00
Vase, lady in bl kimono on side, over-top hdl, rpr, 7"........145.00
Vase, lady in bl/wht kimono, floral panel, dmn shape, 7"........165.00
Vase, man w/basket of rocks in relief, brn/gray, 6¾"........120.00
Vase, 4 boys on front, imp mk, 9½x4¼"........165.00

Textiles

Coat, flowers & insects embr on blk satin, ca 1900, EX........150.00
Handbag, silk emb bird, jade ring hdls, ca 1900, 10", EX........145.00
Kesa, peonies, mc on lt gr silk, Edo Period, 81x44½"........275.00
Kimono, silk, Mt Fuji on bk, EX........225.00
Kimono, wedding; w/tabi & shoes, Japan, 1973, M........950.00
Lady's outfit, silk w/embr florals, 1920s, 3-pc........135.00
Obi, silk brocade, florals/clouds/rosettes, 13x156"........320.00
Robe, gauze, bl w/dragons among clouds, blk borders........110.00
Robe, tapestry-woven dragon on bl ch'i-fu, 1800s........450.00
Scroll, river/pagodas, watercolor on silk, 1600s, 19x103"........1,100.00
Scroll, silk w/HP silver fish & aquatic plants, 1800s, 44"........150.00
Trousers, silk damask w/blk satin cuffs, lady's, 1900........80.00
Wall hanging, silk, lady/child/Fukurokujo, 1900, 112x56"........325.00

Woodblock Prints, Japanese

Beauties, sgn Eisen ga, Oban, 2 prints........250.00

Group of 4 actors on stage, sgn Chikanobu, triptych 225.00
Hokusai, Carrying the Bride, 1820s, lg Oban 550.00
Mountain Village, Yoshida, mat/fr, 15x10" 150.00
Paul Jacoulet, La Mariee, owl seal, 15½x12", EX 300.00
Samurai & Geisha, Oban Tata-e 80.00
Yoshitoshi, 3 Men in Landacape, Oban, triptych 150.00
1 sheet from triptych: garden w/2 females, Qtaguwa, 15x10".......300.00

Miscellaneous

Bird, 24k gold vermeil w/enamel & MOP, 2½x4" 75.00
Bouquet, 4-color Peking glass flowers, celadon pot, 20x16".........150.00
Box, camphorwood, brass fittings, China, 1925, 10x5½" 125.00
Cvg, Guan Yin, cvd/pnt, ornate headdress & halo, 1700s, 22" 700.00
Funerary figures, man, worn, att Tang Dy, 9¾" 225.00
Pipe, silver w/gold shakudo inlay, unsgn, 1800s, 11" 770.00
Pipe, vermeil, 2 dragons wrap stem & bowl, mc enamel, 5".........325.00
Pipe case, lacquer, silver & gold inlay, unsgn, 1800s, 9¾" 880.00
Pipe case, stag antler, peony cvg, Kensai, 1890s, 8½" 800.00
Shop sign, stylized scroll form, pnt/cvd wood, 21x45" 425.00
Tree, pk Peking glass flowers w/gr leaves, celadon pot, 14" 45.00
Yatate, bronze, Biwa form, brush/well in body, 1800s, 6¼" 1,760.00
Yatate, bronze, silver inlay lid, fitted w/brush, 1800s, 7" 440.00
Yatate, bronze/silver, rifle form, 1800s, 5½" 2,420.00
Yatate, cloisonne, florals on hdl, 1800s, 7" 770.00
Yatate, gold/silver inlay hdl: priest, w/brush, 1800s, 7" 550.00

Orrefors

Orrefors Glassworks was founded in the early 1900s in the Swedish province of Smaaland. Utilizing the expertise of designers such as Simon Gate, Edward Hald, Vicki Lindstrand, and Edwin Ohrstrom, it produced art glass of the highest quality. Various techniques were used in achieving the decoration; some were wheel engraved, others were blown through a unique process that formed controlled bubbles or air pockets resulting in unusual patterns and shapes.

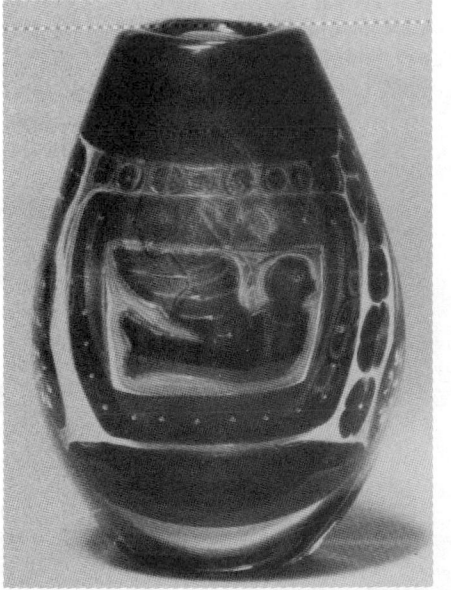

Ariel glass vase, 'Girl and Dove,' air-trap design, geometric border in amber and blue, signed B./Edvin Ohrstrom, ca 1950s, 7", $1,800.00.

Bowl, Graal, int brn geometrics, Hald/Bergkvist, 1920s, 7" 3,000.00
Bowl, suns/stars/comets eng, Hald/H-584.29, '18, 11" +plate.. 2,600.00
Vase, Ariel, gondolier/lady, bl in clear, Ohrstrom, 7" 1,900.00
Vase, Ariel, int bl bubbles, flared cylinder, Lundin, 6" 1,000.00
Vase, Ariel, tiger's faces, brns in clear, Lundin, 7" 3,000.00

Vase, etched nude, cylindrical, Ohrstrom/#2929, 1944, 11" 200.00
Vase, girl w/flowers eng, frost on clear, sgn, 6¼" 95.00
Vase, Graal, clear w/bl freeform swirls, Landberg, 7" 700.00
Vase, Graal, pk floral inclusions, spherical, E Hald, 4" 750.00
Vase, Graal, plants/X-cut, dk/lt bl, Hald/Bergkvist, '20s, 8" 6,000.00

Ott and Brewer

The partnership of Ott and Brewer began in 1865 in Trenton, New Jersey. By 1876 they were making decorated graniteware, parian, and 'ivory porcelain' – similar to Irish belleek though not as fine and of different composition. In 1883, however, experiments toward that end had reached a successful conclusion, and a true belleek body was introduced. It came to be regarded as the finest china ever produced by an American firm. The ware was decorated by various means – hand painting, transfer printing, gilding, and lustre glazing. The company closed in 1893, one of many that failed during that depression. In the listings below, the ware is belleek unless noted otherwise.

Our advisor for this category is Mary Frank Gaston; she is listed in the Directory under Texas.

Basket, thistle on beige matt, gold trim, twig hdl, 6"...................850.00
Bouillon, Cactus, gold thistles & hdls, w/underplate, mk 400.00
Cake plate, Tridacna, gold decor, rare, 9½" 225.00
Creamer & sugar bowl, Tridacna, gold butterfly/thistles, mk 350.00
Cup & saucer, demitasse; Tridacna, forked hdl 125.00
Pitcher, cherries, 6" 110.00
Pitcher, pk/gold water lilies, gold leaves, mk, 8¼x6½"............. 1,400.00
Pitcher, Tridacna, wht w/gold, mauve lustre int, mk, 1¾" 75.00
Rose bowl, gold florals & brush mks, 4".....................................295.00
Teapot, Tridacna, yel w/gold, wht loop hdl, mk, 4" 300.00

Overbeck

The Overbeck Studio was established in 1911 in Cambridge City, Indiana, by four Overbeck sisters. It survived until the last sister died in 1955. Early wares were often decorated with carved designs of stylized animals, birds, or florals with the designs colored to contrast with the background. Others had tooled designs filled in with various colors for a mosaic effect. After 1937, Mary Frances, the last remaining sister, favored handmade figurines with somewhat bizarre features in fanciful combinations of color. Overbeck ware is signed 'OBK.' Large vases from 8" to 12" usually command prices from $1,000 to $3,000 on today's market.

Pin, lavender flower with green leaf, 2", $125.00.

Figurine, afghan hound, sitting, 4-color, 3½", NM.......................200.00
Figurine, boy & girl on fence, w/calf, 4x5" 850.00
Figurine, Dutch boy, 3-color, imp mk, 4".................................135.00
Figurine, gentleman in hat, w/cane, imp mk, 5", NM 155.00

Figurine, hound dog, comical, 3-color, 3½" 240.00
Figurine, Husky dog, wht w/pk tongue, 3x3½", NM.................195.00
Figurine, lady in full dress w/mc shawl, imp mk, 5" 185.00
Figurine, wolverine, dk brn w/wht stripe, 3x5½", NM 200.00
Figurine, woman in full skirt, fur coat/muff, 4" 175.00
Vase, birds in flight, wht on bl, sgn EH, 5½" 1,400.00
Vase, circular motifs cvd in panels, bl/gr, sgn EF, rpr, 6" 800.00
Vase, geese w/in 9 rnd sections, mc on mauve, sgn EH, 6" 1,500.00
Vase, 3 panels w/incising, bl & gr, sgn EH, 4½x5½" 1,000.00
Vase, 3 poppy panels, cream on bl, mk/sgn, 6" 850.00

Overshot

Overshot glass is characterized by the beaded or craggy appearance of its surface. Earlier ware was irregularly textured, while 20th-century examples tend to be more uniform.

Bottle, scent; cranberry, w/stopper, 8½" 250.00
Bowl, gr, shell form, 6" 35.00
Bowl, rubena, clear ruffle, brass ft, 6¾x8¾" 95.00
Jam jar, cranberry, 4½" 150.00
Pitcher, bl, amber reeded hdl, bulbous, rnd mouth, 7½" 110.00
Pitcher, cranberry, w/ice compartment, clear hdl, 11½" 350.00
Pitcher, Swirl, rubena, reeded clear hdl, 7½" 125.00
Pitcher, tankard; cranberry, clear hdl, pewter lid, 9" 175.00
Tumbler, rubena, acid-etched ferns...135.00

Owen, Ben

Ben Owen worked at the Jugtown Pottery of North Carolina (see Jugtown) until it closed in 1959; he continued in the business in his own pottery until 1972. His ware was stamped 'Ben Owen, Master Potter.'

Bowl, brn & wht, 2x5" 35.00
Candle holder, gr, w/drip catcher, sgn, 9½" 200.00
Tumbler, frogskin, sgn Ben Owen, Master Potter, 5¾" 45.00
Tumbler, wht alkaline, imp mk: Ben Owen, Master Potter, 3".......45.00

Pitcher, cobalt on tan, incising, signed, 4", $50.00.

Owens Pottery

J.B. Owens founded his company in Zanesville, Ohio, in 1891, and until 1907, when the company decided to exert most of its energies in the area of tile production, made several quality lines of art pottery. His first line, Utopian, was a standard brown ware with underglaze slip decoration of nature studies, animals, and portraits. A similar line, Lotus, utilized lighter background colors. Henri Deux, introduced in 1900, featured incised Art Nouveau forms inlaid with color. (Be aware that the Brush McCoy Pottery acquired many of Owens' molds and reproduced a line similar to Henri Deux, which they called Navarre.) Other important lines were Opalesce, Rustic, Feroza, Cyrano, and Mission, examples of which are rare today.

The factory burned in 1928, and the company closed shortly thereafter. Values vary according to the quality of the artwork and subject matter. Examples signed by the artist bring higher prices than those that are not signed.

Humidor, Utopian, cigars on brn, mk, 7½" 425.00
Mug, Utopian, cherries on brn, artist sgn, mk, 4½" 150.00
Mug, Utopian, pansy, 4½" 140.00
Tile, stylized floral w/leaves on lt gr, 9" dia, EX 200.00
Vase, bud; Matt Utopian, wild roses on brn, sgn, 13"...................375.00
Vase, Cyrano, brn, slim, unmk, 12" 350.00
Vase, Cyrano, brn & bl, bulbous, long neck, unmk, 8¼" 250.00
Vase, Henri Deux, lady's profile, brn, no hdls, 7" 225.00
Vase, Henri Deux, lady's profile, brn w/gold, hdls, 7x9"..............295.00
Vase, Lotus, mushrooms, gr/wht on gr to gray & pk, 8" 300.00
Vase, Lotus, thistles on bl shaded to cream, #1257, 12"...............350.00
Vase, Matt Utopian, florals on tan, 5" 195.00
Vase, Matt Utopian, grapes on gray, 17¾" 1,150.00
Vase, Owensart, gr matt, 4-ftd, hdls, early JBO mk, 6" 375.00
Vase, Parchment, Hudson type, tan & brn, 5" 250.00
Vase, Soudanese, cactus/flowers, gr/pk on blk gloss, 8" 475.00
Vase, Soudanese, Nouveau florals, gold on blk, slim neck, 10" ...350.00
Vase, Utopian, cloverleaves, #144, 5" 135.00
Vase, Utopian, dog portrait on brn, 10"...800.00
Vase, Utopian, floral, jug form, 5½" 165.00
Vase, Utopian, floral, sgn MC, pillow form, 4x6".........................225.00
Vase, Utopian, head of male lion, MT (M Timberlake), 17"... 5,000.00
Vase, Utopian, oak leaves, twisted mold, sgn CD, 3¾", NM 110.00

Venetian vase, relief face of creature at shoulder, gold glaze, 6", $225.00.

Pacific Clay Products

The Pacific Clay Products Company got its start in the 1920s as a consolidation of several smaller southern California potteries. The main Los Angeles plant had been founded in 1890 to make kitchen stoneware, ollas, and similar items. Terra cotta and brick were later produced.

In 1932 Hostess Ware, a vividly-colored line of dinnerware, was introduced to compete with Bauer's Ring Ware. Coralitos, a lighter-weight, pastel-hued dinnerware line was first marketed in 1937, and a similar but less expensive line called Arcadia soon followed. Art ware including vases, figurines, candlesticks, etc. was produced from 1932 to 1942, at which time the company went into war-related work and pottery manufacture ceased. A limited amount of hand-decorated dinnerware was also made.

Our advisor for this category is Jack Chipman; he is listed in the Directory under California.

Ring-style tumbler, $15.00; Coaster, $6.50; 10½" plate, $15.00; 9½" plate, $12.00; Cup and saucer, $15.00; Large coffee cup, $15.00; Shaker, $5.00.

Bowl, Ring-style, fruit, 6" 10.00
Bowl, Ring-style, 8½" 20.00
Carafe, Ring-style, w/lid 25.00
Chop plate, Ring-style, 12" 30.00
Figurine, nude holds feather, 15½" 55.00
Pitcher, ice lip, tilt-type jug..35.00
Relish tray, Ring-style, 4-part, wood hdl 40.00
Tumbler, Plain, orange, bulbous 15.00
Vase, Art Deco, bl, 7"...25.00
Vase, chartreuse, 11x7" 35.00
Vase, cobalt, 9⅝"..25.00
Vase, pk, #3316..17.50
Vase, turq, 4" 10.00

Paden City

The Paden City Glass Company began operations in 1916 in Paden City, West Virginia. The company's early lines consisted largely of the usual pressed tablewares, but by the 1920s production had expanded to include colored wares in translucent as well as opaque glass in a variety of patterns and styles. The company maintained its high standards of handmade perfection until 1949, when under new management much of the work formerly done by hand was replaced by automation. The Paden City Glass Company closed in 1951; and its earlier wares, the colored patterns in particular, are becoming very collectible. See also Depression Glass.

Bowl, Bees Knees, red, 5¾" 15.00
Bowl, Crow's Foot, red, oval, 9¾"..35.00
Cake stand, Ardith, yel, sq 38.00
Candlestick, Crow's Foot, red, 5½", pr 70.00
Candy box, Crow's Foot, red..80.00
Candy dish, #300 Line, pk 45.00
Candy dish, Crow's Foot, amber, sq, w/lid 35.00
Candy dish, Gazebo, lt bl, tall 75.00
Candy dish, Springtime, pk 45.00
Cheese & cracker set, Peacock & Rose, gr.............................60.00
Compote, mayonnaise; Crow's Foot, red, sq, 6¼" 35.00
Console set, Gazebo etch, 3-pc..115.00
Cordial, Penny Line, red..15.00
Cream soup, Bees Knees, red..12.50
Cream soup, Crow's Foot, amber 9.00
Cream soup, Crow's Foot, red, w/liner 22.00
Creamer & sugar bowl, Crow's Foot, amber 15.00
Cup & saucer, Bees Knees, red 15.00
Cup & saucer, Crow's Foot, amber 7.50
Cup & saucer, Crow's Foot, red...16.00
Decanter, Ardith, pk, w/stopper & chrome tray 100.00
Figurine, dragon swan, 10x6¼"...185.00
Goblet, Penny Line, amethyst, 8-oz.....................................10.00
Ice bucket, Lela Bird, gr 95.00
Mayonnaise, #300 Line, gr, w/ladle 33.00
Mayonnaise, Ardith, yel, w/underplate 35.00
Plate, American Rose, 6"...10.00
Plate, Bees Knees, red, hdls, 10½" 25.00
Plate, Crow's Foot, amber, hdls, sq, 10½"............................12.50
Plate, Crow's Foot, amethyst, 8½" 6.00
Plate, Crow's Foot, blk w/silver, sq, 10" 20.00
Plate, Crow's Foot, red, sq, 6" 3.00
Plate, Crow's Foot, red, sq, 8½" 7.00
Plate, Penny Line, red, 6" 4.00
Plate, Shenandoah Poppy, 9¼"... 5.00
Platter, Crow's Foot, ruby, oval, 11" 38.00
Server, Crow's Foot, red, center hdl 45.00
Server, Gazebo, lt bl, center hdl 35.00
Server, Lucy, cobalt, center hdl 35.00
Shakers, Party Line, amber, flat, pr......................................15.00
Shakers, Party Line, red, flat, pr 45.00
Shakers, Penny Line, cobalt, flat, pr.....................................50.00
Shakers, Penny Line, red, ftd, pr 65.00
Sherbet, Penny Line, amethyst, 3¾" 7.50
Tray, Crow's Foot, red, hdls, 11½" 25.00
Tumbler, Party Line, red, ftd, 5" 13.00
Vase, Blk Forest, gr, 10" 75.00
Wine, Penny Line, red 10.00

Paintings on Ivory

Miniature works of art executed on ivory from the 1800s are assessed by the finesse of the artist, as is any fine painting. Signed examples and portraits with an identifiable subject are usually preferred.

Child in wht dress, in gold fr w/pearls, 2¾x3½" 325.00
Cleo de Merode, sgn Raynol, gilt fr, 3½x2½" 145.00
Countess Gower, ornate gilt metal fr 165.00

General Lafayette, circular brass fr	165.00
General Lafayette, sgn Ledau, ornate ormolu eagle fr	440.00
General reviewing his army, gilt fr	285.00

George and Martha Washington, one signed 'Dupre,' ebonized frames, 3¼" x 2½", $300.00 for the pair.

Harvest scene, Persia, inlaid mosaic fr, 7½x5½"	145.00
Lady in wht dress w/pk sash, gilt metal fr, ca 1790s	475.00
Lady w/gray hair in lg feathered hat, sgn, 3½x2¾"	165.00
Man in red & gr uniform, oval, English, 1800s	300.00
Napoleon, sgn Frie, 3⅜x2⅜"	270.00
1920s gentleman, sgn Wms, in tooled gold fr, 3½x2¾"	275.00

Pairpoint

The Pairpoint Manufacturing Company was built in 1880 in New Bedford, Massachusetts. It was primarily a metalworks whose chief product was coffin fittings. Next door, the Mt. Washington Glassworks made quality glasswares of many varieties. (See Mt. Washington for more information concerning their artware lines.) By 1894 it became apparent to both companies that a merger would be to their best interest.

From the late 1890s until the 1930s, lamps and lamp accessories were an important part of Pairpoint's production. There were three main types of shades, all of which were blown: puffy – blown-out reverse-painted shades (usually floral designs); ribbed – also reverse painted; and scenic – reverse painted with scenes of land or seascapes (usually executed on smooth surfaces, although ribbed scenics may be found occasionally). Cut glass lamps and those with metal overlay panels were also made. Scenic shades were sometimes artist signed; and, although many are unmarked, some are stamped 'Pairpoint Corp.' Blown-out shades may be marked 'Pat July 9, 1907.' Bases were made from bronze, copper, brass, silver, or wood and are always signed.

Because they produced only fancy, handmade artware, the company's sales lagged seriously during the depression; and, as time and tastes changed, their style of product was less in demand. As a result, they never fully recovered; consequently part of the buildings and equipment were sold in 1938. The company reorganized in 1939 under the direction of Robert Gunderson and again specialized in quality hand-blown glassware. Isaac Babbit regained possession of the silver departments, and together they established Gunderson Glassworks, Inc. After WWII, because of a sharp decline in sales, it again became necessary to reorganize. The Gunderson-Pairpoint Glassworks was formed, and the old line of cut, engraved artware was reintroduced. The company moved to East Wareham, Massachusetts, in 1957. But business continued to suffer, and the firm closed only one year later. In 1970, however, new facilities were constructed in Sagamore under the direc-

tion of Robert Bryden, sales manager for the company since the 1950s.

In 1974 the company began to produce lead glass cup plates which were made on commission as fund raisers for various churches and organizations. These are signed with a 'P' in diamond and are becoming quite collectible. See also Napkin Rings.

Key: pwt — paperweight

Glass

Biscuit jar, floral on lt gr, scalloped base, 6x5½"	350.00
Bottle, perfume; bubble body & stopper	125.00
Bowl, cut foliage/etc, flared, 16½"	300.00
Bowl, gr w/clear swan hdls, Gunderson	110.00
Bowl, Myrtle, cut, very heavy, 3½x9½"	475.00
Box, pk, couple HP on lid, 4-ftd egg form, wreath hdls, 7"	500.00
Box, relief florals on pnt burmese, gilt 4-ftd base, 2x4"	385.00
Candlestick, Adelaide, auroria, 12", pr	225.00
Candlestick, Dia Quilt, lav/clear stripes, blk ft, 3½", pr	375.00

Centerpiece set, honey amber cut glass, pair of 12" vases and a 15" bowl, $425.00.

Cocktail, rouge flambe, silver mts, +undertray	120.00
Compote, gr w/clear bubble stem, 6½x10½"	130.00
Compote, Hampton, cut, intaglio florals in panels, 7x8"	150.00
Compote, ruby, bubble stem, 5"	125.00
Cordial, amberina, Gunderson	35.00
Creamer, Delft scene & scrolls, SP lid/rim/hdl, #7906	325.00
Creamer, violets on Crown Milano tones w/gold, 6x4½"	175.00
Cup & saucer, Camelia, reeded peachblow hdl, Gunderson, lg	425.00
Ewer, Delft, rose pk, man walks down path/windmill, 10"	425.00
Ladle, hobstar/strawberry dmn, cut, silver stem/bowl, 15"	750.00
Powder jar, Viscaria, hinged lid, 6" dia	200.00
Smoking stand, Delft, 3 bowls mtd on maple w/brass ft	550.00
Swan, bl, Gunderson, 12x13¾"	350.00
Swan, cranberry w/clear neck & head, 6½x8¾"	250.00
Tazza, Wellington, cut, 5x7"	150.00
Tray, Colias, butterflies/webs, 3-part, 9", +pr 9" sticks	275.00
Vase, cobalt spiral on clear, flared, 9" dia	185.00
Vase, Dia Quilt, cranberry on clear bubble ball stem, 12"	225.00
Vase, lt gr w/eng grapes, bulbous, ftd, 7"	175.00
Vase, ruby, cornucopia, bubble ball stem, 10"	95.00
Wine, Flambeau, orange-red w/silver overlay, blk stem, rare	85.00

Lamps

Boudoir, puffy poppies/roses in basket shade; blk base, 8"	1,800.00
Candle, puffy floral shade on wood std, 10"	500.00
Gone w/the Wind, David the Shepherd on dk gr w/gilt, 25"	1,450.00
Molded/frosted 12" nautilus shade w/prisms; rtcl ftd std	9,000.00
Puffy 10" rosebush sgn shade; 2-light metal base, 19"	7,000.00

Puffy 13" grapes shade; sgn std, 20½" 800.00
Puffy 14" poppy sgn dome shade; cylinder std w/dish ft 16,000.00
Puffy 16" poinsettia bell-form shade; leafy std, 21" 6,000.00
Rvpt 10" chipped ext shade w/sea gulls; sgn std #D8000, 25".. 6,300.00
Rvpt 15" Garden of Allah shade by Durand; sgn Egyptian std.. 1,800.00
Rvpt 17" peacock Exeter shade; fluted bronzed sgn std, 22" 1,200.00
Rvpt 20" golden bird-border shade; fluted urn std 1,900.00
Rvpt 8½" scenic shade; fluted/flaring bronzed std, 15½" 1,100.00

Table lamp, painted on the outside in an autumn scene with butterflies and wildflowers, signed base, 22", $1,850.00.

Pairpoint Limoges

Limoges china china blanks were imported from France in strict accordance with Pairpoint specifications. They were decorated by Pairpoint in designs that ranged from simple to elaborate florals and scenics. These are easily identified – look for the Pairpoint name over a crown with the Limoges name below. You may also find similar ware marked 'Pairpoint Minton.'

Ewer, gold lotus branch hdl, sgn/#d...550.00
Gravy boat, allover Dresden-type decor, #d, w/underplate...........130.00
Plate, mums, gold scroll borders, 10" 145.00
Platter, poppies w/gold, scalloped/rtcl rim, sgn/#d, 14x10"...........225.00
Vase, cherub w/tray of flowers, bk: poppies, hdls, 15" 1,350.00
Vase, mums, 8¼" 350.00

Paper Dolls

No one knows quite how or when paper dolls originated. One belief is that they began in Europe as 'pantins' (jumping jacks) and were frequently worn as part of the costume. By the late 1790s, they were being mass-produced. During the 19th century, most paper dolls portrayed famous dancers and opera stars such as Fanny Elssler and Jenny Lind. In the late 1800s, the Raphael Tuck Publishers of England produced many series of beautiful paper dolls; retail companies used them as advertisements to further the sale of their products. Around the turn of the century, many popular women's magazines began featuring a page of paper dolls.

Most familiar to today's collectors are the books with dolls on cardboard covers and clothes on the inside pages. These made their appearance in the late 1920s and early thirties. The most collectible (and the most valuable) are those representing celebrities, movie stars, and comic-strip characters of the thirties and forties.

Authority Mary Young has compiled an informative book, *Collector's Guide to Paper Dolls*, with current prices; you will find her address in the Directory under Ohio. When no condition is indicated, the dolls listed below are assumed to be in mint, uncut, original condition. Cut sets will be worth about half price, if all dolls and outfits are included and pieces are in very good condition. If dolls were produced in die-cut form, these prices reflect such a set in mint condition with all costumes and accessories.

American Beauties, Reuben H Lilja, #901, 1942 ....17.00
American Family, Grinnell Lithographic, #C1002, 1940...............25.00
American Miss Magic Doll, Parker Bros, 1957 ....15.00
Annette Funicello, cut/in folder, 1960, EX...................................30.00
Ava Gardner, Whitman #119215, 1949, complete, EX.................57.50
Baby Merry, Merry Mfg, #4350, bottle & diaper, 1964 .... 8.00
Betsy Ross, Platt & Munk, #224B, 1963 .... 6.00
Betty & Barbara, Milton Bradley, #4382, 1934.............................18.00
Betty Ann & Her Friends, Platt & Munk, #210.............................30.00
Betty Belle Paper Dolls, Rea-Harrison 25.00
Betty Marie, Londy Card Corporation, #5F, 1932 .... 5.00
Bible Land Children, Near East Foundation, 1934.......................... 8.00
Big Sister, Londy Card Corporation, #5J, 1932 .... 5.00
Blondie, DeJournette Mfg, #R30... 6.00
Bob Hope & Dorothy Lamour, Whitman #976, 1942, EX 165.00
Bobby, Doll To Dress, MS Publishing, #900 ....20.00
Brenda Lee Teenage Celebrity, Lowe #2785, 1961, NM................14.00
Bride & Groom, Magic Wand Corporation, #106 .... 6.00
Buster Brown & Tige, J Ottmann Litho..75.00
Caroline, Magic Wand Corporation, #109......................................18.00
Chanticleer Paper Doll, J Ottmann Litho.......................................75.00
Cinderella, George W Jacobs, 1918 ....50.00
Circus Twins, Nat'l Paper Box Company, #N12-29......................... 5.00
Colonial Dolls, Platt & Munk, #242, 1960.....................................20.00
Connie Francis, Whitman #1956, 1963, EX....................................27.50
Crepe Paper Doll Outfit, Dennison Mfg, #36.................................30.00
Cutie Dolls, Milton Bradley, #4716, 1 doll set...............................25.00
Cutie Paper Dolls, Milton Bradley, #4053......................................15.00
Daisy Dolly, Goldsmith Publishing, #516, 1922.............................17.00
Dancing Priscilla, Gertrude Breed, 1927..17.50
Debbie Dolls, McLoughlin Brothers, #548, 1937 ....25.00
Dennison's Doll Outfit, Dennison Mfg, #31, 1913 ....55.00
Dimple Doll Family, Samuel Gabriel, #D126 ....25.00
Doll Dresses To Color, Samuel Gabriel, #D109.............................15.00
Dolls Across The Sea, Platt & Munk, #228A, 1965 .... 6.00
Dolls' Open House, Platt & Munk, #220, 1963..............................10.00
Dolly May, Selchow & Righter 50.00
Dolly Twins, DeJournette Mfg, #500..10.00
Doris Day, orig folder, 54 outfits (31 are uncut) 50.00
Dress-Up, Reuben H Lilja, #905, 1947..10.00
Dress-Ups, Nutmeg Press, #954 .... 4.00
Elizabeth Taylor, cut-out doll book, 1952, M.................................85.00
Elizabeth Taylor, Whitman #973-10, 1950, EX...............................70.00
Ever-New Doll, Samuel Gabriel, #D115 ....18.00
Fashion Art Dolls, Art Award, #6000 .... 4.00
Fluffy Ruffles, J Ottmann Litho, 1907 ....60.00
Follies Girl, Jackie, Pla-Mor Toy Co, puzzle...................................17.50
Funny Bunnies, McLoughlin Brothers, #553, 1938 ....35.00
Gay Dolls, Platt & Munk, #225A, 1942... 6.00
Gingham Girl Doll, DeJournette Mfg 8.00
Glitter Dolls, Playtime House, #3152..12.00
Going Abroad Dolls, Platt & Munk, #230D, 1937.......................... 8.00
Hansel & Gretel, DeJournette Mfg, #1440 ....18.00

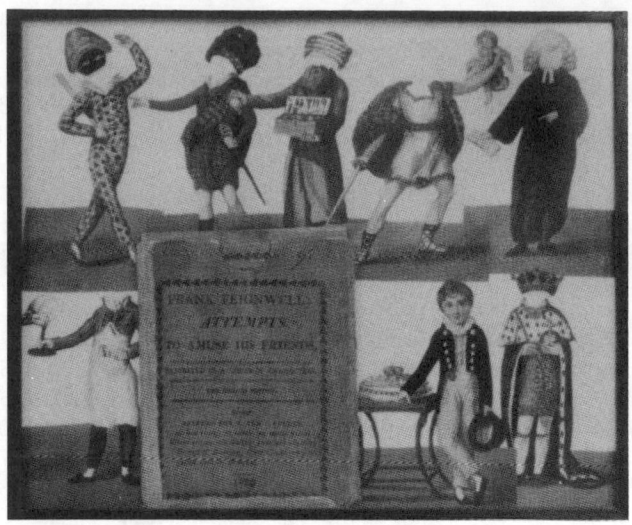

Frank Feignwell, printed for S. & J. Fuller, London, 1810, in 12" x 10" frame, EX, $550.00.

Honey Bun, DeJournette Mfg, #R50	6.00
Jack & Janet Paper Dolls, MH Leavis	12.00
Jackie Onassis, uncut, lg set, NM	75.00
Jane Russell, uncut, 1955, NM	20.00
Jodi, Merry Mfg, #4362	6.00
Junior Miss Dolls, Platt & Munk, #229, 1942	20.00
Let's Play Eskimo, Rand McNally, #211, 1937	15.00
Life Size Doll, Decro Plaks, 1950s	15.00
Little Buntings, Platt & Munk, #370, 1921	30.00
Lovey & Dovey Magic Dolls, Parker Bros, 1951	15.00
Lullaby Twins, Nat'l Paper Box Company, #N10-29	5.00
Lynda-Lou Doll, Lamp Studio	15.00
Madame Hattie, Reuben H Lilja, #908	20.00
Magic Doll, Parker Bros, 1961	8.00
Magic Mary, Milton Bradley, #4010-1, 1966	5.00
Magic Mary Jane, Milton Bradley, #4010-2, 1955	7.00
Magic Princess, Magic Wand Corporation, #1010	8.00
Magna Magic Sue, Children's World Publishing, 1954	6.50
Magnetic Sue, Milton Bradley, #4815, 1947	10.00
Marguerite Clark, Percy Reeves, 1920	45.00
Mary Pickford, Percy Reeves, 1920	45.00
Mary Poppins, Whitman #1977, 1973, EX	27.50
Minard's Liniment Doll, OW Nelson, 20½"	50.00
Mother & Daughter, Reuben H Lilja, #914	12.00
Movieland, Reuben H Lilja, #906, 1947	12.00
Mr & Mrs Hawaii, Schattel's, 1955	10.00
My Doll Jack, Samuel Gabriel, #D78	15.00
My Wardrobe Dolls, Samuel Gabriel, #D100	20.00
Nancy Reagan, uncut, 1983, NM	15.00
New Becky, DeJournette Mfg, #777	12.00
Our America, Samuel Gabriel, #D114	25.00
Our Favorite Dolls, Amlico Publishing	50.00
Paint Me Pretty, Magic Wand Corporation, #1011, 1969	5.00
Paper Doll Bazaar, Samuel Gabriel, #D115	25.00
Paper Doll Outfit, American Toy Works, #102	20.00
Party Dolls, Platt & Munk, #225B, 1942	6.00
Pat Boone, Whitman #1968, 1959, NM	28.00
Peggy, Playtime House, #314	5.00
Peggy & Polly, Milton Bradley, #4374, 1934	18.00
Play Paper Dolls, Samuel Gabriel, #D105	18.00
Princess Elizabeth Magic Doll, Parker Bros	25.00
Rhonda Fleming, Saalfield, 1956, M	45.00

Rita Hayworth, 26 cut outfits	25.00
Roy Rogers & Dale Evans, Whitman #1186, 1950, EX	48.00
Sandra Dee, Saalfield, 2 dolls & 34 outfits, 1959, NM	50.00
School Days, Samuel Gabriel, #D118	25.00
Sewing Set, Dolls To Dress, Cardinal Games, #501	10.00
Shirley Temple, Samuel Gabriel, #303	25.00
Sister Nan, Samuel Gabriel, #D90	25.00
Snow White, J Pressman Toy Corporation, #1214	15.00
Sonja Henie, uncut, 1930s, M	200.00
Stitch & Sew, J Pressman Toy Corporation, #1205	6.00
Sunny The Wonder Doll, Milton Bradley, #4236	8.00
Suzie Sweet, Grinnell Lithographic, #N2009, 1940	25.00
Sweet Sue, Magic Wand Corporation, #108	5.00
Teddy Bear & His Friends, Platt & Munk, #190	40.00
Teddy Bear Paper Doll, J Ottmann Litho	75.00
That Girl, Marlo Thomas, Saalfield #1379, 1967, EX	17.50
Tiny Tiptoe & Her Neighbors, MA Donohue, #85B	40.00
Tony, Merry Mfg, #6501	6.00
Tubby Twinkle, Charles E Graham, #0221	18.00
Wedding Party, Jaymar Specialty, #909	12.00
Wendy Walks, Merry Mfg, #6504, 1965	10.00
Winky Winnie, Jaymar Specialty, #994	12.00

Paperweights

The term 'paperweight' technically refers to any small, heavy object used to hold down loose papers. They have been made from a broad range of materials; many have been sold as souvenirs or given away by retail companies as advertising premiums. But today those attracting the most interest are the antique and contemporary artists' glass weights.

During the mid-1800s, the French factories of St. Louis, Baccarat, and Clichy incorporated millefiori and lampwork into glass domes which were called paperweights. This was done commercially and was probably the result of earlier efforts by Pierre Bigaglia of Venice. These 'baubles' were eagerly snapped up. Weights from the French factories that originally sold for a mere $2.00 to $3.00 are today commanding prices of $500.00 and up, depending on condition and craftsmanship. Many have been damaged but are restored or restorable. Interest waned in the late 1860s, and production nearly came to a halt. Clichy closed in the late 1800s. Baccarat is known to have made weights until about 1910 and again in the 1920s and 1930s. In the early 1950s, a revival of interest in paperweights resulted in renewed production at both Baccarat and St. Louis.

In the United States, production started in the 1850s, a little later than in France; and paperweights continued to be in vogue a little longer. The New England and Sandwich factories along with Millville, New Jersey, are the best-known manufacturers of weights made in the 1920s and 1930s. Today several well-known glass artists such as Kaziun, Whittemore, Ysart, and Stankard are making weights with a floral motif as well as other designs.

Paperweight collecting began with the 19th-century weights, but much knowledge and interest was lost during the period when production drastically declined. During the 1920s, collector-interest began to pick up and by 1950 had intensified to the point that books and articles on the subject began to be published. The Paperweight Collectors' Association was formed in 1953. It has bi-annual conventions, and there are several state and regional associations. Interest in weight collecting shows continuous growth.

Note: Prices do not reflect the usual 10% buyer's fee charged by most auction houses. Furthermore, there are many factors which determine value, particularly of antique weights. Auction-realized prices of contemporary weights are usually other than issue price; 'list price' may be for weights issued earlier and reduced for clearance or influenced by market demand and other factors. The dimension given at the end of the description is diameter.

Key:
A — antique	latt — latticinio
cl — clear	mill — millefiori
con — concentric	o/l — overlay
fct — faceted	pm — pastry mold
gar — garland	pwt — paperweight
grd — ground	sil — silhouette
jsp — jasper	

Ayotte, Rick

Crested Cockatoo pr on bl grd, compound layers, ltd ed	550.00
Lg yel moon/Snow Owl on pine branch, blk grd, ltd ed	550.00
Owl couple on pine limb, #20 of 50, sgn, 1984, 3"	325.00
Red/yel butterfly+yel & wht daffodils, 3½"	350.00
Robin on flowering dogwood, 1⅞"	125.00

Baccarat, Antique

Bl-edge flower in red & wht wallflower gar, star base, 2½"	2,900.00
Bud+7 leaves around purple/yel mill-center pansy, star base	750.00
Close pack mill mushroom w/bl & wht torsade, cl star base	1,600.00
Compound, mill-wing butterfly over flower+bud+6 leaves	3,950.00
Con mill, red/pk/gr/amber in clear, 1⅞"	525.00
Mill on lace w/sil, central flower cane, 3"	1,500.00
Red/wht wallflower+bud+gr leaves, red/wht cane border, fct	2,350.00
Scattered mill/upset muslin grd, 24 canes, sgn/1848, 3"	1,100.00

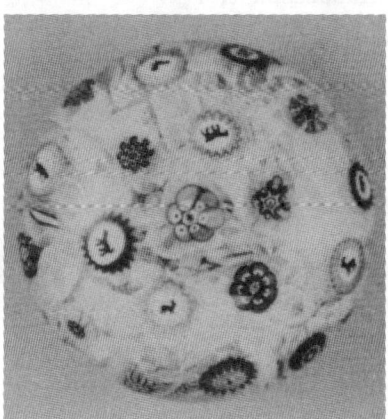

Antique Baccarat, patterned concentric millefiori with eight Gridel animal silhouette canes, all set on white latticinio twists, 3", $950.00.

Sulfide, Caesar profile on ruby, mk, 4"	75.00
Wht clematis+2 purple/wht/bl pansies+red rose, fct, 1850s	11,000.00
5 circles on lg 1 of wht star bundles, arrowhead center, 3"	375.00
6 wht tulip buds, entwined stems, star base, 3⅛"	1,750.00

Baccarat, Modern

Butterfly over wht clematis+ochre bud on teal bl, '77, 3⅛"	325.00
Con mill, bl/pk/red/brn/yel canes, sgn/1970, 3⅛"	150.00
Con mill, lg Gridel pelican w/in 5 rings, 1974, 3⅛"	300.00
Con mill w/lg Gridel swan sil in center, 1974, 3⅛"	190.00
Mill close pack w/sil of Zodiac signs, 1970, 3⅛"	300.00
Pattern mill in 7 groups on wht upset muslin, 1971, 3⅛"	150.00
Sand Dune, 2 peaks over sand-color grd w/mica & gr, 2⅛"	45.00
Scattered mill (w/star cane) on wht upset muslin, '68, 2⅞"	165.00
Scattered mill on wht upset muslin, sgn/1970, 3"	120.00

Stretched cane 6-petal flower+5 leaves on teal, 1971, 3¼"	185.00
Sulphide, Geo WA over ruby, 1/6 fct, 2¾"	180.00
Sulphide, Thos Paine on lt bl, indented ft, 1/6 fct, 2⅞"	40.00
Violet pansy over bl w/blk & brn sand, 1970, 3¼"	240.00
Yel dahlia w/pk center cane+6 leaves on teal, 1970, 3"	245.00
2 lt bl wht-edge flowers/gr leaves on cobalt flash, '72, 3"	110.00

Banford, Bob

Gr leaves/wht 8-petal flower cruciform in cl, sgn, 3"	350.00
Striped snake on pebbly gr w/branch, B cane, 3"	375.00
Yel flower+3 buds/gr leaves on cl, star base, B cane, 2½"	275.00
12-petal cobalt-dot wht flower in cl, star base, B cane, 3"	400.00
12-petal yel/brn wheat flower+bud on star-cut cl grd, 3"	325.00
4 yel/brn-stripe brn-center florals on cobalt, B cane, 3"	325.00

Caithness

Lobster	125.00
Planet, sgn/1970, 3⅛", set of 4	210.00
Sagittarius, wht sil on cl purple, side fct, sgn, 3½"	60.00
Snake, red aventurine+yel/red spots on gr/tan pebbles, 3"	220.00
Trout over sandy grd & petaled flower, sgn/#d, 3"	190.00

Clichy, Antique

Checker, pk/gr rose center+17 canes in latt, 2¼"	1,250.00
Close mill w/florets/tube/stars/etc in bl/wht basket, 2"	850.00
Close mill w/roses/arrows/pm/stars/etc, in wht basket, 3⅛"	2,800.00
Concentric setup canes in pk/wht/gr/red/bl, 1¾"	200.00
Exotic pk-tip wht-petal flower w/pk center swirl, 2½"	3,100.00
Flat bouquet, 3 lg cane flowers (2 pm/1 pk rose), 2¼"	2,600.00
Pattern mill w/wht rose center w/in ring of pm, 2¼"	425.00
Pentagon pattern mill on bl, 3⅛"	1,200.00
Space mill w/central gr floret w/in 9 mc canes on cl, mini	450.00
Spaced con w/21 typical canes, lg center pm on cl, 2⅛"	700.00
Wide bl/wht swirls radiate from ¾" gr/wht rose, 2¼"	1,450.00

Kaziun, Charles

Bottle, scent; red rose in base & stopper, 4½"	2,800.00
Pattern mill, cranberry w/gold grd, star-cane heart, 2"	600.00
Pk-tipped dk red rose, ped base, 2¼"	1,750.00
Red spider lily on gold-dusted dk bl, ped base, 2"	350.00
Wht crimped rose, ped base, 2¾"	1,600.00
Wht/pk spider lily over gold-dusted dk bl, ped base, 2"	325.00
Yel jonquil+3 leaves on wine, 4 star rods as stamin, 2¼"	950.00
Yel/orange-striped snake on emerald w/gold dust, sgn, 2⅜"	750.00

New England Glass

Crown, 26 mc twist ribbons, 2⅝"	850.00
Mill cane nosegay w/4 lt gr leaves on cl, 1¾"	325.00
Scattered mill w/typical canes etc, 2⅜"	50.00
Scramble, tight-packed canes, top fct+honeycomb sides, 2¾"	100.00
Spaced mill canes on dbl wht latt, 2½"	295.00
2 apples+4 leaves in cl, 2½"	950.00
5 lime/orange pears+4 cherries on wht latt swirl, fct, 2⅝"	550.00

Perthshire

Bl/tan pansy on wht upset muslin grd, 1/8 fct, '71, 2⅝"	130.00
Carpet grd, 7 mc animal/bird sil on lt yel mill+6 rosettes	180.00

Christmas angel sil on bl, 1979 ....**175.00**
Circus seal, translucent ruby o/l, 1979 ....**280.00**
Dbl o/l, pk flower on cl, cut base, fcts, '79, 2¼" **190.00**
Fruit, pear/orange/lemon/plums in latt basket, dtd 1980, 2½"......**275.00**
Gar, 7 sil canes: kangaroo/car/rooster/etc on red, '79, 3" **200.00**
Mill butterfly over 3-D stave basket, mini **260.00**
Nosegay, 3 mill flowers+4 leaves on pk/gr latt swirl, 1977 ....**130.00**
Nosegay on latt swirl, sgn/1976 cane on base, 3" **110.00**
Pk/wht flower+bl/wht flower+3 yel flowers on cl, fcts, 3¼" **210.00**
Triple o/l, bl/wht 6-petal flower, top fct+2 8-fct rows, 3" **240.00**
Tudor Rose, mill cane ring on cobalt, sgn/1975, 3¼" **230.00**
2 Pansies over translucent grd w/in 2 mill rings, top fct **300.00**
3 striped flowers on blk, P cane in 1 flower, '78, 3⅛" **275.00**
6-petal pk flower in pk/wht cane basket, cane sgn/'72, 1⅞" **70.00**

Sandwich Glass

Bl 12-petal clematis+bud on wht latt swirl, 2⅞".............................**250.00**
Dbl pk/red clematis+3 leaves & stems, 2½".......................**425.00**
Pk/wht-stripe flower w/cane center+8 leaves on cl, 2⅞" **650.00**
Poinsettia, pk center cane, dewdrop bubbles in cl, 3¼" **675.00**
Red poinsettia on bl jsp, yel/pk/bl center cane, 2⅞".....................**550.00**
12-petal bl poinsettia w/Lutz rose center on pk/wht jsp, 3" **600.00**
4 red cherries in cl, 2¾" **1,250.00**

St Louis, Antique

Cherries/oranges/pear on wht latt swirl **1,750.00**
Con mill, 7 rings mc canes, sq center, 2⅞" **2,200.00**
Crown, red/gr, lg center cane, 2¾" **950.00**
Fruit in wht basket, 3".. **1,500.00**
Lg dahlia, pk w/gr leaves, 2¼" **2,900.00**

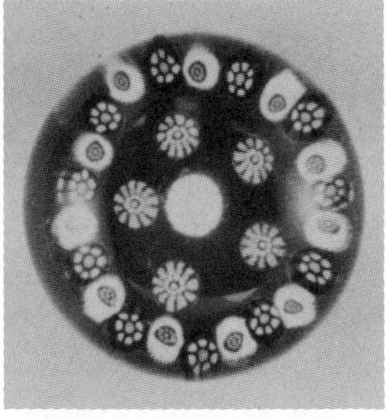

Antique St. Louis, alternating blue and white millefiori outer ring, central white cane within five yellow canes, all on clear, 2½", $300.00.

Mushroom, wht stem, bl torsade, unfct, 3⅛" **2,250.00**
Posy, w/4 canes+leaves in cl, grid-cut base, fct, 2⅜".....................**550.00**
Wht pompom w/gr leaves on swirled pk latt **2,200.00**
Wht pompom+bud+4 gr leaves over pk latt grd **4,850.00**
4-flower mill nosegay w/4 gr leaves, 3-row fcts **950.00**

St. Louis, Modern

Coiled lizard atop, pk/wht o/l w/gilt, hollow, 1980, 3¼" **1,150.00**
Gold inclusion Tutankhamen death mask on orange, cane ring..**340.00**
Lg 5-petal wht mill flower+wht bud/gr stem on orange, 3" **100.00**
Purple/yel pansy on wht upset muslin, 8 fluted fcts, 1980 ....**325.00**
Red/wht lily of valley spray on lt bl, 1/6 fct, 1986, 3"..................**240.00**
Sulphide, eagle on bl, red/wht o/l, etch sgn, 1976, 3¼"................**190.00**
Sulphide, Jimmy Carter on bl, by Poillerat, sgn, 3⅛" **60.00**

Sulphide, Pope John Paul II on amber-flash waffle-cut grd **220.00**
Wht latt basket w/3-D plums/pears/cherries, 1985, 3½" L.............**550.00**
3 red cherries over thick 2-layer wht latt, 1954, 3¼".....................**110.00**
7 flowers on latt basket w/pk & wht twist, 3-color o/l, 3¼"..........**950.00**

Stankard, Paul

Botanical Study, pk/wht flowers, 1980, 3¼" **1,750.00**
Cactus+2 yel flowers+2 buds/roots on bl, sgn A697, '83, 3".........**600.00**
Dogwood, on cobalt, 1975...**700.00**
Jack-in-the-pulpit w/root system, bl grd, 1983................................**800.00**
Lav starflower w/2 leaves+2 buds & roots on plum, sgn, 3" **700.00**
Lav/wht/red/yel flower+3 leaves/roots+2 buds on cobalt, 3" **800.00**
Morning-glory, 2 blooms+bud over lt bl opaque, 3¼" **1,500.00**
Orange Desert Flower, 5+2 brn buds, 1986, 3" **1,100.00**
Pk/yel/wht flowers w/gr leaves on cobalt, B609, 1982, 3" **1,200.00**
Tiger lily w/bulb on bl, 1984 ....**800.00**
Trifloral Bouquet Block, w/dried seed pods, 2¼x2⅜x1¾" **1,000.00**
Wht Marsh Gentian, amethyst grd, 1975 ....**600.00**
Yel Cinquefoil w/3 buds on cobalt, cane sgn, 1975, 2⅜" **500.00**
3 pk/wht/yel lilies+6 pads+4 buds on cobalt, B711, '82, 3" **700.00**

Tarsitano, Debbie

Bouquet: 5 2-tone yel flowers, gr leaves/brn stems, 3¼" **550.00**
Opening Night Bouquet, 3 lg red flowers+3 wht sprigs, 2¾"........**350.00**
Pansy+bud on star base...**575.00**
Striped pk zinnia, 1/6 fct, star base, DT cane, 2¾" **400.00**
3 bl bellflowers w/wht int & leaves on cl, sgn, 2⅝" **425.00**
3 mc flowers in wht-hdld yel basket, star base, sgn, 3¼"...............**550.00**

Trabucco, Victor

Ice block, butterfly w/2 daisies, 1981......................................**450.00**
Nature in Ice, butterfly/daisies, sgn/1981 Proof, 3½" L................**550.00**
Pk flower+2 buds & gr leaves on wht trellis, sgn/1984, 3⅛" **350.00**
Pk rose+4 buds+sm bl & wht flowers on cobalt, 1/6 fct, 3¼" **450.00**
Yel/blk butterfly+pk upright peony & bud, fct, 1984....................**450.00**
2 purple/yel trumpet flowers+stems on cl, VT cane/1984, 3" **325.00**

Whitefriars

Con mill, 1848 in 2nd row, 3⅛" **325.00**
Con rows of cogs & tubes w/central lg pm cane, 3½" **90.00**
Prince Charles, 1969...**50.00**
Random canes on cl, inwardly-tilted cane perimeter, 3½" **350.00**

Whittemore, Francis D.

Bl/wht dahlia w/wht stardust cane center on cl grd, 2⅜"............**375.00**
Bleeding heart+2 buds & 4 leaves on gr flash grd, 2⅜" **350.00**
Mill nosegay on opal, angle-set on ped ft, 1974, 2½" **275.00**
Pk cyclamen+bud on translucent gr grd **300.00**
Purple/pk fuchsia+pk bud, 3-leaf/brn stem on gr flash, 2¼" **275.00**
Wht calla lily on ruby grd, 2¼" **200.00**
15-petal pk flower on 3 leaves, doorknob base, 2x2⅜"................**160.00**
2 pears on violet jsp grd, gr leaves, yel cane sgn, 2⅛" **170.00**
2 yel pears on pk jsp, 2 gr leaves/stems, cane sgn, 2⅛"................**190.00**
3 mushrooms yel/rust/brn w/gr & wht shoots on cobalt, 2½" **170.00**

Ysart, Paul

Crown, 5-petal flower center w/radiating latt on red, 2¾" **475.00**

Gar, striped red fish on sand-color grd, H mk, 2¾" 145.00
Orange/violet fish on bl jsp w/bubbles, Harlan H mk, 2¾" 200.00
Pattern mill, cane set-up on latt & yel tubes, unsgn, 3" 325.00
Pattern mill, ribbons alternate w/cane groups, unsgn, 2½" 110.00

Paul Ysart, ten-petaled pink flower with leafy green stem suspended above blue and white jasper layer, 'PY' cane by stem, 2¾", $400.00.

Pk/bl-stripe cane-center flower+3 leaves on violet, sgn, 3" 400.00
Pk/purple clematis w/in gr & wht latt ribbons, 2⅞" 450.00

Miscellaneous

Bohemian, scattered mill on 3-color upset muslin grd, 2½" 750.00
Chicken, dk amber, molded, 3", NM 150.00
Correia, frosted, frog/lilypad seen through 'window,' 3" 80.00
Gillander, 'moving turtle' on wht cloth, prism fcts, 3" 270.00
J Glass, o/l, flat bouquet on upset muslin, fct, 2¾" 235.00
Orient & Flume, beetle on yel swirl, paper label/1975, 2¾" 50.00
Rosenfeld, Ken; 3 strawberries+wht blossom, sgn/'84, 2½" 160.00
Rosenfeld, Ken; 6 lg flowers, 2-color leaves, sgn/'85, 2⅞" 195.00

Papier-Mache

The art of papier-mache was mainly European. It originated in Paris around the middle of the 18th century and became popular in America during Victorian times. Small items such as boxes, trays, inkwells, frames, etc., as well as extensive ceiling moldings and larger articles of furniture were made. The process involved building layer upon layer of paper soaked in glue, then coaxed into shape over a wood or wire form. When dry it was painted or decorated with gilt or inlays. Inexpensive 20th-century 'notions' were machine processed and mold pressed. See also Christmas; Candy Containers.

Bear on wheels, papier-mache with glass eyes, nodding head, Germany, 7", $245.00.

Table, chinoiserie, 3-shelf, 1850s, 32", EX...................................450.00

Tea board, blk w/gilt-stencil pineapples, 1780s, 24x32"........... 1,500.00
Tiger, life sized, Canton OH, 1930, 36x72", EX...................... 1,400.00
Tray, floral/geometrics, brass hdls, English, 1800s, 23x32"...........750.00
Tray, pheasants w/floral bkground, minor roughage, 23x29" 400.00
Tray on stand, peacocks/flowers, serpentine, 1850, 23" L.............450.00

Paragon

The Paragon China Company has operated in Longton, England, from about 1920 until the present. Their line of finely modeled figurines are attracting favorable collector interest.

Figurine, Lady Isobel, bl cape, gold hat, mk, 7¾x4⅜" 165.00
Figurine, Lady Melanie, figured stole, blk hat, mk, 7" 165.00
Figurine, Paulette, wht hair, holds fan, mk, 6½"...........................145.00
Figurine, Ursula, lady in red dress sits on bench, 6½x4⅛".............165.00

Parian Ware

Parian is hard-paste unglazed porcelain made to resemble marble. First made in the mid-1800s by Staffordshire potters, it was soon after produced in the United States by the U.S. Pottery at Bennington, Vermont. Busts and statuary were favored, but plaques, vases, mugs, and pitchers were also made.

Bowl, water lily relief, Minton 1849 mk, +lid/undertray..............125.00
Bust of Bacchus, grape-strewn hair, on short plinth, 9"................135.00
Bust of Miranda, WC Marshall, Copeland, 11"............................650.00
Figurine, Mercury sits on rock/ties on wings, Pigalle, 22" 700.00
Figurine, Roman Legionnaire preparing for combat, 19" 160.00

Three Graces, attributed to Copeland, after Canova, ca 1850, 21", $400.00.

Jug, molasses; Tyrol, bl/wht, 1864 registry mk, NM.....................235.00
Pitcher, maple leaves, fluted bottom, twist hdl, 9" 100.00
Swan boat w/cherub rider, 8" L, pr...130.00

Parrish, Maxfield

Maxfield Parrish was a painter and illustrator who began his career in the last decade of the 19th century. His work remained prominent until the early 1940s. His most famous painting, *Daybreak*, was published in print form and sold nearly two thousand copies between 1910 and 1930. All prices are for framed prints except for those from the 1960s.

Ad, Fit for a King, Fisk Tires, blk/wht, 1918, 12½x9".............**18.00**
Ad, Goodrich Tires, Sat Evening Post, 1923, 13x10½"................**40.00**
Ad, King & Queen Might Eat Thereof, Jell-O, 1921, 14x10"........**75.00**
Ad, King & Queen Might Eat Thereof, Jell-O, 1921, 9½x6".........**55.00**
Ad, Peter Peter Pumpkin Eater, ca 1920, 14½x10½" **75.00**
Ad, Swifts Premium Ham, ca 1921, fr, 14x11" **125.00**
Book, Arabian Knights, 1929, VG...**115.00**
Book, Dream Days, 1902, EX **115.00**

The Knave of Hearts, illustrated volume, published by Scribner's, NY, ca 1925, 14", **$800.00.**

Book, Wonderbook of Tanglewood Tales, EX................................**135.00**
Booklet, Jell-O, Polly Put the Kettle On, 3 recipes, M...................**45.00**
Bookplate, Arab at the Fire, 7¼x4⅝" **18.00**
Bookplate, Bellerphon at Fountain of Pyrene, 1904, 9¼x6¾"........**24.00**
Bookplate, Gardner & His Vegetables, 1925, 12½x10½" **65.00**
Bookplate, Lady Violette & Prince, ca 1925, 12½x10½" **80.00**
Bookplate, Prince Cododad & His Brothers, 9⅛x6½"...................**18.00**
Bookplate, Villa Gori, ca 1907, 10¼x7" **25.00**
Calendar, Contentment, Edison/Mazda, complete, 1928, sm.......**150.00**
Calendar, Contentment, Edison/Mazda, full pad, fr, lg, M...........**425.00**
Calendar, Dreamlight, Edison/Mazda, complete, 1925, fr, sm......**165.00**
Calendar, Ecstacy, Edison/Mazda, complete, 1930, sm, M..........**190.00**
Calendar, Evening Shadows, 1953, lg, EX.................................**250.00**
Calendar, Golden Hours, Edison/Mazda, complete, 1929, sm......**190.00**
Calendar, Lights of Home, complete, M....................................**175.00**
Calendar, Path to Home, Brown/Bigelow, 1940, 15½x12", EX....**190.00**
Calendar, Reveries, Edison/Mazda, full pad, 1927, fr, 22x14" **425.00**
Calendar, Silent Night, winter scene, 1942, M **165.00**
Calendar, Thy Templed Hills, Brn/Bigelow, 1942, 16x34", NM ..**225.00**
Calendar, Waterfall, Edison/Mazda, complete, 1931, sm **175.00**
Calendar print, Early Autumn, 12x14½"...................................**125.00**
Card, Christmas; Christmas Morning, Brown/Bigelow **15.00**
Card, Christmas; Silent Night, Brown/Bigelow...........................**15.00**
Card, Christmas; When Christmas Comes, Brown/Bigelow, 1947.**15.00**
Card, greeting; Afterglow, Brown/Bigelow, 1977.........................**15.00**
Card, greeting; Twilight Hour/Hilltop Farm, Brn/Bigelow, '51.......**15.00**
Figure, GE Bandi, wooden, jtd, rare...**850.00**
Frontispc, Sinbad Plots...Giant, Collier's, '07, 14x10"...................**75.00**
Magazine, Atlantic Monthly, King & Queen Jell-O ad, 1922........**15.00**
Magazine cover, Collier's, Dawn, May 1906, 14x10" **75.00**
Magazine cover, Collier's, Mama Ox, Mar 1906, 14½x10½"..........**55.00**
Magazine cover, Collier's, Old Man Gardener, June 1906, VG......**55.00**
Magazine cover, Collier's, Old Man Time, Jan 1905, EX **50.00**
Magazine cover, LH Journal, girl skier, June 1930, EX **195.00**
Magazine cover, LH Journal, Pierrot in wht on red, 1912, EX **195.00**
Magazine cover, Life, Happy Fisherman, w/cane pole, 1921 ....**135.00**
Magazine cover, Success, Dec 1901, 14½x10½" **75.00**
Menu, Broadmoor Hotel, rare, M...**250.00**

Playing cards, Dawn, 1918, rare, EX **275.00**
Playing cards, Ecstasy, 1930, EX in G box **225.00**
Playing cards, Egypt, 1933, EX in box **275.00**
Playing cards, Reveries, 1937, VG in box **175.00**
Playing cards, Waterfall, 1931, VG in box **225.00**
Print, Air Castles, ca 1904, 15x11"...**140.00**
Print, Aladdin, 1909, orig fr, 11x13" **100.00**
Print, Arabian Nights, 1929, 15x11"..**75.00**
Print, Arizona, 1930, orig fr, 10x12" **75.00**
Print, Aucassin Seeks for Nicole, 17x11", EX............................**375.00**
Print, Bl & Yel Hose, comic chefs, 1925, orig fr, 12½x14½" **65.00**
Print, Broadmoor, wood fr, 19x15"...**75.00**
Print, Cadmus, 1908, fr, 11x13" **150.00**
Print, Canyon, 1924, orig fr, 13½x16½" **135.00**
Print, Centaur, 1910, orig fr, 12x13½" **165.00**
Print, Chef Serving Tarts, 1925, orig fr, 12x14" **75.00**
Print, Christmas Morning, Brown/Bigelow, 1949, fr, 12x15" **95.00**
Print, Circes Palace, fr, 15½x12½"...**110.00**
Print, Cleopatra, matted & fr, 6½x7½", EX...............................**225.00**
Print, Cleopatra, 1917, fr, 24½x28", EX **750.00**
Print, Daybreak, orig fr w/crown above, 18x30", M **245.00**
Print, Daybreak, orig gesso Duro Craft fr, 6x10" **120.00**
Print, Dinkey Bird, 1904, orig fr, 13½x16½" **140.00**
Print, Dreaming, nude near waterfall, 1928, 18x30" **425.00**
Print, Dreaming, 1928, orig fr, 12½x14½" **190.00**
Print, Enchantment, Edison/Mazda, 1926, orig fr, 18x26", EX.....**375.00**
Print, Evening, nude on rock, 1922, orig fr, 13x16" **165.00**
Print, Eventide, orig folder, 14x10"...**125.00**
Print, Garden of Allah, orig fr, 18x33" **255.00**
Print, Garden of Allah, orig sticker, 16x30" **200.00**
Print, Garden of Allah, 1918, orig fr, 12x21" **165.00**
Print, Golden Hours, cropped, 17½x22½", EX **235.00**
Print, Golden Hours, lg **350.00**
Print, Hilltop, 1926, orig fr, 23x15" **365.00**
Print, Hilltop, 34x23"...**500.00**
Print, Interlude, 1924, 12x14", M **190.00**
Print, King of Blk Isles, 13x14" **90.00**
Print, Lady Violetta, 1925, orig fr, 12½x14½" **70.00**
Print, Lute Players, 1924, 10x18"..**240.00**
Print, Lute Players, 1924, 18x30", M **475.00**
Print, Moonlight, fr, 12x15", M **200.00**
Print, Morning, fr, 13½x16½" **145.00**
Print, Old Glen Mill, 1954, orig fr, 14x18" **275.00**
Print, Page, 1925, orig fr, 12½x14½".......................................**145.00**
Print, Pandora's Box, 1909, fr, 11x13".....................................**165.00**
Print, Peaceful Valley, Brown/Bigelow, 1955, oak fr, 11x11"..........**95.00**
Print, Perfect Day, trimmed, 1943, fr, 14x19" **95.00**
Print, Pierrot's Serenade, 9x11", EX..**165.00**
Print, Polly Put the Kettle On, fr, 8½x10½", M...........................**50.00**
Print, Primitive Man, Edison/Mazda, 1921, orig fr, 17x20" **475.00**
Print, Primitive Man, Edison/Mazda, 1929, fr, 9½x14" **225.00**
Print, Prince Codadad, 9x11"..**125.00**
Print, Reveries, Edison/Mazda, 1927, orig fr, 10½x14½" **285.00**
Print, Reveries, ladies at fountain, 1938, 6x10", NM **85.00**
Print, Reveries, 1926, sm fr, EX...**200.00**
Print, Romance, 1925, orig fr, 19x28" **385.00**
Print, Rubaiyat, 1917, orig fr, 11½x33", EX..............................**430.00**
Print, Sea Nymphs, 1911, orig fr, 7½x9½".................................**55.00**
Print, Sheltering Oaks, 1960, orig fr, 12½x20" **245.00**
Print, Solitude, Edison/Mazda, 11x14" **290.00**
Print, Solitude, Edison/Mazda, 16x19" **390.00**
Print, Stars, nude on rock at dusk, 1926, fr, 21x33".....................**450.00**
Print, Sunrise, 16x22"..**175.00**
Print, The Glen, 1925, orig fr, 13x15" **85.00**

Print, To Autumn, 1904, orig fr, 10x13" **75.00**
Print, Twilight, Brown/Bigelow, 16x19" **75.00**
Print, Twilight, 1935, orig fr, 30x12½" **195.00**
Print, Under Summer Skies, Brown/Bigelow, '50, fr, 16x19" **125.00**
Print, Under Summer Skies, Brown/Bigelow, 11x14", M **75.00**
Print, Wild Geese, 1924, orig fr, 13x17" **140.00**
Puzzle, The Prince, 1925, NM in box **90.00**

Pate-Sur-Pate

Pate-sur-pate, literally paste-on-paste, is a technique whereby relief decorations are built up on a ceramic body by layering several applications of slip, one on the other, until the desired result is achieved. Usually only two colors are used, and the value of a piece is greatly enhanced as more color is added. See also Rousseau, Argy; Walter, A.

Plaque, Bacchante w/grapes, teal w/wht slip, #1886, 9x6½" **1,200.00**
Plaque, Queen Elizabeth, lav w/teal border, 6" dia **165.00**
Plaque, seated maid/cherubs/beehive, L Solon, Mintons, 15".. **2,500.00**
Plaque, Venus w/putti, olive w/wht slip, by F Rhead, 11x7".... **1,200.00**
Screen, pr of winged figures, wht/red/gilt, Mintons, 7" **1,800.00**
Vase, cherub w/net chases butterfly, blk ground, Geo Jones, 6" ...**525.00**
Vase, Cupid & Psyche, wht/teal/gilt, A Birks, Mintons, 8" **2,200.00**
Vase, iris, bk: butterfly, dk bl/wht/gilt, Worcester, 10" **850.00**
Vase, teal/wht putti band, gilt, hdls/ftd, sgn/Mintons, 15".......**1,700.00**

Pattern Glass

Pattern Glass was the first mass-produced fancy tableware in America and was much prized by our ancestors. From the 1840s to the Civil War, it contained a high lead content and is known as 'Flint Glass.' It is exceptionally clear and resonant. Later glass was made with soda lime and is known as non-flint. By the 1890s pattern glass was produced in great volume in thousands of patterns, and colored glass came into vogue. Today the highest prices are often paid for these later patterns flashed with rose, amber, canary, and vaseline; stained ruby; or made in colors of cobalt, green, yellow, amethyst, etc. Demand for pattern glass declined by 1915, and glass fanciers were collecting it by 1930. No other field of antiques offers more diversity in patterns, prices, or pieces than this unique and historical glass that represents the Victorian era in America. For a more thorough study on the subject, we recommend *The Collector's Encyclopedia of Pattern Glass,* by Mollie Helen McCain, available from Collector Books. See also Bread Plates; Cruets; Historical Glass; Salt and Pepper Shakers; Salts, Open; Sugar Shakers; Syrups; specific manufacturers such as Northwood.

Note: Values are given for open sugar bowls and compotes unless noted 'w/lid.'

Actress, bottle, scent; 11" **48.00**
Actress, bowl, ftd, 6" **42.00**
Actress, cheese dish **245.00**
Actress, marmalade jar **125.00**
Actress, pitcher, water; 9" **250.00**
Alabama, butter dish, ruby stained **150.00**
Alabama, creamer **40.00**
Alabama, pitcher, water **78.00**
Almond Thumbprint, butter dish, ruby stained **110.00**
Almond Thumbprint, egg cup, flint **24.00**
Almond Thumbprint, tumbler, flint **38.00**
Almond Thumbprint, wine **12.50**
Amazon, banana stand **67.50**
Amazon, butter dish **55.00**

Amazon, creamer **32.50**
Amazon, pitcher, water **55.00**
Amazon, syrup, etched **48.00**
Amberette, see Klondike
Apollo, bowl, 8" **20.00**
Apollo, butter dish, etched **58.00**
Apollo, compote, w/lid, 6" **55.00**
Apollo, sauce dish, flat **7.50**
Apollo, sugar bowl, w/lid, etched **40.00**
Arched Grape, champagne **50.00**
Argus, bottle, bitters **65.00**
Argus, egg cup **25.00**
Argus, goblet, flint **44.00**

Argus

Argus, mug, appl hdl, flint **65.00**
Argus, pitcher, water; flint, 8¼" **200.00**
Argus, wine **18.00**
Art, biscuit jar, ruby stained **200.00**
Art, compote, w/lid, 9½x6" **50.00**
Art, creamer, rnd **44.00**
Art, plate, 10" **37.50**
Art, tumbler **35.00**
Ashburton, bottle, water; tumble up **100.00**
Ashburton, champagne, cut, flint **78.00**
Ashburton, decanter, flint, qt **65.00**
Ashburton, egg cup, dbl, flint **100.00**
Ashburton, goblet, bbl form, flint **40.00**
Ashburton, tumbler, bar; 6½" **57.00**
Atlas, cake stand, 10" **44.00**
Atlas, pitcher, water; tankard form **60.00**
Atlas, salt cellar, ind **15.00**
Atlas, sugar bowl, w/lid **40.00**
Aurora, creamer **37.50**
Aurora, mug, ruby stained **65.00**
Aurora, tray, ruby stained, 10" dia **47.50**
Aurora, wine, ruby stained **40.00**
Austrian, bowl, rectangular, 8¼" **55.00**
Austrian, cordial **48.00**
Austrian, punch cup **20.00**
Austrian, see also Greentown, Austrian
Austrian, wine **32.00**
Baby Thumbprint, see Dakota
Balder, see Pennsylvania
Baltimore Pear, bread plate, 12½" **65.00**
Baltimore Pear, creamer, oval, ind **28.00**
Baltimore Pear, sugar bowl, w/lid **48.00**
Banner, butter dish **95.00**
Bar & Diamond, celery vase, ruby stained **40.00**
Bar & Diamond, compote, high std, 6" **28.00**
Bar & Diamond, goblet **27.50**

Bar & Diamond, pitcher, tankard form, 10½" 50.00
Barberry, pitcher, water; bulbous 90.00
Barley, celery vase 25.00
Barred Forget-Me-Not, creamer 30.00
Barrel Huber, see Huber
Beaded Band, goblet 25.00
Beaded Dewdrop, see Wisconsin
Beaded Grape Medallion, goblet 30.00
Beaded Loop, see Oregon
Beaded Medallion, butter dish 42.50
Beaded Medallion, goblet 25.00
Beaded Medallion, pitcher, water 100.00
Beaded Medallion, sugar bowl, w/lid 47.50
Beaded Mirror, see Beaded Medallion
Beaded Panel, bowl, 8¼" dia 75.00
Beaded Panel, cruet, w/stopper 170.00
Beaded Panel, plate, 9¼" dia 80.00
Beaded Panel, relish tray, 8½x4" 70.00
Beaded Tulip, creamer 88.00
Beaded Tulip, goblet 37.50
Bearded Head, see Viking
Beehive, goblet, clear 85.00
Bellflower, bowl, oval, rayed base, 9x6" 130.00
Bellflower, champagne, bbl form, single vine 100.00
Bellflower, compote, dome lid, low std, 8½x8", NM 225.00
Bellflower, decanter, dbl vine, w/orig stopper, pt 235.00
Bellflower, egg cup, single vine 40.00
Bellflower, goblet, bbl form, single vine 38.00
Bellflower, goblet, cut 350.00
Bellflower, lamp, fluid; int pattern, milk glass base, 10" 400.00
Bellflower, mug, single vine 195.00
Bellflower, pitcher, flint, dbl vine, appl hdl, 9" 300.00
Bellflower, spill holder 40.00
Bellflower, sweetmeat, single vine, 6" 325.00
Bellflower, syrup, appl hdl, David Baker pat lid 500.00
Bellflower, tumbler, water; dbl vine 100.00
Bellflower, tumbler, whiskey; single vine, 3½" 150.00
Bellflower, wine, bbl form, knop stem, flint 100.00
Bellflower, wine, str sides, plain stem 60.00
Bent Buckle, see New Hampshire
Bevelled Diamond & Star, shakers, pr 15.00
Bigler, champagne 95.00
Bigler, egg cup, dbl 48.00
Bigler, plate, 6" 30.00
Bigler, tumbler, water 48.00
Bird & Fern, see Hummingbird
Bird & Strawberry, sugar bowl, w/lid 75.00
Blaze, creamer, molded hdl 48.00
Bleeding Heart, cake stand, 9½x11" 70.00
Bleeding Heart, sugar bowl, w/lid 55.00
Bleeding Heart, wine, knob stem 165.00
Block, wine, ruby stained 35.00
Block & Fan, cookie jar 68.00
Block & Fan, finger bowl 30.00
Block & Fan, ice tub 45.00
Block & Fan, pitcher, water; ruby stained 130.00
Block & Fan, rose bowl 27.50
Block & Fan, spooner 27.50
Blue Jay, see Cardinal Bird
Bosworth, butter dish 27.50
Bosworth, creamer 20.00
Bosworth, pitcher, water 32.00
Bosworth, wine 18.00
Bow Tie, butter dish 75.00

Bow Tie, butter pat 27.50
Bow Tie, compote, high std, 9¼" 68.00
Bow Tie, goblet 65.00
Bow Tie, salt cellar, master 40.00
Bow Tie, sauce dish, flat 15.00
Broken Column, bowl, 7¼" 28.00
Broken Column, carafe, water 75.00
Broken Column, compote, w/lid, ruby stained, 10" 345.00
Broken Column, compote, 6x5" 37.50
Broken Column, cookie jar 70.00
Broken Column, decanter, 10½" 85.00
Broken Column, pitcher, water; ruby stained 250.00
Broken Column, spooner 28.00
Broken Column, tumbler, water; ruby stained 55.00
Buckle, butter dish 60.00
Buckle, champagne, flint 58.00
Buckle, creamer, ind 27.50
Buckle, goblet 25.00

Buckle

Buckle, goblet, flint 48.00
Buckle, pitcher, water; appl hdl 88.00
Buckle, sugar bowl, w/lid, flint 60.00
Buckle, wine 45.00
Buckle w/Star, cake stand, 9" 36.00
Buckle w/Star, salt cellar 25.00
Buckle w/Star, tumbler, bar 60.00
Bull's Eye, cordial, flint 80.00
Bull's Eye, decanter, bar lip, flint, qt 125.00
Bull's Eye, salt cellar, rectangular, sm 32.00
Bull's Eye, spooner, flint 42.00
Bull's Eye, sugar bowl, w/lid, flint 125.00
Bull's Eye & Daisy, creamer 20.00
Bull's Eye & Daisy, spooner 15.00
Bull's Eye & Daisy, wine, ruby stained 44.00
Bull's Eye & Fan, bowl, berry; 8" 15.00
Bull's Eye & Fan, creamer, 3¼" 15.00
Bull's Eye & Fan, goblet, amethyst stained 27.50
Bull's Eye & Fan, pitcher, water; tankard form 42.50
Bull's Eye & Spearhead, compote, Findlay, 7½" 55.00
Bull's Eye Band, see Reverse Torpedo
Bull's Eye in Heart, see Heart w/Thumbprint
Bull's Eye w/Fleur-de-lis, butter dish 98.00
Bull's Eye w/Fleur-de-lis, creamer 60.00
Bull's Eye w/Fleur-de-lis, decanter, bar lip, flint, pr 350.00
Bull's Eye w/Fleur-de-lis, decanter, marble on stopper, qt 250.00
Bull's Eye w/Fleur-de-lis, sugar bowl 57.50
Button Arches, bowl, ruby stained, 8" 44.00
Button Arches, goblet 25.00
Button Arches, mug, ruby stained 27.50
Button Arches, pitcher, water; tankard form, 11" 125.00
Button Arches, spooner 28.00
Button Arches, sugar bowl, w/lid 32.00
Button Arches, toothpick holder 22.50
Button Arches, tumbler, water 18.00

Cabbage Rose, bottle, bitters; 6½" 98.00
Cabbage Rose, cake stand, 9½" 65.00

Cabbage Rose

Cabbage Rose, champagne 45.00
Cabbage Rose, compote, w/lid, 7½" 90.00
Cabbage Rose, cordial 48.00
Cabbage Rose, egg cup 35.00
Cabbage Rose, pitcher, water; qt 127.50
Cabbage Rose, spooner 25.00
Cable, butter dish 90.00
Cable, creamer 425.00
Cable, goblet 65.00
Cable, spooner 38.00
Cable, sugar bowl, w/lid 98.00
Cable, wine 95.00
Canadian, bread plate, hdls, 10" 48.00
Canadian, celery vase 50.00
Canadian, goblet 55.00
Canadian, pitcher, water 95.00
Cane, creamer, amber 32.00
Cane, finger bowl, amber 22.00
Cane, goblet, vaseline 40.00
Cane, sugar bowl, w/lid, amber 58.00
Cane, tray, water; bl 48.00
Cane, tumbler, vaseline 27.50
Cane, wine 22.00
Cardinal Bird, butter dish 75.00
Cardinal Bird, goblet 33.00
Cardinal Bird, honey dish 20.00
Cardinal Bird, pitcher, water 120.00
Cathedral, cake stand, amber, 10" 50.00
Cathedral, cake stand, bl, 4½x10" 50.00
Cathedral, cruet, amber 95.00
Cathedral, lamp, bl, 12¾" 188.00
Cathedral, relish, fish form, amber 37.50
Cathedral, spooner, vaseline 45.00
Cathedral, wine, amber 37.50
Centennial, see Liberty Bell
Chain, bread plate 28.00
Chain, goblet 20.00
Chain, spooner 22.50
Chain w/Diamonds, see Washington Centennial
Chain w/Star, compote, jelly 18.00
Chain w/Star, creamer 25.00
Chandelier, cake stand, etched, 10" 75.00
Chandelier, creamer 32.00
Chandelier, salt cellar, master; plain 37.50
Chandelier, sauce dish, flat, plain 17.50
Chandelier, tumbler, water 35.00
Chandelier, tumbler, water; etched 38.00
Chrysanthemum Leaf, vase, bulbous w/flutes, Sandwich, 7" 125.00

Church Windows, sugar bowl, w/lid 25.00
Classic, celery vase, open log ft 175.00
Classic, compote, collared, w/lid, 8½" 178.00
Classic, goblet 200.00
Classic, plate, 10" 180.00
Classic, spooner, collared base 88.00
Clear Diagonal Band, pitcher, water 45.00
Coin, see US Coin
Colorado, toothpick holder 30.00
Columbian Coin, butter dish, frosted coins 165.00
Columbian Coin, compote, w/lid, 8" 78.00
Columbian Coin, shakers, frosted coins, pr 95.00
Columbian Coin, spooner, frosted coins 50.00
Columbian Coin, spooner, gold coins 50.00
Columbian Coin, syrup, gold coins 235.00
Comet, creamer 165.00
Comet, goblet, flint 100.00
Comet, tumbler, bar 98.00
Comet, tumbler, water 115.00
Compact, see Snail
Cord & Tassel, butter dish 50.00
Cord & Tassel, pitcher, water 95.00
Cord & Tassel, sugar bowl 25.00
Cord & Tassel, wine 40.00
Croesus, bowl, ftd, gr w/gold, 4x6¾" 68.00
Croesus, butter dish, purple w/gold 220.00
Croesus, cake stand, amethyst, 10" 180.00
Croesus, compote, jelly 22.00
Croesus, creamer, purple 140.00
Croesus, cruet, gr 180.00
Croesus, pitcher, water 80.00
Croesus, pitcher, water; gr w/gold 225.00
Croesus, sauce dish, ftd 17.50
Croesus, sugar bowl, purple w/gold, w/lid, M 160.00
Croesus, toothpick holder 28.00
Croesus, tumbler, water; gr 40.00
Crow's Foot, see Yale
Crown Jewels, see Chandelier
Cryptic, see Zippered Block
Crystal Ball, see Atlas
Crystal Wedding, cake plate, sq, ruby stained 88.00
Crystal Wedding, creamer 48.00
Crystal Wedding, pitcher, milk; rnd 115.00
Crystal Wedding, spooner, amber stained 45.00
Crystal Wedding, vase, twisted, ftd 27.50
Cube w/Fan, see Pineapple & Fan
Cupid & Venus, bread plate, amber, 10½" 110.00
Cupid & Venus, cordial 80.00
Cupid & Venus, cruet 80.00
Cupid & Venus, pitcher, milk 65.00
Cupid & Venus, pitcher, water; amber 200.00
Cupid & Venus, wine 100.00
Currant, butter dish 78.00
Currant, celery vase 38.00
Currant, compote, w/lid, 8" 65.00
Currant, egg cup 18.00
Currant, pitcher, water 75.00
Currant, wine 37.50
Currier & Ives, bowl, oval, 10" 32.00
Currier & Ives, pitcher, milk 62.50
Currier & Ives, plate, 10" 18.00
Currier & Ives, spooner 28.00
Currier & Ives, tray, wine; 9½" 48.00
Currier & Ives, waste bowl 45.00

Curtain, butter dish 55.00
Curtain, creamer 30.00
Curtain, mug 28.00
Curtain, tumbler 18.00
Curtain Tie-Back, butter dish 40.00
Curtain Tie-Back, relish 12.50
Cut Log, bowl, scalloped, 8½" 28.00
Cut Log, cake stand, 10" 70.00
Cut Log, compote, high std, 8¼x6½" 55.00
Cut Log, compote, w/lid, 7½x5½" 48.00
Cut Log, creamer, ind 15.00
Cut Log, olive dish 20.00
Cut Log, sugar bowl, w/lid 50.00
Cut Log, vase, 16" 37.50
Cut Log, wine 25.00
Dahlia, bread tray, oval, hdls 40.00
Dahlia, cake stand, amber, 9" 50.00
Dahlia, champagne, amber 95.00
Dahlia, goblet, bl 50.00
Dahlia, mug..32.00
Dahlia, mug, vaseline, 3⅛" 50.00
Dahlia, pitcher, water; amber 90.00
Dahlia, pitcher, 8½" 60.00
Dahlia, plate, hdls, amber, 9" 25.00
Dahlia, platter, bl 48.00
Dahlia, spooner 27.50
Dahlia, wine, vaseline 45.00
Daisy & Button, bottle, cologne; orig stopper 25.00
Daisy & Button, bowl, oblong, amber, 9¼" 35.00
Daisy & Button, bowl, triangular, bl 48.00
Daisy & Button, butter pat, vaseline 37.50
Daisy & Button, celery vase 32.00
Daisy & Button, creamer 30.00
Daisy & Button, egg cup, amber 18.00
Daisy & Button, inkwell, amber.................................150.00
Daisy & Button, plate, amber, 6" 12.00
Daisy & Button, syrup, amber 60.00
Daisy & Button, tumbler, water....................................17.50
Daisy & Button, tumbler, water; amber 24.00
Daisy & Button, wine 28.00
Daisy & Button w/Crossbar, bread tray 27.50
Daisy & Button w/Crossbar, butter dish 48.00
Daisy & Button w/Crossbar, compote, amber, 4x7" 28.00
Daisy & Button w/Crossbar, goblet, bl 40.00
Daisy & Button w/Crossbar, pitcher, water; amber, 8" ...80.00
Daisy & Button w/Crossbar, spooner, amber 50.00
Daisy & Button w/Thumbprint, bowl, sq, 8" 28.00
Daisy & Button w/Thumbprint, butter dish...................80.00
Daisy & Button w/Thumbprint, finger bowl 20.00
Daisy & Button w/Thumbprint, sauce dish, sq, amber stripe 17.50
Daisy & Button w/Thumbprint, tumbler, amber............24.00
Daisy & Button w/V Ornament, celery vase, amber 38.00
Daisy & Button w/V Ornament, mug, bl 24.00
Daisy & Button w/V Ornament, sauce dish, flat 15.00
Daisy & Button w/V Ornament, sugar bowl, w/lid, bl ...50.00
Dakota, butter dish, etched 70.00
Dakota, celery vase, flat base 35.00
Dakota, compote, 9x8" 58.00
Dakota, mug, ruby stained 36.00
Dakota, pitcher, milk 78.00
Dakota, spooner 35.00
Dakota, sugar bowl, breakfast 20.00
Dakota, waste bowl 60.00
Dakota, wine 25.00

Dart, butter dish 35.00
Dart, pitcher, water 35.00
Dart, tumbler 15.00
Deer & Dog, compote, 8" 170.00
Deer & Dog, marmalade 80.00
Deer & Dog, wine 75.00
Deer & Pine Tree, bread tray, bl, 13x8" 80.00
Deer & Pine Tree, creamer, apple gr 90.00
Deer & Pine Tree, finger bowl 55.00
Deer & Pine Tree, mug, bl, lg 50.00
Delaware, banana boat, gr w/gold, 11¾" 50.00
Delaware, bowl, octagonal, gold trim, 9" 27.50
Delaware, butter dish 58.00
Delaware, butter dish, rose w/gold...............................145.00

Delaware

Delaware, pitcher, water; tankard form, gr w/gold, 9½" 100.00
Delaware, punch cup, gr w/gold....................................38.00
Delaware, spooner 40.00
Delaware, spooner, gr w/gold 55.00
Delaware, vase, gr w/gold, 9½" 80.00
Dew & Raindrop, bowl, berry; 8" 40.00
Dew & Raindrop, creamer...27.50
Dew & Raindrop, spooner 35.00
Dew & Raindrop, wine 17.00
Dewdrop, egg cup, dbl 22.00
Dewdrop, mug, appl hdl 25.00
Dewdrop, tumbler, bl 28.00
Dewey, plate, ftd 17.50
Diagonal Band, pitcher, milk...35.00
Diagonal Band, relish, oval, 6⅞" 15.00
Diagonal Band, wine 25.00
Diagonal Band w/Fan, compote, 7½" 27.50
Diagonal Band w/Fan, sauce dish, ftd 15.00
Diagonal Band w/Fan, shakers, pr 50.00
Diamond & Sunburst, cake stand, 8" 30.00
Diamond & Sunburst, sugar shaker................................24.00
Diamond Horseshoe, see Aurora
Diamond Medallion, see Grand
Diamond Point, bread plate..30.00
Diamond Point, champagne, flint 78.00
Diamond Point, creamer, appl hdl, flint 120.00
Diamond Point, goblet 40.00
Diamond Point, pitcher, water; tankard form, flint, qt...175.00
Diamond Point, syrup, flint..100.00
Diamond Point, tumbler, bar; flint 68.00
Diamond Point w/Ribs, goblet, flint..............................52.50
Diamond Quilted, bowl, amber, 7" 20.00
Diamond Quilted, champagne 20.00
Diamond Quilted, goblet, amethyst 32.00
Diamond Quilted, mug..17.50
Diamond Quilted, salt cellar, vaseline............................18.00
Diamond Quilted, tumbler, bl 44.00
Diamond Quilted, wine 18.00
Diamond Thumbprint, celery vase, scalloped, flint 145.00

Diamond Thumbprint, cup plate 48.00
Diamond Thumbprint, spooner.....................................85.00
Doric, see Feather
Double Leaf & Dart, see Leaf & Dart
Double Wedding Ring, see Wedding Ring
Drapery, creamer..30.00
Drapery, goblet..25.00
Drapery, sugar bowl, w/lid.......................................40.00
Drapery, tumbler..28.00
Drum, creamer 50.00
Egg in Sand, butter dish...50.00
Egg in Sand, pitcher, milk 48.00
Egg in Sand, sauce dish..12.50
Egg in Sand, tumbler 35.00
Egyptian, goblet 40.00
Egyptian, plate, 10"..45.00
Egyptian, sugar bowl 70.00
Elephant, see Jumbo
Emerald Green Herringbone, see Florida
English Hobnail Cross, see Klondike
Esther, butter dish, gr...125.00
Esther, compote, amber stained, 8" 85.00
Esther, compote, jelly; gr w/gold 60.00
Esther, cruet, orig stopper, gr w/gold 200.00

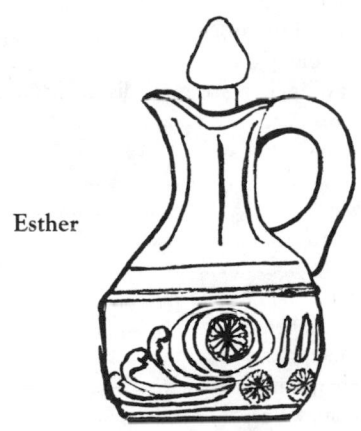

Esther

Esther, goblet 55.00
Esther, relish dish, gr w/gold, 9x5"..............................24.00
Esther, spooner..40.00
Esther, spooner, gr w/gold 55.00
Esther, toothpick holder, gr w/gold...............................95.00
Esther, tray, ice cream; gr w/gold 145.00
Esther, wine...35.00
Etched Dakota, see Dakota
Eureka, bowl, oval, 9"..32.00
Eureka, cordial 40.00
Eureka, sugar bowl, w/lid 50.00
Eureka, wine...32.50
Excelsior, cake stand, flint, 9¼" 155.00
Excelsior, creamer, flint 85.00
Excelsior, mug 28.00
Excelsior, sugar bowl, w/lid, flint 95.00
Eyewinker, celery vase, 6½" 60.00
Eyewinker, creamer..55.00
Eyewinker, tumbler 30.00
Fan w/Diamond, pitcher, water 55.00
Fan w/Diamond, spooner...22.00
Feather, bowl, 7½" 25.00
Feather, celery vase 35.00
Feather, goblet 58.00

Feather, plate, 10"...38.00
Feather, syrup..95.00
Feather, toothpick holder, gr 195.00
Festoon, compote, high std, 8" 60.00
Festoon, relish dish, 9x5½"...36.00
Festoon, sauce dish 7.50
Festoon, waste bowl 35.00
Fine Cut, creamer, bl 40.00
Fine Cut, goblet, vaseline 45.00
Fine Cut, plate, 10"..20.00
Fine Cut, sugar bowl, w/lid 40.00
Fine Cut, wine 15.00
Fine Cut & Block, butter dish, ftd.................................78.00
Fine Cut & Block, cake stand.......................................38.00
Fine Cut & Block, pitcher, water; bl stained.......................95.00
Fine Cut & Block, tumbler, bl 32.00
Fine Cut & Diamond, see Grand
Fine Cut & Feather, see Feather
Fine Cut & Panel, plate, 6" 15.00
Fine Cut & Panel, tumbler, vaseline................................40.00
Fine Cut Medallion, see Austrian & Greentown, Austrian
Fine Rib, butter dish, flint 75.00
Fine Rib, champagne, flint 78.00
Fine Rib, cordial 48.00
Fine Rib, salt cellar, ind 15.00
Fine Rib, tumbler, whiskey; bl 130.00
Fingerprint, see Almond Thumbprint
Fishscale, cake stand, 10"..45.00
Fishscale, compote, high std, 7"...................................35.00
Fishscale, plate, sq, 9" 30.00
Flamingo Habitat, celery vase 48.00
Flamingo Habitat, creamer 40.00
Flamingo Habitat, sugar bowl, w/lid 48.00
Florida, butter dish, gr...52.00
Florida, goblet, gr 45.00
Florida, plate, 9"...15.00
Florida, tumbler, water..18.00
Florida, wine..25.00
Flower Pot, goblet...38.00
Flower Pot, sugar bowl 40.00
Frosted Circle, champagne 60.00
Frosted Circle, punch cup 18.00
Frosted Circle, spooner..35.00
Frosted Leaf, creamer, flint 100.00
Frosted Leaf, salt cellar 40.00
Frosted Leaf, tumbler, ftd..100.00
Frosted Lion, see Lion
Frosted Stork, finger bowl...70.00
Frosted Stork, sauce dish 24.00
Frosted Stork, waste bowl 42.00
Galloway, bowl, ice cream; 3½x11".................................48.00
Galloway, bowl, rectangular, 5¼x3½"...............................12.00
Galloway, butter dish 60.00
Galloway, carafe...78.00
Galloway, finger bowl, 6" 25.00
Galloway, punch cup.. 9.00
Galloway, syrup, ruby stained 130.00
Galloway, tumbler, ruby stained 55.00
Garfield Drape, creamer..48.00
Garfield Drape, goblet...38.00
Garfield Drape, pitcher, water....................................100.00
Garfield Drape, sugar bowl, w/lid 65.00
Gem, see Nailhead
Good Luck, see Horseshoe

Grand, bread plate, 10"..24.00
Grand, compote, w/lid, 5½" 65.00
Grand, plate, 10"..27.50
Grand, waste bowl 32.00
Grand, wine 32.00
Grape & Festoon, butter dish, stippled leaf.............55.00
Grape & Festoon, plate, stippled leaf, 6" 18.00
Grape & Festoon w/Shield, creamer 35.00
Grape & Festoon w/Shield, goblet, w/shield & grapes.........25.00
Grape & Festoon w/Shield, pitcher, water.................70.00
Grape & Festoon w/Shield, spooner 25.00
Grape Band, egg cup..22.00
Grape Band, salt cellar, master 25.00
Grape Band, wine, flint 37.50
Grasshopper, bowl, ftd, 7"..22.00
Grasshopper, creamer..35.00
Grasshopper, pitcher, water; amber 130.00
Grasshopper, sauce dish, ftd, etched 15.00
Grasshopper, sugar bowl, w/lid 44.00
Guardian Angel, see Cupid & Venus
Hairpin, champagne, knop stem 60.00
Hairpin, egg cup..18.00
Hairpin, pitcher, 8"...180.00
Hairpin, tumbler, whiskey; appl hdl, flint 47.50
Halley's Comet, goblet...38.00

Halley's Comet

Halley's Comet, salt cellar 22.00
Halley's Comet, wine..28.00
Hamilton, cake stand 150.00
Hamilton, creamer 68.00
Hamilton, plate, frosted leaf, hdls, 10½"..................60.00
Hamilton, spooner 35.00
Hamilton, tumbler, frosted leaf 130.00
Hamilton, wine, frosted leaf 75.00
Hand, cake stand 50.00
Hand, cordial 80.00
Hand, goblet 45.00
Hand, wine 50.00
Hartley, celery vase, bl...38.00
Hartley, goblet 28.00
Hartley, sauce dish, ftd, amber, 4" 15.00
Hartley, spooner, vaseline 30.00
Heart w/Thumbprint, carafe 75.00
Heart w/Thumbprint, creamer 40.00
Heart w/Thumbprint, goblet 50.00
Heart w/Thumbprint, pitcher, water 70.00
Heart w/Thumbprint, vase, gr w/gold, 6" 70.00
Hearts & Spades, see Medallion
Heavy Panelled Finecut, creamer, 6".........................22.00
Heavy Panelled Finecut, sugar bowl..........................35.00
Heavy Panelled Finecut, tumbler, bar 18.00
Herringbone Band, see Ripple
Herringbone Buttress, see Greentown, Herringbone Buttress
Hexagon Block, tumbler, water; etched, amber stained.................35.00

Hickman, bowl, sq, 7" 15.00
Hickman, butter dish, gr..60.00
Hickman, champagne 22.50
Hickman, creamer, gr 35.00
Hickman, goblet, gr 48.00
Hickman, tumbler...28.00
Hidalgo, celery vase, flat base, amber stained 40.00
Hidalgo, compote, w/lid, 7"..45.00
Hidalgo, goblet, amber stained 40.00
Hidalgo, sugar shaker 45.00
Hidalgo, tumbler, ruby stained...................................30.00
Hinoto, champagne 58.00
Hinoto, salt cellar 38.00
Holbrook, see Pineapple & Fan
Holly, butter dish 155.00
Holly, goblet 95.00
Holly, spooner 65.00
Holly Amber, see Greentown, Holly Amber
Honeycomb, champagne, flint 60.00
Honeycomb, egg cup..22.00
Honeycomb, pitcher, water; flint, 9".........................100.00
Hops & Barley, see Wheat & Barley
Horn of Plenty, bottle, bar; pewter pouring spout, 8" 140.00
Horn of Plenty, celery vase 135.00
Horn of Plenty, goblet...65.00
Horn of Plenty, goblet, flint 77.50
Horn of Plenty, spill holder 50.00
Horseshoe, bread tray, single horseshoe hdls.............35.00
Horseshoe, celery vase 60.00
Horseshoe, creamer, ind...40.00
Horseshoe, salt cellar, ind..20.00
Huber, claret, 10-panel...27.50
Huber, egg cup, single 15.00
Huber, tumbler, water 22.50
Huber, wine, 8-panel..20.00
Hummingbird, bowl, amber, 6"..................................32.00
Hummingbird, creamer, bl..55.00
Hummingbird, pitcher, water; amber 100.00
Hummingbird, pitcher, water; bl................................126.00
Hummingbird, waste bowl..36.00
Idaho, see Snail
Illinois, butter dish, sq, 7" 65.00
Illinois, salt cellar, ind...15.00
Illinois, sugar bowl, w/lid 50.00
Illinois, toothpick holder 30.00
Indian Tree, see Barley
Indiana, see Greentown, Cord Drapery
Indiana Swirl, see Feather
Inverted Fern, compote, 8"..58.00
Inverted Fern, cruet 50.00
Inverted Fern, plate, 6" 25.00
Inverted Fern, sugar bowl, w/lid 80.00
Invincible, bowl, w/lid, 6" dia....................................45.00
Invincible, cruet, w/stopper 170.00
Invincible, spooner 40.00
Invincible, sugar bowl, w/lid 55.00
Iris Column, see Broken Column
Iris w/Meander, creamer, clear w/gold 45.00
Iris w/Meander, see also Opalescent Glass
Iris w/Meander, shaker, clear w/gold 28.00
Iris w/Meander, vase, clear w/gold, 11".....................25.00
Ivy in Snow, cake stand, 10".......................................48.00
Ivy in Snow, pitcher, water 50.00
Ivy in Snow, syrup..72.50

Ivy in Snow, tumbler, ruby stained 48.00
Ivy in Snow, wine 32.00
Jacob's Ladder, butter dish, Maltese Cross finial 70.00
Jacob's Ladder, compote, 7x6" 30.00
Jacob's Ladder, goblet, water; amber 40.00
Jacob's Ladder, pickle dish, Maltese Cross hdl, bl 70.00
Jacob's Ladder, salt cellar, master 30.00
Jacob's Ladder, sugar bowl, w/lid 45.00
Jersey Swirl, compote, high std, bl, 8" 48.00
Jersey Swirl, salt cellar, ind, canary............................20.00
Jersey Swirl, wine 20.00
Jewel w/Dewdrop, creamer...38.00
Jewel w/Dewdrop, pitcher, milk 75.00
Jewel w/Dewdrop, wine, rare 65.00
Jewel w/Moondrop, pitcher, water..............................60.00
Jewelled Moon & Star, carafe 45.00
Jewelled Moon & Star, goblet 20.00
Jewelled Moon & Star, tumbler, water 25.00
Job's Tears, see Art
Jumbo, creamer 200.00
Jumbo, goblet 425.00
Kansas, see Jewel w/Moondrop
Kentucky, cruet 38.00
Kentucky, punch cup, gr 17.50
Kentucky, sugar bowl, w/lid 32.00
Kentucky, toothpick holder, gr 85.00
Kentucky, wine, gr 30.00
King's Crown, castor bottle, ruby stained 65.00
King's Crown, pitcher, water; tankard form, 13" 125.00
King's Crown, punch cup...20.00
King's Crown, toothpick holder 28.00
Klondike, bowl, sq, clear w/amber, 11" 135.00
Klondike, butter dish, frosted w/amber 385.00
Klondike, celery vase, frosted w/amber 195.00
Klondike, relish, frosted w/amber, boat shape, 9x4" 125.00
Klondike, sugar bowl, frosted w/amber 178.00
Kokomo, see Bar & Diamond
La Clede, see Hickman
Lace, see Drapery
Ladder w/Diamonds, shakers, pr 25.00
Ladder w/Diamonds, tumbler, water; ruby stained w/gold.....25.00
Lady Hamilton, egg cup, saucer base 22.00
Lady Hamilton, platter, frosted, 13x9" 30.00
Lady Hamilton, sugar bowl, w/lid 45.00
Late Block, see Red Block
Late Buckle, see Buckle w/Star
Lawrence, see Bull's Eye
Leaf, see Maple Leaf
Leaf & Dart, bowl, low ft, 8¼" 22.50
Leaf & Dart, egg cup 24.00
Leaf & Dart, pitcher, water...90.00
Leaf & Dart, wine 34.00
Leaf Bracket, see Greentown, Leaf Bracket
Leaf Medallion, see Northwood, Leaf Medallion
Liberty, butter dish...45.00
Liberty, wine 18.50
Liberty Bell, butter dish 135.00
Liberty Bell, creamer, reeded appl hdl 95.00
Liberty Bell, goblet..45.00
Liberty Bell, pitcher, water..575.00
Liberty Bell, salt cellar, ind.......................................38.00
Liberty Bell, spoon holder...65.00
Lily of the Valley, creamer, 3-ftd 75.00
Lily of the Valley, egg cup...45.00

Lily of the Valley, sauce dish, flat, 4" 12.00
Lily of the Valley, tumbler, ftd....................................45.00
Lincoln Drape, creamer, flint 150.00
Lincoln Drape, sugar bowl, open................................95.00
Lincoln Drape w/Tassel, salt cellar, master 120.00
Lincoln Drape w/Tassel, syrup 155.00
Lion, butter dish, head finial.....................................100.00
Lion, cake stand..80.00
Lion, champagne 165.00
Lion, compote, lion finial on lid, 13x8".......................185.00
Lion, creamer 65.00

Lion

Lion, goblet..65.00
Lion, pitcher, water; clear hdl, 9" 280.00
Lion, relish 42.50
Lion, sugar bowl, lion finial on lid, 8½" 155.00
Log Cabin, compote, 10½" 285.00
Log Cabin, creamer 125.00
Log Cabin, sugar bowl, w/lid, 8"................................275.00
Long Spear, see Grasshopper
Loop, celery vase, flint..60.00
Loop, creamer, flint 65.00
Loop, goblet, flint 27.00
Loop, tumbler, water...22.00
Loop & Dart, butter dish 48.00
Loop & Dart, cordial, 3¾"...25.00
Loop & Dart, goblet, rnd ornaments............................30.00
Loop & Dart, spooner, flint 35.00
Loop w/Stippled Panels, see Texas
Lotus, see Garden of Eden
Louisiana, creamer 35.00
Louisiana, wine 35.00
Magnet & Grape, compote, high std, 7½" 70.00
Magnet & Grape, sugar bowl, w/lid, flint.....................100.00
Maine, butter dish 45.00
Maine, cake stand, gr, 8½" 55.00
Maine, pitcher, water..90.00
Maple Leaf, bowl, sq, crimped rim, bl, 10" 80.00
Maple Leaf, compote, jelly; gr 42.50
Maple Leaf, creamer 55.00
Maple Leaf, goblet, amber 90.00
Maryland, cake stand, 8" 45.00
Maryland, pickle dish 20.00
Maryland, sugar bowl, w/lid, ruby stained 65.00
Mascotte, bowl, shallow, etched, 2¾x9" 35.00
Mascotte, pitcher, water; etched..................................70.00
Mascotte, tumbler, etched 32.00
Massachusetts, goblet 47.00
Massachusetts, ice cream tray, 8" 18.00
Massachusetts, vase, trumpet form, 6½" 25.00
Melrose, cake stand, 10" 30.00
Melrose, goblet..20.00
Melrose, plate, 8" 12.00
Michigan, bowl, pk stained, 9" 48.00
Michigan, celery vase 32.00
Michigan, shakers, pr 50.00
Minerva, creamer...45.00

Minerva, goblet..80.00
Minerva, marmalade.....................................155.00
Minerva, plate, warrior in center, 10½".............58.00
Minnesota, carafe..40.00
Minnesota, pickle dish.................................12.50
Minnesota, tumbler, water.............................17.50
Minor Block, see Mascotte
Mirror, see Galloway
Missouri, celery vase...................................30.00
Missouri, mug, gr..45.00
Missouri, wine...40.00
Moon & Star, carafe.....................................45.00
Moon & Star, compote, w/lid, high std, 8" 70.00
Moon & Star, goblet....................................35.00
Moon & Star, spill holder.............................50.00
Morning Glory, compote, sauce-dish base, Sandwich, 5x8" 100.00
Morning Glory, egg cup, Sandwich 90.00
Nail, bowl, flat, ruby stained, etched, 6" 47.50
Nail, butter dish 75.00
Nail, cordial 44.00
Nail, tumbler, ruby stained 65.00
Nail, wine..50.00
Nailhead, butter dish 48.00
Nailhead, goblet..24.00
Nailhead, pitcher, flint, 9½"..........................200.00
Nailhead, wine..22.00
New England Pineapple, compote, flint, 4x7".......80.00
New England Pineapple, sugar bowl, w/lid, flint......125.00
New England Pineapple, wine, flint...................140.00
New Hampshire, carafe.................................65.00
New Hampshire, goblet, rose stained 48.00
New Hampshire, punch cup 8.50
New Hampshire, vase, gold trim.......................22.00
New Jersey, goblet......................................32.00
New Jersey, plate, 11"..................................25.00
New Jersey, sauce dish, flat, clear w/gold, 4¼" 10.00
Notched Rib, see Broken Column
Oak Leaf Band, goblet 35.00
Oak Leaf Band, relish 12.00
Oaken Bucket, see Wooden Pail
One Hundred & One, creamer, 4¾" 37.50
One Hundred & One, pitcher, water; bulbous...........115.00
One Hundred & One, sauce dish 18.00
One-O-One, see One Hundred & One
Open Rose, compote, 7½"...............................35.00
Open Rose, pitcher, water 175.00
Open Rose, sugar bowl, w/lid...........................45.00
Open Rose, tumbler.....................................48.00
Oregon, bowl, 2½x7¾"..................................14.00
Oregon, butter dish.....................................55.00
Oregon, creamer, ruby stained 42.50
Oregon, mug, ftd..40.00
Oregon, relish tray, 7½x3¾"............................12.00
Oregon, spooner, ruby stained 58.00
Oregon, tumbler, water; ruby stained 38.00
Oriental, tumbler, water 32.00
Orion, see Cathedral
Palmette, champagne....................................70.00
Palmette, creamer 55.00
Palmette, spooner 32.00
Panelled Daisy, bowl, berry; oval, 8¼x5¾"...........22.00
Panelled Daisy, creamer.................................45.00
Panelled Daisy, goblet...................................27.50
Panelled Dewdrop, butter dish 65.00

Panelled Dewdrop, cordial, 3¼" 30.00
Panelled Dewdrop, sugar bowl, w/lid..................40.00
Panelled Diamond Cut & Fan, see Hartley
Panelled Forget-Me-Not, cake stand, amber, 10" 75.00
Panelled Forget-Me-Not, creamer......................32.00

Panelled Forget-Me-Not

Panelled Forget-Me-Not, pitcher, milk 48.00
Panelled Herringbone, see Florida
Panelled Star & Button, creamer 28.00
Panelled Star & Button, goblet.........................25.00
Panelled Star & Button, spooner........................25.00
Panelled Thistle, butter dish 60.00
Panelled Thistle, candy dish, ftd, sq, 6¼x5"...........35.00
Panelled Thistle, sugar bowl, w/lid....................30.00
Pavonia, compote, jelly.................................40.00
Pavonia, spooner..40.00
Pavonia, sugar bowl, w/lid..............................60.00
Peerless, see Lady Hamilton
Pennsylvania, butter dish 50.00
Pennsylvania, carafe....................................44.00
Pennsylvania, creamer, clear w/gold, 3" 20.00
Pennsylvania, cruet.....................................50.00
Pennsylvania, toothpick holder, gr....................42.00
Pennsylvania, tumbler, clear w/gold...................30.00
Pennsylvania, tumbler, ruby stained...................50.00
Pennsylvania, tumbler, water...........................25.00
Pennsylvania, wine 17.50
Pillar, goblet...50.00
Pillar, tumbler, ale; 6½".................................45.00
Pillow Encircled, butter dish, ruby rosette 68.00
Pillow Encircled, creamer 30.00
Pillow Encircled, tumbler 18.00
Pineapple & Fan, butter dish...........................38.00
Pineapple & Fan, goblet................................17.50
Pineapple & Fan, tumbler, water; gr...................22.50
Pineapple Stem, see Pavonia
Pioneer, see Westward Ho
Pioneer's Victoria, wine tray 16.00
Pleat & Panel, cake stand, sq, 8" 35.00
Pleat & Panel, finger bowl.............................20.00
Pleat & Panel, pitcher, milk............................35.00
Pleat & Panel, sauce dish, ftd..........................15.00
Pleat & Panel, waste bowl..............................25.00
Plume, bowl, 9¼"..22.00
Plume, relish 27.50
Plume, spooner 25.00
Plume, tumbler, water 38.00
Pointed Thumbprint, see Almond Thumbprint
Polar Bear, butter dish, ruby stained 140.00
Polar Bear, tray, water; frosted, 16"...................185.00
Popcorn, cheese dish...................................180.00

Popcorn, goblet, w/ear 50.00
Popcorn, wine 32.00
Portland, carafe, water 40.00
Portland, punch cup 15.00
Portland, sugar bowl, w/lid 42.00
Portland, syrup 85.00
Post, compote, 13½x7½x7½" 125.00
Powder & Shot, goblet, flint 60.00
Powder & Shot, sugar bowl, w/lid 88.00
Pressed Leaf, champagne 24.00
Pressed Leaf, goblet 22.50
Pressed Leaf, wine 35.00
Primrose, cake stand, bl, 10" 68.00
Primrose, celery vase, amber 35.00
Primrose, creamer 30.00
Primrose, relish tray, 8x5¼" 14.00
Princess Feather, compote, low std, w/lid, 8" 110.00
Princess Feather, goblet 35.00
Princess Feather, honey dish 15.00
Princess Feather, sauce dish, bl, flint 30.00
Priscilla, bowl, shallow, 9" 40.00
Priscilla, creamer 40.00
Prism, creamer 58.00
Prism, tumbler, buttermilk 38.00
Prism w/Diamond Points, butter dish 62.50
Prism w/Diamond Points, compote, high std, w/lid, 6" 88.00
Prism w/Diamond Points, wine 48.00
Pygmy, see Torpedo
Queen Anne, butter dish 60.00
Queen Anne, creamer 40.00
Queen Anne, spooner 38.00
Raindrop, cake plate, bl 45.00
Raindrop, creamer, bl 35.00
Recessed Pillared Red Top, see Nail
Red Block, celery vase, 6½" 85.00
Red Block, goblet 40.00
Red Block, wine 38.00
Red Top, see Button Arches
Reverse Torpedo, basket 70.00
Reverse Torpedo, compote, jelly; w/lid 44.00
Reverse Torpedo, pitcher, water; 10" 155.00
Reverse Torpedo, tumbler 50.00
Ribbed Ivy, champagne 125.00
Ribbed Ivy, compote, low std, 8" 75.00

Ribbed Ivy

Ribbed Ivy, egg cup 32.00
Ribbed Ivy, tumbler, bar 95.00
Ribbed Palm, butter dish 85.00
Ribbed Palm, pitcher, water; 9" 245.00
Ribbed Palm, salt cellar, master 38.00
Ribbon, champagne 95.00
Ribbon, cheese dish 140.00
Ribbon, creamer 50.00

Ribbon, pitcher, water 95.00
Ribbon, salt cellar, ind 6.00
Ribbon, sugar bowl, w/lid 60.00
Ribbon Candy, celery vase 32.00
Ribbon Candy, mug 24.00
Ribbon Candy, spooner 25.00
Ribbon Candy, tumbler 27.50
Ripple, creamer 35.00
Ripple, egg cup 20.00
Ripple, goblet 30.00
Ripple, ice tub 50.00
Ripple, spooner 25.00
Ripple, sugar bowl, w/lid 45.00
Ripple, wine 32.50
Ripple Band, see Ripple
Rising Sun, bowl, master berry; pk trim 32.00
Rising Sun, goblet, gr trim 27.50
Rising Sun, wine 18.00
Rochelle, see Princess Feather
Roman Key, butter dish, frosted 88.00
Roman Key, celery vase, frosted 78.00
Roman Key, creamer 120.00
Roman Key, goblet, frosted 50.00
Roman Key, tumbler, bar; frosted 47.50
Roman Rosette, bread platter, 11x9" 30.00
Roman Rosette, cordial 45.00
Roman Rosette, tumbler, lemonade 30.00
Rose in Snow, bowl, ftd, 7" 35.00
Rose in Snow, butter dish, sq 57.50
Rose in Snow, goblet, bl 35.00
Rose in Snow, pitcher, water 85.00
Rose in Snow, sugar bowl, sq, w/lid 44.00
Rose Sprig, cake stand, bl 70.00
Rose Sprig, compote, amber, oval, 7" 35.00
Rose Sprig, sauce dish, ftd, bl 18.00
Rosette, goblet 25.00
Rosette, pitcher, milk 45.00
Rosette, relish, fish form 12.50
Rosette, waste bowl 27.50
Royal Ivy, see Northwood, Royal Ivy
Royal Oak, see Northwood, Royal Oak
Ruby Thumbprint, see King's Crown
Sandwich Star, compote, low std, 8½" 55.00
Sandwich Star, spill holder 55.00
Sandwich Star, spill holder, clambroth 435.00
Sawtooth, creamer, flint 78.00
Sawtooth, salt cellar, master 17.00
Sawtooth, wine, flint 36.00
Sawtooth Band, see Amazon
Scalloped Daisy Red Top, see Button Arches
Scroll w/Flowers, mustard jar 45.00
Sedan, see Panelled Star & Button
Seneca Loop, see Loop
Sequoia, see Heavy Panelled Finecut
Shell & Jewel, cake stand, 5x10" 45.00
Shell & Jewel, sauce dish 7.50
Shell & Tassel, bowl, rectangular, amber 70.00
Shell & Tassel, pickle dish 20.00
Shell & Tassel, plate, oyster 230.00
Shell & Tassel, spooner, rnd 38.00
Shell & Tassel, sugar bowl, rnd 50.00
Sheraton, compote, w/lid, 8" 36.00
Sheraton, goblet, bl 45.00
Sheraton, pitcher, water; bl 90.00

Sheraton, wine..20.00
Shoshone, compote, jelly 18.00
Shoshone, creamer, amber stained.................48.00
Shoshone, toothpick holder, clear w/gold.......32.00
Shovel, syrup 20.00
Shovel, tumbler 15.00
Shrine, pickle dish 18.00
Shrine, sugar bowl, w/lid 48.00
Shrine, tumbler...38.00
Shuttle, champagne 35.00
Shuttle, punch cup 12.50
Shuttle, see also Greentown, Shuttle
Shuttle, shaker...55.00
Shuttle, wine 20.00
Skilton, butter dish, ruby stained 115.00
Skilton, creamer...32.00
Skilton, shakers, pr 48.00
Skilton, tumbler, ruby stained 38.00
Smocking, compote, low std, 7¾"....................55.00
Smocking, creamer, ind 110.00
Snail, butter dish 85.00
Snail, creamer 50.00

Snail

Snail, pitcher, cider 165.00
Snail, shakers, ruby stained, pr 98.00
Snakeskin & Dot, celery vase............................32.00
Snakeskin & Dot, goblet 32.00
Spirea Band, butter dish 36.00
Spirea Band, goblet, amber...............................30.00
Spirea Band, platter, bl, 10½x8".......................40.00
Spirea Band, wine, vaseline...............................32.00
Sprig, celery vase...38.00
Sprig, pitcher, water..55.00
Sprig, sugar bowl, w/lid 50.00
Star Rosetted, cake stand 36.00
Star Rosetted, relish, 3-hdl 12.50
Star Rosetted, sugar bowl, w/lid 45.00
Stars & Stripes, cordial.....................................12.50
Stars & Stripes, pitcher, water..........................38.00
Stars & Stripes, wine 17.50
States, cocktail, flared.......................................24.00
States, creamer...30.00
States, pitcher, water...55.00
States, toothpick holder 40.00
Stedman, champagne 35.00
Stedman, creamer...30.00
Stedman, syrup, 8¼"...98.00
Stedman, wine 45.00
Stippled Chain, celery vase 38.00
Stippled Chain, egg cup 28.00
Stippled Chain, tumbler....................................18.00
Stippled Forget-Me-Not, cup & saucer 36.00
Stippled Forget-Me-Not, pitcher, milk 38.00

Stippled Grape & Festoon, butter dish 55.00
Stippled Grape & Festoon, compote, high std, 8" 48.00
Stippled Grape & Festoon, sugar bowl, w/lid ...55.00
Stippled Ivy, creamer 36.00
Stippled Ivy, egg cup 28.00
Stippled Ivy, salt cellar, master 25.00
Stippled Ivy, sugar bowl, w/lid 36.00
Stippled Panelled Flower, see Maine
Strawberry, creamer 66.00
Strawberry, goblet..42.50
Strawberry, wine 98.00
Sunburst, plate, 7"... 9.00
Sunk Honeycomb, cup & saucer, ruby stained....36.00
Sunk Honeycomb, shakers, pr 14.00
Sunk Honeycomb, shakers, ruby stained, pr 40.00
Sunken Primrose, see Florida
Swan, compote, 8½" 55.00
Swan, creamer 45.00
Swan, mug, ftd 25.00
Swan, sugar bowl, w/lid 125.00
Swirl, see Jersey Swirl
Tape Measure, sauce dish, 4" 7.50
Teardrop & Diamond Block, see Art
Teardrop & Tassel, goblet 135.00
Teardrop & Tassel, relish 40.00
Teardrop & Tassel, sauce dish 18.00
Teardrop & Tassel, see also Greentown, Teardrop & Tassel
Teardrop & Tassel, tumbler...............................38.00
Texas, creamer, ind 18.00
Texas, cruet 68.00
Texas, wine, ruby stained 98.00
Theatrical, see Actress
Thousand Eye, cake stand, 3-knob stem, gr 60.00
Thousand Eye, compote, low std, amber, 9" 35.00
Thousand Eye, creamer, vaseline, ind 42.50
Thousand Eye, egg cup, gr 88.00
Thousand Eye, pitcher, water; 1-gal 85.00
Thousand Eye, spooner, vaseline 44.00
Thousand Eye, sugar bowl, w/lid, vaseline 60.00
Thousand Eye, toothpick holder, amber 35.00
Three Face, bread plate......................................80.00
Three Face, butter dish....................................120.00
Three Face, cake stand, 10"............................150.00
Three Face, cake stand, 11"............................165.00
Three Face, celery vase 85.00
Three Face, champagne, saucer type................150.00
Three Face, claret 150.00
Three Face, compote, w/lid, 10"......................235.00
Three Face, compote, w/lid, 6x4½"...................75.00
Three Face, compote, w/lid, 8½x6".................145.00
Three Face, compote, 7½x6"..............................75.00
Three Face, creamer, mask spout......................130.00
Three Face, goblet..85.00
Three Face, pitcher, water; clear & frosted 450.00
Three Face, salt cellar..48.00
Three Face, spooner...85.00
Three Face, sugar bowl, w/lid 120.00
Three Face, wine 98.00
Thumbprint, see Argus
Thumbprint Band, see Dakota
Thunderbird, see Hummingbird
Torpedo, butter dish..88.00
Torpedo, cup & saucer 60.00
Torpedo, goblet, ruby stained 80.00

Torpedo, pitcher, ruby stained, 8½" 140.00
Torpedo, spooner...45.00
Torpedo, tumbler, water..38.00
Torpedo, tumbler, water; ruby stained 45.00
Tree of Life, bread tray...42.00
Tree of Life, compote, sgn PG Co, 7¾" 78.00
Tree of Life, goblet..45.00
Tree of Life, salt cellar, ftd, gr opaque 98.00
Tree of Life, waste bowl 15.00
Triangular Prism, goblet.......................................18.00
Triple Triangle, creamer, ruby stained 50.00
Triple Triangle, sugar bowl, w/lid..........................80.00
Triple Triangle, wine, ruby stained 45.00
Truncated Cube, creamer, ind 20.00
Truncated Cube, goblet 28.00
Truncated Cube, spooner, ruby stained 48.00
Truncated Cube, wine...36.00
Tulip w/Sawtooth, celery vase, flint 75.00
Tulip w/Sawtooth, champagne 38.00
Tulip w/Sawtooth, decanter, w/bar lip, flint, pt........70.00
Tulip w/Sawtooth, tumbler, flint 32.00
Two Panel, butter dish, amber 50.00
Two Panel, celery vase 24.00
Two Panel, pitcher, water; apple gr........................58.00
Two Panel, spooner, amber 36.00
US Coin, bowl, frosted, 6"....................................225.00
US Coin, cake stand, 10" 235.00
US Coin, champagne, frosted 385.00
US Coin, compote, low std, frosted, 7" 400.00
US Coin, creamer, frosted 350.00
US Coin, mug, frosted 295.00
US Coin, pitcher, water...395.00
US Coin, pitcher, water; frosted.............................575.00
US Coin, spooner 225.00
US Coin, sugar bowl, w/lid, frosted........................400.00
Valencia Waffle, celery vase, yel 36.00
Valencia Waffle, goblet...25.00
Valencia Waffle, pitcher, water; amber 66.00
Valencia Waffle, tumbler, ruby stained 32.00
Vermont, bowl, berry; gr w/gold............................40.00
Vermont, goblet, clear w/gold 45.00
Vermont, see also Custard Glass
Vermont, tumbler 18.00
Viking, butter dish 65.00
Viking, egg cup 38.00
Viking, sugar bowl, w/lid 65.00
Waffle, creamer, ftd..48.00
Waffle, sweetmeat, Sandwich, pr, NM...................175.00
Waffle, tumbler, bar 70.00
Waffle & Thumbprint, egg cup, flint.......................32.00
Waffle & Thumbprint, goblet.................................60.00
Waffle & Thumbprint, tumbler, whiskey; flint 80.00
Washington, claret, flint 140.00
Washington, pitcher, water; flint 245.00
Washington, salt cellar, master; rnd 30.00
Washington Centennial, butter dish........................88.00
Washington Centennial, champagne........................45.00
Washington Centennial, salt cellar, master...............27.50
Wedding Bells, creamer, 4-ftd................................50.00
Wedding Bells, punch cup 17.50
Wedding Bells, spooner...32.00
Wedding Bells, wine 22.50
Wedding Ring, creamer 80.00
Wedding Ring, sauce dish......................................24.00

Wedding Ring, syrup 97.50
Wedding Ring, tumbler 80.00
Westward Ho, butter dish......................................185.00
Westward Ho, celery vase......................................130.00
Westward Ho, creamer...130.00
Westward Ho, mug, rare, 2"...................................225.00
Wheat & Barley, bowl, flat, w/lid, 8".......................40.00
Wheat & Barley, butter dish, bl.............................75.00
Wheat & Barley, pitcher, milk; bl 67.50

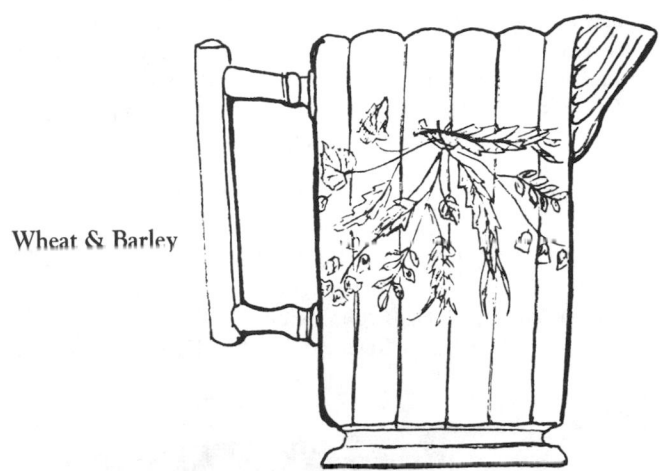

Wheat & Barley

Wheat & Barley, salt cellar, bl...............................37.50
Wheat & Barley, shakers, bl, pr.............................95.00
Wheat & Barley, tumbler 22.00
Wildflower, creamer, amber...................................38.00
Wildflower, pitcher, water 50.00
Wildflower, pitcher, water; amber 55.00
Willow Oak, bowl, w/lid, 7"...................................40.00
Willow Oak, creamer, amber..................................36.00
Willow Oak, sugar bowl, w/lid 40.00
Windflower, celery vase 42.00
Windflower, egg cup 22.50
Windflower, wine 30.00
Wisconsin, cup & saucer 45.00
Wisconsin, pickle dish 25.00
Wisconsin, toothpick holder 40.00
Wooden Pail, creamer, amethyst 80.00
Wooden Pail, spooner, vaseline..............................50.00
Wooden Pail, sugar bowl, amethyst, mini................24.00
X-Ray, butter dish, emerald gr................................70.00
X-Ray, pitcher, water 38.00
X-Ray, toothpick holder 30.00
Yale, cake stand, 9"...50.00
Yale, goblet..35.00
Yale, tumbler 18.00
Zipper, cheese dish 50.00
Zipper, goblet 18.00
Zipper, wine 20.00
Zippered Block, creamer, ruby stained 80.00
Zippered Block, goblet, ruby stained 55.00
Zippered Block, shakers, pr...................................95.00
Zippered Block, sugar bowl, w/lid, ruby stained........100.00
Zippered Block, tumbler, ruby stained 48.00

Paul Revere Pottery

The Saturday Evening Girls were a social group of young Boston ladies who met to pursue various activities, among them pottery making. Their first kiln was bought in 1906, and within a few years it became necessary to move to a larger location. Because their new quarters were near the historical Old North Church, they chose the name Paul Revere Pottery. With very little training, the girls produced only simple ware. Until 1915 the pottery operated at a deficit; then a new building with four kilns was constructed on Nottingham Road. Vases, miniature jugs, children's tea sets, tiles, dinnerware, and lamps were produced, usually in soft matt glazes often decorated with incised, hand-painted designs from nature. Occasional examples in a dark high gloss may also be found.

Several marks were used: 'P.R.P.'; 'S.E.G.'; or the circular device, 'Boston, Paul Revere Pottery' with the horse and rider.

The pottery continued to operate; and, even though their product sold well, the high production costs of the handmade ware caused the pottery to fail in 1946.

Bowl, bl w/chartreuse pockmarks, PRP, 5" **45.00**
Bowl, duck band, wht/gr on bl, SEG/AP, 4" **250.00**
Bowl, gr w/beige rim, SEG, +6⅜" undertray **175.00**
Bowl, gr/gray/cream, Greek Key rim, SEG/FL/449-5-11, 6¾" **175.00**
Bowl, Midnight Ride of Paul Revere, PRP/LS/6-41, 7" **1,900.00**

Bowl, white geese and foliage on blue and green, signed 'SEG A.M. 7-15,' hairline, 5" x 11½", $600.00.

Compote, gun metal, PRP paper label, 12½" dia..........................110.00
Cup & saucer, bl-gr, no decor, PRP.......................................85.00
Cup plate, chick border on cream/yel/blk, unmk, 4¼", EX.........150.00
Egg cup, chick on bl & wht, RTP, SEG/CGT105/5-22, +plate...185.00
Egg cup, chick on mustard yel, unmk, EX................................100.00
Lamp base, dusty rose, SEG/22, 13".....................................325.00
Paperweight, incised figure of P Revere, SEG/TL/7-14, 3" dia.....150.00
Paperweight, swans on bl & wht, octagonal, SEG/7-17, 2½".......225.00
Paperweight, wht bird on bl, sgn, 2½" dia 150.00
Pitcher, hen/chick band w/motto on bl, SEG, 4" 550.00
Planter, irid frieze, bl/gr on bl, SEG/12-18, rpr, 5x9½" L 650.00
Plate, chicks, pk/bl/blk, SEG/EGT/11-17, EX 175.00
Plate, pine cone border, 5-color, SEG/EGT/9-17, 8⅜" 375.00
Plate, rabbits on bl band, SEG/LS, 6" 325.00
Plate, 8 pigs in band, HOS monogram, SEG/FL, 8½" 1,200.00
Teapot, bl & wht, 4⅞", +creamer+handleless cup, SEG, child's..200.00
Trivet, geometrics on gr/brn/bl, sq, SEG/AM/3-14, 5¼" 175.00
Vase, dk bl, molding at rim, paper label, 4⅝" 100.00
Vase, sand beige, bulbous, long slim neck, ftd, PRP/437, 8⅝"........75.00
Vase, scenic band at shoulder on tan, SEG, 4½" 700.00
Vase, tulip band, yel/blk on dk gr, PRP, 4"..................................550.00
Vase, turq, gourd form, SEG/2-19, 4⅛".....................................100.00

Pauline Pottery

Pauline Pottery was made from 1883 to 1888 in Chicago, Ill., from clay imported from the Ohio area. Its founder was Mrs. Pauline Jacobus, who had learned the trade at the Rookwood Pottery. Mrs. Jacobus moved to Edgerton, Wisconsin, to be near a source of suitable clay, thus eliminating shipping expenses. Until 1905 she produced high-quality wares, able to imitate with ease designs and styles of such masters as Wedgwood and Meissen. Her products were sold through leading department stores, and the names of some of these firms may appear on the ware. Not all were marked; and, unless signed by a noted local artist, positive identification is often impossible. Marked examples carry a variety of stamps and signatures: 'Trade Mark' with a crown, 'Pauline Pottery,' and 'Edgerton Art Pottery' are but a few.

Bowl, dogwood on dusty red, trefoil w/3 loop hdls, 9½", EX 150.00
Bowl, yel roses on yel semi-gloss, 3½x9½"...............................250.00
Jug, bamboo reeds, gold on cobalt, 2-spout, 9x9" 200.00
Pitcher, floral, bulbous, ornate hdl, 10" 650.00

Teapot, floral, gold trim, EX, $265.00.

Vase, dk gr drip on dk bl gloss, crown mk, 3½x5" 190.00
Vase, gold-traced bl flowers w/gr leaves, sgn Edwards, 12"...........600.00

Peachblow

Peachblow, made to imitate the colors of the Chinese Peachbloom porcelain, was made by several glasshouses in the late 1800s. Among them were New England Glass; Mt. Washington; Webb; and Hobbs, Brockunier, and Company. Its pink shading was achieved through action of the heat on the gold content of the glass. While New England's peachblow shades from pink to cool white, Mt. Washington's tends to shade from peach to ivory. Although usually glossy, a satin (or acid) finish was also produced, and many pieces were enameled and gilded. In the 1950s, Gunderson-Pairpoint Glassworks initiated the reproduction of Mt. Washington peachblow using an exact duplication of the original formula. Though of recent manufacture, this glass is very collectible. In the listings that follow, the finish is glossy unless noted acid.

Our advisors for this category are Betty and Clarence Maier; they are listed in the Directory under Pennsylvania.

Biscuit jar, gold prunus/mums/butterfly/spider, Webb, 6" 500.00

Biscuit jar, peacock/flowers, mk Meriden Co lid #1569, 7" 550.00
Bottle, scent; florals/butterfly, gold-tone top, Webb, 6x5"............750.00
Bowl, gold prunus flowers/insects, int: butterfly, Webb, 5"..........500.00
Compote, Morning-Glory, baluster stem, Gundersen, 5x5½" 385.00
Cruet, amber twisted hdl & stopper, 6½".....................................650.00
Cruet, wine; florals, French, 11x3⅞"...450.00
Cup & saucer, wht reeded hdl, Gunderson, 2¾x3½" 255.00
Decanter, reeded shell hdl, bulbous, Gunderson, 10x4½" 785.00
Ewer, acid, frosted amber stopper/twist hdls, Wheeling, 9½" 700.00
Ewer, amber rigaree, amber reeded hdl, Wheeling, 10½"........ 2,000.00
Finger bowl, acid, NE Glass, 4¼" dia 375.00
Finger bowl, acid, ruffled, NE Glass, 5"......................................425.00
Finger bowl, florals, ruffled, 2⅞x5"...165.00
Goblet, appl ft, Gunderson...265.00
Jam dish, gold prunus & butterfly, Webb, silver wire fr, 6" 500.00
Mustard jar, acid, pewter lift lid, Wheeling, 2½" 350.00
Mustard jar, ovoid, SP lid, Wheeling, 4½"...................................375.00
Pear, wht cased, Wheeling, ¾" stem, 6¾" 750.00
Pitcher, appl clear hdl, bulbous, 3½x2⅜".....................................295.00
Pitcher, Lincoln Drape, clear reeded hdl, Wheeling, 5½" 600.00
Pitcher, petticoat form, NE Glass, 4½x5"....................................665.00
Pitcher, sq top, Wheeling, 4½"..750.00
Pitcher, sq top, wht hdl, NE Glass, 4½x4¾".................................575.00
Punch cup, appl wht hdl, NE Glass...400.00
Punch cup, ring hdl, Wheeling, 2½x2⅝".......................................300.00
Rose bowl, NE Glass, 4x4"..500.00
Rose bowl, World's Fair, 1893, ribbed, 2½" 325.00
Rose bowl, 8-crimp, cream int, 3x3⅛"...225.00
Shaker, salt; acid, rnd, Wheeling, 2¼" 350.00
Shakers, ribbed, Mt WA, in mk Pairpoint holder 1,600.00
Sherbet, Gunderson..150.00
Spooner, ruffled top, NE Glass, 1880s, 5x3¼" 725.00
Sugar bowl, baluster stem, Gunderson, 3½x4½"............................265.00
Sugar bowl, Wheeling, 2¾x4¼"...400.00
Sugar shaker, gold-tone top, Wheeling 850.00
Sweetmeat, gold prunus/butterfly, cream int, Webb, 4½" 450.00
Toothpick, acid, Wheeling, 2½" 650.00
Toothpick, sq top, NE Glass..450.00
Toothpick, Wheeling, 2½".. 1,500.00
Toothpick, yel coralene seaweed, sq top, 3" 1,500.00
Tumbler, Wheeling, 3¼x2¾"..300.00
Vase, acid, florals w/gold, ruffled, Webb, 11¼", pr 1,200.00
Vase, amber rigaree at stick neck, Wheeling, 8".............................625.00
Vase, birds & flowers, Webb propellor mk, 5x3½"..........................495.00
Vase, dainty floral in brn, heavy gold leaves, Webb, 5", pr 650.00
Vase, gold & silver florals, hdls, Webb, 4½x2½" 365.00
Vase, gold & silver florals, 5", pr...650.00
Vase, gold daisies/leaves/dragonfly, Webb, 7x5¼" 600.00
Vase, gold florals/dragonfly/band, cylindrical, 7x3¼"...................375.00
Vase, gold prunus/lg butterfly, Webb, 8".......................................375.00
Vase, Gunderson, 6½x3¾"..150.00
Vase, raised wht stripes, rolled rim, NE Glass, 2½x2¾" 325.00
Vase, rose bands at shoulder, Gunderson, 6½x3¾" 145.00
Vase, stick neck, NE Glass, 8x4"..885.00
Vase, stick neck, Wheeling, 11" 1,050.00

Peking Glass

The first glasshouse was established in Peking in 1680. It produced glassware made in imitation of porcelain, a more desirable medium to the Chinese. By 1725 multi-layered carving that resulted in a cameo effect lead to the manufacture of a wider range of shapes and colors. The factory was closed from 1736 to 1795, but glass made in Po-shan

and shipped to Peking for finishing continued to be called Peking glass. In addition to the cameo ware, other types were made as well. See also Orientalia; Snuff Bottles.

Bowl, crane/pine trees, gr on wht, 6½" 150.00
Bowl, honeycomb cvg, aqua, 6½" dia 75.00
Jar, horses cvd on yel, fungus clouds on lid, bulbous, 7" 275.00
Vase, crane in pine tree, gr on wht, baluster, 12" 350.00
Vase, cranes/peonies, gr on wht, Ching mk, 14", pr 950.00

Vase, dragons and flaming pearls in high relief, translucent turquoise on white, 12", $2,750.00 for the pair.

Vase, ducks/lotus flowers, red on wht, 9x6", pr............................450.00
Vase, fish amid lotus, red on wht, baluster, ca 1900, 13" 900.00
Vase, flowers/butterfly cvd on dk yel, 14" 250.00
Vase, honeycomb pattern, cobalt cut to wht, 10".........................350.00
Vase, leaves berries, red on wht, ca 1900, 9" 550.00
Vase, peonies, gr on wht, slim form, 12" 250.00
Vase, phoenix birds/sacred fungus clouds, red/wht, late, 10"........150.00
Vase, prunus limbs/narcissus, red on wht, baluster, 9", pr............375.00
Vase, rvpt, 3 flying cranes/pine trees, 12" 85.00
Vase, squirrels/tree cvd on yel, late, 8" 100.00

Peloton

Peloton glass was first made by Wilhelm Kralik in Bohemia in 1880. This unusual art glass was produced by rolling colored threads onto the transparent or opaque glass gather as it was removed from the furnace. Usually more than one color of threading was used, and some items were further decorated with enameling. It was made with both shiny and acid finishes.

Rose bowl, lav-pk, mc strings, oval top, 2¾x3⅜" 195.00
Rose bowl, pk cased, mc strings, clear wishbone ft, 3x2¾"...........225.00
Rose bowl, wht cased, mc strings, wht int, 2⅜" 210.00
Rose bowl, wht opaque, mc strings, clear ft, 4⅛x3½" 195.00
Vase, clear, wht strings, 3⅛"..130.00
Vase, clear w/mc strings, 5 wishbone ft, ruffled, 6½x4"...............455.00
Vase, lav to wht, crystal cased, vertical ribs, 6x4½" 450.00
Vase, mauve cased, mc strings, corset shaped, 6x4½"...................450.00
Vase, mc strings, clear rigaree, 4-point top, 3¾"..........................245.00
Vase, mc strings on ivory, cloverleaf top, 3½" 185.00
Vase, wht, mc strings, corset shape, crimped, 6"..........................450.00
Vase, wht, mc strings, 3-side folded rim, bulb body, 4x5" 295.00

Vase, wht, pastel strings, ribbed, folded-in top, 5"........................325.00
Vase, wht, pastel strings, 5 wishbone ft, ribbed, 7x4" 450.00

Pennsbury

New in the collectibles market, Pennsbury Pottery is drawing quite a following! Established in the 1950s in Morrisville, Pennsylvania, by Henry Below, the company produced dinnerware and novelty items, much of which was sold in gift shops along the Pennsylvania Turnpike. Henry and his wife, Lee, worked for years at the Stangl Pottery before striking out on their own. Lee and her daughter were the artists responsible for many of the early pieces, the birds among them. Pennsbury pottery was hand painted, some in blue on white, some in multicolors on caramel. Pennsylvania Dutch motifs, Amish couples, and barber shop singers were among their most popular decorative themes. Sgraffito, or hand incising, was used extensively. The company marked their wares 'Pennsbury Pottery' or 'Pennsbury Pottery, Morrisville, PA.'

In October of 1969 the company closed; contents of the pottery were sold in December of the following year, and in April of 1971, the buildings burned to the ground. Items marked Pennsbury Glenview or Stumar pottery (or these marks in combination) were made by Glenview after 1969. Pieces manufactured after 1976 were made by the Pennington Pottery. Several of the old molds still exist, and the original Pennsbury Caramel process is still being used on novelty items, some of which are produced by Lewis Brothers, N.J. Pennsbury dinnerware was not continued after the closing. For those wishing to learn more, we recommend *Pennsbury Pottery Video Book 1* and accompanying 1987-88 price guide offered by our advisor Shirley Graff and BA Wellman. He is listed in the Directory under Massachusetts; Mrs. Graff is in Ohio.

Ash tray, Blk Rooster, scalloped, 8"...20.00
Ash tray, Hex, scalloped, 8"..25.00
Ash tray, Lafayette, Baltimore & Ohio RR, oval, 7¾x5¾"............45.00
Ash tray, What Ouches You, rnd...18.00
Bookend, eagle figural, 8¼", pr...75.00
Bowl, divided vegetable; Blk Rooster, 6x9½"................................45.00
Bowl, fruit; Hex, 5"...12.00
Bowl, Red Rooster, 9" 25.00
Bowl, salad; Folkart, 13"...35.00
Bowl, vegetable; rooster, 9½"...30.00
Butter dish, Bird over Heart 30.00
Butter dish, Three Tulips 28.00
Candlestick, hen & rooster figural, rare, 5", pr 75.00
Canister, Folkart, 7½" 48.00
Casserole, Blk Rooster, bulbous, ind...28.00
Casserole, Red Rooster, cylinder, w/lid, 5" dia 35.00
Cigarette box, Hex, 2½x4½"...15.00
Coaster, fish pattern, pretzel shape 18.00
Coffeepot, Hex, 6-cup, 8½"...50.00
Compote, Red Rooster, ftd, 5"...22.00
Creamer & sugar bowl, Amish or Hex, 6", ea set...........................22.00
Cruets, oil & vinegar; Amish, pr...125.00
Cruets, oil & vinegar; Gay Nineties, pr 125.00
Cup & saucer, Hex 15.00
Cup & saucer, Rooster 22.00
Desk basket, Nat'l Enchange Club 30.00
Figurine, Blue Jay...45.00
Figurine, Cardinal..75.00
Figurine, Redstart, 2¾x3½"..45.00
Gravy boat, Folkart...25.00
Mug, beer; Nottingham Fire Co, Oct 19, 1968..............................22.00
Mug, eagle w/banner, 4½"...22.00
Mug, pretzel; Amish..22.00

Mug, Swallow the Insult..22.00
Pen holder, Eagle 45.00
Pie plate, Hex Star..30.00
Pitcher, eagle w/E Pluribus Unum, 6½"...45.00
Pitcher, Folkart, 2½"...12.00
Pitcher, Tulip, 2-qt, 7¼" 55.00
Pitcher, Yel Flower, ½-pt, 3¾" 18.00
Plaque, eagle & ribbon, 6x8"...38.00

Plaque, 8", $35.00.

Plate, Blk Rooster, 10" 25.00
Plate, Christmas, 1970, 8" 25.00
Plate, Folkart or Hex, 6" 6.00
Plate, Homestead, 11" 28.00
Plate, Picking Apples, 8" 20.00
Platter, fish; bl & wht, rnd..30.00
Platter, Hex, 14x11" 30.00
Shakers, Hex, hdls, pr...20.00
Ship, Constitution, med sz 40.00
Ship, steam boat, lg 45.00
Snack set (cup & tray), Folkart or Hex...18.00
Teapot, Blk Rooster, 4-cup..35.00
Tile, Come in w/o Knocking, rnd, 6" 18.00
Tile, You Could Be a Real Stinker, skunk, rnd, 6" 18.00
Tray, Laurel Ridge...25.00
Wall pocket, bellows, 6½x6½"..35.00
Wall pocket, 2 birds over heart, 6½x6½" 35.00

Pens and Pencils

The first metallic writing pen was patented in 1809, and soon machine-produced pens with steel nibs gradually began replacing the quill. The first fountain pen was invented in 1830; but, due to the fact that a suitable metal for the tips had not yet been developed, they were not manufactured commercially until the 1880s. The first successful commercial producers were Waterman in 1884 and Parker with the Lucky Curve in 1888.

The self-filling pen of 1890 featured the soft, interior sack which filled with ink as the metal bar on the outside of the pen was raised and lowered. Variations of the pumping mechanism were tried until 1932 when Parker introduced the Vacumatic, a sackless pen with an internal pump.

Our advisors for this category are Judy and Cliff Lawrence; they are listed in the Directory under Florida. For those seeking additional information, a magazine is published monthly by the Pen Fancier's Club, whose address can be found in the Directory under Clubs, Newsletters, and Catalogs. In the listings that follow, all pens are lever-filled unless otherwise noted.

Key:
AF — aeromatic filler	GPT — gold-plated trim
BF — button filler	HR — hard rubber
CF — cartridge filler	LF — lever filler
CPT — chrome-plated trim	NPT — nickel-plated trim
ED — eyedropper filler	TD — touchdown filler
GFM — gold-filled metal	VF — vacuumatic filler

Ballpoint Pens

Eberhard Faber, 1946, brn/GF cap, EX 65.00
Eversharp, CA, 1946, bl/GF cap, M 95.00
Eversharp, CA, 1947, GFM, EX..125.00
Eversharp, Skyline, CA, 1944, maroon w/striped cap, EX.............50.00
Eversharp, Skyline, CA, 1948, brn/gold striped cap, M 50.00
Reynolds, International, 1945, aluminum, GF clip, EX 150.00
Reynolds, Rocket, 1946, aluminum/chrome clip, EX 85.00
Sheaffer, Stratowriter, 1946, GFM, M..95.00

Fountain Pens

Aiken Lambert, Ebony Beakon Stylographic, 1910, HR, ED, EX ..99.00
Conklin, Crescent Filler #50, 1919, blk-chased HR, EX 395.00
Conklin, Glider, 1940, emerald/pearl marble, M 60.00
Conklin, Glider, 1940, gold/silver marble, LF, EX 40.00
Eversharp, Skyline Presentation, 1946, maroon, GF cap, EX 75.00
F Phaspel, Stylographic, 1910, blk-chased HR, ED, EX..................80.00
John Holland, Hatchet Filler #76, 1918, blk-chased HR, EX 450.00
Moore, #72, 1925, pearl/blk marble, EX.......................................49.00
Parker, Bl Diamond 51, blk, sterling silver cap, VF, EX................150.00
Parker, Bl Diamond 51, 1942, brn, aluminum cap, VF, EX..........125.00
Parker, Challenger, 1935, red pearl, EX.......................................55.00
Parker, Debutante Vacumatic, 1941, gold w/pearl stripe, EX 50.00
Parker, Duofold Jr, 1928, lapis bl marbled, BF, EX 150.00
Parker, Duofold Sr, Big Red, 1924, red HR, BF, EX 395.00
Parker, Heritage 61, 1956, blk, 2-tone rainbow cap, CF, EX 175.00
Parker, Jack Knife Safety #20, 1920, blk HR, EX..........................75.00
Parker, Jack Knife Safety #24, 1919, blk HR w/14k gold, BF, EX .525.00
Parker, Lady Duofold, 1924, red HR, BF, EX................................85.00
Parker, Lady Duofold, 1927, blk HR, BF, EX................................55.00
Parker, Lucky Curve, vest pocket, 1920, GFM, BF, EX 595.00
Parker, Super 21, 1960, gray, chrome cap, CPT, alloy nib, AF, M ..30.00
Parker, Vacumatic, 1934, burgundy w/pearl stripe, VF, EX 200.00
Parker, 51, 1948, bl, Lustraloy top, CPT, M 65.00
Sheaffer, Admiral Snorkel, 1955, gr, TD, M 42.00
Sheaffer, Demonstrater #5-30, 1925, wavy blk HR, EX................225.00
Sheaffer, Feathertouch 500, 1938, gold pearl striped, EX 50.00
Sheaffer, Lifetime, 1925, jade gr marble, EX...............................250.00
Sheaffer, Lifetime Balance Pen, 1932, blk, EX 250.00
Sheaffer, Triumph 500, 1947, red w/pearl stripe, EX......................75.00
Sheaffer, Tuckaway 875, 1948, brn, pump filler, M 60.00
Swan, 1899, blk-chased HR, overfeed nib, ED, EX 250.00
Wahl, 1925, GFM, miniature, EX 42.00
Waterman, Emblem, 1943, blk, EX 195.00
Waterman, Ideal, Patrician, 1932, Nacre, NPT, EX 695.00
Waterman, Ideal #0552½V, 1925, eng GFM, EX 150.00
Waterman, Ideal #14, 1910, blk chased HR, ED, EX 199.00
Waterman, Ideal #52½V, 1918, blk-chased HR, NPT, EX............40.00
Waterman, Ideal #94, 1937, silver/red marble, NPT, EX 125.00

Mechanical Pencils

Eversharp, Repeating Prototype, 1934, GFM, NM 225.00
Jackwin, 1932, pearl/blk marble, M..49.00
Moore, Repeater, 1940, gold-tone metal, EX 25.00
Norma, Super 4-Color, 1935, GFM, EX......................................100.00
Parker, Challenger, 1930, emerald marble, EX...............................32.00
Parker, Duofold Sr, 'Big Bro,' 1924, red HR, EX 195.00
Parker, Duofold Sr, 1932, burgundy/blk marble, EX 175.00
Parker, Duofold Sr, 1932, jade gr marble, EX..............................155.00
Parker, Duofold Sr Deluxe, 1932, Moderne Gr & pearl, EX 160.00
Parker, 1934, silver/blk marble, NPT, EX.....................................35.00
Parker, 51 Demi-Size Repeater, 1948, gray, GF top, EX 30.00
Parker, 51 Repeater, 1954, beige, GF top, M 35.00
Sheaffer, Golf, 1932, pearl/blk marble, EX....................................55.00
Sheaffer, Lifetime, 1925, GFM, EX 32.00
Sheaffer, Lifetime, 1927, jade gr marble, EX................................165.00
Sheaffer, Wht Dot Crest, 1956, blk, GF top, EX............................18.00
Sheaffer, 350, 1938, emerald w/pearl stripe, EX 20.00
Wahl-Eversharp, 1922, blk-chased HR, EX...................................50.00
Wahl-Eversharp, 1925, red-chased HR, EX...................................99.00
Waterman, Ideal, 1925, red mottled HR, EX 95.00
Waterman, Ideal, 1926, olive ripple HR, EX 95.00
Waterman, Stateleigh, 1945, bl, GF top, M 45.00

Sets

Parker, VS, 1947, rust, Lustraloy caps, BF, EX pen/M pencil..........70.00
Parker, 61 Signet, 1960, GFM, CF, EX..190.00
Sheaffer, Feathertouch, 1938, gold w/pearl stripe, EX 95.00
Sheaffer, PFM, 1959, maroon, silver nib, CPT, TD, M 150.00
Sheaffer, Wht Dot Crest Triumph, 1949, blk, GF cap, TD, EX....115.00
Sheaffer, Wht Dot Sentinel Triumph Snorkel, 1954, TD, M 99.00
Sheaffer, Wht Dot Triumph, 1951, gr, TD, M..............................90.00
Sheaffer, Wht Dot Triumph Snorkel, 1954, orange, TD, M...........99.00

Personalities, Fact and Fiction

One of the largest and most popular areas of collecting today, if trade-paper ads and articles be any indication, is character-related memorabilia. Everyone has favorites, whether they be comic-strip personalities or true-life heroes. The earliest comic strip dealt with the adventures of the Yellow Kid, the smiling, bald-headed Oriental boy always in a nightshirt. He was introduced in 1895, a product of the imagination of Richard Fenton Outcault. Today, though very hard to come by, items relating to the Yellow Kid bring premium prices.

In 1902 Buster Brown and Tige, his dog and constant companion (more of Outcault's progenies), made it big in the comics as well as in the world of advertising. Shoe stores appealed to the younger set through merchandising displays that featured them both. Today the items from their earlier years are very collectible.

Though her 1923 introduction was unobtrusively made through only one newspaper, New York's *Daily News,* Little Orphan Annie, the vacant-eyed redhead in the inevitable red dress, was quickly adopted by hordes of readers nationwide; and before the demise of her creator, Harold Gray, in 1968, she starred in her own radio show. She made two feature films, and in 1977 'Annie' was launched on Broadway.

Other early comic figures were Moon Mullins, created in 1923 by Frank Willard; Buck Rogers by Philip Nowlan in 1928; and Betty Boop, the round-faced, innocent-eyed, chubby-cheeked Boop-Boop-a-Doop girl of the early 1930s. Bimbo was her dog and KoKo her clown friend.

Popeye made his debut in 1929 as the spinach-eating sailor with the spindly-limbed girlfriend, Olive Oyl, in the comic strip *Thimble*

Theatre, created by Elzie Segar. He became a film star in 1933 and had his own radio show that during 1936 played three times a week on CBS. He obligingly modeled for scores of toys, dolls, and figurines, and especially those from the thirties are very collectible.

Tarzan, created around 1930 by Edgar Rice Burroughs, and Captain Midnight, by Robert Burtt and Willfred G. Moore, are popular heroes with today's collectors. During the days of radio, Sky King of the Flying Crown Ranch (also created by Burtt and Moore) thrilled boys and girls of the mid-1940s. Hopalong Cassidy, Red Rider, Tom Mix, and the Lone Ranger were only a few of the other 'good guys' always on the side of law and order.

But of all the fictional heroes and comic characters collected today, probably the best loved and most well known is Mickey Mouse. Created in the late 1920s by Walt Disney, Micky (as his name was first spelled) became an instant success with his film debut, Steamboat Willie. His popularity was parlayed through windup toys, watches, figurines, cookie jars, puppets, clothing, and numerous other products. Items from the 1930s are usually copyrighted 'Walt Disney Enterprises'; thereafter, 'Walt Disney Productions' was used. For those interested in Disneyanna, we recommend *Stern's Guide to Disney Collectibles,* available from Collector Books.

Our advisors for this category are Cathy and Norm Vigue; they are listed in the Directory under Massachusetts. See also Autographs; Banks; Big Little Books; Cartoon Books; Children's Books; Comic Books; Cookie Jars; Dolls; Lunch Boxes; Movie Memorabilia; Paper Dolls; Pin-Back Buttons; Posters; Toys.

Addams Family, card game, Milton Bradley, 1965, NM 28.00
Addams Family, Gomez hand puppet, 1965, EX 60.00
Addams Family, jigsaw puzzle, Milton Bradley, 1965, NM 46.00
Alice in Wonderland, phonograph, WDP, RCA, 1950s, EX 48.00
Amos & Andy, ash tray & match holder, plaster, G 25.00
Amos & Andy, puzzle, OK Hotel, premium, orig mailer 45.00
Amos & Andy & Kingfish, cb diecut, 1931, 3x5", 3 for 20.00
Annie Oakley, board game, Milton Bradley, 1950s, EX 32.00
Annie Oakley, costume, 1950s, EX in box 70.00
Atom Ant, kite, 1960s, 38x6" pkg, M 35.00
Bambi & Thumper, planter, ceramic, WDP, 1950s, VG 18.00
Barney Google, color book, 1968, M 10.00
Batman, badge, I'm a Batman Crimefighter, 1966, M on card 18.50
Batman, bank, Batman figural, 1976 ....25.00
Batman, banner, cloth, 1966, M...165.00
Batman, Bat Ray gun, battery operated, MIB 40.00
Batman, Batcave desk lamp, 1977, M 45.00
Batman, Batchute, 42" parachute to mt on bike, M 50.00
Batman, card game, 1966, MIB 35.00
Batman, charm bracelet, 1966, M on card 45.00
Batman, color book, Catwoman cover, Whitman, 1967, NM........18.50
Batman, Colorforms Cartoon Kit, 1976, EX 17.50
Batman, costume, Ben Cooper, 1966, EX 45.00
Batman, doll, Mego, 1976, 12½", MIB...65.00
Batman, doll, Mego, 8", MIB...50.00
Batman, game, Adventures of Caped Crusader, 1973, M 27.50
Batman, gum card set, Topps, 1966, set of 55, NM......................65.00
Batman, hairbrush, Avon, 1976, M...20.00
Batman, mug, ceramic, 1966, M 10.00
Batman, pencil sharpener, figural, 1960s, NM 30.00
Batman, Pepsi glass 15.00
Batman, puppet, 1966, NM...30.00
Batman, radio, 1978, EX..60.00
Batman, sheet, 1960s, twin sz, EX 50.00
Batman, siren, EX in box...25.00
Batman, sticker book, 1966, M 28.00
Batman, talking alarm clock, 1978, NM 60.00

Batman, talking Batmobile, Japan, 1972, MIB..........................145.00
Batman, toothbrush, battery-op, 1974, 7", MIB 15.00
Batman, toothbrush holder 12.50
Batman & Robin, bookends, 1966, 6½", pr....................................225.00
Batman & Robin, flip mask, GE premium, 1966, NM 15.00
Batman & Robin, record, orig die-cut sleeves, pr 25.00
Batman & Robin, table napkins, 10x10", M in pkg........................10.00
Beanie & Cecil, flashlight, M on card 45.00

Beatles, promotional poster for 'Revolver' album, 1966, Capitol Records, 32" x 25", $200.00.

Beatles, belt, Meet the Beatles, plastic buckle, 1960s, M 30.00
Beatles, board game, Flip Your Wig, NM in box 80.00
Beatles, coffee mug, 4 different colors, ea...................................... 6.00
Beatles, color book, 1964, unused 60.00
Beatles, date book w/pictures 20.00
Beatles, diary, unused...25.00
Beatles, dish towel, maroon/blk/wht, 1964, 31x20", EX 125.00
Beatles, George Halloween costume & mask, MIB 145.00
Beatles, John Halloween mask, NM...40.00
Beatles, license plate, 1967, Post, VG...35.00
Beatles, notebook, 3-ring binder, NM...75.00
Beatles, picture sleeve, Can't Buy Me Love 285.00
Beatles, puzzle, Yel Submarine, 19x19", EX in box 35.00
Beatles, record case, cb, for 45 rpm record, VG 75.00
Beatles, Ringo model kit, Revell, unassembled, complete, EX.....165.00
Beatles, scrapbook, 1960s, unused, M 80.00
Beatles, serving tray, metal, pictures/signatures, orig tag 40.00
Beatles, wallet, bl plastic, EX..85.00
Beetle Bailey, board game, 1963, NM...30.00
Beetle Bailey, color book, 1964, M 15.00
Ben Casey, board game, Transogram, EX 30.00
Ben Casey, sweater guard, TV show, 1962, M on card..................15.00
Betty Boop, china set, Fleischer Studios, 1930s, 20-pc, EX.........475.00
Betty Boop, decal sheet, set of 12, 1920s 10.00
Betty Boop, perfume bottle, glass figural, 1930s, 3½" 30.00
Betty Boop & Bimbo, wall pocket, lustre, Fleischer Studios 95.00
Bing Crosby, game, Call Me Lucky, 1954, EX 35.00
Bionic Woman, game, MIB...10.00
Blondie, color book, 1959, M 10.00
Blondie, stationery set, 1950s 26.00
Bobby Benson, code book, 1935, NM 16.50
Buck Jones, air rifle, EX..225.00

Buck Jones, guitar, 1933, VG **175.00**
Buck Rogers, pin, Solar Scouts, gold color, 1", NM........................**48.00**
Buck Rogers, pocket watch, Ingraham, M **525.00**
Buck Rogers, pop-up book, 'Dangerous Mission' pop-up, 1934....**165.00**
Buck Rogers, pop-up book, Strange Adventures in Spider Ship ..**250.00**
Buck Rogers, popgun, blk metal, 1934 ....**85.00**
Buck Rogers, Sonic Ray gun, plastic, +code book, 1950s, NMIB...**55.00**
Buck Rogers, Sonic Ray Signal flashlight, 1950s, EX in box **45.00**

Buck Rogers space suit: shirt, vest, pants, leggings, gun and holster, and a helmet in its own box, $1,800.00; Map of the solar system, Coco Malt premium, ca 1933, 22" x 28", $200.00.

Buck Rogers, spaceman figure, lead 8.00
Bugs Bunny, talking alarm clock, 1974, EX **40.00**
Bugs Bunny & Elmer Fudd, nightlight, '70s, M **15.00**
Bugs Bunny & Porky Pig, color book, 1944, VG **12.50**
Captain America, utility belt kit, Remco, 1979, MIB **12.00**
Captain Crunch, Sea Dog Spy Kit, premium, plastic, 1960s, M.....**12.50**
Captain Kangaroo, color book, 1950s, M....................................**10.00**
Captain Kangaroo, game, Kangadoodles, 1956, MIB......................**35.00**
Captain Kangaroo, game, Let's Build a House, 1954, EX **22.00**
Captain Marvel, flying paper toy, Fawcett, 1944, M in envelope...**20.00**
Captain Marvel, game, Shazam, paper, 1944, M **30.00**
Captain Marvel, magic flute, 1946, M on card **65.00**
Captain Marvel, magic picture, Fawcett, 1945, NM......................**15.00**
Captain Midnight, cup, Ovaltine radio premium, M...................**35.00**
Captain Midnight, Key-O-Matic decoder w/key, '49, M in mailer...**200.00**
Captain Midnight, manual, 1949, M in orig mailer **150.00**
Captain Midnight, membership card & coin................................**35.00**
Captain Universe, frame tray puzzle, 1950s, 11x10", NM **10.00**
Captain Video, Kellog's Premium Space figure.............................**10.00**
Captain Video, puzzle, rocket key chain, 1950s **15.00**
Captain Video, Rocketship pen, 1950s, EX **20.00**
Captain Video, Secret Ray Gun, M **95.00**
Casper the Ghost, figure, jtd paper, 1970s, 18", M in pkg **15.00**
Casper the Ghost, plush doll, 1960s...**20.00**
Charlie Brown, All-Stars Book, 1966, NM...................................**10.00**
Charlie Chaplin, comic/color book, 1915, 13-pg, 10x17", M **110.00**
Charlie Chaplin, figurine, porc, musical, dtd 1973.......................**40.00**
Charlie Chaplin, naughty flasher, store giveaway, 2¼x3½"...........**20.00**
Charlie Chaplin, publicity promo folder, early, 11x17" **10.00**
Charlie McCarthy, bubble gum wrapper **12.00**
Charlie McCarthy, cb puppet, 18", M **40.00**
Charlie McCarthy, cb puppet, 21" **40.00**
Charlie McCarthy, valentine, M **16.00**
Charlie Tuna, radio, w/stand **40.00**

Chilly Willy, card game, Walter Lantz, 1964, MIB........................**14.00**
Cinderella, pop-up book, Cinderella Puppet Show, 1949 ....**25.00**
Cinderella, suitcase, circus motif int, WDP, ca 1950 ....**50.00**
Cinderella, wall clock, Elgin, 1960s **35.00**
Clarabell, push puppet, wood, #186...**60.00**
Dagwood, marionette, wood/plastic, Hazell, 1950s, 14", MIB **25.00**
Dagwood, pencil, 1949, M **12.50**
Dale Evans, Queen of the West cowgirl outfit, MIB **160.00**
Daniel Boone, activity book, Fess Parker, 1964, M **18.50**
Daniel Boone, game, Trail Blazers, Milton Bradley, 1964..............**18.00**
Darth Vader, doll, 1978, 15", MIB **20.00**
Darth Vader, lamp, ceramic, M **40.00**
Davy Crockett, cap rifle, Cohn, 1950s, 33", M in VG case............**38.00**
Davy Crockett, cereal bowl, milk glass, mc graphics, 1950 .... 8.00
Davy Crockett, coonskin cap, WD, MIB.....................................**35.00**
Davy Crockett, flashlight, Fulton Mfg, VG **12.50**
Davy Crockett, game, Frontier Target, 1950s, EX.........................**50.00**
Davy Crockett, jailer's keys & handcuffs, M in orig pkg................**35.00**
Davy Crockett, lamp, compo figural, rpl shade, 1950s, 13", EX **78.00**
Davy Crockett, lariat tie, M in orig pkg **15.00**
Davy Crockett, neckerchief w/leather slide **25.00**
Davy Crockett, pendulum clock **150.00**
Davy Crockett, pillow, 1950s, VG **60.00**
Davy Crockett, shirt, brn fringe, 1950s, NM **11.50**
Dennis the Menace, color book, 1960, M **12.50**
Dennis the Menace, doll, early, NM in box **125.00**
Dennis the Menace, doll, Stuff 'N Lace, NMIB............................**40.00**
Dennis the Menace, game, baseball, MIB **95.00**
Dick Tracy, badge, Inspector General, w/promotional paper **375.00**
Dick Tracy, Cartoon Kit, colorforms, 1962, M in 13x8" box **33.00**
Dick Tracy, Master Detective game, 1961, M in 17x10" box **30.00**
Dick Tracy, pin-bk button, Lieutenant, EX **25.00**
Dick Tracy, puzzle, Man Hunt, Jaymar, '50s, NM, 20x15" box **20.00**
Dick Tracy, suspenders, M on orig card **28.00**
Dionne Quints, bowl, silverplate, EX...**50.00**
Dionne Quints, hand fan, School Days, EX.................................**18.00**
Donald Duck, card game, Disney, 1949, EX in box **15.00**
Donald Duck, cereal bowl, bl Beetleware, WDE, EX....................**25.00**
Donald Duck, doll, cloth, long bill, gr scarf, EX **285.00**
Donald Duck, rocker, wood, 1940s, VG....................................**225.00**
Donald Duck, still bank, pnt pot metal, rare, 7", NM **475.00**
Donald Duck, Tricky Toe Football game, WDP, M **15.00**
Donald Duck, walker, plastic, Marx, 1960s **18.00**
Donnie & Marie, TV show playset, M..**30.00**
Dopey, hand puppet, rubber head, cloth body, 1940s, EX............**38.00**
Dopey, linen book, He Don't Talk None, 1938, EX......................**40.00**
Dr Dolittle, card game, Post premium, 1960s, M in box 9.50
Dr Kildare, Thumpy Stethoscope, NM **20.00**
Dragnet, whistle 8.00
Droopy, color book, 1957, M **13.50**
Dumbo, halloween costume, WD, 1950s, EX **17.50**
Eddie Cantor, magic kit, 1935, EX **20.00**
Elsie the Cow, baby bottle set, 1940s, MIB...............................**100.00**
Elsie the Cow & Elmer, creamer & sugar bowl, orig labels, pr........**75.00**
Elvis Presley, key chain, Elvis Presley Blvd, M 4.00
Elvis Presley, money clip, solid brass.. 5.00
Elvis Presley, pocket knife, dtd 1977, M...................................... 4.00
Elvis Presley, scrap book, pictorial history, 185-pg, 1975 ....**25.00**
Elvis Presley, sideburns, vending-machine stickers, M **10.00**
Felix the Cat, figure, compo, jtd arms, 13", EX.........................**350.00**
Felix the Cat, puzzle, Built-Rite, 1949, 13x10½", NM **15.00**
Ferdinand the Bull, linen book, Whitman, 1936, EX **45.00**
Ferdinand the Bull, linen book, 1939, EX..................................**40.00**
Flash Gordon, inflatable spaceship, MIB **40.00**

Felix the Cat, copyright 1922-1924, 8", $350.00.

Flash Gordon, pep pin, Kellogg's, NM 14.00
Flash Gordon, rocket fighter w/tail fin, windup, 1930s, EX 465.00
Flash Gordon, Solar Commando set, 1950s, M on card 45.00
Flintstones, activity book, Hanna Barbera, 1974, M 10.00
Flintstones, Barney doll, vinyl, w/tag/bag, Dakin, '70, 6" 25.00
Flintstones, colorforms set, 1972, MIB..18.50
Flintstones, Dino push puppet, Kohner, 1950s 10.00
Flintstones, finger puppet, BammBamm, 1972, M on card 6.50
Flintstones, Fred bank, plastic, 1971, 13", NM............................20.00
Flintstones, Fred pedal car, 1960s, 28x24" 48.00
Flintstones, Fred punching figure, bounces bk, 1984, 36" 15.00
Flintstones, game, Stone Age, 1961, EX in box 55.00
Flintstones, Pebbles doll, Dakin 12.50
Flip Wilson, Geraldine doll, mute, EX in orig box 30.00
Flying Nun, board game, NM in VG box 18.00
Frank Buck, club horse pin...40.00
Gabby Hayes, rocking horse...200.00
Gene Autry, bicycle, Monark, ca 1950, 36", EX 1,870.00
Gene Autry, bicycle horn, MIB 75.00
Gene Autry, chaps & vest 40.00
Gene Autry, color book, 1941, lg, NM 35.00
Gene Autry, frame-tray puzzle, 1950s, 15x11", EX 16.50
Gene Autry, game, Bandit Trail, Kenton Hdw, 1939, EX.............125.00
Gene Autry, guitar, Emenee, MIB..80.00
Gene Autry, guitar, Melody Ranch, wood, EX 100.00
Gene Autry, guitar, Roundup, wood, w/case, EX 100.00
Gene Autry, magic slate, M 25.00
Gene Autry, pistol, red grips 65.00
Gene Autry, punch-out book, dtd 1941, NM 225.00
Gene Autry, rubber boots, MIB 125.00
Gene Autry, wrist watch, gun moves, 1948, EX 200.00
Gene Autry, writing tablet, unused 25.00
Get Smart, signal ray gun, M on card...65.00
GI Joe, puzzle, Whitman, 100-pc, 1965, NM 10.00
GI Joe, wrist watch, 1965, M...35.00
Green Hornet, Color Magic Rub-Off, 1966, EX in box..................65.00
Green Hornet, frame-tray puzzles (4), Whitman, 1966, MIB........55.00
Green Hornet, silver plastic flicker ring, 1960, NM 7.50
Green Hornet, Viewmaster, 3 reels, 16-pg booklet, 1966, NM 48.00
Happy Hooligan, brass stick pin, early, 2¼", EX 35.00
Happy Hooligan, nesting toy, M 45.00
Heckle & Jeckle, 3-D target game, MIB 25.00
Henry, color book #1, 1935, VG..35.00

Hoot Gibson, play clothes set, VG in box 29.00
Hopalong Cassidy, autograph book, 6½x5½", NM 21.00
Hopalong Cassidy, badge, Sheriff, brass, 6-point, EX 15.00
Hopalong Cassidy, bedspread, chenille, twin sz, EX 150.00
Hopalong Cassidy, binoculars, decal of HC on Topper, MIB..........55.00
Hopalong Cassidy, birthday napkins, in pkg, 1950 ....12.50
Hopalong Cassidy, board game, 1950, complete in orig box 55.00
Hopalong Cassidy, bottle, poster pnt..14.50
Hopalong Cassidy, button, Tenderfoot, tin litho, NM.....................6.00
Hopalong Cassidy, chenille rug..100.00

Hopalong Cassidy cookie jar, Cookie Coral, brown with decal, 6", $225.00.

Hopalong Cassidy, color book, 1950, oversz, M 28.00
Hopalong Cassidy, compass hat ring, complete w/hat 145.00
Hopalong Cassidy, cowgirl outfit w/clicker pistol, EX 95.00
Hopalong Cassidy, crayon & stencil set, EX in orig box................95.00
Hopalong Cassidy, folder w/writing paper, rare 45.00
Hopalong Cassidy, Frontier Town, in orig box 200.00
Hopalong Cassidy, gum wrapper 30.00
Hopalong Cassidy, gun, Zoomerang, MIB 195.00
Hopalong Cassidy, gun, Zoomerang, NM.....................................80.00
Hopalong Cassidy, gun & holster set, dbl, NM in box 375.00
Hopalong Cassidy, inflatable Topper, 1950s.................................85.00
Hopalong Cassidy, milk bottle, 1-qt 40.00
Hopalong Cassidy, milk bottle cap 4.50
Hopalong Cassidy, mug/plate/bowl, porc, mc decals, M 25.00
Hopalong Cassidy, nightlight, gun & holster, Aladdin 150.00
Hopalong Cassidy, party plates, M in pkg 25.00
Hopalong Cassidy, plate, dinner; milk glass 30.00
Hopalong Cassidy, pnt set, 1950, lg, NMIB 65.00
Hopalong Cassidy, publicity manual, 16-pg, lg 30.00
Hopalong Cassidy, ring, radio promotion, face in horseshoe.........25.00
Hopalong Cassidy, shooting gallery, tin litho, NMIB...................125.00
Hopalong Cassidy, statue, plastic 40.00
Hopalong Cassidy, tie clip, orig ruby eyes, 2", NM 16.00
Hopalong Cassidy, TV book, graphic, 1950, EX 50.00
Hopalong Cassidy, wrist watch, 1950, M in saddle box 350.00
Hopalong Cassidy & Singing Bandit, book & 2 records, NM 27.50
Howdy Doody, Air-O-Doodle, plastic train/boat/plane, 1950s.......22.00
Howdy Doody, bank, ceramic, HD riding pig, 6½x5" 45.00
Howdy Doody, battery ring, plastic face on top, lg, EX 80.00
Howdy Doody, Bee-Nee kit, unused, M in 7x5" box 35.00
Howdy Doody, belt, suede w/embr face 30.00

Howdy Doody, birthday cake set 35.00
Howdy Doody, cap, red felt, 1950s, EX 25.00
Howdy Doody, cup, Ovaltine 30.00
Howdy Doody, doll, compo, 18", NM 140.00
Howdy Doody, doll, compo head & hands, sleep eyes, 1940s.........65.00
Howdy Doody, doll, movable mouth, 1970s, MIB 27.00
Howdy Doody, Fun Book, Whitman, 150+ pgs, 1951, unused 20.00
Howdy Doody, game, Flub-A-Dub Flip-A-Ring, 1955, M in pkg ..22.50
Howdy Doody, game, TV show, Vagran Mfg, MIB 38.00
Howdy Doody, glasses, Bond 10.00
Howdy Doody, handkerchief, 8x8¼" 15.00
Howdy Doody, hat, blk cloth, Howdy's face, Kagran, '50s, NM 22.50
Howdy Doody, ice cream spoon, Kagran, M 12.50
Howdy Doody, lamp, full figure, no shade, 1950s, EX 135.00
Howdy Doody, mask, rubber, orig label, c Bob Smith 75.00
Howdy Doody, pencil case, red vinyl, Kagran, 1950s, M 20.00
Howdy Doody, puppet, pull string, 1977, 24", MIB 45.00
Howdy Doody, record player, Phone-A-Doodle, 1950s, EX 50.00
Howdy Doody, record player, Shura-tone, NY, 7x11x11", EX........25.00
Howdy Doody, ring, 1950 cereal premium 15.00
Howdy Doody, shoe polish, MIB 15.00
Howdy Doody, Teacher Board, M in orig pkg 28.00
Howdy Doody Gang, Welsh jelly glass 15.00
Huckleberry Hound, bank, plastic figural, Knickerbocker, NM 17.50
Huckleberry Hound, doll, stuffed, Knickerbocker, 1959, 13" 10.00
J Fred Muggs, hand puppet, autographed, 1954, MIB 26.00
Jack Armstrong, airplane, paper model, M in orig envelope 30.00
Jack Armstrong, code book, Secret Whistle, premium 20.00
Jack Armstrong, ring, Egyptian, EX.................................45.00
Jack Armstrong, telescope, Explorer, premium, 1938, MIB............22.00
Jackie Gleason/Ralph Kramden, wrist watch, Showtime................35.00
Jackie Kennedy, cologne bottle, milk glass.......................30.00
Jerry Mahoney, ventriloquist dummy, compo, EX 135.00
Jetsons, Fun Pad, Milton Bradley game, 1963, complete, EX 28.00
JF Kennedy, model doll kit, w/rocker/stand, Aurora, '65, EX 22.00
Jiminy Cricket, clicker, premium, WDP 10.00
Joe Carioca, pencil sharpener, Bakelite, hand held.....................35.00
John Wayne, memorial book, Allen Eyles, 1976, EX....................12.00
Johnny Ringo, holster, blk leather, stamped name, EX..................10.00
Katzenjammer Kids, Captain doll, rubber, 1950s, 6" 6.00
Kit Carson, cap pistol, EX...30.00
Kit Carson, color Book, Bill Williams cover, 1957, unused 25.00
Krazy Cat, puzzles, set of 4, Milton Bradley, 1964, NMIB............20.00
Lady & the Tramp, plastic figures, from cereal, WDP, 2", pr 8.50
Lassie, dog, stuffed, w/tag & collar, 1957, 15", M.....................28.00
Lassie, game, Adventures of Lassie, 1955, EX in orig box...............30.00
Laurel & Hardy, drawing set, electric, EX 45.00
Laurel & Hardy, figures, metal, 2½", pr...........................12.50
Leave It to Beaver, game, Ambush, 1959, M 30.00
Liberace, 16" transcript records of 1954 radio program, EX...........20.00
Little Abner, birthday card, 1950, M 11.00
Little Abner, valentine, 1950s, M 13.00
Little Audrey, doll, vinyl, Harvey, 1950s, 13", EX 37.00
Little Lulu, frame-tray puzzle, Whitman 15.00
Little Orphan Annie, decoder, 1936 ....25.00
Little Orphan Annie, decoder, 1939 ....25.00
Little Orphan Annie, decoder, 1940 ....24.00
Little Orphan Annie, mug, plastic, Ovaltine, w/lid, NM 25.00
Little Orphan Annie, pamphlet, Secret Ring, premium..................25.00
Little Orphan Annie, pin, Secret Society 25.00
Little Orphan Annie, puzzle, Famous Comics Mystery, '30s, NM ..32.50
Little Orphan Annie, sheet music, 1931, EX 25.00
Little Orphan Annie, stationery set, Whitman, 1932, EX 48.00
Little Orphan Annie, stove, 2-burner, EX orig 25.00

Little Orphan Annie, tumbler, Beetleware, minor wear................18.00
Little Orphan Annie, wrist watch, New Haven, MIB.................225.00
Little Orphan Annie & Sandy, bank, Applause, 1982 ....10.00
Little Red Riding Hood, plate, tin litho, 1930s, EX 10.00
Lone Ranger, badge, Safety Scout, 1"..............................13.00
Lone Ranger, badge, secret compartment........................30.00
Lone Ranger, binoculars, graphic decals, early, EX 40.00
Lone Ranger, blotter, Bond Bread 15.00
Lone Ranger, book bag, Nat'l Leather Mfg 47.50
Lone Ranger, cap gun, Peg-Leg Pete, mini, 2" L 12.00
Lone Ranger, chewing gum card, 1940, NM 10.00
Lone Ranger, compass, bullet form, 1948, 1", NM.............22.00
Lone Ranger, Deputy Kit, Cheerios premium, 1980, M.......25.00
Lone Ranger, Family Restaurant comic book 8.00
Lone Ranger, figure, Hartland, EX in orig box 225.00
Lone Ranger, filmstrip ring..35.00
Lone Ranger, filmstrip ring w/film/instructions, orig mailer.........175.00
Lone Ranger, flashlight ring, EX......................................40.00
Lone Ranger, frame-tray puzzle, Whitman, 1955, NM 15.00
Lone Ranger, frame-tray puzzle, 1951, NM 14.00
Lone Ranger, game, 1939, EX..38.00
Lone Ranger, guitar, Jefferson, 30", EX............................80.00
Lone Ranger, gun, Hi-Ho Silver, clicker, 1938 ....35.00
Lone Ranger, gun, smoking clicker, plastic, Marx, 1950s, M..........48.00
Lone Ranger, hairbrush, 1939, EX...................................23.00
Lone Ranger, jackknife, compass in hdl, 5½" L in case 15.00
Lone Ranger, Lucky Horse Shoe, rubber 18.00
Lone Ranger, Ped-O-Meter, tin, 3", NM.........................40.00
Lone Ranger, pencil, silver bullet, M 10.00
Lone Ranger, photograph, 7-Up premium 20.00
Lone Ranger, printing set, 1940s, EX in box.....................40.00
Lone Ranger, Range Rider, tin wind-up, Marx, MIB 495.00
Lone Ranger, record player, wood cabinet 185.00
Lone Ranger, ring, Atom Bomb 35.00
Lone Ranger, silver bullet, secret compartment................35.00
Lone Ranger, Six Gun ring, EX 60.00
Lone Ranger, toothbrush holder, compo figural, 1938, NM 45.00
Lone Ranger & Silver, bank, plastic, 1970s, orig tag 18.00
Ludwig Von Drake, tiddlywinks, Disney, MIB 30.00
Maggie & Jiggs, necklace pendant, EX............................25.00
Maggie & Jiggs, paperweight, glass.................................35.00
Maggie & Jiggs, shakers, ceramic, NM, pr.......................45.00
Magilla Gorilla, sticker book, Hanna Barbera, 1974, M 10.00
Man from UNCLE, board game, Ideal, NMIB.................25.00
Man from UNCLE, card game, Illa Kuryakin, rare, NM 20.00
Man from UNCLE, card game, 1965, EX..........................13.50
Man from UNCLE, color book, 1965, 200-pg, M 26.50
Man from UNCLE, flicker ring, EX 8.00
Man from UNCLE, Shooting Arcade, tin litho, Marx, 1966, EX ..70.00
Mandrake the Magician, game, Transogram, 1966, M 25.00
Mary Poppins, figure, plastic windup, Marx, 1965, 8", NM..........20.00
Mary Poppins, paint & crayon set, 1962, 15x12" box, M 15.00
Maverick, cap pistol, single shot, M in pkg......................38.00
Maverick, derringer, cap gun, metal, 3½", M on card.....................30.00
Maverick, frame-tray puzzle, James Garner, 1960, 14x11", pr.........10.00
Maverick, Golden Record, 45 rpm, 1958 ....12.00
Melvin Purvis, Secret Operators Manual, 1939, EX 30.00
Michael Jackson, doll, 1984, 11½".................................10.00
Mickey & Minnie Mouse, clothes/shoe rack, wood, WDP, 42"....425.00
Mickey & Minnie Mouse, pillow, embroidery/pnt, 1931, EX.......125.00
Mickey & Minnie Mouse, pillow, WDP.........................45.00
Mickey & Minnie Mouse, seed packets, 1977, pr 15.00
Mickey & Minnie Mouse, shakers, ceramic, M, pr............30.00
Mickey Mouse, acrobat string toy, paper & wood, WDP............55.00

Mickey Mouse, AM/FM clock radio telephone, GE, 1960s............**48.00**
Mickey Mouse, bank, dime register, tin, 1939, 2½x2½", NM.........**75.00**
Mickey Mouse, bank, plastic, EX color, 12" **15.00**
Mickey Mouse, blotter, 1936, EX **20.00**
Mickey Mouse, book, MM & Boy Thursday, Whitman, 1948........**45.00**
Mickey Mouse, book, The Golden Touch, color plates, 1937, EX .**80.00**
Mickey Mouse, bowl, red Beetleware **20.00**
Mickey Mouse, bubble gum cards, 20 in album, 1930s.................**225.00**
Mickey Mouse, camera, 1940s, NM **150.00**
Mickey Mouse, club house frame-tray puzzle, 1954, EX................**15.00**
Mickey Mouse, dominoes, WDE, 1930s, colorful box **60.00**
Mickey Mouse, figure, bsk, MM riding Pluto, NM **69.00**
Mickey Mouse, film, Full Steam Ahead, 1930s, EX in box.............**10.00**
Mickey Mouse, Library of Games, 1940s **110.00**
Mickey Mouse, linen book, MM & His Friends, 1936, EX...........**185.00**
Mickey Mouse, magazine, Pluto cover, Feb, 1939, EX...................**60.00**
Mickey Mouse, pendant, metal, blk/yel, ca 1935, 1", NM.............**32.00**
Mickey Mouse, pin, wood, MM playing drum, early......................**35.00**
Mickey Mouse, pop-up book, Silly Symphony, EX **200.00**
Mickey Mouse, push plate, brass, orig **125.00**
Mickey Mouse, puzzle, 12-pc, makes a story, 1950s, NM **55.00**
Mickey Mouse, puzzle card, Amaco premium, 1930s, NM **5.00**
Mickey Mouse, radio, wood case, EX **100.00**
Mickey Mouse, starship, battery operated, MIB...............................**65.00**
Mickey Mouse, Target game, WDE, M **100.00**
Mickey Mouse, top, WDE, 1930s, 11", EX **145.00**
Mickey Mouse, tumbler, paper litho on wood, 1930s, 8" **90.00**
Mickey Mouse, valentine, satin-like paper, WDE, 1930s, NM **22.00**
Mickey Mouse, wall clock, red plastic, Elgin, EX............................**30.00**
Mickey Mouse, wrist watch, Ingersoll, 1930s, M in VG box........**900.00**
Mickey Mouse, wrist watch, US Time, 1947, MIB **550.00**
Mickey Mouse & Donald Duck, appointment card, WDE, '30s.....**22.50**
Mickey Mouse Club, drum, tin litho, 11" **35.00**
Mickey Mouse Club, game, Magic Subtractor, MIB **25.00**
Mickey Mouse Club, light-up drawing desk, MIB **25.00**
Mighty Mouse, Skill ballgame, MIB **70.00**
Mighty Mouse/Heckle & Jeckle, target game, 1957, EX................**25.00**
Minnie Mouse, buckle, brass, Award of Merit, rectangular, '33 ..**350.00**
Minnie Mouse, figure, jtd, wood, 1930s, 5½"................................**110.00**
Minnie Mouse, mail bag, WDP, Woolikin Orig, 23x10" **25.00**
Monkees, cake decoration figures, complete....................................**45.00**
Monkees, playing cards, NM in box **18.00**
Monkees, puzzle, 1967, NMIB...**30.00**
Monkees, reflector ring, premium... **8.00**
Moon Mullins, bsk nodder, Germany **75.00**
Moon Mullins, Pillsbury Comicookie Baking Set, 1937, MIB........**35.00**
Mr Ed, talking puppet, 1962, MIB...**60.00**
Mr Spock, model kit, unassembled, 1979, M **20.00**
Munsters, card game, MIB...**65.00**
Our Gang, pencil box, 1930s, EX...**60.00**
Palladin, game, Have Gun Will Travel, 1959, EX in box **55.00**
Peter Pan, game, Adventure, Transogram, NM **38.00**
Peter Pan, punch-out color book, premium, 1947, M **12.50**
Peter Pan, puzzle, Flight to Never Land, WDP, 1950s, MIB........... **8.00**
Pink Panther, gramophone radio, United Artists, MIB...................**25.00**
Pinky Lee, figure, plastic, Marx, 2¾", NM.....................................**38.00**
Pinocchio, cup & saucer, tin...**10.00**
Pinocchio, figure, wood/compo, jtd arms, pre-war, Disney **125.00**
Pinocchio, marionette puppet, 1930s, EX..**65.00**
Pinocchio, music box, wood/compo, 11", VG.................................**50.00**
Pinocchio, xylophone player, Japan, battery-op, EX in box **125.00**
Pinocchio & Gepetto, face masks, Gillette, 1939, EX, pr..............**30.00**
Planet of the Apes, bank, Galen, 1974, 10¾", M **20.00**
Planet of the Apes, board game, photo cover box, 1974, M.........**13.50**

Planet of the Apes, General Aldo model kit, Addar, 1973, M **13.50**
Pluto, figure, Seiberling, complete w/tail, EX **65.00**
Pluto, flashlight, plastic, 4", EX **12.00**
Popeye, Bifbat, 1929, EX..**45.00**
Popeye, book, Popeye Borrows a Baby Nurse, Whitman, #712 ......**40.00**
Popeye, book, Thimble Theatre, #4063, 1935, EX.........................**30.00**
Popeye, figural soap, early, NM **35.00**
Popeye, figure, chalkware, standing, 14", VG................................**125.00**
Popeye, figure, wood, jtd/pnt/stenciled, 1930s, 5", EX.................**46.00**
Popeye, game, Bowl 'Em Down, 1950s, M in VG 19½x15" box.....**29.00**
Popeye, game, Juggler, ca 1929, EX..**30.00**
Popeye, game, Shipwreck, Milton Bradley, 1933 ....**75.00**
Popeye, phonograph, Emerson, 1970s, EX.....................................**45.00**
Popeye, puzzle, Three's a Crowd, Jamar, 100-pc, 1950s, NM **15.00**
Popeye, shirt, 1935, EX...**200.00**
Popeye & Olive Oyl, marionettes, hard plastic, 1950s, 12", pr ...**150.00**
Prince Valiant, game, Valor, Transogram, 1950s, 18x9", MIB **25.00**
Princess Leia, doll, Kenner, 12", EX...**65.00**
Quick Draw McGraw, bubble bath bank, plastic, 1960, NM..........**20.00**
Raggedy Ann & Andy, bowl & plate, 1969....................................**10.00**
Rebel, game, Nick Adams on board & box, Ideal, 1961, NM **40.00**
Red Ryder, frame-tray puzzle, Saalfield, 1951, EX **15.00**
Red Ryder, Good Luck token, JC Penney, brass, M **10.00**
Red Ryder, paint book, 1941, EX..**35.00**
Red Ryder, target game, cb litho, Whitman, 1939, EX in box........**55.00**
Riddler, figural nightlight, 1974, 8", NM **35.00**
Roy Rogers, bank, western boot, metal, NM **30.00**
Roy Rogers, box camera, blk w/silver, 1950s, EX...........................**27.00**
Roy Rogers, cap gun, M **35.00**
Roy Rogers, cap gun, Tuck-A-Way, 3", M on card.........................**32.00**
Roy Rogers, comic book #1, NM...**255.00**
Roy Rogers, Fix-it Chuck Wagon & Jeep, 1950s, NMIB................**85.00**
Roy Rogers, game, Rodeo, 1949 ....**40.00**
Roy Rogers, guitar, heavy cb & wood, w/Trigger & Dale, VG **40.00**
Roy Rogers, gun & holster set, dbl, NM **175.00**
Roy Rogers, harmonica, Riders, VG **12.50**
Roy Rogers, kerchief, Happy Trails, triangular, EX **22.00**
Roy Rogers, mug, face figural **18.00**
Roy Rogers, pencil, King of the Cowboys, 1942, M.......................**11.00**
Roy Rogers, pin-bk button, Happy Trails.. **4.00**
Roy Rogers, slicker, yel & blk, 1950s, M..**45.00**
Roy Rogers, story book album, 22-pg, +2 78 records, RCA, '50.....**37.50**
Roy Rogers, telescope **30.00**
Roy Rogers, tent, M...**250.00**
Roy Rogers, Trigger, plastic blow-up figure for pool.....................**150.00**
Roy Rogers, Yo-Yo, plastic, 1940s **15.00**
Roy Rogers & Trigger, lamp, rotating shade, NM.........................**200.00**
Schmoo, bottle, bl glass, figural, Baldwin Lab/1950s, 7½"............**30.00**
Secret Agent, game, John Drake, Milton Bradley, 1966, MIB **25.00**
Sherlock Holmes, game, Parker Bros, NM......................................**30.00**
Shirley Temple, book, How I Raised ST, Saalfield, 1935, EX.........**40.00**
Shirley Temple, bowl, cobalt glass...**45.00**
Shirley Temple, creamer, cobalt glass **38.00**
Shirley Temple, fountain pen, NM...**95.00**
Shirley Temple, mug, cobalt glass..**48.00**
Shirley Temple, pocket mirror, School Days, dtd 1937................... **5.00**
Shirley Temple, scrapbook, Saalfield, 1938, 12x13", NM..............**90.00**
Shirley Temple, sheet music, Toy Trumpet, EX..............................**20.00**
Shirley Temple, sugar bowl, cobalt glass...**38.00**
Sky King, pen ring, Magni-Glo **35.00**
Sky King, ring, electronic w/4 pictures, EX....................................**70.00**
Sky King, ring, Teleblinker, w/instructions, NM...........................**185.00**
Smitty, color book, McLoughlin Bros, 1932, 24-pg, EX................**45.00**
Snoopy, nodder, Joe Cool, early 1950s, NM **20.00**

Snow White, bank, dime register, WDE, 1939, M **90.00**
Snow White, kaleidoscope, NM...**45.00**
Snow White, sink & refrigerator, Wolverine **50.00**
Snow White, song sheet, WDE, 1937 ....**25.00**
Snow White & 7 Dwarfs, handkerchief, WDE, 9x9".................**20.00**
Snow White & 7 Dwarfs, ironing board, child's sz, EX.............**22.00**
Snow White & 7 Dwarfs, plastic wringer washer windup, 8" **95.00**
Snow White & 7 Dwarfs, soaps, individually boxed, ea **45.00**
Snuffy Smith & Barney book, shakers, EX, pr **38.00**
Sonja Henie, paper dolls, 1930s, uncut, M **95.00**
Sonny & Cher, Theatre Go Round, M **65.00**
Space Patrol, handbook...**150.00**
Space Patrol, Space-O-Phones, MIB **200.00**
Space Ranger, wallet, w/play money & ID card, NM **50.00**
Spark Plug, candy container, glass...**78.00**
Spiderman, Spiderbike, Corgi, lg, EX in box **45.00**
Star Trek, Star Fleet Technical manual, Nov 1975, unused **28.00**
Steve Canyon, goggles/scarf, 1950s, M on card **13.50**
Sugarfoot, post card, color, W Hutchins, 1959, 3½x5½" **8.50**
Superman, costume, Ben Cooper, 1958, MIB..........................**100.00**
Superman, frame-tray puzzle, Whitman, 1966, 10x8", NM **12.00**
Superman, game, Calling Superman, Transogram, 1954, NM........**65.00**
Superman, gum wrapper, 1960s...**8.00**
Superman, pep pin, 1947, EX **5.00**
Superman, Secret Code card, premium, 1940s **20.00**
Superman, wallet, vinyl, 1966 ....**20.00**
Tarzan, book, Ella Cinders, ice cream premium **18.00**
Tarzan, notebook, Mattel Toymakers, loose-leaf, M **25.00**
Tarzan, popsicle coin, Johnny Weissmueller **7.00**
Three Stooges, Larry hand puppet, 1960s, EX **60.00**
Three Stooges, membership kit, Maurer, 1959, NM in envelope.**155.00**
Tin Man of Oz, rubber figure, 7"...**15.00**
Tom Corbett, Atomic Rifle **125.00**
Tom Corbett, flashlight, NM in box **125.00**
Tom Corbett, flashlight badge, Space Cadet, plastic, M................**35.00**
Tom Corbett, frame-tray puzzle, boxed set of 3, EX **45.00**
Tom Corbett, Little Golden book **12.50**
Tom Corbett, punch-out book, Saalfield, 1950s, 14x10", M **35.00**
Tom Corbett, punch-out book, Space Cadet, M **50.00**
Tom Corbett, Space Academy playset, Marx............................**185.00**
Tom Mix, book, Tony & His Pals, hardbk, 1934, EX.....................**18.00**
Tom Mix, cowboy hat, metal, eng name on brim **50.00**
Tom Mix, pocket knife, Straight Shooter, VG...........................**28.00**
Tom Mix, postage stamp, 3-D **6.00**
Tom Mix, postal telegraph set, bl, metal clicker, 1938, EX............**35.00**
Tom Mix, poster, safety concerns for children, 1947, 25x17".........**20.00**
Tom Mix, premiums catalog, Straight Shooter, 1930s **22.00**
Tom Mix, puzzle, ad for Rexall Drugs, orig mailer **35.00**
Tom Mix, story manual, The Life of..., EX **50.00**
Tom Mix, TV set w/1 film, brn plastic, premium, 1949, 1" **35.00**
Tom Mix, watch fob, gold tone **185.00**
Tom Mix, western boots, leather, child's sz, MIB......................**325.00**
Tom Thumb, typewriter, MIB..**15.00**
Tonto, figure, Hartland..**195.00**
Winnie the Poo, baby mug, SP..**25.00**
Woody Woodpecker, figure, red plastic, orig tag, '50s, 5½" **20.00**
Woody Woodpecker, learn-to-draw book, 1958, M **11.50**
Wyatt Erp, cowboy outfit, EX **185.00**
Wyatt Erp, figure, Hartland..**150.00**
Yel Kid, cigarette premium button #80 ....**20.00**
Yogi Bear, bank, plastic figural, Knickerbocker, 1960s, NM..........**10.00**
Yogi Bear, figure, plastic, nose lights up, 1960s, 3", M **8.00**
Yogi Bear, game, Milton Bradley, 1971 ....**15.00**
Zorro, mask, Whip & Ring lariat, Guy Williams on card, M **45.00**

Zorro, paper film strip & viewer **35.00**
007, tarot book, 96-pg, NM **9.00**

Peters and Reed

John Peters and Adam Reed founded their pottery in Zanesville, Ohio, just before the turn of the century, using the local red clay to produce a variety of wares. Moss Aztec, introduced about 1912, has an unglazed exterior with designs molded in high relief and the recesses highlighted with a green wash. Only the interior is glazed to hold water. Pereco (named for Peters, Reed and Company) is glazed in semi-matt blue, maroon, or cream. Orange was also used very early, but such examples are rare. Shapes are simple with in-mold decoration sometimes borrowed from the Moss Aztec line. Wilse Blue is a line of high-gloss medium blue with dark specks on simple shapes. Landsun, characterized by its soft matt multicolor or blue and gray combinations, is decorated either by dripping or by hand brushing in an effect sometimes called Flame or Herringbone. Chromal, in much the same colors as Landsun, may be decorated with a realistic scenic, or the swirling application of colors may merely suggest one. (Brush-McCoy made a very similar line called Chromart. Neither will be marked; and, due to the lack of documented background material available, it may be impossible make a positive identification. Collectors nearly always attribute this type of decoration to Peters and Reed.) Shadow Ware is a glossy, multicolor drip over a harmonious base color. When the base is black, the effect is often iridescent.

Perhaps the most familiar line is the brown high-glaze artware with the 'sprigged'-type designs. Although research has uncovered no positive proof, it is generally accepted as having been made by Peters and Reed. It is interesting to note that many of the artistic shapes in this line are recognizable as those made by Weller, Roseville, and other Zanesville area companies. Other lines include Mirror Black, Persian, and an unidentified line which collectors call Mottled Colors. In this high gloss line, the red clay body often shows through the splashed-on multicolors.

In 1922 the company became known as the Zane Pottery. Peters and Reed retired, and Harry McClelland became president. Charles Chilcote designed new lines, and production of many of the old lines continued. The body of the ware after 1922 was light in color. Marks include the impressed logo or ink stamp 'Zaneware' in a rectangle.

Ash tray, Landsun, bl/wht **35.00**
Bowl, Moss Aztec, pine cones, sgn Ferrell, 3x6¼" **35.00**
Bowl, Sheenware, bl/wht swirls, flared top, #625.....................**35.00**
Ewer, Brn Ware, leafy sprigs, 8½" **75.00**
Jardiniere, Chromal, impressionistic cabin & trees, 6x7"............**150.00**
Jardiniere, Moss Aztec, pine cone relief, #200, 5"....................**55.00**
Jug, Brn Ware, wreath sprigs, 5" **50.00**
Mug, Brn Ware, grape sprigs, ornate hdl, 5½"...........................**55.00**
Pitcher, Brn Ware, grape sprigs, 11½".......................................**95.00**
Teapot, Marbleized, bl/yel/blk/brn, 8", NM **100.00**
Umbrella stand, Moss Aztec, panels w/Grecian woman, 21" **295.00**
Vase, Chromal, house/post fence/trees, bulbous, 7"....................**350.00**
Vase, Chromal, trees/moon/mtns, brn tones, #5, 10"..................**395.00**
Vase, Landsun, bl/brn, ball form, 3" **40.00**
Vase, Landsun, bl/gr/beige/brn, narrow top, #5, 10" **65.00**
Vase, Marbleized, bl/blk/yel, 6" **45.00**
Vase, Moss Aztec, floral relief, 12" **85.00**
Vase, Pereco, gr matt, emb grapes, #49, 12" **60.00**
Vase, Wilse Blue, cherry design, flared, 8" **45.00**
Wall pocket, Egyptian Ware, w/king profile, #83, 9" **85.00**
Wall pocket, Moss Aztec, grapes relief, 8"................................**75.00**
Window box, w/liner, sgn Ferrell, 6x11"....................................**125.00**

Vase, Brown Ware, 10", $85.00.

Pewabic

The Pewabic Pottery was formally established in Detroit, Michigan, in 1907 by Mary Chase Perry Stratton and Horace James Caulkins. The two had worked together since 1903, firing their ware in a small kiln Caulkins had designed especially for use by the dental trade. Always a small operation which relied upon basic equipment and the skill of the workers, they took pride in being commissioned for several important architectural tile installations.

Some of the early artware was glazed a simple matt green; occasionally other colors were added, sometimes in combination, one over the other in a drip effect. Later Stratton developed a lustrous crystalline glaze. The body of the ware was highly fired and extremely hard. Shapes were basic, and decorative modeling, if used at all, was in low relief. Mary Stratton kept the pottery open until her death in 1961. In 1968 it was purchased and reopened by Michigan State University.

Several marks were used over the years: a triangle with 'Revelation Pottery' (for a short time only); 'Pewabic' with five maple leaves; and the impressed circle mark.

Ash tray, pk & gr gloss, triangular, 4" 95.00
Bowl, gr & gray gloss w/dk gr drip, 10" 240.00
Bowl, orange gloss w/dk specks, 1¾x4" 80.00
Cup & saucer, gold-gr irid w/pk highlights, 3x5" 120.00

Shield-back candle holder, brown to yellow, 5", $135.00.

Plate, tree border, gr/bl on cream, mk Pewabic, 10" 475.00
Tile, horse 125.00
Tile, Zodiac, Aries the Ram 125.00
Tile, Zodiac, Pisces the fish 125.00
Vase, aqua/turq drip, bulbous base, 5" 365.00
Vase, bl, 7" 260.00
Vase, blk/dk bl irid w/pk & gold highlights, rnd mk, 5" 550.00
Vase, bud; thick/bubbly bl over blk matt, label, 6x3½" 550.00
Vase, gr w/bl mirror drip, pk/gold highlights, rnd mk, 6" 475.00
Vase, gr/bl metallic w/pk & gold highlights, shouldered, 5" 575.00
Vase, gray-gr irid, bulbous w/short neck, 1910, 6" 250.00
Vase, ivory w/bl irid drip, narrow neck/squat, '05, 6", EX 200.00
Vase, lt brn w/brn drip, squat, 4x7" 375.00
Vase, royal bl, squat, 4½" 250.00
Vase, rust splotchy lustre, bulbous middle, imp mk, 10" 600.00
Vase, tan drip on dk brn, gourd form, semi-circle mk, 5½" 425.00
Vase, thick yel w/pk irid, cvd geometrics, rnd mk, 4" 245.00

Pewter

Pewter is a metal alloy of tin, copper, very small parts of bismuth and/or antimony, and sometimes lead. Very little American pewter contained lead, however, because much of the ware was designed to be used as tableware, and makers were aware that the use of lead could result in poisoning. (Pieces that do contain lead are usually darker in color and heavier than those that have no lead.) Most of the fine examples of American pewter date from 1700 to the 1840s. Many pieces were melted down and recast into bullets during the American Revolution in 1775; this accounts to some extent why examples from this period are quite difficult to find. The pieces that did survive may include buttons, buckles, and writing equipment as well as the tableware we generally think of.

After the Revolution, makers began using antimony as the major alloy with the tin in an effort to regain the popularity of pewter, which glassware and china was beginning to replace in the home. The resulting product, known as britannia, had a lustrous silver-like appearance and was far more durable. While closely related, britannia is a collectible in its own right and should not be confused with pewter.

Key: tm — touchmark

Basin, Blakeslee Barnes, partial tm, minor pitting, 10½" 250.00
Basin, Edward Danforth, strong tm, 8", NM 1,000.00
Basin, Jacob Whitmore, partial tm, rpr, 9", VG 250.00
Basin, Jacob Whitmore, partial tm, 9", NM 550.00
Basin, Love tm, 8", NM..500.00
Basin, Richard Austin, sm pitted areas, 8", EX 200.00
Basin, Samuel Hamlin Sr, partial tm, minor dents, 7¾" 300.00
Basin, Thos Badger, EX tm, 3 old rprs, flaking, 8" 150.00
Basin, unmk Am, rpr/pits/dents, 6½" 50.00
Basin, unmk Am, unreadable tm, normal pitting, 13" 150.00
Beaker, Boardman & Hart, break by hdl, 3", EX 200.00
Beaker, JB Woodbury, EX tm, w/hdl, 3", NM 325.00
Beaker, Samuel Kilburn, minor dents, 3¼" 650.00
Beaker, unreadable tm, possibly English, ftd 75.00
Bedpan, Thos Danforth Boardman, dbl tm/Peabody, 18", EX 200.00
Bottle, nursing; unmk Am, 1 rpr, rare form, 6½", EX 400.00
Candlestick, Ostrander & Norris, w/bobeche, 9¾", NM, pr 750.00
Candlestick, Roswell Gleason, 7", NM.......................................400.00
Caster, Reed & Barton, ftd, dome lid, 7", NM 50.00
Chamberstick, Henry Hopper, line tm, crudely resoldered..........200.00
Charger, David Melville, 3 areas of pitting, rare sz, 14" 400.00
Charger, Nathaniel Austin, tm only fair, pinholes/rprs, 15" 250.00

Charger, Parks Boyd, 3 tm, even wear but VG, 13½" 250.00
Charger, Samuel Hamlin Sr, EX tm, minor pitting, 13½" 850.00
Charger, Thos Badger, deeply pitted, 15" 250.00
Charger, Thos Badger, EX tm, minor wear, 12" 450.00
Charger, Thos Badger, 13½", NM 600.00
Charger, Thos Danforth Boardman, dbl tm, 12", NM 600.00
Coffeepot, Israel Trask, eng band, lighthouse form, 11" 550.00
Coffeepot, Josiah Danforth, minor pitting, 10" 300.00
Coffeepot, Rufus Dunham, lighthouse form, minor dent, 11" 200.00
Coffeepot, Wm Calder, EX tm, lighthouse form, 11" 400.00
Communion token, AC of Hebron, bk: JI 1824, 1", VG...............25.00
Communion tray, Reed & Barton, 11⅛", VG.............................100.00
Cuspidor, Roswell Gleason, minor dents, 8" dia 175.00
Dish, deep; Blakeslee Barns+2-line tm, 13", NM 400.00
Dish, deep; Thos Danforth Boardman, bold tm, 13", EX 350.00
Flagon, Roswell Gleason, tm, 11", NM..................................650.00
Flagon, Thos Danforth Boardman, EX tm, resoldered lid, 12" 400.00
Flagon, unmk European, 12", VG 100.00
Funnel, unmk Am, minor dents, 3¼x3½", VG...........................50.00
Inkstand, W&E tm, sq base w/2 drws, 4¼" 600.00
Lamp, camphene; Capen & Molineux, slight flaking, 6½" 200.00
Lamp, camphene; Henry Hopper, saucer base, dbl burner, 5" 200.00
Lamp, fluid; Roswell Gleason, acorn font, 5¼"..........................400.00
Lamp, hand; Morey & Ober/tm #1, orig camphene burner, 4".....150.00
Lamp, hand; Wm Calder, orig burner, 5½", EX 550.00
Lamp, whale oil; att Israel Trask, orig burner, 6½", NM...............300.00
Lamp, whale oil; att R Gleason, lens mk Pat, tin base, 8½" 425.00
Lamp, whale oil; Freeman Porter, EX tm, 6", EX, pr....................550.00
Lamp, whale oil; Israel Trask, orig burner, 6½", NM 450.00
Lamp, whale oil; Taunton Britannia, orig burner, 6½", pr............400.00
Lamp, whale oil; unmk Am, lemon font, orig burner, 6", pr 650.00
Lamp, whale oil; unmk Am, tall std, orig burner, 5½"..................125.00
Lamp, whale oil; unmk Am, 1½", EX 225.00
Measure, Boardman & Hart/dtd 1838, sgn JD, baluster, 1-qt 500.00
Muff warmer, unmk Am, spherical, many dents, 2½"...................175.00
Mug, Joseph Danforth, VG tm, normal wear, 1-pt...................2,000.00
Mug, Josiah Danforth, strong tm, 1-pt, NM 2,100.00
Mug, Robert Palethorp Jr, partial tm, rpr by hdl, 1-qt, EX 1,000.00
Mug, Samuel Hamlin Sr, VG tm, 1-qt, NM............................2,200.00
Mug, Thos A & Sherman Boardman, str-line tm, 1-qt, VG 300.00
Pitcher, Geo Richardson, EX tm, minor dents/pits/rpr, 2-qt.........200.00
Pitcher, Roswell Gleason, EX tm, w/lid, 1-gal, NM 1,000.00
Pitcher, Sellew & Co, w/lid, 2-qt, NM 800.00
Pitcher, syrup; Henry Homan, lighthouse form, EX tm, 7"...........175.00
Pitcher, syrup; Sellew & Co, lighthouse form, w/lid, 6" 450.00
Pitcher, syrup; unmk Am, lighthouse form, w/lid, 6", NM 150.00
Pitcher, unmk Am, w/lid, several rprs, 2-qt, VG 100.00
Plate, Ashbil Griswold, dbl tm, 2 sm pitted areas, 8", EX 200.00
Plate, Daniel Curtis, EX dbl tm, minor wear, 8" 300.00
Plate, David Melville, EX tm, 8¼", NM 350.00
Plate, Francis Bassett II, EX dbl tm & ID w/crown, 9", EX 1,500.00
Plate, Frederick Bassett, EX tm, smooth brim, 8½", EX 500.00
Plate, Geo Lightner, EX dbl tm, 8", NM.................................350.00
Plate, Harbeson, Phila, 1790s, 8" 210.00
Plate, Hiram Yale, EX dbl tm, 8½", NM 550.00
Plate, Jacob Eggleston, partial dbl tm, minor wear, 9" 600.00
Plate, Jehiel Johnson, EX dbl tm, very minor wear, 8" 650.00
Plate, John Skinner, EX tm/IB, hammered booge, 8", EX 500.00
Plate, John Will, NY, ca 1752-1766, 8½" 1,210.00
Plate, Malcolm McEuen & Son, smooth brim, lt wear, 10" 1,400.00
Plate, R Palethorp, Phila, ca 1820, 8½" 210.00
Plate, Samuel Kilbourne, EX tm, minor scratches, 8½"................300.00
Plate, Samuel Pierce, dbl tm, 8", NM 450.00
Plate, Samuel Pierce, 8", VG..175.00

Plate, Spencer Stafford, normal wear, 8"..................................350.00
Plate, Thos Byles, dbl tm, dents/minor mks, 9".......................1,600.00
Plate, Thos Danforth Boardman, dbl tm, minor wear, 8¼" 200.00
Plate, Thos Danforth II, smooth brim, hammered booge, 9¼" . 1,200.00
Plate, Thos Danforth III, normal wear, 6⅛"..............................500.00
Plate, unmk Am, normal wear, 5¼" 225.00
Pocket mirror, commemorative eng of Lafayette, 1½", EX 350.00

Porringers: Gershom Jones, good touchmark, 5½", $1,500.00; Samuel Danforth, strong touchmark, one small dent, EX, 5", $700.00.

Porringer, Flagg & Homan, 2⅛", EX......................................275.00
Porringer, RG tm of Roswell Gleason, crown hdl, 4", VG 150.00
Porringer, Richard Lee, rare, 2¼" 1,050.00
Porringer, Samuel E Hamlin Jr, EX tm, 4¼", NM......................700.00
Porringer, SG in reverse in bk of crown hdl, rpr, 5½"..................150.00
Porringer, unmk Am, crown hdl, minor pitting, 5⅛" 150.00
Porringer, unmk Am, crown hdl, 4⅝", NM.............................200.00
Porringer, unmk Am, Old English hdl, 3¾"..............................200.00
Pot, Whitlock, Troy, NY, minor dents to base, 11½" 325.00
Salt box, att Geo Coldwell, NY, 1787-1811, shoe form, 3½".......235.00
Salt cellar, master; eagle tm, att TD Boardman, 4-ftd, pr 100.00
Shakers, IH tm, ftd pear form, normal wear, 4", pr......................400.00
Snuff box, Israel Trask, VG tm, minor dents, 3⅜" dia, EX...........200.00
Sugar bowl, Geo Richardson, superb tm, w/lid, 4½", NM 3,500.00
Sugar bowl, Sellew & Co, VG tm, w/lid, 6½", EX 250.00
Tankard, att Samuel Danfort, CT, 1810, S-form hdl, 4¾" 475.00
Teapot, att Samuel Danforth, Hartford, ca 1800, pear form, 6" ..750.00
Teapot, Daniel Curtis, EX tm, worn reguled wood finial, 7¾" 275.00
Teapot, Eben Smith, partial tm, pear form, rpr, 7".......................500.00
Teapot, James H Putnam, partial tm, pigeon-breasted, 9", NM ...150.00
Teapot, JD Locke, clear tm, minor dents, 7" 150.00
Teapot, Leonard Reed & Barton, line tm, 10", EX 125.00
Teapot, Lorenzo L Williams, dbl-line tm, minor dents, 8" 300.00
Teapot, Otis Williams, X quality mk, VG tm, 7¾", NM.............850.00

Phoenix Bird

Blue and white Phoenix Bird china has been produced by various Japanese potteries from the early 1900s. With slight variations, the design features the Japanese bird of paradise and scroll-like vines of Kara-Kusa, or Chinese grass. Although some of their earlier ware is unmarked, the majority is marked in some fashion. More than forty different stamps have been reported, with 'Made in Japan' the one most often found. Newer items, if marked at all, carry a paper label. Compared to the older ware, the coloring of the new is whiter and the blue more harsh; the design is sparse with more ground area showing. Although collectors buy even 'new' pieces, the older is of course more highly prized and valued. For further information we recommend *The Collector's Encyclopedia of Nippon, Third Series*, by Joan Van Patten, whose address is in the Directory under New York.

Bowl, berry; 8¾"	28.00
Bowl, serving; scalloped, 9"	40.00
Bowl, vegetable; scalloped corners, sq, 9"	40.00
Casserole, oval, Japan, w/lid, 2½x6¼x4½"	50.00
Chocolate pot	90.00
Coaster, 3"	18.00
Condensed milk can holder, w/lid	100.00
Cup, custard; mk	15.00
Cup & saucer, demitasse	20.00
Ginger jar, 6"	35.00
Gravy boat, w/attached 8" underplate & lid	65.00
Matchbox, 3"	35.00
Pitcher, milk; 4⅝"	30.00
Plate, dinner; 10"	45.00
Platter, 12¼x8½"	40.00
Shakers, hexagonal, 3", pr	24.00
Shakers, 3¼", pr	32.00
Teapot, mk #19, 5"	55.00
Tray, relish; hdls, 10"	40.00

Phoenix Glass

Founded in 1880 in Monaca, Pennsylvania, the Phoenix Glass Company became one of the country's foremost manufacturers of lighting glass by the early 1900s. Today, however, collectors are primarily interested in the 'Sculptured Artware' produced in the 1930s and 1940s. These beautiful mold-blown pieces are most often found in white milk glass or crystal with various fired-on color treatments or a satin finish.

Phoenix did not mark their 'Sculptured Artware' line; instead, a silver and black or gold and black foil label in the shape of the mythical phoenix bird was used.

Quite often glassware made by the Consolidated Lamp and Glass Company of nearby Coraopolis, Pennsylvania, is mistaken for Phoenix Sculptured Artware. Although the style of the glass is very similar, one distinguishing characteristic is that perhaps 80% of the time Phoenix applied color to the background, leaving the raised design plain in contrast, while Consolidated generally applied color to the raised design and left the background plain. The glassware of both firms is of equal quality and comparable value.

In 1970 Phoenix Glass became a division of Anchor Hocking which in turn was acquired by the Newell Group in 1987. Phoenix has the distinction of being one of the oldest continuously operating glass factories in the United States. For more information, see the section on Consolidated Glass.

Key:
bg — background   mg — milk glass

Aster, vase, yel flowers/gr leaves on wht satin bg, 7"	70.00
Bachelor Button, vase, orchid bg on crystal, 6"	70.00
Cigarette box, lt bl on crystal, w/3 ash trays, 3" & 5½"	90.00
Cosmos, vase, bright yel bg, wht flowers on crystal, 7½"	85.00
Daisy, vase, tan bg on mg, 9¼" dia	145.00
Dancing Girl, vase, lav bg on milk glass, 12"	275.00
Diving Girl, bowl, cadet bl bg on mg, oval, 14"	160.00
Fern, vase, chartreuse bg, MOP fronds on mg, 1976, 7"	35.00

Freesia, vase, crystal satin on sea gr bg, flared, 8"	90.00
Jewel, vase, brn bg on mg, 5"	45.00
Jonquil, vase, all-over MOP on mg, 14" dia	190.00
Lily, vase, orchid bg on crystal satin, cylindrical, 8"	120.00

Vase, Philodendron, cadet blue background on milk glass, 11", $105.00.

Philodendron, vase, gray bg, MOP leaves on mg, 11"	95.00
Pine Cone, vase, (no cones), lt bl on crystal satin, 6½"	85.00
Primrose, vase, tan bg on mg, 8¾"	150.00
Reuben Line, dogwood vase, sea gr on crystal satin, 10"	135.00
Reuben Line, plate, fruit & leaf, dk bl on crystal, 13"	40.00
Strawberry, bowl, wine on milk glass, 10½" +candle holders	180.00
Thistle, vase, mg, 1976 re-issue, 18"	95.00
Tiger Lily, plate, bl bg w/cream satin flowers, 13¾"	150.00
Violets, candy box, cadet bl on mg, 6½" dia	65.00
Water Lily, bowl, wht on crystal, 14", +4¾" candle holders	200.00
Wild Geese, vase, bright bl bg on mg, oval, 9¼"	140.00
Wild Geese, vase, chartreuse, MOP on mg, mk PG Co, 1976	50.00
Wild Rose, vase, lt bl bg, MOP flowers on mg, 10½"	125.00

Lighting

Shade #4529, Rich Cut Stalactite, crystal, 9" L, 3" holder	60.00
Shade #5069, Flame, ruby, 8" L, 3¼" fitter	95.00
Shade #5809, Phoenix Rich Cut Electric Ball, crystal, 8"	125.00
Shade #5884, Twist Electric Bowl, straw opal, 10" dia	60.00
Shade #604, Spot, pk opal, 7" dia, 8" H, 5" fitter	65.00
Shade #6608, Electro, etched floral on crystal, 10" dia	40.00

Miscellaneous

Blackberry, comport, pearl lustre on mg, ftd, w/lid, 8½"	35.00
Lace Dew Drop, banana server, pk on mg, ftd, 11"	45.00
Lace Dew Drop, candlestick, pk on mg, 7", pr	40.00
Lace Dew Drop, goblet, caramel lustre on mg, 7-oz	12.50
Lace Dew Drop, milk jug, caramel lustre on mg, 8"	50.00
Lace Dew Drop, tumbler, antique bl on mg	12.00
Moon & Star, server, pearl lustre on mg, ftd, 11¼"	35.00
Queen Anne, jello mold, star-shaped, crystal	2.00

Phonographs

The phonograph, invented by Thomas Edison in 1877, was the

first practical instrument for recording and reproducing sound. Sound wave vibrations were recorded on a tinfoil-covered cylinder and played back with a needle that ran along the grooves made from the recording, thus reproducing the sound. Other companies further improved Edison's invention, and by 1900 three phonograph companies were in business.

Early models had morning-glory horns; these are especially desirable. The early cylinder players are all of special interest, because after 1910 nearly all models were made to play disk records. By 1925 the hand-cranked players were discontinued and were replaced by electric phonographs.

Our advisor for this category is Steve Oliphant; he is listed in the Directory under California.

Key:
mg — morning-glory   rpd — reproducer
NP — nickel-plated

Busy Bee, cylinder, VG orig..**275.00**
Columbia BS, coin-op, NM **2,500.00**
Columbia Eagle, EX orig...**275.00**
Columbia Grafonola, rnd mahog table **850.00**
Columbia Graphophone, mg horn & stand, ca 1900, EX.............**650.00**
Edison, Chippendale, mahog, disk player **375.00**
Edison Adam, oak..**500.00**
Edison Amberola #1A, oak, NM **1,650.00**
Edison Amberola #30, EX **375.00**
Edison Amberola #75, mahog, EX orig **450.00**
Edison Amberola #75, oak, EX orig **600.00**
Edison Army-Navy, disk player, EX **1,000.00**
Edison Banner Triumph, EX orig **650.00**
Edison Chippendale, oak, disk player, EX orig **500.00**
Edison Fireside, mg horn & cygnet horn, EX orig **775.00**
Edison Gem **450.00**
Edison Home, cylinder, brass horn, EX orig...............**700.00**
Edison Home, 4-min, EX...**450.00**
Edison Home B, 2/4 min, 36" horn, EX orig **750.00**
Edison Standard, under glass cylinder record cabinet **1,500.00**
Edison Standard B **450.00**
Edison Standard D, cylinder, sm repro horn, EX **450.00**
General, child's, crank, dvtl wood case, decals, EX orig **200.00**
Heywood-Wakefield, wicker, EX orig.................... **1,200.00**
Melodograph, w/4 Emerson dbl disc (7") records **195.00**
Mignophone, disk player, outside horn, VG **125.00**
Modernola, mahog, EX orig **600.00**
Multiphone, 24-cylinder, 1900, 84", EX...................**15,000.00**
Psychophone, used by mediums in 1920s, EX **300.00**
RCA, table top, pat 1915, EX, +18 records **225.00**
Reginaphone #150, 15½" d, mahog, outside horn..................**6,000.00**
Victor #130...**450.00**
Victor #16, EX orig...**350.00**
Victor #940E, EX orig **1,000.00**
Victor D, tiger-striped oak & mg horn, EX **1,700.00**
Victor Orthophonic Credenza X, 15½" **900.00**
Victor Schoolhouse, oak horn, EX orig **2,000.00**
Victor VV-IV, oak, table top, EX orig **150.00**

Photographica

Photographic collectibles include not only the cameras and equipment used to 'freeze' special moments in time, but also the photographic images produced by a great variety of processes that have evolved since the daguerrean era of the mid-1800s.

Among the earliest cameras was the sliding box-on-a-box camera. It was focused by sliding one box in and out of the other, thus adjusting the distance of the lens to the ground glass. This was replaced on later models with leather bellows. These were the forerunners of the multi-lens cameras developed in the late 1870s, which were capable of recording many small portraits on a single plate. Double-lens cameras produced stereo images which, when viewed through a device called a stereoscope, achieved a 3-dimensional effect. In 1888 George Eastmann introduced his box camera, the first to utilize roll film. This greatly simplified the process, making it possible for the amateur to enjoy photography as a hobby. Detective cameras, those disguised as books, handbags, etc., are among the most sought after by today's collectors.

Many processes have been used to produce photographic images: daguerreotypes – the most-valued examples being the full-plate which measures 6½" x 8½"; ambrotypes, produced by an early wet-plate process whereby a faint negative image on glass is seen as positive when held against a dark background; and tintypes, contemporaries of ambrotypes, but produced on japanned iron and not as easily damaged.

Other collectible images include carte de visites, known as CDVs, which are portraits printed on paper and produced in quantity. The CDV fad of the 1800s enticed the famous and the unknown alike to pose for these cards, which were circulated among the public to the extent that they became known as 'publics.' When the popularity of CDVs began to wane, a new fascination developed for the cabinet photo, a larger version measuring about 4½" x 6½".

Stereo cards, photos viewed through a device called a stereoscope, are another popular collectible. The glass stereo plates of the mid-1800s and photo prints produced in the darkroom are among the most valuable.

For the most part, good quality images have either maintained or increased in value. Poor quality examples (regardless of rarity) are not selling well. Interest in cameras and stereo equipment is down, and dealers report that often average-priced items that were moving well are often completely overlooked. Though rare items always have a market, collectors seem to be buying only if they are bargain priced.

Our advisor for this category is Roberta Etter; she is listed in the Directory under England. See also Gutta Percha.

Ambrotypes

Half-plate ambrotype, portrait of Bishop Richard Whelon, Western Virginia Diocese of the Catholic Church, 1857, with letter claiming allegiance to Virginia, not to Lincoln, $325.00.

Half plate, CA mining camp outdoor view, men w/tools, EX.. **1,750.00**
Half plate, farmhouse, clothes on line, ME, MOP case **190.00**
Half plate, man w/goatee, full case **50.00**
Whole plate, couple at Niagara Falls, EX tone, case, EX..............**350.00**
Whole plate, 8-member missionary family, Hawaii, 1820s...........**275.00**

4th plate, fireman stands w/knee up, helmet in hand, EX............300.00
4th plate, girl w/drum, tinted, +full case, VG...............................80.00
4th plate, horse & sleigh, driver w/buffalo skins, EX 130.00
4th plate, Louisiana Tiger (soldier w/sword), EX 320.00
4th plate, man w/full beard, tinted, full case, EX.........................40.00
4th plate, New England storefronts, metal mat, half case............150.00
4th plate, Union artillery soldier, wife & daughter, ruby 110.00
6th plate, bagpipe player in full costume, EX 80.00
6th plate, Blk lady in fancy dress, EX...150.00
6th plate, Blk man, seated, Cary, Canal Street, EX 100.00
6th plate, child in plaid, full case, EX...50.00
6th plate, man in reflective pose, trick photo, 1850s, case 60.00
6th plate, Union soldier kneels w/rifle, plastic case 250.00
6th plate, US Marine, frock coat, metal mat/surround, early 150.00
6th plate, US Marine stands in uniform, EX................................110.00
9th plate, Blk boy in jacket/plantation-style hat, cb case 65.00
9th plate, man in suit w/Colt gun, Union & Constitution case...125.00
9th plate, Union soldier in frock coat & kepi, ruby, case 40.00
9th plate, Zouave drummer boy w/cartridge case, ruby, case 275.00
9th plate, 6 Civil War Marines w/weapons, outdoor scene 600.00

Cabinet Photos

Assiniboine Indians, costumes/weapons/homes, 6 for 250.00
Benjamin Harrison, President, Bell, Washington DC 20.00
Billie Johnson, Pony Express rider, sgn 300.00
Captain Jack Crawford, western garb/rifle, sgn 300.00
Charles A Boutelle, Rep from ME, Bell, Washington DC.............20.00
Chief Rain-in-the-Face, Chicago 1893 Expo 1,000.00
Cowboy in chaps, saddle/lasso at side, Kirkland WY, EX 175.00
Gen Francis Cockrell, CSA, Bell 15.00
Gen Geo McClellan, Presidential candidate, Brisbois..................22.00
Girl w/lg doll, Newcomb, Salt Lake City, UT, EX 35.00
James G Blaine, Presidential candidate, Bogardus, NY..................12.00
Lincoln, beardless candidate...40.00
Oliver Wendell Holmes, poet, W Notman, Boston 30.00
Walt Whitman, Gutekunst, Phila, EX..160.00

Cameras

Aiglon, FR sub-miniature, NP w/miniscus lens, +case, EX 275.00
Argus C-3, box style w/flash, 1940, +carrying case, EX.................30.00
Ascot Buckeye, box type, uses plates or roll film, 1896 ....60.00
Autographic 2-C Jr, Kodak, case release & stylus, +case 45.00
Bellieni stereo, Fl:8 lenses, Nancy France, +case, VG 185.00
Brownie #2, Eastman Kodak, in orig Brownie decorated box.........65.00
Brownie #2, 1909, EX in case 35.00
Brownie #3, Eastman, model A, 1903, EX 20.00
Buckeye #3, American Camera Co, wooden folder, 1895 ....100.00
Cameradio, Universal Radio, reflex viewer, 127 film, ca 1949.....120.00
Cirofles TLR, 120 film, 1950s, common 40.00
Conley Jr, folding plate, 4x8" 40.00
Fotron Electronic, 1963, +leather case & instructions 30.00
Hawk-Eye #2A, Eastman Kodak, folding cartridge, 1940s, EX 30.00
Hawk-Eye Detective, Boston Camera, brass knob works bellows.175.00
Hawk-Eye Special #2, box type, tooled leather sides, EX 45.00
Icon Contessa, Zeiss, folding, 35mm, 1950s................................200.00
Kodak #3-C, folds for pocket, rotary shutter, 1885 ....50.00
Kodak Bl Beau Brownie, missing hdl, EX colors 35.00
Komic Kamera, tin windup camera+3 rolls of film, orig box 75.00
Monroe Pocket Poco, folding, 1890s, 3x4" 200.00
Petie, Kunick/Frankfurt, vanity case/camera, 1958, EX 550.00
Plan Primar, Bentzin, folding, 1920s, 6x9 centimeters 45.00
Polyopticon, Hall, Boston, paper board house-shaped box, 6x8" ..80.00

Premo, Eastman Kodak, red bellows, brass lens, 1903, +case 65.00
Ticka, Houghton Ltd, London, pocket watch type, MIB 200.00

#2A Beau Brownie camera, Walter Doren Teague Eastman Kodak, 1927, in leather carrying case, 5" x 3¼" x 6¾", $175.00; Cine Kodak movie camera, Eastman Kodak, 1935, black leather case with chrome attachments, 4¼" x 9⅜", $150.00; Revere Eight movie camera, brown leather and gray enamel case, 1945, 4½" x 4½", $50.00; Jiffy Six-20 camera, Walter Doren Teague, Kodak, 1940, with original cardboard gift box, 6" x 3¼", $40.00; Bantam Special, Walter Doren Teague, Kodak, 1936, black-lacquered metal case, 3" x 4¾", $175.00.

Carte De Visites

Admiral Dupont, Anthony/Brady mt, EX....................................15.00
Albino woman, lady w/wht hair & complexion, G 25.00
Gen Geo A Custer, 3 stars on shoulder bars, Brady, 1865, VG....425.00
Gen Hooker, Anthony/Brady mt w/revenue stamp, EX 20.00
Gen Wm M McCarther, full uniform, Loomis, Boston, EX............60.00
Indian group of 8, visiting Washington, full regalia, early............145.00
Lewis Payne, alias Wood alias Hall arrested..., dtd 1865, EX 600.00
Lincoln & son Tad, book on lap, EX..18.00
Lincoln & Washington, clouds & angels in bkground, EX 15.00
Lincoln & wife, ¾-length, unmk, EX...20.00
Managers of House...Impeachment of A Johnson, Brady, G 185.00
Mary & Frank Littlefingers, 2 dwarfs, Eisemann, NY 20.00
Mrs Tom Thumb (Lavinia W Stratton), elderly, Anthony/Brady ..30.00
Plains Indian squaw & papoose, WH Jackson, card mt, EX 40.00
Sam Houston, vignette portrait, Fredricks, NY, scarce 350.00
Statue of Liberty, JA French, NH, EX...35.00
Tom Thumb (Charles Stratton) & Lavinia Warren, Anthony 15.00
Ulysses S Grant, as General-in-Chief, 4-star, EX...........................27.50
Ulysses S Grant, as Secretary of War, 1862, unmk, EX 17.50
Zouave w/bayonet in full-length portrait, EX 175.00

Daguerreotypes

Half plate, boy & girl stand w/toys, EX......................................160.00
Half plate, CA lumber camp, men & tools, 1850s, full case 800.00
Half plate, child w/toy ram, Fontayne & Porter, Cincinnati........850.00

Half plate, couple w/4 children, leather case 275.00
Half plate, man w/compass, EX 1,800.00
Half plate, officer seated, wife stands w/arm at shoulder, EX 120.00
Half plate, officer seated w/sword, EX.....................................350.00
Half plate, soldier stands, dress uniform/sword/fur hat, EX..........650.00
Whole plate, Gen John Wool, after Buena Vista victory, EX . 4,000.00
4th plate, dog on couch, EX 50.00
4th plate, French soldier w/sword & hat, EX 200.00
4th plate, lady's portrait, Langenheim, Phila, emb label, EX..........80.00
4th plate, Lieutenant from MD, Mexican War, 1847, EX 450.00
4th plate, man in Masonic apron, tinted, EX...............................250.00
4th plate, ME street scene, church at bk, 1850, full case 1,100.00
4th plate, Mexican War officer w/sword, EX 200.00
4th plate, sailing vessel in full sail, G 250.00
6th plate, boy & girl w/long-haired dog, EX 180.00
6th plate, boy w/dog on lap, Schoonmaker Building, NY, VG 175.00
6th plate, druggist w/mortar & pestle, EX 300.00
6th plate, gold miner w/wide-brimmed hat, Vance, CA, VG 450.00
6th plate, Hamilton Canal Buildings/Hump Bridge, NY, EX... 1,000.00
6th plate, Indian lady, patterned dress, hair bk, EX.....................275.00
6th plate, J Phipps, founder of midwest town, 1850s, case 25.00
6th plate, Jenny Lind, tinted close up, in Jenny Lind case 600.00
6th plate, lady seated w/dog, GW Lewis, CT, EX 150.00
6th plate, man w/trophy, some mat oxidation, EX.........................90.00
6th plate, miner/bridge builder at CA bridge, full case 1,000.00
6th plate, post mortem, child w/doll, EX......................................60.00
6th plate, riverboat gamblers at cards, EX 1,500.00
6th plate, tinsmith at work w/tools at table, EX 320.00
6th plate, violinist playing, full case, EX.......................................90.00
9th plate, CA miner w/account book, 1950s, case........................500.00
9th plate, man w/sheaf of papers & map folio, metal mat..............40.00

Photos

Baseball team of USS Maine, albumen, ca 1898, EX 500.00
Charles Sumner, full-figure portrait, albumen, 1874, 16x13" 60.00
Chief Gall, Barry blindstamp, fr, 10x7".......................................350.00
Civil War officers by tent, A Gardner, albumen, 7x9" 150.00
Cotton market, Montgomery AL, silver print, 1910, 8x9" 45.00
Cree canoe on Lac Les Isles, Suffolk, gravure, '26, lg folio 100.00
Flatheads...dance...near Missoula, Curtis, orotone, 11x14" 1,200.00
Gen FJ Gardner, CSA, albumen, orig card mt, EX 95.00
Gen Thomas, in uniform, mtd, albumen, 8½x6½", EX 250.00
Geronimo & Nachez w/Apache band, CS Fly, orig mt, 5x8½". 1,050.00
Indian maid, nude, from bk, Curtis, fr, 10x8" image....................150.00
Jean Harlow, GF Cannon, credits on bk, 7½x9½", EX.................80.00
John Philip Sousa, in uniform, w/baton, albumen, 1898, 6x4".....210.00
Lands of Apsaroke, Curtis, photogravure, 4x8" on 10x12" sheet ..25.00
Lillie Langtry, portrait, sepia, card mt, 8x4" 35.00
Lincoln, Berger, from Brady Gallery, albumen, 5½x4"...................90.00
Mary Pickford, Hartsook, CA, 9½x7½", EX 15.00
Nez Perce Indian school, students outside, albumen, 8x9" 25.00
Nude study, frontal pose, wears necklace, sepia, 1890s, 5x4".........35.00
Pawnee Bill, Taylor, Nashville TN, sgn in margin, 9x6" 170.00
People before 3-story building, Lock, Deadwood SD, albumen......25.00
Piano tuner w/tools at grand piano, sepia, 10x8", EX 30.00
Swampy Cree Indian, Thorndike/Rice trip to Hudson Bay 1899.125.00
Tree cut w/tunnel, wagon emerges, silverprint, 1890, 30x19" 50.00
US Grant, seated in business suit, albumen, 5½x4".......................30.00
West Virginia, church/stone path, 1970s, 8x5", EX 12.50

Stereoscopic Views

In evaluating stereo views, the date and condition are all-impor-

tant. Some views were printed over a thirty- to forty-year period – 'first generation' prices are far higher than later copies. Right now, quality stereo views are at a premium.

Am soldiers in Philippines, Craig carbines, Posey, 1899.................. 8.00
Anton Gregor Rubenstein, pianist/composer, Gurney, EX 17.50
Bound for Klondike Gold Fields, Calikoot Pass, AK, Keystone 30.00
Buffalo Bill on horse aiming rifle, yel Am Scenery mt 35.00
Bull Run Monuments, McCollum & Butterworth, gr mt, EX 7.00
Chippewas/canoes/wigwams, Upton's MN & NW Views, 1870s ..30.00
Cincinnati & Covington Suspension Bridge, Mendenhall, G 10.00
Congregational Church, Emporia KS, 1870s, VG 6.00
French balloon ascension, 17 people on ground, 1860s, EX...........35.00
Geronimo shoots arrow, St Louis Expo, Keystone, EX 35.00
Girl w/4 dolls, Weller #312, VG 10.00
India wharf w/ships at anchor on dock, Joule, early, EX 15.00
Indians before teepee, some in military clothes, 1870s.................40.00
Looking Up 5th Ave, man w/camera on skyscraper, Keystone 40.00
Natural History Building, wing being added, Boston, EX.............. 8.00
President Roosevelt at Yellowstone, 1903, EX.............................20.00
Prospect Point, camera on stand, Niagara scenery.......................30.00
PT Barnum's party at Yosemite Falls, Woodward #556, EX 7.50
Quincy market building, Boston, 1870s, EX 15.00
Sen Sumner collection, Dr Holmes, Wallach, 14 for 25.00
Sioux Indians, 2 seated women, Taylor, St Paul MN, EX 22.00
Tarapin Towers Falls from Goat Island, Langenhiem, 1856, EX.....68.00
Texas Giant Shield Brothers in uniforms, Eisemann, EX 20.00
Train wreck, Hartford CT, 1870s, VG...12.00
Washington Irving's home, Langenhiem, ca 1856, EX 66.00
Washington Street, city after fire, JP Soule, yel mt...................... 7.00
4 Blks holding o'possum, 2 w/shotguns, Kilburn #7026.................10.00

Tintypes

Outdoor view of railroad station at Wakeeney, Kansas, Pacific Express Company labels affix tintype to its mat, 4½" x 6½", $300.00.

Half plate, men in band uniforms, 1 w/major's staff, EX................60.00
Half plate, 3 tennis players in 1880s clothes, EX 220.00
Whole plate, couple in rain gear at falls, EX 45.00
Whole plate, printer & Echo Print #2 Model Press, EX...............380.00
Whole plate, 4 dressmakers w/various tools, 1870s, 7x5", VG 40.00
4th plate, Boston view, minor wrinkling......................................70.00
4th plate, Captain 4th VT Infantry, saber at chest, case 200.00
4th plate, drummer boy, red jacket, stars on lapel, case................345.00
4th plate, Indian lady w/baby, gold touches, EX 145.00

4th plate, Indian lady w/2 children, EX 125.00
4th plate, soldier w/musket w/fixed bayonet, gold touches 160.00
6th plate, Apache w/striped blanket, full figure, EX....................165.00
6th plate, blind man w/dk glasses & cane, VG 20.00
6th plate, Blk mammy w/wht baby in carriage, VG 35.00
6th plate, Brooklin Zouave Redleg, shaved head, case 350.00
6th plate, Civil War officer w/sword/hat/flag, case 110.00
6th plate, Confederate w/bugle/revolver, gutta percha case 200.00
6th plate, Confederate w/feather in hat, gold touches, EX 90.00
6th plate, cowboy in leather clothes, rifle at chest, EX 200.00
6th plate, Dewitt Baseball Club, 9 men in uniforms, EX.............300.00
6th plate, firemen in uniform w/helmets, 3 for 160.00
6th plate, hairlipped man w/bouquet of flowers, EX 40.00
6th plate, Indian War Federal officer in tent scene, EX.................20.00
6th plate, Infantry man w/knapsack/roll/canteen/rifle, case 175.00
6th plate, man w/gun & sword, w/2 girls, EX 75.00
6th plate, Southeastern Indian & agent, rare clothing, EX 80.00
6th plate, tennis player w/racquet, ca 1870s, EX...........................35.00
6th plate, Union Infantryman in slouch hat, armed, cased 110.00
6th plate, Union musician w/horn, epaulettes, EX 75.00
6th plate, Union trooper w/rifle/Bowie knife, case 165.00
6th plate, 1860s man, in Mascher case, EX 125.00
6th plate, 2 KY Confederates seated, ¾ profiles, unarmed 150.00
9th plate, owl (stuffed) on chair, leather case 150.00
9th plate, Union soldier seated w/Colt pistol, EX 75.00
9th plate, Union soldier w/Bowie knife & Starr revolver, EX 130.00

Viewers and Slides

Brewster, mahog, brass lenses, ivory knob, early, VG 250.00
Claudet, maroon leather, brass bbl lenses, late 1840s, EX 525.00
Edison Kinetoscope w/magic lantern, +100 slides 625.00
Enterprise, slide projector, tin/cast metal, pat 1899 ....50.00
Foto Reel, metal, 26 views on reel...35.00
Holmes-Bater Pedestal Stereo Viewer, walnut/mahog, 1850s.........75.00
Keystone Telebinocular, collapsible, book-form box.......................60.00
Magic Lantern, tin w/brass plaque, wood hdl, AT Thompson........85.00
Oraphoscope, hand-held viewer w/metal lens, pat 1889, EX..........45.00
Sawyers Jr Projector, stereoscope viewer, 26 reels, M 30.00
Stereo viewer, burl case/fancy SP moldings, European, EX 170.00
Stereopticon, standard..40.00
Varnished wood/eng aluminum, velvet liner 40.00
Vue de Optique, St Petersburg Russia, ca 1750, EX 185.00
Zeotrope, see movies through slots, 9½" dia, EX 475.00
Zograscope, mahog w/diamond pattern, leaded base, 1780s.........450.00

Miscellaneous

Album, gr plush w/brass trim, inserted fr, Victorian 185.00
Case, MOP, floral, 6th plate, pr..400.00
Case, MOP, river & cottage scene, whole case, EX 700.00
Stanhope, alabaster barrel, Niagara Falls scene...............................30.00
Stanhope, cross, bone, WWI, troups in trenches, ca 1914, EX 55.00
Stanhope, pen, ivory, Crystal Palace Sydenham view, EX..............75.00
Stanhope, pipe, cvd wood, 6 Port Erin views, 1" L, EX 48.00
Stanhope, scent bottle, brass, w/neck chain, 6 views, EX.............150.00
Stanhope, silvery cross on chain, Lord's Prayer inside 25.00
Stanhope, tape measure, bbl form w/ivory finial, 1 view 65.00

Piano Babies

A familiar sight in Victorian parlors, piano babies languished atop shawl-covered pianos in a variety of poses: crawling, sitting, on their tummies, or on their backs playing with their toes. Some babies were nude and some wore gowns. Sizes ranged from about 3" up to 12". The most famous manufacturer of these bisque darlings was the Heubach Brothers of Germany, who nearly always marked their product; see Heubach for more listings. Watch for reproductions.

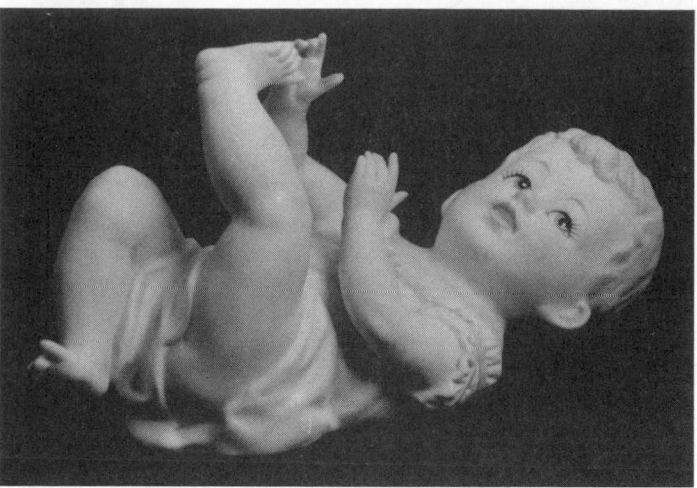

Baby, reclining, unmarked, 8½" long, $125.00.

Blk baby, crawling, Germany, 4"...75.00
Boy, sitting, 6¾" 60.00
Boy & girl, pastels, Andrea, #6161, 12", pr...................................400.00
Boy frowns/holds pig trying to drink from chamber pot, 8½" 400.00
Cowboy hat, boots, holster..48.00
Curly brn wig, wht gown, dog licking face, 3½x2x3" 165.00
Lace-trimmed bonnet, wht & gr gown, 4¼x2¾x4", pr...............195.00
Lying on stomach, flowered gown, 17" L 525.00
Lying on stomach, holds lamb, Germany, 6½" 130.00
Lying on stomach, 8¾" 70.00
Sits, hand to cheek, in yel gown w/roses, Germany, 9½" 650.00
Sits, holds lg cup, left hand raised, Germany, 7x5".....................145.00
Sitting w/drum, bl hat, mk Royal Rudolstadt, 8" 350.00
Thumb to mouth, fine details, unmk, 6x10" 235.00

Picasso Art Pottery

Pablo Picasso created some distinctive pottery during the 1940s, marking the ware with his signature.

Charger, terra cotta, partially glazed with bull in black slip, Madoura, 15", $1,800.00.

Pitcher, Faune Cavalier, horses, over-top hdl, 8½"	5,000.00
Plate, Bouquet a la Pomme, floral, 9¾"	2,800.00
Plate, Joneur de Flute ed Chevre, flutist, 10"	2,800.00
Plate, Poissons, 3 mc stylized fish, 12½x15"	4,600.00
Plate, Tete de Lion, lion's face, sq, 17"	6,000.00
Plate, Visage aux Taches, facial features, 16½"	6,000.00
Roundel, bull's head, Madoura, 10"	1,000.00
Vase, Arenes, bullfight/crowd, 12"	15,000.00
Vase, Chouette Blanche, rooster form, 11½"	4,100.00

Pickard

Founded in 1897 in Chicago, Illinois, the Pickard China Company was originally a decorating studio, importing china blanks from European manufacturers. Some of these early pieces bear the name of those companies as well as Pickard's. Trained artists decorated the wares with hand-painted studies of fruit, florals, birds, and scenics, and often signed their work. In 1915 Pickard introduced a line of 23k gold over a dainty floral-etched ground design. In the 1930s, they began to experiment with the idea of making their own ware and by 1938 had succeeded in developing a formula for fine translucent china. Since 1976 they have issued an annual limited edition Christmas plate. They are now located in Antioch, Illinois.

The company has used various marks: 'Pickard' with double circles; the crown mark; 'Pickard' on a gold maple leaf; and the current mark, the lion and shield. Work signed by Challinor, Marker, and Yeschek is especially valued by today's collectors.

Our advisors for this category are Lois and Milt Steinfeld; they are listed in the Directory under New Jersey.

Bowl, lilies w/much gold, sgn Yeschek, 7½"	165.00
Bowl, tiger lilies, sgn, gold trim, hdls, 5½x7½"	85.00
Bowl, water lilies, sgn S Nessy, sq, mk, 2⅞x7½"	145.00
Cake plate, gold etched florals, 10"	60.00
Candy dish, pk floral/tall trees, sgn Marker, hdls, 6"	120.00
Candy dish, 4 medallions, cobalt w/wht daisies, 5½x6"	70.00
Creamer & sugar bowl, Deserted Garden, sgn Vokral, EX gold	210.00
Jardiniere, leaves, pk on gr w/gold, Hessler, ca 1900 mk, 5½"	275.00

Pitcher, Deserted Garden, signed Challinor, ca 1912-1919, 7½", $475.00.

Pitcher, gold w/water lily band, 6-sided/bulbous, sgn, 8"	250.00
Plate, bellflowers, gilt detail, sgn Vobor, 7¾"	110.00
Plate, Deserted Garden, fruit rim, sgn Yeschek, hdls, 11"	200.00
Plate, Goldenrod & Daisy, wide gold rim, Challinor, 6¾"	75.00

Plate, purple grapes, sgn Hess, gold scallops, 8½"	90.00
Plate, 3 groups of buttercups/pk flowers, sgn Richter, 8"	115.00
Shaker, lemon trees, heavy gold, sgn Tolpin, 1905 mk	35.00
Tea set, bl w/gold etch, 1919 mk, 3-pc	225.00
Toothpick holder, Nouveau decor, gold rim/ft, 1912-19 mk	135.00
Vase, abstract flowers, gold lined on gr to aqua, sgn, 10"	300.00
Vase, florals w/gold, sgn Florence James, basket form	225.00
Vase, forest/moon scenic, sgn Challinor, 9"	410.00
Vase, palm treees by moonlit water, artist sgn, 6½"	275.00

Pickle Castors

Pickle castors, which were both functional and decorative, became popular after the Civil War, reaching their peak about 1885. By 1900 they had virtually disappeared from factory catalogs. Numerous styles were available. They consisted of a decorated, silverplated frame that held either a fancy clear pressed-glass insert or one of decorated art glass – the latter being popular in the more affluent Victorian households and more desirable with collectors today.

In the listings below, the description prior to the semi-colon (;) refers to the jar (insert), and the remainder of the line describes the frame. Where no condition is indicated, the silverplate is assumed to be in very good to excellent condition; glass jars are assumed mint.

Apple Blossom, wht w/mc florals; Northwood ftd fr, +tongs	425.00
Baby Invt T'print, cranberry, HP; slide lid, emb Meriden fr	475.00
Beaded Dart, bl, shell finial; ornate Rogers fr	285.00
Bl cased, gold flowers & bug; R&B SP fr & lid, +tongs	395.00
Block, amber; ornate fr w/face emb on tall legs, +tongs	175.00
Cane, amber; Hartford fr w/trimmed base, +pickle hook	195.00
Cosmos, pigeon blood; SP fr/tongs/lid, 10x4¾"	395.00
Cranberry, HP florals; ftd Wilcox fr, +tongs	325.00
Cranberry, HP florals; ornate cut-out Derby fr, +tongs	395.00
Cranberry, HP peonies, ribbed; Reed & Barton fr, +tongs	450.00
Crown Milano, coral/HP floral, Mt WA; Wilcox fr, +tongs	650.00
Cut, strawberry, dmn points, fans; SP lid, +tongs	110.00
Daisy & Button, topaz; ornate Derby fr, NM	195.00
Daisy & Button w/V band, vaseline; orig fr/lid/tongs, 11"	250.00
Dia Quilt, cranberry; fancy fr, 12", +tongs	300.00
Dia Quilt, rubena, HP florals; ornate Tufts fr, +tongs	495.00
Diamond, topaz; Pacific fr w/swirled decor, +tongs	215.00
Faceted Block, bl; emb fr, +tongs	155.00
Hobnail, peach to rose opal; Meriden fr, +tongs	450.00

Sapphire blue Inverted Thumbprint with applied crystal shells in Wilcox frame with owls, 9¾", $565.00.

Invt T'print, bl, HP florals; unmk fr, +tongs	295.00
Invt T'print, cranberry, bulbous; unmk fr, +tongs	295.00

Invt T'print, cranberry, HP florals; 13½" Tufts fr **395.00**
Leaf Mold, vaseline/cranberry spatter; fancy ftd fr, +tongs...........**395.00**
Melon Ribs, clear & frosted; Rogers fr, +tongs **150.00**
MOP Dia Quilt, pk, HP rose, att Webb; Rogers fr, +fork **400.00**
Panelled Sprig, cranberry; lacy fretwork on Benedict fr **450.00**
Pigeon blood satin w/floral; ornate fr, +tongs, 10" **325.00**
Pine cone, pk cased; ornate SP fr, +tongs, NM **375.00**
Pk satin, HP floral, egg form; ftd orig Tufts fr, +tongs..................**650.00**
Raindrop MOP, rose; SH&M floral-emb fr, +tongs **885.00**
Spanish Lace, cranberry opal; ftd fr w/lid & tongs, NM **450.00**
Swirled Bark, rubena, Mt WA; rstr Pairpoint fr, +tongs **350.00**
Yel, HP dogwood blossoms, Mt W Verona; ornate Pairpoint fr ...**450.00**
Zipper, emerald gr, dbl; SH&M ftd fr, +tongs **295.00**

Pie Birds

Pie birds (also known as pie vents and pie funnels) have been in use since late Victorian times. Placed in the middle of a pie, they serve the dual purpose of supporting the pastry and allowing steam to escape from the pie so that it does not boil over. They come in various, interesting forms.

Our advisor for this category is Alan Pedel; he is listed in the Directory under England.

Blk bird on wht base, ceramic **29.00**
Blk Chef, w/spoon, J Barry/Chicago, Pie-Aire, 1945, 4½".............**35.00**
Blk Piewoman, holds pie, vents through mouth, ceramic **40.00**
British Bobby, vents from helmet, ceramic **35.00**
Duck w/beret on head, ceramic **35.00**
Eggman, ceramic...**35.00**
Mammy, ceramic, 5"...**35.00**
Owl on tree stump, ceramic, EX detail **40.00**
Pillsbury twin, pk, ceramic..**17.00**
2-Headed bird, bake-proof glass, cobalt beak, Scotland.................**39.00**

Pierce, Howard

Howard Pierce opened a studio in Claremont, California, in the mid-1940s where he produced small ceramic models of birds and animals, figurines, and vases, making his molds and decorating his ware with no outside help except for his wife and more recently his daughter. He is best known for his skill at sculpting his models, which he decorates entirely with the airbrush. Early items were incised 'Howard Pierce, Claremont, California,' or stamped 'Howard Pierce Porcelain.' Not all of his ware is marked, however, and some may carry only his initials.

Our advisor for this category is Jack Chipman; he is listed in the Directory under California.

Creche, wht, 1950s...**30.00**
Figurine, African head, 1950s **45.00**
Figurine, bear, brn, 1950s..**15.00**
Figurine, bull, brn, 1950s...**15.00**
Figurine, eagle, blk, 1960s..**35.00**
Figurine, goose, brn & wht, 1950s **25.00**
Figurine, goose, wht, 1950s-1960s, pr **35.00**
Figurine, heron, wht **25.00**
Figurine, penguin, brn, 1950s, pr **35.00**
Figurine, quail mother & 2 young, brn speckled, 3-pc set **45.00**
Figurine, rabbit, brn, sm, 1970s, pr **15.00**
Figurine, ram, recent **15.00**
Figurine, roadrunner, blk, recent, lg **22.00**

Figurine, rooster & hen, brn & wht, 1950s, 9¼", 7¾", pr **35.00**
Figurine, unicorn, recent **18.00**
Figurine, wood duck, brn, 1950s...**15.00**

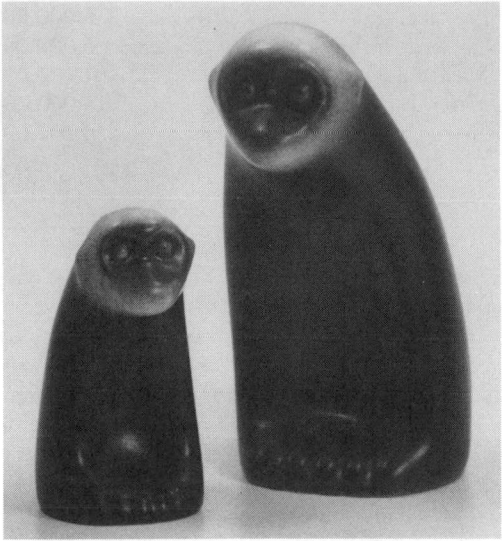

Monkeys, 1950s, scarce, tallest: 6½", $45.00 for the pair.

Vase, Deco girl w/in circular cutout, creche style, gr, sq.................**45.00**
Vase, fish insert, creche style, gr, 8" **35.00**
Vase, wht deer/tree at side, creche style, gr, Claremont, 8" **35.00**

Pietra-Dura

From the Italian Renaissance period, Pietra-dura is a type of mosaic work used for plaques, table tops, frames, etc., that includes small pieces of gemstones, mother-of-pearl, and the like.

Box, 5 mosaic panels, 4½x8" **995.00**
Plaque, country int: man at table talks w/girl, 10x13" **2,200.00**
Plaque, lady in doorway, Italian, 1900s, 12x9" **1,000.00**
Plaque, 2 birds on branches, bl sky, Florentine, 12x10" **2,200.00**
Plaque, 2 men seated w/instruments, Florentine, 9x11" **2,300.00**

Pigeon Blood

Pigeon blood glass, produced in the late 1800s, may be distinguished from other dark red glass by its distinctive orange tint.

Torquay: Jar, 8½", $475.00; Bride's basket, 11" diameter, $635.00; Jar, 8½", $475.00.

Celery, Torquay, emb silver rim..**200.00**
Decanter, Bulging Loops, 8" **48.00**
Pickle castor, HP Coreopsis; Benedict SP fr, all orig, EX **365.00**

Pitcher, clear hdl, 7" 150.00
Pitcher, tankard; Dia Quilt, 10" 175.00
Shakers, Flower Band, pr...135.00
Toothpick holder, Fine Rib...55.00
Top hat, rolled rim, 4x8" 100.00

Pillin

Polia Pillin was born in Poland in 1909; many of her family were artisians and craftsmen. Except for a few weeks of formal instruction at the Hull House in Chicago, Pillin is self-taught in the arts. Her work has been shown in many exhibits, and she has received awards from the Los Angeles County Art Institute, Syracuse Museum, Los Angeles County Fair, and the California State Fair. First interested in oils and watercolors, she has carried the same Byzantine quality over to her pottery. All of her work is signed 'Pillin' or 'W&P Pillin,' both with the loop of the P extended in an arc over the remaining letters of her name.

Bowl, bust portraits & birds on bl, 5½x10½" 300.00
Bowl, bust portraits on blk, 6½x5½" 275.00
Bowl, red abstract, 3¾x5¾" 125.00
Pendant, horse on bl, 2" 40.00
Plate, children w/balloons on yel, 7½" 100.00
Plate, frolicking horses on gr, 7½" 110.00
Vase, birds on gr w/pastels, 5¼" 125.00
Vase, birds on yel, 1½"...50.00
Vase, bust portraits on blk, bulbous, 9½".....................275.00
Vase, bust portraits on gr, bulbous, 8½" 225.00
Vase, fish, pk & gr, squat 75.00
Vase, gr/pastel, bottle form, 11½" 140.00
Vase, horses on pastels, 5¾".......................................165.00
Vase, 3 nudes on bl, 9¼" 300.00
Vase, 3 nudes on pastels, 4½"......................................150.00

Pin-Back Buttons

Most of the advertising buttons made until the 1920s were top-quality, full-color, celluloid-covered buttons termed 'cellos.' Many were issued in sets on related topics featuring historical people and events, animals and birds, and other themes. Several cigarette, gum, and candy companies used buttons as inserts in their products. Usually the name of the company or product was printed on a paper placed in the back of the button and held securely by the pin. Most of the back papers are still in place today, aiding in the identification of the button. Beginning in the 1920s, a large number of buttons were lithographed (printed on metal); these buttons are referred to as 'lithos.' Nearly all advertising buttons are collected today with perhaps these exceptions: common buttons picturing flags of various nations, general labor union buttons denoting the payment of dues, and similar buttons with clever sayings.

Following is a listing of some of the most popular non-political buttons. Values reflect buttons which have designs centered, colors aligned, no fading or yellowing, no spots or stains, and no cracks, splits, or dents. See also Personalities and Political Entourage.

Buster Brown Bread 27.50
Buster Brown Brownbilt Shoes.....................................12.50
Chew Soda Mint Gum..., ball player, rare 450.00
Drink Fan Taz, Memphis TN, baseballs/bat, NM 375.00
Dupont Dynamite 32.00
Edison Mazda Lamp 35.00
Hercules Powder, Keep 'Em Shooting, red/wht/bl, 1910s 22.50
Kitty Kelly, Columbia Broadcasting 7.50

MacArthur, photo, red/wht/bl 8.00
Old Style Lager, kitten & ball 35.00
Papa Knows BVD Best, man w/smile, 3-color, 1940s, NM 3.50
RC Cole Ledgers, Binders & Supplies, red/wht, 1910 ....4.50
Rochester Bicycles 22.00
Rockne of Notre Dame, man in profile, 1930s, NM......................18.00
Sharples Separator, mother & child...............................22.50
St Joseph Co Raccoon Hunters Club, blk/wht, 1938, 1¼", NM 12.00
Uncle Don's Engineers Club, 2 trains, mc, 1930......................15.00
Welcome Trans-Atlantic Fliers 12.50
Winchester Guns, The Topperweins, stained 28.00
Yel Kid, High Admiral Cigarettes, #4, EX 60.00
Zorro, 3½" 32.00

Pink Lustre Ware

Pink lustre was produced by nearly every potter in the Staffordshire district in the 18th and 19th centuries. The application of gold lustre on white or light-colored backgrounds produced pinks, while the same over dark colors developed copper. The wares ranged from hand-painted plaques to transfer-printed dinnerware.

Bowl, divided, mc florals/appl leaves w/gold, mk, 5½x9x11" 135.00
Creamer, scenic, 2½" 45.00
Cup & saucer, handleless; church decor, minor wear 95.00
Cup & saucer, scene w/cows, Queensware 32.00
Jug, house/trees ea side, mfg flaw, 4".............................65.00
Mug, house w/lake transfer..100.00
Plaque, He That Believes Shall Be Saved, 7¾x8¾", EX 85.00

Plate, 6½"; Cup and saucer, $65.00 for the set.

Plate, Scroll & Flowers, ca 1850, 7½" 15.00
Plate, Shepherd Boy, center transfer, deep, 1830s, 7¾" 60.00
Punch bowl, florals/house scene, scenic int, 11"...........................425.00

Pink Pigs

Pink Pigs on cabbage green were made in Germany around the turn of the century. They were sold as souvenirs in train depots, amusement parks, and gift shops. 'Action pigs' (those involved in some amusing activity) are the most valuable, and prices increase with the number of pigs. Though a similar type of figurine was made in white bisque, most serious collectors prefer only the pink ones. They are marked in two ways: 'Germany' in incised letters, and a black ink stamp 'Made in Germany' in a circle.

1 beside gr drum, wall mt match holder 60.00
1 beside stump, camera around neck, toothpick holder..................95.00
1 coming out of cup 65.00
1 coming out of suitcase...85.00
1 coming through gr fence, post at sides, open for flowers..............95.00
1 in case looking through binoculars..85.00
1 in gr Dutch shoe 50.00
1 in gr suitcase bank, head 1 side, bk other, gold trim 75.00
1 in Japanese submarine, Japan imp on both sides.........................125.00
1 in money sack bank 85.00
1 lg pig sitting behind 3" trough 75.00
1 on binoculars, gold trim..95.00
1 on gr trinket dish, leg caught in lobster claw 65.00
1 on horseshoe-shaped dish w/raised 4-leaf clover 65.00
1 on shoulder of gr ink bottle 65.00
1 reclining on horseshoe ash tray 70.00
1 riding train, 4½" 125.00
1 sits, holds orange Boston Baked Beans pot match holder............65.00
1 sitting by purse 75.00
1 sitting in bathtub 90.00
1 sitting on log, mk Germany..80.00
1 standing in gr tub..75.00
1 w/attached toothpick holder 55.00
1 w/front ft in 3-part dish containing 3 dice, 1 ft on dice...............75.00
1 wearing chef's costume, holds frypan, w/basket 95.00

Pig with old-style camera, $100.00.

2, mother & baby in bl blanket in tub, rabbit on board atop 70.00
2, mother in tub gives baby a bottle, lamb looks on, 4x3½" 75.00
2 behind trough, unmk 65.00
2 by eggshell 80.00
2 dancing, in top hat, tux & cane 95.00
2 holding hands in roadster, 4½" L 125.00
2 in bed, Good Night on footboard, 4x3x2½" 145.00
2 in love sit on lg log, 2 openings on tree stump, 7" L..................67.50
2 in purse..75.00
2 on basket, head raising lid, plaque on front 80.00
2 on binoculars, gold trim 115.00
2 on bl container 40.00
2 on cotton bale, 1 peers from hole, 1 over top................................90.00
2 on gr tray...50.00
2 on seesaw on top of pouch bank..75.00
2 on top hat 95.00
3, 1 on lg slipper playing banjo, 2 dancing on side 125.00
3 dressed up on edge of dish...70.00
3 sm pigs behind oval trough, mk, 2¾x2½x1¾" 55.00
3 w/baby carriage, father & 2 babies, Wheeling His Own 75.00

3 w/carriage, mother & 2 babies, Germany.....................................85.00
3 w/coach, mama & babies, More the Merrier...............................85.00

Pisgah Forest

The Pisgah Forest Pottery was established in 1920 near Mount Pisgah in Arden, North Carolina, by Walter B. Stephen, who had worked in previous years at other locations – Nonconnah, Tennessee, and Skyland (the latter from 1913 until 1916). Stephen, who was born in the mountain region near Asheville, was known for his work in the Southern tradition. He produced skillfully executed wares exhibiting an amazing variety of techniques. He operated his business with only two helpers. Recognized today as his most outstanding accomplishment, his Cameo line was decorated by hand in the pate-sur-pate style (similar to Wedgwood Jasper) in such designs as Fiddler and Dog, Spinning Wheel, Covered Wagon, Buffalo Hunt, Mountain Cabin, Square Dancers, Indian Campfire, and Plowman. Stephen is known for other types of wares as well. His crystalline glaze is highly regarded by today's collectors.

At least nine different stamps mark his wares, several of which contain the outline of the potter at the wheel and 'Pisgah Forest.' Stephen died in 1961, but the work was continued by his associates.

Bowl, Cameo, wagon train, sgn Stephen, 4" H............................125.00
Bowl, turq crackle, pk int, 5½" H..17.50
Creamer, Cameo in design, w/fiddler, 4".......................................130.00
Fish plate, Nonconnah in Cameo, dk gr slip, 11½" 150.00
Pitcher, eggplant glaze, potter at wheel, 3½" 30.00
Teapot, Cameo, knob finial, 5"..200.00
Teapot, turq, w/hood, 5"..35.00
Tobacco jar, Nonconnah swirl, swirl clay in buff/brn/bl, 6½".......250.00
Vase, bl crystalline, Ku shape, mk 1948, 7½" 125.00
Vase, Cameo, ox & figure w/wheat, dk gr slip, 18" 250.00
Vase, crystalline, silver/gr w/wht matt, 6½" 100.00
Vase, pnt in Cameo, mk Nonconnah, 8½" 350.00

Vase, ivory crystalline, 5", $200.00.

Vase, turq/wine crackle, 6½" 45.00
Vase, yel ware, pk int, 3", VG 20.00

Pittsburgh Glass

As early as 1797, utility window glass and hollowware were being produced in the Pittsburgh area. Coal had been found in abundance, and it was there that it was first used instead of wood to fuel the glass furnaces. Because of this, as many as 150 glass companies operated there at one time. However, most failed due to the economically disastrous effects of the War of 1812. By the mid-1850s, those that remained were producing a wide range of flint glass items including pattern-molded and free-blown glass, cut and engraved wares, and pressed tableware patterns.

Bottle, bar; canary, 8-panel, long neck w/cap rest, 11" **475.00**
Bottle, pocket; gr-aqua, 12 vertical ribs, tooled mouth, 5¾" **140.00**
Bottle, toilet water; 16-rib, amethyst shaded to purple **1,600.00**
Cake stand, appl dome ft w/folded rim, 8x10" **265.00**
Candlestick, blown & pillar molded, 11¾" **1,300.00**
Candlestick, Dolphin, canary yel, 7", NM, pr **750.00**
Candlestick, Thistle, turq opaque, Bakewell/Pears, 9½" **95.00**
Canister, 3 appl cobalt rings, dome lid, 11" **500.00**
Chestnut flask, amethyst, 19 swirled ribs, att, 6" **725.00**
Compote, eng Greek Key rim w/monogram, cut star ft, 8x8".......**230.00**
Compote, lt custard dolphin base, starch bl shell bowl, 6" **850.00**
Compote, pillar mold, baluster stem, lid, 9x7½", EX...................**175.00**
Compote, pillar mold, 8-rib, wide ft, baluster stem, 7x7" **295.00**
Compote, 20-rib, baluster stem, appl finial, 8x5¾", EX **500.00**

Free-blown cobalt creamer, tooled rim, open pontil, 5½", $625.00.

Decanter, cut flutes, 3 appl rings, umbrella stopper, 10" **125.00**
Jigger, sapphire bl, arched panels, 2⅜", pr......................................**70.00**
Pan, 10-panel, folded rim, pontil, 5¾" **110.00**
Pitcher, blown, appl horizontal rings/hdl, 8" **165.00**
Pitcher, ruby, 12-rib, appl hollow hdl, 1815-40, 4" **395.00**
Pitcher, 9 tooled bands at mouth, 3-rib hdl w/curl, 8½"...............**350.00**
String holder, clear w/cobalt base & finial, 4½x4¾" dia **125.00**
Sugar bowl, clear/wht loops, appl ft, 4½"+witch ball lid **500.00**
Syllabub, cut flutes, knop stem, polished pontil, 4¾" **40.00**
Tumbler, violet, paneled, 3¼", NM..**65.00**
Whiskey taster, pillar mold, 8-rib, cobalt, ftd, rare **145.00**
Wine, cut flat panels/rays, knop stem, polished pontil, 4"..............**25.00**

Plastics

The term 'collectible plastics' is defined as those types produced between 1868 (when synthetic plastics were invented) and the period immediately following WWII. There are several, and we shall mention each one and attempt briefly to acquaint you with their characteristics:

1) Pyroxylin (Celluloid, French Ivory, Pyralin). Chemical name: cellulose nitrate. Earliest form, invented in 1868 by John Wesley Hyatt; highly flammable; yellows with age; much used in toiletry articles. Fairly lightweight, many articles of pyroxylin were made by heating and molding thin sheets.

2) Cellulose Acetate (Tenite, Similoid). Made in attempt to produce a product similar to cellulose nitrate but without the flammability. Had limited use in the costume jewelry trade; most often encountered as car knobs and handles of the thirties and forties. Surfaces tend to crack with age and exposure to light. Always molded, never cast. Colors varied; imitation horn and marble were most popular.

3) Casein Plastics (Ameroid, Galalith, Dorcasine, Casolith). Invented in 1904 using milk proteins. Use limited to buttons and buckles due to warping and lengthy curing time. Made in a wide range of colors; very easy to laminate or to carve from stock rods or sheets, but never molded.

4) Phenol Formaldehyde (Bakelite, Catalin, Marblette, Agatine, Gemstone, Durite, Durez, Prystal). Invented by L.H. Baekland in 1908; used extensively in the thirties. There are two major types: cast and molded. Molded types include Durez and Bakelite, dark-toned, wood-flour filled plastics that were used extensively for early telephones (still used when non-conductivity of heat and electricity is vital). The most popular name in cast phenolics was Catalin, trade name of the American Catalin Corporation of New York. Made in a wide range of colors; widely used for costume jewelry, cutlery handles, decorative boxes, lamps, desk sets, etc. Heavyweight material with a slightly 'greasy' feel; very hard, but can be carved with files, grinding tools, and abrasive cutters. Buffs to high, durable polish. Cast phenolics were used primarily from 1930 to around 1950 when they proved too labor-intensive to be economical.

5) Urea Formaldehyde (Beetleware, Plaskon, Duroware, Hemocoware, Uralite). Invented around 1929, this was lighter in color than phenol formaldehyde, thus used for injection-molded products in pastel colors. Lightweight, not strong; shiny rather than glossy. It cannot be carved and was used mainly for cheap radio and clock cases, never for jewelry.

The period between the two World Wars produced acrylic resins such as Lucite and vinyl. Polystryene made its appearance then, and furfural-phenols were in use in industrial applications. Though a great future was predicted for ethyl cellulose, by the late thirties it was still in the experimental phase. For most purposes, the field of decorative plastics from the first half of the century can be narrowed down to the five major types listed above. Of these, cellulose acetate is rarely encountered. Casein is limited to button and belt buckle manufacture; urea is easily identifiable as a cheap, brittle material. Pyroxylin is the celluloid of which so many vanity sets were made. Molded phenolics such as Bakelite were dark in color and used for utilitarian objects; cast phenolics such as Catalin were used most notably for jewelry (please don't call it Bakelite), cutlery handles, desk sets, and novelties.

Dealers and collectors should beware of reproduction Marblette animal napkin rings (they have no eye rods and no age patina) and molded acrylic bracelets in imitation of carved Catalin ones (look for a seam line or lack of definition in 'carved areas'). As prices rise, copies become more common. 1986 saw the mass-production of inlaid polka-dot bracelets using old-stock findings but without the precision fit (or patina) of the originals.

In 1988 and continuing to the present, a large number of 'collage' pieces appeared in vintage clothing and antique stores on the West and East Coasts. These are over-sized, glued-together assemblages of old Catalin stock parts including buttons with the shanks filed off, poker chips, etc. made into brooches or pendants, sometimes hung on necklaces of re-strung Catalin beads. They can be recognized by their aesthetically jumbled, 'put-together' look; and although some may claim they are 'old,' they are not.

Our advisor for this category is Catherine Yronwode, who also publishes an informative newsletter, *The Collectible Plastics*; she is listed in the Directory under California.

Bakelite

Cigarette box, half-cylinder, rotates open, dk brn..........................**40.00**

Clock, electric, alarm, Deco design, blk..50.00
Clock, mantel, windup alarm, Deco design, dk brn 45.00
Inkwell, streamlined, blk, w/lid..20.00
Penholder, streamlined, blk..15.00
Radio, Majestic #55, dk brn, 1939 ....150.00
Radio, Silvertone Compact, Sears, dk brn, 1936-1937................150.00
Radio, Stewart Warner Varsity College, dk brn, 1938-1939 ....150.00
Roulette wheel, dk brn, 1930s 80.00
Roulette wheel, mc Catalin chips, wood rack, w/box, 1930s 200.00
Watch, lady's handbag; Westclox, blk, 2¾" dia..........................60.00

Catalin

Ash tray, marbleized lt gr, sq, 4½" 14.00
Barometer, Taylor, amber & dk gr, rectangular, 4" 30.00
Bottle opener, chrome plate, red, gr, or amber hdl........................ 5.00
Bracelet, bangle; apple-juice clear, figural bk-cvg.......................150.00
Bracelet, bangle; apple-juice clear, floral bk-cvg.......................130.00
Bracelet, bangle; apple-juice clear, geometric bk-cvg 100.00
Bracelet, bangle; deep cvg, w/rhinestones.................................70.00
Bracelet, bangle; elaborate floral cvg, narrow 28.00
Bracelet, bangle; elaborate floral cvg, wide................................48.00
Bracelet, bangle; lt geometric cvg, narrow 18.00
Bracelet, bangle; lt geometric cvg, wide....................................28.00
Bracelet, bangle; novelty, figural or animal cvg 180.00
Bracelet, bangle; scratch cvd, narrow 10.00
Bracelet, bangle; scratch cvd, w/rhinestones..............................25.00
Bracelet, bangle; scratch cvd, wide 20.00
Bracelet, bangle; stylized floral cvg, narrow 18.00
Bracelet, bangle; stylized floral cvg, wide 30.00
Bracelet, bangle; uncvd, narrow 3.00
Bracelet, bangle; uncvd, wide 8.00
Bracelet, bangle; 12 inlaid polka dots, wide..............................120.00
Bracelet, bangle; 2-color stripes 40.00
Bracelet, bangle; 3-color stripes 50.00
Bracelet, bangle; 4-color (or more) stripes...................................60.00
Bracelet, bangle; 6 inlaid polka dots, narrow 110.00
Bracelet, cellulose acetate chain, 7 cvd figural charms.................100.00
Bracelet, clamper; figural, animal, or novelty applique 200.00
Bracelet, clamper; inlaid geometric designs 120.00
Bracelet, clamper; stylized floral cvg..48.00
Bracelet, clamper; w/inlaid rhinestones......................................32.00
Bracelet, curved/flat links, deeply cvd 50.00
Bracelet, curved/flat links, uncvd 38.00
Bracelet, stretch; orig elastic, Catalin & metal 32.00
Bracelet, stretch; orig elastic, deeply cvd 50.00
Bracelet, stretch; orig elastic, mc, uncvd...................................40.00
Buckle, latch type, mc, novelty or figural applique.......................40.00
Buckle, latch type, mc, stylized floral or geometric, cvd 30.00
Buckle, latch type, mc, uncvd 20.00
Buckle, latch type, 1-color, novelty or figural applique 20.00
Buckle, latch type, 1-color, stylized floral or geometric 10.00
Buckle, latch type, 1-color, uncvd 5.00
Buckle, latch type, 1-color w/rhinestones, Deco...........................20.00
Buckle, slide type, mc, stylized floral or geometric, cvd 20.00
Buckle, slide type, mc, uncvd 10.00
Buckle, slide type, 1-color, stylized floral or geometric, cvd............. 5.00
Buckle, slide type, 1-color, uncvd 3.00
Butter mold, gr/amber/brn, floral cvg, 2½" 32.00
Buttons, card of 6, red or blk laminated, 1½" rod..........................18.00
Buttons, card of 6, scotty, fruit, or cvd floral figural 18.00
Buttons, card of 6, uncvd octagonal, amber, 1" dia 6.00
Cake breaker, CJ Schneider, red, gr, or amber hdl 2.00
Carving set, knife, fork, steel..28.00

Carving set, 3-pc w/wood wall rack..30.00
Checkers, red & blk, full set, in box 30.00
Cheese slicer, scotty hdl, wood & chrome base 10.00
Chess set, hand cvd, red & blk, leather box 150.00
Chopsticks, ivory, pr 3.00
Cigarette box, chrome inserts, cylindrical, 4½" 35.00
Cigarette box, lt gr, wood bottom, rectangular, 5½x3¾" 25.00
Cigarette holder, imitation amber, sterling tip, orig case 25.00
Cigarette holder, long, mc or w/rhinestones 18.00
Cigarette lighter, Arco-Lite devil's head, red or blk 150.00
Cigarette lighter, mc stripes or inlay 30.00

Catalin clock, General Electric Model #3H96, amber, Deco styling, 5½", $50.00.

Clock, New Haven, windup alarm, amber, Deco, 3⅝" 50.00
Clock, Sessions, electric alarm, scalloped case, 4¼" dia 50.00
Clock, Seth Thomas, windup alarm, maroon case, 3½" 40.00
Clock, Westclox, Moonbeam, electric flashing light alarm............50.00
Clothesline, Jigger, red anchors, 10 pins, metal box 8.00
Cocktail recipes, Ben Hur, mtd on drunk, red w/blk base..............38.00
Cocktail recipes, Ben Hur, mtd on fighting roosters.....................40.00
Cork, Ben Hur, w/red fighting roosters, blk base..........................12.00
Corkscrew, chrome, red, gr, or amber hdl....................................10.00
Corn holder, Kob Knobs, diamond shape or lathe trn, 8 +box.......30.00
Crib toy, Tykie Toy, boy, girl, clown, kitten, etc, ea.....................55.00
Crib toy, Tykie Toy, clown or elephant, celluloid head/body..........38.00
Crib toy, Tykie Toy, 11 mc spools on string, 1940s......................30.00
Crib toy, Tykie Toy, 12-1½" rings on 2⅞" ring, 1940s..................30.00
Dice, ivory or red, 2½", pr..15.00
Dice, ivory or red, ¾", pr.. 2.00
Dice cage, metal/red Catalin, blk Lucite base, w/dice 75.00
Dice cup, leather or cork lined 30.00
Dominoes, ivory or blk, full set, w/wood box 25.00
Dominoes, red or gr, full set, w/wood box 40.00
Drawer pull, 1-color, w/pnt inlay stripe....................................... 2.00
Drawer pull, 2-color, octagon, w/inlaid dot.................................. 3.00
Dress clip, mc inlaid Deco design 15.00
Dress clip, novelty, figural, animal, or vegetable 25.00
Dress clip, scratch cvd... 6.00
Dress clip, stylized floral cvg..10.00
Dress clip, 1-color, w/rhinestones, Deco design 12.00
Earrings, lg drop style, pr.. 8.00
Earrings, novelty, figural, animal, or vegetable, pr 14.00
Earrings, stylized floral cvg, pr.. 6.00
Earrings, uncvd disks, pr 3.00
Egg beater, red, gr, or amber hdl...10.00
Flatware, chrome plate, 1-color hdl... 1.00
Flatware, chrome plate, 3-pc matched place setting....................... 5.00

Flatware, stainless, 1-color hdl.. 1.50
Flatware, stainless, 1-color hdl, leatherette box, 36-pc.....50.00
Flatware, stainless, 1-color hdl, 3-pc matched place setting 6.00
Flatware, stainless, 2-color hdl.. 3.00
Flatware, stainless, 2-color hdl, wood box, 36-pc 200.00
Flatware, stainless, 2-color hdl, 3-pc matched place setting 10.00
Gavel, lathe turned, ivory...18.00
Gavel, lathe turned, red, blk, & ivory 25.00
Gavel, lathe turned, red, w/presentation box, dtd 1946 ....28.00
Ice cream scoop, stainless, red hdl.....................................14.00
Inkwell, Carvacraft Great Britain, amber, dbl well.....................75.00
Inkwell, Carvacraft Great Britain, amber, single well 35.00
Knife, cvd red, gr, or amber hdl 4.00
Lamp base, brass & amber, Deco design, 10" 30.00
Lamp base, red, amber, & blk, Deco design, 8" 44.00
Letter opener, blk & amber stripes, Deco design..................10.00
Letter opener, chrome/Catalin, Deco design........................ 6.00
Letter opener, marbleized gr, dagger shape 8.00
Mah-Jong set, tiles, rails, 6-color, complete, w/box............40.00
Manicure set, tube holder, pnt floral design.......................35.00
Manicure set, 4-mini tools in tube, Germany.....................22.00
Memo pad, Carvacraft Great Britain, amber......................20.00
Nail brush, Ducky, duck shape, translucent eye rod...............30.00
Nail brush, marbleized lt gr, 2½x1½".................................. 6.00
Nail brush, Masso, amber octagon, 2" dia.......................... 6.00
Nail brush, turtle shape, dark amber, 3½".........................14.00
Napkin ring, amber, red, or gr, 2" dia band 3.00
Napkin ring, animal or bird, no inlaid eye or ball on head............15.00
Napkin ring, elephant w/ball on head.................................20.00
Napkin ring, lathe turned, amber, red, or gr, 1¾" dia......................4.00
Napkin ring, Mickey Mouse or Donald Duck shape w/decal.........40.00
Napkin ring, rabbit w/inlaid eye rod 20.00
Napkin ring, rocking horse or camel w/inlaid eye rod 45.00
Napkin ring, scotty, w/inlaid eye rod 22.00
Napkin ring set, 6-colors, 2" band, orig box.......................30.00
Necklace, cellulose acetate chain, animal figurals.......................120.00
Necklace, cellulose acetate chain, Deco dangling pcs 56.00
Necklace, cvd red & amber beads, 18".................................35.00
Necklace, uncvd gr beads, 20"...20.00
Ozone generator, Air-Clear, dk amber, streamlined case 40.00
Pencil sharpener, Disney character decal, silhouette shape.............28.00
Pencil sharpener, gun, tank, or plane shape w/decal...................22.00
Pencil sharpener, orange, no decal, ¾x1"............................ 4.00
Pencil sharpener, red, Mickey Mouse decal, ¾x1" 24.00
Pencil sharpener, scotty, red, cvd details, blk base 18.00
Pencil sharpener, scotty, yel, silhouette shape....................10.00
Pencil sharpener, Trylon & Perisphere, 1939 World's Fair 40.00
Penholder, amber & blk striped, Deco design 35.00
Penholder, marbleized amber, Deco design 20.00
Penholder, scotty, red w/blk base 42.00
Picture frame, amber & red Deco design, 6x7" 45.00
Picture frame, red, gr, or amber, sq, 6" 25.00
Pin, animal, resin wash w/glass eye, lg................................60.00
Pin, animal, resin wash w/glass eye, sm 48.00
Pin, animal or vegetable, inlaid or appl in several colors, lg.........110.00
Pin, animal or vegetable, inlaid or appl in several colors, sm 70.00
Pin, animal or vegetable, 1-color, lg 60.00
Pin, animal or vegetable, 1-color, sm 48.00
Pin, mc Deco design, lg...48.00
Pin, mc Deco design, sm...35.00
Pin, novelty or patriotic figural, resin wash/inlay/appl, lg 160.00
Pin, novelty or patriotic figural, resin wash/inlay/appl, sm 95.00
Pin, novelty or patriotic figural, 1-color, lg 80.00
Pin, novelty or patriotic figural, 1-color, sm.....................50.00

Pin, stylized floral cvg, lg 32.00
Pin, stylized floral cvg, sm 20.00
Pin, w/danglers, animal or vegetable, resin wash/inlay/appl........140.00
Pin, w/danglers, animal or vegetable, 1-color 90.00
Pin, w/danglers, geometric form, mc 50.00
Pin, w/danglers, geometric form, 1-color............................30.00
Pin, w/danglers, novelty or patriotic, resin wash/inlay/appl 180.00
Pin, w/danglers, novelty or patriotic, 1-color.....................90.00
Pipe, amber & gr, bowl lined w/clay 15.00
Pitcher, glass, red, gr, or amber hdl, syrup size 8.00
Pocket watch, Debonaire, yel Deco case, 1⅞" dia..............50.00
Poker chip rack, cylindrical, w/50 chips, 2½" 50.00
Poker chip rack, rectangular, w/200 chips, 4" 90.00
Powder box, amber & blk fluted cylinder, 2½" 35.00
Powder box, amber & gr fluted cylinder, 4" 50.00
Radio, Emerson College model, amber or gr, 1938 ....400.00
Radio, Emerson College model, red, 1938 ....425.00
Radio, Fada Streamliner, amber, amber knobs/bezel, 1941 ......450.00
Radio, Fada Streamliner, amber, red knobs/bezel...............475.00
Radio, Fada Streamliner, red, amber knobs/bezel, 1941 ....525.00
Radio, Kadette Klockette, amber, gr, or maroon, 1937........375.00
Radio, Kadette Klockette, red, 1937 ....395.00
Ring, inlaid Deco stripe design, 2-color 30.00
Ring, stylized floral cvg, 1-color 20.00
Ring, uncvd, 1-color 5.00
Ring, uncvd, 2-color 15.00
Ring case, hinged-lid style, amber or maroon 70.00
Ring case, open-top style, amber, red, or blk, Deco design.............50.00
Safety razor, Schick Injector, amber hdl 9.00
Safety razor, Schick Injector, extra blades, orig box, 1939.............20.00
Salad servers, Chase chrome, ivory, blk, or brn, pr 30.00
Salad servers, chrome, red, gr, or amber hdls, pr 10.00
Shakers, ball shape or half-cylinder shape, 1½", pr...........22.00
Shakers, glass, in 3⅛" Catalin holder, pr 14.00
Shakers, mushroom shape, amber & ivory, 1⅞", pr...........19.00
Shakers, stepped cylinder shape, 3½", pr...........................18.00
Shakers, Washington Monument, 3¼", pr...........................18.00
Shaving brush, red, gr, or amber 18.00
Shaving brush, red, gr, or amber, w/holder 22.00
Spatula, stainless, red, gr, or amber hdl 3.00
Spoon, iced tea, chrome, w/Catalin knob, 6-pc set 12.00
Spoon, slotted, stainless, red, gr, or amber hdl 3.00
Steering knob, chrome clamp...12.00
Stirrer, iced tea; Chase, chrome ball/mint leaf, 6-pc set 20.00
Stirrer, iced tea; shovel blade, Catalin hdl, 6-pc set...........24.00
Strainer, red, gr, or amber hdl, 2¾" dia............................ 4.00
Strainer, red, gr, or amber hdl, 5" dia............................... 6.00
Swizzle stick, baseball-bat shape, amber or red.................. 4.00
Swizzle stick holder, amber or red, Rheingold Lager decal 70.00
Thermometer, BT Co, amber & blk, 2¾" dia 34.00
Thermometer, Taylor, amber & dk gr, rectangular, 4"...................42.00
Writing set, blk, amber, or gr marble, Deco, 5-pc, orig box..........150.00

Celluloid

Bracelet, imitation tortoise w/inlaid rhinestones 35.00
Bracelet, snake w/inlaid rhinestones 42.00
Bridge marker, pnt ivoroid animal or figure, France 20.00
Bridge pencil holder, animal, pearlescent ivory on blk 60.00
Buttons, ivoroid or pearlescent, ¾" dia, card of 6.............. 8.00
Carving set, ivoroid, knife/fork/steel, eng blade 30.00
Clock, Greek temple facade, windup alarm, ivoroid 45.00
Dresser set, amberoid & gr marbleized, 7-pc 52.00
Dresser set, ivoroid, 10-pc, w/9" bevel glass mirror 80.00

Dresser set, ivory pearlescent or amberoid, 5-pc 40.00
Flatware, gr pearl on blk hdl, 3-pc set.. 9.00
Flatware, ivoroid hdl, table knife, fork, or spoon, ea...................... 1.00
Hair receiver, ivoroid, pearlescent or amberoid 8.00
Manicure set, ivoroid, pearlescent or amberoid, 10-pc, +case 30.00
Manicure set, ivoroid, 18-pc, roll-up leather case 25.00
Mirror, dresser; ivoroid, cut-out hdl, bevel glass, 8" 18.00
Mirror, dresser; ivoroid, oval bevel glass, 13" 28.00
Mirror, dresser; pearlescent or amberoid, bevel glass, 12" 20.00
Picture frame, easel bk, ivoroid, 2" dia 10.00
Powder box, ivoroid, pearlescent or amberoid 8.00
Shaving stand, ivoroid, 5-pc, w/razor 75.00

Lucite

Bottle, perfume; w/atomizer, rose inclusion....................................10.00
Bracelet, stretch, orig elastic, clear, bk-cvd....................................24.00
Picture frame, Deco, clear, sq, 6"..14.00
Purse, box style, clear or tortoise 22.00
Shakers, translucent red, 4", pr.. 5.00

Playing Cards

Playing cards can be an enjoyable way to trace the course of history. Knowledge of the art, literature, and politics of an era can be gleaned from a study of its playing cards. When royalty lost favor with the people, Kings and Queens were replaced by common people. During the periods of war, generals, officers, and soldiers were favored. In the United States, early examples had portraits of Washington and Adams as opposed to Kings, Indian chiefs instead of Jacks, and goddesses for Queens.

Tarot cards were used in Europe during the 1300s as a game of chance, but in the 18th century they were used to predict the future and were regarded with great reverence.

The backs of cards were of no particular consequence until the 1890s. The marble design used by the French during the late 1800s and the colored wood-cut patterns of the Italians in the 19th century are among the first attempts at decoration. Later the English used cards printed with portraits of royalty. Eventually cards were decorated with a broad range of subjects from reproductions of fine art to advertising.

Although playing cards are becoming a popular collectible, prices are still relatively low. Complete decks of cards printed earlier than the first postage stamp can still be purchased for less than $100. Periodic auction catalogs are available from 'Full House' Antique Playing Cards and Gambling Memorabilia. See the Directory under Clubs, Newsletters and Catalogs for the address.

Key:
C — complete   OB — original box
cts — courts   sz — size
hc — hand colored   XC — extra card
J — joker

Advertising

Anna Held, Queen of 5¢ Cigars, wide, 1900s, 52+J+XC, OB, M ..50.00
Chief Whip Cigarettes, Dutch cts, scenic aces, 52+JJ+XC, MOB .. 5.00
Heineken Beer, aces & Js w/ads, Dutch cts, 52+JJ+XC, OB, M 10.00
Miss Panorama, Xmas 1984, cts/aces: lady stars, 52+JJ, M 20.00
Olifant, elephant cts/aces/Js, Carta Mundi, 52+JJ, OB, M 15.00
Royal Crown Cola, 1945, 52+J, VG in box 20.00
Singer Sewing Machines, linen finish, 1900, 52/no J, EX in box ...25.00
Time Magazine, special cts, 1962, 52+J+XC, EX in box..................50.00

France and Belgium

Automobile photo bks, Biermans, #1308, ca 1900, 52+J, OB, M...10.00
Casanova, Becat art on all, Philibert, 1960, 52+JJ+1, OB, M.....175.00
Fleur-de-lis watermks, Marc, ca 1760, 49 of 52, EX.....................100.00
L'Art Est Magique, Pry, 1970, ltd ed, 36+3Js+#card, M 15.00
Nat'l Leaders, Ghandi & others on bks, 1931, 52+J, OB, M..........16.00
Pour Nos Prisonniers, Van Genechten, WWII, 51 of 52+J, NM ... 6.00
Sobrane, blk ground w/gold edge, ltd production, 52+JJ, M 30.00
Visitor in Courtyard, Van Genechten, 1950s, 52+J+XC, OB, M ... 6.00

Games, No Suit Signs

Astronomical, 4-suited, FG Moon, 1829, 52C, VG 400.00
Chestnut Burrs, Fireside, #1106, 1896, 52+1+rules, EX, OB 15.00
Dondorf's Schwartzer Peter, Dondorf, 1900s, 37C, VG.................50.00
Old Glory, 34-star, Parker Bros, 1899, 52+2XC, VG, OB 40.00
Petit Metamorphoses, France, 1800s, 20 cards, EX, OB 200.00
Sherlock Holmes, Parker Bros, 1904, 56+rules, EX, OB.............20.00
Wiggs, B Books, Atlanta, 1903, 63 of 65+rules, worn, OB.............10.00

Germany, Austria, and Czechoslovakia

Allied Armies, copper eng, Industrie-Comptoir, 1815, 36C, EX..300.00
Dondorf #174, Swiss costume deck, gold corners, 52C, OB, M......30.00
Dondorf #207, 4 Corners of Earth, 52+J, OB, EX........................275.00
Dondorf #304, Spanish suits, ca 1910, 48C, M..............................50.00
Kasino Pikett #0, Piatnik, ca 1900, 32C, orig wrap, M 25.00
Landleben, 1968 repro of 1840 deck, 32+booklet in case...............40.00
Scenic Aces of Portugal, standard cts, Stralsunder, 1910, M..........22.00
Schwerter-Karte, Saxon pattern by Vass, ca 1910, 32C, VG 22.00
1001 Waltzes, Bermann, Graven, 1830s, 32+rule card, OB, VG .500.00

Great Britain

Cupid's Triumph, narrow named, Kirschner, 52, no J, OB, EX.......25.00
Elizabeth II Silver Jubilee, Waddington, sealed, M.........................22.00
Geo V Coronation Special Issue, Worshipful, 1911, 52, OB, EX...75.00
His Majesty's Yacht, Regimental, 52 in worn OB, EX 20.00
Hodges Geographic, hc, 1827, 52C, VG 1,200.00
Simpson-Picadilly, Francois, 1953, 52+J+XC, NM.........................20.00
XIX Olympiad, Mexico City, Worshipful, 1968, dbl, sealed, M 45.00

Italy, Spain, and Latin America

Clemente Roxas, Martinez de Castro, 1810, 47 of 48, EX............400.00
El Navio, La Cubana, 1952 tax stamp, 40C, M in wrapper 30.00
La Campana, La Cubana, 1945, 40C, orig wrapper, M 18.00
Marca Gallo, Jacques, 1930, sealed, M 140.00
Political satire, 104 caricatures, Ortuno, 1973, MIB.......................25.00
Real Fabrica de Madrid, El Leon, dtd 1801, 48C, EX 75.00

Miniatures and Patience

Dondorf, 4 Corners of the Earth, ca 1920, 52+J, VG 50.00
Dondorf #25, Kinder Patience, cts, 53C, 36x54mm 55.00
Jeu Louis XV, Grimaud #542, 52C, 64x43mm, soiled, OB.............22.00
Little Duke, dbl of 1st version, 1900, 104+JJ, metal box, EX 35.00
Mirim, Fr suits, Copag, Brazil, 52+JJ (photo), OB, M..................... 5.00

Souvenir and Expositions

Among Wht Mtns, wide, Chisholm Bros, 52+J+2XC, OB, EX 25.00

Capetown, S Africa, wide scenic, 1900, 52+J (photo), OB, VG....**45.00**
Century of Progress, maroon/gold, 1933, 52+J+2XC, OB, M **15.00**
Columbian Expo, Clark, 1893, 52+J+blank, OB, VG...................**65.00**
Midwinter Expo, 1894, 52+J, rare, EX....................................**225.00**
Nation's Capitol, wide scenic, gold edges, 1909, 52+J, OB, M........**45.00**
Niagara Falls, wide scenic, corner indices, 52+J+XC, EX...............**50.00**
Rocky Mountain, wide scenic, 52+J, ½-OB, EX **40.00**

Tarot and Fortune Telling

Astral Tarot, Mont-Saint-Johns, 1969, 78+lg booklet, OB, M.......**40.00**
Dondorf #345, historic cts, geographic trumps, 78C, OB, M **200.00**
Gentilini Tarrochi, ltd ed, 1975, w/booklet, OB, M **50.00**
Gipsy, Cock drawings, DeLaRue, 1880s, 32+blank+rules, OB, M..**35.00**
Madame Le Normand, McLoughlin, 1990s, 36C, OB, EX **25.00**
Old Witch, ME Ivens, NJ, 1912, 52C+rules, OB, M **25.00**
Rameses Fortune Telling, Goodall, 1890, 52 no J, OB, M..............**25.00**
Tarocco Piemontese #70, Cambissa, Trieste, 1950s, 78C, OB, M ..**10.00**
Tarot Noir, Astrid Larsen, Copenhagen, 1970, 22 trumps, M **25.00**

Transformations

Carte a Rire des Journeaux, 1819, 52C, OB, EX **750.00**
Carte a Rire II...de Theatre, 50 of 50, ½-OB, EX **750.00**
Crowquill, comic cts, Reynolds, 1860, 52C, M...........................**350.00**
Hustling Joe II, USPC, 1895, 52 no J, soiled, OB..........................**175.00**
Kaloprosopian, 2nd ed, hc, Olivatte, 1828, 52, ½-OB, VG **500.00**
Kinney, 1889, full sz, 52+J, EX..**475.00**

Transportation: Airline, Steamship, Railroad

ANA All Nippon Airways, Kuroda, 52+JJ, 120x60mm, M............**18.00**
Army, eng ace of Spades & J, Russell, 1883, 52+J, OB, EX.............**75.00**
Blue Star, London to S America Steamer, 52 no J, soiled, OB.......**10.00**
Canadian Nat'l Railways, Goodall, '05, 52+photo J+XC, OB, M..**35.00**
Esquire Jungle series, pinups, 52+logo J+poem J, ½-OB, EX **25.00**
Ethiopian Airlines, costumed cts, M.. **8.00**
Globe, rnd deck, 1st ed, ca 1850, rare, 52+J, OB, EX...................**140.00**
Intercolonial Railway, wide scenic, Canada, 52+J+XC, OB, EX....**45.00**
Love Scenes, Nelson, 1864, rare, 52C, EX...................................**800.00**
Nat'l Whist #175, USPC, 1922 tax stamp, sealed, M **35.00**
Polish Ocean Lines, POL on aces, 52+JJ, EX.................................**25.00**
Prince Charles, CPH Cook, Hartford, 1897, 46 of 52, VG **45.00**
Queen Elizabeth II, NY Skyline at bk, sealed, M............................ **5.00**
Rovers #20, Kayak bks, Am Playing Cards, ca 1900, 52+J, NM.....**25.00**
Saudia Airlines, 747 in flight to right, plastic, sealed, M.................**25.00**
Triplicate #18, Dougherty, 1878, orig wrapper/tax stamp, M **100.00**
United States Line, wide, early, 52+JJ, OB, VG **65.00**

Political

The most valuable political items are those from any period which relate to a political figure whose term was especially significant or marked by an important event or one whose personality was particularly colorful. Posters, ribbons, badges, photographs, and pin-back buttons are but a few examples of the items popular with collectors of political memorabilia.

Political campaign pin-back buttons were first mass-produced and widely distributed in 1896 for the president-to-be William McKinley and for the first of three unsuccessful attempts by William Jennings Bryan. Pin-back buttons have been used during each presidential campaign ever since and are collected by many people. The most scarce are those used in the presidential campaigns of James Davis in 1924 and

James Cox in 1920.

Our advisor for this category is Paul Longo; he is listed in the Directory under Massachusetts. See also Autographs; Broadsides; Historical Glass; Watch Fobs.

Armband, beardless Lincoln/2 Liberty heads, tissue, 4x11" **170.00**
Armband, Dewey/Bricker, Liberty Bell, 4x14"................................**22.00**
Badge, press; Humphrey, plastic clip-on, M **15.00**
Ballot, Garfield/Arthur, MA, 1889, EX **35.00**
Ballot, Grant/Wilson, NH, 1872, VG...**50.00**
Ballpoint pen, Hubert Humphrey, Minority Whip, US Senator ...**15.00**
Bandana, Harrison/Morton, bl/blk on wht cotton, 20", NM........**120.00**
Bandana, Harrison/Morton, bl/red/wht, flags in corners, 22".......**150.00**
Bandana, Harrison/Morton, 3-color on wht, flags/eagle, 22x25" ..**200.00**
Bandana, McKinley bust, silk w/N&S Am flags, 1899, 23x24" ..**100.00**
Bandana, TR (Teddy Roosevelt), red/blk/wht printed cotton **100.00**
Banner, Blaine/Logan, HP portraits on canvas, 1888, 51x56"....**500.00**
Banner, Garfield/Arthur, cloth, 1880, 56x34", VG **125.00**
Banner, T Roosevelt portrait, full color HP on canvas, 44x51" ..**500.00**
Book, Presidential Election Digest, FDR/Willkie **10.00**
Booklet, Picture Life of Great American, Hoover, 1928, EX **10.00**
Booklet, presidential elections through 1924, 11x14", VG............**20.00**
Broadside, Washington's Farewell Address, silk, 1832, VG..........**200.00**

Broadside, notice of reward for Booth, Surrat, and Harold, April 20, 1865, 24" x 12", EX, $7,000.00.

Bust, Abraham Lincoln, bronze, Pompeian Bronze Co, 12".........**465.00**
Bust, Lincoln on ped, parian, 1860s, 12x8"....................................**80.00**
Bust, McKinley, from walking stick, cast wht metal, 3⅜"...............**30.00**
Bust, Taft, from cane, red cast rubber, St Louis 1888, 2" **125.00**
Bust, Taft, from walking stick, bronze, St Louis 1888, 2¼" **125.00**
Button, Wm Henry Harrison, log cabin, 1840, EX........................**100.00**
Campaign torch, copper, eagle form, dbl spout burners, 23" **400.00**
Campaign torch, tin, halberd shape w/wood hdl, 47", EX..............**85.00**
Campaign torch, tin on wood pole, 48" **50.00**
Campaign torch, tin on wood pole, 54" **50.00**
Cane, McKinley, tin w/horn top, stamped slogan, 33", EX.............**85.00**
Carte de visite, Lincoln, fr w/death notice, 1886, 5x9½" **125.00**
Cartoon, Straw Vote Hat/Harding-1924, sgn Terry G(?), 7x9"......**50.00**

Clock, T Roosevelt/rearing horse, clock below, 1899, 11x9" 130.00
Cup plate, Henry Clay, Sandwich, 1932, EX 40.00
Door stop, CI frog, I croak for the Jackson wagon, 5" L 175.00
Fan, 11 presidents ending w/Z Taylor, ivory/paper, 10½" 1,600.00
Handkerchief, McKinley, Protection, Sound Money, silk, EX 50.00
Hat, JFK convention/campaign, EX 50.00
Kerchief, Herbert Hoover, silk, red/wht/bl trim, 14x16", NM........50.00
Lantern, Grant bust, red/gr/brn paper, 23", VG...........................130.00
Lantern, parade; Lincoln portrait/Union/Freedom, paper, 13".....200.00

Harrison and Cleveland lapel pins, head appears from behind shell by moving a pin on reverse, cardboard and metal, 1888, $100.00 each.

Letter opener, Kennedy Will Win, CA campaign, metal 20.00
Medal, peace; James Madison, proof plaster cast, 1809, EX 100.00
Mug, Bobby (Kennedy) for President, red/wht/bl caricature 12.50
Noisemaker, tin litho, Crow for..., Roosevelt campaign...............100.00
Paperweight, McKinley, bronze, flat relief bust, 3" 25.00
Pencil, Hoover for President, 1928, NM.......................................20.00
Pennant, Woodrow Wilson, felt, red/wht/bl, 29", EX..................125.00
Pin, lapel; Benjamin Harrison, atop red/wht/bl shield, 1888..........65.00
Pin, mourning for Lincoln, gutta percha, EX...............................120.00
Pin, Seymour/Blair ferrotype jugate, silver shell fr, 1¼" 170.00
Pin-bk, Democratic Integrity, 5 portraits & flag, 1984 ....3.50
Pin-bk, Democrats for Willkie, orig, NM.......................................3.00
Pin-bk, Goldwater, In Your Heart You Know He's Right.................4.00
Pin-bk, Johnson for Humphrey, M 5.00
Pin-bk, Ladybird Start Packing, NM..6.00
Pin-bk, McKinley/Hobart photos, mechanical flag 125.00
Pin-bk, Pat for First lady, portrait on wht....................................4.00
Pin-bk, Wilson Inauguration, sepia, 1913, 1¼"............................55.00
Pitcher, For President/Benjamin Harrison, ironstone, 8" 385.00
Plaque, J Garfield in relief, brass, 1881, 29x23", EX 150.00
Plaque, McClellan on horse, walnut fr, brass relief, 22x19" 380.00
Plaque, Washington bust, cast zinc, Houdon's, 1877, 28x24" 300.00
Plate, LBJ, ceramic, natural colors w/gold trim, 9¼", NM.............10.00
Plate, Z Taylor, Our Country Right or Wrong, tin, 4½" 700.00
Poster, Keep Hoover on the Job, 1932, EX 35.00
Poster, Kennedy for President, 1960, M 35.00
Print, Candidates....Clay & Freylinghuysen, Kellogg, EX 300.00
Program; 1948 Republican Convention...15.00
Puppets, Nixon & Agnew, West Germany, pr 30.00
Ring, mourning; Washington, gold band, seed pearls, w/case.15,000.00
Sash, Grant/Colfax, People's Choice, red/wht/bl cloth, 39".........400.00
Sham, B Harrison/flags/eagles, 17x24", EX 130.00

Sham, Roosevelt/Fairbanks, 1904, Protection...Industries, 24" ...125.00
Sticker, Roosevelt/Curley, Vote Straight Democrat, 4x10"............25.00
Stud, Harrison/Morton jugate photo, Cheshire Mfg, 1" 90.00
Tapestry, Kennedy by Wht House & Capitol Bldg, 19x38", EX 20.00
Teddy bear, w/button 'Goodbye Teddy!,' 4" 325.00
Textile, WA/Harrison, shield-shape, Xd flags, 26" W, EX 115.00
Thimble, Hoover, Home, Happiness.. 9.00
Tie clasp, LBJ for the USA, flasher, M 10.00
Tile, McKinley portrait 50.00
Token, Wm H Harrison, bust/log cabin on wht metal, VG...........70.00
Torch/walking stick combo, tin, unscrew knob for wick, 33" 100.00
Trade card, Cleveland/Hendricks, 2½x4½" 10.00
Wallet, WH Harrison in uniform emb on leather, 6½x3½" 250.00
Watch fob, Roosevelt/Fairbanks, 1904..20.00
Watch fob, Taft 1908...25.00
Watercolor, Garfield/Arthur/flag, sgn Baker, 1880, 11x9".............80.00

Pomona

Pomona glass was patented in 1885 by the New England Glass Works. Its characteristics are an etched background of crystal lead glass often decorated with simple designs painted with metallic stains of amber or blue. The etching was first achieved by hand cutting through an acid resist. This method, called first grind, resulted in an uneven feather-like frost effect. Later, to cut production costs, the hand-cut process was discontinued in favor of an acid bath which effected an even frosting. This method is called second grind.

Our advisors for this category are Betty and Clarence Maier; they are listed in the Directory under Pennsylvania.

Bowl, 1st grind, cornflowers, ruffled, 10½" 425.00
Bowl, 2nd grind, ruffled amber rim, 2¾" H...................................62.00
Celery, 1st grind, crimped, EX staining, 5x5½" 375.00
Celery, 2nd grind, daisy variant w/T'print, 20-panel top...............60.00
Creamer, 1st grind, T'print, ruffled, bulbous, 2¾x5" 375.00
Creamer, 2nd grind, cornflowers, clear crimped base, 3x6" 225.00
Creamer & sugar bowl, 2nd grind, Invt T'print 250.00
Cruet, 2nd grind, amber stain, orig stopper 215.00
Cruet, 2nd grind, blueberries, ball stopper, M gold, 5½" 535.00
Finger bowl, 1st grind, 5"...90.00
Finger bowl, 2nd grind, pansy & butterfly, ruffled 225.00
Lamp shade, cornflowers, amber stain, ruffled, 7" dia 295.00
Lamp shade, 1st grind, cornflowers, 5x9"....................................600.00
Pitcher, water; 2nd grind, Dia Quilt, 8½" 150.00
Pitcher, 1st grind, cornflowers, sq top, EX stain, 6¼" 395.00
Pitcher, 2nd grind, cornflowers, slim form, 9", +6 mugs 1,100.00

Pitcher, second grind, enameled florals, 6¾", $265.00.

Punch cup, 1st grind, acanthus leaves, EX stain, 2½"..................**185.00**
Punch cup, 2nd grind, blueberries, EX stain, 2½"........................**225.00**
Punch cup, 2nd grind, Rivulet over expanded dmn, 2¾"............**120.00**
Toothpick holder, 1st grind, tricorn rim.................................**225.00**
Toothpick holder, 1st grind, w/rigaree, 2½"............................**275.00**
Tray, 2nd grind, cornflowers, 12½x7¾".................................**475.00**
Tumbler, lemonade; 2nd grind, Rivulet **185.00**
Tumbler, 2nd grind, bl cornflowers, amber stain......................**150.00**
Vase, 1st grind, amber rim & scalloped base, fan form, 8" **150.00**
Vase, 1st grind, cornflowers, amber trim, fan form, 3x6".............**235.00**
Vase, 1st grind, ovoid w/sq fluted rim, 7".............................**285.00**
Vase, 2nd grind, blueberries, ruffled top, crimped base, 5"...........**550.00**
Vase, 2nd grind, Dia Quilt, lily form, 5" **275.00**

Post Cards

A German by the name of Emmanuel Herrman is credited for inventing the post card, first printed in Austria in 1869. They were eagerly accepted by the Continentals and the English alike, who saw them as a more economical way to send written messages.

Post cards, first sold here in the 1880s, were made in Germany to order by private firms. The first to be printed in the United States were on U.S. government postals. The Columbian Exposition of 1892-1893 served as the spark that ignited the post card phenomenon. Souvenir cards by the thousands were sent to folks back home – expo scenes, transportation themes, animals, birds, and advertising messages became popular. There were patriotic themes, Black themes, and cards for every occasion and holiday. Scenics, cards with small-town railroad depots, and views of U.S. towns (especially photos) are very sought-after.

Some of the earliest post card publishers were Raphael Tuck, Nister and Gabriel. Early 20th-century illustrators such as Frances Brundage, Rose O'Neill, and Ellen Clapsaddle designed cards that are especially sought after today.

Although the post card rage waned at the onset of WWI, they rank today among the most sought-after paper collectibles, second only to stamps.

Even though post cards may be sixty to eighty years old, they must be in good condition. As a worth-accessing factor, condition is second only to subject matter. When no condition is indicated, the items listed below are assumed to be in excellent condition whether used or unused.

Our advisor for this category is Sally Carver; she is listed in the Directory under Massachusetts.

Key:
p/ — publisher   s/ — signed

Attwell, I'll Learn...To Learn Me Music, #488, p/Valentine, VG ... **8.00**
Attwell, Kiss Me Quick, boy & girl before moon, p/Tuck, EX........**12.50**
Attwell, Tis Moon Time, children/moon/owl, p/Tuck, EX **12.50**
Bannister, Blackburn Skuas, bombers/ships, p/Salmon, WWI, VG. **8.00**
Bannister, Defiants & Junkers 88'Ks, p/Salmon, WWI era, EX......**10.00**
Beraud, Bleriot Aeroplane, p/Tuck, #9802, EX **22.00**
Beraud, Kings of the Air, p/Tuck, #9802, oilette, VG....................**20.00**
Boileau, Have a Care, p/Reinthal–Newman, #938, VG **22.00**
Boileau, Out for Fun, lady in brn hat w/ribbon, VG......................**18.00**
Boileau, Priscilla, Puritan girl, p/Reinthal-Newman, #823, VG **18.00**
Brundage, Christmas, girl w/doll amid holly, Gabriel, VG **12.00**
Brundage, Halloween, 4 girls & jack-o'-lantern, Gabriel, VG **12.00**
Brundage, I'm Real Glad, well-dressed girl, Tuck #6373, VG.........**25.00**
Brundage, Telling the News, Dutch boy & girl, p/Tuck, EX...........**22.00**
Brundage, The Night Before..., Blk mom & children, p/Tuck, EX ...**25.00**
Christy, College Seal of Columbia, c 1905, EX **17.50**
Christy, Masks Off!, lady in blk, p/Reinthal-Newman, #945, VG .**12.00**

Christy, Wisconsin University Girl, p/Tuck, #2626, VG **20.00**
Clapsaddle, Birthday Blessings, girls at tea, #5, VG........................**14.00**
Clapsaddle, Christmas, mechanical, children revolve, G..............**30.00**
Clapsaddle, Christmas, Santa listing to child's prayers, VG **7.50**
Clapsaddle, Halloween, blk cat on fence/peeking moon, VG **9.00**
Clapsaddle, kaleidoscope, Joyful Easter, p/Internat'l, VG **28.00**
Clapsaddle, Many Moons of Happiness, Indian lady, 1910s, VG ...**10.00**
Clapsaddle, To My Valentine, boy hands heart to girl, VG **10.00**

Advertising, Coen Bros., 1911 calendar, $8.00.

Coin & Currency, Bulgaria, 15 coins, p/MH Berlin, VG **15.00**
Coin & Currency, Rumanian, 11 coins, p/MH Berlin, EX............**18.00**
Coin & Currency, USSR, 18 coins, p/W Erhard, EX **20.00**
Disney, Alice in Wonderland, ...Why Your Cat..., p/Lester, EX **17.50**
Disney, Alice in Wonderland, Who Are You?..., p/Lester, EX........**17.50**
Drayton, I Should Worry, p/Reinthal-Newman, #497, VG............**27.50**
Drayton, I'm Neutral!, Klever Kard #295, EX..........................**35.00**
Dwig, I'm Just Crazy To Hear Your Voice Again, p/Gross, VG **12.00**
Dwig, Were Having Ticklish Weather, lady/feather, p/Tuck, VG...**15.00**
Dwig, What's the Use...Sleep in Them, p/Gross, VG **12.00**
Ebner, Courtship, girl & boy w/flowers, dolls watch, EX **15.00**
Ebner, Little Mother, couple w/baby, fireplace, & dog, EX **15.00**
Gabriel, Would I Duly Praise You, Miss Liberty, #150, VG...........**15.00**
Gartner/Bender, Halloween, Strange Things You Will See..., EX .**15.00**
Gassaway, Don't Be Afraid I'm Here, p/Rotograph, VG................**10.00**
Gassaway, This Is So Sudden, boy & girl, p/National Art, VG **8.00**
Gibson, Charles Dana; Am Picturesque, Detroit #14050, EX........**14.00**
Gibson, Charles Dana; Love Song, lady/cherubs, Henderson, G **8.00**
Golliwogg, Chaperon, w/boy & girl, p/Faulkner, Fr words, VG......**20.00**
Golliwogg, drives w/doll in roadster, p/London, VG **30.00**
Golliwogg, Teddy, Golly, & Me, Kittens #103, VG.......................**16.00**
Golliwogg, There's Room for Two, p/Tuck, #9982, VG................**15.00**
Grozzi, Falto Silhouetten, lady on skis, #601, EX **15.00**
HBG, Many Happy Returns, boy & girl on phone, #2073, VG **9.00**
Henderson, Fire Engine, to cut out & assemble, #3213, EX...........**60.00**
Henderson, Hospital Ship, to cut out & assemble, #3215, VG......**45.00**
Hold-to-light, Garfield Park, Chicago, p/Koehler, VG..................**30.00**
Hold-to-light, S Station, Boston MA, p/Koehler, #2305L, VG **30.00**
Hold-to-light, Santa w/tree & lantern, text, VG.........................**90.00**
Hold-to-light/cut-out, ...Gefreite Lemburg 23, Juni 1915, EX........**28.00**
Hold-to-light/cut-out, ...Library & New S Church, Koehler **30.00**
Hold-to-light/cut-out, Festund Manur Vor Dem Fall, #58, EX **28.00**
Hopcroft, Homeward Bound, oilette, p/Tuck, #3107, VG.............**12.50**
Innis, John; Army Post Man, scout w/rifle & horse, VG **12.00**
Innis, John; Bad Man, man at house waits for rider, VG **10.00**
King, Atlantic City Girl, c 1907, VG **8.00**

King, Palm Beach girl, c 1907, unused, VG **8.00**
Kirchner, Fan, lady in lowbk dress w/fan, p/Delta, VG **38.00**
Kirschner, Poisson d/Avril, lady feeds fish, VG.............................**38.00**
Koehler, M; lady in gr coat w/blk dog, VG **40.00**
Koehler, M; lady w/lace shawl, unused, EX **40.00**
Kraus, Dan Dix, Cowboy Clown, 101 Ranch, vignettes, VG.........**18.00**
Kraus, Princess Wenona...Rifle Shot..., 101 Ranch, VG **20.00**
Langsdorf, Hook & Ladder Truck Going to Fire, emb, VG **17.50**
Langsdorf, Miss Illinois, lady w/mini train, emb, VG **20.00**
Langsdorf, Musical Coons, alligator border, S-646, EX................**38.00**
Langsdorf, Santa in plane w/toys, not emb, VG...........................**20.00**
Langsdorf, Solid Comfort, alligator border, #S650, VG **30.00**
Langsdorf, State Capitol, Maryland, #6, VG.................................**8.00**
Linen pin-up, Mail & Female, #DG12, EX....................................**10.00**
Linen pin-up, Orchids to You, #DG9, EX......................................**10.00**
Map, France, insert lithos, p/Remy, VG.......................................**12.00**
Map, State of CA, p/Emanuel, EX **10.00**
Martin, exaggerated photo, Giant Apples, VG.............................**10.00**
Mechanical, Hooligans Again, cops in boat, c 1906, VG **15.00**
Mechanical, man's arm hits lady's bk side, 1940s, EX.................**15.00**
Metamorphic Fantasy, Kaiser Bill/His Satanic Majesty, VG..........**38.00**
Payne, Charge!, cavalry in battle, oilette, Tuck, VG.....................**12.50**
Payne, For England Home & Beauty, sailors, Tuck, VG...............**20.00**
Payne, On the Look-out, chromolitho, #120, early Tuck, EX **35.00**
Payne, Review Order, soldiers/horses, oilette, common Tuck, VG.**10.00**
Photo, Auto Laundry-Parking Station, roadsters, EX....................**25.00**
Photo, Chief Daylight, tribal headpc/clothes, EX..........................**15.00**
Photo, Custom Tailor & Dry Cleaner, window scene, EX..............**18.00**
Photo, grocery store int w/Moxie sign, EX **30.00**
Political, A Third Term, Teddy Bear/doll, c 1907, VG...................**30.00**
Political, Kennedy's Summer Home in Hyannisport, chrome, EX ..**5.00**
Political, Martyred Presidents, c/Sheahan, 1908, VG...................**10.00**
Robinson, boy pitching ball, pre-1920, VG **25.00**
Rotary, Geo Hackenschmidt, wrestler w/flexed muscles, VG.........**12.50**
Russell, Painting the Town, cowboys/Chinaman, p/Glacier, VG...**27.50**
Russell, Shell Game, line drawings, p/Glacier, VG **30.00**
Schermele, Kept In at School, bears in schoolroom, p/Tuck, G.....**10.00**
Schermele, Outing, bear family on picnic, p/Salmon, EX..............**14.00**
Sowerby, Favourite Nursery Rhymes, p/Milford, EX, set of 6.........**75.00**
Sowerby, Kingfisher Gr, 2 babes on leaf fish, p/Milford, EX..........**12.00**
Sowerby, Lg White & Caterpillar, p/Milford, EX............................**12.00**
Sports, Forbes Field, triple-fold post card....................................**100.00**
Sports, 1912 Cleveland Indian Team photo, VG............................**40.00**
Sports, 1948 Boston Braves Champion Team, linen, EX.................**10.00**
Stamps, 14+Russian nat'l crest, p/Ottmar-Zieher, EX...................**12.50**
Stevens, woven-in-silk, President Wilson, scarce, VG....................**85.00**
Stevens, woven-in-silk, RMS Arabic, men clasp hands/flags, VG ..**48.00**
Stevens, woven-in-silk, RMS Eturia, men clasp hands/flags, EX ...**48.00**
Stevens, woven-in-silk, Warwick Castle, castle scene, EX **65.00**
Thiele, bride & groom on skates, p/Egemes, VG **20.00**
Thiele, Treffpunkt, soldier salutes lady, VG **17.50**
Tichnor, Defend Our Country, linen, #V10, 1941, EX...................**12.00**
Tichnor, Fenway Park, Boston, ca 1950, EX **10.00**
Tichnor, Let's Go Forward Together, linen, #VI, 1941, EX **10.00**
Transparency, Palais Officiel de l'Algerie, Paris Expo 1900, VG....**30.00**
Tuck, cut-out/paper doll, Le Jazzah, #3397, EX............................**85.00**
Tuck, cut-out/paper doll, Little Geisha, #3394, EX **95.00**
Tuck, Ensign-US Navy, data, #405, VG...**18.00**
Tuck, Girard College, emb crest & vignette, #5028, EX **17.50**
Tuck, HMS Queen Elizabeth, oilette, #8624, G **10.00**
Tuck, Luftschiffe, dirigible, oilette, #500B, 1909, VG...................**20.00**
Tuck, Santa in red w/toys on sleigh, #54, EX **27.50**
Tuck, Trooping the Colors, oilfascisms, #3578, VG, set of 6.........**38.00**
Tuck, Yel Thunder, Indian chiefs, silverette, #6593, EX................**22.00**

Valentine, Rockies, Great Divide, Canadian Patriotic, VG..........**15.00**
Valentine, Victoria, Government Street, Canadian Patriotic, EX.**15.00**
Wain, Dancer's Mascot, cat dancing, VG **32.00**
Wain, Wooing of Kitty, 2 blk cats, photochrome, VG...................**27.50**
Whitney, Halloween, boy w/jack-o'-lantern on stick, EX..............**12.50**
Whitney, Halloween, Just About Now Ghosts Are Due, VG **14.00**
Whitney, Halloween, Wish I Could Celebrate..., 1920s, VG.........**14.00**
Winsch, Santa hides from girl, c 1912, EX **27.50**
Winsch, To My Sweetheart, lady in silk oval center, EX...............**27.50**
Winsch, W/Love, lady & man w/flowers, pk silk, EX **22.00**

Posters

Advertising posters by such French artists as Cheret and Toulouse-Lautrec were used as early as the mid-1800s. Color lithography spurred their popularity. Circus posters by the Strobridge Lithograph Co. are considered to be the finest in their field, though Gibson and Co. Litho, Erie Litho, and Enquirer Job Printing Co. printed fine examples as well. Posters by noted artists such as Mucha, Parrish, and Hohlwein bring high prices. Other considerations are good color, interesting subject matter, and of course, condition. The WWII posters listed below are among the more expensive examples – 80% of those on the market bring less than $50.00. See also Fisher, Harrison; Movie Memorabilia; Political; Rockwell, Norman.

Advertising

Bi-Borax Oriental, Fr laundress, Marcel Clement, fr, 26x34".......**450.00**
Bittmann Cafe, lady w/drink, Knab/Koch, '25, 13x10", M...........**200.00**
Bosch Magnetos, man, speeding car, 1920s, 33x22", EX **250.00**
Carl Jocobi Soap, ladies w/linens, anon, 1890s, 27x16", M **300.00**
Catz Elixer, waitress & man w/glass, Fiocchi, 1896, 41x27", M ..**350.00**
Cognac Cocktails Tobacco, color litho, linen bk, NY, 18x10".....**200.00**
Crow Motor Cars, 4 models shown, text, ca 1915, 40x24", G **320.00**
Cunard Line, steamship, Between NY or Boston..., 29x26", EX ..**220.00**
Cycles Griffon, lady bicyclist, Misti, ca 1900, 63x47" **575.00**
Elgin Watches, country boy w/watch, wood mt, 1910, 23x15" ...**285.00**
Horsford's Bread...Baking Powder, girl on ledge, 24x32" **500.00**
Klaus Caramels, children w/candy, Bonfatti, '27, 55x39", M **325.00**
LA-Pacific Balloon Route, Am Engr Co, early, 1-sheet, EX **300.00**
Luxite Hosiery, beach scene, Phillips, ca 1915, 21x11", NM **150.00**
Mercedes Benz, car/racing wins, Gotschke, '39, 22x33", NM.. **1,100.00**
Millinery, Niagara in Winter, 1890s, EX **25.00**
Monarch Fruits & Vegetables, 1920s, 32x22", EX.......................**85.00**
Nat'l Wax Thread, sewing machine, ca 1870, 22x24¼", EX **150.00**
Pacific Whaling, showing of captive whale, RI, 22x11" **800.00**
Packer's Tar Soap, barber/customer, Rhead, 1897, 17x12", NM...**150.00**
Palmer Tires, Gwendolyn, brunette in robe, 31x25", NM............**325.00**
Parnu, lady diver/resort spa, Blumenfeldt, 1930, 34x25", NM **300.00**
Peach Blossom Tobacco, factory scene, mc, NY, 13x10", NM **320.00**
Raleigh Cigarettes, man smokes on blk, anon, 1935, 18x12", M ...**70.00**
Schofield Bi-Treadle Grind Stone, Cleveland, 22x13½".............**700.00**
Sunlight Soap, lady at board, Metlicovitz, 1900, 54x39", M ... **1,250.00**
Veedol, Valentino pours oil in car, anon, 1925, 39x53", M **675.00**

Circus

B&B, clown acts, German, Strobridge, 1898, 1-sheet, EX **350.00**
B&B, rhino by lake, Strobridge, 1909, 1-sheet, EX **450.00**
B&B, stunt rider, French, Strobridge, ca 1897, 1-sheet, EX........**400.00**
BB & Hutchinson, Australian Cannibal..., 25x37", EX..............**900.00**
Bentley's Old Fashioned Country Circus, Donaldson, 27x38" **400.00**
Buffalo Bill, Indian maiden, by WJ Morgan, ca 1881, 28x15" . **1,400.00**

Buffalo Bill, portrait, vignettes surround, 1888, 25x18" **850.00**
Heely Bors, Boneless Wonders, Strobridge, 1910, full sheet.........**650.00**
Orig Miss Daisy, equestrian, Hoenig, Berlin, 1900, 1-sheet.........**550.00**
PT Barnums New & Greatest..., blk/wht, Thomas, ½-sheet **750.00**
RB World's Greatest Shows, clowns/riders, Courier, 3-sheet........**450.00**
RBB&B, giant clown stands over grounds, 1923, 1-sheet, EX **500.00**
RBB&B, lg cats before audience, EX color, 1920s, 1-sheet, EX....**180.00**
Royal Marionettes, Only...of the Kind..., 1890s, 27x27", EX **550.00**
Sarrasani, owner & Big Top, Geigat, Berlin, ca 1925, 38x29"......**300.00**
Sells Brothers, Romeski Troup, Strobridge, full sheet, EX **320.00**
Tim Mix, Menagerie of Wild Beasts, 1934, 42x28", EX **275.00**

Magic

Ackohr Automatas, man tips hat, Arreis, 1900s, 52x38", M **300.00**
Alexander the Man Who Knows, ca 1915, 42x28", NM **110.00**
Carter Beats the Devil, playing poker, ca 1915, 14x22" **85.00**
Carter the Great, Weird...Wizard, Otis, '20, 81x41", M...............**600.00**
Colini, Clairon's Wedding Eve, Friedlander, '05, 37x27", EX **550.00**
Fak Hongs, cave of devils/etc, anon, 1900s, 76x54", NM.............**775.00**
Fak Hongs, magic scenes, Friedlander, 1916, 38x28", NM...........**425.00**
George, Supreme Master of..., 1930s, 27x41", EX..........................**75.00**
George, Supreme Master..., Buddha/devil, Otis, '29, 27x20", M .**150.00**
Houdini, Master Mystifier, 3-color, 43x110", VG **1,000.00**
Kar-Mi, ghosts/Indians, Nat'l Printing, 1914, 1-sheet.................**200.00**
Karl...Mysteries of Ages, Sphinx, Erie Litho, 28x21", EX **400.00**
Mysterious Dante, Friedlander, 1930s, 37x27", EX.....................**175.00**
New Orleans Minstrels, Welby & Pearl, others, 35x12½", EX.....**120.00**
Powell the Magician, ...Old School, fr, 22x14" **80.00**
Von Arx, Magician/Illusionist, full color, Morgan Litho, EX.......**120.00**
Willard the Wizard, Nights of Enchantment, 22½x8¼", EX........**125.00**

Minstrel

Al G Field, EX color, Donaldson, 1-sheet, VG, pr **140.00**
Blk Patti Troubadors, singer/troupe, Nat'l, 1900, 28x21", EX **275.00**
Carncross Minstrels, Blks w/banjos, 1885, 10x31", EX.................**175.00**
Haverly's Am United Mastadon..., Strobridge, 1900, 1-sheet......**750.00**
IW Baird's Famous..., Zouaves in parade, Armstrong, 1-sheet......**120.00**
JH Haverly Mastadon Minstrels, color, Miner, 1-sheet, EX **180.00**
Johnson & Slavin's Refined..., Courier, 1870s, 28x22" **225.00**
Wm H West's Big...Jubilee, color, Strobridge, 1900, 1-sheet........**280.00**
Wm Murry-Singing & Dancing Comedian, 1903, 26x19" **325.00**

Theatrical

Across the Trail, Wild West scenes, 1-sheet, EX **110.00**
Claudine, girl in Paris street scene, Freres, '10, 33x26", M...........**200.00**
Dixie Girl, Sadie Calhoun, comical, ½-sheet, EX **45.00**
Fetards, draped nude dances, PAL, 1897, 42x24", M **250.00**
Hamlet Festival, Bloom & Burton, Thelander, '54, 39x25", EX ..**150.00**
Hill & Polk Rag Time Coons..., Donaldson, 1-sheet, VG **200.00**
Hottest Coon in Dixie, mc, Goe's Litho, 3-sheet, EX **125.00**
Hoyt's a Bunch of Keys, hotel scene, Forbes, 1-sheet, VG..............**30.00**
Human Hearts, Russell-Morgan, 1901, 1-sheet, EX.......................**50.00**
Human Hearts, winter scene, R Morgan, 1901, 42x80", EX **125.00**
Little Eva's Temptation, full sheet, EX **45.00**
Louise, lovers embrace, Rochegrosse, 1900, 35x25", M **350.00**
Louise Liewellyn Dramatic Soprano, color, 42x80", VG **75.00**
Madame Butterfly, lady in kimono, 1900s, 42x28" **185.00**
Miss Dollar, goddess/Paris cityscape, Gray, 1900, 51x35", NM ..**550.00**
MO Girl, Daisy All Dressed Up, Donaldson, 1900, 30x20 ....**150.00**
Modern Cinderella, Ackermann-Quigley Litho, ½-sheet, EX **175.00**
Old Arkansaw, The Quartet, couples, Donaldson, 42x29", M **225.00**

Orpheum Shoes, Cressy/Dayne, 1900, US Printing,1-sheet, EX **40.00**
Railroad Jack, hobo smoking, color, 1-sheet, EX **55.00**
San Antonio's Siamese Twins, Daisy & Violet Hilton, 43x28½".**160.00**
Sarah Bernhardt in L'Aiglon, ca 1900, 76x28", EX **950.00**
Slaves of Mine, mining scene, Enquirer, 1890, 42x29", EX..........**225.00**
Ten Nights in a Bar Room, Donaldson, 1-sheet, VG **115.00**
Uncle Tom's Cabin, children, Chicago Litho, ½-sheet, EX **45.00**
Valley Forge, Goe's Litho, 1-sheet, 3 w/different scenes..............**210.00**

Travel

Antwerpen-Am, Red Star Line, steamer, Cassiers, '10, 20x30" ...**675.00**

Automobile Club, Georges Gaudy, printed by Affiches d'Art O. de Rycker, Brussels, linen back, 1898, 49" x 35", $1,500.00.

Bermuda, Queen of...steamer, Treidler, '50, 30x40", NM **275.00**
Caribbean, Grace Line, natives dive, Evers, 1949, 23x30", M **200.00**
China, China Airways, city silhouettes, anon, '50, 21x31", M ...**300.00**
Frankreich, for '37 Paris Expo, Cappiello, 1937, 39x25", M **350.00**
French Line, luggage boy/steamship, Walther, 1950, 25x40", M .**150.00**
Germany, Fly Pan Am, castle scene, EM Kauffer, 1953, 28x42" ..**225.00**
Grand Canyon, train/Indians, Bryn, 1938, 14x23", M **150.00**
Los Angeles, Am Airlines, nightscape, Ludikens, '54, 30x39".....**350.00**
Mexico, Am Airlines, man in straw hat/birds, '47, 30x40", M.....**225.00**
Mexico Tomorrow, Via Pan Am, DC3/lady, '37, 40x26", M **225.00**
Night Freight, night train scene, Cuneo, 1946, 50x40", NM **350.00**
NY-CA, Panama Pacific, wht liner in canal, 1920, 27x23", NM.**250.00**
Railway Express for Speed, sgn Burger, 45x60", EX **70.00**
Visit London, See Britain by Rail, anon, 1947, 40x25", NM **165.00**

War

All Together, Enlist in Navy, Reuterdahl, 1-sheet, VG **110.00**
Am Field Service, French soldier, Nuyttens, '17, 30x20", NM **200.00**
Be a Sea Soldier, Marine, Underwood, WWI, 30x20", M............**125.00**
Come On!, WWI soldier/fallen Hun, Whitehead, 30x20", NM ...**75.00**
Do Your Duty, Join...Marines, gun crew, anon, WWI, 30x20", M..**50.00**
E-E-E-Yah Yip Yip..., charging Marine, Falls, WWI, 30x20" **85.00**
Food Will Win War, Hebrew, Chambers, WWI, 30x20", EX.......**325.00**
For Every Fighter a Woman Worker, Treidler, WWI, 1-sheet, EX .**75.00**
Give or We Perish, fearful lady, Benda, WWI, 30x20", M **225.00**
Help Stop This, enemy w/dagger, Treidler, WWI, 30x20", M......**135.00**
Hip Hip Another Ship..., Mengll, WWI, 61x41", VG.................**300.00**

His Home Over There, YMCA, Herter, WWI, 40x28", NM **65.00**
Marine w/flag, JM Flagg, fr, WWI, 42x31", EX.............................**275.00**
My Daddy Bought Me a Bond-Did Yours?, WWI, 30x20", NM **95.00**
New Teacher, Kaiser w/devil as student, Collier, 21x11", M........**125.00**
On Job for Victory, ship builders, Lie, WWI, 56x38", EX............**250.00**
Ring It Again, Liberty Bell, Ketterlinus, 1917, 1-sheet, NM.........**60.00**
Save a Loaf a Week-Help Win the War, anon, WWI, 21x11", M .**95.00**
Teamwork Wins, riveters before flag, Kline, WWI, 41x26", NM.**175.00**
There's Room for You, Fry, British, WWI, 30x20"....................**225.00**
Tidal Wave-July 4, 1918, ships/riders, Cozzens, 30x20", M **150.00**
Together We Win, worker/sailor/soldier, Flagg, WWI, 39x29" **150.00**
Uber Allies, Kaiser as devil on skulls, Collier, 21x11", M.............**125.00**
War Clouds Gather, Army, Woodburn, 1940,1-sheet, NM..........**100.00**
4 Minute Men, Capitol building, WWI, 1-sheet, NM..................**45.00**

Miscellaneous

Artists' Suffrage, Votes for Workers, Winter, 1905, 30x20" **325.00**

Boxing, Wolgast/Nelson bout in 1908, 27" x 42", EX, $900.00.

Japanese Internment, San Francisco CA, US Army, 14x22", M ..**250.00**
Olympic Games Amsterdam, Anrooy, 1928, 39x25", NM **600.00**
Prohibition, Saloon Must Go, Vote..., 1910, 19x12", EX **185.00**
Sports, Ali Frazier, Thrilla in Manilla, Neiman, 22x14", M.........**125.00**
Sports, Deutscher Touring Club, skiers, anon, '12, 34x22", M.....**350.00**
Work Incentive, Have You the Best, anon, 1923, 41x28", NM ..**225.00**
Work Incentive, How Much...Waste, Beebe, '23, 41x28", M **200.00**

Pot Lids

Pot lids were pottery covers for containers that were used for hair dressing, potted meats, etc. The most desirable were decorated with colorful transfer prints under the glaze in a variety of themes, animal and scenic. The first and probably the largest company to manufacture these lids was F & R Pratt of Fenton, Staffordshire, established in the early 1800s. The name or initials of Jesse Austin, their designer, may sometimes be found on exceptional designs. Although few pot lids were made after the 1880s, the firm continued into the 20th century.

American pot lids are very rare. Most have been dug up by collectors searching through sites of early gold rush mining towns in California. Minor rim chips are expected and normally do not detract from listed values.

American

Amandine...Chapped Hands, blk transfer, Bazin & Sargent, 3¼"..**75.00**
Amandine...Chapped Hands, blk transfer, X Bazin, 3⅛", M **50.00**
Bear, blk transfer, Bears Grease, Hauel, 2⅞", EX **125.00**
Bear, blk transfer, Russian Bear's Grease, 3⅜", NM **200.00**
Bust of Franklin, blk transfer, Hauel Perfumer, 3½", VG..............**35.00**
Capitol at WA, blk transfer, Worsley...Perfumer, 3½", M.............**325.00**
Cold Cream, mc transfer, HP Wakelee, sm chip, rare, 3" **130.00**
Dr EJ Coxe's...Copaiva Sarsaparilla, blk transfer, 3¼", EX **190.00**
House of Parliament in London, blk transfer, Hauel, 4⅛", EX.....**475.00**
HP&WC Taylor's...Shaving Compound, blk transfer, 3⅜", NM....**70.00**
Improved Cold Cream of Roses, blk transfer, X Bazin, 2", EX **220.00**
Independence Hall, blk transfer, ...Shaving Compound, 4", M **625.00**
Man shaving, blk transfer, Taylors...Compound, 3⅜", EX **195.00**
Man shaving, blk transfer, Wrights...Compound, 4¼", EX **180.00**
Rousell's...Premium Shaving Cream, blk transfer, 4", NM...........**170.00**
Saponaccous Shaving Compound, red transfer, Hauel, 4⅛", EX ...**80.00**
Steer, blk transfer, Beef Marrow, Hauel Perfumer, 3", EX.............**170.00**
Taylor's Saponaceous Compound, bl transfer, 3⅞", EX **180.00**
2 cows, blk transfer, Liston's Extract of Beef, 1⅞", M **110.00**

English

Bellevue Tavern, Pratt, 4½" **165.00**
Dr Johnson, 4" **365.00**
Letter from Diggings, Fenton, rnd fr, 4" **195.00**
Lobster Sauce, Pratt, #49 ....**100.00**
Pair, card players, Pratt, in rnd walnut fr.....................................**275.00**
Pegwell Bay, Fenton, 4" **185.00**
Pretty Kettle of Fish, Fenton, rnd fr, 4" **165.00**
Revenge **150.00**
Skewbald Horse...**115.00**
Strasberg, city scene, Pratt, #331 ....**125.00**

Uncle Toby, 4¼", $225.00.

Village Wedding **88.00**
Wimbledon 1860, marbled, #223 ....**300.00**
Wolf & Lamb...**95.00**

Potschappel

The Carl Thieme Porcelain Factory has been operating in Potschappel in the East German area from 1872 until the present. Their products are very similar to Dresden and Meissen wares. Our advisor for this category is William Brinkley; he is listed in the Directory under Illinois.

Dish, floral bouquets HP on border/center, 1880s, 10½" L..........125.00
Lamp base, figural reserves/encrusted florals, w/shade, 30" 500.00
Urn, appl florals, figural reserve, mask/scroll hdls, 14" 300.00

Vase, encrusted florals, romantic scenes, Carl Thieme, late 1800s, 12", $500.00 for the pair.

Powder Horns and Shot Flasks

Though powder horns had already been in use for hundreds of years, collectors usually focus on those made after the expansion of the United States westward in the very early 1800s. While some are basic and very simple, others were scrimshawed and highly polished. Especially nice carvings can quickly escalate the value of a horn that has survived intact to as high as $400.00. Those with detailed maps, historical scenes, etc. bring even higher prices.

Metal flasks were introduced in the 1830s; by the middle of the century they were produced in quantity and at prices low enough that they became a viable alternative to the powder horn. Today's collector regards the smaller flasks as the more desirable and valuable, and those made for specific companies bring premium prices.

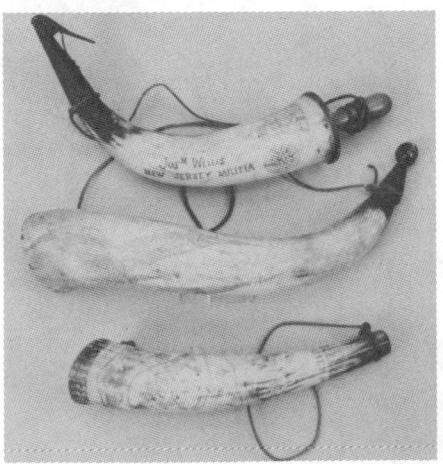

Engraved powder horns: Late engraving, inscribed with name and 'New Jersey Militia,' 14", $150.00; Late engraving, eagle and American flag, 15", $100.00; Late copy with name 'James Wilcox,' missing plug, 11½", $100.00.

Flask, brass, dog's head in sunburst, sporting sz, VG 65.00
Flask, brass, eagle emb, MS Arms Co, pistol sz, EX......................160.00

Flask, brass, fouled anchor/USN emb, lg, EX...............................220.00
Flask, brass, hunting scenes/1776, sporting sz, VG 80.00
Flask, brass, Indian/slain deer emb, sporting sz, EX 210.00
Flask, brass, Peace, eagle/US shield emb, dtd 1858, lg, EX..........200.00
Flask, brass, Public Property, bugle emb, lg, VG 150.00
Flask, brass, Xd pistols/eagle/flags/cannon/etc, mid-sz, VG 100.00
Flask, copper, cupid emb, pistol sz, EX 130.00
Flask, copper, eagle emb, Colt's Pat, pistol sz, EX 210.00
Horn, animals/trees/faces/name/1826, fine eng, 10" 550.00
Horn, cvd wooden end, leather tassel, 11" 250.00
Horn, cvd wooden end, 9"..50.00
Horn, EX detail, trn wooden end & threaded cap, 12" 575.00
Horn, trn wooded end, age crack in end, 14" 190.00
Horn, trn wooden end & threaded tip, 12" 400.00

Pratt

Prattware is a type of relief-molded earthenware with polychrome decoration. Scenic motifs with figures were popular; sometimes captions were added. Jugs are most common; but teapots, tableware, even figurines were made. The term 'Pratt' refers to Wm. Pratt of Lane Delph, who is credited with making the first of this type, though similar wares were made later by other Staffordshire potters.

Figurine, allegorical 'Summer,' on sq base, prof rstr, 10"...............220.00
Figurine, Charity, mother in yel cloak w/baby & 2 children 400.00
Figurine, man in gr toga by column, sacrificing lamb, 1800s........400.00
Pitcher, appl hunting & drinking figures, 7½x7", EX...................200.00
Pitcher, satyr's face/flowers w/silver lustre, 5¼", EX 450.00
Pitcher, 4-color courting scenes, stains, 7¼"...............................700.00
Pitcher, 5-color heart medallions w/children, 5", VG 325.00

Pitcher, embossed medallion with figures, stapled repair, 5", $385.00.

Plate, King Geo IV relief, mc, prof rstr, 8½" 300.00
Sauce boat, duck form, molded feathes, 4-color decor, 4¾" 400.00
Syrup, seashell transfer on beige, pewter lid, 7¼" 155.00
Tea caddy, cherubs/garlands relief, Ann Holms 1798, 5¼" 1,000.00
Teapot, vintage panels, widow Warburton finial, 7", EX.............950.00
Toddy plate, floral relief center, emb rim, mc on wht, 3⅜" 110.00
Wall pocket, cornucopia w/emb 'Summer' child, mc, 9", NM 600.00

Precious Moments

Figurines and bells created by Samuel Butcher and produced by Enesco Co. of Chicago, a division of Stanhome Products, are becoming some of the most sought-after collectibles on today's market. Often referred to as 'America's Hummels,' these pieces endear themselves to many through the inspirational messages they portray. The first twenty-one pieces were made in 1979. These were unmarked and today are the most valuable. Since then they have been marked with a different mark for each year of production – older marks bring the higher prices. Retired figures, especially those from 1981, are also highly valued. A magazine edited by Rosie Wells, our advisor for this category, is available if you want more information. Rosie also publishes the yearly official Secondary Price Guide for these collectibles. She is listed in the Directory under Illinois and again under Clubs, Newsletters, and Catalogs. Items listed below are assumed to be in mint condition and without box.

Bride & Groom, E7267, no mark, set...775.00
Drummer Boy, ornament, 1982, E-2357, hourglass mk 75.00
Drummer Boy, plate, 1982, E-2357, no mk 65.00
God Loveth Cheerful Giver, girl/pups, retired, E-1378, no mk 650.00
God's Speed, jogger, retired, E-3112, fish mark..........................55.00
God's Speed, jogger, retired, E-3112, no mk 95.00
Hello Lord..., boy on telephone, PM811, hourglass mk...............325.00
I Love To Tell the Story, boy w/lamb, PM852, dove mk................50.00
Jesus Is the Light, girl w/candle, retired, E-1373G, no mk 100.00
Jesus Loves Me, Easter Seal figurine, 1988, 104531 .... 1,000.00
Make Me a Blessing, girl w/sick bear, 100102, cedar tree mk 50.00
Praise the Lord..., ice cream boy, retired, E-1374B, no mk...........115.00
Put on a Happy Face, clown, PM822, hourglass mk 140.00
Smile, God Loves You, girl in curlers, PM821, fish mk 170.00
Smile, God Loves You, girl in curlers, PM821, hourglass mk 175.00
Special Event Piece, girl w/balloons, 115231, cedar tree mk..........70.00

Pre-Columbian Artifacts

The term 'pre-Columbian' loosely refers to some time prior to 1492, when Columbus arrived in America. In particular, it indicates pre-1492 artifacts of Central and South America, some of which can be dated as early as 4000 B.C. Artifacts representing the cultures of the Inca, Maya, and Aztec Indians are avidly sought by the collector. These may be made of precious metals and hardstones or pottery. Some were used in rituals and religious rites; some such as bowls and other utensils, though strictly utilitarian, nevertheless convey through form and decoration the craftsmanship of these early tribes.

Beaker, Nazca, molded heads, geometric frieze, 300 AD, 4" 300.00
Bottle, Cajamarca, Blk Ware, geometric/animals, 1000 AD, 9" ..400.00
Bottle, Chimu, Blk Ware, globular, 2 wave bands, 900 AD, 6"....140.00
Bowl, Mayan, Blk Ware, waisted/everted rim/ftd, 600 AD, 4x5" .500.00
Bowl, Mayan, buff pottery, red/blk border, ca 500 AD, 7½".........220.00
Bowl, Mayan, polychrome, monster on side, 600 AD, 5½" H......400.00
Bowl, Miztec, tripod, rattle ft/geometrics, ca 1300 AD, 10"........660.00
Doll, Chimu, Blk Ware, flat profile/arms at chest, 1000 AD, 7" ..145.00
Female, Tlatilco, arms at sides, 1150-550 BC, 3" 440.00
Figure, Jalisco, male seated, pigment traces, 100 BC, 10½" 1,200.00
Jar, Mayan, Blk Ware, glyph reserve, ftd, ca 600 AD, 7¼" 450.00
Jar, Mayan, blk/red stripes on cylinder form, ca 600 AD, 5½".....450.00
Man, Guerrero, gr mottled stone, 700 BC, 6" 600.00
Man, Manabi, warrior w/staff, arm bands, ca 100 BC, 11" 330.00
Pendant, Costa Rican, gold alloy, 1x1" 65.00
Pendant, Costa Rican, gold alloy fertility god, 1x1¾"..................100.00
Pendant, Veraguas, gold, eagle, missing wing, 1200 AD, 3" 660.00
Rattle, Mayan, female w/headdress figural, 750 AD, 7½" 500.00
Vessel, Inca-Chimu, Blk Ware, llama on gourd, 1200 AD, 8½" .375.00
Vessel, Machica, man's head, geometrics on red, 300 AD, 9" 650.00
Vessel, Mochica, Orange Ware, feline head, 300 AD, 7½" 240.00
Vessel, Mochica, Orange Ware, skull w/headdress, 300 AD, 4½"...125.00

Vessel, stirrup; Mochica, female form, slip decor, 300 AD, 8" 380.00
Whistle, Mayan, lady in headdress figural, ca 650 AD, 3" 440.00
Yoke, Mayan, gr granite, seashell decor, ca 750 AD, 15" L 2,750.00

Primitives

Like the mouse that ate the grindstone, so has collectible interest in primitives increased, a little bit at a time, until demand is taking bites instead of nibbles into their availability. Although the term 'primitives' once referred to those survival essentials contrived by our American settlers, it has recently been expanded to include objects needed or desired by succeeding generations – items representing the cabin-n'-cornpatch existence as well as examples of life on larger farms and in towns. Through popular usage, it also respectfully covers what are actually 'country collectibles.'

From the 1600s into the latter 1800s, factories employed carvers, blacksmiths, and other artisans whose handwork contributed to turning out quality items. When buying, 'touchmarks' – a company's name and/or location and maker's or owner's initials – are exciting discoveries.

Primitives are uniquely individual. Following identical forms, results more often than not show typically personal ideas. Using this as a guide (combined with circumstances of age, condition, desire to own, etc.) should lead to a reasonably accurate evaluation. For items not listed, consult comparable examples. Authority Kathryn McNerney has compiled several lovely books on primitives and related topics: *Primitives, Our American Heritage*; *Collectible Blue and White Stoneware*; and *Antique Tools, Our American Heritage*. You will find her address in the Directory under Florida. See also Butter Molds and Stamps; Boxes; Copper; Farm Collectibles; Fireplace Implements; Kitchen Collectibles; Molds; Tinware; Weaving; Woodenware; and Wrought Iron.

Basket tree, walnut, 6 trn arms, EX detail, 37" 800.00
Bed warmer, brass, eng man w/pipe, florals, trn walnut hdl..........525.00
Bed warmer, brass, pierced, trn tiger maple hdl, 41".....................265.00
Bed warmer, brass w/eng floral, trn cherry hdl, 43" 250.00
Bed warmer, brass w/sunburst eng, trn wood hdl, 47" 235.00
Bed warmer, copper, chased lid, trn hdl, 44"................................275.00
Bed warmer, copper, EX floral piercing, trn wood hdl, 1780 ....600.00
Bed warmer, copper, floral emb, trn maple hdl, 45".....................395.00
Bed warmer, tin plate, pierced, brass push knob on lid, 34" 475.00
Bed warmer, wrought iron, tooled brass lid, 37", EX....................450.00
Broom, hearth; rope-twist cvd hdl, 1880s, 34" 85.00
Camp stove, wrought iron, 9" sq, +trn wood hdl..........................375.00

Candle box, pine with original red, Connecticut, early 1700s, 16" long, $2,000.00.

Candle mold, 1-tube, pewter, 15" 100.00
Candle mold, 1-tube, tin, fluted top & bottom, strap hdl.............88.00
Candle mold, 1-tube, tin, makes 10" candles, EX 95.00
Candle mold, 1-tube, tin, makes 9" candles, EX 90.00
Candle mold, 12-tube, pewter w/wick serving device, 14x18". 1,050.00
Candle mold, 12-tube, pine w/pewter tubes, 16x17" 500.00
Candle mold, 2-tube, tin, makes 10" candles, EX 90.00
Candle mold, 24-tube, pewter, in dvtl pine fr, 18x7x20" 1,200.00
Candle mold, 24-tube, tin, battered, 9¾" 115.00
Candle mold, 24-tube, tin, dbl-ear hdls, 10½" 260.00
Candle mold, 25-tube, tin, minor battering, 12" 300.00
Candle mold, 36-tube, tin, w/hdl, 10" 355.00
Candle mold, 4-tube, tin, side hdl, tray top, 10½" 75.00
Candle mold, 6-tube, tin, makes 10" candles, EX 80.00
Candle mold, 8-tube (4 ea side), CI, hinged, Guillon, 11" 250.00
Candle snuffer, iron, scissors-shaped, ftd, early 1800s.....................55.00
Cheese drainer & ladder, Windsor, ½-rnd, sq spindles, 13x22"....220.00
Chestnut roaster, sheet iron w/wrought hdl, Am, 24¾" 300.00
Churn, drum type, wooden, w/lid, 1895, rfn, sm 125.00
Churn, staved, brass bands, porc hdls on lid, +dasher, 23" 150.00
Churn, syllabub; propeller-type blade, flat ring lid, 9½" 65.00
Churn, Union, Mfg in Dixon IL, bentwood body, CI gears...........330.00
Coffee roaster, tin w/slide cover, long wood shaft, 42" 295.00
Cookie mold, iron, urn w/flower, NY State, 2¾x4" 145.00
Cookie peel, hand forged, ram's horn curl, 1-pc, 28½" 250.00
Cranberry scoop, wood & tin w/metal teeth, rfn, 17½x11½".........85.00
Cranberry scoop, wooden tines, rpr bottom, sm, EX 100.00
Dough box, pine, worn red pnt, trn legs, 2-brd lid, 43" 375.00
Dough box, pine/maple, trn/splay legs, Am, 1800, 38" L 350.00
Dough box, pine/poplar, splayed base, dvtl, 31x19x34", EX 295.00
Dough box, popular w/red stain, splay base/trn legs, 35" W 350.00
Dough scraper, copper hdl, half-rnd steel blade, ca 1800...............95.00
Dough scraper, curly maple hdl, steel blade, 7½" 45.00
Dough trough, pine w/orig red, stretcher base, no lid, 47" 750.00
Dough trough, w/lid, 1800s, rfn, 20" L 300.00
Dryer, pierced tin, for 2 boots, used on stove, 12x11x22" 130.00
Ember carrier, wrought iron, flat w/long hdl, 18" 250.00
Foot warmer, birch, drilled holes, dtd 1814, 6½x8x8½" 225.00
Foot warmer, brass, pierced, eng inscription/1723, 7x8x8" 225.00
Foot warmer, pierced tin, mortised fr w/trn posts, 9" L 225.00
Fork, meat; wrought wht steel, 2-tine, ball end, 13¼" 58.00
Grape press, wood, detachable tin strainer, trestle base................150.00
Griddle polisher, fabric covered, trn hdl, 1½x2½" 39.00
Peg board, pine, 23 mortised pins, beaded bottom, 92" L.............200.00
Quilting fr, pine w/gr pnt, 2 ends w/X poles, shoe ft, 102" 195.00
Rack, drying; pine, mortised/pinned, shoe ft, 22x23", EX 325.00
Rack, drying; pine, 2-section, mortised/pinned, 39x55" 150.00
Rack, drying; pine w/worn finish, trn posts/ft/bars, 32x24" 75.00
Rope bed key, wooden clothespin shape w/T-bar hdl, 12x12" 50.00
Scrub board, all wood, cvd hdl on bk, 1800s, 25" 150.00
Sieve, horsehair in bentwood fr w/laced seams, 15" dia................130.00
Spice chest, pumpkin pine, dvtl, 12-drw (3 szs), 18x17" 675.00
Spice chest, walnut, 8-drw, wire nails, trn knobs, 18x9" 175.00
Spoon, cvd cow horn, arched hdl, 9½" 30.00
Spoon, serving; cvd from bone, 10"..29.00
Spoon mold, bronze, 1800s, EX 150.00
Stocking stretcher, wood, 7 rnd holes for drying, 31" 15.00
Sugar nippers, iron, complete 125.00
Sugar nippers, steel, scissors shape, complete, 9½" 130.00
Tinder lighter, flintlock, brass, mk Payne/Poolboro, EX..............800.00
Tinder lighter, flintlock, iron, English, 1700s, EX 600.00
Tinder lighter, flintlock, maple pistol stock, 7½" 925.00
Tinderbox, tin, striker/flint/lid, candle holder atop, 3x4"............475.00
Tinderbox, tin, w/candle holder & flint striker, oval, 7½" 550.00

Trammel, iron, delicately made, early, extends to 28", EX 200.00
Trammel, iron, for lamp, 1700s, extends to 50", NM 300.00
Wagon jack, wood/wrought iron, red/blk pnt, dtd 1793, 17" 115.00
Washboard, hand made, all wood, 25" 45.00
Washboard, wood w/sapphire bl glass scrub surface 135.00
Washing machine, New Era, golden oak, staved w/iron bands 300.00

Prints

The term 'print' may be defined today as almost any image printed on paper by any available method. Examples of collectible old 'prints' are Norman Rockwell magazine covers and Maxfield Parrish posters and calendars. 'Original print' refers to one achieved through the efforts of the artist or under his direct supervision. A 'reproduction' is a print produced by an accomplished print maker who reproduces another artist's print or original work. Thorough study is required on the part of the collector to recognize and appreciate the many variable factors to be considered in evaluating a print. Prices vary from one area of the country to another and are dependent upon new findings regarding the scarcity or abundance of prints as such information may arise. Although each collector of old prints may have their own varying criteria by which to judge condition, for those who deal only rarely in this area or newer collectors, a few guidelines may prove helpful. Staining, though unquestionably detrimental, is nearly always present in some degree and should be weighed against the rarity of the print. Professional cleaning should improve its appearance and at the same time help preserve it. Avoid tears that affect the image; minor margin tears are another matter, especially if the print is a rare one. Moderate 'foxing' (brown spots caused by mold or the fermentation of the rag content of old paper) and light stains from the old frames are not serious unless present in excess. Margin trimming was a common practice; but look for at least ½" to 1½" margins, depending on print size. When no condition is indicated, the items listed below are assumed to be in very good to excellent condition. See also Fisher, Harrison; Parrish, Maxfield; Rockwell, Norman.

Audubon, John J.

Audubon is the best known of American and European wildlife artists. His first series of prints 'Birds of America,' was produced by Robert Havell of London. They were printed on Whitman watermarked paper bearing dates of 1826 to 1838. The Octavo Edition of the same series was printed in three editions, the first by J.T. Bowen under Audubon's direction. There were seven volumes of prints, each 11" x 7", the first five bearing the J.J. Audubon and J.B. Chevalier mark, the last two, J.J. Audubon. They were produced from 1840 through 1871. The Bien Edition prints were full size, made under the direction of Audubon's son and daughter in the late 1850s. Due to the onset of the Civil War, only 105 plates were finished. These are considered to be the most valuable of the reprints of the 'Birds of America' Series.

In the 1950s New York Graphics reproduced the full-color prints through photolithography; and in 1971 the complete set was reprinted by Johnson Reprint Corp. of New York, and Theaturm Orbis Terrarum of Amsterdam. Examples of the latter bear the watermark G. Schut and Zonen.

Although Audubon is best known for his portrayal of birds, one of his less-familiar series, 'Vivaparous Quadrupeds of North America,' portrayed various species of animals. Assembled in corroboration with John Bachman from 1839 until 1851, these prints are 28" x 22" in size.

American Crow, #156, Havell, unfr, 37½x25½" 4,400.00
American Red Fox, #84, Bowen, 10½x6½" 50.00
Arctic Tern, #250, Havell, unfr, 18½x20½" 4,100.00

Barn Owl, #34, Bowen, ca 1850, 10½x6½" 100.00
Black Warrior, #86, Havell, 38¾x25½"................................ 1,500.00
Blue Bird, #113, Havell, unfr, 19⅜x12¼" 3,850.00
Brant Goose, #379, Bowen, ca 1850, unfr, 10½x6½" 70.00
Brown Pelican, #251, Havell, 1833, 37¾x25" 6,600.00
Carolina Titmouse, #160, Havell, 1836, 19½x12¼" 1,900.00
Collared Peccary, #31, Bowen, ca 1850, 10½x6½" 60.00
Columbian Hummingbird, #425, Havell, 1838, unfr, 19x12".. 2,750.00
Cougar, #96, Bowen, ca 1845, unfr, 18x25" 770.00

Common Crow Blackbird, Bein edition, 20" x 28", framed, $1,500.00.

Cuvier's Regulus, #55, Havell, 1834, unfr, 19½x12¼" 1,760.00
Great Tern, #309, Havell, 1836, unfr, 19⅜x15¼" 4,950.00
Ivory-billed Woodpecker, #256, Bowen, ca 1850, 10½x6½" 50.00
Lazuli Finch, #424, Havell, 1838, unfr, 20⅛x13⅜" 1,760.00
Mallard, #385, Bowen, ca 1850, unfr, 10½x6½" 275.00
Marsh Hawk, #356, Havell, 1837, unfr, 37¾x25½" 2,420.00
Pectoral Sandpiper, #294, Havell, 1836, unfr, 12¼x19½" 935.00
Polar Bear, #91, Bowen, 10½x6½" 60.00
Raven, #101, Havell, 1834, unfr, 37½x25¼" 3,850.00
Red-throated Diver, #202, Havell, 1834, unfr, 21x28½" 4,400.00
Rose-breasted Grosbeak, #127, Havell, 1836, unfr, 26x21" 3,300.00
Ruby-throated Hummingbird, #253, Bowen, 1850, 10½x6½" 100.00
Rusty Grackle, #157, Havell, 1836, unfr, 26x20¾" 1,200.00
Sharp-tailed Grouse, #382, Havell, 1837, unfr, 23x29¼" 2,200.00
Song Sparrow, #25, Havell, 1834, unfr, 19½x12¼" 1,100.00
Trumpeter Swan, #383, Bowen, unfr, 10½x6½" 70.00
Turkey Buzzard, #151, Havell, 1836, 37½x25½" 1,760.00
White-headed Eagle, #126, Havell, 1836, unfr, 37½x25½" 3,850.00
Wild Turkey, #287, Bowen, ca 1850, unfr, 10½x6½" 300.00
Wood Wren, #179, Havell, 1836, unfr, 19½x12⅜" 1,540.00
Yellow-winged Sparrow, #130, Havell, 1836, 19½x12¼" 1,540.00

Currier and Ives

    Nathaniel Currier was in business by himself until the late 1850s when he formed a partnership with James Merrit Ives. Currier is given credit for being the first to use the medium to portray newsworthy subjects, and the Currier and Ives views of 19th-century American culture are familiar to us all. Values are given for prints in very good condition; all are colored unless indicated black and white. Unless noted 'NC' (Nathaniel Currier), all prints are published by Currier and Ives.

    Our advisors for this category are Barbara and John Rudisill; they are listed in the Directory under Massachusetts.

Abraham Lincoln, 16th President of US, sm folio 275.00
Adelaide, NC, sm folio..95.00

American Brook Trout, sm folio..325.00
American Country Life, May Morning, NC, lg folio 1,950.00
American Country Life, Pleasures of Winter, NC, lg folio 3,000.00
American Farm Scenes, No 1, NC, lg folio............................. 3,850.00
American Farm Yard, Evening, lg folio 2,750.00
American Frontier Life, On the War-Path, lg folio 4,500.00
American Game Fish, lg folio 2,000.00
American Homestead, Spring, sm folio 400.00
American Scenery, Palenville NY, sm folio 295.00
American Speckled Brook Trout, lg folio................................. 2,000.00
Arguing the Point, NC, lg folio 3,500.00
Autumn Fruits, med folio 400.00
Autumn in New England, Cider Making, lg folio 14,850.00
Base Hit, sm folio...250.00
Battle of Cerro Gordo, NC, sm folio..125.00
Battle of Corinth, MS, Oct 4, 1862, sm folio.............................175.00
Battle of Pea Ridge, March 8th, 1862, sm folio 175.00
Battle of the Wilderness, VA, sm folio 175.00
Beautiful Empress, sm folio...50.00
Beauty of the Atlantic, sm folio 75.00
Black Duck Shooting, sm folio 250.00
Black-Eyed Beauty, sm folio...75.00
Boss of the Road, sm folio...250.00
Boss of the Track, sm folio..250.00
Bound To Smash, sm folio...250.00
Broadway NY, South from the Park, NC, sm folio.................. 1,000.00
Brush for the Lead, NY Flyers on the Snow, lg folio 4,500.00
Buffalo & Chicago, Steam Packet Empire State, NC, sm folio....375.00
Burning of the Henry Clay Near Yonkers, NC, sm folio 350.00
Bustin' a Picnic, sm folio 250.00
California Scenery, Seal Rocks, sm folio 395.00
Camping Out, Some of the Right Sort, NC, lg folio 3,500.00
Canal Scene, Moonlight, sm folio...300.00
Catterskill Falls, sm folio..300.00
Celebrated Horse Geo M Patchen, Champion of Turf, lg folio. 2,500.00
Central Park, The Bridge, sm folio..450.00
Chicago in Flames, sm folio..525.00
Children's Picnic, sm folio..150.00
City of Mexico From..., NC, sm folio...250.00
City of New York, lg folio 5,000.00
Clipper Ship Great Republic, sm folio 500.00
Clipper Ship Red Jacket, sm folio 500.00
Cork River, sm folio..95.00
Cornwallis Is Taken, sm folio 800.00
Cross Matched Team, sm folio 250.00
Darktown Fire Brigade, Investigating a Smoke, sm folio.............250.00
Darktown Fire Brigade, Prize Squirt, sm folio 250.00
Darktown Lawn Party, A Bully Time, sm folio 250.00
Deacon's Mare, sm folio..250.00
Death of Tecumseh, NC, sm folio 95.00
Death of Washington, NC, sm folio 95.00
Death Shot, sm folio..225.00
Distanced, sm folio 250.00
Dusted & Disgusted, sm folio 250.00
Eliza, NC, sm folio..95.00
Ethan Allen & Mate to Wagon, sm folio 300.00
Fall of Richmond VA, sm folio 225.00
Fannie, sm folio...75.00
Feeding the Swans, sm folio 150.00
First Trot of the Season, lg folio... 3,000.00
Foul Tip, sm folio..250.00
Four Seasons of Life, Childhood, lg folio 2,000.00
From Shore to Shore, sm folio 75.00
Frontier Lake, sm folio..295.00

Fruits of the Season, sm folio	150.00
Garfield Family, sm folio	75.00
Gen George McClellan & Staff, sm folio	125.00
Gen John C Breckenridge, sm folio	95.00
Gen Shields at Battle of Winchester VA, sm folio	125.00
Gen US Grant, med folio	125.00
Geo Washington, First Pres of US, NC, sm folio	195.00
George M Dallas, VP of US, NC, sm folio	125.00
Giants Causeway, sm folio	95.00
Girl I Love, sm folio	95.00
God Bless Our School, sm folio	250.00
Got 'Em Both, sm folio	250.00
Grand Nat'l Am Banner, Fillmore/Donnelson, NC, sm folio	275.00
Grand US Centennial Exhibition 1876, sm folio	275.00
Great Eastern, sm folio	325.00
Great Mississippi Steamboat Race, sm folio	800.00
Great West, 1870, sm folio	1,500.00
Happy Family, sm folio	150.00
Harbor for the Night, sm folio	395.00
Harvesting, sm folio	325.00
Hewitt's Quick Step, NC, sm folio	95.00
Hiawatha's Departure, lg folio	350.00
Hiawatha's Wooing, lg folio	350.00
High Bridge at Harlem NY, NC, sm folio	600.00
Home in the Wilderness, sm folio	800.00
Home of Washington, Mt Vernon VA, med folio	250.00
Homeward Bound, NC, sm folio	1,000.00
Horse Car Sports Going to the Chicken Show, sm folio	250.00
Hug Me Closer George..., sm folio	275.00
Hunter's Shanty, In the Adirondacks, lg folio	2,000.00
Ice Cream Racket, Thawing Out, sm folio	250.00
In the Mountains, sm folio	250.00
Infant St John, sm folio	35.00
Ingleside Winter, sm folio	850.00
Ivy Bridge, sm folio	175.00
James K Polk, 11th President of the US, NC, sm folio	125.00
John J Dwyer, Champion of America, med folio	250.00
Julia, NC, sm folio	95.00
Kilkenny Castle, Ireland, sm folio	95.00
LaFayette at Tomb of Washington, NC, sm folio	125.00
Lake Memphremagog, Owl's Head, sm folio	295.00
Lapped on the Last Quarter, sm folio	250.00
Last Shot, lg folio	3,500.00
Laying Back Stiff for a Brush, sm folio	250.00
Life & Age of Man, NC, sm folio	225.00
Life of a Fireman, The Race, Jump Her Boys..., NC, lg folio	3,500.00
Life of Sportsman, Camping in Woods, sm folio	600.00
Life on the Prairie, Buffalo Hunt, lg folio	3,500.00
Light of the Dwelling, sm folio	95.00
Little Brothers, sm folio	95.00
Little Daisy, sm folio	95.00
Little Maggie, sm folio	95.00
Little Manly, sm folio	95.00
Little Pets, sm folio	95.00
Little White Kitties Fishing, sm folio	150.00
Little Willie, sm folio	95.00
Lottie, sm folio	95.00
Lucky Escape, NC, med folio	450.00
Maj Gen Ambrose E Burnside, sm folio	125.00
Maj Gen John C Fremont, sm folio	125.00
Mambrino, sm folio	425.00
Mary, NC, sm folio	95.00
Midnight Race on Mississippi, sm folio	800.00
Millard Fillmore, NC, sm folio	450.00
Miniature Ship Red, White & Blue, sm folio	450.00
Moonlight in Fairyland, sm folio	95.00
Moosehead Lake, sm folio	295.00
Morning Star, sm folio	75.00
Moss Roses & Buds, sm folio	150.00
Mt Holyoke Female Seminary, NC, sm folio	450.00
My Boyhood's Home, sm folio	325.00
My Little White Kittens, sm folio	150.00
My Sweetheart, sm folio	75.00
National Washington Monument, NC, sm folio	400.00
Naval Heroes of the US, NC, beveled fr, sm folio	500.00
New England Home, sm folio	295.00
New Jersey Fox Hunt, Taking Breath, sm folio	250.00
Niagara by Moonlight, med folio	295.00
Niagara Falls From Goat Island, med folio	295.00
Night After the Battle, sm folio	125.00
Noah's Ark, NC, sm folio	250.00
Oh! How Nice, NC, sm folio	195.00
Old Bull Dog on Right Track, med folio	250.00
Old Farm Gate, lg folio	2,500.00
Old Plantation Home, sm folio	800.00
Oregon, NC, sm folio	500.00
Outlet of Niagara River, sm folio	325.00
Pacing King Robert J, sm folio	350.00
Partridge Shooting, NC, med folio	1,200.00
Peerless Beauty, sm folio	75.00
Pioneer Cabin of the Yosemite Valley, sm folio	1,000.00
Positive Process From Negative Result, sm folio	250.00
Poultry Show on a Bust, sm folio	250.00
Prairie Fires of the Great West, sm folio	1,500.00
Prairie Hens, sm folio	400.00
Pride of America, NC, sm folio	150.00
Pride of the Garden, sm folio	150.00
Pursuit, NC	3,500.00
Reconciliation, NC, sm folio	125.00
Renowned Trotter Prince Wilkes Record 2:14¾, lg folio	2,000.00
Return From the Woods, med folio	1,200.00
Rising Family, lg folio	3,500.00
Roses of May, sm folio	150.00
Rural Lake, med folio	425.00
Scenery on Upper Mississippi, Indian Village, sm folio	425.00
Season of Joy, sm folio	225.00
Shooting on the Beach, sm folio	1,200.00
Sisters, NC, sm folio	125.00
Snipe Shooting, NC, lg folio	3,850.00
Soldier's Adieu, NC, sm folio	125.00
Soldier's Return, NC, sm folio	125.00
South Sea Whale Fishery, NC, sm folio	1,500.00
Spirit of the Union, sm folio	195.00
Star Spangled Banner, sm folio	300.00
Steamer Messenger No 2, NC, sm folio	350.00
Steamship Alaska of the Guion Line, sm folio	350.00
Steeple Chase Cracks, sm folio	225.00
Striped Bass, sm folio	250.00
Summer Flowers, sm folio	150.00
Summer in the Country, sm folio	250.00
Summer Night, sm folio	295.00
Surprise, lg folio	3,500.00
Sussex Vale, New Brunswick, sm folio	195.00
Sweet Springtime, med folio	395.00
Through the Pacific, sm folio	1,500.00
To the Memory, NC, sm folio	35.00
Tomb of Gen WH Harrison, NC, sm folio	95.00
Tree of Life, The Christian, NC, sm folio	125.00

Stanch Pointer, original frame, small folio, EX, $450.00.

Trial of Patience, med folio	450.00
Trotters on Snow, sm folio	1,500.00
Trotting Queen Alix, sm folio	350.00
Trotting Stallion Smuggler, 1875, sm folio	350.00
Two Little Fraid Cats, sm folio	150.00
Two To Go, sm folio	250.00
US Frigate Constitution, NC, sm folio	450.00
Valley Falls, VA, sm folio	295.00
Victorious Attack on Fort Fisher NC, Jan 15, 1865, lg folio	2,000.00
View on Long Island NY, lg folio	2,500.00
Village Blacksmith, med folio	800.00
Washington, First in War..., NC, sm folio	125.00
Washington Columns, Yosemite Valley, sm folio	450.00
Western Farmer's Home, sm folio	600.00
Western River Scenery, med folio	1,200.00
Wild Duck Shooting, Good Day's Sport, NC, lg folio	3,500.00
Wild West in Darktown, sm folio	250.00
William R King, VP of US, NC, sm folio	95.00
Wm Henry Harrison, Ninth Pres of US, N Currier, sm folio	150.00
Won by a Foot, sm folio	250.00
Woodcock Shooting, NC, sm folio	600.00
Wreck of the Atlantic, sm folio	295.00
Young America, sm folio	195.00

Erte (Romain de Tirtoff)

Angel, sgn, 1983, 25x37½"	1,980.00
Autumn Song, of Twenties Remembered Suite, '77, 18x13½"	330.00
Brown Boot, sgn, 1974, 13x10"	245.00
Columbine, sgn, 1982	825.00
Coquette, sgn, 1981, 18x13"	770.00
D, from the Alphabet, signed, dtd 1976, 10½x16"	825.00
Dream Voyage, of Twenties Remembered Suite, '77, 13½x18"	1,760.00
Enchanted Melody, sgn, 1974, 42½x30"	1,760.00
Flames of Love, sgn, sgn, 1978, 21½x16"	1,760.00
French Rooster, sgn, 1980, 27x19"	3,000.00
Heat, sgn, 1980, 27x19"	2,200.00
Her Secret Admirers, sgn, 1982, 28x18"	1,760.00
La Serenade, sgn, 15x12"	530.00
Legerete, of Twenties Remembered Again Suite, '78, 18x13½"	440.00
Leo, from the Zodiac, sgn, 1982, 19x14"	330.00
Les Bijoux de Perles, sgn, 1983, 21¼x15½"	880.00
Mirror, sgn, 1979, 20x16"	550.00
Noon, sgn, 1980, 9x9"	330.00
On the Avenue, Metropolis Suite, sgn, 1986, 28½x22½"	2,640.00

Perfume, sgn, 1986, 39x23½"	3,000.00
Princess Lontaine, sgn, 1983, 21½x15½"	715.00
Red Heart, Hearts & Zephyrs, 12x12"	425.00
Riviera, sgn, 1980, 6½x14"	715.00
Spring Shadows, sgn, 1984, 32x31"	1,870.00
Stolen Kisses, sgn, 1982, 22½x17½"	715.00
Summer Breeze, sgn, 1978, 26½x19"	1,300.00
T, from the Alphabet, sgn, dtd 1977, 10½x16"	935.00
Top Hats, sgn, 1975	3,740.00
Twin Sisters, sgn, 1982, 34x49"	3,740.00
Wings of Victory, sgn, 1978, 19x27"	2,975.00

Fox, R. Atkinson

Clipper Ship, #75, 15x19"	60.00
Dreamland, 8x12"	65.00
Garden of Contentment, 1927, 5x6½"	100.00
Garden of Romance, #30, 25x17"	80.00
Good Ship of Adventure, 8x10"	50.00
In My Garden of Dreams, 10x7"	130.00
Memories of Childhood Days, 9x12"	130.00
Poppies, orig fr, 20x15"	68.00
Sentinels of the Pass, 6x10"	60.00
Spring Beauties, 10x16"	80.00
Where Nature Beats in Perfect Tune, 20x16"	150.00
3 Moose, 15x12"	95.00

Venetian Garden, 16" x 19", $65.00.

Gutmann, Bessie Pease

Awakening	65.00
Contentment, 4x7½"	50.00
Daddy's Coming	240.00
Friendly Enemies, girl w/puppy & kitten, fr, 11x14"	48.00
Good Morning, 8½x11½"	125.00
Happy Dreams, orig fr	165.00
Harmony	40.00
Homebuilders	70.00
Little Bit of Heaven, fr, 15x16"	65.00
Love's Blossom, M	40.00
Lovebirds, orig fr, 12x16", EX	95.00
Message of Roses	95.00
Mine	65.00
Miss Flirt, M	40.00
On Dreamland's Border, orig rnd fr	175.00

Sonny Boy, orig fr & mat, hand sgn, 22½x16½" 110.00
Sunbeam 85.00
Sympathy, #804...50.00
Thank You God, 21x14", M 45.00

Homer, Winslow

Approach of the British Pirate Alabama......................150.00
Bathers 200.00
Camping Out in Adirondack Mountains......................200.00
Dinner Horn 200.00
Fishing Party 200.00
Gathering Berries 200.00
Holiday in Camp, soldiers playing football 150.00
Home From the War 150.00
Making Hay 200.00
Noon Recess 200.00
Nooning...200.00
Raid on Sand Swallow Colony.....................................200.00
Sharp Shooter 200.00
Snap the Whip 1,400.00
Spring Blossoms...200.00

Icart, Louis

Louis Icart was a French artist who immortalized the French woman through his etchings, which were widely produced during the 1920s. Most of his post-1920 etchings carry a U.S. copyright notice in the margin as well as Icart's personal intaglio seal.

Autumn Leaves, sgn/blindstamp, #350, 20x16" 1,300.00
Basket of Apples, 1930, sgn, fr, 17½x12½".............. 1,300.00
Bird Seller, sgn/blindstamp, 1929, fr, 19x14" 1,200.00
Black Mask, sgn/blindstamp, 1933, 13x8½" 1,500.00
Blue Buddha, sgn, ca 1924, fr, 16x21" 900.00
Carmen, sgn/blindstamp, ca 1927, fr, 20x13½" 900.00
Coach, sgn/blindstamp, fr, 21½x17½" 1,000.00
Coursing II, sgn/blindstamp, 15½x26"..................... 3,500.00
Dame aux Camelias, sgn/blindstamp, ca 1927, fr, 17x21" 1,100.00
Dear Friends, sgn/blindstamp, ca 1929, fr, 14x11" 1,200.00
Desire, 1926, sgn/annotated #201, fr, 13x19" 1,900.00
Don Juan, sgn/blindstamp, fr, 21x14".........................700.00
Elephants, sgn, ca 1925, fr, 16½x11½", EX.................800.00
Eve, 1928, sgn/blindstamp, fr, 14x19½" 1,900.00
Faust, sgn/blindstamp, ca 1928, fr, 21x13"............... 1,200.00
Four Dears, sgn/blindstamp, ca 1929, fr, 21x15"...... 1,400.00
Four Season's Suite, sgn, ca 1923, fr, 11x7½", set of 4.............. 4,500.00
Girl in Crinoline, sgn/blindstamp, 1937, 23x19" 1,500.00
Girls w/Swans, sgn, 1940, 12½x15½" 5,000.00
Golden Veil, sgn/blindstamp, 1930, 15x20" 2,000.00
Gust of Wind, sgn/blindstamp, 1925, 21x17½" 1,600.00
Horsewoman, sgn/blindstamp, 1948, fr, 26x21½" 7,500.00
Hydrangeas, sgn/blindstamp, fr, 17x21"................... 1,900.00
Intimacy, sgn/blindstamp, 1928, fr, 16x18"............. 1,800.00
La Lettre, orig fr, 16x20" 95.00
Laughing, sgn/blindstamp, 1930, fr, 12x17".............. 1,400.00
Laziness, sgn/epr d'artiste, 1925, fr, 15x19" 1,650.00
Le Bonnet Bleu, orig fr, 16x20" 95.00
Leda & Swan, sgn, 1934, lacquered, fr, 21x31" 7,200.00
Lilies, sgn/blindstamp, 1934, 28x19½" 3,000.00
Little Bo Peep, 1927, sgn/blindstamp, fr, 21x14"...... 2,800.00
Martini, sgn/blindstamp, 1932, fr, 12½x16¾" 4,000.00
Meditation, sgn/blindstamp, 1928, fr, 12x17" 1,750.00
Minuet, sgn/blindstamp, 1929, fr, 21x13".....................900.00

Mockery, sgn/blindstamp, #E55, 16x18" 1,500.00
Muff, sgn/blindstamp, #172, 20½x11½" 1,200.00
Orange Cage, sgn/Estampe Moderne, 1924, fr, 15½x19½"..........550.00
Orange Seller, sgn/blindstamp, #d, minor losses, 19x14" 900.00
Orchids, sgn/blindstamp, 1937, fr, 28x19½" 2,600.00
Perfect Harmony, sgn, 12½x16½".............................. 3,500.00
Puppies, sgn/blindstamp, 1925, fr, 16½x21" 1,150.00
Rainbow, sgn/blindstamp, 1930, fr, 25x17" 1,500.00
Sea Nymph, sgn, 1920, fr, trimmed, 15½x12½" 400.00
Seville, sgn/blindstamp, 1928, fr, 20x13" 1,000.00
Smoke, sgn/blindstamp, 1926, fr, 15x20½" 2,200.00
Spanish Dancer, sgn/blindstamp, 1929, fr, 20½x13"..........950.00
Spanish Nights, sgn/Nuite Espagnole, 1926, fr, 21x13" 900.00
Speed, 1933, fr, 14x24½"...900.00
Speed II, 1933, sgn/blindstamp, fr, minor foxing, 14½x25" 6,000.00
Spilled Milk, sgn, ca 1925, fr, 16½x21" 1,400.00
Storyteller, sgn/blindstamp, fr, 14x17" 1,100.00
Sweet Caress, sgn, fr, 17½x12" 800.00

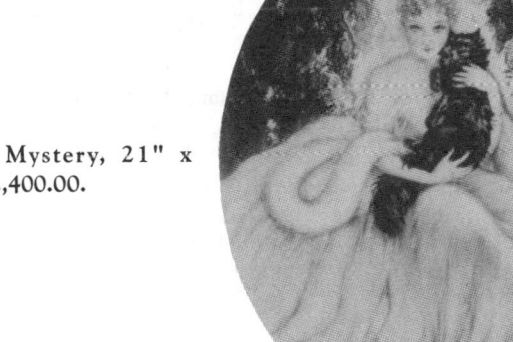

Sweet Mystery, 21" x 16", $2,400.00.

Swing, sgn/blindstamp, 1928, fr, 19½x13½"............. 2,600.00
Symphony in Blue, sgn/blindstamp, 23x19½".......... 1,700.00
Symphony in White, sgn/blindstamp, 'E Artiste,' 20x15½" 2,800.00
Tosca, sgn/blindstamp, #111, 1928, fr, 21x13" 1,200.00
Unmasked, sgn/blindstamp, 1933, 13x8½"..................900.00
Untitled (Blk Lace), sgn, ca 1924, fr, 12x9" 800.00
Untitled (Nude w/Scarf), fr, minor foxing, 14x12" 800.00
Untitled (Woman w/Dog), sgn/blindstamp, #179, 12x9½" 800.00
Venetian Nights, 1926, fr, 21x13" 1,200.00
Winter, 1920, sgn/#d, 10x7½" 1,200.00

Kellogg

Abraham Lincoln 16th Pres, beardless, minor damage, 9x13" 150.00
Battle of Champion Hills MS, May 16, 1863 ....125.00
Battle of Newbern NC, March 14, 1862.....................125.00
Children in the Wood, 13¾x16¾"...............................48.00
James Monroe, walnut fr, 14x17" 100.00
Pope Pius IX, 14¼x18¼" 27.50
Repose...95.00
Tree of Life, color..95.00
Washington, 12½x16¼"...48.00

Kurz and Allison

Louis Kurz founded the Chicago Lithograph Company in 1833.

Among his most notable works were a series of thirty-six Civil War scenes and one hundred illustrations of Chicago architecture. His company was destroyed in the Great Fire of 1871, and in 1880 Kurz formed a partnership with Alexander Allison, an engraver. Until both retired in 1903, they produced hundreds of lithographs in color as well as black and white.

Battle of Monmoth, blk/wht, med folio **40.00**
Battle of Williamsburg VA, lg folio...**200.00**
Battle of Wilson's Creek, Lyon vs McCullough, lg folio.............**200.00**
Declaration of Independence, after Trumbull, lg folio **165.00**
Destruction of Battleship Maine in Havana Harbor, sm folio **70.00**
Execution of Robert Emmet, Hanged...1803, lg folio **175.00**
Fall of Petersburg VA, Gen Grant vs Gen Lee, lg folio **200.00**
Gen Joseph Hooker, bust view, blk/wht, lg folio **90.00**
President McKinley, His Wife & Mother, blk/wht, lg folio **90.00**
Transporting Munitions from Concord...1775, blk/wht, 14x21" **40.00**

McKenney and Hall

Aseola, Seminole chief w/rifle, 1842, 14x20", EX **400.00**
Els-Kwau-Ta-Waw, hand colored, Biddle, 1833, lg folio **140.00**
Jack-O-Pa, Chippewa Chief, Rice & Clark, 1843, lg folio **125.00**
Lappawinze, Delaware Chief, Greenough, 1838, 14x20" **165.00**
Little Crow, Sioux Chief, Greenough, 1838, 14x20" **160.00**
Mon Hongo, Osage woman w/child, Hullmandel, 14x20" **180.00**
Oche Finceco, Creek Chief, Rice & Clark, 1843, 14x20" **195.00**
Pocohontas, Powhatan woman, Rice & Clark, 1842, 14x20" **200.00**
Stumanu, Flat Head boy, Greenough, 1838, 14x20".....................**150.00**
Waa Top E Not, Chippewa, Rice & Clark, 1943, 14x20" **195.00**
Yaha Hojo, Seminole Chief, Rice & Clark, 1843, 14x20" **235.00**

Mucha, Alphonse

Biscuits Lefevre Utile, Flirt, linen bk, 1900, 25x10½" **2,500.00**
Gismonda, from Les Maitres de l'Affiche, 14x5½" **700.00**
Job, fr, 59x40" **6,600.00**
Job, from Les Maitres de l'Affiche, ink sgn, fr, 11½x8¾" **1,800.00**
Lance Parfum Rodo, sgn in plate, 1896, fr, 17x12" **4,000.00**
Leslie Carter, linen bk, 1908, 81x30" **5,700.00**
Lorenzaccio, from Les Maitres de l'Affiche, fr, 14x5½" **700.00**
Lorenzaccio, linen bk, 1896, 41x15"...................................... **1,700.00**
Salome, from L'Estampe Moderne, 1897, fr, 15x12"................ **1,650.00**
Salon des Cent, linen bk, 63½x43" **5,000.00**
Sarah Bernhardt, American Tour, linen bk, 78x30"................. **6,000.00**

Nutting, Wallace

　　Born in 1862, Nutting pursued many careers. His hand-tinted photographs of landscapes and interior scenes are prized by collectors today. He was also a writer, minister, farmer, and a furniture maker, designing reproductions of early American pieces. Collectors of his prints should be aware of rosy-hued, inconsistently bright or dark examples – especially large prints of *An Elaborate Dinner* and *A Chair for John;* these have been reproduced. Prices for large interior prints have recently been on the increase. Those with animals have risen at least 25% in the past few years, and prints with men are commanding extremely high prices. Those with babies and/or adolescent children bring very high prices as well.

　　Our advisor for this category is Milt Steinfeld; he is listed in the Directory under New Jersey.

Among October Birches, 21x18", EX **95.00**
Bag & Baggage, stagecoach, EX **425.00**

Blossom Pasture, sheep...**325.00**
Book Settle, 4x9½"...**175.00**
By a Cottage Door, French scene, uncolored...............................**235.00**
Caherlough, Irish scene w/castle ruins **400.00**
Cold Day, 14x16"..**275.00**
Comfort & the Cat, 14x16" **300.00**
Drying Apples, man w/Uncle Sam-type beard **400.00**
Dykeside Blossoms, 4½x6½"...**110.00**
Eventful Journey, stagecoach..**450.00**
Garden of Larkspur, sgn, dtd 1914, orig fr, 17½x21½" **38.00**
Garden Steps, no signature, 20x16" **125.00**
His Move, man w/beard **585.00**
Hollyhock Cottage, 18x22", EX **135.00**
Home Room, 7½x9½"..**185.00**
Honeymoon Cottage, orig fr, 21x11½" **70.00**
Jersey Banks, 7½x9½" in orig 14x17" fr, M................................**145.00**
Meeting Place **550.00**
Memory of Childhood, fr, 15" **105.00**
Old Tune Revisited, man in red jacket **400.00**
On Dress Parade, old fr, 17x11"...**85.00**
Red, White & Blue, #d label on bk, c 1942, 21x18" **125.00**
Shadowy Orchard Curves, 10x12" **95.00**
Sheffield Basket **340.00**
Sip of Tea, 7½x9½"...**150.00**
Warm Spring Day, orig fr, 16½x23½", M **240.00**
Where Grandma Was Wed, 10x13" **145.00**
Zinnias..**450.00**

Prang, Louis

Battle of Kenesaw Mountain, Prang's Am Litho Co, 15x21½" **110.00**
On the Hudson, Near West Point, 1866, 6x11" **110.00**
Sheridan's Ride, Prang's Am Litho Co, 15x21½"..........................**155.00**
Siege of Vicksburg, Prang's Aquerelle facsimile, 15x22".............**155.00**
Trespassing, 1878, 8x10"...**90.00**

Yard Long

　　Values for yard-longs are given for examples in very good to excellent condition, full length, nicely framed, and with the original glass. To learn more about this popular area of collector interest, we recommend *Those Wonderful Yard-Long Prints and More,* by our advisors W.D. and M.J. Keagy, and C.G. and J.M. Rhoden. They are listed in the Directory under Indiana and Illinois respectively.

American Farming Magazine, sgn WH Lister, 1918, 8x27" **175.00**
Bowles Live Stock Commission, Beauty Among Roses, 1912......**235.00**
Diamond Crystal Salt Co, advertising on bk, dtd 1913 ....**225.00**
Nat'l Stockman & Farmer Magazine, Stockman Bride, 1912.......**225.00**
Pabst, advertising on bk, dtd 1910 ....**175.00**
Pabst, sgn Alfred Everitt Orr, advertising on bk, dtd 1907...........**185.00**
Pabst, sgn CW Henning, advertising on bk, dtd 1907.................**175.00**
Pabst, sgn Stuart Travis, advertising on bk, dtd 1913 ....**175.00**
Pompeian, by Forbes, sgn: Sincerely, Mary Pickford, 1916..........**250.00**
Pompeian, Honeymooning in Alps, sgn Gene Pressler, 1923.......**125.00**
Pompeian, Liberty Girl, by Forbes, 1919....................................**200.00**
Pompeian, man & woman in front of fireplace, 1914 ....**150.00**
Pompeian, The Bride, sgn Rolf Armstrong, 1927 ....**225.00**
Selz Good Shoes, sgn Christy...**250.00**
Walk-Over Shoe Co, girl in boat, 1912, 10x27" **235.00**
Walk-Over Shoe Co, girl in cowgirl outfit, 11x29" **225.00**
Yard of Kittens, sgn Guy Radford..**250.00**
Yard of Pansies, sgn ME Hart **130.00**
Yard of Puppies, c 1903..**225.00**

Purinton

Founded in 1936 in Wellsville, Ohio, Purinton Pottery relocated in 1941 in Shippenville, Pennsylvania, and began producing hand-painted wares that are today attracting the interest of collectors of 'country-type' dinnerware. Using bold brush strokes of vivid color, simple yet attractive patterns such as Apple, Fruits, Tea Rose, and Pennsylvania Dutch were manufactured in tableware sets as well as in many accessory pieces. The pottery closed in 1959.

Our advisor for this category is Pat Dole; she is listed in the Directory under Alabama. Pat is the editor of *The Glaze;* see Clubs, Newsletters, and Catalogs.

Bean pot, Apple, ind	15.00
Bowl, Apple, 12"	24.00
Canister, Apple & Pear	25.00
Canister, tea; Apple	25.00
Canister set, Apple & Pear, on rnd wooden tray, lg sz	35.00
Canister set, Apple & Pear, on rnd wooden tray, med sz	25.00
Chop plate, Maywood, 12"	45.00
Coffeepot, Intaglio, brn	30.00
Cookie jar, Apple & Pear, oval	25.00
Creamer & sugar bowl, Maywood	30.00
Cruet, Apple	25.00
Cruet, Normandy Plaid, pr	15.00
Cup, coffee; Dutch	16.00
Cup & saucer, Normandy Plaid	8.00
Jug, Apple, 5-pt	20.00
Jug, Apple & Pear, Kent	10.00
Jug, Apple & Pear, lg	15.00
Jug, Dutch, 2-pt	12.00
Mug, beer; Intaglio, brn	30.00
Mug, beer; Normandy Plaid	25.00
Night bottle w/tumbler, Apple & Pear, 8"	30.00
Pitcher, utility; Apple	25.00
Pitcher, water; Apple, lg	30.00
Plate, Apple, 12"	20.00
Plate, dinner; Apple	8.00
Plate, dinner; Normandy Plaid	8.00
Plate, salad; Normandy Plaid	5.00
Platter, Intaglio, brn, oval	15.00
Relish, Intaglio, brn, 3-compartment	20.00
Shakers, Apple, jug form, sm, pr	6.00
Shakers, Apple & Pear, pr	6.00
Shakers, Intaglio, brn, jug form, pr	15.00
Snack set, Apple	12.00
Sugar bowl, Apple, hdls	8.00
Teapot, Apple, 2-cup	15.00

Tea set, Ivy pattern, $30.00.

Teapot, Oriental design, 2-cup	15.00
Tumbler, Apple, 12-oz	12.00
Tumbler, Apple & Pear, 6-oz	5.00

Purses

Beaded purses and bags represent an area of collecting interest that is very popular today. Purses from the early 1800s are often decorated with small, brightly-colored glass beads. Cut steel beads were popular in the 1840s and remained stylish until about 1930. Mesh purses are also popular. In the 1820s, mesh was woven. Chain-link mesh came into usage in the 1890s, followed by the enamel mesh bags carried by the flappers in the 1920s. Purses are divided into several categories by (a) construction techniques – whether beaded, embroidered, or a type of needlework; (b) material – fabric or metal; and (c) design and style. Condition is very important. Watch for dry, brittle leather or fragile material. For those interested in learning more, we recommend *Antique Purses, A History, Identification, and Value Guide*, Second Edition, by Richard Holiner, available at your library or local bookstore.

Beaded, faceted/smooth gold & silver metal, metal fr, 5x6½"	60.00
Beaded, floral tapestry, ornate fr, chain hdl, 9x12"	200.00
Beaded, mc Deco florals, chain hdl, 6x11"	265.00
Leather, alligator, leather lining, 1940s, 4x9", EX	20.00
Leather, lizard, fitted leather int, 2 hdls, 1940s, EX	20.00
Leopard skin, clutch style, EX	35.00
Lucite w/rhinestones, clutch style, 1950s, EX	35.00
Mesh, Deco florals, fringed, Whiting & Davis, 3½x6¼"	55.00

Mesh evening bag, colorful designs, $85.00.

Mesh, geometric pattern, fringed, Mandalian, 3¼x6½"	50.00
Mesh, German silver, 5x7"	70.00
Mesh, silver diagonal pattern, Whiting & Davis, 7x12"	200.00
Snakeskin, clutch style, blk, gold clasp, 1940s, 13" L, EX	10.00
Snakeskin, red dye, 4-strand snake hdl, 9½x5"	25.00
Suede, brn w/leather trim & strap, Koret, 1950s, 9x11"	35.00
Velvet, blk w/ornate brocade design, chain hdl, India, 6¾x4"	25.00

Quezal

The Quezal Art Glass and Decorating Company of Brooklyn, New York, was founded in 1901 by Martin Bach. A former Tiffany employee, Bach's glass closely resembled that of his former employer. Most pieces were signed 'Quezal,' a name taken from a Central American bird. After Bach's death in 1920, his son-in-law, Conrad Vohlsing, continued to produce a Quezal-type glass in Elmhurst, New York, which he marked 'Lustre Art Glass.' See also that particular category. Examples listed here are signed unless noted otherwise.

Bowl, gold, tri-fold rim, 5½"..375.00
Bowl vase, gold, ribbed, 2x2½" 575.00
Cup & saucer, amber w/EX irid, scroll hdl, 5" dia saucer.............375.00
Lamp, feathers, gold/wht/cobalt on gold, 2 lily shades, 28" 1,700.00

Lamp base, green and gold pulled feathers on opal glass, reticulated metal platform, 12", $800.00.

Shade, feathers, gr, gold irid int, ribbed, 5½", pr 320.00
Shade, feathers, ivory/gr/gold lustre, 7" 225.00
Shade, gold snakeskin, 5½x4½", pr....................................500.00
Shade, King Tut, gr/silver, chartreuse int, 4½x3"....................475.00
Vase, amber irid w/silver overlay ribbons, 6½" 850.00
Vase, bud; feathers, gr/gold on opal, flat bronze ft, 20" 1,500.00
Vase, bud; orange/gold irid, appl ft, scalloped rim, 12"................425.00
Vase, concentric rings, amber irid/gr opal, long neck, 13"....... 1,300.00
Vase, feathers, gold on amber, opal int, cylindrical, 4¾".............400.00
Vase, feathers, gr below gold striations, gold int, 6" 900.00
Vase, feathers, gr/gold-outlined, heavy, 4¾" 425.00
Vase, feathers/swirls, gold/gr on opal, 9".............................. 2,600.00
Vase, floriform; leaves, gr/opal on gold, #268, 4¾".....................800.00
Vase, gold irid, ribbed, scalloped, 1½" 400.00
Vase, gr w/opal ribs, pulled/swirled gold at rim, 3½" 2,100.00
Vase, jack-in-pulpit; feathers, amber irid/yel, 12" 1,400.00
Vase, jack-in-pulpit; feathers, gr/gold on ivory, 6" 1,650.00
Vase, King Tut, gr irid on gold, baluster, 10"............................ 1,250.00
Vase, rainbow opaque cased, #782, 7".....................................750.00
Vase, swirls, amber/bl/gr/brn striations, 6" 800.00
Vase, swirls, gr irid on gold, 10" 950.00

Quilts

Quilts, while made of necessity, nevertheless represent an art form which expresses the character and the personality of the designer. During the 17th and 18th centuries, quilts were considered a necessary part of a bride's hope chest – the traditional number required to be properly endowed for marriage was a 'baker's dozen'! Quilts were used not only for bed coverings but for curtains, extra insulation, and mattresses as well. The early quilts were made from pieces salvaged from cloth items

that had outlived their original usefulness and from bits left over from sewing projects. Regardless of shape, these scraps were fitted together following no organized lines. The resulting hodge-podge design was called a crazy quilt.

In 1793 Eli Whitney developed the cotton gin; as a result, textile production in America became industrialized. Soon inexpensive fabrics were readily available, and ladies were able to choose from colorful prints and solids to add contrast to their work. Both pieced and appliqued work became popular – pieced quilts were considered utilitarian, while appliqued work was shown with pride of accomplishment at the fair. Today many collectors prize pieced quilts and their intricate geometric patterns above all other types. Many of these designs were given names: Daisy and Oak Leaf, Grandmother's Flower Garden, Log Cabin, and Ocean Wave are only a few. Appliqued quilts involved stitching one piece – carefully cut into a specific form such as a leaf, a flower, or a stylized device – onto either a large one-piece ground fabric or an individual block. Often the background fabric was quilted in a decorative pattern.

Amish women scorned printed calicos as 'worldly' and instead used colorful blocks set with black fabrics to produce a stunning pieced effect. During the Victorian era, the crazy quilt was revived, but the ladies of the 1870s used plush velvets, brocades, silks, and linen patches and embroidered along the seams with feather or chain stitches.

Another type of quilting, highly prized and rare today, is trapunto. These quilts were made by first stitching the outline of the design onto a solid sheet of fabric which was backed with a second having a much looser weave. White was often favored, but color was sometimes used for accent. The design (grapes, flowers, leaves, etc.) was padded through openings made by separating the loose weave of the underneath fabric; a backing was added and the three layers quilted as one.

Besides condition, value is judged on intricacy of pattern, color effect, and craftsmanship. In the listings that follow, examples rated excellent have minor defects.

Key:
dmn — diamond	ms — machine sewn
embr — embroidered	X — cross
hs — hand sewn	

Amish

Blk w/lg red sq center & red binding, EX quilting, 70x70" 260.00
Bow Tie, 5-color, sgn, ms binding, 88x72", EX 1,600.00
Bow Tie, 7-color, hs, 70x65", EX....................................700.00
Chained 4-Patch Variant, 7-color, hs, 82x62", EX 1,700.00
Dmn-in-Sqs, 6-color, ms binding, Lebanon, 86x80, EX........... 1,250.00
Dmn-in-Sqs, sqs in corners, gr/purple/lav, 1940, 80x84", EX 700.00
Dutchman's Puzzle, EX color & quilting, sgn/1940, 70x89" 550.00
Log Cabin, dk colors, 1860s, crib sz, EX................................350.00
Lone Star, mc on blk, S Miller, OH, 1965, crib sz, 43x43" 150.00
Lone Star, reds/yels on bl, by S Miller, OH, ms binding..............475.00
Roman Stripes, dk colors/blk sateen, sgn/1906, 87x66", NM . 5,400.00
9-Sq, maroon/bl/orange, 74x72", VG.................................375.00

Appliqued

Colonial Umbrella Girl, yel/wht, EX quilting, lg.........................365.00
Crib, folk art motifs in wht sqs: animals/scissors/etc.................. 4,700.00
Floral pinwheels, vining borders, pots in corners, NM 1,200.00
Floral wreaths, pots of flowers in corners, EX work, EX...............950.00
Floral wreaths, vining border, gr/brn/goldenrod, 92x94" 475.00
Florals, red/gr, embr initials in center, 1860s, full sz, NM.............750.00
Florals, red/gr/goldenrod, 1875, NM 525.00
Florals, trapunto florals between, sgn/1850, rpr, 82x86" 3,300.00

Florals & medallions, mc calico, homespun bk, 94x92", NM .. **1,900.00**
Flower sprays, yel & gr on wht, EX quilting, lg, NM **600.00**
Log Cabin, red/wht/brn/gold, child's sz, 52x66", VG..................**200.00**
Magnolia branches, mc on wht, gr/wht borders, 1930s, lg, EX.....**495.00**
Oak Leaf, red/bl/gr, ca 1920s, full sz, EX **600.00**
Pinwheels (4), floral border, EX stitching, rpl, 86x88".............**1,600.00**
Poppy, red/gr/gold on wht, queen sz, NM....................................**495.00**
Pots of vines/flowers, pk/gr calico & solids **650.00**
Tulips, cotton sateens on cream, 1930s, lg, NM **440.00**
Tulips, pastels, outline stitches, ca 1900, lg, EX.........................**450.00**
Tulips, red/gr on wht, red border stripe, unused, 96x112" **450.00**
20 gr pots, ea w/different color flower+2 birds, 66x72" **1,400.00**

Mennonite

Bars, tan on bl-gr, feather quilting, 74x78".............................**1,500.00**
Log Cabin & Pineapples, cotton prints/ginghams, 1900s, EX **650.00**
Log Cabin variant, stars/blades, 1860s, 79x79".............................**850.00**
Pinwheels, goldenrod/navy bl on dk brn, bk: bars, 90x90" **500.00**
Rainbow variant, mc bars, 1900s, 84x88", EX..........................**1,600.00**

Pieced

Barn Raising, cotton/calicos, fine quilting, ca 1880, lg, EX..........**400.00**
Birds in the Air, indigo/wht, feather quilting, 1880s, lg **770.00**
Blocks w/bands of flying geese, silk, ca 1890s, full sz, EX............**400.00**
Bow Tie, coral & gold, fine quilting, lg, EX **300.00**
Broken Star, yel/pk on wht, ca 1900, lg, EX.................................**395.00**
Carolina Lily, cream/yel/brn, 85x74", EX.....................................**350.00**
Cookie Cutter, 'sampler' border, PA Dutch, 1860s, lg, EX **500.00**
Courthouse Sq, shrimp/brn/bl, late 1800s, lg, VG **375.00**
Courthouse Steps, bright colors, 1880s, lg, EX **375.00**
Crazy, silks/satins/velvet w/embr, 62x65" **500.00**
Crib, Pineapple, red/wht, overall wear, crib sz, 21x37".................**375.00**
Dbl Wedding Ring, mc, 76x72", EX..**475.00**
Dbl Wedding Ring, pk & lav w/wht, 1930s, lg, NM.....................**450.00**
Dbl Wedding Ring, pk on wht, ca 1900, full sz, EX.....................**400.00**
Devil's Claw, mc, fine quilting, ca 1860, full sz, EX.....................**400.00**
Diagonal bars/dmn stripes, lt/dk bl & wht, minor stains **325.00**
Dmn-in-Sqs, mc calicos, sawtooth border, 79x79", EX **800.00**
Dresden Plate, bls, full sz, 1920s, unused.....................................**500.00**
Dresden Plate, lt bl & wht, ca 1930, full sz, EX **350.00**
Flower Garden, gr border, twin sz, EX, pr.....................................**895.00**
Glower Garden w/Garden Path, bls, 1920s, lg, M **475.00**
Grandmother's Flower Garden, mc, thick, EX quilting, 74x72"...**325.00**
Hearts & Gizzards, pumpkin on wht, hs, 1930s, lg, EX **265.00**
Hole in the Barn Door, yel on wht, full sz, EX..............................**225.00**
Irish Chain, red/wht, overall wear/fading, 76x78" **220.00**
Jacob's Ladder Variant, pk/wht, EX quilting, 1900, lg, EX **325.00**
Kaleidoscope Star, red/bl/gray, 1890, lg, EX.................................**275.00**
Kansas Dust Storm, mc, fine piecing/quilting, 1930s, lg, M **265.00**
Lightning Stripe, brn/red/purple/bl on wht, 1880s, lg, EX **660.00**
Log Cabin, red calico/wht, minor stains, crib sz, 28x40".............**295.00**
Mirror Baskets, purple/wht, dbl-band border, 1890s, sm, EX........**195.00**
Monkey Wrench, bk: 9-Patch, sgn, 31x43" **450.00**
Mosaic look, mc on pk, homespun bk, ms binding, 78x78", EX...**800.00**
North Carolina Lily, bright calicos on wht, 1900, lg, EX **450.00**
Oak Leaf, bl on wht, dmn/feather quilting, 1880s, lg, EX **770.00**
Patchwork, circle-in-sq design, mc prints, 72x78" **195.00**
Patchwork, mc on wht, fine sewing, 1930s, full sz **195.00**
Patchwork, satin/silk/velvet, Am, 1850s, 79x79".........................**250.00**
Patchwork baskets, mc prints on wht, navy sqs w/wht stars **850.00**
Patchwork stars in mc prints on bl & wht, EX.............................**350.00**
Pine Tree, gr on wht, 1900, lg, EX **195.00**

Pinwheels, mc calico on wht/navy, 76x68", EX.........................**475.00**
Pinwheels, pk & wht calico, PA, 1890s, lg, EX **295.00**
Puss in the Corner, red/bl calicos on wht, red binding, 1870s **286.00**
Rose of Sharon, bl/yel/brn on wht, ca 1900, full sz, EX **325.00**
Sampler, house center, different design in ea sq, 76x87"..........**2,600.00**
Schoolhouse, calicos on brn print, no batting, 69x85", EX **400.00**
Seven Sisters Star, mc on wht, ca 1900, full sz, EX......................**575.00**
Spider Web Star, gr/bl/blk, ca 1900, lg, EX..................................**265.00**
Springtime Blossoms, orchid & wht, EX quilting, 103x94", NM.**525.00**
Starflowers, feather wreaths/meandering feathers, 80x90"...........**950.00**
Stars, bl/rose on dk bl, sgn, 78x80", NM......................................**700.00**
Stars, feather-quilted wreath at ea, minor wear, 83x89"...............**195.00**
Stars, made w/8 parallelograms, bl/red, red border, 75x76".........**325.00**
Stars, mc on wht & tan sqs, sawtooth border, sgn, 90x92", EX....**800.00**
Stars, mc on 2-tone goldenrod, red/gr border, 86x86", EX **650.00**
Stars & Blocks, bl/wht, unused, 76x76"...**885.00**
Stars in sqs (16 repeats), red/yel/gr, ms pk binding....................**300.00**
Sweet Gum Leaf, brn/yel/gr on wht, ca 1900, lg, EX...................**395.00**

Tree of Life with Cocheco Mfg. Co. pictorial patches, ca 1866, 71" x 96", $2,250.00.

Triangles, prints/wht on goldenrod, feather stitching, M **350.00**
Tumbling Block, homespun bk, 90x80", EX **650.00**
Tumbling Flowers, red & wht, English, ca 1880, EX **600.00**
Wedding Ring, brightly-colored prints, 82x82" **345.00**
Windmill, med & dk bl on wht, 1930s, EX, lg...............................**225.00**
7 stars in octagon, brn & wht, 82x72", EX **250.00**
9-Patch, bl/gray/wht prints, 82x70", EX.......................................**375.00**
9-Patch, mc calicos, homespun bk, ms binding, 84x84", EX........**560.00**
9-Patch, mc prints w/red centers on lt lav print ground...............**225.00**
9-Patch dmns, zigzag border, dbl scalloped edge, 36x50"............**225.00**
9-Patch/Irish Chain variant, bl/wht, 68x80" **395.00**

Trapunto

Bride's, vines & flowers in urns, 1820s, 88x90" **2,400.00**
Bride's, wht cotton, 1820, wear/rpr/stains **1,100.00**
Wht on wht, vintage/meandering feathers, lt wear, 68x72".....**1,100.00**

Quimper

    Quimper is a type of pottery produced in Quimper, France. A tin enamel-glazed earthenware pottery with hand-painted decoration, it was first produced in the 1600s by the Bousquet and Caussy Factories.

Little of this early ware was marked. By the late 1700s, three factories were operating in the area, all manufacturing the same type of pottery. The Grande Maison de HB, a company formed as a result of a marriage joining the Hubaudiere and Bousquet families, was a major producer of Quimper pottery. They marked their wares with various forms of the 'HB' logo; but of the pottery they produced, collectors value examples marked with the 'HB' within a triangle most highly.

Francois Eloury established another pottery in Quimper in the late 1700s. Under the direction of Charles Porquier, the ware was marked simply 'P.' Adolph Porquier replaced Charles in the 1850s, marking the ware produced during that period with an 'AP' logo.

Jule HenRiot began operations in 1886, using molds he had purchased from Porquier. His mark was 'HR,' and until the twentieth century he was in competition with The Grande Maison de HB. In 1926 he began to mark his wares 'HenRiot Quimper.' In 1968 the two factories merged. They are still in operation under the name Les Faenceries de Quimper. The factory sold in the fall of 1983 to Sarah and Paul Janssens from the United States, making it the first time the owners were not French.

For those interested in learning more about Quimper pottery, we recommend *Quimper: A French Folk Art Faience,* by Sandra V. Bondhus, our advisor for this category, whose address can be found in the Directory under Connecticut.

Bannette, seated couple, decor riche, gold bands, 11x8½" 475.00
Bowl, lady, concentric yel/bl band rim, HQ, 7x2½" 25.00
Bucket, bird & florals, gr glaze, wood hdl, 6" 75.00
Bust, baby, sgn B Savigny, HB Quimper, 5x4" 160.00
Bust, girl in bonnet smiles, sgn Blandin, HQ, 6½x4½"...................85.00
Bust, old man, sideburns, sgn Roger Le Gall, HQ, 7¾" 210.00
Charger, classical scene, Celtic border, HBQ, 1800s, 11¾"..........400.00
Charger, floral center, cartouch rim, HenRiot Quimper, 24" 400.00
Cheese dish, florals, biniou shape, HR Quimper, 10½x8" 550.00
Clock, floral sprays, Baroque style, HB Quimper, 8¾x6" 1,300.00
Compote, lady, ftd cloverleaf form, HB Quimper, 10⅜".............350.00
Cruet, lady & florals, peach-shaped finial, HBQ, 6½"...................95.00
Egg basket, woven look, HB Quimper, 7x9x7", +6 mk egg cups ..500.00
Egg cup, chick, HB...65.00
Egg server, floral, scalloped, center hdl, HQF, 5½x10½" 350.00
Figurine, dancers, Modern Movement, Micheau-Vernez, HQ, 9"..95.00
Figurine, lady digging potatoes, sgn Le Bozec, 16½"....................135.00
Figurine, Le Marche, lady sells pigs to man, Savigny, 12½" 1,500.00
Figurine, St Ann & child, HB Quimper, 13½" 350.00
Figurine, Ste Vierge, F-470, mk HenRiot, 3½"..............................115.00
Flower holder, man/woman, bombe form, HR Quimper, 5x9x4" .850.00
Inkwell, dancers, decor riche, biniou shape, 2½x8x6"..................750.00
Inkwell, florals, heart shape, HB Quimper, 3¼x5x5" 235.00
Inkwell, man smoking pipe, w/insert & lid, sq, 2½x4" 235.00
Jardiniere, fleur-de-lis/musician, decor riche, HBQ, 8x12"...........800.00
Jug, floral wreath around body, sponge hdl/spout, HB, 6x6".........180.00
Pipe rack, shell motif, Breton lady, HR Quimper, 11x6½" 400.00
Pitcher, man lighting pipe figural, Modern Movement, HQ, 5" ..110.00
Pitcher, man w/cane, floral sprays, HenRiot Quimper, 8½" 150.00
Plate, man, concentric yel/bl band rim, HQ, 7½"............................25.00
Platter, couple, rectangular, canted corners, HQF, 13½x10" 300.00
Platter, lady, concentric yel/bl band rim, HQ, 13½" 110.00
Platter, man & lady, fish form, HQ, 10x4½" 275.00
Porringer, man, sponged hdls, HB Quimper, 8¼" 30.00
Sauce boat, w/underplate, lady, mc florals, HBFQ, 4½x9½" 110.00
Tile, lady, bl border, HQF, 4¾" 60.00
Tray, pen, dancing couple, Rococo, HQ, 10¾x7¼" 450.00
Tub, Breton lady, peonies, HBQF, 5x5¾" 85.00
Tub, Breton man, floral sprays, HBQF, 3¾x5" 70.00
Umbrella stand, peacocks/florals, HB Quimper, 10x9½".............200.00

Vase, Breton man/foliage, fan form, HQF, 5x8" 200.00
Vase, dancing couple, dragon figural hdls, HQ, 14¼" 650.00
Vase, man, Ivoire Corbeille, HQ, 8x7" 75.00
Vase, Mayflower w/French tricolors, quintal, HQF, 3½x4" 190.00
Vase, Odetta, geometric band on brn, Deco, 8½" 165.00
Wall pocket, lady, corne shape, 1800s, HB Quimper 275.00
Wall pocket, man/boy at wheel, decor riche, Briec PB, 13" 1,100.00
Wine cask set, portrait bust, 6-cups/stand/spigot, HQF...............200.00

Radford

The Jasperware listed below was made in Zanesville, Ohio, at the A. Radford Pottery Company incorporated there in 1903. This type of ware was first designed and produced in 1896 when Albert Radford worked in Tiffin, Ohio. The Zanesville Jasper, in contrast to the original line, was decorated with Wedgwood-type cameos in relief that were not applied but were formed within the general mold. The only mark found on the ware is a two-digit shape number. The Tiffin Jasper, though not always marked, is sometimes impressed 'Radford Jasper.'

After only a few months Radford sold the plant to Arc-En-Ciel and moved his works to West Virginia. In addition to the regular line of utility wares, several artware lines were also produced there. Among them were Ruko, a standard brown underglaze decorated line; Thera, matt glazed with slip decoration; and Radura, usually done in matt green glazes.

Jasper

Mug, floral relief, lt bl, 4½" 225.00
Pitcher, grapes, Old Man Winter on hdl, #17, 9" 285.00
Vase, angels in relief, bl & blk, 7"...250.00
Vase, lady w/flowers, bk: grapes, #59, 4" 200.00

Jasper vase, eagle and shield, 7½", $295.00.

Miscellaneous

Candle holder, Ruko, floral, sgn/mk, rare, 7" 190.00
Vase, Radura, gr, Nouveau form, 4 long in-mold hdls, rare, 9" ...275.00
Vase, Thera, floral, red on gr matt, rare, 12" 450.00
Vase, Velvety, gr, sgn & mk, rare, 14¼"...395.00

Radios

Vintage radios are becoming very popular. There were thousands of styles and types produced, the most popular of which today are the breadboard and the cathedral. Consoles are usually considered less saleable since their size makes them hard to display and store.

For those wishing to learn more about antique radios, we recommend *The Collector's Guide to Antique Radios*, by Sue and Marty Bunis, available from your local library or book store.

Addison, Bakelite, maroon w/amber trim, 1935, 6x9" 600.00
Atwater Kent #10B, breadboard, rstr 300.00
Atwater Kent #30, EX 60.00
Atwater Kent #35, EX 50.00
Atwater Kent #42, EX 50.00
Atwater Kent #55-C, metal case, table model, EX 75.00
Atwater Kent #9, breadboard, G orig...500.00
Clearfield TRF-6-RC Model D, Sherman Radios of NY, NM 200.00
Coronado #951, battery, wood case 12.50
Crosley #10-137, lt gr, EX..60.00
Crosley #51, G orig..70.00
Crosley Coloradio #10-136-E, blk & chrome, EX 80.00
Crosley Coloradio #11-126, maroon, EX 65.00
Crosley Tombstone #127, 10-tube, 1931, rare, EX 175.00
Crosley Tombstone #515, EX 45.00
Crosley XJ, EX 185.00
Cutting-Washington #11-A, EX 325.00
DeWald, swirled tortoise-shell Bakelite, lyre form/grillwork........440.00
Emerson #561, B Series, brn/gold Bakelite, EX 35.00
Emerson #9-LW-344, brn Bakelite, table model, EX 30.00
Emerson Mickey Mouse, 1930s, EX 450.00
Fada, Bakelite, amber, bullet form, 10½" L 440.00
Fada #1000, Bakelite, butterscotch, 7x10½" 495.00
Fada #1000, Bakelite, ivory w/red dials & hdl, rnded end............700.00
Fada #5F50, Bakelite, amber w/red grill, 8¾" L 600.00
Fada #845, Bakelite, red hdl/knobs on wht, blk dial, 10" L..........465.00
Fada L-56, Bakelite, amber, arched hdl, 7x9" L 700.00
Fada L-56, Bakelite, jade gr, hdld rectangular case, 9" L 800.00

Fada, tortoise-shell brown Bakelite, 10½" long, $660.00; Emerson, Norman Bel Geddes design, red and white Bakelite, 11" long, $1,000.00.

Grundig Majestic, EX 50.00
Hallicrafters S-120, 5-tube, EX...45.00
Hallicrafters S-38-C, 4-band, VG 35.00
Jackson Bell, 7-tube, 1932, EX 175.00
Majestic #15-A, 1932, EX 85.00
Meissner Model 8C Converter, tubes, wood cabinet, EX 25.00
Metrodyne #5, 1925, EX 55.00
Montgomery Wards, plastic airline, twin speakers, 1940s, EX........85.00
Motorola, Bakelite, jade gr w/amber trim, cloth panel, 7x6" 800.00
Nat'l HRO-50-T, w/12 coil sets, EX...100.00
Philco, PT-19 ....30.00
Philco #41-221, wood cabinet, plastic grill, table model, VG 35.00
Philco #461201 ....65.00

Philco #481-141, Bakelite, EX 25.00
Philco #50, cathedral, EX 175.00
Philco #89, cathedral, EX 145.00
Philco Jr, cathedral, EX 150.00
Philco Transitone #51-532, EX 35.00
Radiola #32, from RCA display, never sold, M............................250.00
RCA #6-T, EX 75.00
RCA Radiola #18, w/speaker, NM 240.00
RCA Victor, Catalin, amber, wht knobs, cloth panel, 8" L..........550.00
RCA VIII, battery box ea end, less tubes, EX 220.00
Sentinel #10356, EX 25.00
Sentinel L-28, Bakelite, amber, 7½x11" 495.00
Silvertone #1965, 1934, rstr 85.00
Sinclair, gasoline pump novelty transister, VG 25.00
Spartan #5-A-7, working..40.00
Spartan #500, cloisonne, EX 1,500.00
Thompson Neutrodyne, slant front, EX..100.00
Ward's Airline #93-BR-420-B, EX..65.00
Westinghouse #23, table model, VG 25.00
Westinghouse RA-DA, no tubes, EX orig.......................................125.00
Zenith #6-G-601M, EX orig..45.00
Zenith #6-V-27, EX 120.00
Zenith B-5095, red & wht, VG 30.00
Zenith G-511-Y, blk w/gold front...45.00
Zenith J-402-G, plastic cabinet, uses 1-volt tubes, portable 20.00
Zenith Tombstone #5-S-29, EX...110.00
Zenith Trans-Oceanic #8-G-005-YT, EX 75.00

Railroadiana

Collecting railroad-related memorabilia has become one of America's most popular hobbies. The range of collectible items available is almost endless, considering the fact that more than 175 different railroad lines are represented. Some collectors prefer to specialize in only one, while others attempt to collect at least one item from every railway line known to have existed. For the advanced collector, there is the challenge of locating rarities from short-lived railroads; for the novice, there are abundant keys, buttons, passes, and playing cards. Among the most popular specializations are dining-car collectibles – flatware, glassware, dinnerware, etc., in a wide variety of patterns and styles.

For a more thorough study, we recommend *Railroad Collectibles, Fourth Edition*, by Stanley L. Baker, available at your local library or bookstore. Some of our listings were provided by Shrader's Antiques (see Directory, California).

Key:
BL — bottom logo	RY — railway
BR — brass	SL — side logo
BS — bottom stamped	SM — side marked
C — cast	ST — steel
NP — nickel plated	STMP — stamped
R&B — Reed and Barton	TL — top logo
RR — railroad	TM — top marked

Dinnerware

Ash tray, C&O, Geo Washington, 3x7" 85.00
Ash tray, N&W, Dogwood, 3¾" 45.00
Ash tray, Seaboard, cobalt, rnd 95.00
Bowl, cereal; ATSF, Mimbreno, BS, 5¾" 45.00
Bowl, cereal; B&O, Centenary, 6½"...40.00
Bowl, cereal; CMStP&P, Peacock, 6" 18.00

Bowl, cereal; CMStP&P, Traveler, 6½" 15.00
Bowl, cereal; PRR, Mountain Laurel, 6¼" 15.00
Bowl, cereal; PRR, Purple Laurel, 6½" 25.00
Bowl, cereal; SP, Prairie Mountain Wildflowers, BS, 6" 40.00
Bowl, cereal; UP, Desert Flower, 6½" 28.00
Bowl, cereal; UP, Winged Streamliner, 6½" 35.00
Bowl, cereal; WP, Feather River, 6½" 65.00
Bowl, salad; ATSF, Mimbreno, BS, 8¾" 75.00
Bowl, soup; B&O, Derby, BS, 9¼" 40.00
Bowl, soup; CMStP&P, Traveler, 8" 30.00
Bowl, soup; PRR, Keystone, 9" 35.00
Bowl, soup; UP, Desert Flower, BS, 9" 35.00
Butter pat, ATSF, California Poppy...................................21.50
Butter pat, ATSF, Mimbreno 35.00
Butter pat, B&O, Centenary, BS.......................................45.00
Butter pat, CB&Q, Violets & Daisies 25.00
Butter pat, CMStP&P, Traveler 29.50
Butter pat, CRI&P, El Reno 10.00
Butter pat, D&RG, Blue Adam 18.00
Butter pat, FEC, Mistic 25.00
Butter pat, Pullman, Indian Tree, TM...............................65.00
Butter pat, SP, Prairie Mountain Wildflowers, BS 85.00
Butter pat, UP, Blue & Gold...15.00
Butter pat, UP, Harriman Blue 20.00
Butter pat, UP, Winged Streamliner 21.00
Celery dish, ACL, Flora of the South, BS, 5x10" 95.00
Celery dish, ATSF, California Poppy, 4½x9½" 65.00
Celery dish, B&O, Capitol, TL, 6x11½" 95.00
Celery dish, C&O, Staffordshire, BS, 5x10" 95.00
Celery dish, CB&Q, Violets & Daisies, 5x10"....................60.00
Celery dish, CMStP&P, Galatea, 5x10" 68.00
Celery dish, CMStP&P, Traveler, 5x10" 35.00
Celery dish, NYC, Mercury, 5x10" 35.00
Celery dish, UP, Blue & Gold, 4½x10" 18.00
Cup, bouillon; CB&Q, Violets & Daisies 25.00
Cup, bouillon; WP, Feather River 38.00
Cup & saucer, ATSF, Adobe, cup TL 38.00
Cup & saucer, ATSF, Mimbreno, BS..................................95.00
Cup & saucer, B&O, Centenary, BS 72.00
Cup & saucer, C&O, Homestead, both TL 60.00
Cup & saucer, C&O, Train Ferry, cup SL 75.00
Cup & saucer, CMStP&P, Olympian, both TL.....................95.00
Cup & saucer, CMStP&P, Traveler 65.00
Cup & saucer, CP, Tremblant, both TL...............................72.00
Cup & saucer, D&RG, Blue Adam 55.00
Cup & saucer, demitasse; ATSF, Mimbreno, both BS 125.00
Cup & saucer, demitasse; B&O, Centenary, both BS 62.00
Cup & saucer, demitasse; CP, Brown Maple Leaf, both TM...........75.00
Cup & saucer, demitasse; CP, Tremblant, both TL 85.00
Cup & saucer, demitasse; IC, Coral....................................95.00
Cup & saucer, demitasse; SR, Piedmont 60.00
Cup & saucer, demitasse; UP, Winged Streamliner 55.00
Cup & saucer, GN, Mountains & Flowers, both BS 95.00
Cup & saucer, NYC, Mercury, both TM 62.00
Cup & saucer, PRR, Broadway 75.00
Cup & saucer, SP, Prairie Mountain Wildflowers, both BS 65.00
Cup & saucer, UP, Desert Flower, both BS 85.00
Cup & saucer, UP, Winged Streamliner...............................25.00
Egg cup, ACL, Carolina, BS..35.00
Egg cup, C&NW, Flambeau..18.00
Egg cup, GN, Mountains & Flowers....................................72.00
Egg cup, MP, Eagle, SL...72.00
Egg cup, MStP&SStM, Logan 95.00
Egg cup, UP, Desert Flower..35.00

Egg cup, UP, Winged Streamliner 35.00
Gravy boat, ATSF, California Poppy....................................55.00
Gravy boat, C&O, Chessie...55.00
Gravy boat, FEC, Mistic..35.00
Gravy boat, NYNH&H, Platinum Blue, BS 100.00
Gravy boat, SP, Prairie Mountain Wildflowers, BS..............95.00
Gravy boat, UP, Winged Streamliner..................................55.00
Ice cream shell, ATSF, Adobe, BS.....................................75.00
Ice cream shell, ATSF, Mimbreno, BS 75.00
Ice cream shell, CN, Bonaventure, TL................................42.00
Ice cream shell, UP, Winged Streamliner 32.00
Mustard, ATSF, Mimbreno, BS, w/lid................................150.00
Mustard, D&RG, Blue Adam, slotted, w/lid........................38.00
Mustard, N&W, Coach & Four, slotted, w/lid......................145.00
Pitcher, FEC, Mistic, 7½"...85.00
Pitcher, UP, Winged Streamliner, 6½"................................85.00
Plate, ACL, Carolina, BS, 9"..28.00
Plate, ACL, Flora of the South, BS, 7¾" 75.00
Plate, ATSF, Adobe, TM, 9"...70.00
Plate, ATSF, California Poppy, 10"......................................50.00
Plate, ATSF, California Poppy, 6".......................................28.00
Plate, ATSF, Griffon, 7¾"...65.00
Plate, ATSF, Mimbreno, BS, 7½".......................................65.00
Plate, ATSF, Mimbreno, BS, 9¾".......................................95.00
Plate, B&O, Capitol, TL, 9"...62.00
Plate, B&O, Centenary, BS, 10½"......................................85.00
Plate, B&O, Centenary, BS, 6½".......................................42.00
Plate, C&O, George Washington, BS, 8" 78.00
Plate, CB&Q, Violets & Daisies, BS, 9" 78.00
Plate, CB&Q, Violets & Daisies, 7½".................................22.00
Plate, CMStP&P, Galatea, 8"...62.00
Plate, CMStP&P, Peacock, 6½"...30.00
Plate, CMStP&P, Traveler, 6½"...22.00
Plate, CMStP&P, Traveler, 9½"...65.00
Plate, CN, Toronto, TL, 9"...42.00
Plate, CN, Windsor, BS, 9"..42.00
Plate, CP, Empress, BS, 6½"...55.00
Plate, CP, Tremblant, TL, 9¾"...45.00
Plate, CRI&P, Golden Rocket, TL, 5¾"...............................110.00
Plate, CRI&P, Golden State (oranges), 9" 95.00
Plate, FEC, Carolina, BS, 7½"...72.00
Plate, GN, Glacier, BS, 5½"...65.00
Plate, GN, Mountains & Flowers, BS, 5½" 35.00
Plate, GN, Oriental, 10"..75.00
Plate, GN, Oriental, 7½"...42.00
Plate, N&W, Coach & Four, 9½"..95.00
Plate, N&W, Dogwood, 9¾" 38.00
Plate, N&W, Shenandoah, 9¾"..75.00
Plate, NP, Monad, TL, 7½"..62.00
Plate, NYC, Mercury, 9"..50.00
Plate, NYC, Mohawk, 6½"...30.00
Plate, NYNH&H, Indian Tree, BS, 6½"...............................38.00
Plate, NYNH&H, Indian Tree, BS, 9".................................80.00
Plate, NYNH&H, Platinum Blue, 8½".................................45.00
Plate, PRR, Broadway, BS, 8½"...38.00
Plate, PRR, Keystone, BS, 9"..72.00
Plate, PRR, Mountain Laurel, BS, 8½"...............................28.00
Plate, PRR, Mountain Laurel, 6½".....................................18.00
Plate, Pullman, Indian Tree, TM, 9"...................................72.00
Plate, SAL, Palm Beach, 9"...72.00
Plate, SL&SF, Denmark, 9"...49.00
Plate, SP, Prairie Mountain Wildflowers, BS, 9½" 75.00
Plate, SP, Prairie Mountain Wildflowers, divided, BS, 9¾"...........95.00
Plate, SP, Prairie Mountain Wildflowers, 5½"......................22.00

Plate, SR, Piedmont, 9" 52.00
Plate, UP, Blue & Gold, 10" 40.00
Plate, UP, Challenger, 9½" 88.00
Plate, UP, Desert Flower, 5½" 18.00
Plate, UP, Desert Flower, 9½" 50.00
Plate, UP, Harriman Blue, BS, 6½" 30.00
Plate, UP, Harriman Blue, BS, 9¼" 75.00
Plate, UP, Winged Streamliner, 10½" 48.00
Plate, UP, Winged Streamliner, 6½" 25.00
Plate, WP, Feather River, TL, 5½" 39.00
Plate, WP, Feather River, TL, 7½" 48.00
Platter, ACL, Flora of the South, BS, 8x12" 185.00
Platter, ACL, Palmetto, TL, 8x11¾" 120.00
Platter, ATSF, California Poppy, 5x9" 50.00
Platter, C&O, Centenary, BS, 8¼x11½" 78.00
Platter, C&O, George Washington, no portrait, 8½x6½" 65.00
Platter, CB&Q, Violets & Daisies, 9x6" 75.00
Platter, CMStP&P, Peacock, 8x6¼" 24.00
Platter, CMStP&P, Traveler, 8x6½" 28.00
Platter, D&RGW, Prospector, TL, 11x9½" 52.00
Platter, Erie, Gould, TL, 8½x5½" 95.00
Platter, Erie, Susquehanna, 8½x6" 35.00
Platter, GN, Mountains & Flowers, BS, 7x5" 45.00
Platter, GN, Oriental, BS, 8x6½" 85.00
Platter, L&N, Green Leaf, 10½x7½" 25.00
Platter, MP, Eagle, TL, 10½x7½" 75.00
Platter, MP, St Albans, 10x7" 52.00
Platter, NP, Yellowstone, TL, 8½x7" 65.00
Platter, PRR, Broadway, TL, 8x5½" 38.00
Platter, PRR, Purple Laurel, BS, 9x6½" 45.00
Platter, Pullman, Indian Tree, TM, 8¼x5½" 62.00
Platter, Reading, Stotesbury, BS, 10½x7" 75.00
Platter, SP, Prairie Mountain Wildflowers, BS, 9½x7½" 62.00
Platter, SP, Sunset, TL, 9x6½" 67.00
Platter, UP, Harriman Blue, BS, 10x8" 55.00
Platter, UP, Winged Streamliner, 9x7½" 32.00
Platter, WP, Feather River, TL, 11½x9" 125.00
Platter, WP, Feather River, TL, 9x7½" 65.00
Sugar bowl, GN, Oriental, w/lid 67.00
Sugar bowl, N&W, Coach & Four, w/lid 75.00
Sugar bowl, N&W, Shenandoah, open 45.00
Teapot, ATSF, California Poppy 79.00
Teapot, FEC, Mistic 95.00
Teapot, UP, Winged Streamliner 50.00

Glassware

Ash tray, ATSF, Santa Fe in script, 3x4" 14.00
Ash tray, GN, entwined wht letters, BS, 4" dia 17.50
Ash tray, N&W, gr w/red logo, 4¼" 13.50
Ash tray, SCL, red/bl logo, ftd, early 10.00
Ash tray, Super Chief, turq on clear, 4x5" 8.00
Bottle, medicine; SP, RR Hospital, 3½" 15.00
Bottle, milk; Mopac, buzz saw logo, octagonal, BS, 5x5" 20.00
Cocktail set, UP, mixer+2 roly-poly 2½" tumblers, logo 32.00
Cordial, NYC underlined in wht on side, 3½" 42.00
Cruet, GN, older frosted goat logo 150.00
Goblet, UP, stemmed, tall 17.50
Martini glass, UP 10.00
Martini set, UP, pitcher+2 glasses+1 stirrer, frosted logo 30.00
Mug, BN, gr name/blk slogan, 1972 ....10.00
Shot glass, UP, frosted shield & wht stripe, 2½" 7.50
Tray, canape; SF, map & Chico emb in gold & wht, 14" dia ..47.50
Tumbler, AAR, slant sides, train around top/music, 4" 5.00

M&STLRR table water pitcher, silverplated frame, Albert Pick & Co., 1928, $350.00.

Tumbler, ATSF, Santa Fe, 5½" 10.00
Tumbler, D&H, appl shield logo, 4½" 14.00
Tumbler, EL, roly-poly, 1st Air Condition Commuter, 1969 ..12.00
Tumbler, Erie, amethyst, slant sides, 3¼x3" 35.00
Tumbler, Frisco, bl bearskin, 6-oz 7.50
Tumbler, Long Island, train & track in tunnel, 3¼" 7.50
Tumbler, NYC, flared base, 3" 17.50
Tumbler, NYC, flared base, 5¾" 22.00
Tumbler, PRR, RR scene w/keystone logo, 4½" 11.00
Tumbler, Santa Fe in wht on side, 4½" 4.50
Tumbler, SF, SM, 5½x2½" 12.50
Tumbler, SL&SF, etched Frisco Lines, 4½" 15.00
Tumbler, UP, frosted shield, 4½" 10.00
Wine, CN, etched name, stemmed 22.50
Wine, NYC, 20th Century Limited, stemmed 25.00
Wine, Santa Fe in script, 4½" 22.00

Lamps

Backhead gauge, N&W, Dietz, pre-WWII, unissued 40.00
Berth, Pullman, aluminum, milk glass shade, 1950s, EX 47.50
Berth, Pullman, steel/porc, egg shape, EX, pr 37.50
Caboose wall, Handlan #180, early version, complete, EX 60.00
Camp car, Y&MV, tin, wall mt, Taplin, 10" chimney, EX 40.00
Carman's, Conrail, battery, bl lights, EX 30.00
Inspector's, Oxweld #2155, carbide, EX 65.00
Inspector's, WAB, Oxweld, carbide, NM 80.00
Marker, NYCS, Adlake, sq top, oil, complete, EX, pr 245.00
Marker, Pyle Nat'l, 1 red/3 gr lenses, electrified, M 80.00
Semaphore, NYC&StL, Dressel, SM, gr lens, orig pnt, EX 80.00
Switch, Adlake #1112½, sq top, oil, w/day targets, EX 100.00
Switch, Adlake #1379, glass lenses, no wires/bulb, dwarf, VG ..55.00
Switch, Adlake #1389, glass lenses, no int wiring, sm, EX 60.00
Switch, Dressel, oil, red/gr lenses, steel/CI, EX 160.00
Switch, IC, Adlake, sq top, oil, gr/red lenses, NM 175.00
Switch, L&N, Dressel, oil, SM w/tag, amber/wht lenses, EX ..100.00
Switch, PRR, Adlake, SM PRR Keystone, 1909, EX 145.00
Switch, WRRS #1876, cast steel, ribbed lenses, VG 70.00
Wall, brass, candle type, w/bracket & chimney, unmk, EX 70.00

Lanterns

Adlake #300 Kero, clear unmk globe, short, unfired, M 50.00
ATSF, Dressel Arlington, unmk globe, thumb latch, short, NM ..50.00

B&O, Adlake Reliable, clear etch globe, dbl guard, VG **60.00**
Baltimore Transit, Handlan, 24-hour pot, red 4½" globe, EX **48.00**
C&NW, Adlake 1913 Reliable, unmk fr, tall globe, EX **65.00**
CMStP&P, Adlake #250 Kero, unmk globe, lt pitting, VG **37.50**
Conger Steel, switchman's, battery, rubber grip hdl, EX................**18.00**
D&H, Adlake #250 Kero, etched D&H globe, dome top, EX **45.00**
Dietz 1910 Vesta, clear US globe, tall, EX................................**55.00**
DL&W, Dietz Vesta 1951, red unmk globe, EX........................**45.00**
FW&DC, Adlake #250 Kero, red unmk globe, EX......................**78.00**
GN, Armspear 1925 Adlake, unmk short globe, EX....................**50.00**
I&GN, Handlan 1889, unmk globe, wire bottom, dbl guard, EX.**125.00**
L&N, Adlake Kero, short clear unmk globe, M..........................**55.00**
L&N, Armspear 1913, mk globe, insert pot, 1-guard, tall, EX **150.00**
LI, Armspear 1925 Kero, amber Fresnel globe, EX **75.00**
LV, Dietz Vesta, TM, 4" etched globe, EX **36.00**
MOPAC, Handlan, unmk 4½" globe, cleaned, EX......................**50.00**
N&W, Adlake Kero, unmk globe, dome top, NM **45.00**
N&W, Adlake Reliable, clear unmk globe, tall, VG **35.00**
N&W, Armspear/Adlake Kero, unmk globe, NM **50.00**
NP, Armspear, flat rib, unmk 5⅜" globe, TM fr, EX..................**88.00**
NYC, Adlake #100, unmk tall globe, rpl pot/burner, EX **60.00**
NYC, Dietz Vesta, unmk fr, clear mk globe, NM **47.50**
NYNH&H, Dietz Vesta, bl unmk globe, unfired, M..................**80.00**
NYNH&H, Dietz Vesta, unmk fr, clear mk globe, EX................**65.00**
NYNH&H, Dressel Arlington, cobalt unmk globe, short, M.........**80.00**
P&R, Vesta 1922, mk globe, dome top, early, EX.......................**70.00**
PC, Dressel Arlington, unmk globe, worn logo on lid, M............**57.50**
PRR, Adams & Westlake 1895, bell bottom, tall, EX **150.00**
PRR, Dressel, TM: PRR Keystone, etched globe, red pnt, VG **44.00**
RI, Adams & Westlake 1909, mk globe, dbl guard, insert font **175.00**
SR, Adlake Kero, red unmk Fresnel globe, dtd 1944, EX **35.00**
Star Headlight, NP, battery, EX..**25.00**
Starlite #222, switchman's, battery, plastic body, steel hdl **12.50**

Linens

Bag, laundry; D&RG, blk letters on wht w/drawstring, 36"............**25.00**
Blanket, berth; Pullman, logo in center, 80x52", EX **65.00**
Blanket, Canadian Nat'l, maple leaf logo, Pendleton wool, EX **45.00**
Blanket, CP/CN, beaver or maple leaf logo, NM **45.00**
Blanket, UP, Streamline logo on salmon wool, VG......................**25.00**
Headrest cover, CA Zephyr, button down, train scene, 14x17" **28.00**
Headrest cover, Milwaukee, tan interwoven logo, 12x18" **12.50**
Headrest cover, Rio Grande, brn letters on tan, 12x18"................**20.00**
Headrest cover, UP, interwoven logo in 1" stripe, 14x16" **10.00**
Headrest cover, UP, red Streamliner & logo on 1 end, 18x12" **12.50**
Napkin, Erie Lackawanna, red script on wht, gr border, 21x20" ...**10.00**
Napkin, RI, wht on wht bearskin logo, 1962, 20"............................**10.00**
Napkin, Rio Grand, interwoven wht on wht letters **5.00**
Napkin, Seaboard, Golden State Rte, wht on wht, 21x20"............**10.00**
Napkin, SF, script letters, bl on wht, 15x16" **7.50**
Napkin, UP, wht, 18x20", EX **7.50**
Pillowcase, CA Zephyr, wht, reg sz....................................**15.00**
Sheet, Burlington Rte, STMP logo, twin sz **12.00**
Sheet, RB, Bond Hotel, twin sz......................................**10.00**
Sheet, Rio Grande Mainline, logo STMP on wht, twin sz **5.00**
Tablecloth, Burlington Rte, lg interwoven logo center **25.00**
Tablecloth, CA Zephyr, interwoven logo, oval, 9x6".................**15.00**
Tablecloth, IL Central, diamond logo, wht on salmon, 36x42"......**15.00**
Tablecloth, Rio Grande, 'speed' letters, wht on wht, EX................**15.00**
Tablecloth, SF, interwoven logo, wht on wht, 32" sq, EX..............**25.00**
Tablecloth, WP, lg Feather River Rte logo, EX **25.00**
Towel, dish; Burlington Rte, Safety Is Our Dish, 17x18"................ **6.50**
Towel, dish; Burlington Rte, wide bl stripe, 26x16" **5.00**

Towel, Ft Worth & Denver, narrow bl stripe, 26x12", EX............... **7.50**
Towel, Santa Fe, bl stripe, 26x16" **5.00**
Towel, Santa Fe, wht w/red stripe in center, 1948, 20x17" **12.50**
Towel, Santa Fe, 16 vertical stripes, 1940s, 30x26" **5.00**
Towel, UP, interwoven yel stripe & wings, 10x16" **7.50**
Towel, UP, stamped logo on wht or yel, 17x12", EX **7.50**
Towel, UP, STMP logo, yel, lg **5.00**
Towel, UP, wide bl stripe, 14x16" **8.00**

Locks

Car, L&N, ST, heart shape, allows for seal through hasp, EX.........**20.00**
Signal, DL&W, BR, +unmk ST key, EX **28.00**
Signal, L&N, screw type, w/chain, EX **22.50**
Signal, SAL, ST, screw type, sm **6.50**
Signal, WRRSCo, BR, screw type, sm, NM **7.50**
Switch, AACo, Handlan-Buck, BR, heart shape, no chain, EX ...**50.00**
Switch, ACL, Adlake, ST, w/chain & BR key dtd 1957, EX..........**22.50**
Switch, ATSF, Slaymaker, ST, dtd 1964, w/chain, NM **17.50**
Switch, B&HC, Adlake, BR, modern style, no chain, NM............**30.00**
Switch, B&LE, BR, W/B logo on body, heart shape, EX..............**44.00**
Switch, CI&L, ST, dtd 1916, rpl chain **20.00**
Switch, CI&S, BR, heart shape, w/chain, EX...........................**48.00**
Switch, GN&A, Adlake, ST, 1975, no chain, EX **20.00**
Switch, L&N, Standard, ST, w/chain, NM..............................**12.50**
Switch, Laurinburg & Southern, BR, heart shape, w/key, NM **66.00**
Switch, Miller, BR, heart shape, w/chain, NM **27.50**
Switch, NYC, Adlake, ST, w/chain, NM.................................**16.00**
Switch, NYC, ST, w/chain, M..**17.50**
Switch, P&PU, Adlake, ST, dtd 1977, no chain, EX **15.00**
Switch, PC, Adlake, BR, w/chain, M......................................**26.00**
Switch, PC, Adlake, BR, w/chain & unmk BR key, M................**37.50**
Switch, PRR, Slaymaker, ST, w/chain & unmk BR key, EX **32.00**

Silverplate

Butter pat, Santa Fe, BS, lt wear **20.00**
Carafe, water; D&RG, dtd 1946, 10" **175.00**
Casserole, UP, Deco hdls, 7", VG...**45.00**
Change tray, Santa Fe, fluted edge, BS in English script **47.50**
Change tray, unmk UP, 6" **27.50**
Coffeepot, Soo Line, Reed & Barton, BS, 8-oz.........................**88.00**
Coffeepot, UP, acorn finial, 14-oz...**75.00**
Corn holders, UP, w/rest, Pfheglar Pat 1896, pr **8.00**
Cover, CA Zephyr, pierced Deco hearts, BM, 6¼" **77.50**
Cover, UP, pagoda finial, pierced hearts, Overland logo, EX **65.00**
Crumber, UP, Winged Streamer logo, VG **55.00**
Finger bowl, UP, pierced, BM, 4½" **27.50**
Fork, dinner; B&M, Meriden, TM, EX **26.00**
Fork, dinner; CM, Rex, rare, 7½" **95.00**
Fork, dinner; Santa Fe, Albany, BM, England **16.00**
Fork, pickle; CA Zephyr, Century...**15.00**
Fork, pickle; Fred Harvey, Albany **16.00**
Fork, pickle; NP, Winthrop, BM...**25.00**
Gravy boat, unmk UP, Streamliner logo, 5-oz............................**55.00**
Gravy ladle, SP&S, Gorham, TM, 9" **95.00**
Knife, butter; CA Zephyr, 7" **18.00**
Knife, butter; NP, Silhouette, BM **24.00**
Knife, dinner; CA Zephyr, Century..**16.00**
Knife, dinner; Santa Fe, Albany, TM, England, 10" **15.00**
Knife, luncheon; Santa Fe, Albany, BM, 8½" **12.50**
Mayonnaise holder, UP, w/attached tray, 1947 ....**60.00**
Pitcher, syrup; CA Zephyr, acorn finial, hinged lid, +tray............**100.00**
Pitcher, syrup; UP, w/attached tray, BS, EX **50.00**

Platter, steak; T&P, BS, 10x7" 55.00
Spoon, CA Zephyr, Century 15.00
Spoon, cheese; UP, Reed & Barton, BM 16.00
Spoon, demitasse; Burlington Rte, TM, Reed & Barton 26.00
Spoon, iced tea; CA Zephyr, Century 16.00
Spoon, NP, Route of Great Big Baked Potato, Wallace, EX ...45.00
Spoon, place; D&RGW, American, TM 12.50
Spoon, place; SP, Westfield, Meriden, BS, 1930 ....17.50
Spoon, serving; CA Zephyr, Century 14.50
Spoon, serving; D&RGW, American, TM 15.00
Spoon, serving; N&W, Internat'l, TM, EX 18.00
Spoon, serving; Santa Fe, Albany, BM 12.50
Spoon, soup; CA Zephyr, Century 15.00
Spoon, tablespoon; NP, Embassy, Reed & Barton, TM/BS, 11-oz ..18.00
Spoon, tablespoon; NP, Winthrop......................................17.50
Sugar bowl, GN, for lump sugar, w/lid, BS, SM 175.00
Sugar bowl, Lackawanna, w/lid, BS, 8-oz 55.00
Sugar tongs, UP, TM..60.00
Teaspoon, Santa Fe, Albany, BM 12.50
Tray, Santa Fe, oval, TM, BM, 12x9" 35.00
Tureen, soup; UP, pierced base, lid w/finial, BS, EX 80.00

Miscellaneous

Air horn, Westinghouse, diesel, single chime, ST, rpt, EX ...80.00
Badge, Am Ry Express, gr pnt diamond on silver, early 20.00
Badge, B&Me, sleeping car conductor, blk letters on gold ...65.00
Badge, B&Me, Trainman, NP, M...48.00
Badge, Boston Transit, operator's, enamel on BR, post mt ...7.50
Badge, CMStP&P, dining car waiter, NP shield, pin-bk, 1" ...7.50
Badge, Conrail, Conductor, emb bl letters on gold, lg, 2" ...27.50
Badge, hat; NYC, Motorman 15.00
Badge, hat; UP Brakeman, NP, rnd ends, old, EX 88.00
Badge, lapel; Brotherhood of RR Trainmen, 15-year, 3-color...10.00
Badge, lapel; C&O, conductor's, C over O w/bl enamel 'and'...22.00
Badge, lapel; New England Veterans, enamel on gold, NM ...25.00
Badge, N&NW, Freight Conductor, NP, incised letters, blk pnt ...65.00
Blazer, Amtrak, navy bl, gold buttons, unissued, M 37.50
Book, Bangor & Aroostook, In the Main Woods, 1921, EX ...22.50
Book, 1925 Locomotive Cyclopedia, Newton Gree, reprint, M ...66.00
Booklet, Pullman Accommodations, 1935, 24-pg, G 7.00
Box, telephone bell; oak w/2 brass bells, unmk, EX orig......65.00
Brush, porter's, Pullman, wood, 2-color bristles, 7" 7.50
Builder's plate, Baldsin...Works, ST, 1943, 9½" dia 75.00
Calendar, RDG, daily desktop, orig sheets, 1961, M 100.00
Calendar, Rio Grande, 1949, 24x18", EX 27.50
Call card, Ry Express Agency, blk letters, metal fr, early......100.00
Can, kerosene; N&W, emb letters on side, 1-gal, VG 24.00
Can, kerosene; NYC, Diamond J brand, EX 37.50
Can, oil; PRR, Keystone logo, Handlan, long spout, EX 30.00
Cap, fuel tank; diesel locomotive, cast aluminum, M 7.50
Catalog, Alco-GE 1600 Road Switcher, 1950, 28-pg, VG.......7.50
Cuff guards, Chessie System-Prevent Injuries, pr, M 12.00
Day target, red 4½" lens, for switch lamp, EX 12.50
Decal, West Point Rte, self adhesive, old, 5" dia, unused 10.00
Dominoes, #9 Express, locomotive emb ea tile, 1880s, EX...80.00
Envelopes, PRR, pack of 20, unused......................................4.50
Fire extinguisher, SP, copper & brass, 26½" 65.00
Hard hat, RI, wht w/red bearskin 7.50
Hat, chef's, N&W, paper, unissued, M 6.00
Hat, SCL, police style, Conductor's badge, last issue, M 78.00
Key, caboose; Keyline, BR, cast up shank, M 5.00
Key, L&N, Adlake, BR, NM 16.00
Key, switch; CCC&StL, Fraim #22060, NM 30.00

Conductor's hat, manufactured by Carlson, with 'NP' badge, $85.00.

Key, switch; L&N, Dayton MFG, early mks, fat type, EX 66.00
Key, switch; LS&MS, ST, oiler type, EX................................40.00
Kit, first aid; B&O, metal box w/logo ea side, empty, EX 10.00
Machine, ticket validating; Cosmo #3, VG...........................48.00
Machine, ticket validating; Hill's Centennial, 1950s, EX 48.00
Magazine, N&W, 1925, 3 for..16.00
Magazine, Railway Carmen's Journal, 1929, 6 issues for......22.50
Medallion, Amtrak, coin in plastic case, 10th anniv, 1981, M 12.00
Medallion, WAB, Century of Service to Decatur IL, 1854-1954 ....5.00
Menu, NP, Special Dinner, gr, 1956, 3x4"..............................4.00
Notice, cafe car; WAB, 1924, 5x6" 5.00
Notice, NC&StL, Explosives, fr under glass, NM....................24.00
Oiler, bench; Eagle, long spout screws on, cone base, EX......16.00
Pants, waiter's, CA Zephyr, wht w/purple stripe, EX..............5.00
Pants cuff bands, C&O, elastic, snap lock, pr, M..................12.00
Paperweight, SR, Best Friend of Charleston, metal, 1927.......88.00
Paperweight, West VA Steel & Mfg, ST, rail w/in circle, early 60.00
Pass, annual; Central of GA, 1902, NM 12.00
Pass, annual; NC&StL, w/logo, 1926, NM 6.00
Pass, annual; SR, 1901, M 18.00
Plaque, Lake Shore & Michigan Southern 1914, BR/wood, NM...45.00
Playing cards, C&O, Chessie-Peake, sealed, M 16.00
Portfolio briefcase, SCL, faux-leather, zipper closure, M 5.00
Punch, ticket; NP, minor wear 22.00
Reflector, lamp; car inspector's, Dietz, glass, 4¾" dia, G 10.00
Register, railway equipment, July 1978, complete, NM 6.00
Rule book, N&W, safety, hard cover, 1970s, NM 4.50
Rule book, SCL, vinyl 3-ring binder, emb letters, 1981, M 10.00
Scales, Virginia & Truckee, Waybill, dtd 1891 ....17.50
Seal, boxcar; SR, bright tin, M...1.50
Sign, Railway Express, porc, cream/red on gr, 2-pc, 6x20" 95.00
Sink, wall; Pullman, Adams & Westlake, folding, complete, EX...85.00
Spittoon, Dayton Mfg, NP BR, removable top, EX 95.00
Spittoon, N&W, CI, blk pnt, wht int, station style, EX 95.00
Stationery, PRR, red printing on wht, sheets in orig packet......5.00
Step box, NYC, Morton style, gray w/silver top, much rstr 150.00
Step stool, C&O, safety top, Morton tag, 15x14", EX............150.00
Step stool, CN, metal, rubber top, orig pnt, 14x14", EX 95.00
Step stool, WAB, metal, emb front, EX 150.00
Stickpin, N&W, Safety First, enamel on gold metal, early......27.50
Time card, Silver City, Deming & Pacific, 1883, EX..............22.00
Timetable, ACL, for passengers, purple w/logo, 1960s, EX 5.00
Timetable, D&RG, suburban, 1917, 2½x4" 38.00
Timetable, NYC&H, RW&O Division, 1905, NM 27.50
Timetable, WP, Exposition Flyer, Dec 1, 1944, EX 8.00

Torch, DMICo #2, CI, tall cylinder, screw top, EX **60.00**
Torch, shop; N&W, BM, M..**37.50**
Trust plate, ACL, emb ST, EX orig **17.50**
Wax, Empress, red, ¼-lb stick **2.50**
Wrench, machinist's, N&W, adjustable, ST, 20", EX **15.00**
Wrench, SR, ST, open end, heavy, shop made, EX.......................**12.50**

Razors

As straight razors gain in popularity, prices increase. And with the lure of investment appreciation, the novice or the speculator sometimes find themselves making purchases that later prove to be unwise. It is important to be able to recognize the material of which the handle is made. This has a great bearing on value, and imitations abound. Learn to distinguish between celluloid and genuine ivory. Razors with plain celluloid handles are practically worthless unless the blade carries a desirable trademark. Those with decorations of scrollwork, leaves and vines, or decorative metal on each end fall into the $8 to $12 price range. Even plain ivory-handled razors are not especially valuable unless the blade is well marked and from a good manufacturer. On a more positive note, celluloid-handled razors with designs such as castles, windmills, nudes, deer, alligators, automobiles, horses, cowboys, peacocks, and various kinds of birds, etc., are very desirable – some more than others – and are usually worth from $25 to $50 to collectors. Those with a figural handle such as a fish, shotgun, eagle, or a barber pole might be worth in excess of $100 for an especially nice example. Ivory, on the other hand, is rarely found; if the carvings are well done, clean, undamaged specimens should start at about $100 and escalate according to the intricacy of the design.

Buffalo horn is sometimes mistakenly called bone. It is usually black, translucent tan, or gray. Though plain handles are worth very little, the early heat-molded examples with a motif such as mentioned above often sell for more than $100. In the same range are mother-of-pearl and stag (deer horn) handles; very elaborate designs go even higher, but watch for imitations.

There is one imitation, however, that is highly desirable. That is jigged bone made to look like stag. This material is rough textured and dyed a handsome tan or brown; usually examples with these handles sell in the $40 to $75 range. Razors with wooden handles are very rare, but even those from the 1800s are worth only about $35, since they are usually very plain. 20th-century examples are only valued at around $15. Don't be fooled by buffalo horn colored in imitation of tortoise – and you'll find celluloid imitations, too. Genuine tortoise handles are worth from $25 to $100 depending on age, condition, and workmanship. Sterling razors are valued at $75 and up, but make sure they are marked 'sterling.' Even if you were to mistake aluminum for silver, those with relief-cast designs are worth $50 to $75 – only $20 or so if the design is incised.

Corn razors were made to pare troublesome corns on the feet. They are a bit smaller and if plain worth a little more than full-size razors. Fancy examples are generally not worth as much as their full-size counterparts.

The older blades are wedge-shaped (flat-sided) in cross-section; hollow-ground blades (made after 1880) are concave. Generally speaking, those etched with words are only worth a little more than a plain, common blade. Try to find those with people, places, and things – the more famous, the better.

Key:
cell — celluloid   gw — gold washed
bd — blade

Assy Shaheen, etched bd: Liberty Bell, blk hdl: lady's head............**16.00**

Atlantic Cutlery, faux ivory hdl: eagle/stars/stripes, EX **25.00**
Baker & Sons, gold-etched bd & tang, hdl: nude, EX colors **120.00**
Boker, faux ivory hdl: German silver inlay, etched bd, EX **12.50**
Case Bros Cutlery, etched bd: Apollo, cracked tang, EX **50.00**
Challenge Works, hdl: fishscale & scroll, bd: Our Reliable............**13.00**
Crane Brand, Robert Klass, blk hdl: lady's head/scroll, NMIB **15.00**
Eagle, etch steel bd: camels, cvd bone hdl: birds & acorns...........**180.00**
Elliot, faux ivory hdl: cowboy scene inlay, eng bd, EX................**45.00**
Ern, cell hdl: pine cones & branches, EX colors, VG **48.00**
F Fenny W (crown) R, pressed horn hdl: buffalo, wedge bd.........**135.00**
Frederick Reynolds, etched wedge bd, clear horn hdl, 1850s **28.00**
Geneva, etched bd: Improved Eagle...& eagle, blk cell hdl **20.00**
Geo Korn...Little Valley NY on bd, blk hdl: goddess, EX..............**20.00**
Griffin, blk hdl: Corn Razor in gold, NM in box **36.00**
Harris Goar, etched bd: We sell Elgin watches..., rubber hdl..........**22.00**
Imperial Warranted, etched bd: US Battleship Oregon, EX...........**25.00**
Imperial Warranted, faux ivory hdl, etched bd: eagle, G **20.00**
JA Henckels, cell hdl: horse head w/horseshoe, etched bd............**28.00**
James Barlow & Sons, ivory hdl, polished bd, 1850s, NMIB..........**40.00**
Jas T Scott, faux ivory hdl: stag in forest, narrow bd, G **25.00**
John Pitts Celebrated, horn hdl: 3 rnd pewter inlays, EX............**100.00**
Joseph Elliot Best Damascus Steel, S-shaped ivory hdl, EX **40.00**
Joseph Elliot Silver Steel, wedge bd, blk horn hdl w/pewter **20.00**
Joseph Elliot's Celebrated pressed on hdl, ground bd, 1840s **20.00**
Joseph Rodgers & Sons, etched bd: train, horn hdl, ca 1850 ....**30.00**
Joseph Rodgers & Sons Sheffield, MOP hdl: German silver inlay ..**90.00**
Lafayette Cutlery, faux ivory hdl: windmill scene, rpl tang **16.00**
Le Royal Tranchant etched on bd, faux ivory hdl, VG..................**18.00**
Limbrick Cast Steel, blk horn hdl, no tang, VG............................**28.00**
Max Dorner, Solingen NY, gw tang & bd, blk cell hdl: Dorn **16.00**
Oxford, faux ivory hdl: nude on man's shoulders, EX **25.00**
Packard, orange cell hdl: race car inlay, NM in orig box..............**138.00**
Parkin, horn hdl w/pewter decor, cast steel bd, 1790s, EX **45.00**
Pressed blk horn hdl w/2 figures, wedge bd, ca 1815, EX..............**125.00**
R Imperial, etch bd: Safety/bicycle for 2, cell hdl: stork **16.00**
Red Imp Made in USA by Case, blk hdl w/gr 'reptile skin,' EX **26.00**
Robert Schmidt Solingen, cvd bone hdl, hollow ground bd, EX....**30.00**
Sheffield, etched bd: Celebrated...Steel..., horn hdl, 1850s............**10.00**
Sheffield, etched bd: Champion...G Washington, horn hdl, EX....**20.00**
Silver King, burgundy hdl: emb florals w/gr & silver, EX...............**50.00**
Simmons Hdwe, faux ivory hdl: chief w/tomahawk, etched bd **30.00**
Smith & Hawksley Sheffield, bone hdl: German silver inlay **90.00**
Uncle Sam w/eagle, stars & stripes on cell hdl, EX......................**35.00**
Van Camp Hdwe & Iron, blk cell hdl: Indian chief, etch bd, EX .**77.00**
Wade & Butcher, bd: train scene, blk horn hdl, 1850s, EX **45.00**
Wade & Butcher Sheffield, steel hdl: mc florals, etched bd **120.00**
Warranted Sheffield, horn hdl: eagle in gold, bd: American...........**20.00**
Westfield, Germany, faux ivory hdl: checked w/raised shield.........**50.00**
WH Morley, bd: Damascus in gold, faux ivory hdl: stork **20.00**
WH Morley, burgundy cell hdl: spread-wing eagle, EX **78.00**
WH Morley & Sons, cell hdl: nude on man's shoulders, EX **45.00**
Wilson Hawksworth & Moss, plain ivory hdl, stamped bd, 1830s .**30.00**
Winchester, faux ivory hdl, blued tang, cleaned bd, #8525 ....**65.00**
Wm Elliot, cell hdl: sailboats, red/gr w/blk, unused, M **136.00**
Wm Greaves & Sons Sheaf Works, steel bd, bone hdl, 1840s........**30.00**
Wm Stenton & Son Again Superior, bone hdl: log cabin, 1820s...**36.00**
WR Case & Sons Manganese, wood grain hdl, NM......................**20.00**

Reamers

Reamers have been made in hundreds of styles and colors and by as many manufacturers. Their purpose is to extract the juices from lemons, oranges, and grapefruits. The largest producer of glass reamers was McKee, who pressed their products from many types of glass – custard; delphite and Chalaine blue; opaque white; Skokie green; black; caramel and white opalescent; Seville yellow; and transparent pink, green, and clear. Among these, the black and the caramel opalescents are the most valuable.

The Fry Glass Company also made reamers that are today very collectible. Their vaseline glass juicers with embossed lettering, both the straight-sided and ruffled-top models, are valued at well over $200. The Hazel Atlas Crisscross orange reamer in pink often brings in excess of $225; the same in blue, $200. Hocking produced a light blue orange reamer and, in the same soft hue, a two-piece reamer and measuring cup combination. Both are considered rare and very valuable with currently-quoted estimates at $400 and up for the former and $500 and up for the latter. In addition to the colors mentioned, red glass examples – transparent or slag – are rare and costly.

Among the most valuable ceramic reamers are those made by American potteries. The Spongeband reamer by Red Wing is valued in excess of $350; Coorsite reamers with gold or silver trim are worth $200 and up. Figurals are popular – Mickey Mouse and John Bull may bring $300 to $400. Others range from $45 to $150. Fine china one- and two-piece reamers are also very desirable and command very respectable prices.

A word about reproductions: A series of limited edition reamers is being made by Edna Barnes of Uniontown, Ohio. These are all marked with a 'B' in a circle. Other repoductions have been made from old molds. The most important of these are: Anchor Hocking 2-piece 2-cup measure and top, Gillespie 1-cup measure with reamer top, Westmoreland N-365 with flattened handle, Westmoreland 4-cup measure embossed with orange and lemons, Duboe, Easley's diamonds 1-piece, and spiral 1-piece #202.

Our advisor for this category is Dee Long; she is listed in the Directory under Illinois. For more information concerning reamers and reproductions, contact our advisor or the National Reamer Collectors Association (see Clubs, Newsletters, and Catalogs). Be sure to include SASE when requesting information.

Reference numbers in the ceramic reamer listings correspond with *200 Years of Reamers* by Mary Walker, available at your local library or from the National Reamer Collectors Association.

Ceramic

Clown figural, bl/wht/yel, C-27, 5½"	40.00
Clown figural, gr/wht/orange, C-36, 6½"	45.00
Clown figural, gr/wht/orange/blk, Japan, C-29, 7½"	45.00
Cottage figural, tan/brn/gr, F-56, 5¾"	50.00
Duck figural, gr & yel lustre, F-12	44.00
Florals, Japan, 3-sided, D-54, 3½"	40.00
Leaf base, wht w/gr & gold, D-39, 4½"	50.00
Orange figural, gr leaves, Japan, L-39, 4½"	40.00
Pear figural, gr leaves, bent stem, L-41	40.00
Pear figural, wht w/gr & gold, L-39, 4½"	50.00
Pitcher form, florals, bl/lav on wht, P-29, 8"	35.00
Pitcher form, mc florals, Japan, P-15, 7"	48.00
Pitcher form, yel lustre, L-2, 4"	30.00
Pitcher form, 2 spouts, wht, France, D-85, recent, 3¼"	10.00
Puddinhead figural, gr hat, F-32, 6¼"	130.00

Glass

Federal, loop hdl, paneled, gr, N-350	20.00
Federal, loop hdl, ribbed, pk, N-348	30.00
Federal, tab hdl, ribbed, seed dam, amber, N-238	18.00
Fenton, mc elephant on crystal base, baby's sz, N-104	70.00
Fleur-de-Lis, red/orange slag, N-325	400.00

Hazel Atlas, pitcher+reamer, cobalt/gr/pk, 2-cup, repro	20.00
Hazel Atlas, pitcher+reamer, wht w/trim, N-129, 2-cup	30.00
Hazel Atlas, pitcher+reamer, yel, N-129, 16-oz	250.00
Hazel Atlas, tab hdl, cobalt bl, N-246	250.00

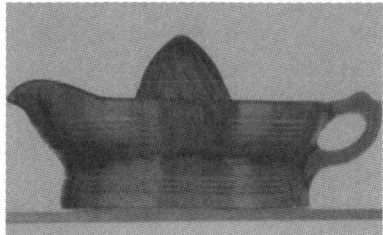

Hazel Atlas Crisscross orange reamer in blue, $200.00.

Hazel Atlas Crisscross, loop hdl, orange reamer, pk, N-342	250.00
Hocking, fruit juice, gr w/decal, 1-qt	20.00
Hocking, LINDSAY, gr, N385-A	425.00
Hocking, pitcher form, Mayfair bl, N-130, 2-cup	850.00
Hocking, ribbed, orange reamer, gr, N-347	15.00
Hocking, vitrock, emb letters/orange reamer, milk glass, N-352	20.00
Jeannette, hex optic, bucket reamer, gr, N-136	40.00
Jeannette, Jennyware, ultramarine, N-310	55.00
Jeannette, loop hdl, dk jadite, N-308, sm	40.00
Jeannette, pitcher+reamer, dk jadite, N-136A	50.00
McKee, emb McK, custard, ftd, N-309, sm	35.00
McKee, grapefruit, Skokie gr, N-358	150.00
Sunkist, emb letters, blk, N-330	350.00
Sunkist, emb letters, dk gr, N-330	200.00
Sunkist, emb letters, wht, N-330	10.00
Sunkist, unemb, jadite, N-329	90.00
US Glass, crystal w/flowers, N-119, 2-pc	25.00
US Glass, Handy Andy, gr, N-120	45.00
US Glass, pitcher+reamer, pk, N-135, 32-oz	150.00
US Glass, pk, N-129, 2-pc, repro	100.00
US Glass, slick hdl, gr	400.00
US Glass, slick hdl, pk	600.00
US Glass, slick or loop hdl, amber, N-119, 2-pc	250.00
Valencia, unemb, amber-pk, N-327	275.00
Westmoreland, crystal w/decor, baby's sz, N-101	40.00
Westmoreland, flattened loop hdl, amber, N-365	350.00
Westmoreland, flattened loop hdl, blk or vaseline, repro	20.00
Westmoreland, flattened loop hdl, crystal w/decor, N-365	55.00
Westmoreland, flattened loop hdl, pk, N-365	85.00
Westmoreland, flattened loop hdl, red or cobalt, repro	20.00

Records

Records of interest to collectors are generally not the million-selling hits by 'superstars.' Very few records by Bing Crosby, for example, are of any more than nominal value, and those that are valuable usually don't even have his name on the label! Collectors today are most interested in records that were made in limited quantities, early works of a performer who later became famous, and those issued in special series or aimed at a limited market. These are bringing prices well in excess of their original cost. The most widely-collected categories are Jazz, Dance Bands, Celebrity, Blues, Rhythm and Blues, Country and Western, Hillbilly, Rockabilly, and Rock 'N Roll.

Note: LPs and EPs (Extended Play 45 rpm) must be in their original jackets, without which they are often unsaleable at any price.

Our advisor for this category is L.R. Docks, author of *American Premium Record Guide*, which lists 50,000 records by over 6,000 artists; you will find his address in the Directory under Texas.

Key:
Bru — Brunswick   Para — Paramount
Ch — Champion   Orch — Orchestra
Col — Columbia   Vi — Victor
Edi — Edison   Vo — Vocalion

Blues, Rhythm and Blues, Rock 'N Roll, Rockabilly

Alexander, Texas; Corn-Bread Blues, Okeh 8511, 78 rpm **25.00**
Amos, Ira; Blue & Disgusted, Modern 817, 78 rpm **15.00**
Arnold, Kokomo; Sissy Man Blues, Decca 7050, 78 rpm................**20.00**
Austin, Mildred; Sing That Song w/Feeling, Ch 15530, 78 rpm....**30.00**
Baines, Houston; Going Home, Blues & Rhythm 7001, 78 rpm....**15.00**
Banjo Joe, Jazz Gypsy Blues, Para 12604, 78 rpm............................**60.00**
Barner, Wiley; My Gal Treats Me Mean, Gennett 6261, 78 rpm ...**50.00**
Batts, Will; Country Woman, Vo 02531, 78 rpm **75.00**
Benbow, Baby; Down Home Girl, Okeh 8098, 78 rpm.................... **8.00**
Big Willie, Bogey Man, Apollo 450, 78 rpm **12.00**
Bill, Georgia; Stomp Down River, Okeh 8936, 78 rpm.............**150.00**
Black, Frankie; Alley Sally Blues, Ch 50049, 78 rpm....................**30.00**
Blue Boys, Memphis Stomp, Okeh 45314, 78 rpm.........................**20.00**
Booker, Charley; Moonrise Blues, Modern 878, 45 rpm................**20.00**
Boze, Calvin; Fish Tail, Aladdin 3110, 45 rpm **9.00**
Brenston, Jackie; Juiced, Chess 1472, 78 rpm...............................**12.00**
Brooks, Dusty; Heaven On Fire, Sun 182, 78 rpm.........................**55.00**
Brown, Eliza; Peddlin' Man, Col 14471-D, 78 rpm.......................**15.00**
Brown, Ora; Jinx Blue, Para 12481, 78 rpm **40.00**
Bunn, Allen; She'll Be Sorry, Apollo 436, 78 rpm........................ **8.00**
Burston, Clara; Pay w/Money, Gennett 7319, 78 rpm **50.00**
Call, Bob; 31 Blues, Bru 7137, 78 rpm **75.00**
Campbell, Bob; Shotgun Blues, Vo 02830, 78 rpm **100.00**
Campbell, Gene; Face To Face Blues, Bru 7206, 78 rpm **60.00**
Carolina Slim, Rag Mama, Acorn 324, 78 rpm **10.00**
Carter, Bunny; Midnight Special Blues, Conqueror 7266, 78 rpm ...**90.00**
Church, Blind Clyde; Number Nine Blues, Victor 23271, 78 rpm...**50.00**
Coley, Kid; Freight Train Blues, Vi 23369, 78 rpm **80.00**
Collins, Sam; Hesitation Blues, Gennett 6379, 78 rpm **120.00**
Collins, Vie; Confessin' Blues, Silverstone 3538, 78 rpm **30.00**
Conway, Ben; Sing Song Blues, Herwin 93014, 78 rpm **80.00**
Crane, Bob; Ghost Woman Blues, Herwin 93018, 78 rpm **120.00**
Dailey, Dusky; Miss Georgia Blues, Vo 04963, 78 rpm **12.00**
Darby, Teddy; Deceiving Blues, Vi 23311, 78 rpm **200.00**
Davis, Walter; Blue Sea Blues, Bluebird 5038, 78 rpm **20.00**
Dee, Mercy; Happy Bachelor, Bayou 013, 78 rpm **10.00**
Dells, Tell the World, Vee Jay 134, 45 rpm....................................**250.00**
Dickson, Pearl; Little Rock Blues, Col 14286-D, 78 rpm **30.00**
Ervin, Leroy; Rock Island Blues, Swing 415, 78 rpm **20.00**
Everetts, Dorothy; Macon Blues, Col 14444-D, 78 rpm..............**30.00**
Ferguson, Troy; College Blues, Col 14483-D, 78 rpm **20.00**
Five Jinks, Cushion Foot, Bluebird 6905, 78 rpm **10.00**
Freezone, Indian Squaw Blues, Para 12803, 78 rpm....................**60.00**
Fuller, Rocky; Soon One Morning, Checker 753, 45 rpm **17.00**
Garner, Cora; Wouldn't Stop Doing It, Col 14659-D, 78 rpm **20.00**
Groovy Trio, Too Late Baby, Groovy 101, 78 rpm **10.00**
Hall, James; Street Walkin' Woman, Vo 04316, 78 rpm **10.00**
Hill, Charlie; Papa Charlie Hill Blues, Gennett 6904, 78 rpm **250.00**
Hill, Robert; G Blues, Bluebird 6795, 78 rpm **25.00**
Hogg, Andrew; Dark Clouds, Crown 122, 78 rpm........................**15.00**
Holley, Rosa; Lookin' for the Blues, Vo 1179, 78 rpm................**60.00**
Hunter, Slim; Big Bill Blues, Superior 2837, 78 rpm..................**60.00**
Hunter Brothers, Stove Pipe Stomp, Superior 2836, 78 rpm.......**60.00**
Hyde, Hattie; Special Question Blues, Vi 23374, 78 rpm.............**60.00**
Jack O' Diamonds, Smiling Blues, Para 12791, 78 rpm **80.00**
Jackson Blue Boys, Sweet Alberta, Col 14397-D, 78 rpm **30.00**

James, Sadie; Mama, Fold Your Hands, Vi 20575, 78 rpm **30.00**
James, Skip; Drunken Spree, Para 13111, 78 rpm........................**250.00**
Jefferson, George; Honey Bee, Bluebird 7926, 78 rpm **10.00**
Kid & Coot, Keyhole Blues, Col 14363-D, 78 rpm......................**20.00**
Knight, Jessie; Nothing But Money, Checker 797, 45 rpm..........**15.00**
Lacy, Rube; Mississippi Jail House Groan, Para 12629, 78 rpm....**120.00**
Lamar, Justine; Always Mine, Decca 7238, 78 rpm...................... **8.00**
Maxwell, Claude; Bad Woman Blues, Sterling 3006, 78 rpm.........**10.00**
McCoy, William; How Long Baby, Col 14393-D, 78 rpm **30.00**
McDavid, Katherine; Underground Blues, Okeh 8295, 78 rpm...**15.00**
Palmes, Frank; Troubled 'Bout My Soul, Para 12893, 78 rpm **100.00**
Pickett, Charlie; Down the Highway, Decca 7707, 78 rpm **20.00**
Quattlebaum, Doug; Lizzie Lou, Gotham 519, 78 rpm **25.00**
Red, Dallas; Cold Blooded Blues, Selective 112, 78 rpm **8.00**
Stewart, Dan; New Orleans Blues, Vo 1536, 78 rpm...................**100.00**
Tarpley, Sam; That Stuff, Ch 16782, 78 rpm **60.00**
Walker, William; I'll Remember You, Gennett 7100, 78 rpm **20.00**

Country and Western

Alexander & Miller, Medley, Supertone 9398, 78 rpm................. **8.00**
Allen Brothers, Reckless Night Blues, Bluebird 5224, 78 rpm **15.00**
Ashley & Foster, Sideline Blues, Vo 02611, 78 rpm **15.00**
Baker, Mr & Mrs; The Newmarket Wreck, Vi 20863, 78 rpm **10.00**
Bang Boys, When Lulu's Gone, Vo 03372, 78 rpm **20.00**
Behrens, Jerry; Drifting Along, Okeh 45535, 78 rpm..................**15.00**
Bird, Connie; Little Mamie, Gennett 6929, 78 rpm......................**30.00**
Brooks, Bob; Red River Valley, Col 15689-D, 78 rpm **8.00**
Cain, Albert; Runnin' Wild, Okeh 45567, 78 rpm **20.00**
Caldwell, Sam; The Prisoner's Lament, Supertone 9185, 78 rpm ..**10.00**
Carpenter, Boyden; The Hobos' Convention, Ch 16519, 78 rpm..**15.00**
Carter Family, No Depression, Bluebird 5242, 78 rpm **10.00**
Clyde Evans Band, How I Got My Gal, Col 15597-D, 78 rpm **15.00**
Darling, Chuck; Harmonica Rag, Bluebird 5285, 78 rpm............... **8.00**
Davis, Eva; Wild Bill Jones, Col 129-D, 78 rpm **8.00**
Davis, Jimmie; Beautiful Texas, Bluebird 5394, 78 rpm..............**10.00**
Delmore Brothers, The Frozen Girl, Bluebird 5338, 78 rpm............**15.00**
Dixon Trio, Carolina Lullaby, Vi 23790, 78 rpm **20.00**
Dodds, Johnny; Cowboy Yodel, Okeh 45560, 78 rpm.................**80.00**
Duncan Sisters, Dusty Roads, Col 15745-D, 78 rpm......................**8.00**
Elk Creek Trio, Silvery Bell, Ch 15584, 78 rpm **8.00**
Elm City Quartet, The Tree Song, Ch 16827, 78 rpm **10.00**
Ferguson, John; Wild Bill Jones, Challenge 324, 78 rpm.............**15.00**
Foley, David; Poor Little Joe, Challenge 394, 78 rpm..................**12.00**
Frazier, Lee; The Ice Man Blues, Ch 16626, 78 rpm **30.00**
Georgia Melody Boys, Cabin Home, Broadway 8119, 78 rpm........**10.00**
Georgia Wildcats, She's Waiting for Me, Vi 23640, 78 rpm...........**30.00**
Green & Russell, Goodnight Waltz, Supertone 9377, 78 rpm **12.00**
Hall Brothers, Spartanburg Jail, Bluebird 7363, 78 rpm **10.00**
Hamblin, Paul; Prairie Maiden, Vi 40280, 78 rpm **15.00**
Hardin, Tex; The Trail to California, Ch 16552, 78 rpm **15.00**
Hill, Bob; He Was a Good Man, Vi 23718, 78 rpm......................**40.00**
Hughey, Dan; Cindy, Ch 15851, 78 rpm.....................................**12.00**
Hurt, Zack; Gambler's Lament, Okeh 45212, 78 rpm.................. **8.00**
Hutchens, John; I Got Mine, Ch 15503, 78 rpm..........................**10.00**
Irwin, Harvey; Sunny Tennessee, Okeh 45052, 78 rpm................ **8.00**
Jack & Bill, The Lonesome Road, Okeh 45368, 78 rpm...............**10.00**
Kelly, Rex; Down by the Railroad Track, Para 3319, 78 rpm.......**20.00**
Kessinger Brothers, Devil's Dream, Bru 256, 78 rpm..................**10.00**
Lane, Duke; Waiting for a Train, Supertone 9496, 78 rpm..........**12.00**
Lewis, Archie; Miss Handy Hanks, Ch 16677, 78 rpm................**20.00**
Long Brothers, Missouri Is Calling, Vi 23637, 78 rpm.................**20.00**
Maddux Family, Stone Rag, Decca 5393, 78 rpm **7.00**
Magnolia Trio, My Carolina Sweetheart, Okeh 45505, 78 rpm **10.00**

Marshall, Charlie; The Old Hitchin' Rail, Vo 03045, 78 rpm......... **8.00**
Martin, John; The Hobo's Pal, Superior 3658, 78 rpm **20.00**
Marvin, Johnny; Go Along Bum, Vi 23728, 78 rpm **10.00**
McCarn, David; Hobo Life, Vi 23532, 78 rpm **40.00**
McDonald Brothers, Poor Little Joe, Vo 5406, 78 rpm...................**12.00**
Miles, Arthur; The Lonely Cowboy, Vi 40156, 78 rpm **12.00**
Monroe Brothers, Katy Cline, Bluebird 6960, 78 rpm **10.00**
Neal, David; Good Old Turnip Greens, Supertone 9184, 78 rpm ..**12.00**
Nichols, Joe & Bob; Red Wing, Crown 3419, 78 rpm **15.00**
Northlanders, Over the Waves, Vo 5274, 78 rpm **10.00**
Oaks, Charlie; Little Mary Phagan, Vo 5069, 78 rpm................ **8.00**
Padgett, Jack; Boogie Woogie Gal, Talent 729, 78 rpm..............**10.00**
Pate, Fiddlin' Ike; Medley, Ch 15085, 78 rpm.............................. **8.00**
Pavey, Phil; Utah Mormon Blues, Okeh 45355, 78 rpm............**12.00**
Pennington, Bess; Jake & May, Vo 5423, 78 rpm **12.00**
Ray Brothers, Mississippi Echoes, Vi 23552, 78 rpm **20.00**
Reeves, Jim; Teardrops of Regret, Macy's 115, 78 rpm **50.00**
Short Brothers, Whistling Coon, Okeh 45206, 78 rpm................**12.00**
Tennessee Travelers, Forked Deer, Ch 15300, 78 rpm **10.00**
Thompson, Ernest; Little Brown Jug, Co 147-D, 78 rpm............**12.00**
Turner, Cal; Only a Tramp, Ch 15587, 78 rpm **18.00**
Walker, Dave; Someone Owns a Cottage, Superior 2688, 78 rpm .**20.00**
White, Fiddlin' Bob; Cripple Creek, Bell 1171, 78 rpm **8.00**

Jazz, Dance Bands, Personalities

Addison, Bernard; Toledo Shuffle, Bluebird 6174, 78 rpm.............**10.00**
Alabama Creole Band, Choo Choo, Claxtonola 40397, 78 rpm....**10.00**
All Star Band, The Blues, Vi 26144, 78 rpm **3.00**
Arkansas Trio, Boll Weevil Blues, Edi 51373, 78 rpm **8.00**
Astaire, Fred; I'd Rather Lead a Band, Bru 7610, 78 rpm **8.00**
Astaire, Fred; Shall We Dance, Col 3166-D, 78 rpm **8.00**
Auburn, Frank; Faithfully Yours, Clarion 5335-C, 78 rpm **7.00**
Auburn, Frank; Me, Clarion 5369-C, 78 rpm **8.00**
Austin, Gene; Dear Old Southland, Decca 1656, 78 rpm..............**12.00**
Babs & Her Brothers, Let's Swing It, Decca 505, 78 rpm.............**10.00**
Bailey, Mildred; Blues in My Heart, Bru 6190, 78 rpm...................**12.00**
Bailey's Dixie Dudes, I'm Satisfied, Gennett 5577, 78 rpm **8.00**
Barrow, Raymond; Walking Blues, Para 12803, 78 rpm...................**60.00**
Beery, Noah; One Little Drink, Bru 4828, 78 rpm **10.00**
Big Aces, Cherry, Okeh 41136, 78 rpm..**18.00**
Blackbirds of Paradise, Muddy Water, Gennett 6211, 78 rpm **150.00**
Blythe's Sinful Five, Pump Tillie Pump, Para 12346, 78 rpm **50.00**
Burris, Johnny; & Orch, Comfy, Gennett 6850, 78 rpm................**20.00**
California Vagabonds, Waitin' for Katy, Gennett 6426, 78 rpm **15.00**
Calloway, Ermine; Do Something, Edi 14024, thin, 78 rpm...........**15.00**
Campus Cut-Ups, Campus Rush, Edi 52649, 78 rpm **12.00**
Carolina Collegians, Wedding Bells, Banner 6316, 78 rpm.............. **8.00**
Casa Loma Orch, White Jazz, Bru 6092, 78 rpm.............................**10.00**
Davenport, Jed; How Long How Long Blues, Vo 1440, 78 rpm **20.00**
Davis, Red Hot Shakin'; It's Red Hot, Para 12703, 78 rpm............**35.00**
Davis, Wilmer; Gut Struggle, Vo 3342, 78 rpm...............................**30.00**
Dixie Four, Five O'Clock Stamp, Para 12674, 78 rpm...................**75.00**
Dodds & Parham, 19th Street Blues, Para 12483, 78 rpm **90.00**
Effros, Bob; Tin Ear, Bru 4620, 78 rpm...**15.00**
Ellington, Duke; Old Man Blues, Bluebird 6450, 78 rpm **15.00**
Ellington, Duke; Tishomingo Blues, Bru 3987, 78 rpm.................**15.00**
English, Peggy; Sweet Man, Vo 15132, 78 rpm.............................. **8.00**
Etting, Ruth; What Is Sweeter, Bru 6671, 78 rpm.......................... **8.00**
Finnie, Ethel; Heart-Breakin' Joe, Emerson 10846, 78 rpm..........**20.00**
Four Spades, Squabblin' Blues, Col 14028-D, 78 rpm...................**10.00**
Frazier, Jake; Jake's Weary Blues, Ajax 17117, 78 rpm **25.00**
Frenchy's String Band, Sunshine Special, Col 14387-D, 78 rpm ...**50.00**
Garnett, Blind Leroy; Louisiana Glide, Para 12879, 78 rpm **60.00**

Georgia Jumpers, California Blues, Col 14603-D, 78 rpm **15.00**
Get-Happy Band, Puddin' Pappa, Col 14099-D, 78 rpm...............**15.00**
Glascoe, Percy; Stomp 'Em Down, Col 14088-D, 78 rpm................ **9.00**
Goodner, Lillian; Chicago Blues, Ajax 17020, 78 rpm...................**15.00**
Goofus Five, Alabamy Bound, Okeh 40292, 78 rpm **10.00**
Halfway House Orch, Snookum, Col 1041-D, 78 rpm......................**20.00**
Hallett, Mal; & Orch, Whose...Are You, Okeh 40573, 78 rpm....... **7.00**
Hamilton, Paul; & Orch, I've Had...Moments, Vo 2708, 78 rpm ..**15.00**
Hanshaw, Annette; Yes Indeedy, Clarion 5093-C, 78 rpm **15.00**
Harlem Footwarmers, Lazy Duke, Okeh 8760, 78 rpm **35.00**
Hawley, Bill; Delores, Vi 21383, 78 rpm..**10.00**
Irvin, Kitty; Copenhagen, Gennett 2592, 78 rpm...........................**30.00**
James, Madelyn; Long Time Blues, Bru 7155, 78 rpm....................**40.00**
Jazz Masters, Bees Knees, Black Swan 2109, 78 rpm.....................**10.00**
Jazz-O-Harmonists, Sensation, Claxtolona 40375, 78 rpm...........**75.00**
Jimmie's Joys, No No Nora, Golden 1858, 78 rpm **100.00**
Kaley, Charles; Alabama Stomp, Col 910-D, 78 rpm......................**10.00**
Karle, Art; & His Boys, Lights Out, Vo 3147, 78 rpm....................**12.00**
Kashman, Betty; Hoochee Miss Lou, Okeh 8942, 78 rpm.............**10.00**
La Palina Broadcasters, Piccolo Pete, Perfect 15205, 78 rpm **8.00**
La Vizzo, Thelma; The Stomps, Para 12250, 78 rpm.....................**75.00**
Lada's Louisiana Lads, Everybody Stomp, Sunset 1149, 78 rpm.....**50.00**
Lampe, Dell; & Orch, Street of Dreams, Crown 3409, 78 rpm **8.00**
Lewis, Alfred; Friday Moan Blues, Vo 1498, 78 rpm **35.00**
Mapp, Eddie; Riding The Blues, QRS 7078, 78 rpm......................**75.00**
Marigold Entertainers, Jealous, Vo 15800, 78 rpm **20.00**
Mariners, Happy Feet, Okeh 41433, 78 rpm...................................**10.00**
Marvin, Johnny; My Pet, Vi 21435, 78 rpm....................................**12.00**
Mater, Frank; Doin' the Raccoon, Harmony 759-H, 78 rpm.......... **8.00**
Memphis Bell-Hops, Li'l Farina, Challenge 134, 78 rpm **40.00**
Memphis Jug Band, Kansas City Blues, Bluebird 5430, 78 rpm......**20.00**
Mills Brothers, Smoke Rings, Bru 6225, 78 rpm **10.00**
Moran & Mack, Foolishments, Col 1929-D, 78 rpm **8.00**
Musical Trio, Beale Street Blues, Madison 1920, 78 rpm................ **8.00**
Neale, Nobby; & Lyons, Al; Go To It, Para 12775, 78 rpm...........**20.00**
Nelson, Jewell; Beating Me Blues, Col 14390-D, 78 rpm **16.00**
New Orleans Blues Band, Big Blues, Varsity 6029, 78 rpm...........**15.00**
New Orleans Five, Memphis Blues, Oriole 371, 78 rpm.................**10.00**
Newtown Pippins, Caroline, Gennett 6741, 78 rpm.......................**20.00**
North-West Melody Boys, Rain, Ch 15365, 78 rpm......................**20.00**
Original Indiana Five, Struttin' Jerry, Banner 6023, 78 rpm..........**10.00**
Payne, Art; & Orch, Oh Maud, Gennett 5631, 78 rpm **12.00**
Perkins, Albert; Levee Man, Ajax 17125, 78 rpm...........................**30.00**
Randall, Clark; & Orch, Drifting Tide, Bru 7436, 78 rpm.............**12.00**
Red Hotters, Gin Houn' Blues, Silverton 3527, 78 rpm................**15.00**
Rhythm Makers, Wabash Blues, Vo 15763, 78 rpm **50.00**
Searcy Trio, Kansas Avenue Blues, Okeh 8360, 78 rpm................**30.00**
Seven Brown Babies, Dicty Blues, Ajax 17011, 78 rpm.................**30.00**
Simeon, Omer; Beau-Koo Jack, Bru 7109, 78 rpm **60.00**
Street, Beale; Washboard Band, Forty & Tight, Vo 1403, 78 rpm ..**75.00**
Tate, Carroll; You Live on in Memory, Vi 21061, 78 rpm **15.00**
Ten Freshmen, Bag O' Blues, Perfect 15235, 78 rpm....................**15.00**
Texas Ten, Charleston, Regal 9835, 78 rpm **8.00**
University Six, Fallin' Down, Harmony 106-H, 78 rpm...................**12.00**
Vagabonds, Ukelele Lady, Gennett 3100, 78 rpm **12.00**
Wallace, Trixie; Copenhagen, Claxtonola 40393, 78 rpm **40.00**
Walters, Eddie; It Must Be Love, Col 2232-D, 78 rpm...................**12.00**

Red Wing

The Red Red Wing Stoneware Company, founded in 1878, took its name from its location in Red Wing, Minnesota. In 1906 the name was changed to the Red Wing Union Stoneware Company after a merger with several of the other local potteries. For the most part they produced utilitarian wares such as flowerpots, crocks, and jugs. Their early 1930s catalogs offered a line of art pottery vases in colored glazes, some of which featured handles modeled after swan's necks, snakes, or female nudes. Other examples were quite simple, often with classic styling. After the addition of their dinnerware lines in 1935, 'Stoneware' was dropped from the name, and the company became known as Red Wing Potteries, Inc. They closed in 1967. For further study we recommend *Red Wing Stoneware, An Identification and Value Guide*, and *Red Wing Collectibles* by Dan and Gail DePasquale and Larry Peterson, available at your local library or bookstore.

Key:
MN — Minnesota   RW — Red Wing
NS — North Star   RWUS — Red Wing Union
                                        Stoneware

Brushware

Bowl, 5"	20.00
Bread crock, sheaves of wheat, w/orig lid, lg	400.00
Flowerpot, ribbons & berries, 10"	50.00
Pitcher, lady w/harp, gr int	105.00
Planter, daffodils	25.00
Planter, geometrics	32.00
Planter, trees, castle, sailboats	22.00
Syrup dispenser	100.00
Umbrella stand, floral	125.00
Vase, acorns, stained, bowl form w/short neck, angle hdls	50.00
Vase, cherub, 1931, tall	75.00

Commercial Art Ware

Ash tray, magnolia, #1019	10.00
Bowl, console; oval, 15x10", +fawn flower frog, #526, 10½"	35.00
Candle holder, #1629	7.00
Candlestick, magnolia, wht, #1226, pr	28.00
Clock, Mammy, electric, M	125.00
Console bowl, magnolia, wht, #1223	27.50
Figurine, lady w/tambourine, 10"	95.00
Flower frog, angel fish, wht	45.00
Planter, gr, yel int, B-1403	10.00
Planter, hat form, bl, #670	6.00
Teapot, chicken figural, yel, #257	32.00
Urn, Grecian motif, #159, 9"	45.00

Vase, pelican handles, orange, ca 1930s, 10", $45.00.

Vase, brn/lav speckles, 75th anniversary sticker, M-1444	15.00
Vase, fish figural, open mouth, bl, #879	38.00
Vase, HP flowers, gray, #1152	22.00
Vase, leaves, gr, 9"	12.00
Vase, Roman scene emb, gr gloss, 2-hdl jug shape, 10"	57.50
Vase/candle holder, yel	12.00
Wall pocket, cornucopia form, yel, #441, 8", pr	22.00
Wall pocket, tan, Red Wing Potteries, #1004	18.00
Wall pocket, violin, M-1484, 13¼"	15.00

Cookie Jars

Bunch of Bananas, bl	32.00
Carousel	195.00
Dutch Girl, yel w/brn trim	55.00
Dutch People, mc on aqua, no mk	70.00
French Baker, tan & brn, mk	60.00
Katrina, yel	60.00
Monk, bl w/dk bl trim	65.00
Monk, yel w/brn trim	65.00
Pineapple, cobalt	45.00

Dinnerware

Bob White, bowl, cereal; Casual shape	9.00
Bob White, butter dish, Casual shape	65.00
Bob White, butter warmer, Casual shape	28.00
Bob White, cruet, Casual shape, w/stopper & stand	270.00
Bob White, cup & saucer, Casual shape	12.00
Bob White, gravy boat, w/lid & warming stand, Casual shape	75.00
Bob White, pitcher, water; Casual shape, 60-oz	30.00
Bob White, plate, bread & butter; Casual shape	5.00
Bob White, plate, dinner; Casual shape	9.00
Bob White, saucer, Casual shape	4.00
Bob White, tray, French bread; Casual shape	75.00
Bob White, water cooler, Casual shape, w/stand	370.00
Capistrano, bowl, divided vegetable; Anniversary shape	12.00
Capistrano, plate, Anniversary shape, 11"	10.00
Capistrano, platter, Anniversary shape, 13½"	13.00
Capistrano, platter, Anniversary shape, 15"	15.00
Capistrano, saucer, Anniversary shape	2.00
Capistrano, spoon rest, Anniversary shape	7.00
Caprice, beverage server, Fancy Free shape	22.00
Country Garden, plate, dinner; Anniversary shape	7.00
Country Garden, platter, Anniversary shape, 15"	9.00
Damask, plate, dinner	4.00
Damask, sugar bowl, w/lid	8.00
Driftwood, bowl, divided vegetable; Anniversary shape	12.00
Driftwood, saucer, Anniversary shape	2.00
Fruit, cup & saucer	7.50
Fruit, plate, 10"	7.50
Fruit, plate, 6"	4.00
Lotus, cup & saucer, gray, Concord shape	6.00
Lotus, plate, dinner; Concord shape	5.00
Lotus, relish, Concord shape	8.00
Lute Song, plate, 10¼"	6.00
Lute Song, shakers, pr	10.00
Magnolia, casserole, Concord shape, w/lid	10.00
Magnolia, cream soup, Concord shape, w/lid	8.00
Magnolia, cup & saucer, Concord shape	10.00
Magnolia, plate, chop; Concord shape	8.00
Magnolia, sauce bowl, Concord shape	4.00
Midnight Rose, platter, 13"	8.00

Morning Glory, bowl, 6" 5.00
Morning Glory, celery tray, 11" 6.00
Morning Glory, creamer & sugar bowl 7.50
Morning Glory, cup & saucer 6.00
Morning Glory, plate, 10" 7.50
Morning Glory, plate, 7" 4.00
Morning Glory, platter, 13" 17.50
Pepe, cup & saucer 10.00
Pepe, plate, dinner 8.00
Pepe, plate, salad.. 5.00
Pink Spice, egg plate, Anniversary shape......................18.00
Plum Blossom, sugar bowl, w/lid, Dynasty shape 12.00
Quartette, pitcher, water; Concord shape 18.00
Quartette, sugar bowl, Concord shape, w/lid 4.00
Random Harvest, butter dish, ¼-lb 12.00
Random Harvest, celery 10.00
Random Harvest, plate, 10½" 6.00
Round-Up, cookie jar 75.00
Round-Up, plate, 10½"...12.00
Round-Up, plate, 6½" 8.50
Tampico, bowl, fruit..10.00
Tampico, plate, 8½" 4.50

Tampico water pitcher,
13", $40.00.

Two Step, bowl, vegetable; w/lid.....................................20.00
Two Step, cup & saucer 5.00
Two Step, gravy boat 10.00
Two Step, plate, 10"... 4.50
Two Step, plate, 8" 3.00
Two Step, platter, 12½" 12.00
Two Step, platter, 15" 14.00
Village Green, coffee server, w/stand, 1-gal 55.00
Village Green, water jar, 2-gal.......................................120.00

Stoneware

Baking dish, bl sponging, open, unmk 75.00
Bean pot, Albany slip, short neck, NS, ½-gal 75.00
Bean pot, bailed, brn/wht, RWUS, ½-gal.......................50.00
Bean pot, Boston style, Albany slip, RW, ½-gal............125.00
Bean pot, Saffron, bl & red sponging, RWUS, 1-gal 200.00
Bottle, hot water; brn, leaf style, RWUS.......................200.00
Bowl, Greek Key, bl & wht, 12"....................................100.00

Bowl, narrow bands, Saffron w/red & bl sponging, 10"..................50.00
Bowl, paneled, mc sponging, 10"....................................100.00
Butter crock, #20 on wht, MN, early, 20-gal...............250.00
Butter crock, Albany slip, low, RW, 5-lb.......................35.00
Butter crock, salt glaze, low, NS (full signature), 2-lb 220.00
Butter crock, salt glaze, low, RW, 10-lb........................55.00
Cap bowl, smooth sides, red & bl sponging, RWUS, 7" 50.00
Cap bowl, 3 horizontal lines, red & bl sponging, RWUS, 7" 60.00
Casserole, Saffron, w/lid, RWUS, lg................................80.00
Chamber pot, bl banded on salt glaze, unmk 65.00
Chamber pot, brn, fancy hdl, RW 85.00
Chamber pot, wht, fancy hdl, RW, 9"..............................75.00
Christmas tree holder, bl stamp on wht, RWUS, early style 325.00
Churn, butterfly/#6 on salt glaze, RW, 6-gal 650.00
Churn, molded, elephant ear leaves/#3 on wht, MN, 3-gal..........450.00
Churn, molded, leaf/#3 on salt glaze, MN, 3-gal...........550.00
Churn, molded, parrot/#3 on salt glaze, MN, 3-gal 2,600.00
Combinette, emb lily/bl bands on salt glaze, unmk 175.00
Cooler, 'drop 8' motif/#5 on salt glaze, crock form, unmk 250.00
Cooler, birch leaves/Ice Water/#3 on salt glaze, unmk, 3-gal.........300.00
Cooler, Daisy/#6 on salt glaze, RW, 6-gal................... 1,300.00
Cooler, flower/Ice Water/#6 on salt glaze, RW, 6-gal............ 3,000.00
Cooler, red wing/Ice Water/#5 on salt glaze, RWUS, 5-gal 275.00
Cooler, red wing/Water Cooler/bl bands on salt glaze, 5-gal 300.00
Crock, 'drop 8' motif/#3 on salt glaze, RW, 3-gal 250.00
Crock, 'P'/#6 on salt glaze, RW, 6-gal...........................225.00
Crock, 'P'/#6 on salt glaze, unmk, 6-gal.......................100.00
Crock, birch leaves/#25 on salt glaze, MN, 25-gal 325.00
Crock, birch leaves/#3 on wht, MN, 3-gal.......................35.00
Crock, butterfly/#20 on salt glaze, RW, 20-gal 325.00
Crock, dbl 'P'/#2 on salt glaze, MN, 2-gal.......................85.00
Crock, dbl 'P'/#3 on salt glaze, MN, 3-gal.....................275.00
Crock, red wing/#12 on wht, RWUS, 12-gal....................60.00
Crock, 1 leaf/#10 on salt glaze, MN, 10-gal..................275.00
Crock, 2 leaves/#25 on 'new' wht, 25-gal.......................150.00
Crock, 4 elephant ear leaves/#20 on wht, MN, 20-gal 150.00
Crock, 4 leaves/#20 on wht, rare MSWCo mk, 20-gal 375.00
Crock, 4 leaves/#25 stamped on wht, 25-gal..................150.00
Cuspidor, bl & wht sponging, unmk 225.00
Cuspidor, brn/wht, MN, lg..300.00
Cuspidor, molded seam, bl & wht sponging, 10" dia 325.00
Cuspidor, molded seam, brn, unmk 65.00
Flowerpot, Albany slip, MN, 7"......................................200.00
Flowerpot, bsk, NS, 12"..40.00
Jar, pantry; red wing/bl band on wht, 1-gal 500.00
Jar, preserve; Albany slip, RW, 2-gal 110.00
Jar, preserve; Albany slip w/salt glaze lid, MN, 2-gal 110.00
Jug, bailed, Albany slip, MN, ½-gal 125.00
Jug, bailed, bl sponging, MN, 1-gal 550.00
Jug, bailed, wht, RWUS, ca 1930, 1-gal 85.00
Jug, bailed, wide mouth, wht, MN, 1-gal 110.00
Jug, beehive threshing; birch leaf/#5 on wht RWUS, 5-gal..........350.00
Jug, beehive threshing; red wing/#5 on wht, RWUS, 5-gal..........375.00
Jug, beehive; birch leaves/#4 on wht, RWUS, 4-gal 225.00
Jug, beehive; elephant ear leaves/#5 on wht, RWUS, 5-gal.........300.00
Jug, beehive; red wing/#3 on wht, RWUS, 3-gal 150.00
Jug, common, wht, MN, 1-gal 50.00
Jug, fancy, bl bands on wht, brn top, MN, 1-pt.............550.00
Jug, fancy, brn/wht, MN, ¼-pt.......................................200.00
Jug, fancy, brn/wht, RW, 1-gal......................................150.00
Jug, fancy, brn/wht, RW, 1-qt..85.00
Jug, molded seam, wide mouth, wht, MN, 1-gal............50.00
Jug, molded seam, wide mouth, wht, RW, 1-gal 35.00

Jug, shoulder; bl bands on wht, cone top, MN, 1-gal	325.00
Jug, shoulder; red wing on wht w/brn pear top, 2-gal	250.00
Jug, shoulder; red wing/#5 on wht w/brn ball top, 5-gal	250.00
Jug, shoulder; wht, birch leaf/#4, pear top, NM, 4-gal	100.00
Jug, shoulder; wht, cone top, RW, ½-gal	70.00
Jug, shoulder; wht, funnel top, MN, 2-gal	50.00
Jug, shoulder; wht, standard top, MN, 1-gal	20.00
Jug, shoulder; wht, standard top, RW, ½-gal	25.00
Jug, syrup; shouldered, cone top, wht, MN, 1-gal	50.00
Jug, syrup; shouldered, pour spout, wht, MN, 1-gal	40.00
Meat roaster, bsk, bail hdl, MN	125.00
Milk pan, Albany slip, MN, ½-pt	50.00
Milk pan, Albany slip, NS, sm	65.00
Milk pan, bl, RW, 3-gal	125.00
Mug, car & plane on bl & wht	75.00
Pie plate, brn, RW	100.00
Pie plate, salt glaze & brn, MN	165.00
Pipkin, brn/wht, MN, 4-pt	225.00
Pipkin, wht, unmk, 2-pt	65.00
Pitcher, Albany slip, bbl form, RWUS	100.00
Pitcher, bl & wht mottle, knob on hdl, RWUS	150.00
Pitcher, bl emb cherry band on wht, med sz	135.00
Pitcher, Dutch boy & girl on bl & wht, RWUS, lg	550.00
Pitcher, emb iris on Albany slip, RWP, lg	75.00
Pitcher, mustard; Albany slip, NS	200.00
Pitcher, mustard; salt glaze, MN	70.00
Pitcher, Russian milk; Albany slip, rnd hdl, ½-gal	65.00
Pitcher, Saffron, RWUS, lg	75.00
Pitcher, Sponge Band, RWUS, sm	150.00
Pitcher & bowl, emb lily on lt bl & wht, RW	450.00
Salt box, Sponge Band, w/lid, hanging, RWUS	550.00
Spittoon, German type, 'cvg'/bl bands on salt glaze, unmk	300.00
Spittoon, German type, 'cvg'/bl bands on wht, unmk	225.00
Spittoon, German type, bl bands on salt glaze, MN	550.00
Spittoon, salt glaze, unsgn	150.00
Success Filter, cobalt stencil on salt glaze, RW, 4-gal	750.00
Success Filter, red wing/bl bands on wht, 4-gal	300.00
Umbrella stand, red & bl sponging, unmk	550.00

Redware

The term redware refers to a type of simple earthenware produced by the Colonists as early as the 1600s. The red clay used in its production was abundant throughout the country, and during the 18th and 19th centuries redware was made in great quantities. Intended for utilitarian purposes such as everyday tableware or use in the dairy, redware was simple in design and decoration. Glazes of various colors were used, and a liquid clay referred to as 'slip' was sometimes applied in patterns such as zigzag lines, daisies, or stars. In the following listings, EX (excellent condition) indicates very minor damage.

Our advisor for this category is Barbara Rosen; she is listed in the Directory under New Jersey.

Bank, apple form, 3½x3½"	165.00
Bank, brn/amber mottle, knob finial, chips, 3⅞"	175.00
Bank, stylized lady in long dress, yel slip motto, 1831, 7"	850.00
Bird whistle, w/finger holes for multiple tones, 2⅜"	165.00
Bottle, wht w/amber & gr splotches, appl floral, 8", EX	225.00
Bowl, milk; yel slip int, European, 6½x14"	65.00
Bowl, milk; yel slip swags, edge chips, 2¼x10"	105.00
Bowl, vegetable; blk mottling over rust, beaded rim, 1810s	225.00
Bowl, yel slip bands w/brn wavy line, 2½x9", VG	350.00
Bowl, yel slip str/wavy lines on gr & dk brn, 11", EX	500.00

Bowl, yel slip waves & simple floral, 2x7"	450.00
Butter print, stylized flower, minor wear/chips, 3¾" dia	375.00
Canteen, brn running glaze, tooled bands, keg form, 5", EX	125.00
Charger, yel slip abstract, coggled, wear/chips, 13"	350.00
Cookie mold, bear, EX details, ca 1810, 3x5"	395.00
Creamer, brn streaks, ribbed strap hdl, 4⅞", EX	125.00
Crock, brn splotches, appl hdls, 9", EX	175.00
Cup, dk brn, strap hdl, details at base, hairline, 3¾"	35.00
Dish, blk, rim spout, strap hdl, 2½x5¾", EX	105.00
Dish, faint W in yel slip, coggled, sm chips, 5"	195.00
Dish, 3-line yel slip waves, coggled, 6" dia	220.00
Dog, open front legs, w/basket, cvd/wht details, 4", EX	2,550.00
Flask, clear w/blk splotch, 7⅜", EX	80.00
Flask, dk brn (blk), 6", EX	75.00
Foot warmer, brn/gr/yel mottle, hole at top, 5x11½x7½"	395.00
Jar, apple butter; gr mottle, ovoid, 7½"	95.00
Jar, brn flecked w/orange & amber mottle, ovoid, 7", pr	180.00
Jar, brn splotches, chips, 6"	85.00
Jar, clear w/brn spots, strap hdl, rpr, 5½"	165.00
Jar, gr & 2-tone brn, ovoid, 4½", EX	85.00
Jar, gr-amber w/brn flecks, 5⅝"	100.00
Jar, yel/brn/blk mottle, bulbous w/wide mouth, hdls, 9½"	200.00
Jug, dk brn, strap hdl, chips, 10½"	165.00
Jug, tan, coiled snake hdl, Little Brn Jug, 5", VG	115.00
Jug, 3 dk splotches on rust, ovoid, 1700s, 8½"	350.00
Lamp, grease; brn, saucer base, strap hdl, 4½", VG	425.00
Lamp, grease; dk brn, 3 coggled rings on std, wide base, 5"	350.00
Lamp, orange, ribbed strap hdl, 5⅜", G	250.00
Loaf pan, closely-spaced yel slip 'rickrack,' 12x15", VG	495.00
Mold, turk's head, wht slip waves, 2½x7½"	100.00
Mug, brn/gr marbleized glaze w/wht slip, strap hdl, 6", VG	825.00
Mug, dk glaze, 2 tooled lines at rim, ribbed hdl, 4", EX	95.00

Plates, sponge decoration on orange-brown, incised rim line, PA, 1840-60, minor glaze loss, 8", $200.00 each.

Pie plate, lt gr w/yel slip decor, coggled, 8", EX	225.00
Pie plate, simple cvg w/yel slip under red mottle, 11", EX	275.00
Pie plate, yel slip on orange clay, rpr chips, 8"	275.00
Pie plate, 3-line yel slip segments, coggled, 10", EX	300.00
Pitcher, brn splotches, mug form, 4⅜", EX	95.00
Pitcher, brn splotches, tooled lines, strap hdl, 8½", EX	225.00
Pitcher, brn streaks on amber, tooled shoulder, ovoid, 10¼"	500.00
Pitcher, dk brn mottle, strap hdl, tooled lines, 3½", EX	85.00
Plate, yel slip flourish, coggled, 11", VG	275.00

Plate, 3-line yel slip flourish, hairlines/chips, 7" **85.00**
Plate, 3-line yel slip lines & waves, smooth rim, 8½", VG...........**175.00**
Plate, 3-line yel slip waves & 'trees,' coggled, 9", EX **300.00**
Pot, amber, rim spout, ribbed strap hdl, 4½", EX **95.00**
Pot, gr mottle, strap hdl, side spout, tooled details, 4⅜" **255.00**
Rooster, by Lester Breininger, PA, sgn/dtd 1973, 3¼" **35.00**

Regal China

Located in Antioch, Illinois, the Regal China Company has been in business since 1938. Products of interest to collectors are James Beam decanters, cookie jars, salt and pepper shakers, and similar novelty items. The Old MacDonald's Farm series listed below are becoming especially collectible. See also Cookie Jars.

Old McDonald's Farm

Butter dish, cow's head **35.00**
Canister, lg...**95.00**
Canister, med **85.00**
Canister, spice; sm **35.00**

Canister, unusual 'Peanuts' label, $120.00.

Jar, grease; pig figural **65.00**
Jar, popcorn; farmer **95.00**
Pitcher, milk; cow's head, gold bell, tankard form **200.00**
Shakers, churn, pr..**18.00**
Shakers, feed sacks w/sheep's head, pr..**35.00**
Shakers, son & daughter, pr..**25.00**
Sugar bowl, rooster, lg...**95.00**
Teapot, duck's head **135.00**

Religious Items

Censer, brass, simple style, no chain, 7½" **40.00**
Chalice, gold/silver/enamel, inscribed, 1890s, 8½" **175.00**
Ciborium, gold-plated brass, cross finial, 5x3½" **65.00**
Crucifix, hand-cvd bone figure of Jesus, bone finials, 19" **250.00**
Engraving, ...Way...to Everlasting Life or...Damnation, 18" **385.00**
Icon, Archangel Michael, Greek, 1700s, 12"................................**400.00**
Icon, St George slays dragon, Russian, 1800s, 19½" **350.00**

Icon, Virgin Mary & Christ Child, Greek, 1700s, 11¾x9¼" **500.00**
Kiddush cup, chased foliage, Continental silver, Russian, 1-oz **75.00**
Kiddush cup, sterling, Russian..**95.00**
Lantern, processional; brass, decor, glass insert, 14" **35.00**
Paten, gold-plated sterling, eng circled cross, 5⅛" dia **75.00**
Rosary, w/cvd ivory Stanhope crucifix **38.00**
Sabbath lamp, silver, 3-hdl, w/shade, Russian, 1880s, 18" **200.00**
Spice tower, sterling, openwork, hinged door, Russian, 9" **265.00**
Taper, w/snuffer, brass fittings, mtd on maple hdl, 41"....................**50.00**
Urn, dull gold color over brass, 14", pr...**25.00**

Russian icon, gold leaf, enamel and tempera on gesso-covered wood panel, 1800s, 38" x 28", $2,000.00.

Restraints

Since the beginning of time, many things from animals to treasures have been held in bondage by hemp, bamboo, chests, chains, shackles, and other constructed devices. Many of these devices were used to hold captives who awaited further torture, as if the restraint wasn't torturous enough. The study and collecting of restraints enables one to learn much about the advancement of civilization in the country or region from which they originated. Such devices at various times in history were made of very heavy metals – so heavy that the wearer could scarcely move about. It has only been in the last sixty years that vast improvements have been made in design and construction that afford the captive some degree of comfort.

Our advisor for this category is Joseph Tanner; he is listed in the Directory under Montana.

Key:
bbl — barrel
d-lb — double lock button
K — key
Kd — keyed
lc — lock case
NST — non-swing through
ST — swing through
stp — stamped

Foreign Handcuffs

Adams, teardrop lc, bbl Kd, NST, usually not stp.........................**150.00**
Australian, Saf Lock, ST, takes pin-tumbler K in side, stp **110.00**
Chubb, NST, English hi-security 10-slider lock mechanism **200.00**
Deutsche Polizei, ST, middle hinge, folds, takes bbl-bit K **100.00**
French Lapegy, ST, alluminum alloys, takes flat bitted K **65.00**
German Clejuso, oval design, ST, dbl-cuff weight, 22-oz **90.00**
German Clejuso, oval design, ST, solid K w/lg bit, stp **80.00**
German Clejuso, sq lc, adjusts/NST, d-lb on side, bbl K **95.00**
German Darby, adjusts, well finished, sm **100.00**

German Hamburg 8, non-adjust NST, center bar/post w/K-way .200.00
Hiatt, English Darby, like US CW Darby, stp Hiatt & #d **55.00**
Hiatt, solid state, 2 separate cuffs joined bk to bk, stp/# **90.00**
Hiatt English non-adjust screw K Darby style, uses screw K **85.00**
Hiatt Figure 8, swings open to insert/withdraw wrists **90.00**
Italian, stp New Police, modern Peerless type, ST, sm bbl K **30.00**
Japanese, stp Chief of Police, modern Peerless type, ST **25.00**
Plug 8, remove plug before inserting external threaded K **150.00**
Spanish, stp Alcyon/Star, modern Peerless type, ST, flat K **65.00**
Spanish, stp Alcyon/Star, modern Peerless type, ST, sm bbl K **45.00**

Foreign Leg Shackles

German Clejuso, sq lc, adjusts/NST, d-bl on side, bbl K **105.00**
German Clejuso Darby type, adjusts/NST/plated, uses screw K ...**125.00**
Hiatt English combo manacles, handcuff/leg irons w/chain **150.00**
Hiatt English non-adjust screw K Darby style, uses screw K **85.00**
Hiatt Plug leg irons, same K-ing as Plug-8 cuffs, w/chain **175.00**

U.S. Handcuffs

American Munitions, modern/rnd, sm bbl Kd, ST bow, stp **45.00**
Bean Patrolman, kidney-bean form, d-lb on lc, NST, stp T **90.00**
Bean-Cobb, sm rnd lc, removable cylinder, d-lb, NST, 1899 ....**80.00**
Civil War padlocking type, various designs w/loop for lock **90.00**
Colt, modern ST bow, sm bbl Kd, stp w/Colt & co name **90.00**
H&R Super, NST, shaft-hinge connector takes hollow titted K **75.00**
Harvard, takes sm bbl K, ST, stp Harvard Lock Co **65.00**
Judd, NST, uses rnd/internally triangular K, stp Mattatuck..........**100.00**
Marlin Daley, NST, bottle-neck form, neck stp, dbl-titted K **150.00**
Mattatuck, NST, propeller-like K-way, stp Mattatuck/etc **85.00**
Peerless, ST, takes sm bbl K, stp Mfg'ered by Peerless Co **40.00**
Peerless, ST, takes sm bbl K, stp Mfg'ered by S&W Co...................**75.00**
Phelps, NST, twist chain between cuffs, Tower look-alike **150.00**
Pratt combo, 1 cuff connects w/nipper/claw, ST, mk Pratt **200.00**
Romer, NST, takes flat K, resembles padlock, stp Romer Co **200.00**
S&W 94 Maximum Security, ST, takes Ace-type K, stp S&W **65.00**
Strauss, ST, takes lg solid bitted K, stp Strauss Eng Co...................**85.00**
Tower, NST, bottom K, solid/flat fitted K goes in cuff edge..........**100.00**
Tower bar cuffs, cuffs serarate by 10-12" steel bar **90.00**
Tower Dbl Lock, NST, takes bbl-bitted K, usually stp Tower **50.00**
Tower Detective Pinkerton, NST, sq lc, bbl-bitted K, no stp **85.00**
Tower Single Lock, NST, bbl-bit K, K-way slanted on lc, sm..........**70.00**
Tower-Bean, NST, sm rnd lc, takes tiny bbl-bitted K, stp...............**70.00**
Walden 'Lady Cuff,' NST, takes sm bbl K, lightweight, stp **200.00**

U.S. Leg Shackles

American Munitions, as handcuffs...**55.00**
Civil War or prison ball & chain, padlocking or rivet type..........**175.00**
H&R Supers, as handcuffs...**200.00**
Harvard, as handcuffs **75.00**
Judd, as handcuffs **110.00**
Oregon boot, break-apart shackle on above ankle support..........**400.00**
Strauss, as handcuffs..**90.00**
Tower, bottom K, as handcuffs **90.00**
Tower ball & chain, leg iron w/chain & 6-lb to 50-lb ball **150.00**
Tower Dbl-Lock, as handcuffs...**75.00**
Tower Detective, as handcuffs **135.00**

Various Other Restraining Devices

African slave Darby-style cuffs, heavy iron/chain, handmade **95.00**
African slave Darby-style leg shackles, heavy/hand forged **150.00**

African slave padlocking or riveted forged iron shackles **125.00**
Darby neck collar, rnd steel loop opens w/screw K **135.00**
English Figure-8 nipper, claws open by lifting top lock tab **65.00**
German Nipper, twist hdl opens/closes cuff, stp Germany/etc **75.00**

Reverse Painting on Glass

Verre eglomise is the technique of painting on the underside of glass. Dating back to the early 1700s, this art became popular in the 19th century when German immigrants chose historical figures and beautiful women as subjects for their reverse glass paintings. Advertising mirrors of this type came into vogue at the turn of the century.

George and Martha Washington, after Gilbert Stuart, in gray, white, black, and flesh tones on gray, 1800s, 30" x 26", $700.00 for the pair.

Basket of flowers, wht on tinsel ground, 7x8" **125.00**
Bearded man w/crown, monk w/child, orig fr, 5x4", pr...............**650.00**
Charlotte, Queen of Great Britain, 1800s, 12¾x9¾" **340.00**
Country scene w/stone bridge & half-timber cottage, 19x27" **125.00**
Gentleman, bust-length, ornate cvd rosewood fr, 6x7" **235.00**
Mourning Queen Charlotte, 1800s, 13½x9½" **220.00**
Napoleon portrait, 12x9" panel, fr **75.00**
Oriental lady w/lg cat, Chinese, 20x28" **140.00**

Richard

Richard, who at one time worked for Galle, made cameo art glass in France during the 1920s. His work was often multi-layered and acid cut with florals and scenics in lovely colors. The ware was marked with his name in relief.

Our advisor for this category is Don Williams; he is listed in the Directory under Iowa.

Cameo

Atomizer, floral, bl on gr, paper label, 5" **325.00**
Atomizer, florals/moth, bl on lemon yel, sgn, 7¾"......................**625.00**
Goblet, landscape/tower, pk on clear/bl frost, knob stem **450.00**
Lamp, 10" shade/base: windmills/river, 2 cuts, rstr, 15" **2,400.00**
Plaque, church/stream in purple, polished, silver fr, 7x9".............**525.00**
Vase, ferns/flowers, blk on orange, 8½" **300.00**
Vase, house/mtns/trees in purple, stick neck, 14" **1,050.00**
Vase, leaves/pods, 2-color gr on yel, ftd, 8" **350.00**
Vase, ships/birds/trees, yel/brn, 4½" **695.00**
Vase, trees/cottage/lake/mtns, lav/yel/wht, 4 cuts, 14"............. **1,500.00**

Vase, scenic in blue and orange, signed, 8", $1,600.00.

Ridgway

As early as 1792, the Ridgway brothers, Job and George, produced fine quality earthenwares in Shelton, Staffordshire, marking their products 'Ridgway, Smith, & Ridgway,' and later, 'Job & George Ridgway.' Around 1800 the brothers split and each had his own firm, both in Shelton. They were joined in the business by various members of the Ridgway family, and in fact their descendants still operate there today.

The two firms created by the split were the Bell Works and the Cauldon Pottery. Bell produced stone china and earthenware decorated with blue transfer printing. Their mark was 'J. & W. Ridgway' or 'J. & W.R.,' until 1848 when 'William Ridgway' was used. The Cauldon Pottery made earthenware, stone china, and high-quality porcelains fine enough to win them the distinction of being appointed potters to the Queen. From 1830 their wares attest to this fact, bearing the Royal Arms mark with 'J.R.' within the crest. In 1840 '& Co.' was added. Most examples of Ridgway's wares found today are transfer-printed historical scenes. See also Staffordshire, Historical; and Flow Blue.

Mustard pot, Coaching Days, 3½", $125.00.

Biscuit jar, Coaching Days, brn rattan hdl, 6½"	230.00
Bowl, Coaching Days, set of 3: 8½x4½", 7x3¾", 6x3⅜"	120.00
Cup & saucer, Coaching Days	35.00
Cup & saucer, Royal Vista	20.00
Mug, Coaching Days, Down the Hill, 4"	20.00
Mug, Coaching Days, silver lustre trim, 2-hdl, mk, 3⅞"	40.00

Mug, Mormon Sq, Salt Lake City, 4½"	45.00
Pitcher, Post Boys, 7"	70.00
Pitcher, stoneware, bl w/emb band, HP flowers, 1835, 11"	160.00
Pitcher, tankard; Coaching Days, 10"	110.00
Plaque, In a Snow Drift, yel, 12"	130.00
Plaque, Taking Up the Mails, yel, 12"	130.00
Plate, chop; Coaching Days, 13½"	125.00
Plate, Coaching Days, 7"	25.00
Platter, Giraffe, med bl transfer, mk Pub 1836, 15", NM	210.00
Tea caddy, Coaching Days, brn, sq, 5¾x4¼"	150.00
Teapot, Coaching Days, 5½"	165.00
Tray, Coaching Days, Christmas Visitor, 12½" dia	125.00
Vase, Coaching Days, 5"	65.00

Rie, Lucie

Lucie Rie was born in Austria in 1902. She moved to London in 1938 and shared her studio with Hans Coper from 1946 to 1958. Her ceramics look modern; however, they are based on shapes from many world cultures dating back to Roman times. Lucie Rie is best known for the use of metallic oxides in her clay and glazes. She specializes in the hand throwing of thin, porcelain bowls, which is a very difficult process. Her works are in the world's best museums. All of her ceramics are impressed with a seal mark on the bottom, a cojoined 'R & L' within a rectangular reserve.

Bowl, bsk, brn matt int, incised lines, wide flare, 8½"	1,200.00
Bowl, copper int, vertical blk lines, funnel form, 8½"	6,000.00
Bowl, gr w/bronze rim, funnel form, 7"	4,000.00
Bowl, incised bands of pk & manganese, conical, 6"	750.00
Bowl, porc, lav w/brn drip at rim & base, cvd fluting, 6"	1,000.00
Bowl, yel, 1975, 5"	600.00
Vase, gold-blk metallic, long neck/sharp shoulder, 9½"	1,500.00
Vase, pk w/bl spirals, stoneware, oval, 1980, 4"	1,100.00

Riviera

Riviera was a line of dinnerware introduced by the Homer Laughlin China Company in 1938. It was sold exclusively by the Murphy Company through their nationwide chain of dime stores. Riviera was unmarked, lightweight, and inexpensive. It was discontinued sometime prior to 1950. Colors are mauve blue, red, yellow, light green, and ivory. On rare occasions, dark blue pieces are found, but this was not a standard color.

Batter set, complete	175.00
Batter set, ivory, w/decals	120.00
Bowl, baker; 9"	15.00
Bowl, cream soup; w/liner, ivory	35.00
Bowl, fruit; 5½"	8.00
Bowl, nappy, 9¼"	14.00
Bowl, oatmeal; 6"	14.00
Butter dish, cobalt, ¼-lb	175.00
Butter dish, other colors, ¼-lb	80.00
Butter dish, turq, ¼-lb	150.00
Butter dish, ½-lb	70.00
Casserole	60.00
Creamer	6.50
Cup & saucer, demitasse; ivory	42.00
Jug, w/lid	70.00
Pitcher, juice; mauve bl	110.00
Plate, deep	13.00
Plate, 10"	20.00

Plate, 6"	5.50
Plate, 7"	7.50
Plate, 9"	12.00
Platter, cobalt, 12"	22.00
Platter, w/closed hdls, 11¼"	14.00
Platter, 11½"	12.00
Sauce boat	15.00
Saucer	3.00
Shakers, pr	12.00
Sugar bowl, w/lid	12.00
Syrup, w/lid	75.00
Teacup	7.50
Teapot	65.00
Tumbler, hdld	48.00
Tumbler, juice	32.00

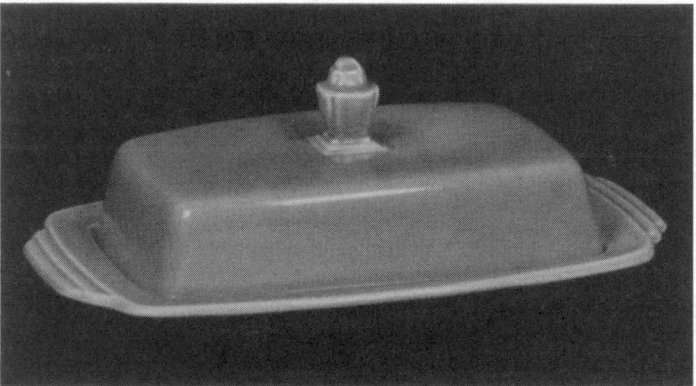

Butter dish, ½-lb, $70.00.

Robertson

Fred H. Robertson, clay expert for the Los Angeles Brick Company and son of Alexander Robertson of the Roblin Pottery, experimented with crystalline glazes as early as 1906. In 1934 Fred and his son George established their own works in Los Angeles, but by 1943 they had moved operations to Hollywood. Though most of their early wares were turned by hand, some were also molded in low relief. Fine crackle glazes and crystallines were developed. The ware was marked with 'Robertson,' 'F.H.R.,' or 'R.,' with the particular location of its manufacture noted. The small pottery closed in 1952.

Our advisor for this category is Jack Chipman; he is listed in the Directory under California.

Box, appl rose on lid, bl, rectangular	150.00
Tile, boy & girl w/duck, blk/wht, 4x4"	95.00
Tile, HP florals, mc, 6x9"	135.00
Vase, bsk, red clay, sgn AWR, 5/05, 3"	200.00
Vase, wht crackle, pillow form, mk Hollywood, 5½x5"	75.00

Robineau

After short-term training in ceramics in 1903, Adelaide Robineau (with the help of her husband Samuel) built a small pottery studio at her home in Syracuse, New York. She was adept at mixing the clay and throwing the ware, which she often decorated by incising designs into the unfired clay. Samuel developed many of the glazes and took charge of the firing process. In 1910 she joined the staff of the American Women's League Pottery at St. Louis, where she designed the famous Scarab Vase. After this pottery failed, she served on the faculty of Syra-

cuse University. Her work was and is today highly acclaimed for the high standards of excellence to which she aspired.

Vase, bright bl crystalline/ochre streaks, #5/357, 3½x5"	5,500.00
Vase, emerald crystals on lime, rpr, 4x6"	1,400.00
Vase, porc experimental, gr crystalline, mk #11, 2¼", EX	350.00

Robj

Robj was the name of a retail store that operated in Paris for only a few years, from about 1925 to 1931. Robj solicited designs from the best French artisans of the period to produce decorative objects for the home. These objects were produced mostly in porcelain but also in glass and earthenware. The most well known are the figural bottles which were particularly popular in the United States. However, Robj also produced tea sets, perfume lamps, chess sets, ash trays, bookends, humidors, powder jars, cigarette boxes, figurines, lamps, and milk pitchers. Robj objects tend to be whimsical, and all embody the Art Deco style.

Our advice for this category comes from Cocktails and Laughter Antiques (Randall Monsen and Rod Baer), whose address is listed in the Directory under Virginia.

Bookends, kneeling Oriental, gilt robe/peaked hat, 8"	1,000.00

Box, Indian head form, stamped Robj Paris, Made in France, 7", $2,400.00 (double the high auction estimate).

Box, head of Arabian princess, gold tracing, 8½" H	1,000.00
Decanter, Blk Mammy, gold trim, Limoges, France, 10"	750.00
Decanter, girl in bonnet w/flower basket, 10½"	400.00
Decanter, Scotsman, 11"	450.00
Decanter, Swiss girl in native dress, gilt trim, 10½"	400.00
Figurine, group of 3 sailors, cream, 11", EX	2,000.00
Lamp shade; frosted glass w/abstract foliage panels, 6" dia	200.00
Tea set, chubby Chinaman in red robe, 5" pot+cr/sug+2 c/s	1,300.00

Roblin

In the late 1800s, Alexander W. Robertson and Linna Irelan established a pottery in San Francisco, combining parts of their respective names to coin the name Roblin. Robertson was responsible for potting and firing the ware, which often reflected his taste for classic styling. Mrs. Irelan did much of the decorating, utilizing almost every method but favoring relief modeling. Mushrooms and lizards were her favorite subjects. Vases were a large part of their production, all of which was made from native California red, buff, and white clays. The ware was well marked with the firm name or the outline of a bear. Roblin Pottery was destroyed in the earthquake of 1906.

Vase, brn bsk, incised line, 3½" **140.00**
Vase, bsk, ftd bulb body w/short neck collar, 3¼".........................**245.00**
Vase, red clay, no glaze, RAPC mk, 4x3¼".................................**200.00**
Vase, wht bsk, cylindrical w/ridges, sgn AWR, mk, 2"..................**150.00**

Rockingham

In the early part of the 19th century, American potters began to favor brown- and buff-burning clays over red because of their durability. The glaze favored by many was Rockingham, which varied from a dark brown mottle to a sponged effect sometimes called tortoise shell. It consisted in part of manganese and various metallic salts and was used by many potters until well into the 20th century. Over the past two years, demand and prices have risen sharply, especially in the east. See also Bennington.

Bottle, book form, Ladies' Companion, corner chip, 5½" **450.00**
Bottle, book form, 6" **250.00**
Bottle, clenched fist form, thumb is spout, 5", NM **225.00**
Bottle, hound's head form, wht slip collar, rprs, 5½" L **200.00**
Bottle, shoe form, emb laces/Ann Reid/1859, 6"........................**300.00**
Bottle, woman half-figure, angels on lower half, 8" **75.00**
Bowl, emb ext, pouring spout, 4½x9¾"......................................**85.00**
Bowl, grapevines emb, str sides, hdls, 5¾x7" **135.00**
Bowl, minor wear, 3x12" dia **175.00**
Cat, free standing front legs, EX detail, poor rprs, 11" **175.00**
Creamer, toby, English, 5½" **135.00**
Creamer, toby, lip chip, 4⅝" **95.00**
Dish, emb scroll borders, corner fans, minor wear, sq, 9" **100.00**
Dish, shaped sides, sq, 8" **125.00**
Dog, seated, free-standing front legs, tooled detail, 10" **475.00**
Doorknob, octagonal, orig metal collar, 2¼" dia..........................**55.00**
Flask, eagles emb, ribbed sides, 7", EX **250.00**
Flask, horses/dismounted riders emb, rpr chips, 7".....................**325.00**
Flask, roses emb, base chips, 6" **100.00**
Flask, roses/vintage emb, 7"..**180.00**

Flask, tavern scenes/vintage emb, base chips/rpr, 6" **150.00**
Inkwell, acanthus leaves emb, paneled, 2¼x3" dia, EX...............**175.00**
Inkwell, spaniel & pup figural, 4", VG.......................................**250.00**
Lion, right paw on ball, stepped base, England, 11" L, EX **275.00**
Mold, turk's head, gr highlights, 8½" dia **150.00**
Pie plate, 11"...**150.00**
Pitcher, anchor emb, 9¾"...**175.00**
Pitcher, bust form: man in Federal hat Wellington/1832, 7"........**125.00**
Pitcher, camel/elephant emb, R Bew Bilston, 7", NM..................**45.00**
Pitcher, cherubs/vintage emb, base flake, 6" **95.00**
Pitcher, emb panels, 9½" **135.00**
Pitcher, Geo WA, emb full-length, Masonic symbols, rpr, 8".......**225.00**
Pitcher, grapes/leaves, branch hdl, Bennington mold, 12" **850.00**
Pitcher, inscr: Mrs John Webb, portraits, frog w/in, 10" **225.00**
Shaving mug, cherubs milk goat emb, edge chips, 4" **115.00**
Shaving mug, toby form, 4¼", EX...**300.00**
Soap dish, oval, 4¾", NM **145.00**
Washboard, yel/brn mottle, minor wear, 10x10" **375.00**

Rockwell, Norman

Norman Rockwell began his career in 1911 at the age of seventeen doing illustrations for a children's book titled *Tell Me Why Stories*. Within a few years he had produced the *Saturday Evening Post* cover that made him one of America's most-beloved artists. Though not well accepted by the professional critics of his day who did not consider his work to be art but 'merely' commercial illustration, Rockwell's popularity grew to the extent that today there is an overwhelming abundance of examples of his work or those related to the theme of one of his illustrations.

Bell, Christmas Medley, Gorham, 1983 ....**32.00**
Book, Norman Rockwell's American, leather bound, ltd ed........**100.00**

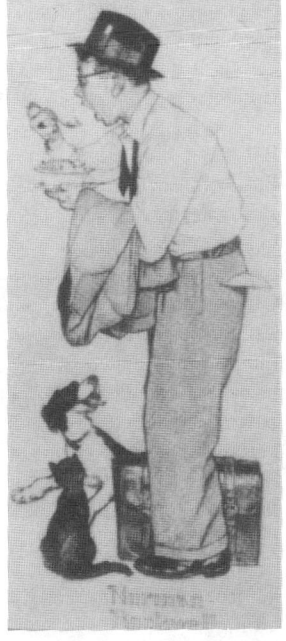

Charcoal and pencil sketch, signed, unframed, 19" x 10", $8,000.00.

Pitcher, medallion portraits, 'To Mrs. John Webb,' figure of a frog in bottom, 10", $225.00; Pitcher, made from Bennington mold, 12", EX, $425.00.

Calendar, Bicentennial, M **20.00**
Fan, Boy Scouts, 1940s, EX **15.00**
Figurine, At the Vets, Gorham **60.00**
Figurine, Checking His List, Museum Collections, Inc.................**80.00**
Figurine, His First Smoke, Goebel **375.00**

Figurine, Independence, Gorham..140.00
Figurine, Jolly Coachman, Gorham 130.00
Figurine, Marriage License, Gorham..105.00
Figurine, Skating, Gorham 800.00
Figurine, The Toymaker, Museum Collections, Inc 88.00
Figurine, Wet Sport, Gorham..85.00
Figurine, Young Love series, Gorham, set of 4 ....950.00
Lithograph, Brooks Robinson, Rawlings, sgn, 24x30" 350.00
Lithograph, You Got To Be Kidden, 24x18" 500.00
Magazine cover, American Boy, Dec, 1916................................32.00
Magazine cover, Collier's, Apr 19, 1919...................................20.00
Magazine cover, Family Circle, Dec, 1968 ....8.00
Magazine cover, Saturday Evening Post, Sept, 1918 ....88.00
Plaque, Freedom From Fear, metal, Curtis Circulation, 11x16" ...300.00
Plate, A Winning Hand 35.00
Plate, Angel w/a Blk Eye 75.00
Plate, Christmas Gift, Royal Devon 95.00
Plate, First Smoke, 1977..60.00
Plate, Looking Out To Sea 115.00
Plate, Scotty Gets His Tree, MIB...150.00
Plate, 50 Years of Canned Beer...35.00
Poster, Freedom From Want, Thanksgiving meal, '43, 40x56", EX .45.00
Poster, Schmidt's Beer, VG 45.00
Stein, Music Lesson 95.00
Stein, Pensive Pals 38.00

Rogers, John

John Rogers (1829-1904) was a machinist from Manchester, New Hampshire, who turned his hobby of sculpting into a financially-successful venture. From the originals he meticulously fashioned of red clay, he had bronze master molds made from which plaster copies were cast. He specialized in five different categories: theatrical, Shakespeare, Civil War, everyday life, and horses. His large detailed groupings portrayed the life and times of the period between 1859 and 1892. When no condition is indicated, examples are assumed to be in very good to excellent condition.

Our advisor for this category is George Humphrey; he is listed in the Directory under Maryland.

Balcony.. 1,200.00
Bath.. 2,000.00
Bushwacker.. 2,000.00
Camp Life 2,000.00
Charity Patient 650.00
Checkers at the Farm..450.00
Council of War 850.00
Elder's Daughter...800.00
Fairy's Whisper, ca 1881 .... 1,400.00
Favored Scholar..425.00
Fetching the Doctor 750.00
Fighting Bob, ca 1889 .... 1,100.00
First Ride..750.00
Football, inscribed, 16x11", NM 800.00
Foundling 625.00
Fugitive Story..900.00
Going for the Cows 425.00
Hide & Seek 775.00
Is It So Nominated in the Bond...375.00
Mail Day 750.00
Neighboring Pews, ca 1884 ....425.00
One More Shot 550.00
Parting Promise...400.00

Peddler at the Fair 825.00
Phrenology at the Fancy Ball, 1886, 20x10" 600.00
Pickett Guard 750.00
Playing Doctor 700.00
Politics 700.00
Returned Volunteer...600.00
Rip Van Winkle at Home 325.00
Rip Van Winkle on the Mountain...400.00
Rip Van Winkle Returned 475.00
Schauchraum & Tatters 475.00
School Days..550.00
School Examination...500.00
Slave Auction 2,000.00
Speak for Yourself, John 475.00
Taking the Oath 425.00
Tap on the Window 500.00
Traveling Magician..750.00
Watch on the Santa Maria 700.00
We Boys 425.00
Weighing the Baby 450.00
Wounded Scout 800.00
Wrestler.. 1,250.00

Coming to the Parson, $375.00.

Rookwood

The Rookwood Pottery Company was established in 1879 in Cincinnati, Ohio. Its founder was Maria Longworth Nichols Storer, daughter of a wealthy family who provided the backing necessary to make such an enterprise possible. Mrs. Storer hired competent ceramic workers who through constant experimentation developed many lines of superior art pottery. While in her employ, Laura Fry invented the airbrush-blending process for which she was issued a patent in 1884. From this, several lines were designed that utilized blended backgrounds.

One of their earlier lines, Standard, was a brown ware decorated with underglaze slip-painted nature studies, animals, portraits, etc. Iris and Sea Green were introduced in 1894 and Vellum, a transparent matglaze line, in 1904. Other lines followed: Ombroso in 1910 and Soft Porcelain in 1915. Many of the early artware lines were signed by the artist. Soon after the turn of the twentieth century, Rookwood manufactured 'production' pieces that relied mainly on molded designs and forms rather than freehand decoration for their esthetic appeal.

The Depression brought on financial difficulties from which the pottery never recovered. Though it continued to operate, the quality of the ware deteriorated, and the pottery was forced to close in 1967.

Unmarked Rookwood is only rarely encountered. Many marks may be found, but the most familiar is the reverse 'RP' monogram. First used in 1886, a flame point was added above it for each succeeding year until 1900. After that, a Roman numeral added below indicated the year of manufacture. Impressed letters that related to the type of clay utilized for the body were also used – G for ginger, O for olive, R for red, S for sage green, W for white, and Y for yellow.

Artware must be judged on an individual basis. Quality of the artwork is a prime factor to consider. Portraits, animals, and birds are worth more than florals; and pieces signed by a particularly renowned artist are highly prized.

Our advisors for this category are Fer-Duc, Inc.; they are listed in the Directory under New York.

Aventurine

Mug, molded line/curl motif at base, lt gr int, 1933, 4¾" **70.00**
Vase, deep red/brn, wide shoulder, flared top, 1940, 7" **165.00**
Vase, floral/leaf, gr on gr, Lorinda Epply, 1920, 11½x4" **1,100.00**

Bisque

Ewer, birds/reeds on pastels, MA Daly, #101A, 1885, 11" **750.00**
Ewer, butterflies, wht/blk on orange to yel, no mk, 11½" **350.00**
Ewer, leaf/branch cvg, lt gray clay, gloss int, 1882, 12" **400.00**
Ewer, leafy vines in gilt, Shirayamadani, 1887, 9½" **350.00**
Lamp base, bamboo/birds, AR Valentien, 1883, 7" **650.00**
Vase, mums on pk, sgn AB Sprague, 1888, 6" **275.00**

Iris

Loving cup, frog/aquatic plants, JD Wareham, 1897, 4½" **1,200.00**
Vase, bachelor buttons, bl on ivory, JD Wareham, 1897, 6" **350.00**
Vase, berries/branches on brn to peach, J Zettel, 1903, 9" **900.00**
Vase, berries/leaves on gray-wht shaded, S Coyne, '03, 3½" **400.00**
Vase, blueberries, Sara Sax, #900C, 1907, 8" **900.00**
Vase, blueberries on shaded gr-gray, I Bishop, 1904, 6" **475.00**
Vase, floral, wht on gray/teal/pk, S Sax, #925C, 1903, 10"...... **1,300.00**
Vase, floral on tan/dk gr, LE Lindeman, #583F, 1903, 5"............ **400.00**
Vase, frieze of crows, lt/dk gr, bottle form, ET Hurley, 7" **800.00**
Vase, iris ea side, wht on shaded gr, C Schmidt, 1908, 10"...... **4,000.00**
Vase, irises, on mc shaded ground, C Schmidt, 1902, 8" **1,750.00**
Vase, lg primrose, wht on shaded bl, I Bishop, 1904, 7" **700.00**
Vase, lg tulip, wht on violet/lt gr, S Sax, 1906, 5½" **700.00**
Vase, mums, peach on brn to cream, I Bishop, 1903, 8x5" **1,000.00**
Vase, orchids, lav on lt gr, C Schmidt, #907, 1903, 10½"........ **1,400.00**
Vase, pansies, wht on lav/bl, S Sax, short neck, 1901, 6¾" **400.00**
Vase, peacock feather on lt bl & gr, C Schmidt, 1911, 8" **4,000.00**
Vase, pond lilies, yel on wht to gr, L Asbury, 1908, 7½" **800.00**
Vase, poppies, red on purple to wht, R Fecheimer, 1903, 6" **725.00**
Vase, school of fish, L Asbury, baluster, 1910, 8"......................... **700.00**
Vase, thistle blossoms on gr & rose, C Schmidt, 1909, 11" **3,800.00**

Jewel Porcelain

Bowl, quilted relief, turq, #6681, 1937, 3x12"................................**70.00**
Vase, bird/magnolia branch on dk bl, S Sax, 1917, 12x8¼" **1,350.00**
Vase, floral band, mc on bl, Arthur Conant, 1922, 8½" **1,000.00**
Vase, florals, gr/pk on cream, MH McDonald, slim, 1943, 6½" ...**225.00**
Vase, florals, pk/blk on cream, P Conant, 1917, 5x7" **700.00**
Vase, florals/ribbon-like leaves, Shirayamadani, 1925, 7x5" **550.00**
Vase, Persian-type floral, bl/gr on turq, sgn, 1920, 18"................**600.00**
Vase, tulips, lav on pk, Shirayamadani, 1940, 7½x3½" **550.00**

Limoges

Basket, birds/grasses, pinched middle, #45, 1885, 12" W **450.00**
Honey jug, mums, brn/wht/gr on red w/gold, #61, 1885, 5" **250.00**

Jardiniere, reeds/birds, gold accents, M Rettig, 1883, 8" **950.00**
Jug, Spanish, reeds/birds, red clay, Wm McDonald, 1882, 12".....**850.00**
Pitcher, brn/blk/wht touches w/gilt, Hirschfield, 1883, 5" **400.00**
Pitcher, clouds/bats/reeds, NJ Hirschfield, 1883, 6½x8"...............**500.00**
Plate, swamp scene, sgn EW, no mk, ca 1881, 8¾" **50.00**

Limoges vase, beetles and leafage on oatmeal with gilt, signed Albert Valentien, 1883, 8", $750.00.

Mat

Bowl, emb leaves & violets on gr, Shirayamadani, 1903, 6½" **325.00**
Bowl, pine cones cvd/rtcl, Shirayamadani, 1907, 3x8".................**260.00**
Jug, geometric lines at shoulder, gr/bl, #1113, 1905, 7½" **350.00**
Loving cup, cvd leaves/vines, gr w/red, CA Duell, 1908, 5½"......**475.00**
Vase, Arts & Crafts tulips, cvd/yel on gr, sgn, 1906, 6"................**425.00**
Vase, butterflies cvg, dk tones, CS Todd, #1839, 1913, 6½" **450.00**
Vase, dandelions, emb/gr on bl, A Pons, 1907, 9½"...................**350.00**
Vase, dragonfly cvg, dk bl/brn, SE Coyne, #911E, 1904, 4" **350.00**
Vase, drip band, red/gr on yel, CS Todd, 1902, 7½"....................**250.00**
Vase, eng floral, brn/ivory on gr, E Barrett, 1934, 5½" **175.00**
Vase, ferns, emb/tan/brn on beige, WE Hentschel, 1927, 14"......**600.00**
Vase, flower cvd on bl mottle, WE Hentschel, 1913, 7" **400.00**
Vase, flowers cvd on brn, CS Todd, cylindrical, 1915, 9".............**125.00**
Vase, flowers/leaves cvg, Arts & Crafts, SE Coyne, 1905, 5".......**290.00**
Vase, lg grapevine cvd on brn/gr, A Pons, 1908, 12x8", NM **950.00**
Vase, mum, cvd/red on yel, open vine at top, HE Wilcox, 8".. **1,800.00**
Vase, sea horses/waves cvg, Shirayamadani, ftd, 1905, 11" **3,000.00**
Vase, wisteria on aqua bl, AR Valentien, #907C, 1899, 14x6". **4,750.00**

Porcelain

Bowl, Deco petals/loops/fans, S Sax, 1926, 2½x13" **1,000.00**
Jardiniere, grape band, purple on bl, L Epply, '21, 9x12" **2,300.00**
Lamp base, brn/gr/rose dripping over wht, baluster, 19" **650.00**
Vase, bldg/deer/trees, gr/bl/brn, J Jensen, 1948, 6½" **1,400.00**
Vase, butterfat, birds/flowers, ET Hurley, 1924, 11½"............... **2,500.00**
Vase, butterfat, blk-lined bird/florals, Jensen, 7"...................... **1,300.00**
Vase, butterfat, leaves/berries, EX art, Holkamp, 10" **650.00**
Vase, deer/abstract floral, Deco, E Barrett, 1945, 7" **875.00**
Vase, fish on dk to lt bl, ET Hurley, baluster, 1944, 6½" **1,650.00**

Vase, floral, wht-gray on Chinese plum, HEW, 1926, 7" **1,950.00**
Vase, floral on lt bl, WE Hentschel, 1920, 7" **360.00**
Vase, floral/birds at wide base on cream, L Epply, '25, 10"....... **1,250.00**
Vase, flowers at shoulder on dk bl, S Sax, 1927, 7x4½" **425.00**
Vase, holly, blk on brn, HE Wilcox, #966, 1930, 6x3½" **250.00**
Vase, hydrangeas on rose/tan/bl, Shirayamadani, 1929, 7½" ... **1,800.00**
Vase, llamas, wht/brn on dk bl & brn, J Jensen, 1933, 7" **1,100.00**
Vase, man/woman/horse/dog/trees/birds, E Barrett, 1944, 8" ... **1,400.00**
Vase, nymphs relief on gray, baluster, #2449, 17", pr **1,900.00**
Vase, pansies on bl, unique overglaze, ET Hurley, 1948, 7" **400.00**
Vase, poppies on salmon, Shirayamadani, 1943, 6½" **1,250.00**
Vase, rose vines, pk on wht, MH McDonald, 1943, #6199F, 4" ...**270.00**
Vase, tulips, HM McDonald, amphora in faux mt, 1937, 5½" **600.00**
Vase, 2 parrots, cvd/pnt, Japanese plum, Shirayamadani, 11".. **5,000.00**
Vase, 3 animals/floral, lt brn/rose/wht, J Jensen, '33, 7" **1,250.00**

Sea Green

Vase, daffodil, S Toohey, 1902, 10¾", Xd/M **1,200.00**
Vase, fish/marine life, ET Hurley, baluster, 1904, 7" **1,100.00**
Vase, floral, S Coyne, 1910, 5½", Xd/M **800.00**
Vase, flying geese at neck, AR Valentien, 1895, 10½" **3,750.00**
Vase, hydrangeas on cobalt to gr, EX art, Sara Sax, 1902, 6"... **1,870.00**
Vase, 2 peacock feathers, CA Baker, exhibition label, 7½" **1,400.00**
Vase, 3 sea gulls/ocean waves/foam, SS/G/S1393, 1898, 6" **3,000.00**
Vase, 4 catfish, med/dk gr, S Laurence, ovoid, 1901, 4"........... **1,200.00**
Vase, 5 lg carp, dk bl/ivory on gr to dk bl, M Daly, 12"............ **4,800.00**

Standard

Basket, floral, Shirayamadani, 1889, #360B, 7x10" **850.00**
Creamer & sugar bowl, holly, ADS, #831, 1899, 2", 2½".............**240.00**
Cup, elfin w/tankard, artist monogram, 1891, 3¾".......................**450.00**
Ewer, detailed floral, sage clay, G Young/L, 1888, 62B, 8".........**325.00**
Ewer, holly, J Zettel, 1898, 8" **375.00**
Ewer, silver overlay/hdl, floral, AM Valentien, 1892, 9½" **2,800.00**
Ewer, 4 pigs at trough, silver overlay/hdl, 1891, 12" **13,000.00**
Humidor, bulldog, collar/leash, sgn LNL, 1903, Xd/M **500.00**
Humidor, Indian woman, S Markland, #672, 1898, rpr, 6½" **425.00**
Jug, bearded Dutchman in hat, H Strafer, 1985, 7" **450.00**
Mug, boy holding hat, Harriet Wilcox, 1892, 5" **625.00**
Mug, boy on stick horse, tree, HE Wilcox, #587, 1892, 4½"........**500.00**
Mug, clover, M Mitchell, 1901, end of hdl wraps body, 6" **250.00**
Mug, floral branch, AM Valentien, curving hdl, 1890, 6" **250.00**
Pitcher, clover/grasses, Artus Van Briggle, 1890, 12" **900.00**
Pitcher, floral, sage clay, EX art, AM Valentien, 1889, 8"............**425.00**
Pitcher, tankard; ear of corn, L Asbury, #775, 1898, 8" **500.00**
Plate, mischievous mouse, Wm McDonald, 1893, 7" **250.00**
Tray, 2 pipes/3 cigars, ET Hurley, #305C, 1902, 9" dia **285.00**
Vase, aquatic flowers, AB Sprague, wide body w/hdls, 10"...........**900.00**
Vase, bud; floral, CC Lindeman, #861, 1901, 6" **230.00**
Vase, Buffalo Hunter Shoshone (Indian boy), OG Reed, 10" . **7,000.00**
Vase, cavalier, EX art, Grace Young, 1903, 8½" **1,100.00**
Vase, clover puffs, AM Valentien, squat/flattened, 1888, 5"........**300.00**
Vase, cloverleaves, C Baker, slim trumpet neck, #617C, 10" **350.00**
Vase, cvd/rtcl palm leaves, HR Strafer, 1893, 5x8" **1,000.00**
Vase, daffodils, MA Daly, strap hdls, 1891, 9"..............................**475.00**
Vase, daffodils, MA Daly, 1902, 11"...**600.00**
Vase, daffodils, S Coyne, several labels, 1901, 10" **900.00**
Vase, fish, AR Valentien, boat form, 1887, 12" L **700.00**
Vase, floral, Irene Bishop, #741C, 1905, 6"...................................**275.00**
Vase, floral, S Toohey, sq/bulbous, 1888, 5½" **300.00**
Vase, floral, sgn ML, dbl-gourd form, 1892, 6½x4½".....................**300.00**
Vase, irises, M Nourse, hdls, #604E, 1891, 6" **600.00**

Vase, leaves, EX art, B Horsfall, #488E, 1894, 6½" **525.00**
Vase, leaves, OG Reed, bulbous w/flared rim, 1897, 7", NM **200.00**
Vase, lilies, orange w/gr leaves, Shirayamadani, 1898, 13" **3,700.00**
Vase, lotus/lily pads, AB Sprague, loop hdls, 1898, 12" **1,000.00**
Vase, Nouveau overlay, nasturtiums, L Van Briggle, 1902, 6" . **2,200.00**
Vase, pansies, Constance Baker, fluted rim/long neck, 10" **250.00**
Vase, poppies, I Bishop, 1902, cylindrical, 10" **375.00**
Vase, portrait of African, lg loop hdls, 1897, 12", NM **2,500.00**
Vase, standing Indian, G Young, EX art, #589D, 1899, 12x4". **8,500.00**

Tiger Eye

Ewer, grape clusters/leaves, amber on orange, ARV, 12" **1,800.00**
Vase, 4 turtles swim upward, paper label, slim form, 11" **3,300.00**

Vellum

Vellum plaque, 'Bank of the River,' signed Fred Rothenbush, original frame, 6" x 9", $2,400.00.

Plaque, birchs/hillside, L Asbury, orig fr/bk, 11x6" **1,800.00**
Plaque, birchs/lake, ET Hurley, 1930s, uncrazed, 8x10", M **5,000.00**
Plaque, edge of lake, L Asbury, orig fr, rare oval, 11x8" **1,800.00**
Plaque, edge of pond/trees, SE Coyne, 1921, 6x8".................... **1,400.00**
Plaque, foggy riverbank w/lone tree, 1912, fr, 5¾x7½" **935.00**
Plaque, Poplars, Lorrinda Epply, orig fr/bk, sight: 8x4½" **1,100.00**
Plaque, Ship Anchored, Lagoon; EX art, Schmidt, '21, 6x8" .. **4,900.00**
Plaque, tall pine/forest/tall mtn, S Sax, fr, 9x14" **3,500.00**
Plaque, Winter Sunset, stream/hills, S Coyne, 1929, 9x14" ... **6,500.00**
Plaque, Winter Twilight, dk bl trees, SE Coyne, 1918, 9x11" . **5,750.00**
Vase, apple blossoms on bl to cream, ET Hurley, 1910, 11" **475.00**
Vase, autumnal birches, dk tones, ET Hurley, 1948, 8½" **1,650.00**
Vase, bayou scene, lg trees on bl, C Schmidt, 1923, 10½"....... **3,000.00**
Vase, bluebirds/wildflowers, ET Hurley, ovoid, 1930, 7".......... **1,200.00**
Vase, bud; rose, pk on shaded bl, M McDonald, 1913, 6" **225.00**
Vase, cherry blossoms, E Diers, 1937, 5½"....................................**450.00**
Vase, crocus, lg/detailed, C Schmidt, baluster, 1926, 8½" **2,000.00**
Vase, dusk w/trees & fence, ET Hurley, #1857DV, '04, 9x4" .. **1,100.00**
Vase, fish on pk to bl crackle, LN Lincoln, 1912, 9½" **300.00**
Vase, fish on shaded bl, ET Hurley, 1910, 7"............................. **1,000.00**
Vase, floral (extensive), Ed Diers, 1925, 8" **1,150.00**

Vase, floral band, violet on peach, EF McDermott, 3x8" 500.00
Vase, floral on lav to yel to gr, L Epply, 1909, 6" 600.00
Vase, hyacinth stalks on lav/bl, Shirayamadani, 1908, 14x5".. 2,750.00
Vase, iris, lg/detailed, C Schmidt, 1926, 9¾" 1,500.00
Vase, lotus flower cvg at rim, Shirayamadani, 1904, 6½x5" 6,700.00
Vase, magnolias, lg/pk on shaded bl, L Epply, 1925, 14x5½" .. 2,250.00
Vase, palm trees/lake, E McDermott, 1916, 8" 800.00
Vase, pansies, bl/gr/tan on bl, E Diers, bulbous, 1929, 6" 475.00
Vase, primroses, pk on bl to pk, F Rothenbusch, 1912, 10" 500.00
Vase, rose, lg/pk on pastels, K Van Horne, 1911, 7"....................375.00
Vase, roses/vines, E Diers, 1907, 9"..550.00
Vase, sailboats, Chas Schmidt, 1921, 9½"............................. 1,100.00
Vase, sailboats (lg), C Schmidt, 1921, 10" 2,800.00
Vase, sailboats (lg) in harbor, C Schmidt, 1924, 7¾" 2,400.00
Vase, sailboats (lg) in harbor, E Diers, 1908, 12" 1,600.00
Vase, sailboats at sea, C Schmidt, 1925, 6½" 800.00
Vase, scenic band at middle on brn, Ed Diers, 1912, 9" 750.00
Vase, scenic on gray/bl, Ed Diers, 1910, 9" 700.00
Vase, snow/trees, pk/yel sky, SE Coyne, 1922, 6" 775.00
Vase, snow/trees/vivid pk sky, E McDermott, #1926, '18, 6"........900.00
Vase, spring scene, bl/mauve/pk, Rothenbusch, 1917, 8x4"........900.00
Vase, springtime woodland, E Diers, ftd cylinder, 1921, 8" 800.00
Vase, storks on lt gr, Shirayamadani, 1904, 10½" 1,100.00
Vase, sweet peas on pk to gray, E Noonan, #950E, 1906, 7" 280.00
Vase, trees/moon/river, EX art, S Coyne, #2033, 12x5½" 2,400.00
Vase, trees/river at dusk, SE Coyne, cylindrical, 1913, 9" 900.00
Vase, wht rose w/yel center on bl, E Diers, 1908, 8"....................700.00
Vase, winding road/trees/mtns, C Schmidt, 1914, 7½"........... 1,700.00
Vase, windswept trees, Rothenbusch, baluster, 1915, 11" 850.00
Vase, woodland river on lt & dk bl, E Diers, 1930, 9" 950.00
Vase, 2 trees on gray to lt yel-gr, L Epply, 1911, 7½" 700.00
Vase, 3 cranes cvd/wht on bl, Shirayamadani, 1904, 9" 2,000.00

Wax Mat

Ash tray, frog on side, gr/brn, triangular, 1928, #2765....................90.00
Bookends, rook on shaped base, bl/gr, 1921, 5" 200.00
Bowl, floral on dk/med rust, L Abel, 1926, 2½x5½", Xd/M 220.00
Jar, pk/gr, #2005, 1920, 8" 100.00

Wax Mat pitcher, floral, signed Louise Abel, griffin handle, 1927, large, $675.00.

Vase, floral, bl/yel on pk, S Coyne, 4-lobed, 1926, 12x4" 500.00
Vase, floral, cvd/pnt on purple & pk, C Todd, 1913, 11" 750.00
Vase, floral, red on yel, L Abel, #2963, 1927, 7½" 260.00
Vase, floral, red on yel, L Abel, 1927, 17"................................ 1,200.00
Vase, floral, turq on red, L Abel, #1918, 1924, 8½" 475.00
Vase, floral, yel/red on cream to bl, S Coyne, 1931, 6" 325.00
Vase, floral (simple), E Barrett, 1926, 8" 350.00
Vase, floral branches, pk/yel on aqua, L Abel, 1924, 8½" 350.00
Vase, floral groups, 4-color on dk bl, L Abel, 1921, 9½" 575.00
Vase, geometric, mc on yel/orange, W Rehm, #2237, 1928, 6" ...390.00
Vase, hibiscus, pk/yel on tan, SE Coyne, 1927, 8½" 400.00
Vase, holly, mc glaze, CS Toddy, #826D, 1914, 6½"....................260.00
Vase, hollyhocks, Shirayamadani, EX art, 1939, 10" 2,200.00
Vase, llamas/deer, thick wht, WE Hentschel, #2918, 1929, 7" . 1,050.00
Vase, poppies/geometrics, Shirayamadani, hdls, 1940, 7" 950.00
Vase, roses, brn-lined on yel, J Harris, 1930, 7", Xd/NM 300.00

Miscellaneous

Ash tray, 1926, bl mat, triangular, #2890, 6" 75.00
Ash tray, 1928, sq w/clown sitting on side, S Toohey, 4x4"..........250.00
Ash tray, 1929, ship, gr/pk mat, #6116, 2½x6½" 85.00
Ash tray, 1957, dk brn metallic, #7143, 1x8"..................................30.00
Bookends, 1922, pelican & turtle, brn mat, #2614, 6x7½" 425.00
Bookends, 1924, rook sits on open book, dk gr, 6½x6" 300.00
Bookends, 1930, winged figures kneel, wht mat, W McD, 6x7" ..420.00
Bowl, 1925, gr gloss, ribbed, w/pelican flower frog, 3x13"...........220.00
Bowl, 1927, semi-nude ea end, L Abel mk, #2923, 7x12½" 330.00
Box, 1929, wht, emb Egyptians, figural final, 6½" dia 225.00
Desk set, 1926, bl mat, L Abel, nude paperweight+5 pcs.............600.00
Humidor, 1925, bl mat, 4½x7" 150.00
Paperweight, zebra, L Abel, yel gloss, #6243, 4" 150.00
Paperweight, 1948, duck, yel/gr, 4½" 130.00
Paperweight, 1952, rooster, mc, Wm McDonald, #6030, 5x4" 180.00
Sign, 1957, ribbon-scroll ends, #2788, 4x14" 500.00
Tile, Faience, 3 trees/road/field, cvd/4-color, Duell, 7x9" 2,600.00
Trivet, 1946, horse head, brn on wht, sgn Am Liberty, 6"............140.00
Vase, bud, 1948, lady figural, gr gloss, #2345, 11" 120.00

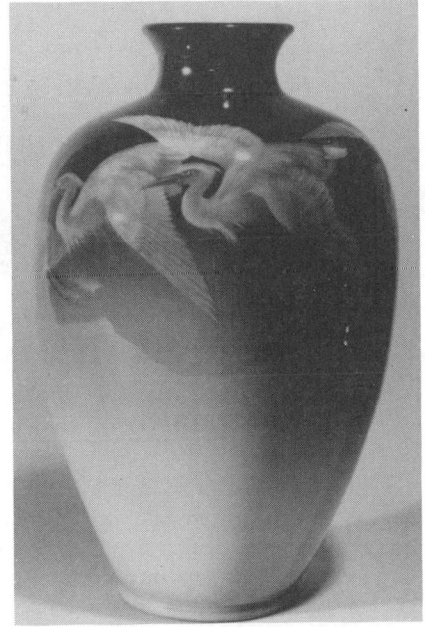

Vase by Carl Schmidt, flock of cranes on shaded green to black ground, drilled base, 16", $8,800.00 at auction.

Vase, bouquet band at shoulder, E Barrett, 1925, 6"....................320.00
Vase, daffodils, EX art, Shirayamadani, 1939, 7"...........................650.00
Vase, dogwood, bl/blk on ivory, J Jensen, #927E, 1931, 7x5".......400.00
Vase, encircling floral branch on aqua, K Jones, 1929, 8x7"........400.00

Vase, gr gloss/orange int, Western Southern 1888-1943, 8" 65.00
Vase, 1884, appl slip flowers on red clay w/gloss, Fry, 6" 600.00
Vase, 1925, butterflies, yel mat, #2072, 6" 65.00

Vase, 1926, wax resist florals, mc on bl, L Abel, 11" 425.00
Vase, 1928, deer/leaves, emb/HP, WE Hentschel, #2918D, 12"...800.00
Vase, 1929, poppies emb, bl on tan clay, #6006, 11½" 180.00
Vase, 1930, dk brn w/irid, classic form, 5" 85.00
Vase, 1930, geometrics, pk/cream w/dk brn drip, Rehm, 7" 350.00
Vase, 1932, bl w/cream drip, tumbler form, 7" 140.00
Vase, 1932, brn w/allover bl crystalline, #6310, 5" 175.00
Vase, 1932, brn w/bl flambe, pk drip & int, #6207, 3" 185.00
Vase, 1932, caramel, bl w/pk drip around top, pk int, 7"..........150.00
Vase, 1932, yel gloss w/bl crystal drip w/in, #6309, 8" 150.00
Vase, 1946, floral/line motif, gr gloss, #6706, 7½" 90.00
Vase, 1946, people, gray/wht w/blk outlines, J Jensen, 7½" 1,550.00

Rorstrand

The Rorstrand Pottery was established in Sweden in 1726 and is today Sweden's oldest existing pottery. The earliest ware, now mostly displayed in Swedish museums, was much like old Delft. Later types were hard-paste porcelains that were enameled and decorated in a peasant style. Contemporary pieces are often described as Swedish Modern. Rorstrand is also famous for their Christmas plates.

Mug, irises, mauve/lav/sea gr, 1900, 6¼" 495.00
Vase, blown-out grapes on wht, leaves form top, rtcl, 13x5"........375.00
Vase, flower on blk, sgn AE 135.00
Vase, magnolia branches on celadon, sgn Algot Erikson, 22" . 2,250.00
Vase, rim shaped w/dandelion heads, tall leaves, 10", NM 800.00

Vase, lavender floral on green and white, baluster form, 9½", $880.00.

Rose Mandarin

Similar in design to Rose Medallion, this Chinese Export porcelain features the pattern of a robed mandarin, often with florals, ladies, genre scenes, or butterflies in polychrome enamels, and sometimes having gold trim. Elaborate in decoration, this pattern was popular from the late 1700s until the early 1840s.

Bowl, fruit; latticework sides, w/11" L undertray.....................1,300.00
Chamberstick, 5½" 400.00
Pitcher, court scene, bulbous, 1850s, 9¾", EX 650.00

Plate, 1920s, 9¾", set of 12.....................................450.00
Punch bowl, w/gilt, 1880s, 6¾x15¾"...............................1,600.00
Vase, celadon, gilt dragon hdls, 16½", VG 450.00

Garden seat, genre scenes, One Hundred Antiques pattern at top, pierced medallions, gilt bosses, ca 1850, hairline, 19", $7,250.00.

Rose Medallion

Rose Medallion is one of the patterns of Chinese export porcelain produced from before 1850 until the second decade of the 20th century. It is decorated in rose colors with panels of florals, birds, and butterflies that form reserves containing Chinese figures. Pre-1850s ware is unmarked and is characterized by quality workmanship and gold trim. From about 1850 until circa 1860, the kilns in Canton did not operate, and no Rose Medallion was made. Post-1860 examples (still unmarked) can often be recognized by the poor quality of the gold trim or its absence. In the 1890s, the ware was often marked 'China'; 'Made in China' was used from 1910 through the 1930s.

Bowl, 1800s, 10" 500.00

Fish bowl, late 1800s, 12" x 14", $850.00.

Chamber pot, button finial on lid, 1880, 7¾" dia, EX................350.00
Fruit basket, rtcl, leaf hdls, 1850s, 9¾x10½", EX 450.00
Fruit platter, shaped rim, ftd, 15x12" 600.00
Jardiniere, 1880, 8¾x10"...650.00
Pitcher, 13" 600.00
Plate, 15" 350.00
Plate, 1800s, 10" 150.00

Plate, 1860s, 8½" 95.00
Platter, mk Made in China, 18" 200.00
Platter, well & tree, 1825, worn, 16½" 350.00
Platter, 6-section design, 16¼" 500.00
Punch bowl, ext/int decor, 1840, 12¾" 1,300.00
Punch bowl, 1830s, 16" 1,650.00
Shrimp dish, shaped panels, floral hdl, 1850s, 10", EX.................450.00
Teapot, wicker hdl, +2 handleless cups in wicker case 250.00
Teapot, 1800s, 6½" 400.00
Tray, quatrefoil, 10½" L...325.00
Umbrella stand, 1800s, 24" 1,900.00
Vase, gold dragon at neck, baluster w/flared neck, 16", pr....... 1,500.00
Vase, gold monkeys at neck, salamanders at shoulder, 24"...........600.00
Vase, many scenes w/figures, 9" 245.00
Vase, 4", pr..100.00
Vase, 6-sided, gold hdls, 6¾" 120.00

Roselane

From the late 1930s until 1973, William and Georgia Fields operated a pottery (first in Pasadena, California; relocating later in Baldwin Park) where they produced various types of novelty items and several lines of bowls, vases, etc. Their ware was sometimes marked with a backstamp (Roselane, Pasadena, Calif.); paper labels were also used.

Figurine, dove, 6", pr 25.00
Figurine, East Indian Dancer, gray, 11" 25.00
Figurine, giraffe, seated, gr, #262, 7"...................15.00
Figurine, roadrunner 15.00
Planter, coolies sit on wall, gray 22.00

Rosemeade

Rosemeade was the name chosen by Wahpeton Pottery Company of Wahpeton, North Dakota, to represent their product. The founders of the company were Laura Meade Taylor and R.J. Hughes, who organized the firm in 1940. It is most noted for small bird and animal figurals, either in high gloss or a Van Briggle-like matt glaze. The ware was marked 'Rosemeade' with an ink stamp or carried a 'Prairie Rose' sticker. The pottery closed in 1961.

Ash tray, mc swirl, 2¼x4" 20.00
Bank, elephant, pk..95.00

Bank, buffalo form, $125.00.

Boot, bl 22.00
Creamer, cow's head, creamery name, pk, 4½" 38.00
Figurine, flamingo..35.00
Figurine, goose, gray, 2", pr 20.00

Flower frog, deer 15.00
Flower frog, fish, bl 25.00
Flower frog, pheasant, mc, 4½" 25.00
Flower frog, stork, 7" 30.00
Hors d'oeuvres, turkey 50.00
Planter, lovebird, dbl 15.00
Planter, squirrel 20.00
Rose bowl, gr shaded, 3" 17.50
Shakers, deer, pr 40.00
Shakers, dogs, orange, sitting up, pr 15.00
Shakers, ducks, orange, pr 25.00
Shakers, fish, tail up, pr 25.00
Shakers, Mexican chihuahuas, pr...........................28.00
Shakers, pelicans, pr 30.00
Shakers, rabbits, pr...25.00
Shakers, raccoons, hands to ears, pr 24.00
Shakers, skunks, pr 20.00
Shakers, tulips, red, pr 22.00
Shakers, turkeys, pr...28.00
Spoon rest, pheasant..29.00
Spoon rest, tulip 27.00
Tumbler, wheat, 5¼" 10.00
Vase, daffodil, dk bl, 4½" 18.00
Vase, fawn, 7½" 20.00
Wall pocket, moon form..10.00
Water can, rabbit 30.00
Wooden shoe 20.00

Rosenthal

In 1879 Phillip Rosenthal established the Rosenthal Porcelain Factory in Selb, Bavaria. Its earliest products were figurines and fine tablewares. The company has continued to operate to the present decade, manufacturing limited edition plates.

Cake plate, mc grapes, scalloped/ruffled edge, 12" 60.00
Creamer & sugar bowl, pate-sur-pate bl cherries 85.00
Cup & saucer, demitasse; Maria 18.00
Ewer, flowers/foliage, mc on dk bl, pottery, spherical, 7" 265.00
Ewer, swags/curving florals overall, mk w/stork, 11" 600.00
Figurine, Boxer dog, old, 9" 240.00

Figural group, marked and signed, 21", $1,100.00.

Figurine, boy dressed as clown..275.00
Figurine, brunette, off-shoulder dress, mandolin, sgn, 17"...........900.00
Figurine, dancers: Hedi/Margot Hopfner in Kaiserwaltz, 12"... 1,300.00
Figurine, elephant, 4½"...26.00
Figurine, fish, wide-eyed, lt bl/gilt/gr, dome base, 9½".................700.00
Figurine, German Shepherd, seated, sgn, 5¾" 150.00
Figurine, nude w/drape on silver base w/gr knop, Wenck, 12" 400.00
Figurine, Oriental dancer, sm Buddha beside, 1919, 16".......... 1,300.00
Figurine, princess & frog, #7333, 11" 275.00
Figurine, princess & frog, 8" 175.00
Figurine, princess by goose, gold egg in hand, Liebermann 225.00
Figurine, stag leaps over bush/2 wolves attack, belleek, 7"..........110.00
Figurine, 2 deer leaping, sgn H Meisel, #d, gr mk, 6½" 315.00
Gravy boat, ivory w/gold borders..55.00
Lamp, yel & wht daisies, HP, 9½".......................................85.00
Mask, frowning man, sgn G Schliepstein, 1920, 9"................ 1,100.00
Mask, lady w/cut-out eyes, arched brows, Schliepstein, 10"..... 1,400.00
Plate, bread & butter; Shadow Rose...................................... 7.00
Platter, Shadow Rose, 12" dia 45.00
Teapot, Shadow Rose...65.00

Roseville

The Roseville Pottery Company was established in 1892 by George F. Young in Roseville, Ohio. Finding their facilities inadequate, the company moved to Zanesville in 1898, erected a new building, and installed the most modern equipment available. By 1900 Young felt ready to enter into the stiffly competitive art pottery market.

Roseville's first art line was called Rozane. Similar to Rookwood's Standard, Rozane featured dark blended backgrounds with slip-painted underglaze artwork of nature studies, portraits, birds, and animals. Azurean, developed in 1902, was a blue and white underglaze art line on a blue blended background. Egypto (1904) featured a matt glaze in a soft shade of old green and was modeled in low relief after examples of ancient Egyptian pottery. Mongol (1904) was a high-gloss oxblood red line after the fashion of the Chinese Sang de Boeuf. Mara (1904), an iridescent lustre line of magenta and rose with intricate patterns developed on the surface or in low relief, successfully duplicated Sicardo's work. These early lines were followed by many others of highest quality: Fudjiyama and Woodland (1905-06) reflected an Oriental theme; Crystalis (1906) was covered with beautiful frost-like crystals. Della Robbia, their most famous line (introduced in 1906), was decorated with designs ranging from florals, animals, and birds to scenes of Viking warriors and Roman gladiators. These designs were accomplished by sgraffito with slip-painted details. Very limited but of great importance to collectors today, Rozane Olympic (1905) was decorated with scenes of Greek mythology on a red ground. Pauleo (1914) was the last of the artware lines. It was varied – over two hundred glazes were recorded – and some pieces were decorated by hand, usually with florals.

During the second decade of the century until the plant closed forty years later, new lines were continually added. Some of the more popular of the middle-period lines were Donatello, 1915; Futura, 1928; Pine Cone, 1931; and Blackberry, 1933. The floral lines of the later years have become highly collectible. Pottery from every era of Roseville production – even its utility ware – attest to an unwavering dedication to quality and artistic merit.

Examples of the fine art pottery lines present the greatest challenge to evaluate. Scarcity is a prime consideration. The quality of artwork varied from one artist to another. Some pieces show fine detail and good color, and naturally this influences their values. Studies of animals and portraits bring higher prices than the floral designs. An artist's signature often increases the value of any item, especially if the artist is one who is well recognized. For further information, consult

The Collector's Encyclopedia of Roseville Pottery, First and Second Series, by Sharon and Bob Huxford.

Our advisors for this category are Janet and Marvin Stofft; they are listed in the Directory under Indiana.

Apple Blossom, basket, #311, 12" 125.00
Apple Blossom, bud vase, hdls, #379, 7" 35.00
Apple Blossom, ewer, #316, 8" 70.00
Apple Blossom, hanging basket 90.00
Apple Blossom, tea set, #371, 3-pc......................................175.00
Apple Blossom, vase, hdls, #381, 6".....................................40.00
Azurean, mug, cherries, sgn/#856.......................................350.00
Azurean, vase, leaves, tiny neck, squat, #80, 3x4½"..................280.00
Baneda, console, hdls, red, 13"...150.00
Baneda, jardiniere, hdls, red, 9½" 300.00
Baneda, vase, red, 5½" 100.00
Bittersweet, basket, #810, 10"...80.00
Bittersweet, cornucopia, #882, 8" 45.00
Bittersweet, ewer, #816, 8" 60.00
Bittersweet, planter, #868, 8" 40.00
Bittersweet, tea set, #871, 3-pc...150.00
Bittersweet, vase, hdls, #883, 8" 55.00
Bittersweet, vase, hdls, #972, 5" 35.00
Blackberry, console bowl, hdls, 13" 175.00
Blackberry, jardiniere, hdls, 6"..200.00
Blackberry, jug, 5"...150.00
Blackberry, vase, hdls, 12½" 400.00
Blackberry, vase, hdls, 4" 110.00
Blackberry, wall pocket, 8¾"..325.00
Bleeding Heart, basket, #360, 10" 125.00
Bleeding Heart, basket, #361, 12" 140.00
Bleeding Heart, ewer, #963, 6"...60.00
Bleeding Heart, ewer, #972, 10"..100.00
Bleeding Heart, pitcher, #1323 ....115.00
Bleeding Heart, vase, hdls, #138, 4"....................................40.00
Burmese, candle holders/bookends, #70-B, blk, pr 160.00
Burmese, candlestick, #75-B, pr 30.00
Bushberry, basket, #372, 12"..165.00
Bushberry, bowl, hdls, #411, 4" 40.00
Bushberry, cornucopia, #153, 6" 35.00
Bushberry, ewer, #1, 6" 50.00
Bushberry, tea set, #2, 3-pc...175.00
Bushberry, wall pocket, #1291, 8" 125.00
Cherry Blossom, bowl, hdls, 5"..135.00
Cherry Blossom, candle holders, hdls, 4", pr...........................175.00
Cherry Blossom, jug vase, hdls, 7"......................................175.00
Cherry Blossom, lamp base..375.00
Cherry Blossom, vase, baluster, 7"......................................175.00
Cherry Blossom, vase, slim form w/hdls, 7½"...........................150.00
Clematis, basket, #388, 8" 50.00
Clematis, basket, #389, 10" 75.00
Clematis, bowl, hdls, #445, 4" 20.00
Clematis, bud vase, hdls, #187, 7" 30.00
Clematis, cookie jar, #3, 10" 125.00
Clematis, cornucopia, #140, 6"...20.00
Clematis, tea set, #5, 3-pc...125.00
Clematis, vase, hdls, #108, 8" 35.00
Clematis, wall pocket, #1295, 8"..80.00
Columbine, basket, #365, 7"..75.00
Columbine, bowl, hdls, #401, 6"...35.00
Columbine, bowl, hdls, #655, 3"...30.00
Columbine, vase, hdls, #20, 8"...40.00
Corinthian, ash tray..55.00
Corinthian, bud vase, dbl, 7" 35.00

Corinthian, compote, 10" dia 60.00
Corinthian, vase, cylindrical, 8" 40.00
Corinthian, vase, wide shoulder, 6" 48.00
Corinthian, vase, 10½" 80.00
Cosmos, basket, bl, 12" 150.00
Cosmos, bowl, #376, 6" 55.00
Cosmos, candle holders, bl, 2½", pr 60.00
Cosmos, ewer, bl, #951, 15" 175.00
Cosmos, vase, #954, 4" 25.00
Crystalis, vase, gr w/crystals, bulbous neck/wide base, 12" 400.00
Crystalis, vase, orange-red crystalline, hdld urn form, 8½" 600.00
Dahlrose, bowl, hdls, 10" 70.00
Dahlrose, bud vase, dbl 50.00
Dahlrose, vase, hdls, 10" 125.00
Dahlrose, vase, hdls, 8" 90.00
Dahlrose, vase, sq, 10" 95.00
Dahlrose, vase, sq, 6" 80.00
Dawn, vase, #826, 6" 50.00
Dawn, vase, #828, 8" 60.00
Dogwood I, vase, 6" 85.00
Dogwood I, wall pocket 125.00
Donatello, jardiniere & pedestal 500.00
Egypto, gate form 35.00
Egypto, pot & liner, 4" 35.00
Egypto, vase, flanged/conical, 3-toed base, 12" 250.00
Egypto, vase, floral emb, bulbous cylinder, seal, 15" ...800.00
Elsie the Cow, bowl, #B3 ....95.00
Elsie the Cow, mug, #B1 ....110.00
Elsie the Cow, plate, #B2, 7½" 150.00
Falline, lamp 450.00
Falline, vase, hdls, 6" 200.00
Falline, vase, hdls, 7" 225.00
Ferella, bowl, red, 12" 225.00
Ferella, console bowl, brn, ftd, 6x12½" 200.00
Ferella, vase, brn, 4" 150.00
Ferella, vase, hdls, brn, 9" 250.00
Ferella, vase, red, 9" 250.00
Florentine, bowl, 9" dia 40.00
Florentine, bud vase, dbl, 6" 50.00
Florentine, compote, ftd, 10" 60.00
Florentine II, sand jar 275.00
Foxglove, candle holder, #1150, 4½", pr 45.00
Foxglove, conch shell, #426, 6" 35.00
Foxglove, cornucopia, #164, 8" 35.00
Foxglove, ewer, #4, 6½" 45.00
Foxglove, ewer, #5, 10" 90.00
Foxglove, vase, hdls, #42, 4" 25.00
Freesia, basket, #391, 8" 80.00
Freesia, bookends, #15, pr 90.00
Freesia, bud vase, #195, 7" 35.00
Freesia, cookie jar, #4, 10" 125.00
Freesia, cornucopia, #198, 8" 30.00
Freesia, ewer, #19, 6" 50.00
Freesia, flowerpot, #670, 5" 40.00
Freesia, pitcher, #20, 10" 65.00
Freesia, tea set, #6, 3-pc 150.00
Freesia, vase, hdls, #122, 8" 60.00
Fuchsia, bowl, hdls, #346, 4" 45.00
Fuchsia, pitcher, #1322, 8" 175.00
Fuchsia, vase, #645, 3" 35.00
Fuchsia, vase, hdls, #895, 7" 75.00
Fuchsia, vase, hdls, #903, 12" 150.00
Futura, bud vase, stacked cones, brn w/mc triangles, 10" 180.00
Futura, hanging basket, M 285.00

Futura, vase, beehive form, tan w/molded gr leaves, 8" 400.00
Futura, vase, stack neck, angle body, long upright hdls, 7" 195.00
Futura, vase, 3-sided cylinder & base, dk/lt bl, 8" 350.00

Futura vases, either style, about $150.00.

Gardenia, basket, #609, 10" 95.00
Gardenia, bowl, #600, 4" 30.00
Gardenia, cornucopia, #621, 6" 35.00
Gardenia, ewer, #616, 6" 50.00
Imperial I, umbrella stand 300.00
Iris, basket, #354, 8" 100.00
Iris, bowl, hdls, #359, 5" 60.00
Iris, planter, #364, 14" 75.00
Iris, vase, #914, 4" 40.00
Iris, wall shelf, 8" 200.00
Ivory II, bowl, Matt Color shape, #550, 6" 30.00
Ivory II, bowl vase, Russco shape, #259, 6" 35.00
Ivory II, candelabra, 5-branch, #1116, 5½", pr 150.00
Ivory II, vase, Carnelian shape, hdls, 10" 50.00
Ixia, basket, #346, 10" 70.00
Ixia, bowl, #387, 6" 50.00
Ixia, vase, #853, 6" 30.00
Jonquil, basket, 9" 150.00
Jonquil, bowl, hdls, 4" 50.00
Jonquil, bowl, hdls, 5½" 60.00
Jonquil, vase, hdls, 8" 95.00
La Rose, bowl, 6" 35.00
La Rose, vase, 10" 125.00
Laurel, bowl, gr, 7" 50.00
Laurel, vase, gold, 6" 70.00
Laurel, vase, gr, 8" 60.00
Luffa, bowl, gr, 4" 50.00
Luffa, vase, brn, 7" 80.00
Luffa, vase, gr, 6" 70.00
Magnolia, cider pitcher, #132, 7" 155.00
Magnolia, cookie jar, #2, 10" 150.00
Magnolia, ewer, #15, 15" 200.00
Magnolia, mug, #3, 3" 60.00
Magnolia, planter, hdls, #389, 8" 50.00
Magnolia, tea set, #4, 3-pc 125.00
Magnolia, vase, #86, 4" 30.00
Mayfair, bowl, #1110, 4" 25.00
Mayfair, pitcher, #1105, 8" 60.00
Mayfair, planter, #1113, 8" 30.00
Mayfair, tankard, #1107, 12" 75.00

Ming Tree, candle holders, #551, pr.................................35.00
Ming Tree, console bowl, hdls, #528, 10".............60.00
Ming Tree, ewer, #516, 10"......................................85.00
Ming Tree, vase, hdls, #582, 8"...............................50.00

Ming Tree basket, #509, 12", $150.00.

Mock Orange, bowl, #900, 4".....................................25.00
Mock Orange, ewer, #916, 6"....................................50.00
Mock Orange, planter, tall, sq..................................45.00
Moderne, lamp, #799, 9"..125.00
Moderne, vase, #794, 7"..35.00
Monticello, basket, bl, 6½"......................................175.00
Monticello, vase, brn, 4"..60.00
Morning-Glory, bowl vase, hdls, 4"......................150.00
Morning-Glory, vase, hdls, 8"................................225.00
Morning-Glory, vase, 12"...325.00
Morning-Glory, vase, 7"...175.00
Mostique, jardiniere & pedestal............................300.00
Mostique, umbrella stand..250.00
Panel, bud vase, dbl...60.00
Panel, fan vase, nude, 6"..185.00
Panel, fan vase, nude, 8"..225.00
Panel, vase, pillow form, 6"......................................65.00
Pasadena, bowl, #L24, 3"..35.00
Pasadena, occasional pc, #526, 7"...........................25.00
Peony, basket, #378, 10"..75.00
Peony, bowl, hdls, #427, 4".......................................25.00
Peony, ewer, #7, 6"...35.00
Peony, tea set, #3, 3-pc...125.00
Peony, vase, hdls, #168, 6".......................................30.00
Peony, vase, hdls, #57, 4"...25.00
Peony, wall pocket, #1293, 8"...................................80.00
Persian, jardiniere, orange band/stylized motif, 6x7"......215.00
Pine Cone, basket, #338, brn, 10".........................200.00
Pine Cone, basket, #408, gr, 6"................................75.00
Pine Cone, boat basket, #410, bl, 10"..................225.00
Pine Cone, bowl, #632, brn, 3".................................50.00
Pine Cone, console bowl, #323, brn, 15".............150.00
Pine Cone, cornucopia, #128, gr, 8".......................55.00
Pine Cone, fan vase, #472, brn, 6"..........................90.00
Pine Cone, planter, #468, brn, 8".............................70.00

Pine Cone, umbrella stand 800.00
Pine Cone, vase, #478, brn, 7"..................................60.00
Poppy, basket, #347, 10"..100.00
Poppy, ewer, #876, 10"...100.00
Poppy, vase, 6½"...60.00
Primrose, bowl, 4"...40.00
Primrose, vase, #765, 8"..70.00
Raymor, bean pot, #195...25.00
Raymor, dinner plate, #152, wht.............................. 8.00
Raymor, salad plate, #154, brn................................. 5.00
Rosecraft Hexagon, vase, bowl form, 4"................85.00
Rosecraft Hexagon, vase, 6"....................................90.00
Rosecraft Vintage, candlestick, 8", pr..................150.00
Rosecraft Vintage, vase, 5"......................................60.00
Rozane, bowl, #927, 2½"..100.00
Rozane, ewer, floral, #852/RP Co, 4½"................130.00
Rozane, jug, floral, #888, 4x5"...............................120.00
Rozane, jug, 7"...265.00
Rozane, tobacco jar, 6"...550.00
Rozane, vase, pillow form, #882, 9"................... 2,775.00
Rozane, vase, 14"...285.00
Rozane Pattern, bud vase, #2, 6".............................30.00
Rozane Pattern, planter, #397, 14".........................35.00
Rozane Pattern, vase, hdls, #398, 6".......................35.00
Rozane 1917, basket, ivory, 11"...............................90.00
Rozane 1917, basket, pk, 6"......................................60.00
Rozane 1917, candlestick, bl, 6", pr.........................65.00
Rozane 1917, compote, gr, 5"...................................70.00
Rozane 1917, spittoon, ivory, 5".............................150.00
Rozane 1917, vase, yel, 7"...50.00
Silhouette, ash tray, #799, turq...............................30.00
Silhouette, basket, #708, turq, 6"............................70.00

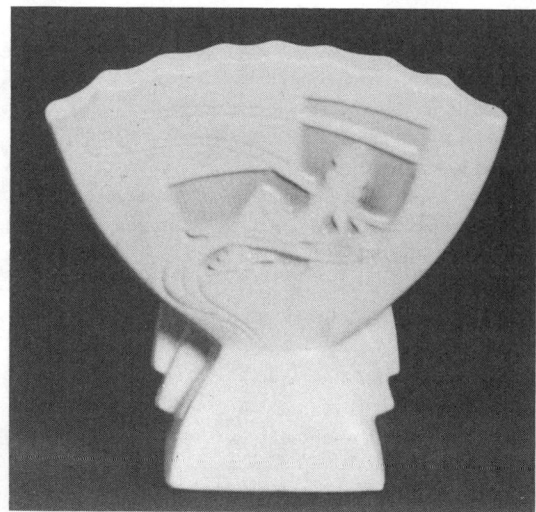

Silhouette, fan vase with nude, #783, 7", $175.00.

Silhouette, basket, #710, rose, 10"..........................50.00
Silhouette, cigarette box, rose.................................35.00
Silhouette, cornucopia, #721, wht, 8".....................30.00
Silhouette, ewer, #716, turq, 6"................................40.00
Silhouette, planter, #731, wht, 14"..........................40.00
Silhouette, vase, #782, brn, 7".................................30.00
Snowberry, ash tray..40.00
Snowberry, basket, #1BK, 7"....................................35.00
Snowberry, bud vase, #1BV, 7"................................30.00
Snowberry, candle holders, #1CS-1, pr...................25.00

Snowberry, console bowl, hdls, #1BL1, 10" 25.00
Snowberry, ewer, #1TK, 6" 45.00
Sunflower, jardiniere, 9" 250.00
Sunflower, vase, 10" 225.00
Sunflower, vase, 6" 90.00
Sunflower, vase, 8" 200.00
Teasel, basket, #349, 10" 100.00
Teasel, bowl, #342, 4" 30.00
Teasel, vase, #348, 6" 35.00
Teasel, vase, hdls, 5" 30.00
Tourmaline, ginger jar 300.00
Tourmaline, planter, bl, 5x12½" 85.00
Tourmaline, vase, bl, 8" 60.00
Tourmaline, vase, hdls, bl, 6" 50.00
Tuscany, candle holders, 4", pr 35.00
Tuscany, console bowl, 11" 40.00
Velmoss II, vase, hdls, bl, 6" 60.00
Velmoss II, vase, hdls, gr, 7" 50.00
Velmoss Scroll, bowl, 2½x9" 50.00
Velmoss Scroll, candlestick, 8", pr 125.00
Velmoss Scroll, compote, 9" dia 80.00
Velmoss Scroll, jardiniere & pedestal, 30" 900.00
Velmoss Scroll, vase, 6" 75.00
Water Lily, basket, #380, 8" 60.00
Water Lily, bowl, hdls, #663, 3" 25.00
Water Lily, cookie jar, #1, 10" 125.00
Water Lily, cornucopia, #178, 8" 40.00
Water Lily, ewer, #10, 6" 35.00
Water Lily, ewer, #12, 15" 175.00
Water Lily, vase, hdls, #81, 12" 80.00
White Rose, basket, #363, 10" 90.00
White Rose, basket, #364, 12" 90.00
White Rose, bowl, hdls, #653, 3" 30.00
White Rose, cornucopia, #143, 6" 25.00
White Rose, ewer, #981, 6" 50.00
White Rose, ewer, #990, 10" 125.00
White Rose, pitcher, #1324 ....70.00
White Rose, tea set, #1-T, 3-pc 150.00
Wincraft, basket, #209, 12" 70.00
Wincraft, circle vase, #1053, 8" 50.00
Wincraft, cornucopia, #222, 8" 22.00
Wincraft, planter set, #1050-51, 6", 3-pc 35.00
Wincraft, tea set, #271, 3-pc 100.00
Wincraft, vase, #282, 8" 35.00
Wisteria, bowl, hdls, 4" 125.00
Wisteria, console bowl, hdls, 12" 150.00
Wisteria, vase, hdls, 10" 275.00
Zephyr Lily, ash tray 35.00
Zephyr Lily, basket, #393, 7" 50.00
Zephyr Lily, bowl, hdls, #671, 4" 30.00
Zephyr Lily, console boat, #475, 10" 40.00
Zephyr Lily, cookie jar, #5, 10" 125.00
Zephyr Lily, cornucopia, #203, 6" 35.00
Zephyr Lily, tea set, #7, 3-pc 150.00
Zephyr Lily, vase, #137, 10" 60.00
Zephyr Lily, vase, hdls, #131, 7" 35.00

Rowland and Marsellus

Though the impressive backstamp seems to suggest otherwise, Rowland and Marsellus were not Staffordshire potters but American importers who commissioned various English companies to supply them with the blue-printed historical ware that had been a popular import

item since the early 1800s. Plates (both flat and with a rolled edge), cups and saucers, pitchers, and platters were sold as souvenirs from 1890 through the 1930s. Though other importers – Bawo & Dotter, and A. C. Bosselman & Co., both of New York City – commissioned the manufacture of similar souvenir items, by far the largest volume carries the R. & M. mark, and Rowland and Marsellus has become a generic term that covers all 20th-century souvenir china of this type. Their mark may be in full or 'R. & M.' in a diamond.

Our advisor for this category is David Ringering; he is listed in the Directory under California.

Key:
s/o — souvenir of   v/o — view of

Rolled edge 10" plate: Tacoma, Washington, Mt. Tacoma (now Mt. Rainier) in center, $55.00.

Plate, Albany NY, s/o, Fort Frederick, State St in 1775, 10" 50.00
Plate, Asbury Park NJ, v/o, Casino, rolled edge, 10" 50.00
Plate, Boston MS, s/o, NY & Brooklyn Bridge, rolled edge, 10" ...45.00
Plate, Butte MT, s/o, Tremont St Mall, rolled edge, 10" 60.00
Plate, Charles Dickens, portrait, rolled edge, 10" 55.00
Plate, Cleveland OH, s/o, Garfield Memorial, rolled edge, 10" 45.00
Plate, Golden Rule Co, co store, rolled edge, 10" 55.00
Plate, Lake Champlain, s/o, Au Sable Chasm, rolled edge, 10" 50.00
Plate, Lewis & Clark Centennial, portrait w/Sacagawea, 10" 55.00
Plate, Mobile AL, s/o, courthouse/Government St, rolled edge.....55.00
Plate, New York NY, s/o, Statue of Liberty, rolled edge, 10" 50.00
Plate, Pittsburgh, s/o, Allegheny Co Courthouse, rolled edge........50.00
Plate, Plymouth Rock MS, s/o, landing of the pilgrims, 10"...........45.00
Plate, Robert Burns, portrait, rolled edge, 10" 55.00
Plate, Syracuse NY, s/o, Indian portrait, rolled edge, 10" 55.00
Plate, Wm Howard Taft/J Sherman, 2 portraits, rolled edge, 10" ...65.00

Royal Bayreuth

Founded in 1794 in Tettau, Bavaria, the Royal Bayreuth firm originally manufactured fine dinnerwares of superior quality. Their figural items, produced from before the turn of the century until the onset of WWI, are highly sought after by today's collectors. Perhaps the most abundantly produced and easily recognized of these are the tomato and lobster pieces. Fruits, flowers, people, animals, birds, and vegetables shapes were also made. Aside from figural items, pitchers, toothpick holders, cups and saucers, humidors and the like were decorated in florals and scenic motifs. Some, such as the very popular Rose Tapestry line, utilized a cloth-like tapestry background. Transfer prints were used as well. Two of the most popular are Sunbonnet Babies and Nursery Rhymes (in particular, those decorated with the complete verse).

Caution: Many pieces were not marked; some were marked 'Deponiert' or 'Registered' only. While marked pieces are the most valued, unmarked items are still very worthwhile.

Our advisors for this category are Larry Brenner from New Hampshire and Dee Hooks from Illinois; they are listed in the Directory under their home states.

Figurals

Ash tray, lobster, bl mk, 6"	42.00
Bowl, cache; oyster & pearl, bl mk, 2x3¾"	57.00
Bowl, lobster, bl mk, w/lid, 4½"	85.00
Bowl, pansy, yel, bl mk, 9"	300.00
Box, card; Devil & Cards, bl mk, scarce	195.00
Candle holder, basset hound, bl mk	335.00
Candle holder, dachshund, bl mk, 4½"	250.00
Celery dish, lobster, bl mk	125.00
Chamberstick, elk, bl mk,7½x4½"	295.00
Chocolate pot, poppy, yel, bl mk	525.00
Cracker jar, poppy, MOP, unmk	350.00
Cup & saucer, coffee; rose, pk, bl mk	265.00
Cup & saucer, demitasse; Devil & Cards, unmk	165.00
Cup & saucer, demitasse; oyster & pearl, bl mk	145.00
Cup & saucer, demitasse; shell, bl mk	90.00
Cup & saucer, Devil & Cards, unmk	175.00
Hatpin holder, dachshund, bl mk	350.00
Hatpin holder, owl, bl mk	475.00
Hatpin holder, poppy, red, bl mk	325.00
Inkwell, elk, bl mk, 2x5"	200.00
Match holder, chimpanzee, wall hanging, bl mk	355.00
Match holder, clown, wall hanging, bl mk	275.00
Mustard, conch shell, bl mk	65.00
Mustard, grapes, wht MOP, bl mk, w/undertray	145.00
Mustard, poppy, red, bl mk & Deponiert, w/spoon	155.00
Pitcher, alligator, bl mk, cream sz	275.00
Pitcher, apple, bl mk, cream sz	150.00
Pitcher, apple, bl mk, cream sz, +sugar bowl, apple, bl mk	300.00
Pitcher, apple, bl mk, lemonade sz, rare	550.00
Pitcher, Art Nouveau, bl mk, cream sz	525.00
Pitcher, bass, bl mk, cream sz	165.00
Pitcher, bear, bl mk, cream sz, rare	625.00
Pitcher, bellringer, bl mk, cream sz	235.00
Pitcher, bull, brn, bl mk, cream sz	160.00

Pitcher, Bell Ringer, marked, 7", $895.00.

Pitcher, bull, red, bl mk, cream sz	150.00
Pitcher, butterfly, wings closed, milk sz	425.00
Pitcher, butterfly, wings open, bl mk, cream sz	295.00
Pitcher, cat, blk, bl mk, cream sz	150.00
Pitcher, cat, calico, bl mk, cream sz	225.00
Pitcher, chick, bl mk, milk sz	350.00
Pitcher, chrysanthemum, pk, bl mk, cream sz	225.00
Pitcher, clown, red, bl mk, cream sz	175.00
Pitcher, coachman, bl mk, cream sz	175.00
Pitcher, coachman, bl mk, water sz	435.00
Pitcher, cockatoo, bl mk, cream sz	325.00
Pitcher, conch shell, lobster hdl, bl mk, water sz	235.00
Pitcher, conch shell, MOP, bl mk, cream sz	55.00
Pitcher, cow's head, brn, bl mk, cream sz, 4"	75.00
Pitcher, crow, blk, bl mk, cream sz	145.00
Pitcher, dachshund, bl mk, cream sz	180.00
Pitcher, dachshund, unmk, water sz	425.00
Pitcher, devil, red, bl mk, cream sz	225.00
Pitcher, Devil & Cards, bl mk, cream sz	145.00
Pitcher, Devil & Cards, bl mk, milk sz	225.00
Pitcher, Devil & Cards, gr mk, 5½"	225.00
Pitcher, Devil & Cards, left-hand, bl mk, 7"	425.00
Pitcher, duck, bl mk, cream sz	145.00
Pitcher, duck, bl mk, water sz	360.00
Pitcher, duck, mk Deponiert, cream sz	125.00
Pitcher, duck, mk Deponiert, milk sz	160.00
Pitcher, eagle, bl mk, cream sz	195.00
Pitcher, eagle, bl mk, milk sz	230.00
Pitcher, elk, bl mk, cream sz	90.00
Pitcher, fish head, bl mk, cream sz	145.00
Pitcher, fish head, unmk, cream sz	85.00
Pitcher, frog, gr, bl mk, cream sz	185.00
Pitcher, girl w/pitcher, red, bl mk, cream sz	275.00
Pitcher, grapes, bl mk, cream sz, +sugar bowl, grapes, bl mk	180.00
Pitcher, grapes, unmk, cream sz	90.00
Pitcher, lamplighter, bl mk, cream sz	180.00
Pitcher, lemon, bl mk, cream sz	145.00
Pitcher, leopard, bl mk, cream sz, rare	750.00
Pitcher, lettuce leaf & lobster, bl mk, cream sz	85.00
Pitcher, lobster, bl mk, cream sz	95.00
Pitcher, maple leaf, bl mk, cream sz	225.00
Pitcher, melon, bl mk, cream sz	175.00
Pitcher, monkey, bl mk, cream sz	250.00
Pitcher, monkey, gr, bl mk, milk sz	385.00
Pitcher, mountain goat, bl mk, cream sz	250.00
Pitcher, mouse, bl mk, cream sz	650.00
Pitcher, murex shell, bl mk, cream sz	100.00
Pitcher, murex shell, MOP, bl mk, cream sz	125.00
Pitcher, oak leaf, bl mk, cream sz	135.00
Pitcher, oak leaf, MOP, bl mk, cream sz	165.00
Pitcher, Old Man of the Mountain, bl mk, cream sz	180.00
Pitcher, orange, bl mk, cream sz	125.00
Pitcher, oyster & pearl, bl mk, cream sz	165.00
Pitcher, pansy, bl mk, cream sz	150.00
Pitcher, parakeet, bl mk, cream sz	220.00
Pitcher, parakeet, unmk, cream sz	140.00
Pitcher, parrot, unmk, water sz	325.00
Pitcher, pelican, bl mk, cream sz	195.00
Pitcher, pig, gray, bl mk, cream sz	495.00
Pitcher, poodle, gray, bl mk, cream sz	225.00
Pitcher, poppy, red, bl mk & Deponiert, cream sz	160.00
Pitcher, poppy, wht, bl mk, cream sz	135.00
Pitcher, robin, bl mk, cream sz	175.00
Pitcher, robin, unmk, 4"	110.00

Pitcher, rooster, bl mk, cream sz 225.00
Pitcher, seal, bl mk, cream sz 225.00
Pitcher, St Bernard, bl mk, cream sz............................195.00
Pitcher, St Bernard, bl mk, milk sz 245.00
Pitcher, St Bernard, bl mk, water sz 450.00
Pitcher, strawberry, bl mk, cream sz 150.00
Pitcher, strawberry, bl mk, milk sz 185.00
Pitcher, strawberry, unmk, cream sz 85.00
Pitcher, sunflower, bl mk, cream sz 295.00
Pitcher, tomato, bl mk, cream sz 65.00
Pitcher, tomato, bl mk, milk sz 170.00
Pitcher, tomato, unmk, cream sz 45.00
Pitcher, turtle, bl mk, cream sz 275.00
Pitcher, water buffalo, bl mk, cream sz 165.00
Pitcher, water buffalo, unmk, 3¾" 85.00
Plate, lettuce leaf, yel flowers, ring hdl, bl mk, 7" 40.00
Shakers, bellringer, unmk, pr 235.00
Shakers, conch shell, bl mk, pr......................................45.00
Shakers, conch shell, MOP, unmk, pr 30.00
Shakers, elk, bl mk, ea 70.00
Shakers, tomato, unmk, pr 40.00
String holder, rooster, wall hanging, bl mk, rare 225.00
Sugar bowl, grape, purple, w/lid, unmk 70.00
Sugar bowl, tomato, w/lid, unmk.....................................40.00
Teapot, apple, bl mk 145.00
Teapot, tomato, bl mk, ftd 105.00
Toothpick holder, Art Nouveau, wht satin, bl mk................275.00
Toothpick holder, elk head, bl mk 95.00
Tray, bread; oak leaf, bl mk, rare 185.00
Tray, dresser; Devil & Cards, bl mk.................................350.00
Tureen, rose, oval, w/lid, bl mk, 6" 250.00

Florals, Scenics, and Series Ware

Basket, Rose Tapestry, 3-color, bl mk, 4x4x2½" 345.00
Basket, Violet Tapestry, bl mk......................................200.00
Bell, Nursery Rhyme, Ring Around the Rosies, bl mk 295.00
Bell, Rose Tapestry, 3-color on gr w/gold, orig clapper 495.00
Bell, Sunbonnet Babies, fishing, bl mk, orig wood clapper 595.00
Bowl, Rose Tapestry, gold border, bl mk, 10½" 135.00
Box, Little Jack Horner, bl mk, kidney shape 125.00
Box, man & lady tapestry, 3-ftd, mk, 4" dia.....................175.00
Box, pheasant & water tapestry, oval, blk mk....................275.00
Box, Rose Tapestry, 3-color, kidney shape, bl mk, 2x4¾x3".........365.00
Box, Snow Babies, bl mk, kidney shape 125.00
Box, stamp; donkey & boy, bl mk, 2x3¾" 85.00
Box, trinket; Jack & the Beanstalk, sq, bl mk, 2½" 115.00
Box, trinket; Sand Babies, bl mk...................................125.00
Candlestick, Sunbonnet Babies, bl mk, 4"..........................175.00
Chamberstick, Devil & Cards, bl mk................................325.00
Chamberstick, Nursery Rhymes, Jack Horner, bl mk 155.00
Chamberstick, Sunbonnet Babies, washing, shield bk, bl mk 425.00
Desk set, Ring Around the Rosies, bl mk, child's, 8-pc 950.00
Dish, Chrysanthemum Tapestry, leaf form, bl mk, 6¾x6¼" 195.00
Dish, Rose Tapestry, leaf form, bl mk 180.00
Flowerpot, Rose Tapestry, bl mk, 2-pc, 4" 550.00
Flowerpot, Sunbonnet Babies, ironing, bl mk, w/insert, 4" 495.00
Hair receiver, goose girl, bl mk...................................125.00
Hair receiver, Rose Tapestry, 3-color, bl mk....................195.00
Hair receiver, Sunbonnet Babies, washing, bl mk.................525.00
Hatpin holder, courting couple tapestry w/gold, bl mk 395.00
Hatpin holder, Rose Tapestry, bl mk, 4½".........................395.00
Humidor, pk roses on lt bl, bl mk 125.00
Match holder, Sunbonnet Babies, sewing, wall hanging, bl mk ...495.00

Mug, yel roses, bl mk, lg 50.00
Nappy, Sunbonnet Babies, bl mk 300.00
Nut cup, Rose Tapestry, 3-color, gr mk, 1¾x3¼" 160.00
Pitcher, floral, bl mk, bulbous, 11" 150.00
Pitcher, girl & 3 geese in pastoral scene, 4" 65.00
Pitcher, goat tapestry, pinched spout, bl mk, cream sz 235.00
Pitcher, hunt scene, bl mk, 3¼" 65.00
Pitcher, musicians, cream sz, +sugar bowl, musicians, bl mk 105.00
Pitcher, Rose Tapestry, bl mk, cream sz, 3½" 255.00
Pitcher, Rose Tapestry, bl mk, milk sz, 5" 285.00
Pitcher, Rose Tapestry, 3-color, tankard, bl mk, cream sz 300.00
Pitcher, Rose Tapestry w/gold, pinched spout, unmk, 4½" 175.00
Pitcher, Sunbonnet Babies, bl mk, milk sz 380.00
Pitcher, Sunbonnet Babies, cleaning, bl mk, 4¼" 235.00
Pitcher, tapestry portrait, mk, 3½" 150.00
Pitcher, 3 cows in pastoral scene, mk, 4" 65.00
Plate, boy w/2 donkeys, farmhouse at bk, bl mk, 12¾"...........145.00
Plate, cake; Rose Tapestry, pierced hdls, bl mk, 9¾" 235.00
Plate, Little Bo Peep, bl mk, 6¼"...................................75.00
Plate, Nursery Rhyme, Little Jack Horner, bl mk, 7¾"............95.00
Plate, Rose Tapestry, 3-color, bl mk, ornate rim, 7½"..........225.00
Plate, Snow Babies, bl mk 100.00
Relish, Rose Tapestry, bl mk, oval bowl shape 195.00
Shakers, Rose Tapestry, 3-color, bl mk, 3½", pr 425.00
Slipper, Rose Tapestry, gold trim, gr mk, 2¾x5" 265.00
Sugar bowl, cow scenic, bl mk 65.00
Toothpick holder, Rose Tapestry, pk, bl mk, 2⅝"................275.00
Toothpick holder, Sunbonnet Babies, bulbous, bl mk 395.00
Tray, dresser; Christmas Rose Tapestry, bl mk 450.00
Tray, Rose Tapestry, rectangular, mk, 11⅛x7⅞" 295.00
Tray, Rose Tapestry, 3-color, bl mk, 11x8" 450.00
Tray, sheep in meadow tapestry, bl mk, 11x8"....................295.00
Vase, bud; Rose Tapestry, bl mk....................................200.00
Vase, castle tapestry, bl mk, 4½" 130.00
Vase, hunt scene, bl mk, 5" 95.00
Vase, Rose Tapestry, 3-color, bl mk, 6¾" 300.00
Vase, Rose Tapestry, 3-color, bulbous, bl mk, 5½" 350.00
Wall pocket, Penny in Pocket Is a Merry Companion, bl mk 165.00
Wall pocket, Sunbonnet Babies, cleaning, bl mk 495.00

Chocolate pot, scenic tapestry with birds, 9", $500.00.

Royal Bonn

Royal Bonn is a fine-paste porcelain, ornately decorated with scenes, portraits, or florals. The factory was established in the mid-1800s in Bonn, Germany; however, most pieces found today are from the latter part of the century.

Biscuit jar, mc florals, SP top/rim/hdl, mk, 7x5½" 110.00
Vase, Dutch ladies scenic, 4-leg ped base, 5¾" 135.00
Vase, florals, sm gold hdl, bulbous, mk, 9½" 175.00
Vase, florals outlined in gold, slim neck, crown mk, 15x10" ... 1,000.00
Vase, iris w/gold, 8", pr 225.00
Vase, lady's portrait, sgn Muller, emb cup neck, hdls, 11" 550.00
Vase, lady's portrait w/gold on brn, Muller, 8¼x8" 550.00
Vase, lg blown-out gold florals, sm HP florals, 5½" 150.00
Vase, man looking out to sea, sgn, mk, 8⅞x7¼" 450.00
Vase, roses, sgn FM, bullet form in 3-leg fr w/masks, 14" 350.00
Vase, stylized gnarled trees/tulips, lav/yel/brn, 19" 700.00

Vase, gnarled trees and tulips, signed Old Dutch #247, 19", $700.00.

Royal Copenhagen

The Royal Copenhagen Manufactory was established in Denmark in about 1775 by Frantz Henrich Muller. When bankruptcy threatened in 1779, the Crown took charge. The fine dinnerware and objects of art produced after that time carries the familiar logo, the crown over three wavy lines. See also Limited Edition Plates.

Bowl, cupid on chariot pulled by 3 maidens in relief, 4x10" 375.00
Candlesticks, floral, bl on wht, lion heads at base, 9", pr 150.00
Figurine, ballet girl, overglaze, #4075.........................575.00
Figurine, Barn Owls, 12½", pr 625.00
Figurine, boy at lunch, #865...........................275.00
Figurine, boy in bl coat w/umbrella, #3556, 7¼" 140.00
Figurine, boy in carnival attire, #4794.....................155.00
Figurine, boy standing at shore, #1186.....................200.00
Figurine, boy w/horn, #3689 ....140.00
Figurine, boy w/teddy bear, #3468 ....275.00
Figurine, boy w/whittling stick, #905 ....350.00
Figurine, child w/accordion, #3667.......................175.00
Figurine, drummer, #3647 ....145.00
Figurine, farm girl, #815 ....415.00
Figurine, Faroe girl holding flowers, overglaze, #12413............ 1,475.00
Figurine, Faroe girl holding flowers, overglaze, #12416............ 1,175.00
Figurine, girl bather w/parasol seated on ped, 9½" 275.00
Figurine, girl dancing, #2444 ....300.00
Figurine, girl seated, knitting, 8½" 150.00

Figurine, girl w/doll, #1938, 5" 245.00
Figurine, girl w/doll, #3539 ....230.00
Figurine, girl w/wht coat, brn umbrella & hat, #1145, 6½"..........110.00
Figurine, goat, recumbent, #466, 11" L....................400.00
Figurine, goose girl, #527, 9¼" 210.00
Figurine, goose girl, #528, 7½" 345.00
Figurine, Hans Clodhopper, #1228 ....415.00
Figurine, Little Mermaid, #4431 ....815.00
Figurine, male fashion designer, #4109 ....200.00
Figurine, nude, kneeling, curling hair, #4424 ....275.00
Figurine, nude, kneels/kisses sitting faun, 1910, 11" 1,100.00
Figurine, nude lying on side, #4703 ....300.00
Figurine, nude sitting on rock, #4027, 5¾" 175.00
Figurine, Pan on tortoise, #858, 4" 195.00
Figurine, Pan playing pipes, #1736.....................245.00
Figurine, Pan rides, pulls ear of bear, 7x4" 220.00
Figurine, Pan w/lizard, #433 ....285.00
Figurine, Pan w/parrot, #752 ....300.00
Figurine, Pan w/snake, #1712........................200.00

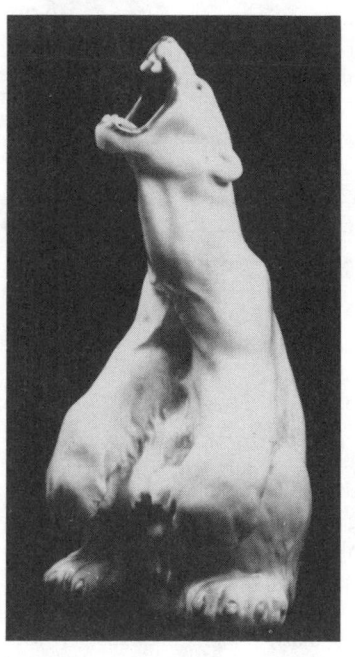

Figure of a polar bear, #502, 13", $275.00.

Figurine, polar bear crouches over pinned gray seal, 8½" 460.00
Figurine, puppy, #259, lg 130.00
Figurine, robin, #2238 ....75.00
Figurine, Sandman, #1145 ....275.00
Figurine, Sandman, overglaze, #1129....................700.00
Figurine, seal, #1441 ....135.00
Figurine, soldier w/dog, #1156.......................475.00
Figurine, soldier w/witch, #1112 ....545.00
Figurine, squirrel eating, #982, #36 on ft 60.00
Figurine, Victorian couple, #1593 ....925.00
Figurine, 2 Amager Girls, #1316......................565.00
Figurine, 2 children, #1761 ....575.00
Figurine, 2 children w/dog, #707 ....300.00
Jar, finial: figure w/bouquet, orange/wht ribbed panels, 17" 600.00
Wall hanging, 3-panel, parrot on branch relief, '50, 16x34".... 1,100.00

Royal Copley

Royal Copley is a decorative type of pottery made by the Spaulding China Company in Sebring, Ohio, from 1942 to 1957. They also produced two other major lines – Royal Windsor and Spaulding. Royal Copley was primarily marketed through five-and-ten cent stores; Royal Windsor and Spaulding were sold through department stores, gift shops, and jobbers.

Items trimmed in gold are worth 25% to 50% more than the same item with no gold trim. Our advisor for this category is Joe Devine; he is listed in the Directory under Iowa.

Creamer, chick, Spaulding, 4¾"	10.00
Creamer & sugar bowl, leaf, yel, open	20.00
Figurine, Chinese girl beside basket, 7¾"	10.00
Figurine, cockatoo, mc, 8¼"	22.50
Figurine, dog & mailbox	15.00
Figurine, hen, #1, 5½"	10.00
Figurine, hen, Royal Windsor, 6½"	12.00
Figurine, kingfisher, red & blk, 5"	15.00
Figurine, macaw on stump, 8¼"	22.00
Figurine, mallard duckling, erect head, 6"	12.00
Figurine, parrot, yel, 8"	25.00
Figurine, rooster, #2, paper label, 6¼"	12.00
Figurine, rooster, 8"	17.50
Figurine, spaniel, brn, 5"	15.00
Figurine, sparrow, 5"	10.00
Figurine, swallow, bl & red, 8"	14.00
Figurine, thrush, bl & yel, 6½"	12.50
Figurine, wren, Spaulding, 3½"	15.00
Piggy bank, Parky	22.00
Pitcher, daffodil, 8"	22.50
Pitcher, floral decal on wht, gold stamp, 6"	12.50
Pitcher, Pome Fruit, 8"	25.00
Planter, bear cub clinging to stump, 8¼"	25.00
Planter, big blossom, gr stamp, 3"	6.00

Bear with mandolin, $37.50; Bear planter, $27.50. (This bear as a bank, $37.50.)

Planter, blk cat & tub	15.00
Planter, blk cat w/pk bow, 8"	25.00
Planter, boy leaning on barrel, 6"	12.50
Planter, bunting, 5"	16.00
Planter, cocker spaniel's head, 5"	10.00
Planter, Colonial man, 8"	25.00
Planter, deer w/fawn, 9"	18.00

Planter, dog pulling wagon, 5¾"	20.00
Planter, duck eating grass, 5"	9.00
Planter, elephant w/ball, paper label, 6"	18.00
Planter, elf beside stump, 6"	18.00
Planter, farm girl, bl, 6½"	8.00
Planter, finch beside lg apple, paper label, 6½"	12.00
Planter, gazelle, 9"	17.50
Planter, girl w/pk hat	15.00
Planter, Indian boy & drum, paper label, 6½"	12.00
Planter, Ivy, dk gr on ivory, paper label, 4"	4.50
Planter, kitten w/ball of red yarn, 8¼"	25.00
Planter, mallard, sitting, paper label, 5"	15.00
Planter, mallard, 7¾"	12.00
Planter, pony, mk, 5¼"	12.00
Planter, pouter pigeon, paper label, 5¾"	12.00
Planter, puppy in basket, 7"	15.00
Planter, puppy w/suitcase, paper label, 7"	20.00
Planter, ram's head, paper label, 6½"	18.00
Planter, rooster, 7¼"	12.00
Planter, tanager by stump, 6¼"	12.00
Planter, teddy bear on stump, 5½"	17.50
Planter, water lily, gr, 6¼"	8.00
Plaque/planter, fruit plate, sgn, 6¾"	12.50
Plaque/planter, mill, Jacob van Ruysdael, 8"	28.00
Smoking set, mallards, 3-pc	30.00
String & scissors holder, bird	22.50
Vase, bamboo, cylindrical, 8"	15.00
Vase, bud; parrot at side of stump vase, 5"	8.00
Vase, Carol's Corsage, cobalt, 7"	12.00
Vase, dragon, ftd, paper label, 5½"	12.00
Vase, fish form, 6"	22.00
Vase, floral decal, stub hdls, 4⅛"	8.00
Vase, floral decal on cream, hdls, gold stamp, 6¼"	8.00
Vase, ivy, dk gr on ivory, ftd, 7"	6.50
Vase, nuthatch, 5½"	12.50
Vase, philodendron, ftd, paper label, 7½"	12.00
Vase/planter, deer, paper label, 7½"	20.00
Wall pocket, bonnet w/flowers	17.00
Wall pocket, dancing lady	35.00

Royal Crown Derby

In the latter 1870s, a new firm, the Derby Crown Porcelain Company Ltd., began operations in Derby, England. Since 1890 when they were appointed Manufacturers of Porcelain to Her Majesty, their fine porcelain wares have been known as Royal Crown Derby. Their earliest wares were marked with a crown over 'Derby'; often a complicated dating code indicated the year of manufacture. After 1890 the 'Royal Crown Derby, England' mark was employed; in 1921 'Made In England' was substituted in the wording. 'Bone China' was added after 1945. See also Derby.

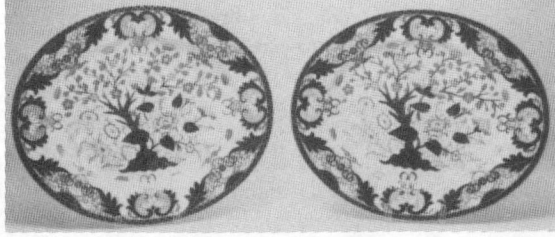

Platters, tree of life motif in Imari palette, 1877-89 mark, 19", $450.00 each.

Cup & saucer, Imari...**75.00**
Ewer, floral & arabesque on Chinese red, 1880s, 7½" **215.00**
Pitcher, florals, mc on ivory, gold hdl, mk, 9" **395.00**
Plate, Imari, 7" **40.00**
Sugar bowl, Imari **135.00**
Vase, bird on floral branch on pk, gilt cat hdls, 1885, 8" **600.00**
Vase, floral branches on yel, rope swags at neck, lid, 19" **950.00**
Vase, florals/gilding allover, jeweled neck, w/stopper, 15"...........**600.00**
Vase, foliage/swags, gilt on cobalt, dome top, lid, 1890, 11" **700.00**

Royal Dux

The Duxer Porzellan Manufactur was established by E. Eichler in 1860. Located in what is now Duchcov, Czechoslovakia, the area was known as Dux, Bohemia, until WWI. The war brought about changes in both the style of the ware as well as the mark. Pre-war pieces were modeled in the Art Nouveau or Greek Classical manner and marked with 'Bohemia' and a pink triangle containing the letter 'E.' They were usually matt glazed in green, brown, and gold. Better pieces were made of porcelain, while the larger items were of pottery. After the war, the ware was marked with the small pink triangle but without the Bohemia designation; 'Made in Czechslovakia' was added. The style became Art Deco, with cobalt blue a dominant color.

Bust, maid, lilies/pads in hair & on decollete dress, 17" **1,000.00**
Bust of Caesar, caramel robe w/pk drape across shoulder, 9" **350.00**
Centerpiece, 2 cupids/maiden ride shell boat on waves, unmk **600.00**
Chess set, porc, 4½" King, ea pc mk, complete **895.00**

Farm girl feeding chickens, pink triangle mark, early 20th Century, restored, 26", $1,500.00.

Figurine, couple dance, gold trim base, pk triangle mk, 9" **350.00**
Figurine, courting couple, seated, pk triangle mk, 7x8"..............**400.00**
Figurine, Deco lady, bl gown/gr hat, swirling skirt, 9" **325.00**
Figurine, Deco lady lifts bl dress to expose leg, 10" **325.00**
Figurine, Dutch girl w/geese, earth tones, 8x10" dia.....................**535.00**
Figurine, lady dancing, swirling dress/coat, wide hat, 10" **350.00**
Figurine, lady on conch shell, 13½" **550.00**
Figurine, lady on rock overlooks pool, pk mk, #537, 11x9" **495.00**
Figurine, lady w/banjo on 8-sided ped, breast exposed, 14" **1,300.00**
Figurine, lady w/basket holds child, old triangle mk, 8½" **395.00**
Figurine, man w/sickle & wheat; lady w/wheat, 1930, 21", pr......**950.00**
Figurine, nude w/drape, standing, 9½" **295.00**
Figurine, Pierrot w/mandolin blows kiss to Pierette, 11"..............**400.00**

Figurine, rhinocerous beetle, pk triangle mk, pr **250.00**
Figurine, senorita, hands on hips, wrapped in shawl, 14" **750.00**
Figurine, waterboy, wht cap/suit, leans on jug, rocks, 22"............**450.00**
Figurine, 2 children w/basket, pk triangle mk, 8½" **395.00**
Tray, girl holds child in corner, cat at ft, mk, 12x9x15" **775.00**
Vase, maid/trees, grisaille on wht, rtcl neck/ft, hdls, 13"............**450.00**
Vase, open limbs/appl leaves/olives on wht w/gilt, 19", pr..........**800.00**
Vase, stylized floral panels, gr on bl, bulbous, 16", pr **350.00**
Vase, water nymph figural, iris hdls, scalloped, 15½" **600.00**
Vase, 2 nymphs at rim, natural colors, sgn M Vavra, 15".............**650.00**
Vase, 3 children w/garland drape at top, 20" **550.00**

Royal Flemish

Royal Flemish was introduced in the late 1880s and was patented in 1894 by the Mt. Washington Glass Company. Transparent glass was enameled with one or several colors and the surface divided by a network of raised lines suggesting leaded glass work. Some pieces were further decorated with enameled florals, birds, or Roman coins.

Our advisors for this category are Betty and Clarence Maier; they are listed in the Directory under Pennsylvania.

Biscuit jar, gold coins & lines on brn tones, 7½" **1,850.00**
Biscuit jar, lg pk roses in scroll panels, SP mk lid, 7¾" **1,100.00**
Biscuit jar, 2 geometric+2 floral panels, crab finial, sq **1,600.00**
Bowl, water lilies/mc leaves, emb gold, brn/gold collar, 4".......**2,000.00**
Ewer, floral, rampant lions around top, brns/gold, 13" **2,000.00**
Pickle castor, mums, yel/wht on frost; Pairpoint fr, 9½"...........**1,265.00**
Rose bowl, asters, wht/bl on brn to clear, 8-scallop, #617........**1,285.00**
Vase, blk disks w/gold florals on brn, stick neck, 12x7"...........**1,800.00**
Vase, peacock, lg/jeweled on lt bl, purple/gold neck, 13" **6,750.00**
Vase, peonies, mc/gold on lt gold, dome lid, bulbous, 11" **2,250.00**
Vase, Roman coins, narrow neck w/tri-fold top, 7½x8"...........**1,650.00**
Vase, Roman coins, sm hdls, 5" sq base, 8½" **3,600.00**
Vase, Roman coins, w/dome lid & hdls, 6½" **2,350.00**

Vase, floral medallions, browns with gold, 9½", $4,500.00.

Royal Haeger, Haeger

In 1871 David Henry Haeger, a young son of German immigrants, purchased a brick factory at Dundee, Illinois, and began an association with the ceramic industry that his descendants have pursued to the present time. Soon their production was expanded to include drainage tile. By 1914 they had ventured into the field of commerical artware. Vases, figurines, lamp bases, and gift items in a pastel matt glaze carried the logo of the company name written over the bar of an 'H.' From 1929 to 1933, they produced a line of dinnerware in solid colors – blue, rose, green, and yellow – which they marketed through Marshall Fields. Royal Haeger, their premium line designed in 1938 by Royal Hickman, and the Flower Ware line (1954 to 1963, marked 'RG' for Royal Garden) are especially desirable with collectors today. Ware produced before the mid-thirties sometimes is found with a paper label; these are also of special interest. A stylized script mark, 'Royal Haeger' in raised lettering, was used during the thirties and forties; later a paper label in the shape of a crown was used. The Macomb plant, built in 1939, primarily made ware for the florist trade. A second plant, built there in 1969, produces lamp bases.

For those interested in learning more about the subject, we recommend *Collecting Royal Haeger*, by our advisors, Lee Garmon and Doris Frizzell; both are listed in the Directory under Illinois.

Ash tray, Abe Lincoln, R-1095, 1818-1968, 7" L 6.00
Ash tray, Jane Addams, R-1098, 1818-1968, 7" L 6.00
Ash tray, Louis Joliet, R-1097, 1818-1968, 7" L 6.00
Ash tray, Stephen A Douglas, 1818-1968, R-1096, 7" L 6.00
Bottle vase, #1919, 10" 5.00
Bowl, console; swan, R-955, 11" 20.00
Candle holders, cornucopia form, R-312, 5½", pr........................12.00
Candlestick, swan, 5¼", pr 20.00
Cigarette lighter, aladdin lamp form 10.00
Figurine, blk-dappled horse, R-402, 5½" 10.00
Figurine, colt, R-103, 8" 12.00
Figurine, Little Brother, R-1254, 11½" 18.00
Figurine, panther, R-683, 18" L 20.00
Flower holder, colt, R-235, 12½" 22.00
Lamp, petal louvre reflector, #5353, 11¼" 25.00
Lamp, TV; bronco, #6105, 11½" L...25.00
Lamp, 2 fawns at base, 24" 32.00
Lamp, 3 plumes w/bow, #5292, 26" 35.00
Pitcher/vase, hdld, #408 ....15.00
Planter, cow, label, Haeger, 4½" 10.00
Planter, dachshund, R-736, 14½" L 25.00
Planter, fawn, R-1913, 7½" 15.00
Planter, fish, R-752, 8½" 12.00
Planter, scottie, #3377, 6" L 8.00
Vase, basket form, R-386, 12" W 22.00
Vase, eagle, #3278, 13" 10.00
Vase, laurel wreath bow, R-303, 12"...20.00
Vase, lg leaf, R-138, 12½" 12.00
Vase, modern dbl loop, R-1500, 8" 10.00
Vase, morning-glory, R-452, 16" 25.00
Vase, Peacock Gladiola, head str, R-31, 15" 50.00
Vase, Peter Pan, R-917, 10"..20.00
Vase, pillow, R-651, 8".. 8.00
Vase, Rose of Sharon, R-580, 9½"..15.00
Vase, running deer, R-706, 15"...22.00
Vase, sailfish, R-901, 6", ea 10.00
Vase, snail shell, R-299, 7" 12.00
Vase, sunflower, R-647, 8"...10.00
Vase, swan form, R-713, 8"..12.00

Royal Rudolstadt

The hard-paste porcelain that has come to be known as Royal

Rudolstadt was produced in Thuringia, Germany, in the early 18th century. Various names and marks have been associated with this pottery – one of the earliest was a hay fork symbol associated with Johann Frederich von Schwarzburg-Rudolstadt, one of the first founders. Variations, some that included an 'R,' were also used. In 1854 Earnst Bohne produced wares that were marked with an anchor and the letters 'EB.' Wares commonly found today are those made during the late 1800s and early twentieth century. These are usually marked with an 'RW' within a shield under a crown and the words 'Crown Rudolstadt.' Items marked 'Germany' were made after 1890.

Our advisor for this category is William Brinkley; he is listed in the Directory under Illinois.

Bowl supported by three cupids, ca 1854-1900, 5" x 10", $285.00.

Chocolate pot, roses, mc on cream w/gold, mk, 9¾x4" 88.00
Figurine, beggar girl holds tambourine, wht, 1905, 5½" 150.00
Figurine, girl feeds birds, copper lustre, 13".................................95.00
Figurine, hunchbk, brn hat/bl pants/floral & red vest, 6" 125.00
Plate, floral w/gold, mk, 6¾" 20.00
Shakers, roses, mk, pr..35.00
Smoker set, dog after cat on fence, mk, 6x6½" 165.00
Teapot, roses, pk on wht w/gold, mk, ind......................................115.00
Vase, gold florals on tree bark, narrow neck, ruffled, 9½" 60.00
Vase floral w/dbl gold hdls, #7190, 16", pr...................................225.00

Royal Vienna

In 1719 Claude Innocentius de Paquier established a hard-paste porcelain factory in Vienna where he made highly ornamental wares similar to the type produced at Meissen. Early wares were usually unmarked; but after 1744, when the factory was purchased by the Empress, the Austrian shield (often called 'beehive') was stamped on under the glaze. In the following listings, values are for hand-painted items unless noted otherwise. Decal-decorated items would be considerably lower.

Note: An influx of Japanese reproductions on the market have influenced values to decline on genuine old Royal Vienna. Buyer beware! On new items, the beehive mark is over the glaze, the weight of the porcelain is heavier, and the decoration is obviously decaled.

Our advisor for this category is Madeleine France; she is listed in the Directory under Florida.

Box, cherub/attendants on lid, red w/much gilt, 6" dia 350.00
Charger, Flora, maid w/flowers, sgn, bl on rose w/gilt, 20" 3,500.00
Plaque, Terpsichores' daughters, Riemer, fr, 18x14½" 6,000.00
Plate, birds in reserve on dk gr, Xd Vs (Vater), 10", pr.................250.00
Plate, lady & knight in shield, Kauffmann, 13" 65.00
Plate, maid's portrait w/in gilt bands on claret, fr, 9" 600.00
Plate, musicians, sgn Jacke, gilt scrolls, cobalt border, 10" 750.00
Plate, portrait, sgn Forster, gilt & cobalt border, 9½" 650.00
Plate, portrait: Edelweifs, on turq/dk bl/gilt, Wagner, 10" 1,000.00
Tray, mythological figures, sgn Stadter, lattice rim, 13" L.............250.00
Urn, floral panels, nymphs/cherubs on maroon decal, 11" 275.00
Urn, maid's portrait on claret, allover gilding/hdls, 24" 8,000.00
Urn, romantic decals on vase & sq base, gr, sgn Stahl, 22" 250.00
Vase, lady's portrait, artist sgn, cobalt w/gold, mk, 11½" 695.00
Vase, lady's portrait in gilt border on cobalt, 12", pr............... 1,650.00
Vase, lady's portrait on cobalt, sgn A Bork, pillow form, 5" 300.00
Vase, portrait of Ruth on cobalt, Wagner, mask hdls, 7" 500.00
Vase, portrait: Reveuse, on gr w/gilt fleurettes, hdls, 10".............700.00

Royal Worcester, Worcester

The Worcester Porcelain Company was deeded in 1751. During the first or Dr. Wall period (so called for one of its proprietors), porcelain with an Oriental influence was decorated in underglaze blue. Useful tablewares represented the largest portion of production, but figurines and decorative items were also made. Very little of the earliest wares were marked and can only be identified by a study of forms, glazes, and the porcelain body, which tends to transmit a greenish cast when held to light. Late in the fifties, a crescent mark was in general use, and rare examples bare a facsimile of the Meissen crossed swords. The first period ended in 1783, and the company went through several changes in ownership during the next eighty years. The years from 1783-1792 are referred to as the Flight period. Marks were a small crescent, a crown with 'Royal,' or an impressed 'Flight.' From 1792-1807, the company was known as Flight and Barr and used the trademark 'F&B' or 'B,' with or without a small cross. From 1807-1813, the company was under the Barr, Flight, and Barr management; this era is recognized as having produced porcelain of the highest quality of artistic decoration. Their mark was 'B.F.B.' From 1813-1840, many marks were used, but the most usual was 'F.B.B.' under a crown to indicate Flight, Barr, and Barr. In 1840 the firm merged with Chamberlain, and in 1852 they were succeeded by Kerr and Binns. The firm became known as Royal Worcester in 1862. Since 1930 Royal Worcester has been considered one of the leaders in the field of limited edition plates and figurines.

Our advisor for this category is William Brinkley; he is listed in the Directory under Illinois.

Basket, gold fleur-de-lis at base of hdl, relief heads, 7" 550.00
Biscuit jar, floral, mc on beige, SP lid/rim/hdl, mk, 6" 285.00
Bowl, bl & wht floral, crescent mk, minor wear, 2¾x6" 400.00
Bowl, floral, bl/wht on cream, scalloped, Dr Wall, 3x9¾" 600.00
Bowl, floral, underglaze bl, emb spiral fluting, mk, 7⅝"................100.00
Bowl, glazed parian, peach/yel, triangular shell form, 4" 110.00
Bowl, pine cone in bl, clam shell border, ca 1780, 9¾" 220.00
Bowl, rtcl scroll panels, jeweled ribs, 1891, 5½" dia 850.00
Candelabrum, girl stands before 3 flower stems, Hadley, 21".... 2,100.00
Candle snuffer, hat shape, pk plume, G-178 ....59.00
Candle snuffer, monk, dtd 1954 ....50.00
Candlestick, lily form w/leaf saucer, gold wash, pr..........................90.00

Coffeepot, fruit still life, L Flexman, +6 c/s, in case................ 2,800.00
Compote, shell bowl, 3-dolphin support, bl/wht, 1880, 8x7".......280.00
Creamer, chinoiserie, bl on wht, Dr Wall crescent mk.................175.00
Creamer & sugar bowl, scalloped neck, serpent hdl, purple mk...195.00
Crocus pot, gold relief birds/floral branches, lobed, 6" W 335.00
Cup & saucer, bl/wht florals, handleless, crescent mk, EX 250.00
Cup & saucer, Bridal Rose 35.00
Cup & saucer, dbl-walled/rtcl scrolls & jewels, 1895, 4½" 495.00
Cup & saucer, demitasse; HP sheep, artist sgn 275.00
Cup & saucer, fruit w/gold trim, miniature 85.00
Cup & saucer, glazed parian, vegetable-form cup/leaf saucer 175.00
Cup & saucer, gnomes working, ca 1904 ....165.00
Cup & saucer, rtcl scrolls, wht/gold, dbl-walled, 1895.................495.00

Dish, Kylin pattern, ca 1775, 7¾", $700.00.

Ewer, bl flowers, gold tracery, salamander hdl, 1887 mk, 9" 435.00
Ewer, floral, mc on beige, gold hdl, 1889 mk, 9¼x3⅛".................275.00
Ewer, floral HP on bulbous basketweave body, gilt hdl, 12" 180.00
Figurine, A Merry New Song 275.00
Figurine, Anne Boleyn, bl gown w/gold trim, holds fan, 8½".......350.00
Figurine, Apple Blossom & Bees, D Doughty, 8", pr 650.00
Figurine, Audubon's Warblers & Palo Verdi, D Doughty, pr ... 4,500.00
Figurine, Babes in the Woods, sisters, 1930s mk, 6" 235.00
Figurine, Bewick's Wrens & Yel Jasmine, D Doughty, 10", pr.. 3,800.00
Figurine, Bl-Grey Gnatcatchers & Dogwood, D Doughty, pr.. 4,500.00
Figurine, boy w/parakeet, #3087, dtd 1950 ....150.00
Figurine, Delicate Cucumbers To Pickle.......................................300.00
Figurine, Dutch boy, Gertner, #3923, 5½"....................................145.00
Figurine, Fortuneteller...285.00
Figurine, Golden Crown Kinglets & Nobel Pine, Doughty, pr . 3,750.00
Figurine, Greenaway boy w/basket, ca 1893, 8½" 525.00
Figurine, Joy & Sorrow, gold trim, 1894 mk, 9⅝", pr 850.00
Figurine, June, gr, lg..285.00
Figurine, Magnolia Warblers & Magnolia, D Doughty, pr 12,500.00
Figurine, Mary Queen of Scots, lav/gold, cape & hood, 8½" 350.00
Figurine, My Favorite 175.00
Figurine, Phoebes & Flame Vine, D Doughty, 9¾", pr 5,500.00
Figurine, Red-Eyed Vireo, D Doughty, 7½", pr............................750.00
Figurine, Scarlet Tanagers & Wht Oak, D Doughty, pr 3,250.00
Figurine, Scotsman, gr jacket/kilts, gold trim, mk, 6" 395.00
Figurine, VA Cardinals & Orange Blossom, D Doughty, pr 8,500.00
Figurine, Vermillion Flycatchers & Pussy Willow, Doughty, pr.. 3,250.00
Figurine, Yankee, Countries of the World Series 395.00
Gravy boat, birds in flight/garden scene, 1750s, 9½" L 850.00
Jar, rtcl foliage, birds/trees reserves, 1890s, 10½" 1,650.00
Jar, rtcl foliage, hexagonal panels, 1890s, 10" 400.00
Jar, rtcl scrolls, gilt/jewels, ftd squat sq, 1892, 4" W 550.00
Jardiniere, palm leaves, gold on royal bl, sgn, 7½x9", pr 595.00

Mug, butterflies/flowers in bl, ca 1775, 4½" 175.00
Mug, roses & mum, bl on wht, ca 1775, 4½" 175.00
Pitcher, Cabbage Leaf/mask, bl/wht florals, ca 1775, 6" 120.00
Pitcher, floral, gold band & bamboo hdl, bottle form, 10" 250.00
Pitcher, floral & foliage on beige, mk, 9" 300.00
Pitcher, floral on beige, dtd 1901, 5½" 245.00
Pitcher, floral on beige w/gold, 1900 mk, 4x2⅝" 88.00
Pitcher, floral on cream w/gold, mask spout, 1895, 3¾" 85.00
Pitcher, owl on branch/moon, gold serpent hdl, ca 1885, 11" 925.00
Pitcher, roses, ornate hdl & spout, mk, 7" 300.00
Plaque, Edward VIII bust, 5" 85.00
Plate, dinner; HP floral, WH Price, #C1167, set of 6 .... 1,500.00
Plate, floral, bl/wht on cream, scalloped, Dr Wall, 7⅝" 525.00

Soup tureen, blue transfer, ca 1880, 17", $250.00.

Sugar shaker, ftd w/sterling lid 100.00
Teapot, bl Oriental transfer, flower finial, Dr Wall, 5¾" 450.00
Teapot, floral & butterfly on beige w/gold, 1874 mk, 5¼"............375.00
Teapot, florals/chinoiserie, Dr Wall, 7⅝" 1,700.00
Tray, floral, mc w/gold, oval, mk Barr Flight Barr, 10"................150.00
Vase, conch chell on ped ft, gold trim, 1888 mk, 8½".................450.00
Vase, egg form on ftd base, openwork at top & on lid, 4½" 560.00
Vase, emb gold berries/vines, cut-out floral hdl, #1137, 3½" 100.00
Vase, emb leaves w/gold on beige, ftd, mk, 3½x3½".................135.00
Vase, floral, mc on beige, fluted trumpet, #1938, 1902, 9"...........225.00
Vase, floral, mc on beige, gold hdls, ped ft, 1898 mk, 7" 225.00
Vase, floral, mc on beige, 1911 mk, 6¾x3"...............................110.00
Vase, floral, mc on beige w/gold, dtd 1897, mk, 6½x2⅝".............110.00
Vase, floral, salamander hdl, ewer form, 1887, mk, 9" 425.00
Vase, floral w/gold, ewer form, 1889 mk, 6¾x4½" 225.00
Vase, floral w/gold, rtcl hdls & neck, ca 1890, 14½" 475.00
Vase, floral w/much gold, florals on hdl, 1896 mk, 9⅝" 325.00
Vase, gold heron/butterfly/serpent hdls, 1882 mk, 8" 500.00
Vase, gold-rayed serrated wheels on yel, 1887 mk, 9" 178.00
Vase, lotus form, twining stem & bud base, 8" 500.00
Vase, nautilus shell on coral-branch base, 1912 mk, mini............225.00
Vase, Persian manner, partial rtcl, ornate hdls, 1887, 26" 3,800.00
Vase, roses on rnd cream body, rtcl neck, ornate hdls, 12"...........550.00
Vase, sheep, blk on cream, att H Davis, rtcl base, 6" 295.00
Vase, shell form, beige w/gold trim, mk, 4x3" 110.00
Wine pot, floral w/gold, funnel on side 295.00

Roycroft

Near the turn of the century, Elbert Hubbard established the Roycroft Printing Shop in East Aurora, New York. Named in honor of two 17th-century printer-bookbinders, the print shop was just the beginning of a community called Roycroft, which came to be known worldwide. Hubbard became a popular personality of the early 1900s, known for his talents in a variety of areas from writing and lecturing to manufacturing. The Roycroft community became a meeting place for people of various capabilities and included shops for the production of furniture, copper, leather items, and a multitude of other wares which were marked with the Roycroft symbol, an 'R' within a circle below a stylized cross. Hubbard lost his life on the Lusitania in 1915; production in the community continued until the Depression.

Interest is escalating in the field of Arts and Crafts in general, and Roycroft items in particular (along with Stickley, Rolfs, etc.) are rapidly appreciating in value. Copper items are evaluated to a large extent by the condition of the original patina that remains.

Key: pcr — polychrome

Book, Book of Roycrofters, 1901, gr suede cover, VG 30.00
Book, Compensation, Emerson, 1904, red suede cover, VG...........25.00
Book, Friendship, Love, & Marriage, Hubbard, 1923, VG 25.00
Book, Homes of the Great, 1928 memorial ed, leatherette cover .40.00
Book, Message to Garcia, 1899, red suede cover, VG....................75.00
Book, Roycroft Shop, A History, 1909, D Hunter cover, VG 45.00
Book, Smoke Over America, 1943, cloth cover, VG.....................25.00
Book, Song of Songs, 1896, EX 350.00
Book stand, Little Journeys, 3-shelf, metal tag, 26" W 600.00
Bookends, hammered copper/brass wash, poppies, #305, VG 300.00
Bookshelf, slat sides/bk, 4-shelf, 38x33x15½" 2,600.00
Bowl, hammered copper, repousse leaves, #238, 4" 280.00
Bowl, hammered copper/pcr, #216, 2½x6", VG 155.00
Bowl, hammered copper/pcr, 4-crimp top, mk, 2½x4", VG...........90.00
Bowl, nut; hammered copper w/floral, #801, +scoop 450.00
Bridal chest, oak, serpentine sides, keyed tenons, 37" L 6,750.00
Candelabrum, brass, 3 cups/twist std, #419, 20", pr, EX 800.00
Candelabrum, hammered copper, twist std+2 scroll arms, 20" 475.00
Candelabrum, hammered copper/pcr, strap w/8 cups, 3x20", pr...525.00
Candle holder, copper, sm curled hdl on drip tray, ftd, 3", NM....110.00
Candlestick, copper, 2-strip std on sq base, 8x3", pr 450.00
Candlestick, copper w/brass stem, copper cup, 9", pr 300.00

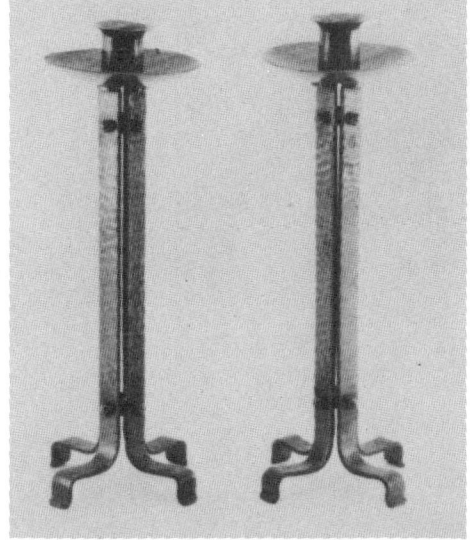

Hammered copper candlesticks, both signed, 12", $650.00 for the pair.

Candlestick, hammered copper/EX patina, 2-stem std, 8", pr 575.00
Card tray, hammered copper, 4 cigarette rests, #1000-C, 6"...........90.00
Catalog, ca 1910, VG...150.00

Desk, fall front over 4 drw, fitted int, #092, 53x36x18" 1,300.00
Dish, hammered copper, 3-lobe rim, center medallion, 8" 150.00
Dish, hammered silver, ftd shell form, 1x5" 300.00
Footstool, side stretchers/extended corner posts, 15x18x12" 325.00
Frame, hammered copper, for desk-top calendar 35.00
Goblets, hammered/silver-washed, 6 on 20" L tray.....................225.00
Humidor, hammered copper, #635, old cleaning, 4", VG.............260.00
Inkwell, copper, 2 wells/central pen tray, #524, 15" L 150.00
Inkwell, hammered copper, hinged, glass pot, mk, 2x3", EX 200.00
Inkwell, hammered copper/pcr, glass pot, bell form, mk, 2½" 160.00
Lamp, hammered copper, dome shade, slim std w/rnd ft, 18" . 1,500.00
Magazine stand #80, splayed sides, orb/leaf cvg, 64x18", EX ... 4,000.00
Shakers, blk orb/gr & rust on ivory, Buffalo, 2¾", pr 250.00
Table, library; Mackmurdo ft, orb mk, revarnished, 30"........... 1,800.00
Table, library; wide stretchers mortised thru legs, 48", EX 900.00
Tabouret #050½, oak, incised Roycroft, 20x12" 750.00
Telephone, planished copper shaft/base, mk, 1905, 12x5"....... 1,700.00
Tray, hammered copper, octagonal, #826, 10", EX 200.00
Tray, hammered copper w/brass wash, octagonal, hdls, 15" 250.00
Vase, Am Beauty, cylinder neck, ftd, 7"..800.00
Vase, Am Beauty, mk/#201, 18" 3,000.00
Vase, bud; hammered copper, ruffled, ftd, mk, 4", EX 90.00
Vase, copper w/appl silver sqs, 4 long buttresses, 8" 2,000.00
Vase, hammered copper, cut-out silver band, varnished, 6" 350.00
Vase, hammered copper, EX orig patina, #220, 4½" 250.00
Vase, hammered copper, has been cleaned, mk, #220, 4" 130.00
Vase, hammered copper, rolled-rim ovoid, orb mk, 4½" 125.00
Vase, hammered copper canister w/appl silver, #203, 6".......... 1,000.00

Rozenburg

Some of the most innovative and original Art Nouveau ceramics were created by the Rozenberg factory at The Hague in The Netherlands between 1885 and 1916. Some pieces are similar to Gouda. Rozenburg also made highly-prized eggshell ware, so called because of its very thin walls; this is eagerly sought after by collectors. T.A.C. Colenbrander was their artistic leader, with Samuel Schellink and J. Kok designing many of the eggshell pieces.

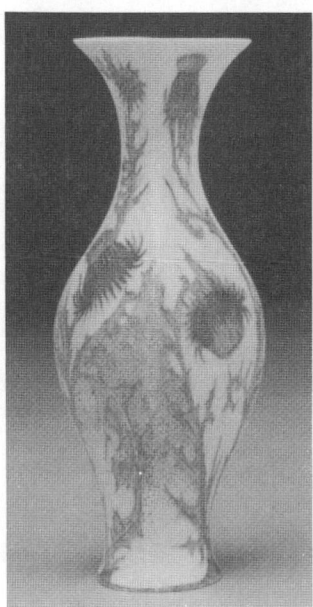

Vase, thistles in red, green, and pink, signed Schellink, 1907, 3¾", $1,000.00.

Bowl, tulips amidst curling/dotted border, irreg sides, 11" 240.00
Cup & saucer, Nouveau floral, octagonal, Van Rossum 500.00

Tile, windmill, pastoral, pictoral fr, sgn Gabriel............................450.00
Vase, earthenware, pansies on yel & lt brn, 13" 800.00
Vase, eggshell, florals, lav on wht & yel, ribbed, 6" 600.00
Vase, mushroom caps/exotic florals, eggshell, paneled, 5" 900.00
Vase, Nouveau florals/vines/waves, long hdls, #DW-366, 15"......900.00

Rubena

Rubena glass was made by several firms in the late 1800s. It is a blown art glass that shades from clear to red. See also Art Glass Baskets; Cruets; Sugar Shakers; Salts; specific manufacturers.

Bottle, scent; gold bands, stippling, cut stopper, unmk, 6¾" 95.00
Pitcher, hobnail, opal, sq top, water sz 500.00
Tray, celery; dragon/floral, vaseline rigaree rim, 12" 200.00
Vase, florals/bl ribbon, cylindrical, ruffled, 11"............................175.00
Vase, jack-in-pulpit; horizontal ribbing, 8¾", pr 200.00
Vase, jack-in-pulpit; opal petal top, 13" 200.00
Vase, printed/etched floral, frosted, ribbed, Mt WA, 6" 275.00
Vase, zinnias/leaves, vertical ribs, 7½" 65.00

Rubena Verde

Rubena Verde glass was introduced in the late 1800s by Hobbs, Brockunier, and Company of Wheeling, West Virginia. Its transparent colors shade from red to green. See also Art Glass Baskets; Cruets; Sugar Shakers; Salts.

Creamer 40.00
Pitcher, Hobbs, 7"...280.00
Shakers, HP florals, pewter lid, 4¼", pr 185.00
Sugar shaker, HP florals, Hobbs Coloratura series 295.00
Tumbler, floral...85.00
Tumbler, Hobnail 150.00
Vase, Drape, bowl form, ped ft, 9¼"..180.00
Vase, jack-in-the-pulpit; appl crystal rigaree spirals, 14".............275.00

Ruby–Stained Souvenirs

Ruby-flashed or ruby-stained glass was made through the application of a thin layer of color over clear. It was used in the manufacture of some early pressed tableware and from the Victorian era well into the 20th century for souvenir items which were often engraved on the spot with the date, location, and buyer's name.

Wine goblet, 5", $30.00; Mug, Button Arches, dated 1906, 3", $45.00.

Creamer, Naomi 50.00
Creamer, Riverside's Victoria 65.00
Cruet, Block & Bull's Eye, World's Fair, 1893 ....200.00
Decanter, Tiny Fine Cut 75.00
Goblet, Beaded Dart Band...................................30.00
Mug, Pulaski, IA, EX..48.00
Plate, Barred Ovals, 5".......................................32.00
Spooner, Henrietta 55.00
Toothpick holder, Beaded Swag 35.00
Tumbler, Diamond Peg, IN, 1910.......................35.00
Tumbler, Lacy Medallion, 1901 ....22.00
Tumbler, Triple Triangle, Niagara Falls, 1892 ......15.00
Wine, Campanula..30.00
Wine, Zipper Slash 35.00

Rugs

Key:

comp — complimentary	mdl — medallion
dmn — diamond	s/a — semi-antique
gb — guard border	

Hooked

Hooked rugs are treasured today for their folk-art appeal. It was a craft that was introduced to this country in about 1830 and flourished its best in the New England states. The prime consideration is not age but artistic appeal. Scenes with animals, buildings, and people; patriotic designs; or whimsical themes are preferred. Condition is, of course, also a factor. Marked examples bearing the stamps of 'Frost and Co.,' 'Abenakee,' 'C.R.,' and 'Ouia' are highly prized. Note: the rugs listed here are rag unless noted otherwise.

Black cat, wool and cotton edged with silk ruching, 1890s, 23" x 31", $1,000.00.

Blk cat on pillow, mc ground, wear/fading/rpr, 20x32" 175.00
Cat+3 kittens on patterned floor, 1900, 27x50", EX 625.00
Dog reclines on rug in reserve on florals, wear/rpr, 37x70" 450.00
Eagle on mc ground, braided border, 1900s, 35x41" 500.00
Eagle w/in Jacobean florals, 45x64" 1,250.00
Floral, mc on blk, sgn binding dtd 1889, 30x45" 235.00
Floral, pastel yarn on beige, 31x54" 200.00
Floral w/garlands on beige, 52x66"......................................180.00
Flowering tree, EX color on tan, minor edge damage, 36x59" 100.00
Folk art flowers/birds, dramatic contrasts, rpr, 40x45" 1,000.00

Horse center, flags/horseshoes/1898 in border, 35x56", EX 2,000.00
Landscape w/house, trees, etc, VG colors, 25x35".......................450.00
Lg group of skaters in Victorian attire, yarns, 30x43" 1,700.00
Stylized design, strong colors, 27x56", VG 225.00
Train on railroad, 30x34", EX 300.00
Tree of Life w/birds etc, 1930, 30x74".....................................350.00
15 sqs, ea w/different animal or floral, worn, 28x46" 325.00
2 greyhound dogs/trees on blk, wear/damage, 29x40" 225.00
2 lions/exotic foliage, E Ross & Co, Toledo OH, rpr, 23x60"......475.00
3 elephants, on saddle blankets: We bring you luck, 30x60".......400.00

Oriental

The Oriental and Eastern rug market has enjoyed a renewal of interest in recent years as collectors have become aware of the fact that some of the semi-antique rugs (those sixty to one hundred years old) may be had at a price within the range of the average buyer.

Arak, mdl/floral sprays, red on cream, 1930, 120x72" 440.00
Belouchistan, latchhook mdl on rust, 1875, 70x45" 750.00
Bidjar, Herati on navy, vine/palmette gb, 48x53" 1,300.00
Fereghan Prayer, silk, flowering urn, lav on tan, 92x50"..........7,000.00
Ghiordes, mdl, gray on red, gray border, 3 gb, 275x135" 3,000.00
Hamadan, Herati on navy, red primary borders, 170x135"......2,860.00
Heriz, mdl/floral sprays on rust, palmette gb, 144x100" 4,200.00
Heriz, vines/palmettes on ivory, navy border, 1929, 130x96" .. 3,800.00
Karabagh, Lenkoran motif, mdl/latchhooks on brn, 140x62".. 3,500.00
Kashan, lobed mdl, red on navy, florals/cartouches, 80x53" 2,000.00
Kazvin, pr of floral mdl on ivory, rose border, 140x100" 2,000.00
Kerman, mdl, rose/celadon, floral border, 1930, 165x140" 1,500.00
Kerman, mdl/floral on rose, floral border, 1920, 160x110" 4,000.00
Kerman, poled mdl/vines/florals on apricot, 140x65" 6,000.00
Mahal, botehs on navy, ivory floral border, 150x86"...............4,400.00
Northwest Persian, latchhook mdl, ivory on dk bl, 80x55" 1,400.00
Oushak, mdl, salmon/gold on cream, 1920, 150x140" 9,000.00
Panderma Pictorial, mosques/trees on beige, 80x50", EX.........300.00
Qashghai, mdl/morgi/geometrics on dk bl, 1900, 140x70" 4,000.00
Sarouk, floral mdl on red, med bl spandrels, 63x48" 600.00
Sarouk, florals on claret, dk bl border, 2 gb, 80x53", EX 900.00

Shirvan, East Caucasus, very fine weave, even wear, late 1800s, 75" x 50" $1,600.00.

Sivas, mdl/vines, red ground, ivory spandrels, 90x60", VG **700.00**
Soumak bagface, rows of hexagons, lt/bk bl, red, 24x20", VG **495.00**
Tabriz, floral mdl on cream, floral spandrels, 150x130"............ **4,000.00**
Tabriz, Herati on navy, red primary border, 6 gb, 140x100"..... **2,500.00**
Tekke Turkoman, 5 rows guls on red, octagon border, 100x54" ...**400.00**
Yazd, floral on dk bl, claret border, 1920, 160x114"................. **2,400.00**
Yuruk prayer, latchhooks on red/navy, dog gb, 55x41"............. **1,200.00**

Miscellaneous

Braided, eagles w/in 2 co-joined circles, 3-color, 47" L.................**495.00**
Penny, mc dmns in wool, wear, some loose circles, 35x66" **175.00**
Table/Penny, wool appl to ticking, hexagonal, 24x41".................**300.00**

Rum Rill

During the early 1930s, the Red Wing Union Stoneware Company of Red Wing, Minnesota, produced pottery for George Rumrill of Little Rock, Arkansas. Rumrill not only designed the ware but marketed it as well. In 1938 when the Shawnee Pottery Company of Zanesville, Ohio, submitted a lower bid, he awarded the contract to them, and they continued to manufacture decorative pottery for Rumrill until the early forties. His designs can be identified by the 'Rum Rill' mark or label.

Jug, ball form, w/cork...**28.00**
Pitcher, ball form, mauve, #50...**20.00**
Vase, bl, #J-7..**20.00**
Vase, wht, bl int, urn shape, hdls, #638 ....**30.00**
Vase, wht, turq int, emb hdls & rings, #640, 7" **18.00**
Vase, wht, 3-hole top, #601...**30.00**

Russel Wright Dinnerware

Russel Wright, one of America's foremost industrial designers, also designed several lines of ceramic dinnerware, glassware, and aluminum ware that are now highly sought-after collectibles.

His most popular dinnerware then and with today's collectors, American Modern, was manufactured by the Steubenville Pottery Company from 1939 until 1959. It was produced in a variety of solid colors in assortments chosen to stay attune with the times.

Casual (his first line sturdy enough to be guaranteed against breakage for ten years from date of purchase) is relatively easy to find today – simply because it has held up so well. During the years of its production, the Casual line was constantly being restyled, some items as many as five times. Early examples were heavily mottled, while later pieces were smoothly glazed and patterned. The ware was marked with Wright's signature and 'China by Iroquois.' It was marketed in fine department stores throughout the country. After 1950 the line was marked 'Iroquois China by Russel Wright.'

To calculate values for items in American Modern, add 25% to the suggested prices in the following listings for examples in the these colors: White, Bean Brown, Black Chutney, Cantaloupe, Cedar Green, and Glacier Blue. In Casual, Brick Red and Aqua items go for around 200% more than any other colors, while those in Avocado Yellow are priced lower than suggested values.

For those wanting to learn more about the subject, we recommend *The Collector's Encyclopedia of Russel Wright Designs*, by our advisor, Ann Kerr. She is listed in the Directory under Ohio.

American Modern

Bowl, divided vegetable..**48.00**

Bowl, lug fruit 6.00
Bowl, lug soup..10.00
Bowl, salad...38.00
Bowl, vegetable; open..15.00
Bowl, vegetable; w/lid, 12" 25.00
Butter dish..95.00
Carafe, w/stopper, rare 95.00
Celery, 13"..22.00
Coffeepot..65.00
Creamer.. 8.00
Cup & saucer 7.50
Cup & saucer, demitasse..18.00
Hostess set, w/cup 45.00
Pickle dish..10.00
Pitcher, w/lid, 7½" 95.00
Pitcher, water 65.00
Plate, bread & butter; 6¼" 4.00
Plate, chop 20.00
Plate, dinner 6.00
Platter, 14½" 17.50
Ramekin, w/lid, ind 85.00
Refrigerator jar..90.00
Relish, divided...45.00
Sauce boat, 8¼" 15.00
Saucer... 3.00
Shakers, pr 12.00
Stack server..80.00
Teapot...45.00
Tumbler, child's..45.00

American Modern, see listings for specific values.

Casual

Bowl, cereal; restyled, 5".. 6.00
Bowl, fruit; 9½-oz, 5½" 5.00
Bowl, salad; 10"..25.00
Bowl, soup; flat, 21-oz, 8⅜" 15.00
Bowl, soup; restyled, 18-oz 15.00
Casserole, deep, 4-qt, 8" 35.00
Casserole, 2-qt 20.00
Coffeepot 65.00
Creamer & sugar bowl, stacking, family sz 27.50
Cup & saucer, 7-oz..10.00
Fry pan, w/lid 35.00
Gravy bowl, 12-oz, 5¼" 8.00
Mug, restyled, tall, 9-oz 35.00
Pepper mill...45.00
Pitcher, water; restyled, 2-qt..................................40.00
Plate, bread & butter; 6½" 3.00
Plate, chop; 13⅝"...20.00

Plate, dessert & salad; 7½" 5.00
Plate, dinner; 10" 6.00
Plate, luncheon; 9½" 5.00
Plate, party; w/cup 35.00
Platter, oval, 10¼" 25.00
Platter, oval, 14½" 20.00
Shakers, stacking, pr 12.00
Sugar bowl, restyled 20.00
Sugar bowl, stacking, 4" 10.00
Teapot, restyled 85.00
Wine, carafe 65.00

Glassware

Old Morgantown, bowl, dessert; smoke 30.00
Old Morgantown, cocktail, chartreuse 22.00
Old Morgantown, goblet, chartreuse 12.00
Old Morgantown, goblet, coral 12.00
Old Morgantown, goblet, gray 20.00
Old Morgantown, goblet, smoke 30.00
Old Morgantown, Madrid, goblet, water; yel 20.00
Old Morgantown, Madrid, parfait, yel 16.00
Old Morgantown, Madrid, wine, yel 22.50
Old Morgantown, sherbet, seafoam 20.00
Old Morgantown, tumbler, cordial 40.00
Old Morgantown, tumbler, iced tea; seafoam 22.00
Old Morgantown, tumbler, pilsner; coral 40.00
Old Morgantown, tumbler, water; chartreuse 20.00
Old Morgantown, wine, chartreuse 20.00
Paden City, tumbler, snow glass 100.00

Highlight

Bowl, cereal..18.00
Bowl, vegetable; oval 35.00
Creamer..18.00
Cup..15.00
Plate, dinner; 10" 15.00
Platter, oval, lg 40.00
Platter, rnd, sm 40.00

Spun Aluminum

Russel Wright's aluminum ware may not have been especially well accepted in its day – it tended to damage easily and seems to have had only limited market appeal – but today's collectors feel quite differently about it, as is apparent in the suggested values noted in the following listings.

Bowl, fruit 65.00
Bowls, nested, 7", 9", 10", set 135.00
Bun warmer, sphere...65.00
Candelabrum, rare, 18x14" 95.00
Canister set, 4-pc 240.00
Casserole, pottery liner, w/lid 125.00
Casserole, walnut hdl, w/lid 95.00
Cheese board, w/cover 75.00
Coffeepot, AD 345.00
Gravy boat, w/ladle & liner, 3-pc 135.00
Humidor, sandwich; w/lid...185.00
Humidor, tobacco; 12" 95.00
Humidor, tobacco; 16" 145.00
Ice bucket, in holder, w/tongs...55.00
Ice pail, rattan hdl, w/tongs, 10" 65.00

Ice pail, rattan hdl, w/tongs, 5" 35.00
Ice pail, rattan hdl, w/tongs, 6½" 45.00
Lemonade set, pitcher/tray/6 tumblers 350.00
Muffin warmer, wire insert, w/lid 85.00
Mug, beverage 35.00
Mug, ponytail hdl 35.00
Peanut scoop 38.00
Pitcher, stick hdl..185.00
Punch set, rolled edge w/8 hanging cups, rare 875.00
Punch set, w/ladle & liner, 8 cups, covered 975.00
Relish, glass insert, 13¼" 145.00
Relish rosette, lg...85.00
Relish rosette, sm 50.00
Shakers, range, pr 65.00
Tea set, on tray..425.00
Tidbit, 2-tier, rattan hdl...65.00
Tray, cork apple w/stem hdl 85.00
Tray, cork ball... 55.00
Vase, sphere, 10½" 95.00
Vase, sphere, 7" 65.00

Miscellaneous

Bauer, vase, ovoid, 6" 165.00
Harker, clock, Clover 45.00
Harker, shakers, Clover, pr 20.00
Ideal, coffeepot, child's 15.00
Iroquois, casserole, 8" 22.00
Iroquois, coffeepot, restyled 70.00
Iroquois Cookware, sauce pan 65.00
Knowles, pitcher, water..45.00
Knowles, platter, oval 25.00
Sterling, ash tray 65.00
Sterling, pitcher, 2-qt..45.00

Russian Art

Before the Revolution in 1917, many jewelers and craftsmen created exquisite marvels of their arts, distinctive in the extravagant detail of their enamel work, jeweled inlays, and use of precious metals. These treasures aptly symbolized the glitter and the romance of the glorious days under the reign of the Tsars of Imperial Russia.

The most famous of these master jewelers was Peter Carl Faberge. Following the tradition of his father, he took over the Faberge workshop in 1870 at the age of twenty-four. His specialties were enamel work, clockwork automated figures, carved animal and human figures of precious or semiprecious stone and his best-known creations, the Imperial Easter Eggs – each of an entirely different design. By the turn of the century, his influence had spread to other countries, and his work was revered by royalty and the very wealthy. The onset of the war marked the end of the era.

Box, cigarette; Niello silver, gold-wash int, 1870s, 5¼"...............200.00
Box, cigarette; silver & enamel, book form, mk, 1900, 4" L.........200.00
Box, lacquer, Gifts from Overseas, sgn Gorelik, 1½x4½x3" 225.00
Box, lacquer, Living Water, sgn Panova, 1½x3½x3" 195.00
Box, lacquer, sleigh ride scene, 1900, 3¼x13" 425.00
Box, silver gilt/enamel, cartouch form, mk ZZ/84, 2¾-oz.............400.00
Box, silver gilt/enamel, rectangular, mk OU/84, 7-oz.................700.00
Box, silver gilt/enamel, swan vignettes, ftd egg form, 5" 500.00
Buckle, belt; silver & enamel, 1800s 1,200.00
Creamer, silver & enamel, mk MC/82, 2-oz 300.00
Cup, vodka; silver, eng, ftd, 1800s, 3½" 550.00

Cup, vodka; silver, eng E, 1800s..............................330.00
Cup, vodka; silver gilt, HP troika scene, mk, 1900, 2"................150.00
Figure, cat, silver, glass cabachon button, 1890s, 4¼" L...............150.00
Figure, dancer, silver, mtd on lapis lazuli/silver base, 3"...............250.00
Fork, dinner; silver, fiddle pattern, 1895, 5 for............................165.00
Pendant, silver gilt/enamel, eagle on egg shape, 1-oz.................185.00
Salt dish, silver gilt/enamel, kvosch form, mk, 1½-oz, pr.............450.00
Shot glass, silver gilt/enamel, mk AH/84................................275.00
Spoon, silver, spiral hdls, mk/84, set of 9, 4-oz.......................200.00
Teapot, silver, floral cartouches, MOP finial, 1871, 7¼"..............325.00

Silver-gilt and enamel cigarette case, cabachon blue stone thumb piece, Dimitri Nicholaev, ca 1910, 301 grams, 4½", $1,300.00.

Sabino

Sabino art glass was produced by Marius-Ernest Sabino in France during the 1920s and '30s. It was made in opalescent, frosted, and colored glass and was designed to reflect the Art Deco style of that era. In 1960 using molds he modeled by hand, Sabino once again began to produce art glass using a special formula he himself developed that was characterized by a golden opalescence. Although the family continued to produce glassware for export after his death in 1971, they were never able to duplicate Sabino's formula.

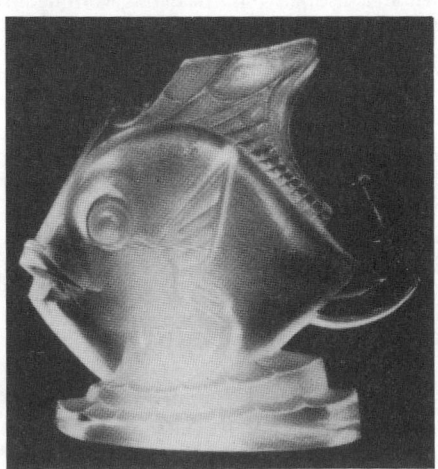

Figure of an angel fish, blue-tinted opalescent, ca 1930s, 4", NM, $225.00.

Bottle, scent; nudes bathing, bl opal, Sabino-Paris, 5½"..............135.00
Bottle, scent; 4 nudes, Deco style, mk, 8"............................165.00
Figurine, butterfly, wings open, sm....................................30.00
Figurine, dove, head up, sm...22.50
Figurine, gazelle, on base, 4½"..100.00
Figurine, heron stands on rectangular base, ca 1930, 7"..............170.00
Figurine, L'Idole, nude sits on tasseled cushion, 1925, 7".........3,800.00

Figurine, Le Reveil, nude, arm up, hair reaches ground, 7".........500.00
Globe, ribbed/scalloped fans, 1930s, 20"...........................3,000.00
Lamp, dome shade resembles cascading water; Gillen std, 17".....880.00
Mirror, octagonal, 10"..25.00
Mirror, oval, 6x4"..15.00
Sconce, lady's head, hair in braids w/flowers, #4684, 14"........2,200.00
Tray, sea urchin, lg...80.00
Tray, sm butterfly, rnd...75.00
Vase, amber w/allover clear & frosted swirls & dots, 13"...........600.00
Vase, Art Nouveau...225.00
Vase, blk, artichoke leaves on sphere, 7"............................800.00
Vase, flower thickets relief, nymph-form hdls, 7½", pr.............700.00
Vase, geometric panels, doves on neck, opal, 8½"...................500.00
Vase, Manta Ray...250.00

Salesman's Samples and Patent Models

Salesman's samples and patent models are often mistaken for toys or homemade folk art pieces. They are instead actual working models made by very skilled craftsmen who worked as model-makers. Patent models were made until the early 1900s. After that, the patent office no longer required a model to grant a patent. The name of the inventor or the model-maker and the date it was built is sometimes noted on the patent model. Salesman's samples were occasionally made by model-makers, but often they were assembled by an employee of the company. These usually carried advertising messages to boost the sale of the product. Though they are still in use today, the most desirable examples date from the 1800s to about 1945.

Many small stoves are incorrectly termed a 'salesman's sample'; remember that no matter how detailed one may be, it must be considered a toy unless accompanied by a carrying case – the indisputable mark of a salesman's sample.

Album, Raphael Tuck Xmas Cards, over 400 in leather case.......500.00
Bathtub, CI, clawfoot, NM..75.00
Bathtub, tin w/worn pnt, 6"..40.00
Bible, 1915, NM...45.00
Box, Jack Daniels, wood, 13x10"......................................40.00
Calendar order book, 1938...25.00
Carte-de-visite photo case, 4 matted examples, EX....................40.00
Cash register, RC Allen, dtd 1958, EX.................................25.00
Chandelier, hanging beads, Victorian style............................90.00
Clothesline, Nu-Way, Elgin IL, 1930s.................................165.00
Coffin, figured wood lid, 15" L.......................................85.00
Decoy, Carry Lite, Milwaukee WI, EX..................................35.00
Dinner pail, Lisk, copper w/worn nickel plate, dents.................40.00
Dishwasher, Youngstown, working model, 1947.......................675.00
Dumbwaiter, Stauffacher, oak case, ca 1890..........................95.00
Farm gate, dbl, wood/metal, functional, 27" W, VG.................200.00
Farm gate, Easy, Pat 1909, in carrying case, 27" L.................145.00
Farm gate, No Sag, wood w/metal fittings, 13x27"...................120.00
Fence, US Poultry, galvanized wire, paper label, 4" roll.............35.00
Floor sweeper, Bissell's Junior, complete w/case, NM................35.00
Food chopper, Rollman Mfg, Mt Joy PA, Pat 06-14-15, EX..........50.00
Food grinder, JP Co, 3"..35.00
Furnace, Front Rank, 3 hinged doors, 4 chambers, NM..............750.00
Furnace, Holland, CI/aluminum, coal burning, 9"......................55.00
Grater, gr & wht mottled granite ware, 3"............................85.00
Grave vault, Clark, cast aluminum, 6½" L.............................40.00
Hand truck, Wrigley in relief, CI, W on ft, 8", VG...................300.00
Hat, Victory, straw, #25-G-2..18.00
Hat box, Dobbs 5th Avenue..10.00
Hitching post, jockey, CI, 10½"..450.00

Ice cream freezer, Peerless Dana Freezer, 7", VG	145.00
Jardiniere on ped, Weller, floral, yel on brn, 8"	750.00
Kitchen cabinet set, General Electric, 10-pc, EX	45.00
Midget Smoker, trade stimulator, w/case, EX	550.00
Monument, Monumental Bronze Co-1885, cast wht metal, 19"	165.00
Pill case, McKesson/Robbins, w/5 sm bottles	45.00
Plow, horse-drawn, wood w/wrought iron fittings, 26", VG	400.00
Plow, South Bend #15, 1-row, pnt pine/steel, 1886, 23½"	1,900.00
Porch swing, wooden slats, 16" L	125.00
Portable Shower Bath-1880, worn mc pnt, pat model, 7½"	165.00
Pump, CI/bronze w/wooden base, worn pnt/minor rust, 30"	120.00
Pump, Cincinnati Co, wood/CI, pnt: Water Purifier, 11", VG	225.00
Punch bowl, bl irid stretch glass, +6 cups, rare	275.00
Railroad trestle, wood, 10"	35.00
Rug, Baseball NY American League, 5¼x5¼"	20.00
Saddle, tooled leather, sides different, model #s, 12", VG	300.00
Sawtooth setter, Buckeye, Pat July '10, CI on wood base, 9"	75.00
Shoe, Tom McAnn, EX	25.00
Soap box, Swifts, w/17 bars, 1920s, 4x12x7", NM	80.00
Spittoon, US Stamping Co...WVA, bl & wht granite ware	750.00
Stalk cutter, brass/iron/steel/wood, adjusts, complex, 20"	1,100.00
Steamer, tin w/copper bottom, w/inserts & spout whistle, 6"	95.00
Stock pen, wood, folds into case, Pat Sept 29 1891, 24" L	150.00
Storm window, Weather Seal, wooden, in case, 20x26½"	15.00
Table, ice cream; porc over CI, Vitrolite top, w/stool	275.00
Tent, 20th century, minor wear, 26x30"	50.00
Threshing machine, wood, galvanized metal/CI mts, 13", EX	425.00
Tin container, Libby's Corn Beef, EX details, 1915, NM	30.00
Tin container, Libby's Salmon, 1920s, EX	20.00
Tool, Best Ho Farm & Garden	20.00
Trimmer, candle wax; SP, mk Pat, 7", +tray	65.00
Waffle iron, Super Maid Cookware, CI w/wood hdls, 7½"	60.00
Wash tub wringer, Horseshoe Brand, wood/CI/rubber, 15" L	75.00
Wind charger, EX	275.00
Windmill, Woodmanse, aluminum/brass/metal, ornate, 30"	2,500.00
Window sash & lock, wood w/CI fittings, 18"	10.00

Hawkes mowing machine, Hoosick, NY, cast iron and wood, working model, in case, $3,250.00.

Salt Glaze

As early as the 1600s, potters used common salt to glaze their stoneware. This was accomplished by heating the salt and introducing it into the kiln at maximum temperature. The resulting gray-white glaze was a thin, pitted surface that resembles the peel of an orange.

Charger, emb star/dot border w/diaper rim, 1760, 15½", EX	400.00
Pitcher, mc landscape of ruins, old rpr, 9"	1,800.00
Plate, emb decor w/rtcl rim, hairline, 10"	800.00
Plate, emb scalloped rim, minor wear, 9⅜"	200.00
Plate, emb scalloped rim, W Pitt Esq, 9"	775.00
Syrup, emb figures in arches, pewter lid, blk transfer, 6⅝"	155.00
Teapot, camel shape, lid is howdah, 5¼", EX	6,100.00
Teapot, Castleford type, bl striping, hinged lid, 5⅝"	800.00
Teapot, emb decor on panels, animal finial, 5⅜", NM	2,250.00
Teapot, emb florals/medallions, swan finial, 6½", EX	1,500.00
Teapot, mc youth & maid, old rpr, 3⅜"	1,800.00
Teapot, medallions, brn on wht, domed rtcl lid, Turner, 6½"	300.00

Salt Shakers

The screw-top salt shaker was invented by John Mason in 1858. In 1871 when salt became more refined, some ceramic shakers were molded with pierced tops. 'Christmas' shakers, so called because of their December 25, 1877, patent date, were fitted with a rotary agitator designed to break up any lumps in the salt. There are four types: Christmas Barrel (rare in cranberry and amethyst); Christmas Panel (rare in colors); Christmas Pearl (opaque, pearly white with painted decor); and Octagon Waffle (clear, thick glass made in three sizes with a rotary agitator, usually having undated tops.) The dated top and patented agitator for the Christmas salt shakers were produced by Dana K. Alden of Boston; the glass bodies were made by the Boston and Sandwich Glass Co. in the late 1870s and 1880s. Identical shakers which have no agitator or dated top are the companion peppers; these fetch about 30% less than the salts on today's markets.

Today much of the interest in collecting is concentrated on art glass, Wave Crest, and custard glass examples. (See also specific categories.) If you would like to learn more about salt shakers, we recommend *The World of Salt Shakers*, by Mildred and Ralph Lechner; their address may be found in the Directory under Virginia. Those interested in novelty shakers will enjoy *Salt and Pepper Shakers*, an illustrated price guide by Helene Guarnaccia, and *The Collector's Encyclopedia of Salt and Pepper Shakers, Figural and Novelty*, by Melva Davern. In the following listing, prices are for single shakers unless noted 'pair.' Values are for old, original shakers. Some of these have been reproduced, and this will be noted in the description.

Acorn, pink to white shading, $45.00; Grape with Vine, pink, rare, $55.00.

Argus Swirl, cranberry	150.00

Barrel, Excelsior, emb Excelsior, pat 1886, rare............................**65.00**
Beaded Dahlia, gr opaque, pr **32.50**
Brittanic, amber flashed, orig lid **37.00**
Bubble, opal lattice pattern, Hobbs/Brockunier, scarce **40.00**
Bulging Petal, bl **25.00**
Button Arches, ruby flashed, pr **40.00**
Challinor's Forget-Me-Not, pk opal, pr **50.00**
Chick head, SP, lime body w/wht mums & gr leaves, Mt WA **375.00**
Christmas Barrel, amber, lid dtd, Dana Alden **100.00**
Christmas Barrel, cobalt, salt w/agitator, +pepper, pr **200.00**
Christmas Barrel, cranberry, salt w/agitator, +pepper, pr **450.00**
Christmas Barrel, cranbery, orig lid & agitator **290.00**
Christmas Barrel, dk amethyst, orig pewter lid & agitator **100.00**
Christmas Barrel, gr, orig lid & agitator, pr **225.00**
Christmas Barrel, peacock bl, salt w/agitator, +pepper, pr............**250.00**
Christmas Panel, amethyst, w/lid & agitator **225.00**
Christmas Panel, cranberry, w/lid & agitator **300.00**
Christmas Panel, dk amethyst, w/lid & agitator **275.00**
Christmas Panel, sapphire bl, w/lid & agitator **225.00**
Circled Scroll, opal colors, gr or bl, ca 1903 ....**80.00**
Cloverleaf, bl opaque, pr **50.00**
Cord & Tassel, gr **20.00**
Cotton Bale, bl opaque **25.00**
Creased Bale, bl opaque **35.00**
Croesus, gr w/VG gold, pr **120.00**
Crossroads, amber, pr **35.00**
Daisy & Fern on Ribbed Swirl, cranberry opal, pr **140.00**
Diamond w/Peg, custard, pr **85.00**
Dice, orig lids, pr **55.00**
Draped Beads, HP milk glass w/beaded panels, Fostoria, 1898 ....**35.00**
Egg in Blossom, Mt WA **45.00**
Fan Band, Dbl; pk cased, pr **70.00**
Fig, violets, wht on cranberry, Mt WA, orig lid **185.00**
Fine Cut, yel, pr **50.00**
Flower & Rain, cased, bl or yel, Mt WA, rare, pr **290.00**
Flower Band, pk cased, pr **85.00**
Forget-Me-Not, milk glass, tall, pr..**45.00**
Geneve, gr w/gold, orig lid..**28.00**
Georgia Gem, custard, souvenir, pr **85.00**
Guttate, milk glass **25.00**
Guttate, pk cased, pr (reproduced) **75.00**
Half Cone, satin, Consolidated Lamp & Glass, 1890s..................**60.00**
Heart, bl opaque, Dithridge, 1894-1897, pr **60.00**
Heart, custard, Dithridge, ca 1894-1897, pr..................................**75.00**
Heart, milk glass, pr **40.00**
Horseshoe, amber, lg, pr..**35.00**
Intaglio, emerald gr w/gold, Northwood, rare, pr..........................**325.00**
Invt Fan & Feather, pk slag, Northwood, 1900s, rare, pr **750.00**
Invt T'print, bl w/HP florals, pr **75.00**
Iris w/Meander, gr w/gold, pr **75.00**
Jefferson Optic, amethyst, HP, pr **65.00**
Leaf & Spear, HP opalware, Wave Crest, pr **165.00**
Leaf Base, ca 1910-1913, pr..**30.00**
Leaf Mold, vaseline spatter, pr..**125.00**
Leaf Overlapping, bl, pr..**40.00**
Leaf Overlapping, pk cased, pr **65.00**
Lobe Four, wht/bl floral on yel, 6-lobed, Mt WA, pr **185.00**
Mitered Diamond Point (Zigzag), milk glass................................**15.00**
MOP Diamond, bl floral branch, Mt WA......................................**295.00**
National's Eureka, ruby stain, pr **65.00**
Nestor, amethyst, gold & enamel, pr..**55.00**
Nestor, bl, no enamel **25.00**
O'Hara Daimond, red flashed, pr..**50.00**
Optic, Hobb's, rubena w/florals, pr..**190.00**

Overlapping Shell, pk **40.00**
Panel, Ten; opaline (gr or bl), rare **80.00**
Panelled Scroll, gr..**20.00**
Panelled Shell, pk cased..**30.00**
Pillar, Ribbed, glossy burmese, Mt WA, rare, pr............................**800.00**
Pillar, Ribbed, satinized burmese, HP florals, Mt WA, rare, pr.....**900.00**
Quilted Phlox, gr cased, Northwood..**30.00**
Reverse Swirl, clear opal **48.00**
Reverse Swirl, cranberry opal, pr **65.00**
Roman Rosette, pr **30.00**
Scroll, gr opaque, ftd **23.00**
Sequoia, bl, in stand, pr..**85.00**
Shoshone, pr **30.00**
Sunset, milk glass **15.00**
Swag w/Brackets, amethyst w/gold, pr..**80.00**
Thousand Eye, bl..**32.00**
Tokyo, clear opal..**35.00**
Torch & Wreath, custard, Dithridge, pr..**85.00**
Wildflower, vaseline (reproduced) **45.00**
Woven Neck, Wave Crest, kitten in grass decor **55.00**

Novelty

Boat, smokestacks are shakers, red/wht, plastic, pr **8.00**
Bride & Groom, Occupied Japan, pr **20.00**
Chipmunks, cartoon-type figures, ceramic, brn gloss, pr............... **8.00**
Clowns on donkeys, ceramic, pr **10.00**
Conestoga wagon & pioneer, ceramic, pr **8.00**
Dog, Mugsy, bl bows around head, ceramic, pr **12.00**
Dutch boy & girl, kissing couple, ceramic, pr **10.00**
Fish, Chicken of the Sea, yel/bl, ceramic, pr **8.00**
Hillbillies taking a snooze, ceramic, pr..**10.00**
Humpty Dumpty & wall, ceramic, pr..**10.00**
Indians, wood grained, ceramic, pr.. **7.00**
Kangaroo w/baby, brn, ceramic, pr **10.00**
Locomotive & coal car, ceramic, pr.. **8.00**
Old-fashioned car, people as shakers, plastic, pr **10.00**
Parakeets on a branch, yel, plastic **10.00**
Policeman & thug, ceramic, pr..**12.00**
Poodle, trimmed w/gingerbread, wht, ceramic, pr.......................... **7.00**
President Kennedy in his rocking chair, ceramic, pr......................**25.00**
Rabbits, ceramic, wht gloss, pr... **8.00**
Revolver, ceramic, brn/blk gloss, pr..**10.00**
Sailor & fish, painted wood, pr... **7.00**
Steam engines, bronze, pr **8.00**
Stork carrying a baby, ceramic, pr **10.00**
Tappan chefs, yel/red, plastic, pr..**10.00**
Toilet, red, plastic, pr **6.00**
World's Fair, New York 1939, orange/bl, plastic, pr **25.00**

Salts, Open

Before salt became refined, processed, and 'free-flowing' as we know it today, it was necessary to serve it in a 'cellar.' An innovation of the early 1800s, the master salt cellar was placed by the host and passed from person to person. Smaller 'individual' salts were a part of each place setting. A small silver spoon was used to sprinkle it onto the food. If you would like to learn more about the subject of salts, we recommend *5,000 Open Salts*, written by William Heacock and our advisor for this category, Patricia Johnson, with many full-color illustrations and current values; you will find Patricia Johnson's address in the Directory under California.

In the listings below, the numbers refer to *Open Salts* by Heacock and Johnson, and *Pressed Glass Salt Dishes* by L.W. and D.B. Neal. Lines with 'repro' within the description reflect values for reproduced salts.

Key:
EPNS — electroplated nickel silver   HM — hallmarked

Cameo, Art Glass, and Miscellaneous

Daum Nancy, windmill scene, HJ-10	750.00
Doulton, Lambeth, sterling HM rim, HJ-1851, ca 1900	65.00
Itaglio, animals or butterfly HP, sgn, HJ-159	55.00
Itaglio, bl, gr, etc..., unsgn, HJ-215	15.00
Millefiori: European, HJ-609, ca 1900, 2" dia	350.00
Monot & Stumpf, HJ-19, ca 1900, ind	85.00
Moorcroft, sterling HM rim, London, HJ-1762, ca 1920	55.00
Mt Washington, HJ-35 to HJ-44, unsgn	90.00
Plique-a-jour, Viking boat, Norway 930S, HJ-83, 2½"	650.00
Royal Doulton, sterling HM rim, HJ-1870, ca 1873	95.00
Sowerby, HJ 385 & HJ-2090, sgn & #d	55.00

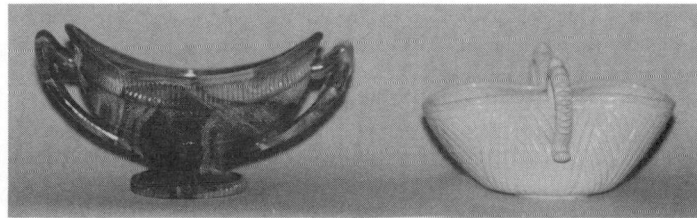

Signed Sowerby: HJ-385, ca 1880, in purple slag, $75.00, in blue slag, $110.00; ca 1878, in cream opaque, $65.00.

Steuben, Calcite, ped ft, HJ-34	200.00
Stevens & Williams, opal w/vaseline ruffles, HJ-72	95.00
Tiffany, bl, ruffled top, sgn, HJ-30	375.00
Tiffany, pulled ears, sgn, HJ-3	275.00
Tiffany, witch's pot, sgn, HJ-1	275.00
Webb, Burmese, HJ-75, ca 1890, 1¾" dia	650.00
Webb, 2-color, sgn, HJ-84	900.00
Wedgwood, sterling rim, sgn, HJ-1850, ca 1897	160.00

China and Porcelain

Austria, HP, mk, HJ-1272, rnd, ind	12.00
Belleek, HP, ruffled top, mk, HJ-1310, rnd, ind	35.00
Celery salt, HP, HJ-1720, ind	10.00
Dresden, attached flowers, HJ-1689, ind	45.00
Elfinware, heavy decor, sgn Germany, HJ-1270, ind	30.00
Elfinware, Japan, HJ-1222, ind	10.00
Elfinware, tub, sgn Germany, HJ-1250, ind	25.00
Elfinware, wheelbarrow, sgn Germany, HJ-1244, ind	65.00
Haviland, HJ-1400, ind	35.00
HP, artist sgn, scalloped ft, HJ-1390, ind	20.00
Limoges, HP, mk, HJ-1275, rnd, ind	12.00
Meissen, HJ-1595, sq, ind	60.00
Nippon, celery salt, HJ-1714, ind	8.00
Nippon, HP, HJ-1365, ind	10.00
Nippon, HP, ped ft, HJ-1495, ind	24.00
Nippon, HP floral tub, HJ-1454, ind	20.00
Pickard, HJ-1569, sq, ind	45.00
Royal Bayreuth, animal decor, ped ft, HJ-1666, ind	135.00
Royal Bayreuth, figural claw, HJ-1667, ind	75.00
Royal Copenhagen, HJ-1332, ind	25.00
Royal Worcester, HJ-1861, ca 1862, ind	120.00

Satsuma, HJ-1931, ca 1940-1960, ind	20.00

Cut Glass

Clark, ped ft, sgn, HJ-3009	30.00
Cranberry, ped ft, etched, HJ-123, ca 1890	85.00
Diamond Point, HJ-3101	10.00
English Strawberry & Diamond Cut, oval tub, HJ-2857	45.00
Faceted, HJ-2919	14.00
Hawkes, sgn, HJ-3064	55.00
Heart, spade, diamond, club, HJ-3034 to HJ-3035, 4 for	225.00
J Hoare, sgn, HJ-3166	45.00
Waterford, ped ft, sgn, HJ-3698, ca 1970	35.00
Waterford type, gr, ped ft, HJ-601, ca 1860	125.00
Waterford type, ped ft, HJ-3699, ca 1860	75.00
Zippered, HJ-3088	12.00

Doubles

Austria Hungary, HM sterling, w/mustard, HJ-751, 1850s, M	350.00
Automobile, pressed glass, mk Pontieux, HJ-3764	55.00
European, pressed glass, plain, HJ-3976 to HJ-3978	25.00
European, 800 sterling, figural, cobalt inserts, HJ-2062	125.00
French, cobalt pressed glass, HJ-2087	55.00
French, pressed glass figural, HJ-3777	35.00
French, sterling HM, cobalt insert, HJ-761, ca 1845	150.00
German, HP porc, HJ-1150	45.00
KPM, figural, porc, HJ-1155 to HJ-1156, ca 1860	295.00
KPM, porc, wht w/gold border, HJ-1142	35.00
Meissen, porc, w/hdl, HJ-1169	125.00
Quimper, porc, sgn, old, HJ-1135	65.00

Lacy Glass

American, non-flint, ca 1920-1940, repro, VG	45.00
Avon, #3506, repro	5.00
French, amber, non-flint, #2117, ca 1920-1940, repro, VG	65.00
Metro Museum of Art, vaseline, bl, etc..., MMA, repro, VG	15.00
Neal BF-1, basket of flowers, #3462, VG	75.00
Neal BF-1B, opal, basket of flowers, chip on leg	125.00
Neal BS-2, opal, Beaded Scroll, Sandwich, NM	150.00
Neal BS-3, chalk wht, Beaded Scroll, Sandwich, EX	350.00
Neal BS-3, dk opaque violet, Beaded Scroll	750.00
Neal BT-2, cobalt, boat, Stourbridge, NM	850.00
Neal BT-8, cobalt, boat, Sandwich, VG	950.00
Neal BT-9, opal, boat, NM	400.00
Neal BT-9, violet, boat, NM	500.00
Neal CD-3, w/lid, NM	700.00
Neal CN-1A, crown, Sandwich, NM	125.00
Neal CT-1A, chariot, Sandwich, VG	125.00
Neal DI-18, divided, French, NM	125.00
Neal DI-4, sapphire, divided, NM	800.00
Neal DI-8, dbl, #3460, roughage on bottom	140.00
Neal DS-11, opal, Strawberry Dmn, Sandwich, NM	420.00
Neal EE-3B, eagles on 4 corners, VG	150.00
Neal EE-3B, opal, eagle, NM	350.00
Neal GA-2, cobalt, Cathedral Windows, leg chipped	100.00
Neal GA-2A, med bl, Gothic Arch, minor chips	400.00
Neal HN-18A, opal, ftd, #4460, VG	250.00
Neal MV-1, dk aqua, sq/ftd, Mt Vernon Glass Co, EX	240.00
Neal NE-1A, wht opaque NE Glass Co, minor roughage	225.00
Neal NE-1A, wht opaque, NE Glass Co, EX	125.00
Neal NE-5, lt gr, NE Glass Co, NM	300.00
Neal OG-2, heart, NE Glass Co, EX	125.00

Neal OG-4, violet-bl, oval, Pittsburgh, EX....................700.00
Neal OL-17, minor chips, 3½" L 45.00
Neal OL-9, oblong, Pittsburgh, EX 275.00
Neal OO-1, dk amethyst, octagonal oblong, Sandwich, EX........425.00
Neal OO-1A, NM....................60.00
Neal OP-1, ftd, Sandwich, EX 200.00
Neal OP-17, oblong, Sandwich, NM 200.00
Neal OP-2, clambroth, ftd oval, Sandwich, NM 300.00
Neal PE-1, beaded base, Providence Flint Glass, NM 100.00
Neal PO-4, cobalt, Peacock Eye, NM 750.00
Neal PR-1C, violet-bl, Peacock Eye, rnd, Sandwich, NM 700.00
Neal RP-17, rnd w/ped base, Sandwich, EX 210.00
Neal SC-16, cobalt, French, EX 1,200.00
Neal SC-6, cobalt, scroll, EX 425.00
Neal SD-2A, Strawberry Dmn, paw ft, Sandwich, NM................50.00
Neal SD-4, Strawberry Dmn, Sandwich, EX 100.00
Neal SD-7, cobalt, Strawberry Dmn, Sandwich, NM................400.00
Neal SL-14, opal, shell, Sandwich, EX 225.00
Neal SN-1B, clambroth, stag's horn, EX....................225.00
Neal WN-1, wagon, Sandwich, EX....................450.00
Taiwan, Mexico, bl or gr, #924, repro 5.00

Pressed Pattern Glass, Clear

Beaded Acorn Leaf Band, HJ-3609, flint, master....................65.00
Bearded Head, HJ-3636, master 40.00
Bird & Berry, sgn Degenhardt, HJ-998, ind 30.00
Bird & Berry, unsgn Degenhardt, HJ-998, ind 12.00
Bow Tie, HJ-2548, ind 25.00
Brazilian, HJ-2572, ind....................15.00
Butterfly, HJ-3539, master 45.00
Chicken, covered, sgn Vallerystahl, HJ-958 to HJ-960, ind 55.00
Daisy & Button, LG Wright, HJ-875 & HJ-876, repro, ind, ea.......5.00
English Hobnail, HJ-2680, ind 8.00
Euchre, HJ-3018 to HJ-3021, ind, ea 12.00
Faceted, HJ-2910, ind 6.00
Heisey, Fandango, HJ-2673, ind 25.00
Heisey, tub, sgn, HJ-2850 ....12.00
Heisey Fancy Loop, HJ-2674, ind 25.00
Horseshoe, HJ-3741, ind....................27.00
Liberty Bell 1776-1876, HJ-2689, ind 55.00
Moon & Star, HJ-3044, 1940s, ind....................15.00
Moon & Star, ped ft, HJ-3044, old, ind....................45.00
Open Plaid, HJ-3567, master....................15.00
Panelled Grape Band, HJ-3516, master....................35.00
Roman Key, HJ-3582, flint, master 55.00
Sawtooth Circle, HJ-3540, master....................25.00
Snail, HJ-2656, ind....................28.00
Stippled Bowl, HJ-3589, flint, master 65.00
Tree of Life, 'SALT,' HJ-3581, master 75.00
Tulip w/Sawtooth, HJ-3621, master 35.00
Turtle, HJ-3758, ind....................35.00
Washington Centennial, HJ-3510, master....................45.00

Pressed Pattern Glass, Colored

Bird & Berry, McKee, vaseline, amber, or bl, HJ-997, ind..........55.00
Daisy & Button Triangle, bl, old, HJ-442, ind 25.00
Jersey Swirl, bl, HJ-426, ind 25.00
Moon & Star, all colors are repros, HJ-870, ind....................5.00
Tub, unmk Heisey, pk or gr, HJ-2850, ind....................25.00
Two-Panel, bl, gr, or amber, HJ-429, ind....................20.00
Two-Panel, bl, gr, or vaseline, HJ-564, master 25.00
Wildflower w/turtle base, amber, HJ-506, master 125.00

Silverplate

American, cobalt liner, mk W&S, HJ-653....................15.00
American, ruby liner, mk Derby, HJ-319 ....65.00
American, Victorian, crackle glass liner, Meriden, HJ-4215 ....85.00
English, ornate, w/babies, gold wash, ca 1880 ....125.00
English, ruby liner, paw ft, ca 1900....................55.00
English, set of 4 w/spoons, ca 1880, MIB 100.00
English, vaseline ruffled Webb insert, HJ-95, ca 1880 ....225.00
European, vaseline ruffled liner, HJ-91, ca 1880....................125.00

Sterling and Continental Silver

Albert Cole, medallion, HJ-4028, ca 1860 ....175.00
American, ped ft, HJ-4034, ca 1930....................35.00
Dutch, cobalt liner, HM, HJ-713, ca 1880, 4-pc set....................300.00
English, gr liner, HJ-379, ind....................75.00
English, ornate, HM, HJ-4164, ca 1899 ....125.00
French, cobalt liner, HM, HJ-720, ca 1845, master 175.00
French, liner & spoon, HJ-3937, ind 135.00
German, HJ-4286, ca 1800, master, pr....................450.00
German 800, HJ-3983....................45.00
Gorham, medallion, ped ft, HJ-3976, ca 1860 ....175.00
Gorham, plain, HJ-3992, ca 1920 ....20.00
Gorham, ruby liner, HJ-323, ca 1890 ....135.00
Russian, chair, HM, HJ-4735, ca 1890....................450.00
Swan, cut glass w/835 sterling wings, old, HJ-4287 ....55.00
Viking, 900, Norway boat, HJ-4260, w/pepper 75.00
Viking, 900, Norway boat, HJ-4260, w/spoon....................35.00

Samplers

American samplers were made as early as the colonial days; even earlier examples from 17th century England still exist today. Changes in style and decorative motif are evident down through the years. Verses were not added until the late 17th century. By the 18th century, samplers were used not only for sewing experience but also as an educational tool. Young ladies, who often signed and dated their work, embroidered numbers and letters of the alphabet and practiced fancy stitches as well. Fruits and flowers were added for borders; birds, animals, and Adam and Eve were popular subjects. Later, houses and other buildings were included. By the 19th century, the American Eagle and the little red schoolhouse had made their appearances.

Adam & Eve/alphanumerics/flowers, sgn/age 11/1824, 12x12" ..300.00
Adam & Eve/verse/crowned lion, 1831, EX work, 14x16", VG...600.00
Alphabets, dtd 1871, 9x12"....................185.00
Alphabets, sgn/1840, homespun, modern fr, 21½x18½" 275.00
Alphabets, strawberry border, sgn/1826, EX color, 20x21" 2,750.00
Alphabets, 3 trees w/birds, sgn/dtd 1790, 7¾x11", NM..............600.00
Alphabets (5 styles)/bldg/verse, sgn/1803, 21x16", NM 3,250.00
Alphabets/Adams & Eve w/snake & trees, sgn/1808, 11x18" 575.00
Alphabets/animals/etc, sgn/1805, wear/holes, 17x13" 400.00
Alphabets/crowns/flowers, sgn/1813, VG color, rpr, 10x12" 350.00
Alphabets/flowers/bldgs, sgn/1893, mahog fr, 21x23"....................300.00
Alphabets/house on hill/trees/crows, sgn/1827, 15x15" 700.00
Alphabets/house/birds/animals, sgn/1848, EX color, 18x18" 475.00
Alphabets/morbid verse, homespun, sgn/1834, 19x19"....................325.00
Alphabets/trees/deer/etc, sgn/1826, EX color, 12x19", EX 675.00
Alphabets/verse/crown, sgn/1768, EX color, 12x17" 775.00
Alphabets/verse/name, sgn/1763, 8x12"....................450.00
Alphabets/vine border/crown, sgn/1821, 11x12"....................300.00
Alphanumerics, bl/gold on linen, 6x20"....................375.00

Alphabet bands and floral border, signed and dated 1787, 11" x 8", $700.00.

Alphanumerics in gray, sgn/1855, 16x15"............................250.00
Animals/trees/verse, sgn/1798, 21x16", EX 550.00
Brick house w/flowers, sgn/1833, 26x22" 2,500.00
Dog/birds/flowers/church, sgn/1872, 16x17", EX....................225.00
Family Record, vine border, sgn/ca 1835, 15x16", VG.................400.00
Floral border, vase of flowers, long verse, 1849, 27x20" 400.00
Floral border/Psalm LXVIII, sgn/1792, 15x16", EX 250.00
Flower basket/verse, sgn/1889, fr, 15¾x20", EX 295.00
Flowering urns/X-stitch trees/verse, sgn/aged 9, unfr, 17" 300.00
Flowers/birds/tree/2 figures, EX work, sgn/1785, 14x15" 700.00
House/landscape/4-line prayer, sgn, 20x16", VG.......................300.00
Lg bldg/verses/strawberry border, sgn/1832, 18x18", EX 2,550.00
Map of MA on homespun, sgn/1810, 9x12", NM 1,900.00
Potted plants/birds/trees, sgn by 8-yr old, unfr, 12x11"................325.00
Stylized floral border/long verse, sgn, 1845, 17x17" 775.00
2 lg houses/flowers/verse, 9x10" 900.00

Sandwich Glass

The Boston and Sandwich Glass Company was founded in 1820 by Deming Jarves in Sandwich, Massachusetts. Their first products were simple cruets, salts, half-pint jugs, and lamps. They were attributed as being one of the first to perfect a method for pressing glass, a step toward the manufacture of the 'lacy' glass which they made until about 1840. Many other types of glass were made there – cut, colored, snakeskin, hobnail, and opalescent among them.

After the Civil War, profits began to dwindle due to the keen competition of the Western factories which were situated in areas rich in natural gas and easily accessible sand and coal deposits. The end came with an unreconcilable wage dispute between the workers and the company, and the factory closed in 1888.

Our advisor for this category is Richard Marden; he is listed in the Directory under New Hampshire. See also Cup Plates; Salts, Open; specific types of glass.

Bowl, lacy, chain border, open hdls, oval, 12" L, EX................ 2,000.00
Bowl, lacy, grape border, w/lid, 6" dia, EX............................825.00
Bowl, lacy, Peacock Eye, 8½", NM.....................................100.00
Bowl, lacy, Peacock Eye/Princess Feather, 12", VG 350.00
Bowl, Loop, canary yel, w/lid, 6½" dia, NM 550.00
Butter dish, Prism, canary yel, 7" dia, M 500.00
Candlestick, Acanthus Leaf, bl/wht opaque, 7¾", M, pr 1,000.00

Candlestick, Acanthus Leaf, bl/wht opaque, 9", NM, pr 1,200.00
Candlestick, Acanthus Leaf, bl/wht opaque, 9½", VG, pr 550.00
Candlestick, columnar, bl/wht opaque, 8½", NM 1,100.00
Candlestick, columnar, clambroth, 9", pr 900.00
Candlestick, dolphin, canary yel, 10", pr, EX 850.00
Candlestick, dolphin, scalloped base, 6⅝" 800.00
Candlestick, hexagonal, bl opaque, 7", pr 800.00
Candlestick, hexagonal, bl/wht opaque, 7½", pr 1,000.00
Candlestick, hexagonal, clambroth, 7½" 150.00
Candlestick, Loop & Petal, canary yel, 7", EX, pr 300.00
Candlestick, Loop & Petal, clambroth, 7", NM, pr....................325.00
Candlestick, miniature, 1⅝", pr 150.00
Chamberstick, hexagonal, miniature, 1"................................250.00
Cup & saucer, lacy, miniature, NM 180.00
Decanter, Ashburton, canary yel, period stopper, qt 600.00
Dish, lacy, eagle, octagonal, 7½", NM 250.00
Dish, lacy, Hairpin, 6", NM..150.00
Egg cup, Diamond Point, w/lid 210.00
Iron, lacy, miniature, NM 150.00
Jar, pomade; bear form, clambroth, Xd paws, lg, VG..................450.00
Jar, pomade; bear form, wht opaque, 3½", NM 575.00
Lamp, Acanthus Leaf, bl/wht opaque, 12", pr 1,200.00
Lamp, Cable in Ring, appl hdl, 2½", M.................................420.00
Lamp, clambroth, dbl brass camphene burner, 6" 375.00
Lamp, cut flint font atop opal 3-dolphin base, 12" 900.00
Lamp, wht w/3-color mottle 3-dolphin base, 11" 5,500.00
Lamp, wht/cranberry cut to clear, marble base, 12" 350.00
Mustard pot, lacy, Peacock Eye, w/lid & undertray, NM 500.00
Pitcher, lacy, miniature, M 100.00
Pitcher, lacy, opal, miniature, EX..125.00
Spill holder, cobalt, loops & stars alternate, NM 750.00
Spill holder, fiery opal, 6-point stars in rows...........................450.00
Spill holder, Sandwich Star, clambroth 350.00
Spill holder, Sandwich Star, clambroth, several blk specks...........275.00
Spill holder, Sandwich Star, electric bl..................................900.00
Sugar bowl, Acanthus & Shield, chalk wht, NM 4,100.00
Tray, lacy, butterfly, 10" L, NM 100.00
Tray, lacy, butterfly, 7" L 70.00
Twine holder, emerald cut to clear, 4⅜" dia, NM 300.00
Vase, amethyst, elongated loops, octagon std, sq base, 9" 1,600.00

Tulip vase, amethyst, 10", $450.00.

Vase, Loop, canary yel, sq ftd base, 9"..................................425.00

Whiskey taster, lacy, silvery opal, shallow ft flake 225.00
Whiskey taster, lacy, teal gr, rare 325.00
Wine glass, Sandwich Star 190.00

Sarreguemines

Sarreguemines, France, is the location of Utzschneider and Company, founded in 1770, producers of majolica, transfer-printed dinnerware, figurines, and novelties which are usually marked 'Sarreguemines.'

Decanter, man astride potato figural, 9½" 110.00
Fountain, 3-part bird carries fish amidst sea foliage, 16" 350.00
Pitcher, character face figural, majolica, 6" 125.00

Portrait pitchers: 8½", $175.00; 5½", $125.00; Matching bank: $75.00.

Pitcher, jester holds stomach, seated on stump, mk, 13" 375.00
Plate, fruit center, majolica, 7½" 30.00
Plate, opera character from Rheingold 55.00
Table, coppered-bronze w/floral majolica inset, 30x28" 1,600.00
Tea service, floral, ornate shapes, ca 1860, 14-pc 500.00
Urn, fluted, gilt/dk bl ribs on cream, ped base, 73" 1,700.00

Satin Glass

Satin glass is simply glassware with a velvety matt finish achieved through the application of an acid bath. This procedure has been used by many companies since the 20th century, both here and abroad, on many types of colored and art glass. See also Mother-of-Pearl.

Biscuit jar, Beaded Drape, lettuce gr, fancy bail, 6x7" 145.00
Bottle, wht, florals, bulbous w/stick neck, 10", pr.........................185.00
Bowl, centerpiece; pk shaded, HP florals, SP ft, 10x12"................325.00
Bowl, fruit; ivory, gold roses/leaves, crimped, 10½" 160.00
Ewer, bl, florals/foliage, melon ribs, angle hdl, 8½", pr................235.00
Ewer, lt gr, florals, pinched spout, 8½" 65.00
Rose bowl, bl overlay, appl jewels, 8-crimp egg form, 3⅛"..............85.00
Rose bowl, bl overlay, HP florals/gold foliage, 8-crimp, 4¼" 110.00
Rose bowl, bl shaded, yel floral, spherical, 6x6" 225.00
Rose bowl, brn shaded, pleated/crimped, Webb, 5¼x6¼" 325.00
Rose bowl, chartreuse gr, appl spatter flower, ftd, 4x3¾" 95.00
Rose bowl, med bl overlay, emb flowers, crimped, 3½" 125.00

Rose bowl, pk, 3 camphor leaf ft, berry pontil, 3½x5".................150.00
Rose bowl, pk shaded, HP florals w/gold, 8-crimp, 3¾"................85.00
Rose bowl, Shell & Seaweed, leaves/berries on bl, 5x6½" 275.00
Rose bowl, yel shaded, HP florals, 8-crimp, petal ft, 5x4" 125.00
Vase, Mat-su-Noke, crystal on shaded pk, ruffled/ftd, 9"..............750.00
Vase, pk to wht overlay w/HP floral, fluted, hdls, 14", pr.............425.00
Vase, rainbow, silver overlay on top/middle/base, 7" 750.00
Vase, tan, pk int, thorn overlay, crimped trumpet form, 15"........225.00
Vase, verre moire, blk/gr/wht w/red verticals, 3 ftd, 10" 275.00
Vase, yel, floral/butterfly, wht cased, crimped rim, 10"................100.00

Satsuma

Satsuma is a type of fine cream crackle-glaze pottery or earthenware made in Japan as early as the 17th century. The earliest wares, made at the original kiln in the Satsuma province, were enameled with only simple florals. By the late 18th century, a floral brocade (or nishikide design) was favored, and similar wares were being made at other kilns under the direction of the Lord of Satsuma. In the early part of the 19th century, a diaper pattern was added to the florals. Gold and silver enamels were used for accents by the latter years of the century.

During the 1850s, as the quality of goods made for export to the western world increased and the style of decoration began to evolve toward becoming more appealing to the Westerners, human forms such as Arhats, Kannon, geisha girls, and Samurai warriors were added.

Today the most valuable pieces are those marked 'Kinkozan,' 'Shuzan,' 'Ryuzan,' and 'Kozan.' The genuine Satsuma 'mon' or mark is a cross within a circle – usually in gold on the body or on the lid, or in red on the base of the ware. Character marks may be included.

Caution: Much of what is termed 'Satsuma' comes from the Showa Period (1926 to the present); it is not true Satsuma but a simulated type, a cheaper pottery with heavy enamel.

Bowl, ceremonial procession, int: garden, 1880s, 2½x5" 750.00
Bowl, genre scenes, int: courtesans flee villagers, 5"....................550.00
Box, dragon/attendants, Shimazu crest, w/8" underplate 450.00
Box, female/fish, demon warriors, lg bird, 3" dia, EX 550.00
Box, floral/processional, int: ceremony, 1880s, 4" dia..................750.00
Cup & saucer, warriors, blk & gold 75.00
Jar, artisans/bk: at court, wide angle body, Kinkozan, 2½" 750.00

Koro, lion mask feet, seated boy playing an instrument as finial, 1890, repairs, 13", $950.00.

Koro, children playing/court scene, 1800s, 4" 1,000.00
Koro, florals/figure scenes, 3-ftd, scroll hdls, 1920, 6½" 250.00
Koro, genre scenes/geometric borders, ftd, 1880s, 3½", EX 325.00
Plate, Lohans, Shimazu crests in border, 1880s, 7½" 100.00
Plate, man/2 dieties, waterfall/emb rocks, Taizan, 7" 400.00
Plate, Shimazu crest/Lohans/dragons, 1900, 6½", pr 250.00
Pot, panels of florals/scenes, hexagonal, 1920s, sgn/mk, 2" 350.00
Teapot, attendants/dragon, lid: Shimazu crest, rpl hdl, 4" 200.00
Teapot, ladies, low angled body, rattan hdl, Kinkozan, 2¼" 475.00
Teapot, Lohans, gilt dragon hdl/spout/finial, 1910, 4" 500.00
Tray, attendants/dragons, Shimazu crest, quatrefoil, 8x12" 350.00
Umbrella stand, courtesans/florals, rtcl decor, late, 25" 250.00
Urn, Samurai, raised gold/enamel, 3-D rooster hdls, 18" 245.00
Vase, attendants, emb dragon around neck, Shimazu crest, 6".....400.00
Vase, butterflies/lilies on bl, bamboo hdls, 11x9" 325.00
Vase, florals/clouds, slip trailed, ring hdls, 1880, 9", pr 250.00
Vase, genre panels on floral ground, scroll hdls, late, 14"............150.00
Vase, haloed Arhats/Kwannon, slip-trailed, 1910, 12½", pr 450.00
Vase, haloed Arhats/Kwannon, 1920s, 9½".................................250.00
Vase, Lohans, Shimazu crest, bulbous, 1880s, 6" 350.00
Vase, Lohans/attendants/dragon, mtd on figural dog, 5¾", NM...750.00
Vase, oval genre scene on blk-ground floral, sq, w/lid, 5".............750.00
Vase, panels of courtesans/Lohans, faint mk, 1900, 3¾", pr 325.00
Vase, panels of flowers/warriors/courtesans, sq form, 12" 700.00
Vase, panels of 3 children/child & old man, 1850s, 7" 425.00
Vase, phoenix bird panels, shi-shi hdls, Awata, 15x8" 325.00
Vase, portrait, mc w/moriage & gold, 9¼" 175.00
Vase, Shimazu crest, emb dragon, 1900, 5½", EX, pr 475.00
Vase, wisteria, purple/red on beige, mks, 1850s, 6", pr 250.00
Vase, wisteria, purple/wht on cream, mk, 8½"..............................145.00

Scales

In today's world of pre-measured and pre-packaged goods, it is difficult to imagine the days when such products as sugar, flour, soap, and candy first had to be weighed by the grocer. The variety of scales used at the turn of the century was highly diverse; at the Philadelphia Exposition in 1876, one company alone displayed over three hundred different weighing devices. Among those found today, brass and iron models are the most common. Those seeking additional information concerning antique scales are encouraged to contact the International Society of Antique Scale Collectors, whose address can be found in the Directory under Clubs, Newsletters, and Catalogs.

Key:
bal — balance   lb — pound
g — gram   NP — nickel plated

Am Family, w/pan, 1906, EX 60.00
Balance, nickel-plated brass, on mahog platform 250.00
Chatillon's, dairy, brass front, 0-120 lb 85.00
Chatillon's, star w/figure, Pat Dec 10, 1867, 0-24 lb 55.00
Chatillon's Balance #2, Pat Jan 26, 1892, 0-50 lb 32.00
Chatillon's Improved Spring Balance, hanging, 0-80 lb 35.00
Chatillon's Improved Spring Balance, 0-100 lb, EX 55.00
Egg grading, graduated brass arm, mtd on board, label 90.00
Exact Weight, candy store, w/weights...75.00
Fairbanks, brass, grain weighing, bushels 275.00
Fairbanks & Greenleaf, grain weighing, brass w/iron mts.............200.00
Forschner, brass, w/pan, lg, EX 98.00
Frary Improved, brass, 16" L 65.00
Hanson Viking, #8910, spring bal, gr pnt steel, 1-100 lb...............35.00

Howe, general store, CI...125.00
Imperial Computing, candy store, brass tray, dtd 1899 ....65.00
Intercept Officer's, brass, on rollers, Cox-Stevens, 12" L...............65.00
Jiffyway, egg grading, brass..18.00
JL Lewellyn, brass, 2 single beams, oak cased, EX 135.00
Landers, brass, w/star, lg...45.00
Pelouze, counter, brass circular face, Pat 1903, EX 90.00
Pelouze, dairy, wht enamel on brass, EX.......................................65.00
Pelouze Supreme, candy store, 0-2 lb, EX 150.00
Pelouze Victor, postal, brass & steel, 1898, 4½x4½" 25.00
Philadelphia Scoop & Scale Co, brass scoop 135.00
PS&T Warranted Balance, brass front, Pat July 8 '89, 0-50 lb 25.00
Standard Computing, butcher's, enamel, EX 75.00
Toledo, candy store, brass pan, EX 135.00
Torsion, bal, w/pans, glass case, 10x19x7", EX.............................150.00
Torsion, prescription, glass & metal fr, box type, 1891, EX..........145.00
Triner Liberty, postal, brass top, EX 55.00
Troemner, Columbian, mahog w/marble top, box type, 8" pans 145.00
Troemner, drugstore, tan marble on brass, 12½x5½x7", EX 150.00
Troemner, oak based bal beam, brass pans, 3x11x5½" 90.00
Voland & Sons, bal, 1800s, 20" 140.00
Wht porc, rnd brass dial, iron hdl & hook, 10½" L 130.00
Wm Dixon #2 Beam, wood & glass sliding door, 13x12½x6" 90.00
WM Welch, prescription, graduated beam, steel, 1880s, 12½" 95.00

Schafer and Vater

Schafer and Vater operated in Volkstadt, Germany, from the last decade of the 1800s until about 1920. They produced novelties such as figural bottles, flasks, vases, etc., marked with an 'R' within a star device.

Vase, Grecian lady with dove, 11", $85.00.

Bottle, smiling pear figural, w/stopper..125.00
Box, Victorian ladies on jasperware, man finial lid, 2x3½" 145.00
Box, 2 googly-eyed boys in oval tub figural, mk, 3x2¾x1⅝" 135.00
Figurine, googly-eyed boy, dog at side, gold trim, mk, 3" 110.00
Figurine, googly-eyed girl on stoop w/book, mk, 4" 110.00
Flask, A Wee Scotch 70.00
Hatpin holder, Egyptian ladies' heads, 4½" 160.00
Hatpin holder, lady w/fan, pk jasperware 145.00
Match holder, cat & kitten, Don't Scratch Me..., 3¾x3¾" 100.00

Match holder, monkeys, comical, w/striker 135.00
Match holder, They will blame..., dog & puddle, 3¼x4"..............130.00
Nodder, goblin, gr, 4"..185.00
Nodder, monkey w/apple in paw, 4¼" 155.00
Pitcher, Blk lady, lg eyes/mouth, mk, 5"..............................150.00
Pitcher, Dutch girl w/basket on bk & keys, mk, 3¾" 70.00
Pitcher, girl w/jug, blk purse, mk, 5"................................70.00
Pitcher, goat w/boutonniere, mk, 5½"..................................85.00
Pitcher, Pierrot, comical 100.00
Vase, girl w/googly eyes reading book, bsk, 7" 100.00

Scheier

The Scheiers began their ceramics careers in the late 1930s and soon thereafter began to teach their craft at the University of New Hampshire. After WWII they cooperated with the Puerto Rican government in establishing a native ceramic industry, an involvement which would continue to influence their designs. In the fifties they retired and moved to Mexico; they currently reside in Arizona.

Bowl, bl, deep, 5" 120.00
Bowl, muted tones on shaded gr, sgraffito portrait, 5x6½" 850.00
Mug, ea w/different animal, blk on ivory, 6½", 6 for 325.00
Vase, lt to dk brn semi-gloss, U-form, hand thrown, 4½" 145.00

Vase, earthenware, impressed leaf forms and stylized faces, in blue and cratered gray matt glazes, by Edwin, signed, 21", $2,750.00.

Schiebe-Alsbach

Founded in Thuringia in the 1840s and still in production today, the Schiebe-Alsbach factory was the first in the area to make porcelain figures on a large scale. Their earliest were devotional Madonnas, though Rococo figures were soon included in their line as well. In 1890 they added groups such as female dancers and dancing couples. By 1894 they were producing Meissen-style figures, lace figures, and historical figures and groups. Now nationalized and incorporated into a larger firm, the factory is Europe's largest manufacturer of this type of ware. Their mark is an 'S' with superimposed crossed lines, today slightly modified from the original.

Figurine, Children's Tea party, AF Kister, 1850s, 6½x10" 350.00
Figurine, Dancing Couple, Dutch boy & girl, 6" 160.00

Figurine, Marshal Bertrand, bl coat, red sash, 10" 160.00
Figurine, Marshal DeBeauharnais, hat w/crescent, 10½" 160.00
Figurine, Marshal Dumouriez, wht pants, coat w/gold, 10" 160.00
Figurine, Marshal Exelmans, bl coat, hand on hip, 10" 160.00
Figurine, Marshal Kellerman, bl coat/wht cockade on hat, 10" ...160.00
Figurine, Marshal Lepic, bl jacket, sword at side, 10" 160.00
Figurine, Marshal Murat, fur-trimmed coat, 10" 160.00
Figurine, Napoleon, long gray coat, 10"............................160.00
Figurine, Napoleon Crossing Alps, on wht horse, 10½"..............325.00
Figurine, Napoleon Crossing Berezina, 9x11"........................495.00
Figurine, News Vendor, man w/papers, 1860 mk, 5½" 125.00
Figurine, Othello before seated girl, 10½x15" 1,350.00
Figurine, Pully on Horse, gr coat/red trousers, 11x9" 450.00

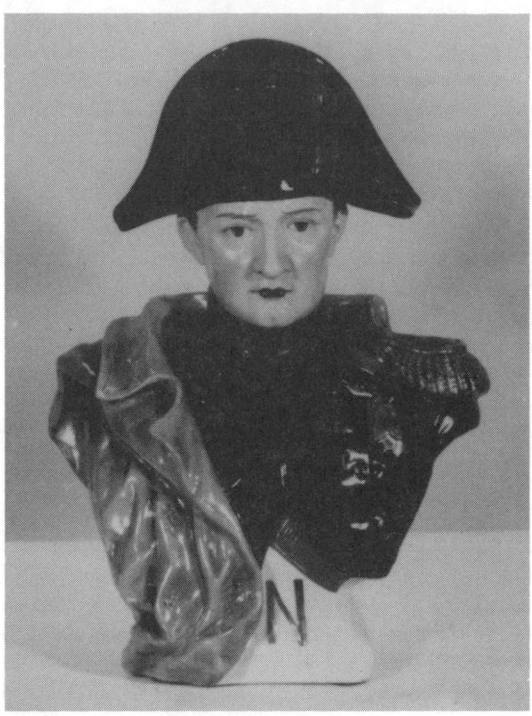

Bust of Napoleon, green tunic, 10½", $250.00.

Schlegelmilch Porcelain

Authority Mary Frank Gaston, who is our advisor, has recently completed the second volume of *The Collector's Encyclopedia of R.S. Prussia* with full-color illustrations and current values. Mold numbers appearing in some of the listings refer to this book. You will find Mrs. Gaston's address in the Directory under Texas.

Key:
BM — blue mark   SM — steeple mark
GM — green mark   RM — red mark

E.S. Germany

Fine chinaware marked 'E.S. Germany' or 'E.S. Prov. Saxe' was produced by E.S. Schlegelmilch at his Suhl factory in the Thuringia region of Prussia from the turn of the century until about 1925.

Cake plate, roses on tan shaded, w/gold, hdls, unmk, 10⅛" 60.00
Ewer, lady smelling rose, mk, 17" 675.00
Pin dish, roses, gold stenciled rim, oval, scalloped, mk............30.00
Pitcher, milk; lady's portrait, florals w/gold, mk, 4½" 100.00

Plate, ladies & cherub w/gold, mk, 6½" **65.00**
Plate, lady & cherub, turq & gold rim, open hdls, mk, 10" **175.00**
Plate, Marie Louise portrait, 4 portrait medallions, unmk, 10" **115.00**
Plate, portrait, scalloped w/cutouts, much gold, mk, 11" **200.00**
Plate, portrait w/flowers & gold, scalloped, hdls, mk, 9½" **125.00**
Sugar bowl, pk primroses, gold tracery, w/lid, mk **40.00**
Tray, dresser; lady w/holly crown on red w/poppies, 8" **150.00**
Tray, dresser; pansies, carnation mold, unmk................................**100.00**
Vase, lady's portrait on pearlized ground, dbl hdls, RM, 12" **350.00**
Vase, man & 2 ladies in portrait, curled hdls, mk, 7½" **200.00**
Vase, tree at sunset, slim, ovoid, mk, 9" **95.00**

R.S. Germany

In 1869 Reinhold Schlegelmilch began to manufacture porcelain in Tillowitz in upper Silesia. He had formerly worked with his brother, Erdmann, in his factory in Suhl in the German province of Thuringia. Both areas were rich in resources necessary for the production of hard-paste porcelain. Wares marked with the name 'Tillowitz' and the accompanying 'R.S. Germany' phrase are attributed to Reinhold. The most common mark is a wreath and star in a solid color under the glaze. Items marked 'R.S. Germany' are usually more simply decorated than R.S. Prussia. Some reflect the Art Deco trend of the 1920s. Certain hand-painted floral decorations and themes such as 'Sheepherder,' 'Man with Horses,' and 'Cottage' are especially valued by collectors – those with a high-gloss finish or on Art Deco shapes in particular. Not all hand-painted items were painted at the factory. Those with an artist's signature but no 'Hand Painted' mark indicate that the blank was decorated outside the factory.

Bowl, apple blossoms, cabbage mold, 9½", $450.00.

Bowl, apple blossoms, gr & wht, BM, 10" **65.00**
Bowl, cabbage leaf, HP florals on gr shaded................................**250.00**
Bowl, floral, gold scrolls/tracery, emb poppies rim, mk, 8½"..........**75.00**
Bowl, roses, mc on cream shaded, gold bands, sq, mk, 9¼" **65.00**
Bowl, roses, wide gold border, factory decor, mk, 10x8" **65.00**
Bowl, snowballs, BM, 9½"..**55.00**
Bowl, tiger lilies on bl to gray, gold rim, scalloped, mk, 10" **65.00**
Cake & ice cream set, wht azaleas, BM, 9-pc **100.00**
Cake plate, pk roses, GM, 8¼" **40.00**
Cake plate, poppies, scalloped rim, BM **35.00**
Cake plate, roses in wicker basket, cut-out hdls, mk, 10" **60.00**

Celery tray, floral w/gold, lily mold, SM, 12¼" **75.00**
Cheese & cracker dish, roses, gold rim, BM................................**75.00**
Chocolate pot, florals on bl to gr, tall, mk, +6 c/s.........................**300.00**
Cracker jar, roses, classic shape, mk, 4½" **145.00**
Dresser set, pk roses, GM, 4-pc...**275.00**
Hatpin holder, daffodils, gr & wht on cream **55.00**
Hatpin holder, roses, brn & yel on cream, mk **55.00**
Mustard, poppy decor, unmk **40.00**
Nappy, hydrangeas on gr w/gold, hdls, triangular, BM..................**40.00**
Pin box, roses, pk on gr, scalloped dmn shape, BM **85.00**
Pitcher, roses, fancy hdl & spout, mk, 5" **75.00**
Plate, bellflowers w/gold pods & scrolls, RM, 10⅝" **140.00**
Plate, dogwood, gold Rococo border, mk, 9½"..............................**40.00**
Plate, lilies, yel on brn shaded, mk, 8"...**35.00**
Plate, palm tree, orange in sky/water, w/gold, mk, 8½" **75.00**
Plate, pk & wht roses w/gr lustre trim, mk, 6½", 4 for **48.00**
Plate, poppies, mk, 8½"..**65.00**
Shaving mug, floral, divided int, mk..**55.00**
Shaving mug, pansies, pk & wht on lt gr, emb floral int, mk..........**85.00**
Sugar bowl, floral, triangle hdls, steeple finial, mk **20.00**
Toothbrush holder, roses on gr shaded, wall mt, 4⅛x4"...............**125.00**
Toothpick holder, pearlized roses at rim, 3-hdl, mk, 2½"................**40.00**
Tray, mc floral w/gold tracery, RM, 11½x7½" **105.00**
Tray, sheepherder & mill scene, hdls, mk, 11½x7¼" **255.00**
Tray, wild roses, gold flowers at edge, mk, 11" L **195.00**
Vase, nightwatch scene, w/gold, GM, 6½" **450.00**

R.S. Poland

'R.S. Poland' is a mark attributed to Reinhold Schlegelmilch's factory in Tillowitz, Silesia.

Bowl, poppies on heart mold, satin finish, 10½"...........................**230.00**
Candlestick, roses, pk & peach w/brn trim, mk, 6¼", pr **195.00**
Candlestick, violets & lilies of the valley, 6" **110.00**
Creamer & sugar bowl, roses, peach on brn/gr, mk......................**150.00**
Planter, pk floral band w/gold, ped ft, 6¾x6½" **230.00**
Plate, dogwood & pine, 8" **95.00**
Relish bowl, dogwood & pine, open hdl, RM **65.00**
Urn, roses, pk/wht on brn, hdls, w/lid, RM, 11½" **800.00**
Vase, crowned crane, salesman's sample, mk, 3½".......................**800.00**
Vase, nightwatch scene on bl/gr, mk, 4" **300.00**
Vase, roses, pk on cobalt, mk, 8¼", pr **225.00**

R.S. Prussia

Art porcelain bearing the mark 'R.S. Prussia' was manufactured by Erdmann and Reinhold Schlegelmilch from the late 1870s to the early 1900s in a Germanic area known until the end of WWI as Prussia. The vast array of mold shapes in combination with a wide variety of decorations is the basis for R.S. Prussia's appeal. Themes can be categorized as figural (usually based on a famous artist's work), birds, florals, portraits, scenics, and animals.

Basket, poppies w/in & w/o, 3-section hdl, RM, 8x9" **350.00**
Berry set, water lilies on water, icicle mold, RM, 7-pc.................**475.00**
Biscuit jar, swallows & water lilies on lav shaded, RM **375.00**
Bowl, acorns, w/gold, acorn mold, RM, 10" **285.00**
Bowl, berry; fruit center, grapes at rim w/gold, RM, 5½" **45.00**
Bowl, berry; magnolias, w/gold, mk, 5½".....................................**30.00**
Bowl, berry; roses, mk, 5½"..**30.00**
Bowl, blown-out floral, 5 turq sections, unmk, 10½"....................**135.00**
Bowl, centerpiece; roses, gold ring hdls, mk, 9½" **350.00**

Bowl, daisies & floral, gold scrolled rim, RM, 10½" 250.00
Bowl, floral, leaf mold, RM, 6½" 155.00
Bowl, floral & gold on bl to gr, plume mold, RM, 10¾" 255.00
Bowl, floral center, cobalt, unmk, 3x10½" 400.00
Bowl, irises, mc on brn shaded, iris mold, RM, 10½" 255.00
Bowl, lilacs on lav shaded, scalloped rim, RM, 2x6¼" 150.00
Bowl, mayonnaise; roses, gold scroll hdl, RM, +6" plate 165.00
Bowl, mc floral, plume mold, RM, 11" 265.00
Bowl, mums on brn shaded, emb sheaves of wheat, RM, 10½" ...150.00
Bowl, old mill scene, earth tones, unmk, 10½" 300.00
Bowl, peafowl, unmk, 10" 1,495.00
Bowl, poppies & roses, blown-out poppies, mk, 10½" 375.00
Bowl, roses, pk & ivory on cream shaded, beaded rim, RM, 10" ..160.00
Bowl, roses, pk & wht, w/gold, carnation mold, RM, 9¾" 285.00
Bowl, roses, pk & yel, w/gold, iris mold, RM, 2⅛x5½" 150.00
Bowl, roses, yel on bl, mk, 10" 210.00
Bowl, roses w/gold, geometric panel-form scallops, RM, 11" 220.00
Bowl, sheepherder scene, tassels & swag mold, RM 800.00
Bowl, snowballs & roses, RM, 10¾" 325.00
Bowl, snowballs & roses, scalloped gold rim, RM, 10½" 275.00
Bowl, snowballs & roses, w/gold, zipper border, RM, 10½" 250.00
Bowl, swans, flowers, & water, 5-dome mold, RM, 11" 350.00
Box, jewel; mc florals, stipple mold, mk, 2½x4½" 90.00
Butter dish, dbl portrait, unmk, 7¾" 600.00
Cake plate, floral w/gold, scalloped, cut-out hdls, RM, 9½" 150.00
Cake plate, florals, emb poppies, gold scrolls, unmk, 10⅝" 110.00
Cake plate, florals w/gold, 6-point & clover mold, mk, 11" 255.00
Cake plate, flower basket w/medallions at rim, RM, 10½" 235.00
Cake plate, flower clusters, gold tracery, unmk, 10¾" 175.00
Cake plate, flower clusters w/gold, hdls, RM, 11" 265.00
Cake plate, jonquils on cobalt w/gold, mk, 10½" 295.00
Cake plate, pk roses, Tiffany border, 11¾", +8 6" plates 495.00
Cake plate, poppies, pk on gr, iris mold, RM, 10¾" 225.00
Cake plate, roses, lily mold, unmk, 9¾" 200.00
Celery tray, roses in center, iris mold, RM, 13x6¼" 225.00
Celery tray, swans on lily pond, unmk, 12⅜" 275.00
Chamberstick, floral, dbl-hdld, saucer base, mk 295.00
Chocolate pot, floral (open/budded) on cream w/gold, mk 215.00
Chocolate pot, hops plant, brns on cream, RM, +6 c/s 600.00
Chocolate pot, hydrangeas, point & clover mold, RM, 10¼" 365.00
Chocolate pot, swan, raspberry mold, mk, 9" 495.00
Chocolate pot, violets w/gold, ball ft & finial, RM, 9¼" 350.00
Coffeepot, dbl portrait, reflecting poppies/daisies, mold #631... 1,200.00
Coffeepot, floral on wht, scalloped rim, +cr/sug & 5 c/s..............650.00
Coffeepot, roses, scalloped base, RM, 9" 300.00
Cracker jar, floral, wht on gr, ruffled edge, RM...........................400.00
Cracker jar, floral w/gold fleur-de-lis, scroll finial, RM.................300.00
Cracker jar, roses, pleat mold, hdls, RM.....................................400.00
Creamer, roses in draped chains on bl w/gold, RM, 2¾" 115.00
Creamer & sugar bowl, castle scene, ped ft, RM, pr 550.00
Creamer & sugar bowl, floral, on gold shaded, unmk...................135.00
Creamer & sugar bowl, poppies, w/gold, ped ft, RM 185.00
Creamer & sugar bowl, white lily, w/gold, ftd, mk 175.00
Cup, mustache; iris & roses, mc on bl w/gold, mk 295.00
Cup, mustache; pheasants & evergreens on wht, RM 265.00
Cup & saucer, church/trees, gold rim decor, RM.........................125.00
Cup & saucer, demitasse; floral, raised gold, ftd, unmk.................45.00
Cup & saucer, demitasse; floral, RM..95.00
Cup & saucer, floral on bl shaded, iris mold, RM 75.00
Cup & saucer, lilies of valley/violets w/gold, RM 95.00
Cup & saucer, mc roses, scalloped rim, blown-out mold, RM 100.00
Cup & saucer, poppies, blown-out mold, RM 100.00
Cup & saucer, roses w/much gold, jewels, RM............................110.00
Hatpin holder, floral, bulbous, unmk 145.00

Dish, water lilies on cobalt, marked, 12" long, $475.00.

Hatpin holder, floral, 3-hdl, RM 325.00
Hatpin holder, hanging baskets, attached tray, RM 275.00
Pitcher, floral, carnation mold, mk, 12" 825.00
Pitcher, lemonade; roses, pk on gr shaded, melon shape, RM 300.00
Pitcher, lilacs, w/gold, scalloped rim, RM, 6" 200.00
Pitcher, tankard; basket of roses on gr & ivory, mk, 9½" 565.00
Pitcher, tankard; carnations, RM, 11½" 650.00
Pitcher, tankard; lady/wht gown, mc flowers/emb swirls, 13" .. 3,500.00
Plaque, mill scene on gr, lav & yel border, unmk, 11¼" 700.00
Plate, carnations, pk & wht on gr, shell mold, RM, 11" 175.00
Plate, floral medallions, 6-point & clover mold, 8½" 165.00
Plate, floral on bl, hdls, mk, 11" 225.00
Plate, iris on shaded bl w/gold, iris mold, mk, 11" 250.00
Plate, Melon Boy, jeweled, RM, 6" 350.00
Plate, Melon Eater, keyhole mold, RM, 6" 550.00
Plate, pansies, mc on turq shaded w/gold, iris mold, RM, 11" 250.00
Plate, pears, grapes, & plums, scalloped, mk, 10¾" 300.00
Plate, poppies & daisies, 6-medallion mold, RM, 11" 155.00
Plate, Queen Louise portrait, RM, 10¼" 985.00
Plate, rose chains, gold scrolled rim, mk, 6" 22.00
Plate, roses w/gold tracery, scalloped, RM, 7" 40.00
Plate, tangerine/grapes/acorns, w/gold, scalloped, unmk, 10".......275.00
Relish, roses w/gold, iris mold, RM, 9½x4½" 125.00
Sauce, floral center, lily mold, mk, 5½", 6 for 95.00
Shaving mug, pheasant & evergreens on wht, RM 395.00
Teapot, floral, wht on gr, RM, +5 c/s 1,150.00
Teapot, floral on aqua to wht w/gold, RM 275.00
Teapot, roses w/gold, fleur-de-lis mold, mk 350.00
Toothpick holder, fruit, unmk 100.00

Tray, Melon Eaters, red mark, 12", $650.00.

Tray, castle scene, brn & orange on yel, mk, 13x8¼" 800.00
Tray, Flora portrait, unmk, 11½" 800.00
Tray, floral, lily mold, unmk, 11¾" 295.00
Tray, floral w/pearl lustre, carnation mold, RM, 11½x7½"...........295.00

Tray, pin; Old Grist Mill, gold beaded rim, red mk, 7" L 325.00
Tray, poppies, feather & plume mold, RM, 12x7½".....................250.00
Tray, roses, 4 portraits in ovals, RM, 10" L.............................450.00
Tray, roses w/gold, carnation mold, RM, 11x7½" 265.00
Tray, swan, swag & tassel mold, RM, 11x7" 475.00
Vase, castle scene on gr shaded, 8¼"......................................635.00
Vase, Dice Players, unmk, 9"...695.00
Vase, florals on cobalt w/gold, steeple mk, 4⅞" 300.00
Vase, florals w/cobalt leaves on cream w/gold, RM, 5" 275.00
Vase, lady w/peacock portrait, dbl hdls, Windsor mk, 8".............400.00
Vase, man going to church scene on brn/gold, RM, 9x4½" 675.00
Vase, Melon Boy, hdls, red mk, 7" 700.00
Vase, pheasant, RM, 6½" 495.00
Vase, portrait, sgn Le Brun, hdls, 9" 750.00

R.S. Tillowitz

R.S. Tillowitz-marked porcelains are attributed to Reinhold Schlegelmilch's factory in Tillowitz, Silesia.

Bowl, berry; dogwood on gr, sm, set of 6 ....100.00
Cake set, fuchsia on gr w/tan shadows, open hdls, 7-pc...............325.00
Creamer & sugar bowl, lilies, wht on shaded gr............................175.00
Mint dish, florals, mk, 7½x5" 95.00
Plate, cherries, 11" 50.00
Plate, roses, peach on cream to brn, mk, 8" 45.00
Tray, floral, bl on gr, much gold, pierced hdls, 8x4" 35.00
Tray, magnolias, w/gold, mk, 8¾x4" 45.00

Schneider

The Schneider Glass Company was founded in 1914 at Epinay-sur-seine, France. They made many types of art glass, some of which sandwiched designs between layers. Other decorative devices were applique and carved work. These were marked 'Charder,' or 'Schneider.' During the twenties, commercial artware was produced with Deco motifs cut by acid through two or three layers and signed 'LeVerre Francais' in script or with a section of inlaid filigrane. See also Le Verre Francais.

Bowl, orange mottle, purple stem, gr ft, 6"....................................198.00
Charger, brn to orange mottle, Ovington, 15½".............................250.00
Compote, amethyst base & stem, peach bowl, bl rim, 7½x6¼"...380.00
Compote, bl & orange mottle, amethyst stem, metal ft, 9x10" ...595.00
Compote, yel to orange mottle, yel/dk purple base, 5" 175.00
Ewer, yel/pk mottle, purple triangular bosses/hdl, 14" 900.00
Pitcher, clear-cased w/mc internal decor, hdl w/rigaree, 7" 225.00
Vase, bl/amethyst/orange mottled ground, sgn, 13½" 445.00
Vase, bl/yel/orange mottle, blk hdls, squat, 6" 500.00
Vase, dk bl w/rust streaks descending from rim, ftd, 15"..............300.00
Vase, ferns, orange on wht mottle, bun ft, Charder, 15" 1,500.00
Vase, grapes, dk amethyst on swirled yel, sgn, 11x7" 1,400.00
Vase, lime w/random bubbles, 10½" 150.00
Vase, orange, flared rim, blown out in metal fr, 7x7½" 450.00
Vase, orange mottle w/HP olive branches at shoulder, 6" 900.00
Vase, orange to mottled royal bl to bl base, slim form, 12" 275.00
Vase, palms, bl on wht, bun ft, Charder, 16" 2,900.00
Vase, pk w/bl vertical trailings, on bl/yel spotted ft, 19" 700.00
Vase, pk/orange sphere, wrought iron ribs, ftd, 8" 600.00
Vase, red/topaz mottle, flat-sided ftd trumpet form, 12" 600.00
Vase, tangerine to lime, trumpet form w/folded rim, 16" 1,200.00
Vase, wine/wht/blk mottle, dmn form w/knob std, rnd ft, 13" 400.00
Vase, yel, 3 vertical crimped applications, ftd, 12½" 550.00

Vase, cameo palm trees, marked Charder, 8", $400.00.

Schoolhouse Collectibles

Schoolhouse collectibles bring to mind memories of a bygone era when the teacher rang the bell to call the youngsters to class in a one-room schoolhouse – where often both the 'hickory stick' and an apple occupied a prominent position on the teacher's desk.

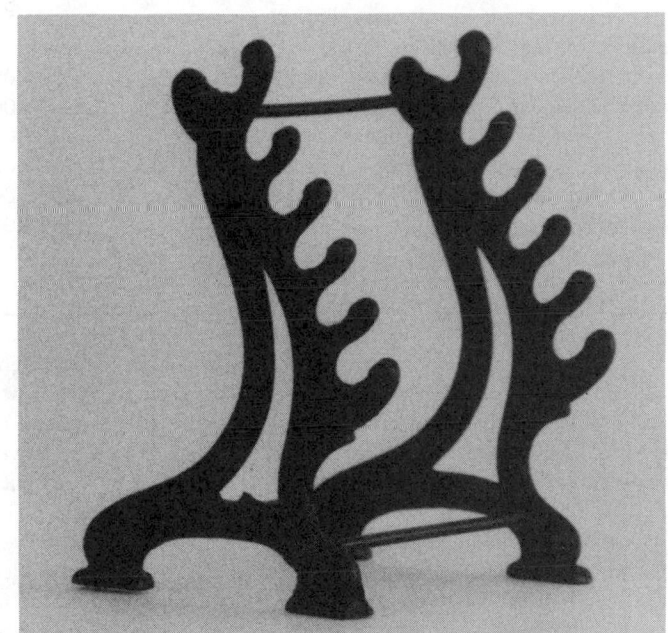

Pencil holder, cast iron, 5½" x 4", $20.00.

Bell, brass, 6"...35.00
Bell, steel spring between bell & wood hdl, 9½" 75.00
Book, Hebrew Grammer, Cambridge, 1763, 83-pg, VG..............800.00
Book, McGuffey's Eclectic Spelling...15.00
Book, Palmer Method of Hand Writing, 64-pg, 1926, 4x8" 15.00
Book, Smith's Arithmetic, 1847, VG..28.00
Cards, ABCs for I Learn To Write, goes around blkboard 12.00
Cards, Kibbe Number Drill, EX 8.50
Desk, teacher's; pine/poplar w/bl pnt, Co Hplwht, VG...............200.00
Eraser, New Atlas Noiseless... 9.00
Game, Rolling Reader 20.00

Globe, CI, paw ft, floor stand, 18" dia globe, VG 120.00
Globe, terrestrial world, Hammond, 1930, mtd on iron stand........50.00
Globe, terrestrial world, Sears Roebuck, 1920, 12", on base 130.00
Ink bottle, for desk well, EX 10.00
Pencil box, HP children/verses, 1850s 95.00
Pencil sharpener, ES Webster, pat 1892....................................125.00
Slate, dbl hinged, red wool binding..40.00
Slate, pegged construction fr 75.00
Slate, walnut fr w/beaded edges, rpr split, 16x12" 85.00
Spelling board, wood w/movable letters, pat 1886, EX.................65.00
Tablet, Golden Rod 7.50
Tablet, Hytone Jet Mail, planes on front....................................11.00

Schoop, Hedi

Swiss-born Hedi Schoop started her ceramics business in North Hollywood in 1940. With a talented crew of about twenty decorators, she produced figurines, figure-vases, console sets, TV lamps, and other decorative housewares – much of which was accented with gold or platinum trim. Schoop's pottery closed after a fire destroyed the building in 1958. Marks are impressed or printed.

Our advisor for this category is Jack Chipman; he is listed in the Directory under California.

Figurine, ballerina w/rings on arms, gold trim, 11" 45.00
Figurine, debutante, flower holder, 12½" 35.00
Figurine, flower girl w/appl flowers, 9" 24.00
Figurine, lady w/basket leads lg poodle, 10" 45.00
Figurine, Oriental boy w/horn, 10"...45.00
Figurine, Oriental man in blk & wht jacket, tall 35.00
Flower holder, Tyrolean girl, 11½" 35.00
Flower holder, 2 girls, hands joined, rare, 8" 85.00
Lamp, TV; Skyscrapers, rare, lg..200.00
Planter, geisha w/umbrella, bl, #223...35.00
Vase, fan form, gold trim, 10"..24.00

Scouting Collectibles

Scouting was founded in England in 1907 by a retired Major General, Lord Robert Baden-Powell. Its purpose is the same today as it was then – to help develop physically strong, mentally alert boys and to teach them basic fundamentals of survival and leadership. The movement soon spread to the United States, and in 1910 a Chicago publisher, William Boyce, set out to establish Scouting in America. The first World Scout Jamboree was held in 1911 in England. Baden-Powell was honored as the Chief Scout of the World. In 1926 he was awarded the Silver Buffalo Award in the United States. He was knighted in 1929 for distinguished military service and for his scouting efforts. Baden-Powell died in 1941. For further reading on the subject, we recommend *Scouting Collectibles* by R.J. Sayers; you will find his address in the Directory under North Carolina.

Book, Cub Scout Rank Books, Bear, Wolf, & Lion, 1931, VG, ea.. 5.00
Book, Golden Anniversary of Scouting, Rockwell illus, '59, VG...10.00
Book, History of the Boy Scouts, Murray, 1937, VG 11.00
Book, Scoutmaster's Handbook, hardbound, 1st ed, 1913-14, VG.20.00
Booklet, Merit Badge Series, brn covers, 1929, VG 5.00
Booklet, Merit Badge Series, red/wht covers, 1940, VG 2.00
Bugle, 1930 Rexcraft Official, w/lanyard & mouthpiece 30.00
Coin, Excelsior Shoe, w/swastika, novelty pc, 1910 .... 7.50
Coin, National Jamboree, silver, 1969, VG 3.00
Coin, Scout Good Luck pc, w/Law & Oath, 1934 era, VG 3.00

Game, Boy Scout Marble Game, 1922, VG 50.00
Game, Boy Scout Ten Pins, 1914, VG.......................................22.00
Game, Boy Scouts at Camp, 40 figures/tents/leaders, VG............100.00
Game, Parker Bros, Game of Boy Scouts, 50 cards/rules, 1912 ......25.00
Game, Scout iron figure, khaki pants, saluting, VG.....................10.00
Game, Scout Mechanical Bank, 1912, VG 1,000.00
Handbook, BSA, red cover, 1st ed, 1911, VG 75.00
Handbook, BSA, Seton-Baden-Powell, 1910, VG 100.00
Knife, sheath; Remington, RH51, w/scabbard, VG 50.00
Knife, utility; Remington, R3333, 4-blade, VG 45.00
Knife, utility; Ulster, w/phillips driver, 4-blade, VG.....................10.00
Medal, MacArthur Gardening Award, red or gr ribbon, 1940 era .25.00
Medal, Scout Contest, 3-color ribbon, various events, 1930, ea 13.00
Medal, Type 1 Eagle, BSA, 3-color ribbon, 1920 era, VG.............75.00
Medal, Type 2 Eagle, BSA, sm eagle, 1927 era, VG 100.00
Medal, Type 3 Eagle, no BSA, in coffin box, 1930 era, VG 40.00
Patch, Eagle on blk felt or wht twill, 1940 era, VG.....................100.00
Patch, Merit badge sash w/35 tan sq badges, 1920 era, VG............50.00
Patch, Official World Jamboree, silk, #d thru 5000, 1924 .... 1,500.00
Patch, Official World Jamboree, 10 various colors, 1937 ....300.00
Patch, Scoutmaster, 1st Class, on tan sq, 1920 era 30.00
Pin, Asst Scoutmaster 1st Class, red enamel, 1920 era, VG 50.00
Pin, Official Boy Scout 1st Class, w/knot, 1917, 3", VG.............500.00
Pin, Official Boy Scout 1st Class, w/knot, 1920, 2", VG.............150.00
Pin, Scoutmaster, gr enamel, rnd, 1945 era, VG..........................10.00
Pin, Scoutmaster 1st Class, gr enamel, 1920 era, VG...................50.00

Scrimshaw

The most desirable examples of the art of scrimshaw can be traced back to the first half of the 19th century to the heyday of the whaling industry. Some voyages lasted for several years, and conditions on board were often dismal. Sailors filled the long hours by carving or engraving designs in whale or walrus ivory. Using the tools of their trade, they created animal figures, boxes, pie crimpers, etc., often emphasizing the lines of their carvings with ink or berry stain. Eskimos also made scrimshaw, sometimes borrowing designs from the sailors who traded with them. See also Powder Horns.

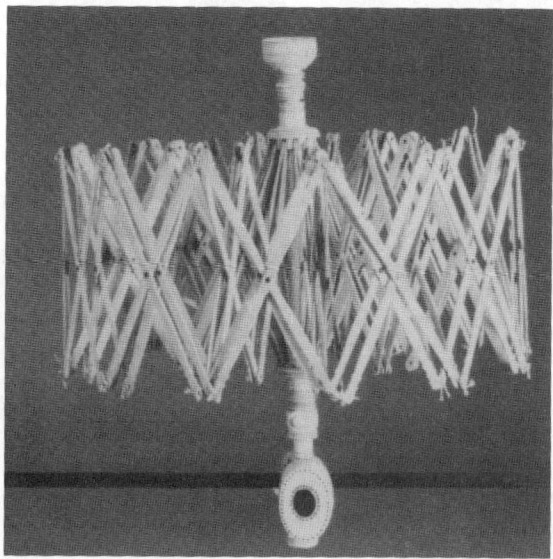

Double swift, clamp made from section of whale's tooth, engraved and colored with portraits of two women and a bird inlaid with bits of silver, oval silver plaque engraved 'C.M.,' 1850s, 17", $3,000.00.

Bank, bureau form, ivory knobs, 1850s, 6x5¾" 600.00
Bodkin, cvd as hand holding baton, whale ivory, 1850s, 3½" 175.00
Bureau, walnut & burl w/ivory drw pulls & inlay, 17x16"........ 1,000.00
Cane, faceted knob, 3 wood rings on whalebone shaft, 1850s 250.00
Cane, ivory knob, rope-cvd/ivory-inlaid hardwood shaft, EX 650.00
Cane, turk's turban knob, tortoise shell/abalone inlay, EX 2,100.00
Cane, walrus ivory fist holds telescope, ebony shaft, 37" 2,250.00
Clothespin, whalebone, 1850s, 4¾" 100.00
Corset busk, Am flags/hearts/flowers, 1850s, 12" 450.00
Corset busk, eng whaling scene, 1825, 13½" 1,100.00
Corset busk, 3 detailed bldgs, 1850s, 15", NM 700.00
Dipper, hdl: ivory/ebony/wood, coconut shell bowl, 16", EX 225.00
Dipper, trn ebony hdl, bone connector, coconut bowl, 17"..........150.00
Fid, turban-knot end, mc detail, from 1 pc whalebone, 13" 400.00
Fid, whalebone, plain, 1825, 12" 90.00
Jagging wheel, lg curved hdl w/opening in end, 8" 400.00
Jagging wheel, lg rtcl hdl end w/star & X-hatching, 8" 800.00
Jagging wheel, rooster form holds wheel/tail is fork, 6" 900.00
Jagging wheel, sperm whale form, tail holds wheel, 1875, 5" 550.00
Jagging wheel, whale ivory, baleen spacer, 6", EX 300.00
Knife box, ivory acorn finials ea end of hdl, drw beneath 550.00
Needle holder, whale ivory, openwork hearts/'SC,' 2x1½" 225.00
Porpoise jaw bones, eng man holding baby, ladies, 17", EX 500.00
Riding crop, lady's, ivory hdl, whalebone shaft, 1850, 36" 125.00
Sewing box, walnut, ivory knobs/abalone inlays, 1-drw, 10"........550.00
Swift, whalebone/ivory, custom metal base, 1850s, 16" 2,500.00
Table, mahog top: inlay ivory/other wood, trn supports, 12"........900.00
Tooth, bird on branch, 1850s, 4½"......................................150.00
Tooth, fleeing couple, bk: soldier w/sword, some mc, 6"...............500.00
Tooth, Indian drawing arrow under palm tree, bk: sailor, 6" 450.00
Tooth, Liberty/eagle/flag, bk: boat/inscription, 5", pr............... 2,750.00
Tooth, nude hunter, +2 other nudes, 1850s, 6", pr 1,900.00
Tooth, portrait of Eliza/Forget Me Not, mc eng, 5", VG 400.00
Tooth, romantic figures/children, mc eng, 1850s, 6", pr 1,100.00
Tooth, ship at anchor, 1850, lg chip at top, 7", EX 1,000.00
Tooth, ships/scenes/foliage/banner/1848, 1850s, 5", EX 600.00
Tooth, Sweet Home/bldg & river, bk: ship/hearts, 1850, 8½" . 2,700.00
Tooth, woman w/lute, lg figure of man, 1850s, 6", pr............... 1,400.00
Tusk, tall flower/eagle/shield/banner/lady, 1875, 17" 600.00
Yardstick, whalebone w/eng #s & lines, 1850s, NM 750.00

Sebastians

Sebastian miniatures were first produced in 1938 by Prescott W. Baston in Marblehead, Massachusetts. Since then more than four hundred have been modeled. These figurines have been sold through gift shops all over the country, primarily in the New England states. In 1976 Baston withdrew his Sebastians from production. Under an agreement with the Lance Corporation of Hudson, Massachusetts, one hundred designs were selected to be produced by that company under Baston's supervision. Those remaining were discontinued. In the short time since then, the older figurines have become very collectible. Price is determined by two factors: 1) in production/out of production; 2) labels – color of oval label, i.e. red, blue, green, etc.; Marblehead label, a green and silver palette-shaped label used until 1977; or no label. If there is no label and the varnish coat is quite yellowed, then it is considered to be of the Marblehead era. Dates are merely copyright dates and have no particular significance in regard to value. (Signed) 'P.W. Baston' should only have impact on price when the signature is an actual autograph – most pieces are manufactured with an imprinted 'P.W. Baston' on the base.

Becky Thatcher, gr label..40.00
Bellringer, gr label, MIB 45.00
Chestnut Hill Mall, Marblehead era..................................225.00
Cleopatra, Marblehead era 225.00
Colonial Blacksmith, bl label 38.00
Gabriel, Marblehead label 130.00
Gathering Tulips...200.00
George Washington, w/cannon, Marblehead label 100.00
Huckleberry Finn, Marblehead label, MIB...............................65.00
Hudson Plaque 200.00
John & Priscilla Alden, ea...75.00
Lincoln, standing, gr label...45.00

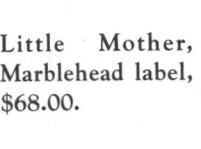

Little Mother, Marblehead label, $68.00.

Lobster Man, sticker, Marblehead label, orig box 85.00
Micawber, 1946..65.00
Minuteman, Marblehead label 75.00
Old Put Enjoys a Licking, M in orig candy box 350.00
Parade Rest, Marblehead label 55.00
Paul Revere, Marblehead label 55.00
Rip Van Winkle, Collector Club issue, MIB 50.00
Rip Van Winkle, Marblehead label, MIB 100.00
Shaker Man & Woman, Marblehead era, pr...........................130.00
Spirit of '76, Marblehead label 68.00
Uncle Sam, gr label 40.00
Weaver & Loom, Marblehead label 55.00
Weighing the Baby, Marblehead label 200.00
Williamsburg Governor & Lady, Marblehead era, pr 150.00
Williamsburg Lady, Marblehead label................................115.00

Sevres

Fine-quality porcelains have been made in Sevres, France, since the early 1700s. Rich ground colors were often hand painted with portraits, scenics, and florals. Some pieces were decorated with transfer prints and decalcomania; many were embellished with heavy gold. These wares are the most respected of all French porcelains. Their style and designs have been widely copied, and some of the items listed below are Sevres-type wares.

Cake plate, bl & aqua mottle, bronze ormolu rims & ft, 12"........250.00
Cup & saucer, dbl-walled/rtcl, gilt stars, 1875, 5" dia 250.00
Figurine, Adieu Au Pays, mother/children, bsk, sgn/mk, 20".......465.00

Plate, Josephine portrait, sgn Dobrie, 1868, 9½" 150.00
Plate, 2 people, gold/gr rim, hdld metal stand, porc stem 345.00
Sugar bowl, rtcl/floral panels, gilt, bamboo hdls, 1877, 5"............220.00
Urn, courting scene/Louis XV portrait, artist sgn, 17" 600.00
Urn, lady's protrait, artist sgn, ormolu mts, w/lid, 8" 350.00

Urns, continuous landscapes with figures, signed L. Malpass, gilt bronze mounts, 22", $1,000.00 for the pair.

Urn, scenic, bk: maid/cherub, gold winged-cherub hdls, 23"... 3,100.00
Vase, cobalt, gilt-ribbed bottle neck w/knob, 1887, 22"..............600.00
Vase, cobalt to lt bl at neck, 12" 250.00
Vase, emb nude/grass, yel/gilt, flat heart shape, hdls, 6"..............300.00
Vase, figural scene in gray, sgn Juramy, ormolu putti, 24" 900.00

Sewer Tile

Whimsies, advertising novelties, and other ornamental items were sometimes made in potteries where the primary product was simply tile.

Mask, 12½", $85.00.

Bank, seated pig, You got me on a diet..., 1967, 10", NM 350.00
Birdhouse, tree bark tooling, 6½"...................................150.00
Boot, red/blk pnt trim, miniature 45.00
Cat, simple tooling, yel slip on face, 9" L...........................225.00
Dog, brn glaze, bold detail/tooling, mfg flaw, 12" 1,400.00
Dog, seated, free-standing, hollow/some tooling, 10" 185.00
Dog, seated, free-standing, solid/well tooled/unglazed, 10" 1,600.00
Dog, seated, red mottle glaze, tooled collar, 9", EX....................135.00
Dog, spaniel pup, seated, 7"...175.00
Frog, incised eyes, sm chip, 8" 70.00
Frog, mk Lonegan, Irondale, 1924, 5"................................150.00
Lamp, stump form, 10½" 125.00
Lion, tooled features, EX details, thin walls, 8½" L, NM 325.00
Planter, cylinder w/allover tooling, lady in 'window,' 21"............200.00
Planter, stump form, appl flowers/birds, 21", EX....................375.00
Planter, stump form, minor edge chips, 11" 100.00
Squirrel, sitting w/nut, cartoon-type face, mk JF, 9" 100.00
Turtle, incised designs, sgn, dtd 1921, 7¼" L 200.00

Sewing Items

This is a field that offers much variety for both beginning and advanced collectors. Some find it interesting to assemble a broad range of the tools used in the needle arts, while others prefer to specialize in thimbles, tatting shuttles, scissors, etc. that show the diversity available in one specific group.

As needlework tools were made for daily use, their design and ornamentation reflected the history of personal fashion as well as historical events and the evolution of manufacturing processes. The various materials that were used and the methods of decorations that were employed provide the collector with exciting possibilities.

Lace bobbins of the English Midlands are an example. Lace-makers learned their craft in childhood and spent their lives working long hours under poor conditions. Their beautifully decorated bobbins, usually made of wood or bone, were embellished with dyes, inlays, intricate carvings, etc. in an effort to add beauty to an often drab existence. Inscribed with names, dates, loving messages, personal and historical events, the bobbins recorded the lives and times of the lace-maker. 'Fairings,' 'Church Windows,' 'Pewter Inlays,' 'Trolly Bobbins,' and 'Cow and Calf' are among the many types available. Although many of the more desirable examples from the 18th and 19th centuries are extremely rare, bobbin-makers of today have mastered the old techniques and are again making beautiful bobbins for comtemporary lace-makers which are eagerly sought by collectors.

There is a wide variance in the value of hand needlework tools due to materials, age, and country of origin. Prices are escalating but unsteady and tend to be regional. Gold, sterling, and enameled items are very high. Also, certain motifs (cherubs, hearts, or unique designs such as male figures and armor) bring higher prices.

Basket, sweet grass, child's, VG 25.00
Bodkin, gilt, for corset 35.00
Book, Shortcuts to Sewing Success, 1945, 66-pg, EX 10.00
Book, Singer Sewing Library, 1930, 4-volume set, EX...................40.00
Box, Tartanware, 5 bone rings & posts, Clark's label, 2x3½".......125.00
Box, thimble holder; velvet over cb, rnd, ca 1820, EX 60.00
Box, wood, cvd lid, Wheeler & Wilson, 1920s, NM 65.00
Buttonhole cutter, mushroom end, trn/tooled shaft, 5½" 130.00
Chatelaine, 5 sewing tools, sterling, all orig............................ 1,500.00
Darner, blk glass, egg form, sterling repousse hdl, 5½".............125.00
Darner, brass, open lyre-shaped hdl, early, unusual, VG.................75.00
Darner, ceramic girl, Darn-It 20.00
Darner, mc spatter glass, blown egg form, 3x4½".....................175.00

Darner, Nailsea, clear w/rose loops, wht int, Pittsburgh, 7".........350.00
Darner, oak, 3-part, mushroom, stick, & ft form, VG...................45.00
Darner, paperweight type, pk lily in egg, bl striated hdl 350.00
Drizzling or raveling tool, celluloid, emb scene, 6", VG 50.00

Buttons, portraits under glass with paste stones in borders, large, $150.00 for the pair.

Emery, apple, red velvet, 1¼" 25.00
Emery, rabbit, velvet cushion, glass eyes, sterling, 1½x2" 125.00
Emery, strawberry, red satin, sterling cap, 2" 65.00
Emery, Victorian scallop shell w/ribbon through bk, M 45.00
Hem gauge, sterling, Deco floral 125.00
Kit, Eastern Star, plastic, w/contents..20.00
Kit, mending; plastic Oriental doll, child's, 1940s.......................35.00
Kit, metal tube, Lydia Pinkham...25.00
Kit, red & wht plastic, ped ft, Mt Angel OR, early 38.00
Kit, red vinyl, zippered, w/complete contents, 1950s...................15.00
Knitting sheath, goosewing type, ornate cvg, ca 1830.................195.00
Lace bobbin, Midlands, ivory, fairing style 125.00
Needle case, Avery, raised florals, flat style, ¾x2".......................95.00
Needle case, Bakelite, doll unscrews at shoulders, NM................45.00
Needle case, celluloid, floral border/crest, book form, '10s.............65.00
Needle case, celluloid, mushroom form, yel w/red cap, 2" 40.00
Needle case, Chinese silver, ornate, ca 1880s 175.00
Needle case, ivory, cvd Alaskan totem, early...............................165.00
Needle case, ivory, serpentine dragon, Victorian, 3½" 165.00
Needle case, vegetable ivory, acorn ends, 2¾" 75.00
Needle case/emery, Transfer Ware, milk can shape, 1910s...........125.00
Oil can, Singer, sm..12.00
Pincushion, beaded red bird on perch w/strawberries, 5x7x9" 130.00
Pincushion, cat form, sterling, Jennings Bros 40.00
Pincushion, china, cartoon dog, polka dots, 1930s 12.00
Pincushion, leather, beaded slipper, 1920s, 5", NM.....................45.00
Pincushion, porc, googly-eyed polka-dot dog...............................17.50
Pincushion, SP, swan, padded top 35.00
Pincushion, velvet, carrot w/ribbon leaves, 1800s, 7" 150.00
Pincushion/tape measure, cowboy nodder, EX.............................65.00
Punch, eyelet; sterling hdl, 3"..37.50
Reel holder, peach enamel on brass, amethyst stone atop, 2" 115.00
Ribbon threader, sterling, floral, 3 in case 135.00
Scissors, buttonhole; brass, pat Sept 1872, 3½".............................37.00
Scissors, embroidery; sterling, relief eng......................................65.00

Scissors, pinking; chrome, lever action, 1939, EX 18.00
Scissors, repousse hdls, sterling, 3½" 65.00
Scissors, sterling, miniature, 1" 30.00
Sewing bird, brass, emb decor, EX clamp & spring, ca 1870 ....225.00
Sewing bird, pat Feb 15, SP, 1 cushion, 1980s repro, EX 75.00
Sewing bird, SP, w/heart key/clamp, pat 1852, 1940s repro 95.00
Sewing bird, SP, w/heart key/clamp, pat 1853, orig...................250.00
Sewing bird, SP, 2 orig cushions, Meriden, ca 1867-1871 ....225.00
Sewing bird, steel, smooth, spring operated, clamps on, 1820s ...220.00
Sharpener, scissors; Rol-It, red celluloid, EX............................. 7.00
Spool, MOP floral top, metal shaft, bone base, 1½" 27.50
Tape measure, bronzed metal, watering can 75.00
Tape measure, celluloid, girl w/dog..65.00
Tape measure, celluloid, gr log form, 2" 65.00
Tape measure, Liberty Bell, ...That Got Kaiser's..., Phila.............75.00
Tape measure, metal, egg w/fly pull, EX 85.00
Tape measure, plastic, gray house, red roof.................................40.00
Tape measure, vegetable ivory, cvd decor, w/pincushion, 4" 125.00
Tatting shuttle, abalone pearl..45.00
Tatting shuttle, celluloid, Lydia Pinkham, M..............................55.00
Tatting shuttle, horn, narrow 65.00
Tatting shuttle, irid mussle shell, aluminum post 68.00
Tatting shuttle, sterling, script initials, Webster mk...................110.00
Thimble, brass, Prudential Life Ins, pre WWII 15.00
Thimble, ivory, scrimshawed ship & flowers, new, EX 15.00
Thimble, Ketcham & McDougal, allover starbursts to rim 65.00
Thimble, Ketcham & McDougal, beads, raised dots on rim...........22.50
Thimble, Ketcham & McDougal, fluted gold band, heavy.............65.00
Thimble, nickel/brass, tailor's, old, lg.......................................12.00
Thimble, Simons, Egyptian border...32.00
Thimble, Simons, emb band, scroll borders 38.00
Thimble, Simons, farm scene, scrolled rim 45.00
Thimble, Simons, wide floral band 35.00
Thimble case, sweet grass, acorn form, VG +sterling thimble........55.00
Thimble case, sweet grass, w/lid & loop, EX 22.00
Thimble stand, Gem Silver Co, triangular, 2½"..........................70.00
Thimble stand, porc, cat w/pk flowers 35.00
Thread caddy, walnut, EX trn detail/finial, pat 1887, 9x9" 65.00
Thread winder, CI, table clamp, ca 1900 ....90.00
Threader, sterling, dbl eng lines, F&B mk, pr 40.00
Tin canister, Tesco Tracing Cloth Powder, 3¼", VG 18.00

Sewing Machines

Child's size, metal and wood, functional, 30", $175.00.

Child's, Betsy Clark, Hallmark Cards, 1976, NMIB **28.00**
Child's, Betsy Ross, gr metal, Deco metal box, VG **50.00**
Child's, Casige, red/tan, British Zone, VG....................................**35.00**
Child's, Casige, steel, scroll decals, pre WWII, EX **55.00**
Child's, Genero Stitch Master, NMIB..**65.00**
Child's, Holly Hobbie, bl plastic, battery op, G **25.00**
Child's, Ideal Sewette, battery op **40.00**
Child's, Kay-An-Ee Sew Master, bl or red metal, US Zone, VG **60.00**
Child's, Little Beauty, CI, Germany, 8x10", EX...........................**150.00**
Child's, Little Comfort, EX **135.00**
Child's, Necchi Supernoval, plastic, red & ivory, VG **25.00**
Gardner, hand crank, EX...**110.00**
New Nat'l, table model, hand crank, much gold, EX **125.00**
New Remington #4, claw ft, EX **105.00**
Singer Sewhandy #20, metal **40.00**
Stitchwell, hand crank/clamp-on, box, HP decor, 5½x6x3¼".......**98.00**
Wheeler & Wilson, pat 1850, Internat'l, complete **795.00**
Wilcox & Gibbs, ft pedal, walnut carrying case, mini, M **495.00**

Shaker Items

The Shaker community was founded in America in 1776 at Niskeyuna, New York, by a small group of English 'Shaking Quakers.' The name referred to a group dance which was part of their religious rites. Their leader was Mother Ann Lee. By 1815 their membership had grown to more than one thousand in eighteen communities as far west as Indiana and Kentucky. But in less than a decade, their numbers began to decline until today only a handful remain.

Their furniture is prized for its originality, simplicity, workmanship, and practicality. Few pieces were signed. Some were carefully finished to enhance the natural wood; a few were painted.

Although other methods were used earlier, most Shaker boxes were of oval construction with overlapping 'fingers' at the seams to prevent buckling as the wood aged. Boxes with original paint fetch double the price of an unpainted box; number of fingers and size should also be considered.

Although the Shakers were responsible for weaving a great number of baskets, their methods are not easily distinguished from those of their outside neighbors, and it is nearly impossible without first-hand knowledge to specifically attribute an example to their manufacture. They were involved in various commercial efforts other than woodworking – among them sheep and dairy farming, sawmills, and pipe and brick making. They were the first to raise crops specifically for seed and to market their product commercially. They perfected a method to recycle paper and were able to produce wrinkle-free fabrics. Prices realized for Shaker artifacts at today's large auctions are very erratic.

Standard two-letter state abbreviations have been used throughout the following listings.

Key:
bj — bootjack
CB — Canterbury
EF — Enfield
NL — New Lebanon

PH — Pleasant Hill
ML — Mt. Lebanon
SDL — Sabbathday Lake
WV — Watervliet

Basket, ash/hickory, rectangular, PH, ca 1850, 15x20x17" **600.00**
Basket, blk ash, dbl hdl, wrapped rim, sgn NF, 11x14½" **300.00**
Basket, cheese; blk ash, Alfred ME, 1840, 7x21"........................**800.00**
Basket, drying; ash, wrapped hdls, 2 runners, 1850, 23" dia **900.00**
Basket, drying; blk ash, sq to rnd form, hdls, 20" dia **600.00**
Basket, gathering; blk ash, cvd hdls, EF, 1850, 11x40x23" **450.00**
Basket, gathering; oak splint, hoop hdl, EF, 1840, 12x32x32"......**900.00**

Basket, sewing; blk ash, 4-pocket, cvd hdls, ME, 1850, 7x15" **600.00**
Basket, sewing; maple splint, natural, sq base, ML, 3½x6"...........**800.00**
Basket, sewing; poplarware, 2 side compartments, SBL................**300.00**

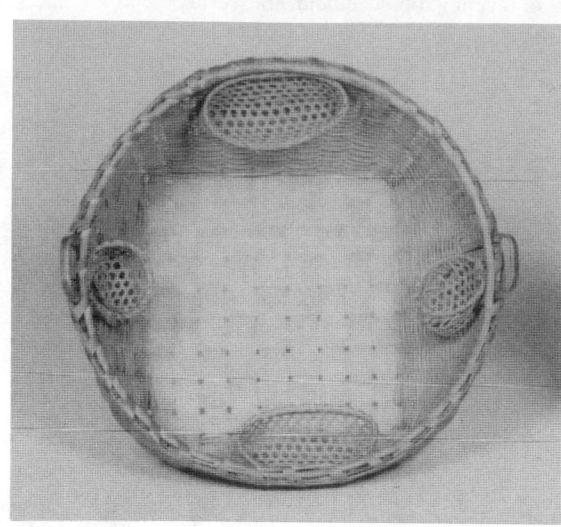

Basket, sewing; splint, four hanging baskets inside, probably from Enfield, 15½", EX, $800.00.

Basket, splint, hoop hdl, attached lid, MA, 1850, 10x9" **600.00**
Basket, wool; ash/maple, cvd dbl hdls, 13x27½x20½" **550.00**
Bottle, gr, Extract of Horehound, NL, orig top, 9¼" **575.00**
Bottle, pickle; clear, rib shoulders, label, Portland, 11½" **550.00**
Bottle filler/funnel, pine/cherry, ML, 1840, 19x15x5" **650.00**
Box, butternut/bird's-eye maple, MOP mt, EF, 1850, 3x8x5" **450.00**
Box, chip; pine/hickory, brn pnt, dvtl, WV, 1840, 14x20x13" . **4,500.00**
Box, chip; pine/hickory, rpt, dvtl, hdl/2 runners, 20x24x15"... **1,800.00**
Box, maple/pine, orig red pnt, 3-finger, SDL, 1830, 2¼x6" **1,750.00**
Box, maple/pine, orig yel pnt, sgn, CB, 1859, 1¾x2⅞"............ **1,100.00**
Box, maple/pine, pnt traces, 3-finger, CB, 1830, 2½x5½" **700.00**
Box, maple/pine, 5-finger, copper nails, Alfred, 1840, 7x12".......**450.00**
Box, natural, stenciled: Lavendar, 4-finger, w/lid, 14" L **875.00**
Box, pine, red stain, dvtl, molded lid, NL, 1830, 7x15x9" **500.00**
Box, pine/cedar, natural, 3-finger, oval, 1½x3⅝".........................**800.00**
Box, pine/maple, orig pnt, 4-finger, Canaan NY, 1820, 4x9"... **4,800.00**
Box, poplarware, kid leather trim, CB, 2¼x4½"...........................**300.00**
Box, seed; orig label, New Gloucester ME, 5½x14x7¼" **700.00**
Box, seed; pine, orig pnt, rpl lid, orig label, ML, 5x22x9"........ **1,100.00**
Box, seed; w/worn ML paper label, 11x24", G..............................**375.00**
Box, sewing; bentwood, satin lining, SDL, 7⅞" L, EX..................**325.00**
Bucket, pine, orig pnt, dmn bail plate, EF, 1840, 7¼x10¼" **450.00**
Bucket, pine, orig pnt, dmn bail plate, w/lid, EF, 8x9¾" **1,000.00**
Candle box, mitered sliding lid, orig pnt, 1800s, 12½x11x21" **295.00**
Candle stand, birch/maple, circle decor, SDL, 1830, 25x16"... **2,100.00**
Candle stand, cherry, rfn, snake legs, NL, 1830, 23x14" dia.... **2,500.00**
Cape, dk bl wool, gray satin trim, MOP buttons, EX....................**250.00**
Carrier, maple, 4-finger, satin lined, SDL, 8x11" dia **400.00**
Carrier, pine/hickory, beveled sides, sq, ML, 1840, 12x10" **400.00**
Carrier, pine/hickory, stain, dvtl, sq, CB, 1830, 10x11" **1,000.00**
Carrier, pine/maple, natural, satin lined, oval, 9x7" **375.00**
Carrier, pine/maple, varnish, 2-finger, CB, 1830, 7x10"..............**900.00**
Carrier, sewing; birch/pine, 4-finger, Alfred ME, 8x11x8" **500.00**
Chair, #0, maple, shawl bar/arms, ML, 1870, 22½" **1,750.00**
Chair, ladderbk w/shawl bar, ML, rfn/rpl rush seat **375.00**
Chair, maple, taped seat, 3-slat, WV, 1820, 37", 4 for **5,000.00**
Chair, maple, yel stain, spindle bk, CB, 1880, 29".......................**700.00**
Chair, rocker, maple/cherry/birch, arms/rush seat, 1850, 42"... **1,800.00**
Chair, rocker #0; maple, dk finish, taped seat, ML, 23" **2,000.00**

Chair, rocker #3; maple, rpt, taped seat, ML, 1870, 34" **400.00**
Chair, rocker #5; maple, taped seat/bk, arms, ML, 1880, 39" **750.00**
Chair, rocker #5; maple, walnut finish, taped seat, ML, 39" **1,300.00**
Chair, rocker #6; maple, varnish, rush seat, ML, 1870, 42" **2,500.00**

Rocker, Mt. Lebanon, late 19th Century, 33", $550.00.

Chair, rocker #7; maple, dk finish, ML, 1900, 41" **1,300.00**
Chair, rocker; maple, orig finish, rush seat, WV, 1820, 39" **900.00**
Chair, rocker; maple, rush seat, scroll arm, NL, 1820, 44" **9,000.00**
Chair, rocker; maple/curly maple, natural, CB, 1820, 39" **1,600.00**
Chair, side #1; maple, varnish, taped seat, ML, 28¼" **1,700.00**
Chair, side; maple/tiger maple, taped seat, NL, 1830, 42" **2,100.00**
Chest, blanket; poplar, orig stain, dvtl drw, NL, 35x41x19".....**3,000.00**
Chest, butternut/poplar, 24-drw/porc knobs, 1840, 42x48" **2,500.00**
Chest, pine, grpt, SDL, w/letter, 31x26x18"............................**3,500.00**
Chest, spice; pine, varnish, 3 drw over 2, 7½x11x5" **650.00**
Churn, pine, bl rpt, sgn Dairy House, ML, 1840, 22½" **550.00**
Cloak, beige wool, pk satin ribbon, doll's, 17" on hanger **375.00**
Cloak, wool, purple w/satin brocade, CB label, 48" +hanger... **1,750.00**
Clothes list, calligraphy, butternut/poplar fr, 1888, 10x9" **1,300.00**
Coffeepot, tin, short/squat, str sides, att, 8" **150.00**
Cupboard, pine, orig pnt, 1-door, 4-shelf, 1830, 55x19x11".... **1,800.00**
Cupboard, pine/walnut, pnt, gallery, 1-drw, 1830, 47x33x15". **5,500.00**
Doll, porc head, kid body, orig clothes, rpl hand, 15".................**600.00**
Dry sink, pine, rfn, panel door, pinned, NL, 1830, 35x32x15".....**900.00**
Flax wheel, oak/maple, natural, Alfred ME, complete, 34x35"....**600.00**
Footstool, #0, maple, varnish, rush seat, ML, 9½x13x10" **500.00**
Hanger, butternut/pine, natural, 3-bar, ML, 1840, 19½x18"........**350.00**
Hanger, clothes; pine, natural, sgn, NL, 1850, 17", 4 for **275.00**
Hanger, clothes; wooden, att, 16", pr **110.00**
Hanger, poplar, walnut stain, 3-bar, PH, 1850, 6¼x14" **450.00**
Hanger, walnut, dk varnish, EF, 1840, 12½x12½" **200.00**
Highchair, maple, foot rail, taped seat, ML, 1880, 33"............. **8,000.00**
Measure, bentwood w/trn hdl, worn patina, 8" hdl, 8", EX..........**100.00**
Measure, oak/pine, natural, SDL, 5x9" dia, 4x8" dia, pr..............**450.00**
Mortar, maple, natural, MA, 1830, 4x3½", +walnut pestle..........**550.00**
Neckerchief, silk, hand woven, hemmed, OH, 1846, 35" **450.00**
Rack, butternut, 2-bar, mortised/tenon, CB, 1830, 32½x14".......**550.00**
Rack, drying; maple, 4-section, orig pnt, EF, 1840s, 60" **1,100.00**
Rack, spool; cherry, 6 cvd horn spindles w/spools, 5x5" dia..... **1,750.00**
Shawl, gray & cream wool, stripe border/fringe, SDL, 64" sq.......**300.00**
Stand, cherry/maple, trn legs, 2 dvtl drw, 1850, 29x20x20"..... **1,500.00**
Stand, cherry/pine, natural, dvtl drw/sq legs, ML, 27x20x18" **950.00**
Stand, cherry/poplar, 1-drw, trn knob, CB, 1840, 28x18x17".. **2,200.00**
Stand, pine/birch, 1-drw, rstr red finish, CB, 27x20x16".............**650.00**

Stand, sewing; butternut/maple, 2-drw, EF, 1840, 28x22x20".. **7,000.00**
Stand, sewing; pine, dvtl drw, trn leg, CB, 1830, 27x18x21"... **1,700.00**
Stand, sewing; pine, varnish, dvtl drw, NL, 1830, 26x18x18" . **3,700.00**
Stand, spool; maple, velvet cushion, 4 spools, Alfred ME............**550.00**
Stand, work; cherry/pine, 1-drw, dvtl, WV, 1830s, 21x16x14"...**900.00**
Stereoscope, butternut/tin/brass, folds, EF, 1872, 15½x5" **300.00**
Stool, pine, 3-step, orange pnt, NL, 1850, rstr, 32x15x15" **1,200.00**
Stove, CI, curved ash catcher, sq legs, 16x33x12" **1,200.00**
Straw press, cherry, varnish, mortised/pegs, ME, 1830, 18x13" **800.00**
Swift, maple, orig mustard pnt, 21"...**450.00**
Table, trestle; cherry, iron braces, NL, 1835, 27x10x35" **5,500.00**
Table, work; birch/cherry, rpt, trn leg, WV, 1820, 26x42x23" **550.00**
Table, work; pine/birch, rnd legs, CB, 1820, 28x63x27" **1,750.00**
Table, work; pine/maple, stain, trn leg, ME, 1820, 28x34x21".. **1,400.00**
Tub, milk; pine, orig bl & cream pnt, EF, 1840, 4¾x9½" **450.00**
Tub, milk; pine, orig pnt, dbl wire hdls, EF, 1840, 5x10" **850.00**
Wardrobe, poplar, paneled door/1-drw, CB, 1840, 69x45x17" . **4,000.00**
Washstand, pine/poplar, 3 dvtl drws, NL, 1860, 39x28x19" **8,000.00**
Wheel, wool; hardwoods, natural, sgn FW, CB, 1820 ....**750.00**
Yarn winder, maple, natural, clock reel, CB, 1839, 37" **550.00**

Shaving Mugs

In the 1860s it became a popular practice for every man who shaved to have his own special shaving mug. Mugs belonging to men who frequented the barber shop for their tonsorial services were often personalized with their owner's name and kept on display on the barber's shelf. Occupational shaving mugs became the high point of individualism during this period. China mugs, mostly made in France, Germany, and Austria, were imported by American barber-supply companies where artists hand painted the occupation or the fraternal or sports affiliation of its customer on the mug. Often his name was added in gold. Because of sanitary rules and restrictions imposed around 1915, these personalized mugs were eventually taken off the barbers' shelves. Today, occupational shaving mugs are the most valuable. Although some are valued by the excellence of the artist, most are priced by the rarity of the subject matter.

Occupational, toll bridge operator, 3½", $265.00.

Birds on branch w/gr foliage, worn gold, EX 40.00
Flow blue, ironstone, Staffordshire, EX..50.00
Fraternal, BPOE, elk scene, mk TPCo, semi-vitreous, VG............65.00
Fraternal, Brotherhood of RR Engineers, EX color & gold, EX......25.00

Fraternal, Knights of Columbus, gold trim, EX 40.00
Fraternal, Knights of Columbus, mc/silver emblem w/gold, T&V..50.00
Fraternal, Knights of Pythias, mc emblem w/gold, T&V Limoges..75.00
Fraternal, Odd Fellows, eye over 3 rings, T&V, EX 110.00
Fraternal, Odd Fellows, Royal China Internat'l, EX 95.00
Fraternal, Sons of Veterans, red/wht/bl ribbon w/gold medal.........95.00
Fraternal, TRA #25299 Hoo Hoo, blk cat w/gold, J&C Bavaria..195.00
Lady's portrait, worn gold, mk Alpha, EX 50.00
Occupational, artist, tools, gold trim, V&D Austria, EX................85.00
Occupational, baker, man making bread, gold trim, #323, EX 700.00
Occupational, butcher, skinning steer, D&C France, EX 500.00
Occupational, butcher, steer, Xd tools ea side, Austria, EX..........150.00
Occupational, cab driver, horse-drawn vehicle & driver, EX 320.00
Occupational, chief of police, gold eagle on shield, EX................250.00
Occupational, drayman, man in horse-drawn wagon w/crates 450.00
Occupational, equipment operator, man at controls, gold trim....110.00
Occupational, farmer, man plows behind horses, J&C Bavaria....150.00
Occupational, florist, hanging plant/curtains, gold trim.................80.00
Occupational, furniture dealer, furniture, gold trim, EX..............150.00
Occupational, gambler, horseshoe & 4-leaf clover, gold trim.......135.00
Occupational, glass blower, 2 men working glass, gold trim..... 1,250.00
Occupational, horse breeder, horses in stalls, D&C France 865.00
Occupational, iceman, man w/tongs by wagon, gold trim, EX 345.00
Occupational, mason, man working cement, Bavaria, EX............525.00
Occupational, minister, church amid village, T&V, EX 125.00
Occupational, minister, church on hill, mk, EX 175.00
Occupational, musician, bugle, fancy gold, D&C France, EX 150.00
Occupational, oilman, oil rigs & house, V&D Austria, EX..........125.00
Occupational, painter, man works on house, mk JP, EX..............600.00
Occupational, printer, hand w/composing stick, T&V Limoges ..125.00
Occupational, railroad man, caboose/man, T&V Limoges, NM..125.00
Occupational, stone mason, tools of trade, gold trim, EX..............75.00
Occupational, sulky driver, trotter scene, Limoges, VG 450.00
Occupational, tailor, man w/pants over arm, T&V Limoges........100.00
Occupational, undertaker, cemetery scene, T&V Limoges, EX ..450.00
Occupational, undertaker, horse-drawn hearse, gold trim, EX 475.00
Occupational, violinist, instrument w/bow, mk DFH/GDM, EX ..110.00
Occupational, waiter, man w/tray of drinks, worn gold, EX 135.00
Patriotic, Am eagle on globe, bl & red bands at base, EX 85.00
Patriotic, flag above gold name, V&D Austria, EX 75.00
Patriotic, flags & flowers, eagle above banner, EX 50.00
Patriotic, flags/shield/eagle/globe/flowers, gold trim, VG 25.50
Personalized signature w/roses, gold rim, EX...............................25.00
Quadruple plated, ornate hdl, Homan Mfg, #2775, pat 1903.......100.00
SP, milk glass insert, scroll hdl, Reed & Barton, VG 35.00
SP, monogrammed milk glass insert, fancy hdl, EX.......................25.00
St Bernard dog on front, pk top rim, Made in Germany, EX 30.00
St Louis Expo 1904, Machinery Building transfer, Austria...........110.00
United Mine Workers, bird trademk, Germany, EX 40.00

Shawnee

The Shawnee Pottery Company operated in Zanesville, Ohio, from 1937 to 1961. They produced inexpensive novelty ware – vases, flowerpots, and figurines – as well as a very successful line of figural cookie jars. These cookie jars and their dinnerware, the Corn Line, are very popular with today's collectors.

For those wanting more information, we recommend *Collecting Shawnee Pottery, A Pictorial Reference and Price Guide*, by Mark Supnick, updated in 1989. His address may be found in the Directory under Florida. In the listings that follow, gold trim may add from 50% to 100% on small items.

Cookie Jars

Add 30% to 50% to listed values for cookie jars with gold trim.

Clown, #12 ....70.00
Dutch Girl or Dutch Boy, #1025 or #1026, w/gold.....................120.00
Elephant, #60 ....45.00
Lucky Elephant, gold trim, USA...90.00
Octagon 25.00
Owl, gold trim, USA..90.00
Puss-N-Boots...60.00
Smiley the Pig..70.00
Winnie the Pig, gold trim 70.00

Corn Line

The utility jar in the Corn Line doubled as a sugar bowl, the small jug as a creamer. A three-piece range set combination comprised of a pair of shakers and the utility jar (used in this instance as a drip jar) was also available.

Bowl, fruit; 6" 25.00
Bowl, mixing; 6½" 25.00
Bowl, soup/cereal 30.00
Butter dish...35.00
Casserole, ind..35.00
Casserole, 1½-qt 50.00
Cookie jar 90.00
Creamer 20.00
Cup 20.00
Dish, 6" 7.00
Jug, 1-qt 50.00
Mug, 8-oz 30.00
Plate, salad; 8"...28.00
Plate, 10"..30.00
Platter, 12"..40.00
Range set, 3-pc...25.00
Saucer.. 8.00
Shaker, lg 20.00
Shaker, sm 12.00
Teapot, 30-oz 50.00
Utility jar 30.00

Miscellaneous

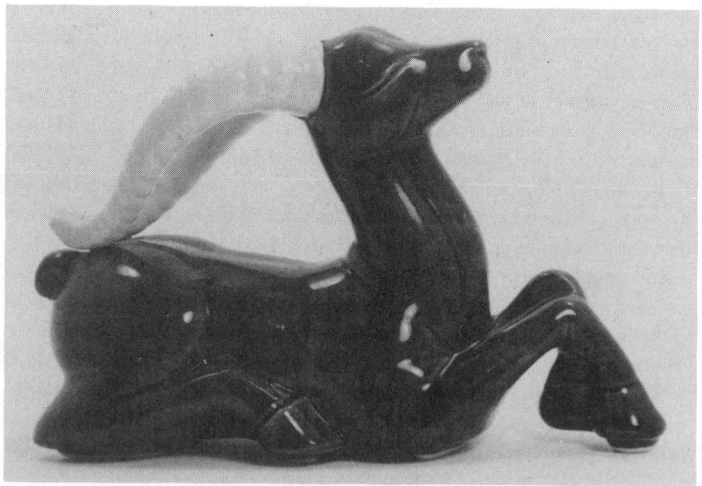

Gazelle, turquoise and white, marked USA #614, $25.00.

Coaster ash tray, paper label, USA #411, 4 for 25.00
Creamer, Puss-N-Boots, pat Puss-N-Boots 16.00
Figurine, gazelle, recumbent, head high, USA #614 ......30.00
Figurine, Oriental w/parasol, USA #601 .... 6.00
Figurine, rabbit, paper label 22.00
Figurine, teddy bear 22.00
Pitcher, Bo Peep, #47 ....35.00
Pitcher, Bo Peep, pat Bo Peep 40.00
Pitcher, emb/pnt florals w/stems, #35 ....14.00
Pitcher, emb/pnt fruit, bulbous, #80 ....22.00
Pitcher, slim form, angle hdl, USA #1168, sm 8.00
Pitcher, Smiley Pig, gold trim, hand decor, pat Smiley..........100.00
Pitcher, Smiley Pig, pat Smiley..........42.00
Planter, bird at side, #767 ....12.00
Planter, bird figural, USA 5.00
Planter, boot figural, USA 6.00
Planter, boy at stump, USA #533 .... 5.00
Planter, Buddha on throne, USA #524 ....12.00
Planter, bull stands beside leaf form dish, Shawnee USA 30.00
Planter, circus animal cage, USA 22.00
Planter, coal stove figural, USA 10.00
Planter, cockatiel, gold trim, Shafer stamp, mk Shawnee #523......12.00
Planter, Conestoga wagon, gold trim, #733 ....28.00
Planter, doe & fawn, gold trim, #669 ....16.00
Planter, doe beside log, #766 ....14.00
Planter, donkey & cart, matt w/gold, USA #538 ....12.00
Planter, donkey pulling cart, mk USA #709 ....14.00
Planter, donkey w/basket on bk, USA #671 ....14.00
Planter, duck, gold trim, stamped Shafer, USA #720 ....20.00
Planter, Dutch children at well, #710 ....12.00
Planter, elephant, USA #759 ....10.00
Planter, elf on shoe, gold trim, Shawnee #765 ....14.00
Planter, emb florals, w/liner, #545 .... 5.00
Planter, fish, open mouth, USA 3.00
Planter, frog on lily pad, #726..........20.00
Planter, frog plays guitar at side of stump, USA..........12.00
Planter, gazelle, gold trim, USA #613 ....25.00
Planter, girl at basket, gold trim, USA #534 ....12.00
Planter, gristmill, #769..........12.00
Planter, high-heel shoe figural, USA.......... 5.00
Planter, highchair, USA #727 ....35.00
Planter, horse figural, #506 ....24.00
Planter, hound & Pekingese dogs, #611 .... 4.00
Planter, hound figural, USA 6.00
Planter, locomotive engine, USA #550 ....20.00
Planter, man w/push cart, emb Rum Carioca, USA #621..........22.00
Planter, mouse w/cheese, USA #705 ....14.00
Planter, Oriental boy pulling rickshaw, USA #539..........10.00
Planter, Oriental w/book, gold trim, USA #574 ....10.00
Planter, Oriential figure beside bowl, USA #701 .... 5.00
Planter, pup on 2-button shoe, USA 7.00
Planter, pup on 3-button shoe, USA 6.00
Planter, push cart, USA #J544P 12.00
Planter, ribbed bowl form w/underplate, #495 .... 8.00
Planter, rocking horse, cold pnt, USA #526 ....16.00
Planter, skunk at side, #512 ....12.00
Planter, terrier dog, USA 10.00
Shakers, Chanticleer, rooster, sm, pr 14.00
Shakers, daisy on wht, unmk, sm, pr 10.00
Shakers, Dutch children, gold trim, pr 35.00
Shakers, flowerpot, gold trim, pr 18.00
Shakers, milk can, paper label, pr..........10.00
Shakers, owl, gr eyes, USA, pr..........16.00
Shakers, Winnie the Pig, lg, pr..........35.00

Teapot, clover blossoms emb/pnt on side, USA..........45.00
Teapot, Granny Anne, USA 45.00
Vase, bow knot at waist, #819 ....14.00
Vase, bud; boy beside cornucopia, USA #1265..........10.00
Vase, bud; gold trim & decals, USA #865 ....20.00
Vase, bud; leaves overlapping, ftd, USA 6.00
Vase, cornucopia, USA #835 .... 7.00
Vase, doe in shadow box, #850 ....12.00
Vase, emb flowers, hdls, USA #875 .... 5.00
Vase, emb philodendron leaves, gold trim, #805 ....24.00
Vase, ewer form w/dolphin hdl, #828 ....14.00
Vase, flower form, USA #1225 ....10.00
Vase, tulip form, gold trim, USA #1115 ....12.00
Vase, tulip form, no gold, USA #1115 .... 8.00
Vase, 2 doves in relief at base, USA #829 ....16.00
Vase, 2 lg leaves form body, ftd, #823..........14.00
Wall pocket, grandfather clock, gold trim, #1261 ....20.00

Shearwater

Since 1928 generations of the Peter, Walter, and James McConnell Anderson families have been producing figurines and art-wares in their studio at Ocean Springs, Mississippi. Their work is difficult to date. Figures from the twenties and thirties won critical acclaim and have continued to be made to the present time. Early marks include a die-stamped 'Shearwater' in a dime-sized circle, a similar ink stamp, and a half-circle mark. Any older item may still be ordered in the same glazes as it was originally produced, so many pieces on the market today may be relatively new. However, the older marks are not currently in use. Retail sales are available at the pottery or by mail order.

Black figures and pirates are usually valued at $35.00 to $50.00.

Pitcher, bl irid, artist sgn, 5" 65.00
Pitcher, ochre, bird hdl, sm lid, 6" 50.00
Teapot, dusty gr, hand trn, appl hdl & spout, imp mk, 6" 60.00
Vase, bl flambe, 5½" 75.00
Vase, gr/brn gloss, bottle form, 6" 25.00

Sheet Music

Sheet music is often collected more for the colorful lithographed covers rather than for the music itself. Transportation songs which have pictures or illustrations of trains, ships, and planes; ragtime tunes which feature popular entertainers such as Al Jolson; or those with Disney characters are among the most valuable. Much of the sheet music on the market today is valued at under $5.00; some of the better examples are listed here.

American Marsaillaise, Michel, blk/wht cover, 1898, EX..........22.00
As Time Goes By, from Casablanca, EX..........20.00
Back to Dixie Land, J Yellen, Starmer cover, 1914, EX 8.00
Battle Cry of Freedom, Root & Cady, Chicago, 1862, VG 55.00
Beautiful Shells, McChesney, Calvert litho, 1886, VG..........12.50
Bunker Hill Quick Step, Prentice, Boston, 1836, VG 40.00
Cazneau's Quick Step, soldier litho by Thayer, 1842, VG..........42.00
Columbia the Gem of the Ocean, color cover, 1843, VG..........22.00
Conover March, Arnold, Expo dedication, 1893, 8-pg, VG 17.50
Darling Boy Is Dead..., Wanless/Whittemore, 1865, 5-pg, VG 15.00
Doncha' Think It's Time?, Elvis cover, 1958, EX..........30.00
Eisenhower March, 1952, M 6.00
Fairy of Wildwood, HA Brown, 1866, 5-pg, VG..........10.00
Footprints on the Snow, Murphy, Detroit, 1866, 5-pg, VG..........15.00

Falling in Love Again, Famous Music Publishing Corp., Dietrich on cover, from Blue Angel, 1930s, $30.00.

For Dixie & Uncle Sam, Brennan/Ball, Starmer cover, 1916, EX..12.00
Freed Man's Lament, Murphy, Detroit, 1868, 5-pg, VG 15.00
Friendly Star, Garland/Kelly cover 8.00
Good-By, But Come Again, Thomas, Peters & Bros, 1867, 6-pg ...15.00
Goodbye France, Berlin, Barbelle mc cover, 1918, EX 7.50
Gypsy Told Me, Henie cover 3.50
Hail Columbia, 4 verses, 1st edition, 1836, EX.............................20.00
I Never Had a Mammy, Duncan Sisters, color cover, 1923 .... 6.00
I Wish I Knew, Grable cover 3.50
Janette, O'Reilley/Thomas, Peters & Bros, 1867, 6-pg 17.50
Kiss Pappa Good Night, Irving/McChesney, 1866, 5-pg 12.50
Leaf by Leaf the Roses Fall, A Vane, 5-pg, 1867, EX.....................17.50
Lucky Lindy, Gilbert/Baer, mc Spirit of St Louis cover, 1927.........14.00
Midnight Flyer, train cover, ET Paull, 1903................................35.00
Missouri Waltz, Shannon/Logan, riverboat cover, 1915, EX 7.50
Moonlight & Shadows, Lamour/Milland cover, 1936 .... 7.00
Mother Is the Battle Over?, stone litho, 1862, VG 45.00
My Belgian Rose, WWI War edition, 7x10".................................10.00
Nelly Was a Lady, SC Foster, Blake cover, 1849, 6-pg, EX.............12.00
Old Time Rag, Madden/Morse, Tom Moore inset mc cover, 1908.12.50
On Yonder Rock Reclining, Endicot litho, 1820s, EX...................22.00
Over the Rainbow, from Wizard of Oz, EX 25.00
Parade March of Union Grays, stone litho, 1862, EX 45.00
President Garfield Memorial March & Song, Root, 1881, EX 15.00
Red Rover, Barbary Pirates litho by Hall & Sons, 1820s, EX.........28.00
Round Hill Quick Step, N Hampden, MA, 1840, EX 32.00
Row Thy Boat Lightly, Woodman/Jameson, 1847, 4-pg, EX 12.50
Sailor's Tear, Pendelton, Boston, 1820s, EX....................................25.00
Smith's March, military litho cover by Hoen, 1848, 5-pg, EX........22.50
Snooky Ookums, Berlin, Pfeiffer cover, 1913, EX 15.00
Sweet Memories of Thee, A Welby/WC Peters, 5-pg, 1849, EX ...15.00
Tipperary Guards March, Starmer, ET Paull cover, 1915, EX 18.00

Shelley

In 1872 Joseph Shelley became partners with James Wileman, owner of Foley China Works, thus creating Wileman & Co., in Stoke-on-Trent. Twelve years later James Wileman withdrew from the company, though the firm continued to use his name until 1925 when it became known as Shelley Potteries, Ltd. Like many successful 19th century English potteries, this firm continued to produce useful household wares as well as dinnerware of considerable note. In 1896 the beautiful Dainty White shape was introduced, and it is regarded by many as synonymous with the name Shelley. In addition to the original Dainty 6-Flute design, other lovely and dainty shapes were produced: 12-Flute, 14-Flute, Leaf, Shell, Queen Anne, and the more modern shapes of Vogue, Regent, and Eve.

Though often overlooked, striking earthenware was produced under the direction of Frederick Rhead and later Walter Slater and his son Eric. Many notable artists contributed their talents in designing unusual, attractive wares: Rowland Morris, Mabel Lucy Attwell, and Hilda Cowham, to name but a few.

In 1966 Allied English Potteries acquired control of the Shelley Company, and by 1967 the last of the exquisite Shelley China had been produced to honor remaining overseas orders. In 1971 Allied English Potteries merged with the Doulton group. The name Shelley China Ltd. still exists, and it has been reported that Royal Doulton has produced trial wares bearing the Shelley backstamp.

Our advisors for this category are Lila and Fred Shrader; they are listed in the Directory under California.

Ash tray, Blue Daisy, gold trim, 3½" 22.50
Ash tray, Blue Rock, 6 flutes, 5" 29.00
Ash tray, Dainty Blue, 3½" 23.50
Bowl, cereal; Dainty Blue, 6 flutes, 6½" 30.00
Bowl, cereal; Harebell, Oleander shape, 6½" 30.00
Bowl, sauce; Blue Rock, 6 flutes, 5½"...25.00
Bowl, sauce; Harebell, Oleander shape, 5½" 22.50
Bowl, sauce; Lilac, 6 flutes, 5½"...23.00
Bowl, vegetable; Begonia, 6 flutes, w/lid, 10½" 105.00
Bowl, vegetable; Bridal Rose, 6 flutes, w/lid, 10½" 110.00
Bowl, vegetable; Dainty Blue, 6 flutes, open, 8½" 65.00
Bowl, vegetable; Harebell, Oleander shape, open, 8½" 60.00
Butter dish, Blue Rock, 6 flutes, oblong...65.00
Butter dish, Blue Rock, 6 flutes, rnd 71.00
Butter dish, Bridal Rose, 6 flutes, rnd...72.50
Butter dish, yel dots on Dainty White, 6 flutes, rnd 75.00
Butter pat, Archway of Roses 18.50
Butter pat, Blue Rock, 6 flutes..22.50
Butter pat, Bridal Rose, Oleander shape 20.00
Butter pat, Bridal Rose, 6 flutes 22.50
Butter pat, Heraldic, 6 flutes...18.50
Butter pat, pk dots on Dainty White, 6 flutes 24.00
Butter pat, Primrose...21.50
Butter pat, Regency, 6 flutes 22.50
Cake plate, Archway of Roses, Queen Anne shape, tab hdls 65.00
Cake plate, Blue Rock, 6 flutes, ftd, 8" 95.00
Cake plate, Bridal Rose, 6 flutes, tab hdls...68.00
Cake plate, Dainty Blue, 6 flutes, ftd, 8" 105.00
Cake plate, Old Sevres, ftd, 8" 95.00
Candle holder, Regency, 6 flutes, 2½", pr..85.00
Candlestick, bl & wht stoneware, 8", pr 125.00
Candy dish, Bridal Rose, 10 flutes, 4½" 21.50
Candy dish, Dainty Pink, 10 flutes, 4½" 22.50
Candy dish, Sheraton, 5"..18.50
Candy dish, yel dots on Dainty White, 6 flutes, 4½" 24.50
Chamberstick, Begonia, w/brass holder, 6" 32.50
Chamberstick, Heavenly Blue, w/brass holder, 6" 35.00
Cheese dish, Regency, 6 flutes, w/lid 125.00
Chocolate pot, Bridal Rose, 6 flutes, 6"...95.00
Chocolate pot, Harebell, Oleander shape, 8" 145.00
Chocolate pot, Heavenly Blue, 6 flutes, 6" 110.00
Chocolate pot, Lily of the Valley, 6 flutes, 8" 115.00

Cigarette holder, Begonia, 6 flutes 22.50
Cigarette holder, Blue Daisy..................................19.00
Cigarette holder, Celandine, 6 flutes 22.50
Coffeepot, Archway of Roses, Queen Anne shape, 9" 100.00
Coffeepot, Blue Daisy, 8-cup 85.00
Coffeepot, Campanula, 6 flutes, 6½" 135.00
Coffeepot, Heavenly Blue, 6 flutes, 8" 150.00
Coffeepot, Heraldic, pear shape, 2-cup 55.00
Coffeepot, Indian Peony, 8-cup 95.00
Coffeepot, Sheraton, 8-cup 85.00
Cream soup, Blue Rock, 6 flutes, w/underplate 50.00
Cream soup, Bridal Rose, Oleander shape, w/underplate 50.00
Cream soup, Dainty White, 6 flutes, w/underplate................45.00
Creamer & sugar bowl, Archway of Roses, Queen Anne, w/lid.....55.00
Creamer & sugar bowl, Blue Rock, 6 flutes, open..................49.50
Creamer & sugar bowl, Bridal Rose, 14 flutes, open..............47.00
Creamer & sugar bowl, Celandine, 6 flutes, open, lg............52.50
Creamer & sugar bowl, Dainty Pink, 6 flutes, w/lid, lg.........65.00
Creamer & sugar bowl, Lily of Valley, 6 flutes, open, w/tray..........75.00
Creamer & sugar bowl, Meissenette, w/lid......................52.50
Creamer & sugar bowl, Regency, 6 flutes, open on tray 72.50
Creamer & sugar bowl, Sheraton, w/lid.........................51.00
Creamer & sugar bowl, Sunrise, Queen Anne shape, w/lid........55.00
Creamer & sugar bowl, Windflower, 6 flutes, w/lid 57.50
Cup & saucer, aqua & wht panels, Queen Anne shape 28.00
Cup & saucer, Begonia, 6 flutes................................45.00
Cup & saucer, Blue Rock, 14 flutes 42.50
Cup & saucer, Celandine, Oleander shape, yel exterior 41.00
Cup & saucer, Daffodil, 6 flutes................................44.50
Cup & saucer, Dainty Blue, farmer-style, lg....................45.00
Cup & saucer, Dainty Pink, 6 flutes 48.50
Cup & saucer, Dainty White, 6 flutes 42.00
Cup & saucer, Daisy, Oleander shape, bl exterior...............42.00
Cup & saucer, demitasse, Blue Rock, 6 flutes 45.00
Cup & saucer, demitasse; Charm.................................27.50
Cup & saucer, demitasse; Dainty Blue, 6 flutes.................46.50
Cup & saucer, demitasse; English Lakes.........................39.50
Cup & saucer, demitasse; Indian Pony...........................44.00
Cup & saucer, demitasse; Lily of the Valley, 6 flutes 45.00
Cup & saucer, demitasse; Old Sevres............................38.50
Cup & saucer, demitasse; Shamrock, 6 flutes....................42.50
Cup & saucer, gold & blk, 14 flutes 44.50
Cup & saucer, Harebell, Oleander shape, bl exterior 42.50
Cup & saucer, Harebell, 14 flutes 44.00

Cup & saucer, Indian Peony, ped ft 44.00
Cup & saucer, Lily of the Valley, 6 flutes 42.00
Cup & saucer, Maytime, gold ft.................................42.50
Cup & saucer, Melody...39.00
Cup & saucer, Morning Glory, 6 flutes 42.50
Cup & saucer, Old Sevres, gold ft 44.00
Cup & saucer, pk dots on Dainty White, 6 flutes 48.50
Cup & saucer, Primrose, 6 flutes...............................42.50
Cup & saucer, Primrose Chintz, w/gold trim.....................42.00
Cup & saucer, Regency, 6 flutes 42.00
Cup & saucer, Rose Pansy Forget-Me-Not, 14 flutes 42.50
Egg cup, Bridal Rose, 6 flutes, sm.............................42.00
Egg cup, Dainty Blue, 6 flutes, lg.............................55.00
Egg cup, Dainty Blue, 6 flutes, sm.............................45.00
Egg cup, Vogue shape, orange & blk Deco design 54.00
Egg cup set, Dainty Blue, 4 sm cups on indented plate 225.00
Gravy boat, Lilac, 6 flutes, w/underplate 75.00
Gravy boat, Rose & Red Daisy, 6 flutes, w/attached underplate 65.00
Jam jar, Harebell, 6 flutes, w/lid & attached underplate 60.00
Jam jar, Lily of the Valley, 6 flutes, w/lid & underplate 65.00
Jam jar, Regency, 6 flutes, w/lid 45.00
Lamp base, Indian Peony, 11"...................................65.00
Mug, Harebell, 6 flutes..45.00
Mug, Harmony...24.50
Mug, Mabel Lucy Atwell, 4½"....................................47.50
Mustard jar, Dainty Blue, w/lid & underplate 58.00
Mustard jar, Stocks, w/lid.....................................42.50
Pitcher, Bridal Rose, 6 flutes, 7".............................71.00
Pitcher, Heavenly Blue, 6 flutes, 6"...........................65.00
Pitcher, Mabel Lucy Atwell, 7".................................72.50
Plate, Archway of Roses, Queen Anne shape, 8" 31.00
Plate, Begonia, 6 flutes, 6"...................................12.50
Plate, Begonia, 6 flutes, 8"...................................24.50
Plate, Blue Rock, Oleander shape, 6½"..........................14.00
Plate, Bridal Rose, Oleander shape, 8" 25.00
Plate, Dainty Blue, 6 flutes, 10¾".............................50.00
Plate, Dainty Mauve, 6 flutes, 8" 30.00
Plate, heraldic design, Prince of Wales, 1936, 10¾"............85.00
Plate, Indian Peony, 10½"......................................45.00
Plate, Lilac, 6 flutes, 10¾"...................................50.00
Plate, Mabel Lucy Atwell, 7½"..................................45.00
Plate, Melody, notched, w/gr trim, 8" 19.50
Plate, Old Sevres, 10½" in ¾" sterling fr......................155.00
Plate, Old Sevres, 6½"...19.50
Plate, Pansy, 6 flutes, 8".....................................29.50
Plate, pk w/gold trim, 6 flutes, 7"............................25.00
Plate, Primrose, 14-flute style, 8"............................28.50
Plate, Regency, 6-flute style, sq, 7½" 25.00
Plate, Sheraton, 10½"..31.50
Plate, yel dots on Dainty White, 6 flutes, 8" 31.50
Platter, Blue Rock, Oleander shape, rnd, 12"...................85.00
Platter, Bridal Rose, 6 flutes, 10" 75.00
Platter, Dainty Blue, 6 flutes, 14"............................95.00
Platter, English Lakes, rnd w/tabs, 10½".......................55.00
Platter, Regency, 6 flutes, 12"................................65.00
Pudding mold, geometric shape, 7" 38.50
Pudding mold, star shape, 5"...................................31.50
Sauce boat, Dainty Blue, 6 flutes, w/underplate................58.00
Snack set, Bridal, 6-flute cup, w/indented 8" sq plate.........55.00
Snack set, Dainty Pink, 6-flute cup, w/indented 8" rnd plate........59.00
Snack set, pk w/gold trim, 6-flute cup w/ind 7" rnd plate 52.00
Snack set, Woodland, cup w/indented 7½" sq plate 52.00
Soup plate, Blue Rock, 6 flutes, 8½"...........................38.00
Soup plate, Bridal Rose, Oleander shape, 8½"...................39.50

Hedgerow cup and saucer, $42.50.

Soup plate, Lilac, 6 flutes, 8½" 39.00
Soup plate, Maytime, w/gold trim, 8" 32.00
Tea & toast, bl w/gold 8-pointed stars, 6 flutes, 6x9" 55.00
Tea & toast, gr w/dk gr dots, 6 flutes, 6x9" 55.00
Tea & toast, Rosebud, 6 flutes, 6x9" tray 52.00
Teapot, Archway of Roses, Queen Anne shape, 7" 75.00
Teapot, Begonia, 6 flutes, 6" 100.00
Teapot, Blue Rock, 6 flutes, 6" 110.00
Teapot, Dainty Blue, Oleander shape, 7" 110.00
Teapot, Mabel Lucy Atwell, mushroom shape 95.00
Teapot, Sheraton, 8-cup 85.00
Teapot, yel dots on Dainty White, 6 flutes, 4" 85.00
Toast rack, Dainty Blue, 6 flutes 55.00
Toast rack, Rosebud 52.50
Toothpick holder, bl dots on Dainty White, 6 flutes 24.00
Toothpick holder, Dainty Blue, 6 flutes.........................28.50
Toothpick holder, Stocks, 6 flutes 22.50
Tray, Dainty Blue, 3-compartment, 13" 195.00
Tray, Regency, 3-compartment, 9" 125.00
Tray, sandwich; Bridal Rose, 6 flutes, 5x12" 64.00
Vase, orange/gr/blk, geometric, 8" 55.00
Vase, red swirl, cylindrical, 8" 45.00
Vase, Rosebud, 6 flutes, 7" 58.00

Shenandoah

The Shenandoah Valley, extending from Virginia to Pennsylvania, is well known for the fine pottery made there from the early 1800s until the turn of the century. It is characterized by bright, clear glazes in a variety of colors used alone or in combination. Many small potteries were involved. Items marked 'Bell' indicate one of the large companies.

Bowl, mixing; fluted sides, gr/burnt umber, 4½x11¼", EX 135.00
Pitcher, redware, wht slip w/dk brn mottle, edge chips, 7" 600.00
Wall pocket, appl birds/floral, mottle/wht on redware, 5⅜" 900.00
Whistle, bird form, wht clay w/appl & tooled detail, 2½" 150.00

Silhouettes

Silhouette portraits were made by positioning the subject between a bright light and a sheet of white drawing paper. The resulting shadow was then traced and cut out, the paper mounted over a contrasting color and framed. The hollow-cut process was simplified by an invention called the Physiognotrace, a device that allowed tracing and cutting to be done in one operation. Experienced silhouette artists could do full-length figures, scenics, ships, or trains free hand. Some of the most famous of these artists were Charles Peale Polk, Charles Wilson Peale, William Bache, Doyle, Edouart, Chamberlain, Brown, and William King. Though not often seen, some silhouettes were drawn or executed in wax. Examples listed here are hollow-cut unless noted.

Key:
bk — backing	p — profile
c/p — cut and pasted	wc — watercolor
fl — full length	

Boy, p, pen/ink details, old blk fr, 4⅛x3⅛" 85.00
Composite pr, p, emb Peale's label, rvpt glass, 13x17", VG..........375.00
Couple, p, identified, Peale/1798, oval fr, 7x5½", pr 350.00
Couple, p, old blk fr, 6½x5½", pr 240.00
Couple+4 children, fl, Edouart, 1836, 19x24" 950.00

Identified couple, she with knitting needles, he with umbrella, on watercolor background, August Edouart, 12" x 10", $1,700.00.

Girl, p, bow at neck, 5⅜x4¾" 90.00
Girl, p, woodblock-printed torso, rvpt, fr, 7x6" 250.00
Girl in bonnet, p, identified, 5½x4¾" 120.00
Lady, bust-length, elaborate bonnet, pen/ink, gilt fr, 4x5" 125.00
Lady, p, emb Peale Museum mk, cloth bk, cherry fr, 2¾x5" 150.00
Lady, p, ink details, verse, Doyle, fr, 6½x5½" 395.00
Lady, p, mahog veneer fr, minor stains, 6¾x5½" 175.00
Lady, p, pen/ink detail, emb brass fr, 5¼x4½" 105.00
Lady, p, worn rvpt glass, brass fr, 6½x5½" 300.00
Lady w/lacy collar, waist-length, pen/ink, reeded fr, 5x4" 275.00
Man, p, gilt highlights, blk lacquered fr, 5½x4⅝" 165.00
Man, p, ink details, brass fr w/gilt, 5x4" 175.00
Man, p, pen/ink detail, sgn Doyle, stained, 5x4" 100.00
Man, p, pnt glass bk, brass fr, 5x4" 65.00
Man holds stove-pipe hat on ink bk, data/sgn JW/1859, 12x6" ...200.00
Young officer, bust-length, wc/ink on paper, 4½x5½", pr 350.00

Silver

Coin Silver

The mark 'Coin Silver' was used after the 1830s to indicate items made with 900 parts of silver to every 1000 parts of content.

A Bancker, NYC; teaspoon, ca 1760 ....175.00
A Coles, NYC; Palace, teaspoon, ca 1860, 6 for..........125.00
AE Warner Jr, Baltimore; mustard pot, cauldron shape, 1870......250.00
AE Warner Jr, Baltimore; salver, repousse rim, 1870 ....325.00
Anthony Rasch, tea service, eng names/1811, 3-pc, 84-oz 4,700.00
AW Cram, salt spoon, shell shape................................25.00
B Wenman, NYC; sugar tongs, ca 1805 ....150.00
Ball, Tompkins & Blk/M Gibney; soup ladle, Fiddle Thread 395.00
Benedict & Scudder, NY; sugar tongs, Basket of Flowers, 1825 ...175.00
Bigelow Bros & Kennard, Boston; Fiddle Thread, sugar shell 35.00
Bigelow Bros & Kennard, Boston; soup spoon, 1845, 7½" 25.00
C Brewer & Co, Middletown; Sheaf of Wheat, sugar tongs, 1925 .175.00
CA Burnette, DE & VA; teaspoon, ca 1820...................29.00
Deodat Williams, tablespoon, monogram, 5-oz, 3 for............70.00
E&D Kensey, julep cup, dented, 4.7-oz, 3½" 250.00

E&D Kensey, julep cup, eng name/1858, minor dents, 3⅝" **400.00**
Emerson & Co, sugar shell **35.00**

Ewer, Lincoln and Reed, ca 1840, 24.5 troy oz., 13", $500.00.

FA Durgin, St Louis; berry spoon, ca 1860 ....**95.00**
Farrington & Hunnewell, Boston; stuffing spoon, 1860..............**425.00**
Gorham & Co, mustard pot, ca 1870 ....**225.00**
Howe & Guion, NYC; tongs, ca 1840 ....**65.00**
HUM, Medallion, ladle **225.00**
J Avery, Preston CT; dessert spoon, ca 1760 ....**495.00**
J Brevoort, NYC, tablespoon, ca 1750 ....**225.00**
J Musgrave, Phila PA; teaspoon, ca 1790s **175.00**
J Sayre, Southampton & NYC; sugar tongs, ca 1810...................**125.00**
J Stanwood, Palmer, & Batchelder, Boston; vase, 1850s **925.00**
J Werne, Louisville KY; julep cup, 3.8-oz, 3½" **400.00**
JJ Monell/CM Wms, coffee set, repousse floral bands, 3-pc **2,100.00**
Jones, Lows, & Ball, Boston; tongs, ca 1835 ....**65.00**
JS Porter, Utica; teaspoon, 1805-49 ....**20.00**
JUP Targee, NYC; teaspoon, ca 1810......................................**45.00**
JW Cusack, Sophie; server, twist hdl, bright-cut floral, 9½" **260.00**
Kirk & Son, Baltimore; chamberstick, repousse, ca 1860............**275.00**
L Moulton, MA & OH; teaspoon, ca 1800 ....**125.00**
Lincoln & Reed, Boston; baby's porringer, 1840s **475.00**
MW Galt-Taylor-Lawrie, stuffing spoon, King pattern.................**595.00**
N Harding, Boston; dessert spoon, ca 1860 ....**35.00**
OD Seymour, Hartford; serving spoon, fiddlebk hdl, 1850, 8½" **35.00**
PO Daniel, Boston MA; teaspoon, 1830s **25.00**
R Fairchild, CT & NY; teaspoon, ca 1760................................**175.00**
RE Smith, Louisville; julep cup...**425.00**
S Haley, tablespoon, ca 1750...**395.00**
Smith & Chamberland, Salem; soup ladle, 11" **210.00**
W Little, Newburyport MA; teaspoon, ca 1760 ....**175.00**
Wolcott & Gelston, Boston; teaspoon, 1820s.............................**22.00**
Zahm & Jackson, Lancaster PA; master butter knife, 1850s...........**55.00**

Flatware

Silver flatware is being collected today either to replace missing pieces of heirloom sets or, in lieu of buying new patterns, by those who admire and appreciate the style and quality of the older ware. Prices vary from dealer to dealer; some pieces are harder to find and are therefore more expensive. Items such as olive spoons, cream ladles, lemon forks, etc., once thought a necessary part of a silver service, may today be slow to sell; as a result, dealers may price them low and make up the difference on items that sell more readily. Many factors enter into evaluation. Popular patterns may be high due to demand though easily found, while scarce patterns may be passed over by collectors who find them difficult to reassemble. See also Tiffany, Silver.

Key:
FH — flat handle   HH — hollow handle

Antique Hammered, berry spoon, Shreve **85.00**
Antique Hammered, cream ladle, Shreve **50.00**
Antique Hammered, gravy ladle, Shreve **70.00**
Antique Hammered, ice cream fork, Shreve..................................**25.00**
Antique Hammered, tablespoon, Shreve **60.00**
Autumn Leaves, teaspoon, Reed & Barton....................................**20.00**
Breton Rose, butter spreader, HH, Internat'l **20.00**
Breton Rose, gravy ladle, Internat'l..**49.00**
Breton Rose, meat fork, Internat'l..**49.00**
Breton Rose, teaspoon, Internat'l **44.00**
Bridal Rose, bouillon, Alvin..**35.00**
Bridal Rose, butter spreader, Alvin...**35.00**
Bridal Rose, cocktail fork, Alvin..**35.00**
Bridal Rose, cold meat fork, Alvin..**95.00**
Bridal Rose, dessert spoon, Alvin...**40.00**
Bridal Rose, dinner fork, Alvin..**55.00**
Bridal Rose, gravy ladle, Alvin...**125.00**
Bridal Rose, jelly spoon, Alvin..**85.00**
Bridal Rose, luncheon knife, Alvin..**50.00**
Bridal Rose, olive spoon, Alvin..**95.00**
Bridal Rose, pickle fork, Alvin..**95.00**
Bridal Rose, pie server, Alvin, 1-pc..**275.00**
Bridal Rose, preserve spoon, Alvin...**135.00**
Bridal Rose, salad fork, Alvin...**75.00**
Bridal Rose, sugar tongs, Alvin, lg..**95.00**
Bridal Rose, teaspoon, Alvin...**35.00**
Bridal Rose, tomato server, Alvin **275.00**
Cameo, pie server, HH, Reed & Barton.......................................**65.00**
Cameo, tablespoon, Reed & Barton...**69.00**
Chateau Rose, cream soup..**26.00**
Chippendale, cocktail fork, Towle...**21.00**
Chippendale, gravy, Towle...**55.00**
Chippendale, iced teaspoon, Towle **28.00**
Chippendale, tablespoon, Towle..**49.00**
Chrysanthemum, cocktail fork, Tiffany.......................................**49.00**
Chrysanthemum, luncheon fork, Tiffany **75.00**
Contessina, bonbon, Towle **20.00**
Contessina, butter spreader, HH, Towle......................................**20.00**
Contessina, cocktail fork, Towle...**25.00**
Contessina, gravy ladle, Towle...**50.00**
Crown Baroque, dinner knife, Internat'l......................................**65.00**
Crown Baroque, tablespoon, Internat'l **115.00**
Dresden Scroll, teaspoon, Lunt..**53.00**
Duke of York, asparagus serving fork, gold washed, Whiting **245.00**
Duke of York, ice cream slice, gold washed, Whiting, 10¾".........**155.00**
Edgewood, butter knife, Internat'l...**45.00**
Edgewood, dinner knife, Internat'l...**40.00**
Edgewood, luncheon fork, Internat'l...**37.50**
Edgewood, rnd soup spoon, Internat'l.......................................**40.00**
Edgewood, tablespoon, Internat'l..**50.00**
Edgewood, teaspoon, Internat'l..**30.00**
El Grandee, fork, 7½"...**67.00**
El Grandee, iced teaspoon **33.00**
El Grandee, knife, 8¾"...**24.00**
El Grandee, teaspoon..**18.00**
Enchantress, butter spreader, FH, Internat'l.................................**20.00**
Enchantress, sugar spoon, Internat'l...**30.00**
Fairfax, butter spreader, HH, Gorham.......................................**27.50**

French Scroll, fork, Gorham, 7¼" 28.00	Lily, luncheon fork, Whiting................65.00
French Scroll, knife, Gorham, 8¾" 22.00	Lily, luncheon knife, Whiting 100.00
French Scroll, salad fork, Gorham 26.00	Lily, salad fork, Whiting 105.00
French Scroll, sugar shell, Gorham 19.00	Lily, sugar tongs, Whiting................95.00
French Scroll, tablespoon, Gorham 38.00	Lily of the Valley, sugar shell, Whiting....59.00
Frontenac, butter spreader, Internat'l...............35.00	Lily of the Valley, tablespoon, Whiting....98.00
Frontenac, fish fork, Internat'l.....................95.00	Madame Jumel, berry spoon, Whiting.......175.00
Frontenac, pie server, Internat'l, 1-pc.............325.00	Madame Jumel, cocktail, Whiting..........28.00
Frontenac, sugar spoon, Internat'l 35.00	Madame Jumel, demitasse spoon, Whiting...29.00
Frontenac, sugar tongs, Internat'l, lg 85.00	Madame Jumel, flat butter spreader, Whiting.....23.00
Georgian, bouillon, Towle 47.00	Madame Jumel, pickle fork, Whiting.......49.00
Georgian, cocktail, Towle 45.00	Madame Jumel, pierced olive spoon, Whiting.....49.00
Grand Colonial, butter spreader, FH, Whiting........16.00	Mary II, berry spoon, Lunt................85.00
Grand Colonial, cocktail, Whiting 18.00	Mary II, butter server, FH, Lunt 20.00
Grand Colonial, fork, Whiting, 7¼" 26.00	Mary II, cream ladle, Lunt................42.50
Grand Colonial, salad fork, Whiting.................24.00	Mary II, gumbo soup spoon, Lunt 35.00
Grand Colonial, teaspoon, Whiting 17.00	Mary II, olive spoon, Lunt................30.00
Grande Baroque, bottle opener, Wallace 49.00	Normandie, bonbon, Wallace...............27.50
Grande Baroque, butter spreader, Wallace 33.00	Normandie, cake server, Wallace...........27.50
Grande Baroque, carving set, Wallace, 2-pc 129.00	Normandie, cold meat server, Wallace......50.00
Grande Baroque, cheese scoop, Wallace 79.00	Normandie, gravy spoon, Wallace..........50.00
Grande Baroque, cocktail fork, Wallace...............40.00	Old Brocade, berry spoon, Towle..........85.00
Grande Baroque, cream soup, Wallace 45.00	Old Brocade, butter knife, Towle 30.00
Grande Baroque, demitasse spoon, Wallace 29.50	Old Brocade, butter spreader, FH, Towle...17.50
Grande Baroque, feeding spoon, Wallace..............25.00	Old Brocade, cake server, Towle...........40.00
Grande Baroque, fish serving set, Wallace, 2-pc......165.00	Old Brocade, cold meat fork, Towle.......70.00
Grande Baroque, iced teaspoon, Wallace..............45.00	Old Brocade, cream ladle, Towle..........40.00
Grande Baroque, ind pastry fork, Wallace............45.00	Old Brocade, cream soup, Towle...........30.00
Grande Baroque, punch ladle, HH, Wallace 450.00	Old Brocade, gravy spoon, Towle..........50.00
Grande Baroque, salad set, Wallace, 2-pc 395.00	Old Brocade, tablespoon, Towle...........50.00
Grande Baroque, serving spoon, Wallace..............69.00	Old English, berry spoon, Towle...........98.00
Grande Baroque, steak knife, HH, Wallace 50.00	Old English, butter spreader, Internat'l....15.00
Grande Baroque, strawberry fork, Wallace............24.50	Old English, cake server, Towle...........115.00
Grande Baroque, tablespoon, Wallace 89.00	Old English, cold meat fork, Internat'l.....35.00
Hunt Club, master butter spreader 27.00	Old English, cream ladle, Internat'l 25.00
Hunt Club, sugar shell.............................27.00	Old English, dessert spoon, Internat'l......25.00
Hunt Club, tablespoon 49.00	Old English, dinner fork, Internat'l........25.00
Intaglio, luncheon fork, Reed & Barton 30.00	Old English, dinner knife, Internat'l 20.00
Intaglio, 5 o'clock spoon, Reed & Barton 15.00	Old English, gravy ladle, Towle...........59.00
King Albert, bonbon...............................26.00	Old English, pie server, Internat'l.........30.00
King Albert, ind butter spreader, FH.................16.00	Old English, sauce ladle, Towle...........49.00
King Albert, master butter spreader 20.00	Old English, 5 o'clock, Internat'l.........10.00
King Albert, sugar shell............................18.00	Old Maryland, ice tong, Kirk..............115.00
King Albert, teaspoon..............................15.00	Old Maryland, meat fork, Kirk 89.00
King Christian, cream soup, Wallace 27.50	Old Master, demitasse spoon, Towle........28.00
King Richard, cream soup, Towle 37.00	Old Master, iced teaspoon, Towle..........33.00
King Richard, gravy ladle, Towle.....................79.00	Old Master, pie server, HH, Towle 47.00
King Richard, sugar tongs, Towle 50.00	Old Master, tomato server, Towle.........70.00
King Richard, tomato server, Towle..................120.00	Old Mirror, berry spoon, Towle...........100.00
Lancaster, ind butter spreader.......................32.00	Old Mirror, butter spreader, FH, Towle....25.00
Lancaster, salad fork 59.00	Old Mirror, cocktail fork, Towle..........20.00
Lancaster, soup ladle 345.00	Old Mirror, cream ladle, Towle...........42.50
Lansdowne, cold meat server, Gorham, lg.............85.00	Old Mirror, gravy spoon, Towle...........59.00
Lansdowne, jelly spoon, Gorham 30.00	Old Mirror, jelly spoon, Towle............40.00
Les Cinq Fleurs, bouillon, Reed & Barton 25.00	Old Mirror, meat fork, Towle.............59.00
Les Cinq Fleurs, cocktail fork, Reed & Barton 27.50	Old Mirror, sauce ladle, Towle...........59.00
Les Cinq Fleurs, cream ladle, Reed & Barton 55.00	Old Mirror, tablespoon, Towle 50.00
Les Cinq Fleurs, ice cream fork, Reed & Barton.......45.00	Olympian, fish serving slice, Tiffany 475.00
Les Cinq Fleurs, ice cream spoon, Reed & Barton......45.00	Onslow, cocktail fork, Tuttle 38.00
Les Cinq Fleurs, 5 o'clock spoon, Reed & Barton......15.00	Onslow, iced teaspoon, Tuttle 56.00
Lily, berry spoon, Whiting..........................260.00	Onslow, steak knife, Tuttle...............59.00
Lily, bouillon spoon, Whiting 55.00	Orange Blossom, bonbon, Alvin 115.00
Lily, cocktail fork, Whiting 45.00	Orange Blossom, bouillon spoon, Alvin 42.50

Orange Blossom, cream ladle, Alvin 97.50
Orange Blossom, dessert spoon, Alvin 50.00
Orange Blossom, dinner knife, Alvin 65.00
Orange Blossom, ind butter spreader, Alvin 40.00
Orange Blossom, lettuce fork, Alvin 175.00
Orange Blossom, master butter spreader, Alvin 42.50
Orange Blossom, tablespoon, Alvin 55.00
Orange Blossom, tea strainer, Alvin 175.00
Pointed Antique, cocktail fork, Reed & Barton 24.00
Pointed Antique, dinner knife, FH, Reed & Barton................35.00
Pointed Antique, ind butter spreader, Reed & Barton 24.00
Pointed Antique, luncheon knife, Reed & Barton 35.00
Polly Lawton, cocktail fork, Manchester..................................12.50
Polly Lawton, cream soup spoon, Manchester 20.00
Polly Lawton, dessert spoon, Manchester 20.00
Polly Lawton, dinner knife, Manchester 15.00
Polly Lawton, salad fork, Manchester 20.00
Polly Lawton, teaspoon, Manchester 12.50
Poppy, bouillon, Gorham..30.00
Poppy, butter spreader, FH, Gorham 25.00
Poppy, cocktail fork, Gorham...30.00
Poppy, crumber, Gorham..250.00
Poppy, dinner fork, Gorham...50.00
Poppy, fish fork, Gorham..45.00
Poppy, luncheon fork, Gorham 30.00
Poppy, olive spoon, Gorham...50.00
Poppy, teaspoon, Gorham...30.00
Prelude, cocktail fork, Internat'l..28.00
Prelude, cream soup, Internat'l...28.75
Prelude, flat butter spreader, Internat'l 21.00
Prelude, iced teaspoon, Internat'l..29.00
Prelude, steak knife, HH, Internat'l...45.00
Prelude, tablespoon, HH, Internat'l...55.00
Rondo, butter spreader, HH, Gorham......................................22.00
Rondo, cream soup, Gorham 33.00
Rondo, meat fork, Gorham 59.00
Rondo, pickle fork, Gorham..29.00
Rondo, sugar shell, Gorham..29.00
Rose Point, berry fork, Wallace 15.00
Rose Point, tablespoon, pierced, Wallace 65.00

Royal Danish, 89 pieces, 101.6 oz. of weighable silver, $1,500.00.

Royal Danish, berry spoon, Internat'l 129.00

Royal Danish, carving set, Internat'l, 2-pc...............................129.00
Royal Danish, cocktail fork, Internat'l.....................................28.50
Royal Danish, demitasse spoon, Internat'l 27.50
Royal Danish, ice cream fork, Internat'l...................................38.00
Royal Danish, lemon fork, Internat'l..28.00
Royal Danish, pickle fork, Internat'l 30.00
Royal Danish, steak knife, Internat'l..50.00
Sonya, butter knife, Internat'l...25.00
Sonya, cream soup, Internat'l..25.00
Sonya, sugar spoon, Internat'l 25.00
Stradivari, bonbon, Wallace..35.00
Stradivari, butter knife, flat, Wallace.......................................35.00
Stradivari, teaspoon, Wallace 18.00
Strasbourg, mustard ladle, Gorham 95.00
Strasbourg, steak knife, Gorham 34.00
Tree of Life, meat fork, Reed & Barton...................................69.00
Versailles, bouillon, Gorham...47.00
Versailles, ice cream fork, Gorham...89.00
Versailles, ice cream knife, Gorham...350.00
Versailles, iced teaspoon, Gorham 95.00
Versailles, luncheon knife, Gorham 95.00
Versailles, tablespoon, Gorham...110.00
Vine, berry spoon, Tiffany..400.00
Vine, conch berry spoon, Tiffany..375.00
Vine, fish serving fork, Tiffany..300.00
Vine, fish serving set, Tiffany..650.00
Vine, ice cream slicer, Tiffany...350.00
Vine, serving spoon, Tiffany..195.00
Vine, sugar sifter, Tiffany..195.00
Washington, cocktail fork, Wallace 20.00
Washington, soup, rnd, Wallace..35.00
Washington, soup ladle, Wallace 175.00
Wave Edge, sugar sifter, Tiffany..195.00
Wave Edge, sugar spoon, Tiffany...85.00
Wave Edge, waffle server, Tiffany 395.00
William & Mary, bonbon, Lunt...30.00
William & Mary, cocktail forks, Lunt.......................................20.00
William & Mary, cold meat spoon, Lunt..................................50.00
William & Mary, demitasse spoon, Lunt 12.50
William & Mary, dessert spoon, Lunt.......................................35.00
William & Mary, tomato server, Lunt.......................................65.00
William & Mary, 5 o'clock spoon, Lunt 15.00

Hollow Ware

Until the middle of the 19th century, the silverware produced in America was custom made on order of the buyer directly from the silversmith. With the rise of industrialization, factories sprung up that manufactured silverware for retailers who often added their trademark to the ware. Silver ore was mined in abundance, and demand spurred production. Changes in style occurred at the whim of fashion. Repousse decoration (relief work) became popular about 1885, reflecting the ostentatious taste of the Victorian era. Later in the century, Greek, Etruscan, and several classic styles found favor. Today the Art Deco styles of this century are very popular with collectors. In the listings that follow, manufacturer's name or trademark is noted first; in lieu of that information, listings are by item. Weight is given in troy ounces. See also Tiffany, Silver.

AE Warner, tureen, chased floral/birds, eng crest, 11x13" 4,250.00
Alvin, dish, shaped rim, 11½" dia 120.00
Alvin, tea set: pot+sug/cr+rnd tray, 36-oz...................................495.00
Am, cake basket, pierced foliate hdl/foliate rim, 1900, 15" 2,600.00

Arthur Hartwell, tea set, stylized flowers, simple, 3-pc **4,900.00**
Arthur Stone, bowl, shaped/ribbed, stamped 'T,' 19-oz, 10".........**300.00**
Arthur Stone, bowl, stylized floral band, rnd ft, 5½" **1,300.00**
Arthur Stone, dish, rnded sq cushion shape, w/lid, 4x6¾".........**800.00**
Arthur Stone, dish, sq shallow form w/rnd corners, 5½" **275.00**
Arthur Stone, pitcher, shouldered, panels w/sm acorns, 9" **2,000.00**
Arthur Stone, tray, stepped rim, pierced hdls, oval, 12" **1,000.00**
Ball/Blk, cake basket, chased florals, regilt, 11x12" **800.00**
Ball/Blk, hot water kettle, repousse, female head hdls, 16"...... **3,000.00**
Bigelow/Kennard, bowl, chased lobster w/appl feelers, 10" **3,500.00**
Bigelow/Kennard, dish, appl insects on folded corners, 5½" **575.00**
Bigelow/Kennard, ftd vegetable dish w/lid, fluted, 69-oz **1,300.00**
Birmingham, muffineer, allover leaf/scroll chasing, 7" **200.00**
Dominick/Haff, basket, gadrooned/pierced rim, 13" L **500.00**
Dominick/Haff, dish, Deco monogram on rim, dome lid, 34-oz...**200.00**
Dominick/Haff, pitcher, flared ft, sqd hdl, monogram, 11" **380.00**
Dominick/Haff, pitcher, sqd, butterflies/foliage, 8" **8,000.00**
Dominick/Haff, platter, Deco monogram on rim, oval, 18" **250.00**
Dominick/Haff, tea set, acanthus hdls, lobed sides, 3-pc.............**800.00**
Eoff/Phyfe, tea caddy, serpentine oval, Chinaman finial **800.00**
European, beaker, eng scroll/mythical beast, dtd 1752, 2¾" **750.00**
Fletcher/Gardner, tea service, c/b ft, acorn finials, 3-pc....... **4,250.00**
Francis Cooper, flagon, inscription on band, 1850s, 12" **1,000.00**
Frank Smith, pitcher, panels w/floral buds, 1910, 8" **275.00**
French, toast server, floral piercing, eng, acanthus hdls **200.00**
Georg Jensen, bowl, Blossom, openwork sides, oval, 8" L **500.00**
Georg Jensen, box, cigarette; dome lid, eng monogram, 5" L.......**300.00**
Georg Jensen, compote, chased leaf/dome rib 8-side base, 5" **225.00**
Georg Jensen, compote, grapevine at ft, hammered, 7½" **2,800.00**
Georg Jensen, compote, openwork foliage stem, ft, w/lid, 5" **600.00**
Georg Jensen, cup, openwork scrolls/beadwork ft, w/lid, 6".....**1,600.00**
Georg Jensen, openwork leafy base, 11" dia...............................**700.00**
Georg Jensen, pitcher, grapevine, band at base, ebony hdl, 9" **4,800.00**
Georg Jensen, pitcher, hammered, Danish style, 11" **3,800.00**
Georg Jensen, plate, appl husks/beading, chased shells, 6"............**300.00**

George Eoff coffeepot, early 1900s, 38-oz., 10", $1,700.00.

George Angell, tray, cyma edge, foliage-eng well w/owl, 10" **625.00**
German, centerpc, shell w/lg mermaid figural, 1900, 15" L **4,500.00**
German, dessert basket, dbl, rectangular hdl, fluted, 12" **2,400.00**
Gorham, ash tray, transportation motif, 'Hands Up,' 6½"............**350.00**
Gorham, bowl, beaded, loop hdls, ftd oval form, 15" L **475.00**
Gorham, bowl, copper/silver crab & trout, ftd, 5½" **800.00**
Gorham, bowl, grapevines appl on everted rim, 1905, 13" **1,200.00**

Gorham, bowl, rtcl, chased/eng, heart shape, 11-oz, 8" **400.00**
Gorham, butter pat, emb waves/fish/etc, sq form, 8 for............ **1,800.00**
Gorham, fruit bowl, vermeil/chased vintage, 1905, 11" **700.00**
Gorham, goblet, pr of children ea side of base, 1869, 7" **450.00**
Gorham, hot water kettle+stand, allover eng, ivory mts, 18" .. **2,100.00**
Gorham, Marlborough, tray, presentation inscription, 15" **575.00**
Gorham, Martele, bowl, floral flange, 4-ftd, mk Codman, 11".. **4,800.00**
Gorham, Martele, cake plate, repousse/chased fuchsias **1,900.00**
Gorham, Martele, pitcher, repousse/chased flowers, 9" **9,000.00**
Gorham, Martele, plate, chased anemone on bossed border, 7" ...**425.00**
Gorham, Martele, vase, emb/chased daisies, wavy rim, 13" **3,500.00**
Gorham, nut cup, pierced w/scrolled edge, set of 12....................**175.00**
Gorham, pan w/lid, emb band w/sea nymphs, matt finish, 10" **600.00**
Gorham, pitcher, appl gilt/copper cherries, emb turkey, 7½" .. **7,500.00**
Gorham, punch bowl, Nouveau bombe form, hdls, 16", +ladle.. **2,100.00**
Gorham, Standish, charger, 38-oz, 14" dia **175.00**
Gorham, tray, repousse flowers & 'H,' serpentine rim, 17" **1,200.00**
Gorham, wine coaster, pierced sides, Rococo style, 5½" **325.00**
Herman Glendenning, bowl, plain panels, repousse ribs, 10" .. **3,000.00**
Hester Bateman, pepper castors, Geo III, eng crest, 4", pr **475.00**
James Woolley, pitcher, shouldered, wide lip, monogram, 6½" **450.00**
Jarvie, pitcher, hexagonally paneled, sgn/#d, 22-oz, 9" **4,000.00**
JE Caldwell, bowl, scroll/floral eng, monogram, 21-oz, pr **350.00**
Joel Hewes, bowl, fluted, 3 ball ft, handmade, 1910, 3x8" **325.00**
John Carter II, salver, Geo II, c/b ft, floral border, 14" **1,200.00**
John Swift, teapot, Geo II, ornate spout/hdl mts, 34-oz........... **3,500.00**
JP Peterson, bowl, pie-crust edge, imp Handmade, 10-oz, 8" **150.00**
Kalo, bowl, lobed rim, appl monogram, oval ft, 9½" W **450.00**
Kalo, bowl, 5-lobed, incurvate, 2x7"..**425.00**
Kalo, tumbler, U-form w/appl monogram, 3½" **75.00**
Kalo, vase, trumpet form, 17-oz, 14" **750.00**
Karl F Leinonen, bowl, hammered, ribbed, 22-oz, 9½"................**450.00**
Kirk, bowl, repousse florals, 9"..**500.00**
Lebkuecher & Co, tray, emb iris, hdls, monogram, 10½" dia **550.00**
Lebolt, vase, flaring repousse/rtcl rim & ft, 1905, 25" **6,000.00**
Liberty & Co, centrpc, hdls, champleve panels, shallow, 12" .. **7,400.00**
Marcus & Co, frame, undulating stone-set flowers, 5x8" **4,000.00**
Martin/Hall & Co, tea/coffee, emb florals, ftd, 88-oz, 3-pc....... **2,200.00**
Meriden, bowl, rtcl floral side panels, 12" dia, 42-oz **900.00**
Meriden, plate, plain w/monogram, 11", set of 12, 236-oz **2,800.00**
Paul Storr, salver, shell/floral border, shell ft, eng, 9" **2,750.00**
Peter Archembo, coffeepot, Geo II, ornate, eng name, 19-oz.. **3,100.00**
R Ruys, canbelabrum, hammered, 4-arm, ca 1930, 7", pr **5,500.00**
Randahl, bowl, dbl ribs, mk Hand Wrought, 15-oz, 9"................**200.00**
Redlich, bread tray, appl rose/ribbon pierced rim, 16", EX...........**600.00**
Reed & Barton, pitcher, Paul Revere style, bulbous, 7½".............**200.00**
Richard Beale, cann, Geo II, chased/repousse foliage, 4¾"..........**900.00**
Robert Abercromby, teapot, Geo II, globular, 11-oz **2,900.00**
Roger Wms, coffeepot, gilt lilies of the valley, slim, 11" **1,700.00**
S Kirk & Son, centerpc, emb/eng leaves, lg hdls, 11x18" **3,000.00**
S Kirk & Son, sweetmeat basket w/lid, repousse, 7x5¾".............**700.00**
Shreve & Co, plate, shaped strapwork border, 6" **85.00**
Shreve & Co, tray, strapwork 'W,' 12½" dia **700.00**
Star/BM, sauce boat, chased florals, shell/hoof ft, 13-oz **425.00**
Theodore B Starr, compote, pierced vintage rims, 12" dia....... **1,200.00**
Thos Brown, bonbon bowl, hammered, scroll ft, 3x4" **300.00**
Whiting, bowl, eng trophies/floral swags, ftd, 8", pr **300.00**
WK Vanderslice, tureen, stag surmount, stag hdls, 7x9"..........**2,400.00**

Silver Lustre Ware

Much of the ware known as silver lustre was produced in the early 1800s in Staffordshire, England. This type of earthenware was entirely covered with the metallic silver glaze. It was most popular prior to 1840, when the technique of electroplating was developed, and silver-plated wares came into vogue. Later in the century, artisans used silver lustre to develop designs on vases and other decorative ware.

Creamer, garlands at top, ped ft, 5¾" 85.00
Cuspidor, lady's; minor wear, 5¼" dia..85.00
Jug, puzzle; rtcl sides, inscribed, ca 1900, 6⅝" 350.00
Mug, child's, lustre rim, brn transfer, 2" 225.00
Pitcher, floral on wht, rust rim, 5½" 45.00
Teapot, ribbed, Queen Anne style, 6"...150.00

Silver Overlay

The silver overlay glass made during the 1800s was decorated with a cut-out pattern of sterling silver applied to the surface of the ware.

Bottle, gr, scrollwork overlay, 5"..250.00
Bottle, silver forms fr for HP floral, 3-sided, Steiff, 10" 675.00
Bowl, banana; florals/scrolls, scalloped/ftd, 4x12½x8½" 65.00
Bowl, fluted rim, cut base, 2½x7½" 45.00
Decanter, hunter & dog on blk glass, pinched sides 175.00
Vase, gr, eng undulating tulips & leaves, trumpet form, 12" 900.00
Vase, gr, ribbed, dogwood overlay mk sterling, 4" 160.00

Silverplate

Silverplated hollowware is fast becoming the focus of attention for many of today's collectors. See also Pairpoint, Silverplate; Railroadiana, Silverplate.

Key:
gw — gold wash   SH&M — Simpson, Hall, &
                                          Miller

Hollow Ware

Basket, appl/cast flowers & branches, twist hdl, SH&M, 8" 500.00
Bowl, fruit; molded fruit hdls, Reed & Barton, 8½x13"................55.00
Box, bright-cut floral lid, shell-emb sides, English, 8" 50.00
Box, emb cherubs/fruit, over copper, hinged, oval, 11¾" L..........450.00
Butter dish, eng glass insert, Meriden Britannia, 1800s.................60.00

Sheffield candelabra, makers Matthew Boulton & Co., ca 1815, 22", $2,500.00 for the pair.

Candle snuffer, repousse hdl, 'ivory' insulator 60.00
Candlestick, repousse scenes/figures, Dutch, 1920s, 12", pr 145.00
Coffeepot, repousse flowers & ribbing, Mead & Robbins, 1845 .....95.00
Compote, Camille, Internat'l, 4¼x6½" 20.00
Condensed milk holder, fox on lid, ad inside lid, rare 60.00
Entree dish, egg/dart border, eng, paw ft, J Dixon, 13" L 250.00
Sauce dish, gadrooned, trn wood hdl, +underplate.........................25.00
Syrup, figural deer heads & hoof ft, sphinx on lid, SH&M 65.00
Tea set, Eternally Yours, 5-pc 395.00
Tray, bright-cut grapes, grape/leaf border & hdls, 28"...................140.00
Tray, gadrooned/pierced border, armorial eng, English, 24".........450.00
Tray, grape/leaf border, bright-cut center, Int'l, 15" 45.00
Tureen, beaded hdls, shell legs, ftd oval, Maple & Co, 15" 800.00
Urn, band w/Pan & other musicians, elongated, German, 28" ...200.00
Vase, bud; Meriden Britannia, ca 1860 ....75.00

Sheffield

Biscuit barrel, c/b ft, Jas Dixon & Sons, ca 1835 ....180.00
Chamberstick, snuffer w/acanthus finial, S-hdl, Boulton, 4½".....350.00
Coasters, gadrooned edge, wood base, Boulton, 6¼", pr.............550.00
Dish, warming; scroll hdls/ft, Boulton, 9½" dia, pr.................. 1,500.00
Spoon, mk J Prime, ca 1840, 12½"...125.00
Tea urn, fluted cover, 4-ftd ped base, English, 15" 450.00
Tea urn, 4-leg base, English, 1700s, 17", NM..............................500.00
Teapot, Georgian style, w/orig stand & burner 275.00
Teapot, strawberry leaf & flower finial, Boulton, 4x10½" 525.00
Tray, foliate hdls, M Boulton, 11" L..275.00
Tray, gadrooned, shell ea end, pineapple finial, ftd, 12" 50.00
Tray, supper; divided, egg/dart border, shells at hdls, 30" 175.00
Urn, paneled, ornate base w/foliage & paw ft, 17" 700.00
Vase, emb cherub heads/floral garlands, Wilkinson, 40", pr 2,000.00
Warmer, fluted columnar supports w/paw ft, Adkin Bros, 14"......200.00

Sinclaire

In 1904 H.P. Sinclaire and Company was founded in Corning, New York. For the first sixteen years of production, Sinclaire used blanks from other glassworks for his cut and engraved designs. In 1920 he established his own glass-blowing factory in Bath, New York. His most popular designs utilize fruits, flowers, and other forms from nature. Most of Sinclaire's glass is unmarked; those that are carry his logo: an 'S' within a wreath with two shields.

Our advisors for this category are Jeanette and Marvin Stofft; they are listed in the Directory under Indiana.

Bowl, chain of hobstars to honeycomb on star base, ftd, 9" 450.00
Candlestick, blk w/10 cut lustres, 9", pr 135.00
Candlestick, cobalt, wht rim, 9½", pr 160.00
Clock, ship's; wheel-cut floral & scrolls, 9½" 1,050.00
Cordial, Greek Key cutting w/starburst base, 3½"..........................30.00
Plate, star center w/radiant threads & 4 floral panels, 10"............325.00
Teapot, wheel-cut floral/leaf, +5 matching cups...........................850.00
Tumbler, copper wheel cut & etched, sgn 27.50
Vase, eng decor, trumpet form, mk, 10" 195.00

Sitzendorf

The Sitzendorf factory began operations in East Germany in the mid 1800s, adopting the name of the city as the name of their company. They produced fine porcelain groups, figurines, etc. in much the same style and quality as Meissen and the Dresden factories. Much of their ware was marked with a crown over the letter 'S.'

Our advisor for this category is William Brinkley; he is listed in the Directory under Illinois.

Bowl, bluebird w/dragonflies, mk, 12"	105.00
Candlestick, cherub w/arm around stick, floral base, mk, 15"	350.00
Clock, lg cupid ea side of rnd dial, basket surmount, 13"	600.00
Figurine, boy & girl pick apples, dog by ladder, 9x7½"	650.00
Figurine, cherub w/wine cup rides blk & wht goat, 6x7"	295.00
Figurine, couple w/Russian wolfhounds, 10x9"	850.00
Figurine, King Henry VIII & 6 wives, 8", set of 7	1,500.00
Figurine, man sits/studies painting, artist/wife flirt, 7x17"	850.00
Figurine, man w/watering can, lady w/flower basket, 9", pr	325.00
Figurine, Monkey Band, ea w/instrument, 6", set of 9	850.00
Figurine, Serenading Couple, she on sofa, he w/violin, 8x9"	750.00
Lamp, 2 lg figures/allover appl roses, rpl shade, 25"	535.00
Vase, cupid aside ball form w/appl flowers, 5½", EX	125.00
Vase, scene w/maid, Kauffman, lg paw ft, 3-hdl, Voight, 8"	225.00

Slag Glass

Slag glass is a marbleized opaque glassware made by several companies from about 1870 until the turn of the century. It is usually found in purple or caramel (see Chocolate Glass), though other colors were also made. Pink is rare and very expensive.

Blue, humidor, drum shape, cap-shaped finial, 6½x5¼"	245.00
Green, sugar bowl, w/lid	95.00
Pink, Invt Fan & Feather, butter dish	550.00
Pink, Invt Fan & Feather, creamer, 4"	450.00
Pink, Invt Fan & Feather, pitcher, 8"	1,400.00
Pink, Invt Fan & Feather, punch cup	285.00
Pink, Invt Fan & Feather, sauce, ftd, 4½" dia	250.00
Pink, Invt Fan & Feather, shakers, pr	750.00
Pink, Invt Fan & Feather, spooner	295.00
Pink, Invt Fan & Feather, sugar bowl, w/lid	650.00
Pink, Invt Fan & Feather, toothpick, 2¼"	600.00
Pink, Invt Fan & Feather, tumbler	400.00
Purple, Beaded Cable, rose bowl	375.00
Purple, Beads & Bark, vase, novelty	45.00
Purple, cake stand, plain, high ped	40.00
Purple, Cherry & Leaf, bowl, 3-section, 5½x7½"	95.00
Purple, Crossbar & Flute, spooner	65.00
Purple, Fan & Leaf, tray, shield form, hdls	85.00
Purple, Flower Petal, spooner	75.00
Purple, Flute, celery dish	90.00
Purple, Oval Medallion, spooner	85.00
Purple, Panelled Flower, spooner	75.00
Purple, pitcher, emb strawberries & leaves, 6¼x3½"	95.00
Red, vase, mc/gold decor at top, 7"	55.00

Smith Bros.

Alfred and Harry Smith founded their glassmaking firm in New Bedford, Massachusetts. They had been formerly associated with the Mt. Washington Glass Works, working there from 1871 to 1875 to aid in establishing a decorating department. Smith glass is valued for its excellent enameled decoration on satin or opalescent glass. Pieces were often marked with a lion in a red shield.

Our advisors for this category are Betty and Clarence Maier; they are listed in the Directory under Pennsylvania.

Bowl, daisies on cream, ribbed, SP rim, lion mk, 10"	225.00

Bowl, pansies, mc on mottled pk & yel, ribbed, 4x9"	300.00
Bowl, pansies on melon ribs, beaded rim, mk, 2½x3"	200.00
Cracker jar, daisies on cream, melon ribs, lion mk	395.00
Cracker jar, pansies, bl on swirled cream, sq, lion mk	875.00
Fernery, violets on glossy wht opal, 9"	650.00
Jar, powder; gold prunus & beading on tan, ribbed, 3½x4"	365.00
Lamp, emb winter scene w/figures on bl, oil burner, 17"	395.00
Rose bowl, daisies/buds/traceries, beaded top, 5x4"	275.00
Rose bowl, pansies on cream, mk, 4¼" H	300.00
Sugar shaker, floral, pear shape, 4"	160.00
Sweetmeat, carnations on melon form, glass lid, 5½" dia	685.00
Sweetmeat, foliage/scrolls, squat, 4-lobed, SP mts, 4½x5"	275.00
Toothpick, floral, ribbed, lion mk, 2¼"	125.00
Vase, bird on branch on pk, conical, mk, 6"	125.00
Vase, bl florals w/gilt leaves, swirled, mk, 6¾"	425.00
Vase, Greenaway-style children on lt gr w/gold, 5¾x3¼"	275.00
Vase, Greenaway-style figures, 3-ring petticoat form, 7"	285.00

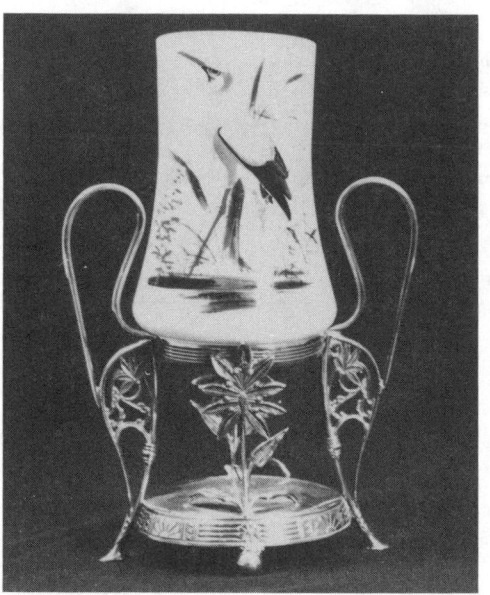

Vase, heron motif, in holder marked Pairpoint, 8", $265.00.

Vase, ivy, flat-sided ovoid, sm rim, lion mk, 4¾", EX	125.00
Vase, leaves, gr/brn/gold on tan, pinched 3 sides, 5x4½"	375.00
Vase, roses, pk/gr on clear, vertical ribs, stick neck, 7"	375.00
Vase, vining leaves on shaded yel, 5x4½"	385.00
Vase, wild roses, bulbous, stick neck, scalloped top, 10¼"	385.00
Vase, wisteria, lav w/gold, dbl pilgrim flask form, 7x8x2"	1,215.00
Vase, wisteria, wht w/gr leaves on brick red, label, 10½"	1,100.00

Snow Babies

During the last quarter of the 19th century, snow babies – little figurals in white snowsuits – originated in Germany. They were made of sugar candy and were often used as decorations for Christmas trees. Later on, they were made of marzipan, a confection of crushed almonds, sugar, and egg whites. Eventually porcelain manufacturers began making them in bisque. They were popular until WWII. These tiny china figures range in size from just over 1" to the very rare jointed babies sometimes nearly 7" tall. Any example brings a very respectable price on the market today. Beware of reproductions.

Babies, 2 stand on lg snowball, 2½"	75.00
Babies slide down brick wall, #6602, 1⅝x2½"	125.00
Baby, jtd, good pnt, impish features, 3"	175.00
Baby, jtd, good pnt, impish features, 4½"	250.00
Baby, riding bear, Japan, 2¾"	38.00

Baby holds baton 110.00
Baby holds camera, 1¾" 125.00
Baby in shell, lg 25.00
Baby on sled pulled by 2 dogs, #7153, 1⅜x3"................60.00
Baby plays tuba, mk Germany, 1½" 75.00
Baby riding polar bear, 2¼" 50.00
Baby slides down hill on champagne bottle, tree in bkground.....145.00
Baby standing w/pr of skis, 2" 75.00
Baby stands on sled, 1¾" 45.00
Baby tumbling on skis, wooden ski & pole, 4"............225.00
Bear, Germany, 1½" 40.00
Bear on skis, Germany 55.00

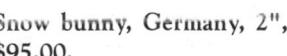
Snow bunny, Germany, 2",
$95.00.

Girl on sled, 2" L...90.00
Girl w/pk pants on sled, 2½" 90.00
Igloo, baby inside, Santa on roof, Germany 85.00
Penguin, Germany, 4" 75.00
Santa climbs down chimney, 3" 90.00
Santa on roof 95.00
Santa skating 95.00
Seal w/ball, 2" 35.00
Snow pup on skies, mk 110.00
Snowman, 1½"...50.00

Snuff Boxes

As early as the 17th century, the Chinese began using snuff. By the early 19th century, the practice had spread to Europe and America. It was used by both the gentlemen and the ladies alike, and expensive snuff boxes and bottles were the earmark of the genteel. Some were of silver or gold set with precious stones or pearls, while others contained music boxes. In the following listings, the dimension noted is length. See also Orientalia, Snuff Bottles.

Brass, Admiral Lord Nelson, printed death record, sm, NM 250.00
Brass, eng All Seeing Eye, arrows/stars/etc, oval, 2¾" 100.00
Burl, nacre inlay lid, 3" L...90.00
Cowrie shell base, silver lid w/1757 coin, Roosevelt, 4"...............800.00
Ivory, cvd as fish emerging from waves, spoon in mouth, 3" 135.00
Ivory, elephant head hdls, trunks hold rings, 3"...........475.00
Papier-mache, group of boys/scholar pnt on lid, 3" dia.................250.00
Papier-mache, lady pnt on blk lacquer lid, 3⅜", EX 95.00
Papier-mache, 2 women pnt on blk lacquer lid, 4" dia 105.00
Peking cameo, flowers/house/mtn, bl on wht, 3" 55.00
Silver, agate inset on lid, Wm IV, Nathaniel Mills, 2¾"...............275.00
Tigereye, front/bk relief-cvd goldfish & foo lion, 3" 90.00
Wht jade, w/brn cvd Oriental man on lg sea creature, 3" 160.00

Soapstone

Soapstone is a soft talc in rock form with a smooth, greasy feel from whence comes its name. In colonial times, it was extracted from out-croppings in large sections with hand saws, carted by oxen to mills, and fashioned into useful domestic articles such as footwarmers, cooking utensils, inkwells, etc. During the early 1800s, it was used to make heating stoves and kitchen sinks. Most familiar today are the carved vases, bookends, and boxes made in China during the Victorian era.

Bookends, potted plant w/bird, 1880s, 5½"....................40.00
Candle holder, florals, 5", pr...55.00
Character stamp, clouds & foo dogs, 5" 50.00
Cvg, Buddha, lotus throne, flame at bk, flecked gr, 10".................70.00
Cvg, foo dogs, wht on dk pedestal, 8x10" 175.00
Cvg, foo lions, female w/pup; male w/Ball of Universe, 6½x5" 75.00
Cvg, Oriental girl holds tray high, EX pnt, on plinth, 13" 85.00
Cvg, 3 monkeys, tan, mk China, 2x3" 55.00
Griddle, for wood stove, primitive.................................22.50
Inkwell, cvd ribbed dome, 4 corner quill holders, sq 150.00
Lamp, table; birds/flowers cvg, vasiform, total height: 41" 500.00
Lamp, table; Guan Yin form, 1900, 13½" 300.00
Screen, 2 peacocks/peonies, 5-color, oblong base, 5½x6½"............40.00
Vase, dbl; brn, joined by floral cvg, 3x6" 100.00
Vase, dbl; peonies/vines/birds, 3-color, 7x9" 125.00
Vase, mums/birds relief on mauve mottle, China, 1900, 8½".......165.00

Soda Fountain Collectibles

As the neighborhood ice cream parlor becomes a thing of the past, soda fountain memorabilia from fancy backbars to ice cream advertising is becoming a popular field of collecting. One area of interest is the glassware used to serve the more elaborate ice cream concoctions. A sundae glass is familiar to us all, but there was also a 'lucky mondae' glass, narrow at the bottom and flaring to a top dimension equal to one scoop. There are footed banana split dishes and soda pop glasses with the name or logo of the beverage company painted on them.

Syrup dispensers, especially those from the teens, are very popular with today's collectors. These had spherical or urn-shaped dispensers and carried names such as Jersey Creme, Buckeye, Cherry Smash, etc.

It is estimated that ice cream dippers may be found in more than 125 different sizes and styles – some bowl shaped or cylindrical, some for making ice cream sandwiches, and even a very rare heart-shaped dipper. (This one was used along with matching heart-shaped ice cream dishes.)

Glass straw holders are very collectible. Clear is the most common color, but they are also found in green and pink; some are made of frosted glass. Early examples were pattern molded; some had matching glass lids – these are the most desirable.

Our advisors for this category are Joyce and Harold Screen; they are listed in the Directory under Maryland. See also Advertising.

Back bar, oak, rstr, 117x150" 3,500.00
Book, equipment & supply; pre-1900, per illus pg..............................75
Book, equipment & supply; 1910-1919, per illus pg 50
Book, formulas & recipes, pre-1910, per pg...................................25
Bottle, seltzer; bl, A Greenberg & Son, NY..................20.00
Bottle, seltzer; gr, Park Drive, Pittsburgh....................25.00
Bottle, syrup; Cherry Smash, w/lid................................125.00
Bottle, syrup; Grapefruit, label under glass, Williams' 1913 ....100.00
Bottle, syrup; root beer, label under glass, w/lid 50.00
Bottle, syrup; vanilla, w/lid 30.00

Carton, Gollams Dairy, rnd, Lebanon PA, 1-gal, EX 7.50
Carton, Peerless Ice Cream Co, Frederick MD, ½-pt, EX................ 7.50
Cone holder, glass, individual 20.00
Cone holder, glass display jars, lift out 250.00
Container, malted milk; Bordens, glass, w/lid 350.00
Container, malted milk; Bordens, steel.....................................175.00
Container, malted milk; Coors 150.00
Container, malted milk; Milkose, glass, aluminum dome lid 85.00
Container, malted milk; Thompson's, dome lid............................175.00
Dipper, banana split; Gilchrist 400.00
Dipper, banana split; United Products 450.00
Dipper, Cold Dog, cylinder..450.00
Dipper, Dover Slicer..400.00
Dipper, Dover Springless...75.00
Dipper, Feller Cone, 3 sections 1,000.00
Dipper, Gilchrist #30, squeeze hdl..75.00
Dipper, Gilchrist #31 ....40.00
Dipper, heart shaped 2,500.00
Dipper, Icy-Pi, wood hdl, EX...200.00
Dipper, Indestructo #4...40.00
Dipper, Keiner-Williams, key release 10.00
Dipper, Kingery, '1-handed,' dtd 1894 ....200.00
Dipper, New Gem 50.00
Dipper, sandwich; Mayer, flat 200.00
Dipper, sandwich; Meyers, curved..225.00
Dish, banana split; clear, ftd 15.00
Dish, banana split; gr, boat type 10.00
Dish, banana split; gr, ftd 25.00
Dish, banana split; Heisey, ftd 35.00
Dish, banana split; pk, ftd...35.00
Dispenser, cup; lily-form glass tube, clamp-on counter type...........48.00
Dispenser, Fowler's Cherry Smash, orig pump......................... 1,500.00
Dispenser, Fowler's Cherry Smash, 5¢ on side 1,300.00
Dispenser, Ginger Mint Julep, ceramic bbl w/long pump 700.00
Dispenser, Ginger-Mint Julep, porc, countertop, EX...................950.00
Dispenser, Hire's, hourglass, w/orig pump 500.00
Dispenser, Jersey-Creme, red & gold letters, 1920, EX 1,200.00
Dispenser, Mission Grapefruit, pk crackle glass 125.00
Dispenser, Mission Orange, lights up, glass & metal, M...............700.00
Dispenser, Orange Crush, orig ball pump, M.............................650.00
Dispenser, Pepsi Cola, bbl form, M... 4,000.00
Dispenser, Pepsi Cola, musical...295.00
Dispenser, Rochester Root Beer, bbl on stump, rpl lid 345.00
Dispenser, Ward's Lemon Crush, orig ball pump 750.00
Dispenser, Ward's Lemon Crush, w/o pump................................350.00

Dispenser, Ward's Orange Crush, rare large size, original pump, ca 1913-19, in mint, unused condition, $1,900.00 at auction.

Fan, Nu-Icy, cb, soda w/beach scene bkground, EX 12.50
Flavor board, rvpt, 1930s 75.00
Flavor board, tin, ca 1900..400.00
Fountain glass, Allen's Red Tame Cherry....................................37.00
Fountain glass, Coke, star on bottom, 1930s............................... 5.00
Fountain glass, Lucky Mondae 25.00
Fountain glass, Pepsi, commemorative, 1970s, 5 for 7.50
Fountain glass, Pepsi, str side, 1950-60s, 10-oz 4.00
Fountain glass, Richardson's Liberty Drinks................................20.00
Fountain glass, Soda Fountain pattern, pk 30.00
Fountain glass, Zipp's Grape-O, grape cluster 25.00
Fountain glass, 7-Up in script, clear 4.50
Fountain glass holder, Agripa, for bell glasses, pat 11-15-21 .... 8.00
Ice Shaver, Peerless, NP brass...600.00
Jar, Johnson's Cold Fudge, bl pottery, w/lid & ladle.....................200.00
Machine, seltzer bottle press; 1920s, EX....................................375.00
Malted milk container, Bordens, aluminum................................30.00
Malted milk container, Coors, aluminum 30.00
Malted milk container, Thompson's, aluminum 30.00
Malted milk container, Thompson's, enamel................................150.00
Milk shake mixer, AC Gilbert..70.00
Milk shake mixer, Albert Pick & Co, marble base, early, EX.......375.00
Milk shake mixer, Anchor Hocking, glass w/vertical arm, sm.........25.00
Milk shake mixer, Gilchrist #22, as found..................................50.00
Milk shake mixer, Gilchrist #22, polished 100.00
Milk shake mixer, Hamilton Beach, marbled base, as found 75.00
Milk shake mixer, Hamilton Beach, porc base, 1920s, NM...........55.00
Milk shake mixer, Hamilton Beach, repolished to brass 200.00
Milk shake mixer, hand-cranked counter model 650.00
Milk shake mixer, hand-cranked floor model 900.00
Milk shake mixer, Hire's, hand crank...500.00
Milk shake mixer, Horlick's, dbl ped, friction drive motor...........300.00
Milk shake mixer, Minute, Made-Rite Mfg, gr pnt, 1930s, VG......75.00
Mug, Armour's Veribest Root Beer, pottery 50.00
Mug, Berry's Famous Root Beer, bl salt glaze.............................100.00
Mug, Richardson's Root Beer emb on glass.................................15.00
Mug, Zipp's Root Beer, dbl bl band, lg.......................................35.00
Sheet Music, Come Have a Soda with Me 5.00
Sheet Music, Oh My, Eskimo Pie, EX.......................................25.00
Sign, Cherry Blossom, tin, red on yel, 18x26" 150.00
Sign, Cherry Blossom, tin, 9x18"...130.00
Sign, Cherry Smash, cb, fits over neck of bottle 38.00
Sign, Meadow Gold Authorized Dealer, oval, 6½x12" 25.00
Soda fountain, marble, box style, Tufts, 1800s, very rare 3,500.00
Soda fountain, portable, SP, Bigelow, 1867, very rare 1,000.00
Soda fountain, w/top, Matthews, 1800s, rstr, very rare 5,000.00
Spoon, Gilchrist #33...25.00
Straw dispenser, Jersey Creme 300.00
Straw dispenser, Jewel Sanitary 250.00
Straw holder, Bloomfield Industries, 1950s.................................30.00
Straw holder, Chrysanthemum Swirl, w/lid 400.00
Straw holder, Edgewood Ware, w/lid...300.00
Straw holder, Fostoria, America pattern, w/lid 200.00
Straw holder, glass, flared base, EX...175.00
Straw holder, Heisey, Colonial pattern, w/lid 225.00
Straw holder, Heisey, open side...500.00
Table, glass display top, swing-out seats, CI 700.00
Table, glass display top, 4 Snug Tite chairs 400.00
Table, marble top, +4 wire chairs 150.00
Table, wood top, +4 wire chairs 100.00
Trade cards, Ice Cream Freezers, ea...12.00
Tray, Merrigan's Ice Cream, When Dreams Come True, EX 250.00
Tray, Murray's Soda Water, rnd...150.00
Tray, Peerless Ice Cream, 2 women & girl...................................450.00

Soft Paste

Soft paste is a low-fired, granular type of porcelain that must be glazed to retain water.

Bowl, cows, bl transfer, 3x7", EX 125.00
Cup & saucer, handleless; emb reeding, florals, scalloped 85.00
Figurine, man pleads w/girl, upset basket, mk, 8x7" 450.00
Jug, floral band in purple lustre resist, 8½", EX.....................275.00
Mug, For My Sweet Girl, emb leaf ends on hdl, 2¾", EX.............275.00
Plate, emb floral rim, mc enamel, 7", NM.............................175.00
Plate, Present for Ann, mc florals, 6¾", NM 250.00
Teapot, gaudy floral, underglaze bl w/yel, 6⅛", EX 500.00
Teapot, strawberries w/purple lustre, 5⅝", EX...........................185.00
Teapot, underglaze bl floral w/red enamel & gilt, rpr, 5" 475.00
Teapot, 2-color floral, minor stains/hairline, 6" 225.00
Tureen, bl feather edge, rose finial, scroll hdls, 5½", EX 285.00

South Jersey Glass

As early as 1739, Caspar Wistar established a factory in Salem County, taking advantage of the large beds of sand suitable for glass blowing and the abundant forests available for fueling his furnaces. Scores of glassworks followed, many of which were short-lived. It is generally conceded that aside from the early works of Wistar and the Harmony Glass Works, which emerged from the Glassboro factory originally founded by the Strangers, the finest quality glassware was blown after 1800. In the 1850s coal was substituted for the wood as fuel. Though a more efficient source of heat, the added cost of transporting the coal inland proved to be the downfall of many of the smaller factories. By the 1800s, many had failed.

Glassware can be attributed to this area through the study of colors, shapes, and decorative devices that were favored there; but because techniques were passed down through generations of South Jersey glass blowers, without specific documentation it is usually impossible to identify the specific factory that produced it.

Candlestick, bl-gr, blown, 8" 350.00
Creamer, dk amber, lily pad decor, ca 1880, 5⅜".................... 3,900.00
Paperweight/doorstop, aqua, turtle form, 6", EX............................85.00
Pitcher, lt gr, threaded neck, appl hdl, att, 9½" 90.00
Pitcher, med gr, ribbed strap hdl w/t'rest, pontil, 4¾" 3,500.00
Vase, aqua w/wht loops, appl creased stem, freeform, 6½" 300.00
Witch ball & stand, clear w/wht loops, 14", pr........................ 2,000.00

Spangle Glass

Spangle glass, also known as Vasa Murrhina, is cased art glass characterized by the metallic flakes embedded in its top layer. It was made both abroad and in the United States during the latter years of the 19th century, and it was reproduced in the 1960s by the Fenton Art Glass Company.

Vasa Murrhina was a New England distributor who sold glassware of this type manufactured by a Dr. Flower of Sandwich, Massachusetts. Flower had purchased the defunct Cape Cod Glassworks in 1885 and used the facilities to operate his own company. Since none of the ware was marked, it is very difficult to attribute specific examples to his manufacture. See also Art Glass Baskets; Fenton.

Basket, bl cased w/silver mica, 8-crimp, thorn hdl, 7½" 175.00
Basket, lt gr w/mica, ribbon candy rim, looped hdl, 7½" 125.00
Bowl, rainbow, ruffled, sq, 5" 150.00

Bowl, rose overlay, ruffled, clear hdls, oval, 6⅝" H.....................235.00
Creamer, red/gr/yel aventurine, clear reed hdl, 5¾" 155.00
Epergne, rose, ormolu dragon supports lily vase, 19x11" 495.00
Pitcher, bl cased w/silver mica, gold-traced flowers, 7"................140.00
Pitcher, cranberry w/gold mica, ruffled, water sz 185.00
Pitcher, crystal w/gold flecks, salmon int, quilted, 9" 125.00
Pitcher, mc spatter w/mica, ruffled, clear reeded hdl, 9" 225.00
Rose bowl, rose w/mica, wht int, 8-crimp, 3⅝x3½"...................110.00
Vase, apricot cased, appl daisy hdls, ruffled, 8", pr 195.00
Vase, autumn spatter w/mica, melon rib, ruffled, 9½x7" 70.00
Vase, bl cased w/silver mica, appl rigaree, 7½" 95.00
Vase, cobalt cased w/silver mica, hdls, 3"................................90.00
Vase, cranberry w/aventurine, swirled ribs, 10" 235.00
Vase, deep rose w/mica, thorn hdls, ewer form, 7½", pr 225.00
Vase, pk cased w/gold mica, appl cherries/rigaree, 8½", pr 550.00
Vase, pk cased w/silver mica, clear hdl, 9⅜x5" 145.00
Vase, red/gr/bl swirl overlay, pear form, 10" 80.00
Vase, rust w/mica, ruffled, melon ribs, 9½" 75.00

Spatter Glass

Spatter glass, characterized by its multicolor 'spatters,' has been made from the late 19th century to the present by American glass houses as well as those abroad. Although it was once thought to have been made entirely by workers at the 'end of the day' from bits and pieces of leftover scrap, it is now known that it was a standard line of production. See also Art Glass Baskets.

Boot, 5-color cased, appl leaf & rigaree, 3¾x4½" 69.00
Creamer, lg molded droplets, decorative metal spout/hdl.............180.00
Pitcher, Invt T'print, maroon & wht, bulbous, clear hdl, 8" 110.00
Pitcher, pk & wht overshot, ruffled top, clear hdl, 8"..................150.00
Pitcher, swirl, pk & yel overlay, clear hdl, 8x6" 135.00
Pitcher, swirl, red/brn/bl/wht, clear hdl, 9" 125.00
Pitcher, yel & wht, gold flowers & hdl, bulbous, 2x1¼" 55.00

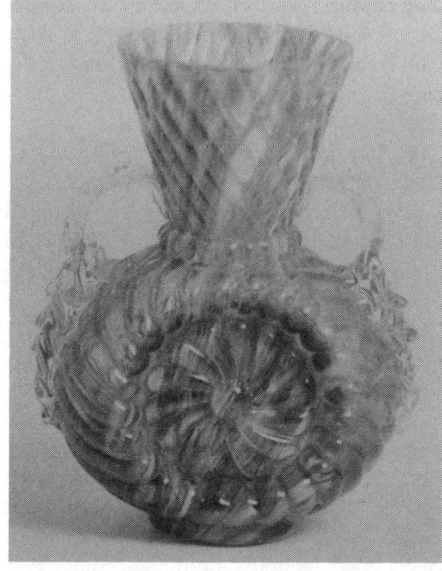

Vase, cranberry and white with clear overlay, 5", $125.00.

Vase, pk/yel/tan swirl, cased, cupped neck, 10", pr......................250.00
Vase, rainbow pastel overlay, clear thorn hdls, 9" 85.00

Spatterware

Spatterware is a general term referring to a type of decoration used by English potters beginning in the late 1700s. Using a brush or a stick, brightly-colored paint was dabbed onto the soft-paste earthenware items, achieving a spattered effect which was often used as a border. Because much of this type of ware was made for export to the United States, some of the subjects in the central design – the schoolhouse and the eagle patterns, for instance – reflect American tastes. Yellow, green, and black spatterware is scarce and highly valued by collectors.

In the descriptions that follow, the color listed after the item indicates the color of the spatter. The central design is identified next, and the color description that follows that refers to the design.

Bowl, bl, fort, 5½", NM	365.00
Bowl, bl, Peacock at Fountain, w/lid, 10½"	245.00
Cow creamer, allover brn spatter, on gr plinth, no cap	350.00
Creamer, bl, house motif, 3⅝"	550.00
Creamer, bl, rose, 3-color, hairline, 4¼"	150.00
Creamer, bl, tulip, 4-color, sm chip, 3½"	250.00

Creamer and sugar bowl, red and blue rainbow spatter, 8", NM, $550.00.

Cup & saucer, allover bl spatter	85.00
Cup & saucer, allover coarse red spatter	125.00
Cup & saucer, allover red/bl mottling	185.00
Cup & saucer, rainbow, red/gr	350.00
Cup & saucer, red, peafowl, 5-color, minor wear	300.00
Cup plate, brn, 4-part flower in bl w/brn specks, 4", NM	120.00
Cup plate, red, 3¾"	25.00
Pitcher, bl, red cowboy scene transfer, sm hairline, 10"	110.00
Pitcher, red, parrot, 3-color, paneled, 7¾", EX	1,050.00
Pitcher, red, peafowl, 4-color, stains/hairline, 5⅜"	450.00
Plate, bl, fort, 3-color, 8¾", EX	350.00
Plate, bl, peafowl, 4-color, bl feather rim, 9⅞"	650.00
Plate, bl, peafowl, 9"	550.00
Plate, bl, thistle, red/gr, minor stains, sm flakes, 9⅜"	375.00
Plate, gr, peafowl, 3-color, 7¾", NM	900.00
Plate, red, peafowl, 4-color, minor stain, 7¾"	380.00
Plate, red, peafowl, 4-color, mk Adams, 7½", VG	275.00
Platter, bl/yel rainbow rim, tulip, 4-color, 16", NM	3,900.00
Sugar bowl, allover bl spatter, rim rpr	95.00
Sugar bowl, bl, house motif, flanged lid, 5¼", EX	750.00
Sugar bowl, bl, mfg flaw/hairline	135.00
Sugar bowl, rainbow, red/bl bars, rim rpr	125.00
Sugar bowl, red, acorn, 4-color, stain, rpr on lid, 4½"	600.00
Tea bowl, purple, acorn, 4-color, minor stain	355.00
Tea bowl & saucer, rainbow, red/yel, red/gr birds, EX	600.00
Tea bowl & saucer, red, peafowl, 5-color, stains/hairline	150.00
Teapot, bl, hex sign	595.00
Teapot, purple, Mourning Tulip, 2 rim rprs, rpr finial	450.00
Teapot, red, peafowl, 4-color, hairline, rpr on lid, 6⅞"	450.00

Spelter

Spelter figurines are cast from commercial zinc and coated with a metallic patina. The result is a product very similar to bronze in appearance, yet much less expensive.

Bookend, girl w/doll, NuArt, pr	35.00
Bust, Nouveau lady, sgn L'Hiver & Tifflano, 8"	135.00
Figurine, dancer, scantily clad, w/tambourine, 27"	495.00
Figurine, dancing nymph, 2 leafy candle arms, Rousseau, 21"	350.00
Figurine, deer pr (1 recumbent), gazing at bronze bird, 14"	220.00
Figurine, Footsteps, mc/ivorene, after Chiparus, 17"	1,500.00
Figurine, mother hugs children who kiss her, Chiparus, 20" L	900.00
Figurine, seated woman, after Pradier, Susse Freres, 17"	300.00
Figurine, warrior w/spear & shield, marble base, 38"	700.00
Pincushion, touring car, USA, 3x1½"	28.00
Pincushion, Victorian slipper, flower buckle, pre 1900, 7x3½"	50.00

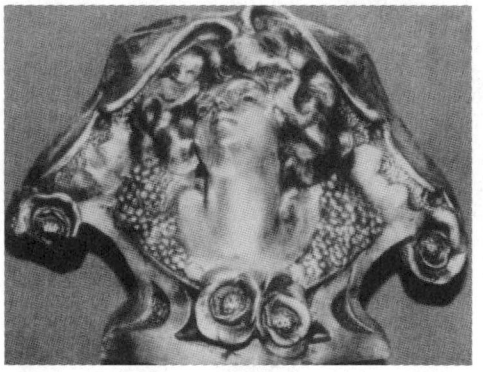

Silver gilt planter in the form of a Bacchante with flowing hair, 9" x 11", $600.00.

Vase, flower w/nude emerging, 20"	395.00

Spode-Copeland

The Spode Works was established in 1770 and continued to operate under that title until 1843. Their earliest products were typical underglaze blue-printed patterns, though basalt was also made. After 1790 a translucent porcelain body was the basis for a line of fine enamel-decorated dinnerware. Stone china was introduced in 1805, often in patterns reflecting an Oriental influence.

In 1833 Wm. Taylor Copeland purchased the company, continuing business in much the same tradition. During the last half of the 19th century, Copeland produced excellent parian figures and groups with such success that many other companies attempted to reproduce his work. He employed famous painters to decorate plaques, vases, and tablewares, many examples of which were signed by the artist. Most of the Copeland wares are marked with one of several variations that incorporate the firm name. Today the company is owned by Royal Worcester Ltd. and operates under the name of Royal Worcester Spode Ltd.

Bowl, fruit; Gainsborough, Spode	15.00
Bowl, vegetable; Tower, bl/wht, w/lid, Copeland	185.00
Bust, Miranda, parian, WC Marshall/mk Crystal Place, 11"	650.00
Coffeepot, Billingsley Rose, 10"	65.00
Cream soup, Tower, bl/wht, w/saucer	25.00
Cup & saucer, demitasse; Buttercup	15.00
Cup & saucer, Wickerdale	17.50

Copeland figural compotes, ca 1880, extensive restorations, 28", $1,000.00 for the pair.

Ewer, Persian motif, jeweling on claret, Copeland, 8" **400.00**
Jardiniere, Chinese Rose, #2/9253, 7x8" **65.00**
Mug, George Washington, Copeland, M...............................**135.00**
Pitcher, nymphs, ivory on bl jasper, Spode, 7½x5" **95.00**
Plate, dinner; Cowslip **20.00**
Plate, red-breasted bird/holly, Copeland, 9½" **95.00**
Platter, Newburyport, 14" **120.00**
Platter, Tower, Copeland, 12¾" **95.00**
Platter, well & tree; Bl Tower, Spode, 23" **200.00**
Relish dish, Italian, med dk bl, England, 1890s, 7¾" **55.00**
Tumbler, hunt scene, wht figures on tan, 4x3" **48.00**
Tureen, river/ruins, med bl transfer, Spode, 14" L, +tray **550.00**
Tureen, Tower, bl/wht, w/underplate **175.00**

Spongeware

Spongeware is a type of factory-made earthenware that was popular during the last quarter of the 19th century. It was decorated by dabbing color onto the drying ware with a sponge, leaving a splotched design at random or in simple patterns. Sometimes a solid band of color was added. The vessel was then covered with a clear glaze and fired at a high temperature. Blue on white is the most preferred combination, but green on ivory, orange on white, or those colors in combination may also occasionally be found.

Bean pot, bl/wht, 'Beans,' hdl, lid chip, 4¼" **600.00**
Bowl, bl on yellowware, gilt scalloped rim, 8"...............................**95.00**
Bowl, bl on yellowware, rim spout, wire bail, 3½x5½" **80.00**
Bowl, bl/brn on cream, 5¾x11" **95.00**
Bowl, bl/tan on cream, 4x7" **55.00**
Bowl, bl/wht, heavy sponging, shaped sides, 8½" L **225.00**
Bowl, bl/wht, lt bl band, hairline, 11½" **135.00**
Bowl, bl/wht, pattern sponging, scalloped hdls, 9" **225.00**
Bowl, bl/wht, str sides, 2¼x7¼" **125.00**
Bowl, bl/wht, wht band/bl stripes, 6x14", EX **175.00**
Bowl, bl/wht, wire bail hdl, int flakes, 4x8¾" **135.00**
Bowl, bl/wht, 2x4½", NM **200.00**
Bowl, bl/wht, 3⅜x7⅝", EX **75.00**

Bowl, bl/wht, 4¾x9¾", VG **65.00**
Butter crock, bl/wht, flat w/str sides, hairline, 4x10" dia **200.00**
Cup & saucer, bl/wht, heavy sponging.....................................**165.00**
Cuspidor, bl/wht, bl stripes, 5x7½" dia...................................**95.00**

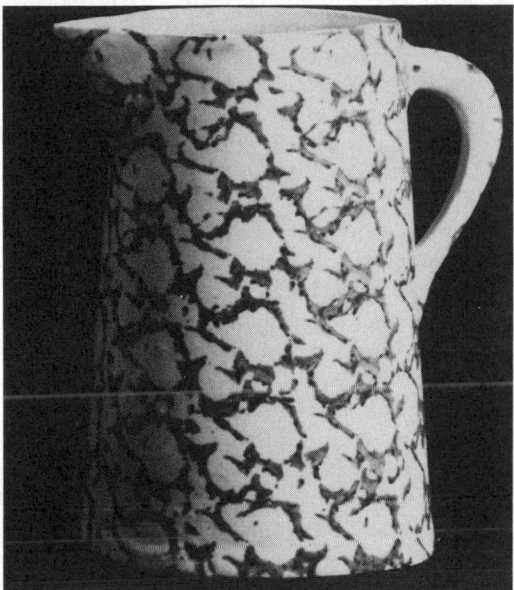

Pitcher, blue sponging on white, 9", M, $435.00.

Pitcher, bl on yellowware, ovoid, 8½"......................................**175.00**
Pitcher, bl/wht, barrel form, sm edge flakes, 8⅜" **300.00**
Pitcher, bl/wht, barrel form, 10" **525.00**
Pitcher, bl/wht, emb arches, 8¾", EX......................................**325.00**
Pitcher, bl/wht, emb bl flower, pattern sponging, 9"....................**600.00**
Pitcher, bl/wht, emb bl flower, str sides, 8⅜" **650.00**
Pitcher, bl/wht, emb floral, str sides, 9" **225.00**
Pitcher, bl/wht, emb medallion of child & dog, 8½", NM **500.00**
Pitcher, bl/wht, heavy sponging, str sides, sm chips, 9" **450.00**
Pitcher, bl/wht, pattern sponging, barrel form, rpr, 10" **150.00**
Pitcher, bl/wht, pattern sponging, barrel form, 8", NM..............**300.00**
Pitcher, bl/wht, pattern sponging, ovoid, 10¾", EX **390.00**
Pitcher, bl/wht, streaky, emb details, 6¾" **225.00**
Pitcher, bl/wht, 3 sponged bands, edge chips, 10½" **100.00**
Pitcher, brn/gr on cream w/blk label: Co-op Grain Co, 4½" **75.00**
Plate, brn/wht, 9", set of 4 ....**140.00**
Platter, bl/wht, 13"...**200.00**
Sauce boat, bl/wht, lion & unicorn mk, 7" L.............................**300.00**
Sugar bowl, bl/wht, undersize lid, 7½", NM **225.00**
Teapot, bl/wht, minor edge flakes, 7" **950.00**
Waste bowl, bl/wht, minor rim flakes, 5" dia **90.00**

Spoons

Souvenir spoons have been popular remembrances since the 1890s. The early hand-wrought examples of the silversmith's art are especially sought and appreciated for their fine craftsmanship. Commemorative, personality-related, advertising, and those with Indian busts or floral designs are only a few of the many types of collectible spoons. In the following listing, spoons are entered by city, character, or occasion.

Key:
B — bowl	FF — full figure
BR — bowl reverse	GW — gold wash
emb — embossed	H — handle
eng — engraved	HR — handle reverse

Albany Capitol emb in B; seal/scenes emb on H; teaspoon.............22.00
Alligator FF H; plain B; mk, teaspoon 27.50
Angel FF H; Mormon Temple emb in B; teaspoon 60.00
Arms of NY emb on H; plain B; Tiffany, teaspoon.......................70.00
Atlanta GA eng in B; ear of corn FF H; teaspoon, EX 16.00
Atlantic City & scenes on H; hotel eng in B; 5½" 37.50
Bar Harbor emb in B; fish FF H; Shepard mk 38.00
Bisbee AZ etched in B; miner w/GW nuggets at ft FF H..............60.00
BPOE Elk & enamel clock on H; plain B; Watson, 1905 ....50.00
Brooklyn emb on H; City of Churches in B; Gorham 60.00
California, Riverside eng in B; pennant H; ca 1905, 4⅞"..............18.00
California emb on H: Cliff House emb in B; Watson, teaspoon.....25.00
California eng in B; bear FF H; Watson 45.00
California on H; US Grant Hotel emb in B; 5½" 20.00
Cannon barrel FF H dtd 1861; emb scene in B; GW, fruit spoon.150.00
Captain Sigsbee on hdl; Battleship Maine emb in B; GW, 4⅜" 5.00
Catalina eng in B; Indian head FF H; mk, teaspoon 27.50
Catskill NY etched in B; Indian FF H; fruit spoon 120.00
Cheyenne & bronco emb on H; plain B; demi 22.50
Chicago fire emb on H; 1892 Auditorium etched in GW B; demi.38.00
Chicago pierced H; plain B; Watson, teaspoon...............................20.00
Civil War soldier FF H; Gettysburg battle scene in B; Gorham ...155.00
Cleopatra's head on twist-stem H; plain B 85.00
Colorado emb on H; Caves of Winds emb in B & BR...................25.00
Colorado Springs etched in B; Indian FF H; teaspoon...................40.00
Columbian Expo on H; anchor on HR; ship in B; demi.................25.00
Columbian Expo symbols on H; ship emb in B; Reed & Barton .140.00
Columbus H; CA Administration Building in B; US Sterling 5.00
Columbus head H; plain B; 4", NM 22.00
Cradle of Liberty/scenes on H; Boston Tea Party scene in B 48.00
Denver CO emb in B; Rainbow Falls scene emb on H; teaspoon...60.00
Edwin Booth portrait on H; Boston etched in B; teaspoon 185.00
Elgin Nat'l Watch Factory on H; factory in B; Shepard 50.00
Evansville IN, Elks Home eng in B; BPOE on H; teaspoon 27.50
Ft Dodge IA eng in B; Indian head H; 5¼", EX.............................22.00
G Clevelend, Nominated...Elected Twice on H; capital in B 145.00
Galveston TX & sailboat emb in GW B; fish/sailboat on H 48.00
Hawaiian figure emb on H; plain B; Towle 20.00
Honolulu, pineapple emb on H; plain B; teaspoon.........................50.00
Illinois emb on H; plain B; Manchester, teaspoon..........................20.00
Indian FF H; emb Providence in B; teaspoon 22.00
Indian FF H; NY subway emb in B; 4¼", EX................................35.00
Indian FF H; squaw & papoose on HR; eng Denver in B; EX 90.00
Indian head H; emb Carmel Mission in B; teaspoon 27.50
Indian maid FF H; State Capitol Albany emb in B; teaspoon 165.00
Indian w/dog on H; Scituate MA etched in B; Lunt, teaspoon......40.00
Jacksonville & flag in B; boy in tree FF H; teaspoon 70.00
Lake Champlain eng in B; NY state seal on H; teaspoon 22.00
Libby Prison War Museum emb in B; plain H; Sterling, 4⅜" 10.00
Lick Observatory, San Jose emb in B; plain H; 5¼", EX................28.00
Long Beach CA eng in B; bear emb on H; Watson, teaspoon.....55.00
Long Beach eng in B; knife/bear H; Watson, teaspoon...................60.00
Longfellow emb on H; Home, Cambridge MA emb in B; Watson.40.00
Los Angeles emb on H; San Gabriel Mission emb in B; EX 22.00
Louisiana Purchase on H; Industries Building in B; EX 37.50
Minnehaha Falls in B; Nouveau woman hdl....................................52.00
Missouri eagle & seal on H; plain B; 5¼", VG...............................22.00
Missouri emb on H; State Building emb in B; teaspoon.................24.50
Montana emb on H; smelters & view emb in B; teaspoon, EX 32.00
Montgomery, AL State Capitol in B; eagle/Xd swords on H 55.00
Mt Hood eng in B; flower forms H; teaspoon 20.00
Mullan ID eng in B; miner panning FF H; teaspoon.......................27.50
Nebraska, Lincoln City pierced H; plain B; 5½" 20.00
New Orleans on H; Cathedral/City Hall on HR; Watson..............30.00

New Orleans on H; tepee/canoe on HR; plain B; Watson 40.00
New Orleans on twist H; Cabilda pnt scene in B; GW overall......50.00
New York emb on H; Statue of Liberty emb in B; teaspoon...........24.00
Niagara Falls emb in B; Indian FF H; Ellis & Co, teaspoon 125.00
Niagara Falls emb in B; Indian finial H; fruit spoon 38.00
Nude FF H; eng Esther & mermaid in B; teaspoon.........................36.00
NY World's Fair emb on H; plain B; Watson, teaspoon...................32.00
Old Point Comfort in B, much detail 45.00
Omaha at base of Indian FF H; plain B; teaspoon 32.00
Oranges emb H; etched Cotton Picker, New Orleans in GW B 50.00
Oriental motif emb on H; bicycle emb in B; Waltham, demi.........40.00
Portland emb in block letters on H; plain B 40.00
Portland emb on H; Mt Hood emb in B; 4", EX.............................17.50
Portland ME, Williston Church emb in B; scroll H; Gorham........32.00
Prospector & nugget FF H; plain B; Meyer & Bros, teaspoon 85.00
Prospector panning FF H; plain B; Meyer & Bros, demi.................50.00
Pueblo CO etched in B; Indian finial on twist H; Watson.............70.00
Redlands CA eng in B; flower forms H; mk, teaspoon 16.00
Salem Witch, Gorham, demi 78.00
Saratoga & Indian emb on H; plain B; Durgin 40.00
Savanna GA, Desoto Hotel on H; tepee/canoe on HR; plain B 35.00
Seattle/chief/totem pole on H; mt Ranier eng in B; teaspoon......22.00
St Louis & Indian head emb on H; plain B; Watson, EX 22.00
St Louis Expo symbols on H; Eads Bridge emb in B; Watson........40.00
Tacoma, Old Bell Tower on H; etch mtn scene in B; teaspoon......40.00
Temple, Salt Lake City, Tabernacle emb in B; Indian FF H 30.00
Toreador FF H; emb Corrida de Torres in B; teaspoon 100.00
Totem pole H of Alaska; Sitka in B 45.00
Utah emb on H; Morman Temple eng in B; mk, teaspoon.............24.00
Utah/seal/angel emb on H; temple emb in B; EX 30.00
Virginia/scenes in GW B; horse & rider on columns form H.......245.00
Wm Penn figural, heavy..60.00
Wm Penn signs treaty on H; Independence Hall in B; demi..........18.00

Sporting Goods

Our advisor for this category is Paul Longo; he is listed in the Directory under Massachusetts. See also Target Balls.

Bank of Jackie Robinson, ca 1950, $325.00.

Baseball, Official American League; sgn by Babe Ruth, 1930s 750.00
Bat, Golden Jubilee Brooklyn Baseball Club, 1883-1933, 24" 200.00
Book, Baseball Encyclopedia, 1956, pocket sz................................. 5.00

Book, score; Kansas City Blues, 1921 ....**25.00**
Booklet, Babe Ruth Story, 10 pgs of photos, some from movie **75.00**
Booklet, Yankee Stadium, stages of construction, 1922-23, EX **50.00**
Boxing cards, full color, cigarette ads, ca 1910, 92 for **350.00**
Brunsometer, measures bowling ball holes, 10x17x13", EX............**35.00**
Card, Geo Dixon, 1891 Featherweight Champ, EX **6.00**
Crow call, JC Higgins, MIB..**35.00**
Duck call, Charles H Perdew...**350.00**
Football, sgn by NY Giants, ca 1960, EX.............................**150.00**
Golf clubs, wooden, early 1900s, 9 clubs in orig bag, EX..............**250.00**
Ice skates, wood, wrought blades w/lg curl, clamp-on, 13" **150.00**
Invitation, Inaugural opening, Phila vs Boston, 1890, printed **450.00**
License, hunting; Illinois resident, red on linen, 1907 ....**50.00**
Newspaper picture, Babe Ruth, Canadian paper, 1928, 11x18" **50.00**
Pass, Boston Braves, brass, silver dollar sz, 1930, NM..................**250.00**
Pencil box, baseball players litho, 1870s, EX **300.00**
Pennant, Brooklyn Dodgers, wht on royal bl, 1952, 24", EX **80.00**
Pennant, Indianapolis Motor Speedway, race cars, 1920s, 24" **75.00**
Pennant, NY Giants Nat'l League, gr/wht, ca 1937, 25", EX **125.00**
Pennant, NY Mets Nat'l...Champions World Series, 1969, 30" **40.00**
Photograph, Babe Ruth, autographed, matted/fr, 5x7", NM **900.00**
Photograph, 1947 NY Yankees, sepia, names below, 12x18" **45.00**
Pin, Jackie Robinson Team for Rockefeller, EX **250.00**
Playing cards, 1932 Olympic games, movie stars on bks **65.00**
Press pin, St Louis Cardinals Japanese Tour, 1958, EX **75.00**
Print, Battle for Championship...King...Mace, 1862, 22x28".......**120.00**
Program, Cincinnati Reds World Series, 1919, EX......................**500.00**
Schedule, Nat'l League, daily, for 1888 season, EX......................**100.00**
Sheet music, Cubs on Parade, c 1907, EX.................................**350.00**
Snooker table, walnut, pearl inlay, 1920s, 5x10", EX **700.00**
Stationery, Dizzy Dean & Falstaff Brewing Corp, 1950s, EX **10.00**
Tag, luggage; Brooklyn Baseball Club, EX................................**75.00**
Turkey call, Roger Latham True Tone **20.00**
Uniform, Oilers, Wayne Gretzky, game used **400.00**
Wristwatch, Babe Ruth Official, color dial, 1948, M in case **400.00**
Writing tablet, Nat'l Game, LaJoie at bat on cover, VG **200.00**

St. Clair

The St. Clair Glass Company began as a small family-oriented operation in Elwood, Indiana, in 1941. Most famous for their lamps, the family made numerous small items of carnival, pink and caramel slag, and custard glass as well. Later, paperweights became popular production pieces; many command considerably high prices on today's market. Weights are stamped and usually dated, while small production pieces are often unmarked.

Dish, bird & berry, cobalt, 2-pc **45.00**
Lamp, paperweight; pk flowers on gr, 12", pr................................**265.00**
Lamp, paperweight; 4 floral segments w/brass spacers, 29" **1,000.00**
Novelty, Liberty Bell, bl carnival, Joe St Clair...............................**18.00**
Paperweight, bell form, 3 mc lilies/bubbles, sgn, 4" **32.00**
Paperweight, pk rose/4 leaves, 1/5 facets, sgn, 3¼"......................**120.00**
Paperweight, pk/opal rose+leaves, 1/5 facets, unsgn, 3½"............**55.00**
Paperweight, swirl, Joe St Clair..**85.00**
Paperweight, Truman...**35.00**
Salt cellar, wheelbarrow, caramel slag, Joe St Clair......................**32.00**
Shot glass, cobalt **18.50**
Toothpick holder, Holly, gr carnival...**45.00**
Toothpick holder, Indian, lustre, Joe St Clair **45.00**
Toothpick holder, Invt Fan & Feather, gr carnival, sgn..................**45.00**
Toothpick holder, owl form, bl opaque, Bob St Clair **15.00**
Town pump, gr, ICGA, Joe St Clair, 1978, mini **24.00**

Staffordshire

Scores of potteries sprang up in England's Staffordshire district in the early 18th century; several remain to the present time. (See also specific companies.) Figurines and groups were made in great numbers; dogs were favorite subjects. Often they were made in pairs, each a mirror image of the other. They varied in heights from 3" or 4" to the largest, measuring 16" to 18". From 1840 until about 1900, portrait figures were produced to represent particular characters, both real and fictional. As a rule, these were never marked.

The Historical ware listed here was made throughout the district; some collectors refer to it as Staffordshire Blue Ware. It was produced as early as 1820; and, because much was exported to America, it was very often decorated with transfers depicting scenic views of well-known American landmarks. Early examples were printed in a deep cobalt. By 1830 a softer blue was favored, and within the next decade black, pink, red, and green prints were used. Although sometimes careless about adding their trademark, many companies used their own border designs that were as individual as their names.

Our advisor for the Historical Blue Ware is Richard Marden; he is listed in the Directory under New Hampshire. See also specific manufacturers.

Key:
blk — black   l/b — light blue
gr — green   m/b — medium blue
d/b — dark blue   m-d/b — medium dark blue

Historical

Bowl, fruit; Zebra, m-d/b, open/sq, Rogers, 9", NM **75.00**
Bowl, Hindu Temple, d/b, wht emb border, Rogers, 10".............**175.00**
Bowl, Near Hudson, Hudson River, brn, 8½".............................**195.00**
Bowl, Pains Hill, Surrey, d/b, beaded rim, Hall, 12", EX **375.00**
Bowl, Regent's Park, d/b, 9¾"..**325.00**
Bowl, Staughton's Church, d/b, Ridgway, 8¼"...........................**375.00**
Bowl, vegetable; Lake George, d/b, Wood, w/lid, 12" L **500.00**
Bowl, Wht Mountain NH, red, Adams, oval, 10¾", NM.............**175.00**
Bowl, Wild Rose, m/b, w/lid, 10" **275.00**
Chamber pot, English cathedral, d/b, rim rpr, 9½" dia............. **2,100.00**
Coffeepot, Lafayette at Franklin's tomb, d/b, 12" **1,250.00**
Coffeepot, MacDonnough's Victory, d/b, Wood, prof rpr, 11" . **1,100.00**
Compote, North Devon, mc floral border, 14" L, EX **600.00**
Creamer, Am & Independence, d/b, Clews, 5" **1,500.00**
Creamer, Comm MacDonnough's Victory, d/b, bbl form, 3½".. **1,550.00**
Creamer, Crow's Nest from Bull Hill, blk, Ridgway, 6½" **95.00**
Cup & saucer, Am eagle on urn, d/b, Clews, tight hairline **195.00**
Cup & saucer, Lafayette at Franklin's Tomb, Wood **145.00**
Cup & saucer, Lafayette at Tomb of Franklin, d/b, E Wood.........**295.00**
Cup & saucer, Washington at Tomb/scroll in hand, d/b, Wood...**325.00**
Cup plate, Am & Independence, d/b, Clews, 3½"........................**375.00**
Cup plate, Am & Independence, full border, d/b, Clews, 4½" **400.00**
Cup plate, boy/cow/church, d/b, 3½" **75.00**
Cup plate, Castle Garden Battery NY, d/b, Wood, 3¾" **350.00**
Cup plate, Columbus, brn, Adams, 4".....................................**75.00**
Cup plate, Consitution Grievances, l/b, 4"..............................**450.00**
Cup plate, Conway NY, l/b, Jackson, 4⅛", NM........................**195.00**
Cup plate, Entrance to Blaize Castle, l/b, 2¾" **75.00**
Cup plate, Kenelworth Priory, l/b, 3⅝".....................................**75.00**
Cup plate, Kenelworth Priory, m/b, 3⅝".....................................**45.00**
Cup plate, Landing of the Fathers, m/b, Wood, 4⅝", EX **200.00**
Cup plate, Scudder's Am Museum, d/b, Stevenson, 4" **1,600.00**
Cup plate, View Near Conway NY, pk, Jackson, 4⅛" **235.00**

Cup plate, Winter View of Pittsfield MA, d/b, Clews, 3⅞".........425.00
Fruit basket, canal scene/ext: wild roses, d/b, 12", +tray.............600.00
Fruit basket, Harewood House+2 views, d/b, rivet rpr, +tray 395.00
Pitcher, Erie Canal, Utica Inscription, d/b, 5¾" 1,400.00
Pitcher, Erie Canal View of Aqueduct Bridge..., d/b, 6½" 1,250.00
Plate, Albany, d/b, 10"..325.00
Plate, America & Independence, d/b, Clews, 10⅝" 300.00
Plate, America & Independence, d/b, Clews, 8" 250.00
Plate, America & Independence, d/b, Clews, 9" 225.00
Plate, Baker's Falls, l/b, Picturesque views, 9" 70.00
Plate, Baltimore & Ohio RR, level, d/b, Wood, 10", EX 500.00
Plate, Battery...NY, blk, minor wear, 8".....................................55.00
Plate, Beach at Brighton, d/b, E Wood & Sons, 10", EX 300.00
Plate, Boston State House, l/b, Enoch Wood, 6½" 135.00
Plate, Boston State House, l/b, Enoch Wood, 7¼" 135.00
Plate, Boston State House, m/b, Wood, 10" 150.00
Plate, British Views, d/b, fruit & flower border, 8¼"....................85.00
Plate, Caledonia, red, mk Adams, 9½"..65.00
Plate, Canterbury Cathedral, d/b, imp Clews, 10".......................125.00
Plate, Cattskill Mountain House, red, Adams, 10¼", NM 80.00
Plate, Chief Justice Marshall Troy, d/b, Wood, 8" 450.00
Plate, Church in City of NY, d/b, Stubbs, 6⅛"............................750.00
Plate, City Hall NY, brn, Jackson, 10½"......................................70.00
Plate, City of Albany, State of NY, d/b, Wood, 10¼"...................425.00
Plate, Commodore MacDonnough's Victory, d/b, Wood, 6½" 350.00
Plate, Consitution Grievances, l/b, 6", EX.................................200.00
Plate, Cupid & Psyche, d/b, Adams, 8" 125.00
Plate, Dam & Water Works, d/b, Henshall, 10" 400.00
Plate, DeWitt Clinton, Late Governor, d/b, 10"..........................450.00
Plate, East View of LaGrange Residence..., d/b, E Wood, 9".......135.00
Plate, Erie Canal at Buffalo, purple, lace border, 10" 95.00
Plate, Erie Canal Views, border of Canal Scenes, d/b, 8½" 650.00
Plate, Erie Canal Views, d/b, rare, 5⅝" 575.00
Plate, Faulkborun Hall, d/b, Stevenson, 10¼" 85.00
Plate, Ft Edwards, Hudson River, blk, Clews, 5¼".......................55.00
Plate, Ft Hamilton, purple, Mellor-Venables, Arms of..., 9" 165.00
Plate, Harvard, d/b, Stevens, 10" 400.00
Plate, Harvard, l/b, Enoch Wood's Celtic Series, 10½" 165.00
Plate, Harvard, sepia, Enoch Wood, 10½" 135.00
Plate, Highlands Hudson River, d/b, Enoch Wood & Son, 5¾" ..450.00
Plate, Insane Hospital Boston, c/s, 7", EX.................................275.00
Plate, Junction of Sacandaga & Hudson River, brn, Clews, 7".......60.00
Plate, King's Chapel, Boston, pk, Adams, commemorative, 10" 85.00
Plate, La Grange, Residence of...Lafayette, d/b, Wood, 10" 145.00
Plate, Landing of Gen Lafayette, d/b, Clews, 10" 325.00
Plate, Landing of Gen Lafayette, d/b, Clews, 9" 300.00
Plate, Landing of Gen Lafayette at Castle Garden, d/b, 5½" 250.00
Plate, Landing of the Fathers, vertical waves, m/b, 10" 150.00
Plate, Monte Video CT, pk, Adams, 7", NM.................................65.00
Plate, Near Hudson, Hudson River, blk, Clews, 8¾", EX 65.00
Plate, Niagara (sheep shearing), d/b, Stevenson, 10" 275.00
Plate, NY, d/b, Mayer, 9¾" 600.00
Plate, NY, pk, Adams, 6", NM...55.00
Plate, NY, pk, Mellor-Venables, Arms of States, 6½"...................145.00
Plate, NY from Brooklyn Heights, d/b, Stevenson, 10", EX 700.00
Plate, NY from Brooklyn Heights, d/b, Stevenson, 10¼" 950.00
Plate, Panshanger, Hertfordshire, d/b, Halls, 5½".......................125.00
Plate, rabbit hunters, d/b transfer, wear/crow's ft, 9" 75.00
Plate, Residence of Late Richard Jordon NJ, l/b, 9", EX..............200.00
Plate, Richmond VA, blk, Jackson, 7", NM 65.00
Plate, Shannon, marine view, m/b, Rogers, 10" 145.00
Plate, Shannondale Springs VA, red, Adams, 7¾", EX 40.00
Plate, St Paul's Church NY, m-d/b, very rare, 6".........................800.00
Plate, State House Boston, l/b, Wood, floral border, 8½".............150.00

Plate, State House Boston, m/b, Rogers, floral border, 10"...........150.00
Plate, Table Rock Niagara, d/b, Wood, glaze wear, 10"................225.00
Plate, The Sea (shipwreck), pk, Adams, 9½", NM 55.00
Plate, toddy; Conway, pk, Jackson, 5", NM 165.00
Plate, toddy; Conway, purple, Jackson, 5" 235.00
Plate, toddy; game birds, d/b, Adams, minor wear, 5"..................50.00
Plate, toddy; Rapids Above Hadley's Falls, blk, 7", EX..................95.00
Plate, toddy; Residence of...Richard Jordon, dk brn, 5¾" 275.00
Plate, Transylvania University, Lexington, Wood, 9".....................335.00
Plate, Tweekenham Surry, d/b, fruit & flower border, 6½" 125.00
Plate, Union Line, d/b, Enoch Wood, 10", EX 400.00
Plate, Union Line, d/b, Wood's irreg shell border, 9", EX 250.00
Plate, View Near Conway, pk, Adams, 9"....................................85.00
Plate, View of Trenton Falls, d/b, Wood, 7½"..............................400.00
Plate, Villa in Regents Park, d/b, Adams, 8¾" 135.00
Plate, Vue d'une Ancienne Abbabye, d/b, Enoch Wood, 9"........135.00
Plate, Vue Prise en Savoie, d/b, Enoch Wood, 7½".....................135.00
Plate, Water Works Philadelphia, blk, rim wear, 9"......................155.00
Plate, Water Works Philadelphia, brn, Jackson, 9".......................80.00
Plate, Winter View of Pittsfield MA, d/b, Clews, 9", EX 225.00
Plate, Wm Penn's Treaty, brn, 7½"..55.00
Platter, Albany, l/b, Meigh, cut corners, 13½" 275.00

Platter, View of the Boston State House with cattle and figures in the foreground, Rogers, 18", $600.00.

Platter, Hudson, Hudson River, blk, Clews, 13" 235.00
Platter, Moose & Hunters, d/b, Hall's Quadruped Series, 15" 550.00
Platter, Norwich Cathedral, Norfolk, d/b, Hall, 11"......................225.00
Platter, Nottingham, d/b, Clews foliage/scroll emb, 19", NM......275.00
Platter, NY From Heights 'Nr' Brooklyn, m-d/b, 16", NM 1,600.00
Platter, Oriental, l/b, Ridgway, 18"...175.00
Platter, Sandusky, d/b, rpr crack/rim chip, 17" 1,200.00
Platter, St Woolston's Kildare Ireland, d/b, Hall, 14½" 400.00
Platter, Theatre Printing House, Oxford, l/b, Ridgway, 19" 475.00
Shaker, classical figures, m/b...85.00
Soup plate, allover floral, d/b, 9½" 95.00
Soup plate, Baltimore & Ohio RR, d/b, Wood, 10" 550.00
Soup plate, Boston State House, Wood, 10" 150.00
Soup plate, Columbus (& men landing), purple, Adams, 10½" 75.00
Soup plate, Dilston Towers..., d/b, Adams, 10", NM 100.00
Soup plate, Erie Canal View of Aqueduct Bridge..., d/b, 10" 650.00
Soup plate, Hannibal (elephants/Alps), m/b, Adams, 10½" 60.00
Soup plate, Oriental scenery, d/b, Adams, sm flakes, 10½" 50.00
Soup plate, Peace & Plenty, d/b, Clews, 10"...............................275.00
Soup plate, Picturesque Views 'Nr' Fishkill, blk, 10½", EX 55.00
Soup plate, Priory, l/b, Alcock, 8½" 23.00

Soup plate, Residence of Late Richard Jordan, red, 9", EX **150.00**
Soup plate, Residence...R Jordan, purple, JH&Co, 10", NM **150.00**
Soup plate, State House, Boston, pk, Jackson, 10" **165.00**
Soup plate, States, d/b, Clews, 10¼"..**275.00**
Sugar bowl, Commodore MacDonnough's Victory, d/b, NM.......**650.00**
Syllabub, sailboats/cottages/church, m-d/b, flatiron hdl **22.00**
Tray, Castle Scenery, m/b, openwork inner border, 10", NM **185.00**
Tray, Luscombe Devonshire, d/b, Hall's Select Views, 8", NM **150.00**
Tureen, Castle Garden Battery NY, d/b, Wood, 16" L **2,100.00**
Tureen, gravy; Chiswick on Thames, d/b, Wood, +ladle/tray . **2,000.00**
Tureen, sauce; Cathedral City, l/b, Wood, +ladle/tray **275.00**
Tureen, sauce; Neptune (ship/lighthouse), l/b, +ladle/tray...........**225.00**
Tureen, soup; Panoramic Scenery, d/b, w/lid, Stevenson, NM **995.00**
Undertray, Hyena, d/b, Wood's Zoological Series, 8" **100.00**

Miscellaneous

Bowl, engine/coal car/4 passenger cars, brn w/mc, 7" **100.00**
Box, trinket; figural hand holds jewel casket **120.00**
Covered dish, bull's head, wht w/yel & brn, 1850s, 8x11" **385.00**
Covered dish, hen on basket, yel, 1850s, 8x11"............................**800.00**
Covered dish, hen on nest, gray/brn, 1850s, 8x11"......................**900.00**
Covered dish, hen on nest, mc, 10" L **285.00**
Covered dish, hen on nest, mc, 12" L **325.00**
Covered dish, hen on nest, mc, 6½" L **285.00**
Creamer, cow form w/pnt florals, floral ground, 6½" L, EX..........**250.00**
Cup, Trust in God/Husbandman's Diligence..., mc, hdls, 4" **110.00**
Cup & saucer, handleless; gaudy 4-color floral, EX........................**40.00**
Cup & saucer, Temperance, red transfer w/pk lustre band.............**35.00**
Cup plate, ships/docks, pk transfer, 4½" **45.00**
Dog, bl, w/lustre & mc enamel, facing pr, 9½", NM....................**350.00**
Dog, red, mc flower basket in mouth, 7½", pr, EX......................**800.00**
Dog, red spots, mc features, minor wear, 4⅜"...............................**135.00**
Dog, red spots, mc features, 3½", NM...**85.00**
Dog, rust spots/gold collars, 1850s, facing pr, 7".........................**450.00**
Dog, spaniel, brn, Singleton, 5"...**95.00**
Dog, spaniel, gray spots, 5¼"...**150.00**
Dog, spaniel, red/orange spots, facing pr, 6¼".............................**275.00**
Dog, spaniel, wht, 13"...**325.00**
Dog, whippet, reclining, 3¼" L, pr **225.00**
Dog, whippet, seated, Ralph Wood type, 1700s, 3¼".....................**800.00**
Figurine, bagpiper in Highland costume, EX pnt, 1860s, 10".......**135.00**
Figurine, boxing match, 'Heenan, Sayers,' 9¼"............................**325.00**
Figurine, boy w/bird's nest & bird, ca 1850, 7¾" **150.00**
Figurine, buck, recumbent, Sherratt-type base, 6", NM **325.00**
Figurine, cat on cushion, blk/wht w/gr collar, 5½" L, pr **1,200.00**
Figurine, cobbler & his wife, ca 1860, 12½", pr............................**500.00**
Figurine, cockerel, EX colors, wood platform, 1800s, 11" **2,000.00**
Figurine, colt, orange/brn/gr, 1785, 3" **1,000.00**
Figurine, cow, grazing, att Sherratt, 1830s, 7" L, EX **550.00**
Figurine, cricket player, 10" **220.00**
Figurine, death of Nelson, 1845, 9"...**300.00**
Figurine, flag dancers, arm in arm, oval base, 1850s, 10" **175.00**
Figurine, Fortitude, Enoch Wood, ca 1800, rpr, 21"................. **2,475.00**
Figurine, girl sewing seed, 4-leaf bocage, att Walton, 6" **275.00**
Figurine, girl sits sidesaddle on rearing pony, 6½".........................**90.00**
Figurine, girl w/animal, 4-leaf bocage, Walton, 6", NM **275.00**
Figurine, girl w/mice & mousetrap, rnd base, 5", NM....................**75.00**
Figurine, Jumbo the elephant, ca 1890, rare, 10" **400.00**
Figurine, lady seated w/cat, 3½" **325.00**
Figurine, lamb, sanded coat, blk spots/yel stripe, 2⅝", NM **75.00**
Figurine, lion, standing, 3¼", EX...**95.00**
Figurine, lovers below floral arbor, 14"..**175.00**
Figurine, man dancing, orange hat/bl jacket, ca 1850, 7½"..........**100.00**

Figures of greyhounds, 11", $400.00 for the pair.

Figurine, man in plumed hat/breeches/knee boots, w/dog, 17" **350.00**
Figurine, man w/jug stands beside lady, ca 1840s, 13" **200.00**
Figurine, monkey holding gr branch, ca 1880, 3½".......................**95.00**
Figurine, officer titled 'G Gordon,' sm rpr chip, 18" **175.00**
Figurine, peasant couple, 13" **125.00**
Figurine, Prince Albert in Order of Garter robes, 1845, 12" **200.00**
Figurine, Queen Victoria, 11" **275.00**
Figurine, Queen Victoria & Prince of Wales, 18", pr...................**550.00**
Figurine, rabbit, tortoise-shell glaze, lying flat, 17", NM..............**750.00**
Figurine, ram, full-curl horns, reclining on grass, 4" **300.00**
Figurine, Red Riding Hood & wolf, 5"...**65.00**
Figurine, sailor leaning on barrel, 1850, 12" **200.00**
Figurine, Scotch couple in serpent-form boat, 8½", NM..............**250.00**
Figurine, Scotsman, 6½"..**80.00**
Figurine, Shakespeare beside pedestal holding script, 8¾"...........**150.00**
Figurine, Uncle Tom & Eva, 1850, 10".......................................**250.00**
Figurine, War, soldier on horse, worn enameling, 11" **275.00**
Figurine, Winter, woman in cloak, mc, ca 1780, 9", EX **350.00**
Figurine, zebra, on foliate oval base, 5x5".....................................**220.00**
Flowerpot, bl lustre band/rust border on ochre, mc motif.............**225.00**
Jug, eagle transfer, rust floral, silver lustre band, 7½".................**650.00**
Jug, gaudy floral, underglaze bl+3 colors, 7½", EX **55.00**
Mug, hunting dogs, lav transfer, Field Sports, 3", EX **120.00**
Plate, California Diggings, blk scene, emb rim, 3", NM **80.00**
Plate, gaudy 4-color floral, 9"...**95.00**
Plate, Gentlemen's Cabin, blk transfer, J&T Edwards, 7" **90.00**
Plate, Temperance, mc meeting scene, emb rim, 5".......................**95.00**
Plate, Worcester Co W/Ag Society...1851, ironstone, 8½" **95.00**
Platter, gaudy roses, 4-color, imp Hall, stains, 15" L **80.00**
Platter, gaudy 5-color floral, stains/wear, 18" L **425.00**
Platter, Jerusalem, red transfer, CJ Mason & Co, 15¾"................**135.00**
Spill holder, deer by tree, free-standing legs, 12", pr....................**500.00**
Sugar bowl, beehive & garden, purple transfer, 6¾", EX **55.00**
Teapot, Fulton's Steamboat/Cadmus, carmen transfer, 6", VG **275.00**
Vase, draped child supports cornucopia, 1800, 9", EX, pr **400.00**
Watch holder, Colonial man on grassy base **165.00**
Whistle, child w/rabbit on lap, 2"..**450.00**
Whistle, hen sitting on brn nest, 3x2", EX **45.00**

Stained Glass

There are many factors to consider in evaluating a window or panel of stained glass art. Besides the obvious factor of condition, intricacy, jeweling, beveling, and the amount of selenium (red, orange, and yellow) present should all be taken into account. Remember, repair work is itself an art and can be very expensive.

Our advisor for this category is Carl Heck; he is listed in the Directory under Colorado.

Lamp, 18" geometric-band shade; gr-pnt std, Chicaco Mosaic.....**900.00**
Window, beveled/slag rectangles, Arts & Crafts, 27x16" **125.00**
Window, clear panels bordered by grapevines, 67x12", 4 for ... **3,700.00**
Window, floral ground w/HP rondel portrait of lady, 14x50"... **1,600.00**
Window, native dancer, pnt/layered detail, LaFarge, 17x13"..**13,000.00**
Window, sq faceted panels, sm jewels, 25x15" **275.00**
Window, stylized floral, ripple glass, bevel border, 24x22" **500.00**

Stanford

The Stanford Company produced a Corn Line, similar to that of the Shawnee Company, that is today becoming very collectible. Most examples are marked, so there should be no difficulty in distinguishing one from the other.

Corn Line, butter dish **45.00**
Corn Line, cookie jar **80.00**
Corn Line, creamer & sugar bowl...**45.00**
Corn Line, shakers, pr..**25.00**
Corn Line, teapot **50.00**

Stangl

In 1910 Johann Martin Stangl joined the Fulper Pottery Company, working there as ceramic chemist and superintendent of the plant. After a brief absence from 1914 until 1919 when he was employed by the Haeger Pottery, Stangl returned to Fulper. He developed glazes for a new line of cigarette boxes, ash trays, vases, figurines, etc. In 1926 J.M. Stangl became president of the company, and by 1946 he and a partner gained total ownership. The Stangl name first appeared on solid-color dinnerware and novelites in 1926. By 1942 a higher grade of hand-decorated and hand-colored dinnerware was made – Fruit, Yellow Tulip, etc. – which was sold in great abundance. During the war years (1940-1946), bird figures were in great demand, since imports were restricted at that time. Stangl created its famous line of birds; these are very collectible today. Stangl ware continued to be produced after J.M. Stangl died in 1972; soon after 1978 the factory closed. Reference: *The Collector's Handbook of Stangl Pottery* by Norma Rehl, published in 1979.

Our advisors for this category are Robert and Nacy Perzel; they are listed in the Directory under New Jersey.

Birds

#3250C, Duck, feeding **40.00**
#3250E, Duck, drinking..**40.00**
#3274, Penguin, Terra Rose...**250.00**
#3275, Turkey **350.00**
#3276, Bluebird, 5"..**85.00**
#3276D, Bluebirds, 8½" **150.00**
#3400, Lovebird **55.00**
#3401, Wren, 3½"...**50.00**
#3401D, Wrens, orig version, 8"...**100.00**
#3402, Oriole **60.00**
#3402D, Orioles, 6", pr..**100.00**
#3405, Cockatoo...**55.00**
#3406, Kingfisher, 3½"...**80.00**
#3406D, Kingfishers, 5"...**110.00**
#3407, Owl **300.00**

Wrens, #3401D, 6½", $100.00.

#3408, Bird of Paradise, 5½"..**80.00**
#3432, Duck, running, 5½" **350.00**
#3444, Cardinal, pk...**65.00**
#3445, Rooster, yel...**125.00**
#3446, Hen **120.00**
#3447, Yellow Warbler, 5" **80.00**
#3448, Blue-Headed Vireo, 4¼"...**70.00**
#3449, Parrot, 6" **150.00**
#3450, Passenger Pigeon, 19" L..**750.00**
#3452, Painted Bunting, 5" **100.00**
#3454, Key West Quail Dove, wht...**250.00**
#3490D, Redstarts **150.00**
#3492, Cock Pheasant...**225.00**
#3580, Green Cockatoo, 8⅞" **100.00**
#3583, Parula Warbler **50.00**
#3584, Cockatoo, sgn Jacob, 11⅜"..**200.00**
#3585, Rufous Hummingbird, 3¼" **50.00**
#3592, Titmouse, 2½"...**50.00**
#3593, Nuthatch...**45.00**
#3596, Grey Cardinal, 4¾"..**65.00**
#3597, Wilson Warbler, 3½" **45.00**
#3599D, Hummingbirds **225.00**
#3627, Rivoli Hummingbird, rose blossom **90.00**
#3628, Rieffer's Hummingbird, 4½"..**125.00**
#3629, Broadtail Hummingbird...**135.00**
#3634, Allen Hummingbird...**48.00**
#3635D, Goldfinches...**200.00**
#3715, Blue Jay, w/peanut **550.00**
#3716, Blue Jay, w/leaf..**550.00**
#3746, Canary, flower on base, 6¼" **150.00**
#3751S, Red-Headed Woodpecker, pk gloss, 6¼"...........................**75.00**
#37515, Red-Headed Woodpecker, red matt, 6¼"...........................**100.00**
#3756D, Audubon Warblers...**85.00**
#3812, Chestnut-Sided Warbler **60.00**
#3813, Grosbeak, 5"..**120.00**
#3815, Western Bluebird..**95.00**
#3850, Yellow Warbler **60.00**
#3851, Red-Breasted Nuthatch, 3¾"...**50.00**
#3852, Swallow..**65.00**
#3924, Yellow-Throated Warbler **50.00**

Miscellaneous

Ash tray, Antique Gold, #3915 ....**18.00**

Ash tray, bathtub; Town & Country, brn 25.00
Ash tray, Canvasback duck, mc on gray, sq, 2x9x9" 45.00
Ash tray, rainbow trout, gray & gr, 9" 55.00
Basket, yel matt, #3228, 7" 40.00
Bowl, divided vegetable; Bella Rosa, 2-part 25.00
Bowl, divided vegetable; Thistle, oval............................35.00
Bowl, First Love, 8" 20.00
Bowl, flower; Colonial Silver, #3410-7, 7" 16.00
Bowl, fruit; Golden Harvest, 5½" 8.00
Bowl, fruit; Thistle, sm............................10.00
Bowl, fruit; Thistle, 12" 45.00
Bowl, Holly, 9¾" 35.00
Bowl, Kiddie Ware, Circus Clown............................20.00
Bowl, lug soup; Golden Harvest 8.00
Bowl, lug soup; Orchard Song 10.00
Bowl, lug soup; Thistle............................10.00
Bowl, Orchard Song, 7½" 25.00
Bowl, vegetable; Town & Country, bl, deep, 1½-qt............................40.00
Butter dish, Starflower............................35.00
Cake plate, Fruit & Flowers, ped ft............................25.00
Candlestick, Antique Gold, #5069, pr............................12.00
Candy dish, Terra Rose, cloverleaf, gr, hdld, #3857 ....15.00
Casserole, First Love 40.00
Casserole, Magnolia............................45.00
Cigarette box, Terra Rose, flowers............................20.00
Clock, Town & Country, electric, 10"............................50.00
Coaster, Thistle, 5" 9.00
Coffee warmer, Golden Harvest 15.00
Creamer, Fruit & Flower............................ 8.00
Creamer, Golden Blossom 6.50
Creamer, Terra Rose, Tulip, yel............................ 8.00
Creamer & sugar bowl, Thistle, w/lid............................15.00
Cup, Kiddie Ware, letter A............................20.00
Cup, Provincial 7.50
Cup & saucer, Blue Daisy 14.00
Cup & saucer, First Love 12.00
Cup & saucer, Garden Flower 13.00
Cup & saucer, Golden Harvest............................10.00
Cup & saucer, Mountain Laurel 10.00
Cup & saucer, Prelude 10.00
Cup & saucer, Thistle 12.00
Cup & saucer, Wild Rose 12.00
Cup & snack plate, Fruit & Flower 15.00
Dish, Kiddie Ware, train motif, 3-compartment 30.00
Gravy boat, Town & Country, yel, w/underplate 35.00
Mug, Stoby; Archie, w/orig hat ash tray, HP, 1930s............................150.00
Mug, Town & Gountry, gr 20.00
Pitcher, Antique Gold, #4060, 5¼"............................12.00
Pitcher, Country Garden, 1-qt............................25.00
Pitcher, Granada Gold, #4053, 12" 125.00
Pitcher, Star Dust, 1-qt............................15.00
Pitcher, Town & Country, gr, 2½-pt 35.00
Planter, swan, Granada Gold, 3" 20.00
Planter, swan form, Antique Gold, #5034, 6" L 25.00
Plate, chop; Thistle, 12½"............................20.00
Plate, chop; Tulip, yel, 12"............................18.00
Plate, Della Ware, Red Cherry, 9¼"............................12.00
Plate, Golden Harvest, 10"............................10.00
Plate, Golden Harvest, 6"............................ 3.00
Plate, Golden Harvest, 8"............................ 9.00
Plate, Kiddie Ware, Ranger Boy 35.00
Plate, Lily, pk, 6"............................ 4.00
Plate, Magnolia, 10"............................10.00
Plate, Mountain Laurel, 10"............................10.00

Plate, Orchard Song, 8" 8.50
Plate, Prelude, 10"............................ 8.00
Plate, Prelude, 8"............................ 6.00
Plate, Starflower, 10"............................11.00
Plate, Thistle, 10"............................10.00
Plate, Thistle, 8"............................ 9.00
Plate, Wild Rose, 10"............................11.00
Relish, Tulip, yel, 9½"............................50.00
Server, Town & Country, blk, center hdl............................12.50
Shakers, Golden Harvest, pr............................10.00
Shakers, Thistle, pr............................15.00
Sign, store; yel tulips, pk tiger lily 125.00
Sugar bowl, Magnolia, w/lid............................10.00
Sugar bowl, Orchard Song, w/lid............................ 8.00
Sugar bowl, Terra Rose, Blue Tulip, w/lid 12.00
Tidbit, Fruit & Flowers, 2-tier 20.00
Tray, yel, 7½x7½"............................ 4.50
Tumbler, bathroom; Town & Country, yel 20.00
Vase, fleur-de-lis, Terra Rose, bl, 6"............................115.00
Vase, horse's head, Terra Rose, bl w/mauve, #3611, 13"............................350.00
Vase, matt gr, leaf hdl, #3104, 7"............................25.00
Vase, orange, #2017, 3" 20.00
Vase, Terra Rose, gr, leaf form, #3441, 10"............................28.00
Vase, Terra Rose, mauve, leaf form, #3442, 6"............................15.00
Wig stand, Blond, w/ceramic base 200.00
Wig stand, Brunette, w/wood base 185.00

Steamship Collectibles

For centuries, ocean-going vessels with their venturesome officers and crews were the catalyst that changed the unknown aspects of our world to the known. Changing economic conditions, unfortunately, have now placed the North American shipping industry in the same jeopardy as the American passenger train. They are becoming a memory. The surge of interest in railroad collectibles and the railroad-related steamship lines has lead collectors to examine the whole spectrum of steamship collectibles.

Our advisors for this category are Lila and Fred Shrader; they are listed in the Directory under California.

Ash tray, Princess, Swedish glass 18.00
Book, Piloting, Seamanship & Small Boat Handling, 1955, EX 15.00
Booklet, Constitution, Let's Talk About SS..., 1957, 15-pg............. 7.00
Booklet, Cunard, Mediterranean Cruise De Luxe, 1927, 63-pg....... 8.50
Booklet, Dollar Line, Orient & Round the World, 1928, M 10.00
Booklet, Hamburg American, winter cruise to Orient, 1897, EX...25.00
Coaster, Rotterdam V, portrait/Statue of Liberty............................ 4.00
Coat hanger, Wht Star Line, wood 4.00
Cuff links, Queen Elizabeth II, enamel on brass, M in case...........24.00
Deck plan, Am Export, 4 Aces, open: 24x36", M 17.50
Deck plan, Queen Elizabeth I, color coded, 1966, M 18.00
Folder, RMS Majestic Wht Star Lines, 1930s, 3x3½", EX............17.50
Hat ribbon, Costa, royal bl w/gold silkscreened letters, 30"............ 6.00
Hot plate, Franconia III, ceramic, gold portrait, 4"............................14.00
Loving cup, Holland Am Line, SP, brass medallion, 5" 12.50
Magazine, French Line, Paris Weekly, Compliments of..., EX......... 2.50
Medallion, Doric/Oceanic, bronze, portraits in relief, 3", M 40.00
Menu, dinner; Queen of Bermuda, April 1949, M 7.50
Menu, RMS Statendam, pirate theme, Jan 1937, EX 17.50
Model, Queen Mary, CI, Triang, 10", EX............................14.00
Paperweight, Majestic I, glass, color portrait, 2x4"............................20.00
Passenger list, Independence, Sunlane Cruise, NY, Aug '62 .... 6.00
Passenger list, RMS Aquitania, WWI vintage, full-color ship 50.00

Pin, Queen Elizabeth I, figural, enamel on brass...........................**14.00**
Pin-bk button, Queen Mary, blk/wht photo portrait, M.................**7.50**
Playing cards, Cunard Lines, 1900, EX in box **25.00**
Post card, Independence/Constitution portrait, unused, NM **10.00**
Postal cover, Queen Elizabeth II, stamped Maiden voyage.............**4.00**
Poster, Baltic-Am Line SS Polonia, lg **195.00**
Print, SS Titanic, w/career write-up in oak fr, 13½x21½"............**225.00**
Program, concert; Canadian Pacific, Montclare, 1930, sm..............**4.00**
Program, Cunard, 1928 ....**7.50**
Publication, Cunard, Crow's Nest, Sept 1957, EX.....................**5.00**
Puzzle, Norwegian Caribbean, Norway portrait, 350-pc.................**12.00**
Rubber stamp, Normandie, portrait, 2x2"..............................**10.00**
Scrapbook, SS Celtic, 70 pgs of ephemera, NY, 1903, EX **120.00**
Ship's paper, Caronia II, Ocean Times, June 1949, EX...................**4.00**
Ship's paper, Franconia III, Ocean Times, July 1971, EX.................**2.50**
Sign, Berengeria Cunard Liner, tin, 1924, 44½x33½", VG.........**200.00**
Sign, Cunard Passenger Fleet, oil on board, 24x36" **115.00**
Soap, Holland Am Line, house logo, orig wrapper, M.....................**4.50**
Stationery, Franconia III portrait, 4 sheets.........................**5.00**
Stationery, Mauretania I, w/Cunard logo, 1 sheet....................**5.00**
Ticket, passenger's, France III, 1971, M in folder...........................**4.00**
Timetable, Kittie Hegler, Cincinnati to Kanawha River packet **7.00**
Vase, bud; Cunard Wht Star, metal, mk Chester EP Co, 7", pr ...**120.00**

Steins

Steins have been made from pottery, pewter, glass, stoneware, and porcelain, from very small up to the four-liter size. They are decorated by etching, in-mold relief, decals, and occasionally they may be hand painted. Some porcelain steins have lithophane bases. Collectors often specialize in a particular type – faience, regimental, or figural – while others limit themselves to the products of only one manufacturer.

Our advisor for this category is Ron Fox; he is listed in the Directory under New York. See also Mettlach.

Key:
L — liter
litho — lithophane
POG — print over glaze
PUG — print under glaze
tl — thumb lift

Character steins: Black Man, porcelain, .5L, small repaired chips, rare, $2,750.00; Gentleman Rabbit, Musterschutz, .5L, $2,500.00; Bison, E. Bohne, .5L, $1,900.00.

Brass & amber glass, ram finial, figural hdl, 1½-L, M...............**1,650.00**
Character, alligator, bsk, Bohne, ½-L, M...........................**695.00**
Character, alligator, porc, Schierholz, faint line, ½-L **580.00**
Character, Alpineman's head, porc, litho lines, ½-L **525.00**

Character, Austrian eagle, blown glass, ½-L, NM **175.00**
Character, barmaid, porc, Schierholz, chip rpr, ½-L **1,235.00**
Character, bearded knight, porc, ½-L, M...........................**880.00**
Character, Bismark as civilian, porc, Schierholz, ½-L, M **1,320.00**
Character, bison, bsk, Bohne, ¼-L, M..............................**850.00**
Character, Caroline, porc, Schierholz, ½-L, M.......................**635.00**
Character, cavalier, pottery, .3-L, M **495.00**
Character, Chinaman's head, porc, ½-L, M..........................**685.00**
Character, clown, stoneware, ½-L, M **635.00**
Character, drunken monkey, porc, Schierholz, ½-L, M **385.00**
Character, dwarf, pottery, DRGM #694, ½-L, M....................**440.00**
Character, eagle, HP on wht over clear glass, flake, ½-L...............**165.00**
Character, fraternal cat, Gerz #60, 1-L, M.........................**385.00**
Character, Frauenkirche tower, porc, inlay lid, ½-L, M **1,210.00**
Character, frog, porc, Schierholz, ½-L, M...........................**935.00**
Character, Indian, bsk, Bohne, faint line, ½-L......................**550.00**
Character, jester, pottery, DRGM #752, minor flakes, 2-L **1,045.00**
Character, lady & lion, pottery, Bavaria, chip/flakes, ½-L............**715.00**
Character, man drinking, blown glass, HP, 1-L, M ....:...........**220.00**
Character, military man, stoneware, ½-L, M.........................**495.00**
Character, Munich child, blown glass, HP, ½-L, M..................**195.00**
Character, Munich child, pewter, normal wear, ½-L **300.00**
Character, Munich child, porc, Joseph Mayer, 1-L, NM **400.00**
Character, Munich child, porc, ½-L, M.............................**270.00**
Character, pickle, porc, Schierholz, hdl line, ½-L **900.00**
Character, pixie, porc, Schierholz, ½-L, M..........................**685.00**
Character, rabbit, copper-plated pewter, rare, ½-L **350.00**
Character, rabbit, porc, Schierholz, ½-L, M **2,650.00**
Character, radish lady, porc, Schierholz, pnt wear, ½-L **1,980.00**
Character, Satan, bsk, Bohne, ½-L, M..............................**635.00**
Character, Scotsman, stoneware, cobalt glazed, ½-L, M **700.00**
Character, skull on book, bsk, Bohne, nose chip, ½-L.................**495.00**
Character, stag, bsk, Bohne, .3-L, M................................**330.00**
Character, student fox, pottery, DRGM #738, split tang, 2-L **825.00**
Character, target girl, porc, faint line/flake, ½-L **745.00**
Character, Turkish man, porc, Schierholz, sm chip rprs, ½-L **685.00**
Character, Von Moltke, porc, Schierholz, ½-L, M **1,320.00**
Character, wealthy German man, stoneware, cobalt, ½-L, EX.....**250.00**
Character, Wilhelm I, stoneware, int chip, ½-L **415.00**
Character, woman photo transfer on porc, ½-L, M **170.00**
Character, woman w/bird, blown milk glass, HP, ¾-L, M............**750.00**
Character, woman w/duck in mouth, pottery, DRGM #692, ½-L .**495.00**
Copper & brass, relief: Christ & Bible scenes, ½-L, EX **225.00**
Faience, bird & floral, Bayreuth, 1740s, mk BK, 1 ¼-L, VG ...**1,980.00**
Faience, Erfurt, sailing ships, 1780s, lines/rpr, ¾-L......................**855.00**
Faience, man w/cane, Thuringen, 1780s, pewter rprs, 1 ¼-L...**1,155.00**
Faience, Nurnberg, Virgin/angel/Holy Spirit, 1740s, 1 ¼-L.....**3,600.00**
Faience, rooster, Ansbach, ca 1760, 1-L, VG.........................**1,430.00**
Glass, blown, bl over clear, glass inlay lid, ½-L, M..................**1,320.00**
Glass, blown, bl stained cut to clear, .3-L, M.........................**440.00**
Glass, blown, cut stag & floral, base rim, 1760s, 2-L, M...............**550.00**
Glass, blown, gr, HP cavalier & knight, 2½-L, M................**440.00**
Glass, blown, gr prism lid, ½-L, NM................................**65.00**
Glass, blown, HP crest, Egerman, anchor mk, 1-L, M.................**770.00**
Glass, blown, HP crest, inlay lid, Egerman, rpl tl, 1-L...............**660.00**
Glass, blown, porc inlay of drinking dog, ½-L, M...................**175.00**
Glass, blown, ruby stain & enamel, Biedermeier period, ½-L **600.00**
Glass, blown, wheel-cut floral, postwar, ½-L, M **25.00**
Glass, blown, wht on cranberry, HP grapes, silver lid, ½-L **880.00**
Glass, blown, woman w/bustle figural lid, ½-L, M..................**465.00**
Glass, mold blown, amber, prism in lid, 1-L, M....................**465.00**
Glass, pressed, amber prism in lid, ½-L **55.00**
Glass, pressed, cranberry prism lid, ½-L, M **55.00**
Hafnerware, glazed, Sausage Krug, 1730, minor flakes, 1½-L **990.00**

Hafnerware, gr glaze, simple form, ca 1700, flakes, ¼-L **660.00**
Hafnerware, relief: folk heart art decor, 1810, 1-L **635.00**
Ivory, cvg: dog chases boar & stag, SP mts, rpr, 1½-L **1,760.00**
Naval, SMS Blitz Wilhelmshaven 1911-14, pottery, 1-L, NM .. **1,000.00**
Occupational, beer barrel wagon driver, porc, ½-L, NM **525.00**
Occupational, coach taxi driver, porc, litho lines, ½-L **525.00**
Occupational, farmer, blown glass, ½-L, M **350.00**
Occupational, farmer's supply house, porc, ½-L, M **440.00**
Occupational, fireman, pottery relief, helmet lid, ½-L **160.00**
Occupational, fireman on 60th birthday, pottery, HP, 2-L, M....**415.00**
Occupational, machinist, porc, ½-L, M **300.00**
Occupational, schoolteacher, porc, ½-L, rare, M **825.00**
Occupational, shoemaker, stoneware, glaze flakes, ½-L.............**355.00**
Pewter, eng: crest & name, old rpr, 1600s, 1-L **465.00**
Pewter, relief: castle scenes, lion tl, EX details, 2-L **550.00**
Pewter, relief: eagle, 4 ball ft, normal wear, 2-L **300.00**
Pewter, relief: Grambrinus, normal wear, ½-L **130.00**
Pewter, relief: target, normal wear, ½-L **110.00**
Porc, football scene, litho lines, ½-L, M **148.00**
Porc, horn shape w/relief boar, Schierholz, ¾-L, NM **715.00**
Porc, HP, strawberry on lid, Dresden, 1-L, M **1,800.00**
Porc, Karl Marx/Socialist Party litho, ½-L, M **290.00**
Porc, knight litho, hdl & base wear, ½-L **247.00**
Porc, relief: dancing couples, HR #131, ½-L, M **415.00**
Porc, relief: florals w/figural hunter inlay, ½-L, NM **148.00**
Porc, royal figures litho, ½-L, M **195.00**
Pottery, enameled: high-wheel bike rider, 3½-L, M.............**850.00**
Pottery, enameled: young couple, 2-L, M.............**330.00**
Pottery, etched: couple, HR #402, ½-L, M **269.00**
Pottery, etched: knights/horses, Marzi & Remy #1620, 1-L, M....**440.00**
Pottery, etched: soccer scene, Merlelbach & Wick, ½-L, M **240.00**
Pottery, POG: men fighting, ½-L, M **105.00**
Pottery, POG: Munich scene, relief Munich lid, ½-L, M **105.00**
Pottery, relief: dance scene, damaged tl, minor wear, 1-L **66.00**
Pottery, relief: drunks, postwar, 1-L, M.............**40.00**
Pottery, relief: guitar player, Gerz, 1-L, M **55.00**
Pottery, relief: Heidelberg, ½-L **110.00**
Pottery, relief: man, Whites Utica #37, 1½-L, M **135.00**
Pottery, relief: monk & men, postwar, ½-L, M.............**28.00**
Pottery, relief: Naval officer/ship, SP lid, rim rpr, ½-L.............**420.00**
Pottery, relief: Prussian/Swede battle scene, ½-L, M.............**170.00**
Pottery, relief: Viking feast, ½-L, M.............**280.00**
Regimental, Garde Train Batl Berlin 1909-11, porc, ½-L, M.......**685.00**
Regimental, Nazi Yager-99th Inft Lindau, porc, ½-L, M.............**525.00**
Regimental, 11 Sea Batl Wilhelmshaven 1907-10, pottery, ½-L . **1,200.00**
Regimental, 12 Pionier Ulm 1910-12, roster, porc, ½-L, M.........**660.00**
Regimental, 14 Ulan St Avold 1905-08, helmet lid, porc, ½-L ..**770.00**
Regimental, 15 Hussar Wandsbek 1906-09, porc, ½-L, M.............**635.00**
Regimental, 2 Chev Regt Dillinger 1890-93, porc, ½-L, M **440.00**
Regimental, 2 Garde Ulan Rerlin 1907-10, pottery, 1-L, M.... **1,100.00**
Regimental, 20 Pionier Metz 1907-09, porc, ½-L, M **465.00**
Regimental, 21 Saxon Ulan Cemnik 1905-08, porc, ½-L, M.......**660.00**
Regimental, 23 Garde Drag Darmstadt 1907-10, ½-L, M **685.00**
Regimental, 3 Eisenbahn Berlin 1908-10, train finial, ½-L **1,540.00**
Regimental, 76 Field Art Freiburg 1903-05, porc, ½-L, M **580.00**
Regimental, 9 Drag Regt Metz 1902-05, pottery, ½-L, M.............**685.00**
Silver, hand hammered, Adam & Eve/Bible scenes, 18"..........**3,410.00**
Silver, relief: floral, waisted form, Sterling, ½-L, M **1,430.00**
SP, relief: outdoor feast, 1-L, EX.............**495.00**
SP brass, relief: children w/animals, ½-L.............**230.00**
SP brass, relief: orgy scene, rare, 1-L **990.00**
Stoneware, appl relief: fox hunt, brass lid, 1800s, 1½-L, VG **250.00**
Stoneware, Bartman Krug, ca 1600, 1½-L, EX **715.00**
Stoneware, building scenes, Westerwald, 1720s, tl rpr, 1-L.......**1,100.00**

Stoneware, cutwork: Kruessen, 1640s, 1700s lid, ½-L, EX **1,100.00**
Stoneware, enameled: Imperial eagle/Frankfurt, '08, ½-L, M.........**250.00**
Stoneware, Munich child scene, relief Munich lid, ½-L, M.........**180.00**
Stoneware, POG: babies drinking, ½-L, M **115.00**
Stoneware, POG: German auto club, matching lid, ½-L, M.........**198.00**
Stoneware, POG: student scenes/crest/roster, ½-L, M **145.00**
Stoneware, POG: Wilhelm II, ½-L, M **285.00**
Stoneware, PUG: Nurnberg, postwar, ½-L.............**66.00**
Stoneware, relief: Bishop on horse, Annaberg, 1680s, 1¼-L ... **3,300.00**
Stoneware, relief: dwarfs ride frogs, ½-L, NM **198.00**
Stoneware, relief: HP monkeys, porc inlay, ½-L, M **180.00**
Stoneware, relief: man w/2 drinking babies, ½-L, M **148.00**
Stoneware, scratch decor/appl relief, Westerwald, 1750s, 1-L . **1,100.00**
Stoneware, slip decor: Bunzlau marriage knot, 1750, 3-L, EX . **1,200.00**
Wood, cvd: florals, ca 1780, minor rpr, 1-L.............**660.00**

Steuben

The Steuben Glass Works of Corning, New York, was founded in 1903 by Frederick Carder and Thomas Hawkes. They made art glass of high quality similar to some of Tiffany's. One of their earliest types was Aurene, a lustrous metallic gold or blue. They also made Verre de Soie, Rosaline, and Silverene as well as other unique types of art glass. In 1918 Steuben became a branch of Corning Glass Works.

In the listings that follow, examples are signed unless noted otherwise. See also Aurene; Cluthra.

Key: ACB — acid cut back

Ash tray, sloping bowl form, sgn, 5" **75.00**
Bottle, scent; cobalt, emb fleur-de-lis, +stopper, #1455 ....**950.00**
Bottle, scent; dk topaz, sq, #6590, w/#7175 stopper, 5" **285.00**
Bottle, scent; Verre de Soie w/Jade Gr stopper, #1455, 4¾" **325.00**
Bowl, amethyst, cut galleons ea side, clear sq base, 20" L........ **1,000.00**
Bowl, amethyst, ribbed, ped ft, 4¾" **125.00**
Bowl, bl, 3 appl ft, sgn Carder, 3x12" **850.00**
Bowl, bl Aurene on Calcite, 12" **495.00**
Bowl, centerpc; Matsu-no-ke, bl appl on clear, #3302.............**550.00**
Bowl, gold Aurene on Calcite, #3200, 2¾x6¼" **180.00**
Bowl, gr on Rosalene base w/3 gr prunts, 9½" dia.............**400.00**
Bowl, Grotesque, amethyst to clear, ruffled/sqd, 4¾".............**425.00**
Bowl, Grotesque, gr to clear, 4-sided freeform, 4¾" **325.00**
Bowl, Grotesque, shaded purple rim, quatrefoil, 4¾" **325.00**
Bowl, Grotesque, 5x9" **250.00**
Bowl, Ivorene, sgn/#7563, 6x13½" L **350.00**
Bowl, Jade Gr, Alabaster base, orig Corning label, 5x12" **375.00**
Bowl, Tyrian, bl-gold lily pads/threading on purple, 5x7½" ...**10,500.00**
Bowl vase, ACB, sea holly, Jade Gr to Alabaster, 7" **550.00**
Buttonhook, amber w/Celeste Bl knob, 5½".............**275.00**
Candlestick, bell form bases, air-trap knop, 8½", pr **375.00**
Candlestick, Jade Gr & Alabaster, unsgn, 11¾" **210.00**
Candlestick, lt amber twist on clear hollow stem, 10", pr **425.00**
Candlestick, Selenium Red, twist stem, sgn, 10" **350.00**
Champagne, Jade Gr, Alabaster twist stem, 5½" **125.00**
Cocktail, lt gr bowl & wafer base, Celeste Bl twist stem **75.00**
Compote, apricot bowl, Alabaster stem & base, 4½" **200.00**
Compote, Verre de Soie, Cyprian edge/bl hdl accents, 10x12"....**800.00**
Creamer & sugar, swirled, Celeste Bl ped ft & hdls.............**450.00**
Cup & saucer, Rosaline, Alabaster hdl, unsgn.............**150.00**
Figurine, Buddha, Pomona Gr on blk plinth, 8½", EX **475.00**
Figurine, Fisherman, Eskimo fishing through ice, 6½" **2,200.00**
Figurine, horse's head, Waugh, 5".............**250.00**
Figurine, penguin, sgn in script, 3½".............**150.00**

Figurine, songbird, sgn, #8112, 4½" L 250.00
Flower holder, creamy ivory crystal, 3-trunk form, 6" 600.00
Goblet, Oriental Poppy, Pomona Gr ped ft, 8" 600.00
Goblet, ribbed bl crystal w/swirl ribbed stem, sgn, 8½" 95.00
Goblet, Rosaline, etched vintage, Alabaster stem/ft, 7½" 425.00
Goblet, Selenium Red, clear stem, sgn, 6½" 195.00
Jar, Rosaline, Alabaster finial & base, 4x3" 300.00
Lamp, ACB, bl Aurene drips on Jade Yel, 4-cherub std, 24" .. 2,395.00
Lamp base, ACB, horses/gold Aurene drips on yel, 17" 3,500.00
Paperweight/doorstop, 5 lg+sm bubbles, 4x5¾" 125.00
Plaque, amber, kneeling nude in bower picks grapes, 9x6" 13,000.00
Plate, Calcite w/gold Aurene casing, stretched edges, 8½" 175.00
Plate, gr, eng leaves/flowers, unmk, 8½" 15.00
Shade, ACB, Ivorene, 5½x8", pr 280.00
Sherbet, Jade Gr, Alabaster stem & ft, 4", +6¼" plate 120.00
Sherbet, Rosaline, Alabaster twist ped ft 150.00
Sherbet, Verre de Soie, eng decor, 3¾" 45.00
Sherbet & underplate, bl Aurene on Calcite.........................275.00
Sugar bowl, bubbly glass, gr reeding at top, 2-hdl, 3¾x4".............85.00
Tazza, Calcite on bl Aurene, 6x6" 800.00
Tazza, Calcite on gold Aurene, 6x6" 375.00
Tazza, Gold Ruby bowl/ped ft, ribbed amber stem, 7" H 350.00
Torchere, Jade Yel trumpet shade; wrought std w/gargoyles 2,200.00
Tumbler, Calcite w/gold Aurene int, set of 8.....................1,200.00
Tumbler, lemonade; Jade Gr, Alabaster hdl, 5¾" 110.00
Vanity set, Rosaline/Alabaster, 3 scent bottles/jar/box 600.00

Jack-in-the-pulpit, cranberry, old mark, ca 1910, 16", $1,100.00.

Vase, ACB, birds/shrubs, Jade Gr to Alabaster, baluster, 9" 1,100.00
Vase, ACB, gold w/textured rose band, sgn/#20170-7½, 7".....1,700.00
Vase, ACB, mums/zigzags, Rose Quartz, flat-side pear, 13" 2,600.00
Vase, ACB, Nedra, gr on Alabaster, bowl form, 7" 1,100.00
Vase, ACB, Oriental flowers, bl Aurene on Jade Yel, 8" 1,900.00
Vase, ACB, pussy willow trees, blk on Jade Wht, ovoid, 6" ...1,200.00
Vase, ACB, trees/geese, wine on frosted Cintra, hdls, 13" 3,300.00
Vase, amethyst, swirled, hexagonal top, clear rnd base, 10".........250.00
Vase, bud; Verre de Soie, eng floral, #2556 shape, 8¼" 175.00
Vase, Calcite, gold int, ftd lily form, 10" 375.00
Vase, Celeste Bl, int ribbing, ped base, 6x4" 100.00
Vase, Celeste Bl w/topaz base, vertical ribs, block mk, 16" 325.00
Vase, controlled bubbles, heavy pk threading, ruffled, 7" 150.00
Vase, cornucopia form, sgn/#7730, 6½", pr...........................200.00
Vase, Dia Quilt, yel w/wht threading at flared rim, 9", NM........125.00
Vase, expanded diamonds, gr-threaded trumpet neck, 14"...........250.00

Vase, gr, swirled, fan form, fleur-de-lis mk, 7¾" 145.00
Vase, gr, 3-lobe, ribbed, ball stem/ft, #6441, sgn, 10" 175.00
Vase, Grotesque, 10" 195.00
Vase, Intarsia, pk on clear, sgn Carder, ftd, 8" 2,500.00
Vase, Ivorene, flared inverted rim on ftd urn form, 12", pr 475.00
Vase, Ivorene, ribbed, ftd, sgn Steuben/Carder, 9" 250.00
Vase, ivory, Jade Blk ft, ribbed, 9" 375.00
Vase, ivory w/blk hdls, baluster form, 11" 700.00
Vase, Jade Gr, #6171, 9x8" 195.00
Vase, Jade Gr, Alabaster ft, slim form, 12½" 150.00
Vase, Jade Gr, Alabaster upright hdls, classic form, 10" 600.00
Vase, Selenium Red, Hawkes vintage-cut border, 12" 150.00
Vase, Selenium Red, wide trumpet form, 7½x8" 150.00
Vase, Silverene, air-trap pattern, bulbous, 12", NM.................700.00
Wine, ribbed crystal, purple swirl stem, mk, +7" underplate 110.00

Stevengraph

A Stevengraph is a small picture made of woven silk resembling an elaborate ribbon, created by Thomas Stevens in England in the latter half of the 1800s. They were matted and framed by Stevens, usually with his name appearing on the mat or, more commonly, the trade announcement on the back of the mat. He also produced silk post cards and bookmarks, all of which have 'Stevens' woven in silk on one of the mitered corners.

Anyone wishing to learn more about Stevengraphs is encouraged to contact the Stevengraph Collectors' Association, whose address can be found in the Directory under Clubs, Newsletters, and Catalogs.

Are You Ready?...135.00
Banner, Am flag, eagle shield, Lincoln portrait 110.00
Bookmark, Birthday Gift 50.00
Bookmark, coach scene 95.00
Bookmark, Geo Washington, 1876 Centennial, M 135.00
Bookmark, Happy May Thy Birthday Be 65.00
Bookmark, Happy New Year..50.00
Bookmark, Home Sweet Home 65.00
Bookmark, Little Bo-Peep 50.00
Bookmark, Moses in the Bullrushes 115.00
Bookmark, Norwich Conn, 250th Anniversary 50.00
Bookmark, Remember Me 65.00
Bookmark, Sir Garibaldi 90.00
Bookmark, To My Father...40.00
Bookmark, Unchanging Love 28.00
Bookmark, Washington's portrait, 9¼" 125.00
Called to the Rescue..125.00
Crystal Palace, orig mat 285.00
Death of Nelson..150.00
Declaration of Independence, from 1893 Columbian Expo 195.00
Finish, The; horserace 145.00
First Touch...365.00
For Life or Death, Heroism on Land, orig mat & fr.................350.00
Fourth Bridge 365.00
Full Cry..145.00
Good Old Days, orig mat & label....................................195.00
Grace Darling 85.00
Lady Godiva Procession, orig mat, EX 125.00
Last Lap, bicycles..265.00
London & York Royal Mailcoach, orig mat, EX 125.00
Present Time..365.00
Procession 175.00
Struggle 150.00
Wellington & Blugher...150.00

The First Train, $595.00.

Stevens and Williams

Stevens and Williams glass was produced at the Brierly Hill Glassworks in Stourbridge, England, for nearly a century, beginning in the 1830s. They were credited with being among the first to develop a method of manufacturing a more affordable type of cameo glass. Other lines were also made – silver deposit, alexandrite, and engraved rock crystal, to name but a few.

Our advisor for this category is Don Williams; he is listed in the Directory under Iowa.

Biscuit jar, pk overlay, appl leaves, SP rim/lid/hdl, 7¾"................275.00
Bottle, scent; bl swirl w/berries, gold trim, 13" 325.00
Bottle, scent; gr, intaglio floral, silver stopper, 8x3" 195.00
Bowl, cream opaque, appl florals, amber ft, rigaree, 4½x5½" 450.00
Bowl, wht w/florals, bl int, amber ft & crimped rim, 6x7½" 325.00
Rose bowl, aqua opal swirl, pleated top, unlined, 3¾x4⅜"..........195.00
Rose bowl, brn shaded to gold, pleated top, 3¼x4⅛" 225.00
Rose bowl, gold prunus on brn, pleated egg form, 6x5½" 475.00
Sherbet, bl w/clear intaglio fruit, 5", +underplate 295.00
Tumbler, amber w/appl pear & apple on branch, 3¾x3¼" 225.00
Vase, bl to wht satin, basketweave, folded/crimped rim, 7" 450.00
Vase, bl/wht/clear stripes, 3-sided, satin ft, 7½" 340.00
Vase, cream, pk int, amber ruffle/ft, appl mc leaves, 6¼" 195.00
Vase, cream, 3 lg amber leaves, amber ruffle top, 7", pr 300.00
Vase, intaglio flowers w/appl centers, Carder, ftd, 10"................745.00
Vase, lav opaque, long cylinder neck w/appl rigaree, 18".............195.00
Vase, MOP, orange/gold swirls, bl int, stick neck, 10"................450.00
Vase, pk, appl amber leaves/pk flowers, ruffled, 6¼x3¾" 150.00
Vase, tan/yel/bl swirl w/enamel decor on bottle neck, 13" 275.00
Vase, wht, pk int, in amber: leaves/acorns/5 ft, 9"........................165.00

Cameo

Vase, floral, bk: fern, wht on red, 13½" 3,600.00
Vase, floral, wht on amber/peach, stick neck w/band, 12"....... 6,000.00
Vase, floral/3 butterflies, wht on med bl, bottle form, 9" 2,500.00

Stickley

Among the leading proponents of the Arts and Crafts Movement, the Stickley brothers – Gustav, Leopold, Charles, Albert, and John George – were at various times and locations involved in designing and producing furniture as well as decorative items for the home. (See Arts and Crafts for further information.)

The oldest of the five Stickley brothers was Gustav; his work is the most highly regarded of all. He developed the style of furniture referred to as Mission. It was strongly influenced by the type of furnishings found in the Spanish missions of California – utilitarian, squarely built, and simple. It was made most often of oak, and decoration was very limited or non-existent. The work of his brothers display adaptations of many of Gustav's ideas and designs. His factory, the Craftsman Shops, operated in Eastwood, New York, from the late 1890s until 1915, when he was forced out of business by larger companies who copied his work and sold it at much lower prices. Among his shopmarks are the early red decal containing a joiner's compass and the words 'Als Ik Kan,' the branded mark with very similar components, and paper labels.

The firm known as Stickley Brothers was located first in Binghampton, New York, and then Grand Rapids, Michigan. Albert and John made the move to Michigan, leaving Charles in Binghamton (where he and an uncle continued the operation under a different name). After several years, John George left the company to rejoin Leopold in New York. (These two later formed their own firm called L. & J.G. Stickley.) The Stickley Brothers Company, under Albert's sole direction, produced furniture that featured fine inlay work, decorative cutouts, and leaned strongly toward a style of Arts and Crafts with an English influence. It was tagged with a paper label 'Made by Stickley Brothers, Grand Rapids' or with a brass plate or decal with the words 'Quaint Furniture,' an English term he chose to refer to his product. In addition to his furniture, he made metal furnishings as well.

The workshops of the L. & J.G. Stickley Company operated under the name 'Onandaga Shops.' Located in Fayetteville, New York, their designs were often all but copies of Gustav's work. Their products were well made and marketed, and their business was very successful. Their marks were decals containing all or a combination of the words Handcraft or Onandaga Shops, along with the brothers' initials and last name. The firm continues in business today.

Note: when only one dimension is given for tables, it is length.

Gustav Stickley

Armchair #312, vertical 5-slat bk, no mk, rpl seat, 6 for 2,700.00
Armchair #376, mahog, spindled high bk/sides, decal, oiled ..11,000.00
Ash tray, hammered copper, 4 repousse hearts on rim, 5½" 185.00
Bed #923, single, head/ft brd: 3 wide slats, branded, EX 1,500.00
Bookcase #703, mahog, 3 glass panels ea door, 58x60", EX 11,000.00
Bookcase #715, 1-door, V-brd bk/chamfered sides, unsgn, 65".. 1,750.00
Bookcase #718, 2-door/24-pane, V-pulls, rfn, 56x54", VG...... 2,500.00
Box #95, shirtwaist; recessed lid panel, cedar lined, 32" 2,500.00
Candelabrum, copper, 2-arm, hammered base, 6x6¾", pr 350.00
Candle holder, hammered copper, dish base, strap hdl, 9x7" 375.00
Cellarette #86, 1-drw/1-do, tray revolves in base, rstr/rfn 1,950.00
Chair #306, ladderbk, rush seat, 35", pr 250.00
Chair #308, rush seat, red decal, 1908, 40" 240.00
Chair #324, fixed back, red decal, new leather/varnish, EX 1,200.00
Chair #349-½, ladderbk, orig tacked leather seat, set of 4 .... 1,950.00
Chest of drw #602, 2 over 4 graduaded drw, sgn, 54x40" 4,250.00
China cabinet #815, 2-door/V-pulls, mk/label, 64x42", EX..... 5,750.00
China cabinet #902, 9-pane door, trapezoidal, no mk, 65x37" 14,000.00
Clock, rectangular oak case w/ldgl window, 14x9x5" 3,000.00
Day bed, 6 vertical slats on high end, ca 1901, no mk, 79" 750.00
Dining table #656, ped base, label, 54" dia, +4 leaves, NM..... 3,850.00
Footstool #302, red decal, orig leather/finish, EX 700.00
Footstool #728, rush seat, orig blk finish, unmk, 17x18x18" ... 1,600.00
Game table #419, pnt chess brd/leather top, unmk, varnished . 3,600.00
Lamp #50, hammered copper base, rpl wicker shade, sgn, 21". 3,450.00
Lantern #205, copper w/heart cutouts, glass cylinder, pr..........6,300.00
Library table #421, heavy post legs, decal, varnished, EX 950.00
Library table #613, hammered pulls, rfn, 30x36" top, VG 1,150.00
Library table #650, hidden drw, decal, rfn, 36", VG 800.00
Magazine rack #79, orig finish, w/decal, EX 1,600.00

Magazine stand, tree of life cvg, for Tobey Co, rfn, 19x14".........800.00
Mirror #68, oak, 3-section, 4 iron hooks, label/rfn, 28x48" 1,500.00
Morris chair #332, 5-slat sides, rope seat, re-uphl/rfn............... 4,100.00
Morris chair #367, slant arms, 18-spindle sides, re-uphl 9,000.00
Morris chair #369, drop arm/5-slat sides, unmk, rfn/uphl 4,500.00
Music stand #674, 5 spindles at side/7 in bk, label, 42" 7,250.00
Office chair #362, revolving, orig leather/finish, no mk................900.00
Piano bench #217, cut-out hdls on solid sides, branded, 37" ... 1,500.00
Plant stand, key-tenoned stretcher, decal, rfn, 20x18x18" 800.00
Porch lantern, 4 amber hammered glass panels, no mk, 22"... 6,000.00
Rocker #311, V-bk, red decal, orig finish/rpl rush seat.................450.00
Settee, cube, 30-spindle bk/15 ea side, mk, rpl seat, 35" 25,000.00
Settee #286, spindle bk/spindles ea side, rfn, unmk, 49x48"...15,000.00
Settle, 49-spindle bk/17 ea side, decal, re-uphl, 78" 45,000.00
Settle #172, experimental, ca 1901-1903, rfn/uphl, 56" L 2,150.00
Settle #225, 2 wide horizontal bk slats, 5-slat sides, 79" 6,000.00
Sideboard #814, strap hinges/V-pulls, plate rail, mk/label....... 4,000.00
Sideboard #891, 3 drw over 1, decal, orig finish/hdw, 48" 3,250.00
Stand, hidden drw/tapered ft, Quaint tag, varnish, 16" top 850.00
Table #611, canted corner 24" top, shelf, no mk, rfn, 29" 1,000.00
Table #633, 40" dia top, arched X-stretchers, decal, EX 3,400.00
Table #638, gate-leg dropleaf/cut corner, label, rfn, 42" 950.00
Table #644, thru tenons/posts, branded, rfn, 30" dia, VG........ 2,400.00
Table #651, stretcher dbl-keyed, label/brand, rfn, 48" L................850.00
Tabouret, arched stretcher, unmk, orig finish, 16x14" dia 475.00
Tabouret #53T, Grueby tile inlay, label, 17" sq top, EX..........15,000.00
Tabouret #601, notched stretchers, no mk, 14" top, VG 400.00
Tabouret #604, w/o thru tenons, paper label, rfn, VG.................750.00
Tankard, hammered copper w/wrought iron hdls, 11" 600.00
Tray, hammered copper/new patina, mk, 13" dia 400.00
Tray #354, copper/new patina, undulating sides, mk, 24x10" 950.00
Umbrella stand #54, 4 posts, open sides, label, rfn, 29"...............425.00
Vase, hammered copper, orig patina, 10½"..................................900.00

L. & J.G. Stickley

Armchair #816, branded mk, orig finish, EX...............................215.00
Book table #516, 7-slat/open-shelf sides, decal, 27" sq top 9,000.00
Bookcase #328, 2 12-pane do, Onandaga Shops, no mk, rpr ... 2,500.00
Bookcase #641, 1-door w/16 panes, gallery, Handcraft, 55" 3,200.00
Catalog, furniture, Art Press Co, 1910, EX.................................100.00

L. & J.G. Stickley flat-top writing desk #503, signed 'The Work of....,' 40" long, $475.00.

Dinner gong, in arched fr w/shoe ft, Handicraft, 34" 8,500.00
Footstool #1292, tacked leather top/7-spindle sides, mk, M 2,750.00
Footstool #391, Handicraft decal, orig finish/leather, 19" 550.00
Grandfather's clock, copper face/glass panel, sgn, rfn, 80"......10,000.00
Lamp table, overhanging 18" dia top, no mk, orig finish 700.00
Magazine rack #547, 4-shelf, flaring sides, Handicraft, 42"...... 1,600.00
Magazine stand #345, 4-shelf, chamfered bk, no mk, rfn, 45" . 1,300.00

Morris chair, 5-slat sides, recovered seat/oiled finish................ 2,000.00
Morris chair #471, 6-slat sides, no mk, new leather, VG 1,300.00
Plaque #344, hammered copper, 4 repousse spades, att, 15" ... 1,800.00
Rocker #401, bent arm, orig cushions/finish, decal, EX.......... 2,550.00
Rocker #475, 2 corbels under 6-slat sides, needs cushion.............950.00
Screen, 3-fold, panels w/prints, slatted base, att, 52x70" 1,100.00
Server #752, 2 lower shelves, Handicraft decal, 38x40" 2,000.00
Settle #263, drop arms, 7-rail bk, no mk, rfn, 77" 2,500.00
Table #578, cut corners/thru tenons, decal, 24" dia, G................650.00
Table #597, hidden drw, Onondaga Shops label, 40", EX 1,050.00
Tabouret, cut corners/thru posts, branded, rfn, 17x15" W...........550.00
Tabouret #515, rimmed/8-sided 20" top, Handicraft, 24" 1,200.00
Tabouret #559, legs mortised thru rfn 8-sided top, no mk 700.00
Tea table #579, arched X-stretchers support 2nd tier, unmk 550.00

Stickley Bros.

Armchair, leather bk/seat, Macmurdo-style ft, rfn, 36"..................85.00
Armchair, vertical 4-slat high-bk, corbels under arms, rfn 210.00
Candlestick #313, brass cylinder w/brass band, 12" 300.00
Catalog, Quaint Furniture, Grand Rapids Eng Co, VG................125.00
Desk, slant top w/gallery, simple inlay, Quaint, 42x36" W 1,100.00
Dining table #2640, 5 str legs, 1 leaf, w/tag, 48" dia, VG......... 1,300.00
Jardiniere, hammered copper, oblongs in relief, #209, 9x12" 475.00
Magazine rack #4602, 5-shelf, slat sides/bk, sgn, 51", EX 900.00
Table #2694, thru tenons, notched ft, sm shelf, 40" dia, VG 575.00
Tabouret, thru tenons, att, rfn, 19x16" dia, VG.............................250.00
Tabouret #314½, thru/top-flush posts, Quaint, 18x15", VG 900.00

Stiegel

Baron Henry Stiegel produced glassware in Pennsylvania as early as 1760, very similar to glass being made concurrently in Germany and England. Without substantiating evidence, it is impossible to positively attribute a specific article to his manufacture. Although he made other types of glass, today the term Stiegel generally refers to any very early ware made in shapes and colors similar to those he is known to have produced – especially that with etched or enameled decoration. It is generally conceded, however, that most glass of this type is of European origin.

Bottle, bride's; 2 lg HP figures, 8½", NM 225.00
Bottle, cordial; mc bird & floral, 6½" 275.00
Bottle, pocket; gray/amethyst tint, daisy in hexagon, 6" 650.00
Bottle, pocket; sapphire bl, right swirl, pontil, 5½".................. 1,050.00
Bowl, cobalt, expanded dmn, rnd ft extension, 4¾".....................525.00
Bowl, emerald, paneled, 5"..500.00
Decanter, tulip plant eng, NM stopper, 12" 475.00
Flask, dk amethyst, sheared lip, pontil, att, ½-pt.........................500.00
Flip, 12-panel, eng geometric band, pontil, 6" 95.00
Goblet, lovebird eng, tooled stem, 6¾" 200.00
Salt, master; cobalt, expanded dmn, rim ground..........................60.00
Sugar bowl, cobalt, 18 vertical ribs, Dia Quilt lid, 4½" 250.00

Stocks and Bonds

Scripophily (scrip-awfully), the collecting of 'worthless' old stocks and bonds, gained recognition as a serious collectible around the mid-1970s. Today there are an estimated 5,000 collectors in the United States and 15,000 world-wide. Collectors who come from numerous business fields mainly enjoy the hobby aspect, though there are those who consider scripophily an investment. Some collectors like the historical significance that certain certificates have. Others prefer the beauty of older stocks and bonds that were printed in various colors with fancy artwork and ornate engravings. Even autograph collectors are found in this field, on the lookout for signed certificates.

Many factors help determine the collector value: autograph value, age of the certificate, the industry represented, whether it is issued or not, its attractiveness, condition, and collector demand. Certificates from the mining, energy, and railroad industries are the most popular with collectors. Other industries or special collecting fields include banking, automobiles, aircraft, and territorials. Serious collectors usually prefer only issued certificates that date from before 1930. Unissued certificates are usually worth one-fourth to one-eighth the value of one that has been issued. A formal collecting organization for scripophilists is known as The Bond & Share Society with an American chapter located in New York City.

In many of the following listings, two-letter state abbreviations immediately follow company name. All are in near-mint condition unless noted otherwise.

Our advisor for this category is Warren Anderson; he is listed in the Directory under Utah.

Key:
cp — coupon   U — unissued
I/C — issued/cancelled   vgn — vignette
I/U — issued/uncancelled

Am-Hawaiian Steamships, steamer/sailing ship vgn, 1906, I/C **32.00**
Arkansas War Bond, 1861, $5, w/10 coupons, I...............................**38.00**
B&O RR, 1900, train vgn, common stock, 7x10", I/C **10.00**
Baltimore & Ohio, 1870s, train vgn, 7x9" **18.00**
Binghamton Copper, AZ/1919, miners vgn, I/C............................**10.00**
Blue Bird Oil, TX/1923, oilfield vgn, bird border, I/U **50.00**
Cedar Falls & Minnesota RR, ca 1864, 3 vgns on gr, U **45.00**
Chicago & Canada Southern RR, 1880, train vgn, U....................**27.50**
City Railway of Dayton OH, 1903, fine artwork, I/C **8.00**
Commerce Exchange Bldg, LA/1928, $1000 bond, eagle vgn, I **6.50**
Confederate States of America, $500, gr print, EX **85.00**
Dayton Street Railway, OH/1909, ornate lettering, 9x11" **10.00**
Easteon Branch RR, ca 1850, bl print on bl, U **9.50**
Flint & Pere Marquette RR, 1881, train/bridge vgn, ABNCo, I **35.00**
Gulf, Mobile & OH, 1945-1954, speeding train vgn, I/U **10.00**
Gulf & Chicago RR, 1903, train/Indian vgn, U **10.00**
IA Central Air Line RR, IA, 1857, plain face stock, 5x7" **25.00**
IL Central RR, 1959, 2 trains & figures in vgn, I **3.50**
Kansas & Texas RR, MO/1903, train vgn, common stock, I/U.......**8.00**
Long Island Nat'l Bank of NY, 1920s, eagle on rock vgn.................**4.00**
Lost Lode Gold Mining, WA, 1898, prospector vgn, I/U **30.00**
Marietta & Cincinnati RR, Chillicothe, dtd 1860 ....**18.00**
MI Central RR, 1896, $5000 registered bond, train vgn, U **32.00**
MO, KS, & TX RR, 1886, sgn Geo Gould, cattle vgn, I/C **18.00**
MO, KS, & TX RR, 1920s, surveyors vgn, I/C **12.50**
New Orleans Great Northern RR, 1913, train vgn, I/C **12.00**
Nuestra Senora del Refugio Silver, CA/1863, vgn, I/C **85.00**
Oconee & Western RR, GA/1893, train vgn, I **35.00**
Ohio Canal, 1842, 4 detailed vgns, I...**180.00**
Old Colony Steamboat, 1889, $5000, steamer vgn, ABNCo, I ...**150.00**
Pacific Mining, CA/1875, ornate artwork, blk on yel, 4x9" **60.00**
Peerless Motor Car, 1930, beehive/factory vgn, I/C.........................**22.00**
Penn-Yann Mining, 1880s, 9 US gold & silver coins vgn, U **50.00**
People's Railway Co of Dayton OH, 1900, streetcar vgn, EX **12.50**
People's Traction Co of Phila, PA/1894, streetcar vgn **10.00**
Sentinel Radio, IL/1945-52, goddess/radio tower vgn, I/U **7.00**
Tuscarora Mines, Elko County NV, 1880s, 4½x9½", U, M............**8.00**
Windsor Oil & Gas, MI/1887, $25 underprint w/gold seal, I/U **35.00**

Stockton

The Stockton Terra Cotta Company was established in 1891 in Stockton, California. In 1879 the name was changed to Stockton Art Pottery Company, and several lines of art pottery, the Rekston line among them, were introduced. Their wares included vases, pitchers, jardinieres, umbrella stands, and teapots – many of which were styled with scrolling ornate handles and graceful shapes. Some examples bear the 'Rekston' mark. The pottery closed in 1902 after a third devastating fire that destroyed their buildings.

Pitcher, gr gloss w/gold trim, very early, mk, 4½" **325.00**
Vase, floral w/tigereye crystals, ruffled/bulbous, 5½" **250.00**
Vase, florals, flattened upright half-moon form, 10x9½".............**375.00**

Stoneware

There are three broad periods of time that collectors of American pottery can look to in evaluating and dating the stoneware and earthenware in their collections. Among the first permanent settlers in America were English and German potters who found a great demand for their individually-turned wares. The early pottery was produced from red and yellow clays scraped from the ground at surface levels. The earthenware made in these potteries was fragile and coated with lead glazes that periodically created health problems for the people who ate or drank from it. There was little stoneware available for sale until the early 1800s, because the clays used in its production were not readily available in many areas and transportation was prohibitively expensive. The opening of the Erie Canal and improved roads brought about a dramatic increase in the accessibility of stoneware clay, and many new potteries began to open in New York and New England.

Collectors have difficulty today locating earthenware and stoneware jugs produced prior to 1840, because few have survived intact. These ovoid or pear-shaped jugs were designed to be used on a daily basis. When cracked or severely chipped, they were quickly discarded.

The value of hand-crafted pottery is often determined by the cobalt decoration it carries. Pieces with elaborate scenes (a chicken pecking corn, a bluebird on a branch, a stag standing near a pine tree, a sailing ship, or people) may easily bring $1,000 to $12,000 at auction.

After the Civil War, there was a need and a national demand for stoneware jugs, crocks, canning jars, churns, spittoons, and a wide variety of other pottery items. The competition among the many potteries reached the point where only the largest could survive. To cut costs, most potteries did away with all but the simplest kinds of decoration on their wares. Time-consuming brush-painted birds or flowers quickly gave way to more simply-executed swirls or numbers and stenciled designs. The coming of home refrigeration and Prohibition in 1919 effectively destroyed the American stoneware industry.

Investment possibilities: 1) Early 19th-century stoneware with elaborate decorations and a potter's mark is expensive and will continue to rise in price. 2) Late 19th century hand-thrown stoneware with simple cobalt swirls or numbers is still reasonably priced and a good investment. 3) Mass-produced stoneware (ca. 1890-1920) is available in large quantities, inexpensive, and has been slowly increasing in price over the last ten years.

Due to the steadily increasing values of decorated stoneware, new stoneware is appearing at antique markets in the east and midwest. Pieces seen so far are crocks (2-gallon and smaller) and batter jugs. These are decorated with cobalt birds, flowers, cows, fish, men, and hearts. The body of the piece is whiter than antique stoneware and the brushed cobalt decoration is paler blue than the old. When a new piece is 'pinged' with the finger, it will ring in a much higher tone than an old one. Some reproduction stoneware is dated on the bottom. The Beaumont Pottery of York, Maine, which produced the 'finest reproduction stoneware of the 20th century,' scratched the date into each piece.

Many skillfully repaired pieces are also surfacing, and prices should reflect that condition. Look for a slight change in color and texture. The use of a black light is also useful in exposing some repairs. Buyer beware! Hint: Buy only from reputable dealers who will guarantee their merchandise.

In the following listings, 'c/s' means 'cobalt on salt glaze'; all decoration described before this abbreviation is in cobalt. See also Bennington.

Bank, mottle/ 'Cora,' brushed, c/s, beehive form, 5", EX..............275.00
Bottle, pig form, Albany slip, 7" L, EX..............275.00
Bottle, pig form, Albany slip w/blk daubs, prof rpr, 5" L 250.00
Bottle, pig form, daubs, c/s, 6", VG..............950.00
Butter stamp, dots/lines, c/s, swirl, brn slip, 4½" 1,400.00
Cheese drainer, brn glaze, cylindrical, 13x6½" 65.00
Churn, bird on leaf/#4, c/s, J Burger Jr, w/top, 16", EX 1,700.00
Churn, floral, brushed, c/s, IM Meade & Co, 24", EX..............275.00
Churn, floral, brushed, c/s, ovoid, 17", EX..............450.00
Cooler, emb bands, c/s, keg shape, 22"..............425.00
Cooler, foliage/cvd horse, c/s, 4-ftd, 8x12"..............750.00
Crock, bird on branch, c/s, Fuller Bros, 11", EX..............250.00
Crock, bird on branch, c/s, Haxstun & Co, 10", EX 425.00
Crock, bird on branch, c/s, Ottman Bros, 12", EX..............450.00
Crock, brushed design, c/s, 13"..............145.00
Crock, eagle, c/s, Hamilton & Jones, hairlines, 11"..............225.00
Crock, floral, brushed, c/s, N Clark Jr, 9"..............200.00
Crock, floral, c/s, Snipe & Son, Albany int, 6x10", NM..............225.00
Crock, floral, quilled, c/s, Haxstun & Co, 11" 200.00
Crock, floral (dbl w/stalk & leaves), c/s, Lyons, 2-gal..............225.00
Crock, floral (dbl), c/s, Lyons, 1-gal, 10", EX..............190.00
Crock, floral (detailed), quilled, c/s, N Clark & Co, 12" 400.00
Crock, floral (EX work), c/s, John Burger, lid, 3-gal, VG 425.00
Crock, floral (lg/triple), c/s, T Harrington-Lyons, 5-gal 650.00
Crock, floral plant (lg/well done), c/s, N Clark, 4-gal, EX 400.00
Crock, floral/#1, c/s, Lyons, 1-gal, NM..............350.00
Crock, floral/leaf (profuse), c/s, pear form, 1-gal..............275.00
Crock, floral/leaves/hdl trim, c/s, WH Farrar, 2-gal, EX..............275.00
Crock, foliage, quilled, c/s, West Troy NY Pottery #3, 11".............250.00
Crock, grapes/leaves, c/s, Lyons, w/lid, 2-gal..............475.00
Crock, leaves, brushed, c/s, JM Hickerson Strasburg VA, 9"........275.00
Crock, leaves (1 striped/1 dotted) c/s, 3-gal..............250.00
Crock, leaves/tendril (detailed), c/s, Lions, no lid, 2-gal..............275.00
Crock, parrot on branch, quilled, c/s, Haxstun, 10x10", NM.......450.00
Crock, rooster, stenciled, c/s, hairlines, 14" 150.00
Crock, tulip plant, c/s, M Woodruff-Cortland, 2-gal, EX 250.00
Crock, tulip/#2, c/s, J Fisher & Co, no lid, 2-gal..............300.00
Crock, turkey, c/s, White's Utica, heavy rim/hdls, 5-gal 1,500.00
Crock, woodcock on branch, c/s, AO Whittemore, 5-gal........ 2,300.00
Crock, 2 birds/flowers/#6, c/s, WA MAC Pottery Works, 12¾" ..450.00
Dog, seated, c/s on paws/collar/eyes, brn highlights, 7½" 800.00
Flask, brush strokes, c/s, flattened ovoid, 9" 1,000.00
Flask, gray salt glaze, cobalt lip, 7½"..............150.00
Flowerpot, floral, c/s, AK Ballard, hdls, 12" 275.00
Inkwell, beading, c/s, brn highlights, N Clark, 6½" dia 1,000.00
Inkwell, gray, dome form, ca 1860 ....80.00
Jar, bird on twig, c/s, W Roberts, 10¾", NM..............350.00
Jar, canning; floral, brushed, c/s, 6½" 145.00
Jar, canning; floral (primitive), brushed, c/s, 8½", EX 100.00
Jar, canning; floral band, c/s, imp I in circle, 11", EX 225.00

Jar, canning; foliage, brushed, c/s, rim chips, 8" 115.00
Jar, canning; stencil: AP Donaghho, c/s, 7¾" 75.00
Jar, canning; stencil: AP Donaghho, sm chips, 5⅜" 175.00
Jar, canning; stencil: From WD Cooper & Bro #7 Dmn, c/s, 8"...200.00
Jar, canning; stencil: Hamilton & Jones, c/s, 10", EX..............150.00
Jar, canning; stencil: James Hamilton, c/s, 10", EX..............100.00
Jar, canning; str/wavy lines, c/s, tooled lines, 7½"..............135.00
Jar, canning; trefoil, brushed, c/s, 10½", NM 125.00
Jar, canning; 3 stripes, brushed, c/s, tapered sides, 8"..............225.00
Jar, canning; 4 stenciled stars, c/s, chipped lip, 6"..............450.00
Jar, floral, brushed, c/s, IM Mead, chips, 14"..............395.00
Jar, floral, brushed, c/s, ovoid, minor stains/chips, 10" 175.00
Jar, floral, brushed, c/s, 15"..............200.00
Jar, floral (EX art)/#3, brushwork, c/s, ovoid, 14" 195.00
Jar, floral (simple), c/s, N Tracy, ear hdls, ovoid, 17"..............700.00
Jar, floral (stylized) ea side, c/s, ovoid, hdls, 14", NM..............300.00
Jar, foliage, brushed, c/s, S Bell & Son Strasburg, 13", EX..........150.00
Jar, grape clusters, c/s, OL & AK Ballard, ovoid, 15" 1,650.00
Jar, laurel wreath, c/s, Stetzenmeyer-Goetzman, ovoid, 12" 500.00
Jar, stencil/freehand eagle & label: Reppert, c/s, 22", NM....... 1,250.00
Jar, stencil: Hamilton & Jones, c/s, 13½"..............150.00
Jar, stencil: TF Reppert successor to...Hamilton, c/s, 12" 300.00
Jar, stencil: Wms & Reppert, c/s, ovoid, 12"..............125.00
Jar, tulips (3 stems), c/s, 10"..............150.00
Jar, vining floral, brushed, c/s, ovoid, appl hdl, 14", EX..............325.00
Jug, bird, c/s, NY Stoneware Co, 2-gal..............400.00
Jug, bird (fan-tailed) on branch, c/s, Whites Utica, 13"..............325.00
Jug, bird on branch, c/s, Barnes & Parkman Store, 14", EX 300.00
Jug, bird on branch, c/s, West Troy Pottery, 11", EX..............625.00
Jug, butterfly, c/s, str sides, 1-gal 160.00
Jug, dragonfly/#2, c/s, J Fisher-Lyons NY, 2-gal..............175.00
Jug, eagle w/banner, c/s, NY Stoneware Co, 2-gal, EX 2,750.00
Jug, feather by #2, c/s, T Harrington-Lyons, 2-gal, EX 225.00
Jug, floral, brushed, c/s, Cowden & Wilcox, 13", NM..............250.00
Jug, floral, brushed, c/s, D Roberts, ovoid, 13", EX..............175.00
Jug, floral, c/s, Peter Fahey, Elm & Pleasants Sts, 2-gal 275.00
Jug, floral (lg/elaborate), c/s, Ottman & Co, 2-gal..............300.00
Jug, floral (lg/long stem), c/s, 15", NM..............300.00
Jug, floral (simple)/#2, c/s, T Harrington-Lyons, 2-gal..............175.00
Jug, floral plant (lg/ornate), c/s, N Clark, ovoid, 3-gal..............375.00
Jug, floral/leaves, c/s, Harrington & Burger, 2-gal..............475.00
Jug, floral/leaves, quilled, c/s, J Burger Jr, 16", NM..............300.00
Jug, floral/2 leaves/#2, c/s, N Clark & Co, ovoid, NM 450.00
Jug, flourish, quilled, c/s, 19"..............75.00
Jug, foliage, brushed, c/s, 13½", NM..............275.00
Jug, foliage, quilled, c/s, JS Taft, 11", NM..............150.00
Jug, harvest; stencil: Osage Rub..., c/s, ME Waite, 10"..............375.00
Jug, hdl highlights, c/s, EH Merill, ovoid, 11" 150.00
Jug, incised dove/hdl trim, c/s, I Seymour Troy, ovoid 1,300.00
Jug, leaf, c/s, faint maker's mk/Hartford, 2-gal, NM..............75.00
Jug, leaves (3)/#2, c/s, Burger & Lang, NM 350.00
Jug, lg tulip, c/s, WH Farrar & Co Geddes NY, 2-gal, EX..........400.00
Jug, Lyons in script, c/s, J Fisher Lyons NY, 2-gal..............150.00
Jug, quillwork name: E Kane, NY & Brooklyn, c/s, 9", NM.........235.00
Jug, rose, c/s, Haxstun & Co, 2-gal, NM..............250.00
Jug, stencil & freehand: James Hamilton & Co, c/s, 14"..............200.00
Jug, 3 men in tavern, stencil, c/s, James Hamilton, 14½" 4,100.00
Jug, 3-masted ship/lighthouse, brushed, c/s, rpr, 13" 1,300.00
Match holder, bands, c/s, emb striker, cone shape, 2¾" 85.00
Mug, floral (incised), c/s, chip/hairline, 6"..............110.00
Mug, lines, c/s, w/pewter lid, 4¼" 135.00
Mug, wht w/red-brn transfer: Gesundheit...Lane Co, 5⅞"..............35.00
Mug, 2 incised bands highlighted in c/s, 4"..............55.00
Mustache cup, brn Albany slip, snake hdl w/sgraffito, 4½"..........125.00

Paperweight, open book form w/Bible verse, c/s, 4¼x5½"............275.00
Pitcher, dog form, nose is spout, Albany slip, 9" 275.00
Pitcher, dragonfly, c/s, 1-gal...................................450.00
Pitcher, floral, brushed, c/s, edge chips, 10½" 285.00
Pitcher, floral, brushed, c/s, JM Harris, chips, 10" 475.00
Pitcher, floral (blurred), c/s, hairlines, 7½" 275.00
Pitcher, floral (EX art), brushed, c/s, 12", EX.............1,000.00
Pitcher, floral (stylized), c/s, FT Wright & Son, 13", EX 500.00
Pitcher, rose, c/s, 1½-gal, EX 400.00
Pitcher, 3-leaf clovers/stems, cobalt on brn, 8"...........500.00

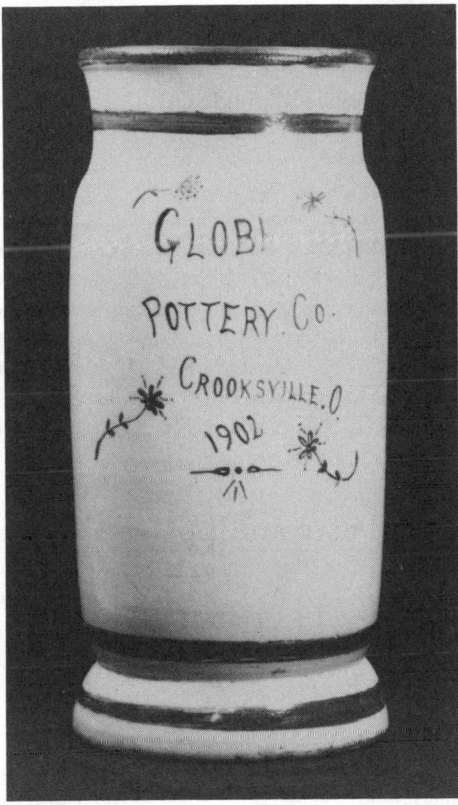

Umbrella stand, Globe Pottery Co., dated 1902, $1,200.00.

Store

Perhaps more more than any other yester-year establishment, the country store evokes the most nostalgic feelings for folks old enough to remember its charms – barrels for coffee, crackers, and big green pickles; candy in a jar for the grocer to weigh on shiny brass scales; beheaded chickens in the meat case outwardly devoid of nothing but feathers. Today, mementos from this segment of Americana are being collected by those who 'lived it' as well as those less fortunate! See also Advertising.

Bag filler, brass, 4¾" 25.00
Bag rack, holds 10 sizes, lt rust, 30x14x8", EX 90.00
Box, 1-drw, Mitchell's Pharmaceutical Products, 2½x11x10" 20.00
Cabinet, display; Old Hickory Shoe Laces, EX...............25.00
Case, wood w/glass sides & top, 11x11½x25" 80.00
Crate opener, Buy Only Arm & Hammer Soda, CI, 13" 22.50
Dispenser, gummed paper; #5, Pat May 14, 1918, CI, EX 25.00
Holder, display; 30 slots for buggy whips, CI, 33¼" W............55.00
Holder, lollypop; Chief Watta Pop, plaster, orig pnt, 10x7".......135.00
Holder, paper sack; Computing Scale Co, Burbs Pat, 31" 260.00
Meat/cheese slicer, oak w/wrought iron hdls, collapsible 115.00
Paper file, spike set in slot in cut-out CI base, 7½" 7.50
Store license, unissued, 1890s............................15.00

Stoves

Antique stoves' desirability is based on two criteria: their utility and their decorative value. It's the latter that adds an 'antique' premium to the basic functional value that could be served just as well by a modern stove. Sheer age is usually irrelevant. Decorative features that enhance desirability include fancy, embossed ornamentation, nickel-plated trim, mica windows, ceramic tiles, and (in cooking stoves) water reservoirs and high warming closets rather than mere high shelves. The less sheet metal and the more cast iron, the better. Look for crisp, sharp designs in preference to those made from worn or damaged and repaired foundry patterns. Stoves with pastel porcelain finish can be very attractive; blue is a favorite, white is least desirable. Chrome trim, rather than nickel, is the mark of a stove too recent to be interesting. Among stove types, base burners (with self-feeding coal magazines) are the most desirable. Then come the upright, cylindrical 'oak' stoves, kitchen ranges, and wood parlors. Potbellies approach the margin of undesirability; laundries and gasoline stoves plunge through it.

In judging condition, look out for deep rust pits, warped or burnt-out parts, unsound firebricks, poorly-fitting parts, poor repairs, and empty mounting holes indicating missing trim. Search meticulously for cracks in the cast iron. Our listings reflect auction prices of completely restored, safe, and functional stoves, unless indicated otherwise.

There's a thin but continuing stream of desirable antique stoves going to the high-priced Pacific Coast market. Interest in antique stoves is least in the Deep South. Demand for wood/coal stoves is strongest in areas where firewood is affordable and storage of it is practical. Demand for antique gas ranges has recently surged, especially in metropolitan markets.

The market for antique stoves is so thin and the variety so bewildering that a consensus on a going price can hardly emerge. They are only worth something to the right individual, and prices realized depend very greatly on who happens to be in the auction crowd. Even an expert's appraisal will usually miss the realized price by a substantial percent.

Base Burners

Acme Sunburst #112, Wehrle Co, Newark OH, M 2,900.00
Art Amherst #15, nickel trim, tiles, 11" urn, 50x25x28".........1,500.00
Detroit Emerald Jewel No 14, mica doors, NP trim, 69", EX ..2,500.00
Favorite #30, Piqua OH, ornate chrome/mica windows, 52" ..1,600.00
No 44, Burdett, Smith & Co, Chicago, swivel top/tiles, 38"........950.00
Waverly #12, Thos Caffney & Co, Boston MA, 40x20x22"....1,350.00

Box Stoves

A Belanger Barge No 14, scrollwork, CI, 1906, sm 300.00
BF&M Co #1, front load, early 1800s, 17x24"..............................100.00
E Eaton No 24, Amherst NH, CI schoolhouse type, 24x38x16" .350.00
Shaker, 1-pc cast body, wrought latch, 1800s, 21x35x14" 275.00
Unknown, parlor type, reeded column sides, 1830s, 25x32x17" ..400.00

Franklin Stoves

Acme #18 Orient 1890, 6 tiles, mica findow, fancy 300.00
Atlanta Franklin #8M, CI, 2 burner, coal/wood, EX 100.00
Muzzy & Co Villa Franklin, fancy CI fireplace, 20x29x19" 150.00

Parlor

Barstow...Boston...NY, cottage type, 1880s, 37"+8" urn 100.00
C Williams, Forest No 19, fancy CI, 1870, 27"+urn 300.00
Co-Op, Sylvan Red Cross #45, CI, Pat 1899 ....200.00

Cool Morning, B&H Radiant Handwarmer, Pat 1893-1894, 33" .350.00
Enterprise/Burnside #20A, CI, potbelly, 48", EX.........................375.00
Gem #15, John F Rathbone, Albany NY, Pat 1877, 38", NM 375.00
Gr Mtn #2, EG Ruggles, W Poultney VT, 1850s, 25+7" urn, EX.375.00
Johnson, Cox, & Fuller Home Parlor No 3, 1852, 25"+10" urn ..300.00
Low & Hicks Revere Air-Tight No 4, Troy NY, 29"+11" urn 275.00
Modern Glenwood Oak No 115, Weir, Tauton MA, 1908, 68" ...300.00
Moores Air Tight Heater No 402B, Joliet IL, Pat...1883, 56" 750.00
Morison/Manning, column type, ornate style, 2 doors, 42" 2,150.00
Oven Parlor #7, Pat 1855, Newberry, Filley, & Co, 34x22x27" ...200.00
PP Stewart L'Hiver No 17, NP trim, 1890s, 57"+12" finial..........450.00
Prat & Perkins Organ No 2, Boston MA, 1852, 36x22x25" 275.00
Rathbone, Sard & Co, Floral Acorn No 38, CI/nickel, fancy 600.00
Standard Lighting Globe Incandescent, Cleveland OH, 29" 250.00
Thos Caffney, Waverly No 12, doors all sides, 1880s, 52" 1,500.00
Tyson Furnace No 1, 2-column, fancy, 36x25" 250.00

Wyer & Noble, Portland; early cast metal fireplace, early 1800s, $1,600.00.

Ranges

Atlantic Grand, Portland, ornate bk shelf, 12x20x18", EX 1,700.00
Detroit Jewel, cabinet, gas, glass door, 1916, VG 400.00
Imperial Clarion No 8-20, CI, high shelf, fancy, 1898 .... 1,500.00
Kalamazoo, coal/wood burner, tan enamel, EX............................250.00
Noyes/Nutter, Star Kineo No 8-20, CI, plain, high shelf............600.00
Portland, Ideal Atlantic 8-20, fancy CI/NP, oven: 11x19x17".. 1,250.00
Quaker Standard No. 8-20, Taunton, CI, high shelf, nickel 700.00
Queen Atlantic, Portland, 1-shelf, simple style, 1930s.................500.00
Rugby, CI/nickel, silver pnt, ornate, 6-burner, high shelf........ 1,600.00
Universal, bl porc CI, high closet, no reservoir, 1924..............2,200.00
Weir, Glenwood C No 280, Taunton MA, oven: 11x18x18"......850.00
Weir, Modern Glenwood E 508, NP trim, oven: 12x20x19"........700.00
Wood/Bishop, New Clarion #8, cabinet base, 1882, 32" 1,500.00
Wood/Bishop, Popular Clarion, scrolled leaf design, 1890s 850.00

Miscellaneous

Fireplace, #116, scrollwork front, 1850s, 33x25x32", EX 200.00
Fireplace, Barstow No 137 Orient 1886, CI, 37x22x32", EX.......900.00
Fireplace, Kineo 16, Noyes-Nutter, Bangor ME, 1870s, 32".........150.00
Fireplace, Magee, Ideal #3, CI, 2 side trivets, 1892, 32x28".........150.00
Griswold, space heater, sheet steel, iron base & top, 27" 88.00
Laundry, Stamford Laundry #20, 4-ring lid, 21½x21x26" 150.00

RR, B&M No 5, CI potbelly, ca 1910, 48x32", EX......................300.00
RR, Union Stove Works, NY, Station Agent, CI potbelly, 46" ...350.00

Stove Manufacturers' Toy Stoves

Buck Jr range, St Louis MO, new body & pnt/recast parts, 26"....850.00
Buck Jr range, St Louis MO, rstr, 26x11¾x15½".....................1,300.00
Charter Oak #503, GF Filley, St Louis MO, 14x12x25", EX ... 2,050.00
Dainty, Reading Stove Works, PA, 7x13x8", VG.........................150.00
Great Majestic Jr, The; Majestic Mfg, 31x16x23", M 5,650.00
Karr range, Belleville IL, bl porc, old model, 21½x9x13" 3,100.00
Little Eva, T Southard, NYC, 8½x14x11", G..............................350.00
Qualified, bl porc w/nickel, Karr, Belleville IL, 1925, EX........ 2,500.00
Qualified, bl porc w/nickel, 1960s repro, EX 2,500.00
Royal American, Bridgeford, Louisville KY, 14x12x20", G..........950.00

Toy Manufacturers' Toy Stoves

Eagle, Hubley, Lancaster PA, nickeled, recast parts......................450.00
Fireplace, unmk/unidentified, nickeled, 7½x7½x2½" 50.00
Little Giant, unmk/unidentified, 7½x8½x11", EX orig 675.00
Novelty, Kenton Hdwe, bl pnt/nickeled trim, rfn, 13x6½x8½" ...600.00
Pet, The; Young Bros, Albany NY, 10½x6x8½" 165.00
Queen, The; unmk/unidentified, copper overlay, 23½", M...... 2,400.00
Rival, J&E Stevens, Cromwell CT, 14x8½x16", M, +2 kettles. 1,350.00
Rival, J&E Stevens, Cromwell CT, 1895, 13x7½x18½", G 240.00
Triumph, Kenton Hdwe, OH, 14x8½x19", G 195.00

Strawberry Soft Paste and Lustre Ware

Strawberry lustre is a general term for pearlware and semi-porcelain decorated with hand-painted strawberries, vines, tendrils, and pink lustre trim. Strawberry soft paste is decorated creamware without the pink lustre trim. Both were made by many manufacturers in England in the 19th century, most of whom never marked their ware.

Coffeepot, lustre, fruit finial on dome lid, 11", NM......................450.00
Coffeepot, soft paste, dome lid, rpr, 12" 1,600.00
Cup & saucer, handleless; early, lustre, NM..............................200.00
Plate, soft paste, Davenport, ca 1810, 6½" 150.00
Platter, lustre, 11" 200.00
Sauce boat, lustre, 6" 165.00
Sugar bowl, lustre, w/lid, early...225.00
Teapot, soft paste, vining rim, rpr finial, 8", EX.........................550.00
Teapot, squat, 1820s, 5", VG...500.00
Teapot, vine border, ftd, 11", NM 525.00
Waste bowl, soft paste, mk Wood...575.00

Stretch Glass

Stretch glass, produced from the early 1900s until after 1930, was made in an effort to emulate the fine art glass of Tiffany and Carder. The glassware was sprayed with a special finish while still hot, and a reheating process caused the coating to contract, leaving a striated, crepe-like iridescence. Northwood, Imperial, Fenton, and the United States Glass Company were the largest manufacturers of this type of glass. See also specific companies.

Bowl, bl, w/flower frog, sm...25.00
Bowl, bl, 3x10" dia...25.00
Bowl, bl w/blk rims, ftd, 2¼x4¾" 25.00
Bowl, paneled, rolled rim, 1½x8¾"..22.50

Box, powder; pk/frosted, elephant finial, 6" 40.00
Compote, 4x5½" 20.00
Pitcher, lemonade; Celeste Bl, cobalt hdl 195.00
Plate, vaseline, octagonal, 6" 12.50
Sherbet, bl, ribbed 28.00
Vase, pk, dolphin hdls, fan form, 6" 60.00
Vase, ribbed int, HP florals/leaves, rolled rim, 6" 30.00

String Holders

Today, if you want to wrap and secure a package, you have a variety of products to choose from: cellophane tape, staples, etc. But in the 1800s, string was about the only available binder; thus the string holder, either the hanging or counter type, was a common and practical item found in most homes and businesses. Chalkware and ceramic figurals from the 1930s and 1940s contrast with the cast and wrought iron examples from the 1800s to make for an interesting collection.

Group of three girls, Japan, $20.00.

Apple w/worm, plaster 28.00
Beehive, CI, 5½x6" 65.00
Blk porter, Fredericksburg Art Pottery, 6½", M 135.00
Cat head, CI, string out top, EX 1,000.00
Cathedral pattern, CI, rnd. 45.00
Chef (wht) w/bottle, ceramic 60.00
Colonial boy, CI, mc pnt, 7", VG 400.00
Dog w/fly, Deco style, ceramic 48.00
Dutch girl, chalk, lg, EX 25.00
Dutch girl ice skater, CI, VG 800.00
Girl's head, ceramic 47.50
Indian man's head, plaster 68.00
Mammy, chalkware, 6" 125.00
Mammy, red turban, checkered dress, pottery, 6¾x6" 110.00
Mechanical, ball runs on track, CI..350.00
Mexican man's head, plaster, sm 28.00
Pull w/me, heart shape, ceramic, Clemenson..................................30.00
Pumpkin face, ceramic 48.00

Sugar Shakers

Sugar shakers (or muffineers, as they were also called) were used during the Victorian era to sprinkle sugar and spice onto breakfast muffins, toast, etc. They were made of art glass, in pressed patterns, and in china. See also specific types and manufacturers.

Acorn, pk shaded opaque 155.00
Acorn, sapphire bl 165.00
Apollo, etched, orig top...75.00
Argus Swirl, peachbloom, Heacock #14 ....175.00
Baby T'print, amberina..200.00
Beatty Rib, bl opal 100.00
Bubble Lattice, cranberry satin, rare 600.00
Bulging Loops, bl cased 215.00
Challinor's Forget-Me-Not, pk 120.00
China, floral spray, pk/wht on wht, unmk...................................50.00
Chrysanthemum Base Swirl, wht speckled 145.00

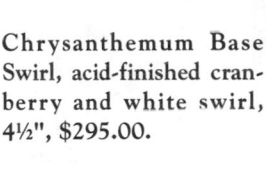

Chrysanthemum Base Swirl, acid-finished cranberry and white swirl, 4½", $295.00.

Coin Spot, cranberry opal, wide waist 150.00
Corn, turq opaque 110.00
Flower & Pleat, clear/frosted 120.00
Horseshoe, amber...80.00
Invt T'print, amber w/decor, pewter collar & lid..........................175.00
Ivory w/prunus blossoms, Hobbs' Coloratura series 145.00
Jewelled Heart, bl, scarce 175.00
Jumbo & Barnum 145.00
Leaf Mold, cranberry & wht w/mica, shiny..................................245.00
Leaf Umbrella, bl cased 250.00
Medallion Sprig, rubena, rare 275.00
Melligo, bl opaque 95.00
Parian Swirl, cranberry, Heacock #221 ....195.00
Parian Swirl, wht opaque, HP roses, Northwood, EX 95.00
Ribbed Pillar, cranberry spatter, frosted 195.00
Ring Neck, cranberry frost spatter 135.00
Rubena, cut panels, SP top, 5½x2¼" 115.00
Tomato figural, ornate top, Mt WA 235.00

Sunderland Lustre

Sunderland lustre was made by various potters in the Sunderland district of England during the 18th and 19th centuries. It is characterized by a splashed-on application of the pink lustre, which results in an effect sometimes referred to as the 'cloud' pattern. Some pieces are transfer printed with scenes, ships, florals, or portraits.

Creamer, blk transfer: Ladies All I Pray..., 2¾" 95.00

Goblet, 4½"..50.00
Jug, blk transfer: N Umberland 74, bk: Masonic poem, 7"..........**425.00**
Jug, 3 transfers: N Umberland/W View of.../wreath, 8½", EX **575.00**
Mug, 2 transfers: Tynemouth Haven/Rest in Heaven, 3½", NM .**175.00**

Mug, Mariner's compass, 5", $375.00.

Pitcher, Old Castle, England, coach/horses in front, 3" **145.00**
Plaque, Prepare To Meet Thy God, w/angel, 6½" dia, NM..........**200.00**
Plaque, Thou God Seest Me, mk Dixon, 7½x8", NM **175.00**
Plaque, Wm Gladstone, gr/gold spatter lustre rim, NM.................**95.00**
Plate, house, ca 1850, 9¼" **80.00**
Toothpick holder, HP florals, yel band......................................**60.00**

Swastika Keramos

Swastika Keramos was a line of artware made by the Owens China Co., of Minerva, Ohio, around 1902-1904. It is characterized either by a coralene type of decoration (similar to the Opalesce line made by the J.B. Owens Pottery Company of Zanesville) or by the application of metallic lustres, usually in simple designs. Shapes are often plain and handles squarish and rather thick, suggestive of the Arts and Crafts style.

Ewer, gold and red dripping glazes, 14", $160.00.

Pitcher, flowers/leaves, red/gr on gold, sm mouth, 11" **170.00**
Vase, landscape, mc, 9" **550.00**
Vase, Nouveau florals, red on gold lustre, 3-hdl, 6x6"..................**185.00**
Vase, Nouveau florals on copper, 6½"......................................**125.00**
Vase, tree trunks, bronzed/gold against red horizon, 10" **600.00**
Vase, trees, gray & rose, squat, 6"..**250.00**
Vase, 3-color LaSa type, bowling pin form, flared top, 14½" **225.00**

Syracuse

Syracuse was a line of fine dinnerware which was made for nearly a century by the Onondaga Pottery Company of Syracuse, New York. Collectors of American dinnerware are focusing their attention on reassembling some of their many lovely patterns. In 1966 the firm became officially known as the Syracuse China Company in order to better identify with the name of their popular chinaware. By 1971 dinnerware geared for use in the home was discontinued, and the company turned to the manufacture of hotel, restaurant, and other types of commercial tableware.

Arcadia, bowl, fruit..**20.00**
Arcadia, bowl, vegetable; oval...**45.00**
Arcadia, bowl, vegetable; w/lid...**85.00**
Arcadia, cream soup set, w/underplate **27.00**
Arcadia, creamer..**30.00**
Arcadia, cup & saucer...**25.00**
Arcadia, cup & saucer, demitasse **25.00**
Arcadia, gravy boat..**65.00**
Arcadia, plate, bread **12.50**
Arcadia, plate, cake **50.00**
Arcadia, plate, dessert..**15.00**
Arcadia, plate, dinner...**20.00**
Arcadia, plate, salad **18.00**
Arcadia, platter, 12" **45.00**
Arcadia, platter, 14" **55.00**
Arcadia, platter, 16" **65.00**
Arcadia, sugar bowl..**35.00**
Bombay, coffeepot **95.00**
Bombay, plate, chop..**85.00**
Bombay, platter, 16"...**65.00**
Bombay, soup, rimmed..**20.00**
Carvel, bowl, vegetable; rnd..**40.00**
Carvel, platter, 14"...**65.00**
Carvel, sugar bowl..**35.00**
Champlain, sugar bowl **18.00**
Champlain, teapot, 7½"...**38.00**
Fusan, bowl, vegetable; w/lid **40.00**
Fusan, gravy boat **25.00**
Fusan, platter, 14" **35.00**
Jefferson, bowl, fruit...**20.00**
Jefferson, bowl, salad..**18.00**
Jefferson, bowl, vegetable; oval..**45.00**
Jefferson, bowl, vegetable; w/lid **95.00**
Jefferson, coffeepot...**95.00**
Jefferson, creamer...**30.00**
Jefferson, cup & saucer **25.00**
Jefferson, gravy boat **65.00**
Jefferson, plate, bread...**15.00**
Jefferson, plate, chop..**85.00**
Jefferson, plate, dinner...**20.00**
Jefferson, platter, 12"..**65.00**
Jefferson, platter, 14"..**75.00**
Jefferson, soup, rimmed..**20.00**

Jefferson, sugar bowl	35.00
Lady Mary, bowl, fruit	20.00
Lady Mary, bowl, vegetable; oval	45.00
Lady Mary, creamer & sugar bowl	75.00
Lady Mary, plate, dinner	20.00
Lady Mary, plate, salad	18.00
Lady Mary, platter, 14"	65.00
Meadow Breeze, cup & saucer	25.00
Meadow Breeze, plate, dinner	20.00
Meadow Breeze, plate, salad	15.00
Plate, Indian in canoe, mk 'Souvenir,' 10"	40.00
Suzanne, bowl, vegetable; w/lid	95.00
Suzanne, creamer & sugar bowl	40.00
Suzanne, cup & saucer	25.00
Suzanne, gravy boat	65.00
Suzanne, plate, bread	10.00
Suzanne, plate, dinner	20.00
Suzanne, plate, salad	15.00
Suzanne, platter, 12"	40.00
Suzanne, platter, 14"	60.00
Whitby, cake plate	65.00
Whitby, cup & saucer	28.00

Syrups

Values are for old, original syrups. Beware of reproductions! See also various manufacturers and specific types of glass.

Alba, wht opaque, HP florals, Dithridge	95.00
Birch Leaf, wht opaque, flint	95.00
Chrysanthemum Base Swirl, wht speckled	165.00
Coin Spot & Swirl, bl opal	150.00
Coin Spot & Swirl, cranberry opal, rare	850.00
Cone, pk cased, squatty, orig top	150.00
Cranberry, ribbed, emb metal top & hdl	175.00
Daisy & Button, sapphire bl, clamp-on lid	175.00
Daisy & Fern, cranberry, swirled, Northwood, rare	400.00
Dbl Daisy, ruby & clear	250.00
Fancy Arches, emerald gr, McKee	175.00
Fishnet & Poppies, milk glass	95.00
Fleur-de-lis & Tassel, pewter hdl, Adams/4 pat mks on lid, 9"	165.00
Florette, pk satin, SP hinged lid & hdl	300.00
Flower & Pleat, clear/frosted	120.00
Frosted Lion, orig dtd pewter lid	300.00
Gonterman Swirl, amber, pewter lid, rare	350.00
Gonterman Swirl, bl & frosted, rare	395.00
Guttate, pk cased, metal lid	250.00
Hercules Pillar, amber	120.00
Hobnail, cranberry opal, pewter lid, 6½"	375.00
Invt T'print, amberina, SP lid/collar/hdl, Mt WA, 5½"	625.00
Leaf Umbrella, mauve cased, pewter lid, rare	575.00
Medallion Sprig, bl	300.00
Parian Swirl, cranberry, rare	335.00
Peace & Plenty, milk glass, orig pewter lid	95.00
Peachblow, amber hdl, Wheeling	1,450.00
Pk & wht spatter, Hobbs' Coloratura series	135.00
Reverse Swirl, cranberry opal	350.00
Ring Band, custard w/EX gold	350.00
Royal Crystal, ruby flashed	135.00
Rubena, threaded top, swirled, gold-tone lid, Northwood	250.00
Rubena to clear, ribbed, clear hdl, 6"	130.00
Shoshone, yel flashed	250.00
Spanish Lace, vaseline opal	195.00

Stoneware, basketweave, English, 1850s, pewter lid, NM	70.00
Thousand Eye, amber	115.00
Torpedo, brass lid	90.00
Truncated Cube, ruby, rare, 7½"	235.00
Valencia Waffle, amber	125.00

Priscilla, green with gold trim, scarce, $350.00.

Target Balls

Prior to 1880 when the clay pigeon was invented, blown glass target balls were used extensively for shotgun competitions. Approximately 2¾" in diameter, these balls were hand-blown into a three-piece mold. All have a ragged hole where the blowpipe was twisted free. Target balls date from approximately 1840 (English) to World War I, although they were most widely used in the 1870-1880 period. Common examples are unmarked except for the blower's code – dots, crude numerals, etc. Some balls are embossed in a dot or diamond pattern so they were more likely to shatter when struck by shot, and some have names and/or patent dates. When evaluating condition, bubbles and other minor manufacturing imperfections are acceptable; cracks are not. The prices below are for mint condition examples.

Black Pitch, CTB Co	250.00
Bogardus' Glass Ball Pat'd April 10 1877, amber	250.00
Bogardus' Glass Ball Pat'd April 10 1877, other than amber	500.00
Emb ribs, amber	150.00
English, shooter emb in 2 rnd panels, clear	300.00
English, shooter emb in 2 rnd panels, gr	300.00
English, shooter emb in 2 rnd panels, purple	300.00
For Hockey's Patent Trap, gr	500.00
Great Western Gun Works, amber	600.00
Gurd & Son, London, Ontario, amber	400.00
Ira Paine's Filled Ball Pat Oct 23 1877, amber	250.00
Ira Paine's Filled Ball Pat Oct 23 1877, amber, set of 10	950.00
Ira Paine's Filled Ball Pat Oct 23 1877, other than amber	500.00
NB Glass Works Perth, other than pale gr	300.00
NB Glass Works Perth, pale gr, almost clear	200.00
Plain, amber	65.00
Plain, clear, w/mold marks	1,000.00
Plain, cobalt	150.00
Plain, purple	150.00
WW Greener St Mary's Works Birm/68 Haymarket London	250.00

Related Memorabilia

Clay birds, Winchester, Pat May 29 1917, 1 flight in box 100.00
Pitch bird, blk, DUVROCK 1.00
Shell, dummy, w/single window, any brand.....................................25.00
Shell, dummy shotgun, Winchester, window w/powder, 6" 100.00
Shell set, dummy, Gamble Stores, 2 window shells, 3 cut out......125.00
Shell set, dummy, Winchester, 5 window shells 125.00
Shell set, dummy shotgun, Peters, 6 window shells+full box 125.00
Shotshell loader, rosewood/brass, Parker Bros, Pat 1884 ....50.00
Target, Am sheet metal, rod ends mk Pat Feb 8 '21, set 25.00
Target, blk japanned sheet metal, Bussy Patentee, London 50.00
Target, BUST-O, blk or wht breakable wafer 20.00
Trap, DUVROCK, w/blk pitch birds...150.00
Trap, MO-SKEET-O, w/birds 150.00

Tea Caddies

Because tea was once regarded as a precious commodity, special boxes called caddies were used to store the tea leaves. They were made from various materials: porcelain, carved and inlaid woods, and metals ranging from painted tin or tole to engraved silver.

Federal mahog w/rectangular maple reserve, 5x9x5" 175.00
George III mahog w/inlay, octagonal, 7x9x5" 450.00
Mahog veneer, brass ft, emb flower basket hdls, 11" L 225.00
Rosewood, Georgian, ivory escutcheon, brass ft/hdls, 7" L 200.00
Rosewood veneer w/satinwood inlay, brass lion ring hdls, 8" 225.00
Silver, Rococo bombe form, ornate ft, Austrian, T&Co, 5".........500.00
Sterling, eng garlands on shoulders, early Durgin mk, 5" 165.00
Tortoise shell, stepped-bk cover, brass ball ft, 7", EX....................200.00

Tea Leaf Ironstone

Tea Leaf Ironstone became popular in the 1880s when middle-class American housewives became bored with the plain white stone china that English potters had been exporting to this country for nearly a century. The original design has been credited to Anthony Shaw of Longport, who decorated the plain ironstone with a hand-painted copper lustre design of bands and leaves. Originally known as Lustre Band and Sprig, the pattern has since come to be known as Tea Leaf Lustre. It was produced with minor variations by many different firms both in England and the United States. By the early 1900s, it had become so commonplace that it had lost much of its appeal.

Our advisors for this category are the owners of Home Place Antiques; their address is listed in the Directory under Illinois.

Bowl, fruit; scalloped, H Burgess, 10" dia 75.00
Bowl, sauce; Wilkinson, 4½" 20.00
Bowl, vegetable; Fish Hook, w/lid, Meakin 125.00
Bowl, vegetable; melon ribbed, sq, open, Grindley, 5" 35.00
Bowl, vegetable; Pepper Leaf, w/lid..225.00
Bowl, vegetable; sq, open, Mellor Taylor, 7¼" 40.00
Butter dish, sq, w/lid & drain, Wedgwood 130.00
Butter pat, rnd, Meakin 14.00
Butter pat, rnd, scalloped, Meakin 15.00
Butter pat, sq, Meakin, 2¾" 15.00
Chamber pot, Cable, no lid, Shaw..145.00
Coffeepot, Bamboo, Meakin 165.00
Coffeepot, Fish Hook, Meakin, lg 175.00
Creamer, beaded hdl, rectangular, East End Pottery, 4¾" 85.00
Cup & saucer, barrel shape, Wedgwood 65.00

Cup & saucer, Chinese shape, Shaw 95.00
Cup & saucer, handleless; Chinese shape, paneled, Shaw.............80.00
Cup & saucer, Pepper Leaf Variant, Elsmore & Forster.................65.00
Cup & saucer, ribbed, Adams, ca 1970 ....35.00
Ewer & basin, Bamboo, Meakin...375.00
Gravy boat, Bamboo, Meakin..55.00
Gravy boat, Fish Hook, Meakin 45.00
Gravy boat, plain, Wedgwood 50.00
Mug, child's sz 195.00
Nappy, plain, rnd, Shaw 18.00
Nappy, plain, sq, Meakin 20.00
Pitcher, Meakin, 6" 95.00
Pitcher, milk; Dolphin, Victory shape, Edwards, 8⅛"...................195.00
Pitcher, milk; Fish Hook, Meakin, 7" 175.00
Plate, bread & butter; Meakin 10.00
Plate, dessert; Meakin..12.00
Plate, dessert; Wilkinson 12.00
Plate, dinner; Pepper Leaf Variant, Elsmore & Forster, 10" 30.00
Plate, luncheon; Pepper Leaf, Elsmore & Forster.........................25.00
Plate, Meakin, 8¾", NM 12.50
Plate, Wedgwood, 7⅝" 12.00
Plate, Wedgwood, 8½" 12.00
Platter, rectangular, ribbed flange, Wedgwood, 15¾x11½" 45.00
Relish dish, Fish Hook, rectangular, Meakin 25.00
Saucer, deep, Meakin, 6" 8.00
Shaving mug, Chinese shape, Shaw..175.00
Shaving mug, Grape, 12-sided, Shaw, 3¼" 155.00
Sugar bowl, Bamboo, Meakin, sm 65.00
Sugar bowl, Cable, open 40.00
Sugar bowl, Fish Hook, Meakin, w/lid, lg 65.00
Sugar bowl, Furnival, no lid 40.00
Sugar bowl, Pepper Leaf, Elsmore & Forster, 7"...........................85.00

Creamer and sugar bowl, child's size, gold trim, Mellor Taylor, $195.00 for the set.

Teapot, Bamboo, Meakin 165.00
Teapot, Chinese shape, paneled, Shaw, late 1850s......................245.00
Teapot, ribbed spout & hdl, scalloped top 185.00
Tureen, soup; Davenport, oval, w/lid, ladle, & underplate 795.00
Tureen, vegetable; plain, rectangular, w/lid, Wedgwood 95.00
Wash bowl & ewer, Burgess 375.00

Teapots

The custom of drinking tea has resulted in the production of many tea-related collectibles; the most popular is the teapot. The first teapots were manufactured in the Chinese village of Vi-Hsing during the late 16th century and were no bigger than the tiny cups previously used for tea drinking. Amazingly, these same tiny teapots are still being used today.

A wide range of teapots can be found by the avid searcher; those most readily available today were produced from about 1870 to the present. Several books have been written solely devoted to teapots, although most are out of print. *An Anthology of British Teapots* by Philip Miller and Michael Berthoud is an extensive work with over 2,000 photographs; it is currently available from Micawber Publications, The Lawns, Church Street, Brosely, Stropshire TF12 5DG for L. 24.95. Another is titled *The Eccentric Teapot*; it is written by Garth Clark and is available at your local bookstore.

Almost every pottery and porcelain manufacturer in Europe as well as in America have produced teapots. Some are purely functional, others decorative and whimsical. Refer to various manufacturers' names for further listings.

Our advisor for this category is Tina Carter; she is listed by her shop name, Hot Tea, in the Directory under California.

Austria Victoria Carlsbad, floral on china	30.00
Dbl spout, earthenware, slip decor, ca 1890	80.00
DM mk, coralene dragon, Japanese, 6-cup	20.00
Ellgreave, Wood & Sons, England, ironstone w/floral	35.00
Flow blue, man sits w/legs outstretched, conical hat, 8x9"	60.00
Grimwades, Royal Winton, England, cozy set, floral hdls	55.00
H&K England, Old English Sampler, 6-cup, EX	45.00
Japan, Tea for Two, man in tux hdl, girl in gown forms pot	45.00
Ming Tea Co, made in Japan, w/label, 1½-cup	15.00
Monterey, made in CA, pk spatter, lg	20.00
Noritake, mk M HP Japan, yel w/flowers, tall, 2-cup	25.00
Pyrex mk, blown glass, etched flowers, 6-cup	45.00

Rabbit figural, natural colors, Germany, att Erphila, $75.00.

S Derbyshire, England, barge, brn, emb mk, lg	75.00
Sadler, pk w/sm flowers, oval, mk, 6-cup	35.00
Spode's Tower, England, bl/wht transfer, London shape, VG	45.00
Sutherland, England, silver lustre, mk, 6-cup	60.00
SYP, 'Simple Yet Perfect,' brn earthenware, ca 1905	95.00
SYP, Wedgwood, bone china, bl/wht/gold, ca 1905-1906	110.00
Wade, Scotty, mk, 1953-1955, 9"	45.00
Wales CM, Charles & Diana, brn pottery, 2½"	75.00
Walt Disney Productions, Snow White w/Dwarfs, musical	50.00

Wedgwood, Jasperware, bl/wht, ca 1784, 2-cup	210.00
WS George, yel w/gold, mk, rnd, 6-cup, EX	18.00

Teco

Teco artware was made by the American Terra Cotta and Ceramic Company, located near Chicago, Illinois. The firm was established in 1886 and until 1901 produced only brick, sewer tile, and other redware. Their early glaze was inspired by the matt green made popular by Grueby. 'Teco Green' was made for nearly ten years. It was similar to Grueby's yet with a subtle silver-gray cast. The company was one of the first in the United States to perfect a true crystalline glaze. The only decoration used was through the modeling and glazing techniques; no hand painting was attempted. Favored motifs were naturalistic leaves and flowers.

The company broadened their lines to include garden pottery and faience tiles and panels. New matt glazes (browns, yellows, blue, and rose) were added to the green in 1910. By 1922 the artware lines were discontinued; the company was sold in 1930.

Values are dictated by size and color of glaze, with examples in colors other than green bringing the higher prices. High-gloss glaze is seldom seen and expensive.

Teco is usually marked with a vertical impressed device comprised of a large 'T' to the left of the remaining three letters.

Bowl, gr, floral at incurvate top, scalloped sides, 9"	235.00
Bowl, gr, stylized leaves, 2x9"	200.00
Bowl, gr w/blk feathering, 6 irregular protrusions, 2½x9"	350.00
Candlestick, lt gr, sqd hdl, 2x5", pr, NM	230.00
Dish, gr, ribbed, str sides/slightly incurvate, 2 mks, 1x5"	120.00
Ewer, brn/yel metallic over wht clay, 4½"	200.00
Mug, gr, emb woven band, 6"	240.00
Mug, gr w/some feathering, thrown/ribbed, cvd hdl, 3½", NM	250.00
Pitcher, dk gr w/much charcoal, 4"	110.00
Pitcher, gr w/gray, extended rim forms split hdl, 8½"	250.00
Vase, blk/ochre/rust w/metallic dust, squat gourd form, 5"	700.00
Vase, bright bl, cylindrical, 8½", NM	425.00
Vase, bright bl, incurvate cylinder, bun ft, 13", NM	750.00
Vase, brn, 2 rim-to-base buttresses form sm neck hdls, 12"	1,100.00
Vase, brn w/blk spots overall, classic form, #248, 6¾"	260.00
Vase, bud; gr w/brn specks, 2 mks/#392, 7"	280.00
Vase, caramel-brn, 4 buttress hdls at long neck, 11x4½"	1,100.00
Vase, dk brn, 2 pinched sides, rectangular top, 3¾"	230.00
Vase, dk gr, blk splotches/whitish cast, tiny opening, 5"	300.00
Vase, goldstone-style crystals on brn, mk, 4"	650.00
Vase, gr, broad body, 8x7"	1,000.00
Vase, gr, bulbous melon base/floriform neck, P197, 10"	1,900.00
Vase, gr, rtcl flange extends to body to form 4 hdls, 6"	1,900.00
Vase, gr, spherical w/sm neck, 5"	245.00
Vase, gr, vertical-rib canister neck, bulging bottom, 6"	500.00
Vase, gr, wide mouth/rnd shoulder, 4-hdl, #267, 6½"	850.00
Vase, gr, wide sq-rim top/bulbous base, 4"	160.00
Vase, gr, 2 rim-to-base buttresses form sm hdls, 5"	525.00
Vase, gr, 2 tiny closed shoulder hdls, 6"	300.00
Vase, gr, 4 long S-curve rim-to-width hdls, 12"	900.00
Vase, gr, 4 rim-to-base buttresses form open neck hdls, 8"	1,200.00
Vase, gr w/dk gray pools at bottom, bulbous, 4½"	350.00
Vase, gr w/feathering, pooled gray at neck, ribbed, mk, 4"	300.00
Vase, gr w/gray, long-stem flowers/leaves, Wm Gates, 8"	450.00
Vase, gr w/gray crystalline top, sgn/#126/2 labels, 3½x4"	350.00
Vase, gr w/gray detail, buttressed floriform, Moureau, 12"	3,000.00
Vase, gr w/gray touches, ribbed, 2½x4"	160.00
Vase, gray, classic form, 5¾"	230.00

Vase, lt brn, 4 in-mold buttresses top to base, slim, 6" 800.00
Vase, lt brn, 4 long open buttresses at stick neck, 7x3" 750.00
Vase, med gr w/some gray, rim-to-shoulder hdls, mk, 9" 600.00
Vase, ochre, emb leaves/blossoms, baluster, 8½" 500.00
Vase, rust, tulip-form top, acquired from ex-employee, 11" 600.00

Teddy Bear Collectibles

The story of Teddy Roosevelt's encounter with the bear cub has been oft recounted with varying degrees of accuracy, so it will suffice to say that it was as a result of this incident in 1902 that the teddy bear got his name. These appealing little creatures are enjoying renewed popularity with collectors today. To one who has not yet succumbed to their obvious charms, one bear seems to look very much like another. How to tell the older ones? Look for long snouts, jointed limbs, large feet and felt paws, long curving arms, and glass or shoe-button eyes. Most old bears have a humped back and are made of mohair stuffed with straw or excelsior. Cute expressions, original clothes, a nice personality, and, of course, good condition add to their value. Some Steiff bears in mint condition may go as high as $100.00 per inch. These are easily recognized by the trademark button within the ear. See also Toys, Steiff.

Bears

Bing, brn/wht mohair, button eyes, long snout, 24", EX 2,500.00
Chad Valley, long gold mohair, jtd body, 23", EX 785.00
Clemens, growler, mohair, jtd body, felt mouth, 1950, 10" 250.00
Fully jtd, mohair, glass eyes, hump, long nose, 20" 325.00
Fully jtd, mohair, glass eyes, hump, 1920s, 21", M....................325.00
German, gold mohair, glass eyes, straw stuffed, 15" 260.00
Hermann, gold mohair, jtd body, straw filled, 1950s, 16" 275.00
Hermann, wht mohair, plastic eyes, embr nose, 1950s, 6"............125.00
Ideal, long auburn mohair, jtd body, 1950s, 23", EX..................235.00
Knickerbocker, brn plush, jtd body, 1930s, 14", EX...................225.00
Petz, growler, honey melange, jtd body, US Zone, 16", EX 235.00
Schuco, gold mohair, metal eyes, 2¼", M..................................195.00
Schuco, orange mohair, for perfume, 3", M 575.00
Schuco, yes/no, tan mohair, glass eyes, 5", EX............................500.00

Steiff Bear, musical, worn, 15½", $3,800.00.

Steiff, brn mohair, straw stuffed, wood in ft, button, 30" 2,200.00
Steiff, chocolate curly mohair, button, 1950s, 24", NM..............265.00
Steiff, cinnamon mohair, button eyes, button, '04, 9½", NM . 1,200.00
Steiff, gold mohair, button eyes, button, 1908, 12", NM 1,650.00
Steiff, gold mohair, button eyes, straw stuffed, 3½", M.................265.00
Steiff, gold mohair, shoebutton eyes, button, 1915, 18", NM.. 1,200.00
Steiff, growler, iron & rubber-wheel base, button, 27", VG 800.00

Steiff, mohair, glass eyes/glasses, button, early, 20" 1,200.00
Steiff, tan mohair, button eyes, rpl nose, button, '08, 15", NM....800.00
Steiff, wht mohair, button eyes, button, 1909, 12", EX 500.00
Steiff, wht mohair, glass eyes, rpl pads, button, 11", G 450.00
Swiss, cinnamon mohair, button eyes, 1915, 17", EX..................575.00

Miscellaneous

Cup & saucer, Roosevelt Bears, EX transfer, +6" plate 110.00
Dish, child's feeding; bears on a seesaw, ceramic 135.00
Plate, Roosevelt Bears, Up San Juan Hill, 7" 145.00
Print, Roosevelt Bears, p MC Sheehan...65.00
Spoon, sterling, bear hdl, eng initials/'08, 5½" 125.00
Tip tray, Roosevelt Bears, 1906, 5x3¾", EX 180.00
Toothpick holder, Teddy & the Bears, souvenir 85.00

Telephones

Since Alexander Graham Bell's first successful telephone communication, the phone itself has undergone a complete evolution in style as well as efficiency. Early models, especially those wall types with ornately carved oak boxes, are of special interest to collectors. Also of value are the candlestick phones from the early part of the century and any related memorabilia.

Automatic Electric, 3-slot coin-op, EX.......................................175.00
Automatic Electric #40, Bakelite, desk style, 1940s, EX................85.00
Danish, French horn style, 1913..55.00
Gray, pay phone, brass direction plate, early, rstr.........................275.00
Kellogg, red-bar desk style 20.00
Kellogg #925, switchboard supply, Deco style, 1920s.................110.00
New England Telegraph & Telephone Co, 2-box, walnut..........500.00
Norwegian, dial phone, old, EX 15.00
Sears & Roebuck, wall style, oak..200.00
Stromberg-Carlson, Bakelite, cradle style, 1920s...........................35.00
Wall crank, wood, ringer box 45.00
Western Electric, candlestick w/dial, brass, Pat 1919 ....165.00
Western Electric, pay, blk-pnt iron, 3-slot, old 175.00
Western Electric, wall intercom, oak 50.00
Western Electric #1315, wood, 26" 240.00
Western Electric 1915 ....95.00

Related Memorabilia

Directory, Fond du Lac, 1925... 8.00
Paperweight, bell figural, cobalt glass, Local & Long... 3"............100.00
Post card, candlestick telephone photo, 1913, NM 6.00
Sign, AT&T Long Lines Department, rvpt, orig copper fr..........500.00
Toy truck, Bell Telephone, pnt CI, Made in USA #2011, 9½" L.125.00
Wall cabinet, holds desk telephone, early 350.00

Telescopes

Old telescopes are still appreciated for the quality of the workmanship and materials that went into their production. Some of the more elaborate styles were covered in leather or ebony and the 'draws' or extensions were often brass.

A Ross, brass & leather, 2-draw, 1800s, 39" 255.00
Brass, 1-draw, VG, 13½" 60.00
Brass & wood, 3-draw, ca 1850, 34", VG 200.00
France, brass & leather, 1-draw, 12", VG 68.00
Harris & Son, Day or Night, 2-draw, leather tube, 38" 200.00

J&A Walker, copper/brass mts, 2-draw, extended: 36" L...............175.00
Pocket type, brass & rosewood, VG 35.00
SIB Solomons, London, cased tripod, ca 1840, EX.....................800.00
Spencer-Browning-Rust, mahog, 1-draw, 1800s, 47" 175.00
T Chapman, Day or Night, 1-draw, fruitwood tube, 30", VG 100.00
US Navy Signalman's, 22 power, in case 450.00

Televisions

Collectible TV's are a quickly moving group of saleable items. TV's made before WWII (circa 1920s – 1940) now sell at $1,000.00 to $10,000.00! Unusual and/or attractive wood and Bakelite sets from 1946 to 1950 usually are worth $20.00 to $200.00; metal mid-1950s televisions sell for $10.00 to $60.00. Old TV's need not work in order to attract a buyer!

Our advisor for this category is Harry Poster; he is listed in the Directory under New Jersey.

Admiral, 14" to 16" Bakelite console, VG 25.00
Admiral #20X122, 10" Bakelite console, EX 225.00
Air King #A-2000, 10" table top, EX...80.00
Andrea #C-VJ12, 12" combination, NM..100.00
Automatic #TV-P490, built-in magnifier, 7" portable, EX 225.00
Bendix #235, 10" pushbutton table top, EX 80.00
Crosley #10-404, 12", EX 70.00
Crosley #9-407, 1949, 12" table top, NM....................................100.00
Fada #880, Deco style, projection console, VG 200.00
Fada #899, 10" console model 90.00
General Electric #803, 10" table top, speaker at top, EX 125.00
Hallicrafters #T-54, 7" metal table top, EX..................................175.00
Motorola #VK-106, console w/stepped top, EX............................125.00

Motorola VT-71, ca 1947, $75.00.

Philco Predicta, on laminated floor base w/4 wood supports........550.00
Philco Safari #H-2010, 1st transistor, EX 125.00
RCA, #630-TS, mass-produced, 10" table top, EX.......................200.00
RCA #CT100, color, 15" screen 400.00
RCA #630TCS, console model, EX..550.00
RCA #721TCS, console model 200.00
Sentinel #400TV, 7" portable, EX 150.00
Sparton #4920, 12" console, EX...45.00
Transvision #7FL, 13 channels, 7" kit w/cabinet, EX 175.00
Westinghouse #H242, electric magnifier, EX 125.00
Zenith Mayflower #28T925, porthole table top, EX......................130.00

Teplitz

Teplitz, in Bohemia, was an active art pottery center at the turn of the century. The Amphora Pottery Works was only one of the firms that operated there. (See Amphora.) Art Nouveau and Art Deco styles were favored, and much of the ware was hand decorated with the primary emphasis on vases and figurines. Items listed here are marked 'Teplitz' or 'Turn,' a nearby city.

Our advisor for this category is Jack Gunsaulus; he is listed in the Directory under Michigan.

Bowl, child pulls rooster's feathers on gr, hdls, 2½x5½" 45.00
Bowl, lily pads, 3-D girl emerges from lotus flower, 8½"..............450.00
Ewer, Noveau floral, purple on wht, red mk, 9" 235.00
Ewer, poppies, purple w/gold on cream, RS&K mk, 9" 75.00
Lamp, mosque; Persian-style decor, Stellmacher, 1880s 185.00
Vase, appl cupid on gr to lav, dbl hdls, rtcl, 16"............................380.00
Vase, cavalier, mc on brn, Stellmacher, hdls, 10" 125.00
Vase, gold dragon at neck on cobalt w/flowers, mk, 17"...............595.00
Vase, gold-traced flowers on cream, 1-hdl, mk Bohemia, 16" 100.00
Vase, Nouveau maid relief panel, mk Brownoakware, 12½" 525.00
Vase, poppies, orange on gr w/gold, ewer form, 17", pr 485.00

Vase, portrait of a lady, ca 1895, 4", $85.00.

Terra Cotta

Terra cotta is a type of earthenware or clay used for statuary, architectural facings, or domestic articles. It is unglazed, baked to durable hardness, and characterized by the color of the body which may range from brick red to buff.

Bust of Mozart, dk brn glaze, mk C&C, 9", NM 40.00
Bust of 18th-century child, mk Le Brun, socle base, 13½" 350.00
Figurine, cupid keeps 2nd bk from flaming heart, 20" 400.00
Figurine, figure well concealed by hooded robe, Samson, 17" . 1,000.00
Figurine, nude, legs about male peacock, sgn Gurdjan, 12" 700.00
Figurine, nude dancer, arms raised, bobbed hair, Luce, 29" 385.00
Pin tray, gr, frog on edge 150.00
Roundel, relief bust of man w/goatee & wide hat, 18" 150.00
Teapot, leaves/appl roundels, lion finial, 6-sided, 6" 5,400.00
Teapot, Oriental scenes, unglazed, 3⅝", EX 1,200.00

Thermometers

Though the collecting of advertising thermometers has been popular for years, only recently have decorative thermometers come into their own as bona fide items of interest and value. Indoor and outdoor decorative models have been manufactured for hundreds of years, yet their relative scarcity enhances their value and interest for the collector. Most American thermometers manufactured early in the 20th century were produced by Taylor (Tycos), and today their thermometers remain the most plentiful on the market. They also serve as the price standards for most historical thermometers.

Insofar as sheer beauty, uniqueness, and scientific accuracy, decorative thermometers are far superior to the ordinary and inexpensive versions which carry advertising. Decorative thermometers run the gamut from plain tin household varieties to the highly ornate creations of Tiffany and Bradley and Hubbard. They have been manufactured from nearly every conceivable material – oak, sterling, brass, and glass being the favorites – and have tested the artistry and technical skills of some of America's finest craftsmen. Ornamental models can be found in free-hanging, wall-mounted, or desk/mantel versions.

Thermometer prices are based on age, ornateness, and whether mercury or alcohol is used as the filler in the tube. Thermometers with damaged, missing, or substitute parts bring greatly reduced prices. Paper scales indicate either replacement of a broken metal scale or a device of lower quality.

Virtually all American-made thermometers available today as collectors' items were made between 1875 and 1940. The Golden Age of decoratives ended in the early 1940s as modern manufacturing processes and materials robbed them of their natural distinctiveness. European thermometers, while of comparable beauty and craftsmanship, have not yet migrated to this country in any great numbers; those produced in America still dominate the buy/sell market.

Our advisor for this category is Warren Harris; he is listed in the Directory under California.

Key:
br — brass	pmc — permacolor
F & C — Fahrenheit and Celsius	sc — scales
F & R — Fahrenheit and Reamer	stl — stainless
mrc — mercury	

Adam Kilt, desk; br portico/scallop roof, F&R sc/mrc, 4½" **42.00**
Alexandre, folding; F&R sc, mrc, 1850s **85.00**
Anonymous, desk; picture fr w/glass, mrc, 1902, 7" **85.00**
Bargess Reversible Box, br sc, oak case, mrc, 5½" **30.00**
Bearskin Ltd, desk; fluted base, brass, brass sc, 6" **150.00**
Bearskin Ltd, wall; metal clip, rnd mcr, 1930, 3x4" **240.00**
Bertrand Mumser, desk; cast/cathedral, months rotate/mrc, 12" **930.00**
BLT-Luce, desk; figural, flared base, br w/br sc, mrc, 6" **75.00**
Bradley & Hubbard, desk; br/ornate lion, br sc/mrc, 9", VG **70.00**
Bradley & Hubbard, scroll bk, steel/cb, Mensh, mrc, 8" **250.00**
Brown Penzance, desk; brn marble, ivory sc, mrc, 6" **75.00**
C Wilder Co, bear & billboard br figural, mrc, 6½" **65.00**
Casella London, wall; maxi/minimum, 2 units, wood, plastic sc .**235.00**
CE Lange, kitchen; The Modern Thermometer, tin, pmc...........**150.00**
Chester, desk; stl sc, sterling bezel, mrc, 2x6" **95.00**
Clark, desk; ivory ped, crown, mrc, 1904, 7" **145.00**
Cloister, inkwell, stl bk & base w/angels at side, 1901..................**975.00**
Creswel, travel; ivory case/mirror, removable sc, mrc, 2½" **2,400.00**
Desk, cvd walrus tusk, 2-tier disk base, inlay sc, 1860, 9"............**220.00**
Dr Dan'l Draper's Self-Recording, metal/glass, 1887, 20" **25.00**
E Berman Co, desk; br/filigree/top scrollwork, mrc, 8" **110.00**
Freeborn, desk; bronze w/lead decor/br sc, mrc, 8"........................**39.00**
G Barnes, oak fold-out box, plastic sc, mrc, 2½"............................**90.00**
G Cooper, desk; bell shape w/cupola, sterling, dial, 2x3" **50.00**
Gloucester Scientific, stl case, glass front, pmc, 42"................. **1,050.00**
Golub, hanging; mahog/br bulb cap, lg sc/red spirit, 9x2" **65.00**
H Lauramark, hanging; gold stipple on boxwood, 0-120, mrc **60.00**
Harriman, P, desk; br ped on griffin, mrc, 9" **48.00**

Hiergelsell Bros, indoor; cabinet/oak bk, bl liquid, #159 ....**65.00**
Hohmann Maurer Co, steel F&C sc & bk, mrc, 12" **27.00**
Honeywell, desk; Bakelite bell base, dial sc, 1935, 3" dia............**95.00**
J Needle, desk; figural, calendar, br w/porc sc, mrc, 6"................**95.00**
Jed Sirrah, hanging; silver, umbrella, mrc, 8" **70.00**
Jedseth Ltd, desk; Mercury figure w/base filigree, mrc, 7"............**90.00**
Jockomo IN, desk; sterling face/br sc, mrc, 1904, 6"......................**65.00**

Kate Greenaway-type figure on ladder, French bronze, 7", $495.00.

Koizumisan, desk; w/br candelabra, rnd mrc tube, 1875, 10" ... **4,000.00**
Nova Products, desk; glass cover over bronze sc, 4"........................**35.00**
Nova Products, desk; rnd, glass encased, dial sc, pat 1923.............**52.00**
Orchard, iron case, br face, w/glass intact, 14"...............................**75.00**
Pairpoint, desk; sterling picture fr, mrc, 1907, 5"..........................**220.00**
Pairpoint, mantel; br, w/angel, sterling sc/mrc, 1904 ....**195.00**
Phila Therm Co, hygrometer; br sc, rotating bezel, 1928 ....**40.00**
Reau, desk; ornate blk bronze, wood F&C sc, mrc..........................**57.00**
Reau, desk; sq incline base, floral top, mrc, 1895 ....**195.00**
S Mitzutani, alabaster ped, candle figural atop, mrc, 15" **100.00**
Short & Mason, recording drum; copper case, 1910......................**78.00**
Slouche, desk; alabaster ped, paper sc inset, mrc, 8x2½"..............**75.00**
Standard, for Fairbanks & Co, rnd, br case, 1886, 7" **70.00**
Standard, hanging; rnd, br rim, -40 to 150, dial.............................**40.00**
Standard, wall; br case, dial counter balance, 1885, 9" **110.00**
Taylor, hanging; ornate wood bk, br sc, 10x7" **50.00**
Taylor, hanging; pnt wood, red spirit, 6x24" **50.00**
Taylor, lady's profile, cvd wood, emb Art Deco, 20½", EX **195.00**
Taylor, wall; blk enameled case, F&R sc on stl, mrc, 12" **35.00**
Taylor, wall; octagonal wood fr/metal sc, red liquid, 5"................**45.00**
Tiffany, desk; horoscope, bronze, mrc, 1907, 4x7" **86.00**
Tycos, incubator hygrometer; glass reservoir, 4x4"........................**16.00**
Tycos, maxi/minimum, japanned tin/br, mrc, T-5452, 8" **85.00**
Tycos-Taylor, outdoor wall; wood fr, red liquid, 27x5"..................**70.00**
Vogue, desk; Victorian, dial, gr, 1931 ....**25.00**
W Pratt, desk; wood inlays, ivory sc, mrc, 1900, 6" **90.00**
Warren Foundries, wall; umbrella w/dragon hdl, br sc, mrc, 12" **90.00**
Wise, desk; Tunbridge, twin columns, mrc, 1870, 5" **1,250.00**
Zeradatha, desk; cast metal, dial w/rotate sc, 1926, 7" **43.00**

Tiffany

Louis Comfort Tiffany was born in 1848 to Charles Lewis and Harriet Young Tiffany of New York. By the time he was eighteen, his father's small dry goods and stationery store had grown and developed into the world-renowned Tiffany and Company.

Preferring the study of art to joining his father in the family business, Louis spent the next six years under the tutelage of noted artists. He returned to America in 1870 and until 1875 painted canvases that focused on European and North African scenes. Deciding the more lucrative approach was in the application of industrial arts and crafts, he opened a decorating studio called Louis C. Tiffany and Co., Associated Artists. He began seriously experimenting with glass, and eschewing traditionally painted-on details, he instead learned to produce glass with qualities that could suggest natural textures and effects. His experiments broadened, and he soon concentrated his efforts on vases, bowls, etc. that came to be considered the highest achievements of the art. Peacock feathers, leaves and vines, flowers and abstracts were developed within the plane of the glass as it was blown. Opalescent and metallic lustres were combined with transparent color to produce stunning effects. Tiffany called his glass Favrile, meaning handmade.

In 1900 he established Tiffany Studios and turned his attention full time to producing art glass, leaded-glass lamp shades, and household wares with metal components. He also designed a complete line of jewelry which was sold through his father's store. He became proficiently accomplished in silverwork and produced such articles as hand mirrors embellished with peacock feather designs set with gems and candlesticks with Favrile glass inserts.

Tiffany's work exemplified the Art Nouveau style of design and decoration, and through his own flamboyant personality and business acumen he perpetrated his tastes onto the American market to the extent that his name became a household word. Tiffany Studios continued to prosper until the second decade of this century when due to changing tastes his influence began to diminish. By 1920 the company had closed.

Serial numbers were assigned to much of Tiffany's work, and letter prefixes indicated the year of manufacture: A-N for 1896-1900, P-Z for 1901-1905. After that, the letter followed the numbers with A-N in use from 1906-1912; P-Z from 1913-1920. O-marked pieces were made especially for friends of relatives; X indicated pieces not made for sale.

Our listings are primarily from the auction houses in the East where Tiffany sells at a premium; our advisor tells us that in other areas of the country many examples may command prices of as much as 50% less. All items are signed unless noted otherwise.

Bronze

Address file, Zodiac, gilt patina, orig paper roll, #1074 .... **1,500.00**
Ash stand, overlapping leaves on std, #1651, 26½" **1,600.00**
Ash stand, swirled rnd base w/knop std, 28" **1,100.00**
Ash tray, gilt patina, ribbed oval, nested set of 4 ....**250.00**
Blotter ends, Grapevine, filigree, 19½", pr **100.00**
Book rack, Abalone, gilt patina, #1177, 14" L **1,100.00**
Bookends, seated Buddha, #1025, 6" **300.00**
Bookends, textured/patinated, abstract silver inlay, 4½" **100.00**

Jewelry box, abalone shell grapes inlaid on lid, #1174, 6½", $900.00.

Box, Grapevine, cream glass insert, 4 ball ft, 4½" L **200.00**
Box, handkerchief; Grapevine, amber slag insert, 2x8x8" **600.00**
Box, Pine Needle, cream glass insert, gilding, 8" L **500.00**
Candelabrum, 2-arm, std w/bud terminal, petal base, 9" **800.00**
Candlestick, rtcl cup w/blown-in slag glass, 13½" **600.00**
Candlestick, 4-leg std, 4 paw ft, gold shades, 17", pr............... **2,300.00**
Candlestick, 7-jewel cup, slim std splits to 4 legs, 10".............. **1,700.00**
Charger, Abalone, gilt patina, #1728, 14" **550.00**
Charger, abstract foliate border, gilt, #1747, 14" **135.00**
Clock, fluted supports w/acorn finials, #2074, 9" **1,800.00**
Clock, Graduate, polychrome/gilt, upward-angled face, 2½" **600.00**
Clock, slanted front, face w/enamel 'tiles,' #360, 5½" **800.00**
Desk set, Abalone, paper rack/inkwell/pen tray/box/opener ... **2,100.00**
Desk set, Venetian, clock/paperweight/bookends+9 pcs.......... **3,700.00**
Fr, Grapevine, beaded borders, cream/amber slag, 14x12" **1,800.00**
Fr, Pine Needle, beaded borders, over gr slag, 9½x8" **1,500.00**
Fr, Pine Needle, easel bk, 15x12", EX **1,400.00**
Fr, Pine Needle, gr glass insert, rstr, 7x6" **100.00**
Fr, Pine Needle, gr glass insert, 12x9½", NM **1,500.00**
Fr, Venetian, gilt, #1682, 12x9" **1,650.00**
Inkstand, Zodiac, gilt patina, #1072...**385.00**
Inkwell, Pine Needle, filigree/glass, #10, 3¾" dia **350.00**
Letter file, Venetian, gilt patina, #1644, 6" **495.00**
Letter file, Zodiac, 3-tier, dk brn patina, 8".................................**400.00**
Letter scale, Grapevine, filigree, #872, 3" **450.00**
Lighter, scarab form, gilt patina, #9395, 4" L.............................**175.00**
Paperweight, bulldog's head, #888, 2" **700.00**
Paperweight, crouching panther, dk patina, #887, 3¾" L **400.00**
Paperweight, reclining lion, gilt dore, 5" L **600.00**
Thermometer, Grapevine, gr glass insert, 8¾" L **550.00**

Glass

Bowl, amber/yel irid, stretched/ruffled/crimped, +7" plate **450.00**
Bowl, bl-gold, ribbed/scalloped, 3x10"..................................... **1,350.00**
Bowl, bl-gold w/gr lily pads, 11", +2-tier frog w/loops.............. **2,600.00**
Bowl, butterscotch pastel, dmn motif, stretch border, 10" **850.00**
Bowl, gold, intaglio leaves, ribbed, low ribbed ped ft, 6" **725.00**
Bowl, gold, ribbed, scalloped, 8" **700.00**
Bowl, gold, ribbed, slender, flared, 7" **450.00**
Bowl, gold, swirl ribbed, 9½" **1,000.00**
Bowl, gold w/intaglio leaves & vines, low std, 2x8" **1,100.00**
Bowl, gr pastel, dmn motif, ped ft, 2x6" **600.00**
Bowl, lt gold w/gold feathers, tiny pulled hdls, 2½x3¾" **700.00**
Bowl, pk pastel, opal dmn pattern spreads to hot pk, 8"..............**550.00**
Bowl, pk pastel, stretch border, opal ped ft, 3¼x11½" **2,450.00**
Bowl, silver-bl w/gr irid foliage, ca 1916, 8"............................ **1,700.00**
Bowl, swirls, bl on orange, pearl int, 4" **525.00**
Bowl, yel pastel, wht dmn motif, 6" **300.00**
Bowl, yel pastel w/rice pattern, 5½", in gold-wash mk fr.......... **1,000.00**
Candle holder, gr pastel, opal rice-pattern ped ft, 3½" **550.00**
Candlestick, bl, gold/purple irid, twist stem/bobeche, 5" **425.00**
Candlestick, gold, 10-rib swirl base, 5", pr **850.00**
Candlestick, rose pastel, short std, opal panels in ft, 3¾" **800.00**
Compote, floriform; wht w/gr feathers, gold ft/int, 5½" **1,600.00**
Compote, gold, scalloped, knob std, 3¾" **400.00**
Compote, gold, stretched/scalloped rim, ftd, 3½x8" **850.00**
Compote, gold, swollen cylindrical std, 11" **1,900.00**
Compote, gold w/EX irid, baluster stem, 3½x6" **225.00**
Compote, gr pastel, wht striations in ft & ring std, 6½" **900.00**
Compote, opal w/gr feathers, gold int, 4x5"...............................**850.00**
Cordial, gold irid, long stem, 5" **290.00**
Decanter, gold, pinched sides, stick neck, sq stopper, 11" **1,600.00**
Finger bowl, gold, intaglio grapes border, 5", +underplate...........**500.00**

Humidor, gold, cushion lid w/rnd finial, 7¾" 1,000.00
Parfait, floriform; opal/clear striped w/bl irid int, 9" 375.00
Plate, gr opal pastel w/internal leafy decor, 8" 500.00
Salt cellar, gold, ribbed, scalloped, 2½" dia, pr 340.00
Shade, bl irid, bell form, 13½" 1,500.00
Sherbet, amber w/gold irid, appl 'thorns,' 3½" 175.00
Sherbet, gr pastel, lt yel ped ft, 4" 275.00
Toothpick holder, gold, pinched sides, 1¾" 220.00
Vase, Agate, irregular ovoid, crude rim, experimental, 6" 3,000.00
Vase, Agate, marbleized brns, ribbed bottle form, unsgn, 5" 240.00
Vase, amber irid, striated gr coils/ribbons, 10½"............. 1,200.00
Vase, amber irid, trumpet form, dome ft, 13" 1,210.00
Vase, amber irid w/rose & bl-gr tinge, faint feathers, 3½" 800.00
Vase, amber w/EX lustre, baluster w/scroll hdls, 13x9" 3,000.00
Vase, amber w/2 gr & gold feathered bands, dbl bulb, 10"....... 1,800.00
Vase, bl, ribbed, trumpet form, in mk bronze base, 12"........... 1,900.00
Vase, bl w/gr leaves & vines, spherical, 2¾"............. 1,650.00
Vase, bl w/purple irid, slim form, in gilt-bronze std, 14" 1,700.00
Vase, bl-gold, bulbous w/flared rim & ped ft, 12" 1,550.00
Vase, bl-gold, scalloped 6½" dia stretch rim, ped ft, 5" 1,100.00
Vase, bl-gold, urn form w/scroll hdl, 4½"............. 925.00
Vase, blk irid w/bl & gr banded swirls, baluster, 5½" 1,900.00
Vase, bright bl w/intaglio leaves & vines, 10"............. 1,650.00
Vase, brn w/bl-gold leaves, dbl-bulb base/stick neck, 12" 4,500.00
Vase, bud; gold, in ftd bronze base, 8¾"............. 400.00
Vase, bud; red w/bl irid zigzags, 6"............. 7,500.00
Vase, cobalt irid w/internal gr heart-leaves, ftd, 6" 2,500.00
Vase, Cypriote, amber/gr/brn textured irid, thick sides, 5" 3,500.00
Vase, dk purple w/silver swirls, gourd form, 3½" 2,000.00
Vase, Egyptian, orange irid, gold neck, 2-color zigzags, 6" 2,300.00
Vase, floriform; amber w/gold irid, ribbed, ped ft, 6x6" 600.00
Vase, floriform; bl-gold ribbed/scalloped bowl, 13½x4½" 2,750.00
Vase, floriform; gold, ribbed, scalloped, 11" 800.00
Vase, floriform; gold, ribbed tulip-form w/petal rim, 9" 1,400.00
Vase, floriform; opal & gold w/gr leaves, dome ft, 18½" 7,000.00
Vase, floriform; opal w/gr feathers, 12¾"............. 3,500.00
Vase, gold, appl lily pads pulled up from ft, #M7382, 3¾" 300.00
Vase, gold, molded oval bosses, fluted neck, label, 6"............. 550.00
Vase, gold, ribbed, spherical w/can neck, 9"............. 1,000.00
Vase, gold, ribbed trumpet form, label, 7"............. 500.00
Vase, gold, trumpet form on knopped rnd ft, 10" 1,200.00
Vase, gold w/gr & wht cameo, intaglio dogwood blooms, 18" . 6,500.00
Vase, gold w/gr hearts & vines, spherical, 2¾" 1,000.00
Vase, gold w/mirror lustre, threaded at waist, 4" 175.00
Vase, internal gold loop-coils/pk spots, pinched sides, 5" 5,500.00
Vase, jack-in-pulpit; gold, frilled rim, label, 17"............. 6,600.00
Vase, jack-in-pulpit; gold, frosted stem, bulbous base, 17"....... 8,000.00
Vase, jack-in-pulpit; gold w/EX lustre, bun ft, 21" 7,600.00
Vase, orange irid w/amber tinge, urn form, 1916, 6" 1,500.00
Vase, pk pastel, yel base, trumpet form, 14" 1,225.00
Vase, red w/yel pull-up swirls, 6 molded petals, 3½" 6,250.00
Vase, tan irid to gold w/pulled decor, 16" 4,600.00
Vase, Tel El Amarna, amber irid w/rust neck, 5"............. 600.00
Vase, Tel El Amarna, gr/brn on gold neck, lt gr body, 8" 5,500.00
Vase, Tel El Amarna, purple neck, gr cased to opal body, 8" ... 4,500.00
Vase, Tel El Amarna, vines, gr on gold, blk/gold neck, 13" 5,700.00
Wine, bl pastel w/wht ferns, 7"............. 500.00
Wine, bl-gold, 3⅜", set of 6............. 1,260.00
Wine, Draped Bead, gold, ftd, 5½"............. 450.00
Wine, gold, flared bowl, 4", set of 6 (4 sgn) 1,200.00

Lamps

Base, bamboo, #1934, 27½" 2,200.00

Base, floor; bronze harp style w/lily buds, 12" base, #425 ....950.00
Base, floor; 4-ftd cushion w/foliage emb, ribbed std, 81" 2,850.00
Base, harp std on fluted cushion ft, #424, 17" 1,000.00
Base, ovoid w/4 fluted paw-ft legs on rnd base, gilt, 14"............800.00
Base, pine needle relief, baluster form, 12½"............. 1,000.00
Base, table, bronze, 3-prong holder for 11½" shade, #431 ....750.00
Base, 2-leg std, ea leg w/2 curved cylinder ft, #396, 22" 3,575.00
Base, 3-leaf circular ft, 3 arms branch from base, 10" 500.00
Boudoir, bl-gold 7" shade/twist ped base, feathered stem 1,850.00
Bridge, ldgl 12" acorn-band shade, EX mottling; std #1410 .... 7,000.00
Candle, gold chimney/dmn-emb shade & std; foliate std #25   1,300.00
Candle, gold flared shade & swirl-rib base, 12", pr 4,400.00
Candle, gold 7" shade on feathered stem, swirl/rib std, 14".........750.00
Chandelier, ldgl, fringed border: 4 rows sm sqs, 24" 9,600.00
Chandelier, ldgl 'Roman,' flared dome, #564, 24½"............. 6,000.00
Chandelier, ldgl brickwork shade, 6-light cluster, 24"............. 8,250.00
Chandelier, ldgl brickwork/1 turtle-bk tile, domical, 21" 4,000.00

20" daffodil shade; #6879 base (EX condition), $27,000.00 at auction.

Desk, amber damascene 7" shade (EX); counter-balance, 13" . 3,500.00
Desk, bronze shade; counter-balance std #637, 13½" 1,500.00
Desk, gold damascene 7" shade (EX); 3-arm std #322, 15" 2,750.00
Desk, gold irid bowl shade; Zodiac std #664, 17" 2,600.00
Desk, gold lily shade on counter-balanced tilting arm, 16"...... 1,700.00
Desk, kappa shell shade; counter-balance std #416 .... 800.00
Desk, linenfold 8" paneled shade; harp std #613, 18½" 3,900.00
Desk, Zodiac, U-form support, dome/octagon base, 13½"........ 1,760.00
Floor, ldgl 24" acorn-band shade; std #1510 w/17" base, 82"..18,000.00
Floor, ldgl 25" Roman helmet shade; std #1564, 64"...............16,000.00
Floor, 6 amber 'blossom' shades; lg 3-D crane on tree std 34,000.00
Hanging, ldgl 12" sq brickwork/bull's eye band shade, 17" 10,000.00
Lily, upright; 8-light, gold shades; organic std #569, 28".........30,000.00
Lily, 10-light, ea gold shade sgn; cvd lily pad std #381............15,000.00
Lily, 12-light, amber shades (1 damaged); lily pad std, 22" 18,000.00
Lily, 12-light, ea gold shade sgn; std #6017 ....28,000.00
Lily, 3-light, gold shades; fluted rnd-base std #319, 13" 4,500.00
Nautilus, ldgl shell shade; bronze dolphin std #634, 14½"....... 3,600.00
Scarab, bl-gr, U-form support, dome base, 4 ball ft, 9"............. 3,850.00
Shade, amber w/strong irid highlights, bowl form, 4x7" 1,800.00
Shade, opal w/stretched gold irid, bowl form, 2½x10" 1,800.00
Shade, paneled fabric, emb grapevines & butterflies, 18"........ 1,760.00
Student, ldgl 12" acorn dome shade w/fringe; oil canister 4,100.00
Table, ldgl 14" acorn shade; broad-rib/3-arm std #333, EX 4,700.00
Table, ldgl 14" acorn shade; bronze 4-ftd std, rpl sockets 4,000.00
Table, ldgl 14" poinsettia shade; std #1556 (EX), 19½" 15,000.00

Table, ldgl 16" acorn shade (EX); urn-form std #D888, 22½" . 7,000.00
Table, ldgl 16" daffodil shade; 3-arm std #25882, 22" 11,500.00
Table, ldgl 16" geometric shade; std #585, 22" 1,650.00
Table, ldgl 16" herringbone shade; 3-arm std #6148, 21".......... 9,000.00
Table, ldgl 16" pomegranate shade; 4-leg oil can std #888 ...... 5,000.00
Table, ldgl 18" clematis shade; bronze sgn std 16,000.00
Table, ldgl 18" pk dogwood-band shade; #531 std.................20,000.00
Table, ldgl 20" acorn-band shade; 4-light library std #681......13,000.00
Table, ldgl 20" daffodil shade; 5-arm twist std (damage).........23,000.00
Table, ldgl 20" daffodil/narcissus shade; std #368, 28"............36,000.00
Table, ldgl 20" dragonfly w/jewels shade; std #358, 25" 33,000.00
Table, ldgl 20" poinsettia-border shade; std #368 ....33,000.00
Table, ldgl 22" geometric shade; std #532, 29" 12,000.00
Table, linenfold 10" shade, abalone on shade & std #604........ 7,000.00
Table, linenfold 24-panel 18" bronze-band shade; std #203 .... 9,500.00

Pottery

Vase, bouquet of Queen Anne's Lace form, bsk, gr int, 8" 1,700.00
Vase, Chinese-style bl-gr gloss w/red dripping, 5½", NM.............350.00
Vase, floral relief, wht bsk w/gr gloss int, slim form, 12" 650.00
Vase, florals emb on cream w/gr drip, #7, 7" 750.00
Vase, hollyhocks relief, mk Bronze Pottery, 17" 3,000.00
Vase, lady slippers emb on cylinder, gr mottle, 12" 3,750.00
Vase, lilies/leaves relief on mint & olive, waisted, 14"............. 1,200.00
Vase, tulips emb on silver-clad bronze, mk Bronze, 7", NM 700.00

Silver

Bonbon server, hdl: child kisses cherub head, 1938, 13½"....... 1,250.00
Bowl, chased vine border, monogram, oval, 12" L, pr.................750.00
Candlestick, smooth std w/moldings, 13", pr, NM 1,800.00
Claret jug, bulbous glass body, lion/shield surmount, 12" 1,100.00
Cocktail shaker, etched palmettes, tapered cylinder, 9" 475.00
Compote, etched floral border, champleve wreath, 8" dia...........900.00
Crumb knife, Persian, monogram, 1872, 4-oz................................325.00
Ladle, Persian, monogram, 1872, 7-oz..450.00
Platter, plated, w/dome, stand, & burner, monogram, 20" L 400.00
Sealing wax set, sq 3-compartment decorated tray w/lighter........800.00
Teapot, ribbed, appl chrysanthemums, ivory mts, 5¾" 1,400.00
Tray, interlaced vine border, monogram, 13" dia 650.00

Miscellaneous

Bracelet, 18k gold, Arts & Crafts style, ca 1958........................ 1,500.00
Clock, gold/silver face w/exposed works, many dials, 78" 24,000.00
Clock, travel; mk 8-Day Swiss Made, orig case, 2½" dia 450.00
Mirror, tile fr: red w/flowers alternate w/bl irid, 22x28" 935.00
Panel, cvd wood nude over cartouch 'Favrile Glass,' 50" 700.00
Panel, ldgl, lily blossom, att, 1900s, 23x13" 7,000.00
Plaque, glass mosaic, portrait of centaur, 16x12" 6,000.00
Plate, English porc, gilt border, retailed by Tiffany, 10" 20.00
Salt cellar, copper w/3-color enamel swirls, ⅞x2" 400.00
Turtle-bk tile, purple/bl irid, in bronze frwork, 8x7" 495.00
Window, ldgl full-length angel in floral field, fr, 48x33".........14,000.00

Tiffin Glass

The Tiffin Glass Company was founded in 1887 in Tiffin, Ohio, one of the many factories composing the U.S. Glass Company. Its early wares consisted of tablewares and decorative items such as lamps and globes. Among the most popular of all Tiffin products was the black satin glass produced there during the 1920s. In 1959 U.S. Glass was sold, and in 1962 the factories closed. The plant was re-opened in 1963 as the Tiffin Art Glass Company. Products from this period were tableware, hand-blown stemware, and other decorative items.

Those interested in learning more about Tiffin glass are encouraged to contact the Tiffin Collectors' Club, whose address can be found in the Directory under Clubs, Newsletters, and Catalogs. See also Black Glass.

Basket, Twilight, sm...70.00
Bonbon, Fuchsia, 3-ftd...45.00
Bowl, Palais Versailles, gold encrusted, 4½"...............................28.00
Bowl, Twilight, heart form..55.00
Candlesticks, twisted, blk satin, pr 45.00
Champagne, Cherokee Rose 18.00
Champagne, Classic, pulled stem 22.00
Champagne, Empire, pk 18.00
Champagne, First Love 18.00
Champagne, Flanders 15.00
Champagne, Flanders, pk 25.00
Champagne, Fontaine, gr 30.00
Champagne, Fontaine, pk..32.00
Champagne, Forever Yours 12.00
Champagne, Fuchsia 18.00
Champagne, June Night 22.00
Champagne, Liege 15.00
Champagne, Palais Versailles, gold encrusted................................35.00
Champagne, Persian Pheasant...30.00
Claret, Cherokee Rose 32.50
Claret, June Night 32.50
Claret, Persian Pheasant...30.00
Cocktail, Cherokee Rose...20.00
Cocktail, Fuchsia 20.00
Cocktail, June Night..20.00
Cocktail, Le Fleur, yel...25.00
Cocktail, Liege...12.00
Cordial, Cherokee Rose..45.00
Cordial, First Love 18.00
Cordial, Flanders, pk..75.00
Cordial, Kilarny..25.00
Cordial, Liege...15.00
Cordial, Palais Versailles, gold encrusted......................................35.00
Cordial, Persian Pheasant 55.00
Cordial, Rambling Rose..35.00
Cordial, True Love..22.50
Creamer, Cerise, ftd 25.00
Creamer, Twilight 55.00
Creamer & sugar bowl, Cerise 50.00
Creamer & sugar bowl, Flanders, ftd 95.00
Creamer & sugar bowl, Fuchsia, flat..45.00
Creamer & sugar bowl, Le Fleur, yel, ftd......................................125.00
Creamer & sugar bowl, Modern Wisteria 75.00
Creamer & sugar bowl, Rosalind, yel 85.00
Cup & saucer, bouillon; Fontaine, gr...60.00
Cup & saucer, Flanders, ftd...35.00
Cup & saucer, Rosalind, yel...35.00
Decanter, cordial; Swedish Modern, cobalt 65.00
Decanter, Flanders, pk..395.00
Finger bowl, Liege 8.00
Flower floater, dbl candle...32.00
Goblet, water; Cerise, #071 ....22.50
Goblet, water; Cherokee Rose...24.00
Goblet, water; Classic...22.00
Goblet, water; First Love 18.00
Goblet, water; Fontaine, gr..40.00

Goblet, water; Fuchsia 21.00
Goblet, water; June Night 20.00
Goblet, water; Liege..17.50
Goblet, water; Palais Versailles, gold encrusted.........35.00
Goblet, water; Persian Pheasant.................................35.00
Goblet, water; Rambling Rose....................................23.00
Goblet, water; Rosalyn, Mandarin Yel 15.00
Goblet, water; Shawl Dancer, pulled stem 15.00
Iced tea, Byzantine, crystal w/blk base......................14.00
Iced tea, Cherokee Rose 20.00
Iced tea, Empire, pk, ftd 22.00
Iced tea, Flanders, pk 40.00
Iced tea, Flanders, yel...25.00
Iced tea, Fuchsia, ftd 22.00
Iced tea, Persian Pheasant, ftd 18.00
Lamp, parrot, red, 13"..225.00
Oyster cocktail, Fuchsia..20.00
Parfait, Classic Dancer..25.00
Parfait, Empire, pk 22.00
Parfait, Flying Nun, gr 40.00
Pitcher, Flanders, pk, w/lid 295.00
Pitcher, Flying Nun, gr, w/lid..................................475.00
Pitcher, Le Fleur, yel, water sz.................................275.00
Pitcher, Twilight, 6" 100.00
Plate, Byzantine, 10½" 35.00
Plate, Empire, pk, 8" 16.00
Plate, Empire, Twilight, 8" 17.50
Plate, Flanders, pk, 6" 12.50
Plate, Flanders, pk, 8" 17.50
Plate, Flanders, yel, 10"..35.00
Plate, Flanders, 10½" 35.00
Plate, Fontaine, gr, 10" 50.00
Plate, Fontaine, gr, 8" 15.00
Plate, Fontaine, Twilight, 8" 18.00
Plate, Fontaine, 8" 15.00
Plate, Le Fleur, yel, 7¼" 10.00
Plate, Palais Versailles, gold encrusted, 8" 28.00
Plate, Rosalind, yel, 10½" 35.00
Plate, Wisteria, pk, 8" 16.00
Relish, Rambling Rose, 3-part 17.50
Rose bowl, Juno, yel, 3-toed, lg 75.00
Saucer, Persian Pheasant.. 6.00
Shade, Fuchsia, 12"..150.00
Shakers, Cerise, pr 75.00
Sherbet, Athione, w/label 6.00
Sherbet, Flying Nun, gr, low.......................................25.00
Sherbet, Fuchsia...15.00
Sherbet, Thistle, yel, 3⅞" 6.00
Sherry, Liege 12.00
Sherry, Persian Pheasant, wide mouth 30.00
Sugar bowl, Flying Nun, gr 65.00
Sugar bowl, Fuchsia, ind 35.00
Sugar bowl, Rambling Rose 25.00
Sundae, Fontaine, gr..25.00
Sundae, Persian Pheasant 30.00
Sundae, Rambling Rose 16.00
Tumbler, juice; Byzantine, ftd...................................15.00
Tumbler, juice; Cherokee Rose, ftd 15.00
Tumbler, juice; Empire, pk, ftd 22.00
Tumbler, juice; Fontaine, gr, ftd 30.00
Tumbler, juice; June Night, ftd, 4"............................15.00
Tumbler, juice; Liege 6.00
Vase, blk satin, blown-out poppies, 5".......................35.00
Vase, bud; Cerise, 10½" 25.00

Vase, bud; June Night, 10½" 45.00
Vase, Fuchsia, beaded, 11"...65.00
Vase, Fuchsia, bulbous, 11".......................................125.00
Vase, Fuchsia, trophy form 95.00
Vase, Swedish Modern, lt amethyst, teardrop form, 8¾"...............35.00

Vase, tomato red on black satin base, paper label, 6" x 7", $75.00.

Wine, Cherokee Rose 20.00
Wine, Fontaine, gr...40.00
Wine, Forever Yours 15.00
Wine, Fuchsia 24.00
Wine, Liege..14.00
Wine, Palais Versailles, gold encrusted 35.00
Wine, Persian Pheasant..35.00
Wine, Psyche, gr..50.00
Wine, Rosalyn, Mandarin Yel 15.00

Tiles

Though originally strictly functional, tiles were being produced in various colors and used as architectural highlights as early as the Ancient Roman Empire. By the 18th century, Dutch tiles were decorated with polychrome landscapes and figures. During the 19th century, there were over a hundred companies in England involved in the manufacture of tile. By the Victorian era, the use of decorative tiles had reached its peak. Special souvenir editions, campaign and portrait tiles, and Art Nouveau motifs with lovely ladies and stylized examples from nature were popular. Today all of these are very collectible. See also specific manufacturers.

CA Art, peacock in grape arbor w/fountain, bl tones, 8x12" 80.00
Columbia Encaustic, floral, cream/brn gloss, 4½" 24.00
Dutch, horse, mulberry/wht, 1700s, fr, 5½" 50.00
Kensington, classic female head, brn, 6" 40.00
Low, Autumn, lady's portrait, bl-gr, 6⅛x4½" 75.00
Low, boy w/book, caramel, imp A in circle on front, 6" 100.00
Low, florals, amber 35.00
Low, geometric florals, yel/gr, 6" 25.00
Low, lady in bonnet, 2 sm faces at bottom, gr/brn, 6" 55.00
Low, Lincoln (no beard) & Washington, c 1895, 4x6", pr...........185.00
Low, portrait of stylish lady, bl-gr, 7⅜x5⅜" 75.00
Low, sheep/European village street, teal bl, sgn AO, 18x10" 900.00

Minton, dog by beehive, ca 1880, 6"...45.00
Minton, King Henry, 6"...65.00
Minton, man carrying scythe, bl on wht, by Wm Wise, 6" 125.00
Pardee, Alice in Wonderland, rabbit, hexagonal, 3½" 110.00
Pilkington, Art Nouveau flower, red, Lewis Day design, 6" 85.00
Pilkington, circus horses & lady trainer, sgn, ca 1940 ....65.00

San Jose Pottery, $75.00.

Trent, floral, tan gloss, 6"...20.00
Walrich, mission motif, rnd, paper label, imp mk, 5" 300.00
Wedgwood, calendar, Dec, brn transfer, boy w/mistletoe 65.00
Wedgwood, Red Riding Hood/wolf, blk/wht, Crane design, 6" ..110.00
Wheeling, kittens, calendar bk, 1948..20.00
Wheeling, koala bear, clothed, in tree, sq, 4½" 50.00
Wheeling, W Crane illus & text in brn/bl/yel transfer, 6" 150.00

Tinware

In the American household of the 17th and 18th centuries, tinware items could be found in abundance, from food containers to foot warmers and mirror frames. Although the first settlers brought much of their tinware with them from Europe, by 1798 sheets of tin plate were being imported from England for use by the growing number of American tinsmiths. Tinwares were often decorated either by piercing or painted designs which were both free-hand and stenciled. (See Toleware.) By the early 1900s, many homes had replaced their old tinware with the more attractive aluminum and graniteware.

In the 19th century, tenth wedding anniversaries were traditionally celebrated by gifts of tin. Couples gave big parties, dressed in their wedding clothes, and reaffirmed their vows before their friends and family who arrived bearing (and often wearing) tin gifts, most of which were quite humorous. Anniversary tin items may include hats, cradles, slippers and shoes, rolling pins, etc. See also Primitives and Kitchen Collectibles.

Anniversary basket, blk pnt, minor rust, 9x10" 45.00
Anniversary sword, 33½"...135.00
Anniversary top hat, rpt w/mc flowers, 6¾" 30.00
Apple roaster, cylindrical, minor rust/rpr, 10" L 275.00
Box, candle; cylindrical, 2 hanging tabs, 17" L, EX 85.00
Box, hinged, oval, early, 2½"..28.00
Box, map; cylindrical, hinged lid, leather thong, 18" L 35.00
Candle snuffer, brn japanning, witch's hat form, 3"........................75.00
Chamberstick, conical snuffer, 9" 185.00

Coal bucket, two lids, repousse stars and scallops, American, 1800s, 14½" x 17", $800.00.

Coffeepot, eng folky eagle/flag/foliage, pnt traces, 12"............. 1,850.00
Coffeepot, rolled rims, Shaker-type filter, 1850s, 11½" 145.00
Coffeepot, short/squat, str sides, att Shakers, 8" 150.00
Colander, pierced triangles, ped base, side hdls, lg, EX................20.00
Cooking reflector, punched/pierced, semicircular, 12" L 135.00
Cream can, arched hdl, inset lid, side hdls, 1850s, 11"..................65.00
Dutch oven, cylindrical, rprs/rpl, 22" L..90.00
Dutch oven, cylindrical, wrought iron spit, lt rust, 18x19" 220.00
Egg coddler, divided lid lifts to pull up egg holder 125.00
Egg poacher, 1-egg, spring hdl, EX 24.00
Egg poacher, 6-egg, spring hdl, EX 45.00
Finial, moon mtd above 3 grad stars, 1900, 29" 500.00
Fish slice, rnded blade w/punched designs, wood hdl 75.00
Helmet, campaign; tin w/gold japanning, torch finial.....................80.00
Ladle, pierced, 17" L 20.00
Lamp, candle; funnel-form base, crimp-top reflector, 11" 325.00
Lamp, dbl bull's eye lens, weighted, pnt traces, 9" 500.00
Lamp filler, brass cap, dtd Apr 2, 1861...65.00
Lighting shelf, emb star, Betty lamp rod/candle shelf, 14"............175.00
Measure, Rumford, 1-cup...17.50
Rum warmer, cone shape, pouring lip, cup base, 1830s 130.00
Sconce, crimped crest, miniature, 5¾" 300.00
Sconce, oblong concave bk, fluted cup & socket, 10", pr........ 3,000.00
Sconce, radiating pattern of mirror glass, 9", VG, pr 900.00
Soap saver, screen wire top & bottom, rnd, EX 22.50
Spittoon, removable top, side hdl, early, 6" base 40.00
Stencil, name/1865, 10x14", EX 140.00
Sugar bowl, rim rolled over wire, 1850s, 3¾x4⅝"..........................55.00
Tea ball, screen wire & dk tin, 1½" dia, 2½" L.............................22.00
Teakettle, slant spout, flat bail, Kreamer, 4x4½" 58.00
Teapot, punched flower-filled pot, drilled for lamp, 11"........... 1,200.00
Toddy warmer, funnel top w/pouring lip, side hdl..........................95.00
Torch, hooded, cylinder font, 2-burner, 12x14"..............................85.00
Wash boiler, w/lid, 12" L 60.00

Tobacciana

Tobacciana is the generally accepted term used to cover a field of collecting that includes smoking pipes, cigar molds, cigarette lighters, humidors – in short, any article having to do with the practice of using tobacco in any form.

Perhaps the most valuable variety of pipes is the meerschaum – hand carved from hydrous magnesium, an opaque white-gray or cream-colored mineral of the soapstone family. (Much of this is today mined in Turkey which has the largest meerschaum deposit in the world, though there are other deposits of lesser significance around the globe.) These figural bowls often portray an elaborately carved mythological character, an animal, or a historical scene. Amber is often used for the stem. Other collectible pipes are corn cob (Missouri Meerschaum) and Indian peace pipes of clay or catlinite. (See American Indian Art.)

Chosen because it was the Indians who first introduced the white man to smoking, the cigar store Indian was a symbol used to identify tobacco stores in the 19th century. The majority of them were hand carved between 1830 and 1900 and are today recognized as some of the finest examples of early wood sculptures. When found they command very high prices.

Our advisor for this category is Chuck Thompson; he is listed in the Directory under Texas. See also Advertising; Snuff Boxes.

Box, cigar; wood, Sear's Golden Jubilee, 1886-1936........................20.00
Case, vesta; enameled silver, Simon & Adler, 1903, 1¾" 1,100.00
Cigar box, brass, emb lid & base, Dutch, 1800, 6½" L 200.00
Cigar box, cb, Rudolph Valentino, 5 for 25¢, EX...........................85.00
Cigar box, Lady Abby, Salina Kansas, EX....................................22.00
Cigar box, The Doctor, All Your Ills Will..., w/drw, VG 85.00
Cigar box opener, Golden's Bl Ribbon Cigar, EX 25.00

Cigar cutter, monkey form, 4½", $135.00.

Cigar holder, cherry amber, 2"...12.00
Cigar holder, meerschaum, cvd lady w/fan, orig leather case..........65.00
Cigar holder, meerschaum, ornate cvg, in case 30.00
Cigar lighter/lamp, rpl globe on emb brass/iron base, 11" 225.00
Cigarette cards, Sweet Caporal cigarettes, 1890s, 27 for 70.00
Cigarette case, silver-gilt w/blk stripe, Cartier, 5" 600.00
Cigarette dispenser/lighter, Blk bartender, Ronson, 7" 1,000.00
Cigarette holder, blk Bakelite, sterling band, 2-pc, 3½" 15.00
Cigarette holder, ivory, cvd dragon, 4"...45.00
Cigarette holder, meerschaum, buxom lady sits on flower, 6" 200.00
Cigarette holder, plastic, gr w/gold, 1950s, 1⅛" 6.00
Cigarette holder, Scandia, cb, plastic, metal ring...........................7.50
Cigarette holder, silver filigree, handcrafted, 3⅛"..........................25.00
Cigarette roller, Cigarola, CI, M 38.00
Coffer, tobacco; pyramidal top, ball finial, CI, 1700s, 3x4x5".....260.00
Cutter, cigar; Champagne, champagne bottle forms base 155.00
Cutter, cigar; Home Insurance 100.00
Cutter, cigar; mechanical windup, John Hay..............................325.00
Cutter, cigar; wood/wire/iron, spring-op counter type, 4x7"...........39.00
Cutter, plug; boy thumbs nose on hdl, CI, Brighton #3, 11" 65.00
Cutter, plug; Griswold Erie #1, CI..125.00

Cutter, plug; Griswold Erie #2, CI, gold japanning......................135.00
Cutter, plug; Old Star, gilt letters, mk Save the Tags.....................90.00
Cutter, plug; shield cutout on bk, Pat 1891..................................35.00
Cutter, plug; stainless steel, Japan, w/tamper 9.50
Cutter, plug; Star, dtd 1885 ....65.00
Flier, Pilot cigar cutter ad, dbl sided, 1800s, EX 37.50
Humidor, clear glass w/thick bevels, Nouveau emb brass lid 85.00
Humidor, flint glass, 14-sided, pewter lid, acorn finial, M 36.00
Humidor, glass, LA Palina-Quality Cigar Since 1896, 6x7"...........45.00
Humidor, SP, pug dog figural, glass eyes, Derby, 6x5x3" 225.00
Humidor, SP, reclining boy finial, hat is match holder.................250.00
Indian w/rifle & pipe, Fine Cigars, CI wheels, 1900s, 68" 4,300.00
Jar, Imperial, Coat of Arms, cube cut 35.00
Lighter, brass, eng Meuse, Argonne, Verdun, France, 1920s 175.00
Lighter, brass, US Nat'l seal, bk: Imperial Crown/eagle..................75.00
Lighter, chrome/brass/enamel, French-style Deco, tall 35.00
Lighter, Scripto V-Liter, dice...10.00
Pipe, briar, MacDuff, British sterling band, EX 16.00
Pipe, burlwood, crest eng on bowl cover, European, 33" 700.00
Pipe, clay, sailor smoking pipe, ca 1800, 6½" 500.00
Pipe, cvd Bakelite Indian head bowl/stem, amber mouthpc, 3" 28.00
Pipe, deer antler stem, wooden bowl: etched moose, Germany, 7".32.00
Pipe, meerschaum, cvd Roman's head bowl, 6", w/orig case 65.00
Pipe, meerschaum, fireman w/hose, rpl stem, EX.........................100.00
Pipe, meerschaum, gartered lady's leg, w/orig case, 4½" 100.00
Pipe, meerschaum, turbaned head, amber stem, Turkey 65.00
Pipe, meerschaum, 3 deer relief, w/orig case, 12" 200.00
Pipe, opium; brass & bronze mts, reed stem, China, w/case 95.00
Pipe reamer, British Buttner, bladed, 1945....................................15.00
Pipe reamer, chrome, bladed, Denmark..10.00
Pipe reamer, Rocket, brass finish, USA..12.00
Pipe reamer, Rough Reamer, Fr sawtooth, cylinder.........................10.00
Pipe reamer, Simplex, bladed, US 7.00
Pipe rest, metal, German Shepherd figural 22.00
Pipe rest, 1911 Renault car..15.00
Pipe tamp, brass, Georgian nutcracker type, mk Vaun, 1800 ......225.00
Pipe tamp, brass, Napolean figural, 1840 ....125.00
Pipe tamp, burl maple, mushroom pestle top, cvd, Am, 6½" 350.00
Pipe/cigar holder, briar, metal nose, dirigible form, Italy 20.00
Snuff spoon, ivory, ca 1800..55.00
Spittoon, bl/wht stoneware, emb scroll, sponging...........................95.00
Spittoon, brass, emb 5-cent Havana Cigars, 10x9".........................65.00
Spittoon, CI, wht enameled, flared top, 8½" dia 50.00
Table lighter, pumpkin form, Bakelite, Strike-A-Lite....................25.00
Table lighter, Ronson, silver & mauve 20.00

Toby Jugs

The delightful jug known as the Toby dates back to the 18th century, when factories in England produced them for export to the American colonies. Named for the character Toby Philpots in the song *The Little Brown Jug*, the Toby was fashioned in the form of a jolly fellow, usually holding a jug of beer and a glass. The earlier examples were made with strict attention to details such as fingernails and teeth. Originally representing only a non-entity, a trend developed to portray well-known individuals such as George II, Napoleon, and Ben Franklin. Among the most-valued Tobies are those produced by Ralph Wood I in the late 1700s. By the mid-1830s, Tobies were being made in America. See also Doulton, Lenox, and Occupied Japan.

Hearty Goodfellow, 4-color sponging, Pratt type, 12", EX....... 1,000.00
Man seated w/jug, sponging, w/lid, Pratt, 1800s, rstr, 10"............400.00
Man w/jug, male figural hdl, att Yorkshire, 1830s, 10", VG.........300.00

Man w/jug, mc clothes, 1780s, 10", EX 1,000.00
Man w/pitcher, 5-color, Davenport type, 1830, 10" 100.00
Napoleon, pk suit, gilt trim, Alfred Evans Phila, 11", NM 350.00
Pearlware, Dr Johnson, 1800, 6¾", EX 400.00
Pearlware, lav coat/turq vest/yel breeches, 1800, rpr, 9¾" 450.00
Postilion, EX molding & color, Pratt, 1700s, 7", EX 2,200.00

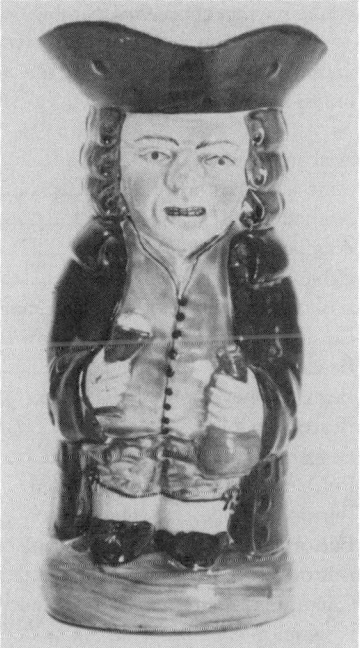

Prattware Toby, ca 1800, 8", EX, $550.00.

Rodney's Sailor, Ralph Wood, 1770s, no lid, 12" 5,700.00
Sailor on sea chest w/emb ship, stump hdl, no lid, 12", EX 200.00
Sailor seated, beaker to lips, holds jug, 1800, rstr, 11" 800.00
Stoneware, bl/brn/yel, Ralph Wood (att), 9½", EX 900.00
Woman, clasped hands, blk jacket/peach apron, 1880, 9¾" 50.00

Toleware

The term 'toleware' originally came from a French term meaning 'sheet iron.' Today it is used to refer to paint-decorated tin items. The earliest toleware was hand painted; by the 1820s, much of it was decorated by means of a stencil. Among the most collectible today are those items painted by the Pennsylvania Dutch in the 1800s. This type of toleware has a very distinctive look. The surface is dull and unvarnished; background colors range from black to cream. Geometrics are quite common, but florals and fruits were also popular motifs. Often gold-stenciled borders were added.

American toleware is usually found in practical, everyday forms – trays, pails, jugs, boxes, and tankards, for instance – while French examples might include candlesticks, wine coolers, jardinieres, etc. Be sure to note color, design, and condition when determining date and value. In the listings that follow, the dimension given for boxes and trays indicates length.

Apple dish, grapes/leaves, gold stencil on red, 3x11" 150.00
Apple dish, red/wht cherry flange, blk center, sq, CT, 12" 800.00
Box, document; floral, mc on dk brn, worn, 8" 150.00
Box, document; floral, mc on dk brn, 1800s, 8¾", NM 750.00
Box, document; floral, 3-color band on brn, rpr, 6¾" 150.00
Box, document; fruit, mc on blk, dome top, 3½x6½" 550.00
Box, document; 3-color florals, yel scrolls on lid, 9", EX 465.00
Box, Friendship stencil, gold on brn, w/hasp, 6½" L 200.00
Box, fruit & foliage, 5-color on brn, hinged lid, 8¼" dia 300.00

Box, gold lettering on orig blk, book shape, 6x4⅜" 550.00
Bucket, A Gift, gold stencil on orig bl, wear, 2" 125.00
Candle holder, floral, mc on brn, ejector slide, 5½", pr 2,700.00
Canister, birds/flowers/hearts on blk, 1820s, 6", VG 75.00
Canister, floral, 3-color on dk japanning, 5½" 95.00
Chocolate pot, floral, gold stencil on tortoise brn, 8½" 1,000.00
Coffeepot, bold floral, gooseneck, sgn/dtd 1838, 10½" 1,550.00
Coffeepot, floral, red/gr on blk, str spout, 12", VG 250.00
Coffeepot, floral (lg/4-color) on dk gr, cone lid, NE, 11" 3,800.00
Creamer, brush strokes, red/yel/gr on dk brn, 4", VG 90.00
Creamer, townscape/cherry band, mc on red, w/lid, NE, 5" 4,800.00
Hot water urn, flowers, dome lid/wreath finial, Europe, 16" 350.00
Mug, floral, red/yel on dk brn, minor wear, 4¼" 275.00
Pitcher, maple syrup; flower stencil on brn, hinged lid 85.00
Taper holder, stripes/vines, yel/gold on blk, 4" 40.00
Tea caddy, floral band, mc on dk brn japanning, wear, 5" 225.00
Tea urn, barnyard, pear form w/lid, Dutch, 1770s, rstr, 18 .... 250.00
Teapot, floral, red & gr on dk brn, 5½", EX 105.00
Tray, bread; floral, all orig, shaped ends, 1800s, 12½" 565.00
Tray, bread; floral rim band on blk, integral hdls, 13" L 200.00
Tray, floral, bronze powder on blk, wear, 13x7" 70.00
Tray, fox hunt scene w/flower border, English, hdls, 30" 200.00
Tray, gold crystallized center, florals on brn, 3x12½x8" 2,050.00
Tray, tavern view, English, 1800s, 30" L 1,100.00
Tray, tea; hunt scene sgn Bligni, 8-sided, EX 66.00
Tray, town w/several bldgs, style of R Porter, 1830s, 22" 1,800.00
Tray, walking & mtd figures by gov't bldg, Oldham St, 28" 700.00
Tumbler, gold stenciled flowers & birds, 1850s, 3x3" 50.00
Wash bowl & pitcher, floral transfers, worn, 12", 13½" dia 65.00

Wall sconces, 3-color floral vine on asphaltum, 13½", $1,800.00 for the pair.

Tools

Before the Civil War, tools for the most part were handmade. Some were primitive to the point of crudeness, while others reflected the skill of those who took pride in their trade. Increasing demand for quality tools and the dawning of the age of industrialization resulted in tools that were mass-produced.

Factors important in evaluating antique tools are scarcity, usefulness, and portability. Those with a manufacturer's mark are worth more than unmarked items. When no condition is indicated, the items listed below are assumed to be in excellent condition. See also Winchester and Keen Kutter. If you would like more information, contact Jim Calison, who is listed in the Directory under New York.

Adze, cooper's; Rochester #7 .... 35.00

Axe, for rifleman's belt 48.00
Brace, boring; R Marple Inventor Sheffield, wood/brass, 15".......135.00
Brace, iron/wood/brass, EX patina, EX detail, 16" L 35.00
Calf weaner, CI, Kant-Suk, dtd '10 ....20.00
Calipers, steel, stamped WTI 1863, sm ft on ea end, 18" 85.00
Cobbler's bench, leather seat, 2 drws, primitive, 45" 875.00
Draw shave, coach maker's, tiger maple, forged blade, 12" 55.00
Hammer, bill poster's, 2-pc take-down, MA, NP joints, 36" 70.00
Hatchet, trade; AA&G Going/Glassport, Penna, pat 1700, EX .150.00
Ice chipper/shaver, Crawford, brass ferrule, wood hdl, 7½" 45.00
Ice shaver, Clawson, Flagtown NJ, rotary hand crank 100.00
Knife, farrier's, Wostenholm...on blade, stag hdl, 4 ....70.00
Level, CI, glass intact, unmk, 6" 25.00
Level, Stanley #41, EX 15.00
Mallet, ship's caulking; lignum vitae or teak, 17½" 80.00
Mallet, wood, lg 8.00
Measure, wire rope; John A Roellings & Sons, EX....................175.00
Pencil, carpenter's, in sterling case 24.00
Plane, Bailey #3 ....35.00
Plane, Bedrock #605 ....18.00
Plane, Bedrock #605½C 65.00
Plane, ship's carpenter's, lignum vitae, eng hdl, 22" 200.00
Plane, ship's carpenter's, rosewood, 17", EX............................75.00
Plane, Stanley, 4-sq, 11½" 50.00
Plane, Stanley #194, MIB..85.00
Plane, Stanley #29 ....25.00
Plane, Stanley #45, w/blades 65.00
Plane, Stanley #55, w/blades, MIB 325.00
Rule, Lufkin #1206, EX 25.00
Rule, Lufkin #781, folding..15.00
Rule, Stanley #32, 4-fold, 72" 20.00
Rule, Stanley #36½R, M 22.50
Rule, Stanley #62, G 12.50
Saw, in mortised & chamfered chestnut fr, 25x34"....................45.00
Scribe, ship's carpenter's, rosewood, 21" 70.00

Scribe, rosewood and brass, 7½", $58.00.

Scribe, shipbuilder's, cherrywood, MOP dmn-shape inlay, 22" 70.00
Shovel, grain; 1-pc cvd wood, open D hdl, ca 1800, 14x36" 240.00
Spoke shave, #66 ....10.00
Spoke shave, shipbuilder's, mahog w/whalebone parts, 11"..........225.00
Square, carpenter's, HD Aupke, steel/rosewood/brass, 20" 45.00
Tool stand, blacksmith's, pine w/leather sides, 17x16x14" 175.00
Tri-square, Stanley, rosewood & brass hdl, pat 3-16-97................10.00
Vise, for making horse collars, wood w/worn pnt, 50" L...........115.00
Vise, saw; pat 1888 ....25.00
Wheel gauge, traveling; wrought iron w/wood hdl, 11"................70.00

Toothpick Holders

Once common on every table, the toothpick holder was relegated

to the china cabinet near the turn of the century. Fortunately, this contributed to their survival; as a result, many are available to collectors today. Because they are small and easily displayed, they are a very popular collectible; and they come in a wide range of prices to fit every budget. The rare ones have been reproduced and, unfortunately, are being offered for sale right along with the originals. (These 'repros' should be priced in the $10.00 to $15.00 range.) So unless you're sure of what you're buying, choose a reputable dealer.

In addition to pattern glass, you'll find examples in china, bisque, art glass, and silverplate. In the listings that follow, items are glass unless noted otherwise.

Alabama..70.00
American, Fostoria 25.00
Arched Ovals, gr w/gold 30.00
Argonaut Shell, custard..275.00
Babies Bootie, bl opal 40.00
Basketweave w/3-D bird on side, amethyst, beaded rim 25.00
Beaded Swag, etched, ruby stain w/EX gold 25.00
Beaded Swirl & Disk, amber..50.00
Beatty Honeycomb, bl opal, 2½x2" 45.00
Beatty Rib, bl opal 35.00
Beggar's Hand, vaseline 25.00
Bull's Eye & Fan, clear w/EX gold 45.00
Button & Bulge, milk glass, decor 50.00
Button Arches, ruby stain (beware of repros) 12.00
Button Panel, clear w/gold..22.00
Cactus, chocolate, Greentown (beware of repros)....................65.00
Champion 28.00
China, HP roses, hdls, Nippon 35.00
Chrysanthemum Leaf Swirl, clear w/gold............................95.00
Church Windows 22.00
Colonial, bl, hdls 25.00
Cordova, ruby stain..55.00
Corset, amber 88.00
Cranberry cracquelle w/appl clear rosettes & enameling.............125.00
Cut Block, ruby stain 28.00
Daisy, frosted..20.00
Daisy & Button, amberina, EX fuchsia coloring, 3"................200.00
Daisy & Button, vaseline, hat form, 2½" 45.00
Daisy & Button w/VT..30.00
Delaware, gr w/EX gold 90.00
Delaware, rose 80.00
Dia Quilt, amberina, tricorn top, 2¼"..............................250.00
Dia Quilt MOP, wht to raspberry, ruffled, sgn Webb............325.00
Dia Quilt MOP, yel, quatrelobe rim, 2¼"..........................350.00
Diamond w/Spearpoint, vaseline opal................................33.00
Empress, gr w/gold..210.00
Esther, clear w/amber 90.00
Fern, cranberry..250.00
Florate, turq opaque..95.00
Flute, mk Heisey 25.00
Four Ladders..25.00
Fruit Panels 30.00
Gaelic, clear w/gold 30.00
Galloway, clear w/gold 20.00
Gathered Knots, sapphire bl, ca 1900 ....125.00
Harvard, gr opaque..35.00
Hickman 30.00
Hobnail, bl opal 25.00
Holly, old..70.00
Horseshoe & Clover, milk glass......................................30.00
Invt T'print, amberina, bulbous base 135.00
Iowa..20.00

Iris w/Meander, bl opal 75.00
Jefferson Optic, bl, souvenir 58.00
Jewel & Dewdrop (Kansas) 50.00
Kentucky, gr...110.00
Little Lobe, bl floral & beading, 'World's Fair 1893,' mk 575.00
Madora 25.00
Maple Leaf, custard with gr & gold decor 650.00
Michigan, bl stain w/yel enameled dots 65.00
Moire MOP, robin's egg bl, frosted leaf ft 235.00
National's Eureka, ruby stain 50.00
New Hampshire, maiden's blush 50.00
Owl, cobalt 18.00
Paddle Wheel & Star..22.00
Panelled Sprig, cranberry w/decor 100.00
Pansy, pk cased..60.00
Pineapple, pk satin...75.00
Plain Scalloped Panel, bl HP flowers 20.00
Pleating, ruby stain..55.00
Portland 20.00
Pretty Maid 55.00
Prince of Wales Plume, clear w/gold, Heisey 120.00
Priscilla 38.00
Reverse Swirl, bl speckled 85.00
Rib & Bead, ruby stain, etched.................................22.00
Ribbed Spiral, vaseline opal 60.00
Scalloped Swirl, ruby stain 30.00

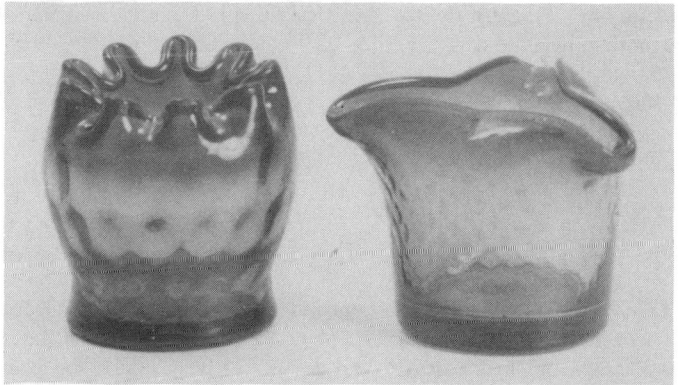

Inverted Thumbprint, amberina, 2¼", $295.00; Venetian Diamond, amberina, 2", $275.00.

Scroll w/Cane Band, amber 60.00
Silverplate, barrel w/spigot/fireman's helmet, Pairpoint.............165.00
Silverplate, dog w/glass eyes & terrier by holder, Tufts.................100.00
Silverplate, man carries barrel on bk, Tufts #2643.....................150.00
Silverplate, pig, glass eyes, pot eng Boston...Beans, Acme 85.00
Silverplate, porcupine figural, quills intact, sgn base.....................40.00
Silverplate, sailor boy shooting cannon, Reed & Barton 350.00
Simplicity Scroll, clear w/gold..................................20.00
Spearpoint Band, ruby flashed 80.00
Stars & Bars, bl, rare...220.00
Sunflower, majolica 95.00
Sweet Sixteen, hdls, Fostoria 35.00
Swinger, ruby stain 20.00
Texas, clear w/gold 35.00
Thompson 77, ruby stain..30.00
Thousand Eye 35.00
Tortoise Shell, tricorner top, Boston & Sandwich 395.00
Trophy, ruby stain 25.00
Truncated Cube, ruby stain 32.00
Ward's Regal, gr...22.00

Widmer 32.00
Wild Bouquet, wht opal w/pastel decor 135.00
Wild Rose w/Scrolling, emerald gr w/EX gold 110.00
Wild Rose w/Scrolling, gr frost w/goofus flower decor 195.00
Windows, cranberry opal 115.00
Wreath & Shell, wht opal w/decor 195.00
Zippered Swirl & Diamond 25.00

Torquay 'Devon Motto' Ware

Torquay is a unique type of pottery made in the South Devon area of England from 1867. At the height of productivity, at least a dozen companies flourished there, producing simple folk pottery from the area's natural red clay. The ware was both wheel-turned and molded and decorated under the glaze with heavy slip resulting in low-relief nature subjects or simple scrollwork.

Three of the best-known of these potteries were: Watcombe (1867-1962); Aller Vale (in operation from the mid-1800s, producing domestic ware and architectural products); and Longpark (1890 until 1957). Watcombe and Aller Vale merged in 1901 and operated until 1962 under the name of Royal Aller Vale and Watcombe Art Pottery.

Perhaps the most famous type of ware potted in this area was Motto Ware, so called because of the verses, proverbs, and quotations that decorated it. This decor was achieved by the sgraffito technique – scratching the letters through the slip to expose the red clay underneath. The most popular decorative devices were cottages, black cockerel, multi-cockerel, and a scrollwork pattern called Scandy. Other popular patterns were Kerswell Daisy, ships, kingfishers, and many other birds on blue ground.

Aller Vale ware may sometimes be found marked 'H.H. and Company,' a firm who assumed ownership from 1897 to 1901. 'Watcombe Torquay' was an impressed mark used from 1884 to 1927.

Those interested in learning more about Torquay are encouraged to contact Jerry and Gerry Kline, members of The Torquay Pottery Collectors' Society, whose address can be found in the Directory under Clubs, Newsletters, and Catalogs.

Toby, Torquay, 2¼", $35.00; Vase, Scandy, Empty barrels make most...,' 2⅜", $45.00; Loving cup, Torquay, Black Cockerel, two handles, 2", $55.00.

Ash tray, Scandy, 'A place for ashes,' oval, 4¾x3¼" 25.00
Bottle, scent; Devonshire Violets, Longpark, crown finial, 4" 30.00
Bottle, scent; Real Devonshire Violets, 3½" 25.00
Bowl, Cottage, Devon, 'Say little but...,' shallow........................30.00
Bowl, porridge; Cottage, 'Rolling stone...,' unmk, 2x4½".........38.00
Candle holder, brn flower on gr band, unmk, motto, 5" 75.00
Candlestick, Blk Cockerel, Longpark, 'Last in bed...,' 3¼" 55.00
Candlestick, Scandy, Longpark, 'Last in bed...,' 3½" 45.00
Cheese dish, Cottage, motto, rectangular top, 5¼x6½" 85.00
Coffeepot, Cottage, Longpark, 'He never fails...,' 6½" 85.00

Condiment holder, w/salt & pepper, egg cup, & mustard, 3½" ...100.00
Creamer, Cottage, unmk, 'Help yourself...,' conical, 2" 30.00
Creamer, sailboat scene, Watcombe, no motto 30.00
Creamer, Watcombe, ped ft, 'Take a little...,' 2¾x3½" 35.00
Cruet, Cottage, Dartmouth, 'Go aisy wi it...,' 8" 45.00
Cup & saucer, Cottage, Watcombe, 'Take a cup of tea' 35.00
Dish, Cockerel, Watcombe, 3-section, motto, 8x8¾" 95.00
Egg cup, 'New laid...,' unmk 20.00
Figurine, classical, Watcombe, terra cotta, 11½" 350.00
Hatpin holder, Scandy, Longpark, 'I'll take care...,' 4½" 65.00
Inkwell, Sailboat, Watcombe, 'Send us a scrape...,' 2¾" 45.00
Inkwell, Scandy, 'Jist a scrip 'o yer pen' 48.00
Inkwell, Scandy, Aller Vale, 'Us be always glad...,' 2¾" 50.00
Jam dish, Cottage, Longpark, ruffled, 'Elp yerzel..., ' ¾x5" 42.00
Jam dish, Cottage, unmk, 'Duee ave zum jam,' 2¼x5" 40.00
Jam dish, Cottage, Watcombe, 'Go easy w/the...,' 3½x3" 40.00
Jam dish, Scandy, unmk, cylindrical, flared, motto..................48.00
Jardiniere, Orchids, gr bkground, 9x7½".............................225.00
Jug, Multi-Cockerel, Longpark, 'The deils aye kind...,' 5" 75.00
Match striker, Cockerel, 'A match for any man,' lg....................55.00
Mug, Kerswell Daisy, Aller Vale, amber, hdls, motto, 4¼"..........55.00
Mug, shaving; Multi-Cockerel, 4x5½" from hdl to spout 95.00
Mug, toby; MIE, 2"...32.00
Mug, toby; Royal Torquay, lg...85.00
Mustard, Thistle, Longpark, 'Frae huntly help yoursel...,' 2" 35.00
Pepper pot, Scandy, flares up from sm ped ft, motto 24.00
Pin tray, Scandy, Watcombe, no motto, 5½" L 28.00
Pitcher, Cottage, motto, 2¼"..28.00
Pitcher, flowers on trellis, unmk, 5½" 50.00
Pitcher, milk; Cottage, Longpark, 'If...be as aisy...,' 5½" 60.00
Pitcher, milk; tadpoles on bbl shape, Watcombe, motto, 5½" 60.00
Pitcher, sailboat, unmk, 'Do the work that's nearest,' 3x3¾"..........35.00
Pitcher, Scandy, unmk, 'Long may yer lum reek,' mini...................35.00
Pitcher, Watcombe, tadpoles, 'Duee ave zum...,' 3½" 40.00
Plate, Kerswell Daisy, Aller Vale, 'Say weel...,' 4½"......................35.00
Plate, sandalwood dots, bl rim, Longpark, 'Tis deeds...,' 3" 30.00
Platter, Multi-Cockerel, 'A place for...,' oval, 10½x7⅜"..............95.00
Pot, gypsy, Cottage, 3-leg, 3¾"..45.00
Salt cellar, Cottage, Lands End, ftd egg shape, 'Pass the...' 35.00
Salt cellar, Thistle, Longpark, 'From Tighnabruaich,' 2x2½" 32.00
Sugar bowl, Cottage, Longpark, ped ft, motto, 3¼"....................45.00
Sugar bowl, Primrose, unmk, low ped, 'Help yerzel tae...' 40.00
Sugar bowl, sailboat scene, Watcombe, 'Sandown there's...' 40.00
Sugar bowl, Scandy, Longpark, 'Elp yerzel tu...,' 2¼x3½"..............45.00
Sugar bowl, shamrock, Watcombe, 'Be careful...,' 1¾".................30.00
Teapot, Cockerel, Longpark, 'Dawntee be fraid aut..,' 4" 75.00
Teapot, Cockerel, Longpark, rnd, 'Duee ave...,' 4¾" 85.00
Toast rack, Cottage, Dartmouth, 'Go aisy...', 7¼" L....................45.00
Toast rack, Cottage, Watcombe, 'Take a...,' 3½" 50.00
Vase, Kingfisher, stamped England, bl glaze, 4½x4" 38.00
Vase, sailboat, Watcombe, 'Beer,' waisted, 3¼x1¾"....................38.00
Vase, sailboat, Watcombe, mc w/bl slip, 7½" 70.00
Vase, Scandy, tricorn, crimped top, 'Be bold,' 1½" 30.00
Vase, wild roses on mauve, Longpark, rippled rim, 3¼" 38.00
Vase, windmill scene, Watcombe, no motto, 6" 70.00

Tortoise Shell Glass

By combining several shades of glass – brown, clear, and yellow – glass manufacturers of the 19th century were able to produce an art glass that closely resembled the shell of the tortoise. Some of this type of glassware was manufactured in Germany. In America it was made by several firms, the most prominent of which was the Boston and Sand-wich Glass Works.

Basket, appl amber thorn twist hdl, 8x5" 90.00
Biscuit jar, ornate SP rim, lid, & hdl.................................110.00
Butter dish 175.00
Cruet, swirl, dk amber stopper...325.00
Ewer, appl amber hdl, 9½" 75.00
Pitcher, appl amber hdl, ground pontil, 7x5½"......................85.00
Pitcher, tricorner, clear reeded hdl, water sz 115.00
Tumbler..60.00
Vase, random fluted top, 10"...125.00

Toys

Toys, obviously, are fun to collect, and those made before WWII also have special investment potential. Lithograph-printed mechanical toys, for instance, are especially popular with today's collectors and steadily continue to increase in value year after year. Condition of any type of toy is critical. They were made for children to play with, and many that have survived to the present are in a well-played-with state, which only serves to enhance the value of those that yet may be found in excellent condition. Authority Richard O'Brien has compiled an informative book, *Collecting Toys*, available at your local library or favorite bookstore. In the listings below, toys are listed by manufacturer's name when at all possible, otherwise by type. Condition is assumed excellent unless noted otherwise. The dimension listed is the greater one – height if the toy is vertical, length if that measurement is larger than height. See also Children's Things; Personalities.

Key:
b/o — battery operated   w/up — windup
NP — nickel plated

Cast Iron

Cast iron toys were made from shortly before the Civil War until the beginning of the 20th century. They are evaluated to a large extent by scarcity, complexity, design, and detail. See next section for examples of cast iron toys listed by company name.

Airplane, 'Lindy' type, minor pnt rstr, 4½", VG 100.00
Boat Tail Racer, VG pnt, missing driver, 8", G.......................150.00
Boy & alligator bell toy, 9", VG......................................1,550.00
Bus, worn pnt, surface rust, 4½", G 50.00
Cannon, eagle symbols at sides, 1½x3¼", EX 75.00
Carriage, European style, EX orig pnt, 9" 250.00
Cement mixer, horse drawn, Made in US, mk 5M, 14" L, EX. 2,000.00
Chariot, emb florals, w/driver & 3 pnt horses, 1900s, 10" 1,000.00
Charlie Chaplin bell toy, steel wheels & fr, 5"..........................750.00
Delivery wagon w/2 horses & driver, G pnt, rpr shaft, 15" 150.00
Digger crane, red pnt, 4½", EX 175.00
Donkey cart, driver w/mechanical arm action, pnt chips, 9" 475.00
Dump truck, bumpers missing, 1920s, 8½", VG 130.00
Elephant doing trick bell toy, w/gong, 8", VG 1,150.00
Fire truck, red, unmk, 7½"..165.00
Friendship Pumper, dbl hose, plunger action, VG pnt, 15" 850.00
Graf Zepplin, worn pnt, lt rust, 5", G.................................100.00
Ice wagon, horse drawn, EX pnt, 8" 200.00
Ice wagon, poor pnt, 14", G 350.00
Mack truck, orig pnt, 4½", NM 125.00
Mack truck, stake side, gr, 5", EX pnt 125.00
Mule kicks bell gong, mechanical, 8", VG 1,000.00

Patrol wagon, pnt wear, 21½", VG **1,250.00**
Police motorcycle & sidecar, G pnt, nickeled wheels, 4", G **60.00**
Pony cart, partial pnt, 4", G **60.00**
Sand & Gravel Wagon, w/2 horses & driver, EX pnt, 15", VG ...**190.00**
Sedan, lt pnt wear, 4", G **40.00**
Speed boat, 3 wheels, worn pnt, lt rust, 5½", VG **90.00**
Tank, WWI, HP, 8", EX **600.00**
Toonerville Trolly, clockwork, Dent, ca 1922, 5", EX **1,200.00**
Tractor w/driver, Fordson, 4" **100.00**
Wild Mule Jack bell toy, lt rust, 8", VG **400.00**
Wrecker, VG pnt, rubber tires, ca 1930, 7"................................**200.00**

Company or Country of Manufacturer

Alps, Sambo, celluloid & tin w/up, 9½", NMIB..........................**145.00**
Alps, Teddy, Balloon Blowing Bear, plush/tin, b/o, 11½", NM.......**60.00**
Arcade, Ford Coupe, CI w/decals/gold stripe, rumble seat, 7"......**450.00**
Arcade, gasoline truck, CI, NP wheels, rpt, 13", G................. **1,000.00**
Arcade, Mack dump truck, CI, rpl driver, missing tires, 12" **400.00**
Arcade, Mack dump truck, tin, EX red pnt, rpl hoist, 12" **450.00**
Arcade, Model T Ford 'Fordor' Sedan, pnt CI, 1924, 6½" **385.00**
Arcade, World's Fair Tram, CI & tin litho, 16½", VG **180.00**
Arnold, Mac motorcycle, tin litho w/up, 7½", EX in box **1,000.00**
Auburn, American Frontier Set #563, MIB................................**110.00**
Bandai, Pontiac Firebird, tin, b/o, scale model, 11", NMIB **135.00**
Bing, battleship, pnt tin, clockwork, ca 1912, 32", EX **4,950.00**
Bing, Jaureguinberry battleship, pnt tin, clockwork, 32" **1,200.00**
Bing, Leviathan ocean liner, pnt int, clockwork, 1925, 39" **1,430.00**
Bing, ocean liner, pnt tin, clockwork, 1912, 26", NM **5,775.00**
Bing, Yel Taxi, tin litho w/up, 9", NM.................................. **3,400.00**
Buddy L, cement mixer, #280, VG...**800.00**

**Buddy L Flivver Delivery Truck #210, minor paint wear, 12",
$550.00.**

Buddy L, Ford Dump Cart, pnt steel, #211, 1924, 12", VG..........**600.00**
Buddy L, sand loader, 1930s, 20", EX.......................................**365.00**
Buddy L, steam shovel, #220, 1923, EX **375.00**
Buddy L, steam shovel, seal decal, #220, 1921, NM **450.00**
Cardini, Flying Ladies, tin litho carousel, '20s, 12", NMIB **3,000.00**
Carpenter, delivery wagon, horse drawn, pat 1881, 12", EX **300.00**
Carpenter, wagon, horse drawn, CI/wood, pat 1880, 17", VG **525.00**
Carter, Pan-Gee the Funny Dancer, tin litho w/up, 7", EX..........**600.00**
Chein, clown in barrel, tin w/up walker, 7½", NM **275.00**
Chein, Disneyland Ferris Wheel, tin litho w/up, 17", EX **435.00**
Chein, duck, tin litho w/up, waddles, 4", EX.............................**48.00**
Chein, Popeye Bag-on-Platform Puncher, tin w/up, 7", EX **1,450.00**

Chein, Popeye Over-Head Punching Bag, tin litho w/up, NM. **3,500.00**
Chein, Ski Ride, tin litho w/up, 19½", NMIB.............................**500.00**
China, hen & chickens, tin litho b/o walker, 10", NMIB..............**80.00**
Clark, horse, pnt sheet metal, CI fr, friction, 14½", VG...............**300.00**
Converse, Fairy Stroller, paper litho on wood, musical, 18".........**550.00**
Corgi, Yel Submarine, MIB **365.00**
Cragstan, fishing polar bear, plush/tin, b/o, 10", NMIB...............**225.00**
Cragstan, squirrel, tin litho w/up, plush tail, 5", EX **75.00**
Daito, Ford 'Edsel' Police Dept car, tin, friction, siren **95.00**
Daito, Ford 'Edsel' Wagon, tin, friction, 13", VG **120.00**
Descamps, lion, leather covered, growls, clockwork, 16", G **275.00**
Dinky, Fire Station Kit #954, MIB **80.00**
Distler, What's Wrong Car, tin litho w/up, 7", NM **1,000.00**
Doepke, Adams grater, orange, VG...**75.00**
Ebo, peacock, tin litho w/up, 10½", EX **400.00**
Fisher-Price, Allie Gator, complete, EX.....................................**50.00**
Fisher-Price, Big Performing Circus, ca 1930s, EX **750.00**
Fisher-Price, Campbell Kids farm truck, EX...............................**55.00**
Fisher-Price, Chick Basket Cart, #302, 1957, EX **45.00**
Fisher-Price, Coon, #172, 1979..**16.00**
Fisher-Price, Dizzy Donkey, #433..**50.00**
Fisher-Price, Farmer on Tractor, #529, 1961 ....**25.00**
Fisher-Price, Fire Engine #720, 1968, EX **25.00**
Fisher-Price, Go 'N Back Mule, keywind, ca 1931, rare **550.00**
Fisher-Price, Hot Diggity, 1934, EX **450.00**
Fisher-Price, Humpty Dumpty, #730, EX **20.00**
Fisher-Price, Lop-Eared Looie, #415 ....**135.00**
Fisher-Price, Mickey Mouse Choo Choo, EX **125.00**
Fisher-Price, Musical Merry-Go-Round, plastic **20.00**
Fisher-Price, Penguin, #786 ....**12.00**
Fisher-Price, Pluto, pop-up toy, early, EX **45.00**
Fisher-Price, Puff #444 Engine, VG..**25.00**
Fisher-Price, Queen Buzy Bee, #444, 1957, EX **30.00**
Fisher-Price, Toot Toot, #643, 1964, EX **25.00**
Fisher-Price, wagon, #171, 1941, VG...**145.00**
Fisher-Price, Woofy Wouser, #700 ....**125.00**
Fleischmann, gunboat T655, HP/stenciled tin w/up, 14", EX . **1,500.00**
Fleischmann, ocean liner, tinplate, 1 stack, EX pnt, 20" **1,750.00**
France, Blk Drummer, tin, felt clothes, Schuco copy, 4" **1,750.00**
France, motorcycle, driver, w/sidecar, w/up, 1920s, M **650.00**
Germany, acrobat tumbler, tin, arm wind, 6½", EX.....................**325.00**
Germany, Blk Mammy w/basket, HP, clockwork, 6⅝", EX..........**950.00**
Germany, boy riding dog, HP, clockwork, 6½", G **950.00**
Germany, Buttercup & Spareribs, tin, pull toy, 1920s, EX....... **1,400.00**
Germany, camouflaged troop carrier, tin litho w/up, 12½", VG...**300.00**
Germany, carousel, 3 horses, tin, clockwork, 1890s, 12" **1,540.00**
Germany, clown seated w/cymbal, HP tin w/up, 6", NM **1,600.00**
Germany, clown w/bell, HP tin w/up, lead ft, 8", EX...................**750.00**
Germany, duck w/young, HP tin w/up, rolls, 10", NM **450.00**
Germany, farmer pulls cart, tin litho & HP w/up, 7½", EX...... **1,250.00**
Germany, lizard, tin litho w/up, spoked wheels, 7½", EX **125.00**
Germany, Maggie & Jiggs, tin litho w/up bobbers, 8", EX........ **2,150.00**
Germany, monkey w/ball, tin litho w/up walker, 3½", EX **125.00**
Germany, motorcycle w/sidecar, pnt tin, clockwork, 1900s, 8" . **2,860.00**
Germany, Nazi on horsebk, tin litho w/up, 5½", EX.....................**850.00**
Germany, Red Riding Hood & Wolf, tin w/up walker, 6½" **1,750.00**
Germany, sailor climber, tin, string pully, 9", EX.......................**150.00**
Germany, Toonerville Trolly, tin litho w/up, 6", NMIB **1,500.00**
Germany, touring car, tin litho, clockwork, 1900s, 8", NM **3,575.00**
Germany, touring car, tin litho, clockwork, 1920s, 8", EX **1,870.00**
Germany, Volkswagon, tin litho w/up, dk gr, 9", NM in box .. **1,200.00**
Gilbert, erector set, #10021 ....**30.00**
Gilbert, erector set, #7½", w/motor, metal case, EX **120.00**
Gilbert, erector set, #8½, Ferris wheel, metal case, G **165.00**

Gilbert, erector set, #9½, w/motor, lg tin box, EX 160.00
Gilbert, Yankee Tank, tin litho, clockwork, 15", EX...................300.00
Girard, Airways Express plane, tin w/up, 12", NMIB.................525.00
Guntherman, poodle jumping rope, tin/cloth, clockwork, 10" 700.00
Hubley, fire engine, CI, orig pnt, rubber tires, mk, 13½", EX.......750.00

Hubley dump coal truck, cast iron and hand painted, repair, repainted, recast wheels, 15", $650.00.

Hubley, grasshopper, CI, articulated action, 4½", EX...................250.00
Hubley, Lindy plane, CI, 4½", EX...150.00
Hubley, motorcycle w/sidecar, CI, clicker, rpt, 9", VG.................650.00
Illco, Pluto, plastic, jumps/barks, b/o, 10½", NMIB........................88.00
Ives, bear, fur covered, stands, clockwork, 9", EX.........................750.00
Japan, boxers, tin litho w/up, separate tin bases, 5" 135.00
Japan, Boy Scout, celluloid, pre-war, 6¼", EX 70.00
Japan, Cadillac, tin, non-mechanical, 1930s, 6", NM 800.00
Japan, circus cyclist, tin w/up, 6½", NMIB 450.00
Japan, Communications Truck, b/o, friction, camo pnt, 12", M ..150.00
Japan, cowboy on donkey, celluloid w/up, 4½" 50.00
Japan, Donald Duck Boxers, celluloid/tin, '30s, 4½", NM....... 1,850.00
Japan, Donald Duck Whirligig, tin litho w/up, '30s, 10½" 4,000.00
Japan, elf w/bass fiddle, tin clicker type w/lever, 4" 32.00
Japan, Frankenstein, tin/cloth, b/o, blushes/pants fall, M 180.00
Japan, Happy Plane, plastic/tin, b/o, 9", NM 55.00
Japan, High Wheel Robot, tin w/up w/plastic gears, 10", MIB 200.00
Japan, Hungry Baby Bear, tin & plush, b/o, 10", NMIB................220.00
Japan, Mickey Mouse on Handcar, tin/plastic, b/o, 10", NM 220.00
Japan, monkey boxer, plush head, tin base, w/up, 8", NM..............85.00
Japan, mouse, tin litho w/up tumbler, rubber tail, 4" 50.00
Japan, native on alligator, tin litho w/up, pre-war, 7"...................175.00
Japan, native w/spear on snake, celluloid w/up, '30s, 18", EX 255.00
Japan, Oriental boy on sled, tin litho w/up, 6½" 185.00
Japan, Pango Pango African Dancer, tin litho w/up, 6", NM 165.00
Japan, Planet Robot, tin litho w/up, 9", MIB................................130.00
Japan, Slurpy Pup, plush/tin, b/o, 8", NMIB 50.00
Japan, Strange Explorer, tank & gorilla, tin litho, b/o, NM 95.00
Joustra, Auto-Obstacle, tin w/up, 2-door car, 6½", NM 120.00
Joustra, trolly bus, tinplate, w/up, b/o lights, 14" 350.00
Katz, Soldiers on Parade, tin litho w/up, 19", EX 655.00
Kellerman, man does leg splits, tin litho, clockwork, 7", EX........650.00
Kenton, Happy Hooligan Police Wagon, CI, w/horses, 18" 3,000.00
Kenton, Overland Circus band wagon, CI, 15½", EX 650.00
Kenton, Overland Circus bear wagon, CI, 14", EX 450.00
Kenton, Phaethon, CI, horse drawn, 16", EX...............................325.00
Kenton, Stanley Canopy-Top Horse-Drawn Surrey, EX 125.00
Knickerbocker, Mother Hen Target Game, 1940s 55.00
Lehmann, Autobus, dbl-decker, tin litho w/up, 8", EX 2,500.00
Lehmann, Balky Mule, tin litho, w/up, 6½", NMIB.....................650.00
Lehmann, Bucking Bronco, tin litho, wheel base, 6", NMIB .. 2,500.00
Lehmann, Dare Devil, tin litho w/up, EX...................................575.00
Lehmann, Ikarus Airplane, orig pilot, keywind, 10½", VG 2,600.00

Lehmann, Lila Hansom Cab, tin, clockwork, 5¾" 1,500.00
Lehmann, Masuyama Rickshaw, man pulls lady, keywind, EX.. 2,000.00
Lehmann, Naughty Boy, tin litho w/up 850.00
Lehmann, Oh My Dancer, tin litho, #685, 9", EX.......................650.00
Lehmann, seal, w/up...275.00
Lehmann, Tut-Tut, tin litho w/up 1,050.00
Lindstrom, Betty Walker, tin litho w/up, 8", EX.........................200.00
Lindstrom, Gold Star Pinball, tin on wood, 1930s, 14x24", EX 40.00
Lindstrom, Sweeping Mammy, w/up walker, #1750, 8", EX 200.00
Linemar, Casper the Ghost Turnover Tank, tin, 4" 275.00
Linemar, Disney Dipsy Car, tin litho w/up, 5½", NMIB 1,000.00
Linemar, Donald Duck Climbing Fireman, tin w/up, 5½", NM ..500.00
Linemar, Donald Duck motorcycle, tin, friction, 4", NM 750.00
Linemar, Donald Duck on trike w/bell, tin w/up, 3½", NM 750.00
Linemar, Flippo Dog, tin litho w/up, 4", NMIB 100.00
Linemar, Goofy Unicyclist, tin litho w/up, M.......................... 1,000.00
Linemar, Ham 'N Sam, tin litho w/up, 1920s, 4½", NMIB...... 2,000.00
Linemar, Ham 'N Sam, tin litho w/up, 1950s, scarce 1,000.00
Linemar, Henry w/ice cream, tin litho w/up, 5½", EX................650.00
Linemar, Hopping Kangaroo, w/up, 1950s, M 125.00
Linemar, Mickey Mouse Acrobat, tin litho, b/o, 8", NMIB.........965.00
Linemar, Mickey Mouse Unicyclist, tin litho w/up, 5", NMIB .. 2,200.00
Linemar, Mike Mallard Climbing Fireman, tin litho w/up, 5½" ..225.00
Linemar, Pinocchio, tin litho w/up walker, 5½", NMIB...............825.00
Linemar, Popeye the Pilot, tin litho w/up, 1950s, rare, 5" 2,500.00
Linemar, Superman Turnover Tank, tin litho w/up, 4", EX..........500.00
Lionel, Mickey Mouse Express Anniversary Car, MIB 450.00
Lionel, troup carrier, tin litho, clockwork, 12 men, 12"........... 1,100.00

Lionel, Mickey Mouse and Santa Car, 6", $1,500.00.

Marklin, construction set, #4, ca 1900, VG.................................325.00
Marklin, German Army horse-drawn wagon soup kitchen, 5-pc....900.00
Martin, Blk man w/orange cart, tin litho w/up, 7½", NM 1,850.00
Martin, bowler, HP tin, clothes, push lever, 1903, 8", NM 3,200.00
Martin, lady chases mouse w/broom, tin clockwork, 1900s, 8".. 2,000.00
Martin, Ma Portiere, tin litho w/up, cloth dressed, 8" 2,750.00
Martin, policeman, HP tin walker, wood baton, 7½", EX 2,750.00
Martin, violin player, tin litho w/up, 1890s 850.00
Marx, Amos & Andy Fresh Air Taxi, tin litho w/up, 7½", EX......... 1,000.00
Marx, Army Staff Car, tin litho w/up, siren, b/o light, 11"...........120.00
Marx, Be Bop, Blk plastic man, tin drum base, '40s, 9½" 200.00
Marx, Big Load Van, tin litho, w/up, 13", VG.............................300.00
Marx, Charleston Trio, tin litho w/up, 9", NMIB 1,500.00
Marx, Charlie McCarthy Drummer, tin, clockwork, 8½", G 750.00
Marx, Dagwood Aeroplane, tin litho w/up, 8½", NMIB 1,250.00
Marx, Dick Tracy Siren Squad Car, tin w/up, b/o light, NM 250.00
Marx, Disney Parade Roadster, plastic/tin litho w/up, 11", M......500.00
Marx, Donald Duck Duet, tin litho w/up, NMIB.................... 1,350.00

Marx, Donald the Drummer, plastic/tin litho w/up, '40s, 10" 385.00
Marx, Dopey, tin litho w/up walker, 8", NMIB.................850.00
Marx, Doughboy Tank, tin litho, clockwork, 9", EX in box.........250.00
Marx, Drummer Boy, tin litho w/up, 18½", EX in orig box..........300.00
Marx, Drummer Boy, tin litho walker, 7½", NMIB 800.00
Marx, Ferdinand the Bull, tin litho w/up, 5½", EX....................200.00
Marx, Flintstones Playset, 1962, MIB.................................350.00
Marx, G-Man Pursuit Car, tin litho w/up, NM in orig box..........850.00
Marx, Honeymoon Express, tin litho base w/train, 9", NMIB 285.00
Marx, Joe Penner, tin litho w/up walker, 8", NMIB 1,400.00
Marx, Komikal Kop, tin litho w/up, 7½", NMIB.......................975.00
Marx, Learn To Drive Car, tin/plastic w/up, 7", NM 75.00
Marx, Main Street Airport, ca 1930s, EX.............................175.00
Marx, Mickey Mouse Plays Xylophone, plastic, 11½", EX...........435.00
Marx, Midget Climbing Fighting Tank, tin litho w/up, 5", NM.....65.00
Marx, Milton Berle Car, tin litho w/up, plastic hat, 5½", EX.......300.00
Marx, Old Jalopy, tin litho, funny quotes allover, 7", EX 175.00
Marx, Old Jalopy, 3-D driver, tin litho w/up, 7", NMIB 250.00
Marx, Pathe Movie Camera, tin, on tripod, wood crank hdl, 6"...145.00
Marx, Peter Rabbit Drives Crazy Car, metal/plastic w/up, MIB...650.00
Marx, Play Away Piano, 1939, NM.................................120.00
Marx, Popeye Express, tin litho w/up walker, 8", EX 500.00
Marx, Popeye the Pilot, tin litho w/up, orig version, 8½" 650.00
Marx, Running Scottie, tin litho w/up, 5", NMIB.....................100.00
Marx, Somsteppa Dancer, tin litho w/up, 8", EX......................500.00
Marx, Sparkling Rocket Fighter Ship, tin litho w/up, 12", M......600.00
Marx, Thor, Super Hero tricycle, vinyl/celluloid/tin, 3½" 120.00
Marx, Tidy Tim Cleanup Man, tin litho w/up, 7½", EX.............500.00
Marx, Tom Corbett Rocket Ship, tin litho w/up, 12", EX............750.00
Marx, Tower Aeroplane, tin litho w/up, 7½", NMIB 220.00
Marx, Turnover Tank, tin litho w/up, 4", NMIB 175.00
Marx, Uncle Wiggly Car, tin litho w/up, 7", NMIB................ 1,000.00
Marx, Watch Me Roll Over Pluto, tin, WDP, 1939, EX 250.00
Marx, Zeppelin, tin & aluminum w/up on string, 10½", NMIB...450.00
Marx, Zippo, Climbing Monkey, tin string climber, 9½", EX.........50.00
Meccano, sports car, pnt metal, clockwork, 1932, 9", EX............440.00
Mengel, Mickey Mouse rocker, pnt wood, ca 1935, 35", EX 465.00
Metalcraft, Heinz Pickles Truck, 1930s, EX..........................350.00
Moko, Clever Joe, Wonderful Acrobat, tin tumbler, 8", NMIB .. 2,750.00
Morrison, Walking Turk, cloth/cb/kid, clockwork, 1862, 10".. 1,320.00
Ohio Art, Hot Job Sea Plane, w/up, MIB 110.00
Planck, pontoon boat, HP tin, ca 1905, 10", VG.................... 2,860.00
Remco, Fire Engine Factory Kit, 1964 ....15.00
Remco, Kindergarten Band on Wheels, 1968, M 30.00
Remco, School Bus Factory Kit, 1964.................................15.00
Schieble, sedan, headlights on fenders, EX pnt, 17"................500.00
Schoenhut, see Toys, Schoenhut

Schuco, Blk man in lg top hat, tin w/up, 5½", EX......................950.00
Schuco, Donald Duck, plastic & tin litho w/up, '50s, 5½"...........745.00
Schuco, Donald Duck, tin litho w/up, 1930s, NMIB 575.00
Schuco, Donald Duck, tin litho w/up walker, '60s, 6", MIB 265.00
Schuco, Dutch boy w/violin, tin litho w/up, felt clothes, 5½" 225.00
Schuco, Electro-Submarino, tin/plastic, b/o, 12", NM 110.00
Schuco, jitterbug monkey w/mouse, tin litho w/up, 4½", NM 225.00
Schuco, monkey, flocked tin, jtd, non-mechanical, 5" 375.00
Schuco, monkey drummer, tin litho w/up, felt clothes, 4" 100.00
Steelcraft, Heinz Pickle Truck, tin litho, b/o, 12" 250.00
Steiff, See Toys, Steiff
Stock, Paddy's Pride, butcher & pig, tin litho w/up, 8", EX..... 1,000.00
Strauss, Ham 'N Sam, tin litho w/up, NMIB 1,350.00
Strauss, Jazzbo Jim Dancer, tin litho w/up, EX in orig box 550.00
Strauss, Jenny the Balking Mule, tin litho w/up, 9", NM............350.00
Strauss, Knock-Out Prize Fighters, tin litho w/up, 7", EX 550.00
Strauss, Leaping Lena, tin litho w/up, EX 450.00
Strauss, Los Angeles Flying Airship, aluminum, 10", NMIB........575.00
Strauss, Parcel Post Truck, tin litho w/up, 1920s 850.00
Strauss, Red Cap Porter, tin litho w/up, 6", NM......................850.00
Strauss, Taxi, w/driver, tin litho w/up, 1920s 750.00
Strauss, Tombo Dancer, tin litho, clockwork, 10¼", EX 650.00
Takara, R2D2 robot, die-cast & plastic, 1978, 5", NM...............325.00
Tandem, military truck, tin litho, clockwork, 2 figures, 18".........275.00
Tootsie Toy, Buck Rogers Battle Cruiser, 1937, NM 200.00
Tootsie Toy, Buck Rogers Venus Duo Destroyer, NM 100.00
Transogram, Little Country Doctor Bag, w/contents, 1961, NM ...35.00
Unique Art, Bombo the Monk, tin litho w/up, 9½", NMIB 175.00
Unique Art, Flying Circus, tin litho w/up, 12", NMIB 1,000.00
Unique Art, GI Joe & His Jouncing Jeep, tin w/up, 7½", NM.....165.00
Unique Art, Howdy Doody Piano, tin litho w/up, 8½", NM .. 1,250.00
Unique Art, Jazzbo Jim, tin litho, clockwork, 10½" 350.00
Unique Art, Jazzbo Jim, tin litho w/up, 9½", NMIB..................550.00
Unique Art, Lil Abner & Band, tin w/up, 4 at piano, 6½", NM..500.00
Unique Art, Lincoln Tunnel, tin w/up, 24", NMIB....................750.00
Utopia, Jackie Gleason Story Stage Theatre, 1955, MIB 150.00
Vega, balancing bear, fur/papier-mache, w/up, 24", VG 1,000.00
Wolverine, car & trailer, tin litho, mechanical, 27", M 150.00
Wolverine, Snow White stove, tin, 11½x11x6½" 58.00
Wolverine, Sunny Andy Zilotone Player, tinplate w/up, 7" 350.00
Wyandotte, SS America, tin litho boat on wheels, 7¼", M..........35.00

Farm Toys

Two-bottom plow, marked SLIK 1952, 9" long, $125.00.

Bulldozer, Tonka, 9", NM 40.00
Manure spreader, McCormick Deering, EX 50.00
Tractor, Allis Chalmers #190, EX.......................................95.00

Shuco wind-up violin-playing clown, 4½", $135.00.

Tractor, Auburn John Deere A, w/man, EX 35.00
Tractor, Cochshutt #540, MIB 500.00
Tractor, Farmall #404, EX 25.00
Tractor, Ford #8600, Ertle, EX pnt 35.00
Tractor, Internat'l Harvester #404, red metal wheels, EX 95.00
Tractor, Massey Harris #44, w/man, EX 35.00
Tractor, Minneapolis-Moline G-1000, NM 200.00
Tractor, Oliver #77, w/man, EX in box 235.00
Tractor & 4 wagons, wood, Peter Mar, 1940s, NM 375.00
Truck, cattle; all metal, Structo, lg, EX 85.00

Guns and Cap Bombs

Though toy guns were patented as early as the 1850s, the cap pistol was not invented until 1870, when paper caps that were primarily developed to detonate muzzleloaders became available. Some of the earlier models were very ornate and were occasionally decorated with figural heads. Most are marked with the name of their manufacturer – Ace, Daisy, Bulldog, Victor, and Excelsior are the most common

Bakelite ball pop rifle, 1950s 35.00
BB pump, eng metal, Chein, 1940s, M 65.00
Beretta, aluminum, Lytle Novelty, 1950s 40.00
Billy the Kid, buffalo on blk grips, 7½", M 30.00
Blk Sambo, CI, cap pistol, 1890s, EX 225.00
Breakaway, tin, revolver, 10¼" 35.00
Brn woodgrain grips, gold hammer & trigger, Daisy, M 40.00
Bulldozer, cap pistol, 6-shot, minor wear, EX 225.00
Cadet Officer's, cork pistol, leather holster, 9½", NM 55.00
Chinese Must Go, cap pistol, CI, minor wear 650.00
Congo Firebug, cap gun, CI, lt rust, EX 650.00
Dagger Derringer 20.00
Electronic Signal, Remco, NM 60.00
G-Men Big Shot repeater, Chein, M on card 38.50
Kit Carson, pistol, pot metal, EX 25.00
Lugar, aluminum, Lytle Novelty, 1950s 35.00
Mauser, aluminum, Lytle Novelty, 1950s 45.00
Monkey w/coconut, cap bomb, CI, lt rust, EX 400.00
Oh Boy, cap gun, CI, 1922, 5½" 25.00
Palladin, 2 horseshoes in brn circle on ivory grips, 9", M 40.00
Pinto, horse head on ivory grips, 8", M 35.00
Pirate, cap gun, dbl barrel, 1950s, 9¾" 35.00
Pony, cap gun, CI, 1923, 5¼" 45.00
Pony Boy, horse head on ivory/brn grips, 9½", M 30.00
Red Ryder, BB gun, Daisy, 1938 ....25.00
Ric-O-Shays, blk grips, Hubley, pat pending, 11½", M 45.00
Snub-Nose .38, aluminum, Lytle Novelty, 1950s 35.00
Stallion-Nichols-38-Jacksonville, Tex-USA, 9½", M 45.00
Star Single Shot, cap gun, cast metal, 7", EX 15.00
Super Sonic, friction gun 25.00
Thundergun, tan & blk marbleized grips, Marx, 12½", M 50.00
Wanted: Dead or Alive, cap gun, 5½", EX 20.00
Western, steer's head on maroon marbleized grips, 8½", M 35.00
Western Colt, aluminum, Lytle Novelty, 1950s 35.00
Wizard Liquid Pistol, NP, lt rust, EX in box 325.00

Pedal Cars and Ride-On Toys

Airplane, sheet metal w/rpt, 3-wheel, pitted/rust, 48" 700.00
Chicken, cast metal w/spring, rpl base, Gametime, 35x23" 60.00
City Fire Dept, red & wht metal, ball-bearing drive, 35" 150.00
Convertible, Mercedes ornament, Ferbedo on spare tire, 43" 950.00
Cow, Saddle Mates, Gametime, CI base w/rpl spring, 32x27" 65.00
Duck, CI w/spring & CI base, Gametime, ride-on, 32x24" 105.00

Elephant, CI w/spring & metal base, ride-on, 31x27", EX 100.00
Fire Chief, 1907, pedal type, NM 3,800.00
Fire engine, Murray OH Mfg, red/wht/bl, pedal type, EX 70.00
Horse, CI, spring & CI base, Gametime, ride-on, 30x29", EX 100.00
Irish Mail, plank seat/fr, wire-spoked wheels, worn, 40" 160.00
Lincoln Zepher, pedal car, 1940, EX 650.00
Mobo Snail, orig pnt w/only minor wear, ride-on, NM 145.00

Pedal airplane by Steelcraft, sheet metal with rubber tires, 46", VG, $2,700.00.

Rabbit, CI w/spring & metal base, Gametime, ride-on, 33x24" ...100.00
Race car, pnt metal, hinged hood, Eureka, 1940s, 51", EX 600.00
Roadster, gr w/blk & yel trim, wear/some rust, 34" L 600.00
Steam roller, w/bell, wood hdl, ride-on, 14x19x8½", VG 85.00
Tricycle, wood w/CI fittings, spoke wheels, wood pedals 400.00
USAF Jeep, rpt 190.00

Penny Toys

Alligator, tin, hinged head/legs/tail, Germany, 4½" 135.00
Beetle, tin, mc pnt, 3 sm wheels, Germany, 3" 115.00
Butterfly, paper litho on tin w/CI wheels, push toy, 1900s 275.00
Coach w/horse & driver, tin litho, EX 175.00
Dump truck w/driver, Germany 135.00
Girl in 2-wheeled goat cart, tin, Germany, 4", EX 325.00
Gnomes sawing wood, Germany 265.00
Man plays pool at end of table, tin, Germany, 4", EX 185.00
Touring car w/people in windows & chaffeur, Germany 135.00
Train, steam engine w/3 cars 225.00

Pipsqueaks

Pipsqueak toys were popular among the Pennsylvania Germans. The earliest had bellows made from sheepskin. Later, cloth replaced the sheepskin, and finally paper bellows were used.

Ball w/pnt comic features on spring legs, silent, 6" 90.00
Bird on spring legs, felt covering/glass eyes, Germany, 9" 95.00
Blk boy in striped cloth costume, glass eyes, silent, 12" 900.00
Buffalo on wheels, wood/leather, squeaker in head, 11", VG 160.00
Cat & kitten, papier-mache, orig pnt, squeaks, 5¾", EX 235.00
Cat w/2 kittens, striped flocking, animated mouth, 7", VG 425.00
Chickens in cage, open door: papier-mache rooster pops up 55.00
Child w/feather tree, cloth/papier-mache/celluloid, silent 165.00
Dog, seated, blk/wht flocking, silent, rpr, 6¾" 90.00
Duck, solid base, working, cracks/edge damage, 6" 100.00
Duck on nest, papier-mache, kid leather bellows, 4½", EX 145.00
Duck on nest, papier-mache, orig pnt, rpr, silent, 5¾" 425.00

Goose on seesaw bellows, papier-mache, squeaks, 6", EX.............200.00
Goose on spring legs, squeaks, glued rprs, 7" 160.00
Jack-in-box, drunk in barrel, papier-mache, 8", VG..................250.00
Pigeon, mc, silent, rprs, 9" 100.00
Rabbit, haircloth, animated ears, glass eyes, silent, 9".................325.00
Rooster, felt/feathers/glass eyes, in wood cage, silent, 7" 65.00
Rooster, papier-mache, orig pnt, rpr, silent, 7¼" 85.00
Rooster on spring legs, mc/gilt, silent, wear/rstr, 8½" 150.00
Turkey-like bird, bright colors, working, 6", VG 150.00

Pull Toys

Bear, haircloth, glass eyes, metal wheels, worn, 17" 350.00
Elephant, haircloth, wood wheels, voice box, 17", VG.................325.00
Goat, tin w/mc pnt, NP bell & wheel, 5" L.................275.00
Horse, cvd wood, 3-color rpt, tack eyes, rpl wheels, 15".................275.00
Horse, haircloth over wood, all orig, MIG, 16", EX 625.00
Horse, laminated wood w/pnt traces, CI wheels, 16" 625.00
Horse, wood w/papier-mache w/worn dapple gray pnt, 9", G.......135.00
Horse & buggy, tin w/worn mc pnt, 7½", EX.................300.00
Lamb, cloth over iron, glass eyes, voice box, rpl ears, 21" 175.00

Schoenhut

Alligator, pnt eyes, regular 450.00
Barny Google, pnt eyes, reduced.................450.00
Buffalo, glass eyes, regular, NM.................275.00
Buffalo, pnt eyes, regular, M.................345.00
Bulldog, pnt eyes, regular, EX.................550.00
Cage wagon, pnt wood, EX.................900.00
Camel, 1-hump, glass eyes, regular, EX.................375.00
Camel, 2-hump, pnt eyes, regular, NM.................350.00
Circus rider, glass eyes, regular 225.00
Clown, glass eyes, regular, EX.................75.00
Clown, pnt eyes, reduced, EX.................70.00
Clown, pnt eyes, regular, NM.................75.00
Cow, pnt eyes, regular, EX.................375.00
Donkey, glass eyes, regular, EX.................120.00

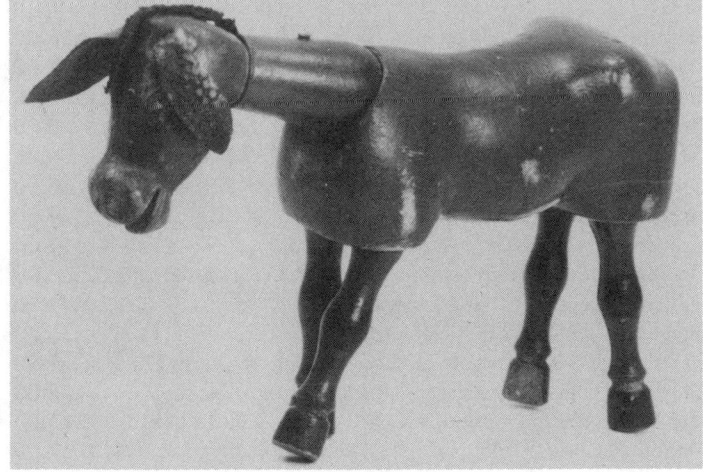

Schoenhut donkey, 6", NM, $160.00.

Donkey, pnt eyes, reduced, EX 65.00
Donkey, pnt eyes, regular, NM 115.00
Dude, pnt eyes, regular.................275.00
Elephant, pnt eyes, reduced, NM.................75.00
Elephant, pnt eyes, regular.................125.00
Giraffe, pnt eyes, regular.................260.00

Goat, glass eyes, regular 250.00
Goose, pnt eyes, regular.................450.00
Hippo, pnt eyes, regular, NM 375.00
Hobo, glass eyes, regular 185.00
Hobo, pnt eyes, regular.................250.00
Horse, brn, pnt eyes, reduced.................95.00
Horse, brn, pnt eyes, regular 160.00
Horse, wht, pnt eyes, regular 175.00
Jiggs, reduced.................450.00
Kangaroo, pnt eyes, regular, NM.................525.00
Lady acrobat, pnt eyes, reduced, VG.................100.00
Lady circus rider, pnt eyes, regular, EX.................225.00
Leopard, pnt eyes, regular.................345.00
Lion, pnt eyes, regular, NM.................350.00
Monkey, pnt eyes, regular.................295.00
Ostrich, pnt eyes, regular, NM.................475.00
Piano, baby grand; 18-key, fold-down top, lg.................275.00
Piano, pnt wood & plastic, 5½x12½", rare, EX.................125.00
Piano, wooden urpight, 20x17x10", EX.................125.00
Pig, pnt eyes, regular.................200.00
Poodle, pnt eyes, regular, EX 165.00
Reindeer, pnt eyes, regular, EX.................600.00
Rhino, pnt eyes, regular, EX 350.00
Ringmaster, pnt eyes, reduced, VG 150.00
Roly poly, clown, musical 195.00
Sea lion, glass eyes, regular, EX 650.00
Sea lion, pnt eyes, regular.................550.00
Speedy Felix, Felix in open car, wooden pull toy, EX 500.00
Tiger, pnt eyes, reduced.................225.00
Tiger, pnt eyes, regular, NM 345.00
Trinity Chimes, paper litho on wood, angel finial, 18", VG.........300.00
Zebra, pnt eyes, regular 1,000.00

Steiff

Margaret Steiff began making her felt stuffed toys in Germany in the late 1800s. The animals she made were tagged with an elephant in a circle. Her first teddy bear, made in 1903, became such a popular seller that she changed her tag to a bear. Felt stuffing was replaced with excelsior and wool; when it became available, foam was used. In addition to the tag, look for the 'Steiff' ribbon and the button inside the ear. For further information we recommend *Teddy Bears and Steiff Animals*, a full-color identification and value guide by Margaret Fox Mandel, available at your local bookstore or public library. See also Teddy Bears.

Afghan, Corso, mohair, chest tag/button, 8½", NM.................165.00
Alligator, velvet, chest tag/button, 21½", EX 175.00
Baboon, Coco, straw stuffed, tag/button, 4", M 90.00
Baboon, sitting, mohair, bl eyes, button, 1950s, 12".................135.00
Badger, Diggy, red & wht mohair, chest tag/button, '50s, 4".........75.00
Bear, Jackie, mohair, button eyes, straw stuffed, 9½", NM.......1,650.00
Bear, Richard Steiff 80th Anniversary, MIB.................225.00
Bear, Zotty, mohair, button eyes, chest tag/button, 8", M 180.00
Cat, Kitty Cat, blk/wht stripes, jtd, tag/button, 4¾", NM.................75.00
Cat, Kolac, mohair, dangling limbs, tag/button, 15½", EX.................565.00
Cat, Tabby, button, 6".................65.00
Cat, Topsi & Tabby, buttons, 2½", ea.................55.00
Chicken, Kiki, red dress, tag/button, 5", NM 300.00
Chipmunk, mohair, jtd head, glass eyes, 1950s, 4", EX 40.00
Cow, w/udder, orig red collar, button, 8x12", NM.................200.00
Dalmation, chest tag/button, 1950s, 4", NM 75.00
Dalmation, wht w/blk spots, chest tag/button, 4", NM.................65.00
Dog, Bully, velvet & mohair, jtd head, button, 6½", EX 75.00

Dog, movable head, long fur, rpl eye, button, 15½", VG 100.00
Dog puppet, wht w/blk eye, brn ear/blk ear, 1908, EX................98.00
Dwarf, Pucky, jtd body, tag/button, 12", NM........................155.00
Dwarf, Pucky, tag/button, 5", M........................48.00
Elephant, Cosy Trampy, gray, collar & bell, tag/button, 8"............88.00
Finch, mohair w/movable horsehair wings, all ID, 4", NM.........220.00
Fox, Foxy, blank button, 3"........................65.00
Fox, Xorry, sitting, button, 5", NM........................95.00
Frog, velveteen, button, 1940s, 3", EX........................55.00
Giraffe, closed mouth, lt yel/orange, button, 1950s, 12", EX 110.00
Gnome, felt, button, 1910, 8", EX 1,000.00
Goat baby, mohair, felt horns, bell, tag/button, 9", EX................75.00
Hedgehog, Joggi, recumbent, mohair, button, 4", EX.................35.00
Kangaroo, Kangoo, felt, no pouch, chest tag, 5½", EX................70.00
Kitty, movable legs & head, no tag, 9x15", EX 150.00
Lion, Leo, sitting, mohair, button, miniature 35.00
Lizard, Lizzy, chest tag, 1½x8", M 165.00
Mickey Mouse, not jtd, orig clothes, ca 1930, 8½", EX 1,200.00

Barclay, Indian, full headdress, pulling bow, sm, NM 12.50
Barclay, Indian w/shield & tomahawk, #251, rstr 8.00
Barclay, lady w/purse, #165, NM.......................14.00
Barclay, machine gunner, prone, cast helmet, #62, NM...............17.50
Barclay, man w/overcoat, #158, NM 7.50
Barclay, pilot, #80, rstr 7.50
Barclay, policeman, arm raised, #186, EX 8.00
Barclay, preacher, holds hat, blk hair, #168, VG........................ 9.00
Barclay, radio operator, tin helmet, no antenna, #147, EX 12.50
Barclay, soldier charging, #234, NM 8.00
Barclay, soldier eating, #112, G........................20.00
Barclay, train mechanic, #162, EX 10.00
Barclay, wounded on crutches, #119, G 12.00
Britains, cowboy w/pistol, movable right arm, EX 7.50
Britains, Indian w/tomahawk, #208, gr tunic, NM 22.00

Steiff, monkey riding Irish Mail, EX, 9", $245.00.

Courtenay, John Fineux defending his master Sir Nicholas Keriel, signed, $1,000.00.

Poodle, Snobby, jtd, gray mohair, chest tag, 5½", M.....................48.00
Rabbit, felt, button, on mk wooden wheels, 12½".......................600.00
Rabbit, Manni, button, 10", NM 150.00
Rabbit, Ossilini, mohair, tag/button, 12", M.......................185.00
Rabbit, Sonny, button, 8" 145.00
Raven, Hucky, straw stuffed, metal ft, chest tag, 6½", M...............90.00
Rooster, mohair & felt, tag/button, 11", NM........................115.00
Wild boar, gr & wht mohair, tusks, button, 1950s, 6x12", EX......175.00

Toy Soldiers

Toy soldiers were popular playthings with children of the 19th century. They were made by many European manufacturers in various sizes until 1848 when a standard size of approximately 1⅓" was established. The most collectible of all toy soldiers were made in England by Britains Ltd. from 1893 to 1966. In America some of the important manufacturers were Barclay, Manoil, Grey, and All-Nu.

Barclay, bugler, tin helmet, long stride, #30, rstr............................ 9.00
Barclay, doctor w/bag, brn, #81, NM.......................12.50
Barclay, drummer, tin helmet, short stride, #32, G 14.00
Barclay, fireman w/axe, #187, rstr.......................14.00
Barclay, flag bearer, tin helmet, short stride, #5, rstr.................13.00
Barclay, girl on skis, #191, EX........................11.00

Elastolin, Doughboy officer, mtd, EX................................36.00
Elastolin, Doughboy officer marching, brn boots, EX...................17.00
French, man for wheelbarrow, #2, EX........................ 9.00
French, man w/pitchfork, #207, EX 5.00
French, peasant girl w/2 baskets, #303, EX 5.00
Grey Iron, boy flying kite, orig kite & string, #3, EX....................18.00
Grey Iron, cowboy, mtd, #57, EX........................24.00
Grey Iron, doughboy, #26, NM........................11.00
Grey Iron, doughboy grenade thrower, #32, G........................20.00
Grey Iron, Legion drummer, #84, NM........................17.50
Grey Iron, US Cavalry officer, mtd, red/wht/bl pnt, #38, G..........25.00
Grey Iron, US Infantry soldier, shoulder arms, #9, early, G............. 7.50
Grey Iron, US Naval officer in whts, G 8.00
Manoil, bugler, 2nd version, #12, EX........................13.00
Manoil, flag bearer, #45, NM........................12.00
Manoil, Indian w/knives, str hair, rstr........................ 9.00
Manoil, man fixing shoe, #149, NM........................24.00
Manoil, man for bench, #131, EX 5.00
Manoil, Navy gunner, #76, rstr........................13.00
Manoil, observer, #51, NM........................18.00
Manoil, soldier w/roll of barbed wire, #119, VG........................18.00
Manoil, stretcher bearer w/medical kit, #58, G........................12.00
Manoil, trooper w/missile, #525, NM........................12.00
Marx, Infantry captain, #36, NM........................11.00

Marx, Infantry private marching, #2, EX **6.00**
Marx, 4-star general, #50, NM **11.00**
Mignot, Assyrian foot soldier w/bow, #2, NM.....................**13.00**
Mignot, Attila, King of the Huns, mtd, #602, M.................**44.00**
Mignot, Gaul, mtd, 2-pc, #200, NM **22.00**
Mignot, Roman foot soldier, NM **10.00**

Trains

Electric trains were produced as early as the late 19th century. Names to look for are Lionel, Ives, and American Flyer.

The following listings were prepared by Bruce C. Greenberg and are taken from his comprehensive publications on Lionel, American Flyer, and Ives trains. The prices presented are the most common versions of each item. In many cases, there are several other variations often having a substantially higher value. Identification numbers given in the listings below actually appear on the item.

Our advisor for this category is Bruce Greenberg; he is listed in the Directory under Maryland.

Key: Std Gauge — Standard Gauge

American Flyer 283, S Gauge engine w/tender, EX......................**45.00**
American Flyer 332DC, S Gauge engine w/tender, EX **350.00**
American Flyer 332DC, S Gauge engine w/tender, G.................**100.00**
American Flyer 360, 361 S Gauge diesels, EX **150.00**
American Flyer 360, 361 S Gauge diesels, G **70.00**
Ives 11, 0 Gauge steam engine w/tender, EX **135.00**
Ives 11, 0 Gauge steam engine w/tender, G **75.00**
Ives 1118, 0 Gauge steam engine w/tender, EX **135.00**
Ives 1118, 0 Gauge steam engine w/tender, G **65.00**
Ives 1132, Wide Gauge steam engine w/tender, 1921-26, EX **850.00**
Ives 1132, Wide Gauge steam engine w/tender, 1921-26, G **325.00**
Ives 3240, 1 Gauge electric engine, 1912-20, EX **950.00**
Ives 3240, 1 Gauge electric engine, 1912-20, G **350.00**
Ives 3241, Wide Gauge electric engine, 1921-25, EX...............**225.00**
Ives 3241, Wide Gauge electric engine, 1921-25, G **85.00**
Ives 3243, Wide Gauge electric engine, 1921-28, EX...............**550.00**
Ives 3243, Wide Gauge electric engine, 1921-28, G **200.00**
Lionel 1668, 0 Gauge steam engine w/tender, 1937-41, EX.........**100.00**
Lionel 1668, 0 Gauge steam engine w/tender, 1937-41, G............**60.00**
Lionel 2037, 0 Gauge steam engine/tender, 1954-55, 57-58, EX .**100.00**
Lionel 2037, 0 Gauge steam engine/tender, 1954-55, 57-58, G **50.00**
Lionel 224, 0 Gauge steam engine w/tender, 1938-42, EX...........**150.00**
Lionel 224, 0 Gauge steam engine w/tender, 1938-42, G **60.00**
Lionel 2343, 0 Gauge diesels, 2 units, EX **650.00**
Lionel 2343, 0 Gauge diesels, 2 units, G.................................**200.00**
Lionel 252, 0 Gauge electric engine, 1926-32, EX **125.00**
Lionel 252, 0 Gauge electric engine, 1926-32, G........................**75.00**
Lionel 380, Std Gauge electric engine, 1923-27, EX...................**400.00**
Lionel 380, Std Gauge electric engine, 1923-27, G **250.00**
Lionel 400E, Std Gauge steam engine, 1931-40, EX...............**2,000.00**
Lionel 400E, Std Gauge steam engine, 1931-40, G....................**950.00**
Lionel 408E, Std Gauge electric engine, 1927-36, EX **1,200.00**
Lionel 408E, Std Gauge electric engine, 1927-36, G **600.00**
Lionel 42, Std Gauge electric engine, 1913-23, rnd hood, EX.....**450.00**
Lionel 42, Std Gauge electric engine, 1913-23, rnd hood, G.......**200.00**
Lionel 50, 027 Gauge gang car, 1955-64, EX **55.00**
Lionel 50, 027 Gauge gang car, 1955-64, G **15.00**
Lionel 58, 027 Gauge rotary snowplow, 1959-61, EX................**400.00**
Lionel 58, 027 Gauge rotary snowplow, 1959-61, G....................**160.00**
Lionel 60, 0 Gauge trolly, 1955-58, EX...................................**275.00**
Lionel 60, 0 Gauge trolly, 1955-58, G **100.00**
Lionel 675, 0 Gauge steam engine w/tender, 1947, EX **115.00**

Lionel 700E, 0 Gauge steam engine w/tender, 1937-42, G....... **1,700.00**
Lionel 726, 0 Gauge steam engine w/tender, 1946-49, EX..........**375.00**
Lionel 726, 0 Gauge steam engine w/tender, 1946-49, G **200.00**
Lionel 773, 0 Gauge steam engine w/tender, 1950, EX........... **1,100.00**
Lionel 773, 0 Gauge steam engine w/tender, 1950, G.................**400.00**
Lionel 8, Std Gauge electric engine, 1925-32, EX.....................**160.00**
Lionel 8, Std Gauge electric engine, 1925-32, G.......................**80.00**

Miscellaneous

Blocks, spelling; litho/emb wood, 9x6¾", EX in orig box...............**60.00**
Blocks, zoo animals, paper litho on wood, set of 8, VG................**575.00**
Bugle, pewter & brass, ceramic mouthpc, 1860s, VG **65.00**
Butcher shop, wood w/papier-mache meat, VG **275.00**
Horse, rocking; dapple-gray, leather saddle, 42", EX **1,100.00**
Horse, rocking; w/jockey, tin w/old rpt, 6½x7" **600.00**
Jack-in-box, cloth-covered spring w/papier-mache face **270.00**
Noah's Ark, 143 mc animals, EX variety/detail, 29" ark......... **3,650.00**
Noah's Ark, 62 mc figures, 22" ark, EX **1,100.00**
Teeter-Totter, Popeye/Olive Oyl, sand toy, tin litho, 9¼" **650.00**
Top, ivory, octagonal, 1¼" dia **65.00**

Trade Signs

Trade signs were popular during the 1800s. They were usually made in an easily recognizable shape that one could mentally associate with the particular type of business it was to represent, especially appropriate in the days when many customers could not read!

Apothecary, mortar/pestle, 3-D, metal w/rpt, 1800s, 27", EX.......**400.00**
Axe, dbl headed, cvd/pnt, 59" L **150.00**
Bait & tackle, cvd/pnt perch lure w/hooks, glass eyes, 32"...........**850.00**
Barber, cvd razor, w/hinged silver blade, 19" L, EX....................**220.00**
Barber, pnt/cvd razor, hinged, 26" L.....................................**200.00**
Bottle w/label: Welch's Grape Juice, wood w/VG pnt, 30" **800.00**
Butcher, cutting tools w/steer atop, CI, old pnt, 20x24" **450.00**
Fan, wood w/mc Chinese figures, Japan, 20" W, EX................ **1,100.00**
Fish, wood, open mouth, w/chain, 6x18", EX............................**525.00**
Fish, wood w/metal fins, glass eyes, very worn pnt, 36" **350.00**
Haberdashery, wrought scroll bracket w/3-D top hat & glove . **4,000.00**

Jack knife, carved and painted, 32" long, $850.00.

Inn, wooden oval in wrought scroll & arrow frwork, 50x65"... **3,500.00**
Locksmith's, wrought iron openwork bracket, key cutout, 39".. **1,500.00**
Lutz Funeral Home, cast brass cornerstone, 10x15" **55.00**

Pocket watch, zinc w/pnt face, 46", VG.....................275.00
Tobacconist, lg porc pipe in iron fr, EX 1,500.00
Watchmaker, pocket watch, sheet zinc faces/CI fr, 30x23".........475.00

Tramp Art

Today considered a type of American folk art, tramp art was made from the late 1800s until after the turn of the century. Often produced by 'tramps' and 'hobos' from wooden materials which could be scavenged (crates and cigar boxes, for instance), articles such as jewelry boxes and picture frames were usually decorated by chip carving and then stained.

Box, mirror in lift lid, worn finish, 8½" L.....................75.00
Box, mirror inserts in lid & sides, 11" L 100.00
Box, red pincushion top, 2 end drws, 10½" L 100.00
Box, 1-drw, hinged lid, scenes under glass, 10x13" 135.00
Box, 2 pyramid forms on hinged lid, cigar label w/in, 9" L.....65.00
Box, 3-tier, geometrics/simple inlay, cvd 'LD,' 20x11" 300.00
Chest, 2-drw, high crest, pnt, 16x10"........................85.00
Chest, 3-drw+shelf, appl hearts/etc, dtd 1912, 10", VG........125.00
Clock case, VG detail, no works or face, 14x14"..............200.00
Dresser, 3-drw, VG detail, swivel mirror, 21x10", VG.........150.00
Frame, gold heart appl ea side, EX detail, 26x20", pr 650.00
Frame, hearts/etc in gilt, detailed, scalloped edge, 20x24".........200.00

Traps

Though of interest to collectors for many years, trap collecting has gained in popularity over the past ten years in particular, causing prices to appreciate rapidly. Traps are usually marked on the pan as to manufacturer, and the condition of these trademarks are important when determining their value. Grading is as follows:

Good: one-half of pan legible.
Very Good: legible in entirety, but light.
Fine: legible in entirety, with strong lettering.
Mint: in like-new, shiny condition.

Our advisor for this category is Boyd Nedry; he is listed in the Directory under Michigan. Prices listed here are for traps in fine condition.

Acme, mousetrap, wood snap.....................................15.00
Allsteal #3, dbl long spring....................................40.00
Arrow #1, single underspring...................................30.00
Bear trap, hand forged, 42" L..................................400.00
Big Stinky, fly trap..20.00
Blizzard, mousetrap, wood snap.................................10.00
Bu-Ro-Des, orchard mouse destroyer, glass 25.00
Bunker, bear trap, unmk, 42" L..............................1,200.00
Champion #3, dbl long spring...................................65.00
Clayton Killer...300.00
Crago Clutch, #4 Missoula Mt...................................285.00
Crescent #2, dbl long spring...................................250.00
Critter Getter, plastic, live mousetrap 5.00
Diamond #H22, dbl long spring 165.00
Diamond #1½, single long spring 18.00
Dicks Ant Destroyer, glass.....................................45.00
Dog Proof, raccoon trap..11.00
Easy Set, metal, mousetrap 15.00
Eclipse #1, dbl under spring...................................68.00

Electrocuter, Ratchford Products, mousetrap....................35.00
Fenn Mark #4, English rodent trap 20.00
Funsten, float trap..250.00
Get-Mor-Mole & Rattrap...12.00
Gibbs Gladiator, rattrap.......................................75.00
Harmon Live Bait, dbl under spring, w/teeth & bait cage.........225.00
Herters, Kodiak bear trap 315.00
Iron Cat, metal, choker-type mousetrap.........................20.00
Joker, wood snap rattrap.......................................18.00
JVJ, Crete Nebraska, gopher trap...............................32.00
Klincher, wood snap mousetrap 8.00
Knock Em Stiff, wood snap mousetrap............................18.00
Little Samson, iron rattrap w/teeth 150.00
Lomar #3, dbl coil spring 15.00
Macabee, gopher trap... 6.00
Master Killer, by WW Stout.....................................150.00
Nash, mole trap, CI..20.00
Newhouse #5, Onieda NY...350.00
Newhouse #6, Animal Trap Co, w/teeth...........................700.00
Oneida Victor #12, single under spring, w/teeth 25.00
Pines, glass roach trap..50.00
Pines, tin & screen fly trap...................................60.00
Quigley, wood snap rattrap.....................................10.00
Rapid Transit, mousetrap.......................................150.00
Safe Setter, metal, single long spring, mousetrap 125.00
Sargent #10, single long spring................................45.00
Schene #4, dbl coil spring.....................................110.00
Stand By, wood snap mousetrap 12.00
Sure Catch, mole trap..10.00
Sure Shut, mousetrap, fits on fruit jar........................38.00
Victor #1, single coil spring, rubber padded jaws 8.00
Victor #3, dbl long spring, brass jaws, w/teeth................150.00
Ward OS, gopher trap...75.00
Woodward, death clamp, 4½".....................................35.00
Ymir, humane trap, Canada 15.00

Trenton

Trenton, New Jersey, was an area that supported several pottery companies from the mid-1800s until the late 1960s. A consolidation of several smaller companies that occurred in the 1890s was called Trenton Potteries Company. Each company produced their own type of wares independent of the others.

Planter, burgundy, 7" 22.00
Urn, yel, classic shape on ped, 7¾" 50.00
Vase, lime gr, 7½" 20.00

Trivets

Although strictly a decorative item today, the original purpose of the trivet was much more practical. They were used to protect table tops from hot serving dishes, and irons heated on the kitchen range were placed on trivets during use to protect work surfaces. The first patent date was 1869; many of the earliest trivets bore portraits of famous people or patriotic designs. Florals, birds, animals, and fruit were other favored motifs.

Watch for remakes of early original designs. Some of these are marked Wilton, Emig, Wright, and Iron Art.

Brass

Foliage, rtcl, wrought iron ft, trn wood hdl, 12½" 155.00
Heart form w/greyhound cutout, 3 cutouts in hdl, 9" 85.00

Iron form, eng flowerpots, heart cutout in hdl base, 10"..................25.00
Iron form, fox & tree cutouts, 8" 165.00
Iron form, lattice work, scroll hdl, 7½" 30.00
Iron form, several heart cutouts, cutout in hdl, 8½" 55.00
Lyre form, wrought legs, trn wood hdl, 12½" 100.00
Pierced, owner's initials, ca 1830..165.00
6-point star in hexagon, 3-ftd, 8½" 65.00

Brass, marked FR, 1884, 10½", $165.00.

Cast Iron

Fruit & flowers, ornate hdl, for sadiron, old 35.00
Jenny Lind emb above hdl...85.00
Lacy, w/Red Riding Hood pattern hdl, ftd, 6¼x11¼"...................250.00
Pinwheel, 2-pc, revolving, 9½" dia 105.00
Rnd w/hearts & star, thistle & pinwheel hdl, Baltimore, 13".......335.00
Star w/in triangular form, Cleveland Foundry 25.00
2 open hearts on geometric grid, 1700s, 4¼x10" 110.00

Wrought Iron

Heart form, 3 penny ft, mk 3 times: JP Seaver, 9", NM 500.00
Heart form, 3-ftd, 1700s, 5x7½"..300.00
Heart form w/geometric center, cast bubous ft, 5" 200.00
Heart form w/lg loop in notch of top, pnt, 6½" 100.00
Heart formed by ram's horn scrolls, scrolled ft, 6" L 325.00
Iron form, 2 'C' scrolls ea side center bar, 8½".............................135.00
Iron form, 3 rickrack strips joined at point, wood hdl, 9"..............85.00
Iron form w/lg O ring, twisted detail & hdl, 12¾".........................125.00
Triangular, good bulbous ft, 5¾"..65.00
Triangular, plain, twisted perimeter, long flat hdl, 10"...................45.00
Triangular, twisted rods, ftd, 1700s, 5x5x6" 75.00
2 spiral ft, 1 plain ft, early, 12" L, EX 275.00
4-legged, ftd, 5½" dia, 8½" hdl 85.00

Miscellaneous

Bronze, iron form, scalloped gallery, wood hdl, 11" 25.00
Copper, scroll ft, hand hammered, wood hdl, 1850s, 10" dia 90.00
Wire, advertising, bl/wht tin litho, 6½" dia 65.00

Trolls

The modern-day version of the troll was designed in 1952 by Helena and Marti Kuuskoski of Tampere, Finland. Those made by Dam and those marked with a horseshoe are among the most valuable, since both are made from the original Kuuskoski design. Many copies have been produced, the best of which are the Wishniks, made by the Uneeda Doll Company. These were first marketed in 1979 and are cur-

rently still available. Troll animals are scarce, and values are rising.

Baby boy, Dam 22.00
Bank, Dam, 7" 45.00
Bank, purple bibs, wht shirt, Denmark, 7".....................................12.50
Batman, all orig, 3" 22.50
Blk-pnt body, Dam, wht hair, orange eyes 17.50
Bobbin' head, Heintz, Germany, 1967 ....50.00
Boy in brn bibs, red hair w/blk tips, red eyes, unmk, 3" 7.50
Bride in gown, wht hair, orange eyes, unmk, 3" 7.50
Cave girl in pk suit, red hair, yel eyes, unmk, 3" 15.00
Cave man, molded eyes, blk hair, sm 35.00
Cow, Dam, sm..30.00
Elephant, Dam, 3" 38.50
Girl in purple tutu, yel hair & eyes, unmk, 3".................................10.00
Graduate, blk gown/hat/shoes, red hair, orange eyes, unmk, 3" 8.00
Grandpa & Grandma, Dam, 1977, 14", pr 30.00
Groom in tuxedo, wht hair & eyes, unmk, 5½" 15.00
Guru, Dam 22.00
Horshoes on ft, Wishnick, 3"... 7.50
Monster, L Khem, gr w/bl hair & gr eyes, pat pend 1964 ....22.50
Nodder, Lucky Schnook, Japan, orig tag...30.00
Nurse, Uneeda, 6" 25.00
Sailor girl, bl hair, orange eyes, unmk, 3" 6.50
Space Troll, gr, 1964 ....30.00
Troll house, orig 55.00

Trunks

In the the days of steamboat voyages, stagecoach journeys, and railroad travel, trunks were used to transport clothing and personal belongings. Some, called 'dome top' or 'turtle backs,' were rounded on top to better accommodate milady's finery. Today, some of the more interesting examples are used in various ways in home decorating. For instance, a flat-topped trunk may become a coffee table, while a smaller dome style may be 'home' for antique dolls or a teddy bear collection.

Vinegar-painted dome-top trunk, green on yellow, 16½", EX, $1,350.00.

Brass/leather/wood fittings, Louis Vuitton, 1920s, 23x40" 175.00
Dome top, sponge pnt, iron bound, 37" L, EX..............................275.00
Immigrant's, oak dome top, rpt/pnt name, brass/iron mts, 47" 300.00
Immigrant's, pine, rose-mulled rpt w/name & 1877, 36" L...........300.00
Immigrant's, pine w/brn grpt, dvtl, wrought hdls, 34" L...............110.00
Immigrant's, pine w/iron corner braces, pnt label, 41" L..............175.00
Immigrant's, scrubbed pine dome top/tooled iron straps, 49".......200.00
Pine, dome top, dvtl, iron bindings, rfn, 40" L 110.00
Pine, hand-wrought metalwork, 1820s, 23x39x24" 250.00

Pine w/blk pnt, dome top, iron bound, 'NY,' 33" L, EX 125.00
Pine w/orig brn grpt, bowed sides & lid, 28" L.............................175.00

Tuthill

The Tuthill Glass Company operated in Middletown, New York, from 1902 to 1923.

Our advisors for this category are Jeanette and Marvin Stofft; their address is listed in the Directory under Indiana.

Bowl, Phlox, 8" 275.00
Bowl, Wild Rose, intaglio, nailhead band, 3-ftd, 7½".................145.00
Bowl, 3 Fruits, scalloped/serrated, shallow, 10" 500.00
Compote, Cosmos, 4x6" 120.00
Compote, geometric & intaglio cut, 7½" 300.00
Pitcher, Phlox, intaglio/lg hobstars, +6 tumblers 750.00
Vase, single stars/X-hatching in dmn shapes, ftd, 12" 450.00
Vase, sweet pea; Wood Lily, deep intaglio, heavy, 4x5½".............325.00

Typewriters

The first commercially successful typewriter was the Sholes and Glidden, introduced in 1874. By 1882 other models appeared, and by the 1890s dozens were on the market. At the time of the First World War, the ranks of typewriter-makers thinned, and by the 1920s only a few survived.

Collectors informally divide typewriter history into the pioneering period, up to about 1890; the classic period, from 1890 to 1920; and the modern period, since 1920. There are two broad classifications of early typewriters: (1) Keyboard machines, in which depression of a key prints a character and via a shift key prints up to three different characters per key. (2) Index machines, in which a chart of all the characters appears on the typewriter; the character is selected by a pointer or dial and is printed by operation of a lever or other device. Even though index typewriters were simpler and more primitive than keyboard machines, they were none-the-less a later development, designed to provide a cheaper alternative to the standard keyboard models that were selling for upwards of $100. Eventually second-hand keyboard typewriters supplied the low-price customer, and index typewriters vanished except as toys. Both classes of typewriters appeared in a great many designs.

It is difficult, if not impossible, to assign standard market prices to early typewriters. Unlike collectors of postage stamps, carnival glass, etc. few people collect typewriters – so there is no active marketplace from which to establish prices. Also, condition is a very important factor, and typewriters can vary infinitely in condition. A third factor to consider is that an early typewriter achieves its value mainly through the skill, effort, and patience of the collector who restores it to its original condition, in which case its purchase price is insignificant. Some unusual-looking early typewriters are not at all rare or valuable, while some very ordinary-looking ones are scarce and could be quite valuable. No general rules apply. When no condition is indicated, the items listed below are assumed to be in excellent, unrestored condition.

Our advisor for this category is Mike Brooks; he is listed in the Directory under California.

American, indicator type, M 85.00
Bing #2, 1926, EX 125.00
Blickensderfer #5, in wood case 150.00
Blickensderfer #7, oak case, EX 60.00
Blickensderfer #8 ....50.00
Blickensderfer Electric 3,000.00
Crandall...1,000.00

Densmore...300.00
Edison, index 2,000.00
Franklin #9, decal of Franklin, 1891, EX 160.00
Hammond #12 ....75.00
Hammond Multiplex, folding, for all nations, M 100.00
Merritt, index, wood cover, instruction label in lid, EX...............375.00
Molle #3..40.00
Monarch, portable 35.00
Morris, index 500.00
O'Dell #2 ....250.00
O'Dell #4, orig box 275.00
Oliver Standard Visible Writer, old upright keys, M 80.00
Royal, dbl glass sides 25.00
Royal #5 ....35.00
Sholes & Glidden, w/decor 2,500.00
Underwood Standard, gr, portable, in orig case, EX 45.00
World, index..100.00
World, last pat date 1886, orig case..200.00

Uhl Pottery

Founded in Evansville, Indiana, in 1849 by German immigrants, the Uhl Pottery was moved to Huntingburg, Indiana, in 1908 because of the more suitable clay available there. They produced stoneware – Acorn Ware jugs, crocks, and bowls – which were marked with the acorn logo and 'Uhl Pottery.' They also made mugs, pitchers, and vases in simple shapes and solid glazes marked with a circular ink stamp containing the name of the pottery and 'Huntingburg, Indiana.' The pottery closed in the mid-1940s. Those seeking additional information about Uhl pottery are encouraged to contact the Uhl Collectors' Society, whose address is listed in the Directory under Clubs, Newsletters, and Catalogs.

Ash tray, acorn, brn, mk 80.00
Ash tray, dog at fire hydrant, brn 160.00
Ash tray, Shell service station ad, brn...60.00
Bowl, batter; pk, mk, 10" 90.00
Bowl, bulb; tulips, bl, mk, #120..50.00
Bowl, chili; bl, mk, 12-oz..35.00
Bowl, dog's feeding; dog emb, mk, #130, 7" 90.00
Candle holder, bl, mk 75.00
Casserole, bl, w/lid, mk, 5-pt 40.00

Chicken waterer, stoneware, 10", $75.00.

Churn, Acorn Ware, w/bails, mk, 3-gal 80.00
Churn, Evansville mk, 3-gal 95.00
Cookie jar, bl, mk, #522 ....120.00
Cookie jar, globe, pk, mk 90.00
Dispenser, ice water; Acorn Ware, 5-gal 165.00
Jar, Acorn Ware, wht, 30-gal 285.00
Jug, Acorn Ware, squat, bail hdl, brn/wht 150.00
Jug, Acorn Ware, 5-gal 50.00
Jug, baseball, 2½" 80.00
Jug, Believe-it-or-not 250.00
Jug, canteen, bl, miniature................................90.00
Jug, cat, tan 65.00
Jug, elephant, blk, mk 85.00
Jug, football, brn, 4" 40.00
Jug, horse head, wht.......................................90.00
Jug, Merry Christmas, 1937, 2½" 200.00
Jug, polar bear, bl, ½-gal, 10" 375.00
Jug, ring, bl, 2½" 180.00
Jug, softball, 3½" 210.00
Miniature, cowboy boots, bl, mk, pr.......................125.00
Miniature, lady's slippers, pk, pr........................160.00
Mug, coffee; bl, mk 65.00
Mug, grape, bl, 12-oz 80.00
Mug, tan, mk, 14-oz 12.00
Pitcher, flagon, bl, mk, 5-pt 120.00
Pitcher, grape, bulbous, bl, #181 ....90.00
Pitcher, grape, bulbous, bl, #184 ....110.00
Pitcher, grape, str sides, bl, mk, 6-pt 120.00
Pitcher, Lincoln, bl, mk, 1-pt, 6" 240.00
Pitcher, Lincoln, bl, mk, ½-pt, 4" 200.00
Pitcher, Lincoln, bl, mk, 2-pt, 8" 250.00
Pitcher, Lincoln, bl, mk, 4-pt, 10" 300.00
Roaster, bl, w/lid, mk, 11"...............................200.00
Teapot, bl, mk, #143......................................300.00
Teapot, pk, mk, #132......................................130.00
Vase, bl, #152, 5"...50.00
Vase, cemetery; bl, 5" 45.00
Vase, cut flower; yel, mk, #117 ....35.00

Unger Brothers

The Art Nouveau silver produced by Unger Brothers, who operated in Newark, New Jersey, from the early 1880s until 1909, is fast becoming very popular with today's collectors. In addition to tableware, they also made brushes, mirrors, powder boxes, and the like for milady's dressing table as well as jewelry and small personal accessories such as match safes and flasks. They often marked their products with a circle seal containing an intertwined 'UB' and '925 fine sterling.' In addition to sterling, a very limited amount of gold was also used. Note: This company made no pewter items; Unger designs may occasionally be found in pewter, but these are copies. Items dated in the mark or signed 'Birmingham' are English (not Unger).

Flour sifter, Duvaine, sm 110.00
Glove stretcher, Love's Dream, 9" 235.00
Locket, Love's Dream, 1½" dia 575.00
Matchsafe, Love's Dream, bk: smooth, sq w/rnded corners...........450.00
Mirror, Love's Dream, long hdl............................750.00
Shoe horn, Love's Dream, w/sterling hdls 150.00
Spoon, Nouveau lady 100.00
Tomato fork, Duvaine......................................185.00
Tray, Love's Dream, 5" dia 350.00
Whisk brush, Love's Dream, worn bristles, hdl 4½x2¾".............265.00

Universal

Universal Potteries Incorporated operated in Cambridge, Ohio, from 1934 to 1956. Many lines of dinnerware and kitchen items were produced in both earthenware and semi-porcelain. In 1956 the emphasis was shifted to the manufacture of floor and wall tiles, and the name was changed to the Oxford Tile Company, Division of Universal Potteries. The plant closed in 1976.

Ballerina, bowl, 5½" 4.00
Ballerina, coffeepot......................................20.00
Ballerina, cup & saucer 6.00
Ballerina, gravy boat 7.50
Ballerina, plate, hdls, 10½"..............................7.50
Ballerina, plate, 9" 5.00
Bittersweet, bowls, stacking set of 3, w/lids.............30.00
Bittersweet, casserole, hdls, w/lid 22.00
Bittersweet, jug, w/lid, lg 25.00
Calico Fruit, jug, utility; w/lid, 8" 25.00
Cameo Ware, cake lifter & spoon 15.00
Cattail, bowl, berry; sm..................................3.50
Cattail, bowl, mixing; 8" 15.00
Cattail, bowl, soup; flat 8.00
Cattail, casserole, hdls, w/lid...........................18.00
Cattail, cup & saucer 10.00
Cattail, fork 10.00
Cattail, jug, batter; metal lid...........................65.00
Cattail, pie server.......................................7.50

Cattail syrup pitcher, 5", $30.00.

Cattail, plate, grill; 9¾"................................12.00
Cattail, plate, 6"...3.00
Cattail, plate, 9"...5.00
Cattail, platter, 11½"....................................8.00
Rodeo, plate, 9¼"...3.00
Rodeo, soup, hdls 3.00
Woodvine, shakers, pr.....................................10.00

Val St. Lambert

Since its inception in Belgium at the turn of the 19th century, the Val St. Lambert Cristalleries has been involved in the production of high quality glass, specializing in cameo.

Our advisor for this category is Don Williams; he is listed in the Directory under Iowa. See also Animal Dishes with Covers.

Paperweight, flat w/impressed frosted eagle	50.00
Vase, bl cut to clear, gold label, 5"	105.00
Vase, bl w/bronze floral overlay, wide base, Belgique, 11"	385.00
Vase, emerald to clear, prism-shaped cuttings, 10"	150.00
Vase, honey w/gray patina, 2 spiral/dot bands, sphere, 7½"	300.00

Cameo

Bowl, floral on gr, incurvate, att, 8x12"	325.00
Vase, berries, ruby on clear, w/gilt, 10"	375.00
Vase, blackberry vines, cut/HP, cylindrical w/wide ft, 10"	700.00
Vase, floral/berries/vines, pk on crystal, 8"	150.00
Vase, gr on clear, Deco style, ca 1900, 7"	450.00
Vase, mums, gold on gr texture, SP floral overlay, 12"	475.00

Valentines

Pagan ritual once held that on Valentine's Day the birds of the air elected to choose their mates; and, as this premise was eagerly adopted by the homo sapien species, romantic poems became a familiar expression of one's intentions. By the mid-1800s, comical hand-colored lithographic and wood-block prints were mass-produced both here and abroad. At the turn of the century, the more romantic, often mechanical German imports forced many American companies out of business. Today's collectors often specialize – comics, post cards, mechanicals, Victorian, Kewpies, Greenaway characters, or those signed by a specific artist are among many well-established categories.

If you're interested in learning more about valentines, we recommend *Tokens of Love* by Roberta Etter; her address is in the Directory under England.

Key
hc — hand colored   p — publisher

Cutwork, affixed hair wreath, verse, 1800s	35.00
Cutwork, circular w/script verse, ca 1900, sm	55.00
Cutwork, heart shaped w/animals in landscape, 5x6"	265.00
Cutwork, hearts/birds/foliage, inscr/1822, fr, 12x16"	1,725.00
Cutwork, octagonal heart design, old fr, 17½x14½"	225.00
Cutwork, pricked border, theorem primroses, verse, 1830s	100.00
Cutwork, watch paper, handmade, 1800s	50.00

Doily, applied pansy, and gold decoration, 1800s, 6" x 4½", $7.00.

Drawing, red/blk ink, figure w/heart-form head, verse, 7x9"	300.00
For One I love, stand-up w/beehive, 1920s, 4"	6.00
Just a Hot Water Bottle, stand-up, 1920s, 5½"	6.00
Lacy w/flowers & children, 1896, M	25.00
Mechanical, boy & girl on scooter, 1920s, 5"	10.00
Mechanical, boy & girl pumping up heart, 1920s, 5"	10.00
Mechanical, boy & girl w/camera, 1920s, 5"	10.00
PA Dutch heart w/Bible quote, 1854	60.00
Popeye, 1943, VG	8.00
Unrequited Love, aquatint vignette, 1940s, series of 14	500.00
You're the Cream in My Coffee, stand-up, 1920s, 5"	5.00

Van Briggle

The Van Briggle Pottery of Colorado Springs, Colorado, was established in 1901 by Artus Van Briggle, whose early career had been shaped by such notables as Karl Langenbeck and Maria Nichols Storer. His quest for several years had been to perfect a completely flat matt glaze; and, upon accomplishing his goal, he opened his pottery. His wife, Anne, worked with him, and they, along with George Young, were responsible for the modeling of the wares. Their work typified the flow and form of the Art Nouveau movement, and the shapes they designed played as important a part in their success as their glazes. Some of their most famous pieces were Despondency, Lorelei, and Toast Cup.

Increasing demand for their work soon made it necessary to add to their quarters as well as their staff. Although much of the ware was eventually made from molds, each piece was carefully trimmed and refined before the glaze was sprayed on. Their most popular colors were Persian Rose, Ming Blue, and Mustard Yellow.

Van Briggle died in 1904, but the work was continued by his wife. New facilities were built and by 1908, in addition to their artware, tiles, gardenware, and commercial lines were added. By the twenties, the emphasis had shifted from art pottery to novelties and commercial wares. As late as 1970, reproductions of some of the early designs continued to be made. Until about 1920, most pieces were marked with the date and shape number; after that the AA mark was used.

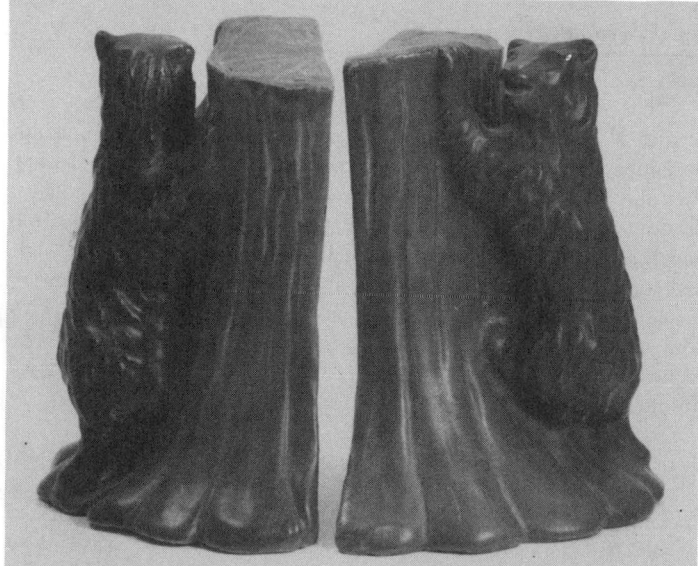

Bookends, Mulberry and Persian Rose, repaired, $375.00 for the pair.

Bookends, squirrel, mulberry, pr	135.00
Bowl, quadrifoil, no panels, Persian Rose, dtd 1916, 3x6¾"	200.00

Bust, Chief Sitting Bull, bl, ltd/#d edition, 11½" 275.00
Bust, Red Cloud, bl, limited/#d edition, 10" 275.00
Paperweight, rabbit, maroon w/bl-gr, 2½x3¼" 45.00
Paperweight, rabbit, Persian Rose, early base, 2½" 65.00
Pitcher, leaves/berries, lt gr, dtd 1904, factory flaws, 10" 850.00
Plate, poppy/swirling leaves, med gr, dtd 1904 (?), 8½" 500.00
Tile, branches, brn w/gr leaves on bl, mk, 6x6" 125.00
Tile, flowers/berries/stem, gray/bl/brn on gr, no mk, 6x6" 125.00
Tile, 3 poppies on edge, dk gr/blk, 6x6" 125.00
Vase, bl-gray, mk, ca 1908-11, 10¾" 975.00
Vase, blk matt, 2 sm in-mold hdls, #240, 1904, 11x4½" 750.00
Vase, bud; lt gr textured semi-gloss, #418, dtd 1906, 8½ 350.00
Vase, curved leaves/stems, dk bl/gr on brn clay, 1908, 4½" 500.00
Vase, Dos Cabezos, bl-gray, dtd 1914, EX glaze, 8x5½" 3,500.00
Vase, floral, gr/purple flecks, #291, 1906, 11" 900.00
Vase, floral/whiplash stems, dk red w/gr, #d, dtd '04, 13" 2,600.00
Vase, florals in relief, bl, modern, 5" 30.00
Vase, geometric floral, rose w/lt gr top, #282, dtd '05, 8" 1,100.00
Vase, Lady of the Lily, lt bl, dtd 1917, 11x10"...........................1,900.00
Vase, leaf band, mauve, bulbous, 1905, 7" 550.00
Vase, leaves, feathered Mustard Yel, #466/dtd 1908-11, 5½" 500.00
Vase, leaves, lt gr on brn clay, #692, dtd 1915, 7½" 260.00
Vase, leaves/blossoms, bl mottle to bl-gr, dtd 1920, 13" 450.00
Vase, Lorelei, bl tones, 1970, 11" 350.00
Vase, Lorelei, burgundy w/dk bl, ca 1925, 10x5" 425.00
Vase, Lorelei, mint to cream, #17, III/1902, EX mold, 10" 21,000.00
Vase, maroon/dk bl, #795, dtd 1920, 5" 280.00
Vase, morning-glories, maroon w/gr-bl, #208, 1904, 12" 4,250.00
Vase, peacock eyes, mossy gr, #201, dtd 1904, 5½"......................800.00
Vase, pendant flower, gr w/red touches, #197, dtd 1903, 6"..... 1,050.00
Vase, poppies, dk maroon w/gr, #794, dtd 1916, 8" 325.00
Vase, prs of stemmed flowers, gr, dtd 1902, 4" 700.00
Vase, raspberry w/gr at top, hdls, #238, 1903, 6x8" 950.00
Vase, recessed 2-leaf stems, powdery wht, ca 1907, 7x4".............425.00
Vase, swirled highly-emb poppy pods, lt gr, dtd '02, 8", NM ... 3,800.00
Vase, swirled leaves, dk bl on dk brn, #662, 1908/11, 11" 750.00
Vase, thick mottled celery gr, #374, dtd 1905, 6x4" 500.00
Vase, tulip band on lower half, lav/dk bl, no mk, 5½x5½"............350.00
Vase, tulips/leaves, maroon w/gr, #844, dtd 1915, 6" 450.00
Vase, twisted leaves form closed hdls, #40, dtd '02, 11x4"....... 2,200.00
Vase, 4 lg leaves at bulbous base, dk gray-gr, '07-12, 9x6"...........425.00

Vance Avon

Although pottery had been made in Tiltonville, Ohio, since about 1880, the ware manufactured there was of little significance until after the turn of the century when the Vance Faience Company was organized for the purpose of producing quality artware. By 1902 the name had been changed to the Avon Faience Company, and late in the same year it and three other West Virginia potteries incorporated to form the Wheeling Potteries Company. The Avon branch operated in Tiltonville until 1905 when production was moved to Wheeling. Art pottery was discontinued.

From the beginning, only skilled craftsmen and trained engineers were hired. Wm. P. Jervis and Frederick Hurten Rhead were among the notable artists responsible for designing some of the early artware. Some of the ware was slip decorated under glaze, while other pieces were molded with high-relief designs. Examples with squeeze-bag decoration by Rhead are obviously forerunners of the Jap Birdimal line he later developed for Weller. Ware was marked 'Vance F. Co.'; 'Avon F. Co., Tiltonville'; or 'Avon W. Pts. Co.'

Jardiniere & ped, landscape/pine trees, squeezebag, 39" 1,700.00

Pitcher, gr, hound hdl, emb animals/grapevines, 12¾", EX 500.00
Vase, flower arranger; brn, 5-hole, Faience mk, 11" 130.00
Vase, 4 mermaids/fish relief, brn/yel mottle, 12" 650.00

Venetian Glass

Venetian glass is a thin, fragile ware usually made in colors, often with internal gold or silver flecks. It was produced on the island of Murano, near Venice, from the 13th century to the early 1900s. Murano-type glassware is always heavier and thicker than the older ware. Art Deco items and items from the fifties often command high prices at auctions in the east.

Our advisor for this category is Madeleine France; she is listed in the Directory under Florida.

Bottle, clear w/wht loopings, amethyst rim/rigaree, 2" L 95.00
Bowl, Deco leaf form w/stem, bl/crystal, 1950s, 8½".....................250.00
Carafe, aventurine fish stopper, mk Murano/Lusardo, 1909 ....75.00
Compote, bl w/gold-flecked ball stem, gold leaf prunts, 8½"..........75.00
Ewer, dolphin figural, gold flecks in amethyst, rigaree, 11"..........110.00
Figurine, dancer, exotic attire, clear w/gold mica, 9", pr...............125.00
Figurine, fish, ruby, gold flecks, 5½x9¾" 125.00
Figurine, lady w/basket, 1900s, 16" 120.00
Figurine, rooster crowing, pk to clear w/gold flecks, 9"................135.00
Figurine, swan, ruby, clear bill & base, 8"....................................55.00
Paperweight, clear bubbly pear w/gr glass inner pear, 1905 ....60.00
Vase, amber drops on mauve frost, ruffled bottle form, 1895 ....195.00
Vase, bl/wht/goldstone/clear spirals, ftd, 5" 65.00
Vase, gr w/gold foil inclusions, Venini/Murano, 5½" 300.00
Vase, handkerchief; mauve cased in wht, Venini/Murano, 4" 220.00
Vase, handkerchief; yel, wht int, Venini/Murano, 8"...................275.00
Vase, quilted, goblet shape w/petal stem, gr w/gold dust, 10½" 48.00
Vase, quilted w/appl berries, flower rigaree, gr w/gold, 10"............55.00
Vase, red spirals, gold-flecked ft, Venini/Murano, 10" 495.00
Wine, latticinio stripes in cranberry/clear/opal/goldstone 75.00

Verlys

Verlys art glass, produced in France after 1931 by the Holophane Company of Verlys, was made in crystal with acid-finished relief work in the Art Deco style. Colored and opalescent glass was also used. In 1935 an American branch was opened in Newark, Ohio, where very similar wares were produced.

French Verlys was signed with one of three mold-impressed script signatures, all containing the company name and country of origin. The American-made glassware was signed 'Verlys' only, either scratched with a diamond-tipped pen or impressed in the mold. There is very little if any difference in value between items produced in France and America. Though some seem to feel that the French should be the higher priced (assuming it to be scarce), many prefer the American-made product.

In June of 1955, about sixteen Verlys molds were leased to the A. H. Heisey Company. Heisey's versions were not signed with the Verlys name; so if an item is unsigned, it is almost certainly a Heisey piece. The molds were returned to Verlys of America in July 1957.

Our advisor for this category is Don Frost; he is listed in the Directory under Oregon.

Bowl, bluebirds & dragonflies, frosted, 12" 120.00
Bowl, chrysanthemums, 10" 125.00
Bowl, fan-tailed goldfish, opal, 2-hdl oval, 20" L.........................600.00
Bowl, poppies, clear/frosted, 13½" 120.00
Bowl, wild ducks, Directoire bl, 13½"...250.00

Centerpiece, 2 doves ea side of sq base, frosted, 12" 125.00
Figurine, pigeon, frosted, 4¼" 285.00
Plaffonier, lt gr, birds dive for fish, iron base, mk Brandt............800.00
Vase, Four Seasons, dtd 1940, 8¼"..350.00
Vase, lovebirds at base, fan form, clear w/tan wash, 4x6½" 120.00
Vase, sunflowers, gray, ftd cylinder, 9"..285.00
Vase, 6 mermaids among seaweed, opal, 10x7"..........................200.00

Vase, Gem, with hard to find flower frog, ca 1930s, $245.00.

Vernon Kilns

Vernon Potteries Ltd. was established by Faye G. Bennison in Vernon, California, in 1931. The name was later changed to Vernon Kilns; until it closed in 1958, dinnerware and figurines were their primary products. Among its wares most sought after by collectors today are items designed by such famous artists as Rockwell Kent, Walt Disney, and Don Blanding.

Our advisor for this category is Maxine Nelson; she is listed in the Directory under California.

Ash tray, Maine the Pine Tree State, red 15.00
Brown-Eyed Susan, casserole, w/lid, 8" 35.00
Brown-Eyed Susan, chowder 5.00
Brown-Eyed Susan, creamer & sugar bowl....................................12.50
Brown-Eyed Susan, plate, 9½"...5.00
Brown-Eyed Susan, shakers, regular, pr 10.00
Chatelaine Jade, cup, ped ft...18.00
Chatelaine Jade, plate, 7½"..10.00
Chatelaine Jade, platter, 16" 38.00
Early California, bowl, fruit; 5½" 4.00
Early California, lug soup.. 5.00
Early California, plate, 7½".. 4.00
Fantasia, bowl, Mushroom, pk, no decor, 12" L 90.00
Fantasia, bowl, Satyr, #124, 1940, 3x6½" 125.00
Fantasia, bowl, Winged Nymph, pk, #112, 2½x12" 125.00
Fantasia, Donkey Unicorn, #16 ....250.00
Fantasia, figurine, Dumbo, #40...95.00
Fantasia, figurine, elephant w/raised trunk, #26, 5⅞"..................350.00
Fantasia, figurine, Ostrich Ballerina, #28 or #29 ....600.00
Fantasia, plate, 10½"..50.00
Fantasia, shakers, Mushroom, 1941, pr 100.00
Fantasia, sugar bowl, w/lid, ind..25.00
Fantasia, vase, Goddess, wht goddess w/lt gr, #126.....................200.00
Fantasia, vase, Pegasus, bl, #127, 12x7½" dia 200.00

Fantasia elephants, $250.00 each.

Gingham, bowl, divided vegetable 12.00
Gingham, bowl, mixing; 4-pc set 65.00
Gingham, bowl, 5½" 4.00
Gingham, chop plate 12.00
Gingham, creamer & sugar bowl, w/lid..12.50
Gingham, plate, 9½"...5.00
Gingham, tumbler 15.00
Hawaiian Flowers, creamer & sugar bowl, w/lid 30.00
Hawaiian Flowers, cup, demitasse 12.00
Hawaiian Flowers, plate, 10½" 15.00
Hawaiian Flowers, saucer... 4.00
Hawaiian Flowers, shakers, pr 15.00
Heavenly Days, bowl, divided vegetable..10.00
Heavenly Days, chowder 5.00
Heavenly Days, coffeepot 20.00
Heavenly Days, cup & saucer 6.00
Heavenly Days, tumbler 12.00
Homespun, bowl, chowder 7.00
Homespun, carafe & stopper 18.00
Homespun, cup & saucer.. 8.00
Homespun, plate, 6" 2.50
Homespun, platter, 12½"..12.50
Lei Lani, chop plate, 14" 40.00
Lei Lani, shakers, pr 12.00
Monterey, bowl, 9" 8.00
Monterey, creamer & sugar bowl...15.00
Monterey, cup & saucer 6.00
Monterey, plate, 10½".. 7.00
Native American, platter, 12" 10.00
Native American, shakers, pr 5.00
Native American, soup bowl 5.00
Organdie, bowl, fruit 5.00
Organdie, bowl, salad; 5½" 8.00
Organdie, bowl, vegetable; w/lid...30.00
Organdie, bowl, 9"..10.00
Organdie, carafe 20.00
Organdie, chop plate, 10" 10.00
Organdie, creamer & sugar bowl, w/lid 12.00
Organdie, gravy boat...12.00
Organdie, mug 10.00
Organdie, pitcher, bulbous, 1-qt...16.00
Organdie, plate, dinner... 6.00
Organdie, plate, salad 4.00

Organdie, platter, oval, 14½" 15.00
Organdie, shakers, pr 7.00
Organdie, sugar bowl, w/lid 10.00
Organdie, teapot, ind 18.00
Organdie, teapot, 6-cup 20.00
Organdie, tumbler, 14-oz 14.00
Plate, Army Air Corps, song, brn, 10¼" 25.00
Plate, Bit of Old England, #4 ....20.00
Plate, Bits of Old New England, Old Dobbin 20.00
Plate, Bits of the Old South, Cotton patch w/Blk figures 28.00
Plate, Bits of the Old West, Barfly..............................20.00
Plate, California Centennial, El Camino Real, 14" 40.00
Plate, Famous Men, Gen Douglas MacArthur, 1942 ....12.00
Plate, French Operas, La Musette de Portici, 8½" 18.00
Plate, New Orleans, Little Theatre of Courtyard, 10" 20.00
Plate, Our American, brn, 9½"...................................45.00
Plate, Republican Convention, San Francisco, 1956 ....65.00
Plate, 175th Anniversary of Walter Baker Co, 1st ed, 1940 ..25.00
Salamina, cup & saucer 50.00
Salamina, plate, 10½" 95.00
Salamina, plate, 14"..150.00
Salamina, plate, 6½"..24.00
Salamina, plate, 7½"..70.00
Salamina, plate, 9½", in pewter fr 125.00
Salamina, saucer 12.50
Salamina, sugar bowl, w/lid, regular 35.00
Salamina, tumbler 30.00
Tam O'Shanter, bowl, salad; ind.................................. 8.00
Tam O'Shanter, carafe, w/stopper................................15.00
Tam O'Shanter, casserole, w/lid, 8"..............................25.00
Tam O'Shanter, plate, 9½" 4.50
Tam O'Shanter, sauce boat 9.00
Tickled Pink, bowl, divided vegetable 12.00
Tickled Pink, coffeepot..22.00
Tickled Pink, creamer & sugar bowl, w/lid 15.00
Tickled Pink, pitcher, sm 8.00
Tickled Pink, plate, 10" 6.00

Verre de Soie

Literally meaning glass of silk, this type of glassware is named for its lovely, almost pearl-like lustre.

Bottle, scent; intaglio flowers/festoons, cylindrical, 8" 300.00
Tumbler, soft irid, sgn Steuben, 4"...................................55.00
Vase, Hawkes cuttings, short neck, 7" 195.00
Vase, quilted, bl threading, flared, 8".............................265.00
Vase, ruffled, 6" 180.00

Viennese Enameled Ware

Clock, putti support & surmount rnd dial, 9½" 600.00
Flask, perfume; mythological figures/cupids, dome lid, 2½" 400.00
Music box, lg/sm urns, panels, glass doors, octagonal, 16" 3,500.00
Tankard, winged caryatid hdl, pineapple finial, scenic, 4" 1,200.00

Villeroy and Boch

The firm of Villeroy and Boch, located in Mettlach, Germany, was brought into being by the 1841 merger of three German factories – the Wallerfangen factory, founded by Nicholas Villeroy in 1787; the Mettlach factory, founded by Jean Francis Boch 1809; and Boch's father's

factory in Septfontaines, established in 1767. Villeroy and Boch produced many varieties of wares, including earthenware with printed underglaze designs which carried the well-known castle mark with the name 'Mettlach.' See also Mettlach.

**Ewer with figural cupid, 13",
$185.00.**

Charger, Meissen castle on Elbe, 12" 175.00
Plaque, child w/bbl, walking steins, sgn Schlitt, 17" dia 425.00
Plate, gaudy floral, 10"..25.00
Plate, old touring car w/passengers, 8½" 45.00
Tile, Oriental fish, 6" 40.00
Tumbler, girl holding pitcher, peacock on tray, #1025 ....60.00

Vistosa

Vistosa was produced from about 1938 through the early forties. It was Taylor, Smith, and Taylor's answer to the very successful Fiesta line of their nearby competitor, Homer Laughlin. Vistosa was made in four solid colors – mango red, cobalt blue, light green, and deep yellow. 'Pie crust' edges and a dainty five-petal flower molded into handles and lid finials made for a very attractive yet nevertheless commercially unsuccessful product.

Bowl, salad 95.00

Creamer and sugar bowl, $27.50.

Cup & saucer 10.00
Egg cup, 3" 22.50
Gravy boat 75.00
Pitcher, red..35.00
Plate, gr, 6" 3.00
Plate, serving, yel, 11" 12.50
Plate, 9" 6.00

Shakers, pr	15.00
Teapot, red	75.00

Volkmar

Charles Volkmar established a workshop in Tremont, New York, in 1882. He produced artware decorated under the glaze in the manner of the early barbotine work done at the Haviland factory in Limoges, France. He relocated in 1888 in Menlo Park, New Jersey, and together with J.T. Smith established the Menlo Park Ceramic Company for the production of art tile. The partnership was dissolved in 1893. From 1895 until 1902, Volkmar located in Corona, New York, first under the name Volkmar Ceramic Company, later as Volkmar and Cory, and for the final six years as Crown Point. During the latter period he made art tile, blue underglaze Delft-type wares, colorful polychrome vases, etc. The Volkmar Kilns were established in 1903 in Metuchen, New Jersey, by Volkmar and his son. Wares were marked with various devices consisting of the Volkmar name, initials, or 'Crown Point Ware.'

Plaque, Washington's Headquarter's, bl & wht, 12"	185.00
Tankard, gr & blk, 7¾"	200.00
Vase, dk gr w/lt gr striations at rim, 4", EX	135.00
Vase, robin's egg bl mottle, collared rim, sgn, 3½x5¼"	150.00

Volkstadt

The Volkstadt Porcelain Factory was established in Thuringia, Germany, about 1760. They continue to operate to the present, often marking their wares with the 'crossed hayfork' device used since the late 1700s.

Our advisor for this category is William Brinkley; he is listed in the Directory under Illinois.

Figurine, artist pnts seated lady in crinoline, 8x9"	525.00
Figurine, ballerina, appl flowers/comb in hair, 5½"	175.00
Figurine, bride & groom, 2 flower girls/page holding train	1,250.00
Figurine, classical maiden & lion, rstr, 5½"	175.00
Figurine, couple by rail watch 2 swans in pond, mk, 8½x9"	575.00
Figurine, girl w/goose, after Antonio Canova, 6"	160.00
Figurine, lady on sofa, man behind w/violin, musical, 9x9½"	1,050.00
Figurine, lady w/flower basket, after Antonio Canova, 6"	140.00
Figurine, lady w/Greek lyre, after Antonio Canova, 6"	140.00
Figurine, lovers seated on Baroque plinth, 7"	395.00
Figurine, man & lady play chess at table, 6x9"	950.00
Figurine, ostrich group, Karla Ens, 7½"	125.00
Vase, lady's portrait on cobalt w/gilt, 12", pr	1,050.00

Von Tury

Studio potter J.F. Von Tury, of Metuchen, New Jersey, began working in 1939 producing architectural tiles, ceramic items for the home, and porcelain artware for exhibition.

Vase, floral/leaf, cobalt/brn/gr on lt bl, 1940s, 15"	60.00
Vase, lt bl w/underglaze decor, pillow form, 8"	25.00

Wade

The Wade Group of Potteries originated in 1810 with a small pottery located in Burslem, England. This pottery, first owned by a Henry Hallen, was eventually taken over by George Wade who opened his own pottery (also in Burslem) in 1867.

Both the Hallen pottery and the original George Wade pottery specialized in ceramic and pottery items for the textile industry, then blooming in northern England. By the early 20th century, the two potteries amalgamated, taking the name of the George Wade Pottery, which in turn became George Wade & Son, Ltd., in 1919.

George Wade's brother, Albert, had interests in two potteries, A.J. Wade, Ltd., and Wade Heath & Co., Ltd., which manufactured decorative tiles, teapots, and other related dinnerware. In 1938 Wade Heath took over the Royal Victoria Pottery in Burslem and began producing a wide range of figurines and other decorative items.

In 1947 a new pottery was opened in Portadown, Northern Ireland, to produce both industrial ceramics and Irish porcelain giftware. In 1958 all the Wade potteries amalgamated, becoming the Wade Group of Potteries. The most recent addition to the group is Wade (PDM) Limited, a marketing arm for the advertising ware made by Wade Heath at the Royal Victoria Pottery. Wade (PDM) Limited was incorporated in 1969. In 1989 the Wade Group of Potteries was bought out by Beauford Engineering. With this takeover, Wade Heath and George Wade & Son Ltd. were combined to form Wade Ceramics. Wade (Ireland) Ltd. and Wade (PDM) Ltd. became subsidiaries of Wade Ceramics.

For those interested in learning more about Wade pottery, we recommend *The World of Wade* by Ian Warner and Mike Posgay; Mr. Warner is listed in the Directory under Canada.

Beefeater Gin, water jug, Wade (PMD) Ltd	24.00
Birdbath, pitcher, 1940s-1950s, ea	65.00
Biscuit barrel, Lattice pattern, ca early 1960s	45.00
Blynkyn, figurine, 1951, 2¼"	50.00
Captain Morgan Rum boat, ash tray, Wade Regicor	40.00
Carnival, figurine, ca 1929, 8"	180.00
Championship dogs, ca 1975-1981, ea	32.00
Charles & Diana wedding, Bell's whiskey decanter, full/boxed	450.00
Charles & Diana wedding, trinket box, 1981	25.00
Dog, pipe rest, ca 1973-1981, ea	25.00
Dr Foster, Red Rose Tea, ca 1971-1979	6.50
Drum Box series, ca 1956-1959, ea	80.00
Gingerbread Man, Red Rose Tea, ca 1971-1979	22.00
Irish Character figurines, ca 1970s-1986, ea	18.00
Leprechaun, pin tray, ca 1956-1986, ea	12.50
Mother Goose, Red Rose Tea, 1971-1979	10.00
Nod, figurine, 1951, 2½"	50.00
Nursery Favourites, ca 1972-1981, ea	18.00
Queen's Jubilee, Bell's whiskey decanter, 1986, full/boxed	180.00
Romance plates, ca 1951-1960, ea	28.00
Snail, from aquarium set, 1975-1980, ea	35.00
Snow White & the Seven Dwarfs, ca 1981-1986, set	450.00
Springtime, George Wade & Son Ltd, ca 1929, 11"	200.00
Tankard, Wade (Ireland) Ltd, 1-pt	28.00
Teapot, Bramble pattern, ca 1950+	45.00
Tom & Jerry, figurines, ca 1973-1979, pr	150.00
TV Pets, ca 1959-1965, ea	35.00
Viking Boat, posy bowl, ca 1959-1965	18.00
Whimsy (old), ca 1953-1959	25.00
Wynkyn, figurine, 1951, 2¾"	50.00

Walley

The Walley Pottery operated in West Sterling, Massachusetts, from 1898 to 1919. Never more than a one-man operation, Walley himself hand crafted all his wares from local clay. The majority of his pottery was simple and unadorned and usually glazed in matt green. On occasion, however, you may find high- and semi-gloss green, as well as matt glazes in blue, cream, brown, and red. The rarest and most desirable examples of his work are those with applied or relief-carved decorations. Some pieces are marked 'WJW.'

Bowl, brn/gr mottle, tooled overlapping leaves, 6x6¾" 550.00
Bowl, copper patina, 2x3½" 250.00
Mug, devil's face pinched on bulbous form, 5½" 700.00
Vase, gr gloss w/red flambe, mk WJW, 6" 160.00
Vase, gray/mauve gloss to matt, collared neck, 4¾x6½" 200.00

Walrath

Frederick Walrath was a studio potter who worked from around the turn of the century until his death in 1920. He was located in Rochester, New York, until 1918 when he became associated with the Newcomb Pottery in New Orleans, Louisiana.

Bowl, brn/gr matt, kneeling woman in center, 6x7" 300.00
Flower holder, nude kneels w/arm extended, wht, 5x5" 375.00
Mug, brn, unmk, 3" 75.00
Pitcher, grapes, purple/gr on wine, 7½", +4 tumblers 770.00
Pitcher, stylized flower, 3-color, loop hdl, 11", NM 350.00
Vase, brn on brn drip, 4" 350.00
Vase, buds & leaves HP on gr, cylindrical, 4¾" 750.00
Vase, floral, muted colors, crystalline on gr, 6½" 700.00

Walter, A.

Almaric Walter was employed from 1904 through 1914 at Verreries Artistiques des Freres Daum in Nancy, France. After 1919 he opened his own business where he continued to make the same type of quality objects d'art in pate-de-verre glass as he had earlier. His pieces are signed A. Walter, Nancy H. Berge Sc.

Ash tray, sm lizard ea side, yel/ochre/tan/blk, 4½" dia 2,000.00
Box, kneeling nude w/bird & snake on lid, yel/blk/ochre, 7"... 7,000.00
Dish, Bacchus in center, gr/purple on yel, sgn Mercier, 7" 2,600.00
Dish, lg lizard on 1 side, gr/blk on streaky yel, 4½" L.............. 7,000.00
Pan, seated, playing pipes, lemon/lime-gr, 3¾" 1,500.00
Paperweight, scarab, gr/brn, atop rnd lime-gr base, 2"............. 1,500.00
Paperweight, snail & branch, mustard/brn/tan, 3" L................ 3,400.00
Paperweight, snake on base, gr/blk on streaky gray, 1¾" 2,000.00
Pendant, berries relief on oval, red on gray, 2¾" L.................. 1,000.00
Pheasant, yel/gr, rectangular base, 7½" 900.00
Sparrow, bl figure on flat base, 4x3¾", NM 1,100.00
Tray, boat form w/lizard on 1 end, yel to gr/mc, 10" L.............. 7,000.00
Tray, grotesque masks in ea solid D-form hdl, 10" L................ 2,000.00
Tray, lg exotic fish on rim, yel/ochres, sgn, 5½" L 4,800.00
Tray, parakeet perched on lip, gr/yel, sgn Berge, 6¾" H 4,000.00
Tray, snail on 1 end, streaky mustard w/gr, 6" L..................... 3,750.00
Vase, floriform, mottled yel, 6" 2,600.00
Woman: Daneuse, emerald/shaded lime, 8", NM..................... 3,400.00

Warwick

The Warwick China Company operated in Wheeling, West Virginia, from 1887 until 1951. They produced both hand-painted and decaled plates, vases, teapots, coffeepots, pitchers, bowls, and jardinieres featuring lovely florals or portraits of beautiful ladies done in luscious colors. Backgrounds were usually blendings of brown and beige,

but ivory was also used (and on rare occasion, pink).

Various marks were employed, all of which incorporate the Warwick name. For a more thorough study of the subject, we recommend *Warwick, A to W* a supplement to *Why Not Warwick* by our advisor, Donald C. Hoffmann; his address can be found in the Directory under Illinois.

Dinnerware

Bowl, cereal; #AB1000 .... **4.00**
Bowl, cereal; #AB9361 .... **1.25**
Bowl, cereal; #AB9486 .... **2.00**
Bowl, cereal; #AB9501 .... **1.75**
Bowl, cereal; #A2002 .... **2.00**
Bowl, cereal; #A2003... **1.25**
Bowl, cereal; #A9229 .... **2.00**
Bowl, cereal; #A9354 .... **1.75**
Bowl, cereal; #A9417 .... **3.00**
Bowl, cereal; #B2001 .... **4.00**
Bowl, cereal; #B2007 .... **1.75**
Creamer & sugar bowl, #AB1000 .... **9.00**
Creamer & sugar bowl, #AB9361 .... **4.50**
Creamer & sugar bowl, #AB9486 .... **6.00**
Creamer & sugar bowl, #AB9501 .... **4.50**
Creamer & sugar bowl, #A2002 .... **8.00**
Creamer & sugar bowl, #A2003 .... **7.50**
Creamer & sugar bowl, #A9229 .... **6.00**
Creamer & sugar bowl, #A9354 .... **5.00**
Creamer & sugar bowl, #A9417 .... **6.50**
Creamer & sugar bowl, #B2001 ....**12.00**
Creamer & sugar bowl, #B2007 .... **6.00**
Cup & saucer, #AB1000 .... **6.00**
Cup & saucer, #AB9361 .... **3.00**
Cup & saucer, #AB9486 .... **4.00**
Cup & saucer, #AB9501 .... **3.00**
Cup & saucer, #A2002.. **4.00**
Cup & saucer, #A2003.. **4.50**
Cup & saucer, #A9229.. **3.25**
Cup & saucer, #A9354.. **2.50**
Cup & saucer, #A9417.. **4.00**
Cup & saucer, #B2001.. **8.00**
Cup & saucer, #B2007.. **2.50**
Plate, #AB1000, 10" **4.00**
Plate, #AB9361, 10" **1.50**
Plate, #AB9486, 10" **2.00**
Plate, #AB9501, 10" **2.00**
Plate, #A2002, 10"... **3.00**
Plate, #A2003, 10"... **2.75**
Plate, #A9229, 10"... **2.50**
Plate, #A9354, 10"... **2.00**
Plate, #A9417, 10"... **3.00**
Plate, #B2001, 10"... **4.00**
Plate, #B2007, 10"... **4.00**
Platter, #AB1000, oval, lg.. **9.00**
Platter, #AB9361, oval, lg.. **3.00**
Platter, #AB9486, oval, lg.. **4.00**
Platter, #AB9501, oval, lg.. **3.00**
Platter, #A2002, oval, lg... **4.50**
Platter, #A2003, oval, lg... **3.25**
Platter, #A9229, oval, lg... **3.00**
Platter, #A9354, oval, lg... **3.00**
Platter, #A9417, oval, lg... **4.50**
Platter, #B2001, oval, lg...**10.00**
Platter, #B2007, oval, lg... **4.00**

Spirit Jugs

Brn, Dickens-type character w/top hat, 6" 185.00
Brn, friar w/wine glass, 6" 180.00
Brn, Indian w/braid, 6" 200.00
Brn, Indian w/full headdress, 6" 400.00
Brn, monk w/red cap, 6" 170.00
Brn, portrait of a Gypsy girl, 6" 200.00
Brn w/Dickens-type character & guitar, 6" 185.00
Brn w/Negro boy & banjo, 6" 215.00

Unique Items

Candle holder, wht w/bl border, ring hdl 70.00
Candle holder, wht w/gold border, no hdl 65.00
Cane stand, brn w/floral decor, 29" 360.00
Humidor, cigar; brn w/bulldog, w/lid, 6¼" 200.00
Humidor, cigar; brn w/monk, w/lid, 6¼" 165.00
Humidor, cigar; brn w/rose hips, w/lid, 6¼" 170.00
Humidor, cigar; Flow Blue, crackle pattern, 8" 220.00
Humidor, tobacco; brn w/bulldog, w/lid, 6¼" 190.00
Humidor, tobacco; brn w/eagle, w/lid, 6¼" 165.00
Humidor, tobacco; brn w/elk, w/lid, 6¼" 165.00
Humidor, tobacco; brn w/monk, w/lid, 6¼" 145.00
Humidor, tobacco; brn w/monk, w/lid, 7" 230.00
Humidor, tobacco; pouch-like, brn w/bulldog, 7¼" 195.00
Humidor, tobacco; pouch-like, brn w/rose hips, 7¼" 160.00
Humidor, tobacco; pouch-like, pk/wht w/floral, 7¼" 185.00
Jardiniere, bl, 14" 95.00
Jardiniere & pedestal, brn w/floral, 45" overall 425.00
Pedestal w/center plate 260.00
Spittoon, brn w/emb design, no decal, 8" 100.00
Spittoon, lady's, pk/wht w/floral decor, 5" 115.00
Umbrella stand, gr to wht w/floral, 30" 375.00

Vase, A Beauty, brn w/hibiscus, 15" 235.00
Vase, A Beauty, tan matt w/flowers, 15" 230.00
Vase, A Beauty, wht w/roses, 15" 300.00
Vase, Bonnie, wht w/roses, 10½" 285.00
Vase, Bouquet #1, brn w/lady in pearls, 11¾" 235.00
Vase, Bouquet #1, brn w/orchids, 11¾" 230.00
Vase, Bouquet #2, brn, Gypsy in red turban/long hair, 10½ 220.00
Vase, Bouquet #2, brn w/flowers, 10½" 150.00
Vase, Bouquet #2, brn w/lady, lg medallion in hair, 10½" 195.00
Vase, Bouquet #2, brn w/Madame Le Brun as adult, 10½" 195.00
Vase, Bouquet #2, brn w/Madame Le Brun as child, 10½" 195.00
Vase, Bouquet #2, brn w/nude portrait, sgn Carreno, 10½" 325.00
Vase, Bouquet #2, brn w/portrait of Countess A Potocka, 10½" 220.00
Vase, Bouquet #2, brn w/portrait of Gypsy, bl turban, 10½" 220.00
Vase, Bouquet #2, brn w/portrait of Gypsy, red turban, 10½" 220.00
Vase, Bouquet #2, brn w/portrait of lady in red cap, 10½" 285.00
Vase, Bouquet #2, brn w/portrait of Madame Re Camier, 10½" 200.00
Vase, Bouquet #2, brn w/portrait of redhead, 10½" 350.00
Vase, Bouquet #2, brn w/portrait of redhead w/roses, 10½" 200.00
Vase, Bouquet #2, brn w/portrait of redhead w/scarf, 10½" 300.00
Vase, Bouquet #2, gr w/roses, 10½" 325.00
Vase, Bouquet #2, portrait of blonde w/peonies, 10½" 240.00
Vase, Canteen, brn w/acorns, 11½" 385.00
Vase, Canteen, brn w/hunting dogs, sgn Beck, 11½" 425.00
Vase, Clytie, brn w/hibiscus, 4¼" 200.00
Vase, Clytie, brn w/peony decor, 6¾" 265.00
Vase, Clytie, red overglaze w/poinsettias, 6¾" 235.00

Vase, Verbenia, brown with floral, 7½", $200.00.

Vase, Clytie, red overglaze w/portrait, 6¾" 240.00
Vase, Dainty, red overglaze w/portrait, 4¼" 200.00
Vase, Den, brn w/portrait, 6½x10" 185.00
Vase, Den, matt finish, brn w/portrait, 6½x10" 210.00
Vase, Den, matt finish, gr w/flowers, 6½x10" 220.00
Vase, Den, red overglaze w/portrait, 6½x10" 195.00
Vase, Duchess, charcoal w/florals, 6x8" 195.00
Vase, Duchess, red overglaze w/poinsettias, 8" 185.00
Vase, Duchess, wht w/birds, 8" 215.00
Vase, Egyptian, brn w/hibiscus, 11¾" 300.00
Vase, Flower, brn w/flowers, 12" 185.00
Vase, Flower, brn w/portrait, 10" 165.00
Vase, Flower, pk w/portrait, 12" 265.00
Vase, Geran, brn w/flowers, 11" 195.00
Vase, Geran, charcoal w/flowers, 11" 225.00
Vase, Lemonade, brn w/fruit, 6½" 195.00
Vase, Lemonade, brn w/portrait, 6½" 210.00
Vase, Lemonade, pk w/portrait, 6½" 315.00
Vase, Lemonade, wht w/flowers, 6½" 200.00
Vase, Lemonade, wht w/fruit, 6½" 200.00
Vase, Lily, brn w/peonies, 9½" 185.00
Vase, Lily, charcoal w/flowers, 9½" 215.00
Vase, Louise, brn w/flowers, 9½" 230.00
Vase, Narcis #2, wht, HP bkground w/geese 425.00
Vase, Poppy, brn w/flowers, 10½" 285.00
Vase, Poppy, charcoal w/floral decor, 10½" 320.00
Vase, Roberta, brn w/monk in red cap, 10" 290.00
Vase, Roberta, red overglaze w/fisherman 320.00
Vase, Tobio Jug #1, brn w/flowers, 7¾" 145.00
Vase, Tobio Jug #1, brn w/monk, 7¾" 150.00
Vase, Tobio Jug #1, brn w/portrait, 7¾" 165.00
Vase, Tobio Jug #2, brn w/Indian, 7" 215.00
Vase, Tobio Jug #2, brn w/monk, 7" 165.00
Vase, Tobio Jug #2, brn w/portrait, 7" 220.00
Vase, Verbenia #1, brn w/hibiscus, 9¼" 175.00
Vase, Verbenia #1, charcoal w/flowers, 9¼" 220.00
Vase, Verbenia #1, wht w/sea gulls 240.00
Vase, Verbenia #2, charcoal w/flowers, 7¼" 215.00
Vase, Verbenia #2, red overglaze w/portrait 220.00
Vase, Verbenia #2, wht w/ducks 240.00

Wash Sets

Before the days of running water, bedrooms were standardly equipped with a wash bowl and pitcher as a matter of necessity. A 'toilet set' was comprised of the pitcher and bowl, toothbrush holder, covered commode, soap dish, shaving dish, and mug. Some sets were even more elaborate. Through everyday usage, the smaller items were often broken, and today it is unusual to find a complete set.

Porcelain sets decorated with florals, fruits, or scenics were produced abroad by Limoges in France; some were imported from Germany and England. During the last quarter of the 1800s and until after the turn of the century, American-made toilet sets were manufactured in abundance. Tin and graniteware sets were also made.

Child's pitcher and bowl, marked Wedgwood Pearl, ca 1840-68, $175.00.

Bl Willow, Myott, 9½" pitcher/bowl/chamber pot 600.00
English, bl-gr florals, pitcher/bowl/toothbrush holder/pot...........350.00
Festoon, med bl transfer, Wedgwood, pitcher/bowl, EX 125.00
Homer Laughlin, pk & yel roses on bl, gold trim, 2-pc 160.00
Imari style, foliage, gilt/orange/bl, 13" pitcher/18" bowl..............700.00
Knowles-Taylor-Knowles, child's, wht w/gold, bowl/pitcher 50.00
Medcina, bl transfer, Staffordshire, pitcher/bowl, rpr 175.00
Mercer Pottery, Trenton NJ, wht w/gold trim, 5-pc, EX 375.00
Minton, child's, gr ivy on cream, 7" pitcher/9½" bowl.................225.00
Palestine, red transfer, English, 10½" pitcher/bowl, EX.................20.00
Rosetti, Royal Doulton, pitcher/bowl 210.00

Watch Fobs

Watch fobs have been popular since the last quarter of the 19th century. They were often made by retail companies to advertise their products. Souvenir, commemorative, and political fobs were also produced. All are popular collectibles today. Beware of modern restrikes and reproductions.

Adams & Ford, shoe on arrowhead, enameled 40.00
American Bakery & Confectionary Union, enameled....................35.00
American Bowling Congress, 1918...15.00
American Boy Scout...48.00
American Legion, 1937 ....15.00
Armour & Co, figural knight's armor...30.00
Armour's, cow head, silver color 35.00
Avery Bulldog, brass, minor wear 75.00
Banigan Rubbers, emb lion 35.00
Baseball game in action, glove/mask on bk, silver, 1900, EX 165.00
Blue Goose, brass/enamel 25.00
Brotherhood Railroad Trainmen, enameled....................................42.50
Bull Dog, manure spreaders 90.00

Bull Moose, EX 20.00
Chi-Namel (paint) 35.00
De Laval, enamel 95.00
Disston Keystone Saw Works, enameled..50.00
Drink Hires, boy..65.00
Drover's Bank, steer head 28.00
E-Z Ola Polish, brass 28.00
Glass Bottle Blowers' Assoc, bottle form.......................................22.50
GOP Elephant 15.00
Grand Council Indiana UCT, enameling, w/strap 15.00
Green River Whiskey, horseshoe 35.00
Hamilton #940, enameled train 58.00
Hamlight Lanterns 88.00
Hog, Sioux City Iowa 135.00
IL State Undertakers Assoc, brass, 1907 ....30.00
Internat'l Harvester, Century of the Reaper....................................40.00
Internat'l Harvester, dbl globe 55.00
Jamestown Expo, Connecticut House 40.00
Jamestown Expo, Powhatan's tomahawk figural 55.00
Jap Rose Soap 38.00
John Deere, shell 175.00
John Deere Centennial 100.00
Keystone Watch Case Co, Columbian Expo, w/case opener 25.00
La Salle Extension University, gilded 15.00
Lion's Stock Remedy, Live Stock Remedy Co, celluloid 65.00
Loom Lodge, enameled...20.00
Magnetic Club, NY, 1913, enameled 22.50
Maine, emb eagle, from Spanish-American War.............................17.50
Masonic cornerstone...38.00
McKinley Monument 20.00
Moon Face Solarine, EX...38.00
Mormon Temple, Salt Lake City 30.00
Munson Warm-Air Furnaces 35.00
Napoleon Flour, w/strap...65.00
Olds Motor Works, Oldsmobile, enameled 85.00
Our Next President Wm H Taft, old strap type 60.00
Pabst Brewing, enameled..125.00
Panama-Pacific Expo, ornate frying pan 50.00
Paris Expo 1889, eng brass 16.00
Peter's Weatherbird Shoes, enameled...45.00
Pharmacy, Cincinnati College, sterling, 1901................................45.00
Philadelphia Lawn Mowers, nickeled brass, oval 45.00
Pierce Arrow, enameled..95.00
Pontiac, Chief of the Sixes...30.00
Red Owl Coal, enameled, oval..85.00
Rumely Oil, pull tractor 195.00
School Shoes, 1898 Expo 27.50
Shapeleigh Hardware, brass, worn..25.00
St Louis Fair, 1904, coins, 3-pc chain fob......................................65.00
St Louis Fair, 1904, crosses, 3-pc chain fob 65.00
Travelers Insurance, Ticket Dept, train, w/strap 75.00
Tyson Ice Cream Freezers...30.00
US Gypsum, 1928...25.00
US Master Brewer's Assoc 55.00
Walch Land Co, enameling on brass, EX 35.00
Women's Auxiliary, Sons of Veterans, Latin, USA, 1883 ....55.00
WWI, Aviators 125.00
XXth Century Heating 22.00

Watch Stands

Watch stands were decorative articles designed with a hook from which to hang a watch. Some displayed the watch as the face of a grandfather clock or as part of an interior scene with figures in period costumes and contemporary furnishings. They were popular products of Staffordshire potters and silver companies as well.

Cabinet w/high crest, bead-trimmed glass door, 1700s, 14" **1,000.00**
Chalkware, recumbent dog atop rectangle case, EX pnt, 11" **900.00**
Pine, glass panel in door w/rnd top, wire hinges, 8½"..................**750.00**
Wreath form, leafy hdl, mc/gilt on Meissen porc, 6½" **285.00**

Watches

First made in the 1500s in Germany, early watches were actually small clocks, suspended from the wrist or belt. By 1700 they had become the approximate shape and size we know today. The first watches produced in America were made in 1810. The well-known Waltham Watch Company was established in 1850, and their inexpensive 'Waterbury' models were produced by the thousands.

Open-face and hunting-case watches of the 1890s were solid gold or gold-filled and were often elaborately decorated in several colors of gold. Gold watches became a status symbol in this decade and were worn by both men and women on chains with fobs or jeweled slides. Ladies sometimes fastened them to their clothing with pins often set with jewels. The chatelaine watch was worn at the waist, only one of several items such as scissors, coin purses, or needle cases, each attached by small chains. During this period, movements and cases could be purchased separately, so inexpensive cases may sometimes be found containing well-jeweled movements, or the contrary may be true.

Most turn-of-the-century watch cases were gold-filled, and these are plentiful today. 18k cases are rare, and 22k cases are very valuable. Sterling cases, though interest in them is on the increase, are not in great demand. For character-related watches, see Personalities.

Key:
adj — adjusted	k/s — key set
brg — bridge plate design	k/w — key wind
d/s — double sunk dial	l/s — lever set
fbd — finger bridge design	mvt — movement
gf — gold-filled	o/f — open face
g/j/s — gold jewel setting	p/s — pendant set
h/c — hunter case	r/g/p — rolled gold plate
HCI#P — heat, cold,	s — size
isochronism & position	s/s — single sunk dial
adjusted	s/w — stem wind
j — jewel	w/g/f — white gold-filled
k — karat	y/g/f — yellow gold-filled

Am Watch Co, 10s, 15j, 20-yr, y/g/f, h/c, s/s **110.00**
Am Watch Co, 12s, 15j, #1894, 14k, h/c, Colonial....................**325.00**
Am Watch Co, 14s, 13j, #1884, 14k, h/c................................**450.00**
Am Watch Co, 16s, 11-15j, #1872, p/s, Park Road **250.00**
Am Watch Co, 16s, 15-16j, #1899, h/c **175.00**
Am Watch Co, 16s, 15j, #1899, s/w, silveroid **70.00**
Am Watch Co, 16s, 16j, #1872, 5-min, coin silver, Repeater.. **3,000.00**
Am Watch Co, 16s, 17j, #1888, Railroader, rare, NM **725.00**
Am Watch Co, 16s, 17j, #1899, s/w **75.00**
Am Watch Co, 16s, 17j, royal nickel case, d/s **60.00**
Am Watch Co, 16s, 17j, 2-tone, Railroad King.......................**325.00**
Am Watch Co, 16s, 19j, #1899, l/s, o/f, HCI5P, Crescent St **135.00**
Am Watch Co, 16s, 19j, #1908, o/f, adj, s/s, RR, Vanguard **175.00**
Am Watch Co, 16s, 21j, #1872, 14k, 3/4-mvt, rare **1,950.00**
Am Watch Co, 16s, 23j, g/j/s, brg, HCI5P, gold train **1,000.00**
Am Watch Co, 18s, #1877, k/w, Excelsior.............................**240.00**
Am Watch Co, 18s, 11j, #1857, h/c, k/w, y/g/f, s/s, Ellery, EX......**150.00**

Am Watch Co, 18s, 11j, #1857, k/w, 1st run, PS Bartlett **575.00**
Am Watch Co, 18s, 15j, #1877, k/w, RE Robbins **275.00**
Am Watch Co, 18s, 15j, silverine, o/f, k/w, Fogg's Pat **125.00**
Am Watch Co, 18s, 17j, #1892, HCI5P, Canadian Railway **400.00**
Am Watch Co, 18s, 17j, #1892, o/f, y/g/f, Railroader, rare..........**850.00**
Am Watch Co, 18s, 17j, #1892, s/w, h/c, PS Bartlett **185.00**
Am Watch Co, 18s, 17j, 25-yr, o/f, y/g/f, s/s, PS Bartlett **185.00**
Am Watch Co, 18s, 19j, #1883, Crescent Street **350.00**
Am Watch Co, 18s, 21j, #1892, o/f, y/g/f, d/s, Crescent St **150.00**
Am Watch Co, 18s, 21j, #1892, s/w, Appleton, Tracy & Co **225.00**
Am Watch Co, 18s, 7j, #1857, k/w, CT Parker, scarce **1,400.00**
Am Watch Co, 18s, 7j, #1877, s/w, Franklin **350.00**
Am Watch Co, 18s, 7j, #1883, Pioneer **175.00**
Auburndale Watch Co, 18s, 7j, k/w, l/s, Lincoln **600.00**
Aurora Watch Co, 18s, k/w, h/c **375.00**
Aurora Watch Co, 18s, 11j, o/f, k/w, h/c................................**350.00**
Ball (Elgin), 18s, 16j, o/f, Commercial Standard **500.00**
Ball (Hamilton), 16s, 17j, #974, o/f, l/s, g/f, nickel plates **200.00**
Ball (Hamilton), 18s, 19j, #999, o/f, l/s, g/f, HCI5P **475.00**
Ball (Hampden), 18s, 17j, o/f, adj, RR, Superior Grade.......... **1,500.00**
Ball (Seth Thomas), 18s, 17j, #3, o/f, l/s, g/j/s, scarce **5,600.00**
Ball (Waltham), 16s, 19j, o/f, Offical Standard **250.00**
Ball (Waltham), 16s, 19j, 14k, o/f, l/s **600.00**
Columbus Watch Co, 18s, 11-15j, k/w, k/s **425.00**
Columbus Watch Co, 18s, 11j, o/f, silveroid case......................**100.00**
Columbus Watch Co, 18s, 15j, o/f, l/s **160.00**
Columbus Watch Co, 18s, 15j, 18k, k/w, k/s **1,300.00**
Columbus Watch Co, 18s, 19j, g/j/s, h/c, 2-tone, grade #105 .. **1,250.00**
Columbus Watch Co, 6s, 15j, 18k, g/j/s, nickel plate **575.00**
Cornell, 18s, 15j, s/w, CM Cady...**450.00**
Dudley, 12s, #3, 14k, o/f, display case, Mason's **2,400.00**
Elgin, 10s, g/f, h/c, mc case **125.00**
Elgin, 10s, h/c, k/w, k/s, s/s, Gail Borden................................**150.00**
Elgin, 12s, 15j, 14k, h/c **425.00**
Elgin, 12s, 17j, g/f, h/c, Lord Elgin **90.00**
Elgin, 12s, 17j, 14k, GM Wheeler..**350.00**
Elgin, 12s, 21j, g/f, h/c, Lord Elgin **175.00**
Elgin, 12s, 7j, 14k, EX **200.00**
Elgin, 16s, 10k, y/g/f, g/j/s, Raymond....................................**225.00**
Elgin, 16s, 11j, g/f, h/c **125.00**
Elgin, 16s, 15j, doctor's, 4th model, 14k, 2nd sweep hand **650.00**
Elgin, 16s, 15j, 14k, h/c **600.00**
Elgin, 16s, 17j, g/j/s, s/w, o/f, BW Raymond **160.00**
Elgin, 16s, 17j, 14k, h/c **600.00**
Elgin, 16s, 19j, 14k, g/j/s, brg, h/c, grade #145, scarce **800.00**
Elgin, 16s, 21j, g/f, h/c **460.00**
Elgin, 16s, 21j, g/f, 3 fbd, grade #72-91, scarce **300.00**
Elgin, 16s, 21j, g/j/s, 3 fbd **285.00**
Elgin, 16s, 21j, o/f, y/g/f, l/s, RR, Father Time **240.00**
Elgin, 16s, 21j, 14k, 3 fbd, Convertible **1,400.00**
Elgin, 17s, k/w, orig case, Leader, grade #59 ....**165.00**
Elgin, 17s, k/w, silveroid **70.00**
Elgin, 18s, 11j, g/f, h/c, k/w, gilded, MG Odgen **165.00**
Elgin, 18s, 15j, g/f, mc dial, Solar W Co **150.00**
Elgin, 18s, 15j, o/f, d/s, RR, silveroid case, Raymond **125.00**
Elgin, 18s, 15j, y/g/f, l/s, s/w, box hinge case **425.00**
Elgin, 18s, 15j, 14k, k/w, k/s, h/c, HL Culver **625.00**
Elgin, 18s, 17j, silveroid, BW Raymond **125.00**
Elgin, 18s, 21j, g/f, h/c, l/s, s/w **135.00**
Elgin, 18s, 21j, o/f, y/g/f, Father Time....................................**200.00**
Elgin, 18s, 23j, y/g/f, 5-position, RR, Veritas **325.00**
Elgin, 6s, 11j, 14k, h/c **275.00**
Elgin, 6s, 15j, 20-yr, y/g/f, h/c, s/s **150.00**
Elgin, 6s, 7j, 10k, h/c **210.00**

Hamilton, #3992B, 16s, 22j, HCI6P **265.00**
Hamilton, #904, 12s, 21j, g/j/s, brg, HCI5P, dbl roller **150.00**
Hamilton, #910, 12s, 17j, 20-yr, y/g/f, o/f, s/s **125.00**
Hamilton, #912, 12s, 17j, adj, dbl roller, ¾-mvt **125.00**
Hamilton, #918, presentation, 14k w/20 diamonds, orig box **600.00**
Hamilton, #920, 12s, 23j, o/f, w/g/f **225.00**
Hamilton, #922MP, 12s, 18k case **800.00**
Hamilton, #925, 18s, 17j, w/g/f, h/c, s/s, l/s **185.00**
Hamilton, #928, 18s, 15j, o/f, y/g/f, s/s **180.00**
Hamilton, #933, 18s, 16j, h/c, nickel plate **825.00**
Hamilton, #938, 18s, 17j, 10k, y/g/f, adj, NAW Co Case **475.00**
Hamilton, #940, 18s, 21j, nickel plate, coin silver, o/f **160.00**
Hamilton, #946, 18s, 23j, o/f, g/j/s, EX **700.00**
Hamilton, #947, 23j, h/c, orig/sgn, EX **5,500.00**
Hamilton, #950, 16s, 23j, o/f, y/g/f, l/s, sgn d/s **400.00**
Hamilton, #965, 16s, 17j, p/s, h/c, brg, scarce **825.00**
Hamilton, #972, 16s, 17j, o/f, y/g/f, g/j/s, d/s, l/s, adj **125.00**
Hamilton, #974, 16s, 17j, 20-yr, y/g/f, o/f, s/s **140.00**
Hamilton, #992, 16s, 21j, o/f, y/g/f, adj, d/s, dbl roller **185.00**
Hamilton, #992B, 16s, 21j, l/s, o/f, ¾-mvt **225.00**
Hampden, 12s, 17j, HCI4P, thin model, Aviator **70.00**
Hampden, 12s, 7j, s/w, o/f **40.00**
Hampden, 16s, 17j, h/c, s/w **200.00**
Hampden, 16s, 17j, o/f, adj **125.00**
Hampden, 16s, 21j, g/j/s, HCI5P/nickel plate, Dueber, ¾-mvt ...**150.00**
Hampden, 16s, 21j, o/f, adj, dbl roller, HCI5P, New Railway **175.00**
Hampden, 16s, 7j, gilded, nickel plate, ¾-mvt **80.00**
Hampden, 18s, 15j, k/w, Hayward **175.00**
Hampden, 18s, 15j, k/w, mk on mvt, Railway **850.00**
Hampden, 18s, 15j, s/w, gilded, JC Perry **100.00**
Hampden, 18s, 16j, gilded, damaskeened, Dueber **125.00**
Hampden, 18s, 17j, adj, h/c, Dueber Grand **150.00**
Hampden, 18s, 17j, nickel plate, Tramway Special **200.00**
Hampden, 18s, 19j, g/j/s, h/c, adj, Dueber **475.00**
Hampden, 18s, 21j, g/j/s, h/c, HCI5P, New Railway **300.00**
Hampden, 18s, 21j, o/f, y/g/f, d/s, HCI5P, l/s, N Am Railway **200.00**
Hampden, 18s, 23j, y/g/f, d/s, adj, New Railway **300.00**
Hampden, 18s, 23j, 14k, h/c, Special Railway **775.00**
Hampden, 18s, 7-11j, k/w, gilded, Springfield **95.00**
Howard, 12s, 23j, 14k, h/c, brg, HCI5P, Series 8 ....**625.00**
Howard, 18s, 17j, 25-yr, y/g/f, o/f **250.00**
Illinois, 0s, 7j, 10k, l/s, h/c **150.00**
Illinois, 12s, 19j, y/g/f, o/f, d/s dial, Elite **110.00**
Illinois, 16s, 17j, adj, ¾-mvt **150.00**
Illinois, 16s, 17j, o/f, d/s, HCI5P, Bunn, EX **225.00**
Illinois, 16s, 17j, o/f, Railway King **250.00**
Illinois, 16s, 19j, o/f, y/g/f, d/s, 60-hr, Sangamo Special **660.00**
Illinois, 16s, 21j, g/j/s, HCI6P, Burlington **240.00**
Illinois, 16s, 21j, g/j/s, o/f, HCI6P, Ariston **600.00**
Illinois, 16s, 21j, h/c, Sangamo Special **1,000.00**
Illinois, 16s, 21j, o/f, d/s, Santa Fe Special **300.00**
Illinois, 16s, 21j, o/f, y/g/f, s/s, Bunn Special **225.00**
Illinois, 16s, 23j, o/f, d/s, RR, heavy decor, Bunn Special **400.00**
Illinois, 18s, 11j, #1, k/w, Alleghany **140.00**
Illinois, 18s, 11j, #3, o/f, s/w, l/s, Comet **150.00**
Illinois, 18s, 11j, Forest City **135.00**
Illinois, 18s, 15j, #1, adj, k/w, k/s, Stuart **900.00**
Illinois, 18s, 15j, #1, h/c, y/g/f, k/w, gilt, Bunn **750.00**
Illinois, 18s, 15j, #1, k/w, h/c, Bunn **950.00**
Illinois, 18s, 15j, k/w, k/s, gilt, Railway Regulator **600.00**
Illinois, 18s, 15j, s/w, silveroid **70.00**
Illinois, 18s, 17j, g/j/s, adj, B&O RR Special **600.00**
Illinois, 18s, 17j, o/f, d/s, adj, silveroid case, Lakeshore **135.00**
Illinois, 18s, 17j, o/f, s/w, 5th pinion, Miller **300.00**

Illinois, 18s, 17j, s/w, nickel plate, coin silver, Bunn **185.00**
Illinois, 18s, 21j, g/j/s, adj, B&O RR Special **800.00**
Illinois, 18s, 21j, g/j/s, g/f, o/f, HCI5P, A Lincoln **325.00**
Illinois, 18s, 21j, g/j/s, HCI5P, Ben Franklin USA **1,400.00**
Illinois, 18s, 21j, 14k, g/j/s, h/c, HCI5P, Bunn Special **1,000.00**
Illinois, 18s, 24j, g/j/s, adj, Chesapeake & Ohio Special **2,250.00**
Illinois, 18s, 26j, Penn Special, orig case **5,900.00**
Illinois, 18s, 7j, #3, Interior **110.00**
Illinois, 18s, 7j, #3, silveroid, America **90.00**
Illinois, 18s, 9-11j, o/f, k/w, s/s, silveroid case, Hoyt **110.00**
Illinois, 8s, 13j, ¾-mvt, Rose LeLand, scarce **240.00**
Ingersoll, 16s, 7j, wht base metal, Reliance **55.00**
Lancaster, 18s, 7j, o/f, k/w, k/s, eng case, New Era **125.00**
Marion US, 18s, h/c, k/w, k/s, ¾-plate, Asa Fuller **375.00**
Marion US, 18s, 15j, nickel plate, h/c, s/w, Henry Randel **360.00**
Melrose Watch Co, 18s, 7j, k/w, k/s **450.00**
New York Watch Co, 15j, wolf's teeth wind **1,500.00**
New York Watch Co, 18s, 7j, k/w, George Sam Rice **175.00**
Rockford, 16s, 17j, brg, HCI3P, dbl roller **175.00**
Rockford, 16s, 21j, #515, y/g/f **200.00**
Rockford, 16s, 21j, o/f, g/j/s, HCI5P, grade #537, scarce **650.00**
Rockford, 18s, 15j, o/f, k/w, silver case **100.00**
Rockford, 18s, 17j, silveroid w/mc dial, fancy mvt/hands **225.00**
Rockford, 18s, 21j, o/f, Railway King **550.00**
Rockford, 18s, 7j, silveroid, o/f, k/w **100.00**
Seth Thomas, 18s, 17j, #2, g/j/s, adj, Henry Molineux **550.00**
Seth Thomas, 18s, 17j, Edgemere **125.00**
Seth Thomas, 18s, 21j, g/j/s, HCI5P, dbl roller **395.00**
Seth Thomas, 18s, 7j, ¾-mvt, bk: eagle/Liberty model **125.00**
South Bend, 12s, 21j, HCI5P, dbl roller, grade #431 ....**110.00**
South Bend, 12s, 21j, orig o/f, d/s, Studebaker **200.00**
South Bend, 18s, 21j, g/j/s, h/c, full plate, grade #328 ....**425.00**
South Bend, 18s, 21j, 14k, h/c **750.00**
Swiss, h/c, 5-min, Repeater **625.00**

Waterford

The The Waterford Glass Company operated in Ireland from the late 1700s until 1851 when the factory closed. One hundred years later (in 1951) another Waterford glassworks was instituted that produced glass similar to the 18th century wares – crystal glass, usually with cut decoration. Today, Waterford is a generic term referring to the type of glass first produced there.

Ash tray, paperweight; allover diamond cuts, heavy **45.00**
Bowl, centerpiece; brilliant cuts, ftd, ca 1950, 7½x9" **945.00**
Bowl, waffle-cut, fine X-hatching, fan-cut rim, oval, 14" **1,375.00**
Champagne, Eileen **325.00**
Compote, paneled fan & sawtooth designs, t'print band, 9" **965.00**
Cordial, Ross Lake **25.00**
Cruet, strawberry leaf/fan cuts, waisted, faceted stopper, 5" **115.00**
Decanter, faceted panels, bulbous, 12" **175.00**
Lamp, old kerosene style, electric, 2-pc, 27" **275.00**
Pitcher, diamond cuts, appl hdl, 10" **195.00**
Plate, diamond-cut center, 8" **95.00**
Wine, diamond & flute cut, star base **32.00**

Watt Pottery

The Watt Pottery Company was incorporated on July 5, 1922, in Perry County, Crooksville, Ohio. Their products were stoneware jars, jugs, milk pans, Dutch pots, mixing bowls (white with blue bands), churns, preserve jars, and chicken waterers, all marked in cobalt with their trademark, 'Acorn.' In 1935 these items were discontinued, and the company began to make free-hand decorated kitchen and ovenware items such as 'Banded' and 'Decorated' mixing bowls, 'spaghetti' bowls, canister sets, covered casseroles, nappies, cookie jars, ice buckets, pitchers, handled French casseroles, bean pots, salad sets, and dog dishes. Bold brush strokes of red and green contrasted with the natural buff color of the glazed body. Several patterns were produced: 'Red Apple,' 'Star Flower,' 'Rooster,' 'Autumn Foliage,' 'Morning Glory,' and 'Tulip.' Other lines were 'Basket Weave' (made in solid colors), 'Wood Grain' (a brown-glazed line), and 'Royal Danish' dinnerware.

Fire destroyed the entire manufacturing plant on October 4, 1965.

Because of the country flavor of the hand-decorated yellowware pieces, Watt Pottery is fast becoming a favorite collectible. Much of the ware was made for advertising premiums and is often found stenciled with the name of a retail company.

Bean pot, Apple, #76	75.00
Bowl, Apple, #05 or #06, ea	35.00
Bowl, Apple, #118, w/hdl, EX	32.00
Bowl, Apple, #39, EX	45.00
Bowl, Apple, #63	40.00

Apple bowl with lid, 6", $65.00.

Bowl, Apple, #64	45.00
Bowl, Apple, #65	55.00
Bowl, Apple, #7 or #8, ea	65.00
Bowl, Apple, #73	45.00
Bowl, Apple, #74	22.00
Bowl, Apple, #9, w/advertising, EX	50.00
Bowl, Pansy, #39	30.00
Bowl, Starflower, #39, w/underplate	100.00
Casserole, Apple, #600, w/lid, EX	65.00
Casserole, Apple, #601, w/lid	65.00
Casserole, Cherry, #53, w/lid	55.00
Casserole, Eagle, #601	150.00
Casserole, French; Apple, #118, EX	85.00
Cookie jar, Apple, #76	75.00
Ice bucket, Apple	95.00
Mug, Apple, #121, EX	95.00
Pie plate, Apple, #33	95.00
Pie plate, Apple, #33, w/advertising	110.00
Pitcher, Apple, #15	40.00
Pitcher, Apple, #15, w/advertising	45.00
Pitcher, Apple, #16, milk sz	40.00
Pitcher, Apple, #16, w/advertising	75.00
Pitcher, Apple, #62, cream sz	40.00
Pitcher, Apple, #62, w/advertising, cream sz	60.00
Pitcher, Apple, #65	40.00
Pitcher, Red Leaves, #15, 5½"	25.00
Pitcher, Rooster, #15	55.00
Pitcher, Starflower, #16	45.00
Pitcher, Starflower, #17, 8¼"	65.00
Pitcher, Tulip, #16	95.00
Pitcher, Tulip, #62, cream sz	50.00
Plate, Dogwood	95.00
Plate, Starflower, 15½"	55.00
Shakers, Apple, #118, EX	85.00
Sugar bowl, Apple, #98, w/advertising	115.00

Wave Crest

Wave Crest is the trademark used on a line of creamy opaque glassware manufactured by the C.F. Monroe Company of New York, who operated there from 1892 until 1916. Vases, boxes, tablewares, and humidors in swirled and blown-out shapes were either hand painted or transfer printed with florals, scenics, or portraits. Many pieces were enhanced with ornately scrolled ormolu handles, feet, or rims. Several marks were used: the black mark, 'Trade Mark Wave Crest'; the red banner mark; and the paper label, 'Wave Crest Ware, Patented Oct. 4, 1892.'

Our advisors for this category are Betty and Clarence Maier; they are listed in the Directory under Pennsylvania.

Bowl, Rococo, HP daises on bl, brass ormolu rim/hdls, 4½"	88.00
Bowl, Swirl, daisies, bl on lt gr, open, ormolu hdls, 7"	160.00
Box, blown-out pansy on lid, brn-red ground, 4" dia	600.00
Box, blown-out shell on lid, bl w/gold scrolls & dots, 6½"	950.00
Box, blown-out shell on lid, w/yel & red flowers, 4" dia	325.00
Box, mtn scene on yel, brass rim, mk, 3¼x4½x3¼"	285.00
Box, Puffy, Cigars, mums on lid, 5x7x7"	700.00
Box, Puffy, clover/daisies, pk on blk, sq, 3½x6½"	300.00
Box, Puffy, Collars & Cuffs, lg pk clover, sq, 7"	900.00
Box, Puffy, courting scene, floral on blk, ormolu ft, 7" H	500.00
Box, Puffy, roses, yel on lt gr, sq, 6½" W	425.00
Box, Rococo, Collars & Cuffs, florals, 4 ormolu ft, 7" dia	900.00
Box, Rococo, Collars & Cuffs, florals, 6x7½" dia	750.00
Box, Rococo, red floral, sq, 3¼"	250.00
Box, Rococo, roses, pk on ivory, 4" dia	190.00
Box, trees/mtn on lt yel, brass rim, 3x3x4½" L	285.00
Box, wild roses, open w/swivel oval mirror, 5½" dia	450.00
Candelabrum, triple branch, bl forget-me-nots, pr	495.00
Card holder, Rococo, rose buds on lt bl, 4 " L	375.00
Cigarette urn, match holder ea side, floral, ormolu base	675.00
Cracker jar, Rococo, floral, base flare, no bail, 6x6"	250.00
Cracker jar, Swirl, bl w/HP florals, SP lid/rim/hdl	345.00
Creamer & sugar, bird on fence/florals on pk, w/lid	265.00
Creamer & sugar, Swirl, floral on gr to wht, SP mts/lid, 3"	325.00
Dish, Swirl, dogwood on lt bl, ormolu rim/hdls, 5½"	95.00
Fernery, Puffy, red flowers, metal insert, 7" dia	175.00
Fernery, Rococo, daisies on pk, metal insert, 7½" dia	250.00
Fernery, Rococo, forget-me-not on pk, metal insert, sq, 5"	180.00
Fernery, Swirl, pk mums, mk, 7" dia	200.00
Jardiniere, bl clematis, cherubs/scrolls on rim band, 8x9"	575.00
Plaque, Venetian scene on cobalt, regilded fr, 9¾" dia	1,000.00
Shakers, Rococo, roses, pk on bl, no mk, pr	225.00
Toothpick holder, florals/beads, ormolu base, pk banner mk	285.00
Vase, bud; floral, fancy ormolu mt, 8"	300.00
Vase, orchids, ornate ormolu, 18"	1,950.00
Vase, pk & bl floral panels, ormolu base & top, sgn, 7½"	400.00
Vase, pk peonies w/gold, 15"	795.00
Vase, Scroll, wild roses, cylindrical, ormolu ftd base, 6"	250.00

Whisk broom holder, florals in shield, ornate ormolu, 10x7".......**985.00**

Weapons

Among the varied areas of specialization within the broad category of weapons, guns are by far the most popular. Muskets are among the earliest firearms; they were large-bore shoulder arms, usually firing black powder with separate loading of powder and shot. Some ignited the charge by flintlock or caplock, while later types used a firing pin with a metallic cartridge. Side arms, referred to as such because they were worn at the side, include pistols and revolvers. Pistols range from early single-shot and multiple barrels to modern types with cartridges held in the handle. Revolvers were supplied with a cylinder that turned to feed a fresh round in front of the barrel breech. Other firearms include shotguns, which fired round or conical bullets and had a smooth inner barrel surface, and rifles, so named because the interior of the barrel contained spiral grooves (rifling) which increased accuracy.

For further study, we recommend *Modern Guns, Eighth Edition*, by Russell Quertermous and Steve Quertermous, available at your local bookstore.

Our advisor for this cateogory is Steve Howard; he is listed in the Directory under California. See also Militaria.

Key:
bbl — barrel	hdw — hardware
cal — caliber	h/s — half stock
conv — conversion	mag — magazine
cyl — cylinder	oct — octagon
f/l — flintlock	p/b — patch box
f/s — full stock	perc — percussion
ga — gauge	

Carbine

Ballard, 44 cal, oct to rnd 22" bbl, EX	1,100.00
Frowith, Civil War perc, w/saddle ring, VG	225.00
Joslyn 1864, 52 cal, inspector's mks, 39", VG	650.00
Maynard, 50 cal perc, inspector's mks, label, 36½", VG	900.00
Remington 14½-R, 38-40 cal, pump action, VG	165.00
Remington 1897, rolling block, VG	300.00
Sharp's 1859, 52 cal, factory conv to cartridge, EX	750.00
Sharps & Hankins, 52 cal, VG plated metal, 24" bbl	500.00
Smith, 50 cal perc, w/case colors & bl, 39", VG	850.00
Spencer, 52 cal, VG plated metal, 22" bbl, VG	850.00
Springfield 1873, 45-70 cal, trapdoor, saddle ring, VG	900.00
Springfield 1884, trapdoor, clear mks, EX	650.00
Starr, 54 cal perc, initialed stock, 38", G	500.00

Musket

Belgium perc, 3 bands w/steel hdw, walnut stock, 56", VG	200.00
Colt 1863, mk lock, bbl dvtl for site, G	350.00
Enfield perc, 58 cal, Tower 1862 on lock, 55", VG	800.00
Harpers Ferry 1819 f/l, f/l & bbl dtd 1819, VG	525.00
Harpers Ferry 1821 f/l, eagle on lock, inspector's mks, 57"	1,600.00
Harpers Ferry 1842 perc, cvd stock, eagle on lock, 58", G	600.00
L Pomeroy 1844 conv perc, eagle/1844/US on lock, 58", VG	550.00
Mid-Eastern f/l, brass bbl bands, 34½" bbl, G	125.00
Pottsdam perc, brass hdw, inspector's mks, 57", G	450.00
Remington 1858, lock/bbl dtd 1858, bbl stamped NJ, VG	435.00
Springfield 1808, US on bbl, initialed stock, 59", VG	1,500.00
Springfield 1848 perc, mk bbl/stock, 34" bbl, G	125.00
Springfield 1863, eagle/signature on lock, 56", G	350.00

Tower-lock 1862 perc, 58 cal, 3 bands, crown mk, VG	450.00
VA 1811 f/l, stamped Richmond 1817, steel hdw, 57", G	2,000.00
VA 1811 perc conv, Richmond 1817 on lock, 57", G	1,300.00
VA 1863 conv perc, steel hdw, mk CSA/Richmond, 56", G	1,050.00
Wiesebaden perc, 38 cal, eng metal, 25" bbl, G	85.00

Pistol

Allen & Thurber pepperbox, 31 cal, dtd 1845, 3½" bbl, VG	375.00
Belgian semi-auto break tip, rubber grips, ca 1890, G	70.00
Colt 1902 sporting auto, 38 cal, rimless, NP, VG	350.00
Cossack Miquelet f/l, 50 cal, ivory ball butt, 13", VG	235.00
Derringer, cased 1-shot perc, 45-cal, mk ELG, 1840s, EX	450.00
Derringer, English perc, dbl bbl & triggers, 7"	145.00
Derringer, English perc, folding trigger guard, 6½"	145.00
English dueling perc conv, 65 cal, oct bbl, ca 1820, VG	245.00
English military f/l, 80 cal, 1-pc stock, ca 1840, 9", EX	335.00

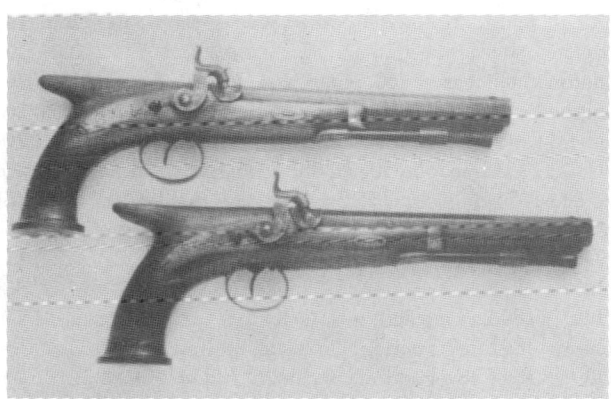

English percussion cap traveling pistols, smooth-bore browned, octagonal barrels engraved 'Liverpool,' gold-inlaid and carved breeches, lockplate signed 'T. Wilson and Co.,' 14", cased with accessories, $1,500.00.

English perc, 50 cal, bk action, walnut stock, oct bbl, VG	115.00
European officer's f/l, 70 cal, walnut stock, oct bbl, 1760s	260.00
European perc, 55 cal, twist bbl, ca 1860, VG	95.00
Forehand & Wadsworth pocket, 22 cal, plated/eng, ivory hdl	150.00
German Dragoon f/l, 72 cal, ca 1720, VG	165.00
German pocket, 41 cal, silver mts, walnut stock, rpl hammer	350.00
Italian perc, 70 cal, 5½" oct bbl, eng lock, 1850s, EX	350.00
Kentland f/l, 58 cal, mk lock, brass bbl, VG	300.00
Manhattan Fire Arms Hero, 34 cal, single shot, G	85.00
Remington 1871 Army rolling block, 50 cal, VG	400.00
Remington 1911 auto, 45 cal, G	275.00
Smith & Wesson #3, 22 cal, single shot, EX	255.00
Spanish 1852 auto, 32 cal, gold inlay on bbl, MOP grips, VG	200.00
Stevens Tip-Up #41, 22 cal, EX	150.00

Revolver

Allen & Wheel Lock Army, 44 cal, VG	550.00
Colt New Line, 22 cal, 7 shot, EX	300.00
Colt Python, 357 mag, w/Bushnell Phantom scope, NM	400.00
Colt 1849 pocket, 31 cal, 5-shot, 4" bbl, VG	450.00
Colt 1849 pocket, 31 cal, 6 shot, cyl scene, 5" bbl, G	400.00
Colt 1849 pocket, 31 cal, 6-shot, cyl scene, 5" bbl, NM	3,000.00
Colt 1851 Navy, 36 cal, eng cyl, silver inlay on grips, VG	825.00
Colt 1851 Navy, 36 cal, faint cyl scene, G	550.00
Colt 1855, 28 cal, side hammer, 3½" oct bbl, VG	400.00

Colt 1860 Army, 44 cal, fluted cyl, Hartford CT on bbl, VG .. **1,100.00**
Colt 1860 Army, 44 cal, rpl bbl, G....................................**300.00**
Colt 1862 Police, 36 cal, 5-shot, fluted cyl, reblued, G................**325.00**
Defender, 25 cal, 5-shot, chrome plate, G.............................**55.00**
Griswold & Gunnison, 36 cal, brass fr & grip strap, G **5,000.00**
Remington New Model Army, 44 cal, inspector's mk, G **425.00**
Smith & Wesson #2, 32 cal, some bl remains, EX.......................**300.00**
Starr 1863 Army, 44 cal, single action, 8" rnd bbl, G **650.00**
Whitney Navy, 36 cal, eng cyl, stamped bbl, VG.......................**500.00**

Rifle

Bridesburg 1861 Contract, mk on lock plate, EX **600.00**
G Kopp 1855, full stock perc, 38 cal, dbl set triggers, 51" **800.00**
German 1926, bolt action, 7mm, VG **125.00**
Half-stock perc, oct bbl, prof rstr, p/b...**200.00**
JB Tubbs, perc target, 40 cal, half stock, G **150.00**
Ky f/l, 44 cal, curly maple f/s, oct bbl, p/b, EX **600.00**
Marlin 336, lever action, 30-30 cal, w/Weaver scope, VG...........**125.00**
M16 practice, hard rubber **25.00**
Remington Gamemaster 760, pump, 243 Winchester cal, NM ..**200.00**
Remington Springfield 1827, rolling block, 50 cal, 36" bbl **285.00**
Springfield Krag 1898, bolt action, 30-40 cal, VG **200.00**
Springfield 1863 trapdoor, 50 cal, dtd 1866, EX **400.00**
Springfield 1873 trapdoor, 45-70 cal, inspector's mks, VG **450.00**
Springfield 1884 trapdoor, 45-70 cal, G...................................**250.00**
US 1917 Eddystone, 30 cal, birch stock, NM **125.00**
Winchester 1873, lever action, 32 cal, 24" oct bbl, VG...............**500.00**
Winchester 1890, pump action, 22 cal, G **200.00**
Winchester 1892, lever action, 25/20 cal, 20" rnd bbl, EX **550.00**
Winchester 1894, lever action, 30 cal, 26" rnd bbl, G **250.00**
Winchester 52 target, 22 cal, VG...**275.00**
Winchester 670, bolt action, 270 cal, w/scope, EX **275.00**
Winchester 70, bolt action, modified 222 cal, reblued, EX **400.00**
Winchester 70, bolt action, 243 cal, M in case............................**500.00**
Winchester 70 Feather Weight, bolt action, 30-36 cal, +scope ...**450.00**
Winchester 94, lever action, 30 cal, EX......................................**500.00**

Shotgun

Belgium, 12 ga, dbl bbl, T Barker on locks, eng plate, G...............**75.00**
Browning, 12 ga, auto-load, gold eng on sides of receiver, EX **500.00**
Browning, 12 ga, standard grade, Belgium made, EX **350.00**
Crescent, 12 ga, dbl bbl, hammer style, bbl mk Belgium steel........**50.00**
GF Stormer-Herzberg, pin fire, 16 ga, dbl bbl, eng plates **400.00**
Hopkins & Allen Forehand, 10 ga, single shot, G........................**125.00**
Ithaca 100, 20 ga, EX **200.00**
J Stevens, 12 ga, single full choke bbl, pump action, G................**100.00**
R Hughes, perc muzzleloader, dbl bbl, much eng, 48", VG **225.00**
Remington, 10 ga, dbl bbl, hammer style, G................................**150.00**
Royal Gun Works, 12 ga, dbl bbl, outside hammers, VG **75.00**
W Parker, muzzleloader, 12 ga, London Fine Twist bbl, G **125.00**
Wards Western Field 10, 10 ga, nylon stock, G **75.00**
Winchester 12, 12 ga, NP steel bbl, modified choke, +case **300.00**
Winchester 12, 12 ga, single bbl w/poly-choke, pump action **300.00**
Winchester 1887, 10 ga, single 28" bbl, lever action, VG...........**250.00**
Winchester 42, 410 ga, full choke bbl, pump action, VG **800.00**
Winchester 50, 12 ga, single 28" bbl w/ventilated rib, EX **300.00**
WW Greener, 12 ga, dbl bbl, eng receiver, G **750.00**

Sword

Ames US Navy, eagle pommel, ivory grip, eng blade, EX **635.00**
Ames US Navy, mk blade, leather sheath, copper rivets **550.00**

Civil War Cavalry, Ames...USA...1863 on blade, brass guard **225.00**
Civil War Cavalry, ebony checkered grip, iron scabbard, G **85.00**
Civil War officer, mk Collins/Hartford/1862, EX, +scabbard .. **1,050.00**
Civil War 1850 Navy, anchors/USN/eagle on blade, VG **900.00**
Civil War 1850 Navy, Horstmann-Sons/Phila, eng blade, VG **900.00**
Confederate Foot Artillery, brass hilt w/fish scales, G................**850.00**
French Cavalry #1822, leather grip w/knot, dtd 1880, EX **125.00**
French Infantry #1855, ebony grip, gilded guard, dtd 1869 ....**85.00**
German, iron hilt, ca 1850, iron scabbard, VG **75.00**
German, sharkskin grip, brass guard, eng blade, mk **75.00**
German hunting, eng hunt scene blade, silver mts, scabbard **175.00**
Japanese police, brass, decor hilt, 1940s, +scabbard **30.00**
Japanese Samurai, mtns scene on tsuba, EX, +lacquer case.........**275.00**
Japanese Samurai, water mk blade, brass eng tsuba, scabbard **350.00**
Japanese WWII, sharkskin grip, leather-wrapped scabbard, G.....**200.00**
Mansfield & Lamb, US 1863 on blade, EX, +iron scabbard.........**375.00**
Nazi dress, swastika inlay on guard/pommel, belt hanger, VG **250.00**
Sons of Union Veterans, brass guard w/insignia, NP scabbard.......**85.00**
Staff & Field officer, eng blade w/gilt, 1940s, VG **750.00**
US Artillery officer, JA Joel/NY, eagle on blade..........................**65.00**
Victorian British officer, Royal Engineers, London, VG..............**175.00**
Wilkinson, brass guard, leather sheath, 22½", VG **150.00**

Weathervanes

The earliest weathervanes were of handmade wrought iron and were generally simple angular silhouettes with a small hole suggesting an eye. Later, copper, zinc, and polychromed wood with features in relief were fashioned into more realistic forms. Ships, horses, fish, Indians, roosters, and angels were popular motifs. In the 19th century, silhouettes were often made from sheet metal. Wooden figures became highly carved and were painted in vivid colors. E.G. Washburne and Company in New York was one of the most prominent manufacturers of weathervanes during the last half of the century.

Two-dimensional sheet metal weathervanes are increasing in value due to the already heady prices of the full-bodied variety. Originality, strength of line, and patination help to determine value. When no condition is indicated, the items listed below are assumed to be in excellent condition.

Key:
fb — full-bodied   f/fb — flattened full-bodied

Rooster, copper with traces of original gold paint underneath, 16½" x 29", $5,500.00.

Auto w/driver, stamped zinc on 34" CI arrow, VG **70.00**
Bull, f/fb copper, 1880s, 19" H, EX...**750.00**
Cow, f/fb gilt copper, no directionals, 1880, 29" L **3,700.00**
Cow, fb copper w/sheet ears, zinc horns, att Cushing, 25" **3,200.00**
Eagle, copper w/raised sheet copper wings, att Jewell, 25" **1,700.00**

Eagle (wings wide) on orb/lg arrow, copper, fb, 43" W, VG **1,000.00**
Fighting cock, f/fb copper, sheet copper tail, 1830s, 18" **4,250.00**
Horse, gilt copper, 43" L, G **2,100.00**
Horse, iron silhouette, 1800s, some rust, 31" L......................**100.00**
Horse, prancing, sheet metal, molded head, Tuckerman, 31" .. **2,100.00**
Horse, running, molded copper, 19x31" **1,300.00**
Horse, running, molded hollow copper, zinc head, 41" L.............**800.00**
Horse, standing, sheet iron silhouette, 8½" L **550.00**
Horse w/jockey, f/fb copper, 33" L, EX................................. **2,600.00**
Horse w/jockey, stylized, sheet metal w/worn pnt, 22x36" **600.00**
Indian w/bow, sheet metal w/VG pnt, 1875, 17" **650.00**
Jockey w/trumpet, wood w/old pnt, Am, 1800s, 41" L **1,750.00**
Locomotive & tender on RR tracks, sheet iron, 1900, 22" **650.00**
Rooster, f/fb copper, zinc tail/ft, urn base, Cushing, 38"........... **1,900.00**
Rooster, fb copper w/zinc legs, sheet copper comb, 12"............. **2,500.00**
Rooster (sm), atop lg arrow, molded copper, losses, 25" **1,100.00**
Rooster (sm), hollow-molded cooper, on zinc banner, 28".............**285.00**
Simple Simon/pieman/dog, iron silhouette, 1940s, 48x54"..........**700.00**
Spanish galleon, copper silhouette, late, 37x46" **400.00**
Steam locomotive, sheet metal cutout, old pnt, 21" L................**875.00**
Tuna fish, wood silhouette, metal fins, pnt traces, 60" L **2,500.00**

Weaving

Early Americans used a variety of tools and a great amount of time to produce the material from which their clothing was made. Soaked and dried flax was broken on a flax brake to remove waste material. It was then tapped and stroked with a scutching knife. Hackles further removed waste and separated the short fibers from the longer ones. Unspun fibers were placed on the distaff on the spinning wheel for processing into yarn. The yarn was then wound around a reel for measuring. Three tools used for this purpose were the niddy-noddy, the reel yarn winder, and the click reel. After it was washed and dyed, the yarn was transferred to a barrel-cage or squirrel-cage swift and fed onto a bobbin winder.

Today, flax wheels are more plentiful than the large wool wheels since they were small and could be more easily stored and preserved. The distaff, an often-discarded or misplaced part of the wheel, is very scarce. French spinners from the Quebec area painted their wheels. Many have been stripped and refinished by those unaware of this fact. Wheels may be very simple or have a great amount of detail, depending upon the owner's ethnic background and the maker's skill.

Bobbin winder, wood, grpt, ca 1830...**225.00**
Hatchel, flax, sgn WT, dtd 46 (1846), 4½x13½" **95.00**
Hatchel, primitive, on pine brd w/cover, 17" L................................**45.00**
Loom light, iron, twisted hanger, 1700s, 13½", EX........................**175.00**
Niddy-noddy, primitive, bent twig-braced ends, 19" L **85.00**
Niddy-noddy, wood, mortised & pinned, worn..............................**55.00**
Reel, floor standing, adjustable rods, old patina, 42" **135.00**
Reel, floor standing, hardwood w/trn legs & spindle, 36".............**350.00**
Shuttle, wood, eng flowers, sgn, 2½x12"......................................**45.00**
Swift, chrome, table clamp, extends to 20" sq **30.00**
Swift, umbrella form, table clamp **95.00**
Swift, wood w/worn orig red & blk pnt, table clamp, 21"............**125.00**
Wheel, flax; distaff/spindle/tin water pan, Europe, 23" **150.00**
Wheel, flax; EX trn, ivory trim, edge damage/rpl, 23x26"............**150.00**
Wheel, flax; 2-color pnt decor, chip cvg, 13" wheel, 36"..............**395.00**
Wheel, spinning; oak w/EX trn detail, rpl distaff, 35" **400.00**
Wheel, spinning; trn legs/spindles, rpl arm, ca 1860, 35" **235.00**
Wheel, spinning; trn members, 3-color stripes, 38"+distaff..........**325.00**
Wheel, wool; horn-banded trn details, 43" wheel..........................**125.00**
Wheel, wool; trn legs/spindles, 48" dia wheel **135.00**

Wheel, wool; 47" wheel, 60" **385.00**
Wool carder, wood bk/hdl, branded Robinson #10, 5x11", pr **25.00**

Webb

Thomas Webb and Sons have been making fine art glass in Stourbridge, England, since 1837. Besides their fine cameo glass, they have also made enameled ware and pieces heavily decorated with applied glass ornaments. The butterfly is a motif that has been so often featured that it tends to suggest Webb as the manufacturer.

Our advisor for this category is Don Williams; he is listed in the Directory under Iowa. See also specific types of glass such as Alexandrite, Burmese, Mother of Pearl, and Peachblow.

Biscuit jar, fruit, pnt/gilt on opal, pink int, SP mts, 8" **400.00**
Biscuit jar, gold prunus on pk satin cased, floral-emb lid..............**350.00**
Biscuit jar, lime/intaglio orange roses, SP mts, 7" **575.00**
Bowl, florals/lg bird on strawberry-pk, ftd metal base, 9"............**215.00**
Bowl, gold prunus/butterfly on brn, tricorn shape, 2½x3"............**325.00**
Decanter, Rock Crystal, spirals/berry prunts/ferns, 11½"..............**900.00**
Ewer, gold branches/3 apples on gr to wht satin, 9x4" **425.00**
Ewer, Rock Crystal, floral panels, ftd, sgn Woodall, 8" **6,500.00**
Ewer, 3-color berries on bl shaded, frosted hdl, 10", pr.................**215.00**
Goblet, panels w/dragons, sgn Fritsche, 4½" **400.00**
Goblet, Rock Crystal, sgn Fritsche, elaborate stem, 12½" **1,300.00**
Lamp, butterfly on gr, brass finger loop, sgn, mini **475.00**
Pitcher, apples on branch, gold on gr shaded, #d, 9x4" **450.00**
Rose bowl, amber, 2" threading at top/eng birds, 6-crimp, 5".......**350.00**
Rose bowl, brn to yel to cream, wht int, pleated top, 5x6"...........**325.00**
Rose bowl, pk overlay w/gold, 4-crimp, spider web mk, 3x3".......**325.00**
Vase, allover mc flowers & orange enameling, gourd form, 8" **425.00**
Vase, bird/prunus/butterfly, yel on bl shaded, 8¼x6¼"................**425.00**
Vase, bronze irid, shouldered, EX color, 7x4" **375.00**
Vase, florals on pk shaded, cup neck on dbl gourd, 9" **245.00**
Vase, gold floral branch on coral overlay, 9x4¼".........................**350.00**
Vase, gold florals on orange overlay, label, 10¼", pr....................**395.00**
Vase, gold florals/bands on brn, cream ped ft, 5⅝x4¼" **225.00**
Vase, gold prunus/butterfly & wht floral on pk satin, 17" **500.00**
Vase, gold prunus/butterfly on gold shaded, 6½", pr....................**600.00**
Vase, gold prunus/dragonfly, mk, 5¼x2¾".................................**295.00**
Vase, Intarsia, free molded, amethyst/gr striations, 6" **650.00**
Vase, Isnik florals/dotted borders HP on peach, gilt, 16" **220.00**
Vase, rose/basketweave intaglio, HP chinoiserie, 8"....................**225.00**
Vase, wht/gold floral/butterfly on maroon, wht int, 9½" **300.00**
Wine, Rock Crystal, panels w/dragons, sgn Hall, 4½", pr.............**600.00**

Cameo

Bottle, scent; clear w/cane cuttings, cameo bird nest, 3¼" **1,700.00**
Bottle, scent; floral, bk: butterfly, wht on red, 2⅜" **700.00**
Bottle, scent; grasses/butterflies, wht on emerald, sq, 11" **3,500.00**
Bottle, scent; roses, wht on red, sq, silver lid, 5¾", NM.......... **1,100.00**
Bottle, scent; sweet peas, wht on red, lay down, 10" **2,500.00**
Bottle, scent; sweet peas/etc, wht on gr, lay down, 11" **2,500.00**
Bottle, smelling salts; floral, wht on bright gr, 3¾"......................**750.00**
Bowl, jasmine, wht on citron, silver beaded rim, 5x8" **950.00**
Cane knob, branches/acorns, wht on blk, ball form, 1½" **500.00**
Card holder, florals, bl on frost, saucer base, 3½" **1,050.00**
Flower bowl, apple blossoms, 4-layer, Gem mk, 4x9"............. **4,000.00**
Serving fork & spoon, 3-color floral, Gorham hdls, 12" **1,900.00**
Tea bowl & saucer, butterflies/florals, red/wht/bl, 3½" **1,200.00**
Vase, apple blossoms, rainbow on DQ MOP, Gem mk, 5x8½" .. **2,000.00**
Vase, apple blossoms/boughs, wht/red on yel, opal int, 10" **7,000.00**

Vase, arabesques, gr/lav/wht on yel, wht int, Gem mk, 6" **22,000.00**
Vase, berries/insect, 4-color, 2" **500.00**
Vase, bud; floral, wht on red; metal base w/3-D lion, 8½" **1,200.00**
Vase, cyclamen, wht on citron, Gem mk, 5½" **1,900.00**

Vase, white floral on red, signed, 11", $3,000.00.

Vase, daisies, red on yel, Gem mk, 5¼" **2,800.00**
Vase, daisies/butterfly, wht on citron, stick neck, 6" **850.00**
Vase, fig leaves/lappet border, pk/gr on ivory, 7½" **4,100.00**
Vase, floral, bl/wht on amber, lg bamboo hdls, Gem mk, 6" ... **8,500.00**
Vase, floral, wht on teal, rnd w/cup-like neck, 5" **1,700.00**
Vase, floral/berries/butterfly, wht on citron, bulbous, 6" **750.00**
Vase, floral/butterflies, wht on cornflower bl, 3¼" **750.00**
Vase, floral/2 butterflies/geometrics, bl/lav/wht, 12" **7,750.00**
Vase, foxglove/butterfly, wht on red, frost int, 24" **16,000.00**
Vase, morning-glories/butterfly, wht on lime, Gem mk, 10" ... **2,050.00**
Vase, nasturtiums, 4-color, bottle form, 4"..................................**675.00**
Vase, oak leaves, wht on pk shaded to bl, 4¼" **2,000.00**
Vase, Oriental brocade, red on yel, opal int, Gem mk, 6" **4,750.00**
Vase, panels w/birds, Oriental motif, faux ivory, 9" **7,500.00**
Vase, petunias, wht on raspberry, 3 loop ft, squat, 4" **2,100.00**
Vase, poppies, bk: butterfly, wht on citron, ovoid, 5" **750.00**
Vase, prunus flowers/leaves, wht on citron, 3"............................**900.00**
Vase, snowdrop flowers, wht on red, Gem mk, 5".................... **1,750.00**
Vase, sunflowers, wht on gr, frost int, Gem mk, 8½" **2,200.00**
Vase, trumpet floral/butterfly, wht on burmese, wht int, 9"..... **7,500.00**
Vase, tubular flowers/pods, wht on dk bl, 10" **4,000.00**
Vase, tulips/leaves, amber on textured clear, ftd, 10" **375.00**
Vase, tulips/leaves, lav on frost, etched silver band, 7" **1,075.00**
Vase, various fruits, cvd as snuff bottle, red/wht, 3¾" **3,500.00**
Vase, vines/buds, amethyst/wht on turq, Gem mk, 8½"........... **7,400.00**
Vase, 2 deer/trees, wht on topaz, sgn Woodall, ftd, 8" **19,000.00**
Whimsey, foo dog, wht & pk on crystal, 1¼x1⅞" **1,700.00**

Wedgwood

Josiah Wedgwood established his pottery in Burslem, England, in 1759. He produced only molded utilitarian earthenwares until 1770 when new facilities were opened at Etruria. It was there he introduced his famous Basalt and Jasperware. Jasperware, an unglazed fine stoneware decorated with classic figures in white relief, was usually produced in blues; but it was also made in ground colors of green, lilac, yellow, black, or white. Occasionally, three or more colors were used in combination. It has been in continuous production to the present day and is the most easily recognized of all the Wedgwood lines. (Jasper is a body of solid color; the term 'Jasper-Dip' refers to ware with a white body that has been dipped in an overlay color. This type, introduced in the late 1700s, is the type most often encountered on today's market.)

Though Wedgwood's Jasperware was highly acclaimed, on a more practical basis his creamware was his greatest success. Due to the ease with which it could be potted and because its lighter weight significantly reduced transportation expenses, Wedgwood was able to offer 'chinaware' at affordable prices. Queen Charlotte was so pleased with the ware that she allowed it to be called 'Queen's Ware.' Most creamware was marked simply 'Wedgwood.' ('Wedgwood & Co.' and 'Wedgewood' are marks of other potters.) From 1769 to 1780, Wedgwood was in partnership with Thomas Bently; artwares of the highest quality bear the mark indicating this partnership.

Moonlight Lustre, an allover splashed-on effect of pink intermingling with gray, brown, or yellow, was made from 1805 to 1815. Porcelain was made, though not to any great extent, from 1812 to 1822. Both of these types of wares were marked 'Wedgwood.' Stone china and Pearlware were made from about 1820 to 1875. Examples of either may be found with a mark to indicate their body type. During the late 1800s, Wedgwood produced some fine parian and majolica. Creamware, hand painted by Emile Lessore, was sold from about 1860 to 1875. From the 20th century, several lines of lustre wares – Butterfly, Dragon, and Fairyland (the latter designed by Miss Makeig-Jones) – have attracted the collector and, as their prices suggest, are highly sought-after and admired.

Nearly all of Wedgwood's wares are clearly marked. 'Wedgwood' was used before 1891, after which time 'England' was added. Most examples marked 'Made In England' were made after 1921. A detailed study of all marks is recommended for accurate dating.

Key:
WW — Wedgwood   WWE — Wedgwood England

Asparagus server, Creamware, WW, ca 1800, 4"............................**135.00**
Beaker, Jasper, dk bl, WW, 3" **135.00**
Bidet, Creamware, WW, 15x34", in 22" mahog case, ca 1830. **1,775.00**
Biscuit jar, Jasper, dk bl, bbl shape, SP trim, WW, 5⅛" **165.00**
Biscuit jar, Jasper, dk bl, classical figures, WW, 5½" **150.00**
Biscuit jar, Jasper, dk bl, ladies/cupids, SP trim, WW, 6½" **175.00**
Biscuit jar, Jasper, gold/blk bands, gilt lid/bail, WW, 7"...............**600.00**
Biscuit jar, Jasper, lav & gr, SP lid & bail, WW, 9" **1,000.00**
Biscuit jar, Jasper, lt bl w/wide dk band, SP mts, WWE, 7"..........**395.00**
Biscuit jar, Jasper, sage gr, fox hunt, WWE, hallmk band.............**400.00**
Biscuit jar, Jasper, sage gr, SP ball ft/mts, WW, 6¾"....................**210.00**
Biscuit jar, Jasper, 3-color, ladies/cupids, WW, 6¼" **585.00**
Biscuit jar, Jasper, 3-color, SP finial, WW, 1882, 7½" **775.00**
Biscuit jar, Jasper, 3-color w/gold, SP lid/rim/hdl, WW, 6⅝"........**895.00**
Biscuit jar, lav, florals, WWE, 7¾x5¼" **725.00**
Biscuit jar, stoneware, dk gr w/wht ivy, WW **345.00**
Bowl, Butterfly Lustre, flame/MOP, silver leaves, WW, 8⅜"........**425.00**
Bowl, Butterfly Lustre, gold/umber, bl/gr int, WWE, 8" **450.00**
Bowl, Dragon Lustre, bl mottle, Portland vase mk, 5⅝"..............**250.00**
Bowl, Dragon Lustre, bl mottle w/gold, MOP int, WW, 5½".......**235.00**
Bowl, Dragon Lustre, bl w/red & gold, gold int, WWE/#d, 9" **550.00**
Bowl, Dragon Lustre, bl/flame, Portland vase mk, 4x9½" **400.00**
Bowl, Fairyland Lustre, Castle on Road, octagonal, WW, 11½".. **4,000.00**
Bowl, Fairyland Lustre, orange ground, 6x10" **1,700.00**
Bowl, ferner; Jasper, buff & blk, 3-ftd, WWE.............................**345.00**
Bowl, Fruit Lustre, bl w/much gold, Portland mk, 3½x8⅛" **550.00**
Bowl, Hummingbird Lustre, bl mottle, Portland vase mk, 3⅞" ...**160.00**
Bowl, Jasper, blk, Dancing Hours, WW, 3x6" **245.00**
Bowl, Jasper, dk bl, WW, 2¾x5" **110.00**

Bowl, Jasper, lt bl, WWE, 2x4¾" 80.00
Bowl, Moonstone, cream, fluted/low, K Murray, 10" 300.00
Bowl, Oriental Lustre, flame, Portland vase mk, 3⅞" 145.00
Bowl, Pearlware, shell form, WW, 1½x8¼" 385.00
Bowl, Pearlware, shell form, WW, 6½x13" 545.00
Box, Dragon Lustre, widow finial, WW, 5½" dia 395.00
Box, Jasper, dk bl, WWE, 3¾x4¾" 155.00
Box, stoneware, olive gr, heart shape, WWE, 2x4½x3½" 195.00
Bust, Basalt, bearded man, WW, 4½" 375.00
Cameo, Jasper, dk bl, lapidary polished, WW, set in MOP/brass .115.00
Cameo, Jasper, gr, Antonia, oval, WW, 1⅝x2" 115.00
Candlestick, Jasper, blk, classical figures, WW, 6x4" 225.00
Candlestick, Jasper, dk bl, MIE, 1½", pr 130.00
Candlestick, Jasper, dk bl, WW, 7" 135.00
Candlestick, Jasper, lt bl, WWE, 7¼" 85.00
Candlestick, Jasper, med bl, ca 1955, 1½", pr 115.00
Cigarette lighter, Jasper, lt gr, MIE 80.00
Clock, Jasper, lt bl, rpl works, WWE, ca 1905 ....465.00
Creamer, Drabware, lt brn, WW, ca 1830, 2½x5" 175.00
Creamer, Jasper, lt bl, St Louis shape, WWE, 2¼x3½" 70.00
Creamer, Jasper, sage gr, WWE, 2¼" 115.00
Creamer & sugar bowl, Basalt, silver rim, WW, ca 1870 ....200.00
Creamer & sugar bowl, Jasper, lt bl, WWE 130.00
Cup, Fairyland Lustre, elves, Portland vase mk, 3½x4⅞" 695.00
Cup & saucer, Basalt, Niagara Falls, WWE 100.00
Cup & saucer, Caneware, blk vintage, WW, ca 1810 ....365.00
Cup & saucer, Creamware, gr floral, WW, ca 1882 ....40.00
Cup & saucer, handleless; Basalt, WW, 2¼x3" 75.00

Ewers, Basalt, first half of 19th century, handle restored, 15", $2,300.00.

Flower frog, Creamware, tree trunk w/holes, WWE, 6" dia 80.00
Ginger jar, Fairyland Lustre, blk/gold on turq, 8" 1,300.00
Hair receiver, Jasper, blk, classical figures, WW, 3½x3¼" 325.00
Honey pot, Caneware, glazed, beehive form, 1830s, 4", EX 225.00
Inkstand, Drabware, florals/gilt trim, 1850s, 8x10", EX.............275.00
Inkstand, Drabware, glazed, WW, ca 1845..........................675.00
Inkwell, Jasper, lt bl, dolphins, brass lid, WW, 6" 500.00
Jar, Jasper, dk bl, WWE, 3x2" dia 95.00
Jardiniere, Jasper, lt bl, WWE, 3½x4" 130.00
Jardiniere, stoneware, olive gr, flared top, WWE, 7½" 435.00
Jug, Drabware, classical ladies, relief molded, 6-sided, WW, 8"....225.00
Lamp, Jasper, lt bl, WW, 10", pr...................................475.00
Loving cup, Jasper, lt bl, 3-hdl, WWE, 4½" 165.00
Match holder, Jasper, dk bl, strike on base, WWE, 2½x2" 75.00

Match holder, Jasper, lt bl, WW, 3¾x6" 135.00
Medallion, Jasper, lt bl, Hadrian, WW, 3" dia 135.00
Medallion, Jasper, med bl, WW, 1800s, 2" dia 135.00
Mug, Shakespeare 400th Anniversary, bone china, WWE.............55.00
Pitcher, Basalt, garlands, mk J Mare, 4¼x2⅝" 175.00
Pitcher, Basalt, rose/shamrock/thistle, WW, 3½" 120.00
Pitcher, Creamware, Josiah Wedgwood, ca 1881 ....135.00
Pitcher, Fallow Deer, bone china, copper lustre, WWE, 1937 .....140.00
Pitcher, Jasper, dk bl, Byerly shape, WW, ca 1840, 4½" 130.00
Pitcher, Jasper, dk bl, ladies/cherubs, bulbous, WW, 5½" 150.00
Pitcher, stoneware, olive gr, Franklin/Washington, WWE, 8½" ..445.00
Pitcher, syrup; Jasper, dk bl, classical ladies, WW, 5¼x3" 145.00
Pitcher, syrup; Jasper, lt bl, WWE, 7½" 85.00
Pitcher, tankard; Jasper, dk bl, classical ladies, WW, 7½" 165.00
Pitcher, tankard; Jasper, dk bl, grapes/ladies, WW, 4x2½" 110.00
Pitcher, tankard; Jasper, dk bl, grapes/ladies, WW, 6⅜" 145.00
Pitcher, tankard; Jasper, dk bl, WW, 5½" 120.00
Plaque, deer in winter, artist sgn, WW, 12⅛" 600.00
Plaque, Jasper, bl, Bacchanalian Boys, WW, ca 1810, 10½" 1,000.00
Plaque, Jasper, dk bl, Dancing Hours, WW, 2½x6" 365.00
Plaque, Jasper, lt bl, Pegasus, fr, WW, 4" 135.00
Plate, bone china, Imari decor, WW, ca 1880, 6¾" dia 45.00
Plate, Creamware, ribbon rim w/gold, WW, dinner sz 50.00
Plate, Creamware, Sleepy Hollow, WWE 40.00
Plate, Drabware, wht vintage border, WW, ca 1810, 6¼" 235.00
Plate, Ivanhoe, Rebecca Repelling the Templar, WW, 10¼" 75.00
Plate, Ivanhoe, Wamba & Gurth the swineherd, WW, 10¼" 75.00
Plate, Jasper, lt bl, Cupid, WWE, 8¾" 88.00
Plate, Millicent Taplin, bone china, platinum lustre, WWE 90.00
Plate, Moonlight Lustre, shell shape, WW, 8¼" 285.00
Plate, Pearlware, Knave of Clubs, WWE, ca 1909................135.00
Platter, Creamware, HP florals, WW, ca 1871 ....135.00
Potpourri, Pearlware, floral, WW, ca 1840 .... 1,880.00
Ring tree, Jasper, dk bl, classical ladies, WW, 2¾x3⅛" 145.00
Shakers, Jasper, med gr, WWE, ca 1958, pr 160.00
Sugar bowl, Jasper, dk bl, w/lid, WW, 2½x4½" 135.00
Sugar bowl, Jasper, dk bl, w/lid, WWE 115.00
Sugar bowl, Jasper, gr, WW, 3½x4⅜" 135.00
Teapot, Basalt, Capri, HP florals, WW, 4x8" 465.00
Teapot, Caneware, basketweave, sheaf of wheat knop, WW, 5" ..245.00
Teapot, Drabware, Gothic style, WW, ca 1840, rpr, 4½x8½" 155.00
Teapot, Jasper, dk bl, WWE, 4½x6¼" 115.00
Teapot, Jasper, sage gr, WW, +cr/sug............................220.00
Teapot, Rosso Antico, blk decor, WW, ca 1810, 4½x9" 545.00
Teapot, Rosso Antico w/rooster, flat sided, 1880s, rstr, 5" 500.00
Trembleuse, stoneware, wht/plain, 2-hdl, w/underdish, 4¼" 200.00
Vase, Basalt, laurel swags, WW, 6"..............................325.00
Vase, Butterfly Lustre, flame int, WW, 8½" 375.00
Vase, Dragon Luster, lt bl, bone china, WWE, 8½" 565.00
Vase, Dragon Lustre, bl w/gold & red, WW, Z4829, 8½" 525.00
Vase, Fairyland Lustre, Torches, A-4968, 11¼" 2,900.00
Vase, Hummingbird Lustre, bl, flame int, WW, 4⅜x2½" 195.00
Vase, Jasper, blk, classical figures, Portland mk, 5x3½" 325.00
Vase, Jasper, blk, Muses, w/lid, WWE, 11½", pr 3,000.00
Vase, Jasper, dk bl, classical ladies, WW, 4⅞" 118.00
Vase, Jasper, dk bl, Cupids as seasons, WW, 5⅛x2¾", pr..........165.00
Vase, Jasper, lav, WW, 7", pr 995.00
Vase, Jasper, lav, WWE, 3¾" 185.00
Vase, Jasper, lt bl, classical figures, Portland mk, 8" 350.00
Vase, Jasper, lt bl, Dancing Hours, w/lid, WW, 8" 995.00
Vase, Jasper, med gr, w/grid, WWE, ca 1958, 6¾" 170.00
Vase, Moonstone, cream, faceted trumpet form, K Murray, 7".....300.00
Vase, Moonstone, cream, rnd w/can neck, K Murray, 8" 500.00
Vase, Victoria Ware, brn/cream gloss, gold trim, hdls, 7½" 395.00

Waste bowl, Jasper, dk bl, classical figures, WW, 2⅜x4⅜" 70.00

Weil Ware

Max Weil came to the United States in the 1940s, settling in California. There he began manufacturing dinnerware, figurines, cookie jars, and wall pockets. American clays were used, and the dinnerware was all hand decorated. Weil died in 1954; the company closed two years later. The last backstamp to be used was the outline of a burro with the words 'Weil Ware – Made in California.'

Ash tray, Bamboo, 5" 5.00
Box, dogwood, wht on gray, oval, 10" 15.00
Coffee server, Bamboo 20.00
Compote, floral, ftd...14.00
Figurine, boy w/wheelbarrow, #4005 ....15.00
Figurine, Buddy, boy, 7" 15.00
Figurine, Dee Lee, girl, 7" 15.00
Figurine, girl, lifted chin, sgraffito floral on skirt, lg.....................30.00
Figurine, girl planter, #3062, 8" 22.00
Figurine, girl planter, artist sgn, #1899, 11" 30.00
Figurine, girl planter, orig sticker, #1733........................25.00
Planter, bust of lady, HP fan in hand, 8" 30.00
Vase, bud; girl w/arms on pillars, 10".............................26.00
Vase, bud; Ming tree, w/coralene, #946, 6"......................22.00
Vase, Ming tree, w/coralene, 8½".....................................35.00
Wall pocket, Oriental girl, #4046 ....22.50

Weller

The Weller Pottery Company was established in Zanesville, Ohio, in 1882, the outgrowth of a small one-kiln log cabin works Sam Weller had operated in Fultonham. Through an association with Wm. Long, he entered the art pottery field in 1895, producing the Lonhuda Ware Long had perfected in Steubenville six years earlier. His famous Louwelsa line was merely a continuation of Lonhuda and was made in at least five hundred different shapes until 1924.

Many fine lines of artware followed under the direction of Charles Babcock Upjohn, Art Director from 1895 to 1904: Dickens Ware (1st Line), underglaze slip decorations on dark backgrounds; Turada, featuring applied ivory bands of delicate openwork on solid dark brown backgrounds; and Aurelian, similar to Louwelsa, but with a brushed-on rather than blended ground.

One of their most famous lines was 2nd Line Dickens, introduced in 1900. Backgrounds, characteristically caramel shading to turquoise matt, were decorated by sgraffito with animals, golfers, monks, Indians, and scenes from Dickens novels. The work is often artist signed. Sicardo, 1903, was a metallic lustre line in tones of rose, blue, green, or purple with flowing Art Nouveau patterns developed within the glaze.

Frederick Hurten Rhead, who worked for Weller in 1903 to 1904, created the prestigious Jap Birdimal line decorated with geisha girls, landscapes, storks, etc., accomplished through application of heavy slip forced through the tiny nozzle of a squeeze bag. Other lines to his credit are L'Art Nouveau, produced both in high-gloss brown and matt pastels, and 3rd Line Dickens, often decorated with Cruikshank's illustrations in relief.

Other early artware lines were Eocean, Floretta, Hunter, Perfecto, Dresden, Etched Matt, and Etna.

In 1920 John Lessel was hired as Art Director, and under his supervision several new lines were created. LaSa, LaMar, Marengo, and Besline attest to his expertise with metallic lustres.

The last of the artware lines and one of the most sought-after by collectors today is Hudson, first made during the early 1920s. Hudson, a semi-matt glazed ware, was beautifully artist decorated on shaded backgrounds with florals, animals, birds, and scenics. Notable artists often signed their work, among them Hester Pillsbury, Dorothy England Laughead, Ruth Axline, Claude Leffler, Sarah Reid McLaughlin, E.L. Pickens, and Mae Timberlake.

During the thirties, Weller produced a line of gardenware and naturalistic life-sized figures of dogs, cats, swans, geese, and playful gnomes.

The depression brought a slow, steady decline in sales, and by 1948 the pottery was closed. For a more thorough study, we recommend *The Collector's Encyclopedia of Weller Pottery* by Sharon and Bob Huxford, available at your local library or bookstore.

Arcadia, fan vase, turq, 8x15" 35.00
Arcola, wall pocket, 11" 85.00
Ardsley, bud vase, 7½" 30.00
Ardsley, candle holders, 3", pr 30.00
Ardsley, vase, 7" 70.00
Athens, vase, 10" 350.00
Atlas, bowl, #C-3, 4" 45.00
Atlas, star dish, #C-2, 2" 25.00
Atlas, vase, 10½" 65.00
Aurelian, ewer, floral, sgn MP, 6" 250.00
Aurelian, jardiniere & pedestal, floral, 38" 1,400.00
Aurelian, lamp, grape clusters, sgn E Roberts, 29" 2,200.00
Aurelian, mug, silver lid, dog, sgn K, 7" 1,400.00
Aurelian, oil banquet lamp, floral, sgn Schnieder, 27"............ 1,500.00
Baldin, bowl, apples, bl, 4" 60.00
Baldin, vase, apples, 5½" 50.00
Barcelona, ewer, 9½" 100.00
Barcelona, oil jar, hdls, 25½" 500.00
Barcelona, vase, hdls, 6½" 75.00
Barcelona, vase, hdls, 8" 80.00
Besline, vase, leaves/berries, orange lustre, 8½" 160.00
Blossom, planter, floral on bl, 4"..15.00
Blue Drapery, planter, 4" 30.00
Blue Drapery, vase, 6" 30.00
Blue Drapery, wall pocket, 9" 65.00
Blue Ware, bud vase, 8" 20.00
Blue Ware, comport, 5½" 80.00
Blue Ware, jardiniere, w/4 angels, 9" 200.00
Bonito, candle holders, 1½", pr 65.00
Bonito, vase, floral, sgn NC, 10" 130.00
Bouquet, console bowl, #B-12, 5x12½"....................................15.00
Bouquet, pitcher, #B-18, 9½" 30.00
Bouquet, vase, #B-15, 5" 15.00
Breton, bowl, brn, 4" 35.00
Breton, vase, brn, 7" 35.00
Brighton, bluebird, #5, 5½" 200.00
Brighton, cardinal, 5½" 225.00
Brighton, crow, 6½" 500.00
Brighton, hanging parrot, spread wings, 15" 1,000.00
Brighton, kingfisher, 6½" 250.00
Brighton, parrot, 12½" 700.00
Brighton, parrot, 7½"...300.00
Brighton, penguins, 5" 400.00
Brighton, rooster, 9½" 900.00
Burntwood, vase, 12" 150.00
Burntwood, vase, 5" 40.00
Burntwood, vase, 8" 80.00
Cactus, camel, brn, 4"...60.00
Cactus, duck, gr, 4½" 60.00

Cactus, monkey, brn, 4"..60.00
Camelot, vase, tan-gold swirls, bulbous w/stick neck, 6"..........135.00
Camelot, vase, 8"..160.00
Cameo, vase, hdls, 5"..25.00
Cameo, vase, sq, 8½"..25.00
Cameo Jewell, jardiniere & pedestal, 33½"..........350.00
Cameo Jewell, umbrella stand, 22"................................400.00
Candis, console, 11x2½"..20.00
Candis, hanging basket, 5½"..40.00
Chase, vase, scene in silver, 12"................................250.00
Chengtu, ginger jar, 12"..120.00
Chengtu, jar, w/lid, 8"..80.00
Chengtu, vase, 12"..75.00
Chengtu, vase, 8"..55.00
Classic, bowl, gr, 11"..15.00
Classic, fan vase, brn, 5"..15.00
Classic, plate, wht, 11½"..15.00
Classic, wall pocket, gr, 6"..15.00
Classic, window box, gr, 4"..15.00
Claywood, bowl, 2"..30.00
Claywood, candle holder, 5"..35.00
Claywood, spittoon, 4½"..100.00
Claywood, vase, 5½"..35.00
Coppertone, ash tray, 6½"..125.00
Coppertone, console, w/frog, 12x3"................................225.00
Coppertone, frog, 4"..85.00
Coppertone, frog w/banjo, 7½"................................400.00
Coppertone, pitcher, fish hdl, 7½"................................400.00
Coppertone, vase, hdls, 10½"..85.00
Coppertone, vase, hdls, 8½"..70.00
Coppertone, vase, 6½"..50.00
Copra, jardiniere, tulips, 8"..70.00
Cornish, bowl, 7½"..25.00
Cornish, jardiniere, 5"..30.00
Creamware, hanging basket, rtcl, 11½"................................100.00
Creamware, planter, w/liner, 11½"................................60.00
Darsie, vase, turq, 5½"..25.00
Darsie, vase, turq, 7½"..35.00
Decorated Creamware, vase, grape cluster, HP, 11½"..........275.00
Delsa, vase, 6"..20.00
Dickens I, bowl, daffodils on dk brn, 9¾"................................135.00
Dickens I, jardiniere, floral, 8"................................200.00
Dickens I, lamp, owl, sgn EA, 14"................................2,000.00
Dickens I, mug, floral, sgn MM, 4½"................................140.00
Dickens II, ewer, duck, 8½"..450.00
Dickens II, ewer, fish, sgn EL Pickens, 11½"................................500.00
Dickens II, mug, grape cluster, 5"................................125.00
Dickens II, pillow vase, old church, wht, 7x8"................................800.00
Dickens II, pitcher, elk, 4"................................200.00
Dickens II, pitcher, monk, 7"................................300.00
Dickens II, tankard, nude, sgn EL Pickens, dtd 1902, 12"..........1,100.00
Dickens II, tobacco jar, The Captain, 7"................................500.00
Dickens II, vase, cavalier, bl, glossy, sgn JH, 13½"................................700.00
Dickens II, vase, floral, 9½"..275.00
Dickens II, vase, geishas, Upjohn/FS, drilled for lamp, 14"..........650.00
Dickens II, vase, Indian, full headdress, Dusenberry, 13"..........950.00
Dickens II, vase, Indian head, pillow form, #352, 5"..........250.00
Dickens II, vase, kitten, 9"..1,100.00
Dickens II, vase, pointer bird dog, sgn EL Pickens, 9"..........850.00
Dickens II, vase, sword duel, hdls, sgn LJB, 5½"................................200.00
Dickens II, vase, wht knight on horse, glossy, sgn Upjohn, 14"...800.00
Dickens III, carafe, w/cup, D Copperfield, sgn R, 14½"..........1,100.00
Dickens III, creamer, Charles Dickens, #0034, 4"................................350.00

Dickens III, ewer, Squeers, sgn LM, 12½"................................650.00
Dickens III, flask vase, Dombey & Son, #0021, 7½"................................600.00
Dickens III, vase, David Copperfield, sgn LS, 10½"................................600.00
Dupont, bowl, Roma glaze, 3"..30.00
Dupont, planter, sq, 3½"..30.00
Elberta, jardiniere, 5½"..50.00
Elberta, nut dish, 3"..25.00
Elberta, vase, 5"..30.00
Eocean, candlestick, grapes on wide base, sgn Ferrell, 9"..........200.00
Eocean, vase, fish, gr/pk on dk gr to lt pk, sgn EG, 11"..........325.00
Eocean, vase, floral, sgn LJB, 11½"................................350.00
Eocean, vase, floral, sgn Mt, 10½"................................125.00
Etched Matt, plaque, lady w/flowing hair, sgn Pickens, 18"..........750.00
Etched Matt, vase, profile portrait of lady, 20½"................................700.00
Etched Matt, vase, 10½"..125.00
Etched Matt, vase, 6½"..70.00
Etna, bowl, mouse, 2½"..185.00
Etna, vase, floral, pk on gray to wht, 11"................................190.00
Etna, vase, floral, 6½"..100.00
Etna, vase, grapes/vines, shouldered, 15"................................500.00
Etna, vase, lizard, 4½"..190.00
Evergreen, vase, 4"..25.00
Fairfield, vase, 9½"..50.00
Flemish, comport, w/lid, 8½"..225.00
Flemish, inkwell..600.00
Flemish, jardiniere, 6"..95.00
Flemish, tub, hdls, 4½"..55.00
Flemish, vase, 6½"..50.00
Fleron, batter pitcher, 11½"..80.00
Fleron, bowl, flared rim, #J-6, 3"..15.00
Fleron, vase, flared rim, 9"..20.00
Florala, candle holders, 5", pr..65.00
Florala, console bowl, 11"..35.00
Florenzo, fan vase, 5½"..30.00
Florenzo, planter, 3½"..35.00
Florenzo, window box, 3"..35.00
Floretta, ewer, grape cluster, 10½"................................135.00
Floretta, vase, grape cluster, 5½"................................75.00
Forest, jardiniere, 4½"..45.00
Forest, pitcher, glossy, 5"..110.00
Forest, teapot, w/lid, glossy, 4½"................................125.00
Forest, tub planter, hdls, shape #3, 3½"................................60.00
Forest, tub planter, 6"..65.00
Forest, window box, 5¼x14½"..250.00
Fruitone, vase, 6"..30.00
Garden Ornaments, gnome on boulder, 18"................................1,600.00
Garden Ornaments, gnome on toadstool, 14"................................1,200.00
Glendale, vase, bird in flight, 6½"................................200.00
Glendale, vase, bird in nest, 12"................................325.00
Glendale, vase, 2 birds on branch, 8½"................................300.00
Gloria, bowl, gr, #G-15, 3½"..25.00
Gloria, ewer, brn, #G-12, 9"..40.00
Goldenglow, bowl, 16x3½"..40.00
Goldenglow, bud vase, 8½"..35.00
Goldenglow, candle holder, triple, 3½"................................40.00
Goldenglow, ginger jar, 8"..90.00
Goldenglow, wall pocket, 11"..55.00
Graystone Garden Ware, jardiniere & pedestal, 28"..........175.00
Greenbriar, pitcher, 10"..80.00
Greenbriar, vase, 6"..40.00
Greenbriar, vase, 8"..70.00
Greora, strawberry pot, 8½"..115.00
Greora, vase, ftd, 4½"..50.00

Hobart flower frog, 8½", $95.00.

Hobart, bowl, 9½x3"	30.00
Hudson, lamp base, bluebird, 14"	350.00
Hudson, vase, floral, bl, 7½"	110.00
Hudson, vase, floral, sgn M Timberlake, 12"	450.00
Hudson, vase, floral, sgn Pillsbury, 12"	400.00
Hudson, vase, fruited branch, hdls, sgn Pillsbury, 13½"	800.00
Hudson, vase, lg florals, sgn Pillsbury, baluster, 15"	800.00
Hudson, vase, lg irises, McLaughlin, 15½"	1,200.00
Hudson, vase, lg sunflower, Pillsbury, hdls, 9x10"	450.00
Hudson, vase, mtn scene, sgn Pillsbury, 8"	800.00
Hudson, vase, pumpkin field, sgn Pillsbury, 8"	1,300.00
Hudson, vase, sailboat scene, sgn McLaughlin, 27½"	6,000.00
Hudson, vase, soldier w/horse on wht, 11½"	1,900.00
Hudson, vase, tiger, 8"	1,100.00
Hudson, vase, trees/mtns, blk outlined, exhibition stamp, 15"	1,800.00
Hudson, vase, 2 birds on branch, 15"	800.00
Hudson-Light, vase, floral, 15"	350.00
Hudson-Perfecto, vase, floral, sgn C Leffler, 9½"	360.00
Hudson-Perfecto, vase, floral, sgn DE, 6½"	135.00
Hudson-Perfecto, vase, irises, purple on lav to pk, mk, 7"	180.00
Hunter, vase, deer, hdls, #343, 6½"	400.00
Hunter, vase, duck, pillow form, 4¾"	400.00
Ivoris, ginger jar, 8½"	40.00
Ivoris, vase, hdls, 7"	35.00
Ivory, bottle vase, 9"	45.00
Ivory, jardiniere, 6½"	45.00
Ivory, planter, sq, 4"	50.00
Ivory, vase, 10½"	70.00
Ivory, wall vase, eagle letter pocket, 9"	165.00

Jap Birdimal mug with geisha and trees, 5½", $600.00.

Ivory, window box, 15½"	60.00
Jap Birdimal, mug, geisha/cat, 5"	550.00
Jap Birdimal, vase, bl trees, 14"	575.00
Kenova, bowl, 3½"	40.00
Kenova, vase, 5½"	75.00
Klyro, bud vase, 7"	35.00
Klyro, candle holder, 9½"	40.00
Klyro, fan vase, 6"	45.00
Klyro, planter, 4"	40.00
Knifewood, bowl, glossy, 4"	80.00
Knifewood, vase, 7"	125.00
L'Art Nouveau, bank, corn, 8"	150.00
L'Art Nouveau, console bowl, glossy, 6x12"	100.00
L'Art Nouveau, ewer, floral, 14½"	125.00
L'Art Nouveau, vase, floral, 8"	85.00
L'Art Nouveau, vase, lady's profile on ftd shell form, 8x7"	160.00
LaMar, vase, mtns/palm trees on dk red, 12"	400.00
LaMar, vase, 6"	100.00
LaSa, lamp, sgn, 8"	230.00
LaSa, vase, trees, EX work & glaze, 13"	450.00
LaSa, vase, trees/mtns on gold, paper label, 11"	400.00
LaSa, vase, 8"	275.00
Lavonia, vase, floral, 9"	15.00
Lido, ewer, turq/bl, 10½"	45.00
Lido, vase, pk, 6"	30.00
Lorbeek, vase, 7"	65.00
Lorbeek, wall pocket, 8½"	65.00
Loru, cornucopia, bl, 4"	15.00
Loru, vase, bl, 8"	15.00
Louella, powder jar, 4"	40.00
Louella, vase, 9½"	40.00
Louwelsa, Blue; lamp base, irises, wht on bl, 10"	550.00
Louwelsa, Blue; vase, daffodils, 7"	485.00
Louwelsa, Blue; vase, sailboat, C Leffler, tall/sq, 11x3"	900.00
Louwelsa, candle holder, floral, sgn HL, 9"	95.00
Louwelsa, ewer, floral, sgn Burgess, 6"	175.00
Louwelsa, humidor, floral, sgn CA, 5½"	380.00
Louwelsa, mug, Black man portrait, 7"	1,400.00
Louwelsa, mug, floral, sgn HM, 8½"	220.00
Louwelsa, mug, monk portrait, 7"	800.00
Louwelsa, pitcher, sgn MT, 5"	150.00
Louwelsa, tankard, grape cluster, sgn Ferrell, 17"	600.00
Louwelsa, tankard, smiling Black man, RG Turner, rstr, 17"	400.00
Louwelsa, vase, chicks, 11½"	1,800.00
Louwelsa, vase, dog, sgn L Blake, 7"	900.00
Louwelsa, vase, floral, sgn HM, 11"	250.00
Louwelsa, vase, floral, sgn VA, 6½"	150.00
Louwelsa, vase, floral, 4"	135.00
Louwelsa, vase, grape cluster & leaves, sgn Lybarger, 17"	800.00
Louwelsa, vase, pansies w/silver overlay, 6½"	2,000.00
Louwelsa, vase, silver overlay vine on florals, sm hdls, 7"	800.00
Louwelsa, vase, 2 kittens, ftd pillow form, 7"	2,050.00
Lustre, bud vase, lt gray, 6"	25.00
Lustre, candlestick, brn, 8"	30.00
Lustre, Cloudburst bowl, 4x9"	50.00
Lustre, wall pocket, 7½"	48.00
Luxor, bud vase, 7½"	12.00
Luxor, vase, 9"	15.00
Malverne, candle holders, 2", pr	40.00
Malverne, pillow vase, leaves, 8½"	45.00
Malverne, vase, leaves, 5½"	25.00
Malverne, wall pocket, leaves, 11"	65.00
Manhattan, vase, hdls, gr leaves, 8"	45.00
Marbleized, bowl, 7"	40.00

Marbleized, vase, 7½"	50.00
Marengo, vase, 8"	185.00
Marvo, bowl, brn, 5"	40.00
Marvo, console bowl, gr, 2½x10"	40.00
Marvo, hanging basket, gr, 5"	75.00
Matt Floretta, tankard, apples, sgn CD, 13½"	450.00
Matt Gr, vase, hexagonal w/angle base, emb 'windows,' 10"	270.00
Melrose, basket, 10"	180.00
Melrose, vase, hdls, 5"	75.00
Mi-Flo, vase, floral, #M-8, 7"	30.00
Minerva, vase, flamingos, 8½"	395.00
Minerva, vase, trees, 13½"	300.00
Mirror Black, bud vase, 5½"	25.00
Mirror Black, wall vase, 6"	30.00
Monochrome, bowl, 2½x10"	25.00
Monochrome, comport, 8"	55.00
Montego, vase, 5"	40.00
Muskota, bowl w/goose, 4½"	200.00
Muskota, fence, 5"	70.00
Muskota, fish & stump, 5"	125.00
Muskota, fish bowl base w/reaching cat, rpr, 10x11"	500.00
Muskota, fishing boy, 6½"	150.00
Muskota, gate w/pots & cats, 7"	400.00
Muskota, girl w/flowers & hat, 9"	150.00
Muskota, girl w/watering can, 7"	200.00
Muskota, kneeling woman, 7½"	150.00
Muskota, nude on rock, 8"	200.00
Neiska, bowl, ftd, bl, 4"	30.00
Noval, comport, 5½"	60.00
Novelty Line, ash tray, 3 pigs, 4"	80.00
Novelty Line, kangaroo & pouch, 5½"	85.00
Novelty Line, tray, fox, 3x7"	135.00
Novelty Line, wall pocket, 10"	85.00
Oak Leaf, basket, #G-1, 7½"	35.00
Oak Leaf, wall pocket, 8½"	40.00
Panella, bowl, ftd, 3½"	25.00
Paragon, bowl/vase, bl, 4½"	40.00
Pastel, planter, #P-10, 6"	40.00
Pastel, planter, #P-5, 4x8"	30.00
Pastel, vase, #P-14, 6½"	20.00
Patra, basket, 5½"	75.00
Patra, vase, hdls, 4½"	50.00
Patricia, pelican planter, 5"	50.00
Patricia, swan planter, 3½"	40.00
Patricia, vase, swan hdls, 8½"	65.00
Pearl, bud vase, 7"	40.00
Pearl, candle holders, 8½", pr	85.00
Pearl, wall vase, 7"	85.00
Perfecto, ewer, floral, #436, sgn HP, 17"	450.00
Pierre, pitcher, brn, 5"	30.00
Pierre, sugar bowl, pk, 2"	15.00
Pierre, teapot, pk, 8½"	60.00
Pumila, vase, 9"	40.00
Ragenda, vase, 12"	40.00
Roba, cornucopia, 5½"	20.00
Roba, ewer, 6"	30.00
Rochelle, vase, floral, sgn TF, 6"	200.00
Roma, bowl, 3"	35.00
Roma, bud vase, dbl, 8½"	35.00
Roma, bud vase, 5"	20.00
Roma, candelabrum, 5-light, 8"	55.00
Roma, comport, 5"	40.00
Roma, console, w/liner, 6½"	60.00
Roma, jardiniere, 5"	22.00

Roma, log planter, 3x10½"	40.00
Roma, tobacco jar, 7½"	200.00
Roma, wall pocket, 7"	50.00
Rosemont, jardiniere, 4½"	100.00
Rosemont, vase, bird on branch, 10½"	300.00
Rudlor, vase, hdls, 9"	15.00
Sabrinian, vase, hdls, 10½"	80.00
Sabrinian, window box, 3½x9"	50.00
Senic, pillow vase, #S-11, 7½"	25.00
Senic, vase, #S-4, 5½"	20.00
Sicard, mug, 3½"	600.00
Sicard, pitcher, hdl center top, boat form, sgn, 3¼x4½"	300.00
Sicard, plaque, butterflies/thorns, sgn front/bk, 12½"	2,800.00
Sicard, vase, berries/leaves, purple/gr, no mk/#6, 5", NM	300.00
Sicard, vase, cloverleaves, maroon/gold, sgn, 5"	500.00
Sicard, vase, daisies, sm rim, shaped cylinder, 9½"	900.00
Sicard, vase, daisies/loose petals, waisted cylinder, 7"	600.00

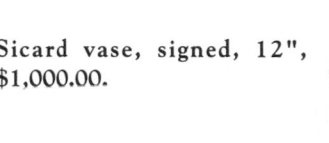

Sicard vase, signed, 12",
$1,000.00.

Sicard, vase, emb floral, gr/purple irid, sgn, 12"	475.00
Sicard, vase, floral, gold on burgundy, 9"	800.00
Sicard, vase, gold snail motif on bl/gr, swirl mold, 8x6"	1,300.00
Sicard, vase, mistletoe, ovoid w/waisted neck, 5"	450.00
Sicard, vase, pillow form, 6½x10"	700.00
Sicard, vase, scrolling leaves, cylinder on wide ft, 13"	1,100.00
Silhouette, vase, fisherboy, sgn Timberlake, 15"	1,400.00
Silvertone, vase, floral, 8½"	125.00
Silvertone, vase, hdls, floral, 11½"	220.00
Softone, bud vase, dbl, pk, 9"	28.00
Softone, planter, bl, 4x8"	35.00
Souevo, bowl, 2½x6½"	50.00
Souevo, vase, 8"	85.00
Sydonia, console, bl/gr, 17x6"	40.00
Sydonia, cornucopia, gr, 8"	25.00
Sydonia, fan vase, bl/gr, 6½"	40.00
Sydonia, planter, bl/gr, 4"	35.00
Sydonia, wall vase, 4-tube, bl, 9½"	30.00
Teakwood, umbrella stand, 21"	325.00
Tivoli, bowl, 2½"	65.00
Trellis, wall shelf, turq, 10½"	55.00
Turada, lamp base, 8"	600.00
Turada, umbrella stand, 21"	650.00
Turkis, vase, 5"	30.00
Tutone, basket, 7½"	85.00
Tutone, planter, 5½"	55.00

Tutone, vase, 11" **70.00**
Tutone, vase, 4" **30.00**
Tutone, wall pocket, 10½" **55.00**
Utility Ware, teapot, pineapple, 6½" **125.00**
Velva, vase, gr, 6" **20.00**
Voile, fan vase, 7" **45.00**
Voile, vase, 9" **60.00**
Warwick, basket, 9" **80.00**
Warwick, bud vase, 7" **30.00**
Warwick, jardiniere, 7" **60.00**
Warwick, pillow vase, 7" **40.00**
Warwick, vase, 4½" **40.00**
Wht & Decorated, lamp base, floral shoulder, 9½x11" **150.00**
Wild Rose, basket, floral, 5½" **15.00**
Wild Rose, vase, hdls, floral, 8½" **20.00**
Woodcraft, bowl, 3" **45.00**
Woodcraft, fan vase, 8" **30.00**
Woodcraft, hanging basket, w/owl, 5½x10" **225.00**
Woodcraft, hanging basket, 6" **60.00**
Woodcraft, owl vase, 16" **600.00**
Woodrose, bowl, 2½x8½" **45.00**
Woodrose, jardiniere, 7" **80.00**
Xenia, vase, floral, red/gr on purple, waisted w/hdls, 7" **300.00**
Zona, baby plate, squirrels in center, rolled ABC rim, 7½" **40.00**
Zona, bowl, apples, 9½" **25.00**
Zona, comport, floral, 5½" **50.00**
Zona, creamer, strutting duck, 3½" **35.00**
Zona, mug, rabbit/bird on branch, 3" **40.00**
Zona, pickle dish, 11" **65.00**
Zona, pitcher, strutting duck, 5½" **60.00**
Zona, pitcher, strutting duck, 7" **60.00**
Zona, salad plate, apples, 7½" **15.00**

West Coast Pottery

Founded in Burbank, California, West Coast Pottery has become known for finely decorated artware and novelties.

Bowl, pk, sq, low, 8" **6.00**
Bowl, shell, pk, 1¼x7¼x5¼" **8.00**
Vase, aqua/pk swirl, abstract hdls **32.00**
Vase, Dutch girl, urn form **28.00**
Vase, shell, turq, #201 ....**7.50**

Western Americana

The collecting of Western Americana encompases a broad spectrum of memorabilia and collectibles. Examples of various areas within the main stream would include the following fields: weapons, bottles, photographs, mining/railroad artifacts, cowboy paraphernalia, farm and ranch implements, maps, barbed wire, tokens, Indian relics, saloon/gambling items, and branding irons. Some of these areas have their own separate listings in this book.

Western Americana is not only a collecting field but is also a collecting *era* with specific boundries. Depending upon which field the collector decides to specialize in, prices can start at a few dollars and run into the hundreds.

There has been an increased amount of focus on Western Americana collectibles in recent years, and there are several books that explore this field. For additional reading, we recommend *Treasury of Frontier Relics* by Les Beitz and *Western Memorabilia* by William Ketchum, Jr. To better understand the complexities of pricing various types of collectibles, read as much as possible concerning the field you prefer. While one strand of barbed wire may be worth $5.00, another may be worth $50.00; the same holds true in all fields.

Our advisor for this category is Warren Anderson; he is listed in the Directory under Utah.

Branding iron, older wooden socket type, EX **15.00**
Bridle, braided horsehair, mc diamond design, EX.............**85.00**
Chaps, bat-wing style w/pockets, EX, pr **175.00**
Chaps, General Leather, tooled belt, EX **200.00**
Chaps, 13 conchos ea leg, EX fringe, unmk **300.00**
Fence tool, wire cutters/staple puller/hammer, 1880s **25.00**
Hitching post, CI, tree form, stubby 'branches,' mk, 62½" **100.00**
Hobbles, leather w/swivel chain **40.00**
Holster, tooled leather, flap style, w/pouch & skirt, sm **35.00**
Map case, lg leather sheet, w/hdl/strap/buckle, 1850s, VG **40.00**
Poster, Life of Buffalo Bill, Custer/horsebk, 1912, 42x28" **440.00**
Rope, horsehair, early, 37 ft **250.00**
Rope, 4-strand braided rawhide, 10 ft **145.00**
Saddle, Great West Saddlery, Calgary Alberta, high bk **350.00**
Saddle, Stockton, tooled seat, 1860s...................................**275.00**
Saddle, tooled leather, western style, 1930s, EX **250.00**
Saddlebags, N Porter, AZ, rnd bottom pouches, silver buckles **195.00**
Spurs, Buerman, drop shank, pr **68.00**
Spurs, Buerman, str shank **65.00**
Spurs, Herculese Bronze, horse heads on sides, pr **175.00**
Spurs, Mexican style silver inlay, 2½" rowels, pr................**90.00**
Spurs, North & Judd, pr..**68.00**
Spurs, plain, narrow heel band, 10 points, 2" rowel, pr, EX **80.00**
Stirrups, brass conquistador type from NM, 1800, 10x4" **145.00**
Stirrups, heart form, wrought iron, 1-pc, early, pr.............**90.00**

Westmoreland

Originally titled the Specialty Glass Company, Westmoreland began operations in East Liverpool, Ohio, producing utility items as well as tableware in milk glass and crystal. When the company moved to Grapeville, PA, in 1890, lamps, vases, covered animal dishes, and decorative plates were introduced. Prior to the 1920s, Westmoreland was a major manufacturer of carnival glass and soon thereafter added a line of lovely reproduction art glass items. High-quality milk glass became their speciality, accounting for about 90% of their production. Black glass was introduced in the 1940s, and later in the decade ruby-stained pieces and items decorated in the Mary Gregory style became popular. By the 1960s, colored glassware was being produced, examples of which are very popular with collectors today.

Early pieces were marked with a paper label; by the 1960s the ware was embossed with a superimposed 'WG.' The last mark was a circle containing 'Westmoreland' around the perimeter and a large 'W' in the center. The company closed in 1985. See also Animal Dishes with Covers and Carnival Glass.

Ash tray, Beaded Grape, milk glass, HP roses & bows, 4"...............**18.00**
Ash tray, Old Quilt, milk glass, 4" **20.00**
Ash tray, Panelled Grape, milk glass, 4" **9.00**
Banana bowl, pk MOP..**30.00**
Banana bowl, Wildflower & Lace, bl **25.00**
Basket, Am Hobnail, lilac opal...**30.00**
Basket, Coral, milk glass **25.00**
Basket, Panelled Grape, milk glass, oval **30.00**
Basket, Panelled Grape, red carnival, ltd ed, lg...................**75.00**
Bowl, Beaded Grape, milk glass, gold trim, ftd, w/lid, 9" **45.00**
Bowl, Beaded Grape, milk glass, sq, ftd, w/lid, 7"................**28.00**

Bowl, Della Robbia, flared, plain, 12" 45.00
Bowl, fruit; Wildflower & Lace, 10" 20.00
Bowl, Old Quilt, milk glass, crimped, ftd, 9" 50.00
Bowl, Old Quilt, milk glass, cupped, ftd, 7" 50.00
Bowl, Old Quilt, milk glass, lipped, rare, 12" 100.00
Bowl, Old Quilt, milk glass, rnd, shallow, 9" 42.50
Bowl, Panelled Grape, milk glass, lipped, 9" 38.00
Bowl, Panelled Grape, milk glass, rnd, shallow, 14"........95.00
Box, Beaded Grape, milk glass, HP roses & bows, ftd, 4" 40.00
Box, trinket; Golden Bouquet, blk 18.00
Butter dish, Old Quilt, milk glass, ¼-lb...................30.00
Cake salver, Old Quilt, milk glass, skirted, 12"...........60.00
Cake salver, Panelled Grape, milk glass, ftd/skirted, 11" ..55.00
Candle holder, Panelled Grape, milk glass, Colonial hdl, 5"..25.00
Candlestick, dolphin hdl, bl opaque, pr....................75.00
Candlestick, Panelled Grape, milk glass w/gold, 4", pr.....35.00
Candlestick, Ring & Petal, milk glass, pr 30.00
Candy dish, Argonaut Shell, ruby, dolphin hdls.............45.00
Candy dish, Della Robbia, scalloped, ftd...................40.00
Candy dish, Old Quilt, milk glass, low ft..................20.00
Candy dish, ruby, #300, 8".................................85.00
Champagne, English Hobnail, short 12.00
Cigar holder, etched, #352.................................15.00
Cocktail, Della Robbia.....................................10.00
Cocktail, English Hobnail 7.00
Compote, Della Robbia, milk glass, ftd.....................26.00

1861 Lincoln Drape covered compote, $150.00 and up.

Compote, Sawtooth, milk glass, w/lid, 15" 115.00
Cookie jar, Grape & Cable, vaseline........................90.00
Cordial, English Hobnail...................................10.00
Creamer & sugar bowl, Della Robbia, colored fruit 30.00
Creamer & sugar bowl, Maple Leaf, blk, repro 18.00
Creamer & sugar bowl, Maple Leaf, sapphire bl 25.00
Creamer & sugar bowl, Old Quilt, milk glass, w/lid.........50.00
Cruet, Princess Feather, pr................................50.00
Cup, Panelled Grape, milk glass............................ 7.50
Cup & saucer, Della Robbia.................................20.00
Cup & saucer, Old Quilt, milk glass........................27.50
Cup & saucer, Panelled Grape, milk glass...................14.00
Dish, covered; bunny w/ptd eggs on lace bottom, lg........175.00
Dish, covered; Lovebirds, milk glass.......................38.00
Dish, covered; Santa in Sleigh, HP.........................40.00
Epergne, Panelled Grape, milk glass, 14", +8½" vase 185.00
Fruit cocktail, Old Quilt, milk glass, 3½".................22.50
Goblet, Panelled Grape, amber, 5¾".........................14.00

Goblet, Panelled Grape, amethyst...........................22.00
Goblet, Panelled Grape, milk glass.........................14.00
Honey dish, Old Quilt, milk glass 22.00
Ice bucket, English Hobnail................................37.00
Jardiniere, Old Quilt, milk glass, str style, 6½".........40.00
Jardiniere, Panelled Grape, milk glass, cupped, ftd, 6½"...25.00
Jardiniere, Panelled Grape, milk glass, ftd, 5"............20.00
Mint dish, Am Hobnail, lilac opal, dbl crimped 18.00
Nappy, Panelled Grape, milk glass, bell shape, 5".........23.00
Pitcher, Old Quilt, blk carnival, exprimental pc, very rare ..75.00
Pitcher, Old Quilt, milk glass, 1-qt, +8 9-oz tumblers 185.00
Pitcher, Old Quilt, milk glass, 3-qt.......................40.00
Planter, Panelled Grape, milk glass, 3x8½"................30.00
Plate, angel w/mandolin, amethyst carnival.................25.00
Plate, Beaded Edge, milk glass, 6"......................... 4.00
Plate, Della Robbia, milk glass, 10½".....................30.00
Plate, English Hobnail, 13½"..............................45.00
Plate, Indian chief, purple carnival 35.00
Plate, kittens, bl opaque..................................32.00
Plate, Panelled Grape, milk glass, 8½"....................15.00
Plate, Zodiac, 14½".......................................55.00
Punch bowl, red carnival, #575, lg........................575.00
Punch set, #1881..500.00
Punch set, Pineapple & Grape, milk glass..................285.00
Punch set, red carnival.................................1,300.00
Relish, English Hobnail, oval, 8" 12.00
Relish, Old Quilt, milk glass, divided, 8"................40.00
Rose bowl, Panelled Grape, milk glass, cupped, ftd, 4".....16.00
Shakers, Lotus, milk glass, pr.............................40.00
Shakers, Panelled Grape, milk glass, sm, pr 15.00
Shakers, Princess Feather, pr 24.00
Sherbet, Della Robbia, 3½"................................ 9.00
Sherbet, Panelled Grape, milk glass, low ft...............17.50
Spooner, Panelled Grape, milk glass, 6"...................28.00
Sweetmeat, Old Quilt, milk glass, w/lid 30.00
Sweetmeat, Wildflower & Lace...............................18.00
Syrup, Old Quilt, milk glass...............................24.00
Toothpick holder, Panelled Grape, milk glass...............15.00
Tray, Panelled Grape, milk glass, oval, 9"................65.00
Tray, serving; Wildflower & Lace, bl MOP 20.00
Tumbler, Beaded Edge, milk glass, ftd 7.50
Tumbler, Della Robbia, milk glass, gold trim, 8-oz.........20.00
Tumbler, iced tea; Della Robbia, ftd.......................16.00
Tumbler, Old Quilt, milk glass, 8-oz.......................14.00
Tumbler, Panelled Grape, milk glass, 8-oz..................16.00
Vase, bud; Am Hobnail, lilac opal 12.00
Vase, bud; Panel, pk.......................................10.00
Vase, jack-in-the-pulpit; Am Hobnail, lilac opal...........35.00
Vase, Old Quilt, milk glass, bell shape, 9"...............48.00
Vase, Old Quilt, milk glass, fan form 22.00
Vase, Panelled Grape, milk glass, bell shape, 11½" 32.00
Vase, Panelled Grape, milk glass, bell shape, 9" 22.50
Vase, swan hdl, milk glass.................................22.50
Vase, swung; Old Quilt, milk glass 30.00
Vase, swung; Panelled Grape, milk glass, 16"..............16.00
Wine, Old Quilt, milk glass................................20.00
Wine, Panelled Grape, amber, 4" 8.00

Western Stoneware Co.

The Western Stoneware Co. was formed in 1906, a merger of seven companies: Monmouth Pottery, Weir Pottery, Macomb Pottery, Macomb Stoneware, D. Culbertson Stoneware, Clinton Stoneware, and Fort Dodge Stoneware. Besides their stoneware products, they also manufactured gardenware and some artware. One by one each branch of the corporation closed, and today only one plant remains, located in Monmouth on the site of the old Weir Pottery.

Bottle, hot water; bl/wht, mk, NM 225.00
Bowl, chili; Marcrest, 6" 3.00
Bowl, flower & flame on tan, brn int, 6" 7.00
Bowl, Marcrest, 8" 10.00
Pitcher, Marcrest, 6" 12.00
Poultry fount, cone shape, 2-pc, wire bail........................25.00
Umbrella stand, raised butterflies on brn 60.00
Water cooler, gray w/bl leaves, w/lid, 8-gal, M................175.00

Wheatley, T. J.

In 1880 after a brief association with the Coultry Works, Thomas J. Wheatley opened his own studio in Cincinnati, Ohio, claiming to have been the first to discover the secret of underglaze slip decoration on an unbaked clay vessel. He applied for and was granted a patent for his process. Demand for his ware increased to the point that several artists were hired to decorate the ware. The company incorporated in 1880 as the Cincinnati Art Pottery, but until 1882 it continued to operate under Wheatley's name. Ware from this period is marked 'T.J. Wheatley' or 'T.J.W. and Co.,' and it may be dated.

Bowl, emb florals, gr matt, mk, 3x8½" 300.00
Vase, emb buds/leaves, gr matt, 4 flared buttresses, 7x9½" 750.00
Vase, emb leaves, gr matt, bulbous top/broad body, 12", EX.... 2,100.00
Vase, emb leaves on hdls/sides, mustard yel, #616, 17½" 1,650.00
Vase, emb stalks & buds, gr matt, bottle form, 8" 275.00
Vase, emb stylized floral, leaves at wide base, gr matt, 10" 475.00
Vase, florals, Limoges style, gray & gr, 7".....................................350.00
Wall pocket, emb ribbed leaves & buds, gr matt, 8x9"..................225.00

Whieldon

Thomas Whieldon was regarded as the finest of the Staffordshire potters of the mid-1700s. He produced marbled and black Egyptian wares, as well as tortoise shell, a mottled brown-glazed earthenware accented with touches of blue and yellow. In 1754 he became a partner of Josiah Wedgwood. Other potters produced similar wares, and today the term Whieldon is used generically.

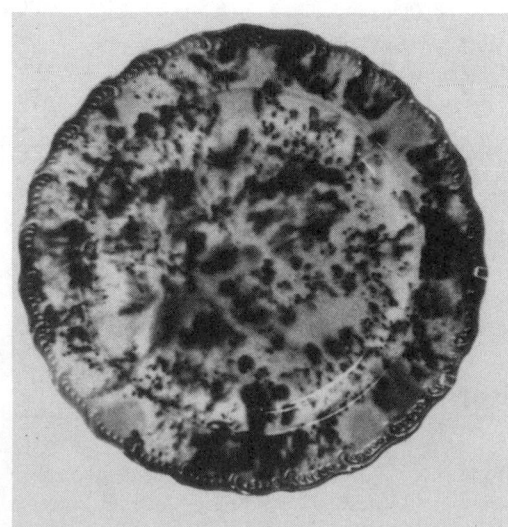

Plate, overall tortoise shell glaze, scalloped, 9", $250.00.

Coffeepot, tortoise shell w/emb leaves, rprs, 9½" 1,300.00
Creamer, gr/brn mottle, stain/hairline, 2¾" 325.00
Dish, leaf shape, bird in tree, polychrome, 8x10", EX 800.00
Pitcher, brn mottle, sm flake/hairline, 5⅝" 550.00
Pitcher, mc mottle, emb pineapple, minor wear, rpl lid, 5½" ... 1,100.00
Plate, emb foliage, polychrome glaze, scalloped, 8", EX 200.00
Plate, tortoise shell, emb scalloped feather rim, 10", EX 300.00
Plate, tortoise shell, emb scalloped rim, 9", EX.........................100.00
Plate, tortoise shell, emb scalloped rim, 9⅜", EX......................350.00
Plate, tortoise shell, 4-color, octagonal, 9¼" 425.00
Plate, tortoise shell w/gr & yel, 6¼", NM 425.00
Tea set, brn mottle, 2¾" pot+sug/cr+4 c/s+caddy, miniature .. 1,600.00
Teapot, bl/brn agate, 3 paw ft, 4", NM 5,400.00
Teapot, brn mottle, appl vintage, rpr lid, 4⅜" 850.00
Teapot, emb cabbage leaves, rabbit finial, mc glaze, 4¾", EX .. 4,150.00
Teapot, emb cauliflower in gr/wht, sm chip, 4" 1,200.00
Teapot, fruit & flowers, polychrome/clear glazes, rpr, 5" 800.00
Teapot, mc stripes, paneled, chinoiserie w/leaf spout, 5¼" 4,400.00
Teapot, tortoise shell, emb leaf designs, minor wear, 4½" 1,500.00
Toby, clear glaze w/brn & gr mottle, sm stains/chip, 9½" 1,400.00

Wicker

Wicker is the basket-like material used in many types of furniture and accessories. It may be made from bamboo cane, rattan, reed, or artificial fibers. It is airy, lightweight, and very popular in hot regions.

Imported from the Orient in the 18th century, it was first manufactured in the United States in about 1850. The elaborate, closely-woven Victorian designs belong to the mid-to-late 1800s, and the simple styles with coarse reedings usually indicate a post-1900 production. Art Deco styles followed in the twenties and thirties.

The most important consideration in buying wicker is condition – it can be restored, but only by a professional. Age is an important factor, but be aware that 'Victorian-style' furniture is being manufactured today.

Armchair, Nouveau styling, Heywood-Wakefield, 1920s.............450.00
Armchair, wide arms/crest rail, Heywood-Wakefield, 33" 700.00
Basket, long cone shape, hdls, hanging, old 40.00
Basket, sewing; tufted lining, brass/enamel thread holder 25.00
Buggy, Heywood-Wakefld, parasol/rubber tires/cord uphl, 38".....425.00
Chair, side; ornate fan bk, pressed seat, fancy apron 175.00
Chaise, wicker legs, openweave apron, simple style 395.00
Conversation bench, early 1900s 425.00
Cradle, doll; swinging, sm..100.00
Cradle, doll; tight weave, w/hood, ca 1920s, lg............................250.00
Desk, 40x36"...350.00
Footstool, sq base, rnd top w/uphl insert, 9½x12" 100.00
Highchair, Victorian, woven braid trim, simple style 200.00
Lamp, openweave shade, gourd base, att Stickley, 24x19" 300.00
Lamp, table; simple, w/shade, 24" 75.00
Rack, magazine; reed, openweave sides, bentwood hdl 130.00
Rocker, loose weave, sq bk w/high armrest 250.00
Rocker, oak/wicker, padded spring seat, very ornate, 1890s 275.00
Rocker, platform; rolled serpentine fr, crown headrest 325.00
Settee, w/arms, heart/scroll bk, sides & legs, 58" 425.00
Stroller, doll; Victorian, high-wheel, orig pnt/upholstery.............495.00
Table, mahog top, lower wicker shelf, flaring legs, 54" 750.00
Table, scrollwork, curved legs, 20x16x16" 120.00
Tea cart, tight weave, bottom shelf, front wheels, top tray...........340.00
Tea cart, 2-tier, simple weave, wood fr, 30x36" L 365.00
Tray, breakfast; w/cup holder, paper rack on side, 1920s.............110.00

Willets

The Willets Manufacturing Company of Trenton, New Jersey, produced a type of belleek porcelain during the late 1880s and 1890s. Examples were often marked with a coiled snake that formed a 'W' with 'Willets' below and 'Belleek' above.

Not all Willets is factory decorated. Items painted by amateurs outside the factory are worth considerably less. In the listings below, all items are belleek unless noted otherwise. For more information, we recommend *American Belleek* with full-color photos and current market values, by Mary Frank Gaston. You will find her address in the Directory under Texas.

Bowl, pk buds, much gold, coral-like hdls, ruffled, mk, 4"	175.00
Chalice, red berries/gr leaves w/gold, mk, 11½"	450.00
Creamer & sugar bowl, floral & gold paste, dragon hdls	225.00
Creamer & sugar bowl, gold Nouveau decor, ped ft, #105	85.00
Cup & saucer, bouillon; Cactus, yel w/gold cactus hdls	345.00
Cup & saucer, demi; floral, gold on ivory, mk	235.00
Cup & saucer, fleur-de-lis & floral w/gold, mk	80.00
Cup & saucer, floral band, mk	65.00
Hatpin holder, gold paste decor	90.00
Hatpin holder, ivory, ribbed, mk, 5¼"	95.00
Muffineer, HP pastel floral band w/gold, mk	110.00
Mug, portraits of lady/cherub, artist sgn, mk, 5¼"	900.00
Pitcher, Seashell, wht/rose w/gold, gold coral hdl, 7½x8½"	995.00
Pitcher, tankard; berries, gold dragon hdl, mask spout, 11½"	250.00
Pitcher, tankard; HP cherries/blkberries, sgn MCM, mk, 14½"	175.00
Pitcher, tankard; roses HP on aqua to lav, ornate hdl, mk, 12"	275.00
Plate, portrait, sgn Bower, scalloped	225.00
Vase, birds of paradise, gold on pk lustre, gr mk, 17"	225.00
Vase, marine scenic, tans & gray, mk, 8"	850.00
Vase, Nouveau nude w/filmy veil, Cooper/1910, snake mk, 15"	850.00
Vase, sterling overlay, Deco-style hdls/neck, mk, 12¾"	325.00
Vase, swans on blk & gray, Deco style, sgn, mk, 16"	450.00

Loving cup, purple with green floral, #488, 8", $225.00.

Willow Ware

Willow Ware, inspired no doubt by the numerous patterns of the blue and white Nanking imports, has been popular since the late 18th century and has been made in as many variations as there were manufacturers. English transfer wares by such notable firms as Allerton and Ridgway are the most sought-after and the most expensive. Japanese potters have been producing Willow-patterned dinnerware since the late 1800s, and American manufacturers have followed suit. Although blue is the color most commonly used, mauve, black, and even multi-color Willow Ware may be found. Complementary glassware, tinware, and linens have also been made.

In addition to 'Allerton' and 'Ridgway,' both companies used the possessive forms of their names in marking their wares (i.e. Allerton's, Ridgway's). For further study, we recommend the book *Blue Willow*, with full-color photos and current prices, by Mary Frank Gaston. You will find her address in the Directory under Texas. In the following listings, if no manufacturer is noted, the ware is unmarked.

Baking dish, Hall China, 2 Temples II Simplified, 3x8"	17.50
Biscuit jar, Adderly mk, Temples II, cane hdl, 4½"	110.00
Biscuit jar, unmk English, SP lid & bail, 7"	165.00
Bone dish, Bourne & Leigh, kidney shape, 6¼"	25.00
Bowl, Booth-Royal Doulton, 8½"	35.00
Bowl, Doulton, scalloped rim, flow bl, 7½"	50.00
Bowl, illegible English mk, knob finial, 3½x9"	80.00
Bowl, salad; unmk Japan, 3½x10", +wood-hdld fork & spoon	65.00
Bowl, unmk England, rtcl sides, hdls, 10"	400.00
Bowl, unmk Japan, for bread rising, 15"	135.00
Bowl, vegetable; Adderly, w/lid, 6x10"	85.00
Bowl, vegetable; Allerton, divided, 7¼"	65.00
Bowl, vegetable; Aynsley & Co, beaded outer rim, 9¼"	50.00
Bowl, vegetable; Ridgway, rnd, w/lid	75.00
Bowl, vegetable; unmk English, rectangular, ftd, 12¼x9¼"	110.00
Butter dish, Josiah Wedgwood, 3½x8"	135.00
Butter dish, unmk, open style w/Butter emb on side, 6½"	65.00
Candelabrum, Shenango, creamic & brass, 11", pr	135.00
Canister, Japan, barrel shape, 4-pc set in graduated szs	220.00
Chamber pot, Doulton, 5½x9¼"	265.00
Chamberstick, Gibson & Sons, scalloped edge w/gold, 5" dia	135.00
Chocolate pot, Japan, w/warming base	95.00
Coaster, unmk English, ad for Yorkshire Relish, 4"	22.50
Coffeepot, mk Japan, 7"	60.00
Coffeepot, unmk graniteware, 6"	75.00
Compote, Copeland, earthenware, Mandarin, Dagger border, 8"	135.00
Cookie jar, McCoy, pitcher form, 8"	37.50
Cream soup, unmk, hdls, 2½x6½"	22.50
Cream soup, Wood & Sons, Canton, hdls, 3"	12.50
Creamer, mk England, scalloped rim, 2"	22.50
Creamer, Shanango, hotel ware, 2½"	17.50
Creamer & sugar bowl, Booth	125.00
Creamer & sugar bowl, Buffalo, w/lid	75.00
Creamer & sugar bowl, unmk Japan, gold trim, 3½"	35.00
Cup, chili; unmk Japan, 4x4½"	22.50
Cup, custard; unmk Homer Laughlin, short ped base, 3"	12.50
Cup & saucer, Booth-Royal Doulton	30.00
Cup & saucer, handleless; unmk, pk	55.00
Cup & saucer, Japan	10.00
Cup & saucer, unmk Japan, brn, 1½" cup, 3¼" saucer	17.50
Dish, unmk English, leaf form, 6"	135.00
Drainer, unmk English, Mandarin, 16"	235.00
Egg cup, Buffalo	25.00
Egg cup, Japan, ped base, 1½"	15.00
Ginger jar, unmk, 5x4"	35.00
Gravy boat, Allerton, scalloped, w/underplate, 7½" L	75.00
Gravy boat, Mandarin, Copeland	75.00
Gravy boat, Shenango, 6"	40.00
Gravy boat, Staffordshire, rectangular, w/underplate	30.00
Horseradish dish, unmk	35.00
Humidor, Carlton Ware, Worcester Variant, ca 1900, 5"	185.00
Invalid feeder, Wood & Sons, 2½x6x2"	110.00
Jardiniere, unmk English, 8½x7"	225.00
Knife rest, unmk English, Traditional border, 4"	65.00
Muffineer, unmk, octagonal body, rnd lid, 5½"	60.00

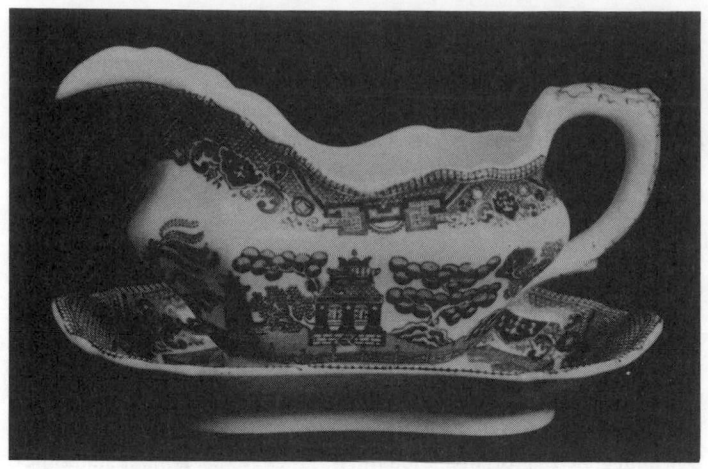

Gravy boat and undertray, Buffalo, $95.00.

Mug, mk Japan, heavy, 4" 22.50
Mug, Sebring Pottery, Temples II, 3½" 12.50
Mustache cup, Minton, gold trim, 2x4" 110.00
Mustard pot, Shenango, 2½" 40.00
Pancake dish, w/lid, Booth's, ca 1906 ....175.00
Pepper mill, unmk, Traditional, 3¾" 110.00
Pie plate, Moriyama, unglazed base for baking, 10" 50.00
Pie server, Made in Japan, 10" 30.00
Pitcher, Allerton, scalloped border, 6" 85.00
Pitcher, Buffalo, bulbous, 7" 85.00
Pitcher, Buffalo, 7" 95.00
Pitcher, Doulton, triangular shape, 6" 135.00
Pitcher, Johnson Bros, red, 6" 45.00
Pitcher, Josiah Wedgwood, mc, 7" 135.00
Pitcher, unmk, simplified Traditional, scalloped, 8" 65.00
Planter, kitten figural, Lipper & Mann Inc, Japan, 9¼" L...165.00
Plate, Buffalo, Traditional center & border, scalloped, 9½"....70.00
Plate, dinner; Meakin 12.00
Plate, grill; German, Traditional motifs, 10¾" 18.00
Plate, Minton, Traditional, scalloped, ca 1860s, 12" 165.00
Plate, Pinder, Bourne & Co, Traditional w/cobalt rim, 9½".....160.00
Plate, unmk, calico, pk, 8" 50.00
Plate, unmk English, Traditional, rtcl rim, 7¼" 165.00
Plate, WT Copeland & Sons, Mandarin, canted corners, 8½" 45.00
Platter, Allerton, 9½" 55.00
Platter, Buffalo, Traditional, scalloped, 11¾" 110.00
Platter, Staffordshire Stone China, hairline, 15" 100.00
Platter, unmk, 11½" 65.00
Pudding mold, mk England, 4¼" 55.00
Relish, WA Adderly, 2-compartment, lug-style hdl, 8" 85.00
Salt cellar, master; unmk English, Traditional, ftd, 2x3" 165.00
Shaving mug, Gibson & Sons, scuttle style, 3¾x5" 220.00
Soap dish & drainer, Doulton w/Made in England, 5½" 165.00
Soup, Wedgwood, hdls, 1940s, +6½" saucer 85.00
Soup plate, Maastrich, 9" 15.00
Soup plate, Shenango, Traditional center & border, 9" 18.00
Syrup, Doulton, flow bl, no lid, 5" 125.00
Syrup & batter jug, Hazel Atlas, frosted, plastic lid, 9", 6" 80.00
Tea set, Ideal Toys, Traditional, plastic, 15-pc 30.00
Teapot, Booth 125.00
Teapot, Buffalo, rnd, lg 150.00
Teapot, Myott, Son & Co, Traditional w/Pictorial border, 8" 75.00
Teapot, N Staffordshire Pottery, 1940s, 4-cup 45.00
Toothpick holder, Buffalo, 1¾" 25.00
Toothpick holder, Josiah Wedgwood, Traditional, 2¼" 45.00

Tumbler, juice; unmk Japan, ceramic 16.00
Tumbler, unmk, clear glass, 5" 10.00
Tumbler, unmk, frosted glass, 5" 22.00
Tureen, unmk English, lid pierced for ladle, ftd, 9x6" 250.00
Vase, Cauldon mk, mc, ovoid, ring hdls, 9" 285.00
Wall pocket, unmk Japan, pitcher form, 6" 27.50
Wash bowl, Wedgwood, 5½x16" 325.00
Waste bowl, Doulton, 3½x6½" 65.00

Winchester

The Winchester Repeating Arms Company lost their important government contract after WWI and of necessity turned to the manufacture of sporting goods, hardware items, tools, etc. to augment their gun production. Between 1920 and 1931, over 7,500 different items, each marked 'Winchester Trademark U.S.A.,' were offered for sale by thousands of Winchester Hardware stores throughout the country. After 1931 the firm became Winchester-Western. See also Knives.

Our advisor for this category is James Anderson; he is listed in the Directory under Minnesota.

Air rifle, #422, M..125.00
Air rifle, boy's, #416..95.00
Air rifle, Winchester MDL 422, M.................................100.00
Badge, Winchester Jr Rifle Corps Pro Marksman 35.00
Baseball glove, EX..275.00
Bicycle, VG+..375.00
Bit, #12..20.00
Box, ranger shell 12.00
Box, repeater shells, 1910s, EX.......................................35.00
Calendar, hunter in duck blind, 1924, 28x14", EX.........625.00
Calendar, store; 1927, VG...250.00
Calendar, store; 1928, EX...350.00
Calendar, 1914, complete, EX 1,200.00
Catalog, pocket; tools, 1923, EX.....................................30.00
Counter change mat, felt, 10½x12½", EX.......................110.00
Dispenser, split shot 50.00
Display case, knife; EX..265.00
Fishing fly, EX on orig card..75.00
Fishing fly rod, VG+...165.00
Fishing reel..65.00
Fishing rod, steel, #5650, NM in orig canvas bag.............90.00
Fishing tackle box, VG...125.00
Flashlight, brass & chrome, 10".......................................35.00
Flashlight, 5-cell, EX..45.00
Flashlight battery 15.00
Folder, shows early store fixtures 25.00
Football helmet, leather, M...325.00
Golf ball 150.00
Golf club, left handed...140.00
Hockey puck...190.00
Household scale 75.00
Knife, celluloid hdl, #2087...90.00
Knife, pearl hdl, #2363...110.00
Knife, stag hdl, #2918...110.00
Knife, stag hdl, Made in Germany, #2967........................95.00
Lawn mower, push type, EX 275.00
Paperweight, 1910 (beware of repros) 55.00
Pencil box...75.00
Plane, #3041...65.00
Plug, 3-hook, EX..185.00
Plug, 5-hook, #9217...225.00

Print, Winchester Hounds, 4 dogs in barn, fr, 32x42", EX 750.00
Radiator plate, identification; brass, for P-40.................................30.00
Rifle, 32-20, 1892, EX 550.00
Screwdriver, #7126, 8" 35.00
Screwdriver, #7160, jeweler's 45.00
Sign, tin, antlers/guns/dead mallards, 1913, 30x35"................. 1,650.00
Split shot, in paper tube, scarce 75.00
Straight razor, EX...85.00
Wrench, lineman's, 12½" 75.00

Three-panel folding arms display, 40", EX, $275.00.

Windmill Weights

Windmill weights were used to protect the windmill's plunger rod from damage during high winds by adding weight that slowed down the speed of the blades.

Buffalo, A-56, gr/brn pnt, 16" L 450.00
Bull, full bodied, CI, no pnt, 13x14" 525.00
Bull, Hanchett, full bodied...500.00
Bull, mk Boss ea side, full bodied, 18-lb 650.00
Horse, bobtail, raised foreleg, 2-part CI casting, 19x21" 3,950.00
Horse, Dempster, bob-tailed, #58, 17x18", EX 350.00
Horse, Dempster, bob-tailed, old rpt, 15½" 300.00
Moon crescent, CI, worn gr pnt, #417, 21-lb, 11x7x2¾" 140.00
Moon crescent, Fairbanks Morse, 1900, 27-lb, 10x6½x3½".........135.00
Rooster, Elgin, CI w/worn red, blk, & wht pnt, 20" 900.00
Rooster, Elgin, U-form base, no pnt, 63-lb, 19½x18" 565.00
Rooster, Elgin #2, no pnt, 34-lb, 16½x15½x4½" 725.00
Rooster, Hummer, orig ball mt, ca 1900, 10x9x1¾" 325.00
Squirrel, Elgin, VG pnt, rare 1,200.00
Star, US Wind Engine, no pnt, 1890s, 14½x14½x3" 400.00
W Form, Althouse Wheeler, WI, ca 1900, 22-lb, 19½x9x2½" ...265.00

Winfield

Founded in Pasadena, California, in 1929, the Winfield Pottery made artware vases as well as dinnerware to order until its closing in 1962. During the 1940s, some of the ware was sub-contracted to American Products of Santa Monica, who used Winfield designs.

Ash tray, leaf form, bl w/wht decor....................................... 5.00
Ash tray, pk w/brn decor, rnd 4.00

Candlestick, tan w/gr int, sq, #225, Pasadena die mk, pr................25.00
Cookie jar, teddy bear on bk on lid, purple drip............................50.00
Shakers, cats, pr 14.00
Vase, iris emb, pk/lt gr on wht clay, #1/44/73, 1931, 6½" 40.00
Water server, wht w/gr palm frond, 3-qt......................................14.00

Wire Ware

Two thousand years B.C. wire was made by cutting sheet metal into strips which were shaped with mallet and file. By the late 13th century, craftsmen in Europe had developed a method of pulling these strips through progressively smaller holes until the desired gauge was obtained. During the Industrial Revolution of the late 1800s, machinery was developed that could produce wire cheaply and easily; and it became a popular commercial commodity. It was used to produce large items such as garden benches and fencing as well as innumerable small pieces for use in the kitchen or on the farm. Beware of reproductions.

Our advisor for this category is Rosella Tinsley; she is listed in the Directory under Kansas.

Apple picker, scalloped top, heavy wire on long pole.....................30.00
Basket, egg; scalloped close-down top, wire hdls, EX....................30.00
Basket, fruit; oval, braided rim, hdls, 2¾x11x6¾" 30.00
Basket, fruit; plate center, heart-shaped hdls, 2¼x7¼"..................78.00
Basket, potato boiling; twisted, loop ft, arched hdl, 4x5"...............95.00
Basket, tulip form, folding, 5½x4½" 40.00
Basket, vegetable; fine wire, bail hdl, ca 1870, 5x7" 35.00
Basket, washing; 2 oval-shaped bowls fit together, hdls.................48.00
Basket, washing; 2-pc ball shape w/diamond design, hdls..............50.00
Beater, batter; curved to fit bowl, wood hdl, EX 15.00
Biscuit pricker, triangular top, twisted, 4½x3" dia 65.00
Bowl, egg; ornate wirework, folds flat, EX................................30.00
Bowl, fine wire, looped ft, cb bottom, 2½x7".............................45.00
Clam lifter, net for draining, spring action, long twist hdl.............25.00
Compote, twisted wire, fancy top hdl, ped base 115.00
Drainer, rnd holder for silverware, ca 1900, 4x15" dia..................50.00
Egg whip, trn wood hdl, EX..20.00
Fork, 3-tine, 15" 10.00
Grater, cheese; rectangular, Xd wires for grating, hdl.................... 7.50
Ladle, lg bowl, long twisted hdl..25.00
Ladle, long trn wood hdl, early, EX 20.00
Pie lifter, 2-prong, wooden Shaker-style hdl 40.00
Pie lifter, 4-prong, spring-action wire hdl, EX...........................37.50
Pie rack, 6-tier, old 65.00
Plant stand, 2-tier, semicircular, 69x46" 550.00
Plant stand, 3-tier, arched top, 56"..175.00
Sieve, trn wood hdl, hook for hanging, 1-qt 6.00
Soap dish, hooks over side of tub 20.00
Spoon, corkscrew design w/dbl-twisted hdl 15.00
Spoon/whip, twisted in crisscross pattern, short wood hdl 8.00

Witch Balls

Witch balls were a Victorian fad touted to be meritorious toward ridding the house of evil spirits, thus warding off sickness and bad luck. Folklore would have it that by wiping the dust and soot from the ball, the spirits were exorcised. It is much more probable, however, considering the fact that such beautiful art glass was used in their making, that the ostensive Victorians perpetrated the myth rather tongue-in-cheek while enjoying them as lovely decorations for their homes.

Aqua w/lg red spots, filled w/plaster of Paris, +vase, 11" 350.00

Aquamarine, opal ribs & loops alternate, 1860s, 3" **100.00**
Clear w/wht loops, +vase, att South Jersey, 14", pr **2,000.00**
Cobalt w/wht loops, +ftd vase, att Pittsburgh, 10" **2,400.00**
Cranberry, 5" **200.00**
Olive gr, +vase, att Saratoga, 4½", NM **600.00**
Plum, 5¼" **80.00**
Tortoise shell, lt amber w/red splotches, ca 1860, 4" **100.00**
Wht opaque, bl/pk flecks, 7" dia **200.00**

Woodcarvings

Wood sculptures represent an important section of American folk art. Wood carvings were made not only by skilled woodworkers such as cabinetmakers, carpenters, etc. but by amateur 'whittlers' as well. They take the form of circus-wagon figures, carousel animals, decoys, busts, figurines, and cigar store Indians. Oriental artists show themselves to have been as proficient with the medium of wood as they were with ivory or hardstone. See also Carousel Animals; Decoys; Tobacciana.

Bird, stylized, simple relief cvg, 2-tone pnt w/gilt, 7" L **185.00**
Bust of Daniel Webster on sq ped, cvd from 1 pc, 17" **650.00**
Eagle, primitive, from single block of pine, 21" **375.00**
Man w/derby, knee-length top coat, sgn/dtd 1910, 12½" **1,300.00**
Ornament, cherub's head w/wings, pnt/laminated oak, 13" H **395.00**
Soldier, primitive, worn pnt, 6", EX **65.00**
Tree w/5 birds on branches, mc pnt, 34" **3,000.00**
Wall bracket, w/eagle support, hand-forged nails, 20x32" **600.00**
Wall shelf, walnut, cvd cherub head/leaves, 17x15" **235.00**

Woodenware

Woodenware (or treenware, as it is sometimes called) generally refers to those wooden items such as spoons, bowls, food molds, etc. that were used in the preparation of food. Common during the 18th and 19th centuries, these wares were designed from a strictly functional viewpoint and were used on a day-to-day basis. With the advent of the Industrial Revolution which brought new materials and products, many of the old woodenwares were simply discarded. Today, original hand-crafted American woodenwares are extremely difficult to find.

Basket, burl, branching hdl, 6x11x9", EX...................................**400.00**
Basket, made from natural growth of burl, 12" L **600.00**
Basket, made from natural growth of burl, 7"................................**85.00**
Basket, ½-bushel; staved, wire bail, 14" dia.................................**85.00**
Bowl, ash, trn from 1 pc, scrubbed int, EX patina, 7x21" **75.00**
Bowl, birch, ca 1800, 4½x13½x24", EX....................................**225.00**
Bowl, bird's eye maple, EX figure, int wear, 13x12½" **145.00**
Bowl, burl, EX figure, filled hole, deep, 7x10".............................**200.00**
Bowl, burl, EX figure, raised rim, cut-out hdls, 7x14", EX............**900.00**
Bowl, burl, EX figure & detail, w/lid, chip/age crack, 5x6" **1,250.00**
Bowl, burl, ftd, w/lid, re-attached finial, 7½x5½".......................**500.00**
Bowl, burl, hdl extensions, oval, 11x15", NM.......................... **2,750.00**
Bowl, burl, natural, 6", EX...**200.00**
Bowl, burl, rfn w/putty in cracks, red stain, 5x14½"...................**350.00**
Bowl, burl, tight grain, worn patina, 2⅜x6½", EX......................**500.00**
Bowl, burl, trn, natural, 6", NM...**500.00**
Bowl, burl, unusually shallow, 15", NM................................... **1,500.00**
Bowl, burl, well formed, 5", M..**200.00**
Bowl, burl, 13", NM... **1,500.00**
Bowl, burl, 7", M..**400.00**
Bowl, chopping; maple, rectangular, 20" L **100.00**
Bowl, gr ext, trn from 1 pc, out of rnd/crack, 8x21" **115.00**

Bowl, sm protruding end hdls, scrubbed, 5x15x25" **145.00**
Bowl, stenciled fruit w/in, oblong, 22" L **210.00**

Burl bowls: 10", $400.00; 14", $975.00.

Bowl, tiger maple, incised lines, re-drilled hole, 24" **1,000.00**
Bowl, trough-like, 20x40" **250.00**
Bowl, walnut, 2x11x10"..**55.00**
Bowl, wild ash grain/some burl, plugged hole, rfn, 5½x12" **150.00**
Bowl, yel-pnt ext, almond shape, scrubbed, 5x14x25" **345.00**
Bowl, 3 rows incised lines, 1700s, 4x8½" **195.00**
Box, staved, interlocking wood band, w/lid, 7x16" **125.00**
Bucket, bentwood, finger-joint lid, swivel hdl, 8x9" **195.00**
Bucket, sugar; staved, copper tacks, varnish, 14x14", VG............**110.00**
Bucket, sugar; staved, interlaced wood bands, pnt, 9x10" **135.00**
Bucket, sugar; staved, wire bail, old patina, 8".............................**90.00**
Bucket, sugar; staved, wooden bail/pegs, old pnt, 11½x12"..........**175.00**
Canteen, trn, keg shape, old red finish, 6½".................................**100.00**
Cheese ladder, maple, 8" center sq **30.00**
Cheese mold, pegged, diamond grooves, 4x1¼x6¼" **175.00**
Chopping block, butcher's, Bally Block Co label, 18" sq, M **275.00**
Chopping block, 3 stout turn legs, worn, 26x32" dia....................**185.00**
Churn, staved, metal bands, trn lid, worn bl pnt, 20", EX **350.00**
Clothespin, handmade, 5 for **7.50**
Cookie brd, flower basket, bk: grapes, beechwood, 10x16" **300.00**
Cookie brd, flower basket cvgs, cherrywood, 6x7".......................**495.00**
Cookie brd, goose, sheep, rooster, 3½x12"..................................**175.00**
Cookie brd, lg Renaissance figure ea side, 23x10", EX **150.00**
Cookie brd, mtd knight, bk: flower basket, sgn, 10x15" **1,500.00**
Cookie brd, pine, inserted pewter mold w/bird & 'FB,' 5x9"........**575.00**
Cookie brd, rooster, bakery label, oval, 3⅜x4" **325.00**
Cookie brd, rooster, simple cvg, worn finish, 7x9" **125.00**
Cookie brd, walnut w/15 cvd designs, 6x10" **375.00**
Cookie brd, 4 different leaves, rfn, 27" L **175.00**
Cranberry scoop, 12x16" **285.00**
Cutting board, maple, maple-leaf form, 1¼x11x13" **65.00**
Dipper, long crooked hdl, crack in bowl, 17½"............................**115.00**
Dish-draining brd, 1-pc, all wood, 19x24", EX **165.00**
Egg cup, ped base, fine grain, joint at rim, pr..............................**120.00**
Fork, cvd, 5-tine, beveled shaft, knob hdl, 18" **130.00**
Funnel, maple sap, wood, 1-pc, trn & cvd, 3½x4" w/2" spout **90.00**
Jar, EX trn detail, ftd, varnish, Pease, w/lid, 5¾".......................**150.00**
Jar, trn, brn patina, w/lid, Pease, cracks/wear, 4½"......................**60.00**
Jar, trn, EX dk brn finish, rpl bail, Pease, 4½".............................**120.00**
Jar, worn orig red sponging, ivory button on lid, 1⅞" **135.00**
Jar, worn orig red sponging, w/lid, 3" **170.00**
Ladle, burl, hook hdl, 10"...**475.00**
Ladle, butter; ash burl, 4x4½" paddle, 9" L **350.00**
Ladle, butter; tiger maple, handmade, 1700s **260.00**
Ladle, fruitwood, bird's head hdl, 8¾"..**550.00**
Ladle, primitive, pot-hook hdl, 15"...**45.00**
Lemon squeezer, maple, 2-part, hinged, 3x3x20".........................**95.00**
Lemon squeezer, on legs, wood base, lg.....................................**195.00**
Marble, burl, 1" dia, pr..**55.00**

Match holder, cvd shell & starflower, pnt, 4½x2½" **300.00**
Noggin, maple, 1-pc, hdld, ca 1800, 5¾" **240.00**
Noggin, maple, 1-pc, 1700s, 5½" **240.00**
Noisemaker, brass trim, 7" L **90.00**
Paddle, butter; burl, hook hdl, 9", EX **150.00**
Paddle, butter; burl, simple design, 7", EX **125.00**
Paddle, butter; curly maple, hook hdl, EX color, 11", VG **125.00**
Paddle, butter; maple w/some curl & bird's eye, 12" **175.00**
Paddle, butter; some burl in bowl, hook hdl, scrubbed, 9" **75.00**
Pastry jigger, crimped wheel, curved hdl, 8" **85.00**
Peel, hardwood w/EX brn patina, 20" **140.00**
Peel, pine, 9½" dia, 17" **75.00**
Peel, tombstone top, long hdl, 42" **220.00**
Pie board/cutting board, pine, lollipop hdl, 19" **230.00**
Piggin, lock-lapped wood hoop, 1 wire hoop, 1830s, 4½x6½" **175.00**
Plate, minor wear, good age, 8½" **225.00**
Plate, 7½" **250.00**
Porringer, cherry, trn, tab hdls, 1810, sm **175.00**
Rolling pin, curly maple, age crack in 1 hdl, 17" L **45.00**
Rolling pin, tiger maple, trn from 1 pc, 20", EX **225.00**
Scoop, apple butter; 1-pc, open D hdl, 6½x8½" **260.00**
Scoop, burl, fiddlehead-like hdl, 8½" **600.00**
Scoop, burl, scroll hdl, sm chip, 8" **750.00**
Scoop, tiger maple, heart-cvd hdl, 9", EX **325.00**
Skimmer, cream; maple, shell shape, 3x4½" **175.00**
Skimmer, shallow, thin, rnd, 1900s, 6x6¼" **95.00**
Smoothing brd, scratched-cvd hex signs/1785, 27" **150.00**
Smoothing brd, simple chip cvg/stamping, 27½" L **135.00**
Smoothing brd, walnut, 2-tone pnt, horse hdl, cvd/1769, 27" **800.00**
Spoon, cvd foliate hdl, EX patina, minor wear, 5½" **90.00**
Spoon, pine, dk patina, 1700s, 15", EX **65.00**
Spoon, short curved effigy hdl, 5½x2½" **260.00**
Spoon/dipper, curly maple, long hdl, 19" **105.00**
Tray, tobacco drying; weathered gray surface, 26x39" **75.00**
Tub, staved, iron bands/hdls, worn mustard pnt, 9x25" **185.00**
Wine, worn orig red sponging, 3⅛" **25.00**

World's Fairs and Expos

Since 1851 and the Crystal Palace Exhibition in London, World's Fairs and Expositions have taken place at a steady pace. Many of them commemorate historical events. The 1904 Louisiana Purchase Exposition, commonly known as the St. Louis World's Fair, celebrated the 100th anniversary of the Louisiana Purchase agreement between Thomas Jefferson and Napoleon in 1803. The 1893 Columbian Exposition, known as The Chicago World's Fair, commemorated the 400th anniversary of the discovery of America by Columbus in 1492. (Both of these fairs were held one year later than originally scheduled.) The multitude of souvenirs from these and similar events have become a growing area of interest to collectors in recent years. Many items have a 'cross-over' interest into other fields: i.e., collectors of post cards and souvenir spoons eagerly search for those from various fairs and expositions.

For additional information, collectors may contact World's Fairs Collectors Society (WFCS), whose address is in the Directory under Clubs, Newsletters, and Catalogs; or our advisor, D.D. Woollard, Jr. His address is listed in the Directory under Missouri.

Key: T&P — Trylon & Perisphere

1876 Centennial, Philadelphia

Diary, general info/laws/populations/etc, 22-pg, 6x3", EX **30.00**
Guide, Centennial Expo, Lawrence, 30+ pgs, 6x9", EX **22.50**
Medal, aluminum, Liberty Bell/Independence Hall, 1½" **30.00**
Medallion, brass, emb...Schuttler...Wagon Works..., 1¼" **15.00**
Medallion, wood, Gen JR Hawley in relief, 2½" dia **75.00**
Purse, leather, stamped letters, 4-compartment, 2½x4" **30.00**
Towel, wht on wht with red borders, 17x29", +3" fringe **60.00**

1893 Columbian, Chicago

Bell, dinner; etched glass, frosted swirl hdl, M **100.00**
Book, Dream City, photographic views, Thompson, 13½x11" **30.00**
Book, Glimpses of..., soft cover, 200+ pgs, 7x5", EX **20.00**
Book, History of..., Major BC Truman, 594-pg, 8x10½", VG **30.00**
Book, Official Guide, soft cover, 192-pg, 5x7½", EX **20.00**
Book, View Album of Chicago, Ward Bros, 6x9½", EX **12.50**
Book, Week at Fair, Rand-McNally, soft red cover, 6x9" **35.00**
Bookmark, Mrs Potter Palmer, Women's Building, VG **75.00**
Cup, ironstone, Fisheries Building/Art Palace, 4x5" **75.00**
Folder, Henry R Worthington Co ads, fold-out map, 14x21" **12.50**
Hat, glass, fully sgn/dtd, Libbey **225.00**
Magazine, Cosmopolitan, Expo edition, Sept 1893, EX **25.00**
Nickel, elongated, 1893 .... **35.00**
Paperweight, brass, Columbus bust **100.00**
Paperweight, glass, Ferris Wheel, sepia scene, 3" dia **75.00**
Playing cards, landing scene, CS Clark, complete, EX **100.00**
Razor, etched blade, blk handles, closed: 6½" **85.00**
Ring, sterling, cross & crown, man's, Gorham, EX **95.00**
Sheet music, Columbus Day Waltz, ships/flags cover, fr **25.00**
Shot glass, Bust of Columbus intaglio in base **50.00**
Spoon, Columbus hdl finial, sailors in bowl, 5¼" **45.00**

Fan, 1893 Columbian Expo, 13", $100.00.

Spoon, demi; Mrs Palmers finial hdl, Children's Home in bowl **45.00**
Spoon, floral hdl, Fisheries Building in bowl, SP, Leonard **12.50**
Spoon, Isabella on hdl, Women's Building emb in bowl, 4¼" **45.00**
Stereoscopic view card, New Educational Series **5.00**
Ticket, Chicago Day, admit the bearer, with stub **20.00**
Ticket, Manhattan Day, admit the bearer, with stub **20.00**

1898 Omaha

Badge, brass, pin-bk, Government Building emb, 2-part **30.00**
Book, Snap Shots of...Expo, soft cover, 40-pg, 7x9" **20.00**
Medallion, brass, heart shaped, Nebraska Building, 1x1¼" **22.50**
Pin-bk, celluloid, Pennsylvania Day, EX **40.00**
Poster, For All the News..., scenes, 29x42", EX **175.00**
Spoon, Administration Building in bowl, lettered hdl, 5½" **35.00**
Spoon, US Government Building in bowl, angel on hdl, 4¼" **22.50**

1901 Pan American

Book, Pan-Am Expo Illus, Arnold, hard cover, 115-pg, 7x10" 32.50
Book, views, soft cover, string-tied, 24-pg, 11x9", EX 22.50
Booklet, Singer Sewing Machines, full color, 4½" 17.50
Cent, Electric Tower, elongated or rolled, EX 15.00
Cup, collapsible; aluminum, emb & eng, 2x2½", EX 20.00
Envelope, buffalo on globe & electric tower, 3x6½" 15.00
Letter opener, brass or bronze, buffalo at hdl finial, 6½" 35.00
Napkin ring, aluminum, emb buffalo, eng florals, 1½" dia 20.00
Paperweight, glass, Government Building, Empire Art, 4" 32.50
Pin-bk, celluloid, mc ladies as N&S Am, 1¼" dia 20.00
Spoon, eng building in bowl, enameled McKinley hdl, sterling.....95.00
Ticket, souvenir; Railroad Day overprinted in red, EX 17.50

1904 St. Louis

Book, History of..., hard cover, 800-pg, 11x14", EX 150.00
Book, Louisiana Purchase Expo, soft cover, 9x11", EX 25.00
Book, Uncle Jeremiah at..., Stevens, 332-pg, 5½x7½" 17.50
Booklet, Singer Sewing Machines, color, 20-pg, 7x5", EX 15.00
Box, jewel; glass w/brass fr & legs, 2¼x2¼x3" 90.00
Card, business; JR Johnson, Supt World's Fair...RR, NM 10.00
Certificate, attendance; color vignette, 9½x12½" 15.00
Cup, collapsible; nickel, Palace of Mines & Metallurgy, 2" 30.00
Fan, cb w/wood hdl, mc scenes, 7½" dia, EX 75.00
Humidor, clear glass, emb design, metal lid, 6x4" dia 50.00
Paperweight, seashells encased in glass, 1½x3½" 17.50
Pocket mirror, celluloid, Palace of Transportation, mc, 2" 75.00
Stein, Festival Hall & Cascades relief, Germany, ½-liter 150.00
Tray, card; aluminum, emb corners, 4x6½", VG 15.00
Tumbler, milk glass, molded designs, 5" 15.00
Watch fob, brass, Government Bldg/MO seal/Jefferson, 3-part......70.00

1905 Lewis and Clark

Card, business; HE Dosch, Commissioner General, 2¼x4" 17.50
Folder, holds 24 post cards, Wolff & O'Brien, EX 17.50
Pin-bk, celluloid, frogs w/umbrella, 1905, 1¾" 40.00
Pin-bk, celluloid, Sighting Pacific 1805, 1903, 1½" 35.00
Post card, night scene on the trail, BB Rich, EX 4.00
Stamps, Expo figures & scenes, sheet of 12, 4½x6½" 15.00
Ticket, Portland Day, Expo scene, Sept 30, 1905, 2½x4" 17.50
Tray, aluminum, Lewis & Clark center, emb border, 6½x4" 17.50

1909 Alaska Yukon Pacific

Book, New York at Alaska Yukon Pacific Expo 35.00
Daily program, 33-pg, 7x10", EX 20.00
Pin, A&P form upper sides of Y, EX 15.00
Post card, Scenic Ferris Wheel, blk/wht photo type 6.00
Spoon, angel w/horn/WM Seward bust on hdl, building in bowl...25.00
Watch fob, NP, 3-part 50.00
Watch fob, strap type, 3 women, mk Official Souvenir 30.00

1915 Panama Pacific

Book, Architecture & Landscape Gardening of Expo, Elder, EX ...27.50
Book, Art of..., Neuhaus, illus, 120+ pages, 6x9", EX 35.00
Book, Balboa on soft cover, illus, 30-pg, 7½x11", VG 15.00
Book, Expo in Colors, soft bk, Reid, 62-pg, 11x9¼", EX 35.00
Book, Official Miniature View, soft bk, Reid, 6x4", EX 15.00
Book, 13th Labor of Hercules on soft cover, 56-pg, 7x10" 17.50
Folder, Official Souvenir #12, Vincent, 22 views, ea 6x4" 15.00

Medallion, enameled, ¾", attached chain w/brass horse on end 15.00
Napkin ring, celluloid, Tower of Jewels, 2x2", EX 20.00
Pin-bk, bl/gold/wht, orig label w/slogan on bk, 1", EX 20.00
Post card album, 10 cards inside, Cardinell-Vincent, EX 17.50
Tablecloth, bl felt, aerial view in center, 16x25" 35.00
Ticket, Good for One Admission, blk & wht, 1⅛x2¾" 15.00

1926 Sesquicentennial

Ash tray, metal, emb Liberty bell, oval, 5½x3¼" 15.00
Book, Liberty Bell on soft cover, 30-pg, 8½x11" 22.50
Booklet, Official Views, Cardinell, 32-pg, EX 15.00
Case, pencil; emb Liberty Bell on leather, calendar, 3x8" 30.00
Certificate, membership; emb seal, 11x8½", EX 30.00
Cloth, fair symbols woven in silver on blk, 15x49", EX 55.00
Fob, 150 Years of Am Independence, bronze, EX 22.50
Invitation, heavy stock, flag in full color EX 30.00
Key, metal, Liberty Bell shape at tip, 2¼" 15.00
Medallion, brass, emb fair symbols, 1½", EX 12.50
Paperweight, metal, Liberty Bell form, 1½x3x3", EX 25.00
Pin-bk, Liberty Bell, 150 Years of Independence, 1" 12.50
Spoon, gold-washed bowl, Independence Hall on hdl, mk, 6" 20.00

1933 Chicago

Mug, Century of Progress, $25.00.

Book, Official Guide, illus, 176-pg, 5½x9¼", EX 17.50
Booklet, Official Pictures, Donnelley, Kaufmann & Fabry, 7x10"..22.50
Booklet, Royal Scot, train/bagpipers cover, 5½x8½", EX 5.00
Bookmark/letter opener, metal, comet logo/1933, 4¼" 12.50
Bracelet, gold metal, comet logo/1933 in center, EX 15.00
Brochure, Safety Glass Mfg, Lefty Grove, EX color 7.50
Brochure, What We Saw in General Motors Exhibit, EX 7.50
Cap, felt, military style, red w/wht letters, EX 50.00
Cent, Sky Ride design, rolled or elongated, Expo mk...........10.00
Cigarette case, comet logo in gold on brn, 2½x3½" 28.00
Key, good luck souvenir, Master Lock, 2" 12.50
Medal, bronze, Ford in script on radiator, 1903-1933, 1⅜" 22.50
Napkin ring, metal, gr on gold, florals/scenes, 1½" dia 20.00
Needle folder, mc buildings ea side, 6½x4½", EX 7.50
Photo, Electrical Building, gold/brn tones, fr, 5½x4½" 20.00
Plate, Blk Forest, A Century of..., bl on wht, Pickard, EX.........40.00
Playing cards, comet logo, Expo mk, complete, EX in box 30.00
Post card folder, 18 views, EX 12.50
Shakers, ceramic, pitcher shape, pr 25.00
Spoon, buildings in lg bowl, emb 5½" hdl, mk Sterling 40.00
Spoon, Century of Progress on hdl w/comet, Gr Duck, EX 12.00
Spoon, view in bowl, comet/building on hdl, SP, 5¾" 10.00
Ticket, lady & buildings, blk print on gr & wht, w/stub 20.00
Ticket, souvenir of Chicago Day, mc, 4¼x2¼", EX 12.50
Tie clip, metal, comet logo & 1934, bar type, EX 12.50

Tray, metal, Travel & Transportation Building, 4½x2½" 10.00
Umbrella, paper w/bamboo spokes, mk wood hdl, 28" dia, EX 35.00

1939 California Golden Gate

Book, Official Guide, illus, 116-pg, 5½x8", EX 20.00
Booklet, aerial view of Treasure Island, RR ads, 24-pg, 8x9" 12.50
Catalog, Department of Fine Arts, 150-pg, 7¼x10", EX.................25.00
Figurine, Sun Tower, dk metal, mk sq base, 4½", EX.................32.50
Folder, 18 color post card views, ea 6x4", EX 12.50
Ice pick, World's Fair 1939 in red & blk on wood hdl, 8"..............20.00
Medal, brass, Golden Gate Bridge design, 1¼"........................10.00
Pencil, mechanical; building/bridge, bl & gold, 10½" 20.00
Spoon, Golden Gate Bridge, nude on hdl, Rodgers, 6" 35.00
Towel, Golden Gate Bridge design, dtd 1939, 27x15", EX 25.00

1939 New York

Book, NYWF Views, Quality Art Novelty Co, 18 pg, 9½x12" 30.00
Book, Official Souvenir Guide & Picture, 130-pg, 9½x12¼".........35.00
Card table, T&P over outline of US, Samson DeLuxe, 30" 150.00
Coin, T&P design, NYWF 1939 World of Tomorrow, elongated...10.00
Folder, Am Air Lines Time Tables & Schedules, 4x9", EX............10.00
Folder, Tichoner, 18 post-card sz views, ea 4½x6"..........................12.50
Jar, jelly; clear Hobnail base, T&P on metal top, 3¼x3½" 55.00
Knife, pocket; 2-blade, T&P/1939 on faux pearl hdl, 3" 30.00
Map, overview of fair, Halifax Insurance, 18x25", EX 10.00
Needle book, Administration Building on cover, 7x4", EX............10.00
Sewing kit, cb box, T&P on gold seal, J&P Coats, 5½x3½" 25.00
Tray, compo, florals in relief, T&P inlay, 9½" dia 27.50

1962 Seattle

Bowl, china, mc fair scenes, 4" dia, in wire hanger..........................10.00
Bowl, china, mc Space Needle, heart shape, rtcl rim, 5"..................10.00
Bowl, china, 4 mc fair scenes, openwork border, 6" dia 10.00
Key chain, attached viewer w/Space Needle, w/mailing tag...........10.00
Medal, Official, 1¼", in orig cb folder w/information, M 10.00
Pin, gilt key through metal heart, gr/lt & dk bl enameling............. 7.50
Tumbler, glass, Boulevards of the World, bl/wht, 5½" 12.50
Tumbler, glass, Space Needle in red & wht w/gold rim, 5½" 12.50

1964 New York

Book, Official Guide, Time-Life, 312-pg, EX.................................15.00
Book, Official Souvenir, mc views, 32-pg, 1965, 7x10" 15.00
Bumper sticker, I've Seen..., bl/orange/wht, 4x8", EX 10.00
Calendar, perpetual, Unisphere/Statue of Liberty, 3", EX.............20.00
Cigarette lighter, NYWF 1964/65 in relief, 2" dia 20.00
Dime, silver, Neutron Irradiated Dime NYWF 1964/65, 2"...........15.00
Game, Official NYWF Children's Card Game, NM in box............17.50
License plate, souvenir, metal, NYWF 1964/65, 6x12", EX............20.00
Map, Official, mc, detailed, Esso, 16x24", EX 5.00
Mug, coffee; china, I Was a Coffee Hound..., dog's head, lg...........12.50
Plate, china, mc Unisphere & scenes, 8" dia 17.50
Puzzle, overall view, cb tray, M Bradley, 10x14", EX....................17.50
Tray, metal, mc scene, 12" dia, EX...12.50

Wrought Iron

Until the middle of the 19th century, almost all the metal hand forged in America was made from a material called wrought iron. When wrought iron rusts it appears grainy, while the mild steel that was used later shows no grain but pits to an orange-peel surface. This is an important aid in determining the age of an ironwork piece.

Broiler, hearth; hdl adjust w/slide, 1700s, NM............................350.00
Broiler, rotary, rnd w/2 wavy lines, 19" L 175.00
Dough scraper, 3¾" W 75.00
Fork, baked potato; dbl, 1-pc, 1830s, 16½" 140.00
Ladle, sgn J Schmidt, copper rivets, ca 1850, 20" 400.00
Lock, 1700s, 4"..95.00
Lock, 1700s, 5¾" 125.00
Miner's lamp, pitted, w/hanger, 4¼"..95.00
Pan, spider; 3-leg base, 7" dia, +10" hdl.....................................85.00
Peel, ram's horn finial, 42" 115.00
Pie crimper, twisted hdl, brass bushing, 7" 125.00
Pipe tongs, scissors type, 1800, EX 200.00
Pot hdl, folding, holds up to 21" dia pot, 1700s 50.00
Rack, utensil; scrolled crest, 6 hooks, 26" L 225.00
Roaster, 6 hooks, short ft, long swivel hdl, rust, 24" L.................185.00
Roasting stand, adjusts, VG detail, tripod/penny ft, 26" H 650.00
Roasting stick, hook ea end rotating bar, long hdl, mk, 24".........185.00
Skewer, long, orig hanger, matched set of 6 ....550.00
Skewer, w/hanger, assorted set of 8...400.00
Skimmer, early, 17", VG 250.00
Skimmer, sgn J Schmidt, iron rivets, curled hdl, 1850s, 20".........450.00
Sugar nippers, 8", VG 150.00
Toaster, hearth; 1700s, NM 350.00
Toaster, hearth; 2 decorative scrolls, 1700s, NM.........................500.00
Trammel, sawtooth, extends from 36"..125.00

Yellowware

Yellowware is most often a plain type of earthenware, so called because of the color of the clay used in its manufacture. Pieces may vary from buff to yellow to nearly brown; the glaze itself is clear. Some yellowware was decorated with blue, white, brown, or black bands; only seldom was it relief molded. Yellowware was made to a large extent in East Liverpool, Ohio, but other Ohio potteries as well as some in Pennsylvania, New Jersey, and Vermont also produced it. Because it was not often marked, it is almost impossible to identify the manufacturer. English yellowware has a harder body composition. There is a growing interest in this type of pottery, and consequently prices are continually increasing.

Bottle, pig form, brn sponging, 8" L 400.00
Bowl, bl sponging, minor hairlines, 7½" 40.00
Bowl, bl stripes, knife-sharpening edge, 5x9" 18.00
Bowl, bl stripes, med 20.00
Bowl, brn & bl bands, 12" 40.00
Bowl, brn band, 15" 95.00
Bowl, brn-sponged splotches, wear/flakes, 6x11½" 65.00
Bowl, brn/gr sponging, emb foliage, 4x9" 65.00
Bowl, flower stencil, nesting set of 5 ....225.00
Bowl, mixing; 3 wht stripes, 3½x8" 23.00
Bowl, plain, heavy & thick, 4x8" 22.00
Bowl, red/bl/brn sponge spatter, 2¾x5¼" 65.00
Bowl, seaweed, bl on wht band, 5x10", EX.................................285.00
Bowl, seaweed/stripes, w/lid, E Liverpool, 8½x9½", EX 575.00
Butter crock, wht stripe 90.00
Casserole, w/lid, late, 8"..35.00
Chamber pot, brn bands, hdld, 6x9½" 65.00
Chamber pot, seaweed/stripes, w/lid, E Liverpool, 10", EX 235.00
Dog, seated, bl mottle, tooled detail on paws, Ohio, 10" 1,150.00
Ink stand, recumbent lion, dk bl glaze, 6x10", VG 750.00

Jar, bl seaweed, brn/wht band, Minerva hdls, lid, 8", EX.............450.00
Jar, heavy running brn/bl/gr glaze, 8", EX, pr 90.00
Lion, dk bl mottle, EX color & detail, Ohio, 9¾" L 825.00
Mold, ear of corn, 6" 85.00
Mold, grape cluster, 3½x6x7" 85.00
Mug, brn sponging, well-shaped hdl, minor flakes, 3¼" 110.00
Mug, brn/wht stripes, professional rpr, 4"..........................115.00
Mug, seaweed/stripes, E Liverpool, minor wear, 3½" 275.00
Paperweight, woman w/lg hat in relief, edge chips, 4" dia 90.00
Pitcher, bl sponging, ovoid, 8½" 175.00
Pitcher, blk/brn/gr sponge spatter, 7", EX..........................95.00
Pitcher, brn splotches/red highlights, tooled bands, 6".............225.00
Pitcher, brn stripes/wht band, professional rpr, 5½" 125.00
Pitcher, gr sponge spatter, 5" 95.00
Pitcher, seaweed/stripes, E Liverpool, wear/sm flakes, 4" 200.00
Pitcher, seaweed/stripes, E Liverpool, 5⅝", NM 220.00
Salt cellar, seaweed, bl on wht band, ftd, E Liverpool, 2¼".........225.00
Salt cellar, seaweed band, ftd, E Liverpool, hairline, 2x3".........275.00
Soap dish+base/insert/lid, wht/blk bands, Green & Smith, 6".....185.00
Teapot, emb motif, long gooseneck, English, 8", NM.................145.00

Pitcher, seaweed motif with brown bands, 5", $325.00.

Zanesville Glass

Glassware was produced in Zanesville, Ohio, from as early as 1815 until 1851. Two companies produced clear and colored hollowware pieces in five characteristic patterns: 1) diamond faceted, 2) broken swirls, 3) vertical swirls, 4) perpendicular fluting, 5) plain, with scalloped or fluted rims and strap handles. The most readily-identified product is perhaps the whiskey bottles made in the vertical swirl pattern, often called globular swirls because of their full, round body. Their necks vary in width; some have a ringed rim and some are collared. They were made in several colors – amber, light green, and light aquamarine are the most common.

Our advisor for this category is Mark Vuono; he is listed in the Directory under Connecticut.

Bottle, club, aqua, 24 swirled ribs, 6¾" 95.00
Bottle, club, aqua, 24 swirled ribs, 8⅜" 145.00
Bottle, club, lt gr, 24-rib swirl/broken ribs, 8", NM 400.00
Bottle, globular, amber, 24 swirled ribs, 8¾".......................625.00
Bottle, globular, aqua, 24 swirled ribs, 7⅝", NM 200.00
Bottle, globular, citron, 24 swirled ribs, 7½", NM 2,200.00
Bottle, globular, gold-amber, 24 swirled ribs, 7" 725.00
Bottle, globular, gold-amber, 24 swirled ribs, 7½", EX 375.00
Bottle, globular, gold-amber, 24 swirled ribs, 9" 900.00
Bottle, globular, honey amber, 24 swirled ribs, 8" 850.00

Bottle, globular, lt gr, 24 swirled ribs, cloudy, 7¾".................. 1,800.00
Bottle, globular, olive-yel, 24 swirled ribs, long neck, 8½" 700.00
Flask, chestnut, amber, 10-dmn, 5¼".............................. 1,200.00
Flask, chestnut, amber, 24 swirled ribs, 5"........................450.00
Flask, chestnut, aqua, 10-dmn, short check in side, 5" 100.00
Flask, chestnut, dk red-amber, 10-dmn, sheared neck, 5" 1,700.00
Flask, chestnut, gold-amber, 24 swirled ribs, 4⅝" 450.00
Flask, chestnut, gold-amber, 24 vertical ribs, 4¾" 425.00
Salt, dk gold-amber, 24 vertical ribs, bulbous, ftd, 3½" 375.00

Zsolnay

Zsolnay pottery has been made at Pecs in Hungary since the mid-1800s. The factory received international attention in 1878 by winning the Grand Prix gold medal at the Paris World Exhibition for their technological innovations and high artistic level. Zsolnay used lead-free high-temperature glazes on his unique 'porcelain-faience' material. The Hungarian, Persian, Turkish, Japanese, and Renaissance motifs were applied with colored glazes which after firing resulted in rich ornamentation almost in relief. In the 1890s Zsolnay introduced iridescent 'eosine' glazes in nearly every color and subsequently adopted the Art Nouveau style. The unique eosine glazes and special application techniques allowed striking artistic designs which brought the factory world-wide fame and recognition. Presently the factory produces porcelain wares and various decorative items such as the red or green iridescent-glazed figurines that are frequently seen on the market today.

Basin, snake about rim, gr irid, 15", ornate CI 42" base........... 2,300.00
Basket, red/wht/gold, rtcl, gold steeple mk, 1890, 9" 450.00
Bowl, triangular, rtcl gold-lined bands, PECS, 5½x8" 300.00
Bowl, 3 3-D bears at side of 'pool,' gold lustre, 8x13" 650.00
Box, chariot scene, gr irid, 4½x5½" dia 90.00
Centerpc, irid gr mottle w/red 3-D parrot ea end, 15" L 1,000.00
Ewer, 2 female figures relief, gr irid, 6" 200.00
Figurine, cubistic rooster, gr irid, 1950s, 7¾" 285.00
Figurine, highly-stylized mother & child, gr irid, 1950s, 8"..........800.00
Figurine, nude Eve, gr/purple, irid, emb mk, 1904, 20" 1,800.00
Figurine, nude leans on draped ped w/urn, gr irid, 10" 400.00
Figurine, owl clutching fish, gold lustre irid, 1925, 13½" 1,400.00
Jug, toga-clad maid at spout/centaur on shoulder, irid, 18" 2,500.00
Pitcher, formed by snake's coiled body, mouth is spout, 9"....... 2,400.00
Pitcher, mc w/exotic birds, dbl walled, rtcl, irid, 1904, 9"........ 1,600.00
Plaque, 2 satyrs/maid in oval w/in rectangle, irid, 11"............ 1,400.00
Plate, leaves form rim, whiplash stems, 3-color irid, 12" 1,400.00
Plate, relief lobster/snake encircle rim, irid, #6103, 12".......... 2,000.00
Vase, bk-to-bk 3-D queen's & king's heads, irid, 1900, 20" 2,500.00
Vase, bl/brn w/red flower, irid, emb steeple mk, 1898, 10" 1,400.00
Vase, brn/gr/red w/gr leaves, irid, looped hdls, 1900, 9½" 1,300.00
Vase, bulb-neck cylinder w/in 3 leafy stalks, gr irid, 19" 400.00
Vase, cobalt/gold/beige, dbl walled, rtcl, steeple mk, 6½" 349.00
Vase, draped lady on bulbus form w/slim neck, gr-gold, 9¼" 250.00
Vase, gourd form/multiple hdls, bl irid, 7" 550.00
Vase, Grecian figures, gold/gr irid, gold castle mk, 6"...............175.00
Vase, lg dbl-loop hdls, paneled indents, ftd ovoid, 13"..............900.00
Vase, mc floral on cream, fully rtcl, sq, hdls, ftd, 9"...................500.00
Vase, mc floral on cream, rtcl, rnd, steeple mk, 1892, 9" 360.00
Vase, peacocks, mc lustres on floral mottled ground, 12" 2,250.00
Vase, red floral in relief on beige, twisted hdls, 1879, 17".........680.00
Vase, sturgeon form, waves at base, pearl lustres, 16".............. 2,800.00
Vase, stylized ferns, red/blk on pearl lustre, 1910, 9½"............. 1,000.00
Vase, stylized trees, gr/yel/lime/poppy, 1900, 13".................... 3,000.00
Vase, trees, river w/boat & swan, mc irid, 1902, 12½" 2,500.00
Vase, volcano w/trees, irid, emb steeple mk, 1900, 8½" 1,700.00

Auction Houses

We wish to thank the following auction houses whose catalogs have been used as sources for pricing information. Many have granted us permission to reproduce their photographs as well.

A-1 Auction Service
P.O. Box 540672, Orlando, Florida 32854;
407-841-6681
Specializing in American antique sales

American West Archives
Anderson, Warren
P.O. Box 100, Cedar City, Utah 84721
26-page illustrated catalog issued quarterly
includes an auction section featuring
scarce and historical early western documents, letters, autographs, stock certificates, and other important ephemera. 1-
year subscription: $10.00

Arman Absentee Auctions
P.O. Box 174, Woodstock, CT 06281; 203-
928-5838
Specializing in American glass, Historical
Staffordshire, English soft paste, paper-
weights

Barrett/Bertoia Auctions & Appraisals
1217 Glenwood Dr., Vineland, NJ 18630;
609-692-4092
Specializing in antique toys and collectibles

Brian Riba
Riba Auctions Inc.
P.O. Box 53, Main St., S. Glastonbury, CT
06073; 203-633-3076

C.E. Guarino
Box 49, Denmark, ME 04022

Col. Doug Allard
P.O. Box 460, St. Ignatius, MT 59865

David Rago
P.O. Box 3592, Station E, Trenton, NJ
08629; 609-585-2546
Specializing in American art pottery and
Arts & Crafts

Doyle, Auctioneers & Appraisers
R.D. 3, Box 137, Osborne Hill Road,
Fishkill, NY 12524; 914-896-9492

Du Mouchelles
409 Jefferson Ave., Detroit, MI 48226

Early Auction Co.
123 Main St., Milford, OH 45150

F.T.S. Inc.
416 Throop St., N. Babylon, NY 11704;
516-669-7232
Specializing in stein auctions with illustrated catalogs

Garths Auctions Inc.
2690 Stratford Rd., Box 369, Delaware,
OH 43015; 614-362-4771

Greenberg Auctions
7566 Main St.
Sykesville, MD 21784

Guernsey's
136 E. 73rd St., New York, NY 10021;
212-794-2280
Specializing in carousel figures

Hake's Americana & Collectibles
Specializing in character and personality
collectibles along with all artifacts of popular culture for over 20 years. To receive a
catalog for their next 3,000-item
mail/phone bid auction, send $3.00 to
Hake's Americana, P.O. Box 1444M,
York, PA 17405

Jack Sellner Auctioneer
P.O. Box 113, Scottsdale, AZ 85252

James D. Julia
P.O. Box 210, Showhegan Rd., Fairfield,
ME 04937

L.R. 'Les' Docks
Box 691035, San Antonio, TX 78269-
1035
Providing occasional mail-order record

auctions, rarely consigned, the only consignments considered are exceptionally
scarce and unusual records

Lloyd Ralston Toys
447 Stratford Rd., Fairfield, CT 06432

Manion's International Auction House,
Inc.
P.O. Box 12214, Kansas City, KS 66112

Maritime Auctions
R.R. 2, Box 45A, York, ME 03909; 207-
363-4247

Milwaukee Auction Galleries, Ltd.
4747 W. Bradley Rd., Milwaukee, WI
53223; 414-355-5054

Nostalgia Co.
21 S. Lake Dr., Hackensack, NJ 07601;
201-488-4536

Phillips
406 E. 79th St., New York City, NY 10021

Rex Stark Auctions
49 Wethersfield Rd., Bellingham, MA
02019

Richard A. Bourne Co. Inc.
Estate Auctioneers & Appraisers
Box 141, Hyannis Port, MA 02647; 617-
775-0797

Roan Inc.
Box 118, R.D. 3, Cogan Station, PA 17728

Robert W. Skinner Inc.
Auctioneers & Appraisers
Rt. 117, Bolton, MA 01740; 617-779-5528

Sally S. Carver Postcard Mail Auctions
179 South St., Chestnut Hill, MA 02167;
617-469-9175
Specializing in all better quality pre-1930
postcards; SASE with correspondence, no

consignments accepted

Sotheby Parke Bernet Inc.
980 Madison Ave., New York City, NY
10021

Weschler's, Adam A. Weschler & Son
905 E. St. N.W., Washington, DC 20004

Willis Henry Auctions
22 Main St., Marshfield, MA 02050

Alabama

Dole, Pat
Editor of *The Glaze*
P.O. Box 4782 Birmingham, 35206; 205-833-9853
Specializing in Purinton pottery

Luckey, Carl
Carl F. Luckey Communications
R.R. 4, Box 301, Lingerlost Tr., Killen, 35645
Freelance writer specializing in art, antiques, and collectibles

Arkansas

Hall, Doris & Burdell
B&B Antiques
P.O. Box 1501, Fairfield Bay, 72088 or 210 W. Sassafras Dr., Morton, IL 61550
Authors of *Morton's Potteries: 99 Years*
Specializing in Morton pottery, American dinnerware, early American pattern glass, historical items, small primitives

Musgrave, Marge
Look Nook Antiques
R.R. 3, Box 352, Mountain Home, 72653; 501-499-5283
Specializing in art glass and colored Victorian glass

Yohe, Darlene
Timberview Antiques
P.O. Box 343, Stuttgart, 72160; 501-673-3437
Specializing in American pattern glass, historical glass, Victorian pattern glass, carnival glass, and custard glass

California

Baker, Mrs. Lillian
15237 Chanera Ave., Gardena, 90249; 213-329-2619
Author Collector Books on antique, collectible, and high-fashion costume jewelry, hatpins and hatpin holders, miniatures

Baker, Roger
Baker's Lady Luck Emporium
Box 620417, Woodside, 94062; 415-851-7188
Specializing in Saloon Americana – advertising, gambling, bar bottles, cigar lighters, match safes, bowie knives, dirks, daggers, barber items: bottles, shaving mugs, razors

Benjamin, Scott
7250 Franklin Ave. #216, Los Angeles, 90046; 213-876-2056
Specializing in gasoline pump globes

Brooks, Mike
7355 Skyline, Oakland, 94611; 415-339-1751
Specializing in typewriters, early televisions

Carter, Tina M.
Hot Tea
882 S. Mollison, El Cajon, 92020; 619-440-5043
Specializing in teapots, tea-related items, tea tins, children's and toy tea sets, coffeepots, etc.

Chamberlain, Jackie
1520 Foothill Blvd., La Canada, 91011; 818-790-5416
Specializing in holiday collectibles, antique reference books, teddy bears, pewter ice cream molds

Chipman, Jack
California Spectrum
Box 1429, Redondo Beach, 90278
Specializing in California and other American ceramics

Enge, Delleen
Franciscan Dinnerware Matching Service
323 E. Matilija, Ste. 112, Ojai, 93023
FAX 1-805-0165

George, Tony
22941 Briarcroft, El Toro, 92630; 714-951-1310
Specializing in watch fobs

Harris, Warren D.
4555 Auburn Blvd., Suite #11, Sacramento, 95841
Specializing in decorative (non-advertising) thermometers

Howard, Steve
101 1st St., Suite 404, Los Altos, 94022; 415-484-4488
Specializing in antique American firearms, Bowie knives, Western Americana

Johnson, Patricia A.
Box 1221, Torrance, 90505
Specializing in open salts

Long, Earnest & Ida
Long's Americana
P.O. Box 90, Mokelumne Hill, 95245; 209-286-1348
Specializing in children's items: toys, banks, games, etc.; publishers of *Dictionary of Toys, Vol. I & II*; *Dictionary of Still Banks*; and *Penny Lane*, a history of antique mechanical toy banks

Malowanczyk, Abby & Wlodek
Collage
931 S. Coast Hwy., Laguna Beach, 92651; 714-494-3940
Specializing in Art Deco and mid-century classic furniture; European art glass, 1930s-60s

Maurer, Oveda L.
Oveda Maurer Antiques
137 Tunstead Ave., San Anselmo, 94960; 415-454-6439
Specializing in 18th-century and early 19th-century American furniture, lighting, pewter, and hearthware

Nelson, Maxine
873 Marigold Ct., Carlsbad, 92009
Specializing in Vernon Kilns

Oliphant, Steve
5255 Allott Ave., Van Nuys, 91401; 818-789-2339
Specializing in phonographs

Pardini, Dick
3107 N. El Dorado St., Dept. SAPG, Stockton, 95204; 209-466-5550
Specializing in California Perfume Company items: buyer and information center Inquiries require LSASE; not necessary if offering items for sale

Ringerling, David
Belle Ringer Antiques
1509 Wilson Terrace, Glendale, 91206; 818-241-8469 or 818-409-8026
Specializing in Rowland and Marsellus, Royal Fenton, Bawo & Dotter, A.C. Bosselman & Co., souvenir china. Feel free to contact David if you have any questions about Rowland and Marsellus china. He will be happy to answer any questions about souvenir china as well.

Shrader, Fred & Lila
Shrader Antiques
2025 Hwy. 199, Crescent City, 95531; 707-458-3525
Specializing in railroad, steamship and other transportation memorabilia; Shelley and select Americana

Stella's Collectibles
Memory Lanes Antique Mall
2451 Frampton St., Harbor City, 90710; 213-316-7198
Also at Westchester Fair Mall & Farmer's Market Showcase Gallery
Specializing in quality glass and china, paperweights, figurines, plates, jewelry

Yronwode, Catherine
6632 Covey Rd., Forestville, 95436; 707-887-2424
Specializing in pre-1950 collectible plastic

Zeder, Audrey
6755 Coralite St. S, Long Beach, 90808 (By appointment only)
Specializing in British Royal Commemorative Souvenirs (mail-order catalog available)
Author of *British Royal Commemoratives* (Wallace Homestead)

Canada

Warner, Ian
P.O. Box 44, Brampton, Ontario, L6V 2K7
Specializing in Wade porcelain and Swanky swigs, author of *The World of Wade*, Co-author: Mike Posgay

Colorado

Heck, Carl
Carl Heck Antiques
Box 8416, Aspen, 81612; 303-925-8011
Specializing in antique stained and beveled glass and Tiffany windows; leaded and reverse-painted lamps

Connecticut

Bondhus, Sandra V.
Box 100, Unionville, 06085; 203-678-1808
Author of *Quimper: A French Folk Art Faience*
Specializing in Quimper pottery

Harned, Denise
P.O. Box 10373, Elmwood, 06133; 203-666-6308, after 9 P.M.
Author of *Griswold Cast Collectibles*.
Specializing in Griswold cast iron and aluminum.

Kilbride, Richard J.
81 Willard Terrace, Stamford, 06903; 203-322-0568
Author of *Art Deco Chrome, The Chase Era* and *Art Deco Chrome, Book 2*

Mayer, Fran
Mechanical Music Center
18 Marshall St., Box 1078, S. Norwalk, 06854; 203-852-1780
Specializing in mechanical musical instruments; illustrated catalogs of items for sale, $5 annual subscription

Rivera, Ted
Box 163, Torrington, 06790; 203-489-4325
Specializing in inkwells and inkstands; co-author of *Inkstands and Inkwells: a Collector's Guide*.

Vuono, Mark
306 Mill Rd., Stamford, 06903; 203-329-8744
Specializing in historical flasks, blown-3-mold glass, blown American glass

Delaware

Davis, Patricia M.
700 Greenhill Ave., Wilmington, 19805; 302-658-2992

District of Columbia

Durham, Ken & Jackie
By appointment
909 26 St. N.W., Washington, DC 20037; 202-338-1342
Specializing in countertop arcade machines, trade stimulators, and vending machines; publish *Coin-Op Newsletter*, 16-page illustrated list: $2

England

Etter, Roberta
Flat 11, Hilton House, 22 Craven Hill Gardens, London, W2 3EE; 01/262-8728

Pedel, Alan
Collectibles from England
Marwood Lee, Barnstaple, Devon, EX31 4EB; 011-44-271-75166 (anytime) Specializing in pie birds, open salts, cat post cards, most other collectibles

Florida

Archer, Dick & Ellie
Artiques
419 Sevilla Dr., St. Augustine, 32086; 904-797-4678
Specializing in Victorian silverplate: figurals, fancy hollowware, and collectibles

Bettinger, Robert
448 E. 7th Ave.
Mt. Dora, 32757
Specializing in American art pottery

deCourtivron, Gael
Cocaholics
4811 Remington Dr., Sarasota, 34234; 813-351-1560
Specializing in Coca-Cola memorabilia
Cocaholics hot line: 813-355-COLA

Dodds, Rebecca
Silver Flute

Box 39644, Ft. Lauderdale, 33339
Specializing in jewelry

Donnelly, Ron
Saturday Matinee
Box 7047, Panama City Beach, 32413
Specializing in Big Little Books, movie posters, premiums, western heroes, character collectibles

France, Madeleine
P.O. Box 15555, Plantation, 33318; 305-584-0009
Specializing in top quality perfume bottles: Lalique, Steuben, Czechoslovakian

Hochman, Gene
Full House
9320 Laurel Green Dr., Boynton Beach, 33437; 407-734-8690
Mail auctions; specializing in antique playing cards, gambling memorabilia

Hudson, Hardy
108 Green Leaf Lane, Altamonte Springs, 32714
Specializing in majolica, American art pottery

Lawrence, Judy & Cliff
1169 Overcash Dr., Dunedin, 34698; 813-734-4742
Specializing in fountain pens and mechanical pencils

Linscott, Len
Line Jewels
3557 Nicklaus Dr., Titusville, 32780
Specializing in glass insulators, Blue Bell paperweights and other telephone items, rare Ball fruit jars and Ball items
SASE required

McNerney, Kathryn
502 Kettering Way, Orange Park, 32073
Author Collector Books on blue and white stoneware, primitives, tools

Supnick, Mark
8524 N.W. 2 St., Coral Springs, 33065; 305-755-3448
Author of *Collecting Hull Pottery's Little Red Riding Hood*
Specializing in American pottery

White, Douglass
Classic Interiors & Antiques
2144 Edgewater Dr., Orlando, 32804; 407-841-6681
Specializing in Fulper, other American art pottery

Georgia

Glenn, Walter
Geode Ltd.
3393 Peachtree Rd., Atlanta, 30326; 404-261-9346
Specializing in Frankart

Joiner, John R.
245 Ashland Trail, Tyrone, 30290; 404-487-3732
Specializing in commercial aviation collectibles

Illinois

Brinkley, Wm. J.
Brinkley Interiors & Galleries

401 S. Washington Ave., McLeansboro, 62859
Specializing in Meissen, Dresden, European porcelains, American porcelains (Cybis)

Broom, Jim
Box 65, Effingham, 62401
Specializing in opalescent pattern glassware

Carley, Tod
Vice President – International Society of Antique Scale Collectors
811 E. Central Rd., Apt. 304, Arlington Heights, 60005
Specializing in scales

Collier, Charles & Gladys
C&G Antiques
Champaign, 217-359-2762
Specializing in china, pattern glass, figurines, Nutting prints, and miscellaneous

Courter, J.W.
R.R. 1, Simpson, 62985; 618-949-3884
Specializing in Aladdin lamps
Author of *Aladdin – The Magic Name in Lamps*, softbound, 180 pages; and *Aladdin Electric Lamps*, hardbound, 154 pages

Danis, John
11028 Raleigh Ct., Rockford, 61111; 815-963-0757
Specializing in R. Lalique

Frizzell, Doris
Doris' Dishes
16 Oakdale Dr., Springfield, 62707; 217-529-3873
Specializing in Royal Haeger, American china and pottery, Depression glass

Garmon, Lee
1529 Whittier St., Springfield, 62704; 217-789-9574
Specializing in Royal Haeger, Royal Hickman, glass animals

Griffith, Woody
4107 White Ash Rd., Crystal Lake, 60014; 815-459-7808
Specializing in Jewel Tea, Noritake, Hall

Grist, Everett
734 12th St., Charleston, 61920
Specializing in marbles

Hall, Doris & Burdell
B&B Antiques
210 W. Sassafras Dr., Morton, 61550 or P.O. Box 1501, Fairfield Bay, Arkansas 72088; Authors of *Morton's Potteries: 99 Years*
Specializing in Morton pottery, American dinnerware, early American pattern glass, historical items, small primitives

Haussmann, Richard A.
Past President, Aurora Historical Society
Aurora, 60507

Hilst, Randy
1221 Florence #4, Pekin, 61554; 309-346-2710
Specializing in old fishing tackle, duck and goose calls

Hoffmann, Pat & Don, Sr.
1291 N. Elmwood Dr., Aurora, 60506; 312-859-3435
Authors of *Warwick, A to W*, a supplement to *Why Not Warwick? China Collectors Guide*
Specializing in Warwick china

Hooks, Dee
Dee's China Shop
Box 142, Lawrenceville, 62439
Specializing in R.S. Prussia, Royal Bayreuth, Haviland, other fine china

Lambrich, Charles
P.O. Box 105
Alton, 62002
Specializing in art glass, porcelain, carnival

Long, Dee
112 S. Center, Lacon, 61540
Specializing in reamers

Lotton, Charles
Specializing in Lotton art glass
Co-author of *Lotton Art Glass*, a comprehensive study with 96 color pages and current values
Available from Antique Publications, P.O. Box 553, Marietta, OH, 45750

Owen, Larry & Sally
Specializing in Morten Studio dogs

Rhoden, Joan & Charles
Memories/Rhoden's Antiques
605 N. Main, Georgetown, 61846; 217-662-8046
Specializing in Heisey and other Elegant Glassware, general line antiques
Co-authors of *Those Wonderful Yard-Long Prints and More*, an illustrated value guide

The Home Place Antiques
Durham, William; Galaway, William
9633 Beaver Valley Rd., Belvidere, 61008; 815-547-5128
Specializing in Tea Leaf and white ironstone

Thomsen, Barry
P.O. Box 7066, Westchester, 60154; 708-409-0909
Specializing in cookie jars

Weldi, Frank John
Weldi-Skinner, Mary
1736 W. Farragut Ave., Chicago, 60640; 312-728-7750
Specializing in American and European art pottery, fine glass, designer collectibles

Wells, Rosalie J. 'Rosie'
R.R. 1, Canton, 61520; 309-668-2565
Publishes magazines & other periodicals for Precious Moments Collectors, Hallmark Ornament Collectors, and Lowell Davis Collectors. She has hosted the International Convention for Precious Moments Collectors each year since 1984. Write for free literature.

Indiana

Boram, Clifford
Antique Stove Information Clearinghouse
417 N. Main St., Monticello, 47960
Inquiries should be accompanied by SASE

and marked 'Urgent' in red

Cummings, Jim
2822 Mariposa, Terre Haute, 47803

Edwards, Bill
423 N. Main, Rushville, 46173
Author Collector Books on carnival glass

Fred, James A.
Antique Radio Labs.
R.R. 1, Box 41, Cutler, 46920; 317-268-2214
Specializing in radios made between 1922 and 1950

Harris, Dave
Hoosier Peddler
5400 S. Webster St., Kokomo, 46902; 317-453-6172
Specializing in advertising, toys

Haun, Ted
2426 N. 700 East, Kokomo, 46901; 317-628-3640
Specializing in American pottery and china, '50s items

Heiss, Virginia
7777 N. Alton Ave., Indianapolis, 46268; 317-875-6797
Specializing in Muncie, AMACO, Brandt Steele, Marblehead, Kenton Hills

Keagy, William & June
P.O. Box 106, Bloomfield 47424; 812-384-3471
Co-authors of *Those Wonderful Yard-Long Prints and More*, an illustrated value guide

Mary Spoerle Antiques
1100 N. Eleanor, Indianapolis, 46214; 317-241-0362

Mary's Antiques
317-861-6878
Specializing in jewelry, glass, china

Miller, Susan
606 E. Wabash Ave., Crawfordsville, 47933; 317-362-0352
Specializing in trolls

Old Storefront Antiques
P.O. Box 357, Dublin, 47335; 317-478-4809
Specializing in country store items, tins, primitives, pharmaceuticals, advertising, etc.
Active in mail order with catalogs available. Information requires LSASE

Ross, Tom & Veda
1917 Sommer Lane, Crawfordsville, 47933; 317-362-5783
Specializing in general line

Scowden, Virgil
303 Lincoln, Williamsport, 47993; 317-762-3408 or 317-762-3178
Antiques museum, general line, tours

Smith, Robert L.; & Susan C.
Antiques Galore & More
644 W. 256th St., Sheridan, 46069; 317-758-6553

Specializing in Victorian furniture and decor; art glass (Loetz, Galle, Daum); art pottery (Weller, Grueby, Teco, Sicard, Marblehead)

Stapp, Charles Dennis
7037 Haynes Rd., Georgetown, 47122
Specializing in knives, straight razors, safety razors

Stofft, Marvin & Jeanette
Marnette Antiques
Tell City, 47586; 812-547-5707
Specializing in Ohio art pottery, cut glass, R.S. Prussia
Buy and sell

Stroble, Jim & Donna
Stroble's Antiques
219-244-7475
Specializing in flow blue and milk glass

Iowa

Addy, Geneva D.
Winterset, 50273; 515-462-3027

Arnbal, Una
Woodland Antiques
236 Trail Ridge Rd., Ames, 50010; 515-292-1005
Specializing in china, glass, Lomonosov figurines

Botts, Rick
2545 S.E. 60th Court, Des Moines, 50317-5099
Publisher of *Jukebox Collector* magazine
Collector of Wurlitzer jukeboxes, sales of jukebox books, service manuals, etc.

DeGood, Hal & Meredith
The Baggage Car
513 Elm St., West Des Moines, IA 50265; 515-225-3070
Specializing in Hallmark collectibles; publishers of Hallmark newsletter

Devine, Dennis; Norman; and Joe
D&D Antique Mall, 1411 3rd St., Council Bluffs, 51503; 712-323-5233 or 712-328-7305
Specializing in furniture, phonographs, collectibles, general line
Joe Devine: Royal Copley collector

Evans, Lorna
Lorna Evans Antiques
Cedar Rapids, 319-366-3102
Specializing in fine country quilts, samplers, early children's items

Jaarsma, Ralph
De Pelikaan Antieks
627 Franklin St., Pella, 50219
Specializing in Dutch antiques

Picek, Louis
Main Street Antiques
110 W. Main St., Box 340, West Branch, 52358
Specializing in folk art, country Americana, the unusual

Rullestad, Frank & Eleanor
Valley Antiques
P.O. Box 65944, West Des Moines, 50265

Williams, Don
Ottumwa, 52501
Specializing in art glass

Kansas

Garton, Wesley & Jan
Wes-Jan Antiques
P.O. Box 780985, Wichita, 67278; 316-778-1948
Specializing in American art pottery, early American flint glass, Deco arts

Robison, Joleen A.
502 Lindley Dr., Lawrence, 66044
Collector Books author on advertising dolls

Sandler, Miles
Maundy International Watches
P.O. Box 13028-SA; 1-800-235-2866
Specializing in watches – antique pocket and vintage wristwatches

Tinsley, Rosella
105 15th St., Osawatomie, 66064 Specializing in primitives, kitchen, farm, woodenware, miscellaneous

Toohey, Marlena
9716 W. 92 Terrace, Overland Park, 66212; 913-599-5936
Specializing in black glass

Kentucky

Florence, Gene
Box 7186H, Lexington, 40522
Author Collector Books on depression glass, Occupied Japan

Johnson, Wes
1725 Dixie Hwy., Box 169001, Louisville, 40256-0001
Specializing in Cracker Jack: toys, point of sale, packages, etc.; Checkers Confection, Schoenhut toys, Victor Toy Oats, Universal Theatre (Chicago), toys

Willis, Roy M.
Heartland of Kentucky Specialties
Box 428, Lebanon Jct., 40150; 502-833-2827 after 6 p.m. EST
Specializing in most brands of decanters, domestic beer steins, and advertising
Open showroom

Louisiana

Deckler, Dorothy & Wade N.
Dottie's Antiques
P.O. Box 1141, St. Francisville, 70775
Specializing in glass

Maine

Hathaway, John
Hathaway's Antiques
Upper Main St., Bryant Pond, 04219; 207-665-2124
Specializing in fruit jars – mail order a specialty

Maryland

Banks, Robert
Stars and Stripes
18901 Gold Mine Court, Brookeville, 20833
Specializing in American flags of historical significance and exceptional design.
Bought and sold

Dennis & George Collectables
O'Brien, Dennis; and Goehring, George
3407 Lake Montebello Dr., Baltimore, 21218; 301-889-3964
Specializing in advertising items, personalities, unusual items

Greenberg, Bruce C., Ph. D.
Greenberg Publishing Company
7566 Main St., Sykesville, 21784
Specializing in toy trains; author and publisher of comprehensive publications on Lionel, American Flyer, and Ives trains

Humphrey, George C.
4392 Prince George Ave., Beltsville, 20705; 301-937-7899
Specializing in John Rogers groups

Screen, Harold & Joyce
2804 Munster Rd., Baltimore, 21234; 301-661-6765
Specializing in soda fountain 'tools of the trade' and paper: catalogs, soda fountain magazines, etc.

Massachusetts

Adams, Charles & Barbara
Middleboro, 02346; 508-947-7277
Specializing in Bennington (brown only)

Carver, Sally S.
179 South St., Chestnut Hill, 02167; 617-469-9175
Author of *The American Postcard Guide to Tuck*; columnist for *Hobbies*; *Collector's News*; *Postcard Collector*; *Antique Trader Price Guide*
Specializing in all better quality antique pre-1930 postcards; yearly postcard mail auctions with illustrated catalogs; SASE required with correspondence

Longo, Paul J.
Paul Longo Americana
Box 490, Chatham Rd., South Orleans, Cape Cod, 02662; 508-255-5482
Specializing in political pins, ribbons, banners, autographs, old stocks and bonds, baseball memorabilia of all types

Morin, Albert
668 Robbins Ave. #23
Dracut, 01826; 508-454-7907
Specializing in miscellaneous Akro Agate and Westite

Owings, K.C., Jr.
Antiques Americana
Box 19, N. Abington 02351; 617-857-1655
Specializing in Civil War, Revolutionary War, autographs, documents, books, antiques

Rudisill, John & Barbara
Rudisill's Alt Print Haus
3 Lakewood, Medfield, 02052; 508-359-2261
Specializing in Currier and Ives

Vigue, Norm & Cathy
62 Bailey St., Stoughton, 02072; 617-344-5441
Buying and selling comic character, TV and western character collectibles

Wellman, BA
#9 Cottage St., Southboro, 01772

Specializing in Ceramic Arts Studio and Pennsbury pottery: price guide and videotape identification guides available

Michigan

Bailey, Lois & Don
Bailey's Antiques
103 E. North St., Tekonsha, 49092; 517-767-4760
Specializing in early American pressed glass

Brown, Rick
Newspaper Collectors Society of America
Box 9134-S, Lansing, 48901; 517-372-8381
Specializing in newspapers

Daly, Robert L.
10341 Jewell Lake Ct., Fenton, 48430
Collector of early American bottles and flasks
Specializing in bitters bottles and historical whiskey flasks

Gunsaulus, Jack
Gray's Gallery
583 W. Ann Arbor Trail, Plymouth, 48170; 313-455-2373
Specializing in porcelain, glass, jewelry, books

Haas, Norman
264 Clizbe Rd., Quincy, 49082; 517-639-8537
Specializing in American art pottery

Nedry, Boyd W.
728 Buth Dr., Comstock Park, 49321; 616-784-1513
Specializing in traps and trap-related items

Newbound, Betty
4567 Chadsworth, Union Lake, 48085
Author Collector Books on Blue Ridge dinnerware
Specializing in collectible china and glass

Minnesota

Anderson, James
Box 12704, New Brighton, 55112; 612-484-3198
Specializing in old fishing lures and reels, also tackle catalogs, posters, calendars

Furst, Steve
4800 Barbara Dr.
Minnetonka, 55343; 612-938-7103
Specializing in Van Briggle

Hoppe, Gordon
10120 32nd Ave. N., Plymouth, 55441; 612-546-7461
Specializing in Roseville, Trenton

Hukriede, Linda
Linda's Caravan
2910 Hwy. 1695, Lot 20, Grand Rapids, 55744; 218-326-3941
Specializing in Fiesta, depression and elegant glass, pottery

Ketcham, Steve
Steve Ketcham Antiques (shows and mail order only)
Box 24114, Edina, 55424; 612-920-4205

Specializing in early American bottles, stoneware, advertising

Podpeskar, Doug
3154 Miller Trunk Rd.
Eveleth, 55734; 218-744-4854
Specializing in Red Wing dinnerware

Riendeau, Dale
Nostalgic Treasures
2910 Hwy. 169 S., Lot 11, Grand Rapids, 55744; 218-326-3626
Specializing in depression glass and pottery.

Schoneck, Steve
P.O. Box 56, Newport, 55055; 612-459-2980
Specializing in Handicraft Guild of Minneapolis, American art pottery, Arts & Crafts

Missouri

Allen, Helen
629 E. 65th Terrace
Kansas City, 64131
Specializing in depression and elegant glass

Bosworth, Dick & Waunita
Kansas City Trade Winds
7307 N.W. 75th St., Kansas City, 64152
Specializing in Fenton glass, American art pottery, Parrish prints

Ford, Pamela Ekey
1104 Holgate Drive
Ballwin, 63021; 314-225-6723
Specializing in Black Cats

Gentry, Bill
2423 Leslie, St. Louis, 63114; 314-427-3715
Specializing in depression glass

Hankins, Doris
5311 N. Walrond, Kansas City, 64119; 816-452-1738
Specializing in pottery

Old World Antiques
1715 Summit, Kansas City, 64108
Branch Location: 4436 State Line Rd.
Kansas City 66103
Specializing in 18th- and 19th-century furniture, paintings, accessories, clocks, medical and scientific instruments, chandeliers, sconces, Sabino

Rhodes, Evelyn
7818 N.E. 54th St. Kansas City, 64119; 816-453-7169
Specializing in American-made dinnerware

Roberts, Brenda
Country Side Antiques
R.R. 2, Marshall, 65340
Specializing in Hull pottery and general line
Author Collector Books on Hull pottery; SASE required

Scott, John and Peggy
Scotty's Antiques
Springfield, 65810; 417-887-2191
Specializing in depression-era glassware and pottery

Smith, Pat
Independence
Author Collector Books doll book series

Stratton, Bill
Blue Buds Antiques
Box 8711; 417-862-4212
Specializing in Akro, pottery, etc.

Wiesehan, Doug
D&R Farm Antiques
4535 Hwy. H, St. Charles, 63301
Specializing in salesman's samples and patent models, antique toys, farm toys, metal farm signs

Woollard, D.D., Jr.
11614 Old St. Charles Rd., Bridgeton, 63044
Specializing in World's Fair & Exposition memorabilia

Montana

Tanner, Joseph & Pamela
Wheeler-Tanner Escapes
P.O. Box 349, Great Falls, 59403; 406-453-4961
Specializing in handcuffs, leg shackles, balls and chains, restraints and padlocks of all kinds (including railroad), locking and non-locking devices

Nebraska

Larsen, Robert V.
3214 19th St., Columbus, 68601
Specializing in old hatpins and hatpin holders

New Hampshire

Brenner, Larry
L. Brenner Antiques
1005 Chestnut St., Manchester, 03104; 603-625-8203
Specializing in Royal Bayreuth

Marden, Richard G.
Box 524, Elm St., Wolfeboro, 03894; 603-569-3209

New Jersey

Bilane, John E. (mail order only, no shop)
2065 Morris Ave., Apt. 109, Union, 07083
Specializing in antique glass cup plates

Perzel, Robert & Nancy
Popkorn
20 Spring St., P.O. Box 1057, Flemington, 08822; 201-782-9631
Specializing in Stangl dinnerware, birds, and artware; depression glass

Poster, Harry
Vintage TVs
Box 1883, S. Hackensack, 07606; 201-794-9606
Specializing in vintage TVs, unusual radios, 1950s items, view master

Rago, David
Box 3592, Station E, Trenton, 08629; 609-585-2546
Specializing in Arts & Crafts, American art pottery

Rosen, Barbara
6 Shoshone Trail, Wayne, 07470
Specializing in figural bottle openers and antique dollhouses

Sight Sound Style
Box 2224, S. Hackensack, 07606
Quarterly newsletter of vintage TVs and collectible radios

Steinfeld, Lois & Milt
633 Westfield Ave., Box 457, Westfield, 07091
Specializing in collectible glass and china, Victorian silverplate, and other small collectibles

Young, Art & Penni
P.O. Box 81, Little Falls, 07424; 201-785-8115
Specializing in Stevengraphs, police and fire badges, police collectibles, photographs

New York

Austin, Bruce A.
716-223-0711 (evenings); 716-475-2879 (days)
Specializing in clocks

Batchelor, Daniel J.
R.D. #3, Box 10, Oswego, 13126; 315-342-1511
Specializing in Pairpoint, Handel, Bradley and Hubbard Lamps

Calison, Jim
Tools of Distinction
Wallkill, 12589; 914-895-8035
Specializing in antique and collectible tools, buying and selling

Doyle, Robert A.
Doyle Auctioneers & Appraisers
R.D. 3, Box 137, Osborne Hill Rd., Fishkill, 12524; 914-896-9492
Thousands of collectibles offered: call for free calendar of upcoming auctions.

Fer-Duc Inc.
Ferrara, Joseph; Leduc, Gerard
Box 1303, Newburgh, 12550; 914-565-5990
Specializing in American art pottery (Ohr, Rookwood, Zanesville), 19th- and 20th-century American paintings

Fox, Ron
F.T.S. Inc.
416 Throop St., N. Babylon, 11704; 516-669-7232
Specializing in steins; auctions with illustrated catalogs and video tapes

Greguire, Helen
Helen's Antiques
103 Trimmer Rd., Hilton, 14468; 716-392-2704
Specializing in graniteware (all colors), carnival glass lamps and shades, carnival glass lighting of all kinds

Laun, H. Thomas & Patricia
Little Century
215 Paul Ave., Syracuse, 13206; 315-437-4156 or 315-654-3244
Summer residence: Box 69-A, Cape Vincent, 13618
Specializing in fire-fighting collectibles

Meisel, Louis K. & Susan P.; Bonanno, Joann
Susan P. Meisel Decorative Arts

133 Prince St., New York City, 10012
Specializing in Clarice Cliff and all 20th-century designs in furniture, jewelry, objects d'art, watches, and toys

Owens, Lowell
Owens' Collectibles
12 Bonnie Ave., New Hartford, 13413
Specializing in beer advertising

Pisello, Faye
577 Lake St., Wilson, 14172
Specializing in Brownies by Palmer Cox

Rifken, Blume J.
Author of *Silhouettes in America – 1790-1840 – a Collector's Guide*
Specializing in American antique silhouettes from 1790 to 1840

Schleifman, Roselle
Ed's Collectibles
16 Vincent Rd., Spring Valley, 10977; 914-356-2121
Specializing in Duncan & Miller

Van Kuren, Ruth & Dale
Ruth & Dale Van Kuren Antiques
5990 Goodrich Rd., Clarence Center, 14032; 716-741-2606
Specializing in Buffalo pottery, general line

Van Patten, Joan F.
Box 102, Rexford, 12148
Author Collector Books on Nippon and Noritake

North Carolina

Ricketts, Bill
Pepper's Deli
126 Cherry St., Black Mountain, 28711
Specializing in items advertising Dr Pepper

Sayers, R.J.
Southeastern Antiques & Appraisals
P.O. Box 629, Brevard, 29712
Specializing in Boy Scout Collectibles, Pisgah Forest pottery, primitive American furniture

Ohio

Baker, Shirley
Shirley's Collectibles
Tiffin, 419-447-9875
Specializing in Tiffin glass

Blair, Betty
Golden Apple Antiques
216 Bridge St., Jackson, 45640; 614-286-4817
Specializing in art pottery, Watt, cookie jars, chocolate molds, general line

Budin, Nicki
Gourmet Antiques Inc.
679 High St., Worthington, 43085; 614-885-1986 and (800)-331-8543
Specializing in Royal Doulton

Calkins, Donald
Calkins Antiques Company
The Hatchery Antique Mall, 7474 Avon, Beldon Rd., Rt. #83, N. Ridgeville, 44039; 216-226-0752
Specializing in American art pottery; interested in buying Cowan and Clewell

DeGenaro, Steve
P.O. Box 5662, Youngstown, 44505; 216-759-7151
Specializing in post-mortem photos, mourning collectibles

De Luca, Mary A.
Red Barn Antiques
5510 W. Lakeshore Dr., Port Clinton, 43452; 419-635-2045
General line

Distel, Ginny
Distel's Antiques
4041 S.C.R. 22, Tiffin, 44883; 419-447-5832
Specializing in Tiffin glass

Dutcher, Phil; Hardy, Sherri
The Antiquary
1325 E. 15th St., Tulsa, 74120; 918-582-2897
Specializing in early Americana, folk art, oil paintings, quilts, early glass china, estate jewelry, Art Nouveau & Deco, Lalique glass, and early silver

Ebner, Rita & John
Cracker Barrel Antiques
P.O. Box 328866, Columbus, 43232
Specializing in door knockers, cast iron bottle openers, doorstops, toy tractors, general line

Ferguson, Maxine
Wayside Antiques
2290 E. Pike, Zanesville, 43701
General line, furniture, dolls, pottery, glass

Forsythe, Ruth A.
Box 327, Galena, 43021
Author of Made in Czechoslovakia

Graff, Shirley
4515 Grafton Rd., Brunswick, 44212
Specializing in Pennsbury pottery

Guenin, Tom
Box 454, Chardon, 44024
Specializing in antique telephones and antique telephone restoration

Hermes, Dianne
5664 W. Harbor Rd., Port Clinton, 43452; 419-635-2495
General line

Hopfinger, Jackie
208 E. 6th
Port Clinton, 43452; 419-732-3268
Specializing in jewelry and general line

Hothem, Lar
Hothem House
Box 458, Lancaster, 43130
Specializing in books about Indians and artifacts

Kaltenbach, Bob & Doris
1756 Brussels, Toledo, 43613; 419-474-4955
Specializing in glassware and jewelry

Kao, Fern
Lustre Pitcher Antiques
Box 312, Bowling Green, 43402; 419-352-5928
Specializing in Shelley china, small antiques

Kerr, Ann
P.O. 437, Sidney, 45365; 513-492-6369
Author of Collector's Encyclopedia of Russel Wright Designs
Specializing in work of Wright, interest in 20th century decorative arts

Kier, Donald A.
2022 Marengo St., Toledo, 43614
Specializing in Victorian art glass, hand-painted china, and autographs

Kitchen, Lorrie
Toledo, 43612; 419-478-3815
Specializing in depression-era glass, Hall china, Fiesta, Blue Ridge, Shawnee

Klender, James & Grace
Town & Country Antiques & Collectibles
P.O. Box 447, Pioneer, 43554; 419-237-2880
Specializing in depression glass, clocks, and general line

Kline, Mr. & Mrs. Jerry & Gerry
604 Orchard View Dr., Maumee, 43537; 419-893-1226
Specializing in collecting Torquay pottery

Little's Antiques
Lorain, 44053; 216-282-2442
Specializing in Heisey glass

Mazzarella, Kathy
527 S. College Dr. Bowling Green, 43402; 419-353-1290
Specializing in British Royalty Commemorative tins

Moore, Carolyn
445 N. Prospect, Bowling Green, 43402
Specializing in primitives, yellowware, graniteware

National Cambridge Collectors Inc.
Box 416, Cambridge, 43725
Specializing in Cambridge glass

National Heisey Glass Museum
Heisey Collectors of America Inc.
6th & Church Sts., P.O. Box 4367, Newark, 43055; 614-345-2932

Nitecki, Vicky
Articles & Old Lace (no shop)
314 Jefferson, Republic, 44867; 419-585-5151
Specializing in quilts, linens, glass, china

Osborne, Ruth
Box 85, Higginsport, 45131; 513-375-6605
Specializing in vintage clothing, lamps, jewelry

Penrose, Donald M. (mail order only)
6351 Garber Rd., Dayton, 45415; 513-890-3728
Specializing in continental porcelains and art glass

Peters, Jeannie L.
Mt. Washington Antiques
3742 Kellogg, Cincinnati, 45226; 513-231-6584
Specializing in sheet music

Pierce, David
27544 Black Road, P.O. Box 248, Danville, 43014
Specializing in Glidden pottery

Piersol, Gary
419-476-7687
Specializing in art glass, Libbey, Nash, flint glass, and porcelain

Rees, Debbie & Bill
Zanesville
Specializing in Watt, blue and white stoneware, Steiff, cookie jars, Roseville pottery

Rosco, Michael
Days Gone By
3351 Lagrange, Toledo, 43608; 419-244-6935
Specializing in quality glass, pottery, old toys, and coin-operated machines

Rouppas, William
Frogtown
Box 822, Toledo
Specializing in medical, dental, and old drugstore items

Tucker, Dan
Toledo, 43612; 419-478-3815
Specializing in depression-era glass, Hall china, Fiesta, Blue Ridge, Shawnee

Walczak, Mary Jo
5312 Brophy Dr., Toledo, 43611
Specializing in dolls and snow babies

Walker, Bunny
Box 502, Bucyrus, 44820; 419-562-8355
Specializing in Steiff teddy bears, penny toys, pottery

Warren, Betty & Bob
II B'z Antiques
3056 Edgebrook Dr., Toledo, 43613; 419-472-7187
Specializing in Degenhart, furniture, and general line

Whitmyer, Margaret & Kenn
Box 30806, Gahanna, 43230
Author Collector Books on children's dishes
Specializing in depression-era collectibles

Wilkins, Juanita
The Bird of Paradise
Lima, 419-227-2163
Specializing in R.S. China, Old Ivory, colored pattern glass, lamps, jewelry

Wood, Mildred
La Petit' Grandmere
Toledo, 419-726-3161
Specializing in perfumes and glassware

Young, Mary
1040 Greenridge Dr., Kettering, 45429
Author Collector Books Collector's Guide to Paper Dolls

Oklahoma

Bess, Phyllis & Tom
Authors of Frankoma Treasures
14535 E. 13th St., Tulsa, 74108; 918-437-7776
Specializing in Frankoma pottery

Cox, David; & Gunter, A.W.
Colonial Antiques
1329 E. 15th St., Tulsa, 74120; 918-585-3865
Specializing in early Americana and accessories, quilts, oil paintings, 18th and 19th century

Moore, Art & Shirley
2161 S. Owasso Place, Tulsa, 74114; 918-747-4164
Specializing in Lu Ray Pastels, depression glass

Willis, Ron L.
2110 Fox Ave., Moore, 73160
Specializing in militaria

Oregon

Bartsch, Henry
Antique Registers
2050 N. Hwy. 101, Rockaway Beach, 97136; 503-355-2932
Specializing in antique cash registers. Co-author of Antique Cash Registers 1880-1920

Carter, Fran
Appointment only
Box 3220, Coos Bay, 97420; 503-888-5780
Specializing in estate sales

Collins, Harriett & Hank
Harriett's Antiques (shows and by appointment only)
192 Janney Lane, Medford, 97501; 503-776-0727
Specializing in children's things

Crapo, Lynda
P.O. Box 1013, Medford, 97501; 503-779-6483
Specializing in Metlox, carnival, Jell-O, Nippon, R.S. Prussia, art glass, toys

Frost, Donald M.
Country Estate Antiques
690 Lower Cleveland Rapids Rd.
Roseburg, 97470; 503-672-7613
Specializing in fine glass and porcelain

Geddes, Marjorie
Beaverton, 503-649-1041
Specializing in sewing items, holidays
Buy and sell

Kelley, Dick & Evelyn
Kelley's Kollectables
P.O. Box 1108, North Bend, 97459; 503-759-3915

Lonsway, Beverly
The Sampler
P.O. Box 1233, 1313 Main, Philomath, 97370; 503-929-5605
Specializing in quilts, primitives, & furniture

Matthews, Skip & Kathy
Aristocratic Attic
344 S.W. 'K' St., Grants Pass, 97526; 503-474-6660
Specializing in toys, books, paper items, and advertising ephemera

Mike & Bev's Antiques
P.O. Box 470, Cottage Grove, 97424; 503-

942-7918
Specializing in Roseville pottery

Miller, Don & Robby
P.O. Box 508, Talent, 97504; 503-535-1231

Morris, Thomas G.
Prize Publishers
49 Monterey Dr., Medford, 97504; author of *The Carnival Chalk Prize*, a pictorial price guide on carnival chalkware figures with brief histories and values for each.

Schroeder, George
Schroeder & Sons Antiques
2908 Hillcrest, Medford, 97501; 503-772-4694
Specializing in sports memorabilia

The Sterling Shop
Box 595, Silverton, 97381; 503-873-6315
Specializing in silver

Pennsylvania

Atkinson, Phil & Karol
903 Apache Trail, Mercer, 16137; 412-475-2490
Specializing in antique advertising, country store collectibles

Barker, J. Allen
Toastermaster Antique Appliances
P.O. Box 592, Hawley, 18428; 717-253-1951
Specializing in electric toasters and appliances

Cerebro
P.O. Box 1221, Lancaster, 17603; 717-656-7875 or 800-69-LABEL
Specializing in antique advertising labels, especially cigar box labels, cigar bands, food labels

Cohen, Bea
Box 825, Easton, 18044-0825; 215-252-1098
Specializing in spatterware, Gaudy Dutch, mocha, chalkware, Dedham, spongeware, Canton, textiles

Damaska, Ron
738 9th Ave, New Brighton, 15066; 412-843-1393
Specializing in match holders

DLK Nostalgia & Collectibles
P.O. Box 5112, Johnstown, 15904
Specializing in corkscrews and openers, Art Deco, clocks, toys, breweriana, miscellaneous

Garvin, Joann
P.O. Box 182, Beaver Falls, 15010; 412-843-3999
Specializing in Fiesta

Gyugyi, Dr. Laszlo
P.O. 17329, Pittsburgh, 15235
Specializing in Zsolnay art pottery

Kelly, Kathy
The Kelly Collection
1621 Princess Ave., Pittsburgh, 15216; 412-561-3379
Buying Phoenix glass and related items,

glass company catalogs, trade journals, Monaca PA post cards

Lindsay, Ralph
P.O. Box 21, New Holland, 17557
Specializing in target balls

Locke, Ken & Phyllis
Locke Art Glass
825 6th St., Patt. Heights, Beaver Falls, 15010; 412-846-4393
Specializing in Locke Art Glass

Maier, Clarence & Betty
Mail order: The Burmese Cruet
Box 432, Montgomeryville, 18936; 215-855-5388
Specializing in Victorian art glass

Posner, Judy
R.D.1, Box 273, Effort, 18330; 717-629-6583
Specializing in figural pottery, cookie jars, salt and peppers, Black memorabilia, Disneyana

Rosso, Philip J. & Philip Jr.
Wholesale Glass Dealers
1815 Trimble Avenue, Port Vue, 15133; 412-678-7352
Specializing in Westmoreland glass

Theofiles, George
Miscellaneous Man
Box 1776, New Freedom, 17349; 717-235-4766 from 10 a.m. to 6 p.m.
Specializing in vintage posters and graphics

Weiser, Pastor Frederick S.
New Oxford, 17350; 717-624-4106
Specializing in frakturs

Rhode Island

Dumont, Louise
579 Old Main St., Coventry, 02816; 401-828-2799
Specializing in cookie jars, pottery: Hull and Shawnee

The Occupied Japan Club
c/o Florence Archambault
29 Freeborn St., Newport, 02840
Publishes monthly newsletter, *The Upside Down World of an O.J. Collector*. Please send SASE when requesting information

Tennessee

Price, Gene
Railroad Antiques
Box 278, Erwin, 37650
Specializing in railroadiana

Texas

Bennett, John
Bennett-Pennington Antiques
Rt. 15, Box 355, Denton, 76205; 817-382-2449
Specializing in Clewell, Teco

Docks, L.R. 'Les'
Shellac Shack; Discollector
Box 691035, San Antonio, 78269-1035
Author of *American Premium Record Guide*
Specializing in vintage records

Gaston, Mary Frank
Box 342, Bryan, 77806
Author Collector Books on china and metals
SASE required

Norris, Kenn
Schoolmaster Auctions
P.O. Box 4830, 208 Kerr St., Sanderson, 79848; 915-345-2640
Specializing in school-related items and barbed wire

Sack, Gordon
10914 Shawnbrook, Houston, 77071; 713-995-6577
Specializing in cartoon books (not comics)

Smith, Allan
1806 Shields Dr., Sherman, 75090; 214-893-3626
Specializing in children's lunch boxes and all types of advertising, especially Coca-Cola, Dr Pepper, Pepsi Cola, RC Cola, Red Goose, Buster Brown Shoes, character tin windup toys, and western stars' items

Thompson, Chuck
Chuck Thompson & Associates
P.O. Box 11652, Houston, 77293
Specializing in memorabilia of poets (collector), writes syndicated column, *Poets Remembered*

Tunks, Greg
150 Hohldale, Houston, 77022
Publisher of *Credit Card Collector* newsletter

Walker, Jimmy & Carol
The Iron Lady
501 N. 5th, Waelder, 78959; 512-665-7166
Specializing in pressing irons

Utah

Anderson, Tim
Box 461, Provo, 84603; 801-226-1787
Specializing in autographs: buys single items or collections – historical, movie stars, Mormons, sports figures, etc.

Anderson, Warren R.
American West Archives
P.O. Box 100, Cedar City, 84721
Specializing in old stock certificates and bonds, western documents and books, financial ephemera, autographs, maps, prints

Vermont

Barry, Kit
143 Main St., Brattleboro, 05301
Author of *The Advertising Trade Card*
Specializing in advertising trade cards and ephemera in general

Virginia

Bradfield, Jeff
Jeff's Antiques
Corner of Rt. 42 & Rt. 257, Dayton, 22821; 703-879-9961
Also located in Rocky's Antique Mall (I-81), Exit 60, Weyers Cave
Specializing in post cards, candy containers, toys, pottery, furniture, lamps, and advertising items

Flanigan, Vicki
Flanigan's Antiques
P.O. Box 1662, Winchester, 22601
Specializing in antique dolls and hand fans

Friend, Terry
R.R. 4, Box 152-D, Galax, 24333; 703-236-9027 after 9:30 p.m. EST
Specializing in coffee mills
SASE required

Lechner, Mildred & Ralph
Box 554, Mechanicsville, 23111
Author Collector Books on salt shakers
Specializing in art and pattern glass salt shakers circa 1870-1940

Monsen, Randall; Baer, Rod
Cocktails & Laughter Antiques
Box 1503, Arlington, 22210; 703-938-2129
Specializing in perfume bottles, Roseville pottery, Art Deco

Reynolds, Charles
Reynolds Toys
2836 Monroe St., Falls Church, 22042; 703-533-1322
Specializing in limited edition mechanical and still banks, figural bottle openers

Washington

Haynes, Bob
House of Haynes Antiques
P.O. Box 6842, Bellevue, 98008; 206-641-5198 or 800-321-5198
Specializing in Royal Doulton and Moorcroft

Rothe, Linda
P.O. Box 27374, Seattle, 98125-1874
Specializing in Black Americana

West Virginia

Fostoria Glass Society of America Inc.
Box 826, Moundsville, 26041
Specializing in Fostoria glass

Wisconsin

Apple, John
John Apple Antiques
1720 College Ave., Racine, 53403; 414-633-3086
Specializing in brass cash registers and parts

Falat, Tim
T&J Antiques
1403A Ahrens, Manitowoc, 54220; 414-683-3958

Fortney, Daniel
Suite 713 Chalet at the River, 823 N. 2nd St., Milwaukee, 53203
Specializing in china and glass

Matzke, Gene
Gene's Badges & Emblems
2345S. 28th St., Milwaukee, 53215; 414-383-8995
Specializing in police badges, patches, leg irons, old police photos, fire badges (old), patches, and memorabilia

Rice, Ferill J.
302 Pheasant Run, Kaukauna, 54130
Specializing in Fenton art glass

American Clay Exchange
800 Murray Dr., El Cajon, CA 92020

American West Archives
Anderson, Warren
P.O. Box 100, Cedar City, Utah, 84721
26-page illustrated catalogs issued quarterly. Has both fixed-price and auction sections offering early western documents, letters, stock certificates, autographs, and other important ephemera. 1-year subscription: $10.00.

Antique & Art Glass Salt Shaker Collectors' Society
c/o Albert Mills, Secretary/Treasurer
348 N. Hamilton St., Painted Post, NY, 14870

Antique Radio Club of America
81 Steeplechase Rd., Devon, PA 19333

Antique Stove Association
Clifford Boram, Secretary
417 N. Main St., Monticello, IN 47960
Inquiries should be accompanied by SASE and marked 'Urgent' in red

Antique Wireless Association
Ormiston Rd., Breesport, NY 14816

Antique Woodworking Power Tool Assn.
Walt Vinoski, Editor/Publisher
P.O. Box 1027, Connellville, PA 15425
Information requires SASE

Arts & Crafts Quarterly
P.O. Box 3592, Station E
Trenton, NJ 08629
1-800-541-5787

Avon Collectors' Club
Western World
c/o Floyd or Ellen Busby
P.O. Box 23785, Dept P
Pleasant Hill, CA 94523
Information requires LSASE

Avon Times
c/o Dwight or Vera Young
P.O. Box 9868, Dept. P
Kansas City, MO 64134
Information requires LSASE

Black Americana Catalogs
Rothe, Linda
P.O. Box 27374 Seattle, WA 98125-1874

British Royal Commemorative Souvenirs
Mail Order Catalog
Audrey Zeder
6755 Coralite St. S, Long Beach, CA 90808

California Perfume Company
For information contact Dick Pardini
3107 North El Dorado St., Dept. SAPG, Stockton, CA 95204
Information requires LSASE; not necessary when offering items for sale

Candy Container Collectors of America
P.O. Box 1088
Washington, PA 15301

Central Florida Insulator Collectors
3557 Nicklaus Dr., Titusville, FL 32780

Chicagoland Antique Advertizing
Slot Machine & Jukebox Gazette
Ken Durham, Editor
P.O. Box 2426, Dept. S, Rockville, MD 20852
20-page newspaper published twice a year, subscription: 4 issues for $10; sample $5

Coin-Op Newsletter
Ken Durham, Publisher
909 26th St. NW, Washington, DC 20037
Subscription (10 issues) $24, sample issue $5

The Cola Clan
Alice Fisher, Treasurer
2084 Continental Drive, N.E., Atlanta, GA 30345

Credit Card Collector newsletter
Greg Tunks, Publisher
150 Hohldale, Houston, TX 77022

Cutting Edge
Adrienne S. Escoe, Editor
P.O. Box 342, Los Alamitos, CA 90720
Published quarterly
Subscription: $2.50 per year, 50¢ for sample

Depression Glass Daze
12135 N. State St., Otisville, MI 48463

Docks, L.R. 'Les'
Shellac Shack
Box 691035, San Antonio, TX, 78269-1035
Send $2 for a 72-page catalog of thousands of 78s that Docks wants to buy, the prices he will pay, and shipping instructions

Doyle Auctioneers & Appraisers
Doyle, Robert A.
R.D. 3, Box 137, Osborne Hill Rd., Fishkill, NY 12524; 914-896-9492
Thousands of collectibles offered: call for free calendar of upcoming auctions

Fenton Art Glass Collectors of America Inc.
Williamstown, WV 26187

Figural Bottle Opener Collectors
c/o Barbara Rosen
6 Shoshone Trail, Wayne, NJ 07470

Fostoria Glass Society of America Inc.
P.O. Box 826, Moundsville, WV 26041

F.T.S. Inc.
416 Throop St., North Babylon, NY, 11704; 516-669-7232
Specializing in stein auctions with illustrated catalogs

Full House Antique Playing Cards & Gambling Memorabilia
9320 Laurel Green Dr., Boynton Beach, FL, 33437; 407-734-8690
Mail auction catalogs; will date and price cards – include SASE

The Glaze, Pottery Collectors Newsletter
P.O. Box 4782, Birmingham, AL 35706

Hake's Americana & Collectibles
Specializing in character and personality collectibles along with artifacts of popular

culture for over 20 years. To receive a catalog for their next 3,000-item mail/phone bid auction, send $3.00 to Hake's Americana, P.O. Box 1444M, York, PA, 17405

The Harrison Fisher Society
c/o Deena Zachritz
Rocking Chair Emporium
123 N. Glassell, Orange, CA 92666; 714-633-5206
Or (correspondence address) P.O. Box 8188, Redlands, CA 92373
Information and research on Harrison Fisher and network of collectors and dealers; publishes annual exchange newsletter

Heisey Collectors of America Inc.
National Heisey Glass Museum
169 W. Church St., Newark, OH 43055; 614-345-2932

Hot Tea, a bi-monthly magazine for teapot collectors
Tina M. Carter, Editor
822 S. Mollison, El Cajon, CA 92020
Annual subscription rate is $10.50; sample: $1.00

Ice Screamer
c/o Ed Marks, Publisher
P.O. Box 5387, Lancaster, PA 17601
Published bimonthly, $15 for 1 year's dues
Annual convention late June

Indiana Historical Radio Society
245 N. Oakland Ave. Indianapolis, IN 46201

International Club for Collectors of Hatpins & Hatpin Holders (ICC of H&HH)
Lillian Baker, Founder
15237 Chanera Ave., Gardena, CA 90249; 213-329-2619
Monthly *Points* newsletter and *Pictorial Journal*

International Society of Antique Scale Collectors
Bob Stein, President
111 North Canal St., Suite 380, Chicago, IL 60606
Publishes quarterly magazine

Jukebox Collector magazine
Rick Botts, Publisher
2545 S.E. 60th Ct. Des Moines, IA 50317-5099

Loose Change Magazine
Jackie Durham, Agent
909 26th St. NW, Washington, DC, 20037; Monthly magazine, subscription: $39 (payable to Jackie Durham)

Mechanical Music Center
Mayer, Fran
18 Marshall St., Box 1078, S. Norwalk, CT 06854; 203-852-1780
Illustrated catalogs of mechanical musical instruments for sale, $5 annual subscription

Mystic Lights of the Aladdin Knights newsletter, bimonthly
c/o J.W. Courter
R.R. 1, Simpson, IL 62985
Information requires LSASE

National Association of Avon Collectors

c/o Bill Armstrong
P.O. Box 68, Dept. P
West Newton, IN 46183
Information requires LSASE

National Association of Miniature Enthusiasts (N.A.M.E.)
Box 2621, Anaheim, CA 92804-0621; (714) 871-NAME

National Blue Ridge Newsletter
Norma Lilly
144 Highland Dr., Blountville, TN 37617
$9 per year (6 issues)

National Cambridge Collectors Inc.
P.O. Box 416, Cambridge, OH 43725

National Graniteware Society
4818 Reamer Rd., Center Point, IA 52213

National Insulator Association #256
3557 Nicklaus Dr., Titusville, FL 32780

National Reamer Association
c/o Dee Long, 112 S. Center, Lacon, IL 61540

New England Society of Open Salt Collectors
Mrs. Ruth Arch, Treasurer
Stoneridge Estates, 9 Casey Circle, Waltham, MA 02154; dues $5

Newspaper Collectors' Society of America
Rick Brown
Box 19134-S, Lansing, MI 48901; 517-372-8381

North American Trap Collectors' Association
21149 NE 212th Ave., Battle Ground, WA 98064
Dues: $7.50 per year; Newsletter published 6 times a year

The Occupied Japan Club
c/o Florence Archambault
29 Freeborn St., Newport, RI 02840
Publishes *The Upside Down World of an O.J. Collector*, a monthly newsletter. Information requires SASE

Old Storefront Antiques
P.O. Box 357, Dublin, IN 47335; 317-478-4809
Publishes catalogs on store items, primitives, advertising, profession-related, etc. Each is available for $1.50 or all 17 for $17 postpaid. Include LSASE

Open Salt Collectors of the Atlantic Regions (O.S.C.A.R.)
Lee Anne Gommer, 56 Northview Dr., Lancaster, PA 17601; dues $5

Open Salt Seekers of the West, Northern California Chapter
Verna Boller, 1552 Bicardy, Stockton, CA 95203; dues $5

Open Salt Seekers of the West, Southern California Chapter
Marie Smith, Treasurer, 4208 Country Club Dr., Bakersville, CA 93306; dues $5

Paperweight Collectors' Association
120 Old Broadway, Garden City Park, NY

11040; 516-741-3090
Chapters in many states and Canada, England, New Zealand, and West Germany.

Pen Fancier's Club
1169 Overcash Dr., Dunedin, FL 34698
Publishes monthly magazine of pens and mechanical pencils
Yearly subscription rate: $35, sample copy: $3

Perfume & Scent Bottle Collectors
Jeane Parris
2022 E. Charleston Blvd., Las Vegas, NV 89104; 702-385-6059
Membership of $15 USA ($30 Foreign) includes an informative quarterly newsletter. Information requires SASE

Postcard Mail Auctions
Run by Sally S. Carver, 179 South St., Chestnut Hill, MA 02167; 617-469-9175
Specializing in all better quality pre-1930 postcards; large illustrated auction published yearly
$5 charge for auction, no consignment accepted

Precious Collectibles, for Precious Moments figurine collectors, *The Ornament Collector* magazine for Hallmark ornaments and other ornament collectors
Rosie Wells, Publisher
R.R. 1, Canton, IL 61520
Write for free literature; publishes *The Secondary Market Price Guide for Precious Moments Collectibles,* and *The Secondary*

Price Guide for Hallmark Ornaments. Each guide is approximately 90 pages. Rosie also has an informational guide for Lowell Davis collectors.

R. Lalique – listings of items for sale
John Danis
11028 Raleigh Ct., Rockford, IL 61111; 815-963-0757

Shawnee Pottery Collectors' Club
P.O. Box 713
New Smyrna Beach, FL 32170-0713
Please send SASE when requesting information package for membership. Optional: Send $3 and SASE to Pamela Curran in care of above address for a copy of the current newsletter.

Table Toppers
1340 West Irving Park Rd., P.O. Box 161, Chicago, 60613; 312-769-3184
Individual membership is $18 per year, which includes *Table Topics,* a bimonthly newsletter for those who appreciate and enjoy spreading information about tabletop collectibles and the multiple ways in which they can be used and enjoyed.

Tea Leaf Club International
P.O. Box 904, Mt. Prospect, IL 60056
Publishes *Tea Leaf Reading* newsletter, sent to all members as part of membership fee
$20 for single membership, $25 for double membership per year

Thermometer Collectors' Club of America
Warren D. Harris, President
4555 Auburn Blvd., Suite #11, Sacramento, CA 95841

Thimble Collectors International
6411 Montego Rd.
Louisville, KY 40228

Three Rivers Depression Era Glass Society
Meetings held 1st Monday of each month at Airport Ramada Inn, Beers School Rd., PA; for more information contact Nancy Zamborsky, 4038 Willett Rd., Pittsburgh, PA 15227; 412-882-1989

Tiffin Glass Collectors
Meetings at Seneca Cty. Museum on 2nd Tuesday of each month
P.O. Box 554, Tiffin, OH 44883

Tops & Bottoms Club
(Rene Lalique perfumes only)
c/o Madeleine France
P.O. Box 15555, Plantation, FL 33318

Torquay Pottery Collectors' Society
Jerry & Gerry Kline, members
604 Orchard View Dr., Maumee, OH 43537

Toy Gun Collectors of America
Jim Buskirk, Secretary and Editor of newsletter
430-B N. Lakeview, Suite 704, Anaheim, CA 92807

The Trade Card Journal
Barry, Kit
A quarterly publication on the social and historical use of trade cards

UHL Collectors' Society
Roger Shelton, President
607 Willow Dr., Shelbyville, IN 46176.
For membership information, contact Sue Uhl Maynard, 3570 Candlewood, Corona, CA 91719
For information concerning a newsletter write to: UHL Collectors Society, P.O. Box 251, Knightstown, IN 46148. Information requires SASE

Vernon Views newsletter
P.O. Box 945, Scottsdale, AZ 85252
Published quarterly beginning with the spring issue, $6 per year

Wheeler-Tanner Escapes
P.O. Box 349, Great Falls, Montana 59403
40-page catalog of magician/escape artist equipment from trick and regulation handcuffs, padlocks, leg sheckles, straight jackets to picks, and pick sets. Books on all of the above and much more. Catalog: $3

World's Fair Collectors' Society, Inc.
P.O. Box 20806, Sarasota, FL 34238; 813-923-2590
Publishes monthly *Fair News* newsletter
Michael R. Pender, Editor
Dues: (Including subscription to *Fair News*)
$12 per year in U.S.A., $13 in Canada, and $20 for overseas members

Books on Antiques and Collectibles

Most of the following books are available from your local book seller or antique dealer, or on loan from your public library. If you are unable to locate certain titles in your area you may order by mail from COLLECTOR BOOKS, P.O. Box 3009, Paducah, KY 42002-3009. Add $2.00 for postage for the first book ordered and $.25 for each additional book. Include item number, title and price when ordering. Allow 14 to 21 days for delivery. All books are well illustrated and contain current values.

Books on Glass and Pottery

1810	American Art Glass, Shuman	$29.95
1517	American Belleek, Gaston	$19.95
2016	Bedroom & Bathroom Glassware of the Depression Years	$19.95
1312	Blue & White Stoneware, McNerney	$9.95
1959	Blue Willow, 2nd Ed., Gaston	$14.95
1627	Children's Glass Dishes, China & Furniture II, Lechler	$19.95
1892	Collecting Royal Haeger, Garmon	$19.95
2017	Collector's Ency. of Depression Glass, Florence, 9th Ed.	$19.95
1373	Collector's Ency of Amercian Dinnerware, Cunningham	$24.95
1812	Collector's Ency. of Fiesta, Huxford	$19.95
1439	Collector's Ency. of Flow Blue China, Gaston	$19.95
1961	Collector's Ency. of Fry Glass, Fry Glass Society	$24.95
2086	Collector's Ency. of Gaudy Dutch & Welsh, Schuman	$14.95
1813	Collector's Encyclopedia of Geisha Girl Porcelain, Litts	$19.95
1915	Collector's Ency. of Hall China, 2nd Ed., Whitmyer	$19.95
1358	Collector's Ency. of McCoy Pottery, Huxford	$19.95
1039	Collector's Ency. of Nippon Porcelain I, Van Patten	$19.95
1350	Collector's Ency. of Nippon Porcelain II, Van Patten	$19.95
1665	Collector's Ency. of Nippon Porcelain III, Van Patten	$24.95
1447	Collector's Ency. of Noritake, Van Patten	$19.95
1038	Collector's Ency. of Occupied Japan, 2nd Ed., Florence	$14.95
1719	Collector's Ency. of Occupied Japan III, Florence	$14.95
2019	Collector's Ency. of Occupied Japan IV, Florence	$14.95
1715	Collector's Ency. of R.S. Prussia II, Gaston	$24.95
1034	Collector's Ency. of Roseville Pottery, Huxford	$19.95
1035	Collector's Ency. of Roseville Pottery, 2nd Ed., Huxford	$19.95
1623	Coll. Guide to Country Stoneware & Pottery, Raycraft	$9.95
2077	Coll. Guide Country Stoneware & Pottery, 2nd Ed., Raycraft	$14.95
1523	Colors in Cambridge, National Cambridge Society	$19.95
1425	Cookie Jars, Westfall	$9.95
1843	Covered Animal Dishes, Grist	$14.95
1844	Elegant Glassware of the Depression Era, 3rd Ed., Florence	$19.95
2024	Kitchen Glassware of the Depression Years, 4th Florence	$19.95
1465	Haviland Collectibles & Art Objects, Gaston	$19.95
1917	Head Vases Id & Value Guide, Cole	$14.95
1392	Majolica Pottery, Katz-Marks	$9.95
1669	Majolica Pottery, 2nd Series, Katz-Marks	$9.95
1919	Pocket Guide to Depression Glass, 6th Ed., Florence	$9.95
1438	Oil Lamps II, Thuro	$19.95
1670	Red Wing Collectibles, DePasquale	$9.95
1440	Red Wing Stoneware, DePasquale	$9.95
1958	So. Potteries Blue Ridge Dinnerware, 3rd Ed., Newbound	$14.95
1889	Standard Carnival Glass, 2nd Ed., Edwards	$24.95
1814	Wave Crest, Glass of C.F. Monroe, Cohen	$29.95
1848	Very Rare Glassware of the Depression Years, Florence	$24.95

Books on Dolls & Toys

1887	American Rag Dolls, Patino	$14.95
2079	Barbie Fashion, Vol. 1, 1959-1967, Eames	$24.95
1749	Black Dolls, Gibbs	$14.95
1514	Character Toys & Collectibles 1st Series, Longest	$19.95
1750	Character Toys & Collectibles, 2nd Series, Longest	$19.95
2021	Collectible Male Action Figures, Manos	$14.95
1529	Collector's Ency. of Barbie Dolls, DeWein	$19.95
1066	Collector's Ency. of Half Dolls, Marion	$29.95
2082	Collector's Guide to Magazine Paper Dolls, Young	$14.95
1891	French Dolls in Color, 3rd Series, Smith	$14.95
1631	German Dolls, Smith	$9.95
1635	Horsman Dolls, Gibbs	$19.95
1067	Madame Alexander Collector's Dolls, Smith	$19.95
2025	Madame Alexander Price Guide #15, Smith	$7.95
1995	Modern Collectors Dolls, Vol. I, Smith	$19.95
1516	Modern Collector's Dolls V, Smith	$19.95

1540	Modern Toys, 1930-1980, Baker	$19.95
2033	Patricia Smith Doll Values, Antique to Modern, 6th ed.,	$9.95
1886	Stern's Guide to Disney	$14.95
1513	Teddy Bears & Steiff Animals, Mandel	$9.95
1817	Teddy Bears & Steiff Animals, 2nd, Mandel	$19.95
2084	Teddy Bears, Steiff Animals, Annalees, 3rd, Mandel	$19.95
2028	Toys, Antique & Collectible, Longest	$14.95
1648	World of Alexander-Kins, Smith	$19.95
1808	Wonder of Barbie, Manos	$9.95
1430	World of Barbie Dolls, Manos	$9.95

Other Collectibles

1457	American Oak Furniture, McNerney	$9.95
1846	Antique & Collectible Marbles, Grist, 2nd Ed.	$9.95
1712	Antique & Collectible Thimbles, Mathis	$19.95
1880	Antique Iron, McNerney	$9.95
1748	Antique Purses, Holiner	$19.95
1868	Antique Tools, Our American Heritage, McNerney	$9.95
2015	Archaic Indian Points & Knives, Edler	$14.95
1426	Arrowheads & Projectile Points, Hothem	$7.95
1278	Art Nouveau & Art Deco Jewelry, Baker	$9.95
1714	Black Collectibles, Gibbs	$19.95
1666	Book of Country, Raycraft	$19.95
1960	Book of Country Vol II, Raycraft	$19.95
1811	Book of Moxie, Potter	$29.95
1128	Bottle Pricing Guide, 3rd Ed., Cleveland	$7.95
1751	Christmas Collectibles, Whitmyer	$19.95
1752	Christmas Ornaments, Johnston	$19.95
1713	Collecting Barber Bottles, Holiner	$24.95
2018	Collector's Ency. of Graniteware, Greguire	$24.95
2083	Collector's Ency. of Russel Wright Designs, Kerr	$19.95
1634	Coll. Ency. of Salt & Pepper Shakers, Davern	$19.95
2020	Collector's Ency. of Salt & Pepper Shakers II, Davern	$19.95
1916	Collector's Guide to Art Deco, Gaston	$14.95
1753	Collector's Guide to Baseball Memorabilia, Raycraft	$14.95
1537	Collector's Guide to Country Baskets, Raycraft	$9.95
1437	Collector's Guide to Country Furniture, Raycraft	$9.95
1842	Collector's Guide to Country Furniture II, Raycraft	$14.95
1962	Collector's Guide to Decoys, Huxford	$14.95
1441	Collector's Guide to Post Cards, Wood	$9.95
1716	Fifty Years of Fashion Jewelry, Baker	$19.95
2022	Flea Market Trader, 6th Ed., Huxford	$9.95
1668	Flint Blades & Proj. Points of the No. Am. Indian, Tully	$24.95
1755	Furniture of the Depression Era, Swedberg	$19.95
2081	Guide to Collecting Cookbooks, Allen	$14.95
1424	Hatpins & Hatpin Holders, Baker	$9.95
1964	Indian Axes & Related Stone Artifacts, Hothem	$14.95
2023	Keen Kutter Collectibles, 2nd Ed., Heuring	$14.95
1181	100 Years of Collectible Jewelry, Baker	$9.95
1965	Pine Furniture, Our Am. Heritage, McNerney	$14.95
2080	Price Guide to Cookbooks & Recipe Leaflets, Dickinson	$9.95
1124	Primitives, Our American Heritage, McNerney	$8.95
1759	Primitives, Our American Heritage, 2nd Series, McNerney	$14.95
2026	Railroad Collectibles, 4th Ed., Baker	$14.95
1632	Salt & Pepper Shakers, Guarnaccia	$9.95
1888	Salt & Pepper Shakers II, Guarnaccia	$14.95
2096	Silverplated Flatware, 4th Ed., Hagan	$14.95
2027	Standard Baseball Card Pr. Gd., Florence	$9.95
1922	Standard Bottle Pr. Gd., Sellari	$14.95
1966	Standard Fine Art Value Guide, Huxford	$29.95
2085	Standard Fine Art Value Guide Vol. 2, Huxford	$29.95
2078	The Old Book Value Guide, 2nd Ed	$19.95
1923	Wanted to Buy	$9.95
1885	Victorian Furniture, McNerney	$9.95